CODE OF FEDERAL REGULATIONS

Title 12
Banks and Banking

Parts 1 to 199

Revised as of January 1, 2019

Containing a codification of documents
of general applicability and future effect

As of January 1, 2019

Published by the Office of the Federal Register
National Archives and Records Administration
as a Special Edition of the Federal Register

Table of Contents

Page

Explanation v

Title 12:

Chapter I—Comptroller of the Currency, Department of the Treasury 3

Finding Aids:

Table of CFR Titles and Chapters 1069

Alphabetical List of Agencies Appearing in the CFR 1089

List of CFR Sections Affected 1099

Cite this Code: CFR

To cite the regulations in this volume use title, part and section number. Thus, 12 CFR 1.1 *refers to title 12, part 1, section 1.*

Explanation

The Code of Federal Regulations is a codification of the general and permanent rules published in the Federal Register by the Executive departments and agencies of the Federal Government. The Code is divided into 50 titles which represent broad areas subject to Federal regulation. Each title is divided into chapters which usually bear the name of the issuing agency. Each chapter is further subdivided into parts covering specific regulatory areas.

Each volume of the Code is revised at least once each calendar year and issued on a quarterly basis approximately as follows:

Title 1 through Title 16 .... as of January 1
Title 17 through Title 27 .... as of April 1
Title 28 through Title 41 .... as of July 1
Title 42 through Title 50 .... as of October 1

The appropriate revision date is printed on the cover of each volume.

LEGAL STATUS

The contents of the Federal Register are required to be judicially noticed (44 U.S.C. 1507). The Code of Federal Regulations is prima facie evidence of the text of the original documents (44 U.S.C. 1510).

HOW TO USE THE CODE OF FEDERAL REGULATIONS

The Code of Federal Regulations is kept up to date by the individual issues of the Federal Register. These two publications must be used together to determine the latest version of any given rule.

To determine whether a Code volume has been amended since its revision date (in this case, January 1, 2019), consult the "List of CFR Sections Affected (LSA)," which is issued monthly, and the "Cumulative List of Parts Affected," which appears in the Reader Aids section of the daily Federal Register. These two lists will identify the Federal Register page number of the latest amendment of any given rule.

EFFECTIVE AND EXPIRATION DATES

Each volume of the Code contains amendments published in the Federal Register since the last revision of that volume of the Code. Source citations for the regulations are referred to by volume number and page number of the Federal Register and date of publication. Publication dates and effective dates are usually not the same and care must be exercised by the user in determining the actual effective date. In instances where the effective date is beyond the cut-off date for the Code a note has been inserted to reflect the future effective date. In those instances where a regulation published in the Federal Register states a date certain for expiration, an appropriate note will be inserted following the text.

OMB CONTROL NUMBERS

The Paperwork Reduction Act of 1980 (Pub. L. 96–511) requires Federal agencies to display an OMB control number with their information collection request.

Many agencies have begun publishing numerous OMB control numbers as amendments to existing regulations in the CFR. These OMB numbers are placed as close as possible to the applicable recordkeeping or reporting requirements.

PAST PROVISIONS OF THE CODE

Provisions of the Code that are no longer in force and effect as of the revision date stated on the cover of each volume are not carried. Code users may find the text of provisions in effect on any given date in the past by using the appropriate List of CFR Sections Affected (LSA). For the convenience of the reader, a "List of CFR Sections Affected" is published at the end of each CFR volume. For changes to the Code prior to the LSA listings at the end of the volume, consult previous annual editions of the LSA. For changes to the Code prior to 2001, consult the List of CFR Sections Affected compilations, published for 1949-1963, 1964-1972, 1973-1985, and 1986-2000.

"[RESERVED]" TERMINOLOGY

The term "[Reserved]" is used as a place holder within the Code of Federal Regulations. An agency may add regulatory information at a "[Reserved]" location at any time. Occasionally "[Reserved]" is used editorially to indicate that a portion of the CFR was left vacant and not accidentally dropped due to a printing or computer error.

INCORPORATION BY REFERENCE

What is incorporation by reference? Incorporation by reference was established by statute and allows Federal agencies to meet the requirement to publish regulations in the Federal Register by referring to materials already published elsewhere. For an incorporation to be valid, the Director of the Federal Register must approve it. The legal effect of incorporation by reference is that the material is treated as if it were published in full in the Federal Register (5 U.S.C. 552(a)). This material, like any other properly issued regulation, has the force of law.

What is a proper incorporation by reference? The Director of the Federal Register will approve an incorporation by reference only when the requirements of 1 CFR part 51 are met. Some of the elements on which approval is based are:

(a) The incorporation will substantially reduce the volume of material published in the Federal Register.

(b) The matter incorporated is in fact available to the extent necessary to afford fairness and uniformity in the administrative process.

(c) The incorporating document is drafted and submitted for publication in accordance with 1 CFR part 51.

What if the material incorporated by reference cannot be found? If you have any problem locating or obtaining a copy of material listed as an approved incorporation by reference, please contact the agency that issued the regulation containing that incorporation. If, after contacting the agency, you find the material is not available, please notify the Director of the Federal Register, National Archives and Records Administration, 8601 Adelphi Road, College Park, MD 20740-6001, or call 202-741-6010.

CFR INDEXES AND TABULAR GUIDES

A subject index to the Code of Federal Regulations is contained in a separate volume, revised annually as of January 1, entitled CFR INDEX AND FINDING AIDS. This volume contains the Parallel Table of Authorities and Rules. A list of CFR titles, chapters, subchapters, and parts and an alphabetical list of agencies publishing in the CFR are also included in this volume.

An index to the text of "Title 3—The President" is carried within that volume.

The Federal Register Index is issued monthly in cumulative form. This index is based on a consolidation of the "Contents" entries in the daily Federal Register.

A List of CFR Sections Affected (LSA) is published monthly, keyed to the revision dates of the 50 CFR titles.

REPUBLICATION OF MATERIAL

There are no restrictions on the republication of material appearing in the Code of Federal Regulations.

INQUIRIES

For a legal interpretation or explanation of any regulation in this volume, contact the issuing agency. The issuing agency's name appears at the top of odd-numbered pages.

For inquiries concerning CFR reference assistance, call 202–741–6000 or write to the Director, Office of the Federal Register, National Archives and Records Administration, 8601 Adelphi Road, College Park, MD 20740-6001 or e-mail *fedreg.info@nara.gov*.

SALES

The Government Publishing Office (GPO) processes all sales and distribution of the CFR. For payment by credit card, call toll-free, 866-512-1800, or DC area, 202-512-1800, M-F 8 a.m. to 4 p.m. e.s.t. or fax your order to 202-512-2104, 24 hours a day. For payment by check, write to: US Government Publishing Office – New Orders, P.O. Box 979050, St. Louis, MO 63197-9000.

ELECTRONIC SERVICES

The full text of the Code of Federal Regulations, the LSA (List of CFR Sections Affected), The United States Government Manual, the Federal Register, Public Laws, Public Papers of the Presidents of the United States, Compilation of Presidential Documents and the Privacy Act Compilation are available in electronic format via *www.ofr.gov*. For more information, contact the GPO Customer Contact Center, U.S. Government Publishing Office. Phone 202-512-1800, or 866-512-1800 (toll-free). E-mail, *ContactCenter@gpo.gov*.

The Office of the Federal Register also offers a free service on the National Archives and Records Administration's (NARA) World Wide Web site for public law numbers, Federal Register finding aids, and related information. Connect to NARA's web site at *www.archives.gov/federal-register*.

The e-CFR is a regularly updated, unofficial editorial compilation of CFR material and Federal Register amendments, produced by the Office of the Federal Register and the Government Publishing Office. It is available at *www.ecfr.gov*.

OLIVER A. POTTS,
Director,
Office of the Federal Register.
January 1, 2019.

THIS TITLE

Title 12—BANKS AND BANKING is composed of ten volumes. The parts in these volumes are arranged in the following order: Parts 1–199, 200–219, 220–229, 230–299, 300–346, 347–599, 600–899, 900–1025, 1026–1099, and 1100–end. The contents of these volumes represent all current regulations codified under this title of the CFR as of January 1, 2019.

For this volume, Ann Worley was Chief Editor. The Code of Federal Regulations publication program is under the direction of John Hyrum Martinez, assisted by Stephen J. Frattini.

Title 12—Banks and Banking

(This book contains parts 1 to 199)

	Part
CHAPTER I—Comptroller of the Currency, Department of the Treasury	1

CHAPTER I—COMPTROLLER OF THE CURRENCY, DEPARTMENT OF THE TREASURY

Part		*Page*
1	Investment securities	7
2	Sales of credit life insurance	14
3	Capital adequacy standards	15
4	Organization and functions, availability and release of information, contracting outreach program, post-employment restrictions for senior examiners	267
5	Rules, policies, and procedures for corporate activities	291
6	Prompt corrective action	402
7	Activities and operations	414
8	Assessment of fees	438
9	Fiduciary activities of national banks	444
10	Municipal securities dealers	456
11	Securities Exchange Act disclosure rules	457
12	Recordkeeping and confirmation requirements for securities transactions	459
13	Government securities sales practices	466
14	Consumer protection in sales of insurance	469
15	[Reserved]	
16	Securities offering disclosure rules	474
19	Rules of practice and procedure	481
21	Minimum security devices and procedures, reports of suspicious activities, and Bank Secrecy Act Compliance Program	521
22	Loans in areas having special flood hazards	526
23	Leasing	533
24	Community and economic development entities, community development projects, and other public welfare investments	537
25	Community Reinvestment Act and interstate deposit production regulations	547
26	Management official interlocks	569
27	Fair housing home loan data system	574
28	International banking activities	585

Part		Page
29	[Reserved]	
30	Safety and soundness standards	599
31	Extensions of credit to insiders and transactions with affiliates	625
32	Lending limits	629
33	[Reserved]	
34	Real estate lending and appraisals	651
35	Disclosure and reporting of CRA-related agreements	681
36	[Reserved]	
37	Debt cancellation contracts and debt suspension agreements	694
38–40	[Reserved]	
41	Fair credit reporting	699
42	[Reserved]	
43	Credit risk retention	705
44	Proprietary trading and certain interests in and relationships with covered funds	746
45	Margin and capital requirements for covered swap entities	790
46	Annual stress test	812
47	Mandatory contractual stay requirements for qualified financial contracts	816
48	Retail foreign exchange transactions	827
49	[Reserved]	
50	Liquidity risk measurement standards	841
51	Receiverships for uninsured national banks	870
52–99	[Reserved]	
100	Rules applicable to savings associations	873
101–107	[Reserved]	
108	Removals, suspensions, and prohibitions where a crime is charged or proven	873
109	Rules of practice and procedure in adjudicatory proceedings	876
110–111	[Reserved]	
112	Rules for investigative proceedings and formal examination proceedings	898
113–127	[Reserved]	
128	Nondiscrimination requirements	901
129–140	[Reserved]	
141	Definitions for regulations affecting Federal savings associations	906
142	[Reserved]	
143	Federal savings associations—grandfathered authority	908
144	Federal mutual savings associations—communication between members	909
145	Federal savings associations—operations	910

Part		*Page*
146–149	[Reserved]	
150	Fiduciary powers of Federal savings associations	912
151	Recordkeeping and confirmation requirements for securities transactions	922
152–154	[Reserved]	
155	Electronic operations of Federal savings associations	930
156	[Reserved]	
157	Deposits	930
158–159	[Reserved]	
160	Lending and investment	931
161	Definitions for regulations affecting all savings associations	948
162	Accounting and disclosure standards	954
163	Savings associations—operations	954
165	Prompt corrective action	967
166	[Reserved]	
167	Capital	970
168	Security procedures	1003
169	Proxies	1005
170–189	[Reserved]	
190	Preemption of State usury laws	1006
191	Preemption of State due-on-sale laws	1011
192	Conversions from mutual to stock form	1015
195	Community reinvestment	1044
196–199	[Reserved]	

PART 1—INVESTMENT SECURITIES

Sec.
1.1 Authority, purpose, scope, and reservation of authority.
1.2 Definitions.
1.3 Limitations on dealing in, underwriting, and purchase and sale of securities.
1.4 Calculation of limits.
1.5 Safe and sound banking practices; credit information required.
1.6 Convertible securities.
1.7 Securities held in satisfaction of debts previously contracted; holding period; disposal; accounting treatment; nonspeculative purpose.
1.8 Nonconforming investments.

INTERPRETATIONS

1.100 Indirect general obligations.
1.110 Taxing powers of a State or political subdivision.
1.120 Prerefunded or escrowed bonds and obligations secured by Type I securities.
1.130 Type II securities; guidelines for obligations issued for university and housing purposes.

AUTHORITY: 12 U.S.C. 1 *et seq.*, 24 (Seventh), and 93a.

SOURCE: 61 FR 63982, Dec. 2, 1996, unless otherwise noted.

§ 1.1 Authority, purpose, scope, and reservation of authority.

(a) *Authority*. This part is issued pursuant to 12 U.S.C. 1 *et seq.*, 12 U.S.C. 24 (Seventh), and 12 U.S.C. 93a.

(b) *Purpose* This part prescribes standards under which national banks may purchase, sell, deal in, underwrite, and hold securities, consistent with the authority contained in 12 U.S.C. 24 (Seventh) and safe and sound banking practices.

(c) *Scope*. The standards set forth in this part apply to national banks and Federal branches of foreign banks.Further, pursuant to 12 U.S.C. 335, State banks that are members of the Federal Reserve System are subject to the same limitations and conditions that apply to national banks in connection with purchasing, selling, dealing in, and underwriting securities and stock. In addition to activities authorized under this part, foreign branches of national banks are authorized to conduct international activities and invest in securities pursuant to 12 CFR part 211.

(d) *Reservation of authority*. The OCC may determine, on a case-by-case basis, that a national bank may acquire an investment security other than an investment security of a type set forth in this part, provided the OCC determines that the bank's investment is consistent with 12 U.S.C. section 24 (Seventh) and with safe and sound banking practices. The OCC will consider all relevant factors, including the risk characteristics of the particular investment in comparison with the risk characteristics of investments that the OCC has previously authorized, and the bank's ability effectively to manage such risks. The OCC may impose limits or conditions in connection with approval of an investment security under this subsection. Investment securities that the OCC determines are permissible in accordance with this paragraph constitute eligible investments for purposes of 12 U.S.C. 24.

[61 FR 63982, Dec. 2, 1996, as amended at 73 FR 22235, Apr. 24, 2008]

§ 1.2 Definitions.

(a) *Capital and surplus* means:

(1) A bank's tier 1 and tier 2 capital calculated under the OCC's risk-based capital standards set forth in 12 CFR part 3, as applicable (or comparable capital guidelines of the appropriate Federal banking agency), as reported in the bank's Consolidated Reports of Condition and Income (Call Report) filed under 12 U.S.C. 161 (or under 12 U.S.C. 1817 in the case of a state member bank); plus

(2) The balance of a bank's allowance for loan and lease losses not included in the bank's Tier 2 capital, for purposes of the calculation of risk-based capital described in paragraph (a)(1) of this section, as reported in the bank's Consolidated Report of Condition and Income filed under 12 U.S.C. 161 (or under 12 U.S.C. 1817 in the case of a state member bank).

(b) *General obligation of a State or political subdivision* means:

(1) An obligation supported by the full faith and credit of an obligor possessing general powers of taxation, including property taxation; or

(2) An obligation payable from a special fund or by an obligor not possessing general powers of taxation, when an obligor possessing general powers of taxation, including property taxation, has unconditionally promised to make payments into the fund or otherwise provide funds to cover all required payments on the obligation.

(c) *Investment company* means an investment company, including a mutual fund, registered under section 8 of the Investment Company Act of 1940, 15 U.S.C. 80a–8.

(d) *Investment grade* means the issuer of a security has an adequate capacity to meet financial commitments under the security for the projected life of the asset or exposure. An issuer has an adequate capacity to meet financial commitments if the risk of default by the obligor is low and the full and timely repayment of principal and interest is expected.

(e) *Investment security* means a marketable debt obligation that is investment grade and not predominately speculative in nature.

(f) *Marketable* means that the security:

(1) Is registered under the Securities Act of 1933, 15 U.S.C. 77a *et seq.;*

(2) Is a municipal revenue bond exempt from registration under the Securities Act of 1933, 15 U.S.C. 77c(a)(2);

(3) Is offered and sold pursuant to Securities and Exchange Commission Rule 144A, 17 CFR 230.144A, and investment grade; or

(4) Can be sold with reasonable promptness at a price that corresponds reasonably to its fair value.

(g) *Municipal bonds* means obligations of a State or political subdivision other than general obligations, and includes limited obligation bonds, revenue bonds, and obligations that satisfy the requirements of section 142(b)(1) of the Internal Revenue Code of 1986 issued by or on behalf of any State or political subdivision of a State, including any municipal corporate instrumentality of 1 or more States, or any public agency or authority of any State or political subdivision of a State.

(h) [Reserved]

(i) *Political subdivision* means a county, city, town, or other municipal corporation, a public authority, and generally any publicly-owned entity that is an instrumentality of a State or of a municipal corporation.

(j) *Type I security* means:

(1) Obligations of the United States;

(2) Obligations issued, insured, or guaranteed by a department or an agency of the United States Government, if the obligation, insurance, or guarantee commits the full faith and credit of the United States for the repayment of the obligation;

(3) Obligations issued by a department or agency of the United States, or an agency or political subdivision of a State of the United States, that represent an interest in a loan or a pool of loans made to third parties, if the full faith and credit of the United States has been validly pledged for the full and timely payment of interest on, and principal of, the loans in the event of non-payment by the third party obligor(s);

(4) General obligations of a State of the United States or any political subdivision thereof; and municipal bonds if the national bank is well capitalized as defined in 12 CFR 6.4;

(5) Obligations authorized under 12 U.S.C. 24 (Seventh) as permissible for a national bank to deal in, underwrite, purchase, and sell for the bank's own account, including qualified Canadian government obligations; and

(6) Other securities the OCC determines to be eligible as Type I securities under 12 U.S.C. 24 (Seventh).

(k) *Type II security* means an investment security that represents:

(1) Obligations issued by a State, or a political subdivision or agency of a State, for housing, university, or dormitory purposes that would not satisfy the definition of Type I securities pursuant to paragraph (j) of § 1.2;

(2) Obligations of international and multilateral development banks and organizations listed in 12 U.S.C. 24 (Seventh);

(3) Other obligations listed in 12 U.S.C. 24 (Seventh) as permissible for a bank to deal in, underwrite, purchase, and sell for the bank's own account, subject to a limitation per obligor of 10 percent of the bank's capital and surplus; and

(4) Other securities the OCC determines to be eligible as Type II securities under 12 U.S.C. 24 (Seventh).

(l) *Type III security* means an investment security that does not qualify as a Type I, II, IV, or V security. Examples of Type III securities include corporate bonds and municipal bonds that do not satisfy the definition of Type I securities pursuant to paragraph (j) of § 1.2 or the definition of Type II securities pursuant to paragraph (k) of § 1.2.

(m) *Type IV security* means:

(1) A small business-related security as defined in section 3(a)(53)(A) of the Securities Exchange Act of 1934, 15 U.S.C. 78c(a)(53)(A), that is fully secured by interests in a pool of loans to numerous obligors.

(2) A commercial mortgage-related security that is offered or sold pursuant to section 4(5) of the Securities Act of 1933, 15 U.S.C. 77d(5), that is investment grade, or a commercial mortgage-related security as described in section 3(a)(41) of the Securities Exchange Act of 1934, 15 U.S.C. 78c(a)(41), that represents ownership of a promissory note or certificate of interest or participation that is directly secured by a first lien on one or more parcels of real estate upon which one or more commercial structures are located and that is fully secured by interests in a pool of loans to numerous obligors.

(3) A residential mortgage-related security that is offered and sold pursuant to section 4(5) of the Securities Act of 1933, 15 U.S.C. 77d(5), that is investment grade, or a residential mortgage-related security as described in section 3(a)(41) of the Securities Exchange Act of 1934, 15 U.S.C. 78c(a)(41)) that does not otherwise qualify as a Type I security.

(n) *Type V security* means a security that is:

(1) Investment grade;

(2) Marketable;

(3) Not a Type IV security; and

(4) Fully secured by interests in a pool of loans to numerous obligors and in which a national bank could invest directly.

[61 FR 63982, Dec. 2, 1996, as amended at 66 FR 34791, July 2, 2001; 77 FR 35257, June 13, 2012; 79 FR 11309, Feb. 28, 2014]

§ 1.3 Limitations on dealing in, underwriting, and purchase and sale of securities.

(a) *Type I securities.* A national bank may deal in, underwrite, purchase, and sell Type I securities for its own account. The amount of Type I securities that the bank may deal in, underwrite, purchase, and sell is not limited to a specified percentage of the bank's capital and surplus.

(b) *Type II securities.* A national bank may deal in, underwrite, purchase, and sell Type II securities for its own account, provided the aggregate par value of Type II securities issued by any one obligor held by the bank does not exceed 10 percent of the bank's capital and surplus. In applying this limitation, a national bank shall take account of Type II securities that the bank is legally committed to purchase or to sell in addition to the bank's existing holdings.

(c) *Type III securities.* A national bank may purchase and sell Type III securities for its own account, provided the aggregate par value of Type III securities issued by any one obligor held by the bank does not exceed 10 percent of the bank's capital and surplus. In applying this limitation, a national bank shall take account of Type III securities that the bank is legally committed to purchase or to sell in addition to the bank's existing holdings.

(d) *Type II and III securities; other investment securities limitations.* A national bank may not hold Type II and III securities issued by any one obligor with an aggregate par value exceeding 10 percent of the bank's capital and surplus. However, if the proceeds of each issue are to be used to acquire and lease real estate and related facilities to economically and legally separate industrial tenants, and if each issue is payable solely from and secured by a first lien on the revenues to be derived from rentals paid by the lessee under net noncancellable leases, the bank may apply the 10 percent investment limitation separately to each issue of a single obligor.

(e) *Type IV securities.* A national bank may purchase and sell Type IV securities for its own account. The amount of the Type IV securities that a bank may purchase and sell is not limited to a specified percentage of the bank's capital and surplus.

(f) *Type V securities.* A national bank may purchase and sell Type V securities for its own account provided that the aggregate par value of Type V securities issued by any one issuer held by the bank does not exceed 25 percent of the bank's capital and surplus. In applying this limitation, a national bank shall take account of Type V securities that the bank is legally committed to purchase or to sell in addition to the bank's existing holdings.

(g) *Securitization.* A national bank may securitize and sell assets that it holds, as a part of its banking business. The amount of securitized loans and obligations that a bank may sell is not limited to a specified percentage of the bank's capital and surplus.

(h) *Pooled investments*—(1) *General.* A national bank may purchase and sell for its own account investment company shares provided that:

(i) The portfolio of the investment company consists exclusively of assets that the national bank may purchase and sell for its own account; and

(ii) The bank's holdings of investment company shares do not exceed the limitations in § 1.4(e).

(2) *Other issuers.* The OCC may determine that a national bank may invest in an entity that is exempt from registration as an investment company under section 3(c)(1) of the Investment Company Act of 1940, provided that the portfolio of the entity consists exclusively of assets that a national bank may purchase and sell for its own account.

(3) Investments made under this paragraph (h) must comply with § 1.5 of this part, conform with applicable published OCC precedent, and must be:

(i) Marketable and investment grade, or

(ii) Satisfy the requirements of § 1.3(i).

(i) *Securities held based on estimates of obligor's performance.* (1) Notwithstanding § 1.2(d) and (e), a national bank may treat a debt security as an investment security for purposes of this part if the security is marketable and the bank concludes, on the basis of estimates that the bank reasonably believes are reliable, that the obligor will be able to satisfy its obligations under that security.

(2) The aggregate par value of securities treated as investment securities under paragraph (i)(1) of this section may not exceed 5 percent of the bank's capital and surplus.

[61 FR 63982, Dec. 2, 1996, as amended at 64 FR 60098, Nov. 4, 1999; 73 FR 22235, Apr. 24, 2008; 77 FR 35257, June 13, 2012]

§ 1.4 Calculation of limits.

(a) *Calculation date.* For purposes of determining compliance with 12 U.S.C. 24 (Seventh) and this part, a bank shall determine its investment limitations as of the most recent of the following dates:

(1) The last day of the preceding calendar quarter; or

(2) The date on which there is a change in the bank's capital category for purposes of 12 U.S.C. 1831o and 12 CFR 6.3.

(b) *Effective date.* (1) A bank's investment limit calculated in accordance with paragraph (a)(1) of this section will be effective on the earlier of the following dates:

(i) The date on which the bank's Consolidated Report of Condition and Income (Call Report) is submitted; or

(ii) The date on which the bank's Consolidated Report of Condition and Income is required to be submitted.

(2) A bank's investment limit calculated in accordance with paragraph (a)(2) of this section will be effective on the date that the limit is to be calculated.

(c) *Authority of OCC to require more frequent calculations.* If the OCC determines for safety and soundness reasons that a bank should calculate its investment limits more frequently than required by paragraph (a) of this section, the OCC may provide written notice to the bank directing the bank to calculate its investment limitations at a more frequent interval. The bank shall thereafter calculate its investment limits at that interval until further notice.

(d) *Calculation of Type III and Type V securities holdings*—(1) *General.* In calculating the amount of its investment in Type III or Type V securities issued by any one obligor, a bank shall aggregate:

(i) Obligations issued by obligors that are related directly or indirectly through common control; and

(ii) Securities that are credit enhanced by the same entity.

(2) *Aggregation by type.* The aggregation requirement in paragraph (d)(1) of this section applies separately to the Type III and Type V securities held by a bank.

(e) *Limit on investment company holdings*—(1) *General.* In calculating the amount of its investment in investment company shares under this part, a bank shall use reasonable efforts to calculate and combine its pro rata share of a particular security in the portfolio of each investment company with the bank's direct holdings of that security. The bank's direct holdings of the particular security and the bank's pro rata interest in the same security in the investment company's portfolio may not, in the aggregate, exceed the investment limitation that would apply to that security.

(2) *Alternate limit for diversified investment companies.* A national bank may elect not to combine its pro rata interest in a particular security in an investment company with the bank's direct holdings of that security if:

(i) The investment company's holdings of the securities of any one issuer do not exceed 5 percent of its total portfolio; and

(ii) The bank's total holdings of the investment company's shares do not exceed the most stringent investment limitation that would apply to any of the securities in the company's portfolio if those securities were purchased directly by the bank.

§ 1.5 Safe and sound banking practices; credit information required.

(a) A national bank shall adhere to safe and sound banking practices and the specific requirements of this part in conducting the activities described in § 1.3. The bank shall consider, as appropriate, the interest rate, credit, liquidity, price, foreign exchange, transaction, compliance, strategic, and reputation risks presented by a proposed activity, and the particular activities undertaken by the bank must be appropriate for that bank.

(b) In conducting these activities, the bank shall determine that there is adequate evidence that an obligor possesses resources sufficient to provide for all required payments on its obligations, or, in the case of securities deemed to be investment securities on the basis of reliable estimates of an obligor's performance, that the bank reasonably believes that the obligor will be able to satisfy the obligation.

(c) Each bank shall maintain records available for examination purposes adequate to demonstrate that it meets the requirements of this part. The bank may store the information in any manner that can be readily retrieved and reproduced in a readable form.

§ 1.6 Convertible securities.

A national bank may not purchase securities convertible into stock at the option of the issuer.

§ 1.7 Securities held in satisfaction of debts previously contracted; holding period; disposal; accounting treatment; non-speculative purpose.

(a) *Securities held in satisfaction of debts previously contracted.* The restrictions and limitations of this part, other than those set forth in paragraphs (b),(c), and (d) of this section, do not apply to securities acquired:

(1) Through foreclosure on collateral;

(2) In good faith by way of compromise of a doubtful claim; or

(3) To avoid loss in connection with a debt previously contracted.

(b) *Holding period.* A national bank holding securities pursuant to paragraph (a) of this section may do so for a period not to exceed five years from the date that ownership of the securities was originally transferred to the bank. The OCC may extend the holding period for up to an additional five years if a bank provides a clearly convincing demonstration as to why an additional holding period is needed.

(c) *Accounting treatment.* A bank shall account for securities held pursuant to paragraph (a) of this section in accordance with Generally Accepted Accounting Principles.

(d) *Non-speculative purpose.* A bank may not hold securities pursuant to paragraph (a) of this section for speculative purposes.

§ 1.8 Nonconforming investments.

(a) A national bank's investment in securities that no longer conform to this part but conformed when made will not be deemed in violation but instead will be treated as nonconforming if the reason why the investment no longer conforms to this part is because:

(1) The bank's capital declines;

(2) Issuers, obligors, or credit-enhancers merge;

(3) Issuers become related directly or indirectly through common control;

(4) The investment securities rules change;

(5) The security no longer qualifies as an investment security; or

(6) Other events identified by the OCC occur.

(b) A bank shall exercise reasonable efforts to bring an investment that is nonconforming as a result of events described in paragraph (a) of this section into conformity with this part unless to do so would be inconsistent with safe and sound banking practices.

INTERPRETATIONS

§ 1.100 Indirect general obligations.

(a) *Obligation issued by an obligor not possessing general powers of taxation.* Pursuant to § 1.2(b), an obligation issued by an obligor not possessing general powers of taxation qualifies as a general obligation of a State or political subdivision for the purposes of 12 U.S.C. 24 (Seventh), if a party possessing general powers of taxation unconditionally promises to make sufficient funds available for all required payments in connection with the obligation.

(b) *Indirect commitment of full faith and credit.* The indirect commitment of the full faith and credit of a State or political subdivision (that possesses general powers of taxation) in support of an obligation may be demonstrated by any of the following methods, alone or in combination, when the State or political subdivision pledges its full faith and credit in support of the obligation.

(1) *Lease/rental agreement.* The lease agreement must be valid and binding on the State or the political subdivision, and the State or political subdivision must unconditionally promise to pay rentals that, together with any other available funds, are sufficient for the timely payment of interest on, and principal of, the obligation. These lease/rental agreement may, for instance, provide support for obligations financing the acquisition or operation of public projects in the areas of education, medical care, transportation, recreation, public buildings, and facilities.

(2) *Service/purchase agreement.* The agreement must be valid and binding on the State or the political subdivision, and the State or political subdivision must unconditionally promise in the agreement to make payments for services or resources provided through or by the issuer of the obligation. These payments, together with any other available funds, must be sufficient for the timely payment of interest on, and principal of, the obligation. An agreement to purchase municipal sewer, water, waste disposal, or electric services may, for instance, provide support for obligations financing the construction or acquisition of facilities supplying those services.

(3) *Refillable debt service reserve fund.* The reserve fund must at least equal the amount necessary to meet the annual payment of interest on, and principal of, the obligation as required by applicable law. The maintenance of a refillable reserve fund may be provided, for instance, by statutory direction for an appropriation, or by statutory automatic apportionment and payment from the State funds of amounts necessary to restore the fund to the required level.

(4) *Other grants or support.* A statutory provision or agreement must unconditionally commit the State or the political subdivision to provide funds which, together with other available funds, are sufficient for the timely payment of interest on, and principal of, the obligation. Those funds may, for instance, be supplied in the form of annual grants or may be advanced whenever the other available revenues are not sufficient for the payment of principal and interest.

§ 1.110 Taxing powers of a State or political subdivision.

(a) An obligation is considered supported by the full faith and credit of a State or political subdivision possessing general powers of taxation when the promise or other commitment of the State or the political subdivision will produce funds, which (together with any other funds available for the purpose) will be sufficient to provide for all required payments on the obligation. In order to evaluate whether a commitment of a State or political subdivision is likely to generate sufficient funds, a bank shall consider the impact of any possible limitations regarding the State's or political subdivision's taxing powers, as well as the availability of funds in view of the projected revenues and expenditures. Quantitative restrictions on the general powers of taxation of the State or political subdivision do not necessarily mean that an obligation is not supported by the full faith and credit of the State or political subdivision. In such case, the bank shall determine the eligibility of obligations by reviewing, on a case-by-case basis, whether tax revenues available under the limited taxing powers are sufficient for the full and timely payment of interest on, and principal of, the obligation. The bank shall use current and reasonable financial projections in calculating the availability of the revenues. An obligation expressly or implicitly dependent upon voter or legislative authorization of appropriations may be considered supported by the full faith and credit of a State or political subdivision if the bank determines, on the basis of past actions by the voters or legislative body in similar situations involving similar types of projects, that it is reasonably probable that the obligor will obtain all necessary appropriations.

(b) An obligation supported exclusively by excise taxes or license fees is not a general obligation for the purposes of 12 U.S.C. 24 (Seventh). Nevertheless, an obligation that is primarily payable from a fund consisting of excise taxes or other pledged revenues qualifies as a "general obligation," if, in the event of a deficiency of those revenues, the obligation is also supported by the general revenues of a State or a political subdivision possessing general powers of taxation.

§ 1.120 Prerefunded or escrowed bonds and obligations secured by Type I securities.

(a) An obligation qualifies as a Type I security if it is secured by an escrow fund consisting of obligations of the United States or general obligations of a State or a political subdivision, and the escrowed obligations produce interest earnings sufficient for the full and timely payment of interest on, and principal of, the obligation.

(b) If the interest earnings from the escrowed Type I securities alone are not sufficient to guarantee the full repayment of an obligation, a promise of a State or a political subdivision possessing general powers of taxation to maintain a reserve fund for the timely payment of interest on, and principal of, the obligation may further support a guarantee of the full repayment of an obligation.

(c) An obligation issued to refund an indirect general obligation may be supported in a number of ways that, in combination, are sufficient at all times to support the obligation with the full faith and credit of the United States or a State or a political subdivision possessing general powers of taxation. During the period following its issuance, the proceeds of the refunding obligation may be invested in U.S. obligations or municipal general obligations that will produce sufficient interest income for payment of principal and interest. Upon the retirement of the outstanding indirect general obligation bonds, the same indirect commitment, such as a lease agreement or a reserve fund, that supported the prior issue, may support the refunding obligation.

§ 1.130 Type II securities; guidelines for obligations issued for university and housing purposes.

(a) *Investment quality.* An obligation issued for housing, university, or dormitory purposes is a Type II security only if it:

(1) Qualifies as an investment security, as defined in § 1.2(e); and

(2) Is issued for the appropriate purpose and by a qualifying issuer.

(b) *Obligation issued for university purposes.* (1) An obligation issued by a State or political subdivision or agency of a State or political subdivision for the purpose of financing the construction or improvement of facilities at or used by a university or a degree-granting college-level institution, or financing loans for studies at such institutions, qualifies as a Type II security. Facilities financed in this manner may include student buildings, classrooms, university utility buildings, cafeterias, stadiums, and university parking lots.

(2) An obligation that finances the construction or improvement of facilities used by a hospital may be eligible as a Type II security, if the hospital is a department or a division of a university, or otherwise provides a nexus with university purposes, such as an affiliation agreement between the university and the hospital, faculty positions of the hospital staff, and training of medical students, interns, residents, and nurses (*e.g.*, a "teaching hospital").

(c) *Obligation issued for housing purposes.* An obligation issued for housing purposes may qualify as a Type II security if the security otherwise meets the criteria for a Type II security.

PART 2—SALES OF CREDIT LIFE INSURANCE

Sec.

2.1 Authority, purpose, and scope.
2.2 Definitions.
2.3 Distribution of credit life insurance income.
2.4 Bonus and incentive plans.
2.5 Bank compensation.

AUTHORITY: 12 U.S.C. 24 (Seventh), 93a, and 1818(n).

SOURCE: 61 FR 51781, Oct. 4, 1996, unless otherwise noted.

§ 2.1 Authority, purpose, and scope.

(a) *Authority.* A national bank may provide credit life insurance to loan customers pursuant to 12 U.S.C. 24 (Seventh).

(b) *Purpose.* The purpose of this part is to set forth the principles and standards that apply to a national bank's provision of credit life insurance and the limitations that apply to the receipt of income from those sales by certain individuals and entities associated with the bank.

(c) *Scope.* This part applies to the provision of credit life insurance by any national bank employee, officer, director, or principal shareholder, and certain entities in which such persons own an interest of more than ten percent.

§ 2.2 Definitions.

(a) *Bank* means a national banking association.

(b) *Credit life insurance* means credit life, health, and accident insurance, sometimes referred to as credit life and disability insurance, and mortgage life and disability insurance.

(c) *Owning an interest* includes:

(1) Ownership through a spouse or minor child;

(2) Ownership through a broker, nominee, or other agent; or

(3) Ownership through any corporation, partnership, association, joint venture, or proprietorship, that is controlled by the director, officer, employee, or principal shareholder of the bank.

(d) *Officer, director, employee, or principal shareholder* includes the spouse and minor children of an officer, director, employee, or principal shareholder.

(e) *Principal shareholder* means any shareholder who directly or indirectly owns or controls an interest of more than ten percent of the bank's outstanding voting securities.

[61 FR 51781, Oct. 4, 1996, as amended at 73 FR 22235, Apr. 24, 2008]

§ 2.3 Distribution of credit life insurance income.

(a) Distribution of credit life insurance income by a national bank must be consistent with the requirements and principles of this section.

(b) It is an unsafe and unsound practice for any director, officer, employee, or principal shareholder of a national bank (including any entity in which this person owns an interest of more than ten percent), who is involved in the sale of credit life insurance to loan customers of the national bank, to take advantage of that business opportunity for personal profit. Recommendations to customers to buy insurance should be based on the benefits of the policy, not the commissions received from the sale.

(c) Except as provided in §§2.4 and 2.5(b), and paragraph (d) of this section, a director, officer, employee, or principal shareholder of a national bank, or an entity in which such person owns an interest of more than ten percent, may not retain commissions or other income from the sale of credit life insurance in connection with any loan made by that bank, and income from credit life insurance sales to loan customers must be credited to the income accounts of the bank.

(d) The requirements of paragraph (c) of this section do not apply to a director, officer, employee, or principal shareholder if:

(1) The person is employed by a third party that has contracted with the bank on an arm's-length basis to sell financial products on bank premises; and

(2) The person is not involved in the bank's credit decision process.

§2.4 Bonus and incentive plans.

A bank employee or officer may participate in a bonus or incentive plan based on the sale of credit life insurance if payments to the employee or officer in any one year do not exceed the greater of:

(a) Five percent of the recipient's annual salary; or

(b) Five percent of the average salary of all loan officers participating in the plan.

§2.5 Bank compensation.

(a) Nothing contained in this part prohibits a bank employee, officer, director, or principal shareholder who holds an insurance agent's license from agreeing to compensate the bank for the use of its premises, employees, or good will. However, the employee, officer, director, or principal shareholder shall turn over to the bank as compensation all income received from the sale of the credit life insurance to the bank's loan customers.

(b) Income derived from credit life insurance sales to loan customers may be credited to an affiliate operating under the Bank Holding Company Act of 1956, 12 U.S.C. 1841 *et seq.*, or to a trust for the benefit of all shareholders, provided that the bank receives reasonable compensation in recognition of the role played by its personnel, premises, and good will in credit life insurance sales. Reasonable compensation generally means an amount equivalent to at least 20 percent of the affiliate's net income attributable to the bank's credit life insurance sales.

PART 3—CAPITAL ADEQUACY STANDARDS

Subpart A—General Provisions

Sec.
3.1 Purpose, applicability, reservations of authority, and timing.
3.2 Definitions.
3.3 Operational requirements for certain exposures.
3.4–3.9 [Reserved]

Subpart B—Capital Ratio Requirements and Buffers

3.10 Minimum capital requirements.
3.11 Capital conservation buffer and countercyclical capital buffer amount.
3.12–3.19 [Reserved]

Subpart C—Definition of Capital

3.20 Capital components and eligibility criteria for regulatory capital instruments.
3.21 Minority interest.
3.22 Regulatory capital adjustments and deductions.
3.23–3.29 [Reserved]

Subpart D—Risk-Weighted Assets—Standardized Approach

3.30 Applicability.

RISK-WEIGHTED ASSETS FOR GENERAL CREDIT RISK

3.31 Mechanics for calculating risk-weighted assets for general credit risk.
3.32 General risk weights.
3.33 Off-balance sheet exposures.
3.34 OTC derivative contracts.
3.35 Cleared transactions.
3.36 Guarantees and credit derivatives: Substitution treatment.
3.37 Collateralized transactions.

RISK-WEIGHTED ASSETS FOR UNSETTLED TRANSACTIONS

3.38 Unsettled transactions.

3.39–3.40 [Reserved]

RISK-WEIGHTED ASSETS FOR SECURITIZATION EXPOSURES

3.41 Operational requirements for securitization exposures.
3.42 Risk-weighted assets for securitization exposures.
3.43 Simplified supervisory formula approach (SSFA) and the gross-up approach.
3.44 Securitization exposures to which the SSFA and gross-up approach do not apply.
3.45 Recognition of credit risk mitigants for securitization exposures.
3.46–3.50 [Reserved]

RISK-WEIGHTED ASSETS FOR EQUITY EXPOSURES

3.51 Introduction and exposure measurement.
3.52 Simple risk-weight approach (SRWA).
3.53 Equity exposures to investment funds.
3.54–3.60 [Reserved]

DISCLOSURES

3.61 Purpose and scope.
3.62 Disclosure requirements.
3.63 Disclosures by national banks or Federal savings associations described in §3.61.
3.64–3.99 [Reserved]

Subpart E—Risk-Weighted Assets—Internal Ratings-Based and Advanced Measurement Approaches

3.100 Purpose, applicability, and principle of conservatism.
3.101 Definitions.
3.102–3.120 [Reserved]

QUALIFICATION

3.121 Qualification process.
3.122 Qualification requirements.
3.123 Ongoing qualification.
3.124 Merger and acquisition transitional arrangements.
3.125–3.130 [Reserved]

RISK-WEIGHTED ASSETS FOR GENERAL CREDIT RISK

3.131 Mechanics for calculating total wholesale and retail risk-weighted assets.
3.132 Counterparty credit risk of repo-style transactions, eligible margin loans, and OTC derivative contracts.
3.133 Cleared transactions.
3.134 Guarantees and credit derivatives: PD substitution and LGD adjustment approaches.
3.135 Guarantees and credit derivatives: Double default treatment.
3.136 Unsettled transactions.
3.137–3.140 [Reserved]

RISK-WEIGHTED ASSETS FOR SECURITIZATION EXPOSURES

3.141 Operational criteria for recognizing the transfer of risk.
3.142 Risk-weighted assets for securitization exposures.
3.143 Supervisory formula approach (SFA).
3.144 Simplified supervisory formula approach (SSFA).
3.145 Recognition of credit risk mitigants for securitization exposures.
3.146–3.150 [Reserved]

RISK-WEIGHTED ASSETS FOR EQUITY EXPOSURES

3.151 Introduction and exposure measurement.
3.152 Simple risk weight approach (SRWA).
3.153 Internal models approach (IMA).
3.154 Equity exposures to investment funds.
3.155 Equity derivative contracts.
3.156–3.160 [Reserved]

RISK-WEIGHTED ASSETS FOR OPERATIONAL RISK

3.161 Qualification requirements for incorporation of operational risk mitigants.
3.162 Mechanics of risk-weighted asset calculation.
3.163–3.170 [Reserved]

DISCLOSURES

3.171 Purpose and scope.
3.172 Disclosure requirements.
3.173 Disclosures by certain advanced approaches national banks and Federal savings associations.
3.174–3.200 [Reserved]

Subpart F—Risk-Weighted Assets—Market Risk

3.201 Purpose, applicability, and reservation of authority.
3.202 Definitions.
3.203 Requirements for application of this subpart F.
3.204 Measure for market risk.
3.205 VaR-based measure.
3.206 Stressed VaR-based measure.
3.207 Specific risk.
3.208 Incremental risk.
3.209 Comprehensive risk.
3.210 Standardized measurement method for specific risk.
3.211 Simplified supervisory formula approach (SSFA).
3.212 Market risk disclosures.
3.213–3.299 [Reserved]

Subpart G—Transition Provisions

3.300 Transitions.

Subpart H—Establishment of Minimum Capital Ratios for an Individual Bank or Individual Federal Savings Association

3.401 Purpose and scope.
3.402 Applicability.
3.403 Standards for determination of appropriate individual minimum capital ratios.
3.404 Procedures.
3.405 Relation to other actions.

Subpart I—Enforcement

3.501 Remedies.

Subpart J—Issuance of a Directive

3.601 Purpose and scope.
3.602 Notice of intent to issue a directive.
3.603 Response to notice.
3.604 Decision.
3.605 Issuance of a directive.
3.606 Change in circumstances.
3.607 Relation to other administrative actions.

Subpart K—Interpretations

3.701 Capital and surplus.

APPENDIX A TO PART 3—RISK-BASED CAPITAL GUIDELINES

APPENDIX B TO PART 3— RISK-BASED CAPITAL GUIDELINES; MARKET RISK

AUTHORITY: 12 U.S.C. 93a, 161, 1462, 1462a, 1463, 1464, 1818, 1828(n), 1828 note, 1831n note, 1835, 3907, 3909, and 5412(b)(2)(B).

SOURCE: 50 FR 10216, Mar. 14, 1985, unless otherwise noted.

Subpart A—General Provisions

SOURCE: 78 FR 62157, 62273, Oct. 11, 2013, unless otherwise noted.

§ 3.1 Purpose, applicability, reservations of authority, and timing.

(a) *Purpose.* This part establishes minimum capital requirements and overall capital adequacy standards for national banks or Federal savings associations. This part includes methodologies for calculating minimum capital requirements, public disclosure requirements related to the capital requirements, and transition provisions for the application of this part.

(b) *Limitation of authority.* Nothing in this part shall be read to limit the authority of the OCC to take action under other provisions of law, including action to address unsafe or unsound practices or conditions, deficient capital levels, or violations of law or regulation, under section 8 of the Federal Deposit Insurance Act.

(c) *Applicability.* Subject to the requirements in paragraphs (d) and (f) of this section:

(1) *Minimum capital requirements and overall capital adequacy standards.* Each national bank or Federal savings association must calculate its minimum capital requirements and meet the overall capital adequacy standards in subpart B of this part.

(2) *Regulatory capital.* Each national bank or Federal savings association must calculate its regulatory capital in accordance with subpart C of this part.

(3) *Risk-weighted assets.* (i) Each national bank or Federal savings association must use the methodologies in subpart D of this part (and subpart F of this part for a market risk national bank or Federal savings association) to calculate standardized total risk-weighted assets.

(ii) Each advanced approaches national bank or Federal savings association must use the methodologies in subpart E (and subpart F of this part for a market risk national bank or Federal savings association) to calculate advanced approaches total risk-weighted assets.

(4) *Disclosures.* (i) Except for an advanced approaches national bank or Federal savings association that is making public disclosures pursuant to the requirements in subpart E of this part, each national bank or Federal savings association with total consolidated assets of $50 billion or more must make the public disclosures described in subpart D of this part.

(ii) Each market risk national bank or Federal savings association must make the public disclosures described in subpart F of this part.

(iii) Each advanced approaches national bank or Federal savings association must make the public disclosures described in subpart E of this part.

(d) *Reservation of authority*—(1) *Additional capital in the aggregate.* The OCC may require a national bank or Federal savings association to hold an amount of regulatory capital greater than otherwise required under this part if the OCC determines that the national bank's or Federal savings association's capital requirements under this part are not commensurate with the national bank's or Federal savings association's credit, market, operational, or other risks.

(2) *Regulatory capital elements.* (i) If the OCC determines that a particular common equity tier 1, additional tier 1, or tier 2 capital element has characteristics or terms that diminish its ability to absorb losses, or otherwise present safety and soundness concerns, the OCC may require the national bank or Federal savings association to exclude all or a portion of such element from common equity tier 1 capital, additional tier 1 capital, or tier 2 capital, as appropriate.

(ii) Notwithstanding the criteria for regulatory capital instruments set forth in subpart C of this part, the OCC may find that a capital element may be included in a national bank's or Federal savings association's common equity tier 1 capital, additional tier 1 capital, or tier 2 capital on a permanent or temporary basis consistent with the loss absorption capacity of the element and in accordance with § 3.20(e).

(3) *Risk-weighted asset amounts.* If the OCC determines that the risk-weighted asset amount calculated under this part by the national bank or Federal savings association for one or more exposures is not commensurate with the risks associated with those exposures, the OCC may require the national bank or Federal savings association to assign a different risk-weighted asset amount to the exposure(s) or to deduct the amount of the exposure(s) from its regulatory capital.

(4) *Total leverage.* If the OCC determines that the total leverage exposure, or the amount reflected in the national bank's or Federal savings association's reported average total consolidated assets, for an on- or off-balance sheet exposure calculated by a national bank or Federal savings association under § 3.10 is inappropriate for the exposure(s) or the circumstances of the national bank or Federal savings association, the OCC may require the national bank or Federal savings association to adjust this exposure amount in the numerator and the denominator for purposes of the leverage ratio calculations.

(5) *Consolidation of certain exposures.* The OCC may determine that the risk-based capital treatment for an exposure or the treatment provided to an entity that is not consolidated on the national bank's or Federal savings association's balance sheet is not commensurate with the risk of the exposure and the relationship of the national bank or Federal savings association to the entity. Upon making this determination, the OCC may require the national bank or Federal savings association to treat the exposure or entity as if it were consolidated on the balance sheet of the national bank or Federal savings association for purposes of determining the national bank's or Federal savings association's risk-based capital requirements and calculating the national bank's or Federal savings association's risk-based capital ratios accordingly. The OCC will look to the substance of, and risk associated with, the transaction, as well as other relevant factors the OCC deems appropriate in determining whether to require such treatment.

(6) *Other reservation of authority.* With respect to any deduction or limitation required under this part, the OCC may require a different deduction or limitation, provided that such alternative deduction or limitation is commensurate with the national bank's or Federal savings association's risk and consistent with safety and soundness.

(e) *Notice and response procedures.* In making a determination under this section, the OCC will apply notice and response procedures in the same manner as the notice and response procedures in § 3.404.

(f) *Timing.* (1) Subject to the transition provisions in subpart G of this part, an advanced approaches national bank or Federal savings association that is not a savings and loan holding company must:

(i) Except as described in paragraph (f)(1)(ii) of this section, beginning on January 1, 2014, calculate advanced approaches total risk-weighted assets in accordance with subpart E and, if applicable, subpart F of this part and, beginning on January 1, 2015, calculate standardized total risk-weighted assets in accordance with subpart D and, if applicable, subpart F of this part;

(ii) From January 1, 2014 to December 31, 2014:

(A) Calculate risk-weighted assets in accordance with the general risk-based capital rules under appendix A to this part and, if applicable, subpart F of this part (national banks), or 12 CFR part 167 and, if applicable, subpart F of this part (Federal savings associations)[1] and substitute such risk-weighted assets for standardized total risk-weighted assets for purposes of §3.10;

(B) If applicable, calculate general market risk equivalent assets in accordance with appendix B to this part, section 4(a)(3) (national banks) and substitute such general market risk equivalent assets for standardized market risk-weighted assets for purposes of §3.20(d)(3); and

(C) Substitute the corresponding provision or provisions of appendix A to this part, and, if applicable, appendix B to this part (national banks), or 12 CFR part 167 (Federal savings associations) for any reference to subpart D of this part in: §3.121(c); §3.124(a) and (b); §3.144(b); §3.154(c) and (d); §3.202(b) (definition of covered position in paragraph (b)(3)(iv)); and §3.211(b);[2]

(iii) Beginning on January 1, 2014, calculate and maintain minimum capital ratios in accordance with subparts A, B, and C of this part, provided, however, that such national bank or Federal savings association must:

(A) From January 1, 2014 to December 31, 2014, maintain a minimum common equity tier 1 capital ratio of 4 percent, a minimum tier 1 capital ratio of 5.5 percent, a minimum total capital ratio of 8 percent, and a minimum leverage ratio of 4 percent; and

(B) From January 1, 2015 to December 31, 2017, an advanced approaches national bank or Federal savings association:

(*1*) Is not required to maintain a supplementary leverage ratio; and

(*2*) Must calculate a supplementary leverage ratio in accordance with §3.10(c), and must report the calculated supplementary leverage ratio on any applicable regulatory reports.

(2) Subject to the transition provisions in subpart G of this part, a national bank or Federal savings association that is not an advanced approaches national bank or Federal savings association or a savings and loan holding company that is an advanced approaches national bank or Federal savings association must:

(i) Beginning on January 1, 2015, calculate standardized total risk-weighted assets in accordance with subpart D, and if applicable, subpart F of this part; and

(ii) Beginning on January 1, 2015, calculate and maintain minimum capital ratios in accordance with subparts A, B and C of this part, provided, however, that from January 1, 2015 to December 31, 2017, a savings and loan holding company that is an advanced approaches national bank or Federal savings association:

(A) Is not required to maintain a supplementary leverage ratio; and

(B) Must calculate a supplementary leverage ratio in accordance with §3.10(c), and must report the calculated supplementary leverage ratio on any applicable regulatory reports.

---

[1] For the purpose of calculating its general risk-based capital ratios from January 1, 2014 to December 31, 2014, an advanced approaches national bank or Federal savings association shall adjust, as appropriate, its risk-weighted asset measure (as that amount is calculated under appendix A to this part, Sec. 3 and, if applicable, subpart F of this part (national banks), or 12 CFR part 167 and, if applicable, subpart F of this part (Federal savings associations) in the general risk-based capital rules) by excluding those assets that are deducted from its regulatory capital under §3.22.

[2] In addition, for purposes of §3.201(c)(3), from January 1, 2014 to December 31, 2014, for any circumstance in which the OCC may require a national bank or Federal savings association to calculate risk-based capital requirements for specific positions or portfolios under subpart D of this part, the OCC will instead require the national bank or Federal savings association to make such calculations according to appendix A to this part and, if applicable, subpart F of this part (national banks), or 12 CFR part 167 and, if applicable, subpart F of this part (Federal savings associations).

(3) Beginning on January 1, 2016, and subject to the transition provisions in subpart G of this part, a national bank or Federal savings association is subject to limitations on distributions and discretionary bonus payments with respect to its capital conservation buffer and any applicable countercyclical capital buffer amount, in accordance with subpart B of this part.

(4) No national bank or Federal savings association that is not an advanced approaches bank or advanced approaches savings association is subject to this part 3 until January 1, 2015.

[78 FR 62157, 62273, Oct. 11, 2013, as amended at 79 FR 57740, Sept. 26, 2014]

§ 3.2 Definitions.

As used in this part:

Additional tier 1 capital is defined in § 3.20(c).

Advanced approaches national bank or Federal savings association means a national bank or Federal savings association that is described in § 3.100(b)(1).

Advanced approaches total risk-weighted assets means:

(1) The sum of:

(i) Credit-risk-weighted assets;

(ii) Credit valuation adjustment (CVA) risk-weighted assets;

(iii) Risk-weighted assets for operational risk; and

(iv) For a market risk national bank or Federal savings association only, advanced market risk-weighted assets; minus

(2) Excess eligible credit reserves not included in the national bank's or Federal savings association's tier 2 capital.

Advanced market risk-weighted assets means the advanced measure for market risk calculated under § 3.204 multiplied by 12.5.

Affiliate with respect to a company, means any company that controls, is controlled by, or is under common control with, the company.

Allocated transfer risk reserves means reserves that have been established in accordance with section 905(a) of the International Lending Supervision Act, against certain assets whose value U.S. supervisory authorities have found to be significantly impaired by protracted transfer risk problems.

Allowances for loan and lease losses (ALLL) means valuation allowances that have been established through a charge against earnings to cover estimated credit losses on loans, lease financing receivables or other extensions of credit as determined in accordance with GAAP. ALLL excludes "allocated transfer risk reserves." For purposes of this part, ALLL includes allowances that have been established through a charge against earnings to cover estimated credit losses associated with off-balance sheet credit exposures as determined in accordance with GAAP.

Asset-backed commercial paper (ABCP) program means a program established primarily for the purpose of issuing commercial paper that is investment grade and backed by underlying exposures held in a bankruptcy-remote special purpose entity (SPE).

Asset-backed commercial paper (ABCP) program sponsor means a national bank or Federal savings association that:

(1) Establishes an ABCP program;

(2) Approves the sellers permitted to participate in an ABCP program;

(3) Approves the exposures to be purchased by an ABCP program; or

(4) Administers the ABCP program by monitoring the underlying exposures, underwriting or otherwise arranging for the placement of debt or other obligations issued by the program, compiling monthly reports, or ensuring compliance with the program documents and with the program's credit and investment policy.

Bank holding company means a bank holding company as defined in section 2 of the Bank Holding Company Act.

Bank Holding Company Act means the Bank Holding Company Act of 1956, as amended (12 U.S.C. 1841 *et seq.*).

Bankruptcy remote means, with respect to an entity or asset, that the entity or asset would be excluded from an insolvent entity's estate in receivership, insolvency, liquidation, or similar proceeding.

Call Report means Consolidated Reports of Condition and Income.

Carrying value means, with respect to an asset, the value of the asset on the balance sheet of the national bank or Federal savings association, determined in accordance with GAAP.

Central counterparty (CCP) means a counterparty (for example, a clearing house) that facilitates trades between counterparties in one or more financial markets by either guaranteeing trades or novating contracts.

CFTC means the U.S. Commodity Futures Trading Commission.

Clean-up call means a contractual provision that permits an originating national bank or Federal savings association or servicer to call securitization exposures before their stated maturity or call date.

Cleared transaction means an exposure associated with an outstanding derivative contract or repo-style transaction that a national bank or Federal savings association or clearing member has entered into with a central counterparty (that is, a transaction that a central counterparty has accepted).

(1) The following transactions are cleared transactions:

(i) A transaction between a CCP and a national bank or Federal savings association that is a clearing member of the CCP where the national bank or Federal savings association enters into the transaction with the CCP for the national bank's or Federal savings association's own account;

(ii) A transaction between a CCP and a national bank or Federal savings association that is a clearing member of the CCP where the national bank or Federal savings association is acting as a financial intermediary on behalf of a clearing member client and the transaction offsets another transaction that satisfies the requirements set forth in §3.3(a);

(iii) A transaction between a clearing member client national bank or Federal savings association and a clearing member where the clearing member acts as a financial intermediary on behalf of the clearing member client and enters into an offsetting transaction with a CCP, provided that the requirements set forth in §3.3(a) are met; or

(iv) A transaction between a clearing member client national bank or Federal savings association and a CCP where a clearing member guarantees the performance of the clearing member client national bank or Federal savings association to the CCP and the transaction meets the requirements of §3.3(a)(2) and (3).

(2) The exposure of a national bank or Federal savings association that is a clearing member to its clearing member client is not a cleared transaction where the national bank or Federal savings association is either acting as a financial intermediary and enters into an offsetting transaction with a CCP or where the national bank or Federal savings association provides a guarantee to the CCP on the performance of the client.[3]

Clearing member means a member of, or direct participant in, a CCP that is entitled to enter into transactions with the CCP.

Clearing member client means a party to a cleared transaction associated with a CCP in which a clearing member acts either as a financial intermediary with respect to the party or guarantees the performance of the party to the CCP.

Collateral agreement means a legal contract that specifies the time when, and circumstances under which, a counterparty is required to pledge collateral to a national bank or Federal savings association for a single financial contract or for all financial contracts in a netting set and confers upon the national bank or Federal savings association a perfected, first-priority security interest (notwithstanding the prior security interest of any custodial agent), or the legal equivalent thereof, in the collateral posted by the counterparty under the agreement. This security interest must provide the national bank or Federal savings association with a right to close-out the financial positions and liquidate the collateral upon an event of default of, or failure to perform by, the counterparty under the collateral agreement. A contract would not satisfy this requirement if the national bank's or Federal savings association's exercise of rights

[3] For the standardized approach treatment of these exposures, see §3.34(e) (OTC derivative contracts) or §3.37(c) (repo-style transactions). For the advanced approaches treatment of these exposures, see §§3.132(c)(8) and (d) (OTC derivative contracts) or §§3.132(b) and 3.132(d) (repo-style transactions) and for calculation of the margin period of risk, see §§3.132(d)(5)(iii)(C) (OTC derivative contracts) and 3.132(d)(5)(iii)(A) (repo-style transactions).

under the agreement may be stayed or avoided:

(1) Under applicable law in the relevant jurisdictions, other than:

(i) In receivership, conservatorship, or resolution under the Federal Deposit Insurance Act, Title II of the Dodd-Frank Act, or under any similar insolvency law applicable to GSEs, or laws of foreign jurisdictions that are substantially similar[4] to the U.S. laws referenced in this paragraph (1)(i) in order to facilitate the orderly resolution of the defaulting counterparty;

(ii) Where the agreement is subject by its terms to any of the laws referenced in paragraph (1)(i) of this definition; or

(2) Other than to the extent necessary for the counterparty to comply with the requirements of part 47, subpart I of part 252, and part 382 of this title 12, as applicable.

Commitment means any legally binding arrangement that obligates a national bank or Federal savings association to extend credit or to purchase assets.

Commodity derivative contract means a commodity-linked swap, purchased commodity-linked option, forward commodity-linked contract, or any other instrument linked to commodities that gives rise to similar counterparty credit risks.

Commodity Exchange Act means the Commodity Exchange Act of 1936 (7 U.S.C. 1 *et seq.*)

Common equity tier 1 capital is defined in § 3.20(b).

Common equity tier 1 minority interest means the common equity tier 1 capital of a depository institution or foreign bank that is:

(1) A consolidated subsidiary of a national bank or Federal savings association; and

(2) Not owned by the national bank or Federal savings association.

Company means a corporation, partnership, limited liability company, depository institution, business trust, special purpose entity, association, or similar organization.

[4] The OCC expects to evaluate jointly with the Board and FDIC whether foreign special resolution regimes meet the requirements of this paragraph.

Control. A person or company *controls* a company if it:

(1) Owns, controls, or holds with power to vote 25 percent or more of a class of voting securities of the company; or

(2) Consolidates the company for financial reporting purposes.

Core capital means tier 1 capital, as calculated in accordance with subpart B of this part.

Corporate exposure means an exposure to a company that is not:

(1) An exposure to a sovereign, the Bank for International Settlements, the European Central Bank, the European Commission, the International Monetary Fund, a multi-lateral development bank (MDB), a depository institution, a foreign bank, a credit union, or a public sector entity (PSE);

(2) An exposure to a GSE;

(3) A residential mortgage exposure;

(4) A pre-sold construction loan;

(5) A statutory multifamily mortgage;

(6) A high volatility commercial real estate (HVCRE) exposure;

(7) A cleared transaction;

(8) A default fund contribution;

(9) A securitization exposure;

(10) An equity exposure; or

(11) An unsettled transaction.

Country risk classification (CRC) with respect to a sovereign, means the most recent consensus CRC published by the Organization for Economic Cooperation and Development (OECD) as of December 31st of the prior calendar year that provides a view of the likelihood that the sovereign will service its external debt.

Covered savings and loan holding company means a top-tier savings and loan holding company other than:

(1) A top-tier savings and loan holding company that is:

(i) A grandfathered unitary savings and loan holding company as defined in section 10(c)(9)(A) of HOLA; and

(ii) As of June 30 of the previous calendar year, derived 50 percent or more of its total consolidated assets or 50 percent of its total revenues on an enterprise-wide basis (as calculated under GAAP) from activities that are not financial in nature under section 4(k) of the Bank Holding Company Act (12 U.S.C. 1842(k));

(2) A top-tier savings and loan holding company that is an insurance underwriting company; or

(3)(i) A top-tier savings and loan holding company that, as of June 30 of the previous calendar year, held 25 percent or more of its total consolidated assets in subsidiaries that are insurance underwriting companies (other than assets associated with insurance for credit risk); and

(ii) For purposes of paragraph (3)(i) of this definition, the company must calculate its total consolidated assets in accordance with GAAP, or if the company does not calculate its total consolidated assets under GAAP for any regulatory purpose (including compliance with applicable securities laws), the company may estimate its total consolidated assets, subject to review and adjustment by the Board.

Credit derivative means a financial contract executed under standard industry credit derivative documentation that allows one party (the protection purchaser) to transfer the credit risk of one or more exposures (reference exposure(s)) to another party (the protection provider) for a certain period of time.

Credit-enhancing interest-only strip (CEIO) means an on-balance sheet asset that, in form or in substance:

(1) Represents a contractual right to receive some or all of the interest and no more than a minimal amount of principal due on the underlying exposures of a securitization; and

(2) Exposes the holder of the CEIO to credit risk directly or indirectly associated with the underlying exposures that exceeds a pro rata share of the holder's claim on the underlying exposures, whether through subordination provisions or other credit-enhancement techniques.

Credit-enhancing representations and warranties means representations and warranties that are made or assumed in connection with a transfer of underlying exposures (including loan servicing assets) and that obligate a national bank or Federal savings association to protect another party from losses arising from the credit risk of the underlying exposures. Credit-enhancing representations and warranties include provisions to protect a party from losses resulting from the default or nonperformance of the counterparties of the underlying exposures or from an insufficiency in the value of the collateral backing the underlying exposures. Credit-enhancing representations and warranties do not include:

(1) Early default clauses and similar warranties that permit the return of, or premium refund clauses covering, 1–4 family residential first mortgage loans that qualify for a 50 percent risk weight for a period not to exceed 120 days from the date of transfer. These warranties may cover only those loans that were originated within 1 year of the date of transfer;

(2) Premium refund clauses that cover assets guaranteed, in whole or in part, by the U.S. Government, a U.S. Government agency or a GSE, provided the premium refund clauses are for a period not to exceed 120 days from the date of transfer; or

(3) Warranties that permit the return of underlying exposures in instances of misrepresentation, fraud, or incomplete documentation.

Credit risk mitigant means collateral, a credit derivative, or a guarantee.

Credit-risk-weighted assets means 1.06 multiplied by the sum of:

(1) Total wholesale and retail risk-weighted assets as calculated under §3.131;

(2) Risk-weighted assets for securitization exposures as calculated under §3.142; and

(3) Risk-weighted assets for equity exposures as calculated under §3.151.

Credit union means an insured credit union as defined under the Federal Credit Union Act (12 U.S.C. 1752 *et seq.*).

Current exposure means, with respect to a netting set, the larger of zero or the fair value of a transaction or portfolio of transactions within the netting set that would be lost upon default of the counterparty, assuming no recovery on the value of the transactions. Current exposure is also called replacement cost.

Current exposure methodology means the method of calculating the exposure amount for over-the-counter derivative contracts in §3.34(a) and exposure at default (EAD) in §3.132(c)(5) or (6), as applicable.

Custodian means a financial institution that has legal custody of collateral provided to a CCP.

Default fund contribution means the funds contributed or commitments made by a clearing member to a CCP's mutualized loss sharing arrangement.

Depository institution means a depository institution as defined in section 3 of the Federal Deposit Insurance Act.

Depository institution holding company means a bank holding company or savings and loan holding company.

Derivative contract means a financial contract whose value is derived from the values of one or more underlying assets, reference rates, or indices of asset values or reference rates. Derivative contracts include interest rate derivative contracts, exchange rate derivative contracts, equity derivative contracts, commodity derivative contracts, credit derivative contracts, and any other instrument that poses similar counterparty credit risks. Derivative contracts also include unsettled securities, commodities, and foreign exchange transactions with a contractual settlement or delivery lag that is longer than the lesser of the market standard for the particular instrument or five business days.

Discretionary bonus payment means a payment made to an executive officer of a national bank or Federal savings association, where:

(1) The national bank or Federal savings association retains discretion as to whether to make, and the amount of, the payment until the payment is awarded to the executive officer;

(2) The amount paid is determined by the national bank or Federal savings association without prior promise to, or agreement with, the executive officer; and

(3) The executive officer has no contractual right, whether express or implied, to the bonus payment.

Distribution means:

(1) A reduction of tier 1 capital through the repurchase of a tier 1 capital instrument or by other means, except when a national bank or Federal savings association, within the same quarter when the repurchase is announced, fully replaces a tier 1 capital instrument it has repurchased by issuing another capital instrument that meets the eligibility criteria for:

(i) A common equity tier 1 capital instrument if the instrument being repurchased was part of the national bank's or Federal savings association's common equity tier 1 capital, or

(ii) A common equity tier 1 or additional tier 1 capital instrument if the instrument being repurchased was part of the national bank's or Federal savings association's tier 1 capital;

(2) A reduction of tier 2 capital through the repurchase, or redemption prior to maturity, of a tier 2 capital instrument or by other means, except when a national bank or Federal savings association, within the same quarter when the repurchase or redemption is announced, fully replaces a tier 2 capital instrument it has repurchased by issuing another capital instrument that meets the eligibility criteria for a tier 1 or tier 2 capital instrument;

(3) A dividend declaration or payment on any tier 1 capital instrument;

(4) A dividend declaration or interest payment on any tier 2 capital instrument if the national bank or Federal savings association has full discretion to permanently or temporarily suspend such payments without triggering an event of default; or

(5) Any similar transaction that the OCC determines to be in substance a distribution of capital.

Dodd-Frank Act means the Dodd-Frank Wall Street Reform and Consumer Protection Act of 2010 (Pub. L. 111–203, 124 Stat. 1376).

Early amortization provision means a provision in the documentation governing a securitization that, when triggered, causes investors in the securitization exposures to be repaid before the original stated maturity of the securitization exposures, unless the provision:

(1) Is triggered solely by events not directly related to the performance of the underlying exposures or the originating national bank or Federal savings association (such as material changes in tax laws or regulations); or

(2) Leaves investors fully exposed to future draws by borrowers on the underlying exposures even after the provision is triggered.

Effective notional amount means for an eligible guarantee or eligible credit derivative, the lesser of the contractual notional amount of the credit risk mitigant and the exposure amount (or EAD for purposes of subpart E of this part) of the hedged exposure, multiplied by the percentage coverage of the credit risk mitigant.

Eligible ABCP liquidity facility means a liquidity facility supporting ABCP, in form or in substance, that is subject to an asset quality test at the time of draw that precludes funding against assets that are 90 days or more past due or in default. Notwithstanding the preceding sentence, a liquidity facility is an eligible ABCP liquidity facility if the assets or exposures funded under the liquidity facility that do not meet the eligibility requirements are guaranteed by a sovereign that qualifies for a 20 percent risk weight or lower.

Eligible clean-up call means a clean-up call that:

(1) Is exercisable solely at the discretion of the originating national bank or Federal savings association or servicer;

(2) Is not structured to avoid allocating losses to securitization exposures held by investors or otherwise structured to provide credit enhancement to the securitization; and

(3)(i) For a traditional securitization, is only exercisable when 10 percent or less of the principal amount of the underlying exposures or securitization exposures (determined as of the inception of the securitization) is outstanding; or

(ii) For a synthetic securitization, is only exercisable when 10 percent or less of the principal amount of the reference portfolio of underlying exposures (determined as of the inception of the securitization) is outstanding.

Eligible credit derivative means a credit derivative in the form of a credit default swap, n^{th}-to-default swap, total return swap, or any other form of credit derivative approved by the OCC, provided that:

(1) The contract meets the requirements of an eligible guarantee and has been confirmed by the protection purchaser and the protection provider;

(2) Any assignment of the contract has been confirmed by all relevant parties;

(3) If the credit derivative is a credit default swap or n^{th}-to-default swap, the contract includes the following credit events:

(i) Failure to pay any amount due under the terms of the reference exposure, subject to any applicable minimal payment threshold that is consistent with standard market practice and with a grace period that is closely in line with the grace period of the reference exposure; and

(ii) Receivership, insolvency, liquidation, conservatorship or inability of the reference exposure issuer to pay its debts, or its failure or admission in writing of its inability generally to pay its debts as they become due, and similar events;

(4) The terms and conditions dictating the manner in which the contract is to be settled are incorporated into the contract;

(5) If the contract allows for cash settlement, the contract incorporates a robust valuation process to estimate loss reliably and specifies a reasonable period for obtaining post-credit event valuations of the reference exposure;

(6) If the contract requires the protection purchaser to transfer an exposure to the protection provider at settlement, the terms of at least one of the exposures that is permitted to be transferred under the contract provide that any required consent to transfer may not be unreasonably withheld;

(7) If the credit derivative is a credit default swap or n^{th}-to-default swap, the contract clearly identifies the parties responsible for determining whether a credit event has occurred, specifies that this determination is not the sole responsibility of the protection provider, and gives the protection purchaser the right to notify the protection provider of the occurrence of a credit event; and

(8) If the credit derivative is a total return swap and the national bank or Federal savings association records net payments received on the swap as net income, the national bank or Federal savings association records offsetting deterioration in the value of the hedged exposure (either through reductions in fair value or by an addition to reserves).

Eligible credit reserves means all general allowances that have been established through a charge against earnings to cover estimated credit losses associated with on- or off-balance sheet wholesale and retail exposures, including the ALLL associated with such exposures, but excluding allocated transfer risk reserves established pursuant to 12 U.S.C. 3904 and other specific reserves created against recognized losses.

Eligible guarantee means a guarantee that:

(1) Is written;

(2) Is either:

(i) Unconditional; or

(ii) A contingent obligation of the U.S. government or its agencies, the enforceability of which is dependent upon some affirmative action on the part of the beneficiary of the guarantee or a third party (for example, meeting servicing requirements);

(3) Covers all or a pro rata portion of all contractual payments of the obligated party on the reference exposure;

(4) Gives the beneficiary a direct claim against the protection provider;

(5) Is not unilaterally cancelable by the protection provider for reasons other than the breach of the contract by the beneficiary;

(6) Except for a guarantee by a sovereign, is legally enforceable against the protection provider in a jurisdiction where the protection provider has sufficient assets against which a judgment may be attached and enforced;

(7) Requires the protection provider to make payment to the beneficiary on the occurrence of a default (as defined in the guarantee) of the obligated party on the reference exposure in a timely manner without the beneficiary first having to take legal actions to pursue the obligor for payment;

(8) Does not increase the beneficiary's cost of credit protection on the guarantee in response to deterioration in the credit quality of the reference exposure;

(9) Is not provided by an affiliate of the national bank or Federal savings association, unless the affiliate is an insured depository institution, foreign bank, securities broker or dealer, or insurance company that:

(i) Does not control the national bank or Federal savings association; and

(ii) Is subject to consolidated supervision and regulation comparable to that imposed on depository institutions, U.S. securities broker-dealers, or U.S. insurance companies (as the case may be); and

(10) For purposes of §§3.141 through 3.145 and subpart D of this part, is provided by an eligible guarantor.

Eligible guarantor means:

(1) A sovereign, the Bank for International Settlements, the International Monetary Fund, the European Central Bank, the European Commission, a Federal Home Loan Bank, Federal Agricultural Mortgage Corporation (Farmer Mac), a multilateral development bank (MDB), a depository institution, a bank holding company, a savings and loan holding company, a credit union, a foreign bank, or a qualifying central counterparty; or

(2) An entity (other than a special purpose entity):

(i) That at the time the guarantee is issued or anytime thereafter, has issued and outstanding an unsecured debt security without credit enhancement that is investment grade;

(ii) Whose creditworthiness is not positively correlated with the credit risk of the exposures for which it has provided guarantees; and

(iii) That is not an insurance company engaged predominately in the business of providing credit protection (such as a monoline bond insurer or reinsurer).

Eligible margin loan means:

(1) An extension of credit where:

(i) The extension of credit is collateralized exclusively by liquid and readily marketable debt or equity securities, or gold;

(ii) The collateral is marked-to-fair value daily, and the transaction is subject to daily margin maintenance requirements; and

(iii) The extension of credit is conducted under an agreement that provides the national bank or Federal savings association the right to accelerate and terminate the extension of credit and to liquidate or set-off collateral promptly upon an event of default, including upon an event of receivership, insolvency, liquidation, conservatorship, or similar proceeding, of the counterparty, provided that, in any such case:

(A) Any exercise of rights under the agreement will not be stayed or avoided under applicable law in the relevant jurisdictions, other than in receivership, conservatorship, or resolution under the Federal Deposit Insurance Act, Title II of the Dodd-Frank Act, or under any similar insolvency law applicable to GSEs,[5] or laws of foreign jurisdictions that are substantially similar[6] to the U.S. laws referenced in this paragraph (1)(iii)(A) in order to facilitate the orderly resolution of the defaulting counterparty; and

(B) The agreement may limit the right to accelerate, terminate, and close-out on a net basis all transactions under the agreement and to liquidate or set-off collateral promptly upon an event of default of the counterparty to the extent necessary for the counterparty to comply with the requirements of part 47, subpart I of part 252, and part 382, of this title 12, as applicable.

(2) In order to recognize an exposure as an eligible margin loan for purposes of this subpart, a national bank or Federal savings association must comply with the requirements of §3.3(b) with respect to that exposure.

Eligible servicer cash advance facility means a servicer cash advance facility in which:

(1) The servicer is entitled to full reimbursement of advances, except that a servicer may be obligated to make non-reimbursable advances for a particular underlying exposure if any such advance is contractually limited to an insignificant amount of the outstanding principal balance of that exposure;

(2) The servicer's right to reimbursement is senior in right of payment to all other claims on the cash flows from the underlying exposures of the securitization; and

(3) The servicer has no legal obligation to, and does not make advances to the securitization if the servicer concludes the advances are unlikely to be repaid.

Employee stock ownership plan has the same meaning as in 29 CFR 2550.407d–6.

Equity derivative contract means an equity-linked swap, purchased equity-linked option, forward equity-linked contract, or any other instrument linked to equities that gives rise to similar counterparty credit risks.

Equity exposure means:

(1) A security or instrument (whether voting or non-voting) that represents a direct or an indirect ownership interest in, and is a residual claim on, the assets and income of a company, unless:

(i) The issuing company is consolidated with the national bank or Federal savings association under GAAP;

(ii) The national bank or Federal savings association is required to deduct the ownership interest from tier 1 or tier 2 capital under this part;

(iii) The ownership interest incorporates a payment or other similar obligation on the part of the issuing company (such as an obligation to make periodic payments); or

(iv) The ownership interest is a securitization exposure;

(2) A security or instrument that is mandatorily convertible into a security or instrument described in paragraph (1) of this definition;

(3) An option or warrant that is exercisable for a security or instrument described in paragraph (1) of this definition; or

(4) Any other security or instrument (other than a securitization exposure) to the extent the return on the security or instrument is based on the performance of a security or instrument described in paragraph (1) of this definition.

ERISA means the Employee Retirement Income and Security Act of 1974 (29 U.S.C. 1001 *et seq.*).

[5] This requirement is met where all transactions under the agreement are (i) executed under U.S. law and (ii) constitute "securities contracts" under section 555 of the Bankruptcy Code (11 U.S.C. 555), qualified financial contracts under section 11(e)(8) of the Federal Deposit Insurance Act, or netting contracts between or among financial institutions under sections 401–407 of the Federal Deposit Insurance Corporation Improvement Act or the Federal Reserve Board's Regulation EE (12 CFR part 231).

[6] The OCC expects to evaluate jointly with the Board and FDIC whether foreign special resolution regimes meet the requirements of this paragraph.

Exchange rate derivative contract means a cross-currency interest rate swap, forward foreign-exchange contract, currency option purchased, or any other instrument linked to exchange rates that gives rise to similar counterparty credit risks.

Executive officer means a person who holds the title or, without regard to title, salary, or compensation, performs the function of one or more of the following positions: President, chief executive officer, executive chairman, chief operating officer, chief financial officer, chief investment officer, chief legal officer, chief lending officer, chief risk officer, or head of a major business line, and other staff that the board of directors of the national bank or Federal savings association deems to have equivalent responsibility.

Expected credit loss (ECL) means:

(1) For a wholesale exposure to a non-defaulted obligor or segment of non-defaulted retail exposures that is carried at fair value with gains and losses flowing through earnings or that is classified as held-for-sale and is carried at the lower of cost or fair value with losses flowing through earnings, zero.

(2) For all other wholesale exposures to non-defaulted obligors or segments of non-defaulted retail exposures, the product of the probability of default (PD) times the loss given default (LGD) times the exposure at default (EAD) for the exposure or segment.

(3) For a wholesale exposure to a defaulted obligor or segment of defaulted retail exposures, the national bank's or Federal savings association's impairment estimate for allowance purposes for the exposure or segment.

(4) Total ECL is the sum of expected credit losses for all wholesale and retail exposures other than exposures for which the national bank or Federal savings association has applied the double default treatment in §3.135.

Exposure amount means:

(1) For the on-balance sheet component of an exposure (other than an available-for-sale or held-to-maturity security, if the national bank or Federal savings association has made an AOCI opt-out election (as defined in §3.22(b)(2)); an OTC derivative contract; a repo-style transaction or an eligible margin loan for which the national bank or Federal savings association determines the exposure amount under §3.37; a cleared transaction; a default fund contribution; or a securitization exposure), the national bank's or Federal savings association's carrying value of the exposure.

(2) For a security (that is not a securitization exposure, equity exposure, or preferred stock classified as an equity security under GAAP) classified as available-for-sale or held-to-maturity if the national bank or Federal savings association has made an AOCI opt-out election (as defined in §3.22(b)(2)), the national bank's or Federal savings association's carrying value (including net accrued but unpaid interest and fees) for the exposure less any net unrealized gains on the exposure and plus any net unrealized losses on the exposure.

(3) For available-for-sale preferred stock classified as an equity security under GAAP if the national bank or Federal savings association has made an AOCI opt-out election (as defined in §3.22(b)(2)), the national bank's or Federal savings association's carrying value of the exposure less any net unrealized gains on the exposure that are reflected in such carrying value but excluded from the national bank's or Federal savings association's regulatory capital components.

(4) For the off-balance sheet component of an exposure (other than an OTC derivative contract; a repo-style transaction or an eligible margin loan for which the national bank or Federal savings association calculates the exposure amount under §3.37; a cleared transaction; a default fund contribution; or a securitization exposure), the notional amount of the off-balance sheet component multiplied by the appropriate credit conversion factor (CCF) in §3.33.

(5) For an exposure that is an OTC derivative contract, the exposure amount determined under §3.34.

(6) For an exposure that is a cleared transaction, the exposure amount determined under §3.35.

(7) For an exposure that is an eligible margin loan or repo-style transaction for which the bank calculates the exposure amount as provided in §3.37, the

exposure amount determined under §3.37.

(8) For an exposure that is a securitization exposure, the exposure amount determined under §3.42.

Federal Deposit Insurance Act means the Federal Deposit Insurance Act (12 U.S.C. 1813).

Federal Deposit Insurance Corporation Improvement Act means the Federal Deposit Insurance Corporation Improvement Act of 1991 (12 U.S.C. 4401).

Financial collateral means collateral:

(1) In the form of:

(i) Cash on deposit with the national bank or Federal savings association (including cash held for the national bank or Federal savings association by a third-party custodian or trustee);

(ii) Gold bullion;

(iii) Long-term debt securities that are not resecuritization exposures and that are investment grade;

(iv) Short-term debt instruments that are not resecuritization exposures and that are investment grade;

(v) Equity securities that are publicly traded;

(vi) Convertible bonds that are publicly traded; or

(vii) Money market fund shares and other mutual fund shares if a price for the shares is publicly quoted daily; and

(2) In which the national bank or Federal savings association has a perfected, first-priority security interest or, outside of the United States, the legal equivalent thereof (with the exception of cash on deposit and notwithstanding the prior security interest of any custodial agent).

Federal savings association means an insured Federal savings association or an insured Federal savings bank chartered under section 5 of the Home Owners' Loan Act of 1933.

Financial institution means:

(1) A bank holding company; savings and loan holding company; nonbank financial institution supervised by the Board under Title I of the Dodd-Frank Act; depository institution; foreign bank; credit union; industrial loan company, industrial bank, or other similar institution described in section 2 of the Bank Holding Company Act; national association, state member bank, or state non-member bank that is not a depository institution; insurance company; securities holding company as defined in section 618 of the Dodd-Frank Act; broker or dealer registered with the SEC under section 15 of the Securities Exchange Act; futures commission merchant as defined in section 1a of the Commodity Exchange Act; swap dealer as defined in section 1a of the Commodity Exchange Act; or security-based swap dealer as defined in section 3 of the Securities Exchange Act;

(2) Any designated financial market utility, as defined in section 803 of the Dodd-Frank Act;

(3) Any entity not domiciled in the United States (or a political subdivision thereof) that is supervised and regulated in a manner similar to entities described in paragraphs (1) or (2) of this definition; or

(4) Any other company:

(i) Of which the national bank or Federal savings association owns:

(A) An investment in GAAP equity instruments of the company with an adjusted carrying value or exposure amount equal to or greater than $10 million; or

(B) More than 10 percent of the company's issued and outstanding common shares (or similar equity interest), and

(ii) Which is predominantly engaged in the following activities:

(A) Lending money, securities or other financial instruments, including servicing loans;

(B) Insuring, guaranteeing, indemnifying against loss, harm, damage, illness, disability, or death, or issuing annuities;

(C) Underwriting, dealing in, making a market in, or investing as principal in securities or other financial instruments; or

(D) Asset management activities (not including investment or financial advisory activities).

(5) For the purposes of this definition, a company is "predominantly engaged" in an activity or activities if:

(i) 85 percent or more of the total consolidated annual gross revenues (as determined in accordance with applicable accounting standards) of the company is either of the two most recent calendar years were derived, directly or indirectly, by the company on a consolidated basis from the activities; or

(ii) 85 percent or more of the company's consolidated total assets (as determined in accordance with applicable accounting standards) as of the end of either of the two most recent calendar years were related to the activities.

(6) Any other company that the OCC may determine is a financial institution based on activities similar in scope, nature, or operation to those of the entities included in paragraphs (1) through (4) of this definition.

(7) For purposes of this part, "financial institution" does not include the following entities:

(i) GSEs;

(ii) Small business investment companies, as defined in section 102 of the Small Business Investment Act of 1958 (15 U.S.C. 662);

(iii) Entities designated as Community Development Financial Institutions (CDFIs) under 12 U.S.C. 4701 *et seq.* and 12 CFR part 1805;

(iv) Entities registered with the SEC under the Investment Company Act of 1940 (15 U.S.C. 80a–1) or foreign equivalents thereof;

(v) Entities to the extent that the national bank's or Federal savings association's investment in such entities would qualify as a community development investment under section 24 (Eleventh) of the National Bank Act; and

(vi) An employee benefit plan as defined in paragraphs (3) and (32) of section 3 of ERISA, a "governmental plan" (as defined in 29 U.S.C. 1002(32)) that complies with the tax deferral qualification requirements provided in the Internal Revenue Code, or any similar employee benefit plan established under the laws of a foreign jurisdiction.

First-lien residential mortgage exposure means a residential mortgage exposure secured by a first lien.

Foreign bank means a foreign bank as defined in §211.2 of the Federal Reserve Board's Regulation K (12 CFR 211.2) (other than a depository institution).

Forward agreement means a legally binding contractual obligation to purchase assets with certain drawdown at a specified future date, not including commitments to make residential mortgage loans or forward foreign exchange contracts.

GAAP means generally accepted accounting principles as used in the United States.

Gain-on-sale means an increase in the equity capital of a national bank or Federal savings association (as reported on [Schedule RC of the Call Report or Schedule HC of the FR Y–9C]) resulting from a traditional securitization (other than an increase in equity capital resulting from the national bank's or Federal savings association's receipt of cash in connection with the securitization or reporting of a mortgage servicing asset on [Schedule RC of the Call Report or Schedule HC of the FRY–9C]).

General obligation means a bond or similar obligation that is backed by the full faith and credit of a public sector entity (PSE).

Government-sponsored enterprise (GSE) means an entity established or chartered by the U.S. government to serve public purposes specified by the U.S. Congress but whose debt obligations are not explicitly guaranteed by the full faith and credit of the U.S. government.

Guarantee means a financial guarantee, letter of credit, insurance, or other similar financial instrument (other than a credit derivative) that allows one party (beneficiary) to transfer the credit risk of one or more specific exposures (reference exposure) to another party (protection provider).

High volatility commercial real estate (HVCRE) exposure means a credit facility that, prior to conversion to permanent financing, finances or has financed the acquisition, development, or construction (ADC) of real property, unless the facility finances:

(1) One- to four-family residential properties;

(2) Real property that:

(i) Would qualify as an investment in community development under 12 U.S.C. 338a or 12 U.S.C. 24 (Eleventh), as applicable, or as a "qualified investment" under 12 CFR parts 25 (national banks) and 195 (Federal savings associations), and

(ii) Is not an ADC loan to any entity described in 12 CFR 25.12(g)(3) (national banks) and 12 CFR 195.12(g)(3) (Federal savings associations), unless it is otherwise described in paragraph (1), (2)(i), (3) or (4) of this definition;

(3) The purchase or development of agricultural land, which includes all land known to be used or usable for agricultural purposes (such as crop and livestock production), provided that the valuation of the agricultural land is based on its value for agricultural purposes and the valuation does not take into consideration any potential use of the land for non-agricultural commercial development or residential development; or

(4) Commercial real estate projects in which:

(i) The loan-to-value ratio is less than or equal to the applicable maximum supervisory loan-to-value ratio in the OCC's real estate lending standards at 12 CFR part 34, subpart D (national banks) and 12 CFR part 160, subparts A and B (Federal savings associations);

(ii) The borrower has contributed capital to the project in the form of cash or unencumbered readily marketable assets (or has paid development expenses out-of-pocket) of at least 15 percent of the real estate's appraised "as completed" value; and

(iii) The borrower contributed the amount of capital required by paragraph (4)(ii) of this definition before the national bank or Federal savings association advances funds under the credit facility, and the capital contributed by the borrower, or internally generated by the project, is contractually required to remain in the project throughout the life of the project. The life of a project concludes only when the credit facility is converted to permanent financing or is sold or paid in full. Permanent financing may be provided by the national bank or Federal savings association that provided the ADC facility as long as the permanent financing is subject to the national bank's or Federal savings association's underwriting criteria for long-term mortgage loans.

Home country means the country where an entity is incorporated, chartered, or similarly established.

Indirect exposure means an exposure that arises from the national bank's or Federal savings association's investment in an investment fund which holds an investment in the national bank's or Federal savings association's own capital instrument or an investment in the capital of an unconsolidated financial institution.

Insurance company means an insurance company as defined in section 201 of the Dodd-Frank Act (12 U.S.C. 5381).

Insurance underwriting company means an insurance company as defined in section 201 of the Dodd-Frank Act (12 U.S.C. 5381) that engages in insurance underwriting activities.

Insured depository institution means an insured depository institution as defined in section 3 of the Federal Deposit Insurance Act.

Interest rate derivative contract means a single-currency interest rate swap, basis swap, forward rate agreement, purchased interest rate option, when-issued securities, or any other instrument linked to interest rates that gives rise to similar counterparty credit risks.

International Lending Supervision Act means the International Lending Supervision Act of 1983 (12 U.S.C. 3907).

Investing bank means, with respect to a securitization, a national bank or Federal savings association that assumes the credit risk of a securitization exposure (other than an originating national bank or Federal savings association of the securitization). In the typical synthetic securitization, the investing national bank or Federal savings association sells credit protection on a pool of underlying exposures to the originating national bank or Federal savings association.

Investment fund means a company:

(1) Where all or substantially all of the assets of the company are financial assets; and

(2) That has no material liabilities.

Investment grade means that the entity to which the national bank or Federal savings association is exposed through a loan or security, or the reference entity with respect to a credit derivative, has adequate capacity to meet financial commitments for the projected life of the asset or exposure. Such an entity or reference entity has adequate capacity to meet financial commitments if the risk of its default is low and the full and timely repayment of principal and interest is expected.

Investment in the capital of an unconsolidated financial institution means a net long position calculated in accordance with §3.22(h) in an instrument that is recognized as capital for regulatory purposes by the primary supervisor of an unconsolidated regulated financial institution and is an instrument that is part of the GAAP equity of an unconsolidated unregulated financial institution, including direct, indirect, and synthetic exposures to capital instruments, excluding underwriting positions held by the national bank or Federal savings association for five or fewer business days.

Investment in the national bank's or Federal savings association's own capital instrument means a net long position calculated in accordance with §3.22(h) in the national bank's or Federal savings association's own common stock instrument, own additional tier 1 capital instrument or own tier 2 capital instrument, including direct, indirect, or synthetic exposures to such capital instruments. An investment in the national bank's or Federal savings association's own capital instrument includes any contractual obligation to purchase such capital instrument.

Junior-lien residential mortgage exposure means a residential mortgage exposure that is not a first-lien residential mortgage exposure.

Main index means the Standard & Poor's 500 Index, the FTSE All-World Index, and any other index for which the national bank or Federal savings association can demonstrate to the satisfaction of the OCC that the equities represented in the index have comparable liquidity, depth of market, and size of bid-ask spreads as equities in the Standard & Poor's 500 Index and FTSE All-World Index.

Market risk national bank or Federal savings association means a national bank or Federal savings association that is described in §3.201(b).

Money market fund means an investment fund that is subject to 17 CFR 270.2a–7 or any foreign equivalent thereof.

Mortgage servicing assets (MSAs) means the contractual rights owned by a national bank or Federal savings association to service for a fee mortgage loans that are owned by others.

Multilateral development bank (MDB) means the International Bank for Reconstruction and Development, the Multilateral Investment Guarantee Agency, the International Finance Corporation, the Inter-American Development Bank, the Asian Development Bank, the African Development Bank, the European Bank for Reconstruction and Development, the European Investment Bank, the European Investment Fund, the Nordic Investment Bank, the Caribbean Development Bank, the Islamic Development Bank, the Council of Europe Development Bank, and any other multilateral lending institution or regional development bank in which the U.S. government is a shareholder or contributing member or which the OCC determines poses comparable credit risk.

National Bank Act means the National Bank Act (12 U.S.C. 24).

Netting set means a group of transactions with a single counterparty that are subject to a qualifying master netting agreement or a qualifying cross-product master netting agreement. For purposes of calculating risk-based capital requirements using the internal models methodology in subpart E of this part, this term does not cover a transaction:

(1) That is not subject to such a master netting agreement; or

(2) Where the national bank or Federal savings association has identified specific wrong-way risk.

Non-significant investment in the capital of an unconsolidated financial institution means an investment in the capital of an unconsolidated financial institution where the national bank or Federal savings association owns 10 percent or less of the issued and outstanding common stock of the unconsolidated financial institution.

N^{th}-to-default credit derivative means a credit derivative that provides credit protection only for the nth-defaulting reference exposure in a group of reference exposures.

Operating entity means a company established to conduct business with clients with the intention of earning a profit in its own right.

Original maturity with respect to an off-balance sheet commitment means the length of time between the date a commitment is issued and:

(1) For a commitment that is not subject to extension or renewal, the stated expiration date of the commitment; or

(2) For a commitment that is subject to extension or renewal, the earliest date on which the national bank or Federal savings association can, at its option, unconditionally cancel the commitment.

Originating national bank or Federal savings association, with respect to a securitization, means a national bank or Federal savings association that:

(1) Directly or indirectly originated or securitized the underlying exposures included in the securitization; or

(2) Serves as an ABCP program sponsor to the securitization.

Over-the-counter (OTC) derivative contract means a derivative contract that is not a cleared transaction. An OTC derivative includes a transaction:

(1) Between a national bank or Federal savings association that is a clearing member and a counterparty where the national bank or Federal savings association is acting as a financial intermediary and enters into a cleared transaction with a CCP that offsets the transaction with the counterparty; or

(2) In which a national bank or Federal savings association that is a clearing member provides a CCP a guarantee on the performance of the counterparty to the transaction.

Performance standby letter of credit (or performance bond) means an irrevocable obligation of a national bank or Federal savings association to pay a third-party beneficiary when a customer (account party) fails to perform on any contractual nonfinancial or commercial obligation. To the extent permitted by law or regulation, performance standby letters of credit include arrangements backing, among other things, subcontractors' and suppliers' performance, labor and materials contracts, and construction bids.

Pre-sold construction loan means any one-to-four family residential construction loan to a builder that meets the requirements of section 618(a)(1) or (2) of the Resolution Trust Corporation Refinancing, Restructuring, and Improvement Act of 1991 (12 U.S.C. 1831n note) and the following criteria:

(1) The loan is made in accordance with prudent underwriting standards, meaning that the national bank or Federal savings association has obtained sufficient documentation that the buyer of the home has a legally binding written sales contract and has a firm written commitment for permanent financing of the home upon completion;

(2) The purchaser is an individual(s) that intends to occupy the residence and is not a partnership, joint venture, trust, corporation, or any other entity (including an entity acting as a sole proprietorship) that is purchasing one or more of the residences for speculative purposes;

(3) The purchaser has entered into a legally binding written sales contract for the residence;

(4) The purchaser has not terminated the contract;

(5) The purchaser has made a substantial earnest money deposit of no less than 3 percent of the sales price, which is subject to forfeiture if the purchaser terminates the sales contract; provided that, the earnest money deposit shall not be subject to forfeiture by reason of breach or termination of the sales contract on the part of the builder;

(6) The earnest money deposit must be held in escrow by the national bank or Federal savings association or an independent party in a fiduciary capacity, and the escrow agreement must provide that in an event of default arising from the cancellation of the sales contract by the purchaser of the residence, the escrow funds shall be used to defray any cost incurred by the national bank or Federal savings association;

(7) The builder must incur at least the first 10 percent of the direct costs of construction of the residence (that is, actual costs of the land, labor, and material) before any drawdown is made under the loan;

(8) The loan may not exceed 80 percent of the sales price of the presold residence; and

(9) The loan is not more than 90 days past due, or on nonaccrual.

Protection amount (P) means, with respect to an exposure hedged by an eligible guarantee or eligible credit derivative, the effective notional amount of the guarantee or credit derivative, reduced to reflect any currency mismatch, maturity mismatch, or lack of restructuring coverage (as provided in § 3.36 or § 3.134, as appropriate).

Publicly-traded means traded on:

(1) Any exchange registered with the SEC as a national securities exchange under section 6 of the Securities Exchange Act; or

(2) Any non-U.S.-based securities exchange that:

(i) Is registered with, or approved by, a national securities regulatory authority; and

(ii) Provides a liquid, two-way market for the instrument in question.

Public sector entity (PSE) means a state, local authority, or other governmental subdivision below the sovereign level.

Qualifying central counterparty (QCCP) means a central counterparty that:

(1)(i) Is a designated financial market utility (FMU) under Title VIII of the Dodd-Frank Act;

(ii) If not located in the United States, is regulated and supervised in a manner equivalent to a designated FMU; or

(iii) Meets the following standards:

(A) The central counterparty requires all parties to contracts cleared by the counterparty to be fully collateralized on a daily basis;

(B) The national bank or Federal savings association demonstrates to the satisfaction of the OCC that the central counterparty:

(*1*) Is in sound financial condition;

(*2*) Is subject to supervision by the Board, the CFTC, or the Securities Exchange Commission (SEC), or, if the central counterparty is not located in the United States, is subject to effective oversight by a national supervisory authority in its home country; and

(*3*) Meets or exceeds the risk-management standards for central counterparties set forth in regulations established by the Board, the CFTC, or the SEC under Title VII or Title VIII of the Dodd-Frank Act; or if the central counterparty is not located in the United States, meets or exceeds similar risk-management standards established under the law of its home country that are consistent with international standards for central counterparty risk management as established by the relevant standard setting body of the Bank of International Settlements; and

(2)(i) Provides the national bank or Federal savings association with the central counterparty's hypothetical capital requirement or the information necessary to calculate such hypothetical capital requirement, and other information the national bank or Federal savings association is required to obtain under §§ 3.35(d)(3) and 3.133(d)(3);

(ii) Makes available to the OCC and the CCP's regulator the information described in paragraph (2)(i) of this definition; and

(iii) Has not otherwise been determined by the OCC to not be a QCCP due to its financial condition, risk profile, failure to meet supervisory risk management standards, or other weaknesses or supervisory concerns that are inconsistent with the risk weight assigned to qualifying central counterparties under §§ 3.35 and 3.133.

(3) Exception. A QCCP that fails to meet the requirements of a QCCP in the future may still be treated as a QCCP under the conditions specified in § 3.3(f).

Qualifying master netting agreement means a written, legally enforceable agreement provided that:

(1) The agreement creates a single legal obligation for all individual transactions covered by the agreement upon an event of default following any stay permitted by paragraph (2) of this definition, including upon an event of receivership, conservatorship, insolvency, liquidation, or similar proceeding, of the counterparty;

(2) The agreement provides the national bank or Federal savings association the right to accelerate, terminate, and close-out on a net basis all transactions under the agreement and to liquidate or set-off collateral promptly upon an event of default, including upon an event of receivership, conservatorship, insolvency, liquidation, or similar proceeding, of the

counterparty, provided that, in any such case:

(i) Any exercise of rights under the agreement will not be stayed or avoided under applicable law in the relevant jurisdictions, other than:

(A) In receivership, conservatorship, or resolution under the Federal Deposit Insurance Act, Title II of the Dodd-Frank Act, or under any similar insolvency law applicable to GSEs, or laws of foreign jurisdictions that are substantially similar[7] to the U.S. laws referenced in this paragraph (2)(i)(A) in order to facilitate the orderly resolution of the defaulting counterparty; or

(B) Where the agreement is subject by its terms to, or incorporates, any of the laws referenced in paragraph (2)(i)(A) of this definition; and

(ii) The agreement may limit the right to accelerate, terminate, and close-out on a net basis all transactions under the agreement and to liquidate or set-off collateral promptly upon an event of default of the counterparty to the extent necessary for the counterparty to comply with the requirements of part 47, subpart I of part 252, and part 382, of this title 12, as applicable.

Regulated financial institution means a financial institution subject to consolidated supervision and regulation comparable to that imposed on the following U.S. financial institutions: Depository institutions, depository institution holding companies, nonbank financial companies supervised by the Board, designated financial market utilities, securities broker-dealers, credit unions, or insurance companies.

Repo-style transaction means a repurchase or reverse repurchase transaction, or a securities borrowing or securities lending transaction, including a transaction in which the national bank or Federal savings association acts as agent for a customer and indemnifies the customer against loss, provided that:

(1) The transaction is based solely on liquid and readily marketable securities, cash, or gold;

(2) The transaction is marked-to-fair value daily and subject to daily margin maintenance requirements;

(3)(i) The transaction is a "securities contract" or "repurchase agreement" under section 555 or 559, respectively, of the Bankruptcy Code (11 U.S.C. 555 or 559), a qualified financial contract under section 11(e)(8) of the Federal Deposit Insurance Act, or a netting contract between or among financial institutions under sections 401–407 of the Federal Deposit Insurance Corporation Improvement Act or the Federal Reserve Board's Regulation EE (12 CFR part 231); or

(ii) If the transaction does not meet the criteria set forth in paragraph (3)(i) of this definition, then either:

(A) The transaction is executed under an agreement that provides the national bank or Federal savings association the right to accelerate, terminate, and close-out the transaction on a net basis and to liquidate or set-off collateral promptly upon an event of default, including upon an event of receivership, insolvency, liquidation, or similar proceeding, of the counterparty, provided that, in any such case:

(*1*) Any exercise of rights under the agreement will not be stayed or avoided under applicable law in the relevant jurisdictions, other than in receivership, conservatorship, or resolution under the Federal Deposit Insurance Act, Title II of the Dodd-Frank Act, or under any similar insolvency law applicable to GSEs, or laws of foreign jurisdictions that are substantially similar[8] to the U.S. laws referenced in this paragraph (3)(ii)(A)(*1*) in order to facilitate the orderly resolution of the defaulting counterparty; and

(*2*) The agreement may limit the right to accelerate, terminate, and close-out on a net basis all transactions under the agreement and to liquidate or set-off collateral promptly upon an event of default of the counterparty to the extent necessary for the counterparty to comply with the requirements of part 47, subpart I

[7] The OCC expects to evaluate jointly with the Board and FDIC whether foreign special resolution regimes meet the requirements of this paragraph.

[8] The OCC expects to evaluate jointly with the Board and FDIC whether foreign special resolution regimes meet the requirements of this paragraph.

of part 252, and part 382, of this title 12, as applicable; or

(B) The transaction is:

(*1*) Either overnight or unconditionally cancelable at any time by the national bank or Federal savings association; and

(*2*) Executed under an agreement that provides the national bank or Federal savings association the right to accelerate, terminate, and close-out the transaction on a net basis and to liquidate or set-off collateral promptly upon an event of counterparty default; and

(4) In order to recognize an exposure as a repo-style transaction for purposes of this subpart, a national bank or Federal savings association must comply with the requirements of § 3.3(e) of this part with respect to that exposure.

Resecuritization means a securitization which has more than one underlying exposure and in which one or more of the underlying exposures is a securitization exposure.

Resecuritization exposure means:

(1) An on- or off-balance sheet exposure to a resecuritization;

(2) An exposure that directly or indirectly references a resecuritization exposure.

(3) An exposure to an asset-backed commercial paper program is not a resecuritization exposure if either:

(i) The program-wide credit enhancement does not meet the definition of a resecuritization exposure; or

(ii) The entity sponsoring the program fully supports the commercial paper through the provision of liquidity so that the commercial paper holders effectively are exposed to the default risk of the sponsor instead of the underlying exposures.

Residential mortgage exposure means an exposure (other than a securitization exposure, equity exposure, statutory multifamily mortgage, or presold construction loan):

(1)(i) That is primarily secured by a first or subsequent lien on one-to-four family residential property; or

(ii) With an original and outstanding amount of $1 million or less that is primarily secured by a first or subsequent lien on residential property that is not one-to-four family; and

(2) For purposes of calculating capital requirements under subpart E of this part, managed as part of a segment of exposures with homogeneous risk characteristics and not on an individual-exposure basis.

Revenue obligation means a bond or similar obligation that is an obligation of a PSE, but which the PSE is committed to repay with revenues from the specific project financed rather than general tax funds.

Savings and loan holding company means a savings and loan holding company as defined in section 10 of the Home Owners' Loan Act (12 U.S.C. 1467a).

Securities and Exchange Commission (SEC) means the U.S. Securities and Exchange Commission.

Securities Exchange Act means the Securities Exchange Act of 1934 (15 U.S.C. 78).

Securitization exposure means:

(1) An on-balance sheet or off-balance sheet credit exposure (including credit-enhancing representations and warranties) that arises from a traditional securitization or synthetic securitization (including a resecuritization), or

(2) An exposure that directly or indirectly references a securitization exposure described in paragraph (1) of this definition.

Securitization special purpose entity (securitization SPE) means a corporation, trust, or other entity organized for the specific purpose of holding underlying exposures of a securitization, the activities of which are limited to those appropriate to accomplish this purpose, and the structure of which is intended to isolate the underlying exposures held by the entity from the credit risk of the seller of the underlying exposures to the entity.

Separate account means a legally segregated pool of assets owned and held by an insurance company and maintained separately from the insurance company's general account assets for the benefit of an individual contract holder. To be a separate account:

(1) The account must be legally recognized as a separate account under applicable law;

(2) The assets in the account must be insulated from general liabilities of the

insurance company under applicable law in the event of the insurance company's insolvency;

(3) The insurance company must invest the funds within the account as directed by the contract holder in designated investment alternatives or in accordance with specific investment objectives or policies; and

(4) All investment gains and losses, net of contract fees and assessments, must be passed through to the contract holder, provided that the contract may specify conditions under which there may be a minimum guarantee but must not include contract terms that limit the maximum investment return available to the policyholder.

Servicer cash advance facility means a facility under which the servicer of the underlying exposures of a securitization may advance cash to ensure an uninterrupted flow of payments to investors in the securitization, including advances made to cover foreclosure costs or other expenses to facilitate the timely collection of the underlying exposures.

Significant investment in the capital of an unconsolidated financial institution means an investment in the capital of an unconsolidated financial institution where the national bank or Federal savings association owns more than 10 percent of the issued and outstanding common stock of the unconsolidated financial institution.

Small Business Act means the Small Business Act (15 U.S.C. 632).

Small Business Investment Act means the Small Business Investment Act of 1958 (15 U.S.C. 682).

Sovereign means a central government (including the U.S. government) or an agency, department, ministry, or central bank of a central government.

Sovereign default means noncompliance by a sovereign with its external debt service obligations or the inability or unwillingness of a sovereign government to service an existing loan according to its original terms, as evidenced by failure to pay principal and interest timely and fully, arrearages, or restructuring.

Sovereign exposure means:

(1) A direct exposure to a sovereign; or

(2) An exposure directly and unconditionally backed by the full faith and credit of a sovereign.

Specific wrong-way risk means wrong-way risk that arises when either:

(1) The counterparty and issuer of the collateral supporting the transaction; or

(2) The counterparty and the reference asset of the transaction, are affiliates or are the same entity.

Standardized market risk-weighted assets means the standardized measure for market risk calculated under §3.204 multiplied by 12.5.

Standardized total risk-weighted assets means:

(1) The sum of:

(i) Total risk-weighted assets for general credit risk as calculated under §3.31;

(ii) Total risk-weighted assets for cleared transactions and default fund contributions as calculated under §3.35;

(iii) Total risk-weighted assets for unsettled transactions as calculated under §3.38;

(iv) Total risk-weighted assets for securitization exposures as calculated under §3.42;

(v) Total risk-weighted assets for equity exposures as calculated under §§3.52 and 3.53; and

(vi) For a market risk national bank or Federal savings association only, standardized market risk-weighted assets; minus

(2) Any amount of the national bank's or Federal savings association's allowance for loan and lease losses that is not included in tier 2 capital and any amount of allocated transfer risk reserves.

Statutory multifamily mortgage means a loan secured by a multifamily residential property that meets the requirements under section 618(b)(1) of the Resolution Trust Corporation Refinancing, Restructuring, and Improvement Act of 1991, and that meets the following criteria:[9]

(1) The loan is made in accordance with prudent underwriting standards;

[9] The types of loans that qualify as loans secured by multifamily residential properties are listed in the instructions for preparation of the Call Report.

(2) The principal amount of the loan at origination does not exceed 80 percent of the value of the property (or 75 percent of the value of the property if the loan is based on an interest rate that changes over the term of the loan) where the value of the property is the lower of the acquisition cost of the property or the appraised (or, if appropriate, evaluated) value of the property;

(3) All principal and interest payments on the loan must have been made on a timely basis in accordance with the terms of the loan for at least one year prior to applying a 50 percent risk weight to the loan, or in the case where an existing owner is refinancing a loan on the property, all principal and interest payments on the loan being refinanced must have been made on a timely basis in accordance with the terms of the loan for at least one year prior to applying a 50 percent risk weight to the loan;

(4) Amortization of principal and interest on the loan must occur over a period of not more than 30 years and the minimum original maturity for repayment of principal must not be less than 7 years;

(5) Annual net operating income (before making any payment on the loan) generated by the property securing the loan during its most recent fiscal year must not be less than 120 percent of the loan's current annual debt service (or 115 percent of current annual debt service if the loan is based on an interest rate that changes over the term of the loan) or, in the case of a cooperative or other not-for-profit housing project, the property must generate sufficient cash flow to provide comparable protection to the national bank or Federal savings association; and

(6) The loan is not more than 90 days past due, or on nonaccrual.

Subsidiary means, with respect to a company, a company controlled by that company.

Synthetic exposure means an exposure whose value is linked to the value of an investment in the national bank's or Federal savings association's own capital instrument or to the value of an investment in the capital of an unconsolidated financial institution.

Synthetic securitization means a transaction in which:

(1) All or a portion of the credit risk of one or more underlying exposures is retained or transferred to one or more third parties through the use of one or more credit derivatives or guarantees (other than a guarantee that transfers only the credit risk of an individual retail exposure);

(2) The credit risk associated with the underlying exposures has been separated into at least two tranches reflecting different levels of seniority;

(3) Performance of the securitization exposures depends upon the performance of the underlying exposures; and

(4) All or substantially all of the underlying exposures are financial exposures (such as loans, commitments, credit derivatives, guarantees, receivables, asset-backed securities, mortgage-backed securities, other debt securities, or equity securities).

Tangible capital means the amount of core capital (tier 1 capital), as calculated in accordance with subpart B of this part, plus the amount of outstanding perpetual preferred stock (including related surplus) not included in tier 1 capital.

Tier 1 capital means the sum of common equity tier 1 capital and additional tier 1 capital.

Tier 1 minority interest means the tier 1 capital of a consolidated subsidiary of a national bank or Federal savings association that is not owned by the national bank or Federal savings association.

Tier 2 capital is defined in §3.20(d).

Total capital means the sum of tier 1 capital and tier 2 capital.

Total capital minority interest means the total capital of a consolidated subsidiary of a national bank or Federal savings association that is not owned by the national bank or Federal savings association.

Total leverage exposure is defined in §3.10(c)(4)(ii) of this part.

Traditional securitization means a transaction in which:

(1) All or a portion of the credit risk of one or more underlying exposures is transferred to one or more third parties other than through the use of credit derivatives or guarantees;

(2) The credit risk associated with the underlying exposures has been separated into at least two tranches reflecting different levels of seniority;

(3) Performance of the securitization exposures depends upon the performance of the underlying exposures;

(4) All or substantially all of the underlying exposures are financial exposures (such as loans, commitments, credit derivatives, guarantees, receivables, asset-backed securities, mortgage-backed securities, other debt securities, or equity securities);

(5) The underlying exposures are not owned by an operating company;

(6) The underlying exposures are not owned by a small business investment company defined in section 302 of the Small Business Investment Act;

(7) The underlying exposures are not owned by a firm an investment in which qualifies as a community development investment under section 24(Eleventh) of the National Bank Act;

(8) The OCC may determine that a transaction in which the underlying exposures are owned by an investment firm that exercises substantially unfettered control over the size and composition of its assets, liabilities, and off-balance sheet exposures is not a traditional securitization based on the transaction's leverage, risk profile, or economic substance;

(9) The OCC may deem a transaction that meets the definition of a traditional securitization, notwithstanding paragraph (5), (6), or (7) of this definition, to be a traditional securitization based on the transaction's leverage, risk profile, or economic substance; and

(10) The transaction is not:

(i) An investment fund;

(ii) A collective investment fund (as defined in 12 CFR 9.18 (national banks), 12 CFR 151.40 (Federal saving associations);

(iii) An employee benefit plan (as defined in paragraphs (3) and (32) of section 3 of ERISA), a "governmental plan" (as defined in 29 U.S.C. 1002(32)) that complies with the tax deferral qualification requirements provided in the Internal Revenue Code, or any similar employee benefit plan established under the laws of a foreign jurisdiction;

(iv) A synthetic exposure to the capital of a financial institution to the extent deducted from capital under § 3.22; or

(v) Registered with the SEC under the Investment Company Act of 1940 (15 U.S.C. 80a–1) or foreign equivalents thereof.

Tranche means all securitization exposures associated with a securitization that have the same seniority level.

Two-way market means a market where there are independent bona fide offers to buy and sell so that a price reasonably related to the last sales price or current bona fide competitive bid and offer quotations can be determined within one day and settled at that price within a relatively short time frame conforming to trade custom.

Unconditionally cancelable means with respect to a commitment, that a national bank or Federal savings association may, at any time, with or without cause, refuse to extend credit under the commitment (to the extent permitted under applicable law).

Underlying exposures means one or more exposures that have been securitized in a securitization transaction.

Unregulated financial institution means, for purposes of § 3.131, a financial institution that is not a regulated financial institution, including any financial institution that would meet the definition of "financial institution" under this section but for the ownership interest thresholds set forth in paragraph (4)(i) of that definition.

U.S. Government agency means an instrumentality of the U.S. Government whose obligations are fully and explicitly guaranteed as to the timely payment of principal and interest by the full faith and credit of the U.S. Government.

Value-at-Risk (VaR) means the estimate of the maximum amount that the value of one or more exposures could decline due to market price or rate movements during a fixed holding period within a stated confidence interval.

Wrong-way risk means the risk that arises when an exposure to a particular counterparty is positively correlated with the probability of default of such counterparty itself.

[78 FR 62157, 62273, Oct. 11, 2013, as amended at 79 FR 44123, July 30, 2014; 79 FR 57740, Sept. 26, 2014; 79 FR 78293, Dec. 30, 2014; 80 FR 41415, July 15, 2015; 82 FR 56661, Nov. 29, 2017]

§3.3 Operational requirements for counterparty credit risk.

For purposes of calculating risk-weighted assets under subparts D and E of this part:

(a) *Cleared transaction.* In order to recognize certain exposures as cleared transactions pursuant to paragraphs (1)(ii), (iii) or (iv) of the definition of "cleared transaction" in §3.2, the exposures must meet the applicable requirements set forth in this paragraph (a).

(1) The offsetting transaction must be identified by the CCP as a transaction for the clearing member client.

(2) The collateral supporting the transaction must be held in a manner that prevents the national bank or Federal savings association from facing any loss due to an event of default, including from a liquidation, receivership, insolvency, or similar proceeding of either the clearing member or the clearing member's other clients. Omnibus accounts established under 17 CFR parts 190 and 300 satisfy the requirements of this paragraph (a).

(3) The national bank or Federal savings association must conduct sufficient legal review to conclude with a well-founded basis (and maintain sufficient written documentation of that legal review) that in the event of a legal challenge (including one resulting from a default or receivership, insolvency, liquidation, or similar proceeding) the relevant court and administrative authorities would find the arrangements of paragraph (a)(2) of this section to be legal, valid, binding and enforceable under the law of the relevant jurisdictions.

(4) The offsetting transaction with a clearing member must be transferable under the transaction documents and applicable laws in the relevant jurisdiction(s) to another clearing member should the clearing member default, become insolvent, or enter receivership, insolvency, liquidation, or similar proceedings.

(b) *Eligible margin loan.* In order to recognize an exposure as an eligible margin loan as defined in §3.2, a national bank or Federal savings association must conduct sufficient legal review to conclude with a well-founded basis (and maintain sufficient written documentation of that legal review) that the agreement underlying the exposure:

(1) Meets the requirements of paragraph (1)(iii) of the definition of eligible margin loan in §3.2, and

(2) Is legal, valid, binding, and enforceable under applicable law in the relevant jurisdictions.

(c) *Qualifying cross-product master netting agreement.* In order to recognize an agreement as a qualifying cross-product master netting agreement as defined in §3.101, a national bank or Federal savings association must obtain a written legal opinion verifying the validity and enforceability of the agreement under applicable law of the relevant jurisdictions if the counterparty fails to perform upon an event of default, including upon receivership, insolvency, liquidation, or similar proceeding.

(d) *Qualifying master netting agreement.* In order to recognize an agreement as a qualifying master netting agreement as defined in §3.2, a national bank or Federal savings association must:

(1) Conduct sufficient legal review to conclude with a well-founded basis (and maintain sufficient written documentation of that legal review) that:

(i) The agreement meets the requirements of paragraph (2) of the definition of qualifying master netting agreement in §3.2; and

(ii) In the event of a legal challenge (including one resulting from default or from receivership, insolvency, liquidation, or similar proceeding) the relevant court and administrative authorities would find the agreement to be legal, valid, binding, and enforceable under the law of the relevant jurisdictions; and

(2) Establish and maintain written procedures to monitor possible changes in relevant law and to ensure that the agreement continues to satisfy the requirements of the definition of qualifying master netting agreement in §3.2.

(e) *Repo-style transaction.* In order to recognize an exposure as a repo-style transaction as defined in §3.2, a national bank or Federal savings association must conduct sufficient legal review to conclude with a well-founded basis (and maintain sufficient written documentation of that legal review) that the agreement underlying the exposure:

(1) Meets the requirements of paragraph (3) of the definition of repo-style transaction in §3.2, and

(2) Is legal, valid, binding, and enforceable under applicable law in the relevant jurisdictions.

(f) *Failure of a QCCP to satisfy the rule's requirements.* If a national bank or Federal savings association determines that a CCP ceases to be a QCCP due to the failure of the CCP to satisfy one or more of the requirements set forth in paragraphs (2)(i) through (2)(iii) of the definition of a QCCP in §3.2, the national bank or Federal savings association may continue to treat the CCP as a QCCP for up to three months following the determination. If the CCP fails to remedy the relevant deficiency within three months after the initial determination, or the CCP fails to satisfy the requirements set forth in paragraphs (2)(i) through (2)(iii) of the definition of a QCCP continuously for a three-month period after remedying the relevant deficiency, a national bank or Federal savings association may not treat the CCP as a QCCP for the purposes of this part until after the national bank or Federal savings association has determined that the CCP has satisfied the requirements in paragraphs (2)(i) through (2)(iii) of the definition of a QCCP for three continuous months.

§§3.4–3.9 [Reserved]

Subpart B—Capital Ratio Requirements and Buffers

SOURCE: 78 FR 62157, 62273, Oct. 11, 2013, unless otherwise noted.

§3.10 Minimum capital requirements.

(a) *Minimum capital requirements.* A national bank or Federal savings association must maintain the following minimum capital ratios:

(1) A common equity tier 1 capital ratio of 4.5 percent.

(2) A tier 1 capital ratio of 6 percent.

(3) A total capital ratio of 8 percent.

(4) A leverage ratio of 4 percent.

(5) For advanced approaches national banks or Federal savings associations, a supplementary leverage ratio of 3 percent.

(6) For Federal savings associations, a tangible capital ratio of 1.5 percent.

(b) *Standardized capital ratio calculations.* Other than as provided in paragraph (c) of this section:

(1) *Common equity tier 1 capital ratio.* A national bank's or Federal savings association's common equity tier 1 capital ratio is the ratio of the national bank's or Federal savings association's common equity tier 1 capital to standardized total risk-weighted assets;

(2) *Tier 1 capital ratio.* A national bank's or Federal savings association's tier 1 capital ratio is the ratio of the national bank's or Federal savings association's tier 1 capital to standardized total risk-weighted assets;

(3) *Total capital ratio.* A national bank's or Federal savings association's total capital ratio is the ratio of the national bank's or Federal savings association's total capital to standardized total risk-weighted assets; and

(4) *Leverage ratio.* A national bank's or Federal savings association's leverage ratio is the ratio of the national bank's or Federal savings association's tier 1 capital to the national bank's or Federal savings association's average total consolidated assets as reported on the national bank's or Federal savings association's Call Report minus amounts deducted from tier 1 capital under §3.22(a), (c) and (d).

(5) *Federal savings association tangible capital ratio.* A Federal savings association's tangible capital ratio is the ratio of the Federal savings association's core capital (tier 1 capital) to average total assets as calculated under this subpart B. For purposes of this paragraph (b)(5), the term "total assets" means "total assets" as defined in part 6, subpart A of this chapter, subject to subpart G of this part.

(c) *Advanced approaches capital ratio calculations.* An advanced approaches national bank or Federal savings association that has completed the parallel run process and received notification from the OCC pursuant to § 3.121(d) must determine its regulatory capital ratios as described in paragraphs (c)(1) through (3) of this section. An advanced approaches national bank or Federal savings association must determine its supplementary leverage ratio in accordance with paragraph (c)(4) of this section, beginning with the calendar quarter immediately following the quarter in which the national bank or Federal savings association meets any of the criteria in § 3.100(b)(1).

(1) *Common equity tier 1 capital ratio.* The national bank's or Federal savings association's common equity tier 1 capital ratio is the lower of:

(i) The ratio of the national bank's or Federal savings association's common equity tier 1 capital to standardized total risk-weighted assets; and

(ii) The ratio of the national bank's or Federal savings association's common equity tier 1 capital to advanced approaches total risk-weighted assets.

(2) *Tier 1 capital ratio.* The national bank's or Federal savings association's tier 1 capital ratio is the lower of:

(i) The ratio of the national bank's or Federal savings association's tier 1 capital to standardized total risk-weighted assets; and

(ii) The ratio of the national bank's or Federal savings association's tier 1 capital to advanced approaches total risk-weighted assets.

(3) *Total capital ratio.* The national bank's or Federal savings association's total capital ratio is the lower of:

(i) The ratio of the national bank's or Federal savings association's total capital to standardized total risk-weighted assets; and

(ii) The ratio of the national bank's or Federal savings association's advanced-approaches-adjusted total capital to advanced approaches total risk-weighted assets. A national bank's or Federal savings association's advanced-approaches-adjusted total capital is the national bank's or Federal savings association's total capital after being adjusted as follows:

(A) An advanced approaches national bank or Federal savings association must deduct from its total capital any allowance for loan and lease losses included in its tier 2 capital in accordance with § 3.20(d)(3); and

(B) An advanced approaches national bank or Federal savings association must add to its total capital any eligible credit reserves that exceed the national bank's or Federal savings association's total expected credit losses to the extent that the excess reserve amount does not exceed 0.6 percent of the national bank's or Federal savings association's credit risk-weighted assets.

(4) *Supplementary leverage ratio.* (i) An advanced approaches national bank's or Federal savings association's supplementary leverage ratio is the ratio of its tier 1 capital to total leverage exposure, the latter which is calculated as the sum of:

(A) The mean of the on-balance sheet assets calculated as of each day of the reporting quarter; and

(B) The mean of the off-balance sheet exposures calculated as of the last day of each of the most recent three months, minus the applicable deductions under § 3.22(a), (c), and (d).

(ii) For purposes of this part, *total leverage exposure* means the sum of the items described in paragraphs (c)(4)(ii)(A) through (H) of this section, as adjusted pursuant to paragraph (c)(4)(ii)(I) for a clearing member national bank or Federal savings association:

(A) The balance sheet carrying value of all of the national bank's or Federal savings association's on-balance sheet assets, *plus* the value of securities sold under a repurchase transaction or a securities lending transaction that qualifies for sales treatment under U.S. GAAP, *less* amounts deducted from tier 1 capital under § 3.22(a), (c), and (d), and *less* the value of securities received in security-for-security repo-style transactions, where the national bank or Federal savings association acts as a securities lender and includes the securities received in its on-balance sheet assets but has not sold or re-hypothecated the securities received;

(B) The PFE for each derivative contract or each single-product netting set of derivative contracts (including a cleared transaction except as provided in paragraph (c)(4)(ii)(I) of this section and, at the discretion of the national bank or Federal savings association, excluding a forward agreement treated as a derivative contract that is part of a repurchase or reverse repurchase or a securities borrowing or lending transaction that qualifies for sales treatment under U.S. GAAP), to which the national bank or Federal savings association is a counterparty as determined under § 3.34, but without regard to § 3.34(b), provided that:

(*1*) A national bank or Federal savings association may choose to exclude the PFE of all credit derivatives or other similar instruments through which it provides credit protection when calculating the PFE under § 3.34, but without regard to § 3.34(b), provided that it does not adjust the net-to-gross ratio (NGR); and

(*2*) A national bank or Federal savings association that chooses to exclude the PFE of credit derivatives or other similar instruments through which it provides credit protection pursuant to paragraph (c)(4)(ii)(B)(*1*) of this section must do so consistently over time for the calculation of the PFE for all such instruments;

(C) The amount of cash collateral that is received from a counterparty to a derivative contract and that has offset the mark-to-fair value of the derivative asset, or cash collateral that is posted to a counterparty to a derivative contract and that has reduced the national bank's or Federal savings association's on-balance sheet assets, unless such cash collateral is all or part of variation margin that satisfies the following requirements:

(*1*) For derivative contracts that are not cleared through a QCCP, the cash collateral received by the recipient counterparty is not segregated (by law, regulation or an agreement with the counterparty);

(*2*) Variation margin is calculated and transferred on a daily basis based on the mark-to-fair value of the derivative contract;

(*3*) The variation margin transferred under the derivative contract or the governing rules for a cleared transaction is the full amount that is necessary to fully extinguish the net current credit exposure to the counterparty of the derivative contracts, subject to the threshold and minimum transfer amounts applicable to the counterparty under the terms of the derivative contract or the governing rules for a cleared transaction;

(*4*) The variation margin is in the form of cash in the same currency as the currency of settlement set forth in the derivative contract, provided that for the purposes of this paragraph, currency of settlement means any currency for settlement specified in the governing qualifying master netting agreement and the credit support annex to the qualifying master netting agreement, or in the governing rules for a cleared transaction;

(*5*) The derivative contract and the variation margin are governed by a qualifying master netting agreement between the legal entities that are the counterparties to the derivative contract or by the governing rules for a cleared transaction, and the qualifying master netting agreement or the governing rules for a cleared transaction must explicitly stipulate that the counterparties agree to settle any payment obligations on a net basis, taking into account any variation margin received or provided under the contract if a credit event involving either counterparty occurs;

(*6*) The variation margin is used to reduce the current credit exposure of the derivative contract, calculated as described in § 3.34(a), and not the PFE; and

(*7*) For the purpose of the calculation of the NGR described in § 3.34(a)(2)(ii)(B), variation margin described in paragraph (c)(4)(ii)(C)(*6*) of this section may not reduce the net current credit exposure or the gross current credit exposure;

(D) The effective notional principal amount (that is, the apparent or stated notional principal amount multiplied by any multiplier in the derivative contract) of a credit derivative, or other similar instrument, through which the national bank or Federal savings association provides credit protection, provided that:

(*1*) The national bank or Federal savings association may reduce the effective notional principal amount of the credit derivative by the amount of any reduction in the mark-to-fair value of the credit derivative if the reduction is recognized in common equity tier 1 capital;

(*2*) The national bank or Federal savings association may reduce the effective notional principal amount of the credit derivative by the effective notional principal amount of a purchased credit derivative or other similar instrument, provided that the remaining maturity of the purchased credit derivative is equal to or greater than the remaining maturity of the credit derivative through which the national bank or Federal savings association provides credit protection and that:

(*i*) With respect to a credit derivative that references a single exposure, the reference exposure of the purchased credit derivative is to the same legal entity and ranks *pari passu* with, or is junior to, the reference exposure of the credit derivative through which the national bank or Federal savings association provides credit protection; or

(*ii*) With respect to a credit derivative that references multiple exposures, the reference exposures of the purchased credit derivative are to the same legal entities and rank *pari passu* with the reference exposures of the credit derivative through which the national bank or Federal savings association provides credit protection, and the level of seniority of the purchased credit derivative ranks *pari passu* to the level of seniority of the credit derivative through which the national bank or Federal savings association provides credit protection;

(*iii*) Where a national bank or Federal savings association has reduced the effective notional amount of a credit derivative through which the national bank or Federal savings association provides credit protection in accordance with paragraph (c)(4)(ii)(D)(*1*) of this section, the national bank or Federal savings association must also reduce the effective notional principal amount of a purchased credit derivative used to offset the credit derivative through which the national bank or Federal savings association provides credit protection, by the amount of any increase in the mark-to-fair value of the purchased credit derivative that is recognized in common equity tier 1 capital; and

(*iv*) Where the national bank or Federal savings association purchases credit protection through a total return swap and records the net payments received on a credit derivative through which the national bank or Federal savings association provides credit protection in net income, but does not record offsetting deterioration in the mark-to-fair value of the credit derivative through which the national bank or Federal savings association provides credit protection in net income (either through reductions in fair value or by additions to reserves), the national bank or Federal savings association may not use the purchased credit protection to offset the effective notional principal amount of the related credit derivative through which the national bank or Federal savings association provides credit protection;

(E) Where a national bank or Federal savings association acting as a principal has more than one repo-style transaction with the same counterparty and has offset the gross value of receivables due from a counterparty under reverse repurchase transactions by the gross value of payables under repurchase transactions due to the same counterparty, the gross value of receivables associated with the repo-style transactions *less* any on-balance sheet receivables amount associated with these repo-style transactions included under paragraph (c)(4)(ii)(A) of this section, unless the following criteria are met:

(*1*) The offsetting transactions have the same explicit final settlement date under their governing agreements;

(*2*) The right to offset the amount owed to the counterparty with the amount owed by the counterparty is legally enforceable in the normal course of business and in the event of receivership, insolvency, liquidation, or similar proceeding; and

(*3*) Under the governing agreements, the counterparties intend to settle net, settle simultaneously, or settle according to a process that is the functional equivalent of net settlement, (that is, the cash flows of the transactions are equivalent, in effect, to a single net amount on the settlement date), where both transactions are settled through the same settlement system, the settlement arrangements are supported by cash or intraday credit facilities intended to ensure that settlement of both transactions will occur by the end of the business day, and the settlement of the underlying securities does not interfere with the net cash settlement;

(F) The counterparty credit risk of a repo-style transaction, including where the national bank or Federal savings association acts as an agent for a repo-style transaction and indemnifies the customer with respect to the performance of the customer's counterparty in an amount limited to the difference between the fair value of the security or cash its customer has lent and the fair value of the collateral the borrower has provided, calculated as follows:

(*1*) If the transaction is not subject to a qualifying master netting agreement, the counterparty credit risk (E*) for transactions with a counterparty must be calculated on a transaction by transaction basis, such that each transaction *i* is treated as its own netting set, in accordance with the following formula, where E_i is the fair value of the instruments, gold, or cash that the national bank or Federal savings association has lent, sold subject to repurchase, or provided as collateral to the counterparty, and C_i is the fair value of the instruments, gold, or cash that the national bank or Federal savings association has borrowed, purchased subject to resale, or received as collateral from the counterparty:

$E_i^* = \max \{0, [E_i - C_i]\}$; and

(*2*) If the transaction is subject to a qualifying master netting agreement, the counterparty credit risk (E*) must be calculated as the greater of zero and the total fair value of the instruments, gold, or cash that the national bank or Federal savings association has lent, sold subject to repurchase or provided as collateral to a counterparty for all transactions included in the qualifying master netting agreement (ΣE_i), *less* the total fair value of the instruments, gold, or cash that the national bank or Federal savings association borrowed, purchased subject to resale or received as collateral from the counterparty for those transactions (ΣC_i), in accordance with the following formula:

$E^* = \max \{0, [\Sigma E_i - \Sigma C_i]\}$

(G) If a national bank or Federal savings association acting as an agent for a repo-style transaction provides a guarantee to a customer of the security or cash its customer has lent or borrowed with respect to the performance of the customer's counterparty and the guarantee is not limited to the difference between the fair value of the security or cash its customer has lent and the fair value of the collateral the borrower has provided, the amount of the guarantee that is greater than the difference between the fair value of the security or cash its customer has lent and the value of the collateral the borrower has provided;

(H) The credit equivalent amount of all off-balance sheet exposures of the national bank or Federal savings association, excluding repo-style transactions, repurchase or reverse repurchase or securities borrowing or lending transactions that qualify for sales treatment under U.S. GAAP, and derivative transactions, determined using the applicable credit conversation factor under §3.33(b), provided, however, that the minimum credit conversion factor that may be assigned to an off-balance sheet exposure under this paragraph is 10 percent; and

(I) For a national bank or Federal savings association that is a clearing member:

(*1*) A clearing member national bank or Federal savings association that guarantees the performance of a clearing member client with respect to a cleared transaction must treat its exposure to the clearing member client as a derivative contract for purposes of determining its total leverage exposure;

(*2*) A clearing member national bank or Federal savings association that guarantees the performance of a CCP with respect to a transaction cleared on behalf of a clearing member client must treat its exposure to the CCP as a derivative contract for purposes of determining its total leverage exposure;

(*3*) A clearing member national bank or Federal savings association that does not guarantee the performance of a CCP with respect to a transaction cleared on behalf of a clearing member client may exclude its exposure to the

CCP for purposes of determining its total leverage exposure;

(*4*) A national bank or Federal savings association that is a clearing member may exclude from its total leverage exposure the effective notional principal amount of credit protection sold through a credit derivative contract, or other similar instrument, that it clears on behalf of a clearing member client through a CCP as calculated in accordance with part (c)(4)(ii)(D); and

(*5*) Notwithstanding paragraphs (c)(4)(ii)(I)(*1*) through (*3*) of this section, a national bank or Federal savings association may exclude from its total leverage exposure a clearing member's exposure to a clearing member client for a derivative contract, if the clearing member client and the clearing member are affiliates and consolidated for financial reporting purposes on the national bank's or Federal savings association's balance sheet.

(5) *Federal savings association tangible capital ratio.* A Federal savings association's tangible capital ratio is the ratio of the Federal savings association's core capital (tier 1 capital) to average total assets as calculated under this subpart B. For purposes of this paragraph (c)(5), the term "total assets" means "total assets" as defined in part 6, subpart A of this chapter, subject to subpart G of this part.

(d) *Capital adequacy.* (1) Notwithstanding the minimum requirements in this part, a national bank or Federal savings association must maintain capital commensurate with the level and nature of all risks to which the national bank or Federal savings association is exposed. The supervisory evaluation of a national bank's or Federal savings association's capital adequacy is based on an individual assessment of numerous factors, including those listed at this section (national banks), 12 CFR 167.3(c) (Federal savings associations).

(2) A national bank or Federal savings association must have a process for assessing its overall capital adequacy in relation to its risk profile and a comprehensive strategy for maintaining an appropriate level of capital.

[78 FR 62157, 62273, Oct. 11, 2013, as amended at 79 FR 57740, Sept. 26, 2014; 80 FR 41415, July 15, 2015]

§3.11 Capital conservation buffer and countercyclical capital buffer amount.

(a) *Capital conservation buffer*—(1) *Composition of the capital conservation buffer.* The capital conservation buffer is composed solely of common equity tier 1 capital.

(2) *Definitions.* For purposes of this section, the following definitions apply:

(i) *Eligible retained income.* The eligible retained income of a national bank or Federal savings association is the national bank's or Federal savings association's net income for the four calendar quarters preceding the current calendar quarter, based on the national bank's or Federal savings association's quarterly Call Reports, net of any distributions and associated tax effects not already reflected in net income.

(ii) *Maximum payout ratio.* The maximum payout ratio is the percentage of eligible retained income that a national bank or Federal savings association can pay out in the form of distributions and discretionary bonus payments during the current calendar quarter. The maximum payout ratio is based on the national bank's or Federal savings association's capital conservation buffer, calculated as of the last day of the previous calendar quarter, as set forth in Table 1 to §3.11.

(iii) *Maximum payout amount.* A national bank's or Federal savings association's maximum payout amount for the current calendar quarter is equal to the national bank's or Federal savings association's eligible retained income, multiplied by the applicable maximum payout ratio, as set forth in Table 1 to §3.11.

(iv) *Private sector credit exposure.* Private sector credit exposure means an exposure to a company or an individual that is not an exposure to a sovereign, the Bank for International Settlements, the European Central Bank, the European Commission, the International Monetary Fund, a MDB, a PSE, or a GSE.

(3) *Calculation of capital conservation buffer.* (i) A national bank's or Federal savings association's capital conservation buffer is equal to the lowest of the following ratios, calculated as of the last day of the previous calendar quarter based on the national bank's or Federal savings association's most recent Call Report:

(A) The national bank's or Federal savings association's common equity tier 1 capital ratio minus the national bank's or Federal savings association's minimum common equity tier 1 capital ratio requirement under § 3.10;

(B) The national bank's or Federal savings association's tier 1 capital ratio minus the national bank's or Federal savings association's minimum tier 1 capital ratio requirement under § 3.10; and

(C) The national bank's or Federal savings association's total capital ratio minus the national bank's or Federal savings association's minimum total capital ratio requirement under § 3.10; or

(ii) Notwithstanding paragraphs (a)(3)(i)(A)–(C) of this section, if the national bank's or Federal savings association's common equity tier 1, tier 1 or total capital ratio is less than or equal to the national bank's or Federal savings association's minimum common equity tier 1, tier 1 or total capital ratio requirement under § 3.10, respectively, the national bank's or Federal savings association's capital conservation buffer is zero.

(4) *Limits on distributions and discretionary bonus payments.* (i) A national bank or Federal savings association shall not make distributions or discretionary bonus payments or create an obligation to make such distributions or payments during the current calendar quarter that, in the aggregate, exceed the maximum payout amount.

(ii) A national bank or Federal savings association with a capital conservation buffer that is greater than 2.5 percent plus 100 percent of its applicable countercyclical capital buffer, in accordance with paragraph (b) of this section, is not subject to a maximum payout amount under this section.

(iii) *Negative eligible retained income.* Except as provided in paragraph (a)(4)(iv) of this section, a national bank or Federal savings association may not make distributions or discretionary bonus payments during the current calendar quarter if the national bank's or Federal savings association's:

(A) Eligible retained income is negative; and

(B) Capital conservation buffer was less than 2.5 percent as of the end of the previous calendar quarter.

(iv) *Prior approval.* Notwithstanding the limitations in paragraphs (a)(4)(i) through (iii) of this section, the OCC may permit a national bank or Federal savings association to make a distribution or discretionary bonus payment upon a request of the national bank or Federal savings association, if the OCC determines that the distribution or discretionary bonus payment would not be contrary to the purposes of this section, or to the safety and soundness of the national bank or Federal savings association. In making such a determination, the OCC will consider the nature and extent of the request and the particular circumstances giving rise to the request.

TABLE 1 TO § 3.11—CALCULATION OF MAXIMUM PAYOUT AMOUNT

Capital conservation buffer	Maximum payout ratio (as a percentage of eligible retained income)
Greater than 2.5 percent plus 100 percent of the national bank's or Federal savings association's applicable countercyclical capital buffer amount.	No payout ratio limitation applies.
Less than or equal to 2.5 percent plus 100 percent of the national bank's or Federal savings association's applicable countercyclical capital buffer amount, and greater than 1.875 percent plus 75 percent of the national bank's or Federal savings association's applicable countercyclical capital buffer amount.	60 percent.
Less than or equal to 1.875 percent plus 75 percent of the national bank's or Federal savings association's applicable countercyclical capital buffer amount, and greater than 1.25 percent plus 50 percent of the national bank's or Federal savings association's applicable countercyclical capital buffer amount.	40 percent.

TABLE 1 TO § 3.11—CALCULATION OF MAXIMUM PAYOUT AMOUNT—Continued

Capital conservation buffer	Maximum payout ratio (as a percentage of eligible retained income)
Less than or equal to 1.25 percent plus 50 percent of the national bank's or Federal savings association's applicable countercyclical capital buffer amount, and greater than 0.625 percent plus 25 percent of the national bank's or Federal savings association's applicable countercyclical capital buffer amount.	20 percent.
Less than or equal to 0.625 percent plus 25 percent of the national bank's or Federal savings association's applicable countercyclical capital buffer amount.	0 percent.

(v) *Other limitations on distributions.* Additional limitations on distributions may apply to a national bank or Federal savings association under subparts H and I of this part; 12 CFR 5.46, 12 CFR part 5, subpart E; 12 CFR part 6.

(b) *Countercyclical capital buffer amount*—(1) *General.* An advanced approaches national bank or Federal savings association must calculate a countercyclical capital buffer amount in accordance with the following paragraphs for purposes of determining its maximum payout ratio under Table 1 to § 3.11.

(i) *Extension of capital conservation buffer.* The countercyclical capital buffer amount is an extension of the capital conservation buffer as described in paragraph (a) of this section.

(ii) *Amount.* An advanced approaches national bank or Federal savings association has a countercyclical capital buffer amount determined by calculating the weighted average of the countercyclical capital buffer amounts established for the national jurisdictions where the national bank's or Federal savings association's private sector credit exposures are located, as specified in paragraphs (b)(2) and (3) of this section.

(iii) *Weighting.* The weight assigned to a jurisdiction's countercyclical capital buffer amount is calculated by dividing the total risk-weighted assets for the national bank's or Federal savings association's private sector credit exposures located in the jurisdiction by the total risk-weighted assets for all of the national bank's or Federal savings association's private sector credit exposures. The methodology a national bank or Federal savings association uses for determining risk-weighted assets for purposes of this paragraph (b) must be the methodology that determines its risk-based capital ratios under § 3.10. Notwithstanding the previous sentence, the risk-weighted asset amount for a private sector credit exposure that is a covered position under subpart F of this part is its specific risk add-on as determined under § 3.210 multiplied by 12.5.

(iv) *Location.* (A) Except as provided in paragraphs (b)(1)(iv)(B) and (b)(1)(iv)(C) of this section, the location of a private sector credit exposure is the national jurisdiction where the borrower is located (that is, where it is incorporated, chartered, or similarly established or, if the borrower is an individual, where the borrower resides).

(B) If, in accordance with subparts D or E of this part, the national bank or Federal savings association has assigned to a private sector credit exposure a risk weight associated with a protection provider on a guarantee or credit derivative, the location of the exposure is the national jurisdiction where the protection provider is located.

(C) The location of a securitization exposure is the location of the underlying exposures, or, if the underlying exposures are located in more than one national jurisdiction, the national jurisdiction where the underlying exposures with the largest aggregate unpaid principal balance are located. For purposes of this paragraph (b), the location of an underlying exposure shall be the location of the borrower, determined consistent with paragraph (b)(1)(iv)(A) of this section.

(2) *Countercyclical capital buffer amount for credit exposures in the United States*—(i) *Initial countercyclical capital buffer amount with respect to credit exposures in the United States.* The initial countercyclical capital buffer amount in the United States is zero.

(ii) *Adjustment of the countercyclical capital buffer amount.* The OCC will adjust the countercyclical capital buffer amount for credit exposures in the United States in accordance with applicable law.[10]

(iii) *Range of countercyclical capital buffer amount.* The OCC will adjust the countercyclical capital buffer amount for credit exposures in the United States between zero percent and 2.5 percent of risk-weighted assets.

(iv) *Adjustment determination.* The OCC will base its decision to adjust the countercyclical capital buffer amount under this section on a range of macroeconomic, financial, and supervisory information indicating an increase in systemic risk including, but not limited to, the ratio of credit to gross domestic product, a variety of asset prices, other factors indicative of relative credit and liquidity expansion or contraction, funding spreads, credit condition surveys, indices based on credit default swap spreads, options implied volatility, and measures of systemic risk.

(v) *Effective date of adjusted countercyclical capital buffer amount*—(A) *Increase adjustment.* A determination by the OCC under paragraph (b)(2)(ii) of this section to increase the countercyclical capital buffer amount will be effective 12 months from the date of announcement, unless the OCC establishes an earlier effective date and includes a statement articulating the reasons for the earlier effective date.

(B) *Decrease adjustment.* A determination by the OCC to decrease the established countercyclical capital buffer amount under paragraph (b)(2)(ii) of this section will be effective on the day following announcement of the final determination or the earliest date permissible under applicable law or regulation, whichever is later.

(vi) *Twelve month sunset.* The countercyclical capital buffer amount will return to zero percent 12 months after the effective date that the adjusted countercyclical capital buffer amount is announced, unless the OCC announces a decision to maintain the adjusted countercyclical capital buffer amount or adjust it again before the expiration of the 12-month period.

(3) *Countercyclical capital buffer amount for foreign jurisdictions.* The OCC will adjust the countercyclical capital buffer amount for private sector credit exposures to reflect decisions made by foreign jurisdictions consistent with due process requirements described in paragraph (b)(2) of this section.

[10] The OCC expects that any adjustment will be based on a determination made jointly by the Board, OCC, and FDIC.

§§3.12–3.19 [Reserved]

Subpart C—Definition of Capital

SOURCE: 78 FR 62157, 62273, Oct. 11, 2013, unless otherwise noted.

§3.20 Capital components and eligibility criteria for regulatory capital instruments.

(a) *Regulatory capital components.* A national bank's or Federal savings association's regulatory capital components are:

(1) Common equity tier 1 capital;

(2) Additional tier 1 capital; and

(3) Tier 2 capital.

(b) *Common equity tier 1 capital.* Common equity tier 1 capital is the sum of the common equity tier 1 capital elements in this paragraph (b), minus regulatory adjustments and deductions in §3.22. The common equity tier 1 capital elements are:

(1) Any common stock instruments (plus any related surplus) issued by the national bank or Federal savings association, net of treasury stock, and any capital instruments issued by mutual banking organizations, that meet all the following criteria:

(i) The instrument is paid-in, issued directly by the national bank or Federal savings association, and represents the most subordinated claim in a receivership, insolvency, liquidation, or similar proceeding of the national bank or Federal savings association;

(ii) The holder of the instrument is entitled to a claim on the residual assets of the national bank or Federal savings association that is proportional with the holder's share of the national bank's or Federal savings association's issued capital after all senior claims have been satisfied in a receivership, insolvency, liquidation, or similar proceeding;

(iii) The instrument has no maturity date, can only be redeemed via discretionary repurchases with the prior approval of the OCC, and does not contain any term or feature that creates an incentive to redeem;

(iv) The national bank or Federal savings association did not create at issuance of the instrument through any action or communication an expectation that it will buy back, cancel, or redeem the instrument, and the instrument does not include any term or feature that might give rise to such an expectation;

(v) Any cash dividend payments on the instrument are paid out of the national bank's or Federal savings association's net income or retained earnings and are not subject to a limit imposed by the contractual terms governing the instrument.

(vi) The national bank or Federal savings association has full discretion at all times to refrain from paying any dividends and making any other distributions on the instrument without triggering an event of default, a requirement to make a payment-in-kind, or an imposition of any other restrictions on the national bank or Federal savings association;

(vii) Dividend payments and any other distributions on the instrument may be paid only after all legal and contractual obligations of the national bank or Federal savings association have been satisfied, including payments due on more senior claims;

(viii) The holders of the instrument bear losses as they occur equally, proportionately, and simultaneously with the holders of all other common stock instruments before any losses are borne by holders of claims on the national bank or Federal savings association with greater priority in a receivership, insolvency, liquidation, or similar proceeding;

(ix) The paid-in amount is classified as equity under GAAP;

(x) The national bank or Federal savings association, or an entity that the national bank or Federal savings association controls, did not purchase or directly or indirectly fund the purchase of the instrument;

(xi) The instrument is not secured, not covered by a guarantee of the national bank or Federal savings association or of an affiliate of the national bank or Federal savings association, and is not subject to any other arrangement that legally or economically enhances the seniority of the instrument;

(xii) The instrument has been issued in accordance with applicable laws and regulations; and

(xiii) The instrument is reported on the national bank's or Federal savings association's regulatory financial statements separately from other capital instruments.

(2) Retained earnings.

(3) Accumulated other comprehensive income (AOCI) as reported under GAAP.[11]

(4) Any common equity tier 1 minority interest, subject to the limitations in § 3.21(c).

(5) Notwithstanding the criteria for common stock instruments referenced above, a national bank's or Federal savings association's common stock issued and held in trust for the benefit of its employees as part of an employee stock ownership plan does not violate any of the criteria in paragraph (b)(1)(iii), paragraph (b)(1)(iv) or paragraph (b)(1)(xi) of this section, provided that any repurchase of the stock is required solely by virtue of ERISA for an instrument of a national bank or Federal savings association that is not publicly-traded. In addition, an instrument issued by a national bank or Federal savings association to its employee stock ownership plan does not violate the criterion in paragraph (b)(1)(x) of this section.

(c) *Additional tier 1 capital.* Additional tier 1 capital is the sum of additional tier 1 capital elements and any related surplus, minus the regulatory adjustments and deductions in § 3.22. Additional tier 1 capital elements are:

(1) Instruments (plus any related surplus) that meet the following criteria:

[11] *See* § 3.22 for specific adjustments related to AOCI.

(i) The instrument is issued and paid-in;

(ii) The instrument is subordinated to depositors, general creditors, and subordinated debt holders of the national bank or Federal savings association in a receivership, insolvency, liquidation, or similar proceeding;

(iii) The instrument is not secured, not covered by a guarantee of the national bank or Federal savings association or of an affiliate of the national bank or Federal savings association, and not subject to any other arrangement that legally or economically enhances the seniority of the instrument;

(iv) The instrument has no maturity date and does not contain a dividend step-up or any other term or feature that creates an incentive to redeem; and

(v) If callable by its terms, the instrument may be called by the national bank or Federal savings association only after a minimum of five years following issuance, except that the terms of the instrument may allow it to be called earlier than five years upon the occurrence of a regulatory event that precludes the instrument from being included in additional tier 1 capital, a tax event, or if the issuing entity is required to register as an investment company pursuant to the Investment Company Act of 1940 (15 U.S.C. 80a–1 *et seq.*). In addition:

(A) The national bank or Federal savings association must receive prior approval from the OCC to exercise a call option on the instrument.

(B) The national bank or Federal savings association does not create at issuance of the instrument, through any action or communication, an expectation that the call option will be exercised.

(C) Prior to exercising the call option, or immediately thereafter, the national bank or Federal savings association must either: Replace the instrument to be called with an equal amount of instruments that meet the criteria under paragraph (b) of this section or this paragraph (c);[12] or demonstrate to the satisfaction of the OCC that following redemption, the national bank or Federal savings association will continue to hold capital commensurate with its risk.

(vi) Redemption or repurchase of the instrument requires prior approval from the OCC.

(vii) The national bank or Federal savings association has full discretion at all times to cancel dividends or other distributions on the instrument without triggering an event of default, a requirement to make a payment-in-kind, or an imposition of other restrictions on the national bank or Federal savings association except in relation to any distributions to holders of common stock or instruments that are pari passu with the instrument.

(viii) Any cash dividend payments on the instrument are paid out of the national bank's or Federal savings association's net income or retained earnings and are not subject to a limit imposed by the contractual terms governing the instrument.

(ix) The instrument does not have a credit-sensitive feature, such as a dividend rate that is reset periodically based in whole or in part on the national bank's or Federal savings association's credit quality, but may have a dividend rate that is adjusted periodically independent of the national bank's or Federal savings association's credit quality, in relation to general market interest rates or similar adjustments.

(x) The paid-in amount is classified as equity under GAAP.

(xi) The national bank or Federal savings association, or an entity that the national bank or Federal savings association controls, did not purchase or directly or indirectly fund the purchase of the instrument.

(xii) The instrument does not have any features that would limit or discourage additional issuance of capital by the national bank or Federal savings association, such as provisions that require the national bank or Federal savings association to compensate holders of the instrument if a new instrument is issued at a lower price during a specified time frame.

[12] Replacement can be concurrent with redemption of existing additional tier 1 capital instruments.

(xiii) If the instrument is not issued directly by the national bank or Federal savings association or by a subsidiary of the national bank or Federal savings association that is an operating entity, the only asset of the issuing entity is its investment in the capital of the national bank or Federal savings association, and proceeds must be immediately available without limitation to the national bank or Federal savings association or to the national bank's or Federal savings association's top-tier holding company in a form which meets or exceeds all of the other criteria for additional tier 1 capital instruments.[13]

(xiv) For an advanced approaches national bank or Federal savings association, the governing agreement, offering circular, or prospectus of an instrument issued after the date upon which the national bank or Federal savings association becomes subject to this part as set forth in § 3.1(f) must disclose that the holders of the instrument may be fully subordinated to interests held by the U.S. government in the event that the national bank or Federal savings association enters into a receivership, insolvency, liquidation, or similar proceeding.

(2) Tier 1 minority interest, subject to the limitations in § 3.21(d), that is not included in the national bank's or Federal savings association's common equity tier 1 capital.

(3) Any and all instruments that qualified as tier 1 capital under the OCC's general risk-based capital rules under appendix A to this part (national banks), 12 CFR part 167 (Federal savings associations) as then in effect, that were issued under the Small Business Jobs Act of 2010[14] or prior to October 4, 2010, under the Emergency Economic Stabilization Act of 2008.[15]

(4) Notwithstanding the criteria for additional tier 1 capital instruments referenced above:

(i) An instrument issued by a national bank or Federal savings association and held in trust for the benefit of its employees as part of an employee stock ownership plan does not violate any of the criteria in paragraph (c)(1)(iii) of this section, provided that any repurchase is required solely by virtue of ERISA for an instrument of a national bank or Federal savings association that is not publicly-traded. In addition, an instrument issued by a national bank or Federal savings association to its employee stock ownership plan does not violate the criteria in paragraph (c)(1)(v) or paragraph (c)(1)(xi) of this section; and

(ii) An instrument with terms that provide that the instrument may be called earlier than five years upon the occurrence of a rating agency event does not violate the criterion in paragraph (c)(1)(v) of this section provided that the instrument was issued and included in a national bank's or Federal savings association's tier 1 capital prior to January 1, 2014, and that such instrument satisfies all other criteria under this § 3.20(c).

(d) *Tier 2 Capital.* Tier 2 capital is the sum of tier 2 capital elements and any related surplus, minus regulatory adjustments and deductions in § 3.22. Tier 2 capital elements are:

(1) Instruments (plus related surplus) that meet the following criteria:

(i) The instrument is issued and paid-in;

(ii) The instrument is subordinated to depositors and general creditors of the national bank or Federal savings association;

(iii) The instrument is not secured, not covered by a guarantee of the national bank or Federal savings association or of an affiliate of the national bank or Federal savings association, and not subject to any other arrangement that legally or economically enhances the seniority of the instrument in relation to more senior claims;

(iv) The instrument has a minimum original maturity of at least five years. At the beginning of each of the last five years of the life of the instrument, the amount that is eligible to be included in tier 2 capital is reduced by 20 percent of the original amount of the instrument (net of redemptions) and is excluded from regulatory capital when the remaining maturity is less than one year. In addition, the instrument must not have any terms or features

[13] *De minimis* assets related to the operation of the issuing entity can be disregarded for purposes of this criterion.

[14] Public Law 111–240; 124 Stat. 2504 (2010).

[15] Public Law 110–343, 122 Stat. 3765 (2008).

that require, or create significant incentives for, the national bank or Federal savings association to redeem the instrument prior to maturity;[16] and

(v) The instrument, by its terms, may be called by the national bank or Federal savings association only after a minimum of five years following issuance, except that the terms of the instrument may allow it to be called sooner upon the occurrence of an event that would preclude the instrument from being included in tier 2 capital, a tax event, or if the issuing entity is required to register as an investment company pursuant to the Investment Company Act of 1940 (15 U.S.C. 80a–1 *et seq.*). In addition:

(A) The national bank or Federal savings association must receive the prior approval of the OCC to exercise a call option on the instrument.

(B) The national bank or Federal savings association does not create at issuance, through action or communication, an expectation the call option will be exercised.

(C) Prior to exercising the call option, or immediately thereafter, the national bank or Federal savings association must either: Replace any amount called with an equivalent amount of an instrument that meets the criteria for regulatory capital under this section;[17] or demonstrate to the satisfaction of the OCC that following redemption, the national bank or Federal savings association would continue to hold an amount of capital that is commensurate with its risk.

(vi) The holder of the instrument must have no contractual right to accelerate payment of principal or interest on the instrument, except in the event of a receivership, insolvency, liquidation, or similar proceeding of the national bank or Federal savings association.

(vii) The instrument has no credit-sensitive feature, such as a dividend or interest rate that is reset periodically based in whole or in part on the national bank's or Federal savings association's credit standing, but may have a dividend rate that is adjusted periodically independent of the national bank's or Federal savings association's credit standing, in relation to general market interest rates or similar adjustments.

(viii) The national bank or Federal savings association, or an entity that the national bank or Federal savings association controls, has not purchased and has not directly or indirectly funded the purchase of the instrument.

(ix) If the instrument is not issued directly by the national bank or Federal savings association or by a subsidiary of the national bank or Federal savings association that is an operating entity, the only asset of the issuing entity is its investment in the capital of the national bank or Federal savings association, and proceeds must be immediately available without limitation to the national bank or Federal savings association or the national bank's or Federal savings association's top-tier holding company in a form that meets or exceeds all the other criteria for tier 2 capital instruments under this section.[18]

(x) Redemption of the instrument prior to maturity or repurchase requires the prior approval of the OCC.

(xi) For an advanced approaches national bank or Federal savings association, the governing agreement, offering circular, or prospectus of an instrument issued after the date on which the advanced approaches national bank or Federal savings association becomes subject to this part under §3.1(f) must disclose that the holders of the instrument may be fully subordinated to interests held by the U.S. government in the event that the national bank or Federal savings association enters into a receivership, insolvency, liquidation, or similar proceeding.

(2) Total capital minority interest, subject to the limitations set forth in

[16] An instrument that by its terms automatically converts into a tier 1 capital instrument prior to five years after issuance complies with the five-year maturity requirement of this criterion.

[17] A national bank or Federal savings association may replace tier 2 capital instruments concurrent with the redemption of existing tier 2 capital instruments.

[18] A national bank or Federal savings association may disregard *de minimis* assets related to the operation of the issuing entity for purposes of this criterion.

§ 3.21(e), that is not included in the national bank's or Federal savings association's tier 1 capital.

(3) ALLL up to 1.25 percent of the national bank's or Federal savings association's standardized total risk-weighted assets not including any amount of the ALLL (and excluding in the case of a market risk national bank or Federal savings association, its standardized market risk-weighted assets).

(4) Any instrument that qualified as tier 2 capital under the OCC's general risk-based capital rules under appendix A to this part, 12 CFR part 167 as then in effect, that were issued under the Small Business Jobs Act of 2010,[19] or prior to October 4, 2010, under the Emergency Economic Stabilization Act of 2008.[20]

(5) For a national bank or Federal savings association that makes an AOCI opt-out election (as defined in paragraph (b)(2) of this section), 45 percent of pretax net unrealized gains on available-for-sale preferred stock classified as an equity security under GAAP and available-for-sale equity exposures.

(6) Notwithstanding the criteria for tier 2 capital instruments referenced above, an instrument with terms that provide that the instrument may be called earlier than five years upon the occurrence of a rating agency event does not violate the criterion in paragraph (d)(1)(v) of this section provided that the instrument was issued and included in a national bank's or Federal savings association's tier 1 or tier 2 capital prior to January 1, 2014, and that such instrument satisfies all other criteria under this paragraph (d).

(e) *OCC approval of a capital element.* (1) A national bank or Federal savings association must receive OCC prior approval to include a capital element (as listed in this section) in its common equity tier 1 capital, additional tier 1 capital, or tier 2 capital unless the element:

(i) Was included in a national bank's or Federal savings association's tier 1 capital or tier 2 capital prior to May 19, 2010 in accordance with the OCC's risk-based capital rules that were effective as of that date and the underlying instrument may continue to be included under the criteria set forth in this section; or

(ii) Is equivalent, in terms of capital quality and ability to absorb losses with respect to all material terms, to a regulatory capital element the OCC determined may be included in regulatory capital pursuant to paragraph (e)(3) of this section.

(2) When considering whether a national bank or Federal savings association may include a regulatory capital element in its common equity tier 1 capital, additional tier 1 capital, or tier 2 capital, the OCC will consult with the Federal Deposit Insurance Corporation and Federal Reserve Board.

(3) After determining that a regulatory capital element may be included in a national bank's or Federal savings association's common equity tier 1 capital, additional tier 1 capital, or tier 2 capital, the OCC will make its decision publicly available, including a brief description of the material terms of the regulatory capital element and the rationale for the determination.

§ 3.21 Minority interest.

(a) *Applicability.* For purposes of § 3.20, a national bank or Federal savings association is subject to the minority interest limitations in this section if:

(1) A consolidated subsidiary of the national bank or Federal savings association has issued regulatory capital that is not owned by the national bank or Federal savings association; and

(2) For each relevant regulatory capital ratio of the consolidated subsidiary, the ratio exceeds the sum of the subsidiary's minimum regulatory capital requirements plus its capital conservation buffer.

(b) *Difference in capital adequacy standards at the subsidiary level.* For purposes of the minority interest calculations in this section, if the consolidated subsidiary issuing the capital is not subject to capital adequacy standards similar to those of the national bank or Federal savings association, the national bank or Federal savings

[19] Public Law 111–240; 124 Stat. 2504 (2010).

[20] Public Law 110–343, 122 Stat. 3765 (2008).

association must assume that the capital adequacy standards of the national bank or Federal savings association apply to the subsidiary.

(c) *Common equity tier 1 minority interest includable in the common equity tier 1 capital of the national bank or Federal savings association.* For each consolidated subsidiary of a national bank or Federal savings association, the amount of common equity tier 1 minority interest the national bank or Federal savings association may include in common equity tier 1 capital is equal to:

(1) The common equity tier 1 minority interest of the subsidiary; minus

(2) The percentage of the subsidiary's common equity tier 1 capital that is not owned by the national bank or Federal savings association, multiplied by the difference between the common equity tier 1 capital of the subsidiary and the lower of:

(i) The amount of common equity tier 1 capital the subsidiary must hold, or would be required to hold pursuant to paragraph (b) of this section, to avoid restrictions on distributions and discretionary bonus payments under §3.11 or equivalent standards established by the subsidiary's home country supervisor; or

(ii)(A) The standardized total risk-weighted assets of the national bank or Federal savings association that relate to the subsidiary multiplied by

(B) The common equity tier 1 capital ratio the subsidiary must maintain to avoid restrictions on distributions and discretionary bonus payments under §3.11 or equivalent standards established by the subsidiary's home country supervisor.

(d) *Tier 1 minority interest includable in the tier 1 capital of the national bank or Federal savings association.* For each consolidated subsidiary of the national bank or Federal savings association, the amount of tier 1 minority interest the national bank or Federal savings association may include in tier 1 capital is equal to:

(1) The tier 1 minority interest of the subsidiary; minus

(2) The percentage of the subsidiary's tier 1 capital that is not owned by the national bank or Federal savings association multiplied by the difference between the tier 1 capital of the subsidiary and the lower of:

(i) The amount of tier 1 capital the subsidiary must hold, or would be required to hold pursuant to paragraph (b) of this section, to avoid restrictions on distributions and discretionary bonus payments under §3.11 or equivalent standards established by the subsidiary's home country supervisor, or

(ii)(A) The standardized total risk-weighted assets of the national bank or Federal savings association that relate to the subsidiary multiplied by

(B) The tier 1 capital ratio the subsidiary must maintain to avoid restrictions on distributions and discretionary bonus payments under §3.11 or equivalent standards established by the subsidiary's home country supervisor.

(e) *Total capital minority interest includable in the total capital of the national bank or Federal savings association.* For each consolidated subsidiary of the national bank or Federal savings association, the amount of total capital minority interest the national bank or Federal savings association may include in total capital is equal to:

(1) The total capital minority interest of the subsidiary; minus

(2) The percentage of the subsidiary's total capital that is not owned by the national bank or Federal savings association multiplied by the difference between the total capital of the subsidiary and the lower of:

(i) The amount of total capital the subsidiary must hold, or would be required to hold pursuant to paragraph (b) of this section, to avoid restrictions on distributions and discretionary bonus payments under §3.11 or equivalent standards established by the subsidiary's home country supervisor, or

(ii)(A) The standardized total risk-weighted assets of the national bank or Federal savings association that relate to the subsidiary multiplied by

(B) The total capital ratio the subsidiary must maintain to avoid restrictions on distributions and discretionary bonus payments under §3.11 or equivalent standards established by the subsidiary's home country supervisor.

§ 3.22 Regulatory capital adjustments and deductions.

(a) *Regulatory capital deductions from common equity tier 1 capital.* A national bank or Federal savings association must deduct from the sum of its common equity tier 1 capital elements the items set forth in this paragraph (a):

(1) Goodwill, net of associated deferred tax liabilities (DTLs) in accordance with paragraph (e) of this section, including goodwill that is embedded in the valuation of a significant investment in the capital of an unconsolidated financial institution in the form of common stock (and that is reflected in the consolidated financial statements of the national bank or Federal savings association), in accordance with paragraph (d) of this section;

(2) Intangible assets, other than MSAs, net of associated DTLs in accordance with paragraph (e) of this section;

(3) Deferred tax assets (DTAs) that arise from net operating loss and tax credit carryforwards net of any related valuation allowances and net of DTLs in accordance with paragraph (e) of this section;

(4) Any gain-on-sale in connection with a securitization exposure;

(5)(i) Any defined benefit pension fund net asset, net of any associated DTL in accordance with paragraph (e) of this section, held by a depository institution holding company. With the prior approval of the OCC, this deduction is not required for any defined benefit pension fund net asset to the extent the depository institution holding company has unrestricted and unfettered access to the assets in that fund.

(ii) For an insured depository institution, no deduction is required.

(iii) A national bank or Federal savings association must risk weight any portion of the defined benefit pension fund asset that is not deducted under paragraphs (a)(5)(i) or (a)(5)(ii) of this section as if the national bank or Federal savings association directly holds a proportional ownership share of each exposure in the defined benefit pension fund.

(6) For an advanced approaches national bank or Federal savings association that has completed the parallel run process and that has received notification from the OCC pursuant to § 3.121(d), the amount of expected credit loss that exceeds its eligible credit reserves; and

(7) With respect to a financial subsidiary, the aggregate amount of the national bank's or Federal savings association's outstanding equity investment, including retained earnings, in its financial subsidiaries (as defined in [12 CFR 5.39 (OCC); 12 CFR 208.77 (Board))]. A national bank or Federal savings association must not consolidate the assets and liabilities of a financial subsidiary with those of the parent bank, and no other deduction is required under paragraph (c) of this section for investments in the capital instruments of financial subsidiaries.

(8)(i) A Federal savings association must deduct the aggregate amount of its outstanding investments (both equity and debt) in, and extensions of credit to, subsidiaries that are not includable subsidiaries as defined in paragraph (a)(8)(iv) of this section and may not consolidate the assets and liabilities of the subsidiary with those of the Federal savings association. Any such deductions shall be deducted from assets and common equity tier 1 except as provided in paragraphs (a)(8)(ii) and (iii) of this section.

(ii) If a Federal savings association has any investments (both debt and equity) in, or extensions or credit to, one or more subsidiaries engaged in any activity that would not fall within the scope of activities in which includable subsidiaries as defined in paragraph (a)(8)(iv) of this section may engage, it must deduct such investments and extensions of credit from assets and, thus, common equity tier 1 in accordance with paragraph (a)(8)(i) of this section.

(iii) If a Federal savings association holds a subsidiary (either directly or through a subsidiary) that is itself a domestic depository institution, the OCC may, in its sole discretion upon determining that the amount of common equity tier 1 that would be required would be higher if the assets and liabilities of such subsidiary were consolidated with those of the parent Federal savings association than the amount that would be required if the parent Federal savings association's investment were deducted pursuant to paragraphs (a)(8)(i) and (ii) of this section, consolidate the assets and liabilities of that subsidiary with those of the parent Federal savings association in calculating the capital adequacy of the parent Federal savings association, regardless of whether the subsidiary would otherwise be an includable subsidiary as defined in paragraph (a)(8)(iv) of this section.

(iv) For purposes of this section, the term includable subsidiary means a subsidiary of a Federal savings association that:

(A) Is engaged solely in activities not impermissible for a national bank;

(B) Is engaged in activities not permissible for a national bank, but only if acting solely as agent for its customers and such agency position is clearly documented in the Federal savings association's files;

(C) Is engaged solely in mortgage-banking activities;

(D)(*1*) Is itself an insured depository institution or a company the sole investment of which is an insured depository institution; and

(*2*) Was acquired by the parent Federal savings association prior to May 1, 1989; or

(E) Was a subsidiary of any Federal savings association existing as a Federal savings association on August 9, 1989:

(*1*) That was chartered prior to October 15, 1982, as a savings bank or a cooperative bank under state law; or

(*2*) That acquired its principal assets from an association that was chartered prior to October 15, 1982, as a savings bank or a cooperative bank under state law.

(b) *Regulatory adjustments to common equity tier 1 capital.* (1) A national bank or Federal savings association must adjust the sum of common equity tier 1 capital elements pursuant to the requirements set forth in this paragraph (b). Such adjustments to common equity tier 1 capital must be made net of the associated deferred tax effects.

(i) A national bank or Federal savings association that makes an AOCI opt-out election (as defined in paragraph (b)(2) of this section), must make the adjustments required under § 3.22(b)(2)(i).

(ii) A national bank or Federal savings association that is an advanced approaches national bank or Federal savings association, and a national bank or Federal savings association that has not made an AOCI opt-out election (as defined in paragraph (b)(2) of this section), must deduct any accumulated net gains and add any accumulated net losses on cash flow hedges included in AOCI that relate to the hedging of items that are not recognized at fair value on the balance sheet.

(iii) A national bank or Federal savings association must deduct any net gain and add any net loss related to changes in the fair value of liabilities that are due to changes in the national bank's or Federal savings association's own credit risk. An advanced approaches national bank or Federal savings association must deduct the difference between its credit spread premium and the risk-free rate for derivatives that are liabilities as part of this adjustment.

(2) *AOCI opt-out election.* (i) A national bank or Federal savings association that is not an advanced approaches national bank or Federal savings association may make a one-time election to opt out of the requirement to include all components of AOCI (with the exception of accumulated net gains and losses on cash flow hedges related to items that are not fair-valued on the balance sheet) in common equity tier 1 capital (AOCI opt-out election). A national bank or Federal savings association that makes an AOCI opt-out election in accordance with this paragraph (b)(2) must adjust common equity tier 1 capital as follows:

(A) Subtract any net unrealized gains and add any net unrealized losses on available-for-sale securities;

(B) Subtract any net unrealized losses on available-for-sale preferred stock classified as an equity security under GAAP and available-for-sale equity exposures;

(C) Subtract any accumulated net gains and add any accumulated net losses on cash flow hedges;

(D) Subtract any amounts recorded in AOCI attributed to defined benefit postretirement plans resulting from the initial and subsequent application of the relevant GAAP standards that pertain to such plans (excluding, at the national bank's or Federal savings association's option, the portion relating to pension assets deducted under paragraph (a)(5) of this section); and

(E) Subtract any net unrealized gains and add any net unrealized losses on held-to-maturity securities that are included in AOCI.

(ii) A national bank or Federal savings association that is not an advanced approaches national bank or Federal savings association must make its AOCI opt-out election in its Call Report filed for the first regulatory reporting period after the date required for such national bank or Federal savings association to comply with subpart A of this part as set forth in § 3.1(f).

(iii) With respect to a national bank or Federal savings association that is not an advanced approaches national bank or Federal savings association, each of its subsidiary banking organizations that is subject to regulatory capital requirements issued by the Board of Governors of the Federal Reserve, the Federal Deposit Insurance Corporation, or the Office of the Comptroller of the Currency[21] must elect the same option as the national bank or Federal savings association pursuant to this paragraph (b)(2).

(iv) With prior notice to the OCC, a national bank or Federal savings association resulting from a merger, acquisition, or purchase transaction and that is not an advanced approaches national bank or Federal savings association may change its AOCI opt-out election in its Call Report filed for the first reporting period after the date required for such national bank or Federal savings association to comply with subpart A of this part as set forth in § 3.1(f) if:

(A) Other than as set forth in paragraph (b)(2)(iv)(C) of this section, the merger, acquisition, or purchase transaction involved the acquisition or purchase of all or substantially all of either the assets or voting stock of another banking organization that is subject to regulatory capital requirements issued by the Board of Governors of the Federal Reserve, the Federal Deposit Insurance Corporation, or the Office of the Comptroller of the Currency;[22]

(B) Prior to the merger, acquisition, or purchase transaction, only one of the banking organizations involved in the transaction made an AOCI opt-out election under this section; and

(C) A national bank or Federal savings association may, with the prior approval of the OCC, change its AOCI opt-out election under this paragraph (b) in the case of a merger, acquisition, or purchase transaction that meets the requirements set forth at paragraph (b)(2)(iv)(B) of this section, but does not meet the requirements of paragraph (b)(2)(iv)(A). In making such a determination, the OCC may consider the terms of the merger, acquisition, or purchase transaction, as well as the extent of any changes to the risk profile, complexity, and scope of operations of the national bank or Federal savings association resulting from the merger, acquisition, or purchase transaction.

(c) *Deductions from regulatory capital related to investments in capital instruments*[23]—(1) *Investment in the national bank's or Federal savings association's own capital instruments.* A national bank or Federal savings association must deduct an investment in the national bank's or Federal savings association's own capital instruments as follows:

(i) A national bank or Federal savings association must deduct an investment in the national bank's or Federal savings association's own common stock instruments from its common equity tier 1 capital elements to the extent such instruments are not excluded from regulatory capital under § 3.20(b)(1);

[21] These rules include the regulatory capital requirements set forth at 12 CFR part 3 (OCC); 12 CFR part 225 (Board); 12 CFR part 325, and 12 CFR part 390 (FDIC).

[22] These rules include the regulatory capital requirements set forth at 12 CFR part 3 (OCC); 12 CFR part 225 (Board); 12 CFR part 325, and 12 CFR part 390 (FDIC).

[23] The national bank or Federal savings association must calculate amounts deducted under paragraphs (c) through (f) of this section after it calculates the amount of ALLL includable in tier 2 capital under § 3.20(d)(3).

(ii) A national bank or Federal savings association must deduct an investment in the national bank's or Federal savings association's own additional tier 1 capital instruments from its additional tier 1 capital elements; and

(iii) A national bank or Federal savings association must deduct an investment in the national bank's or Federal savings association's own tier 2 capital instruments from its tier 2 capital elements.

(2) *Corresponding deduction approach.* For purposes of subpart C of this part, the corresponding deduction approach is the methodology used for the deductions from regulatory capital related to reciprocal cross holdings (as described in paragraph (c)(3) of this section), non-significant investments in the capital of unconsolidated financial institutions (as described in paragraph (c)(4) of this section), and non-common stock significant investments in the capital of unconsolidated financial institutions (as described in paragraph (c)(5) of this section). Under the corresponding deduction approach, a national bank or Federal savings association must make deductions from the component of capital for which the underlying instrument would qualify if it were issued by the national bank or Federal savings association itself, as described in paragraphs (c)(2)(i)–(iii) of this section. If the national bank or Federal savings association does not have a sufficient amount of a specific component of capital to effect the required deduction, the shortfall must be deducted according to paragraph (f) of this section.

(i) If an investment is in the form of an instrument issued by a financial institution that is not a regulated financial institution, the national bank or Federal savings association must treat the instrument as:

(A) A common equity tier 1 capital instrument if it is common stock or represents the most subordinated claim in liquidation of the financial institution; and

(B) An additional tier 1 capital instrument if it is subordinated to all creditors of the financial institution and is senior in liquidation only to common shareholders.

(ii) If an investment is in the form of an instrument issued by a regulated financial institution and the instrument does not meet the criteria for common equity tier 1, additional tier 1 or tier 2 capital instruments under § 3.20, the national bank or Federal savings association must treat the instrument as:

(A) A common equity tier 1 capital instrument if it is common stock included in GAAP equity or represents the most subordinated claim in liquidation of the financial institution;

(B) An additional tier 1 capital instrument if it is included in GAAP equity, subordinated to all creditors of the financial institution, and senior in a receivership, insolvency, liquidation, or similar proceeding only to common shareholders; and

(C) A tier 2 capital instrument if it is not included in GAAP equity but considered regulatory capital by the primary supervisor of the financial institution.

(iii) If an investment is in the form of a non-qualifying capital instrument (as defined in § 3.300(c)), the national bank or Federal savings association must treat the instrument as:

(A) An additional tier 1 capital instrument if such instrument was included in the issuer's tier 1 capital prior to May 19, 2010; or

(B) A tier 2 capital instrument if such instrument was included in the issuer's tier 2 capital (but not includable in tier 1 capital) prior to May 19, 2010.

(3) *Reciprocal cross holdings in the capital of financial institutions.* A national bank or Federal savings association must deduct investments in the capital of other financial institutions it holds reciprocally, where such reciprocal cross holdings result from a formal or informal arrangement to swap, exchange, or otherwise intend to hold each other's capital instruments, by applying the corresponding deduction approach.

(4) *Non-significant investments in the capital of unconsolidated financial institutions.* (i) A national bank or Federal savings association must deduct its non-significant investments in the capital of unconsolidated financial institutions (as defined in § 3.2) that, in the aggregate, exceed 10 percent of the sum

of the national bank's or Federal savings association's common equity tier 1 capital elements minus all deductions from and adjustments to common equity tier 1 capital elements required under paragraphs (a) through (c)(3) of this section (the 10 percent threshold for non-significant investments) by applying the corresponding deduction approach.[24] The deductions described in this section are net of associated DTLs in accordance with paragraph (e) of this section. In addition, a national bank or Federal savings association that underwrites a failed underwriting, with the prior written approval of the OCC, for the period of time stipulated by the OCC, is not required to deduct a non-significant investment in the capital of an unconsolidated financial institution pursuant to this paragraph (c) to the extent the investment is related to the failed underwriting.[25]

(ii) The amount to be deducted under this section from a specific capital component is equal to:

(A) The national bank's or Federal savings association's non-significant investments in the capital of unconsolidated financial institutions exceeding the 10 percent threshold for non-significant investments, multiplied by

(B) The ratio of the national bank's or Federal savings association's non-significant investments in the capital of unconsolidated financial institutions in the form of such capital component to the national bank's or Federal savings association's total non-significant investments in unconsolidated financial institutions.

(5) *Significant investments in the capital of unconsolidated financial institutions that are not in the form of common stock.* A national bank or Federal savings association must deduct its significant investments in the capital of unconsolidated financial institutions that are not in the form of common stock by applying the corresponding deduction approach.[26] The deductions described in this section are net of associated DTLs in accordance with paragraph (e) of this section. In addition, with the prior written approval of the OCC, for the period of time stipulated by the OCC, a national bank or Federal savings association that underwrites a failed underwriting is not required to deduct a significant investment in the capital of an unconsolidated financial institution pursuant to this paragraph (c) if such investment is related to such failed underwriting.

(d) *Items subject to the 10 and 15 percent common equity tier 1 capital deduction thresholds.* (1) A national bank or Federal savings association must deduct from common equity tier 1 capital elements the amount of each of the items set forth in this paragraph (d) that, individually, exceeds 10 percent of the sum of the national bank's or Federal savings association's common equity tier 1 capital elements, less adjustments to and deductions from common equity tier 1 capital required under paragraphs (a) through (c) of this section (the 10 percent common equity tier 1 capital deduction threshold).

(i) DTAs arising from temporary differences that the national bank or Federal savings association could not realize through net operating loss carrybacks, net of any related valuation allowances and net of DTLs, in accordance with paragraph (e) of this section. A national bank or Federal savings association is not required to

[24] With the prior written approval of the OCC, for the period of time stipulated by the OCC, a national bank or Federal savings association is not required to deduct a non-significant investment in the capital instrument of an unconsolidated financial institution pursuant to this paragraph if the financial institution is in distress and if such investment is made for the purpose of providing financial support to the financial institution, as determined by the OCC.

[25] Any non-significant investments in the capital of unconsolidated financial institutions that do not exceed the 10 percent threshold for non-significant investments under this section must be assigned the appropriate risk weight under subparts D, E, or F of this part, as applicable.

[26] With prior written approval of the OCC, for the period of time stipulated by the OCC, a national bank or Federal savings association is not required to deduct a significant investment in the capital instrument of an unconsolidated financial institution in distress which is not in the form of common stock pursuant to this section if such investment is made for the purpose of providing financial support to the financial institution as determined by the OCC.

deduct from the sum of its common equity tier 1 capital elements DTAs (net of any related valuation allowances and net of DTLs, in accordance with § 3.22(e)) arising from timing differences that the national bank or Federal savings association could realize through net operating loss carrybacks. The national bank or Federal savings association must risk weight these assets at 100 percent. For a national bank or Federal savings association that is a member of a consolidated group for tax purposes, the amount of DTAs that could be realized through net operating loss carrybacks may not exceed the amount that the national bank or Federal savings association could reasonably expect to have refunded by its parent holding company.

(ii) MSAs net of associated DTLs, in accordance with paragraph (e) of this section.

(iii) Significant investments in the capital of unconsolidated financial institutions in the form of common stock, net of associated DTLs in accordance with paragraph (e) of this section.[27] Significant investments in the capital of unconsolidated financial institutions in the form of common stock subject to the 10 percent common equity tier 1 capital deduction threshold may be reduced by any goodwill embedded in the valuation of such investments deducted by the national bank or Federal savings association pursuant to paragraph (a)(1) of this section. In addition, with the prior written approval of the OCC, for the period of time stipulated by the OCC, a national bank or Federal savings association that underwrites a failed underwriting is not required to deduct a significant investment in the capital of an unconsolidated financial institution in the form of common stock pursuant to this paragraph (d) if such investment is related to such failed underwriting.

(2) A national bank or Federal savings association must deduct from common equity tier 1 capital elements the items listed in paragraph (d)(1) of this section that are not deducted as a result of the application of the 10 percent common equity tier 1 capital deduction threshold, and that, in aggregate, exceed 17.65 percent of the sum of the national bank's or Federal savings association's common equity tier 1 capital elements, minus adjustments to and deductions from common equity tier 1 capital required under paragraphs (a) through (c) of this section, minus the items listed in paragraph (d)(1) of this section (the 15 percent common equity tier 1 capital deduction threshold). Any goodwill that has been deducted under paragraph (a)(1) of this section can be excluded from the significant investments in the capital of unconsolidated financial institutions in the form of common stock.[28]

(3) For purposes of calculating the amount of DTAs subject to the 10 and 15 percent common equity tier 1 capital deduction thresholds, a national bank or Federal savings association may exclude DTAs and DTLs relating to adjustments made to common equity tier 1 capital under paragraph (b) of this section. A national bank or Federal savings association that elects to exclude DTAs relating to adjustments under paragraph (b) of this section also must exclude DTLs and must do so consistently in all future calculations. A national bank or Federal savings association may change its exclusion preference only after obtaining the prior approval of the OCC.

(e) *Netting of DTLs against assets subject to deduction.* (1) Except as described in paragraph (e)(3) of this section, netting of DTLs against assets that are subject to deduction under this section is permitted, but not required, if the following conditions are met:

[27] With the prior written approval of the OCC, for the period of time stipulated by the OCC, a national bank or Federal savings association is not required to deduct a significant investment in the capital instrument of an unconsolidated financial institution in distress in the form of common stock pursuant to this section if such investment is made for the purpose of providing financial support to the financial institution as determined by the OCC.

[28] The amount of the items in paragraph (d) of this section that is not deducted from common equity tier 1 capital pursuant to this section must be included in the risk-weighted assets of the national bank or Federal savings association and assigned a 250 percent risk weight.

(i) The DTL is associated with the asset; and

(ii) The DTL would be extinguished if the associated asset becomes impaired or is derecognized under GAAP.

(2) A DTL may only be netted against a single asset.

(3) For purposes of calculating the amount of DTAs subject to the threshold deduction in paragraph (d) of this section, the amount of DTAs that arise from net operating loss and tax credit carryforwards, net of any related valuation allowances, and of DTAs arising from temporary differences that the national bank or Federal savings association could not realize through net operating loss carrybacks, net of any related valuation allowances, may be offset by DTLs (that have not been netted against assets subject to deduction pursuant to paragraph (e)(1) of this section) subject to the conditions set forth in this paragraph (e).

(i) Only the DTAs and DTLs that relate to taxes levied by the same taxation authority and that are eligible for offsetting by that authority may be offset for purposes of this deduction.

(ii) The amount of DTLs that the national bank or Federal savings association nets against DTAs that arise from net operating loss and tax credit carryforwards, net of any related valuation allowances, and against DTAs arising from temporary differences that the national bank or Federal savings association could not realize through net operating loss carrybacks, net of any related valuation allowances, must be allocated in proportion to the amount of DTAs that arise from net operating loss and tax credit carryforwards (net of any related valuation allowances, but before any offsetting of DTLs) and of DTAs arising from temporary differences that the national bank or Federal savings association could not realize through net operating loss carrybacks (net of any related valuation allowances, but before any offsetting of DTLs), respectively.

(4) A national bank or Federal savings association may offset DTLs embedded in the carrying value of a leveraged lease portfolio acquired in a business combination that are not recognized under GAAP against DTAs that are subject to paragraph (d) of this section in accordance with this paragraph (e).

(5) A national bank or Federal savings association must net DTLs against assets subject to deduction under this section in a consistent manner from reporting period to reporting period. A national bank or Federal savings association may change its preference regarding the manner in which it nets DTLs against specific assets subject to deduction under this section only after obtaining the prior approval of the OCC.

(f) *Insufficient amounts of a specific regulatory capital component to effect deductions.* Under the corresponding deduction approach, if a national bank or Federal savings association does not have a sufficient amount of a specific component of capital to effect the required deduction after completing the deductions required under paragraph (d) of this section, the national bank or Federal savings association must deduct the shortfall from the next higher (that is, more subordinated) component of regulatory capital.

(g) *Treatment of assets that are deducted.* A national bank or Federal savings association must exclude from standardized total risk-weighted assets and, as applicable, advanced approaches total risk-weighted assets any item deducted from regulatory capital under paragraphs (a), (c), and (d) of this section.

(h) *Net long position.* (1) For purposes of calculating an investment in the national bank's or Federal savings association's own capital instrument and an investment in the capital of an unconsolidated financial institution under this section, the net long position is the gross long position in the underlying instrument determined in accordance with paragraph (h)(2) of this section, as adjusted to recognize a short position in the same instrument calculated in accordance with paragraph (h)(3) of this section.

(2) *Gross long position.* The gross long position is determined as follows:

(i) For an equity exposure that is held directly, the adjusted carrying value as that term is defined in § 3.51(b);

(ii) For an exposure that is held directly and is not an equity exposure or a securitization exposure, the exposure amount as that term is defined in § 3.2;

(iii) For an indirect exposure, the national bank's or Federal savings association's carrying value of the investment in the investment fund, provided that, alternatively:

(A) A national bank or Federal savings association may, with the prior approval of the OCC, use a conservative estimate of the amount of its investment in its own capital instruments or the capital of an unconsolidated financial institution held through a position in an index; or

(B) A national bank or Federal savings association may calculate the gross long position for the national bank's or Federal savings association's own capital instruments or the capital of an unconsolidated financial institution by multiplying the national bank's or Federal savings association's carrying value of its investment in the investment fund by either:

(*1*) The highest stated investment limit (in percent) for investments in the national bank's or Federal savings association's own capital instruments or the capital of unconsolidated financial institutions as stated in the prospectus, partnership agreement, or similar contract defining permissible investments of the investment fund; or

(*2*) The investment fund's actual holdings of own capital instruments or the capital of unconsolidated financial institutions.

(iv) For a synthetic exposure, the amount of the national bank's or Federal savings association's loss on the exposure if the reference capital instrument were to have a value of zero.

(3) *Adjustments to reflect a short position*. In order to adjust the gross long position to recognize a short position in the same instrument, the following criteria must be met:

(i) The maturity of the short position must match the maturity of the long position, or the short position has a residual maturity of at least one year (maturity requirement); or

(ii) For a position that is a trading asset or trading liability (whether on- or off-balance sheet) as reported on the national bank's or Federal savings association's Call Report, if the national bank or Federal savings association has a contractual right or obligation to sell the long position at a specific point in time and the counterparty to the contract has an obligation to purchase the long position if the national bank or Federal savings association exercises its right to sell, this point in time may be treated as the maturity of the long position such that the maturity of the long position and short position are deemed to match for purposes of the maturity requirement, even if the maturity of the short position is less than one year; and

(iii) For an investment in the national bank's or Federal savings association's own capital instrument under paragraph (c)(1) of this section or an investment in a capital of an unconsolidated financial institution under paragraphs (c)(4), (c)(5), and (d)(1)(iii) of this section.

(A) A national bank or Federal savings association may only net a short position against a long position in the national bank's or Federal savings association's own capital instrument under paragraph (c)(1) of this section if the short position involves no counterparty credit risk.

(B) A gross long position in a national bank's or Federal savings association's own capital instrument or in a capital instrument of an unconsolidated financial institution resulting from a position in an index may be netted against a short position in the same index. Long and short positions in the same index without maturity dates are considered to have matching maturities.

(C) A short position in an index that is hedging a long cash or synthetic position in a national bank's or Federal savings association's own capital instrument or in a capital instrument of an unconsolidated financial institution can be decomposed to provide recognition of the hedge. More specifically, the portion of the index that is composed of the same underlying instrument that is being hedged may be used to offset the long position if both the long position being hedged and the short position in the index are reported as a trading asset or trading liability (whether on- or off-balance sheet) on the national bank's or Federal savings association's Call Report, and the hedge is deemed effective by the national bank's or Federal savings association's internal control processes, which have not been found to be inadequate by the OCC.

[78 FR 62157, 62273, Oct. 11, 2013, as amended at 80 FR 41415, July 15, 2015]

§§ 3.23–3.29 [Reserved]

Subpart D—Risk-Weighted Assets—Standardized Approach

SOURCE: 78 FR 62157, 62273, Oct. 11, 2013, unless otherwise noted.

§ 3.30 Applicability.

(a) This subpart sets forth methodologies for determining risk-weighted assets for purposes of the generally applicable risk-based capital requirements for all national banks or Federal savings associations.

(b) Notwithstanding paragraph (a) of this section, a market risk national bank or Federal savings association must exclude from its calculation of risk-weighted assets under this subpart the risk-weighted asset amounts of all covered positions, as defined in subpart F of this part (except foreign exchange positions that are not trading positions, OTC derivative positions, cleared transactions, and unsettled transactions).

RISK-WEIGHTED ASSETS FOR GENERAL CREDIT RISK

§ 3.31 Mechanics for calculating risk-weighted assets for general credit risk.

(a) *General risk-weighting requirements.* A national bank or Federal savings association must apply risk weights to its exposures as follows:

(1) A national bank or Federal savings association must determine the exposure amount of each on-balance sheet exposure, each OTC derivative contract, and each off-balance sheet commitment, trade and transaction-related contingency, guarantee, repo-style transaction, financial standby letter of credit, forward agreement, or other similar transaction that is not:

(i) An unsettled transaction subject to § 3.38;

(ii) A cleared transaction subject to § 3.35;

(iii) A default fund contribution subject to § 3.35;

(iv) A securitization exposure subject to §§ 3.41 through 3.45; or

(v) An equity exposure (other than an equity OTC derivative contract) subject to §§ 3.51 through 3.53.

(2) The national bank or Federal savings association must multiply each exposure amount by the risk weight appropriate to the exposure based on the exposure type or counterparty, eligible guarantor, or financial collateral to determine the risk-weighted asset amount for each exposure.

(b) Total risk-weighted assets for general credit risk equals the sum of the risk-weighted asset amounts calculated under this section.

§ 3.32 General risk weights.

(a) *Sovereign exposures*—(1) *Exposures to the U.S. government.* (i) Notwithstanding any other requirement in this subpart, a national bank or Federal savings association must assign a zero percent risk weight to:

(A) An exposure to the U.S. government, its central bank, or a U.S. government agency; and

(B) The portion of an exposure that is directly and unconditionally guaranteed by the U.S. government, its central bank, or a U.S. government agency. This includes a deposit or other exposure, or the portion of a deposit or other exposure, that is insured or otherwise unconditionally guaranteed by the FDIC or National Credit Union Administration.

(ii) A national bank or Federal savings association must assign a 20 percent risk weight to the portion of an exposure that is conditionally guaranteed by the U.S. government, its central bank, or a U.S. government agency. This includes an exposure, or the portion of an exposure, that is conditionally guaranteed by the FDIC or National Credit Union Administration.

(2) *Other sovereign exposures.* In accordance with Table 1 to § 3.32, a national bank or Federal savings association must assign a risk weight to a sovereign exposure based on the CRC applicable to the sovereign or the sovereign's OECD membership status if

there is no CRC applicable to the sovereign.

TABLE 1 TO § 3.32—RISK WEIGHTS FOR SOVEREIGN EXPOSURES

	Risk weight (in percent)
CRC:	
0–1	0
2	20
3	50
4–6	100
7	150
OECD Member with No CRC	0
Non-OECD Member with No CRC	100
Sovereign Default	150

(3) *Certain sovereign exposures.* Notwithstanding paragraph (a)(2) of this section, a national bank or Federal savings association may assign to a sovereign exposure a risk weight that is lower than the applicable risk weight in Table 1 to § 3.32 if:

(i) The exposure is denominated in the sovereign's currency;

(ii) The national bank or Federal savings association has at least an equivalent amount of liabilities in that currency; and

(iii) The risk weight is not lower than the risk weight that the home country supervisor allows national banks or Federal savings associations under its jurisdiction to assign to the same exposures to the sovereign.

(4) *Exposures to a non-OECD member sovereign with no CRC.* Except as provided in paragraphs (a)(3), (a)(5) and (a)(6) of this section, a national bank or Federal savings association must assign a 100 percent risk weight to an exposure to a sovereign if the sovereign does not have a CRC.

(5) *Exposures to an OECD member sovereign with no CRC.* Except as provided in paragraph (a)(6) of this section, a national bank or Federal savings association must assign a 0 percent risk weight to an exposure to a sovereign that is a member of the OECD if the sovereign does not have a CRC.

(6) *Sovereign default.* A national bank or Federal savings association must assign a 150 percent risk weight to a sovereign exposure immediately upon determining that an event of sovereign default has occurred, or if an event of sovereign default has occurred during the previous five years.

(b) *Certain supranational entities and multilateral development banks (MDBs).* A national bank or Federal savings association must assign a zero percent risk weight to an exposure to the Bank for International Settlements, the European Central Bank, the European Commission, the International Monetary Fund, or an MDB.

(c) *Exposures to GSEs.* (1) A national bank or Federal savings association must assign a 20 percent risk weight to an exposure to a GSE other than an equity exposure or preferred stock.

(2) A national bank or Federal savings association must assign a 100 percent risk weight to preferred stock issued by a GSE.

(d) *Exposures to depository institutions, foreign banks, and credit unions*—(1) *Exposures to U.S. depository institutions and credit unions.* A national bank or Federal savings association must assign a 20 percent risk weight to an exposure to a depository institution or credit union that is organized under the laws of the United States or any state thereof, except as otherwise provided under paragraph (d)(3) of this section.

(2) *Exposures to foreign banks.* (i) Except as otherwise provided under paragraphs (d)(2)(iv) and (d)(3) of this section, a national bank or Federal savings association must assign a risk weight to an exposure to a foreign bank, in accordance with Table 2 to § 3.32, based on the CRC that corresponds to the foreign bank's home country or the OECD membership status of the foreign bank's home country if there is no CRC applicable to the foreign bank's home country.

TABLE 2 TO § 3.32—RISK WEIGHTS FOR EXPOSURES TO FOREIGN BANKS

	Risk weight (in percent)
CRC:	
0–1	20
2	50
3	100
4–7	150
OECD Member with No CRC	20
Non-OECD Member with No CRC	100
Sovereign Default	150

(ii) A national bank or Federal savings association must assign a 20 percent risk weight to an exposure to a foreign bank whose home country is a member of the OECD and does not have a CRC.

(iii) A national bank or Federal savings association must assign a 100 percent risk weight to an exposure to a foreign bank whose home country is not a member of the OECD and does not have a CRC, with the exception of self-liquidating, trade-related contingent items that arise from the movement of goods, and that have a maturity of three months or less, which may be assigned a 20 percent risk weight.

(iv) A national bank or Federal savings association must assign a 150 percent risk weight to an exposure to a foreign bank immediately upon determining that an event of sovereign default has occurred in the bank's home country, or if an event of sovereign default has occurred in the foreign bank's home country during the previous five years.

(3) A national bank or Federal savings association must assign a 100 percent risk weight to an exposure to a financial institution if the exposure may be included in that financial institution's capital unless the exposure is:

(i) An equity exposure;

(ii) A significant investment in the capital of an unconsolidated financial institution in the form of common stock pursuant to § 3.22(d)(iii);

(iii) Deducted from regulatory capital under § 3.22; or

(iv) Subject to a 150 percent risk weight under paragraph (d)(2)(iv) or Table 2 of paragraph (d)(2) of this section.

(e) *Exposures to public sector entities (PSEs)*—(1) *Exposures to U.S. PSEs.* (i) A national bank or Federal savings association must assign a 20 percent risk weight to a general obligation exposure to a PSE that is organized under the laws of the United States or any state or political subdivision thereof.

(ii) A national bank or Federal savings association must assign a 50 percent risk weight to a revenue obligation exposure to a PSE that is organized under the laws of the United States or any state or political subdivision thereof.

(2) *Exposures to foreign PSEs.* (i) Except as provided in paragraphs (e)(1) and (e)(3) of this section, a national bank or Federal savings association must assign a risk weight to a general obligation exposure to a PSE, in accordance with Table 3 to § 3.32, based on the CRC that corresponds to the PSE's home country or the OECD membership status of the PSE's home country if there is no CRC applicable to the PSE's home country.

(ii) Except as provided in paragraphs (e)(1) and (e)(3) of this section, a national bank or Federal savings association must assign a risk weight to a revenue obligation exposure to a PSE, in accordance with Table 4 to § 3.32, based on the CRC that corresponds to the PSE's home country; or the OECD membership status of the PSE's home country if there is no CRC applicable to the PSE's home country.

(3) A national bank or Federal savings association may assign a lower risk weight than would otherwise apply under Tables 3 or 4 to § 3.32 to an exposure to a foreign PSE if:

(i) The PSE's home country supervisor allows banks under its jurisdiction to assign a lower risk weight to such exposures; and

(ii) The risk weight is not lower than the risk weight that corresponds to the PSE's home country in accordance with Table 1 to § 3.32.

TABLE 3 TO § 3.32—RISK WEIGHTS FOR NON-U.S. PSE GENERAL OBLIGATIONS

	Risk weight (in percent)
CRC:	
0–1	20
2	50
3	100
4–7	150
OECD Member with No CRC	20
Non-OECD Member with No CRC	100
Sovereign Default	150

TABLE 4 TO § 3.32—RISK WEIGHTS FOR NON-U.S. PSE REVENUE OBLIGATIONS

	Risk weight (in percent)
CRC:	
0–1	50
2–3	100
4–7	150
OECD Member with No CRC	50
Non-OECD Member with No CRC	100
Sovereign Default	150

(4) *Exposures to PSEs from an OECD member sovereign with no CRC.* (i) A national bank or Federal savings association must assign a 20 percent risk weight to a general obligation exposure to a PSE whose home country is an OECD member sovereign with no CRC.

(ii) A national bank or Federal savings association must assign a 50 percent risk weight to a revenue obligation exposure to a PSE whose home country is an OECD member sovereign with no CRC.

(5) *Exposures to PSEs whose home country is not an OECD member sovereign with no CRC.* A national bank or Federal savings association must assign a 100 percent risk weight to an exposure to a PSE whose home country is not a member of the OECD and does not have a CRC.

(6) A national bank or Federal savings association must assign a 150 percent risk weight to a PSE exposure immediately upon determining that an event of sovereign default has occurred in a PSE's home country or if an event of sovereign default has occurred in the PSE's home country during the previous five years.

(f) *Corporate exposures.* A national bank or Federal savings association must assign a 100 percent risk weight to all its corporate exposures.

(g) *Residential mortgage exposures.* (1) A national bank or Federal savings association must assign a 50 percent risk weight to a first-lien residential mortgage exposure that:

(i) Is secured by a property that is either owner-occupied or rented;

(ii) Is made in accordance with prudent underwriting standards, including standards relating to the loan amount as a percent of the appraised value of the property;

(iii) Is not 90 days or more past due or carried in nonaccrual status; and

(iv) Is not restructured or modified.

(2) A national bank or Federal savings association must assign a 100 percent risk weight to a first-lien residential mortgage exposure that does not meet the criteria in paragraph (g)(1) of this section, and to junior-lien residential mortgage exposures.

(3) For the purpose of this paragraph (g), if a national bank or Federal savings association holds the first-lien and junior-lien(s) residential mortgage exposures, and no other party holds an intervening lien, the national bank or Federal savings association must combine the exposures and treat them as a single first-lien residential mortgage exposure.

(4) A loan modified or restructured solely pursuant to the U.S. Treasury's Home Affordable Mortgage Program is not modified or restructured for purposes of this section.

(h) *Pre-sold construction loans.* A national bank or Federal savings association must assign a 50 percent risk weight to a pre-sold construction loan unless the purchase contract is cancelled, in which case a national bank or Federal savings association must assign a 100 percent risk weight.

(i) *Statutory multifamily mortgages.* A national bank or Federal savings association must assign a 50 percent risk weight to a statutory multifamily mortgage.

(j) *High-volatility commercial real estate (HVCRE) exposures.* A national bank or Federal savings association must assign a 150 percent risk weight to an HVCRE exposure.

(k) *Past due exposures.* Except for a sovereign exposure or a residential mortgage exposure, a national bank or Federal savings association must determine a risk weight for an exposure that is 90 days or more past due or on nonaccrual according to the requirements set forth in this paragraph (k).

(1) A national bank or Federal savings association must assign a 150 percent risk weight to the portion of the exposure that is not guaranteed or that is unsecured.

(2) A national bank or Federal savings association may assign a risk weight to the guaranteed portion of a past due exposure based on the risk weight that applies under § 3.36 if the guarantee or credit derivative meets the requirements of that section.

(3) A national bank or Federal savings association may assign a risk weight to the collateralized portion of a past due exposure based on the risk weight that applies under § 3.37 if the collateral meets the requirements of that section.

(l) *Other assets.* (1) A national bank or Federal savings association must assign a zero percent risk weight to cash owned and held in all offices of the national bank or Federal savings association or in transit; to gold bullion held in the national bank's or Federal savings association's own vaults or held in another depository institution's vaults on an allocated basis, to the extent the gold bullion assets are offset by gold bullion liabilities; and to exposures that arise from the settlement of cash transactions (such as equities, fixed income, spot foreign exchange and spot commodities) with a central counterparty where there is no assumption of ongoing counterparty credit risk by the central counterparty after settlement of the trade and associated default fund contributions.

(2) A national bank or Federal savings association must assign a 20 percent risk weight to cash items in the process of collection.

(3) A national bank or Federal savings association must assign a 100 percent risk weight to DTAs arising from temporary differences that the national bank or Federal savings association could realize through net operating loss carrybacks.

(4) A national bank or Federal savings association must assign a 250 percent risk weight to the portion of each of the following items that is not deducted from common equity tier 1 capital pursuant to § 3.22(d):

(i) MSAs; and

(ii) DTAs arising from temporary differences that the national bank or Federal savings association could not realize through net operating loss carrybacks.

(5) A national bank or Federal savings association must assign a 100 percent risk weight to all assets not specifically assigned a different risk weight under this subpart and that are not deducted from tier 1 or tier 2 capital pursuant to § 3.22.

(6) Notwithstanding the requirements of this section, a national bank or Federal savings association may assign an asset that is not included in one of the categories provided in this section to the risk weight category applicable under the capital rules applicable to bank holding companies and savings and loan holding companies at 12 CFR part 217, provided that all of the following conditions apply:

(i) The national bank or Federal savings association is not authorized to hold the asset under applicable law other than debt previously contracted or similar authority; and

(ii) The risks associated with the asset are substantially similar to the risks of assets that are otherwise assigned to a risk weight category of less than 100 percent under this subpart.

§ 3.33 Off-balance sheet exposures.

(a) *General.* (1) A national bank or Federal savings association must calculate the exposure amount of an off-balance sheet exposure using the credit conversion factors (CCFs) in paragraph (b) of this section.

(2) Where a national bank or Federal savings association commits to provide a commitment, the national bank or Federal savings association may apply the lower of the two applicable CCFs.

(3) Where a national bank or Federal savings association provides a commitment structured as a syndication or participation, the national bank or Federal savings association is only required to calculate the exposure amount for its pro rata share of the commitment.

(4) Where a national bank or Federal savings association provides a commitment, enters into a repurchase agreement, or provides a credit-enhancing representation and warranty, and such commitment, repurchase agreement, or credit-enhancing representation and warranty is not a securitization exposure, the exposure amount shall be no greater than the maximum contractual amount of the commitment, repurchase agreement, or credit-enhancing representation and warranty, as applicable.

(b) *Credit conversion factors*—(1) *Zero percent CCF.* A national bank or Federal savings association must apply a zero percent CCF to the unused portion of a commitment that is unconditionally cancelable by the national bank or Federal savings association.

(2) *20 percent CCF.* A national bank or Federal savings association must apply a 20 percent CCF to the amount of:

(i) Commitments with an original maturity of one year or less that are not unconditionally cancelable by the national bank or Federal savings association; and

(ii) Self-liquidating, trade-related contingent items that arise from the movement of goods, with an original maturity of one year or less.

(3) *50 percent CCF.* A national bank or Federal savings association must apply a 50 percent CCF to the amount of:

(i) Commitments with an original maturity of more than one year that are not unconditionally cancelable by the national bank or Federal savings association; and

(ii) Transaction-related contingent items, including performance bonds, bid bonds, warranties, and performance standby letters of credit.

(4) *100 percent CCF.* A national bank or Federal savings association must apply a 100 percent CCF to the amount of the following off-balance-sheet items and other similar transactions:

(i) Guarantees;

(ii) Repurchase agreements (the off-balance sheet component of which equals the sum of the current fair values of all positions the national bank or Federal savings association has sold subject to repurchase);

(iii) Credit-enhancing representations and warranties that are not securitization exposures;

(iv) Off-balance sheet securities lending transactions (the off-balance sheet component of which equals the sum of the current fair values of all positions the national bank or Federal savings association has lent under the transaction);

(v) Off-balance sheet securities borrowing transactions (the off-balance sheet component of which equals the sum of the current fair values of all non-cash positions the national bank or Federal savings association has posted as collateral under the transaction);

(vi) Financial standby letters of credit; and

(vii) Forward agreements.

§ 3.34 OTC derivative contracts.

(a) *Exposure amount*—(1) *Single OTC derivative contract.* Except as modified by paragraph (b) of this section, the exposure amount for a single OTC derivative contract that is not subject to a qualifying master netting agreement is equal to the sum of the national bank's or Federal savings association's current credit exposure and potential future credit exposure (PFE) on the OTC derivative contract.

(i) *Current credit exposure.* The current credit exposure for a single OTC derivative contract is the greater of the mark-to-fair value of the OTC derivative contract or zero.

(ii) *PFE.* (A) The PFE for a single OTC derivative contract, including an OTC derivative contract with a negative mark-to-fair value, is calculated by multiplying the notional principal amount of the OTC derivative contract by the appropriate conversion factor in Table 1 to § 3.34.

(B) For purposes of calculating either the PFE under this paragraph (a) or the gross PFE under paragraph (a)(2) of this section for exchange rate contracts and other similar contracts in which the notional principal amount is equivalent to the cash flows, notional principal amount is the net receipts to each party falling due on each value date in each currency.

(C) For an OTC derivative contract that does not fall within one of the specified categories in Table 1 to § 3.34, the PFE must be calculated using the appropriate "other" conversion factor.

(D) A national bank or Federal savings association must use an OTC derivative contract's effective notional principal amount (that is, the apparent or stated notional principal amount multiplied by any multiplier in the OTC derivative contract) rather than the apparent or stated notional principal amount in calculating PFE.

(E) The PFE of the protection provider of a credit derivative is capped at the net present value of the amount of unpaid premiums.

TABLE 1 TO § 3.34—CONVERSION FACTOR MATRIX FOR DERIVATIVE CONTRACTS [1]

Remaining maturity [2]	Interest rate	Foreign exchange rate and gold	Credit (investment grade reference asset) [3]	Credit (non-investment-grade reference asset)	Equity	Precious metals (except gold)	Other
One year or less	0.00	0.01	0.05	0.10	0.06	0.07	0.10
Greater than one year and less than or equal to five years	0.005	0.05	0.05	0.10	0.08	0.07	0.12
Greater than five years	0.015	0.075	0.05	0.10	0.10	0.08	0.15

[1] For a derivative contract with multiple exchanges of principal, the conversion factor is multiplied by the number of remaining payments in the derivative contract.

[2] For an OTC derivative contract that is structured such that on specified dates any outstanding exposure is settled and the terms are reset so that the fair value of the contract is zero, the remaining maturity equals the time until the next reset date. For an interest rate derivative contract with a remaining maturity of greater than one year that meets these criteria, the minimum conversion factor is 0.005.

[3] A national bank or Federal savings association must use the column labeled "Credit (investment-grade reference asset)" for a credit derivative whose reference asset is an outstanding unsecured long-term debt security without credit enhancement that is investment grade. A national bank or Federal savings association must use the column labeled "Credit (non-investment-grade reference asset)" for all other credit derivatives.

(2) *Multiple OTC derivative contracts subject to a qualifying master netting agreement.* Except as modified by paragraph (b) of this section, the exposure amount for multiple OTC derivative contracts subject to a qualifying master netting agreement is equal to the sum of the net current credit exposure and the adjusted sum of the PFE amounts for all OTC derivative contracts subject to the qualifying master netting agreement.

(i) *Net current credit exposure.* The net current credit exposure is the greater of the net sum of all positive and negative mark-to-fair values of the individual OTC derivative contracts subject to the qualifying master netting agreement or zero.

(ii) *Adjusted sum of the PFE amounts.* The adjusted sum of the PFE amounts, Anet, is calculated as Anet = (0.4 × Agross) + (0.6 × NGR × Agross),

where:

(A) Agross = the gross PFE (that is, the sum of the PFE amounts as determined under paragraph (a)(1)(ii) of this section for each individual derivative contract subject to the qualifying master netting agreement); and

(B) Net-to-gross Ratio (NGR) = the ratio of the net current credit exposure to the gross current credit exposure. In calculating the NGR, the gross current credit exposure equals the sum of the positive current credit exposures (as determined under paragraph (a)(1)(i) of this section) of all individual derivative contracts subject to the qualifying master netting agreement.

(b) *Recognition of credit risk mitigation of collateralized OTC derivative contracts:* (1) A national bank or Federal savings association may recognize the credit risk mitigation benefits of financial collateral that secures an OTC derivative contract or multiple OTC derivative contracts subject to a qualifying master netting agreement (netting set) by using the simple approach in § 3.37(b).

(2) As an alternative to the simple approach, a national bank or Federal savings association may recognize the credit risk mitigation benefits of financial collateral that secures such a contract or netting set if the financial collateral is marked-to-fair value on a daily basis and subject to a daily margin maintenance requirement by applying a risk weight to the exposure as if it were uncollateralized and adjusting the exposure amount calculated under paragraph (a)(1) or (2) of this section using the collateral haircut approach in § 3.37(c). The national bank or Federal savings association must substitute the exposure amount calculated under paragraph (a)(1) or (2) of this section for ΣE in the equation in § 3.37(c)(2).

(c) *Counterparty credit risk for OTC credit derivatives*—(1) *Protection purchasers.* A national bank or Federal savings association that purchases an OTC credit derivative that is recognized under § 3.36 as a credit risk mitigant for an exposure that is not a covered position under subpart F is not required to compute a separate counterparty credit risk capital requirement under § 3.32 provided that the national bank or Federal savings association does so consistently for all such credit derivatives. The national bank or Federal savings association must either include all or exclude all such credit derivatives that are subject to a qualifying master netting agreement from any measure used to determine counterparty credit risk exposure to all relevant counterparties for risk-based capital purposes.

(2) *Protection providers.* (i) A national bank or Federal savings association that is the protection provider under an OTC credit derivative must treat the OTC credit derivative as an exposure to the underlying reference asset. The national bank or Federal savings association is not required to compute a counterparty credit risk capital requirement for the OTC credit derivative under § 3.32, provided that this treatment is applied consistently for all such OTC credit derivatives. The national bank or Federal savings association must either include all or exclude all such OTC credit derivatives that are subject to a qualifying master netting agreement from any measure used to determine counterparty credit risk exposure.

(ii) The provisions of this paragraph (c)(2) apply to all relevant counterparties for risk-based capital purposes unless the national bank or Federal savings association is treating the OTC credit derivative as a covered position under subpart F, in which case the national bank or Federal savings association must compute a supplemental counterparty credit risk capital requirement under this section.

(d) *Counterparty credit risk for OTC equity derivatives.* (1) A national bank or Federal savings association must treat an OTC equity derivative contract as an equity exposure and compute a risk-weighted asset amount for the OTC equity derivative contract under §§ 3.51 through 3.53 (unless the national bank or Federal savings association is treating the contract as a covered position under subpart F of this part).

(2) In addition, the national bank or Federal savings association must also calculate a risk-based capital requirement for the counterparty credit risk of an OTC equity derivative contract under this section if the national bank or Federal savings association is treating the contract as a covered position under subpart F of this part.

(3) If the national bank or Federal savings association risk weights the contract under the Simple Risk-Weight Approach (SRWA) in § 3.52, the national bank or Federal savings association may choose not to hold risk-based capital against the counterparty credit risk of the OTC equity derivative contract, as long as it does so for all such contracts. Where the OTC equity derivative contracts are subject to a qualified master netting agreement, a national bank or Federal savings association using the SRWA must either include all or exclude all of the contracts from any measure used to determine counterparty credit risk exposure.

(e) *Clearing member national bank's or Federal savings association's exposure amount.* A clearing member national bank's or Federal savings association's exposure amount for an OTC derivative contract or netting set of OTC derivative contracts where the national bank or Federal savings association is either acting as a financial intermediary and enters into an offsetting transaction with a QCCP or where the national bank or Federal savings association provides a guarantee to the QCCP on the performance of the client equals the exposure amount calculated according to paragraph (a)(1) or (2) of this section multiplied by the scaling factor 0.71. If the national bank or Federal savings association determines that a longer period is appropriate, the national bank or Federal savings association must use a larger scaling factor to adjust for a longer holding period as follows:

$$\text{Scaling factor} = \sqrt{\frac{H}{10}}$$

where

H = the holding period greater than five days. Additionally, the OCC may require the national bank or Federal savings association to set a longer holding period if the OCC determines that a longer period is appropriate due to the nature, structure, or characteristics of the transaction or is commensurate with the risks associated with the transaction.

§ 3.35 Cleared transactions.

(a) *General requirements*—(1) *Clearing member clients*. A national bank or Federal savings association that is a clearing member client must use the methodologies described in paragraph (b) of this section to calculate risk-weighted assets for a cleared transaction.

(2) *Clearing members*. A national bank or Federal savings association that is a clearing member must use the methodologies described in paragraph (c) of this section to calculate its risk-weighted assets for a cleared transaction and paragraph (d) of this section to calculate its risk-weighted assets for its default fund contribution to a CCP.

(b) *Clearing member client national banks or Federal savings associations*—(1) *Risk-weighted assets for cleared transactions*. (i) To determine the risk-weighted asset amount for a cleared transaction, a national bank or Federal savings association that is a clearing member client must multiply the trade exposure amount for the cleared transaction, calculated in accordance with paragraph (b)(2) of this section, by the risk weight appropriate for the cleared transaction, determined in accordance with paragraph (b)(3) of this section.

(ii) A clearing member client national bank's or Federal savings association's total risk-weighted assets for cleared transactions is the sum of the risk-weighted asset amounts for all its cleared transactions.

(2) *Trade exposure amount*. (i) For a cleared transaction that is either a derivative contract or a netting set of derivative contracts, the trade exposure amount equals:

(A) The exposure amount for the derivative contract or netting set of derivative contracts, calculated using the methodology used to calculate exposure amount for OTC derivative contracts under § 3.34; plus

(B) The fair value of the collateral posted by the clearing member client national bank or Federal savings association and held by the CCP, clearing member, or custodian in a manner that is not bankruptcy remote.

(ii) For a cleared transaction that is a repo-style transaction or netting set of repo-style transactions, the trade exposure amount equals:

(A) The exposure amount for the repo-style transaction calculated using the methodologies under § 3.37(c); plus

(B) The fair value of the collateral posted by the clearing member client national bank or Federal savings association and held by the CCP, clearing member, or custodian in a manner that is not bankruptcy remote.

(3) *Cleared transaction risk weights*. (i) For a cleared transaction with a QCCP, a clearing member client national bank or Federal savings association must apply a risk weight of:

(A) 2 percent if the collateral posted by the national bank or Federal savings association to the QCCP or clearing member is subject to an arrangement that prevents any losses to the clearing member client national bank or Federal savings association due to the joint default or a concurrent insolvency, liquidation, or receivership proceeding of the clearing member and any other clearing member clients of the clearing member; and the clearing member client national bank or Federal savings association has conducted sufficient legal review to conclude with a well-founded basis (and maintains sufficient written documentation of that legal review) that in the event of a legal challenge (including one resulting from an event of default or from liquidation, insolvency, or receivership proceedings) the relevant court and administrative authorities would find the arrangements to be legal, valid, binding and enforceable under the law of the relevant jurisdictions; or

(B) 4 percent if the requirements of §3.35(b)(3)(A) are not met.

(ii) For a cleared transaction with a CCP that is not a QCCP, a clearing member client national bank or Federal savings association must apply the risk weight appropriate for the CCP according to §3.32.

(4) *Collateral.* (i) Notwithstanding any other requirements in this section, collateral posted by a clearing member client national bank or Federal savings association that is held by a custodian (in its capacity as custodian) in a manner that is bankruptcy remote from the CCP, the custodian, clearing member and other clearing member clients of the clearing member, is not subject to a capital requirement under this section.

(ii) A clearing member client national bank or Federal savings association must calculate a risk-weighted asset amount for any collateral provided to a CCP, clearing member, or custodian in connection with a cleared transaction in accordance with the requirements under §3.32.

(c) *Clearing member national banks or Federal savings associations*—(1) *Risk-weighted assets for cleared transactions.* (i) To determine the risk-weighted asset amount for a cleared transaction, a clearing member national bank or Federal savings association must multiply the trade exposure amount for the cleared transaction, calculated in accordance with paragraph (c)(2) of this section, by the risk weight appropriate for the cleared transaction, determined in accordance with paragraph (c)(3) of this section.

(ii) A clearing member national bank's or Federal savings association's total risk-weighted assets for cleared transactions is the sum of the risk-weighted asset amounts for all of its cleared transactions.

(2) *Trade exposure amount.* A clearing member national bank or Federal savings association must calculate its trade exposure amount for a cleared transaction as follows:

(i) For a cleared transaction that is either a derivative contract or a netting set of derivative contracts, the trade exposure amount equals:

(A) The exposure amount for the derivative contract, calculated using the methodology to calculate exposure amount for OTC derivative contracts under §3.34; plus

(B) The fair value of the collateral posted by the clearing member national bank or Federal savings association and held by the CCP in a manner that is not bankruptcy remote.

(ii) For a cleared transaction that is a repo-style transaction or netting set of repo-style transactions, trade exposure amount equals:

(A) The exposure amount for repo-style transactions calculated using methodologies under §3.37(c); plus

(B) The fair value of the collateral posted by the clearing member national bank or Federal savings association and held by the CCP in a manner that is not bankruptcy remote.

(3) *Cleared transaction risk weight.* (i) A clearing member national bank or Federal savings association must apply a risk weight of 2 percent to the trade exposure amount for a cleared transaction with a QCCP.

(ii) For a cleared transaction with a CCP that is not a QCCP, a clearing member national bank or Federal savings association must apply the risk weight appropriate for the CCP according to §3.32.

(4) *Collateral.* (i) Notwithstanding any other requirement in this section, collateral posted by a clearing member national bank or Federal savings association that is held by a custodian in a manner that is bankruptcy remote from the CCP is not subject to a capital requirement under this section.

(ii) A clearing member national bank or Federal savings association must calculate a risk-weighted asset amount for any collateral provided to a CCP, clearing member, or a custodian in connection with a cleared transaction in accordance with requirements under §3.32.

(d) *Default fund contributions*—(1) *General requirement.* A clearing member national bank or Federal savings association must determine the risk-weighted asset amount for a default fund contribution to a CCP at least quarterly, or more frequently if, in the opinion of the national bank or Federal savings association or the OCC, there is a material change in the financial condition of the CCP.

(2) *Risk-weighted asset amount for default fund contributions to non-qualifying CCPs.* A clearing member national bank's or Federal savings association's risk-weighted asset amount for default fund contributions to CCPs that are not QCCPs equals the sum of such default fund contributions multiplied by 1,250 percent, or an amount determined by the OCC, based on factors such as size, structure and membership characteristics of the CCP and riskiness of its transactions, in cases where such default fund contributions may be unlimited.

(3) *Risk-weighted asset amount for default fund contributions to QCCPs.* A clearing member national bank's or Federal savings association's risk-weighted asset amount for default fund contributions to QCCPs equals the sum of its capital requirement, K_{CM} for each QCCP, as calculated under the methodology set forth in paragraphs (d)(3)(i) through (iii) of this section (Method 1), multiplied by 1,250 percent or in paragraphs (d)(3)(iv) of this section (Method 2).

(i) *Method 1.* The hypothetical capital requirement of a QCCP (K_{CCP}) equals:

$$K_{CCP} = \sum_{clearing\ member\ i} \max\left(EBRM_i - VM_i - IM_i - DF_i ; 0\right) \times RW \times 0.08$$

(A) $EBRM_i$ = the exposure amount for each transaction cleared through the QCCP by clearing member i, calculated in accordance with § 3.34 for OTC derivative contracts and § 3.37(c)(2) for repo-style transactions, provided that:

(*1*) For purposes of this section, in calculating the exposure amount the national bank or Federal savings association may replace the formula provided in § 3.34(a)(2)(ii) with the following: Anet = (0.15 × Agross) + (0.85 × NGR × Agross); and

(*2*) For option derivative contracts that are cleared transactions, the PFE described in § 3.34(a)(1)(ii) must be adjusted by multiplying the notional principal amount of the derivative contract by the appropriate conversion factor in Table 1 to § 3.34 and the absolute value of the option's delta, that is, the ratio of the change in the value of the derivative contract to the corresponding change in the price of the underlying asset.

(*3*) For repo-style transactions, when applying § 3.37(c)(2), the national bank or Federal savings association must use the methodology in § 3.37(c)(3);

(B) VM_i = any collateral posted by clearing member i to the QCCP that it is entitled to receive from the QCCP, but has not yet received, and any collateral that the QCCP has actually received from clearing member i;

(C) IM_i = the collateral posted as initial margin by clearing member i to the QCCP;

(D) DF_i = the funded portion of clearing member i's default fund contribution that will be applied to reduce the QCCP's loss upon a default by clearing member i;

(E) RW = 20 percent, except when the OCC has determined that a higher risk weight is more appropriate based on the specific characteristics of the QCCP and its clearing members; and

(F) Where a QCCP has provided its K_{CCP}, a national bank or Federal savings association must rely on such disclosed figure instead of calculating K_{CCP} under this paragraph (d), unless the national bank or Federal savings association determines that a more conservative figure is appropriate based on the nature, structure, or characteristics of the QCCP.

(ii) For a national bank or Federal savings association that is a clearing member of a QCCP with a default fund supported by funded commitments, K_{CM} equals:

$$K_{CM_i} = \left(1 + \beta \cdot \frac{N}{N-2}\right) \cdot \frac{DF_i}{DF_{CM}} \cdot K^*_{CM}$$

$$K^*_{CM} = \begin{cases} c_2 \cdot \mu \cdot (K_{CCP} - DF') + c_2 \cdot DF'_{CM} & if \quad DF' < K_{CCP} \quad (i) \\ c_2 \cdot (K_{CCP} - DF_{CCP}) + c_1 \cdot (DF' - K_{CCP}) & if \quad DF_{CCP} < K_{CCP} \le DF' \quad (ii) \\ c_1 \cdot DF'_{CM} & if \quad K_{CCP} \le DF_{CCP} \quad (iii) \end{cases}$$

Where

(A) $\beta = \dfrac{A_{Net,1} + A_{Net,2}}{\sum_i A_{Net,i}}$

Subscripts 1 and 2 denote the clearing members with the two largest A_{Net} values. For purposes of this paragraph (d), for derivatives A_{Net} is defined in § 3.34(a)(2)(ii) and for repo-style transactions, A_{Net} means the exposure amount as defined in § 3.37(c)(2) using the methodology in § 3.37(c)(3);

(B) N = the number of clearing members in the QCCP;

(C) DF_{CCP} = the QCCP's own funds and other financial resources that would be used to cover its losses before clearing members' default fund contributions are used to cover losses;

(D) DF_{CM} = funded default fund contributions from all clearing members and any other clearing member contributed financial resources that are available to absorb mutualized QCCP losses;

(E) $DF = DF_{CCP} + DF_{CM}$ (that is, the total funded default fund contribution);

(F) $\overline{DF_i}$ = average $\overline{DF_i}$ = the average funded default fund contribution from an individual clearing member;

(G) $DF'_{CM} = DF_{CM} - 2 \cdot \overline{DF_i} = \sum_i DF_i - 2 \cdot \overline{DF_i}$ (that is, the funded default fund contribution from surviving clearing members assuming that two average clearing members have defaulted and their default fund contributions and initial margins have been used to absorb the resulting losses);

(H) $DF' = DF_{CCP} + DF'_{CM} = DF - 2 \cdot \overline{DF_i}$

(that is, the total funded default fund contributions from the QCCP and the surviving clearing members that are available to mutualize losses, assuming that two average clearing members have defaulted);

(I) $c_1 = Max\left\{\frac{1.6\%}{\left(DF'/K_{CCP}\right)^{0.3}};0.16\%\right\}$

(that is, a decreasing capital factor, between 1.6 percent and 0.16 percent, applied to the excess funded default funds provided by clearing members);

(J) c_2 = 100 percent; and

(K) μ= 1.2;

(iii) (A) For a [BANK] that is a clearing member of a QCCP with a default fund supported by unfunded commitments, K_{CM} equals:

$$K_{CM_i} = \frac{DF_i}{DF_{CM}} \cdot K^*_{CM}$$

Where:

(*1*) DF_i = the national bank's or Federal savings association's unfunded commitment to the default fund;

(*2*) DF_{CM} = the total of all clearing members' unfunded commitment to the default fund; and

(*3*) K^*_{CM} as defined in paragraph (d)(3)(ii) of this section.

(B) For a national bank or Federal savings association that is a clearing member of a QCCP with a default fund supported by unfunded commitments and is unable to calculate K_{CM} using the methodology described in paragraph (d)(3)(iii) of this section, K_{CM} equals:

$$K_{CM_i} = \frac{IM_i}{IM_{CM}} \cdot K^*_{CM}$$

Where:

(*1*) IM_i = the national bank's or Federal savings association's initial margin posted to the QCCP;

(*2*) IM_{CM} = the total of initial margin posted to the QCCP; and

(*3*)K^*_{CM} as defined in paragraph (d)(3)(ii) of this section.

(iv) *Method 2.* A clearing member national bank's or Federal savings association's risk-weighted asset amount for its default fund contribution to a QCCP, RWA_{DF}, equals:

RWA_{DF} = Min {12.5 * DF; 0.18 * TE}

Where:

(A) TE = the national bank's or Federal savings association's trade exposure amount to the QCCP, calculated according to section 35(c)(2);

(B) DF = the funded portion of the national bank's or Federal savings association's default fund contribution to the QCCP.

(4) *Total risk-weighted assets for default fund contributions.* Total risk-weighted assets for default fund contributions is the sum of a clearing member national bank's or Federal savings association's risk-weighted assets for all of its default fund contributions to all CCPs of which the national bank or Federal savings association is a clearing member.

§3.36 Guarantees and credit derivatives: substitution treatment.

(a) *Scope*—(1) *General.* A national bank or Federal savings association may recognize the credit risk mitigation benefits of an eligible guarantee or eligible credit derivative by substituting the risk weight associated with the protection provider for the risk weight assigned to an exposure, as provided under this section.

(2) This section applies to exposures for which:

(i) Credit risk is fully covered by an eligible guarantee or eligible credit derivative; or

(ii) Credit risk is covered on a pro rata basis (that is, on a basis in which the national bank or Federal savings association and the protection provider share losses proportionately) by an eligible guarantee or eligible credit derivative.

(3) Exposures on which there is a tranching of credit risk (reflecting at least two different levels of seniority) generally are securitization exposures subject to §§3.41 through 3.45.

(4) If multiple eligible guarantees or eligible credit derivatives cover a single exposure described in this section, a national bank or Federal savings association may treat the hedged exposure as multiple separate exposures each covered by a single eligible guarantee or eligible credit derivative and may calculate a separate risk-weighted asset amount for each separate exposure as described in paragraph (c) of this section.

(5) If a single eligible guarantee or eligible credit derivative covers multiple hedged exposures described in paragraph (a)(2) of this section, a national bank or Federal savings association must treat each hedged exposure as covered by a separate eligible guarantee or eligible credit derivative and must calculate a separate risk-weighted asset amount for each exposure as described in paragraph (c) of this section.

(b) *Rules of recognition.* (1) A national bank or Federal savings association may only recognize the credit risk mitigation benefits of eligible guarantees and eligible credit derivatives.

(2) A national bank or Federal savings association may only recognize the credit risk mitigation benefits of an eligible credit derivative to hedge an exposure that is different from the credit derivative's reference exposure used for determining the derivative's cash settlement value, deliverable obligation, or occurrence of a credit event if:

(i) The reference exposure ranks *pari passu* with, or is subordinated to, the hedged exposure; and

(ii) The reference exposure and the hedged exposure are to the same legal entity, and legally enforceable cross-default or cross-acceleration clauses are in place to ensure payments under the credit derivative are triggered when the obligated party of the hedged exposure fails to pay under the terms of the hedged exposure.

(c) *Substitution approach*—(1) *Full coverage.* If an eligible guarantee or eligible credit derivative meets the conditions in paragraphs (a) and (b) of this section and the protection amount (P) of the guarantee or credit derivative is greater than or equal to the exposure amount of the hedged exposure, a national bank or Federal savings association may recognize the guarantee or credit derivative in determining the risk-weighted asset amount for the hedged exposure by substituting the risk weight applicable to the guarantor or credit derivative protection provider under § 3.32 for the risk weight assigned to the exposure.

(2) *Partial coverage.* If an eligible guarantee or eligible credit derivative meets the conditions in §§ 3.36(a) and 3.37(b) and the protection amount (P) of the guarantee or credit derivative is less than the exposure amount of the hedged exposure, the national bank or Federal savings association must treat the hedged exposure as two separate exposures (protected and unprotected) in order to recognize the credit risk mitigation benefit of the guarantee or credit derivative.

(i) The national bank or Federal savings association may calculate the risk-weighted asset amount for the protected exposure under § 3.32, where the applicable risk weight is the risk weight applicable to the guarantor or credit derivative protection provider.

(ii) The national bank or Federal savings association must calculate the risk-weighted asset amount for the unprotected exposure under § 3.32, where the applicable risk weight is that of the unprotected portion of the hedged exposure.

(iii) The treatment provided in this section is applicable when the credit risk of an exposure is covered on a partial pro rata basis and may be applicable when an adjustment is made to the effective notional amount of the guarantee or credit derivative under paragraphs (d), (e), or (f) of this section.

(d) *Maturity mismatch adjustment.* (1) A national bank or Federal savings association that recognizes an eligible guarantee or eligible credit derivative in determining the risk-weighted asset amount for a hedged exposure must adjust the effective notional amount of the credit risk mitigant to reflect any maturity mismatch between the hedged exposure and the credit risk mitigant.

(2) A maturity mismatch occurs when the residual maturity of a credit risk mitigant is less than that of the hedged exposure(s).

(3) The residual maturity of a hedged exposure is the longest possible remaining time before the obligated party of the hedged exposure is scheduled to fulfil its obligation on the hedged exposure. If a credit risk mitigant has embedded options that may reduce its term, the national bank or Federal savings association (protection purchaser) must use the shortest possible residual maturity for the credit risk mitigant. If a call is at the discretion of the protection provider, the residual maturity of the credit risk mitigant is at the first call date. If the call is at the discretion of the national bank or Federal savings association (protection purchaser), but the terms of the arrangement at origination of the credit risk mitigant contain a positive incentive for the national bank or Federal savings association to call the transaction before contractual maturity, the remaining time to the first call date is the residual maturity of the credit risk mitigant.

(4) A credit risk mitigant with a maturity mismatch may be recognized only if its original maturity is greater than or equal to one year and its residual maturity is greater than three months.

(5) When a maturity mismatch exists, the national bank or Federal savings association must apply the following adjustment to reduce the effective notional amount of the credit risk mitigant: $Pm = E \times (t - 0.25) / (T - 0.25)$, where:

(i) Pm = effective notional amount of the credit risk mitigant, adjusted for maturity mismatch;

(ii) E = effective notional amount of the credit risk mitigant;

(iii) t = the lesser of T or the residual maturity of the credit risk mitigant, expressed in years; and

(iv) T = the lesser of five or the residual maturity of the hedged exposure, expressed in years.

(e) *Adjustment for credit derivatives without restructuring as a credit event.* If a national bank or Federal savings association recognizes an eligible credit derivative that does not include as a credit event a restructuring of the hedged exposure involving forgiveness or postponement of principal, interest, or fees that results in a credit loss event (that is, a charge-off, specific provision, or other similar debit to the profit and loss account), the national bank or Federal savings association must apply the following adjustment to reduce the effective notional amount of the credit derivative: $Pr = Pm \times 0.60$, where:

(1) Pr = effective notional amount of the credit risk mitigant, adjusted for lack of restructuring event (and maturity mismatch, if applicable); and

(2) Pm = effective notional amount of the credit risk mitigant (adjusted for maturity mismatch, if applicable).

(f) *Currency mismatch adjustment.* (1) If a national bank or Federal savings association recognizes an eligible guarantee or eligible credit derivative that is denominated in a currency different from that in which the hedged exposure is denominated, the national bank or Federal savings association must apply the following formula to the effective notional amount of the guarantee or credit derivative: $Pc = Pr \times (1 - H_{FX})$, where:

(i) Pc = effective notional amount of the credit risk mitigant, adjusted for currency mismatch (and maturity mismatch and lack of restructuring event, if applicable);

(ii) Pr = effective notional amount of the credit risk mitigant (adjusted for maturity mismatch and lack of restructuring event, if applicable); and

(iii) H_{FX} = haircut appropriate for the currency mismatch between the credit risk mitigant and the hedged exposure.

(2) A national bank or Federal savings association must set H_{FX} equal to eight percent unless it qualifies for the use of and uses its own internal estimates of foreign exchange volatility based on a ten-business-day holding period. A national bank or Federal savings association qualifies for the use of its own internal estimates of foreign exchange volatility if it qualifies for the use of its own-estimates haircuts in §3.37(c)(4).

(3) A national bank or Federal savings association must adjust H_{FX} calculated in paragraph (f)(2) of this section upward if the national bank or Federal savings association revalues the guarantee or credit derivative less frequently than once every 10 business days using the following square root of time formula:

$$H_{FX} = 8\% \sqrt{\frac{T_M}{10}}$$, where T_M equals the greater of 10 or the number of days between revaluation.

§3.37 Collateralized transactions.

(a) *General.* (1) To recognize the risk-mitigating effects of financial collateral, a national bank or Federal savings association may use:

(i) The simple approach in paragraph (b) of this section for any exposure; or

(ii) The collateral haircut approach in paragraph (c) of this section for repo-style transactions, eligible margin loans, collateralized derivative contracts, and single-product netting sets of such transactions.

(2) A national bank or Federal savings association may use any approach described in this section that is valid for a particular type of exposure or transaction; however, it must use the same approach for similar exposures or transactions.

(b) *The simple approach*—(1) *General requirements.* (i) A national bank or Federal savings association may recognize the credit risk mitigation benefits of financial collateral that secures any exposure.

(ii) To qualify for the simple approach, the financial collateral must meet the following requirements:

(A) The collateral must be subject to a collateral agreement for at least the life of the exposure;

(B) The collateral must be revalued at least every six months; and

(C) The collateral (other than gold) and the exposure must be denominated in the same currency.

(2) *Risk weight substitution.* (i) A national bank or Federal savings association may apply a risk weight to the portion of an exposure that is secured by the fair value of financial collateral (that meets the requirements of paragraph (b)(1) of this section) based on the risk weight assigned to the collateral under § 3.32. For repurchase agreements, reverse repurchase agreements, and securities lending and borrowing transactions, the collateral is the instruments, gold, and cash the national bank or Federal savings association has borrowed, purchased subject to resale, or taken as collateral from the counterparty under the transaction. Except as provided in paragraph (b)(3) of this section, the risk weight assigned to the collateralized portion of the exposure may not be less than 20 percent.

(ii) A national bank or Federal savings association must apply a risk weight to the unsecured portion of the exposure based on the risk weight applicable to the exposure under this subpart.

(3) *Exceptions to the 20 percent risk-weight floor and other requirements.* Notwithstanding paragraph (b)(2)(i) of this section:

(i) A national bank or Federal savings association may assign a zero percent risk weight to an exposure to an OTC derivative contract that is marked-to-market on a daily basis and subject to a daily margin maintenance requirement, to the extent the contract is collateralized by cash on deposit.

(ii) A national bank or Federal savings association may assign a 10 percent risk weight to an exposure to an OTC derivative contract that is marked-to-market daily and subject to a daily margin maintenance requirement, to the extent that the contract is collateralized by an exposure to a sovereign that qualifies for a zero percent risk weight under § 3.32.

(iii) A national bank or Federal savings association may assign a zero percent risk weight to the collateralized portion of an exposure where:

(A) The financial collateral is cash on deposit; or

(B) The financial collateral is an exposure to a sovereign that qualifies for a zero percent risk weight under § 3.32, and the national bank or Federal savings association has discounted the fair value of the collateral by 20 percent.

(c) *Collateral haircut approach*—(1) *General.* A national bank or Federal savings association may recognize the credit risk mitigation benefits of financial collateral that secures an eligible margin loan, repo-style transaction, collateralized derivative contract, or single-product netting set of such transactions, and of any collateral that secures a repo-style transaction that is included in the national bank's or Federal savings association's VaR-based measure under subpart F of this part by using the collateral haircut approach in this section. A national bank or Federal savings association may use the standard supervisory haircuts in paragraph (c)(3) of this section or, with prior written approval of the OCC, its own estimates of haircuts according to paragraph (c)(4) of this section.

(2) *Exposure amount equation.* A national bank or Federal savings association must determine the exposure amount for an eligible margin loan, repo-style transaction, collateralized derivative contract, or a single-product netting set of such transactions by setting the exposure amount equal to $\max\{0, [(\Sigma E - \Sigma C) + \Sigma(Es \times Hs) + \Sigma(Efx \times Hfx)]\}$, where:

(i)(A) For eligible margin loans and repo-style transactions and netting sets thereof, ΣE equals the value of the exposure (the sum of the current fair values of all instruments, gold, and cash the national bank or Federal savings association has lent, sold subject to repurchase, or posted as collateral to the counterparty under the transaction (or netting set)); and

(B) For collateralized derivative contracts and netting sets thereof, ΣE equals the exposure amount of the OTC derivative contract (or netting set) calculated under § 3.34 (a)(1) or (2).

(ii) ΣC equals the value of the collateral (the sum of the current fair values of all instruments, gold and cash the national bank or Federal savings association has borrowed, purchased subject to resale, or taken as collateral from the counterparty under the transaction (or netting set));

(iii) Es equals the absolute value of the net position in a given instrument or in gold (where the net position in the instrument or gold equals the sum of the current fair values of the instrument or gold the national bank or Federal savings association has lent, sold subject to repurchase, or posted as collateral to the counterparty minus the sum of the current fair values of that same instrument or gold the national bank or Federal savings association has borrowed, purchased subject to resale, or taken as collateral from the counterparty);

(iv) Hs equals the market price volatility haircut appropriate to the instrument or gold referenced in Es;

(v) Efx equals the absolute value of the net position of instruments and cash in a currency that is different from the settlement currency (where the net position in a given currency equals the sum of the current fair values of any instruments or cash in the currency the national bank or Federal savings association has lent, sold subject to repurchase, or posted as collateral to the counterparty minus the sum of the current fair values of any instruments or cash in the currency the national bank or Federal savings association has borrowed, purchased subject to resale, or taken as collateral from the counterparty); and

(vi) Hfx equals the haircut appropriate to the mismatch between the currency referenced in Efx and the settlement currency.

(3) *Standard supervisory haircuts.* (i) A national bank or Federal savings association must use the haircuts for market price volatility (Hs) provided in Table 1 to § 3.37, as adjusted in certain circumstances in accordance with the requirements of paragraphs (c)(3)(iii) and (iv) of this section.

TABLE 1 TO § 3.37—STANDARD SUPERVISORY MARKET PRICE VOLATILITY HAIRCUTS [1]

Residual maturity	Haircut (in percent) assigned based on:						Investment grade securitization exposures (in percent)
	Sovereign issuers risk weight under § 3.32 (in percent) [2]			Non-sovereign issuers risk weight under § 3.32 (in percent)			
	Zero	20 or 50	100	20	50	100	
Less than or equal to 1 year	0.5	1.0	15.0	1.0	2.0	4.0	4.0
Greater than 1 year and less than or equal to 5 years	2.0	3.0	15.0	4.0	6.0	8.0	12.0
Greater than 5 years	4.0	6.0	15.0	8.0	12.0	16.0	24.0
Main index equities (including convertible bonds) and gold				15.0			
Other publicly traded equities (including convertible bonds)				25.0			
Mutual funds				Highest haircut applicable to any security in which the fund can invest.			
Cash collateral held				Zero.			
Other exposure types				25.0			

[1] The market price volatility haircuts in Table 1 to § 3.37 are based on a 10 business-day holding period.

[2] Includes a foreign PSE that receives a zero percent risk weight.

(ii) For currency mismatches, a national bank or Federal savings association must use a haircut for foreign exchange rate volatility (Hfx) of 8.0 percent, as adjusted in certain circumstances under paragraphs (c)(3)(iii) and (iv) of this section.

(iii) For repo-style transactions, a national bank or Federal savings association may multiply the standard supervisory haircuts provided in paragraphs (c)(3)(i) and (ii) of this section by the square root of ½ (which equals 0.707107).

(iv) If the number of trades in a netting set exceeds 5,000 at any time during a quarter, a national bank or Federal savings association must adjust the supervisory haircuts provided in paragraphs (c)(3)(i) and (ii) of this section upward on the basis of a holding period of twenty business days for the following quarter except in the calculation of the exposure amount for purposes of § 3.35. If a netting set contains one or more trades involving illiquid collateral or an OTC derivative that cannot be easily replaced, a national bank or Federal savings association must adjust the supervisory haircuts upward on the basis of a holding period of twenty business days. If over the two previous quarters more than two margin disputes on a netting set have occurred that lasted more than the holding period, then the national bank or Federal savings association must adjust the supervisory haircuts upward for that netting set on the basis of a holding period that is at least two times the minimum holding period for that netting set. A national bank or Federal savings association must adjust the standard supervisory haircuts upward using the following formula:

$$H_A = H_S \sqrt{\frac{T_M}{T_S}}, \text{ where}$$

(A) T_M equals a holding period of longer than 10 business days for eligible margin loans and derivative contracts or longer than 5 business days for repo-style transactions;

(B) H_S equals the standard supervisory haircut; and

(C) T_S equals 10 business days for eligible margin loans and derivative contracts or 5 business days for repo-style transactions.

(v) If the instrument a national bank or Federal savings association has lent, sold subject to repurchase, or posted as collateral does not meet the definition of financial collateral, the national bank or Federal savings association must use a 25.0 percent haircut for market price volatility (H_s).

(4) *Own internal estimates for haircuts.* With the prior written approval of the OCC, a national bank or Federal savings association may calculate haircuts (Hs and Hfx) using its own internal estimates of the volatilities of market prices and foreign exchange rates:

(i) To receive OCC approval to use its own internal estimates, a national bank or Federal savings association must satisfy the following minimum standards:

(A) A national bank or Federal savings association must use a 99th percentile one-tailed confidence interval.

(B) The minimum holding period for a repo-style transaction is five business days and for an eligible margin loan is ten business days except for transactions or netting sets for which paragraph (c)(4)(i)(C) of this section applies. When a national bank or Federal savings association calculates an own-estimates haircut on a T_N-day holding period, which is different from the minimum holding period for the transaction type, the applicable haircut (H_M) is calculated using the following square root of time formula:

$$H_M = H_N \sqrt{\frac{T_M}{T_N}}, \text{ where}$$

(*1*) T_M equals 5 for repo-style transactions and 10 for eligible margin loans;

(*2*) T_N equals the holding period used by the national bank or Federal savings association to derive H_N; and

(*3*) H_N equals the haircut based on the holding period T_N.

(C) If the number of trades in a netting set exceeds 5,000 at any time during a quarter, a national bank or Federal savings association must calculate the haircut using a minimum holding period of twenty business days for the following quarter except in the calculation of the exposure amount for purposes of §3.35. If a netting set contains one or more trades involving illiquid collateral or an OTC derivative that cannot be easily replaced, a national bank or Federal savings association must calculate the haircut using a minimum holding period of twenty business days. If over the two previous quarters more than two margin disputes on a netting set have occurred that lasted more than the holding period, then the national bank or Federal savings association must calculate the haircut for transactions in that netting set on the basis of a holding period that is at least two times the minimum holding period for that netting set.

(D) A national bank or Federal savings association is required to calculate its own internal estimates with inputs calibrated to historical data from a continuous 12-month period that reflects a period of significant financial stress appropriate to the security or category of securities.

(E) A national bank or Federal savings association must have policies and procedures that describe how it determines the period of significant financial stress used to calculate the national bank's or Federal savings association's own internal estimates for haircuts under this section and must be able to provide empirical support for the period used. The national bank or Federal savings association must obtain the prior approval of the OCC for, and notify the OCC if the national bank or Federal savings association makes any material changes to, these policies and procedures.

(F) Nothing in this section prevents the OCC from requiring a national bank or Federal savings association to use a different period of significant financial stress in the calculation of own internal estimates for haircuts.

(G) A national bank or Federal savings association must update its data sets and calculate haircuts no less frequently than quarterly and must also reassess data sets and haircuts whenever market prices change materially.

(ii) With respect to debt securities that are investment grade, a national bank or Federal savings association may calculate haircuts for categories of securities. For a category of securities, the national bank or Federal savings association must calculate the haircut on the basis of internal volatility estimates for securities in that category that are representative of the securities in that category that the national bank or Federal savings association has lent, sold subject to repurchase, posted as collateral, borrowed, purchased subject to resale, or taken as collateral. In determining relevant categories, the national bank or Federal savings association must at a minimum take into account:

(A) The type of issuer of the security;

(B) The credit quality of the security;

(C) The maturity of the security; and

(D) The interest rate sensitivity of the security.

(iii) With respect to debt securities that are not investment grade and equity securities, a national bank or Federal savings association must calculate a separate haircut for each individual security.

(iv) Where an exposure or collateral (whether in the form of cash or securities) is denominated in a currency that differs from the settlement currency, the national bank or Federal savings association must calculate a separate currency mismatch haircut for its net position in each mismatched currency based on estimated volatilities of foreign exchange rates between the mismatched currency and the settlement currency.

(v) A national bank's or Federal savings association's own estimates of market price and foreign exchange rate volatilities may not take into account the correlations among securities and foreign exchange rates on either the exposure or collateral side of a transaction (or netting set) or the correlations among securities and foreign exchange rates between the exposure and collateral sides of the transaction (or netting set).

RISK-WEIGHTED ASSETS FOR UNSETTLED TRANSACTIONS

§ 3.38 Unsettled transactions.

(a) *Definitions.* For purposes of this section:

(1) Delivery-versus-payment (DvP) transaction means a securities or commodities transaction in which the buyer is obligated to make payment only if the seller has made delivery of the securities or commodities and the seller is obligated to deliver the securities or commodities only if the buyer has made payment.

(2) Payment-versus-payment (PvP) transaction means a foreign exchange transaction in which each counterparty is obligated to make a final transfer of one or more currencies only if the other counterparty has made a final transfer of one or more currencies.

(3) A transaction has a normal settlement period if the contractual settlement period for the transaction is equal to or less than the market standard for the instrument underlying the transaction and equal to or less than five business days.

(4) Positive current exposure of a national bank or Federal savings association for a transaction is the difference between the transaction value at the agreed settlement price and the current market price of the transaction, if the difference results in a credit exposure of the national bank or Federal savings association to the counterparty.

(b) *Scope.* This section applies to all transactions involving securities, foreign exchange instruments, and commodities that have a risk of delayed settlement or delivery. This section does not apply to:

(1) Cleared transactions that are marked-to-market daily and subject to daily receipt and payment of variation margin;

(2) Repo-style transactions, including unsettled repo-style transactions;

(3) One-way cash payments on OTC derivative contracts; or

(4) Transactions with a contractual settlement period that is longer than the normal settlement period (which are treated as OTC derivative contracts as provided in § 3.34).

(c) *System-wide failures.* In the case of a system-wide failure of a settlement, clearing system or central counterparty, the OCC may waive risk-based capital requirements for unsettled and failed transactions until the situation is rectified.

(d) *Delivery-versus-payment (DvP) and payment-versus-payment (PvP) transactions.* A national bank or Federal savings association must hold risk-based capital against any DvP or PvP transaction with a normal settlement period if the national bank's or Federal savings association's counterparty has not made delivery or payment within five business days after the settlement date. The national bank or Federal savings association must determine its risk-weighted asset amount for such a transaction by multiplying the positive current exposure of the transaction for the national bank or Federal savings association by the appropriate risk weight in Table 1 to § 3.38.

TABLE 1 TO § 3.38—RISK WEIGHTS FOR UNSETTLED DVP AND PVP TRANSACTIONS

Number of business days after contractual settlement date	Risk weight to be applied to positive current exposure (in percent)
From 5 to 15	100.0
From 16 to 30	625.0
From 31 to 45	937.5
46 or more	1,250.0

(e) *Non-DvP/non-PvP (non-delivery-versus-payment/non-payment-versus-payment) transactions.* (1) A national bank or Federal savings association must hold risk-based capital against any non-DvP/non-PvP transaction with a normal settlement period if the national bank or Federal savings association has delivered cash, securities, commodities, or currencies to its counterparty but has not received its corresponding deliverables by the end of the same business day. The national bank or Federal savings association must continue to hold risk-based capital against the transaction until the national bank or Federal savings association has received its corresponding deliverables.

(2) From the business day after the national bank or Federal savings association has made its delivery until five business days after the counterparty delivery is due, the national bank or Federal savings association must calculate the risk-weighted asset amount for the transaction by treating the current fair value of the deliverables owed to the national bank or Federal savings association as an exposure to the counterparty and using the applicable counterparty risk weight under § 3.32.

(3) If the national bank or Federal savings association has not received its deliverables by the fifth business day after counterparty delivery was due, the national bank or Federal savings association must assign a 1,250 percent risk weight to the current fair value of the deliverables owed to the national bank or Federal savings association.

(f) *Total risk-weighted assets for unsettled transactions.* Total risk-weighted assets for unsettled transactions is the sum of the risk-weighted asset amounts of all DvP, PvP, and non-DvP/non-PvP transactions.

§§ 3.39–3.40 [Reserved]

RISK-WEIGHTED ASSETS FOR SECURITIZATION EXPOSURES

§ 3.41 Operational requirements for securitization exposures.

(a) *Operational criteria for traditional securitizations.* A national bank or Federal savings association that transfers exposures it has originated or purchased to a securitization SPE or other third party in connection with a traditional securitization may exclude the exposures from the calculation of its risk-weighted assets only if each condition in this section is satisfied. A national bank or Federal savings association that meets these conditions must hold risk-based capital against any credit risk it retains in connection with the securitization. A national bank or Federal savings association that fails to meet these conditions must hold risk-based capital against the transferred exposures as if they had not been securitized and must deduct from common equity tier 1 capital any after-tax gain-on-sale resulting from the transaction. The conditions are:

(1) The exposures are not reported on the national bank's or Federal savings association's consolidated balance sheet under GAAP;

(2) The national bank or Federal savings association has transferred to one or more third parties credit risk associated with the underlying exposures;

(3) Any clean-up calls relating to the securitization are eligible clean-up calls; and

(4) The securitization does not:

(i) Include one or more underlying exposures in which the borrower is permitted to vary the drawn amount within an agreed limit under a line of credit; and

(ii) Contain an early amortization provision.

(b) *Operational criteria for synthetic securitizations.* For synthetic securitizations, a national bank or Federal savings association may recognize for risk-based capital purposes the use of a credit risk mitigant to hedge underlying exposures only if each condition in this paragraph (b) is satisfied. A national bank or Federal savings association that meets these conditions must hold risk-based capital against any credit risk of the exposures it retains in connection with the synthetic securitization. A national bank or Federal savings association that fails to meet these conditions or chooses not to recognize the credit risk mitigant for purposes of this section must instead hold risk-based capital against the underlying exposures as if they had not been synthetically securitized. The conditions are:

(1) The credit risk mitigant is:

(i) Financial collateral;

(ii) A guarantee that meets all criteria as set forth in the definition of "eligible guarantee" in § 3.2, except for the criteria in paragraph (3) of that definition; or

(iii) A credit derivative that meets all criteria as set forth in the definition of "eligible credit derivative" in § 3.2, except for the criteria in paragraph (3) of the definition of "eligible guarantee" in § 3.2.

(2) The national bank or Federal savings association transfers credit risk associated with the underlying exposures to one or more third parties, and the terms and conditions in the credit risk mitigants employed do not include provisions that:

(i) Allow for the termination of the credit protection due to deterioration in the credit quality of the underlying exposures;

(ii) Require the national bank or Federal savings association to alter or replace the underlying exposures to improve the credit quality of the underlying exposures;

(iii) Increase the national bank's or Federal savings association's cost of credit protection in response to deterioration in the credit quality of the underlying exposures;

(iv) Increase the yield payable to parties other than the national bank or Federal savings association in response to a deterioration in the credit quality of the underlying exposures; or

(v) Provide for increases in a retained first loss position or credit enhancement provided by the national bank or Federal savings association after the inception of the securitization;

(3) The national bank or Federal savings association obtains a well-reasoned opinion from legal counsel that confirms the enforceability of the credit risk mitigant in all relevant jurisdictions; and

(4) Any clean-up calls relating to the securitization are eligible clean-up calls.

(c) *Due diligence requirements for securitization exposures.* (1) Except for exposures that are deducted from common equity tier 1 capital and exposures subject to § 3.42(h), if a national bank or Federal savings association is unable to demonstrate to the satisfaction of the OCC a comprehensive understanding of the features of a securitization exposure that would materially affect the performance of the exposure, the national bank or Federal savings association must assign the securitization exposure a risk weight of 1,250 percent. The national bank's or Federal savings association's analysis must be commensurate with the complexity of the securitization exposure and the materiality of the exposure in relation to its capital.

(2) A national bank or Federal savings association must demonstrate its comprehensive understanding of a securitization exposure under paragraph (c)(1) of this section, for each securitization exposure by:

(i) Conducting an analysis of the risk characteristics of a securitization exposure prior to acquiring the exposure, and documenting such analysis within three business days after acquiring the exposure, considering:

(A) Structural features of the securitization that would materially impact the performance of the exposure, for example, the contractual cash flow waterfall, waterfall-related triggers, credit enhancements, liquidity enhancements, fair value triggers, the performance of organizations that service the exposure, and deal-specific definitions of default;

(B) Relevant information regarding the performance of the underlying credit exposure(s), for example, the percentage of loans 30, 60, and 90 days past due; default rates; prepayment rates; loans in foreclosure; property types; occupancy; average credit score or other measures of creditworthiness; average LTV ratio; and industry and geographic diversification data on the underlying exposure(s);

(C) Relevant market data of the securitization, for example, bid-ask spread, most recent sales price and historic price volatility, trading volume, implied market rating, and size, depth and concentration level of the market for the securitization; and

(D) For resecuritization exposures, performance information on the underlying securitization exposures, for example, the issuer name and credit quality, and the characteristics and performance of the exposures underlying the securitization exposures; and

(ii) On an on-going basis (no less frequently than quarterly), evaluating, reviewing, and updating as appropriate the analysis required under paragraph (c)(1) of this section for each securitization exposure.

§ 3.42 Risk-weighted assets for securitization exposures.

(a) *Securitization risk weight approaches.* Except as provided elsewhere in this section or in § 3.41:

(1) A national bank or Federal savings association must deduct from common equity tier 1 capital any after-tax gain-on-sale resulting from a securitization and apply a 1,250 percent risk weight to the portion of a CEIO that does not constitute after-tax gain-on-sale.

(2) If a securitization exposure does not require deduction under paragraph (a)(1) of this section, a national bank or Federal savings association may assign a risk weight to the securitization exposure using the simplified supervisory formula approach (SSFA) in accordance with §§ 3.43(a) through 3.43(d) and subject to the limitation under paragraph (e) of this section. Alternatively, a national bank or Federal savings association that is not subject to subpart F of this part may assign a risk weight to the securitization exposure using the gross-up approach in accordance with § 3.43(e), provided, however, that such national bank or Federal savings association must apply either the SSFA or the gross-up approach consistently across all of its securitization exposures, except as provided in paragraphs (a)(1), (a)(3), and (a)(4) of this section.

(3) If a securitization exposure does not require deduction under paragraph (a)(1) of this section and the national bank or Federal savings association cannot, or chooses not to apply the SSFA or the gross-up approach to the exposure, the national bank or Federal savings association must assign a risk weight to the exposure as described in § 3.44.

(4) If a securitization exposure is a derivative contract (other than protection provided by a national bank or Federal savings association in the form of a credit derivative) that has a first priority claim on the cash flows from the underlying exposures (notwithstanding amounts due under interest rate or currency derivative contracts, fees due, or other similar payments), a national bank or Federal savings association may choose to set the risk-weighted asset amount of the exposure equal to the amount of the exposure as determined in paragraph (c) of this section.

(b) *Total risk-weighted assets for securitization exposures.* A national bank's or Federal savings association's total risk-weighted assets for securitization exposures equals the sum of the risk-weighted asset amount for securitization exposures that the national bank or Federal savings association risk weights under §§ 3.41(c), 3.42(a)(1), and 3.43, 3.44, or § 3.45, and paragraphs (e) through (j) of this section, as applicable.

(c) *Exposure amount of a securitization exposure*—(1) *On-balance sheet securitization exposures.* The exposure amount of an on-balance sheet securitization exposure (excluding an available-for-sale or held-to-maturity security where the national bank or Federal savings association has made an AOCI opt-out election under § 3.22(b)(2), a repo-style transaction, eligible margin loan, OTC derivative contract, or cleared transaction) is equal to the carrying value of the exposure.

(2) *On-balance sheet securitization exposures held by a national bank or Federal savings association that has made an AOCI opt-out election.* The exposure amount of an on-balance sheet securitization exposure that is an available-for-sale or held-to-maturity security held by a national bank or Federal savings association that has made an AOCI opt-out election under § 3.22(b)(2) is the national bank's or Federal savings association's carrying value (including net accrued but unpaid interest and fees), less any net unrealized gains on the exposure and plus any net unrealized losses on the exposure.

(3) *Off-balance sheet securitization exposures.* (i) Except as provided in paragraph (j) of this section, the exposure amount of an off-balance sheet securitization exposure that is not a repo-style transaction, eligible margin loan, cleared transaction (other than a

credit derivative), or an OTC derivative contract (other than a credit derivative) is the notional amount of the exposure. For an off-balance sheet securitization exposure to an ABCP program, such as an eligible ABCP liquidity facility, the notional amount may be reduced to the maximum potential amount that the national bank or Federal savings association could be required to fund given the ABCP program's current underlying assets (calculated without regard to the current credit quality of those assets).

(ii) A national bank or Federal savings association must determine the exposure amount of an eligible ABCP liquidity facility for which the SSFA does not apply by multiplying the notional amount of the exposure by a CCF of 50 percent.

(iii) A national bank or Federal savings association must determine the exposure amount of an eligible ABCP liquidity facility for which the SSFA applies by multiplying the notional amount of the exposure by a CCF of 100 percent.

(4) *Repo-style transactions, eligible margin loans, and derivative contracts.* The exposure amount of a securitization exposure that is a repo-style transaction, eligible margin loan, or derivative contract (other than a credit derivative) is the exposure amount of the transaction as calculated under § 3.34 or § 3.37, as applicable.

(d) *Overlapping exposures.* If a national bank or Federal savings association has multiple securitization exposures that provide duplicative coverage to the underlying exposures of a securitization (such as when a national bank or Federal savings association provides a program-wide credit enhancement and multiple pool-specific liquidity facilities to an ABCP program), the national bank or Federal savings association is not required to hold duplicative risk-based capital against the overlapping position. Instead, the national bank or Federal savings association may apply to the overlapping position the applicable risk-based capital treatment that results in the highest risk-based capital requirement.

(e) *Implicit support.* If a national bank or Federal savings association provides support to a securitization in excess of the national bank's or Federal savings association's contractual obligation to provide credit support to the securitization (implicit support):

(1) The national bank or Federal savings association must include in risk-weighted assets all of the underlying exposures associated with the securitization as if the exposures had not been securitized and must deduct from common equity tier 1 capital any after-tax gain-on-sale resulting from the securitization; and

(2) The national bank or Federal savings association must disclose publicly:

(i) That it has provided implicit support to the securitization; and

(ii) The risk-based capital impact to the national bank or Federal savings association of providing such implicit support.

(f) *Undrawn portion of a servicer cash advance facility.* (1) Notwithstanding any other provision of this subpart, a national bank or Federal savings association that is a servicer under an eligible servicer cash advance facility is not required to hold risk-based capital against potential future cash advance payments that it may be required to provide under the contract governing the facility.

(2) For a national bank or Federal savings association that acts as a servicer, the exposure amount for a servicer cash advance facility that is not an eligible servicer cash advance facility is equal to the amount of all potential future cash advance payments that the national bank or Federal savings association may be contractually required to provide during the subsequent 12 month period under the contract governing the facility.

(g) *Interest-only mortgage-backed securities.* Regardless of any other provisions in this subpart, the risk weight for a non-credit-enhancing interest-only mortgage-backed security may not be less than 100 percent.

(h) *Small-business loans and leases on personal property transferred with retained contractual exposure.* (1) Regardless of any other provision of this subpart, a national bank or Federal savings association that has transferred small-business loans and leases on personal property (small-business obligations) with recourse must include in risk-weighted assets only its contractual exposure to the small-business obligations if all the following conditions are met:

(i) The transaction must be treated as a sale under GAAP.

(ii) The national bank or Federal savings association establishes and maintains, pursuant to GAAP, a non-capital reserve sufficient to meet the national bank's or Federal savings association's reasonably estimated liability under the contractual obligation.

(iii) The small-business obligations are to businesses that meet the criteria for a small-business concern established by the Small Business Administration under section 3(a) of the Small Business Act (15 U.S.C. 632 et seq.).

(iv) The national bank or Federal savings association is well capitalized, as defined in 12 CFR 6.4. For purposes of determining whether a national bank or Federal savings association is well capitalized for purposes of this paragraph (h), the national bank's or Federal savings association's capital ratios must be calculated without regard to the capital treatment for transfers of small-business obligations under this paragraph (h).

(2) The total outstanding amount of contractual exposure retained by a national bank or Federal savings association on transfers of small-business obligations receiving the capital treatment specified in paragraph (h)(1) of this section cannot exceed 15 percent of the national bank's or Federal savings association's total capital.

(3) If a national bank or Federal savings association ceases to be well capitalized under 12 CFR 6.4 or exceeds the 15 percent capital limitation provided in paragraph (h)(2) of this section, the capital treatment under paragraph (h)(1) of this section will continue to apply to any transfers of small-business obligations with retained contractual exposure that occurred during the time that the national bank or Federal savings association was well capitalized and did not exceed the capital limit.

(4) The risk-based capital ratios of the national bank or Federal savings association must be calculated without regard to the capital treatment for transfers of small-business obligations specified in paragraph (h)(1) of this section for purposes of:

(i) Determining whether a national bank or Federal savings association is adequately capitalized, undercapitalized, significantly undercapitalized, or critically undercapitalized under the OCC's prompt corrective action regulations; and

(ii) Reclassifying a well-capitalized national bank or Federal savings association to adequately capitalized and requiring an adequately capitalized national bank or Federal savings association to comply with certain mandatory or discretionary supervisory actions as if the national bank or Federal savings association were in the next lower prompt-corrective-action category.

(i) *N^{th}-to-default credit derivatives*—(1) *Protection provider*. A national bank or Federal savings association may assign a risk weight using the SSFA in §3.43 to an nth-to-default credit derivative in accordance with this paragraph (i). A national bank or Federal savings association must determine its exposure in the nth-to-default credit derivative as the largest notional amount of all the underlying exposures.

(2) For purposes of determining the risk weight for an nth-to-default credit derivative using the SSFA, the national bank or Federal savings association must calculate the attachment point and detachment point of its exposure as follows:

(i) The attachment point (parameter A) is the ratio of the sum of the notional amounts of all underlying exposures that are subordinated to the national bank's or Federal savings association's exposure to the total notional amount of all underlying exposures. The ratio is expressed as a decimal value between zero and one. In the case of a first-to-default credit derivative, there are no underlying exposures that are subordinated to the national bank's or Federal savings association's exposure. In the case of a second-or-subsequent-to-default credit derivative, the smallest (n-1) notional amounts of the underlying exposure(s) are subordinated to the national bank's or Federal savings association's exposure.

(ii) The detachment point (parameter D) equals the sum of parameter A plus the ratio of the notional amount of the national bank's or Federal savings association's exposure in the nth-to-default credit derivative to the total notional amount of all underlying exposures. The ratio is expressed as a decimal value between zero and one.

(3) A national bank or Federal savings association that does not use the SSFA to determine a risk weight for its nth-to-default credit derivative must assign a risk weight of 1,250 percent to the exposure.

(4) *Protection purchaser*—(i) *First-to-default credit derivatives.* A national bank or Federal savings association that obtains credit protection on a group of underlying exposures through a first-to-default credit derivative that meets the rules of recognition of § 3.36(b) must determine its risk-based capital requirement for the underlying exposures as if the national bank or Federal savings association synthetically securitized the underlying exposure with the smallest risk-weighted asset amount and had obtained no credit risk mitigant on the other underlying exposures. A national bank or Federal savings association must calculate a risk-based capital requirement for counterparty credit risk according to § 3.34 for a first-to-default credit derivative that does not meet the rules of recognition of § 3.36(b).

(ii) *Second-or-subsequent-to-default credit derivatives.* (A) A national bank or Federal savings association that obtains credit protection on a group of underlying exposures through a nth-to-default credit derivative that meets the rules of recognition of § 3.36(b) (other than a first-to-default credit derivative) may recognize the credit risk mitigation benefits of the derivative only if:

(1) The national bank or Federal savings association also has obtained credit protection on the same underlying exposures in the form of first-through-(n-1)-to-default credit derivatives; or

(2) If n-1 of the underlying exposures have already defaulted.

(B) If a national bank or Federal savings association satisfies the requirements of paragraph (i)(4)(ii)(A) of this section, the national bank or Federal savings association must determine its risk-based capital requirement for the underlying exposures as if the national bank or Federal savings association had only synthetically securitized the underlying exposure with the nth smallest risk-weighted asset amount and had obtained no credit risk mitigant on the other underlying exposures.

(C) A national bank or Federal savings association must calculate a risk-based capital requirement for counterparty credit risk according to § 3.34 for a nth-to-default credit derivative that does not meet the rules of recognition of § 3.36(b).

(j) *Guarantees and credit derivatives other than n^{th}-to-default credit derivatives*—(1) *Protection provider.* For a guarantee or credit derivative (other than an nth-to-default credit derivative) provided by a national bank or Federal savings association that covers the full amount or a pro rata share of a securitization exposure's principal and interest, the national bank or Federal savings association must risk weight the guarantee or credit derivative as if it holds the portion of the reference exposure covered by the guarantee or credit derivative.

(2) *Protection purchaser.* (i) A national bank or Federal savings association that purchases a guarantee or OTC credit derivative (other than an nth-to-default credit derivative) that is recognized under § 3.45 as a credit risk mitigant (including via collateral recognized under § 3.37) is not required to compute a separate counterparty credit risk capital requirement under § 3.31, in accordance with 34(c).

(ii) If a national bank or Federal savings association cannot, or chooses not to, recognize a purchased credit derivative as a credit risk mitigant under § 3.45, the national bank or Federal savings association must determine the exposure amount of the credit derivative under § 3.34.

(A) If the national bank or Federal savings association purchases credit protection from a counterparty that is not a securitization SPE, the national bank or Federal savings association must determine the risk weight for the exposure according to general risk weights under § 3.32.

(B) If the national bank or Federal savings association purchases the credit protection from a counterparty that is a securitization SPE, the national bank or Federal savings association must determine the risk weight for the exposure according to section § 3.42, including § 3.42(a)(4) for a credit derivative that has a first priority claim on the cash flows from the underlying exposures of the securitization SPE (notwithstanding amounts due under interest rate or currency derivative contracts, fees due, or other similar payments).

§ 3.43 Simplified supervisory formula approach (SSFA) and the gross-up approach.

(a) *General requirements for the SSFA.* To use the SSFA to determine the risk weight for a securitization exposure, a national bank or Federal savings association must have data that enables it to assign accurately the parameters described in paragraph (b) of this section. Data used to assign the parameters described in paragraph (b) of this section must be the most currently available data; if the contracts governing the underlying exposures of the securitization require payments on a monthly or quarterly basis, the data used to assign the parameters described in paragraph (b) of this section must be no more than 91 calendar days old. A national bank or Federal savings association that does not have the appropriate data to assign the parameters described in paragraph (b) of this section must assign a risk weight of 1,250 percent to the exposure.

(b) *SSFA parameters.* To calculate the risk weight for a securitization exposure using the SSFA, a national bank or Federal savings association must have accurate information on the following five inputs to the SSFA calculation:

(1) K_G is the weighted-average (with unpaid principal used as the weight for each exposure) total capital requirement of the underlying exposures calculated using this subpart. K_G is expressed as a decimal value between zero and one (that is, an average risk weight of 100 percent represents a value of K_G equal to 0.08).

(2) Parameter W is expressed as a decimal value between zero and one. Parameter W is the ratio of the sum of the dollar amounts of any underlying exposures of the securitization that meet any of the criteria as set forth in paragraphs (b)(2)(i) through (vi) of this section to the balance, measured in dollars, of underlying exposures:

(i) Ninety days or more past due;

(ii) Subject to a bankruptcy or insolvency proceeding;

(iii) In the process of foreclosure;

(iv) Held as real estate owned;

(v) Has contractually deferred payments for 90 days or more, other than principal or interest payments deferred on:

(A) Federally-guaranteed student loans, in accordance with the terms of those guarantee programs; or

(B) Consumer loans, including non-federally-guaranteed student loans, provided that such payments are deferred pursuant to provisions included in the contract at the time funds are disbursed that provide for period(s) of deferral that are not initiated based on changes in the creditworthiness of the borrower; or

(vi) Is in default.

(3) Parameter A is the attachment point for the exposure, which represents the threshold at which credit losses will first be allocated to the exposure. Except as provided in § 3.42(i) for n^{th}-to-default credit derivatives, parameter A equals the ratio of the current dollar amount of underlying exposures that are subordinated to the exposure of the national bank or Federal savings association to the current dollar amount of underlying exposures. Any reserve account funded by the accumulated cash flows from the underlying exposures that is subordinated to the national bank's or Federal savings association's securitization exposure may be included in the calculation of parameter A to the extent that cash is present in the account. Parameter A is expressed as a decimal value between zero and one.

(4) Parameter D is the detachment point for the exposure, which represents the threshold at which credit losses of principal allocated to the exposure would result in a total loss of principal. Except as provided in section

42(i) for n^{th}-to-default credit derivatives, parameter D equals parameter A plus the ratio of the current dollar amount of the securitization exposures that are *pari passu* with the exposure (that is, have equal seniority with respect to credit risk) to the current dollar amount of the underlying exposures. Parameter D is expressed as a decimal value between zero and one.

(5) A supervisory calibration parameter, p, is equal to 0.5 for securitization exposures that are not resecuritization exposures and equal to 1.5 for resecuritization exposures.

(c) *Mechanics of the SSFA.* K_G and W are used to calculate K_A, the augmented value of K_G, which reflects the observed credit quality of the underlying exposures. K_A is defined in paragraph (d) of this section. The values of parameters A and D, relative to K_A determine the risk weight assigned to a securitization exposure as described in paragraph (d) of this section. The risk weight assigned to a securitization exposure, or portion of a securitization exposure, as appropriate, is the larger of the risk weight determined in accordance with this paragraph (c) or paragraph (d) of this section and a risk weight of 20 percent.

(1) When the detachment point, parameter D, for a securitization exposure is less than or equal to K_A, the exposure must be assigned a risk weight of 1,250 percent.

(2) When the attachment point, parameter A, for a securitization exposure is greater than or equal to K_A, the national bank or Federal savings association must calculate the risk weight in accordance with paragraph (d) of this section.

(3) When A is less than K_A and D is greater than K_A, the risk weight is a weighted-average of 1,250 percent and 1,250 percent times K_{SSFA} calculated in accordance with paragraph (d) of this section. For the purpose of this weighted-average calculation:

(i) The weight assigned to 1,250 percent equals $\frac{K_A - A}{D - A}$.

(ii) The weight assigned to 1,250 percent times K_{SSFA} equals $\frac{D - K_A}{D - A}$.

(iii) The risk weight will be set equal to:

$$RW = \left[\left(\frac{K_A - A}{D - A}\right) \cdot 1{,}250\ percent\right] + \left[\left(\frac{D - K_A}{D - A}\right) \cdot 1{,}250\ percent \cdot K_{SSFA}\right]$$

(d) SSFA equation. (1) The [BANK] must define the following parameters:

$$K_A = (1 - W) \cdot K_G + (0.5 \cdot W)$$

$$a = -\frac{1}{p \cdot K_A}$$

$$u = D - K_A$$

$$l = \max(A - K_A, 0)$$

$e = 2.71828$, the base of the natural logarithms.

(2) Then the [BANK] must calculate K_{SSFA} according to the following equation:

$$K_{SSFA} = \frac{e^{a \cdot u} - e^{a \cdot l}}{a(u - l)}$$

(3) The risk weight for the exposure (expressed as a percent) is equal to

$K_{SSFA} \times 1{,}250$.

(e) *Gross-up approach*—(1) *Applicability*. A national bank or Federal savings association that is not subject to subpart F of this part may apply the gross-up approach set forth in this section instead of the SSFA to determine the risk weight of its securitization exposures, provided that it applies the gross-up approach to all of its securitization exposures, except as otherwise provided for certain securitization exposures in §§ 3.44 and 3.45.

(2) To use the gross-up approach, a national bank or Federal savings association must calculate the following four inputs:

(i) Pro rata share, which is the par value of the national bank's or Federal savings association's securitization exposure as a percent of the par value of the tranche in which the securitization exposure resides;

(ii) Enhanced amount, which is the par value of tranches that are more senior to the tranche in which the national bank's or Federal savings association's securitization resides;

(iii) Exposure amount of the national bank's or Federal savings association's securitization exposure calculated under § 3.42(c); and

(iv) Risk weight, which is the weighted-average risk weight of underlying exposures of the securitization as calculated under this subpart.

(3) *Credit equivalent amount.* The credit equivalent amount of a securitization exposure under this section equals the sum of:

(i) The exposure amount of the national bank's or Federal savings association's securitization exposure; and

(ii) The pro rata share multiplied by the enhanced amount, each calculated in accordance with paragraph (e)(2) of this section.

(4) *Risk-weighted assets.* To calculate risk-weighted assets for a securitization exposure under the gross-up approach, a national bank or Federal savings association must apply the risk weight required under paragraph (e)(2) of this section to the credit equivalent amount calculated in paragraph (e)(3) of this section.

(f) *Limitations.* Notwithstanding any other provision of this section, a national bank or Federal savings association must assign a risk weight of not less than 20 percent to a securitization exposure.

§ 3.44 Securitization exposures to which the SSFA and gross-up approach do not apply.

(a) *General requirement.* A national bank or Federal savings association must assign a 1,250 percent risk weight to all securitization exposures to which the national bank or Federal savings association does not apply the SSFA or the gross-up approach under § 3.43, except as set forth in this section.

(b) *Eligible ABCP liquidity facilities.* A national bank or Federal savings association may determine the risk-weighted asset amount of an eligible ABCP liquidity facility by multiplying the exposure amount by the highest risk weight applicable to any of the individual underlying exposures covered by the facility.

(c) *A securitization exposure in a second loss position or better to an ABCP program*—(1) *Risk weighting.* A national bank or Federal savings association may determine the risk-weighted asset amount of a securitization exposure that is in a second loss position or better to an ABCP program that meets the requirements of paragraph (c)(2) of this section by multiplying the exposure amount by the higher of the following risk weights:

(i) 100 percent; and

(ii) The highest risk weight applicable to any of the individual underlying exposures of the ABCP program.

(2) *Requirements.* (i) The exposure is not an eligible ABCP liquidity facility;

(ii) The exposure must be economically in a second loss position or better, and the first loss position must provide significant credit protection to the second loss position;

(iii) The exposure qualifies as investment grade; and

(iv) The national bank or Federal savings association holding the exposure must not retain or provide protection to the first loss position.

§ 3.45 Recognition of credit risk mitigants for securitization exposures.

(a) *General.* (1) An originating national bank or Federal savings association that has obtained a credit risk mitigant to hedge its exposure to a synthetic or traditional securitization that satisfies the operational criteria provided in § 3.41 may recognize the credit risk mitigant under § 3.36 or § 3.37, but only as provided in this section.

(2) An investing national bank or Federal savings association that has obtained a credit risk mitigant to hedge a securitization exposure may recognize the credit risk mitigant under § 3.36 or § 3.37, but only as provided in this section.

(b) *Mismatches.* A national bank or Federal savings association must make any applicable adjustment to the protection amount of an eligible guarantee or credit derivative as required in §3.36(d), (e), and (f) for any hedged securitization exposure. In the context of a synthetic securitization, when an eligible guarantee or eligible credit derivative covers multiple hedged exposures that have different residual maturities, the national bank or Federal savings association must use the longest residual maturity of any of the hedged exposures as the residual maturity of all hedged exposures.

§§3.46–3.50 [Reserved]

RISK-WEIGHTED ASSETS FOR EQUITY EXPOSURES

§3.51 Introduction and exposure measurement.

(a) *General.* (1) To calculate its risk-weighted asset amounts for equity exposures that are not equity exposures to an investment fund, a national bank or Federal savings association must use the Simple Risk-Weight Approach (SRWA) provided in 3.52. A national bank or Federal savings association must use the look-through approaches provided in §3.53 to calculate its risk-weighted asset amounts for equity exposures to investment funds.

(2) A national bank or Federal savings association must treat an investment in a separate account (as defined in §3.2) as if it were an equity exposure to an investment fund as provided in §3.53.

(3) *Stable value protection.* (i) Stable value protection means a contract where the provider of the contract is obligated to pay:

(A) The policy owner of a separate account an amount equal to the shortfall between the fair value and cost basis of the separate account when the policy owner of the separate account surrenders the policy; or

(B) The beneficiary of the contract an amount equal to the shortfall between the fair value and book value of a specified portfolio of assets.

(ii) A national bank or Federal savings association that purchases stable value protection on its investment in a separate account must treat the portion of the carrying value of its investment in the separate account attributable to the stable value protection as an exposure to the provider of the protection and the remaining portion of the carrying value of its separate account as an equity exposure to an investment fund.

(iii) A national bank or Federal savings association that provides stable value protection must treat the exposure as an equity derivative with an adjusted carrying value determined as the sum of paragraphs (b)(1) and (3) of this section.

(b) *Adjusted carrying value.* For purposes of §§3.51 through 3.53, the adjusted carrying value of an equity exposure is:

(1) For the on-balance sheet component of an equity exposure (other than an equity exposure that is classified as available-for-sale where the national bank or Federal savings association has made an AOCI opt-out election under §3.22(b)(2)), the national bank's or Federal savings association's carrying value of the exposure;

(2) For the on-balance sheet component of an equity exposure that is classified as available-for-sale where the national bank or Federal savings association has made an AOCI opt-out election under §3.22(b)(2), the national bank's or Federal savings association's carrying value of the exposure less any net unrealized gains on the exposure that are reflected in such carrying value but excluded from the national bank's or Federal savings association's regulatory capital components;

(3) For the off-balance sheet component of an equity exposure that is not an equity commitment, the effective notional principal amount of the exposure, the size of which is equivalent to a hypothetical on-balance sheet position in the underlying equity instrument that would evidence the same change in fair value (measured in dollars) given a small change in the price of the underlying equity instrument, minus the adjusted carrying value of the on-balance sheet component of the exposure as calculated in paragraph (b)(1) of this section; and

(4) For a commitment to acquire an equity exposure (an equity commitment), the effective notional principal amount of the exposure is multiplied

by the following conversion factors (CFs):

(i) Conditional equity commitments with an original maturity of one year or less receive a CF of 20 percent.

(ii) Conditional equity commitments with an original maturity of over one year receive a CF of 50 percent.

(iii) Unconditional equity commitments receive a CF of 100 percent.

§ 3.52 Simple risk-weight approach (SRWA).

(a) *General.* Under the SRWA, a national bank's or Federal savings association's total risk-weighted assets for equity exposures equals the sum of the risk-weighted asset amounts for each of the national bank's or Federal savings association's individual equity exposures (other than equity exposures to an investment fund) as determined under this section and the risk-weighted asset amounts for each of the national bank's or Federal savings association's individual equity exposures to an investment fund as determined under § 3.53.

(b) *SRWA computation for individual equity exposures.* A national bank or Federal savings association must determine the risk-weighted asset amount for an individual equity exposure (other than an equity exposure to an investment fund) by multiplying the adjusted carrying value of the equity exposure or the effective portion and ineffective portion of a hedge pair (as defined in paragraph (c) of this section) by the lowest applicable risk weight in this paragraph (b).

(1) *Zero percent risk weight equity exposures.* An equity exposure to a sovereign, the Bank for International Settlements, the European Central Bank, the European Commission, the International Monetary Fund, an MDB, and any other entity whose credit exposures receive a zero percent risk weight under § 3.32 may be assigned a zero percent risk weight.

(2) *20 percent risk weight equity exposures.* An equity exposure to a PSE, Federal Home Loan Bank or the Federal Agricultural Mortgage Corporation (Farmer Mac) must be assigned a 20 percent risk weight.

(3) *100 percent risk weight equity exposures.* The equity exposures set forth in this paragraph (b)(3) must be assigned a 100 percent risk weight.

(i) *Community development equity exposures.* An equity exposure that qualifies as a community development investment under section 24 (Eleventh) of the National Bank Act, excluding equity exposures to an unconsolidated small business investment company and equity exposures held through a consolidated small business investment company described in section 302 of the Small Business Investment Act.

(ii) *Effective portion of hedge pairs.* The effective portion of a hedge pair.

(iii) *Non-significant equity exposures.* Equity exposures, excluding significant investments in the capital of an unconsolidated financial institution in the form of common stock and exposures to an investment firm that would meet the definition of a traditional securitization were it not for the application of paragraph (8) of that definition in § 3.2 and has greater than immaterial leverage, to the extent that the aggregate adjusted carrying value of the exposures does not exceed 10 percent of the national bank's or Federal savings association's total capital.

(A) To compute the aggregate adjusted carrying value of a national bank's or Federal savings association's equity exposures for purposes of this section, the national bank or Federal savings association may exclude equity exposures described in paragraphs (b)(1), (b)(2), (b)(3)(i), and (b)(3)(ii) of this section, the equity exposure in a hedge pair with the smaller adjusted carrying value, and a proportion of each equity exposure to an investment fund equal to the proportion of the assets of the investment fund that are not equity exposures or that meet the criterion of paragraph (b)(3)(i) of this section. If a national bank or Federal savings association does not know the actual holdings of the investment fund, the national bank or Federal savings association may calculate the proportion of the assets of the fund that are not equity exposures based on the terms of the prospectus, partnership agreement, or similar contract that defines the fund's permissible investments. If the sum of the investment limits for all exposure classes within the fund exceeds 100 percent, the national bank or Federal savings association must assume for purposes of this section that the investment fund invests to the maximum extent possible in equity exposures.

(B) When determining which of a national bank's or Federal savings association's equity exposures qualify for a 100 percent risk weight under this paragraph (b), a national bank or Federal savings association first must include equity exposures to unconsolidated small business investment companies or held through consolidated small business investment companies described in section 302 of the Small Business Investment Act, then must include publicly traded equity exposures (including those held indirectly through investment funds), and then must include non-publicly traded equity exposures (including those held indirectly through investment funds).

(4) *250 percent risk weight equity exposures.* Significant investments in the capital of unconsolidated financial institutions in the form of common stock that are not deducted from capital pursuant to § 3.22(d) are assigned a 250 percent risk weight.

(5) *300 percent risk weight equity exposures.* A publicly traded equity exposure (other than an equity exposure described in paragraph (b)(7) of this section and including the ineffective portion of a hedge pair) must be assigned a 300 percent risk weight.

(6) *400 percent risk weight equity exposures.* An equity exposure (other than an equity exposure described in paragraph (b)(7)) of this section that is not publicly traded must be assigned a 400 percent risk weight.

(7) *600 percent risk weight equity exposures.* An equity exposure to an investment firm must be assigned a 600 percent risk weight, provided that the investment firm:

(i) Would meet the definition of a traditional securitization were it not for the application of paragraph (8) of that definition; and

(ii) Has greater than immaterial leverage.

(c) *Hedge transactions*—(1) *Hedge pair.* A hedge pair is two equity exposures that form an effective hedge so long as each equity exposure is publicly traded or has a return that is primarily based on a publicly traded equity exposure.

(2) *Effective hedge.* Two equity exposures form an effective hedge if the exposures either have the same remaining maturity or each has a remaining maturity of at least three months; the hedge relationship is formally documented in a prospective manner (that is, before the national bank or Federal savings association acquires at least one of the equity exposures); the documentation specifies the measure of effectiveness (E) the national bank or Federal savings association will use for the hedge relationship throughout the life of the transaction; and the hedge relationship has an E greater than or equal to 0.8. A national bank or Federal savings association must measure E at least quarterly and must use one of three alternative measures of E as set forth in this paragraph (c).

(i) Under the dollar-offset method of measuring effectiveness, the national bank or Federal savings association must determine the ratio of value change (RVC). The RVC is the ratio of the cumulative sum of the changes in value of one equity exposure to the cumulative sum of the changes in the value of the other equity exposure. If RVC is positive, the hedge is not effective and E equals 0. If RVC is negative and greater than or equal to -1 (that is, between zero and -1), then E equals the absolute value of RVC. If RVC is negative and less than -1, then E equals 2 plus RVC.

(ii) Under the variability-reduction method of measuring effectiveness:

$$E = 1 - \frac{\sum_{t=1}^{T} (X_t - X_{t-1})^2}{\sum_{t=1}^{T} (A_t - A_{t-1})^2}, \text{ where}$$

(A) $X_t = A_t - B_t$;

(B) A_t = the value at time t of one exposure in a hedge pair; and

(C) B_t = the value at time t of the other exposure in a hedge pair.

(iii) Under the regression method of measuring effectiveness, E equals the coefficient of determination of a regression in which the change in value of one exposure in a hedge pair is the dependent variable and the change in value of the other exposure in a hedge pair is the independent variable. However, if the estimated regression coefficient is positive, then E equals zero.

(3) The effective portion of a hedge pair is E multiplied by the greater of the adjusted carrying values of the equity exposures forming a hedge pair.

(4) The ineffective portion of a hedge pair is (1–E) multiplied by the greater of the adjusted carrying values of the equity exposures forming a hedge pair.

§ 3.53 Equity exposures to investment funds.

(a) *Available approaches.* (1) Unless the exposure meets the requirements for a community development equity exposure under § 3.52(b)(3)(i), a national bank or Federal savings association must determine the risk-weighted asset amount of an equity exposure to an investment fund under the full look-through approach described in paragraph (b) of this section, the simple modified look-through approach described in paragraph (c) of this section, or the alterative modified look-through approach described paragraph (d) of this section, provided, however, that the minimum risk weight that may be assigned to an equity exposure under this section is 20 percent.

(2) The risk-weighted asset amount of an equity exposure to an investment fund that meets the requirements for a community development equity exposure in § 3.52(b)(3)(i) is its adjusted carrying value.

(3) If an equity exposure to an investment fund is part of a hedge pair and the national bank or Federal savings association does not use the full look-through approach, the national bank or Federal savings association must use the ineffective portion of the hedge pair as determined under § 3.52(c) as the adjusted carrying value for the equity exposure to the investment fund. The risk-weighted asset amount of the effective portion of the hedge pair is equal to its adjusted carrying value.

(b) *Full look-through approach.* A national bank or Federal savings association that is able to calculate a risk-weighted asset amount for its proportional ownership share of each exposure held by the investment fund (as calculated under this subpart as if the proportional ownership share of the adjusted carrying value of each exposure were held directly by the national bank or Federal savings association) may set the risk-weighted asset amount of the national bank's or Federal savings association's exposure to the fund equal to the product of:

(1) The aggregate risk-weighted asset amounts of the exposures held by the fund as if they were held directly by the national bank or Federal savings association; and

(2) The national bank's or Federal savings association's proportional ownership share of the fund.

(c) *Simple modified look-through approach.* Under the simple modified look-through approach, the risk-weighted asset amount for a national bank's or Federal savings association's equity exposure to an investment fund equals the adjusted carrying value of the equity exposure multiplied by the highest risk weight that applies to any exposure the fund is permitted to hold under the prospectus, partnership agreement, or similar agreement that defines the fund's permissible investments (excluding derivative contracts that are used for hedging rather than speculative purposes and that do not constitute a material portion of the fund's exposures).

(d) *Alternative modified look-through approach.* Under the alternative modified look-through approach, a national bank or Federal savings association may assign the adjusted carrying value of an equity exposure to an investment fund on a pro rata basis to different risk weight categories under this subpart based on the investment limits in the fund's prospectus, partnership agreement, or similar contract that defines the fund's permissible investments. The risk-weighted asset amount for the national bank's or Federal savings association's equity exposure to the investment fund equals the sum of each portion of the adjusted carrying value assigned to an exposure type multiplied by the applicable risk weight under this subpart. If the sum of the investment limits for all exposure types within the fund exceeds 100 percent, the national bank or Federal savings association must assume that the fund invests to the maximum extent permitted under its investment limits in the exposure type with the highest applicable risk weight under this subpart and continues to make investments in order of the exposure type with the next highest applicable risk weight under this subpart until the maximum total investment level is reached. If more than one exposure type applies to an exposure, the national bank or Federal savings association must use the highest applicable risk weight. A national bank or Federal savings association may exclude derivative contracts held by the fund that are used for hedging rather than for speculative purposes and do not constitute a material portion of the fund's exposures.

§§ 3.54–3.60 [Reserved]

DISCLOSURES

§ 3.61 Purpose and scope.

Sections 3.61–3.63 of this subpart establish public disclosure requirements related to the capital requirements described in subpart B of this part for a national bank or Federal savings association with total consolidated assets of $50 billion or more as reported on the national bank's or Federal savings association's most recent year-end Call Report that is not an advanced approaches national bank or Federal savings association making public disclosures pursuant to § 3.172. An advanced approaches national bank or Federal savings association that has not received approval from the OCC to exit parallel run pursuant to § 3.121(d) is subject to the disclosure requirements described in §§ 3.62 and 3.63. Such a national bank or Federal savings association must comply with § 3.62 unless it is a consolidated subsidiary of a bank holding company, savings and loan holding company, or depository institution that is subject to these disclosure requirements or a subsidiary of a non-U.S. banking organization that is subject to comparable public disclosure requirements in its home jurisdiction. For purposes of this section, total consolidated assets are determined based on the average of the national bank's or Federal savings association's total consolidated assets in the four most recent quarters as reported on the Call Report; or the average of the national bank's or Federal savings association's total consolidated assets in the most recent consecutive quarters as reported quarterly on the national bank's or Federal savings association's Call Report if the national bank or Federal savings association has not filed such a report for each of the most recent four quarters.

§ 3.62 Disclosure requirements.

(a) A national bank or Federal savings association described in § 3.61 must provide timely public disclosures each calendar quarter of the information in the applicable tables in § 3.63. If a significant change occurs, such that the most recent reported amounts are no longer reflective of the national bank's or Federal savings association's capital adequacy and risk profile, then a brief discussion of this change and its likely impact must be disclosed as soon as practicable thereafter. Qualitative disclosures that typically do not change each quarter (for example, a general summary of the national bank's or Federal savings association's risk management objectives and policies, reporting system, and definitions) may be disclosed annually after the end of the fourth calendar quarter, provided that any significant changes are disclosed in the interim. The national bank's or Federal savings association's management may provide all of the disclosures required by §§ 3.61 through 3.63 in one place on the national bank's or Federal savings association's public Web site or may provide the disclosures in more than one public financial report or other regulatory reports, provided that the national bank or Federal savings association publicly provides a summary table specifically indicating the location(s) of all such disclosures.

(b) A national bank or Federal savings association described in § 3.61 must have a formal disclosure policy approved by the board of directors that addresses its approach for determining the disclosures it makes. The policy must address the associated internal controls and disclosure controls and procedures. The board of directors and senior management are responsible for establishing and maintaining an effective internal control structure over financial reporting, including the disclosures required by this subpart, and must ensure that appropriate review of the disclosures takes place. One or more senior officers of the national bank or Federal savings association must attest that the disclosures meet the requirements of this subpart.

(c) If a national bank or Federal savings association described in § 3.61 concludes that specific commercial or financial information that it would otherwise be required to disclose under this section would be exempt from disclosure by the OCC under the Freedom of Information Act (5 U.S.C. 552), then the national bank or Federal savings association is not required to disclose that specific information pursuant to this section, but must disclose more general information about the subject matter of the requirement, together with the fact that, and the reason why, the specific items of information have not been disclosed.

§ 3.63 Disclosures by national banks or Federal savings associations described in § 3.61.

(a) Except as provided in § 3.62, a national bank or Federal savings association described in § 3.61 must make the disclosures described in Tables 1 through 10 of this section. The national bank or Federal savings association must make these disclosures publicly available for each of the last three years (that is, twelve quarters) or such shorter period beginning on January 1, 2015.

(b) A national bank or Federal savings association must publicly disclose each quarter the following:

(1) Common equity tier 1 capital, additional tier 1 capital, tier 2 capital, tier 1 and total capital ratios, including the regulatory capital elements and all the regulatory adjustments and deductions needed to calculate the numerator of such ratios;

(2) Total risk-weighted assets, including the different regulatory adjustments and deductions needed to calculate total risk-weighted assets;

(3) Regulatory capital ratios during any transition periods, including a description of all the regulatory capital elements and all regulatory adjustments and deductions needed to calculate the numerator and denominator of each capital ratio during any transition period; and

(4) A reconciliation of regulatory capital elements as they relate to its balance sheet in any audited consolidated financial statements.

TABLE 1 TO §3.63—SCOPE OF APPLICATION

Qualitative Disclosures	(a)	The name of the top corporate entity in the group to which subpart D of this part applies.
	(b)	A brief description of the differences in the basis for consolidating entities[1] for accounting and regulatory purposes, with a description of those entities: (1) That are fully consolidated; (2) That are deconsolidated and deducted from total capital; (3) For which the total capital requirement is deducted; and (4) That are neither consolidated nor deducted (for example, where the investment in the entity is assigned a risk weight in accordance with this subpart).
	(c)	Any restrictions, or other major impediments, on transfer of funds or total capital within the group.
	(d)	The aggregate amount of surplus capital of insurance subsidiaries included in the total capital of the consolidated group.
	(e)	The aggregate amount by which actual total capital is less than the minimum total capital requirement in all subsidiaries, with total capital requirements and the name(s) of the subsidiaries with such deficiencies.

[1] Entities include securities, insurance and other financial subsidiaries, commercial subsidiaries (where permitted), and significant minority equity investments in insurance, financial and commercial entities.

TABLE 2 TO §3.63—CAPITAL STRUCTURE

Qualitative Disclosures	(a)	Summary information on the terms and conditions of the main features of all regulatory capital instruments.
Quantitative Disclosures	(b)	The amount of common equity tier 1 capital, with separate disclosure of: (1) Common stock and related surplus; (2) Retained earnings; (3) Common equity minority interest; (4) AOCI; and (5) Regulatory adjustments and deductions made to common equity tier 1 capital.
	(c)	The amount of tier 1 capital, with separate disclosure of: (1) Additional tier 1 capital elements, including additional tier 1 capital instruments and tier 1 minority interest not included in common equity tier 1 capital; and (2) Regulatory adjustments and deductions made to tier 1 capital.
	(d)	The amount of total capital, with separate disclosure of: (1) Tier 2 capital elements, including tier 2 capital instruments and total capital minority interest not included in tier 1 capital; and (2) Regulatory adjustments and deductions made to total capital.

TABLE 3 TO §3.63—CAPITAL ADEQUACY

Qualitative disclosures	(a)	A summary discussion of the national bank's or Federal savings association's approach to assessing the adequacy of its capital to support current and future activities.
Quantitative disclosures	(b)	Risk-weighted assets for: (1) Exposures to sovereign entities; (2) Exposures to certain supranational entities and MDBs; (3) Exposures to depository institutions, foreign banks, and credit unions; (4) Exposures to PSEs; (5) Corporate exposures; (6) Residential mortgage exposures; (7) Statutory multifamily mortgages and pre-sold construction loans; (8) HVCRE loans; (9) Past due loans; (10) Other assets; (11) Cleared transactions; (12) Default fund contributions; (13) Unsettled transactions; (14) Securitization exposures; and (15) Equity exposures.
	(c)	Standardized market risk-weighted assets as calculated under subpart F of this part.
	(d)	Common equity tier 1, tier 1 and total risk-based capital ratios: (1) For the top consolidated group; and (2) For each depository institution subsidiary.
	(e)	Total standardized risk-weighted assets.

TABLE 4 TO § 3.63—CAPITAL CONSERVATION BUFFER

Quantitative Disclosures	(a)	At least quarterly, the national bank or Federal savings association must calculate and publicly disclose the capital conservation buffer as described under § 3.11.
	(b)	At least quarterly, the national bank or Federal savings association must calculate and publicly disclose the eligible retained income of the national bank or Federal savings association, as described under § 3.11.
	(c)	At least quarterly, the national bank or Federal savings association must calculate and publicly disclose any limitations it has on distributions and discretionary bonus payments resulting from the capital conservation buffer framework described under § 3.11, including the maximum payout amount for the quarter.

(c) *General qualitative disclosure requirement.* For each separate risk area described in Tables 5 through 10, the national bank or Federal savings association must describe its risk management objectives and policies, including: Strategies and processes; the structure and organization of the relevant risk management function; the scope and nature of risk reporting and/or measurement systems; policies for hedging and/or mitigating risk and strategies and processes for monitoring the continuing effectiveness of hedges/ mitigants.

TABLE 5 TO § 3.63 [1]—CREDIT RISK: GENERAL DISCLOSURES

Qualitative Disclosures	(a)	The general qualitative disclosure requirement with respect to credit risk (excluding counterparty credit risk disclosed in accordance with Table 6), including the: (1) Policy for determining past due or delinquency status; (2) Policy for placing loans on nonaccrual; (3) Policy for returning loans to accrual status; (4) Definition of and policy for identifying impaired loans (for financial accounting purposes); (5) Description of the methodology that the national bank or Federal savings association uses to estimate its allowance for loan and lease losses, including statistical methods used where applicable; (6) Policy for charging-off uncollectible amounts; and (7) Discussion of the national bank's or Federal savings association's credit risk management policy.
Quantitative Disclosures	(b)	Total credit risk exposures and average credit risk exposures, after accounting offsets in accordance with GAAP, without taking into account the effects of credit risk mitigation techniques (for example, collateral and netting not permitted under GAAP), over the period categorized by major types of credit exposure. For example, national banks or Federal savings associations could use categories similar to that used for financial statement purposes. Such categories might include, for instance (1) Loans, off-balance sheet commitments, and other non-derivative off-balance sheet exposures; (2) Debt securities; and (3) OTC derivatives.[2]
	(c)	Geographic distribution of exposures, categorized in significant areas by major types of credit exposure.[3]
	(d)	Industry or counterparty type distribution of exposures, categorized by major types of credit exposure.
	(e)	By major industry or counterparty type: (1) Amount of impaired loans for which there was a related allowance under GAAP; (2) Amount of impaired loans for which there was no related allowance under GAAP; (3) Amount of loans past due 90 days and on nonaccrual; (4) Amount of loans past due 90 days and still accruing; [4] (5) The balance in the allowance for loan and lease losses at the end of each period, disaggregated on the basis of the national bank's or Federal savings association's impairment method. To disaggregate the information required on the basis of impairment methodology, an entity shall separately disclose the amounts based on the requirements in GAAP; and (6) Charge-offs during the period.

TABLE 5 TO § 3.63 [1]—CREDIT RISK: GENERAL DISCLOSURES—Continued

	(f)	Amount of impaired loans and, if available, the amount of past due loans categorized by significant geographic areas including, if practical, the amounts of allowances related to each geographical area,[5] further categorized as required by GAAP.
	(g)	Reconciliation of changes in ALLL.[6]
	(h)	Remaining contractual maturity delineation (for example, one year or less) of the whole portfolio, categorized by credit exposure.

[1] Table 5 does not cover equity exposures, which should be reported in Table 9.
[2] *See,* for example, ASC Topic 815–10 and 210, as they may be amended from time to time.
[3] Geographical areas may consist of individual countries, groups of countries, or regions within countries. A national bank or Federal savings association might choose to define the geographical areas based on the way the national bank's or Federal savings association's portfolio is geographically managed. The criteria used to allocate the loans to geographical areas must be specified.
[4] A national bank or Federal savings association is encouraged also to provide an analysis of the aging of past-due loans.
[5] The portion of the general allowance that is not allocated to a geographical area should be disclosed separately.
[6] The reconciliation should include the following: A description of the allowance; the opening balance of the allowance; charge-offs taken against the allowance during the period; amounts provided (or reversed) for estimated probable loan losses during the period; any other adjustments (for example, exchange rate differences, business combinations, acquisitions and disposals of subsidiaries), including transfers between allowances; and the closing balance of the allowance. Charge-offs and recoveries that have been recorded directly to the income statement should be disclosed separately.

TABLE 6 TO § 3.63—GENERAL DISCLOSURE FOR COUNTERPARTY CREDIT RISK-RELATED EXPOSURES

Qualitative Disclosures	(a)	The general qualitative disclosure requirement with respect to OTC derivatives, eligible margin loans, and repo-style transactions, including a discussion of: (1) The methodology used to assign credit limits for counterparty credit exposures; (2) Policies for securing collateral, valuing and managing collateral, and establishing credit reserves; (3) The primary types of collateral taken; and (4) The impact of the amount of collateral the national bank or Federal savings association would have to provide given a deterioration in the national bank's or Federal savings association's own creditworthiness.
Quantitative Disclosures	(b)	Gross positive fair value of contracts, collateral held (including type, for example, cash, government securities), and net unsecured credit exposure.[1] A national bank or Federal savings association also must disclose the notional value of credit derivative hedges purchased for counterparty credit risk protection and the distribution of current credit exposure by exposure type.[2]
	(c)	Notional amount of purchased and sold credit derivatives, segregated between use for the national bank's or Federal savings association's own credit portfolio and in its intermediation activities, including the distribution of the credit derivative products used, categorized further by protection bought and sold within each product group.

[1] Net unsecured credit exposure is the credit exposure after considering both the benefits from legally enforceable netting agreements and collateral arrangements without taking into account haircuts for price volatility, liquidity, etc.
[2] This may include interest rate derivative contracts, foreign exchange derivative contracts, equity derivative contracts, credit derivatives, commodity or other derivative contracts, repo-style transactions, and eligible margin loans.

TABLE 7 TO § 3.63—CREDIT RISK MITIGATION [1] [2]

Qualitative Disclosures	(a)	The general qualitative disclosure requirement with respect to credit risk mitigation, including: (1) Policies and processes for collateral valuation and management; (2) A description of the main types of collateral taken by the national bank or Federal savings association; (3) The main types of guarantors/credit derivative counterparties and their creditworthiness; and (4) Information about (market or credit) risk concentrations with respect to credit risk mitigation.
Quantitative Disclosures	(b)	For each separately disclosed credit risk portfolio, the total exposure that is covered by eligible financial collateral, and after the application of haircuts.
	(c)	For each separately disclosed portfolio, the total exposure that is covered by guarantees/credit derivatives and the risk-weighted asset amount associated with that exposure.

[1] At a minimum, a national bank or Federal savings association must provide the disclosures in Table 7 in relation to credit risk mitigation that has been recognized for the purposes of reducing capital requirements under this subpart. Where relevant, national banks or Federal savings associations are encouraged to give further information about mitigants that have not been recognized for that purpose.

[2] Credit derivatives that are treated, for the purposes of this subpart, as synthetic securitization exposures should be excluded from the credit risk mitigation disclosures and included within those relating to securitization (Table 8).

TABLE 8 TO § 3.63—SECURITIZATION

Qualitative Disclosures	(a)	The general qualitative disclosure requirement with respect to a securitization (including synthetic securitizations), including a discussion of: (1) The national bank's or Federal savings association's objectives for securitizing assets, including the extent to which these activities transfer credit risk of the underlying exposures away from the national bank or Federal savings association to other entities and including the type of risks assumed and retained with resecuritization activity; [1] (2) The nature of the risks (e.g. liquidity risk) inherent in the securitized assets; (3) The roles played by the national bank or Federal savings association in the securitization process [2] and an indication of the extent of the national bank's or Federal savings association's involvement in each of them; (4) The processes in place to monitor changes in the credit and market risk of securitization exposures including how those processes differ for resecuritization exposures; (5) The national bank's or Federal savings association's policy for mitigating the credit risk retained through securitization and resecuritization exposures; and (6) The risk-based capital approaches that the national bank or Federal savings association follows for its securitization exposures including the type of securitization exposure to which each approach applies.
	(b)	A list of: (1) The type of securitization SPEs that the national bank or Federal savings association, as sponsor, uses to securitize third-party exposures. The national bank or Federal savings association must indicate whether it has exposure to these SPEs, either on- or off-balance sheet; and (2) Affiliated entities: (i) That the national bank or Federal savings association manages or advises; and (ii) That invest either in the securitization exposures that the national bank or Federal savings association has securitized or in securitization SPEs that the national bank or Federal savings association sponsors.[3]
	(c)	Summary of the national bank's or Federal savings association's accounting policies for securitization activities, including: (1) Whether the transactions are treated as sales or financings; (2) Recognition of gain-on-sale; (3) Methods and key assumptions applied in valuing retained or purchased interests; (4) Changes in methods and key assumptions from the previous period for valuing retained interests and impact of the changes; (5) Treatment of synthetic securitizations; (6) How exposures intended to be securitized are valued and whether they are recorded under subpart D of this part; and (7) Policies for recognizing liabilities on the balance sheet for arrangements that could require the national bank or Federal savings association to provide financial support for securitized assets.
	(d)	An explanation of significant changes to any quantitative information since the last reporting period.
Quantitative Disclosures	(e)	The total outstanding exposures securitized by the national bank or Federal savings association in securitizations that meet the operational criteria provided in § 3.41 (categorized into traditional and synthetic securitizations), by exposure type, separately for securitizations of third-party exposures for which the bank acts only as sponsor.[4]
	(f)	For exposures securitized by the national bank or Federal savings association in securitizations that meet the operational criteria in § 3.41: (1) Amount of securitized assets that are impaired/past due categorized by exposure type; [5] and (2) Losses recognized by the national bank or Federal savings association during the current period categorized by exposure type.[6]
	(g)	The total amount of outstanding exposures intended to be securitized categorized by exposure type.
	(h)	Aggregate amount of:

TABLE 8 TO § 3.63—SECURITIZATION—Continued

		(1) On-balance sheet securitization exposures retained or purchased categorized by exposure type; and (2) Off-balance sheet securitization exposures categorized by exposure type.
	(i)	(1) Aggregate amount of securitization exposures retained or purchased and the associated capital requirements for these exposures, categorized between securitization and resecuritization exposures, further categorized into a meaningful number of risk weight bands and by risk-based capital approach (e.g., SSFA); and (2) Exposures that have been deducted entirely from tier 1 capital, CEIOs deducted from total capital (as described in § 3.42(a)(1), and other exposures deducted from total capital should be disclosed separately by exposure type.
	(j)	Summary of current year's securitization activity, including the amount of exposures securitized (by exposure type), and recognized gain or loss on sale by exposure type.
	(k)	Aggregate amount of resecuritization exposures retained or purchased categorized according to: (1) Exposures to which credit risk mitigation is applied and those not applied; and (2) Exposures to guarantors categorized according to guarantor creditworthiness categories or guarantor name.

[1] The national bank or Federal savings association should describe the structure of resecuritizations in which it participates; this description should be provided for the main categories of resecuritization products in which the national bank or Federal savings association is active.

[2] For example, these roles may include originator, investor, servicer, provider of credit enhancement, sponsor, liquidity provider, or swap provider.

[3] Such affiliated entities may include, for example, money market funds, to be listed individually, and personal and private trusts, to be noted collectively.

[4] "Exposures securitized" include underlying exposures originated by the bank, whether generated by them or purchased, and recognized in the balance sheet, from third parties, and third-party exposures included in sponsored transactions. Securitization transactions (including underlying exposures originally on the bank's balance sheet and underlying exposures acquired by the bank from third-party entities) in which the originating bank does not retain any securitization exposure should be shown separately but need only be reported for the year of inception. Banks are required to disclose exposures regardless of whether there is a capital charge under this part.

[5] Include credit-related other than temporary impairment (OTTI).

[6] For example, charge-offs/allowances (if the assets remain on the bank's balance sheet) or credit-related OTTI of interest-only strips and other retained residual interests, as well as recognition of liabilities for probable future financial support required of the bank with respect to securitized assets.

TABLE 9 TO § 3.63—EQUITIES NOT SUBJECT TO SUBPART F OF THIS PART

Qualitative Disclosures	(a)	The general qualitative disclosure requirement with respect to equity risk for equities not subject to subpart F of this part, including: (1) Differentiation between holdings on which capital gains are expected and those taken under other objectives including for relationship and strategic reasons; and (2) Discussion of important policies covering the valuation of and accounting for equity holdings not subject to subpart F of this part. This includes the accounting techniques and valuation methodologies used, including key assumptions and practices affecting valuation as well as significant changes in these practices.
Quantitative Disclosures	(b)	Value disclosed on the balance sheet of investments, as well as the fair value of those investments; for securities that are publicly traded, a comparison to publicly-quoted share values where the share price is materially different from fair value.
	(c)	The types and nature of investments, including the amount that is: (1) Publicly traded; and (2) Non publicly traded.
	(d)	The cumulative realized gains (losses) arising from sales and liquidations in the reporting period.
	(e)	(1) Total unrealized gains (losses).[1] (2) Total latent revaluation gains (losses).[2] (3) Any amounts of the above included in tier 1 or tier 2 capital.
	(f)	Capital requirements categorized by appropriate equity groupings, consistent with the national bank's or Federal savings association's methodology, as well as the aggregate amounts and the type of equity investments subject to any supervisory transition regarding regulatory capital requirements.

[1] Unrealized gains (losses) recognized on the balance sheet but not through earnings.

[2] Unrealized gains (losses) not recognized either on the balance sheet or through earnings.

TABLE 10 TO § 3.63—INTEREST RATE RISK FOR NON-TRADING ACTIVITIES

Qualitative disclosures	(a)	The general qualitative disclosure requirement, including the nature of interest rate risk for non-trading activities and key assumptions, including assumptions regarding loan prepayments and behavior of non-maturity deposits, and frequency of measurement of interest rate risk for non-trading activities.
Quantitative disclosures	(b)	The increase (decline) in earnings or economic value (or relevant measure used by management) for upward and downward rate shocks according to management's method for measuring interest rate risk for non-trading activities, categorized by currency (as appropriate).

§§ 3.64–3.99 [Reserved]

Subpart E—Risk-Weighted Assets—Internal Ratings-Based and Advanced Measurement Approaches

SOURCE: 78 FR 62157, 62273, Oct. 11, 2013, unless otherwise noted.

§ 3.100 Purpose, applicability, and principle of conservatism.

(a) *Purpose.* This subpart E establishes:

(1) Minimum qualifying criteria for national banks or Federal savings associations using institution-specific internal risk measurement and management processes for calculating risk-based capital requirements; and

(2) Methodologies for such national banks or Federal savings associations to calculate their total risk-weighted assets.

(b) *Applicability.* (1) This subpart applies to a national bank or Federal savings association that:

(i) Has consolidated total assets, as reported on its most recent year-end Call Report equal to $250 billion or more;

(ii) Has consolidated total on-balance sheet foreign exposure on its most recent year-end Federal Financial Institutions Examination Council (FFIEC) 009 Report equal to $10 billion or more (where total on-balance sheet foreign exposure equals total foreign countries cross-border claims on an ultimate-risk basis, plus total foreign countries claims on local residents on an ultimate-risk basis, plus total foreign countries fair value of foreign exchange and derivative products), calculated in accordance with the FFIEC 009 Country Exposure Report;

(iii) Is a subsidiary of a depository institution that uses the advanced approaches pursuant to subpart E of 12 CFR part 3 (OCC), 12 CFR part 217 (Board), or 12 CFR part 325 (FDIC) to calculate its total risk-weighted assets;

(iv) Is a subsidiary of a bank holding company or savings and loan holding company that uses the advanced approaches pursuant to 12 CFR part 217 to calculate its total risk-weighted assets; or

(v) Elects to use this subpart to calculate its total risk-weighted assets.

(2) A national bank or Federal savings association that is subject to this subpart shall remain subject to this subpart unless the OCC determines in writing that application of this subpart is not appropriate in light of the national bank's or Federal savings association's asset size, level of complexity, risk profile, or scope of operations. In making a determination under this paragraph (b), the OCC will apply notice and response procedures in the same manner and to the same extent as the notice and response procedures in 12 CFR 3.404.

(3) A market risk national bank or Federal savings association must exclude from its calculation of risk-weighted assets under this subpart the risk-weighted asset amounts of all covered positions, as defined in subpart F of this part (except foreign exchange positions that are not trading positions, over-the-counter derivative positions, cleared transactions, and unsettled transactions).

(c) *Principle of conservatism.* Notwithstanding the requirements of this subpart, a national bank or Federal savings association may choose not to apply a provision of this subpart to one or more exposures provided that:

(1) The national bank or Federal savings association can demonstrate on an ongoing basis to the satisfaction of the OCC that not applying the provision would, in all circumstances, unambiguously generate a risk-based capital requirement for each such exposure greater than that which would otherwise be required under this subpart;

(2) The national bank or Federal savings association appropriately manages the risk of each such exposure;

(3) The national bank or Federal savings association notifies the OCC in writing prior to applying this principle to each such exposure; and

(4) The exposures to which the national bank or Federal savings association applies this principle are not, in the aggregate, material to the national bank or Federal savings association.

[78 FR 62157, 62273, Oct. 11, 2013, as amended at 80 FR 41415, July 15, 2015]

§ 3.101 Definitions.

(a) Terms that are set forth in § 3.2 and used in this subpart have the definitions assigned thereto in § 3.2.

(b) For the purposes of this subpart, the following terms are defined as follows:

Advanced internal ratings-based (IRB) systems means an advanced approaches national bank's or Federal savings association's internal risk rating and segmentation system; risk parameter quantification system; data management and maintenance system; and control, oversight, and validation system for credit risk of wholesale and retail exposures.

Advanced systems means an advanced approaches national bank's or Federal savings association's advanced IRB systems, operational risk management processes, operational risk data and assessment systems, operational risk quantification systems, and, to the extent used by the national bank or Federal savings association, the internal models methodology, advanced CVA approach, double default excessive correlation detection process, and internal models approach (IMA) for equity exposures.

Backtesting means the comparison of a national bank's or Federal savings association's internal estimates with actual outcomes during a sample period not used in model development. In this context, backtesting is one form of out-of-sample testing.

Benchmarking means the comparison of a national bank's or Federal savings association's internal estimates with relevant internal and external data or with estimates based on other estimation techniques.

Bond option contract means a bond option, bond future, or any other instrument linked to a bond that gives rise to similar counterparty credit risk.

Business environment and internal control factors means the indicators of a national bank's or Federal savings association's operational risk profile that reflect a current and forward-looking assessment of the national bank's or Federal savings association's underlying business risk factors and internal control environment.

Credit default swap (CDS) means a financial contract executed under standard industry documentation that allows one party (the protection purchaser) to transfer the credit risk of one or more exposures (reference exposure(s)) to another party (the protection provider) for a certain period of time.

Credit valuation adjustment (CVA) means the fair value adjustment to reflect counterparty credit risk in valuation of OTC derivative contracts.

Default—For the purposes of calculating capital requirements under this subpart:

(1) *Retail*. (i) A retail exposure of a national bank or Federal savings association is in default if:

(A) The exposure is 180 days past due, in the case of a residential mortgage exposure or revolving exposure;

(B) The exposure is 120 days past due, in the case of retail exposures that are not residential mortgage exposures or revolving exposures; or

(C) The national bank or Federal savings association has taken a full or partial charge-off, write-down of principal, or material negative fair value adjustment of principal on the exposure for credit-related reasons.

(ii) Notwithstanding paragraph (1)(i) of this definition, for a retail exposure held by a non-U.S. subsidiary of the national bank or Federal savings association that is subject to an internal ratings-based approach to capital adequacy consistent with the Basel Committee on Banking Supervision's "International Convergence of Capital Measurement and Capital Standards: A Revised Framework" in a non-U.S. jurisdiction, the national bank or Federal savings association may elect to use the definition of default that is used in that jurisdiction, provided that the national bank or Federal savings association has obtained prior approval from the OCC to use the definition of default in that jurisdiction.

(iii) A retail exposure in default remains in default until the national bank or Federal savings association has reasonable assurance of repayment and performance for all contractual principal and interest payments on the exposure.

(2) *Wholesale.* (i) A national bank's or Federal savings association's wholesale obligor is in default if:

(A) The national bank or Federal savings association determines that the obligor is unlikely to pay its credit obligations to the national bank or Federal savings association in full, without recourse by the national bank or Federal savings association to actions such as realizing collateral (if held); or

(B) The obligor is past due more than 90 days on any material credit obligation(s) to the national bank or Federal savings association.[29]

(ii) An obligor in default remains in default until the national bank or Federal savings association has reasonable assurance of repayment and performance for all contractual principal and interest payments on all exposures of the national bank or Federal savings association to the obligor (other than exposures that have been fully written-down or charged-off).

Dependence means a measure of the association among operational losses across and within units of measure.

Economic downturn conditions means, with respect to an exposure held by the national bank or Federal savings association, those conditions in which the aggregate default rates for that exposure's wholesale or retail exposure subcategory (or subdivision of such subcategory selected by the national bank or Federal savings association) in the exposure's national jurisdiction (or subdivision of such jurisdiction selected by the national bank or Federal savings association) are significantly higher than average.

Effective maturity (M) of a wholesale exposure means:

(1) For wholesale exposures other than repo-style transactions, eligible margin loans, and OTC derivative contracts described in paragraph (2) or (3) of this definition:

(i) The weighted-average remaining maturity (measured in years, whole or fractional) of the expected contractual cash flows from the exposure, using the undiscounted amounts of the cash flows as weights; or

(ii) The nominal remaining maturity (measured in years, whole or fractional) of the exposure.

(2) For repo-style transactions, eligible margin loans, and OTC derivative contracts subject to a qualifying master netting agreement for which the national bank or Federal savings association does not apply the internal models approach in section 132(d), the weighted-average remaining maturity (measured in years, whole or fractional) of the individual transactions subject to the qualifying master netting agreement, with the weight of each individual transaction set equal to the notional amount of the transaction.

(3) For repo-style transactions, eligible margin loans, and OTC derivative contracts for which the national bank or Federal savings association applies the internal models approach in § 3.132(d), the value determined in § 3.132(d)(4).

Eligible double default guarantor, with respect to a guarantee or credit derivative obtained by a national bank or Federal savings association, means:

(1) *U.S.-based entities.* A depository institution, a bank holding company, a savings and loan holding company, or a securities broker or dealer registered

[29] Overdrafts are past due once the obligor has breached an advised limit or been advised of a limit smaller than the current outstanding balance.

with the SEC under the Securities Exchange Act, if at the time the guarantee is issued or anytime thereafter, has issued and outstanding an unsecured debt security without credit enhancement that is investment grade.

(2) *Non-U.S.-based entities.* A foreign bank, or a non-U.S.-based securities firm if the national bank or Federal savings association demonstrates that the guarantor is subject to consolidated supervision and regulation comparable to that imposed on U.S. depository institutions, or securities broker-dealers) if at the time the guarantee is issued or anytime thereafter, has issued and outstanding an unsecured debt security without credit enhancement that is investment grade.

Eligible operational risk offsets means amounts, not to exceed expected operational loss, that:

(1) Are generated by internal business practices to absorb highly predictable and reasonably stable operational losses, including reserves calculated consistent with GAAP; and

(2) Are available to cover expected operational losses with a high degree of certainty over a one-year horizon.

Eligible purchased wholesale exposure means a purchased wholesale exposure that:

(1) The national bank or Federal savings association or securitization SPE purchased from an unaffiliated seller and did not directly or indirectly originate;

(2) Was generated on an arm's-length basis between the seller and the obligor (intercompany accounts receivable and receivables subject to contra-accounts between firms that buy and sell to each other do not satisfy this criterion);

(3) Provides the national bank or Federal savings association or securitization SPE with a claim on all proceeds from the exposure or a pro rata interest in the proceeds from the exposure;

(4) Has an M of less than one year; and

(5) When consolidated by obligor, does not represent a concentrated exposure relative to the portfolio of purchased wholesale exposures.

Expected exposure (EE) means the expected value of the probability distribution of non-negative credit risk exposures to a counterparty at any specified future date before the maturity date of the longest term transaction in the netting set. Any negative fair values in the probability distribution of fair values to a counterparty at a specified future date are set to zero to convert the probability distribution of fair values to the probability distribution of credit risk exposures.

Expected operational loss (EOL) means the expected value of the distribution of potential aggregate operational losses, as generated by the national bank's or Federal savings association's operational risk quantification system using a one-year horizon.

Expected positive exposure (EPE) means the weighted average over time of expected (non-negative) exposures to a counterparty where the weights are the proportion of the time interval that an individual expected exposure represents. When calculating risk-based capital requirements, the average is taken over a one-year horizon.

Exposure at default (EAD) means:

(1) For the on-balance sheet component of a wholesale exposure or segment of retail exposures (other than an OTC derivative contract, a repo-style transaction or eligible margin loan for which the national bank or Federal savings association determines EAD under §3.132, a cleared transaction, or default fund contribution), EAD means the national bank's or Federal savings association's carrying value (including net accrued but unpaid interest and fees) for the exposure or segment less any allocated transfer risk reserve for the exposure or segment.

(2) For the off-balance sheet component of a wholesale exposure or segment of retail exposures (other than an OTC derivative contract, a repo-style transaction or eligible margin loan for which the national bank or Federal savings association determines EAD under §3.132, cleared transaction, or default fund contribution) in the form of a loan commitment, line of credit, trade-related letter of credit, or transaction-related contingency, EAD means the national bank's or Federal savings association's best estimate of net additions to the outstanding

amount owed the national bank or Federal savings association, including estimated future additional draws of principal and accrued but unpaid interest and fees, that are likely to occur over a one-year horizon assuming the wholesale exposure or the retail exposures in the segment were to go into default. This estimate of net additions must reflect what would be expected during economic downturn conditions. For the purposes of this definition:

(i) Trade-related letters of credit are short-term, self-liquidating instruments that are used to finance the movement of goods and are collateralized by the underlying goods.

(ii) Transaction-related contingencies relate to a particular transaction and include, among other things, performance bonds and performance-based letters of credit.

(3) For the off-balance sheet component of a wholesale exposure or segment of retail exposures (other than an OTC derivative contract, a repo-style transaction, or eligible margin loan for which the national bank or Federal savings association determines EAD under § 3.132, cleared transaction, or default fund contribution) in the form of anything other than a loan commitment, line of credit, trade-related letter of credit, or transaction-related contingency, EAD means the notional amount of the exposure or segment.

(4) EAD for OTC derivative contracts is calculated as described in § 3.132. A national bank or Federal savings association also may determine EAD for repo-style transactions and eligible margin loans as described in § 3.132.

Exposure category means any of the wholesale, retail, securitization, or equity exposure categories.

External operational loss event data means, with respect to a national bank or Federal savings association, gross operational loss amounts, dates, recoveries, and relevant causal information for operational loss events occurring at organizations other than the national bank or Federal savings association.

IMM exposure means a repo-style transaction, eligible margin loan, or OTC derivative for which a national bank or Federal savings association calculates its EAD using the internal models methodology of § 3.132(d).

Internal operational loss event data means, with respect to a national bank or Federal savings association, gross operational loss amounts, dates, recoveries, and relevant causal information for operational loss events occurring at the national bank or Federal savings association.

Loss given default (LGD) means:

(1) For a wholesale exposure, the greatest of:

(i) Zero;

(ii) The national bank's or Federal savings association's empirically based best estimate of the long-run default-weighted average economic loss, per dollar of EAD, the national bank or Federal savings association would expect to incur if the obligor (or a typical obligor in the loss severity grade assigned by the national bank or Federal savings association to the exposure) were to default within a one-year horizon over a mix of economic conditions, including economic downturn conditions; or

(iii) The national bank's or Federal savings association's empirically based best estimate of the economic loss, per dollar of EAD, the national bank or Federal savings association would expect to incur if the obligor (or a typical obligor in the loss severity grade assigned by the national bank or Federal savings association to the exposure) were to default within a one-year horizon during economic downturn conditions.

(2) For a segment of retail exposures, the greatest of:

(i) Zero;

(ii) The national bank's or Federal savings association's empirically based best estimate of the long-run default-weighted average economic loss, per dollar of EAD, the national bank or Federal savings association would expect to incur if the exposures in the segment were to default within a one-year horizon over a mix of economic conditions, including economic downturn conditions; or

(iii) The national bank's or Federal savings association's empirically based best estimate of the economic loss, per dollar of EAD, the national bank or Federal savings association would expect to incur if the exposures in the segment were to default within a one-year horizon during economic downturn conditions.

(3) The economic loss on an exposure in the event of default is all material credit-related losses on the exposure (including accrued but unpaid interest or fees, losses on the sale of collateral, direct workout costs, and an appropriate allocation of indirect workout costs). Where positive or negative cash flows on a wholesale exposure to a defaulted obligor or a defaulted retail exposure (including proceeds from the sale of collateral, workout costs, additional extensions of credit to facilitate repayment of the exposure, and drawdowns of unused credit lines) occur after the date of default, the economic loss must reflect the net present value of cash flows as of the default date using a discount rate appropriate to the risk of the defaulted exposure.

Obligor means the legal entity or natural person contractually obligated on a wholesale exposure, except that a national bank or Federal savings association may treat the following exposures as having separate obligors:

(1) Exposures to the same legal entity or natural person denominated in different currencies;

(2)(i) An income-producing real estate exposure for which all or substantially all of the repayment of the exposure is reliant on the cash flows of the real estate serving as collateral for the exposure; the national bank or Federal savings association, in economic substance, does not have recourse to the borrower beyond the real estate collateral; and no cross-default or cross-acceleration clauses are in place other than clauses obtained solely out of an abundance of caution; and

(ii) Other credit exposures to the same legal entity or natural person; and

(3)(i) A wholesale exposure authorized under section 364 of the U.S. Bankruptcy Code (11 U.S.C. 364) to a legal entity or natural person who is a debtor-in-possession for purposes of Chapter 11 of the Bankruptcy Code; and

(ii) Other credit exposures to the same legal entity or natural person.

Operational loss means a loss (excluding insurance or tax effects) resulting from an operational loss event. Operational loss includes all expenses associated with an operational loss event except for opportunity costs, forgone revenue, and costs related to risk management and control enhancements implemented to prevent future operational losses.

Operational loss event means an event that results in loss and is associated with any of the following seven operational loss event type categories:

(1) Internal fraud, which means the operational loss event type category that comprises operational losses resulting from an act involving at least one internal party of a type intended to defraud, misappropriate property, or circumvent regulations, the law, or company policy excluding diversity- and discrimination-type events.

(2) External fraud, which means the operational loss event type category that comprises operational losses resulting from an act by a third party of a type intended to defraud, misappropriate property, or circumvent the law. Retail credit card losses arising from non-contractual, third-party-initiated fraud (for example, identity theft) are external fraud operational losses. All other third-party-initiated credit losses are to be treated as credit risk losses.

(3) Employment practices and workplace safety, which means the operational loss event type category that comprises operational losses resulting from an act inconsistent with employment, health, or safety laws or agreements, payment of personal injury claims, or payment arising from diversity- and discrimination-type events.

(4) Clients, products, and business practices, which means the operational loss event type category that comprises operational losses resulting from the nature or design of a product or from an unintentional or negligent failure to meet a professional obligation to specific clients (including fiduciary and suitability requirements).

(5) Damage to physical assets, which means the operational loss event type category that comprises operational losses resulting from the loss of or damage to physical assets from natural disaster or other events.

(6) Business disruption and system failures, which means the operational

loss event type category that comprises operational losses resulting from disruption of business or system failures.

(7) Execution, delivery, and process management, which means the operational loss event type category that comprises operational losses resulting from failed transaction processing or process management or losses arising from relations with trade counterparties and vendors.

Operational risk means the risk of loss resulting from inadequate or failed internal processes, people, and systems or from external events (including legal risk but excluding strategic and reputational risk).

Operational risk exposure means the 99.9th percentile of the distribution of potential aggregate operational losses, as generated by the national bank's or Federal savings association's operational risk quantification system over a one-year horizon (and not incorporating eligible operational risk offsets or qualifying operational risk mitigants).

Other retail exposure means an exposure (other than a securitization exposure, an equity exposure, a residential mortgage exposure, a pre-sold construction loan, a qualifying revolving exposure, or the residual value portion of a lease exposure) that is managed as part of a segment of exposures with homogeneous risk characteristics, not on an individual-exposure basis, and is either:

(1) An exposure to an individual for non-business purposes; or

(2) An exposure to an individual or company for business purposes if the national bank's or Federal savings association's consolidated business credit exposure to the individual or company is $1 million or less.

Probability of default (PD) means:

(1) For a wholesale exposure to a non-defaulted obligor, the national bank's or Federal savings association's empirically based best estimate of the long-run average one-year default rate for the rating grade assigned by the national bank or Federal savings association to the obligor, capturing the average default experience for obligors in the rating grade over a mix of economic conditions (including economic downturn conditions) sufficient to provide a reasonable estimate of the average one-year default rate over the economic cycle for the rating grade.

(2) For a segment of non-defaulted retail exposures, the national bank's or Federal savings association's empirically based best estimate of the long-run average one-year default rate for the exposures in the segment, capturing the average default experience for exposures in the segment over a mix of economic conditions (including economic downturn conditions) sufficient to provide a reasonable estimate of the average one-year default rate over the economic cycle for the segment.

(3) For a wholesale exposure to a defaulted obligor or segment of defaulted retail exposures, 100 percent.

Qualifying cross-product master netting agreement means a qualifying master netting agreement that provides for termination and close-out netting across multiple types of financial transactions or qualifying master netting agreements in the event of a counterparty's default, provided that the underlying financial transactions are OTC derivative contracts, eligible margin loans, or repo-style transactions. In order to treat an agreement as a qualifying cross-product master netting agreement for purposes of this subpart, a national bank or Federal savings association must comply with the requirements of §3.3(c) of this part with respect to that agreement.

Qualifying revolving exposure (QRE) means an exposure (other than a securitization exposure or equity exposure) to an individual that is managed as part of a segment of exposures with homogeneous risk characteristics, not on an individual-exposure basis, and:

(1) Is revolving (that is, the amount outstanding fluctuates, determined largely by a borrower's decision to borrow and repay up to a pre-established maximum amount, except for an outstanding amount that the borrower is required to pay in full every month);

(2) Is unsecured and unconditionally cancelable by the national bank or Federal savings association to the fullest extent permitted by Federal law; and

(3)(i) Has a maximum contractual exposure amount (drawn plus undrawn) of up to $100,000; or

(ii) With respect to a product with an outstanding amount that the borrower is required to pay in full every month, the total outstanding amount does not in practice exceed $100,000.

(4) A segment of exposures that contains one or more exposures that fails to meet paragraph (3)(ii) of this definition must be treated as a segment of other retail exposures for the 24 month period following the month in which the total outstanding amount of one or more exposures individually exceeds $100,000.

Retail exposure means a residential mortgage exposure, a qualifying revolving exposure, or an other retail exposure.

Retail exposure subcategory means the residential mortgage exposure, qualifying revolving exposure, or other retail exposure subcategory.

Risk parameter means a variable used in determining risk-based capital requirements for wholesale and retail exposures, specifically probability of default (PD), loss given default (LGD), exposure at default (EAD), or effective maturity (M).

Scenario analysis means a systematic process of obtaining expert opinions from business managers and risk management experts to derive reasoned assessments of the likelihood and loss impact of plausible high-severity operational losses. Scenario analysis may include the well-reasoned evaluation and use of external operational loss event data, adjusted as appropriate to ensure relevance to a national bank's or Federal savings association's operational risk profile and control structure.

Total wholesale and retail risk-weighted assets means the sum of:

(1) Risk-weighted assets for wholesale exposures that are not IMM exposures, cleared transactions, or default fund contributions to non-defaulted obligors and segments of non-defaulted retail exposures;

(2) Risk-weighted assets for wholesale exposures to defaulted obligors and segments of defaulted retail exposures;

(3) Risk-weighted assets for assets not defined by an exposure category;

(4) Risk-weighted assets for non-material portfolios of exposures;

(5) Risk-weighted assets for IMM exposures (as determined in §3.132(d));

(6) Risk-weighted assets for cleared transactions and risk-weighted assets for default fund contributions (as determined in §3.133); and

(7) Risk-weighted assets for unsettled transactions (as determined in §3.136).

Unexpected operational loss (UOL) means the difference between the national bank's or Federal savings association's operational risk exposure and the national bank's or Federal savings association's expected operational loss.

Unit of measure means the level (for example, organizational unit or operational loss event type) at which the national bank's or Federal savings association's operational risk quantification system generates a separate distribution of potential operational losses.

Wholesale exposure means a credit exposure to a company, natural person, sovereign, or governmental entity (other than a securitization exposure, retail exposure, pre-sold construction loan, or equity exposure).

Wholesale exposure subcategory means the HVCRE or non-HVCRE wholesale exposure subcategory.

QUALIFICATION

§3.121 Qualification process.

(a) *Timing.* (1) A national bank or Federal savings association that is described in §3.100(b)(1)(i) through (iv) must adopt a written implementation plan no later than six months after the date the national bank or Federal savings association meets a criterion in that section. The implementation plan must incorporate an explicit start date no later than 36 months after the date the national bank or Federal savings association meets at least one criterion under §3.100(b)(1)(i) through (iv). The OCC may extend the start date.

(2) A national bank or Federal savings association that elects to be subject to this appendix under §3.100(b)(1)(v) must adopt a written implementation plan.

(b) *Implementation plan.* (1) The national bank's or Federal savings association's implementation plan must address in detail how the national bank or Federal savings association complies, or plans to comply, with the qualification requirements in § 3.122. The national bank or Federal savings association also must maintain a comprehensive and sound planning and governance process to oversee the implementation efforts described in the plan. At a minimum, the plan must:

(i) Comprehensively address the qualification requirements in § 3.122 for the national bank or Federal savings association and each consolidated subsidiary (U.S. and foreign-based) of the national bank or Federal savings association with respect to all portfolios and exposures of the national bank or Federal savings association and each of its consolidated subsidiaries;

(ii) Justify and support any proposed temporary or permanent exclusion of business lines, portfolios, or exposures from the application of the advanced approaches in this subpart (which business lines, portfolios, and exposures must be, in the aggregate, immaterial to the national bank or Federal savings association);

(iii) Include the national bank's or Federal savings association's self-assessment of:

(A) The national bank's or Federal savings association's current status in meeting the qualification requirements in § 3.122; and

(B) The consistency of the national bank's or Federal savings association's current practices with the OCC's supervisory guidance on the qualification requirements;

(iv) Based on the national bank's or Federal savings association's self-assessment, identify and describe the areas in which the national bank or Federal savings association proposes to undertake additional work to comply with the qualification requirements in § 3.122 or to improve the consistency of the national bank's or Federal savings association's current practices with the OCC's supervisory guidance on the qualification requirements (gap analysis);

(v) Describe what specific actions the national bank or Federal savings association will take to address the areas identified in the gap analysis required by paragraph (b)(1)(iv) of this section;

(vi) Identify objective, measurable milestones, including delivery dates and a date when the national bank's or Federal savings association's implementation of the methodologies described in this subpart will be fully operational;

(vii) Describe resources that have been budgeted and are available to implement the plan; and

(viii) Receive approval of the national bank's or Federal savings association's board of directors.

(2) The national bank or Federal savings association must submit the implementation plan, together with a copy of the minutes of the board of directors' approval, to the OCC at least 60 days before the national bank or Federal savings association proposes to begin its parallel run, unless the OCC waives prior notice.

(c) *Parallel run.* Before determining its risk-weighted assets under this subpart and following adoption of the implementation plan, the national bank or Federal savings association must conduct a satisfactory parallel run. A satisfactory parallel run is a period of no less than four consecutive calendar quarters during which the national bank or Federal savings association complies with the qualification requirements in § 3.122 to the satisfaction of the OCC. During the parallel run, the national bank or Federal savings association must report to the OCC on a calendar quarterly basis its risk-based capital ratios determined in accordance with § 3.10(b)(1) through (3) and § 3.10 (c)(1) through (3). During this period, the national bank's or Federal savings association's minimum risk-based capital ratios are determined as set forth in subpart D of this part.

(d) *Approval to calculate risk-based capital requirements under this subpart.* The OCC will notify the national bank or Federal savings association of the date that the national bank or Federal savings association must begin to use this subpart for purposes of § 3.10 if the OCC determines that:

(1) The national bank or Federal savings association fully complies with all

the qualification requirements in §3.122;

(2) The national bank or Federal savings association has conducted a satisfactory parallel run under paragraph (c) of this section; and

(3) The national bank or Federal savings association has an adequate process to ensure ongoing compliance with the qualification requirements in §3.122.

§3.122 Qualification requirements.

(a) *Process and systems requirements.* (1) A national bank or Federal savings association must have a rigorous process for assessing its overall capital adequacy in relation to its risk profile and a comprehensive strategy for maintaining an appropriate level of capital.

(2) The systems and processes used by a national bank or Federal savings association for risk-based capital purposes under this subpart must be consistent with the national bank's or Federal savings association's internal risk management processes and management information reporting systems.

(3) Each national bank or Federal savings association must have an appropriate infrastructure with risk measurement and management processes that meet the qualification requirements of this section and are appropriate given the national bank's or Federal savings association's size and level of complexity. Regardless of whether the systems and models that generate the risk parameters necessary for calculating a national bank's or Federal savings association's risk-based capital requirements are located at any affiliate of the national bank or Federal savings association, the national bank or Federal savings association itself must ensure that the risk parameters and reference data used to determine its risk-based capital requirements are representative of long run experience with respect to its own credit risk and operational risk exposures.

(b) *Risk rating and segmentation systems for wholesale and retail exposures.* (1)(i) A national bank or Federal savings association must have an internal risk rating and segmentation system that accurately, reliably, and meaningfully differentiates among degrees of credit risk for the national bank's or Federal savings association's wholesale and retail exposures. When assigning an internal risk rating, a national bank or Federal savings association may consider a third-party assessment of credit risk, provided that the national bank's or Federal savings association's internal risk rating assignment does not rely solely on the external assessment.

(ii) If a national bank or Federal savings association uses multiple rating or segmentation systems, the national bank's or Federal savings association's rationale for assigning an obligor or exposure to a particular system must be documented and applied in a manner that best reflects the obligor's or exposure's level of risk. A national bank or Federal savings association must not inappropriately allocate obligors or exposures across systems to minimize regulatory capital requirements.

(iii) In assigning ratings to wholesale obligors and exposures, including loss severity ratings grades to wholesale exposures, and assigning retail exposures to retail segments, a national bank or Federal savings association must use all relevant and material information and ensure that the information is current.

(iv) When assigning an obligor to a PD rating or retail exposure to a PD segment, a national bank or Federal savings association must assess the obligor or retail borrower's ability and willingness to contractually perform, taking a conservative view of projected information.

(2) For wholesale exposures:

(i) A national bank or Federal savings association must have an internal risk rating system that accurately and reliably assigns each obligor to a single rating grade (reflecting the obligor's likelihood of default). A national bank or Federal savings association may elect, however, not to assign to a rating grade an obligor to whom the national bank or Federal savings association extends credit based solely on the financial strength of a guarantor, provided that all of the national bank's or Federal savings association's exposures to the obligor are fully covered by eligible guarantees, the national bank or

Federal savings association applies the PD substitution approach in §3.134(c)(1) to all exposures to that obligor, and the national bank or Federal savings association immediately assigns the obligor to a rating grade if a guarantee can no longer be recognized under this part. The national bank's or Federal savings association's wholesale obligor rating system must have at least seven discrete rating grades for non-defaulted obligors and at least one rating grade for defaulted obligors.

(ii) Unless the national bank or Federal savings association has chosen to directly assign LGD estimates to each wholesale exposure, the national bank or Federal savings association must have an internal risk rating system that accurately and reliably assigns each wholesale exposure to a loss severity rating grade (reflecting the national bank's or Federal savings association's estimate of the LGD of the exposure). A national bank or Federal savings association employing loss severity rating grades must have a sufficiently granular loss severity grading system to avoid grouping together exposures with widely ranging LGDs.

(iii) A national bank or Federal savings association must have an effective process to obtain and update in a timely manner relevant and material information on obligor and exposure characteristics that affect PD, LGD and EAD.

(3) For retail exposures:

(i) A national bank or Federal savings association must have an internal system that groups retail exposures into the appropriate retail exposure subcategory and groups the retail exposures in each retail exposure subcategory into separate segments with homogeneous risk characteristics that provide a meaningful differentiation of risk. The national bank's or Federal savings association's system must identify and group in separate segments by subcategories exposures identified in §3.131(c)(2)(ii) and (iii).

(ii) A national bank or Federal savings association must have an internal system that captures all relevant exposure risk characteristics, including borrower credit score, product and collateral types, as well as exposure delinquencies, and must consider cross-collateral provisions, where present.

(iii) The national bank or Federal savings association must review and, if appropriate, update assignments of individual retail exposures to segments and the loss characteristics and delinquency status of each identified risk segment. These reviews must occur whenever the national bank or Federal savings association receives new material information, but generally no less frequently than quarterly, and, in all cases, at least annually.

(4) The national bank's or Federal savings association's internal risk rating policy for wholesale exposures must describe the national bank's or Federal savings association's rating philosophy (that is, must describe how wholesale obligor rating assignments are affected by the national bank's or Federal savings association's choice of the range of economic, business, and industry conditions that are considered in the obligor rating process).

(5) The national bank's or Federal savings association's internal risk rating system for wholesale exposures must provide for the review and update (as appropriate) of each obligor rating and (if applicable) each loss severity rating whenever the national bank or Federal savings association obtains relevant and material information on the obligor or exposure that affects PD, LGD and EAD, but no less frequently than annually.

(c) *Quantification of risk parameters for wholesale and retail exposures.* (1) The national bank or Federal savings association must have a comprehensive risk parameter quantification process that produces accurate, timely, and reliable estimates of the risk parameters on a consistent basis for the national bank's or Federal savings association's wholesale and retail exposures.

(2) A national bank's or Federal savings association's estimates of PD, LGD, and EAD must incorporate all relevant, material, and available data that is reflective of the national bank's or Federal savings association's actual wholesale and retail exposures and of sufficient quality to support the determination of risk-based capital requirements for the exposures. In particular, the population of exposures in the data used for estimation purposes, the lending standards in use when the data

were generated, and other relevant characteristics, should closely match or be comparable to the national bank's or Federal savings association's exposures and standards. In addition, a national bank or Federal savings association must:

(i) Demonstrate that its estimates are representative of long run experience, including periods of economic downturn conditions, whether internal or external data are used;

(ii) Take into account any changes in lending practice or the process for pursuing recoveries over the observation period;

(iii) Promptly reflect technical advances, new data, and other information as they become available;

(iv) Demonstrate that the data used to estimate risk parameters support the accuracy and robustness of those estimates; and

(v) Demonstrate that its estimation technique performs well in out-of-sample tests whenever possible.

(3) The national bank's or Federal savings association's risk parameter quantification process must produce appropriately conservative risk parameter estimates where the national bank or Federal savings association has limited relevant data, and any adjustments that are part of the quantification process must not result in a pattern of bias toward lower risk parameter estimates.

(4) The national bank's or Federal savings association's risk parameter estimation process should not rely on the possibility of U.S. government financial assistance, except for the financial assistance that the U.S. government has a legally binding commitment to provide.

(5) The national bank or Federal savings association must be able to demonstrate which variables have been found to be statistically significant with regard to EAD. The national bank's or Federal savings association's EAD estimates must reflect its specific policies and strategies with regard to account management, including account monitoring and payment processing, and its ability and willingness to prevent further drawdowns in circumstances short of payment default. The national bank or Federal savings association must have adequate systems and procedures in place to monitor current outstanding amounts against committed lines, and changes in outstanding amounts per obligor and obligor rating grade and per retail segment. The national bank or Federal savings association must be able to monitor outstanding amounts on a daily basis.

(6) At a minimum, PD estimates for wholesale obligors and retail segments must be based on at least five years of default data. LGD estimates for wholesale exposures must be based on at least seven years of loss severity data, and LGD estimates for retail segments must be based on at least five years of loss severity data. EAD estimates for wholesale exposures must be based on at least seven years of exposure amount data, and EAD estimates for retail segments must be based on at least five years of exposure amount data. If the national bank or Federal savings association has relevant and material reference data that span a longer period of time than the minimum time periods specified above, the national bank or Federal savings association must incorporate such data in its estimates, provided that it does not place undue weight on periods of favorable or benign economic conditions relative to periods of economic downturn conditions.

(7) Default, loss severity, and exposure amount data must include periods of economic downturn conditions, or the national bank or Federal savings association must adjust its estimates of risk parameters to compensate for the lack of data from periods of economic downturn conditions.

(8) The national bank's or Federal savings association's PD, LGD, and EAD estimates must be based on the definition of default in §3.101.

(9) If a national bank or Federal savings association uses internal data obtained prior to becoming subject to this subpart E or external data to arrive at PD, LGD, or EAD estimates, the national bank or Federal savings association must demonstrate to the OCC that the national bank or Federal savings association has made appropriate adjustments if necessary to be consistent with the definition of default in

§ 3.101. Internal data obtained after the national bank or Federal savings association becomes subject to this subpart E must be consistent with the definition of default in § 3.101.

(10) The national bank or Federal savings association must review and update (as appropriate) its risk parameters and its risk parameter quantification process at least annually.

(11) The national bank or Federal savings association must, at least annually, conduct a comprehensive review and analysis of reference data to determine relevance of the reference data to the national bank's or Federal savings association's exposures, quality of reference data to support PD, LGD, and EAD estimates, and consistency of reference data to the definition of default in § 3.101.

(d) *Counterparty credit risk model.* A national bank or Federal savings association must obtain the prior written approval of the OCC under § 3.132 to use the internal models methodology for counterparty credit risk and the advanced CVA approach for the CVA capital requirement.

(e) *Double default treatment.* A national bank or Federal savings association must obtain the prior written approval of the OCC under § 3.135 to use the double default treatment.

(f) *Equity exposures model.* A national bank or Federal savings association must obtain the prior written approval of the OCC under § 3.153 to use the internal models approach for equity exposures.

(g) *Operational risk.* (1) Operational risk management processes. A national bank or Federal savings association must:

(i) Have an operational risk management function that:

(A) Is independent of business line management; and

(B) Is responsible for designing, implementing, and overseeing the national bank's or Federal savings association's operational risk data and assessment systems, operational risk quantification systems, and related processes;

(ii) Have and document a process (which must capture business environment and internal control factors affecting the national bank's or Federal savings association's operational risk profile) to identify, measure, monitor, and control operational risk in the national bank's or Federal savings association's products, activities, processes, and systems; and

(iii) Report operational risk exposures, operational loss events, and other relevant operational risk information to business unit management, senior management, and the board of directors (or a designated committee of the board).

(2) *Operational risk data and assessment systems.* A national bank or Federal savings association must have operational risk data and assessment systems that capture operational risks to which the national bank or Federal savings association is exposed. The national bank's or Federal savings association's operational risk data and assessment systems must:

(i) Be structured in a manner consistent with the national bank's or Federal savings association's current business activities, risk profile, technological processes, and risk management processes; and

(ii) Include credible, transparent, systematic, and verifiable processes that incorporate the following elements on an ongoing basis:

(A) *Internal operational loss event data.* The national bank or Federal savings association must have a systematic process for capturing and using internal operational loss event data in its operational risk data and assessment systems.

(*1*) The national bank's or Federal savings association's operational risk data and assessment systems must include a historical observation period of at least five years for internal operational loss event data (or such shorter period approved by the OCC to address transitional situations, such as integrating a new business line).

(*2*) The national bank or Federal savings association must be able to map its internal operational loss event data into the seven operational loss event type categories.

(*3*) The national bank or Federal savings association may refrain from collecting internal operational loss event data for individual operational losses below established dollar threshold amounts if the national bank or Federal savings association can demonstrate to the satisfaction of the OCC that the thresholds are reasonable, do not exclude important internal operational loss event data, and permit the national bank or Federal savings association to capture substantially all the dollar value of the national bank's or Federal savings association's operational losses.

(B) *External operational loss event data.* The national bank or Federal savings association must have a systematic process for determining its methodologies for incorporating external operational loss event data into its operational risk data and assessment systems.

(C) *Scenario analysis.* The national bank or Federal savings association must have a systematic process for determining its methodologies for incorporating scenario analysis into its operational risk data and assessment systems.

(D) *Business environment and internal control factors.* The national bank or Federal savings association must incorporate business environment and internal control factors into its operational risk data and assessment systems. The national bank or Federal savings association must also periodically compare the results of its prior business environment and internal control factor assessments against its actual operational losses incurred in the intervening period.

(3) *Operational risk quantification systems.* (i) The national bank's or Federal savings association's operational risk quantification systems:

(A) Must generate estimates of the national bank's or Federal savings association's operational risk exposure using its operational risk data and assessment systems;

(B) Must employ a unit of measure that is appropriate for the national bank's or Federal savings association's range of business activities and the variety of operational loss events to which it is exposed, and that does not combine business activities or operational loss events with demonstrably different risk profiles within the same loss distribution;

(C) Must include a credible, transparent, systematic, and verifiable approach for weighting each of the four elements, described in paragraph (g)(2)(ii) of this section, that a national bank or Federal savings association is required to incorporate into its operational risk data and assessment systems;

(D) May use internal estimates of dependence among operational losses across and within units of measure if the national bank or Federal savings association can demonstrate to the satisfaction of the OCC that its process for estimating dependence is sound, robust to a variety of scenarios, and implemented with integrity, and allows for uncertainty surrounding the estimates. If the national bank or Federal savings association has not made such a demonstration, it must sum operational risk exposure estimates across units of measure to calculate its total operational risk exposure; and

(E) Must be reviewed and updated (as appropriate) whenever the national bank or Federal savings association becomes aware of information that may have a material effect on the national bank's or Federal savings association's estimate of operational risk exposure, but the review and update must occur no less frequently than annually.

(ii) With the prior written approval of the OCC, a national bank or Federal savings association may generate an estimate of its operational risk exposure using an alternative approach to that specified in paragraph (g)(3)(i) of this section. A national bank or Federal savings association proposing to use such an alternative operational risk quantification system must submit a proposal to the OCC. In determining whether to approve a national bank's or Federal savings association's proposal to use an alternative operational risk quantification system, the OCC will consider the following principles:

(A) Use of the alternative operational risk quantification system will be allowed only on an exception basis, considering the size, complexity, and risk profile of the national bank or Federal savings association;

(B) The national bank or Federal savings association must demonstrate that its estimate of its operational risk exposure generated under the alternative operational risk quantification system is appropriate and can be supported empirically; and

(C) A national bank or Federal savings association must not use an allocation of operational risk capital requirements that includes entities other than depository institutions or the benefits of diversification across entities.

(h) *Data management and maintenance.* (1) A national bank or Federal savings association must have data management and maintenance systems that adequately support all aspects of its advanced systems and the timely and accurate reporting of risk-based capital requirements.

(2) A national bank or Federal savings association must retain data using an electronic format that allows timely retrieval of data for analysis, validation, reporting, and disclosure purposes.

(3) A national bank or Federal savings association must retain sufficient data elements related to key risk drivers to permit adequate monitoring, validation, and refinement of its advanced systems.

(i) *Control, oversight, and validation mechanisms.* (1) The national bank's or Federal savings association's senior management must ensure that all components of the national bank's or Federal savings association's advanced systems function effectively and comply with the qualification requirements in this section.

(2) The national bank's or Federal savings association's board of directors (or a designated committee of the board) must at least annually review the effectiveness of, and approve, the national bank's or Federal savings association's advanced systems.

(3) A national bank or Federal savings association must have an effective system of controls and oversight that:

(i) Ensures ongoing compliance with the qualification requirements in this section;

(ii) Maintains the integrity, reliability, and accuracy of the national bank's or Federal savings association's advanced systems; and

(iii) Includes adequate governance and project management processes.

(4) The national bank or Federal savings association must validate, on an ongoing basis, its advanced systems. The national bank's or Federal savings association's validation process must be independent of the advanced systems' development, implementation, and operation, or the validation process must be subjected to an independent review of its adequacy and effectiveness. Validation must include:

(i) An evaluation of the conceptual soundness of (including developmental evidence supporting) the advanced systems;

(ii) An ongoing monitoring process that includes verification of processes and benchmarking; and

(iii) An outcomes analysis process that includes backtesting.

(5) The national bank or Federal savings association must have an internal audit function or equivalent function that is independent of business-line management that at least annually:

(i) Reviews the national bank's or Federal savings association's advanced systems and associated operations, including the operations of its credit function and estimations of PD, LGD, and EAD;

(ii) Assesses the effectiveness of the controls supporting the national bank's or Federal savings association's advanced systems; and

(iii) Documents and reports its findings to the national bank's or Federal savings association's board of directors (or a committee thereof).

(6) The national bank or Federal savings association must periodically stress test its advanced systems. The stress testing must include a consideration of how economic cycles, especially downturns, affect risk-based capital requirements (including migration across rating grades and segments and the credit risk mitigation benefits of double default treatment).

(j) *Documentation.* The national bank or Federal savings association must adequately document all material aspects of its advanced systems.

[78 FR 62157, 62273, Oct. 11, 2013, as amended at 80 FR 41415, July 15, 2015]

§3.123 Ongoing qualification.

(a) *Changes to advanced systems.* A national bank or Federal savings association must meet all the qualification requirements in §3.122 on an ongoing basis. A national bank or Federal savings association must notify the OCC when the national bank or Federal savings association makes any change to an advanced system that would result in a material change in the national bank's or Federal savings association's advanced approaches total risk-weighted asset amount for an exposure type or when the national bank or Federal savings association makes any significant change to its modeling assumptions.

(b) *Failure to comply with qualification requirements.* (1) If the OCC determines that a national bank or Federal savings association that uses this subpart and that has conducted a satisfactory parallel run fails to comply with the qualification requirements in §3.122, the OCC will notify the national bank or Federal savings association in writing of the national bank's or Federal savings association's failure to comply.

(2) The national bank or Federal savings association must establish and submit a plan satisfactory to the OCC to return to compliance with the qualification requirements.

(3) In addition, if the OCC determines that the national bank's or Federal savings association's advanced approaches total risk-weighted assets are not commensurate with the national bank's or Federal savings association's credit, market, operational, or other risks, the OCC may require such a national bank or Federal savings association to calculate its advanced approaches total risk-weighted assets with any modifications provided by the OCC.

§3.124 Merger and acquisition transitional arrangements.

(a) *Mergers and acquisitions of companies without advanced systems.* If a national bank or Federal savings association merges with or acquires a company that does not calculate its risk-based capital requirements using advanced systems, the national bank or Federal savings association may use subpart D of this part to determine the risk-weighted asset amounts for the merged or acquired company's exposures for up to 24 months after the calendar quarter during which the merger or acquisition consummates. The OCC may extend this transition period for up to an additional 12 months. Within 90 days of consummating the merger or acquisition, the national bank or Federal savings association must submit to the OCC an implementation plan for using its advanced systems for the acquired company. During the period in which subpart D of this part applies to the merged or acquired company, any ALLL, net of allocated transfer risk reserves established pursuant to 12 U.S.C. 3904, associated with the merged or acquired company's exposures may be included in the acquiring national bank's or Federal savings association's tier 2 capital up to 1.25 percent of the acquired company's risk-weighted assets. All general allowances of the merged or acquired company must be excluded from the national bank's or Federal savings association's eligible credit reserves. In addition, the risk-weighted assets of the merged or acquired company are not included in the national bank's or Federal savings association's credit-risk-weighted assets but are included in total risk-weighted assets. If a national bank or Federal savings association relies on this paragraph (a), the national bank or Federal savings association must disclose publicly the amounts of risk-weighted assets and qualifying capital calculated under this subpart for the acquiring national bank or Federal savings association and under subpart D of this part for the acquired company.

(b) *Mergers and acquisitions of companies with advanced systems.* (1) If a national bank or Federal savings association merges with or acquires a company that calculates its risk-based capital requirements using advanced systems, the national bank or Federal savings association may use the acquired company's advanced systems to determine total risk-weighted assets for the merged or acquired company's exposures for up to 24 months after the calendar quarter during which the acquisition or merger consummates. The OCC may extend this transition period for up to an additional 12 months.

Within 90 days of consummating the merger or acquisition, the national bank or Federal savings association must submit to the OCC an implementation plan for using its advanced systems for the merged or acquired company.

(2) If the acquiring national bank or Federal savings association is not subject to the advanced approaches in this subpart at the time of acquisition or merger, during the period when subpart D of this part applies to the acquiring national bank or Federal savings association, the ALLL associated with the exposures of the merged or acquired company may not be directly included in tier 2 capital. Rather, any excess eligible credit reserves associated with the merged or acquired company's exposures may be included in the national bank's or Federal savings association's tier 2 capital up to 0.6 percent of the credit-risk-weighted assets associated with those exposures.

§§ 3.125–3.130 [Reserved]

RISK-WEIGHTED ASSETS FOR GENERAL CREDIT RISK

§ 3.131 Mechanics for calculating total wholesale and retail risk-weighted assets.

(a) *Overview.* A national bank or Federal savings association must calculate its total wholesale and retail risk-weighted asset amount in four distinct phases:

(1) Phase 1—categorization of exposures;

(2) Phase 2—assignment of wholesale obligors and exposures to rating grades and segmentation of retail exposures;

(3) Phase 3—assignment of risk parameters to wholesale exposures and segments of retail exposures; and

(4) Phase 4—calculation of risk-weighted asset amounts.

(b) *Phase 1—Categorization.* The national bank or Federal savings association must determine which of its exposures are wholesale exposures, retail exposures, securitization exposures, or equity exposures. The national bank or Federal savings association must categorize each retail exposure as a residential mortgage exposure, a QRE, or an other retail exposure. The national bank or Federal savings association must identify which wholesale exposures are HVCRE exposures, sovereign exposures, OTC derivative contracts, repo-style transactions, eligible margin loans, eligible purchased wholesale exposures, cleared transactions, default fund contributions, unsettled transactions to which § 3.136 applies, and eligible guarantees or eligible credit derivatives that are used as credit risk mitigants. The national bank or Federal savings association must identify any on-balance sheet asset that does not meet the definition of a wholesale, retail, equity, or securitization exposure, as well as any non-material portfolio of exposures described in paragraph (e)(4) of this section.

(c) *Phase 2—Assignment of wholesale obligors and exposures to rating grades and retail exposures to segments*—(1) *Assignment of wholesale obligors and exposures to rating grades.* (i) The national bank or Federal savings association must assign each obligor of a wholesale exposure to a single obligor rating grade and must assign each wholesale exposure to which it does not directly assign an LGD estimate to a loss severity rating grade.

(ii) The national bank or Federal savings association must identify which of its wholesale obligors are in default.

(2) *Segmentation of retail exposures.* (i) The national bank or Federal savings association must group the retail exposures in each retail subcategory into segments that have homogeneous risk characteristics.

(ii) The national bank or Federal savings association must identify which of its retail exposures are in default. The national bank or Federal savings association must segment defaulted retail exposures separately from non-defaulted retail exposures.

(iii) If the national bank or Federal savings association determines the EAD for eligible margin loans using the approach in § 3.132(b), the national bank or Federal savings association must identify which of its retail exposures are eligible margin loans for which the national bank or Federal savings association uses this EAD approach and must segment such eligible margin loans separately from other retail exposures.

(3) *Eligible purchased wholesale exposures.* A national bank or Federal savings association may group its eligible purchased wholesale exposures into segments that have homogeneous risk characteristics. A national bank or Federal savings association must use the wholesale exposure formula in Table 1 of this section to determine the risk-based capital requirement for each segment of eligible purchased wholesale exposures.

(d) *Phase 3—Assignment of risk parameters to wholesale exposures and segments of retail exposures*—(1) *Quantification process.* Subject to the limitations in this paragraph (d), the national bank or Federal savings association must:

(i) Associate a PD with each wholesale obligor rating grade;

(ii) Associate an LGD with each wholesale loss severity rating grade or assign an LGD to each wholesale exposure;

(iii) Assign an EAD and M to each wholesale exposure; and

(iv) Assign a PD, LGD, and EAD to each segment of retail exposures.

(2) *Floor on PD assignment.* The PD for each wholesale obligor or retail segment may not be less than 0.03 percent, except for exposures to or directly and unconditionally guaranteed by a sovereign entity, the Bank for International Settlements, the International Monetary Fund, the European Commission, the European Central Bank, or a multilateral development bank, to which the national bank or Federal savings association assigns a rating grade associated with a PD of less than 0.03 percent.

(3) *Floor on LGD estimation.* The LGD for each segment of residential mortgage exposures may not be less than 10 percent, except for segments of residential mortgage exposures for which all or substantially all of the principal of each exposure is either:

(i) Directly and unconditionally guaranteed by the full faith and credit of a sovereign entity; or

(ii) Guaranteed by a contingent obligation of the U.S. government or its agencies, the enforceability of which is dependent upon some affirmative action on the part of the beneficiary of the guarantee or a third party (for example, meeting servicing requirements).

(4) *Eligible purchased wholesale exposures.* A national bank or Federal savings association must assign a PD, LGD, EAD, and M to each segment of eligible purchased wholesale exposures. If the national bank or Federal savings association can estimate ECL (but not PD or LGD) for a segment of eligible purchased wholesale exposures, the national bank or Federal savings association must assume that the LGD of the segment equals 100 percent and that the PD of the segment equals ECL divided by EAD. The estimated ECL must be calculated for the exposures without regard to any assumption of recourse or guarantees from the seller or other parties.

(5) *Credit risk mitigation: credit derivatives, guarantees, and collateral.* (i) A national bank or Federal savings association may take into account the risk reducing effects of eligible guarantees and eligible credit derivatives in support of a wholesale exposure by applying the PD substitution or LGD adjustment treatment to the exposure as provided in §3.134 or, if applicable, applying double default treatment to the exposure as provided in §3.135. A national bank or Federal savings association may decide separately for each wholesale exposure that qualifies for the double default treatment under §3.135 whether to apply the double default treatment or to use the PD substitution or LGD adjustment treatment without recognizing double default effects.

(ii) A national bank or Federal savings association may take into account the risk reducing effects of guarantees and credit derivatives in support of retail exposures in a segment when quantifying the PD and LGD of the segment. In doing so, a national bank or Federal savings association must consider all relevant available information.

(iii) Except as provided in paragraph (d)(6) of this section, a national bank or Federal savings association may take into account the risk reducing effects of collateral in support of a wholesale exposure when quantifying the LGD of the exposure, and may take into account the risk reducing effects of collateral in support of retail exposures when quantifying the PD and LGD of the segment. In order to do so, a national bank or Federal savings association must have established internal requirements for collateral management, legal certainty, and risk management processes.

(6) *EAD for OTC derivative contracts, repo-style transactions, and eligible margin loans.* A national bank or Federal savings association must calculate its EAD for an OTC derivative contract as provided in §3.132 (c) and (d). A national bank or Federal savings association may take into account the risk-reducing effects of financial collateral in support of a repo-style transaction or eligible margin loan and of any collateral in support of a repo-style transaction that is included in the national bank's or Federal savings association's VaR-based measure under subpart F of this part through an adjustment to EAD as provided in §3.132(b) and (d). A national bank or Federal savings association that takes collateral into account through such an adjustment to EAD under §3.132 may not reflect such collateral in LGD.

(7) *Effective maturity.* An exposure's M must be no greater than five years and no less than one year, except that an exposure's M must be no less than one day if the exposure is a trade related letter of credit, or if the exposure has an original maturity of less than one year and is not part of a national bank's or Federal savings association's ongoing financing of the obligor. An exposure is not part of a national bank's or Federal savings association's ongoing financing of the obligor if the national bank or Federal savings association:

(i) Has a legal and practical ability not to renew or roll over the exposure in the event of credit deterioration of the obligor;

(ii) Makes an independent credit decision at the inception of the exposure and at every renewal or roll over; and

(iii) Has no substantial commercial incentive to continue its credit relationship with the obligor in the event of credit deterioration of the obligor.

(8) *EAD for exposures to certain central counterparties.* A national bank or Federal savings association may attribute an EAD of zero to exposures that arise from the settlement of cash transactions (such as equities, fixed income, spot foreign exchange, and spot commodities) with a central counterparty where there is no assumption of ongoing counterparty credit risk by the central counterparty after settlement of the trade and associated default fund contributions.

(e) *Phase 4—Calculation of risk-weighted assets*—(1) *Non-defaulted exposures.* (i) A national bank or Federal savings association must calculate the dollar risk-based capital requirement for each of its wholesale exposures to a non-defaulted obligor (except for eligible guarantees and eligible credit derivatives that hedge another wholesale exposure, IMM exposures, cleared transactions, default fund contributions, unsettled transactions, and exposures to which the national bank or Federal savings association applies the double default treatment in §3.135) and segments of non-defaulted retail exposures by inserting the assigned risk parameters for the wholesale obligor and exposure or retail segment into the appropriate risk-based capital formula specified in Table 1 and multiplying the output of the formula (K) by the EAD of the exposure or segment. Alternatively, a national bank or Federal savings association may apply a 300 percent risk weight to the EAD of an eligible margin loan if the national bank or Federal savings association is not able to meet the OCC's requirements for estimation of PD and LGD for the margin loan.

TABLE 1 TO §__.131 – IRB RISK-BASED CAPITAL FORMULAS FOR WHOLESALE EXPOSURES TO NON-DEFAULTED OBLIGORS AND SEGMENTS OF NON-DEFAULTED RETAIL EXPOSURES[1]

Retail	**Capital Requirement (K) Non-Defaulted Exposures**	$K = \left[LGD \times N\left(\frac{N^{-1}(PD) + \sqrt{R} \times N^{-1}(0.999)}{\sqrt{1-R}} \right) - (LGD \times PD) \right]$
	Correlation Factor (R)	For residential mortgage exposures: $R = 0.15$ For qualifying revolving exposures: $R = 0.04$ For other retail exposures: $R = 0.03 + 0.13 \times e^{-35 \times PD}$
Wholesale	**Capital Requirement (K) Non-Defaulted Exposures**	$K = \left[LGD \times N\left(\frac{N^{-1}(PD) + \sqrt{R} \times N^{-1}(0.999)}{\sqrt{1-R}} \right) - (LGD \times PD) \right] \times \left(\frac{1+(M-2.5)\times b}{1-1.5\times b} \right)$
	Correlation Factor (R)	For HVCRE exposures: $R = 0.12 + 0.18 \times e^{-50 \times PD}$ For wholesale exposures to unregulated financial institutions:

$$R = 1.25 \times \left(0.12 + 0.12 \times e^{-50 \times PD}\right)$$

For wholesale exposures to regulated financial institutions with total assets greater than or equal to $100 billion:

$$R = 1.25 \times \left(0.12 + 0.12 \times e^{-50 \times PD}\right)$$

For wholesale exposures other than HVCRE exposures, unregulated financial institutions, and regulated financial institutions with total assets greater than or equal to $100 billion:

$$R = 0.12 + 0.12 \times e^{-50 \times PD}$$

Maturity Adjustment (b)

$$b = (0.11852 - 0.05478 \times \ln(PD))^2$$

[1]N(.) means the cumulative distribution function for a standard normal random variable. N^{-1}(.) means the inverse cumulative distribution function for a standard normal random variable. The symbol e refers to the base of the natural logarithms, and the function ln(.) refers to the natural logarithm of the expression within parentheses. The formulas apply when PD is greater than zero. If PD equals zero, the capital requirement K is set equal to zero.

(ii) The sum of all the dollar risk-based capital requirements for each wholesale exposure to a non-defaulted obligor and segment of non-defaulted retail exposures calculated in paragraph (e)(1)(i) of this section and in § 3.135(e) equals the total dollar risk-based capital requirement for those exposures and segments.

(iii) The aggregate risk-weighted asset amount for wholesale exposures to non-defaulted obligors and segments of non-defaulted retail exposures equals the total dollar risk-based capital requirement in paragraph (e)(1)(ii) of this section multiplied by 12.5.

(2) *Wholesale exposures to defaulted obligors and segments of defaulted retail exposures*—(i) *Not covered by an eligible U.S. government guarantee:* The dollar risk-based capital requirement for each wholesale exposure not covered by an eligible guarantee from the U.S. government to a defaulted obligor and each segment of defaulted retail exposures not covered by an eligible guarantee from the U.S. government equals 0.08 multiplied by the EAD of the exposure or segment.

(ii) *Covered by an eligible U.S. government guarantee:* The dollar risk-based capital requirement for each wholesale exposure to a defaulted obligor covered by an eligible guarantee from the U.S. government and each segment of defaulted retail exposures covered by an eligible guarantee from the U.S. government equals the sum of:

(A) The sum of the EAD of the portion of each wholesale exposure to a defaulted obligor covered by an eligible guarantee from the U.S. government plus the EAD of the portion of each segment of defaulted retail exposures that is covered by an eligible guarantee from the U.S. government and the resulting sum is multiplied by 0.016, and

(B) The sum of the EAD of the portion of each wholesale exposure to a defaulted obligor not covered by an eligible guarantee from the U.S. government plus the EAD of the portion of each segment of defaulted retail exposures that is not covered by an eligible guarantee from the U.S. government and the resulting sum is multiplied by 0.08.

(iii) The sum of all the dollar risk-based capital requirements for each wholesale exposure to a defaulted obligor and each segment of defaulted retail exposures calculated in paragraph (e)(2)(i) of this section plus the dollar risk-based capital requirements each wholesale exposure to a defaulted obligor and for each segment of defaulted retail exposures calculated in paragraph (e)(2)(ii) of this section equals the total dollar risk-based capital requirement for those exposures and segments.

(iv) The aggregate risk-weighted asset amount for wholesale exposures to defaulted obligors and segments of defaulted retail exposures equals the total dollar risk-based capital requirement calculated in paragraph (e)(2)(iii) of this section multiplied by 12.5.

(3) *Assets not included in a defined exposure category.* (i) A national bank or Federal savings association may assign a risk-weighted asset amount of zero to cash owned and held in all offices of the national bank or Federal savings association or in transit and for gold bullion held in the national bank's or Federal savings association's own vaults, or held in another national bank's or Federal savings association's vaults on an allocated basis, to the extent the gold bullion assets are offset by gold bullion liabilities.

(ii) A national bank or Federal savings association must assign a risk-weighted asset amount equal to 20 percent of the carrying value of cash items in the process of collection.

(iii) A national bank or Federal savings association must assign a risk-weighted asset amount equal to 50 percent of the carrying value to a pre-sold construction loan unless the purchase contract is cancelled, in which case a national bank or Federal savings association must assign a risk-weighted asset amount equal to a 100 percent of the carrying value of the pre-sold construction loan.

(iv) The risk-weighted asset amount for the residual value of a retail lease exposure equals such residual value.

(v) The risk-weighted asset amount for DTAs arising from temporary differences that the national bank or Federal savings association could realize through net operating loss carrybacks equals the carrying value, netted in accordance with §3.22.

(vi) The risk-weighted asset amount for MSAs, DTAs arising from temporary timing differences that the national bank or Federal savings association could not realize through net operating loss carrybacks, and significant investments in the capital of unconsolidated financial institutions in the form of common stock that are not deducted pursuant to §3.22(d) equals the amount not subject to deduction multiplied by 250 percent.

(vii) The risk-weighted asset amount for any other on-balance-sheet asset that does not meet the definition of a wholesale, retail, securitization, IMM, or equity exposure, cleared transaction, or default fund contribution and is not subject to deduction under §3.22(a), (c), or (d) equals the carrying value of the asset.

(4) *Non-material portfolios of exposures.* The risk-weighted asset amount of a portfolio of exposures for which the national bank or Federal savings association has demonstrated to the OCC's satisfaction that the portfolio (when combined with all other portfolios of exposures that the national bank or Federal savings association seeks to treat under this paragraph (e)) is not material to the national bank or Federal savings association is the sum of the carrying values of on-balance sheet exposures plus the notional amounts of off-balance sheet exposures in the portfolio. For purposes of this paragraph (e)(4), the notional amount of an OTC

derivative contract that is not a credit derivative is the EAD of the derivative as calculated in § 3.132.

[78 FR 62157, 62273, Oct. 11, 2013, as amended at 80 FR 41416, July 15, 2015]

§ 3.132 Counterparty credit risk of repo-style transactions, eligible margin loans, and OTC derivative contracts.

(a) *Methodologies for collateral recognition.* (1) Instead of an LGD estimation methodology, a national bank or Federal savings association may use the following methodologies to recognize the benefits of financial collateral in mitigating the counterparty credit risk of repo-style transactions, eligible margin loans, collateralized OTC derivative contracts and single product netting sets of such transactions, and to recognize the benefits of any collateral in mitigating the counterparty credit risk of repo-style transactions that are included in a national bank's or Federal savings association's VaR-based measure under subpart F of this part:

(i) The collateral haircut approach set forth in paragraph (b)(2) of this section;

(ii) The internal models methodology set forth in paragraph (d) of this section; and

(iii) For single product netting sets of repo-style transactions and eligible margin loans, the simple VaR methodology set forth in paragraph (b)(3) of this section.

(2) A national bank or Federal savings association may use any combination of the three methodologies for collateral recognition; however, it must use the same methodology for transactions in the same category.

(3) A national bank or Federal savings association must use the methodology in paragraph (c) of this section, or with prior written approval of the OCC, the internal model methodology in paragraph (d) of this section, to calculate EAD for an OTC derivative contract or a set of OTC derivative contracts subject to a qualifying master netting agreement. To estimate EAD for qualifying cross-product master netting agreements, a national bank or Federal savings association may only use the internal models methodology in paragraph (d) of this section.

(4) A national bank or Federal savings association must also use the methodology in paragraph (e) of this section to calculate the risk-weighted asset amounts for CVA for OTC derivatives.

(b) *EAD for eligible margin loans and repo-style transactions*—(1) *General.* A national bank or Federal savings association may recognize the credit risk mitigation benefits of financial collateral that secures an eligible margin loan, repo-style transaction, or single-product netting set of such transactions by factoring the collateral into its LGD estimates for the exposure. Alternatively, a national bank or Federal savings association may estimate an unsecured LGD for the exposure, as well as for any repo-style transaction that is included in the national bank's or Federal savings association's VaR-based measure under subpart F of this part, and determine the EAD of the exposure using:

(i) The collateral haircut approach described in paragraph (b)(2) of this section;

(ii) For netting sets only, the simple VaR methodology described in paragraph (b)(3) of this section; or

(iii) The internal models methodology described in paragraph (d) of this section.

(2) *Collateral haircut approach*—(i) *EAD equation.* A national bank or Federal savings association may determine EAD for an eligible margin loan, repo-style transaction, or netting set by setting EAD equal to max

$$\{0, [(\Sigma E - \Sigma C) + \Sigma(E_s \times H_s) + \Sigma(E_{fx} \times H_{fx})]\},$$

where:

(A) ΣE equals the value of the exposure (the sum of the current fair values of all instruments, gold, and cash the national bank or Federal savings association has lent, sold subject to repurchase, or posted as collateral to the counterparty under the transaction (or netting set));

(B) ΣC equals the value of the collateral (the sum of the current fair values of all instruments, gold, and cash the national bank or Federal savings association has borrowed, purchased subject to resale, or taken as collateral from the counterparty under the transaction (or netting set));

(C) E_s equals the absolute value of the net position in a given instrument or in gold (where the net position in a given instrument or in gold equals the sum of the current fair values of the instrument or gold the national bank or Federal savings association has lent, sold subject to repurchase, or posted as collateral to the counterparty minus the sum of the current fair values of that same instrument or gold the national bank or Federal savings association has borrowed, purchased subject to resale, or taken as collateral from the counterparty);

(D) H_s equals the market price volatility haircut appropriate to the instrument or gold referenced in E_s;

(E) E_{fx} equals the absolute value of the net position of instruments and cash in a currency that is different from the settlement currency (where the net position in a given currency equals the sum of the current fair values of any instruments or cash in the currency the national bank or Federal savings association has lent, sold subject to repurchase, or posted as collateral to the counterparty minus the sum of the current fair values of any instruments or cash in the currency the national bank or Federal savings association has borrowed, purchased subject to resale, or taken as collateral from the counterparty); and

(F) H_{fx} equals the haircut appropriate to the mismatch between the currency referenced in E_{fx} and the settlement currency.

(ii) *Standard supervisory haircuts.* (A) Under the standard supervisory haircuts approach:

(*1*) A national bank or Federal savings association must use the haircuts for market price volatility (H_s) in Table 1 to § 3.132, as adjusted in certain circumstances as provided in paragraphs (b)(2)(ii)(A)(*3*) and (*4*) of this section;

TABLE 1 TO § 3.132—STANDARD SUPERVISORY MARKET PRICE VOLATILITY HAIRCUTS [1]

Residual maturity	Haircut (in percent) assigned based on:						Investment grade securitization exposures (in percent)
	Sovereign issuers risk weight under § 3.32 [2] (in percent)			Non-sovereign issuers risk weight under § 3.32 (in percent)			
	Zero	20 or 50	100	20	50	100	
Less than or equal to 1 year	0.5	1.0	15.0	1.0	2.0	4.0	4.0
Greater than 1 year and less than or equal to 5 years	2.0	3.0	15.0	4.0	6.0	8.0	12.0
Greater than 5 years	4.0	6.0	15.0	8.0	12.0	16.0	24.0
Main index equities (including convertible bonds) and gold	15.0						
Other publicly traded equities (including convertible bonds)	25.0						
Mutual funds	Highest haircut applicable to any security in which the fund can invest.						
Cash collateral held	Zero						
Other exposure types	25.0						

[1] The market price volatility haircuts in Table 1 to § 3.132 are based on a 10 business-day holding period.
[2] Includes a foreign PSE that receives a zero percent risk weight.

(*2*) For currency mismatches, a national bank or Federal savings association must use a haircut for foreign exchange rate volatility (H_{fx}) of 8 percent, as adjusted in certain circumstances as provided in paragraphs (b)(2)(ii)(A)(*3*) and (*4*) of this section.

(*3*) For repo-style transactions, a national bank or Federal savings association may multiply the supervisory haircuts provided in paragraphs (b)(2)(ii)(A)(*1*) and (*2*) of this section by the square root of ½ (which equals 0.707107).

(*4*) A national bank or Federal savings association must adjust the supervisory haircuts upward on the basis of a holding period longer than ten business days (for eligible margin loans) or five business days (for repo-style transactions) where the following conditions apply. If the number of trades in a netting set exceeds 5,000 at any time during a quarter, a national bank or Federal savings association must adjust the supervisory haircuts upward on the basis of a holding period of twenty business days for the following quarter (except when a national bank or Federal savings association is calculating EAD for a cleared transaction under § 3.133). If a netting set contains one or more trades involving illiquid collateral or an OTC derivative that cannot be easily replaced, a national bank or Federal savings association must adjust the supervisory haircuts upward on the basis of a holding period of twenty business days. If over the two previous quarters more than two margin disputes on a netting set have occurred that lasted more than the holding period, then the national bank or Federal savings association must adjust the supervisory haircuts upward for that netting set on the basis of a holding period that is at least two times the minimum holding period for that netting set. A national bank or Federal savings association must adjust the standard supervisory haircuts upward using the following formula:

$$H_A = H_S \sqrt{\frac{T_M}{T_S}}, \text{ where,}$$

(*i*) T_M equals a holding period of longer than 10 business days for eligible margin loans and derivative contracts or longer than 5 business days for repo-style transactions;

(*ii*) H_s equals the standard supervisory haircut; and

(*iii*) T_s equals 10 business days for eligible margin loans and derivative contracts or 5 business days for repo-style transactions.

(*5*) If the instrument a national bank or Federal savings association has lent, sold subject to repurchase, or posted as collateral does not meet the definition of financial collateral, the national bank or Federal savings association must use a 25.0 percent haircut for market price volatility (Hs).

(iii) *Own internal estimates for haircuts.* With the prior written approval of the OCC, a national bank or Federal savings association may calculate haircuts (H_s and H_{fx}) using its own internal estimates of the volatilities of market prices and foreign exchange rates.

(A) To receive OCC approval to use its own internal estimates, a national bank or Federal savings association must satisfy the following minimum quantitative standards:

(*1*) A national bank or Federal savings association must use a 99th percentile one-tailed confidence interval.

(*2*) The minimum holding period for a repo-style transaction is five business days and for an eligible margin loan is ten business days except for transactions or netting sets for which paragraph (b)(2)(iii)(A)(*3*) of this section applies. When a national bank or Federal savings association calculates an own-estimates haircut on a T_N-day holding period, which is different from the minimum holding period for the transaction type, the applicable haircut (H_M) is calculated using the following square root of time formula:

$$H_M = H_N \sqrt{\frac{T_M}{T_N}}, \text{ where}$$

(*i*) T_M equals 5 for repo-style transactions and 10 for eligible margin loans;

(*ii*) T_N equals the holding period used by the national bank or Federal savings association to derive H_N; and

(*iii*) H_N equals the haircut based on the holding period T_N

(*3*) If the number of trades in a netting set exceeds 5,000 at any time during a quarter, a national bank or Federal savings association must calculate the haircut using a minimum holding period of twenty business days for the following quarter (except when a national bank or Federal savings association is calculating EAD for a cleared transaction under § 3.133). If a netting set contains one or more trades involving illiquid collateral or an OTC derivative that cannot be easily replaced, a national bank or Federal savings association must calculate the haircut using a minimum holding period of twenty business days. If over the two previous quarters more than two margin disputes on a netting set have occurred that lasted more than the holding period, then the national bank or Federal savings association must calculate the haircut for transactions in that netting set on the basis of a holding period that is at least two times the minimum holding period for that netting set.

(*4*) A national bank or Federal savings association is required to calculate its own internal estimates with inputs calibrated to historical data from a continuous 12-month period that reflects a period of significant financial stress appropriate to the security or category of securities.

(*5*) A national bank or Federal savings association must have policies and procedures that describe how it determines the period of significant financial stress used to calculate the national bank's or Federal savings association's own internal estimates for haircuts under this section and must be able to provide empirical support for the period used. The national bank or Federal savings association must obtain the prior approval of the OCC for, and notify the OCC if the national bank or Federal savings association makes any material changes to, these policies and procedures.

(*6*) Nothing in this section prevents the OCC from requiring a national bank or Federal savings association to use a different period of significant financial stress in the calculation of own internal estimates for haircuts.

(*7*) A national bank or Federal savings association must update its data sets and calculate haircuts no less frequently than quarterly and must also reassess data sets and haircuts whenever market prices change materially.

(B) With respect to debt securities that are investment grade, a national bank or Federal savings association may calculate haircuts for categories of securities. For a category of securities, the national bank or Federal savings association must calculate the haircut on the basis of internal volatility estimates for securities in that category that are representative of the securities in that category that the national bank or Federal savings association has lent, sold subject to repurchase, posted as collateral, borrowed, purchased subject to resale, or taken as collateral. In determining relevant categories, the national bank or Federal savings association must at a minimum take into account:

(*1*) The type of issuer of the security;

(*2*) The credit quality of the security;

(*3*) The maturity of the security; and

(*4*) The interest rate sensitivity of the security.

(C) With respect to debt securities that are not investment grade and equity securities, a national bank or Federal savings association must calculate a separate haircut for each individual security.

(D) Where an exposure or collateral (whether in the form of cash or securities) is denominated in a currency that differs from the settlement currency, the national bank or Federal savings association must calculate a separate currency mismatch haircut for its net position in each mismatched currency based on estimated volatilities of foreign exchange rates between the mismatched currency and the settlement currency.

(E) A national bank's or Federal savings association's own estimates of market price and foreign exchange rate volatilities may not take into account the correlations among securities and foreign exchange rates on either the exposure or collateral side of a transaction (or netting set) or the correlations among securities and foreign exchange rates between the exposure and collateral sides of the transaction (or netting set).

(3) *Simple VaR methodology.* With the prior written approval of the OCC, a national bank or Federal savings association may estimate EAD for a netting set using a VaR model that meets the requirements in paragraph (b)(3)(iii) of this section. In such event, the national bank or Federal savings association must set EAD equal to max {0, [(ΣE − ΣC) + PFE]}, where:

(i) ΣE equals the value of the exposure (the sum of the current fair values of all instruments, gold, and cash the national bank or Federal savings association has lent, sold subject to repurchase, or posted as collateral to the counterparty under the netting set);

(ii) ΣC equals the value of the collateral (the sum of the current fair values of all instruments, gold, and cash the national bank or Federal savings association has borrowed, purchased subject to resale, or taken as collateral from the counterparty under the netting set); and

(iii) PFE (potential future exposure) equals the national bank's or Federal savings association's empirically based best estimate of the 99th percentile, one-tailed confidence interval for an increase in the value of (ΣE − ΣC) over a five-business-day holding period for repo-style transactions, or over a ten-business-day holding period for eligible margin loans except for netting sets for which paragraph (b)(3)(iv) of this section applies using a minimum one-year historical observation period of price data representing the instruments that the national bank or Federal savings association has lent, sold subject to repurchase, posted as collateral, borrowed, purchased subject to resale, or taken as collateral. The national bank or Federal savings association must validate its VaR model by establishing and maintaining a rigorous and regular backtesting regime.

(iv) If the number of trades in a netting set exceeds 5,000 at any time during a quarter, a national bank or Federal savings association must use a twenty-business-day holding period for the following quarter (except when a national bank or Federal savings association is calculating EAD for a cleared transaction under § 3.133). If a netting set contains one or more trades involving illiquid collateral, a national bank or Federal savings association must use a twenty-business-day holding period. If over the two previous quarters more than two margin disputes on a netting set have occurred that lasted more than the holding period, then the national bank or Federal savings association must set its PFE for that netting set equal to an estimate over a holding period that is at least two times the minimum holding period for that netting set.

(c) *EAD for OTC derivative contracts*—(1) *OTC derivative contracts not subject to a qualifying master netting agreement.* A national bank or Federal savings association must determine the EAD for an OTC derivative contract that is not subject to a qualifying master netting agreement using the current exposure methodology in paragraph (c)(5) of this section or using the internal models methodology described in paragraph (d) of this section. A national bank or Federal savings association may reduce the EAD calculated according to paragraph (c)(5) of this section by the credit valuation adjustment that the national bank or Federal savings association has recognized in its balance sheet valuation of any OTC derivative contracts in the netting set. For purposes of this paragraph (c)(1), the credit valuation adjustment does not include any adjustments to common equity tier 1 capital attributable to changes in the fair value of the national bank's or Federal savings association's liabilities that are due to changes in its own credit risk since the inception of the transaction with the counterparty.

(2) *OTC derivative contracts subject to a qualifying master netting agreement.* A national bank or Federal savings association must determine the EAD for multiple OTC derivative contracts that are subject to a qualifying master netting agreement using the current exposure methodology in paragraph (c)(6) of this section or using the internal models methodology described in paragraph (d) of this section. A national

bank or Federal savings association may reduce the EAD calculated according to paragraph (c)(6) of this section by the credit valuation adjustment that the national bank or Federal savings association has recognized in its balance sheet valuation of any OTC derivative contracts in the netting set. For purposes of this paragraph (c)(2), the credit valuation adjustment does not include any adjustments to common equity tier 1 capital attributable to changes in the fair value of the national bank's or Federal savings association's liabilities that are due to changes in its own credit risk since the inception of the transaction with the counterparty.

(3) *Credit derivatives.* Notwithstanding paragraphs (c)(1) and (c)(2) of this section:

(i) A national bank or Federal savings association that purchases a credit derivative that is recognized under §3.134 or §3.135 as a credit risk mitigant for an exposure that is not a covered position under subpart F of this part is not required to calculate a separate counterparty credit risk capital requirement under this section so long as the national bank or Federal savings association does so consistently for all such credit derivatives and either includes or excludes all such credit derivatives that are subject to a master netting agreement from any measure used to determine counterparty credit risk exposure to all relevant counterparties for risk-based capital purposes.

(ii) A national bank or Federal savings association that is the protection provider in a credit derivative must treat the credit derivative as a wholesale exposure to the reference obligor and is not required to calculate a counterparty credit risk capital requirement for the credit derivative under this section, so long as it does so consistently for all such credit derivatives and either includes all or excludes all such credit derivatives that are subject to a master netting agreement from any measure used to determine counterparty credit risk exposure to all relevant counterparties for risk-based capital purposes (unless the national bank or Federal savings association is treating the credit derivative as a covered position under subpart F of this part, in which case the national bank or Federal savings association must calculate a supplemental counterparty credit risk capital requirement under this section).

(4) *Equity derivatives.* A national bank or Federal savings association must treat an equity derivative contract as an equity exposure and compute a risk-weighted asset amount for the equity derivative contract under §§3.151–3.155 (unless the national bank or Federal savings association is treating the contract as a covered position under subpart F of this part). In addition, if the national bank or Federal savings association is treating the contract as a covered position under subpart F of this part, and under certain other circumstances described in §3.155, the national bank or Federal savings association must also calculate a risk-based capital requirement for the counterparty credit risk of an equity derivative contract under this section.

(5) *Single OTC derivative contract.* Except as modified by paragraph (c)(7) of this section, the EAD for a single OTC derivative contract that is not subject to a qualifying master netting agreement is equal to the sum of the national bank's or Federal savings association's current credit exposure and potential future credit exposure (PFE) on the derivative contract.

(i) *Current credit exposure.* The current credit exposure for a single OTC derivative contract is the greater of the mark-to-fair value of the derivative contract or zero; and

(ii) *PFE.* The PFE for a single OTC derivative contract, including an OTC derivative contract with a negative mark-to-fair value, is calculated by multiplying the notional principal amount of the derivative contract by the appropriate conversion factor in Table 2 to §3.132. For purposes of calculating either the PFE under paragraph (c)(5) of this section or the gross PFE under paragraph (c)(6) of this section for exchange rate contracts and other similar contracts in which the notional principal amount is equivalent to the cash flows, the notional principal amount is the net receipts to each party falling due on each value date in each currency. For any OTC derivative contract that does not fall within one of the specified categories in Table 2 to § 3.132, the PFE must be calculated using the "other" conversion factors. A national bank or Federal savings association must use an OTC derivative contract's effective notional principal amount (that is, its apparent or stated notional principal amount multiplied by any multiplier in the OTC derivative contract) rather than its apparent or stated notional principal amount in calculating PFE. PFE of the protection provider of a credit derivative is capped at the net present value of the amount of unpaid premiums.

TABLE 2 TO § 3.132—CONVERSION FACTOR MATRIX FOR OTC DERIVATIVE CONTRACTS [1]

Remaining maturity [2]	Interest rate	Foreign exchange rate and gold	Credit (investment-grade reference asset) [3]	Credit (non-investment-grade reference asset)	Equity	Precious metals (except gold)	Other
One year or less	0.00	0.01	0.05	0.10	0.06	0.07	0.10
Over one to five years	0.005	0.05	0.05	0.10	0.08	0.07	0.12
Over five years	0.015	0.075	0.05	0.10	0.10	0.08	0.15

[1] For an OTC derivative contract with multiple exchanges of principal, the conversion factor is multiplied by the number of remaining payments in the derivative contract.

[2] For an OTC derivative contract that is structured such that on specified dates any outstanding exposure is settled and the terms are reset so that the fair value of the contract is zero, the remaining maturity equals the time until the next reset date. For an interest rate derivative contract with a remaining maturity of greater than one year that meets these criteria, the minimum conversion factor is 0.005.

[3] A national bank or Federal savings association must use the column labeled "Credit (investment-grade reference asset)" for a credit derivative whose reference asset is an outstanding unsecured long-term debt security without credit enhancement that is investment grade. A national bank or Federal savings association must use the column labeled "Credit (non-investment-grade reference asset)" for all other credit derivatives.

(6) *Multiple OTC derivative contracts subject to a qualifying master netting agreement.* Except as modified by paragraph (c)(7) of this section, the EAD for multiple OTC derivative contracts subject to a qualifying master netting agreement is equal to the sum of the net current credit exposure and the adjusted sum of the PFE exposure for all OTC derivative contracts subject to the qualifying master netting agreement.

(i) *Net current credit exposure.* The net current credit exposure is the greater of:

(A) The net sum of all positive and negative fair values of the individual OTC derivative contracts subject to the qualifying master netting agreement; or

(B) Zero; and

(ii) *Adjusted sum of the PFE.* The adjusted sum of the PFE, A_{net}, is calculated as

$$A_{net} = (0.4 \times A_{gross}) + (0.6 \times NGR \times A_{gross}),$$

where:

(A) A_{gross} = the gross PFE (that is, the sum of the PFE amounts (as determined under paragraph (c)(5)(ii) of this section) for each individual derivative contract subject to the qualifying master netting agreement); and

(B) NGR = the net to gross ratio (that is, the ratio of the net current credit exposure to the gross current credit exposure). In calculating the NGR, the gross current credit exposure equals the sum of the positive current credit exposures (as determined under paragraph (c)(6)(i) of this section) of all individual derivative contracts subject to the qualifying master netting agreement.

(7) *Collateralized OTC derivative contracts.* A national bank or Federal savings association may recognize the credit risk mitigation benefits of financial collateral that secures an OTC derivative contract or single-product netting set of OTC derivatives by factoring the collateral into its LGD estimates for the contract or netting set. Alternatively, a national bank or Federal savings association may recognize the credit risk mitigation benefits of financial collateral that secures such a contract or netting set that is marked-to-market on a daily basis and subject to a daily margin maintenance requirement by estimating an unsecured LGD for the contract or netting set and adjusting the EAD calculated under paragraph (c)(5) or (c)(6) of this section using the collateral haircut approach in paragraph (b)(2) of this section. The

national bank or Federal savings association must substitute the EAD calculated under paragraph (c)(5) or (c)(6) of this section for ΣE in the equation in paragraph (b)(2)(i) of this section and must use a ten-business day minimum holding period ($T_M = 10$) unless a longer holding period is required by paragraph (b)(2)(iii)(A)(*3*) of this section.

(8) *Clearing member national bank's or Federal savings association's EAD.* A clearing member national bank's or Federal savings association's EAD for an OTC derivative contract or netting set of OTC derivative contracts where the national bank or Federal savings association is either acting as a financial intermediary and enters into an offsetting transaction with a QCCP or where the national bank or Federal savings association provides a guarantee to the QCCP on the performance of the client equals the exposure amount calculated according to paragraph (c)(5) or (6) of this section multiplied by the scaling factor 0.71. If the national bank or Federal savings association determines that a longer period is appropriate, it must use a larger scaling factor to adjust for a longer holding period as follows:

$$\text{Scaling factor} = \sqrt{\frac{H}{10}}$$

where

H = the holding period greater than five days. Additionally, the OCC may require the national bank or Federal savings association to set a longer holding period if the OCC determines that a longer period is appropriate due to the nature, structure, or characteristics of the transaction or is commensurate with the risks associated with the transaction.

(d) *Internal models methodology.* (1)(i) With prior written approval from the OCC, a national bank or Federal savings association may use the internal models methodology in this paragraph (d) to determine EAD for counterparty credit risk for derivative contracts (collateralized or uncollateralized) and single-product netting sets thereof, for eligible margin loans and single-product netting sets thereof, and for repo-style transactions and single-product netting sets thereof.

(ii) A national bank or Federal savings association that uses the internal models methodology for a particular transaction type (derivative contracts, eligible margin loans, or repo-style transactions) must use the internal models methodology for all transactions of that transaction type. A national bank or Federal savings association may choose to use the internal models methodology for one or two of these three types of exposures and not the other types.

(iii) A national bank or Federal savings association may also use the internal models methodology for derivative contracts, eligible margin loans, and repo-style transactions subject to a qualifying cross-product netting agreement if:

(A) The national bank or Federal savings association effectively integrates the risk mitigating effects of cross-product netting into its risk management and other information technology systems; and

(B) The national bank or Federal savings association obtains the prior written approval of the OCC.

(iv) A national bank or Federal savings association that uses the internal models methodology for a transaction type must receive approval from the OCC to cease using the methodology for that transaction type or to make a material change to its internal model.

(2) *Risk-weighted assets using IMM.* Under the IMM, a national bank or Federal savings association uses an internal model to estimate the expected exposure (EE) for a netting set and then calculates EAD based on that EE. A national bank or Federal savings association must calculate two EEs and two EADs (one stressed and one

unstressed) for each netting set as follows:

(i) $EAD_{unstressed}$ is calculated using an EE estimate based on the most recent data meeting the requirements of paragraph (d)(3)(vii) of this section;

(ii) $EAD_{stressed}$ is calculated using an EE estimate based on a historical period that includes a period of stress to the credit default spreads of the national bank's or Federal savings association's counterparties according to paragraph (d)(3)(viii) of this section;

(iii) The national bank or Federal savings association must use its internal model's probability distribution for changes in the fair value of a netting set that are attributable to changes in market variables to determine EE; and

(iv) Under the internal models methodology, EAD = Max (0, α × effective EPE − CVA), or, subject to the prior written approval of OCC as provided in paragraph (d)(10) of this section, a more conservative measure of EAD.

(A) CVA equals the credit valuation adjustment that the national bank or Federal savings association has recognized in its balance sheet valuation of any OTC derivative contracts in the netting set. For purposes of this paragraph (d), CVA does not include any adjustments to common equity tier 1 capital attributable to changes in the fair value of the national bank's or Federal savings association's liabilities that are due to changes in its own credit risk since the inception of the transaction with the counterparty.

(B) $$Effective\ EPE_{t_k} = \sum_{k=1}^{n} Effective\ EE_k \times \Delta t_k$$

(that is, effective EPE is the time-weighted average of effective EE where the weights are the proportion that an individual effective EE represents in a one-year time interval) where:

(1) $EffectiveEE_{t_k} = \max\left(EffectiveEE_{t_{k-1}}, EE_{t_k}\right)$ (that is, for a specific date t_k, effective EE is the greater of EE at that date or the effective EE at the previous date); and

(2) t_k represents the kth future time period in the model and there are n time periods represented in the model over the first year, and

(C) α = 1.4 except as provided in paragraph (d)(6) of this section, or when the OCC has determined that the national bank or Federal savings association must set α higher based on the national bank's or Federal savings association's specific characteristics of counterparty credit risk or model performance.

(v) A national bank or Federal savings association may include financial collateral currently posted by the counterparty as collateral (but may not include other forms of collateral) when calculating EE.

(vi) If a national bank or Federal savings association hedges some or all of the counterparty credit risk associated with a netting set using an eligible credit derivative, the national bank or Federal savings association may take the reduction in exposure to the counterparty into account when estimating EE. If the national bank or Federal savings association recognizes this reduction in exposure to the counterparty in its estimate of EE, it must also use its internal model to estimate a separate EAD for the national bank's or Federal savings association's exposure to the protection provider of the credit derivative.

(3) *Prior approval relating to EAD calculation.* To obtain OCC approval to calculate the distributions of exposures upon which the EAD calculation is based, the national bank or Federal savings association must demonstrate to the satisfaction of the OCC that it has been using for at least one year an internal model that broadly meets the following minimum standards, with which the national bank or Federal savings association must maintain compliance:

(i) The model must have the systems capability to estimate the expected exposure to the counterparty on a daily basis (but is not expected to estimate or report expected exposure on a daily basis);

(ii) The model must estimate expected exposure at enough future dates to reflect accurately all the future cash flows of contracts in the netting set;

(iii) The model must account for the possible non-normality of the exposure distribution, where appropriate;

(iv) The national bank or Federal savings association must measure, monitor, and control current counterparty exposure and the exposure to the counterparty over the whole life of all contracts in the netting set;

(v) The national bank or Federal savings association must be able to measure and manage current exposures gross and net of collateral held, where appropriate. The national bank or Federal savings association must estimate expected exposures for OTC derivative contracts both with and without the effect of collateral agreements;

(vi) The national bank or Federal savings association must have procedures to identify, monitor, and control wrong-way risk throughout the life of an exposure. The procedures must include stress testing and scenario analysis;

(vii) The model must use current market data to compute current exposures. The national bank or Federal savings association must estimate model parameters using historical data from the most recent three-year period and update the data quarterly or more frequently if market conditions warrant. The national bank or Federal savings association should consider using model parameters based on forward-looking measures, where appropriate;

(viii) When estimating model parameters based on a stress period, the national bank or Federal savings association must use at least three years of historical data that include a period of stress to the credit default spreads of the national bank's or Federal savings association's counterparties. The national bank or Federal savings association must review the data set and update the data as necessary, particularly for any material changes in its counterparties. The national bank or Federal savings association must demonstrate, at least quarterly, and maintain documentation of such demonstration, that the stress period coincides with increased CDS or other credit spreads of the national bank's or Federal savings association's counterparties. The national bank or Federal savings association must have procedures to evaluate the effectiveness of its stress calibration that include a process for using benchmark portfolios that are vulnerable to the same risk factors as the national bank's or Federal savings association's portfolio. The OCC may require the national bank or Federal savings association to modify its stress calibration to better reflect actual historic losses of the portfolio;

(ix) A national bank or Federal savings association must subject its internal model to an initial validation and annual model review process. The model review should consider whether the inputs and risk factors, as well as the model outputs, are appropriate. As part of the model review process, the national bank or Federal savings association must have a backtesting program for its model that includes a process by which unacceptable model performance will be determined and remedied;

(x) A national bank or Federal savings association must have policies for the measurement, management and control of collateral and margin amounts; and

(xi) A national bank or Federal savings association must have a comprehensive stress testing program that captures all credit exposures to counterparties, and incorporates stress testing of principal market risk factors and creditworthiness of counterparties.

(4) *Calculating the maturity of exposures.* (i) If the remaining maturity of the exposure or the longest-dated contract in the netting set is greater than one year, the national bank or Federal savings association must set M for the exposure or netting set equal to the lower of five years or M(EPE), where:

(A) $$M(EPE) = 1 + \frac{\sum_{t_k > 1\,year}^{maturity} EE_k \times \Delta t_k \times df_k}{\sum_{k=1}^{t_k \le 1\,year} effectiveEE_k \times \Delta t_k \times df_k};$$

(B) df_k is the risk-free discount factor for future time period t_k; and

(C) $\Delta t_k = t_k - t_{k-1}$.

(ii) If the remaining maturity of the exposure or the longest-dated contract in the netting set is one year or less, the national bank or Federal savings association must set M for the exposure or netting set equal to one year, except as provided in § 3.131(d)(7).

(iii) Alternatively, a national bank or Federal savings association that uses an internal model to calculate a one-sided credit valuation adjustment may use the effective credit duration estimated by the model as M(EPE) in place of the formula in paragraph (d)(4)(i) of this section.

(5) *Effects of collateral agreements on EAD.* A national bank or Federal savings association may capture the effect on EAD of a collateral agreement that requires receipt of collateral when exposure to the counterparty increases, but may not capture the effect on EAD of a collateral agreement that requires receipt of collateral when counterparty credit quality deteriorates. Two methods are available to capture the effect of a collateral agreement, as set forth in paragraphs (d)(5)(i) and (ii) of this section:

(i) With prior written approval from the OCC, a national bank or Federal savings association may include the effect of a collateral agreement within its internal model used to calculate EAD. The national bank or Federal savings association may set EAD equal to the expected exposure at the end of the margin period of risk. The margin period of risk means, with respect to a netting set subject to a collateral agreement, the time period from the most recent exchange of collateral with a counterparty until the next required exchange of collateral, plus the period of time required to sell and realize the proceeds of the least liquid collateral that can be delivered under the terms of the collateral agreement and, where applicable, the period of time required to re-hedge the resulting market risk upon the default of the counterparty. The minimum margin period of risk is set according to paragraph (d)(5)(iii) of this section; or

(ii) As an alternative to paragraph (d)(5)(i) of this section, a national bank or Federal savings association that can model EPE without collateral agreements but cannot achieve the higher level of modeling sophistication to model EPE with collateral agreements can set effective EPE for a collateralized netting set equal to the lesser of:

(A) An add-on that reflects the potential increase in exposure of the netting set over the margin period of risk, plus the larger of:

(*1*) The current exposure of the netting set reflecting all collateral held or posted by the national bank or Federal savings association excluding any collateral called or in dispute; or

(*2*) The largest net exposure including all collateral held or posted under the margin agreement that would not trigger a collateral call. For purposes of this section, the add-on is computed as the expected increase in the netting set's exposure over the margin period of risk (set in accordance with paragraph (d)(5)(iii) of this section); or

(B) Effective EPE without a collateral agreement plus any collateral the national bank or Federal savings association posts to the counterparty that exceeds the required margin amount.

(iii) For purposes of this part, including paragraphs (d)(5)(i) and (ii) of this section, the margin period of risk for a netting set subject to a collateral agreement is:

(A) Five business days for repo-style transactions subject to daily remargining and daily marking-to-market, and ten business days for other transactions when liquid financial collateral is posted under a daily margin maintenance requirement, or

(B) Twenty business days if the number of trades in a netting set exceeds 5,000 at any time during the previous quarter (except if the national bank or Federal savings association is calculating EAD for a cleared transaction under §3.133) or contains one or more trades involving illiquid collateral or any derivative contract that cannot be easily replaced. If over the two previous quarters more than two margin disputes on a netting set have occurred that lasted more than the margin period of risk, then the national bank or Federal savings association must use a margin period of risk for that netting set that is at least two times the minimum margin period of risk for that netting set. If the periodicity of the receipt of collateral is N-days, the minimum margin period of risk is the minimum margin period of risk under this paragraph (d) plus N minus 1. This period should be extended to cover any impediments to prompt re-hedging of any market risk.

(C) Five business days for an OTC derivative contract or netting set of OTC derivative contracts where the national bank or Federal savings association is either acting as a financial intermediary and enters into an offsetting transaction with a CCP or where the national bank or Federal savings association provides a guarantee to the CCP on the performance of the client. A national bank or Federal savings association must use a longer holding period if the national bank or Federal savings association determines that a longer period is appropriate. Additionally, the OCC may require the national bank or Federal savings association to set a longer holding period if the OCC determines that a longer period is appropriate due to the nature, structure, or characteristics of the transaction or is commensurate with the risks associated with the transaction.

(6) *Own estimate of alpha.* With prior written approval of the OCC, a national bank or Federal savings association may calculate alpha as the ratio of economic capital from a full simulation of counterparty exposure across counterparties that incorporates a joint simulation of market and credit risk factors (numerator) and economic capital based on EPE (denominator), subject to a floor of 1.2. For purposes of this calculation, economic capital is the unexpected losses for all counterparty credit risks measured at a 99.9 percent confidence level over a one-year horizon. To receive approval, the national bank or Federal savings association must meet the following minimum standards to the satisfaction of the OCC:

(i) The national bank's or Federal savings association's own estimate of alpha must capture in the numerator the effects of:

(A) The material sources of stochastic dependency of distributions of fair values of transactions or portfolios of transactions across counterparties;

(B) Volatilities and correlations of market risk factors used in the joint simulation, which must be related to the credit risk factor used in the simulation to reflect potential increases in volatility or correlation in an economic downturn, where appropriate; and

(C) The granularity of exposures (that is, the effect of a concentration in the proportion of each counterparty's exposure that is driven by a particular risk factor).

(ii) The national bank or Federal savings association must assess the potential model uncertainty in its estimates of alpha.

(iii) The national bank or Federal savings association must calculate the numerator and denominator of alpha in a consistent fashion with respect to modeling methodology, parameter specifications, and portfolio composition.

(iv) The national bank or Federal savings association must review and adjust as appropriate its estimates of the numerator and denominator of alpha on at least a quarterly basis and more frequently when the composition of the portfolio varies over time.

(7) *Risk-based capital requirements for transactions with specific wrong-way risk.* A national bank or Federal savings association must determine if a repo-style transaction, eligible margin loan, bond option, or equity derivative contract or purchased credit derivative to which the national bank or Federal savings association applies the internal models methodology under this paragraph (d) has specific wrong-way risk. If a transaction has specific wrong-way risk, the national bank or Federal savings association must treat the transaction as its own netting set and exclude it from the model described in §3.132(d)(2) and instead calculate the risk-based capital requirement for the transaction as follows:

(i) For an equity derivative contract, by multiplying:

(A) K, calculated using the appropriate risk-based capital formula specified in Table 1 of §3.131 using the PD of the counterparty and LGD equal to 100 percent, by

(B) The maximum amount the national bank or Federal savings association could lose on the equity derivative.

(ii) For a purchased credit derivative by multiplying:

(A) K, calculated using the appropriate risk-based capital formula specified in Table 1 of §3.131 using the PD of the counterparty and LGD equal to 100 percent, by

(B) The fair value of the reference asset of the credit derivative.

(iii) For a bond option, by multiplying:

(A) K, calculated using the appropriate risk-based capital formula specified in Table 1 of §3.131 using the PD of the counterparty and LGD equal to 100 percent, by

(B) The smaller of the notional amount of the underlying reference asset and the maximum potential loss under the bond option contract.

(iv) For a repo-style transaction or eligible margin loan by multiplying:

(A) K, calculated using the appropriate risk-based capital formula specified in Table 1 of §3.131 using the PD of the counterparty and LGD equal to 100 percent, by

(B) The EAD of the transaction determined according to the EAD equation in §3.132(b)(2), substituting the estimated value of the collateral assuming a default of the counterparty for the value of the collateral in Σc of the equation.

(8) *Risk-weighted asset amount for IMM exposures with specific wrong-way risk.* The aggregate risk-weighted asset amount for IMM exposures with specific wrong-way risk is the sum of a national bank's or Federal savings association's risk-based capital requirement for purchased credit derivatives that are not bond options with specific wrong-way risk as calculated under paragraph (d)(7)(ii) of this section, a national bank's or Federal savings association's risk-based capital requirement for equity derivatives with specific wrong-way risk as calculated under paragraph (d)(7)(i) of this section, a national bank's or Federal savings association's risk-based capital requirement for bond options with specific wrong-way risk as calculated under paragraph (d)(7)(iii) of this section, and a national bank's or Federal savings association's risk-based capital requirement for repo-style transactions and eligible margin loans with specific wrong-way risk as calculated under paragraph (d)(7)(iv) of this section, multiplied by 12.5.

(9) *Risk-weighted assets for IMM exposures.* (i) The national bank or Federal savings association must insert the assigned risk parameters for each

counterparty and netting set into the appropriate formula specified in Table 1 of §3.131 and multiply the output of the formula by the $EAD_{unstressed}$ of the netting set to obtain the unstressed capital requirement for each netting set. A national bank or Federal savings association that uses an advanced CVA approach that captures migrations in credit spreads under paragraph (e)(3) of this section must set the maturity adjustment (b) in the formula equal to zero. The sum of the unstressed capital requirement calculated for each netting set equals $K_{unstressed}$.

(ii) The national bank or Federal savings association must insert the assigned risk parameters for each wholesale obligor and netting set into the appropriate formula specified in Table 1 of §3.131 and multiply the output of the formula by the $EAD_{stressed}$ of the netting set to obtain the stressed capital requirement for each netting set. A national bank or Federal savings association that uses an advanced CVA approach that captures migrations in credit spreads under paragraph (e)(6) of this section must set the maturity adjustment (b) in the formula equal to zero. The sum of the stressed capital requirement calculated for each netting set equals $K_{stressed}$.

(iii) The national bank's or Federal savings association's dollar risk-based capital requirement under the internal models methodology equals the larger of $K_{unstressed}$ and $K_{stressed}$. A national bank's or Federal savings association's risk-weighted assets amount for IMM exposures is equal to the capital requirement multiplied by 12.5, plus risk-weighted assets for IMM exposures with specific wrong-way risk in paragraph (d)(8) of this section and those in paragraph (d)(10) of this section.

(10) *Other measures of counterparty exposure.* (i) With prior written approval of the OCC, a national bank or Federal savings association may set EAD equal to a measure of counterparty credit risk exposure, such as peak EAD, that is more conservative than an alpha of 1.4 (or higher under the terms of paragraph (d)(7)(iv)(C) of this section) times the larger of $EPE_{unstressed}$ and $EPE_{stressed}$ for every counterparty whose EAD will be measured under the alternative measure of counterparty exposure. The national bank or Federal savings association must demonstrate the conservatism of the measure of counterparty credit risk exposure used for EAD. With respect to paragraph (d)(10)(i) of this section:

(A) For material portfolios of new OTC derivative products, the national bank or Federal savings association may assume that the current exposure methodology in paragraphs (c)(5) and (c)(6) of this section meets the conservatism requirement of this section for a period not to exceed 180 days.

(B) For immaterial portfolios of OTC derivative contracts, the national bank or Federal savings association generally may assume that the current exposure methodology in paragraphs (c)(5) and (c)(6) of this section meets the conservatism requirement of this section.

(ii) To calculate risk-weighted assets for purposes of the approach in paragraph (d)(10)(i) of this section, the national bank or Federal savings association must insert the assigned risk parameters for each counterparty and netting set into the appropriate formula specified in Table 1 of §3.131, multiply the output of the formula by the EAD for the exposure as specified above, and multiply by 12.5.

(e) *Credit valuation adjustment (CVA) risk-weighted assets*—(1) *In general.* With respect to its OTC derivative contracts, a national bank or Federal savings association must calculate a CVA risk-weighted asset amount for its portfolio of OTC derivative transactions that are subject to the CVA capital requirement using the simple CVA approach described in paragraph (e)(5) of this section or, with prior written approval of the OCC, the advanced CVA approach described in paragraph (e)(6) of this section. A national bank or Federal savings association that receives prior OCC approval to calculate its CVA risk-weighted asset amounts for a class of counterparties using the advanced CVA approach must continue to use that approach for that class of counterparties until it notifies the OCC in writing that the national bank or Federal savings association expects to begin calculating its CVA risk-weighted asset amount using the simple CVA approach. Such notice must include an explanation of the national bank's or Federal savings association's rationale and the date upon which the national bank or Federal savings association will begin to calculate its CVA risk-weighted asset amount using the simple CVA approach.

(2) *Market risk national banks or Federal savings associations.* Notwithstanding the prior approval requirement in paragraph (e)(1) of this section, a market risk national bank or Federal savings association may calculate its CVA risk-weighted asset amount using the advanced CVA approach if the national bank or Federal savings association has OCC approval to:

(i) Determine EAD for OTC derivative contracts using the internal models methodology described in paragraph (d) of this section; and

(ii) Determine its specific risk add-on for debt positions issued by the counterparty using a specific risk model described in § 3.207(b).

(3) *Recognition of hedges.* (i) A national bank or Federal savings association may recognize a single name CDS, single name contingent CDS, any other equivalent hedging instrument that references the counterparty directly, and index credit default swaps (CDS_{ind}) as a CVA hedge under paragraph (e)(5)(ii) of this section or paragraph (e)(6) of this section, provided that the position is managed as a CVA hedge in accordance with the national bank's or Federal savings association's hedging policies.

(ii) A national bank or Federal savings association shall not recognize as a CVA hedge any tranched or n^{th}-to-default credit derivative.

(4) *Total CVA risk-weighted assets.* Total CVA risk-weighted assets is the CVA capital requirement, K_{CVA}, calculated for a national bank's or Federal savings association's entire portfolio of OTC derivative counterparties that are subject to the CVA capital requirement, multiplied by 12.5.

(5) *Simple CVA approach.* (i) Under the simple CVA approach, the CVA capital requirement, K_{CVA}, is calculated according to the following formula:

$$K_{CVA} = 2.33 \times \sqrt{\left(\sum_i 0.5 \times w_i \times \left(M_i \times EAD_i^{total} - M_i^{hedge} \times B_i \right) - \sum_{ind} w_{ind} \times M_{ind} \times B_{ind} \right)^2 + A}$$

Where:

$$A = \sum_i 0.75 \times w_i^2 \times \left(M_i \times EAD_i^{total} - M_i^{hedge} \times B_i \right)^2$$

(A) w_i = the weight applicable to counterparty i under Table 3 to § 3.132;

(B) M_i = the EAD-weighted average of the effective maturity of each netting set with counterparty i (where each netting set's effective maturity can be no less than one year.)

(C) EAD_i^{total} = the sum of the EAD for all netting sets of OTC derivative contracts with counterparty i calculated using the current exposure methodology described in paragraph (c) of this section or the internal models methodology described in paragraph (d) of this section. When the national bank or Federal savings association calculates EAD under paragraph (c) of this section, such EAD may be adjusted for purposes of calculating EAD_i^{total} by multiplying EAD by $(1-\exp(-0.05 \times M_i))/(0.05 \times M_i)$, where "exp" is the exponential function. When the national bank or Federal savings association calculates EAD under paragraph (d) of this section, EAD_i^{total} equals $EAD_{unstressed}$.

(D) M_i^{hedge} = the notional weighted average maturity of the hedge instrument.

(E) B_i = the sum of the notional amounts of any purchased single name CDS referencing counterparty i that is used to hedge CVA risk to counterparty i multiplied by $(1-\exp(-0.05 \times M_i^{hedge}))/(0.05 \times M_i^{hedge})$.

(F) M_{ind} = the maturity of the CDS_{ind} or the notional weighted average maturity of any CDS_{ind} purchased to hedge CVA risk of counterparty *i*.

(G) B_{ind} = the notional amount of one or more CDS_{ind} purchased to hedge CVA risk for counterparty *i* multiplied by $(1\text{-}\exp(-0.05 \times M_{ind}))/(0.05 \times M_{ind})$

(H) w_{ind} = the weight applicable to the CDS_{ind} based on the average weight of the underlying reference names that comprise the index under Table 3 to §3.132.

(ii) The national bank or Federal savings association may treat the notional amount of the index attributable to a counterparty as a single name hedge of counterparty *i* (B_i,) when calculating K_{CVA}, and subtract the notional amount of B_i from the notional amount of the CDS_{ind}. A national bank or Federal savings association must treat the CDS_{ind} hedge with the notional amount reduced by B_i as a CVA hedge.

TABLE 3 TO §3.132—ASSIGNMENT OF COUNTERPARTY WEIGHT

Internal PD (in percent)	Weight w_i (in percent)
0.00–0.07	0.70
>0.070–0.15	0.80
>0.15–0.40	1.00
>0.40–2.00	2.00
>2.00–6.00	3.00
>6.00	10.00

(6) *Advanced CVA approach.* (i) A national bank or Federal savings association may use the VaR model that it uses to determine specific risk under §3.207(b) or another VaR model that meets the quantitative requirements of §§3.205(b) and 3.207(b)(1) to calculate its CVA capital requirement for a counterparty by modeling the impact of changes in the counterparties' credit spreads, together with any recognized CVA hedges, on the CVA for the counterparties, subject to the following requirements:

(A) The VaR model must incorporate only changes in the counterparties' credit spreads, not changes in other risk factors. The VaR model does not need to capture jump-to-default risk;

(B) A national bank or Federal savings association that qualifies to use the advanced CVA approach must include in that approach any immaterial OTC derivative portfolios for which it uses the current exposure methodology in paragraph (c) of this section according to paragraph (e)(6)(viii) of this section; and

(C) A national bank or Federal savings association must have the systems capability to calculate the CVA capital requirement for a counterparty on a daily basis (but is not required to calculate the CVA capital requirement on a daily basis).

(ii) Under the advanced CVA approach, the CVA capital requirement, K_{CVA}, is calculated according to the following formulas:

$$K_{CVA} = 3 \times \left(VaR^{CVA}_{Unstressed} + VaR^{CVA}_{Stressed}\right)$$

where VaR^{CVA}_j is the 99% VaR reflecting changes of CVA_j and fair value of eligible hedges (aggregated across all counterparties and eligible hedges) resulting from simulated changes of credit spreads over a 10-day time horizon. CVA_j for a given counterparty must be calculated according to

$$CVA_j = (LGD_{MKT}) \times \sum_{i=1}^{T} Max\left(0; \exp\left(-\frac{s_{i-1} \times t_{i-1}}{LGD_{MKT}}\right) - \exp\left(-\frac{s_i \times t_i}{LGD_{MKT}}\right)\right) \times \left(\frac{EE_{i-1} \times D_{i-1} + EE_i \times D_i}{2}\right)$$

Where

(A) t_i = the time of the i-th revaluation time bucket starting from $t_0 = 0$.

(B) t_T = the longest contractual maturity across the OTC derivative contracts with the counterparty.

(C) s_i = the CDS spread for the counterparty at tenor t_i used to calculate the CVA for the counterparty. If a CDS spread is not available, the national bank or Federal savings association must use a proxy spread based on the credit quality, industry and region of the counterparty.

(D) LGD_{MKT} = the loss given default of the counterparty based on the spread of a publicly traded debt instrument of the counterparty, or, where a publicly traded debt instrument spread is not available, a proxy spread based on the credit quality, industry, and region of the counterparty. Where no market information and no reliable proxy based on the credit quality, industry, and region of the counterparty are available to determine LGD_{MKT}, a national bank or Federal savings association may use a conservative estimate when determining LGD_{MKT}, subject to approval by the OCC.

(E) EE_i = the sum of the expected exposures for all netting sets with the counterparty at revaluation time t_i, calculated according to paragraphs (e)(6)(iv)(A) and (e)(6)(v)(A) of this section.

(F) D_i = the risk-free discount factor at time t_i, where $D_0 = 1$.

(G) Exp is the exponential function.

(H) The subscript j refers either to a stressed or an unstressed calibration as described in paragraphs (e)(6)(iv) and (v) of this section.

(iii) Notwithstanding paragraphs (e)(6)(i) and (e)(6)(ii) of this section, a national bank or Federal savings association must use the formulas in paragraphs (e)(6)(iii)(A) or (e)(6)(iii)(B) of this section to calculate credit spread sensitivities if its VaR model is not based on full repricing.

(A) If the VaR model is based on credit spread sensitivities for specific tenors, the national bank or Federal savings association must calculate each credit spread sensitivity according to the following formula:

$$\text{Regulatory CS01} = 0.0001 \times t_i \times exp\left(-\frac{s_i \times t_i}{LGD_{MKT}}\right) \times \left(\frac{EE_{i-1} \times D_{i-1} - EE_{i+1} \times D_{i+1}}{2}\right)$$

For the final time bucket i = T, the corresponding formula is

$$\text{Regulatory CS01} = 0.0001 \times t_i \times \exp\left(-\frac{s_i \times t_i}{LGD_{MKT}}\right) \times \left(\frac{EE_{i-1} \times D_{i-1} + EE_T \times D_T}{2}\right)$$

(B) If the VaR model uses credit spread sensitivities to parallel shifts in credit spreads, the [BANK] must calculate each credit spread sensitivity according to the following formula:

$$\text{Regulatory CS01} = 0.0001 \times \sum_{i=1}^{T}\left(t_i \times \exp\left(-\frac{s_i \times t_i}{LGD_{MKT}}\right) - t_{i-1} \times \exp\left(-\frac{s_{i-1} \times t_{i-1}}{LGD_{MKT}}\right)\right) \times \left(\frac{EE_{i-1} \times D_{i-1} + EE_i \times D_i}{2}\right)$$

(iv) To calculate the $CVA_{\text{Unstressed}}$ measure for purposes of paragraph (e)(6)(ii) of this section, the national bank or Federal savings association must:

(A) Use the EE_i calculated using the calibration of paragraph (d)(3)(vii) of this section, except as provided in § 3.132(e)(6)(vi), and

(B) Use the historical observation period required under § 3.205(b)(2).

(v) To calculate the $CVA_{Stressed}$ measure for purposes of paragraph (e)(6)(ii) of this section, the national bank or Federal savings association must:

(A) Use the EE_i calculated using the stress calibration in paragraph (d)(3)(viii) of this section except as provided in paragraph (e)(6)(vi) of this section.

(B) Calibrate VaR model inputs to historical data from the most severe twelve-month stress period contained within the three-year stress period used to calculate EE_i. The OCC may require a national bank or Federal savings association to use a different period of significant financial stress in the calculation of the $CVA_{Stressed}$ measure.

(vi) If a national bank or Federal savings association captures the effect of a collateral agreement on EAD using the method described in paragraph (d)(5)(ii) of this section, for purposes of paragraph (e)(6)(ii) of this section, the national bank or Federal savings association must calculate EE_i using the method in paragraph (d)(5)(ii) of this section and keep that EE constant with the maturity equal to the maximum of:

(A) Half of the longest maturity of a transaction in the netting set, and

(B) The notional weighted average maturity of all transactions in the netting set.

(vii) For purposes of paragraph (e)(6) of this section, the national bank's or Federal savings association's VaR model must capture the basis between the spreads of any CDS_{ind} that is used as the hedging instrument and the hedged counterparty exposure over various time periods, including benign and stressed environments. If the VaR model does not capture that basis, the national bank or Federal savings association must reflect only 50 percent of the notional amount of the CDS_{ind} hedge in the VaR model.

(viii) If a national bank or Federal savings association uses the current exposure methodology described in paragraphs (c)(5) and (c)(6) of this section to calculate the EAD for any immaterial portfolios of OTC derivative contracts, the national bank or Federal savings association must use that EAD as a constant EE in the formula for the calculation of CVA with the maturity equal to the maximum of:

(A) Half of the longest maturity of a transaction in the netting set, and

(B) The notional weighted average maturity of all transactions in the netting set.

[78 FR 62157, 62273, Oct. 11, 2013, as amended at 80 FR 41417, July 15, 2015]

§ 3.133 Cleared transactions.

(a) *General requirements.* (1) A national bank or Federal savings association that is a clearing member client must use the methodologies described in paragraph (b) of this section to calculate risk-weighted assets for a cleared transaction.

(2) A national bank or Federal savings association that is a clearing member must use the methodologies described in paragraph (c) of this section to calculate its risk-weighted assets for cleared transactions and paragraph (d) of this section to calculate its risk-weighted assets for its default fund contribution to a CCP.

(b) *Clearing member client national banks or Federal savings associations*—(1) *Risk-weighted assets for cleared transactions.* (i) To determine the risk-weighted asset amount for a cleared transaction, a national bank or Federal savings association that is a clearing member client must multiply the trade exposure amount for the cleared transaction, calculated in accordance with paragraph (b)(2) of this section, by the risk weight appropriate for the cleared transaction, determined in accordance with paragraph (b)(3) of this section.

(ii) A clearing member client national bank's or Federal savings association's total risk-weighted assets for cleared transactions is the sum of the risk-weighted asset amounts for all of its cleared transactions.

(2) *Trade exposure amount.* (i) For a cleared transaction that is a derivative contract or a netting set of derivative contracts, trade exposure amount

equals the EAD for the derivative contract or netting set of derivative contracts calculated using the methodology used to calculate EAD for OTC derivative contracts set forth in § 3.132(c) or (d), plus the fair value of the collateral posted by the clearing member client national bank or Federal savings association and held by the CCP or a clearing member in a manner that is not bankruptcy remote. When the national bank or Federal savings association calculates EAD for the cleared transaction using the methodology in § 3.132(d), EAD equals $EAD_{unstressed}$.

(ii) For a cleared transaction that is a repo-style transaction or netting set of repo-style transactions, trade exposure amount equals the EAD for the repo-style transaction calculated using the methodology set forth in § 3.132(b)(2), (b)(3), or (d), plus the fair value of the collateral posted by the clearing member client national bank or Federal savings association and held by the CCP or a clearing member in a manner that is not bankruptcy remote. When the national bank or Federal savings association calculates EAD for the cleared transaction under § 3.132(d), EAD equals $EAD_{unstressed}$.

(3) *Cleared transaction risk weights.* (i) For a cleared transaction with a QCCP, a clearing member client national bank or Federal savings association must apply a risk weight of:

(A) 2 percent if the collateral posted by the national bank or Federal savings association to the QCCP or clearing member is subject to an arrangement that prevents any loss to the clearing member client national bank or Federal savings association due to the joint default or a concurrent insolvency, liquidation, or receivership proceeding of the clearing member and any other clearing member clients of the clearing member; and the clearing member client national bank or Federal savings association has conducted sufficient legal review to conclude with a well-founded basis (and maintains sufficient written documentation of that legal review) that in the event of a legal challenge (including one resulting from an event of default or from liquidation, insolvency or receivership proceedings) the relevant court and administrative authorities would find the arrangements to be legal, valid, binding and enforceable under the law of the relevant jurisdictions.

(B) 4 percent, if the requirements of paragraph (b)(3)(i)(A) of this section are not met.

(ii) For a cleared transaction with a CCP that is not a QCCP, a clearing member client national bank or Federal savings association must apply the risk weight applicable to the CCP under § 3.32.

(4) *Collateral.* (i) Notwithstanding any other requirement of this section, collateral posted by a clearing member client national bank or Federal savings association that is held by a custodian (in its capacity as custodian) in a manner that is bankruptcy remote from the CCP, the custodian, clearing member, and other clearing member clients of the clearing member, is not subject to a capital requirement under this section.

(ii) A clearing member client national bank or Federal savings association must calculate a risk-weighted asset amount for any collateral provided to a CCP, clearing member or a custodian in connection with a cleared transaction in accordance with requirements under subparts E or F of this part, as applicable.

(c) *Clearing member national bank or Federal savings association*—(1) *Risk-weighted assets for cleared transactions.* (i) To determine the risk-weighted asset amount for a cleared transaction, a clearing member national bank or Federal savings association must multiply the trade exposure amount for the cleared transaction, calculated in accordance with paragraph (c)(2) of this section by the risk weight appropriate for the cleared transaction, determined in accordance with paragraph (c)(3) of this section.

(ii) A clearing member national bank's or Federal savings association's total risk-weighted assets for cleared transactions is the sum of the risk-weighted asset amounts for all of its cleared transactions.

(2) *Trade exposure amount.* A clearing member national bank or Federal savings association must calculate its trade exposure amount for a cleared transaction as follows:

(i) For a cleared transaction that is a derivative contract or a netting set of derivative contracts, trade exposure amount equals the EAD calculated using the methodology used to calculate EAD for OTC derivative contracts set forth in § 3.132(c) or § 3.132(d), plus the fair value of the collateral posted by the clearing member national bank or Federal savings association and held by the CCP in a manner that is not bankruptcy remote. When the clearing member national bank or Federal savings association calculates EAD for the cleared transaction using the methodology in § 3.132(d), EAD equals $EAD_{unstressed}$.

(ii) For a cleared transaction that is a repo-style transaction or netting set of repo-style transactions, trade exposure amount equals the EAD calculated under §§ 3.132(b)(2), (b)(3), or (d), plus the fair value of the collateral posted by the clearing member national bank or Federal savings association and held by the CCP in a manner that is not bankruptcy remote. When the clearing member national bank or Federal savings association calculates EAD for the cleared transaction under § 3.132(d), EAD equals $EAD_{unstressed}$.

(3) *Cleared transaction risk weights.* (i) A clearing member national bank or Federal savings association must apply a risk weight of 2 percent to the trade exposure amount for a cleared transaction with a QCCP.

(ii) For a cleared transaction with a CCP that is not a QCCP, a clearing member national bank or Federal savings association must apply the risk weight applicable to the CCP according to § 3.32.

(iii) Notwithstanding paragraphs (c)(3)(i) and (ii) of this section, a clearing member national bank or Federal savings association may apply a risk weight of 0 percent to the trade exposure amount for a cleared transaction with a CCP where the clearing member national bank or Federal savings association is acting as a financial intermediary on behalf of a clearing member client, the transaction offsets another transaction that satisfies the requirements set forth in § 3.3(a), and the clearing member national bank or Federal savings association is not obligated to reimburse the clearing member client in the event of the CCP default.

(4) *Collateral.* (i) Notwithstanding any other requirement of this section, collateral posted by a clearing member national bank or Federal savings association that is held by a custodian in a manner that is bankruptcy remote from the CCP is not subject to a capital requirement under this section.

(ii) A clearing member national bank or Federal savings association must calculate a risk-weighted asset amount for any collateral provided to a CCP, clearing member or a custodian in connection with a cleared transaction in accordance with requirements under subparts E or F of this part, as applicable

(d) *Default fund contributions*—(1) *General requirement.* A clearing member national bank or Federal savings association must determine the risk-weighted asset amount for a default fund contribution to a CCP at least quarterly, or more frequently if, in the opinion of the national bank or Federal savings association or the OCC, there is a material change in the financial condition of the CCP.

(2) *Risk-weighted asset amount for default fund contributions to non-qualifying CCPs.* A clearing member national bank's or Federal savings association's risk-weighted asset amount for default fund contributions to CCPs that are not QCCPs equals the sum of such default fund contributions multiplied by 1,250 percent or an amount determined by the OCC, based on factors such as size, structure and membership characteristics of the CCP and riskiness of its transactions, in cases where such default fund contributions may be unlimited.

(3) *Risk-weighted asset amount for default fund contributions to QCCPs.* A clearing member national bank's or Federal savings association's risk-weighted asset amount for default fund contributions to QCCPs equals the sum of its capital requirement, K_{CM} for each QCCP, as calculated under the methodology set forth in paragraph (d)(3)(i) of this section (Method 1), multiplied by 1,250 percent or paragraph (d)(3)(iv) of this section (Method 2).

(i) *Method* 1. The hypothetical capital requirement of a QCCP (K_{CCP}) equals:

$$K_{CCP} = \sum_{clearing\ member\ i} \max\left(EBRM_i - VM_i - IM_i - DF_i; 0\right) \times RW \times 0.08$$

Where

(A) $EBRM_i$ = the EAD for each transaction cleared through the QCCP by clearing member i, calculated using the methodology used to calculate EAD for OTC derivative contracts set forth in § 3.132(c)(5) and § 3.132(c)(6) or the methodology used to calculate EAD for repo-style transactions set forth in § 3.132(b)(2) for repo-style transactions, provided that:

(*1*) For purposes of this section, when calculating the EAD, the national bank or Federal savings association may replace the formula provided in § 3.132(c)(6)(ii) with the following formula:

Anet = $(0.15 \times A_{gross}) + (0.85 \times NGR \times A_{gross})$; and

(*2*) For option derivative contracts that are cleared transactions, the PFE described in § 3.132(c)(5) must be adjusted by multiplying the notional principal amount of the derivative contract by the appropriate conversion factor in Table 2 to § 3.132 and the absolute value of the option's delta, that is, the ratio of the change in the value of the derivative contract to the corresponding change in the price of the underlying asset.

(*3*) For repo-style transactions, when applying § 3.132(b)(2), the national bank or Federal savings association must use the methodology in § 3.132(b)(2)(ii).

(B) VM_i = any collateral posted by clearing member i to the QCCP that it is entitled to receive from the QCCP but has not yet received, and any collateral that the QCCP has actually received from clearing member i;

(C) IM_i = the collateral posted as initial margin by clearing member i to the QCCP;

(D) DF_i = the funded portion of clearing member i's default fund contribution that will be applied to reduce the QCCP's loss upon a default by clearing member i; and

(E) RW = 20 percent, except when the OCC has determined that a higher risk weight is more appropriate based on the specific characteristics of the QCCP and its clearing members; and

(F) Where a QCCP has provided its K_{CCP}, a national bank or Federal savings association must rely on such disclosed figure instead of calculating K_{CCP} under this paragraph (d), unless the national bank or Federal savings association determines that a more conservative figure is appropriate based on the nature, structure, or characteristics of the QCCP.

(ii) For a national bank or Federal savings association that is a clearing member of a QCCP with a default fund supported by funded commitments, K_{CM} equals:

$$K_{CM_i} = \left(1 + \beta \cdot \frac{N}{N-2}\right) \cdot \frac{DF_i}{DF_{CM}} \cdot K^*_{CM}$$

$$K^*_{CM} = \begin{cases} c_2 \cdot \mu \cdot (K_{CCP} - DF') + c_2 \cdot DF'_{CM} & if \quad DF' < K_{CCP} \quad (i) \\ c_2 \cdot (K_{CCP} - DF_{CCP}) + c_1 \cdot (DF' - K_{CCP}) & if \quad DF_{CCP} < K_{CCP} \le DF' \quad (ii) \\ c_1 \cdot DF'_{CM} & if \quad K_{CCP} \le DF_{CCP} \quad (iii) \end{cases}$$

Where

(A) $\beta = \frac{A_{Net,1} + A_{Net,2}}{\sum_i A_{Net,i}}$

Subscripts 1 and 2 denote the clearing members with the two largest A_{Net} values. For purposes of this section, for cleared transactions that are derivatives, A_{Net} is defined using the definition set forth in §___.132(c)(6)(ii) and for cleared transactions that are repo-style transactions, A_{Net} is the EAD equation max {0, [(∑E - ∑C) + ∑(E_s x H_s) + ∑(Efx]} from §___.132(b)(2(i)) using the methodology in §___.132(b)(2)(ii);

(B) N = the number of clearing members in the QCCP;

(C) DF_{CCP} = the QCCP's own funds and other financial resources that would be used to cover its losses before clearing members' default fund contributions are used to cover losses;

(D) DF_{CM} = Funded default fund contributions from all clearing members and any other clearing member contributed financial resources that are available to absorb mutualized QCCP losses;

(E) DF = DF_{CCP} + DF_{CM} (that is, the total funded default fund contribution);

(F) $\overline{DF_i}$ = Average $\overline{DF_i}$ = the average funded default fund contribution from an individual clearing member;

(G) $DF_{CM}^{'} = DF_{CM} - 2 \cdot \overline{DF_i} = \sum_i DF_i - 2 \cdot \overline{DF_i}$ (that is, the funded default fund contribution from surviving clearing members assuming that two average clearing members have defaulted and their default fund contributions and initial margins have been used to absorb the resulting losses);

(H) $DF' = DF_{CCP} + DF_{CM}^{'} = DF - 2 \cdot \overline{DF_i}$

(that is, the total funded default fund contributions from the QCCP and the surviving clearing members that are available to mutualize losses, assuming that two average clearing members have defaulted);

(I) $c_1 = Max\left\{\frac{1.6\%}{\left(DF'/K_{CCP}\right)^{0.3}};0.16\%\right\}$

(that is, a decreasing capital factor, between 1.6 percent and .16 percent, applied to the excess funded default funds provided by clearing members);

(J) c_2 = 100 percent; and

(K) μ= 1.2;

(iii) For a [BANK] that is a clearing member of a QCCP with a default fund supported by unfunded commitments, K_{CM} equals:

$$K_{CM_i} = \frac{DF_i}{DF_{CM}} \cdot K_{CM}^{*}$$

Where:

(A) DF_i = the national bank's or Federal savings association's unfunded commitment to the default fund;

(B) DF_{CM} = the total of all clearing members' unfunded commitments to the default fund; and

(C) K^*_{CM} as defined in paragraph (d)(3)(ii) of this section.

(D) For a national bank or Federal savings association that is a clearing member of a QCCP with a default fund supported by unfunded commitments and that is unable to calculate K_{CM} using the methodology described above in this paragraph (d)(3)(iii), K_{CM} equals:

$$K_{CM_i} = \frac{IM_i}{IM_{CM}} \cdot K_{CM}^{*}$$

Where:

(*1*) IM_i = the national bank's or Federal savings association's initial margin posted to the QCCP;

(*2*) IM_{CM} = the total of initial margin posted to the QCCP; and

(*3*) K^*_{CM} as defined above in this paragraph (d)(3)(iii).

(iv) *Method 2.* A clearing member national bank's or Federal savings association's risk-weighted asset amount for its default fund contribution to a QCCP, RWA_{DF}, equals:

$$RWA_{DF} = Min \{12.5 * DF; 0.18 * TE\}$$

Where:

(A) TE = the national bank's or Federal savings association's trade exposure amount to the QCCP calculated according to section 133(c)(2);

(B) DF = the funded portion of the national bank's or Federal savings association's default fund contribution to the QCCP.

(v) *Total risk-weighted assets for default fund contributions.* Total risk-weighted assets for default fund contributions is the sum of a clearing member national bank's or Federal savings association's risk-weighted assets for all of its default fund contributions to all CCPs of which the national bank or Federal savings association is a clearing member.

[78 FR 62157, 62273, Oct. 11, 2013, as amended at 80 FR 41417, July 15, 2015]

§ 3.134 Guarantees and credit derivatives: PD substitution and LGD adjustment approaches.

(a) *Scope.* (1) This section applies to wholesale exposures for which:

(i) Credit risk is fully covered by an eligible guarantee or eligible credit derivative; or

(ii) Credit risk is covered on a pro rata basis (that is, on a basis in which the national bank or Federal savings association and the protection provider share losses proportionately) by an eligible guarantee or eligible credit derivative.

(2) Wholesale exposures on which there is a tranching of credit risk (reflecting at least two different levels of seniority) are securitization exposures subject to §§ 3.141 through 3.145.

(3) A national bank or Federal savings association may elect to recognize the credit risk mitigation benefits of an eligible guarantee or eligible credit derivative covering an exposure described in paragraph (a)(1) of this section by using the PD substitution approach or the LGD adjustment approach in paragraph (c) of this section or, if the transaction qualifies, using the double default treatment in § 3.135. A national bank's or Federal savings association's PD and LGD for the hedged exposure may not be lower than the PD and LGD floors described in § 3.131(d)(2) and (d)(3).

(4) If multiple eligible guarantees or eligible credit derivatives cover a single exposure described in paragraph (a)(1) of this section, a national bank or Federal savings association may treat the hedged exposure as multiple separate exposures each covered by a single eligible guarantee or eligible credit derivative and may calculate a separate risk-based capital requirement for each separate exposure as described in paragraph (a)(3) of this section.

(5) If a single eligible guarantee or eligible credit derivative covers multiple hedged wholesale exposures described in paragraph (a)(1) of this section, a national bank or Federal savings association must treat each hedged exposure as covered by a separate eligible guarantee or eligible credit derivative and must calculate a separate risk-based capital requirement for each exposure as described in paragraph (a)(3) of this section.

(6) A national bank or Federal savings association must use the same risk parameters for calculating ECL as it uses for calculating the risk-based capital requirement for the exposure.

(b) *Rules of recognition.* (1) A national bank or Federal savings association may only recognize the credit risk mitigation benefits of eligible guarantees and eligible credit derivatives.

(2) A national bank or Federal savings association may only recognize the credit risk mitigation benefits of an eligible credit derivative to hedge an exposure that is different from the credit derivative's reference exposure used for determining the derivative's cash settlement value, deliverable obligation, or occurrence of a credit event if:

(i) The reference exposure ranks *pari passu* (that is, equally) with or is junior to the hedged exposure; and

(ii) The reference exposure and the hedged exposure are exposures to the same legal entity, and legally enforceable cross-default or cross-acceleration clauses are in place to assure payments under the credit derivative are triggered when the obligor fails to pay under the terms of the hedged exposure.

(c) *Risk parameters for hedged exposures*—(1) *PD substitution approach*—(i) *Full coverage.* If an eligible guarantee or eligible credit derivative meets the conditions in paragraphs (a) and (b) of this section and the protection amount (P) of the guarantee or credit derivative is greater than or equal to the EAD of the hedged exposure, a national bank or Federal savings association may recognize the guarantee or credit derivative in determining the national bank's or Federal savings association's risk-based capital requirement for the hedged exposure by substituting the PD associated with the rating grade of the protection provider for the PD associated with the rating grade of the obligor in the risk-based capital formula applicable to the guarantee or credit derivative in Table 1 of § 3.131 and using the appropriate LGD as described in paragraph (c)(1)(iii) of this section. If the national bank or Federal savings association determines that full substitution of the protection provider's PD leads to an inappropriate degree of risk mitigation, the national bank or Federal savings association may substitute a higher PD than that of the protection provider.

(ii) *Partial coverage.* If an eligible guarantee or eligible credit derivative meets the conditions in paragraphs (a) and (b) of this section and P of the guarantee or credit derivative is less than the EAD of the hedged exposure, the national bank or Federal savings association must treat the hedged exposure as two separate exposures (protected and unprotected) in order to recognize the credit risk mitigation benefit of the guarantee or credit derivative.

(A) The national bank or Federal savings association must calculate its risk-based capital requirement for the protected exposure under § 3.131, where PD is the protection provider's PD, LGD is determined under paragraph (c)(1)(iii) of this section, and EAD is P. If the national bank or Federal savings association determines that full substitution leads to an inappropriate degree of risk mitigation, the national bank or Federal savings association may use a higher PD than that of the protection provider.

(B) The national bank or Federal savings association must calculate its risk-based capital requirement for the unprotected exposure under § 3.131, where PD is the obligor's PD, LGD is the hedged exposure's LGD (not adjusted to reflect the guarantee or credit derivative), and EAD is the EAD of the original hedged exposure minus P.

(C) The treatment in paragraph (c)(1)(ii) of this section is applicable when the credit risk of a wholesale exposure is covered on a partial pro rata basis or when an adjustment is made to the effective notional amount of the guarantee or credit derivative under paragraphs (d), (e), or (f) of this section.

(iii) *LGD of hedged exposures.* The LGD of a hedged exposure under the PD substitution approach is equal to:

(A) The lower of the LGD of the hedged exposure (not adjusted to reflect the guarantee or credit derivative) and the LGD of the guarantee or credit derivative, if the guarantee or credit derivative provides the national bank or Federal savings association with the option to receive immediate payout upon triggering the protection; or

(B) The LGD of the guarantee or credit derivative, if the guarantee or credit derivative does not provide the national bank or Federal savings association with the option to receive immediate payout upon triggering the protection.

(2) *LGD adjustment approach*—(i) *Full coverage.* If an eligible guarantee or eligible credit derivative meets the conditions in paragraphs (a) and (b) of this section and the protection amount (P) of the guarantee or credit derivative is greater than or equal to the EAD of the hedged exposure, the national bank's or Federal savings association's risk-

based capital requirement for the hedged exposure is the greater of:

(A) The risk-based capital requirement for the exposure as calculated under § 3.131, with the LGD of the exposure adjusted to reflect the guarantee or credit derivative; or

(B) The risk-based capital requirement for a direct exposure to the protection provider as calculated under § 3.131, using the PD for the protection provider, the LGD for the guarantee or credit derivative, and an EAD equal to the EAD of the hedged exposure.

(ii) *Partial coverage.* If an eligible guarantee or eligible credit derivative meets the conditions in paragraphs (a) and (b) of this section and the protection amount (P) of the guarantee or credit derivative is less than the EAD of the hedged exposure, the national bank or Federal savings association must treat the hedged exposure as two separate exposures (protected and unprotected) in order to recognize the credit risk mitigation benefit of the guarantee or credit derivative.

(A) The national bank's or Federal savings association's risk-based capital requirement for the protected exposure would be the greater of:

(*1*) The risk-based capital requirement for the protected exposure as calculated under § 3.131, with the LGD of the exposure adjusted to reflect the guarantee or credit derivative and EAD set equal to P; or

(*2*) The risk-based capital requirement for a direct exposure to the guarantor as calculated under § 3.131, using the PD for the protection provider, the LGD for the guarantee or credit derivative, and an EAD set equal to P.

(B) The national bank or Federal savings association must calculate its risk-based capital requirement for the unprotected exposure under § 3.131, where PD is the obligor's PD, LGD is the hedged exposure's LGD (not adjusted to reflect the guarantee or credit derivative), and EAD is the EAD of the original hedged exposure minus P.

(3) *M of hedged exposures.* For purposes of this paragraph (c), the M of the hedged exposure is the same as the M of the exposure if it were unhedged.

(d) *Maturity mismatch.* (1) A national bank or Federal savings association that recognizes an eligible guarantee or eligible credit derivative in determining its risk-based capital requirement for a hedged exposure must adjust the effective notional amount of the credit risk mitigant to reflect any maturity mismatch between the hedged exposure and the credit risk mitigant.

(2) A maturity mismatch occurs when the residual maturity of a credit risk mitigant is less than that of the hedged exposure(s).

(3) The residual maturity of a hedged exposure is the longest possible remaining time before the obligor is scheduled to fulfil its obligation on the exposure. If a credit risk mitigant has embedded options that may reduce its term, the national bank or Federal savings association (protection purchaser) must use the shortest possible residual maturity for the credit risk mitigant. If a call is at the discretion of the protection provider, the residual maturity of the credit risk mitigant is at the first call date. If the call is at the discretion of the national bank or Federal savings association (protection purchaser), but the terms of the arrangement at origination of the credit risk mitigant contain a positive incentive for the national bank or Federal savings association to call the transaction before contractual maturity, the remaining time to the first call date is the residual maturity of the credit risk mitigant.[30]

(4) A credit risk mitigant with a maturity mismatch may be recognized only if its original maturity is greater than or equal to one year and its residual maturity is greater than three months.

(5) When a maturity mismatch exists, the national bank or Federal savings association must apply the following adjustment to the effective notional amount of the credit risk mitigant:

$$P_m = E \times (t - 0.25)/(T - 0.25),$$

where:

[30] For example, where there is a step-up in cost in conjunction with a call feature or where the effective cost of protection increases over time even if credit quality remains the same or improves, the residual maturity of the credit risk mitigant will be the remaining time to the first call.

(i) P_m = effective notional amount of the credit risk mitigant, adjusted for maturity mismatch;

(ii) E = effective notional amount of the credit risk mitigant;

(iii) t = the lesser of T or the residual maturity of the credit risk mitigant, expressed in years; and

(iv) T = the lesser of five or the residual maturity of the hedged exposure, expressed in years.

(e) *Credit derivatives without restructuring as a credit event.* If a national bank or Federal savings association recognizes an eligible credit derivative that does not include as a credit event a restructuring of the hedged exposure involving forgiveness or postponement of principal, interest, or fees that results in a credit loss event (that is, a charge-off, specific provision, or other similar debit to the profit and loss account), the national bank or Federal savings association must apply the following adjustment to the effective notional amount of the credit derivative:

$$P_r = P_m \times 0.60,$$

where:

(1) P_r = effective notional amount of the credit risk mitigant, adjusted for lack of restructuring event (and maturity mismatch, if applicable); and

(2) P_m = effective notional amount of the credit risk mitigant adjusted for maturity mismatch (if applicable).

(f) *Currency mismatch.* (1) If a national bank or Federal savings association recognizes an eligible guarantee or eligible credit derivative that is denominated in a currency different from that in which the hedged exposure is denominated, the national bank or Federal savings association must apply the following formula to the effective notional amount of the guarantee or credit derivative:

$$P_c = P_r \times (1 - H_{FX}),$$

where:

(i) P_c = effective notional amount of the credit risk mitigant, adjusted for currency mismatch (and maturity mismatch and lack of restructuring event, if applicable);

(ii) P_r = effective notional amount of the credit risk mitigant (adjusted for maturity mismatch and lack of restructuring event, if applicable); and

(iii) H_{FX} = haircut appropriate for the currency mismatch between the credit risk mitigant and the hedged exposure.

(2) A national bank or Federal savings association must set H_{FX} equal to 8 percent unless it qualifies for the use of and uses its own internal estimates of foreign exchange volatility based on a ten-business-day holding period and daily marking-to-market and remargining. A national bank or Federal savings association qualifies for the use of its own internal estimates of foreign exchange volatility if it qualifies for:

(i) The own-estimates haircuts in § 3.132(b)(2)(iii);

(ii) The simple VaR methodology in § 3.132(b)(3); or

(iii) The internal models methodology in § 3.132(d).

(3) A national bank or Federal savings association must adjust H_{FX} calculated in paragraph (f)(2) of this section upward if the national bank or Federal savings association revalues the guarantee or credit derivative less frequently than once every ten business days using the square root of time formula provided in § 3.132(b)(2)(iii)(A)(*2*).

§ 3.135 Guarantees and credit derivatives: double default treatment.

(a) *Eligibility and operational criteria for double default treatment.* A national bank or Federal savings association may recognize the credit risk mitigation benefits of a guarantee or credit derivative covering an exposure described in § 3.134(a)(1) by applying the double default treatment in this section if all the following criteria are satisfied:

(1) The hedged exposure is fully covered or covered on a pro rata basis by:

(i) An eligible guarantee issued by an eligible double default guarantor; or

(ii) An eligible credit derivative that meets the requirements of § 3.134(b)(2) and that is issued by an eligible double default guarantor.

(2) The guarantee or credit derivative is:

(i) An uncollateralized guarantee or uncollateralized credit derivative (for example, a credit default swap) that provides protection with respect to a single reference obligor; or

(ii) An nth-to-default credit derivative (subject to the requirements of § 3.142(m).

(3) The hedged exposure is a wholesale exposure (other than a sovereign exposure).

(4) The obligor of the hedged exposure is not:

(i) An eligible double default guarantor or an affiliate of an eligible double default guarantor; or

(ii) An affiliate of the guarantor.

(5) The national bank or Federal savings association does not recognize any credit risk mitigation benefits of the guarantee or credit derivative for the hedged exposure other than through application of the double default treatment as provided in this section.

(6) The national bank or Federal savings association has implemented a process (which has received the prior, written approval of the OCC) to detect excessive correlation between the creditworthiness of the obligor of the hedged exposure and the protection provider. If excessive correlation is present, the national bank or Federal savings association may not use the double default treatment for the hedged exposure.

(b) *Full coverage.* If a transaction meets the criteria in paragraph (a) of this section and the protection amount (P) of the guarantee or credit derivative is at least equal to the EAD of the hedged exposure, the national bank or Federal savings association may determine its risk-weighted asset amount for the hedged exposure under paragraph (e) of this section.

(c) *Partial coverage.* If a transaction meets the criteria in paragraph (a) of this section and the protection amount (P) of the guarantee or credit derivative is less than the EAD of the hedged exposure, the national bank or Federal savings association must treat the hedged exposure as two separate exposures (protected and unprotected) in order to recognize double default treatment on the protected portion of the exposure:

(1) For the protected exposure, the national bank or Federal savings association must set EAD equal to P and calculate its risk-weighted asset amount as provided in paragraph (e) of this section; and

(2) For the unprotected exposure, the national bank or Federal savings association must set EAD equal to the EAD of the original exposure minus P and then calculate its risk-weighted asset amount as provided in § 3.131.

(d) *Mismatches.* For any hedged exposure to which a national bank or Federal savings association applies double default treatment under this part, the national bank or Federal savings association must make applicable adjustments to the protection amount as required in § 3.134(d), (e), and (f).

(e) *The double default dollar risk-based capital requirement.* The dollar risk-based capital requirement for a hedged exposure to which a national bank or Federal savings association has applied double default treatment is K_{DD} multiplied by the EAD of the exposure. K_{DD} is calculated according to the following formula:

$$K_{DD} = K_o \times (0.15 + 160 \times PD_g),$$

Where:

(1)

$$K_O = LGD_g \times \left[N\left(\frac{N^{-1}(PD_o) + N^{-1}(0.999)\sqrt{\rho_{os}}}{\sqrt{1-\rho_{os}}} \right) - PD_o \right] \times \left[\frac{1+(M-2.5)\times b}{1-1.5\times b} \right]$$

(2) PD_g = PD of the protection provider.

(3) PD_o = PD of the obligor of the hedged exposure.

(4) LGD_g =

(i) The lower of the LGD of the hedged exposure (not adjusted to reflect the guarantee or credit derivative) and the LGD of the guarantee or credit derivative, if the guarantee or credit derivative provides the national bank or Federal savings association with the option to receive immediate payout on triggering the protection; or

(ii) The LGD of the guarantee or credit derivative, if the guarantee or credit derivative does not provide the national bank or Federal savings association with the option to receive immediate payout on triggering the protection; and

(5) ρ_{os} (asset value correlation of the obligor) is calculated according to the appropriate formula for (R) provided in Table 1 in § 3.131, with PD equal to PD_o.

(6) b (maturity adjustment coefficient) is calculated according to the formula for b provided in Table 1 in § 3.131, with PD equal to the lesser of PD_o and PD_g; and

(7) M (maturity) is the effective maturity of the guarantee or credit derivative, which may not be less than one year or greater than five years.

§ 3.136 Unsettled transactions.

(a) *Definitions.* For purposes of this section:

(1) Delivery-versus-payment (DvP) transaction means a securities or commodities transaction in which the buyer is obligated to make payment only if the seller has made delivery of the securities or commodities and the seller is obligated to deliver the securities or commodities only if the buyer has made payment.

(2) Payment-versus-payment (PvP) transaction means a foreign exchange transaction in which each counterparty is obligated to make a final transfer of one or more currencies only if the other counterparty has made a final transfer of one or more currencies.

(3) A transaction has a normal settlement period if the contractual settlement period for the transaction is equal to or less than the market standard for the instrument underlying the transaction and equal to or less than five business days.

(4) The positive current exposure of a national bank or Federal savings association for a transaction is the difference between the transaction value at the agreed settlement price and the current market price of the transaction, if the difference results in a credit exposure of the national bank or Federal savings association to the counterparty.

(b) *Scope.* This section applies to all transactions involving securities, foreign exchange instruments, and commodities that have a risk of delayed settlement or delivery. This section does not apply to:

(1) Cleared transactions that are subject to daily marking-to-market and daily receipt and payment of variation margin;

(2) Repo-style transactions, including unsettled repo-style transactions (which are addressed in §§ 3.131 and 132);

(3) One-way cash payments on OTC derivative contracts (which are addressed in §§ 3. 131 and 132); or

(4) Transactions with a contractual settlement period that is longer than the normal settlement period (which are treated as OTC derivative contracts and addressed in §§ 3.131 and 132).

(c) *System-wide failures.* In the case of a system-wide failure of a settlement or clearing system, or a central counterparty, the OCC may waive risk-based capital requirements for unsettled and failed transactions until the situation is rectified.

(d) *Delivery-versus-payment (DvP) and payment-versus-payment (PvP) transactions.* A national bank or Federal savings association must hold risk-based capital against any DvP or PvP transaction with a normal settlement period if the national bank's or Federal savings association's counterparty has not made delivery or payment within five business days after the settlement date. The national bank or Federal savings association must determine its risk-weighted asset amount for such a transaction by multiplying the positive current exposure of the transaction for the national bank or Federal savings association by the appropriate risk weight in Table 1 to § 3.136.

TABLE 1 TO § 3.136—RISK WEIGHTS FOR UNSETTLED DVP AND PVP TRANSACTIONS

Number of business days after contractual settlement date	Risk weight to be applied to positive current exposure (in percent)
From 5 to 15	100
From 16 to 30	625
From 31 to 45	937.5
46 or more	1,250

(e) *Non-DvP/non-PvP (non-delivery-versus-payment/non-payment-versus-payment) transactions.* (1) A national bank or Federal savings association must hold risk-based capital against any non-DvP/non-PvP transaction with a normal settlement period if the national bank or Federal savings association has delivered cash, securities, commodities, or currencies to its counterparty but has not received its corresponding deliverables by the end of the same business day. The national bank or Federal savings association must continue to hold risk-based capital against the transaction until the national bank or Federal savings association has received its corresponding deliverables.

(2) From the business day after the national bank or Federal savings association has made its delivery until five business days after the counterparty delivery is due, the national bank or Federal savings association must calculate its risk-based capital requirement for the transaction by treating the current fair value of the deliverables owed to the national bank or Federal savings association as a wholesale exposure.

(i) A national bank or Federal savings association may use a 45 percent LGD for the transaction rather than estimating LGD for the transaction provided the national bank or Federal savings association uses the 45 percent LGD for all transactions described in paragraphs (e)(1) and (2) of this section.

(ii) A national bank or Federal savings association may use a 100 percent risk weight for the transaction provided the national bank or Federal savings association uses this risk weight for all transactions described in paragraphs (e)(1) and (2) of this section.

(3) If the national bank or Federal savings association has not received its deliverables by the fifth business day after the counterparty delivery was due, the national bank or Federal savings association must apply a 1,250 percent risk weight to the current fair value of the deliverables owed to the national bank or Federal savings association.

(f) *Total risk-weighted assets for unsettled transactions.* Total risk-weighted assets for unsettled transactions is the sum of the risk-weighted asset amounts of all DvP, PvP, and non-DvP/non-PvP transactions.

[78 FR 62157, 62273, Oct. 11, 2013, as amended at 80 FR 41417, July 15, 2015]

§§ 3.137–3.140 [Reserved]

RISK-WEIGHTED ASSETS FOR SECURITIZATION EXPOSURES

§ 3.141 Operational criteria for recognizing the transfer of risk.

(a) *Operational criteria for traditional securitizations.* A national bank or Federal savings association that transfers exposures it has originated or purchased to a securitization SPE or other third party in connection with a traditional securitization may exclude the exposures from the calculation of its risk-weighted assets only if each of the conditions in this paragraph (a) is satisfied. A national bank or Federal savings association that meets these conditions must hold risk-based capital against any securitization exposures it retains in connection with the securitization. A national bank or Federal savings association that fails to meet these conditions must hold risk-based capital against the transferred exposures as if they had not been securitized and must deduct from common equity tier 1 capital any after-tax gain-on-sale resulting from the transaction. The conditions are:

(1) The exposures are not reported on the national bank's or Federal savings association's consolidated balance sheet under GAAP;

(2) The national bank or Federal savings association has transferred to one or more third parties credit risk associated with the underlying exposures;

(3) Any clean-up calls relating to the securitization are eligible clean-up calls; and

(4) The securitization does not:

(i) Include one or more underlying exposures in which the borrower is permitted to vary the drawn amount within an agreed limit under a line of credit; and

(ii) Contain an early amortization provision.

(b) *Operational criteria for synthetic securitizations.* For synthetic securitizations, a national bank or

Federal savings association may recognize for risk-based capital purposes under this subpart the use of a credit risk mitigant to hedge underlying exposures only if each of the conditions in this paragraph (b) is satisfied. A national bank or Federal savings association that meets these conditions must hold risk-based capital against any credit risk of the exposures it retains in connection with the synthetic securitization. A national bank or Federal savings association that fails to meet these conditions or chooses not to recognize the credit risk mitigant for purposes of this section must hold risk-based capital under this subpart against the underlying exposures as if they had not been synthetically securitized. The conditions are:

(1) The credit risk mitigant is:

(i) Financial collateral; or

(ii) A guarantee that meets all of the requirements of an eligible guarantee in §3.2 except for paragraph (3) of the definition; or

(iii) A credit derivative that meets all of the requirements of an eligible credit derivative except for paragraph (3) of the definition of eligible guarantee in §3.2.

(2) The national bank or Federal savings association transfers credit risk associated with the underlying exposures to third parties, and the terms and conditions in the credit risk mitigants employed do not include provisions that:

(i) Allow for the termination of the credit protection due to deterioration in the credit quality of the underlying exposures;

(ii) Require the national bank or Federal savings association to alter or replace the underlying exposures to improve the credit quality of the underlying exposures;

(iii) Increase the national bank's or Federal savings association's cost of credit protection in response to deterioration in the credit quality of the underlying exposures;

(iv) Increase the yield payable to parties other than the national bank or Federal savings association in response to a deterioration in the credit quality of the underlying exposures; or

(v) Provide for increases in a retained first loss position or credit enhancement provided by the national bank or Federal savings association after the inception of the securitization;

(3) The national bank or Federal savings association obtains a well-reasoned opinion from legal counsel that confirms the enforceability of the credit risk mitigant in all relevant jurisdictions; and

(4) Any clean-up calls relating to the securitization are eligible clean-up calls.

(c) *Due diligence requirements for securitization exposures.* (1) Except for exposures that are deducted from common equity tier 1 capital and exposures subject to §3.142(k), if a national bank or Federal savings association is unable to demonstrate to the satisfaction of the OCC a comprehensive understanding of the features of a securitization exposure that would materially affect the performance of the exposure, the national bank or Federal savings association must assign a 1,250 percent risk weight to the securitization exposure. The national bank's or Federal savings association's analysis must be commensurate with the complexity of the securitization exposure and the materiality of the position in relation to regulatory capital according to this part.

(2) A national bank or Federal savings association must demonstrate its comprehensive understanding of a securitization exposure under paragraph (c)(1) of this section, for each securitization exposure by:

(i) Conducting an analysis of the risk characteristics of a securitization exposure prior to acquiring the exposure and document such analysis within three business days after acquiring the exposure, considering:

(A) Structural features of the securitization that would materially impact the performance of the exposure, for example, the contractual cash flow waterfall, waterfall-related triggers, credit enhancements, liquidity enhancements, fair value triggers, the performance of organizations that service the position, and deal-specific definitions of default;

(B) Relevant information regarding the performance of the underlying credit exposure(s), for example, the percentage of loans 30, 60, and 90 days past due; default rates; prepayment rates; loans in foreclosure; property types; occupancy; average credit score or other measures of creditworthiness; average loan-to-value ratio; and industry and geographic diversification data on the underlying exposure(s);

(C) Relevant market data of the securitization, for example, bid-ask spreads, most recent sales price and historical price volatility, trading volume, implied market rating, and size, depth and concentration level of the market for the securitization; and

(D) For resecuritization exposures, performance information on the underlying securitization exposures, for example, the issuer name and credit quality, and the characteristics and performance of the exposures underlying the securitization exposures; and

(ii) On an on-going basis (no less frequently than quarterly), evaluating, reviewing, and updating as appropriate the analysis required under this section for each securitization exposure.

§3.142 Risk-weighted assets for securitization exposures.

(a) *Hierarchy of approaches*. Except as provided elsewhere in this section and in §3.141:

(1) A national bank or Federal savings association must deduct from common equity tier 1 capital any after-tax gain-on-sale resulting from a securitization and must apply a 1,250 percent risk weight to the portion of any CEIO that does not constitute after tax gain-on-sale;

(2) If a securitization exposure does not require deduction or a 1,250 percent risk weight under paragraph (a)(1) of this section, the national bank or Federal savings association must apply the supervisory formula approach in §3.143 to the exposure if the national bank or Federal savings association and the exposure qualify for the supervisory formula approach according to §3.143(a);

(3) If a securitization exposure does not require deduction or a 1,250 percent risk weight under paragraph (a)(1) of this section and does not qualify for the supervisory formula approach, the national bank or Federal savings association may apply the simplified supervisory formula approach under §3.144;

(4) If a securitization exposure does not require deduction or a 1,250 percent risk weight under paragraph (a)(1) of this section, does not qualify for the supervisory formula approach in §3.143, and the national bank or Federal savings association does not apply the simplified supervisory formula approach in §3.144, the national bank or Federal savings association must apply a 1,250 percent risk weight to the exposure; and

(5) If a securitization exposure is a derivative contract (other than protection provided by a national bank or Federal savings association in the form of a credit derivative) that has a first priority claim on the cash flows from the underlying exposures (notwithstanding amounts due under interest rate or currency derivative contracts, fees due, or other similar payments), a national bank or Federal savings association may choose to set the risk-weighted asset amount of the exposure equal to the amount of the exposure as determined in paragraph (e) of this section rather than apply the hierarchy of approaches described in paragraphs (a)(1) through (4) of this section.

(b) *Total risk-weighted assets for securitization exposures*. A national bank's or Federal savings association's total risk-weighted assets for securitization exposures is equal to the sum of its risk-weighted assets calculated using §§3.141 through 146.

(c) *Deductions*. A national bank or Federal savings association may calculate any deduction from common equity tier 1 capital for a securitization exposure net of any DTLs associated with the securitization exposure.

(d) *Maximum risk-based capital requirement*. Except as provided in §3.141(c), unless one or more underlying exposures does not meet the definition of a wholesale, retail, securitization, or equity exposure, the total risk-based capital requirement for all securitization exposures held by a single national bank or Federal savings association associated with a single securitization (excluding any risk-based capital requirements that relate to the national bank's or Federal savings association's gain-on-sale or CEIOs associated with the securitization) may not exceed the sum of:

(1) The national bank's or Federal savings association's total risk-based capital requirement for the underlying exposures calculated under this subpart as if the national bank or Federal savings association directly held the underlying exposures; and

(2) The total ECL of the underlying exposures calculated under this subpart.

(e) *Exposure amount of a securitization exposure.* (1) The exposure amount of an on-balance sheet securitization exposure that is not a repo-style transaction, eligible margin loan, OTC derivative contract, or cleared transaction is the national bank's or Federal savings association's carrying value.

(2) Except as provided in paragraph (m) of this section, the exposure amount of an off-balance sheet securitization exposure that is not an OTC derivative contract (other than a credit derivative), repo-style transaction, eligible margin loan, or cleared transaction (other than a credit derivative) is the notional amount of the exposure. For an off-balance-sheet securitization exposure to an ABCP program, such as an eligible ABCP liquidity facility, the notional amount may be reduced to the maximum potential amount that the national bank or Federal savings association could be required to fund given the ABCP program's current underlying assets (calculated without regard to the current credit quality of those assets).

(3) The exposure amount of a securitization exposure that is a repo-style transaction, eligible margin loan, or OTC derivative contract (other than a credit derivative) or cleared transaction (other than a credit derivative) is the EAD of the exposure as calculated in § 3.132 or § 3.133.

(f) *Overlapping exposures.* If a national bank or Federal savings association has multiple securitization exposures that provide duplicative coverage of the underlying exposures of a securitization (such as when a national bank or Federal savings association provides a program-wide credit enhancement and multiple pool-specific liquidity facilities to an ABCP program), the national bank or Federal savings association is not required to hold duplicative risk-based capital against the overlapping position. Instead, the national bank or Federal savings association may assign to the overlapping securitization exposure the applicable risk-based capital treatment under this subpart that results in the highest risk-based capital requirement.

(g) *Securitizations of non-IRB exposures.* Except as provided in § 3.141(c), if a national bank or Federal savings association has a securitization exposure where any underlying exposure is not a wholesale exposure, retail exposure, securitization exposure, or equity exposure, the national bank or Federal savings association:

(1) Must deduct from common equity tier 1 capital any after-tax gain-on-sale resulting from the securitization and apply a 1,250 percent risk weight to the portion of any CEIO that does not constitute gain-on-sale, if the national bank or Federal savings association is an originating national bank or Federal savings association;

(2) May apply the simplified supervisory formula approach in § 3.144 to the exposure, if the securitization exposure does not require deduction or a 1,250 percent risk weight under paragraph (g)(1) of this section;

(3) Must assign a 1,250 percent risk weight to the exposure if the securitization exposure does not require deduction or a 1,250 percent risk weight under paragraph (g)(1) of this section, does not qualify for the supervisory formula approach in § 3.143, and the national bank or Federal savings association does not apply the simplified supervisory formula approach in § 3.144 to the exposure.

(h) *Implicit support.* If a national bank or Federal savings association provides support to a securitization in excess of the national bank's or Federal savings association's contractual obligation to provide credit support to the securitization (implicit support):

(1) The national bank or Federal savings association must calculate a risk-weighted asset amount for underlying exposures associated with the securitization as if the exposures had not been securitized and must deduct from common equity tier 1 capital any after-tax gain-on-sale resulting from the securitization; and

(2) The national bank or Federal savings association must disclose publicly:

(i) That it has provided implicit support to the securitization; and

(ii) The regulatory capital impact to the national bank or Federal savings association of providing such implicit support.

(i) *Undrawn portion of a servicer cash advance facility.* (1) Notwithstanding any other provision of this subpart, a national bank or Federal savings association that is a servicer under an eligible servicer cash advance facility is not required to hold risk-based capital against potential future cash advance payments that it may be required to provide under the contract governing the facility.

(2) For a national bank or Federal savings association that acts as a servicer, the exposure amount for a servicer cash advance facility that is not an eligible servicer cash advance facility is equal to the amount of all potential future cash advance payments that the national bank or Federal savings association may be contractually required to provide during the subsequent 12 month period under the contract governing the facility.

(j) *Interest-only mortgage-backed securities.* Regardless of any other provisions in this part, the risk weight for a non-credit-enhancing interest-only mortgage-backed security may not be less than 100 percent.

(k) *Small-business loans and leases on personal property transferred with recourse.* (1) Notwithstanding any other provisions of this subpart E, a national bank or Federal savings association that has transferred small-business loans and leases on personal property (small-business obligations) with recourse must include in risk-weighted assets only the contractual amount of retained recourse if all the following conditions are met:

(i) The transaction is a sale under GAAP.

(ii) The national bank or Federal savings association establishes and maintains, pursuant to GAAP, a non-capital reserve sufficient to meet the national bank's or Federal savings association's reasonably estimated liability under the recourse arrangement.

(iii) The loans and leases are to businesses that meet the criteria for a small-business concern established by the Small Business Administration under section 3(a) of the Small Business Act (15 U.S.C. 632 *et seq.*); and

(iv) The national bank or Federal savings association is well-capitalized, as defined in 12 CFR 6.4. For purposes of determining whether a national bank or Federal savings association is well capitalized for purposes of this paragraph (k), the national bank's or Federal savings association's capital ratios must be calculated without regard to the capital treatment for transfers of small-business obligations with recourse specified in paragraph (k)(1) of this section.

(2) The total outstanding amount of recourse retained by a national bank or Federal savings association on transfers of small-business obligations subject to paragraph (k)(1) of this section cannot exceed 15 percent of the national bank's or Federal savings association's total capital.

(3) If a national bank or Federal savings association ceases to be well capitalized or exceeds the 15 percent capital limitation in paragraph (k)(2) of this section, the preferential capital treatment specified in paragraph (k)(1) of this section will continue to apply to any transfers of small-business obligations with recourse that occurred during the time that the national bank or Federal savings association was well capitalized and did not exceed the capital limit.

(4) The risk-based capital ratios of a national bank or Federal savings association must be calculated without regard to the capital treatment for transfers of small-business obligations with recourse specified in paragraph (k)(1) of this section.

(l) *N^{th}-to-default credit derivatives*—(1) *Protection provider.* A national bank or Federal savings association must determine a risk weight using the supervisory formula approach (SFA) pursuant to §3.143 or the simplified supervisory formula approach (SSFA) pursuant to §3.144 for an nth-to-default credit derivative in accordance with this paragraph (l). In the case of credit protection sold, a national bank or Federal savings association must determine its exposure in the nth-to-default credit derivative as the largest notional amount of all the underlying exposures.

(2) For purposes of determining the risk weight for an nth-to-default credit derivative using the SFA or the SSFA, the national bank or Federal savings association must calculate the attachment point and detachment point of its exposure as follows:

(i) The attachment point (parameter A) is the ratio of the sum of the notional amounts of all underlying exposures that are subordinated to the national bank's or Federal savings association's exposure to the total notional amount of all underlying exposures. For purposes of the SSFA, parameter A is expressed as a decimal value between zero and one. For purposes of using the SFA to calculate the risk weight for its exposure in an nth-to-default credit derivative, parameter A must be set equal to the credit enhancement level (L) input to the SFA formula. In the case of a first-to-default credit derivative, there are no underlying exposures that are subordinated to the national bank's or Federal savings association's exposure. In the case of a second-or-subsequent-to-default credit derivative, the smallest (n-1) risk-weighted asset amounts of the underlying exposure(s) are subordinated to the national bank's or Federal savings association's exposure.

(ii) The detachment point (parameter D) equals the sum of parameter A plus the ratio of the notional amount of the national bank's or Federal savings association's exposure in the nth-to-default credit derivative to the total notional amount of all underlying exposures. For purposes of the SSFA, parameter W is expressed as a decimal value between zero and one. For purposes of the SFA, parameter D must be set to equal L plus the thickness of tranche T input to the SFA formula.

(3) A national bank or Federal savings association that does not use the SFA or the SSFA to determine a risk weight for its exposure in an nth-to-default credit derivative must assign a risk weight of 1,250 percent to the exposure.

(4) *Protection purchaser*—(i) *First-to-default credit derivatives.* A national bank or Federal savings association that obtains credit protection on a group of underlying exposures through a first-to-default credit derivative that meets the rules of recognition of § 3.134(b) must determine its risk-based capital requirement under this subpart for the underlying exposures as if the national bank or Federal savings association synthetically securitized the underlying exposure with the lowest risk-based capital requirement and had obtained no credit risk mitigant on the other underlying exposures. A national bank or Federal savings association must calculate a risk-based capital requirement for counterparty credit risk according to § 3.132 for a first-to-default credit derivative that does not meet the rules of recognition of § 3.134(b).

(ii) *Second-or-subsequent-to-default credit derivatives.* (A) A national bank or Federal savings association that obtains credit protection on a group of underlying exposures through a nth-to-default credit derivative that meets the rules of recognition of § 3.134(b) (other than a first-to-default credit derivative) may recognize the credit risk mitigation benefits of the derivative only if:

(*1*) The national bank or Federal savings association also has obtained credit protection on the same underlying exposures in the form of first-through-(n-1)-to-default credit derivatives; or

(*2*) If n-1 of the underlying exposures have already defaulted.

(B) If a national bank or Federal savings association satisfies the requirements of paragraph (l)(3)(ii)(A) of this section, the national bank or Federal savings association must determine its risk-based capital requirement for the underlying exposures as if the bank had only synthetically securitized the underlying exposure with the nth smallest risk-based capital requirement and had obtained no credit risk mitigant on the other underlying exposures.

(C) A national bank or Federal savings association must calculate a risk-based capital requirement for counterparty credit risk according to

§3.132 for a nth-to-default credit derivative that does not meet the rules of recognition of §3.134(b).

(m) *Guarantees and credit derivatives other than n^{th}-to-default credit derivatives*—(1) *Protection provider.* For a guarantee or credit derivative (other than an nth-to-default credit derivative) provided by a national bank or Federal savings association that covers the full amount or a pro rata share of a securitization exposure's principal and interest, the national bank or Federal savings association must risk weight the guarantee or credit derivative as if it holds the portion of the reference exposure covered by the guarantee or credit derivative.

(2) *Protection purchaser.* (i) A national bank or Federal savings association that purchases an OTC credit derivative (other than an nth-to-default credit derivative) that is recognized under §3.145 as a credit risk mitigant (including via recognized collateral) is not required to compute a separate counterparty credit risk capital requirement under §3.131 in accordance with §3.132(c)(3).

(ii) If a national bank or Federal savings association cannot, or chooses not to, recognize a purchased credit derivative as a credit risk mitigant under §3.145, the national bank or Federal savings association must determine the exposure amount of the credit derivative under §3.132(c).

(A) If the national bank or Federal savings association purchases credit protection from a counterparty that is not a securitization SPE, the national bank or Federal savings association must determine the risk weight for the exposure according §3.131.

(B) If the national bank or Federal savings association purchases the credit protection from a counterparty that is a securitization SPE, the national bank or Federal savings association must determine the risk weight for the exposure according to this section, including paragraph (a)(5) of this section for a credit derivative that has a first priority claim on the cash flows from the underlying exposures of the securitization SPE (notwithstanding amounts due under interest rate or currency derivative contracts, fees due, or other similar payments.

§3.143 Supervisory formula approach (SFA).

(a) *Eligibility requirements.* A national bank or Federal savings association must use the SFA to determine its risk-weighted asset amount for a securitization exposure if the national bank or Federal savings association can calculate on an ongoing basis each of the SFA parameters in paragraph (e) of this section.

(b) *Mechanics.* The risk-weighted asset amount for a securitization exposure equals its SFA risk-based capital requirement as calculated under paragraph (c) and (d) of this section, multiplied by 12.5.

(c) *The SFA risk-based capital requirement.* (1) If K_{IRB} is greater than or equal to L + T, an exposure's SFA risk-based capital requirement equals the exposure amount.

(2) If K_{IRB} is less than or equal to L, an exposure's SFA risk-based capital requirement is UE multiplied by TP multiplied by the greater of:

(i) $F \cdot T$ (where F is 0.016 for all securitization exposures); or

(ii) $S[L + T] - S[L]$.

(3) If K_{IRB} is greater than L and less than L + T, the national bank or Federal savings association must apply a 1,250 percent risk weight to an amount equal to $UE \cdot TP (K_{IRB} - L)$, and the exposure's SFA risk-based capital requirement is UE multiplied by TP multiplied by the greater of:

(i) $F \cdot (T - (K_{IRB} - L))$ (where F is 0.016 for all other securitization exposures); or

(ii) $S[L + T] - S[K_{IRB}]$.

(d) *The supervisory formula:*

$$(1)\quad S[Y]=\begin{cases} Y & \text{when } Y \le K_{IRB} \\ K_{IRB}+K[Y]-K[K_{IRB}]+\dfrac{d\cdot K_{IRB}}{20}\left(1-e^{\frac{20\cdot(K_{IRB}-Y)}{K_{IRB}}}\right) & \text{when } Y > K_{IRB} \end{cases}$$

$$(2)\quad K[Y]=(1-h)\cdot\left[(1-\beta[Y;a,b])\cdot Y+\beta[Y;a+1,b]\cdot c\right]$$

$$(3)\quad h=\left(1-\frac{K_{IRB}}{EWALGD}\right)^{N}$$

$$(4)\quad a = g \cdot c$$

$$(5)\quad b = g\cdot(1-c)$$

$$(6)\quad c=\frac{K_{IRB}}{1-h}$$

$$(7)\quad g=\frac{(1-c)\cdot c}{f}-1$$

$$(8)\quad f=\frac{v+K_{IRB}^{2}}{1-h}-c^{2}+\frac{(1-K_{IRB})\cdot K_{IRB}-v}{(1-h)\cdot 1000}$$

$$(9)\quad v=K_{IRB}\cdot\frac{(EWALGD-K_{IRB})+.25\cdot(1-EWALGD)}{N}$$

$$(10)\quad d=1-(1-h)\cdot(1-\beta[K_{IRB};a,b]).$$

(11) In these expressions, β [Y; a, b] refers to the cumulative beta distribution with parameters a and b evaluated at Y. In the case where N = 1 and EWALGD = 100 percent, S[Y] in formula (1) must be calculated with K[Y] set equal to the product of K_{IRB} and Y, and d set equal to 1 - K_{IRB}.

(e) *SFA parameters.* For purposes of the calculations in paragraphs (c) and (d) of this section:

(1) *Amount of the underlying exposures (UE).* UE is the EAD of any underlying exposures that are wholesale and retail exposures (including the amount of any funded spread accounts, cash collateral accounts, and other similar funded credit enhancements) plus the amount of any underlying exposures that are securitization exposures (as defined in § 3.142(e)) plus the adjusted carrying value of any underlying exposures that are equity exposures (as defined in § 3.151(b)).

(2) *Tranche percentage (TP).* TP is the ratio of the amount of the national bank's or Federal savings association's securitization exposure to the amount of the tranche that contains the securitization exposure.

(3) *Capital requirement on underlying exposures (K_{IRB}).* (i) K_{IRB} is the ratio of:

(A) The sum of the risk-based capital requirements for the underlying exposures plus the expected credit losses of the underlying exposures (as determined under this subpart E as if the underlying exposures were directly held by the national bank or Federal savings association); to

(B) UE.

(ii) The calculation of K_{IRB} must reflect the effects of any credit risk mitigant applied to the underlying exposures (either to an individual underlying exposure, to a group of underlying exposures, or to all of the underlying exposures).

(iii) All assets related to the securitization are treated as underlying exposures, including assets in a reserve account (such as a cash collateral account).

(4) *Credit enhancement level (L).* (i) L is the ratio of:

(A) The amount of all securitization exposures subordinated to the tranche that contains the national bank's or Federal savings association's securitization exposure; to

(B) UE.

(ii) A national bank or Federal savings association must determine L before considering the effects of any tranche-specific credit enhancements.

(iii) Any gain-on-sale or CEIO associated with the securitization may not be included in L.

(iv) Any reserve account funded by accumulated cash flows from the underlying exposures that is subordinated to the tranche that contains the national bank's or Federal savings association's securitization exposure may be included in the numerator and denominator of L to the extent cash has accumulated in the account. Unfunded reserve accounts (that is, reserve accounts that are to be funded from future cash flows from the underlying exposures) may not be included in the calculation of L.

(v) In some cases, the purchase price of receivables will reflect a discount that provides credit enhancement (for example, first loss protection) for all or certain tranches of the securitization. When this arises, L should be calculated inclusive of this discount if the discount provides credit enhancement for the securitization exposure.

(5) *Thickness of tranche (T).* T is the ratio of:

(i) The amount of the tranche that contains the national bank's or Federal savings association's securitization exposure; to

(ii) UE.

(6) *Effective number of exposures (N).* (i) Unless the national bank or Federal savings association elects to use the formula provided in paragraph (f) of this section,

$$N = \frac{(\sum_i EAD_i)^2}{\sum_i EAD_i^2}$$

where EAD_i represents the EAD associated with the ith instrument in the underlying exposures.

(ii) Multiple exposures to one obligor must be treated as a single underlying exposure.

(iii) In the case of a resecuritization, the national bank or Federal savings association must treat each underlying exposure as a single underlying exposure and must not look through to the originally securitized underlying exposures.

(7) *Exposure-weighted average loss given default (EWALGD).* EWALGD is calculated as:

$$EWALGD = \frac{\sum_i LGD_i \cdot EAD_i}{\sum_i EAD_i}$$

where LGD_i represents the average LGD associated with all exposures to the ith obligor. In the case of a resecuritization, an LGD of 100 percent must be assumed for the underlying exposures that are themselves securitization exposures.

(f) *Simplified method for computing N and EWALGD.* (1) If all underlying exposures of a securitization are retail exposures, a national bank or Federal savings association may apply the SFA using the following simplifications:

(i) h = 0; and

(ii) v = 0.

(2) Under the conditions in §§ 3.143(f)(3) and (f)(4), a national bank or Federal savings association may employ a simplified method for calculating N and EWALGD.

(3) If C_1 is no more than 0.03, a national bank or Federal savings association may set EWALGD = 0.50 if none of the underlying exposures is a securitization exposure, or may set EWALGD = 1 if one or more of the underlying exposures is a securitization exposure, and may set N equal to the following amount:

$$N = \frac{1}{C_1 C_m + \left(\frac{C_m - C_1}{m-1}\right) \max(1 - mC_1, 0)}$$

where:

(i) C_m is the ratio of the sum of the amounts of the 'm' largest underlying exposures to UE; and

(ii) The level of m is to be selected by the national bank or Federal savings association.

(4) Alternatively, if only C_1 is available and C_1 is no more than 0.03, the national bank or Federal savings association may set EWALGD = 0.50 if none of the underlying exposures is a securitization exposure, or may set EWALGD = 1 if one or more of the underlying exposures is a securitization exposure and may set $N = 1/C_1$.

§ 3.144 Simplified supervisory formula approach (SSFA).

(a) *General requirements for the SSFA.* To use the SSFA to determine the risk weight for a securitization exposure, a national bank or Federal savings association must have data that enables it to assign accurately the parameters described in paragraph (b) of this section. Data used to assign the parameters described in paragraph (b) of this section must be the most currently available data; if the contracts governing the underlying exposures of the securitization require payments on a monthly or quarterly basis, the data used to assign the parameters described in paragraph (b) of this section must be no more than 91 calendar days old. A national bank or Federal savings association that does not have the appropriate data to assign the parameters described in paragraph (b) of this section must assign a risk weight of 1,250 percent to the exposure.

(b) *SSFA parameters.* To calculate the risk weight for a securitization exposure using the SSFA, a national bank or Federal savings association must have accurate information on the following five inputs to the SSFA calculation:

(1) K_G is the weighted-average (with unpaid principal used as the weight for each exposure) total capital requirement of the underlying exposures calculated using subpart D of this part. K_G

is expressed as a decimal value between zero and one (that is, an average risk weight of 100 percent represents a value of K_G equal to 0.08).

(2) Parameter W is expressed as a decimal value between zero and one. Parameter W is the ratio of the sum of the dollar amounts of any underlying exposures of the securitization that meet any of the criteria as set forth in paragraphs (b)(2)(i) through (vi) of this section to the balance, measured in dollars, of underlying exposures:

(i) Ninety days or more past due;

(ii) Subject to a bankruptcy or insolvency proceeding;

(iii) In the process of foreclosure;

(iv) Held as real estate owned;

(v) Has contractually deferred payments for 90 days or more, other than principal or interest payments deferred on:

(A) Federally-guaranteed student loans, in accordance with the terms of those guarantee programs; or

(B) Consumer loans, including non-federally-guaranteed student loans, provided that such payments are deferred pursuant to provisions included in the contract at the time funds are disbursed that provide for period(s) of deferral that are not initiated based on changes in the creditworthiness of the borrower; or

(vi) Is in default.

(3) Parameter A is the attachment point for the exposure, which represents the threshold at which credit losses will first be allocated to the exposure. Except as provided in section 142(l) for n^{th}-to-default credit derivatives, parameter A equals the ratio of the current dollar amount of underlying exposures that are subordinated to the exposure of the national bank or Federal savings association to the current dollar amount of underlying exposures. Any reserve account funded by the accumulated cash flows from the underlying exposures that is subordinated to the national bank's or Federal savings association's securitization exposure may be included in the calculation of parameter A to the extent that cash is present in the account. Parameter A is expressed as a decimal value between zero and one.

(4) Parameter D is the detachment point for the exposure, which represents the threshold at which credit losses of principal allocated to the exposure would result in a total loss of principal. Except as provided in section 142(l) for n^{th}-to-default credit derivatives, parameter D equals parameter A plus the ratio of the current dollar amount of the securitization exposures that are *pari passu* with the exposure (that is, have equal seniority with respect to credit risk) to the current dollar amount of the underlying exposures. Parameter D is expressed as a decimal value between zero and one.

(5) A supervisory calibration parameter, p, is equal to 0.5 for securitization exposures that are not resecuritization exposures and equal to 1.5 for resecuritization exposures.

(c) *Mechanics of the SSFA.* K_G and W are used to calculate K_A, the augmented value of K_G, which reflects the observed credit quality of the underlying exposures. K_A is defined in paragraph (d) of this section. The values of parameters A and D, relative to K_A determine the risk weight assigned to a securitization exposure as described in paragraph (d) of this section. The risk weight assigned to a securitization exposure, or portion of a securitization exposure, as appropriate, is the larger of the risk weight determined in accordance with this paragraph (c), paragraph (d) of this section, and a risk weight of 20 percent.

(1) When the detachment point, parameter D, for a securitization exposure is less than or equal to K_A, the exposure must be assigned a risk weight of 1,250 percent;

(2) When the attachment point, parameter A, for a securitization exposure is greater than or equal to K_A, the national bank or Federal savings association must calculate the risk weight in accordance with paragraph (d) of this section;

(3) When A is less than K_A and D is greater than K_A, the risk weight is a weighted-average of 1,250 percent and 1,250 percent times K_{SSFA} calculated in accordance with paragraph (d) of this section. For the purpose of this weighted-average calculation:

(i) The weight assigned to 1,250 percent equals $\frac{K_A - A}{D - A}$; and

(ii) The weight assigned to 1,250 percent times K_{SSFA} equals $\frac{D - K_A}{D - A}$. The risk weight will be set equal to:

$$Risk\ Weight = \left[\left(\frac{K_A - A}{D - A}\right) \cdot 1{,}250\ percent\right] + \left[\left(\frac{D - K_A}{D - A}\right) \cdot 1{,}250\ percent \cdot K_{SSFA}\right]$$

(d) SSFA equation. (1) The [BANK] must define the following parameters:

$$K_A = (1 - W) \cdot K_G + (0.5 \cdot W)$$

$$a = -\frac{1}{p \cdot K_A}$$

$$u = D - K_A$$

$$l = \max(A - K_A, 0)$$

$e = 2.71828$, the base of the natural logarithms.

(2) Then the [BANK] must calculate K_{SSFA} according to the following equation:

$$K_{SSFA} = \frac{e^{a \cdot u} - e^{a \cdot l}}{a(u - l)}$$

(3) The risk weight for the exposure (expressed as a percent) is equal to $K_{SSFA} \times 1{,}250$.

§ 3.145 Recognition of credit risk mitigants for securitization exposures.

(a) *General.* An originating national bank or Federal savings association that has obtained a credit risk mitigant to hedge its securitization exposure to a synthetic or traditional securitization that satisfies the operational criteria in § 3.141 may recognize the credit risk mitigant, but only as provided in this section. An investing national bank or Federal savings association that has obtained a credit risk mitigant to hedge a securitization exposure may recognize the credit risk mitigant, but only as provided in this section.

(b) *Collateral*—(1) *Rules of recognition.* A national bank or Federal savings association may recognize financial collateral in determining the national bank's or Federal savings association's risk-weighted asset amount for a securitization exposure (other than a repo-style transaction, an eligible margin loan, or an OTC derivative contract for which the national bank or Federal savings association has reflected collateral in its determination of exposure amount under §3.132) as follows. The national bank's or Federal savings association's risk-weighted asset amount for the collateralized securitization exposure is equal to the risk-weighted asset amount for the securitization exposure as calculated under the SSFA in §3.144 or under the SFA in §3.143 multiplied by the ratio of adjusted exposure amount (SE*) to original exposure amount (SE),

Where:

(i) SE* = max {0, [SE − C × $(1 - H_s - H_{fx})$]};

(ii) SE = the amount of the securitization exposure calculated under §3.142(e);

(iii) C = the current fair value of the collateral;

(iv) H_s = the haircut appropriate to the collateral type; and

(v) H_{fx} = the haircut appropriate for any currency mismatch between the collateral and the exposure.

(2) Mixed collateral. Where the collateral is a basket of different asset types or a basket of assets denominated in different currencies, the haircut on the basket will be $H = \sum_i a_i H_i$, where a_i is the current fair value of the asset in the basket divided by the current fair value of all assets in the basket and H_i is the haircut applicable to that asset.

(3) *Standard supervisory haircuts.* Unless a national bank or Federal savings association qualifies for use of and uses own-estimates haircuts in paragraph (b)(4) of this section:

(i) A national bank or Federal savings association must use the collateral type haircuts (H_s) in Table 1 to §3.132 of this subpart;

(ii) A national bank or Federal savings association must use a currency mismatch haircut (H_{fx}) of 8 percent if the exposure and the collateral are denominated in different currencies;

(iii) A national bank or Federal savings association must multiply the supervisory haircuts obtained in paragraphs (b)(3)(i) and (ii) of this section by the square root of 6.5 (which equals 2.549510); and

(iv) A national bank or Federal savings association must adjust the supervisory haircuts upward on the basis of a holding period longer than 65 business days where and as appropriate to take into account the illiquidity of the collateral.

(4) *Own estimates for haircuts.* With the prior written approval of the OCC, a national bank or Federal savings association may calculate haircuts using its own internal estimates of market price volatility and foreign exchange volatility, subject to §3.132(b)(2)(iii). The minimum holding period (T_M) for securitization exposures is 65 business days.

(c) *Guarantees and credit derivatives*—(1) *Limitations on recognition.* A national bank or Federal savings association may only recognize an eligible guarantee or eligible credit derivative provided by an eligible guarantor in determining the national bank's or Federal savings association's risk-weighted asset amount for a securitization exposure.

(2) *ECL for securitization exposures.* When a national bank or Federal savings association recognizes an eligible guarantee or eligible credit derivative provided by an eligible guarantor in determining the national bank's or Federal savings association's risk-weighted asset amount for a securitization exposure, the national bank or Federal savings association must also:

(i) Calculate ECL for the protected portion of the exposure using the same risk parameters that it uses for calculating the risk-weighted asset amount of the exposure as described in paragraph (c)(3) of this section; and

(ii) Add the exposure's ECL to the national bank's or Federal savings association's total ECL.

(3) *Rules of recognition.* A national bank or Federal savings association may recognize an eligible guarantee or eligible credit derivative provided by an eligible guarantor in determining the national bank's or Federal savings association's risk-weighted asset amount for the securitization exposure as follows:

(i) *Full coverage.* If the protection amount of the eligible guarantee or eligible credit derivative equals or exceeds the amount of the securitization exposure, the national bank or Federal savings association may set the risk-weighted asset amount for the securitization exposure equal to the risk-weighted asset amount for a direct exposure to the eligible guarantor (as determined in the wholesale risk weight function described in § 3.131), using the national bank's or Federal savings association's PD for the guarantor, the national bank's or Federal savings association's LGD for the guarantee or credit derivative, and an EAD equal to the amount of the securitization exposure (as determined in § 3.142(e)).

(ii) *Partial coverage.* If the protection amount of the eligible guarantee or eligible credit derivative is less than the amount of the securitization exposure, the national bank or Federal savings association may set the risk-weighted asset amount for the securitization exposure equal to the sum of:

(A) *Covered portion.* The risk-weighted asset amount for a direct exposure to the eligible guarantor (as determined in the wholesale risk weight function described in § 3.131), using the national bank's or Federal savings association's PD for the guarantor, the national bank's or Federal savings association's LGD for the guarantee or credit derivative, and an EAD equal to the protection amount of the credit risk mitigant; and

(B) *Uncovered portion.* (*1*) 1.0 minus the ratio of the protection amount of the eligible guarantee or eligible credit derivative to the amount of the securitization exposure); multiplied by

(*2*) The risk-weighted asset amount for the securitization exposure without the credit risk mitigant (as determined in §§ 3.142 through 146).

(4) *Mismatches.* The national bank or Federal savings association must make applicable adjustments to the protection amount as required in § 3.134(d), (e), and (f) for any hedged securitization exposure and any more senior securitization exposure that benefits from the hedge. In the context of a synthetic securitization, when an eligible guarantee or eligible credit derivative covers multiple hedged exposures that have different residual maturities, the national bank or Federal savings association must use the longest residual maturity of any of the hedged exposures as the residual maturity of all the hedged exposures.

§§ 3.146–3.150 [Reserved]

RISK-WEIGHTED ASSETS FOR EQUITY EXPOSURES

§ 3.151 Introduction and exposure measurement.

(a) *General.* (1) To calculate its risk-weighted asset amounts for equity exposures that are not equity exposures to investment funds, a national bank or Federal savings association may apply either the Simple Risk Weight Approach (SRWA) in § 3.152 or, if it qualifies to do so, the Internal Models Approach (IMA) in § 3.153. A national bank or Federal savings association must use the look-through approaches provided in § 3.154 to calculate its risk-weighted asset amounts for equity exposures to investment funds.

(2) A national bank or Federal savings association must treat an investment in a separate account (as defined in § 3.2), as if it were an equity exposure to an investment fund as provided in § 3.154.

(3) *Stable value protection.* (i) Stable value protection means a contract where the provider of the contract is obligated to pay:

(A) The policy owner of a separate account an amount equal to the shortfall between the fair value and cost basis of the separate account when the policy owner of the separate account surrenders the policy, or

(B) The beneficiary of the contract an amount equal to the shortfall between the fair value and book value of a specified portfolio of assets.

(ii) A national bank or Federal savings association that purchases stable value protection on its investment in a separate account must treat the portion of the carrying value of its investment in the separate account attributable to the stable value protection as an exposure to the provider of the protection and the remaining portion of the carrying value of its separate account as an equity exposure to an investment fund.

(iii) A national bank or Federal savings association that provides stable value protection must treat the exposure as an equity derivative with an adjusted carrying value determined as the sum of §3.151(b)(1) and (2).

(b) *Adjusted carrying value.* For purposes of this subpart, the adjusted carrying value of an equity exposure is:

(1) For the on-balance sheet component of an equity exposure, the national bank's or Federal savings association's carrying value of the exposure;

(2) For the off-balance sheet component of an equity exposure, the effective notional principal amount of the exposure, the size of which is equivalent to a hypothetical on-balance sheet position in the underlying equity instrument that would evidence the same change in fair value (measured in dollars) for a given small change in the price of the underlying equity instrument, minus the adjusted carrying value of the on-balance sheet component of the exposure as calculated in paragraph (b)(1) of this section.

(3) For unfunded equity commitments that are unconditional, the effective notional principal amount is the notional amount of the commitment. For unfunded equity commitments that are conditional, the effective notional principal amount is the national bank's or Federal savings association's best estimate of the amount that would be funded under economic downturn conditions.

§3.152 Simple risk weight approach (SRWA).

(a) *General.* Under the SRWA, a national bank's or Federal savings association's aggregate risk-weighted asset amount for its equity exposures is equal to the sum of the risk-weighted asset amounts for each of the national bank's or Federal savings association's individual equity exposures (other than equity exposures to an investment fund) as determined in this section and the risk-weighted asset amounts for each of the national bank's or Federal savings association's individual equity exposures to an investment fund as determined in §3.154.

(b) *SRWA computation for individual equity exposures.* A national bank or Federal savings association must determine the risk-weighted asset amount for an individual equity exposure (other than an equity exposure to an investment fund) by multiplying the adjusted carrying value of the equity exposure or the effective portion and ineffective portion of a hedge pair (as defined in paragraph (c) of this section) by the lowest applicable risk weight in this section.

(1) *Zero percent risk weight equity exposures.* An equity exposure to an entity whose credit exposures are exempt from the 0.03 percent PD floor in §3.131(d)(2) is assigned a zero percent risk weight.

(2) *20 percent risk weight equity exposures.* An equity exposure to a Federal Home Loan Bank or the Federal Agricultural Mortgage Corporation (Farmer Mac) is assigned a 20 percent risk weight.

(3) *100 percent risk weight equity exposures.* The following equity exposures are assigned a 100 percent risk weight:

(i) *Community development equity exposures.* An equity exposure that qualifies as a community development investment under section 24 (Eleventh) of the National Bank Act, excluding equity exposures to an unconsolidated small business investment company and equity exposures held through a consolidated small business investment company described in section 302 of the Small Business Investment Act.

(ii) *Effective portion of hedge pairs.* The effective portion of a hedge pair.

(iii) *Non-significant equity exposures.* Equity exposures, excluding significant investments in the capital of an unconsolidated institution in the form of common stock and exposures to an investment firm that would meet the definition of a traditional securitization were it not for the OCC's application of paragraph (8) of that definition in § 3.2 and has greater than immaterial leverage, to the extent that the aggregate adjusted carrying value of the exposures does not exceed 10 percent of the national bank's or Federal savings association's total capital.

(A) To compute the aggregate adjusted carrying value of a national bank's or Federal savings association's equity exposures for purposes of this section, the national bank or Federal savings association may exclude equity exposures described in paragraphs (b)(1), (b)(2), (b)(3)(i), and (b)(3)(ii) of this section, the equity exposure in a hedge pair with the smaller adjusted carrying value, and a proportion of each equity exposure to an investment fund equal to the proportion of the assets of the investment fund that are not equity exposures or that meet the criterion of paragraph (b)(3)(i) of this section. If a national bank or Federal savings association does not know the actual holdings of the investment fund, the national bank or Federal savings association may calculate the proportion of the assets of the fund that are not equity exposures based on the terms of the prospectus, partnership agreement, or similar contract that defines the fund's permissible investments. If the sum of the investment limits for all exposure classes within the fund exceeds 100 percent, the national bank or Federal savings association must assume for purposes of this section that the investment fund invests to the maximum extent possible in equity exposures.

(B) When determining which of a national bank's or Federal savings association's equity exposures qualifies for a 100 percent risk weight under this section, a national bank or Federal savings association first must include equity exposures to unconsolidated small business investment companies or held through consolidated small business investment companies described in section 302 of the Small Business Investment Act, then must include publicly traded equity exposures (including those held indirectly through investment funds), and then must include non-publicly traded equity exposures (including those held indirectly through investment funds).

(4) *250 percent risk weight equity exposures.* Significant investments in the capital of unconsolidated financial institutions in the form of common stock that are not deducted from capital pursuant to § 3.22(b)(4) are assigned a 250 percent risk weight.

(5) *300 percent risk weight equity exposures.* A publicly traded equity exposure (other than an equity exposure described in paragraph (b)(6) of this section and including the ineffective portion of a hedge pair) is assigned a 300 percent risk weight.

(6) *400 percent risk weight equity exposures.* An equity exposure (other than an equity exposure described in paragraph (b)(6) of this section) that is not publicly traded is assigned a 400 percent risk weight.

(7) *600 percent risk weight equity exposures.* An equity exposure to an investment firm that:

(i) Would meet the definition of a traditional securitization were it not for the OCC's application of paragraph (8) of that definition in § 3.2; and

(ii) Has greater than immaterial leverage is assigned a 600 percent risk weight.

(c) *Hedge transactions*—(1) *Hedge pair.* A hedge pair is two equity exposures that form an effective hedge so long as each equity exposure is publicly traded or has a return that is primarily based on a publicly traded equity exposure.

(2) *Effective hedge.* Two equity exposures form an effective hedge if the exposures either have the same remaining maturity or each has a remaining maturity of at least three months; the hedge relationship is formally documented in a prospective manner (that is, before the national bank or Federal savings association acquires at least one of the equity exposures); the documentation specifies the measure of effectiveness (E) the national bank or Federal savings association will use for the hedge relationship throughout the life of the transaction; and the hedge relationship has an E greater than or equal to 0.8. A national bank or Federal savings association must measure E at least quarterly and must use one of three alternative measures of E:

(i) Under the dollar-offset method of measuring effectiveness, the national bank or Federal savings association must determine the ratio of value change (RVC). The RVC is the ratio of the cumulative sum of the periodic changes in value of one equity exposure to the cumulative sum of the periodic changes in the value of the other equity exposure. If RVC is positive, the hedge is not effective and E equals zero. If RVC is negative and greater than or equal to −1 (that is, between zero and −1), then E equals the absolute value of RVC. If RVC is negative and less than −1, then E equals 2 plus RVC.

(ii) Under the variability-reduction method of measuring effectiveness:

$$E = 1 - \frac{\sum_{t=1}^{T} \left(X_t - X_{t-1}\right)^2}{\sum_{t=1}^{T} \left(A_t - A_{t-1}\right)^2}, \text{ where}$$

(A) $X_t = A_t - B_t$;

(B) $A_t =$ the value at time t of one exposure in a hedge pair; and

(C) $B_t =$ the value at time t of the other exposure in a hedge pair.

(iii) Under the regression method of measuring effectiveness, E equals the coefficient of determination of a regression in which the change in value of one exposure in a hedge pair is the dependent variable and the change in value of the other exposure in a hedge pair is the independent variable. However, if the estimated regression coefficient is positive, then the value of E is zero.

(3) The effective portion of a hedge pair is E multiplied by the greater of the adjusted carrying values of the equity exposures forming a hedge pair.

(4) The ineffective portion of a hedge pair is (1–E) multiplied by the greater of the adjusted carrying values of the equity exposures forming a hedge pair.

§3.153 Internal models approach (IMA).

(a) *General.* A national bank or Federal savings association may calculate its risk-weighted asset amount for equity exposures using the IMA by modeling publicly traded and non-publicly traded equity exposures (in accordance with paragraph (c) of this section) or by modeling only publicly traded equity exposures (in accordance with paragraphs (c) and (d) of this section).

(b) *Qualifying criteria.* To qualify to use the IMA to calculate risk-weighted assets for equity exposures, a national bank or Federal savings association must receive prior written approval from the OCC. To receive such approval, the national bank or Federal savings association must demonstrate to the OCC's satisfaction that the national bank or Federal savings association meets the following criteria:

(1) The national bank or Federal savings association must have one or more models that:

(i) Assess the potential decline in value of its modeled equity exposures;

(ii) Are commensurate with the size, complexity, and composition of the national bank's or Federal savings association's modeled equity exposures; and

(iii) Adequately capture both general market risk and idiosyncratic risk.

(2) The national bank's or Federal savings association's model must produce an estimate of potential losses

for its modeled equity exposures that is no less than the estimate of potential losses produced by a VaR methodology employing a 99th percentile one-tailed confidence interval of the distribution of quarterly returns for a benchmark portfolio of equity exposures comparable to the national bank's or Federal savings association's modeled equity exposures using a long-term sample period.

(3) The number of risk factors and exposures in the sample and the data period used for quantification in the national bank's or Federal savings association's model and benchmarking exercise must be sufficient to provide confidence in the accuracy and robustness of the national bank's or Federal savings association's estimates.

(4) The national bank's or Federal savings association's model and benchmarking process must incorporate data that are relevant in representing the risk profile of the national bank's or Federal savings association's modeled equity exposures, and must include data from at least one equity market cycle containing adverse market movements relevant to the risk profile of the national bank's or Federal savings association's modeled equity exposures. In addition, the national bank's or Federal savings association's benchmarking exercise must be based on daily market prices for the benchmark portfolio. If the national bank's or Federal savings association's model uses a scenario methodology, the national bank or Federal savings association must demonstrate that the model produces a conservative estimate of potential losses on the national bank's or Federal savings association's modeled equity exposures over a relevant long-term market cycle. If the national bank or Federal savings association employs risk factor models, the national bank or Federal savings association must demonstrate through empirical analysis the appropriateness of the risk factors used.

(5) The national bank or Federal savings association must be able to demonstrate, using theoretical arguments and empirical evidence, that any proxies used in the modeling process are comparable to the national bank's or Federal savings association's modeled equity exposures and that the national bank or Federal savings association has made appropriate adjustments for differences. The national bank or Federal savings association must derive any proxies for its modeled equity exposures and benchmark portfolio using historical market data that are relevant to the national bank's or Federal savings association's modeled equity exposures and benchmark portfolio (or, where not, must use appropriately adjusted data), and such proxies must be robust estimates of the risk of the national bank's or Federal savings association's modeled equity exposures.

(c) *Risk-weighted assets calculation for a national bank or Federal savings association using the IMA for publicly traded and non-publicly traded equity exposures.* If a national bank or Federal savings association models publicly traded and non-publicly traded equity exposures, the national bank's or Federal savings association's aggregate risk-weighted asset amount for its equity exposures is equal to the sum of:

(1) The risk-weighted asset amount of each equity exposure that qualifies for a 0 percent, 20 percent, or 100 percent risk weight under § 3.152(b)(1) through (b)(3)(i) (as determined under § 3.152) and each equity exposure to an investment fund (as determined under § 3.154); and

(2) The greater of:

(i) The estimate of potential losses on the national bank's or Federal savings association's equity exposures (other than equity exposures referenced in paragraph (c)(1) of this section) generated by the national bank's or Federal savings association's internal equity exposure model multiplied by 12.5; or

(ii) The sum of:

(A) 200 percent multiplied by the aggregate adjusted carrying value of the national bank's or Federal savings association's publicly traded equity exposures that do not belong to a hedge pair, do not qualify for a 0 percent, 20 percent, or 100 percent risk weight under § 3.152(b)(1) through (b)(3)(i), and are not equity exposures to an investment fund;

(B) 200 percent multiplied by the aggregate ineffective portion of all hedge pairs; and

(C) 300 percent multiplied by the aggregate adjusted carrying value of the national bank's or Federal savings association's equity exposures that are not publicly traded, do not qualify for a 0 percent, 20 percent, or 100 percent risk weight under § 3.152(b)(1) through (b)(3)(i), and are not equity exposures to an investment fund.

(d) *Risk-weighted assets calculation for a national bank or Federal savings association using the IMA only for publicly traded equity exposures.* If a national bank or Federal savings association models only publicly traded equity exposures, the national bank's or Federal savings association's aggregate risk-weighted asset amount for its equity exposures is equal to the sum of:

(1) The risk-weighted asset amount of each equity exposure that qualifies for a 0 percent, 20 percent, or 100 percent risk weight under §§ 3.152(b)(1) through (b)(3)(i) (as determined under § 3.152), each equity exposure that qualifies for a 400 percent risk weight under § 3.152(b)(5) or a 600 percent risk weight under § 3.152(b)(6) (as determined under § 3.152), and each equity exposure to an investment fund (as determined under § 3.154); and

(2) The greater of:

(i) The estimate of potential losses on the national bank's or Federal savings association's equity exposures (other than equity exposures referenced in paragraph (d)(1) of this section) generated by the national bank's or Federal savings association's internal equity exposure model multiplied by 12.5; or

(ii) The sum of:

(A) 200 percent multiplied by the aggregate adjusted carrying value of the national bank's or Federal savings association's publicly traded equity exposures that do not belong to a hedge pair, do not qualify for a 0 percent, 20 percent, or 100 percent risk weight under § 3.152(b)(1) through (b)(3)(i), and are not equity exposures to an investment fund; and

(B) 200 percent multiplied by the aggregate ineffective portion of all hedge pairs.

§ 3.154 Equity exposures to investment funds.

(a) *Available approaches.* (1) Unless the exposure meets the requirements for a community development equity exposure in § 3.152(b)(3)(i), a national bank or Federal savings association must determine the risk-weighted asset amount of an equity exposure to an investment fund under the full look-through approach in paragraph (b) of this section, the simple modified look-through approach in paragraph (c) of this section, or the alternative modified look-through approach in paragraph (d) of this section.

(2) The risk-weighted asset amount of an equity exposure to an investment fund that meets the requirements for a community development equity exposure in § 3.152(b)(3)(i) is its adjusted carrying value.

(3) If an equity exposure to an investment fund is part of a hedge pair and the national bank or Federal savings association does not use the full look-through approach, the national bank or Federal savings association may use the ineffective portion of the hedge pair as determined under § 3.152(c) as the adjusted carrying value for the equity exposure to the investment fund. The risk-weighted asset amount of the effective portion of the hedge pair is equal to its adjusted carrying value.

(b) *Full look-through approach.* A national bank or Federal savings association that is able to calculate a risk-weighted asset amount for its proportional ownership share of each exposure held by the investment fund (as calculated under this subpart E of this part as if the proportional ownership share of each exposure were held directly by the national bank or Federal savings association) may either:

(1) Set the risk-weighted asset amount of the national bank's or Federal savings association's exposure to the fund equal to the product of:

(i) The aggregate risk-weighted asset amounts of the exposures held by the fund as if they were held directly by the national bank or Federal savings association; and

(ii) The national bank's or Federal savings association's proportional ownership share of the fund; or

(2) Include the national bank's or Federal savings association's proportional ownership share of each exposure held by the fund in the national bank's or Federal savings association's IMA.

(c) *Simple modified look-through approach.* Under this approach, the risk-weighted asset amount for a national bank's or Federal savings association's equity exposure to an investment fund equals the adjusted carrying value of the equity exposure multiplied by the highest risk weight assigned according to subpart D of this part that applies to any exposure the fund is permitted to hold under its prospectus, partnership agreement, or similar contract that defines the fund's permissible investments (excluding derivative contracts that are used for hedging rather than speculative purposes and that do not constitute a material portion of the fund's exposures).

(d) *Alternative modified look-through approach.* Under this approach, a national bank or Federal savings association may assign the adjusted carrying value of an equity exposure to an investment fund on a pro rata basis to different risk weight categories assigned according to subpart D of this part based on the investment limits in the fund's prospectus, partnership agreement, or similar contract that defines the fund's permissible investments. The risk-weighted asset amount for the national bank's or Federal savings association's equity exposure to the investment fund equals the sum of each portion of the adjusted carrying value assigned to an exposure class multiplied by the applicable risk weight. If the sum of the investment limits for all exposure types within the fund exceeds 100 percent, the national bank or Federal savings association must assume that the fund invests to the maximum extent permitted under its investment limits in the exposure type with the highest risk weight under subpart D of this part, and continues to make investments in order of the exposure type with the next highest risk weight under subpart D of this part until the maximum total investment level is reached. If more than one exposure type applies to an exposure, the national bank or Federal savings association must use the highest applicable risk weight. A national bank or Federal savings association may exclude derivative contracts held by the fund that are used for hedging rather than for speculative purposes and do not constitute a material portion of the fund's exposures.

§ 3.155 Equity derivative contracts.

(a) Under the IMA, in addition to holding risk-based capital against an equity derivative contract under this part, a national bank or Federal savings association must hold risk-based capital against the counterparty credit risk in the equity derivative contract by also treating the equity derivative contract as a wholesale exposure and computing a supplemental risk-weighted asset amount for the contract under § 3.132.

(b) Under the SRWA, a national bank or Federal savings association may choose not to hold risk-based capital against the counterparty credit risk of equity derivative contracts, as long as it does so for all such contracts. Where the equity derivative contracts are subject to a qualified master netting agreement, a national bank or Federal savings association using the SRWA must either include all or exclude all of the contracts from any measure used to determine counterparty credit risk exposure.

§§ 3.156–3.160 [Reserved]

RISK-WEIGHTED ASSETS FOR OPERATIONAL RISK

§ 3.161 Qualification requirements for incorporation of operational risk mitigants.

(a) *Qualification to use operational risk mitigants.* A national bank or Federal savings association may adjust its estimate of operational risk exposure to reflect qualifying operational risk mitigants if:

(1) The national bank's or Federal savings association's operational risk quantification system is able to generate an estimate of the national bank's or Federal savings association's operational risk exposure (which does not incorporate qualifying operational risk mitigants) and an estimate of the

national bank's or Federal savings association's operational risk exposure adjusted to incorporate qualifying operational risk mitigants; and

(2) The national bank's or Federal savings association's methodology for incorporating the effects of insurance, if the national bank or Federal savings association uses insurance as an operational risk mitigant, captures through appropriate discounts to the amount of risk mitigation:

(i) The residual term of the policy, where less than one year;

(ii) The cancellation terms of the policy, where less than one year;

(iii) The policy's timeliness of payment;

(iv) The uncertainty of payment by the provider of the policy; and

(v) Mismatches in coverage between the policy and the hedged operational loss event.

(b) *Qualifying operational risk mitigants.* Qualifying operational risk mitigants are:

(1) Insurance that:

(i) Is provided by an unaffiliated company that the national bank or Federal savings association deems to have strong capacity to meet its claims payment obligations and the obligor rating category to which the national bank or Federal savings association assigns the company is assigned a PD equal to or less than 10 basis points;

(ii) Has an initial term of at least one year and a residual term of more than 90 days;

(iii) Has a minimum notice period for cancellation by the provider of 90 days;

(iv) Has no exclusions or limitations based upon regulatory action or for the receiver or liquidator of a failed depository institution; and

(v) Is explicitly mapped to a potential operational loss event;

(2) Operational risk mitigants other than insurance for which the OCC has given prior written approval. In evaluating an operational risk mitigant other than insurance, the OCC will consider whether the operational risk mitigant covers potential operational losses in a manner equivalent to holding total capital.

§3.162 Mechanics of risk-weighted asset calculation.

(a) If a national bank or Federal savings association does not qualify to use or does not have qualifying operational risk mitigants, the national bank's or Federal savings association's dollar risk-based capital requirement for operational risk is its operational risk exposure minus eligible operational risk offsets (if any).

(b) If a national bank or Federal savings association qualifies to use operational risk mitigants and has qualifying operational risk mitigants, the national bank's or Federal savings association's dollar risk-based capital requirement for operational risk is the greater of:

(1) The national bank's or Federal savings association's operational risk exposure adjusted for qualifying operational risk mitigants minus eligible operational risk offsets (if any); or

(2) 0.8 multiplied by the difference between:

(i) The national bank's or Federal savings association's operational risk exposure; and

(ii) Eligible operational risk offsets (if any).

(c) The national bank's or Federal savings association's risk-weighted asset amount for operational risk equals the national bank's or Federal savings association's dollar risk-based capital requirement for operational risk determined under sections 162(a) or (b) multiplied by 12.5.

§§3.163–3.170 [Reserved]

DISCLOSURES

§3.171 Purpose and scope.

§§3.171 through 3.173 establish public disclosure requirements related to the capital requirements of a national bank or Federal savings association that is an advanced approaches national bank or Federal savings association.

§3.172 Disclosure requirements.

(a) A national bank or Federal savings association that is an advanced approaches national bank or Federal savings association that has completed the parallel run process and that has received notification from the OCC pursuant to section 121(d) of subpart E of this part must publicly disclose each quarter its total and tier 1 risk-based capital ratios and their components as calculated under this subpart (that is, common equity tier 1 capital, additional tier 1 capital, tier 2 capital, total qualifying capital, and total risk-weighted assets).

(b) A national bank or Federal savings association that is an advanced approaches national bank or Federal savings association that has completed the parallel run process and that has received notification from the OCC pursuant to section 121(d) of subpart E of this part must comply with paragraph (c) of this section unless it is a consolidated subsidiary of a bank holding company, savings and loan holding company, or depository institution that is subject to these disclosure requirements or a subsidiary of a non-U.S. banking organization that is subject to comparable public disclosure requirements in its home jurisdiction.

(c)(1) A national bank or Federal savings association described in paragraph (b) of this section must provide timely public disclosures each calendar quarter of the information in the applicable tables in §3.173. If a significant change occurs, such that the most recent reported amounts are no longer reflective of the national bank's or Federal savings association's capital adequacy and risk profile, then a brief discussion of this change and its likely impact must be disclosed as soon as practicable thereafter. Qualitative disclosures that typically do not change each quarter (for example, a general summary of the national bank's or Federal savings association's risk management objectives and policies, reporting system, and definitions) may be disclosed annually after the end of the fourth calendar quarter, provided that any significant changes to these are disclosed in the interim. Management may provide all of the disclosures required by this subpart in one place on the national bank's or Federal savings association's public Web site or may provide the disclosures in more than one public financial report or other regulatory reports, provided that the national bank or Federal savings association publicly provides a summary table specifically indicating the location(s) of all such disclosures.

(2) A national bank or Federal savings association described in paragraph (b) of this section must have a formal disclosure policy approved by the board of directors that addresses its approach for determining the disclosures it makes. The policy must address the associated internal controls and disclosure controls and procedures. The board of directors and senior management are responsible for establishing and maintaining an effective internal control structure over financial reporting, including the disclosures required by this subpart, and must ensure that appropriate review of the disclosures takes place. One or more senior officers of the national bank or Federal savings association must attest that the disclosures meet the requirements of this subpart.

(3) If a national bank or Federal savings association described in paragraph (b) of this section believes that disclosure of specific commercial or financial information would prejudice seriously its position by making public information that is either proprietary or confidential in nature, the national bank or Federal savings association is not required to disclose those specific items, but must disclose more general information about the subject matter of the requirement, together with the fact that, and the reason why, the specific items of information have not been disclosed.

(d)(1) A national bank or Federal savings association that meets any of the criteria in §3.100(b)(1) before January 1, 2015, must publicly disclose each quarter its supplementary leverage ratio and the components thereof (that is, tier 1 capital and total leverage exposure) as calculated under subpart B of this part, beginning with the first quarter in 2015. This disclosure requirement applies without regard to whether the national bank or Federal savings association has completed the parallel run process and received notification from the OCC pursuant to §3.121(d).

(2) A national bank or Federal savings association that meets any of the criteria in §3.100(b)(1) on or after January 1, 2015, must publicly disclose each

quarter its supplementary leverage ratio and the components thereof (that is, tier 1 capital and total leverage exposure) as calculated under subpart B of this part beginning with the calendar quarter immediately following the quarter in which the national bank or Federal savings association becomes an advanced approaches national bank or Federal savings association. This disclosure requirement applies without regard to whether the national bank or Federal savings association has completed the parallel run process and has received notification from the OCC pursuant to § 3.121(d).

[78 FR 62157, 62273, Oct. 11, 2013, as amended at 79 FR 57743, Sept. 26, 2014; 80 FR 41417, July 15, 2015]

§ 3.173 Disclosures by certain advanced approaches national banks or Federal savings associations.

(a)(1) An advanced approaches national bank or Federal savings association described in § 3.172(b) must make the disclosures described in Tables 1 through 12 to § 3.173.

(2) An advanced approaches national bank or Federal savings association that is required to publicly disclose its supplementary leverage ratio pursuant to § 3.172(d) must make the disclosures required under Table 13 to § 3.173, unless the national bank or Federal savings association is a consolidated subsidiary of a bank holding company, savings and loan holding company, or depository institution that is subject to these disclosures requirements or a subsidiary of a non-U.S. banking organization that is subject to comparable public disclosure requirements in its home jurisdiction.

(3) The disclosures described in Tables 1 through 12 to § 3.173 must be made publicly available for twelve consecutive quarters beginning on January 1, 2014, or a shorter period, as applicable, for the quarters after the national bank or Federal savings association has completed the parallel run process and received notification from the OCC pursuant to § 3.121(d). The disclosures described in Table 13 to § 3.173 must be made publicly available for twelve consecutive quarters beginning on January 1, 2015, or a shorter period, as applicable, for the quarters after the national bank or Federal savings association becomes subject to the disclosure of the supplementary leverage ratio pursuant to §§ 3.172(d) and 3.173(a)(2).

TABLE 1 TO § 3.173—SCOPE OF APPLICATION

Qualitative disclosures	(a)	The name of the top corporate entity in the group to which subpart E of this part applies.
	(b)	A brief description of the differences in the basis for consolidating entities[1] for accounting and regulatory purposes, with a description of those entities: (1) That are fully consolidated; (2) That are deconsolidated and deducted from total capital; (3) For which the total capital requirement is deducted; and (4) That are neither consolidated nor deducted (for example, where the investment in the entity is assigned a risk weight in accordance with this subpart).
	(c)	Any restrictions, or other major impediments, on transfer of funds or total capital within the group.
Quantitative disclosures	(d)	The aggregate amount of surplus capital of insurance subsidiaries included in the total capital of the consolidated group.
	(e)	The aggregate amount by which actual total capital is less than the minimum total capital requirement in all subsidiaries, with total capital requirements and the name(s) of the subsidiaries with such deficiencies.

[1] Such entities include securities, insurance and other financial subsidiaries, commercial subsidiaries (where permitted), and significant minority equity investments in insurance, financial and commercial entities.

TABLE 2 TO § 3.173—CAPITAL STRUCTURE

Qualitative disclosures	(a)	Summary information on the terms and conditions of the main features of all regulatory capital instruments.
Quantitative disclosures	(b)	The amount of common equity tier 1 capital, with separate disclosure of: (1) Common stock and related surplus; (2) Retained earnings;

TABLE 2 TO § 3.173—CAPITAL STRUCTURE—Continued

		(3) Common equity minority interest; (4) AOCI (net of tax) and other reserves; and (5) Regulatory adjustments and deductions made to common equity tier 1 capital.
	(c)	The amount of tier 1 capital, with separate disclosure of: (1) Additional tier 1 capital elements, including additional tier 1 capital instruments and tier 1 minority interest not included in common equity tier 1 capital; and (2) Regulatory adjustments and deductions made to tier 1 capital.
	(d)	The amount of total capital, with separate disclosure of: (1) Tier 2 capital elements, including tier 2 capital instruments and total capital minority interest not included in tier 1 capital; and (2) Regulatory adjustments and deductions made to total capital.

TABLE 3 TO § 3.173—CAPITAL ADEQUACY

Qualitative disclosures	(a)	A summary discussion of the national bank's or Federal savings association's approach to assessing the adequacy of its capital to support current and future activities.
Quantitative disclosures	(b)	Risk-weighted assets for credit risk from: (1) Wholesale exposures; (2) Residential mortgage exposures; (3) Qualifying revolving exposures; (4) Other retail exposures; (5) Securitization exposures; (6) Equity exposures: (7) Equity exposures subject to the simple risk weight approach; and (8) Equity exposures subject to the internal models approach.
	(c)	Standardized market risk-weighted assets and advanced market risk-weighted assets as calculated under subpart F of this part: (1) Standardized approach for specific risk; and (2) Internal models approach for specific risk.
	(d)	Risk-weighted assets for operational risk.
	(e)	Common equity tier 1, tier 1 and total risk-based capital ratios: (1) For the top consolidated group; and (2) For each depository institution subsidiary.
	(f)	Total risk-weighted assets.

TABLE 4 TO § 3.173—CAPITAL CONSERVATION AND COUNTERCYCLICAL CAPITAL BUFFERS

Qualitative disclosures	(a)	The national bank or Federal savings association must publicly disclose the geographic breakdown of its private sector credit exposures used in the calculation of the countercyclical capital buffer.
Quantitative disclosures	(b)	At least quarterly, the national bank or Federal savings association must calculate and publicly disclose the capital conservation buffer and the countercyclical capital buffer as described under § 3.11 of subpart B.
	(c)	At least quarterly, the national bank or Federal savings association must calculate and publicly disclose the buffer retained income of the national bank or Federal savings association, as described under § 3.11 of subpart B.
	(d)	At least quarterly, the national bank or Federal savings association must calculate and publicly disclose any limitations it has on distributions and discretionary bonus payments resulting from the capital conservation buffer and the countercyclical capital buffer framework described under § 3.11 of subpart B, including the maximum payout amount for the quarter.

(b) *General qualitative disclosure requirement*. For each separate risk area described in Tables 5 through 12 to § 3.173, the national bank or Federal savings association must describe its risk management objectives and policies, including:

(1) Strategies and processes;

(2) The structure and organization of the relevant risk management function;

(3) The scope and nature of risk reporting and/or measurement systems; and

(4) Policies for hedging and/or mitigating risk and strategies and processes for monitoring the continuing effectiveness of hedges/mitigants.

TABLE 5[1] TO § 3.173—CREDIT RISK: GENERAL DISCLOSURES

Qualitative disclosures	(a)	The general qualitative disclosure requirement with respect to credit risk (excluding counterparty credit risk disclosed in accordance with Table 7 to § 3.173), including: (1) Policy for determining past due or delinquency status; (2) Policy for placing loans on nonaccrual; (3) Policy for returning loans to accrual status; (4) Definition of and policy for identifying impaired loans (for financial accounting purposes). (5) Description of the methodology that the entity uses to estimate its allowance for loan and lease losses, including statistical methods used where applicable; (6) Policy for charging-off uncollectible amounts; and (7) Discussion of the national bank's or Federal savings association's credit risk management policy
Quantitative disclosures	(b)	Total credit risk exposures and average credit risk exposures, after accounting offsets in accordance with GAAP,[2] without taking into account the effects of credit risk mitigation techniques (for example, collateral and netting not permitted under GAAP), over the period categorized by major types of credit exposure. For example, national banks or Federal savings associations could use categories similar to that used for financial statement purposes. Such categories might include, for instance: (1) Loans, off-balance sheet commitments, and other non-derivative off-balance sheet exposures; (2) Debt securities; and (3) OTC derivatives.
	(c)	Geographic[3] distribution of exposures, categorized in significant areas by major types of credit exposure.
	(d)	Industry or counterparty type distribution of exposures, categorized by major types of credit exposure.
	(e)	By major industry or counterparty type: (1) Amount of impaired loans for which there was a related allowance under GAAP; (2) Amount of impaired loans for which there was no related allowance under GAAP; (3) Amount of loans past due 90 days and on nonaccrual; (4) Amount of loans past due 90 days and still accruing;[4] (5) The balance in the allowance for loan and lease losses at the end of each period, disaggregated on the basis of the entity's impairment method. To disaggregate the information required on the basis of impairment methodology, an entity shall separately disclose the amounts based on the requirements in GAAP; and (6) Charge-offs during the period.
	(f)	Amount of impaired loans and, if available, the amount of past due loans categorized by significant geographic areas including, if practical, the amounts of allowances related to each geographical area,[5] further categorized as required by GAAP.
	(g)	Reconciliation of changes in ALLL.[6]
	(h)	Remaining contractual maturity breakdown (for example, one year or less) of the whole portfolio, categorized by credit exposure.

[1] Table 5 to § 3.173 does not cover equity exposures, which should be reported in Table 9.
[2] *See*, for example, ASC Topic 815–10 and 210–20 as they may be amended from time to time.
[3] Geographical areas may comprise individual countries, groups of countries, or regions within countries. A national bank or Federal savings association might choose to define the geographical areas based on the way the company's portfolio is geographically managed. The criteria used to allocate the loans to geographical areas must be specified.
[4] A national bank or Federal savings association is encouraged also to provide an analysis of the aging of past-due loans.
[5] The portion of the general allowance that is not allocated to a geographical area should be disclosed separately.
[6] The reconciliation should include the following: A description of the allowance; the opening balance of the allowance; charge-offs taken against the allowance during the period; amounts provided (or reversed) for estimated probable loan losses during the period; any other adjustments (for example, exchange rate differences, business combinations, acquisitions and disposals of subsidiaries), including transfers between allowances; and the closing balance of the allowance. Charge-offs and recoveries that have been recorded directly to the income statement should be disclosed separately.

TABLE 6 TO § 3.173—CREDIT RISK: DISCLOSURES FOR PORTFOLIOS SUBJECT TO IRB RISK-BASED CAPITAL FORMULAS

Qualitative disclosures	(a)	Explanation and review of the: (1) Structure of internal rating systems and if the national bank or Federal savings association considers external ratings, the relation between internal and external ratings;

TABLE 6 TO § 3.173—CREDIT RISK: DISCLOSURES FOR PORTFOLIOS SUBJECT TO IRB RISK-BASED CAPITAL FORMULAS—Continued

		(2) Use of risk parameter estimates other than for regulatory capital purposes; (3) Process for managing and recognizing credit risk mitigation (see Table 8 to § 3.173); and (4) Control mechanisms for the rating system, including discussion of independence, accountability, and rating systems review.
	(b)	Description of the internal ratings process, provided separately for the following: (1) Wholesale category; (2) Retail subcategories; (i) Residential mortgage exposures; (ii) Qualifying revolving exposures; and (iii) Other retail exposures. For each category and subcategory above the description should include: (A) The types of exposure included in the category/subcategories; and (B) The definitions, methods and data for estimation and validation of PD, LGD, and EAD, including assumptions employed in the derivation of these variables.[1]
Quantitative disclosures: risk assessment.	(c)	(1) For wholesale exposures, present the following information across a sufficient number of PD grades (including default) to allow for a meaningful differentiation of credit risk:[2] (i) Total EAD;[3] (ii) Exposure-weighted average LGD (percentage); (iii) Exposure-weighted average risk weight; and (iv) Amount of undrawn commitments and exposure-weighted average EAD including average drawdowns prior to default for wholesale exposures. (2) For each retail subcategory, present the disclosures outlined above across a sufficient number of segments to allow for a meaningful differentiation of credit risk.
Quantitative disclosures: historical results.	(d)	Actual losses in the preceding period for each category and subcategory and how this differs from past experience. A discussion of the factors that impacted the loss experience in the preceding period—for example, has the national bank or Federal savings association experienced higher than average default rates, loss rates or EADs.
	(e)	The national bank's or Federal savings association's estimates compared against actual outcomes over a longer period.[4] At a minimum, this should include information on estimates of losses against actual losses in the wholesale category and each retail subcategory over a period sufficient to allow for a meaningful assessment of the performance of the internal rating processes for each category/subcategory.[5] Where appropriate, the national bank or Federal savings association should further decompose this to provide analysis of PD, LGD, and EAD outcomes against estimates provided in the quantitative risk assessment disclosures above.[6]

[1] This disclosure item does not require a detailed description of the model in full—it should provide the reader with a broad overview of the model approach, describing definitions of the variables and methods for estimating and validating those variables set out in the quantitative risk disclosures below. This should be done for each of the four category/subcategories. The national bank or Federal savings association must disclose any significant differences in approach to estimating these variables within each category/subcategories.

[2] The PD, LGD and EAD disclosures in Table 6 (c) to § 3.173 should reflect the effects of collateral, qualifying master netting agreements, eligible guarantees and eligible credit derivatives as defined under this part. Disclosure of each PD grade should include the exposure-weighted average PD for each grade. Where a national bank or Federal savings association aggregates PD grades for the purposes of disclosure, this should be a representative breakdown of the distribution of PD grades used for regulatory capital purposes.

[3] Outstanding loans and EAD on undrawn commitments can be presented on a combined basis for these disclosures.

[4] These disclosures are a way of further informing the reader about the reliability of the information provided in the "quantitative disclosures: Risk assessment" over the long run. The disclosures are requirements from year-end 2010; in the meantime, early adoption is encouraged. The phased implementation is to allow a national bank or Federal savings association sufficient time to build up a longer run of data that will make these disclosures meaningful.

[5] This disclosure item is not intended to be prescriptive about the period used for this assessment. Upon implementation, it is expected that a national bank or Federal savings association would provide these disclosures for as long a set of data as possible—for example, if a national bank or Federal savings association has 10 years of data, it might choose to disclose the average default rates for each PD grade over that 10-year period. Annual amounts need not be disclosed.

[6] A national bank or Federal savings association must provide this further decomposition where it will allow users greater insight into the reliability of the estimates provided in the "quantitative disclosures: Risk assessment." In particular, it must provide this information where there are material differences between its estimates of PD, LGD or EAD compared to actual outcomes over the long run. The national bank or Federal savings association must also provide explanations for such differences.

TABLE 7 TO § 3.173—GENERAL DISCLOSURE FOR COUNTERPARTY CREDIT RISK OF OTC DERIVATIVE CONTRACTS, REPO-STYLE TRANSACTIONS, AND ELIGIBLE MARGIN LOANS

Qualitative Disclosures	(a)	The general qualitative disclosure requirement with respect to OTC derivatives, eligible margin loans, and repo-style transactions, including: (1) Discussion of methodology used to assign economic capital and credit limits for counterparty credit exposures; (2) Discussion of policies for securing collateral, valuing and managing collateral, and establishing credit reserves; (3) Discussion of the primary types of collateral taken; (4) Discussion of policies with respect to wrong-way risk exposures; and (5) Discussion of the impact of the amount of collateral the national bank or Federal savings association would have to provide if the national bank or Federal savings association were to receive a credit rating downgrade.
Quantitative Disclosures	(b)	Gross positive fair value of contracts, netting benefits, netted current credit exposure, collateral held (including type, for example, cash, government securities), and net unsecured credit exposure.[1] Also report measures for EAD used for regulatory capital for these transactions, the notional value of credit derivative hedges purchased for counterparty credit risk protection, and, for national banks or Federal savings associations not using the internal models methodology in § 3.132(d) , the distribution of current credit exposure by types of credit exposure.[2]
	(c)	Notional amount of purchased and sold credit derivatives, segregated between use for the national bank's or Federal savings association's own credit portfolio and for its intermediation activities, including the distribution of the credit derivative products used, categorized further by protection bought and sold within each product group.
	(d)	The estimate of alpha if the national bank or Federal savings association has received supervisory approval to estimate alpha.

[1] Net unsecured credit exposure is the credit exposure after considering the benefits from legally enforceable netting agreements and collateral arrangements, without taking into account haircuts for price volatility, liquidity, etc.

[2] This may include interest rate derivative contracts, foreign exchange derivative contracts, equity derivative contracts, credit derivatives, commodity or other derivative contracts, repo-style transactions, and eligible margin loans.

TABLE 8 TO § 3.173—CREDIT RISK MITIGATION [1] [2]

Qualitative disclosures	(a)	The general qualitative disclosure requirement with respect to credit risk mitigation, including: (1) Policies and processes for, and an indication of the extent to which the national bank or Federal savings association uses, on- or off-balance sheet netting; (2) Policies and processes for collateral valuation and management; (3) A description of the main types of collateral taken by the national bank or Federal savings association; (4) The main types of guarantors/credit derivative counterparties and their creditworthiness; and (5) Information about (market or credit) risk concentrations within the mitigation taken.
Quantitative disclosures	(b)	For each separately disclosed portfolio, the total exposure (after, where applicable, on- or off-balance sheet netting) that is covered by guarantees/credit derivatives.

[1] At a minimum, a national bank or Federal savings association must provide the disclosures in Table 8 in relation to credit risk mitigation that has been recognized for the purposes of reducing capital requirements under this subpart. Where relevant, national banks or Federal savings associations are encouraged to give further information about mitigants that have not been recognized for that purpose.

[2] Credit derivatives and other credit mitigation that are treated for the purposes of this subpart as synthetic securitization exposures should be excluded from the credit risk mitigation disclosures (in Table 8 to § 3.173) and included within those relating to securitization (in Table 9 to § 3.173).

TABLE 9 TO § 3.173—SECURITIZATION

Qualitative disclosures	(a)	The general qualitative disclosure requirement with respect to securitization (including synthetic securitizations), including a discussion of:

TABLE 9 TO § 3.173—SECURITIZATION—Continued

		(1) The national bank's or Federal savings association's objectives for securitizing assets, including the extent to which these activities transfer credit risk of the underlying exposures away from the national bank or Federal savings association to other entities and including the type of risks assumed and retained with resecuritization activity; [1] (2) The nature of the risks (e.g. liquidity risk) inherent in the securitized assets; (3) The roles played by the national bank or Federal savings association in the securitization process [2] and an indication of the extent of the national bank's or Federal savings association's involvement in each of them; (4) The processes in place to monitor changes in the credit and market risk of securitization exposures including how those processes differ for resecuritization exposures; (5) The national bank's or Federal savings association's policy for mitigating the credit risk retained through securitization and resecuritization exposures; and (6) The risk-based capital approaches that the national bank or Federal savings association follows for its securitization exposures including the type of securitization exposure to which each approach applies.
	(b)	A list of: (1) The type of securitization SPEs that the national bank or Federal savings association, as sponsor, uses to securitize third-party exposures. The national bank or Federal savings association must indicate whether it has exposure to these SPEs, either on- or off-balance sheet; and (2) Affiliated entities: (i) That the national bank or Federal savings association manages or advises; and (ii) That invest either in the securitization exposures that the national bank or Federal savings association has securitized or in securitization SPEs that the national bank or Federal savings association sponsors.[3]
	(c)	Summary of the national bank's or Federal savings association's accounting policies for securitization activities, including: (1) Whether the transactions are treated as sales or financings; (2) Recognition of gain-on-sale; (3) Methods and key assumptions and inputs applied in valuing retained or purchased interests; (4) Changes in methods and key assumptions and inputs from the previous period for valuing retained interests and impact of the changes; (5) Treatment of synthetic securitizations; (6) How exposures intended to be securitized are valued and whether they are recorded under subpart E of this part; and (7) Policies for recognizing liabilities on the balance sheet for arrangements that could require the national bank or Federal savings association to provide financial support for securitized assets.
	(d)	An explanation of significant changes to any of the quantitative information set forth below since the last reporting period.
Quantitative disclosures	(e)	The total outstanding exposures securitized [4] by the national bank or Federal savings association in securitizations that meet the operational criteria in § 3.141 (categorized into traditional/synthetic), by underlying exposure type [5] separately for securitizations of third-party exposures for which the bank acts only as sponsor.
	(f)	For exposures securitized by the national bank or Federal savings association in securitizations that meet the operational criteria in § 3.141: (1) Amount of securitized assets that are impaired [6]/past due categorized by exposure type; and (2) Losses recognized by the national bank or Federal savings association during the current period categorized by exposure type.[7]
	(g)	The total amount of outstanding exposures intended to be securitized categorized by exposure type.
	(h)	Aggregate amount of: (1) On-balance sheet securitization exposures retained or purchased categorized by exposure type; and (2) Off-balance sheet securitization exposures categorized by exposure type.

TABLE 9 TO §3.173—SECURITIZATION—Continued

	(i)	(1) Aggregate amount of securitization exposures retained or purchased and the associated capital requirements for these exposures, categorized between securitization and resecuritization exposures, further categorized into a meaningful number of risk weight bands and by risk-based capital approach (e.g. SA, SFA, or SSFA). (2) Aggregate amount disclosed separately by type of underlying exposure in the pool of any: (i) After-tax gain-on-sale on a securitization that has been deducted from common equity tier 1 capital: And (ii) Credit-enhancing interest-only strip that is assigned a 1,250 percent risk weight.
	(j)	Summary of current year's securitization activity, including the amount of exposures securitized (by exposure type), and recognized gain or loss on sale by asset type.
	(k)	Aggregate amount of resecuritization exposures retained or purchased categorized according to: (1) Exposures to which credit risk mitigation is applied and those not applied; and (2) Exposures to guarantors categorized according to guarantor creditworthiness categories or guarantor name.

[1] The national bank or Federal savings association must describe the structure of resecuritizations in which it participates; this description must be provided for the main categories of resecuritization products in which the national bank or Federal savings association is active.

[2] For example, these roles would include originator, investor, servicer, provider of credit enhancement, sponsor, liquidity provider, or swap provider.

[3] For example, money market mutual funds should be listed individually, and personal and private trusts, should be noted collectively.

[4] "Exposures securitized" include underlying exposures originated by the bank, whether generated by them or purchased, and recognized in the balance sheet, from third parties, and third-party exposures included in sponsored transactions. Securitization transactions (including underlying exposures originally on the bank's balance sheet and underlying exposures acquired by the bank from third-party entities) in which the originating bank does not retain any securitization exposure should be shown separately but need only be reported for the year of inception.

[5] A national bank or Federal savings association is required to disclose exposures regardless of whether there is a capital charge under this part.

[6] A national bank or Federal savings association must include credit-related other than temporary impairment (OTTI).

[7] For example, charge-offs/allowances (if the assets remain on the bank's balance sheet) or credit-related OTTI of I/O strips and other retained residual interests, as well as recognition of liabilities for probable future financial support required of the bank with respect to securitized assets.

TABLE 10 TO §3.173—OPERATIONAL RISK

Qualitative disclosures	(a)	The general qualitative disclosure requirement for operational risk.
	(b)	Description of the AMA, including a discussion of relevant internal and external factors considered in the national bank's or Federal savings association's measurement approach.
	(c)	A description of the use of insurance for the purpose of mitigating operational risk.

TABLE 11 TO §3.173—EQUITIES NOT SUBJECT TO SUBPART F OF THIS PART

Qualitative disclosures	(a)	The general qualitative disclosure requirement with respect to the equity risk of equity holdings not subject to subpart F of this part, including: (1) Differentiation between holdings on which capital gains are expected and those held for other objectives, including for relationship and strategic reasons; and (2) Discussion of important policies covering the valuation of and accounting for equity holdings not subject to subpart F of this part. This includes the accounting methodology and valuation methodologies used, including key assumptions and practices affecting valuation as well as significant changes in these practices.
Quantitative disclosures	(b)	Carrying value on the balance sheet of equity investments, as well as the fair value of those investments.
	(c)	The types and nature of investments, including the amount that is: (1) Publicly traded; and (2) Non-publicly traded.
	(d)	The cumulative realized gains (losses) arising from sales and liquidations in the reporting period.
	(e)	(1) Total unrealized gains (losses) [1] (2) Total latent revaluation gains (losses) [2] (3) Any amounts of the above included in tier 1 and/or tier 2 capital.

TABLE 11 TO § 3.173—EQUITIES NOT SUBJECT TO SUBPART F OF THIS PART—Continued

	(f)	Capital requirements categorized by appropriate equity groupings, consistent with the national bank's or Federal savings association's methodology, as well as the aggregate amounts and the type of equity investments subject to any supervisory transition regarding total capital requirements.[3]

[1] Unrealized gains (losses) recognized in the balance sheet but not through earnings.
[2] Unrealized gains (losses) not recognized either in the balance sheet or through earnings.
[3] This disclosure must include a breakdown of equities that are subject to the 0 percent, 20 percent, 100 percent, 300 percent, 400 percent, and 600 percent risk weights, as applicable.

TABLE 12 TO § 3.173—INTEREST RATE RISK FOR NON-TRADING ACTIVITIES

Qualitative disclosures	(a)	The general qualitative disclosure requirement, including the nature of interest rate risk for non-trading activities and key assumptions, including assumptions regarding loan prepayments and behavior of non-maturity deposits, and frequency of measurement of interest rate risk for non-trading activities.
Quantitative disclosures	(b)	The increase (decline) in earnings or economic value (or relevant measure used by management) for upward and downward rate shocks according to management's method for measuring interest rate risk for non-trading activities, categorized by currency (as appropriate).

(c) Except as provided in § 3.172(b), a national bank or Federal savings association described in § 3.172(d) must make the disclosures described in Table 13 to § 3.173; provided, however, the disclosures required under this paragraph are required without regard to whether the national bank or Federal savings association has completed the parallel run process and has received notification from the OCC pursuant to § 3.121(d). The national bank or Federal savings association must make these disclosures publicly available beginning on January 1, 2015.

TABLE 13 TO § 3.173—SUPPLEMENTARY LEVERAGE RATIO

	Dollar amounts in thousands			
	Tril	Bil	Mil	Thou
Part 1: Summary comparison of accounting assets and total leverage exposure				
1 Total consolidated assets as reported in published financial statements.				
2 Adjustment for investments in banking, financial, insurance or commercial entities that are consolidated for accounting purposes but outside the scope of regulatory consolidation.				
3 Adjustment for fiduciary assets recognized on balance sheet but excluded from total leverage exposure.				
4 Adjustment for derivative exposures.				
5 Adjustment for repo-style transactions.				
6 Adjustment for off-balance sheet exposures (that is, conversion to credit equivalent amounts of off-balance sheet exposures).				
7 Other adjustments.				
8 Total leverage exposure.				
Part 2: Supplementary leverage ratio				
On-balance sheet exposures				
1 On-balance sheet assets (excluding on-balance sheet assets for repo-style transactions and derivative exposures, but including cash collateral received in derivative transactions).				
2 LESS: Amounts deducted from tier 1 capital.				
3 Total on-balance sheet exposures (excluding on-balance sheet assets for repo-style transactions and derivative exposures, but including cash collateral received in derivative transactions) (sum of lines 1 and 2).				
Derivative exposures				
4 Replacement cost for derivative exposures (that is, net of cash variation margin).				

TABLE 13 TO § 3.173—SUPPLEMENTARY LEVERAGE RATIO—Continued

	Dollar amounts in thousands			
	Tril	Bil	Mil	Thou
5 Add-on amounts for potential future exposure (PFE) for derivative exposures.				
6 Gross-up for cash collateral posted if deducted from the on-balance sheet assets, except for cash variation margin.				
7 LESS: Deductions of receivable assets for cash variation margin posted in derivative transactions, if included in on-balance sheet assets.				
8 LESS: Exempted CCP leg of client-cleared transactions.				
9 Effective notional principal amount of sold credit protection.				
10 LESS: Effective notional principal amount offsets and PFE adjustments for sold credit protection.				
11 Total derivative exposures (sum of lines 4 to 10).				
Repo-style transactions				
12 On-balance sheet assets for repo-style transactions, except include the gross value of receivables for reverse repurchase transactions. Exclude from this item the value of securities received in a security-for-security repo-style transaction where the securities lender has not sold or re-hypothecated the securities received. Include in this item the value of securities that qualified for sales treatment that must be reversed.				
13 LESS: Reduction of the gross value of receivables in reverse repurchase transactions by cash payables in repurchase transactions under netting agreements.				
14 Counterparty credit risk for all repo-style transactions.				
15 Exposure for repo-style transactions where a banking organization acts as an agent.				
16 Total exposures for repo-style transactions (sum of lines 12 to 15).				
Other off-balance sheet exposures				
17 Off-balance sheet exposures at gross notional amounts.				
18 LESS: Adjustments for conversion to credit equivalent amounts.				
19 Off-balance sheet exposures (sum of lines 17 and 18).				
Capital and total leverage exposure				
20 Tier 1 capital.				
21 Total leverage exposure (sum of lines 3, 11, 16 and 19).				
Supplementary leverage ratio				
22 Supplementary leverage ratio	(in percent)			

[78 FR 62157, 62273, Oct. 11, 2013, as amended at 79 FR 57743, Sept. 26, 2014; 80 FR 41418, July 15, 2015]

§§ 3.174–3.200 [Reserved]

Subpart F—Risk-Weighted Assets—Market Risk

SOURCE: 78 FR 62157, 62273, Oct. 11, 2013, unless otherwise noted.

§ 3.201 Purpose, applicability, and reservation of authority.

(a) *Purpose.* This subpart F establishes risk-based capital requirements for national banks or Federal savings associations with significant exposure to market risk, provides methods for these national banks or Federal savings associations to calculate their standardized measure for market risk and, if applicable, advanced measure for market risk, and establishes public disclosure requirements.

(b) *Applicability.* (1) This subpart F applies to any national bank or Federal savings association with aggregate trading assets and trading liabilities (as reported in the national bank's or

Federal savings association's most recent quarterly [regulatory report]), equal to:

(i) 10 percent or more of quarter-end total assets as reported on the most recent quarterly [Call Report or FR Y–9C]; or

(ii) $1 billion or more.

(2) The OCC may apply this subpart to any national bank or Federal savings association if the OCC deems it necessary or appropriate because of the level of market risk of the national bank or Federal savings association or to ensure safe and sound banking practices.

(3) The OCC may exclude a national bank or Federal savings association that meets the criteria of paragraph (b)(1) of this section from application of this subpart if the OCC determines that the exclusion is appropriate based on the level of market risk of the national bank or Federal savings association and is consistent with safe and sound banking practices.

(c) *Reservation of authority* (1) The OCC may require a national bank or Federal savings association to hold an amount of capital greater than otherwise required under this subpart if the OCC determines that the national bank's or Federal savings association's capital requirement for market risk as calculated under this subpart is not commensurate with the market risk of the national bank's or Federal savings association's covered positions. In making determinations under paragraphs (c)(1) through (c)(3) of this section, the OCC will apply notice and response procedures generally in the same manner as the notice and response procedures set forth in 12 CFR 3.404.

(2) If the OCC determines that the risk-based capital requirement calculated under this subpart by the national bank or Federal savings association for one or more covered positions or portfolios of covered positions is not commensurate with the risks associated with those positions or portfolios, the OCC may require the national bank or Federal savings association to assign a different risk-based capital requirement to the positions or portfolios that more accurately reflects the risk of the positions or portfolios.

(3) The OCC may also require a national bank or Federal savings association to calculate risk-based capital requirements for specific positions or portfolios under this subpart, or under subpart D or subpart E of this part, as appropriate, to more accurately reflect the risks of the positions.

(4) Nothing in this subpart limits the authority of the OCC under any other provision of law or regulation to take supervisory or enforcement action, including action to address unsafe or unsound practices or conditions, deficient capital levels, or violations of law.

§ 3.202 Definitions.

(a) Terms set forth in § 3.2 and used in this subpart have the definitions assigned thereto in § 3.2.

(b) For the purposes of this subpart, the following terms are defined as follows:

Backtesting means the comparison of a national bank's or Federal savings association's internal estimates with actual outcomes during a sample period not used in model development. For purposes of this subpart, backtesting is one form of out-of-sample testing.

Commodity position means a position for which price risk arises from changes in the price of a commodity.

Corporate debt position means a debt position that is an exposure to a company that is not a sovereign entity, the Bank for International Settlements, the European Central Bank, the European Commission, the International Monetary Fund, a multilateral development bank, a depository institution, a foreign bank, a credit union, a public sector entity, a GSE, or a securitization.

Correlation trading position means:

(1) A securitization position for which all or substantially all of the value of the underlying exposures is based on the credit quality of a single company for which a two-way market exists, or on commonly traded indices based on such exposures for which a two-way market exists on the indices; or

(2) A position that is not a securitization position and that hedges a position described in paragraph (1) of this definition; and

(3) A correlation trading position does not include:

(i) A resecuritization position;

(ii) A derivative of a securitization position that does not provide a pro rata share in the proceeds of a securitization tranche; or

(iii) A securitization position for which the underlying assets or reference exposures are retail exposures, residential mortgage exposures, or commercial mortgage exposures.

Covered position means the following positions:

(1) A trading asset or trading liability (whether on- or off-balance sheet),[31] as reported on Call Report, that meets the following conditions:

(i) The position is a trading position or hedges another covered position;[32] and

(ii) The position is free of any restrictive covenants on its tradability or the national bank or Federal savings association is able to hedge the material risk elements of the position in a two-way market;

(2) A foreign exchange or commodity position, regardless of whether the position is a trading asset or trading liability (excluding any structural foreign currency positions that the national bank or Federal savings association chooses to exclude with prior supervisory approval); and

(3) Notwithstanding paragraphs (1) and (2) of this definition, a covered position does not include:

(i) An intangible asset, including any servicing asset;

(ii) Any hedge of a trading position that the OCC determines to be outside the scope of the national bank's or Federal savings association's hedging strategy required in paragraph (a)(2) of § 3.203;

(iii) Any position that, in form or substance, acts as a liquidity facility that provides support to asset-backed commercial paper;

(iv) A credit derivative the national bank or Federal savings association recognizes as a guarantee for risk-weighted asset amount calculation purposes under subpart D or subpart E of this part;

(v) Any position that is recognized as a credit valuation adjustment hedge under § 3.132(e)(5) or § 3.132(e)(6), except as provided in § 3.132(e)(6)(vii);

(vi) Any equity position that is not publicly traded, other than a derivative that references a publicly traded equity and other than a position in an investment company as defined in and registered with the SEC under the Investment Company Act of 1940 (15 U.S.C. 80a–1 *et seq.*), provided that all the underlying equities held by the investment company are publicly traded;

(vii) Any equity position that is not publicly traded, other than a derivative that references a publicly traded equity and other than a position in an entity not domiciled in the United States (or a political subdivision thereof) that is supervised and regulated in a manner similar to entities described in paragraph (3)(vi) of this definition;

(viii) Any position a national bank or Federal savings association holds with the intent to securitize; or

(ix) Any direct real estate holding.

Debt position means a covered position that is not a securitization position or a correlation trading position and that has a value that reacts primarily to changes in interest rates or credit spreads.

Default by a sovereign entity has the same meaning as the term sovereign default under § 3.2.

Equity position means a covered position that is not a securitization position or a correlation trading position and that has a value that reacts primarily to changes in equity prices.

Event risk means the risk of loss on equity or hybrid equity positions as a result of a financial event, such as the announcement or occurrence of a company merger, acquisition, spin-off, or dissolution.

Foreign exchange position means a position for which price risk arises from changes in foreign exchange rates.

General market risk means the risk of loss that could result from broad market movements, such as changes in the general level of interest rates, credit

[31] Securities subject to repurchase and lending agreements are included as if they are still owned by the lender.

[32] A position that hedges a trading position must be within the scope of the bank's hedging strategy as described in paragraph (a)(2) of section 203 of this subpart.

spreads, equity prices, foreign exchange rates, or commodity prices.

Hedge means a position or positions that offset all, or substantially all, of one or more material risk factors of another position.

Idiosyncratic risk means the risk of loss in the value of a position that arises from changes in risk factors unique to that position.

Incremental risk means the default risk and credit migration risk of a position. Default risk means the risk of loss on a position that could result from the failure of an obligor to make timely payments of principal or interest on its debt obligation, and the risk of loss that could result from bankruptcy, insolvency, or similar proceeding. Credit migration risk means the price risk that arises from significant changes in the underlying credit quality of the position.

Market risk means the risk of loss on a position that could result from movements in market prices.

Resecuritization position means a covered position that is:

(1) An on- or off-balance sheet exposure to a resecuritization; or

(2) An exposure that directly or indirectly references a resecuritization exposure in paragraph (1) of this definition.

Securitization means a transaction in which:

(1) All or a portion of the credit risk of one or more underlying exposures is transferred to one or more third parties;

(2) The credit risk associated with the underlying exposures has been separated into at least two tranches that reflect different levels of seniority;

(3) Performance of the securitization exposures depends upon the performance of the underlying exposures;

(4) All or substantially all of the underlying exposures are financial exposures (such as loans, commitments, credit derivatives, guarantees, receivables, asset-backed securities, mortgage-backed securities, other debt securities, or equity securities);

(5) For non-synthetic securitizations, the underlying exposures are not owned by an operating company;

(6) The underlying exposures are not owned by a small business investment company described in section 302 of the Small Business Investment Act;

(7) The underlying exposures are not owned by a firm an investment in which qualifies as a community development investment under section 24(Eleventh) of the National Bank Act;

(8) The OCC may determine that a transaction in which the underlying exposures are owned by an investment firm that exercises substantially unfettered control over the size and composition of its assets, liabilities, and off-balance sheet exposures is not a securitization based on the transaction's leverage, risk profile, or economic substance;

(9) The OCC may deem an exposure to a transaction that meets the definition of a securitization, notwithstanding paragraph (5), (6), or (7) of this definition, to be a securitization based on the transaction's leverage, risk profile, or economic substance; and

(10) The transaction is not:

(i) An investment fund;

(ii) A collective investment fund (as defined in [12 CFR 208.34 (Board), 12 CFR 9.18 (OCC)]);

(iii) An employee benefit plan as defined in paragraphs (3) and (32) of section 3 of ERISA, a "governmental plan" (as defined in 29 U.S.C. 1002(32)) that complies with the tax deferral qualification requirements provided in the Internal Revenue Code, or any similar employee benefit plan established under the laws of a foreign jurisdiction; or

(iv) Registered with the SEC under the Investment Company Act of 1940 (15 U.S.C. 80a–1 *et seq.*) or foreign equivalents thereof.

Securitization position means a covered position that is:

(1) An on-balance sheet or off-balance sheet credit exposure (including credit-enhancing representations and warranties) that arises from a securitization (including a resecuritization); or

(2) An exposure that directly or indirectly references a securitization exposure described in paragraph (1) of this definition.

Sovereign debt position means a direct exposure to a sovereign entity.

Specific risk means the risk of loss on a position that could result from factors other than broad market movements and includes event risk, default risk, and idiosyncratic risk.

Structural position in a foreign currency means a position that is not a trading position and that is:

(1) Subordinated debt, equity, or minority interest in a consolidated subsidiary that is denominated in a foreign currency;

(2) Capital assigned to foreign branches that is denominated in a foreign currency;

(3) A position related to an unconsolidated subsidiary or another item that is denominated in a foreign currency and that is deducted from the national bank's or Federal savings association's tier 1 or tier 2 capital; or

(4) A position designed to hedge a national bank's or Federal savings association's capital ratios or earnings against the effect on paragraphs (1), (2), or (3) of this definition of adverse exchange rate movements.

Term repo-style transaction means a repo-style transaction that has an original maturity in excess of one business day.

Trading position means a position that is held by the national bank or Federal savings association for the purpose of short-term resale or with the intent of benefiting from actual or expected short-term price movements, or to lock in arbitrage profits.

Two-way market means a market where there are independent bona fide offers to buy and sell so that a price reasonably related to the last sales price or current bona fide competitive bid and offer quotations can be determined within one day and settled at that price within a relatively short time frame conforming to trade custom.

Value-at-Risk (VaR) means the estimate of the maximum amount that the value of one or more positions could decline due to market price or rate movements during a fixed holding period within a stated confidence interval.

§3.203 Requirements for application of this subpart F.

(a) *Trading positions*—(1) *Identification of trading positions.* A national bank or Federal savings association must have clearly defined policies and procedures for determining which of its trading assets and trading liabilities are trading positions and which of its trading positions are correlation trading positions. These policies and procedures must take into account:

(i) The extent to which a position, or a hedge of its material risks, can be marked-to-market daily by reference to a two-way market; and

(ii) Possible impairments to the liquidity of a position or its hedge.

(2) *Trading and hedging strategies.* A national bank or Federal savings association must have clearly defined trading and hedging strategies for its trading positions that are approved by senior management of the national bank or Federal savings association.

(i) The trading strategy must articulate the expected holding period of, and the market risk associated with, each portfolio of trading positions.

(ii) The hedging strategy must articulate for each portfolio of trading positions the level of market risk the national bank or Federal savings association is willing to accept and must detail the instruments, techniques, and strategies the national bank or Federal savings association will use to hedge the risk of the portfolio.

(b) *Management of covered positions*—(1) *Active management.* A national bank or Federal savings association must have clearly defined policies and procedures for actively managing all covered positions. At a minimum, these policies and procedures must require:

(i) Marking positions to market or to model on a daily basis;

(ii) Daily assessment of the national bank's or Federal savings association's ability to hedge position and portfolio risks, and of the extent of market liquidity;

(iii) Establishment and daily monitoring of limits on positions by a risk control unit independent of the trading business unit;

(iv) Daily monitoring by senior management of information described in paragraphs (b)(1)(i) through (b)(1)(iii) of this section;

(v) At least annual reassessment of established limits on positions by senior management; and

(vi) At least annual assessments by qualified personnel of the quality of market inputs to the valuation process, the soundness of key assumptions, the reliability of parameter estimation in pricing models, and the stability and accuracy of model calibration under alternative market scenarios.

(2) *Valuation of covered positions.* The national bank or Federal savings association must have a process for prudent valuation of its covered positions that includes policies and procedures on the valuation of positions, marking positions to market or to model, independent price verification, and valuation adjustments or reserves. The valuation process must consider, as appropriate, unearned credit spreads, close-out costs, early termination costs, investing and funding costs, liquidity, and model risk.

(c) *Requirements for internal models.* (1) A national bank or Federal savings association must obtain the prior written approval of the OCC before using any internal model to calculate its risk-based capital requirement under this subpart.

(2) A national bank or Federal savings association must meet all of the requirements of this section on an ongoing basis. The national bank or Federal savings association must promptly notify the OCC when:

(i) The national bank or Federal savings association plans to extend the use of a model that the OCC has approved under this subpart to an additional business line or product type;

(ii) The national bank or Federal savings association makes any change to an internal model approved by the OCC under this subpart that would result in a material change in the national bank's or Federal savings association's risk-weighted asset amount for a portfolio of covered positions; or

(iii) The national bank or Federal savings association makes any material change to its modeling assumptions.

(3) The OCC may rescind its approval of the use of any internal model (in whole or in part) or of the determination of the approach under § 3.209(a)(2)(ii) for a national bank's or Federal savings association's modeled correlation trading positions and determine an appropriate capital requirement for the covered positions to which the model would apply, if the OCC determines that the model no longer complies with this subpart or fails to reflect accurately the risks of the national bank's or Federal savings association's covered positions.

(4) The national bank or Federal savings association must periodically, but no less frequently than annually, review its internal models in light of developments in financial markets and modeling technologies, and enhance those models as appropriate to ensure that they continue to meet the OCC's standards for model approval and employ risk measurement methodologies that are most appropriate for the national bank's or Federal savings association's covered positions.

(5) The national bank or Federal savings association must incorporate its internal models into its risk management process and integrate the internal models used for calculating its VaR-based measure into its daily risk management process.

(6) The level of sophistication of a national bank's or Federal savings association's internal models must be commensurate with the complexity and amount of its covered positions. A national bank's or Federal savings association's internal models may use any of the generally accepted approaches, including but not limited to variance-covariance models, historical simulations, or Monte Carlo simulations, to measure market risk.

(7) The national bank's or Federal savings association's internal models must properly measure all the material risks in the covered positions to which they are applied.

(8) The national bank's or Federal savings association's internal models must conservatively assess the risks arising from less liquid positions and positions with limited price transparency under realistic market scenarios.

(9) The national bank or Federal savings association must have a rigorous

and well-defined process for re-estimating, re-evaluating, and updating its internal models to ensure continued applicability and relevance.

(10) If a national bank or Federal savings association uses internal models to measure specific risk, the internal models must also satisfy the requirements in paragraph (b)(1) of §3.207.

(d) *Control, oversight, and validation mechanisms.* (1) The national bank or Federal savings association must have a risk control unit that reports directly to senior management and is independent from the business trading units.

(2) The national bank or Federal savings association must validate its internal models initially and on an ongoing basis. The national bank's or Federal savings association's validation process must be independent of the internal models' development, implementation, and operation, or the validation process must be subjected to an independent review of its adequacy and effectiveness. Validation must include:

(i) An evaluation of the conceptual soundness of (including developmental evidence supporting) the internal models;

(ii) An ongoing monitoring process that includes verification of processes and the comparison of the national bank's or Federal savings association's model outputs with relevant internal and external data sources or estimation techniques; and

(iii) An outcomes analysis process that includes backtesting. For internal models used to calculate the VaR-based measure, this process must include a comparison of the changes in the national bank's or Federal savings association's portfolio value that would have occurred were end-of-day positions to remain unchanged (therefore, excluding fees, commissions, reserves, net interest income, and intraday trading) with VaR-based measures during a sample period not used in model development.

(3) The national bank or Federal savings association must stress test the market risk of its covered positions at a frequency appropriate to each portfolio, and in no case less frequently than quarterly. The stress tests must take into account concentration risk (including but not limited to concentrations in single issuers, industries, sectors, or markets), illiquidity under stressed market conditions, and risks arising from the national bank's or Federal savings association's trading activities that may not be adequately captured in its internal models.

(4) The national bank or Federal savings association must have an internal audit function independent of business-line management that at least annually assesses the effectiveness of the controls supporting the national bank's or Federal savings association's market risk measurement systems, including the activities of the business trading units and independent risk control unit, compliance with policies and procedures, and calculation of the national bank's or Federal savings association's measures for market risk under this subpart. At least annually, the internal audit function must report its findings to the national bank's or Federal savings association's board of directors (or a committee thereof).

(e) *Internal assessment of capital adequacy.* The national bank or Federal savings association must have a rigorous process for assessing its overall capital adequacy in relation to its market risk. The assessment must take into account risks that may not be captured fully in the VaR-based measure, including concentration and liquidity risk under stressed market conditions.

(f) *Documentation.* The national bank or Federal savings association must adequately document all material aspects of its internal models, management and valuation of covered positions, control, oversight, validation and review processes and results, and internal assessment of capital adequacy.

§3.204 Measure for market risk.

(a) *General requirement.* (1) A national bank or Federal savings association must calculate its standardized measure for market risk by following the steps described in paragraph (a)(2) of this section. An advanced approaches national bank or Federal savings association also must calculate an advanced measure for market risk by following the steps in paragraph (a)(2) of this section.

(2) *Measure for market risk.* A national bank or Federal savings association must calculate the standardized measure for market risk, which equals the sum of the VaR-based capital requirement, stressed VaR-based capital requirement, specific risk add-ons, incremental risk capital requirement, comprehensive risk capital requirement, and capital requirement for *de minimis* exposures all as defined under this paragraph (a)(2), (except, that the national bank or Federal savings association may not use the SFA in section 210(b)(2)(vii)(B) of this subpart for purposes of this calculation)[, plus any additional capital requirement established by the OCC]. An advanced approaches national bank or Federal savings association that has completed the parallel run process and that has received notifications from the OCC pursuant to § 3.121(d) also must calculate the advanced measure for market risk, which equals the sum of the VaR-based capital requirement, stressed VaR-based capital requirement, specific risk add-ons, incremental risk capital requirement, comprehensive risk capital requirement, and capital requirement for *de minimis* exposures as defined under this paragraph (a)(2) [, plus any additional capital requirement established by the OCC].

(i) *VaR-based capital requirement.* A national bank's or Federal savings association's VaR-based capital requirement equals the greater of:

(A) The previous day's VaR-based measure as calculated under § 3.205; or

(B) The average of the daily VaR-based measures as calculated under § 3.205 for each of the preceding 60 business days multiplied by three, except as provided in paragraph (b) of this section.

(ii) *Stressed VaR-based capital requirement.* A national bank's or Federal savings association's stressed VaR-based capital requirement equals the greater of:

(A) The most recent stressed VaR-based measure as calculated under § 3.206; or

(B) The average of the stressed VaR-based measures as calculated under § 3.206 for each of the preceding 12 weeks multiplied by three, except as provided in paragraph (b) of this section.

(iii) *Specific risk add-ons.* A national bank's or Federal savings association's specific risk add-ons equal any specific risk add-ons that are required under § 3.207 and are calculated in accordance with § 3.210.

(iv) *Incremental risk capital requirement.* A national bank's or Federal savings association's incremental risk capital requirement equals any incremental risk capital requirement as calculated under section 208 of this subpart.

(v) *Comprehensive risk capital requirement.* A national bank's or Federal savings association's comprehensive risk capital requirement equals any comprehensive risk capital requirement as calculated under section 209 of this subpart.

(vi) *Capital requirement for de minimis exposures.* A national bank's or Federal savings association's capital requirement for *de minimis* exposures equals:

(A) The absolute value of the fair value of those *de minimis* exposures that are not captured in the national bank's or Federal savings association's VaR-based measure or under paragraph (a)(2)(vi)(B) of this section; and

(B) With the prior written approval of the OCC, the capital requirement for any *de minimis* exposures using alternative techniques that appropriately measure the market risk associated with those exposures.

(b) *Backtesting.* A national bank or Federal savings association must compare each of its most recent 250 business days' trading losses (excluding fees, commissions, reserves, net interest income, and intraday trading) with the corresponding daily VaR-based measures calibrated to a one-day holding period and at a one-tail, 99.0 percent confidence level. A national bank or Federal savings association must begin backtesting as required by this paragraph (b) no later than one year after the later of January 1, 2014 and the date on which the national bank or Federal savings association becomes subject to this subpart. In the interim, consistent with safety and soundness principles, a national bank or Federal savings association subject to this subpart as of January 1, 2014 should continue to follow backtesting procedures in accordance with the OCC's supervisory expectations.

(1) Once each quarter, the national bank or Federal savings association must identify the number of exceptions (that is, the number of business days for which the actual daily net trading loss, if any, exceeds the corresponding daily VaR-based measure) that have occurred over the preceding 250 business days.

(2) A national bank or Federal savings association must use the multiplication factor in Table 1 to § 3.204 that corresponds to the number of exceptions identified in paragraph (b)(1) of this section to determine its VaR-based capital requirement for market risk under paragraph (a)(2)(i) of this section and to determine its stressed VaR-based capital requirement for market risk under paragraph (a)(2)(ii) of this section until it obtains the next quarter's backtesting results, unless the OCC notifies the national bank or Federal savings association in writing that a different adjustment or other action is appropriate.

TABLE 1 TO § 3.204—MULTIPLICATION FACTORS BASED ON RESULTS OF BACKTESTING

Number of exceptions	Multiplication factor
4 or fewer	3.00
5	3.40
6	3.50
7	3.65
8	3.75
9	3.85
10 or more	4.00

§ 3.205 VaR-based measure.

(a) *General requirement.* A national bank or Federal savings association must use one or more internal models to calculate daily a VaR-based measure of the general market risk of all covered positions. The daily VaR-based measure also may reflect the national bank's or Federal savings association's specific risk for one or more portfolios of debt and equity positions, if the internal models meet the requirements of paragraph (b)(1) of § 3.207. The daily VaR-based measure must also reflect the national bank's or Federal savings association's specific risk for any portfolio of correlation trading positions that is modeled under § 3.209. A national bank or Federal savings association may elect to include term repo-style transactions in its VaR-based measure, provided that the national bank or Federal savings association includes all such term repo-style transactions consistently over time.

(1) The national bank's or Federal savings association's internal models for calculating its VaR-based measure must use risk factors sufficient to measure the market risk inherent in all covered positions. The market risk categories must include, as appropriate, interest rate risk, credit spread risk, equity price risk, foreign exchange risk, and commodity price risk. For material positions in the major currencies and markets, modeling techniques must incorporate enough segments of the yield curve—in no case less than six—to capture differences in volatility and less than perfect correlation of rates along the yield curve.

(2) The VaR-based measure may incorporate empirical correlations within and across risk categories, provided the national bank or Federal savings association validates and demonstrates the reasonableness of its process for measuring correlations. If the VaR-based measure does not incorporate empirical correlations across risk categories, the national bank or Federal savings association must add the separate measures from its internal models used to calculate the VaR-based measure for the appropriate market risk categories (interest rate risk, credit spread risk, equity price risk, foreign exchange rate risk, and/or commodity price risk) to determine its aggregate VaR-based measure.

(3) The VaR-based measure must include the risks arising from the nonlinear price characteristics of options positions or positions with embedded optionality and the sensitivity of the fair value of the positions to changes in the volatility of the underlying rates, prices, or other material risk factors. A

national bank or Federal savings association with a large or complex options portfolio must measure the volatility of options positions or positions with embedded optionality by different maturities and/or strike prices, where material.

(4) The national bank or Federal savings association must be able to justify to the satisfaction of the OCC the omission of any risk factors from the calculation of its VaR-based measure that the national bank or Federal savings association uses in its pricing models.

(5) The national bank or Federal savings association must demonstrate to the satisfaction of the OCC the appropriateness of any proxies used to capture the risks of the national bank's or Federal savings association's actual positions for which such proxies are used.

(b) *Quantitative requirements for VaR-based measure.* (1) The VaR-based measure must be calculated on a daily basis using a one-tail, 99.0 percent confidence level, and a holding period equivalent to a 10-business-day movement in underlying risk factors, such as rates, spreads, and prices. To calculate VaR-based measures using a 10-business-day holding period, the national bank or Federal savings association may calculate 10-business-day measures directly or may convert VaR-based measures using holding periods other than 10 business days to the equivalent of a 10-business-day holding period. A national bank or Federal savings association that converts its VaR-based measure in such a manner must be able to justify the reasonableness of its approach to the satisfaction of the OCC.

(2) The VaR-based measure must be based on a historical observation period of at least one year. Data used to determine the VaR-based measure must be relevant to the national bank's or Federal savings association's actual exposures and of sufficient quality to support the calculation of risk-based capital requirements. The national bank or Federal savings association must update data sets at least monthly or more frequently as changes in market conditions or portfolio composition warrant. For a national bank or Federal savings association that uses a weighting scheme or other method for the historical observation period, the national bank or Federal savings association must either:

(i) Use an effective observation period of at least one year in which the average time lag of the observations is at least six months; or

(ii) Demonstrate to the OCC that its weighting scheme is more effective than a weighting scheme with an average time lag of at least six months representing the volatility of the national bank's or Federal savings association's trading portfolio over a full business cycle. A national bank or Federal savings association using this option must update its data more frequently than monthly and in a manner appropriate for the type of weighting scheme.

(c) A national bank or Federal savings association must divide its portfolio into a number of significant subportfolios approved by the OCC for subportfolio backtesting purposes. These subportfolios must be sufficient to allow the national bank or Federal savings association and the OCC to assess the adequacy of the VaR model at the risk factor level; the OCC will evaluate the appropriateness of these subportfolios relative to the value and composition of the national bank's or Federal savings association's covered positions. The national bank or Federal savings association must retain and make available to the OCC the following information for each subportfolio for each business day over the previous two years (500 business days), with no more than a 60-day lag:

(1) A daily VaR-based measure for the subportfolio calibrated to a one-tail, 99.0 percent confidence level;

(2) The daily profit or loss for the subportfolio (that is, the net change in price of the positions held in the portfolio at the end of the previous business day); and

(3) The p-value of the profit or loss on each day (that is, the probability of observing a profit that is less than, or a loss that is greater than, the amount reported for purposes of paragraph (c)(2) of this section based on the model used to calculate the VaR-based measure described in paragraph (c)(1) of this section).

§ 3.206 Stressed VaR-based measure.

(a) *General requirement.* At least weekly, a national bank or Federal savings association must use the same internal model(s) used to calculate its VaR-based measure to calculate a stressed VaR-based measure.

(b) *Quantitative requirements for stressed VaR-based measure.* (1) A national bank or Federal savings association must calculate a stressed VaR-based measure for its covered positions using the same model(s) used to calculate the VaR-based measure, subject to the same confidence level and holding period applicable to the VaR-based measure under § 3.205, but with model inputs calibrated to historical data from a continuous 12-month period that reflects a period of significant financial stress appropriate to the national bank's or Federal savings association's current portfolio.

(2) The stressed VaR-based measure must be calculated at least weekly and be no less than the national bank's or Federal savings association's VaR-based measure.

(3) A national bank or Federal savings association must have policies and procedures that describe how it determines the period of significant financial stress used to calculate the national bank's or Federal savings association's stressed VaR-based measure under this section and must be able to provide empirical support for the period used. The national bank or Federal savings association must obtain the prior approval of the OCC for, and notify the OCC if the national bank or Federal savings association makes any material changes to, these policies and procedures. The policies and procedures must address:

(i) How the national bank or Federal savings association links the period of significant financial stress used to calculate the stressed VaR-based measure to the composition and directional bias of its current portfolio; and

(ii) The national bank's or Federal savings association's process for selecting, reviewing, and updating the period of significant financial stress used to calculate the stressed VaR-based measure and for monitoring the appropriateness of the period to the national bank's or Federal savings association's current portfolio.

(4) Nothing in this section prevents the OCC from requiring a national bank or Federal savings association to use a different period of significant financial stress in the calculation of the stressed VaR-based measure.

§ 3.207 Specific risk.

(a) *General requirement.* A national bank or Federal savings association must use one of the methods in this section to measure the specific risk for each of its debt, equity, and securitization positions with specific risk.

(b) *Modeled specific risk.* A national bank or Federal savings association may use models to measure the specific risk of covered positions as provided in paragraph (a) of section 205 of this subpart (therefore, excluding securitization positions that are not modeled under section 209 of this subpart). A national bank or Federal savings association must use models to measure the specific risk of correlation trading positions that are modeled under § 3.209.

(1) *Requirements for specific risk modeling.* (i) If a national bank or Federal savings association uses internal models to measure the specific risk of a portfolio, the internal models must:

(A) Explain the historical price variation in the portfolio;

(B) Be responsive to changes in market conditions;

(C) Be robust to an adverse environment, including signaling rising risk in an adverse environment; and

(D) Capture all material components of specific risk for the debt and equity positions in the portfolio. Specifically, the internal models must:

(*1*) Capture event risk and idiosyncratic risk; and

(*2*) Capture and demonstrate sensitivity to material differences between positions that are similar but not identical and to changes in portfolio composition and concentrations.

(ii) If a national bank or Federal savings association calculates an incremental risk measure for a portfolio of debt or equity positions under section 208 of this subpart, the national bank or Federal savings association is not required to capture default and credit migration risks in its internal models used to measure the specific risk of those portfolios.

(2) *Specific risk fully modeled for one or more portfolios.* If the national bank's or Federal savings association's VaR-based measure captures all material aspects of specific risk for one or more of its portfolios of debt, equity, or correlation trading positions, the national bank or Federal savings association has no specific risk add-on for those portfolios for purposes of paragraph (a)(2)(iii) of § 3.204.

(c) *Specific risk not modeled.* (1) If the national bank's or Federal savings association's VaR-based measure does not capture all material aspects of specific risk for a portfolio of debt, equity, or correlation trading positions, the national bank or Federal savings association must calculate a specific-risk add-on for the portfolio under the standardized measurement method as described in § 3.210.

(2) A national bank or Federal savings association must calculate a specific risk add-on under the standardized measurement method as described in § 3.210 for all of its securitization positions that are not modeled under § 3.209.

§ 3.208 Incremental risk.

(a) *General requirement.* A national bank or Federal savings association that measures the specific risk of a portfolio of debt positions under § 3.207(b) using internal models must calculate at least weekly an incremental risk measure for that portfolio according to the requirements in this section. The incremental risk measure is the national bank's or Federal savings association's measure of potential losses due to incremental risk over a one-year time horizon at a one-tail, 99.9 percent confidence level, either under the assumption of a constant level of risk, or under the assumption of constant positions. With the prior approval of the OCC, a national bank or Federal savings association may choose to include portfolios of equity positions in its incremental risk model, provided that it consistently includes such equity positions in a manner that is consistent with how the national bank or Federal savings association internally measures and manages the incremental risk of such positions at the portfolio level. If equity positions are included in the model, for modeling purposes default is considered to have occurred upon the default of any debt of the issuer of the equity position. A national bank or Federal savings association may not include correlation trading positions or securitization positions in its incremental risk measure.

(b) *Requirements for incremental risk modeling.* For purposes of calculating the incremental risk measure, the incremental risk model must:

(1) Measure incremental risk over a one-year time horizon and at a one-tail, 99.9 percent confidence level, either under the assumption of a constant level of risk, or under the assumption of constant positions.

(i) A constant level of risk assumption means that the national bank or Federal savings association rebalances, or rolls over, its trading positions at the beginning of each liquidity horizon over the one-year horizon in a manner that maintains the national bank's or Federal savings association's initial risk level. The national bank or Federal savings association must determine the frequency of rebalancing in a manner consistent with the liquidity horizons of the positions in the portfolio. The liquidity horizon of a position or set of positions is the time required for a national bank or Federal savings association to reduce its exposure to, or hedge all of its material risks of, the position(s) in a stressed market. The liquidity horizon for a position or set of positions may not be less than the shorter of three months or the contractual maturity of the position.

(ii) A constant position assumption means that the national bank or Federal savings association maintains the same set of positions throughout the one-year horizon. If a national bank or Federal savings association uses this assumption, it must do so consistently across all portfolios.

(iii) A national bank's or Federal savings association's selection of a constant position or a constant risk assumption must be consistent between the national bank's or Federal savings association's incremental risk model and its comprehensive risk model described in section 209 of this subpart, if applicable.

(iv) A national bank's or Federal savings association's treatment of liquidity horizons must be consistent between the national bank's or Federal savings association's incremental risk model and its comprehensive risk model described in section 209, if applicable.

(2) Recognize the impact of correlations between default and migration events among obligors.

(3) Reflect the effect of issuer and market concentrations, as well as concentrations that can arise within and across product classes during stressed conditions.

(4) Reflect netting only of long and short positions that reference the same financial instrument.

(5) Reflect any material mismatch between a position and its hedge.

(6) Recognize the effect that liquidity horizons have on dynamic hedging strategies. In such cases, a national bank or Federal savings association must:

(i) Choose to model the rebalancing of the hedge consistently over the relevant set of trading positions;

(ii) Demonstrate that the inclusion of rebalancing results in a more appropriate risk measurement;

(iii) Demonstrate that the market for the hedge is sufficiently liquid to permit rebalancing during periods of stress; and

(iv) Capture in the incremental risk model any residual risks arising from such hedging strategies.

(7) Reflect the nonlinear impact of options and other positions with material nonlinear behavior with respect to default and migration changes.

(8) Maintain consistency with the national bank's or Federal savings association's internal risk management methodologies for identifying, measuring, and managing risk.

(c) *Calculation of incremental risk capital requirement.* The incremental risk capital requirement is the greater of:

(1) The average of the incremental risk measures over the previous 12 weeks; or

(2) The most recent incremental risk measure.

§ 3.209 Comprehensive risk.

(a) *General requirement.* (1) Subject to the prior approval of the OCC, a national bank or Federal savings association may use the method in this section to measure comprehensive risk, that is, all price risk, for one or more portfolios of correlation trading positions.

(2) A national bank or Federal savings association that measures the price risk of a portfolio of correlation trading positions using internal models must calculate at least weekly a comprehensive risk measure that captures all price risk according to the requirements of this section. The comprehensive risk measure is either:

(i) The sum of:

(A) The national bank's or Federal savings association's modeled measure of all price risk determined according to the requirements in paragraph (b) of this section; and

(B) A surcharge for the national bank's or Federal savings association's modeled correlation trading positions equal to the total specific risk add-on for such positions as calculated under section 210 of this subpart multiplied by 8.0 percent; or

(ii) With approval of the OCC and provided the national bank or Federal savings association has met the requirements of this section for a period of at least one year and can demonstrate the effectiveness of the model through the results of ongoing model validation efforts including robust benchmarking, the greater of:

(A) The national bank's or Federal savings association's modeled measure of all price risk determined according to the requirements in paragraph (b) of this section; or

(B) The total specific risk add-on that would apply to the bank's modeled correlation trading positions as calculated under section 210 of this subpart multiplied by 8.0 percent.

(b) *Requirements for modeling all price risk.* If a national bank or Federal savings association uses an internal model to measure the price risk of a portfolio of correlation trading positions:

(1) The internal model must measure comprehensive risk over a one-year time horizon at a one-tail, 99.9 percent confidence level, either under the assumption of a constant level of risk, or under the assumption of constant positions.

(2) The model must capture all material price risk, including but not limited to the following:

(i) The risks associated with the contractual structure of cash flows of the position, its issuer, and its underlying exposures;

(ii) Credit spread risk, including nonlinear price risks;

(iii) The volatility of implied correlations, including nonlinear price risks such as the cross-effect between spreads and correlations;

(iv) Basis risk;

(v) Recovery rate volatility as it relates to the propensity for recovery rates to affect tranche prices; and

(vi) To the extent the comprehensive risk measure incorporates the benefits of dynamic hedging, the static nature of the hedge over the liquidity horizon must be recognized. In such cases, a national bank or Federal savings association must:

(A) Choose to model the rebalancing of the hedge consistently over the relevant set of trading positions;

(B) Demonstrate that the inclusion of rebalancing results in a more appropriate risk measurement;

(C) Demonstrate that the market for the hedge is sufficiently liquid to permit rebalancing during periods of stress; and

(D) Capture in the comprehensive risk model any residual risks arising from such hedging strategies;

(3) The national bank or Federal savings association must use market data that are relevant in representing the risk profile of the national bank's or Federal savings association's correlation trading positions in order to ensure that the national bank or Federal savings association fully captures the material risks of the correlation trading positions in its comprehensive risk measure in accordance with this section; and

(4) The national bank or Federal savings association must be able to demonstrate that its model is an appropriate representation of comprehensive risk in light of the historical price variation of its correlation trading positions.

(c) *Requirements for stress testing.* (1) A national bank or Federal savings association must at least weekly apply specific, supervisory stress scenarios to its portfolio of correlation trading positions that capture changes in:

(i) Default rates;

(ii) Recovery rates;

(iii) Credit spreads;

(iv) Correlations of underlying exposures; and

(v) Correlations of a correlation trading position and its hedge.

(2) *Other requirements.* (i) A national bank or Federal savings association must retain and make available to the OCC the results of the supervisory stress testing, including comparisons with the capital requirements generated by the national bank's or Federal savings association's comprehensive risk model.

(ii) A national bank or Federal savings association must report to the OCC promptly any instances where the stress tests indicate any material deficiencies in the comprehensive risk model.

(d) *Calculation of comprehensive risk capital requirement.* The comprehensive risk capital requirement is the greater of:

(1) The average of the comprehensive risk measures over the previous 12 weeks; or

(2) The most recent comprehensive risk measure.

§ 3.210 Standardized measurement method for specific risk

(a) *General requirement.* A national bank or Federal savings association must calculate a total specific risk add-on for each portfolio of debt and equity positions for which the national bank's or Federal savings association's VaR-based measure does not capture all material aspects of specific risk and for all securitization positions that are not modeled under § 3.209. A national bank or Federal savings association must calculate each specific risk add-on in accordance with the requirements of this section. Notwithstanding any other definition or requirement in this subpart, a position that would have qualified as a debt position or an equity position but for the fact that it qualifies as a correlation trading position under paragraph (2) of the definition of correlation trading position in §3.202, shall be considered a debt position or an equity position, respectively, for purposes of this section 210 of this subpart.

(1) The specific risk add-on for an individual debt or securitization position that represents sold credit protection is capped at the notional amount of the credit derivative contract. The specific risk add-on for an individual debt or securitization position that represents purchased credit protection is capped at the current fair value of the transaction plus the absolute value of the present value of all remaining payments to the protection seller under the transaction. This sum is equal to the value of the protection leg of the transaction.

(2) For debt, equity, or securitization positions that are derivatives with linear payoffs, a national bank or Federal savings association must assign a specific risk-weighting factor to the fair value of the effective notional amount of the underlying instrument or index portfolio, except for a securitization position for which the national bank or Federal savings association directly calculates a specific risk add-on using the SFA in paragraph (b)(2)(vii)(B) of this section. A swap must be included as an effective notional position in the underlying instrument or portfolio, with the receiving side treated as a long position and the paying side treated as a short position. For debt, equity, or securitization positions that are derivatives with nonlinear payoffs, a national bank or Federal savings association must risk weight the fair value of the effective notional amount of the underlying instrument or portfolio multiplied by the derivative's delta.

(3) For debt, equity, or securitization positions, a national bank or Federal savings association may net long and short positions (including derivatives) in identical issues or identical indices. A national bank or Federal savings association may also net positions in depositary receipts against an opposite position in an identical equity in different markets, provided that the national bank or Federal savings association includes the costs of conversion.

(4) A set of transactions consisting of either a debt position and its credit derivative hedge or a securitization position and its credit derivative hedge has a specific risk add-on of zero if:

(i) The debt or securitization position is fully hedged by a total return swap (or similar instrument where there is a matching of swap payments and changes in fair value of the debt or securitization position);

(ii) There is an exact match between the reference obligation of the swap and the debt or securitization position;

(iii) There is an exact match between the currency of the swap and the debt or securitization position; and

(iv) There is either an exact match between the maturity date of the swap and the maturity date of the debt or securitization position; or, in cases where a total return swap references a portfolio of positions with different maturity dates, the total return swap maturity date must match the maturity date of the underlying asset in that portfolio that has the latest maturity date.

(5) The specific risk add-on for a set of transactions consisting of either a debt position and its credit derivative hedge or a securitization position and its credit derivative hedge that does not meet the criteria of paragraph (a)(4) of this section is equal to 20.0 percent of the capital requirement for the side of the transaction with the higher specific risk add-on when:

(i) The credit risk of the position is fully hedged by a credit default swap or similar instrument;

(ii) There is an exact match between the reference obligation of the credit derivative hedge and the debt or securitization position;

(iii) There is an exact match between the currency of the credit derivative hedge and the debt or securitization position; and

(iv) There is either an exact match between the maturity date of the credit derivative hedge and the maturity date of the debt or securitization position; or, in the case where the credit derivative hedge has a standard maturity date:

(A) The maturity date of the credit derivative hedge is within 30 business days of the maturity date of the debt or securitization position; or

(B) For purchased credit protection, the maturity date of the credit derivative hedge is later than the maturity date of the debt or securitization position, but is no later than the standard maturity date for that instrument that immediately follows the maturity date of the debt or securitization position. The maturity date of the credit derivative hedge may not exceed the maturity date of the debt or securitization position by more than 90 calendar days.

(6) The specific risk add-on for a set of transactions consisting of either a debt position and its credit derivative hedge or a securitization position and its credit derivative hedge that does not meet the criteria of either paragraph (a)(4) or (a)(5) of this section, but in which all or substantially all of the price risk has been hedged, is equal to the specific risk add-on for the side of the transaction with the higher specific risk add-on.

(b) *Debt and securitization positions.* (1) The total specific risk add-on for a portfolio of debt or securitization positions is the sum of the specific risk add-ons for individual debt or securitization positions, as computed under this section. To determine the specific risk add-on for individual debt or securitization positions, a national bank or Federal savings association must multiply the absolute value of the current fair value of each net long or net short debt or securitization position in the portfolio by the appropriate specific risk-weighting factor as set forth in paragraphs (b)(2)(i) through (b)(2)(vii) of this section.

(2) For the purpose of this section, the appropriate specific risk-weighting factors include:

(i) *Sovereign debt positions.* (A) In accordance with Table 1 to §3.210, a national bank or Federal savings association must assign a specific risk-weighting factor to a sovereign debt position based on the CRC applicable to the sovereign, and, as applicable, the remaining contractual maturity of the position, or if there is no CRC applicable to the sovereign, based on whether the sovereign entity is a member of the OECD. Notwithstanding any other provision in this subpart, sovereign debt positions that are backed by the full faith and credit of the United States are treated as having a CRC of 0.

TABLE 1 TO §3.210—SPECIFIC RISK-WEIGHTING FACTORS FOR SOVEREIGN DEBT POSITIONS

	Specific risk-weighting factor (in percent)	
CRC:		
0–1	0.0	
2–3	Remaining contractual maturity of 6 months or less	0.25
	Remaining contractual maturity of greater than 6 and up to and including 24 months.	1.0
	Remaining contractual maturity exceeds 24 months	1.6
4–6	8.0	
7	12.0	
OECD Member with No CRC	0.0	
Non-OECD Member with No CRC	8.0	
Sovereign Default	12.0	

(B) Notwithstanding paragraph (b)(2)(i)(A) of this section, a national bank or Federal savings association may assign to a sovereign debt position a specific risk-weighting factor that is lower than the applicable specific risk-weighting factor in Table 1 to §3.210 if:

(*1*) The position is denominated in the sovereign entity's currency;

(*2*) The national bank or Federal savings association has at least an equivalent amount of liabilities in that currency; and

(*3*) The sovereign entity allows banks under its jurisdiction to assign the lower specific risk-weighting factor to the same exposures to the sovereign entity.

(C) A national bank or Federal savings association must assign a 12.0 percent specific risk-weighting factor to a sovereign debt position immediately upon determination a default has occurred; or if a default has occurred within the previous five years.

(D) A national bank or Federal savings association must assign a 0.0 percent specific risk-weighting factor to a sovereign debt position if the sovereign entity is a member of the OECD and does not have a CRC assigned to it, except as provided in paragraph (b)(2)(i)(C) of this section.

(E) A national bank or Federal savings association must assign an 8.0 percent specific risk-weighting factor to a sovereign debt position if the sovereign is not a member of the OECD and does not have a CRC assigned to it, except as provided in paragraph (b)(2)(i)(C) of this section.

(ii) *Certain supranational entity and multilateral development bank debt positions.* A national bank or Federal savings association may assign a 0.0 percent specific risk-weighting factor to a debt position that is an exposure to the Bank for International Settlements, the European Central Bank, the European Commission, the International Monetary Fund, or an MDB.

(iii) *GSE debt positions.* A national bank or Federal savings association must assign a 1.6 percent specific risk-weighting factor to a debt position that is an exposure to a GSE. Notwithstanding the foregoing, a national bank or Federal savings association must assign an 8.0 percent specific risk-weighting factor to preferred stock issued by a GSE.

(iv) *Depository institution, foreign bank, and credit union debt positions.* (A) Except as provided in paragraph (b)(2)(iv)(B) of this section, a national bank or Federal savings association must assign a specific risk-weighting factor to a debt position that is an exposure to a depository institution, a foreign bank, or a credit union, in accordance with Table 2 to §3.210, based on the CRC that corresponds to that entity's home country or the OECD membership status of that entity's home country if there is no CRC applicable to the entity's home country, and, as applicable, the remaining contractual maturity of the position.

TABLE 2 TO §3.210—SPECIFIC RISK-WEIGHTING FACTORS FOR DEPOSITORY INSTITUTION, FOREIGN BANK, AND CREDIT UNION DEBT POSITIONS

	Specific risk-weighting factor (in percent)	
CRC 0–2 or OECD Member with No CRC	Remaining contractual maturity of 6 months or less	0.25
	Remaining contractual maturity of greater than 6 and up to and including 24 months.	1.0
	Remaining contractual maturity exceeds 24 months	1.6
CRC 3	8.0	
CRC 4–7	12.0	
Non-OECD Member with No CRC	8.0	
Sovereign Default	12.0	

(B) A national bank or Federal savings association must assign a specific risk-weighting factor of 8.0 percent to a debt position that is an exposure to a depository institution or a foreign bank that is includable in the depository institution's or foreign bank's regulatory capital and that is not subject to deduction as a reciprocal holding under §3.22.

(C) A national bank or Federal savings association must assign a 12.0 percent specific risk-weighting factor to a debt position that is an exposure to a foreign bank immediately upon determination that a default by the foreign bank's home country has occurred or if a default by the foreign bank's home country has occurred within the previous five years.

(v) *PSE debt positions.* (A) Except as provided in paragraph (b)(2)(v)(B) of this section, a national bank or Federal savings association must assign a specific risk-weighting factor to a debt position that is an exposure to a PSE in accordance with Tables 3 and 4 to § 3.210 depending on the position's categorization as a general obligation or revenue obligation based on the CRC that corresponds to the PSE's home country or the OECD membership status of the PSE's home country if there is no CRC applicable to the PSE's home country, and, as applicable, the remaining contractual maturity of the position, as set forth in Tables 3 and 4 of this section.

(B) A national bank or Federal savings association may assign a lower specific risk-weighting factor than would otherwise apply under Tables 3 and 4 of this section to a debt position that is an exposure to a foreign PSE if:

(*1*) The PSE's home country allows banks under its jurisdiction to assign a lower specific risk-weighting factor to such position; and

(*2*) The specific risk-weighting factor is not lower than the risk weight that corresponds to the PSE's home country in accordance with Tables 3 and 4 of this section.

(C) A national bank or Federal savings association must assign a 12.0 percent specific risk-weighting factor to a PSE debt position immediately upon determination that a default by the PSE's home country has occurred or if a default by the PSE's home country has occurred within the previous five years.

TABLE 3 TO § 3.210—SPECIFIC RISK-WEIGHTING FACTORS FOR PSE GENERAL OBLIGATION DEBT POSITIONS

	General obligation specific risk-weighting factor (in percent)	
CRC 0–2 or OECD Member with No CRC	Remaining contractual maturity of 6 months or less	0.25
	Remaining contractual maturity of greater than 6 and up to and including 24 months.	1.0
	Remaining contractual maturity exceeds 24 months	1.6
CRC 3	8.0	
CRC 4–7	12.0	
Non-OECD Member with No CRC	8.0	
Sovereign Default	12.0	

TABLE 4 TO § 3.210—SPECIFIC RISK-WEIGHTING FACTORS FOR PSE REVENUE OBLIGATION DEBT POSITIONS

	Revenue obligation specific risk-weighting factor (in percent)	
CRC 0–1 or OECD Member with No CRC	Remaining contractual maturity of 6 months or less	0.25
	Remaining contractual maturity of greater than 6 and up to and including 24 months.	1.0
	Remaining contractual maturity exceeds 24 months	1.6
CRC 2–3	8.0	
CRC 4–7	12.0	
Non-OECD Member with No CRC	8.0	
Sovereign Default	12.0	

(vi) *Corporate debt positions.* Except as otherwise provided in paragraph (b)(2)(vi)(B) of this section, a national bank or Federal savings association must assign a specific risk-weighting factor to a corporate debt position in accordance with the investment grade methodology in paragraph (b)(2)(vi)(A) of this section.

(A) *Investment grade methodology.* (*1*) For corporate debt positions that are exposures to entities that have issued and outstanding publicly traded instruments, a national bank or Federal savings association must assign a specific risk-weighting factor based on the category and remaining contractual maturity of the position, in accordance with Table 5 to §3.210. For purposes of this paragraph (b)(2)(vi)(A)(*1*), the national bank or Federal savings association must determine whether the position is in the investment grade or not investment grade category.

TABLE 5 TO §3.210—SPECIFIC RISK-WEIGHTING FACTORS FOR CORPORATE DEBT POSITIONS UNDER THE INVESTMENT GRADE METHODOLOGY

Category	Remaining contractual maturity	Specific risk-weighting factor (in percent)
Investment Grade	6 months or less	0.50
	Greater than 6 and up to and including 24 months	2.00
	Greater than 24 months	4.00
Non-investment Grade		12.00

(*2*) A national bank or Federal savings association must assign an 8.0 percent specific risk-weighting factor for corporate debt positions that are exposures to entities that do not have publicly traded instruments outstanding.

(B) *Limitations.* (*1*) A national bank or Federal savings association must assign a specific risk-weighting factor of at least 8.0 percent to an interest-only mortgage-backed security that is not a securitization position.

(*2*) A national bank or Federal savings association shall not assign a corporate debt position a specific risk-weighting factor that is lower than the specific risk-weighting factor that corresponds to the CRC of the issuer's home country, if applicable, in table 1 of this section.

(vii) *Securitization positions.* (A) General requirements. (*1*) A national bank or Federal savings association that is not an advanced approaches national bank or Federal savings association must assign a specific risk-weighting factor to a securitization position using either the simplified supervisory formula approach (SSFA) in paragraph (b)(2)(vii)(C) of this section (and §3.211) or assign a specific risk-weighting factor of 100 percent to the position.

(*2*) A national bank or Federal savings association that is an advanced approaches national bank or Federal savings association must calculate a specific risk add-on for a securitization position in accordance with paragraph (b)(2)(vii)(B) of this section if the national bank or Federal savings association and the securitization position each qualifies to use the SFA in §3.143. A national bank or Federal savings association that is an advanced approaches national bank or Federal savings association with a securitization position that does not qualify for the SFA under paragraph (b)(2)(vii)(B) of this section may assign a specific risk-weighting factor to the securitization position using the SSFA in accordance with paragraph (b)(2)(vii)(C) of this section or assign a specific risk-weighting factor of 100 percent to the position.

(*3*) A national bank or Federal savings association must treat a short securitization position as if it is a long securitization position solely for calculation purposes when using the SFA in paragraph (b)(2)(vii)(B) of this section or the SSFA in paragraph (b)(2)(vii)(C) of this section.

(B) *SFA.* To calculate the specific risk add-on for a securitization position using the SFA, a national bank or Federal savings association that is an advanced approaches national bank or Federal savings association must set the specific risk add-on for the position equal to the risk-based capital requirement as calculated under §3.143.

(C) *SSFA.* To use the SSFA to determine the specific risk-weighting factor for a securitization position, a national bank or Federal savings association must calculate the specific risk-weighting factor in accordance with § 3.211.

(D) *N^th-to-default credit derivatives.* A national bank or Federal savings association must determine a specific risk add-on using the SFA in paragraph (b)(2)(vii)(B) of this section, or assign a specific risk-weighting factor using the SSFA in paragraph (b)(2)(vii)(C) of this section to an nth-to-default credit derivative in accordance with this paragraph (b)(2)(vii)(D), regardless of whether the national bank or Federal savings association is a net protection buyer or net protection seller. A national bank or Federal savings association must determine its position in the nth-to-default credit derivative as the largest notional amount of all the underlying exposures.

(*1*) For purposes of determining the specific risk add-on using the SFA in paragraph (b)(2)(vii)(B) of this section or the specific risk-weighting factor for an nth-to-default credit derivative using the SSFA in paragraph (b)(2)(vii)(C) of this section the national bank or Federal savings association must calculate the attachment point and detachment point of its position as follows:

(*i*) The attachment point (parameter A) is the ratio of the sum of the notional amounts of all underlying exposures that are subordinated to the national bank's or Federal savings association's position to the total notional amount of all underlying exposures. For purposes of the SSFA, parameter A is expressed as a decimal value between zero and one. For purposes of using the SFA in paragraph (b)(2)(vii)(B) of this section to calculate the specific add-on for its position in an nth-to-default credit derivative, parameter A must be set equal to the credit enhancement level (L) input to the SFA formula in section 143 of this subpart. In the case of a first-to-default credit derivative, there are no underlying exposures that are subordinated to the national bank's or Federal savings association's position. In the case of a second-or-subsequent-to-default credit derivative, the smallest (n-1) notional amounts of the underlying exposure(s) are subordinated to the national bank's or Federal savings association's position.

(*ii*) The detachment point (parameter D) equals the sum of parameter A plus the ratio of the notional amount of the national bank's or Federal savings association's position in the nth-to-default credit derivative to the total notional amount of all underlying exposures. For purposes of the SSFA, parameter A is expressed as a decimal value between zero and one. For purposes of using the SFA in paragraph (b)(2)(vii)(B) of this section to calculate the specific risk add-on for its position in an nth-to-default credit derivative, parameter D must be set to equal the L input plus the thickness of tranche T input to the SFA formula in § 3.143 of this subpart.

(*2*) A national bank or Federal savings association that does not use the SFA in paragraph (b)(2)(vii)(B) of this section to determine a specific risk-add on, or the SSFA in paragraph (b)(2)(vii)(C) of this section to determine a specific risk-weighting factor for its position in an nth-to-default credit derivative must assign a specific risk-weighting factor of 100 percent to the position.

(c) *Modeled correlation trading positions.* For purposes of calculating the comprehensive risk measure for modeled correlation trading positions under either paragraph (a)(2)(i) or (a)(2)(ii) of § 3.209, the total specific risk add-on is the greater of:

(1) The sum of the national bank's or Federal savings association's specific risk add-ons for each net long correlation trading position calculated under this section; or

(2) The sum of the national bank's or Federal savings association's specific risk add-ons for each net short correlation trading position calculated under this section.

(d) *Non-modeled securitization positions.* For securitization positions that are not correlation trading positions and for securitizations that are correlation trading positions not modeled under § 3.209, the total specific risk add-on is the greater of:

(1) The sum of the national bank's or Federal savings association's specific risk add-ons for each net long securitization position calculated under this section; or

(2) The sum of the national bank's or Federal savings association's specific risk add-ons for each net short securitization position calculated under this section.

(e) *Equity positions.* The total specific risk add-on for a portfolio of equity positions is the sum of the specific risk add-ons of the individual equity positions, as computed under this section. To determine the specific risk add-on of individual equity positions, a national bank or Federal savings association must multiply the absolute value of the current fair value of each net long or net short equity position by the appropriate specific risk-weighting factor as determined under this paragraph (e):

(1) The national bank or Federal savings association must multiply the absolute value of the current fair value of each net long or net short equity position by a specific risk-weighting factor of 8.0 percent. For equity positions that are index contracts comprising a well-diversified portfolio of equity instruments, the absolute value of the current fair value of each net long or net short position is multiplied by a specific risk-weighting factor of 2.0 percent.[33]

(2) For equity positions arising from the following futures-related arbitrage strategies, a national bank or Federal savings association may apply a 2.0 percent specific risk-weighting factor to one side (long or short) of each position with the opposite side exempt from an additional capital requirement:

(i) Long and short positions in exactly the same index at different dates or in different market centers; or

(ii) Long and short positions in index contracts at the same date in different, but similar indices.

(3) For futures contracts on main indices that are matched by offsetting positions in a basket of stocks comprising the index, a national bank or Federal savings association may apply a 2.0 percent specific risk-weighting factor to the futures and stock basket positions (long and short), provided that such trades are deliberately entered into and separately controlled, and that the basket of stocks is comprised of stocks representing at least 90.0 percent of the capitalization of the index. A main index refers to the Standard & Poor's 500 Index, the FTSE All-World Index, and any other index for which the national bank or Federal savings association can demonstrate to the satisfaction of the OCC that the equities represented in the index have liquidity, depth of market, and size of bid-ask spreads comparable to equities in the Standard & Poor's 500 Index and FTSE All-World Index.

(f) *Due diligence requirements for securitization positions.* (1) A national bank or Federal savings association must demonstrate to the satisfaction of the OCC a comprehensive understanding of the features of a securitization position that would materially affect the performance of the position by conducting and documenting the analysis set forth in paragraph (f)(2) of this section. The national bank's or Federal savings association's analysis must be commensurate with the complexity of the securitization position and the materiality of the position in relation to capital.

(2) A national bank or Federal savings association must demonstrate its comprehensive understanding for each securitization position by:

(i) Conducting an analysis of the risk characteristics of a securitization position prior to acquiring the position and document such analysis within three business days after acquiring position, considering:

(A) Structural features of the securitization that would materially impact the performance of the position, for example, the contractual cash flow waterfall, waterfall-related triggers, credit enhancements, liquidity enhancements, fair value triggers, the performance of organizations that service the position, and deal-specific definitions of default;

(B) Relevant information regarding the performance of the underlying credit exposure(s), for example, the percentage of loans 30, 60, and 90 days past due; default rates; prepayment

[33] A portfolio is well-diversified if it contains a large number of individual equity positions, with no single position representing a substantial portion of the portfolio's total fair value.

rates; loans in foreclosure; property types; occupancy; average credit score or other measures of creditworthiness; average loan-to-value ratio; and industry and geographic diversification data on the underlying exposure(s);

(C) Relevant market data of the securitization, for example, bid-ask spreads, most recent sales price and historical price volatility, trading volume, implied market rating, and size, depth and concentration level of the market for the securitization; and

(D) For resecuritization positions, performance information on the underlying securitization exposures, for example, the issuer name and credit quality, and the characteristics and performance of the exposures underlying the securitization exposures.

(ii) On an on-going basis (no less frequently than quarterly), evaluating, reviewing, and updating as appropriate the analysis required under paragraph (f)(1) of this section for each securitization position.

§ 3.211 Simplified supervisory formula approach (SSFA).

(a) *General requirements.* To use the SSFA to determine the specific risk-weighting factor for a securitization position, a national bank or Federal savings association must have data that enables it to assign accurately the parameters described in paragraph (b) of this section. Data used to assign the parameters described in paragraph (b) of this section must be the most currently available data; if the contracts governing the underlying exposures of the securitization require payments on a monthly or quarterly basis, the data used to assign the parameters described in paragraph (b) of this section must be no more than 91 calendar days old. A national bank or Federal savings association that does not have the appropriate data to assign the parameters described in paragraph (b) of this section must assign a specific risk-weighting factor of 100 percent to the position.

(b) *SSFA parameters.* To calculate the specific risk-weighting factor for a securitization position using the SSFA, a national bank or Federal savings association must have accurate information on the five inputs to the SSFA calculation described in paragraphs (b)(1) through (b)(5) of this section.

(1) K_G is the weighted-average (with unpaid principal used as the weight for each exposure) total capital requirement of the underlying exposures calculated using subpart D. K_G is expressed as a decimal value between zero and one (that is, an average risk weight of 100 percent represents a value of K_G equal to 0.08).

(2) Parameter W is expressed as a decimal value between zero and one. Parameter W is the ratio of the sum of the dollar amounts of any underlying exposures of the securitization that meet any of the criteria as set forth in paragraphs (b)(2)(i) through (vi) of this section to the balance, measured in dollars, of underlying exposures:

(i) Ninety days or more past due;

(ii) Subject to a bankruptcy or insolvency proceeding;

(iii) In the process of foreclosure;

(iv) Held as real estate owned;

(v) Has contractually deferred payments for 90 days or more, other than principal or interest payments deferred on:

(A) Federally-guaranteed student loans, in accordance with the terms of those guarantee programs; or

(B) Consumer loans, including non-federally-guaranteed student loans, provided that such payments are deferred pursuant to provisions included in the contract at the time funds are disbursed that provide for period(s) of deferral that are not initiated based on changes in the creditworthiness of the borrower; or

(vi) Is in default.

(3) Parameter A is the attachment point for the position, which represents the threshold at which credit losses will first be allocated to the position. Except as provided in § 3.210(b)(2)(vii)(D) for n^{th}-to-default credit derivatives, parameter A equals the ratio of the current dollar amount of underlying exposures that are subordinated to the position of the national bank or Federal savings association to the current dollar amount of underlying exposures. Any reserve account funded by the accumulated cash flows from the underlying exposures that is subordinated to the position that contains the national bank's or Federal

savings association's securitization exposure may be included in the calculation of parameter A to the extent that cash is present in the account. Parameter A is expressed as a decimal value between zero and one.

(4) Parameter D is the detachment point for the position, which represents the threshold at which credit losses of principal allocated to the position would result in a total loss of principal. Except as provided in §3.210(b)(2)(vii)(D) for n^{th}-to-default credit derivatives, parameter D equals parameter A plus the ratio of the current dollar amount of the securitization positions that are *pari passu* with the position (that is, have equal seniority with respect to credit risk) to the current dollar amount of the underlying exposures. Parameter D is expressed as a decimal value between zero and one.

(5) A supervisory calibration parameter, p, is equal to 0.5 for securitization positions that are not resecuritization positions and equal to 1.5 for resecuritization positions.

(c) *Mechanics of the SSFA.* K_G and W are used to calculate K_A, the augmented value of K_G, which reflects the observed credit quality of the underlying exposures. K_A is defined in paragraph (d) of this section. The values of parameters A and D, relative to K_A determine the specific risk-weighting factor assigned to a position as described in this paragraph (c) and paragraph (d) of this section. The specific risk-weighting factor assigned to a securitization position, or portion of a position, as appropriate, is the larger of the specific risk-weighting factor determined in accordance with this paragraph (c), paragraph (d) of this section, and a specific risk-weighting factor of 1.6 percent.

(1) When the detachment point, parameter D, for a securitization position is less than or equal to K_A, the position must be assigned a specific risk-weighting factor of 100 percent.

(2) When the attachment point, parameter A, for a securitization position is greater than or equal to K_A, the national bank or Federal savings association must calculate the specific risk-weighting factor in accordance with paragraph (d) of this section.

(3) When A is less than K_A and D is greater than K_A, the specific risk-weighting factor is a weighted-average of 1.00 and K_{SSFA} calculated under paragraphs (c)(3)(i) and (c)(3)(ii) of this section. For the purpose of this calculation:

(i) The weight assigned to 1.00 equals

(ii) The weight assigned to K_{SSFA} equals $\frac{D - K_A}{D - A}$. The specific risk-weighting factor is equal to:

$$SRWF = 100 \cdot \left[\left(\frac{K_A - A}{D - A} \right) \cdot 1.00 \right] + \left[\left(\frac{D - K_A}{D - A} \right) \cdot K_{SSFA} \right]$$

(d) SSFA equation. (1) The [BANK] must define the following parameters:

$$K_A = (1 - W) \cdot K_G + (0.5 \cdot W)$$

$$a = -\frac{1}{p \cdot K_A}$$

$$u = D - K_A$$

$$l = \max(A - K_A, 0)$$

$e = 2.71828$, the base of the natural logarithms.

(2) Then the [BANK] must calculate K_{SSFA} according to the following formula:

$$K_{SSFA} = \frac{e^{a \cdot u} - e^{a \cdot l}}{a(u - l)}$$

(3) The specific risk-weighting factor for the position (expressed as a percent) is equal to $K_{SSFA} \times 100$.

§ 3.212 Market risk disclosures.

(a) *Scope.* A national bank or Federal savings association must comply with this section unless it is a consolidated subsidiary of a bank holding company or a depository institution that is subject to these requirements or of a non-U.S. banking organization that is subject to comparable public disclosure requirements in its home jurisdiction. A national bank or Federal savings association must make timely public disclosures each calendar quarter. If a significant change occurs, such that the most recent reporting amounts are no longer reflective of the national bank's or Federal savings association's capital adequacy and risk profile, then a brief discussion of this change and its likely impact must be provided as soon as practicable thereafter. Qualitative disclosures that typically do not change each quarter may be disclosed annually, provided any significant changes are disclosed in the interim. If a national bank or Federal savings association believes that disclosure of specific commercial or financial information would prejudice seriously its position by making public certain information that is either proprietary or confidential in nature, the national bank or Federal savings association is not required to disclose these specific items, but must disclose more general information about the subject matter of the requirement, together with the fact that, and the reason why, the specific items of information have not been disclosed. The national bank's or Federal savings association's management may provide all of the disclosures required by this section in one place on the national bank's or Federal savings association's public Web site or may provide the disclosures in more than one public financial report or other regulatory reports, provided that the national bank or Federal savings association publicly provides a summary table specifically indicating the location(s) of all such disclosures.

(b) *Disclosure policy.* The national bank or Federal savings association must have a formal disclosure policy approved by the board of directors that addresses the national bank's or Federal savings association's approach for determining its market risk disclosures. The policy must address the associated internal controls and disclosure controls and procedures. The board of directors and senior management must ensure that appropriate verification of the disclosures takes place and that effective internal controls and disclosure controls and procedures are maintained. One or more senior officers of the national bank or Federal savings association must attest that the disclosures meet the requirements of this subpart, and the board of directors and senior management are responsible for establishing and maintaining an effective internal control structure over financial reporting, including the disclosures required by this section.

(c) *Quantitative disclosures.* (1) For each material portfolio of covered positions, the national bank or Federal savings association must provide timely public disclosures of the following information at least quarterly:

(i) The high, low, and mean VaR-based measures over the reporting period and the VaR-based measure at period-end;

(ii) The high, low, and mean stressed VaR-based measures over the reporting period and the stressed VaR-based measure at period-end;

(iii) The high, low, and mean incremental risk capital requirements over the reporting period and the incremental risk capital requirement at period-end;

(iv) The high, low, and mean comprehensive risk capital requirements over the reporting period and the comprehensive risk capital requirement at period-end, with the period-end requirement broken down into appropriate risk classifications (for example, default risk, migration risk, correlation risk);

(v) Separate measures for interest rate risk, credit spread risk, equity price risk, foreign exchange risk, and commodity price risk used to calculate the VaR-based measure; and

(vi) A comparison of VaR-based estimates with actual gains or losses experienced by the national bank or Federal savings association, with an analysis of important outliers.

(2) In addition, the national bank or Federal savings association must disclose publicly the following information at least quarterly:

(i) The aggregate amount of on-balance sheet and off-balance sheet securitization positions by exposure type; and

(ii) The aggregate amount of correlation trading positions.

(d) *Qualitative disclosures.* For each material portfolio of covered positions, the national bank or Federal savings association must provide timely public disclosures of the following information at least annually after the end of the fourth calendar quarter, or more frequently in the event of material changes for each portfolio:

(1) The composition of material portfolios of covered positions;

(2) The national bank's or Federal savings association's valuation policies, procedures, and methodologies for covered positions including, for securitization positions, the methods and key assumptions used for valuing such positions, any significant changes since the last reporting period, and the impact of such change;

(3) The characteristics of the internal models used for purposes of this subpart. For the incremental risk capital requirement and the comprehensive risk capital requirement, this must include:

(i) The approach used by the national bank or Federal savings association to determine liquidity horizons;

(ii) The methodologies used to achieve a capital assessment that is consistent with the required soundness standard; and

(iii) The specific approaches used in the validation of these models;

(4) A description of the approaches used for validating and evaluating the accuracy of internal models and modeling processes for purposes of this subpart;

(5) For each market risk category (that is, interest rate risk, credit spread risk, equity price risk, foreign exchange risk, and commodity price risk), a description of the stress tests applied to the positions subject to the factor;

(6) The results of the comparison of the national bank's or Federal savings association's internal estimates for purposes of this subpart with actual outcomes during a sample period not used in model development;

(7) The soundness standard on which the national bank's or Federal savings association's internal capital adequacy assessment under this subpart is based, including a description of the methodologies used to achieve a capital adequacy assessment that is consistent with the soundness standard;

(8) A description of the national bank's or Federal savings association's processes for monitoring changes in the credit and market risk of securitization positions, including how those processes differ for resecuritization positions; and

(9) A description of the national bank's or Federal savings association's policy governing the use of credit risk mitigation to mitigate the risks of securitization and resecuritization positions.

§§ 3.213–3.299 [Reserved]

Subpart G—Transition Provisions

SOURCE: 78 FR 62157, 62273, Oct. 11, 2013, unless otherwise noted.

§ 3.300 Transitions.

(a) *Capital conservation and countercyclical capital buffer.* (1) From January 1, 2014 through December 31, 2015, a national bank or Federal savings association is not subject to limits on distributions and discretionary bonus payments under § 3.11 of subpart B of this part notwithstanding the amount of its capital conservation buffer or any applicable countercyclical capital buffer amount.

(2) Beginning January 1, 2016 through December 31, 2018 a national bank's or Federal savings association's maximum payout ratio shall be determined as set forth in Table 1 to § 3.300.

TABLE 1 TO § 3.300

Transition period	Capital conservation buffer	Maximum payout ratio (as a percentage of eligible retained income)
Calendar year 2016.	Greater than 0.625 percent (plus 25 percent of any applicable countercyclical capital buffer amount).	No payout ratio limitation applies under this section.
	Less than or equal to 0.625 percent (plus 25 percent of any applicable countercyclical capital buffer amount), and greater than 0.469 percent (plus 17.25 percent of any applicable countercyclical capital buffer amount).	60 percent.
	Less than or equal to 0.469 percent (plus 17.25 percent of any applicable countercyclical capital buffer amount), and greater than 0.313 percent (plus 12.5 percent of any applicable countercyclical capital buffer amount).	40 percent.
	Less than or equal to 0.313 percent (plus 12.5 percent of any applicable countercyclical capital buffer amount), and greater than 0.156 percent (plus 6.25 percent of any applicable countercyclical capital buffer amount).	20 percent.
	Less than or equal to 0.156 percent (plus 6.25 percent of any applicable countercyclical capital buffer amount).	0 percent.
Calendar year 2017.	Greater than 1.25 percent (plus 50 percent of any applicable countercyclical capital buffer amount).	No payout ratio limitation applies under this section.
	Less than or equal to 1.25 percent (plus 50 percent of any applicable countercyclical capital buffer amount), and greater than 0.938 percent (plus 37.5 percent of any applicable countercyclical capital buffer amount).	60 percent.
	Less than or equal to 0.938 percent (plus 37.5 percent of any applicable countercyclical capital buffer amount), and greater than 0.625 percent (plus 25 percent of any applicable countercyclical capital buffer amount).	40 percent.

TABLE 1 TO § 3.300—Continued

Transition period	Capital conservation buffer	Maximum payout ratio (as a percentage of eligible retained income)
	Less than or equal to 0.625 percent (plus 25 percent of any applicable countercyclical capital buffer amount), and greater than 0.313 percent (plus 12.5 percent of any applicable countercyclical capital buffer amount).	20 percent.
	Less than or equal to 0.313 percent (plus 12.5 percent of any applicable countercyclical capital buffer amount).	0 percent.
Calendar year 2018.	Greater than 1.875 percent (plus 75 percent of any applicable countercyclical capital buffer amount).	No payout ratio limitation applies under this section.
	Less than or equal to 1.875 percent (plus 75 percent of any applicable countercyclical capital buffer amount), and greater than 1.406 percent (plus 56.25 percent of any applicable countercyclical capital buffer amount).	60 percent.
	Less than or equal to 1.406 percent (plus 56.25 percent of any applicable countercyclical capital buffer amount), and greater than 0.938 percent (plus 37.5 percent of any applicable countercyclical capital buffer amount).	40 percent.
	Less than or equal to 0.938 percent (plus 37.5 percent of any applicable countercyclical capital buffer amount), and greater than 0.469 percent (plus 18.75 percent of any applicable countercyclical capital buffer amount).	20 percent.
	Less than or equal to 0.469 percent (plus 18.75 percent of any applicable countercyclical capital buffer amount).	0 percent.

(b) *Regulatory capital adjustments and deductions.* Beginning January 1, 2014 for an advanced approaches national bank or Federal savings association, and beginning January 1, 2015 for a national bank or Federal savings association that is not an advanced approaches national bank or Federal savings association, and in each case through December 31, 2017, a national bank or Federal savings association must make the capital adjustments and deductions in § 3.22 in accordance with the transition requirements in this paragraph (b). Beginning January 1, 2018, a national bank or Federal savings association must make all regulatory capital adjustments and deductions in accordance with § 3.22.

(1) *Transition deductions from common equity tier 1 capital.* Beginning January 1, 2014 for an advanced approaches national bank or Federal savings association, and beginning January 1, 2015 for a national bank or Federal savings association that is not an advanced approaches national bank or Federal savings association, and in each case through December 31, 2017, a national bank or Federal savings association, must make the deductions required under § 3.22(a)(1)–(8) from common equity tier 1 or tier 1 capital elements in accordance with the percentages set forth in Table 2 and Table 3 to § 3.300.

(i) A national bank or Federal savings association must deduct the following items from common equity tier 1 and additional tier 1 capital in accordance with the percentages set forth in Table 2 to § 3.300: goodwill (§ 3.22(a)(1)), DTAs that arise from net operating loss and tax credit carryforwards (§ 3.22(a)(3)), a gain-on-sale in connection with a securitization exposure (§ 3.22(a)(4)), defined benefit pension fund assets (§ 3.22(a)(5)), expected credit loss that exceeds eligible credit reserves (for advanced approaches national banks or Federal savings associations that have completed the parallel run process and that have received notifications from the OCC pursuant to § 3.121(d) of subpart E) and financial subsidiaries (§ 3.22(a)(7)), and nonincludable subsidiaries of a Federal savings association (§ 3.22(a)(8)).

TABLE 2 TO § 3.300

Transition period	Transition deductions under § 3.22(a)(1) and (7)	Transition deductions under § 3.22(a)(3)–(6) and (8)	
	Percentage of the deductions from common equity tier 1 capital	Percentage of the deductions from common equity tier 1 capital	Percentage of the deductions from tier 1 capital
Calendar year 2014	100	20	80
Calendar year 2015	100	40	60
Calendar year 2016	100	60	40
Calendar year 2017	100	80	20
Calendar year 2018, and thereafter	100	100	0

(ii) A national bank or Federal savings association must deduct from common equity tier 1 capital any intangible assets other than goodwill and MSAs in accordance with the percentages set forth in Table 3 to § 3.300.

(iii) A national bank or Federal savings association must apply a 100 percent risk-weight to the aggregate amount of intangible assets other than goodwill and MSAs that are not required to be deducted from common equity tier 1 capital under this section.

TABLE 3 TO § 3.300

Transition period	Transition deductions under § 3.22(a)(2)—percentage of the deductions from common equity tier 1 capital
Calendar year 2014	20
Calendar year 2015	40
Calendar year 2016	60
Calendar year 2017	80
Calendar year 2018, and thereafter	100

(2) *Transition adjustments to common equity tier 1 capital.* Beginning January 1, 2014 for an advanced approaches national bank or Federal savings association, and beginning January 1, 2015 for a national bank or Federal savings association that is not an advanced approaches national bank or Federal savings association, and in each case through December 31, 2017, a national bank or Federal savings association, must allocate the regulatory adjustments related to changes in the fair value of liabilities due to changes in the national bank's or Federal savings association's own credit risk (*§ 3*.22(b)(1)(iii)) between common equity tier 1 capital and tier 1 capital in accordance with the percentages set forth in Table 4 to § 3.300.

(i) If the aggregate amount of the adjustment is positive, the national bank or Federal savings association must allocate the deduction between common equity tier 1 and tier 1 capital in accordance with Table 4 to § 3.300.

(ii) If the aggregate amount of the adjustment is negative, the national bank or Federal savings association must add back the adjustment to common equity tier 1 capital or to tier 1 capital, in accordance with Table 4 to § 3.300.

TABLE 4 TO § 3.300

Transition period	Transition adjustments under § 3.22(b)(2)	
	Percentage of the adjustment applied to common equity tier 1 capital	Percentage of the adjustment applied to tier 1 capital
Calendar year 2014	20	80
Calendar year 2015	40	60
Calendar year 2016	60	40
Calendar year 2017	80	20
Calendar year 2018, and thereafter	100	0

(3) *Transition adjustments to AOCI for an advanced approaches national bank or Federal savings association and a national bank or Federal savings association that has not made an AOCI opt-out election under § 3.22(b)(2).* Beginning January 1, 2014 for an advanced approaches national bank or Federal savings association, and beginning January 1, 2015 for a national bank or Federal savings association that is not an advanced approaches national bank or Federal savings association that has not made an AOCI opt-out election under § 3.22(b)(2), and in each case through December 31, 2017, a national bank or Federal savings association must adjust common equity tier 1 capital with respect to the transition AOCI adjustment amount (transition AOCI adjustment amount):

(i) The transition AOCI adjustment amount is the aggregate amount of a national bank's or Federal savings association's:

(A) Unrealized gains on available-for-sale securities that are preferred stock classified as an equity security under GAAP or available-for-sale equity exposures, plus

(B) Net unrealized gains or losses on available-for-sale securities that are not preferred stock classified as an equity security under GAAP or available-for-sale equity exposures, plus

(C) Any amounts recorded in AOCI attributed to defined benefit post-retirement plans resulting from the initial and subsequent application of the relevant GAAP standards that pertain to such plans (excluding, at the national bank's or Federal savings association's option, the portion relating to pension assets deducted under section 22(a)(5)), plus

(D) Accumulated net gains or losses on cash flow hedges related to items that are reported on the balance sheet at fair value included in AOCI, plus

(E) Net unrealized gains or losses on held-to-maturity securities that are included in AOCI.

(ii) A national bank or Federal savings association must make the following adjustment to its common equity tier 1 capital:

(A) If the transition AOCI adjustment amount is positive, the appropriate amount must be deducted from common equity tier 1 capital in accordance with Table 5 to § 3.300.

(B) If the transition AOCI adjustment amount is negative, the appropriate amount must be added back to common equity tier 1 capital in accordance with Table 5 to § 3.300.

TABLE 5 TO § 3.300

Transition period	Percentage of the transition AOCI adjustment amount to be applied to common equity tier 1 capital
Calendar year 2014	80
Calendar year 2015	60
Calendar year 2016	40
Calendar year 2017	20
Calendar year 2018 and thereafter	0

(iii) A national bank or Federal savings association may include in tier 2 capital the percentage of unrealized gains on available-for-sale preferred stock classified as an equity security under GAAP and available-for-sale equity exposures as set forth in Table 6 to § 3.300.

TABLE 6 TO § 3.300

Transition period	Percentage of unrealized gains on available-for-sale preferred stock classified as an equity security under GAAP and available-for-sale equity exposures that may be included in tier 2 capital
Calendar year 2014	36
Calendar year 2015	27
Calendar year 2016	18
Calendar year 2017	9
Calendar year 2018 and thereafter	0

(4) *Additional transition deductions from regulatory capital.* Except as provided in paragraph (b)(5) of this section:

(i) Beginning January 1, 2014 for an advanced approaches national bank or Federal savings association, and beginning January 1, 2015 for a national bank or Federal savings association that is not an advanced approaches national bank or Federal savings association, and in each case through December 31, 2017, a national bank or Federal savings association, must use Table 7 to § 3.300 to determine the amount of investments in capital instruments and the items subject to the 10 and 15 percent common equity tier 1 capital deduction thresholds (§ 3.22(d)) (that is, MSAs, DTAs arising from temporary differences that the national bank or Federal savings association could not realize through net operating loss carrybacks, and significant investments in the capital of unconsolidated financial institutions in the form of common stock) that must be deducted from common equity tier 1 capital.

(ii) Beginning January 1, 2014 for an advanced approaches national bank or Federal savings association, and beginning January 1, 2015 for a national bank or Federal savings association that is not an advanced approaches national bank or Federal savings association, and in each case through December 31, 2017, a national bank or Federal savings association must apply a 100 percent risk weight to the aggregate amount of the items subject to the 10 and 15 percent common equity tier 1 capital deduction thresholds that are not deducted under this section. As set forth in § 3.22(d)(2), beginning January 1, 2018, a national bank or Federal savings association must apply a 250 percent risk weight to the aggregate amount of the items subject to the 10 and 15 percent common equity tier 1 capital deduction thresholds that are not deducted from common equity tier 1 capital.

TABLE 7 TO § 3.300

Transition period	Transitions for deductions under § 3.22(c) and (d)—percentage of additional deductions from regulatory capital
Calendar year 2014	20
Calendar year 2015	40
Calendar year 2016	60
Calendar year 2017	80
Calendar year 2018 and thereafter	100

(iii) For purposes of calculating the transition deductions in this paragraph (b)(4) beginning January 1, 2014 for an advanced approaches national bank or Federal savings association, and beginning January 1, 2015 for a national bank or Federal savings association that is not an advanced approaches national bank or Federal savings association, and in each case through December 31, 2017, a national bank's or Federal savings association's 15 percent common equity tier 1 capital deduction threshold for MSAs, DTAs arising from temporary differences that the national bank or Federal savings association could not realize through net operating loss carrybacks, and significant investments in the capital of unconsolidated financial institutions in the form of common stock is equal to 15 percent of the sum of the national bank's or Federal savings association's common equity tier 1 elements, after regulatory adjustments and deductions required under § 3.22(a) through (c) (transition 15 percent common equity tier 1 capital deduction threshold).

(iv) Beginning January 1, 2018, a national bank or Federal savings association must calculate the 15 percent common equity tier 1 capital deduction threshold in accordance with § 3.22(d).

(5) *Special transition provisions for non-significant investments in the capital of unconsolidated financial institutions, significant investments in the capital of unconsolidated financial institutions that are not in the form of common stock, MSAs, DTAs arising from temporary differences that the national bank or Federal savings association could not realize through net operating loss carrybacks, and significant investments in the capital of unconsolidated financial institutions in the form of common stock.* Beginning January 1, 2018, a national bank or Federal savings association that is not an advanced approaches national bank or Federal savings association must continue to apply the transition provisions described in paragraphs (b)(4)(i), (ii), and (iii) of this section applicable to calendar year 2017 to items that are subject to deduction under § 3.22(c)(4), (c)(5), and (d), respectively.

(c) *Non-qualifying capital instruments.*

(1)–(3) [Reserved]

(4) *Depository institutions.* (i) Beginning on January 1, 2014, a depository institution that is an advanced approaches national bank or Federal savings association, and beginning on January 1, 2015, all other depository institutions, may include in regulatory capital debt or equity instruments issued prior to September 12, 2010 that do not meet the criteria for additional tier 1

or tier 2 capital instruments in § 3.20 but that were included in tier 1 or tier 2 capital respectively as of September 12, 2010 (non-qualifying capital instruments issued prior to September 12, 2010) up to the percentage of the outstanding principal amount of such non-qualifying capital instruments as of January 1, 2014 in accordance with Table 9 to § 3.300.

(ii) Table 9 to § 3.300 applies separately to tier 1 and tier 2 non-qualifying capital instruments.

(iii) The amount of non-qualifying capital instruments that cannot be included in additional tier 1 capital under this section may be included in tier 2 capital without limitation, provided that the instruments meet the criteria for tier 2 capital instruments under § 3.20(d).

TABLE 9 TO § 3.300

Transition period (calendar year)	Percentage of non-qualifying capital instruments includable in additional tier 1 or tier 2 capital
Calendar year 2014	80
Calendar year 2015	70
Calendar year 2016	60
Calendar year 2017	50
Calendar year 2018	40
Calendar year 2019	30
Calendar year 2020	20
Calendar year 2021	10
Calendar year 2022 and thereafter	0

(d) *Minority interest*—(1) *Surplus minority interest*—(i) *Advanced approaches national bank or Federal savings association surplus minority interest.* Beginning January 1, 2014 through December 31, 2017, an advanced approaches national bank or Federal savings association may include in common equity tier 1 capital, tier 1 capital, or total capital the percentage of the common equity tier 1 minority interest, tier 1 minority interest, and total capital minority interest outstanding as of January 1, 2014, that exceeds any common equity tier 1 minority interest, tier 1 minority interest, or total capital minority interest includable under § 3.21 (surplus minority interest), respectively, as set forth in Table 10 to § 3.300.

(ii) *Non-advanced approaches national bank and Federal savings association surplus minority interest.* A national bank or Federal savings association that is not an advanced approaches national bank or Federal savings association may include in common equity tier 1 capital, tier 1 capital, or total capital 20 percent of the common equity tier 1 minority interest, tier 1 minority interest and total capital minority interest outstanding as of January 1, 2014, that exceeds any common equity tier 1 minority interest, tier 1 minority interest, or total capital minority interest includable under § 3.21 (surplus minority interest), respectively.

(2) *Non-qualifying minority interest.* Beginning January 1, 2014 for an advanced approaches national bank or Federal savings association, and beginning January 1, 2015 for a national bank or Federal savings association that is not an advanced approaches national bank or Federal savings association, and in each case through December 31, 2017, a national bank or Federal savings association may include in tier 1 capital or total capital the percentage of the tier 1 minority interest and total capital minority interest outstanding as of January 1, 2014 that does not meet the criteria for additional tier 1 or tier 2 capital instruments in § 3.20 (non-qualifying minority interest), as set forth in Table 10 to § 3.300.

TABLE 10 TO § 3.300

Transition period	Percentage of the amount of surplus or non-qualifying minority interest that can be included in regulatory capital during the transition period
Calendar year 2014	80
Calendar year 2015	60
Calendar year 2016	40
Calendar year 2017	20
Calendar year 2018 and thereafter	0

(e) *Prompt corrective action.* For purposes of 12 CFR part 6, a national bank or Federal savings association must calculate its capital measures and tangible equity ratio in accordance with the transition provisions in this section.

[78 FR 62157, 62273, Oct. 11, 2013, as amended at 82 FR 55315, Nov. 21, 2017]

Subpart H—Establishment of Minimum Capital Ratios for an Individual Bank or Individual Federal Savings Association

SOURCE: 78 FR 62269, Oct. 11, 2013, unless otherwise noted.

§ 3.401 Purpose and scope.

The rules and procedures specified in this subpart are applicable to a proceeding to establish required minimum capital ratios that would otherwise be applicable to a national bank or Federal savings association under subpart B of this part. The OCC is authorized under 12 U.S.C. 1464(s)(2) and 3907(a)(2) to establish such minimum capital requirements for a national bank or Federal savings association as the OCC, in its discretion, deems appropriate in light of the particular circumstances at that national bank or Federal savings association. Proceedings under this subpart also may be initiated to require a national bank or Federal savings association having capital ratios above those set forth in subpart B of this part, or other legal authority to continue to maintain those higher ratios.

§ 3.402 Applicability.

The OCC may require higher minimum capital ratios for an individual national bank or Federal savings association in view of its circumstances. For example, higher capital ratios may be appropriate for:

(a) A newly chartered national bank or Federal savings association;

(b) A national bank or Federal savings association receiving special supervisory attention;

(c) A national bank or Federal savings association that has, or is expected to have, losses resulting in capital inadequacy;

(d) A national bank or Federal savings association with significant exposure due to the risks from concentrations of credit, certain risks arising from nontraditional activities, or management's overall inability to monitor and control financial and operating risks presented by concentrations of credit and nontraditional activities;

(e) A national bank or Federal savings association with significant exposure to declines in the economic value of its capital due to changes in interest rates;

(f) A national bank or Federal savings association with significant exposure due to fiduciary or operational risk;

(g) A national bank or Federal savings association exposed to a high degree of asset depreciation, or a low level of liquid assets in relation to short term liabilities;

(h) A national bank or Federal savings association exposed to a high volume of, or particularly severe, problem loans;

(i) A national bank or Federal savings association that is growing rapidly, either internally or through acquisitions; or

(j) A national bank or Federal savings association that may be adversely affected by the activities or condition of its holding company, affiliate(s), or other persons or institutions, including chain banking organizations, with which it has significant business relationships.

§ 3.403 Standards for determination of appropriate individual minimum capital ratios.

The appropriate minimum capital ratios for an individual national bank or Federal savings association cannot be determined solely through the application of a rigid mathematical formula or wholly objective criteria. The decision is necessarily based in part on subjective judgment grounded in agency expertise. The factors to be considered in the determination will vary in each case and may include, for example:

(a) The conditions or circumstances leading to the OCC's determination that higher minimum capital ratios are appropriate or necessary for the national bank or Federal savings association;

(b) The exigency of those circumstances or potential problems;

(c) The overall condition, management strength, and future prospects of the national bank or Federal savings association and, if applicable, its holding company and/or affiliate(s);

(d) The national bank's or Federal savings association's liquidity, capital, risk asset and other ratios compared to the ratios of its peer group; and

(e) The views of the national bank's or Federal savings association's directors and senior management.

§ 3.404 Procedures.

(a) *Notice.* When the OCC determines that minimum capital ratios above those set forth in subpart B of this part or other legal authority are necessary or appropriate for a particular national bank or Federal savings association, the OCC will notify the national bank or Federal savings association in writing of the proposed minimum capital ratios and the date by which they should be reached (if applicable) and will provide an explanation of why the ratios proposed are considered necessary or appropriate for the national bank or Federal savings association.

(b) *Response.* (1) The national bank or Federal savings association may respond to any or all of the items in the notice. The response should include any matters which the national bank or Federal savings association would have the OCC consider in deciding whether individual minimum capital ratios should be established for the national bank or Federal savings association, what those capital ratios should be, and, if applicable, when they should be achieved. The response must be in writing and delivered to the designated OCC official within 30 days after the date on which the national bank or Federal savings association received the notice. The OCC may shorten the time period when, in the opinion of the OCC, the condition of the national bank or Federal savings association so requires, provided that the national bank or Federal savings association is informed promptly of the new time period, or with the consent of the national bank or Federal savings association. In its discretion, the OCC may extend the time period for good cause.

(2) Failure to respond within 30 days or such other time period as may be specified by the OCC shall constitute a waiver of any objections to the proposed minimum capital ratios or the deadline for their achievement.

(c) *Decision.* After the close of the national bank's or Federal savings association's response period, the OCC will decide, based on a review of the national bank's or Federal savings association's response and other information concerning the national bank or Federal savings association, whether individual minimum capital ratios should be established for the national bank or Federal savings association and, if so, the ratios and the date the requirements will become effective. The national bank or Federal savings association will be notified of the decision in writing. The notice will include an explanation of the decision, except for a decision not to establish individual minimum capital requirements for the national bank or Federal savings association.

(d) *Submission of plan.* The decision may require the national bank or Federal savings association to develop and submit to the OCC, within a time period specified, an acceptable plan to reach the minimum capital ratios established for the national bank or Federal savings association by the date required.

(e) *Change in circumstances.* If, after the OCC's decision in paragraph (c) of this section, there is a change in the circumstances affecting the national bank's or Federal savings association's capital adequacy or its ability to reach the required minimum capital ratios by the specified date, the national bank or Federal savings association may propose to the OCC, or the OCC may propose to the national bank or Federal savings association, a change in the minimum capital ratios for the national bank or Federal savings association, the date when the minimums must be achieved, or the national bank's or Federal savings association's plan (if applicable). The OCC may decline to consider proposals that are not based on a significant change in circumstances or are repetitive or frivolous. Pending a decision on reconsideration, the OCC's original decision and any plan required under that decision shall continue in full force and effect.

§ 3.405 Relation to other actions.

In lieu of, or in addition to, the procedures in this subpart, the required minimum capital ratios for a national bank or Federal savings association may be established or revised through a written agreement or cease and desist proceedings under 12 U.S.C. 1818 (b) or (c) (12 CFR 19.0 through 19.21 for national banks and 12 CFR part 109 for Federal savings associations) or as a condition for approval of an application.

Subpart I—Enforcement

SOURCE: 78 FR 62269, Oct. 11, 2013, unless otherwise noted.

§ 3.501 Remedies.

A national bank or Federal savings association that does not have or maintain the minimum capital ratios applicable to it, whether required in subpart B of this part, in a decision pursuant to subpart H of this part, in a written agreement or temporary or final order under 12 U.S.C. 1818 (b) or (c), or in a condition for approval of an application, or a national bank or Federal savings association that has failed to submit or comply with an acceptable plan to attain those ratios, will be subject to such administrative action or sanctions as the OCC considers appropriate. These sanctions may include the issuance of a Directive pursuant to subpart J of this part or other enforcement action, assessment of civil money penalties, and/or the denial, conditioning, or revocation of applications. A national bank's or Federal savings association's failure to achieve or maintain minimum capital ratios in subpart B of this part may also be the basis for an action by the Federal Deposit Insurance Corporation to terminate Federal deposit insurance. See 12 CFR part 308, subpart F.

Subpart J—Issuance of a Directive

SOURCE: 78 FR 62269, Oct. 11, 2013, unless otherwise noted.

§ 3.601 Purpose and scope.

(a) This subpart is applicable to proceedings by the OCC to issue a directive under 12 U.S.C. 3907(b)(2) or 12 U.S.C. 1464(s), as appropriate. A directive is an order issued to a national bank or Federal savings association that does not have or maintain capital at or above the minimum ratios set forth in subpart B of this part, or established for the national bank or Federal savings association under subpart H of this part, by a written agreement under 12 U.S.C. 1818(b), or as a condition for approval of an application. A directive may order the national bank or Federal savings association to:

(1) Achieve the minimum capital ratios applicable to it by a specified date;

(2) Adhere to a previously submitted plan to achieve the applicable capital ratios;

(3) Submit and adhere to a plan acceptable to the OCC describing the means and time schedule by which the national bank or Federal savings association shall achieve the applicable capital ratios;

(4) Take other action, such as reduction of assets or the rate of growth of assets, or restrictions on the payment of dividends, to achieve the applicable capital ratios; or

(5) A combination of any of these or similar actions.

(b) A directive issued under this rule, including a plan submitted under a directive, is enforceable in the same manner and to the same extent as an effective and outstanding cease and desist order which has become final as defined in 12 U.S.C. 1818(k). Violation of a directive may result in assessment of civil money penalties in accordance with 12 U.S.C. 3909(d).

§ 3.602 Notice of intent to issue a directive.

The OCC will notify a national bank or Federal savings association in writing of its intention to issue a directive. The notice will state:

(a) Reasons for issuance of the directive; and

(b) The proposed contents of the directive.

§ 3.603 Response to notice.

(a) A national bank or Federal savings association may respond to the notice by stating why a directive should not be issued and/or by proposing alternative contents for the directive. The response should include any matters which the national bank or Federal savings association would have the OCC consider in deciding whether to issue a directive and/or what the contents of the directive should be. The response may include a plan for achieving the minimum capital ratios applicable to the national bank or Federal savings association. The response must be in writing and delivered to the designated OCC official within 30 days after the date on which the national bank or Federal savings association received the notice. The OCC may shorten the 30-day time period:

(1) When, in the opinion of the OCC, the condition of the national bank or Federal savings association so requires, provided that the national bank or Federal savings association shall be informed promptly of the new time period;

(2) With the consent of the national bank or Federal savings association; or

(3) When the national bank or Federal savings association already has advised the OCC that it cannot or will not achieve its applicable minimum capital ratios.

(b) In its discretion, the OCC may extend the time period for good cause.

(c) Failure to respond within 30 days or such other time period as may be specified by the OCC shall constitute a waiver of any objections to the proposed directive.

§3.604 Decision.

After the closing date of the national bank's or Federal savings association's response period, or receipt of the national bank's or Federal savings association's response, if earlier, the OCC will consider the national bank's or Federal savings association's response, and may seek additional information or clarification of the response. Thereafter, the OCC will determine whether or not to issue a directive, and if one is to be issued, whether it should be as originally proposed or in modified form.

§3.605 Issuance of a directive.

(a) A directive will be served by delivery to the national bank or Federal savings association. It will include or be accompanied by a statement of reasons for its issuance.

(b) A directive is effective immediately upon its receipt by the national bank or Federal savings association, or upon such later date as may be specified therein, and shall remain effective and enforceable until it is stayed, modified, or terminated by the OCC.

§3.606 Change in circumstances.

Upon a change in circumstances, a national bank or Federal savings association may request the OCC to reconsider the terms of its directive or may propose changes in the plan to achieve the national bank's or Federal savings association's applicable minimum capital ratios. The OCC also may take such action on its own motion. The OCC may decline to consider requests or proposals that are not based on a significant change in circumstances or are repetitive or frivolous. Pending a decision on reconsideration, the directive and plan shall continue in full force and effect.

§3.607 Relation to other administrative actions.

A directive may be issued in addition to, or in lieu of, any other action authorized by law, including cease and desist proceedings, civil money penalties, or the conditioning or denial of applications. The OCC also may, in its discretion, take any action authorized by law, in lieu of a directive, in response to a national bank's or Federal savings association's failure to achieve or maintain the applicable minimum capital ratios.

Subpart K—Interpretations

SOURCE: 78 FR 62272, Oct. 11, 2013, unless otherwise noted.

§3.701 Capital and surplus.

For purposes of determining statutory limits that are based on the amount of a national bank's *capital* and/or *surplus*, the provisions of this section are to be used, rather than the definitions of capital contained in subparts A through J of this part.

(a) *Capital.* The term *capital* as used in provisions of law relating to the capital of national banks shall include the amount of common stock outstanding and unimpaired plus the amount of perpetual preferred stock outstanding and unimpaired.

(b) *Capital Stock.* The term *capital stock* as used in provisions of law relating to the capital stock of national banks, other than 12 U.S.C. 101, 177, and 178 shall have the same meaning as the term *capital* set forth in paragraph (a) of this section.

(c) *Surplus.* The term *surplus* as used in provisions of law relating to the surplus of national banks means the sum of paragraphs (c)(1), (2), (3), and (4) of this section:

(1) Capital surplus; undivided profits; reserves for contingencies and other capital reserves (excluding accrued dividends on perpetual and limited life preferred stock); net worth certificates issued pursuant to 12 U.S.C. 1823(i); minority interests in consolidated subsidiaries; and allowances for loan and lease losses; minus intangible assets;

(2) Mortgage servicing assets;

(3) Mandatory convertible debt to the extent of 20 percent of the sum of paragraphs (a) and (c)(1) and (2) of this section;

(4) Other mandatory convertible debt, limited life preferred stock and subordinated notes and debentures to the extent set forth in paragraph (f)(2) of this section.

(d) *Unimpaired surplus fund.* The term *unimpaired surplus fund* as used in provisions of law relating to the unimpaired surplus fund of national banks shall have the same meaning as the term *surplus* set forth in paragraph (c) of this section.

(e) *Definitions.* (1) *Allowance for loan and lease losses* means the balance of the valuation reserve on December 31, 1968, plus additions to the reserve charged to operations since that date, less losses charged against the allowance net of recoveries.

(2) *Capital surplus* means the total of those accounts reflecting:

(i) Amounts paid in in excess of the par or stated value of capital stock;

(ii) Amounts contributed to the national bank other than for capital stock;

(iii) Amounts transferred from undivided profits pursuant to 12 U.S.C. 60; and

(iv) Other amounts transferred from undivided profits.

(3) *Intangible assets* means those purchased assets that are to be reported as intangible assets in accordance with the *Instructions—Consolidated Reports of Condition and Income* (Call Report).

(4) *Limited life preferred stock* means preferred stock which has a maturity or which may be redeemed at the option of the holder.

(5) *Mandatory convertible debt* means subordinated debt instruments which unqualifiedly require the issuer to exchange either common or perpetual preferred stock for such instruments by a date at or before the maturity of the instrument. The maturity of these instruments must be 12 years or less. In addition, the instrument must meet the requirements of paragraphs (f)(1)(i) through (v) of this section for subordinated notes and debentures or other requirements published by the OCC.

(6) *Minority interest in consolidated subsidiaries* means the portion of equity capital accounts of all consolidated subsidiaries of the national bank that is allocated to minority shareholders of such subsidiaries.

(7) *Mortgage servicing assets* means the national bank-owned rights to service for a fee mortgage loans that are owned by others.

(8) *Perpetual preferred stock* means preferred stock that does not have a stated maturity date and cannot be redeemed at the option of the holder.

(f) *Requirements and restrictions: Limited life preferred stock, mandatory convertible debt, and other subordinated debt*—(1) *Requirements.* Issues of limited life preferred stock and subordinated notes and debentures (except mandatory convertible debt) shall have original weighted average maturities of at least five years to be included in the definition of *surplus.* In addition, a subordinated note or debenture must also:

(i) Be subordinated to the claims of depositors;

(ii) State on the instrument that it is not a deposit and is not insured by the FDIC;

(iii) Be unsecured;

(iv) Be ineligible as collateral for a loan by the issuing national bank;

(v) Provide that once any scheduled payments of principal begin, all scheduled payments shall be made at least annually and the amount repaid in each year shall be no less than in the prior year; and

(vi) Provide that no prepayment (including payment pursuant to an acceleration clause or redemption prior to maturity) shall be made without prior OCC approval unless the national bank remains an eligible bank, as defined in 12 CFR 5.3(g), after the prepayment.

(2) *Restrictions.* The total amount of mandatory convertible debt not included in paragraph (c)(3) of this section, limited life preferred stock, and subordinated notes and debentures considered as surplus is limited to 50 percent of the sum of paragraphs (a) and (c) (1), (2) and (3) of this section.

(3) *Reservation of authority.* The OCC expressly reserves the authority to waive the requirements and restrictions set forth in paragraphs (f)(1) and (2) of this section, in order to allow the inclusion of other limited life preferred stock, mandatory convertible notes and subordinated notes and debentures in the capital base of any national bank for capital adequacy purposes or for purposes of determining statutory limits. The OCC further expressly reserves the authority to impose more stringent conditions than those set forth in paragraphs (f)(1) and (2) of this section to exclude any component of tier 1 or tier 2 capital, in whole or in part, as part of a national bank's capital and surplus for any purpose.

(g) *Transitional rules.* (1) Equity commitment notes approved by the OCC as capital and issued prior to April 15, 1985, may continue to be included in paragraph (c)(3) of this section. All other instruments approved by the OCC as capital and issued prior to April 15, 1985, are to be included in paragraph (c)(4) of this section.

(2) Intangible assets (other than mortgage servicing assets) purchased prior to April 15, 1985, and accounted for in accordance with OCC instructions, may continue to be included as surplus up to 25 percent of the sum of paragraphs (a) and (c)(1) of this section.

APPENDIX A TO PART 3—RISK-BASED CAPITAL GUIDELINES

Section 1. Purpose, Applicability of Guidelines, and Definitions.

(a) *Purpose.* (1) An important function of the Office of the Comptroller of the Currency (*OCC*) is to evaluate the adequacy of capital maintained by each national bank. Such an evaluation involves the consideration of numerous factors, including the riskiness of a bank's assets and off-balance sheet items. This appendix A implements the OCC's risk-based capital guidelines. The risk-based capital ratio derived from those guidelines is more systematically sensitive to the credit risk associated with various bank activities than is a capital ratio based strictly on a bank's total balance sheet assets. A bank's risk-based capital ratio is obtained by dividing its capital base (as defined in section 2 of this appendix A) by its risk-weighted assets (as calculated pursuant to section 3 of this appendix A). These guidelines were created within the framework established by the report issued by the Committee on Banking Regulations and Supervisory Practices in July 1988. The OCC believes that the risk-based capital ratio is a useful tool in evaluating the capital adequacy of all national banks, not just those that are active in the international banking system.

(2) The purpose of this appendix A is to explain precisely (i) how a national bank's risk-based capital ratio is determined and (ii) how these risk-based capital guidelines are applied to national banks. The OCC will review these guidelines periodically for possible adjustments commensurate with its experience with the risk-based capital ratio and with changes in the economy, financial markets and domestic and international banking practices.

(b) *Applicability.* (1) The risk-based capital ratio derived from these guidelines is an important factor in the OCC's evaluation of a bank's capital adequacy. However, since this measure addresses only credit risk, the 8% minimum ratio should not be viewed as the level to be targeted, but rather as a floor. The final supervisory judgment on a bank's capital adequacy is based on an individualized assessment of numerous factors, including those listed in 12 CFR 3.10. With respect to the consideration of these factors, the OCC will give particular attention to any bank with significant exposure to declines in the economic value of its capital due to changes in interest rates. As a result, it may differ from the conclusion drawn from an isolated comparison of a bank's risk-based capital ration to the 8% minimum specified in these guidelines. In addition to the standards established by these risk-based capital guidelines, all national banks must maintain a minimum capital-to-total assets ratio in accordance with the provisions of 12 CFR part 3.

(2) Effective December 31, 1990, these risk-based capital guidelines will apply to all national banks. In the interim, banks must maintain minimum capital-to-total assets ratios as required by 12 CFR part 3, and should begin preparing for the implementation of these risk-based capital guidelines. In this regard, each national bank that does not currently meet the final minimum ratio established in section 4(b)(1) of this appendix A should begin planning for achieving that standard.

(3) These risk-based capital guidelines will not be applied to federal branches and agencies of foreign banks.

(c) *Definitions.* For purposes of this appendix A, the following definitions apply:

(1) *Adjusted carrying value* means, for purposes of section 2(c)(5) of this appendix A, the aggregate value that investments are carried on the balance sheet of the bank reduced by any unrealized gains on the investments that are reflected in such carrying value but excluded from the bank's Tier 1 capital and reduced by any associated deferred tax liabilities. For example, for investments held as available-for-sale (AFS), the adjusted carrying value of the investments would be the aggregate carrying value of the investments (as reflected on the consolidated balance sheet of the bank) less any unrealized gains on those investments that are included in other comprehensive income and that are not reflected in Tier 1 capital, and less any associated deferred tax liabilities. Unrealized losses on AFS nonfinancial equity investments must be deducted from Tier 1 capital in accordance with section 1(c)(10) of this appendix A. The treatment of small business investment companies that are consolidated for accounting purposes under generally accepted accounting principles is discussed in section 2(c)(5)(ii) of this appendix A. For investments in a nonfinancial company that is consolidated for accounting purposes, the bank's adjusted carrying value of the investment is determined under the equity method of accounting (net of any intangibles associated with the investment that are deducted from the bank's Tier 1 capital in accordance with section 2(c)(2) of this appendix A). Even though the assets of the nonfinancial company are consolidated for accounting purposes, these assets (as well as the credit equivalent amounts of the company's off-balance sheet items) are excluded from the bank's risk-weighted assets.

(2) *Allowances for loan and lease losses* means the balance of the valuation reserve on December 31, 1968, plus additions to the reserve charged to operations since that date, less losses charged against the allowance net of recoveries.

(3) *Asset-backed commercial paper program* means a program that primarily issues externally rated commercial paper backed by assets or other exposures held in a bankruptcy-remote, special-purpose entity.

(4) *Asset-backed commercial paper sponsor* means a bank that:

(i) Establishes an asset-backed commercial paper program;

(ii) Approves the sellers permitted to participate in an asset-backed commercial paper program;

(iii) Approves the asset pools to be purchased by an asset-backed commercial paper program; or

(iv) Administers the asset-backed commercial paper program by monitoring the assets, arranging for debt placement, compiling monthly reports, or ensuring compliance with the program documents and with the program's credit and investment policy.

(5) *Associated company* means any corporation, partnership, business trust, joint venture, association or similar organization in which a national bank directly or indirectly holds a 20 to 50 percent ownership interest.

(6) *Banking and finance subsidiary* means any subsidiary of a national bank that engages in banking- and finance-related activities.

(7) *Cash items in the process of collection* means checks or drafts in the process of collection that are drawn on another depository institution, including a central bank, and that are payable immediately upon presentation in the country in which the reporting bank's office that is clearing or collecting the check or draft is located; U.S. Government checks that are drawn on the United States Treasury or any other U.S. Government or Government-sponsored agency and that are payable immediately upon presentation; broker's security drafts and commodity or bill-of-lading drafts payable immediately upon presentation in the United States or the country in which the reporting bank's office that is handling the drafts is located; and unposted debits.

(8) *Central government* means the national governing authority of a country; it includes the departments, ministries and agencies of the central government and the central bank. The U.S. Central Bank includes the 12 Federal Reserve Banks. The definition of central government does not include the following: State, provincial, or local governments; commercial enterprises owned by the central government, which are entities engaged in activities involving trade, commerce, or profit that are generally conducted or performed in the private sector of the United States economy; and non-central government entities whose obligations are guaranteed by the central government.

(9) *Commitment* means any arrangement that obligates a national bank to: (i) Purchase loans or securities; or (ii) extend credit

in the form of loans or leases, participations in loans or leases, overdraft facilities, revolving credit facilities, home equity lines of credit, liquidity facilities, or similar transactions.

(10) *Common stockholders' equity* means common stock, common stock surplus, undivided profits, capital reserves, and adjustments for the cumulative effect of foreign currency translation, less net unrealized holding losses on available-for-sale equity securities with readily determinable fair values.

(11) *Conditional guarantee* means a contingent obligation of the United States Government or its agencies, or the central government of an OECD country, the validity of which to the beneficiary is dependent upon some affirmative action—*e.g.*, servicing requirements—on the part of the beneficiary of the guarantee or a third party.

(12) *Deferred tax assets* means the tax consequences attributable to tax carryforwards and deductible temporary differences. Tax carryforwards are deductions or credits that cannot be used for tax purposes during the current period, but can be carried forward to reduce taxable income or taxes payable in a future period or periods. Temporary differences are financial events or transactions that are recognized in one period for financial statement purposes, but are recognized in another period or periods for income tax purposes. Deductible temporary differences are temporary differences that result in a reduction of taxable income in a future period or periods.

(13) *Derivative contract* means generally a financial contract whose value is derived from the values of one or more underlying assets, reference rates or indexes of asset values. Derivative contracts include interest rate, foreign exchange rate, equity, precious metals and commodity contracts, or any other instrument that poses similar credit risks.

(14) *Depository institution* means a financial institution that engages in the business of banking; that is recognized as a bank by the bank supervisory or monetary authorities of the country of its incorporation and the country of its principal banking operations; that receives deposits to a substantial extent in the regular course of business; and that has the power to accept demand deposits. In the U.S., this definition encompasses all federally insured offices of commercial banks, mutual and stock savings banks, savings or building and loan associations (stock and mutual), cooperative banks, credit unions, and international banking facilities of domestic depository institution. Bank holding companies are excluded from this definition. For the purposes of assigning risk weights, the differentiation between OECD depository institutions and non-OECD depository institutions is based on the country of incorporation. Claims on branches and agencies of foreign banks located in the United States are to be categorized on the basis of the parent bank's country of incorporation.

(15) *Equity investment* means, for purposes of section 1(c)(19) and section 2(c)(5) of this appendix A, any equity instrument including warrants and call options that give the holder the right to purchase an equity instrument, any equity feature of a debt instrument (such as a warrant or call option), and any debt instrument that is convertible into equity. An investment in any other instrument, including subordinated debt or other types of debt instruments, may be treated as an equity investment if the OCC determines that the instrument is the functional equivalent of equity or exposes the bank to essentially the same risks as an equity instrument.

(16) *Exchange rate contracts* include: Cross-currency interest rate swaps; forward foreign exchange rate contracts; currency options purchased; and any similar instrument that, in the opinion of the OCC, gives rise to similar risks.

(17) *Goodwill* is an intangible asset that represents the excess of the cost of an acquired entity over the net of the amounts assigned to assets acquired and liabilities assumed.

(18) *Intangible assets* include mortgage and non-mortgage servicing assets (but exclude any interest only (IO) strips receivable related to these mortgage and nonmortgage servicing assets), purchased credit card relationships, goodwill, favorable leaseholds, and core deposit value.

(19) *Interest rate contracts* include: Single currency interest rate swaps; basis swaps; forward rate agreements; interest rate options purchased; forward forward deposits accepted; and any similar instrument that, in the opinion of the OCC, gives rise to similar risks, including when-issued securities.

(20) *Liquidity facility* means a legally binding commitment to provide liquidity to various types of transactions, structures or programs. A liquidity facility that supports asset-backed commercial paper, in any amount, by lending to, or purchasing assets from any structure, program, or conduit constitutes an *asset-backed commercial paper liquidity facility*.

(21) *Multifamily residential property* means any residential property consisting of five or more dwelling units including apartment buildings, condominiums, cooperatives, and other similar structures primarily for residential use, but not including hospitals, nursing homes, or other similar facilities.

(22) *Nationally recognized statistical rating organization (NRSRO)* means an entity recognized by the Division of Market Regulation of the Securities and Exchange Commission (or any successor Division) (Commission or SEC) as a nationally recognized statistical

rating organization for various purposes, including the Commission's uniform net capital requirements for brokers and dealers.

(23) *Nonfinancial equity investment* means any equity investment held by a bank in a nonfinancial company through a small business investment company (SBIC) under section 302(b) of the Small Business Investment Act of 1958 (15 U.S.C. 682(b)) or under the portfolio investment provisions of Regulation K (12 CFR 211.8(c)(3)). An equity investment made under section 302(b) of the Small Business Investment Act of 1958 in a SBIC that is not consolidated with the bank is treated as a nonfinancial equity investment in the manner provided in section 2(c)(5)(ii)(C) of this appendix A. A nonfinancial company is an entity that engages in any activity that has not been determined to be permissible for a bank to conduct directly or to be financial in nature or incidental to financial activities under section 4(k) of the Bank Holding Company Act (12 U.S.C. 1843(k)).

(24) The *OECD-based group of countries* comprises all full members of the Organization for Economic Cooperation and Development (OECD) regardless of entry date, as well as countries that have concluded special lending arrangements with the International Monetary Fund (IMF) associated with the IMF's General Arrangements to Borrow,[1] but excludes any country that has rescheduled its external sovereign debt within the previous five years. These countries are hereinafter referred to as *OECD countries.* A rescheduling of external sovereign debt generally would include any renegotiation of terms arising from a country's inability or unwillingness to meet its external debt service obligations, but generally would not include renegotiations of debt in the normal course of business, such as a renegotiation to allow the borrower to take advantage of a decline in interest rates or other change in market conditions.

(25) *Original maturity* means, with respect to a commitment, the earliest possible date after a commitment is made on which the commitment is scheduled to expire (*i.e.*, it will reach its stated maturity and cease to be binding on either party), *provided that* either:

(i) The commitment is not subject to extension or renewal and will actually expire on its stated expiration date; or

(ii) If the commitment is subject to extension or renewal beyond its stated expiration date, the stated expiration date will be deemed the original maturity only if the extension or renewal must be based upon terms and conditions independently negotiated in good faith with the customer at the time of the extension or renewal and upon a new, *bona fide* credit analysis utilizing current information on financial condition and trends.

(26) *Preferred stock* includes the following instruments: (i) *Convertible preferred stock,* which means preferred stock that is mandatorily convertible into either common or perpetual preferred stock; (ii) *Intermediate-term preferred stock,* which means preferred stock with an original maturity of at least five years, but less than 20 years; (iii) *Long-term preferred stock,* which means preferred stock with an original maturity of 20 years or more; and (iv) *Perpetual preferred stock,* which means preferred stock without a fixed maturity date that cannot be redeemed at the option of the holder, and that has no other provisions that will require future redemption of the issue. For purposes of these instruments, preferred stock that can be redeemed at the option of the holder is deemed to have an *original maturity* of the earliest possible date on which it may be so redeemed.

(27) *Public-sector entities* include states, local authorities and governmental subdivisions below the central government level in an OECD country. In the United States, this definition encompasses a state, county, city, town, or other municipal corporation, a public authority, and generally any publicly-owned entity that is an instrumentality of a state or municipal corporation. This definition does not include commercial companies owned by the public sector.[1a]

(28) *Reciprocal holdings of bank capital instruments* means cross-holdings or other formal or informal arrangements in which two or more banking organizations swap, exchange, or otherwise agree to hold each other's capital instruments. This definition does not include holdings of capital instruments issued by other banking organizations that were taken in satisfaction of debts previously contracted, provided that the reporting national bank has not held such instruments for more than five years or a longer period approved by the OCC.

(29) *Replacement cost* means, with respect to interest rate and exchange rate contracts, the loss that would be incurred in the event of a counterparty default, as measured by

---

[1] As of November 1995, the OECD included the following countries: Australia, Austria, Belgium, Canada, Denmark, Finland, France, Germany, Greece, Iceland, Ireland, Italy, Japan, Luxembourg, Mexico, the Netherlands, New Zealand, Norway, Portugal, Spain, Sweden, Switzerland, Turkey, the United Kingdom, and the United States; and Saudi Arabia had concluded special lending arrangements with the IMF associated with the IMF's General Arrangements to Borrow.

[1a] *See* Definition (5), *Central government,* for further explanation of commercial companies owned by the public sector.

the net cost of replacing the contract at the current market value. If default would result in a theoretical profit, the replacement value is considered to be zero. The mark-to-market process should incorporate changes in both interest rates and counterparty credit quality.

(30) *Residential properties* means houses, condominiums, cooperative units, and manufactured homes. This definition does not include boats or motor homes, even if used as a primary residence.

(31) *Risk-weighted assets* means the sum of total risk-weighted balance sheet assets and the total of risk-weighted off-balance sheet credit equivalent amounts. Risk-weighted balance sheet and off-balance sheet assets are calculated in accordance with section 3 of this appendix A.

(32) *State* means any one of the several states of the United States of America, the District of Columbia, Puerto Rico, and the territories and possessions of the United States.

(33) *Subsidiary* means any corporation, partnership, business trust, joint venture, association or similar organization in which a national bank directly or indirectly holds more than a 50% ownership interest. This definition does not include ownership interests that were taken in satisfaction of debts previously contracted, provided that the reporting bank has not held the interest for more than five years or a longer period approved by the OCC.

(34) *Total capital* means the sum of a national bank's core (Tier 1) and qualifying supplementary (Tier 2) capital elements.

(35) *Unconditionally cancelable* means, with respect to a commitment-type lending arrangement, that the bank may, at any time, with or without cause, refuse to advance funds or extend credit under the facility. In the case of home equity lines of credit, the bank is deemed able to unconditionally cancel the commitment if it can, at its option, prohibit additional extensions of credit, reduce the line, and terminate the commitment to the full extent permitted by relevant Federal law.

(36) *United States Government or its agencies* means an instrumentality of the U.S. Government whose debt obligations are fully and explicitly guaranteed as to the timely payment of principal and interest by the full faith and credit of the United States Government.

(37) *United States Government-sponsored agency* means an agency originally established or chartered to serve public purposes specified by the United States Congress, but whose obligations are not explicitly guaranteed by the full faith and credit of the United States Government.

(38) *Walkaway clause* means a provision in a bilateral netting contract that permits a nondefaulting counterparty to make a lower payment than it would make otherwise under the bilateral netting contract, or no payment at all, to a defaulter or the estate of a defaulter, even if the defaulter or the estate of the defaulter is a net creditor under the bilateral netting contract.

Section 2. Components of Capital.

A national bank's qualifying capital base consists of two types of capital—core (Tier 1) and supplementary (Tier 2).

(a) *Tier 1 Capital.* The following elements comprise a national bank's Tier 1 capital:

(1) Common stockholders' equity;

(2) Noncumulative perpetual preferred stock and related surplus; and [2]

(3) Minority interests in the equity accounts of consolidated subsidiaries, except that the following are not included in Tier 1 capital or total capital:

(i) Minority interests in a small business investment company or investment fund that holds nonfinancial equity investments and minority interests in a subsidiary that is engaged in a nonfinancial activities and is held under one of the legal authorities listed in section 1(c)(23) of this appendix A.

(ii) [Reserved]

(b) *Tier 2 Capital.* The following elements comprise a national bank's Tier 2 capital:

(1) Allowance for loan and lease losses, up to a maximum of 1.25% of risk-weighted assets, [3] subject to the transition rules in section 4(a)(2) of this appendix A;

(2) Cumulative perpetual preferred stock, long-term preferred stock, convertible preferred stock, and any related surplus, without limit, if the issuing national bank has the option to defer payment of dividends on

---

[2] Preferred stock issues where the dividend is reset periodically based upon current market conditions and the bank's current credit rating, including but not limited to, auction rate, money market or remarketable preferred stock, are assigned to Tier 2 capital, regardless of whether the dividends are cumulative or noncumulative.

[3] The amount of the allowance for loan and lease losses that may be included in capital is based on a percentage of risk-weighted assets. The gross sum of risk-weighted assets used in this calculation includes all risk-weighted assets, with the exception of the assets required to be deducted under section 3 in establishing risk-weighted assets (*i.e.*, the assets required to be deducted from capital under section 2(c)) of this appendix. A banking organization may deduct reserves for loan and lease losses in excess of the amount permitted to be included as capital, as well as allocated transfer risk reserves and reserves held against other real estate owned, from the gross sum of risk-weighted assets in computing the denominator of the risk-based capital ratio.

these instruments. For long-term preferred stock, the amount that is eligible to be included as Tier 2 capital is reduced by 20% of the original amount of the instrument (net of redemptions) at the beginning of each of the last five years of the life of the instrument;

(3) Hybrid capital instruments, without limit. Hybrid capital instruments are those instruments that combine certain characteristics of debt and equity, such as perpetual debt. To be included as Tier 2 capital, these instruments must meet the following criteria:[4]

(i) The instrument must be unsecured, subordinated to the claims of depositors and general creditors, and fully paid-up;

(ii) The instrument must not be redeemable at the option of the holder prior to maturity, except with the prior approval of the OCC;

(iii) The instrument must be available to participate in losses while the issuer is operating as a going concern (in this regard, the instrument must automatically convert to common stock or perpetual preferred stock, if the sum of the retained earnings and capital surplus accounts of the issuer shows a negative balance); and

(iv) The instrument must provide the option for the issuer to defer principal and interest payments, if

(A) The issuer does not report a net profit for the most recent combined four quarters, and

(B) The issuer eliminates cash dividends on its common and preferred stock.

(4) Term subordinated debt instruments, and intermediate-term preferred stock and related surplus are included in Tier 2 capital, but only to a maximum of 50% of Tier 1 capital as calculated after deductions pursuant to section 2(c) of this appendix. To be considered capital, term subordinated debt instruments shall meet the requirements of §3.100(f)(1). However, pursuant to 12 CFR 5.47, the OCC may, in some cases, require that the subordinated debt be approved by the OCC before the subordinated debt may qualify as Tier 2 capital or may require prior approval for any prepayment (including payment pursuant to an acceleration clause or redemption prior to maturity) of the subordinated debt. Also, at the beginning of each of the last five years for the life of either type of instrument, the amount that is eligible to be included as Tier 2 capital is reduced by 20% of the original amount of that instrument (net of redemptions).

(5) Up to 45 percent of the pretax net unrealized holding gains (that is, the excess, if any, of the fair value over historical cost) on available-for-sale equity securities with readily determinable fair values.[5] Unrealized gains (losses) on other types of assets, such as bank premises and available-for-sale debt securities, are not included in Tier 2 capital, but the OCC may take these unrealized gains (losses) into account as additional factors when assessing a bank's overall capital adequacy.

(c) *Deductions from Capital.* The following items are deducted from the appropriate portion of a national bank's capital base when calculating its risk-based capital ratio:

(1) *Deductions from Tier 1 Capital.* The following items are deducted from Tier 1 capital before the Tier 2 portion of the calculation is made:

(i) Goodwill;

(ii) Other intangible assets, except as provided in section 2(c)(2) of this appendix A;

(iii) Deferred tax assets, except as provided in section 2(c)(3) and (2)(c)(6) of this appendix A, that are dependent upon future taxable income, which exceed the lesser of either:

(A) The amount of deferred tax assets that the bank could reasonably expect to realize within one year of the quarter-end Call Report, based on its estimate of future taxable income for that year; or

(B) 10% of Tier 1 capital, net of goodwill and all intangible assets other than purchased credit card relationships, mortgage servicing assets and non-mortgage servicing assets; and

(iv) Credit-enhancing interest-only strips (as defined in section 4(a)(2) of this appendix A), as provided in section 2(c)(4).

(v) Nonfinancial equity investments as provided by section 2(c)(5) of this appendix A.

(2) *Qualifying intangible assets.* Subject to the following conditions, mortgage servicing assets, nonmortgage servicing assets[6] and

[4] Mandatory convertible debt instruments that meet the requirements of 12 CFR 3.100(e)(5), or that have been previously approved as capital by the OCC, are treated as qualifying hybrid capital instruments.

[5] The OCC reserves the authority to exclude all or a portion of unrealized gains from Tier 2 capital if the OCC determines that the equity securities are not prudently valued.

[6] Intangible assets are defined to exclude IO strips receivable related to these mortgage and non-mortgage servicing assets. See section 1(c)(18) of this appendix A. Consequently, IO strips receivable related to mortgage and non-mortgage servicing assets are not required to be deducted under section 2(c)(2) of this appendix A. However, credit-enhancing interest-only strips as defined in section 4(a)(2) are deducted from Tier 1 capital in accordance with section 2(c)(4) of this appendix A. Any non credit-enhancing IO strips receivable are subject to a 100% risk weight under section 3(a)(4) of this appendix A.

purchased credit card relationships need not be deducted from Tier 1 capital:

(i) The total of all intangible assets that are included in Tier 1 capital is limited to 100 percent of Tier 1 capital, of which no more than 25 percent of Tier 1 capital can consist of purchased credit card relationships and non-mortgage servicing assets in the aggregate. Calculation of these limitations must be based on Tier 1 capital net of goodwill and all other identifiable intangibles, other than purchased credit card relationships, mortgage servicing assets and non-mortgage servicing assets.

(ii) Banks must value each intangible asset included in Tier 1 capital at least quarterly at the lesser of:

(A) 90 percent of the fair value of each intangible asset, determined in accordance with section 2(c)(2)(iii) of this appendix A; or

(B) 100 percent of the remaining unamortized book value.

(iii) The quarterly determination of the current fair value of the intangible asset must include adjustments for any significant changes in original valuation assumptions, including changes in prepayment estimates.

(3) *Deferred tax assets*—(i) *Net unrealized gains and losses on available-for-sale securities.* Net unrealized gains and losses on available-for-sale securities. Before calculating the amount of deferred tax assets subject to the limit in section 2(c)(1)(iii) of this appendix A, a bank may eliminate the deferred tax effects of any net unrealized holding gains and losses on available-for-sale debt securities. Banks report these net unrealized holding gains and losses in their Call Reports as a separate component of equity capital, but exclude them from the definition of common stockholders' equity for regulatory capital purposes. A bank that adopts a policy to deduct these amounts must apply that approach consistently in all future calculations of the amount of disallowed deferred tax assets under section 2(c)(1)(iii) of this appendix A.

(ii) *Consolidated groups.* The amount of deferred tax assets that a bank can realize from taxes paid in prior carryback years and from reversals of existing taxable temporary differences generally would not be deducted from capital. However, for a bank that is a member of a consolidated group (for tax purposes), the amount of carryback potential a bank may consider in calculating the limit on deferred tax assets under section 2(c)(1)(iii) of this appendix A, may not exceed the amount that the bank could reasonably expect to have refunded by its parent holding company.

(iii) *Estimated future taxable income.* Estimated future taxable income does not include net operating loss carryforwards to be used during that year or the amount of existing temporary differences expected to reverse within the year. A bank may use future taxable income projections for their closest fiscal year, provided it adjusts the projections for any significant changes that occur or that it expects to occur. Such projections must include the estimated effect of tax planning strategies that the bank expects to implement to realize net operating losses or tax credit carryforwards that will otherwise expire during the year.

(4) *Credit-enhancing interest-only strips.* Credit-enhancing interest-only strips, whether purchased or retained, that exceed 25% of Tier 1 capital must be deducted from Tier 1 capital. Purchased and retained credit-enhancing interest-only strips, on a non-tax adjusted basis, are included in the total amount that is used for purposes of determining whether a bank exceeds its Tier 1 capital.

(i) The 25% limitation on credit-enhancing interest-only strips will be based on Tier 1 capital net of goodwill and all identifiable intangibles, other than purchased credit card relationships, mortgage servicing assets and non-mortgage servicing assets.

(ii) Banks must value each credit-enhancing interest-only strip included in Tier 1 capital at least quarterly. The quarterly determination of the current fair value of the credit-enhancing interest-only strip must include adjustments for any significant changes in original valuation assumptions, including changes in prepayment estimates.

(5) *Nonfinancial equity investments—(i) General.* (A) A bank must deduct from its Tier 1 capital the appropriate percentage, as determined in accordance with Table A, of the adjusted carrying value of all nonfinancial equity investments held by the bank and its subsidiaries.

TABLE A—DEDUCTION FOR NONFINANCIAL EQUITY INVESTMENTS

Aggregate adjusted carrying value of all nonfinancial equity investments held directly or indirectly by banks (as a percentage of the Tier 1 capital of the bank) [1]	Deduction from Tier 1 Capital (as a percentage of the adjusted carrying value of the investment)
Less than 15 percent	8.0 percent.
Greater than or equal to 15 percent but less than 25 percent	12.0 percent.

TABLE A—DEDUCTION FOR NONFINANCIAL EQUITY INVESTMENTS—Continued

Aggregate adjusted carrying value of all nonfinancial equity investments held directly or indirectly by banks (as a percentage of the Tier 1 capital of the bank) [1]	Deduction from Tier 1 Capital (as a percentage of the adjusted carrying value of the investment)
Greater than or equal to 25 percent	25.0 percent.

[1] For purposes of calculating the adjusted carrying value of nonfinancial equity investments as a percentage of Tier 1 capital, Tier 1 capital is defined as the sum of the Tier 1 capital elements net of goodwill and net of all identifiable intangible assets other than mortgage servicing assets, nonmortgage servicing assets and purchased credit card relationships, but prior to the deduction for disallowed mortgage servicing assets, disallowed nonmortgage servicing assets, disallowed purchased credit card relationships, disallowed credit-enhancing interest only strips (both purchased and retained), disallowed deferred tax assets, and nonfinancial equity investments.

(B) Deductions for nonfinancial equity investments must be applied on a marginal basis to the portions of the adjusted carrying value of nonfinancial equity investments that fall within the specified ranges of the bank's Tier 1 capital. For example, if the adjusted carrying value of all nonfinancial equity investments held by a bank equals 20 percent of the Tier 1 capital of the bank, then the amount of the deduction would be 8 percent of the adjusted carrying value of all investments up to 15 percent of the bank's Tier 1 capital, and 12 percent of the adjusted carrying value of all investments equal to, or in excess of, 15 percent of the bank's Tier 1 capital.

(C) The total adjusted carrying value of any nonfinancial equity investment that is subject to deduction under section 2(c)(5) of this appendix A is excluded from the bank's weighted risk assets for purposes of computing the denominator of the bank's risk-based capital ratio. For example, if 8 percent of the adjusted carrying value of a nonfinancial equity investment is deducted from Tier 1 capital, the entire adjusted carrying value of the investment will be excluded from risk-weighted assets in calculating the denominator of the risk-based capital ratio.

(D) Banks engaged in equity investment activities, including those banks with a high concentration in nonfinancial equity investments (e.g., in excess of 50 percent of Tier 1 capital), will be monitored and may be subject to heightened supervision, as appropriate, by the OCC to ensure that such banks maintain capital levels that are appropriate in light of their equity investment activities, and the OCC may impose a higher capital charge in any case where the circumstances, such as the level of risk of the particular investment or portfolio of investments, the risk management systems of the bank, or other information, indicate that a higher minimum capital requirement is appropriate.

(ii) *Small business investment company investments.* (A) Notwithstanding section 2(c)(5)(i) of this appendix A, no deduction is required for nonfinancial equity investments that are made by a bank or its subsidiary through a SBIC that is consolidated with the bank, or in a SBIC that is not consolidated with the bank, to the extent that such investments, in the aggregate, do not exceed 15 percent of the Tier 1 capital of the bank. Except as provided in paragraph (c)(5)(ii)(B) of this section, any nonfinancial equity investment that is held through or in a SBIC and not deducted from Tier 1 capital will be assigned to the 100 percent risk-weight category and included in the bank's consolidated risk-weighted assets.

(B) If a bank has an investment in a SBIC that is consolidated for accounting purposes but the SBIC is not wholly owned by the bank, the adjusted carrying value of the bank's nonfinancial equity investments held through the SBIC is equal to the bank's proportionate share of the SBIC's adjusted carrying value of its equity investments in nonfinancial companies. The remainder of the SBIC's adjusted carrying value (*i.e.*, the minority interest holders' proportionate share) is excluded from the risk-weighted assets of the bank.

(C) If a bank has an investment in a SBIC that is not consolidated for accounting purposes and has current information that identifies the percentage of the SBIC's assets that are equity investments in nonfinancial companies, the bank may reduce the adjusted carrying value of its investment in the SBIC proportionately to reflect the percentage of the adjusted carrying value of the SBIC's assets that are not equity investments in nonfinancial companies. The amount by which the adjusted carrying value of the bank's investment in the SBIC is reduced under this paragraph will be risk weighted at 100 percent and included in the bank's risk-weighted assets.

(D) To the extent the adjusted carrying value of all nonfinancial equity investments that the bank holds through a consolidated SBIC or in a nonconsolidated SBIC equals or exceeds, in the aggregate, 15 percent of the Tier 1 capital of the bank, the appropriate percentage of such amounts, as set forth in Table A, must be deducted from the bank's Tier 1 capital. In addition, the aggregate adjusted carrying value of all nonfinancial equity investments held through a consolidated SBIC and in a nonconsolidated SBIC (including any nonfinancial equity investments for which no deduction is required) must be included in determining, for purposes of Table A the total amount of nonfinancial equity investments held by the bank in relation to its Tier 1 capital.

(iii) *Nonfinancial equity investments excluded.* (A) Notwithstanding section 2(c)(5)(i) and (ii) of this appendix A, no deduction from Tier 1 capital is required for the following:

(1) Nonfinancial equity investments (or portion of such investments) made by the bank prior to March 13, 2000, and continuously held by the bank since March 13, 2000.

(2) Nonfinancial equity investments made on or after March 13, 2000, pursuant to a legally binding written commitment that was entered into by the bank prior to March 13, 2000, and that required the bank to make the investment, if the bank has continuously held the investment since the date the investment was acquired.

(3) Nonfinancial equity investments received by the bank through a stock split or stock dividend on a nonfinancial equity investment made prior to March 13, 2000, provided that the bank provides no consideration for the shares or interests received, and the transaction does not materially increase the bank's proportional interest in the nonfinancial company.

(4) Nonfinancial equity investments received by the bank through the exercise on or after March 13, 2000, of an option, warrant, or other agreement that provides the bank with the right, but not the obligation, to acquire equity or make an investment in a nonfinancial company, if the option, warrant, or other agreement was acquired by the bank prior to March 13, 2000, and the bank provides no consideration for the nonfinancial equity investments.

(B) Any excluded nonfinancial equity investments described in section 2(c)(5)(iii)(A) of this appendix A must be included in determining the total amount of nonfinancial equity investments held by the bank in relation to its Tier 1 capital for purposes of Table A. In addition, any excluded nonfinancial equity investments will be risk weighted at 100 percent and included in the bank's risk-weighted assets.

(6) *Netting of Deferred Tax Liability.* (i) Banks may elect to deduct the following assets from Tier 1 capital on a basis that is net of any associated deferred tax liability:

(A) Goodwill;

(B) Intangible assets acquired due to a nontaxable purchase business combination, except banks may not elect to deduct from Tier 1 capital on a basis that is net of any associated deferred tax liability, regardless of the method by which they were acquired:

(*1*) Purchased credit card relationships; and

(*2*) Servicing assets that are includable in Tier 1 capital;

(C) Disallowed servicing assets;

(D) Disallowed credit-enhancing interest-only strips; and

(E) Nonfinancial equity investments, as defined in section 1(c)(1) of this appendix A.

(ii) Deferred tax liabilities netted in this manner cannot also be netted against deferred tax assets when determining the amount of deferred tax assets that are dependent upon future taxable income as calculated under section 2(c)(1)(iii) of this appendix A.

(7) *Deductions from total capital.* The following assets are deducted from total capital:

(i) Investments, both equity and debt, in unconsolidated banking and finance subsidiaries that are deemed to be capital of the subsidiary;[7] and

(ii) Reciprocal holdings of bank capital instruments.

Section 3. Risk Categories/Weights for On-Balance Sheet Assets and Off-Balance Sheet Items

The denominator of the risk-based capital ratio, *i.e.*, a national bank's risk-weighted assets,[8] is derived by assigning that bank's assets and off-balance sheet items to one of the four risk categories detailed in section 3(a) of this appendix A. Each category has a specific risk weight. Before an off-balance sheet item is assigned a risk weight, it is converted to an on-balance sheet credit equivalent amount in accordance with section 3(b) of this appendix A. The risk weight assigned to a particular asset or on-balance sheet credit equivalent amount determines the percentage of that asset/credit equivalent that is included in the denominator of the bank's risk-based capital ratio. Any asset deducted from a bank's capital in computing the numerator of the risk-based capital ratio is not included as part of the bank's risk-weighted assets.

Some of the assets on a bank's balance sheet may represent an indirect holding of a pool of assets, *e.g.*, mutual funds, that encompasses more than one risk weight within the pool. In those situations, the bank may assign the asset to the risk category applicable to the highest risk-weighted asset that pool is permitted to hold pursuant to its stated investment objectives in the fund's prospectus. Alternatively, the bank may assign the asset on a pro rata basis to different risk categories according to the investment

[7] The OCC may require deduction of investments in other subsidiaries and associated companies, on a case-by-case basis.

[8] The OCC reserves the right to require a bank to compute its risk-based capital ratio on the basis of average, rather than period-end, risk-weighted assets when necessary to carry out the purposes of these guidelines.

limits in the fund's prospectus. In either case, the minimum risk weight that may be assigned to such a pool is 20%. If a bank assigns the asset on a pro rata basis, and the sum of the investment limits in the fund's prospectus exceeds 100%, the bank must assign the highest pro rata amounts of its total investment to the higher risk category. If, in order to maintain a necessary degree of liquidity, the fund is permitted to hold an insignificant amount of its assets in short-term, highly-liquid securities of superior credit quality (that do not qualify for a preferential risk weight), such securities generally will not be taken into account in determining the risk category into which the bank's holding in the overall pool should be assigned. The prudent use of hedging instruments by a fund to reduce the risk of its assets will not increase the risk weighting of the investment in that fund above the 20% category. However, if a fund engages in any activities that are deemed to be speculative in nature or has any other characteristics that are inconsistent with the preferential risk weighting assigned to the fund's assets, the bank's investment in the fund will be assigned to the 100% risk category. More detail on the treatment of mortgage-backed securities is provided in section 3(a)(3)(vi) of this appendix A.

(a) *On-Balance Sheet Assets.* The following are the risk categories/weights for on-balance sheet assets.

(1) *Zero percent risk weight.* (i) Cash, including domestic and foreign currency owned and held in all offices of a national bank or in transit. Any foreign currency held by a national bank should be converted into U.S. dollar equivalents.

(ii) Deposit reserves and other balances at Federal Reserve Banks.

(iii) Securities issued by, and other direct claims on, the United States Government or its agencies, or the central government of an OECD country.

(iv) That portion of assets directly and unconditionally guaranteed by the United States Government or its agencies, or the central government of an OECD country. [9]

(v) That portion of local currency claims on, or unconditionally guaranteed by, central governments of non-OECD countries, to the extent the bank has liabilities in that currency. Any amount of such claims that exceeds the amount of the bank's liabilities in that currency is assigned to the 100% risk category of section 3(a)(4) of this appendix.

(vi) Gold bullion held in the bank's own vaults or in another bank's vaults on an allocated basis, to the extent it is backed by gold bullion liabilities.

(vii) The book value of paid-in Federal Reserve Bank stock.

(viii) That portion of assets and off-balance sheet transactions [9a] collateralized by cash or securities issued or directly and unconditionally guaranteed by the United States Government or its agencies, or the central government of an OECD country, provided that: [9b]

(A) The bank maintains control over the collateral:

(*1*) If the collateral consists of cash, the cash must be held on deposit by the bank or by a third-party for the account of the bank;

(*2*) If the collateral consists of OECD government securities, then the OECD government securities must be held by the bank or by a third-party acting on behalf of the bank;

(B) The bank maintains a daily positive margin of collateral fully taking into account any change in the market value of the collateral held as security;

(C) Where the bank is acting as a customer's agent in a transaction involving the loan or sale of securities that is collateralized by cash or OECD government securities delivered to the bank, any obligation by the bank to indemnify the customer is limited to no more than the difference between the market value of the securities lent and the market value of the collateral received, and any reinvestment risk associated with the collateral is borne by the customer; and

(D) The transaction involves no more than minimal risk.

(ix) Asset-backed commercial paper (ABCP) that is:

(A) Purchased by the bank on or after September 19, 2008, from a Securities and Exchange Commission (SEC)-registered open-end investment company that holds itself out as a money market mutual fund under SEC Rule 2a–7 (17 CFR 270.2a–7); and

---

[9] For the treatment of privately-issued mortgage-backed securities where the underlying pool is comprised solely of mortgage-related securities issued by GNMA, *see infra* note 10.

[9a] See footnote 22 in section 3(b)(5)(iii) of this appendix A (collateral held against derivative contracts).

[9b] Assets and off-balance sheet transactions collateralized by securities issued or guaranteed by the United States Government or its agencies, or the central government of an OECD country include, but are not limited to, securities lending transactions, repurchase agreements, collateralized letters of credit, such as reinsurance letters of credit, and other similar financial guarantees. Swaps, forwards, futures, and options transactions are also eligible, if they meet the collateral requirements. However, the OCC may at its discretion require that certain collateralized transactions be risk weighted at 20 percent if they involve more than a minimal risk.

(B) Pledged by the bank to a Federal Reserve Bank to secure financing from the ABCP lending facility (AMLF) established by the Federal Reserve Board on September 19, 2008.

(2) *20 percent risk weight.* (i) All claims on depository institutions incorporated in an OECD country, and all assets backed by the full faith and credit of depository institutions incorporated in an OECD country. This includes the credit equivalent amount of participations in commitments and standby letters of credit sold to other depository institutions incorporated in an OECD country, but only if the originating bank remains liable to the customer or beneficiary for the full amount of the commitment or standby letter of credit. Also included in this category are the credit equivalent amounts of risk participations in bankers' acceptances conveyed to other depository institutions incorporated in an OECD country. However, bank-issued securities that qualify as capital of the issuing bank are not included in this risk category, but are assigned to the 100% risk category of section 3(a)(4) of this appendix A.

(ii) Claims on, or guaranteed by depository institutions, other than the central bank, incorporated in a non-OECD country, with a residual maturity of one year or less.

(iii) Cash items in the process of collection.

(iv) That portion of assets collateralized by cash or by securities issued or directly and unconditionally guaranteed by the United States Government or its agencies, or the central government of an OECD country, that does not qualify for the zero percent risk-weight category.

(v) That portion of assets conditionally guaranteed by the United States Government or its agencies, or the central government of an OECD country.

(vi) Securities issued by, or other direct claims on, United States Government-sponsored agencies.

(vii) That portion of assets guaranteed by United States Government-sponsored agencies.[10]

(viii) That portion of assets collateralized by the current market value of securities issued or guaranteed by United States Government-sponsored agencies.

(ix) Claims representing general obligations of any public-sector entity in an OECD country, and that portion of any claims guaranteed by any such public-sector entity. In the U.S., these obligations must meet the requirements of 12 CFR 1.2(b).

(x) Claims on, or guaranteed by, official multilateral lending institutions or regional development institutions in which the United States Government is a shareholder or contributing member.[11]

(xi) That portion of assets collateralized by the current market value of securities issued by official multilateral lending institutions or regional development institutions in which the United States Government is a shareholder or contributing member.

(xii) That portion of local currency claims conditionally guaranteed by central governments of non-OECD countries, to the extent the bank has local currency liabilities in that country. Any amount of such claims that exceeds the amount of the bank's local currency liabilities is assigned to the 100% risk category of section 3(a)(4) of this appendix.

(xiii) Claims on, or guaranteed by, a securities firm incorporated in an OECD country, that satisfies the following conditions:

(A) If the securities firm is incorporated in the United States, then the firm must be a broker-dealer that is registered with the SEC and must be in compliance with the SEC's net capital regulation (17 CFR 240.15c3(1)).

(B) If the securities firm is incorporated in any other OECD country, then the bank must be able to demonstrate that the firm is subject to consolidated supervision and regulation, including its subsidiaries, comparable

---

[10] Privately issued mortgage-backed securities, *e.g.*, CMOs and REMICs, where the underlying pool is comprised solely of mortgage-related securities issued by GNMA, FNMA and FHLMC, will be treated as an indirect holding of the underlying assets and assigned to the 20% risk category of this section 3(a)(2). If the underlying pool is comprised of assets which attract different risk weights, *e.g.*, FNMA securities and conventional mortgages, the bank should generally assign the security to the highest risk category appropriate for any asset in the pool. However, on a case-by-case basis, the OCC may allow the bank to assign the security proportionately to the various risk categories based on the proportion in which the risk categories are represented by the composition cash flows of the underlying pool of assets. Before the OCC will consider a request to proportionately risk-weight such a security, the bank must have current information for the reporting date that details the composition and cash flows of the underlying pool of assets. Furthermore, before a mortgage-related security will receive a risk weight lower than 100%, it must meet the criteria set forth in section 3(a)(3)(vi) of this appendix A.

[11] These institutions include, but are not limited to, the International Bank for Reconstruction and Development (World Bank), the Inter-American Development Bank, the Asian Development Bank, the African Development Bank, the European Investments Bank, the International Monetary Fund and the Bank for International Settlements.

to that imposed on depository institutions in OECD countries; such regulation must include risk-based capital standards comparable to those applied to depository institutions under the Basel Capital Accord.[11a]

(C) The securities firm, whether incorporated in the United States or another OECD country, must also have a long-term credit rating in accordance with section 3(a)(2)(xiii)(C)(*1*) of this appendix A; a parent company guarantee in accordance with section 3(a)(2)(xiii)(C)(*2*) of this appendix A; or a collateralized claim in accordance with section 3(a)(2)(xiii)(C)(*3*) of this appendix A. Claims representing capital of a securities firm must be risk weighted at 100 percent in accordance with section 3(a)(4) of this appendix A.

(*1*) *Credit rating.* The securities firm must have either a long-term issuer credit rating or a credit rating on at least one issue of long-term unsecured debt, from a NRSRO that is in one of the three highest investment-grade categories used by the NRSRO. If the securities firm has a credit rating from more than one NRSRO, the lowest credit rating must be used to determine the credit rating under this paragraph.

(*2*) *Parent company guarantee.* The claim on, or guaranteed by, the securities firm must be guaranteed by the firm's parent company, and the parent company must have either a long-term issuer credit rating or a credit rating on at least one issue of long-term unsecured debt, from a NRSRO that is in one of the three highest investment-grade categories used by the NRSRO.

(*3*) *Collateralized claim.* The claim on the securities firm must be collateralized subject to all of the following requirements:

(*i*) The claim must arise from a reverse repurchase/repurchase agreement or securities lending/borrowing contract executed using standard industry documentation.

(*ii*) The collateral must consist of debt or equity securities that are liquid and readily marketable.

(*iii*) The claim and collateral must be marked-to-market daily.

(*iv*) The claim must be subject to daily margin maintenance requirements under standard industry documentation.

(*v*) The contract from which the claim arises can be liquidated, terminated, or accelerated immediately in bankruptcy or similar proceedings, and the security or collateral agreement will not be stayed or avoided under the applicable law of the relevant jurisdiction. To be exempt from the automatic stay in bankruptcy in the United States, the claim must arise from a securities contract or a repurchase agreement under section 555 or 559, respectively, of the Bankruptcy Code (11 U.S.C. 555 or 559), a qualified financial contract under section 11(e)(8) of the Federal Deposit Insurance Act (12 U.S.C. 1821(e)(8)), or a netting contract between or among financial institutions under sections 401–407 of the Federal Deposit Insurance Corporation Improvement Act of 1991 (912 U.S.C. 4407), or the Regulation EE (12 CFR part 231).

(3) *50 percent risk weight.* (i) Revenue obligations of any public-sector entity in an OECD country for which the underlying obligor is the public-sector entity, but which are repayable solely from the revenues generated by the project financed through the issuance of the obligations.

(ii) The credit equivalent amount of derivative contracts, calculated in accordance with section 3(b)(5) of this appendix A, that do not qualify for inclusion in a lower risk category.

(iii) Loans secured by first mortgages on one-to-four family residential properties, either owner occupied or rented, provided that such loans are not otherwise 90 days or more past due, or on nonaccrual or restructured. It is presumed that such loans will meet the prudent underwriting standards. For the purposes of the risk-based capital guidelines, a loan modified on a permanent or trial basis solely pursuant to the U.S. Department of Treasury's Home Affordable Mortgage Program will not be considered to have been restructured. If a bank holds a first lien and junior lien on a one-to-four family residential property and no other party holds an intervening lien, the transaction is treated as a single loan secured by a first lien for the purposes of both determining the loan-to-value ratio and assigning a risk weight to the transaction. Furthermore, residential property loans made for the purpose of construction financing are assigned to the 100% risk category of section 3(a)(4) of this appendix A; however, these loans may be included in the 50% risk category of this section 3(a)(3) of this appendix A if they are subject to a legally binding sales contract and satisfy the requirements of section 3(a)(3)(iv) of this appendix A.

(iv) Loans to residential real estate builders for one-to-four family residential property construction, if the bank obtains sufficient documentation demonstrating that the buyer of the home intends to purchase the home (*i.e.*, a legally binding written sales contract) and has the ability to obtain a mortgage loan sufficient to purchase the home (*i.e.*, a firm written commitment for permanent financing of the home upon completion), subject to the following additional criteria:

[11a] *See* Accord on International Convergence of Capital Measurement and Capital Standards as adopted by the Basle Committee on Banking Regulations and Supervisory Practices (renamed as the Basel Committee on Banking Supervision), dated July 1988 (amended 1998).

(A) The builder must incur at least the first 10% of the direct costs (*i.e.*, actual costs of the land, labor, and material) before any drawdown is made under the construction loan and the construction loan may not exceed 80% of the sales price of the resold home;

(B) The individual purchaser has made a substantial "earnest money deposit" of no less than 3% of the sales price of the home that must be subject to forfeiture by the individual purchaser if the sales contract is terminated by the individual purchaser; however, the earnest money deposit shall not be subject to forfeiture by reason of breach or termination of the sales contract on the part of the builder;

(C) The earnest money deposit must be held in escrow by the bank financing the builder or by an independent party in a fiduciary capacity; the escrow agreement must provide that in the event of default the escrow funds must be used to defray any cost incurred relating to any cancellation of the sales contract by the buyer;

(D) If the individual purchaser terminates the contract or if the loan fails to satisfy any other criterion under this section, then the bank must immediately recategorize the loan at a 100% risk weight and must accurately report the loan in the bank's next quarterly Consolidated Reports of Condition and Income (Call Report);

(E) The individual purchaser must intend that the home will be owner-occupied;

(F) The loan is made by the bank in accordance with prudent underwriting standards;

(G) The loan is not more than 90 days past due, or on nonaccrual; and

(H) The purchaser is an individual(s) and not a partnership, joint venture, trust, corporation, or any other entity (including an entity acting as a sole proprietorship) that is purchasing one or more of the homes for speculative purposes.

(v) Loans secured by a first mortgage on multifamily residential properties: [11b]

(A) The amortization of principal and interest occurs in not more than 30 years;

(B) The minimum original maturity for repayment of principal is not less than 7 years;

(C) All principal and interest payments have been made on a timely basis in accordance with the terms of the loan for at least one year immediately preceding the risk weighting of the loan in the 50% risk weight category, and the loan is not otherwise 90 days or more past due, or on nonaccrual status;

(D) The loan is made in accordance with all applicable requirements and prudent underwriting standards;

(E) If the rate of interest does not change over the term of the loan:

(I) The current loan amount outstanding does not exceed 80% of the current value of the property, as measured by either the value of the property at origination of the loan (which is the lower of the purchase price or the value as determined by the initial appraisal, or if appropriate, the initial evaluation) or the most current appraisal, or if appropriate, the most current evaluation; and

(II) In the most recent fiscal year, the ratio of annual net operating income generated by the property (before payment of any debt service on the loan) to annual debt service on the loan is not less than 120%;[11c]

(F) If the rate of interest changes over the term of the loan:

(I) The current loan amount outstanding does not exceed 75% of the current value of the property, as measured by either the value of the property at origination of the loan (which is the lower of the purchase price or the value as determined by the initial appraisal, or if appropriate, the initial evaluation) or the most current appraisal, or if appropriate, the most current evaluation; and

(II) In the most recent fiscal year, the ratio of annual net operating income generated by the property (before payment of

---

[11b] The portion of multifamily residential property loans that is sold subject to a pro rata loss sharing arrangement may be treated by the selling bank as sold to the extent that the sales agreement provides for the purchaser of the loan to share in any loss incurred on the loan on a pro rata basis with the selling bank. The portion of multifamily residential property loans sold subject to any loss sharing arrangement other than *pro rata* sharing of the loss shall be accorded the same treatment as any other asset sold under an agreement to repurchase or sold with recourse under section 4(b) of this appendix A.

[11c] For the purposes of the debt service requirements in sections 3(a)(3)(v)(E)(II) and 3(a)(3)(v)(F)(II) of this appendix A, other forms of debt service coverage that generate sufficient cash flows to provide comparable protection to the institution may be considered for (a) a loan secured by cooperative housing or (b) a multifamily residential property loan if the purpose of the loan is for the development or purchase of multifamily residential property primarily intended to provide low- to moderate-income housing, including special operating reserve accounts or special operating subsidies provided by federal, state, local or private sources. However, the OCC reserves the right, on a case-by-case basis, to review the adequacy of any other forms of comparable debt service coverage relied on by the bank.

any debt service on the loan) to annual debt service on the loan is not less than 115%; and

(G) If the loan was refinanced by the borrower:

(I) All principal and interest payments on the loan being refinanced which were made in the preceding year prior to refinancing shall apply in determining the one-year timely payment requirement under paragraph (a)(3)(v)(C) of this section; and

(II) The net operating income generated by the property in the preceding year prior to refinancing shall apply in determining the applicable debt service requirements under paragraphs (a)(3)(v)(E) and (a)(3)(v)(F) of this section.

(vi) Privately-issued mortgage-backed securities, *i.e.* those that do not carry the guarantee of a government or government-sponsored agency, if the privately-issued mortgage-backed securities are at the time the mortgage-backed securities are originated fully secured by or otherwise represent a sufficiently secure interest in mortgages that qualify for the 50% risk weight under paragraphs (a)(3) (iii), (iv) and (v) of this section,[12] provided that they meet the following criteria:

(A) The underlying assets must be held by an independent trustee that has a first priority, perfected security interest in the underlying assets for the benefit of the holders of the security;

(B) The holder of the security must have an undivided pro rata ownership interest in the underlying assets or the trust that issues the security must have no liabilities unrelated to the issued securities;

(C) The trust that issues the security must be structured such that the cash flows from the underlying assets fully meet the cash flows requirements of the security without undue reliance on any reinvestment income; and

(D) There must not be any material reinvestment risk associated with any funds awaiting distribution to the holder of the security.

(4) *100 percent risk weight.* All other assets not specified above,[12a] including:

(i) Claims on or guaranteed by depository institutions incorporated in a non-OECD country, as well as claims on the central bank of a non-OECD country, with a residual maturity exceeding one year.

(ii) All non-local currency claims on non-OECD central governments, as well as local currency claims on non-OECD central governments that are not included in section 3(a)(1)(v) of this appendix A.

(iii) Asset-or mortgage backed securities that are externally rated are risk weighted in accordance with section 4(d) of this appendix A.

(iv) All stripped mortgage-backed securities, including interest only portions (IOs), principal only portions (POs) and other similar instruments, regardless of the issuer or guarantor.

(v) Obligations issued by any state or any political subdivision thereof for the benefit of a private party or enterprise where that party or enterprise, rather than the issuing state or political subdivision, is responsible for the timely payment of principal and interest on the obligation, *e.g.*, industrial development bonds.

(vi) Claims on commercial enterprises owned by non-OECD and OECD central governments.

(vii) Any investment in an unconsolidated subsidiary that is not required to be deducted from total capital pursuant to section 2(c)(3) of this appendix A.

(viii) Instruments issued by depository institutions incorporated in OECD and non-OECD countries that qualify as capital of the issuer.

(ix) Investments in fixed assets, premises, and other real estate owned.

(x) Claims representing capital of a securities firm notwithstanding section 3(a)(2)(xiii) of this appendix A. [Reserved]

(xi) Subject to the requirements below, a bank may assign an asset not included in the categories above to the risk weight category applicable under the capital guidelines for bank holding companies (see 12 CFR part 225, appendix A), provided that all of the following conditions apply:

(A) The bank is not authorized to hold the asset under applicable law other than debt previously contracted or similar authority; and

(B) The risks associated with the asset are substantially similar to the risks of assets

[12] If all of the underlying mortgages in the pool do not qualify for the 50% risk weight, the bank should generally assign the entire value of the security to the 100% risk category of section 3(a)(4) of this appendix A; however, on a case-by-case basis, the OCC may allow the bank to assign only the portion of the security which represents an interest in, and the cash flows of, nonqualifying mortgages to the 100% risk category, with the remainder being assigned a risk weight of 50%. Before the OCC will consider a request to risk weight a mortgage-backed security on a proportionate basis, the bank must have current information for the reporting date that details the composition and cash flows of the underlying pool of mortgages.

[12a] A bank subject to the market risk capital requirements pursuant to appendix B of this part 3 may calculate the capital requirement for qualifying securities borrowing transactions pursuant to section 3(a)(1)(ii) of appendix B of this part 3.

that are otherwise assigned to a risk weight category less than 100 percent under this appendix.

(6) *Other variable interest entities subject to consolidation.* If a bank is required to consolidate the assets of a variable interest entity under generally accepted accounting principles, the bank must assess a risk-based capital charge based on the appropriate risk weight of the consolidated assets in accordance with sections 3(a) and 4 of this appendix A. Any direct credit substitutes and recourse obligations (including residual interests), and loans that a bank may provide to such a variable interest entity are not subject to a capital charge under section 4 of this appendix A.

(b) *Off-Balance Sheet Activities.* The risk weight assigned to an off-balance sheet item is determined by a two-step process. First, the face amount of the off-balance sheet item is multiplied by the appropriate credit conversion factor specified in this section. This calculation translates the face amount of an off-balance sheet item into an on-balance sheet credit equivalent amount. Second, the resulting credit equivalent amount is then assigned to the proper risk category using the criteria regarding obligors, guarantors, and collateral listed in section 3(a) of this appendix A, or external credit rating in accordance with section 4(d), if applicable. Collateral and guarantees are applied to the face amount of an off-balance sheet item; however, with respect to derivative contracts under section 3(b)(5) of this appendix A, collateral and guarantees are applied to the credit equivalent amounts of such derivative contracts. The following are the credit conversion factors and the off-balance sheet items to which they apply. However, direct credit substitutes, recourse obligations, and securities issued in connection with asset securitizations are treated as described in section 4 of this appendix A.

(1) *100 percent credit conversion factor.* (i) [Reserved][13]

(ii) Risk participations purchased in bankers' acceptances;

(iii) [Reserved][14]

(iv) Contingent obligations with a certain draw down, *e.g.*, legally binding agreements to purchase assets as a specified future date.

(v) Indemnification of customers whose securities the bank has lent as agent. If the customer is not indemnified against loss by the bank, the transaction is excluded from the risk-based capital calculation.[15]

(2) *50 percent credit conversion factor.* (i) Transaction-related contingencies including, among other things, performance bonds and performance-based standby letters of credit related to a particular transaction.[16] To the extent permitted by law or regulation, performance-based standby letters of credit include such things as arrangements backing subcontractors' and suppliers' performance, labor and materials contracts, and construction bids;

(ii) Unused portion of commitments with an original maturity exceeding one-year;[17] however, commitments that are asset-backed commercial paper liquidity facilities must satisfy the eligibility requirements under section 3(b)(6)(ii) of this appendix A;

(iii) Revolving underwriting facilities, note issuance facilities, and similar arrangements pursuant to which the bank's customer can issue short-term debt obligations in its own name, but for which the bank has a legally binding commitment to either:

(A) Purchase the obligations the customer is unable to sell by a stated date; or

(B) Advance funds to its customer, if the obligations cannot be sold.

(3) *20 percent credit conversion factor.* (i) Trade-related contingencies. These are short-term self-liquidating instruments used to finance the movement of goods and are collateralized by the underlying shipment. A commercial letter of credit is an example of such an instrument.

(4) *10 percent credit conversion factor.* Unused portion of asset-backed commercial paper liquidity facilities with an original maturity of one year or less that satisfy the eligibility requirements under section 3(b)(6)(ii) of this appendix A.

(5) *Zero percent credit conversion factor.* (i) Unused portion of commitments with an original maturity of one year or less, but excluding any asset-backed commercial paper liquidity facilities;

---

[13] [Reserved]

[14] [Reserved]

[15] When a bank lends its own securities, the transaction is treated as a loan. When a bank lends its own securities or, acting as agent, agrees to indemnify a customer, the transaction is assigned to the risk weight appropriate to the obligor or collateral that is delivered to the lending or indemnifying institution or to an independent custodian acting on their behalf.

[16] For purposes of this section 3(b)(2)(i), a "performance-based standby letter of credit" is any letter of credit, or similar arrangement, however named or described, which represents an irrevocable obligation to the beneficiary on the part of the issuer to make payment on account of any default by the account party in the performance of a non-financial or commercial obligation. Participations in performance-based standby letters of credit are treated in accordance with section 4 of this appendix A.

[17] Participations in commitments are treated in accordance with section 4 of this appendix A.

(ii) Unused portion of commitments with an original maturity of greater than one year, if they are unconditionally cancelable[18] at any time at the option of the bank and the bank has the contractual right to make, and in fact does make, either—

(A) A separate credit decision based upon the borrower's current financial condition, before each drawing under the lending facility; or

(B) An annual (or more frequent) credit review based upon the borrower's current financial condition to determine whether or not the lending facility should be continued; and

(iii) The unused portion of retail credit card lines or other related plans that are unconditionally cancelable by the bank in accordance with applicable law.

(6) *Liquidity facility provided to asset-backed commercial paper.* (i) *Noneligible asset-backed commercial paper liquidity facilities treated as recourse or direct credit substitute.* Unused portion of asset-backed commercial paper liquidity facilities that do not meet the criteria for an eligible liquidity facility provided to asset-backed commercial paper in accordance with section 3(b)(6)(ii) of this appendix A must be treated as recourse or as a direct credit substitute, and assessed the appropriate risk-based capital charge in accordance with section 4 of this appendix A.

(ii) *Eligible asset-backed commercial paper liquidity facility.* Except as provided in section 3(b)(6)(iii) of this appendix A, in order for the unused portion of an asset-backed commercial paper liquidity facility to be eligible for either the 50 percent or 10 percent credit conversion factors under section 3(b)(2)(ii) or 3(b)(4) of this appendix A, the asset-backed commercial paper liquidity facility must satisfy the following criteria:

(A) At the time of draw, the asset-backed commercial paper liquidity facility must be subject to an asset quality test that:

(*1*) Precludes funding of assets that are 90 days or more past due or in default; and

(*2*) If the assets that an asset-backed commercial paper liquidity facility is required to fund are externally rated securities at the time they are transferred into the program, the asset-backed commercial paper liquidity facility must be used to fund only securities that are externally rated investment grade at the time of funding. If the assets are not externally rated at the time they are transferred into the program, then they are not subject to this investment grade requirement.

(B) The asset-backed commercial paper liquidity facility must provide that, prior to any draws, the bank's funding obligation is reduced to cover only those assets that satisfy the funding criteria under the asset quality test as provided in section 3(b)(6)(ii)(A) of this appendix A.

(iii) *Exception to eligibility requirements for assets guaranteed by the United States Government or its agencies, or the central government of an OECD country.* Notwithstanding the eligibility requirements for asset-backed commercial paper program liquidity facilities in section 3(b)(6)(ii), the unused portion of an asset-backed commercial paper liquidity facility may still qualify for either the 50 percent or 10 percent credit conversion factors under section 3(b)(2)(ii) or 3(b)(4) of this appendix A, if the assets required to be funded by the asset-back commercial paper liquidity facility are guaranteed, either conditionally or unconditionally, by the United States Government or its agencies, or the central government of an OECD country.

(iv) *Transition period for asset-backed commercial paper liquidity facilities.* Notwithstanding the eligibility requirements for asset-backed commercial paper program liquidity facilities in section 3(b)(6)(i) of this appendix A, the unused portion of an asset-backed commercial paper liquidity will be treated as eligible liquidity facilities pursuant to section 3(b)(6)(ii) of this appendix A regardless of their compliance with the definition of eligible liquidity facilities until September 30, 2005. On that date and thereafter, the unused portions of asset-backed commercial paper liquidity facilities that do not meet the eligibility requirements in section 3(b)(6)(i) of this appendix A will be treated as recourse obligations or direct credit substitutes.

(7) *Derivative contracts*—(i) *Calculation of credit equivalent amounts.* The credit equivalent amount of a derivative contract equals the sum of the current credit exposure and the potential future credit exposure of the derivative contract. The calculation of credit equivalent amounts must be measured in U.S. dollars, regardless of the currency or currencies specified in the derivative contract.

(A) *Current credit exposure.* The current credit exposure for a single derivative contract is determined by the mark-to-market value of the derivative contract. If the mark-to-market value is positive, then the current credit exposure equals that mark-to-market value. If the mark-to-market is zero or negative, then the current credit exposure is zero. The current credit exposure for multiple derivative contracts executed with a single counterparty and subject to a qualifying bilateral netting contract is determined as provided by section 3(b)(5)(ii)(A) of this appendix A.

(B) *Potential future credit exposure.* The potential future credit exposure for a single derivative contract, including a derivative contract with negative mark-to-market value, is

[18] See section 1(c)(26) of appendix A to this part.

calculated by multiplying the notional principal[19] of the derivative contract by one of the credit conversion factors in Table A—Conversion Factor Matrix of this appendix A, for the appropriate category.[20] The potential future credit exposure for gold contracts shall be calculated using the foreign exchange rate conversion factors. For any derivative contract that does not fall within one of the specified categories in Table A—Conversion Factor Matrix of this appendix A, the potential future credit exposure shall be calculated using the other commodity conversion factors. Subject to examiner review, banks should use the effective rather than the apparent or stated notional amount in calculating the potential future credit exposure. The potential future credit exposure for multiple derivatives contracts executed with a single counterparty and subject to a qualifying bilateral netting contract is determined as provided by section 3(b)(5)(ii)(A) of this appendix A.

TABLE B—CONVERSION FACTOR MATRIX[1]

Remaining maturity[2]	Interest rate	Foreign exchange rate and gold	Equity[2]	Precious metals	Other commodity
One year or less	0.0	1.0	6.0	7.0	10.0
Over one to five years	0.5	5.0	8.0	7.0	12.0
Over five years	1.5	7.5	10.0	8.0	15.0

[1] For derivative contracts with multiple exchanges of principal, the conversion factors are multiplied by the number of remaining payments in the derivative contract.

[2] For derivative contracts that automatically reset to zero value following a payment, the remaining maturity equals the time until the next payment. However, interest rate contracts with remaining maturities of greater than one year shall be subject to a minimum conversion factor of 0.5 percent.

(ii) *Derivative contracts subject to a qualifying bilateral netting contract*—(A) *Netting calculation.* The credit equivalent amount for multiple derivative contracts executed with a single counterparty and subject to a qualifying bilateral netting contract as provided by section (3)(b)(5)(ii)(B) of this appendix A is calculated by adding the net current credit exposure and the adjusted sum of the potential future credit exposure for all derivative contracts subject to the qualifying bilateral netting contract.

(*1*) *Net current credit exposure.* The net current credit exposure is the net sum of all positive and negative mark-to-market values of the individual derivative contracts subject to a qualifying bilateral netting contract. If the net sum of the mark-to-market value is positive, then the net current credit exposure equals that net sum of the mark-to-market value. If the net sum of the mark-to-market value is zero or negative, then the net current credit exposure is zero.

(*2*) *Adjusted sum of the potential future credit exposure.* The adjusted sum of the potential future credit exposure is calculated as:

$$A_{net} = 0.4 \times A_{gross} + (0.6 \times NGR \times A_{gross})$$

A_{net} is the adjusted sum of the potential future credit exposure, A_{gross} is the gross potential future credit exposure, and NGR is the net to gross ratio. A_{gross} is the sum of the potential future credit exposure (as determined under section 3(b)(5)(i)(B) of this appendix A) for each individual derivative contract subject to the qualifying bilateral netting contract. The NGR is the ratio of the net current credit exposure to the gross current credit exposure. In calculating the NGR, the gross current credit exposure equals the sum of the positive current credit exposures (as determined under section 3(b)(5)(i)(A) of this appendix A) of all individual derivative contracts subject to the qualifying bilateral netting contract.

(B) *Qualifying bilateral netting contract.* In determining the current credit exposure for multiple derivative contracts executed with a single counterparty, a bank may net derivative contracts subject to a qualifying bilateral netting contract by offsetting positive and negative mark-to-market values, provided that:

(*1*) The qualifying bilateral netting contract is in writing.

(*2*) The qualifying bilateral netting contract is not subject to a walkaway clause.

[19] For purposes of calculating either the potential future credit exposure under section 3(b)(5)(i)(B) of this appendix A or the gross potential future credit exposure under section 3(b)(5)(ii)(A)(2) of this appendix A for foreign exchange contracts and other similar contracts in which the notional principal is equivalent to the cash flows, total notional principal is the net receipts to each party falling due on each value date in each currency.

[20] No potential future credit exposure is calculated for single currency interest rate swaps in which payments are made based upon two floating indices, so-called floating/floating or basis swaps; the credit equivalent amount is measured solely on the basis of the current credit exposure.

(*3*) The qualifying bilateral netting contract creates a single legal obligation for all individual derivative contracts covered by the qualifying bilateral netting contract. In effect, the qualifying bilateral netting contract must provide that the bank would have a single claim or obligation either to receive or to pay only the net amount of the sum of the positive and negative mark-to-market values on the individual derivative contracts covered by the qualifying bilateral netting contract. The single legal obligation for the net amount is operative in the event that a counterparty, or a counterparty to whom the qualifying bilateral netting contract has been assigned, fails to perform due to any of the following events: default, insolvency, bankruptcy, or other similar circumstances.

(*4*) The bank obtains a written and reasoned legal opinion(s) that represents, with a high degree of certainty, that in the event of a legal challenge, including one resulting from default, insolvency, bankruptcy, or similar circumstances, the relevant court and administrative authorities would find the bank's exposure to be the net amount under:

(*i*) The law of the jurisdiction in which the counterparty is chartered or the equivalent location in the case of noncorporate entities, and if a branch of the counterparty is involved, then also under the law of the jurisdiction in which the branch is located;

(*ii*) The law of the jurisdiction that governs the individual derivative contracts covered by the bilateral netting contract; and

(*iii*) The law of the jurisdiction that governs the qualifying bilateral netting contract.

(*5*) The bank establishes and maintains procedures to monitor possible changes in relevant law and to ensure that the qualifying bilateral netting contract continues to satisfy the requirement of this section.

(*6*) The bank maintains in its files documentation adequate to support the netting of a derivative contract.[21]

(iii) *Risk weighting.* Once the bank determines the credit equivalent amount for a derivative contract or a set of derivative contracts subject to a qualifying bilateral netting contract, the bank assigns that amount to the risk weight category appropriate to the counterparty, or, if relevant, the nature of any collateral or guarantee.[22] However, the maximum weight that will be applied to the credit equivalent amount of such derivative contract(s) is 50 percent.

(iv) *Exceptions.* The following derivative contracts are not subject to the above calculation, and therefore, are not part of the denominator of a national bank's risk-based capital ratio:

(A) An exchange rate contract with an original maturity of 14 calendar days or less;[23] and

(B) A derivative contract that is traded on an exchange requiring the daily payment of any variations in the market value of the contract.

Section 4. Recourse, Direct Credit Substitutes and Positions in Securitizations

(a) *Definitions.* For purposes of this section 4 of this appendix A, the following definitions apply:

(1) *Credit derivative* means a contract that allows one party (the protection purchaser) to transfer the credit risk of an asset or off-balance sheet credit exposure to another party (the protection provider). The value of a credit derivative is dependent, at least in part, on the credit performance of a "reference asset."

(2) *Credit-enhancing interest-only strip* means an on-balance sheet asset that, in form or in substance:

(i) Represents the contractual right to receive some or all of the interest due on transferred assets; and

(ii) Exposes the bank to credit risk directly or indirectly associated with the transferred assets that exceeds its *pro rata* claim on the assets whether through subordination provisions or other credit enhancing techniques.

(3) *Credit-enhancing representations and warranties* means representations and warranties that are made or assumed in connection with a transfer of assets (including loan servicing assets) and that obligate a bank to protect

---

[21] By netting individual derivative contracts for the purpose of calculating its credit equivalent amount, a bank represents that documentation adequate to support the netting of a set of derivative contract is in the bank's files and available for inspection by the OCC. Upon determination by the OCC that a bank's files are inadequate or that a qualifying bilateral netting contract may not be legally enforceable in any one of the bodies of law described in section 3(b)(5)(ii)(B)(*3*)(*i*) through (*iii*) of this appendix A, the underlying derivative contracts may not be netted for the purposes of this section.

[22] Derivative contracts are an exception to the general rule of applying collateral and guarantees to the face value of off-balance sheet items. The sufficiency of collateral and guarantees is determined on the basis of the credit equivalent amount of derivative contracts. However, collateral and guarantees held against a qualifying bilateral netting contract is not recognized for capital purposes unless it is legally available for all contracts included in the qualifying bilateral netting contract.

[23] Notwithstanding section 3(b)(5)(B) of this appendix A, gold contracts do not qualify for this exception.

investors from losses arising from credit risk in the assets transferred or the loans serviced. Credit-enhancing representations and warranties include promises to protect a party from losses resulting from the default or nonperformance of another party or from an insufficiency in the value of the collateral. Credit-enhancing representations and warranties do not include:

(i) Early-default clauses and similar warranties that permit the return of, or premium refund clauses covering, 1–4 family residential first mortgage loans (as described in section 3(a)(3)(iii) of this appendix A) for a period not to exceed 120 days from the date of transfer. These warranties may cover only those loans that were originated within 1 year of the date of transfer;

(ii) Premium refund clauses that cover assets guaranteed, in whole or in part, by the U.S. Government, a U.S. Government agency, or a U.S. Government-sponsored enterprise, provided the premium refund clauses are for a period not to exceed 120 days from the date of transfer; or

(iii) Warranties that permit the return of assets in instances of fraud, misrepresentation or incomplete documentation.

(4) *Direct credit substitute* means an arrangement in which a bank assumes, in form or in substance, credit risk associated with an on- or off-balance sheet asset or exposure that was not previously owned by the bank (third-party asset) and the risk assumed by the bank exceeds the *pro rata* share of the bank's interest in the third-party asset. If a bank has no claim on the third-party asset, then the bank's assumption of any credit risk is a direct credit substitute. Direct credit substitutes include:

(i) Financial standby letters of credit that support financial claims on a third party that exceed a bank's *pro rata* share in the financial claim;

(ii) Guarantees, surety arrangements, credit derivatives and similar instruments backing financial claims that exceed a bank's *pro rata* share in the financial claim;

(iii) Purchased subordinated interests that absorb more than their *pro rata* share of losses from the underlying assets;

(iv) Credit derivative contracts under which the bank assumes more than its *pro rata* share of credit risk on a third-party asset or exposure;

(v) Loans or lines of credit that provide credit enhancement for the financial obligations of a third party;

(vi) Purchased loan servicing assets if the servicer is responsible for credit losses or if the servicer makes or assumes credit-enhancing representations and warranties with respect to the loans serviced. Mortgage servicer case advances that meet the conditions of section 4(a)(8)(i) and (ii) of this appendix A, are not direct credit substitutes;

(vii) Clean-up calls on third-party assets. Clean-up calls that are 10% or less of the original pool balance and that are exercisable at the option of the bank are not direct credit substitutes; and

(viii) Unused portion of noneligible asset-backed commercial paper liquidity facilities.

(5) *Externally rated* means that an instrument or obligation has received a credit rating from at least one nationally recognized statistical rating organization.

(6) *Face amount* means the notional principal, or face value, amount of an off-balance sheet item; the amortized cost of an asset not held for trading purposes; and the fair value of a trading asset.

(7) *Financial asset* means cash or other monetary instrument, evidence of debt, evidence of an ownership interest in an entity, or a contract that conveys a right to receive or exchange cash or another financial instrument from another party.

(8) *Financial standby letter of credit* means a letter of credit or similar arrangement that represents an irrevocable obligation to a third-party beneficiary:

(i) To repay money borrowed by, or advanced to, or for the account of, a second party (the account party); or

(ii) To make payment on behalf of the account party, in the event that the account party fails to fulfill its obligation to the beneficiary.

(9) *Mortgage servicer cash advance* means funds that a residential mortgage servicer advances to ensure an uninterrupted flow of payments, including advances made to cover foreclosure costs or other expenses to facilitate the timely collection of the loan. A mortgage servicer cash advance is not a recourse obligation or a direct credit substitute if:

(i) The servicer is entitled to full reimbursement and this right is not subordinated to other claims on the cash flows from the underlying asset pool; or

(ii) For any one loan, the servicer's obligation to make nonreimbursable advances is contractually limited to an insignificant amount of the outstanding principal amount of that loan.

(10) *Nationally recognized statistical rating organization (NRSRO)* means an entity recognized by the Division of Market Regulation of the Securities and Exchange Commission (or any successor Division) (Commission) as a nationally recognized statistical rating organization for various purposes, including the Commission's uniform net capital requirements for brokers and dealers.

(11) *Recourse* means a bank's retention, in form or in substance, of any credit risk directly or indirectly associated with an asset it has sold that exceeds a *pro rata* share of that bank's claim on the asset. If a bank has no claim on a sold asset, then the retention

of any credit risk is recourse. A recourse obligation typically arises when a bank transfers assets and retains an explicit obligation to repurchase assets or to absorb losses due to a default on the payment of principal or interest or any other deficiency in the performance of the underlying obligor or some other party. Recourse may also exist implicitly if a bank provides credit enhancement beyond any contractual obligation to support assets it has sold. The following are examples of recourse arrangements:

(i) Credit-enhancing representations and warranties made on transferred assets;

(ii) Loan servicing assets retained pursuant to an agreement under which the bank will be responsible for losses associated with the loans serviced. Mortgage servicer cash advances that meet the conditions of section 4(a)(9)(i) and (ii) of this appendix A, are not recourse arrangements;

(iii) Retained subordinated interests that absorb more than their *pro rata* share of losses from the underlying assets;

(iv) Assets sold under an agreement to repurchase, if the assets are not already included on the balance sheet;

(v) Loan strips sold without contractual recourse where the maturity of the transferred portion of the loan is shorter than the maturity of the commitment under which the loan is drawn;

(vi) Credit derivatives issued that absorb more than the bank's pro rata share of losses from the transferred assets;

(vii) Clean-up calls. Clean-up calls that are 10% or less of the original pool balance and that are exercisable at the option of the bank are not recourse arrangements; and

(viii) Noneligible asset-backed commercial paper liquidity facilities.

(12) *Residual interest* means any on-balance sheet asset that represents an interest (including a beneficial interest) created by a transfer that qualifies as a sale (in accordance with generally accepted accounting principles) of financial assets, whether through a securitization or otherwise, and that exposes a bank to any credit risk directly or indirectly associated with the transferred asset that exceeds a *pro rata* share of that bank's claim on the asset, whether through subordination provisions or other credit enhancement techniques. Residual interests generally include credit-enhancing interest-only strips, spread accounts, cash collateral accounts, retained subordinated interests (and other forms of overcollateralization) and similar assets that function as a credit enhancement. Residual interests further include those exposures that, in substance, cause the bank to retain the credit risk of an asset or exposure that had qualified as a residual interest before it was sold. Residual interests generally do not include interests purchased from a third party.

(13) *Risk participation* means a participation in which the originating party remains liable to the beneficiary for the full amount of an obligation (*e.g.* a direct credit substitute) notwithstanding that another party has acquired a participation in that obligation.

(14) *Securitization* means the pooling and repackaging by a special purpose entity of assets or other credit exposures that can be sold to investors. Securitization includes transactions that create stratified credit risk positions whose performance is dependent upon an underlying pool of credit exposures, including loans and commitments.

(15) *Structured finance program* means a program where receivable interests and asset-backed securities issued by multiple participants are purchased by a special purpose entity that repackages those exposures into securities that can be sold to investors. Structured finance programs allocate credit risks, generally, between the participants and credit enhancement provided to the program.

(16) *Traded position* means a position retained, assumed or issued in connection with a securitization that is externally rated, where there is a reasonable expectation that, in the near future, the rating will be relied upon by:

(i) Unaffiliated investors to purchase the position; or

(ii) An unaffiliated third party to enter into a transaction involving the position, such as a purchase, loan or repurchase agreement.

(b) *Credit equivalent amounts and risk weights of recourse obligations and direct credit substitutes*—(1) *Credit-equivalent amount.* Except as otherwise provided, the credit-equivalent amount for a recourse obligation or direct credit substitute is the full amount of the credit-enhanced assets for which the bank directly or indirectly retains or assumes credit risk multiplied by a 100% conversion factor.

(2) *Risk-weight factor.* To determine the bank's risk-weighted assets for off-balance sheet recourse obligations and direct credit substitutes, the credit equivalent amount is assigned to the risk category appropriate to the obligor in the underlying transaction, after considering any associated guarantees or collateral. For a direct credit substitute that is an on-balance sheet asset (*e.g.*, a purchased subordinated security), a bank must calculate risk-weighted assets using the amount of the direct credit substitute and the full amount of the assets it supports, *i.e.*, all the more senior positions in the structure.

(c) *Credit equivalent amount and risk weight of participations in, and syndications of, direct credit substitutes.* The credit equivalent amount for a participation interest in, or syndication of, a direct credit substitute is calculated and risk weighted as follows:

(1) In the case of a direct credit substitute in which a bank has conveyed a risk participation, the full amount of the assets that are supported by the direct credit substitute is converted to a credit equivalent amount using a 100% conversion factor. The *pro rata* share of the credit equivalent amount that has been conveyed through a risk participation is then assigned to whichever risk-weight category is lower: the risk-weight category appropriate to the obligor in the underlying transaction, after considering any associated guarantees or collateral, or the risk-weight category appropriate to the party acquiring the participation. The *pro rata* share of the credit equivalent amount that has not been participated out is assigned to the risk-weight category appropriate to the obligor after considering any associated guarantees or collateral.

(2) In the case of a direct credit substitute in which the bank has acquired a risk participation, the acquiring bank's *pro rata* share of the direct credit substitute is multiplied by the full amount of the assets that are supported by the direct credit substitute and converted using a 100% credit conversion factor. The resulting credit equivalent amount is then assigned to the risk-weight category appropriate to the obligor in the underlying transaction, after considering any associated guarantees or collateral.

(3) In the case of a direct credit substitute that takes the form of a syndication where each bank or participating entity is obligated only for its *pro rata* share of the risk and there is no recourse to the originating entity, each bank's credit equivalent amount will be calculated by multiplying only its *pro rata* share of the assets supported by the direct credit substitute by a 100% conversion factor. The resulting credit equivalent amount is then assigned to the risk-weight category appropriate to the obligor in the underlying transaction, after considering any associated guarantees or collateral.

(d) *Externally rated positions: credit-equivalent amounts and risk weights*—(1) *Traded positions.* With respect to a recourse obligation, direct credit substitute, residual interest (other than a credit-enhancing interest-only strip) or asset- or mortgage-backed security that is a "traded position" and that has received an external rating on a long-term position that is one grade below investment grade or better or a short-term position that is investment grade, the bank may multiply the face amount of the position by the appropriate risk weight, determined in accordance with Tables C or D of this appendix A.[24] If a traded position receives more than one external rating, the lowest single rating will apply.

TABLE C

Long-term rating category	Examples	Risk weight (In percent)
Highest or second highest investment grade	AAA, AA	20
Third highest investment grade	A	50
Lowest investment grade	BBB	100
One category below investment grade	BB	200

TABLE D

Short-term rating category	Examples	Risk weight (In percent)
Highest investment grade	A–1, P–1	20
Second highest investment grade	A–2, P–2	50
Lowest investment grade	A–3, P–3	100

(2) *Non-traded positions.* A recourse obligation, direct credit substitute, residual interest (but not a credit-enhancing interest-only strip) or asset- or mortgage-backed security extended in connection with a securitization that is not a "traded position" may be assigned a risk weight in accordance with section 4(d)(1) of this appendix A if:

(i) It has been externally rated by more than one NRSRO;

(ii) It has received an external rating on a long-term position that is one category below investment grade or better or a short-term position that is investment grade by all NRSROs providing a rating;

(iii) The ratings are publicly available; and

(iv) The ratings are based on the same criteria used to rate traded positions.

If the ratings are different, the lowest rating will determine the risk category to which

[24] Stripped mortgage-backed securities or other similar instruments, such as interest-only or principal-only strips, that are not credit enhancing must be assigned to the 100% risk category.

the recourse obligation, residual interest or direct credit substitute will be assigned.

(e) *Senior positions not externally rated.* For a recourse obligation, direct credit substitute, residual interest or asset- or mortgage-backed security that is not externally rated but is senior or preferred in all features to a traded position (including collateralization and maturity), a bank may apply a risk weight to the face amount of the senior position in accordance with section 4(d)(1) of this appendix A, based upon the traded position, subject to any current or prospective supervisory guidance and the bank satisfying the OCC that this treatment is appropriate. This section will apply only if the traded position provides substantive credit support to the unrated position until the unrated position matures.

(f) *Residual Interests*—(1) *Concentration limit on credit-enhancing interest-only strips.* In addition to the capital requirement provided by section 4(f)(2) of this appendix A, a bank must deduct from Tier 1 capital all credit-enhancing interest-only strips in excess of 25 percent of Tier 1 capital in accordance with section 2(c)(2)(iv) of this appendix A.

(2) *Credit-enhancing interest-only strip capital requirement.* After applying the concentration limit to credit-enhancing interest-only strips in accordance with section (f)(1), a bank must maintain risk-based capital for a credit-enhancing interest-only strip equal to the remaining amount of the credit-enhancing interest-only strip (net of any existing associated deferred tax liability), even if the amount of risk-based capital required to be maintained exceeds the full risk-based capital requirement for the assets transferred. Transactions that, in substance, result in the retention of credit risk associated with a transferred credit-enhancing interest-only strip will be treated as if the credit-enhancing interest-only strip was retained by the bank and not transferred.

(3) *Other residual interests capital requirement.* Except as provided in sections (d) or (e) of this section, a bank must maintain risk-based capital for a residual interest (excluding a credit-enhancing interest-only strip) equal to the face amount of the residual interest that is retained on the balance sheet (net of any existing associated deferred tax liability), even if the amount of risk-based capital required to be maintained exceeds the full risk-based capital requirement for the assets transferred. Transactions that, in substance, result in the retention of credit risk associated with a transferred residual interest will be treated as if the residual interest was retained by the bank and not transferred.

(4) *Residual interests and other recourse obligations.* Where the aggregate capital requirement for residual interests (including credit-enhancing interest-only strips) and recourse obligations arising from the same transfer of assets exceed the full risk-based capital requirement for those assets, a bank must maintain risk-based capital equal to the greater of the risk-based capital requirement for the residual interest as calculated under sections 4(f)(1) through (3) of this appendix A or the full risk-based capital requirement for the assets transferred.

(g) *Positions that are not rated by an NRSRO.* A position (but not a residual interest) extended in connection with a securitization and that is not rated by an NRSRO may be risk-weighted based on the bank's determination of the credit rating of the position, as specified in Table E of this appendix A, multiplied by the face amount of the position. In order to qualify for this treatment, the bank's system for determining the credit rating of the position must meet one of the three alternative standards set out in section 4(g)(1)through (3) of this appendix A.

TABLE E

Rating category	Examples	Risk weight (In percent)
Investment grade	BBB, or better	100
One category below investment grade	BB	200

(1) *Internal risk rating used for asset-backed programs.* A direct credit substitute (but not a purchased credit-enhancing interest-only strip) is assumed by a bank in connection with an asset-backed commercial paper program sponsored by the bank and the bank is able to demonstrate to the satisfaction of the OCC, prior to relying upon its use, that the bank's internal credit risk rating system is adequate. Adequate internal credit risk rating systems usually contain the following criteria:

(i) The internal credit risk system is an integral part of the bank's risk management system that explicitly incorporates the full range of risks arising from a bank's participation in securitization activities;

(ii) Internal credit ratings are linked to measurable outcomes, such as the probability that the position will experience any loss, the position's expected loss given default, and the degree of variance in losses given default on that position;

(iii) The bank's internal credit risk system must separately consider the risk associated with the underlying loans or borrowers, and the risk associated with the structure of a particular securitization transaction;

(iv) The bank's internal credit risk system must identify gradations of risk among "pass" assets and other risk positions;

(v) The bank must have clear, explicit criteria that are used to classify assets into each internal risk grade, including subjective factors;

(vi) The bank must have independent credit risk management or loan review personnel assigning or reviewing the credit risk ratings;

(vii) An internal audit procedure should periodically verify that internal risk ratings are assigned in accordance with the bank's established criteria.

(viii) The bank must monitor the performance of the internal credit risk ratings assigned to nonrated, nontraded direct credit substitutes over time to determine the appropriateness of the initial credit risk rating assignment and adjust individual credit risk ratings, or the overall internal credit risk ratings system, as needed; and

(ix) The internal credit risk system must make credit risk rating assumptions that are consistent with, or more conservative than, the credit risk rating assumptions and methodologies of NRSROs.

(2) *Program Ratings.* A direct credit substitute or recourse obligation (but not a residual interest) is assumed or retained by a bank in connection with a structured finance program and a NRSRO has reviewed the terms of the program and stated a rating for positions associated with the program. If the program has options for different combinations of assets, standards, internal credit enhancements and other relevant factors, and the NRSRO specifies ranges of rating categories to them, the bank may apply the rating category applicable to the option that corresponds to the bank's position. In order to rely on a program rating, the bank must demonstrate to the OCC's satisfaction that the credit risk rating assigned to the program meets the same standards generally used by NRSROs for rating traded positions. The bank must also demonstrate to the OCC's satisfaction that the criteria underlying the NRSRO's assignment of ratings for the program are satisfied for the particular position. If a bank participates in a securitization sponsored by another party, the OCC may authorize the bank to use this approach based on a program rating obtained by the sponsor of the program.

(3) *Computer Program.* The bank is using an acceptable credit assessment computer program to determine the rating of a direct credit substitute or recourse obligation (but not a residual interest) extended in connection with a structured finance program. A NRSRO must have developed the computer program and the bank must demonstrate to the OCC's satisfaction that ratings under the program correspond credibly and reliably with the rating of traded positions.

(h) *Limitations on risk-based capital requirements*—(1) *Low-level exposure rule.* If the maximum contractual exposure to loss retained or assumed by a bank is less than the effective risk-based capital requirement, as determined in accordance with section 4(b) of this appendix A, for the asset supported by the bank's position, the risk based capital required under this appendix A is limited to the bank's contractual exposure, less any recourse liability account established in accordance with generally accepted accounting principles. This limitation does not apply when a bank provides credit enhancement beyond any contractual obligation to support assets that it has sold.

(2) *Related on-balance sheet assets.* If an asset is included in the calculation of the risk-based capital requirement under this section 4 of this appendix A and also appears as an asset on a bank's balance sheet, the asset is risk-weighted only under this section 4 of this appendix A, except in the case of loan servicing assets and similar arrangements with embedded recourse obligations or direct credit substitutes. In that case, both the on-balance sheet servicing assets and the related recourse obligations or direct credit substitutes must both be separately risk weighted and incorporated into the risk-based capital calculation.

(i) *Alternative Capital Calculation for Small Business Obligations*—(1) *Definitions.* For purposes of this section 4(i):

(i) *Qualified bank* means a bank that:

(A) Is well capitalized as defined in 12 CFR 6.4 without applying the capital treatment described in this section 4(i), or

(B) Is adequately capitalized as defined in 12 CFR 6.4 without applying the capital treatment described in this section 4(i) and has received written permission from the appropriate district office of the OCC to apply the capital treatment described in this section 4(i).

(ii) *Recourse* has the meaning given to such term under generally accepted accounting principles.

(iii) *Small business* means a business that meets the criteria for a small business concern established by the Small Business Administration in 13 CFR part 121 pursuant to 15 U.S.C. 632.

(2) *Capital and reserve requirements.* Notwithstanding the risk-based capital treatment outlined in section 2(c)(4) and any other subsection (other than subsection (i)) of this section 4, with respect to a transfer of a small business loan or a lease of personal property with recourse that is a sale under generally accepted accounting principles, a

qualified bank may elect to apply the following treatment:

(i) The bank establishes and maintains a non-capital reserve under generally accepted accounting principles sufficient to meet the reasonable estimated liability of the bank under the recourse arrangement; and

(ii) For purposes of calculating the bank's risk-based capital ratio, the bank includes only the face amount of its recourse in its risk-weighted assets.

(3) *Limit on aggregate amount of recourse.* The total outstanding amount of recourse retained by a qualified bank with respect to transfers of small business loans and leases of personal property and included in the risk-weighted assets of the bank as described in section 4(i)(2) of this appendix A may not exceed 15 percent of the bank's total capital after adjustments and deductions, unless the OCC specifies a greater amount by order.

(4) *Bank that ceases to be qualified or that exceeds aggregate limit.* If a bank ceases to be a qualified bank or exceeds the aggregate limit in section 4(i)(3) of this appendix A, the bank may continue to apply the capital treatment described in section 4(i)(2) of this appendix A to transfers of small business loans and leases of personal property that occurred when the bank was qualified and did not exceed the limit.

(5) *Prompt Corrective Action not affected.* (i) A bank shall compute its capital without regard to this section 4(i) for purposes of prompt corrective action (12 U.S.C. 1831o and 12 CFR part 6) unless the bank is an adequately or well capitalized bank (without applying the capital treatment described in this section 4(i)) and, after applying the capital treatment described in this section 4(i), the bank would be well capitalized.

(ii) A bank shall compute its capital without regard to this section 4(i) for purposes of 12 U.S.C. 1831o(g) regardless of the bank's capital level.

Section 5. Optional transition provisions related to the implementation of consolidation requirements under FAS 167.

(a) This section 5 provides optional transition provisions for a national bank that is required for financial and regulatory reporting purposes, as a result of its implementation of Statement of Financial Accounting Standards No. 167, *Amendments to FASB Interpretation No. 46(R)* (FAS 167), to consolidate certain variable interest entities (VIEs) as defined under United States generally accepted accounting principles (GAAP). These transition provisions apply through the end of the fourth quarter following the date of a bank's implementation of FAS 167 (implementation date).

(b) *Exclusion period.* (1) *Exclusion of risk-weighted assets for the first and second quarters.* For the first two quarters after the implementation date (exclusion period), including for the two calendar quarter-end regulatory report dates within those quarters, a bank may exclude from risk-weighted assets:

(i) Subject to the limitations in paragraph (d) of this section 5, assets held by a VIE, provided that the following conditions are met:

(A) The VIE existed prior to the implementation date;

(B) The bank did not consolidate the VIE on its balance sheet for calendar quarter-end regulatory report dates prior to the implementation date;

(C) The bank must consolidate the VIE on its balance sheet beginning as of the implementation date as a result of its implementation of FAS 167; and

(D) The bank excludes all assets held by VIEs described in paragraphs (b)(1)(i)(A) through (C) of this section 5; and

(ii) Subject to the limitations of paragraph (d) of this section 5, assets held by a VIE that is a consolidated asset-backed commercial paper (ABCP) program, provided that the following conditions are met:

(A) The bank is the sponsor of the ABCP program;

(B) Prior to the implementation date, the bank consolidated the VIE onto its balance sheet under GAAP and excluded the VIE's assets from the bank's risk-weighted assets; and

(C) The bank chooses to exclude all assets held by ABCP program VIEs described in paragraphs (b)(1)(ii)(A) and (B) of this section 5.

(2) *Risk-weighted assets during exclusion period.* During the exclusion period, including the two calendar quarter-end regulatory report dates within the exclusion period, a bank adopting the optional provisions of this paragraph (b) of this section 5 must calculate risk-weighted assets for its contractual exposures to the VIEs referenced in paragraph (b)(1) of this section 5 on the implementation date and include this calculated amount in its risk-weighted assets. Such contractual exposures may include direct-credit substitutes, recourse obligations, residual interests, liquidity facilities, and loans.

(3) *Inclusion of ALLL in Tier 2 capital for the first and second quarters.* During the exclusion period, including for the two calendar quarter-end regulatory report dates within the exclusion period, a bank that excludes VIE assets from risk-weighted assets pursuant to paragraph (b)(1) of this section may include in Tier 2 capital the full amount of the allowance for loan and lease losses (ALLL) calculated as of the implementation date that is attributable to the assets it excludes pursuant to paragraph (b)(1) of this section 5 (inclusion amount). The amount of ALLL includable in Tier 2 capital in accordance with this paragraph shall not be subject to the limitations set forth in section 2(b)(1) of this appendix A.

(c) *Phase-in period.* (1) *Exclusion amount.* For purposes of this paragraph (c), exclusion amount is defined as the amount of risk-weighted assets excluded in paragraph (b)(1) of this section as of the implementation date.

(2) *Risk-weighted assets during the third and fourth quarters.* A bank that excludes assets of consolidated VIEs from risk-weighted assets pursuant to paragraph (b)(1) of this section may, for the third and fourth quarters after the implementation date (phase-in period), including for the two calendar quarter-end regulatory report dates within those quarters, exclude from risk-weighted assets 50 percent of the exclusion amount, provided that the bank may not include in risk-weighted assets pursuant to this paragraph an amount less than the aggregate risk-weighted assets calculated pursuant to paragraph (b)(2) of this section.

(3) *Inclusion of ALLL in Tier 2 capital during the third and fourth quarters.* A bank that excludes assets of consolidated VIEs from risk-weighted assets pursuant to paragraph (c)(2) of this section may, for the phase-in period, include in Tier 2 capital 50 percent of the inclusion amount it included in Tier 2 capital during the exclusion period, notwithstanding the limit on including ALLL in Tier 2 capital in section 2(b)(1) of this appendix A.

(d) *Implicit recourse limitation.* Notwithstanding any other provision in this section 5, assets held by a VIE to which the bank has provided recourse through credit enhancement beyond any contractual obligation to support assets it has sold may not be excluded from risk-weighted assets.

[54 FR 4177, Jan. 27, 1989]

EDITORIAL NOTE: For FEDERAL REGISTER citations affecting appendix A, see the List of CFR Sections Affected, which appears in the Finding Aids section of the printed volume and at *www.govinfo.gov.*

APPENDIX B TO PART 3—RISK-BASED CAPITAL GUIDELINES; MARKET RISK

Section 1 Purpose, Applicability, and Reservation of Authority
Section 2 Definitions
Section 3 Requirements for Application of the Market Risk Capital Rule
Section 4 Adjustments to the Risk-Based Capital Ratio Calculations
Section 5 VaR-based Measure
Section 6 Stressed VaR-based Measure
Section 7 Specific Risk
Section 8 Incremental Risk
Section 9 Comprehensive Risk
Section 10 Standardized Measurement Method for Specific Risk
Section 11 Simplified Supervisory Formula Approach
Section 12 Market Risk Disclosures

Section 1. Purpose, Applicability, and Reservation of Authority

(a) *Purpose.* This appendix establishes risk-based capital requirements for banks with significant exposure to market risk and provides methods for these banks to calculate their risk-based capital requirements for market risk. This appendix supplements and adjusts the risk-based capital calculations under appendix A to this part and appendix C to this part and establishes public disclosure requirements.

(b) *Applicability.* (1) This appendix applies to any bank with aggregate trading assets and trading liabilities (as reported in the bank's most recent quarterly Consolidated Reports of Condition and Income (Call Report)), equal to:

(i) 10 percent or more of quarter-end total assets as reported on the most recent quarterly Call Report; or

(ii) $1 billion or more.

(2) The OCC may apply this appendix to any bank if the OCC deems it necessary or appropriate because of the level of market risk of the bank or to ensure safe and sound banking practices.

(3) The OCC may exclude a bank that meets the criteria of paragraph (b)(1) of this section from application of this appendix if the OCC determines that the exclusion is appropriate based on the level of market risk of the bank and is consistent with safe and sound banking practices.

(c) *Reservation of authority.* (1) The OCC may require a bank to hold an amount of capital greater than otherwise required under this appendix if the OCC determines that the bank's capital requirement for market risk as calculated under this appendix is not commensurate with the market risk of the bank's covered positions. In making determinations under paragraphs (c)(1) through (c)(3) of this section, the OCC will apply notice and response procedures generally in the same manner as the notice and response procedures set forth in [12 CFR 3.12, 12 CFR 263.202, 12 CFR 325.6(c), 12 CFR 567.3(d)].

(2) If the OCC determines that the risk-based capital requirement calculated under this appendix by the bank for one or more covered positions or portfolios of covered positions is not commensurate with the risks associated with those positions or portfolios, the OCC may require the bank to assign a different risk-based capital requirement to the positions or portfolios that more accurately reflects the risk of the positions or portfolios.

(3) The OCC may also require a bank to calculate risk-based capital requirements for specific positions or portfolios under this appendix, or under appendix C to this part or appendix A to this part, as appropriate, to more accurately reflect the risks of the positions.

(4) Nothing in this appendix limits the authority of the OCC under any other provision of law or regulation to take supervisory or enforcement action, including action to address unsafe or unsound practices or conditions, deficient capital levels, or violations of law.

Section 2. Definitions

For purposes of this appendix, the following definitions apply:

Affiliate with respect to a company means any company that controls, is controlled by, or is under common control with, the company.

Backtesting means the comparison of a bank's internal estimates with actual outcomes during a sample period not used in model development. For purposes of this appendix, backtesting is one form of out-of-sample testing.

Bank holding company is defined in section 2(a) of the Bank Holding Company Act of 1956 (12 U.S.C. 1841(a)).

Commodity position means a position for which price risk arises from changes in the price of a commodity.

Company means a corporation, partnership, limited liability company, depository institution, business trust, special purpose entity, association, or similar organization.

Control A person or company controls a company if it:

(1) Owns, controls, or holds with power to vote 25 percent or more of a class of voting securities of the company; or

(2) Consolidates the company for financial reporting purposes.

Corporate debt position means a debt position that is an exposure to a company that is not a sovereign entity, the Bank for International Settlements, the European Central Bank, the European Commission, the International Monetary Fund, a multilateral development bank, a depository institution, a foreign bank, a credit union, a public sector entity, a government-sponsored entity, or a securitization.

Correlation trading position means:

(1) A securitization position for which all or substantially all of the value of the underlying exposures is based on the credit quality of a single company for which a two-way market exists, or on commonly traded indices based on such exposures for which a two-way market exists on the indices; or

(2) A position that is not a securitization position and that hedges a position described in paragraph (1) of this definition; and

(3) A correlation trading position does not include:

(i) A resecuritization position;

(ii) A derivative of a securitization position that does not provide a pro rata share in the proceeds of a securitization tranche; or

(iii) A securitization position for which the underlying assets or reference exposures are retail exposures, residential mortgage exposures, or commercial mortgage exposures.

Country risk classification (CRC) for a sovereign entity means the consensus CRC published from time to time by the Organization for Economic Cooperation and Development that provides a view of the likelihood that the sovereign entity will service its external debt.

Covered position means the following positions:

(1) A trading asset or trading liability (whether on- or off-balance sheet),[43] as reported on Schedule RC–D of the Call Report or Schedule HC–D of the FR Y–9C, that meets the following conditions:

(i) The position is a trading position or hedges another covered position;[44] and

(ii) The position is free of any restrictive covenants on its tradability or the bank is able to hedge the material risk elements of the position in a two-way market;

(2) A foreign exchange or commodity position, regardless of whether the position is a trading asset or trading liability (excluding any structural foreign currency positions that the bank chooses to exclude with prior supervisory approval); and

(3) Notwithstanding paragraphs (1) and (2) of this definition, a covered position does not include:

(i) An intangible asset, including any servicing asset;

(ii) Any hedge of a trading position that the OCC determines to be outside the scope of the bank's hedging strategy required in paragraph (a)(2) of section 3 of this appendix;

(iii) Any position that, in form or substance, acts as a liquidity facility that provides support to asset-backed commercial paper;

(iv) A credit derivative the bank recognizes as a guarantee for risk-weighted asset amount calculation purposes under appendix C to this part or appendix A to this part;

(v) Any equity position that is not publicly traded, other than a derivative that references a publicly traded equity;

(vi) Any position a bank holds with the intent to securitize; or

(vii) Any direct real estate holding.

Credit derivative means a financial contract executed under standard industry documentation that allows one party (the protection purchaser) to transfer the credit risk of one or more exposures (reference exposure(s)) to another party (the protection provider).

---

[43] Securities subject to repurchase and lending agreements are included as if they are still owned by the lender.

[44] A position that hedges a trading position must be within the scope of the bank's hedging strategy as described in paragraph (a)(2) of section 3 of this appendix.

Credit union means an insured credit union as defined under the Federal Credit Union Act (12 U.S.C. 1752).

Default by a sovereign entity means noncompliance by the sovereign entity with its external debt service obligations or the inability or unwillingness of a sovereign entity to service an existing obligation according to its original contractual terms, as evidenced by failure to pay principal and interest timely and fully, arrearages, or restructuring.

Debt position means a covered position that is not a securitization position or a correlation trading position and that has a value that reacts primarily to changes in interest rates or credit spreads.

Depository institution is defined in section 3 of the Federal Deposit Insurance Act (12 U.S.C. 1813).

Equity position means a covered position that is not a securitization position or a correlation trading position and that has a value that reacts primarily to changes in equity prices.

Event risk means the risk of loss on equity or hybrid equity positions as a result of a financial event, such as the announcement or occurrence of a company merger, acquisition, spin-off, or dissolution.

Foreign bank means a foreign bank as defined in § 211.2 of the Federal Reserve Board's Regulation K (12 CFR 211.2), other than a depository institution.

Foreign exchange position means a position for which price risk arises from changes in foreign exchange rates.

General market risk means the risk of loss that could result from broad market movements, such as changes in the general level of interest rates, credit spreads, equity prices, foreign exchange rates, or commodity prices.

General obligation means a bond or similar obligation that is guaranteed by the full faith and credit of states or other political subdivisions of a sovereign entity.

Government-sponsored entity (GSE) means an entity established or chartered by the U.S. government to serve public purposes specified by the U.S. Congress but whose debt obligations are not explicitly guaranteed by the full faith and credit of the U.S. government.

Hedge means a position or positions that offset all, or substantially all, of one or more material risk factors of another position.

Idiosyncratic risk means the risk of loss in the value of a position that arises from changes in risk factors unique to that position.

Incremental risk means the default risk and credit migration risk of a position. Default risk means the risk of loss on a position that could result from the failure of an obligor to make timely payments of principal or interest on its debt obligation, and the risk of loss that could result from bankruptcy, insolvency, or similar proceeding. Credit migration risk means the price risk that arises from significant changes in the underlying credit quality of the position.

Investment grade means that the entity to which the bank is exposed through a loan or security, or the reference entity with respect to a credit derivative, has adequate capacity to meet financial commitments for the projected life of the asset or exposure. Such an entity or reference entity has adequate capacity to meet financial commitments if the risk of its default is low and the full and timely repayment of principal and interest is expected.

Market risk means the risk of loss on a position that could result from movements in market prices.

Multilateral development bank means the International Bank for Reconstruction and Development, the Multilateral Investment Guarantee Agency, the International Finance Corporation, the Inter-American Development Bank, the Asian Development Bank, the African Development Bank, the European Bank for Reconstruction and Development, the European Investment Bank, the European Investment Fund, the Nordic Investment Bank, the Caribbean Development Bank, the Islamic Development Bank, the Council of Europe Development Bank, and any other multilateral lending institution or regional development bank in which the U.S. government is a shareholder or contributing member or which the OCC determines poses comparable credit risk.

Nth-to-default credit derivative means a credit derivative that provides credit protection only for the nth-defaulting reference exposure in a group of reference exposures.

Over-the-counter (OTC) derivative means a derivative contract that is not traded on an exchange that requires the daily receipt and payment of cash-variation margin.

Public sector entity (PSE) means a state, local authority, or other governmental subdivision below the sovereign entity level.

Publicly traded means traded on:

(1) Any exchange registered with the SEC as a national securities exchange under section 6 of the Securities Exchange Act of 1934 (15 U.S.C. 78f); or

(2) Any non-U.S.-based securities exchange that:

(i) Is registered with, or approved by, a national securities regulatory authority; and

(ii) Provides a liquid, two-way market for the instrument in question.

Qualifying securities borrowing transaction means a cash-collateralized securities borrowing transaction that meets the following conditions:

(1) The transaction is based on liquid and readily marketable securities;

(2) The transaction is marked-to-market daily;

(3) The transaction is subject to daily margin maintenance requirements; and

(4)(i) The transaction is a securities contract for the purposes of section 555 of the Bankruptcy Code (11 U.S.C. 555), a qualified financial contract for the purposes of section 11(e)(8) of the Federal Deposit Insurance Act (12 U.S.C. 1821(e)(8)), or a netting contract between or among financial institutions for the purposes of sections 401–407 of the Federal Deposit Insurance Corporation Improvement Act of 1991 (12 U.S.C. 4401–4407) or the Board's Regulation EE (12 CFR part 231); or

(ii) If the transaction does not meet the criteria in paragraph (4)(i) of this definition, either:

(A) The bank has conducted sufficient legal review to reach a well-founded conclusion that:

(*1*) The securities borrowing agreement executed in connection with the transaction provides the bank the right to accelerate, terminate, and close-out on a net basis all transactions under the agreement and to liquidate or set off collateral promptly upon an event of counterparty default, including in a bankruptcy, insolvency, or other similar proceeding of the counterparty; and

(*2*) Under applicable law of the relevant jurisdiction, its rights under the agreement are legal, valid, binding, and enforceable and any exercise of rights under the agreement will not be stayed or avoided; or

(B) The transaction is either overnight or unconditionally cancelable at any time by the bank, and the bank has conducted sufficient legal review to reach a well-founded conclusion that:

(*1*) The securities borrowing agreement executed in connection with the transaction provides the bank the right to accelerate, terminate, and close-out on a net basis all transactions under the agreement and to liquidate or set off collateral promptly upon an event of counterparty default; and

(*2*) Under the law governing the agreement, its rights under the agreement are legal, valid, binding, and enforceable.

Resecuritization means a securitization in which one or more of the underlying exposures is a securitization position.

Resecuritization position means a covered position that is:

(1) An on- or off-balance sheet exposure to a resecuritization; or

(2) An exposure that directly or indirectly references a resecuritization exposure in paragraph (1) of this definition.

Revenue obligation means a bond or similar obligation, including loans and leases, that is an obligation of a state or other political subdivision of a sovereign entity, but for which the government entity is committed to repay with revenues from the specific project financed rather than with general tax funds.

SEC means the U.S. Securities and Exchange Commission.

Securitization means a transaction in which:

(1) All or a portion of the credit risk of one or more underlying exposures is transferred to one or more third parties;

(2) The credit risk associated with the underlying exposures has been separated into at least two tranches that reflect different levels of seniority;

(3) Performance of the securitization exposures depends upon the performance of the underlying exposures;

(4) All or substantially all of the underlying exposures are financial exposures (such as loans, commitments, credit derivatives, guarantees, receivables, asset-backed securities, mortgage-backed securities, other debt securities, or equity securities);

(5) For non-synthetic securitizations, the underlying exposures are not owned by an operating company;

(6) The underlying exposures are not owned by a small business investment company described in section 302 of the Small Business Investment Act of 1958 (15 U.S.C. 682); and

(7) The underlying exposures are not owned by a firm an investment in which qualifies as a community development investment under 12 U.S.C. 24 (Eleventh).

(8) The OCC may determine that a transaction in which the underlying exposures are owned by an investment firm that exercises substantially unfettered control over the size and composition of its assets, liabilities, and off-balance sheet exposures is not a securitization based on the transaction's leverage, risk profile, or economic substance.

(9) The OCC may deem an exposure to a transaction that meets the definition of a securitization, notwithstanding paragraph (5), (6), or (7) of this definition, to be a securitization based on the transaction's leverage, risk profile, or economic substance.

Securitization position means a covered position that is:

(1) An on-balance sheet or off-balance sheet credit exposure (including credit-enhancing representations and warranties) that arises from a securitization (including a resecuritization); or

(2) An exposure that directly or indirectly references a securitization exposure described in paragraph (1) of this definition.

Sovereign debt position means a direct exposure to a sovereign entity.

Sovereign entity means a central government (including the U.S. government) or an agency, department, ministry, or central bank of a central government.

Sovereign of incorporation means the country where an entity is incorporated, chartered, or similarly established.

Specific risk means the risk of loss on a position that could result from factors other than broad market movements and includes event risk, default risk, and idiosyncratic risk.

Structural position in a foreign currency means a position that is not a trading position and that is:

(1) Subordinated debt, equity, or minority interest in a consolidated subsidiary that is denominated in a foreign currency;

(2) Capital assigned to foreign branches that is denominated in a foreign currency;

(3) A position related to an unconsolidated subsidiary or another item that is denominated in a foreign currency and that is deducted from the bank's tier 1 and tier 2 capital; or

(4) A position designed to hedge a bank's capital ratios or earnings against the effect on paragraphs (1), (2), or (3) of this definition of adverse exchange rate movements.

Term repo-style transaction means a repurchase or reverse repurchase transaction, or a securities borrowing or securities lending transaction, including a transaction in which the bank acts as agent for a customer and indemnifies the customer against loss, that has an original maturity in excess of one business day, provided that:

(1) The transaction is based solely on liquid and readily marketable securities or cash;

(2) The transaction is marked-to-market daily and subject to daily margin maintenance requirements;

(3) The transaction is executed under an agreement that provides the bank the right to accelerate, terminate, and close-out the transaction on a net basis and to liquidate or set off collateral promptly upon an event of default (including bankruptcy, insolvency, or similar proceeding) of the counterparty, provided that, in any such case, any exercise of rights under the agreement will not be stayed or avoided under applicable law in the relevant jurisdictions;[45] and

(4) The bank has conducted and documented sufficient legal review to conclude with a well-founded basis that the agreement meets the requirements of paragraph (3) of this definition and is legal, valid, binding, and enforceable under applicable law in the relevant jurisdictions.

Tier 1 capital is defined in appendix A to this part or appendix C to this part, as applicable.

Tier 2 capital is defined in appendix A to this part or appendix C to this part, as applicable.

Trading position means a position that is held by the bank for the purpose of short-term resale or with the intent of benefiting from actual or expected short-term price movements, or to lock in arbitrage profits.

Two-way market means a market where there are independent bona fide offers to buy and sell so that a price reasonably related to the last sales price or current bona fide competitive bid and offer quotations can be determined within one day and settled at that price within a relatively short time frame conforming to trade custom.

Underlying exposure means one or more exposures that have been securitized in a securitization transaction.

Value-at-Risk (VaR) means the estimate of the maximum amount that the value of one or more positions could decline due to market price or rate movements during a fixed holding period within a stated confidence interval.

Section 3. Requirements for Application of the Market Risk Capital Rule

(a) *Trading positions.* (1) *Identification of trading positions.* A bank must have clearly defined policies and procedures for determining which of its trading assets and trading liabilities are trading positions and which of its trading positions are correlation trading positions. These policies and procedures must take into account:

(i) The extent to which a position, or a hedge of its material risks, can be marked-to-market daily by reference to a two-way market; and

(ii) Possible impairments to the liquidity of a position or its hedge.

(2) *Trading and hedging strategies.* A bank must have clearly defined trading and hedging strategies for its trading positions that are approved by senior management of the bank.

(i) The trading strategy must articulate the expected holding period of, and the market risk associated with, each portfolio of trading positions.

(ii) The hedging strategy must articulate for each portfolio of trading positions the level of market risk the bank is willing to accept and must detail the instruments, techniques, and strategies the bank will use to hedge the risk of the portfolio.

(b) *Management of covered positions.* (1) *Active management.* A bank must have clearly defined policies and procedures for actively managing all covered positions. At a minimum, these policies and procedures must require:

[45] This requirement is met where all transactions under the agreement are (i) executed under U.S. law and (ii) constitute "securities contracts" or "repurchase agreements" under section 555 or 559, respectively, of the Bankruptcy Code (11 U.S.C. 555 or 559), qualified financial contracts under section 11(e)(8) of the Federal Deposit Insurance Act (12 U.S.C. 1821(e)(8)), or netting contracts between or among financial institutions under sections 401–407 of the Federal Deposit Insurance Corporation Improvement Act of 1991 (12 U.S.C. 4407), or the Federal Reserve Board's Regulation EE (12 CFR part 231).

(i) Marking positions to market or to model on a daily basis;

(ii) Daily assessment of the bank's ability to hedge position and portfolio risks, and of the extent of market liquidity;

(iii) Establishment and daily monitoring of limits on positions by a risk control unit independent of the trading business unit;

(iv) Daily monitoring by senior management of information described in paragraphs (b)(1)(i) through (b)(1)(iii) of this section;

(v) At least annual reassessment of established limits on positions by senior management; and

(vi) At least annual assessments by qualified personnel of the quality of market inputs to the valuation process, the soundness of key assumptions, the reliability of parameter estimation in pricing models, and the stability and accuracy of model calibration under alternative market scenarios.

(2) *Valuation of covered positions.* The bank must have a process for prudent valuation of its covered positions that includes policies and procedures on the valuation of positions, marking positions to market or to model, independent price verification, and valuation adjustments or reserves. The valuation process must consider, as appropriate, unearned credit spreads, close-out costs, early termination costs, investing and funding costs, liquidity, and model risk.

(c) *Requirements for internal models.* (1) A bank must obtain the prior written approval of the OCC before using any internal model to calculate its risk-based capital requirement under this appendix.

(2) A bank must meet all of the requirements of this section on an ongoing basis. The bank must promptly notify the OCC when:

(i) The bank plans to extend the use of a model that the OCC has approved under this appendix to an additional business line or product type;

(ii) The bank makes any change to an internal model approved by the OCC under this appendix that would result in a material change in the bank's risk-weighted asset amount for a portfolio of covered positions; or

(iii) The bank makes any material change to its modeling assumptions.

(3) The OCC may rescind its approval of the use of any internal model (in whole or in part) or of the determination of the approach under section 9(a)(2)(ii) of this appendix for a bank's modeled correlation trading positions and determine an appropriate capital requirement for the covered positions to which the model would apply, if the OCC determines that the model no longer complies with this appendix or fails to reflect accurately the risks of the bank's covered positions.

(4) The bank must periodically, but no less frequently than annually, review its internal models in light of developments in financial markets and modeling technologies, and enhance those models as appropriate to ensure that they continue to meet the OCC's standards for model approval and employ risk measurement methodologies that are most appropriate for the bank's covered positions.

(5) The bank must incorporate its internal models into its risk management process and integrate the internal models used for calculating its VaR-based measure into its daily risk management process.

(6) The level of sophistication of a bank's internal models must be commensurate with the complexity and amount of its covered positions. A bank's internal models may use any of the generally accepted approaches, including but not limited to variance-covariance models, historical simulations, or Monte Carlo simulations, to measure market risk.

(7) The bank's internal models must properly measure all the material risks in the covered positions to which they are applied.

(8) The bank's internal models must conservatively assess the risks arising from less liquid positions and positions with limited price transparency under realistic market scenarios.

(9) The bank must have a rigorous and well-defined process for re-estimating, re-evaluating, and updating its internal models to ensure continued applicability and relevance.

(10) If a bank uses internal models to measure specific risk, the internal models must also satisfy the requirements in paragraph (b)(1) of section 7 of this appendix.

(d) *Control, oversight, and validation mechanisms.* (1) The bank must have a risk control unit that reports directly to senior management and is independent from the business trading units.

(2) The bank must validate its internal models initially and on an ongoing basis. The bank's validation process must be independent of the internal models' development, implementation, and operation, or the validation process must be subjected to an independent review of its adequacy and effectiveness. Validation must include:

(i) An evaluation of the conceptual soundness of (including developmental evidence supporting) the internal models;

(ii) An ongoing monitoring process that includes verification of processes and the comparison of the bank's model outputs with relevant internal and external data sources or estimation techniques; and

(iii) An outcomes analysis process that includes backtesting. For internal models used to calculate the VaR-based measure, this process must include a comparison of the changes in the bank's portfolio value that would have occurred were end-of-day positions to remain unchanged (therefore, excluding fees, commissions, reserves, net interest income, and intraday trading) with VaR-based measures during a sample period not used in model development.

(3) The bank must stress test the market risk of its covered positions at a frequency appropriate to each portfolio, and in no case less frequently than quarterly. The stress tests must take into account concentration risk (including but not limited to concentrations in single issuers, industries, sectors, or markets), illiquidity under stressed market conditions, and risks arising from the bank's trading activities that may not be adequately captured in its internal models.

(4) The bank must have an internal audit function independent of business-line management that at least annually assesses the effectiveness of the controls supporting the bank's market risk measurement systems, including the activities of the business trading units and independent risk control unit, compliance with policies and procedures, and calculation of the bank's measures for market risk under this appendix. At least annually, the internal audit function must report its findings to the bank's board of directors (or a committee thereof).

(e) *Internal assessment of capital adequacy.* The bank must have a rigorous process for assessing its overall capital adequacy in relation to its market risk. The assessment must take into account risks that may not be captured fully in the VaR-based measure, including concentration and liquidity risk under stressed market conditions.

(f) *Documentation.* The bank must adequately document all material aspects of its internal models, management and valuation of covered positions, control, oversight, validation and review processes and results, and internal assessment of capital adequacy.

Section 4. Adjustments to the Risk-Based Capital Ratio Calculations

(a) *Risk-based capital ratio denominators.* A bank must calculate its general risk-based capital ratio denominator by following the steps described in paragraphs (a)(1) through (a)(4) of this section. A bank subject to appendix C to this part must use its general risk-based capital ratio denominator for purposes of determining its total risk-based capital ratio and its tier 1 risk-based capital ratio under section 3(a)(2)(ii) and section 3(a)(3)(ii), respectively, of appendix C to this part, provided that the bank may not use the supervisory formula approach (SFA) in section 10(b)(2)(vii)(B) of this appendix for purposes of this calculation. A bank subject to appendix C to this part also must calculate an advanced risk-based capital ratio denominator by following the steps in paragraphs (a)(1) through (a)(4) of this section for purposes of determining its total risk-based capital ratio and its tier 1 risk-based capital ratio under sections 3(a)(2)(i) and section 3(a)(3)(i), respectively, of appendix C to this part.

(1) *Adjusted risk-weighted assets.* (i) The bank must calculate:

(A) General adjusted risk-weighted assets, which equals risk-weighted assets as determined in accordance with appendix A to this part with the adjustments in paragraphs (a)(1)(ii) and, if applicable, (a)(1)(iii) of this section; and

(B) For a bank subject to appendix C to this part, advanced adjusted risk-weighted assets, which equal risk-weighted assets as determined in accordance with appendix C to this part with the adjustments in paragraph (a)(1)(ii) of this section.

(ii) For purposes of calculating its general and advanced adjusted risk-weighted assets under paragraphs (a)(1)(i)(A) and (a)(1)(i)(B) of this section, respectively, the bank must exclude the risk-weighted asset amounts of all covered positions (except foreign exchange positions that are not trading positions and over-the-counter derivative positions).

(iii) For purposes of calculating its general adjusted risk-weighted assets under paragraph (a)(1)(i)(A) of this section, a bank may exclude receivables that arise from the posting of cash collateral and are associated with qualifying securities borrowing transactions to the extent the receivable is collateralized by the market value of the borrowed securities.

(2) *Measure for market risk.* The bank must calculate the general measure for market risk (except, as provided in paragraph (a) of this section, that the bank may not use the SFA in section 10(b)(2)(vii)(B) of this appendix for purposes of this calculation), which equals the sum of the VaR-based capital requirement, stressed VaR-based capital requirement, specific risk add-ons, incremental risk capital requirement, comprehensive risk capital requirement, and capital requirement for *de minimis* exposures all as defined under this paragraph (a)(2). A bank subject to appendix C to this part also must calculate the advanced measure for market risk, which equals the sum of the VaR-based capital requirement, stressed VaR-based capital requirement, specific risk add-ons, incremental risk capital requirement, comprehensive risk capital requirement, and capital requirement for *de minimis* exposures as defined under this paragraph (a)(2).

(i) *VaR-based capital requirement.* A bank's VaR-based capital requirement equals the greater of:

(A) The previous day's VaR-based measure as calculated under section 5 of this appendix; or

(B) The average of the daily VaR-based measures as calculated under section 5 of this appendix for each of the preceding 60 business days multiplied by three, except as provided in paragraph (b) of this section.

(ii) *Stressed VaR-based capital requirement.* A bank's stressed VaR-based capital requirement equals the greater of:

(A) The most recent stressed VaR-based measure as calculated under section 6 of this appendix; or

(B) The average of the stressed VaR-based measures as calculated under section 6 of this appendix for each of the preceding 12 weeks multiplied by three, except as provided in paragraph (b) of this section.

(iii) *Specific risk add-ons.* A bank's specific risk add-ons equal any specific risk add-ons that are required under section 7 of this appendix and are calculated in accordance with section 10 of this appendix.

(iv) *Incremental risk capital requirement.* A bank's incremental risk capital requirement equals any incremental risk capital requirement as calculated under section 8 of this appendix.

(v) *Comprehensive risk capital requirement.* A bank's comprehensive risk capital requirement equals any comprehensive risk capital requirement as calculated under section 9 of this appendix.

(vi) *Capital requirement for de minimis exposures.* A bank's capital requirement for *de minimis* exposures equals:

(A) The absolute value of the market value of those *de minimis* exposures that are not captured in the bank's VaR-based measure or under paragraph (a)(2)(vi)(B) of this section; and

(B) With the prior written approval of the OCC, the capital requirement for any *de minimis* exposures using alternative techniques that appropriately measure the market risk associated with those exposures.

(3) *Market risk equivalent assets.* The bank must calculate general market risk equivalent assets as the general measure for market risk (as calculated in paragraph (a)(2) of this section) multiplied by 12.5. A bank subject to appendix C to this part also must calculate advanced market risk equivalent assets as the advanced measure for market risk (as calculated in paragraph (a)(2) of this section) multiplied by 12.5.

(4) *Denominator calculation.* (i) The bank must add general market risk equivalent assets (as calculated in paragraph (a)(3) of this section) to general adjusted risk-weighted assets (as calculated in paragraph (a)(1)(i) of this section). The resulting sum is the bank's general risk-based capital ratio denominator.

(ii) A bank subject to appendix C to this part must add advanced market risk equivalent assets (as calculated in paragraph (a)(3) of this section) to advanced adjusted risk-weighted assets (as calculated in paragraph (a)(1)(i) of this section). The resulting sum is the bank's advanced risk-based capital ratio denominator.

(b) *Backtesting.* A bank must compare each of its most recent 250 business days' trading losses (excluding fees, commissions, reserves, net interest income, and intraday trading) with the corresponding daily VaR-based measures calibrated to a one-day holding period and at a one-tail, 99.0 percent confidence level. A bank must begin backtesting as required by this paragraph no later than one year after the later of January 1, 2013, and the date on which the bank becomes subject to this appendix. In the interim, consistent with safety and soundness principles, a bank subject to this appendix as of its effective date should continue to follow backtesting procedures in accordance with the OCC's supervisory expectations.

(1) Once each quarter, the bank must identify the number of exceptions (that is, the number of business days for which the actual daily net trading loss, if any, exceeds the corresponding daily VaR-based measure) that have occurred over the preceding 250 business days.

(2) A bank must use the multiplication factor in table 1 of this appendix that corresponds to the number of exceptions identified in paragraph (b)(1) of this section to determine its VaR-based capital requirement for market risk under paragraph (a)(2)(i) of this section and to determine its stressed VaR-based capital requirement for market risk under paragraph (a)(2)(ii) of this section until it obtains the next quarter's backtesting results, unless the OCC notifies the bank in writing that a different adjustment or other action is appropriate.

TABLE 1—MULTIPLICATION FACTORS BASED ON RESULTS OF BACKTESTING

Number of exceptions	Multiplication factor
4 or fewer	3.00
5	3.40
6	3.50
7	3.65
8	3.75
9	3.85
10 or more	4.00

Section 5. VaR-Based Measure

(a) *General requirement.* A bank must use one or more internal models to calculate daily a VaR-based measure of the general market risk of all covered positions. The daily VaR-based measure also may reflect the bank's specific risk for one or more portfolios of debt and equity positions, if the internal models meet the requirements of paragraph (b)(1) of section 7 of this appendix. The daily VaR-based measure must also reflect the bank's specific risk for any portfolio of correlation trading positions that is modeled under section 9 of this appendix. A bank may elect to include term repo-style transactions in its VaR-based measure, provided that the bank includes all such term repo-style transactions consistently over time.

(1) The bank's internal models for calculating its VaR-based measure must use risk factors sufficient to measure the market risk inherent in all covered positions. The market risk categories must include, as appropriate, interest rate risk, credit spread risk, equity price risk, foreign exchange risk, and commodity price risk. For material positions in the major currencies and markets, modeling techniques must incorporate enough segments of the yield curve—in no case less than six—to capture differences in volatility and less than perfect correlation of rates along the yield curve.

(2) The VaR-based measure may incorporate empirical correlations within and across risk categories, provided the bank validates and demonstrates the reasonableness of its process for measuring correlations. If the VaR-based measure does not incorporate empirical correlations across risk categories, the bank must add the separate measures from its internal models used to calculate the VaR-based measure for the appropriate market risk categories (interest rate risk, credit spread risk, equity price risk, foreign exchange rate risk, and/or commodity price risk) to determine its aggregate VaR-based measure.

(3) The VaR-based measure must include the risks arising from the nonlinear price characteristics of options positions or positions with embedded optionality and the sensitivity of the market value of the positions to changes in the volatility of the underlying rates, prices, or other material risk factors. A bank with a large or complex options portfolio must measure the volatility of options positions or positions with embedded optionality by different maturities and/or strike prices, where material.

(4) The bank must be able to justify to the satisfaction of the OCC the omission of any risk factors from the calculation of its VaR-based measure that the bank uses in its pricing models.

(5) The bank must demonstrate to the satisfaction of the OCC the appropriateness of any proxies used to capture the risks of the bank's actual positions for which such proxies are used.

(b) *Quantitative requirements for VaR-based measure.* (1) The VaR-based measure must be calculated on a daily basis using a one-tail, 99.0 percent confidence level, and a holding period equivalent to a 10-business-day movement in underlying risk factors, such as rates, spreads, and prices. To calculate VaR-based measures using a 10-business-day holding period, the bank may calculate 10-business-day measures directly or may convert VaR-based measures using holding periods other than 10 business days to the equivalent of a 10-business-day holding period. A bank that converts its VaR-based measure in such a manner must be able to justify the reasonableness of its approach to the satisfaction of the OCC.

(2) The VaR-based measure must be based on a historical observation period of at least one year. Data used to determine the VaR-based measure must be relevant to the bank's actual exposures and of sufficient quality to support the calculation of risk-based capital requirements. The bank must update data sets at least monthly or more frequently as changes in market conditions or portfolio composition warrant. For a bank that uses a weighting scheme or other method for the historical observation period, the bank must either:

(i) Use an effective observation period of at least one year in which the average time lag of the observations is at least six months; or

(ii) Demonstrate to the OCC that its weighting scheme is more effective than a weighting scheme with an average time lag of at least six months representing the volatility of the bank's trading portfolio over a full business cycle. A bank using this option must update its data more frequently than monthly and in a manner appropriate for the type of weighting scheme.

(c) A bank must divide its portfolio into a number of significant subportfolios approved by the OCC for subportfolio backtesting purposes. These subportfolios must be sufficient to allow the bank and the OCC to assess the adequacy of the VaR model at the risk factor level; the OCC will evaluate the appropriateness of these subportfolios relative to the value and composition of the bank's covered positions. The bank must retain and make available to the OCC the following information for each subportfolio for each business day over the previous two years (500 business days), with no more than a 60-day lag:

(1) A daily VaR-based measure for the subportfolio calibrated to a one-tail, 99.0 percent confidence level;

(2) The daily profit or loss for the subportfolio (that is, the net change in price of the positions held in the portfolio at the end of the previous business day); and

(3) The p-value of the profit or loss on each day (that is, the probability of observing a profit that is less than, or a loss that is greater than, the amount reported for purposes of paragraph (c)(2) of this section based on the model used to calculate the VaR-based measure described in paragraph (c)(1) of this section).

Section 6. Stressed VaR-Based Measure

(a) *General requirement.* At least weekly, a bank must use the same internal model(s) used to calculate its VaR-based measure to calculate a stressed VaR-based measure.

(b) *Quantitative requirements for stressed VaR-based measure.* (1) A bank must calculate a stressed VaR-based measure for its covered positions using the same model(s) used to calculate the VaR-based measure, subject to the same confidence level and holding period applicable to the VaR-based measure under section 5 of this appendix, but with model inputs calibrated to historical data from a continuous 12-month period that reflects a period of significant financial stress appropriate to the bank's current portfolio.

(2) The stressed VaR-based measure must be calculated at least weekly and be no less than the bank's VaR-based measure.

(3) A bank must have policies and procedures that describe how it determines the period of significant financial stress used to calculate the bank's stressed VaR-based measure under this section and must be able to provide empirical support for the period used. The bank must obtain the prior approval of the OCC for, and notify the OCC if the bank makes any material changes to, these policies and procedures. The policies and procedures must address:

(i) How the bank links the period of significant financial stress used to calculate the stressed VaR-based measure to the composition and directional bias of its current portfolio; and

(ii) The bank's process for selecting, reviewing, and updating the period of significant financial stress used to calculate the stressed VaR-based measure and for monitoring the appropriateness of the period to the bank's current portfolio.

(4) Nothing in this section prevents the OCC from requiring a bank to use a different period of significant financial stress in the calculation of the stressed VaR-based measure.

Section 7. Specific Risk

(a) *General requirement.* A bank must use one of the methods in this section to measure the specific risk for each of its debt, equity, and securitization positions with specific risk.

(b) *Modeled specific risk.* A bank may use models to measure the specific risk of covered positions as provided in paragraph (a) of section 5 of this appendix (therefore, excluding securitization positions that are not modeled under section 9 of this appendix). A bank must use models to measure the specific risk of correlation trading positions that are modeled under section 9 of this appendix.

(1) *Requirements for specific risk modeling.* (i) If a bank uses internal models to measure the specific risk of a portfolio, the internal models must:

(A) Explain the historical price variation in the portfolio;

(B) Be responsive to changes in market conditions;

(C) Be robust to an adverse environment, including signaling rising risk in an adverse environment; and

(D) Capture all material components of specific risk for the debt and equity positions in the portfolio. Specifically, the internal models must:

(*1*) Capture event risk and idiosyncratic risk;

(*2*) Capture and demonstrate sensitivity to material differences between positions that are similar but not identical and to changes in portfolio composition and concentrations.

(ii) If a bank calculates an incremental risk measure for a portfolio of debt or equity positions under section 8 of this appendix, the bank is not required to capture default and credit migration risks in its internal models used to measure the specific risk of those portfolios.

(2) *Specific risk fully modeled for one or more portfolios.* If the bank's VaR-based measure captures all material aspects of specific risk for one or more of its portfolios of debt, equity, or correlation trading positions, the bank has no specific risk add-on for those portfolios for purposes of paragraph (a)(2)(iii) of section 4 of this appendix.

(c) *Specific risk not modeled.* (1) If the bank's VaR-based measure does not capture all material aspects of specific risk for a portfolio of debt, equity, or correlation trading positions, the bank must calculate a specific-risk add-on for the portfolio under the standardized measurement method as described in section 10 of this appendix.

(2) A bank must calculate a specific risk add-on under the standardized measurement method as described in section 10 of this appendix for all of its securitization positions that are not modeled under section 9 of this appendix.

Section 8. Incremental Risk

(a) *General requirement.* A bank that measures the specific risk of a portfolio of debt positions under section 7(b) of this appendix using internal models must calculate at least weekly an incremental risk measure for that portfolio according to the requirements in this section. The incremental risk measure is the bank's measure of potential losses due to incremental risk over a one-year time horizon at a one-tail, 99.9 percent confidence level, either under the assumption of a constant level of risk, or under the assumption of constant positions. With the prior approval of the OCC, a bank may choose to include portfolios of equity positions in its incremental risk model, provided that it consistently includes such equity positions in a manner that is consistent with how the bank internally measures and manages the incremental risk of such positions at the portfolio level. If equity positions are included in the model, for modeling purposes default is considered to have occurred upon the default of any debt of the issuer of the equity position. A bank may not include correlation trading positions or securitization positions in its incremental risk measure.

(b) *Requirements for incremental risk modeling.* For purposes of calculating the incremental risk measure, the incremental risk model must:

(1) Measure incremental risk over a one-year time horizon and at a one-tail, 99.9 percent confidence level, either under the assumption of a constant level of risk, or under the assumption of constant positions.

(i) A constant level of risk assumption means that the bank rebalances, or rolls over, its trading positions at the beginning of each liquidity horizon over the one-year horizon in a manner that maintains the bank's initial risk level. The bank must determine the frequency of rebalancing in a manner consistent with the liquidity horizons of the positions in the portfolio. The liquidity horizon of a position or set of positions is the time required for a bank to reduce its exposure to, or hedge all of its material risks of, the position(s) in a stressed market. The liquidity horizon for a position or set of positions may not be less than the shorter of three months or the contractual maturity of the position.

(ii) A constant position assumption means that the bank maintains the same set of positions throughout the one-year horizon. If a bank uses this assumption, it must do so consistently across all portfolios.

(iii) A bank's selection of a constant position or a constant risk assumption must be consistent between the bank's incremental risk model and its comprehensive risk model described in section 9 of this appendix, if applicable.

(iv) A bank's treatment of liquidity horizons must be consistent between the bank's incremental risk model and its comprehensive risk model described in section 9 of this appendix, if applicable.

(2) Recognize the impact of correlations between default and migration events among obligors.

(3) Reflect the effect of issuer and market concentrations, as well as concentrations that can arise within and across product classes during stressed conditions.

(4) Reflect netting only of long and short positions that reference the same financial instrument.

(5) Reflect any material mismatch between a position and its hedge.

(6) Recognize the effect that liquidity horizons have on dynamic hedging strategies. In such cases, a bank must:

(i) Choose to model the rebalancing of the hedge consistently over the relevant set of trading positions;

(ii) Demonstrate that the inclusion of rebalancing results in a more appropriate risk measurement;

(iii) Demonstrate that the market for the hedge is sufficiently liquid to permit rebalancing during periods of stress; and

(iv) Capture in the incremental risk model any residual risks arising from such hedging strategies.

(7) Reflect the nonlinear impact of options and other positions with material nonlinear behavior with respect to default and migration changes.

(8) Maintain consistency with the bank's internal risk management methodologies for identifying, measuring, and managing risk.

(c) *Calculation of incremental risk capital requirement.* The incremental risk capital requirement is the greater of:

(1) The average of the incremental risk measures over the previous 12 weeks; or

(2) The most recent incremental risk measure.

Section 9. Comprehensive Risk

(a) *General requirement.* (1) Subject to the prior approval of the OCC, a bank may use the method in this section to measure comprehensive risk, that is, all price risk, for one or more portfolios of correlation trading positions.

(2) A bank that measures the price risk of a portfolio of correlation trading positions using internal models must calculate at least weekly a comprehensive risk measure that captures all price risk according to the requirements of this section. The comprehensive risk measure is either:

(i) The sum of:

(A) The bank's modeled measure of all price risk determined according to the requirements in paragraph (b) of this section; and

(B) A surcharge for the bank's modeled correlation trading positions equal to the total specific risk add-on for such positions as calculated under section 10 of this appendix multiplied by 8.0 percent; or

(ii) With approval of the OCC and provided the bank has met the requirements of this section for a period of at least one year and can demonstrate the effectiveness of the model through the results of ongoing model validation efforts including robust benchmarking, the greater of:

(A) The bank's modeled measure of all price risk determined according to the requirements in paragraph (b) of this section; or

(B) The total specific risk add-on that would apply to the bank's modeled correlation trading positions as calculated under section 10 of this appendix multiplied by 8.0 percent.

(b) *Requirements for modeling all price risk.* If a bank uses an internal model to measure the price risk of a portfolio of correlation trading positions:

(1) The internal model must measure comprehensive risk over a one-year time horizon

at a one-tail, 99.9 percent confidence level, either under the assumption of a constant level of risk, or under the assumption of constant positions.

(2) The model must capture all material price risk, including but not limited to the following:

(i) The risks associated with the contractual structure of cash flows of the position, its issuer, and its underlying exposures;

(ii) Credit spread risk, including nonlinear price risks;

(iii) The volatility of implied correlations, including nonlinear price risks such as the cross-effect between spreads and correlations;

(iv) Basis risk;

(v) Recovery rate volatility as it relates to the propensity for recovery rates to affect tranche prices; and

(vi) To the extent the comprehensive risk measure incorporates the benefits of dynamic hedging, the static nature of the hedge over the liquidity horizon must be recognized. In such cases, a bank must:

(A) Choose to model the rebalancing of the hedge consistently over the relevant set of trading positions;

(B) Demonstrate that the inclusion of rebalancing results in a more appropriate risk measurement;

(C) Demonstrate that the market for the hedge is sufficiently liquid to permit rebalancing during periods of stress; and

(D) Capture in the comprehensive risk model any residual risks arising from such hedging strategies;

(3) The bank must use market data that are relevant in representing the risk profile of the bank's correlation trading positions in order to ensure that the bank fully captures the material risks of the correlation trading positions in its comprehensive risk measure in accordance with this section; and

(4) The bank must be able to demonstrate that its model is an appropriate representation of comprehensive risk in light of the historical price variation of its correlation trading positions.

(c) *Requirements for stress testing*. (1) A bank must at least weekly apply specific, supervisory stress scenarios to its portfolio of correlation trading positions that capture changes in:

(i) Default rates;

(ii) Recovery rates;

(iii) Credit spreads;

(iv) Correlations of underlying exposures; and

(v) Correlations of a correlation trading position and its hedge.

(2) Other requirements. (i) A bank must retain and make available to the OCC the results of the supervisory stress testing, including comparisons with the capital requirements generated by the bank's comprehensive risk model.

(ii) A bank must report to the OCC promptly any instances where the stress tests indicate any material deficiencies in the comprehensive risk model.

(d) *Calculation of comprehensive risk capital requirement*. The comprehensive risk capital requirement is the greater of:

(1) The average of the comprehensive risk measures over the previous 12 weeks; or

(2) The most recent comprehensive risk measure.

Section 10. Standardized Measurement Method for Specific Risk

(a) *General requirement*. A bank must calculate a total specific risk add-on for each portfolio of debt and equity positions for which the bank's VaR-based measure does not capture all material aspects of specific risk and for all securitization positions that are not modeled under section 9 of this appendix. A bank must calculate each specific risk add-on in accordance with the requirements of this section. Notwithstanding any other definition or requirement in this appendix, a position that would have qualified as a debt position or an equity position but for the fact that it qualifies as a correlation trading position under paragraph (2) of the definition of correlation trading position, shall be considered a debt position or an equity position, respectively, for purposes of this section 10.

(1) The specific risk add-on for an individual debt or securitization position that represents sold credit protection is capped at the notional amount of the credit derivative contract. The specific risk add-on for an individual debt or securitization position that represents purchased credit protection is capped at the current market value of the transaction plus the absolute value of the present value of all remaining payments to the protection seller under the transaction. This sum is equal to the value of the protection leg of the transaction.

(2) For debt, equity, or securitization positions that are derivatives with linear payoffs, a bank must assign a specific risk-weighting factor to the market value of the effective notional amount of the underlying instrument or index portfolio, except for a securitization position for which the bank directly calculates a specific risk add-on using the SFA in paragraph (b)(2)(vii)(B) of this section. A swap must be included as an effective notional position in the underlying instrument or portfolio, with the receiving side treated as a long position and the paying side treated as a short position. For debt, equity, or securitization positions that are derivatives with nonlinear payoffs, a bank must risk weight the market value of the effective notional amount of the underlying instrument or portfolio multiplied by the derivative's delta.

(3) For debt, equity, or securitization positions, a bank may net long and short positions (including derivatives) in identical issues or identical indices. A bank may also net positions in depositary receipts against an opposite position in an identical equity in different markets, provided that the bank includes the costs of conversion.

(4) A set of transactions consisting of either a debt position and its credit derivative hedge or a securitization position and its credit derivative hedge has a specific risk add-on of zero if:

(i) The debt or securitization position is fully hedged by a total return swap (or similar instrument where there is a matching of swap payments and changes in market value of the debt or securitization position);

(ii) There is an exact match between the reference obligation of the swap and the debt or securitization position;

(iii) There is an exact match between the currency of the swap and the debt or securitization position; and

(iv) There is either an exact match between the maturity date of the swap and the maturity date of the debt or securitization position; or, in cases where a total return swap references a portfolio of positions with different maturity dates, the total return swap maturity date must match the maturity date of the underlying asset in that portfolio that has the latest maturity date.

(5) The specific risk add-on for a set of transactions consisting of either a debt position and its credit derivative hedge or a securitization position and its credit derivative hedge that does not meet the criteria of paragraph (a)(4) of this section is equal to 20.0 percent of the capital requirement for the side of the transaction with the higher specific risk add-on when:

(i) The credit risk of the position is fully hedged by a credit default swap or similar instrument;

(ii) There is an exact match between the reference obligation of the credit derivative hedge and the debt or securitization position;

(iii) There is an exact match between the currency of the credit derivative hedge and the debt or securitization position; and

(iv) There is either an exact match between the maturity date of the credit derivative hedge and the maturity date of the debt or securitization position; or, in the case where the credit derivative hedge has a standard maturity date:

(A) The maturity date of the credit derivative hedge is within 30 business days of the maturity date of the debt or securitization position; or

(B) For purchased credit protection, the maturity date of the credit derivative hedge is later than the maturity date of the debt or securitization position, but is no later than the standard maturity date for that instrument that immediately follows the maturity date of the debt or securitization position. The maturity date of the credit derivative hedge may not exceed the maturity date of the debt or securitization position by more than 90 calendar days.

(6) The specific risk add-on for a set of transactions consisting of either a debt position and its credit derivative hedge or a securitization position and its credit derivative hedge that does not meet the criteria of either paragraph (a)(4) or (a)(5) of this section, but in which all or substantially all of the price risk has been hedged, is equal to the specific risk add-on for the side of the transaction with the higher specific risk add-on.

(b) *Debt and securitization positions.* (1) The total specific risk add-on for a portfolio of debt or securitization positions is the sum of the specific risk add-ons for individual debt or securitization positions, as computed under this section. To determine the specific risk add-on for individual debt or securitization positions, a bank must multiply the absolute value of the current market value of each net long or net short debt or securitization position in the portfolio by the appropriate specific risk-weighting factor as set forth in paragraphs (b)(2)(i) through (b)(2)(vii) of this section.

(2) For the purpose of this section, the appropriate specific risk-weighting factors include:

(i) *Sovereign debt positions.* (A) *In general.* A bank must assign a specific risk-weighting factor to a sovereign debt position based on the CRC applicable to the sovereign entity and, as applicable, the remaining contractual maturity of the position, in accordance with table 2. Sovereign debt positions that are backed by the full faith and credit of the United States are treated as having a CRC of 0.

TABLE 2—SPECIFIC RISK-WEIGHTING FACTORS FOR SOVEREIGN DEBT POSITIONS

		Specific risk-weighting factor	Percent
	0–1		0.0
		Remaining contractual maturity of 6 months or less.	0.25

TABLE 2—SPECIFIC RISK-WEIGHTING FACTORS FOR SOVEREIGN DEBT POSITIONS—Continued

CRC of Sovereign	2–3	Remaining contractual maturity of greater than 6 and up to and including 24 months.	1.0
		Remaining contractual maturity exceeds 24 months.	1.6
	4–6		8.0
	7		12.0
No CRC			8.0
Default by the Sovereign Entity			12.0

(B) Notwithstanding paragraph (b)(2)(i)(A) of this section, a bank may assign to a sovereign debt position a specific risk-weighting factor that is lower than the applicable specific risk-weighting factor in table 2 if:

(*1*) The position is denominated in the sovereign entity's currency;

(*2*) The bank has at least an equivalent amount of liabilities in that currency; and

(*3*) The sovereign entity allows banks under its jurisdiction to assign the lower specific risk-weighting factor to the same exposures to the sovereign entity.

(C) A bank must assign a 12.0 percent specific risk-weighting factor to a sovereign debt position immediately upon determination that a default has occurred; or if a default has occurred within the previous five years.

(D) A bank must assign an 8.0 percent specific risk-weighting factor to a sovereign debt position if the sovereign entity does not have a CRC assigned to it, unless the sovereign debt position must be assigned a higher specific risk-weighting factor under paragraph (b)(2)(i)(C) of this section.

(ii) *Certain supranational entity and multilateral development bank debt positions.* A bank may assign a 0.0 percent specific risk-weighting factor to a debt position that is an exposure to the Bank for International Settlements, the European Central Bank, the European Commission, the International Monetary Fund, or an MDB.

(iii) *GSE debt positions.* A bank must assign a 1.6 percent specific risk-weighting factor to a debt position that is an exposure to a GSE. Notwithstanding the foregoing, a bank must assign an 8.0 percent specific risk-weighting factor to preferred stock issued by a GSE.

(iv) *Depository institution, foreign bank, and credit union debt positions.* (A) Except as provided in paragraph (b)(2)(iv)(B) of this section, a bank must assign a specific risk-weighting factor to a debt position that is an exposure to a depository institution, a foreign bank, or a credit union using the specific risk-weighting factor that corresponds to that entity's sovereign of incorporation and, as applicable, the remaining contractual maturity of the position, in accordance with table 3.

TABLE 3—SPECIFIC RISK-WEIGHTING FACTORS FOR DEPOSITORY INSTITUTION, FOREIGN BANK, AND CREDIT UNION DEBT POSITIONS

		Specific risk-weighting factor	Percent
CRC of Sovereign	0–2	Remaining contractual maturity of 6 months or less.	0.25
		Remaining contractual maturity of greater than 6 and up to and including 24 months.	1.0
		Remaining contractual maturity exceeds 24 months.	1.6
	3		8.0
	4–7		12.0
No CRC			8.0
Default by the Sovereign Entity			12.0

(B) A bank must assign a specific risk-weighting factor of 8.0 percent to a debt position that is an exposure to a depository institution or a foreign bank that is includable in the depository institution's or foreign bank's regulatory capital and that is not subject to deduction as a reciprocal holding under the appendix A to this part.

(C) A bank must assign a 12.0 percent specific risk-weighting factor to a debt position that is an exposure to a foreign bank immediately upon determination that a default by the foreign bank's sovereign of incorporation has occurred or if a default by the foreign bank's sovereign of incorporation has occurred within the previous five years.

(v) *PSE debt positions.* (A) Except as provided in paragraph (b)(2)(v)(B) of this section, a bank must assign a specific risk-weighting factor to a debt position that is an exposure to a PSE based on the specific risk-weighting factor that corresponds to the PSE's sovereign of incorporation and to the position's categorization as a general obligation or revenue obligation and, as applicable, the remaining contractual maturity of the position, as set forth in tables 4 and 5.

(B) A bank may assign a lower specific risk-weighting factor than would otherwise apply under tables 4 and 5 to a debt position that is an exposure to a foreign PSE if:

(*1*) The PSE's sovereign of incorporation allows banks under its jurisdiction to assign a lower specific risk-weighting factor to such position; and

(*2*) The specific risk-weighting factor is not lower than the risk weight that corresponds to the PSE's sovereign of incorporation in accordance with tables 4 and 5.

(C) A bank must assign a 12.0 percent specific risk-weighting factor to a PSE debt position immediately upon determination that a default by the PSE's sovereign of incorporation has occurred or if a default by the PSE's sovereign of incorporation has occurred within the previous five years.

TABLE 4—SPECIFIC RISK-WEIGHTING FACTORS FOR PSE GENERAL OBLIGATION DEBT POSITIONS

		General obligation specific risk-weighting factor (in percent)	Percent
CRC of Sovereign	0–2	Remaining contractual maturity of 6 months or less.	0.25
		Remaining contractual maturity of greater than 6 and up to and including 24 months.	1.0
		Remaining contractual maturity exceeds 24 months.	1.6
	3		8.0
	4–7		12.0
No CRC			8.0
Default by the Sovereign Entity			12.0

TABLE 5—SPECIFIC RISK-WEIGHTING FACTORS FOR PSE REVENUE OBLIGATION DEBT POSITIONS

		Revenue obligation specific risk-weighting factor	Percent
CRC of Sovereign	0–1	Remaining contractual maturity of 6 months or less.	0.25
		Remaining contractual maturity of greater than 6 and up to and including 24 months.	1.0
		Remaining contractual maturity exceeds 24 months.	1.6
	2–3		8.0
	4–7		12.0
No CRC			8.0
Default by the Sovereign Entity			12.0

(vi) *Corporate debt positions.* Except as otherwise provided in paragraph (b)(2)(vi)(B), a bank must assign a specific risk-weighting factor to a corporate debt position in accordance with the investment grade methodology in paragraph (b)(2)(vi)(A) of this section.

(A) *Investment grade methodology.* (*1*) For corporate debt positions that are exposures to entities that have issued and outstanding publicly traded instruments, a bank must assign a specific risk-weighting factor based on the category and remaining contractual maturity of the position, in accordance with table 6. For purposes of this paragraph (A), the bank must determine whether the position is in the investment grade or not investment grade category.

TABLE 6—SPECIFIC RISK-WEIGHTING FACTORS FOR CORPORATE DEBT POSITIONS UNDER THE INVESTMENT GRADE METHODOLOGY

Category	Remaining contractual maturity	Specific risk-weighting factor (in percent)
Investment Grade	6 months or less	0.50
	Greater than 6 and up to and including 24 months	2.00
	Greater than 24 months	4.00
Not-investment Grade		12.00

(*2*) A bank must assign an 8.0 percent specific risk-weighting factor for corporate debt positions that are exposures to entities that do not have publicly traded instruments outstanding.

(B) *Limitations.* (*1*) A bank must assign a specific risk-weighting factor of at least 8.0 percent to an interest-only mortgage-backed security that is not a securitization position.

(*2*) A bank shall not assign a corporate debt position a specific risk-weighting factor that is lower than the specific risk-weighting factor that corresponds to the CRC of the issuer's sovereign of incorporation in table 1.

(vii) *Securitization positions.* (A) *General requirements.* (*1*) A bank that does not use the appendix C to this part must assign a specific risk-weighting factor to a securitization position using either the simplified supervisory formula approach (SSFA) in accordance with section 11 of this appendix or assign a specific risk-weighting factor of 100 percent to the position.

(*2*) A bank that uses appendix C to this part must calculate a specific risk add-on for a securitization position using the SFA in section 45 of appendix C to this part and in accordance with paragraph (b)(2)(vii)(B) of this section if the bank and the securitization position each qualifies to use the SFA under appendix C to this part. A bank that uses appendix C to this part and that has a securitization position that does not qualify for the SFA may assign a specific risk-weighting factor to the securitization position using the SSFA in accordance with section 11 of this appendix or assign a specific risk-weighting factor of 100 percent to the position.

(*3*) A bank must treat a short securitization position as if it is a long securitization position solely for calculation purposes when using the SFA in paragraph (b)(2)(vii)(B) or the SSFA in section 11 of this appendix.

(B) *SFA.* To calculate the specific risk add-on for a securitization position using the SFA, a bank that is subject to appendix C to this part must set the specific risk add-on for the position equal to the risk-based capital requirement, calculated under section 45 of appendix C to this part.

(C) *SSFA.* To use the SSFA to determine the specific risk-weighting factor for a securitization position, a bank must calculate the specific risk-weighting factor in accordance with section 11 of this appendix.

(D) *Nth-to-default credit derivatives.* A bank must determine a specific risk add-on using the SFA in paragraph (b)(2)(vii)(B), or assign a specific risk-weighting factor using the SSFA in section 11 of this appendix to an nth-to-default credit derivative in accordance with this paragraph (D), irrespective of whether the bank is a net protection buyer or net protection seller. A bank must determine its position in the nth-to-default credit derivative as the largest notional dollar amount of all the underlying exposures.

(*1*) For purposes of determining the specific risk add-on using the SFA in paragraph (b)(2)(vii)(B) or the specific risk-weighting factor for an nth-to-default credit derivative using the SSFA in section 11 of this appendix, the bank must calculate the attachment point and detachment point of its position as follows:

(*i*) The attachment point (parameter A) is the ratio of the sum of the notional amounts of all underlying exposures that are subordinated to the bank's position to the total notional amount of all underlying exposures. For purposes of using the SFA to calculate the specific add-on for its position in an nth-to-default credit derivative, parameter A must be set equal to *the credit enhancement level* (L) input to the SFA formula. In the case of a first-to-default credit derivative, there are no underlying exposures that are subordinated to the bank's position. In the case of a second-or-subsequent-to-default credit derivative, the smallest (n-1) notional amounts of the underlying exposure(s) are subordinated to the bank's position.

(*ii*) The detachment point (parameter D) equals the sum of parameter A plus the ratio of the notional amount of the bank's position in the nth-to-default credit derivative to the total notional amount of all underlying exposures. For purposes of using the SFA to calculate the specific risk add-on for its position in an nth-to-default credit derivative, parameter D must be set to equal L plus the *thickness of tranche* (T) input to the SFA formula.

(*2*) A bank that does not use the SFA to determine a specific risk-add on, or the SSFA to determine a specific risk-weighting factor for its position in an nth-to-default credit derivative must assign a specific risk-weighting factor of 100 percent to the position.

(c) *Modeled correlation trading positions.* For purposes of calculating the comprehensive risk measure for modeled correlation trading positions under either paragraph (a)(2)(i) or (a)(2)(ii) of section 9 of this appendix, the total specific risk add-on is the greater of:

(1) The sum of the bank's specific risk add-ons for each net long correlation trading position calculated under this section; or

(2) The sum of the bank's specific risk add-ons for each net short correlation trading position calculated under this section.

(d) *Non-modeled securitization positions.* For securitization positions that are not correlation trading positions and for securitizations that are correlation trading positions not modeled under section 9 of this appendix, the total specific risk add-on is the greater of:

(1) The sum of the bank's specific risk add-ons for each net long securitization position calculated under this section; or

(2) The sum of the bank's specific risk add-ons for each net short securitization position calculated under this section.

(e) *Equity positions.* The total specific risk add-on for a portfolio of equity positions is the sum of the specific risk add-ons of the individual equity positions, as computed under this section. To determine the specific risk add-on of individual equity positions, a bank must multiply the absolute value of the current market value of each net long or net short equity position by the appropriate specific risk-weighting factor as determined under this paragraph:

(1) The bank must multiply the absolute value of the current market value of each net long or net short equity position by a specific risk-weighting factor of 8.0 percent. For equity positions that are index contracts comprising a well-diversified portfolio of equity instruments, the absolute value of the current market value of each net long or net short position is multiplied by a specific risk-weighting factor of 2.0 percent.[46]

(2) For equity positions arising from the following futures-related arbitrage strategies, a bank may apply a 2.0 percent specific risk-weighting factor to one side (long or short) of each position with the opposite side exempt from an additional capital requirement:

(i) Long and short positions in exactly the same index at different dates or in different market centers; or

(ii) Long and short positions in index contracts at the same date in different, but similar indices.

(3) For futures contracts on main indices that are matched by offsetting positions in a basket of stocks comprising the index, a bank may apply a 2.0 percent specific risk-weighting factor to the futures and stock basket positions (long and short), provided that such trades are deliberately entered into and separately controlled, and that the basket of stocks is comprised of stocks representing at least 90.0 percent of the capitalization of the index. A main index refers to the Standard & Poor's 500 Index, the FTSE All-World Index, and any other index for which the bank can demonstrate to the satisfaction of the OCC that the equities represented in the index have liquidity, depth of market, and size of bid-ask spreads comparable to equities in the Standard & Poor's 500 Index and FTSE All-World Index.

(f) *Due diligence requirements.* (1) A bank must demonstrate to the satisfaction of the OCC a comprehensive understanding of the features of a securitization position that would materially affect the performance of the position by conducting and documenting the analysis set forth in paragraph (f)(2) of this section. The bank's analysis must be commensurate with the complexity of the securitization position and the materiality of the position in relation to capital.

(2) To support the demonstration of its comprehensive understanding, for each securitization position a bank must:

(i) Conduct an analysis of the risk characteristics of a securitization position prior to acquiring the position and document such analysis within three business days after acquiring the position, considering:

(A) Structural features of the securitization that would materially impact the performance of the position, for example, the contractual cash flow waterfall, waterfall-related triggers, credit enhancements, liquidity enhancements, market value triggers, the performance of organizations that

---

[46] A portfolio is well-diversified if it contains a large number of individual equity positions, with no single position representing a substantial portion of the portfolio's total market value.

service the position, and deal-specific definitions of default;

(B) Relevant information regarding the performance of the underlying credit exposure(s), for example, the percentage of loans 30, 60, and 90 days past due; default rates; prepayment rates; loans in foreclosure; property types; occupancy; average credit score or other measures of creditworthiness; average loan-to-value ratio; and industry and geographic diversification data on the underlying exposure(s);

(C) Relevant market data of the securitization, for example, bid-ask spreads, most recent sales price and historical price volatility, trading volume, implied market rating, and size, depth and concentration level of the market for the securitization; and

(D) For resecuritization positions, performance information on the underlying securitization exposures, for example, the issuer name and credit quality, and the characteristics and performance of the exposures underlying the securitization exposures; and

(ii) On an on-going basis (no less frequently than quarterly), evaluate, review, and update as appropriate the analysis required under paragraph (f)(1) of this section for each securitization position.

Section 11. Simplified Supervisory Formula Approach

(a) *General requirements.* To use the SSFA to determine the specific risk-weighting factor for a securitization position, a bank must have data that enables it to assign accurately the parameters described in paragraph (b) of this section. Data used to assign the parameters described in paragraph (b) of this section must be the most currently available data and no more than 91 calendar days old. A bank that does not have the appropriate data to assign the parameters described and defined, for purposes of this section, in paragraph (b) of this section must assign a specific risk-weighting factor of 100 percent to the position.

(b) *SSFA parameters.* To calculate the specific risk-weighting factor for a securitization position using the SSFA, a bank must have accurate information on the five inputs to the SSFA calculation described in paragraphs (b)(1) through (b)(5) of this section:

(1) K_G is the weighted-average (with unpaid principal used as the weight for each exposure) total capital requirement of the underlying exposures calculated using appendix A to this part. K_G is expressed as a decimal value between zero and 1 (that is, an average risk weight of 100 percent represents a value of K_G equal to .08).

(2) Parameter W is expressed as a decimal value between zero and one. Parameter W is the ratio of the sum of the dollar amounts of any underlying exposures within the securitized pool that meet any of the criteria as set forth in paragraphs (i) through (vi) of this paragraph (b)(2) to the ending balance, measured in dollars, of underlying exposures:

(i) Ninety days or more past due;

(ii) Subject to a bankruptcy or insolvency proceeding;

(iii) In the process of foreclosure;

(iv) Held as real estate owned;

(v) Has contractually deferred interest payments for 90 days or more; or

(vi) Is in default.

(3) Parameter A is the attachment point for the position, which represents the threshold at which credit losses will first be allocated to the position. Parameter A equals the ratio of the current dollar amount of underlying exposures that are subordinated to the position of the bank to the current dollar amount of underlying exposures. Any reserve account funded by the accumulated cash flows from the underlying exposures that is subordinated to the position that contains the bank's securitization exposure may be included in the calculation of parameter A to the extent that cash is present in the account. Parameter A is expressed as a decimal value between zero and one.

(4) Parameter D is the detachment point for the position, which represents the threshold at which credit losses of principal allocated to the position would result in a total loss of principal. Parameter D equals parameter A plus the ratio of the current dollar amount of the securitization positions that are *pari passu* with the position (that is, have equal seniority with respect to credit risk) to the current dollar amount of the underlying exposures. Parameter D is expressed as a decimal value between zero and one.

(5) A supervisory calibration parameter, p, is equal to 0.5 for securitization positions that are not resecuritization positions and equal to 1.5 for resecuritization positions.

(c) *Mechanics of the SSFA.* K_G and W are used to calculate K_A, the augmented value of K_G, which reflects the observed credit quality of the underlying pool of exposures. K_A is defined in paragraph (d) of this section. The values of parameters A and D, relative to K_A determine the specific risk-weighting factor assigned to a position as described in this paragraph and paragraph (d) of this section. The specific risk-weighting factor assigned to a securitization position, or portion of a position, as appropriate, is the larger of the specific risk-weighting factor determined in accordance with this paragraph and paragraph (d) of this section and a specific risk-weighting factor of 1.6 percent.

(1) When the detachment point, parameter D, for a securitization position is less than or equal to K_A, the position must be assigned a specific risk-weighting factor of 100 percent.

(2) When the attachment point, parameter A, for a securitization position is greater

than or equal to K_A, the bank must calculate the specific risk-weighting factor in accordance with paragraph (d) of this section.

(3) When A is less than K_A and D is greater than K_A, the specific risk-weighting factor is a weighted-average of 1.00 and K_{SSFA} calculated in accordance with paragraph (d) of this section, but with the parameter A revised to be set equal to K_A. For the purpose of this weighted-average calculation:

(i) The weight assigned to 1.00 equals $\frac{K_A - A}{D - A}$.

(ii) The weight assigned to K_{SSFA} equals $\frac{D - K_A}{D - A}$. The specific risk-weighting factor will be set equal to:

$$SRWF = 100 \times \left[\left(\frac{K_A - A}{D - A}\right) \times 1.00\right] + \left[\left(\frac{D - K_A}{D - A}\right) \times K_{SSFA}\right]$$

(d) SSFA equation. (1) The [bank] must define the following parameters:

$$K_A = (1 - W) \cdot K_G + (0.5 \cdot W)$$

$$a = -\frac{1}{p \cdot K_A}$$

$$u = D - K_A$$

$$l = A - K_A$$

$e = 2.71828$, the base of the natural logarithms.

(2) Then the [bank] must calculate K_{SSFA} according to the following equation:

$$K_{SSFA} = \frac{e^{a \cdot u} - e^{a \cdot l}}{a(u - l)}$$

(3) The specific risk-weighting factor for the position (expressed as a percent) is equal to $K_{SSFA} \times 100$.

Section 12. Market Risk Disclosures

(a) *Scope.* A bank must comply with this section unless it is a consolidated subsidiary of a bank holding company or a depository institution that is subject to these requirements or of a non-U.S. banking organization that is subject to comparable public disclosure requirements in its home jurisdiction. A bank must make quantitative disclosures publicly each calendar quarter. If a significant change occurs, such that the most recent reporting amounts are no longer reflective of the bank's capital adequacy and risk profile, then a brief discussion of this change and its likely impact must be provided as soon as practicable thereafter. Qualitative disclosures that typically do not change each quarter may be disclosed annually, provided any significant changes are disclosed in the interim. If a bank believes that disclosure of specific commercial or financial information would prejudice seriously its position by making public certain information that is either proprietary or confidential in nature, the bank is not required to disclose these specific items, but must disclose more general information about the subject matter of the requirement, together with the fact that, and the reason why, the specific items of information have not been disclosed.

(b) *Disclosure policy.* The bank must have a formal disclosure policy approved by the board of directors that addresses the bank's approach for determining its market risk disclosures. The policy must address the associated internal controls and disclosure controls and procedures. The board of directors and senior management must ensure that appropriate verification of the disclosures takes place and that effective internal controls and disclosure controls and procedures are maintained. One or more senior officers of the bank must attest that the disclosures meet the requirements of this appendix, and the board of directors and senior management are responsible for establishing and maintaining an effective internal control structure over financial reporting, including the disclosures required by this section.

(c) *Quantitative disclosures.*

(1) For each material portfolio of covered positions, the bank must disclose publicly the following information at least quarterly:

(i) The high, low, and mean VaR-based measures over the reporting period and the VaR-based measure at period-end;

(ii) The high, low, and mean stressed VaR-based measures over the reporting period and the stressed VaR-based measure at period-end;

(iii) The high, low, and mean incremental risk capital requirements over the reporting period and the incremental risk capital requirement at period-end;

(iv) The high, low, and mean comprehensive risk capital requirements over the reporting period and the comprehensive risk capital requirement at period-end, with the period-end requirement broken down into appropriate risk classifications (for example, default risk, migration risk, correlation risk);

(v) Separate measures for interest rate risk, credit spread risk, equity price risk, foreign exchange risk, and commodity price risk used to calculate the VaR-based measure; and

(vi) A comparison of VaR-based estimates with actual gains or losses experienced by the bank, with an analysis of important outliers.

(2) In addition, the bank must disclose publicly the following information at least quarterly:

(i) The aggregate amount of on-balance sheet and off-balance sheet securitization positions by exposure type; and

(ii) The aggregate amount of correlation trading positions.

(d) *Qualitative disclosures.* For each material portfolio of covered positions, the bank must disclose publicly the following information at least annually, or more frequently in the event of material changes for each portfolio:

(1) The composition of material portfolios of covered positions;

(2) The bank's valuation policies, procedures, and methodologies for covered positions including, for securitization positions, the methods and key assumptions used for valuing such positions, any significant changes since the last reporting period, and the impact of such change;

(3) The characteristics of the internal models used for purposes of this appendix. For the incremental risk capital requirement and the comprehensive risk capital requirement, this must include:

(i) The approach used by the bank to determine liquidity horizons;

(ii) The methodologies used to achieve a capital assessment that is consistent with the required soundness standard; and

(iii) The specific approaches used in the validation of these models;

(4) A description of the approaches used for validating and evaluating the accuracy of internal models and modeling processes for purposes of this appendix;

(5) For each market risk category (that is, interest rate risk, credit spread risk, equity price risk, foreign exchange risk, and commodity price risk), a description of the stress tests applied to the positions subject to the factor;

(6) The results of the comparison of the bank's internal estimates for purposes of this appendix with actual outcomes during a sample period not used in model development;

(7) The soundness standard on which the bank's internal capital adequacy assessment under this appendix is based, including a description of the methodologies used to achieve a capital adequacy assessment that is consistent with the soundness standard;

(8) A description of the bank's processes for monitoring changes in the credit and market risk of securitization positions, including how those processes differ for resecuritization positions; and

(8) A description of the bank's policy governing the use of credit risk mitigation to mitigate the risks of securitization and resecuritization positions.

[77 FR 53112, Aug. 30, 2012]

PART 4—ORGANIZATION AND FUNCTIONS, AVAILABILITY AND RELEASE OF INFORMATION, CONTRACTING OUTREACH PROGRAM, POST-EMPLOYMENT RESTRICTIONS FOR SENIOR EXAMINERS

Subpart A—Organization and Functions

Sec.
4.1 Purpose.
4.2 Office of the Comptroller of the Currency.
4.3 Comptroller of the Currency.
4.4 Washington office and web site.
4.5 Other OCC supervisory offices.
4.6 Frequency of examination of national banks and Federal savings associations.
4.7 Frequency of examination of Federal agencies and branches.

Subpart B—Availability of Information Under the Freedom of Information Act

4.11 Purpose and scope.
4.12 Information available under the FOIA.
4.13 Publication in the Federal Register.
4.14 Public inspection in an electronic format.
4.15 How to request records.
4.16 Predisclosure notice for confidential commercial information.
4.17 FOIA request fees.
4.18 How to track a FOIA request.

Subpart C—Release of Non-Public OCC Information

4.31 Purpose and scope.
4.32 Definitions.
4.33 Requirements for a request of records or testimony.
4.34 Where to submit a request.
4.35 Consideration of requests.
4.36 Disclosure of non-public OCC information.
4.37 Persons and entities with access to OCC information; prohibition on dissemination.
4.38 Restrictions on dissemination of released information.
4.39 Notification of parties and procedures for sharing and using OCC records in litigation.
4.40 Fees for services.

APPENDIX A TO SUBPART C OF PART 4—MODEL STIPULATION FOR PROTECTIVE ORDER AND MODEL PROTECTIVE ORDER

Subpart D—Minority-, Women-, and Individuals With Disabilities-Owned Business Contracting Outreach Program; Contracting for Goods and Services

4.61 Purpose.
4.62 Definitions.
4.63 Policy.
4.64 Promotion.
4.65 Certification.
4.66 Oversight and monitoring.

Subpart E—One-Year Restrictions on Post-Employment Activities of Senior Examiners

4.72 Scope and purpose.
4.73 Definitions.
4.74 One-year post-employment restrictions.
4.75 Waivers.
4.76 Penalties.

AUTHORITY: 5 U.S.C. 301, 552; 12 U.S.C. 1, 93a, 161, 481, 482, 484(a), 1442, 1462a, 1463, 1464 1817(a), 1818, 1820, 1821, 1831m, 1831p–1, 1831o, 1833e, 1867, 1951 *et seq.*, 2601 *et seq.*, 2801 *et seq.*, 2901 *et seq.*, 3101 *et seq.*, 3401 *et seq.*, 5321, 5412, 5414; 15 U.S.C. 77uu(b), 78q(c)(3); 18 U.S.C. 641, 1905, 1906; 29 U.S.C. 1204; 31 U.S.C. 5318(g)(2), 9701; 42 U.S.C. 3601; 44 U.S.C. 3506, 3510; E.O. 12600 (3 CFR, 1987 Comp., p. 235).

SOURCE: 60 FR 57322, Nov. 15, 1995, unless otherwise noted.

Subpart A—Organization and Functions

§4.1 Purpose.

This subpart describes the organization and functions of the Office of the Comptroller of the Currency (OCC), and provides the OCC's principal addresses.

§4.2 Office of the Comptroller of the Currency.

The OCC is charged with assuring the safety and soundness of, and compliance with laws and regulations, fair access to financial services, and fair treatment of customers by, the institutions and other persons subject to its jurisdiction. The OCC examines, supervises, and regulates national banks, Federal branches and agencies of foreign banks, and Federal savings associations to carry out this mission. The OCC also issues rules and regulations applicable to state savings associations.

[76 FR 43561, July 21, 2011]

§ 4.3 Comptroller of the Currency.

The Comptroller of the Currency (Comptroller), as head of the OCC, is responsible for all OCC programs and functions. The Comptroller is appointed by the President, by and with the advice and consent of the Senate, for a term of five years. The Comptroller serves as a member of the board of the Federal Deposit Insurance Corporation, a member of the Financial Stability Oversight Council, a member of the Federal Financial Institutions Examination Council, and a member of the board of the Neighborhood Reinvestment Corporation. The Comptroller is advised and assisted by OCC staff, who perform the duties and functions that the Comptroller directs.

[60 FR 57322, Nov. 15, 1995, as amended at 76 FR 43561, July 21, 2011]

§ 4.4 Washington office and web site.

The Washington office of the OCC is the main office and headquarters of the OCC. The Washington office directs OCC policy, oversees OCC operations, and is responsible for the direct supervision of certain national banks and Federal savings associations, including the largest national banks and the largest Federal savings associations (through the Large Bank Supervision Department); other national banks and Federal savings associations requiring special supervision; and Federal branches and agencies of foreign banks (through the Large Bank Supervision Department). The Washington office is located at 400 7th Street SW., Washington, DC 20219. The OCC's Web site is at *http://www.occ.gov*.

[76 FR 43561, July 21, 2011, as amended at 79 FR 15641, Mar. 21, 2014]

§ 4.5 Other OCC supervisory offices.

(a) *Midsize Bank Supervision (MBS).* Midsize Bank Supervision is responsible for supervising midsize national banks and Federal savings associations that present unique supervisory challenges based on size, complexity, and/or product line. MBS also supervises credit card and certain other special purpose banks. MBS is headquartered in Chicago, IL and located at 1 South Wacker Drive, Suite 2000, Chicago, IL 60606.

(b) *District offices.* Each district office of the OCC is responsible for the direct supervision of the national banks and Federal savings associations in its district, with the exception of the national banks and Federal savings associations supervised by the Washington office pursuant to § 4.4 of this part or Midsize Bank Supervision pursuant to § 4.5(a). The four district offices cover the United States, Puerto Rico, the Virgin Islands, Guam, American Samoa, and the Northern Mariana Islands. The geographical composition of each district follows:

District	Office location	Geographical composition
Northeastern District	Office of the Comptroller of the Currency, 340 Madison Avenue, 5th Floor, New York, NY 10173–0002.	Connecticut, Delaware, District of Columbia, northeast Kentucky, Maine, Maryland, Massachusetts, New Hampshire, New Jersey, New York, North Carolina, Pennsylvania, Puerto Rico, Rhode Island, South Carolina, Vermont, the Virgin Islands, Virginia, and West Virginia.
Central District	Office of the Comptroller of the Currency, One Financial Place, Suite 2700, 440 South LaSalle Street, Chicago, IL 60605.	Illinois, Indiana, central and southern Kentucky, Michigan, northern and eastern Minnesota, eastern Missouri, North Dakota, Ohio, and Wisconsin.
Southern District	Office of the Comptroller of the Currency, 500 North Akard Street, Suite 1600, Dallas, TX 75201.	Alabama, Arkansas, Florida, Georgia, Louisiana, Mississippi, Oklahoma, Tennessee, and Texas.
Western District	Office of the Comptroller of the Currency, 1225 17th Street, Suite 300, Denver, CO 80202.	Alaska, American Samoa, Arizona, California, Colorado, Guam, Hawaii, Idaho, Iowa, Kansas, southwestern Minnesota, western Missouri, Montana, Nebraska, Nevada, New Mexico, Northern Mariana Islands, Oregon, South Dakota, Utah, Washington, and Wyoming.

(c) *Field offices and other supervisory offices.* Field offices and other supervisory offices support the bank and savings association supervision responsibilities of the district offices.

[80 FR 28414, May 18, 2015]

§ 4.6 Frequency of examination of national banks and Federal savings associations.

(a) *General.* The OCC examines national banks and Federal savings associations pursuant to authority conferred by 12 U.S.C. 481 (with respect to national banks) and 1463(a)(1) and 1464 (with respect to Federal savings associations) and the requirements of 12 U.S.C. 1820(d) (with respect to national banks and Federal savings associations). The OCC is required to conduct a full-scope, on-site examination of every national bank and Federal savings association at least once during each 12-month period.

(b) *18-month rule for certain small institutions.* The OCC may conduct a full-scope, on-site examination of a national bank or a Federal savings association at least once during each 18-month period, rather than each 12-month period as provided in paragraph (a) of this section, if the following conditions are satisfied:

(1) The bank or Federal savings association has total assets of less than $3 billion;

(2) The bank or Federal savings association is well capitalized as defined in part 6 of this chapter;

(3) At the most recent examination;

(i) The bank or Federal savings association was assigned a rating of 1 or 2 for management as part of the bank's or association's rating under the Uniform Financial Institutions Rating System; and

(ii) The bank or Federal savings association was assigned a composite rating of 1 or 2 under the Uniform Financial Institutions Rating System;

(4) The bank or Federal savings association currently is not subject to a formal enforcement proceeding or order by the FDIC, OCC, OTS or the Federal Reserve System; and

(5) No person acquired control of the bank or Federal savings association during the preceding 12-month period in which a full-scope, on-site examination would have been required but for this section.

(c) *Authority to conduct more frequent examinations.* This section does not limit the authority of the OCC to examine any national bank or Federal savings association as frequently as the agency deems necessary.

[81 FR 10068, Feb. 29, 2016, as amended at 83 FR 43965, Aug. 29, 2018]

§ 4.7 Frequency of examination of Federal agencies and branches.

(a) *General.* The OCC examines Federal agencies and Federal branches (as these entities are defined in § 28.11 (g) and (h), respectively, of this chapter) pursuant to the authority conferred by 12 U.S.C. 3105(c)(1)(C). Except as noted in paragraph (b) of this section, the OCC will conduct a full-scope, on-site examination of every Federal branch and agency at least once during each 12-month period.

(b) *18-month rule for certain small institutions*—(1) *Mandatory standards.* The OCC may conduct a full-scope, on-site examination at least once during each 18-month period, rather than each 12-month period as provided in paragraph (a) of this section, if the Federal branch or agency:

(i) Has total assets of less than $3 billion;

(ii) Has received a composite ROCA supervisory rating (which rates risk management, operational controls, compliance, and asset quality) of 1 or 2 at its most recent examination;

(iii) Satisfies the requirements of either paragraph (b)(1)(iii)(A) or (B) of this section:

(A) The foreign bank's most recently reported capital adequacy position consists of, or is equivalent to, common equity tier 1, tier 1 and total risk-based capital ratios that satisfy the definition of "well capitalized" set forth at 12 CFR 6.4, respectively, on a consolidated basis; or

(B) The branch or agency has maintained on a daily basis, over the past three quarters, eligible assets in an amount not less than 108 percent of the preceding quarter's average third party liabilities (determined consistent with applicable federal and state law), and sufficient liquidity is currently available to meet its obligations to third parties;

(iv) Is not subject to a formal enforcement action or order by the Federal Reserve Board, the Federal Deposit Insurance Corporation, or the OCC; and

(v) Has not experienced a change in control during the preceding 12-month period in which a full-scope, on-site examination would have been required but for this section.

(2) *Discretionary standards.* In determining whether a Federal branch or agency that meets the standards of paragraph (b)(1) of this section should not be eligible for an 18-month examination cycle pursuant to this paragraph (b), the OCC may consider additional factors, including whether:

(i) Any of the individual components of the ROCA rating of the Federal branch or agency is rated "3" or worse;

(ii) The results of any off-site supervision indicate a deterioration in the condition of the Federal branch or agency;

(iii) The size, relative importance, and role of a particular office when reviewed in the context of the foreign bank's entire U.S. operations otherwise necessitate an annual examination; and

(iv) The condition of the foreign bank gives rise to such a need.

(c) *Authority to conduct more frequent examinations.* Nothing in paragraph (a) or (b) of this section limits the authority of the OCC to examine any Federal branch or agency as frequently as the OCC deems necessary.

[81 FR 10068, Feb. 29, 2016, as amended at 83 FR 43965, Aug. 29, 2018]

Subpart B—Availability of Information Under the Freedom of Information Act

§ 4.11 Purpose and scope.

(a) *Purpose.* This subpart sets forth the standards, policies, and procedures that the OCC applies in administering the Freedom of Information Act (FOIA) (5 U.S.C. 552) to facilitate the OCC's interaction with the banking and savings association industries and the public.

(b) *Scope.* (1) This subpart describes the information that the FOIA requires the OCC to disclose to the public (§ 4.12), and the three methods by which the OCC discloses that information under the FOIA (§§ 4.13, 4.14, and 4.15).

(2) This subpart also sets forth predisclosure notice procedures that the OCC follows, in accordance with Executive Order 12600 (3 CFR, 1987 Comp., p. 235), when the OCC receives a request under § 4.15 for disclosure of records that arguably are exempt from disclosure as confidential commercial information (§ 4.16). Finally, this subpart describes the fees that the OCC assesses for the services it renders in providing information under the FOIA (§ 4.17).

(3) This subpart does not apply to a request for records pursuant to the Privacy Act (5 U.S.C. 552a). A person requesting records from the OCC pursuant to the Privacy Act should refer to 31 CFR part 1, subpart C, and appendix J of subpart C.

[60 FR 57322, Nov. 15, 1995, as amended at 76 FR 43561, July 21, 2011; 81 FR 94244, Dec. 23, 2016]

§ 4.12 Information available under the FOIA.

(a) *General.* Except as otherwise provided by the FOIA, OCC and Office of Thrift Supervision (OTS) records are available to the public.

(b) *Exemptions from availability.* The following records, or portions thereof, are exempt from disclosure under the FOIA:

(1) A record that is specifically authorized, under criteria established by an Executive order, to be kept secret in the interest of national defense or foreign policy, and that is properly classified pursuant to that Executive order;

(2) A record relating solely to the internal personnel rules and practices of an agency;

(3) A record specifically exempted from disclosure by statute (other than 5 U.S.C. 552b), provided that the statute requires that the matters be withheld from the public in such a manner as to leave no discretion on the issue; establishes particular criteria for withholding, or refers to particular types of matters to be withheld; and, if enacted after the date of enactment of the

OPEN FOIA Act of 2009, specifically cites to 5 U.S.C. 552(b)(3);

(4) A record that is privileged or contains trade secrets, or commercial or financial information, furnished in confidence, that relates to the business, personal, or financial affairs of any person (see §4.16 for notice requirements regarding disclosure of confidential commercial information);

(5) An intra-agency or interagency memorandum or letter not routinely available by law to a private party in litigation, including memoranda, reports, and other documents prepared by OCC employees, and records of deliberations and discussions at meetings of OCC employees, provided that the deliberative process privilege shall not apply to records created 25 years or more before the date on which the records were requested;

(6) A personnel, medical, or similar record, including a financial record, or any portion thereof, where disclosure would constitute a clearly unwarranted invasion of personal privacy;

(7) A record or information compiled for law enforcement purposes, but only to the extent that the OCC reasonably believes that producing the record or information may:

(i) Interfere with enforcement proceedings;

(ii) Deprive a person of the right to a fair trial or an impartial adjudication;

(iii) Constitute an unwarranted invasion of personal privacy;

(iv) Disclose the identity of a confidential source, including a State, local, or foreign agency or authority, or any private institution that furnished information on a confidential basis;

(v) Disclose information furnished by a confidential source, in the case of a record or information compiled by a criminal law enforcement authority in the course of a criminal investigation, or by an agency conducting a lawful national security intelligence investigation;

(vi) Disclose techniques and procedures for law enforcement investigations or prosecutions, or disclose guidelines for law enforcement investigations or prosecutions if such disclosure reasonably could be expected to risk circumvention of the law; or

(vii) Endanger the life or physical safety of any individual;

(8) A record contained in or related to an examination, operating, or condition report prepared by, on behalf of, or for the use of the OCC or any other agency responsible for regulating or supervising financial institutions; and

(9) A record containing or relating to geological and geophysical information and data, including maps, concerning wells.

(c) *Discretionary disclosure of exempt records.* Even if a record is exempt under paragraph (b) of this section, the OCC may elect, on a case-by-case basis, not to apply the exemption to the requested record. The OCC's election not to apply an exemption to a requested record has no precedential significance as to the application or nonapplication of the exemption to any other requested record, regardless of who requests the record or when the OCC receives the request. The OCC will provide predisclosure notice to submitters of confidential commercial information in accordance with §4.16.

(d) *Segregability.* If the OCC determines that full disclosure of a requested record is not possible, the OCC considers whether partial disclosure of information is possible and takes reasonable steps necessary to segregate and release nonexempt information. The OCC will note the location and extent of any deletion, and identify the FOIA exemption under which material has been deleted, on the released portion of the material, unless doing so would harm an interest protected by the exemption under paragraph (b) of this section pursuant to which the deletion was made. Where technically feasible, the amount of information redacted and the exemption pursuant to which the redaction was made will be indicated at the site(s) of the deletion.

[60 FR 57322, Nov. 15, 1995, as amended at 75 FR 17850, Apr. 8, 2010; 76 FR 43561, July 21, 2011; 81 FR 94244, Dec. 23, 2016]

§4.13 Publication in the Federal Register.

The OCC publishes certain documents in the FEDERAL REGISTER for the guidance of the public, including the following:

(a) Proposed and final rules; and

(b) Certain notices and policy statements of concern to the general public.

§ 4.14 Public inspection in an electronic format.

(a) *Available information.* Subject to the exemptions listed in § 4.12(b), the OCC makes the following information available for public inspection in an electronic format:

(1) Any final order, agreement, or other enforceable document issued in the adjudication of an OCC enforcement case, including a final order published pursuant to 12 U.S.C. 1818(u);

(2) Any final opinion issued in the adjudication of an OCC enforcement case;

(3) Any statement of general policy or interpretation of general applicability not published in the FEDERAL REGISTER;

(4) Any administrative staff manual or instruction to staff that may affect a member of the public as such;

(5) A current index identifying the information referred to in paragraphs (a)(1) through (a)(4) of this section issued, adopted, or promulgated after July 4, 1967;

(6) A list of available OCC publications;

(7) A list of forms available from the OCC, and specific forms and instructions; [1]

(8) Any public Community Reinvestment Act performance evaluation;

(9) Any public securities-related filing required under parts 11, 16, 194 or 197 of this chapter;

(10) Any public comment letter regarding a proposed rule;

(11) Any records, regardless of form or format, that have been released to any person under 5 U.S.C. 552(a)(3) provided that:

(i) The OCC determines that, because of the nature of their subject matter, the records are or are likely to become the subject of subsequent requests for substantially the same records; or

(ii) The records have been requested three or more times;

(12) Reference materials or a guide for requesting records or information from the OCC, including an index of all major OCC information systems, a description of major information and record locator systems maintained by the OCC, and a handbook for obtaining various types and categories of public information from the OCC pursuant to FOIA and chapter 35 of title 44;

(13) The public file (as defined in 12 CFR 5.9) with respect to a pending application described in part 5 of this chapter; and

(14) Any OTS information similar to that listed in paragraphs (a)(1) through (a)(13) of this section, to the extent this information is in the possession of the OCC.

(b) *Redaction of identifying details.* To the extent necessary to prevent an invasion of personal privacy, the OCC may redact identifying details from any information described in paragraph (a) of this section before making the information available for public inspection in an electronic format.

(c) *Addresses.* The information described in paragraphs (a)(1) through (14) of this section is available from the Chief FOIA Officer, Communications Division, Office of the Comptroller of the Currency, 400 7th Street SW., Washington, DC 20219. The information described in paragraph (a)(13) of this section in the case of both national banks and Federal savings associations is available from the Licensing Manager at the appropriate district office at the address listed in § 4.5(a), or in the case of national banks and Federal savings associations supervised by the Large Bank Supervision Department, from the Large Bank Licensing Expert, Licensing Division, Office of the Comptroller of the Currency, 400 7th Street SW., Washington, DC 20219.

[60 FR 57322, Nov. 15, 1995, as amended at 76 FR 43561, July 21, 2011; 79 FR 15641, Mar. 21, 2014; 81 FR 94244, Dec. 23, 2016]

§ 4.15 How to request records.

(a) *Available information.* Subject to the exemptions described in § 4.12(b), any OCC record is available to any person upon specific request in accordance with this section.

---

[1] Some forms and instructions that national banks and Federal savings associations use are not available from the OCC. The OCC will provide information on where persons may obtain these forms and instructions upon request.

(b) *Where to submit request or appeal*—(1) *General.* Except as provided in paragraph (b)(2) of this section, a person requesting a record or filing an administrative appeal must submit the request or appeal:

(i) Through the OCC's FOIA Web portal at *https://foia-pal.occ.gov/palMain.aspx;*

(ii) Through the consolidated online request portal maintained by the Office of Management and Budget pursuant to 5 U.S.C. 552(m)(1); or

(iii) Under this section to the Chief FOIA Officer, Communications Division, Office of the Comptroller of the Currency, 400 7th Street SW., Washington, DC 20219.

(2) *Exceptions*—(i) *Records at the Federal Deposit Insurance Corporation.* A person requesting any of the following records, other than blank forms (see § 4.14(a)(7)), must submit the request to the FDIC, Legal Division, FOIA/PA Group, 550–17th Street NW., Washington, DC 20429, or fax to (703) 562–2797:

(A) Consolidated Report of Condition and Income (FFIEC 031, 032, 033, 034);

(B) Annual Report of Trust Assets (FFIEC 001);

(C) Uniform Bank Performance Report; and

(D) Special Report.

(ii) *Records of another agency.* When the OCC receives a request for records in its possession that another Federal agency either generated or provided to the OCC, the OCC promptly informs the requester and immediately forwards the request to that agency for processing in accordance with that agency's regulations.

(c) *Request for records*—(1) *Contact information and what the request for records must include.* A person requesting records under this section must state, in writing:

(i) The requester's full name, address, telephone number and, at the requester's option, electronic mail address.

(ii) A reasonable description of the records sought (including sufficient detail to enable OCC employees who are familiar with the subject matter of the request to locate the records with a reasonable amount of effort);

(iii) A statement agreeing to pay all fees that the OCC assesses under § 4.17;

(iv) A description of how the requester intends to use the records, if a requester seeks placement in a lower fee category (i.e., a fee category other than "commercial use requester") under § 4.17; and

(v) Whether the requester prefers the OCC to deliver a copy of the records or to allow the requester to inspect the records at the appropriate OCC office.

(2) *Initial determination.* The Comptroller or the Comptroller's delegate initially determines whether to grant a request for OCC records and notifies the requester, in accordance with the time limits set forth in paragraph (f) of this section, of the determination and the reasons therefore and of the right to seek assistance from the OCC's FOIA Public Liaison.

(3) *If request is granted.* If the OCC grants a request for records, in whole or in part, the OCC promptly discloses the records in one of two ways, depending on the requester's stated preference:

(i) The OCC may deliver a copy of the records to the requester. If the OCC delivers a copy of the records to the requester, the OCC duplicates the records at reasonable and proper times that do not interfere with their use by the OCC or preclude other persons from making inspections; or

(ii) The OCC may allow the requester to inspect the records at reasonable and proper times that do not interfere with their use by the OCC or preclude other persons from making inspections. If the OCC allows the requester to inspect the records, the OCC may place a reasonable limit on the number of records that a person may inspect during a day.

(4) *If request is denied.* If the OCC denies a request for records, in whole or in part, the OCC will notify the requester in writing. The notification is dated and contains a brief statement of the reasons for the denial, sets forth the name and title or position of the official making the decision, advises the requester of the right to seek dispute resolution services from the OCC's FOIA Public Liaison or the Office of Government Information Services, and

advises the requester of the right to appeal to the Comptroller of the Currency in accordance with paragraph (d) of this section.

(d) *Administrative appeal of a denial*—(1) *Procedure.* A requester must submit an administrative appeal of denial of a request for records in writing within 90 days after the date of the initial determination. The appeal must include the circumstances and arguments supporting disclosure of the requested records.

(2) *Appellate determination.* The Comptroller or the Comptroller's delegate determines whether to grant an appeal of a denial of a request for OCC records.

(3) *If appeal is granted.* If the OCC grants an appeal, in whole or in part, the OCC treats the request as if it were originally granted, in whole or in part, by the OCC in accordance with paragraph (c)(3) of this section.

(4) *If appeal is denied.* If the OCC denies an appeal, in whole or in part, the OCC notifies the requester in writing. The notification contains a brief statement of the reasons for the denial, sets forth the name and title or position of the official making the decision, and advises the requester of the right to judicial review of the denial under 5 U.S.C. 552(a)(4)(B).

(e) *Judicial review*—(1) *General.* If the OCC denies an appeal pursuant to paragraph (d) of this section, or if the OCC fails to make a determination within the time limits specified in paragraph (f) of this section, the requester may commence an action to compel disclosure of records, pursuant to 5 U.S.C. 552(a)(4)(B), in the United States district court in:

(i) The district where the requester resides;

(ii) The district where the requester's principal place of business is located;

(iii) The district where the records are located; or

(iv) The District of Columbia.

(2) *Service of process.* In commencing an action described in paragraph (e)(1) of this section, the requester, in addition to complying with the Federal Rules of Civil Procedure (28 U.S.C. appendix) for service upon the United States or agencies thereof, must serve process on the Chief Counsel or the Chief Counsel's delegate at the following location: Office of the Comptroller of the Currency, 400 7th Street, SW., Washington, DC 20219.

(f) *Time limits for responding to FOIA requests.* (1) The OCC makes an initial determination to grant or deny a request for records within 20 days (excluding Saturdays, Sundays, and holidays) after the date of receipt of the request, as described in paragraph (g) of this section, except as stated in paragraph (f)(3) of this section.

(2) *Appeal.* The OCC makes a determination to grant or deny an administrative appeal within 20 business days after the date of receipt of the appeal, as described in paragraph (g) of this section, except as stated in paragraph (f)(3) of this section.

(3) *Extension of time.* The time limits set forth in paragraphs (f)(1) and (2) of this section may be extended as follows:

(i) *In unusual circumstances.* The OCC may extend the time limits in unusual circumstances for a maximum of 10 business days. If the OCC extends the time limits, the OCC provides written notice to the person making the request or appeal, containing the reason for the extension and the date on which the OCC expects to make a determination. Unusual circumstances exist when the OCC requires additional time to:

(A) Search for and collect the requested records from field facilities or other buildings that are separate from the office processing the request or appeal;

(B) Search for, collect, and appropriately examine a voluminous amount of requested records;

(C) Consult with another agency that has a substantial interest in the determination of the request; or

(D) Allow two or more components of the OCC that have substantial interest in the determination of the request to consult with each other;

(ii) *By agreement.* A requester may agree to extend the time limits for any amount of time;

(iii) *By judicial action.* If a requester commences an action pursuant to paragraph (e) of this section for failure to comply with the time limits set forth in this paragraph (f), a court with jurisdiction may, pursuant to 5 U.S.C.

552(a)(6)(C), allow the OCC additional time to complete the review of the records requested, or

(iv) *Tolling of time limits.* (A) The OCC may toll the 20-day time period to:

(*1*) Make one request for additional information from the requester; or

(*2*) Clarify the applicability or amount of any fees, if necessary, with the requester.

(B) The tolling period ends upon the OCC's receipt of requested information from the requester or resolution of the fee issue.

(4) *Requests that require more than a 10-day extension to process.* If the OCC determines unusual circumstances apply to a request for records, and the OCC determines it cannot respond to the request within the 10-day extension set forth in paragraph (f)(3)(i) of this section, the OCC will:

(i) Notify the requester that the request cannot be processed within the time limit set forth in paragraph (f)(3)(i) of this section;

(ii) Provide the requester with an opportunity to limit the scope of the request so that it may be processed within that 10-day period or to arrange with the OCC an alternative time frame for processing the request or a modified request;

(iii) Make available the FOIA Public Liaison, who shall assist in the resolution of any disputes between the requester and the OCC; and

(iv) Notify the requester of the right of the requester to seek dispute resolution services from the Office of Government Information Services.

(g) *Date of receipt of request or appeal.* The date of receipt of a request for records or an appeal is the date that Disclosure Services, Communications Division receives a request that satisfies the requirements of paragraph (c)(1) or (d)(1) of this section, except as provided in §4.17(d).

(h) *Dispute resolution services.* Requesters with concerns about the handling of their FOIA requests may contact the FOIA Public Liaison or the Office of Government Information Services for dispute resolution services.

(1) To apply for dispute resolution assistance from the FOIA Public Liaison, requesters should submit a written request to the FOIA Public Liaison, Communications Division, Office of the Comptroller of the Currency, 400 7th Street SW., Washington, DC 20219.

(2) For dispute resolution services through the Office of Government Services, requesters should contact the Office of Government Services as set forth at 36 CFR 1250.32.

[60 FR 57322, Nov. 15, 1995, as amended at 75 FR 17850, Apr. 8, 2010; 76 FR 43562, July 21, 2011; 79 FR 15641, Mar. 21, 2014; 81 FR 94245, Dec. 23, 2016]

§4.16 Predisclosure notice for confidential commercial information.

(a) *Definitions.* For purposes of this section, the following definitions apply:

(1) *Confidential commercial information* means records that arguably contain material exempt from release under Exemption 4 of the FOIA (5 U.S.C. 552(b)(4); §4.12(b)(4)), because disclosure reasonably could cause substantial competitive harm to the submitter.

(2) *Submitter* means any person or entity that provides confidential commercial information to the OCC. This term includes corporations, State governments, foreign governments, and banks and their employees, officers, directors, and principal shareholders.

(b) *Notice to submitter*—(1) *When provided.* In accordance with Executive Order 12600 (3 CFR, 1987 Comp., p. 235), when the OCC receives a request under §4.15(c) or, where appropriate, an appeal under §4.15(d) for disclosure of confidential commercial information, the OCC provides a submitter with prompt written notice of the receipt of that request (except as provided in paragraph (b)(2) of this section) in the following circumstances:

(i) With respect to confidential commercial information submitted to the OCC or to the Federal Home Loan Bank Board, the predecessor of the OTS, prior to January 1, 1988, if:

(A) The records are less than 10 years old and the submitter designated the information as confidential commercial information;

(B) The OCC reasonably believes that disclosure of the information may cause substantial competitive harm to the submitter; or

(C) The information is subject to a prior express commitment of confidentiality from the OCC or the Federal Home Loan Bank Board, the predecessor of the OTS; and

(ii) With respect to confidential commercial information submitted to the OCC or to the OTS (or the Federal Home Loan Bank Board, its predecessor agency) on or after January 1, 1988, if:

(A) The submitter in good faith designated the information as confidential commercial information;

(B) The OCC or the OTS (or the Federal Home Loan Bank Board, its predecessor agency) designated the class of information to which the requested information belongs as confidential commercial information; or

(C) The OCC reasonably believes that disclosure of the information may cause substantial competitive harm to the submitter.

(2) *Exceptions*. The OCC generally does not provide notice under paragraph (b)(1) of this section if the OCC determines that:

(i) It will not disclose the information;

(ii) The information already has been disclosed officially to the public;

(iii) The OCC is required by law (other than 5 U.S.C. 552) to disclose the information;

(iv) The OCC or the OTS (or the Federal Home Loan Bank Board, its predecessor agency) acquired the information in the course of a lawful investigation of a possible violation of criminal law;

(v) The submitter had an opportunity to designate the requested information as confidential commercial information at the time of submission of the information or a reasonable time thereafter and did not do so, unless the OCC has substantial reason to believe that disclosure of the information would result in competitive harm; or

(vi) The OCC determines that the submitter's designation under paragraph (b)(1)(ii)(A) of this section is frivolous; in such case, however, the OCC will provide the submitter with written notice of any final administrative determination to disclose the information at least 10 business days prior to the date that the OCC intends to disclose the information.

(3) *Content of notice*. The OCC either describes in the notice the exact nature of the confidential commercial information requested or includes with the notice copies of the records or portions of records containing that information.

(4) *Expiration of notice period*. The OCC provides notice under this paragraph (b) with respect to information that the submitter designated under paragraph (b)(1)(ii)(A) of this section only for a period of 10 years after the date of the submitter's designation, unless the submitter requests and justifies to the OCC's satisfaction a specific notice period of greater duration.

(5) *Certification of confidentiality*. If possible, the submitter should support the claim of confidentiality with a statement or certification that the requested information is confidential commercial information that the submitter has not disclosed to the public. This statement should be prepared by an officer or authorized representative if the submitter is a corporation or other entity.

(c) *Notice to requester*. If the OCC provides notice to a submitter under paragraph (b) of this section, the OCC notifies the person requesting confidential commercial information (requester) that it has provided notice to the submitter. The OCC also advises the requester that if there is a delay in its decision whether to grant or deny access to the information sought, the delay may be considered a denial of access to the information, and that the requester may proceed with an administrative appeal or seek judicial review. However, the requester may agree to a voluntary extension of time to allow the OCC to review the submitter's objection to disclosure (see § 4.15(f)(3)(ii)).

(d) *Opportunity to object to disclosure*. Within 10 days after receiving notice under paragraph (b) of this section, the submitter may provide the OCC with a detailed statement of objection to disclosure of the information. That statement must specify the grounds for withholding any of the information under any exemption of the FOIA. Any statement that the submitter provides under this paragraph (d) may be subject to disclosure under the FOIA.

(e) *Notice of intent to disclose*. The OCC considers carefully a submitter's objection and specific grounds for nondisclosure prior to determining whether to disclose the requested information. If the OCC decides to disclose information over the objection of the submitter, the OCC provides to the submitter, with a copy to the requester, a written notice that includes:

(1) A statement of the OCC's reasons for not sustaining the submitter's objections to disclosure;

(2) A description of the information to be disclosed;

(3) The anticipated disclosure date, which is not less than 10 business days after the OCC mails the written notice required under this paragraph (e); and

(4) A statement that the submitter must notify the OCC immediately if the submitter intends to seek injunctive relief.

(f) *Notice of requester's lawsuit*. Whenever the OCC receives service of process indicating that a requester has brought suit seeking to compel the OCC to disclose information covered by paragraph (b)(1) of this section, the OCC promptly notifies the submitter.

[60 FR 57322, Nov. 15, 1995, as amended at 76 FR 43561, July 21, 2011]

§ 4.17 FOIA request fees.

(a) *Definitions*. For purposes of this section, the following definitions apply:

(1) *Actual costs* means those expenditures that the OCC incurs in providing services (including searching for, reviewing, and duplicating records) in response to a request for records under § 4.15.

(2) *Search* means the process of locating a record in response to a request, including page-by-page or line-by-line identification of material within a record. The OCC may perform a search manually or by electronic means.

(3) *Review* means the process of examining a record located in response to a request to determine which portions of that record should be released. It also includes processing a record for disclosure.

(4) *Duplication* means the process of copying a record in response to a request. A copy may take the form of a paper copy, microform, audiovisual materials, or machine readable material (e.g., magnetic tape or disk), among others.

(5) *Commercial use requester* means a person who seeks records for a use or purpose that furthers the commercial, trade, or profit interests of the requester or the person on whose behalf the request is made.

(6) *Educational institution requester* means a person who seeks records on behalf of a public or private educational institution, including a preschool, an elementary or secondary school, an institution of undergraduate or graduate higher education, an institution of professional education, or an institution of vocational education that operates a program of scholarly research.

(7) *Noncommercial scientific institution requester* means a person who is not a "commercial use requester," as that term is defined in paragraph (a)(5) of this section, and who seeks records on behalf of an institution operated solely for the purpose of conducting scientific research, the results of which are not intended to promote any particular product or industry.

(8) *Requester who is a representative of the news media* means any person who, or entity that, gathers information of potential interest to a segment of the public, uses editorial skills to turn the raw materials into a distinct work, and distributes that work to an audience. A freelance journalist shall be regarded as working for a news media entity if the person can demonstrate a solid basis for expecting publication through that entity, whether or not the journalist is actually employed by that entity. A publication contract is one example of a basis for expecting publication that ordinarily would satisfy this standard. The OCC also may consider the past publication record of the requester in determining whether she or he qualifies as a "representative of the news media."

(b) *Fees*—(1) *General*. The hourly and per page rate that the OCC generally charges requesters is set forth in the "Notice of Comptroller of the Currency Fees" (Notice) described in 12 CFR 8.8. Any interested person may request a copy of the Notice from the OCC by mail or may obtain a copy at the location described in §4.14(c). The OCC may contract with a commercial service to search for, duplicate, or disseminate records, provided that the OCC determines that the fee assessed upon a requester is no greater than if the OCC performed the tasks itself. The OCC does not contract out responsibilities that the FOIA provides that the OCC alone may discharge, such as determining the applicability of an exemption or whether to waive or reduce a fee.

(2) *Fee categories.* The OCC assesses a fee based on the fee category in which the OCC places the requester. If the request states how the requester intends to use the requested records (see §4.15(c)(1)(iv)), the OCC may place the requester in a lower fee category; otherwise, the OCC categorizes the requester as a "commercial use requester." If the OCC reasonably doubts the requester's stated intended use, or if that use is not clear from the request, the OCC may place the requester in the "commercial use" category or may seek additional clarification. The fee categories are as follows:

(i) *Commercial use requesters.* The OCC assesses a fee for a requester in this category for the actual cost of search, review, and duplication. A requester in this category does not receive any free search, review, or duplication services.

(ii) *Educational institution requesters, noncommercial scientific institution requesters, and requesters who are representatives of the news media.* The OCC assesses a fee for a requester in this category for the actual cost of duplication. A requester in this category receives 100 free pages.

(iii) *All other requesters.* The OCC assesses a fee for a requester who does not fit into either of the above categories for the actual cost of search and duplication. A requester in this category receives 100 free pages and two hours of free search time.

(3) *Special services.* The OCC may, in its discretion, accommodate a request for special services. The OCC may recover the actual cost of providing any special services.

(4) *Waiving or reducing a fee.* The OCC may waive or reduce a fee under this section whenever, in its opinion, disclosure of records is in the public interest because the disclosure:

(i) Is likely to contribute significantly to public understanding of the operations or activities of the government; and

(ii) Is not primarily in the commercial interest of the requester.

(5) *Fee for unsuccessful search.* The OCC may assess a fee for time spent searching for records, even if the OCC does not locate the records requested.

(6) *No fee if the time limit passes and the OCC has not responded to the request.* The OCC will not assess search or duplication fees, as applicable, if it fails to respond to a requester's FOIA request within the time limits specified under 5 U.S.C. 552(a)(6) and 12 CFR 4.15(f), except as follows:

(i) *Unusual circumstances*—(A) *General.* If the OCC has determined that unusual circumstances (as defined in 5 U.S.C. 552(a)(6)(B) and §4.15(f)(3)(i)) apply and the OCC provides timely written notice to the requester in accordance with 5 U.S.C. 552(a)(6)(B), the OCC may assess search or duplication fees, as applicable, for an additional 10 days. If the OCC fails to comply with the extended time limit, the OCC will not assess any search or duplication fees, as applicable.

(B) *Voluminous Requests.* Notwithstanding paragraph (b)(6)(i)(A) of this section, if the OCC has determined that unusual circumstances (as defined in 5 U.S.C. 552(a)(6)(B) and §4.15(f)(3)(i)) apply and more than 5,000 pages are necessary to respond to the request, the OCC may assess search or duplication fees, as appropriate, if the OCC provides a timely written notice to the requester in accordance with 5 U.S.C. 552(a)(6)(B) and discusses with the requester via written mail, electronic mail, or telephone (or makes not less than three good-faith attempts to do so) how the requester could effectively limit the scope of the request in accordance with 5 U.S.C. 552(a)(6)(B)(ii).

(ii) *In exceptional circumstances.* If a court has determined that exceptional circumstances (as defined in 5 U.S.C. 552(a)(6)(C)) apply to the processing of a request, the OCC may assess search or duplication fees, as applicable, for the length of time provided by the court order.

(c) *Payment of fees*—(1) *General.* The OCC generally assesses a fee when it delivers the records in response to the request, if any. A requester must send payment within 30 calendar days of the billing date to the Financial Management, Accounts Receivable, Office of the Comptroller of the Currency, 400 7th Street SW., Washington, DC 20219.

(2) *Fee likely to exceed $25.* If the OCC estimates that a fee is likely to exceed $25, the OCC notifies the requester of the estimated fee, unless the requester has indicated in advance a willingness to pay a fee as high as the estimated fee. If so notified by the OCC, the requester may confer with OCC employees to revise the request to reflect a lower fee.

(3) *Fee likely to exceed $250.* If the OCC estimates that a fee is likely to exceed $250, the OCC notifies the requester of the estimated fee. In this circumstance, the OCC may require, as a condition to processing the request, that the requester:

(i) Provide satisfactory assurance of full payment, if the requester has a history of prompt payment; or

(ii) Pay the estimated fee in full, if the requester does not have a history of prompt payment.

(4) *Failure to pay a fee.* If the requester fails to pay a fee within 30 days of the date of the billing, the OCC may require, as a condition to processing any further request, that the requester pay any unpaid fee, plus interest (as provided in paragraph (c)(5) of this section), and any estimated fee in full for that further request.

(5) *Interest on unpaid fee.* The OCC may assess interest charges on an unpaid fee beginning on the 31st day following the billing date. The OCC charges interest at the rate prescribed in 31 U.S.C. 3717.

(d) *Tolling of time limits.* Under the circumstances described in paragraphs (c) (2), (3), and (4) of this section, the time limits set forth in §4.15(f) (*i.e.*, 20 business days from the receipt of a request for records and 20 business days from the receipt of an administrative appeal, plus any permissible extension) begin only after the OCC receives a revised request under paragraph (c)(2) of this section, an assurance of payment under paragraph (c)(3)(i) of this section, or the required payments under paragraph (c)(3)(i) or (c)(4) of this section.

(e) *Aggregating requests.* When the OCC reasonably believes that a requester or group of requesters is attempting to break a request into a series of requests for the purpose of evading the assessment of a fee, the OCC may aggregate the requests and assess a fee accordingly.

[60 FR 57322, Nov. 15, 1995, as amended at 75 FR 17850, Apr. 8, 2010; 79 FR 15641, Mar. 21, 2014; 81 FR 94245, Dec. 23, 2016]

§4.18 How to track a FOIA request.

(a) *Tracking number*—(1) *Internet requests.* The OCC will issue a tracking number to all FOIA requesters automatically upon receipt of the request (as described in §4.15(g)) by the OCC's Communications Division via the OCC's Freedom of Information Request Portal, *https://foia-pal.occ.gov/palMain.aspx.* The tracking number will be sent via electronic mail to the requester.

(2) *If a requester does not have Internet access.* The OCC will issue a tracking number to FOIA requesters without Internet access within 5 days of the receipt of the request (as described in §4.15(g)) in the OCC's Communications Division. The OCC will mail the tracking number to the requester's physical address, as provided in the FOIA request.

(b) *Status of request.* FOIA requesters may track the progress of their requests via the OCC's Freedom of Information Request Portal, *https://foia-pal.occ.gov/palMain.aspx.* Requesters without Internet access may continue to contact the Chief FOIA Officer, Communications Division, Office of the Comptroller of the Currency, at (202) 649–6700 to check the status of their FOIA request(s).

[76 FR 43562, July 21, 2011, as amended at 79 FR 15641, Mar. 21, 2014; 80 FR 28414, May 18, 2015; 81 FR 94246, Dec. 23, 2016]

Subpart C—Release of Non-Public OCC Information

§4.31 Purpose and scope.

(a) *Purpose.* The purposes of this subpart are to:

(1) Afford an orderly mechanism for the OCC to process expeditiously requests for non-public OCC information; to address the release of non-public OCC information without a request; and, when appropriate, for the OCC to assert evidentiary privileges in litigation;

(2) Recognize the public's interest in obtaining access to relevant and necessary information and the countervailing public interest of maintaining the effectiveness of the OCC supervisory process and appropriate confidentiality of OCC supervisory information;

(3) Ensure that the OCC's information is used in a manner that supports the public interest and the interests of the OCC;

(4) Ensure that OCC resources are used in the most efficient manner consistent with the OCC's statutory mission;

(5) Minimize burden on national banks, Federal savings associations, the public, and the OCC;

(6) Limit the expenditure of government resources for private purposes; and

(7) Maintain the OCC's impartiality among private litigants.

(b) *Scope.* (1) This subpart applies to requests for, and dissemination of, non-public OCC information, including requests for records or testimony arising out of civil lawsuits and administrative proceedings to which the OCC is not a party and the release of non-public OCC information without a specific request. Lawsuits and administrative proceedings to which the OCC is not a party include proceedings in which a Federal agency is a party in opposition to the private requester.

(2) This subpart does not apply to:

(i) A request for a record or testimony in a proceeding in which the OCC is a party; or

(ii) A request for a record that is required to be disclosed under the Freedom of Information Act (FOIA) (5 U.S.C. 552), as described in § 4.12.

(3) A request for a record or testimony made by the Board of Governors of the Federal Reserve System, the Federal Deposit Insurance Corporation, a government agency of the United States or a foreign government, a state agency with authority to investigate violations of criminal law, or a state bank or state savings association regulatory agency is governed solely by § 4.37(c).

(4) For purposes of §§ 4.35(a)(1), 4.36(a) and 4.37(c) of this part, the OCC's decision to disclose records or testimony involving a Suspicious Activity Report (SAR) filed pursuant to the regulations implementing 12 U.S.C. 5318(g), or any information that would reveal the existence of a SAR, is governed by 12 CFR 21.11(k).

(5) This subpart does not apply to requests for non-public information filed with the Office of Thrift Supervision (OTS) before July 21, 2011. These requests are subject to the rules of the OTS in effect on July 20, 2011.

[60 FR 57322, Nov. 15, 1995, as amended at 63 FR 62929, Nov. 10, 1998; 64 FR 29216, June 1, 1999; 75 FR 75576, Dec. 3, 2010; 76 FR 43562, July 21, 2011]

§ 4.32 Definitions.

(a) *Complete request* means a request containing sufficient information to allow the OCC to make an informed decision.

(b) *Non-public OCC information.* Non-public OCC information:

(1) Means information that the OCC is not required to release under the FOIA (5 U.S.C. 552) or that the OCC has not yet published or made available pursuant to 12 U.S.C. 1818(u) and includes:

(i) A record created or obtained:

(A) By the OCC in connection with the OCC's performance of its responsibilities, such as a record concerning supervision, licensing, regulation, and examination of a national bank, a Federal savings association, a bank holding company, a savings and loan holding company, or an affiliate; or

(B) By the OTS in connection with the OTS's performance of its responsibilities, such as a record concerning supervision, licensing, regulation, and examination of a Federal savings association, a savings and loan holding company, or an affiliate;

(ii) A record compiled by the OCC or the OTS in connection with either agency's enforcement responsibilities;

(iii) A report of examination, supervisory correspondence, an investigatory file compiled by the OCC or OTS in connection with an investigation, and any internal agency memorandum, whether the information is in the possession of the OCC or some other individual or entity;

(iv) Confidential OCC information obtained by a third party or otherwise incorporated in the records of a third party, including another government agency;

(v) Testimony from, or an interview with, a current or former OCC employee, officer, or agent or a former OTS employee, officer, or agent concerning information acquired by that person in the course of his or her performance of official duties with the OCC or OTS or due to that person's official status at the OCC or OTS; and

(vi) Confidential information relating to operating and no longer operating national banks, Federal savings associations, and savings and loan holding companies as well as their subsidiaries and their affiliates.

(2) Is the property of the Comptroller.

(c) *Relevant* means could contribute substantially to the resolution of one or more specifically identified issues in the case.

(d) *Show a compelling need* means, in support of a request for testimony, demonstrate with as much detail as is necessary under the circumstances, that the requested information is relevant and that the relevant material contained in the testimony is not available from any other source. Sources, without limitation, include the books and records of other persons or entities and non-public OCC records that have been, or might be, released.

(e) *Supervised entity* includes a national bank or Federal savings association, a subsidiary of a national bank or Federal savings association, or a Federal branch or agency of a foreign bank licensed by the OCC as defined under 12 CFR 28.11(g) and (h), or any other entity supervised by the OCC.

(f) *Testimony* means an interview or sworn testimony on the record.

[60 FR 57322, Nov. 15, 1995, as amended at 63 FR 62929, Nov. 10, 1998; 64 FR 29216, June 1, 1999; 75 FR 75576, Dec. 3, 2010; 76 FR 43562, July 21, 2011]

§ 4.33 Requirements for a request of records or testimony.

(a) *Generally*—(1) *Form of request.* A person seeking non-public OCC information must submit a request in writing to the OCC. The requester must explain, in as detailed a description as is necessary under the circumstances, the bases for the request and how the requested non-public OCC information relates to the issues in the lawsuit or matter.

(2) *Expedited request.* A requester seeking a response in less than 60 days must explain why the request was not submitted earlier and why the OCC should expedite the request.

(3) *Request arising from adversarial matters.* Where the requested information is to be used in connection with an adversarial matter:

(i) The OCC generally will require that the lawsuit or administrative action has been filed before it will consider the request;

(ii) The request must include:

(A) A copy of the complaint or other pleading setting forth the assertions in the case;

(B) The caption and docket number of the case;

(C) The name, address, and phone number of counsel to each party in the case; and

(D) A description of any prior judicial decisions or pending motions in the case that may bear on the asserted relevance of the requested information;

(iii) The request must also:

(A) Show that the information is relevant to the purpose for which it is sought;

(B) Show that other evidence reasonably suited to the requester's needs is not available from any other source;

(C) Show that the need for the information outweighs the public interest considerations in maintaining the confidentiality of the OCC information and outweighs the burden on the OCC to produce the information;

(D) Explain how the issues in the case and the status of the case warrant that the OCC allow disclosure; and

(E) Identify any other issue that may bear on the question of waiver of privilege by the OCC.

(b) *Request for records.* If the request is for a record, the requester must adequately describe the record or records sought by type and date.

(c) *Request for testimony*—(1) *Generally.* A requester seeking testimony:

(i) Must show a compelling need for the requested information; and

(ii) Should request OCC testimony with sufficient time to obtain the testimony in deposition form.

(2) *Trial or hearing testimony.* A requester seeking testimony at a trial or hearing must show that a deposition would not suffice.

§ 4.34 Where to submit a request.

(a) *A request for non-public OCC information.* A person requesting information under this subpart, requesting authentication of a record under § 4.39(d), or submitting a notification of the issuance of a subpoena or compulsory process under § 4.37, shall send the request or notification to: Office of the Comptroller of the Currency, 400 7th Street, SW., Washington, DC 20219, Attention: Director, Litigation Division.

(b) *Combined requests for non-public and other OCC information.* A person requesting public OCC information and non-public OCC information under this subpart may submit a combined request for both to the address in paragraph (a) of this section. If a requester decides to submit a combined request under this section, the OCC will process the combined request under this subpart and not under subpart B of this part (FOIA).

(c) *Request by government agencies.* A request made pursuant to § 4.37(c) must be submitted:

(1) In a civil action, to the Director of the OCC's Litigation Division at the Washington office; or

(2) In a criminal action, to the appropriate district counsel or the Director of the OCC's Enforcement and Compliance Division at the Washington office.

[60 FR 57322, Nov. 15, 1995, as amended at 64 FR 29216, June 1, 1999; 79 FR 15641, Mar. 21, 2014]

§ 4.35 Consideration of requests.

(a) *In general*—(1) *OCC discretion.* The OCC decides whether to release non-public OCC information based on its weighing of all appropriate factors including the requestor's fulfilling of the requirements enumerated in § 4.33. Each decision is at the sole discretion of the Comptroller or the Comptroller's delegate and is a final agency decision. OCC action on a request for non-public OCC information exhausts administrative remedies for discovery of the information.

(2) *Bases for denial.* The OCC may deny a request for non-public OCC information for reasons that include the following:

(i) The requester was unsuccessful in showing that the information is relevant to the pending matter;

(ii) The requester seeks testimony and the requestor did not show a compelling need for the information;

(iii) The request arises from an adversarial matter and other evidence reasonably suited to the requester's need is available from another source;

(iv) A lawsuit or administrative action has not yet been filed and the request was made in connection with potential litigation;

(v) The production of the information would be contrary to the public interest or unduly burdensome to the OCC; or

(vi) When prohibited by law.

(3) *Additional information.* A requester must submit a complete request. The OCC may require the requester to provide additional information to complete a request. Consistent with the purposes stated in § 4.31, the OCC may inquire into the circumstances of any case underlying the request and rely on sources of information other than the requester, including other parties.

(4) *Time required by the OCC to respond.* The OCC generally will process requests in the order in which they are received. The OCC will notify the requester in writing of the final decision. Absent exigent or unusual circumstances, the OCC will respond to a request within 60 days from the date that the OCC receives a request that it deems a complete request. Consistent

with § 4.33(a)(2), the OCC weighs a request to respond to provide information in less than 60 days against the unfairness to other requesters whose pending requests may be delayed and the burden imposed on the OCC by the expedited processing.

(5) *Notice to subject national banks and Federal savings associations.* Following receipt of a request for non-public OCC information, the OCC generally notifies the national bank or Federal savings association that is the subject of the requested information, unless the OCC, in its discretion, determines that to do so would advantage or prejudice any of the parties in the matter at issue.

(b) *Testimony.* (1) The OCC generally will not authorize a current OCC employee to provide expert or opinion evidence for a private party.

(2) The OCC may restrict the scope of any authorized testimony and may act to ensure that the scope of testimony given by the OCC employee adheres to the scope authorized by the OCC.

(3) Once a request for testimony has been submitted, and before the requested testimony occurs, a party to the relevant case, who did not join in the request and who wishes to question the witness beyond the scope of testimony sought by the request, shall timely submit the party's own request for OCC information pursuant to this subpart.

(4) The OCC may offer the requester the employee's written declaration in lieu of testimony.

(c) *Release of non-public OCC information by others.* In appropriate cases, the OCC may respond to a request for information by authorizing a party to the case who is in possession of non-public OCC information to release the information to the requester. An OCC authorization to release records does not preclude the party in possession from asserting its own privilege, arguing that the records are not relevant, or asserting any other argument for which it has standing to protect the records from release.

[60 FR 57322, Nov. 15, 1995, 75 FR 75576, Dec. 3, 2010; 76 FR 43563, July 21, 2011]

§ 4.36 Disclosure of non-public OCC information.

(a) *Discretionary disclosure of non-public OCC information.* The OCC may make non-public OCC information available to a supervised entity and to other persons, that in the sole discretion of the Comptroller may be necessary or appropriate, without a request for records or testimony.

(b) *OCC policy.* It is the OCC's policy regarding non-public OCC information that such information is confidential and privileged. Accordingly, the OCC will not normally disclose this information to third parties.

(c) *Conditions and limitations.* The OCC may impose any conditions or limitations on disclosures under this section, including the restrictions on dissemination contained in § 4.38, that it determines are necessary to effect the purposes of this section.

(d) *Unauthorized disclosures prohibited.* All non-public OCC information remains the property of the OCC. No supervised entity, government agency, person, or other party to whom the information is made available, or any officer, director, employee, or agent thereof, may disclose non-public OCC information without the prior written permission of the OCC, except in published statistical material that does not disclose, either directly or when used in conjunction with other publicly available information, the affairs of any individual, corporation, or other entity. Except as authorized by the OCC, no person obtaining access to non-public OCC information under this section may make a copy of the information and no person may remove non-public OCC information from the premises of the institution, agency, or other party in authorized possession of the information.

[63 FR 62929, Nov. 10, 1998, as amended at 64 FR 29216, June 1, 1999]

§ 4.37 Persons and entities with access to OCC information; prohibition on dissemination.

(a) *Current and former OCC employees or agents; former OTS employees or agents*—(1) *Generally.* Except as authorized by this subpart or otherwise by the

OCC, no current or former OCC employee or agent or former OTS employee or agent, may, in any manner, disclose or permit the disclosure of any non-public OCC information to anyone other than an employee or agent of the Comptroller for use in the performance of OCC duties.

(2) *Duty of person served.* Any current or former OCC employee or agent or former OTS employee or agent, subpoenaed or otherwise requested to provide information covered by this subpart must immediately notify the OCC as provided in this paragraph. The OCC may intervene, attempt to have the compulsory process withdrawn, and register appropriate objections when a current or former OCC employee or agent or former OTS employee or agent, receives a subpoena and the subpoena requires the current or former employee or agent to appear or produce OCC information. If necessary, the current or former employee or agent must appear as required and respectfully decline to produce the information sought, citing this subpart as authority and United States ex rel. Touhy v. Ragen, 340 U.S. 462 (1951). The current or former OCC employee or agent or former OTS employee or agent, must immediately notify the OCC if subpoenaed or otherwise asked for non-public OCC information:

(i) In a civil action, by notifying the Director of the OCC's Litigation Division at the Washington office; or

(ii) In a criminal action, by notifying the appropriate district counsel for current and former district employees or agents; or the Director of the OCC's Enforcement and Compliance Division at the Washington office, for current and former Washington employees or agents and former OTS employees or agents.

(b) *Non-OCC employees or entities*—(1) *Generally.* (i) Without OCC approval, no person, national bank, Federal savings association, or other entity, including one in lawful possession of non-public OCC information under paragraph (b)(2) of this section, may disclose information covered by this subpart in any manner, except:

(A) After the requester has sought the information from the OCC pursuant to the procedures set forth in this subpart; and

(B) As ordered by a Federal court in a judicial proceeding in which the OCC has had the opportunity to appear and oppose discovery.

(ii) Any person who discloses or uses non-public OCC information except as expressly permitted by the Comptroller of the Currency or as ordered by a Federal court, under paragraph (b)(1)(i) of this section, may be subject to the penalties provided in 18 U.S.C. 641.

(2) *Exception for national banks and Federal savings associations.* When necessary or appropriate for business purposes, a national bank, Federal savings association, or holding company, or any director, officer, or employee thereof, may disclose non-public OCC information, including information contained in, or related to, OCC reports of examination, to a person or organization officially connected with the bank or Federal savings association as officer, director, employee, attorney, auditor, or independent auditor. A national bank, Federal savings association, or holding company or a director, officer, or employee thereof, may also release non-public OCC information to a consultant under this paragraph if the consultant is under a written contract to provide services to the bank or Federal savings association and the consultant has a written agreement with the bank or Federal savings association in which the consultant:

(i) States its awareness of, and agreement to abide by, the prohibition on the dissemination of non-public OCC information contained in paragraph (b)(1) of this section; and

(ii) Agrees not to use the non-public OCC information for any purpose other than as provided under its contract to provide services to the bank or Federal savings association.

(3) *Duty of person or entity served.* Any person, national bank, Federal savings association, or other entity served with a request, subpoena, order, motion to compel, or other judicial or administrative process to provide non-public OCC information shall:

(i) Immediately notify the Director of the OCC's Litigation Division at the Washington, DC office and inform the Director of all relevant facts, including the documents and information requested, so that the OCC may intervene in the judicial or administrative action if appropriate;

(ii) Inform the requester of the substance of these rules and, in particular, of the obligation to follow the request procedures in §§4.33 and 4.34; and

(iii) At the appropriate time, inform the court or tribunal that issued the process of the substance of these rules.

(4) *Actions of the OCC following notice of service.* Following receipt of notice pursuant to paragraph (b)(3) of this section, the OCC may direct the requester to comply with §§4.33 and 4.34, intervene in the judicial or administrative action, attempt to have the compulsory process withdrawn, or register other appropriate objections.

(5) *Return of records.* The OCC may require any person in possession of OCC records to return the records to the OCC.

(c) *Disclosure to government agencies.* When not prohibited by law, the Comptroller may make available to the Board of Governors of the Federal Reserve System, the Federal Deposit Insurance Corporation, and, in the Comptroller's sole discretion, to certain other government agencies of the United States and foreign governments, state agencies with authority to investigate violations of criminal law, and state bank and state savings association regulatory agencies, a copy of a report of examination, testimony, or other non-public OCC information for their use, when necessary, in the performance of their official duties. All non-public OCC information made available pursuant to this paragraph is OCC property, and the OCC may condition its use on appropriate confidentiality protections, including the mechanisms identified in §4.38.

(d) *Intention of OCC not to waive rights.* The possession by any of the entities or individuals described in paragraphs (a), (b), and (c) of this section of non-public OCC information does not constitute a waiver by the OCC of its right to control, or impose limitations on, the subsequent use and dissemination of the information.

[60 FR 57322, Nov. 15, 1995. Redesignated and amended at 63 FR 62929, Nov. 10, 1998; 64 FR 29217, June 1, 1999; 75 FR 75576, Dec. 3, 2010; 76 FR 43563, July 21, 2011]

§4.38 Restrictions on dissemination of released information.

(a) *Records.* The OCC may condition a decision to release non-public OCC information on entry of a protective order by the court or administrative tribunal presiding in the particular case or, in non-adversarial matters, on a written agreement of confidentiality. In a case in which a protective order has already been entered, the OCC may condition approval for release of non-public OCC information upon the inclusion of additional or amended provisions in the protective order. The OCC may authorize a party who obtained records for use in one case to provide them to another party in another case.

(b) *Testimony.* The OCC may condition its authorization of deposition testimony on an agreement of the parties to appropriate limitations, such as an agreement to keep the transcript of the testimony under seal or to make the transcript available only to the parties, the court, and the jury. Upon request or on its own initiative, the OCC may allow use of a transcript in other litigation. The OCC may require the requester, at the requester's expense, to furnish the OCC with a copy of the transcript. The OCC employee whose deposition was transcribed does not waive his or her right to review the transcript and to note errors.

[60 FR 57322, Nov. 15, 1995. Redesignated at 63 FR 62929, Nov. 10, 1998]

§4.39 Notification of parties and procedures for sharing and using OCC records in litigation.

(a) *Responsibility of litigants to notify parties of a request for testimony.* Upon submitting a request to the OCC for the testimony of an OCC employee or former OCC or OTS employee, the requester shall notify all other parties to the case that a request has been submitted.

(b) *Responsibility of litigants to share released records.* The requester shall promptly notify other parties to a case of the release of non-public OCC information obtained pursuant to this subpart, and, upon entry of a protective order, shall provide copies of OCC information, including OCC information obtained pursuant to § 4.15, to the other parties.

(c) *Retrieval and destruction of released records.* At the conclusion of an action:

(1) The requester shall retrieve any non-public OCC information from the court's file as soon as the court no longer requires the information;

(2) Each party shall destroy the non-public OCC information covered by the protective order; and

(3) Each party shall certify to the OCC that the non-public OCC information covered by the protective order has been destroyed.

(d) *Authentication for use as evidence.* Upon request, the OCC authenticates released records to facilitate their use as evidence. Requesters who require authenticated records or certificates of nonexistence of records should, as early as possible, request certificates from the OCC's Litigation Division pursuant to § 4.34(a).

[60 FR 57322, Nov. 15, 1995. Redesignated at 63 FR 62929, Nov. 10, 1998; 76 FR 43563, July 21, 2011]

§ 4.40 Fees for services.

(a) *Fees for records search, copying, and certification.* The requester shall pay a fee to the OCC, or to a commercial copier under contract to the OCC, for any records search, copying, or certification in accordance with the standards specified in § 4.17. The OCC may require a requester to remit payment prior to providing the requested information.

(b) *Witness fees and mileage.* A person whose request for testimony of a current OCC employee is approved shall, upon completion of the testimonial appearance, tender promptly to the OCC payment for the witness fees and mileage. The litigant shall compute these amounts in accordance with 28 U.S.C. 1821. A litigant whose request for testimony of a former OCC employee is approved shall tender promptly to the witness any witness fees or mileage due in accordance with 28 U.S.C. 1821.

[60 FR 57322, Nov. 15, 1995. Redesignated at 63 FR 62929, Nov. 10, 1998]

Appendix A to Subpart C of Part 4—Model Stipulation for Protective Order and Model Protective Order

I. Model Stipulation

CASE CAPTION

Model Stipulation for Protective Order

Whereas, counsel for __________ have applied to the Comptroller of the Currency (hereinafter "Comptroller") pursuant to 12 CFR part 4, Subpart C, for permission to have made available, in connection with the captioned action, certain records; and

Whereas, such records are deemed by the Comptroller to be confidential and privileged, pursuant to 12 U.S.C. 481, 1463(a)(1), 1464(a)(1) and 1464(d)(1)(B)(i); 5 U.S.C. 552(b)(8); 18 U.S.C. 641, 1906; and 12 CFR 4.12, and part 4, Subpart C; and

Whereas, following consideration by the Comptroller of the application of the above described party, the Comptroller has determined that the particular circumstances of the captioned action warrant making certain possibly relevant records as denoted in appendix "A" to this Stipulation [records to be specified by type and date] available to the parties in this action, provided that appropriate protection of their confidentiality can be secured;

Therefore, it is hereby stipulated by and between the parties hereto, through their respective attorneys that they will be bound by the following protective order which may be entered by the Court without further notice.

Dated this __________ day of __________, 19___.

____

Attorney for Plaintiff

____

Attorney for Defendant

II. Model Protective Order

CASE CAPTION

Model Protective Order

Whereas, counsel for __________ have applied to the Comptroller of the Currency (hereinafter Comptroller") pursuant to 12 CFR part 4, Subpart C, for permission to have made available, in connection with the captioned action, certain records; and

Whereas, such records are deemed by the Comptroller to be confidential and privileged, pursuant to 12 U.S.C. 481, 1463(a)(1), 1464(a)(1) and 1464(d)(1)(B)(i); 5 U.S.C. 552(b)(8); 18 U.S.C. 641, 1906; and 12 CFR 4.12, and part 4, Subpart C;

Whereas, following consideration by the Comptroller of the application of the above described party, the Comptroller has determined that the particular circumstances of the captioned action warrant making certain possibly relevant records available to the parties in this action, provided that appropriate protection of their confidentiality can be secured;

Now, Therefore, it is Ordered That:

1. The records, as denoted in appendix "A" to the Stipulation for this Protective Order, upon being furnished [or released for use] by the Comptroller, shall be disclosed only to the parties to this action, their counsel, and the court [and the jury].

2. The parties to this action and their counsel shall keep such records and any information contained in such records confidential and shall in no way divulge the same to any person or entity, except to such experts, consultants and non-party witnesses to whom the records and their contents shall be disclosed, solely for the purpose of properly preparing for and trying the action.

3. No person to whom information and records covered by this Order are disclosed shall make any copies or otherwise use such information or records or their contents for any purpose whatsoever, except in connection with this action.

4. Any party or other person who wishes to use the information or records or their contents in any other action shall make a separate application to the Comptroller pursuant to 12 CFR part 4, Subpart C.

5. Should any records covered by this Order be filed with the Court or utilized as exhibits at depositions in the captioned action, or should information or records or their contents covered by this Order be disclosed in the transcripts of depositions or the trial in the captioned action, such records, exhibits and transcripts shall be filed in sealed envelopes or other sealed containers marked with the title of this action, identifying each document and article therein and bearing a statement substantially in the following form:

CONFIDENTIAL

Pursuant to the Order of the Court dated ________ this envelope containing the above-identified papers filed by (the name of the party) is not to be opened nor the contents thereof displayed or revealed except to the parties to this action or their counsel or by further Order of the Court.

6. FOR JURY TRIAL: Any party offering any of the records into evidence shall offer only those pages, or portions thereof, that are relevant and material to the issues to be decided in the action and shall block out any portion of any page that contains information not relevant or material. Furthermore, the name of any person or entity contained on any page of the records who is not a party to this action, or whose name is not otherwise relevant or material to the action, shall be blocked out prior to the admission of such page into evidence. Any disagreement regarding what portion of any page that should be blocked out in this manner shall be resolved by the Court *in camera*, and the Court shall decide its admissibility into evidence.

7. At the conclusion of this action, all parties shall certify to the Comptroller that the records covered by this Order have been destroyed. Furthermore, counsel for ________, pursuant to 12 CFR 4.39(c), shall retrieve any records covered by this Order that may have been filed with the Court.

So Ordered:

____

Judge

Date

[60 FR 57322, Nov. 15, 1995, as amended at 64 FR 29217, June 1, 1999]

Subpart D—Minority- , Women- , and Individuals With Disabilities-Owned Business Contracting Outreach Program; Contracting for Goods and Services

§4.61 Purpose.

Pursuant to the Financial Institutions Reform, Recovery, and Enforcement Act of 1989, Sec. 1216(c), Pub. L. 101–73, 103 Stat. 183, 529 (12 U.S.C. 1833e(c)) and consistent with the Rehabilitation Act of 1973, as amended (29 U.S.C. 701 *et seq.*), this subpart establishes the OCC Minority- , Women- , and Individuals with Disabilities-Owned Business Contracting Outreach Program (Outreach Program). The Outreach Program is intended to ensure that firms owned and operated by minorities, women, and individuals with disabilities have the opportunity to participate, to the maximum extent possible, in all contracting activities of the OCC.

§4.62 Definitions.

(a) *Minority- and/or women-owned (small and large) businesses and entities owned by minorities and women (MWOB)* means firms at least 51 percent unconditionally-owned by one or more members of a minority group or by one or more women who are citizens of the United States. In the case of publicly-owned companies, at least 51 percent of each class of voting stock must be unconditionally-owned by one or more members of a minority group or by one or more women who are citizens of the United States. In the case of a partnership, at least 51 percent of the partnership interest must be unconditionally-owned by one or more members of a minority group or by one or more women who are citizens of the United States. Additionally, for the foregoing cases, the management and daily business operations must be controlled by one or more such individuals.

(b) *Minority* means any African American, Native American (*i.e.*, American Indian, Eskimo, Aleut and Native Hawaiian), Hispanic American, Asian-Pacific American, or Subcontinent-Asian American.

(c) *Individual with disabilities-owned (small and large) businesses and entities owned by individuals with disabilities (IDOB)* means firms at least 51 percent unconditionally-owned by one or more members who are individuals with disabilities and citizens of the United States. In the case of publicly-owned companies, at least 51 percent of each class of voting stock must be unconditionally-owned by one or more members who are individuals with disabilities and who are citizens of the United States. In the case of a partnership, at least 51 percent of the partnership interest must be unconditionally-owned by one or more members who are individuals with disabilities and citizens of the United States. Additionally, for the foregoing cases, the management and daily business operations must be controlled by one or more such individuals.

(d) *Individual with disabilities* means any person who has a physical or mental impairment that substantially limits one or more of such person's major life activities, has a record of such an impairment, or is regarded as having such an impairment. For purposes of this part, it does not include an individual who is currently engaging in the illegal use of drugs nor an individual who has a currently contagious disease or infection and who, by reason of such disease or infection, would constitute a direct threat to the health or safety of other individuals or who, by reason of the currently contagious disease or infection, is unable to perform the duties of the job as defined by the IDOB.

(e) *Unconditional ownership* means ownership that is not subject to conditions or similar arrangements which cause the benefits of the Outreach Program to accrue to persons other than the participating MWOB or IDOB.

§ 4.63 Policy.

The OCC's policy is to ensure that MWOBs and IDOBs have the opportunity to participate, to the maximum extent possible, in contracts awarded by the OCC. The OCC awards contracts consistent with the principles of full and open competition and best value acquisition, and with the concept of contracting for agency needs at the lowest practicable cost. The OCC ensures that MWOBs and IDOBs have the opportunity to participate fully in all contracting activities that the OCC enters into for goods and services, whether generated by the headquarters office in Washington, DC, or any other office of the OCC. Contracting opportunities may include small purchase awards, contracts above the small purchase threshold, and delivery orders issued against other governmental agency contracts.

§ 4.64 Promotion.

(a) *Scope*. The OCC, under the direction of the Deputy Comptroller for Resource Management, engages in promotion and outreach activities designed to identify MWOBs and IDOBs capable of providing goods and services needed by the OCC, to facilitate interaction between the OCC and the MWOBs and IDOBs community, and to indicate the OCC's commitment to doing business with that community. The Outreach Program is designed to facilitate OCC's participation in business promotion events sponsored by other government agencies and attended by minorities, women and individuals with disabilities. Once the OCC has identified a prospective participant, it will assist the minority- or women-owned business or individual with disabilities-owned business in understanding the OCC's needs and contracting process.

(b) *Outreach activities*. OCC's Outreach Program includes the following:

(1) Obtaining various lists and directories of MWOBs and IDOBs maintained by government agencies;

(2) Contacting appropriate firms for participation in the OCC's Outreach Program;

(3) Participating in business promotion events comprised of or attended by MWOBs and IDOBs to explain OCC contracting opportunities and to obtain names of potential MWOBs and IDOBs;

(4) Ensuring that the OCC contracting staff understands and actively promotes this Outreach Program; and

(5) Registering MWOBs and IDOBs in the Department of the Treasury's database to facilitate their participation in the competitive procurement process for OCC contracts. This database is used by OCC procurement staff to identify firms to be solicited for OCC procurements.

§4.65 Certification.

(a) *Objective.* To preserve the integrity and foster the Outreach Program's objectives, each prospective MWOB or IDOB must demonstrate that it meets the ownership and control requirements for participation in the Outreach Program.

(b) *MWOB.* A prospective MWOB may demonstrate its eligibility for participation in the Outreach Program by:

(1) Submitting a valid MWOB certification received from another government agency whose definition of MWOB is substantially similar to that specified in §4.62(a);

(2) Self-certifying MWOB ownership status by filing with the OCC a completed and signed certification form as prescribed by the Federal Acquisition Regulation, 48 CFR 53.301–129; or

(3) Submitting a valid MWOB certification received from the Small Business Administration.

(c) *IDOB.* A prospective IDOB may demonstrate its eligibility for participation in the Outreach Program by:

(1) Submitting a valid IDOB certification received from another government agency whose definition of IDOB is substantially similar to that specified in §4.62(c); or

(2) Self-certifying IDOB ownership status by filing with the OCC a completed and signed certification as prescribed in the Federal Acquisition Regulation, 48 CFR 53.301–129, and adding an additional certifying statement to read as follows:

I certify that I am an individual with disabilities as defined in 12 CFR 4.62(d), and that my firm, (Name of Firm) qualifies as an individual with disabilities-owned business as defined in 12 CFR 4.62(c).

§4.66 Oversight and monitoring.

The Deputy Comptroller for Resource Management shall appoint an Outreach Program Manager, who shall appoint an Outreach Program Specialist. The Outreach Program Manager is primarily responsible for program advocacy, oversight and monitoring.

Subpart E—One-Year Restrictions on Post-Employment Activities of Senior Examiners

SOURCE: 70 FR 69637, Nov. 17, 2005, unless otherwise noted.

§4.72 Scope and purpose.

This subpart describes those OCC examiners who are subject to the post-employment restrictions set forth in section 10(k) of the Federal Deposit Insurance Act (FDI Act) (12 U.S.C. 1820(k)) and implements those restrictions for officers and employees of the OCC.

§4.73 Definitions.

For purposes of this subpart:

Bank holding company means any company that controls a bank (as provided in section 2 of the Bank Holding Company Act of 1956 (12 U.S.C. 1841 *et seq.*)).

Consultant. For purposes of this subpart, a consultant for a national bank, savings association, bank holding company, savings and loan holding company, or other company shall include only an individual who works directly on matters for, or on behalf of, such bank, savings association, bank holding company, savings and loan holding company, or other company.

Control has the meaning given in section 2 of the Bank Holding Company Act (12 U.S.C. 1841(a)) or in section 10 of the Home Owners' Loan Act (12 U.S.C. 1467a), as applicable under the circumstances. For purposes of this subpart, a foreign bank shall be deemed to control any branch or agency of the foreign bank.

Depository institution has the meaning given in section 3 of the FDI Act (12 U.S.C. 1813(c)). For purposes of this subpart, a depository institution includes an uninsured branch or agency of a foreign bank, if such branch or agency is located in any State.

Federal Reserve means the Board of Governors of the Federal Reserve System and the Federal Reserve Banks.

Foreign bank means any foreign bank or company described in section 8(a) of the International Banking Act of 1978 (12 U.S.C. 3106(a)).

Insured depository institution has the meaning given in section 3 of the FDI Act (12 U.S.C. 1813(c)(2)).

National bank means a national banking association or a Federal branch or agency of a foreign bank.

Savings association has the meaning given in section 3 of the FDI Act (12 U.S.C. 1813(b)(1)).

Savings and loan holding company means any company that controls a savings association or any other company that is a savings and loan holding company (as provided in section 10 of the Home Owners' Loan Act (12 U.S.C. 1467a)).

Senior examiner. For purposes of this subpart, an officer or employee of the OCC is considered to be the "senior examiner" for a particular national bank or savings association if—

(1) The officer or employee has been authorized by the OCC to conduct examinations on behalf of the OCC;

(2) The officer or employee has been assigned continuing, broad, and lead responsibility for examining the national bank or savings association; and

(3) The officer's or employee's responsibilities for examining the national bank or savings association—

(i) Represent a substantial portion of the officer's or employee's assigned responsibilities; and

(ii) Require the officer or employee to interact routinely with officers or employees of the national bank or savings association, or its affiliates."

[70 FR 69637, Nov. 17, 2005, as amended at 76 FR 43563, July 21, 2011]

§4.74 One-year post-employment restrictions.

An officer or employee of the OCC who serves as the senior examiner of a national bank or savings association for two or more months during the last twelve months of such individual's employment with the OCC may not, within one year after leaving the employment of the OCC, knowingly accept compensation as an employee, officer, director or consultant from the national bank, savings association, or any company (including a bank holding company or savings and loan holding company) that controls the national bank or savings association.

[76 FR 43564, July 21, 2011]

§4.75 Waivers.

The post-employment restrictions set forth in section 10(k) of the FDI Act (12 U.S.C. 1820(k)) and §4.74 do not apply to any officer or employee of the OCC, or any former officer or employee of the OCC, if the Comptroller of the Currency certifies, in writing and on a case-by-case basis, that granting the individual a waiver of the restrictions would not affect the integrity of the OCC's supervisory program.

[76 FR 43564, July 21, 2011]

§4.76 Penalties.

(a) *Penalties under section 10(k) of FDI Act (12 U.S.C. 1820(k)).* If a senior examiner of a national bank or savings association, after leaving the employment of the OCC, accepts compensation as an employee, officer, director, or consultant from that bank, savings association, or any company (including a bank holding company or savings and loan holding company) that controls that bank or savings association in violation of §4.74, then the examiner shall, in accordance with section 10(k)(6) of the FDI Act (12 U.S.C. 1820(k)(6)), be subject to one of the following penalties—

(1) An order—

(i) Removing the individual from office or prohibiting the individual from further participation in the affairs of the relevant national bank, savings association, bank holding company, savings and loan holding company, or other company that controls such institution for a period of up to five years; and

(ii) Prohibiting the individual from participating in the affairs of any insured depository institution for a period of up to five years; or

(2) A civil monetary penalty of not more than $250,000.

(b) *Enforcement by appropriate Federal banking agency.* Violations of § 4.74 shall be administered or enforced by the appropriate Federal banking agency for the depository institution or depository institution holding company that provided compensation to the former senior examiner. For purposes of this paragraph, the appropriate Federal banking agency for a company that is not a depository institution or depository institution holding company shall be the Federal banking agency that formerly employed the senior examiner.

(c) *Scope of prohibition orders.* Any senior examiner who is subject to an order issued under paragraph (a) of this section shall, as required by 12 U.S.C. 1820(k)(6)(B), be subject to paragraphs (6) and (7) of section 8(e) of the FDI Act (12 U.S.C. 1818(e)(6)–(7)) in the same manner and to the same extent as a person subject to an order issued under section 8(e).

(d) *Procedures.* The procedures applicable to actions under paragraph (a) of this section are provided in section 10(k)(6) of the FDI Act (12 U.S.C. 1820(k)(6)) and in 12 CFR part 19.

(e) *Remedies not exclusive.* The OCC may seek both of the penalties described in paragraph (a) of this section. In addition, a senior examiner who accepts compensation as described in § 4.74 may be subject to other administrative, civil or criminal remedies or penalties as provided in law.

[60 FR 57322, Nov. 15, 1995, as amended at 76 FR 43564, July 21, 2011]

PART 5—RULES, POLICIES, AND PROCEDURES FOR CORPORATE ACTIVITIES

Sec.

5.1 Scope.

Subpart A—Rules of General Applicability

5.2 Rules of general applicability.
5.3 Definitions.
5.4 Filing required.
5.5 Filing fees.
5.6 [Reserved]
5.7 Investigations.
5.8 Public notice.
5.9 Public availability.
5.10 Comments.
5.11 Hearings and other meetings.
5.12 Computation of time.
5.13 Decisions.

Subpart B—Initial Activities

5.20 Organizing a national bank or Federal savings association.
5.21 Federal mutual savings association charter and bylaws.
5.22 Federal stock savings association charter and bylaws.
5.23 Conversion to become a Federal savings association.
5.24 Conversion to become a national bank.
5.25 Conversion from a national bank or Federal savings association to a state bank or state savings association.
5.26 Fiduciary powers of national banks and Federal savings associations.

Subpart C—Expansion of Activities

5.30 Establishment, acquisition, and relocation of a branch of a national bank.
5.31 Establishment, acquisition, and relocation of a branch and establishment of an agency office of a Federal savings association.
5.32 Expedited procedures for certain reorganizations of a national bank.
5.33 Business combinations involving a national bank or Federal savings association.
5.34 Operating subsidiaries of a national bank.
5.35 Bank service company investments by a national bank or Federal savings association investment.
5.36 Other equity investments by a national bank.
5.37 Investment in national bank or Federal savings association premises.
5.38 Operating subsidiaries of a Federal savings association.
5.39 Financial subsidiaries of a national bank.

Subpart D—Other Changes in Activities and Operations

5.40 Change in location of a main office of a national bank or home office of a Federal savings association.
5.42 Corporate title of a national bank or Federal savings association.

5.45 Increases in permanent capital of a Federal stock savings association.
5.46 Changes in permanent capital of a national bank.
5.47 Subordinated debt issued by a national bank.
5.48 Voluntary liquidation of a national bank or Federal savings association.
5.50 Change in control of a national bank or Federal savings association; reporting of stock loans.
5.51 Changes in directors and senior executive officers of a national bank or Federal savings association.
5.52 Change of address of a national bank or Federal savings association.
5.53 Substantial asset change by a national bank or Federal savings association.
5.55 Capital distributions by Federal savings associations.
5.56 Inclusion of subordinated debt securities and mandatorily redeemable preferred stock as Federal savings association supplementary (tier 2) capital.
5.58 Pass-through investments by a Federal savings association.
5.59 Service corporations of Federal savings associations.

Subpart E—Payment of Dividends by National Banks

5.60 Authority, scope, and exceptions to rules of general applicability.
5.61 Definitions.
5.62 Date of declaration of dividend.
5.63 Capital limitation under 12 U.S.C. 56.
5.64 Earnings limitation under 12 U.S.C. 60.
5.65 Restrictions on undercapitalized institutions.
5.66 Dividends payable in property other than cash.
5.67 Fractional shares.

Subpart F—Federal Branches and Agencies

5.70 Federal branches and agencies.

AUTHORITY: 12 U.S.C. 1 *et seq.*, 24a, 93a, 215a–2, 215a–3, 481, 1462a, 1463, 1464, 2901 *et seq.*, 3907, and 5412(b)(2)(B).

SOURCE: 61 FR 60363, Nov. 27, 1996, unless otherwise noted.

§5.1 Scope.

This part establishes rules, policies and procedures of the Office of the Comptroller of the Currency (OCC) for corporate activities and transactions involving national banks and Federal savings associations. It contains information on rules of general and specific applicability, where and how to file, and requirements and policies applicable to filings. This part also establishes the corporate filing procedures for Federal branches and agencies of foreign banks.

[80 FR 28414, May 18, 2015]

Subpart A—Rules of General Applicability

SOURCE: 80 FR 28414, May 18, 2015, unless otherwise noted.

§5.2 Rules of general applicability.

(a) *In general.* The rules in this subpart apply to all sections in this part unless otherwise stated.

(b) *Exceptions.* The OCC may adopt materially different procedures for a particular filing, or class of filings, in exceptional circumstances or for unusual transactions, after providing notice of the change to the applicant and to any other party that the OCC determines should receive notice.

(c) *Comptroller's Licensing Manual.* The "Comptroller's Licensing Manual" provides additional filing guidance, including policies and procedures. This Manual and sample forms are available on the OCC's Internet Web page at *www.occ.gov.*

(d) *Electronic filing.* The OCC encourages electronic filing for all filings. The Comptroller's Licensing Manual describes the OCC's electronic filing procedures.

§5.3 Definitions.

As used in this part:

(a) *Applicant* means a person or entity that submits a notice or application to the OCC under this part.

(b) *Application* means a submission requesting OCC approval to engage in various corporate activities and transactions.

(c) *Appropriate OCC licensing office* means the OCC office that is responsible for processing applications or notices to engage in various corporate activities or transactions, as described at *www.occ.gov.*

(d) *Appropriate OCC supervisory office* means the OCC office that is responsible for the supervision of a national bank or Federal savings association, as described in subpart A of 12 CFR part 4.

(e) *Capital and surplus* means:

(1) A bank's or Federal savings association's tier 1 and tier 2 capital calculated under the OCC's risk-based capital standards set forth in 12 CFR part 3, as applicable, as reported in the bank's or savings association's Consolidated Reports of Condition and Income (Call Reports) filed under 12 U.S.C. 161 or 12 U.S.C. 1464(v), respectively; plus

(2) The balance of the national bank's or Federal savings association's allowance for loan and lease losses not included in the institution's tier 2 capital, for purposes of the calculation of risk-based capital reported in the institution's Call Reports, described in paragraph (e)(1) of this section.

(f) *Depository institution* means any bank or savings association.

(g) *Eligible bank or eligible savings association* means a national bank or Federal savings association that:

(1) Is well capitalized as defined in 12 CFR 6.4;

(2) Has a composite rating of 1 or 2 under the Uniform Financial Institutions Rating System (CAMELS);

(3) Has a Community Reinvestment Act (CRA), 12 U.S.C. 2901 *et seq.*, rating of "Outstanding" or "Satisfactory," if applicable;

(4) Has a consumer compliance rating of 1 or 2 under the Uniform Interagency Consumer Compliance Rating System; and

(5) Is not subject to a cease and desist order, consent order, formal written agreement, or Prompt Corrective Action directive (*see* 12 CFR part 6, subpart B) or, if subject to any such order, agreement, or directive, is informed in writing by the OCC that the bank or savings association may be treated as an "eligible bank or eligible savings association" for purposes of this part.

(h) *Eligible depository institution* means:

(1) With respect to a national bank, a state bank or a Federal or state savings association that meets the criteria for an "eligible bank or eligible savings association" under §5.3(g) and is FDIC-insured; and

(2) With respect to a Federal savings association, a state or national bank or a state savings association that meets the criteria for an "eligible bank or eligible savings association" under §5.3(g) and is FDIC-insured.

(i) *Filing* means an application or notice submitted to the OCC under this part.

(j) *Notice*, in general, means a submission notifying the OCC that a national bank or Federal savings association intends to engage in or has commenced certain corporate activities or transactions. The specific meaning of *notice* depends on the context of the rule in which it is used and may require the filer to obtain prior OCC approval before engaging in the activity or transaction, may provide the OCC with authority to disapprove the notice, or may be informational requiring no official OCC action.

(k) *Principal city* means an area designated as a "principal city" by the Office of Management and Budget.

(l) *Short-distance relocation* means moving the premises of a branch or main office of a national bank or a branch or home office of a Federal savings association within a:

(1) One thousand foot-radius of the site if the branch, main office, or home office is located within a principal city of an MSA;

(2) One-mile radius of the site if the branch, main office, or home office is not located within a principal city, but is located within an MSA; or

(3) Two-mile radius of the site if the branch, main office, or home office is not located within an MSA.

§5.4 Filing required.

(a) *Filing*. A depository institution shall file an application or notice with the OCC to engage in corporate activities and transactions as described in this part.

(b) *Availability of forms*. Forms and instructions for filing are available on the OCC's Internet Web page at *www.occ.gov.*

(c) *Other agency's applications or filings*. At the request of the applicant, the OCC may accept an application or other filing submitted to another Federal agency that covers the proposed action or transaction and contains substantially the same information as required by the OCC. The OCC also may require the applicant to submit supplemental information.

(d) *Where to file*. An applicant should address a filing or other submission under this part to the appropriate OCC licensing office or appropriate OCC supervisory office, unless the OCC advises an applicant otherwise. Relevant addresses are listed on the OCC's Internet Web page at *www.occ.gov*.

(e) *Incorporation of other material.* An applicant may incorporate any material contained in any other application or filing filed with the OCC or other Federal agency by reference, provided that the material is attached to the application and is current and responsive to the information requested by the OCC. The filing must clearly indicate that the information is so incorporated and include a cross-reference to the information incorporated.

(f) *Prefiling meeting.* When submitting an application to the OCC, an applicant is encouraged to contact the appropriate OCC licensing office to determine the need for a prefiling meeting. The OCC decides whether to require a prefiling meeting on a case-by-case basis. Submission of a draft business plan or other relevant information before any prefiling meeting may expedite the filing review process. Information on model business plans can be found in the Comptroller's Licensing Manual.

§ 5.5 Filing fees.

(a) *Procedure.* An applicant shall submit the appropriate filing fee, if any, in connection with its filing. Filing fees may be paid by check, money order, cashier's check, or wire transfer. Additional information on filing fees, including where to file, can be found in the Comptroller's Licensing Manual. The OCC generally does not refund the filing fees.

(b) *Fee schedule.* The OCC publishes a fee schedule in the "Notice of Comptroller of the Currency Fees," as described in 12 CFR 8.8.

§ 5.6 [Reserved]

§ 5.7 Investigations.

(a) *Authority.* The OCC may examine or investigate and evaluate facts related to a filing to the extent necessary to reach an informed decision.

(b) *Fees.* As described in 12 CFR 8.6, the OCC may assess fees for investigations or examinations conducted under paragraph (a) of this section. The OCC publishes a fee schedule in the "Notice of Comptroller of the Currency Fees," as described in 12 CFR 8.8.

§ 5.8 Public notice.

(a) *In general.* An applicant shall publish a public notice of its filing in a newspaper of general circulation in the community in which the applicant proposes to engage in business, on the date of filing, or as soon as practicable before or after the date of filing. This notice shall be published in the English language but if the OCC determines that the primary language of a significant number of adult residents of the community is a language other than English, the OCC may require that an additional notice(s) simultaneously be published in the community in the appropriate language(s).

(b) *Contents of the public notice.* The public notice shall state that a filing is being made, the date of the filing, the name and address of the applicant, the subject matter of the filing (including the name of the institution that is the subject of the filing), that the public may submit comments to the appropriate OCC licensing office, the address of the appropriate OCC licensing office where comments should be sent, the closing date of the public comment period (if known at the time of publication of the notice), that the public portion of the filing is available on request, that the public may find information about the filing (including the closing date of the comment period) in the OCC's Weekly Bulletin available at *www.occ.gov*, and any other information that the OCC requires.

(c) *Confirmation of public notice.* Promptly following publication, the applicant shall mail or otherwise deliver to the appropriate OCC licensing office a statement containing the date of publication, the name and address of the newspaper that published the public notice, a copy of the public notice, and any other information that the OCC requires.

(d) *Multiple transactions.* The OCC may consider more than one transaction, or a series of transactions, to be a single filing for purposes of the publication requirements of this section. When filing a single public notice for multiple transactions, the applicant shall explain in the notice how the transactions are related.

(e) *Joint public notices accepted.* Upon the request of an applicant, for a transaction subject to a public notice requirement of both the OCC and another Federal agency, the OCC may accept publication of a single joint notice containing the information required by both the OCC and the other Federal agency, provided that the notice states that comments must be submitted to both the OCC and, if applicable, the other Federal agency.

(f) *Public notice by the OCC.* In addition to the foregoing, the OCC may require or give public notice and request comment on any filing and in any manner the OCC determines appropriate for the particular filing.

(g) *New public notice.* At the OCC's discretion, an applicant may be required to publish a new public notice if:

(1) The applicant submits either a revised filing or new or additional information related to a filing;

(2) A major issue of law or change in circumstance arises after a filing; or

(3) The OCC determines that a new public notice is appropriate.

[80 FR 28414, May 18, 2015, as amended at 82 FR 8103, Jan. 23, 2017]

§5.9 Public availability.

(a) *In general.* The OCC provides a copy of the public file to any person who requests it. A requestor should submit a written request for the public file concerning a pending filing to the appropriate OCC licensing office. A requestor should submit a written request for the public file concerning a decided or closed filing to the OCC's Freedom of Information Act Officer, Communications Division, at the address listed on *www.occ.gov.* The OCC may impose a fee in accordance with 12 CFR 4.17 and at the rate the OCC publishes in the "Notice of Comptroller of the Currency Fees," described in 12 CFR 8.8.

(b) *Public file.* A public file consists of the portions of the filing, supporting data, supplementary information, and information submitted by interested persons, to the extent that those documents have not been afforded confidential treatment. Applicants and other interested persons may request that confidential treatment be afforded information submitted to the OCC pursuant to paragraph (c) of this section.

(c) *Confidential treatment.* The applicant or an interested person submitting information may request that specific information be treated as confidential under the Freedom of Information Act, 5 U.S.C. 552 (*see* 12 CFR 4.12(b)). A submitter should draft its request for confidential treatment narrowly to extend only to those portions of a document it considers confidential. If a submitter requests confidential treatment for information that the OCC does not consider to be confidential, the OCC may include that information in the public file after providing notice to the submitter. Moreover, at its own initiative, the OCC may determine that certain information should be treated as confidential and withhold that information from the public file. A person requesting information withheld from the public file should submit the request to the OCC's Freedom of Information Act Officer, Communications Division, under the procedures described in 12 CFR part 4, subpart B. That request may be subject to the predisclosure notice procedures of 12 CFR 4.16.

§5.10 Comments.

(a) *Submission of comments.* During the comment period, any person may submit written comments on a filing to the appropriate OCC licensing office.

(b) *Comment period*—(1) *In general.* Unless otherwise stated, the comment period is 30 days after publication of the public notice required by §5.8(a). If a new public notice is required under §5.8(g), the OCC may require a new comment period of up to 30 days after publication of the new public notice.

(2) *Extension.* The OCC may extend a comment period if:

(i) The applicant fails to file all required publicly available information on a timely basis to permit review by interested persons or makes a request for confidential treatment not granted by the OCC that delays the public availability of that information;

(ii) Any person requesting an extension of time satisfactorily demonstrates to the OCC that additional time is necessary to develop factual information that the OCC determines is necessary to consider the application; or

(iii) The OCC determines that other extenuating circumstances exist.

(3) *Applicant response.* The OCC may give the applicant an opportunity to respond to comments received.

§ 5.11 Hearings and other meetings.

(a) *Hearing requests.* Prior to the end of the comment period, any person may submit to the appropriate OCC office a written request for a hearing on a filing. The request must describe the nature of the issues or facts to be presented and the reasons why written submissions would be insufficient to make an adequate presentation of those issues or facts to the OCC. A person requesting a hearing shall simultaneously submit a copy of the request to the applicant.

(b) *Action on a hearing request.* The OCC may grant or deny a request for a hearing and may limit the issues to those it deems relevant or material. The OCC generally grants a hearing request only if the OCC determines that written submissions would be insufficient or that a hearing would otherwise benefit the decision-making process. The OCC also may order a hearing if it concludes that a hearing would be in the public interest.

(c) *Denial of a hearing request.* If the OCC denies a hearing request, it shall notify the person requesting the hearing of the reason for the denial.

(d) *OCC procedures prior to the hearing*—(1) *Notice of hearing.* The OCC issues a Notice of Hearing if it grants a request for a hearing or orders a hearing because it is in the public interest. The OCC sends a copy of the Notice of Hearing to the applicant, to the person requesting the hearing, and anyone else requesting a copy. The Notice of Hearing states the subject and date of the filing, the time and place of the hearing, and the issues to be addressed. The OCC may limit the issues considered at a hearing to those it determines are relevant or material.

(2) *Presiding officer.* The OCC appoints a presiding officer to conduct the hearing. The presiding officer is responsible for all procedural questions not governed by this section.

(e) *Participation in the hearing.* Any person who wishes to appear (participant) shall notify the appropriate OCC licensing office of his or her intent to participate in the hearing within 10 days from the date the OCC issues the Notice of Hearing. At least five days before the hearing, each participant shall submit to the appropriate OCC licensing office, the applicant, and any other person the OCC requires, the names of witnesses and one copy of each exhibit the participant intends to present.

(f) *Hearing transcripts.* The OCC arranges for a hearing transcript. The person requesting the hearing may be required to bear the cost of one copy of the transcript for his or her use.

(g) *Conduct of the hearing*—(1) *Presentations.* Subject to the rulings of the presiding officer, the applicant and participants may make opening statements and present witnesses, material, and data.

(2) *Information submitted.* A person presenting documentary material shall furnish one copy to the OCC and one copy to the applicant and each participant.

(3) *Laws not applicable to hearings.* The Administrative Procedure Act (5 U.S.C. 551 *et seq.*), the Federal Rules of Evidence (28 U.S.C. appendix), the Federal Rules of Civil Procedure (28 U.S.C. Rule 1 *et seq.*), and the OCC's Rules of Practice and Procedure (12 CFR part 19) do not apply to hearings under this section.

(h) *Closing the hearing record.* At the applicant's or participant's request, the OCC may keep the hearing record open for up to 14 days following the OCC's receipt of the transcript. The OCC resumes processing the filing after the record closes.

(i) *Other meetings*—(1) *Public meetings.* The OCC may arrange for a public meeting in connection with an application, either upon receipt during the comment period of a written request for such a meeting or upon the OCC's own initiative, if the OCC finds that written submissions are insufficient to address facts or issues raised in the application or otherwise determines that a meeting will benefit the decision-making process. Public meetings will be arranged and presided over by a presiding officer.

(2) *Private meetings.* The OCC may arrange a meeting with an applicant or other interested parties to clarify and narrow the issues and to facilitate the resolution of the issues.

(3) *Issues at meetings.* The OCC may limit the issues considered at a meeting to those it determines are relevant or material.

(4) *Meeting format.* The OCC may conduct a meeting in the format that it determines is appropriate, including a telephone conference, a face-to-face meeting, or a more formal meeting.

§5.12 Computation of time.

In computing the period of days, the OCC does not include the day of the act or event (*e.g.*, the date an application is received by the OCC) from which the period begins to run. When the last day of a time period is a Saturday, Sunday, or Federal holiday, the time period runs until the end of the next day that is not a Saturday, Sunday or Federal holiday.

§5.13 Decisions.

(a) *In general.* The OCC may approve, conditionally approve, or deny a filing after appropriate review and consideration of the record. In reviewing a filing, the OCC may consider the activities, resources, or condition of an affiliate of the applicant that may reasonably reflect on or affect the applicant. It also may consider information available from any source, including any comments submitted by interested parties or views expressed by interested parties at meetings with the OCC.

(1) *Conditional approval.* The OCC may impose conditions on any approval, including to address a significant supervisory, CRA (if applicable), or compliance concern, if the OCC determines that the conditions are necessary or appropriate to ensure that approval is consistent with relevant statutory and regulatory standards and OCC policies thereunder and safe and sound banking practices.

(2) *Expedited review.* The OCC grants eligible banks and eligible savings associations expedited review within a specified time after filing or commencement of the public comment period.

(i) The OCC may extend the expedited review period or remove a filing from expedited review procedures if it concludes that the filing, or an adverse comment regarding the filing, presents a significant supervisory, CRA (if applicable), or compliance concern, or raises a significant legal or policy issue, requiring additional OCC review. The OCC will provide the applicant with a written explanation if it decides not to process an application from an eligible bank or eligible savings association under expedited review pursuant to this paragraph.

(ii) Adverse comments that the OCC determines do not raise a significant supervisory, CRA (if applicable), or compliance concern, or a significant legal or policy issue, or are frivolous, filed primarily as a means of delaying action on the filing, or that raise a CRA concern that the OCC determines has been satisfactorily resolved, do not affect the OCC's decision under paragraph (a)(2)(i) of this section. The OCC considers a CRA concern to have been satisfactorily resolved if the OCC previously reviewed (*e.g.*, in an examination or an application) a concern presenting substantially the same issue in substantially the same assessment area during substantially the same time, and the OCC determines that the concern would not warrant denial or imposition of a condition on approval of the application.

(iii) If a bank or savings association files an application for any activity or transaction that is dependent upon the approval of another application under this part, or if requests for approval for more than one activity or transaction are combined in a single application under applicable sections of this part, none of the subject applications may be deemed approved upon expiration of the applicable time periods, unless all of the applications are subject to expedited review procedures and the longest of the time periods expires without the OCC issuing a decision or notifying the bank or savings association that the filings are not eligible for expedited review under the standards in paragraph (a)(2)(i) of this section.

(b) *Denial.* The OCC may deny a filing if:

(1) A significant supervisory, CRA (if applicable), or compliance concern exists with respect to the applicant;

(2) Approval of the filing is inconsistent with applicable law, regulation, or OCC policy thereunder; or

(3) The applicant fails to provide information requested by the OCC that is necessary for the OCC to make an informed decision.

(c) *Required information and abandonment of filing.* A filing must contain information required by the applicable section set forth in this part. To the extent necessary to evaluate an application, the OCC may require an applicant to provide additional information. The OCC may deem a filing abandoned if information required or requested by the OCC in connection with the filing is not furnished within the time period specified by the OCC. The OCC may return an application without a decision if it finds the filing to be materially deficient. A filing is materially deficient if it lacks sufficient information for the OCC to make a determination under the applicable statutory or regulatory criteria.

(d) *Notification of final disposition.* The OCC notifies the applicant, and any person who makes a written request, of the final disposition of a filing, including confirmation of an expedited review under this part. If the OCC denies a filing, the OCC notifies the applicant in writing of the reasons for the denial.

(e) *Publication of decision.* The OCC will issue a public decision when a decision represents a new or changed policy or presents issues of general interest to the public or the banking industry. In rendering its decisions, the OCC may elect not to disclose information that the OCC deems to be private or confidential.

(f) *Appeal.* An applicant may file an appeal of an OCC decision in writing with the Deputy Comptroller for Licensing or with the Ombudsman at the address listed on *www.occ.gov.* In the event that the Deputy Comptroller for Licensing was the deciding official of the matter appealed, or was involved personally and substantially in the matter, the appeal may be referred instead to the Chief Counsel or the Ombudsman.

(g) *Extension of time.* When the OCC approves or conditionally approves a filing, the OCC generally gives the applicant a specified period of time to commence that new or expanded activity. The OCC does not generally grant an extension of the time specified to commence a new or expanded corporate activity approved under this part, unless the OCC determines that the delay is beyond the applicant's control.

(h) *Nullifying a decision*—(1) *Material misrepresentation or omission.* An applicant shall certify that any filing or supporting material submitted to the OCC contains no material misrepresentations or omissions. The OCC may review and verify any information filed in connection with a notice or an application. If the OCC discovers a material misrepresentation or omission after the OCC has rendered a decision on the filing, the OCC may nullify its decision. Any person responsible for any material misrepresentation or omission in a filing or supporting materials may be subject to enforcement action and other penalties, including criminal penalties provided in 18 U.S.C. 1001.

(2) *Other nullifications.* The OCC may nullify any decision on a filing that is:

(i) Contrary to law, regulation, or OCC policy thereunder; or

(ii) Granted due to clerical or administrative error, or a material mistake of law or fact.

Subpart B—Initial Activities

§ 5.20 Organizing a national bank or Federal savings association.

(a) *Authority.* 12 U.S.C. 21, 22, 24(Seventh), 26, 27, 92a, 93a, 1814(b), 1816, 1462a, 1463, 1464, 2903, and 5412(b)(2)(B).

(b) *Licensing requirements.* Any person desiring to establish a national bank or a Federal savings association shall submit an application and obtain prior OCC approval. An existing national bank or Federal savings association desiring to change the purpose of its charter shall submit an application and obtain prior OCC approval.

(c) *Scope.* This section describes the procedures and requirements governing

OCC review and approval of an application to establish a national bank or a Federal stock or mutual savings association, including a national bank or a Federal savings association with a special purpose. Information regarding an application to establish an interim national bank or an interim Federal savings association solely to facilitate a business combination is set forth in § 5.33. This section also describes the requirements for an existing national bank or Federal savings association to change the purpose of its charter and refers such institutions to § 5.53 for the procedures to follow.

(d) *Definitions.* For purposes of this section:

(1) *Bankers' bank* means a bank owned exclusively (except to the extent directors' qualifying shares are required by law) by other depository institutions or depository institution holding companies (as that term is defined in section 3 of the Federal Deposit Insurance Act, 12 U.S.C. 1813), the activities of which are limited by its articles of association exclusively to providing services to or for other depository institutions, their holding companies, and the officers, directors, and employees of such institutions and companies, and to providing correspondent banking services at the request of other depository institutions or their holding companies.

(2) *Control* means with respect to an application to establish a national bank, control as used in section 2 of the Bank Holding Company Act, 12 U.S.C. 1841(a)(2), and with respect to an application to establish a Federal savings association, control as used in section 10 of the Home Owners' Loan Act, 12 U.S.C. 1467a(a)(2).

(3) *Final approval* means the OCC action issuing a charter and authorizing a national bank or Federal savings association to open for business.

(4) *Holding company* means any company that controls or proposes to control a national bank or a Federal savings association whether or not the company is a bank holding company under section 2 of the Bank Holding Company Act, 12 U.S.C. 1841(a)(1), or a savings and loan holding company under section 10 of the Home Owners' Loan Act, 12 U.S.C. 1467a.

(5) *Lead depository institution* means the largest depository institution controlled by a bank holding company or savings and loan holding company based on a comparison of the average total assets controlled by each depository institution as reported in its Consolidated Report of Condition and Income required to be filed for the immediately preceding four calendar quarters.

(6) *Institution* means either a national bank or Federal savings association.

(7) *Organizing group* means five or more persons acting on their own behalf, or serving as representatives of a sponsoring holding company, who apply to the OCC for a national bank or Federal savings association charter.

(8) *Preliminary approval* means a decision by the OCC permitting an organizing group to go forward with the organization of the proposed national bank or Federal savings association. A preliminary approval generally is subject to certain conditions that an applicant must satisfy before the OCC will grant final approval.

(e) *Requirements*—(1) *In general.* (i) The OCC charters a national bank under the authority of the National Bank Act of 1864, as amended, 12 U.S.C. 1 *et seq.* The bank may be a special purpose bank that limits its activities to fiduciary activities or to any other activities within the business of banking. A special purpose bank that conducts activities other than fiduciary activities must conduct at least one of the following three core banking functions: Receiving deposits; paying checks; or lending money. The name of a proposed national bank must include the word "national."

(ii) The OCC charters a Federal savings association under the authority of section 5 of the Home Owners' Loan Act, 12 U.S.C. 1464, which in an application to establish a Federal savings association requires the OCC to consider:

(A) Whether the applicants are persons of good character and responsibility;

(B) Whether a necessity exists for the association in the community to be served;

(C) Whether there is a reasonable probability of the association's usefulness and success; and

(D) Whether the association can be established without undue injury to properly conducted existing local savings associations and home financing institutions.

(iii) In determining whether to approve an application to establish a national bank or Federal savings association, the OCC verifies that the proposed national bank or Federal savings association has complied with the following requirements. A national bank or a Federal savings association shall:

(A) File either articles of association (for a national bank), or a charter and by-laws (for a Federal savings association) with the OCC;

(B) In the case of an application to establish a national bank, file an organization certificate containing specified information with the OCC;

(C) Ensure that all capital stock is paid in, or in the case of a Federal mutual savings association, ensure that at least a minimum amount of capital is paid in; and

(D) Have at least five elected directors.

(2) *Community Reinvestment Act.* (i) Twelve CFR part 25 requires the OCC to take into account a proposed insured national bank's description of how it will meet its CRA objectives.

(ii) Twelve CFR part 195 requires the OCC to take into account a proposed insured Federal savings association description of how it will meet its CRA objectives.

(3) *Federal Deposit Insurance.* Preliminary approval for an application to establish a Federal savings association will be conditioned on the savings association applying for and receiving approval for deposit insurance from the Federal Deposit Insurance Corporation (FDIC). Final approval for an application to establish a Federal savings association will not be issued until receipt by the OCC of written confirmation by the FDIC that the accounts of the Federal savings association will be insured by the FDIC.

(f) *Policy*—(1) *In general.* In determining whether to approve an application to establish a national bank or Federal savings association, the OCC is guided by the following principles:

(i) Maintaining a safe and sound banking system;

(ii) Encouraging a national bank or Federal savings association to provide fair access to financial services by helping to meet the credit needs of its entire community;

(iii) Ensuring compliance with laws and regulations; and

(iv) Promoting fair treatment of customers including efficiency and better service.

(2) *Policy considerations.* (i) In evaluating an application to establish a national bank or Federal savings association, the OCC considers whether the proposed institution:

(A) Has organizers who are familiar with national banking laws and regulations or Federal savings association laws and regulations, respectively;

(B) Has competent management, including a board of directors, with ability and experience relevant to the types of services to be provided;

(C) Has capital that is sufficient to support the projected volume and type of business;

(D) Can reasonably be expected to achieve and maintain profitability;

(E) Will be operated in a safe and sound manner; and

(F) Does not have a title that misrepresents the nature of the institution or the services it offers.

(ii) In evaluating an application to establish a Federal savings association, the OCC considers whether the proposed Federal savings association will be operated as a qualified thrift lender under section 10(m) of the Home Owners' Loan Act, 12 U.S.C. 1467a(m).

(iii) The OCC may also consider additional factors listed in section 6 of the Federal Deposit Insurance Act, 12 U.S.C. 1816, including the risk to the Federal deposit insurance fund, and whether the proposed institution's corporate powers are consistent with the purposes of the Federal Deposit Insurance Act, the National Bank Act, and the Home Owners' Loan Act, as applicable.

(3) *OCC evaluation.* The OCC evaluates a proposed institution's organizing group and its business plan or operating plan together. The OCC's judgment concerning one may affect the evaluation of the other. An organizing group and its business plan or operating plan must be stronger in markets

where economic conditions are marginal or competition is intense.

(g) *Organizing group*—(1) *In general.* Strong organizing groups generally include diverse business and financial interests and community involvement. An organizing group must have the experience, competence, willingness, and ability to be active in directing the proposed institution's affairs in a safe and sound manner. The institution's initial board of directors generally is comprised of many, if not all, of the organizers. The business plan or operating plan and other information supplied in the application must demonstrate an organizing group's collective ability to establish and operate a successful national bank or Federal savings association in the economic and competitive conditions of the market to be served. Each organizer should be knowledgeable about the business plan or operating plan. A poor business plan or operating plan reflects adversely on the organizing group's ability, and the OCC generally denies applications with poor business plans or operating plans.

(2) *Management selection.* The initial board of directors must select competent senior executive officers before the OCC grants final approval. Early selection of executive officers, especially the chief executive officer, contributes favorably to the preparation and review of a business plan or operating plan that is accurate, complete, and appropriate for the type of national bank or Federal savings association proposed and its market, and reflects favorably upon an application. As a condition of the charter approval, the OCC retains the right to object to and preclude the hiring of any officer, or the appointment or election of any director, for a two-year period from the date the institution commences business, or longer as appropriate.

(3) *Financial resources.* (i) Each organizer must have a history of responsibility, personal honesty, and integrity. Personal wealth is not a prerequisite to become an organizer or director of a national bank or Federal savings association. However, directors' stock purchases, or, in the case of a Federal mutual savings association, capital contributions, individually and in the aggregate, should reflect a financial commitment to the success of the institution that is reasonable in relation to their individual and collective financial strength. A director should not have to depend on institution dividends, fees, or other compensation to satisfy financial obligations.

(ii) Because directors are often the primary source of additional capital for an institution not affiliated with a holding company, it is desirable that the proposed directors of the national bank or Federal savings association, as a group, be able to supply or have a realistic plan to enable the institution to obtain capital when needed.

(iii) Any financial or other business arrangement, direct or indirect, between the organizing group or other insiders and the proposed national bank or Federal savings association must be on nonpreferential terms.

(4) *Organizational expenses.* (i) Organizers are expected to contribute time and expertise to the organization of the national bank or Federal savings association. Organizers should not bill excessive charges to the institution for professional and consulting services or unduly rely upon these fees as a source of income.

(ii) A proposed national bank or Federal savings association shall not pay any fee that is contingent upon an OCC decision. Such action generally is grounds for denial of the application or withdrawal of preliminary approval. Organizational expenses for denied applications are the sole responsibility of the organizing group.

(5) *Sponsor's experience and support.* A sponsor must be financially able to support the new institution's operations and to provide or locate capital when needed. The OCC primarily considers the financial and managerial resources of the sponsor and the sponsor's record of performance, rather than the financial and managerial resources of the organizing group, if an organizing group is sponsored by:

(i) An existing holding company;

(ii) Individuals currently affiliated with other depository institutions; or

(iii) Individuals who, in the OCC's view, are otherwise collectively experienced in banking and have demonstrated the ability to work together effectively.

(h) *Business plan or Operating plan*—(1) *In general.* (i) Organizers of a proposed national bank or Federal savings association shall submit a business plan or operating plan that adequately addresses the statutory and policy considerations set forth in paragraphs (e) and (f)(2) of this section. In the case of a proposed Federal savings association the plan must also specifically address meeting qualified thrift lender requirements. The plan must reflect sound banking principles and demonstrate realistic assessments of risk in light of economic and competitive conditions in the market to be served.

(ii) The OCC may offset deficiencies in one factor by strengths in one or more other factors. However, deficiencies in some factors, such as unrealistic earnings prospects, may have a negative influence on the evaluation of other factors, such as capital adequacy, or may be serious enough by themselves to result in denial. The OCC considers inadequacies in a business plan or operating plan to reflect negatively on the organizing group's ability to operate a successful institution.

(2) *Earnings prospects.* The organizing group shall submit *pro forma* balance sheets and income statements as part of the business plan or operating plan. The OCC reviews all projections for reasonableness of assumptions and consistency with the business plan or operating plan.

(3) *Management.* (i) The organizing group shall include in the business plan or operating plan information sufficient to permit the OCC to evaluate the overall management ability of the organizing group. If the organizing group has limited banking experience or community involvement, the senior executive officers must be able to compensate for such deficiencies.

(ii) The organizing group may not hire an officer or elect or appoint a director if the OCC objects to that person at any time prior to the date the institution commences business.

(4) *Capital.* A proposed bank or Federal savings association must have sufficient initial capital, net of any organizational expenses that will be charged to the institution's capital after it begins operations, to support the institution's projected volume and type of business.

(5) *Community service.* (i) The business plan or operating plan must indicate the organizing group's knowledge of and plans for serving the community. The organizing group shall evaluate the banking needs of the community, including its consumer, business, nonprofit, and government sectors. The business plan or operating plan must demonstrate how the proposed national bank or Federal savings association responds to those needs consistent with the safe and sound operation of the institution. The provisions of this paragraph may not apply to an application to organize an institution for a special purpose.

(ii) As part of its business plan or operating plan, the organizing group shall submit a statement that demonstrates its plans to achieve CRA objectives.

(iii) Because community support is important to the long-term success of a national bank or Federal savings association, the organizing group shall include plans for attracting and maintaining community support.

(6) *Safety and soundness.* The business plan or operating plan must demonstrate that the organizing group (and the sponsoring company, if any), is aware of, and understands, applicable depository institution laws and regulations, and safe and sound banking operations and practices. The OCC will deny an application that does not meet these safety and soundness requirements.

(7) *Fiduciary powers.* The business plan or operating plan must indicate if the proposed institution intends to exercise fiduciary powers. The information required by § 5.26 shall be filed with the charter application. A separate application is not required.

(i) *Procedures*—(1) *Prefiling meeting.* The OCC normally requires a prefiling meeting with the organizers of a proposed national bank or Federal savings association before the organizers file an application. Organizers should be familiar with the OCC's chartering policy and procedural requirements in the Comptroller's Licensing Manual before the prefiling meeting. The prefiling meeting normally is held in the district office where the application will be filed but may be held at another location at the request of the applicant.

(2) *Business plan or operating plan.* An organizing group shall file a business plan or operating plan that addresses the subjects discussed in paragraph (h) of this section.

(3) *Contact person.* The organizing group shall designate a contact person to represent the organizing group in all contacts with the OCC. The contact person shall be an organizer and proposed director of the new national bank or Federal savings association, except a representative of the sponsor or sponsors may serve as contact person if an application is sponsored by an existing holding company, individuals currently affiliated with other depository institutions, or individuals who, in the OCC's view, are otherwise collectively experienced in banking and have demonstrated the ability to work together effectively.

(4) *Decision notification.* The OCC notifies the spokesperson and other interested persons in writing of its decision on an application.

(5) *Activities.* (i) Before the OCC grants final approval, a proposed national bank or Federal savings association must be established as a legal entity. A national bank becomes a legal entity after it has filed its organization certificate and articles of association with the OCC as required by law. A Federal savings association becomes a legal entity after it has filed its proposed charter and bylaws with the OCC. A proposed national bank may offer and sell securities prior to OCC preliminary approval of the proposed national bank's charter application, provided that the proposed national bank has filed articles of association, an organization certificate, and a completed charter application and the bank complies with paragraph (i)(5)(iii) of this section. A proposed Federal stock savings association may offer and sell securities prior to OCC preliminary approval of the proposed Federal stock savings association's charter application, provided that the proposed Federal stock savings association has filed a proposed charter, bylaws, and a completed charter application and the Federal stock savings association complies with paragraph (i)(5)(iii) of this section.

(ii)(A) After the OCC grants preliminary approval, the organizing group shall elect a board of directors, take steps necessary to organize the proposed national bank or Federal savings association and prepare it for commencing business.

(B) A proposed national bank may not conduct the business of banking until the OCC grants final approval and issues a charter. A proposed Federal savings association may not commence business until the OCC grants final approval and issues a charter, which shall be in the form provided in this part.

(iii) For all capital obtained through a public offering a proposed national bank or Federal savings association shall use an offering circular that complies with the OCC's securities offering regulations, 12 CFR part 16 or part 197, as applicable. All securities of a particular class in the initial offering shall be sold at the same price.

(iv) A national bank or Federal savings association in organization shall raise its capital before it commences business. Preliminary approval expires if the proposed national bank or Federal savings association does not raise the required capital within 12 months from the date the OCC grants preliminary approval. Preliminary approval expires if the proposed national bank or Federal savings association does not commence business within 18 months from the date of preliminary approval, unless the OCC grants an extension. If preliminary approval expires, all cash collected on subscriptions shall be returned.

(j) *Expedited review.* An application to establish a full-service national bank or Federal savings association that is sponsored by a bank holding company or savings and loan holding company whose lead depository institution is an eligible bank or eligible savings association is deemed preliminarily approved by the OCC as of the 15th day after the close of the public comment period or the 45th day after the filing is received by the OCC, whichever is later, unless the OCC:

(1) Notifies the applicant prior to that date that the filing is not eligible for expedited review, or the expedited review process is extended, under § 5.13(a)(2); or

(2) Notifies the applicant prior to that date that the OCC has determined that the proposed bank will offer banking services that are materially different than those offered by the lead depository institution.

(k) *National bankers' banks*—(1) *Activities and customers*. In addition to the other requirements of this section, when an organizing group seeks to organize a national bankers' bank, the organizing group shall list in the application the anticipated activities and customers or clients of the proposed national bankers' bank.

(2) *Waiver of requirements*. At the organizing group's request, the OCC may waive requirements that are applicable to national banks in general if those requirements are inappropriate for a national bankers' bank and would impede its ability to provide desired services to its market. An applicant must submit a request for a waiver with the application and must support the request with adequate justification and legal analysis. A national bankers' bank that is already in operation may also request a waiver. The OCC cannot waive statutory provisions that specifically apply to national bankers' banks pursuant to 12 U.S.C. 27(b)(1).

(3) *Investments*. A national bank or Federal savings association may invest up to 10 percent of its capital and surplus in a bankers' bank and may own five percent or less of any class of a bankers' bank's voting securities.

(l) *Special purpose institutions*—(1) *In general*. An applicant for a national bank or Federal savings association charter that will limit its activities to fiduciary activities, credit card operations, or another special purpose shall adhere to established charter procedures with modifications appropriate for the circumstances as determined by the OCC. An applicant for a national bank or Federal savings association charter that will have a community development focus shall also adhere to established charter procedures with modifications appropriate for the circumstances as determined by the OCC. A national bank that seeks to invest in a bank or savings association with a community development focus must comply with applicable requirements of 12 CFR part 24. A Federal savings association that seeks to invest in a bank or savings association with a community development focus must comply with § 160.36 or any other applicable requirements.

(2) *Changes in charter purpose*. An existing national bank or Federal savings association whose activities are limited to a special purpose that desires to change to another special purpose, to add another special purpose, or to no longer be limited to a special purpose charter shall submit an application and obtain prior OCC approval under § 5.53. An existing national bank or Federal savings association whose activities are not limited that desires to limit its activities and become a special purpose institution shall submit an application and obtain prior OCC approval under § 5.53.

[80 FR 28418, May 18, 2015, as amended at 82 FR 8103, Jan. 23, 2017]

§ 5.21 Federal mutual savings association charter and bylaws.

(a) *Authority*. 12 U.S.C. 1462a, 1463, 1464, and 2901 *et seq*.

(b) *Licensing requirements*. A Federal mutual savings association must file an application, notice, or other filing as prescribed by this section when adopting or amending its charter or bylaws.

(c) *Scope*. This section describes the procedures and requirements governing charters and bylaws for Federal mutual savings associations.

(d) *Exceptions to rules of general applicability*. Notwithstanding any other provision of this part, §§ 5.8 through 5.11 shall not apply to this section.

(e) *Charter form*. Except as provided in paragraphs (f) and (g) of this section, a Federal mutual savings association shall have a charter in the following form. A charter for a Federal mutual savings bank shall substitute the term "savings bank" for "association." The term "trustee" may be substituted for the term "director." Associations adopting this charter with existing borrower members must grandfather those borrower members who were members as of the date of issuance of the new charter by the OCC. Such borrowers shall have one vote for the period of time such borrowings are in existence.

Federal Mutual Charter

Section 1. Corporate title. The full corporate title of the Federal savings association is ______.

Section 2. Office. The home office shall be located in ______ [city, state].

Section 3. Duration. The duration of the association is perpetual.

Section 4. Purpose and powers. The purpose of the association is to pursue any or all of the lawful objectives of a Federal mutual savings association chartered under section 5 of the Home Owners' Loan Act and to exercise all the express, implied, and incidental powers conferred thereby and by all acts amendatory thereof and supplemental thereto, subject to the Constitution and laws of the United States as they are now in effect, or as they may hereafter be amended, and subject to all lawful and applicable rules, regulations, and orders of the Office of the Comptroller of the Currency ("OCC").

Section 5. Capital. The association may raise capital by accepting payments on savings and demand accounts and by any other means authorized by the OCC.

Section 6. Members. All holders of the association's savings, demand, or other authorized accounts are members of the association. In the consideration of all questions requiring action by the members of the association, each holder of an account shall be permitted to cast one vote for each $100, or fraction thereof, of the withdrawal value of the member's account. No member, however, shall cast more than 1,000 votes. All accounts shall be nonassessable.

Section 7. Directors. The association shall be under the direction of a board of directors. The authorized number of directors shall not be fewer than five nor more than fifteen persons, as fixed in the association's bylaws, except that the number of directors may be decreased to a number less than five or increased to a number greater than fifteen with the prior approval of the OCC.

Section 8. Capital, surplus, and distribution of earnings. The association shall maintain for the purpose of meeting losses the amount of capital required by section 5 of the Home Owners' Loan Act and by regulations of the OCC. The association shall distribute net earnings on its accounts on such basis and in accordance with such terms and conditions as may from time to time be authorized by the OCC: *Provided,* That the association may establish minimum-balance requirements for accounts to be eligible for distribution of earnings. All holders of accounts of the association shall be entitled to equal distribution of assets, *pro rata* to the value of their accounts, in the event of voluntary or involuntary liquidation, dissolution, or winding up of the association. Moreover, in any such event, or in any other situation in which the priority of such accounts is in controversy, all such accounts shall, to the extent of their withdrawal value, be debts of the association having the same priority as the claims of general creditors of the association not having priority (other than any priority arising or resulting from consensual subordination) over other general creditors of the association.

Section 9. Amendment of charter. Adoption of any preapproved charter amendment shall be effective after such preapproved amendment has been approved by the members at a legal meeting. Any other amendment, addition, change, or repeal of this charter must be approved by the OCC prior to approval by the members at a legal meeting, and shall be effective upon filing with the OCC in accordance with regulatory procedures.

Attest: ______

Secretary of the Association

By: ______

President or Chief Executive Officer of the Association

Attest: ______

Deputy Comptroller for Licensing

By: ______

Comptroller of the Currency

Effective Date: ______

(f) *Charter amendments.* In order to adopt a charter amendment, a Federal mutual savings association must comply with the following requirements:

(1) *Board of directors approval.* The board of directors of the association must adopt a resolution proposing the charter amendment that states the text of such amendment;

(2) *Form of filing*—(i) *Application requirement.* If the proposed charter amendment would: Render more difficult or discourage a merger, proxy contest, the assumption of control by a mutual account holder of the association, or the removal of incumbent management; or involve a significant issue of law or policy; then, the association shall file the proposed amendment and obtain the prior approval of the OCC.

(ii) *Notice requirement.* If the proposed charter amendment does not involve a provision that would be covered by paragraph (f)(2)(i) of this section and is permissible under all applicable laws, rules and regulations, then the association shall submit the proposed amendment to the appropriate OCC licensing office, at least 30 days prior to the effective date of the proposed charter amendment.

(g) *Approval.* Any charter amendment filed pursuant to paragraph (f)(2)(ii) of this section shall automatically be approved 30 days from the date of filing of such amendment, provided that the association follows the requirements of its charter in adopting such amendment. This automatic approval does not apply if, prior to the expiration of such 30-day period, the OCC notifies the association that such amendment is rejected or that such amendment is deemed to be filed under the provisions of paragraph (f)(2)(i) of this section. In addition, notwithstanding anything in paragraph (f) of this section to the contrary, the following charter amendments, including the adoption of the Federal mutual charter as set forth in paragraph (e) of this section, shall be effective and deemed approved at the time of adoption, if adopted without change and filed with the OCC, within 30 days after adoption, provided the association follows the requirements of its charter in adopting such amendments:

(1) *Purpose and powers.* Add a second paragraph to section 4, as follows:

Section 4. Purpose and powers. * * * The association shall have the express power: (i) To act as fiscal agent of the United States when designated for that purpose by the Secretary of the Treasury, under such regulations as the Secretary may prescribe, to perform all such reasonable duties as fiscal agent of the United States as may be required, and to act as agent for any other instrumentality of the United States when designated for that purpose by any such instrumentality; (ii) To sue and be sued, complain and defend in any court of law or equity; (iii) To have a corporate seal, affixed by imprint, facsimile or otherwise; (iv) To appoint officers and agents as its business shall require and allow them suitable compensation; (v) To adopt bylaws not inconsistent with the Constitution or laws of the United States and rules and regulations adopted thereunder and under this Charter; (vi) To raise capital, which shall be unlimited, by accepting payments on savings, demand, or other accounts, as are authorized by rules and regulations made by the OCC, and the holders of all such accounts or other accounts as shall, to such extent as may be provided by such rules and regulations, be members of the association and shall have such voting rights and such other rights as are thereby provided; (vii) To issue notes, bonds, debentures, or other obligations, or securities, provided by or under any provision of Federal statute as from time to time is in effect; (viii) To provide for redemption of insured accounts; (ix) To borrow money without limitation and pledge and otherwise encumber any of its assets to secure its debts; (x) To lend and otherwise invest its funds as authorized by statute and the rules and regulations of the OCC; (xi) To wind up and dissolve, merge, consolidate, convert, or reorganize; (xii) To purchase, hold, and convey real estate and personalty consistent with its objects, purposes, and powers; (xiii) To mortgage or lease any real estate and personalty and take such property by gift, devise, or bequest; and (xiv) To exercise all powers conferred by law. In addition to the foregoing powers expressly enumerated, this association shall have power to do all things reasonably incident to the accomplishment of its express objects and the performance of its express powers.

(2) *Title change.* A Federal mutual savings association that has complied with § 5.42 may amend its charter by substituting a new corporate title in section 1.

(3) *Home office.* A Federal mutual savings association may amend its charter by substituting a new home office in section 2, if it has complied with applicable requirements of § 5.40.

(4) *Maximum number of votes.* A Federal mutual savings association may amend its charter by substituting any number of votes per member between 1 and 1000 in section 6.

(h) *Reissuance of charter.* A Federal mutual savings association that has amended its charter may apply to have its charter, including the amendments, reissued by the OCC. Such request for reissuance should be filed at the appropriate OCC licensing office and contain signatures required under paragraph (e) of this section, together with such supporting documents as may be needed to demonstrate that the amendments were properly adopted.

(i) *Availability of chartering documents.* A Federal mutual savings association shall cause a true copy of its charter and bylaws and all amendments thereto to be available to accountholders at all times in each office of the savings association, and shall upon request deliver to any accountholders a copy of such charter and bylaws or amendments thereto.

(j) *Bylaws for Federal mutual savings associations*—(1) *In general.* A Federal mutual savings association shall operate under bylaws that contain provisions that comply with all requirements specified by the OCC in this paragraph and that are not otherwise inconsistent with the provisions of this paragraph, the association's charter, and all other applicable laws, rules, and regulations *provided that*, a bylaw provision inconsistent with the provisions of this paragraph may be adopted with the approval of the OCC. Bylaws may be adopted, amended or repealed by a majority of the votes cast by the members at a legal meeting or a majority of the association's board of directors. The bylaws for a Federal mutual savings bank shall substitute the term "savings bank" for "association". The term "trustee" may be substituted for the term "director".

(2) *Requirements.* The following requirements are applicable to Federal mutual savings associations:

(i) *Annual meetings of members.* (A) An association shall provide for and conduct an annual meeting of its members for the election of directors and at which any other business of the association may be conducted. Such meeting shall be held at any convenient place the board of directors may designate, and at a date and time within 150 days after the end of the association's fiscal year.

(B) At each annual meeting, the officers shall make a full report of the financial condition of the association and of its progress for the preceding year and shall outline a program for the succeeding year.

(ii) *Special meetings of members.* Procedures for calling any special meeting of the members and for conducting such a meeting shall be set forth in the bylaws. The board of directors of the association or the holders of 10 percent or more of the voting capital shall be entitled to call a special meeting. For purposes of this paragraph, "voting capital" means FDIC-insured deposits as of the voting record date.

(iii) *Notice of meeting of members.* Notice specifying the date, time, and place of the annual or any special meeting and adequately describing any business to be conducted shall be published for two successive weeks immediately prior to the week in which such meeting shall convene in a newspaper of general circulation in the city or county in which the principal place of business of the association is located, or mailed postage prepaid at least 15 days and not more than 45 days prior to the date on which such meeting shall convene to each of its members of record. A similar notice shall be posted in a conspicuous place in each of the offices of the association during the 14 days immediately preceding the date on which such meeting shall convene. The bylaws may permit a member to waive in writing any right to receive personal delivery of the notice. When any meeting is adjourned for 30 days or more, notice of the adjournment and reconvening of the meeting shall be given as in the case of the original meeting.

(iv) *Fixing of record date.* The bylaws shall provide for the fixing of a record date and a method for determining from the books of the association the members entitled to vote. Such date shall be not more than 60 days nor fewer than 10 days prior to the date on which the action, requiring such determination of members, is to be taken. The same determination shall apply to any adjourned meeting.

(v) *Member quorum.* Any number of members present and voting, represented in person or by proxy, at a regular or special meeting of the members shall constitute a quorum. A majority of all votes cast at any meeting of the members shall determine any question, unless otherwise required by regulation. At any adjourned meeting, any business may be transacted that might have been transacted at the meeting as originally called. Members present at a duly constituted meeting may continue to transact business until adjournment.

(vi) *Voting by proxy.* Procedures shall be established for voting at any annual or special meeting of the members by proxy pursuant to the rules and regulations of the OCC. Proxies may be given telephonically or electronically as long as the holder uses a procedure for verifying the identity of the member.

All proxies with a term greater than eleven months or solicited at the expense of the association must run to the board of directors as a whole, or to a committee appointed by a majority of such board.

(vii) *Communications between members.* Provisions relating to communications between members shall be consistent with § 144.8 of this chapter. No member, however, shall have the right to inspect or copy any portion of any books or records of a Federal mutual savings association containing:

(A) A list of depositors in or borrowers from such association;

(B) Their addresses;

(C) Individual deposit or loan balances or records; or

(D) Any data from which such information could be reasonably constructed.

(viii) *Number of directors, membership.* The bylaws shall set forth a specific number of directors, not a range. The number of directors shall be not fewer than five nor more than fifteen, unless a higher or lower number has been authorized by the OCC. Each director of the association shall be a member of the association. Directors may be elected for periods of one to three years and until their successors are elected and qualified, but if a staggered board is chosen, provision shall be made for the election of approximately one-third or one-half of the board each year, as appropriate. State-chartered savings banks converting to Federal savings banks may include alternative provisions for the election and term of office of directors so long as such provisions are authorized by the OCC, and provide for compliance with the standard provisions of this paragraph no later than six years after the conversion to a Federal savings association.

(ix) *Meetings of the board.* The board of directors shall determine the place, frequency, time, procedure for notice, which shall be at least 24 hours unless waived by the directors, and waiver of notice for all regular and special meetings. The board also may permit telephonic or electronic participation at meetings. The bylaws may provide for action to be taken without a meeting if unanimous written consent is obtained for such action. A majority of the authorized directors shall constitute a quorum for the transaction of business. The act of a majority of the directors present at any meeting at which there is a quorum shall be the act of the board.

(x) *Officers, employees and agents.* (A) The bylaws shall contain provisions regarding the officers of the association, their functions, duties, and powers. The officers of the association shall consist of a president, one or more vice presidents, a secretary, and a treasurer or comptroller, each of whom shall be elected annually by the board of directors. Such other officers and assistant officers and agents as may be deemed necessary may be elected or appointed by the board of directors or chosen in such other manner as may be prescribed in the bylaws. Any two or more offices may be held by the same person, except the offices of president and secretary.

(B) Any officer may be removed by the board of directors with or without cause, but such removal, other than for cause, shall be without prejudice to the contractual rights, if any, of the person so removed. Termination for cause, for purposes of this §§ 5.21 and 5.22, shall include termination because of the person's personal dishonesty, incompetence, willful misconduct, breach of fiduciary duty involving personal profit, intentional failure to perform stated duties, willful violation of any law, rule, or regulation (other than traffic violations or similar offenses) or final cease and desist order, or material breach of any provision of an employment contract.

(xi) *Vacancies, resignation or removal of directors.* In the event of a vacancy on the board, the board of directors may, by their affirmative vote, fill such vacancy, even if the remaining directors constitute less than a quorum. A director elected to fill a vacancy shall be elected to serve only until the next election of directors by the members. The bylaws shall set out the procedure for the resignation of a director. Directors may be removed only for cause, as defined in § 5.21(j)(2)(x)(B), by a vote of the holders of a majority of the shares then entitled to vote at an election of directors.

(xii) *Powers of the board.* The board of directors shall have the power to exercise any and all of the powers of the association not expressly reserved by the charter to the members.

(xiii) *Nominations for directors.* The bylaws shall provide that nominations for directors may be made at the annual meeting by any member and shall be voted upon, except, however, the bylaws may require that nominations by a member must be submitted to the secretary and then prominently posted in the principal place of business, at least 10 days prior to the date of the annual meeting. However, if such provision is made for prior submission of nominations by a member, then the bylaws must provide for a nominating committee, which, except in the case of a nominee substituted as a result of death or other incapacity, must submit nominations to the secretary and have such nominations similarly posted at least 15 days prior to the date of the annual meeting.

(xiv) *New business.* The bylaws shall provide procedures for the introduction of new business at the annual meeting.

(xv) *Amendment.* Bylaws may include any provision for their amendment that would be consistent with applicable law, rules, and regulations and adequately addresses its subject and purpose.

(A) Amendments shall be effective:

(*1*) After approval by a majority vote of the authorized board, or by a majority of the vote cast by the members of the association at a legal meeting; and

(*2*) After receipt of any applicable regulatory approval.

(B) When an association fails to meet its quorum requirement, solely due to vacancies on the board, the bylaws may be amended by an affirmative vote of a majority of the sitting board.

(xvi) *Miscellaneous.* The bylaws may also address any other subjects necessary or appropriate for effective operation of the association.

(3) *Form of filing*—(i) *Application requirement.* (A) Any bylaw amendment shall be submitted to the appropriate OCC licensing office for OCC approval if it would render more difficult or discourage a merger, proxy contest, the assumption of control by a mutual account holder of the association, or the removal of incumbent management; involve a significant issue of law or policy, including indemnification, conflicts of interest, and limitations on director or officer liability; or be inconsistent with the requirements of this paragraph or with applicable laws, rules, regulations, or the association's charter.

(B) For purposes of paragraph (j)(3) of this section, bylaw provisions that adopt the language of the OCC's model or optional bylaws, if adopted without change, and filed with the OCC within 30 days after adoption, are effective upon adoption.

(ii) *Filing requirement.* If the proposed bylaw amendment does not involve a provision that would be covered by paragraph (j)(3)(i)(A) of this section, then the association shall submit the amendment to the appropriate OCC licensing office at least 30 days prior to the date the bylaw amendment is to be adopted by the association.

(iii) *Corporate governance procedures.* A Federal mutual association may elect to follow the corporate governance procedures of the laws of the state where the home office of the institution is located, provided that such procedures may be elected only to the extent not inconsistent with applicable Federal statutes, regulations, and safety and soundness, and such procedures are not of the type described in paragraph (j)(3)(i)(A) of this section. If this election is selected, a Federal mutual association shall designate in its bylaws the provision or provisions from the body of law selected for its corporate governance procedures, and shall file a copy of such bylaws, which are effective upon adoption, within 30 days after adoption. The submission shall indicate, where not obvious, why the bylaw provisions meet the requirements stated in paragraph (j)(3)(i)(A) of this section.

(4) *Effectiveness.* Any bylaw amendment filed pursuant to paragraph (j)(3)(ii) of this section shall automatically be effective 30 days from the date of filing of such amendment, provided that the association follows the requirements of its charter and bylaws in adopting such amendment. This automatic effective date does not apply if, prior to the expiration of such 30-day

period, the OCC notifies the association that such amendment is rejected or that such amendment requires an application to be filed pursuant to paragraph (j)(3)(i) of this section.

(5) *Effect of subsequent charter or bylaw change.* Notwithstanding any subsequent change to its charter or bylaws, the authority of a Federal mutual savings association to engage in any transaction shall be determined only by the association's charter or bylaws then in effect.

[80 FR 28421, May 18, 2015, as amended at 82 FR 8103, Jan. 23, 2017]

§ 5.22 Federal stock savings association charter and bylaws.

(a) *Authority.* 12 U.S.C. 1462a, 1463, 1464, and 2901 *et seq.*

(b) *Licensing requirements.* A Federal stock savings association must file an application, notice, or other filing as prescribed by this section when adopting or amending its charter or bylaws.

(c) *Scope.* This section describes the procedures and requirements governing charters and bylaws for Federal stock savings associations.

(d) *Exceptions to rules of general applicability.* Notwithstanding any other provision of this part, §§ 5.8 through 5.11 shall not apply to this section.

(e) *Charter form.* The charter of a Federal stock association shall be in the following form, except as provided in this section. An association that has converted from the mutual form pursuant to part 192 of this chapter shall include in its charter a section establishing a liquidation account as required by § 192.3(c)(13) of this chapter. A charter for a Federal stock savings bank shall substitute the term "savings bank" for "association." Charters may also include any preapproved optional provision contained in this section.

Federal Stock Charter

Section 1. Corporate title. The full corporate title of the association is ____.

Section 2. Office. The home office shall be located in ____ [city, state].

Section 3. Duration. The duration of the association is perpetual.

Section 4. Purpose and powers. The purpose of the association is to pursue any or all of the lawful objectives of a Federal savings association chartered under section 5 of the Home Owners' Loan Act and to exercise all of the express, implied, and incidental powers conferred thereby and by all acts amendatory thereof and supplemental thereto, subject to the Constitution and laws of the United States as they are now in effect, or as they may hereafter be amended, and subject to all lawful and applicable rules, regulations, and orders of the Office of the Comptroller of the Currency ("OCC").

Section 5. Capital stock. The total number of shares of all classes of the capital stock that the association has the authority to issue is ____, all of which shall be common stock of par [or if no par is specified then shares shall have a stated] value of ____ per share. The shares may be issued from time to time as authorized by the board of directors without the approval of its shareholders, except as otherwise provided in this Section 5 or to the extent that such approval is required by governing law, rule, or regulation. The consideration for the issuance of the shares shall be paid in full before their issuance and shall not be less than the par [or stated] value. Neither promissory notes nor future services shall constitute payment or part payment for the issuance of shares of the association. The consideration for the shares shall be cash, tangible or intangible property (to the extent direct investment in such property would be permitted to the association), labor, or services actually performed for the association, or any combination of the foregoing. In the absence of actual fraud in the transaction, the value of such property, labor, or services, as determined by the board of directors of the association, shall be conclusive. Upon payment of such consideration, such shares shall be deemed to be fully paid and nonassessable. In the case of a stock dividend, that part of the retained earnings of the association that is transferred to common stock or paid-in capital accounts upon the issuance of shares as a stock dividend shall be deemed to be the consideration for their issuance.

Except for shares issued in the initial organization of the association or in connection with the conversion of the association from the mutual to stock form of capitalization, no shares of capital stock (including shares issuable upon conversion, exchange, or exercise of other securities) shall be issued, directly or indirectly, to officers, directors, or controlling persons of the association other than as part of a general public offering or as qualifying shares to a director, unless the issuance or the plan under which they would be issued has been approved by a majority of the total votes eligible to be cast at a legal meeting. The holders of the common stock shall exclusively possess all voting power. Each holder of shares of common stock shall be entitled to one vote for each share held by such holder, except as to the cumulation of votes for the election of directors, unless the charter provides that there shall be no such cumulative voting. Subject to any provision for a liquidation account, in the event of any liquidation, dissolution, or winding up of the association, the holders of the common stock shall be entitled, after payment or provision for payment of all debts and liabilities of the association, to receive the remaining assets of the association available for distribution, in cash or in kind. Each share of common stock shall have the same relative rights as and be identical in all respects with all the other shares of common stock.

Section 6. Preemptive rights. Holders of the capital stock of the association shall not be entitled to preemptive rights with respect to any shares of the association which may be issued.

Section 7. Directors. The association shall be under the direction of a board of directors. The authorized number of directors, as stated in the association's bylaws, shall not be fewer than five nor more than fifteen except when a greater or lesser number is approved by the OCC.

Section 8. Amendment of charter. Except as provided in Section 5, no amendment, addition, alteration, change or repeal of this charter shall be made, unless such is proposed by the board of directors of the association, approved by the shareholders by a majority of the votes eligible to be cast at a legal meeting, unless a higher vote is otherwise required, and approved or preapproved by the OCC.

Attest: ____________________
Secretary of the Association

By: ____________________
President or Chief Executive Officer of the Association

Attest: ____________________
Deputy Comptroller for Licensing

By: ____________________
Comptroller of the Currency

Effective Date: ____________________

(f) *Charter amendments.* In order to adopt a charter amendment, a Federal stock savings association must comply with the following requirements:

(1) *Board of directors approval.* The board of directors of the association must adopt a resolution proposing the charter amendment that states the text of such amendment;

(2) *Form of filing*—(i) *Application requirement.* If the proposed charter amendment would render more difficult or discourage a merger, tender offer, or proxy contest, the assumption of control by a holder of a block of the association's stock, the removal of incumbent management, or involve a significant issue of law or policy, the association shall file the proposed amendment and shall obtain the prior approval of the OCC; and

(ii) *Notice requirement.* If the proposed charter amendment does not involve a provision that would be covered by paragraph (f)(2)(i) of this section and such amendment is permissible under all applicable laws, rules or regulations, then the association shall submit the proposed amendments to the appropriate OCC licensing office, at least 30 days prior to the date the proposed charter amendment is to be mailed for consideration by the association's shareholders.

(g) *Approval.* Any charter amendment filed pursuant to paragraph (f)(2)(ii) of this section shall automatically be approved 30 days from the date of filing of such amendment, provided that the association follows the requirements of its charter in adopting such amendment, unless prior to the expiration of such 30-day period the OCC notifies the association that such amendment is rejected or that such amendment is deemed to be filed under the provisions of paragraph (f)(2)(i) of this section. In addition, the following charter amendments, including the adoption of the Federal stock charter as set forth in paragraph (e) of this section, shall be approved at the time of adoption, if adopted without change and filed with the OCC within 30 days after adoption, provided the association follows the requirements of its charter in adopting such amendments:

(1) *Title change.* A Federal stock association that has complied with §5.42 of this chapter may amend its charter by substituting a new corporate title in section 1.

(2) *Home office.* A Federal savings association may amend its charter by substituting a new home office in section 2, if it has complied with applicable requirements of §5.40.

(3) *Number of shares of stock and par value.* A Federal stock association may amend Section 5 of its charter to change the number of authorized shares of stock, the number of shares within each class of stock, and the par or stated value of such shares.

(4) *Capital stock.* A Federal stock association may amend its charter by revising Section 5 to read as follows:

Section 5. Capital stock. The total number of shares of all classes of capital stock that the association has the authority to issue is ____, of which ____ shall be common stock of par [or if no par value is specified the stated] value of ____ per share and of which [list the number of each class of preferred and the par or if no par value is specified the stated value per share of each such class]. The shares may be issued from time to time as authorized by the board of directors without further approval of shareholders, except as otherwise provided in this Section 5 or to the extent that such approval is required by governing law, rule, or regulation. The consideration for the issuance of the shares shall be paid in full before their issuance and shall not be less than the par [or stated] value. Neither promissory notes nor future services shall constitute payment or part payment for the issuance of shares of the association. The consideration for the shares shall be cash, tangible or intangible property (to the extent direct investment in such property would be permitted), labor, or services actually performed for the association, or any combination of the foregoing. In the absence of actual fraud in the transaction, the value of such property, labor, or services, as determined by the board of directors of the association, shall be conclusive. Upon payment of such consideration, such shares shall be deemed to be fully paid and nonassessable. In the case of a stock dividend, that part of the retained earnings of the association that is transferred to common stock or paid-in capital accounts upon the issuance of shares as a stock dividend shall be deemed to be the consideration for their issuance.

Except for shares issued in the initial organization of the association or in connection with the conversion of the association from the mutual to the stock form of capitalization, no shares of capital stock (including shares issuable upon conversion, exchange, or exercise of other securities) shall be issued, directly or indirectly, to officers, directors, or controlling persons of the association other than as part of a general public offering or as qualifying shares to a director, unless their issuance or the plan under which they would be issued has been approved by a majority of the total votes eligible to be cast at a legal meeting.

Nothing contained in this Section 5 (or in any supplementary sections hereto) shall entitle the holders of any class of a series of capital stock to vote as a separate class or series or to more than one vote per share, except as to the cumulation of votes for the election of directors, unless the charter otherwise provides that there shall be no such cumulative voting: *Provided,* That this restriction on voting separately by class or series shall not apply:

i. To any provision which would authorize the holders of preferred stock, voting as a class or series, to elect some members of the board of directors, less than a majority thereof, in the event of default in the payment of dividends on any class or series of preferred stock;

ii. To any provision that would require the holders of preferred stock, voting as a class or series, to approve the merger or consolidation of the association with another corporation or the sale, lease, or conveyance (other than by mortgage or pledge) of properties or business in exchange for securities of a corporation other than the association if the preferred stock is exchanged for securities of such other corporation: *Provided,* That no provision may require such approval for transactions undertaken with the assistance or pursuant to the direction of the OCC or the Federal Deposit Insurance Corporation;

iii. To any amendment which would adversely change the specific terms of any class or series of capital stock as set forth in this Section 5 (or in any supplementary sections hereto), including any amendment which would create or enlarge any class or series ranking prior thereto in rights and preferences. An amendment which increases the number of authorized shares of any class or series of capital stock, or substitutes the surviving association in a merger or consolidation for the association, shall not be considered to be such an adverse change.

A description of the different classes and series (if any) of the association's capital stock and a statement of the designations, and the relative rights, preferences, and limitations of the shares of each class of and series (if any) of capital stock are as follows:

A. *Common stock.* Except as provided in this Section 5 (or in any supplementary sections thereto) the holders of the common stock shall exclusively possess all voting power. Each holder of shares of the common stock shall be entitled to one vote for each share held by each holder, except as to the cumulation of votes for the election of directors, unless the charter otherwise provides that there shall be no such cumulative voting.

Whenever there shall have been paid, or declared and set aside for payment, to the holders of the outstanding shares of any class of stock having preference over the common stock as to the payment of dividends, the full amount of dividends and of sinking fund, retirement fund, or other retirement payments, if any, to which such holders are respectively entitled in preference to the common stock, then dividends may be paid on the common stock and on any class or series of stock entitled to participate therewith as to dividends out of any assets legally available for the payment of dividends.

In the event of any liquidation, dissolution, or winding up of the association, the holders of the common stock (and the holders of any class or series of stock entitled to participate with the common stock in the distribution of assets) shall be entitled to receive, in cash or in kind, the assets of the association available for distribution remaining after: (i) Payment or provision for payment of the association's debts and liabilities; (ii) distributions or provision for distributions in settlement of its liquidation account; and (iii) distributions or provision for distributions to holders of any class or series of stock having preference over the common stock in the liquidation, dissolution, or winding up of the association. Each share of common stock shall have the same relative rights as and be identical in all respects with all the other shares of common stock.

B. *Preferred stock.* The association may provide in supplementary sections to its charter for one or more classes of preferred stock, which shall be separately identified. The shares of any class may be divided into and issued in series, with each series separately designated so as to distinguish the shares thereof from the shares of all other series and classes. The terms of each series shall be set forth in a supplementary section to the charter. All shares of the same class shall be identical except as to the following relative rights and preferences, as to which there may be variations between different series:

a. The distinctive serial designation and the number of shares constituting such series;

b. The dividend rate or the amount of dividends to be paid on the shares of such series, whether dividends shall be cumulative and, if so, from which date(s), the payment date(s) for dividends, and the participating or other special rights, if any, with respect to dividends;

c. The voting powers, full or limited, if any, of shares of such series;

d. Whether the shares of such series shall be redeemable and, if so, the price(s) at which, and the terms and conditions on which, such shares may be redeemed;

e. The amount(s) payable upon the shares of such series in the event of voluntary or involuntary liquidation, dissolution, or winding up of the association;

f. Whether the shares of such series shall be entitled to the benefit of a sinking or retirement fund to be applied to the purchase or redemption of such shares, and if so entitled, the amount of such fund and the manner of its application, including the price(s) at which such shares may be redeemed or purchased through the application of such fund;

g. Whether the shares of such series shall be convertible into, or exchangeable for, shares of any other class or classes of stock of the association and, if so, the conversion price(s) or the rate(s) of exchange, and the adjustments thereof, if any, at which such conversion or exchange may be made, and any other terms and conditions of such conversion or exchange.

h. The price or other consideration for which the shares of such series shall be issued; and

i. Whether the shares of such series which are redeemed or converted shall have the status of authorized but unissued shares of serial preferred stock and whether such shares may be reissued as shares of the same or any other series of serial preferred stock.

Each share of each series of serial preferred stock shall have the same relative rights as and be identical in all respects with all the other shares of the same series.

The board of directors shall have authority to divide, by the adoption of supplementary charter sections, any authorized class of preferred stock into series, and, within the limitations set forth in this section and the remainder of this charter, fix and determine the relative rights and preferences of the shares of any series so established.

Prior to the issuance of any preferred shares of a series established by a supplementary charter section adopted by the board of directors, the association shall file with the OCC a dated copy of that supplementary section of this charter established and designating the series and fixing and determining the relative rights and preferences thereof.

(5) *Limitations on subsequent issuances.* A Federal stock association may amend its charter to require shareholder approval of the issuance or reservation of common stock or securities convertible into common stock under circumstances which would require shareholder approval under the rules of the New York Stock Exchange if the shares were then listed on the New York Stock Exchange.

(6) *Cumulative voting.* A Federal stock association may amend its charter by substituting the following sentence for the second sentence in the third paragraph of Section 5: "Each holder of shares of common stock shall be entitled to one vote for each share held by such holder and there shall be no right to cumulate votes in an election of directors."

(7) *Anti-takeover provisions following mutual to stock conversion.* Notwithstanding the law of the state in which the association is located, a Federal stock association may amend its charter by renumbering existing sections as appropriate and adding a new section 8 as follows:

Section 8. Certain Provisions Applicable for Five Years. Notwithstanding anything contained in the Association's charter or bylaws to the contrary, for a period of [specify number of years up to five] years from the date of completion of the conversion of the Association from mutual to stock form, the following provisions shall apply:

A. *Beneficial Ownership Limitation.* No person shall directly or indirectly offer to acquire or acquire the beneficial ownership of more than 10 percent of any class of an equity security of the association. This limitation shall not apply to a transaction in which the association forms a holding company without change in the respective beneficial ownership interests of its stockholders other than pursuant to the exercise of any dissenter and appraisal rights, the purchase of shares by underwriters in connection with a public offering, or the purchase of less than 25 percent of a class of stock by a tax-qualified employee stock benefit plan as defined in § 192.25 of the OCC's regulations.

In the event shares are acquired in violation of this section 8, all shares beneficially owned by any person in excess of 10 percent shall be considered "excess shares" and shall not be counted as shares entitled to vote and shall not be voted by any person or counted as voting shares in connection with any matters submitted to the stockholders for a vote.

For purposes of this section 8, the following definitions apply:

1. The term "person" includes an individual, a group acting in concert, a corporation, a partnership, an association, a joint stock company, a trust, an unincorporated organization or similar company, a syndicate or any other group formed for the purpose of acquiring, holding or disposing of the equity securities of the association.

2. The term "offer" includes every offer to buy or otherwise acquire, solicitation of an offer to sell, tender offer for, or request or invitation for tenders of, a security or interest in a security for value.

3. The term "acquire" includes every type of acquisition, whether effected by purchase, exchange, operation of law or otherwise.

4. The term "acting in concert" means (a) knowing participation in a joint activity or conscious parallel action towards a common goal whether or not pursuant to an express agreement, or (b) a combination or pooling of voting or other interests in the securities of an issuer for a common purpose pursuant to any contract, understanding, relationship, agreement or other arrangements, whether written or otherwise.

B. *Cumulative Voting Limitation.* Stockholders shall not be permitted to cumulate their votes for election of directors.

C. *Call for Special Meetings.* Special meetings of stockholders relating to changes in control of the association or amendments to its charter shall be called only upon direction of the board of directors.

(h) *Anti-takeover provisions.* The OCC may grant approval to a charter amendment not listed in paragraph (g) of this section regarding the acquisition by any person or persons of its equity securities provided that the association shall file as part of its application for approval an opinion, acceptable to the OCC, of counsel independent from the association that the proposed charter provision would be permitted to be adopted by a corporation chartered by the state in which the principal office of the association is located. Any such provision must be consistent with applicable statutes, regulations, and OCC policies. Further, any such provision that would have the effect of rendering more difficult a change in control of the association and would require for any corporate action (other than the removal of directors) the affirmative vote of a larger percentage of shareholders than is required by this part, shall not be effective unless adopted by a percentage of shareholder vote at least equal to the highest percentage that would be required to take any action under such provision.

(i) *Reissuance of charter.* A Federal stock association that has amended its charter may apply to have its charter, including the amendments, reissued by the OCC. Such requests for reissuance should be filed with the appropriate OCC licensing office, and contain signatures required under (c) of this part, together with such supporting documents as needed to demonstrate that the amendments were properly adopted.

(j) *Bylaws for Federal stock savings associations*—(1) *In general.* Bylaws may be adopted, amended or repealed by either a majority of the votes cast by the shareholders at a legal meeting or a majority of the board of directors. A bylaw provision inconsistent with paragraph (k), (l), (m) or (n) of this section may be adopted only with the approval of the OCC.

(2) *Form of filing*—(i) *Application requirement.* (A) Any bylaw amendment shall be submitted to the OCC for approval if it would:

(*1*) Render more difficult or discourage a merger, tender offer, or proxy contest, the assumption of control by a holder of a large block of the association's stock, or the removal of incumbent management; or

(*2*) Be inconsistent with paragraphs (k) through (n) of this section, with applicable laws, rules, regulations or the association's charter or involve a significant issue of law or policy, including indemnification, conflicts of interest, and limitations on director or officer liability.

(B) Bylaw provisions that adopt the language of the OCC's model or optional bylaws, if adopted without change, and filed with the OCC within 30 days after adoption, are effective upon adoption.

(ii) *Filing requirement.* If the proposed bylaw amendment does not involve a provision that would be covered by paragraph (j)(2)(i) or (iii) of this section and is permissible under all applicable laws, rules, or regulations, then the association shall submit the amendment to the OCC at least 30 days prior to the date the bylaw amendment is to be adopted by the association.

(iii) *Corporate governance procedures.* A Federal stock association may elect to follow the corporate governance procedures of: The laws of the state where the home office of the association is located; the laws of the state where the association's holding company, if any, is incorporated or chartered; Delaware General Corporation law; or The Model Business Corporation Act, provided that such procedures may be elected to the extent not inconsistent with applicable Federal statutes and regulations and safety and soundness, and such procedures are not of the type described in paragraph (j)(2)(i) of this section. If this election is selected, a Federal stock association shall designate in its bylaws the provision or provisions from the body or bodies of law selected for its corporate governance procedures, and shall file a copy of such bylaws, which are effective upon adoption, within 30 days after adoption. The submission shall indicate, where not obvious, why the bylaw provisions meet the requirements stated in paragraph (j)(2)(i) of this section.

(3) *Effectiveness.* Any bylaw amendment filed pursuant to paragraph (j)(2)(ii) of this section shall automatically be effective 30 days from the date of filing of such amendment, provided that the association follows the requirements of its charter and bylaws in adopting such amendment, unless prior to the expiration of such 30-day period the OCC notifies the association that such amendment is rejected or that such amendment requires an application to be filed pursuant to paragraph (j)(2)(i) of this section.

(4) *Effect of subsequent charter or bylaw change.* Notwithstanding any subsequent change to its charter or bylaws, the authority of a Federal savings association to engage in any transaction shall be determined only by the association's charter or bylaws then in effect.

(k) *Shareholders of Federal stock savings associations*—(1) *Shareholder meetings.* A meeting of the shareholders of the association for the election of directors and for the transaction of any other business of the association shall be held annually within 150 days after the end of the association's fiscal year. Unless otherwise provided in the association's charter, special meetings of the shareholders may be called by the board of directors or on the request of the holders of 10 percent or more of the shares entitled to vote at the meeting, or by such other persons as may be specified in the bylaws of the association. All annual and special meetings of shareholders shall be held at any convenient place the board of directors may designate.

(2) *Notice of shareholder meetings.* Written notice stating the place, day, and hour of the meeting and the purpose or purposes for which the meeting is called shall be delivered not fewer than 20 nor more than 50 days before the date of the meeting, either personally or by mail, by or at the direction of the chairman of the board, the president, the secretary, or the directors, or other persons calling the meeting, to each shareholder of record entitled to vote at such meeting. If mailed, such notice shall be deemed to be delivered when deposited in the mail, addressed to the shareholder at the address appearing on the stock transfer books or records of the association as of the record date prescribed in paragraph (i)(3) of this section, with postage thereon prepaid. When any shareholders' meeting, either annual or special, is adjourned for 30 days or more, notice of the adjourned meeting shall

be given as in the case of an original meeting. Notwithstanding anything in this section, however, a Federal stock association that is wholly owned shall not be subject to the shareholder notice requirement.

(3) *Fixing of record date.* For the purpose of determining shareholders entitled to notice of or to vote at any meeting of shareholders or any adjournment thereof, or shareholders entitled to receive payment of any dividend, or in order to make a determination of shareholders for any other proper purpose, the board of directors shall fix in advance a date as the record date for any such determination of shareholders. Such date in any case shall be not more than 60 days and, in case of a meeting of shareholders, not less than 10 days prior to the date on which the particular action, requiring such determination of shareholders, is to be taken. When a determination of shareholders entitled to vote at any meeting of shareholders has been made as provided in this section, such determination shall apply to any adjournment thereof.

(4) *Voting lists.* (i) At least 20 days before each meeting of the shareholders, the officer or agent having charge of the stock transfer books for the shares of the association shall make a complete list of the stockholders of record entitled to vote at such meeting, or any adjournments thereof, arranged in alphabetical order, with the address and the number of shares held by each. This list of shareholders shall be kept on file at the home office of the association and shall be subject to inspection by any shareholder of record or the stockholder's agent during the entire time of the meeting. The original stock transfer book shall constitute *prima facie* evidence of the stockholders entitled to examine such list or transfer books or to vote at any meeting of stockholders. Notwithstanding anything in this section, however, a Federal stock association that is wholly owned shall not be subject to the voting list requirements.

(ii) In lieu of making the shareholders list available for inspection by any shareholders as provided in paragraph (j)(4)(i) of this section, the board of directors may perform such acts as required by paragraphs (a) and (b) of Rule 14a–7 of the General Rules and Regulations under the Securities and Exchange Act of 1934 (17 CFR 240.14a–7) as may be duly requested in writing, with respect to any matter which may be properly considered at a meeting of shareholders, by any shareholder who is entitled to vote on such matter and who shall defray the reasonable expenses to be incurred by the association in performance of the act or acts required.

(5) *Shareholder quorum.* A majority of the outstanding shares of the association entitled to vote, represented in person or by proxy, shall constitute a quorum at a meeting of shareholders. The shareholders present at a duly organized meeting may continue to transact business until adjournment, notwithstanding the withdrawal of enough shareholders to leave less than a quorum. If a quorum is present, the affirmative vote of the majority of the shares represented at the meeting and entitled to vote on the subject matter shall be the act of the stockholders, unless the vote of a greater number of stockholders voting together or voting by classes is required by law or the charter. Directors, however, are elected by a plurality of the votes cast at an election of directors.

(6) *Shareholder voting*—(i) *Proxies.* Unless otherwise provided in the association's charter, at all meetings of shareholders, a shareholder may vote in person or by proxy executed in writing by the shareholder or by a duly authorized attorney in fact. Proxies may be given telephonically or electronically as long as the holder uses a procedure for verifying the identity of the shareholder. Proxies solicited on behalf of the management shall be voted as directed by the shareholder or, in the absence of such direction, as determined by a majority of the board of directors. No proxy shall be valid more than eleven months from the date of its execution except for a proxy coupled with an interest.

(ii) *Shares controlled by association.* Neither treasury shares of its own stock held by the association nor shares held by another corporation, if a majority of the shares entitled to vote for the election of directors of such other corporation are held by the association, shall be voted at any meeting or counted in determining the total number of outstanding shares at any given time for purposes of any meeting.

(7) *Nominations and new business submitted by shareholders.* Nominations for directors and new business submitted by shareholders shall be voted upon at the annual meeting if such nominations or new business are submitted in writing and delivered to the secretary of the association at least five days prior to the date of the annual meeting. Ballots bearing the names of all the persons nominated shall be provided for use at the annual meeting.

(8) *Informal action by stockholders.* If the bylaws of the association so provide, any action required to be taken at a meeting of the stockholders, or any other action that may be taken at a meeting of the stockholders, may be taken without a meeting if consent in writing has been given by all the stockholders entitled to vote with respect to the subject matter.

(l) *Board of directors*—(1) *General powers and duties.* The business and affairs of the association shall be under the direction of its board of directors. Directors need not be stockholders unless the bylaws so require.

(2) *Number and term.* The bylaws shall set forth a specific number of directors, not a range. The number of directors shall be not fewer than five nor more than fifteen, unless a higher or lower number has been authorized by the OTS, prior to July 21, 2011 or the OCC. Directors shall be elected for a term of one to three years and until their successors are elected and qualified. If a staggered board is chosen, the directors shall be divided into two or three classes as nearly equal in number as possible and one class shall be elected by ballot annually.

(3) *Regular meetings.* The board of directors shall determine the place, frequency, time and procedure for notice of regular meetings.

(4) *Quorum.* A majority of the number of directors shall constitute a quorum for the transaction of business at any meeting of the board of directors. The act of the majority of the directors present at a meeting at which a quorum is present shall be the act of the board of directors, unless a greater number is prescribed by regulation of the OCC.

(5) *Vacancies.* Any vacancy occurring in the board of directors may be filled by the affirmative vote of a majority of the remaining directors although less than a quorum of the board of directors. A director elected to fill a vacancy shall be elected to serve only until the next election of directors by the shareholders. Any directorship to be filled by reason of an increase in the number of directors may be filled by election by the board of directors for a term of office continuing only until the next election of directors by the shareholders.

(6) *Removal or resignation of directors.* (i) At a meeting of shareholders called expressly for that purpose, any director may be removed only for cause, as termination for cause is defined in § 5.21(j)(2)(x)(B), by a vote of the holders of a majority of the shares then entitled to vote at an election of directors. Associations may provide for procedures regarding resignations in the bylaws.

(ii) If less than the entire board is to be removed, no one of the directors may be removed if the votes cast against the removal would be sufficient to elect a director if then cumulatively voted at an election of the class of directors of which such director is a part.

(iii) Whenever the holders of the shares of any class are entitled to elect one or more directors by the provisions of the charter or supplemental sections thereto, the provisions of this section shall apply, in respect to the removal of a director or directors so elected, to the vote of the holders of the outstanding shares of that class and not to the vote of the outstanding shares as a whole.

(7) *Executive and other committees.* The board of directors, by resolution adopted by a majority of the full board, may designate from among its members an executive committee and one or more other committees. No committee shall have the authority of the board of directors with reference to: The declaration of dividends; the amendment of the charter or bylaws of the association; recommending to the stockholders a plan of merger, consolidation,

or conversion; the sale, lease, or other disposition of all, or substantially all, of the property and assets of the association otherwise than in the usual and regular course of its business; a voluntary dissolution of the association; a revocation of any of the foregoing; or the approval of a transaction in which any member of the executive committee, directly or indirectly, has any material beneficial interest. The designation of any committee and the delegation of authority thereto shall not operate to relieve the board of directors, or any director, of any responsibility imposed by law or regulation.

(8) *Notice of special meetings.* Written notice of at least 24 hours regarding any special meeting of the board of directors or of any committee designated thereby shall be given to each director in accordance with the bylaws, although such notice may be waived by the director. The attendance of a director at a meeting shall constitute a waiver of notice of such meeting, except where a director attends a meeting for the express purpose of objecting to the transaction of any business because the meeting is not lawfully called or convened. Neither the business to be transacted at, nor the purpose of, any meeting need be specified in the notice or waiver of notice of such meeting. The bylaws may provide for electronic participation at a meeting.

(9) *Action without a meeting.* Any action required or permitted to be taken by the board of directors at a meeting may be taken without a meeting if a consent in writing, setting forth the actions so taken, shall be signed by all of the directors.

(10) *Presumption of assent.* A director of the association who is present at a meeting of the board of directors at which action on any association matter is taken shall be presumed to have assented to the action taken unless his or her dissent or abstention shall be entered in the minutes of the meeting or unless a written dissent to such action shall be filed with the person acting as the secretary of the meeting before the adjournment thereof or shall be forwarded by registered mail to the secretary of the association within five days after the date on which a copy of the minutes of the meeting is received. Such right to dissent shall not apply to a director who voted in favor of such action.

(11) *Age limitation on directors.* A Federal association may provide a bylaw on age limitation for directors. Bylaws on age limitations must comply with all Federal laws, rules and regulations.

(m) *Officers*—(1) *Positions.* The officers of the association shall be a president, one or more vice presidents, a secretary, and a treasurer or comptroller, each of whom shall be elected by the board of directors. The board of directors may also designate the chairman of the board as an officer. The offices of the secretary and treasurer or comptroller may be held by the same person and the vice president may also be either the secretary or the treasurer or comptroller. The board of directors may designate one or more vice presidents as executive vice president or senior vice president.

(2) *Removal.* Any officer may be removed by the board of directors whenever in its judgment the best interests of the association will be served thereby; but such removal, other than for cause, as termination for cause is defined in § 5.21(j)(2)(x)(B), shall be without prejudice to the contractual rights, if any, of the person so removed. Employment contracts shall conform with 12 CFR 163.39.

(3) *Age limitation on officers.* A Federal association may provide a bylaw on age limitation for officers. Bylaws on age limitations must comply with all Federal laws, rules, and regulations.

(n) *Certificates for shares and their transfer*—(1) *Certificates for shares.* Certificates representing shares of capital stock of the association shall be in such form as shall be determined by the board of directors and approved by the OCC. The name and address of the person to whom the shares are issued, with the number of shares and date of issue, shall be entered on the stock transfer books of the association. All certificates surrendered to the association for transfer shall be cancelled and no new certificate shall be issued until the former certificate for a like number of shares shall have been surrendered and cancelled, except that in the case of a lost or destroyed certificate a new certificate may be issued upon such terms and indemnity to the association as the board of directors may prescribe.

(2) *Transfer of shares.* Transfer of shares of capital stock of the association shall be made only on its stock transfer books. Authority for such transfer shall be given only by the holder of record or by a legal representative, who shall furnish proper evidence of such authority, or by an attorney authorized by a duly executed power of attorney and filed with the association. The transfer shall be made only on surrender for cancellation of the certificate for the shares. The person in whose name shares of capital stock stand on the books of the association shall be deemed by the association to be the owner for all purposes.

[80 FR 28425, May 18, 2015, as amended at 82 FR 8103, Jan. 23, 2017]

§ 5.23 Conversion to become a Federal savings association.

(a) *Authority.* 12 U.S.C. 35, 1462a, 1463, 1464, 1467a, 2903, and 5412(b)(2)(B).

(b) *Scope.* (1) This section describes procedures and standards governing OCC review and approval of an application by a mutual depository institution to convert to a Federal mutual savings association or an application by a stock depository institution to convert to a Federal stock savings association.

(2) As used in this section, depository institution means any commercial bank (including a private bank), a savings bank, a trust company, a savings and loan association, a building and loan association, a homestead association, a cooperative bank, an industrial bank or a credit union, chartered in the United States and having its principal office located in the United States.

(c) *Licensing requirements.* A depository institution that is mutual in form ("mutual depository institution") shall submit an application and obtain prior OCC approval to convert to a Federal mutual savings association. A stock depository institution shall submit an application and obtain prior OCC approval to convert to a Federal stock savings association. At the time of conversion, the applicant must have deposits insured by the Federal Deposit Insurance Corporation (FDIC). An institution that is not already insured by the FDIC must apply to the FDIC, and obtain FDIC approval, for deposit insurance before converting.

(d) *Conversion of a mutual depository institution or a stock depository institution to a Federal savings association*—(1) *Policy.* Consistent with the OCC's chartering policy, it is OCC policy to allow conversion to a Federal savings association charter by another financial institution that can operate safely and soundly as a Federal savings association in compliance with applicable laws, regulations, and policies. This includes consideration of the factors set out in section 5(e) of the Home Owners' Loan Act, 12 U.S.C. 1464(e). The converting financial institution must obtain all necessary regulatory and shareholder or member approvals. The OCC may deny an application by any mutual depository institution or stock depository institution to convert to a Federal mutual savings association charter or Federal stock association charter, respectively, on the basis of the standards for denial set forth in § 5.13(b) or when conversion would permit the applicant to escape supervisory action by its current regulators.

(2) *Procedures*—(i) *Prefiling communications.* The applicant should consult with the appropriate OCC licensing office prior to filing if it anticipates that its application will raise unusual or complex issues. If a prefiling meeting is appropriate, it will normally be held in the OCC licensing office where the application will be filed, but may be held at another location at the request of the applicant.

(ii) *Application.* A mutual depository institution or a stock depository institution shall submit its application to convert to a Federal mutual savings association or Federal stock depository association, respectively, to the appropriate OCC licensing office and shall send a copy of the application to its current appropriate Federal banking agency. The application must:

(A) Be signed by the president or other duly authorized officer;

(B) Identify each branch that the resulting financial institution expects to operate after conversion;

(C) Include the institution's most recent audited financial statements (if any);

(D) Include the latest report of condition and report of income (the most recent daily statement of condition will suffice if the institution does not file these reports);

(E) Unless otherwise advised by the OCC in a prefiling communication, include an opinion of counsel that, in the case of state-chartered institutions, the conversion is not in contravention of applicable state law, or in the case of Federally-chartered institutions, the conversion is not in contravention of applicable Federal law;

(F) State whether the institution wishes to exercise fiduciary powers after the conversion;

(G) Identify all subsidiaries, service corporation investments, bank service company investments, and other equity investments that will be retained following the conversion, and provide the information and analysis of the subsidiaries' activities and the service corporation investments and other equity investments that would be required if the converting mutual institution or stock institution were a Federal mutual savings association or Federal stock savings association, respectively, establishing each subsidiary or making each service corporation or other equity investment pursuant to § 5.35, § 5.36, § 5.38, or § 5.59, or other applicable law and regulation;

(H) Identify any nonconforming assets (including nonconforming subsidiaries) and nonconforming activities that the institution engages in, and describe the plans to retain or divest those assets and activities;

(I) Include a business plan if the converting institution has been operating for less than three years, plans to make significant changes to its business after the conversion, or at the request of the OCC;

(J) Include a list of all outstanding conditions or other requirements imposed by the institution's current appropriate Federal banking agency and, if applicable, current state bank supervisor or state attorney-general in any cease and desist order, written agreement, other formal enforcement order, memorandum of understanding, approval of any application, notice or request, commitment letter, board resolution, or in any other manner, including the converting institution's analysis whether any such actions prohibit conversion under 12 U.S.C. 35, and the converting institution's plans regarding adhering to such conditions and requirements after conversion; and

(K) If the converting institution does not meet the qualified thrift lender test of 12 U.S.C. 1467a(m), include a plan to achieve compliance within a reasonable period of time and a request for an exception from the OCC.

(iii) The OCC may permit a Federal savings association to retain nonconforming assets of a converting institution for the time period prescribed by the OCC following a conversion, subject to conditions and an OCC determination of the carrying value of the retained assets consistent with the requirements of section 5(c) of the HOLA relating to loans and investments. The OCC may permit a Federal savings association to continue nonconforming activities of a converting institution for the time period prescribed by the OCC following a conversion, subject to conditions.

(iv) Approval for an institution to convert to a Federal savings association expires if the conversion has not occurred within six months of the OCC's approval of the application, unless the OCC grants an extension of time.

(v) When the OCC determines that the applicant has satisfied all statutory and regulatory requirements and any other conditions, the OCC issues a charter. The charter provides that the institution is authorized to begin conducting business as a Federal mutual savings association or a Federal stock savings association as of a specified date.

(3) *Exceptions to rules of general applicability.* Sections 5.8, 5.10, and 5.11 do not apply to this section. However, if the OCC concludes that an application presents significant or novel policy, supervisory, or legal issues, the OCC may determine that any or all parts of §§ 5.8, 5.10, and 5.11 apply.

(4) *Expedited review.* An application by an eligible national bank to convert

to a Federal savings association charter is deemed approved by the OCC as of the 60th day after the filing is received by the OCC, unless the OCC notifies the applicant prior to that date that the filing is not eligible for expedited review under §5.13(a)(2).

(e) *Conversion of a mutual depository institution to a Federal mutual savings association—supplemental rules.* In addition to the rules and procedures set forth in paragraph (d) of this section, an applicant converting from a mutual depository institution to a Federal mutual savings association shall comply with the following: After a Federal charter is issued to a converting institution, the association's members shall after due notice, or upon a valid adjournment of a previous legal meeting, hold a meeting to elect directors and take care of all other actions necessary to fully effectuate the conversion and operate the association in accordance with law and these rules and regulations. Immediately thereafter, the board of directors shall meet, elect officers, and transact any other appropriate business.

(f) *Conversion of a national bank to a Federal stock savings association—supplemental rules*—(1) *Additional procedures.* A national bank may convert to a Federal stock savings association. In addition to the rules and procedures set forth in paragraph (d) of this section, a national bank that desires to convert to a Federal stock savings association shall follow the requirements and procedures set forth in 12 U.S.C. 214a as if it were converting to a state bank and include in its application information demonstrating compliance with the applicable requirements of 12 U.S.C. 214a.

(2) *Termination and change of status.* The appropriate OCC licensing office provides instructions to the converting national bank for terminating its status as a national bank and beginning its status as a Federal savings association.

(g) *Continuation of business and entity.* The existence of the converting institution shall continue in the resulting Federal savings association. The resulting Federal savings association shall be considered the same business and entity as the converting institution, although as to rights, powers, and duties, the resulting Federal savings association is a Federal savings association. Any and all of the assets and other property (whether real, personal, mixed, tangible or intangible, including choses in action, rights, and credits) of the converting institution become assets and property of the resulting Federal savings association when the conversion occurs. Similarly, any and all of the obligations and debts of and claims against the converting institution become obligations and debts of and claims against the Federal savings association when the conversion occurs.

[80 FR 28430, May 18, 2015]

§5.24 Conversion to become a national bank.

(a) *Authority.* 12 U.S.C. 35, 93a, 214a, 214b, 214c, and 2903.

(b) *Licensing requirements.* A state bank, a stock state savings association, or a Federal stock savings association shall submit an application and obtain prior OCC approval to convert to a national bank charter. A Federal mutual savings association that plans to convert to a national bank must first convert to a Federal stock savings association under 12 CFR part 192.

(c) *Scope.* (1) This section describes procedures and standards governing OCC review and approval of an application by a state bank, a stock state savings association, or a Federal stock savings association to convert to a national bank charter.

(2) As used in this section, *state bank* includes a state bank as defined in 12 U.S.C. 214(a).

(d) *Policy.* Consistent with the OCC's chartering policy, it is OCC policy to allow conversion to a national bank charter by another financial institution that can operate safely and soundly as a national bank in compliance with applicable laws, regulations, and policies. A converting financial institution also must obtain all necessary regulatory and shareholder approvals. The OCC may deny an application by any state bank, stock state savings association, and any Federal stock savings association to convert to a national bank charter on the basis of the standards for denial set forth in §5.13(b), or when conversion would permit the applicant to escape supervisory action by its current regulators.

(e) *Procedures*—(1) *Prefiling communications.* The applicant should consult with the appropriate OCC licensing office prior to filing if it anticipates that its application will raise unusual or complex issues. If a prefiling meeting is appropriate, it will normally be held at the OCC licensing office where the application will be filed, but may be held at another location at the request of the applicant.

(2) *Application.* A state bank, a stock state savings association, or a Federal stock savings association shall submit its application to convert to a national bank to the appropriate OCC licensing office and send a copy to its current appropriate Federal banking agency. The application must:

(i) Be signed by the president or other duly authorized officer;

(ii) Identify each branch that the resulting bank expects to operate after conversion;

(iii) Include the institution's most recent audited financial statements (if any);

(iv) Include the latest report of condition and report of income (the most recent daily statement of condition will suffice if the institution does not file these reports);

(v) Unless otherwise advised by the OCC in a prefiling communication, include an opinion of counsel that, in the case of a state bank, the conversion is not in contravention of applicable state law, or in the case of a Federal stock savings association, the conversion is not in contravention of applicable Federal law;

(vi) State whether the institution wishes to exercise fiduciary powers after the conversion;

(vii) Identify all subsidiaries, bank service company investments, and other equity investments that will be retained following the conversion, and provide the information and analysis of the subsidiaries' activities, the bank service company investments, and the other equity investments that would be required if the converting bank or savings association were a national bank establishing each subsidiary or making each bank service company investment or other equity investment pursuant to §5.34, §5.35, §5.36, §5.39, 12 CFR part 1, or other applicable law and regulation;

(viii) Identify any nonconforming assets (including nonconforming subsidiaries) and nonconforming activities that the institution engages in and describe the plans to retain or divest those assets and activities;

(ix) Include a business plan if the converting institution has been operating for fewer than three years, plans to make significant changes to its business after the conversion, or at the request of the OCC; and

(x) List all outstanding conditions or other requirements imposed by the institution's current appropriate Federal banking agency and, if applicable, current state bank supervisor or state attorney-general in any cease and desist order, written agreement, other formal enforcement order, memorandum of understanding, approval of any application, notice or request, commitment letter, board resolution, or in any other manner, including the converting institution's analysis whether the conversion is prohibited under 12 U.S.C. 35, and state the institution's plans regarding adhering to such conditions or requirements after conversion.

(3) The OCC may permit a national bank to retain nonconforming assets of a state bank or stock state savings association, subject to conditions and an OCC determination of the carrying value of the retained assets, pursuant to 12 U.S.C. 35. The OCC may permit a national bank to continue nonconforming activities of a state bank or stock state savings association, or to retain the nonconforming assets or nonconforming activities of a Federal stock savings association, for a reasonable period of time following a conversion, subject to conditions imposed by the OCC.

(4) Approval for an institution to convert to a national bank expires if the conversion has not occurred within six months of the OCC's approval of the application, unless the OCC grants an extension of time.

(5) When the OCC determines that the applicant has satisfied all statutory and regulatory requirements, including those set forth in 12 U.S.C. 35, and any other conditions, the OCC

issues a charter certificate. The certificate provides that the institution is authorized to begin conducting business as a national bank as of a specified date.

(f) *Conversion of a Federal stock savings association to a national bank—supplemental rules*—(1) *Additional information.* A Federal stock savings association may convert to a national bank. In addition to the rules and procedures set forth in paragraph (e) of this section, a Federal stock savings association that desires to convert to a national bank shall include in its application information demonstrating compliance with applicable laws regarding the permissibility, requirements, and procedures for conversions, including any applicable stockholder or account holder approval requirements.

(2) *Termination and change of status.* The appropriate OCC licensing office provides instructions to the converting Federal stock savings association for terminating its status as a Federal stock savings association and beginning its status as a national bank.

(g) *Exceptions to rules of general applicability.* Sections 5.8, 5.10, and 5.11 do not apply to this section. However, if the OCC concludes that an application presents significant or novel policy, supervisory, or legal issues, the OCC may determine that any or all of §§ 5.8, 5.10, and 5.11 apply.

(h) *Expedited review.* An application by an eligible savings association to convert to a national bank charter is deemed approved by the OCC as of the 60th day after the filing is received by the OCC, unless the OCC notifies the applicant prior to that date that the filing is not eligible for expedited review under § 5.13(a)(2).

(i) *Continuation of business and corporate entity.* The corporate existence of the converting institution shall continue in the resulting national bank. The resulting national bank shall be considered the same business and corporate entity as the converting institution, although as to rights, powers, and duties, the resulting national bank is a national bank. Any and all of the assets and other property (whether real, personal, mixed, tangible or intangible, including choses in action, rights, and credits) of the converting institution become assets and property of the resulting national bank when the conversion occurs. Similarly, any and all of the obligations and debts of and claims against the converting institution become obligations and debts of and claims against the national bank when the conversion occurs.

[80 FR 28432, May 18, 2015]

§ 5.25 Conversion from a national bank or Federal savings association to a state bank or state savings association.

(a) *Authority.* 12 U.S.C. 93a, 214a, 214b, 214c, 214d, 1462a, 1463, 1464, and 5412(b)(2)(B).

(b) *Licensing requirement.* A national bank shall give notice to the OCC before converting to a state bank (including a state bank as defined in 12 U.S.C. 214(a)) or a state savings association. A Federal savings association shall give notice to the OCC before converting to a state savings association or a state bank. A Federal mutual savings association that plans to convert to a stock state bank must first convert to a Federal stock savings association under 12 CFR part 192.

(c) *Scope.* This section describes the procedures for a national bank seeking to convert to a state bank or a state savings association or for a Federal savings association seeking to convert to a state savings association or a state bank.

(d) *Procedures*—(1) *National banks.* A national bank may convert to a state bank (including a state bank as defined in 214(a)) or a state savings association in accordance with 12 U.S.C. 214a and 214c, without prior OCC approval, subject to compliance with 12 U.S.C. 214d. Termination of a national bank's status as a national bank occurs upon the bank's completion of the requirements of 12 U.S.C. 214a, and upon the OCC's receipt of the bank's national bank charter in connection with the consummation of the conversion.

(2) *Federal savings associations.* A Federal savings association may convert to a state savings association or to a state bank, without prior OCC approval, subject to compliance with 12 U.S.C. 1464(i)(6). Termination of a Federal savings association's status as a Federal savings association occurs

upon receipt of the Federal savings association's charter in connection with the consummation of the conversion.

(3) *Notice of intent.* (i) A national bank that desires to convert to a state bank (including a state bank as defined in 214(a)) or state savings association, or a Federal savings association that desires to convert to a state savings association or a state bank, shall submit a notice of intent to convert to the appropriate OCC licensing office. The national bank or Federal savings association shall file this notice with the OCC at the time it files a conversion application with the appropriate state authority or the prospective appropriate Federal banking agency. The national bank or Federal savings association also shall transmit a copy of the conversion application to the prospective appropriate Federal banking agency if it has not already done so.

(ii) The notice shall include:

(A) A copy of the conversion application; and

(B) An analysis demonstrating that the conversion is in compliance with laws of the applicable jurisdictions regarding the permissibility, requirements, and procedures for conversions, including any applicable stockholder or account holder approval requirements.

(4) *Consultation.* The OCC may consult with the appropriate state authorities or the prospective appropriate Federal banking agency regarding the proposed conversion.

(5) *Termination of status.* After receipt of the notice, the appropriate OCC licensing office provides instructions to the national bank or Federal savings association for terminating its status as a national bank or Federal savings association.

(e) *Exceptions to rules of general applicability.* Sections 5.5 through 5.8 and 5.10 through 5.13 do not apply to this section.

[80 FR 28433, May 18, 2015]

§ 5.26 Fiduciary powers of national banks and Federal savings associations.

(a) *Authority.* 12 U.S.C. 92a and 1462a, 1463, 1464(n), and 5412(b)(2)(B).

(b) *Licensing requirements.* A national bank or Federal savings association must submit an application and obtain prior approval from, or in certain circumstances file a notice with, the OCC in order to exercise fiduciary powers. No approval or notice is required in the following circumstances:

(1) Where two or more national banks consolidate or merge, and any of the national banks has, prior to the consolidation or merger, received OCC approval to exercise fiduciary powers and that approval is in force at the time of the consolidation or merger, the resulting national bank may exercise fiduciary powers in the same manner and to the same extent as the national bank to which approval was originally granted;

(2) Where two or more Federal savings associations consolidate or merge, and any of the Federal savings associations has, prior to the consolidation or merger, received approval from the OCC or the Office of Thrift Supervision to exercise fiduciary powers and that approval is in force at the time of the consolidation or merger, the resulting Federal savings association may exercise fiduciary powers in the same manner and to the same extent as the Federal savings association to which approval was originally granted;

(3) Where a national bank with prior OCC approval to exercise fiduciary powers is the resulting bank in a merger or consolidation with a state bank, state savings association, or Federal savings association and the national bank will exercise fiduciary powers in the same manner and to the same extent to which approval was originally granted; and

(4) Where a Federal savings association with prior approval from the OCC or the Office of Thrift Supervision to exercise fiduciary powers is the resulting savings association in a merger or consolidation with a state bank, state savings association, or national bank and the Federal savings association will exercise fiduciary powers in the same manner and to the same extent to which approval was originally granted.

(c) *Scope.* This section sets forth the procedures governing OCC review and approval of an application, and in certain cases the filing of a notice, by a national bank or Federal savings association to exercise fiduciary powers.

Fiduciary activities of national banks are subject to the provisions of 12 CFR part 9. Fiduciary activities of Federal savings associations are subject to the provisions of 12 CFR part 150.

(d) *Policy*. The exercise of fiduciary powers is primarily a management decision of the national bank or Federal savings association. The OCC generally permits a national bank or Federal savings association to exercise fiduciary powers if the bank or savings association is operating in a satisfactory manner, the proposed activities comply with applicable statutes and regulations, and the bank or savings association retains qualified fiduciary management.

(e) *Procedure*—(1) *In general*. The following institutions must obtain approval from the OCC in order to exercise fiduciary powers:

(i) A national bank or Federal savings association without fiduciary powers:

(ii) A national bank without fiduciary powers that desires to exercise fiduciary powers as the resulting bank after merging with a state bank, state savings association, or Federal savings association with fiduciary powers or a Federal savings association without fiduciary powers that desires to exercise fiduciary powers as the resulting savings association after merging with a state bank, state savings association or national bank with fiduciary powers;

(iii) A national bank that results from the conversion of a state bank or a state or Federal savings association that was exercising fiduciary powers prior to the conversion or a Federal savings association that results from a conversion of a state or national bank or a state savings association that was exercising fiduciary powers prior to the conversion; and

(iv) A national bank or Federal savings association that has received approval from the OCC to exercise limited fiduciary powers that desires to exercise full fiduciary powers.

(2) *Application*. (i) Except as provided in paragraph (e)(2)(ii) of this section, a national bank or Federal savings association that desires to exercise fiduciary powers shall submit to the OCC an application requesting approval. The application must contain:

(A) A statement requesting full or limited powers (specifying which powers);

(B) A statement that the capital and surplus of the national bank or Federal savings association is not less than the capital and surplus required by state law of state banks, trust companies, and other corporations exercising comparable fiduciary powers;

(C) Sufficient biographical information on proposed trust management personnel to enable the OCC to assess their qualifications;

(D) A description of the locations where the national bank or Federal savings association will conduct fiduciary activities;

(E) If requested by the OCC, an opinion of counsel that the proposed activities do not violate applicable Federal or state law, including citations to applicable law; and

(F) Any other information necessary to enable the OCC to sufficiently assess the factors described in paragraph (e)(2)(iii) of this section.

(ii) If approval to exercise fiduciary powers is desired in connection with any other transaction subject to an application under this part, the applicant covered under paragraph (e)(1)(ii), (e)(1)(iii), or (e)(1)(iv) of this section may include a request for approval of fiduciary powers, including the information required by paragraph (e)(2)(i) of this section, as part of its other application. The OCC does not require a separate application requesting approval to exercise fiduciary powers under these circumstances.

(iii) When reviewing any application filed under this section, the OCC considers factors such as the following:

(A) The financial condition of the national bank or Federal savings association;

(B) The adequacy of the national bank's or Federal savings association's capital and surplus and whether it is sufficient under the circumstances and not less than the capital and surplus required by state law or state banks, trust companies, and other corporations exercising comparable fiduciary powers;

(C) The character and ability of proposed trust management, including qualifications, experience, and competency. The OCC must approve any trust management change the bank or savings association makes prior to commencing trust activities;

(D) The adequacy of the proposed business plan, if applicable;

(E) The needs of the community to be served; and

(F) Any other factors or circumstances that the OCC considers proper.

(3) *Expedited review.* An application by an eligible national bank or eligible Federal savings association to exercise fiduciary powers is deemed approved by the OCC as of the 30th day after the application is received by the OCC, unless the OCC notifies the bank or savings association prior to that date that the filing is not eligible for expedited review under § 5.13(a)(2).

(4) *Permit.* Approval of an application under this section constitutes a permit under 12 U.S.C. 92a for national banks and 12 U.S.C. 1464(n) for Federal savings associations to conduct the fiduciary powers requested in the application.

(5) *Notice required.* A national bank or Federal savings association that has ceased to conduct previously approved fiduciary powers for 18 consecutive months must provide the OCC with a notice describing the nature and manner of the activities proposed to be conducted and containing the information required by paragraph (e)(2)(i) of this section 60 days prior to commencing any fiduciary activity.

(6) *Notice of fiduciary activities in additional states.* (i) No further application under this section is required when a national bank or Federal savings association with existing OCC approval to exercise fiduciary powers plans to engage in any of the activities specified in § 9.7(d) of this chapter or to conduct activities ancillary to its fiduciary business, in a state in addition to the state described in the application for fiduciary powers that the OCC has approved.

(ii) Unless the national bank or Federal savings association provides notice through other means (such as a merger application), the national bank or Federal savings association shall provide written notice to the OCC no later than 10 days after it begins to engage in any of the activities specified in § 9.7(d) of this chapter in a state in addition to the state described in the application for fiduciary powers that the OCC has approved. The written notice must identify the new state or states involved, identify the fiduciary activities to be conducted, and describe the extent to which the activities differ materially from the fiduciary activities the national bank or Federal savings association previously conducted.

(iii) No notice is required if the national bank or Federal savings association is conducting only activities ancillary to its fiduciary business through a trust representative office or otherwise.

(7) *Exceptions to rules of general applicability.* Sections 5.8, 5.10, and 5.11 do not apply to this section. However, if the OCC concludes that an application presents significant or novel policy, supervisory, or legal issues, the OCC may determine that any or all parts of §§ 5.8, 5.10, and 5.11 apply.

(8) *Expiration of approval.* Approval expires if a national bank or Federal savings association does not commence fiduciary activities within 18 months from the date of approval, unless the OCC grants an extension of time.

[80 FR 28433, May 18, 2015]

Subpart C—Expansion of Activities

§ 5.30 Establishment, acquisition, and relocation of a branch of a national bank.

(a) *Authority.* 12 U.S.C. 1–42 and 2901–2907.

(b) *Licensing requirements.* A national bank shall submit an application and obtain prior OCC approval in order to establish or relocate a branch.

(c) *Scope*—(1) *In general.* This section describes the procedures and standards governing OCC review and approval of an application by a national bank to establish a new branch or to relocate a branch.

(2) *Branch established through a conversion or business combination.* The standards of this section governing review and approval of applications by the OCC and, as applicable, 12 U.S.C. 36(b), but not the application procedures set forth in this section, apply to

branches acquired or retained in a conversion approved under 12 CFR 5.24 or a business combination approved under §5.33. A branch acquired or retained in a conversion or business combination is subject to the application procedures set forth in §§5.24 or 5.33.

(d) *Definitions*—(1) *Branch* includes any branch bank, branch office, branch agency, additional office, or any branch place of business established by a national bank in the United States or its territories at which deposits are received, checks paid, or money lent.

(i) A branch established by a national bank includes a mobile facility, temporary facility, intermittent facility, drop box or a seasonal agency as described in 12 U.S.C. 36(c).

(ii) A facility otherwise described in this paragraph (d)(1) is not a branch if:

(A) The bank establishing the facility does not permit members of the public to have physical access to the facility for purposes of making deposits, paying checks, or borrowing money (*e.g.*, an office established by the bank that receives deposits only through the mail); or

(B) It is located at the site of, or is an extension of, an approved main office or branch office of the national bank. The OCC determines whether a facility is an extension of an existing main office or branch office on a case-by-case basis. For this purpose, the OCC will consider a drive-in or pedestrian facility located within 500 feet of a public entrance to an existing main office or branch office to be an extension of the existing main office or branch office, provided the functions performed at the drive-in or pedestrian facility are limited to functions that are ordinarily performed at a teller window.

(iii) A branch does not include an automated teller machine (ATM), a remote service unit (such as an automated loan machine or personal computer used in providing financial services), a loan production office, a deposit production office, a trust office, an administrative office, a data processing office, or any other office that does not engage in any of the activities in paragraph (d)(1) of this section.

(2) *Home state* means the state in which the national bank's main office is located.

(3) *Intermittent branch* means a branch that is operated by a national bank for one or more limited periods of time to provide branch banking services at a specified recurring event, on the grounds or premises where the event is held or at a fixed site adjacent to the grounds or premises where the event is held, and exclusively during the occurrence of the event. Examples of an intermittent branch include the operation of a branch on the campus of, or at a fixed site adjacent to the campus of, a specific college during school registration periods; or the operation of a branch during a state fair on state fairgrounds or at a fixed site adjacent to the fairgrounds.

(4) *Messenger service* has the meaning set forth in 12 CFR 7.1012.

(5) *Mobile branch* is a branch of a national bank, other than a messenger service branch, that does not have a single, permanent site, and includes a vehicle that travels to various public locations to enable customers to conduct their banking business. A mobile branch may provide services at various regularly scheduled locations or it may be open at irregular times and locations such as at county fairs, sporting events, or school registration periods. A branch license is needed for each mobile unit.

(6) *Temporary branch* means a branch of a national bank that is located at a fixed site and which, from the time of its opening, is scheduled to, and will, permanently close no later than a certain date (not longer than one year after the branch is first opened) specified in the branch application and the public notice.

(e) *Policy*. In determining whether to approve an application to establish or relocate a branch, the OCC is guided by the following principles:

(1) Maintaining a safe and sound banking system;

(2) Encouraging a national bank to provide fair access to financial services by helping to meet the credit needs of its entire community;

(3) Ensuring compliance with laws and regulations; and

(4) Promoting fair treatment of customers including efficiency and better service.

(f) *Procedures*—(1) *In general.* Except as provided in paragraph (f)(2) of this section, each national bank proposing to establish a branch shall submit to the appropriate OCC licensing office a separate application for each proposed branch.

(2) *Messenger services.* A national bank may request approval, through a single application, for multiple messenger services to serve the same general geographic area. (*See* 12 CFR 7.1012). Unless otherwise required by law, the bank need not list the specific locations to be served.

(3) *Jointly established branches.* If a national bank proposes to establish a branch jointly with one or more national banks or other depository institutions, only one of the national banks must submit a branch application. The national bank submitting the application may act as agent for all national banks in the group of depository institutions proposing to share the branch. The application must include the name and main office address of each national bank in the group.

(4) *Intermittent branches.* Prior to operating an intermittent branch, a national bank shall file a branch application and publish notice in accordance with § 5.8, both of which shall identify the event at which the branch will be operated; designate a location for operation of the branch which shall be on the grounds or premises at which the event is held or on a fixed site adjacent to those grounds or premises; and specify the approximate time period during which the event will be held and during which the branch will operate, including whether operation of the branch will be on an annual or otherwise recurring basis. If the branch is approved, then the bank need not obtain approval each time it seeks to operate the branch in accordance with the original application and approval.

(5) *Authorization.* The OCC authorizes operation of the branch when all requirements and conditions for opening are satisfied.

(6) *Expedited review.* An application submitted by an eligible bank to establish or relocate a branch is deemed approved by the OCC as of the 15th day after the close of the applicable public comment period or the 45th day after the filing is received by the OCC (or in the case of a short-distance relocation the 30th day after the filing is received by the OCC), whichever is later, unless the OCC notifies the bank prior to that date that the filing is not eligible for expedited review, or the expedited review process is extended, under § 5.13(a)(2). An application to establish or relocate more than one branch is deemed approved by the OCC as of the 15th day after the close of the last public comment period.

(g) *Interstate branches.* A national bank that seeks to establish and operate a *de novo* branch in any state other than the bank's home state or a state in which the bank already has a branch shall satisfy the standards and requirements of 12 U.S.C. 36(g).

(h) *Exceptions to rules of general applicability.* (1) A national bank filing an application for a mobile branch or messenger service branch shall publish a public notice, as described in § 5.8, in the communities in which the bank proposes to engage in business.

(2) The comment period on an application to engage in a short-distance relocation is 15 days.

(3) The OCC may waive or reduce the public notice and comment period, as appropriate, with respect to an application to establish a branch to restore banking services to a community affected by a disaster or to temporarily replace banking facilities where, because of an emergency, the bank cannot provide services or must curtail banking services.

(4) The OCC may waive or reduce the public notice and comment period, as appropriate, for an application by a national bank with a CRA rating of Satisfactory or better to establish a temporary branch which, if it were established by a state bank to operate in the manner proposed, would be permissible under state law without state approval.

(i) *Expiration of approval.* Approval expires if a branch has not commenced business within 18 months after the date of approval unless the OCC grants an extension.

(j) *Branch closings.* A national bank shall comply with the requirements of

12 U.S.C. 1831r–1 with respect to procedures for branch closings.

[80 FR 28435, May 18, 2015]

§5.31 Establishment, acquisition, and relocation of a branch and establishment of an agency office of a Federal savings association.

(a) *Authority.* 12 U.S.C. 1462a, 1463, 1464. 2901–2907 and 5412(b)(2)(B).

(b) *Licensing requirements.* A Federal savings association shall submit an application and obtain prior OCC approval in order to establish or relocate a branch or to establish an agency office or conduct additional activities at an agency office, if required under this section.

(c) *Scope*—(1) *In general.* This section describes the procedures and standards governing OCC review and approval of an application by a Federal savings association to establish a new branch or to relocate a branch and the circumstances in which a Federal savings association may establish or relocate a branch without application to the OCC. It also describes the authority of a Federal savings association to establish an agency office.

(2) *Branch established through a conversion or business combination.* The standards of this section governing review and approval of applications by the OCC, but not the application procedures set forth in this section, apply to branches acquired or retained in a conversion approved under 12 CFR 5.23 or a business combination approved under 12 CFR 5.33. A branch acquired or retained in a conversion or business combination is subject to the application procedures set forth in §5.23 or §5.33.

(3) *Branching by savings associations in the District of Columbia.* This section also implements section 5(m) of the HOLA, 12 U.S.C. 1464(m), addressing branching by savings associations in the District of Columbia.

(d) *Definitions.* (1) A *branch office* of a Federal savings association for purposes of this section is a branch office as defined in 12 CFR 145.92(a).

(2) *Home state* means the state in which the Federal savings association's home office is located.

(e) *Policy.* In determining whether to approve an application to establish or relocate a branch, the OCC is guided by the following principles:

(1) Maintaining a safe and sound banking system;

(2) Encouraging a Federal savings association to provide fair access to financial services by helping to meet the credit needs of its entire community;

(3) Ensuring compliance with laws and regulations; and

(4) Promoting fair treatment of customers including efficiency and better service.

(f) *Procedures*—(1) *Application requirements.* (i) Except as provided in paragraph (f)(2) of this section, each Federal savings association proposing to establish or relocate a branch shall submit to the appropriate OCC licensing office a separate application for each proposed branch.

(ii) *Authorization.* The OCC authorizes operation of the branch when all requirements and conditions for opening are satisfied.

(iii) *Expedited review.* If an application to establish or relocate a branch is required of an eligible Federal savings association, the application is deemed approved by the OCC as of the 15th day after the close of the applicable public comment period or the 45th day after the filing is received by the OCC, whichever is later, unless the OCC notifies the savings association prior to that date that the filing is not eligible for expedited review, or the expedited review process is extended, under §5.13(a)(2). An application to establish or relocate more than one branch is deemed approved by the OCC as of the 15th day after the close of the last public comment period.

(2) *Exceptions.* Except as provided in paragraph (j) of this section, a Federal savings association is not required to submit an application and receive OCC approval under the following circumstances:

(i) *Drive-in or pedestrian offices.* A Federal savings association may establish a drive-in or pedestrian office that is located within 500 feet of a public entrance to its existing home or branch office, provided the functions performed at the office are limited to functions that are ordinarily performed at a teller window.

(ii) *Short-distance relocation.* A Federal savings association may change the permanent location of an existing branch office to a site that is within the market area and short-distance location area, as defined in § 5.3(l).

(iii) *Highly rated Federal savings associations.* A Federal savings association that is an eligible savings association as defined in § 5.3(g) may change the permanent location of, or establish a new, branch office if it meets all of the following requirements:

(A) It published a public notice under § 5.8 of its intent to change the location of the branch office or establish a new branch office. The public notice must be published at least 35 days before the proposed action establishment or relocation. If the notice is published more than 12 months before the proposed action, the publication is invalid.

(B) If the Federal savings association intends to change the location of an existing branch office, it must post a notice of its intent in a prominent location in the existing office to be relocated. This notice must be posted for 30 days from the date of publication of the initial public notice described in paragraph (f)(2)(iii)(A) of this section.

(C)(*1*) No person files a comment opposing the proposed action within 30 days after the date of the publication of the public notice; or

(*2*) A person files a comment opposing the proposed action and the OCC determines that the comment raises issues that are not relevant to the approval standards for an application for a branch or that OCC action in response to the comment is not required.

(3) *Notice of branch opening.* If a Federal savings association is not required to file an application to establish or relocate a branch pursuant to paragraph (f)(2)(iii) of this section, the Federal savings association shall file a notice with the OCC with the date the branch was established or relocated and the address of the branch within 10 days after the opening of the branch.

(g) *Exceptions to rules of general applicability.* (1) The OCC may waive or reduce the public notice and comment period, as appropriate, with respect to an application to establish a branch to restore banking services to a community affected by a disaster or to temporarily replace banking facilities where, because of an emergency, the savings association cannot provide services or must curtail banking services.

(2) The OCC may waive or reduce the public notice and comment period, as appropriate, for an application by a Federal savings association with a CRA rating of Satisfactory or better to establish a temporary branch which, if it were established by a state bank to operate in the manner proposed, would be permissible under state law without state approval.

(h) *Expiration of approval.* Approval expires if a branch has not commenced business within 18 months after the date of approval unless the OCC grants an extension.

(i) *Branch closings.* A Federal savings association shall comply with the applicable requirements of 12 U.S.C. 1831r–1 with respect to procedures for branch closings.

(j) *Section 5(m) of the HOLA.* (1) Under section 5(m)(1) of the HOLA (12 U.S.C. 1464(m)(1)), no savings association may establish or move any branch in the District of Columbia or move its principal office in the District of Columbia without the OCC's prior written approval.

(2) Any Federal savings association that must obtain approval of the OCC under 12 U.S.C. 1464(m)(1) shall follow the application procedures of this section. Any state savings association that must obtain approval of the OCC under 12 U.S.C. 1464(m)(1) shall follow the application procedures of this section as if it were a Federal savings association.

(k) *Agency offices*—(1) *In general.* A Federal savings association may establish or maintain an agency office to engage in one or more of the following activities:

(i) Servicing, originating, or approving loans and contracts;

(ii) Managing or selling real estate owned by the Federal savings association; and

(iii) Conducting fiduciary activities or activities ancillary to the association's fiduciary business in compliance with § 5.26(e).

(2) *Additional services*—(i) *In general.* A Federal savings association may request, and the OCC may approve, any

service not listed in paragraph (k)(1) of this section, except for payment on savings accounts.

(ii) *Application required.* A Federal savings association desiring to engage in such additional services shall submit an application to the appropriate OCC licensing office.

(iii) *Exceptions to rules of general applicability.* Sections 5.8, 5.10, and 5.11 do not apply to filings under this paragraph (k)(2). However, if the OCC concludes that an application presents significant or novel policy, supervisory, or legal issues, the OCC may determine that some or all provisions in §§ 5.8, 5.10, and 5.11 apply.

(3) *Records.* A Federal savings association must maintain records of all business it transacts at an agency office. It must maintain these records at the agency office, and must transmit copies to a home or branch office.

[80 FR 28436, May 18, 2015]

§ 5.32 Expedited procedures for certain reorganizations of a national bank.

(a) *Authority.* 12 U.S.C. 93a and 215a–2.

(b) *Scope.* This section prescribes the procedures for OCC review and approval of a national bank's reorganization to become a subsidiary of a bank holding company or a company that will, upon consummation of such reorganization, become a bank holding company. For purposes of this section, a "bank holding company" means any company that owns or controls a national bank, or will own or control one as a result of the reorganization.

(c) *Licensing requirements.* A national bank shall submit an application to, and obtain approval from, the OCC prior to participating in a reorganization described in paragraph (b) of this section.

(d) *Procedures*—(1) *General.* An application filed in accordance with this section shall be deemed approved on the 30th day after the OCC receives the application, unless the OCC notifies the bank otherwise. Approval is subject to the condition that the bank provide the OCC with 60 days' prior notice of any significant deviation from the bank's business plan or any significant deviation from the proposed changes to the bank's business plan described in the bank's plan of reorganization.

(2) *Reorganization plan.* The application must include a reorganization plan that:

(i) Specifies the manner in which the reorganization shall be carried out;

(ii) Is approved by a majority of the entire board of directors of the national bank;

(iii) Specifies:

(A) The amount and type of consideration that the bank holding company will provide to the shareholders of the reorganizing bank for their shares of stock of the bank;

(B) The date as of which the rights of each shareholder to participate in that exchange will be determined; and

(C) The manner in which the exchange will be carried out;

(iv) Is submitted to the shareholders of the reorganizing bank at a meeting to be held at the call of the directors in accordance with the procedures prescribed in connection with a merger of a national bank under section 3 of the National Bank Consolidation and Merger Act, 12 U.S.C. 215a(a)(2); and

(v) Describes any changes to the bank's business plan resulting from the reorganization.

(3) *Financial and managerial resources and future prospects.* In reviewing an application under this section, the OCC will consider the impact of the proposed affiliation on the financial and managerial resources and future prospects of the national bank.

(4) *Exceptions to rules of general applicability.* Sections 5.8, 5.10, and 5.11 do not apply to this section. However, if the OCC concludes that an application presents significant or novel policy, supervisory, or legal issues, the OCC may determine that some or all provisions in §§ 5.8, 5.10, and 5.11 apply.

(e) *Rights of dissenting shareholders.* Any shareholder of a bank who has voted against an approved reorganization at the meeting referred to in paragraph (d)(2)(iv) of this section, or who has given notice of dissent in writing to the presiding officer at or prior to that meeting, is entitled to receive the value of his or her shares by providing a written request to the bank within 30 days after the consummation of the reorganization, as provided by section 3 of the National Bank Consolidation and Merger Act, 12 U.S.C. 215a(b) and (c), for the merger of a national bank.

(f) *Approval under the Bank Holding Company Act.* This section does not affect the applicability of the Bank Holding Company Act of 1956. Applicants shall indicate in their application the status of any application required to be filed with the Board of Governors of the Federal Reserve System.

(g) *Expiration of approval.* Approval expires if a national bank has not completed the reorganization within one year of the date of approval.

(h) *Adequacy of disclosure.* (1) An applicant shall inform shareholders of all material aspects of a reorganization and comply with applicable requirements of the Federal securities laws, including the OCC's securities regulations at 12 CFR part 11.

(2) Any applicant not subject to the registration provisions of the Securities Exchange Act of 1934 shall submit the proxy materials or information statements it uses in connection with the reorganization to the appropriate OCC licensing office no later than when the materials are sent to the shareholders.

[68 FR 70129, Dec. 17, 2003, as amended at 80 FR 28437, May 18, 2015]

§ 5.33 Business combinations involving a national bank or Federal savings association.

(a) *Authority.* 12 U.S.C. 24(Seventh), 93a, 181, 214a, 214b, 215, 215a, 215a–1, 215a–3, 215b, 215c, 1462a, 1463, 1464, 1467a, 1828(c), 1831u, 2903, and 5412(b)(2)(B).

(b) *Scope.* This section sets forth the provisions governing business combinations and the standards for:

(1) OCC review and approval of an application by a national bank or a Federal savings association for a business combination resulting in a national bank or Federal savings association; and

(2) Requirements of notices and other procedures for national banks and Federal savings associations involved in other combinations in which a national bank or Federal savings association is not the resulting institution.

(c) *Licensing requirements.* As prescribed by this section, a national bank or Federal savings association shall submit an application and obtain prior OCC approval for a business combination when the resulting institution is a national bank or Federal savings association. As prescribed by this section, a national bank or Federal savings association shall give notice to the OCC prior to engaging in an other combination where the resulting institution will not be a national bank or Federal savings association.[1] A national bank shall submit an application and obtain prior OCC approval for any merger between the national bank and one or more of its nonbank affiliates.

(d) *Definitions.* For purposes of this section:

(1) *Bank* means any national bank or any state bank.

(2) *Business combination* means:

(i) Any merger or consolidation between a national bank or a Federal savings association and one or more depository institutions or state trust companies, in which the resulting institution is a national bank or Federal savings association;

(ii) In the case of a Federal savings association, any merger or consolidation with a credit union in which the resulting institution is a Federal savings association;

(iii) In the case of a national bank, any merger between a national bank and one or more of its nonbank affiliates;

(iv) The acquisition by a national bank or a Federal savings association of all, or substantially all, of the assets of another depository institution; or

(v) The assumption by a national bank or a Federal savings association of any deposit liabilities of another insured depository institution or any deposit accounts or other liabilities of a credit union or any other institution that will become deposits at the national bank or Federal savings association.

(3) *Business reorganization* means either:

(i) A business combination between eligible banks and eligible savings associations, or between an eligible bank or an eligible savings association and

[1] Other combination transactions do not require an application under this section. However, some may require an application under 12 CFR 5.53.

an eligible depository institution, that are controlled by the same holding company or that will be controlled by the same holding company prior to the combination; or

(ii) A business combination between an eligible bank or an eligible savings association and an interim national bank or interim Federal savings association chartered in a transaction in which a person or group of persons exchanges its shares of the eligible bank or eligible savings association for shares of a newly formed holding company and receives after the transaction substantially the same proportional share interest in the holding company as it held in the eligible bank or eligible savings association (except for changes in interests resulting from the exercise of dissenters' rights), and the reorganization involves no other transactions involving the bank or savings association.

(4) *Company* means a corporation, limited liability company, partnership, business trust, association, or similar organization.

(5) For business combinations under paragraphs (g)(4) and (5) of this section, a company or shareholder is deemed to *control* another company if:

(i) Such company or shareholder, directly or indirectly, or acting through one or more other persons owns, controls, or has power to vote 25 percent or more of any class of voting securities of the other company, or

(ii) Such company or shareholder controls in any manner the election of a majority of the directors or trustees of the other company. No company shall be deemed to own or control another company by virtue of its ownership or control of shares in a fiduciary capacity.

(6) *Credit union* means a financial institution subject to examination by the National Credit Union Administration Board.

(7) *Home state* means, with respect to a national bank, the state in which the main office of the national bank is located and, with respect to a state bank, the state by which the bank is chartered.

(8) *Interim national bank or interim Federal savings association* means a national bank or Federal savings association that does not operate independently but exists solely as a vehicle to accomplish a business combination.

(9) *Nonbank affiliate* of a national bank means any company (other than a bank or Federal savings association) that controls, is controlled by, or is under common control with the national bank.

(10) *Other combination* means:

(i) Any merger or consolidation between a national bank or a Federal savings association and one or more depository institutions or state trust companies, in which the resulting institution is not a national bank or Federal savings association;

(ii) In the case of a Federal stock savings association, any merger or consolidation with a credit union in which the resulting institution is a credit union;

(iii) The transfer by a national bank or a Federal savings association of any deposit liabilities to another insured depository institution, a credit union or any other institution; or

(iv) The acquisition by a national bank or a Federal savings association of all, or substantially all, of the assets, or the assumption of all or substantially all of the liabilities, of any company other than a depository institution.

(11) *Savings association* and *state savings association* have the meaning set forth in section 3(b)(1) of the Federal Deposit Insurance Act, 12 U.S.C. 1813(b)(1).

(12) *State trust company* means a trust company organized under state law that is not engaged in the business of receiving deposits, other than trust funds.

(e) *Policy*—(1) *Factors*—(i) *In general.* When the OCC evaluates any application for a business combination, the OCC considers the following factors:

(A) The capital level of any resulting national bank or Federal savings association

(B) The conformity of the transaction to applicable law, regulation, and supervisory policies;

(C) The purpose of the transaction;

(D) The impact of the transaction on safety and soundness of the national bank or Federal savings association; and

(E) The effect of the transaction on the national bank's or Federal savings association's shareholders (or members in the case of a mutual savings association), depositors, other creditors, and customers.

(ii) *Bank Merger Act*. When the OCC evaluates an application for a business combination under the Bank Merger Act, the OCC also considers the following factors:

(A) *Competition*. (*1*) The OCC considers the effect of a proposed business combination on competition. The applicant shall provide a competitive analysis of the transaction, including a definition of the relevant geographic market or markets. An applicant may refer to the Comptroller's Licensing Manual for procedures to expedite its competitive analysis.

(*2*) The OCC will deny an application for a business combination if the combination would result in a monopoly or would be in furtherance of any combination or conspiracy to monopolize or attempt to monopolize the business of banking in any part of the United States. The OCC also will deny any proposed business combination whose effect in any section of the United States may be substantially to lessen competition, or tend to create a monopoly, or which in any other manner would be in restraint of trade, unless the probable effects of the transaction in meeting the convenience and needs of the community clearly outweigh the anticompetitive effects of the transaction. For purposes of weighing against anticompetitive effects, a business combination may have favorable effects in meeting the convenience and needs of the community if the depository institution being acquired has limited long-term prospects, or if the resulting national bank or Federal savings association will provide significantly improved, additional, or less costly services to the community.

(B) *Financial and managerial resources and future prospects*. The OCC considers the financial and managerial resources and future prospects of the existing or proposed institutions.

(C) *Convenience and needs of community*. The OCC considers the probable effects of the business combination on the convenience and needs of the community served. The applicant shall describe these effects in its application, including any planned office closings or reductions in services following the business combination and the likely impact on the community. The OCC also considers additional relevant factors, including the resulting national bank's or Federal savings association's ability and plans to provide expanded or less costly services to the community.

(D) *Money laundering*. The OCC considers the effectiveness of any insured depository institution involved in the business combination in combating money laundering activities, including in overseas branches.

(E) *Financial stability*. The OCC considers the risk to the stability of the United States banking and financial system.

(F) *Deposit concentration limit*. The OCC will not approve a transaction that would violate the deposit concentration limit in 12 U.S.C. 1828(c)(13) for certain interstate merger transactions.

(iii) *Community Reinvestment Act*. When the OCC evaluates an application for a business combination under the Community Reinvestment Act, the OCC also considers the performance of the applicant and the other depository institutions involved in the business combination in helping to meet the credit needs of the relevant communities, including low- and moderate-income neighborhoods, consistent with safe and sound banking practices.

(2) *Acquisition and retention of branches*. An applicant shall disclose the location of any branch it will acquire and retain in a business combination, including approved but unopened branches. The OCC considers the acquisition and retention of a branch under the standards set out in §5.30 or §5.31, as applicable, but it does not require a separate application.

(3) *Subsidiaries*. (i) An applicant must identify any subsidiary, financial subsidiary investment, bank service company investment, service corporation investment, or other equity investment to be acquired in a business combination and state the activities of each subsidiary or other company in which

the applicant would be acquiring an investment. The OCC does not require a separate application or notice under §§ 5.34, 5.35, 5.36, 5.38, 5.39, 5.58, and 5.59.

(ii) An national bank applicant proposing to acquire, through a business combination, a subsidiary, financial subsidiary investment, bank service company investment, service corporation investment, or other equity investment of any entity other than a national bank must provide the same information and analysis of the subsidiary's activities, or of the investment, that would be required if the applicant were establishing the subsidiary, or making such investment, pursuant to § 5.34, § 5.35, § 5.36, or § 5.39.

(iii) A Federal savings association applicant proposing to acquire, through a business combination, a subsidiary, bank service company investment, service corporation investment, or other equity investment of any entity other than a Federal savings association must provide the same information and analysis of the subsidiary's activities, or of the investment, that would be required if the applicant were establishing the subsidiary, or making such investment, pursuant to § 5.35, § 5.38, § 5.58, or § 5.59.

(4) *Interim national bank or interim Federal savings association*—(i) *Application.* An applicant for a business combination that plans to use an interim national bank or interim Federal savings association to accomplish the transaction shall file an application to organize an interim national bank or interim Federal savings association as part of the application for the related business combination.

(ii) *Conditional approval.* The OCC grants conditional preliminary approval to form an interim national bank or interim Federal savings association when it acknowledges receipt of the application for the related business combination.

(iii) *Corporate status.* An interim national bank or interim Federal savings association becomes a legal entity and may enter into legally valid agreements when it has filed, and the OCC has accepted, the interim national bank's duly executed articles of association and organization certificate or the Federal savings association's charter and bylaws. OCC acceptance occurs:

(A) On the date the OCC advises the interim national bank that its articles of association and organization certificate are acceptable or advises the interim Federal savings association that its charter and bylaws are acceptable; or

(B) On the date the interim national bank files articles of association and an organization certificate that conform to the form for those documents provided by the OCC in the Comptroller's Licensing Manual or the date the interim Federal savings association files a charter and bylaws that conform to the requirements set out in this part 5.

(iv) *Other corporate procedures.* An applicant should consult the Comptroller's Licensing Manual to determine what other information is necessary to complete the chartering of the interim national bank as a national bank or the interim Federal savings association as a Federal savings association.

(5) *Nonconforming assets.* (i) An applicant shall identify any nonconforming activities and assets, including nonconforming subsidiaries, of other institutions involved in the business combination that will not be disposed of or discontinued prior to consummation of the transaction. The OCC generally requires a national bank or Federal savings association to divest or conform nonconforming assets, or discontinue nonconforming activities, within a reasonable time following the business combination.

(ii) Any resulting Federal savings association shall conform to the requirements of sections 5(c) and 10(m) of the Home Owners' Loan Act (12 U.S.C. 1464(c) and 1467a(m)) within the time period prescribed by the OCC.

(6) *Fiduciary powers.* (i) An applicant shall state whether the resulting national bank or Federal savings association intends to exercise fiduciary powers pursuant to § 5.26(b).

(ii) If an applicant intends to exercise fiduciary powers after the combination and requires OCC approval for such powers, the applicant must include the information required under § 5.26(e)(2).

(7) *Expiration of approval.* Approval of a business combination, and conditional approval to form an interim national bank or interim Federal savings association, if applicable, expires if the business combination is not consummated within six months after the date of OCC approval, unless the OCC grants an extension of time.

(8) *Adequacy of disclosure.* (i) An applicant shall inform shareholders of all material aspects of a business combination and shall comply with any applicable requirements of the Federal securities laws and securities regulations of the OCC. Accordingly, an applicant shall ensure that all proxy and information statements prepared in connection with a business combination do not contain any untrue or misleading statement of a material fact, or omit to state a material fact necessary in order to make the statements made, in the light of the circumstances under which they were made, not misleading.

(ii) A national bank or Federal savings association applicant with one or more classes of securities subject to the registration provisions of section 12(b) or (g) of the Securities Exchange Act of 1934, 15 U.S.C. 78 l (b) or 78 l (g), shall file preliminary proxy material or information statements for review with the Director, Securities and Corporate Practices Division, OCC, Washington, DC 20219. Any other applicant shall submit the proxy materials or information statements it uses in connection with the combination to the appropriate OCC licensing office no later than when the materials are sent to the shareholders.

(f) *Exceptions to rules of general applicability*—(1) *National bank or Federal savings association applicant*—(i) *In general.* Sections 5.8, 5.10, and 5.11 do not apply to this section. However, if the OCC concludes that an application presents significant or novel policy, supervisory, or legal issues, the OCC may determine that some or all provisions in §§ 5.8, 5.10 and 5.11 apply.

(ii) *Statutory notice.* If an application is subject to the Bank Merger Act or to another statute that requires notice to the public, a national bank or Federal savings association applicant shall follow the public notice requirements contained in 12 U.S.C. 1828(c)(3) or the other statute and sections 5.8(b) through 5.8(e), 5.10, and 5.11.

(2) *Interim national bank or interim Federal savings association.* Sections 5.8, 5.10, and 5.11 do not apply to an application to organize an interim national bank or interim Federal savings association. However, if the OCC concludes that an application presents significant or novel policy, supervisory, or legal issues, the OCC may determine that any or all parts of §§ 5.8, 5.10, and 5.11 apply. The OCC treats an application to organize an interim national bank or interim Federal savings association as part of the related application to engage in a business combination and does not require a separate public notice and public comment process.

(3) *State bank, or state savings association, state trust company, or credit union as resulting institution.* Sections 5.7 through 5.13 do not apply to transactions covered by paragraphs (g)(6) or (g)(7) of this section.

(g) *Provisions governing consolidations and mergers with different types of entities*—(1) *Consolidations and mergers under 12 U.S.C. 215 or 215a of a national bank with other national banks and state banks as defined in 12 U.S.C. 215b(1) resulting in a national bank.* (i) A national bank entering into a consolidation or merger authorized pursuant to 12 U.S.C. 215 or 215a, respectively, is subject to the approval procedures and requirements with respect to treatment of dissenting shareholders set forth in those provisions.

(ii) Any national bank that will not be the resulting bank in a consolidation or merger under 12 U.S.C. 215 or 215a shall provide a notice to the OCC under paragraph (k) of this section.

(2) *Consolidations and mergers of a national bank with Federal savings associations under 12 U.S.C. 215c resulting in a national bank.* (i) With the approval of the OCC, any national bank and any Federal savings association may consolidate or merge with a national bank as the resulting institution by complying with the following procedures:

(A) A national bank entering into the consolidation or merger shall follow the procedures of 12 U.S.C. 215 or 215a, respectively, as if the Federal savings association were a national bank.

(B)(*1*) A Federal savings association entering into the consolidation or merger shall comply with the requirements of paragraph (n) of this section and follow the procedures set out in paragraph (o) of this section and shall provide a notice to the OCC under paragraph (k) of this section.

(*2*) For purposes of this paragraph (g)(2), a combination in which a national bank acquires all or substantially all of the assets, or assumes all or substantially all of the liabilities, of a Federal savings association shall be treated as a consolidation for the Federal savings association.

(ii)(A) National bank shareholders who dissent from a plan to consolidate may receive in cash the value of their national bank shares if they comply with the requirements of 12 U.S.C. 215 as if the Federal savings association were a national bank.

(B) Federal savings association shareholders who dissent from a plan to merge or consolidate may receive in cash the value of their Federal savings association shares if they comply with the requirements of 12 U.S.C. 215 or 215a as if the Federal savings association were a national bank.

(C) The OCC will conduct an appraisal or reappraisal of the value of the national bank or Federal savings association held by dissenting shareholders in accordance with the provisions of 12 U.S.C. 215 or 215a, as applicable, except that the costs and expenses of any appraisal or reappraisal may be apportioned and assessed by the Comptroller as he or she may deem equitable against all or some of the parties. In making this determination the Comptroller shall consider whether any party has acted arbitrarily or not in good faith in respect to the rights provided by this paragraph.

(iii) The consolidation or merger agreement must address the effect upon, and the terms of the assumption of, any liquidation account of any participating institution by the resulting institution.

(3) *Consolidation or merger of a Federal savings association with another Federal savings association, a national bank, a state bank, a state savings bank, a state savings association, a state trust company, or a credit union resulting in a Federal savings association.* (i) With the approval of the OCC, a Federal savings association may consolidate or merge with another Federal savings association, a national bank, a state bank, a state savings association, a state trust company, or a credit union with the Federal savings association as the resulting institution by complying with the following procedures:

(A)(*1*) The applicant Federal savings association shall comply with the requirements of paragraph (n) of this section and follow the procedures set out in paragraph (o) of this section.

(*2*) For purposes of this paragraph (g)(3), a combination in which a Federal savings association acquires all or substantially all of the assets, or assumes all or substantially all of the liabilities, of another other participating institution shall be treated as a consolidation for the acquiring Federal savings association and as a consolidation by a Federal savings association whose assets are acquired, if any.

(B)(*1*) A national bank entering into a merger or consolidation with a Federal savings association when the resulting institution will be a Federal savings association shall comply with the requirements of 12 U.S.C. 214a and 12 U.S.C. 214c as if the Federal savings association were a state bank. However, for these purposes the references in 12 U.S.C. 214c to "law of the State in which such national banking association is located" and "any State authority" mean "laws and regulations governing Federal savings associations" and "Office of the Comptroller of the Currency" respectively. The national bank also shall provide a notice to the OCC under paragraph (k) of this section.

(*2*) National bank shareholders who dissent from a plan to merge or consolidate may receive in cash the value of their national bank shares if they comply with the requirements of 12 U.S.C. 214a as if the Federal savings association were a state bank. The OCC will conduct an appraisal or reappraisal of the value of the national bank shares held by dissenting shareholders in accordance with the provisions of 12 U.S.C. 214a, except that the costs and expenses of any appraisal or reappraisal may be apportioned and assessed by the Comptroller as he or she may deem equitable against all or some of the parties. In making this determination the Comptroller shall consider whether any party has acted arbitrarily or not in good faith in respect to the rights provided by this paragraphs.

(C)(*1*) A Federal savings association entering into a merger or consolidation with another Federal savings association when the resulting institution will be the other Federal savings association shall comply with the requirements of paragraph (n) of this section and the procedures of paragraph (o) of this section and shall provide a notice to the OCC under paragraph (k) of this section.

(*2*) Federal savings association shareholders who dissent from a plan to merge or consolidate may receive in cash the value of their Federal savings association shares if they comply with the requirements of 12 U.S.C. 214a as if the other Federal savings association were a state bank. The OCC will conduct an appraisal or reappraisal of the value of the Federal savings association shares held by dissenting shareholders in accordance with the provisions of 12 U.S.C. 214a, except that the costs and expenses of any appraisal or reappraisal may be apportioned and assessed by the Comptroller as he or she may deem equitable against all or some of the parties. In making this determination the Comptroller shall consider whether any party has acted arbitrarily or not in good faith in respect to the rights provided by this paragraph.

(*3*) The plan of merger or consolidation must provide the manner of disposing of the shares of the resulting Federal savings association not taken by the dissenting shareholders of the Federal savings association.

(D)(*1*) A state bank, state savings association, state trust company, or credit union entering into a consolidation or merger with a Federal savings association when the resulting institution will be a Federal savings association shall follow the procedures for such consolidations or mergers set out in the law of the state or other jurisdiction under which the state bank, state savings association, state trust company, or credit union is organized.

(*2*) The rights of dissenting shareholders and appraisal of dissenters' shares of stock in the state bank, state savings association, or state trust company, entering into the consolidation or merger shall be determined in the manner prescribed by the law of the state or other jurisdiction under which the state bank, state savings association, or state trust company is organized.

(ii) The consolidation or merger agreement must address the effect upon, and the terms of the assumption of, any liquidation account of any participating institution by the resulting institution.

(4) *Mergers of a national bank with its nonbank affiliates under 12 U.S.C. 215a–3 resulting in a national bank.* (i) With the approval of the OCC, a national bank may merge with one or more of its nonbank affiliates, with the national bank as the resulting institution, in accordance with the provisions of this paragraph, provided that the law of the state or other jurisdiction under which the nonbank affiliate is organized allows the nonbank affiliate to engage in such mergers. If the national bank is an insured bank, the transaction is also subject to approval by the FDIC under the Bank Merger Act, 12 U.S.C. 1828(c).

(ii) A national bank entering into the merger shall follow the procedures of 12 U.S.C. 215a as if the nonbank affiliate were a state bank, except as otherwise provided herein.

(iii) A nonbank affiliate entering into the merger shall follow the procedures for such mergers set out in the law of the state or other jurisdiction under which the nonbank affiliate is organized.

(iv) The rights of dissenting shareholders and appraisal of dissenters' shares of stock in the nonbank affiliate entering into the merger shall be determined in the manner prescribed by the law of the state or other jurisdiction under which the nonbank affiliate is organized.

(v) The corporate existence of each institution participating in the merger shall be continued in the resulting national bank, and all the rights, franchises, property, appointments, liabilities, and other interests of the participating institutions shall be transferred to the resulting national bank, as set forth in 12 U.S.C. 215a(a), (e), and (f) in the same manner and to the same extent as in a merger between a national bank and a state bank under 12 U.S.C. 215a(a), as if the nonbank affiliate were a state bank.

(5) *Mergers of an uninsured national bank with its nonbank affiliates under 12 U.S.C. 215a–3 resulting in a nonbank affiliate.* (i) With the approval of the OCC, a national bank that is not an insured bank as defined in 12 U.S.C. 1813(h) may merge with one or more of its nonbank affiliates, with the nonbank affiliate as the resulting entity, in accordance with the provisions of this paragraph, provided that the law of the state or other jurisdiction under which the nonbank affiliate is organized allows the nonbank affiliate to engage in such mergers.

(ii) A national bank entering into the merger shall follow the procedures of 12 U.S.C. 214a, as if the nonbank affiliate were a state bank, except as otherwise provided in this section.

(iii) A nonbank affiliate entering into the merger shall follow the procedures for such mergers set out in the law of the state or other jurisdiction under which the nonbank affiliate is organized.

(iv)(A) National bank shareholders who dissent from an approved plan to merge may receive in cash the value of their national bank shares if they comply with the requirements of 12 U.S.C. 214a as if the nonbank affiliate were a state bank. The OCC may conduct an appraisal or reappraisal of dissenters' shares of stock in a national bank involved in the merger if all parties agree that the determination is final and binding on each party and agree on how the total expenses of the OCC in making the appraisal will be divided among the parties and paid to the OCC.

(B) The rights of dissenting shareholders and appraisal of dissenters' shares of stock in the nonbank affiliate involved in the merger shall be determined in the manner prescribed by the law of the state or other jurisdiction under which the nonbank affiliate is organized.

(v) The corporate existence of each entity participating in the merger shall be continued in the resulting nonbank affiliate, and all the rights, franchises, property, appointments, liabilities, and other interests of the participating national bank shall be transferred to the resulting nonbank affiliate as set forth in 12 U.S.C. 214b, in the same manner and to the same extent as in a merger between a national bank and a state bank under 12 U.S.C. 214a, as if the nonbank affiliate were a state bank.

(6) *Consolidation or merger under 12 U.S.C. 214a of a national bank with a state bank resulting in a state bank as defined in 12 U.S.C. 214(a)*—(i) *Policy.* Prior OCC approval is not required for the merger or consolidation of a national bank with a state bank as defined in 12 U.S.C. 214(a) Termination of a national bank's existence and status as a national banking association is automatic, and its charter cancelled, upon completion of the statutory and regulatory requirements for engaging in the consolidation or merger and consummation of the consolidation or merger.

(ii) *Procedures.* A national bank desiring to merge or consolidate with a state bank as defined in 12 U.S.C. 214(a) when the resulting institution will be a state bank shall comply with the requirements and follow the procedures of 12 U.S.C. 214a and 214c and shall provide notice to the OCC under paragraph (k) of this section.

(iii) *Dissenters' rights and appraisal procedures.* National bank shareholders who dissent from a plan to merge or consolidate may receive in cash the value of their national bank shares if they comply with the requirements of 12 U.S.C. 214a. The OCC conducts an appraisal or reappraisal of the value of the national bank shares held by dissenting shareholders as provided for in 12 U.S.C. 214a.

(iv) *Liquidation account.* The consolidation or merger agreement must address the effect upon, and the terms of the assumption of, any liquidation account of any participating institution by the resulting institution.

(7) *Consolidation or merger of a Federal savings association with a state bank, state savings bank, state savings association, state trust company, or credit union resulting in a state bank, state savings bank, state savings association, state trust company, or credit union*—(i) *Policy.* Prior OCC approval is not required for the merger or consolidation of a Federal savings association with a state bank, state savings bank, state savings association, state trust company, or credit union when the resulting institution will be a state institution or credit union. Termination of a national bank's or Federal savings association's existence and status as a national banking association or Federal savings association is automatic, and its charter cancelled, upon completion of the statutory and regulatory requirements for engaging in the consolidation or merger and consummation of the consolidation or merger.

(ii) *Procedures.* (A) A Federal savings association desiring to merge or consolidate with a state bank, state savings bank, state savings association, state trust company, or credit union when the resulting institution will be a state institution or credit union shall comply with the requirements of paragraph (n) of this section and the procedures of paragraph (o) of this section and shall provide notice to the OCC under paragraph (k) of this section.

(B) For purposes of this paragraph (g)(7), a combination in which a state bank, state savings bank, state savings association, state trust company, or credit union acquires all or substantially all of the assets, or assumes all or substantially all of the liabilities, of a Federal savings association shall be treated as a consolidation by the Federal savings association.

(iii) *Dissenters' rights and appraisal procedures.* (A) Federal savings association shareholders who dissent from a plan to merge or consolidate may receive in cash the value of their Federal savings association shares if they comply with the requirements of 12 U.S.C. 214a as if the Federal savings association were a national bank. The OCC conducts an appraisal or reappraisal of the value of the Federal savings association shares held by dissenting shareholders only if all parties agree that the determination will be final and binding. The parties shall also agree on how the total expenses of the OCC in making the appraisal will be divided among the parties and paid to the OCC.

(B) The plan of merger or consolidation must provide the manner of disposing of the shares of the resulting state institution not taken by the dissenting shareholders of the Federal savings association.

(iv) *Liquidation account.* The consolidation or merger agreement must address the effect upon, and the terms of the assumption of, any liquidation account of any participating institution by the resulting institution.

(h) *Interstate combinations under 12 U.S.C. 1831u.* A business combination between insured banks with different home states under the authority of 12 U.S.C. 1831u must satisfy the standards and requirements and comply with the procedures of 12 U.S.C. 1831u and either 12 U.S.C. 215, 215a, and 215a–1, as applicable, if the resulting bank is a national bank, or 12 U.S.C. 214a, 214b, and 214c if the resulting bank is a state bank. For purposes of 12 U.S.C. 1831u, the acquisition of a branch without the acquisition of all or substantially all of the assets of a bank is treated as the acquisition of a bank whose home state is the state in which the branch is located.

(i) *Expedited review for business reorganizations and streamlined applications.* A filing that qualifies as a business reorganization as defined in paragraph (d)(3) of this section, or a filing that qualifies as a streamlined application as described in paragraph (j) of this section, is deemed approved by the OCC as of the 15th day after the close of the comment period, unless the OCC notifies the applicant that the filing is not eligible for expedited review, or the expedited review process is extended, under § 5.13(a)(2). An application under this paragraph must contain all necessary information for the OCC to determine if it qualifies as a business reorganization or streamlined application.

(j) *Streamlined applications.* (1) An applicant may qualify for a streamlined business combination application in the following situations:

(i) At least one party to the transaction is an eligible bank or eligible Federal savings association, and all other parties to the transaction are eligible banks, eligible Federal savings associations, or eligible depository institutions, the resulting national bank or resulting Federal savings association will be well capitalized immediately following consummation of the transaction, and the total assets of the target institution are no more than 50 percent of the total assets of the acquiring bank or Federal savings association, as reported in each institution's Consolidated Report of Condition and Income filed for the quarter immediately preceding the filing of the application;

(ii) The acquiring bank or Federal savings association is an eligible bank or eligible Federal savings association, the target bank or savings association is not an eligible bank, eligible Federal savings association, or an eligible depository institution, the resulting national bank or resulting Federal savings association will be well capitalized immediately following consummation of the transaction, and the applicants in a prefiling communication request and obtain approval from the appropriate OCC licensing office to use the streamlined application;

(iii) The acquiring bank or Federal savings association is an eligible bank or eligible Federal savings association, the target bank or savings association is not an eligible bank, eligible Federal savings association, or an eligible depository institution, the resulting bank or resulting Federal savings association will be well capitalized immediately following consummation of the transaction, and the total assets acquired do not exceed 10 percent of the total assets of the acquiring national bank or acquiring Federal savings association, as reported in each institution's Consolidated Report of Condition and Income filed for the quarter immediately preceding the filing of the application; or

(iv) In the case of a transaction under paragraph (g)(4) of this section, the acquiring bank is an eligible bank, the resulting national bank will be well capitalized immediately following consummation of the transaction, the applicants in a prefiling communication request and obtain approval from the appropriate OCC licensing office to use the streamlined application, and the total assets acquired do not exceed 10 percent of the total assets of the acquiring national bank, as reported in the bank's Consolidated Report of Condition and Income filed for the quarter immediately preceding the filing of the application.

(2) Notwithstanding paragraph (j)(1) of this section, an applicant does not qualify for a streamlined business combination application if the transaction is part of a conversion under part 192 of this chapter.

(3) When a business combination qualifies for a streamlined application, the applicant should consult the Comptroller's Licensing Manual to determine the abbreviated application information required by the OCC. The OCC encourages prefiling communications between the applicants and the appropriate OCC licensing office before filing under paragraph (j) of this section.

(k) *Exit notice to OCC*—(1) *Notice required.* As provided in paragraphs (g)(1)(ii), (g)(2)(i)(B), (g)(3)(i)(B)(*1*), (g)(3)(i)(C)(*1*), (g)(6)(ii), and (g)(7)(ii) of this section, a national bank or Federal savings association engaging in a consolidation or merger in which it is not the applicant and the resulting institution must file a notice rather than an application to the appropriate OCC licensing office advising of its intention.

(2) *Timing of notice.* The national bank or Federal savings association shall submit the notice at the time the application to merge or consolidate is filed with the responsible agency under the Bank Merger Act, 12 U.S.C. 1828(c), or if there is no such filing then no later than 30 days prior to the effective date of the merger or consolidation.

(3) *Content of notice.* The notice shall include the following:

(i)(A) A short description of the material features of the transaction, the identity of the acquiring institution, the identity of the state or Federal regulator to whom the application was made, and the date of the application; or

(B) A copy of a filing made with another Federal or state regulatory agency seeking approval from that agency for the transaction under the Bank Merger Act or other applicable statute;

(ii) The planned consummation date for the transaction;

(iii) Information to demonstrate compliance by the national bank or Federal savings association with applicable requirements to engage in the transactions (*e.g.*, board approval or shareholder or accountholder requirements); and

(iv) If the national bank or Federal savings association submitting the notice maintains a liquidation account established pursuant to part 192 of this chapter, the notice must state that the resulting institution will assume such liquidation account.

(4) *Termination of status.* The national bank or Federal savings association shall advise the OCC when the transaction is about to be consummated. Termination of a national bank's or Federal savings association's existence and status as a national banking association or Federal savings association is automatic, and its charter cancelled, upon completion of the statutory and regulatory requirements and consummation of the consolidation or merger. When the national bank or Federal savings association files the notice under paragraph (k)(2) of this section, the OCC provides instructions to the national bank or Federal savings association for terminating its status as a national bank or Federal savings, including surrendering its charter to the OCC immediately after consummation of the transaction.

(5) *Expiration.* If the action contemplated by the notice is not completed within six months after the OCC's receipt of the notice, a new notice must be submitted to the OCC, unless the OCC grants an extension of time.

(l) *Mergers and consolidations; transfer of assets and liabilities to the resulting institution.* (1) In any consolidation or merger in which the resulting institution is a national bank or Federal savings association, on the effective date of the merger or consolidation, all assets and property (real, personal and mixed, tangible and intangible, choses in action, rights, and credits) then owned by each participating institution or which would inure to any of them, shall, immediately by operation of law and without any conveyance, transfer, or further action, become the property of the resulting national bank or Federal savings association. The resulting national bank or Federal savings association shall be deemed to be a continuation of the entity of each participating institution, the rights and obligations of which shall succeed to such rights and obligations and the duties and liabilities connected therewith.

(2) The authority in paragraph (l)(1) of this section is in addition to any authority granted by applicable statutes for specific transactions and is subject to the National Bank Act, the Home Owners' Loan Act, and other applicable statutes.

(m) *Certification of combination; effective date.* (1) When a national bank or Federal savings association is the applicant and will be the resulting entity in a consolidation or merger, after receiving approval from the OCC, it shall complete any remaining steps needed to complete the transaction, provide the OCC with a certification that all other required regulatory or shareholder approvals have been obtained, and inform the OCC of the planned consummation date.

(2) When the transaction is consummated, the applicant shall notify the OCC of the consummation date. The OCC will issue a letter certifying that the combination was effective on the date specified in the applicant's notice.

(n) *Authority for and certain limits on business combinations and other transactions by Federal savings associations.* (1) Federal savings associations may enter into business combinations only in accordance with this section, the Bank Merger Act, and sections 5(d)(3)(A) and 10(s) of the Home Owners' Loan Act.

(2) A Federal savings association may consolidate or merge with another depository institution, a state trust company or a credit union, or may engage in another business combination listed in paragraphs (d)(2)(iv) and (v) of this section, or may engage in an other

combination listed in paragraph (d)(10), provided that:

(i) The combination is in compliance with, and receives all approvals required under, any applicable statutes and regulations;

(ii) Any resulting Federal savings association meets the requirements for insurance of accounts; and

(iii) If any combining savings association is a mutual savings association, the resulting institution shall be a mutually held depository institution that is insured by the FDIC, unless:

(A) The transaction is approved under part 192 governing mutual to stock conversions; or

(B) The transaction involves a mutual holding company reorganization under 12 U.S.C. 1467a(o) or a similar transaction under state law.

(3) Where the resulting institution is a Federal mutual savings association, the OCC may approve a temporary increase in the number of directors of the resulting institution provided that the association submits a plan for bringing the board of directors into compliance with the requirements of § 5.21(e) within a reasonable period of time.

(4)(i) The Federal savings associations described in paragraph (n)(4)(ii) of this section below must provide affected accountholders with a notice of a proposed account transfer and an option of retaining the account in the transferring Federal savings association. The notice must allow affected accountholders at least 30 days to consider whether to retain their accounts in the transferring Federal savings association.

(ii) The following savings associations must provide the notices:

(A) A Federal mutual savings association transferring account liabilities to an institution the accounts of which are not insured by the Deposit Insurance Fund or the National Credit Union Share Insurance Fund; and

(B) Any Federal mutual savings association transferring account liabilities to a stock form depository institution.

(o) *Procedural requirements for Federal savings association approval of combinations*—(1) *Board approval.* Before a Federal savings association files a notice or application for any consolidation or merger, the combination and combination agreement must be approved by majority vote of the entire board of each constituent Federal savings association in the case of Federal stock savings associations or a two-thirds vote of the entire board of each constituent Federal savings association in the case of Federal mutual savings associations;

(2) *Change of name or home office.* If the name the resulting Federal savings association or the location of the home office of the resulting Federal savings association will be changed as a result of the business combination, the resulting Federal savings association shall amend its charter accordingly;

(3) *Shareholder vote*—(i) *General rule.* Except as otherwise provided in this paragraph (o)(3), an affirmative vote of two-thirds of the outstanding voting stock of any constituent Federal stock savings association shall be required for approval of a consolidation or merger. If any class of shares is entitled to vote as a class pursuant to § 152.4 of this part, an affirmative vote of a majority of the shares of each voting class and two-thirds of the total voting shares shall be required. The required vote shall be taken at a meeting of the savings association.

(ii) *General exception.* Stockholders of the resulting Federal stock savings association need not authorize a consolidation or merger if:

(A) It does not involve an interim Federal savings association or an interim state savings association;

(B) The association's charter is not changed;

(C) Each share of stock outstanding immediately prior to the effective date of the consolidation or merger is to be an identical outstanding share or a treasury share of the resulting Federal stock savings association after such effective date; and

(D) Either:

(*1*) No shares of voting stock of the resulting Federal stock savings association and no securities convertible into such stock are to be issued or delivered under the plan of combination, or

(*2*) The authorized unissued shares or the treasury shares of voting stock of the resulting Federal stock savings association to be issued or delivered under the plan of combination, plus those initially issuable upon conversion of any securities to be issued or delivered under such plan, do not exceed 15 percent of the total shares of voting stock of such association outstanding immediately prior to the effective date of the consolidation or merger.

(iii) *Exceptions for certain combinations involving an interim association.* Stockholders of a Federal stock savings association need not authorize by a two-thirds affirmative vote consolidations or mergers involving an interim Federal savings association or interim state savings association when the resulting Federal stock savings association is acquired pursuant to the regulations of the Board of Governors of the Federal Reserve System at 12 CFR 238.15(e) (relating to the creation of a savings and loan holding company by a savings association). In those cases, an affirmative vote of 50 percent of the shares of the outstanding voting stock of the Federal stock savings association plus one affirmative vote shall be required. If any class of shares is entitled to vote as a class pursuant to §5.22(g), an affirmative vote of 50 percent of the shares of each voting class plus one affirmative vote shall be required. The required votes shall be taken at a meeting of the association.

(4) *Mutual member vote.* Notwithstanding any other provision of this section, the OCC may require that a consolidation, merger or other business combination be submitted to the voting members of any mutual savings association participating in the proposed transaction at duly called meetings and that the transaction, to be effective, must be approved by such voting members.

[80 FR 28437, May 18, 2015, as amended at 82 FR 8103, Jan. 23, 2017]

§5.34 Operating subsidiaries of a national bank.

(a) *Authority.* 12 U.S.C. 24 (Seventh), 24a, 25b, 93a, 3101 *et seq.*

(b) *Licensing requirements.* A national bank must file an application or notice as prescribed in this section to acquire or establish an operating subsidiary, or to commence a new activity in an existing operating subsidiary.

(c) *Scope.* This section sets forth authorized activities and application or notice procedures for national banks engaging in activities through an operating subsidiary. The procedures in this section do not apply to financial subsidiaries authorized under §5.39. Unless provided otherwise, this section applies to a Federal branch or agency that acquires, establishes, or maintains any subsidiary that a national bank is authorized to acquire or establish under this section in the same manner and to the same extent as if the Federal branch or agency were a national bank, except that the ownership interest required in paragraphs (e)(2) and (e)(5)(i)(B) of this section shall apply to the parent foreign bank of the Federal branch or agency and not to the Federal branch or agency. The OCC may, at any time, limit a national bank's investment in an operating subsidiary or may limit or refuse to permit any activities in an operating subsidiary for supervisory, legal, or safety and soundness reasons.

(d) *Definitions.* For purposes of this section:

(1) *Authorized product* means a product that would be defined as insurance under section 302(c) of the Gramm-Leach-Bliley Act (Pub. L. 106–102, 113 Stat. 1338, 1407) (GLBA) (15 U.S.C. 6712) that, as of January 1, 1999, the OCC had determined in writing that national banks may provide as principal or national banks were in fact lawfully providing the product as principal, and as of that date no court of relevant jurisdiction had, by final judgment, overturned a determination by the OCC that national banks may provide the product as principal. An authorized product does not include title insurance, or an annuity contract the income of which is subject to treatment under section 72 of the Internal Revenue Code of 1986 (26 U.S.C. 72).

(2) *Well capitalized* means the capital level described in 12 CFR 6.4 or, in the case of a Federal branch or agency, the capital level described in 12 CFR 4.7(b)(1)(iii).

(3) *Well managed* means, unless otherwise determined in writing by the OCC:

(i) In the case of a national bank:

(A) The national bank has received a composite rating of 1 or 2 under the

Uniform Financial Institutions Rating System in connection with its most recent examination; or

(B) In the case of any national bank that has not been examined, the existence and use of managerial resources that the OCC determines are satisfactory.

(ii) In the case of a Federal branch or agency:

(A) The Federal branch or agency has received a composite ROCA supervisory rating (which rates risk management, operational controls, compliance, and asset quality) of 1 or 2 at its most recent examination; or

(B) In the case of a Federal branch or agency that has not been examined, the existence and use of managerial resources that the OCC determines are satisfactory.

(e) *Standards and requirements*—(1) *Authorized activities*. (i) A national bank may conduct in an operating subsidiary activities that are permissible for a national bank to engage in directly either as part of, or incidental to, the business of banking, as determined by the OCC, or otherwise under other statutory authority, including:

(A) Providing authorized products as principal; and

(B) Providing title insurance as principal if the national bank or subsidiary thereof was actively and lawfully underwriting title insurance before November 12, 1999, and no affiliate of the national bank (other than a subsidiary) provides insurance as principal. A subsidiary may not provide title insurance as principal if the state had in effect before November 12, 1999, a law which prohibits any person from underwriting title insurance with respect to real property in that state.

(ii) In addition to OCC authorization, before it begins business an operating subsidiary also must comply with other laws applicable to it and its proposed business, including applicable licensing or registration requirements, if any, such as registration requirements under securities laws.

(2) *Qualifying subsidiaries*. (i) An operating subsidiary in which a national bank may invest includes a corporation, limited liability company, limited partnership, or similar entity if:

(A) The bank has the ability to control the management and operations of the subsidiary, and no other person or entity exercises effective operating control over the subsidiary or has the ability to influence the subsidiary's operations to an extent equal to or greater than that of the bank;

(B) The parent bank owns and controls more than 50 percent of the voting (or similar type of controlling) interest of the operating subsidiary, or the parent bank otherwise controls the operating subsidiary and no other party controls a percentage of the voting (or similar type of controlling) interest of the operating subsidiary greater than the bank's interest; and

(C) The operating subsidiary is consolidated with the bank under generally accepted accounting principles (GAAP).

(ii) However, the following subsidiaries are not operating subsidiaries subject to this section:

(A) A subsidiary in which the bank's investment is made pursuant to specific authorization in a statute or OCC regulation (*e.g.*, a bank service company under 12 U.S.C. 1861 *et seq.*, a financial subsidiary under section 5136A of the Revised Statutes (12 U.S.C. 24a), or a community development corporation subsidiary under 12 U.S.C. 24 (Eleventh) and part 24; and

(B) A subsidiary in which the bank has acquired, in good faith, shares through foreclosure on collateral, by way of compromise of a doubtful claim, or to avoid a loss in connection with a debt previously contracted.

(iii) Notwithstanding the requirements of paragraph (e)(2)(i) of this section,

(A) A national bank must have reasonable policies and procedures to preserve the limited liability of the bank and its operating subsidiaries; and

(B) OCC regulations shall not be construed as requiring a national bank and its operating subsidiaries to operate as a single entity.

(3) *Examination and supervision*. An operating subsidiary conducts activities authorized under this section pursuant to the same authorization, terms

and conditions that apply to the conduct of such activities by its parent national bank, unless otherwise specifically provided by statute, regulation, or published OCC policy, including sections 1044 and 1045 of the Dodd-Frank Wall Street Reform and Consumer Protection Act (12 U.S.C. 25b) with respect to the application of state law. If the OCC determines that the operating subsidiary is operating in violation of law, regulation, or written condition, or in an unsafe or unsound manner or otherwise threatens the safety or soundness of the bank, the OCC will direct the bank or operating subsidiary to take appropriate remedial action, which may include requiring the bank to divest or liquidate the operating subsidiary, or discontinue specified activities. OCC authority under this paragraph is subject to the limitations and requirements of section 45 of the Federal Deposit Insurance Act (12 U.S.C. 1831v) and section 115 of the Gramm-Leach-Bliley Act (12 U.S.C. 1820a).

(4) *Consolidation of figures*—(i) *National banks.* Pertinent book figures of the parent national bank and its operating subsidiary shall be combined for the purpose of applying statutory or regulatory limitations when combination is needed to effect the intent of the statute or regulation, *e.g.*, for purposes of 12 U.S.C. 56, 59, 60, 84, and 371d.

(ii) *Federal branches or agencies.* Transactions conducted by all of a foreign bank's Federal branches and agencies and state branches and agencies, and their operating subsidiaries, shall be combined for the purpose of applying any limitation or restriction as provided in 12 CFR 28.14.

(5) *Procedures*—(i) *Application required.* (A) Except for an operating subsidiary that qualifies for the notice procedures in paragraph (e)(5)(ii) of this section or is exempt from application or notice requirements under paragraph (e)(5)(vi) of this section, a national bank must first submit an application to, and receive prior approval from, the OCC to establish or acquire an operating subsidiary or to perform a new activity in an existing operating subsidiary.

(B) The application must explain, as appropriate, how the bank "controls" the enterprise, describing in full detail structural arrangements where control is based on factors other than bank ownership of more than 50 percent of the voting interest of the subsidiary and the ability to control the management and operations of the subsidiary by holding voting interests sufficient to select the number of directors needed to control the subsidiary's board and to select and terminate senior management. In the case of a limited partnership or limited liability company that does not qualify for the notice procedures set forth in paragraph (e)(5)(ii) of this section, the bank must provide a statement explaining why it is not eligible. The application also must include a complete description of the bank's investment in the subsidiary, the proposed activities of the subsidiary, the organizational structure and management of the subsidiary, the relations between the bank and the subsidiary, and other information necessary to adequately describe the proposal. To the extent that the application relates to the initial affiliation of the bank with a company engaged in insurance activities, the bank must describe the type of insurance activity in which the company is engaged and has present plans to conduct. The bank must also list for each state the lines of business for which the company holds, or will hold, an insurance license, indicating the state where the company holds a resident license or charter, as applicable. The application must state whether the operating subsidiary will conduct any activity at a location other than the main office or a previously approved branch of the bank. The OCC may require an applicant to submit a legal analysis if the proposal is novel, unusually complex, or raises substantial unresolved legal issues. In these cases, the OCC encourages applicants to have a prefiling meeting with the OCC. Any bank receiving approval under this paragraph is deemed to have agreed that the subsidiary will conduct the activity in a manner consistent with published OCC guidance.

(ii) *Notice process only for certain qualifying filings.* (A) Except for an operating subsidiary that is exempt from application or notice procedures under paragraph (e)(5)(vi) of this section, a national bank that is "well capitalized" and "well managed" may establish or acquire an operating subsidiary, or perform a new activity in an existing operating subsidiary, by providing the appropriate OCC licensing office written notice prior to, or within 10 days after, acquiring or establishing the subsidiary, or commencing the new activity, if:

(*1*) The activity is listed in paragraph (e)(5)(v) of this section;

(*2*) The entity is a corporation, limited liability company, or limited partnership; and

(*3*) The bank:

(*i*) Has the ability to control the management and operations of the subsidiary by holding voting interests sufficient to select the number of directors needed to control the subsidiary's board and to select and terminate senior management (or, in the case of a limited partnership or a limited liability company, has the ability to control the management and operations of the subsidiary by controlling the selection and termination of senior management), and no other person or entity exercises effective operating control over the subsidiary or has the ability to influence the subsidiary's operations to an extent equal to or greater than the bank's;

(*ii*) Holds more than 50 percent of the voting, or equivalent, interests in the subsidiary, and, in the case of a limited partnership or limited liability company, the bank or an operating subsidiary thereof is the sole general partner of the limited partnership or the sole managing member of the limited liability company, provided that under the partnership agreement or limited liability company agreement, limited partners or other limited liability company members have no authority to bind the partnership or limited liability company by virtue solely of their status as limited partners or members; and

(*iii*) Is required to consolidate its financial statements with those of the subsidiary under generally accepted accounting principles (GAAP).

(B) The written notice must include a complete description of the bank's investment in the subsidiary and of the activity conducted and a representation and undertaking that the activity will be conducted in accordance with OCC policies contained in guidance issued by the OCC regarding the activity. To the extent that the notice relates to the initial affiliation of the bank with a company engaged in insurance activities, the bank must describe the type of insurance activity in which the company is engaged and has present plans to conduct. The bank also must list for each state the lines of business for which the company holds, or will hold, an insurance license, indicating the state where the company holds a resident license or charter, as applicable. Any bank receiving approval under this paragraph is deemed to have agreed that the subsidiary will conduct the activity in a manner consistent with published OCC guidance.

(iii) *Exceptions to rules of general applicability*. Sections 5.8, 5.10, and 5.11 do not apply to this section. However, if the OCC concludes that an application presents significant or novel policy, supervisory, or legal issues, the OCC may determine that some or all provisions in §§ 5.8, 5.10, and 5.11 apply.

(iv) *OCC review and approval*. The OCC reviews a national bank's application to determine whether the proposed activities are legally permissible under Federal banking laws and to ensure that the proposal is consistent with safe and sound banking practices and OCC policy and does not endanger the safety or soundness of the parent national bank. As part of this process, the OCC may request additional information and analysis from the applicant.

(v) *Activities eligible for notice*. The following activities qualify for the notice procedures in paragraph (e)(5)(ii) of this section, provided the activity is conducted pursuant to the same terms and conditions as would be applicable if the activity were conducted directly by a national bank:

(A) Holding and managing assets acquired by the parent bank or its operating subsidiaries, including investment assets and property acquired by the bank through foreclosure or otherwise in good faith to compromise a doubtful claim, or in the ordinary course of collecting a debt previously contracted;

(B) Providing services to or for the bank or its affiliates, including accounting, auditing, appraising, advertising and public relations, and financial advice and consulting;

(C) Making loans or other extensions of credit, and selling money orders, savings bonds, and travelers checks;

(D) Purchasing, selling, servicing, or warehousing loans or other extensions of credit, or interests therein;

(E) Providing courier services between financial institutions;

(F) Providing management consulting, operational advice, and services for other financial institutions;

(G) Providing check guaranty, verification and payment services;

(H) Providing data processing, data warehousing and data transmission products, services, and related activities and facilities, including associated equipment and technology, for the bank or its affiliates;

(I) Acting as investment adviser (including an adviser with investment discretion) or financial adviser or counselor to governmental entities or instrumentalities, businesses, or individuals, including advising registered investment companies and mortgage or real estate investment trusts, furnishing economic forecasts or other economic information, providing investment advice related to futures and options on futures, and providing consumer financial counseling;

(J) Providing tax planning and preparation services;

(K) Providing financial and transactional advice and assistance, including advice and assistance for customers in structuring, arranging, and executing mergers and acquisitions, divestitures, joint ventures, leveraged buyouts, swaps, foreign exchange, derivative transactions, coin and bullion, and capital restructurings;

(L) Underwriting and reinsuring credit related insurance to the extent permitted under section 302 of the GLBA (15 U.S.C. 6712);

(M) Leasing of personal property and acting as an agent or adviser in leases for others;

(N) Providing securities brokerage or acting as a futures commission merchant, and providing related credit and other related services;

(O) Underwriting and dealing, including making a market, in bank permissible securities and purchasing and selling as principal, asset backed obligations;

(P) Acting as an insurance agent or broker, including title insurance to the extent permitted under section 303 of the GLBA (15 U.S.C. 6713);

(Q) Reinsuring mortgage insurance on loans originated, purchased, or serviced by the bank, its subsidiaries, or its affiliates, provided that if the subsidiary enters into a quota share agreement, the subsidiary assumes less than 50 percent of the aggregate insured risk covered by the quota share agreement. A "quota share agreement" is an agreement under which the reinsurer is liable to the primary insurance underwriter for an agreed upon percentage of every claim arising out of the covered book of business ceded by the primary insurance underwriter to the reinsurer;

(R) Acting as a finder pursuant to 12 CFR 7.1002 to the extent permitted by published OCC precedent for national banks; [2]

(S) Offering correspondent services to the extent permitted by published OCC precedent for national banks;

(T) Acting as agent or broker in the sale of fixed or variable annuities;

(U) Offering debt cancellation or debt suspension agreements;

(V) Providing real estate settlement, closing, escrow, and related services; and real estate appraisal services for the subsidiary, parent bank, or other financial institutions;

(W) Acting as a transfer or fiscal agent;

(X) Acting as a digital certification authority to the extent permitted by published OCC precedent for national banks, subject to the terms and conditions contained in that precedent;

(Y) Providing or selling public transportation tickets, event and attraction tickets, gift certificates, prepaid phone cards, promotional and advertising material, postage stamps, and Electronic

[2] *See, e.g.*, the OCC's monthly publication "Interpretations and Actions." Beginning with the May 1996 issue, the OCC's Web site provides access to electronic versions of "Interpretations and Actions" (*www.occ.gov*).

Benefits Transfer (EBT) script, and similar media, to the extent permitted by published OCC precedent for national banks, subject to the terms and conditions contained in that precedent;

(Z) Providing data processing, and data transmission services, facilities (including equipment, technology, and personnel), databases, advice and access to such services, facilities, databases and advice, for the parent bank and for others, pursuant to 12 CFR 7.5006 to the extent permitted by published OCC precedent for national banks;

(AA) Providing bill presentment, billing, collection, and claims-processing services;

(BB) Providing safekeeping for personal information or valuable confidential trade or business information, such as encryption keys, to the extent permitted by published OCC precedent for national banks;

(CC) Providing payroll processing;

(DD) Providing branch management services;

(EE) Providing merchant processing services except when the activity involves the use of third parties to solicit or underwrite merchants; and

(FF) Performing administrative tasks involved in benefits administration.

(vi) *No application or notice required.* A national bank may acquire or establish an operating subsidiary, or perform a new activity in an existing operating subsidiary, without filing an application or providing notice to the OCC, if the bank is well managed and well capitalized and the:

(A) Activities of the new subsidiary are limited to those activities previously reported by the bank in connection with the establishment or acquisition of a prior operating subsidiary;

(B) Activities in which the new subsidiary will engage continue to be legally permissible for the subsidiary;

(C) Activities of the new subsidiary will be conducted in accordance with any conditions imposed by the OCC in approving the conduct of these activities for any prior operating subsidiary of the bank; and

(D) The standards set forth in paragraphs (e)(5)(ii)(A)(*2*) and (*3*) of this section are satisfied.

(vii) *Fiduciary powers.* (A) If an operating subsidiary proposes to accept fiduciary appointments for which fiduciary powers are required, such as acting as trustee or executor, then the national bank must have fiduciary powers under 12 U.S.C. 92a and the subsidiary also must have its own fiduciary powers under the law applicable to the subsidiary.

(B) Unless the subsidiary is a registered investment adviser, if an operating subsidiary proposes to exercise investment discretion on behalf of customers or provide investment advice for a fee, the national bank must have prior OCC approval to exercise fiduciary powers pursuant to § 5.26 and 12 CFR part 9.

(viii) *Expiration of approval.* Approval expires if the national bank has not established or acquired the operating subsidiary, or commenced the new activity in an existing operating subsidiary within 12 months after the date of the approval, unless the OCC shortens or extends the time period.

(6) *Grandfathered operating subsidiaries.* Notwithstanding the requirements for a qualifying operating subsidiary in paragraph (e)(2) of this section and unless otherwise notified by the OCC with respect to a particular operating subsidiary, an entity that a national bank lawfully acquired or established as an operating subsidiary before April 24, 2008 may continue to operate as a national bank operating subsidiary under this section, provided that the bank and the operating subsidiary were, and continue to be, conducting authorized activities in compliance with the standards and requirements applicable when the bank established or acquired the operating subsidiary.

(7) *Annual Report on Operating Subsidiaries*—(i) *Filing requirement.* Each national bank shall prepare and file with the OCC an Annual Report on Operating Subsidiaries containing the information set forth in paragraph (e)(7)(ii) of this section for each of its operating subsidiaries that:

(A) Is not functionally regulated within the meaning of section 5(c)(5) of the Bank Holding Company Act of 1956, as amended (12 U.S.C. 1844(c)(5)); and

(B) Does business directly with consumers in the United States. For purposes of paragraph (e)(7) of this section, an operating subsidiary, or any subsidiary thereof, does business directly with consumers if, in the ordinary course of its business, it provides products or services to individuals to be used primarily for personal, family, or household purposes.

(ii) *Information required.* The Annual Report on Operating Subsidiaries must contain the following information for each covered operating subsidiary listed:

(A) The name and charter number of the parent national bank;

(B) The name (include any "dba" (doing business as), abbreviated names, or trade names used to identify the operating subsidiary when it does business directly with consumers), mailing address (include the street address or post office box, city, state, and zip code), email address (if any), and telephone number of the operating subsidiary;

(C) The principal place of business of the operating subsidiary, if different from the address provided pursuant to paragraph (e)(7)(ii)(B) of this section; and

(D) The lines of business in which the operating subsidiary is doing business directly with consumers by designating the appropriate code contained in appendix B (NAICS Activity Codes for Commonly Reported Activities) to the Instructions for Preparation of Report of Changes in Organizational Structure, Form FR Y–10, a copy of which is set forth on the OCC's Internet Web page at *www.occ.gov.* If the operating subsidiary is engaged in an activity not set forth in this list, a national bank shall report the code 0000 and provide a brief description of the activity.

(iii) *Filing time frames and availability of information.* Each national bank's Annual Report on Operating Subsidiaries shall contain information current as of December 31st for the year prior to the year the report is filed. The national bank shall submit its Annual Report on Operating Subsidiaries on or before January 31st each year. The national bank may submit the Annual Report on Operating Subsidiaries electronically or in another format prescribed by the OCC. The OCC will make available to the public the information contained in the Annual Report on Operating Subsidiaries at *www.helpwithmybank.gov.*

[80 FR 28444, May 18, 2015]

§ 5.35 Bank service company investments by a national bank or Federal savings association investment.

(a) *Authority.* 12 U.S.C. 93a, 1462a, 1463, 1464, 1861–1867, 5412(b)(2)(B).

(b) *Licensing requirements.* Except where otherwise provided, a national bank or Federal savings association shall submit a notice and obtain prior OCC approval to invest in the equity of a bank service company or to perform new activities in an existing bank service company.

(c) *Scope.* This section describes the procedures and requirements regarding OCC review and approval of a notice by a national bank or Federal savings association to invest in the equity of a bank service company. The OCC may, at any time, limit a national bank's or Federal savings association's investment in a bank service company or may limit or refuse to permit any activities in any bank service company for which a national bank or Federal savings association is the principal investor for supervisory, legal, or safety and soundness reasons.

(d) *Definitions*—(1) *Bank service company* means a corporation or limited liability company organized to provide services authorized by the Bank Service Company Act, 12 U.S.C. 1861 *et seq.*, all of whose capital stock is owned by one or more insured depository institutions in the case of a corporation, or all of the members of which are one or more insured depository institutions in the case of a limited liability company.

(2) *Limited liability company* means any company, partnership, trust, or similar business entity organized under the law of a state (as defined in section 3 of the Federal Deposit Insurance Act) which provides that a member or manager of such company is not personally liable for a debt, obligation, or liability of the company solely by reason of being, or acting as, a member or manager of such company.

(3) *Depository institution* for purposes of this section, means, except when such term appears in connection with the term 'insured depository institution', an insured bank (as defined in section 3 of the Federal Deposit Insurance Act), a savings association (as defined in section 3 of the Federal Deposit Insurance Act), a financial institution subject to examination by the appropriate Federal banking agency or the National Credit Union Administration Board, or a financial institution the accounts or deposits of which are insured or guaranteed under state law and are eligible to be insured by the Federal Deposit Insurance Corporation or the National Credit Union Administration Board.

(4) *Insured depository institution*, for purposes of this section, has the same meaning as in section 3 of the Federal Deposit Insurance Act.

(5) *Invest* includes making any advance of funds to a bank service company, whether by the purchase of stock, the making of a loan, or otherwise, except a payment for rent earned, goods sold and delivered, or services rendered before the payment was made.

(6) *Principal investor* means the insured depository institution that has the largest amount invested in the equity of a bank service company. In any case where two or more insured depository institutions have equal amounts invested and no other insured depository institution has a larger amount invested, the bank service company shall designate one of those insured depository institutions as its principal investor.

(e) *Standards and requirements.* A national bank or Federal savings association may invest in a bank service company that conducts activities described in paragraphs (f)(3) and (f)(4) of this section and activities (other than taking deposits) permissible for the national bank or Federal savings association and other insured depository institution shareholders or members of the bank service company.

(f) *Procedures*—(1) *OCC notice and approval required.* Except as provided in paragraphs (f)(3) and (f)(4) of this section, a national bank or Federal savings association that intends to invest in the equity of a bank service company, or to perform new activities in an existing bank service company, must submit a notice to and receive prior approval from the OCC. The notice must include the information required by paragraph (g) of this section. The OCC approves or denies a proposed investment within 60 days after the filing is received by the OCC, unless the OCC notifies the bank prior to that date that the filing presents a significant supervisory or compliance concern, or raises a significant legal or policy issue.

(2) *Expedited review for certain activities.* (i) A notice to invest in the equity of a bank service company, or to perform new activities in an existing bank service company, that meets the requirements of this paragraph is deemed approved by the OCC as of the 30th day after the notice is received by the OCC, unless the OCC notifies the filer prior to that date that the filing is not eligible for expedited review or the expedited review process is extended. Any bank or savings association making an investment pursuant to this paragraph is deemed to have agreed that the bank service company will conduct the activity in a manner consistent with the published OCC guidance.

(ii) A notice is eligible for expedited review if all of the following requirements are met:

(A) The national bank or Federal savings association is "well capitalized" and "well managed" as defined in § 5.34(d) or § 5.38(d), as applicable; and

(B) The bank service company engages only in activities that are permissible for the bank service company under 12 U.S.C. 1864 and that are listed in § 5.34(e)(5)(v) or § 5.38(e)(5)(v), as applicable.

(3) *Investments requiring no approval or notice.* A national bank or Federal savings association does not need to submit a notice or obtain OCC approval to invest in a bank service company, or to perform a new activity in an existing bank service company, if the bank service company will provide only the following services only for depository institutions: Check and deposit posting and sorting; computation and posting of interest and other credits and charges; preparation and mailing of

checks, statements, notices, and similar items; or any other clerical, bookkeeping, accounting, statistical, or similar functions.

(4) *Federal Reserve approval.* A national bank or Federal savings association also may, with the approval of the Board of Governors of the Federal Reserve System (Federal Reserve Board), invest in the equity of a bank service company that provides any other service (except deposit taking) that the Federal Reserve Board has determined, by regulation, to be permissible for a bank holding company under 12 U.S.C. 1843(c)(8).

(5) *Exceptions to rules of general applicability.* Sections 5.8, 5.10, and 5.11 do not apply to a request for approval to invest in a bank service company. However, if the OCC concludes that an application presents significant or novel policy, supervisory, or legal issues, the OCC may determine that any or all provisions of §§ 5.8, 5.10, and 5.11 apply.

(g) *Required information.* A notice required under paragraph (f)(1) of this section must contain the following:

(1) The name and location of the bank service company;

(2) A complete description of the activities the bank service company will conduct and a representation and undertaking that the activities will be conducted in accordance with OCC guidance. To the extent the notice relates to the initial affiliation of the national bank or Federal savings association with a company engaged in insurance activities, the national bank or Federal savings association should describe the type of insurance activity that the company is engaged in and has present plans to conduct. The national bank or Federal savings association also must list for each state the lines of business for which the company holds, or will hold, an insurance license, indicating the state where the company holds a resident license or charter, as applicable;

(3) A complete description of the national bank's or Federal savings association's investment in the bank service company and information demonstrating that the national bank or Federal savings association will comply with the investment limitations of paragraph (i) of this section; and

(4) Information demonstrating that the bank service company will perform only those services that each insured depository institution shareholder or member is authorized to perform under applicable Federal or state law and will perform such services only at locations in a state in which each such shareholder or member is authorized to perform such services unless performing services that are authorized by the Federal Reserve Board under the authority of 12 U.S.C. 1865(b).

(h) *Examination and supervision.* Each bank service company in which a national bank or Federal savings association is the principal investor is subject to examination and supervision by the OCC in the same manner and to the same extent as that national bank or Federal savings association. OCC authority under this paragraph is subject to the limitations and requirements of section 45 of the Federal Deposit Insurance Act (12 U.S.C. 1831v) and section 115 of the Gramm-Leach-Bliley Act (12 U.S.C. 1820a).

(i) *Investment limitations.* A national bank or Federal savings association may not invest more than 10 percent of its capital and surplus in a bank service company. In addition, the national bank's or Federal savings association's total investments in all bank service companies may not exceed five percent of the national bank's or Federal savings association's total assets.

[80 FR 28448, May 18, 2015]

§ 5.36 Other equity investments by a national bank.

(a) *Authority.* 12 U.S.C. 1 *et seq.*, 24(Seventh), and 93a.

(b) *Scope.* National banks are permitted to make various types of equity investments pursuant to 12 U.S.C. 24(Seventh) and other statutes. These investments are in addition to those subject to §§ 5.34, 5.35, and 5.37. This section describes the procedure governing the filing of the application or notice that the OCC requires in connection with certain of these investments. Other permissible equity investments may be reviewed on a case-by-case basis by the OCC.

(c) *Definitions.* For purposes of this § 5.36:

(1) *Enterprise* means any corporation, limited liability company, partnership, trust, or similar business entity.

(2) *Well capitalized* means the capital level described in 12 CFR 6.4.

(3) *Well managed* has the meaning set forth in § 5.34(d)(3).

(d) *Procedure.* (1) A national bank must provide the appropriate OCC licensing office with written notice within ten days after making an equity investment in the following:

(i) An agricultural credit corporation;

(ii) A savings association eligible to be acquired under section 13 of the Federal Deposit Insurance Act (12 U.S.C. 1823); and

(iii) Any other equity investment that may be authorized by statute after February 12, 1990, if not covered by other applicable OCC regulation.

(2) The written notice required by paragraph (d)(1) of this section must include a description, and the amount, of the bank's investment.

(3) The OCC reserves the right to require additional information as necessary.

(e) *Non-controlling investments; notice procedure.* Unless the procedures governing a national bank's non-controlling investment are prescribed by OCC rules implementing a separate legal authorization of the investment and except as provided in paragraphs (f) and (g) of this section, a national bank may make a non-controlling investment, directly or through its operating subsidiary, in an enterprise that engages in the activities described in paragraph (e)(2) of this section by filing a written notice. The bank must file this written notice with the appropriate OCC licensing office no later than 10 days after making the investment. The written notice must:

(1) Describe the structure of the investment and the activity or activities conducted by the enterprise in which the bank is investing. To the extent the notice relates to the initial affiliation of the bank with a company engaged in insurance activities, the bank should describe the type of insurance activity that the company is engaged in and has present plans to conduct. The bank must also list for each state the lines of business for which the company holds, or will hold, an insurance license, indicating the state where the company holds a resident license or charter, as applicable;

(2) State which paragraphs of § 5.34(e)(5)(v) describe the activity or activities, or state that, and describe how, the activity is substantively the same as that contained in published OCC precedent approving a non-controlling investment by a national bank or its operating subsidiary, state that the activity will be conducted in accordance with the same terms and conditions applicable to the activity covered by the precedent, and provide the citation to the applicable precedent;

(3) Certify that the bank is well managed and well capitalized at the time of the investment;

(4) Describe how the bank has the ability to prevent the enterprise from engaging in activities that are not set forth in § 5.34(e)(5)(v) or not contained in published OCC precedent approving a non-controlling investment by a national bank or its operating subsidiary, or how the bank otherwise has the ability to withdraw its investment;

(5) Describe how the investment is convenient and useful to the bank in carrying out its business and not a mere passive investment unrelated to the bank's banking business;

(6) Certify that the bank's loss exposure is limited as a legal matter and that the bank does not have unlimited liability for the obligations of the enterprise; and

(7) Certify that the enterprise in which the bank is investing agrees to be subject to OCC supervision and examination, subject to the limitations and requirements of section 45 of the Federal Deposit Insurance Act (12 U.S.C. 1831v) and section 115 of the Gramm-Leach-Bliley Act (12 U.S.C. 1820a).

(f) *Non-controlling investment; application procedure.* Unless the procedures governing a national bank's non-controlling investment are prescribed by OCC rules implementing a separate legal authorization of the investment, a national bank must file an application and obtain prior approval before making or acquiring, either directly or through an operating subsidiary, a non-controlling investment in an enterprise if the non-controlling investment does not qualify for the notice procedure set forth in paragraph (e) of this section because the bank is unable to make the representation required by paragraph (e)(2) or the certification required by paragraph (e)(3) of this section. The application must include the information required in paragraphs (e)(1) and (e)(4) through (e)(7) of this section and (e)(2) or (e)(3), as appropriate. If the bank is unable to make the representation set forth in paragraph (e)(2) of this section, the bank's application must explain why the activity in which the enterprise engages is a permissible activity for a national bank and why the applicant should be permitted to hold a non-controlling investment in an enterprise engaged in that activity. A bank may not make a non-controlling investment if it is unable to make the representations and certifications specified in paragraphs (e)(1) and (e)(4) through (e)(7) of this section.

(g) *Non-controlling investments in entities holding assets in satisfaction of debts previously contracted.* Certain non-controlling investments may be eligible for expedited treatment where the bank's investment is in an entity holding assets in satisfaction of debts previously contracted or the bank acquires shares of a company in satisfaction of debts previously contracted.

(1) *Notice required.* A national bank that is well capitalized and well managed may acquire a non-controlling investment, directly or through its operating subsidiary, in an enterprise that engages in the activities of holding and managing assets acquired by the parent bank through foreclosure or otherwise in good faith to compromise a doubtful claim, or in the ordinary course of collecting a debt previously contracted, by filing a written notice in accordance with this paragraph (g)(1). The activities of the enterprise must be conducted pursuant to the same terms and conditions as would be applicable if the activity were conducted directly by a national bank. The bank must file the written notice with the appropriate OCC licensing office no later than 10 days after making the non-controlling investment. This notice must include a complete description of the bank's investment in the enterprise and the activities conducted, a description of how the bank plans to divest the non-controlling investment or the underlying assets within applicable statutory time frames, and a representation and undertaking that the bank will conduct the activities in accordance with OCC policies contained in guidance issued by the OCC regarding the activities. Any national bank receiving approval under this paragraph (g)(1) is deemed to have agreed that the enterprise will conduct the activity in a manner consistent with published OCC guidance.

(2) *No notice or application required.* A national bank is not required to file a notice or application under this § 5.36 if it acquires a non-controlling investment in shares of a company through foreclosure or otherwise in good faith to compromise a doubtful claim, or in the ordinary course of collecting a debt previously contracted.

(h) *Non-controlling investments by Federal branches.* A Federal branch that satisfies the well capitalized and well managed standards in 12 CFR 4.7(b)(1)(iii) and § 5.34(d)(3)(ii) may make a non-controlling investment in accordance with paragraph (e) of this section in the same manner and subject to the same conditions and requirements as a national bank, and subject to any additional requirements that may apply under 12 CFR 28.10(c).

(i) *Exceptions to rules of general applicability.* Sections 5.8, 5.9, 5.10, and 5.11 of this part do not apply to filings for other equity investments.

[61 FR 60363, Nov. 27, 1996, as amended at 65 FR 12913, Mar. 10, 2000; 65 FR 41560, July 6, 2000; 68 FR 70698, Dec. 19, 2003; 73 FR 22239, Apr. 24, 2008; 79 FR 11310, Feb. 28, 2014; 80 FR 28449, May 18, 2015]

§ 5.37 Investment in national bank or Federal savings association premises.

(a) *Authority.* 12 U.S.C. 29, 93a, 317d, 1464(c)(2), 1464(c)(4)(B), 1828(m), and 5412(b)(2)(B).

(b) *Scope*. This section addresses a national bank's or Federal savings association's investment in banking premises and other premises-related investments, loans, or indebtedness. This section also sets forth the quantitative investment limitations and procedures governing the OCC's review and approval of an application by a national bank or Federal savings association to invest in these premises.

(c) *Definitions*. The following definitions apply for purposes of this section.

(1) *Banking premises* includes:

(i) Premises that are owned and occupied (or to be occupied, if under construction) by a national bank or Federal savings association, its respective branches, or its consolidated subsidiaries;

(ii) Capitalized leases and leasehold improvements, vaults, and fixed machinery and equipment;

(iii) Remodeling costs to existing premises;

(iv) Real estate acquired and intended, in good faith, for use in future expansion; or

(v) Parking facilities that are used by customers or employees of the national bank or Federal savings association.

(2) *Capital stock* means, for national banks and Federal stock savings associations, the amount of common stock outstanding and unimpaired plus the amount of perpetual preferred stock outstanding and unimpaired. With respect to Federal mutual savings associations, "capital stock" should be read to mean the amount of the association's retained earnings.

(3) *Capital and surplus* means:

(i) A national bank's or Federal savings association's tier 1 and tier 2 capital calculated under 12 CFR part 3, as applicable, as reported in the bank's or savings association's Consolidated Reports of Condition and Income (Call Reports) filed under 12 U.S.C. 161 or 12 U.S.C. 1464(v), respectively; plus

(ii) The balance of a national bank's or Federal savings association's allowance for loan and lease losses not included in the bank's or savings association's tier 2 capital, for purposes of the calculation of risk-based capital described in paragraph (c)(3)(i) of this section, as reported in the national bank's or Federal savings association's Call Reports filed under 12 U.S.C. 161 or 1464(v), respectively.

(d) *Procedure*—(1) *Premises application*—(i) *When required*. A national bank or Federal savings association shall submit an application to the appropriate OCC supervisory office to invest in banking premises, or in the stock, bonds, debentures, or other such obligations of any corporation holding the premises of the national bank or Federal savings association, or to make loans to or upon the security of the stock of such corporation, if the aggregate of all such investments and loans, together with the indebtedness incurred by any such corporation that is an affiliate of the national bank or Federal savings association, as defined in 12 U.S.C. 221a or 12 U.S.C. 1462, respectively, will exceed the amount of the capital stock of the national bank or Federal savings association, or, in the case of a Federal mutual savings association the amount of retained earnings.

(ii) *Contents of premises application*. The application must include:

(A) A description of the national bank's or Federal savings association's present investment in banking premises;

(B) The investment in banking premises that the national bank or Federal savings association intends to make, and the business reason for making the investment; and

(C) The amount by which the national bank's or Federal savings association's aggregate investment will exceed the amount of the national bank's or Federal stock savings association's capital stock, or, in the case of a Federal mutual savings association, the amount of retained earnings.

(2) *Approval of premises application*. An application from a national bank or Federal savings association to invest in banking premises or in certain banking premises-related investments, loans or indebtedness, as described in paragraph (d)(1)(i) of this section, is deemed approved as of the 30th day after the filing is received by the OCC, unless the OCC notifies the national bank or Federal savings association prior to that date that the filing presents a significant supervisory or compliance concern, or raises a significant legal or

policy issue. An approval for a specified amount under this section remains valid up to that amount until the OCC notifies the national bank or Federal savings association otherwise.

(3) *Premises notice process*—(i) *General rule.* Notwithstanding paragraph (d)(1)(i) of this section, a national bank or Federal savings association that is rated 1 or 2 under the Uniform Financial Institutions Rating System (CAMELS) may make an aggregate investment in banking premises up to 150 percent of the national bank's or Federal savings association's capital and surplus without the OCC's prior approval, provided that the national bank or Federal savings association is well capitalized as defined in 12 CFR part 6 and will continue to be well capitalized after the investment or loan is made. However, the national bank or Federal savings association shall notify the appropriate OCC supervisory office in writing of the investment within 30 days after the investment or loan is made. The written notice must include a description of the national bank's or Federal savings association's investment or loan.

(ii) *Exception.* If a Federal savings association that would otherwise be eligible for the premises notice process described in paragraph (d)(3)(i) of this section proposes to establish or acquire a subsidiary to make an investment in banking premises, or if investing in banking premises would be a new activity for such a subsidiary, the Federal savings association would not be eligible for the premises notice process and would be required to comply with the provisions of § 5.59 in the case of a service corporation, or § 5.38 in the case of an operating subsidiary.

(4) *Service corporation.* A Federal savings association that invests in banking premises through a service corporation is not subject to the premises application and premises notice requirements of paragraph (d) of this section; however, it must include this investment when calculating the quantitative limitations in paragraph (d) of this section, and must comply with 12 CFR 5.59.

(5) *Exceptions to rules of general applicability.* Sections 5.8, 5.10, and 5.11 do not apply to this section. However, if the OCC concludes that an application presents significant or novel policy, supervisory, or legal issues, the OCC may determine that any or all parts of §§ 5.8, 5.10, and 5.11 apply.

[80 FR 28449, May 18, 2015]

§ 5.38 Operating subsidiaries of a Federal savings association.

(a) *Authority.* 12 U.S.C. 1462a, 1463, 1464, 1465, 1828, 5412(b)(2)(B).

(b) *Licensing requirements.* When required by section 18(m) of the Federal Deposit Insurance Act, a Federal savings association must file an application as prescribed in this section to acquire or establish an operating subsidiary, or to commence a new activity in an existing operating subsidiary.

(c) *Scope.* This section sets forth authorized activities and application procedures for Federal savings associations engaging in activities through an operating subsidiary. The OCC may, at any time, limit a Federal savings association's investment in an operating subsidiary or may limit or refuse to permit any activities in an operating subsidiary for supervisory, legal, or safety and soundness reasons.

(d) *Definitions.* For purposes of this section:

(1) *Well capitalized* means the capital level described in 12 CFR 6.4.

(2) *Well managed* means, unless otherwise determined in writing by the OCC:

(i) The Federal savings association has received a composite rating of 1 or 2 under the Uniform Financial Institutions Rating System in connection with its most recent examination; or

(ii) In the case of any Federal savings association that has not been examined, the existence and use of managerial resources that the OCC determines are satisfactory.

(e) *Standards and requirements*—(1) *Authorized activities.* (i) A Federal savings association may conduct in an operating subsidiary activities that are permissible for a Federal savings association to engage in directly.

(ii) In addition to OCC authorization, before it begins business an operating subsidiary also must comply with other laws applicable to it and its proposed business, including applicable licensing or registration requirements, if any, such as registration requirements under securities laws.

(2) *Qualifying subsidiaries.* (i) An operating subsidiary in which a Federal savings association may invest includes a corporation, limited liability company, limited partnership, or similar entity if:

(A) The savings association has the ability to control the management and operations of the subsidiary, and no other person or entity exercises effective operating control over the subsidiary or has the ability to influence the subsidiary's operations to an extent equal to or greater than that of the savings association;

(B) The parent savings association owns and controls more than 50 percent of the voting (or similar type of controlling) interest of the operating subsidiary, or the parent savings association otherwise controls the operating subsidiary and no other party controls a percentage of the voting (or similar type of controlling) interest of the operating subsidiary greater than the savings association's interest; and

(C) The operating subsidiary is consolidated with the savings association under generally accepted accounting principles (GAAP).

(ii) Subject to the requirements in this section, a Federal savings association may hold another insured depository institution as an operating subsidiary.

(iii) However, the following subsidiaries are not operating subsidiaries subject to this section:

(A) A subsidiary in which the savings association's investment is made pursuant to specific authorization in a statute or OCC regulation (*e.g.*, a service corporation under 12 U.S.C. 1464(c)(4) or a bank service company under 12 U.S.C. 1861 *et seq.*); and

(B) A subsidiary in which the savings association has acquired, in good faith, shares through foreclosure on collateral, by way of compromise of a doubtful claim, or to avoid a loss in connection with a debt previously contracted.

(iv) Notwithstanding the requirements of paragraph (e)(2)(i) of this section:

(A) A Federal savings association must have reasonable policies and procedures to preserve the limited liability of the savings association and its operating subsidiaries; and

(B) OCC regulations shall not be construed as requiring a Federal savings association and its operating subsidiaries to operate as a single entity.

(3) *Examination and supervision.* An operating subsidiary conducts activities authorized under this section pursuant to the same authorization, terms and conditions that apply to the conduct of such activities by its parent Federal savings association, unless otherwise specifically provided by statute, regulation, or published OCC policy, including sections 1045 and 1046 of the Dodd-Frank Wall Street Reform and Consumer Protection Act (12 U.S.C. 25b and 1465) with respect to the application of state law. If the OCC determines that the operating subsidiary is operating in violation of law, regulation, or written condition, or in an unsafe or unsound manner or otherwise threatens the safety or soundness of the savings association, the OCC will direct the savings association or operating subsidiary to take appropriate remedial action, which may include requiring the savings association to divest or liquidate the operating subsidiary, or discontinue specified activities. OCC authority under this paragraph is subject to the limitations and requirements of section 45 of the Federal Deposit Insurance Act (12 U.S.C. 1831v) and section 115 of the Gramm-Leach-Bliley Act (12 U.S.C. 1820a).

(4) *Consolidation of figures.* (i) Except as provided in paragraph (e)(4)(ii) of this section, pertinent book figures of the parent Federal savings association and its operating subsidiary shall be combined for the purpose of applying statutory or regulatory limitations when combination is needed to effect the intent of the statute or regulation, *e.g.*, for purposes of 12 U.S.C. 1464(c) and 1464(u).

(ii) Consolidation for purposes of calculating portfolio assets and qualified thrift investments is subject to 12 U.S.C. 1467a(m)(5).

(5) *Procedures*—(i) *Application required.* (A) A Federal savings association must first submit an application to, and receive prior approval from, the OCC to establish or acquire an operating subsidiary, or to perform a new

activity in an existing operating subsidiary.

(B) The application must explain, as appropriate, how the savings association "controls" the enterprise, describing in full detail structural arrangements where control is based on factors other than savings association ownership of more than 50 percent of the voting interest of the subsidiary and the ability to control the management and operations of the subsidiary by holding voting interests sufficient to select the number of directors needed to control the subsidiary's board and to select and terminate senior management. In the case of a limited partnership or limited liability company that does not qualify for the expedited review procedure set forth in paragraph (e)(5)(ii) of this section, the savings association must provide a statement explaining why it is not eligible. The application also must include a complete description of the savings association's investment in the subsidiary, the proposed activities of the subsidiary, the organizational structure and management of the subsidiary, the relations between the savings association and the subsidiary, and other information necessary to adequately describe the proposal. To the extent that the application relates to the initial affiliation of the savings association with a company engaged in insurance activities, the savings association must describe the type of insurance activity in which the company is engaged and has present plans to conduct. The savings association must also list for each state the lines of business for which the company holds, or will hold, an insurance license, indicating the state where the company holds a resident license or charter, as applicable. The application must state whether the operating subsidiary will conduct any activity at a location other than the home office or a previously approved branch of the savings association. The OCC may require an applicant to submit a legal analysis if the proposal is novel, unusually complex, or raises substantial unresolved legal issues. In these cases, the OCC encourages applicants to have a prefiling meeting with the OCC. Any savings association receiving approval under this paragraph is deemed to have agreed that the subsidiary will conduct the activity in a manner consistent with published OCC guidance.

(ii) *Expedited review*. (A) An application to establish or acquire an operating subsidiary, or to perform a new activity in an existing operating subsidiary, that meets the requirements of this paragraph is deemed approved by the OCC as of the 30th day after the filing is received by the OCC, unless the OCC notifies the applicant prior to that date that the filing is not eligible for expedited review, or the expedited review process is extended under § 5.13(a)(2). Any savings association receiving approval under this paragraph is deemed to have agreed that the subsidiary will conduct the activity in a manner consistent with published OCC guidance.

(B) An application is eligible for expedited review if all of the following requirements are met:

(*1*) The savings association is "well capitalized" and "well managed";

(*2*) The activity is listed in paragraph (e)(5)(v) this section;

(*3*) The entity is a corporation, limited liability company, or limited partnership; and

(*4*) The savings association:

(*i*) Has the ability to control the management and operations of the subsidiary by holding voting interests sufficient to select the number of directors needed to control the subsidiary's board and to select and terminate senior management (or, in the case of a limited partnership or a limited liability company, has the ability to control the management and operations of the subsidiary by controlling the selection and termination of senior management), and no other person or entity has the ability to control the management or operations of the subsidiary;

(*ii*) Holds more than 50 percent of the voting, or equivalent, interests in the subsidiary, and, in the case of a limited partnership or limited liability company, the savings association or an operating subsidiary thereof is the sole general partner of the limited partnership or the sole managing member of the limited liability company, provided that under the partnership agreement or limited liability company agreement, limited partners or other limited liability company members have no authority to bind the partnership or limited liability company by virtue solely of their status as limited partners or members; and

(*iii*) Is required to consolidate its financial statements with those of the subsidiary under generally accepted accounting principles (GAAP). An applicant proposing to qualify for expedited review must include in the application all necessary information showing the application meets the requirements.

(iii) *Exceptions to rules of general applicability.* Sections 5.8, 5.10, and 5.11 do not apply to this section. However, if the OCC concludes that an application presents significant or novel policy, supervisory, or legal issues, the OCC may determine that some or all provisions in §§ 5.8, 5.10, and 5.11 apply.

(iv) *OCC review and approval.* The OCC reviews a Federal savings association's application to determine whether the proposed activities are legally permissible under Federal savings association law and to ensure that the proposal is consistent with safe and sound banking practices and OCC policy and does not endanger the safety or soundness of the parent Federal savings association. As part of this process, the OCC may request additional information and analysis from the applicant.

(v) *Activities eligible for expedited review.* The following activities qualify for the expedited review procedures in paragraph (e)(5)(ii) of this section, provided the activity is conducted pursuant to the same terms and conditions as would be applicable if the activity were conducted directly by a Federal savings association:

(A) Holding and managing assets acquired by the parent savings association or its operating subsidiaries, including investment assets and property acquired by the savings association through foreclosure or otherwise in good faith to compromise a doubtful claim, or in the ordinary course of collecting a debt previously contracted;

(B) Providing services to or for the savings association or its affiliates, including accounting, auditing, appraising, advertising and public relations, and financial advice and consulting;

(C) Making loans or other extensions of credit, and selling money orders and travelers checks;

(D) Purchasing, selling, servicing, or warehousing loans or other extensions of credit, or interests therein;

(E) Providing management consulting, operational advice, and services for other financial institutions;

(F) Providing check payment services;

(G) Acting as investment adviser (including an adviser with investment discretion) or financial adviser or counselor to governmental entities or instrumentalities, businesses, or individuals, including advising registered investment companies and mortgage or real estate investment trusts;

(H) Providing financial and transactional advice and assistance, including advice and assistance for customers in structuring, arranging, and executing mergers and acquisitions, divestitures, joint ventures, leveraged buyouts, swaps, foreign exchange, derivative transactions, coin and bullion, and capital restructurings;

(I) Underwriting and reinsuring credit life and disability insurance;

(J) Leasing of personal property;

(K) Providing securities brokerage;

(L) Underwriting and dealing, including making a market, in savings association permissible securities and purchasing and selling as principal, asset backed obligations;

(M) Acting as an insurance agent or broker for credit life, disability, and unemployment insurance; single property interest insurance; and title insurance;

(N) Offering correspondent services to the extent permitted by published OCC precedent for Federal savings associations;

(O) Acting as agent or broker in the sale of fixed annuities;

(P) Offering debt cancellation or debt suspension agreements;

(Q) Providing escrow services;

(R) Acting as a transfer agent; and

(S) Providing or selling postage stamps.

(vi) *Redesignation.* A Federal savings association that proposes to redesignate a service corporation as an operating subsidiary must submit a notification to the OCC at least 30 days prior to the redesignation date. The notification must include a description of how the redesignated service corporation meets all of the requirements of this section to be an operating subsidiary, a resolution of the savings association's board of directors approving the redesignation, and the proposed effective date of the redesignation. The savings association may effect the redesignation on the proposed date unless the OCC notifies the savings association otherwise prior to that date. The OCC may require an application if the redesignation presents policy, supervisory, or legal issues.

(vii) *Fiduciary powers.* (A) If an operating subsidiary proposes to accept fiduciary appointments for which fiduciary powers are required, such as acting as trustee or executor, then the Federal savings association must have fiduciary powers under 12 U.S.C. 1464(n) and the subsidiary also must have its own fiduciary powers under the law applicable to the subsidiary.

(B) Unless the subsidiary is a registered investment adviser, if an operating subsidiary proposes to exercise investment discretion on behalf of customers or provide investment advice for a fee, the Federal savings association must have prior OCC approval to exercise fiduciary powers pursuant to § 5.26 (or a predecessor provision) and 12 CFR part 150.

(viii) *Expiration of approval.* Approval expires if the Federal savings association has not established or acquired the operating subsidiary, or commenced the new activity in an existing operating subsidiary within 12 months after the date of the approval, unless the OCC shortens or extends the time period.

(6) *Grandfathered operating subsidiaries.* Notwithstanding the requirements for a qualifying operating subsidiary in paragraph (e)(2) of this section and unless otherwise notified by the OCC with respect to a particular operating subsidiary, an entity that a Federal savings association lawfully acquired or established as an operating subsidiary before May 18, 2015, may continue to operate as a Federal savings association operating subsidiary under this section, provided that the savings association and the operating subsidiary were, and continue to be, conducting authorized activities in compliance with the standards and requirements applicable when the savings association established or acquired the operating subsidiary.

(7) *Issuances of securities by operating subsidiaries.* An operating subsidiary shall not state or imply that the securities it issues are covered by Federal deposit insurance. An operating subsidiary shall not issue any security the payment, maturity, or redemption of which may be accelerated upon the condition that the controlling Federal savings association is insolvent or has been placed into receivership. For as long as any securities are outstanding, the controlling Federal savings association must maintain all records generated through each securities issuance in the ordinary course of business, including but not limited to a copy of the prospectus, offering circular, or similar document concerning such issuance, and make such records available for examination by the OCC.

[80 FR 28450, May 18, 2015]

§ 5.39 Financial subsidiaries of a national bank.

(a) *Authority.* 12 U.S.C. 93a and section 121 of Public Law 106–102, 113 Stat. 1338, 1373.

(b) *Approval requirements.* A national bank must file a notice as prescribed in this section prior to acquiring a financial subsidiary or engaging in activities authorized pursuant to section 5136A(a)(2)(A)(i) of the Revised Statutes (12 U.S.C. 24a) through a financial subsidiary. When a financial subsidiary proposes to conduct a new activity permitted under § 5.34, the bank shall follow the procedures in § 5.34(e)(5) instead of paragraph (i) of this section.

(c) *Scope.* This section sets forth authorized activities, approval procedures, and, where applicable, conditions for national banks engaging in activities through a financial subsidiary.

(d) *Definitions.* For purposes of this § 5.39:

(1) *Affiliate* has the meaning set forth in section 2 of the Bank Holding Company Act of 1956 (12 U.S.C. 1841), except that the term "affiliate" for purposes of paragraph (h)(5) of this section shall

have the meaning set forth in sections 23A or 23B of the Federal Reserve Act (12 U.S.C. 371c and 371c–1), as implemented by Regulation W, 12 CFR part 223, as applicable.

(2) *Appropriate Federal banking agency* has the meaning set forth in section 3 of the Federal Deposit Insurance Act (12 U.S.C. 1813).

(3) *Company* has the meaning set forth in section 2 of the Bank Holding Company Act of 1956 (12 U.S.C. 1841), and includes a limited liability company (LLC).

(4) *Control* has the meaning set forth in section 2 of the Bank Holding Company Act of 1956 (12 U.S.C. 1841).

(5) *Eligible debt* means unsecured long-term debt that is:

(i) Not supported by any form of credit enhancement, including a guaranty or standby letter of credit; and

(ii) Not held in whole or in any significant part by any affiliate, officer, director, principal shareholder, or employee of the bank or any other person acting on behalf of or with funds from the bank or an affiliate of the bank.

(6) *Financial subsidiary* means any company that is controlled by one or more insured depository institutions, other than a subsidiary that:

(i) Engages solely in activities that national banks may engage in directly and that are conducted subject to the same terms and conditions that govern the conduct of these activities by national banks; or

(ii) A national bank is specifically authorized to control by the express terms of a Federal statute (other than section 5136A of the Revised Statutes), and not by implication or interpretation, such as by section 25 of the Federal Reserve Act (12 U.S.C. 601–604a), section 25A of the Federal Reserve Act (12 U.S.C. 611–631), or the Bank Service Company Act (12 U.S.C. 1861 *et seq.*)

(7) *Insured depository institution* has the meaning set forth in section 3 of the Federal Deposit Insurance Act (12 U.S.C. 1813).

(8) *Long term debt* means any debt obligation with an initial maturity of 360 days or more.

(9) *Subsidiary* has the meaning set forth in section 2 of the Bank Holding Company Act of 1956 (12 U.S.C. 1841).

(10) *Tangible equity* has the meaning set forth in 12 CFR 6.2.

(11) *Well capitalized* with respect to a depository institution means the capital level designated as "well capitalized" by the institution's appropriate Federal banking agency pursuant to section 38 of the Federal Deposit Insurance Act (12 U.S.C. 1831o).

(12) *Well managed* means:

(i) Unless otherwise determined in writing by the appropriate Federal banking agency, the institution has received a composite rating of 1 or 2 under the Uniform Financial Institutions Rating System (or an equivalent rating under an equivalent rating system) in connection with the most recent examination or subsequent review of the depository institution and, at least a rating of 2 for management, if such a rating is given; or

(ii) In the case of any depository institution that has not been examined by its appropriate Federal banking agency, the existence and use of managerial resources that the appropriate Federal banking agency determines are satisfactory.

(e) *Authorized activities.* A financial subsidiary may engage only in the following activities:

(1) Activities that are financial in nature and activities incidental to a financial activity, authorized pursuant to 5136A(a)(2)(A)(i) of the Revised Statutes (12 U.S.C. 24a) (to the extent not otherwise permitted under paragraph (e)(2) of this section), including:

(i) Lending, exchanging, transferring, investing for others, or safeguarding money or securities;

(ii) Engaging as agent or broker in any state for purposes of insuring, guaranteeing, or indemnifying against loss, harm, damage, illness, disability, death, defects in title, or providing annuities as agent or broker;

(iii) Providing financial, investment, or economic advisory services, including advising an investment company as defined in section 3 of the Investment Company Act (15 U.S.C. 80a–3);

(iv) Issuing or selling instruments representing interests in pools of assets permissible for a bank to hold directly;

(v) Underwriting, dealing in, or making a market in securities;

(vi) Engaging in any activity that the Board of Governors of the Federal Reserve System has determined, by order or regulation in effect on November 12, 1999, to be so closely related to banking or managing or controlling banks as to be a proper incident thereto (subject to the same terms and conditions contained in the order or regulation, unless the order or regulation is modified by the Board of Governors of the Federal Reserve System);

(vii) Engaging, in the United States, in any activity that a bank holding company may engage in outside the United States and the Board of Governors of the Federal Reserve System has determined, under regulations prescribed or interpretations issued pursuant to section 4(c)(13) of the Bank Holding Company Act of 1956 (12 U.S.C. 1843(c)(13)) as in effect on November 11, 1999, to be usual in connection with the transaction of banking or other financial operations abroad; and

(viii) Activities that the Secretary of the Treasury in consultation with the Board of Governors of the Federal Reserve System, as provided in section 5136A of the Revised Statutes, determines to be financial in nature or incidental to a financial activity; and

(2) Activities that may be conducted by an operating subsidiary pursuant to § 5.34.

(f) *Impermissible activities.* A financial subsidiary may not engage as principal in the following activities:

(1) Insuring, guaranteeing, or indemnifying against loss, harm, damage, illness, disability or death, or defects in title (except to the extent permitted under sections 302 or 303(c) of the Gramm-Leach-Bliley Act (GLBA)), 113 Stat. 1407–1409, (15 U.S.C. 6712 or 15 U.S.C. 6713) or providing or issuing annuities the income of which is subject to tax treatment under section 72 of the Internal Revenue Code (26 U.S.C. 72);

(2) Real estate development or real estate investment, unless otherwise expressly authorized by law; and

(3) Activities authorized for bank holding companies by section 4(k)(4)(H) or (I) (12 U.S.C. 1843) of the Bank Holding Company Act, except activities authorized under section 4(k)(4)(H) that may be permitted in accordance with section 122 of the GLBA, 113 Stat. 1381.

(g) *Qualifications.* A national bank may, directly or indirectly, control a financial subsidiary or hold an interest in a financial subsidiary only if:

(1) The national bank and each depository institution affiliate of the national bank are well capitalized and well managed;

(2) The aggregate consolidated total assets of all financial subsidiaries of the national bank do not exceed the lesser of 45 percent of the consolidated total assets of the parent bank or $50 billion (or such greater amount as is determined according to an indexing mechanism jointly established by regulation by the Secretary of the Treasury and the Board of Governors of the Federal Reserve System); and

(3) If the national bank is one of the 100 largest insured banks, determined on the basis of the bank's consolidated total assets at the end of the calendar year, the bank has not fewer than one issue of outstanding debt that meets such standards of creditworthiness or other criteria as the Secretary of the Treasury and the Federal Reserve Board may jointly establish pursuant to Section 5136A of title LXII of the Revised Statutes (12 U.S.C. 24a).

(4) Paragraph (g)(3) of this section does not apply if the financial subsidiary is engaged solely in activities in an agency capacity.

(h) *Safeguards.* The following safeguards apply to a national bank that establishes or maintains a financial subsidiary:

(1) For purposes of determining regulatory capital the national bank may not consolidate the assets and liabilities of a financial subsidiary with those of the bank and must deduct the aggregate amount of its outstanding equity investment, including retained earnings, in its financial subsidiaries from regulatory capital as provided by § 3.22(a)(7) of this chapter;

(2) Any published financial statement of the national bank shall, in addition to providing information prepared in accordance with generally accepted accounting principles, separately present financial information for the bank in the manner provided in paragraph (h)(1) of this section;

(3) The national bank must have reasonable policies and procedures to preserve the separate corporate identity and limited liability of the bank and the financial subsidiaries of the bank;

(4) The national bank must have procedures for identifying and managing financial and operational risks within the bank and the financial subsidiary that adequately protect the national bank from such risks;

(5) Except for a subsidiary of a bank that is considered a financial subsidiary under paragraph (a)(6) of this section solely because the subsidiary engages in the sale of insurance as agent or broker in a manner that is not permitted for national banks, sections 23A and 23B of the Federal Reserve Act (12 U.S.C. 371c and 371c–1), as implemented by Regulation W, 12 CFR part 223, apply to transactions involving a financial subsidiary in the following manner:

(i) A financial subsidiary shall be deemed to be an affiliate of the bank and shall not be deemed to be a subsidiary of the bank;

(ii) The restrictions contained in section 23A(a)(1)(A) of the Federal Reserve Act shall not apply with respect to covered transactions between a bank and any individual financial subsidiary of the bank;

(iii) A bank's purchase of or investment in a security issued by a financial subsidiary of the bank must be valued at the greater of:

(A) The total amount of consideration given (including liabilities assumed) by the bank, reduced to reflect amortization of the security to the extent consistent with GAAP, or

(B) The carrying value of the security (adjusted so as not to reflect the bank's *pro rata* portion of any earnings retained or losses incurred by the financial subsidiary after the bank's acquisition of the security).

(iv) Any purchase of, or investment in, the securities of a financial subsidiary of a bank by an affiliate of the bank will be considered to be a purchase of or investment in such securities by the bank;

(v) Any extension of credit to a financial subsidiary of a bank by an affiliate of the bank is treated as an extension of credit by the bank to the financial subsidiary if the extension of credit is treated as capital of the financial subsidiary under any Federal or State law, regulation, or interpretation applicable to the subsidiary; and

(vi) Any other extension of credit by an affiliate of a bank to a financial subsidiary of the bank may be considered an extension of credit by the bank to the financial subsidiary if the Board of Governors of the Federal Reserve System determines that such treatment is necessary or appropriate to prevent evasions of the Federal Reserve Act and the GLBA.

(6) A financial subsidiary shall be deemed a subsidiary of a bank holding company and not a subsidiary of the bank for purposes of the anti-tying prohibitions set forth in 12 U.S.C. 1971 *et seq*.

(i) *Procedures to engage in activities through a financial subsidiary*. A national bank that intends, directly or indirectly, to acquire control of, or hold an interest in, a financial subsidiary, or to commence a new activity in an existing financial subsidiary, must obtain OCC approval through the procedures set forth in paragraph (i)(1) or (i)(2) of this section.

(1) *Certification with subsequent notice*. (i) At any time, a national bank may file a "Financial Subsidiary Certification" with the appropriate OCC licensing office listing the bank's depository institution affiliates and certifying that the bank and each of those affiliates is well capitalized and well managed.

(ii) Thereafter, at such time as the bank seeks OCC approval to acquire control of, or hold an interest in, a new financial subsidiary, or commence a new activity authorized under section 5136A(a)(2)(A)(i) of the Revised Statutes (12 U.S.C. 24a) in an existing subsidiary, the bank may file a written notice with the appropriate OCC licensing office at the time of acquiring control of, or holding an interest in, a financial subsidiary, or commencing such activity in an existing subsidiary. The written notice must be labeled "Financial Subsidiary Notice" and must:

(A) State that the bank's Certification remains valid;

(B) Describe the activity or activities conducted by the financial subsidiary.

To the extent the notice relates to the initial affiliation of the bank with a company engaged in insurance activities, the bank should describe the type of insurance activity that the company is engaged in and has present plans to conduct. The bank must also list for each state the lines of business for which the company holds, or will hold, an insurance license, indicating the state where the company holds a resident license or charter, as applicable;

(C) Cite the specific authority permitting the activity to be conducted by the financial subsidiary. (Where the authority relied on is an agency order or interpretation under section 4(c)(8) or 4(c)(13), respectively, of the Bank Holding Company Act of 1956, a copy of the order or interpretation should be attached);

(D) Certify that the bank will be well capitalized after making adjustments required by paragraph (h)(1) of this section;

(E) Demonstrate the aggregate consolidated total assets of all financial subsidiaries of the national bank do not exceed the lesser of 45 percent of the bank's consolidated total assets or $50 billion (or the increased level established by the indexing mechanism); and

(F) If applicable, certify that the bank meets the eligible debt requirement in paragraph (g)(3) of this section.

(2) *Combined certification and notice.* A national bank may file a combined certification and notice with the appropriate OCC licensing office at least five business days prior to acquiring control of, or holding an interest in, a financial subsidiary, or commencing a new activity authorized pursuant to section 5136A(a)(2)(A)(i) of the Revised Statutes in an existing subsidiary. The written notice must be labeled "Financial Subsidiary Certification and Notice" and must:

(i) List the bank's depository institution affiliates and certify that the bank and each depository institution affiliate of the bank is well capitalized and well managed;

(ii) Describe the activity or activities to be conducted in the financial subsidiary. To the extent the notice relates to the initial affiliation of the bank with a company engaged in insurance activities, the bank should describe the type of insurance activity that the company is engaged in and has present plans to conduct. The bank must also list for each state the lines of business for which the company holds, or will hold, an insurance license, indicating the state where the company holds a resident license or charter, as applicable;

(iii) Cite the specific authority permitting the activity to be conducted by the financial subsidiary. (Where the authority relied on is an agency order or interpretation under section 4(c)(8) or 4(c)(13), respectively, of the Bank Holding Company Act of 1956, a copy of the order or interpretation should be attached);

(iv) Certify that the bank will remain well capitalized after making the adjustments required by paragraph (h)(1) of this section;

(v) Demonstrate the aggregate consolidated total assets of all financial subsidiaries of the national bank do not exceed the lesser of 45% of the bank's consolidated total assets or $50 billion (or the increased level established by the indexing mechanism); and

(vi) If applicable, certify that the bank meets the eligible debt requirement in paragraph (g)(3) of this section.

(3) *Exceptions to rules of general applicability.* Sections 5.8, 5.10, 5.11, and 5.13 do not apply to activities authorized under this section.

(4) *Community Reinvestment Act (CRA).* A national bank may not apply under this paragraph (i) to commence a new activity authorized under section 5136A(a)(2)(A)(i) of the Revised Statutes (12 U.S.C. 24a), or directly or indirectly acquire control of a company engaged in any such activity, if the bank or any of its insured depository institution affiliates received a CRA rating of less than "satisfactory record of meeting community credit needs" on its most recent CRA examination prior to when the bank would file a notice under this section.

(j) *Failure to continue to meet certain qualification requirements*—(1) *Qualifications and safeguards.* A national bank, or, as applicable, its affiliated depository institutions, must continue to satisfy the qualification requirements set forth in paragraphs (g)(1) and (2) of this section and the safeguards in paragraphs (h)(1), (2), (3) and (4) of this section following its acquisition of control of, or an interest in, a financial subsidiary. A national bank that fails to continue to satisfy these requirements will be subject to the following procedures and requirements:

(i) The OCC shall give notice to the national bank and, in the case of an affiliated depository institution to that depository institution's appropriate Federal banking agency, promptly upon determining that the national bank, or, as applicable, its affiliated depository institution, does not continue to meet the requirements in paragraph (g)(1) or (2) of this section or the safeguards in paragraph (h)(1), (2), (3), or (4) of this section. The bank shall be deemed to have received such notice three business days after mailing of the letter by the OCC;

(ii) Not later than 45 days after receipt of the notice under paragraph (j)(1)(i) of this section, or any additional time as the OCC may permit, the national bank shall execute an agreement with the OCC to comply with the requirements in paragraphs (g)(1) and (2) and (h)(1), (2), (3), and (4) of this section;

(iii) The OCC may impose limitations on the conduct or activities of the national bank or any subsidiary of the national bank as the OCC determines appropriate under the circumstances and consistent with the purposes of section 5136A of the Revised Statutes; and

(iv) The OCC may require a national bank to divest control of a financial subsidiary if the national bank does not correct the conditions giving rise to the notice within 180 days after receipt of the notice provided under paragraph (j)(1)(i) of this section.

(2) *Eligible debt requirement.* A national bank that does not continue to meet the qualification requirement set forth in paragraph (g)(3) of this section, applicable where the bank's financial subsidiary is engaged in activities other than solely in an agency capacity, may not directly or through a subsidiary, purchase or acquire any additional equity capital of any such financial subsidiary until the bank meets the requirement in paragraph (g)(3) of this section. For purposes of this paragraph (j)(2), the term "equity capital" includes, in addition to any equity investment, any debt instrument issued by the financial subsidiary if the instrument qualifies as capital of the subsidiary under Federal or state law, regulation, or interpretation applicable to the subsidiary.

(k) *Examination and supervision.* A financial subsidiary is subject to examination and supervision by the OCC, subject to the limitations and requirements of section 45 of the Federal Deposit Insurance Act (12 U.S.C. 1831v) and section 115 of the GLBA (12 U.S.C. 1820a).

[65 FR 12914, Mar. 10, 2000, as amended at 73 FR 22240, Apr. 24, 2008; 77 FR 35258, June 13, 2012; 78 FR 62275, Oct. 11, 2013; 79 FR 11310, Feb. 28, 2014; 80 FR 28452, May 18, 2015]

Subpart D—Other Changes in Activities and Operations

§5.40 Change in location of a main office of a national bank or home office of a Federal savings association.

(a) *Authority.* 12 U.S.C. 30, 93a, 1462a, 1463, 1464, 1828, 2901–2907 and 5412(b)(2)(B).

(b) *Scope.* This section describes OCC procedures and approval standards for an application or a notice by a national bank to change the location of its main office or by a Federal savings association to change the location of its home office.[3] A national bank or Federal savings association shall follow the procedures described in paragraph (c) of this

[3] A national bank's main office is the place identified in the bank's original organization certificate under 12 U.S.C. 22 or the subsequent location to which the main office has been changed under this §5.40, 12 U.S.C. 30(b), or other applicable law, as reflected in the national bank's amended articles of association. A Federal savings association's home office is the office identified as such in the savings association's original charter or the subsequent location to which the home office has been changed under this §5.40, or other applicable law, as reflected in the savings association's amended charter. These terms are functionally the same but are used in our regulations in order to be consistent with the relevant statutes that govern national

Continued

section to relocate its main office or home office, as applicable.

(c) *Licensing requirements and procedures*—(1) *Main office or home office relocation to an authorized branch location within city, town, or village limits.* A national bank or Federal savings association may change the location of its main office or home office, as applicable, to an authorized branch location (approved or existing branch site) within the limits of the same city, town, or village. The national bank or Federal savings association shall give prior notice to the appropriate OCC licensing office before the relocation. The notice must include the new address of the main office or home office, as applicable, and the effective date of the relocation.

(2) *To any other location*—(i) *National banks.* A national bank shall submit an application to the appropriate OCC licensing office and obtain prior OCC approval to relocate its main office to any other location in the city, town, or village in which the main office of the bank is located other than an authorized branch location or to any other location within 30 miles of the limits of such city, town, or village. If relocating the main office outside the limits of its city, town, or village, a national bank shall also obtain the approval of shareholders owning two-thirds of the voting stock of the bank and shall amend its articles of association.

(ii) *Federal savings associations.* A Federal savings association shall submit an application to the appropriate OCC licensing office and obtain prior OCC approval to relocate its home office to any location other than an authorized branch location within the city, town, or village in which the home office of the savings association is located. If relocating the home office outside the limits of its city, town, or village, a Federal savings association shall obtain any shareholder approval required under its charter for such relocation and shall amend its charter.

(3) *Establishment of a branch at site of former main office or home office.* A national bank or Federal savings association desiring to establish a branch at its former main office or home office location, as applicable, shall follow the provisions of § 5.30 or § 5.31, respectively.

(4) *Expedited review.* A main office or home office relocation application submitted by an eligible national bank or eligible Federal savings association under paragraph (c)(2) of this section is deemed approved by the OCC as of the 15th day after the close of the public comment period or the 45th day after the filing is received by the OCC (or in the case of a short-distance relocation the 30th day after the filing is received by the OCC), whichever is later, unless the OCC notifies the bank or savings association prior to that time that the filing is not eligible for expedited review, or the expedited review period is extended, under § 5.13(a)(2).

(5) *Exceptions to rules of general applicability.* (i) Sections 5.8, 5.9, 5.10, and 5.11 do not apply to a main office or home office relocation to an authorized branch location within the limits of the city, town, or village as described in paragraph (c)(1) of this section. However, if the OCC concludes that the notice under paragraph (c)(1) of this section presents a significant or novel policy, supervisory, or legal issue, the OCC may determine that any or all parts of §§ 5.8, 5.9, 5.10, and 5.11 apply.

(ii) The comment period on any application filed under paragraph (c)(2) of this section to engage in a short-distance relocation of a main office or home office is 15 days.

(d) *Expiration of approval.* Approval expires if the national bank or Federal savings association has not opened its main office or home office, as applicable, at the relocated site within 18 months of the date of approval, unless the OCC grants an extension.

[80 FR 28452, May 18, 2015]

§ 5.42 Corporate title of a national bank or Federal savings association.

(a) *Authority.* 12 U.S.C. 21a, 30, 93a, 1462a, 1463, 1464, 1467a, 2901 *et. seq.* and, 5412(b)(2)(B).

(b) *Scope.* This section describes the method by which a national bank or Federal savings association may change its corporate title.

---

banks and Federal savings associations, respectively.

(c) *Standards.* (1) A national bank or Federal savings association may change its corporate title provided that the new title complies with applicable laws, including 18 U.S.C. 709, regarding false advertising and the misuse of names to indicate a Federal agency, and any applicable OCC guidance.

(2) For a national bank, the new title must include the word "national."

(d) *Procedures*—(1) *Notice process.* A national bank or Federal savings association shall promptly notify the appropriate OCC licensing office if it changes its corporate title. The notice must contain the old and new titles and the effective date of the change.

(2) *Amendment to articles of association.* A national bank whose corporate title is specified in its articles of association shall amend its articles, in accordance with the procedures of 12 U.S.C. 21a, to change its title.

(3) *Amendment to charter.* A Federal savings association shall change its title by amending its charter in accordance with 12 CFR 5.21 or 5.22, as applicable.

(4) *Exceptions to rules of general applicability.* Sections 5.8, 5.9, 5.10, 5.11, and 5.13(a) do not apply to a national bank or Federal savings association's change of corporate title. However, if the OCC concludes that the application presents a significant or novel policy, supervisory, or legal issue, the OCC may determine that any or all parts of §§ 5.8, 5.9, 5.10, 5.11, and 5.13(a) apply.

[80 FR 28453, May 18, 2015]

§ 5.45 Increases in permanent capital of a Federal stock savings association.

(a) *Authority.* 12 U.S.C. 1462a, 1463, 1464, 1467a, 1831o and 5412(b)(2)(B).

(b) *Licensing requirements.* Generally a Federal savings association is not required to apply for an increase in capital unless the method of increase itself requires a filing (such as issuance of a new class of stock). However, in certain circumstances, a Federal stock savings association is required to submit an application and obtain OCC approval.

(c) *Scope.* This section describes procedures and standards relating to a transaction resulting in an increase in a Federal stock savings association's permanent capital.

(d) *Exceptions to rules of general applicability.* Sections 5.8, 5.10, and 5.11 do not apply to increases in a Federal stock savings association's permanent capital.

(e) *Definitions.* For the purposes of this section the following definitions apply:

(1) *Capital plan* means a plan describing the manner and schedule by which a Federal savings association will attain specified capital levels or ratios and a capital restoration plan filed with the OCC under 12 U.S.C. 1831o and 12 CFR 6.5.

(2) *Capital stock* means the total amount of common stock and preferred stock.

(3) *Capital surplus* means the total of:

(i) The amount paid in on capital stock in excess of the par or stated value;

(ii) Direct capital contributions representing the amounts paid in to the Federal stock savings association other than for capital stock;

(iii) The amount transferred from retained net income; and

(iv) The amount transferred from retained net income reflecting stock dividends.

(4) *Permanent capital* means the sum of capital stock and capital surplus.

(5) *Retained net income* means the net income of a specified period less the amount of all dividends and other capital distributions declared in that period.

(f) *Policy.* In determining whether to approve a proposed increase in a Federal stock savings association's permanent capital, the OCC considers whether the change is:

(1) Consistent with law, regulation, and OCC policy thereunder;

(2) Provides an adequate capital structure; and

(3) If appropriate, complies with the savings association's capital plan.

(g) *Procedures*—(1) *When prior approval is required.* A Federal stock savings association must submit an application to the appropriate OCC licensing office and obtain prior OCC approval to increase its permanent capital if the savings association is:

(i) Required to receive OCC approval pursuant to letter, order, directive, written agreement or otherwise;

(ii) Selling common or preferred stock for consideration other than cash; or

(iii) Receiving a material noncash contribution to capital surplus.

(2) *Content of application.* The application must:

(i) Describe the type and amount of the proposed change in permanent capital and explain the reason for the change;

(ii) In the case of a material noncash contribution to capital, provide a description of the method of valuing the contribution; and

(iii) State if the savings association is subject to a capital plan with the OCC and how the proposed change would conform to a capital plan or if a capital plan is otherwise required in connection with the proposed change in permanent capital.

(3) *Expedited review.* An eligible savings association's application is deemed approved by the OCC 15 days after the date the OCC receives the application, unless the OCC notifies the savings association prior to that date that the application is not eligible for expedited review, or the expedited review process is extended, under § 5.13(a)(2).

(4) *Notice of increase.* (i) If prior approval is required pursuant to this paragraph (g), after a savings association completes an increase in capital it shall submit a notice to the appropriate OCC licensing office. The notice must contain:

(A) The amount, including the par value of the stock, and effective date of the increase;

(B) A certification that the funds have been paid in, if applicable; and

(C) A statement that the savings association has complied with all laws, regulations and conditions imposed by the OCC.

(5) *Expiration of approval.* Approval expires if a Federal savings association has not completed its change in permanent capital within one year of the date of approval.

(h) *Offers and sales of stock.* A savings association shall comply with the Securities Offering Disclosure Rules in 12 CFR part 197 for offers and sales of common and preferred stock.

(i) *Shareholder approval.* A savings association shall obtain the necessary shareholder approval required by statute for any change in its permanent capital.

[80 FR 28453, May 18, 2015, as amended at 82 FR 8104, Jan. 23, 2017]

§ 5.46 Changes in permanent capital of a national bank.

(a) *Authority.* 12 U.S.C. 21a, 51a, 51b, 51b–1, 52, 56, 57, 59, 60, and 93a.

(b) *Licensing requirements.* A national bank shall submit an application and obtain OCC approval to decrease its permanent capital. Generally, a national bank need only submit a notice to increase its permanent capital, although, in certain circumstances, a national bank shall be required to submit an application and obtain OCC approval.

(c) *Scope.* This section describes procedures and standards relating to a transaction resulting in a change in a national bank's permanent capital.

(d) *Exceptions to rules of general applicability.* Sections 5.8, 5.10, and 5.11 do not apply to changes in a national bank's permanent capital.

(e) *Definitions.* For the purposes of this section the following definitions apply:

(1) *Capital plan* means a plan describing the manner and schedule by which a national bank will attain specified capital levels or ratios and a capital restoration plan filed with the OCC under 12 U.S.C. 1831o and 12 CFR 6.5.

(2) *Capital stock* means the total amount of common stock and preferred stock.

(3) *Capital surplus* means the total of:

(i) The amount paid in on capital stock in excess of the par or stated value;

(ii) Direct capital contributions representing the amounts paid in to the national bank other than for capital stock;

(iii) The amount transferred from undivided profits; and

(iv) The amount transferred from undivided profits reflecting stock dividends.

(4) *Permanent capital* means the sum of capital stock and capital surplus.

(f) *Policy*. In determining whether to approve a proposed change to a national bank's permanent capital, the OCC considers whether the change is:

(1) Consistent with law, regulation, and OCC policy thereunder;

(2) Provides an adequate capital structure; and

(3) If appropriate, complies with the bank's capital plan.

(g) *Increases in permanent capital*—(1) *Approval*—(i) *Prior approval not required*. If a national bank is not required to file an application and obtain prior approval under paragraph (g)(1)(ii) of this section, the bank need not submit an application. It must submit the notice of capital increase under paragraph (i)(3) of this section. The increase in capital is deemed approved by the OCC as of the date the increase was made, once the bank has filed the notice of capital increase and the OCC certifies the increase, as provided in paragraph (i)(3).

(ii) *Prior approval required*. A national bank must submit an application under paragraph (i)(1) of this section and obtain prior OCC approval to increase its permanent capital if the bank is:

(A) Required to receive OCC approval pursuant to letter, order, directive, written agreement or otherwise;

(B) Selling common or preferred stock for consideration other than cash; or

(C) Receiving a material noncash contribution to capital surplus. The bank also must submit the notice of capital increase under paragraph (i)(3) of this section.

(2) *Preferred stock*. Notwithstanding paragraph (g)(1)(i) of this section, in the case of a sale of preferred stock, the national bank shall also submit provisions in the articles of association concerning preferred stock dividends, voting and conversion rights, retirement of the stock, and rights to exercise control over management to the appropriate OCC licensing office prior to the sale of the preferred stock. The provisions will be deemed approved by the OCC within 15 days of its receipt, unless the OCC notifies the applicant otherwise, including a statement of the reason for the delay.

(h) *Decreases in permanent capital*. A national bank shall submit an application and obtain prior approval under paragraph (i)(1) or (i)(2) of this section for any reduction of its permanent capital.

(i) *Procedures*—(1) *Prior approval*. A national bank proposing to make a change in its permanent capital that requires prior OCC approval under paragraphs (g) or (h) of this section shall submit an application to the appropriate OCC licensing office. The application must:

(i) Describe the type and amount of the proposed change in permanent capital and explain the reason for the change;

(ii) In the case of a reduction in capital, provide a schedule detailing the present and proposed capital structure;

(iii) In the case of a material noncash contribution to capital, provide a description of the method of valuing the contribution; and

(iv) State if the bank is subject to a capital plan with the OCC and how the proposed change would conform to a capital plan or if a capital plan is otherwise required in connection with the proposed change in permanent capital.

(2) *Expedited review*. An eligible bank's application is deemed approved by the OCC 15 days after the date the OCC receives the application described in paragraph (i)(1) of this section, unless the OCC notifies the bank prior to that date that the application is not eligible for expedited review, or the expedited review process is extended, under §5.13(a)(2). An eligible bank seeking to decrease its capital may request OCC approval for up to four consecutive quarters. An eligible bank may decrease its capital pursuant to such a plan only if the bank maintains its eligible bank status before and after each decrease in its capital.

(3) *Notice of increase*. (i) After a bank completes an increase in capital it shall submit a notice to the appropriate OCC licensing office. The notice must be acknowledged before a notary public by the bank's president, vice president, or cashier and contain:

(A) A description of the transaction, unless already provided pursuant to paragraph (i)(1) of this section;

(B) The amount, including the par value of the stock, and effective date of the increase;

(C) A certification that the funds have been paid in, if applicable;

(D) A certified copy of the amendment to the articles of association, if required; and

(E) A statement that the bank has complied with all laws, regulations and conditions imposed by the OCC.

(ii) After it receives the notice of capital increase, the OCC issues a certification specifying the amount of the increase and the effective date (*i.e.*, the date on which the increase occurred). In the case of a capital increase for which prior approval was not required pursuant to paragraph (g)(1)(i), the increase is deemed certified by the OCC seven days after receipt of the notice if the OCC has not issued a certification prior to that date.

(4) *Notice of decrease.* A national bank that decreases its capital in accordance with paragraphs (i)(1) or (i)(2) of this section shall notify the appropriate OCC licensing office following the completion of the transaction.

(5) *Expiration of approval.* Approval expires if a national bank has not completed its change in permanent capital within one year of the date of approval.

(6) *Exception for accounting adjustments.* (i) Changes to the permanent capital accounts that result solely from application of U.S. generally accepted accounting principles are not subject to the prior approval or notice requirements in paragraph (i)(1), (3), or (4) of this section, as applicable.

(ii) Within 30 days after the end of the quarter in which the adjustment occurred, a bank must notify the OCC if the accounting adjustment resulted in an increase or decrease to permanent capital in an amount greater than 5% of the bank's total permanent capital prior to the adjustments; or, if the bank is subject to a letter, order, directive, written agreement, or otherwise related to changes in permanent capital. The notification must include the amount and description of the adjustment, including the applicable provision of U.S. GAAP.

(j) *Offers and sales of stock.* A national bank shall comply with the Securities Offering Disclosure Rules in 12 CFR part 16 for offers and sales of common and preferred stock.

(k) *Shareholder approval.* A national bank shall obtain the necessary shareholder approval required by statute for any change in its permanent capital.

[80 FR 28454, May 18, 2015, as amended at 82 FR 8104, Jan. 23, 2017]

§ 5.47 Subordinated debt issued by a national bank.

(a) *Authority.* 12 U.S.C. 93a, 1831o, and 3907.

(b) *Scope.* This section sets forth the requirements applicable to all subordinated debt notes issued by national banks and the procedures for OCC review and approval of a national bank's application to issue or prepay subordinated debt and a notice to include subordinated debt in tier 2 capital.

(c) *Definitions.* The following definitions apply to this section:

Capital plan means a plan describing the means and schedule by which a national bank will attain specified capital levels or ratios, including a capital restoration plan filed with the OCC under 12 U.S.C. 1831o and 12 CFR 6.5.

Original maturity means the stated maturity of the subordinated debt note. If the subordinated debt note does not have a stated maturity, then original maturity means the earliest possible date the subordinated debt note may be redeemed, repurchased, prepaid, terminated, or otherwise retired by the national bank pursuant to the terms of the subordinated debt note.

Payment on subordinated debt means principal and interest, and premium, if any.

Tier 2 capital has the same meaning as set forth in 12 CFR 3.20(d).

(d) *Requirements for issuance of subordinated debt.* A national bank issuing subordinated debt must satisfy the requirements of this paragraph (d).

(1) *Minimum terms.* The terms of any subordinated debt note issued by a national bank must:

(i) Have a minimum original maturity of at least five years;

(ii) Not be a deposit and not insured by the Federal Deposit Insurance Corporation (FDIC);

(iii) Be subordinated to the claims of depositors;

(iv) Be unsecured, which would include prohibiting the establishment of any legally enforceable fund earmarked for payment of the subordinated debt note through:

(A) A sinking fund; or

(B) A compensating balance or any other funds or assets subject to a legal right of offset, as defined by applicable state law;

(v) Be ineligible as collateral for a loan by the issuing national bank;

(vi) Provide that once any scheduled payments of principal begin, all scheduled payments shall be made at least annually and the amount repaid in each year shall be no less than in the prior year; and

(vii) Provide that, where applicable, no payment (including payment pursuant to an acceleration clause, redemption prior to maturity, repurchase, or exercising a call option) shall be made without prior OCC approval.

(2) *Corporate authority.* A subordinated debt note must not include any provision or covenant that unduly restricts or otherwise acts to unduly limit the authority of a national bank or interferes with the OCC's supervision of the national bank. Specifically, this would include a provision or covenant that:

(i) Maintains a certain minimum amount in its capital accounts or other metric, such as minimum capital assets, liquidity, or loan ratios;

(ii) Unreasonably restricts a national bank's ability to raise additional capital through the issuance of additional subordinated debt or other regulatory capital instruments;

(iii) Provides for default and acceleration of the subordinated debt as the result of a change in control, if such change in control results from the OCC's exercise of its statutory authority to require a national bank to sell stock in that national bank, enter into a merger or consolidation, or be acquired by a bank holding company;

(iv) Requires the prior approval of a purchaser or holder of the subordinated debt note in the case of a voluntary merger by a national bank where the resulting institution:

(A) Assumes the due and punctual performance of all conditions of the subordinated debt note and agreement; and

(B) Is not in default of the various covenants of the subordinated debt; and

(v) Provides for default and acceleration of the subordinated debt as the result of a default by a subsidiary (including a limited liability company) of the national bank, unless:

(A) There is a separate agreement between the subsidiary and the purchaser of the national bank's subordinated debt note; and

(B) Such agreement has been reviewed and approved by the OCC.

(3) *Disclosure requirements.* (i) A national bank must disclose clearly on the face of any subordinated debt note the following language in all capital letters:

(A) THIS OBLIGATION IS NOT A DEPOSIT AND IS NOT INSURED BY THE FEDERAL DEPOSIT INSURANCE CORPORATION; and

(B) THIS OBLIGATION IS SUBORDINATED TO CLAIMS OF DEPOSITORS AND GENERAL CREDITORS, IS UNSECURED, AND IS INELIGIBLE AS COLLATERAL FOR A LOAN BY [INSERT NAME OF ISSUING NATIONAL BANK].

(ii) A national bank must disclose clearly and accurately in the subordinated debt note:

(A) The order and level of subordination, and in addition to being subordinated to the claims of depositors, provide that, at a minimum, the subordinated debt note is subordinate and junior in its right of payment to the obligations of all creditors, including both secured and unsecured or general creditors, except those specifically designated as ranking on a parity with, or subordinated to, the subordinated debt note;

(B) A general description of the OCC's regulatory authority with respect to a national bank in danger of insolvency that includes:

(*1*) With respect to insolvency, that the FDIC, acting as receiver, has authority to transfer a national bank's obligation under the subordinated debt note and to supersede or void any default, acceleration, or subordination that may have occurred;

(*2*) If a national bank that is "undercapitalized" as defined by applicable law fails to satisfactorily implement a required capital restoration plan, the national bank may be subject to all the additional restrictions and requirements applicable to a "significantly undercapitalized" institution, as defined by applicable law, including being required to sell shares in the national bank, being acquired by a depository institution holding company, or being merged or consolidated with another depository institution, and this authority supersedes and voids any defaults that may have occurred; and

(*3*) If a national bank is "critically undercapitalized," as defined by applicable law, the national bank is prohibited from making principal or interest payments on the subordinated debt note without prior regulatory approval; and

(C) A description of the OCC's authority under 12 CFR 3.11 to limit distributions, including interest payments on any tier 2 capital instrument if the national bank has full discretion to permanently or temporarily suspend such payments without triggering an event of default.

(iii) A national bank must comply with the Securities Offering Disclosure Rules in 12 CFR part 16.

(e) *Additional requirements to qualify as tier 2 capital.* In order to qualify as tier 2 capital, a national bank's subordinated debt must meet the requirements in 12 CFR 3.20(d), including, for an advanced approaches national bank, the disclosure requirement in 12 CFR 3.20(d)(1)(xi).

(f) *Process and procedures*—(1) *Issuance of subordinated debt*—(i) *Approval*—(A) *Eligible bank.* An eligible bank is required to receive prior approval from the OCC to issue any subordinated debt, in accordance with paragraph (g)(1)(i) of this section, if:

(*1*) The national bank will not continue to be an eligible bank after the transaction;

(*2*) The OCC has previously notified the national bank that prior approval is required; or

(*3*) Prior approval is required by law.

(B) *National bank not an eligible bank.* A national bank that is not an eligible bank must receive prior OCC approval to issue any subordinated debt, in accordance with paragraph (g)(1)(i) of this section.

(ii) *Notice to include subordinated debt in tier 2 capital.* All national banks must notify the OCC, in accordance with paragraph (h) of this section, within ten days after issuing subordinated debt that is to be counted as tier 2 capital. Where a national bank's application to issue subordinated debt has been deemed to be approved, in accordance with paragraph (g)(2)(i) of this section, the national bank must notify the OCC, pursuant to paragraph (h) of this section, after issuance of the subordinated debt. A national bank may not include subordinated debt as tier 2 capital unless the national bank has filed the notice with the OCC and received notification from the OCC that the subordinated debt issued by the national bank qualifies as tier 2 capital.

(2) *Prepayment of subordinated debt*—(i) *Subordinated debt not included in tier 2 capital*—(A) *Eligible bank.* An eligible bank is required to receive prior approval from the OCC to prepay any subordinated debt that is not included in tier 2 capital (including acceleration, repurchase, redemption prior to maturity, and exercising a call option), in accordance with paragraph (g)(1)(ii) of this section, only if:

(*1*) The national bank will not be an eligible bank after the transaction;

(*2*) The OCC has previously notified the national bank that prior approval is required;

(*3*) Prior approval is required by law; or

(*4*) The amount of the proposed prepayment is equal to or greater than one percent of the national bank's total capital, as defined in 12 CFR 3.2.

(B) *National bank not an eligible bank.* A national bank that is not an eligible bank must receive prior OCC approval to prepay any subordinated debt that is not included in tier 2 capital (including acceleration, repurchase, redemption prior to maturity, and exercising a call option), in accordance with paragraph (g)(1)(ii) of this section.

(ii) *Subordinated debt included in tier 2 capital*—(A) *General.* Notwithstanding paragraph (f)(2)(i)(B) of this section, all national banks must receive prior OCC approval to prepay subordinated debt included in tier 2 capital, in accordance with paragraph (g)(1)(ii)(A) of this section.

(B) *Call option.* Notwithstanding this paragraph (f)(2)(ii)(A) of this section, a national bank must receive prior OCC approval to prepay subordinated debt included in tier 2 capital, in accordance with paragraph (g)(2)(ii)(B) of this section, when the prepayment is a result of exercising a call option.

(g) *Prior approval procedure*—(1) *Application*—(i) *Issuance of subordinated debt.* A national bank required to obtain OCC approval before issuing subordinated debt shall submit an application to the appropriate OCC licensing office. The application must include:

(A) A description of the terms and amount of the proposed issuance;

(B) A statement of whether the national bank is subject to a capital plan or required to file a capital plan with the OCC and, if so, how the proposed change conforms to the capital plan;

(C) A copy of the proposed subordinated note format and note agreement; and

(D) A statement that the subordinated debt issue complies with all applicable laws and regulations.

(ii) *Prepayment of subordinated debt*—(A) *General.* A national bank required to obtain OCC approval before prepaying subordinated debt, pursuant to paragraph (f)(2) of this section, shall submit an application to the appropriate OCC licensing office. The application must include:

(*1*) A description of the terms and amount of the proposed prepayment;

(*2*) A statement of whether the national bank is subject to a capital plan or required to file a capital plan with the OCC and, if so, how the proposed change conforms to the capital plan; and

(*3*) A copy of the subordinated debt instrument the national bank is proposing to prepay.

(B) *Call option.* (*1*) Before prepaying subordinated debt if the prepayment is in the form of a call option, a national bank is required to obtain OCC approval, pursuant to paragraph (g)(2)(ii) of this section, by submitting an application to the appropriate OCC licensing office.

(*2*) In addition to the information required in this paragraph (g)(1)(ii)(A) of this section, the application must include:

(*i*) A statement explaining why the national bank believes that following the proposed prepayment the national bank would continue to hold an amount of capital commensurate with its risk; or

(*ii*) A description of the replacement capital instrument that meets the criteria for tier 1 or tier 2 capital under 12 CFR 3.20, including the amount of such instrument, and the time frame for issuance.

(iii) *Additional information.* The OCC reserves the right to request additional relevant information, as appropriate.

(2) *Approval*—(i) *General.* The application is deemed approved by the OCC as of the 30th day after the filing is received by the OCC, unless the OCC notifies the national bank prior to that date that the filing presents a significant supervisory, or compliance concern, or raises a significant legal or policy issue.

(ii) *Call option.* Notwithstanding this paragraph (g)(2)(i) of this section, if the application for prior approval is for prepayment in the form of a call option, the national bank must receive affirmative approval from the OCC to exercise the call option. If the OCC requires the national bank to replace the subordinated debt, the national bank must receive affirmative approval that the replacement capital instrument meets the criteria for tier 1 or tier 2 capital under 12 CFR 3.20 and must issue the replacement instrument prior to exercising the call option, or immediately thereafter.[4]

(iii) *Tier 2 capital.* Following notification to the OCC pursuant to paragraph (f)(1)(ii) of this section that the national bank has issued the subordinated debt, the OCC will notify the national bank whether the subordinated debt qualifies as tier 2 capital.

(iv) *Expiration of approval.* Approval expires if a national bank does not complete the sale of the subordinated debt within one year of approval.

(h) *Notice procedure for inclusion in tier 2 capital.* (1) All national banks shall

[4] A national bank may replace tier 2 capital instruments concurrent with the redemption of existing tier 2 capital instruments.

notify the appropriate OCC licensing office in writing within ten days after issuing subordinated debt that it intends to include as tier 2 capital. A national bank may not include such subordinated debt in tier 2 capital unless the national bank has received notification from the OCC that the subordinated debt qualifies as tier 2 capital.

(2) The notice must include:

(i) The terms of the issuance;

(ii) The amount and date of receipt of funds;

(iii) A copy of the final subordinated note format and note agreement; and

(iv) A statement that the issuance complies with all applicable laws and regulations.

(i) *Exceptions to rules of general applicability.* Sections 5.8, 5.10, and 5.11 do not apply to transactions governed by this section.

[79 FR 75421, Dec. 18, 2014, as amended at 80 FR 28455, May 18, 2015]

§ 5.48 Voluntary liquidation of a national bank or Federal savings association.

(a) *Authority.* 12 U.S.C. 93a, 181, 182, 1463, 1464, and 5412(b)(1)(B).

(b) *Licensing requirements.* A national bank or a Federal savings association considering going into voluntary liquidation shall provide preliminary notice to the OCC. The bank or savings association shall also file a notice with the OCC once a liquidation plan is definite. The bank or savings association may not begin liquidation unless the OCC has notified it that the OCC does not object to the liquidation plan.

(c) *Exceptions to rules of general applicability.* Sections 5.8, 5.10, and 5.11 do not apply to a voluntary liquidation. However, if the OCC concludes that the notice presents significant or novel policy, supervisory or legal issues, the OCC may determine that any or all parts of §§ 5.8, 5.10, and 5.11 apply.

(d) *Standards*—(1) *In general.* In reviewing a proposed liquidation plan, the OCC will consider:

(i) The purpose of the liquidation;

(ii) Its impact on the safety and soundness of the national bank or Federal savings association; and

(iii) Its impact on the bank's or savings association's depositors, other creditors, and customers.

(2) *National banks.* For national banks, the OCC also will review liquidation plans for compliance with 12 U.S.C. 181 and 182.

(3) *Federal mutual savings associations.* For Federal mutual savings associations, the OCC also will assess the advisability of, and alternatives to, liquidation and the effect of liquidation on all concerned.

(e) *Procedure*—(1) *Preliminary notice of voluntary liquidation.* A national bank or Federal savings association that is considering going into voluntary liquidation shall provide preliminary notice to the appropriate OCC licensing office.

(2) *Submission of liquidation plan and nonobjection.* (i) After a national bank or Federal savings association provides preliminary notice under paragraph (e)(1) of this section, if the bank or savings association plans to proceed with liquidation, it shall submit a voluntary liquidation plan to the OCC. A liquidation plan may be effected in whole or part through purchase and assumption transactions.

(ii) The national bank or Federal savings association must receive the OCC's non-objection to the liquidation plan before beginning the liquidation.

(3) *Notice upon commencing liquidation*—(i) *In general.* When the board of directors and the shareholders of a solvent national bank or Federal savings association, or in the case of a Federal mutual savings association, the board of directors and the members, have voted to voluntarily liquidate, the bank or savings association shall:

(A) File a notice with the appropriate OCC licensing office; and

(B) provide notice to depositors, other known creditors, and known claimants of the bank or savings association.

(ii) *National banks.* A vote to liquidate a national bank must comply with 12 U.S.C. 181. In addition, a national bank shall publish notice in accordance with 12 U.S.C. 182.

(iii) *Federal savings associations.* A Federal savings association shall publish public notice if so directed by the OCC.

(4) *Report of condition.* The national bank's or Federal savings association's liquidating agent or committee shall

submit a report to the appropriate OCC licensing office at the start of liquidation showing the bank's or savings association's balance sheet as of the start of liquidation. The liquidating national bank or Federal savings association shall submit reports of the condition of its commercial, trust, and other departments to the appropriate OCC licensing office by filing the quarterly Consolidated Reports of Condition and Income (Call Reports).

(5) *Report of progress.* The national bank's or Federal savings association's liquidating agent or committee shall submit a "Report of Progress of Liquidation" annually to the appropriate OCC licensing office until the liquidation is complete.

(6) *Final report.* The national bank's or Federal savings association's liquidating agent or committee shall submit a final report at the conclusion of liquidation showing that all creditors have been satisfied, remaining assets have been distributed to shareholders, resolutions to dissolve the bank or savings association have been adopted, and the bank or savings association has been dissolved. The national bank or Federal savings association also shall return its charter certificate to the OCC.

(f) *Expedited liquidations in connection with acquisitions*—(1) *In general.* When an acquiring depository institution in a business combination purchases all the assets, and assumes all the liabilities, including all contingent liabilities, of a target national bank or Federal savings association, the target national bank or Federal savings association may be dissolved immediately after the combination. However, if any liabilities will remain in the target national bank or Federal savings association, then the standard liquidation procedures apply. This paragraph (f) does not apply to dissolutions of Federal mutual savings associations, which are subject to the standard liquidation procedures.

(2) *Procedure.* After its board of directors and shareholders have voted to liquidate and the national bank or Federal savings association has notified the appropriate OCC licensing office of its plans, the bank or savings association may surrender its charter and dissolve immediately, if:

(i) The acquiring depository institution certifies to the OCC that it has purchased all the assets and assumed all the liabilities, including all contingent liabilities, of the national bank or Federal savings association in liquidation; and

(ii) The acquiring depository institution and the national bank or Federal savings association in liquidation have published notice that the bank or savings association will dissolve after the purchase and assumption to the acquiror. This notice shall be included in the notice and publication for the purchase and assumption required under the Bank Merger Act, 12 U.S.C. 1828(c).

[80 FR 28455, May 18, 2015, as amended at 82 FR 8104, Jan. 23, 2017]

§ 5.50 Change in control of a national bank or Federal savings association; reporting of stock loans.

(a) *Authority.* 12 U.S.C. 93a, 1817(j), and 1831aa.

(b) *Licensing requirements.* Any person seeking to acquire control of a national bank or Federal savings association shall provide 60 days prior written notice of a change in control to the OCC, except where otherwise provided in this section.

(c) *Scope*—(1) *In general.* This section describes the procedures and standards governing OCC review of notices for a change in control of a national bank or Federal savings association and reports of stock loans.

(2) *Exempt transactions.* The following transactions are not subject to the requirements of this section:

(i) The acquisition of additional shares of a national bank or Federal savings association by a person who:

(A) Has, continuously since March 9, 1979, (or since that institution commenced business, if later) held power to vote 25 percent or more of the voting securities of that bank or Federal savings association; or

(B) Under paragraph (f)(2)(ii) of this section, would be presumed to have controlled that bank or Federal savings association continuously since March 9, 1979, if the transaction will not result in that person's direct or indirect ownership or power to vote 25 percent or more of any class of voting securities of the national bank or Federal savings association; or, in other cases, where the OCC determines that the person has controlled the bank or savings association continuously since March 9, 1979;

(ii) Unless the OCC otherwise provides in writing, the acquisition of additional shares of a national bank or Federal savings association by a person who has lawfully acquired and maintained continuous control of the bank or Federal savings association under paragraph (f) of this section after complying with the procedures and filing the notice required by this section;

(iii) A transaction subject to approval under section 3 of the Bank Holding Company Act, 12 U.S.C. 1842, section 18(c) of Federal Deposit Insurance Act, 12 U.S.C. 1828(c), or section 10 of the Home Owners' Loan Act (HOLA), 12 U.S.C. 1467a;

(iv) Any transaction described in section 2(a)(5) or 3(a) (A) or (B) of the Bank Holding Company Act, 12 U.S.C. 1841(a)(5) and 1842(a) (A) and (B), by a person described in those provisions;

(v) A customary one-time proxy solicitation or receipt of *pro rata* stock dividends; and

(vi) The acquisition of shares of a foreign bank that has a Federally licensed branch in the United States. This exemption does not extend to the reports and information required under paragraph (i) of this section.

(3) *Prior notice exemption.* The following transactions are not subject to the prior notice requirements of this section but are otherwise subject to this section, including filing a notice and paying the appropriate filing fee, within 90 calendar days after the transaction occurs:

(i) The acquisition of control as a result of acquisition of voting shares of a national bank or Federal savings association through testate or intestate succession;

(ii) The acquisition of control as a result of acquisition of voting shares of a national bank or Federal savings association as a bona fide gift;

(iii) The acquisition of voting shares of a national bank or Federal savings association resulting from a redemption of voting securities;

(iv) The acquisition of control of a national bank or Federal savings association as a result of actions by third parties (including the sale of securities) that are not within the control of the acquiror; and

(v) The acquisition of control as a result of the acquisition of voting shares of a national bank or Federal savings association in satisfaction of a debt previously contracted in good faith.

(A) "Good faith" means that a person must either make, renew, or acquire a loan secured by voting securities of a national bank or Federal savings association in advance of any knowledge of a default or of the substantial likelihood that a default is forthcoming. A person who purchases a previously defaulted loan, or a loan for which there is a substantial likelihood of default, secured by voting securities of a national bank or Federal savings association may not rely on this paragraph (c)(3)(v) to foreclose on that loan, seize or purchase the underlying collateral, and acquire control of the national bank or Federal savings association without complying with the prior notice requirements of this section.

(B) To ensure compliance with this section, the acquiror of a defaulted loan secured by a controlling amount of a national bank's or a Federal savings association's voting securities shall file a notice prior to the time the loan is acquired unless the acquiror can demonstrate to the satisfaction of the OCC that the voting securities are not the anticipated source of repayment for the loan.

(d) *Definitions.* As used in this section:

(1) *Acquire* when used in connection with the acquisition of stock of a national bank or Federal savings association means obtaining ownership, control, power to vote, or sole power of disposition of stock, directly or indirectly or through one or more transactions or subsidiaries, through purchase, assignment, transfer, pledge, exchange, succession, or other disposition of voting stock, including:

(i) An increase in percentage ownership resulting from a redemption, repurchase, reverse stock split or a similar transaction involving other securities of the same class, and

(ii) The acquisition of stock by a group of persons and/or companies acting in concert, which shall be deemed to occur upon formation of such group.

(2) *Acting in concert* means:

(i) Knowing participation in a joint activity or parallel action towards a common goal of acquiring control whether or not pursuant to an express agreement; or

(ii) A combination or pooling of voting or other interests in the securities of an issuer for a common purpose pursuant to any contract, understanding, relationship, agreement, or other arrangement, whether written or otherwise.

(3) *Company* means any corporation, partnership, trust, association, joint venture, pool, syndicate, unincorporated organization, joint-stock company or similar organization.

(4) *Control* means the power, directly or indirectly, to direct the management or policies of a national bank or Federal savings association or to vote 25 percent or more of any class of voting securities of a national bank or Federal savings association.

(5) *Controlling shareholder* means any person who directly or indirectly or acting in concert with one or more persons or companies, or together with members of his or her immediate family, owns, controls, or holds with power to vote 10 percent or more of the voting stock of a company or controls in any manner the election or appointment of a majority of the company's board of directors.

(6) *Federal savings association* means a Federal savings association or a Federal savings bank chartered under section 5 of the HOLA.

(7) *Immediate family* includes a person's spouse, father, mother, stepfather, stepmother, brother, sister, stepbrother, stepsister, children, stepchildren, grandparent, grandchildren, father-in-law, mother-in-law, brother-in-law, sister-in-law, son-in-law, daughter-in-law, and the spouse of any of the forgoing.

(8) Insured *depository institution* means an insured depository institution as defined in 12 U.S.C. 1813(c)(2).

(9) *Management official* means any president, chief executive officer, chief operating officer, vice president, director, partner, or trustee, or any other person who performs or has a representative or nominee performing similar policymaking functions, including executive officers of principal business units or divisions or subsidiaries who perform policymaking functions, for a national bank, savings association, or a company, whether or not incorporated.

(10) *Notice* means a filing by a person in accordance with paragraph (f) of this section.

(11) *Person* means an individual or a corporation, partnership, trust, association, joint venture, pool, syndicate, sole proprietorship, unincorporated organization, or any other form of entity, and includes voting trusts and voting agreements and any group of persons acting in concert.

(12) *Similar organization* for purposes of paragraph (d)(3) of this section means a combination of parties with the potential for or practical likelihood of continuing rather than temporary existence, where the parties thereto have knowingly and voluntarily associated for a common purpose pursuant to identifiable and binding relationships which govern the parties with respect to either:

(i) The transferability and voting of any stock or other indicia of participation in another entity, or

(ii) Achievement of a common or shared objective, such as to collectively manage or control another entity.

(13) *Stock* means common or preferred stock, general or limited partnership shares or interests, or similar interests.

(14) *Voting securities* means:

(i) Shares of stock, if the shares or interests, by statute, charter, or in any manner, allow the holder to vote for or select directors (or persons exercising similar functions) of the issuing national bank or Federal savings association, or to vote on or to direct the conduct of the operations or other significant policies of the issuing national bank or Federal savings association. However, preferred stock or similar interests are not voting securities if:

(A) Any voting rights associated with the shares or interests are limited solely to voting rights customarily provided by statute regarding matters that would significantly affect the rights or preference of the security or other interest. This includes the issuance of additional amounts of classes of senior securities, the modification of the terms of the security or interest, the dissolution of the issuing national bank, or the payment of dividends by the issuing national bank or Federal savings association when preferred dividends are in arrears;

(B) The shares or interests are a passive investment or financing device and do not otherwise provide the holder with control over the issuing national bank or Federal savings association; and

(C) The shares or interests do not allow the holder by statute, charter, or in any manner, to select or to vote for the selection of directors (or persons exercising similar functions) of the issuing national bank or Federal savings association.

(ii) Securities, other instruments, or similar interests that are immediately convertible, at the option of the owner or holder thereof, into voting securities.

(e) *Policy*—(1) *In general.* The OCC seeks to enhance and maintain public confidence in the banking system by preventing a change in control of a national bank or Federal savings association that could have serious adverse effects on a national bank's or Federal savings association's financial stability or management resources, the interests of the bank's or Federal savings association's customers, the Deposit Insurance Fund, or competition.

(2) *Acquisitions subject to the Bank Holding Company Act.* (i) If corporations, partnerships, certain trusts, associations, and similar organizations, that are not already bank holding companies, are not required to secure prior Federal Reserve Board approval to acquire control of a bank under section 3 of the Bank Holding Company Act, 12 U.S.C. 1842, other than indirectly through the acquisition of shares of a bank holding company, they are subject to the notice requirements of this section.

(ii) Certain transactions, including foreclosures by depository institutions and other institutional lenders, fiduciary acquisitions by depository institutions, and increases of majority holdings by bank holding companies, are described in sections 2(a)(5)(D) and 3(a)(A) and (B) of the Bank Holding Company Act, 12 U.S.C. 1841(a)(5)(D) and 12 U.S.C. 1842(a) (A) and (B), but do not require the Federal Reserve Board's prior approval. For purposes of this section, they are considered subject to section 3 of the Bank Holding Company Act, 12 U.S.C. 1842, and do not require either a prior or subsequent notice to the OCC under this section.

(3) *Assessing financial condition.* In assessing the financial condition of the acquiring person, the OCC weighs any debt servicing requirements in light of the acquiring person's overall financial strength; the institution's earnings performance, asset condition, capital adequacy, and future prospects; and the likelihood of the acquiring party making unreasonable demands on the resources of the institution.

(f) *Procedures*—(1) *Exceptions to rules of general applicability.* Sections 5.8(a), 5.9, 5.10, 5.11, and 5.13(a) through (f) do not apply to filings under this section. When complying with § 5.8(b) no address is required for a notice filed by one or more individuals under this section.

(2) *Who must file.* (i) Any person seeking to acquire the power, directly or indirectly, to direct the management or policies, or to vote 25 percent or more of a class of voting securities of a national bank or Federal savings association, shall file a notice with the OCC 60 days prior to the proposed acquisition, unless the acquisition is exempt under paragraph (c)(2) of this section.

(ii) The following persons shall be presumed to be acting in concert for purposes of this section:

(A) A company and any controlling shareholder, partner, trustee or management official of such company if both the company and the person own stock in the national bank or Federal savings association;

(B) A person and the members of the person's immediate family;

(C) Companies under common control;

(D) Persons that have made, or propose to make, a joint filing under section 13 or 14 of the Securities Exchange Act of 1934, and the rules thereunder promulgated by the Securities and Exchange Commission;

(E) A person or company will be presumed to be acting in concert with any trust for which such person or company serves as trustee, except that a tax-qualified employee stock benefit plan as defined in § 192.25 of this chapter shall not be presumed to be acting in concert with its trustee or person acting in a similar fiduciary capacity solely for the purposes of determining whether to combine the holdings of a plan and its trustee or fiduciary; and

(F) Persons that are parties to any agreement, contract, understanding, relationship, or other arrangement, whether written or otherwise, regarding the acquisition, voting or transfer of control of voting securities of a national bank or Federal savings association, other than through a revocable proxy in connection with a proxy solicitation for the purposes of conducting business at a regular or special meeting of the institution, if the proxy terminates within a reasonable period after the meeting.

(iii) The OCC presumes, unless rebutted, that an acquisition or other disposition of voting securities through which any person proposes to acquire ownership of, or the power to vote, 10 percent or more of a class of voting securities of a national bank or Federal savings association is an acquisition by a person of the power to direct the bank's or savings association's management or policies if:

(A) The securities to be acquired or voted are subject to the registration requirements of section 12 of the Securities Exchange Act of 1934, 15 U.S.C. 781; or

(B) Immediately after the transaction no other person will own or have the power to vote a greater proportion of that class of voting securities.

(iv) The OCC will consider a rebuttal of the presumption of control where the person or company intends to have no more than one representative on the board of directors of the national bank or Federal savings association.

(v) The presumption of control may not be rebutted if the total equity investment by the person or company in the national bank or Federal savings association, including 15 percent or more of any class of voting securities, equals or exceeds one third of the total equity of the national bank or Federal savings association.

(vi) Other transactions resulting in a person's control of less than 25 percent of a class of voting securities of a national bank or Federal savings association are not deemed by the OCC to result in control for purposes of this section.

(vii) If two or more persons, not acting in concert, each propose to acquire simultaneously equal percentages of 10 percent or more of a class of a national bank's or Federal savings association's voting securities, and either the acquisitions are of a class of securities subject to the registration requirements of section 12 of the Securities Exchange Act of 1934, 15 U.S.C. 781, or immediately after the transaction no other shareholder of the national bank or Federal savings association would own or have the power to vote a greater percentage of the class, each of the acquiring persons shall either file a notice or rebut the presumption of control.

(viii) An acquiring person may seek to rebut a presumption established in paragraph (f)(2)(ii) or (iii) of this section by presenting relevant information in writing to the appropriate OCC licensing office. The OCC shall respond in writing to any person that seeks to rebut the presumption of control or the presumption of concerted action. No rebuttal filing is effective unless the OCC indicates in writing that the information submitted has been found to be sufficient to rebut the presumption of control.

(3) *Filings*. (i) The OCC does not accept a notice of a change in control unless it is technically complete, *i.e.*, the information provided is responsive to every item listed in the notice form and is accompanied by the appropriate fee.

(A) The notice must contain the information required under 12 U.S.C. 1817(j)(6)(A), and the information prescribed in the Interagency Biographical and Financial Report. This form is available on the OCC's Internet Web page, *www.occ.gov*. The OCC may waive any of the informational requirements of the notice if the OCC determines that it is in the public interest.

(B) When the acquiring person is an individual, or group of individuals acting in concert, the requirement to provide personal financial data may be satisfied with a current statement of assets and liabilities and an income summary, together with a statement of any material changes since the date of the statement or summary. However, the OCC may require additional information, if appropriate.

(ii) The OCC has 60 days from the date it declares the notice to be technically complete to review the notice.

(A) When the OCC declares a notice technically complete, the appropriate OCC licensing office sends a letter of acknowledgment to the applicant indicating the technically complete date.

(B) As set forth in paragraph (g) of this section, the applicant shall publish an announcement within 10 days of filing the notice with the OCC. The publication of the announcement triggers a 20-day public comment period. The OCC may waive or shorten the public comment period if an emergency exists. The OCC also may shorten the comment period for other good cause. The OCC may act on a proposed change in control prior to the expiration of the public comment period if the OCC makes a written determination that an emergency exists.

(C) An applicant shall notify the OCC immediately of any material changes in a notice submitted to the OCC, including changes in financial or other conditions that may affect the OCC's decision on the filing.

(iii) Within the 60-day period, the OCC may inform the applicant that the acquisition has been disapproved, has not been disapproved, or that the OCC will extend the 60-day review period for up to an additional 30 days. The period or the OCC's review of a notice may be further extended not to exceed two additional times for not more than 45 days each time if:

(A) The OCC determines that any acquiring party has not furnished all the information required under this part;

(B) In the OCC's judgment, any material information submitted is substantially inaccurate;

(C) The OCC has been unable to complete an investigation of each acquirer because of any delay caused by, or the inadequate cooperation of, such acquirer; or

(D) The OCC determines that additional time is needed to investigate and determine that no acquiring party has a record of failing to comply with the requirements of subchapter II of chapter 53 of title 31 of the United States Code.

(iv) The applicant may request a hearing by the OCC within 10 days of receipt of a disapproval (*see* 12 CFR part 19, subpart H, for hearing initiation procedures). Following final agency action under 12 CFR part 19, further review by the courts is available. (*See* 12 U.S.C. 1817(j)(5).)

(4) *Conditional actions.* The OCC may impose conditions on its action not to disapprove a notice to assure satisfaction of the relevant statutory criteria for non-objection to a notice.

(5) *Disapproval of notice.* The OCC may disapprove a notice if it finds that any of the following factors exist:

(i) The proposed acquisition of control would result in a monopoly or would be in furtherance of any combination or conspiracy to monopolize or to attempt to monopolize the business of banking in any part of the United States;

(ii) The effect of the proposed acquisition of control in any section of the country may be substantially to lessen competition or to tend to create a monopoly or the proposed acquisition of control would in any other manner be in restraint of trade, and the anticompetitive effects of the proposed acquisition of control are not clearly outweighed in the public interest by the probable effect of the transaction in meeting the convenience and needs of the community to be served;

(iii) Either the financial condition of any acquiring person or the future prospects of the institution is such as might jeopardize the financial stability of the bank or Federal savings association or prejudice the interests of the depositors of the bank or Federal savings association;

(iv) The competence, experience, or integrity of any acquiring person, or of any of the proposed management personnel, indicates that it would not be in the interest of the depositors of the bank or Federal savings association, or in the interest of the public, to permit that person to control the bank or Federal savings association;

(v) An acquiring person neglects, fails, or refuses to furnish the OCC all the information it requires; or

(vi) The OCC determines that the proposed transaction would result in an adverse effect on the Deposit Insurance Fund.

(6) *Disapproval notification.* If the OCC disapproves a notice, it will notify the proposed acquiring person in writing within three days after the decision containing a statement of the basis for disapproval.

(g) *Disclosure*—(1) *Announcement.* The applicant shall publish an announcement in a newspaper of general circulation in the community where the affected national bank or Federal savings association is located within 10 days of filing. The OCC may authorize a delayed announcement if an immediate announcement would not be in the public interest.

(i) In addition to the information required by § 5.8(b), the announcement must include the name of the national bank or Federal savings association named in the notice and the comment period (*i.e.*, 20 days from the date of the announcement). The announcement also must state that the public portion of the notice is available upon request.

(ii) Notwithstanding any other provisions of this paragraph (g), if the OCC determines in writing that an emergency exists and that the announcement requirements of this paragraph (g) would seriously threaten the safety and soundness of the national bank or Federal savings association to be acquired, including situations where the OCC must act immediately in order to prevent the probable failure of a national bank or Federal savings association, the OCC may waive or shorten the publication requirement.

(2) *Release of information.* (i) Upon the request of any person, the OCC releases the information provided in the public portion of the notice and makes it available for public inspection and copying as soon as possible after a notice has been filed. In certain circumstances the OCC may determine that the release of the information would not be in the public interest. In addition, the OCC makes a public announcement of a technically complete notice, the disposition of the notice, and the consummation date of the transaction, if applicable, in the OCC's "Weekly Bulletin."

(ii) The OCC handles requests for the non-public portion of the notice as requests under the Freedom of Information Act, 5 U.S.C. 552, and other applicable law.

(h) *Reporting requirement.* After the consummation of the change in control, the national bank or Federal savings association shall notify the OCC in writing of any changes or replacements of its chief executive officer or of any director occurring during the 12-month period beginning on the date of consummation. This notice must be filed within 10 days of such change or replacement and must include a statement of the past and current business and professional affiliations of the new chief executive officers or directors.

(i) *Reporting of stock loans*—(1) *Requirements.* (i) Any foreign bank, or any affiliate thereof, shall file a consolidated report with the appropriate OCC supervisory office of the national bank or Federal savings association if the foreign bank or any affiliate thereof, has credit outstanding to any person or group of persons that, in the aggregate, is secured, directly or indirectly, by 25 percent or more of any class of voting securities of the same national bank or Federal savings association.

(ii) The foreign bank, or any affiliate thereof, shall also file a copy of the report with its appropriate OCC supervisory office if that office is different from the national bank's or Federal savings association's appropriate OCC supervisory office. If the foreign bank, or any affiliate thereof, is not supervised by the OCC, it shall file a copy of the report filed with the OCC with its appropriate Federal banking agency.

(iii) Any shares of the national bank or Federal savings association held by the foreign bank, or any affiliate thereof, as principal must be included in the calculation of the number of shares in which the foreign bank or any affiliate thereof has a security interest for purposes of paragraph (h)(1)(i) of this section.

(2) *Definitions.* For purposes of this paragraph (i):

(i) *Foreign bank and affiliate* have the same meanings as in section 1 of the International Banking Act of 1978, 12 U.S.C. 3101.

(ii) *Credit outstanding* includes any loan or extension of credit; the issuance of a guarantee, acceptance, or letter of credit, including an endorsement or standby letter of credit; and any other type of transaction that extends credit or financing to a person or group of persons.

(iii) *Group of persons* includes any number of persons that a foreign bank, or an affiliate thereof, has reason to believe:

(A) Are acting together, in concert, or with one another to acquire or control shares of the same insured national bank or Federal savings association, including an acquisition of shares of the same national bank or Federal savings association at approximately the same time under substantially the same terms; or

(B) Have made, or propose to make, a joint filing under 15 U.S.C. 78m regarding ownership of the shares of the same depository institution.

(3) *Exceptions.* Compliance with paragraph (i)(1) of this section is not required if:

(i) The person or group of persons referred to in paragraph (h)(1) of this section has disclosed the amount borrowed and the security interest therein to the appropriate OCC licensing office in connection with a notice filed under this section or any other application filed with the appropriate OCC licensing office as a substitute for a notice under this section, such as for a national bank or Federal savings association charter; or

(ii) The transaction involves a person or group of persons that has been the owner or owners of record of the stock for a period of one year or more or, if the transaction involves stock issued by a newly chartered bank or Federal savings association, before the bank's or Federal savings association's opening.

(4) *Report requirements.* (i) The consolidated report must indicate the number and percentage of shares securing each applicable extension of credit, the identity of the borrower, and the number of shares held as principal by the foreign bank and any affiliate thereof.

(ii) The foreign bank and all affiliates thereof shall file the consolidated report in writing within 30 days of the date on which the foreign bank or affiliate thereof first believes that the security for any outstanding credit consists of 25 percent or more of any class of voting securities of a national bank or Federal savings association.

(5) *Other reporting requirements.* A foreign bank or any affiliate thereof, supervised by the OCC and required to report credit outstanding secured by the shares of a depository institution to another Federal banking agency also shall file a copy of the report with its appropriate OCC supervisory office.

[80 FR 28456, May 18, 2015, as amended at 82 FR 8104, Jan. 23, 2017]

§ 5.51 Changes in directors and senior executive officers of a national bank or Federal savings association.

(a) *Authority.* 12 U.S.C. 1831i and 12 U.S.C. 5412(b)(2)(B).

(b) *Scope.* This section describes the circumstances when a national bank or a Federal savings association must notify the OCC of a change in its directors and senior executive officers, and the OCC's authority to disapprove those notices.

(c) *Definitions*—(1) *Director* means an individual who serves on the board of directors of a national bank or a Federal savings association, except:

(i) A director of a foreign bank that operates a Federal branch; and

(ii) An advisory director who does not have the authority to vote on matters before the board of directors or any committee of the board of directors and provides solely general policy advice to the board of directors or any committee.

(2) *Federal savings association* means a Federal savings association or Federal savings bank chartered under 12 U.S.C. 1464.

(3) *National bank* includes a Federal branch for purposes of this section only.

(4) *Senior executive officer* means the president, chief executive officer, chief operating officer, chief financial officer, chief lending officer, chief investment officer, and any other individual the OCC identifies in writing to the national bank or Federal savings association who exercises significant influence over, or participates in, major policy making decisions of the national bank or Federal savings association without regard to title, salary, or compensation. The term also includes employees of entities retained by a national bank or Federal savings association to perform such functions in lieu of directly hiring the individuals, and, with respect to a Federal branch operated by a foreign bank, the individual functioning as the chief managing official of the Federal branch.

(5) *Technically complete notice* means a notice that provides all the information requested in paragraph (e)(2) of this section, including complete explanations where material issues arise regarding the competence, experience, character, or integrity of proposed directors or senior executive officers, and any additional information that the OCC may request following a determination that the notice was not technically complete.

(6) *Technically complete notice date* means the date on which the OCC has received a technically complete notice.

(7) *Troubled condition* means a national bank or Federal savings association that

(i) Has a composite rating of 4 or 5 under the Uniform Financial Institutions Rating System (CAMELS);

(ii) Is subject to a cease and desist order, a consent order, or a formal written agreement, unless otherwise informed in writing by the OCC; or

(iii) Is informed in writing by the OCC that, based on information pertaining to such national bank or Federal savings association, it has been designated in "troubled condition" for purposes of this section.

(d) *Prior notice.* A national bank or Federal savings association shall provide written notice to the OCC at least 90 calendar days before adding or replacing any member of its board of directors, employing any individual as a senior executive officer of the national bank or Federal savings association, or changing the responsibilities of any senior executive officer so that the individual would assume a different senior executive officer position, if:

(1) The national bank or Federal savings association is not in compliance with minimum capital requirements, as prescribed in 12 CFR part 3 or is otherwise in troubled condition; or

(2) The OCC determines, in writing, in connection with the review by the agency of the plan required under section 38 of the Federal Deposit Insurance Act (12 U.S.C. 1831o), or otherwise, that such prior notice is appropriate.

(e) *Procedures*—(1) *Filing notice.* A national bank or Federal savings association shall file a notice with its appropriate supervisory office. When a national bank or Federal savings association files a notice, the individual to whom the filing pertains shall attest to the validity of the information pertaining to that individual. The 90-day review period begins on the technically complete notice date.

(2) *Content of notice.* (i) The notice must include:

(A) The information required under 12 U.S.C. 1817(j)(6)(A), and the information prescribed in the Interagency Notice of Change in Director or Senior Executive Officer, the biographical and certification portions of the Interagency Biographical and Financial Report ("IBFR"), and unless otherwise determined by the OCC in writing, the financial portion of the IBFR. These forms are available from the OCC;

(B) Legible fingerprints of the individual, except that fingerprints are not required for any individual who, within the three years immediately preceding the initial submission date of the notice currently under review, has been the subject of a notice filed with the OCC or the OTS pursuant to 12 U.S.C. 1831i, or this section, and has previously submitted fingerprints; and

(C) Such other information required by the OCC.

(ii) *Modification of content requirements.* The OCC may require or accept other information in place of the content requirements in paragraph (e)(2)(i) of this section.

(3) *Requests for additional information.* (i) Following receipt of a technically complete notice, the OCC may request additional information. Such request must be in writing, must explain why the information is needed, and must specify a time period during which the information must be provided.

(ii) If the national bank or Federal savings association cannot provide the information requested by the OCC within the time specified in paragraph (e)(3)(i) of this section, the national bank or Federal savings association may request in writing that the OCC suspend processing of the notice. The OCC will advise the national bank or Federal savings association in writing whether the suspension request is granted and, if granted, the length of the suspension.

(iii) If the national bank or Federal savings association fails to provide the requested information within the time specified in paragraphs (e)(3)(i) or (ii) of this section, the OCC may deem the filing abandoned under § 5.13(c) or may review the notice based on the information provided.

(4) *Notice of disapproval.* The OCC may disapprove an individual proposed as a member of the board of directors or as a senior executive officer if the OCC determines on the basis of the individual's competence, experience, character, or integrity that it would not be in the best interests of the depositors of the national bank or Federal savings association or the public to permit the individual to be employed by, or associated with, the national bank or Federal savings association. The OCC must send a written notice of disapproval to both the national bank or Federal savings association and the individual stating the basis for disapproval.

(5) *Notice of intent not to disapprove.* An individual proposed as a member of the board of directors or as a senior executive officer may begin service before the expiration of the review period if the OCC notifies the individual and the national bank or Federal savings association in writing that the OCC does not disapprove the proposed director or senior executive officer and all other applicable legal requirements are satisfied.

(6) *Waiver of prior notice*—(i) *Waiver request.* (A) A national bank or Federal savings association may send a letter to the appropriate supervisory office requesting a waiver of the prior notice requirement.

(B) The OCC may grant the waiver if it issues a written finding that:

(*1*) Delay could adversely affect the safety and soundness of the national bank or Federal savings association;

(*2*) Delay would not be in the public interest; or

(*3*) Other extraordinary circumstances justify waiver of prior notice.

(C) The OCC will determine the length of the waiver on a case-by-case basis. All waivers that the OCC grants under this paragraph (e)(6) are subject to the condition that the national bank or Federal savings association shall file a technically complete notice under this section within the time period specified by the OCC.

(D) Subject to paragraph (e)(6)(i)(C) of this section, the proposed individual may assume the position on an interim basis until the earliest of the following events:

(*1*) The individual and the national bank or the Federal savings association receive a notice of intent not to disapprove, at which time the individual may assume the position on a permanent basis, provided all other applicable legal requirements are satisfied;

(*2*) The individual and the national bank or the Federal savings association receive a notice of disapproval within 90 calendar days after the submission of a technically complete notice. In this event the individual shall immediately resign from the position upon receipt of the notice of disapproval and may assume the position on a permanent basis only if the notice of disapproval is reversed on appeal and all other applicable legal requirements are satisfied; or

(*3*) The OCC does not act within 90 calendar days after the submission of a technically complete notice. In this event, the individual may assume the position on a permanent basis 91 calendar days after the submission of a technically complete notice.

(E) If the technically complete notice is not filed within the time period specified in the waiver, the proposed individual shall immediately resign his or her position. Thereafter, the individual may assume the position only after a technically complete notice has been filed, all other applicable requirements are satisfied, and:

(*1*) The national bank or the Federal savings association receives a notice of intent not to disapprove;

(*2*) The review period expires; or

(*3*) A notice of disapproval has been overturned on appeal as set forth in paragraph (f) of this section.

(F) Notwithstanding the grant of a waiver, the OCC has authority to issue a notice of disapproval within 30 days of the expiration of such waiver.

(ii) *Automatic waiver.* An individual who has been elected to the board of directors of a national bank or Federal savings association may serve as a director on an interim basis before a notice has been filed under this section, provided the individual was not nominated by management, and the national bank or Federal savings association submits a notice under this section not later than seven days after the individual has been notified of the election. The individual may serve on an interim basis until the occurrence of the earliest of the events described in paragraphs (e)(6)(i)(D)(*1*), (*2*), or (*3*) of this section.

(7) *Commencement of service.* An individual proposed as a member of the board of directors or as a senior executive officer who satisfies all other applicable legal requirements may assume the office on a permanent basis:

(i) Prior to the expiration of the review period, only if the OCC notifies the national bank or Federal savings association in writing that the OCC does not disapprove the proposed director or senior executive officer pursuant to paragraph (e)(5) of this section; or

(ii) Following the expiration of the review period, unless:

(A) The OCC issues a written notice of disapproval during the review period; or

(B) The national bank or Federal savings association does not provide additional information within the time period required by the OCC pursuant to paragraph (e)(3) of this section and the OCC deems the notice to be abandoned pursuant to § 5.13(c).

(8) *Exceptions to rules of general applicability.* Sections 5.8, 5.10, 5.11, and 5.13(a) through (f) do not apply to a notice for a change in directors and senior executive officers, except that § 5.13(c) shall apply to the extent provided for in paragraphs (e)(3)(iii) and (e)(7) of this section.

(f) *Appeal.* (1) If the national bank or Federal savings association, the proposed individual, or both, disagree with a disapproval, they may seek review by appealing the disapproval to the Comptroller, or an authorized delegate, within 15 days of the receipt of the notice of disapproval. The national bank or Federal savings association or the individual may appeal on the grounds that the reasons for disapproval are contrary to fact or insufficient to justify disapproval. The appellant shall submit all documents and written arguments that the appellant wishes to be considered in support of the appeal.

(2) The Comptroller, or an authorized delegate, may designate an appellate official who was not previously involved in the decision leading to the appeal at issue. The Comptroller, an authorized delegate, or the appellate official considers all information submitted with the original notice, the material before the OCC official who made the initial decision, and any information submitted by the appellant at the time of the appeal.

(3) The Comptroller, an authorized delegate, or the appellate official shall independently determine whether the reasons given for the disapproval are contrary to fact or insufficient to justify the disapproval. If either is determined to be the case, the Comptroller, an authorized delegate, or the appellate official may reverse the disapproval.

(4) Upon completion of the review, the Comptroller, an authorized delegate, or the appellate official shall notify the appellant in writing of the decision. If the original decision is reversed, the individual may assume the position in the national bank or Federal savings association for which he or she was proposed.

[80 FR 28460, May 18, 2015]

§ 5.52 Change of address of a national bank or Federal savings association.

(a) *Authority*. 12 U.S.C. 93a, 161, 481, 1462a, 1463, 1464 and 5412(b)(2)(B).

(b) *Scope*. This section describes the obligation of a national bank or a Federal savings association to notify the OCC of any change in its address.

(c) *Notice process*. (1) Any national bank with a change in the address of its main office or in its post office box or a Federal savings association with a change in the address of its home office or post office box shall send a written notice to the appropriate OCC licensing office.

(2) No notice is required if the change in address results from a transaction approved under this part or if notice has been provided pursuant to § 5.40(b) with respect to the relocation of a main office or home office to a branch location in the same city, town or village.

(d) *Exceptions to rules of general applicability*. Sections 5.8, 5.9, 5.10, 5.11, and 5.13 do not apply to changes in a national bank's or Federal savings association's address.

[80 FR 28462, May 18, 2015]

§ 5.53 Substantial asset change by a national bank or Federal savings association.

(a) *Authority*. 12 U.S.C. 93a, 1818, 1462a, 1463, 1464, 1467a, and 5412(b)(2)(B).

(b) *Scope*. This section requires a national bank or a Federal savings association to obtain the approval of the OCC for a substantial asset change.

(c) *Definition*—(1) *In general*. Except as provide in paragraph (c)(2) of this section, *substantial asset change* means:

(i) The sale or other disposition of all, or substantially all, of the national bank's or Federal savings association's assets in a transaction or a series of transactions;

(ii) After having sold or disposed of all, or substantially all, of its assets, subsequent purchases or other acquisitions or other expansions of the national bank's or Federal savings association's operations;

(iii) Any other purchases, acquisitions or other expansions of operations that are part of a plan to increase the size of the national bank or Federal savings association by more than 25 percent in a one year period;

(iv) Any other material increase or decrease in the size of the national bank or Federal savings association or a material alteration in the composition of the types of assets or liabilities of the national bank or Federal savings association (including the entry or exit of business lines), on a case-by-case basis, as determined by the OCC; or

(v) Any change in the purpose of the charter of the national bank or Federal savings association as described in § 5.20(l)(2).

(2) *Exceptions*. The term "substantial asset change" does not include, and this section does not apply, to a change in composition of all, or substantially all, of a bank's or savings association's assets:

(i) That the bank or savings association undertakes in response to direction from the OCC (*e.g.*, in an enforcement action pursuant to 12 U.S.C. 1818);

(ii) That is part of a voluntary liquidation under 12 CFR 5.48, if the bank or savings association in liquidation has obtained the OCC's non-objection to its plan of liquidation under 12 CFR 5.48 and has stipulated in its notice of liquidation to the OCC that its liquidation will be completed, the bank or savings association dissolved and its charter returned to the OCC within one year of the date it filed the notice of liquidation, unless the OCC extends the time period;

(iii) That occurs as a result of a bank's or savings association's ordinary and ongoing business of originating and securitizing loans; or

(iv) That are subject to OCC approval under another application to the OCC.

(d) *Procedures*—(1) *Consultation*. A national bank or Federal savings association considering a transaction or series of transactions that may constitute a material change under paragraph (c)(1)(iv) of this section must consult with the appropriate OCC supervisory office for a determination whether the OCC will require an application under this section. In determining whether to require an application, the OCC considers the size and nature of the transaction and the condition of the institutions involved.

(2) *Approval requirement.* A national bank or Federal savings association must file an application and obtain the prior written approval of the OCC before engaging in a substantial asset change.

(3) *Factors*—(i) *In general.* (A) In determining whether to approve an application under paragraph (d)(1) of this section, the OCC considers the following factors:

(*1*) The capital level of any resulting national bank or Federal savings association;

(*2*) The conformity of the transaction to applicable law, regulation, and supervisory policies;

(*3*) The purpose of the transaction;

(*4*) The impact of the transaction on safety and soundness of the national bank or Federal savings association; and

(*5*) The effect of the transaction on the national bank or Federal savings association's shareholders, depositors, other creditors, and customers.

(B) The OCC may deny the application if the transaction would have a negative effect in any of these respects.

(ii) *Additional factors.* The OCC's review of any substantial asset change that involves the purchase or other acquisition or other expansions of the bank's or savings association's operations or that involves a change in the purpose of the bank's or association's charter, as described in § 5.20(l)(2), will include, in addition to the foregoing factors, the factors governing the organization of a bank or savings association under § 5.20.

(e) *Exceptions to rules of general applicability.* Sections 5.8, 5.10, and 5.11 do not apply with respect to applications filed pursuant to this section. However, if the OCC concludes that an application presents significant or novel policy, supervisory, or legal issues, the OCC may determine that some or all of the provisions of §§ 5.8, 5.10, and 5.11 apply.

[80 FR 28462, May 18, 2015, as amended at 82 FR 8104, Jan. 23, 2017]

§ 5.55 Capital distributions by Federal savings associations.

(a) *Authority.* 12 U.S.C. 1462a, 1463, 1464, 1467a, 1831o, and 5412(b)(2)(B).

(b) *Licensing requirements.* A Federal savings association must file an application or notice before making a capital distribution, as provided in this section.

(c) *Scope.* This section applies to all capital distributions by a Federal savings association and sets forth the procedures and standards relating to a capital distribution.

(d) *Definitions.* The following definitions apply to this section:

(1) *Affiliate* means an affiliate, as defined under regulations of the Board of Governors of the Federal Reserve System regarding transactions with affiliates, 12 CFR part 223 (Regulation W).

(2) *Capital* means total capital, as computed under 12 CFR part 3.

(3) *Capital distribution* means:

(i) A distribution of cash or other property to owners of a Federal savings association made on account of their ownership, but excludes:

(A) Any dividend consisting only of the shares of the savings association or rights to purchase the shares; or

(B) If the savings association is a Federal mutual savings association, any payment that the savings association is required to make under the terms of a deposit instrument and any other amount paid on deposits that the OCC determines is not a distribution for the purposes of this section;

(ii) A Federal savings association's payment to repurchase, redeem, retire or otherwise acquire any of its shares or other ownership interests; any payment to repurchase, redeem, retire, or otherwise acquire debt instruments included in its total capital under 12 CFR part 3; and any extension of credit to finance an affiliate's acquisition of the savings association's shares or interests;

(iii) Any direct or indirect payment of cash or other property to owners or affiliates made in connection with a corporate restructuring. This includes the Federal savings association's payment of cash or property to shareholders of another association or to shareholders of its holding company to acquire ownership in that association, other than by a distribution of shares;

(iv) Any other distribution charged against a Federal savings association's capital accounts if the savings association would not be well capitalized, as set forth in 12 CFR 6.4, following the distribution; and

(v) Any transaction that the OCC determines, by order or regulation, to be in substance a distribution of capital.

(4) *Net income* means a Federal savings association's net income computed in accordance with generally accepted accounting principles (GAAP).

(5) *Retained net income* means a Federal savings association's net income for a specified period less total capital distributions declared in that period.

(6) *Shares* means common and preferred stock, and any options, warrants, or other rights for the acquisition of such stock. The term "share" also includes convertible securities upon their conversion into common or preferred stock. The term does not include convertible debt securities prior to their conversion into common or preferred stock or other securities that are not equity securities at the time of a capital distribution.

(e) *Filing requirements*—(1) *Application required.* A Federal savings association must file an application with the OCC if:

(i) The savings association is not an eligible savings association;

(ii) The total amount of all of the savings association's capital distributions (including the proposed capital distribution) for the applicable calendar year exceeds its net income for that year to date plus retained net income for the preceding two years;

(iii) The savings association would not be at least adequately capitalized, as set forth in 12 CFR 6.4, following the distribution; or

(iv) The savings association's proposed capital distribution would violate a prohibition contained in any applicable statute, regulation, or agreement between the savings association and the OCC or the OTS, or violate a condition imposed on the savings association in an application or notice approved by the OCC or the OTS.

(2) *Notice required.* Unless it is required to file an application under paragraph (e)(1) of this section, a Federal savings association that is an eligible savings association must file a notice with the OCC if:

(i) The savings association would not remain well capitalized, as set forth under 12 CFR 6.4, or would otherwise not remain an eligible savings association following the distribution;

(ii) The savings association's proposed capital distribution would reduce the amount of or retire any part of its common or preferred stock or retire any part of debt instruments such as notes or debentures included in capital under 12 CFR part 3 (other than regular payments required under a debt instrument approved under § 5.56);

(iii) The savings association's proposed capital distribution is payable in property other than cash;

(iv) The savings association is a direct or indirect subsidiary of a mutual savings and loan holding company; or

(v) The savings association is a direct or indirect subsidiary of a company that is not a savings and loan holding company.

(3) *No prior notice required.* A Federal savings association does not need to file a notice or an application with the OCC before making a capital distribution if the Federal savings association is not required to file an application under paragraph (e)(1) or a notice under paragraph (e)(2) of this section.

(4) *Informational copy of notice required.* If the Federal savings association is a subsidiary of a savings and loan holding company that is filing a notice with the Board of Governors of the Federal Reserve System (Board) for a dividend solely under 12 U.S.C. 1467a(f) and not also under 12 U.S.C. 1467a(o)(11), and neither an application under paragraph (e)(1) nor a notice under paragraph (e)(2) of this section is required, then the savings association must provide an informational copy to the OCC of the notice filed with the Board, at the same time the notice is filed with the Board.

(f) *Filing format*—(1) *Contents.* The notice or application must:

(i) Be in narrative form;

(ii) Include all relevant information concerning the proposed capital distribution, including the amount, timing, and type of distribution; and

(iii) Demonstrate compliance with paragraph (h) of this section.

(2) *Schedules.* The notice or application may include a schedule proposing capital distributions over a specified period, not to exceed 12 months.

(3) *Combined filings.* A Federal savings association may combine the notice or application required under paragraph (e) of this section with any other notice or application, if the capital distribution is a part of, or is proposed in connection with, another transaction requiring a notice or application under this chapter. If submitting a combined filing, the Federal savings association must state that the related notice or application is intended to serve as a notice or application under this section.

(g) *Filing procedures*—(1) *Application.* When a Federal savings association is required to file an application under paragraph (e)(1) of this section, it must file the application at least 30 days before the proposed declaration of dividend or approval of the proposed capital distribution by its board of directors. The Federal savings association shall not effect the proposed declaration of dividend or approval of the proposed capital distribution unless it has received prior written approval of the OCC.

(2) *Prior notice with expedited review.* A Federal savings association that is an eligible savings association and that is required to file a notice under paragraph (e)(2) must file the notice at least 30 days before the proposed declaration of dividend or approval of the proposed capital distribution by its board of directors. The notice is deemed approved by the OCC upon the expiration of 30 days after the filing date of the notice unless, before the expiration of that time period, the OCC notifies the Federal savings association that:

(i) Additional information is required to supplement the notice;

(ii) The notice is not eligible for expedited review, or the expedited reviewed process is extended, under 5.13(a)(2); or

(iii) The notice is disapproved.

(h) *OCC review of capital distributions.* The OCC reviews applications and notices submitted pursuant to paragraphs (g)(1) and (g)(2) of this section. The OCC may disapprove the notice or deny the application in whole or in part, if it makes any of the following determinations:

(1) The Federal savings association will be undercapitalized, significantly undercapitalized, or critically undercapitalized as set forth in 12 CFR 6.4, as applicable, following the capital distribution. If so, the OCC will determine if the capital distribution is permitted under 12 U.S.C. 1831o(d)(1)(B).

(2) The proposed capital distribution raises safety or soundness concerns.

(3) The proposed capital distribution violates a prohibition contained in any statute, regulation, agreement between the Federal savings association and the OCC or the OTS, or a condition imposed on the Federal savings association in an application or notice approved by the OCC or the OTS. If so, the OCC will determine whether it may permit the capital distribution notwithstanding the prohibition or condition.

(i) *Exceptions to rules of general applicability.* Sections 5.8, 5.10, and 5.11 do not apply to capital distributions made by Federal savings associations.

[80 FR 28463, May 18, 2015]

§ 5.56 Inclusion of subordinated debt securities and mandatorily redeemable preferred stock as Federal savings association supplementary (tier 2) capital.

(a) *Scope and definitions.* (1) A Federal savings association must comply with this section in order to include subordinated debt securities or mandatorily redeemable preferred stock ("covered securities") in tier 2 capital under 12 CFR 3.20(d) and to prepay covered securities included in tier 2 capital. A savings association that does not include covered securities in tier 2 capital is not required to comply with this section. Covered securities not included in tier 2 capital are subject to the requirements of § 163.80 of this chapter.

(2) For purposes of this section, mandatorily redeemable preferred stock means mandatorily redeemable preferred stock that was issued before July 23, 1985 or issued pursuant to regulations and memoranda of the Federal Home Loan Bank Board and approved in writing by the Federal Savings and Loan Insurance Corporation for inclusion as regulatory capital before or after issuance.

(b) *Application and notice procedures*—(1) *Application or notice to include covered securities in tier 2 capital*—(i) *Application.* Unless a Federal savings association is an eligible savings association filing a notice under paragraph (b)(1)(ii) of this section, it must file an application seeking the OCC's approval of the inclusion of covered securities in tier 2 capital. The savings association may file its application before or after it issues covered securities, but may not include covered securities in tier 2 capital until the OCC approves the application.

(ii) *Notice with expedited review.* An eligible savings association must file a notice seeking the OCC's approval of the inclusion of covered securities in tier 2 capital. The savings association may file its notice before or after it issues covered securities, but may not include covered securities in tier 2 capital until the OCC approves the notice. The OCC is deemed to have approved the notice upon the expiration of 30 days after the filing date of the notice unless, before the expiration of that time period, the OCC notifies the Federal savings association that

(A) Additional information is required to supplement the notice;

(B) The notice is not eligible for expedited review, or the expedited reviewed process is extended, under § 5.13(a)(2); or

(C) The OCC denies the notice.

(iii) *Securities offering rules.* A savings association also must comply with the securities offering rules at 12 CFR part 197 by filing an offering circular for a proposed issuance of covered securities, unless the offering qualifies for an exemption under that part.

(2) *Application required to prepay covered securities included in tier 2 capital*—(i) *In general.* A Federal savings association must file an application to, and receive prior approval from, the OCC before prepaying covered securities included in tier 2 capital. For purposes of this requirement, prepayment includes acceleration of a covered security, repurchase of a covered security, redemption of a covered security prior to maturity, and exercising a call option in connection with a covered security.

(ii) *Prepayment in the form of a call option.* (A) If the prepayment will be in the form of a call option, the application must include:

(*1*) A statement explaining why the Federal savings association believes that following the proposed prepayment the savings association would continue to hold an amount of capital commensurate with its risk; or

(*2*) A description of the replacement capital instrument that meets the criteria for tier 1 or tier 2 capital under 12 CFR 3.20, including the amount of such instrument, and the time frame for issuance.

(B) Notwithstanding paragraph (b)(1)(ii) of this section, if the OCC conditions approval of prepayment in the form of a call option on a requirement that a Federal savings association must replace the covered security with a covered security of an equivalent amount that satisfies the requirements for a tier 1 or tier 2 instrument, the savings association must file an application to issue the replacement covered security and must receive prior OCC approval.

(c) *General requirements.* A covered security issued under this section must satisfy the requirements for tier 2 capital in 12 CFR 3.20(d).

(d) *Securities requirements for inclusion in tier 2 capital.* To be included in tier 2 capital, covered securities must satisfy the requirements in 12 CFR 3.20(d). In addition, such covered securities must meet the following requirements:

(1) *Form.* (i) Each certificate evidencing a covered security must:

(A) Bear the following legend on its face, in bold type: "This security is *not* a savings account or deposit and it is *not* insured by the United States or any agency or fund of the United States;"

(B) State that the security is subordinated on liquidation, as to principal, interest, and premium, to all claims against the savings association that have the same priority as savings accounts or a higher priority;

(C) State that the security is not secured by the savings association's assets or the assets of any affiliate of the savings association. An affiliate means any person or company that controls, is controlled by, or is under common control with the savings association;

(D) State that the security is not eligible collateral for a loan by the savings association;

(E) State the prohibition on the payment of dividends or interest at 12 U.S.C. 1828(b) and, in the case of subordinated debt securities, state the prohibition on the payment of principal and interest at 12 U.S.C. 1831o(h), 12 CFR 3.11, and any other relevant restrictions;

(F) For subordinated debt securities, state or refer to a document stating the terms under which the savings association may prepay the obligation; and

(G) Where applicable, state or refer to a document stating that the savings association must obtain OCC's prior approval before the acceleration of payment of principal or interest on subordinated debt securities, redemption of subordinated debt securities prior to maturity, repurchase of subordinated debt securities, or exercising a call option in connection with a subordinated debt security.

(ii) A Federal savings association must include such additional statements as the OCC may prescribe for certificates, purchase agreements, indentures, and other related documents.

(2) *Indenture.* (i) Except as provided in paragraph (d)(2)(ii) of this section, a Federal savings association must use an indenture for subordinated debt securities. If the aggregate amount of subordinated debt securities publicly offered (excluding sales in a non-public offering as defined in 12 CFR 197.4) and sold in any consecutive 12-month or 36-month period exceeds $5,000,000 or $10,000,000 respectively (or such lesser amount that the Securities and Exchange Commission shall establish by rule or regulation under 15 U.S.C. 77ddd), the indenture must provide for the appointment of a trustee other than the savings association or an affiliate of the savings association (as defined in paragraph (d)(1)(i)(C) of this section) and for collective enforcement of the security holders' rights and remedies.

(ii) A Federal savings association is not required to use an indenture if the subordinated debt securities are sold only to accredited investors, as that term is defined in 15 U.S.C. 77d(6). A savings association must have an indenture that meets the requirements of paragraph (d)(2)(i) of this section in place before any debt securities for which an exemption from the indenture requirement is claimed, are transferred to any non-accredited investor. If a savings association relies on this exemption from the indenture requirement, it must place a legend on the debt securities indicating that an indenture must be in place before the debt securities are transferred to any non-accredited investor.

(e) *Review by the OCC.* (1) In reviewing notices and applications under this section, the OCC will consider whether:

(i) The issuance of the covered securities is authorized under applicable laws and regulations and is consistent with the savings association's charter and bylaws;

(ii) The savings association is at least adequately capitalized under 12 CFR 6.4 and meets the regulatory capital requirements at 12 CFR 3.10;

(iii) The savings association is or will be able to service the covered securities;

(iv) The covered securities are consistent with the requirements of this section;

(v) The covered securities and related transactions sufficiently transfer risk from the Deposit Insurance Fund; and

(vi) The OCC has no objection to the issuance based on the savings association's overall policies, condition, and operations.

(2) The OCC's approval is conditioned upon no material changes to the information disclosed in the application or notice submitted to the OCC. The OCC may impose such additional requirements or conditions as it may deem necessary to protect purchasers, the savings association, the OCC, or the Deposit Insurance Fund.

(f) *Amendments.* If a Federal savings association amends the covered securities or related documents following the completion of the OCC's review, it must obtain the OCC's approval under this section before it may include the amended securities in tier 2 capital.

(g) *Sale of covered securities.* The Federal savings association must complete the sale of covered securities within one year after the OCC's approval under this section. A savings association may request an extension of the offering period by filing a written request with the OCC. The savings association must demonstrate good cause for the extension and file the request at least 30 days before the expiration of the offering period or any extension of the offering period.

(h) *Issuance of a replacement regulatory capital instrument in connection with exercising a call option.* Pursuant to 12 CFR 3.20(d)(1)(v)(C), the OCC may require a Federal savings association seeking prior approval to exercise a call option in connection with a covered security included in tier 2 capital to issue a replacement covered security of an equivalent amount that qualifies as tier 1 or tier 2 capital under 12 CFR 3.20. If the OCC imposes such a requirement, the savings association must complete the sale of such covered prior to, or immediately after, the prepayment.[5]

(i) *Reports.* A Federal savings association must file the following information with the OCC within 30 days after the savings association completes the sale of covered securities includable as tier 2 capital. If the savings association filed its application or notice following the completion of the sale, it must submit this information with its application or notice:

(1) A written report indicating the number of purchasers, the total dollar amount of securities sold, the net proceeds received by the savings association from the issuance, and the amount of covered securities, net of all expenses, to be included as tier 2 capital;

(2) Three copies of an executed form of the securities and a copy of any related documents governing the issuance or administration of the securities; and

(3) A certification by the appropriate executive officer indicating that the savings association complied with all applicable laws and regulations in connection with the offering, issuance, and sale of the securities.

[80 FR 28464, May 18, 2015]

§ 5.58 Pass-through investments by a Federal savings association.

(a) *Authority.* 12 U.S.C. 1462a, 1463, 1464, 1828, 5412(b)(2)(B).

(b) *Scope.* Federal savings associations are permitted to make various types of equity investments pursuant to 12 U.S.C. 1464 and other statutes, including pass-through investments authorized under 12 CFR 160.32(a). These investments are in addition to those subject to §§ 5.35, 5.37, 5.38, and 5.59. This section describes the procedure governing the filing of the application or notice that the OCC requires in connection with certain of these investments. The OCC may review other permissible equity investments on a case-by-case basis.

(c) *Licensing requirements.* A Federal savings association must file a notice or application as prescribed in this section to make a pass-through investment authorized under 12 CFR 160.32(a).

(d) *Definitions.* For purposes of this section:

(1) *Enterprise* means any corporation, limited liability company, partnership, trust, or similar business entity.

(2) *Well capitalized* means the capital level described in 12 CFR 6.4.

(3) *Well managed* has the meaning set forth in § 5.38(d)(2) for Federal savings associations.

(e) *Pass-through investments; notice procedure.* A Federal savings association may make a pass-through investment, directly or through its operating subsidiary, in an enterprise that engages in the activities described in paragraph (e)(2) of this section by filing a written notice. The Federal savings association must file this written notice with the appropriate OCC licensing

[5] A Federal savings association may replace tier 2 capital instruments concurrent with the redemption of existing tier 2 capital instruments.

office no later than 10 days after making the investment. The written notice must:

(1) Describe the structure of the investment and the activity or activities conducted by the enterprise in which the Federal savings association is investing. To the extent the notice relates to the initial affiliation of the Federal savings association with a company engaged in insurance activities, the savings association should describe the type of insurance activity that the company is engaged in and has present plans to conduct. The Federal savings association must also list for each state the lines of business for which the company holds, or will hold, an insurance license, indicating the state where the company holds a resident license or charter, as applicable;

(2) State:

(i) Which paragraphs of § 5.38(e)(5)(v) describe the activity; or

(ii) State that, and describe how, the activity is substantively the same as that contained in published OCC precedent for Federal savings associations, including published former OTS precedent, approving a pass-through investment by a Federal savings association or its operating subsidiary, state that the activity will be conducted in accordance with the same terms and conditions applicable to the activity covered by the precedent, and provide the citation to the applicable precedent;

(3) Certify that the Federal savings association is well managed and well capitalized at the time of the investment;

(4) Describe how the Federal savings association has the ability to prevent the enterprise from engaging in an activity that is not set forth in § 5.38(e)(5)(v) or not contained in published OCC precedent for Federal savings associations, including published former OTS precedent, approving a pass-through investment by a Federal savings association or its operating subsidiary, or how the savings association otherwise has the ability to withdraw its investment;

(5) Describe how the investment is convenient and useful to the Federal savings association in carrying out its business and not a mere passive investment unrelated to the savings association's banking business;

(6) Certify that the Federal savings association's loss exposure is limited as a legal matter and that the savings association does not have unlimited liability for the obligations of the enterprise; and

(7) Certify that the enterprise in which the Federal savings association is investing agrees to be subject to OCC supervision and examination, subject to the limitations and requirements of section 45 of the Federal Deposit Insurance Act (12 U.S.C. 1831v) and section 115 of the Gramm-Leach-Bliley Act (12 U.S.C. 1820a).

(f) *Pass-through investments; application procedure*—(1) *Investments not qualifying for notice procedure.* A Federal savings association must file an application and obtain prior approval before making or acquiring, either directly or through an operating subsidiary, a pass-through investment in an enterprise if the pass-through investment does not qualify for the notice procedure set forth in paragraph (e) of this section because the savings association is unable to make the representation required by paragraph (e)(2) or the certification required by paragraph (e)(3) of this section. The application must include the information required in paragraphs (e)(1) and (e)(4) through (e)(7) of this section and paragraphs (e)(2) or (e)(3) of this section, as appropriate. If the Federal savings association is unable to make the representation set forth in paragraph (e)(2) of this section, the savings association's application must explain why the activity in which the enterprise engages is a permissible activity for a Federal savings association and why the applicant should be permitted to hold a pass-through investment in an enterprise engaged in that activity. A Federal savings association may not make a pass-through investment if it is unable to make the representations and certifications specified in paragraphs (e)(1) and (e)(4) through (e)(7) of this section.

(2) *Investments requiring a filing under 12 U.S.C. 1828(m).* Notwithstanding any other provision in this section, if an enterprise in which a Federal savings association proposes to invest would be

a subsidiary of the Federal savings association for purposes of 12 U.S.C. 1828(m) and the enterprise would not be an operating subsidiary or a service corporation, the Federal savings association must file an application with the OCC under this paragraph (f)(2) at least 30 days prior to making the investment and obtain prior approval from the OCC before making the investment. The application must include the information required in paragraphs (e)(1) and (e)(4) through (e)(7) of this section and paragraphs (e)(2) or (e)(3) of this section, if applicable. If the Federal savings association is unable to make the representation set forth in paragraph (e)(2) of this section, the savings association's application must explain why the activity in which the enterprise engages is a permissible activity for a Federal savings association and why the applicant should be permitted to hold a pass-through investment in an enterprise engaged in that activity. A Federal savings association may not make a pass-through investment if it is unable to make the representations and certifications specified in paragraphs (e)(1) and (e)(4) through (e)(7) of this section.

(g) *Pass-through investments in entities holding assets in satisfaction of debts previously contracted.* Certain pass-through investments may be eligible for expedited treatment where the Federal savings association's investment is in an entity holding assets in satisfaction of debts previously contracted or the savings association acquires shares of a company in satisfaction of debts previously contracted.

(1) *Notice required.* A Federal savings association that is well capitalized and well managed may acquire a pass-through investment, directly or through its operating subsidiary, in an enterprise that engages in the activities of holding and managing assets acquired by the parent savings association through foreclosure or otherwise in good faith to compromise a doubtful claim, or in the ordinary course of collecting a debt previously contracted, by filing a written notice in accordance with this paragraph (g)(1)(i). The activities of the enterprise must be conducted pursuant to the same terms and conditions as would be applicable if the activity were conducted directly by a Federal savings association. The Federal savings association must file the written notice with the appropriate OCC licensing office no later than 10 days after making the pass-through investment. This notice must include a complete description of the Federal savings association's investment in the enterprise and the activities conducted, a description of how the savings association plans to divest the pass-through investment or the underlying assets within applicable statutory time frames, and a representation and undertaking that the savings association will conduct the activities in accordance with OCC policies contained in guidance issued by the OCC regarding the activities. Any Federal savings association receiving approval under this paragraph (g)(1)(i) is deemed to have agreed that the enterprise will conduct the activity in a manner consistent with published OCC guidance.

(2) *No notice or application required.* A Federal savings association is not required to file a notice or application under this § 5.58 if it acquires a non-controlling investment in shares of a company through foreclosure or otherwise in good faith to compromise a doubtful claim, or in the ordinary course of collecting a debt previously contracted.

(h) *Additional exception to filing requirement.* A Federal savings association may make a pass-through investment without filing a notice or application to the OCC if all of the following conditions are met:

(1) The investment is in an investment company the portfolio of which consists exclusively of assets that the Federal savings association may hold directly;

(2) The Federal savings association is not investing more than 10 percent of its total capital in one company;

(3) The book value of the Federal savings association's aggregate non-controlling investments does not exceed 25 percent of its total capital after making the investment;

(4) The investment would not give Federal savings association direct or indirect control of the company; and

(5) The Federal savings association's liability is limited to the amount of its investment.

(i) *Exceptions to rules of general applicability.* Sections 5.8, 5.9, 5.10, and 5.11 of this part do not apply to filings for pass-through investments.

[80 FR 28466, May 18, 2015]

§ 5.59 Service corporations of Federal savings associations.

(a) *Authority.* 12 U.S.C. 1462a, 1463, 1464, 1828, 5412(b)(2)(B).

(b) *Licensing requirements.* When required by section 18(m) of the Federal Deposit Insurance Act, a Federal savings association must file an application as prescribed in this section to:

(1) Acquire or establish a service corporation; or

(2) Commence a new activity in an existing service corporation subsidiary.

(c) *Scope.* This section sets forth the OCC's requirements regarding service corporations of Federal savings associations, and sets forth procedures governing OCC review and approval of filings by Federal savings associations to establish or acquire service corporations and filings by Federal savings associations to conduct new activities in existing service corporation subsidiaries, pursuant to the authority provided in section 5(c)(4)(B) of the Home Owners' Loan Act, 12 U.S.C. 1464(c)(4)(B).

(d) *Definitions*—(1) *Control* has the meaning set forth at 12 U.S.C. 1841 and the Federal Reserve Board's regulations thereunder, at 12 CFR part 225.

(2) *GAAP-consolidated subsidiary* means a service corporation in which a Federal savings association has a direct or indirect ownership interest and whose assets are consolidated with those of the savings association for purposes of reporting under generally accepted accounting principles (GAAP).

(3) *Ownership interest* means any equity interest in a business organization, including stock, limited or general partnership interests, or shares in a limited liability company.

(4) *Service corporation* means any entity that satisfies all of the requirements for service corporations in 12 U.S.C. 1464(c)(4)(B) and this part, and that is designated by the investing Federal savings association as a service corporation pursuant to this section. A service corporation may be a first-tier service corporation of a Federal savings association or may be a lower-tier service corporation.

(5) *Service corporation subsidiary* means a service corporation of a Federal savings association that is controlled by that savings association.

(e) *Standards and requirements*—(1) *Ownership.* Only Federal or state-chartered savings associations with home offices in the state where the relevant Federal savings association has its home office may have an ownership interest in a first-tier service corporation. A Federal savings association need not have any minimum percentage ownership interest or have control of a service corporation in order to designate an entity as a service corporation.

(2) *Geographic restrictions.* A first-tier service corporation must be organized under the laws of the state where the relevant Federal savings association's home office is located.

(3) *Authorized activities.* A service corporation may engage in any of the designated permissible service corporation activities listed in paragraph (f) of this section, subject to any applicable filing requirement under paragraph (h) of this section. In addition, a Federal savings association may request OCC approval for a service corporation to engage in any other activity reasonably related to the activities of financial institutions.

(4) *Investment limitations.* A Federal savings association's investment in service corporations is subject to the limitations set forth in paragraph (g) of this section. The assets of a Federal savings association's service corporations are not subject to the investment limitations applicable to the savings association under section 5(c) of the HOLA.

(5) *Form of organization.* A service corporation may be organized as a corporation, or may be organized in any other organizational form that provides the same protections as the corporate form of organization, including limited liability.

(6) *Qualified thrift lender test.* In accordance with 12 U.S.C. 1467a(m)(5), a

Federal savings association may determine whether to consolidate the assets of a particular service corporation for purposes of calculating qualified thrift investments. If a service corporation's assets are not consolidated with the assets of the Federal savings association for that purpose, the savings association's investment in the service corporation will be considered in calculating the savings association's qualified thrift investments.

(7) *Supervisory, legal or safety or soundness considerations.* (i) Each service corporation must be well managed and operate safely and soundly. In addition, each service corporation must pursue financial policies that are safe and consistent with the purposes of savings associations. Each service corporation must maintain sufficient liquidity to ensure its safe and sound operation.

(ii) The OCC may, at any time, limit a Federal savings association's investment in a service corporation, or limit or refuse to permit any activity of a service corporation, for supervisory, legal, or safety or soundness reasons.

(8) *Separate corporate identity.* Federal savings associations and service corporations thereof must be operated in a manner that demonstrates to the public that each maintains a separate corporate existence. Each must operate so that:

(i) Their respective business transactions, accounts, and records are not intermingled;

(ii) Each observes the formalities of their separate corporate procedures;

(iii) Each is held out to the public as a separate enterprise; and

(iv) Unless the parent Federal savings association has guaranteed a loan to the service corporation, all borrowings by the service corporation indicate that the savings association is not liable.

(9) *Issuances of securities by service corporations.* A service corporation shall not state or imply that the securities it issues are covered by Federal deposit insurance. A service corporation subsidiary shall not issue any security the payment, maturity, or redemption of which may be accelerated upon the condition that the controlling Federal savings association is insolvent or has been placed into receivership. For as long as any securities are outstanding, the controlling Federal savings association must maintain all records generated through each securities issuance in the ordinary course of business, including but not limited to a copy of the prospectus, offering circular, or similar document concerning such issuance, and make such records available for examination by the OCC.

(10) *Certain pre-existing non-controlling investments.* A Federal savings association that made a non-controlling investment in a service corporation before May 18, 2015, but did not submit a filing under 12 U.S.C. 1828(m) with respect to such service corporation investment, is not required to file a service corporation application with respect to such investment pursuant to paragraph (b), provided that the Federal savings association does not acquire additional stock or similar interests in the service corporation, and the service corporation does not engage in any activities in which it was not engaged as of May 18, 2015.

(f) *Authorized service corporation activities.* Subject to the prior filing requirements set forth in paragraph (h) of this section and the provisions of paragraph (e)(3) of this section, a service corporation may engage in the following activities:

(1) *Any activity that all Federal savings associations may conduct directly.*

(2) *Business and professional services.* Service corporations may engage in the following activities only when such activities are limited to financial documents or financial clients or are generally finance-related:

(i) Accounting or internal audit;

(ii) Advertising, market research and other marketing;

(iii) Clerical;

(iv) Consulting;

(v) Courier;

(vi) Data processing;

(vii) Data storage facilities operation and related services;

(viii) Office supplies, furniture, and equipment purchasing and distribution;

(ix) Personnel benefit program development or administration;

(x) Printing and selling forms that require Magnetic Ink Character Recognition (MICR) encoding;

(xi) Relocation of personnel;

(xii) Research studies and surveys;

(xiii) Software development and systems integration; and

(xiv) Remote service unit operation, leasing, ownership or establishment.

(3) *Credit-related activities.* (i) Abstracting;

(ii) Acquiring and leasing personal property;

(iii) Appraising;

(iv) Collection agency;

(v) Credit analysis;

(vi) Check or credit card guaranty and verification;

(vii) Escrow agent or trustee (under deeds of trust, including executing and delivery of conveyances, reconveyances and transfers of title); and

(viii) Loan inspection.

(4) *Consumer services.* (i) Financial advice or consulting;

(ii) Foreign currency exchange;

(iii) Home ownership counseling;

(iv) Income tax return preparation;

(v) Postal services;

(vi) Stored value instrument sales;

(vii) Welfare benefit distribution;

(viii) Check printing and related services; and

(ix) Remote service unit operation, leasing, ownership, or establishment.

(5) *Real estate related services.* (i) Acquiring real estate for prompt development or subdivision, for construction of improvements, for resale or leasing to others for such construction, or for use as manufactured home sites, in accordance with a prudent program of property development;

(ii) Acquiring improved real estate or manufactured homes to be held for rental or resale, for remodeling, renovating or demolishing and rebuilding for resale or rental, or to be used for offices and related facilities of a stockholder of the service corporation;

(iii) Maintaining and managing real estate; and

(iv) Real estate brokerage for property owned by a savings association that owns capital stock of the service corporation, or a lower-tier service corporation in which the service corporation invests.

(6) *Securities activities, liquidity management, and coins.* (i) Execution of transactions in securities on an agency or riskless principal basis solely upon the order and for the account of customers or the provision of investment advice. The service corporation must register with the Securities and Exchange Commission and state securities regulators, as required by applicable Federal and state law and regulations;

(ii) Liquidity management;

(iii) Issuing notes, bonds, debentures, or other obligations or securities; and

(iv) Purchase or sale of coins issued by the U.S. Treasury.

(7) *Investments.* (i) Tax-exempt bonds used to finance residential real property for family units;

(ii) Tax-exempt obligations of public housing agencies used to finance housing projects with rental assistance subsidies;

(iii) Small business investment companies and new markets venture capital companies licensed by the U.S. Small Business Administration;

(iv) Rural business investment companies licensed by the U.S. Department of Agriculture; and

(v) Investing in savings accounts of an investing thrift.

(8) *Community development investments.* Community and economic development or public welfare investments that are permissible under part 24 of this chapter.

(9) *Charitable activities.* Establishing or acquiring a corporation that is recognized by the Internal Revenue Service as organized for charitable purposes under 26 U.S.C. 501(c)(3) of the Internal Revenue Code and making a reasonable contribution to capitalize it, *provided* that the corporation engages exclusively in activities designed to promote the well-being of communities in which the owners of the service corporation operate.

(10) *Activities conducted as agent.* Activities conducted on behalf of a customer on other than an "as principal" basis.

(11) *Incidental activities.* Activities reasonably incident to those listed in paragraphs (f)(1) through (f)(10) of this section if the service corporation engages in those activities.

(g) *Limitations on investments in service corporations*—(1) *In general.* Under the authority of section 5(c)(4)(B) of the HOLA, a Federal savings association may invest up to 3 percent of its assets in the capital stock, obligations, and other securities of service corporations. Any investment that would cause a Federal savings association's investment in service corporations, in the aggregate, to exceed 2 percent of assets, or made while the savings association's investments in service corporations exceeds 2 percent of assets, must serve primarily community, inner city, or community and economic development or public welfare purposes consistent with § 24.6 of this chapter. A Federal savings association must designate the investments serving those purposes.

(2) *Loans.* In addition to the amounts that a Federal savings association may invest under paragraph (g)(1) of this section, and to the extent that a Federal savings association has authority under other provisions of section 5(c) of the HOLA and parts 5 and 160 of this chapter, and available capacity within any applicable investment limits, a Federal savings association may make loans to any service corporation subject to the following conditions:

(i) Loans to service corporations other than a GAAP-consolidated subsidiary are subject to the lending limits in part 32 of this chapter.

(ii) The OCC may limit the amount of loans to any service corporation where safety and soundness considerations warrant such action.

(3) *Definition.* For purposes of this paragraph, the terms "loans" and "obligations" include all loans and other debt instruments (except accounts payable incurred in the ordinary course of business and paid within 60 days) and all guarantees or take-out commitments of such loans or debt instruments.

(4) *GAAP-consolidated subsidiaries.* Both debt and equity investments in service corporations that are GAAP-consolidated subsidiaries are considered investments in subsidiaries for purposes of 12 CFR part 3.

(h) *Filing requirements*—(1) *Application.* (i) When required by section 18(m) of the Federal Deposit Insurance Act, a Federal savings association must file an application at least 30 days before:

(A) Acquiring or establishing a service corporation; or

(B) Commencing a new activity in an existing service corporation subsidiary.

(ii) The application must include a complete description of the savings association's investment in the service corporation, the proposed activities of the service corporation, the organizational structure and management of the service corporation, the relations between the savings association and the service corporation, and other information necessary to adequately describe the proposal. If the service corporation proposes to engage in insurance activities, the savings association must describe the type of insurance activity in which the service corporation proposes to engage. The savings association must also list for each state the lines of business for which the company holds, or will hold, an insurance license, indicating the state where the service corporation holds a resident license or charter, as applicable. The OCC may require an applicant to submit a legal analysis if the proposal is novel, unusually complex, or raises substantial unresolved legal issues. In these cases, the OCC encourages applicants to have a prefiling meeting with the OCC. Any savings association receiving approval under this paragraph is deemed to have agreed that the service corporation will conduct the activity in a manner consistent with published OCC guidance.

(2) *Expedited review.* (i) An application to establish or acquire a service corporation, or to perform a new activity in an existing service corporation subsidiary, that meets the requirements of this paragraph is deemed approved by the OCC as of the 30th day after the filing is received by the OCC, unless the OCC notifies the applicant prior to that date that the filing is not eligible for expedited review under 5.13(a)(2). Any savings association receiving approval under this paragraph is deemed to have agreed that the service corporation will conduct the activity in a manner consistent with published OCC guidance.

(ii) An application is eligible for expedited review if the following requirements are met:

(A) The savings association is "well capitalized" and "well managed"; and

(B) The service corporation engages only in one or more of the preapproved activities listed in §5.59(f).

(3) *OCC review and approval.* The OCC reviews a Federal savings association's application to determine whether the proposal is legally permissible and to ensure that the proposal is consistent with the requirements of this section, safe and sound banking practices and OCC policy and does not endanger the safety or soundness of the parent Federal savings association. As part of this process, the OCC may request additional information and analysis from the applicant.

(4) *Redesignation.* A Federal savings association that proposes to redesignate an operating subsidiary as a service corporation must submit a notification to the OCC at least 30 days prior to the redesignation date. The notification must include a description of how the redesignated entity will meet all of the requirements of this section, a resolution of the savings association's board of directors approving the redesignation, and the proposed effective date of the redesignation. The savings association may effect the redesignation on the proposed date unless the OCC notifies the savings association otherwise prior to that date. The OCC may require an application if the redesignation presents policy, supervisory, or legal issues.

(5) *Exception to rules of general applicability.* Sections 5.8, 5.10 and 5.11 do not apply to this section. However, if the OCC concludes that an application presents significant or novel policy, supervisory, or legal issues, the OCC may determine that some or all provisions in §§5.8, 5.10, and 5.11 apply.

(i) *Exercise of salvage powers through service corporations.* (1) In accordance with this section, a Federal savings association may exercise its salvage power to make a contribution or a loan (including a guarantee of a loan made by any other person) to a service corporation ("salvage investment") that exceeds the maximum amount otherwise permitted under law or regulation. A Federal savings association must notify the appropriate supervisory office at least 30 days before making such a salvage investment. The notification must demonstrate:

(i) The salvage investment protects the savings association's interest in the service corporation;

(ii) The salvage investment is consistent with safety and soundness; and

(iii) The savings association considered alternatives to the salvage investment and determined that such alternatives would not adequately satisfy paragraphs (i)(1)(i) and (ii) of this section.

(2) If the OCC notifies the Federal savings association within 30 days of the filing of the notification that the notification presents supervisory concerns, or raises significant issues of law or policy, the Federal savings association must apply for and receive the OCC's prior written approval before making the salvage investment.

(3) If a service corporation is a GAAP-consolidated subsidiary, the salvage investment will be considered an investment in a subsidiary for purposes of 12 CFR part 3.

(j) *Failure to comply with the requirements applicable to service corporations.* If a service corporation fails to meet any of the requirements of this section, the Federal savings association must notify the appropriate OCC licensing office. Unless the Federal savings association is otherwise advised by the OCC, if the service corporation cannot comply with the requirements of this section within 90 days of failing to meet such requirements, or otherwise resolve such failure to comply with this section, the Federal savings association must promptly dispose of its investment in the service corporation.

[80 FR 28467, May 18, 2015]

Subpart E—Payment of Dividends by National Banks

§5.60 Authority, scope, and exceptions to rules of general applicability.

(a) *Authority.* 12 U.S.C. 56, 60, and 93a.

(b) *Scope.* Except as otherwise provided, the restrictions in this subpart apply to the declaration and payment of all dividends by a national bank, including dividends paid in property. However, the provisions contained in §5.64 do not apply to dividends paid in stock of the bank.

(c) *Exceptions to the rules of general applicability*. Sections 5.8, 5.10, and 5.11 do not apply to this subpart.

§ 5.61 Definitions.

For the purposes of subpart E, the following definitions apply:

(a) *Capital stock, capital surplus,* and *permanent capital* have the same meaning as set forth in § 5.46.

(b) *Retained net income* means the net income of a specified period less the total amount of all dividends declared in that period.

§ 5.62 Date of declaration of dividend.

A national bank shall use the date a dividend is declared for the purposes of determining compliance with this subpart.

§ 5.63 Capital limitation under 12 U.S.C. 56.

(a) *General limitation*. Except as provided by 12 U.S.C. 59 and § 5.46, a national bank may not withdraw, or permit to be withdrawn, either in the form of a dividend or otherwise, any portion of its permanent capital. Further, a national bank may not declare a dividend in excess of undivided profits.

(b) *Preferred stock*. The provisions of 12 U.S.C. 56 do not apply to dividends on preferred stock. However, if the undivided profits of the national bank are not sufficient to cover a proposed dividend on preferred stock, the proposed dividend constitutes a reduction in capital subject to 12 U.S.C. 59 and § 5.46.

§ 5.64 Earnings limitation under 12 U.S.C. 60.

(a) *Definitions*. As used in this section, the term "current year" means the calendar year in which a national bank declared, or proposes to declare, a dividend. The term "current year minus one" means the year immediately preceding the current year. The term "current year minus two" means the year that is two years prior to the current year. The term "current year minus three" means the year that is three years prior to the current year. The term "current year minus four" means the year that is four years prior to the current year.

(b) *Dividends from undivided profits*. Subject to 12 U.S.C. 56 and this subpart, the directors of a national bank may declare and pay dividends of so much of the undivided profits as they judge to be expedient.

(c) *Earnings limitations under 12 U.S.C. 60*—(1) *General rule*. For purposes of 12 U.S.C. 60, unless approved by the OCC in accordance with paragraph (c)(3) of this section, a national bank may not declare a dividend if the total amount of all dividends (common and preferred), including the proposed dividend, declared by the national bank in any current year exceeds the total of the national bank's net income for the current year to date, combined with its retained net income of current year minus one and current year minus two, less the sum of any transfers required by the OCC and any transfers required to be made to a fund for the retirement of any preferred stock.

(2) *Excess dividends in prior periods*. (i) If in current year minus one or current year minus two the bank declared dividends in excess of that year's net income, the excess shall not reduce retained net income for the three-year period specified in paragraph (c)(1) of this section, provided that the amount of excess dividends can be offset by retained net income in current year minus three or current year minus four. If the bank declared dividends in excess of net income in current year minus one, the excess is offset by retained net income in current year minus three and then by retained net income in current year minus two. If the bank declared dividends in excess of net income in current year minus two, the excess is first offset by retained net income in current year minus four and then by retained net income in current year minus three.

(ii) If the bank's retained net income in current year minus three and current year minus four was insufficient to offset the full amount of the excess dividends declared, as calculated in accordance with paragraph (c)(2)(i) of this section, then the amount that is not offset will reduce the retained net income available to pay dividends in the current year.

(iii) The calculation in paragraph (c)(2) of this section shall apply only to retained net loss that results from dividends declared in excess of a single year's net income and does not apply to other types of current earnings deficits.

(3) *Prior approval required*. A national bank may declare a dividend in excess of the amount described in paragraph (c) of this section, provided that the dividend is approved by the OCC. A national bank shall submit a request for prior approval of a dividend under 12 U.S.C. 60 to the appropriate OCC supervisory office.

(d) *Surplus surplus*. Any amount in capital surplus in excess of capital stock (referred to as "surplus surplus") may be transferred to undivided profits and available as dividends, provided:

(1) The bank can demonstrate that the amount came from earnings in prior periods, excluding the effect of any stock dividend; and

(2) The board of directors of the bank approves the transfer of the amount from capital surplus to undivided profits.

[73 FR 22241, Apr. 24, 2008, as amended at 80 FR 28470, May 18, 2015]

§ 5.65 Restrictions on undercapitalized institutions.

Notwithstanding any other provision in this subpart, a national bank may not declare or pay any dividend if, after making the dividend, the national bank would be "undercapitalized" as defined in 12 CFR part 6.

§ 5.66 Dividends payable in property other than cash.

In addition to cash dividends, directors of a national bank may declare dividends payable in property, with the approval of the OCC. A national bank shall submit a request for prior approval of a noncash dividend to the appropriate OCC licensing office. Even though the property distributed has been previously charged down or written off entirely, the dividend is equivalent to a cash dividend in an amount equal to the actual current value of the property. Before the dividend is declared, the bank should show the excess of the actual value over book value on the books of the national bank as a recovery, and the dividend should then be declared in the amount of the full book value (equivalent to the actual current value) of the property being distributed.

[61 FR 60363, Nov. 27, 1996, as amended at 82 FR 8104, Jan. 23, 2017]

§ 5.67 Fractional shares.

To avoid complicated recordkeeping in connection with fractional shares, a national bank issuing additional stock by stock dividend, upon consolidation or merger, or otherwise, may adopt arrangements such as the following to preclude the issuance of fractional shares. The bank may:

(a) Issue scripts or warrants for trading;

(b) Make reasonable arrangements to provide those to whom fractional shares would otherwise be issued an opportunity to realize at a fair price upon the fraction not being issued through its sale, or the purchase of the additional fraction required for a full share, if there is an established and active market in the national bank's stock;

(c) Remit the cash equivalent of the fraction not being issued to those to whom fractional shares would otherwise be issued. The cash equivalent is based on the market value of the stock, if there is an established and active market in the national bank's stock. In the absence of such a market, the cash equivalent is based on a reliable and disinterested determination as to the fair market value of the stock if such stock is available; or

(d) Sell full shares representing all the fractions at public auction, or to the highest bidder after having solicited and received sealed bids from at least three licensed stock brokers. The national bank shall distribute the proceeds of the sale *pro rata* to shareholders who otherwise would be entitled to the fractional shares.

Subpart F—Federal Branches and Agencies

§ 5.70 Federal branches and agencies.

(a) *Authority*. 12 U.S.C. 93a and 3101 *et seq.*

(b) *Scope*. This subpart describes the filing requirements for corporate activities and transactions involving

Federal branches and agencies of foreign banks. Substantive rules and policies for specific applications are contained in 12 CFR part 28.

(c) *Definitions.* For purposes of this subpart:

(1) To *establish* a Federal branch or agency means to:

(i) Open and conduct business through an initial or additional Federal branch or agency;

(ii) Acquire directly, through merger, consolidation, or similar transaction with another foreign bank, the operations of a Federal branch or agency that is open and conducting business;

(iii) Acquire a Federal branch or agency through the acquisition of a foreign bank subsidiary that will cease to operate in the same corporate form following the acquisition;

(iv) Convert a state branch or state agency operated by a foreign bank, or a commercial lending company controlled by a foreign bank, into a Federal branch or agency;

(v) Relocate a Federal branch or agency within a state or from one state to another; or

(vi) Convert a Federal agency or a limited Federal branch into a Federal branch.

(2) *Federal branch* includes a limited Federal branch unless otherwise provided.

(d) *Filing requirements*—(1) *General.* Unless otherwise provided in 12 CFR part 28, a Federal branch or agency shall comply with the applicable requirements of this part.

(2) *Applications.* A foreign bank shall submit an application and obtain prior approval from the OCC before it:

(i) Establishes a Federal branch or agency; or

(ii) Exercises fiduciary powers at a Federal branch. A foreign bank may submit an application to exercise fiduciary powers at the time of filing an application for a Federal branch license or at any subsequent date.

[61 FR 60363, Nov. 27, 1996, as amended at 68 FR 70698, Dec. 19, 2003]

PART 6—PROMPT CORRECTIVE ACTION

Subpart A—Capital Categories

Sec.
6.1 Authority, purpose, scope, other supervisory authority, disclosure of capital categories, and transition procedures.
6.2 Definitions.
6.3 Notice of capital category.
6.4 Capital measures and capital category definition.
6.5 Capital restoration plan.
6.6 Mandatory and discretionary supervisory actions.

Subpart B—Directives To Take Prompt Corrective Action

6.20 Scope.
6.21 Notice of intent to issue a directive.
6.22 Response to notice.
6.23 Decision and issuance of a prompt corrective action directive.
6.24 Request for modification or rescission of directive.
6.25 Enforcement of directive.

AUTHORITY: 12 U.S.C. 93a, 1831o, 5412(b)(2)(B).

SOURCE: 78 FR 62275, Oct. 11, 2013, unless otherwise noted.

Subpart A—Capital Categories

§ 6.1 Authority, purpose, scope, other supervisory authority, disclosure of capital categories, and transition procedures.

(a) *Authority.* This part is issued by the Office of the Comptroller of the Currency (OCC) pursuant to section 38 (section 38) of the Federal Deposit Insurance Act (FDI Act) as added by section 131 of the Federal Deposit Insurance Corporation Improvement Act of 1991 (Pub. L. 102–242, 105 Stat. 2236 (1991)) (12 U.S.C. 1831o).

(b) *Purpose.* Section 38 of the FDI Act establishes a framework of supervisory actions for insured depository institutions that are not adequately capitalized. The principal purpose of this subpart is to define, for insured national banks and insured Federal savings associations, the capital measures and capital levels, and for insured Federal branches, comparable asset-based measures and levels, that are used for determining the supervisory actions authorized under section 38 of the FDI

Act. This part 6 also establishes procedures for submission and review of capital restoration plans and for issuance and review of directives and orders pursuant to section 38.

(c) *Scope.* This subpart implements the provisions of section 38 of the FDI Act as they apply to insured national banks, insured Federal branches, and insured Federal savings associations. Certain of these provisions also apply to officers, directors, and employees of these insured institutions. Other provisions apply to any company that controls an insured national bank, insured Federal branch, or insured Federal savings association and to the affiliates of an insured national bank, insured Federal branch, or insured Federal savings association.

(d) *Other supervisory authority.* Neither section 38 nor this part in any way limits the authority of the OCC under any other provision of law to take supervisory actions to address unsafe or unsound practices, deficient capital levels, violations of law, unsafe or unsound conditions, or other practices. Action under section 38 of the FDI Act and this part may be taken independently of, in conjunction with, or in addition to any other enforcement action available to the OCC, including issuance of cease and desist orders, capital directives, approval or denial of applications or notices, assessment of civil money penalties, or any other actions authorized by law.

(e) *Disclosure of capital categories.* The assignment of an insured national bank, insured Federal branch, or insured Federal savings association under this subpart within a particular capital category is for purposes of implementing and applying the provisions of section 38. Unless permitted by the OCC or otherwise required by law, no national bank or Federal savings association may state in any advertisement or promotional material its capital category under this subpart or that the OCC or any other Federal banking agency has assigned the national bank or Federal savings association to a particular capital category.

(f) *Transition procedures*—(1) *Definitions applicable before January 1, 2015, for certain national banks and Federal savings associations.* Before January 1, 2015, notwithstanding any other requirement in this subpart and with respect to any national bank that is not an advanced approaches bank and any Federal savings association that is not an advanced approaches Federal savings association:

(i) The definitions of leverage ratio, tangible equity, tier 1 capital, tier 1 risk-based capital, and total risk-based capital as calculated or defined under appendix A to part 3 of this chapter, remain in effect for purposes of this subpart; and

(ii) The definition of total assets means quarterly average total assets as reported in a national bank's or Federal savings association's Consolidated Reports of Condition and Income (Call Report), minus intangible assets except mortgage servicing assets as provided in the definition of tangible equity. The OCC reserves the right to require a national bank or Federal savings association to compute and maintain its capital ratios on the basis of actual, rather than average, total assets when computing tangible equity.

(2) *Timing.* On January 1, 2015 and thereafter, the calculation of the definitions of common equity tier 1 capital, the common equity tier 1 risk-based capital ratio, the leverage ratio, the supplementary leverage ratio, tangible equity, tier 1 capital, the tier 1 risk-based capital ratio, total assets, total leverage exposure, the total risk-based capital ratio, and total risk-weighted assets under this subpart is subject to the timing provisions at 12 CFR §3.1(f) and the transitions at 12 CFR part 3, subpart G.

§6.2 Definitions.

For purposes of this subpart, except as modified in this section or unless the context otherwise requires, the terms used have the same meanings as set forth in section 38 and section 3 of the FDI Act.

Advanced approaches national bank or advanced approaches Federal savings association means a national bank or Federal savings association that is subject to subpart E of part 3 of this chapter.

Common equity tier 1 capital means common equity tier 1 capital, as defined in accordance with the OCC's definition in subpart A of part 3 of this chapter.

Common equity tier 1 risk-based capital ratio means the ratio of common equity tier 1 capital to total risk-weighted assets, as calculated in accordance with subpart B of part 3 of this chapter, as applicable.

Control. (1) *Control* has the same meaning assigned to it in section 2 of the Bank Holding Company Act (12 U.S.C. 1841), and the term controlled shall be construed consistently with the term control.

(2) *Exclusion for fiduciary ownership.* No insured depository institution or company controls another insured depository institution or company by virtue of its ownership or control of shares in a fiduciary capacity. Shares shall not be deemed to have been acquired in a fiduciary capacity if the acquiring insured depository institution or company has sole discretionary authority to exercise voting rights with respect thereto.

(3) *Exclusion for debts previously contracted.* No insured depository institution or company controls another insured depository institution or company by virtue of its ownership or control of shares acquired in securing or collecting a debt previously contracted in good faith, until two years after the date of acquisition. The two-year period may be extended at the discretion of the appropriate Federal banking agency for up to three one-year periods.

Controlling person means any person having control of an insured depository institution and any company controlled by that person.

Federal savings association means an insured Federal savings association or an insured Federal savings bank chartered under section 5 of the Home Owners' Loan Act of 1933.

Leverage ratio means the ratio of tier 1 capital to average total consolidated assets, as calculated in accordance with subpart B of part 3 of this chapter.[30]

Management fee means any payment of money or provision of any other thing of value to a company or individual for the provision of management services or advice to the national bank or Federal savings association or related overhead expenses, including payments related to supervisory, executive, managerial, or policymaking functions, other than compensation to an individual in the individual's capacity as an officer or employee of the national bank or Federal savings association.

National bank means all insured national banks and all insured Federal branches, except where otherwise provided in this subpart.

Supplementary leverage ratio means the ratio of tier 1 capital to total leverage exposure, as calculated in accordance with subpart B of part 3 of this chapter.

Tangible equity means the amount of tier 1 capital, as calculated in accordance with subpart B of part 3 of this chapter, plus the amount of outstanding perpetual preferred stock (including related surplus) not included in tier 1 capital.[31]

Tier 1 capital means the amount of tier 1 capital as defined in subpart B of part 3 of this chapter.[32]

---

[30] Before January 1, 2015, the leverage ratio of a national bank or Federal savings association that is not an advanced approaches national bank or advanced approaches Federal savings association is the ratio of tier 1 capital to average total consolidated assets, as calculated in accordance with appendix A to part 3 of this chapter.

[31] Before January 1, 2015, the tangible equity of a national bank or Federal savings association that is not an advanced approaches national bank or advanced approaches Federal savings association is the amount of tier 1 capital elements as defined in appendix A to part 3 of this chapter, plus the amount of outstanding cumulative perpetual preferred stock (including related surplus) minus all intangible assets except mortgage servicing assets to the extent permitted in tier 1 capital, as calculated in accordance with appendix A to part 3 of this chapter. The OCC reserves the right to require a national bank or Federal savings association to compute and maintain its capital ratios on the basis of actual, rather than average, total assets when computing tangible equity.

[32] Before January 1, 2015, the tier 1 capital of a national bank or Federal savings association that is not an advanced approaches

Tier 1 risk-based capital ratio means the ratio of tier 1 capital to risk-weighted assets, as calculated in accordance with subpart B of part 3 of this chapter.[33]

Total assets means quarterly average total assets as reported in a national bank's or Federal savings association's Consolidated Reports of Condition and Income (Call Report), minus any deductions as provided in § 3.22(a), (c), and (d) of this chapter. The OCC reserves the right to require a national bank or Federal savings association to compute and maintain its capital ratios on the basis of actual, rather than average, total assets when computing tangible equity.[34]

Total leverage exposure means the total leverage exposure, as calculated in accordance with subpart B of part 3 of this chapter.

Total risk-based capital ratio means the ratio of total capital to total risk-weighted assets, as calculated in accordance with subpart B of part 3 of this chapter.[35]

Total risk-weighted assets means standardized total risk-weighted assets, and for an advanced approaches national bank or advanced approaches Federal savings association also includes advanced approaches total risk-weighted assets, as defined in subpart B of part 3 of this chapter.

§ 6.3 Notice of capital category.

(a) *Effective date of determination of capital category.* A national bank or Federal savings association shall be deemed to be within a given capital category for purposes of section 38 of the FDI Act and this part as of the date the national bank or Federal savings association is notified of, or is deemed to have notice of, its capital category pursuant to paragraph (b) of this section.

(b) *Notice of capital category.* A national bank or Federal savings association shall be deemed to have been notified of its capital levels and its capital category as of the most recent date:

(1) A Consolidated Reports of Condition and Income (Call Report) is required to be filed with the OCC;

(2) A final report of examination is delivered to the national bank or Federal savings association; or

(3) Written notice is provided by the OCC to the national bank or Federal savings association of its capital category for purposes of section 38 of the FDI Act and this part or that the national bank's or Federal savings association's capital category has changed pursuant to paragraph (c) of this section, or § 6.4(e) and with respect to national banks, subpart M of part 19 of this chapter, and with respect to Federal savings associations § 165.8 of this chapter.

---

national bank or advanced approaches Federal savings association (as an advanced approaches national bank or advanced approaches Federal savings association is defined in this § 6.2) is calculated in accordance with appendix A to part 3 of this chapter.

[33] Before January 1, 2015, the tier 1 risk-based capital ratio of a national bank or Federal savings association that is not an advanced approaches national bank or advanced approaches Federal savings association (as an advanced approaches national bank or advanced approaches Federal savings association is defined in this § 6.2) is calculated in accordance with appendix A to part 3 of this chapter.

[34] Before January 1, 2015, total assets means, for a national bank or Federal savings association that is not an advanced approaches national bank or advanced approaches Federal savings association (as an advanced approaches national bank or advanced approaches Federal savings association is defined in this § 6.2), quarterly average total assets as reported in a bank's or savings association's Call Report, minus all intangible assets except mortgage servicing assets to the extent permitted in tier 1 capital, as calculated in accordance with appendix A to part 3 of this chapter. The OCC reserves the right to require a national bank or Federal savings association to compute and maintain its capital ratios on the basis of actual, rather than average, total assets when computing tangible equity.

[35] Before January 1, 2015, the total risk-based capital ratio of a national bank or Federal savings association that is not an advanced approaches national bank or advanced approaches Federal savings association (as an advanced approaches national bank or advanced approaches Federal savings association is defined in this § 6.2) is calculated in accordance with appendix A to part 3 of this chapter.

(c) *Adjustments to reported capital levels and capital category*—(1) *Notice of adjustment by national bank or Federal savings association.* A national bank or Federal savings association shall provide the OCC with written notice that an adjustment to the national bank's or Federal savings association's capital category may have occurred no later than 15 calendar days following the date that any material event has occurred that would cause the national bank or Federal savings association to be placed in a lower capital category from the category assigned to the national bank or Federal savings association for purposes of section 38 and this part on the basis of the national bank's or Federal savings association's most recent Call Report or report of examination.

(2) *Determination to change capital category.* After receiving notice pursuant to paragraph (c)(1) of this section, the OCC shall determine whether to change the capital category of the national bank or Federal savings association and shall notify the national bank or Federal savings association of the OCC's determination.

§ 6.4 Capital measures and capital category definition.

(a) *Capital measures*—(1) *Capital measures applicable before January 1, 2015.* On or before December 31, 2014, for purposes of section 38 and this part, the relevant capital measures for all national banks and Federal savings associations are:

(i) Total Risk-Based Capital Measure: the total risk-based capital ratio;

(ii) Tier 1 Risk-Based Capital Measure: the tier 1 risk-based capital ratio; and

(iii) Leverage Measure: the leverage ratio.

(2) *Capital measures applicable on and after January 1, 2015.* On January 1, 2015 and thereafter, for purposes of section 38 and this part, the relevant capital measures are:

(i) Total Risk-Based Capital Measure: the total risk-based capital ratio;

(ii) Tier 1 Risk-Based Capital Measure: the tier 1 risk-based capital ratio;

(iii) Common Equity Tier 1 Capital Measure: the common equity tier 1 risk-based capital ratio; and

(iv) The Leverage Measure:

(A) The leverage ratio; and

(B) With respect to an advanced approaches national bank or advanced approaches Federal savings association, on January 1, 2018, and thereafter, the supplementary leverage ratio.

(b) *Capital categories applicable before January 1, 2015.* On or before December 31, 2014, for purposes of the provisions of section 38 and this part, a national bank or Federal savings association shall be deemed to be:

(1) *Well capitalized* if:

(i) Total Risk-Based Capital Measure: the national bank or Federal savings association has a total risk-based capital ratio of 10.0 percent or greater;

(ii) Tier 1 Risk-Based Capital Measure: the national bank or Federal savings association has a tier 1 risk-based capital ratio of 6.0 percent or greater;

(iii) Leverage Ratio: the national bank or Federal savings association has a leverage ratio of 5.0 percent or greater; and

(iv) The national bank or Federal savings association is not subject to any written agreement, order or capital directive, or prompt corrective action directive issued by the OCC or the former OTS pursuant to section 8 of the FDI Act, the International Lending Supervision Act of 1983 (12 U.S.C. 3907), the Home Owners' Loan Act (12 U.S.C. 1464(t)(6)(A)(ii)), or section 38 of the FDI Act, or any regulation thereunder, to meet and maintain a specific capital level for any capital measure.

(2) *Adequately capitalized* if:

(i) Total Risk-Based Capital Measure: the national bank or Federal savings association has a total risk-based capital ratio of 8.0 percent or greater;

(ii) Tier 1 Risk-Based Capital Measure: the national bank or Federal savings association has a tier 1 risk-based capital ratio of 4.0 percent or greater;

(iii) Leverage Ratio:

(A) The national bank or Federal savings association has a leverage ratio of 4.0 percent or greater; or

(B) The national bank or Federal savings association has a leverage ratio of 3.0 percent or greater if the national bank or Federal savings association is rated composite 1 under the CAMELS rating system in the most recent examination of the national bank and or Federal savings association; and

(iv) Does not meet the definition of a "well capitalized" national bank or Federal savings association.

(3) *Undercapitalized* if:

(i) Total Risk-Based Capital Measure: the national bank or Federal savings association has a total risk-based capital ratio of less than 8.0 percent; or

(ii) Tier 1 Risk-Based Capital Measure: the national bank or Federal savings association has a tier 1 risk-based capital ratio of less than 4.0 percent; or

(iii) Leverage Ratio:

(A) Except as provided in paragraph (b)(2)(iii)(B) of this section, the national bank or Federal savings association has a leverage ratio of less than 4.0 percent; or

(B) The national bank or Federal savings association has a leverage ratio of less than 3.0 percent, if the national bank or Federal savings association is rated composite 1 under the CAMELS rating system in the most recent examination of the national bank or Federal savings association.

(4) *Significantly undercapitalized* if:

(i) Total Risk-Based Capital Measure: the national bank or Federal savings association has a total risk-based capital ratio of less than 6.0 percent; or

(ii) Tier 1 Risk-Based Capital Measure: the national bank or Federal savings association has a tier 1 risk-based capital ratio of less than 3.0 percent; or

(iii) Leverage Ratio: the national bank or Federal savings association has a leverage ratio of less than 3.0 percent.

(5) *Critically undercapitalized* if the national bank or Federal savings association has a ratio of tangible equity to total assets that is equal to or less than 2.0 percent.

(c) *Capital categories applicable on and after January 1, 2015.* On January 1, 2015, and thereafter, for purposes of the provisions of section 38 and this part, a national bank or Federal savings association shall be deemed to be:

(1) *Well capitalized* if:

(i) Total Risk-Based Capital Measure: the national bank or Federal savings association has a total risk-based capital ratio of 10.0 percent or greater;

(ii) Tier 1 Risk-Based Capital Measure: the national bank or Federal savings association has a tier 1 risk-based capital ratio of 8.0 percent or greater;

(iii) Common Equity Tier 1 Capital Measure: the national bank or Federal savings association has a common equity tier 1 risk-based capital ratio of 6.5 percent or greater;

(iv) Leverage Measure:

(A) The national bank or Federal savings association has a leverage ratio of 5.0 percent or greater; and

(B) With respect to a national bank or Federal savings association that is a subsidiary of a U.S. top-tier bank holding company that has more than $700 billion in total assets as reported on the company's most recent Consolidated Financial Statement for Bank Holding Companies (FR Y–9C) or more than $10 trillion in assets under custody as reported on the company's most recent Banking Organization Systemic Risk Report (Y–15), on Jan. 1, 2018 and thereafter, the national bank or Federal savings association has a supplementary leverage ratio of 6.0 percent or greater; and

(v) The national bank or Federal savings association is not subject to any written agreement, order or capital directive, or prompt corrective action directive issued by the OCC pursuant to section 8 of the FDI Act, the International Lending Supervision Act of 1983 (12 U.S.C. 3907), the Home Owners' Loan Act (12 U.S.C. 1464(t)(6)(A)(ii)), or section 38 of the FDI Act, or any regulation thereunder, to meet and maintain a specific capital level for any capital measure.

(2) *Adequately capitalized* if:

(i) Total Risk-Based Capital Measure: the national bank or Federal savings association has a total risk-based capital ratio of 8.0 percent or greater;

(ii) Tier 1 Risk-Based Capital Measure: the national bank or Federal savings association has a tier 1 risk-based capital ratio of 6.0 percent or greater;

(iii) Common Equity Tier 1 Capital Measure: the national bank or Federal savings association has a common equity tier 1 risk-based capital ratio of 4.5 percent or greater;

(iv) Leverage Measure:

(A) The national bank or Federal savings association has a leverage ratio of 4.0 percent or greater; and

(B) With respect to an advanced approaches national bank or advanced approaches Federal savings association, on January 1, 2018 and thereafter, the national bank or Federal savings association has an supplementary leverage ratio of 3.0 percent or greater; and

(v) The national bank or Federal savings association does not meet the definition of a "well capitalized" national bank or Federal savings association.

(3) *Undercapitalized* if:

(i) Total Risk-Based Capital Measure: the national bank or Federal savings association has a total risk-based capital ratio of less than 8.0 percent;

(ii) Tier 1 Risk-Based Capital Measure: the national bank or Federal savings association has a tier 1 risk-based capital ratio of less than 6.0 percent;

(iii) Common Equity Tier 1 Capital Measure: the national bank or Federal savings association has a common equity tier 1 risk-based capital ratio of less than 4.5 percent; or

(iv) Leverage Measure:

(A) The national bank or Federal savings association has a leverage ratio of less than 4.0 percent; or

(B) With respect to an advanced approaches national bank or advanced approaches Federal savings association, on January 1, 2018, and thereafter, the national bank or Federal savings association has a supplementary leverage ratio of less than 3.0 percent.

(4) *Significantly undercapitalized* if:

(i) Total Risk-Based Capital Measure: the national bank or Federal savings association has a total risk-based capital ratio of less than 6.0 percent;

(ii) Tier 1 Risk-Based Capital Measure: the national bank or Federal savings association has a tier 1 risk-based capital ratio of less than 4.0 percent;

(iii) Common Equity Tier 1 Capital Measure: the national bank or Federal savings association has a common equity tier 1 risk-based capital ratio of less than 3.0 percent; or

(iv) Leverage Ratio: the national bank or Federal savings association has a leverage ratio of less than 3.0 percent.

(5) *Critically undercapitalized* if the national bank or Federal savings association has a ratio of tangible equity to total assets that is equal to or less than 2.0 percent.

(d) *Capital categories for insured Federal branches.* For purposes of the provisions of section 38 of the FDI Act and this part, an insured Federal branch shall be deemed to be:

(1) *Well capitalized* if the insured Federal branch:

(i) Maintains the pledge of assets required under 12 CFR 347.209; and

(ii) Maintains the eligible assets prescribed under 12 CFR 347.210 at 108 percent or more of the preceding quarter's average book value of the insured branch's third-party liabilities; and

(iii) Has not received written notification from:

(A) The OCC to increase its capital equivalency deposit pursuant to § 28.15 of this chapter, or to comply with asset maintenance requirements pursuant to § 28.20 of this chapter; or

(B) The FDIC to pledge additional assets pursuant to 12 CFR 347.209 or to maintain a higher ratio of eligible assets pursuant to 12 CFR 347.210.

(2) *Adequately capitalized* if the insured Federal branch:

(i) Maintains the pledge of assets prescribed under 12 CFR 347.209;

(ii) Maintains the eligible assets prescribed under 12 CFR 347.210 at 106 percent or more of the preceding quarter's average book value of the insured branch's third-party liabilities; and

(iii) Does not meet the definition of a well capitalized insured Federal branch.

(3) *Undercapitalized* if the insured Federal branch:

(i) Fails to maintain the pledge of assets required under 12 CFR 347.209; or

(ii) Fails to maintain the eligible assets prescribed under 12 CFR 347.210 at 106 percent or more of the preceding quarter's average book value of the insured branch's third-party liabilities.

(4) *Significantly undercapitalized* if it fails to maintain the eligible assets prescribed under 12 CFR 347.210 at 104 percent or more of the preceding quarter's average book value of the insured Federal branch's third-party liabilities.

(5) *Critically undercapitalized* if it fails to maintain the eligible assets prescribed under 12 CFR 347.210 at 102 percent or more of the preceding quarter's

average book value of the insured Federal branch's third-party liabilities.

(e) *Reclassification based on supervisory criteria other than capital.* The OCC may reclassify a well capitalized national bank or Federal savings association as adequately capitalized and may require an adequately capitalized or an undercapitalized national bank or Federal savings association to comply with certain mandatory or discretionary supervisory actions as if the national bank or Federal savings association were in the next lower capital category (except that the OCC may not reclassify a significantly undercapitalized national bank or Federal savings association as critically undercapitalized) (each of these actions are hereinafter referred to generally as reclassifications) in the following circumstances:

(1) *Unsafe or unsound condition.* The OCC has determined, after notice and opportunity for hearing pursuant to subpart M of part 19 of this chapter with respect to national banks and §165.8 of this chapter with respect to Federal savings associations, that the national bank or Federal savings association is in unsafe or unsound condition; or

(2) *Unsafe or unsound practice.* The OCC has determined, after notice and opportunity for hearing pursuant to subpart M of part 19 of this chapter with respect to national banks and §165.8 of this chapter with respect to Federal savings associations, that in the most recent examination of the national bank or Federal savings association, the national bank or Federal savings association received, and has not corrected a less-than-satisfactory rating for any of the categories of asset quality, management, earnings, or liquidity.

[78 FR 62275, Oct. 11, 2013, as amended at 79 FR 24539, May 1, 2014]

§6.5 Capital restoration plan.

(a) *Schedule for filing plan*—(1) *In general.* A national bank or Federal savings association shall file a written capital restoration plan with the OCC within 45 days of the date that the national bank or Federal savings association receives notice or is deemed to have notice that the national bank or Federal savings association is undercapitalized, significantly undercapitalized, or critically undercapitalized, unless the OCC notifies the national bank or Federal savings association in writing that the plan is to be filed within a different period. An adequately capitalized national bank or Federal savings association that has been required, pursuant to §6.4 and subpart M of part 19 of this chapter with respect to national banks, and §§6.4 and 165.8 of this chapter with respect to Federal savings associations, to comply with supervisory actions as if the national bank or Federal savings association were undercapitalized is not required to submit a capital restoration plan solely by virtue of the reclassification.

(2) *Additional capital restoration plans.* Notwithstanding paragraph (a)(1) of this section, a national bank or Federal savings association that has already submitted and is operating under a capital restoration plan approved under section 38 and this subpart is not required to submit an additional capital restoration plan based on a revised calculation of its capital measures or a reclassification of the institution pursuant to §6.4 and subpart M of part 19 of this chapter with respect to national banks and §§6.4 and 165.8 of this chapter with respect to Federal savings associations, unless the OCC notifies the national bank or Federal savings association that it must submit a new or revised capital plan. A national bank or Federal savings association that is notified that it must submit a new or revised capital restoration plan shall file the plan in writing with the OCC within 45 days of receiving such notice, unless the OCC notifies the national bank or Federal savings association in writing that the plan must be filed within a different period.

(b) *Contents of plan.* All financial data submitted in connection with a capital restoration plan shall be prepared in accordance with the instructions provided on the Call Report, unless the OCC instructs otherwise. The capital restoration plan shall include all of the information required to be filed under section 38(e)(2) of the FDI Act. A national bank or Federal savings association that is required to submit a capital restoration plan as the result of a reclassification of the national bank or Federal savings association, pursuant to § 6.4 and subpart M of part 19 of this chapter with respect to national banks, and §§ 6.4 and 165.8 of this chapter with respect to Federal savings associations, shall include a description of the steps the national bank or Federal savings association will take to correct the unsafe or unsound condition or practice. No plan shall be accepted unless it includes any performance guarantee described in section 38(e)(2)(C) of that Act by each company that controls the national bank or Federal savings association.

(c) *Review of capital restoration plans.* Within 60 days after receiving a capital restoration plan under this subpart, the OCC shall provide written notice to the national bank or Federal savings association of whether the plan has been approved. The OCC may extend the time within which notice regarding approval of a plan shall be provided.

(d) *Disapproval of capital restoration plan.* If a capital restoration plan is not approved by the OCC, the national bank or Federal savings association shall submit a revised capital restoration plan within the time specified by the OCC. Upon receiving notice that its capital restoration plan has not been approved, any undercapitalized national bank or Federal savings association (as defined in § 6.4) shall be subject to all of the provisions of section 38 and this part applicable to significantly undercapitalized institutions. These provisions shall be applicable until such time as a new or revised capital restoration plan submitted by the national bank or Federal savings association has been approved by the OCC.

(e) *Failure to submit a capital restoration plan.* A national bank or Federal savings association that is undercapitalized (as defined in § 6.4) and that fails to submit a written capital restoration plan within the period provided in this section shall, upon the expiration of that period, be subject to all of the provisions of section 38 and this part applicable to significantly undercapitalized national banks or Federal savings associations.

(f) *Failure to implement a capital restoration plan.* Any undercapitalized national bank or Federal savings association that fails, in any material respect, to implement a capital restoration plan shall be subject to all of the provisions of section 38 and this part applicable to significantly undercapitalized national banks or Federal savings associations.

(g) *Amendment of capital restoration plan.* A national bank or Federal savings association that has submitted an approved capital restoration plan may, after prior written notice to and approval by the OCC, amend the plan to reflect a change in circumstance. Until such time as a proposed amendment has been approved, the national bank or Federal savings association shall implement the capital restoration plan as approved prior to the proposed amendment.

(h) *Notice to FDIC.* Within 45 days of the effective date of OCC approval of a capital restoration plan, or any amendment to a capital restoration plan, the OCC shall provide a copy of the plan or amendment to the Federal Deposit Insurance Corporation.

(i) *Performance guarantee by companies that control a national bank or Federal savings association*—(1) *Limitation on liability*—(i) *Amount limitation.* The aggregate liability under the guarantee provided under section 38 and this subpart for all companies that control a specific national bank or Federal savings association that is required to submit a capital restoration plan under this subpart shall be limited to the lesser of:

(A) An amount equal to 5.0 percent of the national bank's or Federal savings association's total assets at the time the national bank or Federal savings association was notified or deemed to have notice that the national bank or Federal savings association was undercapitalized; or

(B) The amount necessary to restore the relevant capital measures of the national bank or Federal savings association to the levels required for the national bank or Federal savings association to be classified as adequately capitalized, as those capital measures and levels are defined at the time that the national bank or Federal savings association initially fails to comply with a capital restoration plan under this subpart.

(ii) *Limit on duration.* The guarantee and limit of liability under section 38 and this subpart shall expire after the OCC notifies the national bank or Federal savings association that it has remained adequately capitalized for each of four consecutive calendar quarters. The expiration or fulfillment by a company of a guarantee of a capital restoration plan shall not limit the liability of the company under any guarantee required or provided in connection with any capital restoration plan filed by the same national bank or Federal savings association after expiration of the first guarantee.

(iii) *Collection on guarantee.* Each company that controls a given national bank or Federal savings association shall be jointly and severally liable for the guarantee for such national bank or Federal savings association as required under section 38 and this subpart, and the OCC may require payment of the full amount of that guarantee from any or all of the companies issuing the guarantee.

(2) *Failure to provide guarantee.* In the event that a national bank or Federal savings association that is controlled by any company submits a capital restoration plan that does not contain the guarantee required under section 38(e)(2) of the FDI Act, the national bank or Federal savings association shall, upon submission of the plan, be subject to the provisions of section 38 and this part that are applicable to national banks or Federal savings associations that have not submitted an acceptable capital restoration plan.

(3) *Failure to perform guarantee.* Failure by any company that controls a national bank or Federal savings association to perform fully its guarantee of any capital plan shall constitute a material failure to implement the plan for purposes of section 38(f) of the FDI Act. Upon such failure, the national bank or Federal savings association shall be subject to the provisions of section 38 and this part that are applicable to national banks or Federal savings associations that have failed in a material respect to implement a capital restoration plan.

(j) *Enforcement of capital restoration plan.* The failure of a national bank or Federal savings association to implement, in any material respect, a capital restoration plan required under section 38 and this section shall subject the national bank or Federal savings association to the assessment of civil money penalties pursuant to section 8(i)(2)(A) of the FDI Act.

§6.6 Mandatory and discretionary supervisory actions.

(a) *Mandatory supervisory actions*—(1) *Provisions applicable to all national banks and Federal savings associations.* All national banks and Federal savings associations are subject to the restrictions contained in section 38(d) of the FDI Act on payment of distributions and management fees.

(2) *Provisions applicable to undercapitalized, significantly undercapitalized, and critically undercapitalized national banks or Federal savings associations.* Immediately upon receiving notice or being deemed to have notice, as provided in §6.3, that the national bank or Federal savings association is undercapitalized, significantly undercapitalized, or critically undercapitalized, the national bank or Federal savings association shall become subject to the provisions of section 38 of the FDI Act:

(i) Restricting payment of distributions and management fees (section 38(d));

(ii) Requiring that the OCC monitor the condition of the national bank or Federal savings association (section 38(e)(1));

(iii) Requiring submission of a capital restoration plan within the schedule established in this subpart (section 38(e)(2));

(iv) Restricting the growth of the national bank's or Federal savings association's assets (section 38(e)(3)); and

(v) Requiring prior approval of certain expansion proposals (section 38(e)(4)).

(3) *Additional provisions applicable to significantly undercapitalized, and critically undercapitalized national banks or Federal savings associations.* In addition to the provisions of section 38 of the FDI Act described in paragraph (a)(2) of this section, immediately upon receiving notice or being deemed to have notice, as provided in this subpart, that the national bank or Federal savings

association is significantly undercapitalized, or critically undercapitalized, or that the national bank or Federal savings association is subject to the provisions applicable to institutions that are significantly undercapitalized because it has failed to submit or implement, in any material respect, an acceptable capital restoration plan, the national bank or Federal savings association shall become subject to the provisions of section 38 of the FDI Act that restrict compensation paid to senior executive officers of the institution (section 38(f)(4)).

(4) *Additional provisions applicable to critically undercapitalized national banks or Federal savings associations.* In addition to the provisions of section 38 of the FDI Act described in paragraphs (a)(2) and (3) of this section, immediately upon receiving notice or being deemed to have notice, as provided in § 6.3, that the national bank or Federal savings association is critically undercapitalized, the national bank or Federal savings association shall become subject to the provisions of section 38 of the FDI Act:

(i) Restricting the activities of the national bank or Federal savings association (section 38 (h)(1)); and

(ii) Restricting payments on subordinated debt of the national bank or Federal savings association (section 38 (h)(2)).

(b) *Discretionary supervisory actions.* In taking any action under section 38 that is within the OCC's discretion to take in connection with a national bank or Federal savings association that is deemed to be undercapitalized, significantly undercapitalized, or critically undercapitalized, or has been reclassified as undercapitalized or significantly undercapitalized; an officer or director of such national bank or Federal savings association; or a company that controls such national bank or Federal savings association, the OCC shall follow the procedures for issuing directives under subpart B of this part and subpart N of part 19 of this chapter with respect to national banks and subpart B of this part and § 165.9 of this chapter with respect to Federal savings associations, unless otherwise provided in section 38 of the FDI Act or this part.

Subpart B—Directives To Take Prompt Corrective Action

§ 6.20 Scope.

The rules and procedures set forth in this subpart apply to insured national banks, insured Federal branches, Federal savings associations, and senior executive officers and directors of national banks and Federal savings associations that are subject to the provisions of section 38 of the Federal Deposit Insurance Act (section 38) and subpart A of this part.

§ 6.21 Notice of intent to issue a directive.

(a) *Notice of intent to issue a directive*—(1) *In general.* The OCC shall provide an undercapitalized, significantly undercapitalized, or critically undercapitalized national bank or Federal savings association prior written notice of the OCC's intention to issue a directive requiring such national bank, Federal savings association, or company to take actions or to follow proscriptions described in section 38 that are within the OCC's discretion to require or impose under section 38 of the FDI Act, including section 38(e)(5), (f)(2), (f)(3), or (f)(5). The national bank or Federal savings association shall have such time to respond to a proposed directive as provided under § 6.22.

(2) *Immediate issuance of final directive.* If the OCC finds it necessary in order to carry out the purposes of section 38 of the FDI Act, the OCC may, without providing the notice prescribed in paragraph (a)(1) of this section, issue a directive requiring a national bank or Federal savings association immediately to take actions or to follow proscriptions described in section 38 that are within the OCC's discretion to require or impose under section 38 of the FDI Act, including section 38(e)(5), (f)(2), (f)(3), or (f)(5). A national bank or Federal savings association that is subject to such an immediately effective directive may submit a written appeal of the directive to the OCC. Such an appeal must be received by the OCC within 14 calendar days of the issuance of the directive, unless the OCC permits a longer period. The OCC shall consider any such appeal, if filed in a

timely matter, within 60 days of receiving the appeal. During such period of review, the directive shall remain in effect unless the OCC, in its sole discretion, stays the effectiveness of the directive.

(b) *Contents of notice.* A notice of intention to issue a directive shall include:

(1) A statement of the national bank's or Federal savings association's capital measures and capital levels;

(2) A description of the restrictions, prohibitions or affirmative actions that the OCC proposes to impose or require;

(3) The proposed date when such restrictions or prohibitions would be effective or the proposed date for completion of such affirmative actions; and

(4) The date by which the national bank or Federal savings association subject to the directive may file with the OCC a written response to the notice.

§ 6.22 Response to notice.

(a) *Time for response.* A national bank or Federal savings association may file a written response to a notice of intent to issue a directive within the time period set by the OCC. The date shall be at least 14 calendar days from the date of the notice unless the OCC determines that a shorter period is appropriate in light of the financial condition of the national bank or Federal savings association or other relevant circumstances.

(b) *Content of response.* The response should include:

(1) An explanation why the action proposed by the OCC is not an appropriate exercise of discretion under section 38;

(2) Any recommended modification of the proposed directive; and

(3) Any other relevant information, mitigating circumstances, documentation, or other evidence in support of the position of the national bank or Federal savings association regarding the proposed directive.

(c) *Failure to file response.* Failure by a national bank or Federal savings association to file with the OCC, within the specified time period, a written response to a proposed directive shall constitute a waiver of the opportunity to respond and shall constitute consent to the issuance of the directive.

§ 6.23 Decision and issuance of a prompt corrective action directive.

(a) *OCC consideration of response.* After considering the response, the OCC may:

(1) Issue the directive as proposed or in modified form;

(2) Determine not to issue the directive and so notify the national bank or Federal savings association; or

(3) Seek additional information or clarification of the response from the national bank or Federal savings association, or any other relevant source.

(b) [Reserved]

§ 6.24 Request for modification or rescission of directive.

Any national bank or Federal savings association that is subject to a directive under this subpart may, upon a change in circumstances, request in writing that the OCC reconsider the terms of the directive, and may propose that the directive be rescinded or modified. Unless otherwise ordered by the OCC, the directive shall continue in place while such request is pending before the OCC.

§ 6.25 Enforcement of directive.

(a) *Judicial remedies.* Whenever a national bank or Federal savings association fails to comply with a directive issued under section 38, the OCC may seek enforcement of the directive in the appropriate United States district court pursuant to section 8(i)(1) of the FDI Act.

(b) *Administrative remedies.* Pursuant to section 8(i)(2)(A) of the FDI Act, the OCC may assess a civil money penalty against any national bank or Federal savings association that violates or otherwise fails to comply with any final directive issued under section 38 and against any institution-affiliated party who participates in such violation or noncompliance.

(c) *Other enforcement action.* In addition to the actions described in paragraphs (a) and (b) of this section, the OCC may seek enforcement of the provisions of section 38 or this part through any other judicial or administrative proceeding authorized by law.

PART 7—ACTIVITIES AND OPERATIONS

Subpart A—National Bank and Federal Savings Association Powers

Sec.
7.1000 National bank or Federal savings association ownership of property.
7.1001 National bank acting as general insurance agent.
7.1002 National bank acting as finder.
7.1003 Money lent by a national bank at banking offices or at facilities other than banking offices.
7.1004 Loans originating at facilities other than banking offices of a national bank.
7.1005 Credit decisions at other than banking offices of a national bank.
7.1006 Loan agreement providing for a national bank share in profits, income, or earnings or for stock warrants.
7.1007 National Bank Acceptances.
7.1008 Preparation by a national bank of income tax returns for customers or public.
7.1009 National bank holding collateral stock as nominee.
7.1010 Postal service by national bank.
7.1011 National bank acting as payroll issuer.
7.1012 Establishment, operation, or use of a messenger service by a national bank.
7.1014 Sale of money orders at nonbanking outlets by a national bank.
7.1015 National bank receipt of stock from a small business investment company.
7.1016 Independent undertakings issued by a national bank to pay against documents.
7.1017 National bank as guarantor or surety on indemnity bond.
7.1018 National bank automatic payment plan accounts.
7.1020 Purchase of open accounts by a national bank.
7.1021 National bank participation in financial literacy programs.
7.1022 National banks' authority to buy and sell exchange, coin, and bullion.
7.1023 Federal savings associations, prohibition on industrial or commercial metal dealing or investing.

Subpart B—National Bank Corporate Practices

7.2000 Corporate governance procedures.
7.2001 Notice of shareholders' meetings.
7.2002 Director or attorney as proxy.
7.2003 Annual meeting for election of directors.
7.2004 Honorary directors or advisory boards.
7.2005 Ownership of stock necessary to qualify as director.
7.2006 Cumulative voting in election of directors.
7.2007 Filling vacancies and increasing board of directors other than by shareholder action.
7.2008 Oath of directors.
7.2009 Quorum of the board of directors; proxies not permissible.
7.2010 Directors' responsibilities.
7.2011 Compensation plans.
7.2012 President as director; chief executive officer.
7.2013 Fidelity bonds covering officers and employees.
7.2014 Indemnification of institution-affiliated parties.
7.2015 Cashier.
7.2016 Restricting transfer of stock and record dates.
7.2017 Facsimile signatures on bank stock certificates.
7.2018 Lost stock certificates.
7.2019 Loans secured by a bank's own shares.
7.2020 Acquisition and holding of shares as treasury stock.
7.2021 Preemptive rights.
7.2022 Voting trusts.
7.2023 Reverse stock splits.
7.2024 Staggered terms for national bank directors and size of bank board.

Subpart C—Operations

7.3000 National bank hours and closings.
7.3001 Sharing national bank or Federal association space and employees.

Subpart D—Preemption

7.4000 Visitorial powers with respect to national banks.
7.4001 Charging interest by national banks at rates permitted competing institutions; charging interest to corporate borrowers.
7.4002 National bank charges.
7.4003 Establishment and operation of a remote service unit by a national bank.
7.4004 Establishment and operation of a deposit production office by a national bank.
7.4005 Combination of national bank loan production office, deposit production office, and remote service unit.
7.4006 [Reserved]
7.4007 Deposit-taking by national banks.
7.4008 Lending by national banks.
7.4009 [Reserved]
7.4010 Applicability of state law and visitorial powers to Federal savings associations and subsidiaries.

Subpart E—National Bank Electronic Activities

7.5000 Scope.

7.5001 Electronic activities that are part of, or incidental to, the business of banking.
7.5002 Furnishing of products and services by electronic means and facilities.
7.5003 Composite authority to engage in electronic activities.
7.5004 Sale of excess electronic capacity and by-products.
7.5005 National bank acting as digital certification authority.
7.5006 Data processing.
7.5007 Correspondent services.
7.5008 Location of national bank conducting electronic activities.
7.5009 Location under 12 U.S.C. 85 of national banks operating exclusively through the Internet.
7.5010 Shared electronic space.

AUTHORITY: 12 U.S.C. 1 *et seq.*, 25b, 29, 71, 71a, 92, 92a, 93, 93a, 95(b)(1), 371, 371d, 481, 484, 1463, 1464, 1465, 1818, 1828(m) and 5412(b)(2)(B).

SOURCE: 61 FR 4862, Feb. 9, 1996, unless otherwise noted.

Subpart A—National Bank and Federal Savings Association Powers

§ 7.1000 National bank or Federal savings association ownership of property.

(a) *Investment in real estate necessary for the transaction of business*—(1) *In general.* A national bank or Federal savings association may invest in real estate that is necessary for the transaction of its business.

(2) *Type of real estate.* Real estate investments permissible under this section include:

(i) Premises that are owned and occupied (or to be occupied, if under construction) by the national bank or Federal savings association, or its respective branches or consolidated subsidiaries;

(ii) Real estate acquired and intended, in good faith, for use in future expansion;

(iii) Parking facilities that are used by customers or employees of the national bank or Federal savings association, or its respective branches or consolidated subsidiaries;

(iv) Residential property for the use of officers or employees of the national bank or Federal savings association who are:

(A) Located in remote areas where suitable housing at a reasonable price is not readily available; or

(B) Temporarily assigned to a foreign country, including foreign nationals temporarily assigned to the United States; and

(v) Property for the use of national bank or Federal savings association officers, employees, or customers, or for the temporary lodging of such persons in areas where suitable commercial lodging is not readily available, provided that the purchase and operation of the property qualifies as a deductible business expense for Federal tax purposes.

(3) *Permissible means of holding.* (i) A national bank or Federal savings association may acquire and hold real estate under this paragraph (a) by any reasonable and prudent means, including ownership in fee, a leasehold estate, or in an interest in a cooperative. The national bank or Federal savings association may hold this real estate directly or through one or more subsidiaries. The national bank or Federal savings association may organize a banking premises subsidiary as a corporation, partnership, or similar entity (*e.g.*, a limited liability company).

(ii) A Federal savings association also may acquire and hold banking premises through a service corporation in accordance with 12 CFR 5.59.

(b) *Fixed assets.* A national bank or Federal savings association may own fixed assets necessary for the transaction of its business, such as fixtures, furniture, and data processing equipment.

(c) *Investment in banking premises*—(1) *Investment limitation.* Twelve CFR 5.37(d)(1)(i) and (d)(3)(i) provide quantitative investment limitations that govern when OCC approval is required for a national bank or Federal savings association to invest in banking premises.

(2) *Premises approval.* (i) A national bank or Federal savings association shall seek approval from the OCC in accordance with 12 CFR 5.37(d).

(ii) A Federal savings association that invests in banking premises through a service corporation shall comply with the quantitative limitations in 12 CFR 5.37(d) and, to the extent applicable, 12 CFR 5.59.

(3) *Option to purchase.* An unexercised option to purchase banking premises or

stock in a corporation holding banking premises is not an investment in banking premises. However, a national bank or Federal savings association seeking to exercise such an option must comply with the requirements in 12 CFR 5.37(d).

(d) *Future national bank or Federal savings association expansion.* A national bank or Federal savings association normally should use real estate acquired for future national bank or Federal savings association expansion within five years. After holding such real estate for one year, the national bank or Federal savings association shall state, by resolution of its board of directors or an appropriately authorized bank or savings association official or subcommittee of the board, definite plans for its use. The resolution or other official action must be available for inspection by OCC examiners.

(e) *Transition.* If, on May 18, 2015, a Federal savings association holds an investment in real estate, fixed assets, banking premises, or other real property that complies with the legal requirements in effect prior to May 18, 2015, but would violate any provision of this section or §5.37, the savings association may continue to hold such investment in accordance with the prior legal requirements. However, a Federal savings association that holds such an investment shall not modify, expand or improve this investment, except for routine maintenance, without the prior approval of the appropriate OCC supervisory office.

[80 FR 28470, May 18, 2015]

§7.1001 National bank acting as general insurance agent.

Pursuant to 12 U.S.C. 92, a national bank may act as an agent for any fire, life, or other insurance company in any place the population of which does not exceed 5,000 inhabitants. This provision is applicable to any office of a national bank when the office is located in a community having a population of less than 5,000, even though the principal office of such bank is located in a community whose population exceeds 5,000.

§7.1002 National bank acting as finder.

(a) *General.* It is part of the business of banking under 12 U.S.C. 24(Seventh) for a national bank to act as a finder, bringing together interested parties to a transaction.

(b) *Permissible finder activities.* A national bank that acts as a finder may identify potential parties, make inquiries as to interest, introduce or arrange contacts or meetings of interested parties, act as an intermediary between interested parties, and otherwise bring parties together for a transaction that the parties themselves negotiate and consummate. The following list provides examples of permissible finder activities. This list is illustrative and not exclusive; the OCC may determine that other activities are permissible pursuant to a national bank's authority to act as a finder.

(1) Communicating information about providers of products and services, and proposed offering prices and terms to potential markets for these products and services;

(2) Communicating to the seller an offer to purchase or a request for information, including forwarding completed applications, application fees, and requests for information to third-party providers;

(3) Arranging for third-party providers to offer reduced rates to those customers referred by the bank;

(4) Providing administrative, clerical, and record keeping functions related to the bank's finder activity, including retaining copies of documents, instructing and assisting individuals in the completion of documents, scheduling sales calls on behalf of sellers, and conducting market research to identify potential new customers for retailers;

(5) Conveying between interested parties expressions of interest, bids, offers, orders, and confirmations relating to a transaction;

(6) Conveying other types of information between potential buyers, sellers, and other interested parties; and

(7) Establishing rules of general applicability governing the use and operation of the finder service, including rules that:

(i) Govern the submission of bids and offers by buyers, sellers, and other interested parties that use the finder service and the circumstances under which the finder service will pair bids and offers submitted by buyers, sellers, and other interested parties; and

(ii) Govern the manner in which buyers, sellers, and other interested parties may bind themselves to the terms of a specific transaction.

(c) *Limitation.* The authority to act as a finder does not enable a national bank to engage in brokerage activities that have not been found to be permissible for national banks.

(d) *Advertisement and fee.* Unless otherwise prohibited by Federal law, a national bank may advertise the availability of, and accept a fee for, the services provided pursuant to this section.

[67 FR 35004, May 17, 2002]

§ 7.1003 Money lent by a national bank at banking offices or at facilities other than banking offices.

(a) *General.* For purposes of what constitutes a branch within the meaning of 12 U.S.C. 36(j) and 12 CFR 5.30, "money" is deemed to be "lent" only at the place, if any, where the borrower in-person receives loan proceeds directly from bank funds:

(1) From the lending bank or its operating subsidiary; or

(2) At a facility that is established by the lending bank or its operating subsidiary.

(b) *Receipt of bank funds representing loan proceeds.* Loan proceeds directly from bank funds may be received by a borrower in person at a place that is not the bank's main office and is not licensed as a branch without violating 12 U.S.C. 36, 12 U.S.C. 81 and 12 CFR 5.30, provided that a third party is used to deliver the funds and the place is not established by the lending bank or its operating subsidiary. A third party includes a person who satisfies the requirements of § 7.1012(c)(2), or one who customarily delivers loan proceeds directly from bank funds under accepted industry practice, such as an attorney or escrow agent at a real estate closing.

§ 7.1004 Loans originating at facilities other than banking offices of a national bank.

(a) *General.* A national bank may use the services of, and compensate persons not employed by, the bank for originating loans.

(b) *Approval.* An employee or agent of a national bank or of its operating subsidiary may originate a loan at a site other than the main office or a branch office of the bank. This action does not violate 12 U.S.C. 36 and 12 U.S.C. 81 if the loan is approved and made at the main office or a branch office of the bank or at an office of the operating subsidiary located on the premises of, or contiguous to, the main office or branch office of the bank.

§ 7.1005 Credit decisions at other than banking offices of a national bank.

A national bank and its operating subsidiary may make a credit decision regarding a loan application at a site other than the main office or a branch office of the bank without violating 12 U.S.C. 36 and 12 U.S.C. 81, provided that "money" is not deemed to be "lent" at those other sites within the meaning of § 7.1003.

§ 7.1006 Loan agreement providing for a national bank share in profits, income, or earnings or for stock warrants.

A national bank may take as consideration for a loan a share in the profit, income, or earnings from a business enterprise of a borrower. A national bank also may take as consideration for a loan a stock warrant issued by a business enterprise of a borrower, provided that the bank does not exercise the warrant. The share or stock warrant may be taken in addition to, or in lieu of, interest. The borrower's obligation to repay principal, however, may not be conditioned upon the value of the profit, income, or earnings of the business enterprise or upon the value of the warrant received.

§ 7.1007 National Bank Acceptances.

A national bank is not limited in the character of acceptances it may make in financing credit transactions. Bankers' acceptances may be used for such purpose, since the making of acceptances is an essential part of banking authorized by 12 U.S.C. 24.

§ 7.1008 Preparation by a national bank of income tax returns for customers or public.

A national bank may assist its customers in preparing their tax returns, either gratuitously or for a fee.

[68 FR 70131, Dec. 17, 2003]

§ 7.1009 National bank holding collateral stock as nominee.

A national bank that accepts stock as collateral for a loan may have such stock transferred to the bank's name as nominee.

§ 7.1010 Postal service by national bank.

(a) *General.* A national bank may maintain and operate a postal substation on banking premises and receive income from it. The services performed by the substation are those permitted under applicable rules of the United States Postal Service and may include meter stamping of letters and packages, and the sale of related insurance. The bank may advertise, develop, and extend the services of the substation for the purpose of attracting customers to the bank.

(b) *Postal regulations.* A national bank operating a postal substation shall do so in accordance with the rules and regulations of the United States Postal Service. The national bank shall keep the books and records of the substation separate from those of other banking operations. Under 39 U.S.C. 404 and any regulations issued pursuant thereto, the United States Postal Service may inspect the books and records of the substation.

§ 7.1011 National bank acting as payroll issuer.

A national bank may disburse to an employee of a customer payroll funds deposited with the bank by that customer. The bank may disburse those funds by direct payment to the employee, by crediting an account in the employee's name at the disbursing bank, or by forwarding funds to another institution in which an employee maintains an account.

§ 7.1012 Establishment, operation, or use of a messenger service by a national bank.

(a) *Definition.* For purposes of this section, a "messenger service" means any service, such as a courier service or armored car service, used by a national bank and its customers to pick up from, and deliver to, specific customers at locations such as their homes or offices, items relating to transactions between the bank and those customers.

(b) *Pick-up and delivery of items constituting nonbranching activities.* Pursuant to 12 U.S.C. 24 (Seventh), a national bank may establish and operate a messenger service, or use, with its customers, a third party messenger service. The bank may use the messenger service to transport items relevant to the bank's transactions with its customers without regard to the branching limitations set forth in 12 U.S.C. 36, provided the service does not engage in branching functions within the meaning of 12 U.S.C. 36(j). In establishing or using such a facility, the national bank may establish terms, conditions, and limitations consistent with this section and appropriate to assure compliance with safe and sound banking practices.

(c) *Pick-up and delivery of items constituting branching functions by a messenger service established by a third party.* (1) Pursuant to 12 U.S.C. 24 (Seventh), a national bank and its customers may use a messenger service to pick up from, and deliver to customers items that relate to branching functions within the meaning of 12 U.S.C. 36, provided the messenger service is established and operated by a third party. In using such a facility, a national bank may establish terms, conditions, and limitations, consistent with this section and appropriate to assure compliance with safe and sound banking practices.

(2) The OCC reviews whether a messenger service is established by a third party on a case-by-case basis, considering all of the circumstances. However, a messenger service is clearly established by a third party if:

(i) A party other than the national bank owns or rents the messenger service and its facilities and employs the persons who provide the service;

(ii)(A) The messenger service retains the discretion to determine in its own business judgment which customers and geographic areas it will serve; or

(B) If the messenger service and the bank are under common ownership or control, the messenger service actually provides its services to the general public, including other depository institutions, and retains the discretion to determine in its own business judgment which customers and geographic areas it will serve;

(iii) The messenger service maintains ultimate responsibility for scheduling, movement, and routing;

(iv) The messenger service does not operate under the name of the bank, and the bank and the messenger service do not advertise, or otherwise represent, that the bank itself is providing the service, although the bank may advertise that its customers may use one or more third party messenger services to transact business with the bank;

(v) The messenger service assumes responsibility for the items during transit and for maintaining adequate insurance covering thefts, employee fidelity, and other in-transit losses; and

(vi) The messenger service acts as the agent for the customer when the items are in transit. The bank deems items intended for deposit to be deposited when credited to the customer's account at the bank's main office, one of its branches, or another permissible facility, such as a back office facility that is not a branch. The bank deems items representing withdrawals to be paid when the items are given to the messenger service.

(3) A national bank may defray all or part of the costs incurred by a customer in transporting items through a messenger service. Payment of those costs may only cover expenses associated with each transaction involving the customer and the messenger service. The national bank may impose terms, conditions, and limitations that it deems appropriate with respect to the payment of such costs.

(d) *Pickup and delivery of items pertaining to branching activities where the messenger service is established by the national bank.* A national bank may establish and operate a messenger service to transport items relevant to the bank's transactions with its customers if such transactions constitute one or more branching functions within the meaning of 12 U.S.C. 36(j), provided the bank receives approval to establish a branch pursuant to 12 CFR 5.30.

[61 FR 4862, Feb. 9, 1996, as amended at 64 FR 60098, Nov. 4, 1999]

§ 7.1014 Sale of money orders at nonbanking outlets by a national bank.

A national bank may designate bonded agents to sell the bank's money orders at nonbanking outlets. The responsibility of both the bank and its agent should be defined in a written agreement setting forth the duties of both parties and providing for remuneration of the agent. The bank's agents need not report on sales and transmit funds from the nonbanking outlets more frequently than at the end of the third business day following receipt of the funds.

§ 7.1015 National bank receipt of stock from a small business investment company.

A national bank may purchase the stock of a small business investment company (SBIC) (*see* 15 U.S.C. 682(b)), and may receive the benefits of such stock ownership (*e.g.*, stock dividends). The receipt and retention of a dividend by a national bank from an SBIC in the form of stock of a corporate borrower of the SBIC is not a purchase of stock within the meaning of 12 U.S.C. 24 (Seventh).

§ 7.1016 Independent undertakings issued by a national bank to pay against documents.

(a) *General authority*. A national bank may issue and commit to issue letters of credit and other independent undertakings within the scope of the applicable laws or rules of practice recognized by law.[1] Under such letters of credit

[1] Examples of such laws or rules of practice include: The applicable version of Article 5 of the Uniform Commercial Code (UCC) (1962, as amended 1990) or revised Article 5 of the UCC (as amended 1995) (available from West

Continued

and other independent undertakings, the bank's obligation to honor depends upon the presentation of specified documents and not upon nondocumentary conditions or resolution of questions of fact or law at issue between the applicant and the beneficiary. A national bank may also confirm or otherwise undertake to honor or purchase specified documents upon their presentation under another person's independent undertaking within the scope of such laws or rules.

(b) *Safety and soundness considerations*—(1) *Terms*. As a matter of safe and sound banking practice, banks that issue independent undertakings should not be exposed to undue risk. At a minimum, banks should consider the following:

(i) The independent character of the undertaking should be apparent from its terms (such as terms that subject it to laws or rules providing for its independent character);

(ii) The undertaking should be limited in amount;

(iii) The undertaking should:

(A) Be limited in duration; or

(B) Permit the bank to terminate the undertaking either on a periodic basis (consistent with the bank's ability to make any necessary credit assessments) or at will upon either notice or payment to the beneficiary; or

(C) Entitle the bank to cash collateral from the applicant on demand (with a right to accelerate the applicant's obligations, as appropriate); and

(iv) The bank either should be fully collateralized or have a post-honor right of reimbursement from the applicant or from another issuer of an independent undertaking. Alternatively, if the bank's undertaking is to purchase documents of title, securities, or other valuable documents, the bank should obtain a first priority right to realize on the documents if the bank is not otherwise to be reimbursed.

(2) *Additional considerations in special circumstances*. Certain undertakings require particular protections against credit, operational, and market risk:

(i) In the event that the undertaking is to honor by delivery of an item of value other than money, the bank should ensure that market fluctuations that affect the value of the item will not cause the bank to assume undue market risk;

(ii) In the event that the undertaking provides for automatic renewal, the terms for renewal should be consistent with the bank's ability to make any necessary credit assessments prior to renewal;

(iii) In the event that a bank issues an undertaking for its own account, the underlying transaction for which it is issued must be within the bank's authority and comply with any safety and soundness requirements applicable to that transaction.

(3) *Operational expertise*. The bank should possess operational expertise that is commensurate with the sophistication of its independent undertaking activities.

(4) *Documentation*. The bank must accurately reflect the bank's undertakings in its records, including any acceptance or deferred payment or other absolute obligation arising out of its contingent undertaking.

(c) *Coverage*. An independent undertaking within the meaning of this section is not subject to the provisions of § 7.1017.

[61 FR 4862, Feb. 9, 1996, as amended at 64 FR 60099, Nov. 4, 1999; 68 FR 70131, Dec. 17, 2003; 73 FR 22241, Apr. 24, 2008]

Publishing Co., 1/800/328–4880); the Uniform Customs and Practice for Documentary Credits (International Chamber of Commerce (ICC) Publication No. 600 or any applicable prior version) (available from ICC Publishing, Inc., 212/206–1150; *http://www.iccwbo.org*); the Supplements to UCP 500 & 600 for Electronic Presentation (eUCP v. 1.0 & 1.1) (Supplements to the Uniform Customs and Practices for Documentary Credits for Electronic Presentation) (available from ICC Publishing, Inc., 212/206–1150; *http://www.iccwbo.org)* International Standby Practices (ISP98) (ICC Publication No. 590) (available from the Institute of International Banking Law & Practice, 301/869–9840; *http://www.iiblp.org*); the United Nations Convention on Independent Guarantees and Standby Letters of Credit (adopted by the U.N. General Assembly in 1995 and signed by the U.S. in 1997) (available from the U.N. Commission on International Trade Law, 212/963–5353); and the Uniform Rules for Bank-to-Bank Reimbursements Under Documentary Credits (ICC Publication No. 525) (available from ICC Publishing, Inc., 212/206–1150; *http://www.iccwbo.org*); as any of the foregoing may be amended from time to time.

§ 7.1017 National bank as guarantor or surety on indemnity bond.

(a) A national bank may lend its credit, bind itself as a surety to indemnify another, or otherwise become a guarantor (including, pursuant to 12 CFR 28.4, guaranteeing the deposits and other liabilities of its Edge corporations and Agreement corporations and of its corporate instrumentalities in foreign countries), if:

(1) The bank has a substantial interest in the performance of the transaction involved (for example, a bank, as fiduciary, has a sufficient interest in the faithful performance by a cofiduciary of its duties to act as surety on the bond of such cofiduciary); or

(2) The transaction is for the benefit of a customer and the bank obtains from the customer a segregated deposit that is sufficient in amount to cover the bank's total potential liability. A segregated deposit under this section includes collateral:

(i) In which the bank has perfected its security interest (for example, if the collateral is a printed security, the bank must have obtained physical control of the security, and, if the collateral is a book entry security, the bank must have properly recorded its security interest); and

(ii) That has a market value, at the close of each business day, equal to the bank's total potential liability and is composed of:

(A) Cash;

(B) Obligations of the United States or its agencies;

(C) Obligations fully guaranteed by the United States or its agencies as to principal and interest; or

(D) Notes, drafts, or bills of exchange or bankers' acceptances that are eligible for rediscount or purchase by a Federal Reserve Bank; or

(iii) That has a market value, at the close of each business day, equal to 110 percent of the bank's total potential liability and is composed of obligations of a State or political subdivision of a State.

(b) In addition to paragraph (a) of this section, a national bank may guarantee obligations of a customer, subsidiary or affiliate that are financial in character, provided the amount of the bank's financial obligation is reasonably ascertainable and otherwise consistent with applicable law.

[61 FR 4862, Feb. 9, 1996, as amended at 64 FR 60099, Nov. 4, 1999; 73 FR 22241, Apr. 24, 2008]

§ 7.1018 National bank automatic payment plan accounts.

A national bank may, for the benefit and convenience of its savings depositors, adopt an automatic payment plan under which a savings account will earn dividends at the current rate paid on regular savings accounts. The depositor, upon reaching a previously designated age, receives his or her accumulated savings and earned interest in installments of equal amounts over a specified period.

§ 7.1020 Purchase of open accounts by a national bank.

(a) *General.* The purchase of open accounts is a part of the business of banking and within the power of a national bank.

(b) *Export transactions.* A national bank may purchase open accounts in connection with export transactions; the accounts should be protected by insurance such as that provided by the Foreign Credit Insurance Association and the Export-Import Bank.

§ 7.1021 National bank participation in financial literacy programs.

A national bank may participate in a financial literacy program on the premises of, or at a facility used by, a school. The school premises or facility will not be considered a branch of the bank if:

(a) The bank does not establish and operate the school premises or facility on which the financial literacy program is conducted; and

(b) The principal purpose of the financial literacy program is educational. For example, a program is educational if it is designed to teach students the principles of personal economics or the benefits of saving for the future, and is not designed for the purpose of profit-making.

[66 FR 34791, July 2, 2001]

§ 7.1022 National banks' authority to buy and sell exchange, coin, and bullion.

(a) In this section, *industrial or commercial metal* means metal (including an alloy) in a physical form primarily suited to industrial or commercial use, for example, copper cathodes.

(b) *Scope of authorization.* Section 24(Seventh) of the National Bank Act authorizes national banks to buy and sell exchange, coin, and bullion. Industrial or commercial metal is not exchange, coin, and bullion within the meaning of this authorization.

(c) *Buying and selling metal as part of or incidental to the business of banking.* Section 24(Seventh) authorizes national banks to engage in activities that are part of, or incidental to, the business of banking. Buying and selling industrial or commercial metal for the purpose of dealing or investing in that metal is not part of or incidental to the business of banking pursuant to section 24(Seventh). Accordingly, national banks may not acquire industrial or commercial metal for purposes of dealing or investing.

(d) *Other authorities not affected.* This section shall not be construed to preclude a national bank from acquiring or selling metal in connection with its incidental authority to foreclose on loan collateral, compromise doubtful claims, or avoid loss in connection with a debt previously contracted. This section also shall not be construed to preclude a national bank from buying and selling physical metal to hedge a derivative for which that metal is the reference asset so long as the amount of the physical metal used for hedging purposes is nominal.

(e) *Nonconforming holdings.* National banks that hold industrial or commercial metal as a result of dealing or investing in that metal shall dispose of such metal as soon as practicable, but not later than one year from the effective date of this regulation. The OCC may grant up to four separate one-year extensions to dispose of industrial or commercial metal if a national bank makes a good faith effort to dispose of the metal and retention of the metal for an additional year is not inconsistent with the safe and sound operation of the bank.

[81 FR 96360, Dec. 30, 2016]

§ 7.1023 Federal savings associations, prohibition on industrial or commercial metal dealing or investing.

(a) In this section, *industrial or commercial metal* means metal (including an alloy) in a physical form primarily suited to industrial or commercial use, for example, copper cathodes.

(b) Federal savings associations may not deal or invest in industrial or commercial metal.

(c) *Other authorities not affected.* This section shall not be construed to preclude a federal savings association from acquiring or selling metal in connection with its authority to foreclose on loan collateral, compromise doubtful claims, or avoid loss in connection with a debt previously contracted.

(d) *Nonconforming holdings.* Federal savings associations that hold industrial or commercial metal as a result of dealing or investing in that metal shall dispose of such metal as soon as practicable, but not later than one year from the effective date of this regulation. The OCC may grant up to four separate one-year extensions to dispose of industrial or commercial metal if a federal savings association makes a good faith effort to dispose of the metal and retention of the metal for an additional year is not inconsistent with safe and sound operation of the association.

[81 FR 96360, Dec. 30, 2016]

Subpart B—National Bank Corporate Practices

§ 7.2000 Corporate governance procedures.

(a) *General.* A national bank proposing to engage in a corporate governance procedure shall comply with applicable Federal banking statutes and regulations, and safe and sound banking practices.

(b) *Other sources of guidance.* To the extent not inconsistent with applicable Federal banking statutes or regulations, or bank safety and soundness, a national bank may elect to follow the corporate governance procedures of the law of the state in which the main office of the bank is located, the law of the state in which the holding company of the bank is incorporated, the Delaware General Corporation Law, Del. Code Ann. tit. 8 (1991, as amended 1994, and as amended thereafter), or the Model Business Corporation Act (1984, as amended 1994, and as amended thereafter). A national bank shall designate in its bylaws the body of law selected for its corporate governance procedures.

(c) *No-objection procedures.* The OCC also considers requests for its staff's position on the ability of a national bank to engage in a particular corporate governance procedure in accordance with the no-objection procedures set forth in Banking Circular 205 or any subsequently published agency procedures.[2] Requests should demonstrate how the proposed practice is not inconsistent with applicable Federal statutes or regulations, and is consistent with safe and sound banking practices.

[61 FR 4862, Feb. 9, 1996, as amended at 79 FR 15641, Mar. 21, 2014; 80 FR 28471, May 18, 2015]

§ 7.2001 Notice of shareholders' meetings.

A national bank must mail shareholders notice of the time, place, and purpose of all shareholders' meetings at least 10 days prior to the meeting by first class mail, unless the OCC determines that an emergency circumstance exists. Where a national bank is a wholly-owned subsidiary, the sole shareholder is permitted to waive notice of the shareholder's meeting. The articles of association, bylaws, or law applicable to a national bank may require a longer period of notice.

§ 7.2002 Director or attorney as proxy.

Any person or group of persons, except the bank's officers, clerks, tellers, or bookkeepers, may be designated to act as proxy. The bank's directors or attorneys may act as proxy if they are not also employed as an officer, clerk, teller or bookkeeper of the bank.

[2] Available upon request from the OCC Communications Division, 400 7th Street SW., Washington, DC 20219, (202) 649–6700.

§ 7.2003 Annual meeting for election of directors.

When the day fixed for the regular annual meeting of the shareholders falls on a legal holiday in the state in which the bank is located, the shareholders' meeting shall be held, and the directors elected, on the next following banking day.

§ 7.2004 Honorary directors or advisory boards.

A national bank may appoint honorary or advisory members of a board of directors to act in advisory capacities without voting power or power of final decision in matters concerning the business of the bank. Any listing of honorary or advisory directors must distinguish between them and the bank's board of directors or indicate their advisory status.

§ 7.2005 Ownership of stock necessary to qualify as director.

(a) *General.* A national bank director must own a qualifying equity interest in a national bank or a company that has control of a national bank. The director must own the qualifying equity interest in his or her own right and meet a certain minimum threshold ownership.

(b) *Qualifying equity interest*—(1) *Minimum required equity interest.* For purposes of this section, a qualifying equity interest includes common or preferred stock of the bank or of a company that controls the bank that has not less than an aggregate par value of $1,000, an aggregate shareholders' equity of $1,000, or an aggregate fair market value of $1,000.

(i) The value of the common or preferred stock held by a national bank director is valued as of the date purchased or the date on which the individual became a director, whichever value is greater.

(ii) In the case of a company that owns more than one national bank, a director may use his or her equity interest in the controlling company to satisfy, in whole or in part, the equity interest requirement for any or all of the controlled national banks.

(iii) Upon request, the OCC may consider whether other interests in a company controlling a national bank constitute an interest equivalent to $1,000 par value of national bank stock.

(2) *Joint ownership and tenancy in common.* Shares held jointly or as a tenant in common are qualifying shares held by a director in his or her own right only to the extent of the aggregate value of the shares which the director would be entitled to receive on dissolution of the joint tenancy or tenancy in common.

(3) *Shares in a living trust.* Shares deposited by a person in a living trust (inter vivos trust) as to which the person is a trustee and retains an absolute power of revocation are shares owned by the person in his or her own right.

(4) *Other arrangements*—(i) *Shares held through retirement plans and similar arrangements.* A director may hold his or her qualifying interest through a profit-sharing plan, individual retirement account, retirement plan, or similar arrangement, if the director retains beneficial ownership and legal control over the shares.

(ii) *Shares held subject to buyback agreements.* A director may acquire and hold his or her qualifying interest pursuant to a stock repurchase or buyback agreement with a transferring shareholder under which the director purchases the qualifying shares subject to an agreement that the transferring shareholder will repurchase the shares when, for any reason, the director ceases to serve in that capacity. The agreement may give the transferring shareholder a right of first refusal to repurchase the qualifying shares if the director seeks to transfer ownership of the shares to a third person.

(iii) *Assignment of right to dividends or distributions.* A director may assign the right to receive all dividends or distributions on his or her qualifying shares to another, including a transferring shareholder, if the director retains beneficial ownership and legal control over the shares.

(iv) *Execution of proxy.* A director may execute a revocable or irrevocable proxy authorizing another, including a transferring shareholder, to vote his or her qualifying shares, provided the director retains beneficial ownership and legal control over the shares.

(c) *Non-qualifying ownership.* The following are not shares held by a director in his or her own right:

(1) Shares pledged by the holder to secure a loan. However, all or part of the funds used to purchase the required qualifying equity interest may be borrowed from any party, including the bank or its affiliates;

(2) Shares purchased subject to an absolute option vested in the seller to repurchase the shares within a specified period; and

(3) Shares deposited in a voting trust where the depositor surrenders:

(i) Legal ownership (depositor ceases to be registered owner of the stock);

(ii) Power to vote the stock or to direct how it shall be voted; or

(iii) Power to transfer legal title to the stock.

[61 FR 4862, Feb. 9, 1996, as amended at 64 FR 60099, Nov. 4, 1999]

§ 7.2006 Cumulative voting in election of directors.

When electing directors, a shareholder shall have as many votes as the number of directors to be elected multiplied by the number of the shareholder's shares. If permitted by the national bank's articles of association, the shareholder may cast all these votes for one candidate or distribute the votes among as many candidates as the shareholder chooses. If, after the first ballot, subsequent ballots are necessary to elect directors, a shareholder may not vote shares that he or she has already fully cumulated and voted in favor of a successful candidate.

[61 FR 4862, Feb. 9, 1996, as amended at 73 FR 22241, Apr. 24, 2008]

§ 7.2007 Filling vacancies and increasing board of directors other than by shareholder action.

(a) *Increasing board of directors.* If authorized by the bank's articles of association, between shareholder meetings a majority of the board of directors may increase the number of the bank's directors within the limits specified in 12 U.S.C. 71a. The board of directors may increase the number of directors only by up to two directors, when the number of directors last elected by shareholders was 15 or fewer, and by up to four directors, when the number of directors last elected by shareholders was 16 or more.

(b) *Vacancies.* If a vacancy occurs on the board of directors, including a vacancy resulting from an increase in the number of directors, the vacancy may be filled by the shareholders, a majority of the board of directors remaining in office, or, if the directors remaining in office constitute fewer than a quorum, by an affirmative vote of a majority of all the directors remaining in office.

§ 7.2008 Oath of directors.

(a) *Administration of the oath.* A notary public, including one who is a director but not an officer of the national bank, may administer the oath of directors. Any person, other than an officer of the bank, having an official seal and authorized by the state to administer oaths, may also administer the oath.

(b) *Execution of the oath.* Each director shall execute either a joint or individual oath at the first meeting of the board of directors that the director attends after the director is appointed or elected. A director shall take another oath upon re-election, notwithstanding uninterrupted service. Appropriate sample oaths may be found in the Charter Booklet of the Comptroller's Licensing Manual available at *www.occ.gov.*

(c) *Filing and recordkeeping.* A national bank must file the original executed oaths of directors with the appropriate OCC licensing office, as defined in 12 CFR 5.3(c), and retain a copy in the bank's records.

[61 FR 4862, Feb. 9, 1996, as amended at 64 FR 60099, Nov. 4, 1999; 82 FR 8104, Jan. 23, 2017]

§ 7.2009 Quorum of the board of directors; proxies not permissible.

A national bank shall provide in its articles of association or bylaws that for the transaction of business, a quorum of the board of directors is at least a majority of the entire board then in office. A national bank director may not vote by proxy.

§ 7.2010 Directors' responsibilities.

The business and affairs of the bank shall be managed by or under the direction of the board of directors. The board of directors should refer to OCC published guidance for additional information regarding responsibilities of directors.

§ 7.2011 Compensation plans.

Consistent with safe and sound banking practices and the compensation provisions of 12 CFR part 30, a national bank may adopt compensation plans, including, among others, the following:

(a) *Bonus and profit-sharing plans.* A national bank may adopt a bonus or profit-sharing plan designed to ensure adequate remuneration of bank officers and employees.

(b) *Pension plans.* A national bank may provide employee pension plans and make reasonable contributions to the cost of the pension plan.

(c) *Employee stock option and stock purchase plans.* A national bank may provide employee stock option and stock purchase plans.

§ 7.2012 President as director; chief executive officer.

Pursuant to 12 U.S.C. 76, the president of a national bank must be a member of the board of directors, but a director other than the president may be elected chairman of the board. A person other than the president may serve as chief executive officer, and this person is not required to be a director of the bank.

§ 7.2013 Fidelity bonds covering officers and employees.

(a) *Adequate coverage.* All officers and employees of a national bank or Federal savings association must have adequate fidelity bond coverage. The failure of directors to require bonds with adequate sureties and in sufficient amount may make the directors liable for any losses that the bank or savings association sustains because of the absence of such bonds. Directors should not serve as sureties on such bonds. Directors should consider whether agents who have access to assets of the bank or savings association should also have fidelity bond coverage.

(b) *Factors.* The board of directors of the national bank or Federal savings association, or a committee thereof, must determine the amount of such coverage, premised upon a consideration of factors, including:

(1) Internal auditing safeguards employed;

(2) Number of employees;

(3) Amount of deposit liabilities; and

(4) Amount of cash and securities normally held by the bank or savings association.

[61 FR 4862, Feb. 9, 1996, as amended at 82 FR 8104, Jan. 23, 2017]

§ 7.2014 Indemnification of institution-affiliated parties.

(a) *Administrative proceedings or civil actions initiated by Federal banking agencies.* A national bank may only make or agree to make indemnification payments to an institution-affiliated party with respect to an administrative proceeding or civil action initiated by any Federal banking agency, that are reasonable and consistent with the requirements of 12 U.S.C. 1828(k) and the implementing regulations thereunder. The term "institution-affiliated party" has the same meaning as set forth at 12 U.S.C. 1813(u).

(b) *Administrative proceeding or civil actions not initiated by a Federal banking agency*—(1) *General.* In cases involving an administrative proceeding or civil action not initiated by a Federal banking agency, a national bank may indemnify an institution-affiliated party for damages and expenses, including the advancement of expenses and legal fees, in accordance with the law of the state in which the main office of the bank is located, the law of the state in which the bank's holding company is incorporated, or the relevant provisions of the Model Business Corporation Act (1984, as amended 1994, and as amended thereafter), or Delaware General Corporation Law, Del. Code Ann. tit. 8 (1991, as amended 1994, and as amended thereafter), provided such payments are consistent with safe and sound banking practices. A national bank shall designate in its bylaws the body of law selected for making indemnification payments under this paragraph.

(2) *Insurance premiums.* A national bank may provide for the payment of reasonable premiums for insurance covering the expenses, legal fees, and liability of institution-affiliated parties to the extent that the expenses, fees, or liability could be indemnified under paragraph (b)(1) of this section.

§ 7.2015 Cashier.

A national bank's bylaws, board of directors, or a duly designated officer may assign some or all of the duties previously performed by the bank's cashier to its president, chief executive officer, or any other officer.

§ 7.2016 Restricting transfer of stock and record dates.

(a) *Conditions for stock transfer.* Under 12 U.S.C. 52, a national bank may impose conditions upon the transfer of its stock reasonably calculated to simplify the work of the bank with respect to stock transfers, voting at shareholders' meetings, and related matters and to protect it against fraudulent transfers.

(b) *Record dates.* A national bank may close its stock records for a reasonable period to ascertain shareholders for voting purposes. The board of directors may fix a record date for determining the shareholders entitled to notice of, and to vote at, any meeting of shareholders. The record date should be in reasonable proximity to the date that notice is given to the shareholders of the meeting.

§ 7.2017 Facsimile signatures on bank stock certificates.

The president and cashier, or other officers authorized by the bank's bylaws, shall sign each national bank stock certificate. The signatures may be manual or facsimile, including electronic means of signature. Each certificate must be sealed with the seal of the association.

§ 7.2018 Lost stock certificates.

If a national bank does not provide for replacing lost, stolen, or destroyed stock certificates in its articles of association or bylaws, the bank may adopt procedures in accordance with § 7.2000.

§ 7.2019 Loans secured by a bank's own shares.

(a) *Permitted agreements, relating to bank shares.* A national bank may require a borrower holding shares of the bank to execute agreements:

(1) Not to pledge, give away, transfer, or otherwise assign such shares;

(2) To pledge such shares at the request of the bank when necessary to prevent loss; and

(3) To leave such shares in the bank's custody.

(b) *Use of capital notes and debentures.* A national bank may not make loans secured by a pledge of the bank's own capital notes and debentures. Such notes and debentures must be subordinated to the claims of depositors and other creditors of the issuing bank, and are, therefore, capital instruments within the purview of 12 U.S.C. 83.

§ 7.2020 Acquisition and holding of shares as treasury stock.

(a) *Acquisition of outstanding shares.* Pursuant to 12 U.S.C. 59, including the requirements for prior approval by the bank's shareholders and the OCC imposed by that statute, a national bank may acquire its outstanding shares and hold them as treasury stock, if the acquisition and retention of the shares is, and continues to be, for a legitimate corporate purpose.

(b) *Legitimate corporate purpose.* Examples of legitimate corporate purposes include the acquisition and holding of treasury stock to:

(1) Have shares available for use in connection with employee stock option, bonus, purchase, or similar plans;

(2) Sell to a director for the purpose of acquiring qualifying shares;

(3) Purchase a director's qualifying shares upon the cessation of the director's service in that capacity if there is no ready market for the shares;

(4) Reduce the number of shareholders in order to qualify as a Subchapter S corporation; and

(5) Reduce costs associated with shareholder communications and meetings.

(c) *Prohibition.* It is not a legitimate corporate purpose to acquire or hold treasury stock on speculation about changes in its value.

[64 FR 60099, Nov. 4, 1999]

§ 7.2021 Preemptive rights.

A national bank in its articles of association must grant or deny preemptive rights to the bank's shareholders. Any amendment to a national bank's articles of association which modifies such preemptive rights must be approved by a vote of the holders of two-thirds of the bank's outstanding voting shares.

§ 7.2022 Voting trusts.

The shareholders of a national bank may establish a voting trust under the applicable law of a state selected by the participants and designated in the trust agreement, provided the implementation of the trust is consistent with safe and sound banking practices.

§ 7.2023 Reverse stock splits.

(a) *Authority to engage in reverse stock splits.* A national bank may engage in a reverse stock split if the transaction serves a legitimate corporate purpose and provides adequate dissenting shareholders' rights.

(b) *Legitimate corporate purpose.* Examples of legitimate corporate purposes include a reverse stock split to:

(1) Reduce the number of shareholders in order to qualify as a Subchapter S corporation; and

(2) Reduce costs associated with shareholder communications and meetings.

[64 FR 60099, Nov. 4, 1999]

§ 7.2024 Staggered terms for national bank directors and size of bank board.

(a) *Staggered terms.* Any national bank may adopt bylaws that provide for staggering the terms of its directors. National banks shall provide the OCC with copies of any bylaws so amended.

(b) *Maximum term.* Any national bank director may hold office for a term that does not exceed three years.

(c) *Number of directors.* A national bank's board of directors shall consist of no fewer than 5 and no more than 25 members. A national bank may, after notice to the OCC, increase the size of its board of directors above the 25 member limit. A national bank seeking to increase the number of its directors must notify the OCC any time the proposed size would exceed 25 directors. The bank's notice shall specify the reason(s) for the increase in the size of the board of directors beyond the statutory limit.

[68 FR 70131, Dec. 17, 2003]

Subpart C—Operations

§ 7.3000 National bank hours and closings.

(a) *Bank hours.* A national bank's board of directors should review its banking hours, and, independently of any other bank, take appropriate action to establish a schedule of banking hours.

(b) *Emergency closings.* Pursuant to 12 U.S.C. 95(b)(1), the Comptroller of the Currency (Comptroller), a state, or a legally authorized state official may declare a day a legal holiday if emergency conditions exist. That day is a legal holiday for national banks or their offices in the affected geographic area (*i.e.*, throughout the country, in a state, or in part of a state). Emergency conditions include natural disasters and civil and municipal emergencies (*e.g.*, severe flooding, or a power emergency declared by a local power company or government requesting that businesses in the affected area close). The Comptroller issues a proclamation authorizing the emergency closing in accordance with 12 U.S.C. 95 at the time of the emergency condition, or soon thereafter. When the Comptroller, a State, or a legally authorized State official declares a legal holiday due to emergency conditions, a national bank may temporarily limit or suspend operations at its affected offices. Alternatively, the national bank may continue its operations unless the Comptroller by written order directs otherwise.

(c) *Ceremonial closings.* A state or a legally authorized state official may declare a day a legal holiday for ceremonial reasons. When a state or a legally authorized state official declares a day to be a legal holiday for ceremonial reasons, a national bank may choose to remain open or to close.

(d) *Liability.* A national bank should assure that all liabilities or other obligations under the applicable law due to the bank's closing are satisfied.

[61 FR 4862, Feb. 9, 1996, as amended at 66 FR 34791, July 2, 2001]

§ 7.3001 Sharing national bank or Federal association space and employees.

(a) *Sharing space.* A national bank or Federal savings association may:

(1) Lease excess space on national bank or Federal savings association premises to one or more other businesses (including other financial institutions);

(2) Share space jointly held with one or more other businesses; or

(3) Offer its services in space owned by or leased to other businesses.

(b) *Sharing employees.* When sharing space with other businesses as described in paragraph (a) of this section, a national bank or Federal savings association may provide, under one or more written agreements between the national bank or Federal savings association, the other businesses, and their employees, that:

(1) A national bank or Federal savings association employee may act as agent for the other business; or

(2) An employee of the other business may act as agent for the national bank or Federal savings association.

(c) *Supervisory conditions.* When a national bank or Federal savings association engages in arrangements of the types listed in paragraphs (a) and (b) of this section, the national bank or Federal savings association shall ensure that:

(1) The other business is conspicuously, accurately, and separately identified;

(2) Shared employees clearly and fully disclose the nature of their agency relationship to customers of the national bank or Federal savings association and of the other businesses so that customers will know the identity of the national bank, Federal savings association, or other business that is providing the product or service;

(3) The arrangement does not constitute a joint venture or partnership with the other business under applicable state law;

(4) All aspects of the relationship between the national bank or Federal

savings association and the other business are conducted at arm's length, unless a special arrangement is warranted because the other business is a subsidiary of the national bank or Federal savings association;

(5) Security issues arising from the activities of the other business on the premises are addressed;

(6) The activities of the other business do not adversely affect the safety and soundness of the national bank or Federal savings association;

(7) The shared employees or the entity for which they perform services are duly licensed or meet qualification requirements of applicable statutes and regulations pertaining to agents or employees of such other business; and

(8) The assets and records of the parties are segregated.

(d) *Other legal requirements*. When entering into arrangements of the types described in paragraphs (a) and (b) of this section, and in conducting operations pursuant to those arrangements, a national bank or Federal savings association must ensure that each arrangement complies with all applicable laws and regulations. If the arrangement involves an affiliate or a shareholder, director, officer or employee of the national bank or Federal savings association:

(1) The national bank or Federal savings association must ensure compliance with all applicable statutory and regulatory provisions governing national bank or Federal savings association transactions with these persons or entities;

(2) The parties must comply with all applicable fiduciary duties; and

(3) The parties, if they are in competition with each other, must consider limitations, if any, imposed by applicable antitrust laws.

(e) *Transition*. If, on May 18, 2015, a Federal savings association shares space or employees with another business under an agreement that complies with the legal requirements that were in effect prior to May 18, 2015, but which would violate any provision of this section, the Federal savings association may continue sharing under the existing agreement but it may not amend, renew, or extend the agreement without prior approval of the appropriate OCC supervisory office.

[80 FR 28471, May 18, 2015]

Subpart D—Preemption

§ 7.4000 Visitorial powers with respect to national banks.

(a) *General rule*. (1) Under 12 U.S.C. 484, only the OCC or an authorized representative of the OCC may exercise visitorial powers with respect to national banks. State officials may not exercise visitorial powers with respect to national banks, such as conducting examinations, inspecting or requiring the production of books or records of national banks, or prosecuting enforcement actions, except in limited circumstances authorized by federal law. However, production of a bank's records (other than non-public OCC information under 12 CFR part 4, subpart C) may be required under normal judicial procedures.

(2) For purposes of this section, visitorial powers include:

(i) Examination of a bank;

(ii) Inspection of a bank's books and records;

(iii) Regulation and supervision of activities authorized or permitted pursuant to federal banking law; and

(iv) Enforcing compliance with any applicable Federal or state laws concerning those activities, including through investigations that seek to ascertain compliance through production of non-public information by the bank, except as otherwise provided in paragraphs (a), (b), and (c) of this section.

(3) Unless otherwise provided by Federal law, the OCC has exclusive visitorial authority with respect to the content and conduct of activities authorized for national banks under Federal law.

(b) *Exclusion*. In accordance with the decision of the Supreme Court in *Cuomo* v. *Clearing House Assn., L. L. C.*, 129 S. Ct. 2710 (2009), an action against a national bank in a court of appropriate jurisdiction brought by a state attorney general (or other chief law enforcement officer) to enforce an applicable law against a national bank and to seek relief as authorized by such law is not an exercise of visitorial powers under 12 U.S.C. 484.

(c) *Exceptions to the general rule.* Under 12 U.S.C. 484, the OCC's exclusive visitorial powers are subject to the following exceptions:

(1) *Exceptions authorized by Federal law.* National banks are subject to such visitorial powers as are provided by Federal law. Examples of laws vesting visitorial power in other governmental entities include laws authorizing state or other Federal officials to:

(i) Inspect the list of shareholders, provided that the official is authorized to assess taxes under state authority (12 U.S.C. 62; this section also authorizes inspection of the shareholder list by shareholders and creditors of a national bank);

(ii) Review, at reasonable times and upon reasonable notice to a bank, the bank's records solely to ensure compliance with applicable state unclaimed property or escheat laws upon reasonable cause to believe that the bank has failed to comply with those laws (12 U.S.C. 484(b));

(iii) Verify payroll records for unemployment compensation purposes (26 U.S.C. 3305(c));

(iv) Ascertain the correctness of Federal tax returns (26 U.S.C. 7602);

(v) Enforce the Fair Labor Standards Act (29 U.S.C. 211); and

(vi) Functionally regulate certain activities, as provided under the Gramm-Leach-Bliley Act, Pub. L. 106–102, 113 Stat. 1338 (Nov. 12, 1999).

(2) *Exception for courts of justice.* National banks are subject to such visitorial powers as are vested in the courts of justice. This exception pertains to the powers inherent in the judiciary.

(3) *Exception for Congress.* National banks are subject to such visitorial powers as shall be, or have been, exercised or directed by Congress or by either House thereof or by any committee of Congress or of either House duly authorized.

(d) *Report of examination.* The report of examination made by an OCC examiner is designated solely for use in the supervision of the bank. The bank's copy of the report is the property of the OCC and is loaned to the bank and any holding company thereof solely for its confidential use. The bank's directors, in keeping with their responsibilities both to depositors and to shareholders, should thoroughly review the report. The report may be made available to other persons only in accordance with the rules on disclosure in 12 CFR part 4.

[61 FR 4862, Feb. 9, 1996, as amended at 64 FR 60100, Nov. 4, 1999; 69 FR 1904, Jan. 13, 2004; 76 FR 43565, July 21, 2011]

§ 7.4001 Charging interest by national banks at rates permitted competing institutions; charging interest to corporate borrowers.

(a) *Definition.* The term "interest" as used in 12 U.S.C. 85 includes any payment compensating a creditor or prospective creditor for an extension of credit, making available of a line of credit, or any default or breach by a borrower of a condition upon which credit was extended. It includes, among other things, the following fees connected with credit extension or availability: numerical periodic rates, late fees, creditor-imposed not sufficient funds (NSF) fees charged when a borrower tenders payment on a debt with a check drawn on insufficient funds, overlimit fees, annual fees, cash advance fees, and membership fees. It does not ordinarily include appraisal fees, premiums and commissions attributable to insurance guaranteeing repayment of any extension of credit, finders' fees, fees for document preparation or notarization, or fees incurred to obtain credit reports.

(b) *Authority.* A national bank located in a state may charge interest at the maximum rate permitted to any state-chartered or licensed lending institution by the law of that state. If state law permits different interest charges on specified classes of loans, a national bank making such loans is subject only to the provisions of state law relating to that class of loans that are material to the determination of the permitted interest. For example, a national bank may lawfully charge the highest rate permitted to be charged by a state-licensed small loan company, without being so licensed, but subject to state law limitations on the size of loans made by small loan companies.

(c) *Effect on state definitions of interest.* The Federal definition of the term "interest" in paragraph (a) of this section does not change how interest is defined by the individual states (nor how the state definition of interest is used) solely for purposes of state law. For example, if late fees are not "interest" under state law where a national bank is located but state law permits its most favored lender to charge late fees, then a national bank located in that state may charge late fees to its intrastate customers. The national bank may also charge late fees to its interstate customers because the fees are interest under the Federal definition of interest and an allowable charge under state law where the national bank is located. However, the late fees would not be treated as interest for purposes of evaluating compliance with state usury limitations because state law excludes late fees when calculating the maximum interest that lending institutions may charge under those limitations.

(d) *Usury.* A national bank located in a state the law of which denies the defense of usury to a corporate borrower may charge a corporate borrower any rate of interest agreed upon by a corporate borrower.

[61 FR 4862, Feb. 9, 1996, as amended at 66 FR 34791, July 2, 2001]

§ 7.4002 National bank charges.

(a) *Authority to impose charges and fees.* A national bank may charge its customers non-interest charges and fees, including deposit account service charges.

(b) *Considerations.* (1) All charges and fees should be arrived at by each bank on a competitive basis and not on the basis of any agreement, arrangement, undertaking, understanding, or discussion with other banks or their officers.

(2) The establishment of non-interest charges and fees, their amounts, and the method of calculating them are business decisions to be made by each bank, in its discretion, according to sound banking judgment and safe and sound banking principles. A national bank establishes non-interest charges and fees in accordance with safe and sound banking principles if the bank employs a decision-making process through which it considers the following factors, among others:

(i) The cost incurred by the bank in providing the service;

(ii) The deterrence of misuse by customers of banking services;

(iii) The enhancement of the competitive position of the bank in accordance with the bank's business plan and marketing strategy; and

(iv) The maintenance of the safety and soundness of the institution.

(c) *Interest.* Charges and fees that are "interest" within the meaning of 12 U.S.C. 85 are governed by § 7.4001 and not by this section.

(d) *State law.* The OCC applies preemption principles derived from the United States Constitution, as interpreted through judicial precedent, when determining whether State laws apply that purport to limit or prohibit charges and fees described in this section.

(e) *National bank as fiduciary.* This section does not apply to charges imposed by a national bank in its capacity as a fiduciary, which are governed by 12 CFR part 9.

[66 FR 34791, July 2, 2001]

§ 7.4003 Establishment and operation of a remote service unit by a national bank.

A remote service unit (RSU) is an automated facility, operated by a customer of a bank, that conducts banking functions, such as receiving deposits, paying withdrawals, or lending money. A national bank may establish and operate an RSU pursuant to 12 U.S.C. 24(Seventh). An RSU includes an automated teller machine, automated loan machine, automated device for receiving deposits, personal computer, telephone, and other similar electronic devices. An RSU may be equipped with a telephone or televideo device that allows contact with bank personnel. An RSU is not a "branch" within the meaning of 12 U.S.C. 36(j), and is not subject to state geographic or operational restrictions or licensing laws.

[64 FR 60100, Nov. 4, 1999, as amended at 80 FR 28472, May 18, 2015]

§ 7.4004 Establishment and operation of a deposit production office by a national bank.

(a) *General rule.* A national bank or its operating subsidiary may engage in deposit production activities at a site other than the main office or a branch of the bank. A deposit production office (DPO) may solicit deposits, provide information about deposit products, and assist persons in completing application forms and related documents to open a deposit account. A DPO is not a branch within the meaning of 12 U.S.C. 36(j) and 12 CFR 5.30(d)(1) so long as it does not receive deposits, pay withdrawals, or make loans. All deposit and withdrawal transactions of a bank customer using a DPO must be performed by the customer, either in person at the main office or a branch office of the bank, or by mail, electronic transfer, or a similar method of transfer.

(b) *Services of other persons.* A national bank may use the services of, and compensate, persons not employed by the bank in its deposit production activities.

[64 FR 60100, Nov. 4, 1999]

§ 7.4005 Combination of national bank loan production office, deposit production office, and remote service unit.

A location at which a national bank operates a loan production office (LPO), a deposit production office (DPO), and a remote service unit (RSU) is not a "branch" within the meaning of 12 U.S.C. 36(j) by virtue of that combination. Since an LPO, DPO, or RSU is not, individually, a branch under 12 U.S.C. 36(j), any combination of these facilities at one location does not create a branch.

[64 FR 60100, Nov. 4, 1999]

§ 7.4006 [Reserved]

§ 7.4007 Deposit-taking by national banks.

(a) *Authority of national banks.* A national bank may receive deposits and engage in any activity incidental to receiving deposits, including issuing evidence of accounts, subject to such terms, conditions, and limitations prescribed by the Comptroller of the Currency and any other applicable Federal law.

(b) *Applicability of state law.* A national bank may exercise its deposit-taking powers without regard to state law limitations concerning:

(1) Abandoned and dormant accounts;[3]

(2) Checking accounts;

(3) Disclosure requirements;

(4) Funds availability;

(5) Savings account orders of withdrawal;

(6) State licensing or registration requirements (except for purposes of service of process); and

(7) Special purpose savings services;[4]

(c) *State laws that are not preempted.* State laws on the following subjects are not inconsistent with the deposit-taking powers of national banks and apply to national banks to the extent consistent with the decision of the Supreme Court in *Barnett Bank of Marion County, N.A.* v. *Nelson, Florida Insurance Commissioner, et al.* 517 U.S. 25 (1996):

(1) Contracts;

(2) Torts;

(3) Criminal law;[5]

(4) Rights to collect debts;

(5) Acquisition and transfer of property;

(6) Taxation;

(7) Zoning; and

(8) Any other law that the OCC determines to be applicable to national banks in accordance with the decision of the Supreme Court in *Barnett Bank of Marion County, N.A.* v. *Nelson, Florida*

[3] This does not apply to state laws of the type upheld by the United States Supreme Court in *Anderson Nat'l Bank* v. *Luckett*, 321 U.S. 233 (1944), which obligate a national bank to "pay [deposits] to the persons entitled to demand payment according to the law of the state where it does business." *Id.* at 248–249.

[4] State laws purporting to regulate national bank fees and charges are addressed in 12 CFR 7.4002.

[5] But see the distinction drawn by the Supreme Court in *Easton* v. *Iowa*, 188 U.S. 220, 238 (1903), where the Court stated that "[u]ndoubtedly a state has the legitimate power to define and punish crimes by general laws applicable to all persons within its jurisdiction * * *. But it is without lawful power to make such special laws applicable to banks organized and operating under the laws of the United States." *Id.* at 239 (holding that Federal law governing the operations of national banks preempted a state criminal law prohibiting insolvent banks from accepting deposits).

Insurance Commissioner, et al. 517 U.S. 25 (1996), or that is made applicable by Federal law.

[69 FR 1916, Jan. 13, 2004, as amended at 76 FR 43565, July 21, 2011]

§ 7.4008 Lending by national banks.

(a) *Authority of national banks.* A national bank may make, sell, purchase, participate in, or otherwise deal in loans and interests in loans that are not secured by liens on, or interests in, real estate, subject to such terms, conditions, and limitations prescribed by the Comptroller of the Currency and any other applicable Federal law.

(b) *Standards for loans.* A national bank shall not make a consumer loan subject to this § 7.4008 based predominantly on the bank's realization of the foreclosure or liquidation value of the borrower's collateral, without regard to the borrower's ability to repay the loan according to its terms. A bank may use any reasonable method to determine a borrower's ability to repay, including, for example, the borrower's current and expected income, current and expected cash flows, net worth, other relevant financial resources, current financial obligations, employment status, credit history, or other relevant factors.

(c) *Unfair and deceptive practices.* A national bank shall not engage in unfair or deceptive practices within the meaning of section 5 of the Federal Trade Commission Act, 15 U.S.C. 45(a)(1), and regulations promulgated thereunder in connection with loans made under this § 7.4008.

(d) *Applicability of state law.* A national bank may make non-real estate loans without regard to state law limitations concerning:

(1) Licensing, registration (except for purposes of service of process), filings, or reports by creditors;

(2) The ability of a creditor to require or obtain insurance for collateral or other credit enhancements or risk mitigants, in furtherance of safe and sound banking practices;

(3) Loan-to-value ratios;

(4) The terms of credit, including the schedule for repayment of principal and interest, amortization of loans, balance, payments due, minimum payments, or term to maturity of the loan, including the circumstances under which a loan may be called due and payable upon the passage of time or a specified event external to the loan;

(5) Escrow accounts, impound accounts, and similar accounts;

(6) Security property, including leaseholds;

(7) Access to, and use of, credit reports;

(8) Disclosure and advertising, including laws requiring specific statements, information, or other content to be included in credit application forms, credit solicitations, billing statements, credit contracts, or other credit-related documents;

(9) Disbursements and repayments; and

(10) Rates of interest on loans.[6]

(e) *State laws that are not preempted.* State laws on the following subjects are not inconsistent with the non-real estate lending powers of national banks and apply to national banks to the extent consistent with the decision of the Supreme Court in *Barnett Bank of Marion County, N.A.* v. *Nelson, Florida Insurance Commissioner, et al.*, 517 U.S. 25 (1996):

(1) Contracts;

(2) Torts;

(3) Criminal law;[7]

(4) Rights to collect debts;

(5) Acquisition and transfer of property;

(6) Taxation;

(7) Zoning; and

(8) Any other law that the OCC determines to be applicable to national banks in accordance with the decision of the Supreme Court in *Barnett Bank of Marion County, N.A.* v. *Nelson, Florida Insurance Commissioner, et al.*, 517 U.S. 25 (1996) or that is made applicable by Federal law.

[69 FR 1916, Jan. 13, 2004, as amended at 76 FR 43565, July 21, 2011]

---

[6] The limitations on charges that comprise rates of interest on loans by national banks are determined under Federal law. *See* 12 U.S.C. 85; 12 CFR 7.4001. State laws purporting to regulate national bank fees and charges that do not constitute interest are addressed in 12 CFR 7.4002.

[7] See *supra* note 5 regarding the distinction drawn by the Supreme Court in *Easton* v. *Iowa*, 188 U.S. 220, 238 (1903).

§ 7.4009 [Reserved]

§ 7.4010 Applicability of state law and visitorial powers to Federal savings associations and subsidiaries.

(a) In accordance with section 1046 of the Dodd-Frank Wall Street Reform and Consumer Protection Act (12 U.S.C. 25b), Federal savings associations and their subsidiaries shall be subject to the same laws and legal standards, including regulations of the OCC, as are applicable to national banks and their subsidiaries, regarding the preemption of state law.

(b) In accordance with section 1047 of the Dodd-Frank Wall Street Reform and Consumer Protection Act (12 U.S.C. 1465), the provisions of section 5136C(i) of the Revised Statutes regarding visitorial powers apply to Federal savings associations and their subsidiaries to the same extent and in the same manner as if they were national banks or national bank subsidiaries.

[76 FR 43566, July 21, 2011]

Subpart E—National Bank Electronic Activities

SOURCE: 67 FR 35004, May 17, 2002, unless otherwise noted.

§ 7.5000 Scope.

This subpart applies to a national bank's use of technology to deliver services and products consistent with safety and soundness.

§ 7.5001 Electronic activities that are part of, or incidental to, the business of banking.

(a) *Purpose.* This section identifies the criteria that the OCC uses to determine whether an electronic activity is authorized as part of, or incidental to, the business of banking under 12 U.S.C. 24 (Seventh) or other statutory authority.

(b) *Restrictions and conditions on electronic activities.* The OCC may determine that activities are permissible under 12 U.S.C. 24 (Seventh) or other statutory authority only if they are subject to standards or conditions designed to provide that the activities function as intended and are conducted safely and soundly, in accordance with other applicable statutes, regulations, or supervisory policies.

(c) *Activities that are part of the business of banking.* (1) An activity is authorized for national banks as part of the business of banking if the activity is described in 12 U.S.C. 24 (Seventh) or other statutory authority. In determining whether an electronic activity is part of the business of banking, the OCC considers the following factors:

(i) Whether the activity is the functional equivalent to, or a logical outgrowth of, a recognized banking activity;

(ii) Whether the activity strengthens the bank by benefiting its customers or its business;

(iii) Whether the activity involves risks similar in nature to those already assumed by banks; and

(iv) Whether the activity is authorized for state-chartered banks.

(2) The weight accorded each factor set out in paragraph (c)(1) of this section depends on the facts and circumstances of each case.

(d) *Activities that are incidental to the business of banking.* (1) An electronic banking activity is authorized for a national bank as incidental to the business of banking if it is convenient or useful to an activity that is specifically authorized for national banks or to an activity that is otherwise part of the business of banking. In determining whether an activity is convenient or useful to such activities, the OCC considers the following factors:

(i) Whether the activity facilitates the production or delivery of a bank's products or services, enhances the bank's ability to sell or market its products or services, or improves the effectiveness or efficiency of the bank's operations, in light of risks presented, innovations, strategies, techniques and new technologies for producing and delivering financial products and services; and

(ii) Whether the activity enables the bank to use capacity acquired for its banking operations or otherwise avoid economic loss or waste.

(2) The weight accorded each factor set out in paragraph (d)(1) of this section depends on the facts and circumstances of each case.

(3) In addition to the electronic activities specifically permitted in § 7.5004 (sale of excess electronic capacity and by-products) and § 7.5006 (incidental non-financial data processing), the OCC has determined that the following electronic activities are incidental to the business of banking, pursuant to this section. This list of activities is illustrative and not exclusive; the OCC may determine that other activities are permissible pursuant to this authority.

(i) Web site development where incidental to other banking services;

(ii) Internet access and e-mail provided on a non-profit basis as a promotional activity;

(iii) Advisory and consulting services on electronic activities where the services are incidental to customer use of electronic banking services; and

(iv) Sale of equipment that is convenient or useful to customer's use of related electronic banking services, such as specialized terminals for scanning checks that will be deposited electronically by wholesale customers of banks under the Check Clearing for the 21st Century Act, Public Law 108–100 (12 U.S.C. 5001–5018) (the Check 21 Act).

[61 FR 4862, Feb. 9, 1996, as amended at 73 FR 22242, Apr. 24, 2008]

§ 7.5002 Furnishing of products and services by electronic means and facilities.

(a) *Use of electronic means and facilities.* A national bank may perform, provide, or deliver through electronic means and facilities any activity, function, product, or service that it is otherwise authorized to perform, provide, or deliver, subject to § 7.5001(b) and applicable OCC guidance. The following list provides examples of permissible activities under this authority. This list is illustrative and not exclusive; the OCC may determine that other activities are permissible pursuant to this authority.

(1) Acting as an electronic finder by:

(i) Establishing, registering, and hosting commercially enabled web sites in the name of sellers;

(ii) Establishing hyperlinks between the bank's site and a third-party site, including acting as a "virtual mall" by providing a collection of links to web sites of third-party vendors, organized by-product type and made available to bank customers;

(iii) Hosting an electronic marketplace on the bank's Internet web site by providing links to the web sites of third-party buyers or sellers through the use of hypertext or other similar means;

(iv) Hosting on the bank's servers the Internet web site of:

(A) A buyer or seller that provides information concerning the hosted party and the products or services offered or sought and allows the submission of interest, bids, offers, orders and confirmations relating to such products or services; or

(B) A governmental entity that provides information concerning the services or benefits made available by the governmental entity, assists persons in completing applications to receive such services or benefits and permits persons to transmit their applications for such services or benefits;

(v) Operating an Internet web site that permits numerous buyers and sellers to exchange information concerning the products and services that they are willing to purchase or sell, locate potential counter-parties for transactions, aggregate orders for goods or services with those made by other parties, and enter into transactions between themselves;

(vi) Operating a telephone call center that provides permissible finder services; and

(vii) Providing electronic communications services relating to all aspects of transactions between buyers and sellers;

(2) Providing electronic bill presentment services;

(3) Offering electronic stored value systems;

(4) Safekeeping for personal information or valuable confidential trade or business information, such as encryption keys; and

(5) Issuing electronic letters of credit within the scope of 12 CFR 7.1016.

(b) *Applicability of guidance and requirements not affected.* When a national bank performs, provides, or delivers through electronic means and facilities an activity, function, product, or service that it is otherwise authorized to perform, provide, or deliver, the electronic activity is not exempt from the regulatory requirements and supervisory guidance that the OCC would apply if the activity were conducted by non-electronic means or facilities.

(c) *State laws.* As a general rule, and except as provided by Federal law, State law is not applicable to a national bank's conduct of an authorized activity through electronic means or facilities if the State law, as applied to the activity, would be preempted pursuant to traditional principles of Federal preemption derived from the Supremacy Clause of the U.S. Constitution and applicable judicial precedent. Accordingly, State laws that stand as an obstacle to the ability of national banks to exercise uniformly their Federally authorized powers through electronic means or facilities, are not applicable to national banks.

[61 FR 4862, Feb. 9, 1996, as amended at 73 FR 22242, Apr. 24, 2008]

§ 7.5003 Composite authority to engage in electronic activities.

Unless otherwise prohibited by Federal law, a national bank may engage in an electronic activity that is comprised of several component activities if each of the component activities is itself part of or incidental to the business of banking or is otherwise permissible under Federal law.

§ 7.5004 Sale of excess electronic capacity and by-products.

(a) A national bank may, in order to optimize the use of the bank's resources or avoid economic loss or waste, market and sell to third parties electronic capacities legitimately acquired or developed by the bank for its banking business.

(b) With respect to acquired equipment or facilities, legitimate excess electronic capacity that may be sold to others can arise in a variety of situations, including the following:

(1) Due to the characteristics of the desired equipment or facilities available in the market, the capacity of the most practical optimal equipment or facilities available to meet the bank's requirements exceeds its present needs;

(2) The acquisition and retention of additional capacity, beyond present needs, reasonably may be necessary for planned future expansion or to meet the expected future banking needs during the useful life of the equipment;

(3) Requirements for capacity fluctuate because a bank engages in batch processing of banking transactions or because a bank must have capacity to meet peak period demand with the result that the bank has periods when its capacity is underutilized; and

(4) After the initial acquisition of capacity thought to be fully needed for banking operations, the bank experiences either a decline in level of the banking operations or an increase in the efficiency of the banking operations using that capacity.

(c) Types of electronic capacity in equipment or facilities that banks may have legitimately acquired and that may be sold to third parties if excess to the bank's needs for banking purposes include:

(1) Data processing services;

(2) Production and distribution of non-financial software;

(3) Providing periodic back-up call answering services;

(4) Providing full Internet access;

(5) Providing electronic security system support services;

(6) Providing long line communications services; and

(7) Electronic imaging and storage.

(d) A national bank may sell to third parties electronic by-products legitimately acquired or developed by the bank for its banking business. Examples of electronic by-products that banks may have legitimately acquired that may be sold to third parties if excess to the bank's needs include:

(1) Software acquired (not merely licensed) or developed by the bank for banking purposes or to support its banking business; and

(2) Electronic databases, records, or media (such as electronic images) developed by the bank for or during the performance of its permissible data processing activities.

§ 7.5005 National bank acting as digital certification authority.

(a) It is part of the business of banking under 12 U.S.C. 24(Seventh) for a national bank to act as a certificate authority and to issue digital certificates verifying the identity of persons associated with a particular public/private key pair. As part of this service, the bank may also maintain a listing or repository of public keys.

(b) A national bank may issue digital certificates verifying attributes in addition to identity of persons associated with a particular public/private key pair where the attribute is one for which verification is part of or incidental to the business of banking. For example, national banks may issue digital certificates verifying certain financial attributes of a customer as of the current or a previous date, such as account balance as of a particular date, lines of credit as of a particular date, past financial performance of the customer, and verification of customer relationship with the bank as of a particular date.

(c) When a national bank issues a digital certificate relating to financial capacity under this section, the bank shall include in that certificate an express disclaimer stating that the bank does not thereby promise or represent that funds will be available or will be advanced for any particular transaction.

§ 7.5006 Data processing.

(a) *Eligible activities.* It is part of the business of banking under 12 U.S.C. 24(Seventh) for a national bank to provide data processing, and data transmission services, facilities (including equipment, technology, and personnel), data bases, advice and access to such services, facilities, data bases and advice, for itself and for others, where the data is banking, financial, or economic data, and other types of data if the derivative or resultant product is banking, financial, or economic data. For this purpose, economic data includes anything of value in banking and financial decisions.

(b) *Other data.* A national bank also may perform the activities described in paragraph (a) of this section for itself and others with respect to additional types of data to the extent convenient or useful to provide the data processing services described in paragraph (a), including where reasonably necessary to conduct those activities on a competitive basis. The total revenue attributable to the bank's data processing activities under this section must be derived predominantly from processing the activities described in paragraph (a) of this section.

(c) *Software for performance of authorized banking functions.* A national bank may produce, market, or sell software that performs services or functions that the bank could perform directly, as part of the business of banking.

[61 FR 4862, Feb. 9, 1996, as amended at 73 FR 22242, Apr. 24, 2008]

§ 7.5007 Correspondent services.

It is part of the business of banking for a national bank to offer as a correspondent service to any of its affiliates or to other financial institutions any service it may perform for itself. The following list provides examples of electronic activities that banks may offer correspondents under this authority. This list is illustrative and not exclusive; the OCC may determine that other activities are permissible pursuant to this authority.

(a) The provision of computer networking packages and related hardware;

(b) Data processing services;

(c) The sale of software that performs data processing functions;

(d) The development, operation, management, and marketing of products and processing services for transactions conducted at electronic terminal devices;

(e) Item processing services and related software;

(f) Document control and record keeping through the use of electronic imaging technology;

(g) The provision of Internet merchant hosting services for resale to merchant customers;

(h) The provision of communication support services through electronic means; and

(i) Digital certification authority services.

§ 7.5008 Location of a national bank conducting electronic activities.

A national bank shall not be considered located in a State solely because it physically maintains technology, such as a server or automated loan center, in that state, or because the bank's products or services are accessed through electronic means by customers located in the state.

§ 7.5009 Location under 12 U.S.C. 85 of national banks operating exclusively through the Internet.

For purposes of 12 U.S.C. 85, the main office of a national bank that operates exclusively through the Internet is the office identified by the bank under 12 U.S.C. 22(Second) or as relocated under 12 U.S.C. 30 or other appropriate authority.

§ 7.5010 Shared electronic space.

National banks that share electronic space, including a co-branded web site, with a bank subsidiary, affiliate, or another third-party must take reasonable steps to clearly, conspicuously, and understandably distinguish between products and services offered by the bank and those offered by the bank's subsidiary, affiliate, or the third-party.

PART 8—ASSESSMENT OF FEES

Sec.
8.1 Scope and application.
8.2 Semiannual assessment.
8.6 Fees for special examinations and investigations.
8.7 Payment of interest on delinquent assessments and examination and investigation fees.
8.8 Notice of Comptroller of the Currency Fees.

AUTHORITY: 12 U.S.C. 16, 93a, 481, 482, 1467, 1831c, 1867, 3102, 3108, and 5412(b)(2)(B); and 15 U.S.C. 78c and 78*l*.

§ 8.1 Scope and application.

The assessments contained in this part are made pursuant to the authority contained in 12 U.S.C. 16, 93a, 481, 482, 1467, 1831c, 1867, 3102, and 3108; and 15 U.S.C. 78c and 78*l*.

[76 FR 43566, July 21, 2011]

§ 8.2 Semiannual assessment.

(a) Each national bank and each Federal savings association shall pay to the Comptroller of the Currency a semiannual assessment fee, due by March 31 and September 30 of each year, for the six-month period beginning on January 1 and July 1 before each payment date. The Comptroller of the Currency will calculate the amount due under this section and provide a notice of assessments to each national bank and each Federal savings association no later than 7 business days prior to collection on March 31 and September 30 of each year. In setting assessments, the Comptroller of the Currency may take into account the nature and scope of the activities of a national bank or Federal savings association, the amount and type of assets that the entity holds, the financial and managerial condition of the entity, and any other factor the Comptroller of the Currency determines is appropriate, as provided by 12 U.S.C. 16. The semiannual assessment will be calculated as follows:

If the bank's or Federal savings association's total assets (consolidated domestic and foreign subsidiaries) are:		The semiannual assessment is:		
Over—	But not over—	This amount—base amount	Plus marginal rates	Of excess over—
Column A	Column B	Column C	Column D	Column E
Million (dollars)	Million (dollars)	(dollars)		Million (dollars)
0	2	X1	0	
2	20	X2	Y1	2
20	100	X3	Y2	20
100	200	X4	Y3	100
200	1,000	X5	Y4	200
1,000	2,000	X6	Y5	1,000
2,000	6,000	X7	Y6	2,000
6,000	20,000	X8	Y7	6,000
20,000	40,000	X9	Y8	20,000
40,000	250,000	X10	Y9	40,000
250,000	....	X11	Y10	250,000

(1) Every national bank and every Federal savings association falls into one of the asset-size brackets denoted by Columns A and B. A bank's or Federal savings association's semiannual assessment is composed of two parts. The first part is the calculation of a base amount of the assessment, which is computed on the assets of the bank or Federal savings association up to the lower endpoint (Column A) of the bracket in which it falls. This base amount of the assessment is calculated by the OCC in Column C.

(2) The second part is the calculation of assessments due on the remaining assets of the bank or Federal savings association in excess of Column E. The excess is assessed at the marginal rate shown in Column D.

(3) The total semiannual assessment is the amount in Column C, plus the amount of the bank's or Federal savings association's assets in excess of Column E times the marginal rate in Column D:

Assessments = C + [(Assets − E) × D].

(4) Each year, the OCC may index the marginal rates in Column D to adjust for the percent change in the level of prices, as measured by changes in the Gross Domestic Product Implicit Price Deflator (GDPIPD) for each June-to-June period. The OCC may at its discretion adjust marginal rates by amounts other than the percentage change in the GDPIPD. The OCC will also adjust the amounts in Column C to reflect any change made to the marginal rate.

(5) The specific marginal rates and complete assessment schedule will be published in the "Notice of Comptroller of the Currency Fees," provided for at § 8.8 of this part. Each semiannual assessment is based upon the total assets shown in the national bank's or Federal savings association's most recent "Consolidated Reports of Condition and Income" (Call Report) or "Thrift Financial Report," as appropriate, preceding the payment date. Each bank or Federal savings association subject to the jurisdiction of the Comptroller of the Currency on the date of the second or fourth quarterly Call Report or Thrift Financial Report, as appropriate, required by the Office under 12 U.S.C. 161 and 12 U.S.C. 1464(v) is subject to the full assessment for the next six month period.

(6)(i) Notwithstanding any other provision of this part, the OCC may reduce the semiannual assessment for each non-lead bank or non-lead Federal savings association by a percentage that it will specify in the "Notice of Comptroller of the Currency Fees" described in § 8.8.

(ii) For purposes of this paragraph (a)(6):

(A) *Lead bank* or *lead Federal savings association* means the largest national bank or Federal savings association controlled by a company, based on a comparison of the total assets held by each national bank or Federal savings association controlled by that company as reported in each bank's or Federal savings association's Call Report or Thrift Financial Report, as appropriate, filed for the quarter immediately preceding the payment of a semiannual assessment.

(B) *Non-lead bank* or *non-lead Federal savings association* means a national bank or Federal savings association that is not the lead bank or lead Federal savings association controlled by a company that controls two or more national banks or Federal savings associations.

(C) *Control* and *company* with respect to national banks have the same meanings as these terms have in sections 2(a)(2) and 2(b), respectively, of the Bank Holding Company Act of 1956 (12 U.S.C. 1841(a)(2) and (b)).

(D) *Control* and *company* with respect to Federal savings associations have the same meanings as these terms have in section 10(a) of the Home Owners' Loan Act (12 U.S.C. 1467a(a).

(b)(1) Each Federal branch and each Federal agency shall pay to the Comptroller of the Currency a semiannual assessment fee, due by March 31 and September 30 of each year, for the six month period beginning on January 1 and July 1 before each payment date. The Comptroller of the Currency will calculate the amount due under this section and provide a notice of assessments to each national bank no later than 7 business days prior to March 31 and September 30 of each year.

(2) The amount of the semiannual assessment paid by each Federal branch and Federal agency shall be computed at the same rate as provided in the Table in 12 CFR 8.2(a); however, only the total domestic assets of the Federal branch or agency shall be subject to assessment.

(3) Each semiannual assessment of each Federal branch or agency is based upon the total assets shown in the Federal branch's or agency's Call Report most recently preceding the payment date. Each Federal branch or agency subject to the jurisdiction of the OCC on the date of the second and fourth Call Reports is subject to the full assessment for the next six-month period.

(4)(i) Notwithstanding any other provision of this part, the OCC may reduce the semiannual assessment for each non-lead Federal branch or agency by an amount that it will specify in the "Notice of Comptroller of the Currency Fees" described in § 8.8.

(ii) For purposes of this paragraph (b)(4):

(A) *Lead Federal branch or agency* means the largest Federal branch or agency of a foreign bank, based on a comparison of the total assets held by each Federal branch or agency of that foreign bank as reported in each Federal branch's or agency's Call Report filed for the quarter immediately preceding the payment of a semiannual assessment.

(B) *Non-lead Federal branch or agency* means a Federal branch or agency that is not the lead Federal branch or agency of a foreign bank that controls two or more Federal branches or agencies.

(c) *Additional assessment for independent credit card banks and independent credit card Federal savings associations*—(1) *General rule.* In addition to the assessment calculated according to paragraph (a) of this section, each independent credit card bank and independent credit card Federal savings association will pay an assessment based on receivables attributable to credit card accounts owned by the bank or Federal savings association. This assessment will be computed by adding to its asset-based assessment an additional amount determined by its level of receivables attributable. The dollar amount of the additional assessment will be published in the "Notice of Comptroller of the Currency of Fees," described at § 8.8.

(2) *Independent credit card banks and independent credit card Federal savings associations affiliated with full-service national banks or Federal savings associations.* The OCC will assess an independent credit card bank and an independent credit card Federal savings association in accordance with paragraph (c)(1) of this section, notwithstanding that the bank or Federal savings association is affiliated with a full-service national bank or full service Federal savings association, if the OCC concludes that the affiliation is intended to evade this part.

(3) *Definitions.* For purposes of this paragraph (c), the following definitions apply:

(i) *Affiliate,* with respect to national banks, has the same meaning as this term has in 12 U.S.C. 221a(b).

(ii) *Affiliate,* with respect to Federal savings associations, has the same meaning as in 12 U.S.C. 1462(9).

(iii) *Engaged primarily in card operations* means a bank described in section 2(c)(2)(F) of the Bank Holding Company Act (12 U.S.C. 1841(c)(2)(F)) or a bank or a Federal savings association whose ratio of total gross receivables attributable to the bank's or Federal savings association's balance sheet assets exceeds 50%.

(iv) *Full-service national bank* is a national bank that generates more than 50% of its interest and non-interest income from activities other than credit card operations or trust activities and is authorized according to its charter to engage in all types of permissible banking activities.

(v) *Full-service Federal savings association* is a Federal savings association that generates more than 50% of its interest and non-interest income from activities other than credit card operations or trust activities and is authorized according to its charter to engage in all types of activities permissible for Federal savings associations.

(vi) *Independent credit card bank* is a national bank that engages primarily in credit card operations and is not affiliated with a full-service national bank.

(vii) *Independent credit card Federal savings association* is a Federal savings association that engages primarily in credit card operations and is not affiliated with a full-service Federal savings association.

(viii) *Receivables attributable* is the total amount of outstanding balances due on credit card accounts owned by an independent credit card bank or an independent credit card Federal savings association (the receivables attributable to those accounts) on the last day of the assessment period, minus receivables retained on the bank's or Federal savings association's balance sheet as of that day.

(4) *Reports of receivables attributable.* Independent credit card banks and independent credit card Federal savings associations will report receivables attributable data to the OCC semiannually at a time specified by the OCC.

(d) *Surcharge based on the condition of the bank or Federal savings association.* Subject to any limit that the OCC prescribes in the "Notice of Comptroller of the Currency Fees," the OCC shall apply a surcharge to the semiannual assessment computed in accordance with paragraphs (a) through (c) of this section. This surcharge will be determined by multiplying the semiannual assessment computed in accordance with paragraphs (a) through (c) of this section by—

(1) 1.5, in the case of any bank or Federal savings association that receives a composite rating of 3 under the Uniform Financial Institutions Rating System (UFIRS) and any Federal branch or agency that receives a composite rating of 3 under the ROCA rating system (which rates risk management, operational controls, compliance, and asset quality) at its most recent examination; and

(2) 2.0, in the case of any bank or Federal savings association that receives a composite UFIRS rating of 4 or 5 and any Federal branch or agency that receives a composite rating of 4 or 5 under the ROCA rating system at its most recent examination.

[76 FR 43566, July 21, 2011, as amended at 79 FR 38772, July 9, 2014]

§ 8.6 Fees for special examinations and investigations.

(a) *Fees.* Pursuant to the authority contained in 12 U.S.C. 16, 481, 482, 1467, and 1831c, the Office of the Comptroller of the Currency may assess a fee for:

(1) Examining the fiduciary activities of national banks and Federal savings associations and related entities;

(2) Conducting special examinations and investigations of national banks, Federal branches or agencies of foreign banks, and Federal savings associations;

(3) Conducting special examinations and investigations of an entity with respect to its performance of activities described in section 7(c) of the Bank Service Company Act (12 U.S.C. 1867(c)) if the OCC determines that assessment of the fee is warranted with regard to a particular bank or Federal savings association because of the high risk or unusual nature of the activities performed; the significance to the bank's or Federal saving association's operations and income of the activities performed; or the extent to which the bank or Federal savings association has sufficient systems, controls, and personnel to adequately monitor, measure, and control risks arising from such activities;

(4) Conducting special examinations and investigations of affiliates of national banks, Federal savings associations, and Federal branches or agencies of foreign banks;

(5) Conducting examinations and investigations made pursuant to 12 CFR part 5, Rules, Policies, and Procedures for Corporate Activities; and

(6) Conducting examinations of depository-institution permissible activities of nondepository institution subsidiaries of depository institution holding companies pursuant to section 605(a) of the Dodd-Frank Wall Street Reform and Consumer Protection Act (12 U.S.C. 1831c).

(b) *Notice of Comptroller of the Currency fees.* The OCC publishes the fee schedule for fiduciary activities, special examinations and investigations, examinations of affiliates and examinations related to corporate activities in the "Notice of Comptroller of the Currency Fees" described in § 8.8.

(c) *Additional assessments on trust banks and trust Federal savings associations*—(1) *Independent trust banks and independent trust Federal savings associations.* The assessment of independent trust banks and independent trust Federal savings associations will include a fiduciary and related asset component, in addition to the assessment calculated according to §8.2 of this part, as follows:

(i) *Minimum fee.* All independent trust banks and independent trust Federal savings associations will pay a minimum fee, to be provided in the "Notice of Comptroller of the Currency Fees."

(ii) *Additional amount for independent trust banks and independent trust Federal savings associations with fiduciary and related assets in excess of $1 billion.* Independent trust banks and independent trust Federal savings associations with fiduciary and related assets in excess of $1 billion will pay an amount that exceeds the minimum fee. The amount to be paid will be calculated by multiplying the amount of fiduciary and related assets by a rate or rates provided by the OCC in the "Notice of Comptroller of the Currency Fees."

(iii) *Surcharge based on the condition of the bank or of the Federal savings association.* Subject to any limit that the OCC prescribes in the "Notice of Comptroller of the Currency Fees," the OCC shall adjust the semiannual assessment computed in accordance with paragraphs (c)(1)(i) and (ii) of this section by multiplying that figure by 1.5 for each independent trust bank and independent trust Federal savings association that receives a composite rating of 3 under the Uniform Financial Institutions Rating System (UFIRS) at its most recent examination and by 2.0 for each bank that receives a composite UFIRS rating of 4 or 5 at such examination.

(2) *Trust banks affiliated with full-service national banks and trust Federal savings associations affiliated with full-service Federal savings associations.* The OCC will assess a trust bank and a trust Federal savings association in accordance with paragraph (c)(1) of this section, notwithstanding that the bank is affiliated with a full-service national bank, or that the Federal savings association is affiliated with a full-service Federal savings association, if the OCC concludes that the affiliation is intended to evade the assessment regulation.

(3) *Definitions.* For purposes of this paragraph (c) of this section, the following definitions apply:

(i) *Affiliate,* with respect to a national bank, has the same meaning as this term has in 12 U.S.C. 221a(b);

(ii) *Affiliate,* with respect to Federal savings associations, has the same meaning as in 12 U.S.C. 1462(9).

(iii) *Full-service national bank* is a national bank that generates more than 50% of its interest and non-interest income from activities other than credit card operations or trust activities and is authorized according to its charter to engage in all types of permissible banking activities.

(iv) *Full-service Federal savings association* is a Federal savings association that generates more than 50% of its interest and non-interest income from activities other than credit card operations or trust activities and is authorized according to its charter to engage in all types of activities permissible for Federal savings associations.

(v) *Independent trust bank* is a national bank that has trust powers, does not primarily offer full-service banking, and is not affiliated with a full-service national bank;

(vi) *Independent trust Federal savings association* is a Federal savings association that has trust powers, does not primarily offer full-service banking, and is not affiliated with a full-service Federal savings association; and

(vii) *Fiduciary and related assets* are those assets reported on Schedule RC–T of FFIEC Forms 031 and 041, Line 10 (columns A and B) and Line 11 (column B), any successor form issued by the FFIEC, and any other fiduciary and related assets defined in the "Notice of Comptroller of the Currency Fees."

[76 FR 43568, July 21, 2011, as amended at 76 FR 43568, July 7, 2011; 82 FR 8104, Jan. 23, 2017]

§8.7 Payment of interest on delinquent assessments and examination and investigation fees.

(a) Each national bank, each Federal branch, each Federal agency, and each Federal savings association shall pay to the Comptroller of the Currency interest on its delinquent payments of semiannual assessments. In addition, each national bank, each Federal savings association, and each entity with a trust department examined by the Comptroller of the Currency and each institution that is the subject of a special examination or investigation conducted by the Comptroller of the Currency shall pay to the Comptroller of the Currency interest on its delinquent payments of examination and investigation fees. Semiannual assessment payments will be considered delinquent if they are received after the time for payment specified in §8.2. Examination and investigation fees will be considered delinquent if not received by the Comptroller of the Currency within 30 calendar days of the invoice date.

(b) In the event that an entity that is required to make semiannual assessment payments or trust examination fee payments believes that the notice of assessments prepared by the Comptroller of the Currency contains an error of miscalculation, the entity may provide the Comptroller of the Currency with a written request for a revised assessment notice and a refund of any overpayments. Any such request for a revised notice and refund must be made after timely payment of the semiannual assessment under the dates specified in §8.2.

(1) Refund the amount of the overpayment or

(2) Provide notice of its unwillingness to accept the request for a revised notice of assessments. In the latter instance, the Comptroller of the Currency and the entity claiming the overpayment shall thereafter attempt to reach agreement on the amount, if any, to be refunded; the Comptroller of the Currency shall refund this amount within 30 calendar days of such agreement.

The Comptroller of the Currency shall be considered delinquent if it fails to return an overpayment in accordance with the time limitations specified in this paragraph (b). The Comptroller of the Currency shall pay interest on any such delinquent payments.

(c) Interest on delinquent payments, as described in paragraphs (a) and (b) of this section, will be assessed beginning the first calendar day on which payment is considered delinquent, and on each calendar day thereafter up to and including the day payment is received. Interest will be simple interest, calculated for each day payment is delinquent by multiplying the daily equivalent of the applicable interest rate by the amount delinquent. The rate of interest will be the United States Treasury Department's current value of funds rate (the "TFRM rate"); that rate is issued under the Treasury Fiscal Requirements Manual and is published quarterly in the FEDERAL REGISTER. The interest rates applicable to a delinquent payment will be determined as follows:

(1) For delinquent days occurring from January 1 to March 31, the rate will be the TFRM rate that is published the preceding December for the first quarter of the ensuing year.

(2) For delinquent days occurring from April 1 to June 30, the rate will be the TFRM rate that is published the preceding March for the second quarter of that year.

(3) For delinquent days occurring from July 1 to September 30, the rate will be the TFRM rate that is published the preceding June for the third quarter of that year.

(4) For delinquent days occurring from October 1 to December 31, the rate will be the TFRM rate that is published the preceding September for the fourth quarter of that year.

[48 FR 30599, July 1, 1983. Redesignated and amended at 49 FR 50605, Dec. 31, 1984; 70 FR 69643, Nov. 17, 2005; 76 FR 43568, July 21, 2011]

§8.8 Notice of Comptroller of the Currency Fees.

(a) *December notice of fees.* A "Notice of Office of the Comptroller of the Currency Fees and Assessments" (Notice of Fees) shall be published no later than the first business day in December of each year for fees to be charged by the OCC during the upcoming year. These fees will be effective January 1 of that upcoming year.

(b) *Interim and amended notice of fees.* The OCC may issue a notice of "Interim Office of the Comptroller of the Currency Fees and Assessments" or a notice of "Amended Office of the Comptroller of the Currency Fees and

Assessments" from time to time throughout the year as necessary. Interim or amended notices will be effective 30 days after issuance.

[79 FR 38772, July 9, 2014]

PART 9—FIDUCIARY ACTIVITIES OF NATIONAL BANKS

REGULATIONS

Sec.
9.1 Authority, purpose, and scope.
9.2 Definitions.
9.3 Approval requirements.
9.4 Administration of fiduciary powers.
9.5 Policies and procedures.
9.6 Review of fiduciary accounts.
9.7 Multi-state fiduciary operations.
9.8 Recordkeeping.
9.9 Audit of fiduciary activities.
9.10 Fiduciary funds awaiting investment or distribution.
9.11 Investment of fiduciary funds.
9.12 Self-dealing and conflicts of interest.
9.13 Custody of fiduciary assets.
9.14 Deposit of securities with state authorities.
9.15 Fiduciary compensation.
9.16 Receivership or voluntary liquidation of bank.
9.17 Surrender or revocation of fiduciary powers.
9.18 Collective investment funds.
9.20 Transfer agents.

INTERPRETATIONS

9.100 Acting as indenture trustee and creditor.
9.101 Providing investment advice for a fee.

AUTHORITY: 12 U.S.C. 24 (Seventh), 92a, and 93a; 15 U.S.C. 78q, 78q–1, and 78w.

SOURCE: 61 FR 68554, Dec. 30, 1996, unless otherwise noted.

REGULATIONS

§ 9.1 Authority, purpose, and scope.

(a) *Authority.* The Office of the Comptroller of the Currency (OCC) issues this part pursuant to its authority under 12 U.S.C. 24 (Seventh), 92a, and 93a, and 15 U.S.C. 78q, 78q–1, and 78w.

(b) *Purpose.* The purpose of this part is to set forth the standards that apply to the fiduciary activities of national banks.

(c) *Scope.* This part applies to all national banks that act in a fiduciary capacity, as defined in § 9.2(e). This part also applies to all Federal branches of foreign banks to the same extent as it applies to national banks.

§ 9.2 Definitions.

For the purposes of this part, the following definitions apply:

(a) *Affiliate* has the same meaning as in 12 U.S.C. 221a(b).

(b) *Applicable law* means the law of a state or other jurisdiction governing a national bank's fiduciary relationships, any applicable Federal law governing those relationships, the terms of the instrument governing a fiduciary relationship, or any court order pertaining to the relationship.

(c) *Custodian under a uniform gifts to minors act* means a fiduciary relationship established pursuant to a state law substantially similar to the Uniform Gifts to Minors Act or the Uniform Transfers to Minors Act as published by the American Law Institute.

(d) *Fiduciary account* means an account administered by a national bank acting in a fiduciary capacity.

(e) *Fiduciary capacity* means: trustee, executor, administrator, registrar of stocks and bonds, transfer agent, guardian, assignee, receiver, or custodian under a uniform gifts to minors act; investment adviser, if the bank receives a fee for its investment advice; any capacity in which the bank possesses investment discretion on behalf of another; or any other similar capacity that the OCC authorizes pursuant to 12 U.S.C. 92a.

(f) *Fiduciary officers and employees* means all officers and employees of a national bank to whom the board of directors or its designee has assigned functions involving the exercise of the bank's fiduciary powers.

(g) *Fiduciary powers* means the authority the OCC permits a national bank to exercise pursuant to 12 U.S.C. 92a.

(h) *Guardian* means the guardian or conservator, by whatever name used by state law, of the estate of a minor, an incompetent person, an absent person, or a person over whose estate a court has taken jurisdiction, other than under bankruptcy or insolvency laws.

(i) *Investment discretion* means, with respect to an account, the sole or shared authority (whether or not that authority is exercised) to determine what securities or other assets to purchase or sell on behalf of the account. A bank that delegates its authority over investments and a bank that receives delegated authority over investments are both deemed to have investment discretion.

(j) *Trust office* means an office of a national bank, other than a main office or a branch, at which the bank engages in one or more of the activities specified in § 9.7(d). Pursuant to 12 U.S.C. 36(j), a trust office is not a "branch" for purposes of 12 U.S.C. 36, unless it is also an office at which deposits are received, or checks paid, or money lent.

(k) *Trust representative office* means an office of a national bank, other than a main office, branch, or trust office, at which the bank performs activities ancillary to its fiduciary business, but does not engage in any of the activities specified in § 9.7(d). Examples of ancillary activities include advertising, marketing, and soliciting for fiduciary business; contacting existing or potential customers, answering questions, and providing information about matters related to their accounts; acting as a liaison between the trust office and the customer (*e.g.*, forwarding requests for distribution or changes in investment objectives, or forwarding forms and funds received from the customer); inspecting or maintaining custody of fiduciary assets or holding title to real property. This list is illustrative and not comprehensive. Other activities may also be "ancillary activities" for the purposes of this definition. Pursuant to 12 U.S.C. 36(j), a trust representative office is not a "branch" for purposes of 12 U.S.C. 36, unless it is also an office at which deposits are received, or checks paid, or money lent.

[61 FR 68554, Dec. 30, 1996, as amended at 66 FR 34797, July 2, 2001]

§ 9.3 Approval requirements.

(a) A national bank may not exercise fiduciary powers unless it obtains prior approval from the OCC to the extent required under 12 CFR 5.26.

(b) A national bank that has obtained the OCC s approval to exercise fiduciary powers is not required to obtain the OCC s prior approval to engage in any of the activities specified in § 9.7(d) in a new state or to conduct, in a new state, activities that are ancillary to its fiduciary business. Instead, the national bank must follow the notice procedures prescribed by 12 CFR 5.26(e).

(c) A person seeking approval to organize a special-purpose national bank limited to fiduciary powers shall file an application with the OCC pursuant to 12 CFR 5.20.

[61 FR 68554, Dec. 30, 1996, as amended at 66 FR 34798, July 2, 2001]

§ 9.4 Administration of fiduciary powers.

(a) *Responsibilities of the board of directors.* A national bank's fiduciary activities shall be managed by or under the direction of its board of directors. In discharging its responsibilities, the board may assign any function related to the exercise of fiduciary powers to any director, officer, employee, or committee thereof.

(b) *Use of other personnel.* The national bank may use any qualified personnel and facilities of the bank or its affiliates to perform services related to the exercise of its fiduciary powers, and any department of the bank or its affiliates may use fiduciary officers, employees, and facilities to perform services unrelated to the exercise of fiduciary powers, to the extent not prohibited by applicable law.

(c) *Agency agreements.* Pursuant to a written agreement, a national bank exercising fiduciary powers may perform services related to the exercise of fiduciary powers for another bank or other entity, and may purchase services related to the exercise of fiduciary powers from another bank or other entity.

(d) *Bond requirement.* A national bank shall ensure that all fiduciary officers and employees are adequately bonded.

§ 9.5 Policies and procedures.

A national bank exercising fiduciary powers shall adopt and follow written policies and procedures adequate to maintain its fiduciary activities in compliance with applicable law. Among other relevant matters, the policies and procedures should address, where appropriate, the bank's:

(a) Brokerage placement practices;

(b) Methods for ensuring that fiduciary officers and employees do not use material inside information in connection with any decision or recommendation to purchase or sell any security;

(c) Methods for preventing self-dealing and conflicts of interest;

(d) Selection and retention of legal counsel who is readily available to advise the bank and its fiduciary officers and employees on fiduciary matters; and

(e) Investment of funds held as fiduciary, including short-term investments and the treatment of fiduciary funds awaiting investment or distribution.

§ 9.6 Review of fiduciary accounts.

(a) *Pre-acceptance review.* Before accepting a fiduciary account, a national bank shall review the prospective account to determine whether it can properly administer the account.

(b) *Initial post-acceptance review.* Upon the acceptance of a fiduciary account for which a national bank has investment discretion, the bank shall conduct a prompt review of all assets of the account to evaluate whether they are appropriate for the account.

(c) *Annual review.* At least once during every calendar year, a bank shall conduct a review of all assets of each fiduciary account for which the bank has investment discretion to evaluate whether they are appropriate, individually and collectively, for the account.

§ 9.7 Multi-state fiduciary operations.

(a) *Acting in a fiduciary capacity in more than one state.* Pursuant to 12 U.S.C. 92a and this section, a national bank may act in a fiduciary capacity in any state. If a national bank acts, or proposes to act, in a fiduciary capacity in a particular state, the bank may act in the following specific capacities:

(1) Any of the eight fiduciary capacities expressly listed in 12 U.S.C. 92a(a), unless the state prohibits its own state banks, trust companies, and other corporations that compete with national banks in that state from acting in that capacity; and

(2) Any other fiduciary capacity the state permits for its own state banks, trust companies, or other corporations that compete with national banks in that state.

(b) *Serving customers in other states.* While acting in a fiduciary capacity in one state, a national bank may market its fiduciary services to, and act as fiduciary for, customers located in any state, and it may act as fiduciary for relationships that include property located in other states. The bank may use a trust representative office for this purpose.

(c) *Offices in more than one state.* A national bank with fiduciary powers may establish trust offices or trust representative offices in any state.

(d) *Determination of the state referred to in 12 U.S.C. 92a.* For each fiduciary relationship, the state referred to in section 92a is the state in which the bank acts in a fiduciary capacity for that relationship. A national bank acts in a fiduciary capacity in the state in which it accepts the fiduciary appointment, executes the documents that create the fiduciary relationship, and makes discretionary decisions regarding the investment or distribution of fiduciary assets. If these activities take place in more than one state, then the state in which the bank acts in a fiduciary capacity for section 92a purposes is the state that the bank designates from among those states.

(e) *Application of state law*—(1) *State laws used in section 92a.* The state laws that apply to a national bank's fiduciary activities by virtue of 12 U.S.C. 92a are the laws of the state in which the bank acts in a fiduciary capacity.

(2) *Other state laws.* Except for the state laws made applicable to national banks by virtue of 12 U.S.C. 92a, state laws limiting or establishing preconditions on the exercise of fiduciary powers are not applicable to national banks.

[66 FR 34798, July 2, 2001]

§ 9.8 Recordkeeping.

(a) *Documentation of accounts.* A national bank shall adequately document the establishment and termination of each fiduciary account and shall maintain adequate records for all fiduciary accounts.

(b) *Retention of records.* A national bank shall retain records described in paragraph (a) of this section for a period of three years from the later of the termination of the account or the termination of any litigation relating to the account.

(c) *Separation of records.* A national bank shall ensure that records described in paragraph (a) of this section are separate and distinct from other records of the bank.

§9.9 Audit of fiduciary activities.

(a) *Annual audit.* At least once during each calendar year, a national bank shall arrange for a suitable audit (by internal or external auditors) of all significant fiduciary activities, under the direction of its fiduciary audit committee, unless the bank adopts a continuous audit system in accordance with paragraph (b) of this section. The bank shall note the results of the audit (including significant actions taken as a result of the audit) in the minutes of the board of directors.

(b) *Continuous audit.* In lieu of performing annual audits under paragraph (a) of this section, a national bank may adopt a continuous audit system under which the bank arranges for a discrete audit (by internal or external auditors) of each significant fiduciary activity (*i.e.*, on an activity-by-activity basis), under the direction of its fiduciary audit committee, at an interval commensurate with the nature and risk of that activity. Thus, certain fiduciary activities may receive audits at intervals greater or less than one year, as appropriate. A bank that adopts a continuous audit system shall note the results of all discrete audits performed since the last audit report (including significant actions taken as a result of the audits) in the minutes of the board of directors at least once during each calendar year .

(c) *Fiduciary audit committee.* A national bank's fiduciary audit committee must consist of a committee of the bank's directors or an audit committee of an affiliate of the bank. However, in either case, the committee:

(1) Must not include any officers of the bank or an affiliate who participate significantly in the administration of the bank's fiduciary activities; and

(2) Must consist of a majority of members who are not also members of any committee to which the board of directors has delegated power to manage and control the fiduciary activities of the bank.

§9.10 Fiduciary funds awaiting investment or distribution.

(a) *In general.* With respect to a fiduciary account for which a national bank has investment discretion or discretion over distributions, the bank may not allow funds awaiting investment or distribution to remain uninvested and undistributed any longer than is reasonable for the proper management of the account and consistent with applicable law. With respect to a fiduciary account for which a national bank has investment discretion, the bank shall obtain for funds awaiting investment or distribution a rate of return that is consistent with applicable law.

(b) *Self-deposits*—(1) *In general.* A national bank may deposit funds of a fiduciary account that are awaiting investment or distribution in the commercial, savings, or another department of the bank, unless prohibited by applicable law. To the extent that the funds are not insured by the Federal Deposit Insurance Corporation, the bank shall set aside collateral as security, under the control of appropriate fiduciary officers and employees, in accordance with paragraph (b)(2) of this section. The market value of the collateral set aside must at all times equal or exceed the amount of the uninsured fiduciary funds.

(2) *Acceptable collateral.* A national bank may satisfy the collateral requirement of paragraph (b)(1) of this section with any of the following:

(i) Direct obligations of the United States, or other obligations fully guaranteed by the United States as to principal and interest;

(ii) Securities that qualify as eligible for investment by national banks pursuant to 12 CFR part 1;

(iii) Readily marketable securities of the classes in which state banks, trust companies, or other corporations exercising fiduciary powers are permitted to invest fiduciary funds under applicable state law;

(iv) Surety bonds, to the extent they provide adequate security, unless prohibited by applicable law; and

(v) Any other assets that qualify under applicable state law as appropriate security for deposits of fiduciary funds.

(c) *Affiliate deposits.* A national bank, acting in its fiduciary capacity, may deposit funds of a fiduciary account that are awaiting investment or distribution with an affiliated insured depository institution, unless prohibited by applicable law. A national bank may set aside collateral as security for a deposit by or with an affiliate of fiduciary funds awaiting investment or distribution, unless prohibited by applicable law.

§9.11 Investment of fiduciary funds.

A national bank shall invest funds of a fiduciary account in a manner consistent with applicable law.

§9.12 Self-dealing and conflicts of interest.

(a) *Investments for fiduciary accounts*—(1) *In general.* Unless authorized by applicable law, a national bank may not invest funds of a fiduciary account for which a national bank has investment discretion in the stock or obligations of, or in assets acquired from: the bank or any of its directors, officers, or employees; affiliates of the bank or any of their directors, officers, or employees; or individuals or organizations with whom there exists an interest that might affect the exercise of the best judgment of the bank.

(2) *Additional securities investments.* If retention of stock or obligations of the bank or its affiliates in a fiduciary account is consistent with applicable law, the bank may:

(i) Exercise rights to purchase additional stock (or securities convertible into additional stock) when offered pro rata to stockholders; and

(ii) Purchase fractional shares to complement fractional shares acquired through the exercise of rights or the receipt of a stock dividend resulting in fractional share holdings.

(b) *Loans, sales, or other transfers from fiduciary accounts*—(1) *In general.* A national bank may not lend, sell, or otherwise transfer assets of a fiduciary account for which a national bank has investment discretion to the bank or any of its directors, officers, or employees, or to affiliates of the bank or any of their directors, officers, or employees, or to individuals or organizations with whom there exists an interest that might affect the exercise of the best judgment of the bank, unless:

(i) The transaction is authorized by applicable law;

(ii) Legal counsel advises the bank in writing that the bank has incurred, in its fiduciary capacity, a contingent or potential liability, in which case the bank, upon the sale or transfer of assets, shall reimburse the fiduciary account in cash at the greater of book or market value of the assets;

(iii) As provided in §9.18(b)(8)(iii) for defaulted investments; or

(iv) Required in writing by the OCC.

(2) *Loans of funds held as trustee.* Notwithstanding paragraph (b)(1) of this section, a national bank may not lend to any of its directors, officers, or employees any funds held in trust, except with respect to employee benefit plans in accordance with the exemptions found in section 408 of the Employee Retirement Income Security Act of 1974 (29 U.S.C. 1108).

(c) *Loans to fiduciary accounts.* A national bank may make a loan to a fiduciary account and may hold a security interest in assets of the account if the transaction is fair to the account and is not prohibited by applicable law.

(d) *Sales between fiduciary accounts.* A national bank may sell assets between any of its fiduciary accounts if the transaction is fair to both accounts and is not prohibited by applicable law.

(e) *Loans between fiduciary accounts.* A national bank may make a loan between any of its fiduciary accounts if the transaction is fair to both accounts and is not prohibited by applicable law.

§9.13 Custody of fiduciary assets.

(a) *Control of fiduciary assets.* A national bank shall place assets of fiduciary accounts in the joint custody or control of not fewer than two of the fiduciary officers or employees designated for that purpose by the board of directors. A national bank may maintain the investments of a fiduciary account off-premises, if consistent with applicable law and if the bank maintains adequate safeguards and controls. A bank that is deemed a fiduciary based solely on its capacity as investment advisor, as that capacity is defined in §9.101(a), and has no other fiduciary capacity as enumerated in §9.2(e) is not required to serve as custodian when offering those fiduciary services.

(b) *Separation of fiduciary assets.* A national bank shall keep the assets of fiduciary accounts separate from the assets of the bank. A national bank shall keep the assets of each fiduciary account separate from all other accounts or shall identify the investments as the property of a particular account, except as provided in §9.18.

[61 FR 68554, Dec. 30, 1996, as amended at 82 FR 8105, Jan. 23, 2017]

§9.14 Deposit of securities with state authorities.

(a) *In general.* If state law requires corporations acting in a fiduciary capacity to deposit securities with state authorities for the protection of private or court trusts, then before a national bank acts as a private or court-appointed trustee in that state, it shall make a similar deposit with state authorities. If the state authorities refuse to accept the deposit, the bank shall deposit the securities with the Federal Reserve Bank or Federal Home Loan Bank of the district in which the national bank is located, to be held for the protection of private or court trusts to the same extent as if the securities had been deposited with state authorities.

(b) *Acting in a fiduciary capacity in more than one state.* If a national bank acts in a fiduciary capacity in more than one state, the bank may compute the amount of securities that are required to be deposited for each state on the basis of the amount of assets for which the bank is acting in a fiduciary capacity at offices located in that state. If state law requires a deposit of securities on a basis other than assets (*e.g.*, a requirement to deposit a fixed amount or an amount equal to a percentage of capital), the bank may compute the amount of deposit required in that state on a pro-rated basis, according to the proportion of fiduciary assets for which the bank is acting in a fiduciary capacity at offices located in that state.

[61 FR 68554, Dec. 30, 1996, as amended at 66 FR 34798, July 2, 2001; 82 FR 8105, Jan. 23, 2017]

§9.15 Fiduciary compensation.

(a) *Compensation of bank.* If the amount of a national bank's compensation for acting in a fiduciary capacity is not set or governed by applicable law, the bank may charge a reasonable fee for its services.

(b) *Compensation of co-fiduciary officers and employees.* A national bank may not permit any officer or employee to retain any compensation for acting as a co-fiduciary with the bank in the administration of a fiduciary account, except with the specific approval of the bank's board of directors.

§9.16 Receivership or voluntary liquidation of bank.

If the OCC appoints a receiver for an uninsured national bank, or if a national bank places itself in voluntary liquidation, the receiver or liquidating agent shall promptly close or transfer to a substitute fiduciary all fiduciary accounts, in accordance with OCC instructions and the orders of the court having jurisdiction.

§9.17 Surrender or revocation of fiduciary powers.

(a) *Surrender.* In accordance with 12 U.S.C. 92a(j), a national bank seeking to surrender its fiduciary powers shall file with the OCC a certified copy of the resolution of its board of directors evidencing that intent. If, after appropriate investigation, the OCC is satisfied that the bank has been discharged from all fiduciary duties, the OCC will provide written notice that the bank is no longer authorized to exercise fiduciary powers.

(b) *Revocation.* If the OCC determines that a national bank has unlawfully or unsoundly exercised, or has failed for a period of five consecutive years to exercise its fiduciary powers, the Comptroller may, in accordance with the provisions of 12 U.S.C. 92a(k), revoke the bank's fiduciary powers.

§ 9.18 Collective investment funds.

(a) *In general.* Where consistent with applicable law, a national bank may invest assets that it holds as fiduciary in the following collective investment funds: [1]

(1) A fund maintained by the bank, or by one or more affiliated banks, [2] exclusively for the collective investment and reinvestment of money contributed to the fund by the bank, or by one or more affiliated banks, in its capacity as trustee, executor, administrator, guardian, or custodian under a uniform gifts to minors act.

(2) A fund consisting solely of assets of retirement, pension, profit sharing, stock bonus or other trusts that are exempt from Federal income tax.

(i) A national bank may invest assets of retirement, pension, profit sharing, stock bonus, or other trusts exempt from Federal income tax and that the bank holds in its capacity as trustee in a collective investment fund established under paragraph (a)(1) or (a)(2) of this section.

(ii) A national bank may invest assets of retirement, pension, profit sharing, stock bonus, or other employee benefit trusts exempt from Federal income tax and that the bank holds in any capacity (including agent), in a collective investment fund established under this paragraph (a)(2) if the fund itself qualifies for exemption from Federal income tax.

(b) *Requirements.* A national bank administering a collective investment fund authorized under paragraph (a) of this section shall comply with the following requirements:

(1) *Written plan.* The bank shall establish and maintain each collective investment fund in accordance with a written plan (Plan) approved by a resolution of the bank's board of directors or by a committee authorized by the board. The bank shall make a copy of the Plan available either for public inspection at its main office during all banking hours or on its Web site and shall provide a written or electronic copy of the Plan to any person who requests it. The Plan must contain appropriate provisions, not inconsistent with this part, regarding the manner in which the bank will operate the fund, including provisions relating to:

(i) Investment powers and policies with respect to the fund;

(ii) Allocation of income, profits, and losses;

(iii) Fees and expenses that will be charged to the fund and to participating accounts;

(iv) Terms and conditions governing the admission and withdrawal of participating accounts;

(v) Audits of participating accounts;

(vi) Basis and method of valuing assets in the fund;

(vii) Expected frequency for income distribution to participating accounts;

(viii) Minimum frequency for valuation of fund assets;

(ix) Amount of time following a valuation date during which the valuation must be made;

(x) Bases upon which the bank may terminate the fund; and

(xi) Any other matters necessary to define clearly the rights of participating accounts.

(2) *Fund management.* A bank administering a collective investment fund shall have exclusive management thereof, except as a prudent person might delegate responsibilities to others. [3]

[1] In determining whether investing fiduciary assets in a collective investment fund is proper, the bank may consider the fund as a whole and, for example, shall not be prohibited from making that investment because any particular asset is nonincome producing.

[2] A fund established pursuant to this paragraph (a)(1) that includes money contributed by entities that are affiliates under 12 U.S.C. 221a(b), but are not members of the same affiliated group, as defined at 26 U.S.C. 1504, may fail to qualify for tax-exempt status under the Internal Revenue Code. *See* 26 U.S.C. 584.

[3] If a fund, the assets of which consist solely of Individual Retirement Accounts, Keogh Accounts, or other employee benefit accounts that are exempt from taxation, is registered under the Investment Company Act of 1940 (15 U.S.C. 80a–1 *et seq.*), the fund will not be deemed in violation of this paragraph (b)(2) as a result of its compliance with section 10(c) of the Investment Company Act of 1940 (15 U.S.C. 80a–10(c)).

(3) *Proportionate interests.* Each participating account in a collective investment fund must have a proportionate interest in all the fund's assets.

(4) *Valuation*—(i) *Frequency of valuation.* A bank administering a collective investment fund shall determine the value of the fund's readily marketable assets at least once every three months. A bank shall determine the value of the fund's assets that are not readily marketable at least once a year.

(ii) *General method of valuation.* Except as provided in paragraph (b)(4)(iii) of this section, a bank shall value each fund asset at mark-to-market value as of the date set for valuation, unless the bank cannot readily ascertain mark-to-market value, in which case the bank shall use a fair value determined in good faith.

(iii) *Short-term investment funds (STIFs) method of valuation.* A bank may value a STIF's assets on a cost basis, rather than mark-to-market value as provided in paragraph (b)(4)(ii) of this section, for purposes of admissions and withdrawals, if the Plan includes appropriate provisions, consistent with this part, requiring the STIF to:

(A) Operate with a stable net asset value of $1.00 per participating interest as a primary fund objective;

(B) Maintain a dollar-weighted average portfolio maturity of 60 days or less and a dollar-weighted average portfolio life maturity of 120 days or less as determined in the same manner as is required by the Securities and Exchange Commission pursuant to Rule 2a–7 for money market mutual funds (17 CFR 270.2a–7);

(C) Accrue on a straight-line or amortized basis the difference between the cost and anticipated principal receipt on maturity;

(D) Hold the STIF's assets until maturity under usual circumstances;

(E) Adopt portfolio and issuer qualitative standards and concentration restrictions;

(F) Adopt liquidity standards that include provisions to address contingency funding needs;

(G) Adopt shadow pricing procedures that:

(*1*) Require the bank to calculate the extent of difference, if any, of the mark-to-market net asset value per participating interest using available market quotations (or an appropriate substitute that reflects current market conditions) from the STIF's amortized cost price per participating interest, at least on a calendar week basis and more frequently as determined by the bank when market conditions warrant; and

(*2*) Require the bank, in the event the difference calculated pursuant to this subparagraph exceeds $0.005 per participating interest, to take action to reduce dilution of participating interests or other unfair results to participating accounts in the STIF;

(H) Adopt procedures for stress testing the STIF's ability to maintain a stable net asset value per participating interest that shall provide for:

(*1*) The periodic stress testing, at least on a calendar month basis and at such intervals as an independent risk manager or a committee responsible for the STIF's oversight that consists of members independent from the STIF's investment management determines appropriate and reasonable in light of current market conditions;

(*2*) Stress testing based upon hypothetical events that include, but are not limited to, a change in short-term interest rates, an increase in participant account withdrawals, a downgrade of or default on portfolio securities, and the widening or narrowing of spreads between yields on an appropriate benchmark the STIF has selected for overnight interest rates and commercial paper and other types of securities held by the STIF;

(*3*) A stress testing report on the results of such testing to be provided to the independent risk manager or the committee responsible for the STIF's oversight that consists of members independent from the STIF's investment management that shall include: the date(s) on which the testing was performed; the magnitude of each hypothetical event that would cause the difference between the STIF's mark-to-market net asset value calculated using available market quotations (or appropriate substitutes which reflect current market conditions) and its net asset value per participating interest calculated using amortized cost to exceed $0.005; and an assessment by the bank of the STIF's ability to withstand the events (and concurrent occurrences of those events) that are reasonably likely to occur within the following year; and

(*4*) Reporting adverse stress testing results to the bank's senior risk management that is independent from the STIF's investment management.

(I) Adopt procedures that require a bank to disclose to STIF participants and to the OCC's Asset Management Group, Credit & Market Risk Division, within five business days after each calendar month-end, the fund's total assets under management (securities and other assets including cash, minus liabilities); the fund's mark-to-market and amortized cost net asset values both with and without capital support agreements; the dollar-weighted average portfolio maturity; the dollar-weighted average portfolio life maturity of the STIF as of the last business day of the prior calendar month; and for each security held by the STIF as of the last business day of the prior calendar month:

(*1*) The name of the issuer;

(*2*) The category of investment;

(*3*) The Committee on Uniform Securities Identification Procedures (CUSIP) number or other standard identifier;

(*4*) The principal amount;

(*5*) The maturity date for purposes of calculating dollar-weighted average portfolio maturity;

(*6*) The final legal maturity date (taking into account any maturity date extensions that may be effected at the option of the issuer) if different from the maturity date for purposes of calculating dollar-weighted average portfolio maturity;

(*7*) The coupon or yield; and

(*8*) The amortized cost value;

(J) Adopt procedures that require a bank that administers a STIF to notify the OCC's Asset Management Group, Credit & Market Risk Division, prior to or within one business day thereafter of the following:

(*1*) Any difference exceeding $0.0025 between the net asset value and the mark-to-market value of a STIF participating interest as calculated using the method set forth in paragraph (b)(4)(iii)(G)(*1*) of this section;

(*2*) When a STIF has re-priced its net asset value below $0.995 per participating interest;

(*3*) Any withdrawal distribution-in-kind of the STIF's participating interests or segregation of portfolio participants;

(*4*) Any delays or suspensions in honoring STIF participating interest withdrawal requests;

(*5*) Any decision to formally approve the liquidation, segregation of assets or portfolios, or some other liquidation of the STIF; or

(*6*) In those situations when a bank, its affiliate, or any other entity provides a STIF financial support, including a cash infusion, a credit extension, a purchase of a defaulted or illiquid asset, or any other form of financial support in order to maintain a stable net asset value per participating interest;

(K) Adopt procedures that in the event a STIF has re-priced its net asset value below $0.995 per participating interest, the bank administering the STIF shall calculate, admit, and withdraw the STIF's participating interests at a price based on the mark-to-market net asset value; and

(L) Adopt procedures that, in the event a bank suspends or limits withdrawals and initiates liquidation of the STIF as a result of redemptions, require the bank to:

(*1*) Determine that the extent of the difference between the STIF's amortized cost per participating interest and its mark-to-market net asset value per participating interest may result in material dilution of participating interests or other unfair results to participating accounts;

(*2*) Formally approve the liquidation of the STIF; and

(*3*) Facilitate the fair and orderly liquidation of the STIF to the benefit of all STIF participants.

(5) *Admission and withdrawal of accounts*—(i) *In general.* A bank administering a collective investment fund shall admit an account to or withdraw an account from the fund only on the basis of the valuation described in paragraph (b)(4) of this section.

(ii) *Prior request or notice.* A bank administering a collective investment fund may admit an account to or withdraw an account from a collective investment fund only if the bank has approved a request for or a notice of intention of taking that action on or before the valuation date on which the admission or withdrawal is based. No requests or notices may be canceled or countermanded after the valuation date.

(iii) *Prior notice period for withdrawals from funds with assets not readily marketable.* A bank administering a collective investment fund described in paragraph (a)(2) of this section that is invested primarily in real estate or other assets that are not readily marketable, may require a prior notice period, not to exceed one year, for withdrawals.

(iv) *Method of distributions.* A bank administering a collective investment fund shall make distributions to accounts withdrawing from the fund in cash, ratably in kind, a combination of cash and ratably in kind, or in any other manner consistent with applicable law in the state in which the bank maintains the fund.

(v) *Segregation of investments.* If an investment is withdrawn in kind from a collective investment fund for the benefit of all participants in the fund at the time of the withdrawal but the investment is not distributed ratably in kind, the bank shall segregate and administer it for the benefit ratably of all participants in the collective investment fund at the time of withdrawal.

(6) *Audits and financial reports*—(i) *Annual audit.* At least once during each 12-month period, a bank administering a collective investment fund shall arrange for an audit of the collective investment fund by auditors responsible only to the board of directors of the bank.[4]

[4] If a fund, the assets of which consist solely of Individual Retirement Accounts, Keogh Accounts, or other employee benefit accounts that are exempt from taxation, is registered under the Investment Company Act of 1940 (15 U.S.C. 80a–1 *et seq.*), the fund will not be deemed in violation of this paragraph (b)(6)(i) as a result of its compliance with section 10(c) of the Investment Company Act of 1940 (15 U.S.C. 80a–10(c)), if the bank has access to the audit reports of the fund.

(ii) *Financial report.* At least once during each 12-month period, a bank administering a collective investment fund shall prepare a financial report of the fund based on the audit required by paragraph (b)(6)(i) of this section. The report must disclose the fund's fees and expenses in a manner consistent with applicable law in the state in which the bank maintains the fund. This report must contain a list of investments in the fund showing the cost and current market value of each investment, and a statement covering the period after the previous report showing the following (organized by type of investment):

(A) A summary of purchases (with costs);

(B) A summary of sales (with profit or loss and any other investment changes);

(C) Income and disbursements; and

(D) An appropriate notation of any investments in default.

(iii) *Limitation on representations.* A bank may include in the financial report a description of the fund's value on previous dates, as well as its income and disbursements during previous accounting periods. A bank may not publish in the financial report any predictions or representations as to future performance. In addition, with respect to funds described in paragraph (a)(1) of this section, a bank may not publish the performance of individual funds other than those administered by the bank or its affiliates.

(iv) *Availability of the report.* A bank administering a collective investment fund shall provide a copy of the financial report, or shall provide notice that a copy of the report is available upon request without charge, to each person who ordinarily would receive a regular periodic accounting with respect to each participating account. The bank may provide a copy of the financial report to prospective customers. In addition, the bank shall provide a copy of the report upon request to any person for a reasonable charge.

(7) *Advertising restriction.* A bank may not advertise or publicize any fund authorized under paragraph (a)(1) of this section, except in connection with the advertisement of the general fiduciary services of the bank.

(8) *Self-dealing and conflicts of interest.* A national bank administering a collective investment fund must comply with the following (in addition to § 9.12):

(i) *Bank interests.* A bank administering a collective investment fund may not have an interest in that fund other than in its fiduciary capacity. If, because of a creditor relationship or otherwise, the bank acquires an interest in a participating account, the participating account must be withdrawn on the next withdrawal date. However, a bank may invest assets that it holds as fiduciary for its own employees in a collective investment fund.

(ii) *Loans to participating accounts.* A bank administering a collective investment fund may not make any loan on the security of a participant's interest in the fund. An unsecured advance to a fiduciary account participating in the fund until the time of the next valuation date does not constitute the acquisition of an interest in a participating account by the bank.

(iii) *Purchase of defaulted investments.* A bank administering a collective investment fund may purchase for its own account any defaulted investment held by the fund (in lieu of segregating the investment in accordance with paragraph (b)(5)(v) of this section) if, in the judgment of the bank, the cost of segregating the investment is excessive in light of the market value of the investment. If a bank elects to purchase a defaulted investment, it shall do so at the greater of market value or the sum of cost and accrued unpaid interest.

(9) *Management fees.* A bank administering a collective investment fund may charge a reasonable fund management fee only if:

(i) The fee is permitted under applicable law (and complies with fee disclosure requirements, if any) in the state in which the bank maintains the fund; and

(ii) The amount of the fee does not exceed an amount commensurate with the value of legitimate services of tangible benefit to the participating fiduciary accounts that would not have been provided to the accounts were they not invested in the fund.

(10) *Expenses.* A bank administering a collective investment fund may charge reasonable expenses incurred in operating the collective investment fund, to the extent not prohibited by applicable law in the state in which the bank maintains the fund. However, a bank shall absorb the expenses of establishing or reorganizing a collective investment fund.

(11) *Prohibition against certificates.* A bank administering a collective investment fund may not issue any certificate or other document representing a direct or indirect interest in the fund, except to provide a withdrawing account with an interest in a segregated investment.

(12) *Good faith mistakes.* The OCC will not deem a bank's mistake made in good faith and in the exercise of due care in connection with the administration of a collective investment fund to be a violation of this part if, promptly after the discovery of the mistake, the bank takes whatever action is practicable under the circumstances to remedy the mistake.

(c) *Other collective investments.* In addition to the collective investment funds authorized under paragraph (a) of this section, a national bank may collectively invest assets that it holds as fiduciary, to the extent not prohibited by applicable law, as follows:

(1) *Single loans or obligations.* In the following loans or obligations, if the bank's only interest in the loans or obligations is its capacity as fiduciary:

(i) A single real estate loan, a direct obligation of the United States, or an obligation fully guaranteed by the United States, or a single fixed amount security, obligation, or other property, either real, personal, or mixed, of a single issuer; or

(ii) A variable amount note of a borrower of prime credit, if the bank uses the note solely for investment of funds held in its fiduciary accounts.

(2) *Mini-funds.* In a fund maintained by the bank for the collective investment of cash balances received or held by a bank in its capacity as trustee, executor, administrator, guardian, or custodian under a uniform gifts to minors act, that the bank considers too small to be invested separately to advantage. The total assets in the fund

must not exceed $1,500,000 and the number of participating accounts must not exceed 100. The OCC shall adjust this $1,500,000 threshold amount on January 1 of every year by the percentage increase in the Consumer Price Index for Urban Wage Earners and Clerical Workers (CPI-W) that was in effect on the preceding June 1, rounded to the nearest $100 increment, and make this adjusted amount available to the public.

(3) *Trust funds of corporations and closely-related settlors.* In any investment specifically authorized by the instrument creating the fiduciary account or a court order, in the case of trusts created by a corporation, including its affiliates and subsidiaries, or by several individual settlors who are closely related.

(4) *Other authorized funds.* In any collective investment authorized by applicable law, such as investments pursuant to a state pre-need funeral statute.

(5) *Special exemption funds.* In any other manner described by the bank in a written plan approved by the OCC.[5] In order to obtain a special exemption, a bank shall submit to the OCC a written plan that sets forth:

(i) The reason that the proposed fund requires a special exemption;

(ii) The provisions of the proposed fund that are inconsistent with paragraphs (a) and (b) of this section;

(iii) The provisions of paragraph (b) of this section for which the bank seeks an exemption; and

(iv) The manner in which the proposed fund addresses the rights and interests of participating accounts.

[61 FR 68554, Dec. 30, 1996, as amended at 68 FR 70131, Dec. 17, 2003; 77 FR 61237, Oct. 9, 2012; 82 FR 8105, Jan. 23, 2017]

§ 9.20 Transfer agents.

(a)(1) *Registration.* An application for registration under Section 17A(c) of the Securities Exchange Act of 1934 of a transfer agent for which the OCC is the appropriate regulatory agency, as defined in section 3(a)(34)(B) of the Securities Exchange Act of 1934, shall be filed with the OCC on FFIEC Form TA-1, in accordance with the instructions contained therein. Registration shall become effective 30 days after the date an application on Form TA-1 is filed unless the OCC accelerates, denies, or postpones such registration in accordance with section 17A(c) of the Securities Exchange Act of 1934.

(2) *Amendments to registration.* Within 60 days following the date on which any information reported on Form TA-1 becomes inaccurate, misleading, or incomplete, the registrant shall file an amendment on FFIEC Form TA-1 correcting the inaccurate, misleading, or incomplete information. The filing of an amendment to an application for registration as a transfer agent under this section, which registration has not become effective, shall postpone the effective date of the registration for 30 days following the date on which the amendment is filed unless the OCC accelerates, denies, or postpones the registration in accordance with Section 17A(c) of the Securities Exchange Act of 1934.

(3) *Withdrawal from registration.* Any registered national bank transfer agent that ceases to engage in activities that require registration under Section 17A(c) of the Securities Exchange Act of 1934 may file a written notice of withdrawal from registration with the OCC. Deregistration shall be effective 60 days after filing.

(4) *Reports.* Every registration or amendment filed under this section shall constitute a report or application within the meaning of Sections 17, 17A(c), and 32(a) of the Securities Exchange Act of 1934.

(b) *Operational and reporting requirements.* The rules adopted by the Securities and Exchange Commission pursuant to Section 17A of the Securities Exchange Act of 1934 prescribing operational and reporting requirements for transfer agents apply to the domestic activities of registered national bank transfer agents.

[73 FR 22242, Apr. 24, 2008]

[5] Any institution that must comply with this section in order to receive favorable tax treatment under 26 U.S.C. 584 (namely, any corporate fiduciary) may seek OCC approval of special exemption funds in accordance with this paragraph (c)(5).

INTERPRETATIONS

§ 9.100 Acting as indenture trustee and creditor.

With respect to a debt securities issuance, a national bank may act both as indenture trustee and as creditor until 90 days after default, if the bank maintains adequate controls to manage the potential conflicts of interest.

§ 9.101 Providing investment advice for a fee.

(a) *In general.* The term "fiduciary capacity" at § 9.2(e) is defined to include "investment adviser, if the bank receives a fee for its investment advice." In other words, if a bank is providing investment advice for a fee, then it is acting in a fiduciary capacity. For purposes of that definition, "investment adviser" generally means a national bank that provides advice or recommendations concerning the purchase or sale of specific securities, such as a national bank engaged in portfolio advisory and management activities (including acting as investment adviser to a mutual fund). Additionally, the qualifying phrase "if the bank receives a fee for its investment advice" excludes those activities in which the investment advice is merely incidental to other services.

(b) *Specific activities*—(1) *Full-service brokerage.* Engaging in full-service brokerage may entail providing investment advice for a fee, depending upon the commission structure and specific facts. Full-service brokerage involves investment advice for a fee if a nonbank broker engaged in that activity is considered an investment adviser under the Investment Advisers Act of 1940 (15 U.S.C. 80b–1 *et seq.*).

(2) *Activities not involving investment advice for a fee.* The following activities generally do not entail providing investment advice for a fee:

(i) Financial advisory and counseling activities, including strategic planning of a financial nature, merger and acquisition advisory services, advisory and structuring services related to project finance transactions, and providing market economic information to customers in general;

(ii) Client-directed investment activities (*i.e.*, the bank has no investment discretion) where investment advice and research may be made available to the client, but the fee does not depend on the provision of investment advice;

(iii) Investment advisory activities incidental to acting as a municipal securities dealer;

(iv) Real estate management services provided to other financial institutions;

(v) Real estate consulting services, including acting as a finder in locating, analyzing, and making recommendations regarding the purchase of property, and making recommendations concerning the sale of property;

(vi) Advisory activities concerning bridge loans;

(vii) Advisory activities for homeowners' associations;

(viii) Advisory activities concerning tax planning and structuring; and

(ix) Investment advisory activities authorized by the OCC under 12 U.S.C. 24(Seventh) as incidental to the business of banking.

[63 FR 6473, Feb. 9, 1998]

PART 10—MUNICIPAL SECURITIES DEALERS

Sec.
10.1 Scope.
10.2 Filing requirements.

AUTHORITY: 12 U.S.C. 93a, 481, 1462a, 1463, 1464(c), 1818, and 5412(b)(2)(B); 15 U.S.C. 78o–4(c)(5) and 78q–78w.

SOURCE: 63 FR 29094, May 28, 1998, unless otherwise noted.

§ 10.1 Scope.

This part applies to:

(a) Any national bank or Federal savings association and separately identifiable department or division of a national bank or Federal savings association (collectively, a national bank or Federal savings association) that acts as a municipal securities dealer, as that term is defined in section 3(a)(30) of the Securities Exchange Act of 1934 (15 U.S.C. 78c(a)(30)); and

(b) Any person who is associated or will be associated with a national bank or Federal savings association in the capacity of a municipal securities principal or a municipal securities representative, as those terms are defined in Rule G–3 of the Municipal Securities Rulemaking Board (MSRB). MSRB rules may be obtained at *www.msrb.org*.

[63 FR 29094, May 28, 1998, as amended at 73 FR 22242, Apr. 24, 2008; 82 FR 8105, Jan. 23, 2017]

§ 10.2 Filing requirements.

(a) A national bank or Federal savings association shall use Form MSD–4 (Uniform Application for Municipal Securities Principal or Municipal Securities Representative Associated with a Bank Municipal Securities Dealer) for obtaining the information required by MSRB Rule G–7(b) from a person identified in § 10.1(b). A national bank or Federal savings association receiving a completed MSD–4 form from a person identified in § 10.1(b) must submit this form to the OCC before permitting the person to be associated with it as a municipal securities principal or a municipal securities representative.

(b) A national bank or Federal savings association shall submit Form MSD–5 (Uniform Termination Notice for Municipal Securities Principal or Municipal Securities Representative Associated with a Bank Municipal Securities Dealer) to the OCC within 30 days of terminating a person's association with the national bank or Federal savings association as a municipal securities principal or municipal securities representative.

(c) Forms MSD–4 and MSD–5, with instructions, may be obtained at *http://www.banknet.gov/*.

[63 FR 29094, May 28, 1998, as amended at 63 FR 71343, Dec. 24, 1998; 79 FR 15641, Mar. 21, 2014; 82 FR 8105, Jan. 23, 2017]

PART 11—SECURITIES EXCHANGE ACT DISCLOSURE RULES

Sec.

11.1 Authority.
11.2 Reporting requirements for registered national banks and Federal savings associations.
11.3 Filing requirements and inspection of documents.
11.4 Filing fees.

AUTHORITY: 12 U.S.C. 93a, 1462a, 1463, 1464 and 5412(b)(2)(B); 15 U.S.C. 78j–1(m), 78m, 78n, 78p, 78w, 78l, 7241, 7242, 7243, 7244, 7261, 7262, 7264, and 7265.

SOURCE: 57 FR 46084, Oct. 7, 1992; 57 FR 54499, Nov. 19, 1992, unless otherwise noted.

§ 11.1 Authority.

The Office of the Comptroller of the Currency (OCC) is vested with the powers, functions, and duties otherwise vested in the Securities and Exchange Commission (SEC) to administer and enforce the provisions of sections 10A(m), 12, 13, 14(a), 14(c), 14(d), 14(f), and 16 of the Securities Exchange Act of 1934, as amended (Exchange Act) (15 U.S.C. 78j–1(m), 78l, 78m, 78n(a), 78n(c), 78n(d), 78n(f), and 78p), and sections 302, 303, 304, 306, 401(b), 404, 406, and 407 of the Sarbanes-Oxley Act of 2002 (Sarbanes-Oxley Act), as amended (15 U.S.C. 7241, 7242, 7243, 7244, 7261, 7262, 7264, and 7265), for national banks and Federal savings associations with one or more classes of securities subject to the registration provisions of sections 12(b) and (g) of the Exchange Act (registered national banks or registered Federal savings associations). Further, the OCC has general rulemaking authority under 12 U.S.C. 93a, 1462a, 1463, and 1464, to promulgate rules and regulations concerning the activities of national banks and Federal savings associations.

[82 FR 8105, Jan. 23, 2017]

§ 11.2 Reporting requirements for registered national banks and Federal savings associations.

(a) *Filing, disclosure and other requirements*—(1) *General.* Except as otherwise provided in this section, a national bank or Federal savings association whose securities are subject to registration pursuant to section 12(b) or section 12(g) of the Exchange Act (15 U.S.C. 78l(b) and (g)) shall comply with the rules, regulations, and forms adopted by the SEC pursuant to:

(i) Sections 10A(m), 12, 13, 14(a), 14(c), 14(d), 14(f), and 16 of the Exchange Act (15 U.S.C. 78j–1(m), 78l, 78m, 78n(a), (c), (d) and (f), and 78p); and

(ii) Sections 302, 303, 304, 306, 401(b), 404, 406, and 407 of the Sarbanes-Oxley Act (codified at 15 U.S.C. 7241, 7242, 7243, 7244, 7261, 7262, 7264, and 7265).

(2) [Reserved]

(b) *References to the Securities Exchange Commission, SEC, or Commission.* Any references to the "Securities and

Exchange Commission," the "SEC," or the "Commission" in the rules, regulations and forms described in paragraph (a)(1) of this section with respect to securities issued by registered national banks or registered Federal savings associations shall be deemed to refer to the OCC unless the context otherwise requires.

(c) *References to registration requirements.* For national banks and Federal savings associations, any references to registration requirements under the Securities Act of 1933 and its accompanying rules in the rules, regulations, and forms described in paragraph (a)(1) of this section mean the registration requirements in 12 CFR part 16.

(d) *Emerging growth company eligibility*—(1) *General.* A national bank or Federal savings association that meets the criteria to qualify as an emerging growth company under section 3(a)(80) of the Exchange Act (15 U.S.C. 78c(a)(80)) shall be eligible for treatment as an emerging growth company for purposes of any rule, regulation or form described in paragraph (a)(1) of this section, except as provided in paragraph (d)(3) of this section.

(2) *Opt-in right.* With respect to an exemption provided to a national bank or Federal savings association that is an emerging growth company under this part, the bank or savings association may choose to forgo such exemption and instead comply with the requirements that apply to a bank or savings association that is not an emerging growth company.

(3) *Exclusions.* A national bank or Federal savings association that otherwise meets the definition of emerging growth company in section 3(a)(80) of the Exchange Act (15 U.S.C. 78c(a)(80)) shall not be considered an emerging growth company for purposes of this part if:

(i) The first sale of its common equity securities pursuant to an effective registration statement or offering circular occurred on or before December 8, 2011; or

(ii) It has reached the last day of its fiscal year following the fifth anniversary of the date of the first sale of its common equity securities pursuant to an effective registration statement or offering circular.

[82 FR 8105, Jan. 23, 2017]

§ 11.3 Filing requirements and inspection of documents.

(a) *Filing requirements*—(1)(i) *In general.* Except as otherwise provided in this section, all papers required to be filed with the OCC pursuant to the Exchange Act or regulations thereunder shall be submitted to the Securities and Corporate Practices Division of the OCC electronically at *http://www.banknet.gov/*. Documents may be signed electronically using the signature provision in SEC Rule 12b–11 (17 CFR 240.12b–11).

(ii) *Electronic filing exception.* If a national bank or Federal savings association experiences unanticipated technical difficulties preventing the timely preparation and submission of an electronic filing, other than the filings described in paragraph (a)(3)(ii) of this section, the bank may, upon notice to the OCC's Securities and Corporate Practices Division, file the subject filing in paper format no later than one business day after the date on which the filing was to be made. Paper filings should be submitted to the Securities and Corporate Practices Division, Office of the Comptroller of the Currency at the address provided at *www.occ.gov*.

(2) *Statements filed pursuant to section 16(a) of the 1934 Act.* Statements required under section 16(a) of the 1934 Act shall be filed electronically, as directed by the OCC.

(3) *Date of filing*—(i) *General.* The date of filing is the date the OCC receives the filing, provided the person, bank, or savings association submitting the filing has complied with all applicable requirements. An electronic filing that is submitted on a business day by direct transmission commencing on or before 5:30 p.m. Eastern Standard or Daylight Savings Time, whichever is currently in effect, would be deemed received by the OCC on the same business day. An electronic filing that is submitted by direct transmission commencing after 5:30 p.m. Eastern Standard or Daylight Savings Time, whichever is currently in effect, or on a Saturday, Sunday, or Federal holiday,

would be deemed received by the OCC on the next business day.

(ii) *Beneficial ownership filings*. An electronic filing of a statement required under section 16(a) of the 1934 Act that is submitted by direct transmission on or before 10 p.m. Eastern Standard Time or Eastern Daylight Savings Time, whichever is currently in effect, shall be deemed filed on the same business day.

(iii) *Adjustment of filing date*. If an electronic filer in good faith attempts to file a document pursuant to this part in a timely manner but the filing is delayed due to technical difficulties beyond the electronic filer's control, the electronic filer may request that the OCC adjust the filing date of such document. The OCC may grant the request if it appears that such adjustment is appropriate and consistent with the public interest and the protection of investors.

(b) Copies of registration statements, definitive proxy solicitation materials, reports, and annual reports to shareholders required by this part (exclusive of exhibits) are available from the Disclosure Officer, Communications Division, Office of the Comptroller of the Currency, at the address listed on *www.occ.gov*.

[60 FR 57332, Nov. 15, 1995, as amended at 68 FR 54984, Sept. 22, 2003; 70 FR 46404, Aug. 10, 2005; 79 FR 15641, Mar. 21, 2014; 82 FR 8106, Jan. 23, 2017]

§ 11.4 Filing fees.

(a) The OCC may require filing fees to accompany certain filings made under this part before it will accept the filing. The OCC provides an applicable fee schedule for such filings in the "Notice of Comptroller of the Currency Fees" described in 12 CFR 8.8.

(b) Fees must be paid by check payable to the Comptroller of the Currency or by other means acceptable to the OCC.

[57 FR 46084, Oct. 7, 1992; 57 FR 54499, Nov. 19, 1992, as amended at 60 FR 57332, Nov. 15, 1995; 82 FR 8106, Jan. 23, 2017]

PART 12—RECORDKEEPING AND CONFIRMATION REQUIREMENTS FOR SECURITIES TRANSACTIONS

Sec.

12.1 Authority, purpose, and scope.
12.2 Definitions.
12.3 Recordkeeping.
12.4 Content and time of notification.
12.5 Notification by agreement; alternative forms and times of notification.
12.6 Fees.
12.7 Securities trading policies and procedures.
12.8 Waivers.
12.9 Settlement of securities transactions.

AUTHORITY: 12 U.S.C. 24, 92a, and 93a.

SOURCE: 61 FR 63965, Dec. 2, 1996, unless otherwise noted.

§ 12.1 Authority, purpose, and scope.

(a) *Authority*. This part is issued pursuant to 12 U.S.C. 24, 92a, and 93a.

(b) *Purpose*. This part establishes rules, policies, and procedures applicable to recordkeeping and confirmation requirements for certain securities transactions effected by national banks for customers.

(c) *Scope*—(1) *General*. Any security transaction effected for a customer by a national bank is subject to this part, except as provided by paragraph (c)(2) of this section. This part applies to a national bank effecting transactions in government securities. This part also applies to municipal securities transactions by a national bank that is not registered as a "municipal securities dealer" with the Securities and Exchange Commission (SEC). *See* 15 U.S.C. 78c(a)(30) and 78o-4. This part, as well as 12 CFR part 9, applies to securities transactions effected by a national bank as fiduciary.

(2) *Exceptions*—(i) *Small number of transactions*. The requirements of §§ 12.3(a)(2) through (4) and 12.7(a)(1) through (3) do not apply to a national bank having an average of fewer than 200 securities transactions per year for customers over the prior three calendar year period. The calculation of this average does not include transactions in government securities.

(ii) *Government securities*. The recordkeeping requirements of § 12.3 do not apply to national banks effecting fewer than 500 government securities brokerage transactions per year. This exception does not apply to government securities dealer transactions by national banks. *See* 17 CFR 404.4(a).

(iii) *Municipal securities.* This part does not apply to transactions in municipal securities conducted by a national bank registered with the SEC as a "municipal securities dealer" as defined in title 15 U.S.C. 78c(a)(30). See 15 U.S.C. 78o–4.

(iv) *Foreign branches.* This part does not apply to securities transactions conducted by a foreign branch of a national bank.

(v) *Transactions effected by registered broker/dealers.* This part does not apply to securities transactions effected by a broker or dealer registered with the SEC where the SEC-registered broker or dealer directly provides the customer a confirmation; including, transactions effected by a national bank employee when acting as an employee of an SEC-registered broker/dealer.

(3) *Safe and sound operations.* Notwithstanding paragraph (c)(2) of this section, every national bank conducting securities transactions for customers shall maintain effective systems of records and controls regarding their customer securities transactions to ensure safe and sound operations. The systems maintained must clearly and accurately reflect appropriate information and provide an adequate basis for an audit.

[61 FR 63965, Dec. 2, 1996, as amended at 82 FR 8106, Jan. 23, 2017]

§ 12.2 Definitions.

(a) *Asset-backed security* means a security that is primarily serviced by the cashflows of a discrete pool of receivables or other financial assets, either fixed or revolving, that by their terms convert into cash within a finite time period plus any rights or other assets designed to assure the servicing or timely distribution of proceeds to the security holders.

(b) *Collective investment fund* means any fund established pursuant to 12 CFR 9.18.

(c) *Completion of the transaction* means:

(1) In the case of a customer who purchases a security through or from a national bank, except as provided in paragraph (c)(2) of this section, the time when the customer pays the bank any part of the purchase price, or, if payment is made by a bookkeeping entry, the time when the bank makes the bookkeeping entry for any part of the purchase price;

(2) In the case of a customer who purchases a security through or from a national bank and who makes payment for the security prior to the time when payment is requested or notification is given that payment is due, the time when the bank delivers the security to or into the account of the customer;

(3) In the case of a customer who sells a security through or to a national bank, except as provided in paragraph (c)(4) of this section, if the security is not in the custody of the bank at the time of sale, the time when the security is delivered to the bank, and if the security is in the custody of the bank at the time of sale, the time when the bank transfers the security from the account of the customer;

(4) In the case of a customer who sells a security through or to a national bank and who delivers the security to the bank prior to the time when delivery is requested or notification is given that delivery is due, the time when the bank makes payment to or into the account of the customer.

(d) *Crossing of buy and sell orders* means a security transaction in which the same bank acts as agent for both the buyer and the seller.

(e) *Customer* means any person or account, including any agency, trust, estate, guardianship, or other fiduciary account for which a national bank makes or participates in making the purchase or sale of securities, but does not include a broker, dealer, bank acting as a broker or dealer, bank acting as the fiduciary of an account, bank as trustee acting as shareholder of record for the purchase or sale of securities, or issuer of securities that are the subject of the transaction.

(f) *Debt security* means any security, such as a bond, debenture, note, or any other similar instrument that evidences a liability of the issuer (including any security of this type that is convertible into stock or a similar security) and fractional or participation interests in one or more of any of the foregoing. This definition does not include securities issued by an investment company registered under the Investment Company Act of 1940, 15 U.S.C. 80a–1 *et seq.*

(g) *Government security* means:

(1) A security that is a direct obligation of, or obligation guaranteed as to principal and interest by, the United States;

(2) A security that is issued or guaranteed by a corporation in which the United States has a direct or indirect interest and which is designated by the Secretary of the Treasury for exemption as necessary or appropriate in the public interest or for the protection of investors;

(3) A security issued or guaranteed as to principal and interest by any corporation whose securities are designated, by statute specifically naming the corporation, to constitute exempt securities within the meaning of the laws administered by the SEC; or

(4) Any put, call, straddle, option, or privilege on a security described in paragraph (g)(1), (2), or (3) of this section, other than a put, call, straddle, option, or privilege:

(i) That is traded on one or more national securities exchanges; or

(ii) For which quotations are disseminated through an automated quotation system operated by a registered securities association.

(h) *Investment discretion* means that, with respect to an account, a bank directly or indirectly:

(1) Is authorized to determine what securities or other property shall be purchased or sold by or for the account; or

(2) Makes decisions as to what securities or other property shall be purchased or sold by or for the account even though some other person may have responsibility for these investment decisions.

(i) *Municipal security* means:

(1) A security that is a direct obligation of, or an obligation guaranteed as to principal or interest by, a State or any political subdivision, or any agency or instrumentality of a State or any political subdivision;

(2) A security that is a direct obligation of, or an obligation guaranteed as to principal or interest by, any municipal corporate instrumentality of one or more States; or

(3) A security that is an industrial development bond.

(j) *Periodic plan* means:

(1) A written authorization for a national bank to act as agent to purchase or sell for a customer a specific security or securities, in a specific amount (calculated in security units or dollars) or to the extent of dividends and funds available, at specific time intervals, and setting forth the commission or charges to be paid by the customer or the manner of calculating them. These plans include dividend reinvestment plans, automatic investment plans, and employee stock purchase plans.

(2) Any prearranged, automatic transfer or "sweep" of funds from a deposit account to purchase a security, or any prearranged, automatic redemption or sale of a security with the funds being transferred into a deposit account (including cash management sweep services).

(k) *Security:* (1) Means any note, stock, treasury stock, bond, debenture, certificate of interest or participation in any profit-sharing agreement or in any oil, gas, or other mineral royalty or lease, any collateral-trust certificate, preorganization certificate or subscription, transferable share, investment contract, voting-trust certificate, and any put, call, straddle, option, or privilege on any security or group or index of securities (including any interest therein or based on the value thereof), or, in general, any instrument commonly known as a "security"; or any certificate of interest or participation in, temporary or interim certificate for, receipt for, or warrant or right to subscribe to or purchase, any of the foregoing;

(2) Does not mean currency; any note, draft, bill of exchange, or banker's acceptance which has a maturity at the time of issuance not exceeding nine months, exclusive of days of grace, or any renewal thereof, the maturity of which is likewise limited; a deposit or share account in a Federal or State chartered depository institution; a loan participation; a letter of credit or other form of bank indebtedness incurred in the ordinary course of

business; units of a collective investment fund; interests in a variable amount note in accordance with 12 CFR 9.18; U.S. Savings Bonds; or any other instrument the OCC determines does not constitute a security for purposes of this part.

[61 FR 63965, Dec. 2, 1996, as amended at 82 FR 8106, Jan. 23, 2017]

§ 12.3 Recordkeeping.

(a) *General rule.* A national bank effecting securities transactions for customers shall maintain the following records for at least three years:

(1) *Chronological records.* An itemized daily record of each purchase and sale of securities maintained in chronological order, and including:

(i) Account or customer name for which each transaction was effected;

(ii) Description of the securities;

(iii) Unit and aggregate purchase or sale price;

(iv) Trade date; and

(v) Name or other designation of the broker/dealer or other person from whom the securities were purchased or to whom the securities were sold;

(2) *Account records.* Account records for each customer, reflecting:

(i) Purchases and sales of securities;

(ii) Receipts and deliveries of securities;

(iii) Receipts and disbursements of cash; and

(iv) Other debits and credits pertaining to transactions in securities;

(3) *Memorandum order.* A separate memorandum (order ticket) of each order to purchase or sell securities (whether executed or canceled), including:

(i) Account or customer name for which the transaction was effected;

(ii) Type of order (market order, limit order, or subject to special instructions);

(iii) Time the trader or other bank employee responsible for effecting the transaction received the order;

(iv) Time the trader placed the order with the broker/dealer, or if there was no broker/dealer, time the order was executed or canceled;

(v) Price at which the order was executed; and

(vi) Name of the broker/dealer utilized;

(4) *Record of broker/dealers.* A record of all broker/dealers selected by the bank to effect securities transactions and the amount of commissions paid or allocated to each broker during the calendar year; and

(5) *Notifications.* A copy of the written notification required by §§ 12.4 and 12.5.

(b) *Manner of maintenance.* The records required by this section must clearly and accurately reflect the information required and provide an adequate basis for the audit of the information. Record maintenance may include the use of automated or electronic records provided the records are easily retrievable, readily available for inspection, and capable of being reproduced in a hard copy. A national bank may contract with a third-party service provider to maintain the records, provided that the bank maintains effective oversight of the third-party service provider to ensure the records meet the requirements of this section.

[61 FR 63965, Dec. 2, 1996, as amended at 82 FR 8106, Jan. 23, 2017]

§ 12.4 Content and time of notification.

Unless a national bank elects to provide notification by one of the means specified in § 12.5, a national bank effecting a securities transaction for a customer shall give or send to the customer either of the following types of notifications at or before completion of the transaction or, if the bank uses a registered broker/dealer's confirmation, within one business day from the bank's receipt of the registered broker/dealer's confirmation:

(a) *Written notification.* A written notification disclosing:

(1) Name of the bank;

(2) Name of the customer;

(3) Capacity in which the bank acts (i.e., as agent for the customer, as agent for both the customer and some other person, as principal for its own account, or in any other capacity);

(4) Date and time of execution, or a statement that the bank will furnish the time of execution within a reasonable time upon written request of the customer, and the identity, price, and number of shares or units (or principal amount in the case of debt securities) of the security purchased or sold by the customer;

(5) Amount of any remuneration that the customer has provided or is to provide any broker/dealer, directly or indirectly, in connection with the transaction;

(6)(i) Amount of any remuneration that the bank has received or will receive from the customer, and the source and amount of any other remuneration that the bank has received or will receive in connection with the transaction; unless:

(A) The bank and its customer have determined remuneration pursuant to a written agreement; or

(B) In the case of government securities and municipal securities, the bank received the remuneration in other than an agency transaction.

(ii) If the bank elects not to disclose the source and amount of remuneration it has or will receive from a party other than the customer pursuant to paragraph (a)(6)(i) of this section, the written notification must disclose whether the bank has received or will receive remuneration from a party other than the customer, and that the bank will furnish within a reasonable time the source and amount of this remuneration upon written request of the customer. This election is not available, however, if, with respect to a purchase, the bank was participating in a distribution of that security; or, with respect to a sale, the bank was participating in a tender offer for that security;

(7) Name of the registered broker/dealer utilized; or where there is no registered broker/dealer, the name of the person from whom the security was purchased or to whom the security was sold, or a statement that the bank will furnish this information within a reasonable time upon written request from the customer;

(8) In the case of any transaction in a debt security subject to redemption before maturity, a statement to the effect that the debt security may be redeemed in whole or in part before maturity, that the redemption could affect the yield represented and that additional information is available upon request;

(9) In the case of a transaction in a debt security effected exclusively on the basis of a dollar price:

(i) The dollar price at which the transaction was effected; and

(ii) The yield to maturity calculated from the dollar price, unless the transaction is for a debt security that either:

(A) Has a maturity date that may be extended by the issuer thereof, with a variable interest payable thereon; or

(B) Is an asset-backed security that represents an interest in or is secured by a pool of receivables or other financial assets that continuously are subject to prepayment;

(10) In the case of a transaction in a debt security effected on the basis of yield:

(i) The yield at which the transaction was effected, including the percentage amount and its characterization (e.g., current yield, yield to maturity, or yield to call) and if effected at yield to call, the type of call, the call date, and call price;

(ii) The dollar price calculated from the yield at which the transaction was effected; and

(iii) If effected on a basis other than yield to maturity and the yield to maturity is lower than the represented yield, the yield to maturity as well as the represented yield, unless the transaction is for a debt security that either:

(A) Has a maturity date that may be extended by the issuer thereof, with a variable interest rate payable thereon; or

(B) Is an asset-backed security that represents an interest in or is secured by a pool of receivables or other financial assets that continuously are subject to prepayment;

(11) In the case of a transaction in a debt security that is an asset-backed security, which represents an interest in or is secured by a pool of receivables or other financial assets that continuously are subject to prepayment, a statement indicating that the actual yield of the asset-backed security may vary according to the rate at which the underlying receivables or other financial assets are prepaid and a statement that information concerning the factors that affect yield (including at a minimum estimated yield, weighted average life, and the prepayment assumptions underlying yield) will be

furnished upon written request of the customer; and

(12) In the case of a transaction in a debt security, other than a government security, that the security is unrated by a nationally recognized statistical rating organization, if that is the case; or

(b) *Copy of the registered broker/dealer's confirmation.* A copy of the confirmation of a registered broker/dealer relating to the securities transaction, which the bank may direct the registered broker/dealer to send directly to the customer; and, if the customer or any other source will provide remuneration to the bank in connection with the transaction and a written agreement between the bank and the customer does not determine the remuneration, a statement of the source and amount of any remuneration that the customer or any other source is to provide the bank.

[61 FR 63965, Dec. 2, 1996, as amended at 82 FR 8106, Jan. 23, 2017]

§ 12.5 Notification by agreement; alternative forms and times of notification.

A national bank may elect to use the following notification procedures as an alternative to complying with § 12.4:

(a) *Notification by agreement.* A national bank effecting a securities transaction for an account in which the bank does not exercise investment discretion shall give or send written notification at the time and in the form agreed to in writing by the bank and customer, provided that the agreement makes clear the customer's right to receive the written notification pursuant to § 12.4 (a) or (b) at no additional cost to the customer.

(b) *Trust transactions.* A national bank effecting a securities transaction for an account in which the bank exercises investment discretion other than in an agency capacity shall give or send written notification within a reasonable time if a person having the power to terminate the account, or, if there is no such person, any person holding a vested beneficial interest in the account, requests written notification pursuant to § 12.4 (a) or (b). Otherwise, notification is not required.

(c) *Agency transactions.* (1) A national bank effecting a securities transaction for an account in which the bank exercises investment discretion in an agency capacity shall give or send, not less than once every three months, an itemized statement to each customer that specifies the funds and securities in the custody or possession of the bank at the end of the period and all debits, credits and transactions in the customer's account during the period.

(2) If requested by the customer, the bank shall give or send written notification to the customer pursuant to § 12.4 (a) or (b) within a reasonable time.

(d) *Collective investment fund transactions.* A national bank effecting a securities transaction for a collective investment fund shall follow 12 CFR 9.18.

(e) *Periodic plan transactions.* (1) A national bank effecting a securities transaction for a periodic plan (except for a cash management sweep service) shall give or send to its customer not less than once every three months, a written statement showing:

(i) The customer's funds and securities in the custody or possession of the bank;

(ii) All service charges and commissions paid by the customer in connection with the transaction; and

(iii) All other debits and credits of the customer's account involved in the transaction.

(2) A national bank effecting a securities transaction for a cash management sweep service or other periodic plan as defined in § 12.2(j)(2) shall give or send its customer a written statement, in the same form as under paragraph (e)(1) of this section, for each month in which a purchase or sale of a security takes place in a deposit account and not less than once every three months if there are no securities transactions in the account, subject to any other applicable laws and regulations.

(3) Upon written request of the customer, the bank shall give or send the information described in § 12.4 (a) or (b), except that the bank need not provide to the customer any information relating to remuneration paid in connection with the transaction when the

remuneration is paid by a source other than the customer.

§ 12.6 Fees.

A national bank may charge a reasonable fee for providing notification pursuant to § 12.5(b), (c), and (e). A national bank may not charge a fee for providing notification pursuant to § 12.4 or § 12.5 (a) and (d).

§ 12.7 Securities trading policies and procedures.

(a) *Policies and procedures; reports of securities trading.* A national bank effecting securities transactions for customers shall maintain and adhere to policies and procedures that:

(1) Assign responsibility for supervision of all officers or employees who:

(i) Transmit orders to or place orders with registered broker/dealers;

(ii) Execute transactions in securities for customers; or

(iii) Process orders for notification or settlement purposes, or perform other back office functions with respect to securities transactions effected for customers. Policies and procedures for personnel described in this paragraph (a)(1)(iii) must provide for supervision and reporting lines that are separate from supervision and reporting lines for personnel described in paragraphs (a)(1) (i) and (ii) of this section;

(2) Provide for the fair and equitable allocation of securities and prices to accounts when the bank receives orders for the same security at approximately the same time and places the orders for execution either individually or in combination;

(3) Provide for the crossing of buy and sell orders on a fair and equitable basis to the parties to the transaction, where permissible under applicable law; and

(4) Require bank officers and employees to report to the bank, within the deadline specified in SEC rule 17j–1 (17 CFR 270.17j–1) for quarterly transaction reports, all personal transactions in securities made by them or on their behalf in which they have a beneficial interest, if the officers and employees:

(i) Make investment recommendations or decisions for the accounts of customers;

(ii) Participate in the determination of the recommendations or decisions; or

(iii) In connection with their duties, obtain information concerning which securities are purchased, sold, or recommended for purchase or sale by the bank.

(b) *Required information.* The report required under paragraph (a)(4) of this section must contain the following information:

(1) The date of the transaction, the title and number of shares, and the principal amount of each security involved;

(2) The nature of the transaction (i.e. purchase, sale, or other type of acquisition or disposition);

(3) The price at which the transaction was effected; and

(4) The name of the registered broker, registered dealer, or bank with or through whom the transaction was effected.

(c) *Report not required.* This section does not require a bank officer or employee to report transactions if:

(1) The officer or employee has no direct or indirect influence or control over the transaction;

(2) The transaction is in mutual fund shares;

(3) The transaction is in government securities; or

(4) The transactions involve an aggregate amount of purchases and sales per officer or employee of $10,000 or less during the calendar quarter.

(d) *Additional reporting requirement.* A national bank that acts as an investment adviser to an investment company is subject to the requirements of SEC Rule 17j–1 (17 CFR 270.17j–1) issued under the Investment Company Act of 1940. SEC Rule 17j–1 requires an "access person" of the investment adviser to report certain personal securities transactions to the investment adviser for review by the Securities and Exchange Commission. "Access person" includes directors, officers, and certain employees of the investment adviser. The reporting requirement under paragraph (a)(4) of this section is a separate requirement from any applicable requirements under SEC Rule 17j–1. However, an "access person" required to file a report with a national bank pursuant to SEC Rule 17j–1 need not file a separate report under paragraph (a)(4) of this section if the required information is the same.

[61 FR 63965, Dec. 2, 1996, as amended at 73 FR 22243, Apr. 24, 2008; 82 FR 8107, Jan. 23, 2017]

§ 12.8 Waivers.

A national bank may file a written request with the OCC for waiver of one or more of the requirements set forth in §§ 12.2 through 12.7, either in whole or in part. The OCC may grant a waiver from the requirements of this part to any national bank, or any class of national banks, with regard to a specific transaction or a specific class of transactions.

§ 12.9 Settlement of securities transactions.

(a) All contracts effected or entered into by a national bank for the purchase or sale of a security (other than an exempted security as defined in 15 U.S.C. 78c(a)(12), government security, municipal security, commercial paper, bankers' acceptances, or commercial bills) shall provide for completion of the transaction within the number of business days in the standard settlement cycle followed by registered broker dealers in the United States, unless otherwise agreed to by the parties at the time of the transaction. The number of business days in the standard settlement cycle shall be determined by reference to paragraph (a) of SEC Rule 15c6–1, 17 CFR 240.15c6–1(a).

(b) Paragraphs (a) and (c) of this section do not apply to contracts:

(1) For the purchase or sale of limited partnership interests that are not listed on an exchange or for which quotations are not disseminated through an automated quotation system of a registered securities association;

(2) For the purchase or sale of securities that the SEC may from time to time, taking into account then existing market practices, exempt by order from the requirements of paragraph (a) of SEC Rule 15c6–1, 17 CFR 240.15c6–1(a), either unconditionally or on specified terms and conditions, if the SEC determines that an exemption is consistent with the public interest and the protection of investors.

(c) Paragraph (a) of this section does not apply to contracts for the sale for cash of securities that are priced after 4:30 p.m. Eastern time on the date the securities are priced and that are sold by an issuer to an underwriter pursuant to a firm commitment underwritten offering registered under the Securities Act of 1933, 15 U.S.C. 77a *et seq.*, or sold to an initial purchaser by a national bank participating in the offering. A national bank shall not effect or enter into a contract for the purchase or sale of the securities that provides for payment of funds and delivery of securities later than the fourth business day after the date of the contract unless otherwise expressly agreed to by the parties at the time of the transaction.

(d) For purposes of paragraphs (a) and (c) of this section, the parties to a contract are deemed to have expressly agreed to an alternate date for payment of funds and delivery of securities at the time of the transaction for a contract for the sale for cash of securities pursuant to a firm commitment offering if the managing underwriter and the issuer have agreed to the date for all securities sold pursuant to the offering and the parties to the contract have not expressly agreed to another date for payment of funds and delivery of securities at the time of the transaction.

[61 FR 63965, Dec. 2, 1996, as amended at 82 FR 8107, Jan. 23, 2017; 83 FR 26349, June 7, 2018]

PART 13—GOVERNMENT SECURITIES SALES PRACTICES

Sec.
13.1 Scope.
13.2 Definitions.
13.3 Business conduct.
13.4 Recommendations to customers.
13.5 Customer information.

INTERPRETATIONS

13.100 Obligations concerning institutional customers.

AUTHORITY: 12 U.S.C. 1 *et seq.*, and 93a; 15 U.S.C. 78o–5.

SOURCE: 62 FR 13283, Mar. 19, 1997, unless otherwise noted.

§ 13.1 Scope.

This part applies to national banks that have filed notice as, or are required to file notice as, government securities brokers or dealers pursuant to section 15C of the Securities Exchange Act (15 U.S.C. 78o–5) and Department of the Treasury rules under section 15C (17 CFR 400.1(d) and part 401).

§ 13.2 Definitions.

(a) *Bank that is a government securities broker or dealer* means a national bank that has filed notice, or is required to file notice, as a government securities broker or dealer pursuant to section 15C of the Securities Exchange Act (15 U.S.C. 78o–5) and Department of the Treasury rules under section 15C (17 CFR 400.1(d) and part 401).

(b) *Customer* does not include a broker or dealer or a government securities broker or dealer.

(c) *Government security* has the same meaning as this term has in section 3(a)(42) of the Securities Exchange Act of 1934 (15 U.S.C. 78c(a)(42)).

(d) *Non-institutional customer* means any customer other than:

(1) A bank, savings association, insurance company, or registered investment company;

(2) An investment adviser registered under section 203 of the Investment Advisers Act of 1940 (15 U.S.C. 80b–3); or

(3) Any entity (whether a natural person, corporation, partnership, trust, or otherwise) with total assets of at least $50 million.

§ 13.3 Business conduct.

A bank that is a government securities broker or dealer shall observe high standards of commercial honor and just and equitable principles of trade in the conduct of its business as a government securities broker or dealer.

§ 13.4 Recommendations to customers.

In recommending to a customer the purchase, sale or exchange of a government security, a bank that is a government securities broker or dealer shall have reasonable grounds for believing that the recommendation is suitable for the customer upon the basis of the facts, if any, disclosed by the customer as to the customer's other security holdings and as to the customer's financial situation and needs.

§ 13.5 Customer information.

Prior to the execution of a transaction recommended to a non-institutional customer, a bank that is a government securities broker or dealer shall make reasonable efforts to obtain information concerning:

(a) The customer's financial status;

(b) The customer's tax status;

(c) The customer's investment objectives; and

(d) Such other information used or considered to be reasonable by the bank in making recommendations to the customer.

INTERPRETATIONS

§ 13.100 Obligations concerning institutional customers.

(a) As a result of broadened authority provided by the Government Securities Act Amendments of 1993 (15 U.S.C. 78o–3 and 78o–5), the OCC is adopting sales practice rules for the government securities market, a market with a particularly broad institutional component. Accordingly, the OCC believes it is appropriate to provide further guidance to banks on their suitability obligations when making recommendations to institutional customers.

(b) The OCC's suitability rule (§ 13.4) is fundamental to fair dealing and is intended to promote ethical sales practices and high standards of professional conduct. Banks' responsibilities include having a reasonable basis for recommending a particular security or strategy, as well as having reasonable grounds for believing the recommendation is suitable for the customer to whom it is made. Banks are expected to meet the same high standards of competence, professionalism, and good faith regardless of the financial circumstances of the customer.

(c) In recommending to a customer the purchase, sale, or exchange of any government security, the bank shall have reasonable grounds for believing that the recommendation is suitable for the customer upon the basis of the facts, if any, disclosed by the customer as to the customer's other security holdings and financial situation and needs.

(d) The interpretation in this section concerns only the manner in which a bank determines that a recommendation is suitable for a particular institutional customer. The manner in which a bank fulfills this suitability obligation will vary, depending on the nature of the customer and the specific transaction. Accordingly, the interpretation in this section deals only with guidance regarding how a bank may fulfill customer-specific suitability obligations under § 13.4.[1]

(e) While it is difficult to define in advance the scope of a bank's suitability obligation with respect to a specific institutional customer transaction recommended by a bank, the OCC has identified certain factors that may be relevant when considering compliance with § 13.4. These factors are not intended to be requirements or the only factors to be considered but are offered merely as guidance in determining the scope of a bank's suitability obligations.

(f) The two most important considerations in determining the scope of a bank's suitability obligations in making recommendations to an institutional customer are the customer's capability to evaluate investment risk independently and the extent to which the customer is exercising independent judgement in evaluating a bank's recommendation. A bank must determine, based on the information available to it, the customer's capability to evaluate investment risk. In some cases, the bank may conclude that the customer is not capable of making independent investment decisions in general. In other cases, the institutional customer may have general capability, but may not be able to understand a particular type of instrument or its risk. This is more likely to arise with relatively new types of instruments, or those with significantly different risk or volatility characteristics than other investments generally made by the institution. If a customer is either generally not capable of evaluating investment risk or lacks sufficient capability to evaluate the particular product, the scope of a bank's customer-specific obligations under § 13.4 would not be diminished by the fact that the bank was dealing with an institutional customer. On the other hand, the fact that a customer initially needed help understanding a potential investment need not necessarily imply that the customer did not ultimately develop an understanding and make an independent investment decision.

(g) A bank may conclude that a customer is exercising independent judgement if the customer's investment decision will be based on its own independent assessment of the opportunities and risks presented by a potential investment, market factors and other investment considerations. Where the bank has reasonable grounds for concluding that the institutional customer is making independent investment decisions and is capable of independently evaluating investment risk, then a bank's obligations under § 13.4 for a particular customer are fulfilled.[2] Where a customer has delegated decision-making authority to an agent, such as an investment advisor or a bank trust department, the interpretation in this section shall be applied to the agent.

(h) A determination of capability to evaluate investment risk independently will depend on an examination of the customer's capability to make its own investment decisions, including the resources available to the customer to make informed decisions. Relevant considerations could include:

(1) The use of one or more consultants, investment advisers, or bank trust departments;

(2) The general level of experience of the institutional customer in financial markets and specific experience with the type of instruments under consideration;

[1] The interpretation in this section does not address the obligation related to suitability that requires that a bank have "* * * a 'reasonable basis' to believe that the recommendation could be suitable for at least some customers." *In the Matter of the Application of F.J. Kaufman and Company of Virginia and Frederick J. Kaufman, Jr.*, 50 SEC 164 (1989).

[2] See footnote 1 in paragraph (d) of this section.

(3) The customer's ability to understand the economic features of the security involved;

(4) The customer's ability to independently evaluate how market developments would affect the security; and

(5) The complexity of the security or securities involved.

(i) A determination that a customer is making independent investment decisions will depend on the nature of the relationship that exists between the bank and the customer.

Relevant considerations could include:

(1) Any written or oral understanding that exists between the bank and the customer regarding the nature of the relationship between the bank and the customer and the services to be rendered by the bank;

(2) The presence or absence of a pattern of acceptance of the bank's recommendations;

(3) The use by the customer of ideas, suggestions, market views and information obtained from other government securities brokers or dealers or market professionals, particularly those relating to the same type of securities; and

(4) The extent to which the bank has received from the customer current comprehensive portfolio information in connection with discussing recommended transactions or has not been provided important information regarding its portfolio or investment objectives.

(j) Banks are reminded that these factors are merely guidelines that will be utilized to determine whether a bank has fulfilled its suitability obligation with respect to a specific institutional customer transaction and that the inclusion or absence of any of these factors is not dispositive of the determination of suitability. Such a determination can only be made on a case-by-case basis taking into consideration all the facts and circumstances of a particular bank/customer relationship, assessed in the context of a particular transaction.

(k) For purposes of the interpretation in this section, an institutional customer shall be any entity other than a natural person. In determining the applicability of the interpretation in this section to an institutional customer, the OCC will consider the dollar value of the securities that the institutional customer has in its portfolio and/or under management. While the interpretation in this section is potentially applicable to any institutional customer, the guidance contained in this section is more appropriately applied to an institutional customer with at least $10 million invested in securities in the aggregate in its portfolio and/or under management.

PART 14—CONSUMER PROTECTION IN SALES OF INSURANCE

Sec.
14.10 Purpose and scope.
14.20 Definitions.
14.30 Prohibited practices.
14.40 What a covered person must disclose.
14.50 Where insurance activities may take place.
14.60 Qualification and licensing requirements for insurance sales personnel.
APPENDIX A TO PART 14—CONSUMER GRIEVANCE PROCESS

AUTHORITY: 12 U.S.C. 1 *et seq.*, 24(Seventh), 92, 93a, 1462a, 1463, 1464, 1818, 1831x, and 5412(b)(2)(B).

SOURCE: 65 FR 75839, Dec. 4, 2000, unless otherwise noted.

§ 14.10 Purpose and scope.

(a) *General rule.* This part establishes consumer protections in connection with retail sales practices, solicitations, advertising, or offers of any insurance product or annuity to a consumer by:

(1) Any national bank or Federal savings association; or

(2) Any other person that is engaged in such activities at an office of the national bank or Federal savings association, or on behalf of the national bank or Federal savings association.

(b) *Application to operating subsidiaries.* For purposes of § 5.34(e)(3) of this chapter for national banks and § 5.38(e)(3) of this chapter for Federal savings associations, an operating subsidiary is subject to this part only to the extent that it sells, solicits, advertises, or offers insurance products or annuities at an office of a national bank or Federal savings association, or on behalf of a national bank or Federal savings association.

[79 FR 28398, May 16, 2014, as amended at 80 FR 28472, May 18, 2015]

§ 14.20 Definitions.

As used in this part:

(a) *Affiliate* means a company that controls, is controlled by, or is under common control with another company.

(b) *Bank* means a national bank or a Federal branch, or agency of a foreign bank as defined in section 1 of the International Banking Act of 1978 (12 U.S.C. 3101, *et seq.*)

(c) *Company* means any corporation, partnership, business trust, association or similar organization, or any other trust (unless by its terms the trust must terminate within twenty-five years or not later than twenty-one years and ten months after the death of individuals living on the effective date of the trust). It does not include any corporation the majority of the shares of which are owned by the United States or by any State, or a qualified family partnership, as defined in section 2(o)(10) of the Bank Holding Company Act of 1956, as amended (12 U.S.C. 1841(o)(10)).

(d) *Consumer* means an individual who purchases, applies to purchase, or is solicited to purchase from a covered person insurance products or annuities primarily for personal, family, or household purposes.

(e) *Control* of a company has the same meaning as in section 3(w)(5) of the Federal Deposit Insurance Act (12 U.S.C. 1813(w)(5)).

(f)(1) *Covered person* means:

(i) A bank;

(ii) A Federal savings association; or

(iii) Any other person only when the person sells, solicits, advertises, or offers an insurance product or annuity to a consumer at an office of the bank or Federal savings association or on behalf of a bank or Federal savings association.

(2) For purposes of this definition, activities on behalf of a bank or Federal savings association include activities where a person, whether at an office of the bank or Federal savings association or at another location sells, solicits, advertises, or offers an insurance product or annuity and at least one of the following applies:

(i) The person represents to a consumer that the sale, solicitation, advertisement, or offer of any insurance product or annuity is by or on behalf of the bank or Federal savings association;

(ii) The bank or Federal savings association refers a consumer to a seller of insurance products or annuities and the bank or Federal savings association has a contractual arrangement to receive commissions or fees derived from a sale of an insurance product or annuity resulting from that referral; or

(iii) Documents evidencing the sale, solicitation, advertising, or offer of an insurance product or annuity identify or refer to the bank or Federal savings association.

(g) *Domestic violence* means the occurrence of one or more of the following acts by a current or former family member, household member, intimate partner, or caretaker:

(1) Attempting to cause or causing or threatening another person physical harm, severe emotional distress, psychological trauma, rape, or sexual assault;

(2) Engaging in a course of conduct or repeatedly committing acts toward another person, including following the person without proper authority, under circumstances that place the person in reasonable fear of bodily injury or physical harm;

(3) Subjecting another person to false imprisonment; or

(4) Attempting to cause or causing damage to property so as to intimidate or attempt to control the behavior of another person.

(h) *Electronic media* includes any means for transmitting messages electronically between a covered person and a consumer in a format that allows visual text to be displayed on equipment, for example, a personal computer monitor.

(i) *Office* means the premises of a bank or Federal savings association where retail deposits are accepted from the public.

(j) *Federal savings association means* a Federal savings association or Federal savings bank chartered under section 5 of the Home Owners' Loan Act (12 U.S.C. 1464).

(k) *Subsidiary* has the same meaning as in section 3(w)(4) of the Federal Deposit Insurance Act (12 U.S.C. 1813(w)(4)).

[65 FR 75839, Dec. 4, 2000, as amended at 79 FR 28398, May 16, 2014]

§ 14.30 Prohibited practices.

(a) *Anticoercion and antitying rules.* A covered person may not engage in any practice that would lead a consumer to believe that an extension of credit, in violation of section 106(b) of the Bank Holding Company Act Amendments of 1970 (12 U.S.C. 1972) or section 5(q) of the Home Owners' Loan Act (12 U.S.C. 1464(q)), is conditional upon either:

(1) The purchase of an insurance product or annuity from the bank, Federal savings association, or any of their affiliates; or

(2) An agreement by the consumer not to obtain, or a prohibition on the consumer from obtaining, an insurance product or annuity from an unaffiliated entity.

(b) *Prohibition on misrepresentations generally.* A covered person may not engage in any practice or use any advertisement at any office of, or on behalf of, the bank, Federal savings association, or a subsidiary of the bank or Federal savings association that could mislead any person or otherwise cause a reasonable person to reach an erroneous belief with respect to:

(1) The fact that an insurance product or annuity sold or offered for sale by a covered person or any subsidiary of the bank or Federal savings association is not backed by the Federal government, the bank, or the Federal savings association, or the fact that the insurance product or annuity is not insured by the Federal Deposit Insurance Corporation (FDIC);

(2) In the case of an insurance product or annuity that involves investment risk, the fact that there is an investment risk, including the potential that principal may be lost and that the product may decline in value; or

(3) In the case of a bank, Federal savings association, or subsidiary of the bank or Federal savings association at which insurance products or annuities are sold or offered for sale, the fact that:

(i) The approval of an extension of credit to a consumer by the bank, Federal savings association, or subsidiary may not be conditioned on the purchase of an insurance product or annuity by the consumer from the bank, Federal savings association, or a subsidiary of the bank or Federal savings association; and

(ii) The consumer is free to purchase the insurance product or annuity from another source.

(c) *Prohibition on domestic violence discrimination.* A covered person may not sell or offer for sale, as principal, agent, or broker, any life or health insurance product if the status of the applicant or insured as a victim of domestic violence or as a provider of services to victims of domestic violence is considered as a criterion in any decision with regard to insurance underwriting, pricing, renewal, or scope of coverage of such product, or with regard to the payment of insurance claims on such product, except as required or expressly permitted under State law.

[65 FR 75839, Dec. 4, 2000, as amended at 79 FR 28398, May 16, 2014]

§ 14.40 What a covered person must disclose.

(a) *Insurance disclosures.* In connection with the initial purchase of an insurance product or annuity by a consumer from a covered person, a covered person must disclose to the consumer, except to the extent the disclosure would not be accurate, that:

(1) The insurance product or annuity is not a deposit or other obligation of, or guaranteed by, the bank, Federal savings association, or an affiliate of the bank or Federal savings association;

(2) The insurance product or annuity is not insured by the FDIC or any other agency of the United States, the bank, Federal savings association, or (if applicable) an affiliate of the bank or Federal savings association; and

(3) In the case of an insurance product or annuity that involves an investment risk, there is investment risk associated with the product, including the possible loss of value.

(b) *Credit disclosure.* In the case of an application for credit in connection with which an insurance product or annuity is solicited, offered, or sold, a covered person must disclose that the bank or Federal savings association may not condition an extension of credit on either:

(1) The consumer's purchase of an insurance product or annuity from the bank, Federal savings association, or any of their affiliates; or

(2) The consumer's agreement not to obtain, or a prohibition on the consumer from obtaining, an insurance product or annuity from an unaffiliated entity.

(c) *Timing and method of disclosures*—(1) *In general.* The disclosures required by paragraph (a) of this section must be provided orally and in writing before the completion of the initial sale of an insurance product or annuity to a consumer. The disclosure required by paragraph (b) of this section must be made orally and in writing at the time the consumer applies for an extension of credit in connection with which an insurance product or annuity is solicited, offered, or sold.

(2) *Exception for transactions by mail.* If a sale of an insurance product or annuity is conducted by mail, a covered person is not required to make the oral disclosures required by paragraph (a) of this section. If a covered person takes an application for credit by mail, the covered person is not required to make the oral disclosure required by paragraph (b).

(3) *Exception for transactions by telephone.* If a sale of an insurance product or annuity is conducted by telephone, a covered person may provide the written disclosures required by paragraph (a) of this section by mail within 3 business days beginning on the first business day after the sale, excluding Sundays and the legal public holidays specified in 5 U.S.C. 6103(a). If a covered person takes an application for credit by telephone, the covered person may provide the written disclosure required by paragraph (b) of this section by mail, provided the covered person mails it to the consumer within three days beginning the first business day after the application is taken, excluding Sundays and the legal public holidays specified in 5 U.S.C. 6103(a).

(4) *Electronic form of disclosures.* (i) Subject to the requirements of section 101(c) of the Electronic Signatures in Global and National Commerce Act (15 U.S.C. 7001(c)), a covered person may provide the written disclosures required by paragraph (a) and (b) of this section through electronic media instead of on paper, if the consumer affirmatively consents to receiving the disclosures electronically and if the disclosures are provided in a format that the consumer may retain or obtain later, for example, by printing or storing electronically (such as by downloading).

(ii) Any disclosures required by paragraphs (a) or (b) of this section that are provided by electronic media are not required to be provided orally.

(5) *Disclosures must be readily understandable.* The disclosures provided shall be conspicuous, simple, direct, readily understandable, and designed to call attention to the nature and significance of the information provided. For instance, a covered person may use the following disclosures in visual media, such as television broadcasting, ATM screens, billboards, signs, posters and written advertisements and promotional materials, as appropriate and consistent with paragraphs (a) and (b) of this section:

- NOT A DEPOSIT
- NOT FDIC-INSURED
- NOT INSURED BY ANY FEDERAL GOVERNMENT AGENCY
- NOT GUARANTEED BY THE [BANK] [FEDERAL SAVINGS ASSOCIATION]
- MAY GO DOWN IN VALUE

(6) *Disclosures must be meaningful.* (i) A covered person must provide the disclosures required by paragraphs (a) and (b) of this section in a meaningful form. Examples of the types of methods that could call attention to the nature and significance of the information provided include:

(A) A plain-language heading to call attention to the disclosures;

(B) A typeface and type size that are easy to read;

(C) Wide margins and ample line spacing;

(D) Boldface or italics for key words; and

(E) Distinctive type style, and graphic devices, such as shading or sidebars, when the disclosures are combined with other information.

(ii) A covered person has not provided the disclosures in a meaningful form if the covered person merely states to the consumer that the required disclosures are available in printed material, but does not provide the printed material when required and does not orally disclose the information to the consumer when required.

(iii) With respect to those disclosures made through electronic media for which paper or oral disclosures are not required, the disclosures are not meaningfully provided if the consumer may bypass the visual text of the disclosures before purchasing an insurance product or annuity.

(7) *Consumer acknowledgment.* A covered person must obtain from the consumer, at the time a consumer receives the disclosures required under paragraphs (a) or (b) of this section, or at the time of the initial purchase by the consumer of an insurance product or annuity, a written acknowledgment by the consumer that the consumer received the disclosures. A covered person may permit a consumer to acknowledge receipt of the disclosures electronically or in paper form. If the disclosures required under paragraphs (a) or (b) of this section are provided in connection with a transaction that is conducted by telephone, a covered person must:

(i) Obtain an oral acknowledgment of receipt of the disclosures and maintain sufficient documentation to show that the acknowledgment was given; and

(ii) Make reasonable efforts to obtain a written acknowledgment from the consumer.

(d) *Advertisements and other promotional material for insurance products or annuities.* The disclosures described in paragraph (a) of this section are required in advertisements and promotional material for insurance products or annuities unless the advertisements and promotional materials are of a general nature describing or listing the services or products offered by the bank or Federal savings association.

[65 FR 75839, Dec. 4, 2000, as amended at 79 FR 28398, May 16, 2014]

§ 14.50 Where insurance activities may take place.

(a) *General rule.* A bank or Federal savings association must, to the extent practicable, keep the area where the bank or Federal savings association conducts transactions involving insurance products or annuities physically segregated from areas where retail deposits are routinely accepted from the general public, identify the areas where insurance product or annuity sales activities occur, and clearly delineate and distinguish those areas from the areas where the bank's or Federal savings association's retail deposit-taking activities occur.

(b) *Referrals.* Any person who accepts deposits from the public in an area where such transactions are routinely conducted in the bank or Federal savings association may refer a consumer who seeks to purchase an insurance product or annuity to a qualified person who sells that product only if the person making the referral receives no more than a one-time, nominal fee of a fixed dollar amount for each referral that does not depend on whether the referral results in a transaction.

[65 FR 75839, Dec. 4, 2000, as amended at 79 FR 28399, May 16, 2014]

§ 14.60 Qualification and licensing requirements for insurance sales personnel.

A bank or Federal savings association may not permit any person to sell or offer for sale any insurance product or annuity in any part of its office or on its behalf, unless the person is at all times appropriately qualified and licensed under applicable State insurance licensing standards with regard to the specific products being sold or recommended.

[65 FR 75839, Dec. 4, 2000, as amended at 79 FR 28399, May 16, 2014]

APPENDIX A TO PART 14—CONSUMER GRIEVANCE PROCESS

Any consumer who believes that any bank, Federal savings association, or any other person selling, soliciting, advertising, or offering insurance products or annuities to the consumer at an office of the bank, Federal savings association or on behalf of the bank or Federal savings association has violated the requirements of this part should contact the Customer Assistance Group, Office of the Comptroller of the Currency, (800) 613–6743, 1301 McKinney Street, Suite 3450, Houston, Texas 77010–3031, or *www.helpwithmybank.gov*.

[79 FR 28399, May 16, 2014]

PART 15 [RESERVED]

PART 16—SECURITIES OFFERING DISCLOSURE RULES

Sec.

16.1 Authority, purpose, and scope.
16.2 Definitions.
16.3 Registration statement and prospectus requirements.
16.4 Communications not deemed an offer.
16.5 Exemptions.
16.6 Sales of nonconvertible debt.
16.7 Nonpublic offerings.
16.8 Small issues.
16.9 Securities offered and sold in holding company dissolution.
16.10 Sales of securities at an office of a Federal savings association.
16.15 Form and content.
16.16 Effectiveness.
16.17 Filing requirements and inspection of documents.
16.18 Use of prospectus.
16.19 Withdrawal or abandonment.
16.30 Request for interpretive advice or no-objection letter.
16.31 Escrow requirement.
16.32 Fraudulent transactions and unsafe or unsound practices.
16.33 Filing fees.

AUTHORITY: 12 U.S.C. 1 *et seq.*, 93a, 1462a, 1463, 1464, and 5412(b)(2)(B).

SOURCE: 59 FR 54798, Nov. 2, 1994, unless otherwise noted.

§ 16.1 Authority, purpose, and scope.

(a) *Authority.* This part is issued under the rulemaking authority of the Comptroller of the Currency (OCC) for national banks in 12 U.S.C. 1 *et seq.*, and 93a, and for Federal savings associations in 12 U.S.C. 1462a, 1463, 1464, and 5412(b)(2)(B).

(b) *Purpose.* This part sets forth rules governing the offer and sale of securities issued by a national bank or Federal savings association.

(c) *Scope.* This part applies to offers and sales of national bank or Federal savings association securities by issuers, underwriters, and dealers.

[59 FR 54798, Nov. 2, 1994, as amended at 82 FR 8107, Jan. 23, 2017]

§ 16.2 Definitions.

For purposes of this part, the following definitions apply:

(a) *Accredited investor* means the same as in SEC Rule 501(a) (17 CFR 230.501(a)).

(b) *Dealer* means the same as in section 2(a)(12) of the Securities Act (15 U.S.C. 77b(a)(12)).

(c) *Exchange Act* means the Securities Exchange Act of 1934 (15 U.S.C. 78a *et seq.*).

(d) *Insured depository institution* means the same as in section 3(c)(2) of the Federal Deposit Insurance Act (12 U.S.C. 1813(c)(2)).

(e) *Federal savings association* means an existing Federal savings association chartered under section 5 of the Home Owners' Loan Act (HOLA) (12 U.S.C. 1464 *et seq.*) or a Federal savings association in organization.

(f) *Investment grade* means the issuer of a security has an adequate capacity to meet financial commitments under the security for the projected life of the asset or exposure. An issuer has an adequate capacity to meet financial commitments if the risk of default by the obligor is low and the full and timely repayment of principal and interest is expected.

(g) *Issuer* means a national bank or Federal savings association that issues or proposes to issue any security.

(h) *National bank* means an existing national bank, a national bank in organization, or a Federal branch or agency of a foreign bank.

(i) *Nonconvertible debt* means a general obligation of the national bank or Federal savings association, whether senior or subordinated, that is not convertible into any class of common or preferred stock or any derivative thereof.

(j) *Person* means the same as in section 2(a)(2) of the Securities Act (15 U.S.C. 77b(a)(2)) and includes a national bank and a Federal savings association.

(k) *Prospectus* means an offering document that includes the information required by section 10(a) of the Securities Act (15 U.S.C. 77j(a)).

(l) *Registration statement* means a filing that includes the prospectus and other information required by section 7 of the Securities Act (15 U.S.C. 77g).

(m) *Sale, sell, offer to sell, offer for sale,* and *offer* mean the same as in section 2(a)(3) of the Securities Act (15 U.S.C. 77b(a)(3)).

(n) *SEC* means the Securities and Exchange Commission. When used in the rules, regulations, or forms of the SEC referred to in this part, the term "SEC" shall be deemed to refer to the OCC.

(o) *Securities Act* means the Securities Act of 1933 (15 U.S.C. 77a *et seq.*).

(p) *Security* means the same as in section 2(a)(1) of the Securities Act (15 U.S.C. 77b(a)(1)).

(q) *Underwriter* means the same as in section 2(a)(11) of the Securities Act (15 U.S.C. 77b(a)(11)). SEC Rules 137, 140, 141, 142, and 144 (17 CFR 230.137, 230.140, 230.141, 230.142, and 230.144) (which apply to section 2(a)(11) of the Securities Act) apply to this part.

[59 FR 54798, Nov. 2, 1994, as amended at 73 FR 22243, Apr. 24, 2008; 77 FR 35258, June 13, 2012; 82 FR 8107, Jan. 23, 2017]

§ 16.3 Registration statement and prospectus requirements.

(a) No person shall offer or sell, directly or indirectly, any national bank or Federal savings association issued security unless:

(1) A registration statement for the security meeting the requirements of § 16.15 of this part has been filed with and declared effective by the OCC pursuant to this part, and the offer or sale is accompanied or preceded by a prospectus that has been filed with and declared effective by the OCC as a part of that registration statement; or

(2) An exemption is available under § 16.5 of this part.

(b) Notwithstanding paragraph (a) of this section, securities of a national bank or Federal savings association may be offered through the use of a preliminary prospectus before a registration statement and prospectus for the securities have been declared effective by the OCC if:

(1) A registration statement including the preliminary prospectus has been filed with the OCC;

(2) The preliminary prospectus contains the information required by § 16.15 of this part except for the omission of information with respect to the offering price, underwriting discounts or commissions, discounts or commissions to dealers, amount of proceeds, conversion rates, call prices, or other matters dependent upon the offering price; and

(3) A copy of the prospectus as declared effective containing the information specified in paragraph (b)(2) of this section is furnished to each purchaser prior to or simultaneously with the sale of the security.

(c) SEC Rule 174 (17 CFR 230.174—Delivery of prospectus by dealers; Exemptions under section 4(a)(3) of the Act) applies to transactions by dealers in national bank and Federal savings association issued securities.

[59 FR 54798, Nov. 2, 1994, as amended at 82 FR 8107, Jan. 23, 2017]

§ 16.4 Communications not deemed an offer.

(a) The OCC will not deem the following communications to be an offer under § 16.3 of this part:

(1) Prior to the filing of a registration statement, any notice of a proposed offering that satisfies the requirements of SEC Rule 135 (17 CFR 230.135);

(2) Subsequent to the filing of a registration statement, any notice, circular, advertisement, letter, or other communication published or transmitted to any person that satisfies the requirements of SEC Rule 134 (17 CFR 230.134);

(3) Subsequent to the filing of a registration statement, any oral offer of securities covered by that registration statement;

(4) Subsequent to the filing of a registration statement, any summary prospectus that is filed as a part of that registration statement and satisfies the requirements of SEC Rule 431 (17 CFR 230.431);

(5) Subsequent to the effective date of a registration statement, any written communication if it is proved that each recipient of the communication

simultaneously or previously received a written prospectus meeting the requirements of section 10(a) of the Securities Act (15 U.S.C. 77j(a)) and § 16.15 of this part that was filed with and declared effective by the OCC;

(6) A notice of a proposed unregistered offering that satisfies the requirements of SEC Rule 135c (17 CFR 230.135c); and

(7) A communication that satisfies the requirements of SEC Rule 138 or 139 (17 CFR 230.138 or 230.139).

(b) The OCC may request that communications not deemed an offer under paragraph (a) of this section be submitted to the OCC.

(c) The OCC may prohibit the publication or distribution of any communication not deemed an offer under paragraph (a) of this section if necessary to protect the investing public.

[59 FR 54798, Nov. 2, 1994, as amended at 82 FR 8107, Jan. 23, 2017]

§ 16.5 Exemptions.

The registration statement and prospectus requirements of § 16.3 do not apply to an offer or sale of national bank or Federal savings association securities:

(a) If the securities are exempt from registration under section 3 of the Securities Act (15 U.S.C. 77c), but only by reason of an exemption other than section 3(a)(2) (exemption for bank securities), section 3(a)(5) (exemption for savings association securities), section 3(a)(11) (exemption for intrastate offerings), and section 3(a)(12) (exemption for bank holding company formation) of the Securities Act.

(b) In a transaction exempt from registration under section 4 of the Securities Act (15 U.S.C. 77d). SEC Rules 152 and 152a (17 CFR 230.152 and 230.152a) (which apply to sections 4(a)(2) and 4(a)(1) of the Securities Act) apply to this part;

(c) In a transaction that satisfies the requirements of § 16.7 of this part;

(d) In a transaction that satisfies the requirements of § 16.8 of this part;

(e) In a transaction that satisfies the requirements of SEC Rule 144, 144A, or 236 (17 CFR 230.144, 230.144A, or 230.236);

(f) In a transaction that satisfies the requirements of SEC Rule 701 (17 CFR 230.701);

(g) In a transaction that is an offer or sale occurring outside the United States under SEC Regulation S (17 CFR part 230, Regulation S—Rules Governing Offers and Sales Made Outside the United States Without Registration Under the Securities Act of 1933); or

(h) In a transaction that satisfies the requirements of § 16.9 of this part.

[59 FR 54798, Nov. 2, 1994; 59 FR 67153, Dec. 29, 1994, as amended at 73 FR 22243, Apr. 24, 2008; 82 FR 8107, Jan. 23, 2017]

§ 16.6 Sales of nonconvertible debt.

(a) The OCC will deem offers or sales of national bank or Federal savings association issued nonconvertible debt to be in compliance with §§ 16.3 and 16.15(a) and (b) of this part if all of the following requirements are met:

(1) The national bank or Federal savings association issuing the debt has securities registered under the Exchange Act or is a subsidiary of a holding company that has securities registered under the Exchange Act;

(2) The debt is offered and sold only to accredited investors;

(3) The debt is sold in minimum denominations of $250,000 and each note or debenture, if issued in certificate form, is legended to provide that it cannot be exchanged for notes or debentures of the national bank or Federal savings association in smaller denominations;

(4) The debt is investment grade.

(5) Prior to or simultaneously with the sale of the debt, each purchaser receives an offering document that contains a description of the terms of the debt, the use of proceeds, and method of distribution, and incorporates the national bank's or Federal savings association's latest Consolidated Reports of Condition and Income (Call Report) and the national bank's, Federal savings association's, or the holding company's Forms 10–K, 10–Q, and 8–K (17 CFR part 249) filed under the Exchange Act; and

(6) The offering document and any amendments are filed with the OCC no later than the fifth business day after they are first used.

(b) Offers or sales of nonconvertible debt issued by a federal branch or agency of a foreign bank need not need comply with the requirements of paragraph (a)(1) of this section, if the federal branch or agency provides the OCC the information specified in SEC Rule 12g3–2(b) (17 CFR 240.12g3–2(b)) and provides purchasers the information specified in SEC Rule 144A(d)(4)(i) (17 CFR 230.144A(d)(4)(i)). A federal branch or agency that provides the OCC the information specified in SEC Rule 12g3–2(b) need not incorporate that information by reference into the offering document provided to purchasers pursuant to paragraph (a)(5) of this section. However, the federal branch or agency must make that information available to the potential purchasers upon request. The OCC will make the information available for public inspection.

[59 FR 54798, Nov. 2, 1994, as amended at 73 FR 22243, Apr. 24, 2008; 77 FR 35258, June 13, 2012; 82 FR 8107, Jan. 23, 2017]

§ 16.7 Nonpublic offerings.

(a) The OCC will deem offers and sales of national bank or Federal savings association issued securities that meet all of the following requirements to be exempt from the registration and prospectus requirements of § 16.3 pursuant to § 16.5(c) of this part:

(1) All the securities are offered and sold in a transaction that satisfies the requirements of SEC Regulation D (17 CFR part 230, Regulation D—Rules Governing the Limited Offer and Sale of Securities Without Registration Under the Securities Act of 1933); and

(2) Each purchaser who is not an accredited investor either alone or with its purchaser representative(s) has the knowledge and experience in financial and business matters that it is capable of evaluating the merits and risks of the prospective investment, or the issuer reasonably believes immediately prior to making any sale that the purchaser comes within this description.

(b) All subsequent sales of national bank or Federal savings association issued securities subject to the limitations on resale of SEC Regulation D (17 CFR part 230, Regulation D—Rules Governing the Limited Offer and Sale of Securities Without Registration Under the Securities Act of 1933) must be made pursuant to SEC Rule 144 (17 CFR 230.144), SEC Rule 144A (17 CFR 230.144A), another exemption from registration under the Securities Act referenced in § 16.5 of this part, or in accordance with the registration and prospectus requirements of § 16.3 of this part.

(c) No offer or sale of national bank or Federal savings association issued securities shall be made in reliance on SEC Regulation D (17 CFR part 230, Regulation D—Rules Governing the Limited Offer and Sale of Securities Without Registration Under the Securities Act of 1933) without compliance with paragraphs (a)(1) and (a)(2) of this section.

[59 FR 54798, Nov. 2, 1994, as amended at 73 FR 22243, Apr. 24, 2008; 82 FR 8108, Jan. 23, 2017]

§ 16.8 Small issues.

(a) The OCC will deem offers and sales of national bank or Federal savings association issued securities that satisfy the requirements of SEC Regulation A (17 CFR part 230, Regulation A—Conditional Small Issues Exemption) to be exempt from the registration and prospectus requirements of § 16.3 pursuant to § 16.5(d) of this part.

(b) A filer should consult the SEC's Securities Act Industry Guide 3—Statistical Disclosure by Bank Holding Companies (17 CFR 229.801(c) and 231) and requirement 7 (Loans) of Rule 9–03 of SEC Regulation S-X (17 CFR 230.9–03) for guidance on appropriate disclosures when preparing offering documents to be filed with the OCC pursuant to Regulation A.

[59 FR 54798, Nov. 2, 1994, as amended at 82 FR 8108, Jan. 23, 2017]

§ 16.9 Securities offered and sold in holding company dissolution.

Offers and sales of national bank or Federal savings association issued securities in connection with the dissolution of the holding company of the national bank or Federal savings association are exempt from the registration and prospectus requirements of § 16.3 pursuant to § 16.5(h), provided all of the following requirements are met:

(a) The offer and sale of national bank or Federal savings association issued securities occurs solely as part of a dissolution in which the security holders exchange their shares of stock in a holding company that had no significant assets other than securities of the bank or savings association, for bank or savings association stock;

(b) The security holders receive, after the dissolution, substantially the same proportional share interests in the national bank or Federal savings association as they held in the holding company;

(c) The rights and interests of the security holders in the national bank or Federal savings association are substantially the same as those in the holding company prior to the transaction; and

(d) The national bank or Federal savings association has substantially the same assets and liabilities as the holding company had on a consolidated basis prior to the transaction.

[73 FR 22243, Apr. 24, 2008, as amended at 82 FR 8108, Jan. 23, 2017]

§ 16.10 Sales of securities at an office of a Federal savings association.

Sales of securities of a Federal savings association or its affiliates at an office of a Federal savings association may be made only in accordance with the provisions of 12 CFR 163.76. For the purpose of this section, "affiliate" has the same meaning as in 12 CFR 161.4.

[82 FR 8108, Jan. 23, 2017]

§ 16.15 Form and content.

(a) Any registration statement filed pursuant to this part must be on the form for registration (17 CFR part 239) that the national bank or Federal savings association would be eligible to use were it required to register the securities under the Securities Act and must meet the requirements of the SEC regulations referred to in the applicable form for registration. A filer should consult the SEC's Securities Act Industry Guide 3—Statistical Disclosure by Bank Holding Companies (17 CFR 229.801(c) and 231) for guidance on appropriate disclosures when preparing registration statements.

(b) Any registration statement or amendment filed pursuant to this part must comply with the requirements of SEC Regulation C (17 CFR part 230, Regulation C—Registration), except to the extent those requirements conflict with specific requirements of this part.

(c) In addition to the information expressly required to be included in the registration statement by paragraphs (a) and (b) of this section, the registration statement must include any additional material information that is necessary to make the required statements, in light of the circumstances under which they are made, not misleading.

(d) Notwithstanding paragraph (a) of this section, the registration statement for securities issued by a national bank or Federal savings association that is not in compliance with the regulatory capital requirements set forth in 12 CFR part 3, as applicable must be on the Form S–1 (17 CFR part 239) registration statement under the Securities Act.

(e) Notwithstanding paragraph (a) of this section, a national bank or Federal savings association in organization pursuant to § 5.20 of this chapter shall not be required to include audited financial statements as part of its registration statement for the offer and sale of its securities, unless the OCC determines that factors particular to the proposal indicate that inclusion of such statements would be in the interest of investors or would further the safe and sound operation of a national bank or Federal savings association.

[59 FR 54798, Nov. 2, 1994, as amended at 73 FR 12010, Mar. 6, 2008; 79 FR 11312, Feb. 28, 2014; 82 FR 8108, Jan. 23, 2017]

§ 16.16 Effectiveness.

(a) Registration statements and amendments filed with the OCC pursuant to this part will become effective in accordance with sections 8(a) and (c) of the Securities Act (15 U.S.C. 77h(a) and (c)) and SEC Regulation C (17 CFR part 230, Regulation C—Registration).

(b) The OCC will deem registration statements and amendments that become effective pursuant to paragraph (a) of this section to be declared effective. If the OCC deems a registration statement to be declared effective, the OCC will also deem the prospectus that was filed as a part of that registration statement to be declared effective.

[59 FR 54798, Nov. 2, 1994, as amended at 82 FR 8108, Jan. 23, 2017]

§ 16.17 Filing requirements and inspection of documents.

(a) Except as otherwise provided in this section, all registration statements, offering documents, amendments, notices, or other documents must be filed with the OCC's Securities and Corporate Practices Division electronically at *http://www.banknet.gov/*. Documents may be signed electronically using the signature provision in SEC Rule 402 (17 CFR 230.402).

(b) All registration statements, offering documents, amendments, notices, or other documents relating to a national bank or Federal savings association in organization must be filed with the appropriate district office of the OCC at *http://www.banknet.gov/*.

(c) Where this part refers to a section of the Securities Act or the Exchange Act or an SEC rule that requires the filing of a notice or other document with the SEC, that notice or other document must be filed with the OCC.

(d) Provided the person filing the document has complied with all requirements regarding the filing, including the submission of any fee required under § 16.33, the date of filing of the document is the date the OCC receives the filing. An electronic filing that is submitted on a business day by direct transmission commencing on or before 5:30 p.m. Eastern Standard or Daylight Savings Time, whichever is currently in effect, would be deemed received by the OCC on the same business day. An electronic filing that is submitted by direct transmission commencing after 5:30 p.m. Eastern Standard or Daylight Savings Time, whichever is currently in effect, or on a Saturday, Sunday, or Federal holiday, would be deemed received by the OCC on the next business day. If an electronic filer in good faith attempts to file a document with the OCC in a timely manner but the filing is delayed due to technical difficulties beyond the electronic filer's control, the electronic filer may request that the OCC adjust the filing date of such document. The OCC may grant the request if it appears that such adjustment is appropriate and consistent with the public interest and the protection of investors.

(e) Notwithstanding paragraph (d) of this section, any registration statement or any post-effective amendment thereto filed pursuant to SEC Rule 462(b) (17 CFR 230.462(b)) shall be deemed received by the OCC on the same business day if its submission commenced on or before 10 p.m. Eastern Standard Time or Eastern Daylight Savings Time, whichever is currently in effect, and on the next business day if its submission commenced after 10 p.m. Eastern Standard or Daylight Savings Time, whichever is currently in effect, or any time on a Saturday, Sunday, or Federal holiday.

(f) If a national bank or Federal savings association experiences unanticipated technical difficulties preventing the timely preparation and submission of an electronic filing, the bank or savings association may, upon notice to the OCC's Securities and Corporate Practices Division or district office, as appropriate, file the subject filing in paper format no later than one business day after the date on which the filing was to be made. Paper filings should be submitted to the OCC's Securities and Corporate Practices Division or appropriate district office, at the address provided at *www.occ.gov*.

(g) Any filing of amendments or revisions must include two copies, one of which must be marked to indicate clearly and precisely, by underlining or in some other appropriate manner, the changes made.

(h) The OCC will make available for public inspection copies of the registration statements, offering documents, amendments, exhibits, notices or reports filed pursuant to this part at the address identified in § 4.14 of this chapter.

[82 FR 8108, Jan. 23, 2017]

§ 16.18 Use of prospectus.

(a) No person shall use a prospectus or amendment declared effective by the OCC more than nine months after the effective date unless the information contained in the prospectus or amendment is as of a date not more than 16 months prior to the date of use.

(b) If any event arises, or change in fact occurs, after the effective date and that event or change in fact, individually or in the aggregate, results in the prospectus containing any untrue statement of material fact, or omitting to state a material fact necessary in order to make statements made in the prospectus not misleading under the circumstances, then no person shall use the prospectus that has been declared effective under this part until an amendment reflecting the event or change has been filed with and declared effective by the OCC.

§ 16.19 Withdrawal or abandonment.

(a) Any registration statement, amendment, or exhibit may be withdrawn prior to the effective date. A withdrawal must be signed and state the grounds upon which it is made. The OCC will not remove any withdrawn document from its files, but will mark the document *Withdrawn upon the request of the registrant on (date).*

(b) When a registration statement or amendment has been on file with the OCC for a period of nine months and has not become effective, the OCC may, in its discretion, determine whether the filing has been abandoned. Before determining that a filing has been abandoned, the OCC will notify the filer that the filing is out of date and must either be amended to comply with the applicable requirements of this part or be withdrawn within 30 days after the date of notice. When a filing is abandoned, the OCC will not remove the filing from its files but will mark the filing *Declared abandoned by the OCC on (date).*

§ 16.30 Request for interpretive advice or no-objection letter.

Any person requesting interpretive advice or a no-objection letter from the OCC with respect to any provision of this part shall:

(a) File a copy of the request, including any supporting attachments, with the OCC's Securities and Corporate Practices Division at the address provided at *www.occ.gov*;

(b) Identify or describe the provisions of this part to which the request relates, the participants in the proposed transaction, and the reasons for the request; and

(c) Include with the request a legal opinion as to each legal issue raised and an accounting opinion as to each accounting issue raised.

[59 FR 54798, Nov. 2, 1994, as amended at 82 FR 8109, Jan. 23, 2017]

§ 16.31 Escrow requirement.

The OCC may require that any funds received in connection with an offer or sale of securities be held in an independent escrow account at an unrelated insured depository institution when the use of an escrow account is in the best interests of shareholders.

§ 16.32 Fraudulent transactions and unsafe or unsound practices.

(a) No person in the offer or sale of national bank or Federal savings association securities shall directly or indirectly:

(1) Employ any device, scheme or artifice to defraud;

(2) Make any untrue statement of a material fact or omit to state a material fact necessary in order to make the statements made, in light of the circumstances under which they were made, not misleading; or

(3) Engage in any act, practice, or course of business which operates as a fraud or deceit upon any person, in connection with the purchase or sale of any security of a national bank or Federal savings association.

(b) Nothing in this section limits the applicability of section 17 of the Securities Act (15 U.S.C. 77q) or section 10(b) of the Exchange Act (15 U.S.C. 78j) or Rule 10b–5 promulgated thereunder (17 CFR 240.10b–5).

(c) Any violation of this section also constitutes an unsafe or unsound practice under 12 U.S.C. 1818.

(d) SEC Rule 175 (17 CFR 230.175—Liability for certain statements by issuers) applies to this part.

[59 FR 54798, Nov. 2, 1994, as amended at 82 FR 8109, Jan. 23, 2017]

§ 16.33 Filing fees.

(a) The OCC may require filing fees to accompany certain filings made under this part before it will accept those filings. The OCC provides an applicable fee schedule in the *Notice of Comptroller of the Currency Fees* published pursuant to § 8.8 of this chapter.

(b) Filing fees must be paid by check payable to the Comptroller of the Currency or by other means acceptable to the OCC.

[82 FR 8109, Jan. 23, 2017]

PART 19—RULES OF PRACTICE AND PROCEDURE

Subpart A—Uniform Rules of Practice and Procedure

Sec.
19.1 Scope.
19.2 Rules of construction.
19.3 Definitions.
19.4 Authority of the Comptroller.
19.5 Authority of the administrative law judge.
19.6 Appearance and practice in adjudicatory proceedings.
19.7 Good faith certification.
19.8 Conflicts of interest.
19.9 Ex parte communications.
19.10 Filing of papers.
19.11 Service of papers.
19.12 Construction of time limits.
19.13 Change of time limits.
19.14 Witness fees and expenses.
19.15 Opportunity for informal settlement.
19.16 OCC's right to conduct examination.
19.17 Collateral attacks on adjudicatory proceeding.
19.18 Commencement of proceeding and contents of notice.
19.19 Answer.
19.20 Amended pleadings.
19.21 Failure to appear.
19.22 Consolidation and severance of actions.
19.23 Motions.
19.24 Scope of document discovery.
19.25 Request for document discovery from parties.
19.26 Document subpoenas to nonparties.
19.27 Deposition of witness unavailable for hearing.
19.28 Interlocutory review.
19.29 Summary disposition.
19.30 Partial summary disposition.
19.31 Scheduling and prehearing conferences.
19.32 Prehearing submissions.
19.33 Public hearings.
19.34 Hearing subpoenas.
19.35 Conduct of hearings.
19.36 Evidence.
19.37 Post-hearing filings.
19.38 Recommended decision and filing of record.
19.39 Exceptions to recommended decision.
19.40 Review by the Comptroller.
19.41 Stays pending judicial review.

Subpart B—Procedural Rules for OCC Adjudications

19.100 Filing documents.
19.101 Delegation to OFIA.

Subpart C—Removals, Suspensions, and Prohibitions When a Crime Is Charged or a Conviction is Obtained

19.110 Scope.
19.111 Suspension, removal, or prohibition.
19.112 Informal hearing.
19.113 Recommended and final decisions.

Subpart D—Exemption Hearings Under Section 12(h) of the Securities Exchange Act of 1934

19.120 Scope.
19.121 Application for exemption.
19.122 Newspaper notice.
19.123 Informal hearing.
19.124 Decision of the Comptroller.

Subpart E—Disciplinary Proceedings Involving the Federal Securities Laws

19.130 Scope.
19.131 Notice of charges and answer.
19.132 Disciplinary orders.
19.135 Applications for stay or review of disciplinary actions imposed by registered clearing agencies.

Subpart F—Civil Money Penalty Authority Under the Securities Laws

19.140 Scope.

Subpart G—Cease-and-Desist Authority Under the Securities Laws

19.150 Scope.

Subpart H—Change in Bank Control

19.160 Scope.
19.161 Notice of disapproval and hearing initiation.

Subpart I—Discovery Depositions and Subpoenas

19.170 Discovery depositions.
19.171 Deposition subpoenas.

Subpart J—Formal Investigations

19.180 Scope.
19.181 Confidentiality of formal investigations.
19.182 Order to conduct a formal investigation.
19.183 Rights of witnesses.

19.184 Service of subpoena and payment of witness expenses.

Subpart K—Parties and Representational Practice Before the OCC; Standards of Conduct

19.190 Scope.
19.191 Definitions.
19.192 Sanctions relating to conduct in an adjudicatory proceeding.
19.193 Censure, suspension or debarment.
19.194 Eligibility of attorneys and accountants to practice.
19.195 Incompetence.
19.196 Disreputable conduct.
19.197 Initiation of disciplinary proceeding.
19.198 Conferences.
19.199 Proceedings under this subpart.
19.200 Effect of suspension, debarment or censure.
19.201 Petition for reinstatement.

Subpart L—Equal Access to Justice Act

19.210 Scope.

Subpart M—Procedures for Reclassifying a Bank Based on Criteria Other Than Capital

19.220 Scope.
19.221 Reclassification of a bank based on unsafe or unsound condition or practice.
19.222 Request for rescission of reclassification.

Subpart N—Order To Dismiss a Director or Senior Executive Officer

19.230 Scope.
19.231 Order to dismiss a director or senior executive officer.

Subpart O—Civil Money Penalty Adjustments

19.240 Inflation adjustments.

Subpart P—Removal, Suspension, and Debarment of Accountants From Performing Audit Services

19.241 Scope.
19.242 Definitions.
19.243 Removal, suspension, or debarment.
19.244 Automatic removal, suspension, or debarment.
19.245 Notice of removal, suspension, or debarment.
19.246 Petition for reinstatement.

AUTHORITY: 5 U.S.C. 504, 554–557; 12 U.S.C. 93(b), 93a, 164, 481, 504, 1817, 1818, 1820, 1831m, 1831o, 1832, 1884, 1972, 3102, 3108(a), 3110, 3909, and 4717; 15 U.S.C. 78(h) and (i), 78o–4(c), 78o–5, 78q–1, 78s, 78u, 78u–2, 78u–3, 78w, and 1639e; 28 U.S.C. 2461 note; 31 U.S.C. 330 and 5321; and 42 U.S.C. 4012a.

SOURCE: 56 FR 38028, Aug. 9, 1991, unless otherwise noted.

Subpart A—Uniform Rules of Practice and Procedure

§ 19.1 Scope.

This subpart prescribes Uniform Rules of practice and procedure applicable to adjudicatory proceedings required to be conducted on the record after opportunity for a hearing under the following statutory provisions:

(a) Cease-and-desist proceedings under section 8(b) of the Federal Deposit Insurance Act ("FDIA") (12 U.S.C. 1818(b));

(b) Removal and prohibition proceedings under section 8(e) of the FDIA (12 U.S.C. 1818(e));

(c) Change-in-control proceedings under section 7(j)(4) of the FDIA (12 U.S.C. 1817(j)(4)) to determine whether the Office of the Comptroller of the Currency ("OCC") should issue an order to approve or disapprove a person's proposed acquisition of an institution;

(d) Proceedings under section 15C(c)(2) of the Securities Exchange Act of 1934 ("Exchange Act") (15 U.S.C. 78o–5), to impose sanctions upon any government securities broker or dealer or upon any person associated or seeking to become associated with a government securities broker or dealer for which the OCC is the appropriate agency;

(e) Assessment of civil money penalties by the OCC against institutions, institution-affiliated parties, and certain other persons for which it is the appropriate agency for any violation of:

(1) Any provision of law referenced in 12 U.S.C. 93, or any regulation issued thereunder, and certain unsafe or unsound practices and breaches of fiduciary duty, pursuant to 12 U.S.C. 93;

(2) Sections 22 and 23 of the Federal Reserve Act ("FRA"), or any regulation issued thereunder, and certain unsafe or unsound practices and breaches of fiduciary duty, pursuant to 12 U.S.C. 504 and 505;

(3) Section 106(b) of the Bank Holding CompanyAmendments of 1970, pursuant to 12 U.S.C. 1972(2)(F);

(4) Any provision of the Change in Bank Control Act of 1978 or any regulation or order issued thereunder, and certain unsafe or unsound practices and breaches of fiduciary duty, pursuant to 12 U.S.C. 1817(j)(16);

(5) Any provision of the International Lending Supervision Act of 1983 ("ILSA"), or any rule, regulation or order issued thereunder, pursuant to 12 U.S.C. 3909;

(6) Any provision of the International Banking Act of 1978 ("IBA"), or any rule, regulation or order issued thereunder, pursuant to 12 U.S.C. 3108;

(7) Section 5211 of the Revised Statutes (12 U.S.C. 161), pursuant to 12 U.S.C. 164;

(8) Certain provisions of the Exchange Act, pursuant to section 21B of the Exchange Act (15 U.S.C. 78u–2);

(9) Section 1120 of the Financial Institutions Reform, Recovery, and Enforcement Act of 1989 ("FIRREA") (12 U.S.C. 3349), or any order or regulation issued thereunder;

(10) The terms of any final or temporary order issued under section 8 of the FDIA or any written agreement executed by the OCC, the terms of any condition imposed in writing by the OCC in connection with the grant of an application or request, certain unsafe or unsound practices, breaches of fiduciary duty, or any law or regulation not otherwise provided herein, pursuant to 12 U.S.C. 1818(i)(2);

(11) Any provision of law referenced in section 102(f) of the Flood Disaster Protection Act of 1973 (42 U.S.C. 4012a(f)) or any order or regulation issued thereunder; and

(12) Any provision of law referenced in 31 U.S.C. 5321 or any order or regulation issued thereunder;

(f) Remedial action under section 102(g) of the Flood Disaster Protection Act of 1973 (42 U.S.C. 4012a(g));

(g) Removal, prohibition, and civil monetary penalty proceedings under section 10(k) of the FDI Act (12 U.S.C. 1820(k)) for violations of the post-employment restrictions imposed by that section; and

(h) This subpart also applies to all other adjudications required by statute to be determined on the record after opportunity for an agency hearing, unless otherwise specifically provided for in the Local Rules.

[56 FR 38028, Aug. 9, 1991, as amended at 61 FR 20334, May 6, 1996; 70 FR 69638, Nov. 17, 2005]

§ 19.2 Rules of construction.

For purposes of this part:

(a) Any term in the singular includes the plural, and the plural includes the singular, if such use would be appropriate;

(b) Any use of a masculine, feminine, or neuter gender encompasses all three, if such use would be appropriate;

(c) The term *counsel* includes a non-attorney representative; and

(d) Unless the context requires otherwise, a party's counsel of record, if any, may, on behalf of that party, take any action required to be taken by the party.

§ 19.3 Definitions.

For purposes of this part, unless explicitly stated to the contrary:

(a) *Administrative law judge* means one who presides at an administrative hearing under authority set forth at 5 U.S.C. 556.

(b) *Adjudicatory proceeding* means a proceeding conducted pursuant to these rules and leading to the formulation of a final order other than a regulation.

(c) *Comptroller* means the Comptroller of the Currency or a person delegated to perform the functions of the Comptroller of the Currency under this part.

(d) *Decisional employee* means any member of the Comptroller's or administrative law judge's staff who has not engaged in an investigative or prosecutorial role in a proceeding and who may assist the Comptroller or the administrative law judge, respectively, in preparing orders, recommended decisions, decisions, and other documents under the Uniform Rules.

(e) *Enforcement Counsel* means any individual who files a notice of appearance as counsel on behalf of the OCC in an adjudicatory proceeding.

(f) *Final order* means an order issued by the Comptroller with or without the consent of the affected institution or the institution-affiliated party, that has become final, without regard to the pendency of any petition for reconsideration or review.

(g) *Institution* includes any national bank or Federal branch or agency of a foreign bank.

(h) *Institution-affiliated party* means any institution- affiliated party as that term is defined in section 3(u) of the FDIA (12 U.S.C. 1813(u)).

(i) *Local Rules* means those rules promulgated by the OCC in the subparts of this part excluding subpart A.

(j) *OCC* means the Office of the Comptroller of the Currency.

(k) *OFIA* means the Office of Financial Institution Adjudication, the executive body charged with overseeing the administration of administrative enforcement proceedings for the OCC, the Board of Governors of the Federal Reserve System ("Board of Governors"), the Federal Deposit Insurance Corporation ("FDIC"), the Office of Thrift Supervision ("OTS"), and the National Credit Union Administration ("NCUA").

(l) *Party* means the OCC and any person named as a party in any notice.

(m) *Person* means an individual, sole proprietor, partnership, corporation, unincorporated association, trust, joint venture, pool, syndicate, agency or other entity or organization, including an institution as defined in paragraph (g) of this section.

(n) *Respondent* means any party other than the OCC.

(o) *Uniform Rules* means those rules in subpart A of this part that are common to the OCC, the Board of Governors, the FDIC, the OTS, and the NCUA.

(p) *Violation* includes any action (alone or with another or others) for or toward causing, bringing about, participating in, counseling, or aiding or abetting a violation.

[56 FR 38028, Aug. 9, 1991, as amended at 73 FR 22243, Apr. 24, 2008]

§ 19.4 Authority of the Comptroller.

The Comptroller may, at any time during the pendency of a proceeding, perform, direct the performance of, or waive performance of, any act which could be done or ordered by the administrative law judge.

§ 19.5 Authority of the administrative law judge.

(a) *General rule.* All proceedings governed by this part shall be conducted in accordance with the provisions of chapter 5 of title 5 of the United States Code. The administrative law judge shall have all powers necessary to conduct a proceeding in a fair and impartial manner and to avoid unnecessary delay.

(b) *Powers.* The administrative law judge shall have all powers necessary to conduct the proceeding in accordance with paragraph (a) of this section, including the following powers:

(1) To administer oaths and affirmations;

(2) To issue subpoenas, subpoenas duces tecum, and protective orders, as authorized by this part, and to quash or modify any such subpoenas and orders;

(3) To receive relevant evidence and to rule upon the admission of evidence and offers of proof;

(4) To take or cause depositions to be taken as authorized by this subpart;

(5) To regulate the course of the hearing and the conduct of the parties and their counsel;

(6) To hold scheduling and/or prehearing conferences as set forth in § 19.31;

(7) To consider and rule upon all procedural and other motions appropriate in an adjudicatory proceeding, provided that only the Comptroller shall have the power to grant any motion to dismiss the proceeding or to decide any other motion that results in a final determination of the merits of the proceeding;

(8) To prepare and present to the Comptroller a recommended decision as provided herein;

(9) To recuse himself or herself by motion made by a party or on his or her own motion;

(10) To establish time, place and manner limitations on the attendance of the public and the media for any public hearing; and

(11) To do all other things necessary and appropriate to discharge the duties of a presiding officer.

[56 FR 38028, Aug. 9, 1991; 56 FR 41726, Aug. 22, 1991]

§ 19.6 Appearance and practice in adjudicatory proceedings.

(a) *Appearance before the OCC or an administrative law judge*—(1) *By attorneys.* Any member in good standing of the bar of the highest court of any state, commonwealth, possession, territory of the United States, or the District of Columbia may represent others before the OCC if such attorney is not currently suspended or debarred from practice before the OCC.

(2) *By non-attorneys.* An individual may appear on his or her own behalf; a member of a partnership may represent the partnership; a duly authorized officer, director, or employee of any government unit, agency, institution, corporation or authority may represent that unit, agency, institution, corporation or authority if such officer, director, or employee is not currently suspended or debarred from practice before the OCC.

(3) *Notice of appearance.* Any individual acting as counsel on behalf of a party, including the Comptroller, shall file a notice of appearance with OFIA at or before the time that the individual submits papers or otherwise appears on behalf of a party in the adjudicatory proceeding. The notice of appearance must include a written declaration that the individual is currently qualified as provided in paragraph (a)(1) or (a)(2) of this section and is authorized to represent the particular party. By filing a notice of appearance on behalf of a party in an adjudicatory proceeding, the counsel agrees and represents that he or she is authorized to accept service on behalf of the represented party and that, in the event of withdrawal from representation, he or she will, if required by the administrative law judge, continue to accept service until new counsel has filed a notice of appearance or until the represented party indicates that he or she will proceed on a *pro se* basis.

(b) *Sanctions.* Dilatory, obstructionist, egregious, contemptuous or contumacious conduct at any phase of any adjudicatory proceeding may be grounds for exclusion or suspension of counsel from the proceeding.

[56 FR 38028, Aug. 9, 1991; 56 FR 41726, Aug. 22, 1991; 56 FR 63551, Dec. 4, 1991; 61 FR 20334, May 6, 1996]

§ 19.7 Good faith certification.

(a) *General requirement.* Every filing or submission of record following the issuance of a notice shall be signed by at least one counsel of record in his or her individual name and shall state that counsel's address and telephone number. A party who acts as his or her own counsel shall sign his or her individual name and state his or her address and telephone number on every filing or submission of record.

(b) *Effect of signature.* (1) The signature of counsel or a party shall constitute a certification that: the counsel or party has read the filing or submission of record; to the best of his or her knowledge, information, and belief formed after reasonable inquiry, the filing or submission of record is well-grounded in fact and is warranted by existing law or a good faith argument for the extension, modification, or reversal of existing law; and the filing or submission of record is not made for any improper purpose, such as to harass or to cause unnecessary delay or needless increase in the cost of litigation.

(2) If a filing or submission of record is not signed, the administrative law judge shall strike the filing or submission of record, unless it is signed promptly after the omission is called to the attention of the pleader or movant.

(c) *Effect of making oral motion or argument.* The act of making any oral motion or oral argument by any counsel or party constitutes a certification that to the best of his or her knowledge, information, and belief formed after reasonable inquiry, his or her statements are well-grounded in fact and are warranted by existing law or a good faith argument for the extension, modification, or reversal of existing law, and are not made for any improper purpose, such as to harass or to cause unnecessary delay or needless increase in the cost of litigation.

§ 19.8 Conflicts of interest.

(a) *Conflict of interest in representation.* No person shall appear as counsel for another person in an adjudicatory proceeding if it reasonably appears that such representation may be materially limited by that counsel's responsibilities to a third person or by the counsel's own interests. The administrative law judge may take corrective measures at any stage of a proceeding to cure a conflict of interest in representation, including the issuance of an order limiting the scope of representation or disqualifying an individual from appearing in a representative capacity for the duration of the proceeding.

(b) *Certification and waiver.* If any person appearing as counsel represents two or more parties to an adjudicatory proceeding or also represents a nonparty on a matter relevant to an issue in the proceeding, counsel must certify in writing at the time of filing the notice of appearance required by § 19.6(a):

(1) That the counsel has personally and fully discussed the possibility of conflicts of interest with each such party and non-party; and

(2) That each such party and nonparty waives any right it might otherwise have had to assert any known conflicts of interest or to assert any nonmaterial conflicts of interest during the course of the proceeding.

[56 FR 38028, Aug. 9, 1991, as amended at 61 FR 20334, May 6, 1996]

§ 19.9 Ex parte communications.

(a) *Definition*—(1) *Ex parte communication* means any material oral or written communication relevant to the merits of an adjudicatory proceeding that was neither on the record nor on reasonable prior notice to all parties that takes place between:

(i) An interested person outside the OCC (including such person's counsel); and

(ii) The administrative law judge handling that proceeding, the Comptroller, or a decisional employee.

(2) *Exception.* A request for status of the proceeding does not constitute an ex parte communication.

(b) *Prohibition of ex parte communications.* From the time the notice is issued by the Comptroller until the date that the Comptroller issues his or her final decision pursuant to § 19.40(c):

(1) No interested person outside the OCC shall make or knowingly cause to be made an ex parte communication to the Comptroller, the administrative law judge, or a decisional employee; and

(2) The Comptroller, administrative law judge, or decisional employee shall not make or knowingly cause to be made to any interested person outside the OCC any ex parte communication.

(c) *Procedure upon occurrence of ex parte communication.* If an ex parte communication is received by the administrative law judge, the Comptroller or any other person identified in paragraph (a) of this section, that person shall cause all such written communications (or, if the communication is oral, a memorandum stating the substance of the communication) to be placed on the record of the proceeding and served on all parties. All other parties to the proceeding shall have an opportunity, within ten days of receipt of service of the ex parte communication, to file responses thereto and to recommend any sanctions, in accordance with paragraph (d) of this section, that they believe to be appropriate under the circumstances.

(d) *Sanctions.* Any party or his or her counsel who makes a prohibited ex parte communication, or who encourages or solicits another to make any such communication, may be subject to any appropriate sanction or sanctions imposed by the Comptroller or the administrative law judge including, but not limited to, exclusion from the proceedings and an adverse ruling on the issue which is the subject of the prohibited communication.

(e) *Separation of functions.* Except to the extent required for the disposition of ex parte matters as authorized by law, the administrative law judge may not consult a person or party on any matter relevant to the merits of the adjudication, unless on notice and opportunity for all parties to participate. An employee or agent engaged in the performance of investigative or prosecuting functions for the OCC in a case may not, in that or a factually related case, participate or advise in the decision, recommended decision, or agency review of the recommended decision under § 19.40, except as witness or counsel in public proceedings.

[56 FR 38028, Aug. 9, 1991, as amended at 60 FR 30184, June 8, 1995]

§ 19.10 Filing of papers.

(a) *Filing.* Any papers required to be filed, excluding documents produced in response to a discovery request pursuant to §§ 19.25 and 19.26, shall be filed with OFIA, except as otherwise provided.

(b) *Manner of filing.* Unless otherwise specified by the Comptroller or the administrative law judge, filing may be accomplished by:

(1) Personal service;

(2) Delivering the papers to a reliable commercial courier service, overnight delivery service, or to the U.S. Post Office for Express Mail delivery;

(3) Mailing the papers by first class, registered, or certified mail; or

(4) Transmission by electronic media, only if expressly authorized, and upon any conditions specified, by the Comptroller or the administrative law judge. All papers filed by electronic media shall also concurrently be filed in accordance with paragraph (c) of this section.

(c) *Formal requirements as to papers filed*—(1) *Form.* All papers filed must set forth the name, address, and telephone number of the counsel or party making the filing and must be accompanied by a certification setting forth when and how service has been made on all other parties. All papers filed must be double-spaced and printed or typewritten on 8½ × 11 inch paper, and must be clear and legible.

(2) *Signature.* All papers must be dated and signed as provided in § 19.7.

(3) *Caption.* All papers filed must include at the head thereof, or on a title page, the name of the OCC and of the filing party, the title and docket number of the proceeding, and the subject of the particular paper.

(4) *Number of copies.* Unless otherwise specified by the Comptroller or the administrative law judge, an original and one copy of all documents and papers shall be filed, except that only one copy of transcripts of testimony and exhibits shall be filed.

§ 19.11 Service of papers.

(a) *By the parties.* Except as otherwise provided, a party filing papers shall serve a copy upon the counsel of record for all other parties to the proceeding so represented, and upon any party not so represented.

(b) *Method of service.* Except as provided in paragraphs (c)(2) and (d) of this section, a serving party shall use one or more of the following methods of service:

(1) Personal service;

(2) Delivering the papers to a reliable commercial courier service, overnight delivery service, or to the U.S. Post Office for Express Mail delivery;

(3) Mailing the papers by first class, registered, or certified mail; or

(4) Transmission by electronic media, only if the parties mutually agree. Any papers served by electronic media shall also concurrently be served in accordance with the requirements of § 19.10(c).

(c) *By the Comptroller or the administrative law judge.* (1) All papers required to be served by the Comptroller or the administrative law judge upon a party who has appeared in the proceeding in accordance with § 19.6 shall be served by any means specified in paragraph (b) of this section.

(2) If a party has not appeared in the proceeding in accordance with § 19.6, the Comptroller or the administrative law judge shall make service by any of the following methods:

(i) By personal service;

(ii) If the person to be served is an individual, by delivery to a person of suitable age and discretion at the physical location where the individual resides or works;

(iii) If the person to be served is a corporation or other association, by delivery to an officer, managing or general agent, or to any other agent authorized by appointment or by law to receive service and, if the agent is one authorized by statute to receive service and the statute so requires, by also mailing a copy to the party;

(iv) By registered or certified mail addressed to the person's last known address; or

(v) By any other method reasonably calculated to give actual notice.

(d) *Subpoenas.* Service of a subpoena may be made:

(1) By personal service;

(2) If the person to be served is an individual, by delivery to a person of

suitable age and discretion at the physical location where the individual resides or works;

(3) By delivery to an agent, which, in the case of a corporation or other association, is delivery to an officer, managing or general agent, or to any other agent authorized by appointment or by law to receive service and, if the agent is one authorized by statute to receive service and the statute so requires, by also mailing a copy to the party;

(4) By registered or certified mail addressed to the person's last known address; or

(5) By any other method reasonably calculated to give actual notice.

(e) *Area of service.* Service in any state, territory, possession of the United States, or the District of Columbia, on any person or company doing business in any state, territory, possession of the United States, or the District of Columbia, or on any person as otherwise provided by law, is effective without regard to the place where the hearing is held, provided that if service is made on a foreign bank in connection with an action or proceeding involving one or more of its branches or agencies located in any state, territory, possession of the United States, or the District of Columbia, service shall be made on at least one branch or agency so involved.

[56 FR 38028, Aug. 9, 1991, as amended at 61 FR 20334, May 6, 1996]

§ 19.12 Construction of time limits.

(a) *General rule.* In computing any period of time prescribed by this subpart, the date of the act or event that commences the designated period of time is not included. The last day so computed is included unless it is a Saturday, Sunday, or Federal holiday. When the last day is a Saturday, Sunday, or Federal holiday, the period runs until the end of the next day that is not a Saturday, Sunday, or Federal holiday. Intermediate Saturdays, Sundays, and Federal holidays are included in the computation of time. However, when the time period within which an act is to be performed is ten days or less, not including any additional time allowed for in paragraph (c) of this section, intermediate Saturdays, Sundays, and Federal holidays are not included.

(b) *When papers are deemed to be filed or served.* (1) Filing and service are deemed to be effective:

(i) In the case of personal service or same day commercial courier delivery, upon actual service;

(ii) In the case of overnight commercial delivery service, U.S. Express Mail delivery, or first class, registered, or certified mail, upon deposit in or delivery to an appropriate point of collection;

(iii) In the case of transmission by electronic media, as specified by the authority receiving the filing, in the case of filing, and as agreed among the parties, in the case of service.

(2) The effective filing and service dates specified in paragraph (b)(1) of this section may be modified by the Comptroller or administrative law judge in the case of filing or by agreement of the parties in the case of service.

(c) *Calculation of time for service and filing of responsive papers.* Whenever a time limit is measured by a prescribed period from the service of any notice or paper, the applicable time limits are calculated as follows:

(1) If service is made by first class, registered, or certified mail, add three calendar days to the prescribed period;

(2) If service is made by express mail or overnight delivery service, add one calendar day to the prescribed period; or

(3) If service is made by electronic media transmission, add one calendar day to the prescribed period, unless otherwise determined by the Comptroller or the administrative law judge in the case of filing, or by agreement among the parties in the case of service.

[56 FR 38028, Aug. 9, 1991, as amended at 61 FR 20335, May 6, 1996]

§ 19.13 Change of time limits.

Except as otherwise provided by law, the administrative law judge may, for good cause shown, extend the time limits prescribed by the Uniform Rules or by any notice or order issued in the proceedings. After the referral of the case to the Comptroller pursuant to § 19.38, the Comptroller may grant extensions of the time limits for good cause shown. Extensions may be granted at the motion of a party after notice and opportunity to respond is afforded all non-moving parties or on the Comptroller's or the administrative law judge's own motion.

§ 19.14 Witness fees and expenses.

Witnesses subpoenaed for testimony or depositions shall be paid the same fees for attendance and mileage as are paid in the United States district courts in proceedings in which the United States is a party, provided that, in the case of a discovery subpoena addressed to a party, no witness fees or mileage need be paid. Fees for witnesses shall be tendered in advance by the party requesting the subpoena, except that fees and mileage need not be tendered in advance where the OCC is the party requesting the subpoena. The OCC shall not be required to pay any fees to, or expenses of, any witness not subpoenaed by the OCC.

§ 19.15 Opportunity for informal settlement.

Any respondent may, at any time in the proceeding, unilaterally submit to Enforcement Counsel written offers or proposals for settlement of a proceeding, without prejudice to the rights of any of the parties. No such offer or proposal shall be made to any OCC representative other than Enforcement Counsel. Submission of a written settlement offer does not provide a basis for adjourning or otherwise delaying all or any portion of a proceeding under this part. No settlement offer or proposal, or any subsequent negotiation or resolution, is admissible as evidence in any proceeding.

§ 19.16 OCC's right to conduct examination.

Nothing contained in this subpart limits in any manner the right of the OCC to conduct any examination, inspection, or visitation of any institution or institution-affiliated party, or the right of the OCC to conduct or continue any form of investigation authorized by law.

§ 19.17 Collateral attacks on adjudicatory proceeding.

If an interlocutory appeal or collateral attack is brought in any court concerning all or any part of an adjudicatory proceeding, the challenged adjudicatory proceeding shall continue without regard to the pendency of that court proceeding. No default or other failure to act as directed in the adjudicatory proceeding within the times prescribed in this subpart shall be excused based on the pendency before any court of any interlocutory appeal or collateral attack.

[56 FR 38028, Aug. 9, 1991; 56 FR 41726, Aug. 22, 1991]

§ 19.18 Commencement of proceeding and contents of notice.

(a) *Commencement of proceeding.* (1)(i) Except for change-in-control proceedings under section 7(j)(4) of the FDIA, 12 U.S.C. 1817(j)(4), a proceeding governed by this subpart is commenced by issuance of a notice by the Comptroller.

(ii) The notice must be served by the Comptroller upon the respondent and given to any other appropriate financial institution supervisory authority where required by law.

(iii) The notice must be filed with OFIA.

(2) Change-in control proceedings under section 7(j)(4) of the FDIA (12 U.S.C. 1817(j)(4)) commence with the issuance of an order by the Comptroller.

(b) *Contents of notice.* The notice must set forth:

(1) The legal authority for the proceeding and for the OCC's jurisdiction over the proceeding;

(2) A statement of the matters of fact or law showing that the OCC is entitled to relief;

(3) A proposed order or prayer for an order granting the requested relief;

(4) The time, place, and nature of the hearing as required by law or regulation;

(5) The time within which to file an answer as required by law or regulation;

(6) The time within which to request a hearing as required by law or regulation; and

(7) That the answer and/or request for a hearing shall be filed with OFIA.

§ 19.19 Answer.

(a) *When.* Within 20 days of service of the notice, respondent shall file an answer as designated in the notice. In a civil money penalty proceeding, respondent shall also file a request for a hearing within 20 days of service of the notice.

(b) *Content of answer.* An answer must specifically respond to each paragraph or allegation of fact contained in the notice and must admit, deny, or state that the party lacks sufficient information to admit or deny each allegation of fact. A statement of lack of information has the effect of a denial. Denials must fairly meet the substance of each allegation of fact denied; general denials are not permitted. When a respondent denies part of an allegation, that part must be denied and the remainder specifically admitted. Any allegation of fact in the notice which is not denied in the answer must be deemed admitted for purposes of the proceeding. A respondent is not required to respond to the portion of a notice that constitutes the prayer for relief or proposed order. The answer must set forth affirmative defenses, if any, asserted by the respondent.

(c) *Default*—(1) *Effect of failure to answer.* Failure of a respondent to file an answer required by this section within the time provided constitutes a waiver of his or her right to appear and contest the allegations in the notice. If no timely answer is filed, Enforcement Counsel may file a motion for entry of an order of default. Upon a finding that no good cause has been shown for the failure to file a timely answer, the administrative law judge shall file with the Comptroller a recommended decision containing the findings and the relief sought in the notice. Any final order issued by the Comptroller based upon a respondent's failure to answer is deemed to be an order issued upon consent.

(2) *Effect of failure to request a hearing in civil money penalty proceedings.* If respondent fails to request a hearing as required by law within the time provided, the notice of assessment constitutes a final and unappealable order.

§ 19.20 Amended pleadings.

(a) *Amendments.* The notice or answer may be amended or supplemented at any stage of the proceeding. The respondent must answer an amended notice within the time remaining for the respondent's answer to the original notice, or within ten days after service of the amended notice, whichever period is longer, unless the Comptroller or administrative law judge orders otherwise for good cause.

(b) *Amendments to conform to the evidence.* When issues not raised in the notice or answer are tried at the hearing by express or implied consent of the parties, they will be treated in all respects as if they had been raised in the notice or answer, and no formal amendments are required. If evidence is objected to at the hearing on the ground that it is not within the issues raised by the notice or answer, the administrative law judge may admit the evidence when admission is likely to assist in adjudicating the merits of the action and the objecting party fails to satisfy the administrative law judge that the admission of such evidence would unfairly prejudice that party's action or defense upon the merits. The administrative law judge may grant a continuance to enable the objecting party to meet such evidence.

[61 FR 20335, May 6, 1996]

§ 19.21 Failure to appear.

Failure of a respondent to appear in person at the hearing or by a duly authorized counsel constitutes a waiver of respondent's right to a hearing and is deemed an admission of the facts as alleged and consent to the relief sought in the notice. Without further proceedings or notice to the respondent, the administrative law judge shall file with the Comptroller a recommended decision containing the findings and the relief sought in the notice.

§ 19.22 Consolidation and severance of actions.

(a) *Consolidation.* (1) On the motion of any party, or on the administrative law judge's own motion, the administrative law judge may consolidate, for some or all purposes, any two or more proceedings, if each such proceeding involves or arises out of the same transaction, occurrence or series of transactions or occurrences, or involves at least one common respondent or a material common question of law or fact, unless such consolidation would cause unreasonable delay or injustice.

(2) In the event of consolidation under paragraph (a)(1) of this section, appropriate adjustment to the prehearing schedule must be made to avoid unnecessary expense, inconvenience, or delay.

(b) *Severance.* The administrative law judge may, upon the motion of any party, sever the proceeding for separate resolution of the matter as to any respondent only if the administrative law judge finds that:

(1) Undue prejudice or injustice to the moving party would result from not severing the proceeding; and

(2) Such undue prejudice or injustice would outweigh the interests of judicial economy and expedition in the complete and final resolution of the proceeding.

§ 19.23 Motions.

(a) *In writing.* (1) Except as otherwise provided herein, an application or request for an order or ruling must be made by written motion.

(2) All written motions must state with particularity the relief sought and must be accompanied by a proposed order.

(3) No oral argument may be held on written motions except as otherwise directed by the administrative law judge. Written memoranda, briefs, affidavits or other relevant material or documents may be filed in support of or in opposition to a motion.

(b) *Oral motions.* A motion may be made orally on the record unless the administrative law judge directs that such motion be reduced to writing.

(c) *Filing of motions.* Motions must be filed with the administrative law judge, except that following the filing of the recommended decision, motions must be filed with the Comptroller.

(d) *Responses.* (1) Except as otherwise provided herein, within ten days after service of any written motion, or within such other period of time as may be established by the administrative law judge or the Comptroller, any party may file a written response to a motion. The administrative law judge shall not rule on any oral or written motion before each party has had an opportunity to file a response.

(2) The failure of a party to oppose a written motion or an oral motion made on the record is deemed a consent by that party to the entry of an order substantially in the form of the order accompanying the motion.

(e) *Dilatory motions.* Frivolous, dilatory or repetitive motions are prohibited. The filing of such motions may form the basis for sanctions.

(f) *Dispositive motions.* Dispositive motions are governed by §§ 19.29 and 19.30.

§ 19.24 Scope of document discovery.

(a) *Limits on discovery.* (1) Subject to the limitations set out in paragraphs (b), (c), and (d) of this section, a party to a proceeding under this subpart may obtain document discovery by serving a written request to produce documents. For purposes of a request to produce documents, the term "documents" may be defined to include drawings, graphs, charts, photographs, recordings, data stored in electronic form, and other data compilations from which information can be obtained, or translated, if necessary, by the parties through detection devices into reasonably usable form, as well as written material of all kinds.

(2) Discovery by use of deposition is governed by subpart I of this part.

(3) Discovery by use of interrogatories is not permitted.

(b) *Relevance.* A party may obtain document discovery regarding any matter, not privileged, that has material relevance to the merits of the pending action. Any request to produce documents that calls for irrelevant material, that is unreasonable, oppressive, excessive in scope, unduly burdensome, or repetitive of previous requests, or that seeks to obtain privileged documents will be denied or modified. A request is unreasonable, oppressive, excessive in scope, or unduly burdensome if, among other things, it fails to include justifiable limitations on the time period covered and the geographic locations to be searched, the time provided to respond in the request is inadequate, or the request calls for copies of documents to be delivered to the requesting party and fails to include the requestor's written agreement to pay in advance for the copying, in accordance with § 19.25.

(c) *Privileged matter.* Privileged documents are not discoverable. Privileges include the attorney-client privilege, work-product privilege, any government's or government agency's deliberative process privilege, and any other privileges the Constitution, any applicable act of Congress, or the principles of common law provide.

(d) *Time limits.* All discovery, including all responses to discovery requests, shall be completed at least 20 days prior to the date scheduled for the commencement of the hearing, except as provided in the Local Rules. No exceptions to this time limit shall be permitted, unless the administrative law judge finds on the record that good cause exists for waiving the requirements of this paragraph.

[56 FR 38028, Aug. 9, 1991, as amended at 61 FR 20335, May 6, 1996]

§ 19.25 Request for document discovery from parties.

(a) *General rule.* Any party may serve on any other party a request to produce for inspection any discoverable documents that are in the possession, custody, or control of the party upon whom the request is served. The request must identify the documents to be produced either by individual item or by category, and must describe each item and category with reasonable particularity. Documents must be produced as they are kept in the usual course of business or must be organized to correspond with the categories in the request.

(b) *Production or copying.* The request must specify a reasonable time, place, and manner for production and performing any related acts. In lieu of inspecting the documents, the requesting party may specify that all or some of the responsive documents be copied and the copies delivered to the requesting party. If copying of fewer than 250 pages is requested, the party to whom the request is addressed shall bear the cost of copying and shipping charges. If a party requests 250 pages or more of copying, the requesting party shall pay for the copying and shipping charges. Copying charges are the current per-page copying rate imposed by 12 CFR part 4 implementing the Freedom of Information Act (5 U.S.C. 552). The party to whom the request is addressed may require payment in advance before producing the documents.

(c) *Obligation to update responses.* A party who has responded to a discovery request with a response that was complete when made is not required to supplement the response to include documents thereafter acquired, unless the responding party learns that:

(1) The response was materially incorrect when made; or

(2) The response, though correct when made, is no longer true and a failure to amend the response is, in substance, a knowing concealment.

(d) *Motions to limit discovery.* (1) Any party that objects to a discovery request may, within ten days of being served with such request, file a motion in accordance with the provisions of § 19.23 to strike or otherwise limit the request. If an objection is made to only a portion of an item or category in a request, the portion objected to shall be specified. Any objections not made in accordance with this paragraph and § 19.23 are waived.

(2) The party who served the request that is the subject of a motion to strike or limit may file a written response within five days of service of the motion. No other party may file a response.

(e) *Privilege.* At the time other documents are produced, the producing party must reasonably identify all documents withheld on the grounds of privilege and must produce a statement of the basis for the assertion of privilege. When similar documents that are protected by deliberative process, attorney work-product, or attorney-client privilege are voluminous, these documents may be identified by category instead of by individual document. The administrative law judge retains discretion to determine when the identification by category is insufficient.

(f) *Motions to compel production.* (1) If a party withholds any documents as privileged or fails to comply fully with a discovery request, the requesting party may, within ten days of the assertion of privilege or of the time the failure to comply becomes known to the requesting party, file a motion in accordance with the provisions of §19.23 for the issuance of a subpoena compelling production.

(2) The party who asserted the privilege or failed to comply with the request may file a written response to a motion to compel within five days of service of the motion. No other party may file a response.

(g) *Ruling on motions.* After the time for filing responses pursuant to this section has expired, the administrative law judge shall rule promptly on all motions filed pursuant to this section. If the administrative law judge determines that a discovery request, or any of its terms, calls for irrelevant material, is unreasonable, oppressive, excessive in scope, unduly burdensome, or repetitive of previous requests, or seeks to obtain privileged documents, he or she may deny or modify the request, and may issue appropriate protective orders, upon such conditions as justice may require. The pendency of a motion to strike or limit discovery or to compel production is not a basis for staying or continuing the proceeding, unless otherwise ordered by the administrative law judge. Notwithstanding any other provision in this part, the administrative law judge may not release, or order a party to produce, documents withheld on grounds of privilege if the party has stated to the administrative law judge its intention to file a timely motion for interlocutory review of the administrative law judge's order to produce the documents, and until the motion for interlocutory review has been decided.

(h) *Enforcing discovery subpoenas.* If the administrative law judge issues a subpoena compelling production of documents by a party, the subpoenaing party may, in the event of noncompliance and to the extent authorized by applicable law, apply to any appropriate United States district court for an order requiring compliance with the subpoena. A party's right to seek court enforcement of a subpoena shall not in any manner limit the sanctions that may be imposed by the administrative law judge against a party who fails to produce subpoenaed documents.

[56 FR 38028, Aug. 9, 1991, as amended at 61 FR 20335, May 6, 1996]

§ 19.26 Document subpoenas to nonparties.

(a) *General rules.* (1) Any party may apply to the administrative law judge for the issuance of a document discovery subpoena addressed to any person who is not a party to the proceeding. The application must contain a proposed document subpoena and a brief statement showing the general relevance and reasonableness of the scope of documents sought. The subpoenaing party shall specify a reasonable time, place, and manner for making production in response to the document subpoena.

(2) A party shall only apply for a document subpoena under this section within the time period during which such party could serve a discovery request under §19.24(d). The party obtaining the document subpoena is responsible for serving it on the subpoenaed person and for serving copies on all parties. Document subpoenas may be served in any state, territory, or possession of the United States, the District of Columbia, or as otherwise provided by law.

(3) The administrative law judge shall promptly issue any document subpoena requested pursuant to this section. If the administrative law judge determines that the application does not set forth a valid basis for the issuance of the subpoena, or that any of its terms are unreasonable, oppressive, excessive in scope, or unduly burdensome, he or she may refuse to issue the subpoena or may issue it in a modified form upon such conditions as may be consistent with the Uniform Rules.

(b) *Motion to quash or modify.* (1) Any person to whom a document subpoena is directed may file a motion to quash or modify such subpoena, accompanied by a statement of the basis for quashing or modifying the subpoena. The movant shall serve the motion on all parties, and any party may respond to such motion within ten days of service of the motion.

(2) Any motion to quash or modify a document subpoena must be filed on the same basis, including the assertion of privilege, upon which a party could object to a discovery request under § 19.25(d), and during the same time limits during which such an objection could be filed.

(c) *Enforcing document subpoenas.* If a subpoenaed person fails to comply with any subpoena issued pursuant to this section or any order of the administrative law judge which directs compliance with all or any portion of a document subpoena, the subpoenaing party or any other aggrieved party may, to the extent authorized by applicable law, apply to an appropriate United States district court for an order requiring compliance with so much of the document subpoena as the administrative law judge has not quashed or modified. A party's right to seek court enforcement of a document subpoena shall in no way limit the sanctions that may be imposed by the administrative law judge on a party who induces a failure to comply with subpoenas issued under this section.

§ 19.27 Deposition of witness unavailable for hearing.

(a) *General rules.* (1) If a witness will not be available for the hearing, a party desiring to preserve that witness' testimony for the record may apply in accordance with the procedures set forth in paragraph (a)(2) of this section, to the administrative law judge for the issuance of a subpoena, including a subpoena duces tecum, requiring the attendance of the witness at a deposition. The administrative law judge may issue a deposition subpoena under this section upon showing that:

(i) The witness will be unable to attend or may be prevented from attending the hearing because of age, sickness or infirmity, or will otherwise be unavailable;

(ii) The witness' unavailability was not procured or caused by the subpoenaing party;

(iii) The testimony is reasonably expected to be material; and

(iv) Taking the deposition will not result in any undue burden to any other party and will not cause undue delay of the proceeding.

(2) The application must contain a proposed deposition subpoena and a brief statement of the reasons for the issuance of the subpoena. The subpoena must name the witness whose deposition is to be taken and specify the time and place for taking the deposition. A deposition subpoena may require the witness to be deposed at any place within the country in which that witness resides or has a regular place of employment or such other convenient place as the administrative law judge shall fix.

(3) Any requested subpoena that sets forth a valid basis for its issuance must be promptly issued, unless the administrative law judge on his or her own motion, requires a written response or requires attendance at a conference concerning whether the requested subpoena should be issued.

(4) The party obtaining a deposition subpoena is responsible for serving it on the witness and for serving copies on all parties. Unless the administrative law judge orders otherwise, no deposition under this section shall be taken on fewer than ten days' notice to the witness and all parties. Deposition subpoenas may be served in any state, territory, possession of the United States, or the District of Columbia, on any person or company doing business in any state, territory, possession of the United States, or the District of Columbia, or as otherwise permitted by law.

(b) *Objections to deposition subpoenas.* (1) The witness and any party who has not had an opportunity to oppose a deposition subpoena issued under this section may file a motion with the administrative law judge to quash or modify the subpoena prior to the time for compliance specified in the subpoena, but not more than ten days after service of the subpoena.

(2) A statement of the basis for the motion to quash or modify a subpoena issued under this section must accompany the motion. The motion must be served on all parties.

(c) *Procedure upon deposition.* (1) Each witness testifying pursuant to a deposition subpoena must be duly sworn, and each party shall have the right to examine the witness. Objections to questions or documents must be in short form, stating the grounds for the objection. Failure to object to questions or documents is not deemed a waiver except where the ground for the objection might have been avoided if the objection had been timely presented. All questions, answers, and objections must be recorded.

(2) Any party may move before the administrative law judge for an order compelling the witness to answer any questions the witness has refused to answer or submit any evidence the witness has refused to submit during the deposition.

(3) The deposition must be subscribed by the witness, unless the parties and the witness, by stipulation, have waived the signing, or the witness is ill, cannot be found, or has refused to sign. If the deposition is not subscribed by the witness, the court reporter taking the deposition shall certify that the transcript is a true and complete transcript of the deposition.

(d) *Enforcing subpoenas.* If a subpoenaed person fails to comply with any order of the administrative law judge which directs compliance with all or any portion of a deposition subpoena under paragraph (b) or (c)(3) of this section, the subpoenaing party or other aggrieved party may, to the extent authorized by applicable law, apply to an appropriate United States district court for an order requiring compliance with the portions of the subpoena that the administrative law judge has ordered enforced. A party's right to seek court enforcement of a deposition subpoena in no way limits the sanctions that may be imposed by the administrative law judge on a party who fails to comply with, or procures a failure to comply with, a subpoena issued under this section.

§ 19.28 Interlocutory review.

(a) *General rule.* The Comptroller may review a ruling of the administrative law judge prior to the certification of the record to the Comptroller only in accordance with the procedures set forth in this section and § 19.23.

(b) *Scope of review.* The Comptroller may exercise interlocutory review of a ruling of the administrative law judge if the Comptroller finds that:

(1) The ruling involves a controlling question of law or policy as to which substantial grounds exist for a difference of opinion;

(2) Immediate review of the ruling may materially advance the ultimate termination of the proceeding;

(3) Subsequent modification of the ruling at the conclusion of the proceeding would be an inadequate remedy; or

(4) Subsequent modification of the ruling would cause unusual delay or expense.

(c) *Procedure.* Any request for interlocutory review shall be filed by a party with the administrative law judge within ten days of his or her ruling and shall otherwise comply with § 19.23. Any party may file a response to a request for interlocutory review in accordance with § 19.23(d). Upon the expiration of the time for filing all responses, the administrative law judge shall refer the matter to the Comptroller for final disposition.

(d) *Suspension of proceeding.* Neither a request for interlocutory review nor any disposition of such a request by the Comptroller under this section suspends or stays the proceeding unless otherwise ordered by the administrative law judge or the Comptroller.

§ 19.29 Summary disposition.

(a) *In general.* The administrative law judge shall recommend that the Comptroller issue a final order granting a motion for summary disposition if the undisputed pleaded facts, admissions, affidavits, stipulations, documentary evidence, matters as to which official notice may be taken, and any other evidentiary materials properly submitted in connection with a motion for summary disposition show that:

(1) There is no genuine issue as to any material fact; and

(2) The moving party is entitled to a decision in its favor as a matter of law.

(b) *Filing of motions and responses.* (1) Any party who believes there is no genuine issue of material fact to be determined and that he or she is entitled to a decision as a matter of law may move at any time for summary disposition in its favor of all or any part of the proceeding. Any party, within 20 days after service of such a motion, or within such time period as allowed by the administrative law judge, may file a response to such motion.

(2) A motion for summary disposition must be accompanied by a statement of the material facts as to which the moving party contends there is no genuine issue. Such motion must be supported by documentary evidence, which may take the form of admissions in pleadings, stipulations, depositions, investigatory depositions, transcripts, affidavits and any other evidentiary materials that the moving party contends support his or her position. The motion must also be accompanied by a brief containing the points and authorities in support of the contention of the moving party. Any party opposing a motion for summary disposition must file a statement setting forth those material facts as to which he or she contends a genuine dispute exists. Such opposition must be supported by evidence of the same type as that submitted with the motion for summary disposition and a brief containing the points and authorities in support of the contention that summary disposition would be inappropriate.

(c) *Hearing on motion.* At the request of any party or on his or her own motion, the administrative law judge may hear oral argument on the motion for summary disposition.

(d) *Decision on motion.* Following receipt of a motion for summary disposition and all responses thereto, the administrative law judge shall determine whether the moving party is entitled to summary disposition. If the administrative law judge determines that summary disposition is warranted, the administrative law judge shall submit a recommended decision to that effect to the Comptroller. If the administrative law judge finds that no party is entitled to summary disposition, he or she shall make a ruling denying the motion.

§ 19.30 Partial summary disposition.

If the administrative law judge determines that a party is entitled to summary disposition as to certain claims only, he or she shall defer submitting a recommended decision as to those claims. A hearing on the remaining issues must be ordered. Those claims for which the administrative law judge has determined that summary disposition is warranted will be addressed in the recommended decision filed at the conclusion of the hearing.

§ 19.31 Scheduling and prehearing conferences.

(a) *Scheduling conference.* Within 30 days of service of the notice or order commencing a proceeding or such other time as parties may agree, the administrative law judge shall direct counsel for all parties to meet with him or her in person at a specified time and place prior to the hearing or to confer by telephone for the purpose of scheduling the course and conduct of the proceeding. This meeting or telephone conference is called a "scheduling conference." The identification of potential witnesses, the time for and manner of discovery, and the exchange of any prehearing materials including witness lists, statements of issues, stipulations, exhibits and any other materials may also be determined at the scheduling conference.

(b) *Prehearing conferences.* The administrative law judge may, in addition to the scheduling conference, on his or her own motion or at the request of any party, direct counsel for the parties to meet with him or her (in person or by telephone) at a prehearing conference to address any or all of the following:

(1) Simplification and clarification of the issues;

(2) Stipulations, admissions of fact, and the contents, authenticity and admissibility into evidence of documents;

(3) Matters of which official notice may be taken;

(4) Limitation of the number of witnesses;

(5) Summary disposition of any or all issues;

(6) Resolution of discovery issues or disputes;

(7) Amendments to pleadings; and

(8) Such other matters as may aid in the orderly disposition of the proceeding.

(c) *Transcript.* The administrative law judge, in his or her discretion, may require that a scheduling or prehearing conference be recorded by a court reporter. A transcript of the conference and any materials filed, including orders, becomes part of the record of the proceeding. A party may obtain a copy of the transcript at his or her expense.

(d) *Scheduling or prehearing orders.* At or within a reasonable time following the conclusion of the scheduling conference or any prehearing conference, the administrative law judge shall serve on each party an order setting forth any agreements reached and any procedural determinations made.

§ 19.32 Prehearing submissions.

(a) Within the time set by the administrative law judge, but in no case later than 14 days before the start of the hearing, each party shall serve on every other party, his or her:

(1) Prehearing statement;

(2) Final list of witnesses to be called to testify at the hearing, including name and address of each witness and a short summary of the expected testimony of each witness;

(3) List of the exhibits to be introduced at the hearing along with a copy of each exhibit; and

(4) Stipulations of fact, if any.

(b) Effect of failure to comply. No witness may testify and no exhibits may be introduced at the hearing if such witness or exhibit is not listed in the prehearing submissions pursuant to paragraph (a) of this section, except for good cause shown.

§ 19.33 Public hearings.

(a) *General rule.* All hearings shall be open to the public, unless the Comptroller, in the Comptroller's discretion, determines that holding an open hearing would be contrary to the public interest. Within 20 days of service of the notice or, in the case of change-in-control proceedings under section 7(j)(4) of the FDIA (12 U.S.C. 1817(j)(4)), within 20 days from service of the hearing order, any respondent may file with the Comptroller a request for a private hearing, and any party may file a reply to such a request. A party must serve on the administrative law judge a copy of any request or reply the party files with the Comptroller. The form of, and procedure for, these requests and replies are governed by § 19.23. A party's failure to file a request or a reply constitutes a waiver of any objections regarding whether the hearing will be public or private.

(b) *Filing document under seal.* Enforcement Counsel, in his or her discretion, may file any document or part of a document under seal if disclosure of the document would be contrary to the public interest. The administrative law judge shall take all appropriate steps to preserve the confidentiality of such documents or parts thereof, including closing portions of the hearing to the public.

[56 FR 38028, Aug. 9, 1991, as amended at 61 FR 20336, May 6, 1996]

§ 19.34 Hearing subpoenas.

(a) *Issuance.* (1) Upon application of a party showing general relevance and reasonableness of scope of the testimony or other evidence sought, the administrative law judge may issue a subpoena or a subpoena *duces tecum* requiring the attendance of a witness at the hearing or the production of documentary or physical evidence at the hearing. The application for a hearing subpoena must also contain a proposed subpoena specifying the attendance of a witness or the production of evidence from any state, territory, or possession of the United States, the District of Columbia, or as otherwise provided by law at any designated place where the hearing is being conducted. The party making the application shall serve a copy of the application and the proposed subpoena on every other party.

(2) A party may apply for a hearing subpoena at any time before the commencement of a hearing. During a hearing, a party may make an application for a subpoena orally on the record before the administrative law judge.

(3) The administrative law judge shall promptly issue any hearing subpoena requested pursuant to this section. If the administrative law judge determines that the application does not set forth a valid basis for the issuance of the subpoena, or that any

of its terms are unreasonable, oppressive, excessive in scope, or unduly burdensome, he or she may refuse to issue the subpoena or may issue it in a modified form upon any conditions consistent with this subpart. Upon issuance by the administrative law judge, the party making the application shall serve the subpoena on the person named in the subpoena and on each party.

(b) *Motion to quash or modify.* (1) Any person to whom a hearing subpoena is directed or any party may file a motion to quash or modify the subpoena, accompanied by a statement of the basis for quashing or modifying the subpoena. The movant must serve the motion on each party and on the person named in the subpoena. Any party may respond to the motion within ten days of service of the motion.

(2) Any motion to quash or modify a hearing subpoena must be filed prior to the time specified in the subpoena for compliance but not more than ten days after the date of service of the subpoena upon the movant.

(c) *Enforcing subpoenas.* If a subpoenaed person fails to comply with any subpoena issued pursuant to this section or any order of the administrative law judge which directs compliance with all or any portion of a document subpoena, the subpoenaing party or any other aggrieved party may seek enforcement of the subpoena pursuant to § 19.26(c).

[56 FR 38028, Aug. 9, 1991, as amended at 61 FR 20336, May 6, 1996]

§ 19.35 Conduct of hearings.

(a) *General rules.* (1) Hearings shall be conducted so as to provide a fair and expeditious presentation of the relevant disputed issues. Each party has the right to present its case or defense by oral and documentary evidence and to conduct such cross examination as may be required for full disclosure of the facts.

(2) Order of hearing. Enforcement Counsel shall present its case-in-chief first, unless otherwise ordered by the administrative law judge, or unless otherwise expressly specified by law or regulation. Enforcement Counsel shall be the first party to present an opening statement and a closing statement, and may make a rebuttal statement after the respondent's closing statement. If there are multiple respondents, respondents may agree among themselves as to their order of presentation of their cases, but if they do not agree, the administrative law judge shall fix the order.

(3) Examination of witnesses. Only one counsel for each party may conduct an examination of a witness, except that in the case of extensive direct examination, the administrative law judge may permit more than one counsel for the party presenting the witness to conduct the examination. A party may have one counsel conduct the direct examination and another counsel conduct re-direct examination of a witness, or may have one counsel conduct the cross examination of a witness and another counsel conduct the re-cross examination of a witness.

(4) Stipulations. Unless the administrative law judge directs otherwise, all stipulations of fact and law previously agreed upon by the parties, and all documents, the admissibility of which have been previously stipulated, will be admitted into evidence upon commencement of the hearing.

(b) *Transcript.* The hearing must be recorded and transcribed. The reporter will make the transcript available to any party upon payment by that party to the reporter of the cost of the transcript. The administrative law judge may order the record corrected, either upon motion to correct, upon stipulation of the parties, or following notice to the parties upon the administrative law judge's own motion.

[56 FR 38028, Aug. 9, 1991, as amended at 61 FR 20336, May 6, 1996]

§ 19.36 Evidence.

(a) *Admissibility.* (1) Except as is otherwise set forth in this section, relevant, material, and reliable evidence that is not unduly repetitive is admissible to the fullest extent authorized by the Administrative Procedure Act and other applicable law.

(2) Evidence that would be admissible under the Federal Rules of Evidence is admissible in a proceeding conducted pursuant to this subpart.

(3) Evidence that would be inadmissible under the Federal Rules of Evidence may not be deemed or ruled to be inadmissible in a proceeding conducted pursuant to this subpart if such evidence is relevant, material, reliable and not unduly repetitive.

(b) *Official notice.* (1) Official notice may be taken of any material fact which may be judicially noticed by a United States district court and any material information in the official public records of any Federal or state government agency.

(2) All matters officially noticed by the administrative law judge or the Comptroller shall appear on the record.

(3) If official notice is requested or taken of any material fact, the parties, upon timely request, shall be afforded an opportunity to object.

(c) *Documents.* (1) A duplicate copy of a document is admissible to the same extent as the original, unless a genuine issue is raised as to whether the copy is in some material respect not a true and legible copy of the original.

(2) Subject to the requirements of paragraph (a) of this section, any document, including a report of examination, supervisory activity, inspection or visitation, prepared by an appropriate Federal financial institutions regulatory agency or by a state regulatory agency, is admissible either with or without a sponsoring witness.

(3) Witnesses may use existing or newly created charts, exhibits, calendars, calculations, outlines or other graphic material to summarize, illustrate, or simplify the presentation of testimony. Such materials may, subject to the administrative law judge's discretion, be used with or without being admitted into evidence.

(d) *Objections.* (1) Objections to the admissibility of evidence must be timely made and rulings on all objections must appear on the record.

(2) When an objection to a question or line of questioning propounded to a witness is sustained, the examining counsel may make a specific proffer on the record of what he or she expected to prove by the expected testimony of the witness either by representation of counsel or by direct interrogation of the witness.

(3) The administrative law judge shall retain rejected exhibits, adequately marked for identification, for the record, and transmit such exhibits to the Comptroller.

(4) Failure to object to admission of evidence or to any ruling constitutes a waiver of the objection.

(e) *Stipulations.* The parties may stipulate as to any relevant matters of fact or the authentication of any relevant documents. Such stipulations must be received in evidence at a hearing and are binding on the parties with respect to the matters therein stipulated.

(f) *Depositions of unavailable witnesses.* (1) If a witness is unavailable to testify at a hearing, and that witness has testified in a deposition to which all parties in a proceeding had notice and an opportunity to participate, a party may offer as evidence all or any part of the transcript of the deposition, including deposition exhibits, if any.

(2) Such deposition transcript is admissible to the same extent that testimony would have been admissible had that person testified at the hearing, provided that if a witness refused to answer proper questions during the depositions, the administrative law judge may, on that basis, limit the admissibility of the deposition in any manner that justice requires.

(3) Only those portions of a deposition received in evidence at the hearing constitute a part of the record.

§ 19.37 Post-hearing filings.

(a) *Proposed findings and conclusions and supporting briefs.* (1) Using the same method of service for each party, the administrative law judge shall serve notice upon each party that the certified transcript, together with all hearing exhibits and exhibits introduced but not admitted into evidence at the hearing, has been filed. Any party may file with the administrative law judge proposed findings of fact, proposed conclusions of law, and a proposed order within 30 days following service of this notice by the administrative law judge or within such longer period as may be ordered by the administrative law judge.

(2) Proposed findings and conclusions must be supported by citation to any

relevant authorities and by page references to any relevant portions of the record. A post-hearing brief may be filed in support of proposed findings and conclusions, either as part of the same document or in a separate document. Any party who fails to file timely with the administrative law judge any proposed finding or conclusion is deemed to have waived the right to raise in any subsequent filing or submission any issue not addressed in such party's proposed finding or conclusion.

(b) *Reply briefs.* Reply briefs may be filed within 15 days after the date on which the parties' proposed findings, conclusions, and order are due. Reply briefs must be strictly limited to responding to new matters, issues, or arguments raised in another party's papers. A party who has not filed proposed findings of fact and conclusions of law or a post-hearing brief may not file a reply brief.

(c) *Simultaneous filing required.* The administrative law judge shall not order the filing by any party of any brief or reply brief in advance of the other party's filing of its brief.

[56 FR 38028, Aug. 9, 1991, as amended at 61 FR 20336, May 6, 1996]

§ 19.38 Recommended decision and filing of record.

(a) *Filing of recommended decision and record.* Within 45 days after expiration of the time allowed for filing reply briefs under § 19.37(b), the administrative law judge shall file with and certify to the Comptroller, for decision, the record of the proceeding. The record must include the administrative law judge's recommended decision, recommended findings of fact, recommended conclusions of law, and proposed order; all prehearing and hearing transcripts, exhibits, and rulings; and the motions, briefs, memoranda, and other supporting papers filed in connection with the hearing. The administrative law judge shall serve upon each party the recommended decision, findings, conclusions, and proposed order.

(b) *Filing of index.* At the same time the administrative law judge files with and certifies to the Comptroller for final determination the record of the proceeding, the administrative law judge shall furnish to the Comptroller a certified index of the entire record of the proceeding. The certified index shall include, at a minimum, an entry for each paper, document or motion filed with the administrative law judge in the proceeding, the date of the filing, and the identity of the filer. The certified index shall also include an exhibit index containing, at a minimum, an entry consisting of exhibit number and title or description for: Each exhibit introduced and admitted into evidence at the hearing; each exhibit introduced but not admitted into evidence at the hearing; each exhibit introduced and admitted into evidence after the completion of the hearing; and each exhibit introduced but not admitted into evidence after the completion of the hearing.

[61 FR 20336, May 6, 1996]

§ 19.39 Exceptions to recommended decision.

(a) *Filing exceptions.* Within 30 days after service of the recommended decision, findings, conclusions, and proposed order under § 19.38, a party may file with the Comptroller written exceptions to the administrative law judge's recommended decision, findings, conclusions or proposed order, to the admission or exclusion of evidence, or to the failure of the administrative law judge to make a ruling proposed by a party. A supporting brief may be filed at the time the exceptions are filed, either as part of the same document or in a separate document.

(b) *Effect of failure to file or raise exceptions.* (1) Failure of a party to file exceptions to those matters specified in paragraph (a) of this section within the time prescribed is deemed a waiver of objection thereto.

(2) No exception need be considered by the Comptroller if the party taking exception had an opportunity to raise the same objection, issue, or argument before the administrative law judge and failed to do so.

(c) *Contents.* (1) All exceptions and briefs in support of such exceptions must be confined to the particular matters in, or omissions from, the administrative law judge's recommendations to which that party takes exception.

(2) All exceptions and briefs in support of exceptions must set forth page or paragraph references to the specific parts of the administrative law judge's recommendations to which exception is taken, the page or paragraph references to those portions of the record relied upon to support each exception, and the legal authority relied upon to support each exception.

§ 19.40 Review by the Comptroller.

(a) *Notice of submission to the Comptroller.* When the Comptroller determines that the record in the proceeding is complete, the Comptroller shall serve notice upon the parties that the proceeding has been submitted to the Comptroller for final decision.

(b) *Oral argument before the Comptroller.* Upon the initiative of the Comptroller or on the written request of any party filed with the Comptroller within the time for filing exceptions, the Comptroller may order and hear oral argument on the recommended findings, conclusions, decision, and order of the administrative law judge. A written request by a party must show good cause for oral argument and state reasons why arguments cannot be presented adequately in writing. A denial of a request for oral argument may be set forth in the Comptroller's final decision. Oral argument before the Comptroller must be on the record.

(c) *Comptroller's final decision.* (1) Decisional employees may advise and assist the Comptroller in the consideration and disposition of the case. The final decision of the Comptroller will be based upon review of the entire record of the proceeding, except that the Comptroller may limit the issues to be reviewed to those findings and conclusions to which opposing arguments or exceptions have been filed by the parties.

(2) The Comptroller shall render a final decision within 90 days after notification of the parties that the case has been submitted for final decision, or 90 days after oral argument, whichever is later, unless the Comptroller orders that the action or any aspect thereof be remanded to the administrative law judge for further proceedings. Copies of the final decision and order of the Comptroller shall be served upon each party to the proceeding, upon other persons required by statute, and, if directed by the Comptroller or required by statute, upon any appropriate state or Federal supervisory authority.

§ 19.41 Stays pending judicial review.

The commencement of proceedings for judicial review of a final decision and order of the Comptroller may not, unless specifically ordered by the Comptroller or a reviewing court, operate as a stay of any order issued by the Comptroller. The Comptroller may, in his or her discretion, and on such terms as he or she finds just, stay the effectiveness of all or any part of an order pending a final decision on a petition for review of that order.

Subpart B—Procedural Rules for OCC Adjudications

§ 19.100 Filing documents.

All materials required to be filed with or referred to the Comptroller or the administrative law judge in any proceeding under this part must be filed with the Hearing Clerk, Office of the Comptroller of the Currency, 400 7th Street, SW., Washington, DC 20219. Filings to be made with the Hearing Clerk include the notice and answer; motions and responses to motions; briefs; the record filed by the administrative law judge after the issuance of a recommended decision; the recommended decision filed by the administrative law judge following a motion for summary disposition; referrals by the administrative law judge of motions for interlocutory review; exceptions and requests for oral argument; and any other papers required to be filed with the Comptroller or the administrative law judge under this part.

[68 FR 48265, Aug. 13, 2002, as amended at 73 FR 22243, Apr. 24, 2008; 79 FR 15641, Mar. 21, 2014]

§ 19.101 Delegation to OFIA.

Unless otherwise ordered by the Comptroller, administrative adjudications subject to subpart A of this part shall be conducted by an administrative law judge assigned to OFIA.

Subpart C—Removals, Suspensions, and Prohibitions When a Crime Is Charged or a Conviction is Obtained

§ 19.110 Scope.

This subpart applies to informal hearings afforded to any institution-affiliated party who has been suspended or removed from office or prohibited from further participation in the affairs of any depository institution pursuant to 12 U.S.C. 1818(g) by a notice or order issued by the Comptroller.

[56 FR 38028, Aug. 9, 1991, as amended at 73 FR 22243, Apr. 24, 2008]

§ 19.111 Suspension, removal, or prohibition.

The Comptroller may serve a notice of suspension or order of removal or prohibition pursuant to 12 U.S.C. 1818(g) on an institution-affiliated party. A copy of such notice or order will be served on any depository institution that the subject of the notice or order is affiliated with at the time the notice or order is issued, whereupon the institution-affiliated party involved must immediately cease service to, or participation in the affairs of, that depository institution and, if so determined by the OCC, any other depository institution. The notice or order will indicate the basis for suspension, removal or prohibition and will inform the institution-affiliated party of the right to request in writing, to be received by the OCC within 30 days from the date that the institution-affiliated party was served with such notice or order, an opportunity to show at an informal hearing that continued service to or participation in the conduct of the affairs of any depository institution has not posed, does not pose, or is not likely to pose a threat to the interests of the depositors of, or has not threatened, does not threaten, or is not likely to threaten to impair public confidence in, any relevant depository institution. The written request must be sent by certified mail to, or served personally with a signed receipt on, the District Deputy Comptroller in the OCC district in which the bank in question is located; if the bank is supervised by Large Bank Supervision, to the Senior Deputy Comptroller for Large Bank Supervision for the Office of the Comptroller of the Currency; if the bank is supervised by Mid-Size/Community Bank Supervision, to the Senior Deputy Comptroller for Mid-Size/Community Bank Supervision for the Office of the Comptroller of the Currency; or if the institution-affiliated party is no longer affiliated with a particular national bank, to the Deputy Comptroller for Special Supervision, Washington, DC 20219. The request must state specifically the relief desired and the grounds on which that relief is based. For purposes of this section, the term *depository institution* means any depository institution of which the petitioner is or was an institution-affiliated party at the time at which the notice or order was issued by the Comptroller.

[73 FR 22243, Apr. 24, 2008]

§ 19.112 Informal hearing.

(a) *Issuance of hearing order.* After receipt of a request for hearing, the District Deputy Comptroller, the Senior Deputy Comptroller for Large Bank Supervision, the Senior Deputy Comptroller for Mid-Size/Community Bank Supervision, or the Deputy Comptroller for Special Supervision, as appropriate, must notify the petitioner requesting the hearing, the OCC's Enforcement and Compliance Division, and the appropriate OCC District Counsel of the date, time, and place fixed for the hearing. The hearing must be scheduled to be held not later than 30 days from the date when a request for hearing is received unless the time is extended in response to a written request of the petitioner. The District Deputy Comptroller, the Senior Deputy Comptroller for Large Bank Supervision, the Senior Deputy Comptroller for Mid-Size/Community Bank Supervision, or the Deputy Comptroller for Special Supervision,, as appropriate, may extend the hearing date only for a specific period of time and must take appropriate action to ensure that the hearing is not unduly delayed.

(b) *Appointment of presiding officer.* the District Deputy Comptroller, the Senior Deputy Comptroller for Large Bank Supervision, the Senior Deputy Comptroller for Mid-Size/Community

Bank Supervision, or the Deputy Comptroller for Special Supervision, as appropriate, must appoint one or more OCC employees as the presiding officer to conduct the hearing. The presiding officer(s) may not have been involved in the proceeding, a factually related proceeding, or the underlying enforcement action in a prosecutorial or investigative role.

(c) *Waiver of oral hearing*—(1) *Petitioner.* When the petitioner requests a hearing, the petitioner may elect to have the matter determined by the presiding officer solely on the basis of written submissions by serving on the District Deputy Comptroller, the Senior Deputy Comptroller for Large Bank Supervision, the Senior Deputy Comptroller for Mid-Size/Community Bank Supervision, or the Deputy Comptroller for Special Supervision, as appropriate, and all parties, a signed document waiving the statutory right to appear and make oral argument. The petitioner must present the written submissions to the presiding officer, and serve the other parties, not later than ten days prior to the date fixed for the hearing, or within such shorter time period as the presiding officer may permit.

(2) *OCC.* The OCC may respond to the petitioner's submissions by presenting the presiding officer with a written response, and by serving the other parties, not later than the date fixed for the hearing, or within such other time period as the presiding officer may require.

(d) *Hearing procedures*—(1) *Conduct of hearing.* Hearings under this subpart are not subject to the provisions of subpart A of this part or the adjudicative provisions of the Administrative Procedure Act (5 U.S.C. 554–557).

(2) *Powers of the presiding officer.* The presiding officer shall determine all procedural issues that are governed by this subpart. The presiding officer may also permit or limit the number of witnesses and impose time limitations as he or she deems reasonable. The informal hearing will not be governed by the formal rules of evidence. All oral presentations, when permitted, and documents deemed by the presiding officer to be relevant and material to the proceeding and not unduly repetitious will be considered. The presiding officer may ask questions of any person participating in the hearing and may make any rulings reasonably necessary to facilitate the effective and efficient operation of the hearing.

(3) *Presentation.* (i) The OCC may appear and the petitioner may appear personally or through counsel at the hearing to present relevant written materials and oral argument. Except as permitted in paragraph (c) of this section, each party, including the OCC, must file a copy of any affidavit, memorandum, or other written material to be presented at the hearing with the presiding officer and must serve the other parties not later than ten days prior to the hearing or within such shorter time period as permitted by the presiding officer.

(ii) If the petitioner or the appointed OCC attorney desires to present oral testimony or witnesses at the hearing, he or she must file a written request with the presiding officer not later than ten days prior to the hearing, or within a shorter time period as permitted by the presiding officer. The names of proposed witnesses should be included, along with the general nature of the expected testimony, and the reasons why oral testimony is necessary. The presiding officer generally will not admit oral testimony or witnesses unless a specific and compelling need is demonstrated. Witnesses, if admitted, shall be sworn.

(iii) In deciding on any suspension, the presiding officer shall not consider the ultimate question of the guilt or innocence of the individual with respect to the criminal charges which are outstanding. In deciding on any removal, the presiding officer shall not consider challenges to or efforts to impeach the validity of the conviction. The presiding officer may consider facts in either situation, however, which show the nature of the events on which the indictment or conviction was based.

(4) *Record.* A transcript of the proceedings may be taken if the petitioner requests a transcript and agrees to pay all expenses or if the presiding officer determines that the nature of the case warrants a transcript. The presiding officer may order the record to be kept

open for a reasonable period following the hearing, not to exceed five business days, to permit the petitioner or the appointed OCC attorney to submit additional documents for the record. Thereafter, no further submissions may be accepted except for good cause shown.

[56 FR 38028, Aug. 9, 1991, as amended at 61 FR 20337, May 6, 1996; 73 FR 22244, Apr. 24, 2008]

§ 19.113 Recommended and final decisions.

(a) The presiding officer must issue a recommended decision to the Comptroller within 20 days of the conclusion of the hearing or, when the petitioner has waived an oral hearing, within 20 days of the date fixed for the hearing. The presiding officer must serve promptly a copy of the recommended decision on the parties to the proceeding. The decision must include a summary of the facts and arguments of the parties.

(b) Each party may, within ten days of being served with the presiding officer's recommended decision, submit to the Comptroller comments on the recommended decision.

(c) Within 60 days of the conclusion of the hearing or, when the petitioner has waived an oral hearing, within 60 days from the date fixed for the hearing, the Comptroller must notify the petitioner by registered mail whether the suspension or removal from office, and prohibition from participation in any manner in the affairs of any depository institution, will be affirmed, terminated, or modified. The Comptroller's decision must include a statement of reasons supporting the decision. The Comptroller's decision is a final and unappealable order.

(d) A finding of not guilty or other disposition of the charge on which a notice of suspension was based does not preclude the Comptroller from thereafter instituting removal proceedings pursuant to section 8(e) of the FDIA (12 U.S.C. 1818(e)) and subpart: A of this part.

(e) A removal or prohibition by order remains in effect until terminated by the Comptroller. A suspension or prohibition by notice remains in effect until the criminal charge is disposed of or until terminated by the Comptroller.

(f) A suspended or removed individual may petition the Comptroller to reconsider the decision any time after the expiration of a 12-month period from the date of the decision, but no petition for reconsideration may be made within 12 months of a previous petition. The petition must state specifically the relief sought and the grounds therefor, and may be accompanied by a supporting memorandum and any other documentation the petitioner wishes to have considered. No hearing need be granted on the petition for reconsideration.

[56 FR 38028, Aug. 9, 1991, as amended at 61 FR 20337, May 6, 1996; 73 FR 22244, Apr. 24, 2008]

Subpart D—Exemption Hearings Under Section 12(h) of the Securities Exchange Act of 1934

§ 19.120 Scope.

The rules in this subpart apply to informal hearings that may be held by the Comptroller to determine whether, pursuant to authority in sections 12 (h) and (i) of the Exchange Act (15 U.S.C. 78*l* (h) and (i)), to exempt in whole or in part an issuer or a class of issuers from the provisions of section 12(g), or from section 13 or 14 of the Exchange Act (15 U.S.C. 78*l*(g), 78m or 78n), or whether to exempt from section 16 of the Exchange Act (15 U.S.C. 78p) any officer, director, or beneficial owner of securities of an issuer. The only issuers covered by this subpart are banks whose securities are registered pursuant to section 12(g) of the Exchange Act (15 U.S.C. 78*l*(g)). The Comptroller may deny an application for exemption without a hearing.

§ 19.121 Application for exemption.

An issuer or an individual (officer, director or shareholder) may submit a written application for an exemption order to the Securities and Corporate Practices Division, Office of the Comptroller of the Currency, Washington, DC 20219. The application must specify the type of exemption sought and the reasons therefor, including an explanation of why an exemption would not be inconsistent with the public interest or the protection of investors. The Securities and Corporate Practices Division shall inform the applicant in writing whether a hearing will be held to consider the matter.

§ 19.122 Newspaper notice.

Upon being informed that an application will be considered at a hearing, the applicant shall publish a notice one time in a newspaper of general circulation in the community where the issuer's main office is located. The notice must state: the name and title of any individual applicants; the type of exemption sought; the fact that a hearing will be held; and a statement that interested persons may submit to the Securities and Corporate Practices Division, Office of the Comptroller of the Currency, Washington, DC 20219, within 30 days from the date of the newspaper notice, written comments concerning the application and a written request for an opportunity to be heard. The applicant shall promptly furnish a copy of the notice to the Securities and Corporate Practices Division, and to bank shareholders.

§ 19.123 Informal hearing.

(a) *Conduct of proceeding.* The adjudicative provisions of the Administrative Procedure Act, formal rules of evidence and subpart A of this part do not apply to hearings conducted under this subpart, except as provided in § 19.100(b).

(b) *Notice of hearing.* Following the comment period, the Comptroller shall send a notice which fixes a date, time and place for hearing to each applicant and to any person who has requested an opportunity to be heard.

(c) *Presiding officer.* The Comptroller shall designate a presiding officer to conduct the hearing. The presiding officer shall determine all procedural questions not governed by this subpart and may limit the number of witnesses and impose time and presentation limitations as are deemed reasonable. At the conclusion of the informal hearing, the presiding officer shall issue a recommended decision to the Comptroller as to whether the exemption should issue. The decision shall include a summary of the facts and arguments of the parties.

(d) *Attendance.* The applicant and any person who has requested an opportunity to be heard may attend the hearing, with or without counsel. The hearing shall be open to the public. In addition, the applicant and any other hearing participant may introduce oral testimony through such witnesses as the presiding officer shall permit.

(e) *Order of presentation.* (1) The applicant may present an opening statement of a length decided by the presiding officer. Then each of the hearing participants, or one among them selected with the approval of the presiding officer, may present an opening statement. The opening statement should summarize concisely what the applicant and each participant intends to show.

(2) The applicant shall have an opportunity to make an oral presentation of facts and materials or submit written materials for the record. One or more of the hearing participants may make an oral presentation or a written submission.

(3) After the above presentations, the applicant, followed by one or more of the hearing participants, may make concise summary statements reviewing their position.

(f) *Witnesses.* The obtaining and use of witnesses is the responsibility of the parties afforded the hearing. All witnesses shall be present on their own volition, but any person appearing as a witness may be questioned by each applicant, any hearing participant, and the presiding officer. Witnesses shall be sworn unless otherwise directed by the presiding officer.

(g) *Evidence.* The presiding officer may exclude data or materials deemed to be improper or irrelevant. Formal rules of evidence do not apply. Documentary material must be of a size consistent with ease of handling and filing. The presiding officer may determine the number of copies that must be furnished for purposes of the hearing.

(h) *Transcript.* A transcript of each proceeding will be arranged by the OCC, with all expenses, including the furnishing of a copy to the presiding officer, being borne by the applicant.

§ 19.124 Decision of the Comptroller.

Following the conclusion of the hearing and the submission of the record and the presiding officer's recommended decision to the Comptroller for decision, the Comptroller shall notify the applicant and all persons who have so requested in writing of the final disposition of the application. Exemptions granted must be in the form of an order which specifies the type of exemption granted and its terms and conditions.

Subpart E—Disciplinary Proceedings Involving the Federal Securities Laws

§ 19.130 Scope.

(a) Except as provided in this subpart, subpart A of this part applies to proceedings by the Comptroller to determine whether, pursuant to authority contained in sections 15B(c)(5), 15C(c)(2)(A), 17A(c)(3), and 17A(c)(4)(C) of the Exchange Act (15 U.S.C. 78o–4(c)(5), 78o–5(c)(2)(A), 78q–1(c)(3)(A), and 78q–1(c)(4)(C)), to take disciplinary action against the following:

(1) A bank which is a municipal securities dealer, or any person associated or seeking to become associated with such a municipal securities dealer;

(2) A bank which is a government securities broker or dealer, or any person associated with such government securities broker or dealer; or

(3) A bank which is a transfer agent, or any person associated or seeking to become associated with such transfer agent.

(b) In addition to the issuance of disciplinary orders after opportunity for hearing, the Comptroller or the Comptroller's delegate may issue and serve any notices and temporary or permanent cease-and-desist orders and take any actions that are authorized by section 8 of the FDIA (12 U.S.C. 1818), sections 15B(c)(5), 15C(c)(2)(B), and 17A(d)(2) of the Exchange Act, and other subparts of this part against the following:

(1) The parties listed in paragraph (a) of this section; and

(2) A bank which is a clearing agency.

(c) Nothing in this subpart impairs the powers conferred on the Comptroller by other provisions of law.

§ 19.131 Notice of charges and answer.

(a) Proceedings are commenced when the Comptroller serves a notice of charges on a bank or associated person. The notice must indicate the type of disciplinary action being contemplated and the grounds therefor, and fix a date, time and place for hearing. The hearing must be set for a date at least 30 days after service of the notice. A party served with a notice of charges may file an answer as prescribed in § 19.19. Any party who fails to appear at a hearing personally or by a duly authorized representative shall be deemed to have consented to the issuance of a disciplinary order.

(b) All proceedings under this subpart must be commenced, and the notice of charges must be filed, on a public basis, unless otherwise ordered by the Comptroller. Pursuant to § 19.33(a), a request for a private hearing may be filed within 20 days of service of the notice.

§ 19.132 Disciplinary orders.

(a) In the event of consent, or if on the record filed by the administrative law judge, the Comptroller finds that any act or omission or violation specified in the notice of charges has been established, the Comptroller may serve on the bank or persons concerned a disciplinary order, as provided in the Exchange Act. The order may:

(1) Censure, limit the activities, functions or operations, or suspend or revoke the registration of a bank which is a municipal securities dealer;

(2) Censure, suspend or bar any person associated or seeking to become associated with a municipal securities dealer;

(3) Censure, limit the activities, functions or operations, or suspend or bar a bank which is a government securities broker or dealer;

(4) Censure, limit the activities, functions or operations, or suspend or bar any person associated with a government securities broker or dealer;

(5) Deny registration to, limit the activities, functions, or operations or suspend or revoke the registration of a bank which is a transfer agent; or

(6) Censure or limit the activities or functions, or suspend or bar, any person associated or seeking to become associated with a transfer agent.

(b) A disciplinary order is effective when served on the party or parties involved and remains effective and enforceable until it is stayed, modified, terminated, or set aside by action of the Comptroller or a reviewing court.

§ 19.135 Applications for stay or review of disciplinary actions imposed by registered clearing agencies.

(a) *Stays.* The rules adopted by the Securities and Exchange Commission (SEC) pursuant to section 19 of the Securities Exchange Act of 1934 (15 U.S.C. 78s) regarding applications by persons for whom the SEC is the appropriate regulatory agency for stays of disciplinary sanctions or summary suspensions imposed by registered clearing agencies (17 CFR 240.19d–2) apply to applications by national banks. References to the "Commission" are deemed to refer to the "OCC."

(b) *Reviews.* The regulations adopted by the SEC pursuant to section 19 of the Securities Exchange Act of 1934 (15 U.S.C. 78s) regarding applications by persons for whom the SEC is the appropriate regulatory agency for reviews of final disciplinary sanctions, denials of participation, or prohibitions or limitations of access to services imposed by registered clearing agencies (17 CFR 240.19d–3(a)–(f)) apply to applications by national banks. References to the "Commission" are deemed to refer to the "OCC."

[61 FR 68559, Dec. 30, 1996]

Subpart F—Civil Money Penalty Authority Under the Securities Laws

§ 19.140 Scope.

(a) Except as provided in this subpart, subpart A of this part applies to proceedings by the Comptroller to determine whether, pursuant to authority contained in section 21B of the Exchange Act (15 U.S.C. 78u–2), in proceedings commenced pursuant to sections 15B, 15C, and 17A of the Exchange Act (15 U.S.C. 78o–4, 78o–5, or 78q–1) for which the OCC is the appropriate regulatory agency under section 3(a)(34) of the Exchange Act (15 U.S.C. 78c(a)(34)), the Comptroller may impose a civil money penalty against the following:

(1) A bank which is a municipal securities dealer, or any person associated or seeking to become associated with such a municipal securities dealer;

(2) A bank which is a government securities broker or dealer, or any person associated with such government securities broker or dealer; or

(3) A bank which is a transfer agent, or any person associated or seeking to become associated with such transfer agent.

(b) All proceedings under this subpart must be commenced, and the notice of assessment must be filed, on a public basis, unless otherwise ordered by the Comptroller. Pursuant to § 19.33(a), any request for a private hearing must be filed within 20 days of service of the notice.

Subpart G—Cease-and-Desist Authority Under the Securities Laws

§ 19.150 Scope.

(a) Except as provided in this subpart, subpart A of this part applies to proceedings by the Comptroller to determine whether, pursuant to authority contained in sections 12(i) and 21C of the Exchange Act (15 U.S.C. 78*l*(i) and 78u–3), the Comptroller may initiate cease-and-desist proceedings against a national bank for violations of sections 12, 13, 14(a), 14(c), 14(d), 14(f), and 16 of the Exchange Act or regulations or rules issued thereunder (15 U.S.C. 78*l*, 78m, 78n(a), 78n(c), 78n(d), 78n(f), and 78p) .

(b) All proceedings under this subpart must be commenced, and the notice of charges must be filed, on a public basis, unless otherwise ordered by the Comptroller. Pursuant to § 19.33(a), any request for a private hearing must be filed within 20 days of service of the notice.

Subpart H—Change in Bank Control

§ 19.160 Scope.

(a) Section 7(j) of the FDIA (12 U.S.C. 1817(j)) provides that no person may acquire control of an insured depository institution unless the appropriate Federal bank regulatory agency has been given prior written notice of the proposed acquisition. If, after investigating and soliciting comment on the proposed acquisition, the agency decides that the acquisition should be disapproved, the agency shall mail a written notification to the proposed acquiring person in writing within three days of the decision. The party can then request an agency hearing on the proposed acquisition. The OCC's procedures for reviewing notices of proposed acquisitions in change-in-control proceedings are set forth in § 5.50 of this chapter.

(b) Unless otherwise provided in this subpart, the rules in subpart A of this part set forth the procedures applicable to requests for OCC hearings.

[56 FR 38028, Aug. 9, 1991, as amended at 61 FR 20337, May 6, 1996]

§ 19.161 Notice of disapproval and hearing initiation.

(a) *Notice of disapproval.* The OCC's written disapproval of a proposed acquisition of control of a national bank must:

(1) Contain a statement of the basis for the disapproval; and

(2) Indicate that the filer may request a hearing.

(b) *Hearing request.* Following receipt of a notice of disapproval, a filer may request a hearing on the proposed acquisition. A hearing request must:

(1) Be in writing; and

(2) Be filed with the Hearing Clerk of the OCC within ten days after service on the filer of the notice of disapproval. If a filer fails to request a hearing with a timely written request, the notice of disapproval constitutes a final and unappealable order.

(c) *Hearing order.* Following receipt of a hearing request, the Comptroller shall issue, within 20 days, an order that sets forth:

(1) The legal authority for the proceeding and for the OCC's jurisdiction over the proceeding;

(2) The matters of fact or law upon which the disapproval is based; and

(3) The requirement for filing an answer to the hearing order with OFIA within 20 days after service of the hearing order.

(d) *Answer.* An answer to a hearing order must specifically deny those portions of the order that are disputed. Those portions of the order that the filer does not specifically deny are deemed admitted by the filer. Any hearing under this subpart is limited to those portions of the order that are specifically denied.

(e) *Effect of failure to answer.* Failure of a filer to file an answer within 20 days after service of the hearing order constitutes a waiver of the filer's right to appear and contest the allegations in the hearing order. If a filer does not file a timely answer, enforcement counsel may file a motion for entry of an order of default. Upon a finding that no good cause has been shown for the failure to file a timely answer, the administrative law judge shall file with the Comptroller a recommended decision containing the findings and the relief sought in the hearing order. Any final order issued by the Comptroller based upon a filer's failure to answer is deemed to be an order issued upon consent and is a final and unappealable order.

[61 FR 20337, May 6, 1996]

Subpart I—Discovery Depositions and Subpoenas

§ 19.170 Discovery depositions.

(a) *General rule.* In any proceeding instituted under or subject to the provisions of subpart A of this part, a party may take the deposition of an expert, or of a person, including another party, who has direct knowledge of matters that are non-privileged, relevant, and material to the proceeding, and where there is need for the deposition. The deposition of experts shall be limited to those experts who are expected to testify at the hearing.

(b) *Notice.* A party desiring to take a deposition shall give reasonable notice in writing to the deponent and to every other party to the proceeding. The notice must state the time and place for taking the deposition, and the name and address of the person to be deposed.

(c) *Time limits.* A party may take depositions at any time after the commencement of the proceeding, but no later than ten days before the scheduled hearing date, except with permission of the administrative law judge for good cause shown.

(d) *Conduct of the deposition.* The witness must be duly sworn, and each party will have the right to examine the witness with respect to all non-privileged, relevant, and material matters of which the witness has factual, direct, and personal knowledge. Objections to questions or exhibits must be in short form and must state the grounds for the objection. Failure to object to questions or exhibits is not a waiver except where the grounds for the objection might have been avoided if the objection had been timely presented.

(e) *Recording the testimony*—(1) *Generally.* The party taking the deposition must have a certified court reporter record the witness's testimony:

(i) By stenotype machine or electronic sound recording device;

(ii) Upon agreement of the parties, by any other method; or

(iii) For good cause and with leave of the administrative law judge, by any other method.

(2) *Cost.* The party taking the deposition must bear the cost of the recording and transcribing the witness's testimony.

(3) *Transcript.* Unless the parties agree that a transcription is not necessary, the court reporter must provide a transcript of the witness's testimony to the party taking the deposition and must make a copy of the transcript available to each party upon payment by that party of the cost of the copy.

(f) *Protective orders.* At any time after notice of a deposition has been given, a party may file a motion for the issuance of a protective order. Such protective order may prohibit, terminate, or limit the scope or manner of the taking of a deposition. The administrative law judge shall grant such protective order upon a showing of sufficient grounds, including that the deposition:

(1) Is unreasonable, oppressive, excessive in scope, or unduly burdensome;

(2) Involves privileged, irrelevant, or immaterial matters;

(3) Involves unwarranted attempts to pry into a party's preparation for trial; or

(4) Is being conducted in bad faith or in such manner as to unreasonably annoy, embarrass, or oppress the witness.

(g) *Fees.* Deposition witnesses, including expert witnesses, shall be paid the same expenses in the same manner as are paid witnesses in the district courts of the United States in proceedings in which the United States is a party. Expenses in accordance with this paragraph shall be paid by the party seeking to take the deposition.

[56 FR 38028, Aug. 9, 1991, as amended at 61 FR 20338, May 6, 1996]

§ 19.171 Deposition subpoenas.

(a) *Issuance.* At the request of a party, the administrative law judge shall issue a subpoena requiring the attendance of a witness at a discovery deposition under paragraph (a) of this section. The attendance of a witness may be required from any place in any state or territory that is subject to the jurisdiction of the United States or as otherwise permitted by law.

(b) *Service*—(1) *Methods of service.* The party requesting the subpoena must serve it on the person named therein, or on that person's counsel, by any of the methods identified in § 19.11(d).

(2) *Proof of service.* The party serving the subpoena must file proof of service with the administrative law judge.

(c) *Motion to quash.* A person named in a subpoena may file a motion to quash or modify the subpoena. A statement of the reasons for the motion must accompany it and a copy of the motion must be served on the party which requested the subpoena. The motion must be made prior to the time for compliance specified in the subpoena and not more than ten days after the date of service of the subpoena, or if the subpoena is served within 15 days of the hearing, within five days after the date of service.

(d) *Enforcement of deposition subpoena.* Enforcement of a deposition subpoena shall be in accordance with the procedures of § 19.27(d).

[56 FR 38028, Aug. 9, 1991, as amended at 61 FR 20338, May 6, 1996]

Subpart J—Formal Investigations

§ 19.180 Scope.

This subpart and § 19.8 apply to formal investigations initiated by order of the Comptroller or the Comptroller's delegate and pertain to the exercise of powers specified in 12 U.S.C. 481, 1818(n) and 1820(c), and section 21 of the Exchange Act (15 U.S.C. 78u). This subpart does not restrict or in any way affect the authority of the Comptroller to conduct examinations into the affairs or ownership of banks and their affiliates.

§ 19.181 Confidentiality of formal investigations.

Information or documents obtained in the course of a formal investigation are confidential and may be disclosed only in accordance with the provisions of part 4 of this chapter.

§ 19.182 Order to conduct a formal investigation.

A formal investigation begins with the issuance of an order signed by the Comptroller or the Comptroller's delegate. The order must designate the person or persons who will conduct the investigation. Such persons are authorized, among other things, to issue subpoenas duces tecum, to administer oaths, and receive affirmations as to any matter under investigation by the Comptroller. Upon application and for good cause shown, the Comptroller may limit, modify, or withdraw the order at any stage of the proceedings.

§ 19.183 Rights of witnesses.

(a) Any person who is compelled or requested to furnish testimony, documentary evidence, or other information with respect to any matter under formal investigation shall, on request, be shown the order initiating the investigation.

(b) Any person who, in a formal investigation, is compelled to appear and testify, or who appears and testifies by request or permission of the Comptroller, may be accompanied, represented, and advised by counsel. The right to be accompanied, represented, and advised by counsel means the right of a person testifying to have an attorney present at all times while testifying and to have the attorney—

(1) Advise the person before, during and after the conclusion of testimony;

(2) Question the person briefly at the conclusion of testimony to clarify any of the answers given; and

(3) Make summary notes during the testimony solely for the use of the person.

(c) Any person who has given or will give testimony and counsel representing the person may be excluded from the proceedings during the taking of testimony of any other witness.

(d) Any person who is compelled to give testimony is entitled to inspect any transcript that has been made of the testimony but may not obtain a copy if the Comptroller's representatives conducting the proceedings have cause to believe that the contents should not be disclosed pending completion of the investigation.

(e) Any designated representative conducting an investigative proceeding shall report to the Comptroller any instances where a person has been guilty of dilatory, obstructionist or insubordinate conduct during the course of the proceeding or any other instance involving a violation of this part. The Comptroller may take such action as the circumstances warrant, including exclusion of the offending individual or individuals from participation in the proceedings.

§ 19.184 Service of subpoena and payment of witness expenses.

(a) *Methods of service.* Service of a subpoena may be made by any of the methods identified in § 19.11(d).

(b) *Expenses.* A witness who is subpoenaed will be paid the same expenses in the same manner as witnesses in the district courts of the United States. The expenses need not be tendered at the time a subpoena is served.

[61 FR 20338, May 6, 1996]

Subpart K—Parties and Representational Practice Before the OCC; Standards of Conduct

§ 19.190 Scope.

This subpart contains rules relating to parties and representational practice before the OCC. This subpart includes the imposition of sanctions by the administrative law judge, any other presiding officer appointed pursuant to subparts C and D of this part, or the Comptroller against parties or their counsel in an adjudicatory proceeding under this part. This subpart also covers other disciplinary sanctions—censure, suspension or debarment—against individuals who appear before the OCC in a representational capacity either in an adjudicatory proceeding under this part or in any other matters connected with presentations to the OCC relating to a client's rights, privileges, or liabilities. This representation includes, but is not limited to, the practice of attorneys and accountants. Employees of the OCC are not subject to disciplinary proceedings under this subpart.

[56 FR 38028, Aug. 9, 1991; 56 FR 41726, Aug. 22, 1991]

§ 19.191 Definitions.

As used in §§ 19.190 through 19.201, the following terms shall have the meaning given in this section unless the context otherwise requires:

(a) *Practice before the OCC* includes any matters connected with presentations to the OCC or any of its officers or employees relating to a client's rights, privileges or liabilities under laws or regulations administered by the OCC. Such matters include, but are not limited to, representation of a client in an adjudicatory proceeding under this part; the preparation of any statement, opinion or other paper or document by an attorney, accountant, or other licensed professional which is filed with, or submitted to, the OCC, on behalf of another person in, or in connection with, any application, notification, report or document; the representation of a person at conferences, hearings and meetings; and the transaction of other business before the OCC on behalf of another person. The term "practice before the OCC" does not include work prepared for a bank solely at its request for use in the ordinary course of its business.

(b) *Attorney* means any individual who is a member in good standing of the bar of the highest court of any state, possession, territory, commonwealth, of the United States or the District of Columbia.

(c) *Accountant* means any individual who is duly qualified to practice as a certified public accountant or a public accountant in any state, possession, territory, commonwealth of the United States, or the District of Columbia.

§ 19.192 Sanctions relating to conduct in an adjudicatory proceeding.

(a) *General rule.* Appropriate sanctions may be imposed when any party or person representing a party in an adjudicatory proceeding under this part has failed to comply with an applicable statute, regulation, or order, and that failure to comply:

(1) Constitutes contemptuous conduct;

(2) Materially injures or prejudices another party in terms of substantive injury, incurring additional expenses including attorney's fees, prejudicial delay, or otherwise;

(3) Is a clear and unexcused violation of an applicable statute, regulation, or order; or

(4) Unduly delays the proceeding.

(b) *Sanctions.* Sanctions which may be imposed include any one or more of the following:

(1) Issuing an order against the party;

(2) Rejecting or striking any testimony or documentary evidence offered, or other papers filed, by the party;

(3) Precluding the party from contesting specific issues or findings;

(4) Precluding the party from offering certain evidence or from challenging or contesting certain evidence offered by another party;

(5) Precluding the party from making a late filing or conditioning a late filing on any terms that are just; and

(6) Assessing reasonable expenses, including attorney's fees, incurred by any other party as a result of the improper action or failure to act.

(c) *Procedure for imposition of sanctions.* (1) Upon the motion of any party, or on his or her own motion, the administrative law judge or other presiding officer may impose sanctions in accordance with this section. The administrative law judge or other presiding officer shall submit to the Comptroller for final ruling any sanction entering a final order that determines the case on the merits.

(2) No sanction authorized by this section, other than refusal to accept late filings, shall be imposed without prior notice to all parties and an opportunity for any party against whom sanctions would be imposed to be heard. Such opportunity to be heard may be on such notice, and the response may be in such form as the administrative law judge or other presiding officer directs. The administrative law judge or other presiding officer may limit the opportunity to be heard to an opportunity of a party or a party's representative to respond orally immediately after the act or inaction covered by this section is noted by the administrative law judge or other presiding officer.

(3) Requests for the imposition of sanctions by any party, and the imposition of sanctions, are subject to interlocutory review pursuant to § 19.25 in the same manner as any other ruling.

(d) *Section not exclusive.* Nothing in this section shall be read as precluding the administrative law judge or other presiding officer or the Comptroller from taking any other action, or imposing any restriction or sanction, authorized by applicable statute or regulation.

§ 19.193 Censure, suspension or debarment.

The Comptroller may censure an individual or suspend or debar such individual from practice before the OCC if he or she is incompetent in representing a client's rights or interest in a significant matter before the OCC; or engages, or has engaged, in disreputable conduct; or refuses to comply with the rules and regulations in this part; or with intent to defraud in any manner, willfully and knowingly deceives, misleads, or threatens any client or prospective client. The suspension or debarment of an individual may be initiated only upon a finding by the Comptroller that the basis for the disciplinary action is sufficiently egregious.

§ 19.194 Eligibility of attorneys and accountants to practice.

(a) *Attorneys.* Any attorney who is qualified to practice as an attorney and is not currently under suspension or debarment pursuant to this subpart may practice before the OCC.

(b) *Accountants.* Any accountant who is qualified to practice as a certified public accountant or public accountant and is not currently under suspension or debarment by the OCC may practice before the OCC.

§ 19.195 Incompetence.

Incompetence in the representation of a client's rights and interests in a significant matter before the OCC is grounds for suspension or debarment. The term "incompetence" encompasses conduct that reflects a lack of the knowledge, judgment and skill that a professional would ordinarily and reasonably be expected to exercise in adequately representing the rights and interests of a client. Such conduct includes, but is not limited to:

(a) Handling a matter which the individual knows or should know that he or she is not competent to handle, without associating with a professional who is competent to handle such matter.

(b) Handling a matter without adequate preparation under the circumstances.

(c) Neglect in a matter entrusted to him or her.

§ 19.196 Disreputable conduct.

Disreputable conduct for which an individual may be censured, debarred, or suspended from practice before the OCC includes:

(a) Willfully or recklessly violating or willfully or recklessly aiding and abetting the violation of any provision of the Federal banking or applicable securities laws or the rules and regulations thereunder or conviction of any offense involving dishonesty or breach of trust;

(b) Knowingly or recklessly giving false or misleading information, or participating in any way in the giving of false information to the OCC or any officer or employee thereof, or to any tribunal authorized to pass upon matters administered by the OCC in connection with any matter pending or likely to be pending before it. The term "information" includes facts or other statements contained in testimony, financial statements, applications for enrollment, affidavits, declarations, or any other document or written or oral statement;

(c) Directly or indirectly attempting to influence, or offering or agreeing to attempt to influence, the official action of any officer or employee of the OCC by the use of threats, false accusations, duress or coercion, by the offer of any special inducement or promise of advantage or by the bestowing of any gift, favor, or thing of value.

(d) Disbarment or suspension from practice as an attorney, or debarment or suspension from practice as a certified public accountant or public accountant, by any duly constituted authority of any state, possession, or commonwealth of the United States, or the District of Columbia for the conviction of a felony or misdemeanor involving moral turpitude in matters relating to the supervisory responsibilities of the OCC, where the conviction has not been reversed on appeal.

(e) Knowingly aiding or abetting another individual to practice before the OCC during that individual's period of suspension, debarment, or ineligibility.

(f) Contemptuous conduct in connection with practice before the OCC, and knowingly making false accusations and statements, or circulating or publishing malicious or libelous matter.

(g) Suspension, debarment or removal from practice before the Board of Governors, the FDIC, the OTS, the Securities and Exchange Commission, the Commodity Futures Trading Commission, or any other Federal or state agency; and

(h) Willful violation of any of the regulations contained in this part.

[56 FR 38028, Aug. 9, 1991, as amended at 68 FR 48265, Aug. 13, 2003]

§ 19.197 Initiation of disciplinary proceeding.

(a) *Receipt of information.* An individual, including any employee of the OCC, who has reason to believe that an individual practicing before the OCC in a representative capacity has engaged in any conduct that would serve as a basis for censure, suspension or debarment under § 19.192, may make a report thereof and forward it to the OCC or to such person as may be delegated responsibility for such matters by the Comptroller.

(b) *Censure without formal proceeding.* Upon receipt of information regarding an individual's qualification to practice before the OCC, the Comptroller or the Comptroller's delegate may, after giving the individual notice and opportunity to respond, censure such individual.

(c) *Institution of formal disciplinary proceeding.* When the Comptroller has reason to believe that any individual who practices before the OCC in a representative capacity has engaged in conduct that would serve as a basis for censure, suspension or debarment under § 19.192, the Comptroller may, after giving the individual notice and opportunity to respond, institute a formal disciplinary proceeding against such individual. The proceeding will be conducted pursuant to § 19.199 and initiated by a complaint which names the individual as a respondent and is signed by the Comptroller or the Comptroller's delegate. Except in cases of willfulness, or when time, the nature of the proceeding, or the public interest do not permit, a proceeding under this section may not be commenced until the respondent has been informed, in writing, of the facts or conduct which warrant institution of a proceeding and the respondent has been accorded the opportunity to comply with all lawful requirements or take whatever action may be necessary to remedy the conduct that is the basis for the commencement of the proceeding.

[56 FR 38028, Aug. 9, 1991; 56 FR 46667, Sept. 13, 1991]

§ 19.198 Conferences.

(a) *General.* The Comptroller may confer with a proposed respondent concerning allegations of misconduct or other grounds for censure, debarment or suspension, regardless of whether a proceeding for debarment or suspension has been commenced. If a conference results in a stipulation in connection with a proceeding in which the individual is the respondent, the stipulation may be entered in the record at the request of either party to the proceeding.

(b) *Resignation or voluntary suspension.* In order to avoid the institution of, or a decision in, a debarment or suspension proceeding, a person who practices before the OCC may consent to suspension from practice. At the discretion of the Comptroller, the individual may be suspended or debarred in accordance with the consent offered.

§ 19.199 Proceedings under this subpart.

Any hearing held under this subpart is held before an administrative law judge pursuant to procedures set forth in subpart A of this part. The Comptroller or the Comptroller's delegate shall appoint a person to represent the OCC in the hearing. Any person having prior involvement in the matter which is the basis for the suspension or debarment proceeding is disqualified from representing the OCC in the hearing. The hearing will be closed to the public unless the Comptroller on his or her own initiative, or on the request of a party, otherwise directs. The administrative law judge shall issue a recommended decision to the Comptroller who shall issue the final decision and order. The Comptroller may censure, debar or suspend an individual, or take such other disciplinary action as the Comptroller deems appropriate.

§ 19.200 Effect of suspension, debarment or censure.

(a) *Debarment.* If the final order against the respondent is for debarment, the individual may not practice before the OCC unless otherwise permitted to do so by the Comptroller.

(b) *Suspension.* If the final order against the respondent is for suspension, the individual may not practice before the OCC during the period of suspension.

(c) *Censure.* If the final order against the respondent is for censure, the individual may be permitted to practice before the OCC, but such individual's future representations may be subject to conditions designed to promote high standards of conduct. If a written letter of censure is issued, a copy will be maintained in the OCC's files.

(d) *Notice of debarment or suspension.* Upon the issuance of a final order for suspension or debarment, the Comptroller shall give notice of the order to appropriate officers and employees of the OCC and to interested departments and agencies of the Federal government. The Comptroller or the Comptroller's delegate shall also give notice to the appropriate authorities of the state in which any debarred or suspended individual is or was licensed to practice.

§ 19.201 Petition for reinstatement.

At the expiration of the period of time designated in the order of debarment, the Comptroller may entertain a petition for reinstatement from any person debarred from practice before the OCC. The Comptroller may grant reinstatement only if satisfied that the petitioner is likely to act in accordance with the regulations in this part, and that granting reinstatement would not be contrary to the public interest. Any request for reinstatement shall be limited to written submissions unless the Comptroller, in his or her discretion, affords the petitioner a hearing.

Subpart L—Equal Access to Justice Act

§ 19.210 Scope.

The Equal Access to Justice Act regulations applicable to formal OCC adjudicatory proceedings under this part are set forth at 31 CFR part 6.

Subpart M—Procedures for Reclassifying a Bank Based on Criteria Other Than Capital

SOURCE: 57 FR 44895, Sept. 29, 1992, unless otherwise noted.

§19.220 Scope.

This subpart applies to the procedures afforded to any bank that has been reclassified to a lower capital category by a notice or order issued by the OCC pursuant to section 38 of the Federal Deposit Insurance Act and this part.

§19.221 Reclassification of a bank based on unsafe or unsound condition or practice.

(a) *Issuance of notice of proposed reclassification*—(1) *Grounds for reclassification.* (i) Pursuant to §6.4 of this chapter, the OCC may reclassify a well capitalized bank as adequately capitalized or subject an adequately capitalized bank or undercapitalized bank to the supervisory actions applicable to the next lower capital category if:

(A) The OCC determines that the bank is in an unsafe or unsound condition; or

(B) The OCC deems the bank to be engaging in an unsafe or unsound practice and not to have corrected the deficiency.

(ii) Any action pursuant to this paragraph (a)(1) shall hereinafter be referred to as "reclassification."

(2) *Prior notice to institution.* Prior to taking action pursuant to §6.4 of this chapter, the OCC shall issue and serve on the bank a written notice of the OCC's intention to reclassify the bank.

(b) *Contents of notice.* A notice of intention to reclassify a bank based on unsafe or unsound condition will include:

(1) A statement of the bank's capital measures and capital levels and the category to which the bank would be reclassified;

(2) The reasons for reclassification of the bank;

(3) The date by which the bank subject to the notice of reclassification may file with the OCC a written appeal of the proposed reclassification and a request for a hearing, which shall be at least 14 calendar days from the date of service of the notice unless the OCC determines that a shorter period is appropriate in light of the financial condition of the bank or other relevant circumstances.

(c) *Response to notice of proposed reclassification.* A bank may file a written response to a notice of proposed reclassification within the time period set by the OCC. The response should include:

(1) An explanation of why the bank is not in unsafe or unsound condition or otherwise should not be reclassified;

(2) Any other relevant information, mitigating circumstances, documentation, or other evidence in support of the position of the bank or company regarding the reclassification.

(d) *Failure to file response.* Failure by a bank to file, within the specified time period, a written response with the OCC to a notice of proposed reclassification shall constitute a waiver of the opportunity to respond and shall constitute consent to the reclassification.

(e) *Request for hearing and presentation of oral testimony or witnesses.* The response may include a request for an informal hearing before the OCC under this section. If the bank desires to present oral testimony or witnesses at the hearing, the bank shall include a request to do so with the request for an informal hearing. A request to present oral testimony or witnesses shall specify the names of the witnesses and the general nature of their expected testimony. Failure to request a hearing shall constitute a waiver of any right to a hearing, and failure to request the opportunity to present oral testimony or witnesses shall constitute a waiver of any right to present oral testimony or witnesses.

(f) *Order for informal hearing.* Upon receipt of a timely written request that includes a request for a hearing, the OCC shall issue an order directing an informal hearing to commence no later than 30 days after receipt of the request, unless the OCC allows further time at the request of the bank. The hearing shall be held in Washington, DC or at such other place as may be designated by the OCC, before a presiding officer(s) designated by the OCC to conduct the hearing.

(g) *Hearing procedures.* (1) The bank shall have the right to introduce relevant written materials and to present oral argument at the hearing. The bank may introduce oral testimony and present witnesses only if expressly authorized by the OCC or the presiding officer(s). Neither the provisions of the

Administrative Procedure Act (5 U.S.C. 554–557) governing adjudications required by statute to be determined on the record nor the Uniform Rules of Practice and Procedure in subpart A of this part apply to an informal hearing under this section unless the OCC orders that such procedures shall apply.

(2) The informal hearing shall be recorded, and a transcript furnished to the bank upon request and payment of the cost thereof. Witnesses need not be sworn, unless specifically requested by a party or the presiding officer(s). The presiding officer(s) may ask questions of any witness.

(3) The presiding officer(s) may order that the hearing be continued for a reasonable period (normally five business days) following completion of oral testimony or argument to allow additional written submissions to the hearing record.

(h) *Recommendation of presiding officer(s).* Within 20 calendar days following the date the hearing and the record on the proceeding are closed, the presiding officer(s) shall make a recommendation to the OCC on the reclassification.

(i) *Time for decision.* Not later than 60 calendar days after the date the record is closed or the date of the response in a case where no hearing was requested, the OCC will decide whether to reclassify the bank and notify the bank of the OCC's decision.

§ 19.222 Request for rescission of reclassification.

Any bank that has been reclassified under part 6 of this chapter and this subpart, may, upon a change in circumstances, request in writing that the OCC reconsider the reclassification, and may propose that the reclassification be rescinded and that any directives issued in connection with the reclassification be modified, rescinded, or removed. Unless otherwise ordered by the OCC, the bank shall remain subject to the reclassification and to any directives issued in connection with that reclassification while such request is pending before the OCC.

Subpart N—Order To Dismiss a Director or Senior Executive Officer

SOURCE: 57 FR 44896, Sept. 29, 1992, unless otherwise noted.

§ 19.230 Scope.

This subpart applies to informal hearings afforded to any director or senior executive officer dismissed pursuant to an order issued under 12 U.S.C. 1831o and part 6 of this chapter.

§ 19.231 Order to dismiss a director or senior executive officer.

(a) *Service of notice.* When the OCC issues and serves a directive on a bank pursuant to subpart B of part 6 of this chapter requiring the bank to dismiss from office any director or senior executive officer under section 38(f)(2)(F)(ii) of the FDI Act, the OCC shall also serve a copy of the directive, or the relevant portions of the directive where appropriate, upon the person to be dismissed.

(b) *Response to directive*—(1) *Request for reinstatement.* A director or senior executive officer who has been served with a directive under paragraph (a) of this section (Respondent) may file a written request for reinstatement. The request for reinstatement shall be filed within 10 calendar days of the receipt of the directive by the Respondent, unless further time is allowed by the OCC at the request of the Respondent.

(2) *Contents of request; informal hearing.* The request for reinstatement shall include reasons why the Respondent should be reinstated, and may include a request for an informal hearing before the OCC or its designee under this section. If the Respondent desires to present oral testimony or witnesses at the hearing, the Respondent shall include a request to do so with the request for an informal hearing. The request to present oral testimony or witnesses shall specify the names of the witnesses and the general nature of their expected testimony. Failure to request a hearing shall constitute a waiver of any right to a hearing and failure to request the opportunity to present oral testimony or witnesses shall constitute a waiver of any right

or opportunity to present oral testimony or witnesses.

(3) *Effective date.* Unless otherwise ordered by the OCC, the dismissal shall remain in effect while a request for reinstatement is pending.

(c) *Order for informal hearing.* Upon receipt of a timely written request from a Respondent for an informal hearing on the portion of a directive requiring a bank to dismiss from office any director or senior executive officer, the OCC shall issue an order directing an informal hearing to commence no later than 30 days after receipt of the request, unless the Respondent requests a later date. The hearing shall be held in Washington, DC, or at such other place as may be designated by the OCC, before a presiding officer(s) designated by the OCC to conduct the hearing.

(d) *Hearing procedures.* (1) A Respondent may appear at the hearing personally or through counsel. A Respondent shall have the right to introduce relevant written materials and to present oral argument. A Respondent may introduce oral testimony and present witnesses only if expressly authorized by the OCC or the presiding officer(s). Neither the provisions of the Administrative Procedure Act governing adjudications required by statute to be determined on the record nor the Uniform Rules of Practice and Procedure in subpart A of this part apply to an informal hearing under this section unless the OCC orders that such procedures shall apply.

(2) The informal hearing shall be recorded, and a transcript furnished to the Respondent upon request and payment of the cost thereof. Witnesses need not be sworn, unless specifically requested by a party or the presiding officer(s). The presiding officer(s) may ask questions of any witness.

(3) The presiding officer(s) may order that the hearing be continued for a reasonable period (normally five business days) following completion of oral testimony or argument to allow additional written submissions to the hearing record.

(e) *Standard for review.* A Respondent shall bear the burden of demonstrating that his or her continued employment by or service with the bank would materially strengthen the bank's ability:

(1) To become adequately capitalized, to the extent that the directive was issued as a result of the bank's capital level or failure to submit or implement a capital restoration plan; and

(2) To correct the unsafe or unsound condition or unsafe or unsound practice, to the extent that the directive was issued as a result of classification of the bank based on supervisory criteria other than capital, pursuant to section 38(g) of the FDI Act.

(f) *Recommendation of presiding officer.* Within 20 calendar days following the date the hearing and the record on the proceeding are closed, the presiding officer(s) shall make a recommendation to the OCC concerning the Respondent's request for reinstatement with the bank.

(g) *Time for decision.* Not later than 60 calendar days after the date the record is closed or the date of the response in a case where no hearing was requested, the OCC shall grant or deny the request for reinstatement and notify the Respondent of the OCC's decision. If the OCC denies the request for reinstatement, the OCC shall set forth in the notification the reasons for the OCC's action.

Subpart O—Civil Money Penalty Adjustments

SOURCE: 65 FR 77252, Dec. 11, 2000, unless otherwise noted.

§ 19.240 Inflation adjustments.

(a) *Statutory formula to calculate inflation adjustments.* The OCC is required by statute to annually adjust for inflation the maximum amount of each civil money penalty within its jurisdiction to administer. The inflation adjustment is calculated by multiplying the maximum dollar amount of the civil money penalty for the previous calendar year by the cost-of-living inflation adjustment multiplier provided annually by the Office of Management and Budget and rounding the total to the nearest dollar.

(b) *Notice of inflation adjustments.* The OCC will publish notice in the FEDERAL REGISTER of the maximum penalties which may be assessed on an annual basis on or before January 15 of each calendar year based on the formula in paragraph (a) of this section, for penalties assessed on, or after, the date of publication of the most recent notice related to conduct occurring on, or after, November 2, 2015.

[83 FR 1518, Jan. 12, 2018]

Subpart P—Removal, Suspension, and Debarment of Accountants From Performing Audit Services

SOURCE: 68 FR 48265, Aug. 13, 2003, unless otherwise noted.

§ 19.241 Scope.

This subpart, which implements section 36(g)(4) of the Federal Deposit Insurance Act (FDI Act) (12 U.S.C. 1831m(g)(4)), provides rules and procedures for the removal, suspension, or debarment of independent public accountants and their accounting firms from performing independent audit and attestation services required by section 36 of the FDI Act (12 U.S.C. 1831m) for insured national banks and Federal branches and agencies of foreign banks.

[73 FR 22244, Apr. 24, 2008]

§ 19.242 Definitions.

As used in this subpart, the following terms shall have the meaning given below unless the context requires otherwise:

(a) *Accounting firm* means a corporation, proprietorship, partnership, or other business firm providing audit services.

(b) *Audit services* means any service required to be performed by an independent public accountant by section 36 of the FDIA and 12 CFR part 363, including attestation services.

(c) *Independent public accountant (accountant)* means any individual who performs or participates in providing audit services.

§ 19.243 Removal, suspension, or debarment.

(a) *Good cause for removal, suspension, or debarment*—(1) *Individuals*. The Comptroller may remove, suspend, or debar an independent public accountant from performing audit services for insured national banks that are subject to section 36 of the FDIA if, after service of a notice of intention and opportunity for hearing in the matter, the Comptroller finds that the accountant:

(i) Lacks the requisite qualifications to perform audit services;

(ii) Has knowingly or recklessly engaged in conduct that results in a violation of applicable professional standards, including those standards and conflicts of interest provisions applicable to accountants through the Sarbanes-Oxley Act of 2002, Pub. L. 107–204, 116 Stat. 745 (2002) (Sarbanes-Oxley Act), and developed by the Public Company Accounting Oversight Board and the Securities and Exchange Commission;

(iii) Has engaged in negligent conduct in the form of:

(A) A single instance of highly unreasonable conduct that results in a violation of applicable professional standards in circumstances in which an accountant knows, or should know, that heightened scrutiny is warranted; or

(B) Repeated instances of unreasonable conduct, each resulting in a violation of applicable professional standards, that indicate a lack of competence to perform audit services;

(iv) Has knowingly or recklessly given false or misleading information, or knowingly or recklessly participated in any way in the giving of false or misleading information, to the OCC or any officer or employee of the OCC;

(v) Has engaged in, or aided and abetted, a material and knowing or reckless violation of any provision of the Federal banking or securities laws or the rules and regulations thereunder, or any other law;

(vi) Has been removed, suspended, or debarred from practice before any Federal or state agency regulating the banking, insurance, or securities industries, other than by an action listed in § 19.244, on grounds relevant to the provision of audit services; or

(vii) Is suspended or debarred for cause from practice as an accountant by any duly constituted licensing authority of any state, possession, commonwealth, or the District of Columbia.

(2) *Accounting firms.* If the Comptroller determines that there is good cause for the removal, suspension, or debarment of a member or employee of an accounting firm under paragraph (a)(1) of this section, the Comptroller also may remove, suspend, or debar such firm or one or more offices of such firm. In considering whether to remove, suspend, or debar a firm or an office thereof, and the term of any sanction against a firm under this section, the Comptroller may consider, for example:

(i) The gravity, scope, or repetition of the act or failure to act that constitutes good cause for the removal, suspension, or debarment;

(ii) The adequacy of, and adherence to, applicable policies, practices, or procedures for the accounting firm's conduct of its business and the performance of audit services;

(iii) The selection, training, supervision, and conduct of members or employees of the accounting firm involved in the performance of audit services;

(iv) The extent to which managing partners or senior officers of the accounting firm have participated, directly, or indirectly through oversight or review, in the act or failure to act; and

(v) The extent to which the accounting firm has, since the occurrence of the act or failure to act, implemented corrective internal controls to prevent its recurrence.

(3) *Limited scope orders.* An order of removal, suspension (including an immediate suspension), or debarment may, at the discretion of the Comptroller, be made applicable to a particular national bank or class of national banks.

(4) *Remedies not exclusive.* The remedies provided in this subpart are in addition to any other remedies the OCC may have under any other applicable provisions of law, rule, or regulation.

(b) *Proceedings to remove, suspend, or debar*—(1) *Initiation of formal removal, suspension, or debarment proceedings.* The Comptroller may initiate a proceeding to remove, suspend, or debar an accountant or accounting firm from performing audit services by issuing a written notice of intention to take such action that names the individual or firm as a respondent and describes the nature of the conduct that constitutes good cause for such action.

(2) *Hearings under paragraph (b) of this section.* An accountant or firm named as a respondent in the notice issued under paragraph (b)(1) of this section may request a hearing on the allegations in the notice. Hearings conducted under this paragraph shall be conducted in the same manner as other hearings under the Uniform Rules of Practice and Procedure (12 CFR part 19, subpart A).

(c) *Immediate suspension from performing audit services*—(1) *In general.* If the Comptroller serves a written notice of intention to remove, suspend, or debar an accountant or accounting firm from performing audit services, the Comptroller may, with due regard for the public interest and without a preliminary hearing, immediately suspend such accountant or firm from performing audit services for insured national banks, if the Comptroller:

(i) Has a reasonable basis to believe that the accountant or firm has engaged in conduct (specified in the notice served on the accountant or firm under paragraph (b) of this section) that would constitute grounds for removal, suspension, or debarment under paragraph (a) of this section;

(ii) Determines that immediate suspension is necessary to avoid immediate harm to an insured depository institution or its depositors or to the depository system as a whole; and

(iii) Serves such respondent with written notice of the immediate suspension.

(2) *Procedures.* An immediate suspension notice issued under this paragraph will become effective upon service. Such suspension will remain in effect until the date the Comptroller dismisses the charges contained in the notice of intention, or the effective date of a final order of removal, suspension, or debarment issued by the Comptroller to the respondent.

(3) *Petition for stay.* Any accountant or firm immediately suspended from performing audit services in accordance with paragraph (c)(1) of this section may, within 10 calendar days after service of the notice of immediate suspension, file with the Office of the

Comptroller of the Currency, Washington, DC 20219 for a stay of such immediate suspension. If no petition is filed within 10 calendar days, the immediate suspension shall remain in effect.

(4) *Hearing on petition.* Upon receipt of a stay petition, the Comptroller will designate a presiding officer who shall fix a place and time (not more than 10 calendar days after receipt of the petition, unless extended at the request of petitioner) at which the immediately suspended party may appear, personally or through counsel, to submit written materials and oral argument. Any OCC employee engaged in investigative or prosecuting functions for the OCC in a case may not, in that or a factually related case, serve as a presiding officer or participate or advise in the decision of the presiding officer or of the OCC, except as witness or counsel in the proceeding. In the sole discretion of the presiding officer, upon a specific showing of compelling need, oral testimony of witnesses may also be presented. In hearings held pursuant to this paragraph there shall be no discovery and the provisions of §§ 19.6 through 19.12, 19.16, and 19.21 of this part shall apply.

(5) *Decision on petition.* Within 30 calendar days after the hearing, the presiding officer shall issue a decision. The presiding officer will grant a stay upon a demonstration that a substantial likelihood exists of the respondent's success on the issues raised by the notice of intention and that, absent such relief, the respondent will suffer immediate and irreparable injury, loss, or damage. In the absence of such a demonstration, the presiding officer will notify the parties that the immediate suspension will be continued pending the completion of the administrative proceedings pursuant to the notice.

(6) *Review of presiding officer's decision.* The parties may seek review of the presiding officer's decision by filing a petition for review with the presiding officer within 10 calendar days after service of the decision. Replies must be filed within 10 calendar days after the petition filing date. Upon receipt of a petition for review and any reply, the presiding officer shall promptly certify the entire record to the Comptroller. Within 60 calendar days of the presiding officer's certification, the Comptroller shall issue an order notifying the affected party whether or not the immediate suspension should be continued or reinstated. The order shall state the basis of the Comptroller's decision.

§ 19.244 Automatic removal, suspension, and debarment.

(a) An independent public accountant or accounting firm may not perform audit services for insured national banks if the accountant or firm:

(1) Is subject to a final order of removal, suspension, or debarment (other than a limited scope order) issued by the Board of Governors of the Federal Reserve System, the Federal Deposit Insurance Corporation, or the Office of Thrift Supervision under section 36 of the FDIA.

(2) Is subject to a temporary suspension or permanent revocation of registration or a temporary or permanent suspension or bar from further association with any registered public accounting firm issued by the Public Company Accounting Oversight Board or the Securities and Exchange Commission under sections 105(c)(4)(A) or (B) of the Sarbanes-Oxley Act (15 U.S.C. 7215(c)(4)(A) or (B)); or

(3) Is subject to an order of suspension or denial of the privilege of appearing or practicing before the Securities and Exchange Commission.

(b) Upon written request, the Comptroller, for good cause shown, may grant written permission to such accountant or firm to perform audit services for national banks. The request shall contain a concise statement of the action requested. The Comptroller may require the applicant to submit additional information.

§ 19.245 Notice of removal, suspension or debarment.

(a) *Notice to the public.* Upon the issuance of a final order for removal, suspension, or debarment of an independent public accountant or accounting firm from providing audit services, the Comptroller shall make the order publicly available and provide notice of the order to the other Federal banking agencies.

(b) *Notice to the Comptroller by accountants and firms.* An accountant or accounting firm that provides audit services to a national bank must provide the Comptroller with written notice of:

(1) Any currently effective order or other action described in §19.243(a)(1)(vi) through (a)(1)(vii) or §19.244(a)(2) through (a)(3); and

(2) Any currently effective action by the Public Company Accounting Oversight Board under sections 105(c)(4)(C) or (G) of the Sarbanes-Oxley Act) (15 U.S.C. 7215(c)(4)(C) or (G)).

(c) *Timing of notice.* Written notice required by this paragraph shall be given no later than 15 calendar days following the effective date of an order or action, or 15 calendar days before an accountant or firm accepts an engagement to provide audit services, whichever date is earlier.

§19.246 Petition for reinstatement.

(a) *Form of petition.* Unless otherwise ordered by the Comptroller, a petition for reinstatement by an independent public accountant, an accounting firm, or an office of a firm that was removed, suspended, or debarred under §19.243 may be made in writing at any time. The request shall contain a concise statement of the action requested. The Comptroller may require the applicant to submit additional information.

(b) *Procedure.* A petitioner for reinstatement under this section may, in the sole discretion of the Comptroller, be afforded a hearing. The accountant or firm shall bear the burden of going forward with a petition and proving the grounds asserted in support of the petition. In reinstatement proceedings, the person seeking reinstatement shall bear the burden of going forward with an application and proving the grounds asserted in support of the application. The Comptroller may, in his sole discretion, direct that any reinstatement proceeding be limited to written submissions. The removal, suspension, or debarment shall continue until the Comptroller, for good cause shown, has reinstated the petitioner or until the suspension period has expired. The filing of a petition for reinstatement shall not stay the effectiveness of the removal, suspension, or debarment of an accountant or firm.

PART 21—MINIMUM SECURITY DEVICES AND PROCEDURES, REPORTS OF SUSPICIOUS ACTIVITIES, AND BANK SECRECY ACT COMPLIANCE PROGRAM

Subpart A—Minimum Security Devices and Procedures

Sec.

21.1 Purpose and scope of subpart A of this part.
21.2 Designation of security officer.
21.3 Security program.
21.4 Report.

Subpart B—Reports of Suspicious Activities

21.11 Suspicious Activity Report.

Subpart C—Procedures for Monitoring Bank Secrecy Act Compliance

21.21 Procedures for monitoring Bank Secrecy Act (BSA) compliance.

AUTHORITY: 12 U.S.C. 1, 93a, 1462a, 1463, 1464, 1818, 1881–1884, and 3401–3422; 31 U.S.C. 5318.

Subpart A—Minimum Security Devices and Procedures

SOURCE: 56 FR 29564, June 28, 1991, unless otherwise noted.

§21.1 Purpose and scope of subpart A of this part.

(a) This subpart is issued by the Comptroller of the Currency pursuant to section 3 of the Bank Protection Act of 1968 (12 U.S.C. 1882) and is applicable to all national banking associations. It requires each bank to adopt appropriate security procedures to discourage robberies, burglaries, and larcenies and to assist in identifying and apprehending persons who commit such acts.

(b) It is the responsibility of a bank's board of directors to comply with this regulation and ensure that a security program which equals or exceeds the standards prescribed by this part is developed and implemented for the bank's main office and branches (as the term "branch" is used in 12 U.S.C. 36).

[56 FR 29564, June 28, 1991, as amended at 73 FR 22244, Apr. 24, 2008]

§ 21.2 Designation of security officer.

Within 30 days after the opening of a new bank, the Bank's board of directors shall designate a security officer who shall have the authority, subject to the approval of the board of directors, for immediately developing and administering a written security program to protect each banking office from robberies, burglaries, and larcenies and to assist in identifying and apprehending persons who commit such acts.

(Approval by the Office of Management and Budget under control number 1557–0180)

§ 21.3 Security program.

(a) *Contents of security program.* The security program shall:

(1) Establish procedures for opening and closing for business and for the safekeeping of all currency, negotiable securities, and similar valuables at all times;

(2) Establish procedures that will assist in identifying persons committing crimes against the institution and that will preserve evidence that may aid in their identification or conviction; such procedures may include, but are not limited to:

(i) Using identification devices, such as prerecorded serial-numbered bills, or chemical and electronic devices;

(ii) Maintaining a camera that records activity in the banking office; and

(iii) Retaining a record of any robbery, burglary or larceny committed or attempted against a banking office;

(3) Provide for initial and periodic training of employees in their responsibilities under the security program and in proper employee conduct during and after a robbery; and

(4) Provide for selecting, testing, operating and maintaining appropriate security devices, as specified in paragraph (b) of this section.

(b) *Security devices.* Each national bank shall have, at a minimum, the following security devices:

(1) A means of protecting cash or other liquid assets, such as a vault, safe, or other secure space;

(2) A lighting system for illuminating, during the hours of darkness, the area around the vault, if the vault is visible from outside the banking office;

(3) Tamper-resistant locks on exterior doors and exterior windows designed to be opened;

(4) An alarm system or other appropriate device for promptly notifying the nearest responsible law enforcement officers of an attempted or perpetrated robbery, burglary or larceny; and

(5) Such other devices as the security officer determines to be appropriate, taking into consideration:

(i) The incidence of crimes against financial institutions in the area;

(ii) The amount of currency or other valuables exposed to robbery, burglary, or larceny;

(iii) The distance of the banking office from the nearest responsible law enforcement officers and the time required for such law enforcement officers ordinarily to arrive at the banking office;

(iv) The cost of the security devices;

(v) Other security measures in effect at the banking office; and

(vi) The physical characteristics of the banking office structure and its surroundings.

§ 21.4 Report.

The security officer for a national bank shall report at least annually to the bank's board of directors on the effectiveness of the security program. The substance of such report shall be reflected in the minutes of the Board meeting in which it is given.

(Approved by the Office of Management and Budget under control number 1557–0180)

Subpart B—Reports of Suspicious Activities

§ 21.11 Suspicious Activity Report.

(a) *Purpose and scope.* This section ensures that national banks file a Suspicious Activity Report when they detect a known or suspected violation of Federal law or a suspicious transaction related to a money laundering activity or a violation of the Bank Secrecy Act. This section applies to all national banks as well as any Federal branches and agencies of foreign banks licensed or chartered by the OCC.

(b) *Definitions.* For the purposes of this section:

(1) *FinCEN* means the Financial Crimes Enforcement Network of the Department of the Treasury.

(2) *Institution-affiliated party* means any institution-affiliated party as that term is defined in sections 3(u) and 8(b)(5) of the Federal Deposit Insurance Act (12 U.S.C. 1813(u) and 1818(b)(5)).

(3) *SAR* means a Suspicious Activity Report.

(c) *SARs required.* A national bank shall file a SAR with the appropriate Federal law enforcement agencies and the Department of the Treasury on the form prescribed by the OCC and in accordance with the form's instructions. The bank shall send the completed SAR to FinCEN in the following circumstances:

(1) *Insider abuse involving any amount.* Whenever the national bank detects any known or suspected Federal criminal violation, or pattern of criminal violations, committed or attempted against the bank or involving a transaction or transactions conducted through the bank, where the bank believes that it was either an actual or potential victim of a criminal violation, or series of criminal violations, or that the bank was used to facilitate a criminal transaction, and the bank has a substantial basis for identifying one of its directors, officers, employees, agents or other institution-affiliated parties as having committed or aided in the commission of a criminal act, regardless of the amount involved in the violation.

(2) *Violations aggregating $5,000 or more where a suspect can be identified.* Whenever the national bank detects any known or suspected Federal criminal violation, or pattern of criminal violations, committed or attempted against the bank or involving a transaction or transactions conducted through the bank and involving or aggregating $5,000 or more in funds or other assets where the bank believes that it was either an actual or potential victim of a criminal violation, or series of criminal violations or that it was used to facilitate a criminal transaction, and the bank has a substantial basis for identifying a possible suspect or group of suspects. If it is determined prior to filing this report that the identified suspect or group of suspects has used an alias, then information regarding the true identity of the suspect or group of suspects, as well as alias identifiers, such as drivers' license or social security numbers, addresses and telephone numbers, must be reported.

(3) *Violations aggregating $25,000 or more regardless of potential suspects.* Whenever the national bank detects any known or suspected Federal criminal violation, or pattern of criminal violations, committed or attempted against the bank or involving a transaction or transactions conducted through the bank and involving or aggregating $25,000 or more in funds or other assets where the bank believes that it was either an actual or potential victim of a criminal violation, or series of criminal violations, or that the bank was used to facilitate a criminal transaction, even though there is no substantial basis for identifying a possible suspect or group of suspects.

(4) *Transactions aggregating $5,000 or more that involve potential money laundering or violate the Bank Secrecy Act.* Any transaction (which for purposes of this paragraph (c)(4) means a deposit, withdrawal, transfer between accounts, exchange of currency, loan, extension of credit, or purchase or sale of any stock, bond, certificate of deposit, or other monetary instrument or investment security, or any other payment, transfer, or delivery by, through, or to a financial institution, by whatever means effected) conducted or attempted by, at or through the national bank and involving or aggregating $5,000 or more in funds or other assets, if the bank knows, suspects, or has reason to suspect that:

(i) The transaction involves funds derived from illegal activities or is intended or conducted in order to hide or disguise funds or assets derived from illegal activities (including, without limitation, the ownership, nature, source, location, or control of such funds or assets) as part of a plan to violate or evade any law or regulation or to avoid any transaction reporting requirement under Federal law;

(ii) The transaction is designed to evade any regulations promulgated under the Bank Secrecy Act; or

(iii) The transaction has no business or apparent lawful purpose or is not the sort in which the particular customer would normally be expected to engage, and the institution knows of no reasonable explanation for the transaction after examining the available facts, including the background and possible purpose of the transaction.

(d) *Time for reporting.* A national bank is required to file a SAR no later than 30 calendar days after the date of the initial detection of facts that may constitute a basis for filing a SAR. If no suspect was identified on the date of detection of the incident requiring the filing, a national bank may delay filing a SAR for an additional 30 calendar days to identify a suspect. In no case shall reporting be delayed more than 60 calendar days after the date of initial detection of a reportable transaction. In situations involving violations requiring immediate attention, such as when a reportable violation is ongoing, the financial institution shall immediately notify, by telephone, an appropriate law enforcement authority and the OCC in addition to filing a timely SAR.

(e) *Reports to state and local authorities.* National banks are encouraged to file a copy of the SAR with state and local law enforcement agencies where appropriate.

(f) *Exceptions.* (1) A national bank need not file a SAR for a robbery or burglary committed or attempted that is reported to appropriate law enforcement authorities.

(2) A national bank need not file a SAR for lost, missing, counterfeit, or stolen securities if it files a report pursuant to the reporting requirements of 17 CFR 240.17f–1.

(g) *Retention of records.* A national bank shall maintain a copy of any SAR filed and the original or business record equivalent of any supporting documentation for a period of five years from the date of the filing of the SAR. Supporting documentation shall be identified and maintained by the bank as such, and shall be deemed to have been filed with the SAR. A national bank shall make all supporting documentation available to appropriate law enforcement agencies upon request.

(h) *Notification to board of directors*—(1) *Generally.* Whenever a national bank files a SAR pursuant to this section, the management of the bank shall promptly notify its board of directors, or a committee of directors or executive officers designated by the board of directors to receive notice.

(2) *Suspect is a director or executive officer.* If the bank files a SAR pursuant to paragraph (c) of this section and the suspect is a director or executive officer, the bank may not notify the suspect, pursuant to 31 U.S.C. 5318(g)(2), but shall notify all directors who are not suspects.

(i) *Compliance.* Failure to file a SAR in accordance with this section and the instructions may subject the national bank, its directors, officers, employees, agents, or other institution-affiliated parties to supervisory action.

(j) *Obtaining SARs.* A national bank may obtain SARs and the Instructions from the appropriate OCC District Office listed in 12 CFR part 4.

(k) *Confidentiality of SARs.* A SAR, and any information that would reveal the existence of a SAR, are confidential, and shall not be disclosed except as authorized in this paragraph (k).

(1) *Prohibition on disclosure by national banks*—(i) *General rule.* No national bank, and no director, officer, employee, or agent of a national bank, shall disclose a SAR or any information that would reveal the existence of a SAR. Any national bank, and any director, officer, employee, or agent of any national bank that is subpoenaed or otherwise requested to disclose a SAR, or any information that would reveal the existence of a SAR, shall decline to produce the SAR or such information, citing this section and 31 U.S.C. 5318(g)(2)(A)(i), and shall notify the following of any such request and the response thereto:

(A) Director, Litigation Division, Office of the Comptroller of the Currency; and

(B) The Financial Crimes Enforcement Network (FinCEN).

(ii) *Rules of construction.* Provided that no person involved in any reported suspicious transaction is notified that the transaction has been reported, this paragraph (k)(1) shall not be construed as prohibiting:

(A) The disclosure by a national bank, or any director, officer, employee or agent of a national bank of:

(*1*) A SAR, or any information that would reveal the existence of a SAR, to the OCC, FinCEN, or any Federal, State, or local law enforcement agency; or

(*2*) The underlying facts, transactions, and documents upon which a SAR is based, including, but not limited to, disclosures:

(*i*) To another financial institution, or any director, officer, employee or agent of a financial institution, for the preparation of a joint SAR; or

(*ii*) In connection with certain employment references or termination notices, to the full extent authorized in 31 U.S.C. 5318(g)(2)(B); or

(B) The sharing by a national bank, or any director, officer, employee, or agent of a national bank, of a SAR, or any information that would reveal the existence of a SAR, within the bank's corporate organizational structure for purposes consistent with title II of the Bank Secrecy Act as determined by regulation or in guidance.

(2) *Prohibition on disclosure by the OCC.* The OCC will not, and no officer, employee or agent of the OCC, shall disclose a SAR, or any information that would reveal the existence of a SAR, except as necessary to fulfill official duties consistent with title II of the Bank Secrecy Act. For purposes of this section, official duties shall not include the disclosure of a SAR, or any information that would reveal the existence of a SAR, in response to a request for use in a private legal proceeding or in response to a request for disclosure of non-public OCC information under 12 CFR 4.33.

(l) *Limitation on liability.* A national bank and any director, officer, employee or agent of a national bank that makes a voluntary disclosure of any possible violation of law or regulation to a government agency or makes a disclosure pursuant to this section or any other authority, including a disclosure made jointly with another financial institution, shall be protected from liability to any person for any such disclosure, or for failure to provide notice of such disclosure to any person identified in the disclosure, or both, to the full extent provided by 31 U.S.C. 5318(g)(3).

[61 FR 4337, Feb. 5, 1996, as amended at 75 FR 75583, Dec. 3, 2010]

Subpart C—Procedures for Monitoring Bank Secrecy Act Compliance

§ 21.21 Procedures for monitoring Bank Secrecy Act (BSA) compliance.

(a) *Purpose.* This subpart is issued to assure that all national banks and savings associations establish and maintain procedures reasonably designed to assure and monitor their compliance with the requirements of subchapter II of chapter 53 of title 31, United States Code, and the implementing regulations promulgated thereunder by the Department of the Treasury at 31 CFR Chapter X.

(b) *Definition of savings association.* For purposes of this subpart C, the term *savings association* means a savings association as defined in section 3 of the Federal Deposit Insurance Act (FDI Act), the deposits of which are insured by the Federal Deposit Insurance Corporation. It includes a Federal savings association or Federal savings bank, chartered under section 5 of the FDI Act, or a building and loan, savings and loan, or homestead association, or a cooperative bank (other than a cooperative bank which is a state bank as defined in section 3(a)(2) of the FDI Act) organized and operating according to the laws of the state in which it is chartered or organized, or a corporation (other than a bank as defined in section 3(a)(1) of the FDI Act) that the Board of Directors of the Federal Deposit Insurance Corporation and the Comptroller jointly determine to be operating substantially in the same manner as a savings association.

(c) *Establishment of a BSA compliance program*—(1) *Program requirement.* Each national bank and each savings association shall develop and provide for the continued administration of a program reasonably designed to assure and monitor compliance with the recordkeeping and reporting requirements set forth in subchapter II of chapter 53 of title 31, United States Code and the implementing regulations issued by the Department of the Treasury at 31 CFR Chapter X. The compliance program must be written, approved by the national bank's or savings association's board of directors, and reflected in the minutes of the national bank or savings association.

(2) *Customer identification program.* Each national bank and each savings association is subject to the requirements of 31 U.S.C. 5318(l) and the implementing regulations jointly promulgated by the OCC and the Department of the Treasury at 31 CFR 1020.220, which require a customer identification program to be implemented as part of the BSA compliance program required under this section.

(d) *Contents of compliance program.* The compliance program shall, at a minimum:

(1) Provide for a system of internal controls to assure ongoing compliance;

(2) Provide for independent testing for compliance to be conducted by national bank or savings association personnel or by an outside party;

(3) Designate an individual or individuals responsible for coordinating and monitoring day-to-day compliance; and

(4) Provide training for appropriate personnel.

(Approved by the Office of Management and Budget under control number 1557–0180)

[52 FR 2859, Jan. 27, 1987, as amended at 68 FR 25111, May 9, 2003; 76 FR 6687, Feb. 8, 2011; 79 FR 28399, May 16, 2014]

PART 22—LOANS IN AREAS HAVING SPECIAL FLOOD HAZARDS

Sec.

22.1 Purpose and scope.
22.2 Definitions.
22.3 Requirement to purchase flood insurance where available.
22.4 Exemptions.
22.5 Escrow requirement.
22.6 Required use of standard flood hazard determination form.
22.7 Force placement of flood insurance.
22.8 Determination fees.
22.9 Notice of special flood hazards and availability of Federal disaster relief assistance.
22.10 Notice of servicer's identity.
APPENDIX A TO PART 22—SAMPLE FORM OF NOTICE OF SPECIAL FLOOD HAZARDS AND AVAILABILITY OF FEDERAL DISASTER RELIEF ASSISTANCE
APPENDIX B TO PART 22—SAMPLE CLAUSE FOR OPTION TO ESCROW FOR OUTSTANDING LOANS

AUTHORITY: 12 U.S.C. 93a, 1462a, 1463, 1464, and 5412(b)(2)(B); 42 U.S.C. 4012a, 4104a, 4104b, 4106, and 4128.

SOURCE: 80 FR 43240, July 21, 2015, unless otherwise noted.

§ 22.1 Purpose and scope.

(a) *Purpose.* The purpose of this part is to implement the requirements of the National Flood Insurance Act of 1968 and the Flood Disaster Protection Act of 1973, as amended (42 U.S.C. 4001–4129).

(b) *Scope.* This part, except for §§ 22.6 and 22.8, applies to loans secured by buildings or mobile homes located or to be located in areas determined by the Administrator of the Federal Emergency Management Agency to have special flood hazards. Sections 22.6 and 22.8 apply to loans secured by buildings or mobile homes, regardless of location.

§ 22.2 Definitions.

For purposes of this part:

(a) *Act* means the National Flood Insurance Act of 1968, as amended (42 U.S.C. 4001–4129).

(b) *Administrator of FEMA* means the Administrator of the Federal Emergency Management Agency.

(c) *Building* means a walled and roofed structure, other than a gas or liquid storage tank, that is principally above ground and affixed to a permanent site, and a walled and roofed structure while in the course of construction, alteration, or repair.

(d) *Community* means a State or a political subdivision of a State that has zoning and building code jurisdiction over a particular area having special flood hazards.

(e) *Designated loan* means a loan secured by a building or mobile home that is located or to be located in a special flood hazard area in which flood insurance is available under the Act.

(f) *Federal savings association* means, for purposes of this part, a Federal savings association as that term is defined in 12 U.S.C. 1813(b)(2) and any service corporations thereof.

(g) *Mobile home* means a structure, transportable in one or more sections, that is built on a permanent chassis and designed for use with or without a permanent foundation when attached to the required utilities. The term *mobile home* does not include a recreational vehicle. For purposes of this part, the term *mobile home* means a mobile home on a permanent foundation. The term *mobile home* includes a manufactured home as that term is used in the NFIP.

(h) *National bank* means a national bank or a Federal branch or agency of a foreign bank.

(i) *NFIP* means the National Flood Insurance Program authorized under the Act.

(j) *Residential improved real estate* means real estate upon which a home or other residential building is located or to be located.

(k) *Servicer* means the person responsible for:

(1) Receiving any scheduled, periodic payments from a borrower under the terms of a loan, including amounts for taxes, insurance premiums, and other charges with respect to the property securing the loan; and

(2) Making payments of principal and interest and any other payments from the amounts received from the borrower as may be required under the terms of the loan.

(l) *Special flood hazard area* means the land in the flood plain within a community having at least a one percent chance of flooding in any given year, as designated by the Administrator of FEMA.

(m) *Table funding* means a settlement at which a loan is funded by a contemporaneous advance of loan funds and an assignment of the loan to the person advancing the funds.

§ 22.3 Requirement to purchase flood insurance where available.

(a) *In general.* A national bank or Federal savings association shall not make, increase, extend, or renew any designated loan unless the building or mobile home and any personal property securing the loan is covered by flood insurance for the term of the loan. The amount of insurance must be at least equal to the lesser of the outstanding principal balance of the designated loan or the maximum limit of coverage available for the particular type of property under the Act. Flood insurance coverage under the Act is limited to the building or mobile home and any personal property that secures a loan and not the land itself.

(b) *Table funded loans.* A national bank or Federal savings association that acquires a loan from a mortgage broker or other entity through table funding shall be considered to be making a loan for the purposes of this part.

§ 22.4 Exemptions.

The flood insurance requirement prescribed by § 22.3 does not apply with respect to:

(a) Any State-owned property covered under a policy of self-insurance satisfactory to the Administrator of FEMA, who publishes and periodically revises the list of States falling within this exemption;

(b) Property securing any loan with an original principal balance of $5,000 or less and a repayment term of one year or less; or

(c) Any structure that is a part of any residential property but is detached from the primary residential structure of such property and does not serve as a residence. For purposes of this paragraph (c):

(1) "A structure that is a part of a residential property" is a structure used primarily for personal, family, or household purposes, and not used primarily for agricultural, commercial, industrial, or other business purposes;

(2) A structure is "detached" from the primary residential structure if it is not joined by any structural connection to that structure; and

(3) "Serve as a residence" shall be based upon the good faith determination of the national bank or Federal

savings association that the structure is intended for use or actually used as a residence, which generally includes sleeping, bathroom, or kitchen facilities.

§ 22.5 Escrow requirement.

(a) *In general*—(1) *Applicability.* Except as provided in paragraphs (a)(2) or (c) of this section, a national bank or a Federal savings association, or a servicer acting on its behalf, shall require the escrow of all premiums and fees for any flood insurance required under § 22.3(a) for any designated loan secured by residential improved real estate or a mobile home that is made, increased, extended, or renewed on or after January 1, 2016, payable with the same frequency as payments on the designated loan are required to be made for the duration of the loan.

(2) *Exceptions.* Paragraph (a)(1) of this section does not apply if:

(i) The loan is an extension of credit primarily for business, commercial, or agricultural purposes;

(ii) The loan is in a subordinate position to a senior lien secured by the same residential improved real estate or mobile home for which the borrower has obtained flood insurance coverage that meets the requirements of § 22.3(a);

(iii) Flood insurance coverage for the residential improved real estate or mobile home is provided by a policy that:

(A) Meets the requirements of § 22.3(a);

(B) Is provided by a condominium association, cooperative, homeowners association, or other applicable group; and

(C) The premium for which is paid by the condominium association, cooperative, homeowners association, or other applicable group as a common expense;

(iv) The loan is a home equity line of credit;

(v) The loan is a nonperforming loan, which is a loan that is 90 or more days past due and remains nonperforming until it is permanently modified or until the entire amount past due, including principal, accrued interest, and penalty interest incurred as the result of past due status, is collected or otherwise discharged in full; or

(vi) The loan has a term of no longer than 12 months.

(3) *Duration of exception.* If a national bank or Federal savings association, or a servicer acting its behalf, determines at any time during the term of a designated loan secured by residential improved real estate or a mobile home that is made, increased, extended, or renewed on or after January 1, 2016, that an exception under paragraph (a)(2) of this section does not apply, then the bank or savings association, or the servicer acting on its behalf, shall require the escrow of all premiums and fees for any flood insurance required under § 22.3(a) as soon as reasonably practicable and, if applicable, shall provide any disclosure required under section 10 of the Real Estate Settlement Procedures Act of 1974 (12 U.S.C. 2609) (RESPA).

(4) *Escrow account.* The national bank or Federal savings association, or a servicer acting on its behalf, shall deposit the flood insurance premiums and fees on behalf of the borrower in an escrow account. This escrow account will be subject to escrow requirements adopted pursuant to section 10 of RESPA, which generally limits the amount that may be maintained in escrow accounts for certain types of loans and requires escrow account statements for those accounts, only if the loan is otherwise subject to RESPA. Following receipt of a notice from the Administrator of FEMA or other provider of flood insurance that premiums are due, the national bank or Federal savings association, or a servicer acting on its behalf, shall pay the amount owed to the insurance provider from the escrow account by the date when such premiums are due.

(b) *Notice.* For any loan for which a national bank or Federal savings association is required to escrow under paragraphs (a)(1) or (c)(2) of this section or may be required to escrow under paragraphs (a)(3) of this section during the term of the loan, the national bank or Federal savings association, or a servicer acting on its behalf, shall mail or deliver a written notice with the notice provided under § 22.9 informing the borrower that the national bank or Federal savings association is required to escrow all premiums and fees for required flood insurance, using language that is substantially similar to model clauses on the escrow requirement in appendix A to this part.

(c) *Small lender exception*—(1) *Qualification.* Except as may be required under applicable State law, paragraphs (a), (b), and (d) of this section do not apply to a national bank or Federal savings association:

(i) That has total assets of less than $1 billion as of December 31 of either of the two prior calendar years; and

(ii) On or before July 6, 2012:

(A) Was not required under Federal or State law to deposit taxes, insurance premiums, fees, or any other charges in an escrow account for the entire term of any loan secured by residential improved real estate or a mobile home; and

(B) Did not have a policy of consistently and uniformly requiring the deposit of taxes, insurance premiums, fees, or any other charges in an escrow account for any loans secured by residential improved real estate or a mobile home.

(2) *Change in status.* If a national bank or Federal savings association previously qualified for the exception in paragraph (c)(1) of this section, but no longer qualifies for the exception because it had assets of $1 billion or more for two consecutive calendar year ends, the national bank or Federal savings association must escrow premiums and fees for flood insurance pursuant to paragraph (a) of this section for any designated loan made, increased, extended, or renewed on or after July 1 of the first calendar year of changed status.

(d) *Option to escrow*—(1) *In general.* A national bank or Federal savings association, or a servicer acting on its behalf, shall offer and make available to the borrower the option to escrow all premiums and fees for any flood insurance required under § 22.3 for any loan secured by residential improved real estate or a mobile home that is outstanding on January 1, 2016, or July 1 of the first calendar year in which the national bank or Federal savings association has had a change in status pursuant to paragraph (c)(2) of this section, unless:

(i) The loan or the national bank or Federal savings association qualifies for an exception from the escrow requirement under paragraphs (a)(2) or (c) of this section, respectively;

(ii) The borrower is already escrowing all premiums and fees for flood insurance for the loan; or

(iii) The national bank or Federal savings association is required to escrow flood insurance premiums and fees pursuant to paragraph (a) of this section.

(2) *Notice.* For any loan subject to paragraph (d) of this section, the national bank or Federal savings association, or a servicer acting on its behalf, shall mail or deliver to the borrower no later than June 30, 2016, or September 30 of the first calendar year in which the national bank or Federal savings association has had a change in status pursuant to paragraph (c)(2) of this section, a notice in writing, or if the borrower agrees, electronically, informing the borrower of the option to escrow all premiums and fees for any required flood insurance and the method(s) by which the borrower may request the escrow, using language similar to the model clause in appendix B.

(3) *Timing.* The national bank or Federal savings association or the servicer acting on its behalf, must begin escrowing premiums and fees for flood insurance as soon as reasonably practicable after the bank or savings association, or servicer, receives the borrower's request to escrow.

[80 FR 43243, July 21, 2015]

§ 22.6 Required use of standard flood hazard determination form.

(a) *Use of form.* A national bank or Federal savings association shall use the standard flood hazard determination form developed by the Administrator of FEMA when determining whether the building or mobile home offered as collateral security for a loan is or will be located in a special flood hazard area in which flood insurance is available under the Act. The standard flood hazard determination form may be used in a printed, computerized, or electronic manner. A national bank or Federal savings association may obtain the standard flood hazard determination form from FEMA's Web site at *www.fema.gov.*

(b) *Retention of form.* A national bank or Federal savings association shall retain a copy of the completed standard flood hazard determination form, in either hard copy or electronic form, for the period of time the bank or savings association owns the loan.

§ 22.7 Force placement of flood insurance.

(a) *Notice and purchase of coverage.* If a national bank or Federal savings association, or a servicer acting on behalf of the bank or savings association, determines at any time during the term of a designated loan, that the building or mobile home and any personal property securing the designated loan is not covered by flood insurance or is covered by flood insurance in an amount less than the amount required under § 22.3, then the national bank or Federal savings association, or a servicer acting on its behalf, shall notify the borrower that the borrower should obtain flood insurance, at the borrower's expense, in an amount at least equal to the amount required under § 22.3, for the remaining term of the loan. If the borrower fails to obtain flood insurance within 45 days after notification, then the national bank or Federal savings association, or its servicer, shall purchase insurance on the borrower's behalf. The national bank or Federal savings association, or its servicer, may charge the borrower for the cost of premiums and fees incurred in purchasing the insurance, including premiums or fees incurred for coverage beginning on the date on which flood insurance coverage lapsed or did not provide a sufficient coverage amount.

(b) *Termination of force-placed insurance*—(1) *Termination and refund.* Within 30 days of receipt by a national bank or Federal savings association, or by a servicer acting on its behalf, of a confirmation of a borrower's existing flood insurance coverage, the national bank or Federal savings association, or its servicer, shall:

(i) Notify the insurance provider to terminate any insurance purchased by the national bank or Federal savings association, or its servicer, under paragraph (a) of this section; and

(ii) Refund to the borrower all premiums paid by the borrower for any insurance purchased by the national bank or Federal savings association, or by its servicer, under paragraph (a) of this section during any period during which the borrower's flood insurance coverage and the insurance coverage purchased by the national bank or Federal savings association, or its servicer, were each in effect, and any related fees charged to the borrower with respect to the insurance purchased by the national bank or Federal savings association, or its servicer, during such period.

(2) *Sufficiency of demonstration.* For purposes of confirming a borrower's existing flood insurance coverage under paragraph (b) of this section, a national bank or Federal savings association, or a servicer acting on its behalf, shall accept from the borrower an insurance policy declarations page that includes the existing flood insurance policy number and the identity of, and contact information for, the insurance company or agent.

§ 22.8 Determination fees.

(a) *General.* Notwithstanding any Federal or State law other than the Flood Disaster Protection Act of 1973, as amended (42 U.S.C. 4001–4129), any national bank or Federal savings association, or a servicer acting on behalf of the national bank or Federal savings association, may charge a reasonable fee for determining whether the building or mobile home securing the loan is located or will be located in a special flood hazard area. A determination fee may also include, but is not limited to, a fee for life-of-loan monitoring.

(b) *Borrower fee.* The determination fee authorized by paragraph (a) of this section may be charged to the borrower if the determination:

(1) Is made in connection with a making, increasing, extending, or renewing of the loan that is initiated by the borrower;

(2) Reflects the Administrator of FEMA's revision or updating of flood plain areas or flood-risk zones;

(3) Reflects the Administrator of FEMA's publication of a notice or compendium that:

(i) Affects the area in which the building or mobile home securing the loan is located; or

(ii) By determination of the Administrator of FEMA, may reasonably require a determination whether the building or mobile home securing the loan is located in a special flood hazard area; or

(4) Results in the purchase of flood insurance coverage by the lender, or its servicer, on behalf of the borrower under §22.7.

(c) *Purchaser or transferee fee.* The determination fee authorized by paragraph (a) of this section may be charged to the purchaser or transferee of a loan in the case of the sale or transfer of the loan.

§22.9 Notice of special flood hazards and availability of Federal disaster relief assistance.

(a) *Notice requirement.* When a national bank or Federal savings association makes, increases, extends, or renews a loan secured by a building or a mobile home located or to be located in a special flood hazard area, the bank or savings association shall mail or deliver a written notice to the borrower and to the servicer in all cases whether or not flood insurance is available under the Act for the collateral securing the loan.

(b) *Contents of notice.* The written notice must include the following information:

(1) A warning, in a form approved by the Administrator of FEMA, that the building or the mobile home is or will be located in a special flood hazard area;

(2) A description of the flood insurance purchase requirements set forth in section 102(b) of the Flood Disaster Protection Act of 1973, as amended (42 U.S.C. 4012a(b));

(3) A statement, where applicable, that flood insurance coverage is available from private insurance companies that issue standard flood insurance policies on behalf of the NFIP or directly from the NFIP;

(4) A statement that flood insurance that provides the same level of coverage as a standard flood insurance policy under the NFIP also may be available from a private insurance company that issues policies on behalf of the company;

(5) A statement that the borrower is encouraged to compare the flood insurance coverage, deductibles, exclusions, conditions, and premiums associated with flood insurance policies issued on behalf of the NFIP and policies issued on behalf of private insurance companies and that the borrower should direct inquiries regarding the availability, cost, and comparisons of flood insurance coverage to an insurance agent; and

(6) A statement whether Federal disaster relief assistance may be available in the event of damage to the building or mobile home caused by flooding in a Federally declared disaster.

(c) *Timing of notice.* The national bank or Federal savings association shall provide the notice required by paragraph (a) of this section to the borrower within a reasonable time before the completion of the transaction, and to the servicer as promptly as practicable after the bank or savings association provides notice to the borrower and in any event no later than the time the bank or savings association provides other similar notices to the servicer concerning hazard insurance and taxes. Notice to the servicer may be made electronically or may take the form of a copy of the notice to the borrower.

(d) *Record of receipt.* The national bank or Federal savings association shall retain a record of the receipt of the notices by the borrower and the servicer for the period of time it owns the loan.

(e) *Alternate method of notice.* Instead of providing the notice to the borrower required by paragraph (a) of this section, a national bank or Federal savings association may obtain satisfactory written assurance from a seller or lessor that, within a reasonable time before the completion of the sale or lease transaction, the seller or lessor has provided such notice to the purchaser or lessee. The national bank or Federal savings association shall retain a record of the written assurance from the seller or lessor for the period of time it owns the loan.

(f) *Use of sample form of notice.* A national bank or Federal savings association will be considered to be in compliance with the requirement for notice to the borrower of this section by providing written notice to the borrower containing the language presented in appendix A to this part within a reasonable time before the completion of the transaction. The notice presented in appendix A to this part satisfies the borrower notice requirements of the Act.

[80 FR 43240, July 21, 2015, as amended at 80 FR 43244, July 21, 2015]

§ 22.10 Notice of servicer's identity.

(a) *Notice requirement.* When a national bank or Federal savings association makes, increases, extends, renews, sells, or transfers a loan secured by a building or mobile home located or to be located in a special flood hazard area, it shall notify the Administrator of FEMA (or the Administrator's designee) in writing of the identity of the servicer of the loan. The Administrator of FEMA has designated the insurance provider to receive the national bank's or Federal savings association's notice of the servicer's identity. This notice may be provided electronically if electronic transmission is satisfactory to the Administrator of FEMA's designee.

(b) *Transfer of servicing rights.* The national bank or Federal savings association shall notify the Administrator of FEMA (or the Administrator's designee) of any change in the servicer of a loan described in paragraph (a) of this section within 60 days after the effective date of the change. This notice may be provided electronically if electronic transmission is satisfactory to the Administrator of FEMA's designee. Upon any change in the servicing of a loan described in paragraph (a) of this section, the duty to provide notice under this paragraph (b) shall transfer to the transferee servicer.

Appendix A to Part 22—Sample Form of Notice of Special Flood Hazards and Availability of Federal Disaster Relief Assistance

Notice of Special Flood Hazards and Availability of Federal Disaster Relief Assistance

We are giving you this notice to inform you that:

The building or mobile home securing the loan for which you have applied is or will be located in an area with special flood hazards.

The area has been identified by the Administrator of the Federal Emergency Management Agency (FEMA) as a special flood hazard area using FEMA's *Flood Insurance Rate Map* or the *Flood Hazard Boundary Map* for the following community: _____. This area has a one percent (1%) chance of a flood equal to or exceeding the base flood elevation (a 100-year flood) in any given year. During the life of a 30-year mortgage loan, the risk of a 100-year flood in a special flood hazard area is 26 percent (26%).

Federal law allows a lender and borrower jointly to request the Administrator of FEMA to review the determination of whether the property securing the loan is located in a special flood hazard area. If you would like to make such a request, please contact us for further information.

___The community in which the property securing the loan is located participates in the National Flood Insurance Program (NFIP). Federal law will not allow us to make you the loan that you have applied for if you do not purchase flood insurance. The flood insurance must be maintained for the life of the loan. If you fail to purchase or renew flood insurance on the property, Federal law authorizes and requires us to purchase the flood insurance for you at your expense.

• At a minimum, flood insurance purchased must cover *the lesser of:*

(1) the outstanding principal balance of the loan; *or*

(2) the maximum amount of coverage allowed for the type of property under the NFIP.

Flood insurance coverage under the NFIP is limited to the building or mobile home and any personal property that secures your loan and not the land itself.

• Federal disaster relief assistance (usually in the form of a low-interest loan) may be available for damages incurred in excess of your flood insurance if your community's participation in the NFIP is in accordance with NFIP requirements.

• Although you may not be required to maintain flood insurance on all structures, you may still wish to do so, and your mortgage lender may still require you to do so to protect the collateral securing the mortgage.

If you choose not to maintain flood insurance on a structure and it floods, you are responsible for all flood losses relating to that structure.

Availability of Private Flood Insurance Coverage

Flood insurance coverage under the NFIP may be purchased through an insurance agent who will obtain the policy either directly through the NFIP or through an insurance company that participates in the NFIP. Flood insurance that provides the same level of coverage as a standard flood insurance policy under the NFIP may be available from private insurers that do not participate in the NFIP. You should compare the flood insurance coverage, deductibles, exclusions, conditions, and premiums associated with flood insurance policies issued on behalf of the NFIP and policies issued on behalf of private insurance companies and contact an insurance agent as to the availability, cost, and comparisons of flood insurance coverage.

[Escrow Requirement for Residential Loans

Federal law may require a lender or its servicer to escrow all premiums and fees for flood insurance that covers any residential building or mobile home securing a loan that is located in an area with special flood hazards. If your lender notifies you that an escrow account is required for your loan, then you must pay your flood insurance premiums and fees to the lender or its servicer with the same frequency as you make loan payments for the duration of your loan. These premiums and fees will be deposited in the escrow account, which will be used to pay the flood insurance provider.]

____Flood insurance coverage under the NFIP is not available for the property securing the loan because the community in which the property is located does not participate in the NFIP. In addition, if the non-participating community has been identified for at least one year as containing a special flood hazard area, properties located in the community will not be eligible for Federal disaster relief assistance in the event of a Federally declared flood disaster.

[80 FR 43244, July 21, 2015]

APPENDIX B TO PART 22—SAMPLE CLAUSE FOR OPTION TO ESCROW FOR OUTSTANDING LOANS

Escrow Option Clause

You have the option to escrow all premiums and fees for the payment on your flood insurance policy that covers any residential building or mobile home that is located in an area with special flood hazards and that secures your loan. If you choose this option:

• Your payments will be deposited in an escrow account to be paid to the flood insurance provider.

• The escrow amount for flood insurance will be added to the regular mortgage payment that you make to your lender or its servicer.

• The payments you make into the escrow account will accumulate over time and the funds will be used to pay your flood insurance policy when your lender or servicer receives a notice from your flood insurance provider that the flood insurance premium is due.

To choose this option, follow the instructions below. If you have any questions about the option, contact [Insert Name of Lender or Servicer] at [Insert Contact Information].

[Insert Instructions for Selecting to Escrow]

[80 FR 43244, July 21, 2015]

PART 23—LEASING

Subpart A—General Provisions

Sec.
23.1 Authority, purpose, and scope.
23.2 Definitions.
23.3 Lease requirements.
23.4 Investment in personal property.
23.5 Requirement for separate records.
23.6 Application of lending limits; restrictions on transactions with affiliates.

Subpart B—CEBA Leases

23.10 General rule.
23.11 Lease term.
23.12 Transition rule.

Subpart C—Section 24(Seventh) Leases

23.20 General rule.
23.21 Estimated residual value.
23.22 Transition rule.

AUTHORITY: 12 U.S.C. 1 *et seq.*, 24(Seventh), 24(Tenth), and 93a.

SOURCE: 61 FR 66560, Dec. 18, 1996, unless otherwise noted.

Subpart A—General Provisions

§ 23.1 Authority, purpose, and scope.

(a) *Authority.* A national bank may engage in personal property lease financing transactions pursuant to 12 U.S.C. 24(Seventh) or 12 U.S.C. 24(Tenth).

(b) *Purpose.* The purpose of this part is to set forth standards for personal property lease financing transactions authorized for national banks.

(c) *Scope.* This part applies to the acquisition of personal property by a national bank for the purpose of, or in connection with, the leasing of that property.

§ 23.2 Definitions.

(a) *Affiliate* means an affiliate as described in § 23.6.

(b) *Capital and surplus* means:

(1) A bank's tier 1 and tier 2 capital calculated under the OCC's risk-based capital standards set forth in 12 CFR part 3, as applicable, as reported in the bank's Consolidated Reports of Condition and Income (Call Report) filed under 12 U.S.C. 161; plus

(2) The balance of a bank's allowance for loan and lease losses not included in the bank's Tier 2 capital, for purposes of the calculation of risk-based capital described in paragraph (b)(1) of this section, as reported in the bank's Consolidated Report of Condition and Income filed under 12 U.S.C. 161.

(c) *CEBA Lease* means a personal property lease authorized under 12 U.S.C. 24(Tenth).

(d) *Conforming lease* means:

(1) A CEBA Lease that conforms with the requirements of subparts A and B of this part; or

(2) A Section 24(Seventh) Lease that conforms with the requirements of subparts A and C of this part.

(e) *Full-payout lease* means a lease in which the national bank reasonably expects to realize the return of its full investment in the leased property, plus the estimated cost of financing the property over the term of the lease, from:

(1) Rentals;

(2) Estimated tax benefits; and

(3) The estimated residual value of the property at the expiration of the lease term.

(f) *Net lease* means a lease under which the national bank will not, directly or indirectly, provide or be obligated to provide for:

(1) Servicing, repair, or maintenance of the leased property during the lease term;

(2) Parts or accessories for the leased property;

(3) Loan of replacement or substitute property while the leased property is being serviced;

(4) Payment of insurance for the lessee, except where the lessee has failed in its contractual obligation to purchase or maintain required insurance; or

(5) Renewal of any license or registration for the property unless renewal by the bank is necessary to protect its interest as owner or financier of the property.

(g) *Off-lease property* means property that reverts to a national bank's possession or control upon the expiration of a lease or upon the default of the lessee.

(h) *Section 24(Seventh) Lease* means a personal property lease authorized under 12 U.S.C. 24(Seventh).

[61 FR 66560, Dec. 18, 1996, as amended at 79 FR 11312, Feb. 28, 2014]

§ 23.3 Lease requirements.

(a) *General requirements.* A national bank may acquire personal property for the purpose of, or in connection with leasing that property, and may engage in activities incidental thereto, if the lease qualifies as a full-payout lease and a net lease.

(b) *Exceptions*—(1) *Change in condition.* If, in good faith, a national bank believes that there has been a change in condition that threatens its financial position by increasing its exposure to loss, then the bank may:

(i) Take reasonable and appropriate action, including the actions specified in § 23.2(f), to salvage or protect the value of the leased property or its interests arising under the lease; and

(ii) Acquire or perfect title to the leased property pursuant to any existing rights.

(2) *Provisions to protect the bank's interests.* A national bank may include any provision in a lease, or make any additional agreement, to protect its financial position or investment in the event of a change in conditions that would increase its exposure to loss.

(3) *Arranging for services by a third party.* A national bank may arrange for a third party to provide any of the services enumerated in § 23.2(f) to the lessee at the expense of the lessee.

§ 23.4 Investment in personal property.

(a) *General rule.* A national bank may acquire specific property to be leased only after the bank has entered into:

(1) A conforming lease;

(2) A legally binding written agreement that indemnifies the bank against loss in connection with its acquisition of the property; or

(3) A legally binding written commitment to enter into a conforming lease.

(b) *Exception.* A national bank may acquire property to be leased without complying with the requirements of paragraph (a) of this section, if:

(1) The acquisition of the property is consistent with the leasing business then conducted by the bank or is consistent with a business plan for expansion of the bank's existing leasing business or for entry into the leasing business; and

(2) The bank's aggregate investment in property held pursuant to this paragraph (b) does not exceed 15 percent of the bank's capital and surplus.

(c) *Holding period.* At the expiration of the lease (including any renewals or extensions with the same lessee), or in the event of a default on a lease agreement prior to the expiration of the lease term, a national bank shall either liquidate the off-lease property or re-lease it under a conforming lease as soon as practicable. Liquidation or re-lease must occur not later than five years from the date that the bank acquires the legal right to possession or control of the property, except the OCC may extend the period for up to an additional five years, if the bank provides a clearly convincing demonstration why any additional holding period is necessary. The bank must value off-lease property at the lower of current fair market value or book value promptly after the property becomes off-lease property.

(d) *Bridge or interim leases.* During the holding period allowed by paragraph (c) of this section, a national bank may enter into a short-term bridge or interim lease pending the liquidation of off-lease property or the re-lease of the property under a conforming lease. A short-term bridge or interim lease must be a net lease, but need not comply with any requirement of subpart B or C of this part.

§ 23.5 Requirement for separate records.

If a national bank enters into both CEBA Leases and Section 24(Seventh) Leases, the bank's records must distinguish the CEBA Leases from the Section 24(Seventh) Leases.

§ 23.6 Application of lending limits; restrictions on transactions with affiliates.

All lease entered into pursuant to this part is subject to the lending limits prescribed by 12 U.S.C. 84, as implemented by 12 CFR part 32, or, if the lessee is an affiliate of the bank, to the restrictions on transactions with affiliates prescribed by 12 U.S.C. 371c and 371c–1 and Regulation W, 12 CFR part 223. The OCC may also determine that other limits or restrictions apply. The term affiliate means an affiliate as defined in 12 U.S.C. 371c or 371c–1, as implemented by Regulation W, 12 CFR part 223, as applicable. For the purpose of measuring compliance with the lending limits prescribed by 12 U.S.C. 84 as implemented by part 32, a national bank records the investment in a lease net of any nonrecourse debt the bank has incurred to finance the acquisition of the leased asset.

[61 FR 66560, Dec. 18, 1996, as amended at 73 FR 22244, Apr. 24, 2008]

Subpart B—CEBA Leases

§ 23.10 General rule.

Pursuant to 12 U.S.C. 24(Tenth) a national bank may invest in tangible personal property, including vehicles, manufactured homes, machinery, equipment, or furniture, for the purpose of, or in connection with leasing that property, if the aggregate book value of the property does not exceed 10 percent of the bank's consolidated assets and the related lease is a conforming lease. For the purpose of measuring compliance with the 10 percent limit prescribed by this section, a national bank records the investment in a lease entered into pursuant to this subpart net of any nonrecourse debt the bank has incurred to finance the acquisition of the leased asset.

§ 23.11 Lease term.

A CEBA Lease must have an initial term of not less than 90 days. A national bank may acquire property subject to an existing lease with a remaining maturity of less than 90 days if, at its inception, the lease was a conforming lease.

§ 23.12 Transition rule.

(a) *General rule.* A CEBA Lease entered into prior to July 22, 1991, may continue to be administered in accordance with the lease terms in effect as of that date. For purposes of applying the lending limits and the restrictions on transactions with affiliates described in § 23.6, however, a national bank that enters into a new extension of credit to a customer, including a lease, on or after July 22, 1991, shall include all outstanding leases regardless of the date on which they were made.

(b) *Renewal of non-conforming leases.* A national bank may renew a CEBA Lease that was entered into prior to July 22, 1991, and that is not a conforming lease only if the following conditions are satisfied:

(1) The bank entered into the CEBA Lease in good faith;

(2) The expiring lease contains a binding agreement requiring that the bank renew the lease at the lessee's option, and the bank cannot reasonably avoid its commitment to do so; and

(3) The bank determines in good faith, and demonstrates by appropriate documentation, that renewal of the lease is necessary to avoid financial loss and to recover its investment in, and its cost of financing, the leased property.

Subpart C—Section 24(Seventh) Leases

§ 23.20 General rule.

Pursuant to 12 U.S.C. 24(Seventh) a national bank may invest in tangible or intangible personal property, including vehicles, manufactured homes, machinery, equipment, furniture, patents, copyrights, and other intellectual property, for the purpose of, or in connection with leasing that property, if the related lease is a conforming lease representing a noncancelable obligation of the lessee (notwithstanding the possible early termination of that lease).

§ 23.21 Estimated residual value.

(a) *Recovery of investment and costs.* A national bank's estimate of the residual value of the property that the bank relies upon to satisfy the requirements of a full-payout lease, for purposes of this subpart:

(1) Must be reasonable in light of the nature of the leased property and all circumstances relevant to the transaction; and

(2) Any unguaranteed amount must not exceed 25 percent of the original cost of the property to the bank or the percentage for a particular type of property specified in published OCC guidance.

(b) *Estimated residual value subject to guarantee.* The amount of any estimated residual value guaranteed by the manufacturer, the lessee, or other third party may exceed 25 percent of the original cost of the property if the bank determines, and demonstrates by appropriate documentation, that the guarantor has the resources to meet the guarantee and the guarantor is not an affiliate of the bank.

(c) *Leases to government entities.* A bank's calculations of estimated residual value in connection with leases of personal property to Federal, State, or local governmental entities may be based on future transactions or renewals that the bank reasonably anticipates will occur.

[61 FR 66560, Dec. 18, 1996, as amended at 66 FR 34792, July 2, 2001]

§ 23.22 Transition rule.

(a) *Exclusion.* A Section 24(Seventh) Lease entered into prior to June 12, 1979, may continue to be administered in accordance with the lease terms in effect as of that date. For purposes of applying the lending limits and the restrictions on transactions with affiliates described in § 23.6, however, a national bank that enters into a new extension of credit to a customer, including a lease, on or after June 12, 1979, shall include all outstanding leases regardless of the date on which they were made.

(b) *Renewal of non-conforming leases.* A national bank may renew a Section

24(Seventh) Lease that was entered into prior to June 12, 1979, and that is not a conforming lease only if the following conditions are satisfied:

(1) The bank entered into the Section 24(Seventh) Lease in good faith;

(2) The expiring lease contains a binding agreement requiring that the bank renew the lease at the lessee's option, and the bank cannot reasonably avoid its commitment to do so; and

(3) The bank determines in good faith, and demonstrates by appropriate documentation, that renewal of the lease is necessary to avoid financial loss and to recover its investment in, and its cost of financing, the leased property.

PART 24—COMMUNITY AND ECONOMIC DEVELOPMENT ENTITIES, COMMUNITY DEVELOPMENT PROJECTS, AND OTHER PUBLIC WELFARE INVESTMENTS

Sec.

24.1 Authority, purpose, and OMB control number.
24.2 Definitions.
24.3 Public welfare investments.
24.4 Investment limits.
24.5 Public welfare investment after-the-fact notice and prior procedures.
24.6 Examples of qualifying public welfare investments.
24.7 Examination, records, and remedial action.
APPENDIX 1 TO PART 24—CD-1—NATIONAL BANK COMMUNITY DEVELOPMENT (PART 24) INVESTMENTS

AUTHORITY: 12 U.S.C. 24(Eleventh), 93a, 481 and 1818.

SOURCE: 61 FR 49660, Sept. 23, 1996, unless otherwise noted.

§ 24.1 Authority, purpose, and OMB control number.

(a) *Authority*. The Office of the Comptroller of the Currency (OCC) issues this part pursuant to its authority under 12 U.S.C. 24(Eleventh), 93a, and 481.

(b) *Purpose*. This part implements 12 U.S.C. 24 (Eleventh). It is the OCC's policy to encourage a national bank to make investments described in § 24.3, consistent with safety and soundness. This part provides the standards and procedures that apply to these investments.

(c) *OMB control number*. The collection of information requirements contained in this part were approved by the Office of Management and Budget under OMB control number 1557–0194.

(d) A national bank that makes loans or investments that are authorized under both 12 U.S.C. 24 (Eleventh) and other provisions of the Federal banking laws may do so under such other provisions without regard to the provisions of 12 U.S.C. 24 (Eleventh) or this part.

(e) Investments made, or written commitments to make investments made, prior to October 13, 2006, pursuant to 12 U.S.C. 24 (Eleventh) and this part, continue to be subject to the statutes and regulations in effect prior to the enactment of the Financial Services Regulatory Relief Act of 2006 (Pub. L. 109–351).

[61 FR 49660, Sept. 23, 1996, as amended at 64 FR 70990, Dec. 20, 1999; 68 FR 48775, Aug. 15, 2003; 73 FR 22244, Apr. 24, 2008]

§ 24.2 Definitions.

For purposes of this part, the following definitions apply:

(a) *Adequately capitalized* has the same meaning as adequately capitalized in 12 CFR 6.4.

(b) *Capital and surplus* means:

(1) A bank's tier 1 and tier 2 capital calculated under the OCC's risk-based capital standards set forth in 12 CFR part 3, as applicable, as reported in the bank's Consolidated Reports of Condition and Income (Call Report) as filed under 12 U.S.C. 161; plus

(2) The balance of a bank's allowance for loan and lease losses not included in the bank's tier 2 capital, for purposes of the calculation of risk-based capital described in paragraph (b)(1) of this section, as reported in the bank's Call Report as filed under 12 U.S.C. 161.

(c) *Community and economic development entity* (CEDE) means an entity that makes investments or conducts activities that primarily benefit low- and moderate-income individuals, low- and moderate-income areas, or other areas targeted by a governmental entity for redevelopment, or would receive consideration as "qualified investments" under 12 CFR 25.23. The following is a non-exclusive list of examples of the types of entities that may be CEDEs:

(1) National bank community development corporation subsidiaries;

(2) Private or nonbank community development corporations;

(3) CDFI Fund-certified Community Development Financial Institutions or Community Development Entities;

(4) Limited liability companies or limited partnerships;

(5) Community development loan funds or lending consortia;

(6) Community development real estate investment trusts;

(7) Business development companies;

(8) Community development closed-end mutual funds;

(9) Non-diversified closed-end investment companies; and

(10) Community development venture or equity capital funds.

(d) *Community development Project (CD Project)* means a project to make an investment that meets the requirements of § 24.3.

(e) *Eligible bank* means, for purposes of § 24.5, a national bank that:

(1) Is well capitalized;

(2) Has a composite rating of 1 or 2 under the Uniform Financial Institutions Rating System;

(3) Has a Community Reinvestment Act (CRA) rating of "Outstanding" or "Satisfactory"; and

(4) Is not subject to a cease and desist order, consent order, formal written agreement, or Prompt Corrective Action directive (*see* 12 CFR part 6, subpart B) or, if subject to any such order, agreement or directive, is informed in writing by the OCC that the bank may be treated as an "eligible bank" for purposes of this part.

(f) *Low-income and moderate-income* have the same meanings as "low-income" and "moderate-income" in 12 CFR 25.12(m).

(g) *Significant risk to the deposit insurance fund* means a substantial probability that any Federal deposit insurance fund could suffer a loss.

(h) *Small business* means a business, including a small farm or minority-owned small business, that meets the qualifications for Small Business Administration Development Company or Small Business Investment Company loan programs in 13 CFR 121.301.

(i) *Well capitalized* has the same meaning as well capitalized in 12 CFR 6.4.

[61 FR 49660, Sept. 23, 1996, as amended at 68 FR 48775, Aug. 15, 2003; 73 FR 22244, Apr. 24, 2008; 73 FR 46534, Aug. 11, 2008; 79 FR 11312, Feb. 28, 2014]

§ 24.3 Public welfare investments.

A national bank or national bank subsidiary may make an investment directly or indirectly under this part if the investment primarily benefits low- and moderate income individuals, low- and moderate income areas, or other areas targeted by a governmental entity for redevelopment, or the investment would receive consideration under 12 CFR 25.23 as a "qualified investment."

[73 FR 46534, Aug. 11, 2008]

§ 24.4 Investment limits.

(a) *Limits on aggregate outstanding investments.* A national bank's aggregate outstanding investments under this part may not exceed 5 percent of its capital and surplus, unless the bank is at least adequately capitalized and the OCC determines, by written approval of a written request by the bank to exceed the 5 percent limit, that a higher amount of investments will not pose a significant risk to the deposit insurance fund. In no case may a bank's aggregate outstanding investments under this part exceed 15 percent of its capital and surplus. When calculating the aggregate amount of its aggregate outstanding investments under this part, a national bank should follow generally accepted accounting principles, unless otherwise directed or permitted in writing by the OCC for prudential or safety and soundness reasons.

(b) *Limited liability.* A national bank may not make an investment under this part that would expose the bank to unlimited liability.

[61 FR 49660, Sept. 23, 1996, as amended at 64 FR 70991, Dec. 20, 1999; 68 FR 48776, Aug. 15, 2003; 73 FR 22244, Apr. 24, 2008]

§ 24.5 Public welfare investment after-the-fact notice and prior approval procedures.

(a) *After-the-fact notice of public welfare investments.* (1) Subject to § 24.4(a), an eligible bank may make an investment authorized by 12 U.S.C. 24 (Eleventh) and this part without prior notification to, or approval by, the OCC if the bank follows the after-the-fact notice procedures described in this section.

(2) An eligible bank shall provide an after-the-fact notification of an investment, within 10 working days after it makes the investment, to the Community Affairs Department, Office of the Comptroller of the Currency, Washington, DC 20219. The after-the-fact notification may also be e-mailed to *CommunityAffairs@occ.treas.gov*, faxed to (202) 649–5709, or provided electronically via National BankNet at *www.occ.gov*.

(3) The bank's after-the-fact-notice must include:

(i) A description of the bank's investment;

(ii) The amount of the investment;

(iii) The percentage of the bank's capital and surplus represented by the investment that is the subject of the notice and by the bank's aggregate outstanding public welfare investments and commitments, including the investment that is the subject of the notice; and

(iv) A statement certifying that the investment complies with the requirements of §§ 24.3 and 24.4.

(4) A bank may satisfy the notice requirements of paragraph (3) of this section by completing form CD–1, attached as appendix 1 to this part.

(5) A national bank that is not an eligible bank but that is at least adequately capitalized, and has a composite rating of at least 3 with improving trends under the Uniform Financial Institutions Rating System, may submit a letter to the Community Affairs Department requesting authority to submit after-the-fact notices of its investments. The Community Affairs Department considers these requests on a case-by-case basis.

(6) Notwithstanding the provisions of this section, a bank may not submit an after-the-fact notice of an investment if:

(i) The investment involves properties carried on the bank's books as "other real estate owned"; or

(ii) The OCC determines, in published guidance, that the investment is inappropriate for after-the-fact notice.

(b) *Investments requiring prior approval.* (1) If a national bank does not meet the requirements for after-the-fact investment notification set forth in this part, the bank must submit an investment proposal to the Community Affairs Department, Office of the Comptroller of the Currency, Washington, DC 20219. The investment proposal may also be e-mailed to *CommunityAffairs@occ.treas.gov*, faxed to (202) 874–4652, or submitted electronically via National BankNet at *www.occ.gov*. The bank may use form CD–1, attached to this part as appendix 1, to satisfy this requirement.

(2) The bank's investment proposal must include:

(i) A description of the bank's investment;

(ii) The amount of the investment;

(iii) The percentage of the bank's capital and surplus represented by the proposed investment and by the bank's aggregate outstanding public welfare investments and commitments, including the proposed investment; and

(iv) A statement certifying that the investment complies with the requirements of §§ 24.3 and 24.4.

(3) In reviewing a proposal, the OCC considers the following factors and other available information:

(i) Whether the investment satisfies the requirements of §§ 24.3 and 24.4;

(ii) Whether the investment is consistent with the safe and sound operation of the bank; and

(iii) Whether the investment is consistent with the requirements of this part and the OCC's policies.

(4) Unless otherwise notified in writing by the OCC, and subject to § 24.4(a), the proposed investment is deemed approved after 30 calendar days from the date on which the OCC receives the bank's investment proposal.

(5) The OCC, by notifying the bank, may extend its period for reviewing the investment proposal. If so notified, the bank may make the investment only with the OCC's written approval.

(6) The OCC may impose one or more conditions in connection with its approval of an investment under this part. All approvals are subject to the

condition that a national bank must conduct the approved activity in a manner consistent with any published guidance issued by the OCC regarding the activity.

[61 FR 49660, Sept. 23, 1996, as amended at 64 FR 70991, Dec. 20, 1999; 68 FR 48776, Aug. 15, 2003; 73 FR 22245, Apr. 24, 2008; 79 FR 15641, Mar. 21, 2014; 80 FR 28472, May 18, 2015]

§ 24.6 Examples of qualifying public welfare investments.

Investments that primarily support the following types of activities are examples of investments that meet the requirements of § 24.3:

(a) Affordable housing activities, including:

(1) Investments in an entity that finances, acquires, develops, rehabilitates, manages, sells, or rents housing primarily for low- and moderate-income individuals;

(2) Investments in a project that develops or operates transitional housing for the homeless;

(3) Investments in a project that develops or operates special needs housing for disabled or elderly low- and moderate-income individuals; and

(4) Investments in a project that qualifies for the Federal low-income housing tax credit;

(b) Economic development and job creation investments, including:

(1) Investments that finance small businesses (including equity or debt financing and investments in an entity that provides loan guarantees) that are located in low- and moderate-income areas or other targeted redevelopment areas or that produce or retain permanent jobs, the majority of which are held by low- and moderate-income individuals;

(2) Investments that finance small businesses or small farms, including minority- and women-owned small businesses or small farms, that, although not located in low- and moderate-income areas or targeted redevelopment areas, create a significant number of permanent jobs for low- and moderate-income individuals;

(3) Investments in an entity that acquires, develops, rehabilitates, manages, sells, or rents commercial or industrial property that is located in a low- and moderate-income area or targeted redevelopment area and occupied primarily by small businesses, or that is occupied primarily by small businesses that produce or retain permanent jobs, the majority of which are held by low- and moderate-income individuals; and

(4) Investments in low- and moderate-income areas or targeted redevelopment areas that produce or retain permanent jobs, the majority of which are held by low- and moderate-income individuals;

(c) Investments in CEDEs, including:

(1) Investments in a national bank that has been approved by the OCC as a national bank with a community development focus;

(2) Investments in a community development financial institution, as defined in 12 U.S.C. 4742(5);

(3) Investments in a CEDE that is eligible to receive New Markets tax credits under 26 U.S.C. 45D; and

(d) Other public welfare investments, including:

(1) Investments that provide credit counseling, financial literacy, job training, community development research, and similar technical assistance for non-profit community development organizations, low- and moderate-income individuals or areas or targeted redevelopment areas, or small businesses, including minority- and women-owned small businesses, located in low- and moderate-income areas or that produce or retain permanent jobs, the majority of which are held by low- and moderate-income individuals;

(2) Investments of a type approved by the Federal Reserve Board under 12 CFR 208.22 for state member banks that are consistent with the requirements of § 24.3;

(3) Investments of a type determined by the OCC to be permissible under this part; and

(4) Investments in minority- and women-owned depository institutions that serve primarily low- and moderate-income individuals or low- and moderate-income areas or targeted redevelopment areas.

[68 FR 48776, Aug. 15, 2003, as amended at 73 FR 22245, Apr. 24, 2008; 73 FR 46534, Aug. 11, 2008]

§ 24.7 Examination, records, and remedial action.

(a) *Examination.* National bank investments under this part are subject to the examination provisions of 12 U.S.C. 481.

(b) *Records.* Each national bank shall maintain in its files information adequate to demonstrate that its investments meet the standards set out in § 24.3 of this part, including, where applicable, the criteria of 12 CFR 25.23, and that the bank is otherwise in compliance with the requirements of this part.

(c) *Remedial action.* If the OCC finds that an investment under this part is in violation of law or regulation, is inconsistent with the safe and sound operation of the bank, or poses a significant risk to a Federal deposit insurance fund, the national bank shall take appropriate remedial action as determined by the OCC.

[61 FR 49660, Sept. 23, 1996, as amended at 68 FR 48777, Aug. 15, 2003]

APPENDIX 1 TO PART 24—CD–1—NATIONAL BANK COMMUNITY DEVELOPMENT (PART 24) INVESTMENTS

Comptroller of the Currency
Administrator of National Banks

CD-1 – National Bank Community Development (Part 24) Investments

For Official Use Only

OMB Number
1557-0194

A national bank or national bank subsidiary may make an investment directly or indirectly designed primarily to promote the public welfare under the community development investment authority in 12 USC 24(Eleventh) and its implementing regulation 12 CFR 24 (Part 24). Part 24 contains the OCC standards for determining whether an investment is designed to promote the public welfare and procedures that apply to those investments. National banks must submit the completed form to provide an after-the-fact notice or to request prior approval of a public welfare investment to the Community Affairs Department, Office of the Comptroller of the Currency, Washington, DC 20219. Please contact the Community Affairs Department at (202) 649-6420 or CommunityAffairs@occ.treas.gov for more information.

PLEASE PROVIDE THE FOLLOWING INFORMATION ABOUT THE INVESTING BANK.

Bank name:	Mailing address *(street or P.O. box)*:
Bank charter number:	City, State, ZIP Code:
Telephone number:	Fax number:
E-mail address:	URL:

CONTACT FOR INFORMATION:

Name of bank contact responsible for form's information:	Name of bank contact responsible for CD investment (if different):
Mailing address *(street or P.O. box)*:	Mailing address *(street or P.O. box)*:
City, State, ZIP Code:	City, State, ZIP Code:
Telephone number:	Telephone number:
Fax number:	Fax number:
E-mail address:	E-mail address:

PLEASE INDICATE THE PROCESS THE BANK REQUESTS BY CHECKING THE APPROPRIATE BOX, BELOW.

After-the-fact notice (12 CFR 24.5(a)) - complete sections 1 and 2. ☐

Prior approval (12 CFR 24.5(b)) - complete section 2. ☐

CD-1 (Expiration Date: 07/31/2016)

Section 1 – After-The-Fact Notice Only (12 CFR 24.5(a))

A bank may provide an after-the-fact notice of its Part 24 investment if the bank responds affirmatively to all of the following requirements.

The bank is "well-capitalized," as defined in 12 CFR 24.2(i). Yes ☐ No ☐

The bank has a composite rating of 1 or 2 under the Uniform Financial Institutions Rating System. Yes ☐ No ☐

The bank's most recent Community Reinvestment Act rating is satisfactory or outstanding. Yes ☐ No ☐

The bank is not under a cease and desist order, consent order, formal written agreement, or Prompt Corrective Action directive.

Yes ☐ No ☐

Including this investment, the bank's aggregate outstanding investments and commitments under Part 24 do not exceed 5 percent of its capital and surplus, unless the OCC has provided written approval of a written request by the bank allowing the bank to provide after-the-fact notices for investments that would raise the aggregate amount of the bank's Part 24 investments beyond 5 percent of its capital and surplus.

Yes ☐ No ☐

The investment does not involve properties carried on the bank's books as "other real estate owned." Yes ☐ No ☐

The OCC has not determined, in published guidance, that the investment is inappropriate for the after-the-fact notification.

Yes ☐ No ☐

Has the bank responded affirmatively to all of the above requirements in order to provide an after-the-fact notice of its Part 24 investment? [The OCC may have provided written notification that the bank may submit Part 24 after-the-fact notices. If so, please provide the date or a copy of the OCC's written notification.]

Yes ☐ (The bank may make an investment authorized by 12 USC 24(Eleventh) and this part and notify the OCC within 10 working days by submitting a completed after-the-fact notice.)

No ☐ (The bank must seek prior OCC approval of its investment and submit a completed investment proposal before making the investment.)

(To complete the after-the-fact notice process or to request prior OCC approval, please proceed to section 2 of this form.)

Section 2 — All Requests

1. **Please indicate how the bank's investment is consistent with Part 24 requirements for public welfare investments, under 12 CFR 24.3.**

   a. Check at least one of the following that applies to the bank's investment:

   The investment primarily benefits low- and moderate-income individuals. ☐

   The investment primarily benefits low- and moderate-income areas. ☐

   The investment primarily benefits other areas targeted by a governmental entity for redevelopment. ☐

   The investment would receive consideration under 12 CFR 25.23 as a "qualified investment" for purposes of the Community Reinvestment Act. ☐

2. **Please indicate how the bank's investment is consistent with Part 24 requirements for investment limits under 12 CFR 24.4 by responding to the following questions.**

   a. Dollar amount of the bank's investment that is the subject of this submission: ____________

   b. Percentage of the bank's capital and surplus represented by the bank's investment that is the subject of this submission: ____________ %.

   c. Percentage of the bank's capital and surplus represented by the aggregate outstanding Part 24 investments and commitments, including this investment: ____________ %.

   d. Does this investment expose the bank to unlimited liability?

   Yes ☐ (This investment cannot be made under Part 24.)

   No ☐

3. **Please attach a brief description of the bank's investment. (*See* 12 CFR 24.5(a)(3)(i) and (b)(2)(i)). Include the following information in the description.**

   a. The name of the community and economic development entity (CEDE) into which the bank's investment has been (or will be) made.

   b. The type of bank investment (equity, debt, or other).

   c. The activity or activities of the CEDE in which the bank has invested (or will invest). (*See* examples of qualifying investment activities described in 12 CFR 24.6 (a), (b), (c), and (d).)

   d. How the investment is structured so that it does not expose the bank to unlimited liability, such as by describing the structure of the CEDE (*e.g.*, CDC subsidiary, multi-bank CDC, multi-investor CDC, limited partnership, limited liability company, community development bank, community development financial institution, community development entity, community development venture capital fund, community development lending consortia, community development closed-end mutual funds, non-diversified closed-end investment companies, or any other CEDE) and by providing any other relevant information.

   e. The geographic area served by the CEDE.

f. The total funding or other support by community development partners involved in the project (*e.g.*, government or public agencies, nonprofits, other investors), if known.

g. Supplemental information (*e.g.*, prospectus, annual report, Web address that contains information about the CEDE in which the investment is or will be made), if available.

4. Evidence of qualification is readily available for examination purposes.

The bank maintains information concerning this investment in a form readily accessible and available for examination that supports the certifications contained in this form and demonstrates that the investment meets the standards set out in 12 CFR 24.3, including, where applicable, the criteria of 12 CFR 25.23.

Yes ☐ No ☐

5. Certification

The undersigned hereby certifies that the foregoing information in this form is accurate and complete. It is further certified that the undersigned is authorized to file this form on Part 24 investments for the bank.

Name: ______________________________

Title: ______________________________

Signature: ______________________________

Date: ______________________________

Form **Part 24** Page 5

THE SPACE BELOW MAY BE USED TO DESCRIBE THE BANK'S CD INVESTMENT AS REQUESTED IN SECTION 2, QUESTION 3.

CD-1 (Expiration Date: 07/31/2016)

[80 FR 28472, May 18, 2015; 80 FR 34039, June 15, 2015]

PART 25—COMMUNITY REINVESTMENT ACT AND INTERSTATE DEPOSIT PRODUCTION REGULATIONS

REGULATIONS

Subpart A—General

Sec.
25.11 Authority, purposes, and scope.
25.12 Definitions.

Subpart B—Standards for Assessing Performance

25.21 Performance tests, standards, and ratings, in general.
25.22 Lending test.
25.23 Investment test.
25.24 Service test.
25.25 Community development test for wholesale or limited purpose banks.
25.26 Small bank performance standards.
25.27 Strategic plan.
25.28 Assigned ratings.
25.29 Effect of CRA performance on applications.

Subpart C—Records, Reporting, and Disclosure Requirements

25.41 Assessment area delineation.
25.42 Data collection, reporting, and disclosure.
25.43 Content and availability of public file.
25.44 Public notice by banks.
25.45 Publication of planned examination schedule.

Subpart D [Reserved]

Subpart E—Prohibition Against Use of Interstate Branches Primarily for Deposit Production

25.61 Purpose and scope.
25.62 Definitions.
25.63 Loan-to-deposit ratio screen.
25.64 Credit needs determination.
25.65 Sanctions.

APPENDIX A TO PART 25—RATINGS
APPENDIX B TO PART 25—CRA NOTICE

AUTHORITY: 12 U.S.C. 21, 22, 26, 27, 30, 36, 93a, 161, 215, 215a, 481, 1814, 1816, 1828(c), 1835a, 2901 through 2908, and 3101 through 3111.

SOURCE: 43 FR 47146, Oct. 12, 1978, unless otherwise noted.

REGULATIONS

Subpart A—General

§25.11 Authority, purposes, and scope.

(a) *Authority and OMB control number*—(1) *Authority.* The authority for subparts A, B, C, D, and E is 12 U.S.C. 21, 22, 26, 27, 30, 36, 93a, 161, 215, 215a, 481, 1814, 1816, 1828(c), 1835a, 2901 through 2907, and 3101 through 3111.

(2) *OMB control number.* The information collection requirements contained in this part were approved by the Office of Management and Budget under the provisions of 44 U.S.C. 3501 *et seq.* and have been assigned OMB control number 1557–0160.

(b) *Purposes.* In enacting the Community Reinvestment Act (CRA), the Congress required each appropriate Federal financial supervisory agency to assess an institution's record of helping to meet the credit needs of the local communities in which the institution is chartered, consistent with the safe and sound operation of the institution, and to take this record into account in the agency's evaluation of an application for a deposit facility by the institution. This part is intended to carry out the purposes of the CRA by:

(1) Establishing the framework and criteria by which the Office of the Comptroller of the Currency (OCC) assesses a bank's record of helping to meet the credit needs of its entire community, including low- and moderate-income neighborhoods, consistent with the safe and sound operation of the bank; and

(2) Providing that the OCC takes that record into account in considering certain applications.

(c) *Scope*—(1) *General.* This part applies to all banks except as provided in paragraphs (c)(2) and (c)(3) of this section.

(2) *Federal branches and agencies.* (i) This part applies to all insured Federal branches and to any Federal branch that is uninsured that results from an acquisition described in section 5(a)(8) of the International Banking Act of 1978 (12 U.S.C. 3103(a)(8)).

(ii) Except as provided in paragraph (c)(2)(i) of this section, this part does not apply to Federal branches that are uninsured, limited Federal branches, or

Federal agencies, as those terms are defined in part 28 of this chapter.

(3) *Certain special purpose banks.* This part does not apply to special purpose banks that do not perform commercial or retail banking services by granting credit to the public in the ordinary course of business, other than as incident to their specialized operations. These banks include banker's banks, as defined in 12 U.S.C. 24 (Seventh), and banks that engage only in one or more of the following activities: providing cash management controlled disbursement services or serving as correspondent banks, trust companies, or clearing agents.

[60 FR 22178, May 4, 1995, as amended at 62 FR 47734, Sept. 10, 1997]

§ 25.12 Definitions.

For purposes of this part, the following definitions apply:

(a) *Affiliate* means any company that controls, is controlled by, or is under common control with another company. The term "control" has the meaning given to that term in 12 U.S.C. 1841(a)(2), and a company is under common control with another company if both companies are directly or indirectly controlled by the same company.

(b) *Area median income* means:

(1) The median family income for the MSA, if a person or geography is located in an MSA, or for the metropolitan division, if a person or geography is located in an MSA that has been subdivided into metropolitan divisions; or

(2) The statewide nonmetropolitan median family income, if a person or geography is located outside an MSA.

(c) *Assessment area* means a geographic area delineated in accordance with § 25.41.

(d) *Automated teller machine (ATM)* means an automated, unstaffed banking facility owned or operated by, or operated exclusively for, the bank at which deposits are received, cash dispersed, or money lent.

(e) *Bank* means a national bank (including a Federal branch as defined in part 28 of this chapter) with Federally insured deposits, except as provided in § 25.11(c).

(f) *Branch* means a staffed banking facility authorized as a branch, whether shared or unshared, including, for example, a mini-branch in a grocery store or a branch operated in conjunction with any other local business or nonprofit organization.

(g) *Community development* means:

(1) Affordable housing (including multifamily rental housing) for low- or moderate-income individuals;

(2) Community services targeted to low- or moderate-income individuals;

(3) Activities that promote economic development by financing businesses or farms that meet the size eligibility standards of the Small Business Administration's Development Company or Small Business Investment Company programs (13 CFR 121.301) or have gross annual revenues of $1 million or less; or

(4) Activities that revitalize or stabilize—

(i) Low-or moderate-income geographies;

(ii) Designated disaster areas; or

(iii) Distressed or underserved nonmetropolitan middle-income geographies designated by the Board of Governors of the Federal Reserve System, Federal Deposit Insurance Corporation, and OCC, based on—

(A) Rates of poverty, unemployment, and population loss; or

(B) Population size, density, and dispersion. Activities revitalize and stabilize geographies designated based on population size, density, and dispersion if they help to meet essential community needs, including needs of low- and moderate-income individuals.

(h) *Community development loan* means a loan that:

(1) Has as its primary purpose community development; and

(2) Except in the case of a wholesale or limited purpose bank:

(i) Has not been reported or collected by the bank or an affiliate for consideration in the bank's assessment as a home mortgage, small business, small farm, or consumer loan, unless the loan is for a multifamily dwelling (as defined in § 1003.2(n) of this title); and

(ii) Benefits the bank's assessment area(s) or a broader statewide or regional area that includes the bank's assessment area(s).

(i) *Community development service* means a service that:

(1) Has as its primary purpose community development;

(2) Is related to the provision of financial services; and

(3) Has not been considered in the evaluation of the bank's retail banking services under § 25.24(d).

(j) *Consumer loan* means a loan to one or more individuals for household, family, or other personal expenditures. A consumer loan does not include a home mortgage, small business, or small farm loan. Consumer loans include the following categories of loans:

(1) *Motor vehicle loan,* which is a consumer loan extended for the purchase of and secured by a motor vehicle;

(2) *Credit card loan,* which is a line of credit for household, family, or other personal expenditures that is accessed by a borrower's use of a "credit card," as this term is defined in § 1026.2 of this title;

(3) *Other secured consumer loan,* which is a secured consumer loan that is not included in one of the other categories of consumer loans; and

(4) *Other unsecured consumer loan,* which is an unsecured consumer loan that is not included in one of the other categories of consumer loans.

(k) *Geography* means a census tract delineated by the United States Bureau of the Census in the most recent decennial census.

(l) *Home mortgage loan* means a closed-end mortgage loan or an open-end line of credit as these terms are defined under § 1003.2 of this title, and that is not an excluded transaction under § 1003.3(c)(1) through (10) and (13) of this title.

(m) *Income level* includes:

(1) *Low-income,* which means an individual income that is less than 50 percent of the area median income, or a median family income that is less than 50 percent, in the case of a geography.

(2) *Moderate-income,* which means an individual income that is at least 50 percent and less than 80 percent of the area median income, or a median family income that is at least 50 and less than 80 percent, in the case of a geography.

(3) *Middle-income,* which means an individual income that is at least 80 percent and less than 120 percent of the area median income, or a median family income that is at least 80 and less than 120 percent, in the case of a geography.

(4) *Upper-income,* which means an individual income that is 120 percent or more of the area median income, or a median family income that is 120 percent or more, in the case of a geography.

(n) *Limited purpose bank* means a bank that offers only a narrow product line (such as credit card or motor vehicle loans) to a regional or broader market and for which a designation as a limited purpose bank is in effect, in accordance with § 25.25(b).

(o) *Loan location.* A loan is located as follows:

(1) A consumer loan is located in the geography where the borrower resides;

(2) A home mortgage loan is located in the geography where the property to which the loan relates is located; and

(3) A small business or small farm loan is located in the geography where the main business facility or farm is located or where the loan proceeds otherwise will be applied, as indicated by the borrower.

(p) *Loan production office* means a staffed facility, other than a branch, that is open to the public and that provides lending-related services, such as loan information and applications.

(q) *Metropolitan division* means a metropolitan division as defined by the Director of the Office of Management and Budget.

(r) *MSA* means a metropolitan statistical area as defined by the Director of the Office of Management and Budget.

(s) *Nonmetropolitan area* means any area that is not located in an MSA.

(t) *Qualified investment* means a lawful investment, deposit, membership share, or grant that has as its primary purpose community development.

(u) *Small bank*—(1) *Definition. Small bank* means a bank that, as of December 31 of either of the prior two calendar years, had assets of less than $1.284 billion. *Intermediate small bank* means a small bank with assets of at least $321 million as of December 31 of both of the prior two calendar years and less than $1.284 billion as of December 31 of either of the prior two calendar years.

(2) *Adjustment.* The dollar figures in paragraph (u)(1) of this section shall be adjusted annually and published by the OCC, based on the year-to-year change in the average of the Consumer Price Index for Urban Wage Earners and Clerical Workers, not seasonally adjusted, for each twelve-month period ending in November, with rounding to the nearest million.

(v) *Small business loan* means a loan included in "loans to small businesses" as defined in the instructions for preparation of the Consolidated Report of Condition and Income.

(w) *Small farm loan* means a loan included in "loans to small farms" as defined in the instructions for preparation of the Consolidated Report of Condition and Income.

(x) *Wholesale bank* means a bank that is not in the business of extending home mortgage, small business, small farm, or consumer loans to retail customers, and for which a designation as a wholesale bank is in effect, in accordance with § 25.25(b).

[60 FR 22178, May 4, 1995, as amended at 60 FR 66050, Dec. 20, 1995; 61 FR 21363, May 10, 1996; 69 FR 41186, July 8, 2004; 70 FR 44266, Aug. 2, 2005; 71 FR 78336, Dec. 29, 2006; 72 FR 72573, Dec. 21, 2007; 73 FR 78154, Dec. 22, 2008; 74 FR 68663, Dec. 29, 2009; 75 FR 79285, Dec. 20, 2010; 75 FR 82218, Dec. 30, 2010; 76 FR 79530, Dec. 22, 2011; 77 FR 75523, Dec. 21, 2012; 80 FR 81164, Dec. 29, 2015; 82 FR 55742, Nov. 24, 2017; 83 FR 66603, Dec. 27, 2018]

Subpart B—Standards for Assessing Performance

SOURCE: 60 FR 22180, May 4, 1995, unless otherwise noted.

§ 25.21 Performance tests, standards, and ratings, in general.

(a) *Performance tests and standards.* The OCC assesses the CRA performance of a bank in an examination as follows:

(1) *Lending, investment, and service tests.* The OCC applies the lending, investment, and service tests, as provided in §§ 25.22 through 25.24, in evaluating the performance of a bank, except as provided in paragraphs (a)(2), (a)(3), and (a)(4) of this section.

(2) *Community development test for wholesale or limited purpose banks.* The OCC applies the community development test for a wholesale or limited purpose bank, as provided in § 25.25, except as provided in paragraph (a)(4) of this section.

(3) *Small bank performance standards.* The OCC applies the small bank performance standards as provided in § 25.26 in evaluating the performance of a small bank or a bank that was a small bank during the prior calendar year, unless the bank elects to be assessed as provided in paragraphs (a)(1), (a)(2), or (a)(4) of this section. The bank may elect to be assessed as provided in paragraph (a)(1) of this section only if it collects and reports the data required for other banks under § 25.42.

(4) *Strategic plan.* The OCC evaluates the performance of a bank under a strategic plan if the bank submits, and the OCC approves, a strategic plan as provided in § 25.27.

(b) *Performance context.* The OCC applies the tests and standards in paragraph (a) of this section and also considers whether to approve a proposed strategic plan in the context of:

(1) Demographic data on median income levels, distribution of household income, nature of housing stock, housing costs, and other relevant data pertaining to a bank's assessment area(s);

(2) Any information about lending, investment, and service opportunities in the bank's assessment area(s) maintained by the bank or obtained from community organizations, state, local, and tribal governments, economic development agencies, or other sources;

(3) The bank's product offerings and business strategy as determined from data provided by the bank;

(4) Institutional capacity and constraints, including the size and financial condition of the bank, the economic climate (national, regional, and local), safety and soundness limitations, and any other factors that significantly affect the bank's ability to provide lending, investments, or services in its assessment area(s);

(5) The bank's past performance and the performance of similarly situated lenders;

(6) The bank's public file, as described in § 25.43, and any written comments about the bank's CRA performance submitted to the bank or the OCC; and

(7) Any other information deemed relevant by the OCC.

(c) *Assigned ratings.* The OCC assigns to a bank one of the following four ratings pursuant to § 25.28 and appendix A of this part: "outstanding"; "satisfactory"; "needs to improve"; or "substantial noncompliance" as provided in 12 U.S.C. 2906(b)(2). The rating assigned by the OCC reflects the bank's record of helping to meet the credit needs of its entire community, including low- and moderate-income neighborhoods, consistent with the safe and sound operation of the bank.

(d) *Safe and sound operations.* This part and the CRA do not require a bank to make loans or investments or to provide services that are inconsistent with safe and sound operations. To the contrary, the OCC anticipates banks can meet the standards of this part with safe and sound loans, investments, and services on which the banks expect to make a profit. Banks are permitted and encouraged to develop and apply flexible underwriting standards for loans that benefit low- or moderate-income geographies or individuals, only if consistent with safe and sound operations.

(e) *Low-cost education loans provided to low-income borrowers.* In assessing and taking into account the record of a bank under this part, the OCC considers, as a factor, low-cost education loans originated by the bank to borrowers, particularly in its assessment area(s), who have an individual income that is less than 50 percent of the area median income. For purposes of this paragraph, "low-cost education loans" means any education loan, as defined in section 140(a)(7) of the Truth in Lending Act (15 U.S.C. 1650(a)(7)) (including a loan under a state or local education loan program), originated by the bank for a student at an "institution of higher education," as that term is generally defined in sections 101 and 102 of the Higher Education Act of 1965 (20 U.S.C. 1001 and 1002) and the implementing regulations published by the U.S. Department of Education, with interest rates and fees no greater than those of comparable education loans offered directly by the U.S. Department of Education. Such rates and fees are specified in section 455 of the Higher Education Act of 1965 (20 U.S.C. 1087e).

(f) *Activities in cooperation with minority- or women-owned financial institutions and low-income credit unions.* In assessing and taking into account the record of a nonminority-owned and nonwomen-owned bank under this part, the OCC considers as a factor capital investment, loan participation, and other ventures undertaken by the bank in cooperation with minority- and women-owned financial institutions and low-income credit unions. Such activities must help meet the credit needs of local communities in which the minority- and women-owned financial institutions and low-income credit unions are chartered. To be considered, such activities need not also benefit the bank's assessment area(s) or the broader statewide or regional area that includes the bank's assessment area(s).

[60 FR 22180, May 4, 1995, as amended at 75 FR 61044, Oct. 4, 2010]

§ 25.22 Lending test.

(a) *Scope of test.* (1) The lending test evaluates a bank's record of helping to meet the credit needs of its assessment area(s) through its lending activities by considering a bank's home mortgage, small business, small farm, and community development lending. If consumer lending constitutes a substantial majority of a bank's business, the OCC will evaluate the bank's consumer lending in one or more of the following categories: motor vehicle, credit card, other secured, and other unsecured loans. In addition, at a bank's option, the OCC will evaluate one or more categories of consumer lending, if the bank has collected and maintained, as required in § 25.42(c)(1), the data for each category that the bank elects to have the OCC evaluate.

(2) The OCC considers originations and purchases of loans. The OCC will also consider any other loan data the bank may choose to provide, including data on loans outstanding, commitments and letters of credit.

(3) A bank may ask the OCC to consider loans originated or purchased by consortia in which the bank participates or by third parties in which the bank has invested only if the loans

meet the definition of community development loans and only in accordance with paragraph (d) of this section. The OCC will not consider these loans under any criterion of the lending test except the community development lending criterion.

(b) *Performance criteria.* The OCC evaluates a bank's lending performance pursuant to the following criteria:

(1) *Lending activity.* The number and amount of the bank's home mortgage, small business, small farm, and consumer loans, if applicable, in the bank's assessment area(s);

(2) *Geographic distribution.* The geographic distribution of the bank's home mortgage, small business, small farm, and consumer loans, if applicable, based on the loan location, including:

(i) The proportion of the bank's lending in the bank's assessment area(s);

(ii) The dispersion of lending in the bank's assessment area(s); and

(iii) The number and amount of loans in low-, moderate-, middle-, and upper-income geographies in the bank's assessment area(s);

(3) *Borrower characteristics.* The distribution, particularly in the bank's assessment area(s), of the bank's home mortgage, small business, small farm, and consumer loans, if applicable, based on borrower characteristics, including the number and amount of:

(i) Home mortgage loans to low-, moderate-, middle-, and upper-income individuals;

(ii) Small business and small farm loans to businesses and farms with gross annual revenues of $1 million or less;

(iii) Small business and small farm loans by loan amount at origination; and

(iv) Consumer loans, if applicable, to low-, moderate-, middle-, and upper-income individuals;

(4) *Community development lending.* The bank's community development lending, including the number and amount of community development loans, and their complexity and innovativeness; and

(5) *Innovative or flexible lending practices.* The bank's use of innovative or flexible lending practices in a safe and sound manner to address the credit needs of low- or moderate-income individuals or geographies.

(c) *Affiliate lending.* (1) At a bank's option, the OCC will consider loans by an affiliate of the bank, if the bank provides data on the affiliate's loans pursuant to § 25.42.

(2) The OCC considers affiliate lending subject to the following constraints:

(i) No affiliate may claim a loan origination or loan purchase if another institution claims the same loan origination or purchase; and

(ii) If a bank elects to have the OCC consider loans within a particular lending category made by one or more of the bank's affiliates in a particular assessment area, the bank shall elect to have the OCC consider, in accordance with paragraph (c)(1) of this section, all the loans within that lending category in that particular assessment area made by all of the bank's affiliates.

(3) The OCC does not consider affiliate lending in assessing a bank's performance under paragraph (b)(2)(i) of this section.

(d) *Lending by a consortium or a third party.* Community development loans originated or purchased by a consortium in which the bank participates or by a third party in which the bank has invested:

(1) Will be considered, at the bank's option, if the bank reports the data pertaining to these loans under § 25.42(b)(2); and

(2) May be allocated among participants or investors, as they choose, for purposes of the lending test, except that no participant or investor:

(i) May claim a loan origination or loan purchase if another participant or investor claims the same loan origination or purchase; or

(ii) May claim loans accounting for more than its percentage share (based on the level of its participation or investment) of the total loans originated by the consortium or third party.

(e) *Lending performance rating.* The OCC rates a bank's lending performance as provided in appendix A of this part.

[60 FR 22180, May 4, 1995, as amended at 82 FR 55742, Nov. 24, 2017]

§ 25.23 Investment test.

(a) *Scope of test.* The investment test evaluates a bank's record of helping to meet the credit needs of its assessment area(s) through qualified investments that benefit its assessment area(s) or a broader statewide or regional area that includes the bank's assessment area(s).

(b) *Exclusion.* Activities considered under the lending or service tests may not be considered under the investment test.

(c) *Affiliate investment.* At a bank's option, the OCC will consider, in its assessment of a bank's investment performance, a qualified investment made by an affiliate of the bank, if the qualified investment is not claimed by any other institution.

(d) *Disposition of branch premises.* Donating, selling on favorable terms, or making available on a rent-free basis a branch of the bank that is located in a predominantly minority neighborhood to a minority depository institution or women's depository institution (as these terms are defined in 12 U.S.C. 2907(b)) will be considered as a qualified investment.

(e) *Performance criteria.* The OCC evaluates the investment performance of a bank pursuant to the following criteria:

(1) The dollar amount of qualified investments;

(2) The innovativeness or complexity of qualified investments;

(3) The responsiveness of qualified investments to credit and community development needs; and

(4) The degree to which the qualified investments are not routinely provided by private investors.

(f) *Investment performance rating.* The OCC rates a bank's investment performance as provided in appendix A of this part.

§ 25.24 Service test.

(a) *Scope of test.* The service test evaluates a bank's record of helping to meet the credit needs of its assessment area(s) by analyzing both the availability and effectiveness of a bank's systems for delivering retail banking services and the extent and innovativeness of its community development services.

(b) *Area(s) benefitted.* Community development services must benefit a bank's assessment area(s) or a broader statewide or regional area that includes the bank's assessment area(s).

(c) *Affiliate service.* At a bank's option, the OCC will consider, in its assessment of a bank's service performance, a community development service provided by an affiliate of the bank, if the community development service is not claimed by any other institution.

(d) *Performance criteria—retail banking services.* The OCC evaluates the availability and effectiveness of a bank's systems for delivering retail banking services, pursuant to the following criteria:

(1) The current distribution of the bank's branches among low-,

moderate-, middle-, and upper-income geographies;

(2) In the context of its current distribution of the bank's branches, the bank's record of opening and closing branches, particularly branches located in low- or moderate-income geographies or primarily serving low- or moderate-income individuals;

(3) The availability and effectiveness of alternative systems for delivering retail banking services (*e.g.*, ATMs, ATMs not owned or operated by or exclusively for the bank, banking by telephone or computer, loan production offices, and bank-at-work or bank-by-mail programs) in low- and moderate-income geographies and to low- and moderate-income individuals; and

(4) The range of services provided in low-, moderate-, middle-, and upper-income geographies and the degree to which the services are tailored to meet the needs of those geographies.

(e) *Performance criteria—community development services.* The OCC evaluates community development services pursuant to the following criteria:

(1) The extent to which the bank provides community development services; and

(2) The innovativeness and responsiveness of community development services.

(f) *Service performance rating.* The OCC rates a bank's service performance as provided in appendix A of this part.

§ 25.25 Community development test for wholesale or limited purpose banks.

(a) *Scope of test.* The OCC assesses a wholesale or limited purpose bank's record of helping to meet the credit needs of its assessment area(s) under the community development test through its community development lending, qualified investments, or community development services.

(b) *Designation as a wholesale or limited purpose bank.* In order to receive a designation as a wholesale or limited purpose bank, a bank shall file a request, in writing, with the OCC, at least three months prior to the proposed effective date of the designation. If the OCC approves the designation, it remains in effect until the bank requests revocation of the designation or until one year after the OCC notifies the bank that the OCC has revoked the designation on its own initiative.

(c) *Performance criteria.* The OCC evaluates the community development performance of a wholesale or limited purpose bank pursuant to the following criteria:

(1) The number and amount of community development loans (including originations and purchases of loans and other community development loan data provided by the bank, such as data on loans outstanding, commitments, and letters of credit), qualified investments, or community development services;

(2) The use of innovative or complex qualified investments, community development loans, or community development services and the extent to which the investments are not routinely provided by private investors; and

(3) The bank's responsiveness to credit and community development needs.

(d) *Indirect activities.* At a bank's option, the OCC will consider in its community development performance assessment:

(1) Qualified investments or community development services provided by an affiliate of the bank, if the investments or services are not claimed by any other institution; and

(2) Community development lending by affiliates, consortia and third parties, subject to the requirements and limitations in § 25.22(c) and (d).

(e) *Benefit to assessment area(s)*—(1) *Benefit inside assessment area(s).* The OCC considers all qualified investments, community development loans, and community development services that benefit areas within the bank's assessment area(s) or a broader statewide or regional area that includes the bank's assessment area(s).

(2) *Benefit outside assessment area(s).* The OCC considers the qualified investments, community development loans, and community development services that benefit areas outside the bank's assessment area(s), if the bank has adequately addressed the needs of its assessment area(s).

(f) *Community development performance rating.* The OCC rates a bank's community development performance as provided in appendix A of this part.

§ 25.26 Small bank performance standards.

(a) *Performance criteria*—(1) *Small banks that are not intermediate small banks.* The OCC evaluates the record of a small bank that is not, or that was not during the prior calendar year, an intermediate small bank, of helping to meet the credit needs of its assessment area(s) pursuant to the criteria set forth in paragraph (b) of this section.

(2) *Intermediate small banks.* The OCC evaluates the record of a small bank that is, or that was during the prior calendar year, an intermediate small bank, of helping to meet the credit needs of its assessment area(s) pursuant to the criteria set forth in paragraphs (b) and (c) of this section.

(b) *Lending test.* A small bank's lending performance is evaluated pursuant to the following criteria:

(1) The bank's loan-to-deposit ratio, adjusted for seasonal variation, and, as appropriate, other lending-related activities, such as loan originations for sale to the secondary markets, community development loans, or qualified investments;

(2) The percentage of loans and, as appropriate, other lending-related activities located in the bank's assessment area(s);

(3) The bank's record of lending to and, as appropriate, engaging in other

lending-related activities for borrowers of different income levels and businesses and farms of different sizes;

(4) The geographic distribution of the bank's loans; and

(5) The bank's record of taking action, if warranted, in response to written complaints about its performance in helping to meet credit needs in its assessment area(s).

(c) *Community development test.* An intermediate small bank's community development performance also is evaluated pursuant to the following criteria:

(1) The number and amount of community development loans;

(2) The number and amount of qualified investments;

(3) The extent to which the bank provides community development services; and

(4) The bank's responsiveness through such activities to community development lending, investment, and services needs.

(d) *Small bank performance rating.* The OCC rates the performance of a bank evaluated under this section as provided in appendix A of this part.

[70 FR 44266, Aug. 2, 2005, as amended at 71 FR 78336, Dec. 29, 2006; 72 FR 72573, Dec. 21, 2007]

§ 25.27 Strategic plan.

(a) *Alternative election.* The OCC will assess a bank's record of helping to meet the credit needs of its assessment area(s) under a strategic plan if:

(1) The bank has submitted the plan to the OCC as provided for in this section;

(2) The OCC has approved the plan;

(3) The plan is in effect; and

(4) The bank has been operating under an approved plan for at least one year.

(b) *Data reporting.* The OCC's approval of a plan does not affect the bank's obligation, if any, to report data as required by § 25.42.

(c) *Plans in general*—(1) *Term.* A plan may have a term of no more than five years, and any multi-year plan must include annual interim measurable goals under which the OCC will evaluate the bank's performance.

(2) *Multiple assessment areas.* A bank with more than one assessment area may prepare a single plan for all of its assessment areas or one or more plans for one or more of its assessment areas.

(3) *Treatment of affiliates.* Affiliated institutions may prepare a joint plan if the plan provides measurable goals for each institution. Activities may be allocated among institutions at the institutions' option, provided that the same activities are not considered for more than one institution.

(d) *Public participation in plan development.* Before submitting a plan to the OCC for approval, a bank shall:

(1) Informally seek suggestions from members of the public in its assessment area(s) covered by the plan while developing the plan;

(2) Once the bank has developed a plan, formally solicit public comment on the plan for at least 30 days by publishing notice in at least one newspaper of general circulation in each assessment area covered by the plan; and

(3) During the period of formal public comment, make copies of the plan available for review by the public at no cost at all offices of the bank in any assessment area covered by the plan and provide copies of the plan upon request for a reasonable fee to cover copying and mailing, if applicable.

(e) *Submission of plan.* The bank shall submit its plan to the OCC at least three months prior to the proposed effective date of the plan. The bank shall also submit with its plan a description of its informal efforts to seek suggestions from members of the public, any written public comment received, and, if the plan was revised in light of the comment received, the initial plan as released for public comment.

(f) *Plan content*—(1) *Measurable goals.* (i) A bank shall specify in its plan measurable goals for helping to meet the credit needs of each assessment area covered by the plan, particularly the needs of low- and moderate-income geographies and low- and moderate-income individuals, through lending, investment, and services, as appropriate.

(ii) A bank shall address in its plan all three performance categories and, unless the bank has been designated as a wholesale or limited purpose bank, shall emphasize lending and lending-related activities. Nevertheless, a different emphasis, including a focus on one or more performance categories, may be appropriate if responsive to the characteristics and credit needs of its assessment area(s), considering public comment and the bank's capacity and constraints, product offerings, and business strategy.

(2) *Confidential information.* A bank may submit additional information to the OCC on a confidential basis, but the goals stated in the plan must be sufficiently specific to enable the public and the OCC to judge the merits of the plan.

(3) *Satisfactory and outstanding goals.* A bank shall specify in its plan measurable goals that constitute "satisfactory" performance. A plan may specify measurable goals that constitute "outstanding" performance. If a bank submits, and the OCC approves, both "satisfactory" and "outstanding" performance goals, the OCC will consider the bank eligible for an "outstanding" performance rating.

(4) *Election if satisfactory goals not substantially met.* A bank may elect in its plan that, if the bank fails to meet substantially its plan goals for a satisfactory rating, the OCC will evaluate the bank's performance under the lending, investment, and service tests, the community development test, or the small bank performance standards, as appropriate.

(g) *Plan approval*—(1) *Timing.* The OCC will act upon a plan within 60 calendar days after the OCC receives the complete plan and other material required under paragraph (e) of this section. If the OCC fails to act within this time period, the plan shall be deemed approved unless the OCC extends the review period for good cause.

(2) *Public participation.* In evaluating the plan's goals, the OCC considers the public's involvement in formulating the plan, written public comment on the plan, and any response by the bank to public comment on the plan.

(3) *Criteria for evaluating plan.* The OCC evaluates a plan's measurable goals using the following criteria, as appropriate:

(i) The extent and breadth of lending or lending-related activities, including, as appropriate, the distribution of loans among different geographies, businesses and farms of different sizes, and individuals of different income levels, the extent of community development lending, and the use of innovative or flexible lending practices to address credit needs;

(ii) The amount and innovativeness, complexity, and responsiveness of the bank's qualified investments; and

(iii) The availability and effectiveness of the bank's systems for delivering retail banking services and the extent and innovativeness of the bank's community development services.

(h) *Plan amendment.* During the term of a plan, a bank may request the OCC to approve an amendment to the plan on grounds that there has been a material change in circumstances. The bank shall develop an amendment to a previously approved plan in accordance with the public participation requirements of paragraph (d) of this section.

(i) *Plan assessment.* The OCC approves the goals and assesses performance under a plan as provided for in appendix A of this part.

[60 FR 22180, May 4, 1995, as amended at 60 FR 66050, Dec. 20, 1995; 69 FR 41186, July 8, 2004]

§ 25.28 Assigned ratings.

(a) *Ratings in general.* Subject to paragraphs (b) and (c) of this section, the OCC assigns to a bank a rating of "outstanding," "satisfactory," "needs to improve," or "substantial noncompliance" based on the bank's performance under the lending, investment and service tests, the community development test, the small bank performance standards, or an approved strategic plan, as applicable.

(b) *Lending, investment, and service tests.* The OCC assigns a rating for a bank assessed under the lending, investment, and service tests in accordance with the following principles:

(1) A bank that receives an "outstanding" rating on the lending test receives an assigned rating of at least "satisfactory";

(2) A bank that receives an "outstanding" rating on both the service test and the investment test and a rating of at least "high satisfactory" on the lending test receives an assigned rating of "outstanding"; and

(3) No bank may receive an assigned rating of "satisfactory" or higher unless it receives a rating of at least "low satisfactory" on the lending test.

(c) *Effect of evidence of discriminatory or other illegal credit practices.* (1) The OCC's evaluation of a bank's CRA performance is adversely affected by evidence of discriminatory or other illegal credit practices in any geography by the bank or in any assessment area by any affiliate whose loans have been considered as part of the bank's lending performance. In connection with any type of lending activity described in §25.22(a), evidence of discriminatory or other credit practices that violate an applicable law, rule, or regulation includes, but is not limited to:

(i) Discrimination against applicants on a prohibited basis in violation, for example, of the Equal Credit Opportunity Act or the Fair Housing Act;

(ii) Violations of the Home Ownership and Equity Protection Act;

(iii) Violations of section 5 of the Federal Trade Commission Act;

(iv) Violations of section 8 of the Real Estate Settlement Procedures Act; and

(v) Violations of the Truth in Lending Act provisions regarding a consumer's right of rescission.

(2) In determining the effect of evidence of practices described in paragraph (c)(1) of this section on the bank's assigned rating, the OCC considers the nature, extent, and strength of the evidence of the practices; the policies and procedures that the bank (or affiliate, as applicable) has in place to prevent the practices; any corrective action that the bank (or affiliate, as applicable) has taken or has committed to take, including voluntary corrective action resulting from self-assessment; and any other relevant information.

[43 FR 47146, Oct. 12, 1978, as amended at 70 FR 44266, Aug. 2, 2005]

§25.29 Effect of CRA performance on applications.

(a) *CRA performance.* Among other factors, the OCC takes into account the record of performance under the CRA of each applicant bank in considering an application for:

(1) The establishment of a domestic branch;

(2) The relocation of the main office or a branch;

(3) Under the Bank Merger Act (12 U.S.C. 1828(c)), the merger or consolidation with or the acquisition of assets or assumption of liabilities of an insured depository institution; and

(4) The conversion of an insured depository institution to a national bank charter.

(b) *Charter application.* An applicant (other than an insured depository institution) for a national bank charter shall submit with its application a description of how it will meet its CRA objectives. The OCC takes the description into account in considering the application and may deny or condition approval on that basis.

(c) *Interested parties.* The OCC takes into account any views expressed by interested parties that are submitted in accordance with the OCC's procedures set forth in part 5 of this chapter in considering CRA performance in an application listed in paragraphs (a) and (b) of this section.

(d) *Denial or conditional approval of application.* A bank's record of performance may be the basis for denying or conditioning approval of an application listed in paragraph (a) of this section.

(e) *Insured depository institution.* For purposes of this section, the term "insured depository institution" has the meaning given to that term in 12 U.S.C. 1813.

Subpart C—Records, Reporting, and Disclosure Requirements

SOURCE: 60 FR 22184, May 4, 1995, unless otherwise noted.

§25.41 Assessment area delineation.

(a) *In general.* A bank shall delineate one or more assessment areas within which the OCC evaluates the bank's record of helping to meet the credit needs of its community. The OCC does not evaluate the bank's delineation of its assessment area(s) as a separate performance criterion, but the OCC reviews the delineation for compliance with the requirements of this section.

(b) *Geographic area(s) for wholesale or limited purpose banks.* The assessment area(s) for a wholesale or limited purpose bank must consist generally of one or more MSAs or metropolitan divisions (using the MSA or metropolitan division boundaries that were in effect as of January 1 of the calendar year in which the delineation is made) or one or more contiguous political subdivisions, such as counties, cities, or towns, in which the bank has its main office, branches, and deposit-taking ATMs.

(c) *Geographic area(s) for other banks.* The assessment area(s) for a bank other than a wholesale or limited purpose bank must:

(1) Consist generally of one or more MSAs or metropolitan divisions (using the MSA or metropolitan division boundaries that were in effect as of January 1 of the calendar year in which the delineation is made) or one or more contiguous political subdivisions, such as counties, cities, or towns; and

(2) Include the geographies in which the bank has its main office, its branches, and its deposit-taking ATMs, as well as the surrounding geographies in which the bank has originated or purchased a substantial portion of its loans (including home mortgage loans, small business and small farm loans, and any other loans the bank chooses, such as those consumer loans on which the bank elects to have its performance assessed).

(d) *Adjustments to geographic area(s).* A bank may adjust the boundaries of its assessment area(s) to include only the portion of a political subdivision that it reasonably can be expected to serve. An adjustment is particularly appropriate in the case of an assessment area that otherwise would be extremely large, of unusual configuration, or divided by significant geographic barriers.

(e) *Limitations on the delineation of an assessment area.* Each bank's assessment area(s):

(1) Must consist only of whole geographies;

(2) May not reflect illegal discrimination;

(3) May not arbitrarily exclude low- or moderate-income geographies, taking into account the bank's size and financial condition; and

(4) May not extend substantially beyond an MSA boundary or beyond a state boundary unless the assessment area is located in a multistate MSA. If a bank serves a geographic area that extends substantially beyond a state boundary, the bank shall delineate separate assessment areas for the areas in each state. If a bank serves a geographic area that extends substantially beyond an MSA boundary, the bank shall delineate separate assessment areas for the areas inside and outside the MSA.

(f) *Banks serving military personnel.* Notwithstanding the requirements of this section, a bank whose business predominantly consists of serving the needs of military personnel or their dependents who are not located within a defined geographic area may delineate its entire deposit customer base as its assessment area.

(g) *Use of assessment area(s).* The OCC uses the assessment area(s) delineated by a bank in its evaluation of the bank's CRA performance unless the OCC determines that the assessment area(s) do not comply with the requirements of this section.

[60 FR 22184, May 4, 1995, as amended at 69 FR 41186, July 8, 2004]

§ 25.42 Data collection, reporting, and disclosure.

(a) *Loan information required to be collected and maintained.* A bank, except a small bank, shall collect, and maintain in machine readable form (as prescribed by the OCC) until the completion of its next CRA examination, the following data for each small business or small farm loan originated or purchased by the bank:

(1) A unique number or alpha-numeric symbol that can be used to identify the relevant loan file;

(2) The loan amount at origination;

(3) The loan location; and

(4) An indicator whether the loan was to a business or farm with gross annual revenues of $1 million or less.

(b) *Loan information required to be reported.* A bank, except a small bank or a bank that was a small bank during the prior calendar year, shall report annually by March 1 to the OCC in machine readable form (as prescribed by the OCC) the following data for the prior calendar year:

(1) *Small business and small farm loan data.* For each geography in which the bank originated or purchased a small business or small farm loan, the aggregate number and amount of loans:

(i) With an amount at origination of $100,000 or less;

(ii) With amount at origination of more than $100,000 but less than or equal to $250,000;

(iii) With an amount at origination of more than $250,000; and

(iv) To businesses and farms with gross annual revenues of $1 million or less (using the revenues that the bank considered in making its credit decision);

(2) *Community development loan data.* The aggregate number and aggregate amount of community development loans originated or purchased; and

(3) *Home mortgage loans.* If the bank is subject to reporting under part 1003 of this title, the location of each home mortgage loan application, origination, or purchase outside the MSAs in which the bank has a home or branch office (or outside any MSA) in accordance with the requirements of part 1003 of this title.

(c) *Optional data collection and maintenance*—(1) *Consumer loans.* A bank may collect and maintain in machine readable form (as prescribed by the OCC) data for consumer loans originated or purchased by the bank for consideration under the lending test. A bank may maintain data for one or more of the following categories of consumer loans: motor vehicle, credit card, other secured, and other unsecured. If the bank maintains data for loans in a certain category, it shall maintain data for all loans originated or purchased within that category. The bank shall maintain data separately for each category, including for each loan:

(i) A unique number or alpha-numeric symbol that can be used to identify the relevant loan file;

(ii) The loan amount at origination or purchase;

(iii) The loan location; and

(iv) The gross annual income of the borrower that the bank considered in making its credit decision.

(2) *Other loan data.* At its option, a bank may provide other information concerning its lending performance, including additional loan distribution data.

(d) *Data on affiliate lending.* A bank that elects to have the OCC consider loans by an affiliate, for purposes of the lending or community development test or an approved strategic plan, shall collect, maintain, and report for those loans the data that the bank would have collected, maintained, and reported pursuant to paragraphs (a), (b), and (c) of this section had the loans been originated or purchased by the bank. For home mortgage loans, the bank shall also be prepared to identify the home mortgage loans reported under part 1003 of this title by the affiliate.

(e) *Data on lending by a consortium or a third party.* A bank that elects to have the OCC consider community development loans by a consortium or third party, for purposes of the lending or community development tests or an approved strategic plan, shall report for those loans the data that the bank would have reported under paragraph (b)(2) of this section had the loans been originated or purchased by the bank.

(f) *Small banks electing evaluation under the lending, investment, and service tests.* A bank that qualifies for evaluation under the small bank performance standards but elects evaluation under the lending, investment, and service tests shall collect, maintain, and report the data required for other banks pursuant to paragraphs (a) and (b) of this section.

(g) *Assessment area data.* A bank, except a small bank or a bank that was a small bank during the prior calendar year, shall collect and report to the OCC by March 1 of each year a list for each assessment area showing the geographies within the area.

(h) *CRA Disclosure Statement.* The OCC prepares annually for each bank that reports data pursuant to this section a CRA Disclosure Statement that contains, on a state-by-state basis:

(1) For each county (and for each assessment area smaller than a county) with a population of 500,000 persons or fewer in which the bank reported a small business or small farm loan:

(i) The number and amount of small business and small farm loans reported as originated or purchased located in low-, moderate-, middle-, and upper-income geographies;

(ii) A list grouping each geography according to whether the geography is low-, moderate-, middle-, or upper-income;

(iii) A list showing each geography in which the bank reported a small business or small farm loan; and

(iv) The number and amount of small business and small farm loans to businesses and farms with gross annual revenues of $1 million or less;

(2) For each county (and for each assessment area smaller than a county) with a population in excess of 500,000 persons in which the bank reported a small business or small farm loan:

(i) The number and amount of small business and small farm loans reported as originated or purchased located in geographies with median income relative to the area median income of less than 10 percent, 10 or more but less than 20 percent, 20 or more but less than 30 percent, 30 or more but less than 40 percent, 40 or more but less than 50 percent, 50 or more but less than 60 percent, 60 or more but less than 70 percent, 70 or more but less than 80 percent, 80 or more but less than 90 percent, 90 or more but less than 100 percent, 100 or more but less than 110 percent, 110 or more but less than 120 percent, and 120 percent or more;

(ii) A list grouping each geography in the county or assessment area according to whether the median income in the geography relative to the area median income is less than 10 percent, 10 or more but less than 20 percent, 20 or more but less than 30 percent, 30 or more but less than 40 percent, 40 or more but less than 50 percent, 50 or more but less than 60 percent, 60 or more but less than 70 percent, 70 or more but less than 80 percent, 80 or more but less than 90 percent, 90 or more but less than 100 percent, 100 or more but less than 110 percent, 110 or more but less than 120 percent, and 120 percent or more;

(iii) A list showing each geography in which the bank reported a small business or small farm loan; and

(iv) The number and amount of small business and small farm loans to businesses and farms with gross annual revenues of $1 million or less;

(3) The number and amount of small business and small farm loans located inside each assessment area reported by the bank and the number and amount of small business and small farm loans located outside the assessment area(s) reported by the bank; and

(4) The number and amount of community development loans reported as originated or purchased.

(i) *Aggregate disclosure statements.* The OCC, in conjunction with the Board of Governors of the Federal Reserve System and the Federal Deposit Insurance Corporation, prepares annually, for each MSA or metropolitan division (including an MSA or metropolitan division that crosses a state boundary) and the nonmetropolitan portion of each state, an aggregate disclosure statement of small business and small farm lending by all institutions subject to reporting under this part or parts 195, 228, or 345 of this title. These disclosure statements indicate, for each geography, the number and amount of all small business and small farm loans originated or purchased by reporting institutions, except that the OCC may adjust the form of the disclosure if necessary, because of special circumstances, to protect the privacy of a borrower or the competitive position of an institution.

(j) *Central data depositories.* The OCC makes the aggregate disclosure statements, described in paragraph (i) of this section, and the individual bank CRA Disclosure Statements, described in paragraph (h) of this section, available to the public at central data depositories. The OCC publishes a list of the depositories at which the statements are available.

[60 FR 22184, May 4, 1995, as amended at 69 FR 41186, July 8, 2004; 80 FR 81164, Dec. 29, 2015; 82 FR 55742, Nov. 24, 2017]

§ 25.43 Content and availability of public file.

(a) *Information available to the public.* A bank shall maintain a public file that includes the following information:

(1) All written comments received from the public for the current year and each of the prior two calendar

years that specifically relate to the bank's performance in helping to meet community credit needs, and any response to the comments by the bank, if neither the comments nor the responses contain statements that reflect adversely on the good name or reputation of any persons other than the bank or publication of which would violate specific provisions of law;

(2) A copy of the public section of the bank's most recent CRA Performance Evaluation prepared by the OCC. The bank shall place this copy in the public file within 30 business days after its receipt from the OCC;

(3) A list of the bank's branches, their street addresses, and geographies;

(4) A list of branches opened or closed by the bank during the current year and each of the prior two calendar years, their street addresses, and geographies;

(5) A list of services (including hours of operation, available loan and deposit products, and transaction fees) generally offered at the bank's branches and descriptions of material differences in the availability or cost of services at particular branches, if any. At its option, a bank may include information regarding the availability of alternative systems for delivering retail banking services (*e.g.*, ATMs, ATMs not owned or operated by or exclusively for the bank, banking by telephone or computer, loan production offices, and bank-at-work or bank-by-mail programs);

(6) A map of each assessment area showing the boundaries of the area and identifying the geographies contained within the area, either on the map or in a separate list; and

(7) Any other information the bank chooses.

(b) *Additional information available to the public*—(1) *Banks other than small banks*. A bank, except a small bank or a bank that was a small bank during the prior calendar year, shall include in its public file the following information pertaining to the bank and its affiliates, if applicable, for each of the prior two calendar years:

(i) If the bank has elected to have one or more categories of its consumer loans considered under the lending test, for each of these categories, the number and amount of loans:

(A) To low-, moderate-, middle-, and upper-income individuals;

(B) Located in low-, moderate-, middle-, and upper-income census tracts; and

(C) Located inside the bank's assessment area(s) and outside the bank's assessment area(s); and

(ii) The bank's CRA Disclosure Statement. The bank shall place the statement in the public file within three business days of its receipt from the OCC.

(2) *Banks required to report Home Mortgage Disclosure Act (HMDA) data*. A bank required to report home mortgage loan data pursuant part 1003 of this title shall include in its public file a written notice that the institution's HMDA Disclosure Statement may be obtained on the Consumer Financial Protection Bureau's (Bureau's) Web site at *www.consumerfinance.gov/hmda*. In addition, a bank that elected to have the OCC consider the mortgage lending of an affiliate shall include in its public file the name of the affiliate and a written notice that the affiliate's HMDA Disclosure Statement may be obtained at the Bureau's Web site. The bank shall place the written notice(s) in the public file within three business days after receiving notification from the Federal Financial Institutions Examination Council of the availability of the disclosure statement(s).

(3) *Small banks*. A small bank or a bank that was a small bank during the prior calendar year shall include in its public file:

(i) The bank's loan-to-deposit ratio for each quarter of the prior calendar year and, at its option, additional data on its loan-to-deposit ratio; and

(ii) The information required for other banks by paragraph (b)(1) of this section, if the bank has elected to be evaluated under the lending, investment, and service tests.

(4) *Banks with strategic plans*. A bank that has been approved to be assessed under a strategic plan shall include in its public file a copy of that plan. A bank need not include information submitted to the OCC on a confidential basis in conjunction with the plan.

(5) *Banks with less than satisfactory ratings.* A bank that received a less than satisfactory rating during its most recent examination shall include in its public file a description of its current efforts to improve its performance in helping to meet the credit needs of its entire community. The bank shall update the description quarterly.

(c) *Location of public information.* A bank shall make available to the public for inspection upon request and at no cost the information required in this section as follows:

(1) At the main office and, if an interstate bank, at one branch office in each state, all information in the public file; and

(2) At each branch:

(i) A copy of the public section of the bank's most recent CRA Performance Evaluation and a list of services provided by the branch; and

(ii) Within five calendar days of the request, all the information in the public file relating to the assessment area in which the branch is located.

(d) *Copies.* Upon request, a bank shall provide copies, either on paper or in another form acceptable to the person making the request, of the information in its public file. The bank may charge a reasonable fee not to exceed the cost of copying and mailing (if applicable).

(e) *Updating.* Except as otherwise provided in this section, a bank shall ensure that the information required by this section is current as of April 1 of each year.

[60 FR 22184, May 4, 1995, as amended at 80 FR 81164, Dec. 29, 2015; 82 FR 55742, Nov. 24, 2017]

§ 25.44 Public notice by banks.

A bank shall provide in the public lobby of its main office and each of its branches the appropriate public notice set forth in appendix B of this part. Only a branch of a bank having more than one assessment area shall include the bracketed material in the notice for branch offices. Only a bank that is an affiliate of a holding company shall include the next to the last sentence of the notices. A bank shall include the last sentence of the notices only if it is an affiliate of a holding company that is not prevented by statute from acquiring additional banks.

§ 25.45 Publication of planned examination schedule.

The OCC publishes at least 30 days in advance of the beginning of each calendar quarter a list of banks scheduled for CRA examinations in that quarter.

Subpart D [Reserved]

Subpart E—Prohibition Against Use of Interstate Branches Primarily for Deposit Production

SOURCE: 62 FR 47734, Sept. 10, 1997, unless otherwise noted.

§ 25.61 Purpose and scope.

(a) *Purpose.* The purpose of this subpart is to implement section 109 (12 U.S.C. 1835a) of the Riegle-Neal Interstate Banking and Branching Efficiency Act of 1994 (Interstate Act).

(b) *Scope.* (1) This subpart applies to any national bank that has operated a covered interstate branch for a period of at least one year, and any foreign bank that has operated a covered interstate branch that is a Federal branch for a period of at least one year.

(2) This subpart describes the requirements imposed under 12 U.S.C. 1835a, which requires the appropriate Federal banking agencies (the OCC, the Board of Governors of the Federal Reserve System, and the Federal Deposit Insurance Corporation) to prescribe uniform rules that prohibit a bank from using any authority to engage in interstate branching pursuant to the Interstate Act, or any amendment made by the Interstate Act to any other provision of law, primarily for the purpose of deposit production.

§ 25.62 Definitions.

For purposes of this subpart, the following definitions apply:

(a) *Bank* means, unless the context indicates otherwise:

(1) A national bank; and

(2) A foreign bank as that term is defined in 12 U.S.C. 3101(7) and 12 CFR 28.11(j).

(b) *Covered interstate branch* means:

(1) Any branch of a national bank, and any Federal branch of a foreign bank, that:

(i) Is established or acquired outside the bank's home State pursuant to the interstate branching authority granted by the Interstate Act or by any amendment made by the Interstate Act to any other provision of law; or

(ii) Could not have been established or acquired outside of the bank's home State but for the establishment or acquisition of a branch described in paragraph (b)(1)(i) of this section; and

(2) Any bank or branch of a bank controlled by an out-of-State bank holding company.

(c) *Federal branch* means Federal branch as that term is defined in 12 U.S.C. 3101(6) and 12 CFR 28.11(i).

(d) *Home State* means:

(1) With respect to a State bank, the State that chartered the bank;

(2) With respect to a national bank, the State in which the main office of the bank is located;

(3) With respect to a bank holding company, the State in which the total deposits of all banking subsidiaries of such company are the largest on the later of:

(i) July 1, 1966; or

(ii) The date on which the company becomes a bank holding company under the Bank Holding Company Act;

(4) With respect to a foreign bank:

(i) For purposes of determining whether a U.S. branch of a foreign bank is a covered interstate branch, the home State of the foreign bank as determined in accordance with 12 U.S.C. 3103(c) and 12 CFR 28.11(o); and

(ii) For purposes of determining whether a branch of a U.S. bank controlled by a foreign bank is a covered interstate branch, the State in which the total deposits of all banking subsidiaries of such foreign bank are the largest on the later of:

(A) July 1, 1966; or

(B) The date on which the foreign bank becomes a bank holding company under the Bank Holding Company Act.

(e) *Host State* means a State in which a covered interstate branch is established or acquired.

(f) *Host state loan-to-deposit ratio* generally means, with respect to a particular host state, the ratio of total loans in the host state relative to total deposits from the host state for all banks (including institutions covered under the definition of "bank" in 12 U.S.C. 1813(a)(1)) that have that state as their home state, as determined and updated periodically by the appropriate Federal banking agencies and made available to the public.

(g) *Out-of-State bank holding company* means, with respect to any State, a bank holding company whose home State is another State.

(h) *State* means state as that term is defined in 12 U.S.C. 1813(a)(3).

(i) *Statewide loan-to-deposit ratio* means, with respect to a bank, the ratio of the bank's loans to its deposits in a state in which the bank has one or more covered interstate branches, as determined by the OCC.

[62 FR 47734, Sept. 10, 1997, as amended at 67 FR 38847, June 6, 2002; 67 FR 46842, July 17, 2002]

§25.63 Loan-to-deposit ratio screen.

(a) *Application of screen.* Beginning no earlier than one year after a covered interstate branch is acquired or established, the OCC will consider whether the bank's statewide loan-to-deposit ratio is less than 50 percent of the relevant host State loan-to-deposit ratio.

(b) *Results of screen.* (1) If the OCC determines that the bank's statewide loan-to-deposit ratio is 50 percent or more of the host state loan-to-deposit ratio, no further consideration under this subpart is required.

(2) If the OCC determines that the bank's statewide loan-to-deposit ratio is less than 50 percent of the host state loan-to-deposit ratio, or if reasonably available data are insufficient to calculate the bank's statewide loan-to-deposit ratio, the OCC will make a credit needs determination for the bank as provided in §25.64.

[62 FR 47734, Sept. 10, 1997, as amended at 67 FR 38848, June 6, 2002]

§25.64 Credit needs determination.

(a) *In general.* The OCC will review the loan portfolio of the bank and determine whether the bank is reasonably helping to meet the credit needs of the communities in the host state that are served by the bank.

(b) *Guidelines.* The OCC will use the following considerations as guidelines when making the determination pursuant to paragraph (a) of this section:

(1) Whether covered interstate branches were formerly part of a failed or failing depository institution;

(2) Whether covered interstate branches were acquired under circumstances where there was a low loan-to-deposit ratio because of the nature of the acquired institution's business or loan portfolio;

(3) Whether covered interstate branches have a high concentration of commercial or credit card lending, trust services, or other specialized activities, including the extent to which the covered interstate branches accept deposits in the host state;

(4) The CRA ratings received by the bank, if any;

(5) Economic conditions, including the level of loan demand, within the communities served by the covered interstate branches;

(6) The safe and sound operation and condition of the bank; and

(7) The OCC's CRA regulations (subparts A through D of this part) and interpretations of those regulations.

§ 25.65 Sanctions.

(a) *In general.* If the OCC determines that a bank is not reasonably helping to meet the credit needs of the communities served by the bank in the host state, and that the bank's statewide loan-to-deposit ratio is less than 50 percent of the host state loan-to-deposit ratio, the OCC:

(1) May order that a bank's covered interstate branch or branches be closed unless the bank provides reasonable assurances to the satisfaction of the OCC, after an opportunity for public comment, that the bank has an acceptable plan under which the bank will reasonably help to meet the credit needs of the communities served by the bank in the host state; and

(2) Will not permit the bank to open a new branch in the host state that would be considered to be a covered interstate branch unless the bank provides reasonable assurances to the satisfaction of the OCC, after an opportunity for public comment, that the bank will reasonably help to meet the credit needs of the community that the new branch will serve.

(b) *Notice prior to closure of a covered interstate branch.* Before exercising the OCC's authority to order the bank to close a covered interstate branch, the OCC will issue to the bank a notice of the OCC's intent to order the closure and will schedule a hearing within 60 days of issuing the notice.

(c) *Hearing.* The OCC will conduct a hearing scheduled under paragraph (b) of this section in accordance with the provisions of 12 U.S.C. 1818(h) and 12 CFR part 19.

Appendix A to Part 25—Ratings

(a) *Ratings in general.* (1) In assigning a rating, the OCC evaluates a bank's performance under the applicable performance criteria in this part, in accordance with §§ 25.21 and 25.28. This includes consideration of low-cost education loans provided to low-income borrowers and activities in cooperation with minority- or women-owned financial institutions and low-income credit unions, as well as adjustments on the basis of evidence of discriminatory or other illegal credit practices.

(2) A bank's performance need not fit each aspect of a particular rating profile in order to receive that rating, and exceptionally strong performance with respect to some aspects may compensate for weak performance in others. The bank's overall performance, however, must be consistent with safe and sound banking practices and generally with the appropriate rating profile as follows.

(b) *Banks evaluated under the lending, investment, and service tests*—(1) *Lending performance rating.* The OCC assigns each bank's lending performance one of the five following ratings.

(i) *Outstanding.* The OCC rates a bank's lending performance "outstanding" if, in general, it demonstrates:

(A) Excellent responsiveness to credit needs in its assessment area(s), taking into account the number and amount of home mortgage, small business, small farm, and consumer loans, if applicable, in its assessment area(s);

(B) A substantial majority of its loans are made in its assessment area(s);

(C) An excellent geographic distribution of loans in its assessment area(s);

(D) An excellent distribution, particularly in its assessment area(s), of loans among individuals of different income levels and businesses (including farms) of different sizes, given the product lines offered by the bank;

(E) An excellent record of serving the credit needs of highly economically disadvantaged areas in its assessment area(s), low-income individuals, or businesses (including farms) with gross annual revenues of $1 million or less, consistent with safe and sound operations;

(F) Extensive use of innovative or flexible lending practices in a safe and sound manner to address the credit needs of low- or moderate-income individuals or geographies; and

(G) It is a leader in making community development loans.

(ii) *High satisfactory.* The OCC rates a bank's lending performance "high satisfactory" if, in general, it demonstrates:

(A) Good responsiveness to credit needs in its assessment area(s), taking into account the number and amount of home mortgage, small business, small farm, and consumer loans, if applicable, in its assessment area(s);

(B) A high percentage of its loans are made in its assessment area(s);

(C) A good geographic distribution of loans in its assessment area(s);

(D) A good distribution, particularly in its assessment area(s), of loans among individuals of different income levels and businesses (including farms) of different sizes, given the product lines offered by the bank;

(E) A good record of serving the credit needs of highly economically disadvantaged areas in its assessment area(s), low-income individuals, or businesses (including farms) with gross annual revenues of $1 million or less, consistent with safe and sound operations;

(F) Use of innovative or flexible lending practices in a safe and sound manner to address the credit needs of low- or moderate-income individuals or geographies; and

(G) It has made a relatively high level of community development loans.

(iii) *Low satisfactory.* The OCC rates a bank's lending performance "low satisfactory" if, in general, it demonstrates:

(A) Adequate responsiveness to credit needs in its assessment area(s), taking into account the number and amount of home mortgage, small business, small farm, and consumer loans, if applicable, in its assessment area(s);

(B) An adequate percentage of its loans are made in its assessment area(s);

(C) An adequate geographic distribution of loans in its assessment area(s);

(D) An adequate distribution, particularly in its assessment area(s), of loans among individuals of different income levels and businesses (including farms) of different sizes, given the product lines offered by the bank;

(E) An adequate record of serving the credit needs of highly economically disadvantaged areas in its assessment area(s), low-income individuals, or businesses (including farms) with gross annual revenues of $1 million or less, consistent with safe and sound operations;

(F) Limited use of innovative or flexible lending practices in a safe and sound manner to address the credit needs of low- or moderate-income individuals or geographies; and

(G) It has made an adequate level of community development loans.

(iv) *Needs to improve.* The OCC rates a bank's lending performance "needs to improve" if, in general, it demonstrates:

(A) Poor responsiveness to credit needs in its assessment area(s), taking into account the number and amount of home mortgage, small business, small farm, and consumer loans, if applicable, in its assessment area(s);

(B) A small percentage of its loans are made in its assessment area(s);

(C) A poor geographic distribution of loans, particularly to low- or moderate-income geographies, in its assessment area(s);

(D) A poor distribution, particularly in its assessment area(s), of loans among individuals of different income levels and businesses (including farms) of different sizes, given the product lines offered by the bank;

(E) A poor record of serving the credit needs of highly economically disadvantaged areas in its assessment area(s), low-income individuals, or businesses (including farms) with gross annual revenues of $1 million or less, consistent with safe and sound operations;

(F) Little use of innovative or flexible lending practices in a safe and sound manner to address the credit needs of low- or moderate-income individuals or geographies; and

(G) It has made a low level of community development loans.

(v) *Substantial noncompliance.* The OCC rates a bank's lending performance as being in "substantial noncompliance" if, in general, it demonstrates:

(A) A very poor responsiveness to credit needs in its assessment area(s), taking into account the number and amount of home mortgage, small business, small farm, and consumer loans, if applicable, in its assessment area(s);

(B) A very small percentage of its loans are made in its assessment area(s);

(C) A very poor geographic distribution of loans, particularly to low- or moderate-income geographies, in its assessment area(s);

(D) A very poor distribution, particularly in its assessment area(s), of loans among individuals of different income levels and businesses (including farms) of different sizes, given the product lines offered by the bank;

(E) A very poor record of serving the credit needs of highly economically disadvantaged areas in its assessment area(s), low-income individuals, or businesses (including farms) with gross annual revenues of $1 million or less, consistent with safe and sound operations;

(F) No use of innovative or flexible lending practices in a safe and sound manner to address the credit needs of low- or moderate-income individuals or geographies; and

(G) It has made few, if any, community development loans.

(2) *Investment performance rating.* The OCC assigns each bank's investment performance one of the five following ratings.

(i) *Outstanding.* The OCC rates a bank's investment performance "outstanding" if, in general, it demonstrates:

(A) An excellent level of qualified investments, particularly those that are not routinely provided by private investors, often in a leadership position;

(B) Extensive use of innovative or complex qualified investments; and

(C) Excellent responsiveness to credit and community development needs.

(ii) *High satisfactory.* The OCC rates a bank's investment performance "high satisfactory" if, in general, it demonstrates:

(A) A significant level of qualified investments, particularly those that are not routinely provided by private investors, occasionally in a leadership position;

(B) Significant use of innovative or complex qualified investments; and

(C) Good responsiveness to credit and community development needs.

(iii) *Low satisfactory.* The OCC rates a bank's investment performance "low satisfactory" if, in general, it demonstrates:

(A) An adequate level of qualified investments, particularly those that are not routinely provided by private investors, although rarely in a leadership position;

(B) Occasional use of innovative or complex qualified investments; and

(C) Adequate responsiveness to credit and community development needs.

(iv) *Needs to improve.* The OCC rates a bank's investment performance "needs to improve" if, in general, it demonstrates:

(A) A poor level of qualified investments, particularly those that are not routinely provided by private investors;

(B) Rare use of innovative or complex qualified investments; and

(C) Poor responsiveness to credit and community development needs.

(v) *Substantial noncompliance.* The OCC rates a bank's investment performance as being in "substantial noncompliance" if, in general, it demonstrates:

(A) Few, if any, qualified investments, particularly those that are not routinely provided by private investors;

(B) No use of innovative or complex qualified investments; and

(C) Very poor responsiveness to credit and community development needs.

(3) *Service performance rating.* The OCC assigns each bank's service performance one of the five following ratings.

(i) *Outstanding.* The OCC rates a bank's service performance "outstanding" if, in general, the bank demonstrates:

(A) Its service delivery systems are readily accessible to geographies and individuals of different income levels in its assessment area(s);

(B) To the extent changes have been made, its record of opening and closing branches has improved the accessibility of its delivery systems, particularly in low- or moderate-income geographies or to low- or moderate-income individuals;

(C) Its services (including, where appropriate, business hours) are tailored to the convenience and needs of its assessment area(s), particularly low- or moderate-income geographies or low- or moderate-income individuals; and

(D) It is a leader in providing community development services.

(ii) *High satisfactory.* The OCC rates a bank's service performance "high satisfactory" if, in general, the bank demonstrates:

(A) Its service delivery systems are accessible to geographies and individuals of different income levels in its assessment area(s);

(B) To the extent changes have been made, its record of opening and closing branches has not adversely affected the accessibility of its delivery systems, particularly in low- and moderate-income geographies and to low- and moderate-income individuals;

(C) Its services (including, where appropriate, business hours) do not vary in a way that inconveniences its assessment area(s), particularly low- and moderate-income geographies and low- and moderate-income individuals; and

(D) It provides a relatively high level of community development services.

(iii) *Low satisfactory.* The OCC rates a bank's service performance "low satisfactory" if, in general, the bank demonstrates:

(A) Its service delivery systems are reasonably accessible to geographies and individuals of different income levels in its assessment area(s);

(B) To the extent changes have been made, its record of opening and closing branches has generally not adversely affected the accessibility of its delivery systems, particularly in low- and moderate-income geographies and to low- and moderate-income individuals;

(C) Its services (including, where appropriate, business hours) do not vary in a way that inconveniences its assessment area(s), particularly low- and moderate-income geographies and low- and moderate-income individuals; and

(D) It provides an adequate level of community development services.

(iv) *Needs to improve.* The OCC rates a bank's service performance "needs to improve" if, in general, the bank demonstrates:

(A) Its service delivery systems are unreasonably inaccessible to portions of its assessment area(s), particularly to low- or moderate-income geographies or to low- or moderate-income individuals;

(B) To the extent changes have been made, its record of opening and closing branches has adversely affected the accessibility its delivery systems, particularly in low- or moderate-income geographies or to low- or moderate-income individuals;

(C) Its services (including, where appropriate, business hours) vary in a way that inconveniences its assessment area(s), particularly low- or moderate-income geographies or low- or moderate-income individuals; and

(D) It provides a limited level of community development services.

(v) *Substantial noncompliance*. The OCC rates a bank's service performance as being in "substantial noncompliance" if, in general, the bank demonstrates:

(A) Its service delivery systems are unreasonably inaccessible to significant portions of its assessment area(s), particularly to low- or moderate-income geographies or to low- or moderate-income individuals;

(B) To the extent changes have been made, its record of opening and closing branches has significantly adversely affected the accessibility of its delivery systems, particularly in low- or moderate-income geographies or to low- or moderate-income individuals;

(C) Its services (including, where appropriate, business hours) vary in a way that significantly inconveniences its assessment area(s), particularly low- or moderate-income geographies or low- or moderate-income individuals; and

(D) It provides few, if any, community development services.

(c) *Wholesale or limited purpose banks*. The OCC assigns each wholesale or limited purpose bank's community development performance one of the four following ratings.

(1) *Outstanding*. The OCC rates a wholesale or limited purpose bank's community development performance "outstanding" if, in general, it demonstrates:

(i) A high level of community development loans, community development services, or qualified investments, particularly investments that are not routinely provided by private investors;

(ii) Extensive use of innovative or complex qualified investments, community development loans, or community development services; and

(iii) Excellent responsiveness to credit and community development needs in its assessment area(s).

(2) *Satisfactory*. The OCC rates a wholesale or limited purpose bank's community development performance "satisfactory" if, in general, it demonstrates:

(i) An adequate level of community development loans, community development services, or qualified investments, particularly investments that are not routinely provided by private investors;

(ii) Occasional use of innovative or complex qualified investments, community development loans, or community development services; and

(iii) Adequate responsiveness to credit and community development needs in its assessment area(s).

(3) *Needs to improve*. The OCC rates a wholesale or limited purpose bank's community development performance as "needs to improve" if, in general, it demonstrates:

(i) A poor level of community development loans, community development services, or qualified investments, particularly investments that are not routinely provided by private investors;

(ii) Rare use of innovative or complex qualified investments, community development loans, or community development services; and

(iii) Poor responsiveness to credit and community development needs in its assessment area(s).

(4) *Substantial noncompliance*. The OCC rates a wholesale or limited purpose bank's community development performance in "substantial noncompliance" if, in general, it demonstrates:

(i) Few, if any, community development loans, community development services, or qualified investments, particularly investments that are not routinely provided by private investors;

(ii) No use of innovative or complex qualified investments, community development loans, or community development services; and

(iii) Very poor responsiveness to credit and community development needs in its assessment area(s).

(d) *Banks evaluated under the small bank performance standards*—(1) *Lending test ratings*. (i) *Eligibility for a satisfactory lending test rating*. The OCC rates a small bank's lending performance "satisfactory" if, in general, the bank demonstrates:

(A) A reasonable loan-to-deposit ratio (considering seasonal variations) given the bank's size, financial condition, the credit needs of its assessment area(s), and taking into account, as appropriate, other lending-related activities such as loan originations for sale to the secondary markets and community development loans and qualified investments;

(B) A majority of its loans and, as appropriate, other lending-related activities, are in its assessment area;

(C) A distribution of loans to and, as appropriate, other lending-related activities for individuals of different income levels (including low- and moderate-income individuals) and businesses and farms of different sizes that is reasonable given the demographics of the bank's assessment area(s);

(D) A record of taking appropriate action, when warranted, in response to written complaints, if any, about the bank's performance in helping to meet the credit needs of its assessment area(s); and

(E) A reasonable geographic distribution of loans given the bank's assessment area(s).

(ii) *Eligibility for an "outstanding" lending test rating.* A small bank that meets each of the standards for a "satisfactory" rating under this paragraph and exceeds some or all of those standards may warrant consideration for a lending test rating of "outstanding."

(iii) *Needs to improve or substantial noncompliance ratings.* A small bank may also receive a lending test rating of "needs to improve" or "substantial noncompliance" depending on the degree to which its performance has failed to meet the standard for a "satisfactory" rating.

(2) *Community development test ratings for intermediate small banks*—(i) *Eligibility for a satisfactory community development test rating.* The OCC rates an intermediate small bank's community development performance "satisfactory" if the bank demonstrates adequate responsiveness to the community development needs of its assessment area(s) through community development loans, qualified investments, and community development services. The adequacy of the bank's response will depend on its capacity for such community development activities, its assessment area's need for such community development activities, and the availability of such opportunities for community development in the bank's assessment area(s).

(ii) *Eligibility for an outstanding community development test rating.* The OCC rates an intermediate small bank's community development performance "outstanding" if the bank demonstrates excellent responsiveness to community development needs in its assessment area(s) through community development loans, qualified investments, and community development services, as appropriate, considering the bank's capacity and the need and availability of such opportunities for community development in the bank's assessment area(s).

(iii) *Needs to improve or substantial noncompliance ratings.* An intermediate small bank may also receive a community development test rating of "needs to improve" or "substantial noncompliance" depending on the degree to which its performance has failed to meet the standards for a "satisfactory" rating.

(3) *Overall rating*—(i) *Eligibility for a satisfactory overall rating.* No intermediate small bank may receive an assigned overall rating of "satisfactory" unless it receives a rating of at least "satisfactory" on both the lending test and the community development test.

(ii) *Eligibility for an outstanding overall rating.* (A) An intermediate small bank that receives an "outstanding" rating on one test and at least "satisfactory" on the other test may receive an assigned overall rating of "outstanding."

(B) A small bank that is not an intermediate small bank that meets each of the standards for a "satisfactory" rating under the lending test and exceeds some or all of those standards may warrant consideration for an overall rating of "outstanding." In assessing whether a bank's performance is "outstanding," the OCC considers the extent to which the bank exceeds each of the performance standards for a "satisfactory" rating and its performance in making qualified investments and its performance in providing branches and other services and delivery systems that enhance credit availability in its assessment area(s).

(iii) *Needs to improve or substantial noncompliance overall ratings.* A small bank may also receive a rating of "needs to improve" or "substantial noncompliance" depending on the degree to which its performance has failed to meet the standards for a "satisfactory" rating.

(e) *Strategic plan assessment and rating*—(1) *Satisfactory goals.* The OCC approves as "satisfactory" measurable goals that adequately help to meet the credit needs of the bank's assessment area(s).

(2) *Outstanding goals.* If the plan identifies a separate group of measurable goals that substantially exceed the levels approved as "satisfactory," the OCC will approve those goals as "outstanding."

(3) *Rating.* The OCC assesses the performance of a bank operating under an approved plan to determine if the bank has met its plan goals:

(i) If the bank substantially achieves its plan goals for a satisfactory rating, the OCC will rate the bank's performance under the plan as "satisfactory."

(ii) If the bank exceeds its plan goals for a satisfactory rating and substantially achieves its plan goals for an outstanding rating, the OCC will rate the bank's performance under the plan as "outstanding."

(iii) If the bank fails to meet substantially its plan goals for a satisfactory rating, the OCC will rate the bank as either "needs to improve" or "substantial noncompliance," depending on the extent to which it falls short of its plan goals, unless the bank elected in its plan to be rated otherwise, as provided in §25.27(f)(4).

[60 FR 22186, May 4, 1995, as amended at 70 FR 44267, Aug. 2, 2005; 75 FR 61044, Oct. 4, 2010]

APPENDIX B TO PART 25—CRA NOTICE

(a) *Notice for main offices and, if an interstate bank, one branch office in each state.*

COMMUNITY REINVESTMENT ACT NOTICE

Under the Federal Community Reinvestment Act (CRA), the Comptroller of the Currency evaluates our record of helping to meet the credit needs of this community consistent with safe and sound operations. The Comptroller also takes this record into account when deciding on certain applications submitted by us.

Your involvement is encouraged.

You are entitled to certain information about our operations and our performance under the CRA, including, for example, information about our branches, such as their location and services provided at them; the public section of our most recent CRA Performance Evaluation, prepared by the Comptroller; and comments received from the public relating to our performance in helping to meet community credit needs, as well as our responses to those comments. You may review this information today.

At least 30 days before the beginning of each quarter, the Comptroller publishes a nationwide list of the banks that are scheduled for CRA examination in that quarter. This list is available from the Deputy Comptroller (address). You may send written comments about our performance in helping to meet community credit needs to (name and address of official at bank) and Deputy Comptroller (address). Your letter, together with any response by us, will be considered by the Comptroller in evaluating our CRA performance and may be made public.

You may ask to look at any comments received by the Deputy Comptroller. You may also request from the Deputy Comptroller an announcement of our applications covered by the CRA filed with the Comptroller. We are an affiliate of (name of holding company), a bank holding company. You may request from the (title of responsible official), Federal Reserve Bank of ________ (address) an announcement of applications covered by the CRA filed by bank holding companies.

(b) *Notice for branch offices.*

COMMUNITY REINVESTMENT ACT NOTICE

Under the Federal Community Reinvestment Act (CRA), the Comptroller of the Currency evaluates our record of helping to meet the credit needs of this community consistent with safe and sound operations. The Comptroller also takes this record into account when deciding on certain applications submitted by us.

Your involvement is encouraged.

You are entitled to certain information about our operations and our performance under the CRA. You may review today the public section of our most recent CRA evaluation, prepared by the Comptroller, and a list of services provided at this branch. You may also have access to the following additional information, which we will make available to you at this branch within five calendar days after you make a request to us: (1) A map showing the assessment area containing this branch, which is the area in which the Comptroller evaluates our CRA performance in this community; (2) information about our branches in this assessment area; (3) a list of services we provide at those locations; (4) data on our lending performance in this assessment area; and (5) copies of all written comments received by us that specifically relate to our CRA performance in this assessment area, and any responses we have made to those comments. If we are operating under an approved strategic plan, you may also have access to a copy of the plan.

[If you would like to review information about our CRA performance in other communities served by us, the public file for our entire bank is available at (name of office located in state), located at (address).]

At least 30 days before the beginning of each quarter, the Comptroller publishes a nationwide list of the banks that are scheduled for CRA examination in that quarter. This list is available from the Deputy Comptroller (address). You may send written comments about our performance in helping to meet community credit needs to (name and address of official at bank) and Deputy Comptroller (address). Your letter, together with any response by us, will be considered by the Comptroller in evaluating our CRA performance and may be made public.

You may ask to look at any comments received by the Deputy Comptroller. You may also request from the Deputy Comptroller an announcement of our applications covered by the CRA filed with the Comptroller. We are an affiliate of (name of holding company), a bank holding company. You may request from the (title of responsible official), Federal Reserve Bank of ________ (address) an announcement of applications covered by the CRA filed by bank holding companies.

[60 FR 22189, May 4, 1995]

PART 26—MANAGEMENT OFFICIAL INTERLOCKS

Sec.

26.1 Authority, purpose, and scope.
26.2 Definitions.
26.3 Prohibitions.
26.4 Interlocking relationships permitted by statute.
26.5 Small market share exemption.
26.6 General exemption.
26.7 Change in circumstances.

26.8 Enforcement.

AUTHORITY: 12 U.S.C. 1, 93a, 1462a, 1463, 1464, 3201–3208, 5412(b)(2)(B).

SOURCE: 61 FR 40300, Aug. 2, 1996, unless otherwise noted.

§ 26.1 Authority, purpose, and scope.

(a) *Authority*. This part is issued under the provisions of the Depository Institution Management Interlocks Act (Interlocks Act) (12 U.S.C. 3201 *et seq*.), as amended, and the OCC's general rulemaking authority for national banks in 12 U.S.C. 93a and Federal savings associations in 12 U.S.C. 1462a and 5412(b)(2)(B).

(b) *Purpose*. The purpose of the Interlocks Act and this part is to foster competition by generally prohibiting a management official from serving two nonaffiliated depository organizations in situations where the management interlock likely would have an anticompetitive effect.

(c) *Scope*. This part applies to management officials of national banks, Federal savings associations, and their affiliates.

[73 FR 22251, Apr. 24, 2008, as amended at 79 FR 28399, May 16, 2014]

§ 26.2 Definitions.

For purposes of this part, the following definitions apply:

(a) *Affiliate*. (1) The term *affiliate* has the meaning given in section 202 of the Interlocks Act (12 U.S.C. 3201). For purposes of that section 202, shares held by an individual include shares held by members of his or her immediate family. "Immediate family" means spouse, mother, father, child, grandchild, sister, brother, or any of their spouses, whether or not any of their shares are held in trust.

(2) For purposes of section 202(3)(B) of the Interlocks Act (12 U.S.C. 3201(3)(B)), an affiliate relationship involving a national bank or Federal savings association based on common ownership does not exist if the OCC determines, after giving the affected persons the opportunity to respond, that the asserted affiliation was established in order to avoid the prohibitions of the Interlocks Act and does not represent a true commonality of interest between the depository organizations. In making this determination, the OCC considers, among other things, whether a person, including members of his or her immediate family, whose shares are necessary to constitute the group, owns a nominal percentage of the shares of one of the organizations and the percentage is substantially disproportionate to that person's ownership of shares in the other organization.

(b) *Area median income* means:

(1) The median family income for the metropolitan statistical area (MSA), if a depository organization is located in an MSA; or

(2) The statewide nonmetropolitan median family income, if a depository organization is located outside an MSA.

(c) *Community* means a city, town, or village, and contiguous or adjacent cities, towns, or villages.

(d) *Contiguous or adjacent cities, towns, or villages* means cities, towns, or villages whose borders touch each other or whose borders are within 10 road miles of each other at their closest points. The property line of an office located in an unincorporated city, town, or village is the boundary line of that city, town, or village for the purpose of this definition.

(e) *Depository holding company* means a bank holding company or a savings and loan holding company (as more fully defined in section 202 of the Interlocks Act (12 U.S.C. 3201)) having its principal office located in the United States.

(f) *Depository institution* means a commercial bank (including a private bank), a savings bank, a trust company, a savings and loan association, a building and loan association, a homestead association, a cooperative bank, an industrial bank, or a credit union, chartered under the laws of the United States and having a principal office located in the United States. Additionally, a United States office, including a branch or agency, of a foreign commercial bank is a depository institution.

(g) *Depository institution affiliate* means a depository institution that is an affiliate of a depository organization.

(h) *Depository organization* means a depository institution or a depository holding company.

(i) *Low- and moderate-income areas* means census tracts (or, if an area is not in a census tract, block numbering areas delineated by the United States Bureau of the Census) where the median family income is less than 100 percent of the area median income.

(j) *Management official.* (1) The term *management official* means:

(i) A director;

(ii) An advisory or honorary director of a depository institution with total assets of $100 million or more;

(iii) A senior executive officer as that term is defined in 12 CFR 5.51(c)(3);

(iv) A branch manager;

(v) A trustee of a depository organization under the control of trustees; and

(vi) Any person who has a representative or nominee serving in any of the capacities in this paragaph (j)(1).

(2) The term *management official* does not include:

(i) A person whose management functions relate exclusively to the business of retail merchandising or manufacturing;

(ii) A person whose management functions relate principally to the business outside the United States of a foreign commercial bank; or

(iii) A person described in the provisos of section 202(4) of the Interlocks Act (12 U.S.C. 3201(4)) (referring to an officer of a State-chartered savings bank, cooperative bank, or trust company that neither makes real estate mortgage loans nor accepts savings).

(k) *Office* means a principal or branch office of a depository institution located in the United States. *Office* does not include a representative office of a foreign commercial bank, an electronic terminal, or a loan production office.

(l) *Person* means a natural person, corporation, or other business entity.

(m) *Relevant metropolitan statistical area (RMSA)* means an MSA, a primary MSA, or a consolidated MSA that is not comprised of designated primary MSAs to the extent that these terms are defined and applied by the Office of Management and Budget.

(n) *Representative or nominee* means a natural person who serves as a management official and has an obligation to act on behalf of another person with respect to management responsibilities. The OCC will find that a person has an obligation to act on behalf of another person only if the first person has an agreement, express or implied, to act on behalf of the second person with respect to management responsibilities. The OCC will determine, after giving the affected persons an opportunity to respond, whether a person is a *representative or nominee.*

(o) *Total assets.* (1) The term *total assets* means assets measured on a consolidated basis and reported in the most recent fiscal year-end Consolidated Report of Condition and Income.

(2) The term *total assets* does not include:

(i) Assets of a diversified savings and loan holding company as defined by section 10(a)(1)(F) of the Home Owners' Loan Act (12 U.S.C. 1467a(a)(1)(F)) other than the assets of its depository institution affiliate;

(ii) Assets of a bank holding company that is exempt from the prohibitions of section 4 of the Bank Holding Company Act of 1956 pursuant to an order issued under section 4(d) of that Act (12 U.S.C. 1843(d)) other than the assets of its depository institution affiliate; or

(iii) Assets of offices of a foreign commercial bank other than the assets of its United States branch or agency.

(p) *United States* means the United States of America, any State or territory of the United States of America, the District of Columbia, Puerto Rico, Guam, American Samoa, and the Virgin Islands.

[61 FR 40300, Aug. 2, 1996, as amended at 64 FR 51678, Sept. 24, 1999; 72 FR 1276, Jan. 11, 2007; 73 FR 22251, Apr. 24, 2008; 79 FR 28399, May 16, 2014]

§ 26.3 Prohibitions.

(a) *Community.* A management official of a depository organization may not serve at the same time as a management official of an unaffiliated depository organization if the depository organizations in question (or a depository institution affiliate thereof) have offices in the same community.

(b) *RMSA.* A management official of a depository organization may not serve at the same time as a management official of an unaffiliated depository organization if the depository organizations in question (or a depository institution affiliate thereof) have offices in the same RMSA and each depository organization has total assets of $50 million or more.

(c) *Major assets.* A management official of a depository organization with total assets exceeding $2.5 billion (or any affiliate of such an organization) may not serve at the same time as a management official of an unaffiliated depository organization with total assets exceeding $1.5 billion (or any affiliate of such an organization), regardless of the location of the two depository organizations. The OCC will adjust these thresholds, as necessary, based on the year-to-year change in the average of the Consumer Price Index for the Urban Wage Earners and Clerical Workers, not seasonally adjusted, with rounding to the nearest $100 million. The OCC will announce the revised thresholds by publishing a final rule without notice and comment in the FEDERAL REGISTER.

[61 FR 40300, Aug. 2, 1996, as amended at 64 FR 51678, Sept. 24, 1999; 72 FR 1276, Jan. 11, 2007]

§ 26.4 Interlocking relationships permitted by statute.

The prohibitions of § 26.3 do not apply in the case of any one or more of the following organizations or to a subsidiary thereof:

(a) A depository organization that has been placed formally in liquidation, or which is in the hands of a receiver, conservator, or other official exercising a similar function;

(b) A corporation operating under section 25 or section 25A of the Federal Reserve Act (12 U.S.C. 601 *et seq.* and 12 U.S.C. 611 *et seq.*, respectively) (Edge Corporations and Agreement Corporations);

(c) A credit union being served by a management official of another credit union;

(d) A depository organization that does not do business within the United States except as an incident to its activities outside the United States;

(e) A State-chartered savings and loan guaranty corporation;

(f) A Federal Home Loan Bank or any other bank organized solely to serve depository institutions (a bankers' bank) or solely for the purpose of providing securities clearing services and services related thereto for depository institutions and securities companies;

(g) A depository organization that is closed or is in danger of closing as determined by the appropriate Federal depository institutions regulatory agency and is acquired by another depository organization. This exemption lasts for five years, beginning on the date the depository organization is acquired; and

(h)(1) A diversified savings and loan holding company (as defined in section 10(a)(1)(F) of the Home Owners' Loan Act (12 U.S.C. 1467a(a)(1)(F)) with respect to the service of a director of such company who also is a director of an unaffiliated depository organization if:

(i) Both the diversified savings and loan holding company and the unaffiliated depository organization notify their appropriate Federal depository institutions regulatory agency at least 60 days before the dual service is proposed to begin; and

(ii) The appropriate regulatory agency does not disapprove the dual service before the end of the 60-day period.

(2) The OCC may disapprove a notice of proposed service if it finds that:

(i) The service cannot be structured or limited so as to preclude an anticompetitive effect in financial services in any part of the United States;

(ii) The service would lead to substantial conflicts of interest or unsafe or unsound practices; or

(iii) The notificant failed to furnish all the information required by the OCC.

(3) The OCC may require that any interlock permitted under this paragraph (h) be terminated if a change in circumstances occurs with respect to one of the interlocked depository organizations that would have provided a basis for disapproval of the interlock during the notice period.

(i) Any savings association that has issued stock in connection with a qualified stock issuance pursuant to section 10(q) of the HOLA, as provided by section 205(9) of the Interlocks Act (12 U.S.C. 3204(9)).

(j) A management official or prospective management official of a depository organization may enter into an otherwise prohibited interlocking relationship with a Federal savings association for a period of up to 10 years if such relationship is approved by the Federal Deposit Insurance Corporation pursuant to section 13(k)(1)(A)(v) of the Federal Deposit Insurance Act, as amended (12 U.S.C. 1823(k)(1)(A)(v)).

[61 FR 40300, Aug. 2, 1996, as amended at 79 FR 28399, May 16, 2014]

§ 26.5 Small market share exemption.

(a) *Exemption.* A management interlock that is prohibited by § 26.3 is permissible, if:

(1) The interlock is not prohibited by § 26.3(c); and

(2) The depository organizations (and their depository institution affiliates) hold, in the aggregate, no more than 20 percent of the deposits in each RMSA or community in which both depository organizations (or their depository institution affiliates) have offices. The amount of deposits shall be determined by reference to the most recent annual Summary of Deposits published by the FDIC for the RMSA or community.

(b) *Confirmation and records.* Each depository organization must maintain records sufficient to support its determination of eligibility for the exemption under paragraph (a) of this section, and must reconfirm that determination on an annual basis.

[64 FR 51678, Sept. 24, 1999]

§ 26.6 General exemption.

(a) *Exemption.* The OCC may by order issued following receipt of an application, exempt an interlock from the prohibitions in § 26.3 if the OCC finds that the interlock would not result in a monopoly or substantial lessening of competition and would not present safety and soundness concerns.

(b) *Presumptions.* In reviewing an application for an exemption under this section, the OCC will apply a rebuttable presumption that an interlock will not result in a monopoly or substantial lessening of competition if the depository organization seeking to add a management official:

(1) Primarily serves low-and moderate-income areas;

(2) Is controlled or managed by persons who are members of a minority group, or women;

(3) Is a depository institution that has been chartered for less than two years; or

(4) Is deemed to be in "troubled condition" as defined in 12 CFR 5.51(c)(6).

(c) *Duration.* (1) Unless a specific expiration period is provided in the OCC approval, an exemption permitted by paragraph (a) of this section may continue so long as it does not result in either:

(i) A monopoly or substantial lessening of competition; or

(ii) An unsafe or unsound condition.

(2) If the OCC grants an interlock exemption in reliance upon a presumption under paragraph (b) of this section, the interlock may continue for three years, unless otherwise provided by the OCC in writing.

[64 FR 51678, Sept. 24, 1999, as amended at 79 FR 28399, May 16, 2014]

§ 26.7 Change in circumstances.

(a) *Termination.* A management official shall terminate his or her service or apply for an exemption if a change in circumstances causes the service to become prohibited. A change in circumstances may include an increase in asset size of an organization, a change in the delineation of the RMSA or community, the establishment of an office, an increase in the aggregate deposits of the depository organization, or an acquisition, merger, consolidation, or any reorganization of the ownership structure of a depository organization that causes a previously permissible interlock to become prohibited.

(b) *Transition period.* A management official described in paragraph (a) of this section may continue to serve the depository organization involved in the interlock for 15 months following the date of the change in circumstances. The OCC may shorten this period under appropriate circumstances.

[61 FR 40300, Aug. 2, 1996, as amended at 64 FR 51678, Sept. 24, 1999]

§ 26.8 Enforcement.

Except as provided in this section, the OCC administers and enforces the Interlocks Act with respect to national banks, Federal savings associations, and their affiliates, and may refer any case of a prohibited interlocking relationship involving these entities to the Attorney General of the United States to enforce compliance with the Interlocks Act and this part. If an affiliate of a national bank or Federal savings association is subject to the primary regulation of another Federal depository organization supervisory agency, then the OCC does not administer and enforce the Interlocks Act with respect to that affiliate.

[73 FR 22251, Apr. 24, 2008, as amended at 79 FR 28399, May 16, 2014]

PART 27—FAIR HOUSING HOME LOAN DATA SYSTEM

Sec.
27.1 Scope and OMB control number.
27.2 Definitions.
27.3 Recordkeeping requirements.
27.4 Inquiry/Application Log.
27.5 Record retention period.
27.6 Substitute monitoring program.
27.7 Availability, submission and use of data.

APPENDIX I TO PART 27—MONTHLY HOME LOAN ACTIVITY FORMAT
APPENDIX II TO PART 27—INFORMATION FOR GOVERNMENT MONITORING PURPOSES
APPENDIX III TO PART 27—FAIR HOUSING LENDING INQUIRY/APPLICATION LOG SHEET
APPENDIX IV TO PART 27—HOME LOAN DATA SUBMISSION

AUTHORITY: 5 U.S.C. 301; 12 U.S.C. 1 *et seq.*, 93a, 161, 481, and 1818; 15 U.S.C. 1691 *et seq.;* 42 U.S.C. 3601 *et seq.;* 12 CFR part 202.

SOURCE: 44 FR 63089, Nov. 2, 1979, unless otherwise noted.

§ 27.1 Scope and OMB control number.

(a) *Scope.* This part applies to the activities of national banks and their subsidiaries, which make home loans for the purpose of purchasing, construction-permanent financing, or refinancing of residential real property.

(b) *OMB control number.* The collection of information requirements contained in this part were approved by the Office of Management and Budget under OMB control number 1557–0160.

[49 FR 11825, Mar. 28, 1984, as amended at 73 FR 22251, Apr. 24, 2008]

§ 27.2 Definitions.

For the purpose of this part, including all forms and instructions issued for use under this part:

(a) *Applicant* means a natural person, including a co-applicant, who makes an application.

(b) *Application* means an oral in-person or written request for an extension of credit for a home loan that is made in accordance with procedures established by a bank for the type of credit requested.

(c) *Bank* means a national bank and any subsidiaries of a national bank.

(d) *Completed application* means an application in connection with which a bank has received all the information that it regularly obtains and considers in evaluating the amount and type of credit requested.

(e) *Decision center* means the place where home loan applications are accepted or rejected.

(f) *Home loan* means a real estate loan for the purchase, permanent financing for construction, or the refinancing of residential real property which the applicant intends to occupy as a principal residence.

(g) *Inquirer* means a natural person who makes an inquiry.

(h) *Inquiry* means a written or an oral in-person request for information about the terms of a home loan by a natural person on his/her own behalf which is received on a bank's premises by any person at the bank who customarily receives or is authorized to receive such requests. Telephonic communications do not constitute an inquiry for purposes of this part.

(i) *Real estate loan* means any loan secured by real estate where the bank relies upon such real estate as the primary security for the loan. Where the bank in its judgment relies substantially upon other factors, such as the general credit standing of the borrower, guaranties, or security other than real estate, the loan does not constitute a real estate loan, although as a matter of prudent banking practice it may also be secured by real estate.

(1) A loan made in reliance upon the security of a mobile home will not be considered a real estate loan, although as a prudent banking practice the security interest is recorded or otherwise perfected as if the mobile home were real estate. For purposes of this part, a loan made in reliance upon the security of a mobile home and the parcel of land to which it is permanently affixed will be considered a real estate loan.

(2) Where the bank relies substantially on the insurance guaranty of a governmental agency in making a loan, it does not constitute a real estate loan except for the purposes of §27.4 of this part (Inquiry/Application Log).

(j) *Residential real property* means improved real property (not vacant land) used or intended to be used for residential purposes, including single family homes, dwellings for from two to four families, and individual units of condominiums and cooperatives.

[44 FR 63089, Nov. 2, 1979, as amended at 73 FR 22251, Apr. 24, 2008]

§27.3 Recordkeeping requirements.

(a) *Quarterly recordkeeping requirement.* (1) A bank that is required to collect data on home loans under part 203 of this title shall present the data on Federal Reserve Form FR HMDA-LAR or in an automated format in accordance with the instructions, except that:

(i) A bank shall maintain the reason(s) it denied a loan application, using the codes provided in part 203 of this title; and

(ii) A bank shall record all information required by this paragraph and part 203 of this title within 30 calendar days after the end of each calendar quarter.

(2) A bank that receives 50 or more home loan applications a year, as measured by the previous calendar year, and that is not required to collect data under paragraph (a)(1) of this section, shall record and maintain for each decision center the following information on home loan activity:

(i) Number of applications received for each of the following: Purchase; construction-permanent; refinance.

(ii) Number of loans closed for each of the following: Purchase; construction-permanent; refinance.

(iii) Number of loans denied for each of the following: Purchase; construction-permanent; refinance.

(iv) Number of loans withdrawn by applicant, for each of the following: Purchase; construction-permanent; refinance.

(3) The information required to be maintained under paragraph (a)(2) of this section shall be updated quarterly, within 30 calendar days after the end of each calendar quarter, in a format consistent with the bank's recordkeeping procedures.

(4) A bank exempted under paragraph (a)(2) of this section shall be covered by that requirement beginning the month following any quarter in which their average monthly volume of home loan applications exceeds four applications per month. Banks which are subject to this paragraph may discontinue keeping this information beginning the month following two consecutive quarters in which their average monthly volume of home loan applications drops to four or fewer applications per month. A bank which is otherwise exempted under this paragraph may be required upon notification received from the Comptroller, to record and maintain such information where there is cause to believe that the bank is not in compliance with the fair housing laws based on prior examinations and/or has substantive consumer complaints, among other factors.

(5) A bank required to maintain information under paragraph (a)(2) or (a)(4) of this section may choose to comply with the quarterly recordkeeping requirement by maintaining information in accordance with paragraph (a)(1) of this section.

(b) *Information required on applications for home loan.s* (1) Each bank shall attempt to obtain all of the information listed below, as part of completed applications for home loans:

(i) Loan Amount requested by the applicant(s).

(ii) Interest rate requested by the applicant(s).

(iii) Number of months requested to maturity by the applicant(s).

(iv) Location. Complete street address, city, county, state and zip code of the dwelling which will secure the loan.

(v) Number of residential units (1–4) of the dwelling which will secure the loan.

(vi) Year built. The year in which the dwelling which will secure the loan was built. If the exact year is unknown, approximate to the nearest decade.

(vii) Purpose of the loan. Purchase; refinance; or construction-permanent.

(viii) Name and present address of applicant(s).

(ix) Age of applicant(s).

(x) Marital status of applicant(s) using the categories married, unmarried and separated.

(xi) Number of years employed in present line of work or profession for the applicant(s).

(xii) Years on present job. Number of continuous years employed by the current employer of the applicant(s). For self-employed persons, the number of continuous years self-employed.

(xiii) Gross total monthly income of each applicant, comprising the sum of normal base salary, wages, overtime pay, bonuses, commissions, dividends, interest, rental income, retirement or disability income and income from part-time employment. For self-employed persons, include the average or normal monthly income. Include alimony, separate maintenance and child support income information only if the applicant has been advised that such information need not be provided and nevertheless elects to have it considered.

(xiv) Proposed monthly housing payment, comprising the sum of principal and interest. The bank may also include insurance, real estate taxes and any monthly assessments for home owner dues or condominium fees, and/or utilities if the bank considers these factors in computing housing costs. However, if the bank includes any of these factors for computing the monthly housing payment, it must do so consistently. When a bank changes its regular practice, such change and its effective date should be identifiable with respect to the bank's new policy.

(xv) Purchase price. Sales price or approximate current market value of the property which will secure the loan.

(xvi) Applicant's or applicants' total monthly payments on all outstanding liabilities. Include installment debts, real estate loans and any alimony, child support or separate maintenance payments. Exclude any payments on liabilities which will be satisfied upon sale of real estate owned or upon refinancing of property associated with this application.

(xvii) Net worth. Applicant's or applicants' total assets, including cash checking and savings accounts, stocks and bonds, cash value of life insurance, value of real estate owned, net worth of business owned, automobile, furniture and personal property and other assets, minus total liabilities, including installment debts, automobile loans, real estate loans, and any other debts, including stock pledges.

(xviii) Date of application. The date on which a signed application is received by the bank.

(xix) Sex of applicant(s).

(xx) Race/national origin of applicant(s) using the categories: American Indian or Alaskan Native; Asian or Pacific Islander; Black, not of Hispanic origin; White, not of Hispanic origin; Hispanic; Other.

(2) Information on race/national origin and sex.

(i) Disclosure to applicant.

(A) In collecting the information required under § 27.3(b)(1) (xix) and (xx), the bank shall advise an applicant, either orally or in writing, that:

(*1*) The information on race/national origin and sex is requested by the Federal Government if this loan is related to a home loan, in order to monitor the lender's compliance with equal credit opportunity and fair housing laws;

(*2*) The applicant is not required to furnish the information but is encouraged to do so. The law provides that a lender may neither discriminate on the basis of this information, nor on whether the applicant chooses to furnish it;

(*3*) However, if the applicant chooses not to furnish it, Federal regulations require the lender to note race and sex on the basis of visual observation or surname.

(B) Banks which use the Federal Home Loan Mortgage Corporation/Federal National Mortgage Association (FHLMC/FNMA) insert form ("Information for Government Monitoring

Purposes") requesting this information will be in compliance with paragraph (b)(2)(i) of this section. A copy of the insert form is set forth in appendix II.

(ii) If the applicant does not voluntarily provide the information on sex and race/national origin which the bank is required to record and maintain under §27.3(b)(1) (xix) and (xx), the bank shall request the applicant to note that fact (by initials or otherwise) on the application, and the bank shall provide the information based on visual observation or surname. If the applicant does not voluntarily provide the information and does not initial or otherwise note that fact, the bank shall initial, or otherwise note that fact on the application, as well as provide the information based on visual observation or surname.

(c) *Additional information required in the loan file.* In addition to the information required by §27.3(b), each bank shall maintain the following information in each of its home loan files:

(1) If an appraisal is completed:

(i) The appraised value; and

(ii) The census tract number, where available, for those properties which are in a Standard Metropolitan Statistical Area (SMSA) in which the bank has a home office or branch office.

(2) Disposition of loan application. The disposition of the completed applications using the following categories:

(i) Withdrawn before terms were offered;

(ii) Withdrawn after terms were offered;

(iii) Denied;

(iv) Terms offered and accepted by applicant(s).

(3) If final terms are offered, whether or not accepted:

(i) The loan amount.

(ii) Whether private mortgage insurance is required, and if so, the terms of the insurance.

(iii) Whether a deposit balance is required, and if so, the amount.

(iv) The note (simple) interest rate.

(v) The number of months to maturity of the loan offered.

(vi) Points. The loan origination or discount fee(s) charged to the buyer, computed as a percentage of the loan amount.

(4) Commitment date. The date final terms were offered.

(5) The type of mortgage using the following categories: Standard Fixed Payment; Variable Rate; Graduated Payment; Rollover; Other.

(6) The name or identification of the bank office where the application was submitted.

(7) Whenever credit is denied, copy(s) of the Equal Credit Opportunity Act credit notice and statement of credit denial.

(8) Any additional information used by the bank in determining whether or not to extend credit, or in establishing the terms, including, but not limited to, credit reports, employment verification forms, Federal Income Tax Forms, availability of insurance, and the complete appraisal.

[44 FR 63089, Nov. 2, 1979, as amended at 59 FR 26415, May 20, 1994]

§27.4 Inquiry/Application Log.

(a) The Comptroller, among other things, may require a bank to maintain a Fair Housing Inquiry/Application Log ("Log"), based upon, but not limited to, one or more of the following causes:

(1) There is reason(s) to believe that the bank may be prescreening or otherwise engaging in discriminatory practices on a prohibited basis.

(2) Complaints filed with the Comptroller or letters in the Community Reinvestment Act file are found to be substantive in nature, indicating that the bank's home lending practices are, or may be, discriminatory.

(3) Analysis of the data compiled by the bank under the provisions of the Home Mortgage Disclosure Act (12 U.S.C. 2801 *et seq.* and Regulation C of the Federal Reserve Board, 12 CFR part 203) indicates a pattern of significant variation in the number of home loans between census tracts with similar incomes and home ownership levels, differentiated only by race or national origin (i.e., possible racial redlining).

(b) The Comptroller, when requiring the maintenance of a Log, will specify in writing:

(1) The location(s) where the information shall be obtained;

(2) The length of time it shall be maintained;

(3) The frequency with which it shall be submitted to the Comptroller; and

(4) The reason(s) for imposing this requirement.

(c) A bank which has been directed by the Comptroller to maintain a Log shall obtain and note all of the following information regarding each inquiry or application for the extension of a home loan and each inquiry or application for a government insured home loan (not otherwise included in this part):

(1) Date of application or inquiry.

(2) Type of loan using the categories: purchase, construction-permanent; refinance; and government insured by type of insurance, *i.e.*, FHA, VA, and FmHA (if applicable).

(3) Indication of whether the entry refers to an application or an inquiry.

(4) Case identification (either a unique number which permits the application file to be located, or the name(s) and address(es) of the applicant(s)).

(5) Race/national origin of the inquirer(s) or applicant(s) using the categories: American Indian or Alaskan Native; Asian or Pacific Islander; Black, not of Hispanic origin; White, not of Hispanic origin; Hispanic; Other. In the case of inquiries, this item shall be noted on the basis of visual observation or surname(s) only. In the case of applications, the information shall be obtained pursuant to § 27.3(b)(2).

(6) *Location*. Complete street address, city, county, state and zip code of the property which will secure the extension of credit. The census tract shall also be recorded when the property is located in an SMSA in which the bank has a home office or branch office.

(d) The information required under § 27.4(c), of this part, shall be recorded and maintained on the form set forth in appendix III. Additional information may be recorded and maintained at the bank's discretion.

[44 FR 63089, Nov. 2, 1979, as amended at 59 FR 26415, May 20, 1994]

§ 27.5 Record retention period.

(a) Each bank shall retain the records required under § 27.3 for 25 months after the bank notifies an applicant of action taken on an application, or after withdrawal of an application. This requirement also applies to records of home loans which are originated by the bank and subsequently sold.

(b) The Comptroller of the Currency may, by written notice to a bank, extend the retention period.

§ 27.6 Substitute monitoring program.

The recordkeeping provisions of § 27.3 constitute a substitute monitoring program as authorized under § 202.13(d) of Regulation B of the Federal Reserve Board (12 CFR 202.13(d)). A bank collecting the data in compliance with § 27.3 of this part will be in compliance with the requirements of § 202.13 of Regulation B.

§ 27.7 Availability, submission and use of data.

(a) Each bank shall make all information collected under §§ 27.3 and 27.4 available for review at the bank to national bank examiners upon request.

(b) Prior to a scheduled bank examination, the Comptroller may request the information maintained under § 27.3(a). A bank required to maintain information under § 27.3(a)(2) shall submit the information to the Comptroller on the form prescribed in appendix I of this part. A bank which is exempt from maintaining the information required under § 27.3(a) shall notify the Comptroller of this fact in writing within 30 calendar days of its receipt of the Comptroller's request.

(c) If, upon review of the information maintained under § 27.3(a), the Comptroller determines that statistical analysis prior to examination is warranted, the bank will be notified.

(1) Within 30 calendar days after receipt of notification from the Comptroller, the bank shall submit, for application records specified by the Comptroller, completed Home Loan Data Submission Forms (set forth as appendix IV). The Comptroller may, upon the request of a bank and for good reason, extend the 30-day period.

(2) The number of Home Loan Data Submission Forms requested by the Comptroller will not exceed 250 per *decision center*, or 2,000 per bank with multiple *decision centers*, unless there is cause to believe that a bank is not in compliance with fair housing laws

based on examination findings or substantiated complaints, among other factors.

(3) A bank with fewer than 75 home loan applications in the preceding year will not be required to submit such forms unless:

(i) The home loan activity is concentrated in the few months preceding the request for data, indicating the likelihood of increased activity over the subsequent year, or

(ii) There is cause to believe that a bank is not in compliance with the fair housing laws based on prior examinations and/or complaints, among other factors.

(d) If there is cause to believe that a bank is in noncompliance with fair housing laws, the Comptroller may require submission of additional Home Loan Data Submission Forms. The Comptroller may also require submission of the information maintained under §27.3(a) and Home Loan Data Submission Forms at more frequent intervals than specified in paragraphs (b) and (c) of this section.

[44 FR 63089, Nov. 2, 1979, as amended at 59 FR 26415, May 20, 1994]

APPENDIX I TO PART 27—MONTHLY HOME LOAN ACTIVITY FORMAT

Appendix I

BANK NAME		COMPTROLLER OF THE CURRENCY MONTHLY HOME LOAN ACTIVITY FORMAT	DECISION CENTER NAME	NUMBER
OCC CHARTER #	TOTAL NUMBER OF DECISION CENTERS		ADDRESS	PHONE NO.
PERSON RESPONSIBLE FOR COMPLETING THIS FORM AND PHONE NO.			PRINCIPAL SERVICE AREA (e.g. State, SMSA, County, City or Part Thereof)	

____ YEAR	HOME LOAN APPLICATIONS											
	PURCHASE				CONSTRUCTION—PERMANENT				REFINANCE			
MONTH	No. Received	No. Closed	No. Rejected	No. Withdrawn	No. Received	No. Closed	No. Rejected	No. Withdrawn	No. Received	No. Closed	No. Rejected	No. Withdrawn
JANUARY												
FEBRUARY												
MARCH												
APRIL												
MAY												
JUNE												
JULY												
AUGUST												
SEPTEMBER												
OCTOBER												
NOVEMBER												
DECEMBER												
TOTAL												

Appendix II to Part 27—Information for Government Monitoring Purposes

The following language is approved by the Comptroller of the Currency and will satisfy the requirements of 12 CFR part 27. It may be inserted to complete the "Information for Government Monitoring Purposes" section of the Residential Loan Application Form (FHLMC Form 65/FNMA 1003) or may be used separately. This information may also be provided orally by the applicant.

The following information is requested by the Federal Government if this loan is related to a dwelling, in order to monitor the lender's compliance with equal credit opportunity and fair housing laws. You are not required to furnish this information, but are encourage to do so. The law provides that a lender may neither discriminate on the basis of this information, nor on whether you choose to furnish it. However, if you choose not to furnish it, under Federal regulations this lender is required to note race and sex on the basis of visual observation or surname. If you do not wish to furnish the above information, please initial below.

Borrower

I do not wish to furnish this information (initial)_______.

Race/National Origin

☐ American Indian or Alaskan Native
☐ Asian or Pacific Islander
☐ Black, not of Hispanic origin
☐ Hispanic
☐ White, not of Hispanic origin
☐ Other (specify)_______

Sex

☐ Female
☐ Male

Co-borrower

I do not wish to furnish this information (initial)_______.

Race/National Origin

☐ American Indian or Alaskan Native
☐ Asian or Pacific Islander
☐ Black, not of Hispanic origin
☐ Hispanic
☐ White, not of Hispanic origin
☐ Other (specify)_______

Sex

☐ Female
☐ Male

[59 FR 26415, May 20, 1994]

APPENDIX III TO PART 27—FAIR HOUSING LENDING INQUIRY/APPLICATION LOG SHEET

Appendix III

Bank Name	OCC Charter No.	COMPTROLLER OF THE CURRENCY FAIR HOUSING LENDING INQUIRY/APPLICATION LOG SHEET	City
Branch, Office or Subsidiary Name			County State
Name of Person Responsible For Form	Phone Number		SMSA

INSTRUCTIONS: Use the codes listed below. Indicate by an asterisk (*) if the information recorded is the banker's observation rather than the borrower's statement.

Race Codes: W - White, not of Hispanic origin; I - American Indian or Alaskan Native; A - Asian or Pacific Islander; B - Black, not of Hispanic origin; H - Hispanic; O - Other

Type of Loan: P - Purchase; R - Refinance; C - Construction-Permanent; F - FHA (Federal Housing Admin); V - VA (Veteran's Administration); M - FMHA (Farmers Home Administration)

Date of Application or Inquiry	Type of Loan Code	Inquiry or Application (I) or (A)	Case Identification (Case Number or Name/Address)	Inquirer or Applicant		Co-Inquirer or Co-Applicant		LOCATION OF PROPERTY WHICH WILL SECURE LOAN			
				Sex (M or F)	Race Code	Sex (M or F)	Race Code	Street & Number, City, State	County	Zip Code	Census Tract

[59 FR 26417, May 20, 1994]

APPENDIX IV TO PART 27—HOME LOAN DATA SUBMISSION

Appendix IV

COMPTROLLER OF THE CURRENCY
HOME LOAN DATA SUBMISSION

NAME OF BANK ____________________

CHARTER NUMBER ______________ (1-5)
DECISION CENTER NO. ______________ (6-9)

(Enter dollar amount as whole dollars)

APPLICATION FORM

1. Application file Number _ _ _ _ _ _ _ _ _ _ _ _ (10-21)
2. Amount of Loan Requested $ _ _ _ , _ _ _ (22-27)
3. Number of Months Requested to Maturity _ _ _ (28-30)
4. County _ _ _ _ _ _ _ (31-37)
5. State _ _ (38-39)
6. Number of Units 1 ☐ 2 ☐ 3 ☐ 4 ☐ (40)
7. Year House Was Built _ _ _ _ (41-44)
8. Purpose of Loan 1 ☐ Purchase 2 ☐ Construction-Permanent 3 ☐ Refinance (45)

Applicant	
9. Age _ _ (46-47)	11. Co-Applicant? 1 ☐ Yes 2 ☐ No (49) (If #11 is No, proceed to #14)
10. Marital Status (48)	12. Age _ _ (50-51)
1 ☐ Married 2 ☐ Separated 3 ☐ Unmarried (includes single divorced, widowed)	13. Marital Status (52) 1 ☐ Married 2 ☐ Separated 3 ☐ Unmarried (includes single divorced, widowed)

14. Applicant Gross Monthly Income $ _ _ _ , _ _ _ . (53-58)
15. Co-Applicant Gross Monthly Income $ _ _ _ , _ _ _ . (59-64)
16. Proposed Monthly Housing Payments $ _ _ , _ _ _ . (65-69)
17. Purchase/Sales Price $ _ _ _ , _ _ _ . (70-75)
18. Other Total Monthly Payments $ _ _ _ , _ _ _ (76-81)

Applicant	Co-Applicant? (If none, proceed to #23)
19. Race (82) 1 ☐ American Indian or Alaskan Native 2 ☐ Asian or Pacific Islander 3 ☐ Black, not of Hispanic origin 4 ☐ White, not of Hispanic origin 5 ☐ Hispanic 6 ☐ Other	21. Race (84) 1 ☐ American Indian or Alaskan Native 2 ☐ Asian or Pacific Islander 3 ☐ Black, not of Hispanic origin 4 ☐ White, not of Hispanic origin 5 ☐ Hispanic 6 ☐ Other
20. Sex 1 ☐ Female 2 ☐ Male (83)	22. Sex 1 ☐ Female 2 ☐ Male (85)

23. Bank Relationship at Subject Bank (86)

1 ☐ Current Banking Relationship 2 ☐ **Past Banking Relationship**
3 ☐ No Banking Relationship 4 ☐ **Unable to Determine**

Appraisal

24. Census Tract _ _ _ _ . _ _ . (87-92)
25. Appraised Value $ _ _ _ , _ _ _ . **(93-98)**

Action Taken

26. Description of Action (99)

1 ☐ Withdrawn Before Terms Were Offered
2 ☐ Denied
} **(If checked, skip remaining questions)**

3 ☐ Withdrawn After Terms Were Offered
4 ☐ Approved and Loan Closed
} **(If checked, complete remaining questions)**

Terms of Mortgage or of Mortgage Offer

27. Committment Date _ _ / _ _ / _ _ (100-105)
M M D D Y Y

28. Type of Mortgage (106)

1 ☐ Standard Fixed Payment 2 ☐ **Variable Rate**
3 ☐ Graduated Payment 4 ☐ **Roll-Over** 5 ☐ **Other**

29. Private Mortgage Insurance Required? (107)

1 ☐ No 2 ☐ Yes

30. Loan Amount $ _ _ _ , _ _ _ . (108-113)

31. Note (Simple) Interest Rate _ _ . _ _ % (114-117)

32. Points to Buyer _ . _ _ (118-120)

33. Months to Maturity _ _ _ (121-123)

34. Downpayment Amount $ _ _ _ , _ _ _ . (124-129)

[59 FR 31925, June 21, 1994]

PART 28—INTERNATIONAL BANKING ACTIVITIES

Subpart A—Foreign Operations of National Banks

Sec.
28.1 Authority, purpose, and scope.
28.2 Definitions.
28.3 Filing requirements for foreign operations of a national bank.
28.4 Permissible activities.
28.5 Filing of notice.

Subpart B—Federal Branches and Agencies of Foreign Banks

28.10 Authority, purpose, and scope.
28.11 Definitions.
28.12 Approval of a Federal branch or agency.
28.13 Permissible activities.
28.14 Limitations based upon capital of a foreign bank.
28.15 Capital equivalency deposits.
28.16 Deposit-taking by an uninsured Federal branch.
28.17 Notice of change in activity or operations.
28.18 Recordkeeping and reporting.
28.19 Enforcement.
28.20 Maintenance of assets.
28.21 Service of process.
28.22 Voluntary liquidation.
28.23 Procedures for closing of some of a foreign bank's Federal branches and/or agencies.
28.24 Termination of a Federal branch or agency.
28.25 Change in control.
28.26 Loan production offices.

Subpart C—International Lending Supervision

28.50 Authority, purpose, and scope.
28.51 Definitions.
28.52 Allocated transfer risk reserve.
28.53 Accounting for fees on international loans.
28.54 Reporting and disclosure of international assets.

AUTHORITY: 12 U.S.C. 1 *et seq.*, 24(Seventh), 93a, 161, 602, 1818, 3101 *et seq.*, and 3901 *et seq.*

SOURCE: 61 FR 19532, May 2, 1996, unless otherwise noted.

Subpart A—Foreign Operations of National Banks

§ 28.1 Authority, purpose, and scope.

(a) *Authority.* This subpart is issued pursuant to 12 U.S.C. 1 *et seq.*, 24(Seventh), 93a, and 602.

(b) *Purpose.* This subpart sets forth filing requirements for national banks that engage in international operations and clarifies permissible foreign activities of national banks.

(c) *Scope.* This subpart applies to any national bank that engages in international operations through a foreign branch, or acquires an interest in an Edge corporation, Agreement corporation, foreign bank, or certain other foreign organizations.

§ 28.2 Definitions.

For purposes of this subpart:

(a) *Agreement corporation* means a corporation having an agreement or undertaking with the Board of Governors of the Federal Reserve System (FRB) under section 25 of the Federal Reserve Act (FRA), 12 U.S.C. 601 through 604a.

(b) *Edge corporation* means a corporation that is organized under section 25A of the FRA, 12 U.S.C. 611 through 631.

(c) *Foreign bank* means an organization that:

(1) Is organized under the laws of a foreign country;

(2) Engages in the business of banking;

(3) Is recognized as a bank by the bank supervisory or monetary authority of the country of its organization or principal banking operations;

(4) Receives deposits to a substantial extent in the regular course of its business; and

(5) Has the power to accept demand deposits.

(d) *Foreign branch* means an office of a national bank (other than a representative office) that is located outside the United States at which banking or financing business is conducted.

(e) *Foreign country* means one or more foreign nations, and includes the overseas territories, dependencies, and insular possessions of those nations and of the United States, and the Commonwealth of Puerto Rico.

[61 FR 19532, May 2, 1996, as amended at 61 FR 60387, Nov. 27, 1996]

§ 28.3 Filing requirements for foreign operations of a national bank.

(a) *Notice requirement.* A national bank shall notify the OCC when it:

(1) Files an application, notice, or report with the FRB to:

(i) Establish or open a foreign branch;

(ii) Acquire or divest of an interest in, or close, an Edge corporation, Agreement corporation, foreign bank, or other foreign organization; or

(2) Opens a foreign branch, and no application or notice is required by the FRB for such transaction.

(b) *Other applications and notices accepted.* In lieu of a notice under paragraph (a)(1) of this section, the OCC may accept a copy of an application, notice, or report submitted to another Federal agency that covers the proposed action and contains substantially the same information required by the OCC.

(c) *Additional information.* A national bank shall furnish the OCC with any additional information the OCC may require in connection with the national bank's foreign operations.

[61 FR 19532, May 2, 1996, as amended at 68 FR 70699, Dec. 19, 2003]

§ 28.4 Permissible activities.

(a) *General.* Subject to the applicable approval process, if any, a national bank may engage in any activity in a foreign country that is:

(1) Permissible for a national bank in the United States; and

(2) Usual in connection with the business of banking in the country where it transacts business.

(b) *Additional activities.* In addition to its general banking powers, a national bank may engage in any activity in a foreign country that is permissible under the FRB's Regulation K, 12 CFR part 211.

(c) *Foreign operations guarantees.* A national bank may guarantee the deposits and other liabilities of its Edge corporations and Agreement corporations and of its corporate instrumentalities in foreign countries.

§ 28.5 Filing of notice.

(a) *Where to file.* A national bank shall file any notice or submission required under this subpart with the appropriate supervisory office of the OCC.

(b) *Availability of forms.* Individual forms and instructions for filings are available from the appropriate supervisory office of the OCC.

[61 FR 19532, May 2, 1996, as amended at 68 FR 70699, Dec. 19, 2003]

Subpart B—Federal Branches and Agencies of Foreign Banks

§ 28.10 Authority, purpose, and scope.

(a) *Authority.* This subpart is issued pursuant to the authority in the International Banking Act of 1978 (IBA), 12 U.S.C. 3101 *et seq.*, and 12 U.S.C. 93a.

(b) *Purpose—Purpose and scope.* This subpart implements the IBA pertaining to the licensing, supervision, and operations of Federal branches and agencies in the United States. For corporate procedures pertaining to Federal branches and agencies, refer to 12 CFR part 5.

(c) *Scope.* This subpart applies to all Federal branches and agencies of foreign banks. Nothing in the OCC's rules relieves a Federal branch or agency from complying with requirements that are imposed by the FRB under Regulation K (12 CFR part 211) or otherwise imposed in accordance with applicable law.

[61 FR 19532, May 2, 1996, as amended at 61 FR 60387, Nov. 27, 1996; 68 FR 70699, Dec. 19, 2003]

§ 28.11 Definitions.

For purposes of this subpart:

(a) *Affiliate* means any entity that controls, is controlled by, or is under common control with another entity.

(b) *Agreement corporation* means a corporation having an agreement or undertaking with the FRB under section 25 of the FRA, 12 U.S.C. 601 through 604a.

(c) *Capital equivalency deposit* means a deposit by a Federal branch or agency in a member bank as described in section 4 of the IBA, 12 U.S.C. 3102(g).

(d) *Control.* An entity controls another entity if the entity directly or indirectly controls or has the power to vote 25 percent or more of any class of voting securities of the other entity or controls in any manner the election of a majority of the directors or trustees of the other entity.

(e) *Edge corporation* means a corporation that is organized under section

25A of the FRA, 12 U.S.C. 611 through 631.

(f) *Establish a Federal branch or agency* means to:

(1) Open and conduct business through an initial or additional Federal branch or agency;

(2) Acquire directly or indirectly through merger, consolidation, or similar transaction with another foreign bank, the operations of a Federal branch or agency that is open and conducting business;

(3) Acquire a Federal branch or agency through the acquisition of a foreign bank subsidiary that will cease to operate in the same corporate form following the acquisition;

(4) Convert a state branch or agency operated by a foreign bank, or a commercial lending company controlled by a foreign bank, into a Federal branch or agency;

(5) Relocate a Federal branch or agency within a state or from one state to another; or

(6) Convert a Federal agency or a limited Federal branch into a Federal branch.

(g) *Federal agency* means an office or place of business, licensed by the OCC and operated by a foreign bank in any state, that may engage in the business of banking, including maintaining credit balances, cashing checks, and lending money, but may not accept deposits from citizens or residents of the United States. Obligations may not be considered credit balances unless they are:

(1) Incidental to, or arise out of the exercise of, other lawful banking powers;

(2) To serve a specific purpose;

(3) Not solicited from the general public;

(4) Not used to pay routine operating expenses in the United States such as salaries, rent, or taxes;

(5) Withdrawn within a reasonable period of time after the specific purpose for which they were placed has been accomplished; and

(6) Drawn upon in a manner reasonable in relation to the size and nature of the account.

(h) *Federal branch* means an office or place of business, licensed by the OCC and operated by a foreign bank in any state, that may engage in the business of banking, including accepting deposits, that is not a Federal agency as defined in paragraph (h) of this section. Unless otherwise provided, the references in this subpart B of part 28 to a Federal branch include a limited Federal branch.

(i) *Foreign bank* means an organization that is organized under the laws of a foreign country, a territory of the United States, Puerto Rico, Guam, American Samoa, or the Virgin Islands, and that engages directly in the business of banking in a foreign country.

(j) *Foreign business* means any entity, including a corporation, partnership, sole proprietorship, association, foundation or trust that is organized under the laws of a foreign country, or any United States entity that is controlled by a foreign entity or foreign national.

(k) *Foreign country* means one or more foreign nations, and includes the overseas territories, dependencies, and insular possessions of those nations and of the United States, and the Commonwealth of Puerto Rico.

(l) *Home country* means the country in which the foreign bank is chartered or incorporated.

(m) *Home country supervisor* means the governmental entity or entities in the foreign bank's home country responsible for supervising and regulating the foreign bank.

(n) *Home state* of a foreign bank means the state in which the foreign bank has a branch, agency, subsidiary commercial lending company, or subsidiary bank. If a foreign bank has an office in more than one state, the home state of the foreign bank is the state that is selected to be the home state by the foreign bank or, in default of the foreign bank's selection, by the FRB.

(o) *Immediate family member of an individual* means the spouse, father, mother, brother, sister, son, or daughter of that individual.

(p) *Initial deposit* means the first deposit transaction between a depositor and the Federal branch made on or after July 1, 1996. The initial deposit may be placed into different deposit accounts or into different kinds of deposit accounts, such as demand, savings, or time accounts. Deposit accounts that are held by a depositor in the same right and capacity may be added together for the purpose of determining the dollar amount of the initial deposit. *First deposit* means the deposit made when there is no current deposit relationship between the depositor and the Federal branch.

(q) *International banking facility* means a set of asset and liability accounts segregated on the books and records of a depository institution, a United States branch or agency of a foreign bank, or an Edge corporation or Agreement corporation, that includes only international banking facility time deposits and extensions of credit.

(r) *Large United States business* means any business entity including a corporation, company, partnership, sole proprietorship, association, foundation or trust that is organized under the laws of the United States or any state thereof, and has:

(1) Securities registered on a national securities exchange or quoted on the National Association of Securities Dealers Automated Quotation System; or

(2) More than $1 million in annual gross revenues for the fiscal year immediately preceding the year of the initial deposit.

(s) *Limited Federal branch* means a Federal branch that may receive only those deposits permissible for an Edge corporation to receive.

(t) *Managed or controlled* by a Federal branch or agency means that a majority of the responsibility for business decisions, including decisions with regard to lending, asset management, funding, or liability management, or the responsibility for recordkeeping of assets or liabilities for a non-United States office, resides at the Federal branch or agency. For purposes of this definition, forwarding data or information of offshore operations gathered or compiled by the United States office in the normal course of business to the parent foreign bank does not constitute recordkeeping.

(u) *Manual* has the same meaning as in 12 CFR 5.2(c).

(v) *Parent foreign bank senior management* means individuals at the executive level of the parent foreign bank who are responsible for supervising and authorizing activities of the Federal branch or agency.

(w) *Person* means an individual or a corporation, government, partnership, association, or any other entity.

(x) *State* means any state of the United States and the District of Columbia.

(y) *United States bank* means a bank organized under the laws of the United States or any state.

[61 FR 19532, May 2, 1996, as amended at 61 FR 60387, Nov. 27, 1996; 68 FR 70699, Dec. 19, 2003; 73 FR 22251, Apr. 24, 2008]

§ 28.12 Approval of a Federal branch or agency.

(a) *Approval and licensing requirements*—(1) *General.* Except as otherwise provided in this section, a foreign bank shall submit an application to, and obtain prior approval from, the OCC before it:

(i) Establishes a Federal branch or agency; or

(ii) Exercises fiduciary powers at a Federal branch.

(2) *Licensing.* A foreign bank must receive a license from the OCC to open and operate its initial Federal branch or agency in the United States. A foreign bank that has a license to operate and is operating a full-service Federal branch need not obtain a new license for any additional Federal branches or agencies, or to upgrade or downgrade its operations in an existing Federal branch or agency. A foreign bank that only has a license to operate and is operating a limited Federal branch or Federal agency need not obtain a new license for any additional limited Federal branches or Federal agencies, or to convert a limited Federal branch into a Federal agency or a Federal agency into a limited Federal branch.

(b) *Standards for approval.* Generally, in reviewing an application by a foreign bank to establish a Federal branch or agency, the OCC considers:

(1) The financial and managerial resources and future prospects of the applicant foreign bank and the Federal branch or agency;

(2) Whether the foreign bank has furnished to the OCC the information the OCC requires to assess the application adequately, and provided the OCC with adequate assurances that information will be made available to the OCC on the operations or activities of the foreign bank or any of its affiliates that the OCC deems necessary to determine and enforce compliance with the IBA and other applicable Federal banking statutes;

(3) Whether the foreign bank and its United States affiliates are in compliance with applicable United States law;

(4) The convenience and needs of the community to be served and the effects of the proposal on competition in the domestic and foreign commerce of the United States;

(5) With respect to an application to establish a Federal branch or agency outside of the foreign bank's home state, whether the foreign bank is subject to comprehensive supervision or regulation on a consolidated basis by its home country supervisor. The OCC, in its discretion, also may consider whether the foreign bank is subject to comprehensive supervision or regulation on a consolidated basis by its home country supervisor when reviewing any other type of application to establish a Federal branch or agency; and

(6) Whether the home country supervisor has consented to the proposed establishment of the Federal branch or agency.

(c) *Comprehensive supervision or regulation on a consolidated basis.* In determining whether a foreign bank is subject to comprehensive supervision or regulation on a consolidated basis, the OCC reviews various factors, including whether the foreign bank is supervised or regulated in a manner so that its home country supervisor receives sufficient information on the worldwide operations of the foreign bank to assess the foreign bank's overall financial condition and compliance with laws and regulations as specified in the FRB's Regulation K, 12 CFR 211.24.

(d) *Conditions on approval.* The OCC may impose conditions on its approval including a condition permitting future termination of activities based on the inability of the foreign bank to provide information on its activities, or those of its affiliate, that the OCC deems necessary to determine and enforce compliance with United States banking laws.

(e) *Expedited review.* Unless the OCC concludes that the filing presents significant supervisory or compliance concerns, or raises significant legal or policy issues, the OCC generally processes the following filings by an eligible foreign bank, as defined in paragraph (f) of this section, under expedited review procedures:

(1) *Intrastate relocations.* An application submitted by an eligible foreign bank to relocate a Federal branch or agency within a state is deemed approved by the OCC as of the seventh day after the close of the applicable public comment period in 12 CFR part 5, unless the OCC notifies the bank prior to that date that the filing is not eligible for expedited review.

(2) *Written notice for an additional intrastate Federal branch or agency.* (i) In a case where a foreign bank seeks to establish intrastate an additional Federal branch or agency, the foreign bank shall provide written notice 30 days in advance of the establishment of the intrastate Federal branch or agency.

(ii) The OCC may waive the 30-day period required under paragraph (e)(2)(i) of this section if immediate action is required. The OCC also may suspend the notice period or require an application if the notification raises significant policy or supervisory concerns.

(3) *Expedited approval procedures for an interstate Federal branch or agency.* An application submitted by an eligible foreign bank to establish and operate a de novo Federal branch or agency in any state outside the home state of the foreign bank is deemed conditionally approved by the OCC as of the 15th day after the close of the applicable public comment period, or the 45th day after the filing is received by the OCC, whichever is later, unless the OCC notifies the foreign bank prior to that date that the filing is not eligible for expedited review. In the event that the FRB has approved the application prior to the expiration of the period, then the OCC's approval shall be deemed a final approval.

(4) *Conversions.* An application submitted by an eligible foreign bank to

establish a Federal branch or agency as defined in 12 CFR 28.11(f)(4) or (f)(6) is deemed approved by the OCC as of the 30th day after the OCC receives the filing, unless the OCC notifies the foreign bank prior to that date that the filing is not eligible for expedited review.

(5) *Fiduciary powers.* An application submitted by an eligible foreign bank to exercise fiduciary powers at an established Federal branch is deemed approved by the OCC 30 days after filing with the OCC, unless the OCC notifies the bank prior to that date that the filing is not eligible for expedited review.

(6) *Other filings.* Any other application submitted by an eligible foreign bank may be approved by the OCC on an expedited basis as described in the Manual.

(f) *Eligible foreign bank.* For purposes of this section, a foreign bank is an eligible foreign bank if each Federal branch and agency of the foreign bank or, if the foreign bank has no Federal branches or agencies and is engaging in an establishment of a Federal branch or agency as defined in 12 CFR 28.11(f)(4), each state branch and agency:

(1) Has a composite rating of 1 or 2 under the interagency rating system for United States branches and agencies of foreign banks;

(2) Is not subject to a cease and desist order, consent order, formal written agreement, Prompt Corrective Action directive (*see* 12 CFR part 6) or, if subject to such order, agreement, or directive, is informed in writing by the OCC that the Federal branch or agency may be treated as an "eligible foreign bank" for purposes of this section; and

(3) Has, if applicable, a Community Reinvestment Act (CRA), 12 U.S.C. 2906, rating of "Outstanding" or "Satisfactory".

(g) *After-the-fact approval.* Unless otherwise provided by the OCC, a foreign bank proposing to establish a Federal branch or agency through the acquisition of, or merger or consolidation with, a foreign bank that has an office in the United States, may proceed with the transaction before an application to establish the Federal branch or agency has been filed or acted upon, if the applicant:

(1) Gives the OCC reasonable advance notice of the proposed acquisition, merger, or consolidation;

(2) Prior to consummation of the acquisition, merger, or consolidation, commits in writing to comply with the OCC application procedures within a reasonable period of time, or has already submitted an application; and

(3) Commits in writing to abide by the OCC's decision on the application, including a decision to terminate activities of the Federal branch or agency.

(h) *After-the-fact notice for an eligible foreign bank.* Unless otherwise provided by the OCC, a foreign bank proposing to establish a Federal branch or agency through the acquisition of, or merger or consolidation with, a foreign bank that has an existing U.S. bank subsidiary or a Federal or state branch or agency may proceed with the transaction and provide after-the-fact notice to the OCC within 14 days of the transaction, if:

(1) The resulting bank is an "eligible foreign bank" under paragraph (f) of this section; and

(2) No Federal branch established by the transaction accepts deposits that are insured by the FDIC pursuant to the Federal Deposit Insurance Act (12 U.S.C. 1811 *et seq.*).

(i) *Contraction of operations.* A foreign bank shall provide written notice to the OCC within 10 days after converting a Federal branch into a limited Federal branch or Federal agency.

(j) *Procedures for approval.* A foreign bank shall file an application for approval pursuant to this section in accordance with 12 CFR part 5 and the Manual. The OCC reserves the right to adopt materially different procedures for a particular filing, or class of filings, pursuant to 12 CFR 5.2(b).

(k) *Other applications accepted.* As provided in 12 CFR 5.4(c), the OCC may accept an application or other filing submitted to another U.S. Government agency that covers the proposed activity or transaction and contains substantially the same information as required by the OCC.

[61 FR 19532, May 2, 1996, as amended at 68 FR 70699, Dec. 19, 2003; 73 FR 22251, Apr. 24, 2008]

§ 28.13 Permissible activities.

(a) *Applicability of laws*—(1) *General.* Except as otherwise provided by the IBA, other Federal laws or regulations, or otherwise determined by the OCC, the operations of a foreign bank at a Federal branch or agency shall be conducted with the same rights and privileges and subject to the same duties, restrictions, penalties, liabilities, conditions, and limitations that would apply if the Federal branch or agency were a national bank operating at the same location.

(2) *Parent foreign bank senior management approval.* Unless otherwise provided by the OCC, any provision in law, regulation, policy, or procedure that requires a national bank to obtain the approval of its board of directors will be deemed to require a Federal branch or agency to obtain the approval of parent foreign bank senior management.

(b) *Management of shell branches*—(1) *Federal branches and agencies.* A Federal branch or agency of a foreign bank shall not manage, through an office of the foreign bank that is located outside the United States and that is managed or controlled by that Federal branch or agency, any type of activity that a United States bank is not permitted to manage at any branch or subsidiary of the United States bank that is located outside the United States.

(2) *Activities managed in foreign branches or subsidiaries of United States banks.* The types of activities referred to in paragraph (b)(1) of this section include the types of activities authorized to a United States bank by state or Federal charters, regulations issued by chartering or regulatory authorities, and other United States banking laws. However, United States procedural or quantitative requirements that may be applicable to the conduct of those activities by United States banks do not apply.

(c) *Additional guidance regarding permissible activities.* For purposes of section 7(h) of the IBA, 12 U.S.C. 3105(h), the OCC may issue opinions, interpretations, or rulings regarding permissible activities of Federal branches.

§ 28.14 Limitations based upon capital of a foreign bank.

(a) *General.* Any limitation or restriction based upon the capital of a national bank shall be deemed to refer, as applied to a Federal branch or agency, to the dollar equivalent of the capital of the foreign bank.

(b) *Calculation.* Unless otherwise provided by the OCC, a foreign bank must calculate its capital in a manner consistent with 12 CFR part 3, subpart C, for purposes of this section.

(c) *Aggregation.* The foreign bank shall aggregate business transacted by all Federal branches and agencies with the business transacted by all state branches and state agencies controlled by the foreign bank in determining its compliance with limitations based upon the capital of the foreign bank. The foreign bank shall designate one Federal branch or agency office in the United States to maintain consolidated information so that the OCC can monitor compliance.

[61 FR 19532, May 2, 1996, as amended at 79 FR 11312, Feb. 28, 2014]

§ 28.15 Capital equivalency deposits.

(a) *Capital equivalency deposits*—(1) *General.* For purposes of section 4(g) of the IBA, 12 U.S.C. 3102(g), unless otherwise provided by the OCC, a foreign bank's capital equivalency deposits (CED) must consist of:

(i) Investment securities eligible for investment by national banks;

(ii) United States dollar deposits payable in the United States or payable in any other Group of Ten country;

(iii) Certificates of deposit, payable in the United States, and banker's acceptances, provided that, in either case, the issuer has an adequate capacity to meet financial commitments for the projected life of the asset or exposure. An issuer has an adequate capacity to meet financial commitments if the risk of default by the obligor is low and the full and timely repayment of principal and interest is expected;

(iv) Repurchase agreements; or

(v) Other similar assets permitted by the OCC to qualify to be included in the CED.

(2) *Legal requirements.* The agreement with the depository bank to hold the

CED and the amount of the deposit must comply with the requirements in section 4(g) of the IBA, 12 U.S.C. 3102(g). If a foreign bank has more than one Federal branch or agency in a state, it shall determine the CED and the amount of liabilities requiring capital equivalency coverage on an aggregate basis for all the foreign bank's Federal branches or agencies in that state.

(3) *Exceptions.* In determining the amount of the CED, the OCC excludes liabilities of an international banking facility (IBF) to third parties and of a Federal branch of a foreign bank to an IBF. The OCC may exclude liabilities from repurchase agreements on a case-by-case basis.

(b) *Increase in capital equivalency deposits.* For prudential or supervisory reasons, the OCC may require, in individual cases or otherwise, that a foreign bank increase its CED above the minimum amount. For example, the OCC may require an increase if a Federal branch or agency of the foreign bank increases its leverage through the establishment, acquisition, or maintenance of an operating subsidiary.

(c) *Value of assets.* The obligations referred to in paragraph (a) of this section must be valued at principal amount or market value, whichever is lower.

(d) *Deposit arrangements.* A foreign bank should require its depository bank to segregate its CED on the depository bank's books and records. The funds deposited and obligations referred to in paragraph (a) of this section that are placed in safekeeping at a depository bank to satisfy a foreign bank's CED requirement:

(1) May not be reduced in value below the minimum required for that branch or agency without the prior approval of the OCC, but in no event below the statutory minimum;

(2) Must be maintained pursuant to an agreement prescribed by the OCC that shall be a written agreement entered into with the OCC for purposes of section 8 of the Federal Deposit Insurance Act, 12 U.S.C. 1818; and

(3) Must be free from any lien, charge, right of setoff, credit, or preference in connection with any claim of the depository bank against the foreign bank.

(e)(1) *Deposit and Consolidation.* As provided in 12 U.S.C. 3102(g), a foreign bank with a Federal branch or agency shall deposit its CED into an account in a bank that is located in the state in which the Federal branch or agency is located. For this purpose, such depository bank is considered to be located in those states in which it has its main office or a branch. A foreign bank with Federal branches or agencies in more than one state may consolidate some or all of its CEDs into one such account.

(2) *Calculation.* The total amount of the consolidated CED shall continue to be calculated on an office-by-office basis.

(f) *Maintenance of capital equivalency ledger account.* Each Federal branch or agency shall maintain a capital equivalency account and keep records of the amount of liabilities requiring capital equivalency coverage in a manner and form prescribed by the OCC.

[61 FR 60363, Nov. 27, 1996, as amended at 66 FR 49098, Sept. 26, 2001; 67 FR 4326, Jan. 30, 2002; 67 FR 41620, June 19, 2002; 68 FR 70700, Dec. 19, 2003; 77 FR 35258, June 13, 2012]

§ 28.16 Deposit-taking by an uninsured Federal branch.

(a) *Policy.* In carrying out this section, the OCC shall consider the importance of according foreign banks competitive opportunities equal to those of United States banks and the availability of credit to all sectors of the United States economy, including international trade finance.

(b) *General.* An uninsured Federal branch may accept initial deposits of less than the standard maximum deposit insurance amount as defined in 12 U.S.C. 1821(a)(1)(E) only from:

(1) Individuals who are not citizens or residents of the United States at the time of the initial deposit;

(2) Individuals who are not citizens of the United States, but are residents of the United States, and are employed by a foreign bank, foreign business, foreign government, or recognized international organization;

(3) Persons (including immediate family members of an individual) to

whom the branch or foreign bank (including any affiliate thereof) has extended credit or provided other nondeposit banking services within the past 12 months, or with whom the branch or foreign bank has a written agreement to extend credit or provide such services within 12 months after the date of the initial deposit;

(4) Foreign businesses and large United States businesses;

(5) Foreign governmental units, including political subdivisions, and recognized international organizations;

(6) Federal and state governmental units, including political subdivisions and agencies thereof;

(7) Persons who are depositing funds in connection with the issuance of a financial instrument by the branch for transmission of funds, or transmission of funds by any electronic means;

(8) Persons who may deposit funds with an Edge corporation as provided in the FRB's Regulation K, 12 CFR 211.6, including persons engaged in certain international business activities; and

(9) Any other depositor if:

(i) The aggregate amount of deposits received from those depositors does not exceed, on an average daily basis, 1 percent of the average of the branch's deposits for the last 30 days of the most recent calendar quarter, excluding deposits of other offices, branches, agencies, or wholly owned subsidiaries of the foreign bank; and

(ii) The branch does not solicit deposits from the general public by advertising, display of signs, or similar activity designed to attract the attention of the general public.

(c) *Application for an exemption.* A foreign bank may apply to the OCC for an exemption to permit an uninsured Federal branch to accept or maintain deposit accounts that are not listed in paragraph (b) of this section. The request should describe:

(1) The types, sources, and estimated amounts of such deposits and explain why the OCC should grant an exemption; and

(2) How the exemption maintains and furthers the policies described in paragraph (a) of this section.

(d) *Aggregation of deposits.* For purposes of paragraph (b)(9) of this section, a foreign bank that has more than one Federal branch in the same state may aggregate deposits in all of its Federal branches in that state, but exclude deposits of other branches, agencies or wholly owned subsidiaries of the bank. The Federal branch shall compute the average amount by using the sum of deposits as of the close of business of the last 30 calendar days ending with and including the last day of the calendar quarter, divided by 30. The Federal branch shall maintain records of the calculation until its next examination by the OCC.

(e) *Notification to depositors.* A Federal branch that accepts deposits pursuant to this section shall provide notice to depositors pursuant to 12 CFR 346.207, which generally requires that the Federal branch conspicuously display a sign at the branch and include a statement on each signature card, passbook, and instrument evidencing a deposit that the deposit is not insured by the Federal Deposit Insurance Corporation (FDIC).

(f) *Transition period.* (1) An uninsured Federal branch may maintain a deposit lawfully accepted under the exemptions existing prior to July 1, 1996 if the deposit would qualify for an exemption under paragraph (b) of this section, except for the fact that the deposit was made before July 1, 1996.

(2) If a deposit lawfully accepted under the exemption existing prior to July 1, 1996 would not qualify for an exemption under paragraph (b) or (c) of this section, the uninsured Federal branch must terminate the deposit no later than:

(i) In the case of time deposits, the maturity of a time deposit or October 1, 1996, whichever is longer; or

(ii) In the case of all other deposits, five years after July 1, 1996.

(g) *Insured banks in United States territories.* For purposes of this section, the term "foreign bank" does not include any bank organized under the laws of any territory of the United States, Puerto Rico, Guam, American Samoa, or the Virgin Islands whose deposits are insured by the FDIC pursuant to the Federal Deposit Insurance Act, 12 U.S.C. 1811 *et seq.*

[61 FR 19532, May 2, 1996, as amended at 68 FR 70131, Dec. 17, 2003; 68 FR 70700, Dec. 19, 2003; 76 FR 43569, July 21, 2011]

§ 28.17 Notice of change in activity or operations.

Notice. A Federal branch or agency shall notify the OCC if:

(a) It changes its corporate title;

(b) It changes its mailing address;

(c) It converts to a state branch, state agency, or representative office; or

(d) The parent foreign bank changes the designation of its home state.

§ 28.18 Recordkeeping and reporting.

(a) *General.* A Federal branch or agency shall comply with applicable recordkeeping and reporting requirements that apply to national banks and with any additional requirements that may be prescribed by the OCC. A Federal branch or agency, and the parent foreign bank, shall furnish information relating to the affairs of the parent foreign bank and its affiliates that the OCC may from time to time request.

(b) *Regulatory reports filed with other agencies.* A foreign bank operating a Federal branch or agency in the United States shall provide the OCC with a copy of reports filed with other Federal regulatory agencies that are designated in guidance issued by the OCC.

(c) *Maintenance of accounts, books, and records.* (1) Each Federal branch or agency shall maintain a set of accounts and records reflecting its transactions that are separate from those of the foreign bank and any other branch or agency. The Federal branch or agency shall keep a set of accounts and records in English sufficient to permit the OCC to examine the condition of the Federal branch or agency and its compliance with applicable laws and regulations. The Federal branch or agency shall promptly provide any additional records requested by the OCC for examination or supervisory purposes.

(2) A foreign bank with more than one Federal branch or agency in a state shall designate one of those offices to maintain consolidated asset, liability, and capital equivalency accounts for all Federal branches or agencies in that state.

(3) A foreign bank with a Federal branch or agency in more than one state that consolidates its CEDs into one account in accordance with § 28.15(e) shall designate a participating Federal branch or agency to maintain consolidated asset, liability, and capital equivalency account information for all Federal branches and agencies covered by the consolidated deposit. A foreign bank with a consolidated CED shall maintain a book entry accounting of assets designated under the consolidated CED for each office of that foreign bank.

[61 FR 19532, May 2, 1996, as amended at 68 FR 70700, Dec. 19, 2003]

§ 28.19 Enforcement.

As provided by section 13 of the IBA, 12 U.S.C. 3108(b), the OCC may enforce compliance with the requirements of the IBA, other applicable banking laws, and OCC regulations or orders under section 8 of the Federal Deposit Insurance Act, 12 U.S.C. 1818. This enforcement authority is in addition to any other remedies otherwise provided by the IBA or any other law.

§ 28.20 Maintenance of assets.

(a) *General rule.* (1) For prudential, supervisory, or enforcement reasons, the OCC may require a foreign bank to hold certain assets in the state in which its Federal branch or agency is located. Those assets may only consist of currency, bonds, notes, debentures, drafts, bills of exchange, or other evidence of indebtedness including loan participation agreements or certificates, or other obligations payable in the United States or in United States funds or, with the approval of the OCC, funds freely convertible into United States funds.

(2) If the OCC requires asset maintenance, the amount of assets held by a foreign bank shall be prescribed by the OCC after consideration of the aggregate amount of liabilities of the Federal branch or agency, payable at or through the Federal branch or agency. To determine the aggregate amount of liabilities for purposes of this section, the foreign bank shall include bankers' acceptances, but exclude liabilities to

the head office and any other branches, offices, agencies, subsidiaries, and affiliates of the foreign bank.

(b) *Valuation.* For the purposes of this section, marketable securities must be valued at principal amount or market value, whichever is lower.

(c) *Credits.* In determining compliance with the asset maintenance requirements, the OCC will give the Federal branch or agency credit for:

(1) Capital equivalency deposits maintained pursuant to § 28.15;

(2) Reserves required to be maintained by the Federal branch or agency pursuant to the FRB's authority under 12 U.S.C. 3105(a); and

(3) Assets pledged, and surety bonds payable, to the FDIC to secure the payment of domestic deposits.

(d) *Exclusions.* In determining eligible assets for purposes of this section, the Federal branch or agency shall exclude:

(1) Any amount due from the head office or any other branch, office, agency, subsidiary, or affiliate of the foreign bank;

(2) Any classified asset;

(3) Any asset that, in the determination of the OCC, is not supported by sufficient credit information;

(4) Any deposit with a bank in the United States, unless that bank has executed a valid waiver of offset agreement;

(5) Any asset not in the Federal branch's actual possession unless the branch holds title to the asset and maintains records sufficient to enable independent verification of the branch's ownership of the asset, as determined at the most recent examination; and

(6) Any other particular asset or class of assets as provided by the OCC, based on a case-by-case assessment of the risks associated with the asset.

(e) *International banking facility.* Unless specifically exempted by the OCC, the eligible assets and liabilities of any international banking facility operated through the Federal branch or agency must be included in the computation of eligible assets and liabilities for purposes of this section.

[61 FR 19532, May 2, 1996, as amended at 68 FR 70700, Dec. 19, 2003]

§ 28.21 Service of process.

A foreign bank operating at any Federal branch or agency is subject to service of process at the location of the Federal branch or agency.

§ 28.22 Voluntary liquidation.

(a) *Procedures to close all Federal branches and agencies.* Unless otherwise provided, in cases in which a foreign bank proposes to close all of its Federal branches or agencies, the foreign bank shall comply with applicable requirements in 12 CFR 5.48 and the Manual, including requirements that apply to an expedited liquidation of an insured Federal branch.

(b) *Notice to customers and creditors.* A foreign bank shall publish notice of the impending closure of each Federal branch or agency for a period of two months in every issue of a local newspaper where the Federal branch or agency is located. If only weekly publication is available, the notice must be published for nine consecutive weeks.

(c) *Report of condition.* The Federal branch or agency shall submit a Report of Assets and Liabilities of United States Branches and Agencies of Foreign Banks as of the close of the last business day prior to the start of liquidation of the Federal branch or agency. This report must include a certified maturity schedule of all remaining liabilities, if any.

(d) *Return of certificate.* The Federal branch or agency shall return the Federal branch or agency license certificate within 30 days of closure to the public.

(e) *Reports of examination.* The Federal branch or agency shall send the OCC certification that all of its Reports of Examination have been destroyed or return its Reports of Examination to the OCC.

[61 FR 19532, May 2, 1996, as amended at 68 FR 70700, Dec. 19, 2003]

§ 28.23 Procedures for closing of some of a foreign bank's Federal branches and/or agencies.

In cases where § 28.22 does not apply, and a foreign bank is closing one or more, but not all, of its Federal branches and/or agencies, it shall follow the procedures set forth in 12

U.S.C. 1831r–1(a) and (b) (branch closings).

[68 FR 70700, Dec. 19, 2003]

§ 28.24 Termination of a Federal branch or agency.

(a) *Grounds for termination.* The OCC may revoke the authority of a foreign bank to operate a Federal branch or agency if:

(1) The OCC determines that there is reasonable cause to believe that the foreign bank has violated or failed to comply with any of the provisions of the IBA, other applicable Federal laws or regulations, or orders of the OCC;

(2) A conservator is appointed for the foreign bank, or a similar proceeding is initiated in the foreign bank's home country;

(3) One or more grounds for receivership, including insolvency, as specified in 12 U.S.C. 3102(j), exists;

(4) One or more grounds for termination, including unsafe and unsound practices, insufficiency or dissipation of assets, concealment of books and records, a money laundering conviction, or other grounds as specified in 12 U.S.C. 191, exists; or

(5) The OCC receives a recommendation from the FRB, pursuant to 12 U.S.C. 3105(e)(5), that the license of a Federal branch or agency be terminated.

(b) *Procedures*—(1) *Notice and hearing.* Except as otherwise provided in this section, the OCC may issue an order to terminate the license of a Federal branch or agency after providing notice to the Federal branch or agency and after providing an opportunity for a hearing.

(2) *Procedures for hearing.* The OCC shall conduct a hearing under this section pursuant to the OCC's Rules of Practice and Procedure in 12 CFR part 19.

(3) *Expedited procedure.* The OCC may act without providing an opportunity for a hearing if it determines that expeditious action is necessary in order to protect the public interest. When the OCC finds that it is necessary to act without providing an opportunity for a hearing, the OCC in its sole discretion, may:

(i) Provide the Federal branch or agency with notice of the intended termination order;

(ii) Grant the Federal branch or agency an opportunity to present a written submission opposing issuance of the order; or

(iii) Take any other action designed to provide the Federal branch or agency with notice and an opportunity to present its views concerning the termination order.

[61 FR 19532, May 2, 1996. Redesignated at 68 FR 70700, Dec. 19, 2003]

§ 28.25 Change in control.

(a) *After-the-fact notice.* In cases in which no other filing is required under subpart B of this part, a foreign bank that operates a Federal branch or agency shall inform the OCC in writing of the direct or indirect acquisition of control of the foreign bank by any person or entity, or group of persons or entities acting in concert, within 14 calendar days after the foreign bank becomes aware of a change in control.

(b) *Additional information.* The foreign bank shall furnish the OCC with any additional information the OCC may require in connection with the acquisition of control.

[68 FR 70701, Dec. 19, 2003]

§ 28.26 Loan production offices.

A Federal branch may establish lending offices, make credit decisions, and engage in other representational activities at a site other than a Federal branch office, subject to the same rights, privileges, requirements and limitations that apply to national banks under 12 CFR 7.1003, 7.1004, and 7.1005.

[68 FR 70701, Dec. 19, 2003]

Subpart C—International Lending Supervision

§ 28.50 Authority, purpose, and scope.

(a) *Authority.* This subpart is issued pursuant to 12 U.S.C. 1 *et seq.*, 93a, 161, and 1818; and the International Lending Supervision Act of 1983 (Pub. L. 98–181, title IX, 97 Stat. 1153, 12 U.S.C. 3901 *et seq.*).

(b) *Purpose.* This subpart implements the requirements of the International Lending Supervision Act of 1983 (12 U.S.C. 3901 *et seq.*),

(c) *Scope.* This subpart requires national banks to establish reserves against the risks presented in certain international assets and sets forth the accounting for various fees received by the banks when making international loans.

[61 FR 19532, May 2, 1996, as amended at 73 FR 22251, Apr. 24, 2008]

§28.51 Definitions.

For the purposes of this subpart:

(a) *Banking institution* means a national bank.

(b) *Federal banking agencies* means the OCC, the FRB, and the FDIC.

(c) *International assets* means those assets required to be included in banking institutions' *Country Exposure Report* forms (FFIEC 009).

(d) *International loan* means a loan as defined in the instructions to the *Report of Condition and Income* for the respective banking institution (FFIEC 031, 032, 033 and 034) and made to a foreign government, or to an individual, a corporation, or other entity not a citizen of, resident in, or organized or incorporated in the United States.

(e) *Restructured international loan* means a loan that meets the following criteria:

(1) The borrower is unable to service the existing loan according to its terms and is a resident of a foreign country in which there is a generalized inability of public and private sector obligors to meet their external debt obligations on a timely basis because of a lack of, or restraints on the availability of, needed foreign exchange in the country; and

(2) The terms of the existing loan are amended to reduce stated interest or extend the schedule of payments; or

(3) A new loan is made to, or for the benefit of, the borrower, enabling the borrower to service or refinance the existing debt.

(f) *Transfer risk* means the possibility that an asset cannot be serviced in the currency of payment because of a lack of, or restraints on the availability of, needed foreign exchange in the country of the obligor.

[61 FR 19532, May 2, 1996, as amended at 63 FR 57048, Oct. 26, 1998; 73 FR 22251, Apr. 24, 2008]

§28.52 Allocated transfer risk reserve.

(a) *Establishment of allocated transfer risk reserve.* A banking institution shall establish an allocated transfer risk reserve (ATRR) for specified international assets when required by the OCC in accordance with this section.

(b) *Procedures and standards*—(1) *Joint agency determination.* At least annually, the Federal banking agencies shall determine jointly, based on the standards set forth in paragraph (b)(2) of this section, the following:

(i) Which international assets subject to transfer risk warrant establishment of an ATRR;

(ii) The amount of the ATRR for the specified assets; and

(iii) Whether an ATRR established for specified assets may be reduced.

(2) *Standards for requiring ATRR*—(i) *Evaluation of assets.* The Federal banking agencies shall apply the following criteria in determining whether an ATRR is required for particular international assets:

(A) Whether the quality of a banking institution's assets has been impaired by a protracted inability of public or private obligors in a foreign country to make payments on their external indebtedness as indicated by such factors, among others, as whether:

(*1*) Such obligors have failed to make full interest payments on external indebtedness;

(*2*) Such obligors have failed to comply with the terms of any restructured indebtedness; or

(*3*) A foreign country has failed to comply with any International Monetary Fund or other suitable adjustment program; or

(B) Whether no definite prospects exist for the orderly restoration of debt service.

(ii) *Determination of amount of ATRR.* (A) In determining the amount of the ATRR, the Federal banking agencies shall consider:

(*1*) The length of time the quality of the asset has been impaired;

(*2*) Recent actions taken to restore debt service capability;

(*3*) Prospects for restored asset quality; and

(*4*) Such other factors as the Federal banking agencies may consider relevant to the quality of the asset.

(B) The initial year's provision for the ATRR shall be 10 percent of the principal amount of each specified international asset, or such greater or lesser percentage determined by the Federal banking agencies. Additional provision, if any, for the ATRR in subsequent years shall be 15 percent of the principal amount of each specified international asset, or such greater or lesser percentage determined by the Federal banking agencies.

(3) *Notification.* Based on the joint agency determinations under paragraph (b)(1) of this section, the OCC shall notify each banking institution holding assets subject to an ATRR:

(i) Of the amount of the ATRR to be established by the institution for specified international assets; and

(ii) That an ATRR to be established for specified assets may be reduced.

(c) *Accounting treatment of ATRR*—(1) *Charge to current income.* A banking institution shall establish an ATRR by a charge to current income and the amounts so charged shall not be included in the banking institution's capital or surplus.

(2) *Separate accounting.* A banking institution shall account for an ATRR separately from the Allowance for Possible Loan Losses, and shall deduct the ATRR from "gross loans and leases" to arrive at "net loans and leases." The ATRR must be established for each asset subject to the ATRR in the percentage amount specified.

(3) *Consolidation.* A banking institution shall establish an ATRR, as required, on a consolidated basis. Consolidation should be in accordance with the procedures and tests of significance set forth in the instructions for preparation of *Consolidated Reports of Condition and Income* (FFIEC 031, 032, 033 and 034). For bank holding companies, the consolidation shall be in accordance with the principles set forth in the "Instructions to the Bank Holding Company Financial Supplement to Report F.R. Y–6" (Form F.R. Y–9). Edge corporations and Agreement corporations engaged in banking shall report in accordance with instructions for preparation of the Report of Condition for Edge corporations and Agreement corporations (Form F.R. 2886b).

(4) *Alternative accounting treatment.* A banking institution need not establish an ATRR if it writes down in the period in which the ATRR is required, or has written down in prior periods, the value of the specified international assets in the requisite amount for each such asset. For purposes of this paragraph, international assets may be written down by a charge to the Allowance for Possible Loan Losses or a reduction in the principal amount of the asset by application of interest payments or other collections on the asset. However, the Allowance for Possible Loan Losses must be replenished in such amount necessary to restore it to a level which adequately provides for the estimated losses inherent in the banking institution's loan portfolio.

(5) *Reduction of ATRR.* A banking institution may reduce an ATRR when notified by the OCC or, at any time, by writing down such amount of the international asset for which the ATRR was established.

§ 28.53 Accounting for fees on international loans.

(a) *Restrictions on fees for restructured international loans.* No banking institution shall charge, in connection with the restructuring of an international loan, any fee exceeding the administrative costs of the restructuring unless it amortizes the amount of the fee exceeding the administrative cost over the effective life of the loan.

(b) *Accounting treatment.* Subject to paragraph (a) of this section, a banking institution is to account for fees in accordance with generally accepted accounting principles.

[63 FR 57048, Oct. 26, 1998]

§ 28.54 Reporting and disclosure of international assets.

(a) *Requirements.* (1) Pursuant to section 907(a) of the International Lending Supervision Act of 1983 (title IX, Pub. L. 98–181, 97 Stat. 1153, 12 U.S.C. 3906)

(ILSA) a banking institution shall submit to the OCC, at least quarterly, information regarding the amounts and composition of its holdings of international assets.

(2) Pursuant to section 907(b) of ILSA (12 U.S.C. 3906), a banking institution shall submit to the OCC information regarding concentrations in its holdings of international assets that are material in relation to total assets and to capital of the institution, such information to be made publicly available by the OCC on request.

(b) *Procedures.* The format, content, and reporting and filing dates of the reports required under paragraph (a) of this section shall be determined jointly by the Federal banking agencies. The requirements to be prescribed by the agencies may include changes to existing reporting forms (such as the Country Exposure Report, FFIEC 009) or such other requirements as the agencies deem appropriate. The agencies also may determine to exempt from the requirements of paragraph (a) of this section banking institutions that, in the agencies' judgment, have *de minimis* holdings of international assets.

(c) *Reservation of authority.* Nothing contained in this part shall preclude the OCC from requiring from a banking institution such additional or more frequent information on the institution's holdings of international assets as the OCC may consider necessary.

PART 29 [RESERVED]

PART 30—SAFETY AND SOUNDNESS STANDARDS

Sec.

30.1 Scope.
30.2 Purpose.
30.3 Determination and notification of failure to meet safety and soundness standards and request for compliance plan.
30.4 Filing of safety and soundness compliance plan.
30.5 Issuance of orders to correct deficiencies and to take or refrain from taking other actions.
30.6 Enforcement of orders.
APPENDIX A TO PART 30—INTERAGENCY GUIDELINES ESTABLISHING STANDARDS FOR SAFETY AND SOUNDNESS
APPENDIX B TO PART 30—INTERAGENCY GUIDELINES ESTABLISHING INFORMATION SECURITY STANDARDS
APPENDIX C TO PART 30—OCC GUIDELINES ESTABLISHING STANDARDS FOR RESIDENTIAL MORTGAGE LENDING PRACTICES
APPENDIX D TO PART 30—OCC GUIDELINES ESTABLISHING HEIGHTENED STANDARDS FOR CERTAIN LARGE INSURED NATIONAL BANKS, INSURED FEDERAL SAVINGS ASSOCIATIONS, AND INSURED FEDERAL BRANCHES
APPENDIX E TO PART 30—OCC GUIDELINES ESTABLISHING STANDARDS FOR RECOVERY PLANNING BY CERTAIN LARGE INSURED NATIONAL BANKS, INSURED FEDERAL SAVINGS ASSOCIATIONS, AND INSURED FEDERAL BRANCHES

AUTHORITY: 12 U.S.C. 1, 93a, 371, 1462a, 1463, 1464, 1467a, 1818, 1828, 1831p-1, 1881–1884, 3102(b) and 5412(b)(2)(B); 15 U.S.C. 1681s, 1681w, 6801, and 6805(b)(1).

SOURCE: 60 FR 35680, July 10, 1995, unless otherwise noted.

EDITORIAL NOTE: Nomenclature changes to part 30 appear at 69 FR 77616, Dec. 28, 2004.

§ 30.1 Scope.

(a) The rules set forth in this part and the standards set forth in appendices A, B, C, D, and E to this part apply to national banks, Federal savings associations, and Federal branches of foreign banks that are subject to the provisions of section 39 of the Federal Deposit Insurance Act (section 39)(12 U.S.C. 1831p–1).

(b) The standards set forth in appendix B to this part also apply to uninsured national banks, Federal branches and Federal agencies of foreign banks, and the subsidiaries of any national bank, Federal savings association, and Federal branch and Federal agency of a foreign bank (except brokers, dealers, persons providing insurance, investment companies, and investment advisers). Violation of these standards may be an unsafe and unsound practice within the meaning of 12 U.S.C. 1818.

[66 FR 8633, Feb. 1, 2001, as amended at 70 FR 6332, Feb. 7, 2005; 79 FR 54543, Sept. 11, 2014; 81 FR 66800, Sept. 29, 2016]

§ 30.2 Purpose.

Section 39 of the FDI Act, 12 U.S.C. 1831p–1, requires the Office of the Comptroller of the Currency (OCC) to establish safety and soundness standards. Pursuant to section 39, a national bank or Federal savings association may be required to submit a compliance plan if it is not in compliance with a safety and soundness standard prescribed by guideline under section 39(a) or (b). An enforceable order under section 8 of the FDI Act, 12 U.S.C. 1818(b), may be issued if, after being notified that it is in violation of a safety and soundness standard prescribed under section 39, the national bank or Federal savings association fails to submit an acceptable compliance plan or fails in any material respect to implement an accepted plan. This part establishes procedures for requiring submission of a compliance plan and issuing an enforceable order pursuant to section 39. The Interagency Guidelines Establishing Standards for Safety and Soundness are set forth in appendix A to this part, and the Interagency Guidelines Establishing Information Security Standards are set forth in appendix B to this part. The OCC Guidelines Establishing Standards for Residential Mortgage Lending Practices are set forth in appendix C to this part. The OCC Guidelines Establishing Heightened Standards for Certain Large Insured National Banks, Insured Federal Savings Associations, and Insured Federal Branches are set forth in appendix D to this part. The OCC Guidelines Establishing Standards for Recovery Planning by Certain Large Insured National Banks, Insured Federal Savings Associations, and Insured Federal Branches are set forth in appendix E to this part.

[60 FR 35680, July 10, 1995, as amended at 63 FR 55488, Oct. 15, 1998; 64 FR 52641, Sept. 30, 1999; 66 FR 8633, Feb. 1, 2001; 70 FR 6332, Feb. 7, 2005; 79 FR 54543, Sept. 11, 2014; 81 FR 66800, Sept. 29, 2016]

§ 30.3 Determination and notification of failure to meet safety and soundness standards and request for compliance plan.

(a) *Determination.* The OCC may, based upon an examination, inspection, or any other information that becomes available to the OCC, determine that a national bank or Federal savings association has failed to satisfy the safety and soundness standards contained in the Interagency Guidelines Establishing Standards for Safety and Soundness set forth in appendix A to this part, the Interagency Guidelines Establishing Standards for Safeguarding Customer Information set forth in appendix B to this part, the OCC Guidelines Establishing Standards for Residential Mortgage Lending Practices set forth in appendix C to this part, the OCC Guidelines Establishing Heightened Standards for Certain Large Insured National Banks, Insured Federal Savings Associations, and Insured Federal Branches set forth in appendix D to this part, or the OCC Guidelines Establishing Standards for Recovery Planning by Certain Large Insured National Banks, Insured Federal Savings Associations, and Insured Federal Branches set forth in appendix E to this part.

(b) *Request for compliance plan.* If the OCC determines that a national bank or Federal savings association has failed to satisfy a safety and soundness standard pursuant to paragraph (a) of this section, the OCC may request, by letter or through a report of examination, the submission of a compliance plan and the bank or savings association shall be deemed to have notice of the deficiency three days after mailing of the letter by the OCC or delivery of the report of examination.

[60 FR 35680, July 10, 1995, as amended at 63 FR 55488, Oct. 15, 1998; 64 FR 52641, Sept. 30, 1999; 66 FR 8633, Feb. 1, 2001; 70 FR 6332, Feb. 7, 2005; 79 FR 54543, Sept. 11, 2014; 81 FR 66800, Sept. 29, 2016]

§ 30.4 Filing of safety and soundness compliance plan.

(a) *Schedule for filing compliance plan*—(1) *In general.* A national bank or Federal savings association shall file a written safety and soundness compliance plan with the OCC within 30 days of receiving a request for a compliance plan pursuant to § 30.3(b) unless the OCC notifies the bank or savings association in writing that the plan is to be filed within a different period.

(2) *Other plans.* If a national bank or Federal savings association is obligated to file, or is currently operating under, a capital restoration plan submitted pursuant to section 38 of the FDI Act (12 U.S.C. 1831o), a cease-and-desist order entered into pursuant to section 8 of the FDI Act (12 U.S.C.

1818(b)), a formal or informal agreement, or a response to a report of examination or report of inspection, it may, with the permission of the OCC, submit a compliance plan under this section as part of that plan, order, agreement, or response, subject to the deadline provided in paragraph (a) of this section.

(b) *Contents of plan.* The compliance plan shall include a description of the steps the national bank or Federal savings association will take to correct the deficiency and the time within which those steps will be taken.

(c) *Review of safety and soundness compliance plans.* Within 30 days after receiving a safety and soundness compliance plan under this part, the OCC shall provide written notice to the national bank or Federal savings association of whether the plan has been approved or seek additional information from the bank or savings association regarding the plan. The OCC may extend the time within which notice regarding approval of a plan will be provided.

(d) *Failure to submit or implement a compliance plan*—(1) *Supervisory actions.* If a national bank or Federal savings association fails to submit an acceptable plan within the time specified by the OCC or fails in any material respect to implement a compliance plan, then the OCC shall, by order, require the bank or savings association to correct the deficiency and may take further actions provided in section 39(e)(2)(B). Pursuant to section 39(e)(3), the OCC may be required to take certain actions if the national bank or Federal savings association commenced operations or experienced a change in control within the previous 24-month period, or the bank or savings association experienced extraordinary growth during the previous 18-month period.

(2) *Extraordinary growth.* For purposes of paragraph (d)(1) of this section, extraordinary growth means an increase in assets of more than 7.5 percent during any quarter within the 18-month period preceding the issuance of a request for submission of a compliance plan, by a national bank or Federal savings association that is not well capitalized for purposes of section 38 of the FDI Act. For purposes of calculating an increase in assets, assets acquired through merger or acquisition approved pursuant to the Bank Merger Act (12 U.S.C. 1828(c)) will be excluded.

(e) *Amendment of compliance plan.* A national bank or Federal savings association that has filed an approved compliance plan may, after prior written notice to and approval by the OCC, amend the plan to reflect a change in circumstance. Until such time as a proposed amendment has been approved, the bank or savings association shall implement the compliance plan as previously approved.

[60 FR 35680, July 10, 1995, as amended at 79 FR 54543, Sept. 11, 2014]

§ 30.5 Issuance of orders to correct deficiencies and to take or refrain from taking other actions.

(a) *Notice of intent to issue order*—(1) *In general.* The OCC shall provide a national bank or Federal savings association prior written notice of the OCC's intention to issue an order requiring the bank or savings association to correct a safety and soundness deficiency or to take or refrain from taking other actions pursuant to section 39 of the FDI Act. The national bank or Federal savings association shall have such time to respond to a proposed order as provided by the OCC under paragraph (c) of this section.

(2) *Immediate issuance of final order.* If the OCC finds it necessary in order to carry out the purposes of section 39 of the FDI Act, the OCC may, without providing the notice prescribed in paragraph (a)(1) of this section, issue an order requiring a national bank or Federal savings association immediately to take actions to correct a safety and soundness deficiency or take or refrain from taking other actions pursuant to section 39. A national bank or Federal savings association that is subject to such an immediately effective order may submit a written appeal of the order to the OCC. Such an appeal must be received by the OCC within 14 calendar days of the issuance of the order, unless the OCC permits a longer period. The OCC shall consider any such appeal, if filed in a timely manner, within 60 days of receiving the appeal. During such period of review, the order

shall remain in effect unless the OCC, in its sole discretion, stays the effectiveness of the order.

(b) *Content of notice.* A notice of intent to issue an order shall include:

(1) A statement of the safety and soundness deficiency or deficiencies that have been identified at the national bank or Federal savings association;

(2) A description of any restrictions, prohibitions, or affirmative actions that the OCC proposes to impose or require;

(3) The proposed date when such restrictions or prohibitions would be effective or the proposed date for completion of any required action; and

(4) The date by which the national bank or Federal savings association subject to the order may file with the OCC a written response to the notice.

(c) *Response to notice*—(1) *Time for response.* A national bank or Federal savings association may file a written response to a notice of intent to issue an order within the time period set by the OCC. Such a response must be received by the OCC within 14 calendar days from the date of the notice unless the OCC determines that a different period is appropriate in light of the safety and soundness of the national bank or Federal savings association or other relevant circumstances.

(2) *Content of response.* The response should include:

(i) An explanation why the action proposed by the OCC is not an appropriate exercise of discretion under section 39;

(ii) Any recommended modification of the proposed order; and

(iii) Any other relevant information, mitigating circumstances, documentation, or other evidence in support of the position of the national bank or Federal savings association regarding the proposed order.

(d) *Agency consideration of response.* After considering the response, the OCC may:

(1) Issue the order as proposed or in modified form;

(2) Determine not to issue the order and so notify the national bank or Federal savings association; or

(3) Seek additional information or clarification of the response from the national bank or Federal savings association, or any other relevant source.

(e) *Failure to file response.* Failure by a national bank or Federal savings association to file with the OCC, within the specified time period, a written response to a proposed order shall constitute a waiver of the opportunity to respond and shall constitute consent to the issuance of the order.

(f) *Request for modification or rescission of order.* Any national bank or Federal savings association that is subject to an order under this part may, upon a change in circumstances, request in writing that the OCC reconsider the terms of the order, and may propose that the order be rescinded or modified. Unless otherwise ordered by the OCC, the order shall continue in place while such request is pending before the OCC.

[60 FR 35680, July 10, 1995, as amended at 79 FR 54544, Sept. 11, 2014]

§ 30.6 Enforcement of orders.

(a) *Judicial remedies.* Whenever a national bank or Federal savings association fails to comply with an order issued under section 39, the OCC may seek enforcement of the order in the appropriate United States district court pursuant to section 8(i)(1) of the FDI Act, 12 U.S.C. 1818(i)(1).

(b) *Failure to comply with order.* Pursuant to section 8(i)(2)(A) of the FDI Act, 12 U.S.C. 1818(i)(2)(A), the OCC may assess a civil money penalty against any national bank or Federal savings association that violates or otherwise fails to comply with any final order issued under section 39 and against any institution-affiliated party who participates in such violation or noncompliance.

(c) *Other enforcement action.* In addition to the actions described in paragraphs (a) and (b) of this section, the OCC may seek enforcement of the provisions of section 39 or this part through any other judicial or administrative proceeding authorized by law.

[60 FR 35680, July 10, 1995, as amended at 79 FR 54544, Sept. 11, 2014]

Appendix A to Part 30—Interagency Guidelines Establishing Standards for Safety and Soundness

Table of Contents

I. Introduction

A. Preservation of existing authority.
B. Definitions.

II. Operational and Managerial Standards

A. Internal controls and information systems.
B. Internal audit system.
C. Loan documentation.
D. Credit underwriting.
E. Interest rate exposure.
F. Asset growth.
G. Asset quality.
H. Earnings.
I. Compensation, fees and benefits.

III. Prohibition on Compensation That Constitutes an Unsafe and Unsound Practice

A. Excessive compensation.
B. Compensation leading to material financial loss.

I. Introduction

i. Section 39 of the Federal Deposit Insurance Act[1] (FDI Act) requires each Federal banking agency (collectively, the agencies) to establish certain safety and soundness standards by regulation or by guideline for all insured depository institutions. Under section 39, the agencies must establish three types of standards: (1) Operational and managerial standards; (2) compensation standards; and (3) such standards relating to asset quality, earnings, and stock valuation as they determine to be appropriate.

ii. Section 39(a) requires the agencies to establish operational and managerial standards relating to: (1) Internal controls, information systems and internal audit systems, in accordance with section 36 of the FDI Act (12 U.S.C. 1831m); (2) loan documentation; (3) credit underwriting; (4) interest rate exposure; (5) asset growth; and (6) compensation, fees, and benefits, in accordance with subsection (c) of section 39. Section 39(b) requires the agencies to establish standards relating to asset quality, earnings, and stock valuation that the agencies determine to be appropriate.

iii. Section 39(c) requires the agencies to establish standards prohibiting as an unsafe and unsound practice any compensatory arrangement that would provide any executive officer, employee, director, or principal shareholder of the institution with excessive compensation, fees or benefits and any compensatory arrangement that could lead to material financial loss to an institution. Section 39(c) also requires that the agencies establish standards that specify when compensation is excessive.

iv. If an agency determines that an institution fails to meet any standard established by guideline under subsection (a) or (b) of section 39, the agency may require the institution to submit to the agency an acceptable plan to achieve compliance with the standard. In the event that an institution fails to submit an acceptable plan within the time allowed by the agency or fails in any material respect to implement an accepted plan, the agency must, by order, require the institution to correct the deficiency. The agency may, and in some cases must, take other supervisory actions until the deficiency has been corrected.

v. The agencies have adopted amendments to their rules and regulations to establish deadlines for submission and review of compliance plans.[2]

vi. The following Guidelines set out the safety and soundness standards that the agencies use to identify and address problems at insured depository institutions before capital becomes impaired. The agencies believe that the standards adopted in these Guidelines serve this end without dictating how institutions must be managed and operated. These standards are designed to identify potential safety and soundness concerns and ensure that action is taken to address those concerns before they pose a risk to the deposit insurance funds.

A. *Preservation of Existing Authority*

Neither section 39 nor these Guidelines in any way limits the authority of the agencies to address unsafe or unsound practices, violations of law, unsafe or unsound conditions, or other practices. Action under section 39 and these Guidelines may be taken independently of, in conjunction with, or in addition to any other enforcement action available to the agencies. Nothing in these Guidelines

[1] Section 39 of the Federal Deposit Insurance Act (12 U.S.C. 1831p–1) was added by section 132 of the Federal Deposit Insurance Corporation Improvement Act of 1991 (FDICIA), Pub. L. 102–242, 105 Stat. 2236 (1991), and amended by section 956 of the Housing and Community Development Act of 1992, Pub. L. 102–550, 106 Stat. 3895 (1992) and section 318 of the Riegle Community Development and Regulatory Improvement Act of 1994, Pub. L. 103–325, 108 Stat. 2160 (1994).

[2] For the Office of the Comptroller of the Currency, these regulations appear at 12 CFR part 30; for the Board of Governors of the Federal Reserve System, these regulations appear at 12 CFR part 263; and for the Federal Deposit Insurance Corporation, these regulations appear at 12 CFR part 308, subpart R and 12 CFR part 391, subpart B.

limits the authority of the FDIC pursuant to section 38(i)(2)(F) of the FDI Act (12 U.S.C. 1831(o)) and part 325 of title 12 of the Code of Federal Regulations.

B. *Definitions*

1. *In general.* For purposes of these Guidelines, except as modified in the Guidelines or unless the context otherwise requires, the terms used have the same meanings as set forth in sections 3 and 39 of the FDI Act (12 U.S.C. 1813 and 1831p–1).

2. *Board of directors,* in the case of a state-licensed insured branch of a foreign bank and in the case of a Federal branch of a foreign bank, means the managing official in charge of the insured foreign branch.

3. *Compensation* means all direct and indirect payments or benefits, both cash and non-cash, granted to or for the benefit of any executive officer, employee, director, or principal shareholder, including but not limited to payments or benefits derived from an employment contract, compensation or benefit agreement, fee arrangement, perquisite, stock option plan, postemployment benefit, or other compensatory arrangement.

4. *Director* shall have the meaning described in 12 CFR 215.2(c).[3]

5. *Executive officer* shall have the meaning described in 12 CFR 215.2(d).[4]

6. *Principal shareholder* shall have the meaning described in 12 CFR 215.2(*l*).[5]

II. OPERATIONAL AND MANAGERIAL STANDARDS

A. *Internal controls and information systems.* An institution should have internal controls and information systems that are appropriate to the size of the institution and the nature, scope and risk of its activities and that provide for:

1. An organizational structure that establishes clear lines of authority and responsibility for monitoring adherence to established policies;

2. Effective risk assessment;

3. Timely and accurate financial, operational and regulatory reports;

4. Adequate procedures to safeguard and manage assets; and

5. Compliance with applicable laws and regulations.

B. *Internal audit system.* An institution should have an internal audit system that is appropriate to the size of the institution and the nature and scope of its activities and that provides for:

1. Adequate monitoring of the system of internal controls through an internal audit function. For an institution whose size, complexity or scope of operations does not warrant a full scale internal audit function, a system of independent reviews of key internal controls may be used;

2. Independence and objectivity;

3. Qualified persons;

4. Adequate testing and review of information systems;

5. Adequate documentation of tests and findings and any corrective actions;

6. Verification and review of management actions to address material weaknesses; and

7. Review by the institution's audit committee or board of directors of the effectiveness of the internal audit systems.

C. *Loan documentation.* An institution should establish and maintain loan documentation practices that:

1. Enable the institution to make an informed lending decision and to assess risk, as necessary, on an ongoing basis;

2. Identify the purpose of a loan and the source of repayment, and assess the ability of the borrower to repay the indebtedness in a timely manner;

3. Ensure that any claim against a borrower is legally enforceable;

4. Demonstrate appropriate administration and monitoring of a loan; and

5. Take account of the size and complexity of a loan.

D. *Credit underwriting.* An institution should establish and maintain prudent credit underwriting practices that:

1. Are commensurate with the types of loans the institution will make and consider the terms and conditions under which they will be made;

2. Consider the nature of the markets in which loans will be made;

3. Provide for consideration, prior to credit commitment, of the borrower's overall financial condition and resources, the financial responsibility of any guarantor, the nature and value of any underlying collateral, and the borrower's character and willingness to repay as agreed;

4. Establish a system of independent, ongoing credit review and appropriate communication to management and to the board of directors;

5. Take adequate account of concentration of credit risk; and

6. Are appropriate to the size of the institution and the nature and scope of its activities.

E. *Interest rate exposure.* An institution should:

[3] In applying these definitions for savings associations, pursuant to 12 U.S.C. 1464, savings associations shall use the terms "savings association" and "insured savings association" in place of the terms "member bank" and "insured bank".

[4] See footnote 3 in section I.B.4. of this appendix.

[5] See footnote 3 in section I.B.4. of this appendix.

1. Manage interest rate risk in a manner that is appropriate to the size of the institution and the complexity of its assets and liabilities; and

2. Provide for periodic reporting to management and the board of directors regarding interest rate risk with adequate information for management and the board of directors to assess the level of risk.

F. *Asset growth.* An institution's asset growth should be prudent and consider:

1. The source, volatility and use of the funds that support asset growth;

2. Any increase in credit risk or interest rate risk as a result of growth; and

3. The effect of growth on the institution's capital.

G. *Asset quality.* An insured depository institution should establish and maintain a system that is commensurate with the institution's size and the nature and scope of its operations to identify problem assets and prevent deterioration in those assets. The institution should:

1. Conduct periodic assetquality reviews to identify problem assets;

2. Estimate the inherent losses in those assets and establish reserves that are sufficient to absorb estimated losses;

3. Compare problem asset totals to capital;

4. Take appropriate corrective action to resolve problem assets;

5. Consider the size and potential risks of material asset concentrations; and

6. Provide periodic asset reports with adequate information for management and the board of directors to assess the level of asset risk.

H. *Earnings.* An insured depository institution should establish and maintain a system that is commensurate with the institution's size and the nature and scope of its operations to evaluate and monitor earnings and ensure that earnings are sufficient to maintain adequate capital and reserves. The institution should:

1. Compare recent earnings trends relative to equity, assets, or other commonly used benchmarks to the institution's historical results and those of its peers;

2. Evaluate the adequacy of earnings given the size, complexity, and risk profile of the institution's assets and operations;

3. Assess the source, volatility, and sustainability of earnings, including the effect of nonrecurring or extraordinary income or expense;

4. Take steps to ensure that earnings are sufficient to maintain adequate capital and reserves after considering the institution's asset quality and growth rate; and

5. Provide periodic earnings reports with adequate information for management and the board of directors to assess earnings performance.

I. *Compensation, fees and benefits.* An institution should maintain safeguards to prevent the payment of compensation, fees, and benefits that are excessive or that could lead to material financial loss to the institution.

III. PROHIBITION ON COMPENSATION THAT CONSTITUTES AN UNSAFE AND UNSOUND PRACTICE

A. Excessive Compensation

Excessive compensation is prohibited as an unsafe and unsound practice. Compensation shall be considered excessive when amounts paid are unreasonable or disproportionate to the services performed by an executive officer, employee, director, or principal shareholder, considering the following:

1. The combined value of all cash and noncash benefits provided to the individual;

2. The compensation history of the individual and other individuals with comparable expertise at the institution;

3. The financial condition of the institution;

4. Comparable compensation practices at comparable institutions, based upon such factors as asset size, geographic location, and the complexity of the loan portfolio or other assets;

5. For postemployment benefits, the projected total cost and benefit to the institution;

6. Any connection between the individual and any fraudulent act or omission, breach of trust or fiduciary duty, or insider abuse with regard to the institution; and

7. Any other factors the agencies determines to be relevant.

B. Compensation Leading to Material Financial Loss

Compensation that could lead to material financial loss to an institution is prohibited as an unsafe and unsound practice.

[60 FR 35678, 35682, July 10, 1995, as amended at 61 FR 43950, Aug. 27, 1996; 79 FR 54544, Sept. 11, 2014]

APPENDIX B TO PART 30—INTERAGENCY GUIDELINES ESTABLISHING INFORMATION SECURITY STANDARDS

TABLE OF CONTENTS

I. Introduction
A. Scope
B. Preservation of Existing Authority
C. Definitions
II. Standards for Safeguarding Customer Information
A. Information Security Program
B. Objectives
III. Development and Implementation of Customer Information Security Program
A. Involve the Board of Directors
B. Assess Risk
C. Manage and Control Risk
D. Oversee Service Provider Arrangements

E. Adjust the Program
F. Report to the Board
G. Implement the Standards
I. Introduction

The Interagency Guidelines Establishing Information Security Standards (Guidelines) set forth standards pursuant to section 39 of the Federal Deposit Insurance Act (section 39, codified at 12 U.S.C. 1831p–1), and sections 501 and 505(b), codified at 15 U.S.C. 6801 and 6805(b) of the Gramm-Leach Bliley Act. These Guidelines address standards for developing and implementing administrative, technical, and physical safeguards to protect the security, confidentiality, and integrity of customer information. These Guidelines also address standards with respect to the proper disposal of consumer information, pursuant to sections 621 and 628 of the Fair Credit Reporting Act (15 U.S.C. 1681s and 1681w).

A. *Scope*. The Guidelines apply to customer information maintained by or on behalf of entities over which the OCC has authority. Such entities, referred to as "the national bank or Federal savings association," are national banks, Federal savings associations, Federal branches and Federal agencies of foreign banks, and any subsidiaries of such entities (except brokers, dealers, persons providing insurance, investment companies, and investment advisers). The Guidelines also apply to the proper disposal of consumer information by or on behalf of such entities.

B. *Preservation of Existing Authority*. Neither section 39 nor these Guidelines in any way limit the authority of the OCC to address unsafe or unsound practices, violations of law, unsafe or unsound conditions, or other practices. The OCC may take action under section 39 and these Guidelines independently of, in conjunction with, or in addition to, any other enforcement action available to the OCC.

C. *Definitions*. 1. Except as modified in the Guidelines, or unless the context otherwise requires, the terms used in these Guidelines have the same meanings as set forth in sections 3 and 39 of the Federal Deposit Insurance Act (12 U.S.C. 1813 and 1831p–1).

2. For purposes of the Guidelines, the following definitions apply:

a. *Board of directors*, in the case of a branch or agency of a foreign bank, means the managing official in charge of the branch or agency.

b. *Consumer information* means any record about an individual, whether in paper, electronic, or other form, that is a consumer report or is derived from a consumer report and that is maintained or otherwise possessed by or on behalf of the national bank or Federal savings association for a business purpose. Consumer information also means a compilation of such records. The term does not include any record that does not identify an individual.

i. *Examples*. (1) *Consumer information* includes:

(A) A consumer report that a national bank or Federal savings association obtains;

(B) Information from a consumer report that the national bank or Federal savings association obtains from its affiliate after the consumer has been given a notice and has elected not to opt out of that sharing;

(C) Information from a consumer report that the national bank or Federal savings association obtains about an individual who applies for but does not receive a loan, including any loan sought by an individual for a business purpose;

(D) Information from a consumer report that the national bank or Federal savings association obtains about an individual who guarantees a loan (including a loan to a business entity); or

(E) Information from a consumer report that the national bank or Federal savings association obtains about an employee or prospective employee.

(2) *Consumer information* does not include:

(A) Aggregate information, such as the mean credit score, derived from a group of consumer reports; or

(B) Blind data, such as payment history on accounts that are not personally identifiable, that may be used for developing credit scoring models or for other purposes.

c. *Consumer report* has the same meaning as set forth in the Fair Credit Reporting Act, 15 U.S.C. 1681a(d).

d. *Customer* means any customer of the national bank or Federal savings association as defined in 12 CFR 1016.3(i).

e. *Customer information* means any record containing nonpublic personal information, as defined in 12 CFR 1016.3(p), about a customer, whether in paper, electronic, or other form, that is maintained by or on behalf of the national bank or Federal savings association.

f. *Customer information systems* means any methods used to access, collect, store, use, transmit, protect, or dispose of customer information.

g. *Service provider* means any person or entity that maintains, processes, or otherwise is permitted access to customer information or consumer information through its provision of services directly to the national bank or Federal savings association.

II. STANDARDS FOR INFORMATION SECURITY

A. *Information Security Program*. Each national bank or Federal savings association shall implement a comprehensive written information security program that includes administrative, technical, and physical safeguards appropriate to the size and complexity of the national bank or Federal savings association and the nature and scope of its activities. While all parts of the national bank or Federal savings association are not required to implement a uniform set of policies, all elements of the information security program must be coordinated.

B. *Objectives.* A national bank's or Federal savings association's information security program shall be designed to:

1. Ensure the security and confidentiality of customer information;

2. Protect against any anticipated threats or hazards to the security or integrity of such information;

3. Protect against unauthorized access to or use of such information that could result in substantial harm or inconvenience to any customer; and

4. Ensure the proper disposal of customer information and consumer information.

III. DEVELOPMENT AND IMPLEMENTATION OF INFORMATION SECURITY PROGRAM

A. *Involve the Board of Directors.* The board of directors or an appropriate committee of the board of each national bank or Federal savings association shall:

1. Approve the national bank's or Federal savings association's written information security program; and

2. Oversee the development, implementation, and maintenance of the national bank's or Federal savings association's information security program, including assigning specific responsibility for its implementation and reviewing reports from management.

B. *Assess Risk.* Each national bank or Federal savings association shall:

1. Identify reasonably foreseeable internal and external threats that could result in unauthorized disclosure, misuse, alteration, or destruction of customer information or customer information systems.

2. Assess the likelihood and potential damage of these threats, taking into consideration the sensitivity of customer information.

3. Assess the sufficiency of policies, procedures, customer information systems, and other arrangements in place to control risks.

C. *Manage and Control Risk.* Each national bank or Federal savings association shall:

1. Design its information security program to control the identified risks, commensurate with the sensitivity of the information as well as the complexity and scope of the national bank's or Federal savings association's activities. Each national bank or Federal savings association must consider whether the following security measures are appropriate for the national bank or Federal savings association and, if so, adopt those measures the national bank or Federal savings association concludes are appropriate:

a. Access controls on customer information systems, including controls to authenticate and permit access only to authorized individuals and controls to prevent employees from providing customer information to unauthorized individuals who may seek to obtain this information through fraudulent means.

b. Access restrictions at physical locations containing customer information, such as buildings, computer facilities, and records storage facilities to permit access only to authorized individuals;

c. Encryption of electronic customer information, including while in transit or in storage on networks or systems to which unauthorized individuals may have access;

d. Procedures designed to ensure that customer information system modifications are consistent with the national bank's or Federal savings association's information security program;

e. Dual control procedures, segregation of duties, and employee background checks for employees with responsibilities for or access to customer information;

f. Monitoring systems and procedures to detect actual and attempted attacks on or intrusions into customer information systems;

g. Response programs that specify actions to be taken when the national bank or Federal savings association suspects or detects that unauthorized individuals have gained access to customer information systems, including appropriate reports to regulatory and law enforcement agencies; and

h. Measures to protect against destruction, loss, or damage of customer information due to potential environmental hazards, such as fire and water damage or technological failures.

2. Train staff to implement the national bank's or Federal savings association's information security program.

3. Regularly test the key controls, systems and procedures of the information security program. The frequency and nature of such tests should be determined by the national bank's or Federal savings association's risk assessment. Tests should be conducted or reviewed by independent third parties or staff independent of those that develop or maintain the security programs.

4. Develop, implement, and maintain, as part of its information security program, appropriate measures to properly dispose of customer information and consumer information in accordance with each of the requirements of this paragraph III.

D. *Oversee Service Provider Arrangements.* Each national bank or Federal savings association shall:

1. Exercise appropriate due diligence in selecting its service providers;

2. Require its service providers by contract to implement appropriate measures designed to meet the objectives of these Guidelines; and

3. Where indicated by the national bank's or Federal savings association's risk assessment, monitor its service providers to confirm that they have satisfied their obligations as required by section D.2. As part of this monitoring, a national bank or Federal savings association should review audits, summaries of test results, or other equivalent evaluations of its service providers.

E. *Adjust the Program.* Each national bank or Federal savings association shall monitor, evaluate, and adjust, as appropriate, the information security program in light of any relevant changes in technology, the sensitivity of its customer information, internal or external threats to information, and the national bank's or Federal savings association's own changing business arrangements, such as mergers and acquisitions, alliances and joint ventures, outsourcing arrangements, and changes to customer information systems.

F. *Report to the Board.* Each national bank or Federal savings association shall report to its board or an appropriate committee of the board at least annually. This report should describe the overall status of the information security program and the national bank's or Federal savings association's compliance with these Guidelines. The reports should discuss material matters related to its program, addressing issues such as: risk assessment; risk management and control decisions; service provider arrangements; results of testing; security breaches or violations and management's responses; and recommendations for changes in the information security program.

G. *Implement the Standards.* 1. *Effective date.* Each national bank or Federal savings association must implement an information security program pursuant to these Guidelines by July 1, 2001.

2. *Two-year grandfathering of agreements with service providers.* Until July 1, 2003, a contract that a national bank or Federal savings association has entered into with a service provider to perform services for it or functions on its behalf satisfies the provisions of section III.D., even if the contract does not include a requirement that the servicer maintain the security and confidentiality of customer information, as long as the national bank or Federal savings association entered into the contract on or before March 5, 2001.

3. *Effective date for measures relating to the disposal of consumer information.* Each national bank or Federal savings association must satisfy these Guidelines with respect to the proper disposal of consumer information by July 1, 2005.

4. *Exception for existing agreements with service providers relating to the disposal of consumer information.* Notwithstanding the requirement in paragraph III.G.3., a national bank's or Federal savings association's contracts with its service providers that have access to consumer information and that may dispose of consumer information, entered into before July 1, 2005, must comply with the provisions of the Guidelines relating to the proper disposal of consumer information by July 1, 2006.

SUPPLEMENT A TO APPENDIX B TO PART 30—INTERAGENCY GUIDANCE ON RESPONSE PROGRAMS FOR UNAUTHORIZED ACCESS TO CUSTOMER INFORMATION AND CUSTOMER NOTICE

I. BACKGROUND

This Guidance[1] interprets section 501(b) of the Gramm-Leach-Bliley Act ("GLBA") and the Interagency Guidelines Establishing Information Security Standards (the "Security Guidelines")[2] and describes response programs, including customer notification procedures, that a financial institution should develop and implement to address unauthorized access to or use of customer information that could result in substantial harm or inconvenience to a customer. The scope of, and definitions of terms used in, this Guidance are identical to those of the Security Guidelines. For example, the term "customer information" is the same term used in the Security Guidelines, and means any record containing nonpublic personal information about a customer, whether in paper, electronic, or other form, maintained by or on behalf of the institution.

A. Interagency Security Guidelines

Section 501(b) of the GLBA required the Agencies to establish appropriate standards for financial institutions subject to their jurisdiction that include administrative, technical, and physical safeguards, to protect the security and confidentiality of customer information. Accordingly, the Agencies issued Security Guidelines requiring every financial institution to have an information security program designed to:

1. Ensure the security and confidentiality of customer information;

---

[1] This Guidance was jointly issued by the Board of Governors of the Federal Reserve System (Board), the Federal Deposit Insurance Corporation (FDIC), the Office of the Comptroller of the Currency (OCC), and the Office of Thrift Supervision (OTS). Pursuant to 12 U.S.C. 5412, the OTS is no longer a party to this Guidance.

[2] 12 CFR part 30, app. B (OCC); 12 CFR part 208, app. D–2 and part 225, app. F (Board); and 12 CFR part 364, app. B and 12 CFR 391.5 (FDIC). The "Interagency Guidelines Establishing Information Security Standards" were formerly known as "The Interagency Guidelines Establishing Standards for Safeguarding Customer Information."

2. Protect against any anticipated threats or hazards to the security or integrity of such information; and

3. Protect against unauthorized access to or use of such information that could result in substantial harm or inconvenience to any customer.

B. Risk Assessment and Controls

1. The Security Guidelines direct every financial institution to assess the following risks, among others, when developing its information security program:

a. Reasonably foreseeable internal and external threats that could result in unauthorized disclosure, misuse, alteration, or destruction of customer information or customer information systems;

b. The likelihood and potential damage of threats, taking into consideration the sensitivity of customer information; and

c. The sufficiency of policies, procedures, customer information systems, and other arrangements in place to control risks.[3]

2. Following the assessment of these risks, the Security Guidelines require a financial institution to design a program to address the identified risks. The particular security measures an institution should adopt will depend upon the risks presented by the complexity and scope of its business. At a minimum, the financial institution is required to consider the specific security measures enumerated in the Security Guidelines,[4] and adopt those that are appropriate for the institution, including:

a. Access controls on customer information systems, including controls to authenticate and permit access only to authorized individuals and controls to prevent employees from providing customer information to unauthorized individuals who may seek to obtain this information through fraudulent means;

b. Background checks for employees with responsibilities for access to customer information; and

c. Response programs that specify actions to be taken when the financial institution suspects or detects that unauthorized individuals have gained access to customer information systems, including appropriate reports to regulatory and law enforcement agencies.[5]

C. Service Providers

The Security Guidelines direct every financial institution to require its service providers by contract to implement appropriate measures designed to protect against unauthorized access to or use of customer information that could result in substantial harm or inconvenience to any customer.[6]

II. RESPONSE PROGRAM

Millions of Americans, throughout the country, have been victims of identity theft.[7] Identity thieves misuse personal information they obtain from a number of sources, including financial institutions, to perpetrate identity theft. Therefore, financial institutions should take preventative measures to safeguard customer information against attempts to gain unauthorized access to the information. For example, financial institutions should place access controls on customer information systems and conduct background checks for employees who are authorized to access customer information.[8] However, every financial institution should also develop and implement a risk-based response program to address incidents of unauthorized access to customer information in customer information systems[9] that occur nonetheless. A response program should be a key part of an institution's information security program.[10] The program

---

[3] *See* Security Guidelines, III.B.

[4] *See* Security Guidelines, III.C.

[5] *See* Security Guidelines, III.C.

[6] *See* Security Guidelines, II.B. and III.D. Further, the Agencies note that, in addition to contractual obligations to a financial institution, a service provider may be required to implement its own comprehensive information security program in accordance with the Safeguards Rule promulgated by the Federal Trade Commission ("FTC"), 16 CFR part 314.

[7] The FTC estimates that nearly 10 million Americans discovered they were victims of some form of identity theft in 2002. *See* The Federal Trade Commission, *Identity Theft Survey Report*, (September 2003), available at *http://www.ftc.gov/os/2003/09/synovatereport.pdf*.

[8] Institutions should also conduct background checks of employees to ensure that the institution does not violate 12 U.S.C. 1829, which prohibits an institution from hiring an individual convicted of certain criminal offenses or who is subject to a prohibition order under 12 U.S.C. 1818(e)(6).

[9] Under the Guidelines, an institution's *customer information systems* consist of all of the methods used to access, collect, store, use, transmit, protect, or dispose of customer information, including the systems maintained by its service providers. *See* Security Guidelines, I.C.2.d.

[10] *See* FFIEC Information Technology Examination Handbook, Information Security Booklet, Dec. 2002 available at *http://www.ffiec.gov/ffiecinfobase/html_pages/infosec_book_frame.htm*. Federal Reserve SR 97–32, Sound Practice Guidance for Information Security for Networks, Dec. 4, 1997; OCC Bulletin 2000–14, "Infrastructure Threats—

Continued

should be appropriate to the size and complexity of the institution and the nature and scope of its activities.

In addition, each institution should be able to address incidents of unauthorized access to customer information in customer information systems maintained by its domestic and foreign service providers. Therefore, consistent with the obligations in the Guidelines that relate to these arrangements, and with existing guidance on this topic issued by the Agencies, [11] an institution's contract with its service provider should require the service provider to take appropriate actions to address incidents of unauthorized access to the financial institution's customer information, including notification to the institution as soon as possible of any such incident, to enable the institution to expeditiously implement its response program.

A. Components of a Response Program

1. At a minimum, an institution's response program should contain procedures for the following:

a. Assessing the nature and scope of an incident, and identifying what customer information systems and types of customer information have been accessed or misused;

b. Notifying its primary Federal regulator as soon as possible when the institution becomes aware of an incident involving unauthorized access to or use of *sensitive* customer information, as defined below;

c. Consistent with the Agencies' Suspicious Activity Report ("SAR") regulations, [12] notifying appropriate law enforcement authorities, in addition to filing a timely SAR in situations involving Federal criminal violations requiring immediate attention, such as when a reportable violation is ongoing;

d. Taking appropriate steps to contain and control the incident to prevent further unauthorized access to or use of customer information, for example, by monitoring, freezing, or closing affected accounts, while preserving records and other evidence;[13] and

e. Notifying customers when warranted.

2. Where an incident of unauthorized access to customer information involves customer information systems maintained by an institution's service providers, it is the responsibility of the financial institution to notify the institution's customers and regulator. However, an institution may authorize or contract with its service provider to notify the institution's customers or regulator on its behalf.

III. CUSTOMER NOTICE

Financial institutions have an affirmative duty to protect their customers' information against unauthorized access or use. Notifying customers of a security incident involving the unauthorized access or use of the customer's information in accordance with the standard set forth below is a key part of that duty. Timely notification of customers is important to manage an institution's reputation risk. Effective notice also may reduce an institution's legal risk, assist in maintaining good customer relations, and enable the institution's customers to take steps to protect themselves against the consequences of identity theft. When customer notification is warranted, an institution may not forgo notifying its customers of an incident because the institution believes that it may be potentially embarrassed or inconvenienced by doing so.

A. Standard for Providing Notice

When a financial institution becomes aware of an incident of unauthorized access to sensitive customer information, the institution should conduct a reasonable investigation to promptly determine the likelihood that the information has been or will be misused. If the institution determines that misuse of its information about a customer has occurred or is reasonably possible, it should notify the affected customer as soon as possible. Customer notice may be delayed if an appropriate law enforcement agency determines that notification will interfere with a criminal investigation and

---

Intrusion Risks" (May 15, 2000), for additional guidance on preventing, detecting, and responding to intrusions into financial institution computer systems.

[11] *See* Federal Reserve SR Ltr. 13–19, Guidance on Managing Outsourcing Risk, Dec. 5, 2013; OCC Bulletin 2013–29, "Third-Party Relationships—Risk Management Guidance," Oct. 30, 2013; and FDIC FIL 68–99, Risk Assessment Tools and Practices for Information System Security, July 7, 1999.

[12] An institution's obligation to file a SAR is set out in the Agencies' SAR regulations and Agency guidance. *See* 12 CFR 21.11 (national banks, Federal branches and agencies); 12 CFR 163.180 (Federal savings associations); 12 CFR 208.62 (State member banks); 12 CFR 211.5(k) (Edge and agreement corporations); 12 CFR 211.24(f) (uninsured State branches and agencies of foreign banks); 12 CFR 225.4(f) (bank holding companies and their nonbank subsidiaries); 12 CFR part 353 (State non-member banks); and 12 CFR 390.355 (state savings associations). National banks and Federal savings associations must file SARs in connection with computer intrusions and other computer crimes. *See* OCC Bulletin 2000–14, "Infrastructure Threats—Intrusion Risks" (May 15, 2000); *see also* Federal Reserve SR 01–11, Identity Theft and Pretext Calling, Apr. 26, 2001.

[13] *See* FFIEC Information Technology Examination Handbook, Information Security Booklet, Dec. 2002, pp. 68–74.

provides the institution with a written request for the delay. However, the institution should notify its customers as soon as notification will no longer interfere with the investigation.

1. Sensitive Customer Information

Under the Guidelines, an institution must protect against unauthorized access to or use of customer information that could result in substantial harm or inconvenience to any customer. Substantial harm or inconvenience is most likely to result from improper access to *sensitive customer information* because this type of information is most likely to be misused, as in the commission of identity theft. For purposes of this Guidance, *sensitive customer information* means a customer's name, address, or telephone number, in conjunction with the customer's social security number, driver's license number, account number, credit or debit card number, or a personal identification number or password that would permit access to the customer's account. *Sensitive customer information* also includes any combination of components of customer information that would allow someone to log onto or access the customer's account, such as user name and password or password and account number.

2. Affected Customers

If a financial institution, based upon its investigation, can determine from its logs or other data precisely which customers' information has been improperly accessed, it may limit notification to those customers with regard to whom the institution determines that misuse of their information has occurred or is reasonably possible. However, there may be situations where the institution determines that a group of files has been accessed improperly, but is unable to identify which specific customers' information has been accessed. If the circumstances of the unauthorized access lead the institution to determine that misuse of the information is reasonably possible, it should notify all customers in the group.

B. Content of Customer Notice

1. Customer notice should be given in a clear and conspicuous manner. The notice should describe the incident in general terms and the type of customer information that was the subject of unauthorized access or use. It also should generally describe what the institution has done to protect the customers' information from further unauthorized access. In addition, it should include a telephone number that customers can call for further information and assistance.[14] The notice also should remind customers of the need to remain vigilant over the next twelve to twenty-four months, and to promptly report incidents of suspected identity theft to the institution. The notice should include the following additional items, when appropriate:

a. A recommendation that the customer review account statements and immediately report any suspicious activity to the institution;

b. A description of fraud alerts and an explanation of how the customer may place a fraud alert in the customer's consumer reports to put the customer's creditors on notice that the customer may be a victim of fraud;

c. A recommendation that the customer periodically obtain credit reports from each nationwide credit reporting agency and have information relating to fraudulent transactions deleted;

d. An explanation of how the customer may obtain a credit report free of charge; and

e. Information about the availability of the FTC's online guidance regarding steps a consumer can take to protect against identity theft. The notice should encourage the customer to report any incidents of identity theft to the FTC, and should provide the FTC's Web site address and toll-free telephone number that customers may use to obtain the identity theft guidance and report suspected incidents of identity theft.[15]

2. The Agencies encourage financial institutions to notify the nationwide consumer reporting agencies prior to sending notices to a large number of customers that include contact information for the reporting agencies.

C. Delivery of Customer Notice

Customer notice should be delivered in any manner designed to ensure that a customer can reasonably be expected to receive it. For example, the institution may choose to contact all customers affected by telephone or

[14] The institution should, therefore, ensure that it has reasonable policies and procedures in place, including trained personnel, to respond appropriately to customer inquiries and requests for assistance.

[15] Currently, the FTC Web site for the ID Theft brochure and the FTC Hotline phone number are *http://www.consumer.gov/idtheft* and 1–877–IDTHEFT. The institution may also refer customers to any materials developed pursuant to section 151(b) of the FACT Act (educational materials developed by the FTC to teach the public how to prevent identity theft).

by mail, or by electronic mail for those customers for whom it has a valid e-mail address and who have agreed to receive communications electronically.

[66 FR 8633, Feb. 1, 2001, as amended at 69 FR 77616, Dec. 28, 2004; 70 FR 15751, 15753, Mar. 29, 2005; 71 FR 5780, Feb. 3, 2006; 79 FR 54544, Sept. 11, 2014]

APPENDIX C TO PART 30—OCC GUIDELINES ESTABLISHING STANDARDS FOR RESIDENTIAL MORTGAGE LENDING PRACTICES

TABLE OF CONTENTS

I. Introduction
- A. Scope
- B. Preservation of Existing Authority
- C. Relationship to Other Legal Requirements
- D. Definitions

II. Standards for Residential Mortgage Lending Practices
- A. General
- B. Objectives

III. Implementation of Residential Mortgage Lending Standards
- A. Avoidance of Particular Loan Terms, Conditions, and Features
- B. Prudent Consideration of Certain Loan Terms, Conditions and Features
- C. Enhanced Care To Avoid Abusive Loan Terms, Conditions, and Features in Certain Mortgages
- D. Avoidance of Consumer Misunderstanding
- E. Purchased and Brokered Loans
- F. Monitoring and Corrective Action

I. INTRODUCTION

i. These OCC Guidelines for Residential Mortgage Lending Practices (Guidelines) set forth standards pursuant to Section 39 of the Federal Deposit Insurance Act, 12 U.S.C. 1831p–1 (Section 39). The Guidelines are designed to protect against involvement by national banks, Federal savings associations, Federal branches and Federal agencies of foreign banks, and their respective operating subsidiaries (together, "national banks and Federal savings associations"), either directly or through loans that they purchase or make through intermediaries, in predatory or abusive residential mortgage lending practices that are injurious to their respective customers and that expose the national bank or Federal savings association to credit, legal, compliance, reputation, and other risks. The Guidelines focus on the substance of activities and practices, not the creation of policies. The Guidelines are enforceable under Section 39 in accordance with the procedures prescribed by the regulations in 12 CFR part 30.

ii. As the OCC has previously indicated in guidance to national banks and in rulemaking proceedings (OCC Advisory Letters 2003–2 and 2003–3 (Feb. 21, 2003)), many of the abusive practices commonly associated with predatory mortgage lending, such as loan flipping and equity stripping, will involve conduct that likely violates the Federal Trade Commission Act's (FTC Act) prohibition against unfair or deceptive acts or practices. 15 U.S.C. 45. In addition, loans that involve violations of the FTC Act, or mortgage loans based predominantly on the foreclosure or liquidation value of the borrower's collateral without regard to the borrower's ability to repay the loan according to its terms, will involve violations of OCC regulations governing real estate lending activities, 12 CFR 34.3 (Lending Rules).

iii. In addition, national banks, Federal savings associations, and their respective operating subsidiaries must comply with the requirements and Guidelines affecting appraisals of residential mortgage loans and appraiser independence. 12 CFR part 34, subpart C, and the Interagency Appraisal and Evaluation Guidelines (OCC Bulletin 2010–42 (December 10, 2010). For example, engaging in a practice of influencing the independent judgment of an appraiser with respect to a valuation of real estate that is to be security for a residential mortgage loan would violate applicable standards.

iv. Targeting inappropriate credit products and unfair loan terms to certain borrowers also may entail conduct that violates the FTC Act, as well as the Equal Credit Opportunity Act (ECOA) and the Fair Housing Act (FHA). 15 U.S.C. 1691 *et seq.* 42 U.S.C. 3601 *et seq.* For example, "steering" a consumer to a loan with higher costs rather than to a comparable loan offered by the national bank or Federal savings association with lower costs for which the consumer could qualify, on a prohibited basis such as the borrower's race, national origin, age, gender, or marital status, would be unlawful.

v. OCC regulations also prohibit national banks and their operating subsidiaries from providing lump sum, single premium fees for debt cancellation contracts and debt suspension agreements in connection with residential mortgage loans. 12 CFR 37.3(c)(2). Some lending practices and loan terms, including financing single premium credit insurance and the use of mandatory arbitration clauses, also may significantly impair the eligibility of a residential mortgage loan for purchase in the secondary market.

vi. Finally, OCC regulations and supervisory guidance on fiduciary activities and asset management address the need for national banks and Federal savings associations to perform due diligence and exercise appropriate control with regard to trustee activities. *See* 12 CFR 9.6 (a), in the case of national banks, and 12 CFR 150.200, in the case of Federal savings associations, and the

Comptroller's Handbook on Asset Management. For example, national banks and Federal savings associations should exercise appropriate diligence to minimize potential reputation risks when they undertake to act as trustees in mortgage securitizations.

A. *Scope*. These Guidelines apply to the residential mortgage lending activities of national banks, Federal savings associations, Federal branches and Federal agencies of foreign banks, and operating subsidiaries of such entities (except brokers, dealers, persons providing insurance, investment companies, and investment advisers).

B. *Preservation of Existing Authority*. Neither Section 39 nor these Guidelines in any way limits the authority of the OCC to address unsafe or unsound practices or conditions, unfair or deceptive practices, or other violations of law. The OCC may take action under Section 39 and these Guidelines independently of, in conjunction with, or in addition to any other enforcement action available to the OCC.

C. *Relationship to Other Legal Requirements*. Actions by a national bank or Federal savings association in connection with residential mortgage lending that are inconsistent with these Guidelines or Appendix A to this part 30 may also constitute unsafe or unsound practices for purposes of section 8 of the Federal Deposit Insurance Act, 12 U.S.C. 1818, unfair or deceptive practices for purposes of section 5 of the FTC Act, 15 U.S.C. 45, and the OCC's Lending Rules, 12 CFR 34.3 (Lending Rules) and Real Estate Lending Standards, 12 CFR part 34, subpart D, in the case of national banks, and 12 CFR 160.100 and 160.101, in the case of Federal savings associations, or violations of the ECOA and FHA.

D. *Definitions*.

1. Except as modified in these Guidelines, or unless the context otherwise requires, the terms used in these Guidelines have the same meanings as set forth in sections 3 and 39 of the Federal Deposit Insurance Act, 12 U.S.C. 1813 and 1831p–1.

2. For purposes of these Guidelines, the following definitions apply:

a. *Residential mortgage loan* means any loan or other extension of credit made to one or more individuals for personal, family, or household purposes secured by an owner-occupied 1–4 family residential dwelling, including a cooperative unit or mobile home.

b. *National bank or Federal savings association* means any national bank, Federal savings association, Federal branch or Federal agency of a foreign bank, and any operating subsidiary thereof that is subject to these Guidelines.

II. Standards for Residential Mortgage Lending Practices

A. *General*. A national bank's or Federal savings association's residential mortgage lending activities should reflect standards and practices consistent with and appropriate to the size and complexity of the bank or savings association and the nature and scope of its lending activities.

B. *Objectives*. A national bank's or Federal savings association's residential mortgage lending activities should reflect standards and practices that:

1. Enable the national bank or Federal savings association to effectively manage the credit, legal, compliance, reputation, and other risks associated with the bank's or savings association's consumer residential mortgage lending activities.

2. Effectively prevent the national bank or Federal savings association from becoming engaged in abusive, predatory, unfair, or deceptive practices, directly, indirectly through mortgage brokers or other intermediaries, or through purchased loans.

III. Implementation of Residential Mortgage Lending Standards

A. *Avoidance of Particular Loan Terms, Conditions, and Features*. A national bank or Federal savings association should not become involved, directly or indirectly in residential mortgage lending activities involving abusive, predatory, unfair or deceptive lending practices, including, but not limited to:

1. *Equity Stripping and Fee Packing*. Repeat refinancings where a borrower's equity is depleted as a result of financing excessive fees for the loan or ancillary products.

2. *Loan Flipping*. Repeat refinancings under circumstances where the relative terms of the new and refinanced loan and the cost of the new loan do not provide a tangible economic benefit to the borrower.

3. *Refinancing of Special Mortgages*. Refinancing of a special subsidized mortgage that contains terms favorable to the borrower with a loan that does not provide a tangible economic benefit to the borrower relative to the refinanced loan.

4. *Encouragement of Default*. Encouraging a borrower to breach a contract and default on an existing loan prior to and in connection with the consummation of a loan that refinances all or part of the existing loan.

B. *Prudent Consideration of Certain Loan Terms, Conditions and Features*. Certain loan terms, conditions and features, may, under particular circumstances, be susceptible to abusive, predatory, unfair or deceptive practices, yet may be appropriate and acceptable risk mitigation measures, consistent with safe and sound lending, and benefit customers under other circumstances. A national bank or Federal savings association should prudently consider the circumstances, including the characteristics of a targeted market and applicable consumer and safety and soundness safeguards, under which the national bank or Federal savings association will engage directly or indirectly in making residential mortgage loans with the following loan terms, conditions and features:

1. Financing single premium credit life, disability or unemployment insurance.

2. Negative amortization, involving a payment schedule in which regular periodic payments cause the principal balance to increase.

3. Balloon payments in short-term transactions.

4. Prepayment penalties that are not limited to the early years of the loan, particularly in subprime loans.

5. Interest rate increases upon default at a level not commensurate with risk mitigation.

6. Call provisions permitting the national bank or Federal savings association to accelerate payment of the loan under circumstances other than the borrower's default under the credit agreement or to mitigate the bank's or savings association's exposure to loss.

7. Absence of an appropriate assessment and documentation of the consumer's ability to repay the loan in accordance with its terms, commensurate with the type of loan, as required by appendix A of this part.

8. Mandatory arbitration clauses or agreements, particularly if the eligibility of the loan for purchase in the secondary market is thereby impaired.

9. Pricing terms that result in the loan's being subject to the provisions of the Home Ownership and Equity Protection Act. 15 U.S.C. 1639 *et seq.*

10. Original principal balance of the loan in excess of appraised value.

11. Payment schedules that consolidate more than two periodic payments and pay them in advance from the loan proceeds.

12. Payments to home improvement contractors under a home improvement contract from the proceeds of a residential mortgage loan other than by an instrument payable to the consumer, jointly to the consumer and the contractor, or through an independent third party escrow agent.

C. *Enhanced Care to Avoid Abusive Loan Terms, Conditions, and Features in Certain Mortgages.* A national bank or Federal savings association may face heightened risks when it solicits or offers loans to consumers who are not financially sophisticated, have language barriers, or are elderly, or have limited or poor credit histories, are substantially indebted, or have other characteristics that limit their credit choices. In connection with such consumers, a national bank or Federal savings association should exercise enhanced care if it employs the residential mortgage loan terms, conditions, and features described in paragraph B of this section III, and should also apply appropriate heightened internal controls and monitoring to any line of business that does so.

D. *Avoidance of Consumer Misunderstanding.* A national bank's or Federal savings association's residential mortgage lending activities should include provision of timely, sufficient, and accurate information to a consumer concerning the terms and costs, risks, and benefits of the loan. Consumers should be provided with information sufficient to draw their attention to these key terms.

E. *Purchased and Brokered Loans.* With respect to consumer residential mortgage loans that the national bank or Federal savings association purchases, or makes through a mortgage broker or other intermediary, the national bank or Federal savings association's residential mortgage lending activities should reflect standards and practices consistent with those applied by the bank or savings association in its direct lending activities and include appropriate measures to mitigate risks, such as the following:

1. Criteria for entering into and continuing relationships with intermediaries and originators, including due diligence requirements.

2. Underwriting and appraisal requirements.

3. Standards related to total loan compensation and total compensation of intermediaries, including maximum rates, points, and other charges, and the use of overages and yield-spread premiums, structured to avoid providing an incentive to originate loans with predatory or abusive characteristics.

4. Requirements for agreements with intermediaries and originators, including with respect to risks identified in the due diligence process, compliance with appropriate national bank or Federal savings association policies, procedures and practices and with applicable law (including remedies for failure to comply), protection of the national bank or Federal savings association against risk, and termination procedures.

5. Loan documentation procedures, management information systems, quality control reviews, and other methods through which the national bank or Federal savings association will verify compliance with agreements, bank or savings association policies, and applicable laws, and otherwise retain appropriate oversight of mortgage origination functions, including loan sourcing, underwriting, and loan closings.

6. Criteria and procedures for the national bank or Federal savings association to take appropriate corrective action, including modification of loan terms and termination of the relationship with the intermediary or originator in question.

F. *Monitoring and Corrective Action.* A national bank's or Federal savings association's consumer residential mortgage lending activities should include appropriate monitoring of compliance with applicable law and the bank's or savings association's lending standards and practices, periodic monitoring and evaluation of the nature, quantity and resolution of customer complaints, and appropriate evaluation of the effectiveness of the bank's or savings association's standards and practices in accomplishing the objectives set forth in these Guidelines. The bank's or savings association's activities also should include appropriate steps for taking corrective action in response to failures to comply with applicable law and the bank's or savings association's lending standards, and for making adjustments to the bank's or savings association's activities as may be appropriate to enhance their effectiveness or to reflect changes in business practices, market conditions, or the bank's or savings association's lines of business, residential mortgage loan programs, or customer base.

[70 FR 6332, Feb. 7, 2005, as amended at 79 FR 54544, Sept. 11, 2014]

APPENDIX D TO PART 30—OCC GUIDELINES ESTABLISHING HEIGHTENED STANDARDS FOR CERTAIN LARGE INSURED NATIONAL BANKS, INSURED FEDERAL SAVINGS ASSOCIATIONS, AND INSURED FEDERAL BRANCHES

TABLE OF CONTENTS

I. Introduction
- A. Scope
- B. Compliance Date
- C. Reservation of Authority
- D. Preservation of Existing Authority
- E. Definitions

II. Standards For Risk Governance Framework
- A. Risk Governance Framework
- B. Scope of Risk Governance Framework
- C. Roles and Responsibilities
- 1. Role and Responsibilities of Front Line Units
- 2. Role and Responsibilities of Independent Risk Management
- 3. Role and Responsibilities of Internal Audit
- D. Strategic Plan
- E. Risk Appetite Statement
- F. Concentration and Front Line Unit Risk Limits
- G. Risk Appetite Review, Monitoring, and Communication Processes
- H. Processes Governing Risk Limit Breaches
- I. Concentration Risk Management
- J. Risk Data Aggregation and Reporting
- K. Relationship of Risk Appetite Statement, Concentration Risk Limits, and Front Line Unit Risk Limits to Other Processes
- L. Talent Management Processes
- M. Compensation and Performance Management Programs

III. Standards for Board of Directors
- A. Require an Effective Risk Governance Framework
- B. Provide Active Oversight of Management
- C. Exercise Independent Judgment
- D. Include Independent Directors
- E. Provide Ongoing Training to All Directors
- F. Self-Assessments

I. INTRODUCTION

1. The OCC expects a covered bank, as that term is defined in paragraph I.E. to establish and implement a risk governance framework to manage and control the covered bank's risk-taking activities.

2. This appendix establishes minimum standards for the design and implementation of a covered bank's risk governance framework and minimum standards for the covered bank's board of directors in providing oversight to the framework's design and implementation (Guidelines). These standards are in addition to any other applicable requirements in law or regulation.

3. A covered bank may use its parent company's risk governance framework in its entirety, without modification, if the framework meets these minimum standards, the risk profiles of the parent company and the covered bank are substantially the same as set forth in paragraph I.4. of these Guidelines, and the covered bank has demonstrated through a documented assessment that its risk profile and its parent company's risk profile are substantially the same. The assessment should be conducted at least annually, in conjunction with the review and update of the risk governance framework performed by independent risk management, as set forth in paragraph II.A. of these Guidelines.

4. A parent company's and covered bank's risk profiles are substantially the same if, as reported on the covered bank's Federal Financial Institutions Examination Council Consolidated Reports of Condition and Income (Call Reports) for the four most recent consecutive quarters, the covered bank's average total consolidated assets, as calculated according to paragraph I.A. of these Guidelines, represent 95 percent or more of the parent company's average total consolidated assets.[1] A covered bank that does not satisfy this test may submit a written analysis to the OCC for consideration and approval that

[1] For a parent company, average total consolidated assets means the average of the parent company's total consolidated assets, as reported on the parent company's Form FR Y–9C to the Board of Governors of the Federal Reserve System, or equivalent regulatory report, for the four most recent consecutive quarters.

demonstrates that the risk profile of the parent company and the covered bank are substantially the same based upon other factors not specified in this paragraph.

5. Subject to paragraph I.6. of these Guidelines, a covered bank should establish its own risk governance framework when the parent company's and covered bank's risk profiles are not substantially the same. The covered bank's framework should ensure that the covered bank's risk profile is easily distinguished and separate from that of its parent for risk management and supervisory reporting purposes and that the safety and soundness of the covered bank is not jeopardized by decisions made by the parent company's board of directors and management.

6. When the parent company's and covered bank's risk profiles are not substantially the same, a covered bank may, in consultation with the OCC, incorporate or rely on components of its parent company's risk governance framework when developing its own risk governance framework to the extent those components are consistent with the objectives of these Guidelines.

A. *Scope*

These Guidelines apply to any bank, as that term is defined in paragraph I.E. of these Guidelines, with average total consolidated assets equal to or greater than $50 billion. In addition, these Guidelines apply to any bank with average total consolidated assets less than $50 billion if that institution's parent company controls at least one covered bank. For a covered bank, average total consolidated assets means the average of the covered bank's total consolidated assets, as reported on the covered bank's Call Reports, for the four most recent consecutive quarters.

B. *Compliance Date*

1. *Initial compliance.* The date on which a covered bank should comply with the Guidelines is set forth below:

(a) A covered bank with average total consolidated assets, as calculated according to paragraph I.A. of these Guidelines, equal to or greater than $750 billion as of November 10, 2014 should comply with these Guidelines on November 10, 2014;

(b) A covered bank with average total consolidated assets, as calculated according to paragraph I.A. of these Guidelines, equal to or greater than $100 billion but less than $750 billion as of November 10, 2014 should comply with these Guidelines within six months from November 10, 2014;

(c) A covered bank with average total consolidated assets, as calculated according to paragraph I.A. of these Guidelines, equal to or greater than $50 billion but less than $100 billion as of November 10, 2014 should comply with these Guidelines within 18 months from November 10, 2014;

(d) A covered bank with average total consolidated assets, as calculated according to paragraph I.A. of these Guidelines, less than $50 billion that is a covered bank because that bank's parent company controls at least one other covered bank as of November 10, 2014 should comply with these Guidelines on the date that such other covered bank should comply; and

(e) A covered bank that does not come within the scope of these Guidelines on November 10, 2014, but subsequently becomes subject to the Guidelines because average total consolidated assets, as calculated according to paragraph I.A. of these Guidelines, are equal to or greater than $50 billion after November 10, 2014, should comply with these Guidelines within 18 months from the as-of date of the most recent Call Report used in the calculation of the average.

C. *Reservation of Authority*

1. The OCC reserves the authority to apply these Guidelines, in whole or in part, to a bank that has average total consolidated assets less than $50 billion, if the OCC determines such bank's operations are highly complex or otherwise present a heightened risk as to warrant the application of these Guidelines;

2. The OCC reserves the authority, for each covered bank, to extend the time for compliance with these Guidelines or modify these Guidelines; or

3. The OCC reserves the authority to determine that compliance with these Guidelines should no longer be required for a covered bank. The OCC would generally make the determination under this paragraph I.C.3. if a covered bank's operations are no longer highly complex or no longer present a heightened risk. In determining whether a covered bank's operations are highly complex or present a heightened risk, the OCC will consider the following factors: Complexity of products and services, risk profile, and scope of operations.

4. When exercising the authority in this paragraph I.C., the OCC will apply notice and response procedures, when appropriate, in the same manner and to the same extent as the notice and response procedures in 12 CFR 3.404.

D. *Preservation of Existing Authority*

Neither section 39 of the Federal Deposit Insurance Act (12 U.S.C. 1831p–1) nor these Guidelines in any way limits the authority of the OCC to address unsafe or unsound practices or conditions or other violations of law. The OCC may take action under section 39 and these Guidelines independently of, in conjunction with, or in addition to any other enforcement action available to the OCC.

E. *Definitions*

1. *Bank* means any insured national bank, insured Federal savings association, or insured Federal branch of a foreign bank.

2. *Chief Audit Executive* means an individual who leads internal audit and is one level below the Chief Executive Officer in a covered bank's organizational structure.

3. *Chief Risk Executive* means an individual who leads an independent risk management unit and is one level below the Chief Executive Officer in a covered bank's organizational structure. A covered bank may have more than one Chief Risk Executive.

4. *Control*. A parent company *controls* a covered bank if it:

(a) Owns, controls, or holds with power to vote 25 percent or more of a class of voting securities of the covered bank; or

(b) Consolidates the covered bank for financial reporting purposes.

5. *Covered bank* means any bank:

(a) With average total consolidated assets, as calculated according to paragraph I.A. of these Guidelines, equal to or greater than $50 billion;

(b) With average total consolidated assets less than $50 billion if that bank's parent company controls at least one covered bank; or

(c) With average total consolidated assets less than $50 billion, if the OCC determines such bank's operations are highly complex or otherwise present a heightened risk as to warrant the application of these Guidelines pursuant to paragraph I.C. of these Guidelines.

6. *Front Line Unit*. (a) Except as provided in paragraph (b) of this definition, *front line unit* means any organizational unit or function thereof in a covered bank that is accountable for a risk in paragraph II.B. of these Guidelines that:

(i) Engages in activities designed to generate revenue or reduce expenses for the parent company or covered bank;

(ii) Provides operational support or servicing to any organizational unit or function within the covered bank for the delivery of products or services to customers; or

(iii) Provides technology services to any organizational unit or function covered by these Guidelines.

(b) *Front line unit* does not ordinarily include an organizational unit or function thereof within a covered bank that provides legal services to the covered bank.

7. *Independent risk management* means any organizational unit within a covered bank that has responsibility for identifying, measuring, monitoring, or controlling aggregate risks. Such units maintain independence from front line units through the following reporting structure:

(a) The board of directors or the board's risk committee reviews and approves the risk governance framework;

(b) Each Chief Risk Executive has unrestricted access to the board of directors and its committees to address risks and issues identified through independent risk management's activities;

(c) The board of directors or its risk committee approves all decisions regarding the appointment or removal of the Chief Risk Executive(s) and approves the annual compensation and salary adjustment of the Chief Risk Executive(s); and

(d) No front line unit executive oversees any independent risk management unit.

8. *Internal audit* means the organizational unit within a covered bank that is designated to fulfill the role and responsibilities outlined in 12 CFR part 30, Appendix A, II.B. Internal audit maintains independence from front line units and independent risk management through the following reporting structure:

(a) The Chief Audit Executive has unrestricted access to the board's audit committee to address risks and issues identified through internal audit's activities;

(b) The audit committee reviews and approves internal audit's overall charter and audit plans;

(c) The audit committee approves all decisions regarding the appointment or removal and annual compensation and salary adjustment of the Chief Audit Executive;

(d) The audit committee or the Chief Executive Officer oversees the Chief Audit Executive's administrative activities; and

(e) No front line unit executive oversees internal audit.

9. *Parent company* means the top-tier legal entity in a covered bank's ownership structure.

10. *Risk appetite* means the aggregate level and types of risk the board of directors and management are willing to assume to achieve a covered bank's strategic objectives and business plan, consistent with applicable capital, liquidity, and other regulatory requirements.

11. *Risk profile* means a point-in-time assessment of a covered bank's risks, aggregated within and across each relevant risk category, using methodologies consistent with the risk appetite statement described in paragraph II.E. of these Guidelines.

II. Standards for Risk Governance Framework

A. *Risk Governance Framework*. A covered bank should establish and adhere to a formal, written risk governance framework that is designed by independent risk management and approved by the board of directors or the board's risk committee. The risk governance framework should include delegations of authority from the board of directors to management committees and executive officers as well as the risk limits established for material activities. Independent risk management should review and update the risk governance framework at least annually, and as often as needed to address improvements in industry risk management practices and changes in the covered bank's risk profile caused by emerging risks, its strategic plans, or other internal and external factors.

B. *Scope of Risk Governance Framework.* The risk governance framework should cover the following risk categories that apply to the covered bank: Credit risk, interest rate risk, liquidity risk, price risk, operational risk, compliance risk, strategic risk, and reputation risk.

C. *Roles and Responsibilities.* The risk governance framework should include well-defined risk management roles and responsibilities for front line units, independent risk management, and internal audit.[2] The roles and responsibilities for each of these organizational units should be:

1. *Role and Responsibilities of Front Line Units.* Front line units should take responsibility and be held accountable by the Chief Executive Officer and the board of directors for appropriately assessing and effectively managing all of the risks associated with their activities. In fulfilling this responsibility, each front line unit should, either alone or in conjunction with another organizational unit that has the purpose of assisting a front line unit:

(a) Assess, on an ongoing basis, the material risks associated with its activities and use such risk assessments as the basis for fulfilling its responsibilities under paragraphs II.C.1.(b) and (c) of these Guidelines and for determining if actions need to be taken to strengthen risk management or reduce risk given changes in the unit's risk profile or other conditions;

(b) Establish and adhere to a set of written policies that include front line unit risk limits as discussed in paragraph II.F. of these Guidelines. Such policies should ensure risks associated with the front line unit's activities are effectively identified, measured, monitored, and controlled, consistent with the covered bank's risk appetite statement, concentration risk limits, and all policies established within the risk governance framework under paragraphs II.C.2.(c) and II.G. through K. of these Guidelines;

(c) Establish and adhere to procedures and processes, as necessary, to maintain compliance with the policies described in paragraph II.C.1.(b) of these Guidelines;

(d) Adhere to all applicable policies, procedures, and processes established by independent risk management;

(e) Develop, attract, and retain talent and maintain staffing levels required to carry out the unit's role and responsibilities effectively, as set forth in paragraphs II.C.1.(a) through (d) of these Guidelines;

(f) Establish and adhere to talent management processes that comply with paragraph II.L. of these Guidelines; and

(g) Establish and adhere to compensation and performance management programs that comply with paragraph II.M. of these Guidelines.

2. *Role and Responsibilities of Independent Risk Management.* Independent risk management should oversee the covered bank's risk-taking activities and assess risks and issues independent of front line units. In fulfilling these responsibilities, independent risk management should:

(a) Take primary responsibility and be held accountable by the Chief Executive Officer and the board of directors for designing a comprehensive written risk governance framework that meets these Guidelines and is commensurate with the size, complexity, and risk profile of the covered bank;

(b) Identify and assess, on an ongoing basis, the covered bank's material aggregate risks and use such risk assessments as the basis for fulfilling its responsibilities under paragraphs II.C.2.(c) and (d) of these Guidelines and for determining if actions need to be taken to strengthen risk management or reduce risk given changes in the covered bank's risk profile or other conditions;

(c) Establish and adhere to enterprise policies that include concentration risk limits. Such policies should state how aggregate risks within the covered bank are effectively identified, measured, monitored, and controlled, consistent with the covered bank's risk appetite statement and all policies and processes established within the risk governance framework under paragraphs II.G. through K. of these Guidelines;

[2] These roles and responsibilities are in addition to any roles and responsibilities set forth in Appendices A, B, and C to Part 30. Many of the risk management practices established and maintained by a covered bank to meet these standards, including loan review and credit underwriting and administration practices, should be components of its risk governance framework, within the construct of the three distinct units identified herein. In addition, existing OCC guidance sets forth standards for establishing risk management programs for certain risks, *e.g.*, compliance risk management. These risk-specific programs should also be considered components of the risk governance framework, within the context of the three units described in paragraph II.C. of these Guidelines.

(d) Establish and adhere to procedures and processes, as necessary, to ensure compliance with the policies described in paragraph II.C.2.(c) of these Guidelines;

(e) Identify and communicate to the Chief Executive Officer and the board of directors or the board's risk committee:

(i) Material risks and significant instances where independent risk management's assessment of risk differs from that of a front line unit; and

(ii) Significant instances where a front line unit is not adhering to the risk governance framework, including instances when front line units do not meet the standards set forth in paragraph II.C.1. of these Guidelines;

(f) Identify and communicate to the board of directors or the board's risk committee:

(i) Material risks and significant instances where independent risk management's assessment of risk differs from the Chief Executive Officer; and

(ii) Significant instances where the Chief Executive Officer is not adhering to, or holding front line units accountable for adhering to, the risk governance framework;

(g) Develop, attract, and retain talent and maintain staffing levels required to carry out its role and responsibilities effectively, as set forth in paragraphs II.C.2.(a) through (f) of these Guidelines;

(h) Establish and adhere to talent management processes that comply with paragraph II.L. of these Guidelines; and

(i) Establish and adhere to compensation and performance management programs that comply with paragraph II.M. of these Guidelines.

3. *Role and Responsibilities of Internal Audit.* In addition to meeting the standards set forth in appendix A of part 30, internal audit should ensure that the covered bank's risk governance framework complies with these Guidelines and is appropriate for the size, complexity, and risk profile of the covered bank. In carrying out its responsibilities, internal audit should:

(a) Maintain a complete and current inventory of all of the covered bank's material processes, product lines, services, and functions, and assess the risks, including emerging risks, associated with each, which collectively provide a basis for the audit plan described in paragraph II.C.3.(b) of these Guidelines;

(b) Establish and adhere to an audit plan that is periodically reviewed and updated that takes into account the covered bank's risk profile, emerging risks, and issues, and establishes the frequency with which activities should be audited. The audit plan should require internal audit to evaluate the adequacy of and compliance with policies, procedures, and processes established by front line units and independent risk management under the risk governance framework. Significant changes to the audit plan should be communicated to the board's audit committee;

(c) Report in writing, conclusions and material issues and recommendations from audit work carried out under the audit plan described in paragraph II.C.3.(b) of these Guidelines to the board's audit committee. Internal audit's reports to the audit committee should also identify the root cause of any material issues and include:

(i) A determination of whether the root cause creates an issue that has an impact on one organizational unit or multiple organizational units within the covered bank; and

(ii) A determination of the effectiveness of front line units and independent risk management in identifying and resolving issues in a timely manner;

(d) Establish and adhere to processes for independently assessing the design and ongoing effectiveness of the risk governance framework on at least an annual basis. The independent assessment should include a conclusion on the covered bank's compliance with the standards set forth in these Guidelines;[3]

(e) Identify and communicate to the board's audit committee significant instances where front line units or independent risk management are not adhering to the risk governance framework;

(f) Establish a quality assurance program that ensures internal audit's policies, procedures, and processes comply with applicable regulatory and industry guidance, are appropriate for the size, complexity, and risk profile of the covered bank, are updated to reflect changes to internal and external risk factors, emerging risks, and improvements in industry internal audit practices, and are consistently followed;

(g) Develop, attract, and retain talent and maintain staffing levels required to effectively carry out its role and responsibilities, as set forth in paragraphs II.C.3.(a) through (f) of these Guidelines;

(h) Establish and adhere to talent management processes that comply with paragraph II.L. of these Guidelines; and

(i) Establish and adhere to compensation and performance management programs that comply with paragraph II.M. of these Guidelines.

D. *Strategic Plan.* The Chief Executive Officer should be responsible for the development of a written strategic plan with input from front line units, independent risk management, and internal audit. The board of directors should evaluate and approve the strategic plan and monitor management's efforts

[3] The annual independent assessment of the risk governance framework may be conducted by internal audit, an external party, or internal audit in conjunction with an external party.

to implement the strategic plan at least annually. The strategic plan should cover, at a minimum, a three-year period and:

1. Contain a comprehensive assessment of risks that currently have an impact on the covered bank or that could have an impact on the covered bank during the period covered by the strategic plan;

2. Articulate an overall mission statement and strategic objectives for the covered bank, and include an explanation of how the covered bank will achieve those objectives;

3. Include an explanation of how the covered bank will update, as necessary, the risk governance framework to account for changes in the covered bank's risk profile projected under the strategic plan; and

4. Be reviewed, updated, and approved, as necessary, due to changes in the covered bank's risk profile or operating environment that were not contemplated when the strategic plan was developed.

E. *Risk Appetite Statement.* A covered bank should have a comprehensive written statement that articulates the covered bank's risk appetite and serves as the basis for the risk governance framework. The risk appetite statement should include both qualitative components and quantitative limits. The qualitative components should describe a safe and sound risk culture and how the covered bank will assess and accept risks, including those that are difficult to quantify. Quantitative limits should incorporate sound stress testing processes, as appropriate, and address the covered bank's earnings, capital, and liquidity. The covered bank should set limits at levels that take into account appropriate capital and liquidity buffers and prompt management and the board of directors to reduce risk before the covered bank's risk profile jeopardizes the adequacy of its earnings, liquidity, and capital.[4]

F. *Concentration and Front Line Unit Risk Limits.* The risk governance framework should include concentration risk limits and, as applicable, front line unit risk limits, for the relevant risks. Concentration and front line unit risk limits should limit excessive risk taking and, when aggregated across such units, provide that these risks do not exceed the limits established in the covered bank's risk appetite statement.

G. *Risk Appetite Review, Monitoring, and Communication Processes.* The risk governance framework should require:[5]

1. Review and approval of the risk appetite statement by the board of directors or the board's risk committee at least annually or more frequently, as necessary, based on the size and volatility of risks and any material changes in the covered bank's business model, strategy, risk profile, or market conditions;

2. Initial communication and ongoing reinforcement of the covered bank's risk appetite statement throughout the covered bank in a manner that causes all employees to align their risk-taking decisions with applicable aspects of the risk appetite statement;

3. Monitoring by independent risk management of the covered bank's risk profile relative to its risk appetite and compliance with concentration risk limits and reporting on such monitoring to the board of directors or the board's risk committee at least quarterly;

4. Monitoring by front line units of compliance with their respective risk limits and reporting to independent risk management at least quarterly; and

5. When necessary due to the level and type of risk, monitoring by independent risk management of front line units' compliance with front line unit risk limits, ongoing communication with front line units regarding adherence to these limits, and reporting of any concerns to the Chief Executive Officer and the board of directors or the board's risk committee, as set forth in paragraphs II.C.2.(e) and (f) of these Guidelines, all at least quarterly.

H. *Processes Governing Risk Limit Breaches.* A covered bank should establish and adhere to processes that require front line units and independent risk management, in conjunction with their respective responsibilities, to:

1. Identify breaches of the risk appetite statement, concentration risk limits, and front line unit risk limits;

2. Distinguish breaches based on the severity of their impact on the covered bank;

3. Establish protocols for when and how to inform the board of directors, front line unit management, independent risk management, internal audit, and the OCC of a risk limit breach that takes into account the severity of the breach and its impact on the covered bank;

[4] Where possible, covered banks should establish aggregate risk appetite limits that can be disaggregated and applied at the front line unit level. However, where this is not possible, covered banks should establish limits that reasonably reflect the aggregate level of risk that the board of directors and executive management are willing to accept.

[5] With regard to paragraphs 3., 4., and 5. in this paragraph II.G., the frequency of monitoring and reporting should be performed more often, as necessary, based on the size and volatility of risks and any material change in the covered bank's business model, strategy, risk profile, or market conditions.

4. Include in the protocols established in paragraph II.H.3. of these Guidelines the requirement to provide a written description of how a breach will be, or has been, resolved; and

5. Establish accountability for reporting and resolving breaches that include consequences for risk limit breaches that take into account the magnitude, frequency, and recurrence of breaches.

I. *Concentration Risk Management*. The risk governance framework should include policies and supporting processes appropriate for the covered bank's size, complexity, and risk profile for effectively identifying, measuring, monitoring, and controlling the covered bank's concentrations of risk.

J. *Risk Data Aggregation and Reporting*. The risk governance framework should include a set of policies, supported by appropriate procedures and processes, designed to provide risk data aggregation and reporting capabilities appropriate for the size, complexity, and risk profile of the covered bank, and to support supervisory reporting requirements. Collectively, these policies, procedures, and processes should provide for:

1. The design, implementation, and maintenance of a data architecture and information technology infrastructure that support the covered bank's risk aggregation and reporting needs during normal times and during times of stress;

2. The capturing and aggregating of risk data and reporting of material risks, concentrations, and emerging risks in a timely manner to the board of directors and the OCC; and

3. The distribution of risk reports to all relevant parties at a frequency that meets their needs for decision-making purposes.

K. *Relationship of Risk Appetite Statement, Concentration Risk Limits, and Front Line Unit Risk Limits to Other Processes*. A covered bank's front line units and independent risk management should incorporate at a minimum the risk appetite statement, concentration risk limits, and front line unit risk limits into the following:

1. Strategic and annual operating plans;

2. Capital stress testing and planning processes;

3. Liquidity stress testing and planning processes;

4. Product and service risk management processes, including those for approving new and modified products and services;

5. Decisions regarding acquisitions and divestitures; and

6. Compensation and performance management programs.

L. *Talent Management Processes*. A covered bank should establish and adhere to processes for talent development, recruitment, and succession planning to ensure that management and employees who are responsible for or influence material risk decisions have the knowledge, skills, and abilities to effectively identify, measure, monitor, and control relevant risks. The board of directors or an appropriate committee of the board should:

1. Appoint a Chief Executive Officer and appoint or approve the appointment of a Chief Audit Executive and one or more Chief Risk Executives with the skills and abilities to carry out their roles and responsibilities within the risk governance framework;

2. Review and approve a written talent management program that provides for development, recruitment, and succession planning regarding the individuals described in paragraph II.L.1. of these Guidelines, their direct reports, and other potential successors; and

3. Require management to assign individuals specific responsibilities within the talent management program, and hold those individuals accountable for the program's effectiveness.

M. *Compensation and Performance Management Programs*. A covered bank should establish and adhere to compensation and performance management programs that comply with any applicable statute or regulation and are appropriate to:

1. Ensure the Chief Executive Officer, front line units, independent risk management, and internal audit implement and adhere to an effective risk governance framework;

2. Ensure front line unit compensation plans and decisions appropriately consider the level and severity of issues and concerns identified by independent risk management and internal audit, as well as the timeliness of corrective action to resolve such issues and concerns;

3. Attract and retain the talent needed to design, implement, and maintain an effective risk governance framework; and

4. Prohibit any incentive-based payment arrangement, or any feature of any such arrangement, that encourages inappropriate risks by providing excessive compensation or that could lead to material financial loss.

III. Standards for Board of Directors

A. *Require an Effective Risk Governance Framework*. Each member of a covered bank's board of directors should oversee the covered bank's compliance with safe and sound banking practices. The board of directors should also require management to establish and implement an effective risk governance framework that meets the minimum standards described in these Guidelines. The board of directors or the board's risk committee should approve any significant changes to the risk governance framework and monitor compliance with such framework.

B. *Provide Active Oversight of Management*. A covered bank's board of directors should actively oversee the covered bank's risk-taking activities and hold management accountable for adhering to the risk governance framework. In providing active oversight, the board of directors may rely on risk assessments and reports prepared by independent risk management and internal audit to support the board's ability to question, challenge, and when necessary, oppose recommendations and decisions made by management that could cause the covered bank's risk profile to exceed its risk appetite or jeopardize the safety and soundness of the covered bank.

C. *Exercise Independent Judgment.* When providing active oversight under paragraph III.B. of these Guidelines, each member of the board of directors should exercise sound, independent judgment.

D. *Include Independent Directors.* To promote effective, independent oversight of the covered bank's management, at least two members of the board of directors:[6]

1. Should not be an officer or employee of the parent company or covered bank and has not been an officer or employee of the parent company or covered bank during the previous three years;

2. Should not be a member of the immediate family, as defined in §225.41(b)(3) of the Board of Governors of the Federal Reserve System's Regulation Y (12 CFR 225.41(b)(3)), of a person who is, or has been within the last three years, an executive officer of the parent company or covered bank, as defined in §215.2(e)(1) of Regulation O (12 CFR 215.2(e)(1)); and

3. Should qualify as an independent director under the listing standards of a national securities exchange, as demonstrated to the satisfaction of the OCC.

E. *Provide Ongoing Training to All Directors.* The board of directors should establish and adhere to a formal, ongoing training program for all directors. This program should consider the directors' knowledge and experience and the covered bank's risk profile. The program should include, as appropriate, training on:

1. Complex products, services, lines of business, and risks that have a significant impact on the covered bank;

2. Laws, regulations, and supervisory requirements applicable to the covered bank; and

3. Other topics identified by the board of directors.

F. *Self-Assessments.* A covered bank's board of directors should conduct an annual self-assessment that includes an evaluation of its effectiveness in meeting the standards in section III of these Guidelines.

[6] This provision does not supersede other regulatory requirements regarding the composition of the Board that apply to Federal savings associations. These institutions must continue to comply with such other requirements.

[79 FR 54545, Sept. 11, 2014]

Appendix E to Part 30—OCC Guidelines Establishing Standards for Recovery Planning by Certain Large Insured National Banks, Insured Federal Savings Associations, and Insured Federal Branches

Published at 83 FR 66607, Dec. 27, 2018.

Table of Contents

I. Introduction
A. Scope
B. Compliance date
C. Reservation of authority
D. Preservation of existing authority
E. Definitions
II. Recovery Plan
A. Recovery plan
B. Elements of recovery plan
1. Overview of covered bank
2. Triggers
3. Options for recovery
4. Impact assessments
5. Escalation procedures
6. Management reports
7. Communication procedures
8. Other information
C. Relationship to other processes; coordination with other plans
III. Management's and Board of Directors' Responsibilities
A. Management
B. Board of directors

I. Introduction

A. *Scope.* This appendix applies to a covered bank, as defined in paragraph I.E.3. of this appendix.

B. *Compliance date.*

1. A covered bank with average total consolidated assets, calculated according to paragraph I.E.1. of this appendix, equal to or greater than $750 billion as of January 1, 2017 should comply with this appendix within 6 months from January 1, 2017.

2. A covered bank with average total consolidated assets, calculated according to paragraph I.E.1. of this appendix, equal to or greater than $100 billion but less than $750 billion as of January 1, 2017 should comply with this appendix within 12 months from January 1, 2017.

3. A covered bank with average total consolidated assets, calculated according to paragraph I.E.1. of this appendix, equal to or greater than $50 billion but less than $100 billion as of January 1, 2017 should comply with

this appendix within 18 months from January 1, 2017.

4. A bank with average total consolidated assets, calculated according to paragraph I.E.1. of this appendix, of less than $50 billion as of January 1, 2017 but which subsequently becomes a covered bank should comply with this appendix within 18 months of becoming a covered bank.

C. *Reservation of authority.*

1. The OCC reserves the authority:

a. To apply this appendix, in whole or in part, to a bank that has average total consolidated assets of less than $50 billion, if the OCC determines such bank is highly complex or otherwise presents a heightened risk that warrants the application of this appendix; or

b. To determine that compliance with this appendix should not be required for a covered bank. The OCC will generally make this determination if a covered bank's operations are no longer highly complex or no longer present a heightened risk.

2. In determining whether a bank or covered bank is highly complex or presents a heightened risk, the OCC will consider the bank's size, risk profile, scope of operations, activities, and complexity, including the complexity of its organizational and legal entity structure. Before exercising the authority reserved by paragraph I.C.1. of this appendix, the OCC will apply notice and response procedures in the same manner and to the same extent as the notice and response procedures in 12 CFR 3.404.

D. *Preservation of existing authority.* Neither section 39 of the Federal Deposit Insurance Act (12 U.S.C. 1831p–1) nor this appendix in any way limits the authority of the OCC to address unsafe or unsound practices or conditions or other violations of law. The OCC may take action under section 39 and this appendix independently of, in conjunction with, or in addition to any other enforcement action available to the OCC.

E. *Definitions.*

1. *Average total consolidated assets* means the average total consolidated assets of the bank or the covered bank, as reported on the bank's or the covered bank's Consolidated Reports of Condition and Income for the four most recent consecutive quarters.

2. *Bank* means any insured national bank, insured Federal savings association, or insured Federal branch of a foreign bank.

3. *Covered bank* means any bank:

a. With average total consolidated assets equal to or greater than $50 billion;

b. With average total consolidated assets of less than $50 billion if the bank was previously a covered bank, unless the OCC determines otherwise; or

c. With average total consolidated assets less than $50 billion, if the OCC determines that such bank is highly complex or otherwise presents a heightened risk as to warrant the application of this appendix pursuant to paragraph I.C.1.a. of this appendix.

4. *Recovery* means timely and appropriate action that a covered bank takes to remain a going concern when it is experiencing or is likely to experience considerable financial or operational stress. A covered bank in recovery has not yet deteriorated to the point where liquidation or resolution is imminent.

5. *Recovery plan* means a plan that identifies triggers and options for responding to a wide range of severe internal and external stress scenarios to restore a covered bank that is in recovery to financial strength and viability in a timely manner. The options should maintain the confidence of market participants, and neither the plan nor the options may assume or rely on any extraordinary government support.

6. *Trigger* means a quantitative or qualitative indicator of the risk or existence of severe stress, the breach of which should always be escalated to senior management or the board of directors (or appropriate committee of the board of directors), as appropriate, for purposes of initiating a response. The breach of any trigger should result in timely notice accompanied by sufficient information to enable management of the covered bank to take corrective action.

II. Recovery Plan

A. *Recovery plan.* Each covered bank should develop and maintain a recovery plan that is specific to that covered bank and appropriate for its individual size, risk profile, activities, and complexity, including the complexity of its organizational and legal entity structure.

B. *Elements of recovery plan.* A recovery plan under paragraph II.A. of this appendix should include the following elements:

1. *Overview of covered bank.* A recovery plan should describe the covered bank's overall organizational and legal entity structure, including its material entities, critical operations, core business lines, and core management information systems. The plan should describe interconnections and interdependencies (i) across business lines within the covered bank, (ii) with affiliates in a bank holding company structure, (iii) between a covered bank and its foreign subsidiaries, and (iv) with critical third parties.

2. *Triggers.* A recovery plan should identify triggers that appropriately reflect the covered bank's particular vulnerabilities.

3. *Options for recovery.* A recovery plan should identify a wide range of credible options that a covered bank could undertake to restore financial strength and viability, thereby allowing the bank to continue to operate as a going concern and to avoid liquidation or resolution. A recovery plan should explain how the covered bank would carry out each option and describe the timing required for carrying out each option.

The recovery plan should specifically identify the recovery options that require regulatory or legal approval.

4. *Impact assessments.* For each recovery option, a covered bank should assess and describe how the option would affect the covered bank. This impact assessment and description should specify the procedures the covered bank would use to maintain the financial strength and viability of its material entities, critical operations, and core business lines for each recovery option. For each option, the recovery plan's impact assessment should address the following:

a. The effect on the covered bank's capital, liquidity, funding, and profitability;

b. The effect on the covered bank's material entities, critical operations, and core business lines, including reputational impact; and

c. Any legal or market impediment or regulatory requirement that must be addressed or satisfied in order to implement the option.

5. *Escalation procedures.* A recovery plan should clearly outline the process for escalating decision-making to senior management or the board of directors (or an appropriate committee of the board of directors), as appropriate, in response to the breach of any trigger. The recovery plan should also identify the departments and persons responsible for executing the decisions of senior management or the board of directors (or an appropriate committee of the board of directors).

6. *Management reports.* A recovery plan should require reports that provide senior management or the board of directors (or an appropriate committee of the board of directors) with sufficient data and information to make timely decisions regarding the appropriate actions necessary to respond to the breach of a trigger.

7. *Communication procedures.* A recovery plan should provide that the covered bank notify the OCC of any significant breach of a trigger and any action taken or to be taken in response to such breach and should explain the process for deciding when a breach of a trigger is significant. A recovery plan also should address when and how the covered bank will notify persons within the organization and other external parties of its action under the recovery plan. The recovery plan should specifically identify how the covered bank will obtain required regulatory or legal approvals.

8. *Other information.* A recovery plan should include any other information that the OCC communicates in writing directly to the covered bank regarding the covered bank's recovery plan.

C. *Relationship to other processes; coordination with other plans.* The covered bank should integrate its recovery plan into its risk governance functions. The covered bank also should align its recovery plan with its other plans, such as its strategic; operational (including business continuity); contingency; capital (including stress testing); liquidity; and resolution planning. The covered bank's recovery plan should be specific to that covered bank. The covered bank also should coordinate its recovery plan with any recovery and resolution planning efforts by the covered bank's holding company, so that the plans are consistent with and do not contradict each other.

III. Management's and Board of Directors' Responsibilities

The recovery plan should address the following management and board responsibilities:

A. *Management.* Management should review the recovery plan at least annually and in response to a material event. It should revise the plan as necessary to reflect material changes in the covered bank's size, risk profile, activities, and complexity, as well as changes in external threats. This review should evaluate the organizational structure and its effectiveness in facilitating a recovery.

B. *Board of directors.* The board is responsible for overseeing the covered bank's recovery planning process. The board of directors (or an appropriate committee of the board of directors) of a covered bank should review and approve the recovery plan at least annually, and as needed to address significant changes made by management.

[81 FR 66800, Sept. 29, 2016]

Effective Date Note: At 83 FR 66607, Dec. 27, 2018, appendix E to part 30 was amended by:

a. Removing the phrase "$50 billion" and adding in its place the phrase "$250 billion" everywhere that it appears;

b. Revising section I.B.1;

c. Removing section I.B.2 and I.B.3;

d. Redesignating section I.B.4 as section I.B.2;

e. In newly redesignated section I.B.2:

i. Removing "January 1, 2017" and adding in its place the words "January 28, 2019"; and

ii. Removing the phrase "18 months" and adding in its place the phrase "12 months", effective Jan. 28, 2019. For the convenience of the user, the revised text is set forth as follows:

APPENDIX E TO PART 30—OCC GUIDELINES ESTABLISHING STANDARDS FORRECOVERY PLANNING BY CERTAIN LARGE INSURED NATIONAL BANKS, INSUREDFEDERAL SAVINGS ASSOCIATIONS, AND INSURED FEDERAL BRANCHES

* * * * *

I. * * *

B. * * *

1. A covered bank with average total consolidated assets, calculated according to paragraph I.E.1. of this appendix, equal to or greater than $250 billion as of January 28, 2019 should be in compliance with this appendix on January 28, 2019.

* * * * *

PART 31—EXTENSIONS OF CREDIT TO INSIDERS AND TRANSACTIONS WITH AFFILIATES

Sec.
31.1 Authority.
31.2 Insider lending restrictions and reporting requirements.
31.3 Affiliate transactions requirements.
APPENDIX A TO PART 31—INTERPRETATIONS: DEPOSITS BETWEEN AFFILIATED BANKS
APPENDIX B TO PART 31—COMPARISON OF SELECTED PROVISIONS OF PARTS 32 AND 215

AUTHORITY: 12 U.S.C. 93a, 375a(4), 375b(3), 1463, 1467a(d), 1468, 1817(k), and 5412(b)(2)(B).

SOURCE: 61 FR 54536, Oct. 21, 1996, unless otherwise noted.

§31.1 Authority.

This part is issued pursuant to 12 U.S.C. 93a, 375a(4), 375b(3), 1463, 1467a(d), 1468, 1817(k), and 5412(b)(2)(B), as amended.

[82 FR 8109, Jan. 23, 2017]

§31.2 Insider lending restrictions and reporting requirements.

(a) *General rule.* National banks, Federal savings associations, and their insiders shall comply with the provisions contained in 12 CFR part 215 (Regulation O).

(b) *Enforcement.* The Comptroller of the Currency administers and enforces insider lending standards and reporting requirements as they apply to national banks, Federal savings associations, and their insiders.

[61 FR 54536, Oct. 21, 1996, as amended at 82 FR 8109, Jan. 23, 2017]

§31.3 Affiliate transactions requirements.

(a) *General rule.* National banks and Federal savings associations shall comply with the provisions contained in 12 CFR part 223 (Regulation W).

(b) *Enforcement.* The Comptroller of the Currency administers and enforces affiliate transactions requirements as they apply to national banks and Federal savings associations.

(c) *Standard for exemptions.* The OCC may, by order, exempt transactions or relationships of a national bank or Federal savings association from the requirements of section 23A and section 11 of the Home Owners' Loan Act (HOLA), as applicable, and 12 CFR part 223 if:

(1) The OCC, jointly with the Federal Reserve Board, finds the exemption to be in the public interest and consistent with the purposes of section 23A or section 11 of the HOLA, as applicable; and

(2) The FDIC, within 60 days of receiving notice of such joint finding, does not object in writing to the finding based on a determination that the exemption presents an unacceptable risk to the Deposit Insurance Fund.

(d) *Procedures for exemptions.* A national bank or Federal savings association may request an exemption from the requirements of section 23A or section 11 of the HOLA, as applicable, and 12 CFR part 223 for a national bank or Federal savings association by submitting a written request to the Deputy Comptroller for Licensing with a copy to the appropriate Federal Reserve Bank. Such a request must:

(1) Describe in detail the transaction or relationship for which the national bank or Federal savings association seeks exemption;

(2) Explain why the OCC should exempt the transaction or relationship;

(3) Explain how the exemption would be in the public interest and consistent with the purposes of section 23A or section 11 of the HOLA, as applicable; and

(4) Explain why the exemption does not present an unacceptable risk to the Deposit Insurance Fund.

[82 FR 8109, Jan. 23, 2017]

Appendix A to Part 31—Interpretations: Deposits Between Affiliated Banks

a. *General rule.* A deposit made by a bank in an affiliated bank is treated as a loan or extension of credit to the affiliate bank under 12 U.S.C. 371c, as this statute is implemented by the Federal Reserve Board's Regulation W, 12 CFR part 223. Thus, unless an exemption from Regulation W is available, these deposits must be secured in accordance with 12 CFR 223.14. However, a national bank may not pledge assets to secure private deposits unless otherwise permitted by law (*see, e.g.*, 12 U.S.C. 90 (permitting collateralization of deposits of public funds); 12 U.S.C. 92a (trust funds); and 25 U.S.C. 156 and 162a (Native American funds)). Thus, unless one of the exceptions to 12 CFR part 223 noted in paragraph b. of this interpretation applies, unless another exception applies that enables a bank to meet the collateral requirements of §223.14, or unless a party other than the bank in which the deposit is made can legally offer and does post the required collateral, a national bank may not:

1. Make a deposit in an affiliated national bank;

2. Make a deposit in an affiliated State-chartered bank unless the affiliated State-chartered bank can legally offer collateral for the deposit in conformance with applicable State law and 12 CFR 223.14; or

3. Receive deposits from an affiliated bank.

b. *Exceptions.* The restrictions of 12 CFR part 223 (other than 12 CFR 223.13, which requires affiliate transactions to be consistent with safe and sound banking practices) do not apply to deposits:

1. Made in an affiliated depository institution or affiliated foreign bank provided that the deposit represents an ongoing, working balance maintained in the ordinary course of correspondent business. *See* 12 CFR 223.42(a); or

2. Made in an affiliated, insured depository institution that meets the requirements of the "sister bank" exemption under 12 CFR 223.41(a) or (b).

[73 FR 22251, Apr. 24, 2008]

Appendix B to Part 31—Comparison of Selected Provisions of Parts 32 and 215

Note: This appendix compares certain provisions of 12 CFR part 32 with those of 12 CFR part 215. As used in this appendix, the term "bank" refers to both national banks and Federal savings associations.

Definition of "Loan or Extension of Credit"

Renewals	In most cases, the two definitions of "loan or extension of credit" are equivalent. A difference exists, however, in the treatment of renewals. Under part 215, a renewal of a loan to an "insider" (which, unless noted otherwise, includes a bank's executive officers, directors, principal shareholders, and "related interests" of such persons) is considered to be an extension of credit. Under part 32, renewals generally are not considered to be an extension of credit if the bank exercises reasonable efforts, consistent with safe and sound banking practices, to bring the loan into conformance with the lending limit. Renewals would be considered an extension of credit under part 32, however, if new funds are advanced to the borrower, a new borrower replaces the original borrower, or the OCC determines that the renewal was undertaken to evade the lending limits.
Commitments to extend credit...	A binding commitment to make a loan is treated as an extension of credit under part 215. Under part 32, a commitment to make a loan will not be treated as an extension of credit if the amount of the commitment exceeds the lending limit. Rather, the commitment will be deemed a "nonqualifying commitment" under part 32 and advances may be made thereunder only if the advance, together with all other outstanding loans to the borrower, will not exceed the bank's lending limit.

Overdrafts	An advance by means of an overdraft (except for an intraday overdraft) generally is considered to be an extension of credit under both parts 32 and 215. However, indebtedness in amounts up to $5,000 is excluded from the definition of "extension of credit" under part 215 if the indebtedness arises pursuant to a written, preauthorized, interest-bearing plan or written, preauthorized transfer of funds from another account. Under part 215, if an overdraft is not made pursuant to this type of plan or transfer, a bank is prohibited from paying an overdraft of an insider (which, in this case, includes only an executive officer or director of the insider's bank) unless the overdraft is inadvertent, in amounts not exceeding $1,000, outstanding for not more than 5 business days, and subject to the bank's standard overdraft fee. Part 32 does not contain these exceptions for overdrafts, and simply treats overdrafts (except for intraday overdrafts) as extensions of credit subject to lending limits.
Guarantees	Generally speaking, guarantees are included in the part 215 definition of "extension of credit" but are not included in the definition of "extension of credit" in part 32 unless other criteria are satisfied. Part 215 applies to any transaction as a result of which an insider becomes obligated to pay money to a bank, whether the obligation arises (i) directly or indirectly, (ii) because of an endorsement on an obligation or otherwise, or (iii) by any means whatsoever. Accordingly, a loan guaranteed by an insider will be deemed to have been made to that insider. In contrast, part 32 does not consider a loan on which someone signs as guarantor as having been made to the guarantor unless that person is deemed to be a borrower under the "direct benefit" or "common enterprise" tests (*see* discussion of these tests in the discussion of the "General Rule" under "Combination/Attribution Rules," below).
	EXCLUSIONS TO DEFINITION
Funds advanced for taxes, etc., necessary to preserve collateral or that are incidental to indebtedness.	Both rules exclude funds advanced for items such as taxes, insurance, or other expenses related to existing indebtedness. However, part 32 includes these advances for the purpose of determining whether subsequent loans meet the lending limit, whereas part 215 excludes these advances for all purposes. Part 215 contains no such requirement.
Loan participations.	Both rules exclude loan participations if the participation is without recourse. However, part 32 elaborates on this exclusion by requiring that the participation result in a *pro rata* sharing of credit risk proportionate to the respective interests of the originating and participating lenders. Part 32 also requires the originating bank, if funding the entire loan, to receive funding from the participants before the close of the next business day. Otherwise, the portion funded will be treated as a loan by the originating bank to the underlying borrower, and may be treated as a "nonconforming" loan rather than a violation if (i) the originating bank had an agreement with the participating bank that reduced the loan to an amount within the originating bank's lending limit, (ii) the participating bank reconfirmed its participation and the originating bank had no knowledge of information that would permit the participating bank to withhold its participation, and (iii) the participation was to be funded by close of business of the originating bank's next business day.
Acquisition of debt through merger or foreclosure.	Under part 215, a note or other evidence of indebtedness acquired through a merger is excluded from the definition of "extension of credit." Under part 32, the indebtedness is deemed to be a loan or extension of credit. However, if a loan that conformed with part 32 when originally made exceeds the lending limits following a merger after the loan is aggregated with other extensions of credit to the same borrower, the loan will not be deemed to be a lending limits violation. Rather, the loan will be treated as "nonconforming," and the bank will have to exercise reasonable efforts to bring the loan into compliance unless to do so would be inconsistent with safe and sound banking practices.

Credit card indebtedness.	An insider may incur up to $15,000 in debt on a credit card or similar open-end credit plan offered by the insider's bank without the debt counting as an extension of credit under part 215. The terms of the credit card or other credit plan must be no more favorable than those offered by the bank to the general public. Part 32 does not exclude credit card debt from the lending limits.
	COMBINATION/ ATTRIBUTION RULES
General rule	Under part 215, a loan will be attributed to an insider if the loan proceeds are "transferred to," or used for the "tangible economic benefit of," the insider or if the loan is made to a "related interest" of the insider. Under part 32, a loan will be attributed to another person when either (i) the proceeds of the loan are to be used for the direct benefit of the other person or (ii) a common enterprise exists between the borrower and the other person. The "transfer" test and "tangible economic benefit" test of part 215 are substantially the same as the "direct benefit" test of part 32. Under each of these tests, a loan will be attributed to another person where the proceeds are transferred to the other person, unless the proceeds are used in a *bona fide* arm's length transaction to acquire property, goods, or services. However, the "related interest" test of part 215 and the "common enterprise" test under part 32 will lead to different results in many instances. Under part 215, a "related interest" is a company or a political or campaign committee that is "controlled" by an insider. Part 215 defines "control" as meaning, generally speaking, that someone owns or controls at least 25 percent of a class of voting securities of a company, controls the election of a majority of the company's directors, or can "exercise a controlling influence" over the company. Part 32 uses the same definition of "control" in the "common enterprise" test, but a mere finding of "control" is not, by itself, a sufficient basis to find that a common enterprise exists. Part 32 will attribute a loan under the "common enterprise" test if the borrowers are under common control (including where one of the persons in question controls the other) *and* there is "substantial financial interdependence" between the borrowers (*i.e.*, where at least 50 percent of the gross receipts or expenditures of one borrower comes from transactions with the other). If there is not both common control and substantial financial interdependence, the OCC will not attribute a loan under the "common enterprise" test unless (i) the expected source of repayment for a loan is the same for each borrower and neither borrower has another source of income from which the loan may be repaid, (ii) two people borrow to acquire a business of which they will own a majority of the voting securities, or (iii) OCC determines that a common enterprise exists based on facts and circumstances of a particular transaction.
Loans to corporate groups.	Both parts 32 and 215 will consider a loan that was made to a corporation to have been made to a third person if the tests identified in the previous discussion of the "General Rule" are satisfied. If these tests are not met, parts 32 and 215 still may require attribution, but the circumstances when this will occur and the consequences of attribution under these circumstances differ under the two rules. Under part 215, a loan to a corporation will be deemed to have been made to an insider if the corporation is a "related interest" of the insider (*i.e.*, the insider owns at least 25% percent of a class of voting shares of the company, controls the election of a majority of the company's directors, or has the power to exercise a controlling influence over the company). Under part 32, a loan to an individual or company will not be considered to have been made to a corporate group unless a "person" (which includes individuals and companies) owns more than 50% of the voting shares of a company. If a loan is found to have been made to a related interest of an insider under part 215, the loan must comply with all of the insider lending restrictions of part 215. If a loan is found to have been made to a corporate group under part 32, the loan, when aggregated with all other loans to that corporate group, generally may not exceed 50% of the bank's capital and surplus.

[61 FR 54536, Oct. 21, 1996, as amended at 73 FR 22251, Apr. 24, 2008; 82 FR 8109, Jan. 23, 2017]

PART 32—LENDING LIMITS

Sec.
32.1 Authority, purpose and scope.
32.2 Definitions.
32.3 Lending limits.
32.4 Calculation of lending limits.
32.5 Combination rules.
32.6 Nonconforming loans and extensions of credit.
32.7 Residential real estate loans, small business loans, and small farm loans ("Supplemental Lending Limits Program").
32.8 Temporary funding arrangements in emergency situations.
32.9 Credit exposure arising from derivative and securities financing transactions.
APPENDIX A TO PART 32—INTERPRETATIONS

AUTHORITY: 12 U.S.C. 1 *et seq.*, 12 U.S.C. 84, 93a, 1462a, 1463, 1464(u), 5412(b)(2)(B), and 15 U.S.C. 1639h.

SOURCE: 60 FR 8532, Feb. 15, 1995, unless otherwise noted.

§32.1 Authority, purpose and scope.

(a) *Authority.* This part is issued pursuant to 12 U.S.C. 1 *et seq.*, 12 U.S.C. 84, 93a, 1462a, 1463, 1464(u), and 5412(b)(2)(B).

(b) *Purpose.* The purpose of this part is to protect the safety and soundness of national banks and savings associations by preventing excessive loans to one person, or to related persons that are financially dependent, and to promote diversification of loans and equitable access to banking services.

(c) *Scope.* (1) Except as provided by paragraphs (c) and (d) of this section, this part applies to all loans and extensions of credit made by national banks and their domestic operating subsidiaries and to all loans and extensions of credit made by savings associations, their operating subsidiaries, and their service corporations that are consolidated under Generally Accepted Accounting Principles (GAAP). For purposes of this part, the term "savings association" includes Federal savings associations and state savings associations, as those terms are defined in 12 U.S.C. 1813(b).

(2) This part does not apply to loans or extensions of credit made to the bank's or savings association's:

(i) Affiliates, as that term is defined in 12 U.S.C. 371c(b)(1) and (e), as implemented by 12 CFR 223.2(a) (Regulation W);

(ii) Operating subsidiaries;

(iii) Edge Act or Agreement Corporation subsidiaries; or

(iv) Any other subsidiary consolidated with the bank or savings association under GAAP.

(3) The lending limits in this part are separate and independent from the investment limits prescribed by 12 U.S.C. 24 (Seventh) or 12 U.S.C. 1464(c), as applicable, and 12 CFR Part 1 and 12 CFR 160.30, and a national bank or savings association may make loans or extensions of credit to one borrower up to the full amount permitted by this part and also hold eligible securities of the same obligor up to the full amount permitted under 12 U.S.C. 24 (Seventh) or 12 U.S.C. 1464(c), as applicable, and 12 CFR part 1 and 12 CFR 160.30.

(4) Loans and extensions of credit to executive officers, directors and principal shareholders of national banks, savings associations, and their related interests are subject to limits prescribed by 12 U.S.C. 375a and 375b in addition to the lending limits established by 12 U.S.C. 84 or 12 U.S.C. 1464(u) as applicable, and this part.

(5) In addition to the foregoing, loans and extensions of credit must be consistent with safe and sound banking practices.

(d) *Temporary exception.* The requirements of this part shall not apply to the credit exposure arising from a derivative transaction or securities financing transaction until October 1, 2013.

[60 FR 8532, Feb. 15, 1995, as amended at 73 FR 22251, Apr. 24, 2008; 77 FR 37275, June 21, 2012; 77 FR 76842, Dec. 31, 2012; 78 FR 37943, June 25, 2013]

§32.2 Definitions.

(a) *Appropriate Federal banking agency* has the same meaning as in 12 U.S.C. 1813(q).

(b) *Borrower* means a person who is named as a borrower or debtor in a loan or extension of credit; a person to whom a national bank or savings association has credit exposure arising from a derivative transaction or a securities financing transaction, entered by the bank or savings association; or any other person, including a drawer, endorser, or guarantor, who is deemed to be a borrower under the "direct benefit" or the "common enterprise" tests set forth in § 32.5.

(c) *Capital and surplus* means—

(1) A national bank's or savings association's Tier 1 and Tier 2 capital calculated under the risk-based capital standards applicable to the institution as reported in the bank's or savings association's Consolidated Reports of Condition and Income (Call Report); plus

(2) The balance of a national bank's or savings association's allowance for loan and lease losses not included in the bank's or savings association's Tier 2 capital, for purposes of the calculation of risk-based capital described in paragraph (c)(1) of this section, as reported in the bank's or savings association's Call Report.

(d) *Close of business* means the time at which a national bank or savings association closes its accounting records for the business day.

(e) *Consumer* means the user of any products, commodities, goods, or services, whether leased or purchased, but does not include any person who purchases products or commodities for resale or fabrication into goods for sale.

(f) *Consumer paper* means paper relating to automobiles, mobile homes, residences, office equipment, household items, tuition fees, insurance premium fees, and similar consumer items. Consumer paper also includes paper covering the lease (where the national bank or savings association is not the owner or lessor) or purchase of equipment for use in manufacturing, farming, construction, or excavation.

(g) *Contractual commitment to advance funds.* (1) The term includes a national bank's or savings association's obligation to—

(i) Make payment (directly or indirectly) to a third person contingent upon default by a customer of the bank or savings association in performing an obligation and to make such payment in keeping with the agreed upon terms of the customer's contract with the third person, or to make payments upon some other stated condition;

(ii) Guarantee or act as surety for the benefit of a person;

(iii) Advance funds under a qualifying commitment to lend, as defined in paragraph (t) of this section, and

(iv) Advance funds under a standby letter of credit as defined in paragraph (ee) of this section, a put, or other similar arrangement.

(2) The term does not include commercial letters of credit and similar instruments where the issuing bank or savings association expects the beneficiary to draw on the issuer, that do not guarantee payment, and that do not provide for payment in the event of a default by a third party.

(h) *Control* is presumed to exist when a person directly or indirectly, or acting through or together with one or more persons—

(1) Owns, controls, or has the power to vote 25 percent or more of any class of voting securities of another person;

(2) Controls, in any manner, the election of a majority of the directors, trustees, or other persons exercising similar functions of another person; or

(3) Has the power to exercise a controlling influence over the management or policies of another person.

(i) *Credit derivative* has the same meaning as this term has in 12 CFR 3.2.

(j) *Current market value* means the bid or closing price listed for an item in a regularly published listing or an electronic reporting service.

(k) *Derivative transaction* includes any transaction that is a contract, agreement, swap, warrant, note, or option that is based, in whole or in part, on the value of, any interest in, or any quantitative measure or the occurrence of any event relating to, one or more commodities, securities, currencies, interest or other rates, indices, or other assets.

(l) *Effective margining arrangement* means a master legal agreement governing derivative transactions between a bank or savings association and a counterparty that requires the counterparty to post, on a daily basis, variation margin to fully collateralize that amount of the bank's or savings association's net credit exposure to the counterparty that exceeds $25 million created by the derivative transactions covered by the agreement.

(m) *Eligible credit derivative* means a single-name credit derivative or a standard, non-tranched index credit derivative provided that:

(1) The derivative contract meets the requirements of an eligible guarantee, as defined in 12 CFR 3.2, and has been confirmed by the protection purchaser and the protection provider;

(2) Any assignment of the derivative contract has been confirmed by all relevant parties;

(3) If the credit derivative is a credit default swap, the derivative contract includes the following credit events:

(i) Failure to pay any amount due under the terms of the reference exposure, subject to any applicable minimal payment threshold that is consistent with standard market practice and with a grace period that is closely in line with the grace period of the reference exposure; and

(ii) Bankruptcy, insolvency, restructuring (for obligors not subject to bankruptcy or insolvency), or inability of the obligor on the reference exposure to pay its debts, or its failure or admission in writing of its inability generally to pay its debts as they become due, and similar events;

(4) The terms and conditions dictating the manner in which the derivative contract is to be settled are incorporated into the contract;

(5) If the derivative contract allows for cash settlement, the contract incorporates a robust valuation process to estimate loss with respect to the derivative reliably and specifies a reasonable period for obtaining post-credit event valuations of the reference exposure;

(6) If the derivative contract requires the protection purchaser to transfer an exposure to the protection provider at settlement, the terms of at least one of the exposures that is permitted to be transferred under the contract provides that any required consent to transfer may not be unreasonably withheld; and

(7) If the credit derivative is a credit default swap, the derivative contract clearly identifies the parties responsible for determining whether a credit event has occurred, specifies that this determination is not the sole responsibility of the protection provider, and gives the protection purchaser the right to notify the protection provider of the occurrence of a credit event.

(n) *Eligible national bank or eligible savings association* means a national bank or saving association that:

(1) Is well capitalized as defined in the prompt corrective action rules applicable to the institution; and

(2) Has a composite rating of 1 or 2 under the Uniform Financial Institutions Rating System in connection with the national bank's or savings association's most recent examination or subsequent review, with at least a rating of 2 for asset quality and for management.

(o) *Eligible protection provider* means:

(1) A sovereign entity (a central government, including the U.S. government; an agency; department; ministry; or central bank);

(2) The Bank for International Settlements, the International Monetary Fund, the European Central Bank, the European Commission, or a multilateral development bank;

(3) A Federal Home Loan Bank;

(4) The Federal Agricultural Mortgage Corporation;

(5) A depository institution, as defined in section 3 of the Federal Deposit Insurance Act, 12 U.S.C. 1813(c);

(6) A bank holding company, as defined in section 2 of the Bank Holding Company Act, as amended, 12 U.S.C. 1841;

(7) A savings and loan holding company, as defined in section 10 of the Home Owners' Loan Act, 12 U.S.C. 1467a;

(8) A securities broker or dealer registered with the SEC under the Securities Exchange Act of 1934, 15 U.S.C. 78o et seq;

(9) An insurance company that is subject to the supervision of a State insurance regulator;

(10) A foreign banking organization;

(11) A non-U.S.-based securities firm or a non-U.S.-based insurance company that is subject to consolidated supervision and regulation comparable to that imposed on U.S. depository institutions, securities broker-dealers, or insurance companies; and

(12) A qualifying central counterparty;

(p) *Financial instrument* means stocks, notes, bonds, and debentures traded on a national securities exchange, OTC margin stocks as defined in Regulation

U, 12 CFR part 221, commercial paper, negotiable certificates of deposit, bankers' acceptances, and shares in money market and mutual funds of the type that issue shares in which national banks or savings associations may perfect a security interest. Financial instruments may be denominated in foreign currencies that are freely convertible to U.S. dollars. The term "financial instrument" does not include mortgages.

(q) *Loans and extensions of credit* means a national bank's or savings association's direct or indirect advance of funds to or on behalf of a borrower based on an obligation of the borrower to repay the funds or repayable from specific property pledged by or on behalf of the borrower; and any credit exposure, as determined pursuant to § 32.9, arising from a derivative transaction or a securities financing transaction.

(1) Loans or extensions of credit for purposes of 12 U.S.C. 84 or 12 U.S.C. 1464(u), as applicable, and this part include—

(i) A contractual commitment to advance funds, as defined in paragraph (g) of this section;

(ii) A maker or endorser's obligation arising from a national bank's or savings association's discount of commercial paper;

(iii) A national bank's or savings association's purchase of third-party paper subject to an agreement that the seller will repurchase the paper upon default or at the end of a stated period. The amount of the bank's or savings association's loan is the total unpaid balance of the paper owned by the bank or savings association less any applicable dealer reserves retained by the bank or savings association and held by the bank or savings association as collateral security. Where the seller's obligation to repurchase is limited, the bank's or savings association's loan is measured by the total amount of the paper the seller may ultimately be obligated to repurchase. A national bank's or savings association's purchase of third party paper without direct or indirect recourse to the seller is not a loan or extension of credit to the seller;

(iv) An overdraft, whether or not prearranged, but not an intra-day overdraft for which payment is received before the close of business of the national bank or savings association that makes the funds available;

(v) The sale of Federal funds with a maturity of more than one business day, but not Federal funds with a maturity of one day or less or Federal funds sold under a continuing contract; and

(vi) Loans or extensions of credit that have been charged off on the books of the national bank or savings association in whole or in part, unless the loan or extension of credit—

(A) Is unenforceable by reason of discharge in bankruptcy;

(B) Is no longer legally enforceable because of expiration of the statute of limitations or a judicial decision;

(C) Is no longer legally enforceable for other reasons, provided that the bank or savings association maintains sufficient records to demonstrate that the loan is unenforceable.

(2) The following items do not constitute loans or extensions of credit for purposes of 12 U.S.C. 84 or 12 U.S.C. 1464(u), as applicable, and this part—

(i) Additional funds advanced for the benefit of a borrower by a national bank or savings association for payment of taxes, insurance, utilities, security, and maintenance and operating expenses necessary to preserve the value of real property securing the loan, consistent with safe and sound banking practices, but only if the advance is for the protection of the bank's or savings association's interest in the collateral, and provided that such amounts must be treated as an extension of credit if a new loan or extension of credit is made to the borrower;

(ii) Accrued and discounted interest on an existing loan or extension of credit, including interest that has been capitalized from prior notes and interest that has been advanced under terms and conditions of a loan agreement;

(iii) Financed sales of a national bank's or savings association's own assets, including Other Real Estate Owned, if the financing does not put the bank or savings association in a worse position than when the bank or savings association held title to the assets;

(iv) A renewal or restructuring of a loan as a new "loan or extension of credit," following the exercise by a national bank or savings association of reasonable efforts, consistent with safe and sound banking practices, to bring the loan into conformance with the lending limit, unless new funds are advanced by the national bank or savings association to the borrower (except as permitted by § 32.3(b)(5)), or a new borrower replaces the original borrower, or unless the appropriate Federal banking agency determines that a renewal or restructuring was undertaken as a means to evade the bank's or savings association's lending limit;

(v) Amounts paid against uncollected funds in the normal process of collection;

(vi)(A) That portion of a loan or extension of credit sold as a participation by a national bank or savings association on a nonrecourse basis, provided that the participation results in a pro rata sharing of credit risk proportionate to the respective interests of the originating and participating lenders. Where a participation agreement provides that repayment must be applied first to the portions sold, a pro rata sharing will be deemed to exist only if the agreement also provides that, in the event of a default or comparable event defined in the agreement, participants must share in all subsequent repayments and collections in proportion to their percentage participation at the time of the occurrence of the event.

(B) When an originating national bank or savings association funds the entire loan, it must receive funding from the participants before the close of business of its next business day. If the participating portions are not received within that period, then the portions funded will be treated as a loan by the originating bank or savings association to the borrower. If the portions so attributed to the borrower exceed the originating bank's or savings association's lending limit, the loan may be treated as nonconforming subject to § 32.6, rather than a violation, if:

(*1*) The originating national bank or savings association had a valid and unconditional participation agreement with a participant or participants that was sufficient to reduce the loan to within the originating bank's or savings association's lending limit;

(*2*) The participant reconfirmed its participation and the originating national bank or savings association had no knowledge of any information that would permit the participant to withhold its participation; and

(*3*) The participation was to be funded by close of business of the originating national bank's or savings association's next business day; and

(vii) That portion of one or more loans or extensions of credit, not to exceed 10 percent of capital and surplus, with respect to which the national bank or savings association has purchased protection in the form of a single-name credit derivative that meets the requirements of § 32.2(m)(1) through (7) from an eligible protection provider if the reference obligor is the same legal entity as the borrower in the loan or extension of credit and the maturity of the protection purchased equals or exceeds the maturity of the loan or extension of credit.

(r) *Person* means an individual; sole proprietorship; partnership; joint venture; association; trust; estate; business trust; corporation; limited liability company; not-for-profit corporation; sovereign government or agency, instrumentality, or political subdivision thereof; or any similar entity or organization; and

(s) *Qualifying central counterparty* has the same meaning as this term has in 12 CFR 3.2.

(t) *Qualifying commitment to lend* means a legally binding written commitment to lend that, when combined with all other outstanding loans and qualifying commitments to a borrower, was within the national bank's or savings association's lending limit when entered into, and has not been disqualified.

(1) In determining whether a commitment is within the national bank's or savings association's lending limit when made, the bank or savings association may deduct from the amount of the commitment the amount of any legally binding loan participation commitments that are issued concurrent

with the bank's or savings association's commitment and that would be excluded from the definition of "loan or extension of credit" under paragraph (q)(2)(vi) of this section.

(2) If the national bank or savings association subsequently chooses to make an additional loan and that subsequent loan, together with all outstanding loans and qualifying commitments to a borrower, exceeds the bank's or savings association's applicable lending limit at that time, the bank's or savings association's qualifying commitments to the borrower that exceed the bank's or savings association's lending limit at that time are deemed to be permanently disqualified, beginning with the most recent qualifying commitment and proceeding in reverse chronological order. When a commitment is disqualified, the entire commitment is disqualified and the disqualified commitment is no longer considered a "loan or extension of credit." Advances of funds under a disqualified or non-qualifying commitment may only be made to the extent that the advance, together with all other outstanding loans to the borrower, do not exceed the bank's or savings association's lending limit at the time of the advance, calculated pursuant to § 32.4.

(u) *Qualifying master netting agreement* has the same meaning as this term has in 12 CFR 3.2.

(v) *Readily marketable collateral* means financial instruments and bullion that are salable under ordinary market conditions with reasonable promptness at a fair market value determined by quotations based upon actual transactions on an auction or similarly available daily bid and ask price market.

(w) *Readily marketable staple* means an article of commerce, agriculture, or industry, such as wheat and other grains, cotton, wool, and basic metals such as tin, copper and lead, in the form of standardized interchangeable units, that is easy to sell in a market with sufficiently frequent price quotations.

(1) An article comes within this definition if—

(i) The exact price is easy to determine; and

(ii) The staple itself is easy to sell at any time at a price that would not be considerably less than the amount at which it is valued as collateral.

(2) Whether an article qualifies as a readily marketable staple is determined on the basis of the conditions existing at the time the loan or extension of credit that is secured by the staples is made.

(x) *Residential housing units* mean:

(1) Homes (including a dwelling unit in a multi-family residential property such as a condominium or a cooperative);

(2) Combinations of homes and business property (*i.e.*, a home used in part for business);

(3) Other real estate used for primarily residential purposes other than a home (but which may include homes);

(4) Combinations of such real estate and business property involving only minor business use (*i.e.*, where no more than 20 percent of the total appraised value of the real estate is attributable to the business use);

(5) Farm residences and combinations of farm residences and commercial farm real estate;

(6) Property to be improved by the construction of such structures; or

(7) Leasehold interests in the above real estate.

(y) *Residential real estate loan* means a loan or extension of credit that is secured by 1–4 family residential real estate.

(z) *Sale of Federal funds* means any transaction between depository institutions involving the transfer of immediately available funds resulting from credits to deposit balances at Federal Reserve Banks, or from credits to new or existing deposit balances due from a correspondent depository institution.

(aa) *Securities financing transaction means* a repurchase agreement, reverse repurchase agreement, securities lending transaction, or securities borrowing transaction.

(bb) *Security* has the same meaning as in section 3(a)(10) of the Securities Exchange Act of 1934 (15 U.S.C. 78c(a)(10)).

(cc) *Small business loan* means a loan or extension of credit "secured by nonfarm nonresidential properties" or "a commercial or industrial loan'' as defined in the instructions for preparation of the Consolidated Report of Condition and Income.

(dd) *Small farm loans or extensions of credit* means ''loans to small farms,'' as defined in the instructions for preparation of the Consolidated Report of Condition and Income.

(ee) *Standby letter of credit* means any letter of credit, or similar arrangement, that represents an obligation to the beneficiary on the part of the issuer:

(1) To repay money borrowed by or advanced to or for the account of the account party;

(2) To make payment on account of any indebtedness undertaken by the account party; or

(3) To make payment on account of any default by the account party in the performance of an obligation.

[60 FR 8532, Feb. 15, 1995, as amended at 63 FR 15746, Apr. 1, 1998; 66 FR 31120, June 11, 2001; 66 FR 55072, Nov. 1, 2001; 69 FR 51357, Aug. 19, 2004; 77 FR 37275, June 21, 2012; 77 FR 37277, June 21, 2012; 78 FR 37944, June 25, 2013; 79 FR 11312, Feb. 28, 2014; 80 FR 28479, May 18, 2015]

§32.3 Lending limits.

(a) *Combined general limit.* A national bank's or savings association's total outstanding loans and extensions of credit to one borrower may not exceed 15 percent of the bank's or savings association's capital and surplus, plus an additional 10 percent of the bank's or savings association's capital and surplus, if the amount that exceeds the bank's or savings association's 15 percent general limit is fully secured by readily marketable collateral, as defined in §32.2(v). To qualify for the additional 10 percent limit, the bank or savings association must perfect a security interest in the collateral under applicable law and the collateral must have a current market value at all times of at least 100 percent of the amount of the loan or extension of credit that exceeds the bank's or savings association's 15 percent general limit.

(b) *Loans subject to special lending limits.* The following loans or extensions of credit are subject to the lending limits set forth below. When loans and extensions of credit qualify for more than one special lending limit, the special limits are cumulative.

(1) *Loans secured by bills of lading or warehouse receipts covering readily marketable staples.* (i) A national bank's or savings association's loans or extensions of credit to one borrower secured by bills of lading, warehouse receipts, or similar documents transferring or securing title to readily marketable staples, as defined in §32.2(w), may not exceed 35 percent of the bank's or savings association's capital and surplus in addition to the amount allowed under the bank's or savings association's combined general limit. The market value of the staples securing the loan must at all times equal at least 115 percent of the amount of the outstanding loan that exceeds the bank's or savings association's combined general limit.

(ii) Staples that qualify for this special limit must be nonperishable, may be refrigerated or frozen, and must be fully covered by insurance if such insurance is customary. Whether a staple is non-perishable must be determined on a case-by-case basis because of differences in handling and storing commodities.

(iii) This special limit applies to a loan or extension of credit arising from a single transaction or secured by the same staples, provided that the duration of the loan or extension of credit is:

(A) Not more than ten months if secured by nonperishable staples; or

(B) Not more than six months if secured by refrigerated or frozen staples.

(iv) The holder of the warehouse receipts, order bills of lading, documents qualifying as documents of title under the Uniform Commercial Code, or other similar documents, must have control and be able to obtain immediate possession of the staple so that the bank or savings association is able to sell the underlying staples and promptly transfer title and possession to a purchaser if default should occur on a loan secured by such documents. The existence of a brief notice period, or similar procedural requirements under applicable law, for the disposal of the collateral will not affect the eligibility of the instruments for this special limit.

(A) Field warehouse receipts are an acceptable form of collateral when issued by a duly bonded and licensed grain elevator or warehouse having exclusive possession and control of the staples even though the grain elevator or warehouse is maintained on the premises of the owner of the staples.

(B) Warehouse receipts issued by the borrower-owner that is a grain elevator or warehouse company, duly-bonded and licensed and regularly inspected by state or Federal authorities, may be considered eligible collateral under this provision only when the receipts are registered with an independent registrar whose consent is required before the staples may be withdrawn from the warehouse.

(2) *Discount of installment consumer paper*. (i) A national bank's or savings association's loans and extensions of credit to one borrower that arise from the discount of negotiable or nonnegotiable installment consumer paper, as defined at §32.2(f), that carries a full recourse endorsement or unconditional guarantee by the person selling the paper, may not exceed 10 percent of the bank's or savings association's capital and surplus in addition to the amount allowed under the bank's or savings association's combined general limit. An unconditional guarantee may be in the form of a repurchase agreement or separate guarantee agreement. A condition reasonably within the power of the bank or savings association to perform, such as the repossession of collateral, will not make conditional an otherwise unconditional guarantee.

(ii) Where the seller of the paper offers only partial recourse to the bank or savings association, the lending limits of this section apply to the obligation of the seller to the bank or savings association, which is measured by the total amount of paper the seller may be obligated to repurchase or has guaranteed.

(iii) Where the bank or savings association is relying primarily upon the maker of the paper for payment of the loans or extensions of credit and not upon any full or partial recourse endorsement or guarantee by the seller of the paper, the lending limits of this section apply only to the maker. The bank or savings association must substantiate its reliance on the maker with—

(A) Records supporting the bank's or savings association's independent credit analysis of the maker's ability to repay the loan or extension of credit, maintained by the bank or savings association or by a third party that is contractually obligated to make those records available for examination purposes; and

(B) A written certification by an officer of the bank or savings association authorized by the bank's or savings association's board of directors or any designee of that officer, that the bank or savings association is relying primarily upon the maker to repay the loan or extension of credit.

(iv) Where paper is purchased in substantial quantities, the records, evaluation, and certification must be in a form appropriate for the class and quantity of paper involved. The bank or savings association may use sampling techniques, or other appropriate methods, to independently verify the reliability of the credit information supplied by the seller.

(3) *Loans secured by documents covering livestock*. (i) A national bank's or savings association's loans or extensions of credit to one borrower secured by shipping documents or instruments that transfer or secure title to or give a first lien on livestock may not exceed 10 percent of the bank's or savings association's capital and surplus in addition to the amount allowed under the bank's or savings association's combined general limit. The market value of the livestock securing the loan must at all times equal at least 115 percent of the amount of the outstanding loan that exceeds the bank's or savings association's combined general limit. For purposes of this subsection, the term "livestock" includes dairy and beef cattle, hogs, sheep, goats, horses, mules, poultry and fish, whether or not held for resale.

(ii) The bank or savings association must maintain in its files an inspection and valuation for the livestock pledged that is reasonably current, taking into account the nature and frequency of turnover of the livestock to which the documents relate, but in any case not more than 12 months old.

(iii) Under the laws of certain states, persons furnishing pasturage under a grazing contract may have a lien on the livestock for the amount due for pasturage. If a lien that is based on pasturage furnished by the lienor prior to the bank's or savings association's loan or extension of credit is assigned to the bank or savings association by a recordable instrument and protected against being defeated by some other lien or claim, by payment to a person other than the bank or savings association, or otherwise, it will qualify under this exception provided the amount of the perfected lien is at least equal to the amount of the loan and the value of the livestock is at no time less than 115 percent of the portion of the loan or extension of credit that exceeds the bank's or savings association's combined general limit. When the amount due under the grazing contract is dependent upon future performance, the resulting lien does not meet the requirements of the exception.

(4) *Loans secured by dairy cattle.* A national bank's or savings association's loans and extensions of credit to one borrower that arise from the discount by dealers in dairy cattle of paper given in payment for the cattle may not exceed 10 percent of the bank's or savings association's capital and surplus in addition to the amount allowed under the bank's or savings association's combined general limit. To qualify, the paper—

(i) Must carry the full recourse endorsement or unconditional guarantee of the seller; and

(ii) Must be secured by the cattle being sold, pursuant to liens that allow the bank or savings association to maintain a perfected security interest in the cattle under applicable law.

(5) *Additional advances to complete project financing pursuant to renewal of a qualifying commitment to lend.* A national bank or savings association may renew a qualifying commitment to lend, as defined by § 32.2(t), and complete funding under that commitment if all of the following criteria are met—

(i) The completion of funding is consistent with safe and sound banking practices and is made to protect the position of the bank or savings association;

(ii) The completion of funding will enable the borrower to complete the project for which the qualifying commitment to lend was made; and

(iii) The amount of the additional funding does not exceed the unfunded portion of the bank's or savings association's qualifying commitment to lend.

(c) *Loans not subject to the lending limits.* The following loans or extensions of credit are not subject to the lending limits of 12 U.S.C. 84, or 12 U.S.C. 1464(u), as applicable, of this part.

(1) *Loans arising from the discount of commercial or business paper.* (i) Loans or extensions of credit arising from the discount of negotiable commercial or business paper that evidences an obligation to the person negotiating the paper. The paper—

(A) Must be given in payment of the purchase price of commodities purchased for resale, fabrication of a product, or any other business purpose that may reasonably be expected to provide funds for payment of the paper; and

(B) Must bear the full recourse endorsement of the owner of the paper, except that paper discounted in connection with export transactions, that is transferred without recourse, or with limited recourse, must be supported by an assignment of appropriate insurance covering the political, credit, and transfer risks applicable to the paper, such as insurance provided by the Export-Import Bank.

(ii) A failure to pay principal or interest on commercial or business paper when due does not result in a loan or extension of credit to the maker or endorser of the paper; however, the amount of such paper thereafter must be counted in determining whether additional loans or extensions of credit to the same borrower may be made within the limits of 12 U.S.C. 84 or 12 U.S.C. 1464(u), as applicable, and this part.

(2) *Bankers' acceptances.* A national bank's or savings association's acceptance of drafts eligible for rediscount under 12 U.S.C. 372 and 373 or 12 U.S.C. 1464(c)(1)(M), as applicable, or a national bank's or savings association's purchase of acceptances created by

other banks or savings associations that are eligible for rediscount under those sections; but not including—

(i) A national bank's or savings association's acceptance of drafts ineligible for rediscount (which constitutes a loan by the bank or savings association to the customer for whom the acceptance was made, in the amount of the draft);

(ii) A national bank's or savings association's purchase of ineligible acceptances created by other banks or savings associations (which constitutes a loan from the purchasing bank or savings association to the accepting bank or savings association, in the amount of the purchase price); and

(iii) A national bank's or savings association's purchase of its own acceptances (which constitutes a loan to the bank's or savings association's customer for whom the acceptance was made, in the amount of the purchase price).

(3)(i) *Loans secured by U.S. obligations.* Loans or extensions of credit, or portions thereof, to the extent fully secured by the current market value of:

(A) Bonds, notes, certificates of indebtedness, or Treasury bills of the United States or by similar obligations fully guaranteed as to principal and interest by the United States;

(B) Loans to the extent guaranteed as to repayment of principal by the full faith and credit of the U.S. government, as set forth in paragraph (c)(4)(ii) of this section.

(ii) To qualify a loan or extension of credit under paragraph (c)(3)(i) of this section, the national bank or savings association must perfect a security interest in the collateral under applicable law.

(4) *Loans to or guaranteed by a Federal agency.* (i) Loans or extensions of credit to any department, agency, bureau, board, commission, or establishment of the United States or any corporation wholly owned directly or indirectly by the United States.

(ii) Loans or extensions of credit, including portions thereof, to the extent secured by unconditional takeout commitments or guarantees of any of the foregoing governmental entities. The commitment or guarantee—

(A) Must be payable in cash or its equivalent within 60 days after demand for payment is made;

(B) Is considered unconditional if the protection afforded the national bank or savings association is not substantially diminished or impaired if loss should result from factors beyond the bank's or savings association's control. Protection against loss is not materially diminished or impaired by procedural requirements, such as an agreement to pay on the obligation only in the event of default, including default over a specific period of time, a requirement that notification of default be given within a specific period after its occurrence, or a requirement of good faith on the part of the bank or savings association.

(5) *Loans to or guaranteed by general obligations of a State or political subdivision.* (i) A loan or extension of credit to a State or political subdivision that constitutes a general obligation of the State or political subdivision, as defined in part 1 of this chapter, and for which the lending national bank or savings association has an opinion of counsel or the opinion of that State Attorney General, or other State legal official with authority to opine on the obligation in question, that the loan or extension of credit is a valid and enforceable general obligation of the borrower; and

(ii) A loan or extension of credit, including portions thereof, to the extent guaranteed or secured by a general obligation of a State or political subdivision and for which the lending bank or savings association has an opinion of counsel or the opinion of that State Attorney General, or other State legal official with authority to opine on the guarantee or collateral in question, that the guarantee or collateral is a valid and enforceable general obligation of that public body.

(6) *Loans secured by segregated deposit accounts.* Loans or extensions of credit, including portions thereof, to the extent secured by a segregated deposit account in the lending national bank or savings association, provided a security interest in the deposit has been perfected under applicable law.

(i) Where the deposit is eligible for withdrawal before the secured loan matures, the bank or savings association must establish internal procedures to prevent release of the security without the lending bank's or savings association's prior consent.

(ii) A deposit that is denominated and payable in a currency other than that of the loan or extension of credit that it secures may be eligible for this exception if the currency is freely convertible to U.S. dollars.

(A) This exception applies to only that portion of the loan or extension of credit that is covered by the U.S. dollar value of the deposit.

(B) The lending bank or savings association must establish procedures to periodically revalue foreign currency deposits to ensure that the loan or extension of credit remains fully secured at all times.

(7) *Loans to financial institutions with the approval of the appropriate Federal banking agency.* Loans or extensions of credit to any financial institution or to any receiver, conservator, superintendent of banks, or other agent in charge of the business and property of a financial institution when an emergency situation exists and a national bank or savings association is asked to provide assistance to another financial institution, and the loan is approved by the appropriate Federal banking agency. For purposes of this paragraph, financial institution means a commercial bank, savings bank, trust company, savings association, or credit union.

(8) *Loans to the Student Loan Marketing Association.* Loans or extensions of credit to the Student Loan Marketing Association.

(9) *Loans to industrial development authorities.* A loan or extension of credit to an industrial development authority or similar public entity created to construct and lease a plant facility, including a health care facility, to an industrial occupant will be deemed a loan to the lessee, provided that—

(i) The national bank or savings association evaluates the creditworthiness of the industrial occupant before the loan is extended to the authority;

(ii) The authority's liability on the loan is limited solely to whatever interest it has in the particular facility;

(iii) The authority's interest is assigned to the bank or savings association as security for the loan or the industrial occupant issues a promissory note to the bank or savings association that provides a higher order of security than the assignment of a lease; and

(iv) The industrial occupant's lease rentals are assigned and paid directly to the bank or savings association.

(10) *Loans to leasing companies.* A loan or extension of credit to a leasing company for the purpose of purchasing equipment for lease will be deemed a loan to the lessee, provided that—

(i) The national bank or savings association evaluates the creditworthiness of the lessee before the loan is extended to the leasing corporation;

(ii) The loan is without recourse to the leasing corporation;

(iii) The bank or savings association is given a security interest in the equipment and in the event of default, may proceed directly against the equipment and the lessee for any deficiency resulting from the sale of the equipment;

(iv) The leasing corporation assigns all of its rights under the lease to the bank or savings association;

(v) The lessee's lease payments are assigned and paid to the bank or savings association; and

(vi) The lease terms are subject to the same limitations that would apply to a national bank or savings association acting as a lessor.

(11) *Credit Exposures arising from transactions financing certain government securities.* Credit exposures arising from securities financing transactions in which the securities financed are Type I securities, as defined in 12 CFR 1.2(j), in the case of national banks, or securities listed in section 5(c)(1)(C), (D), (E), and (F) of HOLA and general obligations of a state or subdivision as listed in section 5(c)(1)(H) of HOLA, 12 U.S.C. 1464(c)(1)(C), (D), (E), (F), and (H), in the case of savings associations.

(12) *Intraday credit exposures.* Intraday credit exposures arising from a derivative transaction or securities financing transaction.

(d) *Special lending limits for savings associations*—(1) *$500,000 exception for savings associations.* If a savings association's aggregate lending limitation calculated under paragraph (a) of this section is less than $500,000, notwithstanding this limitation in paragraph (a) of this section, such savings association may have total loans and extensions of credit, for any purpose, to one borrower outstanding at one time not to exceed $500,000.

(2) *Loans by savings associations to develop domestic residential housing units.* (i) Subject to paragraph (d)(2)(ii) of this section, a savings association may make loans to one borrower to develop domestic residential housing units, not to exceed the lesser of $30,000,000 or 30 percent of the savings association's unimpaired capital and unimpaired surplus, including all loans and extensions of credit subject to paragraph (a) of this section, *provided that:*

(A) The savings association is, and continues to be, in compliance with 12 CFR part 3, part 390, subpart Z, or part 324, as applicable;

(B) Upon application by a savings association under paragraph (d)(2)(iv) of this section, the appropriate Federal banking agency permits, subject to conditions it may impose, the savings association to use the higher limit set forth under this paragraph (d)(2)(i);

(C) The loans and extensions of credit made under this paragraph (d)(2)(i) to all borrowers do not, in aggregate, exceed 150 percent of the savings association's unimpaired capital and unimpaired surplus; and

(D) The loans and extensions of credit made under this paragraph (d)(2)(i) comply with the applicable loan-to-value requirements.

(ii) The authority of a savings association to make a loan or extension of credit under the exception in paragraph (d)(2)(i) of this section ceases immediately upon the association's failure to comply with any one of the requirements set forth in paragraph (d)(2)(i) of this section or any condition(s) set forth in an order issued by the appropriate Federal banking agency under paragraphs (d)(2)(i)(B) and (d)(2)(iv) of this section.

(iii) As used in this section, the term "*to develop*" includes each of the various phases necessary to produce housing units as an end product, such as acquisition, development and construction; development and construction; construction; rehabilitation; and conversion; and the term "*domestic*" includes units within the fifty states, the District of Columbia, Puerto Rico, the Virgin Islands, Guam, and the Pacific Islands;

(iv) *Procedures*—(A) *Federal savings associations*—(*1*) *Application.* A Federal savings association must submit an application to, and receive approval from, the appropriate OCC supervisory office before using the higher limit set forth under paragraph (d)(2)(i) of this section. The supervisory office may approve a completed application if it finds that approval is consistent with safety and soundness. To be deemed complete, the application must include:

(*i*) If applicable, certification that the savings association is an "eligible savings association";

(*ii*) A demonstration that the savings association meets the requirements of paragraphs (d)(2)(i)(A), (C), and (D) of this section;

(*iii*) A copy of a written resolution by a majority of the savings association's board of directors approving the use of the limits provided in paragraphs (d)(2)(i) of this section, and confirming the terms and conditions for use of this lending authority; and

(*iv*) A description of how the board will exercise its continuing responsibility to oversee the use of this lending authority.

(*2*) *Expedited review.* An application by an eligible savings association is deemed approved as of the 30th day after the application is received by the OCC, unless before that date the OCC informs the savings association it must obtain prior written approval from the OCC.

(B) *State savings associations.* A state savings association shall seek approval to use the higher limit set forth under paragraph (d)(2)(i) of this section from its appropriate Federal banking agency, under the rules and procedures established by the appropriate Federal banking agency.

(3) *Commercial paper and corporate debt securities.* In addition to the

amount allowed under the savings association's combined general limit, a savings association may invest up to 10 percent of unimpaired capital and unimpaired surplus in the obligations of one issuer evidenced by commercial paper or corporate debt securities that are, as of the date of purchase, investment grade.

[60 FR 8532, Feb. 15, 1995, as amended at 63 FR 15746, Apr. 1, 1998; 66 FR 31120, June 11, 2001; 66 FR 35072, Nov. 1, 2001; 77 FR 37277, June 21, 2012; 79 FR 11312, Feb. 28, 2014; 80 FR 28479, May 18, 2015]

§ 32.4 Calculation of lending limits.

(a) *Calculation date.* For purposes of determining compliance with 12 U.S.C. 84, and 12 U.S.C. 1464(u), as applicable, and this part, a national bank or savings association shall determine its lending limit as of the most recent of the following dates:

(1) The last day of the preceding calendar quarter; or

(2) The date on which there is a change in the bank's or savings association's capital category for purposes of 12 U.S.C. 1831o and 12 CFR 6.3 or 12 CFR 324.402, as applicable.

(b) *Effective date.* (1) A national bank's or savings association's lending limit calculated in accordance with paragraph (a)(1) of this section will be effective as of the earlier of the following dates:

(i) The date on which the bank's or savings association's Call Report is submitted; or

(ii) The date on which the bank's or savings association's Call Report is required to be submitted.

(2) A national bank's or savings association's lending limit calculated in accordance with paragraph (a)(2) of this section will be effective on the date that the limit is to be calculated.

(c) *More frequent calculations.* If the appropriate Federal banking agency determines for safety and soundness reasons that a national bank or savings association should calculate its lending limit more frequently than required by paragraph (a) of this section, the appropriate Federal banking agency may provide written notice to the national bank or savings association directing it to calculate its lending limit at a more frequent interval, and the national bank or savings association shall thereafter calculate its lending limit at that interval until further notice.

[63 FR 15746, Apr. 1, 1998, as amended at 77 FR 37278, June 21, 2012; 79 FR 11312, Feb. 28, 2014]

§ 32.5 Combination rules.

(a) *General rule.* Loans or extensions of credit to one borrower will be attributed to another person and each person will be deemed a borrower—

(1) When proceeds of a loan or extension of credit are to be used for the direct benefit of the other person, to the extent of the proceeds so used; or

(2) When a common enterprise is deemed to exist between the persons.

(b) *Direct benefit.* The proceeds of a loan or extension of credit to a borrower will be deemed to be used for the direct benefit of another person and will be attributed to the other person when the proceeds, or assets purchased with the proceeds, are transferred to another person, other than in a bona fide arm's length transaction where the proceeds are used to acquire property, goods, or services.

(c) *Common enterprise.* A common enterprise will be deemed to exist and loans to separate borrowers will be aggregated:

(1) When the expected source of repayment for each loan or extension of credit is the same for each borrower and neither borrower has another source of income from which the loan (together with the borrower's other obligations) may be fully repaid. An employer will not be treated as a source of repayment under this paragraph because of wages and salaries paid to an employee, unless the standards of paragraph (c)(2) of this section are met;

(2) When loans or extensions of credit are made—

(i) To borrowers who are related directly or indirectly through common control, including where one borrower is directly or indirectly controlled by another borrower; and

(ii) Substantial financial interdependence exists between or among the borrowers. Substantial financial interdependence is deemed to exist when 50 percent or more of one borrower's gross receipts or gross expenditures (on an annual basis) are derived from transactions with the other borrower. Gross receipts and expenditures include gross revenues/expenses, intercompany loans, dividends, capital contributions, and similar receipts or payments;

(3) When separate persons borrow from a national bank or savings association to acquire a business enterprise of which those borrowers will own more than 50 percent of the voting securities or voting interests, in which case a common enterprise is deemed to exist between the borrowers for purposes of combining the acquisition loans; or

(4) When the appropriate Federal banking agency determines, based upon an evaluation of the facts and circumstances of particular transactions, that a common enterprise exists.

(d) *Special rule for loans to a corporate group*. (1) Loans or extensions of credit by a national bank or savings association to a corporate group may not exceed 50 percent of the bank's or savings association's capital and surplus. This limitation applies only to loans subject to the combined general limit. A corporate group includes a person and all of its subsidiaries. For purposes of this paragraph, a corporation or a limited liability company is a subsidiary of a person if the person owns or beneficially owns directly or indirectly more than 50 percent of the voting securities or voting interests of the corporation or company.

(2) Except as provided in paragraph (d)(1) of this section, loans or extensions of credit to a person and its subsidiary, or to different subsidiaries of a person, are not combined unless either the direct benefit or the common enterprise test is met.

(e) *Special rules for loans to partnerships, joint ventures, and associations*—(1) *Partnership loans*. Loans or extensions of credit to a partnership, joint venture, or association are deemed to be loans or extensions of credit to each member of the partnership, joint venture, or association. This rule does not apply to limited partners in limited partnerships or to members of joint ventures or associations if the partners or members, by the terms of the partnership or membership agreement, are not held generally liable for the debts or actions of the partnership, joint venture, or association, and those provisions are valid under applicable law.

(2) *Loans to partners*. (i) Loans or extensions of credit to members of a partnership, joint venture, or association are not attributed to the partnership, joint venture, or association unless either the direct benefit or the common enterprise tests are met. Both the direct benefit and common enterprise tests are met between a member of a partnership, joint venture or association and such partnership, joint venture or association, when loans or extensions of credit are made to the member to purchase an interest in the partnership, joint venture or association.

(ii) Loans or extensions of credit to members of a partnership, joint venture, or association are not attributed to other members of the partnership, joint venture, or association unless either the direct benefit or common enterprise test is met.

(f) *Loans to foreign governments, their agencies, and instrumentalities*—(1) *Aggregation*. Loans and extensions of credit to foreign governments, their agencies, and instrumentalities will be aggregated with one another only if the loans or extensions of credit fail to meet either the means test or the purpose test at the time the loan or extension of credit is made.

(i) The means test is satisfied if the borrower has resources or revenue of its own sufficient to service its debt obligations. If the government's support (excluding guarantees by a central government of the borrower's debt) exceeds the borrower's annual revenues from other sources, it will be presumed that the means test has not been satisfied.

(ii) The purpose test is satisfied if the purpose of the loan or extension of credit is consistent with the purposes of the borrower's general business.

(2) *Documentation*. In order to show that the means and purpose tests have been satisfied, a national bank or savings association must, at a minimum, retain in its files the following items:

(i) A statement (accompanied by supporting documentation) describing the legal status and the degree of financial and operational autonomy of the borrowing entity;

(ii) Financial statements for the borrowing entity for a minimum of three years prior to the date the loan or extension of credit was made or for each year that the borrowing entity has been in existence, if less than three;

(iii) Financial statements for each year the loan or extension of credit is outstanding;

(iv) The national bank's or savings association's assessment of the borrower's means of servicing the loan or extension of credit, including specific reasons in support of that assessment. The assessment shall include an analysis of the borrower's financial history, its present and projected economic and financial performance, and the significance of any financial support provided to the borrower by third parties, including the borrower's central government; and

(v) A loan agreement or other written statement from the borrower which clearly describes the purpose of the loan or extension of credit. The written representation will ordinarily constitute sufficient evidence that the purpose test has been satisfied. However, when, at the time the funds are disbursed, the bank or savings association knows or has reason to know of other information suggesting that the borrower will use the proceeds in a manner inconsistent with the written representation, it may not, without further inquiry, accept the representation.

(3) *Restructured loans*—(i) *Non-combination rule.* Notwithstanding paragraphs (a) through (e) of this section, when previously outstanding loans and other extensions of credit to a foreign government, its agencies, and instrumentalities (i.e., public-sector obligors) that qualified for a separate lending limit under paragraph (f)(1) of this section are consolidated under a central obligor in a qualifying restructuring, such loans will not be aggregated and attributed to the central obligor. This includes any substitution in named obligors, solely because of the restructuring. Such loans (other than loans originally attributed to the central obligor in their own right) will not be considered obligations of the central obligor and will continue to be attributed to the original public-sector obligor for purposes of the lending limit.

(ii) *Qualifying restructuring.* Loans and other extensions of credit to a foreign government, its agencies, and instrumentalities will qualify for the non-combination process under paragraph (f)(3)(i) of this section only if they are restructured in a sovereign debt restructuring approved by the appropriate Federal banking agency, upon request by a national bank or savings association for application of the non combination rule. The factors that the appropriate Federal banking agency will use in making this determination include, but are not limited to, the following:

(A) Whether the restructuring involves a substantial portion of the total commercial bank loans outstanding to the foreign government, its agencies, and instrumentalities;

(B) Whether the restructuring involves a substantial number of the foreign country's external commercial bank creditors;

(C) Whether the restructuring and consolidation under a central obligor is being done primarily to facilitate external debt management; and

(D) Whether the restructuring includes features of debt or debt-service reduction.

(iii) *50 percent aggregate limit.* With respect to any case in which the non-combination process under paragraph (f)(3)(i) of this section applies, a national bank's or savings association's loans and other extensions of credit to a foreign government, its agencies and instrumentalities, (including restructured debt) shall not exceed, in the aggregate, 50 percent of the bank's or savings association's capital and surplus.

[60 FR 8532, Feb. 15, 1995, as amended at 77 FR 37279, June 21, 2012]

§ 32.6 Nonconforming loans and extensions of credit.

(a) A loan or extension of credit, within a national bank's or savings association's legal lending limit when made, will not be deemed a violation but will be treated as nonconforming if the loan or extension of credit is no longer in conformity with the bank's or savings association's lending limit because—

(1) The bank's or savings association's capital has declined, borrowers have subsequently merged or formed a common enterprise, lenders have merged, or the lending limit or capital rules have changed;

(2) Collateral securing the loan to satisfy the requirements of a lending limit exception has declined in value; or

(3) In the case of a credit exposure arising from a transaction identified in § 32.9(a) and measured by the Model Method specified in § 32.9(b)(1)(i) or § 32.9 (c)(1)(i), the Current Exposure Method specified in § 32.9(b)(1)(iii), or the Basel Collateral Haircut Method specified in § 32.9(c)(1)(iii), the credit exposure subject to the lending limits of 12 U.S.C. 84 or 12 U.S.C. 1464(u), as applicable, or this part increases after execution of the transaction.

(b) A national bank or savings association must use reasonable efforts to bring a loan or extension of credit that is nonconforming as a result of paragraph (a)(1) or (a)(3) of this section into conformity with the bank's or savings association's lending limit unless to do so would be inconsistent with safe and sound banking practices.

(c) A national bank or savings association must bring a loan that is nonconforming as a result of circumstances described in paragraph (a)(2) of this section into conformity with the bank's or savings association's lending limit within 30 calendar days, except when judicial proceedings, regulatory actions or other extraordinary circumstances beyond the bank's or savings association's control prevent it from taking action.

[77 FR 37279, June 21, 2012, as amended at 78 FR 37944, June 25, 2013]

§ 32.7 Residential real estate loans, small business loans, and small farm loans ("Supplemental Lending Limits Program").

(a) *Residential real estate, small business, and small farm loans.* (1) In addition to the amount that a national bank or savings association may lend to one borrower under § 32.3, an eligible national bank or eligible savings association may make residential real estate loans or extensions of credit to one borrower in the lesser of the following two amounts: 10 percent of its capital and surplus; or the percent of its capital and surplus, in excess of 15 percent, that a State bank or savings association is permitted to lend under the State lending limit that is available for residential real estate loans or unsecured loans in the State where the main office of the national bank or savings association is located. Any such loan or extension of credit must be secured by a perfected first-lien security interest in 1–4 family real estate in an amount that does not exceed 80 percent of the appraised value of the collateral at the time the loan or extension of credit is made.

(2) In addition to the amount that a national bank or savings association may lend to one borrower under § 32.3, an eligible national bank or eligible savings association may make small business loans or extensions of credit to one borrower in the lesser of the following two amounts: 10 percent of its capital and surplus; or the percent of its capital and surplus, in excess of 15 percent, that a state bank is permitted to lend under the state lending limit that is available for small business loans or unsecured loans in the state where the main office of the national bank or home office of the savings association is located.

(3) In addition to the amount that a national bank or savings association may lend to one borrower under § 32.3, an eligible national bank or eligible savings association may make small farm loans or extensions of credit to one borrower in the lesser of the following two amounts: 10 percent of its capital and surplus; or the percent of its capital and surplus, in excess of 15 percent, that a State bank or savings association is permitted to lend under the State lending limit that is available for small farm loans or unsecured loans in the State where the main office of the national bank or savings association is located.

(4) The total outstanding amount of a national bank's or savings association's loans and extensions of credit to one borrower made under § 32.3(a) and (b), together with loans and extensions

of credit to the borrower made pursuant to paragraphs (a)(1), (2), and (3) of this section, shall not exceed 25 percent of the bank's or savings association's capital and surplus.

(5) The total outstanding amount of a national bank's or savings association's loans and extensions of credit to all of its borrowers made pursuant to the supplemental lending limits provided in paragraphs (a)(1), (2), and (3) of this section may not exceed 100 percent of the bank's or savings association's capital and surplus.

(b) *Application process.* An eligible national bank or eligible savings association must submit an application to, and receive approval from, its supervisory office before using the supplemental lending limits in paragraphs (a)(1), (2), and (3) of this section. The supervisory office may approve a completed application if it finds that approval is consistent with safety and soundness. To be deemed complete, the application must include:

(1) Certification that the bank or savings association is an "eligible bank" or "eligible savings association";

(2) Citations to relevant State laws or regulations;

(3) A copy of a written resolution by a majority of the bank's or savings association's board of directors approving the use of the limits provided in paragraphs (a)(1), (2), and (3) of this section, and confirming the terms and conditions for use of this lending authority; and

(4) A description of how the board will exercise its continuing responsibility to oversee the use of this lending authority.

(c) *Duration of approval.* Except as provided in paragraph (d) of this section, a bank or savings association that has received appropriate Federal banking agency approval may continue to make loans and extensions of credit under the supplemental lending limits in paragraphs (a)(1), (2), and (3) of this section, provided the bank or savings association remains an "eligible bank" or "eligible savings association."

(d) *Discretionary termination of authority.* The appropriate Federal banking agency may rescind a bank's or savings association's authority to use the supplemental lending limits in paragraphs (a)(1), (2), and (3) of this section based upon concerns about credit quality, undue concentrations in the bank's or savings association's portfolio of residential real estate, small business, or small farm loans, or concerns about the bank's or savings association's overall credit risk management systems and controls. The bank or savings association must cease making new loans or extensions of credit in reliance on the supplemental lending limits upon receipt of written notice from the appropriate Federal banking agency that its authority has been rescinded.

(e) *Existing loans.* Any loans or extensions of credit made by a bank or savings association under the supplemental lending limits in paragraphs (a)(1), (2), and (3) of this section, that were in compliance with this section when made, will not be deemed a lending limit violation and will not be treated as nonconforming under §32.6.

[66 FR 31120, June 11, 2001, as amended at 69 FR 32436, June 10, 2004; 69 FR 51357, Aug. 19, 2004; 72 FR 31444, June 7, 2007; 77 FR 37279, June 21, 2012; 80 FR 28479, May 18, 2015]

§32.8 Temporary funding arrangements in emergency situations.

In addition to the amount that a national bank or savings association may lend to one borrower under §32.3 of this part, an eligible bank or eligible savings association with the written approval of the appropriate Federal banking agency may make loans and extensions of credit to one borrower subject to a special temporary lending limit established by the appropriate Federal banking agency, where the appropriate Federal banking agency determines that such loans and extensions of credit are essential to address an emergency situation, such as critical financial markets stability, will be of short duration, will be reduced in amount in a timeframe and manner acceptable to the appropriate Federal banking agency, and do not present unacceptable risk. In granting approval for such a special temporary lending limit, the appropriate Federal banking agency will impose supervisory oversight and reporting measures that it determines are appropriate to monitor compliance with the foregoing standards as set forth in this paragraph.

[73 FR 14924, Mar. 20, 2008, as amended at 77 FR 37280, June 21, 2012]

§ 32.9 Credit exposure arising from derivative and securities financing transactions.

(a) *Scope.* This section sets forth the rules for calculating the credit exposure arising from a derivative transaction or a securities financing transaction entered into by a national bank or savings association for purposes of determining the bank's or savings association's lending limit pursuant to 12 U.S.C. 84 or 12 U.S.C. 1464(u), as applicable, and this part.

(b) *Derivative transactions*—(1) *Non-credit derivatives.* Subject to paragraphs (b)(2), (b)(3) and (b)(4) of this section, a national bank or savings association shall calculate the credit exposure to a counterparty arising from a derivative transaction by one of the following methods. Subject to paragraph (b)(4) of this section, a national bank or savings association shall use the same method for calculating counterparty credit exposure arising from all of its derivative transactions.

(i) *Model Method*—(A) *Credit exposure.* The credit exposure of a derivative transaction under the Internal Model Method shall equal the sum of the current credit exposure of the derivative transaction and the potential future credit exposure of the derivative transaction.

(B) *Calculation of current credit exposure.* A bank or savings association shall determine its current credit exposure by the mark-to-market value of the derivative contract. If the mark-to-market value is positive, then the current credit exposure equals that mark-to-market value. If the mark to market value is zero or negative, than the current credit exposure is zero.

(C) *Calculation of potential future credit exposure.* (*1*) A bank or savings association shall calculate its potential future credit exposure by using either:

(*i*) An internal model the use of which has been approved in writing for purposes of 12 CFR 3.132(d) or 324.132(d), as appropriate, provided that the bank or savings association provides prior written notice to the appropriate Federal banking agency of its use for purposes of this section; or

(*ii*) Any other appropriate model the use of which has been approved in writing for purposes of this section by the appropriate Federal banking agency.

(*2*) Any substantive revisions to a model made after the bank or savings association has provided notice of the use of the model to the appropriate Federal banking agency pursuant to paragraph (b)(1)(i)(C)(*1*)(*i*) of this section or after the appropriate Federal banking agency has approved the use of the model pursuant to paragraph (b)(1)(i)(C)(*1*)(*ii*) of this section must be approved by the agency before a bank or savings association may use the revised model for purposes of this part.

(D) *Net credit exposure.* A bank or savings association that calculates its credit exposure by using the Internal Model Method pursuant to this paragraph (b)(1)(i) may net credit exposures of derivative transactions arising under the same qualifying master netting agreement.

(ii) *Conversion Factor Matrix Method.* The credit exposure arising from a derivative transaction under the Conversion Factor Matrix Method shall equal and remain fixed at the potential future credit exposure of the derivative transaction which shall equal the product of the notional amount of the derivative transaction and a fixed multiplicative factor determined by reference to Table 1 of this section.

TABLE 1—CONVERSION FACTOR MATRIX FOR CALCULATING POTENTIAL FUTURE CREDIT EXPOSURE [1]

Original maturity [2]	Interest rate	Foreign exchange rate and gold	Equity	Other [3] (includes commodities and precious metals except gold)
1 year or less	.015	.015	.20	.06
Over 1 to 3 years	.03	.03	.20	.18
Over 3 to 5 years	.06	.06	.20	.30
Over 5 to 10 years	.12	.12	.20	.60

TABLE 1—CONVERSION FACTOR MATRIX FOR CALCULATING POTENTIAL FUTURE CREDIT EXPOSURE [1]—Continued

Original maturity [2]	Interest rate	Foreign exchange rate and gold	Equity	Other [3] (includes commodities and precious metals except gold)
Over ten years	.30	.30	.20	1.0

[1] For an OTC derivative contract with multiple exchanges of principal, the conversion factor is multiplied by the number of remaining payments in the derivative contract.

[2] For an OTC derivative contract that is structured such that on specified dates any outstanding exposure is settled and the terms are reset so that the market value of the contract is zero, the remaining maturity equals the time until the next reset date. For an interest rate derivative contract with a remaining maturity of greater than one year that meets these criteria, the minimum conversion factor is 0.005.

[3] Transactions not explicitly covered by any other column in the Table are to be treated as "Other."

(iii) *Current Exposure Method.* The credit exposure arising from a derivative transaction (other than a credit derivative transaction) under the Current Exposure Method shall be calculated pursuant to 12 CFR 3.132(c)(5), (6), and (7) or 324.132(c)(5), (6), and (7), as appropriate.

(2) *Credit Derivatives*—(i) *Counterparty exposure*—(A) *In general.* Notwithstanding paragraph (b)(1) of this section and subject to paragraph (b)(2)(i)(B) of this section, a national bank or savings association that uses the Conversion Factor Matrix Method or the Current Exposure Method, or that uses the Model Method without entering an effective margining arrangement as defined in § 32.2(l), shall calculate the counterparty credit exposure arising from credit derivatives entered by the bank or savings association by adding the net notional value of all protection purchased from the counterparty on each reference entity.

(B) *Special rule for certain effective margining arrangements.* A bank or savings association must add the EMA threshold amount to the counterparty credit exposure arising from credit derivatives calculated under the Model Method. The *EMA threshold* is the amount under an effective margining arrangement with respect to which the counterparty is not required to post variation margin to fully collateralize the amount of the bank's or savings association's net credit exposure to the counterparty.

(ii) *Reference entity exposure.* A national bank or savings association shall calculate the credit exposure to a reference entity arising from credit derivatives entered into by the bank or savings association by adding the net notional value of all protection sold on the reference entity. A bank or savings association may reduce its exposure to a reference entity by the amount of any eligible credit derivative purchased on that reference entity from an eligible protection provider.

(3) *Special rule for central counterparties.* (i) In addition to amounts calculated under § 32.9(b)(1) and (2), the measure of counterparty exposure to a central counterparty shall also include the sum of the initial margin posted by the bank or savings association, plus any contributions made by it to a guaranty fund at the time such contribution is made.

(ii) Paragraph (b)(3)(i) of this section does not apply to a national bank or saving association that uses an internal model pursuant to paragraph (b)(1)(i) of this section if such model reflects the initial margin and any contributions to a guaranty fund.

(4) *Mandatory or alternative method.* The appropriate Federal banking agency may in its discretion require or permit a national bank or savings association to use a specific method or methods set forth in paragraph (b)(1) of this section to calculate the credit exposure arising from all derivative transactions or any specific, or category of, derivative transactions if it finds, in its discretion, that such method is consistent with the safety and soundness of the bank or savings association.

(c) *Securities financing transactions*—(1) *In general.* Except as provided by paragraph (c)(2) of this section, a national bank or savings association shall calculate the credit exposure arising from a securities financing transaction by one of the following methods. A national bank or savings association shall use the same method for calculating credit exposure arising from all of its securities financing transactions.

(i) *Model Method.* (A) A national bank or savings association may calculate the credit exposure of a securities financing transaction by using either:

(*1*) An internal model the use of which has been approved in writing by the appropriate Federal banking agency for purposes of 12 CFR 3.132(b) or 324.132(b), as appropriate, provided the bank or savings association provides prior written notice to the appropriate Federal banking agency of its use for purposes of this section; or

(*2*) Any other appropriate model the use of which has been approved in writing for purposes of this section by the appropriate Federal banking agency.

(B) Any substantive revisions to a model made after the bank or savings association has provided notice of the use of the model to the appropriate Federal banking agency pursuant to paragraph (c)(1)(i)(A)(*1*) of this section or after the appropriate Federal banking agency has approved the use of the model pursuant to paragraph (c)(1)(i)(A)(*2*) of this section must be approved by the agency before a bank or savings association may use the revised model for purposes of part 32.

(ii) *Basic Method.* A national bank or savings association may calculate the credit exposure of a securities financing transaction as follows:

(A) *Repurchase agreement.* The credit exposure arising from a repurchase agreement shall equal and remain fixed at the market value at execution of the transaction of the securities transferred to the other party less cash received.

(B) *Securities lending— (1) Cash collateral transactions.* The credit exposure arising from a securities lending transaction where the collateral is cash shall equal and remain fixed at the market value at execution of the transaction of securities transferred less cash received.

(*2*) *Non-cash collateral transactions.* The credit exposure arising from a securities lending transaction where the collateral is other securities shall equal and remain fixed as the product of the higher of the two haircuts associated with the two securities, as determined in Table 2 of this section, and the higher of the two par values of the securities. Where more than one security is provided as collateral, the applicable haircut is the higher of the haircut associated with the security lent and the notional-weighted average of the haircuts associated with the securities provided as collateral.

(C) *Reverse repurchase agreements.* The credit exposure arising from a reverse repurchase agreement shall equal and remain fixed as the product of the haircut associated with the collateral received, as determined in Table 2 of this section, and the amount of cash transferred.

(D) *Securities borrowing—(1) Cash collateral transactions.* The credit exposure arising from a securities borrowed transaction where the collateral is cash shall equal and remain fixed as the product of the haircut on the collateral received, as determined in Table 2 of this section, and the amount of cash transferred to the other party.

(*2*) *Non-cash collateral transactions.* The credit exposure arising from a securities borrowed transaction where the collateral is other securities shall equal and remain fixed as the product of the higher of the two haircuts associated with the two securities, as determined in Table 2 of this section, and the higher of the two par values of the securities. Where more than one security is provided as collateral, the applicable haircut is the higher of the haircut associated with the security borrowed and the notional-weighted average of the haircuts associated with the securities provided as collateral.

TABLE 2—COLLATERAL HAIRCUTS

SOVEREIGN ENTITIES		
	Residual maturity	Haircut without currency mismatch [1]

TABLE 2—COLLATERAL HAIRCUTS—Continued

OECD Country Risk Classification[2] 0–1	≤1 year	0.005.
	>1 year, ≤5 years	0.02.
	>5 years	0.04.
OECD Country Risk Classification 2–3	≤1 year	0.01.
	>1 year, ≤5 years	0.03.
	>5 years	0.06.
CORPORATE AND MUNICIPAL BONDS THAT ARE BANK-ELIGIBLE INVESTMENTS		
	Residual maturity for debt securities	Haircut without currency mismatch
All	≤1 year	0.02.
All	>1 year, ≤5 years	0.06.
All	>5 years	0.12.
OTHER ELIGIBLE COLLATERAL		
Main index[3] equities (including convertible bonds)		0.15.
Other publicly-traded equities (including convertible bonds)		0.25.
Mutual funds		Highest haircut applicable to any security in which the fund can invest.
Cash collateral held		0.

[1] In cases where the currency denomination of the collateral differs from the currency denomination of the credit transaction, an additional 8 percent haircut will apply.

[2] OECD Country Risk Classification means the country risk classification as defined in Article 25 of the OECD's February 2011 Arrangement on Officially Supported Export Credits Arrangement.

[3] Main index means the Standard & Poor's 500 Index, the FTSE All-World Index, and any other index for which the covered company can demonstrate to the satisfaction of the Federal Reserve that the equities represented in the index have comparable liquidity, depth of market, and size of bid-ask spreads as equities in the Standard & Poor's 500 Index and FTSE All-World Index.

(iii) *Basel Collateral Haircut Method.* A national bank or savings association may calculate the credit exposure of a securities financing transaction pursuant to 12 CFR 3.132(b)(2)(i) and (ii) or 324.132(b)(2)(i) and (ii), as appropriate.

(2) *Mandatory or alternative method.* The appropriate Federal banking agency may in its discretion require or permit a national bank or savings association to use a specific method or methods set forth in paragraph (c)(1) of this section to calculate the credit exposure arising from all securities financing transactions or any specific, or category of, securities financing transactions if the appropriate Federal banking agency finds, in its discretion, that such method is consistent with the safety and soundness of the bank or savings association.

[77 FR 37280, June 21, 2012, as amended at 78 FR 37944, June 25, 2013; 79 FR 11312, Feb. 28, 2014]

APPENDIX A TO PART 32—INTERPRETATIONS

Section 1. Interrelation of General Limitation With Exception for Loans To Develop Domestic Residential Housing Units

1. The §32.3(d)(2) exception for loans to one borrower to develop domestic residential housing units is characterized in the regulation as an "alternative" limit. This exceptional $30,000,000 or 30 percent limitation does not operate in addition to the 15 percent General Limitation or the 10 percent additional amount a savings association may loan to one borrower secured by readily marketable collateral, but serves as the uppermost limitation on a savings association's lending to any one person once a savings association employs this exception.

Example: Savings Association A's lending limitation as calculated under the 15 percent General Limitation is $800, 000. If Savings Association A lends Y $800,000 for commercial purposes, Savings Association A cannot lend Y an additional $1,600,000, or 30 percent of capital and surplus, to develop residential housing units under the paragraph §32.3(d)(2) exception. The §32.3(d)(2) exception operates as the uppermost limitation on all lending to one borrower (for savings associations that may employ this exception) and includes any amounts loaned to the same borrower under the General Limitation. Savings Association A, therefore, may lend only an additional $800,000 to Y, provided § 32.3(d)(2) prerequisites have been met. The amount loaned under the authority of the General Limitation ($800,000), when added to the amount loaned under the exception ($800,000), yields a sum that does not exceed the 30 percent uppermost limitation ($1,600,000).

2. a. This result does not change even if the facts are altered to assume that some or all of the $800,000 amount of lending permissible under the General Limitation's 15 percent basket is not used, or is devoted to the development of domestic residential housing units.

b. In other words, using the above example, if Savings Association A lends Y $400,000 for commercial purposes and $300,000 for residential purposes—both of which would be permitted under its $800,000 General Limitation—Savings Association A's remaining permissible lending to Y would be: first, an additional $100,000 under the General Limitation, and then another $800,000 to develop domestic residential housing units if the savings association meets the paragraph § 32.3(d)(2) prerequisites. (The latter is $800,000 because in no event may the total lending to Y exceed 30 percent of unimpaired capital and unimpaired surplus). If Savings Association A did not lend Y the remaining $100,000 permissible under the General Limitation, its permissible loans to develop domestic residential housing units under § 32.3(d)(2) would be $900,000 instead of $800,000 (the total loans to Y would still equal $1,600,000).

3. In short, under the § 32.3(d)(2) exception, the 30 percent or $30,000,000 limit will always operate as the uppermost limitation, unless the savings association does not avail itself of the exception and merely relies upon its General Limitation.

Section 2. Interrelationship Between the General Limitation and the 150 Percent Aggregate Limit on Loans to All Borrowers To Develop Domestic Residential Housing Units

Numerous questions have been received regarding the allocation of loans between the different lending limit "baskets," *i.e.*, the 15 percent General Limitation basket and the 30 percent Residential Development basket. In general, the inquiries concern the manner in which a savings association may "move" a loan from the General Limitation basket to the Residential Development basket. The following example is intended to provide guidance:

Example: Savings Association A's General Limitation under § 32.3(a) is $15 million. In January, Savings Association A makes a $10 million loan to Borrower to develop domestic residential housing units. At the time the loan was made, Savings Association A had not received approval under an order issued by the appropriate Federal banking agency to avail itself of the residential development exception to lending limits. Therefore, the $10 million loan is made under Savings Association A's General Limitation.

2. In June, Savings Association A receives authorization to lend under the Residential Development exception. In July, Savings Association A lends $3 million to Borrower to develop domestic residential housing units. In August, Borrower seeks an additional $12 million commercial loan from Savings Association A. Savings Association A cannot make the loan to Borrower, however, because it already has an outstanding $10 million loan to Borrower that counts against Savings Association A's General Limitation of $15 million. Thus, Savings Association A may lend only up to an additional $5 million to Borrower under the General Limitation.

3. However, Savings Association A may be able to reallocate the $10 million loan it made to Borrower in January to its Residential Development basket provided that: (1) Savings Association A has obtained authority under an order issued by the appropriate Federal banking agency to avail itself of the additional lending authority for residential development and maintains compliance with all prerequisites to such lending authority; (2) the original $10 million loan made in January constitutes a loan to develop domestic residential housing units as defined; and (3) the housing unit(s) constructed with the funds from the January loan remain in a stage of "development" at the time Savings Association A reallocates the loan to the domestic residential housing basket. The project must be in a stage of acquisition, development, construction, rehabilitation, or conversion in order for the loan to be reallocated.

4. If Savings Association A is able to reallocate the $10 million loan made to Borrower in January to its Residential Development basket, it may make the $12 million commercial loan requested by Borrower in August. Once the January loan is reallocated to the Residential Development basket, however, the $10 million loan counts towards Savings Association A's 150 percent aggregate limitation on loans to all borrowers under the residential development basket (§ 32.3(d)(2)).

5. If Savings Association A reallocates the January loan to its domestic residential housing basket and makes an additional $12 million commercial loan to Borrower, Savings Association A's totals under the respective limitations would be: $12 million under the General Limitation; and $13 million

under the Residential Development limitation. The full $13 million residential development loan counts toward Savings Association A's aggregate 150 percent limitation.

[77 FR 37282, June 21, 2012]

PART 33 [RESERVED]

PART 34—REAL ESTATE LENDING AND APPRAISALS

Subpart A—General

Sec.
34.1 Purpose and scope.
34.2 Definitions.
34.3 General rule.
34.4 Applicability of state law.
34.5 Due-on-sale clauses.

Subpart B—Adjustable-Rate Mortgages

34.20 Definitions.
34.21 General rule.
34.22 Index.
34.23 Prepayment fees.
34.24 Nonfederally chartered commercial banks.
34.25 Transition rule.

Subpart C—Appraisals

34.41 Authority, purpose, and scope.
34.42 Definitions.
34.43 Appraisals required; transactions requiring a State certified or licensed appraiser.
34.44 Minimum appraisal standards.
34.45 Appraiser independence.
34.46 Professional association membership; competency.
34.47 Enforcement.

Subpart D—Real Estate Lending Standards

34.61 Purpose and scope.
34.62 Real estate lending standards.
APPENDIX A TO SUBPART D OF PART 34—INTERAGENCY GUIDELINES FOR REAL ESTATE LENDING

Subpart E—Other Real Estate Owned

34.81 Definitions.
34.82 Holding period.
34.83 Disposition of real estate.
34.84 [Reserved]
34.85 Appraisal requirements.
34.86 Additional expenditures and notification.
34.87 Accounting treatment.

Subpart F [Reserved]

Subpart G—Appraisals for Higher-Priced Mortgage Loans

34.201 Authority, purpose, and scope.
34.202 Definitions applicable to higher-priced mortgage loans.
34.203 Appraisals for higher-priced mortgage loans.
APPENDIX A TO SUBPART G OF PART 34—HIGHER-PRICED MORTGAGE LOAN APPRAISAL SAFE HARBOR REVIEW
APPENDIX B TO SUBPART G OF PART 34—ILLUSTRATIVE WRITTEN SOURCE DOCUMENTS FOR HIGHER-PRICED MORTGAGE LOAN APPRAISAL RULES
APPENDIX C TO SUBPART G OF PART 34—OCC INTERPRETATIONS

Subpart H—Appraisal Management Company Minimum Requirements

34.210 Authority, purpose, and scope.
34.211 Definitions.
34.212 Appraiser panel—annual size calculation.
34.213 Appraisal management company registration.
34.214 Ownership limitations for State-registered appraisal management companies.
34.215 Requirements for Federally regulated appraisal management companies.
34.216 Information to be presented to the Appraisal Subcommittee by participating States.

AUTHORITY: 12 U.S.C. 1 *et seq.*, 25b, 29, 93a, 371, 1462a, 1463, 1464, 1465, 1701j–3, 1828(o), 3331 *et seq.*, 5101 *et seq.*, and 5412(b)(2)(B) and 15 U.S.C. 1639h.

Subpart A—General

SOURCE: 61 FR 11300, Mar. 20, 1996, unless otherwise noted.

§ 34.1 Purpose and scope.

(a) *Purpose*. The purpose of this part is to set forth standards for real estate-related lending and associated activities by national banks.

(b) *Scope*. This part applies to national banks and their operating subsidiaries as provided in 12 CFR 5.34. For the purposes of 12 U.S.C. 371 and subparts A and B of this part, loans secured by liens on interests in real estate include loans made upon the security of condominiums, leaseholds, cooperatives, forest tracts, land sales contracts, and construction project loans. Construction project loans are not subject to subparts A and B of this part, however, if they have a maturity not exceeding 60 months and are made to finance the construction of either:

(1) A building where there is a valid and binding agreement entered into by a financially responsible lender or other party to advance the full amount of the bank's loan upon completion of the building; or

(2) A residential or farm building.

§ 34.2 Definitions.

(a) *Due-on-sale clause* means any clause that gives the lender or any assignee or transferee of the lender the power to declare the entire debt payable if all or part of the legal or equitable title or an equivalent contractual interest in the property securing the loan is transferred to another person, whether by deed, contract, or otherwise.

(b) *State* means any State of the United States of America, the District of Columbia, Puerto Rico, the Virgin Islands, the Northern Mariana Islands, American Samoa, and Guam.

(c) *State law limitations* means any State statute, regulation, or order of any State agency, or judicial decision interpreting State law.

§ 34.3 General rule.

(a) A national bank may make, arrange, purchase, or sell loans or extensions of credit, or interests therein, that are secured by liens on, or interests in, real estate (real estate loans), subject to 12 U.S.C. 1828(o) and such restrictions and requirements as the Comptroller of the Currency may prescribe by regulation or order.

(b) A national bank shall not make a consumer loan subject to this subpart based predominantly on the bank's realization of the foreclosure or liquidation value of the borrower's collateral, without regard to the borrower's ability to repay the loan according to its terms. A bank may use any reasonable method to determine a borrower's ability to repay, including, for example, the borrower's current and expected income, current and expected cash flows, net worth, other relevant financial resources, current financial obligations, employment status, credit history, or other relevant factors.

(c) A national bank shall not engage in unfair or deceptive practices within the meaning of section 5 of the Federal Trade Commission Act, 15 U.S.C. 45(a)(1), and regulations promulgated thereunder in connection with loans made under this part.

[68 FR 70131, Dec. 17, 2003, as amended at 69 FR 1917, Jan. 13, 2004]

§ 34.4 Applicability of state law.

(a) A national bank may make real estate loans under 12 U.S.C. 371 and § 34.3, without regard to state law limitations concerning:

(1) Licensing, registration (except for purposes of service of process), filings, or reports by creditors;

(2) The ability of a creditor to require or obtain private mortgage insurance, insurance for other collateral, or other credit enhancements or risk mitigants, in furtherance of safe and sound banking practices;

(3) Loan-to-value ratios;

(4) The terms of credit, including schedule for repayment of principal and interest, amortization of loans, balance, payments due, minimum payments, or term to maturity of the loan, including the circumstances under which a loan may be called due and payable upon the passage of time or a specified event external to the loan;

(5) The aggregate amount of funds that may be loaned upon the security of real estate;

(6) Escrow accounts, impound accounts, and similar accounts;

(7) Security property, including leaseholds;

(8) Access to, and use of, credit reports;

(9) Disclosure and advertising, including laws requiring specific statements, information, or other content to be included in credit application forms, credit solicitations, billing statements, credit contracts, or other credit-related documents;

(10) Processing, origination, servicing, sale or purchase of, or investment or participation in, mortgages;

(11) Disbursements and repayments;

(12) Rates of interest on loans;[1]

---

[1] The limitations on charges that comprise rates of interest on loans by national banks are determined under Federal law. *See* 12 U.S.C. 85 and 1735f–7a; 12 CFR 7.4001. State laws purporting to regulate national bank

(13) Due-on-sale clauses except to the extent provided in 12 U.S.C. 1701j–3 and 12 CFR part 591; and

(14) Covenants and restrictions that must be contained in a lease to qualify the leasehold as acceptable security for a real estate loan.

(b) State laws on the following subjects are not inconsistent with the real estate lending powers of national banks and apply to national banks to the extent consistent with the decision of the Supreme Court in *Barnett Bank of Marion County, N.A.* v. *Nelson, Florida Insurance Commissioner, et al.*, 517 U.S. 25 (1996):

(1) Contracts;

(2) Torts;

(3) Criminal law;[2]

(4) Homestead laws specified in 12 U.S.C. 1462a(f);

(5) Rights to collect debts;

(6) Acquisition and transfer of real property;

(7) Taxation;

(8) Zoning; and

(9) Any other law that the OCC determines to be applicable to national banks in accordance with the decision of the Supreme Court in *Barnett Bank of Marion County, N.A.* v. *Nelson, Florida Insurance Commissioner, et al.*, 517 U.S. 25 (1996), or that is made applicable by Federal law.

[69 FR 1917, Jan. 13, 2004, as amended at 76 FR 43569, July 21, 2011]

§ 34.5 Due-on-sale clauses.

A national bank may make or acquire a loan or interest therein, secured by a lien on real property, that includes a due-on-sale clause. Except as set forth in 12 U.S.C. 1701j–3(d) (which contains a list of transactions in which due-on-sale clauses may not be enforced), due-on-sale clauses in loans, whenever originated, will be valid and enforceable, notwithstanding any State law limitations to the contrary. For the purposes of this section, the term real property includes residential dwellings such as condominium units, cooperative housing units, and residential manufactured homes.

§ 34.6 Applicability of state law to Federal savings associations and subsidiaries.

In accordance with section 1046 of the Dodd-Frank Wall Street Reform and Consumer Protection Act (12 U.S.C. 25b), Federal savings associations and their subsidiaries shall be subject to the same laws and legal standards, including regulations of the OCC, as are applicable to national banks and their subsidiaries, regarding the preemption of state law.

[76 FR 43569, July 21, 2011]

Subpart B—Adjustable-Rate Mortgages

SOURCE: 61 FR 11301, Mar. 20, 1996, unless otherwise noted.

§ 34.20 Definitions.

Adjustable-rate mortgage (ARM) loan means an extension of credit made to finance or refinance the purchase of, and secured by a lien on, a one-to-four family dwelling, including a condominium unit, cooperative housing unit, or residential manufactured home, where the lender, pursuant to an agreement with the borrower, may adjust the rate of interest from time to time. An ARM loan does not include fixed-rate extensions of credit that are payable at the end of a term that, when added to any terms for which the bank has promised to renew the loan, is shorter than the term of the amortization schedule.

§ 34.21 General rule.

(a) *Authorization.* A national bank and its subsidiaries may make, sell, purchase, participate in, or otherwise

---

fees and charges that do not constitute interest are addressed in 12 CFR 7.4002.

[2] But see the distinction drawn by the Supreme Court in *Easton* v. *Iowa*, 188 U.S. 220, 238 (1903), where the Court stated that "[u]ndoubtedly a state has the legitimate power to define and punish crimes by general laws applicable to all persons within its jurisdiction * * *. But it is without lawful power to make such special laws applicable to banks organized and operating under the laws of the United States." *Id.* at 239 (holding that Federal law governing the operations of national banks preempted a state criminal law prohibiting insolvent banks from accepting deposits).

deal in ARM loans and interests therein without regard to any State law limitations on those activities.

(b) *Purchase of loans not in compliance.* Except as provided in paragraph (c) of this section, a national bank may purchase or participate in ARM loans that were not made in accordance with this part, provided such purchases are consistent with safe and sound banking practices as described in published OCC guidance, including appropriate diligence regarding the quality and characteristics of the loans, and other applicable regulations.

(c) *Purchase of loans from a subsidiary or affiliate.* ARM loans purchased, in whole or in part, from a subsidiary or affiliate must comply with this part and with other applicable regulations, and be consistent with safe and sound banking practices as described in published OCC guidance, including appropriate diligence regarding the quality and characteristics of the loans. For purposes of this paragraph, the terms affiliate and subsidiary have the same meaning as in 12 U.S.C. 371c.

[61 FR 11300, Mar. 20, 1996, as amended at 73 FR 22251, Apr. 24, 2008]

§ 34.22 Index.

(a) *In general.* If a national bank makes an ARM loan to which 12 CFR 226.19(b) applies (*i.e.*, the annual percentage rate of a loan may increase after consummation, the term exceeds one year, and the consumer's principal dwelling secures the indebtedness), the loan documents must specify an index or combination of indices to which changes in the interest rate will be linked. This index must be readily available to, and verifiable by, the borrower and beyond the control of the bank. A national bank may use as an index any measure of rates of interest that meets these requirements. The index may be either single values of the chosen measure or a moving average of the chosen measure calculated over a specified period. A national bank also may increase the interest rate in accordance with applicable loan documents specifying the amount of the increase and the times at which, or circumstances under which, it may be made. A national bank may decrease the interest rate at any time.

(b) *Exception.* Thirty days after filing a notice with the OCC, a national bank may use an index other than one described in paragraph (a) of this section unless, within that 30-day period, the OCC has notified the bank that the notice presents supervisory concerns or raises significant issues of law or policy. If the OCC provides such notice to the bank, the bank may not use that index unless it applies for and receives the OCC's prior written approval.

[61 FR 11300, Mar. 20, 1996, as amended at 73 FR 22251, Apr. 24, 2008]

§ 34.23 Prepayment fees.

A national bank offering or purchasing ARM loans may impose fees for prepayments notwithstanding any State law limitations to the contrary. For purposes of this section, prepayments do not include:

(a) Payments that exceed the required payment amount to avoid or reduce negative amortization; or

(b) Principal payments, in excess of those necessary to retire the outstanding debt over the remaining loan term at the then-current interest rate, that are made in accordance with rules governing the determination of monthly payments contained in the loan documents.

§ 34.24 Nonfederally chartered commercial banks.

Pursuant to 12 U.S.C. 3803(a), a State chartered commercial bank may make ARM loans in accordance with the provisions of this subpart. For purposes of this section, the term "State" shall have the same meaning as set forth in § 34.2(b).

§ 34.25 Transition rule.

If, on October 1, 1988, a national bank had made a loan or binding commitment to lend under an ARM loan program that complied with the requirements of 12 CFR part 29 in effect prior to October 1, 1988 (see 12 CFR Parts 1 to 199, revised as of January 1, 1988) but would have violated any of the provisions of this subpart, the national bank may continue to administer the loan or binding commitment to lend in accordance with that loan program. All ARM loans or binding commitments to make

ARM loans that a national bank entered into after October 1, 1988, must comply with all provisions of this subpart.

Subpart C—Appraisals

SOURCE: 55 FR 34696, Aug. 24, 1990, unless otherwise noted.

§ 34.41 Authority, purpose, and scope.

(a) *Authority.* This subpart is issued by the Office of the Comptroller of the Currency (the OCC) under 12 U.S.C. 1, 93a, 1462a, 1463, 1464, 1828(m), 5412(b)(2)(B), and title XI of the Financial Institutions Reform, Recovery, and Enforcement Act of 1989 (FIRREA) (Pub. L. 101–73, 103 Stat. 183 (1989)), 12 U.S.C. 3331 *et seq.*

(b) *Purpose and scope.* (1) Title XI of FIRREA provides protection for federal financial and public policy interests in real estate-related transactions by requiring real estate appraisals used in connection with federally related transactions to be performed in writing, in accordance with uniform standards, by appraisers whose competency has been demonstrated and whose professional conduct will be subject to effective supervision. This subpart implements the requirements of title XI, and applies to all federally related transactions entered into by the OCC or by institutions regulated by the OCC (*regulated institutions*).

(2) This subpart:

(i) Identifies which real estate-related financial transactions require the services of an appraiser;

(ii) Prescribes which categories of federally related transactions shall be appraised by a State certified appraiser and which by a State licensed appraiser; and

(iii) Prescribes minimum standards for the performance of real estate appraisals in connection with federally related transactions under the jurisdiction of the OCC.

[55 FR 34696, Aug. 24, 1990, as amended at 79 FR 28400, May 16, 2014]

§ 34.42 Definitions.

(a) *Appraisal* means a written statement independently and impartially prepared by a qualified appraiser setting forth an opinion as to the market value of an adequately described property as of a specific date(s), supported by the presentation and analysis of relevant market information.

(b) *Appraisal Foundation* means the Appraisal Foundation established on November 30, 1987, as a not-for-profit corporation under the laws of Illinois.

(c) *Appraisal Subcommittee* means the Appraisal Subcommittee of the Federal Financial Institutions Examination Council.

(d) *Business loan* means a loan or extension of credit to any corporation, general or limited partnership, business trust, joint venture, pool, syndicate, sole proprietorship, or other business entity.

(e) *Commercial real estate transaction* means a real estate-related financial transaction that is not secured by a single 1-to-4 family residential property.

(f) *Complex 1-to-4 family residential property appraisal* means one in which the property to be appraised, the form of ownership, or market conditions are atypical.

(g) *Federally related transaction* means any real estate-related financial transaction entered into on or after August 9, 1990, that:

(1) The OCC or any of its regulated institutions engages in or contracts for; and

(2) Requires the services of an appraiser.

(h) *Market value* means the most probable price which a property should bring in a competitive and open market under all conditions requisite to a fair sale, the buyer and seller each acting prudently and knowledgeably, and assuming the price is not affected by undue stimulus. Implicit in this definition is the consummation of a sale as of a specified date and the passing of title from seller to buyer under conditions whereby:

(1) Buyer and seller are typically motivated;

(2) Both parties are well informed or well advised, and acting in what they consider their own best interests;

(3) A reasonable time is allowed for exposure in the open market;

(4) Payment is made in terms of cash in U.S. dollars or in terms of financial arrangements comparable thereto; and

(5) The price represents the normal consideration for the property sold unaffected by special or creative financing or sales concessions granted by anyone associated with the sale.

(i) *Real estate* or *real property* means an identified parcel or tract of land, with improvements, and includes easements, rights of way, undivided or future interests, or similar rights in a tract of land, but does not include mineral rights, timber rights, growing crops, water rights, or similar interests severable from the land when the transaction does not involve the associated parcel or tract of land.

(j) *Real estate-related financial transaction* means any transaction involving:

(1) The sale, lease, purchase, investment in or exchange of real property, including interests in property, or the financing thereof; or

(2) The refinancing of real property or interests in real property; or

(3) The use of real property or interests in property as security for a loan or investment, including mortgage-backed securities.

(k) *State certified appraiser* means any individual who has satisfied the requirements for certification in a State or territory whose criteria for certification as a real estate appraiser currently meet the minimum criteria for certification issued by the Appraiser Qualifications Board of the Appraisal Foundation. No individual shall be a State certified appraiser unless such individual has achieved a passing grade upon a suitable examination administered by a State or territory that is consistent with and equivalent to the Uniform State Certification Examination issued or endorsed by the Appraiser Qualifications Board of the Appraisal Foundation. In addition, the Appraisal Subcommittee must not have issued a finding that the policies, practices, or procedures of the State or territory are inconsistent with title XI of FIRREA. The OCC may, from time to time, impose additional qualification criteria for certified appraisers performing appraisals in connection with federally related transactions within its jurisdiction.

(l) *State licensed appraiser* means any individual who has satisfied the requirements for licensing in a State or territory where the licensing procedures comply with title XI of FIRREA and where the Appraisal Subcommittee has not issued a finding that the policies, practices, or procedures of the State or territory are inconsistent with title XI. The OCC may, from time to time, impose additional qualification criteria for licensed appraisers performing appraisals in connection with federally related transactions within its jurisdiction.

(m) *Tract development* means a project of five units or more that is constructed or is to be constructed as a single development.

(n) *Transaction value* means:

(1) For loans or other extensions of credit, the amount of the loan or extension of credit;

(2) For sales, leases, purchases, and investments in or exchanges of real property, the market value of the real property interest involved; and

(3) For the pooling of loans or interests in real property for resale or purchase, the amount of the loan or market value of the real property calculated with respect to each such loan or interest in real property.

[55 FR 34696, Aug. 24, 1990, as amended at 57 FR 12202, Apr. 9, 1992; 59 FR 29499, June 7, 1994; 79 FR 28400, May 16, 2014; 83 FR 15035, Apr. 9, 2018]

§ 34.43 Appraisals required; transactions requiring a State certified or licensed appraiser.

(a) *Appraisals required.* An appraisal performed by a State certified or licensed appraiser is required for all real estate-related financial transactions except those in which:

(1) The transaction value is $250,000 or less;

(2) A lien on real estate has been taken as collateral in an abundance of caution;

(3) The transaction is not secured by real estate;

(4) A lien on real estate has been taken for purposes other than the real estate's value;

(5) The transaction is a business loan that:

(i) Has a transaction value of $1 million or less; and

(ii) Is not dependent on the sale of, or rental income derived from, real estate as the primary source of repayment;

(6) A lease of real estate is entered into, unless the lease is the economic equivalent of a purchase or sale of the leased real estate;

(7) The transaction involves an existing extension of credit at the lending institution, provided that:

(i) There has been no obvious and material change in market conditions or physical aspects of the property that threatens the adequacy of the institution's real estate collateral protection after the transaction, even with the advancement of new monies; or

(ii) There is no advancement of new monies, other than funds necessary to cover reasonable closing costs;

(8) The transaction involves the purchase, sale, investment in, exchange of, or extension of credit secured by, a loan or interest in a loan, pooled loans, or interests in real property, including mortgaged-backed securities, and each loan or interest in a loan, pooled loan, or real property interest met OCC regulatory requirements for appraisals at the time of origination;

(9) The transaction is wholly or partially insured or guaranteed by a United States government agency or United States government sponsored agency;

(10) The transaction either:

(i) Qualifies for sale to a United States government agency or United States government sponsored agency; or

(ii) Involves a residential real estate transaction in which the appraisal conforms to the Federal National Mortgage Association or Federal Home Loan Mortgage Corporation appraisal standards applicable to that category of real estate;

(11) The regulated institution is acting in a fiduciary capacity and is not required to obtain an appraisal under other law;

(12) The OCC determines that the services of an appraiser are not necessary in order to protect Federal financial and public policy interests in real estate-related financial transactions or to protect the safety and soundness of the institution; or

(13) The transaction is a commercial real estate transaction that has a transaction value of $500,000 or less.

(b) *Evaluations required.* For a transaction that does not require the services of a State certified or licensed appraiser under paragraph (a)(1), (a)(5), (a)(7), or (a)(13) of this section, the institution shall obtain an appropriate evaluation of real property collateral that is consistent with safe and sound banking practices.

(c) *Appraisals to address safety and soundness concerns.* The OCC reserves the right to require an appraisal under this subpart whenever the agency believes it is necessary to address safety and soundness concerns.

(d) *Transactions requiring a State certified appraiser*—(1) *All transactions of $1,000,000 or more.* All federally related transactions having a transaction value of $1,000,000 or more shall require an appraisal prepared by a State certified appraiser.

(2) *Commercial real estate transactions of more than $500,000.* All federally related transactions that are commercial real estate transactions having a transaction value of more than $500,000 shall require an appraisal prepared by a State certified appraiser.

(3) *Complex residential transactions of $250,000 or more.* All complex 1-to-4 family residential property appraisals rendered in connection with federally related transactions shall require a State certified appraiser if the transaction value is $250,000 or more. A regulated institution may presume that appraisals of 1-to-4 family residential properties are not complex, unless the institution has readily available information that a given appraisal will be complex. The regulated institution shall be responsible for making the final determination whether the appraisal is complex. If during the course of the appraisal a licensed appraiser identifies factors that would result in the property, form of ownership, or market conditions being considered atypical, then either:

(i) The regulated institution may ask the licensed appraiser to complete the appraisal and have a certified appraiser approve and co-sign the appraisal; or

(ii) The institution may engage a certified appraiser to complete the appraisal.

(e) *Transactions requiring either a State certified or licensed appraiser.* All appraisals for federally related transactions not requiring the services of a State certified appraiser shall be prepared by either a State certified appraiser or a State licensed appraiser.

[55 FR 34696, Aug. 24, 1990, as amended at 57 FR 12202, Apr. 9, 1992; 59 FR 29499, June 7, 1994; 79 FR 28400, May 16, 2014; 83 FR 15035, Apr. 9, 2018]

§ 34.44 Minimum appraisal standards.

For federally related transactions, all appraisals shall, at a minimum:

(a) Conform to generally accepted appraisal standards as evidenced by the Uniform Standards of Professional Appraisal Practice (USPAP) promulgated by the Appraisal Standards Board of the Appraisal Foundation, (*www.appraisalfoundation.org*), unless principles of safe and sound banking require compliance with stricter standards;

(b) Be written and contain sufficient information and analysis to support the institution's decision to engage in the transaction;

(c) Analyze and report appropriate deductions and discounts for proposed construction or renovation, partially leased buildings, non-market lease terms, and tract developments with unsold units;

(d) Be based upon the definition of market value as set forth in this subpart; and

(e) Be performed by State licensed or certified appraisers in accordance with requirements set forth in this subpart.

[59 FR 29500, June 7, 1994, as amended at 79 FR 28400, May 16, 2014]

§ 34.45 Appraiser independence.

(a) *Staff appraisers.* If an appraisal is prepared by a staff appraiser, that appraiser must be independent of the lending, investment, and collection functions and not involved, except as an appraiser, in the federally related transaction, and have no direct or indirect interest, financial or otherwise, in the property. If the only qualified persons available to perform an appraisal are involved in the lending, investment, or collection functions of the regulated institution, the regulated institution shall take appropriate steps to ensure that the appraisers exercise independent judgment. Such steps include, but are not limited to, prohibiting an individual from performing an appraisal in connection with federally related transactions in which the appraiser is otherwise involved and prohibiting directors and officers from participating in any vote or approval involving assets on which they performed an appraisal.

(b) *Fee appraisers.* (1) If an appraisal is prepared by a fee appraiser, the appraiser shall be engaged directly by the regulated institution or its agent, and have no direct or indirect interest, financial or otherwise, in the property or the transaction.

(2) A regulated institution also may accept an appraisal that was prepared by an appraiser engaged directly by another financial services institution, if:

(i) The appraiser has no direct or indirect interest, financial or otherwise, in the property or the transaction; and

(ii) The regulated institution determines that the appraisal conforms to the requirements of this subpart and is otherwise acceptable.

[55 FR 34696, Aug. 24, 1990, as amended at 59 FR 29500, June 7, 1994]

§ 34.46 Professional association membership; competency.

(a) *Membership in appraisal organizations.* A State certified appraiser or a State licensed appraiser may not be excluded from consideration for an assignment for a federally related transaction solely by virtue of membership or lack of membership in any particular appraisal organization.

(b) *Competency.* All staff and fee appraisers performing appraisals in connection with federally related transactions must be State certified or licensed, as appropriate. However, a State certified or licensed appraiser may not be considered competent solely by virtue of being certified or licensed. Any determination of competency shall be based upon the individual's experience and educational background as they relate to the particular appraisal assignment for which he or she is being considered.

§ 34.47 Enforcement.

Institutions and institution-affiliated parties, including staff appraisers and fee appraisers, may be subject to removal and/or prohibition orders, cease and desist orders, and the imposition of civil money penalties pursuant to the Federal Deposit Insurance Act, 12 U.S.C. 1811 *et seq.*, as amended, or other applicable law.

Subpart D—Real Estate Lending Standards

SOURCE: 57 FR 62889, Dec. 31, 1992, unless otherwise noted.

§ 34.61 Purpose and scope.

This subpart, issued pursuant to section 304 of the Federal Deposit Insurance Corporation Improvement Act of 1991, 12 U.S.C. 1828(o), prescribes standards for real estate lending to be used by national banks in adopting internal real estate lending policies.

§ 34.62 Real estate lending standards.

(a) Each national bank shall adopt and maintain written policies that establish appropriate limits and standards for extensions of credit that are secured by liens on or interests in real estate, or that are made for the purpose of financing permanent improvements to real estate.

(b)(1) Real estate lending policies adopted pursuant to this section must:

(i) Be consistent with safe and sound banking practices;

(ii) Be appropriate to the size of the institution and the nature and scope of its operations; and

(iii) Be reviewed and approved by the bank's board of directors at least annually.

(2) The lending policies must establish:

(i) Loan portfolio diversification standards;

(ii) Prudent underwriting standards, including loan-to-value limits, that are clear and measurable;

(iii) Loan administration procedures for the bank's real estate portfolio; and

(iv) Documentation, approval, and reporting requirements to monitor compliance with the bank's real estate lending policies.

(c) Each national bank must monitor conditions in the real estate market in its lending area to ensure that its real estate lending policies continue to be appropriate for current market conditions.

(d) The real estate lending policies adopted pursuant to this section should reflect consideration of the Interagency Guidelines for Real Estate Lending Policies established by the Federal bank and thrift supervisory agencies.

APPENDIX A TO SUBPART D OF PART 34—INTERAGENCY GUIDELINES FOR REAL ESTATE LENDING

The agencies' regulations require that each insured depository institution adopt and maintain a written policy that establishes appropriate limits and standards for all extensions of credit that are secured by liens on or interests in real estate or made for the purpose of financing the construction of a building or other improvements.[1] These guidelines are intended to assist institutions in the formulation and maintenance of a real estate lending policy that is appropriate to the size of the institution and the nature and scope of its individual operations, as well as satisfies the requirements of the regulation.

Each institution's policies must be comprehensive, and consistent with safe and sound lending practices, and must ensure that the institution operates within limits and according to standards that are reviewed and approved at least annually by the board of directors. Real estate lending is an integral part of many institutions' business plans and, when undertaken in a prudent manner, will not be subject to examiner criticism.

LOAN PORTFOLIO MANAGEMENT CONSIDERATIONS

The lending policy should contain a general outline of the scope and distribution of the institution's credit facilities and the manner in which real estate loans are made, serviced, and collected. In particular, the institution's policies on real estate lending should:

[1] The agencies have adopted a uniform rule on real estate lending. See 12 CFR part 365 (FDIC); 12 CFR part 208, subpart C (FRB); 12 CFR part 34, subpart D (OCC); and 12 CFR 563.100–101 (OTS).

• Identify the geographic areas in which the institution will consider lending.

• Establish a loan portfolio diversification policy and set limits for real estate loans by type and geographic market (e.g., limits on higher risk loans).

• Identify appropriate terms and conditions by type of real estate loan.

• Establish loan origination and approval procedures, both generally and by size and type of loan.

• Establish prudent underwriting standards that are clear and measurable, including loan-to-value limits, that are consistent with these supervisory guidelines.

• Establish review and approval procedures for exception loans, including loans with loan-to-value percentages in excess of supervisory limits.

• Establish loan administration procedures, including documentation, disbursement, collateral inspection, collection, and loan review.

• Establish real estate appraisal and evaluation programs.

• Require that management monitor the loan portfolio and provide timely and adequate reports to the board of directors.

The institution should consider both internal and external factors in the formulation of its loan policies and strategic plan. Factors that should be considered include:

• The size and financial condition of the institution.

• The expertise and size of the lending staff.

• The need to avoid undue concentrations of risk.

• Compliance with all real estate related laws and regulations, including the Community Reinvestment Act, anti-discrimination laws, and for savings associations, the Qualified Thrift Lender test.

• Market conditions.

The institution should monitor conditions in the real estate markets in its lending area so that it can react quickly to changes in market conditions that are relevant to its lending decisions. Market supply and demand factors that should be considered include:

• Demographic indicators, including population and employment trends.

• Zoning requirements.

• Current and projected vacancy, construction, and absorption rates.

• Current and projected lease terms, rental rates, and sales prices, including concessions.

• Current and projected operating expenses for different types of projects.

• Economic indicators, including trends and diversification of the lending area.

• Valuation trends, including discount and direct capitalization rates.

UNDERWRITING STANDARDS

Prudently underwritten real estate loans should reflect all relevant credit factors, including:

• The capacity of the borrower, or income from the underlying property, to adequately service the debt.

• The value of the mortgaged property.

• The overall creditworthiness of the borrower.

• The level of equity invested in the property.

• Any secondary sources of repayment.

• Any additional collateral or credit enhancements (such as guarantees, mortgage insurance or takeout commitments).

The lending policies should reflect the level of risk that is acceptable to the board of directors and provide clear and measurable underwriting standards that enable the institution's lending staff to evaluate these credit factors. The underwriting standards should address:

• The maximum loan amount by type of property.

• Maximum loan maturities by type of property.

• Amortization schedules.

• Pricing structure for different types of real estate loans.

• Loan-to-value limits by type of property.

For development and construction projects, and completed commercial properties, the policy should also establish, commensurate with the size and type of the project or property:

• Requirements for feasibility studies and sensitivity and risk analyses (*e.g.*, sensitivity of income projections to changes in economic variables such as interest rates, vacancy rates, or operating expenses).

• Minimum requirements for initial investment and maintenance of hard equity by the borrower (*e.g.*, cash or unencumbered investment in the underlying property).

• Minimum standards for net worth, cash flow, and debt service coverage of the borrower or underlying property.

• Standards for the acceptability of and limits on non-amortizing loans.

• Standards for the acceptability of and limits on the use of interest reserves.

• Pre-leasing and pre-sale requirements for income-producing property.

• Pre-sale and minimum unit release requirements for non-income-producing property loans.

• Limits on partial recourse or nonrecourse loans and requirements for guarantor support.

• Requirements for takeout commitments.

• Minimum covenants for loan agreements.

LOAN ADMINISTRATION

The institution should also establish loan administration procedures for its real estate portfolio that address:

• Documentation, including:

Type and frequency of financial statements, including requirements for verification of information provided by the borrower;

Type and frequency of collateral evaluations (appraisals and other estimates of value).

• Loan closing and disbursement.
• Payment processing.
• Escrow administration.
• Collateral administration.
• Loan payoffs.
• Collections and foreclosure, including:

Delinquency follow-up procedures;
Foreclosure timing;
Extensions and other forms of forbearance;
Acceptance of deeds in lieu of foreclosure.

• Claims processing (*e.g.*, seeking recovery on a defaulted loan covered by a government guaranty or insurance program).
• Servicing and participation agreements.

SUPERVISORY LOAN-TO-VALUE LIMITS

Institutions should establish their own internal loan-to-value limits for real estate loans. These internal limits should not exceed the following supervisory limits:

Loan category	Loan-to-value limit (percent)
Raw land	65
Land development	75
Construction:	
Commercial, multifamily,[1] and other nonresidential	80
1- to 4-family residential	85
Improved property	85
Owner-occupied 1- to 4-family and home equity	([2])

[1] Multifamily construction includes condominiums and cooperatives.

[2] A loan-to-value limit has not been established for permanent mortgage or home equity loans on owner-occupied, 1- to 4-family residential property. However, for any such loan with a loan-to-value ratio that equals or exceeds 90 percent at origination, an institution should require appropriate credit enhancement in the form of either mortgage insurance or readily marketable collateral.

The supervisory loan-to-value limits should be applied to the underlying property that collateralizes the loan. For loans that fund multiple phases of the same real estate project (e.g., a loan for both land development and construction of an office building), the appropriate loan-to-value limit is the limit applicable to the final phase of the project funded by the loan; however, loan disbursements should not exceed actual development or construction outlays. In situations where a loan is fully cross-collateralized by two or more properties or is secured by a collateral pool of two or more properties, the appropriate maximum loan amount under supervisory loan-to-value limits is the sum of the value of each property, less senior liens, multiplied by the appropriate loan-to-value limit for each property. To ensure that collateral margins remain within the supervisory limits, lenders should redetermine conformity whenever collateral substitutions are made to the collateral pool.

In establishing internal loan-to-value limits, each lender is expected to carefully consider the institution-specific and market factors listed under "Loan Portfolio Management Considerations," as well as any other relevant factors, such as the particular subcategory or type of loan. For any subcategory of loans that exhibits greater credit risk than the overall category, a lender should consider the establishment of an internal loan-to-value limit for that subcategory that is lower than the limit for the overall category.

The loan-to-value ratio is only one of several pertinent credit factors to be considered when underwriting a real estate loan. Other credit factors to be taken into account are highlighted in the "Underwriting Standards" section above. Because of these other factors, the establishment of these supervisory limits should not be interpreted to mean that loans at these levels will automatically be considered sound.

LOANS IN EXCESS OF THE SUPERVISORY LOAN-TO-VALUE LIMITS

The agencies recognize that appropriate loan-to-value limits vary not only among categories of real estate loans but also among individual loans. Therefore, it may be appropriate in individual cases to originate or purchase loans with loan-to-value ratios in excess of the supervisory loan-to-value limits, based on the support provided by other credit factors. Such loans should be identified in the institutions's records, and their aggregate amount reported at least quarterly to the institution's board of directors. (See additional reporting requirements described under "Exceptions to the General Policy.")

The aggregate amount of all loans in excess of the supervisory loan-to-value limits should not exceed 100 percent of total capital.[2] Moreover, within the aggregate limit,

[2] For the state member banks, the term "total capital" means "total risk-based capital" as defined in appendix A to 12 CFR part 208. For insured state non-member banks, "total capital" refers to that term described in table I of appendix A to 12 CFR part 325. For national banks, the term "total capital" is defined at 12 CFR 3.2(e). For savings associations, the term "total capital" is defined at 12 CFR 567.5(c).

Continued

total loans for all commercial, agricultural, multifamily or other non-1-to-4 family residential properties should not exceed 30 percent of total capital. An institution will come under increased supervisory scrutiny as the total of such loans approaches these levels.

In determining the aggregate amount of such loans, institutions should: (a) Include all loans secured by the same property if any one of those loans exceeds the supervisory loan-to-value limits; and (b) include the recourse obligation of any such loan sold with recourse. Conversely, a loan should no longer be reported to the directors as part of aggregate totals when reduction in principal or senior liens, or additional contribution of collateral or equity (e.g., improvements to the real property securing the loan), bring the loan-to-value ratio into compliance with supervisory limits.

EXCLUDED TRANSACTIONS

The agencies also recognize that there are a number of lending situations in which other factors significantly outweigh the need to apply the supervisory loan-to-value limits. These include:

- Loans guaranteed or insured by the U.S. government or its agencies, provided that the amount of the guaranty or insurance is at least equal to the portion of the loan that exceeds the supervisory loan-to-value limit.
- Loans backed by the full faith and credit of a State government, provided that the amount of the assurance is at least equal to the portion of the loan that exceeds the supervisory loan-to-value limit.
- Loans guaranteed or insured by a State, municipal or local government, or an agency thereof, provided that the amount of the guaranty or insurance is at least equal to the portion of the loan that exceeds the supervisory loan-to-value limit, and provided that the lender has determined that the guarantor or insurer has the financial capacity and willingness to perform under the terms of the guaranty or insurance agreement.
- Loans that are to be sold promptly after origination, without recourse, to a financially responsible third party.
- Loans that are renewed, refinanced, or restructured without the advancement of new funds or an increase in the line of credit (except for reasonable closing costs), or loans that are renewed, refinanced, or restructured in connection with a workout situation, either with or without the advancement of new funds, where consistent with safe and sound banking practices and part of a clearly defined and well-documented program to achieve orderly liquidation of the debt, reduce risk of loss, or maximize recovery on the loan.
- Loans that facilitate the sale of real estate acquired by the lender in the ordinary course of collecting a debt previously contracted in good faith.
- Loans for which a lien on or interest in real property is taken as additional collateral through an abundance of caution by the lender (e.g., the institution takes a blanket lien on all or substantially all of the assets of the borrower, and the value of the real property is low relative to the aggregate value of all other collateral).
- Loans, such as working capital loans, where the lender does not rely principally on real estate as security and the extension of credit is not used to acquire, develop, or construct permanent improvements on real property.
- Loans for the purpose of financing permanent improvements to real property, but not secured by the property, if such security interest is not required by prudent underwriting practice.

EXCEPTIONS TO THE GENERAL LENDING POLICY

Some provision should be made for the consideration of loan requests from creditworthy borrowers whose credit needs do not fit within the institution's general lending policy. An institution may provide for prudently underwritten exceptions to its lending policies, including loan-to-value limits, on a loan-by-loan basis. However, any exceptions from the supervisory loan-to-value limits should conform to the aggregate limits on such loans discussed above.

The board of directors is responsible for establishing standards for the review and approval of exception loans. Each institution should establish an appropriate internal process for the review and approval of loans that do not conform to its own internal policy standards. The approval of any such loan should be supported by a written justification that clearly sets forth all of the relevant credit factors that support the underwriting decision. The justification and approval documents for such loans should be maintained as a part of the permanent loan file. Each institution should monitor compliance with its real estate lending policy and individually report exception loans of a significant size to its board of directors.

The cross-references in the first paragraph of this footnote were originally adopted in an interagency rulemaking and are out of date as a result of revisions to capital rules implementing the Basel III Capital Framework. *See* 57 FR 63889 (December 31, 1992). For national banks and Federal savings associations, the term "total capital" is defined at 12 CFR 3.2, 3.2(e), or 167.5, as applicable. *See* 78 FR 62018 (October 11, 2013).

SUPERVISORY REVIEW OF REAL ESTATE LENDING POLICIES AND PRACTICES

The real estate lending policies of institutions will be evaluated by examiners during the course of their examinations to determine if the policies are consistent with safe and sound lending practices, these guidelines, and the requirements of the regulation. In evaluating the adequacy of the institution's real estate lending policies and practices, examiners will take into consideration the following factors:

- The nature and scope of the institution's real estate lending activities.
- The size and financial condition of the institution.
- The quality of the institution's management and internal controls.
- The expertise and size of the lending and loan administration staff.
- Market conditions.

Lending policy exception reports will also be reviewed by examiners during the course of their examinations to determine whether the institutions' exceptions are adequately documented and appropriate in light of all of the relevant credit considerations. An excessive volume of exceptions to an institution's real estate lending policy may signal a weakening of its underwriting practices, or may suggest a need to revise the loan policy.

DEFINITIONS

For the purposes of these Guidelines:

Construction loan means an extension of credit for the purpose of erecting or rehabilitating buildings or other structures, including any infrastructure necessary for development.

Extension of credit or *loan* means:

(1) The total amount of any loan, line of credit, or other legally binding lending commitment with respect to real property; and

(2) The total amount, based on the amount of consideration paid, of any loan, line of credit, or other legally binding lending commitment acquired by a lender by purchase, assignment, or otherwise.

Improved property loan means an extension of credit secured by one of the following types of real property:

(1) Farmland, ranchland or timberland committed to ongoing management and agricultural production;

(2) 1- to 4-family residential property that is not owner-occupied;

(3) Residential property containing five or more individual dwelling units;

(4) Completed commercial property; or

(5) Other income-producing property that has been completed and is available for occupancy and use, except income-producing owner-occupied 1- to 4-family residential property.

Land development loan means an extension of credit for the purpose of improving unimproved real property prior to the erection of structures. The improvement of unimproved real property may include the laying or placement of sewers, water pipes, utility cables, streets, and other infrastructure necessary for future development.

Loan origination means the time of inception of the obligation to extend credit (i.e., when the last event or prerequisite, controllable by the lender, occurs causing the lender to become legally bound to fund an extension of credit).

Loan-to-value or *loan-to-value ratio* means the percentage or ratio that is derived at the time of loan origination by dividing an extension of credit by the total value of the property(ies) securing or being improved by the extension of credit plus the amount of any readily marketable collateral and other acceptable collateral that secures the extension of credit. The total amount of all senior liens on or interests in such property(ies) should be included in determining the loan-to-value ratio. When mortgage insurance or collateral is used in the calculation of the loan-to-value ratio, and such credit enhancement is later released or replaced, the loan-to-value ratio should be recalculated.

Other acceptable collateral means any collateral in which the lender has a perfected security interest, that has a quantifiable value, and is accepted by the lender in accordance with safe and sound lending practices. Other acceptable collateral should be appropriately discounted by the lender consistent with the lender's usual practices for making loans secured by such collateral. Other acceptable collateral includes, among other items, unconditional irrevocable standby letters of credit for the benefit of the lender.

Owner-occupied, when used in conjunction with the term *1- to 4-family residential property* means that the owner of the underlying real property occupies at least one unit of the real property as a principal residence of the owner.

Readily marketable collateral means insured deposits, financial instruments, and bullion in which the lender has a perfected interest. Financial instruments and bullion must be salable under ordinary circumstances with reasonable promptness at a fair market value determined by quotations based on actual transactions, on an auction or similarly available daily bid and ask price market. Readily marketable collateral should be appropriately discounted by the lender consistent with the lender's usual practices for making loans secured by such collateral.

Value means an opinion or estimate, set forth in an appraisal or evaluation, whichever may be appropriate, of the market value of real property, prepared in accordance with the agency's appraisal regulations and guidance. For loans to purchase an existing property, the term "value" means the lesser of the actual acquisition cost or the estimate of value.

1- to 4-family residential property means property containing fewer than five individual dwelling units, including manufactured homes permanently affixed to the underlying property (when deemed to be real property under State law).

[57 FR 62896, Dec. 31, 1992; 58 FR 4460, Jan. 14, 1993, as amended at 79 FR 11312, Feb. 28, 2014]

Subpart E—Other Real Estate Owned

SOURCE: 61 FR 11301, Mar. 20, 1996, unless otherwise noted.

§ 34.81 Definitions.

(a) *Capital and surplus* means:

(1) A bank's tier 1 and tier 2 capital calculated under the OCC's risk-based capital standards set forth in 12 CFR part 3, as applicable, as reported in the bank's Consolidated Reports of Condition and Income (Call Report) as filed under 12 U.S.C. 161; plus

(2) The balance of a bank's allowance for loan and lease losses not included in the bank's tier 2 capital, for purposes of the calculation of risk-based capital described in paragraph (a)(1) of this section, as reported in the bank's Call Report.

(b) *Debts previously contracted (DPC) real estate* means real estate (including capitalized and operating leases) acquired by a national bank through any means in full or partial satisfaction of a debt previously contracted.

(c) *Former banking premises* means real estate (including capitalized and operating leases) for which banking use no longer is contemplated. This includes real estate originally acquired for future expansion that no longer will be used for expansion or other banking purposes.

(d) *Market value* means the value determined in accordance with subpart C of this part.

(e) *Other real estate owned (OREO)* means:

(1) DPC real estate; and

(2) Former banking premises.

(f) *Recorded investment amount* means:

(1) For loans, the recorded loan balance, as determined by generally accepted accounting principles; and

(2) For former banking premises, the net book value.

[61 FR 11301, Mar. 20, 1996, as amended at 79 FR 11313, Feb. 28, 2014]

§ 34.82 Holding period.

(a) *Holding period for OREO.* A national bank shall dispose of OREO at the earliest time that prudent judgment dictates, but not later than the end of the holding period (or an extension thereof) permitted by 12 U.S.C. 29.

(b) *Commencement of holding period.* The holding period begins on the date that:

(1) Ownership of the property is originally transferred to a national bank;

(2) A bank completes relocation from former banking premises to new banking premises or ceases to use the former banking premises without relocating; or

(3) A bank decides not to use real estate acquired for future bank expansion.

(c) *Effect of statutory redemption period.* For DPC real estate that is subject to a redemption period imposed under State law, the holding period begins at the expiration of that redemption period.

§ 34.83 Disposition of real estate.

(a) *Disposition.* A national bank may comply with its obligation to dispose of real estate under 12 U.S.C. 29 in the following ways:

(1) With respect to OREO in general:

(i) By entering into a transaction that is a sale under generally accepted accounting principles;

(ii) By entering into a transaction that involves a loan guaranteed or insured by the United States government or by an agency of the United States government or a loan eligible for purchase by a Federally-sponsored instrumentality that purchases loans; or

(iii) By selling the property pursuant to a land contract or a contract for deed;

(2) With respect to DPC real estate, by retaining the property for its own use as bank premises or by transferring it to a subsidiary or affiliate for use in the business of the subsidiary or affiliate;

(3) With respect to a capitalized or operating lease:

(i) By obtaining an assignment or a coterminous sublease. If a national bank enters into a sublease that is not coterminous, the period during which the master lease must be divested will be suspended for the duration of the sublease, and will begin running again upon termination of the sublease. A national bank holding a lease as OREO may enter into an extension of the lease that would exceed the holding period referred to in §34.82 if the extension meets the following criteria:

(A) The extension is necessary in order to sublease the master lease;

(B) The national bank, prior to entering into the extension, has a firm commitment from a prospective subtenant to sublease the property; and

(C) The term of the extension is reasonable and does not materially exceed the term of the sublease;

(ii) Should the OCC determine that a bank has entered into a lease, extension of a lease, or a sublease for the purpose of real estate speculation in violation of 12 U.S.C. 29 and this part, the OCC will take appropriate measures to address the violation, which may include requiring the bank to take immediate steps to divest the lease or sublease; and

(4) With respect to a transaction that does not qualify as a disposition under paragraphs (a)(1) through (3) of this section, by receiving or accumulating from the purchaser an amount in a down payment, principal and interest payments, and private mortgage insurance totalling at least 10 percent of the sales price, as measured in accordance with generally accepted accounting principles.

(b) *Disposition efforts and documentation.* A national bank shall make diligent and ongoing efforts to dispose of each parcel of OREO, and shall maintain documentation adequate to reflect those efforts.

§34.84 [Reserved]

§34.85 Appraisal requirements.

(a) *General.* (1) Upon transfer to OREO, a national bank shall substantiate the parcel's market value by obtaining either:

(i) An appraisal in accordance with subpart C of this part; or

(ii) An appropriate evaluation when the recorded investment amount is equal to or less than the threshold amount in subpart C of this part.

(2) A national bank shall develop a prudent real estate collateral evaluation policy that allows the bank to monitor the value of each parcel of OREO in a manner consistent with prudent banking practice.

(b) *Exception.* If a national bank has a valid appraisal or an appropriate evaluation obtained in connection with a real estate loan and in accordance with subpart C of this part, then the bank need not obtain another appraisal or evaluation when it acquires ownership of the property.

(c) *Sales of OREO.* A national bank need not obtain a new appraisal or evaluation when selling OREO if the sale is consummated based on a valid appraisal or an appropriate evaluation.

§34.86 Additional expenditures and notification.

(a) *Additional expenditures on OREO.* For OREO that is a development or improvement project, a national bank may make advances to complete the project if the advances:

(1) Are reasonably calculated to reduce any shortfall between the parcel's market value and the bank's recorded investment amount;

(2) Are not made for the purpose of speculation in real estate; and

(3) Are consistent with safe and sound banking practices.

(b) *Notification procedures.* (1) A national bank shall notify the appropriate supervisory office at least 30 days before implementing a development or improvement plan for OREO when the sum of the plan's estimated cost and the bank's current recorded investment amount (including any unpaid prior liens on the property) exceeds 10 percent of the bank's capital and surplus. A national bank need notify the OCC under this paragraph (b)(1) only once. A national bank need not notify the OCC that the bank intends to re-fit an existing building for new tenants or to make normal repairs and incur maintenance costs to protect the value of the collateral.

(2) The required notification must demonstrate that the additional expenditure is consistent with the conditions and limitations in paragraph (a) of this section.

(3) Unless informed otherwise, the bank may implement the proposed plan on the thirty-first day (or sooner, if notified by the OCC) following receipt by the OCC of the bank's notification, subject to any conditions imposed by the OCC.

§ 34.87 Accounting treatment.

A national bank shall account for OREO, and sales of OREO, in accordance with the Instructions for the preparation of the Consolidated Reports of Condition and Income.

Subpart F [Reserved]

Subpart G—Appraisals for Higher-Priced Mortgage Loans

SOURCE: 78 FR 10432, Feb. 13, 2013, unless otherwise noted.

§ 34.201 Authority, purpose and scope.

(a) *Authority.* This subpart is issued by the Office of the Comptroller of the Currency under 12 U.S.C. 93a, 12 U.S.C. 1463, 1464 and 15 U.S.C. 1639h.

(b) *Purpose.* The OCC adopts this subpart pursuant to the requirements of section 129H of the Truth in Lending Act (15 U.S.C. 1639h) which provides that a creditor, including a national bank or operating subsidiary, a Federal branch or agency or a Federal savings association or operating subsidiary, may not extend credit in the form of a higher-risk mortgage without complying with the requirements of section 129H of the Truth in Lending Act (15 U.S.C. 1639h) and this subpart G. The definition of a higher-risk mortgage in section 129H is consistent with the definition of a higher-priced mortgage loan under Regulation Z, 12 CFR part 1026. Specifically, 12 CFR 1026.35 defines a higher-priced mortgage loan as a closed-end consumer credit transaction secured by the consumer's principal dwelling with an annual percentage rate that exceeds the average prime offer rate for a comparable transaction as of the date the interest rate is set:

(1) By 1.5 or more percentage points, for a loan secured by a first lien with a principal obligation at consummation that does not exceed the limit in effect as of the date the transaction's interest rate is set for the maximum principal obligation eligible for purchase by Freddie Mac;

(2) By 2.5 or more percentage points, for a loan secured by a first lien with a principal obligation at consummation that exceeds the limit in effect as of the date the transaction's interest rate is set for the maximum principal obligation eligible for purchase by Freddie Mac; or

(3) By 3.5 or more percentage points, for a loan secured by a subordinate lien.

(c) *Scope.* This subpart applies to higher-priced mortgage loan transactions entered into by national banks and their operating subsidiaries, Federal branches and agencies and Federal savings associations and operating subsidiaries of savings associations.

(d) *Official Interpretations.* Appendix C to this subpart sets out OCC Interpretations of the requirements imposed by the OCC pursuant to this subpart.

§ 34.202 Definitions applicable to higher-priced mortgage loans.

(a) Consummation has the same meaning as in 12 CFR 1026.2(a)(13).

(b) Creditor has the same meaning as in 12 CFR 1026.2(a)(17).

(c) Higher-priced mortgage loan has the same meaning as in 12 CFR 1026.35(a)(1).

(d) Reverse mortgage has the same meaning as in 12 CFR 1026.33(a).

[78 FR 10432, Feb. 13, 2013, as amended at 78 FR 78579, Dec. 26, 2013]

§ 34.203 Appraisals for higher-priced mortgage loans.

(a) *Definitions.* For purposes of this section:

(1) *Certified or licensed appraiser* means a person who is certified or licensed by the State agency in the State in which the property that secures the transaction is located, and who performs the appraisal in conformity with the Uniform Standards of Professional Appraisal Practice and

the requirements applicable to appraisers in title XI of the Financial Institutions Reform, Recovery, and Enforcement Act of 1989, as amended (12 U.S.C. 3331 *et seq.*), and any implementing regulations, in effect at the time the appraiser signs the appraiser's certification.

(2) *Credit risk* means the financial risk that a consumer will default on a loan.

(3) *Manufactured home* has the same meaning as in 24 CFR 3280.2.

(4) *Manufacturer's invoice* means a document issued by a manufacturer and provided with a manufactured home to a retail dealer that separately details the wholesale (base) prices at the factory for specific models or series of manufactured homes and itemized options (large appliances, built-in items and equipment), plus actual itemized charges for freight from the factory to the dealer's lot or the homesite (including any rental of wheels and axles) and for any sales taxes to be paid by the dealer. The invoice may recite such prices and charges on an itemized basis or by stating an aggregate price or charge, as appropriate, for each category.

(5) *National Registry* means the database of information about State certified and licensed appraisers maintained by the Appraisal Subcommittee of the Federal Financial Institutions Examination Council.

(6) *New manufactured home* means a manufactured home that has not been previously occupied.

(7) *State agency* means a "State appraiser certifying and licensing agency" recognized in accordance with section 1118(b) of the Financial Institutions Reform, Recovery, and Enforcement Act of 1989 (12 U.S.C. 3347(b)) and any implementing regulations.

(b) *Exemptions.* Unless otherwise specified, the requirements in paragraph (c) through (f) of this section do not apply to the following types of transactions:

(1) A loan that satisfies the criteria of a qualified mortgage as defined pursuant to 15 U.S.C. 1639c.

(2) An extension of credit for which the amount of credit extended is equal to or less than the applicable threshold amount, which is adjusted every year to reflect increases in the Consumer Price Index for Urban Wage Earners and Clerical Workers, as applicable, and published in the OCC official interpretations to this paragraph (b)(2).

(3) A transaction secured by a mobile home, boat, or trailer.

(4) A transaction to finance the initial construction of a dwelling.

(5) A loan with a maturity of 12 months or less, if the purpose of the loan is a "bridge" loan connected with the acquisition of a dwelling intended to become the consumer's principal dwelling.

(6) A reverse-mortgage transaction subject to 12 CFR 1026.33(a).

(7) An extension of credit that is a refinancing secured by a first lien, with refinancing defined as in 12 CFR 1026.20(a) (except that the creditor need not be the original creditor or a holder or servicer of the original obligation), provided that the refinancing meets the following criteria:

(i) Either—

(A) The credit risk of the refinancing is retained by the person that held the credit risk of the existing obligation and there is no commitment, at consummation, to transfer the credit risk to another person; or

(B) The refinancing is insured or guaranteed by the same Federal government agency that insured or guaranteed the existing obligation;

(ii) The regular periodic payments under the refinance loan do not—

(A) Cause the principal balance to increase;

(B) Allow the consumer to defer repayment of principal; or

(C) Result in a balloon payment, as defined in 12 CFR 1026.18(s)(5)(i); and

(iii) The proceeds from the refinancing are used solely to satisfy the existing obligation and to pay amounts attributed solely to the costs of the refinancing; and

(8) A transaction secured by:

(i) A new manufactured home and land, but the exemption shall only apply to the requirement in paragraph (c)(1) of this section that the appraiser conduct a physical visit of the interior of the new manufactured home; or

(ii) A manufactured home and not land, for which the creditor obtains one of the following and provides a copy to the consumer no later than three business days prior to consummation of the transaction—

(A) For a new manufactured home, the manufacturer's invoice for the manufactured home securing the transaction, provided that the date of manufacture is no earlier than 18 months prior to the creditor's receipt of the consumer's application for credit;

(B) A cost estimate of the value of the manufactured home securing the transaction obtained from an independent cost service provider; or

(C) A valuation, as defined in 12 CFR 1026.42(b)(3), of the manufactured home performed by a person who has no direct or indirect interest, financial or otherwise, in the property or transaction for which the valuation is performed and has training in valuing manufactured homes.

(c) *Appraisals required*—(1) *In general.* Except as provided in paragraph (b) of this section, a creditor shall not extend a higher-priced mortgage loan to a consumer without obtaining, prior to consummation, a written appraisal of the property to be mortgaged. The appraisal must be performed by a certified or licensed appraiser who conducts a physical visit of the interior of the property that will secure the transaction.

(2) *Safe harbor.* A creditor obtains a written appraisal that meets the requirements for an appraisal required under paragraph (c)(1) of this section if the creditor:

(i) Orders that the appraiser perform the appraisal in conformity with the Uniform Standards of Professional Appraisal Practice and title XI of the Financial Institutions Reform, Recovery, and Enforcement Act of 1989, as amended (12 U.S.C. 3331 *et seq.*), and any implementing regulations in effect at the time the appraiser signs the appraiser's certification;

(ii) Verifies through the National Registry that the appraiser who signed the appraiser's certification was a certified or licensed appraiser in the State in which the appraised property is located as of the date the appraiser signed the appraiser's certification;

(iii) Confirms that the elements set forth in appendix A to this subpart are addressed in the written appraisal; and

(iv) Has no actual knowledge contrary to the facts or certifications contained in the written appraisal.

(d) *Additional appraisal for certain higher-priced mortgage loans*—(1) *In general.* Except as provided in paragraphs (b) and (d)(7) of this section, a creditor shall not extend a higher-priced mortgage loan to a consumer to finance the acquisition of the consumer's principal dwelling without obtaining, prior to consummation, two written appraisals, if:

(i) The seller acquired the property 90 or fewer days prior to the date of the consumer's agreement to acquire the property and the price in the consumer's agreement to acquire the property exceeds the seller's acquisition price by more than 10 percent; or

(ii) The seller acquired the property 91 to 180 days prior to the date of the consumer's agreement to acquire the property and the price in the consumer's agreement to acquire the property exceeds the seller's acquisition price by more than 20 percent.

(2) *Different certified or licensed appraisers.* The two appraisals required under paragraph (d)(1) of this section may not be performed by the same certified or licensed appraiser.

(3) *Relationship to general appraisal requirements.* If two appraisals must be obtained under paragraph (d)(1) of this section, each appraisal shall meet the requirements of paragraph (c)(1) of this section.

(4) *Required analysis in the additional appraisal.* One of the two required appraisals must include an analysis of:

(i) The difference between the price at which the seller acquired the property and the price that the consumer is obligated to pay to acquire the property, as specified in the consumer's agreement to acquire the property from the seller;

(ii) Changes in market conditions between the date the seller acquired the property and the date of the consumer's agreement to acquire the property; and

(iii) Any improvements made to the property between the date the seller acquired the property and the date of the consumer's agreement to acquire the property.

(5) *No charge for the additional appraisal.* If the creditor must obtain two appraisals under paragraph (d)(1) of this section, the creditor may charge the consumer for only one of the appraisals.

(6) *Creditor's determination of prior sale date and price*—(i) *Reasonable diligence.* A creditor must obtain two written appraisals under paragraph (d)(1) of this section unless the creditor can demonstrate by exercising reasonable diligence that the requirement to obtain two appraisals does not apply. A creditor acts with reasonable diligence if the creditor bases its determination on information contained in written source documents, such as the documents listed in appendix B to this subpart.

(ii) *Inability to determine prior sale date or price—modified requirements for additional appraisal.* If, after exercising reasonable diligence, a creditor cannot determine whether the conditions in paragraphs (d)(1)(i) and (d)(1)(ii) are present and therefore must obtain two written appraisals in accordance with paragraphs (d)(1) through (d)(5) of this section, one of the two appraisals shall include an analysis of the factors in paragraph (d)(4) of this section only to the extent that the information necessary for the appraiser to perform the analysis can be determined.

(7) *Exemptions from the additional appraisal requirement.* The additional appraisal required under paragraph (d)(1) of this section shall not apply to extensions of credit that finance a consumer's acquisition of property:

(i) From a local, State or Federal government agency;

(ii) From a person who acquired title to the property through foreclosure, deed-in-lieu of foreclosure, or other similar judicial or non-judicial procedure as a result of the person's exercise of rights as the holder of a defaulted mortgage loan;

(iii) From a non-profit entity as part of a local, State, or Federal government program under which the non-profit entity is permitted to acquire title to single-family properties for resale from a seller who acquired title to the property through the process of foreclosure, deed-in-lieu of foreclosure, or other similar judicial or non-judicial procedure;

(iv) From a person who acquired title to the property by inheritance or pursuant to a court order of dissolution of marriage, civil union, or domestic partnership, or of partition of joint or marital assets to which the seller was a party;

(v) From an employer or relocation agency in connection with the relocation of an employee;

(vi) From a servicemember, as defined in 50 U.S.C. App. 511(1), who received a deployment or permanent change of station order after the servicemember purchased the property;

(vii) Located in an area designated by the President as a federal disaster area, if and for as long as the Federal financial institutions regulatory agencies, as defined in 12 U.S.C. 3350(6), waive the requirements in title XI of the Financial Institutions Reform, Recovery, and Enforcement Act of 1989, as amended (12 U.S.C. 3331 *et seq.*), and any implementing regulations in that area; or

(viii) Located in a rural county, as defined in 12 CFR 1026.35(b)(2)(iv)(A).

(e) *Required disclosure*—(1) *In general.* Except as provided in paragraph (b) of this section, a creditor shall disclose the following statement, in writing, to a consumer who applies for a higher-priced mortgage loan: "We may order an appraisal to determine the property's value and charge you for this appraisal. We will give you a copy of any appraisal, even if your loan does not close. You can pay for an additional appraisal for your own use at your own cost." Compliance with the disclosure requirement in Regulation B, 12 CFR 1002.14(a)(2), satisfies the requirements of this paragraph.

(2) *Timing of disclosure.* The disclosure required by paragraph (e)(1) of this section shall be delivered or placed in the mail no later than the third business day after the creditor receives the consumer's application for a higher-priced mortgage loan subject to this section. In the case of a loan that is not a higher-priced mortgage loan subject to this section at the time of application, but becomes a higher-priced mortgage loan subject to this section after application, the disclosure shall be delivered or placed in the mail not later than the

third business day after the creditor determines that the loan is a higher-priced mortgage loan subject to this section.

(f) *Copy of appraisals*—(1) *In general.* Except as provided in paragraph (b) of this section, a creditor shall provide to the consumer a copy of any written appraisal performed in connection with a higher-priced mortgage loan pursuant to paragraphs (c) and (d) of this section.

(2) *Timing.* A creditor shall provide to the consumer a copy of each written appraisal pursuant to paragraph (f)(1) of this section:

(i) No later than three business days prior to consummation of the loan; or

(ii) In the case of a loan that is not consummated, no later than 30 days after the creditor determines that the loan will not be consummated.

(3) *Form of copy.* Any copy of a written appraisal required by paragraph (f)(1) of this section may be provided to the applicant in electronic form, subject to compliance with the consumer consent and other applicable provisions of the Electronic Signatures in Global and National Commerce Act (E-Sign Act) (15 U.S.C. 7001 *et seq.*).

(4) *No charge for copy of appraisal.* A creditor shall not charge the consumer for a copy of a written appraisal required to be provided to the consumer pursuant to paragraph (f)(1) of this section.

(g) *Relation to other rules.* The rules in this section 34.203 were adopted jointly by the Board of Governors of the Federal Reserve System (the Board), the OCC, the Federal Deposit Insurance Corporation, the National Credit Union Administration, the Federal Housing Finance Agency, and the Consumer Financial Protection Bureau (Bureau). These rules are substantively identical to the Board's and the Bureau's higher-priced mortgage loan appraisal rules published separately in 12 CFR 226.43 (for the Board) and 12 CFR 1026.35(a) and (c) (for the Bureau).

[78 FR 10432, Feb. 13, 2013, as amended at 78 FR 78579, 78580, Dec. 26, 2013]

APPENDIX A TO SUBPART G OF PART 34—HIGHER-PRICED MORTGAGE LOAN APPRAISAL SAFE HARBOR REVIEW

To qualify for the safe harbor provided in §34.203(c)(2), a creditor must confirm that the written appraisal:

1. Identifies the creditor who ordered the appraisal and the property and the interest being appraised.
2. Indicates whether the contract price was analyzed.
3. Addresses conditions in the property's neighborhood.
4. Addresses the condition of the property and any improvements to the property.
5. Indicates which valuation approaches were used, and includes a reconciliation if more than one valuation approach was used.
6. Provides an opinion of the property's market value and an effective date for the opinion.
7. Indicates that a physical property visit of the interior of the property was performed, as applicable..
8. Includes a certification signed by the appraiser that the appraisal was prepared in accordance with the requirements of the Uniform Standards of Professional Appraisal Practice.
9. Includes a certification signed by the appraiser that the appraisal was prepared in accordance with the requirements of title XI of the Financial Institutions Reform, Recovery and Enforcement Act of 1989, as amended (12 U.S.C. 3331 *et seq.*), and any implementing regulations.

[78 FR 10432, Feb. 13, 2013, as amended at 78 FR 78580, Dec. 26, 2013]

APPENDIX B TO SUBPART G OF PART 34—ILLUSTRATIVE WRITTEN SOURCE DOCUMENTS FOR HIGHER-PRICED MORTGAGE LOAN APPRAISAL RULES

A creditor acts with reasonable diligence under §34.203(d)(6)(i) if the creditor bases its determination on information contained in written source documents, such as:

1. A copy of the recorded deed from the seller.
2. A copy of a property tax bill.
3. A copy of any owner's title insurance policy obtained by the seller.
4. A copy of the RESPA settlement statement from the seller's acquisition (*i.e.*, the HUD–1 or any successor form).
5. A property sales history report or title report from a third-party reporting service.
6. Sales price data recorded in multiple listing services.
7. Tax assessment records or transfer tax records obtained from local governments.
8. A written appraisal performed in compliance with §34.203(c)(1) for the same transaction.

9. A copy of a title commitment report detailing the seller's ownership of the property, the date it was acquired, or the price at which the seller acquired the property.

10. A property abstract.

APPENDIX C TO SUBPART G OF PART 34—OCC INTERPRETATIONS

SECTION 34.202—DEFINITIONS APPLICABLE TO HIGHER-PRICED MORTGAGE LOANS

1. *Staff Interpretations.* Section 34.202 incorporates definitions from Regulation Z, 12 CFR part 1026. These OCC Interpretations of 12 CFR part 34, subpart G, incorporate the Official Staff Interpretations to the Bureau's Regulation Z associated with those definitions, at 12 CFR part 1026, Supplement I.

SECTION 34.203—APPRAISALS FOR HIGHER-PRICED MORTGAGE LOANS

34.203(a) Definitions.

34.203(a)(1) Certified or licensed appraiser.

1. *USPAP.* The Uniform Standards of Professional Appraisal Practice (USPAP) are established by the Appraisal Standards Board of the Appraisal Foundation (as defined in 12 U.S.C. 3350(9)). Under §34.203(a)(1), the relevant USPAP standards are those found in the edition of USPAP in effect at the time the appraiser signs the appraiser's certification.

2. *Appraiser's certification.* The appraiser's certification refers to the certification that must be signed by the appraiser for each appraisal assignment. This requirement is specified in USPAP Standards Rule 2–3.

3. *FIRREA title XI and implementing regulations.* The relevant regulations are those prescribed under section 1110 of the Financial Institutions Reform, Recovery, and Enforcement Act of 1989 (FIRREA), as amended (12 U.S.C. 3339), that relate to an appraiser's development and reporting of the appraisal in effect at the time the appraiser signs the appraiser's certification. Paragraph (3) of FIRREA section 1110 (12 U.S.C. 3339(3)), which relates to the review of appraisals, is not relevant for determining whether an appraiser is a certified or licensed appraiser under §34.203(a)(1).

34.203(b) Exemptions.

1. *Compliance with title XI of the Financial Institutions Reform, Recovery, and Enforcement Act of 1989 (FIRREA).* Section 34.203(b) provides exemptions solely from the requirements of §34.203(c) through (f). Institutions subject to the requirements of FIRREA and its implementing regulations that make a loan qualifying for an exemption under §34.203(b) must still comply with appraisal and evaluation requirements under FIRREA and its implementing regulations.

34.203(b)(1) Exemptions

Paragraph 34.203(b)(1)

1. *Qualified mortgage criteria.* Under §34.203(b)(1), a loan is exempt from the appraisal requirements of §34.203 if either:

i. The loan is—(1) subject to the ability-to-repay requirements of the Consumer Financial Protection Bureau (Bureau) in 12 CFR 1026.43 as a "covered transaction" (defined in 12 CFR 1026.43(b)(1)) and (2) a qualified mortgage pursuant to the Bureau's rules or, for loans insured, guaranteed, or administered by the U.S. Department of Housing and Urban Development (HUD), U.S. Department of Veterans Affairs (VA), U.S. Department of Agriculture (USDA), or Rural Housing Service (RHS), a qualified mortgage pursuant to applicable rules prescribed by those agencies (but only once such rules are in effect; otherwise, the Bureau's definition of a qualified mortgage applies to those loans); or

ii. The loan is—(1) not subject to the Bureau's ability-to-repay requirements in 12 CFR 1026.43 as a "covered transaction" (defined in 12 CFR 1026.43(b)(1)), but (2) meets the criteria for a qualified mortgage in the Bureau's rules or, for loans insured, guaranteed, or administered by HUD, VA, USDA, or RHS, meets the criteria for a qualified mortgage in the applicable rules prescribed by those agencies (but only once such rules are in effect; otherwise, the Bureau's criteria for a qualified mortgage applies to those loans). To explain further, loans enumerated in 12 CFR 1026.43(a) are not "covered transactions" under the Bureau's ability-to-repay requirements in 12 CFR 1026.43, and thus cannot be qualified mortgages (entitled to a rebuttable presumption or safe harbor of compliance with the ability-to-repay requirements of 12 CFR 1026.43, *see, e.g.*, 12 CFR 1026.43(e)(1)). These include an extension of credit made pursuant to a program administered by a Housing Finance Agency, as defined under 24 CFR 266.5, or pursuant to a program authorized by sections 101 and 109 of the Emergency Economic Stabilization Act of 2008. *See* 12 CFR 1026.43(a)(3)(iv) and (vi). They also include extensions of credit made by a creditor identified in 12 CFR 1026.43(a)(3)(v). However, these loans are eligible for the exemption in §34.203(b)(1) if they meet the Bureau's qualified mortgage criteria in 12 CFR 1026.43(e)(2), (4), (5), or (6) or 12 CFR 1026.43(f) (including limits on when loans must be consummated) or, for loans that are insured, guaranteed, or administered by HUD, VA, USDA, or RHS, in applicable rules prescribed by those agencies (but only once such rules are in effect; otherwise, the Bureau's criteria for a qualified mortgage applies to those loans). For example, assume that HUD has prescribed rules to define loans insured under its programs that are qualified mortgages and those rules are in effect. Assume further that a creditor designated as a Community Development Financial Institution, as defined under 12 CFR 1805.104(h), originates a loan insured by the Federal Housing Administration, which is a part of HUD. The loan is not a "covered transaction" and thus is not a qualified mortgage. *See* 12 CFR 1026.43(a)(3)(v)(A) and (b)(1). Nonetheless, the transaction is eligible for an exemption from the appraisal requirements of § 34.203(b)(1) if it meets the qualified mortgage criteria in HUD's rules. Nothing in § 34.203(b)(1) alters the definition of a qualified mortgage under regulations of the Bureau, HUD, VA, USDA, or RHS.

Paragraph 34.203(b)(2)

1. *Threshold amount*. For purposes of § 34.203(b)(2), the threshold amount in effect during a particular period is the amount stated in comment 203(b)(2)–3 for that period. The threshold amount is adjusted effective January 1 of each year by any annual percentage increase in the Consumer Price Index for Urban Wage Earners and Clerical Workers (CPI–W) that was in effect on the preceding June 1. Comment 203(b)(2)–3 will be amended to provide the threshold amount for the upcoming year after the annual percentage change in the CPI–W that was in effect on June 1 becomes available. Any increase in the threshold amount will be rounded to the nearest $100 increment. For example, if the annual percentage increase in the CPI–W would result in a $950 increase in the threshold amount, the threshold amount will be increased by $1,000. However, if the annual percentage increase in the CPI–W would result in a $949 increase in the threshold amount, the threshold amount will be increased by $900.

2. *No increase in the CPI–W*. If the CPI–W in effect on June 1 does not increase from the CPI–W in effect on June 1 of the previous year, the threshold amount effective the following January 1 through December 31 will not change from the previous year. When this occurs, for the years that follow, the threshold is calculated based on the annual percentage change in the CPI–W applied to the dollar amount that would have resulted, after rounding, if decreases and any subsequent increases in the CPI–W had been taken into account.

i. *Net increases*. If the resulting amount calculated, after rounding, is greater than the current threshold, then the threshold effective January 1 the following year will increase accordingly.

ii. *Net decreases*. If the resulting amount calculated, after rounding, is equal to or less than the current threshold, then the threshold effective January 1 the following year will not change, but future increases will be calculated based on the amount that would have resulted.

3. *Threshold*. For purposes of § 34.203(b)(2), the threshold amount in effect during a particular period is the amount stated below for that period.

i. From January 18, 2014, through December 31, 2014, the threshold amount is $25,000.

ii. From January 1, 2015, through December 31, 2015, the threshold amount is $25,500.

iii. From January 1, 2016, through December 31, 2016, the threshold amount is $25,500.

iv. From January 1, 2017, through December 31, 2017, the threshold amount is $25,500.

v. From January 1, 2018, through December 31, 2018, the threshold amount is $26,000.

vi. From January 1, 2019, through December 31, 2019, the threshold amount is $26,700.

4. *Qualifying for exemption—in general*. A transaction is exempt under § 34.203(b)(2) if the creditor makes an extension of credit at consummation that is equal to or below the threshold amount in effect at the time of consummation.

5. *Qualifying for exemption—subsequent changes*. A transaction does not meet the condition for an exemption under § 34.203(b)(2) merely because it is used to satisfy and replace an existing exempt loan, unless the amount of the new extension of credit is equal to or less than the applicable threshold amount. For example, assume a closed-end loan that qualified for a § 34.203(b)(2) exemption at consummation in year one is refinanced in year ten and that the new loan amount is greater than the threshold amount in effect in year ten. In these circumstances, the creditor must comply with all of the applicable requirements of § 34.203 with respect to the year ten transaction if the original loan is satisfied and replaced by the new loan, unless another exemption from the requirements of § 34.203 applies. *See* § 34.203(b) and (d)(7).

Paragraph 34.203(b)(3).

1. *Secured by a mobile home*. For purposes of the exemption in § 34.203(b)(3), a mobile home does not include a manufactured home, as defined in § 34.203(a)(2).

Paragraph 34.203(b)(4).

1. *Construction-to-permanent loans*. Section 34.203 does not apply to a transaction to finance the initial construction of a dwelling. This exclusion applies to a construction-only loan as well as to the construction phase of a construction-to-permanent loan. Section 34.203 does apply, however, to permanent financing that replaces a construction loan, whether the permanent financing is extended by the same or a different creditor, unless the permanent financing is otherwise exempt from the requirements of § 34.203. *See* § 34.203(b). When a construction loan may be permanently financed by the same creditor, the general disclosure requirements for closed-end credit pursuant to Regulation Z (12 CFR 1026.17) provide that the creditor may give either one combined disclosure for

both the construction financing and the permanent financing, or a separate set of disclosures for each of the two phases as though they were two separate transactions. *See* 12 CFR 1026.17(c)(6)(ii) and the Official Staff Interpretations to the Bureau's Regulation Z, comment 17(c)(6)–2. Which disclosure option a creditor elects under § 1026.17(c)(6)(ii) does not affect the determination of whether the permanent phase of the transaction is subject to § 34.203. When the creditor discloses the two phases as separate transactions, the annual percentage rate for the permanent phase must be compared to the average prime offer rate for a transaction that is comparable to the permanent financing to determine coverage under § 34.203. When the creditor discloses the two phases as a single transaction, a single annual percentage rate, reflecting the appropriate charges from both phases, must be calculated for the transaction in accordance with 12 CFR 1026.35(a)(1) (incorporated into 12 CFR part 34, subpart G by § 34.202) and appendix D to 12 CFR part 1026. The annual percentage rate must be compared to the average prime offer rate for a transaction that is comparable to the permanent financing to determine coverage under § 34.203. If the transaction is determined to be a higher-priced mortgage loan not otherwise exempt under § 34.203(b), only the permanent phase is subject to the requirements of § 34.203.

2. *Financing initial construction*. The exemption for construction loans in § 34.203(b)(4) applies to temporary financing of the construction of a dwelling that will be replaced by permanent financing once construction is complete. The exemption does not apply, for example, to loans to finance the purchase of manufactured homes that have not been or are in the process of being built when the financing obtained by the consumer at that time is permanent. *See* § 34.203(b)(8).

Paragraph 34.203(b)(7)

Paragraph 34.203(b)(7)(i)(A)

1. *Same credit risk holder*. The requirement that the holder of the credit risk on the existing obligation and the refinancing be the same applies to situations in which an entity bears the financial responsibility for the default of a loan by either holding the loan in its portfolio or guaranteeing payments of principal and any interest to investors in a mortgage-backed security in which the loan is pooled. *See* § 34.203(a)(2) (defining "credit risk"). For example, a credit risk holder could be a bank that bears the credit risk on the existing obligation by holding the loan in the bank's portfolio. Another example of a credit risk holder would be a government-sponsored enterprise that bears the risk of default on a loan by guaranteeing the payment of principal and any interest on a loan to investors in a mortgage-backed security. The holder of credit risk under § 34.203(b)(7)(i)(A) does not mean individual investors in a mortgage-backed security or providers of private mortgage insurance.

2. *Same credit risk holder—illustrations*. Illustrations of the credit risk holder of the existing obligation continuing to be the credit risk holder of the refinancing include, but are not limited to, the following:

i. The existing obligation is held in the portfolio of a bank, thus the bank holds the credit risk. The bank arranges to refinance the loan and also will hold the refinancing in its portfolio. If the refinancing otherwise meets the requirements for an exemption under § 34.203(b)(7), the transaction will qualify for the exemption because the credit risk holder is the same for the existing obligation and the refinance transaction. In this case, the exemption would apply regardless of whether the bank arranged to refinance the loan directly or indirectly, such as through the servicer or subservicer on the existing obligation.

ii. The existing obligation is held in the portfolio of a government-sponsored enterprise (GSE), thus the GSE holds the credit risk. The existing obligation is then refinanced by the servicer of the loan and immediately transferred to the GSE. The GSE pools the refinancing in a mortgage-backed security guaranteed by the GSE, thus the GSE holds the credit risk on the refinance loan. If the refinance transaction otherwise meets the requirements for an exemption under § 34.203(b)(7), the transaction will qualify for the exemption because the credit risk holder is the same for the existing obligation and the refinance transaction. In this case, the exemption would apply regardless of whether the existing obligation was refinanced by the servicer or subservicer on the existing obligation (acting as a "creditor" under 12 CFR 1026.2(a)(17)) or by a different creditor.

3. *Forward commitments*. A creditor may make a mortgage loan that will be sold or otherwise transferred pursuant to an agreement that has been entered into at or before the time the transaction is consummated. Such an agreement is sometimes known as a "forward commitment." A refinance loan does not satisfy the requirement of § 34.203(b)(7)(i)(A) if the loan will be acquired pursuant to a forward commitment, such that the credit risk on the refinance loan will transfer to a person who did not hold the credit risk on the existing obligation.

Paragraph 34.203(b)(7)(ii)

1. *Regular periodic payments*. Under § 34.203(b)(7)(ii), the regular periodic payments on the refinance loan must not: Result in an increase of the principal balance (negative amortization); allow the consumer to defer repayment of principal (*see* 12 CFR 1026.43, and the Official Staff Interpretations

to the Bureau's Regulation Z, comment 43(e)(2)(i)–2); or result in a balloon payment. Thus, the terms of the legal obligation must require the consumer to make payments of principal and interest on a monthly or other periodic basis that will repay the loan amount over the loan term. Except for payments resulting from any interest rate changes after consummation in an adjustable-rate or step-rate mortgage, the periodic payments must be substantially equal. For an explanation of the term "substantially equal," *see* 12 CFR 1026.43, the Official Staff Interpretations to the Bureau's Regulation Z, comment 43(c)(5)(i)–4. In addition, a single-payment transaction is not a refinancing meeting the requirements of § 34.203(b)(7) because it does not require "regular periodic payments."

Paragraph 34.203(b)(7)(iii)

1. *Permissible use of proceeds.* The exemption for a refinancing under § 34.203(b)(7) is available only if the proceeds from the refinancing are used exclusively for the existing obligation and amounts attributed solely to the costs of the refinancing. The existing obligation includes the unpaid principal balance of the existing first lien loan, any earned unpaid finance charges, and any other lawful charges related to the existing loan. For guidance on the meaning of refinancing costs, *see* 12 CFR 1026.23, the Official Staff Interpretations to the Bureau's Regulations Z, comment 23(f)–4. If the proceeds of a refinancing are used for other purposes, such as to pay off other liens or to provide additional cash to the consumer for discretionary spending, the transaction does not qualify for the exemption for a refinancing under § 34.203(b)(7) from the appraisal requirements in § 34.203.

For applications received on or after July 18, 2015

Paragraph 34.203(b)(8)

Paragraph 34.203(b)(8)(i)

1. *Secured by new manufactured home and land—physical visit of the interior.* A transaction secured by a new manufactured home and land is subject to the requirements of § 34.203(c) through (f) except for the requirement in § 34.203(c)(1) that the appraiser conduct a physical inspection of the interior of the property. Thus, for example, a creditor of a loan secured by a new manufactured home and land could comply with § 34.203(c)(1) by obtaining an appraisal conducted by a state-certified or -licensed appraiser based on plans and specifications for the new manufactured home and an inspection of the land on which the property will be sited, as well as any other information necessary for the appraiser to complete the appraisal assignment in conformity with the Uniform Standards of Professional Appraisal Practice and the requirements of FIRREA and any implementing regulations.

Paragraph 34.203(b)(8)(ii)

1. *Secured by a manufactured home and not land.* Section 34.203(b)(8)(ii) applies to a higher-priced mortgage loan secured by a manufactured home and not land, regardless of whether the home is titled as realty by operation of state law.

Paragraph 34.203(b)(8)(ii)(B)

1. *Independent.* A cost service provider from which the creditor obtains a manufactured home unit cost estimate under § 34.203(b)(8)(ii)(B) is "independent" if that person is not affiliated with the creditor in the transaction, such as by common corporate ownership, and receives no direct or indirect financial benefits based on whether the transaction is consummated.

2. *Adjustments.* The requirement that the cost estimate be from an independent cost service provider does not prohibit a creditor from providing a cost estimate that reflects adjustments to account for factors such as special features, condition or location. However, the requirement that the estimate be obtained from an independent cost service provider means that any adjustments to the estimate must be based on adjustment factors available as part of the independent cost service used, with associated values that are determined by the independent cost service.

Paragraph 34.203(b)(8)(ii)(C)

1. *Interest in the property.* A person has a direct or indirect in the property if, for example, the person has any ownership or reasonably foreseeable ownership interest in the manufactured home. To illustrate, a person who seeks a loan to purchase the manufactured home to be valued has a reasonably foreseeable ownership interest in the property.

2. *Interest in the transaction.* A person has a direct or indirect interest in the transaction if, for example, the person or an affiliate of that person also serves as a loan officer of the creditor or otherwise arranges the credit transaction, or is the retail dealer of the manufactured home. A person also has a prohibited interest in the transaction if the person is compensated or otherwise receives financial or other benefits based on whether the transaction is consummated.

3. *Training in valuing manufactured homes.* Training in valuing manufactured homes includes, for example, successfully completing a course in valuing manufactured homes offered by a state or national appraiser association or receiving job training from an employer in the business of valuing manufactured homes.

4. *Manufactured home valuation—example.* A valuation in compliance with § 34.203(b)(8)(ii)(C) would include, for example, an appraisal of the manufactured home

in accordance with the appraisal requirements for a manufactured home classified as personal property under the Title I Manufactured Home Loan Insurance Program of the U.S. Department of Housing and Urban Development, pursuant to section 2(b)(10) of the National Housing Act, 12 U.S.C. 1703(b)(10).

34.203(c)(1) In general.

1. *Written appraisal—electronic transmission.* To satisfy the requirement that the appraisal be "written," a creditor may obtain the appraisal in paper form or via electronic transmission.

34.203(c)(2) Safe harbor.

1. *Safe harbor.* A creditor that satisfies the safe harbor conditions in §34.203(c)(2)(i) through (iv) complies with the appraisal requirements of §34.203(c)(1). A creditor that does not satisfy the safe harbor conditions in §34.203(c)(2)(i) through (iv) does not necessarily violate the appraisal requirements of §34.203(c)(1).

2. *Appraiser's certification.* For purposes of §34.203(c)(2), the appraiser's certification refers to the certification specified in item 9 of appendix A to this subpart. *See also* comment 34.203(a)(1)–2.

Paragraph 34.203(c)(2)(iii).

1. *Confirming elements in the appraisal.* To confirm that the elements in appendix A to this subpart are included in the written appraisal, a creditor need not look beyond the face of the written appraisal and the appraiser's certification.

34.203(d) Additional appraisal for certain higher-priced mortgage loans.

1. *Acquisition.* For purposes of §34.203(d), the terms "acquisition" and "acquire" refer to the acquisition of legal title to the property pursuant to applicable State law, including by purchase.

34.203(d)(1) In general.

1. *Appraisal from a previous transaction.* An appraisal that was previously obtained in connection with the seller's acquisition or the financing of the seller's acquisition of the property does not satisfy the requirements to obtain two written appraisals under §34.203(d)(1).

2. *90-day, 180-day calculation.* The time periods described in §34.203(d)(1)(i) and (ii) are calculated by counting the day after the date on which the seller acquired the property, up to and including the date of the consumer's agreement to acquire the property that secures the transaction. For example, assume that the creditor determines that date of the consumer's acquisition agreement is October 15, 2012, and that the seller acquired the property on April 17, 2012. The first day to be counted in the 180-day calculation would be April 18, 2012, and the last day would be October 15, 2012. In this case, the number of days from April 17 would be 181, so an additional appraisal is not required.

3. *Date seller acquired the property.* For purposes of §34.203(d)(1)(i) and (ii), the date on which the seller acquired the property is the date on which the seller became the legal owner of the property pursuant to applicable State law.

4. *Date of the consumer's agreement to acquire the property.* For the date of the consumer's agreement to acquire the property under §34.203(d)(1)(i) and (ii), the creditor should use the date on which the consumer and the seller signed the agreement provided to the creditor by the consumer. The date on which the consumer and the seller signed the agreement might not be the date on which the consumer became contractually obligated under State law to acquire the property. For purposes of §34.203(d)(1)(i) and (ii), a creditor is not obligated to determine whether and to what extent the agreement is legally binding on both parties. If the dates on which the consumer and the seller signed the agreement differ, the creditor should use the later of the two dates.

5. *Price at which the seller acquired the property.* The price at which the seller acquired the property refers to the amount paid by the seller to acquire the property. The price at which the seller acquired the property does not include the cost of financing the property.

6. *Price the consumer is obligated to pay to acquire the property.* The price the consumer is obligated to pay to acquire the property is the price indicated on the consumer's agreement with the seller to acquire the property. The price the consumer is obligated to pay to acquire the property from the seller does not include the cost of financing the property. For purposes of §34.203(d)(1)(i) and (ii), a creditor is not obligated to determine whether and to what extent the agreement is legally binding on both parties. *See also* comment 34.203(d)(1)–4.

34.203(d)(2) Different certified or licensed appraisers.

1. *Independent appraisers.* The requirements that a creditor obtain two separate appraisals under §34.203(d)(1), and that each appraisal be conducted by a different licensed or certified appraiser under §34.203(d)(2), indicate that the two appraisals must be conducted independently of each other. If the two certified or licensed appraisers are affiliated, such as by being employed by the same appraisal firm, then whether they have conducted the appraisal independently of each other must be determined based on the facts and circumstances of the particular case known to the creditor.

34.203(d)(3) Relationship to general appraisal requirements.

1. *Safe harbor.* When a creditor is required to obtain an additional appraisal under §34.203(d)(1), the creditor must comply with the requirements of both §34.203(c)(1) and §34.203(d)(2) through (5) for that appraisal. The creditor complies with the requirements of §34.203(c)(1) for the additional appraisal if

the creditor meets the safe harbor conditions in § 34.203(c)(2) for that appraisal.

34.203(d)(4) Required analysis in the additional appraisal.

1. *Determining acquisition dates and prices used in the analysis of the additional appraisal.* For guidance on identifying the date on which the seller acquired the property, see comment 34.203(d)(1)–3. For guidance on identifying the date of the consumer's agreement to acquire the property, see comment 34.203(d)(1)–4. For guidance on identifying the price at which the seller acquired the property, see comment 34.203(d)(1)–5. For guidance on identifying the price the consumer is obligated to pay to acquire the property, see comment 34.203(d)(1)–6.

34.203(d)(5) No charge for additional appraisal.

1. *Fees and mark-ups.* The creditor is prohibited from charging the consumer for the performance of one of the two appraisals required under § 34.203(d)(1), including by imposing a fee specifically for that appraisal or by marking up the interest rate or any other fees payable by the consumer in connection with the higher-priced mortgage loan.

34.203(d)(6) Creditor's determination of prior sale date and price.

34.203(d)(6)(i) In general.

1. *Estimated sales price.* If a written source document describes the seller's acquisition price in a manner that indicates that the price described is an estimated or assumed amount and not the actual price, the creditor should look at an alternative document to satisfy the reasonable diligence standard in determining the price at which the seller acquired the property.

2. *Reasonable diligence—oral statements insufficient.* Reliance on oral statements of interested parties, such as the consumer, seller, or mortgage broker, does not constitute reasonable diligence under § 34.203(d)(6)(i).

3. *Lack of information and conflicting information—two appraisals required.* If a creditor is unable to demonstrate that the requirement to obtain two appraisals under § 34.203(d)(1) does not apply, the creditor must obtain two written appraisals before extending a higher-priced mortgage loan subject to the requirements of § 34.203 *See also* comment 34.203(d)(6)(ii)–1. For example:

i. Assume a creditor orders and reviews the results of a title search, which shows that a prior sale occurred between 91 and 180 days ago, but not the price paid in that sale. Thus, based on the title search, the creditor would not be able to determine whether the price the consumer is obligated to pay under the consumer's acquisition agreement is more than 20 percent higher than the seller's acquisition price, pursuant to § 34.203(d)(1)(ii). Before extending a higher-priced mortgage loan subject to the appraisal requirements of § 34.203, the creditor must either: perform additional diligence to ascertain the seller's acquisition price and, based on this information, determine whether two written appraisals are required; or obtain two written appraisals in compliance with § 34.203(d)(6). *See also* comment 34.203(d)(6)(ii)–1.

ii. Assume a creditor reviews the results of a title search indicating that the last recorded purchase was more than 180 days before the consumer's agreement to acquire the property. Assume also that the creditor subsequently receives a written appraisal indicating that the seller acquired the property between 91 and 180 days before the consumer's agreement to acquire the property. In this case, unless one of these sources is clearly wrong on its face, the creditor would not be able to determine whether the seller acquired the property within 180 days of the date of the consumer's agreement to acquire the property from the seller, pursuant to § 34.203(d)(1)(ii). Before extending a higher-priced mortgage loan subject to the appraisal requirements of § 34.203, the creditor must either: perform additional diligence to ascertain the seller's acquisition date and, based on this information, determine whether two written appraisals are required; or obtain two written appraisals in compliance with § 34.203(d)(6). *See also* comment 34.203(d)(6)(ii)–1.

34.203(d)(6)(ii) Inability to determine prior sales date or price—modified requirements for additional appraisal.

1. *Required analysis.* In general, the additional appraisal required under § 34.203(d)(1) should include an analysis of the factors listed in § 34.203(d)(4)(i) through (iii). However, if, following reasonable diligence, a creditor cannot determine whether the conditions in § 34.203(d)(1)(i) or (ii) are present due to a lack of information or conflicting information, the required additional appraisal must include the analyses required under § 34.203(d)(4)(i) through (iii) only to the extent that the information necessary to perform the analyses is known. For example, assume that a creditor is able, following reasonable diligence, to determine that the date on which the seller acquired the property occurred between 91 and 180 days prior to the date of the consumer's agreement to acquire the property. However, the creditor is unable, following reasonable diligence, to determine the price at which the seller acquired the property. In this case, the creditor is required to obtain an additional written appraisal that includes an analysis under § 34.203(d)(4)(ii) and (iii) of the changes in market conditions and any improvements made to the property between the date the seller acquired the property and the date of the consumer's agreement to acquire the property. However, the creditor is not required to obtain an additional written appraisal that includes analysis under § 34.203(d)(4)(i) of the difference between the

price at which the seller acquired the property and the price that the consumer is obligated to pay to acquire the property.

34.203(d)(7) Exemptions from the additional appraisal requirement.

Paragraph 34.203(d)(7)(iii).

1. *Non-profit entity.* For purposes of § 34.203(d)(7)(iii), a "non-profit entity" is a person with a tax exemption ruling or determination letter from the Internal Revenue Service under section 501(c)(3) of the Internal Revenue Code of 1986 (12 U.S.C. 501(c)(3)).

Paragraph 34.203(d)(7)(viii).

1. *Bureau table of rural counties.* The Bureau publishes on its Web site a table of rural counties under 12 CFR 1026.35(b)(2)(iv)(A) for each calendar year by the end of that calendar year. *See* Official Staff Interpretations to the Bureau's Regulation Z, comment 35(b)(2)(iv)–1. A property securing an HPML subject to § 34.203 is in a rural county under § 34.203(d)(7)(viii) if the county in which the property is located is on the table of rural counties most recently published by the Bureau. For example, for a transaction occurring in 2015, assume that the Bureau most recently published a table of rural counties at the end of 2014. The property securing the transaction would be located in a rural county for purposes of § 34.203(d)(7)(viii) if the county is on the table of rural counties published by the Bureau at the end of 2014.

34.203(e) Required disclosure.

34.203(e)(1) In general.

1. *Multiple applicants.* When two or more consumers apply for a loan subject to this section, the creditor is required to give the disclosure to only one of the consumers.

2. *Appraisal independence requirements not affected.* Nothing in the text of the consumer notice required by § 34.203(e)(1) should be construed to affect, modify, limit, or supersede the operation of any legal, regulatory, or other requirements or standards relating to independence in the conduct of appraisals or restrictions on the use of borrower-ordered appraisals by creditors.

34.203(f) Copy of appraisals.

34.203(f)(1) In general.

1. *Multiple applicants.* When two or more consumers apply for a loan subject to this section, the creditor is required to give the copy of each required appraisal to only one of the consumers.

34.203(f)(2) Timing.

1. "*Provide.*" For purposes of the requirement to provide a copy of the appraisal within a specified time under § 34.203(f)(2), "provide" means "deliver." Delivery occurs three business days after mailing or delivering the copies to the last-known address of the applicant, or when evidence indicates actual receipt by the applicant (which, in the case of electronic receipt, must be based upon consent that complies with the E-Sign Act), whichever is earlier.

2. *No waiver.* Regulation B, 12 CFR 1002.14(a)(1), allowing the consumer to waive the requirement that the appraisal copy be provided three business days before consummation, does not apply to higher-priced mortgage loans subject to § 34.203. A consumer of a higher-priced mortgage loan subject to § 34.203 may not waive the timing requirement to receive a copy of the appraisal under § 34.203(f)(2).

34.203(f)(4) No charge for copy of appraisal.

1. *Fees and mark-ups.* The creditor is prohibited from charging the consumer for any copy of an appraisal required to be provided under § 34.203(f)(1), including by imposing a fee specifically for a required copy of an appraisal or by marking up the interest rate or any other fees payable by the consumer in connection with the higher-priced mortgage loan.

APPENDIX B—ILLUSTRATIVE WRITTEN SOURCE DOCUMENTS FOR HIGHER-PRICED MORTGAGE LOAN APPRAISAL RULES

1. *Title commitment report.* The "title commitment report" is a document from a title insurance company describing the property interest and status of its title, parties with interests in the title and the nature of their claims, issues with the title that must be resolved prior to closing of the transaction between the parties to the transfer, amount and disposition of the premiums, and endorsements on the title policy. This document is issued by the title insurance company prior to the company's issuance of an actual title insurance policy to the property's transferee and/or creditor financing the transaction. In different jurisdictions, this instrument may be referred to by different terms, such as a title commitment, title binder, title opinion, or title report.

[78 FR 10432, Feb. 13, 2013, as amended at 78 FR 78580, Dec. 26, 2013; 79 FR 78298, Dec. 30, 2014; 80 FR 73945, Nov. 27, 2015; 81 FR 86254, Nov. 30, 2016; 82 FR 51974, Nov. 9, 2017; 83 FR 59274, Nov. 23, 2018]

Subpart H—Appraisal Management Company Minimum Requirements

SOURCE: 80 FR 32679, June 9, 2015, unless otherwise noted.

§ 34.210 Authority, purpose, and scope.

(a) *Authority.* This subpart is issued by the Office of the Comptroller of the Currency under 12 U.S.C. 93a and Title XI of the Financial Institutions Reform, Recovery, and Enforcement Act (FIRREA), as amended by the Dodd-

Frank Wall Street Reform and Consumer Protection Act (the Dodd-Frank Act) (Pub. L. 111–203, 124 Stat. 1376 (2010)), 12 U.S.C. 3331 *et seq.*

(b) *Purpose.* The purpose of this subpart is to implement sections 1109, 1117, 1121, and 1124 of FIRREA Title XI, 12 U.S.C. 3338, 3346, 3350, and 3353.

(c) *Scope.* This subpart applies to States and to appraisal management companies (AMCs) providing appraisal management services in connection with consumer credit transactions secured by a consumer's principal dwelling or securitizations of those transactions.

(d) *Rule of construction.* Nothing in this subpart should be construed to prevent a State from establishing requirements in addition to those in this subpart. In addition, nothing in this subpart should be construed to alter guidance in, and applicability of, the Interagency Appraisal and Evaluation Guidelines[3] or other relevant agency guidance that cautions banks, bank holding companies, Federal savings associations, state savings associations, and credit unions, as applicable, that each such entity is accountable for overseeing the activities of third-party service providers and ensuring that any services provided by a third party comply with applicable laws, regulations, and supervisory guidance applicable directly to the financial institution.

§ 34.211 Definitions.

For purposes of this subpart:

(a) *Affiliate* has the meaning provided in 12 U.S.C. 1841.

(b) *AMC National Registry* means the registry of State-registered AMCs and Federally regulated AMCs maintained by the Appraisal Subcommittee.

(c)(1) *Appraisal management company* (AMC) means a person that:

(i) Provides appraisal management services to creditors or to secondary mortgage market participants, including affiliates;

(ii) Provides such services in connection with valuing a consumer's principal dwelling as security for a consumer credit transaction or incorporating such transactions into securitizations; and

(iii) Within a given 12-month period, as defined in § 34.212(d), oversees an appraiser panel of more than 15 State-certified or State-licensed appraisers in a State or 25 or more State-certified or State-licensed appraisers in two or more States, as described in § 34.212;

(2) An AMC does not include a department or division of an entity that provides appraisal management services only to that entity.

(d) *Appraisal management services* means one or more of the following:

(1) Recruiting, selecting, and retaining appraisers;

(2) Contracting with State-certified or State-licensed appraisers to perform appraisal assignments;

(3) Managing the process of having an appraisal performed, including providing administrative services such as receiving appraisal orders and appraisal reports, submitting completed appraisal reports to creditors and secondary market participants, collecting fees from creditors and secondary market participants for services provided, and paying appraisers for services performed; and

(4) Reviewing and verifying the work of appraisers.

(e) *Appraiser panel* means a network, list or roster of licensed or certified appraisers approved by an AMC to perform appraisals as independent contractors for the AMC. Appraisers on an AMC's "appraiser panel" under this part include both appraisers accepted by the AMC for consideration for future appraisal assignments in covered transactions or for secondary mortgage market participants in connection with covered transactions and appraisers engaged by the AMC to perform one or more appraisals in covered transactions or for secondary mortgage market participants in connection with covered transactions. An appraiser is an independent contractor for purposes of this subpart if the appraiser is treated as an independent contractor by the AMC for purposes of Federal income taxation.

(f) *Appraisal Subcommittee* means the Appraisal Subcommittee of the Federal Financial Institutions Examination Council.

[3] *See http://www.occ.gov/news-issuances/bulletins/2010/bulletin-2010-42.html.*

(g) *Consumer credit* means credit offered or extended to a consumer primarily for personal, family, or household purposes.

(h) *Covered transaction* means any consumer credit transaction secured by the consumer's principal dwelling.

(i) *Creditor* means:

(1) A person who regularly extends consumer credit that is subject to a finance charge or is payable by written agreement in more than four installments (not including a down payment), and to whom the obligation is initially payable, either on the face of the note or contract, or by agreement when there is no note or contract.

(2) A person regularly extends consumer credit if the person extended credit (other than credit subject to the requirements of 12 CFR 1026.32) more than 5 times for transactions secured by a dwelling in the preceding calendar year. If a person did not meet these numerical standards in the preceding calendar year, the numerical standards shall be applied to the current calendar year. A person regularly extends consumer credit if, in any 12-month period, the person originates more than one credit extension that is subject to the requirements of 12 CFR 1026.32 or one or more such credit extensions through a mortgage broker.

(j) *Dwelling* means:

(1) A residential structure that contains one to four units, whether or not that structure is attached to real property. The term includes an individual condominium unit, cooperative unit, mobile home, and trailer, if it is used as a residence.

(2) A consumer can have only one "principal" dwelling at a time. Thus, a vacation or other second home would not be a principal dwelling. However, if a consumer buys or builds a new dwelling that will become the consumer's principal dwelling within a year or upon the completion of construction, the new dwelling is considered the principal dwelling for purposes of this section.

(k) *Federally regulated AMC* means an AMC that is owned and controlled by an insured depository institution, as defined in 12 U.S.C. 1813 and regulated by the Office of the Comptroller of the Currency, the Board of Governors of the Federal Reserve System, or the Federal Deposit Insurance Corporation.

(l) *Federally related transaction regulations* means regulations established by the Office of the Comptroller of the Currency, the Board of Governors of the Federal Reserve System, the Federal Deposit Insurance Corporation, or the National Credit Union Administration, pursuant to sections 1112, 1113, and 1114 of FIRREA Title XI, 12 U.S.C. 3341–3343.

(m) *Person* means a natural person or an organization, including a corporation, partnership, proprietorship, association, cooperative, estate, trust, or government unit.

(n) *Secondary mortgage market participant* means a guarantor or insurer of mortgage-backed securities, or an underwriter or issuer of mortgage-backed securities. Secondary mortgage market participant only includes an individual investor in a mortgage-backed security if that investor also serves in the capacity of a guarantor, insurer, underwriter, or issuer for the mortgage-backed security.

(o) *States* mean the 50 States and the District of Columbia and the territories of Guam, Mariana Islands, Puerto Rico, and the U.S. Virgin Islands.

(p) *Uniform Standards of Professional Appraisal Practice* (USPAP) means the appraisal standards promulgated by the Appraisal Standards Board of the Appraisal Foundation.

§ 34.212 Appraiser panel—annual size calculation.

For purposes of determining whether, within a 12-month period, an AMC oversees an appraiser panel of more than 15 State-certified or State-licensed appraisers in a State or 25 or more State-certified or State-licensed appraisers in two or more States pursuant to § 34.211(c)(1)(iii)—

(a) An appraiser is deemed part of the AMC's appraiser panel as of the earliest date on which the AMC:

(1) Accepts the appraiser for the AMC's consideration for future appraisal assignments in covered transactions or for secondary mortgage market participants in connection with covered transactions; or

(2) Engages the appraiser to perform one or more appraisals on behalf of a

creditor for a covered transaction or secondary mortgage market participant in connection with covered transactions.

(b) An appraiser who is deemed part of the AMC's appraiser panel pursuant to paragraph (a) of this section is deemed to remain on the panel until the date on which the AMC:

(1) Sends written notice to the appraiser removing the appraiser from the appraiser panel, with an explanation of its action; or

(2) Receives written notice from the appraiser asking to be removed from the appraiser panel or notice of the death or incapacity of the appraiser.

(c) If an appraiser is removed from an AMC's appraiser panel pursuant to paragraph (b) of this section, but the AMC subsequently accepts the appraiser for consideration for future assignments or engages the appraiser at any time during the twelve months after the AMC's removal, the removal will be deemed not to have occurred, and the appraiser will be deemed to have been part of the AMC's appraiser panel without interruption.

(d) The period for purposes of counting appraisers on an AMC's appraiser panel may be the calendar year or a 12-month period established by law or rule of each State with which the AMC is required to register.

§ 34.213 Appraisal management company registration.

Each State electing to register AMCs pursuant to paragraph (b)(1) of this section must:

(a) Establish and maintain within the State appraiser certifying and licensing agency a licensing program that is subject to the limitations set forth in § 34.214 and with the legal authority and mechanisms to:

(1) Review and approve or deny an AMC's application for initial registration;

(2) Review and renew or review and deny an AMC's registration periodically;

(3) Examine the books and records of an AMC operating in the State and require the AMC to submit reports, information, and documents;

(4) Verify that the appraisers on the AMC's appraiser panel hold valid State certifications or licenses, as applicable;

(5) Conduct investigations of AMCs to assess potential violations of applicable appraisal-related laws, regulations, or orders;

(6) Discipline, suspend, terminate, or deny renewal of the registration of an AMC that violates applicable appraisal-related laws, regulations, or orders; and

(7) Report an AMC's violation of applicable appraisal-related laws, regulations, or orders, as well as disciplinary and enforcement actions and other relevant information about an AMC's operations, to the Appraisal Subcommittee.

(b) Impose requirements on AMCs that are not owned and controlled by an insured depository institution and not regulated by a Federal financial institutions regulatory agency to:

(1) Register with and be subject to supervision by the State appraiser certifying and licensing agency;

(2) Engage only State-certified or State-licensed appraisers for Federally related transactions in conformity with any Federally related transaction regulations;

(3) Establish and comply with processes and controls reasonably designed to ensure that the AMC, in engaging an appraiser, selects an appraiser who is independent of the transaction and who has the requisite education, expertise, and experience necessary to competently complete the appraisal assignment for the particular market and property type;

(4) Direct the appraiser to perform the assignment in accordance with USPAP; and

(5) Establish and comply with processes and controls reasonably designed to ensure that the AMC conducts its appraisal management services in accordance with the requirements of section 129E(a) through (i) of the Truth in Lending Act, 15 U.S.C. 1639e(a) through (i), and regulations thereunder.

§ 34.214 Ownership limitations for State-registered appraisal management companies.

(a) *Appraiser certification or licensing of owners.* (1) An AMC subject to State registration pursuant to § 34.213 shall not be registered by a State or included on the AMC National Registry if such AMC, in whole or in part, directly or indirectly, is owned by any person who has had an appraiser license or certificate refused, denied, cancelled, surrendered in lieu of revocation, or revoked in any State for a substantive cause, as determined by the appropriate State appraiser certifying and licensing agency.

(2) An AMC subject to State registration pursuant to § 34.213 is not barred by paragraph (a)(1) of this section from being registered by a State or included on the AMC National Registry if the license or certificate of the appraiser with an ownership interest was not revoked for a substantive cause and has been reinstated by the State or States in which the appraiser was licensed or certified.

(b) *Good moral character of owners.* An AMC shall not be registered by a State if any person that owns more than 10 percent of the AMC—

(1) Is determined by the State appraiser certifying and licensing agency not to have good moral character; or

(2) Fails to submit to a background investigation carried out by the State appraiser certifying and licensing agency.

§ 34.215 Requirements for Federally regulated appraisal management companies.

(a) *Requirements in providing services.* To provide appraisal management services for a creditor or secondary mortgage market participant relating to a covered transaction, a Federally regulated AMC must comply with the requirements in § 34.213(b)(2) through (5).

(b) *Ownership limitations.* (1) A Federally regulated AMC shall not be included on the AMC National Registry if such AMC, in whole or in part, directly or indirectly, is owned by any person who has had an appraiser license or certificate refused, denied, cancelled, surrendered in lieu of revocation, or revoked in any State for a substantive cause, as determined by the Appraisal Subcommittee.

(2) A Federally regulated AMC is not barred by this paragraph (b) from being included on the AMC National Registry if the license or certificate of the appraiser with an ownership interest was not revoked for a substantive cause and has been reinstated by the State or States in which the appraiser was licensed or certified.

(c) *Reporting information for the AMC National Registry.* A Federally regulated AMC must report to the State or States in which it operates the information required to be submitted by the State to the Appraisal Subcommittee, pursuant to the Appraisal Subcommittee's policies regarding the determination of the AMC National Registry fee, including but not necessarily limited to the collection of information related to the limitations set forth in this section, as applicable.

§ 34.216 Information to be presented to the Appraisal Subcommittee by participating States.

Each State electing to register AMCs for purposes of permitting AMCs to provide appraisal management services relating to covered transactions in the State must submit to the Appraisal Subcommittee the information required to be submitted by Appraisal Subcommittee regulations or guidance concerning AMCs that operate in the State.

PART 35—DISCLOSURE AND REPORTING OF CRA-RELATED AGREEMENTS

Sec.

35.1 Purpose and scope of this part.
35.2 Definition of covered agreement.
35.3 CRA communications.
35.4 Fulfillment of the CRA.
35.5 Related agreements considered a single agreement.
35.6 Disclosure of covered agreements.
35.7 Annual reports.
35.8 Release of information under FOIA.
35.9 Compliance provisions.
35.10 Transition provisions.
35.11 Other definitions and rules of construction used in this part.

AUTHORITY: 12 U.S.C. 1, 93a, 1462a, 1463, 1464, 1831y, and 5412(b)(2)(B).

SOURCE: 66 FR 2084, Jan. 10, 2001, unless otherwise noted.

§ 35.1 Purpose and scope of this part.

(a) *General.* This part implements section 711 of the Gramm-Leach-Bliley

Act (12 U.S.C. 1831y). That section requires any nongovernmental entity or person, insured depository institution, or affiliate of an insured depository institution that enters into a covered agreement to—

(1) Make the covered agreement available to the public and the appropriate Federal banking agency; and

(2) File an annual report with the appropriate Federal banking agency concerning the covered agreement.

(b) *Scope of this part.* The provisions of this part apply to—

(1) A national bank and its subsidiaries;

(2) A Federal savings association and its subsidiaries; and

(3) Nongovernmental entities or persons (NGEPs) that enter into covered agreements with any entity listed in paragraphs (b)(1) or (b)(2) of this section.

(c) *Relation to Community Reinvestment Act.* This part does not affect in any way the Community Reinvestment Act of 1977 (CRA) (12 U.S.C. 2901 *et seq.*), part 25 (Community Reinvestment Act and Interstate Deposit Production Regulations) or part 195 (Community Reinvestment) of this chapter, or the OCC's interpretations or administration of that Act or these regulations.

(d) *Examples.* (1) The examples in this part are not exclusive. Compliance with an example, to the extent applicable, constitutes compliance with this part.

(2) Examples in a paragraph illustrate only the issue described in the paragraph and do not illustrate any other issues that may arise in this part.

[66 FR 2084, Jan. 10, 2001, as amended at 79 FR 28400, May 16, 2014]

§ 35.2 Definition of covered agreement.

(a) *General definition of covered agreement.* A covered agreement is any contract, arrangement, or understanding that meets all of the following criteria—

(1) The agreement is in writing.

(2) The parties to the agreement include—

(i) One or more insured depository institutions or affiliates of an insured depository institution; and

(ii) One or more NGEPs.

(3) The agreement provides for the insured depository institution or any affiliate to—

(i) Provide to one or more individuals or entities (whether or not parties to the agreement) cash payments, grants, or other consideration (except loans) that have an aggregate value of more than $10,000 in any calendar year; or

(ii) Make to one or more individuals or entities (whether or not parties to the agreement) loans that have an aggregate principal amount of more than $50,000 in any calendar year.

(4) The agreement is made pursuant to, or in connection with, the fulfillment of the CRA, as defined in § 35.4.

(5) The agreement is with a NGEP that has had a CRA communication as described in § 35.3 prior to entering into the agreement.

(b) *Examples concerning written arrangements or understandings*—(1) *Example 1.* A NGEP meets with an insured depository institution and states that the institution needs to make more community development investments in the NGEP's community. The NGEP and insured depository institution do not reach an agreement concerning the community development investments the institution should make in the community, and the parties do not reach any mutual arrangement or understanding. Two weeks later, the institution unilaterally issues a press release announcing that it has established a general goal of making $100 million of community development grants in low- and moderate-income neighborhoods served by the insured depository institution over the next 5 years. The NGEP is not identified in the press release. The press release is not a written arrangement or understanding.

(2) *Example 2.* A NGEP meets with an insured depository institution and states that the institution needs to offer new loan programs in the NGEP's community. The NGEP and the insured depository institution reach a mutual arrangement or understanding that the institution will provide additional loans in the NGEP's community. The institution tells the NGEP that it will issue a press release announcing the program. Later, the insured depository

institution issues a press release announcing the loan program. The press release incorporates the key terms of the understanding reached between the NGEP and the insured depository institution. The written press release reflects the mutual arrangement or understanding of the NGEP and the insured depository institution and is, therefore, a written arrangement or understanding.

(3) *Example 3.* An NGEP sends a letter to an insured depository institution requesting that the institution provide a $15,000 grant to the NGEP. The insured depository institution responds in writing and agrees to provide the grant in connection with its annual grant program. The exchange of letters constitutes a written arrangement or understanding.

(c) *Loan agreements that are not covered agreements.* A covered agreement does not include—

(1) Any individual loan that is secured by real estate; or

(2) Any specific contract or commitment for a loan or extension of credit to an individual, business, farm, or other entity, or group of such individuals or entities, if—

(i) The funds are loaned at rates that are not substantially below market rates; and

(ii) The loan application or other loan documentation does not indicate that the borrower intends or is authorized to use the borrowed funds to make a loan or extension of credit to one or more third parties.

(d) *Examples concerning loan agreements*—(1) *Example 1.* An insured depository institution provides an organization with a $1 million loan that is documented in writing and is secured by real estate owned or to-be-acquired by the organization. The agreement is an individual mortgage loan and is exempt from coverage under paragraph (c)(1) of this section, regardless of the interest rate on the loan or whether the organization intends or is authorized to re-loan the funds to a third party.

(2) *Example 2.* An insured depository institution commits to provide a $500,000 line of credit to a small business that is documented by a written agreement. The loan is made at rates that are within the range of rates offered by the institution to similarly situated small businesses in the market and the loan documentation does not indicate that the small business intends or is authorized to re-lend the borrowed funds. The agreement is exempt from coverage under paragraph (c)(2) of this section.

(3) *Example 3.* An insured depository institution offers small business loans that are guaranteed by the Small Business Administration (SBA). A small business obtains a $75,000 loan, documented in writing, from the institution under the institution's SBA loan program. The loan documentation does not indicate that the borrower intends or is authorized to re-lend the funds. Although the rate charged on the loan is well below that charged by the institution on commercial loans, the rate is within the range of rates that the institution would charge a similarly situated small business for a similar loan under the SBA loan program. Accordingly, the loan is not made at substantially below market rates and is exempt from coverage under paragraph (c)(2) of this section.

(4) *Example 4.* A bank holding company enters into a written agreement with a community development organization that provides that insured depository institutions owned by the bank holding company will make $250 million in small business loans in the community over the next 5 years. The written agreement is not a specific contract or commitment for a loan or an extension of credit and, thus, is not exempt from coverage under paragraph (c)(2) of this section. Each small business loan made by the insured depository institution pursuant to this general commitment would, however, be exempt from coverage if the loan is made at rates that are not substantially below market rates and the loan documentation does not indicate that the borrower intended or was authorized to re-lend the funds.

(e) *Agreements that include exempt loan agreements.* If an agreement includes a loan, extension of credit or loan commitment that, if documented separately, would be exempt under paragraph (c) of this section, the exempt loan, extension of credit or loan commitment may be excluded for purposes of determining whether the agreement is a covered agreement.

(f) *Determining annual value of agreements that lack schedule of disbursements.* For purposes of paragraph (a)(3) of this section, a multi-year agreement that does not include a schedule for the disbursement of payments, grants, loans or other consideration by the insured depository institution or affiliate, is considered to have a value in the first year of the agreement equal to all payments, grants, loans and other consideration to be provided at any time under the agreement.

[66 FR 2084, Jan. 10, 2001, as amended at 79 FR 28400, May 16, 2014]

§ 35.3 CRA communications.

(a) *Definition of CRA communication.* A CRA communication is any of the following—

(1) Any written or oral comment or testimony provided to a Federal banking agency concerning the adequacy of the performance under the CRA of the insured depository institution, any affiliated insured depository institution, or any CRA affiliate.

(2) Any written comment submitted to the insured depository institution that discusses the adequacy of the performance under the CRA of the institution and must be included in the institution's CRA public file.

(3) Any discussion or other contact with the insured depository institution or any affiliate about—

(i) Providing (or refraining from providing) written or oral comments or testimony to any Federal banking agency concerning the adequacy of the performance under the CRA of the insured depository institution, any affiliated insured depository institution, or any CRA affiliate;

(ii) Providing (or refraining from providing) written comments to the insured depository institution that concern the adequacy of the institution's performance under the CRA and must be included in the institution's CRA public file; or

(iii) The adequacy of the performance under the CRA of the insured depository institution, any affiliated insured depository institution, or any CRA affiliate.

(b) *Discussions or contacts that are not CRA communications*—(1) *Timing of contacts with a Federal banking agency.* An oral or written communication with a Federal banking agency is not a CRA communication if it occurred more than 3 years before the parties entered into the agreement.

(2) *Timing of contacts with insured depository institutions and affiliates.* A communication with an insured depository institution or affiliate is not a CRA communication if the communication occurred—

(i) More than 3 years before the parties entered into the agreement, in the case of any written communication;

(ii) More than 3 years before the parties entered into the agreement, in the case of any oral communication in which the NGEP discusses providing (or refraining from providing) comments or testimony to a Federal banking agency or written comments that must be included in the institution's CRA public file in connection with a request to, or agreement by, the institution or affiliate to take (or refrain from taking) any action that is in fulfillment of the CRA; or

(iii) More than 1 year before the parties entered into the agreement, in the case of any other oral communication not described in paragraph (b)(2)(ii).

(3) *Knowledge of communication by insured depository institution or affiliate.* (i) A communication is only a CRA communication under paragraph (a) of this section if the insured depository institution or its affiliate has knowledge of the communication under this paragraph (b)(3)(ii) or (b)(3)(iii) of this section.

(ii) *Communication with insured depository institution or affiliate.* An insured depository institution or affiliate has knowledge of a communication by the NGEP to the institution or its affiliate under this paragraph only if one of the following representatives of the insured depository institution or any affiliate has knowledge of the communication—

(A) An employee who approves, directs, authorizes, or negotiates the agreement with the NGEP; or

(B) An employee designated with responsibility for compliance with the CRA or executive officer if the employee or executive officer knows that the institution or affiliate is negotiating, intends to negotiate, or has been informed by the NGEP that it expects to request that the institution or affiliate negotiate an agreement with the NGEP.

(iii) *Other communications.* An insured depository institution or affiliate is deemed to have knowledge of—

(A) Any testimony provided to a Federal banking agency at a public meeting or hearing;

(B) Any comment submitted to a Federal banking agency that is conveyed in writing by the agency to the insured depository institution or affiliate; and

(C) Any written comment submitted to the insured depository institution that must be and is included in the institution's CRA public file.

(4) *Communication where NGEP has knowledge.* A NGEP has a CRA communication with an insured depository institution or affiliate only if any of the following individuals has knowledge of the communication—

(i) A director, employee, or member of the NGEP who approves, directs, authorizes, or negotiates the agreement with the insured depository institution or affiliate;

(ii) A person who functions as an executive officer of the NGEP and who knows that the NGEP is negotiating or intends to negotiate an agreement with the insured depository institution or affiliate; or

(iii) Where the NGEP is an individual, the NGEP.

(c) *Examples of CRA communications*—(1) *Examples of actions that are CRA communications.* The following are examples of CRA communications. These examples are not exclusive and assume that the communication occurs within the relevant time period as described in paragraph (b)(1) or (b)(2) of this section and the appropriate representatives have knowledge of the communication as specified in paragraphs (b)(3) and (b)(4) of this section.

(i) *Example 1.* A NGEP files a written comment with a Federal banking agency that states than an insured depository institution successfully addresses the credit needs of its community. The written comment is in response to a general request from the agency for comments on an application of the insured depository institution to open a new branch and a copy of the comment is provided to the institution.

(ii) *Example 2.* A NGEP meets with an executive officer of an insured depository institution and states that the institution must improve its CRA performance.

(iii) *Example 3.* A NGEP meets with an executive officer of an insured depository institution and states that the institution needs to make more mortgage loans in low- and moderate-income neighborhoods in its community.

(iv) *Example 4.* A bank holding company files an application with a Federal banking agency to acquire an insured depository institution. Two weeks later, the NGEP meets with an executive officer of the bank holding company to discuss the adequacy of the performance under the CRA of the target insured depository institution. The insured depository institution was an affiliate of the bank holding company at the time the NGEP met with the target institution. (*See* §35.11(a).) Accordingly, the NGEP had a CRA communication with an affiliate of the bank holding company.

(2) *Examples of actions that are not CRA communications.* The following are examples of actions that are not by themselves CRA communications. These examples are not exclusive.

(i) *Example 1.* A NGEP provides to a Federal banking agency comments or testimony concerning an insured depository institution or affiliate in response to a direct request by the agency for comments or testimony from that NGEP. Direct requests for comments or testimony do not include a general invitation by a Federal banking agency for comments or testimony from the public in connection with a CRA performance evaluation of, or application for a deposit facility (as defined in section 803 of the CRA (12 U.S.C. 2902(3)) by, an insured depository institution or an application by a company to acquire an insured depository institution.

(ii) *Example 2.* A NGEP makes a statement concerning an insured depository institution or affiliate at a widely attended conference or seminar regarding a general topic. A public or private meeting, public hearing, or other meeting regarding one or more specific institutions, affiliates or transactions involving an application for a deposit facility is not considered a widely attended conference or seminar.

(iii) *Example 3.* A NGEP, such as a civil rights group, community group providing housing and other services in low- and moderate-income neighborhoods, veterans organization, community theater group, or youth organization, sends a fundraising letter to insured depository institutions and to other businesses in its community. The letter encourages all businesses in the community to meet their obligation to assist in making the local community a better place to live and work by supporting the fundraising efforts of the NGEP.

(iv) *Example 4.* A NGEP discusses with an insured depository institution or affiliate whether particular loans, services, investments, community development activities, or other activities are generally eligible for consideration by a Federal banking agency under the CRA. The NGEP and insured depository institution or affiliate do not discuss the adequacy of the CRA performance of the insured depository institution or affiliate.

(v) *Example 5.* A NGEP engaged in the sale or purchase of loans in the secondary market sends a general offering circular to financial institutions offering to sell or purchase a portfolio of loans. An insured depository institution that receives the offering circular discusses with the NGEP the types of loans included in the loan pool, whether such loans are generally eligible for consideration under the CRA, and which loans are made to borrowers in the institution's local community. The NGEP and insured depository institution do not discuss the adequacy of the institution's CRA performance.

(d) *Multiparty covered agreements*—(1) A NGEP that is a party to a covered agreement that involves multiple NGEPs is not required to comply with the requirements of this part if—

(i) The NGEP has not had a CRA communication; and

(ii) No representative of the NGEP identified in paragraph (b)(4) of this section has knowledge at the time of the agreement that another NGEP that is a party to the agreement has had a CRA communication.

(2) An insured depository institution or affiliate that is a party to a covered agreement that involves multiple insured depository institutions or affiliates is not required to comply with the disclosure and annual reporting requirements in §§ 35.6 and 35.7 if—

(i) No NGEP that is a party to the agreement has had a CRA communication concerning the insured depository institution or any affiliate; and

(ii) No representative of the insured depository institution or any affiliate identified in paragraph (b)(3) of this section has knowledge at the time of the agreement that an NGEP that is a party to the agreement has had a CRA communication concerning any other insured depository institution or affiliate that is a party to the agreement.

§ 35.4 Fulfillment of the CRA.

(a) *List of factors that are in fulfillment of the CRA.* Fulfillment of the CRA, for purposes of this part, means the following list of factors—

(1) *Comments to a Federal banking agency or included in CRA public file.* Providing or refraining from providing written or oral comments or testimony to any Federal banking agency concerning the performance under the CRA of an insured depository institution or CRA affiliate that is a party to the agreement or an affiliate of a party to the agreement or written comments that are required to be included in the CRA public file of any such insured depository institution; or

(2) *Activities given favorable CRA consideration.* Performing any of the following activities if the activity is of the type that is likely to receive favorable consideration by a Federal banking agency in evaluating the performance under the CRA of the insured depository institution that is a party to the agreement or an affiliate of a party to the agreement—

(i) Home-purchase, home-improvement, small business, small farm, community development, and consumer lending, as described in § 25.22 (12 CFR 25.22), including loan purchases, loan commitments, and letters of credit;

(ii) Making investments, deposits, or grants, or acquiring membership shares, that have as their primary purpose community development, as described in § 25.23 (12 CFR 25.23);

(iii) Delivering retail banking services, as described in § 25.24(d) (12 CFR 25.24(d));

(iv) Providing community development services, as described in § 25.24(e) (12 CFR 25.24(e));

(v) In the case of a wholesale or limited-purpose insured depository institution, community development lending, including originating and purchasing loans and making loan commitments and letters of credit, making qualified investments, or providing community development services, as described in § 25.25(c) (12 CFR 25.25(c));

(vi) In the case of a small insured depository institution, any lending or other activity described in § 25.26(a) (12 CFR 25.26(a)); or

(vii) In the case of an insured depository institution that is evaluated on the basis of a strategic plan, any element of the strategic plan, as described in § 25.27(f) (12 CFR 25.27(f)).

(b) *Agreements relating to activities of CRA affiliates.* An insured depository institution or affiliate that is a party to a covered agreement that concerns any activity described in paragraph (a) of this section of a CRA affiliate must, prior to the time the agreement is entered into, notify each NGEP that is a party to the agreement that the agreement concerns a CRA affiliate.

§ 35.5 Related agreements considered a single agreement.

The following rules must be applied in determining whether an agreement is a covered agreement under § 35.2.

(a) *Agreements entered into by same parties.* All written agreements to which an insured depository institution or an affiliate of the insured depository institution is a party shall be considered to be a single agreement if the agreements—

(1) Are entered into with the same NGEP;

(2) Were entered into within the same 12-month period; and

(3) Are each in fulfillment of the CRA.

(b) *Substantively related contracts.* All written contracts to which an insured depository institution or an affiliate of the insured depository institution is a party shall be considered to be a single agreement, without regard to whether the other parties to the contracts are the same or whether each such contract is in fulfillment of the CRA, if the contracts were negotiated in a coordinated fashion and a NGEP is a party to each contract.

§ 35.6 Disclosure of covered agreements.

(a) *Applicability date.* This section applies only to covered agreements entered into after November 12, 1999.

(b) *Disclosure of covered agreements to the public*—(1) *Disclosure required.* Each NGEP and each insured depository institution or affiliate that enters into a covered agreement must promptly make a copy of the covered agreement available to any individual or entity upon request.

(2) *Nondisclosure of confidential and proprietary information permitted.* In responding to a request for a covered agreement from any individual or entity under paragraph (b)(1) of this section, a NGEP, insured depository institution, or affiliate may withhold from public disclosure confidential or proprietary information that the party believes the relevant supervisory agency could withhold from disclosure under the Freedom of Information Act (5 U.S.C. 552 *et seq.*) (FOIA).

(3) *Information that must be disclosed.* Notwithstanding paragraph (b)(2) of this section, a party must disclose any of the following information that is contained in a covered agreement—

(i) The names and addresses of the parties to the agreement;

(ii) The amount of any payments, fees, loans, or other consideration to be made or provided by any party to the agreement;

(iii) Any description of how the funds or other resources provided under the agreement are to be used;

(iv) The term of the agreement (if the agreement establishes a term); and

(v) Any other information that the relevant supervisory agency determines is not properly exempt from public disclosure.

(4) *Request for review of withheld information.* Any individual or entity may request that the relevant supervisory agency review whether any information in a covered agreement withheld by a party must be disclosed. Any requests for agency review of withheld information must be filed, and will be processed in accordance with, the relevant supervisory agency's rules concerning the availability of information (*see* subpart B of part 4 of the OCC's rules regarding the availability of information under the Freedom of Information Act (12 CFR part 4, subpart B).

(5) *Duration of obligation.* The obligation to disclose a covered agreement to the public terminates 12 months after the end of the term of the agreement.

(6) *Reasonable copy and mailing fees.* Each NGEP and each insured depository institution or affiliate may charge an individual or entity that requests a copy of a covered agreement a reasonable fee not to exceed the cost of copying and mailing the agreement.

(7) *Use of CRA public file by insured depository institution or affiliate.* An insured depository institution and any affiliate of an insured depository institution may fulfill its obligation under this paragraph (b) by placing a copy of the covered agreement in the insured depository institution's CRA public file if the institution makes the agreement available in accordance with the procedures set forth in § 25.43 (12 CFR 25.43);

(c) *Disclosure by NGEPs of covered agreements to the relevant supervisory agency.* (1) Each NGEP that is a party to a covered agreement must provide the following within 30 days of receiving a request from the relevant supervisory agency—

(i) A complete copy of the agreement; and

(ii) In the event the NGEP proposes the withholding of any information contained in the agreement in accordance with paragraph (b)(2) of this section, a public version of the agreement that excludes such information and an explanation justifying the exclusions. Any public version must include the information described in paragraph (b)(3) of this section.

(2) The obligation of a NGEP to provide a covered agreement to the relevant supervisory agency terminates 12 months after the end of the term of the covered agreement.

(d) *Disclosure by insured depository institution or affiliate of covered agreements to the relevant supervisory agency*—(1) *In general.* Within 60 days of the end of each calendar quarter, each insured depository institution and affiliate must provide each relevant supervisory agency with—

(i)(A) A complete copy of each covered agreement entered into by the insured depository institution or affiliate during the calendar quarter; and

(B) In the event the institution or affiliate proposes the withholding of any information contained in the agreement in accordance with paragraph (b)(2) of this section, a public version of the agreement that excludes such information (other than any information described in paragraph (b)(3) of this section) and an explanation justifying the exclusions; or

(ii) A list of all covered agreements entered into by the insured depository institution or affiliate during the calendar quarter that contains—

(A) The name and address of each insured depository institution or affiliate that is a party to the agreement;

(B) The name and address of each NGEP that is a party to the agreement;

(C) The date the agreement was entered into;

(D) The estimated total value of all payments, fees, loans and other consideration to be provided by the institution or any affiliate of the institution under the agreement; and

(E) The date the agreement terminates.

(2) *Prompt filing of covered agreements contained in list required.* (i) If an insured depository institution or affiliate files a list of the covered agreements entered into by the institution or affiliate pursuant to paragraph (d)(1)(ii) of this section, the institution or affiliate must provide any relevant supervisory agency a complete copy and public version of any covered agreement referenced in the list within 7 calendar

days of receiving a request from the agency for a copy of the agreement.

(ii) The obligation of an insured depository institution or affiliate to provide a covered agreement to the relevant supervisory agency under this paragraph (d)(2) terminates 36 months after the end of the term of the agreement.

(3) *Joint filings.* In the event that 2 or more insured depository institutions or affiliates are parties to a covered agreement, the insured depository institution(s) and affiliate(s) may jointly file the documents required by this paragraph (d). Any joint filing must identify the insured depository institution(s) and affiliate(s) for whom the filings are being made.

§ 35.7 Annual reports.

(a) *Applicability date.* This section applies only to covered agreements entered into on or after May 12, 2000.

(b) *Annual report required.* Each NGEP and each insured depository institution or affiliate that is a party to a covered agreement must file an annual report with each relevant supervisory agency concerning the disbursement, receipt, and uses of funds or other resources under the covered agreement.

(c) *Duration of reporting requirement*—(1) *NGEPs.* A NGEP must file an annual report for a covered agreement for any fiscal year in which the NGEP receives or uses funds or other resources under the agreement.

(2) *Insured depository institutions and affiliates.* An insured depository institution or affiliate must file an annual report for a covered agreement for any fiscal year in which the institution or affiliate—

(i) Provides or receives any payments, fees, or loans under the covered agreement that must be reported under paragraphs (e)(1)(iii) and (iv) of this section; or

(ii) Has data to report on loans, investments, and services provided by a party to the covered agreement under the covered agreement under paragraph (e)(1)(vi) of this section.

(d) *Annual reports filed by NGEP*—(1) *Contents of report.* The annual report filed by a NGEP under this section must include the following—

(i) The name and mailing address of the NGEP filing the report;

(ii) Information sufficient to identify the covered agreement for which the annual report is being filed, such as by providing the names of the parties to the agreement and the date the agreement was entered into or by providing a copy of the agreement;

(iii) The amount of funds or resources received under the covered agreement during the fiscal year; and

(iv) A detailed, itemized list of how any funds or resources received by the NGEP under the covered agreement were used during the fiscal year, including the total amount used for—

(A) Compensation of officers, directors, and employees;

(B) Administrative expenses;

(C) Travel expenses;

(D) Entertainment expenses;

(E) Payment of consulting and professional fees; and

(F) Other expenses and uses (specify expense or use).

(2) *More detailed reporting of uses of funds or resources permitted*—(i) *In general.* If a NGEP allocated and used funds received under a covered agreement for a specific purpose, the NGEP may fulfill the requirements of paragraph (d)(1)(iv) of this section with respect to such funds by providing—

(A) A brief description of each specific purpose for which the funds or other resources were used; and

(B) The amount of funds or resources used during the fiscal year for each specific purpose.

(ii) *Specific purpose defined.* A NGEP allocates and uses funds for a specific purpose if the NGEP receives and uses the funds for a purpose that is more specific and limited than the categories listed in paragraph (d)(1)(iv) of this section.

(3) *Use of other reports.* The annual report filed by a NGEP may consist of or incorporate a report prepared for any other purpose, such as the Internal Revenue Service Return of Organization Exempt From Income Tax on Form 990, or any other Internal Revenue Service form, state tax form, report to members or shareholders, audited or unaudited financial statements, audit report, or other report, so long as the annual report filed by the

NGEP contains all of the information required by this paragraph (d).

(4) *Consolidated reports permitted.* A NGEP that is a party to 2 or more covered agreements may file with each relevant supervisory agency a single consolidated annual report covering all the covered agreements. Any consolidated report must contain all the information required by this paragraph (d). The information reported under paragraphs (d)(1)(iv) and (d)(2) of this section may be reported on an aggregate basis for all covered agreements.

(5) *Examples of annual report requirements for NGEPs*—(i) *Example 1.* A NGEP receives an unrestricted grant of $15,000 under a covered agreement, includes the funds in its general operating budget and uses the funds during its fiscal year. The NGEP's annual report for the fiscal year must provide the name and mailing address of the NGEP, information sufficient to identify the covered agreement, and state that the NGEP received $15,000 during the fiscal year. The report must also indicate the total expenditures made by the NGEP during the fiscal year for compensation, administrative expenses, travel expenses, entertainment expenses, consulting and professional fees, and other expenses and uses. The NGEP's annual report may provide this information by submitting an Internal Revenue Service Form 990 that includes the required information. If the Internal Revenue Service Form does not include information for all of the required categories listed in this part, the NGEP must report the total expenditures in the remaining categories either by providing that information directly or by providing another form or report that includes the required information.

(ii) *Example 2.* An organization receives $15,000 from an insured depository institution under a covered agreement and allocates and uses the $15,000 during the fiscal year to purchase computer equipment to support its functions. The organization's annual report must include the name and address of the organization, information sufficient to identify the agreement, and a statement that the organization received $15,000 during the year. In addition, since the organization allocated and used the funds for a specific purpose that is more narrow and limited than the categories of expenses included in the detailed, itemized list of expenses, the organization would have the option of providing either the total amount it used during the year for each category of expenses included in paragraph (d)(1)(iv) of this section, or a statement that it used the $15,000 to purchase computer equipment and a brief description of the equipment purchased.

(iii) *Example 3.* A community group receives $50,000 from an insured depository institution under a covered agreement. During its fiscal year, the community group specifically allocates and uses $5,000 of the funds to pay for a particular business trip and uses the remaining $45,000 for general operating expenses. The group's annual report for the fiscal year must include the name and address of the group, information sufficient to identify the agreement, and a statement that the group received $50,000. Because the group did not allocate and use all of the funds for a specific purpose, the group's annual report must provide the total amount of funds it used during the year for each category of expenses included in paragraph (d)(1)(iv) of this section. The group's annual report also could state that it used $5,000 for a particular business trip and include a brief description of the trip.

(iv) *Example 4.* A community development organization is a party to two separate covered agreements with two unaffiliated insured depository institutions. Under each agreement, the organization receives $15,000 during its fiscal year and uses the funds to support its activities during that year. If the organization elects to file a consolidated annual report, the consolidated report must identify the organization and the two covered agreements, state that the organization received $15,000 during the fiscal year under each agreement, and provide the total amount that the organization used during the year for each category of expenses included in paragraph (d)(1)(iv) of this section.

(e) *Annual report filed by insured depository institution or affiliate*—(1) *General.* The annual report filed by an insured depository institution or affiliate must include the following—

(i) The name and principal place of business of the insured depository institution or affiliate filing the report;

(ii) Information sufficient to identify the covered agreement for which the annual report is being filed, such as by providing the names of the parties to the agreement and the date the agreement was entered into or by providing a copy of the agreement;

(iii) The aggregate amount of payments, aggregate amount of fees, and aggregate amount of loans provided by the insured depository institution or affiliate under the covered agreement to any other party to the agreement during the fiscal year;

(iv) The aggregate amount of payments, aggregate amount of fees, and aggregate amount of loans received by the insured depository institution or affiliate under the covered agreement from any other party to the agreement during the fiscal year;

(v) A general description of the terms and conditions of any payments, fees, or loans reported under paragraphs (e)(1)(iii) and (iv) of this section, or, in the event such terms and conditions are set forth—

(A) In the covered agreement, a statement identifying the covered agreement and the date the agreement (or a list identifying the agreement) was filed with the relevant supervisory agency; or

(B) In a previous annual report filed by the insured depository institution or affiliate, a statement identifying the date the report was filed with the relevant supervisory agency; and

(vi) The aggregate amount and number of loans, aggregate amount and number of investments, and aggregate amount of services provided under the covered agreement to any individual or entity not a party to the agreement—

(A) By the insured depository institution or affiliate during its fiscal year; and

(B) By any other party to the agreement, unless such information is not known to the insured depository institution or affiliate filing the report or such information is or will be contained in the annual report filed by another party under this section.

(2) *Consolidated reports permitted*—(i) *Party to multiple agreements.* An insured depository institution or affiliate that is a party to 2 or more covered agreements may file a single consolidated annual report with each relevant supervisory agency concerning all the covered agreements.

(ii) *Affiliated entities party to the same agreement.* An insured depository institution and its affiliates that are parties to the same covered agreement may file a single consolidated annual report relating to the agreement with each relevant supervisory agency for the covered agreement.

(iii) *Content of report.* Any consolidated annual report must contain all the information required by this paragraph (e). The amounts and data required to be reported under paragraphs (e)(1)(iv) and (vi) of this section may be reported on an aggregate basis for all covered agreements.

(f) *Time and place of filing*—(1) *General.* Each party must file its annual report with each relevant supervisory agency for the covered agreement no later than six months following the end of the fiscal year covered by the report.

(2) *Alternative method of fulfilling annual reporting requirement for a NGEP.* (i) A NGEP may fulfill the filing requirements of this section by providing the following materials to an insured depository institution or affiliate that is a party to the agreement no later than six months following the end of the NGEP's fiscal year—

(A) A copy of the NGEP's annual report required under paragraph (d) of this section for the fiscal year; and

(B) Written instructions that the insured depository institution or affiliate promptly forward the annual report to the relevant supervisory agency or agencies on behalf of the NGEP.

(ii) An insured depository institution or affiliate that receives an annual report from a NGEP pursuant to paragraph (f)(2)(i) of this section must file the report with the relevant supervisory agency or agencies on behalf of the NGEP within 30 days.

§ 35.8 Release of information under FOIA.

The OCC will make covered agreements and annual reports available to the public in accordance with the Freedom of Information Act (5 U.S.C. 552 *et seq.*) and the OCC's rules regarding the availability of information under the Freedom of Information Act (12 CFR part 4, subpart B). A party to a covered agreement may request confidential treatment of proprietary and confidential information in a covered agreement or an annual report under those procedures.

§ 35.9 Compliance provisions.

(a) *Willful failure to comply with disclosure and reporting obligations.* (1) If the OCC determines that a NGEP has willfully failed to comply in a material way with § 35.6 or § 35.7, the OCC will notify the NGEP in writing of that determination and provide the NGEP a period of 90 days (or such longer period as the OCC finds to be reasonable under the circumstances) to comply.

(2) If the NGEP does not comply within the time period established by the OCC, the agreement shall thereafter be unenforceable by that NGEP by operation of section 48 of the Federal Deposit Insurance Act (12 U.S.C. 1831y).

(3) The OCC may assist any insured depository institution or affiliate that is a party to a covered agreement that is unenforceable by a NGEP by operation of section 48 of the Federal Deposit Insurance Act (12 U.S.C. 1831y) in identifying a successor to assume the NGEP's responsibilities under the agreement.

(b) *Diversion of funds.* If a court or other body of competent jurisdiction determines that funds or resources received under a covered agreement have been diverted contrary to the purposes of the covered agreement for an individual's personal financial gain, the OCC may take either or both of the following actions—

(1) Order the individual to disgorge the diverted funds or resources received under the agreement;

(2) Prohibit the individual from being a party to any covered agreement for a period not to exceed 10 years.

(c) *Notice and opportunity to respond.* Before making a determination under paragraph (a)(1) of this section, or taking any action under paragraph (b) of this section, the OCC will provide written notice and an opportunity to present information to the OCC concerning any relevant facts or circumstances relating to the matter.

(d) *Inadvertent or de minimis errors.* Inadvertent or de minimis errors in annual reports or other documents filed with the OCC under §§ 35.6 or 35.7 will not subject the reporting party to any penalty.

(e) *Enforcement of provisions in covered agreements.* No provision of this part shall be construed as authorizing the OCC to enforce the provisions of any covered agreement.

§ 35.10 Transition provisions.

(a) *Disclosure of covered agreements entered into before the effective date of this part.* The following disclosure requirements apply to covered agreements that were entered into after November 12, 1999, and that terminated before April 1, 2001.

(1) *Disclosure to the public.* Each NGEP and each insured depository institution or affiliate that was a party to the agreement must make the agreement available to the public under § 35.6 until at least April 1, 2002.

(2) *Disclosure to the relevant supervisory agency.* (i) Each NGEP that was a party to the agreement must make the agreement available to the relevant supervisory agency under § 35.6 until at least April 1, 2002.

(ii) Each insured depository institution or affiliate that was a party to the agreement must, by June 30, 2001, provide each relevant supervisory agency either—

(A) A copy of the agreement under § 35.6(d)(1)(i); or

(B) The information described in § 35.6(d)(1)(ii) for each agreement.

(b) *Filing of annual reports that relate to fiscal years ending on or before December 31, 2000.* In the event that a NGEP, insured depository institution or affiliate has any information to report under § 35.7 for a fiscal year that ends on or before December 31, 2000, and that concerns a covered agreement entered into between May 12, 2000, and

December 31, 2000, the annual report for that fiscal year must be provided no later than June 30, 2001, to—

(1) Each relevant supervisory agency; or

(2) In the case of a NGEP, to an insured depository institution or affiliate that is a party to the agreement in accordance with § 35.7(f)(2).

§ 35.11 Other definitions and rules of construction used in this part.

(a) *Affiliate.* "Affiliate" means—

(1) Any company that controls, is controlled by, or is under common control with another company; and

(2) For the purpose of determining whether an agreement is a covered agreement under § 35.2, an "affiliate" includes any company that would be under common control or merged with another company on consummation of any transaction pending before a Federal banking agency at the time—

(i) The parties enter into the agreement; and

(ii) The NGEP that is a party to the agreement makes a CRA communication, as described in § 35.3.

(b) *Control.* "Control" is defined in section 2(a) of the Bank Holding Company Act (12 U.S.C. 1841(a)).

(c) *CRA affiliate.* A "CRA affiliate" of an insured depository institution is any company that is an affiliate of an insured depository institution to the extent, and only to the extent, that the activities of the affiliate were considered by the appropriate Federal banking agency when evaluating the CRA performance of the institution at its most recent CRA examination prior to the agreement. An insured depository institution or affiliate also may designate any company as a CRA affiliate at any time prior to the time a covered agreement is entered into by informing the NGEP that is a party to the agreement of such designation.

(d) *CRA public file.* "CRA public file" means the public file maintained by an insured depository institution and described in § 25.43 (12 CFR 25.43).

(e) *Executive officer.* The term "executive officer" has the same meaning as in § 215.2(e)(1) of Regulation O issued by the Board of Governors of the Federal Reserve System (12 CFR 215.2(e)(1)). In applying this definition under this part to a Federal savings association, the phrase "Federal savings association" shall be used in place of the term "bank."

(f) *Federal banking agency; appropriate Federal banking agency.* The terms "Federal banking agency" and "appropriate Federal banking agency" have the same meanings as in section 3 of the Federal Deposit Insurance Act (12 U.S.C. 1813).

(g) *Fiscal year.* (1) The fiscal year for a NGEP that does not have a fiscal year shall be the calendar year.

(2) Any NGEP, insured depository institution, or affiliate that has a fiscal year may elect to have the calendar year be its fiscal year for purposes of this part.

(h) *Insured depository institution.* "Insured depository institution" has the same meaning as in section 3 of the Federal Deposit Insurance Act (12 U.S.C. 1813).

(i) *NGEP.* "NGEP" means a nongovernmental entity or person.

(j) *Nongovernmental entity or person*—(1) *General.* A "nongovernmental entity or person" is any partnership, association, trust, joint venture, joint stock company, corporation, limited liability corporation, company, firm, society, other organization, or individual.

(2) *Exclusions.* A nongovernmental entity or person does not include—

(i) The United States government, a state government, a unit of local government (including a county, city, town, township, parish, village, or other general-purpose subdivision of a state) or an Indian tribe or tribal organization established under Federal, state or Indian tribal law (including the Department of Hawaiian Home Lands), or a department, agency, or instrumentality of any such entity;

(ii) A federally-chartered public corporation that receives Federal funds appropriated specifically for that corporation;

(iii) An insured depository institution or affiliate of an insured depository institution; or

(iv) An officer, director, employee, or representative (acting in his or her capacity as an officer, director, employee, or representative) of an entity listed in paragraphs (j)(2)(i) through (iii) of this section.

(k) *Party.* The term "party" with respect to a covered agreement means each NGEP and each insured depository institution or affiliate that entered into the agreement.

(l) *Relevant supervisory agency.* The "relevant supervisory agency" for a covered agreement means the appropriate Federal banking agency for—

(1) Each insured depository institution (or subsidiary thereof) that is a party to the covered agreement;

(2) Each insured depository institution (or subsidiary thereof) or CRA affiliate that makes payments or loans or provides services that are subject to the covered agreement; and

(3) Any company (other than an insured depository institution or subsidiary thereof) that is a party to the covered agreement.

(m) *Term of agreement.* An agreement that does not have a fixed termination date is considered to terminate on the last date on which any party to the agreement makes any payment or provides any loan or other resources under the agreement, unless the relevant supervisory agency for the agreement otherwise notifies each party in writing.

[66 FR 2084, Jan. 10, 2001, as amended at 79 FR 28400, May 16, 2014]

PART 36 [RESERVED]

PART 37—DEBT CANCELLATION CONTRACTS AND DEBT SUSPENSION AGREEMENTS

Sec.

37.1 Authority, purpose, and scope.
37.2 Definitions.
37.3 Prohibited practices.
37.4 Refunds of fees in the event of termination or prepayment of the covered loan.
37.5 Method of payment of fees.
37.6 Disclosures.
37.7 Affirmative election to purchase and acknowledgment of receipt of disclosures required.
37.8 Safety and soundness requirement.
APPENDIX A TO PART 37—SHORT FORM DISCLOSURES
APPENDIX B TO PART 37—LONG FORM DISCLOSURES

AUTHORITY: 12 U.S.C. 1 *et seq.*, 24(Seventh), 93a, 1818.

SOURCE: 67 FR 58976, Sept. 19, 2002, unless otherwise noted.

§ 37.1 Authority, purpose, and scope.

(a) *Authority.* A national bank is authorized to enter into debt cancellation contracts and debt suspension agreements and charge a fee therefor, in connection with extensions of credit that it makes, pursuant to 12 U.S.C. 24(Seventh).

(b) *Purpose.* This part sets forth the standards that apply to debt cancellation contracts and debt suspension agreements entered into by national banks. The purpose of these standards is to ensure that national banks offer and implement such contracts and agreements consistent with safe and sound banking practices, and subject to appropriate consumer protections.

(c) *Scope.* This part applies to debt cancellation contracts and debt suspension agreements entered into by national banks in connection with extensions of credit they make. National banks' debt cancellation contracts and debt suspension agreements are governed by this part and applicable Federal law and regulations, and not by part 14 of this chapter or by State law.

§ 37.2 Definitions.

For purposes of this part:

(a) *Actuarial method* means the method of allocating payments made on a debt between the amount financed and the finance charge pursuant to which a payment is applied first to the accumulated finance charge and any remainder is subtracted from, or any deficiency is added to, the unpaid balance of the amount financed.

(b) *Bank* means a national bank and a Federal branch or Federal agency of a foreign bank as those terms are defined in part 28 of this chapter.

(c) *Closed-end credit* means consumer credit other than open-end credit as defined in this section.

(d) *Contract* means a debt] cancellation contract or a debt suspension agreement.

(e) *Customer* means an individual who obtains an extension of credit from a bank primarily for personal, family or household purposes.

(f) *Debt cancellation contract* means a loan term or contractual arrangement modifying loan terms under which a bank agrees to cancel all or part of a customer's obligation to repay an extension of credit from that bank upon the occurrence of a specified event. The agreement may be separate from or a part of other loan documents.

(g) *Debt suspension agreement* means a loan term or contractual arrangement modifying loan terms under which a bank agrees to suspend all or part of a customer's obligation to repay an extension of credit from that bank upon the occurrence of a specified event. The agreement may be separate from or a part of other loan documents. The term *debt suspension agreement* does not include loan payment deferral arrangements in which the triggering event is the borrower's unilateral election to defer repayment, or the bank's unilateral decision to allow a deferral of repayment.

(h) *Open-end credit* means consumer credit extended by a bank under a plan in which:

(1) The bank reasonably contemplates repeated transactions;

(2) The bank may impose a finance charge from time to time on an outstanding unpaid balance; and

(3) The amount of credit that may be extended to the customer during the term of the plan (up to any limit set by the bank) is generally made available to the extent that any outstanding balance is repaid.

(i) *Residential mortgage loan* means a loan secured by 1–4 family, residential real property.

§37.3 Prohibited practices.

(a) *Anti-tying.* A national bank may not extend credit nor alter the terms or conditions of an extension of credit conditioned upon the customer entering into a debt cancellation contract or debt suspension agreement with the bank.

(b) *Misrepresentations generally.* A national bank may not engage in any practice or use any advertisement that could mislead or otherwise cause a reasonable person to reach an erroneous belief with respect to information that must be disclosed under this part.

(c) *Prohibited contract terms.* A national bank may not offer debt cancellation contracts or debt suspension agreements that contain terms:

(1) Giving the bank the right unilaterally to modify the contract unless:

(i) The modification is favorable to the customer and is made without additional charge to the customer; or

(ii) The customer is notified of any proposed change and is provided a reasonable opportunity to cancel the contract without penalty before the change goes into effect; or

(2) Requiring a lump sum, single payment for the contract payable at the outset of the contract, where the debt subject to the contract is a residential mortgage loan.

§37.4 Refunds of fees in the event of termination or prepayment of the covered loan.

(a) *Refunds.* If a debt cancellation contract or debt suspension agreement is terminated (including, for example, when the customer prepays the covered loan), the bank shall refund to the customer any unearned fees paid for the contract unless the contract provides otherwise. A bank may offer a customer a contract that does not provide for a refund only if the bank also offers that customer a *bona fide* option to purchase a comparable contract that provides for a refund.

(b) *Method of calculating refund.* The bank shall calculate the amount of a refund using a method at least as favorable to the customer as the actuarial method.

§37.5 Method of payment of fees.

Except as provided in §37.3(c)(2), a bank may offer a customer the option of paying the fee for a contract in a single payment, provided the bank also offers the customer a *bona fide* option of paying the fee for that contract in monthly or other periodic payments. If the bank offers the customer the option to finance the single payment by adding it to the amount the customer is borrowing, the bank must also disclose to the customer, in accordance with §37.6, whether and, if so, the time period during which, the customer may cancel the agreement and receive a refund.

§ 37.6 Disclosures.

(a) *Content of short form of disclosures.* The short form of disclosures required by this part must include the information described in appendix A to this part that is appropriate to the product offered. Short form disclosures made in a form that is substantially similar to the disclosures in appendix A to this part will satisfy the short form disclosure requirements of this section.

(b) *Content of long form of disclosures.* The long form of disclosures required by this part must include the information described in appendix B to this part that is appropriate to the product offered. Long form disclosures made in a form that is substantially similar to the disclosures in appendix B to this part will satisfy the long form disclosure requirements of this section.

(c) *Disclosure requirements; timing and method of disclosures*—(1) *Short form disclosures.* The bank shall make the short form disclosures orally at the time the bank first solicits the purchase of a contract.

(2) *Long form disclosures.* The bank shall make the long form disclosures in writing before the customer completes the purchase of the contract. If the initial solicitation occurs in person, then the bank shall provide the long form disclosures in writing at that time.

(3) *Special rule for transactions by telephone.* If the contract is solicited by telephone, the bank shall provide the short form disclosures orally and shall mail the long form disclosures, and, if appropriate, a copy of the contract to the customer within 3 business days, beginning on the first business day after the telephone solicitation.

(4) *Special rule for solicitations using written mail inserts or "take one" applications.* If the contract is solicited through written materials such as mail inserts or "take one" applications, the bank may provide only the short form disclosures in the written materials if the bank mails the long form disclosures to the customer within 3 business days, beginning on the first business day after the customer contacts the bank to respond to the solicitation, subject to the requirements of § 37.7(c).

(5) *Special rule for electronic transactions.* The disclosures described in this section may be provided through electronic media in a manner consistent with the requirements of the Electronic Signatures in Global and National Commerce Act, 15 U.S.C. 7001 *et seq.*

(d) *Form of disclosures*—(1) *Disclosures must be readily understandable.* The disclosures required by this section must be conspicuous, simple, direct, readily understandable, and designed to call attention to the nature and significance of the information provided.

(2) *Disclosures must be meaningful.* The disclosures required by this section must be in a meaningful form. Examples of methods that could call attention to the nature and significance of the information provided include:

(i) A plain-language heading to call attention to the disclosures;

(ii) A typeface and type size that are easy to read;

(iii) Wide margins and ample line spacing;

(iv) Boldface or italics for key words; and

(v) Distinctive type style, and graphic devices, such as shading or sidebars, when the disclosures are combined with other information.

(e) *Advertisements and other promotional material for debt cancellation contracts and debt suspension agreements.* The short form disclosures are required in advertisements and promotional material for contracts unless the advertisements and promotional materials are of a general nature describing or listing the services or products offered by the bank.

§ 37.7 Affirmative election to purchase and acknowledgment of receipt of disclosures required.

(a) *Affirmative election and acknowledgment of receipt of disclosures.* Before entering into a contract the bank must obtain a customer's written affirmative election to purchase a contract and written acknowledgment of receipt of the disclosures required by § 37.6(b). The election and acknowledgment information must be conspicuous, simple, direct, readily understandable, and designed to call attention to their significance. The election and acknowledgment satisfy these standards if they conform with the requirements in § 37.6(d) of this part.

(b) *Special rule for telephone solicitations.* If the sale of a contract occurs by telephone, the customer's affirmative election to purchase may be made orally, provided the bank:

(1) Maintains sufficient documentation to show that the customer received the short form disclosures and then affirmatively elected to purchase the contract;

(2) Mails the affirmative written election and written acknowledgment, together with the long form disclosures required by §37.6 of this part, to the customer within 3 business days after the telephone solicitation, and maintains sufficient documentation to show it made reasonable efforts to obtain the documents from the customer; and

(3) Permits the customer to cancel the purchase of the contract without penalty within 30 days after the bank has mailed the long form disclosures to the customer.

(c) *Special rule for solicitations using written mail inserts or "take one" applications.* If the contract is solicited through written materials such as mail inserts or "take one" applications and the bank provides only the short form disclosures in the written materials, then the bank shall mail the acknowledgment of receipt of disclosures, together with the long form disclosures required by §37.6 of this part, to the customer within 3 business days, beginning on the first business day after the customer contacts the bank or otherwise responds to the solicitation. The bank may not obligate the customer to pay for the contract until after the bank has received the customer's written acknowledgment of receipt of disclosures unless the bank:

(1) Maintains sufficient documentation to show that the bank provided the acknowledgment of receipt of disclosures to the customer as required by this section;

(2) Maintains sufficient documentation to show that the bank made reasonable efforts to obtain from the customer a written acknowledgment of receipt of the long form disclosures; and

(3) Permits the customer to cancel the purchase of the contract without penalty within 30 days after the bank has mailed the long form disclosures to the customer.

(d) *Special rule for electronic election.* The affirmative election and acknowledgment may be made electronically in a manner consistent with the requirements of the Electronic Signatures in Global and National Commerce Act, 15 U.S.C. 7001 *et seq.*

[67 FR 58976, Sept. 19, 2002, as amended at 73 FR 22252, Apr. 24, 2008]

§37.8 Safety and soundness requirements.

A national bank must manage the risks associated with debt cancellation contracts and debt suspension agreements in accordance with safe and sound banking principles. Accordingly, a national bank must establish and maintain effective risk management and control processes over its debt cancellation contracts and debt suspension agreements. Such processes include appropriate recognition and financial reporting of income, expenses, assets and liabilities, and appropriate treatment of all expected and unexpected losses associated with the products. A bank also should assess the adequacy of its internal control and risk mitigation activities in view of the nature and scope of its debt cancellation contract and debt suspension agreement programs.

Appendix A to Part 37—Short Form Disclosures

• This product is optional

Your purchase of [PRODUCT NAME] is optional. Whether or not you purchase [PRODUCT NAME] will not affect your application for credit or the terms of any existing credit agreement you have with the bank.

• Lump sum payment of fee

[Applicable if a bank offers the option to pay the fee in a single payment]

[Prohibited where the debt subject to the contract is a residential mortgage loan]

You may choose to pay the fee in a single lump sum or in [monthly/quarterly] payments. Adding the lump sum of the fee to the amount you borrow will increase the cost of [PRODUCT NAME].

• Lump sum payment of fee with no refund

[Applicable if a bank offers the option to pay the fee in a single payment for a no-refund DCC]

[Prohibited where the debt subject to the contract is a residential mortgage loan]

You may choose [PRODUCT NAME] with a refund provision or without a refund provision. Prices of refund and no-refund products are likely to differ.

• Refund of fee paid in lump sum

[Applicable where the customer pays the fee in a single payment and the fee is added to the amount borrowed]
[Prohibited where the debt subject to the contract is a residential mortgage loan]

[Either:] (1) You may cancel [PRODUCT NAME] at any time and receive a refund; or (2) You may cancel [PRODUCT NAME] within ___ days and receive a full refund; or (3) If you cancel [PRODUCT NAME] you will not receive a refund.

• Additional disclosures

We will give you additional information before you are required to pay for [PRODUCT NAME]. [If applicable]: This information will include a copy of the contract containing the terms of [PRODUCT NAME].

• Eligibility requirements, conditions, and exclusions

There are eligibility requirements, conditions, and exclusions that could prevent you from receiving benefits under [PRODUCT NAME].

[Either:] You should carefully read our additional information for a full explanation of the terms of [PRODUCT NAME] *or* You should carefully read the contract for a full explanation of the terms of [PRODUCT NAME].

APPENDIX B TO PART 37—LONG FORM DISCLOSURES

• This product is optional

Your purchase of [PRODUCT NAME] is optional. Whether or not you purchase [PRODUCT NAME] will not affect your application for credit or the terms of any existing credit agreement you have with the bank.

• Explanation of debt suspension agreement

[Applicable if the contract has a debt suspension feature]

If [PRODUCT NAME] is activated, your duty to pay the loan principal and interest to the bank is only suspended. You must fully repay the loan after the period of suspension has expired. [If applicable]: This includes interest accumulated during the period of suspension.

• Amount of fee

[For closed-end credit]: The total fee for [PRODUCT NAME] is ___.

[For open-end credit, either:] (1) The monthly fee for [PRODUCT NAME] is based on your account balance each month multiplied by the unit-cost, which is ___; *or* (2) The formula used to compute the fee is ___].

• Lump sum payment of fee

[Applicable if a bank offers the option to pay the fee in a single payment]
[Prohibited where the debt subject to the contract is a residential mortgage loan]

You may choose to pay the fee in a single lump sum or in [monthly/quarterly] payments. Adding the lump sum of the fee to the amount you borrow will increase the cost of [PRODUCT NAME].

• Lump sum payment of fee with no refund

[Applicable if a bank offers the option to pay the fee in a single payment for a no-refund DCC]
[Prohibited where the debt subject to the contract is a residential mortgage loan]

You have the option to purchase [PRODUCT NAME] that includes a refund of the unearned portion of the fee if you terminate the contract or prepay the loan in full prior to the scheduled termination date. Prices of refund and no-refund products may differ.

• Refund of fee paid in lump sum

[Applicable where the customer pays the fee in a single payment and the fee is added to the amount borrowed]
[Prohibited where the debt subject to the contract is a residential mortgage loan]

[Either:] (1) You may cancel [PRODUCT NAME] at any time and receive a refund; or (2) You may cancel [PRODUCT NAME] within ___ days and receive a full refund; or (3) If you cancel [PRODUCT NAME] you will not receive a refund.

• Use of card or credit line restricted

[Applicable if the contract restricts use of card or credit line when customer activates protection]

If [PRODUCT NAME] is activated, you will be unable to incur additional charges on the credit card or use the credit line.

• Termination of [PRODUCT NAME]

[Either]: (1) You have no right to cancel [PRODUCT NAME]; *or* (2) You have the right to cancel [PRODUCT NAME] in the following circumstances: ___.

[And either]: (1) The bank has no right to cancel [PRODUCT NAME]; *or* (2)The bank has the right to cancel [PRODUCT NAME] in the following circumstances: ___.

• Eligibility requirements, conditions, and exclusions

There are eligibility requirements, conditions, and exclusions that could prevent you from receiving benefits under [PRODUCT NAME].

[Either]: (1) The following is a summary of the eligibility requirements, conditions, and exclusions. [The bank provides a summary of any eligibility requirements, conditions, and exclusions]; *or* (2) You may find a complete explanation of the eligibility requirements, conditions, and exclusions in paragraphs ___ of the [PRODUCT NAME] agreement.

PARTS 38–40 [RESERVED]

PART 41—FAIR CREDIT REPORTING

Subparts A–H [Reserved]

Subpart I—Proper Disposal of Records Containing Consumer Information

Sec.
41.80–41.82 [Reserved]
41.83 Proper disposal of records containing consumer information.

Subpart J—Identity Theft Red Flags

41.90 Duties regarding the detection, prevention, and mitigation of identity theft.
41.91 Duties of card issuers regarding changes of address.
41.92 Examples.
APPENDIXES A–I TO PART 41 [RESERVED]
APPENDIX J TO PART 41—INTERAGENCY GUIDELINES ON IDENTITY THEFT DETECTION, PREVENTION, AND MITIGATION

AUTHORITY: 12 U.S.C. 1 *et seq.*, 24(Seventh), 93a, 1462a, 1463, 1464, 1818, 1828, 1831p–1, 1881–1884, and 5412(b)(2)(B); 15 U.S.C. 1681m, 1681s, 1681t, and 1681w.

SOURCE: 69 FR 77616, Dec. 28, 2004, unless otherwise noted.

Subparts A–H [Reserved]

Subpart I—Proper Disposal of Records Containing Consumer Information

§§41.80–41.82 [Reserved]

§41.83 Proper disposal of records containing consumer information.

(a) *Definitions as used in this section.* (1) *Consumer* means an individual.

(2) *Federal savings association* means a Federal savings association or an operating subsidiary of a Federal savings association.

(3) *National bank* means a national bank, an operating subsidiary of a national bank, or a Federal branch or agency of a foreign bank.

(b) *In general.* Each national bank or Federal savings association must properly dispose of any consumer information that it maintains or otherwise possesses in accordance with the Interagency Guidelines Establishing Information Security Standards, as set forth in appendix B to 12 CFR part 30, to the extent that the bank or savings association is covered by the scope of the Guidelines.

(c) *Rule of construction.* Nothing in this section shall be construed to:

(1) Require a national bank or Federal savings association to maintain or destroy any record pertaining to a consumer that is not imposed under any other law; or

(2) Alter or affect any requirement imposed under any other provision of law to maintain or destroy such a record.

[79 FR 28400, May 16, 2014]

Subpart J—Identity Theft Red Flags

SOURCE: 72 FR 63753, Nov. 9, 2007, unless otherwise noted.

§41.90 Duties regarding the detection, prevention, and mitigation of identity theft.

(a) *Scope.* This section applies to a financial institution or creditor that is a national bank; a Federal savings association; a Federal branch or agency of a foreign bank; or an operating subsidiary of any of these institutions that is not a functionally regulated subsidiary within the meaning of section 5(c)(5) of the Bank Holding Company Act of 1956, as amended (12 U.S.C. 1844(c)(5)).

(b) *Definitions.* For purposes of this section and appendix J, the following definitions apply:

(1) *Account* means a continuing relationship established by a person with a financial institution or creditor to obtain a product or service for personal, family, household or business purposes. Account includes:

(i) An extension of credit, such as the purchase of property or services involving a deferred payment; and

(ii) A deposit account.

(2) The term *board of directors* includes:

(i) In the case of a branch or agency of a foreign bank, the managing official in charge of the branch or agency; and

(ii) In the case of any other creditor that does not have a board of directors, a designated employee at the level of senior management.

(3) *Covered account* means:

(i) An account that a financial institution or creditor offers or maintains, primarily for personal, family, or household purposes, that involves or is designed to permit multiple payments or transactions, such as a credit card account, mortgage loan, automobile loan, margin account, cell phone account, utility account, checking account, or savings account; and

(ii) Any other account that the financial institution or creditor offers or maintains for which there is a reasonably foreseeable risk to customers or to the safety and soundness of the financial institution or creditor from identity theft, including financial, operational, compliance, reputation, or litigation risks.

(4) *Credit* has the same meaning as in 15 U.S.C. 1681a(r)(5).

(5) *Creditor* has the same meaning as in 15 U.S.C. 1681m(e)(4).

(6) *Customer* means a person that has a covered account with a financial institution or creditor.

(7) *Financial institution* has the same meaning as in 15 U.S.C. 1681a(t).

(8) *Identity theft* has the same meaning as in 12 CFR 1022.3(h).

(9) *Person* means any individual, partnership, corporation, trust, estate, cooperative, association, government, or governmental subdivision or agency, or other entity.

(10) *Red Flag* means a pattern, practice, or specific activity that indicates the possible existence of identity theft.

(11) *Service provider* means a person that provides a service directly to the financial institution or creditor.

(c) *Periodic Identification of Covered Accounts.* Each financial institution or creditor must periodically determine whether it offers or maintains covered accounts. As a part of this determination, a financial institution or creditor must conduct a risk assessment to determine whether it offers or maintains covered accounts described in paragraph (b)(3)(ii) of this section, taking into consideration:

(1) The methods it provides to open its accounts;

(2) The methods it provides to access its accounts; and

(3) Its previous experiences with identity theft.

(d) *Establishment of an Identity Theft Prevention Program*—(1) *Program requirement.* Each financial institution or creditor that offers or maintains one or more covered accounts must develop and implement a written Identity Theft Prevention Program (Program) that is designed to detect, prevent, and mitigate identity theft in connection with the opening of a covered account or any existing covered account. The Program must be appropriate to the size and complexity of the financial institution or creditor and the nature and scope of its activities.

(2) *Elements of the Program.* The Program must include reasonable policies and procedures to:

(i) Identify relevant Red Flags for the covered accounts that the financial institution or creditor offers or maintains, and incorporate those Red Flags into its Program;

(ii) Detect Red Flags that have been incorporated into the Program of the financial institution or creditor;

(iii) Respond appropriately to any Red Flags that are detected pursuant to paragraph (d)(2)(ii) of this section to prevent and mitigate identity theft; and

(iv) Ensure the Program (including the Red Flags determined to be relevant) is updated periodically, to reflect changes in risks to customers and to the safety and soundness of the financial institution or creditor from identity theft.

(e) *Administration of the Program.* Each financial institution or creditor that is required to implement a Program must provide for the continued administration of the Program and must:

(1) Obtain approval of the initial written Program from either its board of directors or an appropriate committee of the board of directors;

(2) Involve the board of directors, an appropriate committee thereof, or a designated employee at the level of senior management in the oversight, development, implementation and administration of the Program;

(3) Train staff, as necessary, to effectively implement the Program; and

(4) Exercise appropriate and effective oversight of service provider arrangements.

(f) *Guidelines.* Each financial institution or creditor that is required to implement a Program must consider the guidelines in appendix J of this part and include in its Program those guidelines that are appropriate.

[72 FR 63753, Nov. 9, 2007, as amended at 79 FR 28400, May 16, 2014]

§ 41.91 Duties of card issuers regarding changes of address.

(a) *Scope.* This section applies to an issuer of a debit or credit card (card issuer) that is a national bank; a Federal savings association; a Federal branch or agency of a foreign bank; or an operating subsidiary of any of these institutions that is not a functionally regulated subsidiary within the meaning of section 5(c)(5) of the Bank Holding Company Act of 1956, as amended (12 U.S.C. 1844(c)(5)).

(b) *Definitions.* For purposes of this section:

(1) *Cardholder* means a consumer who has been issued a credit or debit card.

(2) *Clear and conspicuous* means reasonably understandable and designed to call attention to the nature and significance of the information presented.

(3) *Consumer* means an individual.

(c) *Address validation requirements.* A card issuer must establish and implement reasonable policies and procedures to assess the validity of a change of address if it receives notification of a change of address for a consumer's debit or credit card account and, within a short period of time afterwards (during at least the first 30 days after it receives such notification), the card issuer receives a request for an additional or replacement card for the same account. Under these circumstances, the card issuer may not issue an additional or replacement card, until, in accordance with its reasonable policies and procedures and for the purpose of assessing the validity of the change of address, the card issuer:

(1)(i) Notifies the cardholder of the request:

(A) At the cardholder's former address; or

(B) By any other means of communication that the card issuer and the cardholder have previously agreed to use; and

(ii) Provides to the cardholder a reasonable means of promptly reporting incorrect address changes; or

(2) Otherwise assesses the validity of the change of address in accordance with the policies and procedures the card issuer has established pursuant to § 41.90 of this part.

(d) *Alternative timing of address validation.* A card issuer may satisfy the requirements of paragraph (c) of this section if it validates an address pursuant to the methods in paragraph (c)(1) or (c)(2) of this section when it receives an address change notification, before it receives a request for an additional or replacement card.

(e) *Form of notice.* Any written or electronic notice that the card issuer provides under this paragraph must be clear and conspicuous and provided separately from its regular correspondence with the cardholder.

[72 FR 63753, Nov. 9, 2007, as amended at 79 FR 28401, May 16, 2014]

§ 41.92 Examples.

The examples in appendix J and supplement A to appendix J are not exclusive. Compliance with an example, to the extent applicable, constitutes compliance with this subpart. Examples in a paragraph illustrate only the issue described in the paragraph and do not illustrate any other issue that may arise in this subpart.

[79 FR 28401, May 16, 2014]

APPENDIXES A–I TO PART 41 [RESERVED]

APPENDIX J TO PART 41—INTERAGENCY GUIDELINES ON IDENTITY THEFT DETECTION, PREVENTION, AND MITIGATION

Section 41.90 of this part requires each financial institution and creditor that offers or maintains one or more covered accounts, as defined in § 41.90(b)(3) of this part, to develop and provide for the continued administration of a written Program to detect, prevent, and mitigate identity theft in connection with the opening of a covered account or any existing covered account. These guidelines are intended to assist financial institutions and creditors in the formulation and maintenance of a Program that satisfies the requirements of § 41.90 of this part.

I. The Program

In designing its Program, a financial institution or creditor may incorporate, as appropriate, its existing policies, procedures, and other arrangements that control reasonably foreseeable risks to customers or to the safety and soundness of the financial institution or creditor from identity theft.

II. Identifying Relevant Red Flags

(a) *Risk Factors.* A financial institution or creditor should consider the following factors in identifying relevant Red Flags for covered accounts, as appropriate:

(1) The types of covered accounts it offers or maintains;

(2) The methods it provides to open its covered accounts;

(3) The methods it provides to access its covered accounts; and

(4) Its previous experiences with identity theft.

(b) *Sources of Red Flags.* Financial institutions and creditors should incorporate relevant Red Flags from sources such as:

(1) Incidents of identity theft that the financial institution or creditor has experienced;

(2) Methods of identity theft that the financial institution or creditor has identified that reflect changes in identity theft risks; and

(3) Applicable supervisory guidance.

(c) *Categories of Red Flags.* The Program should include relevant Red Flags from the following categories, as appropriate. Examples of Red Flags from each of these categories are appended as supplement A to this appendix J.

(1) Alerts, notifications, or other warnings received from consumer reporting agencies or service providers, such as fraud detection services;

(2) The presentation of suspicious documents;

(3) The presentation of suspicious personal identifying information, such as a suspicious address change;

(4) The unusual use of, or other suspicious activity related to, a covered account; and

(5) Notice from customers, victims of identity theft, law enforcement authorities, or other persons regarding possible identity theft in connection with covered accounts held by the financial institution or creditor.

III. Detecting Red Flags

The Program's policies and procedures should address the detection of Red Flags in connection with the opening of covered accounts and existing covered accounts, such as by:

(a) Obtaining identifying information about, and verifying the identity of, a person opening a covered account, for example, using the policies and procedures regarding identification and verification set forth in the Customer Identification Program rules implementing 31 U.S.C. 5318(l); and

(b) Authenticating customers, monitoring transactions, and verifying the validity of change of address requests, in the case of existing covered accounts.

IV. Preventing and Mitigating Identity Theft

The Program's policies and procedures should provide for appropriate responses to the Red Flags the financial institution or creditor has detected that are commensurate with the degree of risk posed. In determining an appropriate response, a financial institution or creditor should consider aggravating factors that may heighten the risk of identity theft, such as a data security incident that results in unauthorized access to a customer's account records held by the financial institution, creditor, or third party, or notice that a customer has provided information related to a covered account held by the financial institution or creditor to someone fraudulently claiming to represent the financial institution or creditor or to a fraudulent website. Appropriate responses may include the following:

(a) Monitoring a covered account for evidence of identity theft;

(b) Contacting the customer;

(c) Changing any passwords, security codes, or other security devices that permit access to a covered account;

(d) Reopening a covered account with a new account number;

(e) Not opening a new covered account;

(f) Closing an existing covered account;

(g) Not attempting to collect on a covered account or not selling a covered account to a debt collector;

(h) Notifying law enforcement; or

(i) Determining that no response is warranted under the particular circumstances.

V. Updating the Program

Financial institutions and creditors should update the Program (including the Red Flags determined to be relevant) periodically, to reflect changes in risks to customers or to the safety and soundness of the financial institution or creditor from identity theft, based on factors such as:

(a) The experiences of the financial institution or creditor with identity theft;

(b) Changes in methods of identity theft;

(c) Changes in methods to detect, prevent, and mitigate identity theft;

(d) Changes in the types of accounts that the financial institution or creditor offers or maintains; and

(e) Changes in the business arrangements of the financial institution or creditor, including mergers, acquisitions, alliances, joint ventures, and service provider arrangements.

VI. Methods for Administering the Program

(a) *Oversight of Program.* Oversight by the board of directors, an appropriate committee of the board, or a designated employee at the level of senior management should include:

(1) Assigning specific responsibility for the Program's implementation;

(2) Reviewing reports prepared by staff regarding compliance by the financial institution or creditor with §41.90 of this part; and

(3) Approving material changes to the Program as necessary to address changing identity theft risks.

(b) *Reports.* (1) *In general.* Staff of the financial institution or creditor responsible for development, implementation, and administration of its Program should report to the board of directors, an appropriate committee of the board, or a designated employee at the level of senior management, at least annually, on compliance by the financial institution or creditor with §41.90 of this part.

(2) *Contents of report.* The report should address material matters related to the Program and evaluate issues such as: the effectiveness of the policies and procedures of the financial institution or creditor in addressing the risk of identity theft in connection with the opening of covered accounts and with respect to existing covered accounts; service provider arrangements; significant incidents involving identity theft and management's response; and recommendations for material changes to the Program.

(c) *Oversight of service provider arrangements.* Whenever a financial institution or creditor engages a service provider to perform an activity in connection with one or more covered accounts the financial institution or creditor should take steps to ensure that the activity of the service provider is conducted in accordance with reasonable policies and procedures designed to detect, prevent, and mitigate the risk of identity theft. For example, a financial institution or creditor could require the service provider by contract to have policies and procedures to detect relevant Red Flags that may arise in the performance of the service provider's activities, and either report the Red Flags to the financial institution or creditor, or to take appropriate steps to prevent or mitigate identity theft.

VII. Other Applicable Legal Requirements

Financial institutions and creditors should be mindful of other related legal requirements that may be applicable, such as:

(a) For financial institutions and creditors that are subject to 31 U.S.C. 5318(g), filing a Suspicious Activity Report in accordance with applicable law and regulation;

(b) Implementing any requirements under 15 U.S.C. 1681c–1(h) regarding the circumstances under which credit may be extended when the financial institution or creditor detects a fraud or active duty alert;

(c) Implementing any requirements for furnishers of information to consumer reporting agencies under 15 U.S.C. 1681s–2, for example, to correct or update inaccurate or incomplete information, and to not report information that the furnisher has reasonable cause to believe is inaccurate; and

(d) Complying with the prohibitions in 15 U.S.C. 1681m on the sale, transfer, and placement for collection of certain debts resulting from identity theft.

Supplement A to Appendix J

In addition to incorporating Red Flags from the sources recommended in section II.b. of the Guidelines in appendix J of this part, each financial institution or creditor may consider incorporating into its Program, whether singly or in combination, Red Flags from the following illustrative examples in connection with covered accounts:

Alerts, Notifications or Warnings from a Consumer Reporting Agency

1. A fraud or active duty alert is included with a consumer report.

2. A consumer reporting agency provides a notice of credit freeze in response to a request for a consumer report.

3. A consumer reporting agency provides a notice of address discrepancy, as defined in 12 CFR 1022.82(b) of this part.

4. A consumer report indicates a pattern of activity that is inconsistent with the history and usual pattern of activity of an applicant or customer, such as:

a. A recent and significant increase in the volume of inquiries;

b. An unusual number of recently established credit relationships;

c. A material change in the use of credit, especially with respect to recently established credit relationships; or

d. An account that was closed for cause or identified for abuse of account privileges by a financial institution or creditor.

Suspicious Documents

5. Documents provided for identification appear to have been altered or forged.

6. The photograph or physical description on the identification is not consistent with the appearance of the applicant or customer presenting the identification.

7. Other information on the identification is not consistent with information provided by the person opening a new covered account or customer presenting the identification.

8. Other information on the identification is not consistent with readily accessible information that is on file with the financial institution or creditor, such as a signature card or a recent check.

9. An application appears to have been altered or forged, or gives the appearance of having been destroyed and reassembled.

Suspicious Personal Identifying Information

10. Personal identifying information provided is inconsistent when compared against external information sources used by the financial institution or creditor. For example:

a. The address does not match any address in the consumer report; or

b. The Social Security Number (SSN) has not been issued, or is listed on the Social Security Administration's Death Master File.

11. Personal identifying information provided by the customer is not consistent with other personal identifying information provided by the customer. For example, there is a lack of correlation between the SSN range and date of birth.

12. Personal identifying information provided is associated with known fraudulent activity as indicated by internal or third-party sources used by the financial institution or creditor. For example:

a. The address on an application is the same as the address provided on a fraudulent application; or

b. The phone number on an application is the same as the number provided on a fraudulent application.

13. Personal identifying information provided is of a type commonly associated with fraudulent activity as indicated by internal or third-party sources used by the financial institution or creditor. For example:

a. The address on an application is fictitious, a mail drop, or a prison; or

b. The phone number is invalid, or is associated with a pager or answering service.

14. The SSN provided is the same as that submitted by other persons opening an account or other customers.

15. The address or telephone number provided is the same as or similar to the address or telephone number submitted by an unusually large number of other persons opening accounts or by other customers.

16. The person opening the covered account or the customer fails to provide all required personal identifying information on an application or in response to notification that the application is incomplete.

17. Personal identifying information provided is not consistent with personal identifying information that is on file with the financial institution or creditor.

18. For financial institutions and creditors that use challenge questions, the person opening the covered account or the customer cannot provide authenticating information beyond that which generally would be available from a wallet or consumer report.

Unusual Use of, or Suspicious Activity Related to, the Covered Account

19. Shortly following the notice of a change of address for a covered account, the institution or creditor receives a request for a new, additional, or replacement card or a cell phone, or for the addition of authorized users on the account.

20. A new revolving credit account is used in a manner commonly associated with known patterns of fraud. For example:

a. The majority of available credit is used for cash advances or merchandise that is easily convertible to cash (e.g., electronics equipment or jewelry); or

b. The customer fails to make the first payment or makes an initial payment but no subsequent payments.

21. A covered account is used in a manner that is not consistent with established patterns of activity on the account. There is, for example:

a. Nonpayment when there is no history of late or missed payments;

b. A material increase in the use of available credit;

c. A material change in purchasing or spending patterns;

d. A material change in electronic fund transfer patterns in connection with a deposit account; or

e. A material change in telephone call patterns in connection with a cellular phone account.

22. A covered account that has been inactive for a reasonably lengthy period of time is used (taking into consideration the type of account, the expected pattern of usage and other relevant factors).

23. Mail sent to the customer is returned repeatedly as undeliverable although transactions continue to be conducted in connection with the customer's covered account.

24. The financial institution or creditor is notified that the customer is not receiving paper account statements.

25. The financial institution or creditor is notified of unauthorized charges or transactions in connection with a customer's covered account.

Notice From Customers, Victims of Identity Theft, Law Enforcement Authorities, or Other Persons Regarding Possible Identity Theft in Connection With Covered Accounts Held by the Financial Institution or Creditor

26. The financial institution or creditor is notified by a customer, a victim of identity theft, a law enforcement authority, or any other person that it has opened a fraudulent account for a person engaged in identity theft.

[72 FR 63754, Nov. 9, 2007, as amended at 74 FR 22642, May 14, 2009; 76 FR 6688, Feb. 8, 2011; 79 FR 28401, May 16, 2014]

PART 42 [RESERVED]

PART 43—CREDIT RISK RETENTION

Subpart A—Authority, Purpose, Scope and Definitions

Sec.
43.1 Authority, purpose, scope, and reservation of authority.
43.2 Definitions.

Subpart B—Credit Risk Retention

43.3 Base risk retention requirement.
43.4 Standard risk retention.
43.5 Revolving pool securitizations.
43.6 Eligible ABCP conduits.
43.7 Commercial mortgage-backed securities.
43.8 Federal National Mortgage Association and Federal Home Loan Mortgage Corporation ABS.
43.9 Open market CLOs.
43.10 Qualified tender option bonds.

Subpart C—Transfer of Risk Retention

43.11 Allocation of risk retention to an originator.
43.12 Hedging, transfer and financing prohibitions.

Subpart D—Exceptions and Exemptions

43.13 Exemption for qualified residential mortgages.
43.14 Definitions applicable to qualifying commercial loans, qualifying commercial real estate loans, and qualifying automobile loans.
43.15 Qualifying commercial loans, commercial real estate loans, and automobile loans.
43.16 Underwriting standards for qualifying commercial loans.
43.17 Underwriting standards for qualifying CRE loans.
43.18 Underwriting standards for qualifying automobile loans.
43.19 General exemptions.
43.20 Safe harbor for certain foreign-related transactions.
43.21 Additional exemptions.
43.22 Periodic review of the QRM definition, exempted three-to-four unit residential mortgage loans, and community-focused residential mortgage exemption.

AUTHORITY: 12 U.S.C. 1 *et seq.*, 93a, 161, 1464, 1818, 5412(b)(2)(B), and 15 U.S.C. 78o-11.

SOURCE: 79 FR 77740, 77764, Dec. 24, 2014, unless otherwise noted.

Subpart A—Authority, Purpose, Scope and Definitions

§43.1 Authority, purpose, scope, and reservation of authority.

(a) *Authority*. This part is issued under the authority of 12 U.S.C. 1 *et seq.*, 93a, 161, 1464, 1818, 5412(b)(2)(B), and 15 U.S.C. 78o-11.

(b) *Purpose*. (1) This part requires securitizers to retain an economic interest in a portion of the credit risk for any asset that the securitizer, through the issuance of an asset-backed security, transfers, sells, or conveys to a third party. This part specifies the permissible types, forms, and amounts of credit risk retention, and it establishes certain exemptions for securitizations collateralized by assets that meet specified underwriting standards.

(2) Nothing in this part shall be read to limit the authority of the OCC to take supervisory or enforcement action, including action to address unsafe or unsound practices or conditions, or violations of law.

(c) *Scope*. This part applies to any securitizer that is a national bank, a Federal savings association, a Federal branch or agency of a foreign bank, or a subsidiary thereof.

(d) *Compliance dates*. Compliance with this part is required:

(1) With respect to any securitization transaction collateralized by residential mortgages, on and after December 24, 2015; and

(2) With respect to any other securitization transaction, on and after December 24, 2016.

[79 FR 77764, Dec. 24, 2014]

§43.2 Definitions.

For purposes of this part, the following definitions apply:

ABS interest means:

(1) Any type of interest or obligation issued by an issuing entity, whether or not in certificated form, including a security, obligation, beneficial interest or residual interest (other than an uncertificated regular interest in a REMIC that is held by another REMIC, where both REMICs are part of the same structure and a single REMIC in that structure issues ABS interests to investors, or a non-economic residual

interest issued by a REMIC), payments on which are primarily dependent on the cash flows of the collateral owned or held by the issuing entity; and

(2) Does not include common or preferred stock, limited liability interests, partnership interests, trust certificates, or similar interests that:

(i) Are issued primarily to evidence ownership of the issuing entity; and

(ii) The payments, if any, on which are not primarily dependent on the cash flows of the collateral held by the issuing entity; and

(3) Does not include the right to receive payments for services provided by the holder of such right, including servicing, trustee services and custodial services.

Affiliate of, or a person *affiliated* with, a specified person means a person that directly, or indirectly through one or more intermediaries, controls, or is controlled by, or is under common control with, the person specified.

Appropriate Federal banking agency has the same meaning as in section 3 of the Federal Deposit Insurance Act (12 U.S.C. 1813).

Asset means a self-liquidating financial asset (including but not limited to a loan, lease, mortgage, or receivable).

Asset-backed security has the same meaning as in section 3(a)(79) of the Securities Exchange Act of 1934 (15 U.S.C. 78c(a)(79)).

Collateral means, with respect to any issuance of ABS interests, the assets that provide the cash flow and the servicing assets that support such cash flow for the ABS interests irrespective of the legal structure of issuance, including security interests in assets or other property of the issuing entity, fractional undivided property interests in the assets or other property of the issuing entity, or any other property interest in or rights to cash flow from such assets and related servicing assets. Assets or other property *collateralize* an issuance of ABS interests if the assets or property serve as collateral for such issuance.

Commercial real estate loan has the same meaning as in § 43.14.

Commission means the Securities and Exchange Commission.

Control including the terms "controlling," "controlled by" and "under common control with":

(1) Means the possession, direct or indirect, of the power to direct or cause the direction of the management and policies of a person, whether through the ownership of voting securities, by contract, or otherwise.

(2) Without limiting the foregoing, a person shall be considered to control another person if the first person:

(i) Owns, controls or holds with power to vote 25 percent or more of any class of voting securities of the other person; or

(ii) Controls in any manner the election of a majority of the directors, trustees or persons performing similar functions of the other person.

Credit risk means:

(1) The risk of loss that could result from the failure of the borrower in the case of a securitized asset, or the issuing entity in the case of an ABS interest in the issuing entity, to make required payments of principal or interest on the asset or ABS interest on a timely basis;

(2) The risk of loss that could result from bankruptcy, insolvency, or a similar proceeding with respect to the borrower or issuing entity, as appropriate; or

(3) The effect that significant changes in the underlying credit quality of the asset or ABS interest may have on the market value of the asset or ABS interest.

Creditor has the same meaning as in 15 U.S.C. 1602(g).

Depositor means:

(1) The person that receives or purchases and transfers or sells the securitized assets to the issuing entity;

(2) The sponsor, in the case of a securitization transaction where there is not an intermediate transfer of the assets from the sponsor to the issuing entity; or

(3) The person that receives or purchases and transfers or sells the securitized assets to the issuing entity in the case of a securitization transaction where the person transferring or selling the securitized assets directly to the issuing entity is itself a trust.

Eligible horizontal residual interest means, with respect to any securitization transaction, an ABS interest in the issuing entity:

(1) That is an interest in a single class or multiple classes in the issuing entity, provided that each interest meets, individually or in the aggregate, all of the requirements of this definition;

(2) With respect to which, on any payment date or allocation date on which the issuing entity has insufficient funds to satisfy its obligation to pay all contractual interest or principal due, any resulting shortfall will reduce amounts payable to the eligible horizontal residual interest prior to any reduction in the amounts payable to any other ABS interest, whether through loss allocation, operation of the priority of payments, or any other governing contractual provision (until the amount of such ABS interest is reduced to zero); and

(3) That, with the exception of any non-economic REMIC residual interest, has the most subordinated claim to payments of both principal and interest by the issuing entity.

Eligible horizontal cash reserve account means an account meeting the requirements of § 43.4(b).

Eligible vertical interest means, with respect to any securitization transaction, a single vertical security or an interest in each class of ABS interests in the issuing entity issued as part of the securitization transaction that constitutes the same proportion of each such class.

Federal banking agencies means the Office of the Comptroller of the Currency, the Board of Governors of the Federal Reserve System, and the Federal Deposit Insurance Corporation.

GAAP means generally accepted accounting principles as used in the United States.

Issuing entity means, with respect to a securitization transaction, the trust or other entity:

(1) That owns or holds the pool of assets to be securitized; and

(2) In whose name the asset-backed securities are issued.

Majority-owned affiliate of a person means an entity (other than the issuing entity) that, directly or indirectly, majority controls, is majority controlled by or is under common majority control with, such person. For purposes of this definition, majority control means ownership of more than 50 percent of the equity of an entity, or ownership of any other controlling financial interest in the entity, as determined under GAAP.

Originator means a person who:

(1) Through an extension of credit or otherwise, creates an asset that collateralizes an asset-backed security; and

(2) Sells the asset directly or indirectly to a securitizer or issuing entity.

REMIC has the same meaning as in 26 U.S.C. 860D.

Residential mortgage means:

(1) A transaction that is a covered transaction as defined in § 1026.43(b) of Regulation Z (12 CFR 1026.43(b)(1));

(2) Any transaction that is exempt from the definition of "covered transaction" under § 1026.43(a) of Regulation Z (12 CFR 1026.43(a)); and

(3) Any other loan secured by a residential structure that contains one to four units, whether or not that structure is attached to real property, including an individual condominium or cooperative unit and, if used as a residence, a mobile home or trailer.

Retaining sponsor means, with respect to a securitization transaction, the sponsor that has retained or caused to be retained an economic interest in the credit risk of the securitized assets pursuant to subpart B of this part.

Securitization transaction means a transaction involving the offer and sale of asset-backed securities by an issuing entity.

Securitized asset means an asset that:

(1) Is transferred, sold, or conveyed to an issuing entity; and

(2) Collateralizes the ABS interests issued by the issuing entity.

Securitizer means, with respect to a securitization transaction, either:

(1) The depositor of the asset-backed securities (if the depositor is not the sponsor); or

(2) The sponsor of the asset-backed securities.

Servicer means any person responsible for the management or collection of the securitized assets or making allocations or distributions to holders of the ABS interests, but does not include a trustee for the issuing entity or the asset-backed securities that makes allocations or distributions to holders of the ABS interests if the trustee receives such allocations or distributions from a servicer and the trustee does not otherwise perform the functions of a servicer.

Servicing assets means rights or other assets designed to assure the servicing or timely distribution of proceeds to ABS interest holders and rights or other assets that are related or incidental to purchasing or otherwise acquiring and holding the issuing entity's securitized assets. Servicing assets include amounts received by the issuing entity as proceeds of securitized assets, including proceeds of rights or other assets, whether as remittances by obligors or as other recoveries.

Single vertical security means, with respect to any securitization transaction, an ABS interest entitling the sponsor to a specified percentage of the amounts paid on each class of ABS interests in the issuing entity (other than such single vertical security).

Sponsor means a person who organizes and initiates a securitization transaction by selling or transferring assets, either directly or indirectly, including through an affiliate, to the issuing entity.

State has the same meaning as in Section 3(a)(16) of the Securities Exchange Act of 1934 (15 U.S.C. 78c(a)(16)).

United States or U.S. means the United States of America, including its territories and possessions, any State of the United States, and the District of Columbia.

Wholly-owned affiliate means a person (other than an issuing entity) that, directly or indirectly, wholly controls, is wholly controlled by, or is wholly under common control with, another person. For purposes of this definition, "wholly controls" means ownership of 100 percent of the equity of an entity.

Subpart B—Credit Risk Retention

§ 43.3 Base risk retention requirement.

(a) *Base risk retention requirement.* Except as otherwise provided in this part, the sponsor of a securitization transaction (or majority-owned affiliate of the sponsor) shall retain an economic interest in the credit risk of the securitized assets in accordance with any one of §§ 43.4 through 43.10. Credit risk in securitized assets required to be retained and held by any person for purposes of compliance with this part, whether a sponsor, an originator, an originator-seller, or a third-party purchaser, except as otherwise provided in this part, may be acquired and held by any of such person's majority-owned affiliates (other than an issuing entity).

(b) *Multiple sponsors.* If there is more than one sponsor of a securitization transaction, it shall be the responsibility of each sponsor to ensure that at least one of the sponsors of the securitization transaction (or at least one of their majority-owned or wholly-owned affiliates, as applicable) retains an economic interest in the credit risk of the securitized assets in accordance with any one of § 43.4, § 43.5, § 43.8, § 43.9, or § 43.10.

§ 43.4 Standard risk retention.

(a) *General requirement.* Except as provided in §§ 43.5 through 43.10, the sponsor of a securitization transaction must retain an eligible vertical interest or eligible horizontal residual interest, or any combination thereof, in accordance with the requirements of this section.

(1) If the sponsor retains only an eligible vertical interest as its required risk retention, the sponsor must retain an eligible vertical interest in a percentage of not less than 5 percent.

(2) If the sponsor retains only an eligible horizontal residual interest as its required risk retention, the amount of the interest must equal at least 5 percent of the fair value of all ABS interests in the issuing entity issued as a part of the securitization transaction, determined using a fair value measurement framework under GAAP.

(3) If the sponsor retains both an eligible vertical interest and an eligible horizontal residual interest as its required risk retention, the percentage of the fair value of the eligible horizontal residual interest and the percentage of the eligible vertical interest must equal at least five.

(4) The percentage of the eligible vertical interest, eligible horizontal residual interest, or combination thereof retained by the sponsor must be determined as of the closing date of the securitization transaction.

(b) *Option to hold base amount in eligible horizontal cash reserve account.* In lieu of retaining all or any part of an eligible horizontal residual interest under paragraph (a) of this section, the sponsor may, at closing of the securitization transaction, cause to be established and funded, in cash, an eligible horizontal cash reserve account in the amount equal to the fair value of such eligible horizontal residual interest or part thereof, provided that the account meets all of the following conditions:

(1) The account is held by the trustee (or person performing similar functions) in the name and for the benefit of the issuing entity;

(2) Amounts in the account are invested only in cash and cash equivalents; and

(3) Until all ABS interests in the issuing entity are paid in full, or the issuing entity is dissolved:

(i) Amounts in the account shall be released only to:

(A) Satisfy payments on ABS interests in the issuing entity on any payment date on which the issuing entity has insufficient funds from any source to satisfy an amount due on any ABS interest; or

(B) Pay critical expenses of the trust unrelated to credit risk on any payment date on which the issuing entity has insufficient funds from any source to pay such expenses and:

(*1*) Such expenses, in the absence of available funds in the eligible horizontal cash reserve account, would be paid prior to any payments to holders of ABS interests; and

(*2*) Such payments are made to parties that are not affiliated with the sponsor; and

(ii) Interest (or other earnings) on investments made in accordance with paragraph (b)(2) of this section may be released once received by the account.

(c) *Disclosures.* A sponsor relying on this section shall provide, or cause to be provided, to potential investors, under the caption "Credit Risk Retention", a reasonable period of time prior to the sale of the asset-backed securities in the securitization transaction the following disclosures in written form and within the time frames set forth in this paragraph (c):

(1) *Horizontal interest.* With respect to any eligible horizontal residual interest held under paragraph (a) of this section, a sponsor must disclose:

(i) A reasonable period of time prior to the sale of an asset-backed security issued in the same offering of ABS interests,

(A) The fair value (expressed as a percentage of the fair value of all of the ABS interests issued in the securitization transaction and dollar amount (or corresponding amount in the foreign currency in which the ABS interests are issued, as applicable)) of the eligible horizontal residual interest that the sponsor expects to retain at the closing of the securitization transaction. If the specific prices, sizes, or rates of interest of each tranche of the securitization are not available, the sponsor must disclose a range of fair values (expressed as a percentage of the fair value of all of the ABS interests issued in the securitization transaction and dollar amount (or corresponding amount in the foreign currency in which the ABS interests are issued, as applicable)) of the eligible horizontal residual interest that the sponsor expects to retain at the close of the securitization transaction based on a range of bona fide estimates or specified prices, sizes, or rates of interest of each tranche of the securitization. A sponsor disclosing a range of fair values based on a range of bona fide estimates or specified prices, sizes or rates of interest of each tranche of the securitization must also disclose the method by which it determined any range of prices, tranche sizes, or rates of interest.

(B) A description of the material terms of the eligible horizontal residual interest to be retained by the sponsor;

(C) A description of the valuation methodology used to calculate the fair values or range of fair values of all classes of ABS interests, including any portion of the eligible horizontal residual interest retained by the sponsor;

(D) All key inputs and assumptions or a comprehensive description of such key inputs and assumptions that were used in measuring the estimated total fair value or range of fair values of all classes of ABS interests, including the eligible horizontal residual interest to be retained by the sponsor.

(E) To the extent applicable to the valuation methodology used, the disclosure required in paragraph (c)(1)(i)(D) of this section shall include, but should not be limited to, quantitative information about each of the following:

(*1*) Discount rates;

(*2*) Loss given default (recovery);

(*3*) Prepayment rates;

(*4*) Default rates;

(*5*) Lag time between default and recovery; and

(*6*) The basis of forward interest rates used.

(F) The disclosure required in paragraphs (c)(1)(i)(C) and (D) of this section shall include, at a minimum, descriptions of all inputs and assumptions that either could have a material impact on the fair value calculation or would be material to a prospective investor's ability to evaluate the sponsor's fair value calculations. To the extent the disclosure required in this paragraph (c)(1) includes a description of a curve or curves, the description shall include a description of the methodology that was used to derive each curve and a description of any aspects or features of each curve that could materially impact the fair value calculation or the ability of a prospective investor to evaluate the sponsor's fair value calculation. To the extent a sponsor uses information about the securitized assets in its calculation of fair value, such information shall not be as of a date more than 60 days prior to the date of first use with investors; provided that for a subsequent issuance of ABS interests by the same issuing entity with the same sponsor for which the securitization transaction distributes amounts to investors on a quarterly or less frequent basis, such information shall not be as of a date more than 135 days prior to the date of first use with investors; provided further, that the balance or value (in accordance with the transaction documents) of the securitized assets may be increased or decreased to reflect anticipated additions or removals of assets the sponsor makes or expects to make between the cut-off date or similar date for establishing the composition of the asset pool collateralizing such asset-backed security and the closing date of the securitization.

(G) A summary description of the reference data set or other historical information used to develop the key inputs and assumptions referenced in paragraph (c)(1)(i)(D) of this section, including loss given default and default rates;

(ii) A reasonable time after the closing of the securitization transaction:

(A) The fair value (expressed as a percentage of the fair value of all of the ABS interests issued in the securitization transaction and dollar amount (or corresponding amount in the foreign currency in which the ABS are issued, as applicable)) of the eligible horizontal residual interest the sponsor retained at the closing of the securitization transaction, based on actual sale prices and finalized tranche sizes;

(B) The fair value (expressed as a percentage of the fair value of all of the ABS interests issued in the securitization transaction and dollar amount (or corresponding amount in the foreign currency in which the ABS are issued, as applicable)) of the eligible horizontal residual interest that the sponsor is required to retain under this section; and

(C) To the extent the valuation methodology or any of the key inputs and assumptions that were used in calculating the fair value or range of fair values disclosed prior to sale and required under paragraph (c)(1)(i) of this section materially differs from the methodology or key inputs and assumptions used to calculate the fair value at the time of closing, descriptions of those material differences.

(iii) If the sponsor retains risk through the funding of an eligible horizontal cash reserve account:

(A) The amount to be placed (or that is placed) by the sponsor in the eligible horizontal cash reserve account at closing, and the fair value (expressed as a percentage of the fair value of all of the ABS interests issued in the securitization transaction and dollar amount (or corresponding amount in the foreign currency in which the ABS interests are issued, as applicable)) of the eligible horizontal residual interest that the sponsor is required to fund through the eligible horizontal cash reserve account in order for such account, together with other retained interests, to satisfy the sponsor's risk retention requirement;

(B) A description of the material terms of the eligible horizontal cash reserve account; and

(C) The disclosures required in paragraphs (c)(1)(i) and (ii) of this section.

(2) *Vertical interest.* With respect to any eligible vertical interest retained under paragraph (a) of this section, the sponsor must disclose:

(i) A reasonable period of time prior to the sale of an asset-backed security issued in the same offering of ABS interests,

(A) The form of the eligible vertical interest;

(B) The percentage that the sponsor is required to retain as a vertical interest under this section; and

(C) A description of the material terms of the vertical interest and the amount that the sponsor expects to retain at the closing of the securitization transaction.

(ii) A reasonable time after the closing of the securitization transaction, the amount of the vertical interest the sponsor retained at closing, if that amount is materially different from the amount disclosed under paragraph (c)(2)(i) of this section.

(d) *Record maintenance.* A sponsor must retain the certifications and disclosures required in paragraphs (a) and (c) of this section in its records and must provide the disclosure upon request to the Commission and its appropriate Federal banking agency, if any, until three years after all ABS interests are no longer outstanding.

§43.5 Revolving pool securitizations.

(a) *Definitions.* For purposes of this section, the following definitions apply:

Revolving pool securitization means an issuing entity that is established to issue on multiple issuance dates more than one series, class, subclass, or tranche of asset-backed securities that are collateralized by a common pool of securitized assets that will change in composition over time, and that does not monetize excess interest and fees from its securitized assets.

Seller's interest means an ABS interest or ABS interests:

(1) Collateralized by the securitized assets and servicing assets owned or held by the issuing entity, other than the following that are not considered a component of seller's interest:

(i) Servicing assets that have been allocated as collateral only for a specific series in connection with administering the revolving pool securitization, such as a principal accumulation or interest reserve account; and

(ii) Assets that are not eligible under the terms of the securitization transaction to be included when determining whether the revolving pool securitization holds aggregate securitized assets in specified proportions to aggregate outstanding investor ABS interests issued; and

(2) That is *pari passu* with each series of investor ABS interests issued, or partially or fully subordinated to one or more series in identical or varying amounts, with respect to the allocation of all distributions and losses with respect to the securitized assets prior to early amortization of the revolving securitization (as specified in the securitization transaction documents); and

(3) That adjusts for fluctuations in the outstanding principal balance of the securitized assets in the pool.

(b) *General requirement.* A sponsor satisfies the risk retention requirements of §43.3 with respect to a securitization transaction for which the issuing entity is a revolving pool securitization if the sponsor maintains a seller's interest of not less than 5 percent of the aggregate unpaid principal balance of all outstanding investor ABS interests in the issuing entity.

(c) *Measuring the seller's interest.* In measuring the seller's interest for purposes of meeting the requirements of paragraph (b) of this section:

(1) The unpaid principal balance of the securitized assets for the numerator of the 5 percent ratio shall not include assets of the types excluded from the definition of seller's interest in paragraph (a) of this section;

(2) The aggregate unpaid principal balance of outstanding investor ABS interests in the denominator of the 5 percent ratio may be reduced by the amount of funds held in a segregated principal accumulation account for the repayment of outstanding investor ABS interests, if:

(i) The terms of the securitization transaction documents prevent funds in the principal accumulation account from being applied for any purpose other than the repayment of the unpaid principal of outstanding investor ABS interests; and

(ii) Funds in that account are invested only in the types of assets in which funds held in an eligible horizontal cash reserve account pursuant to § 43.4 are permitted to be invested;

(3) If the terms of the securitization transaction documents set minimum required seller's interest as a proportion of the unpaid principal balance of outstanding investor ABS interests for one or more series issued, rather than as a proportion of the aggregate outstanding investor ABS interests in all outstanding series combined, the percentage of the seller's interest for each such series must, when combined with the percentage of any minimum seller's interest set by reference to the aggregate outstanding investor ABS interests, equal at least 5 percent;

(4) The 5 percent test must be determined and satisfied at the closing of each issuance of ABS interests to investors by the issuing entity, and

(i) At least monthly at a seller's interest measurement date specified under the securitization transaction documents, until no ABS interest in the issuing entity is held by any person not a wholly-owned affiliate of the sponsor; or

(ii) If the revolving pool securitization fails to meet the 5 percent test as of any date described in paragraph (c)(4)(i) of this section, and the securitization transaction documents specify a cure period, the 5 percent test must be determined and satisfied within the earlier of the cure period, or one month after the date described in paragraph (c)(4)(i).

(d) *Measuring outstanding investor ABS interests.* In measuring the amount of outstanding investor ABS interests for purposes of this section, ABS interests held for the life of such ABS interests by the sponsor or its wholly-owned affiliates may be excluded.

(e) *Holding and retention of the seller's interest; legacy trusts.* (1) Notwithstanding § 43.12(a), the seller's interest, and any offsetting horizontal retention interest retained pursuant to paragraph (g) of this section, must be retained by the sponsor or by one or more wholly-owned affiliates of the sponsor, including one or more depositors of the revolving pool securitization.

(2) If one revolving pool securitization issues collateral certificates representing a beneficial interest in all or a portion of the securitized assets held by that securitization to another revolving pool securitization, which in turn issues ABS interests for which the collateral certificates are all or a portion of the securitized assets, a sponsor may satisfy the requirements of paragraphs (b) and (c) of this section by retaining the seller's interest for the assets represented by the collateral certificates through either of the revolving pool securitizations, so long as both revolving pool securitizations are retained at the direction of the same sponsor or its wholly-owned affiliates.

(3) If the sponsor retains the seller's interest associated with the collateral certificates at the level of the revolving pool securitization that issues those collateral certificates, the proportion of the seller's interest required by paragraph (b) of this section retained at that level must equal the proportion that the principal balance of the securitized assets represented by the collateral certificates bears to the principal balance of the securitized assets in the revolving pool securitization that issues the ABS interests, as of each measurement date required by paragraph (c) of this section.

(f) *Offset for pool-level excess funding account.* The 5 percent seller's interest required on each measurement date by paragraph (c) of this section may be reduced on a dollar-for-dollar basis by the balance, as of such date, of an excess funding account in the form of a segregated account that:

(1) Is funded in the event of a failure to meet the minimum seller's interest requirements or other requirement to maintain a minimum balance of securitized assets under the securitization transaction documents by distributions otherwise payable to the holder of the seller's interest;

(2) Is invested only in the types of assets in which funds held in a horizontal cash reserve account pursuant to §43.4 are permitted to be invested; and

(3) In the event of an early amortization, makes payments of amounts held in the account to holders of investor ABS interests in the same manner as payments to holders of investor ABS interests of amounts received on securitized assets.

(g) *Combined seller's interests and horizontal interest retention.* The 5 percent seller's interest required on each measurement date by paragraph (c) of this section may be reduced to a percentage lower than 5 percent to the extent that, for all series of investor ABS interests issued after the applicable effective date of this §43.5, the sponsor, or notwithstanding §43.12(a) a wholly-owned affiliate of the sponsor, retains, at a minimum, a corresponding percentage of the fair value of ABS interests issued in each series, in the form of one or more of the horizontal residual interests meeting the requirements of paragraphs (h) or (i).

(h) *Residual ABS interests in excess interest and fees.* The sponsor may take the offset described in paragraph (g) of this section for a residual ABS interest in excess interest and fees, whether certificated or uncertificated, in a single or multiple classes, subclasses, or tranches, that meets, individually or in the aggregate, the requirements of this paragraph (h);

(1) Each series of the revolving pool securitization distinguishes between the series' share of the interest and fee cash flows and the series' share of the principal repayment cash flows from the securitized assets collateralizing the revolving pool securitization, which may according to the terms of the securitization transaction documents, include not only the series' ratable share of such cash flows but also excess cash flows available from other series;

(2) The residual ABS interest's claim to any part of the series' share of the interest and fee cash flows for any interest payment period is subordinated to all accrued and payable interest due on the payment date to more senior ABS interests in the series for that period, and further reduced by the series' share of losses, including defaults on principal of the securitized assets collateralizing the revolving pool securitization (whether incurred in that period or carried over from prior periods) to the extent that such payments would have been included in amounts payable to more senior interests in the series;

(3) The revolving pool securitization continues to revolve, with one or more series, classes, subclasses, or tranches of asset-backed securities that are collateralized by a common pool of assets that change in composition over time; and

(4) For purposes of taking the offset described in paragraph (g) of this section, the sponsor determines the fair value of the residual ABS interest in excess interest and fees, and the fair value of the series of outstanding investor ABS interests to which it is subordinated and supports using the fair value measurement framework under GAAP, as of:

(i) The closing of the securitization transaction issuing the supported ABS interests; and

(ii) The seller's interest measurement dates described in paragraph (c)(4) of this section, except that for these periodic determinations the sponsor must update the fair value of the residual ABS interest in excess interest and fees for the numerator of the percentage ratio, but may at the sponsor's option continue to use the fair values determined in (h)(4)(i) for the outstanding investor ABS interests in the denominator.

(i) *Offsetting eligible horizontal residual interest.* The sponsor may take the offset described in paragraph (g) of this section for ABS interests that would meet the definition of eligible horizontal residual interests in § 43.2 but for the sponsor's simultaneous holding of subordinated seller's interests, residual ABS interests in excess interests and fees, or a combination of the two, if:

(1) The sponsor complies with all requirements of paragraphs (b) through (e) of this section for its holdings of subordinated seller's interest, and paragraph (h) for its holdings of residual ABS interests in excess interests and fees, as applicable;

(2) For purposes of taking the offset described in paragraph (g) of this section, the sponsor determines the fair value of the eligible horizontal residual interest as a percentage of the fair value of the outstanding investor ABS interests in the series supported by the eligible horizontal residual interest, determined using the fair value measurement framework under GAAP:

(i) As of the closing of the securitization transaction issuing the supported ABS interests; and

(ii) Without including in the numerator of the percentage ratio any fair value based on:

(A) The subordinated seller's interest or residual ABS interest in excess interest and fees;

(B) the interest payable to the sponsor on the eligible horizontal residual interest, if the sponsor is including the value of residual ABS interest in excess interest and fees pursuant to paragraph (h) of this section in taking the offset in paragraph (g) of this section; and,

(C) the principal payable to the sponsor on the eligible horizontal residual interest, if the sponsor is including the value of the seller's interest pursuant to paragraphs (b) through (f) of this section and distributions on that seller's interest are available to reduce charge-offs that would otherwise be allocated to reduce principal payable to the offset eligible horizontal residual interest.

(j) *Specified dates.* A sponsor using data about the revolving pool securitization's collateral, or ABS interests previously issued, to determine the closing-date percentage of a seller's interest, residual ABS interest in excess interest and fees, or eligible horizontal residual interest pursuant to this § 43.5 may use such data prepared as of specified dates if:

(1) The sponsor describes the specified dates in the disclosures required by paragraph (k) of this section; and

(2) The dates are no more than 60 days prior to the date of first use with investors of disclosures required for the interest by paragraph (k) of this section, or for revolving pool securitizations that make distributions to investors on a quarterly or less frequent basis, no more than 135 days prior to the date of first use with investors of such disclosures.

(k) *Disclosure and record maintenance*—(1) *Disclosure.* A sponsor relying on this section shall provide, or cause to be provided, to potential investors, under the caption "Credit Risk Retention" the following disclosure in written form and within the time frames set forth in this paragraph (k):

(i) A reasonable period of time prior to the sale of an asset-backed security, a description of the material terms of the seller's interest, and the percentage of the seller's interest that the sponsor expects to retain at the closing of the securitization transaction, measured in accordance with the requirements of this § 43.5, as a percentage of the aggregate unpaid principal balance of all outstanding investor ABS interests issued, or as a percentage of the aggregate unpaid principal balance of outstanding investor ABS interests for one or more series issued, as required by the terms of the securitization transaction;

(ii) A reasonable time after the closing of the securitization transaction, the amount of seller's interest the sponsor retained at closing, if that amount is materially different from the amount disclosed under paragraph (k)(1)(i) of this section; and

(iii) A description of the material terms of any horizontal residual interests offsetting the seller's interest in accordance with paragraphs (g), (h), and (i) of this section; and

(iv) Disclosure of the fair value of those horizontal residual interests retained by the sponsor for the series being offered to investors and described in the disclosures, as a percentage of the fair value of the outstanding investor ABS interests issued, described in the same manner and within the same timeframes required for disclosure of the fair values of eligible horizontal residual interests specified in § 43.4(c).

(2) *Adjusted data.* Disclosures required by this paragraph (k) to be made a reasonable period of time prior to the sale of an asset-backed security of the amount of seller's interest, residual ABS interest in excess interest and fees, or eligible horizontal residual interest may include adjustments to the amount of securitized assets for additions or removals the sponsor expects to make before the closing date and adjustments to the amount of outstanding investor ABS interests for expected increases and decreases of those interests under the control of the sponsor.

(3) *Record maintenance.* A sponsor must retain the disclosures required in paragraph (k)(1) of this section in its records and must provide the disclosure upon request to the Commission and its appropriate Federal banking agency, if any, until three years after all ABS interests are no longer outstanding.

(l) *Early amortization of all outstanding series.* A sponsor that organizes a revolving pool securitization that relies on this § 43.5 to satisfy the risk retention requirements of § 43.3, does not violate the requirements of this part if its seller's interest falls below the level required by § 43. 5 after the revolving pool securitization commences early amortization, pursuant to the terms of the securitization transaction documents, of all series of outstanding investor ABS interests, if:

(1) The sponsor was in full compliance with the requirements of this section on all measurement dates specified in paragraph (c) of this section prior to the commencement of early amortization;

(2) The terms of the seller's interest continue to make it *pari passu* with or subordinate in identical or varying amounts to each series of outstanding investor ABS interests issued with respect to the allocation of all distributions and losses with respect to the securitized assets;

(3) The terms of any horizontal interest relied upon by the sponsor pursuant to paragraph (g) to offset the minimum seller's interest amount continue to require the interests to absorb losses in accordance with the terms of paragraph (h) or (i) of this section, as applicable; and

(4) The revolving pool securitization issues no additional ABS interests after early amortization is initiated to any person not a wholly-owned affiliate of the sponsor, either at the time of issuance or during the amortization period.

§ 43.6 Eligible ABCP conduits.

(a) *Definitions.* For purposes of this section, the following additional definitions apply:

100 percent liquidity coverage means an amount equal to the outstanding balance of all ABCP issued by the conduit plus any accrued and unpaid interest without regard to the performance of the ABS interests held by the ABCP conduit and without regard to any credit enhancement.

ABCP means asset-backed commercial paper that has a maturity at the time of issuance not exceeding 397 days, exclusive of days of grace, or any renewal thereof the maturity of which is likewise limited.

ABCP conduit means an issuing entity with respect to ABCP.

Eligible ABCP conduit means an ABCP conduit, *provided that:*

(1) The ABCP conduit is bankruptcy remote or otherwise isolated for insolvency purposes from the sponsor of the ABCP conduit and from any intermediate SPV;

(2) The ABS interests acquired by the ABCP conduit are:

(i) ABS interests collateralized solely by assets originated by an originator-seller and by servicing assets;

(ii) Special units of beneficial interest (or similar ABS interests) in a trust or special purpose vehicle that retains legal title to leased property underlying leases originated by an originator-seller that were transferred to an intermediate SPV in connection with a securitization collateralized solely by such leases and by servicing assets;

(iii) ABS interests in a revolving pool securitization collateralized solely by assets originated by an originator-seller and by servicing assets; or

(iv) ABS interests described in paragraph (2)(i), (ii), or (iii) of this definition that are collateralized, in whole or in part, by assets acquired by an originator-seller in a business combination that qualifies for business combination accounting under GAAP, and, if collateralized in part, the remainder of such assets are assets described in paragraph (2)(i), (ii), or (iii) of this definition; and

(v) Acquired by the ABCP conduit in an initial issuance by or on behalf of an intermediate SPV:

(A) Directly from the intermediate SPV,

(B) From an underwriter of the ABS interests issued by the intermediate SPV, or

(C) From another person who acquired the ABS interests directly from the intermediate SPV;

(3) The ABCP conduit is collateralized solely by ABS interests acquired from intermediate SPVs as described in paragraph (2) of this definition and servicing assets; and

(4) A regulated liquidity provider has entered into a legally binding commitment to provide 100 percent liquidity coverage (in the form of a lending facility, an asset purchase agreement, a repurchase agreement, or other similar arrangement) to all the ABCP issued by the ABCP conduit by lending to, purchasing ABCP issued by, or purchasing assets from, the ABCP conduit in the event that funds are required to repay maturing ABCP issued by the ABCP conduit. With respect to the 100 percent liquidity coverage, in the event that the ABCP conduit is unable for any reason to repay maturing ABCP issued by the issuing entity, the liquidity provider shall be obligated to pay an amount equal to any shortfall, and the total amount that may be due pursuant to the 100 percent liquidity coverage shall be equal to 100 percent of the amount of the ABCP outstanding at any time plus accrued and unpaid interest (amounts due pursuant to the required liquidity coverage may not be subject to credit performance of the ABS interests held by the ABCP conduit or reduced by the amount of credit support provided to the ABCP conduit and liquidity support that only funds performing loans or receivables or performing ABS interests does not meet the requirements of this section).

Intermediate SPV means a special purpose vehicle that:

(1)(i) Is a direct or indirect wholly-owned affiliate of the originator-seller; or

(ii) Has nominal equity owned by a trust or corporate service provider that specializes in providing independent ownership of special purpose vehicles, and such trust or corporate service provider is not affiliated with any other transaction parties;

(2) Is bankruptcy remote or otherwise isolated for insolvency purposes from the eligible ABCP conduit and from each originator-seller and each majority-owned affiliate in each case that, directly or indirectly, sells or transfers assets to such intermediate SPV;

(3) Acquires assets from the originator-seller that are originated by the originator-seller or acquired by the originator-seller in the acquisition of a business that qualifies for business combination accounting under GAAP or acquires ABS interests issued by another intermediate SPV of the originator-seller that are collateralized solely by such assets; and

(4) Issues ABS interests collateralized solely by such assets, as applicable.

Originator-seller means an entity that originates assets and sells or transfers those assets, directly or through a majority-owned affiliate, to an intermediate SPV, and includes (except for the purposes of identifying the sponsorship and affiliation of an intermediate SPV pursuant to this § 43.6) any affiliate of the originator-seller that, directly or indirectly, majority controls, is majority controlled by or is under common majority control with, the originator-seller. For purposes of this definition, majority control means ownership of more than 50 percent of the equity of an entity, or ownership of any other controlling financial interest in the entity, as determined under GAAP.

Regulated liquidity provider means:

(1) A depository institution (as defined in section 3 of the Federal Deposit Insurance Act (12 U.S.C. 1813));

(2) A bank holding company (as defined in 12 U.S.C. 1841), or a subsidiary thereof;

(3) A savings and loan holding company (as defined in 12 U.S.C. 1467a), provided all or substantially all of the holding company's activities are permissible for a financial holding company under 12 U.S.C. 1843(k), or a subsidiary thereof; or

(4) A foreign bank whose home country supervisor (as defined in §211.21 of the Federal Reserve Board's Regulation K (12 CFR 211.21)) has adopted capital standards consistent with the Capital Accord of the Basel Committee on Banking Supervision, as amended, and that is subject to such standards, or a subsidiary thereof.

(b) *In general.* An ABCP conduit sponsor satisfies the risk retention requirement of §43.3 with respect to the issuance of ABCP by an eligible ABCP conduit in a securitization transaction if, for each ABS interest the ABCP conduit acquires from an intermediate SPV:

(1) An originator-seller of the intermediate SPV retains an economic interest in the credit risk of the assets collateralizing the ABS interest acquired by the eligible ABCP conduit in the amount and manner required under §43.4 or §43.5; and

(2) The ABCP conduit sponsor:

(i) Approves each originator-seller permitted to sell or transfer assets, directly or indirectly, to an intermediate SPV from which an eligible ABCP conduit acquires ABS interests;

(ii) Approves each intermediate SPV from which an eligible ABCP conduit is permitted to acquire ABS interests;

(iii) Establishes criteria governing the ABS interests, and the securitized assets underlying the ABS interests, acquired by the ABCP conduit;

(iv) Administers the ABCP conduit by monitoring the ABS interests acquired by the ABCP conduit and the assets supporting those ABS interests, arranging for debt placement, compiling monthly reports, and ensuring compliance with the ABCP conduit documents and with the ABCP conduit's credit and investment policy; and

(v) Maintains and adheres to policies and procedures for ensuring that the requirements in this paragraph (b) of this section have been met.

(c) *Originator-seller compliance with risk retention.* The use of the risk retention option provided in this section by an ABCP conduit sponsor does not relieve the originator-seller that sponsors ABS interests acquired by an eligible ABCP conduit from such originator-seller's obligation to comply with its own risk retention obligations under this part.

(d) *Disclosures*—(1) *Periodic disclosures to investors.* An ABCP conduit sponsor relying upon this section shall provide, or cause to be provided, to each purchaser of ABCP, before or contemporaneously with the first sale of ABCP to such purchaser and at least monthly thereafter, to each holder of commercial paper issued by the ABCP conduit, in writing, each of the following items of information, which shall be as of a date not more than 60 days prior to date of first use with investors:

(i) The name and form of organization of the regulated liquidity provider that provides liquidity coverage to the eligible ABCP conduit, including a description of the material terms of such liquidity coverage, and notice of any failure to fund.

(ii) With respect to each ABS interest held by the ABCP conduit:

(A) The asset class or brief description of the underlying securitized assets;

(B) The standard industrial category code (SIC Code) for the originator-seller that will retain (or has retained) pursuant to this section an interest in the securitization transaction; and

(C) A description of the percentage amount of risk retention pursuant to the rule by the originator-seller, and whether it is in the form of an eligible horizontal residual interest, vertical interest, or revolving pool securitization seller's interest, as applicable.

(2) *Disclosures to regulators regarding originator-sellers.* An ABCP conduit sponsor relying upon this section shall provide, or cause to be provided, upon request, to the Commission and its appropriate Federal banking agency, if any, in writing, all of the information required to be provided to investors in paragraph (d)(1) of this section, and the

name and form of organization of each originator-seller that will retain (or has retained) pursuant to this section an interest in the securitization transaction.

(e) *Sale or transfer of ABS interests between eligible ABCP conduits.* At any time, an eligible ABCP conduit that acquired an ABS interest in accordance with the requirements set forth in this section may transfer, and another eligible ABCP conduit may acquire, such ABS interest, if the following conditions are satisfied:

(1) The sponsors of both eligible ABCP conduits are in compliance with this section; and

(2) The same regulated liquidity provider has entered into one or more legally binding commitments to provide 100 percent liquidity coverage to all the ABCP issued by both eligible ABCP conduits.

(f) *Duty to comply.* (1) The ABCP conduit sponsor shall be responsible for compliance with this section.

(2) An ABCP conduit sponsor relying on this section:

(i) Shall maintain and adhere to policies and procedures that are reasonably designed to monitor compliance by each originator-seller which is satisfying a risk retention obligation in respect of ABS interests acquired by an eligible ABCP conduit with the requirements of paragraph (b)(1) of this section; and

(ii) In the event that the ABCP conduit sponsor determines that an originator-seller no longer complies with the requirements of paragraph (b)(1) of this section, shall:

(A) Promptly notify the holders of the ABCP, and upon request, the Commission and its appropriate Federal banking agency, if any, in writing of:

(*1*) The name and form of organization of any originator-seller that fails to retain risk in accordance with paragraph (b)(1) of this section and the amount of ABS interests issued by an intermediate SPV of such originator-seller and held by the ABCP conduit;

(*2*) The name and form of organization of any originator-seller that hedges, directly or indirectly through an intermediate SPV, its risk retention in violation of paragraph (b)(1) of this section and the amount of ABS interests issued by an intermediate SPV of such originator-seller and held by the ABCP conduit; and

(*3*) Any remedial actions taken by the ABCP conduit sponsor or other party with respect to such ABS interests; and

(B) Take other appropriate steps pursuant to the requirements of paragraphs (b)(2)(iv) and (v) of this section which may include, as appropriate, curing any breach of the requirements in this section, or removing from the eligible ABCP conduit any ABS interest that does not comply with the requirements in this section.

§ 43.7 Commercial mortgage-backed securities.

(a) *Definitions.* For purposes of this section, the following definition shall apply:

Special servicer means, with respect to any securitization of commercial real estate loans, any servicer that, upon the occurrence of one or more specified conditions in the servicing agreement, has the right to service one or more assets in the transaction.

(b) *Third-party purchaser.* A sponsor may satisfy some or all of its risk retention requirements under § 43.3 with respect to a securitization transaction if a third party (or any majority-owned affiliate thereof) purchases and holds for its own account an eligible horizontal residual interest in the issuing entity in the same form, amount, and manner as would be held by the sponsor under § 43.4 and all of the following conditions are met:

(1) *Number of third-party purchasers.* At any time, there are no more than two third-party purchasers of an eligible horizontal residual interest. If there are two third-party purchasers, each third-party purchaser's interest must be *pari passu* with the other third-party purchaser's interest.

(2) *Composition of collateral.* The securitization transaction is collateralized solely by commercial real estate loans and servicing assets.

(3) *Source of funds.* (i) Each third-party purchaser pays for the eligible horizontal residual interest in cash at the closing of the securitization transaction.

(ii) No third-party purchaser obtains financing, directly or indirectly, for the purchase of such interest from any other person that is a party to, or an affiliate of a party to, the securitization transaction (including, but not limited to, the sponsor, depositor, or servicer other than a special servicer affiliated with the third-party purchaser), other than a person that is a party to the transaction solely by reason of being an investor.

(4) *Third-party review.* Each third-party purchaser conducts an independent review of the credit risk of each securitized asset prior to the sale of the asset-backed securities in the securitization transaction that includes, at a minimum, a review of the underwriting standards, collateral, and expected cash flows of each commercial real estate loan that is collateral for the asset-backed securities.

(5) *Affiliation and control rights.* (i) Except as provided in paragraph (b)(5)(ii) of this section, no third-party purchaser is affiliated with any party to the securitization transaction (including, but not limited to, the sponsor, depositor, or servicer) other than investors in the securitization transaction.

(ii) Notwithstanding paragraph (b)(5)(i) of this section, a third-party purchaser may be affiliated with:

(A) The special servicer for the securitization transaction; or

(B) One or more originators of the securitized assets, as long as the assets originated by the affiliated originator or originators collectively comprise less than 10 percent of the unpaid principal balance of the securitized assets included in the securitization transaction at the cut-off date or similar date for establishing the composition of the securitized assets collateralizing the asset-backed securities issued pursuant to the securitization transaction.

(6) *Operating Advisor.* The underlying securitization transaction documents shall provide for the following:

(i) The appointment of an operating advisor (the Operating Advisor) that:

(A) Is not affiliated with other parties to the securitization transaction;

(B) Does not directly or indirectly have any financial interest in the securitization transaction other than in fees from its role as Operating Advisor; and

(C) Is required to act in the best interest of, and for the benefit of, investors as a collective whole;

(ii) Standards with respect to the Operating Advisor's experience, expertise and financial strength to fulfill its duties and responsibilities under the applicable transaction documents over the life of the securitization transaction;

(iii) The terms of the Operating Advisor's compensation with respect to the securitization transaction;

(iv) When the eligible horizontal residual interest has been reduced by principal payments, realized losses, and appraisal reduction amounts (which reduction amounts are determined in accordance with the applicable transaction documents) to a principal balance of 25 percent or less of its initial principal balance, the special servicer for the securitized assets must consult with the Operating Advisor in connection with, and prior to, any material decision in connection with its servicing of the securitized assets, including, without limitation:

(A) Any material modification of, or waiver with respect to, any provision of a loan agreement (including a mortgage, deed of trust, or other security agreement);

(B) Foreclosure upon or comparable conversion of the ownership of a property; or

(C) Any acquisition of a property.

(v) The Operating Advisor shall have adequate and timely access to information and reports necessary to fulfill its duties under the transaction documents, including all reports made available to holders of ABS interests and third-party purchasers, and shall be responsible for:

(A) Reviewing the actions of the special servicer;

(B) Reviewing all reports provided by the special servicer to the issuing entity or any holder of ABS interests;

(C) Reviewing for accuracy and consistency with the transaction documents calculations made by the special servicer; and

(D) Issuing a report to investors (including any third-party purchasers)

and the issuing entity on a periodic basis concerning:

(*1*) Whether the Operating Advisor believes, in its sole discretion exercised in good faith, that the special servicer is operating in compliance with any standard required of the special servicer in the applicable transaction documents; and

(*2*) Which, if any, standards the Operating Advisor believes, in its sole discretion exercised in good faith, the special servicer has failed to comply.

(vi)(A) The Operating Advisor shall have the authority to recommend that the special servicer be replaced by a successor special servicer if the Operating Advisor determines, in its sole discretion exercised in good faith, that:

(*1*) The special servicer has failed to comply with a standard required of the special servicer in the applicable transaction documents; and

(*2*) Such replacement would be in the best interest of the investors as a collective whole; and

(B) If a recommendation described in paragraph (b)(6)(vi)(A) of this section is made, the special servicer shall be replaced upon the affirmative vote of a majority of the outstanding principal balance of all ABS interests voting on the matter, with a minimum of a quorum of ABS interests voting on the matter. For purposes of such vote, the applicable transaction documents shall specify the quorum and may not specify a quorum of more than the holders of 20 percent of the outstanding principal balance of all ABS interests in the issuing entity, with such quorum including at least three ABS interest holders that are not affiliated with each other.

(7) *Disclosures*. The sponsor provides, or causes to be provided, to potential investors a reasonable period of time prior to the sale of the asset-backed securities as part of the securitization transaction and, upon request, to the Commission and its appropriate Federal banking agency, if any, the following disclosure in written form under the caption "Credit Risk Retention":

(i) The name and form of organization of each initial third-party purchaser that acquired an eligible horizontal residual interest at the closing of a securitization transaction;

(ii) A description of each initial third-party purchaser's experience in investing in commercial mortgage-backed securities;

(iii) Any other information regarding each initial third-party purchaser or each initial third-party purchaser's retention of the eligible horizontal residual interest that is material to investors in light of the circumstances of the particular securitization transaction;

(iv) The fair value (expressed as a percentage of the fair value of all of the ABS interests issued in the securitization transaction and dollar amount (or corresponding amount in the foreign currency in which the ABS interests are issued, as applicable)) of the eligible horizontal residual interest that will be retained (or was retained) by each initial third-party purchaser, as well as the amount of the purchase price paid by each initial third-party purchaser for such interest;

(v) The fair value (expressed as a percentage of the fair value of all of the ABS interests issued in the securitization transaction and dollar amount (or corresponding amount in the foreign currency in which the ABS interests are issued, as applicable)) of the eligible horizontal residual interest in the securitization transaction that the sponsor would have retained pursuant to § 43.4 if the sponsor had relied on retaining an eligible horizontal residual interest in that section to meet the requirements of § 43.3 with respect to the transaction;

(vi) A description of the material terms of the eligible horizontal residual interest retained by each initial third-party purchaser, including the same information as is required to be disclosed by sponsors retaining horizontal interests pursuant to § 43.4;

(vii) The material terms of the applicable transaction documents with respect to the Operating Advisor, including without limitation:

(A) The name and form of organization of the Operating Advisor;

(B) A description of any material conflict of interest or material potential conflict of interest between the Operating Advisor and any other party to the transaction;

(C) The standards required by paragraph (b)(6)(ii) of this section and a description of how the Operating Advisor satisfies each of the standards; and

(D) The terms of the Operating Advisor's compensation under paragraph (b)(6)(iii) of this section; and

(viii) The representations and warranties concerning the securitized assets, a schedule of any securitized assets that are determined not to comply with such representations and warranties, and what factors were used to make the determination that such securitized assets should be included in the pool notwithstanding that the securitized assets did not comply with such representations and warranties, such as compensating factors or a determination that the exceptions were not material.

(8) *Hedging, transfer and pledging*—(i) *General rule.* Except as set forth in paragraph (b)(8)(ii) of this section, each third-party purchaser and its affiliates must comply with the hedging and other restrictions in §43.12 as if it were the retaining sponsor with respect to the securitization transaction and had acquired the eligible horizontal residual interest pursuant to §43.4; provided that, the hedging and other restrictions in §43.12 shall not apply on or after the date that each CRE loan (as defined in §43.14) that serves as collateral for outstanding ABS interests has been defeased. For purposes of this section, a loan is deemed to be defeased if:

(A) cash or cash equivalents of the types permitted for an eligible horizontal cash reserve account pursuant to §43.4 whose maturity corresponds to the remaining debt service obligations, have been pledged to the issuing entity as collateral for the loan and are in such amounts and payable at such times as necessary to timely generate cash sufficient to make all remaining debt service payments due on such loan; and

(B) the issuing entity has an obligation to release its lien on the loan.

(ii) *Exceptions*—(A) *Transfer by initial third-party purchaser or sponsor.* An initial third-party purchaser that acquired an eligible horizontal residual interest at the closing of a securitization transaction in accordance with this section, or a sponsor that acquired an eligible horizontal residual interest at the closing of a securitization transaction in accordance with this section, may, on or after the date that is five years after the date of the closing of the securitization transaction, transfer that interest to a subsequent third-party purchaser that complies with paragraph (b)(8)(ii)(C) of this section. The initial third-party purchaser shall provide the sponsor with complete identifying information for the subsequent third-party purchaser.

(B) *Transfer by subsequent third-party purchaser.* At any time, a subsequent third-party purchaser that acquired an eligible horizontal residual interest pursuant to this section may transfer its interest to a different third-party purchaser that complies with paragraph (b)(8)(ii)(C) of this section. The transferring third-party purchaser shall provide the sponsor with complete identifying information for the acquiring third-party purchaser.

(C) *Requirements applicable to subsequent third-party purchasers.* A subsequent third-party purchaser is subject to all of the requirements of paragraphs (b)(1), (b)(3) through (5), and (b)(8) of this section applicable to third-party purchasers, provided that obligations under paragraphs (b)(1), (b)(3) through (5), and (b)(8) of this section that apply to initial third-party purchasers at or before the time of closing of the securitization transaction shall apply to successor third-party purchasers at or before the time of the transfer of the eligible horizontal residual interest to the successor third-party purchaser.

(c) *Duty to comply.* (1) The retaining sponsor shall be responsible for compliance with this section by itself and for compliance by each initial or subsequent third-party purchaser that acquired an eligible horizontal residual interest in the securitization transaction.

(2) A sponsor relying on this section:

(i) Shall maintain and adhere to policies and procedures to monitor each third-party purchaser's compliance with the requirements of paragraphs (b)(1), (b)(3) through (5), and (b)(8) of this section; and

(ii) In the event that the sponsor determines that a third-party purchaser no longer complies with one or more of the requirements of paragraphs (b)(1), (b)(3) through (5), or (b)(8) of this section, shall promptly notify, or cause to be notified, the holders of the ABS interests issued in the securitization transaction of such noncompliance by such third-party purchaser.

§ 43.8 Federal National Mortgage Association and Federal Home Loan Mortgage Corporation ABS.

(a) *In general.* A sponsor satisfies its risk retention requirement under this part if the sponsor fully guarantees the timely payment of principal and interest on all ABS interests issued by the issuing entity in the securitization transaction and is:

(1) The Federal National Mortgage Association or the Federal Home Loan Mortgage Corporation operating under the conservatorship or receivership of the Federal Housing Finance Agency pursuant to section 1367 of the Federal Housing Enterprises Financial Safety and Soundness Act of 1992 (12 U.S.C. 4617) with capital support from the United States; or

(2) Any limited-life regulated entity succeeding to the charter of either the Federal National Mortgage Association or the Federal Home Loan Mortgage Corporation pursuant to section 1367(i) of the Federal Housing Enterprises Financial Safety and Soundness Act of 1992 (12 U.S.C. 4617(i)), provided that the entity is operating with capital support from the United States.

(b) *Certain provisions not applicable.* The provisions of § 43.12(b), (c), and (d) shall not apply to a sponsor described in paragraph (a)(1) or (2) of this section, its affiliates, or the issuing entity with respect to a securitization transaction for which the sponsor has retained credit risk in accordance with the requirements of this section.

(c) *Disclosure.* A sponsor relying on this section shall provide to investors, in written form under the caption "Credit Risk Retention" and, upon request, to the Federal Housing Finance Agency and the Commission, a description of the manner in which it has met the credit risk retention requirements of this part.

§ 43.9 Open market CLOs.

(a) *Definitions.* For purposes of this section, the following definitions shall apply:

CLO means a special purpose entity that:

(i) Issues debt and equity interests, and

(ii) Whose assets consist primarily of loans that are securitized assets and servicing assets.

CLO-eligible loan tranche means a term loan of a syndicated facility that meets the criteria set forth in paragraph (c) of this section.

CLO manager means an entity that manages a CLO, which entity is registered as an investment adviser under the Investment Advisers Act of 1940, as amended (15 U.S.C. 80b-1 *et seq.*), or is an affiliate of such a registered investment adviser and itself is managed by such registered investment adviser.

Commercial borrower means an obligor under a corporate credit obligation (including a loan).

Initial loan syndication transaction means a transaction in which a loan is syndicated to a group of lenders.

Lead arranger means, with respect to a CLO-eligible loan tranche, an institution that:

(i) Is active in the origination, structuring and syndication of commercial loan transactions (as defined in § 43.14) and has played a primary role in the structuring, underwriting and distribution on the primary market of the CLO-eligible loan tranche.

(ii) Has taken an allocation of the funded portion of the syndicated credit facility under the terms of the transaction that includes the CLO-eligible loan tranche of at least 20 percent of the aggregate principal balance at origination, and no other member (or members affiliated with each other) of the syndication group that funded at origination has taken a greater allocation; and

(iii) Is identified in the applicable agreement governing the CLO-eligible loan tranche; represents therein to the holders of the CLO-eligible loan tranche and to any holders of participation interests in such CLO-eligible loan tranche that such lead arranger satisfies the requirements of paragraph (i) of this definition and, at the time of initial funding of the CLO-eligible tranche, will satisfy the requirements of paragraph (ii) of this definition; further represents therein (solely for the purpose of assisting such holders to determine the eligibility of such CLO-eligible loan tranche to be held by an open market CLO) that in the reasonable judgment of such lead arranger, the terms of such CLO-eligible loan tranche are consistent with the requirements of paragraphs (c)(2) and (3) of this section; and covenants therein to such holders that such lead arranger will fulfill the requirements of paragraph (c)(1) of this section.

Open market CLO means a CLO:

(i) Whose assets consist of senior, secured syndicated loans acquired by such CLO directly from the sellers thereof in open market transactions and of servicing assets,

(ii) That is managed by a CLO manager, and

(iii) That holds less than 50 percent of its assets, by aggregate outstanding principal amount, in loans syndicated by lead arrangers that are affiliates of the CLO or the CLO manager or originated by originators that are affiliates of the CLO or the CLO manager.

Open market transaction means:

(i) Either an initial loan syndication transaction or a secondary market transaction in which a seller offers senior, secured syndicated loans to prospective purchasers in the loan market on market terms on an arm's length basis, which prospective purchasers include, but are not limited to, entities that are not affiliated with the seller, or

(ii) A reverse inquiry from a prospective purchaser of a senior, secured syndicated loan through a dealer in the loan market to purchase a senior, secured syndicated loan to be sourced by the dealer in the loan market.

Secondary market transaction means a purchase of a senior, secured syndicated loan not in connection with an initial loan syndication transaction but in the secondary market.

Senior, secured syndicated loan means a loan made to a commercial borrower that:

(i) Is not subordinate in right of payment to any other obligation for borrowed money of the commercial borrower,

(ii) Is secured by a valid first priority security interest or lien in or on specified collateral securing the commercial borrower's obligations under the loan, and

(iii) The value of the collateral subject to such first priority security interest or lien, together with other attributes of the obligor (including, without limitation, its general financial condition, ability to generate cash flow available for debt service and other demands for that cash flow), is adequate (in the commercially reasonable judgment of the CLO manager exercised at the time of investment) to repay the loan and to repay all other indebtedness of equal seniority secured by such first priority security interest or lien in or on the same collateral, and the CLO manager certifies, on or prior to each date that it acquires a loan constituting part of a new CLO-eligible tranche, that it has policies and procedures to evaluate the likelihood of repayment of loans acquired by the CLO and it has followed such policies and procedures in evaluating each CLO-eligible loan tranche.

(b) *In general.* A sponsor satisfies the risk retention requirements of § 43.3 with respect to an open market CLO transaction if:

(1) The open market CLO does not acquire or hold any assets other than CLO-eligible loan tranches that meet the requirements of paragraph (c) of this section and servicing assets;

(2) The governing documents of such open market CLO require that, at all times, the assets of the open market CLO consist of senior, secured syndicated loans that are CLO-eligible loan tranches and servicing assets;

(3) The open market CLO does not invest in ABS interests or in credit derivatives other than hedging transactions that are servicing assets to hedge risks of the open market CLO;

(4) All purchases of CLO-eligible loan tranches and other assets by the open market CLO issuing entity or through

a warehouse facility used to accumulate the loans prior to the issuance of the CLO's ABS interests are made in open market transactions on an arms-length basis;

(5) The CLO manager of the open market CLO is not entitled to receive any management fee or gain on sale at the time the open market CLO issues its ABS interests.

(c) *CLO-eligible loan tranche.* To qualify as a CLO-eligible loan tranche, a term loan of a syndicated credit facility to a commercial borrower must have the following features:

(1) A minimum of 5 percent of the face amount of the CLO-eligible loan tranche is retained by the lead arranger thereof until the earliest of the repayment, maturity, involuntary and unscheduled acceleration, payment default, or bankruptcy default of such CLO-eligible loan tranche, provided that such lead arranger complies with limitations on hedging, transferring and pledging in § 43.12 with respect to the interest retained by the lead arranger.

(2) Lender voting rights within the credit agreement and any intercreditor or other applicable agreements governing such CLO-eligible loan tranche are defined so as to give holders of the CLO-eligible loan tranche consent rights with respect to, at minimum, any material waivers and amendments of such applicable documents, including but not limited to, adverse changes to the calculation or payments of amounts due to the holders of the CLO-eligible tranche, alterations to *pro rata* provisions, changes to voting provisions, and waivers of conditions precedent; and

(3) The pro rata provisions, voting provisions, and similar provisions applicable to the security associated with such CLO-eligible loan tranches under the CLO credit agreement and any intercreditor or other applicable agreements governing such CLO-eligible loan tranches are not materially less advantageous to the holder(s) of such CLO-eligible tranche than the terms of other tranches of comparable seniority in the broader syndicated credit facility.

(d) *Disclosures.* A sponsor relying on this section shall provide, or cause to be provided, to potential investors a reasonable period of time prior to the sale of the asset-backed securities in the securitization transaction and at least annually with respect to the information required by paragraph (d)(1) of this section and, upon request, to the Commission and its appropriate Federal banking agency, if any, the following disclosure in written form under the caption "Credit Risk Retention":

(1) *Open market CLOs.* A complete list of every asset held by an open market CLO (or before the CLO's closing, in a warehouse facility in anticipation of transfer into the CLO at closing), including the following information:

(i) The full legal name, Standard Industrial Classification (SIC) category code, and legal entity identifier (LEI) issued by a utility endorsed or otherwise governed by the Global LEI Regulatory Oversight Committee or the Global LEI Foundation (if an LEI has been obtained by the obligor) of the obligor of the loan or asset;

(ii) The full name of the specific loan tranche held by the CLO;

(iii) The face amount of the entire loan tranche held by the CLO, and the face amount of the portion thereof held by the CLO;

(iv) The price at which the loan tranche was acquired by the CLO; and

(v) For each loan tranche, the full legal name of the lead arranger subject to the sales and hedging restrictions of § 43.12; and

(2) *CLO manager.* The full legal name and form of organization of the CLO manager.

§ 43.10 Qualified tender option bonds.

(a) *Definitions.* For purposes of this section, the following definitions shall apply:

Municipal security or *municipal securities* shall have the same meaning as the term "municipal securities" in Section 3(a)(29) of the Securities Exchange Act of 1934 (15 U.S.C. 78c(a)(29)) and any rules promulgated pursuant to such section.

Qualified tender option bond entity means an issuing entity with respect to tender option bonds for which each of the following applies:

(i) Such entity is collateralized solely by servicing assets and by municipal securities that have the same municipal issuer and the same underlying obligor or source of payment (determined without regard to any third-party credit enhancement), and such municipal securities are not subject to substitution.

(ii) Such entity issues no securities other than:

(A) A single class of tender option bonds with a preferred variable return payable out of capital that meets the requirements of paragraph (b) of this section, and

(B) One or more residual equity interests that, in the aggregate, are entitled to all remaining income of the issuing entity.

(C) The types of securities referred to in paragraphs (ii)(A) and (B) of this definition must constitute asset-backed securities.

(iii) The municipal securities held as assets by such entity are issued in compliance with Section 103 of the Internal Revenue Code of 1986, as amended (the "IRS Code", 26 U.S.C. 103), such that the interest payments made on those securities are excludable from the gross income of the owners under Section 103 of the IRS Code.

(iv) The terms of all of the securities issued by the entity are structured so that all holders of such securities who are eligible to exclude interest received on such securities will be able to exclude that interest from gross income pursuant to Section 103 of the IRS Code or as "exempt-interest dividends" pursuant to Section 852(b)(5) of the IRS Code (26 U.S.C. 852(b)(5)) in the case of regulated investment companies under the Investment Company Act of 1940, as amended.

(v) Such entity has a legally binding commitment from a regulated liquidity provider as defined in §43.6(a), to provide a 100 percent guarantee or liquidity coverage with respect to all of the issuing entity's outstanding tender option bonds.

(vi) Such entity qualifies for monthly closing elections pursuant to IRS Revenue Procedure 2003–84, as amended or supplemented from time to time.

Tender option bond means a security which has features which entitle the holders to tender such bonds to the issuing entity for purchase at any time upon no more than 397 days' notice, for a purchase price equal to the approximate amortized cost of the security, plus accrued interest, if any, at the time of tender.

(b) *Risk retention options.* Notwithstanding anything in this section, the sponsor with respect to an issuance of tender option bonds may retain an eligible vertical interest or eligible horizontal residual interest, or any combination thereof, in accordance with the requirements of §43.4. In order to satisfy its risk retention requirements under this section, the sponsor with respect to an issuance of tender option bonds by a qualified tender option bond entity may retain:

(1) An eligible vertical interest or an eligible horizontal residual interest, or any combination thereof, in accordance with the requirements of §43.4; or

(2) An interest that meets the requirements set forth in paragraph (c) of this section; or

(3) A municipal security that meets the requirements set forth in paragraph (d) of this section; or

(4) Any combination of interests and securities described in paragraphs (b)(1) through (b)(3) of this section such that the sum of the percentages held in each form equals at least five.

(c) *Tender option termination event.* The sponsor with respect to an issuance of tender option bonds by a qualified tender option bond entity may retain an interest that upon issuance meets the requirements of an eligible horizontal residual interest but that upon the occurrence of a "tender option termination event" as defined in Section 4.01(5) of IRS Revenue Procedure 2003–84, as amended or supplemented from time to time will meet the requirements of an eligible vertical interest.

(d) *Retention of a municipal security outside of the qualified tender option bond entity.* The sponsor with respect to an issuance of tender option bonds by a qualified tender option bond entity may satisfy its risk retention requirements under this Section by holding municipal securities from the same issuance of municipal securities deposited in the qualified tender option bond entity, the face value of which retained municipal securities is equal to 5 percent of the face value of the municipal securities deposited in the qualified tender option bond entity.

(e) *Disclosures*. The sponsor shall provide, or cause to be provided, to potential investors a reasonable period of time prior to the sale of the asset-backed securities as part of the securitization transaction and, upon request, to the Commission and its appropriate Federal banking agency, if any, the following disclosure in written form under the caption "Credit Risk Retention":

(1) The name and form of organization of the qualified tender option bond entity;

(2) A description of the form and subordination features of such retained interest in accordance with the disclosure obligations in § 43.4(c);

(3) To the extent any portion of the retained interest is claimed by the sponsor as an eligible horizontal residual interest (including any interest held in compliance with § 43.10(c)), the fair value of that interest (expressed as a percentage of the fair value of all of the ABS interests issued in the securitization transaction and as a dollar amount);

(4) To the extent any portion of the retained interest is claimed by the sponsor as an eligible vertical interest (including any interest held in compliance with § 43.10(c)), the percentage of ABS interests issued represented by the eligible vertical interest; and

(5) To the extent any portion of the retained interest claimed by the sponsor is a municipal security held outside of the qualified tender option bond entity, the name and form of organization of the qualified tender option bond entity, the identity of the issuer of the municipal securities, the face value of the municipal securities deposited into the qualified tender option bond entity, and the face value of the municipal securities retained by the sponsor or its majority-owned affiliates and subject to the transfer and hedging prohibition.

(f) *Prohibitions on Hedging and Transfer*. The prohibitions on transfer and hedging set forth in § 43.12, apply to any interests or municipal securities retained by the sponsor with respect to an issuance of tender option bonds by a qualified tender option bond entity pursuant to of this section.

Subpart C—Transfer of Risk Retention

§ 43.11 Allocation of risk retention to an originator.

(a) *In general*. A sponsor choosing to retain an eligible vertical interest or an eligible horizontal residual interest (including an eligible horizontal cash reserve account), or combination thereof under § 43.4, with respect to a securitization transaction may offset the amount of its risk retention requirements under § 43.4 by the amount of the eligible interests, respectively, acquired by an originator of one or more of the securitized assets if:

(1) At the closing of the securitization transaction:

(i) The originator acquires the eligible interest from the sponsor and retains such interest in the same manner and proportion (as between horizontal and vertical interests) as the sponsor under § 43.4, as such interest was held prior to the acquisition by the originator;

(ii) The ratio of the percentage of eligible interests acquired and retained by the originator to the percentage of eligible interests otherwise required to be retained by the sponsor pursuant to § 43.4, does not exceed the ratio of:

(A) The unpaid principal balance of all the securitized assets originated by the originator; to

(B) The unpaid principal balance of all the securitized assets in the securitization transaction;

(iii) The originator acquires and retains at least 20 percent of the aggregate risk retention amount otherwise required to be retained by the sponsor pursuant to § 43.4; and

(iv) The originator purchases the eligible interests from the sponsor at a price that is equal, on a dollar-for-dollar basis, to the amount by which the sponsor's required risk retention is reduced in accordance with this section, by payment to the sponsor in the form of:

(A) Cash; or

(B) A reduction in the price received by the originator from the sponsor or depositor for the assets sold by the originator to the sponsor or depositor for inclusion in the pool of securitized assets.

(2) *Disclosures.* In addition to the disclosures required pursuant to §43.4(c), the sponsor provides, or causes to be provided, to potential investors a reasonable period of time prior to the sale of the asset-backed securities as part of the securitization transaction and, upon request, to the Commission and its appropriate Federal banking agency, if any, in written form under the caption "Credit Risk Retention", the name and form of organization of any originator that will acquire and retain (or has acquired and retained) an interest in the transaction pursuant to this section, including a description of the form and amount (expressed as a percentage and dollar amount (or corresponding amount in the foreign currency in which the ABS interests are issued, as applicable)) and nature (*e.g.*, senior or subordinated) of the interest, as well as the method of payment for such interest under paragraph (a)(1)(iv) of this section.

(3) *Hedging, transferring and pledging.* The originator and each of its affiliates complies with the hedging and other restrictions in §43.12 with respect to the interests retained by the originator pursuant to this section as if it were the retaining sponsor and was required to retain the interest under subpart B of this part.

(b) *Duty to comply.* (1) The retaining sponsor shall be responsible for compliance with this section.

(2) A retaining sponsor relying on this section:

(i) Shall maintain and adhere to policies and procedures that are reasonably designed to monitor the compliance by each originator that is allocated a portion of the sponsor's risk retention obligations with the requirements in paragraphs (a)(1) and (3) of this section; and

(ii) In the event the sponsor determines that any such originator no longer complies with any of the requirements in paragraphs (a)(1) and (3) of this section, shall promptly notify, or cause to be notified, the holders of the ABS interests issued in the securitization transaction of such noncompliance by such originator.

§43.12 Hedging, transfer and financing prohibitions.

(a) *Transfer.* Except as permitted by §43.7(b)(8), and subject to §43.5, a retaining sponsor may not sell or otherwise transfer any interest or assets that the sponsor is required to retain pursuant to subpart B of this part to any person other than an entity that is and remains a majority-owned affiliate of the sponsor and each such majority-owned affiliate shall be subject to the same restrictions.

(b) *Prohibited hedging by sponsor and affiliates.* A retaining sponsor and its affiliates may not purchase or sell a security, or other financial instrument, or enter into an agreement, derivative or other position, with any other person if:

(1) Payments on the security or other financial instrument or under the agreement, derivative, or position are materially related to the credit risk of one or more particular ABS interests that the retaining sponsor (or any of its majority-owned affiliates) is required to retain with respect to a securitization transaction pursuant to subpart B of this part or one or more of the particular securitized assets that collateralize the asset-backed securities issued in the securitization transaction; and

(2) The security, instrument, agreement, derivative, or position in any way reduces or limits the financial exposure of the sponsor (or any of its majority-owned affiliates) to the credit risk of one or more of the particular ABS interests that the retaining sponsor (or any of its majority-owned affiliates) is required to retain with respect to a securitization transaction pursuant to subpart B of this part or one or more of the particular securitized assets that collateralize the asset-backed securities issued in the securitization transaction.

(c) *Prohibited hedging by issuing entity.* The issuing entity in a securitization transaction may not purchase or sell a security or other financial instrument, or enter into an agreement, derivative or position, with any other person if:

(1) Payments on the security or other financial instrument or under the agreement, derivative or position are materially related to the credit risk of one or more particular ABS interests that the retaining sponsor for the transaction (or any of its majority-owned affiliates) is required to retain with respect to the securitization transaction pursuant to subpart B of this part; and

(2) The security, instrument, agreement, derivative, or position in any way reduces or limits the financial exposure of the retaining sponsor (or any of its majority-owned affiliates) to the credit risk of one or more of the particular ABS interests that the sponsor (or any of its majority-owned affiliates) is required to retain pursuant to subpart B of this part.

(d) *Permitted hedging activities.* The following activities shall not be considered prohibited hedging activities under paragraph (b) or (c) of this section:

(1) Hedging the interest rate risk (which does not include the specific interest rate risk, known as spread risk, associated with the ABS interest that is otherwise considered part of the credit risk) or foreign exchange risk arising from one or more of the particular ABS interests required to be retained by the sponsor (or any of its majority-owned affiliates) under subpart B of this part or one or more of the particular securitized assets that underlie the asset-backed securities issued in the securitization transaction; or

(2) Purchasing or selling a security or other financial instrument or entering into an agreement, derivative, or other position with any third party where payments on the security or other financial instrument or under the agreement, derivative, or position are based, directly or indirectly, on an index of instruments that includes asset-backed securities if:

(i) Any class of ABS interests in the issuing entity that were issued in connection with the securitization transaction and that are included in the index represents no more than 10 percent of the dollar-weighted average (or corresponding weighted average in the currency in which the ABS interests are issued, as applicable) of all instruments included in the index; and

(ii) All classes of ABS interests in all issuing entities that were issued in connection with any securitization transaction in which the sponsor (or any of its majority-owned affiliates) is required to retain an interest pursuant to subpart B of this part and that are included in the index represent, in the aggregate, no more than 20 percent of the dollar-weighted average (or corresponding weighted average in the currency in which the ABS interests are issued, as applicable) of all instruments included in the index.

(e) *Prohibited non-recourse financing.* Neither a retaining sponsor nor any of its affiliates may pledge as collateral for any obligation (including a loan, repurchase agreement, or other financing transaction) any ABS interest that the sponsor is required to retain with respect to a securitization transaction pursuant to subpart B of this part unless such obligation is with full recourse to the sponsor or affiliate, respectively.

(f) *Duration of the hedging and transfer restrictions*—(1) *General rule.* Except as provided in paragraph (f)(2) of this section, the prohibitions on sale and hedging pursuant to paragraphs (a) and (b) of this section shall expire on or after the date that is the latest of:

(i) The date on which the total unpaid principal balance (if applicable) of the securitized assets that collateralize the securitization transaction has been reduced to 33 percent of the total unpaid principal balance of the securitized assets as of the cut-off date or similar date for establishing the composition of the securitized assets collateralizing the asset-backed securities issued pursuant to the securitization transaction;

(ii) The date on which the total unpaid principal obligations under the ABS interests issued in the securitization transaction has been reduced to 33 percent of the total unpaid principal obligations of the ABS interests at closing of the securitization transaction; or

(iii) Two years after the date of the closing of the securitization transaction.

(2) *Securitizations of residential mortgages.* (i) If all of the assets that collateralize a securitization transaction subject to risk retention under this part are residential mortgages, the prohibitions on sale and hedging pursuant to paragraphs (a) and (b) of this section shall expire on or after the date that is the later of:

(A) Five years after the date of the closing of the securitization transaction; or

(B) The date on which the total unpaid principal balance of the residential mortgages that collateralize the securitization transaction has been reduced to 25 percent of the total unpaid principal balance of such residential mortgages at the cut-off date or similar date for establishing the composition of the securitized assets collateralizing the asset-backed securities issued pursuant to the securitization transaction.

(ii) Notwithstanding paragraph (f)(2)(i) of this section, the prohibitions on sale and hedging pursuant to paragraphs (a) and (b) of this section shall expire with respect to the sponsor of a securitization transaction described in paragraph (f)(2)(i) of this section on or after the date that is seven years after the date of the closing of the securitization transaction.

(3) *Conservatorship or receivership of sponsor.* A conservator or receiver of the sponsor (or any other person holding risk retention pursuant to this part) of a securitization transaction is permitted to sell or hedge any economic interest in the securitization transaction if the conservator or receiver has been appointed pursuant to any provision of federal or State law (or regulation promulgated thereunder) that provides for the appointment of the Federal Deposit Insurance Corporation, or an agency or instrumentality of the United States or of a State as conservator or receiver, including without limitation any of the following authorities:

(i) 12 U.S.C. 1811;

(ii) 12 U.S.C. 1787;

(iii) 12 U.S.C. 4617; or

(iv) 12 U.S.C. 5382.

(4) *Revolving pool securitizations.* The provisions of paragraphs (f)(1) and (2) are not available to sponsors of revolving pool securitizations with respect to the forms of risk retention specified in §43.5.

Subpart D—Exceptions and Exemptions

§43.13 Exemption for qualified residential mortgages.

(a) *Definitions.* For purposes of this section, the following definitions shall apply:

Currently performing means the borrower in the mortgage transaction is not currently thirty (30) days or more past due, in whole or in part, on the mortgage transaction.

Qualified residential mortgage means a "qualified mortgage" as defined in section 129C of the Truth in Lending Act (15 U.S.C.1639c) and regulations issued thereunder, as amended from time to time.

(b) *Exemption.* A sponsor shall be exempt from the risk retention requirements in subpart B of this part with respect to any securitization transaction, if:

(1) All of the assets that collateralize the asset-backed securities are qualified residential mortgages or servicing assets;

(2) None of the assets that collateralize the asset-backed securities are asset-backed securities;

(3) As of the cut-off date or similar date for establishing the composition of the securitized assets collateralizing the asset-backed securities issued pursuant to the securitization transaction, each qualified residential mortgage collateralizing the asset-backed securities is currently performing; and

(4)(i) The depositor with respect to the securitization transaction certifies that it has evaluated the effectiveness of its internal supervisory controls with respect to the process for ensuring that all assets that collateralize the asset-backed security are qualified residential mortgages or servicing assets and has concluded that its internal supervisory controls are effective; and

(ii) The evaluation of the effectiveness of the depositor's internal supervisory controls must be performed, for each issuance of an asset-backed security in reliance on this section, as of a date within 60 days of the cut-off date or similar date for establishing the composition of the asset pool collateralizing such asset-backed security; and

(iii) The sponsor provides, or causes to be provided, a copy of the certification described in paragraph (b)(4)(i) of this section to potential investors a reasonable period of time prior to the sale of asset-backed securities in the issuing entity, and, upon request, to the Commission and its appropriate Federal banking agency, if any.

(c) *Repurchase of loans subsequently determined to be non-qualified after closing.* A sponsor that has relied on the exemption provided in paragraph (b) of this section with respect to a securitization transaction shall not lose such exemption with respect to such transaction if, after closing of the securitization transaction, it is determined that one or more of the residential mortgage loans collateralizing the asset-backed securities does not meet all of the criteria to be a qualified residential mortgage *provided that:*

(1) The depositor complied with the certification requirement set forth in paragraph (b)(4) of this section;

(2) The sponsor repurchases the loan(s) from the issuing entity at a price at least equal to the remaining aggregate unpaid principal balance and accrued interest on the loan(s) no later than 90 days after the determination that the loans do not satisfy the requirements to be a qualified residential mortgage; and

(3) The sponsor promptly notifies, or causes to be notified, the holders of the asset-backed securities issued in the securitization transaction of any loan(s) included in such securitization transaction that is (or are) required to be repurchased by the sponsor pursuant to paragraph (c)(2) of this section, including the amount of such repurchased loan(s) and the cause for such repurchase.

§ 43.14 Definitions applicable to qualifying commercial loans, qualifying commercial real estate loans, and qualifying automobile loans.

The following definitions apply for purposes of §§ 43.15 through 43.18:

Appraisal Standards Board means the board of the Appraisal Foundation that develops, interprets, and amends the Uniform Standards of Professional Appraisal Practice (USPAP), establishing generally accepted standards for the appraisal profession.

Automobile loan:

(1) Means any loan to an individual to finance the purchase of, and that is secured by a first lien on, a passenger car or other passenger vehicle, such as a minivan, van, sport-utility vehicle, pickup truck, or similar light truck for personal, family, or household use; and

(2) Does not include any:

(i) Loan to finance fleet sales;

(ii) Personal cash loan secured by a previously purchased automobile;

(iii) Loan to finance the purchase of a commercial vehicle or farm equipment that is not used for personal, family, or household purposes;

(iv) Lease financing;

(v) Loan to finance the purchase of a vehicle with a salvage title; or

(vi) Loan to finance the purchase of a vehicle intended to be used for scrap or parts.

Combined loan-to-value (CLTV) ratio means, at the time of origination, the sum of the principal balance of a first-lien mortgage loan on the property, plus the principal balance of any junior-lien mortgage loan that, to the creditor's knowledge, would exist at the closing of the transaction and that is secured by the same property, divided by:

(1) For acquisition funding, the lesser of the purchase price or the estimated market value of the real property based on an appraisal that meets the requirements set forth in § 43.17(a)(2)(ii); or

(2) For refinancing, the estimated market value of the real property based on an appraisal that meets the requirements set forth in § 43.17(a)(2)(ii).

Commercial loan means a secured or unsecured loan to a company or an individual for business purposes, other than any:

(1) Loan to purchase or refinance a one-to-four family residential property;

(2) Commercial real estate loan.

Commercial real estate (CRE) loan means:

(1) A loan secured by a property with five or more single family units, or by nonfarm nonresidential real property, the primary source (50 percent or more) of repayment for which is expected to be:

(i) The proceeds of the sale, refinancing, or permanent financing of the property; or

(ii) Rental income associated with the property;

(2) Loans secured by improved land if the obligor owns the fee interest in the land and the land is leased to a third party who owns all improvements on the land, and the improvements are nonresidential or residential with five or more single family units; and

(3) Does not include:

(i) A land development and construction loan (including 1- to 4-family residential or commercial construction loans);

(ii) Any other land loan; or

(iii) An unsecured loan to a developer.

Debt service coverage (DSC) ratio means:

(1) For qualifying leased CRE loans, qualifying multi-family loans, and other CRE loans:

(i) The annual NOI less the annual replacement reserve of the CRE property at the time of origination of the CRE loan(s) divided by

(ii) The sum of the borrower's annual payments for principal and interest (calculated at the fully-indexed rate) on any debt obligation.

(2) For commercial loans:

(i) The borrower's EBITDA as of the most recently completed fiscal year divided by

(ii) The sum of the borrower's annual payments for principal and interest on all debt obligations.

Debt to income (DTI) ratio means the borrower's total debt, including the monthly amount due on the automobile loan, divided by the borrower's monthly income.

Earnings before interest, taxes, depreciation, and amortization (EBITDA) means the annual income of a business before expenses for interest, taxes, depreciation and amortization are deducted, as determined in accordance with GAAP.

Environmental risk assessment means a process for determining whether a property is contaminated or exposed to any condition or substance that could result in contamination that has an adverse effect on the market value of the property or the realization of the collateral value.

First lien means a lien or encumbrance on property that has priority over all other liens or encumbrances on the property.

Junior lien means a lien or encumbrance on property that is lower in priority relative to other liens or encumbrances on the property.

Leverage ratio means the borrower's total debt divided by the borrower's EBITDA.

Loan-to-value (LTV) ratio means, at the time of origination, the principal balance of a first-lien mortgage loan on the property divided by:

(1) For acquisition funding, the lesser of the purchase price or the estimated market value of the real property based on an appraisal that meets the requirements set forth in § 43.17(a)(2)(ii); or

(2) For refinancing, the estimated market value of the real property based on an appraisal that meets the requirements set forth in § 43.17(a)(2)(ii).

Model year means the year determined by the manufacturer and reflected on the vehicle's Motor Vehicle Title as part of the vehicle description.

Net operating income (NOI) refers to the income a CRE property generates for the owner after all expenses have been deducted for federal income tax purposes, except for depreciation, debt service expenses, and federal and state income taxes, and excluding any unusual and nonrecurring items of income.

Operating affiliate means an affiliate of a borrower that is a lessor or similar party with respect to the commercial real estate securing the loan.

Payments-in-kind means payments of accrued interest that are not paid in cash when due, and instead are paid by increasing the principal balance of the loan or by providing equity in the borrowing company.

Purchase money security interest means a security interest in property that secures the obligation of the obligor incurred as all or part of the price of the property.

Purchase price means the amount paid by the borrower for the vehicle net of any incentive payments or manufacturer cash rebates.

Qualified tenant means:

(1) A tenant with a lease who has satisfied all obligations with respect to the property in a timely manner; or

(2) A tenant who originally had a lease that subsequently expired and currently is leasing the property on a month-to-month basis, has occupied the property for at least three years prior to the date of origination, and has satisfied all obligations with respect to the property in a timely manner.

Qualifying leased CRE loan means a CRE loan secured by commercial nonfarm real property, other than a multifamily property or a hotel, inn, or similar property:

(1) That is occupied by one or more qualified tenants pursuant to a lease agreement with a term of no less than one (1) month; and

(2) Where no more than 20 percent of the aggregate gross revenue of the property is payable from one or more tenants who:

(i) Are subject to a lease that will terminate within six months following the date of origination; or

(ii) Are not qualified tenants.

Qualifying multi-family loan means a CRE loan secured by any residential property (excluding a hotel, motel, inn, hospital, nursing home, or other similar facility where dwellings are not leased to residents):

(1) That consists of five or more dwelling units (including apartment buildings, condominiums, cooperatives and other similar structures) primarily for residential use; and

(2) Where at least 75 percent of the NOI is derived from residential rents and tenant amenities (including income from parking garages, health or swim clubs, and dry cleaning), and not from other commercial uses.

Rental income means:

(1) Income derived from a lease or other occupancy agreement between the borrower or an operating affiliate of the borrower and a party which is not an affiliate of the borrower for the use of real property or improvements serving as collateral for the applicable loan; and

(2) Other income derived from hotel, motel, dormitory, nursing home, assisted living, mini-storage warehouse or similar properties that are used primarily by parties that are not affiliates or employees of the borrower or its affiliates.

Replacement reserve means the monthly capital replacement or maintenance amount based on the property type, age, construction and condition of the property that is adequate to maintain the physical condition and NOI of the property.

Salvage title means a form of vehicle title branding, which notes that the vehicle has been severely damaged and/or deemed a total loss and uneconomical to repair by an insurance company that paid a claim on the vehicle.

Total debt, with respect to a borrower, means:

(1) In the case of an automobile loan, the sum of:

(i) All monthly housing payments (rent- or mortgage-related, including property taxes, insurance and home owners association fees); and

(ii) Any of the following that is dependent upon the borrower's income for payment:

(A) Monthly payments on other debt and lease obligations, such as credit card loans or installment loans, including the monthly amount due on the automobile loan;

(B) Estimated monthly amortizing payments for any term debt, debts with other than monthly payments and debts not in repayment (such as deferred student loans, interest-only loans); and

(C) Any required monthly alimony, child support or court-ordered payments; and

(2) In the case of a commercial loan, the outstanding balance of all long-term debt (obligations that have a remaining maturity of more than one year) and the current portion of all debt that matures in one year or less.

Total liabilities ratio means the borrower's total liabilities divided by the sum of the borrower's total liabilities and equity, less the borrower's intangible assets, with each component determined in accordance with GAAP.

Trade-in allowance means the amount a vehicle purchaser is given as a credit at the purchase of a vehicle for the fair exchange of the borrower's existing vehicle to compensate the dealer for some portion of the vehicle purchase price, not to exceed the highest trade-in value of the existing vehicle, as determined by a nationally recognized automobile pricing agency and based on the manufacturer, year, model, features, mileage, and condition of the vehicle, less the payoff balance of any outstanding debt collateralized by the existing vehicle.

Uniform Standards of Professional Appraisal Practice (USPAP) means generally accepted standards for professional appraisal practice issued by the Appraisal Standards Board of the Appraisal Foundation.

§43.15 Qualifying commercial loans, commercial real estate loans, and automobile loans.

(a) *General exception for qualifying assets.* Commercial loans, commercial real estate loans, and automobile loans that are securitized through a securitization transaction shall be subject to a 0 percent risk retention requirement under subpart B, provided that the following conditions are met:

(1) The assets meet the underwriting standards set forth in §43.16 (qualifying commercial loans), §43.17 (qualifying CRE loans), or §43.18 (qualifying automobile loans) of this part, as applicable;

(2) The securitization transaction is collateralized solely by loans of the same asset class and by servicing assets;

(3) The securitization transaction does not permit reinvestment periods; and

(4) The sponsor provides, or causes to be provided, to potential investors a reasonable period of time prior to the sale of asset-backed securities of the issuing entity, and, upon request, to the Commission, and to its appropriate Federal banking agency, if any, in written form under the caption "Credit Risk Retention", a description of the manner in which the sponsor determined the aggregate risk retention requirement for the securitization transaction after including qualifying commercial loans, qualifying CRE loans, or qualifying automobile loans with 0 percent risk retention.

(b) *Risk retention requirement.* For any securitization transaction described in paragraph (a) of this section, the percentage of risk retention required under §43.3(a) is reduced by the percentage evidenced by the ratio of the unpaid principal balance of the qualifying commercial loans, qualifying CRE loans, or qualifying automobile loans (as applicable) to the total unpaid principal balance of commercial loans, CRE loans, or automobile loans (as applicable) that are included in the pool of assets collateralizing the asset-backed securities issued pursuant to the securitization transaction (the qualifying asset ratio); provided that:

(1) The qualifying asset ratio is measured as of the cut-off date or similar date for establishing the composition of the securitized assets collateralizing the asset-backed securities issued pursuant to the securitization transaction;

(2) If the qualifying asset ratio would exceed 50 percent, the qualifying asset ratio shall be deemed to be 50 percent; and

(3) The disclosure required by paragraph (a)(4) of this section also includes descriptions of the qualifying commercial loans, qualifying CRE loans, and qualifying automobile loans (qualifying assets) and descriptions of the assets that are not qualifying assets, and the material differences between the group of qualifying assets and the group of assets that are not qualifying assets with respect to the composition of each group's loan balances, loan terms, interest rates, borrower credit information, and characteristics of any loan collateral.

(c) *Exception for securitizations of qualifying assets only.* Notwithstanding other provisions of this section, the risk retention requirements of subpart B of this part shall not apply to securitization transactions where the transaction is collateralized solely by servicing assets and either qualifying commercial loans, qualifying CRE loans, or qualifying automobile loans.

(d) *Record maintenance.* A sponsor must retain the disclosures required in paragraphs (a) and (b) of this section and the certifications required in §§ 43.16(a)(8), 43.17(a)(10), and 43.18(a)(8), as applicable, in its records until three years after all ABS interests issued in the securitization are no longer outstanding. The sponsor must provide the disclosures and certifications upon request to the Commission and the sponsor's appropriate Federal banking agency, if any.

§ 43.16 Underwriting standards for qualifying commercial loans.

(a) *Underwriting, product and other standards.* (1) Prior to origination of the commercial loan, the originator:

(i) Verified and documented the financial condition of the borrower:

(A) As of the end of the borrower's two most recently completed fiscal years; and

(B) During the period, if any, since the end of its most recently completed fiscal year;

(ii) Conducted an analysis of the borrower's ability to service its overall debt obligations during the next two years, based on reasonable projections;

(iii) Determined that, based on the previous two years' actual performance, the borrower had:

(A) A total liabilities ratio of 50 percent or less;

(B) A leverage ratio of 3.0 or less; and

(C) A DSC ratio of 1.5 or greater;

(iv) Determined that, based on the two years of projections, which include the new debt obligation, following the closing date of the loan, the borrower will have:

(A) A total liabilities ratio of 50 percent or less;

(B) A leverage ratio of 3.0 or less; and

(C) A DSC ratio of 1.5 or greater.

(2) Prior to, upon or promptly following the inception of the loan, the originator:

(i) If the loan is originated on a secured basis, obtains a perfected security interest (by filing, title notation or otherwise) or, in the case of real property, a recorded lien, on all of the property pledged to collateralize the loan; and

(ii) If the loan documents indicate the purpose of the loan is to finance the purchase of tangible or intangible property, or to refinance such a loan, obtains a first lien on the property.

(3) The loan documentation for the commercial loan includes covenants that:

(i) Require the borrower to provide to the servicer of the commercial loan the borrower's financial statements and supporting schedules on an ongoing basis, but not less frequently than quarterly;

(ii) Prohibit the borrower from retaining or entering into a debt arrangement that permits payments-in-kind;

(iii) Impose limits on:

(A) The creation or existence of any other security interest or lien with respect to any of the borrower's property that serves as collateral for the loan;

(B) The transfer of any of the borrower's assets that serve as collateral for the loan; and

(C) Any change to the name, location or organizational structure of the borrower, or any other party that pledges collateral for the loan;

(iv) Require the borrower and any other party that pledges collateral for the loan to:

(A) Maintain insurance that protects against loss on the collateral for the commercial loan at least up to the amount of the loan, and that names the originator or any subsequent holder of the loan as an additional insured or loss payee;

(B) Pay taxes, charges, fees, and claims, where non-payment might give rise to a lien on any collateral;

(C) Take any action required to perfect or protect the security interest and first lien (as applicable) of the originator or any subsequent holder of the loan in any collateral for the commercial loan or the priority thereof, and to defend any collateral against claims adverse to the lender's interest;

(D) Permit the originator or any subsequent holder of the loan, and the servicer of the loan, to inspect any collateral for the commercial loan and the books and records of the borrower; and

(E) Maintain the physical condition of any collateral for the commercial loan.

(4) Loan payments required under the loan agreement are:

(i) Based on level monthly payments of principal and interest (at the fully indexed rate) that fully amortize the debt over a term that does not exceed five years from the date of origination; and

(ii) To be made no less frequently than quarterly over a term that does not exceed five years.

(5) The primary source of repayment for the loan is revenue from the business operations of the borrower.

(6) The loan was funded within the six (6) months prior to the cut-off date or similar date for establishing the composition of the securitized assets collateralizing the asset-backed securities issued pursuant to the securitization transaction.

(7) At the cut-off date or similar date for establishing the composition of the securitized assets collateralizing the asset-backed securities issued pursuant to the securitization transaction, all payments due on the loan are contractually current.

(8)(i) The depositor of the asset-backed security certifies that it has evaluated the effectiveness of its internal supervisory controls with respect to the process for ensuring that all qualifying commercial loans that collateralize the asset-backed security and that reduce the sponsor's risk retention requirement under §43.15 meet all of the requirements set forth in paragraphs (a)(1) through (7) of this section and has concluded that its internal supervisory controls are effective;

(ii) The evaluation of the effectiveness of the depositor's internal supervisory controls referenced in paragraph (a)(8)(i) of this section shall be performed, for each issuance of an asset-backed security, as of a date within 60 days of the cut-off date or similar date for establishing the composition of the asset pool collateralizing such asset-backed security; and

(iii) The sponsor provides, or causes to be provided, a copy of the certification described in paragraph (a)(8)(i) of this section to potential investors a reasonable period of time prior to the sale of asset-backed securities in the issuing entity, and, upon request, to its appropriate Federal banking agency, if any.

(b) *Cure or buy-back requirement.* If a sponsor has relied on the exception provided in §43.15 with respect to a qualifying commercial loan and it is subsequently determined that the loan did not meet all of the requirements set forth in paragraphs (a)(1) through (7) of this section, the sponsor shall not lose the benefit of the exception with respect to the commercial loan if the depositor complied with the certification requirement set forth in paragraph (a)(8) of this section and:

(1) The failure of the loan to meet any of the requirements set forth in paragraphs (a)(1) through (7) of this section is not material; or

(2) No later than 90 days after the determination that the loan does not meet one or more of the requirements of paragraphs (a)(1) through (7) of this section, the sponsor:

(i) Effectuates cure, establishing conformity of the loan to the unmet requirements as of the date of cure; or

(ii) Repurchases the loan(s) from the issuing entity at a price at least equal to the remaining principal balance and accrued interest on the loan(s) as of the date of repurchase.

(3) If the sponsor cures or repurchases pursuant to paragraph (b)(2) of this section, the sponsor must promptly notify, or cause to be notified, the holders of the asset-backed securities issued in the securitization transaction of any loan(s) included in such securitization transaction that is required to be cured or repurchased by the sponsor pursuant to paragraph (b)(2) of this section, including the principal amount of such loan(s) and the cause for such cure or repurchase.

§43.17 Underwriting standards for qualifying CRE loans.

(a) *Underwriting, product and other standards.* (1) The CRE loan must be secured by the following:

(i) An enforceable first lien, documented and recorded appropriately pursuant to applicable law, on the commercial real estate and improvements;

(ii)(A) An assignment of:

(*1*) Leases and rents and other occupancy agreements related to the commercial real estate or improvements or the operation thereof for which the borrower or an operating affiliate is a lessor or similar party and all payments under such leases and occupancy agreements; and

(*2*) All franchise, license and concession agreements related to the commercial real estate or improvements or the operation thereof for which the borrower or an operating affiliate is a lessor, licensor, concession granter or similar party and all payments under such other agreements, whether the assignments described in this paragraph (a)(1)(ii)(A)(*2*) are absolute or are stated to be made to the extent permitted by the agreements governing the applicable franchise, license or concession agreements;

(B) An assignment of all other payments due to the borrower or due to any operating affiliate in connection with the operation of the property described in paragraph (a)(1)(i) of this section; and

(C) The right to enforce the agreements described in paragraph (a)(1)(ii)(A) of this section and the agreements under which payments under paragraph (a)(1)(ii)(B) of this section are due against, and collect amounts due from, each lessee, occupant or other obligor whose payments were assigned pursuant to paragraphs (a)(1)(ii)(A) or (B) of this section upon a breach by the borrower of any of the terms of, or the occurrence of any other event of default (however denominated) under, the loan documents relating to such CRE loan; and

(iii) A security interest:

(A) In all interests of the borrower and any applicable operating affiliate in all tangible and intangible personal property of any kind, in or used in the operation of or in connection with, pertaining to, arising from, or constituting, any of the collateral described in paragraphs (a)(1)(i) or (ii) of this section; and

(B) In the form of a perfected security interest if the security interest in such property can be perfected by the filing of a financing statement, fixture filing, or similar document pursuant to the law governing the perfection of such security interest;

(2) Prior to origination of the CRE loan, the originator:

(i) Verified and documented the current financial condition of the borrower and each operating affiliate;

(ii) Obtained a written appraisal of the real property securing the loan that:

(A) Had an effective date not more than six months prior to the origination date of the loan by a competent and appropriately State-certified or State-licensed appraiser;

(B) Conforms to generally accepted appraisal standards as evidenced by the USPAP and the appraisal requirements[1] of the Federal banking agencies; and

(C) Provides an "as is" opinion of the market value of the real property, which includes an income approach;[2]

(iii) Qualified the borrower for the CRE loan based on a monthly payment amount derived from level monthly payments consisting of both principal and interest (at the fully-indexed rate) over the term of the loan, not exceeding 25 years, or 30 years for a qualifying multi-family property;

(iv) Conducted an environmental risk assessment to gain environmental information about the property securing the loan and took appropriate steps to mitigate any environmental liability determined to exist based on this assessment;

(v) Conducted an analysis of the borrower's ability to service its overall debt obligations during the next two years, based on reasonable projections (including operating income projections for the property);

(vi)(A) Determined that based on the two years' actual performance immediately preceding the origination of the loan, the borrower would have had:

(*1*) A DSC ratio of 1.5 or greater, if the loan is a qualifying leased CRE loan, net of any income derived from a tenant(s) who is not a qualified tenant(s);

(*2*) A DSC ratio of 1.25 or greater, if the loan is a qualifying multi-family property loan; or

(*3*) A DSC ratio of 1.7 or greater, if the loan is any other type of CRE loan;

---

[1] 12 CFR part 34, subpart C (OCC); 12 CFR part 208, subpart E, and 12 CFR part 225, subpart G (Board); and 12 CFR part 323 (FDIC).

[2] See USPAP, Standard 1.

(B) If the borrower did not own the property for any part of the last two years prior to origination, the calculation of the DSC ratio, for purposes of paragraph (a)(2)(vi)(A) of this section, shall include the property's operating income for any portion of the two-year period during which the borrower did not own the property;

(vii) Determined that, based on two years of projections, which include the new debt obligation, following the origination date of the loan, the borrower will have:

(A) A DSC ratio of 1.5 or greater, if the loan is a qualifying leased CRE loan, net of any income derived from a tenant(s) who is not a qualified tenant(s);

(B) A DSC ratio of 1.25 or greater, if the loan is a qualifying multi-family property loan; or

(C) A DSC ratio of 1.7 or greater, if the loan is any other type of CRE loan.

(3) The loan documentation for the CRE loan includes covenants that:

(i) Require the borrower to provide the borrower's financial statements and supporting schedules to the servicer on an ongoing basis, but not less frequently than quarterly, including information on existing, maturing and new leasing or rent-roll activity for the property securing the loan, as appropriate; and

(ii) Impose prohibitions on:

(A) The creation or existence of any other security interest with respect to the collateral for the CRE loan described in paragraphs (a)(1)(i) and (a)(1)(ii)(A) of this section, except as provided in paragraph (a)(4) of this section;

(B) The transfer of any collateral for the CRE loan described in paragraph (a)(1)(i) or (a)(1)(ii)(A) of this section or of any other collateral consisting of fixtures, furniture, furnishings, machinery or equipment other than any such fixture, furniture, furnishings, machinery or equipment that is obsolete or surplus; and

(C) Any change to the name, location or organizational structure of any borrower, operating affiliate or other pledgor unless such borrower, operating affiliate or other pledgor shall have given the holder of the loan at least 30 days advance notice and, pursuant to applicable law governing perfection and priority, the holder of the loan is able to take all steps necessary to continue its perfection and priority during such 30-day period.

(iii) Require each borrower and each operating affiliate to:

(A) Maintain insurance that protects against loss on collateral for the CRE loan described in paragraph (a)(1)(i) of this section for an amount no less than the replacement cost of the property improvements, and names the originator or any subsequent holder of the loan as an additional insured or lender loss payee;

(B) Pay taxes, charges, fees, and claims, where non-payment might give rise to a lien on collateral for the CRE loan described in paragraphs (a)(1)(i) and (ii) of this section;

(C) Take any action required to:

(*1*) Protect the security interest and the enforceability and priority thereof in the collateral described in paragraphs (a)(1)(i) and (a)(1)(ii)(A) of this section and defend such collateral against claims adverse to the originator's or any subsequent holder's interest; and

(*2*) Perfect the security interest of the originator or any subsequent holder of the loan in any other collateral for the CRE loan to the extent that such security interest is required by this section to be perfected;

(D) Permit the originator or any subsequent holder of the loan, and the servicer, to inspect any collateral for the CRE loan and the books and records of the borrower or other party relating to any collateral for the CRE loan;

(E) Maintain the physical condition of collateral for the CRE loan described in paragraph (a)(1)(i) of this section;

(F) Comply with all environmental, zoning, building code, licensing and other laws, regulations, agreements, covenants, use restrictions, and proffers applicable to collateral for the CRE loan described in paragraph (a)(1)(i) of this section;

(G) Comply with leases, franchise agreements, condominium declarations, and other documents and agreements relating to the operation of collateral for the CRE loan described in paragraph (a)(1)(i) of this section, and to not modify any material terms and conditions of such agreements over the term of the loan without the consent of the originator or any subsequent holder of the loan, or the servicer; and

(H) Not materially alter collateral for the CRE loan described in paragraph (a)(1)(i) of this section without the consent of the originator or any subsequent holder of the loan, or the servicer.

(4) The loan documentation for the CRE loan prohibits the borrower and each operating affiliate from obtaining a loan secured by a junior lien on collateral for the CRE loan described in paragraph (a)(1)(i) or (a)(1)(ii)(A) of this section, unless:

(i) The sum of the principal amount of such junior lien loan, plus the principal amount of all other loans secured by collateral described in paragraph (a)(1)(i) or (a)(1)(ii)(A) of this section, does not exceed the applicable CLTV ratio in paragraph (a)(5) of this section, based on the appraisal at origination of such junior lien loan; or

(ii) Such loan is a purchase money obligation that financed the acquisition of machinery or equipment and the borrower or operating affiliate (as applicable) pledges such machinery and equipment as additional collateral for the CRE loan.

(5) At origination, the applicable loan-to-value ratios for the loan are:

(i) LTV less than or equal to 65 percent and CLTV less than or equal to 70 percent; or

(ii) LTV less than or equal to 60 percent and CLTV less than or equal to 65 percent, if an appraisal used to meet the requirements set forth in paragraph (a)(2)(ii) of this section used a direct capitalization rate, and that rate is less than or equal to the sum of:

(A) The 10-year swap rate, as reported in the Federal Reserve's H.15 Report (or any successor report) as of the date concurrent with the effective date of such appraisal; and

(B) 300 basis points.

(iii) If the appraisal required under paragraph (a)(2)(ii) of this section included a direct capitalization method using an overall capitalization rate, that rate must be disclosed to potential investors in the securitization.

(6) All loan payments required to be made under the loan agreement are:

(i) Based on level monthly payments of principal and interest (at the fully indexed rate) to fully amortize the debt over a term that does not exceed 25 years, or 30 years for a qualifying multifamily loan; and

(ii) To be made no less frequently than monthly over a term of at least ten years.

(7) Under the terms of the loan agreement:

(i) Any maturity of the note occurs no earlier than ten years following the date of origination;

(ii) The borrower is not permitted to defer repayment of principal or payment of interest; and

(iii) The interest rate on the loan is:

(A) A fixed interest rate;

(B) An adjustable interest rate and the borrower, prior to or concurrently with origination of the CRE loan, obtained a derivative that effectively results in a fixed interest rate; or

(C) An adjustable interest rate and the borrower, prior to or concurrently with origination of the CRE loan, obtained a derivative that established a cap on the interest rate for the term of the loan, and the loan meets the underwriting criteria in paragraphs (a)(2)(vi) and (vii) of this section using the maximum interest rate allowable under the interest rate cap.

(8) The originator does not establish an interest reserve at origination to fund all or part of a payment on the loan.

(9) At the cut-off date or similar date for establishing the composition of the securitized assets collateralizing the asset-backed securities issued pursuant to the securitization transaction, all payments due on the loan are contractually current.

(10)(i) The depositor of the asset-backed security certifies that it has evaluated the effectiveness of its internal supervisory controls with respect to the process for ensuring that all qualifying CRE loans that collateralize the asset-backed security and that reduce the sponsor's risk retention requirement under § 43.15 meet all of the requirements set forth in paragraphs (a)(1) through (9) of this section and has concluded that its internal supervisory controls are effective;

(ii) The evaluation of the effectiveness of the depositor's internal supervisory controls referenced in paragraph (a)(10)(i) of this section shall be performed, for each issuance of an asset-backed security, as of a date within 60 days of the cut-off date or similar date for establishing the composition of the asset pool collateralizing such asset-backed security;

(iii) The sponsor provides, or causes to be provided, a copy of the certification described in paragraph (a)(10)(i) of this section to potential investors a reasonable period of time prior to the sale of asset-backed securities in the issuing entity, and, upon request, to its appropriate Federal banking agency, if any; and

(11) Within two weeks of the closing of the CRE loan by its originator or, if sooner, prior to the transfer of such CRE loan to the issuing entity, the originator shall have obtained a UCC lien search from the jurisdiction of organization of the borrower and each operating affiliate, that does not report, as of the time that the security interest of the originator in the property described in paragraph (a)(1)(iii) of this section was perfected, other higher priority liens of record on any property described in paragraph (a)(1)(iii) of this section, other than purchase money security interests.

(b) *Cure or buy-back requirement.* If a sponsor has relied on the exception provided in § 43.15 with respect to a qualifying CRE loan and it is subsequently determined that the CRE loan did not meet all of the requirements set forth in paragraphs (a)(1) through (9) and (a)(11) of this section, the sponsor shall not lose the benefit of the exception with respect to the CRE loan if the depositor complied with the certification requirement set forth in paragraph (a)(10) of this section, and:

(1) The failure of the loan to meet any of the requirements set forth in paragraphs (a)(1) through (9) and (a)(11) of this section is not material; or;

(2) No later than 90 days after the determination that the loan does not meet one or more of the requirements of paragraphs (a)(1) through (9) or (a)(11) of this section, the sponsor:

(i) Effectuates cure, restoring conformity of the loan to the unmet requirements as of the date of cure; or

(ii) Repurchases the loan(s) from the issuing entity at a price at least equal to the remaining principal balance and accrued interest on the loan(s) as of the date of repurchase.

(3) If the sponsor cures or repurchases pursuant to paragraph (b)(2) of this section, the sponsor must promptly notify, or cause to be notified, the holders of the asset-backed securities issued in the securitization transaction of any loan(s) included in such securitization transaction that is required to be cured or repurchased by the sponsor pursuant to paragraph (b)(2) of this section, including the principal amount of such repurchased loan(s) and the cause for such cure or repurchase.

§ 43.18 Underwriting standards for qualifying automobile loans.

(a) *Underwriting, product and other standards.* (1) Prior to origination of the automobile loan, the originator:

(i) Verified and documented that within 30 days of the date of origination:

(A) The borrower was not currently 30 days or more past due, in whole or in part, on any debt obligation;

(B) Within the previous 24 months, the borrower has not been 60 days or more past due, in whole or in part, on any debt obligation;

(C) Within the previous 36 months, the borrower has not:

(*1*) Been a debtor in a proceeding commenced under Chapter 7 (Liquidation), Chapter 11 (Reorganization), Chapter 12 (Family Farmer or Family Fisherman plan), or Chapter 13 (Individual Debt Adjustment) of the U.S. Bankruptcy Code; or

(*2*) Been the subject of any federal or State judicial judgment for the collection of any unpaid debt;

(D) Within the previous 36 months, no one-to-four family property owned by the borrower has been the subject of any foreclosure, deed in lieu of foreclosure, or short sale; or

(E) Within the previous 36 months, the borrower has not had any personal property repossessed;

(ii) Determined and documented that the borrower has at least 24 months of credit history; and

(iii) Determined and documented that, upon the origination of the loan, the borrower's DTI ratio is less than or equal to 36 percent.

(A) For the purpose of making the determination under paragraph (a)(1)(iii) of this section, the originator must:

(*1*) Verify and document all income of the borrower that the originator includes in the borrower's effective monthly income (using payroll stubs, tax returns, profit and loss statements, or other similar documentation); and

(*2*) On or after the date of the borrower's written application and prior to origination, obtain a credit report regarding the borrower from a consumer reporting agency that compiles and maintain files on consumers on a nationwide basis (within the meaning of 15 U.S.C. 1681a(p)) and verify that all outstanding debts reported in the borrower's credit report are incorporated into the calculation of the borrower's DTI ratio under paragraph (a)(1)(iii) of this section;

(2) An originator will be deemed to have met the requirements of paragraph (a)(1)(i) of this section if:

(i) The originator, no more than 30 days before the closing of the loan, obtains a credit report regarding the borrower from a consumer reporting agency that compiles and maintains files on consumers on a nationwide basis (within the meaning of 15 U.S.C. 1681a(p));

(ii) Based on the information in such credit report, the borrower meets all of the requirements of paragraph (a)(1)(i) of this section, and no information in a credit report subsequently obtained by the originator before the closing of the loan contains contrary information; and

(iii) The originator obtains electronic or hard copies of the credit report.

(3) At closing of the automobile loan, the borrower makes a down payment from the borrower's personal funds and trade-in allowance, if any, that is at least equal to the sum of:

(i) The full cost of the vehicle title, tax, and registration fees;

(ii) Any dealer-imposed fees;

(iii) The full cost of any additional warranties, insurance or other products purchased in connection with the purchase of the vehicle; and

(iv) 10 percent of the vehicle purchase price.

(4) The originator records a first lien securing the loan on the purchased vehicle in accordance with State law.

(5) The terms of the loan agreement provide a maturity date for the loan that does not exceed the lesser of:

(i) Six years from the date of origination; or

(ii) 10 years minus the difference between the current model year and the vehicle's model year.

(6) The terms of the loan agreement:

(i) Specify a fixed rate of interest for the life of the loan;

(ii) Provide for a level monthly payment amount that fully amortizes the amount financed over the loan term;

(iii) Do not permit the borrower to defer repayment of principal or payment of interest; and

(iv) Require the borrower to make the first payment on the automobile loan within 45 days of the loan's contract date.

(7) At the cut-off date or similar date for establishing the composition of the securitized assets collateralizing the asset-backed securities issued pursuant to the securitization transaction, all payments due on the loan are contractually current; and

(8)(i) The depositor of the asset-backed security certifies that it has evaluated the effectiveness of its internal supervisory controls with respect to the process for ensuring that all qualifying automobile loans that collateralize the asset-backed security and that reduce the sponsor's risk retention requirement under § 43.15 meet all of the requirements set forth in paragraphs (a)(1) through (7) of this section and has concluded that its internal supervisory controls are effective;

(ii) The evaluation of the effectiveness of the depositor's internal supervisory controls referenced in paragraph (a)(8)(i) of this section shall be performed, for each issuance of an asset-backed security, as of a date within 60 days of the cut-off date or similar date for establishing the composition of the asset pool collateralizing such asset-backed security; and

(iii) The sponsor provides, or causes to be provided, a copy of the certification described in paragraph (a)(8)(i) of this section to potential investors a reasonable period of time prior to the sale of asset-backed securities in the issuing entity, and, upon request, to its appropriate Federal banking agency, if any.

(b) *Cure or buy-back requirement.* If a sponsor has relied on the exception provided in § 43.15 with respect to a qualifying automobile loan and it is subsequently determined that the loan did not meet all of the requirements set forth in paragraphs (a)(1) through (7) of this section, the sponsor shall not lose the benefit of the exception with respect to the automobile loan if the depositor complied with the certification requirement set forth in paragraph (a)(8) of this section, and:

(1) The failure of the loan to meet any of the requirements set forth in paragraphs (a)(1) through (7) of this section is not material; or

(2) No later than ninety (90) days after the determination that the loan does not meet one or more of the requirements of paragraphs (a)(1) through (7) of this section, the sponsor:

(i) Effectuates cure, establishing conformity of the loan to the unmet requirements as of the date of cure; or

(ii) Repurchases the loan(s) from the issuing entity at a price at least equal to the remaining principal balance and accrued interest on the loan(s) as of the date of repurchase.

(3) If the sponsor cures or repurchases pursuant to paragraph (b)(2) of this section, the sponsor must promptly notify, or cause to be notified, the holders of the asset-backed securities issued in the securitization transaction of any loan(s) included in such securitization transaction that is required to be cured or repurchased by the sponsor pursuant to paragraph (b)(2) of this section, including the principal amount of such loan(s) and the cause for such cure or repurchase.

§ 43.19 General exemptions.

(a) *Definitions.* For purposes of this section, the following definitions shall apply:

Community-focused residential mortgage means a residential mortgage exempt from the definition of "covered transaction" under § 1026.43(a)(3)(iv) and (v) of the CFPB's Regulation Z (12 CFR 1026.43(a)).

First pay class means a class of ABS interests for which all interests in the class are entitled to the same priority of payment and that, at the time of closing of the transaction, is entitled to repayments of principal and payments of interest prior to or pro-rata with all other classes of securities collateralized by the same pool of first-lien residential mortgages, until such class has no principal or notional balance remaining.

Inverse floater means an ABS interest issued as part of a securitization transaction for which interest or other income is payable to the holder based on a rate or formula that varies inversely to a reference rate of interest.

Qualifying three-to-four unit residential mortgage loan means a mortgage loan that is:

(i) Secured by a dwelling (as defined in 12 CFR 1026.2(a)(19)) that is owner occupied and contains three-to-four housing units;

(ii) Is deemed to be for business purposes for purposes of Regulation Z under 12 CFR part 1026, supplement I, paragraph 3(a)(5)(i); and

(iii) Otherwise meets all of the requirements to qualify as a qualified mortgage under § 1026.43(e) and (f) of Regulation Z (12 CFR 1026.43(e) and (f)) as if the loan were a covered transaction under that section.

(b) This part shall not apply to:

(1) *U.S. Government-backed securitizations.* Any securitization transaction that:

(i) Is collateralized solely by residential, multifamily, or health care facility mortgage loan assets that are insured or guaranteed (in whole or in part) as to the payment of principal and interest by the United States or an agency of the United States, and servicing assets; or

(ii) Involves the issuance of asset-backed securities that:

(A) Are insured or guaranteed as to the payment of principal and interest by the United States or an agency of the United States; and

(B) Are collateralized solely by residential, multifamily, or health care facility mortgage loan assets or interests in such assets, and servicing assets.

(2) *Certain agricultural loan securitizations.* Any securitization transaction that is collateralized solely by loans or other assets made, insured, guaranteed, or purchased by any institution that is subject to the supervision of the Farm Credit Administration, including the Federal Agricultural Mortgage Corporation, and servicing assets;

(3) *State and municipal securitizations.* Any asset-backed security that is a security issued or guaranteed by any State, or by any political subdivision of a State, or by any public instrumentality of a State that is exempt from the registration requirements of the Securities Act of 1933 by reason of section 3(a)(2) of that Act (15 U.S.C. 77c(a)(2)); and

(4) *Qualified scholarship funding bonds.* Any asset-backed security that meets the definition of a qualified scholarship funding bond, as set forth in section 150(d)(2) of the Internal Revenue Code of 1986 (26 U.S.C. 150(d)(2)).

(5) *Pass-through resecuritizations.* Any securitization transaction that:

(i) Is collateralized solely by servicing assets, and by asset-backed securities:

(A) For which credit risk was retained as required under subpart B of this part; or

(B) That were exempted from the credit risk retention requirements of this part pursuant to subpart D of this part;

(ii) Is structured so that it involves the issuance of only a single class of ABS interests; and

(iii) Provides for the pass-through of all principal and interest payments received on the underlying asset-backed securities (net of expenses of the issuing entity) to the holders of such class.

(6) *First-pay-class securitizations.* Any securitization transaction that:

(i) Is collateralized solely by servicing assets, and by first-pay classes of asset-backed securities collateralized by first-lien residential mortgages on properties located in any state:

(A) For which credit risk was retained as required under subpart B of this part; or

(B) That were exempted from the credit risk retention requirements of this part pursuant to subpart D of this part;

(ii) Does not provide for any ABS interest issued in the securitization transaction to share in realized principal losses other than pro rata with all other ABS interests issued in the securitization transaction based on the current unpaid principal balance of such ABS interests at the time the loss is realized;

(iii) Is structured to reallocate prepayment risk;

(iv) Does not reallocate credit risk (other than as a consequence of reallocation of prepayment risk); and

(v) Does not include any inverse floater or similarly structured ABS interest.

(7) *Seasoned loans.* (i) Any securitization transaction that is collateralized solely by servicing assets, and by seasoned loans that meet the following requirements:

(A) The loans have not been modified since origination; and

(B) None of the loans have been delinquent for 30 days or more.

(ii) For purposes of this paragraph, a *seasoned loan* means:

(A) With respect to asset-backed securities collateralized by residential mortgages, a loan that has been outstanding and performing for the longer of:

(*1*) A period of five years; or

(*2*) Until the outstanding principal balance of the loan has been reduced to 25 percent of the original principal balance.

(*3*) Notwithstanding paragraphs (b)(7)(ii)(A)(*1*) and (*2*) of this section, any residential mortgage loan that has been outstanding and performing for a period of at least seven years shall be deemed a seasoned loan.

(B) With respect to all other classes of asset-backed securities, a loan that has been outstanding and performing for the longer of:

(*1*) A period of at least two years; or

(*2*) Until the outstanding principal balance of the loan has been reduced to

33 percent of the original principal balance.

(8) *Certain public utility securitizations.* (i) Any securitization transaction where the asset-back securities issued in the transaction are secured by the intangible property right to collect charges for the recovery of specified costs and such other assets, if any, of an issuing entity that is wholly owned, directly or indirectly, by an investor owned utility company that is subject to the regulatory authority of a State public utility commission or other appropriate State agency.

(ii) For purposes of this paragraph:

(A) *Specified cost* means any cost identified by a State legislature as appropriate for recovery through securitization pursuant to specified cost recovery legislation; and

(B) *Specified cost recovery legislation* means legislation enacted by a State that:

(*1*) Authorizes the investor owned utility company to apply for, and authorizes the public utility commission or other appropriate State agency to issue, a financing order determining the amount of specified costs the utility will be allowed to recover;

(*2*) Provides that pursuant to a financing order, the utility acquires an intangible property right to charge, collect, and receive amounts necessary to provide for the full recovery of the specified costs determined to be recoverable, and assures that the charges are non-bypassable and will be paid by customers within the utility's historic service territory who receive utility goods or services through the utility's transmission and distribution system, even if those customers elect to purchase these goods or services from a third party; and

(*3*) Guarantees that neither the State nor any of its agencies has the authority to rescind or amend the financing order, to revise the amount of specified costs, or in any way to reduce or impair the value of the intangible property right, except as may be contemplated by periodic adjustments authorized by the specified cost recovery legislation.

(c) *Exemption for securitizations of assets issued, insured or guaranteed by the United States.* This part shall not apply to any securitization transaction if the asset-backed securities issued in the transaction are:

(1) Collateralized solely by obligations issued by the United States or an agency of the United States and servicing assets;

(2) Collateralized solely by assets that are fully insured or guaranteed as to the payment of principal and interest by the United States or an agency of the United States (other than those referred to in paragraph (b)(1)(i) of this section) and servicing assets; or

(3) Fully guaranteed as to the timely payment of principal and interest by the United States or any agency of the United States;

(d) *Federal Deposit Insurance Corporation securitizations.* This part shall not apply to any securitization transaction that is sponsored by the Federal Deposit Insurance Corporation acting as conservator or receiver under any provision of the Federal Deposit Insurance Act or of Title II of the Dodd-Frank Wall Street Reform and Consumer Protection Act.

(e) *Reduced requirement for certain student loan securitizations.* The 5 percent risk retention requirement set forth in §43.4 shall be modified as follows:

(1) With respect to a securitization transaction that is collateralized solely by student loans made under the Federal Family Education Loan Program ("FFELP loans") that are guaranteed as to 100 percent of defaulted principal and accrued interest, and servicing assets, the risk retention requirement shall be 0 percent;

(2) With respect to a securitization transaction that is collateralized solely by FFELP loans that are guaranteed as to at least 98 percent but less than 100 percent of defaulted principal and accrued interest, and servicing assets, the risk retention requirement shall be 2 percent; and

(3) With respect to any other securitization transaction that is collateralized solely by FFELP loans, and servicing assets, the risk retention requirement shall be 3 percent.

(f) *Community-focused lending securitizations.* (1) This part shall not apply to any securitization transaction if the asset-backed securities issued in the transaction are collateralized solely by community-focused residential mortgages and servicing assets.

(2) For any securitization transaction that includes both community-focused residential mortgages and residential mortgages that are not exempt from risk retention under this part, the percent of risk retention required under § 43.4(a) is reduced by the ratio of the unpaid principal balance of the community-focused residential mortgages to the total unpaid principal balance of residential mortgages that are included in the pool of assets collateralizing the asset-backed securities issued pursuant to the securitization transaction (the community-focused residential mortgage asset ratio); provided that:

(i) The community-focused residential mortgage asset ratio is measured as of the cut-off date or similar date for establishing the composition of the pool assets collateralizing the asset-backed securities issued pursuant to the securitization transaction; and

(ii) If the community-focused residential mortgage asset ratio would exceed 50 percent, the community-focused residential mortgage asset ratio shall be deemed to be 50 percent.

(g) *Exemptions for securitizations of certain three-to-four unit mortgage loans.* A sponsor shall be exempt from the risk retention requirements in subpart B of this part with respect to any securitization transaction if:

(1)(i) The asset-backed securities issued in the transaction are collateralized solely by qualifying three-to-four unit residential mortgage loans and servicing assets; or

(ii) The asset-backed securities issued in the transaction are collateralized solely by qualifying three-to-four unit residential mortgage loans, qualified residential mortgages as defined in § 43.13, and servicing assets.

(2) The depositor with respect to the securitization provides the certifications set forth in § 43.13(b)(4) with respect to the process for ensuring that all assets that collateralize the asset-backed securities issued in the transaction are qualifying three-to-four unit residential mortgage loans, qualified residential mortgages, or servicing assets; and

(3) The sponsor of the securitization complies with the repurchase requirements in § 43.13(c) with respect to a loan if, after closing, it is determined that the loan does not meet all of the criteria to be either a qualified residential mortgage or a qualifying three-to-four unit residential mortgage loan, as appropriate.

(h) *Rule of construction.* Securitization transactions involving the issuance of asset-backed securities that are either issued, insured, or guaranteed by, or are collateralized by obligations issued by, or loans that are issued, insured, or guaranteed by, the Federal National Mortgage Association, the Federal Home Loan Mortgage Corporation, or a Federal home loan bank shall not on that basis qualify for exemption under this part.

§ 43.20 Safe harbor for certain foreign-related transactions.

(a) *Definitions.* For purposes of this section, the following definition shall apply:

U.S. person means:

(i) Any of the following:

(A) Any natural person resident in the United States;

(B) Any partnership, corporation, limited liability company, or other organization or entity organized or incorporated under the laws of any State or of the United States;

(C) Any estate of which any executor or administrator is a U.S. person (as defined under any other clause of this definition);

(D) Any trust of which any trustee is a U.S. person (as defined under any other clause of this definition);

(E) Any agency or branch of a foreign entity located in the United States;

(F) Any non-discretionary account or similar account (other than an estate or trust) held by a dealer or other fiduciary for the benefit or account of a U.S. person (as defined under any other clause of this definition);

(G) Any discretionary account or similar account (other than an estate or trust) held by a dealer or other fiduciary organized, incorporated, or (if an individual) resident in the United States; and

(H) Any partnership, corporation, limited liability company, or other organization or entity if:

(*1*) Organized or incorporated under the laws of any foreign jurisdiction; and

(*2*) Formed by a U.S. person (as defined under any other clause of this definition) principally for the purpose of investing in securities not registered under the Act; and

(ii) "U.S. person(s)" does not include:

(A) Any discretionary account or similar account (other than an estate or trust) held for the benefit or account of a person not constituting a U.S. person (as defined in paragraph (i) of this section) by a dealer or other professional fiduciary organized, incorporated, or (if an individual) resident in the United States;

(B) Any estate of which any professional fiduciary acting as executor or administrator is a U.S. person (as defined in paragraph (i) of this section) if:

(*1*) An executor or administrator of the estate who is not a U.S. person (as defined in paragraph (i) of this section) has sole or shared investment discretion with respect to the assets of the estate; and

(*2*) The estate is governed by foreign law;

(C) Any trust of which any professional fiduciary acting as trustee is a U.S. person (as defined in paragraph (i) of this section), if a trustee who is not a U.S. person (as defined in paragraph (i) of this section) has sole or shared investment discretion with respect to the trust assets, and no beneficiary of the trust (and no settlor if the trust is revocable) is a U.S. person (as defined in paragraph (i) of this section);

(D) An employee benefit plan established and administered in accordance with the law of a country other than the United States and customary practices and documentation of such country;

(E) Any agency or branch of a U.S. person (as defined in paragraph (i) of this section) located outside the United States if:

(*1*) The agency or branch operates for valid business reasons; and

(*2*) The agency or branch is engaged in the business of insurance or banking and is subject to substantive insurance or banking regulation, respectively, in the jurisdiction where located;

(F) The International Monetary Fund, the International Bank for Reconstruction and Development, the Inter-American Development Bank, the Asian Development Bank, the African Development Bank, the United Nations, and their agencies, affiliates and pension plans, and any other similar international organizations, their agencies, affiliates and pension plans.

(b) *In general.* This part shall not apply to a securitization transaction if all the following conditions are met:

(1) The securitization transaction is not required to be and is not registered under the Securities Act of 1933 (15 U.S.C. 77a *et seq.*);

(2) No more than 10 percent of the dollar value (or equivalent amount in the currency in which the ABS interests are issued, as applicable) of all classes of ABS interests in the securitization transaction are sold or transferred to U.S. persons or for the account or benefit of U.S. persons;

(3) Neither the sponsor of the securitization transaction nor the issuing entity is:

(i) Chartered, incorporated, or organized under the laws of the United States or any State;

(ii) An unincorporated branch or office (wherever located) of an entity chartered, incorporated, or organized under the laws of the United States or any State; or

(iii) An unincorporated branch or office located in the United States or any State of an entity that is chartered, incorporated, or organized under the laws of a jurisdiction other than the United States or any State; and

(4) If the sponsor or issuing entity is chartered, incorporated, or organized under the laws of a jurisdiction other than the United States or any State, no more than 25 percent (as determined based on unpaid principal balance) of the assets that collateralize the ABS interests sold in the securitization transaction were acquired by the sponsor or issuing entity, directly or indirectly, from:

(i) A majority-owned affiliate of the sponsor or issuing entity that is chartered, incorporated, or organized under the laws of the United States or any State; or

(ii) An unincorporated branch or office of the sponsor or issuing entity that is located in the United States or any State.

(c) *Evasions prohibited.* In view of the objective of these rules and the policies underlying Section 15G of the Exchange Act, the safe harbor described in paragraph (b) of this section is not available with respect to any transaction or series of transactions that, although in technical compliance with paragraphs (a) and (b) of this section, is part of a plan or scheme to evade the requirements of section 15G and this part. In such cases, compliance with section 15G and this part is required.

§ 43.21 Additional exemptions.

(a) *Securitization transactions.* The federal agencies with rulewriting authority under section 15G(b) of the Exchange Act (15 U.S.C. 78o-11(b)) with respect to the type of assets involved may jointly provide a total or partial exemption of any securitization transaction as such agencies determine may be appropriate in the public interest and for the protection of investors.

(b) *Exceptions, exemptions, and adjustments.* The Federal banking agencies and the Commission, in consultation with the Federal Housing Finance Agency and the Department of Housing and Urban Development, may jointly adopt or issue exemptions, exceptions or adjustments to the requirements of this part, including exemptions, exceptions or adjustments for classes of institutions or assets in accordance with section 15G(e) of the Exchange Act (15 U.S.C. 78o-11(e)).

§ 43.22 Periodic review of the QRM definition, exempted three-to-four unit residential mortgage loans, and community-focused residential mortgage exemption.

(a) The Federal banking agencies and the Commission, in consultation with the Federal Housing Finance Agency and the Department of Housing and Urban Development, shall commence a review of the definition of qualified residential mortgage in § 43.13, a review of the community-focused residential mortgage exemption in § 43.19(f), and a review of the exemption for qualifying three-to-four unit residential mortgage loans in § 43.19(g):

(1) No later than four years after the effective date of the rule (as it relates to securitizers and originators of asset-backed securities collateralized by residential mortgages), five years following the completion of such initial review, and every five years thereafter; and

(2) At any time, upon the request of any Federal banking agency, the Commission, the Federal Housing Finance Agency or the Department of Housing and Urban Development, specifying the reason for such request, including as a result of any amendment to the definition of qualified mortgage or changes in the residential housing market.

(b) The Federal banking agencies, the Commission, the Federal Housing Finance Agency and the Department of Housing and Urban Development shall publish in the FEDERAL REGISTER notice of the commencement of a review and, in the case of a review commenced under paragraph (a)(2) of this section, the reason an agency is requesting such review. After completion of any review, but no later than six months after the publication of the notice announcing the review, unless extended by the agencies, the agencies shall jointly publish a notice disclosing the determination of their review. If the agencies determine to amend the definition of qualified residential mortgage, the agencies shall complete any required rulemaking within 12 months of publication in the FEDERAL REGISTER of such notice disclosing the determination of their review, unless extended by the agencies.

PART 44—PROPRIETARY TRADING AND CERTAIN INTERESTS IN AND RELATIONSHIPS WITH COVERED FUNDS

Subpart A—Authority and Definitions

Sec.
44.1 Authority, purpose, scope, and relationship to other authorities.
44.2 Definitions.

Subpart B—Proprietary Trading

44.3 Prohibition on proprietary trading.

44.4 Permitted underwriting and market making-related activities.
44.5 Permitted risk-mitigating hedging activities.
44.6 Other permitted proprietary trading activities.
44.7 Limitations on permitted proprietary trading activities.
44.8–44.9 [Reserved]

Subpart C—Covered Fund Activities and Investments

44.10 Prohibition on acquiring or retaining an ownership interest in and having certain relationships with a covered fund.
44.11 Permitted organizing and offering, underwriting, and market making with respect to a covered fund.
44.12 Permitted investment in a covered fund.
44.13 Other permitted covered fund activities and investments.
44.14 Limitations on relationships with a covered fund.
44.15 Other limitations on permitted covered fund activities and investments.
44.16 Ownership of interests in and sponsorship of issuers of certain collateralized debt obligations backed by trust-preferred securities.
44.17–44.19 [Reserved]

Subpart D—Compliance Program Requirement; Violations

44.20 Program for compliance; reporting.
44.21 Termination of activities or investments; penalties for violations.

APPENDIX A TO PART 44—REPORTING AND RECORDKEEPING REQUIREMENTS FOR COVERED TRADING ACTIVITIES
APPENDIX B TO PART 44—ENHANCED MINIMUM STANDARDS FOR COMPLIANCE PROGRAMS

AUTHORITY: 7 U.S.C. 27 *et seq.*, 12 U.S.C. 1, 24, 92a, 93a, 161, 1461, 1462a, 1463, 1464, 1467a, 1813(q), 1818, 1851, 3101 3102, 3108, 5412.

SOURCE: 79 FR 5779, 5804, Jan. 31, 2014, unless otherwise noted.

Subpart A—Authority and Definitions

§44.1 Authority, purpose, scope, and relationship to other authorities.

(a) *Authority.* This part is issued by the OCC under section 13 of the Bank Holding Company Act of 1956, as amended (12 U.S.C. 1851).

(b) *Purpose.* Section 13 of the Bank Holding Company Act establishes prohibitions and restrictions on proprietary trading and on investments in or relationships with covered funds by certain banking entities, including national banks, Federal branches and agencies of foreign banks, Federal savings associations, and certain subsidiaries thereof. This part implements section 13 of the Bank Holding Company Act by defining terms used in the statute and related terms, establishing prohibitions and restrictions on proprietary trading and on investments in or relationships with covered funds, and explaining the statute's requirements.

(c) *Scope.* This part implements section 13 of the Bank Holding Company Act with respect to banking entities for which the OCC is authorized to issue regulations under section 13(b)(2) of the Bank Holding Company Act (12 U.S.C. 1851(b)(2)) and take actions under section 13(e) of that Act (12 U.S.C. 1851(e)). These include national banks, Federal branches and Federal agencies of foreign banks, Federal savings associations, Federal savings banks, and any of their respective subsidiaries (except a subsidiary for which there is a different primary financial regulatory agency, as that term is defined in this part).

(d) *Relationship to other authorities.* Except as otherwise provided under section 13 of the Bank Holding Company Act or this part, and notwithstanding any other provision of law, the prohibitions and restrictions under section 13 of the Bank Holding Company Act and this part shall apply to the activities and investments of a banking entity identified in paragraph (c) of this section, even if such activities and investments are authorized for the banking entity under other applicable provisions of law.

(e) *Preservation of authority.* Nothing in this part limits in any way the authority of the OCC to impose on a banking entity identified in paragraph (c) of this section additional requirements or restrictions with respect to any activity, investment, or relationship covered under section 13 of the Bank Holding Company Act or this part, or additional penalties for violation of this part provided under any other applicable provision of law.

[79 FR 5804, Jan. 31, 2014]

§ 44.2 Definitions.

Unless otherwise specified, for purposes of this part:

(a) *Affiliate* has the same meaning as in section 2(k) of the Bank Holding Company Act of 1956 (12 U.S.C. 1841(k)).

(b) *Bank holding company* has the same meaning as in section 2 of the Bank Holding Company Act of 1956 (12 U.S.C. 1841).

(c) *Banking entity.* (1) Except as provided in paragraph (c)(2) of this section, *banking entity* means:

(i) Any insured depository institution;

(ii) Any company that controls an insured depository institution;

(iii) Any company that is treated as a bank holding company for purposes of section 8 of the International Banking Act of 1978 (12 U.S.C. 3106); and

(iv) Any affiliate or subsidiary of any entity described in paragraphs (c)(1)(i), (ii), or (iii) of this section.

(2) Banking entity does not include:

(i) A covered fund that is not itself a banking entity under paragraphs (c)(1)(i), (ii), or (iii) of this section;

(ii) A portfolio company held under the authority contained in section 4(k)(4)(H) or (I) of the BHC Act (12 U.S.C. 1843(k)(4)(H), (I)), or any portfolio concern, as defined under 13 CFR 107.50, that is controlled by a small business investment company, as defined in section 103(3) of the Small Business Investment Act of 1958 (15 U.S.C. 662), so long as the portfolio company or portfolio concern is not itself a banking entity under paragraphs (c)(1)(i), (ii), or (iii) of this section; or

(iii) The FDIC acting in its corporate capacity or as conservator or receiver under the Federal Deposit Insurance Act or Title II of the Dodd-Frank Wall Street Reform and Consumer Protection Act.

(d) *Board* means the Board of Governors of the Federal Reserve System.

(e) *CFTC* means the Commodity Futures Trading Commission.

(f) *Dealer* has the same meaning as in section 3(a)(5) of the Exchange Act (15 U.S.C. 78c(a)(5)).

(g) *Depository institution* has the same meaning as in section 3(c) of the Federal Deposit Insurance Act (12 U.S.C. 1813(c)).

(h) *Derivative.* (1) Except as provided in paragraph (h)(2) of this section, *derivative* means:

(i) Any swap, as that term is defined in section 1a(47) of the Commodity Exchange Act (7 U.S.C. 1a(47)), or security-based swap, as that term is defined in section 3(a)(68) of the Exchange Act (15 U.S.C. 78c(a)(68));

(ii) Any purchase or sale of a commodity, that is not an excluded commodity, for deferred shipment or delivery that is intended to be physically settled;

(iii) Any foreign exchange forward (as that term is defined in section 1a(24) of the Commodity Exchange Act (7 U.S.C. 1a(24)) or foreign exchange swap (as that term is defined in section 1a(25) of the Commodity Exchange Act (7 U.S.C. 1a(25));

(iv) Any agreement, contract, or transaction in foreign currency described in section 2(c)(2)(C)(i) of the Commodity Exchange Act (7 U.S.C. 2(c)(2)(C)(i));

(v) Any agreement, contract, or transaction in a commodity other than foreign currency described in section 2(c)(2)(D)(i) of the Commodity Exchange Act (7 U.S.C. 2(c)(2)(D)(i)); and

(vi) Any transaction authorized under section 19 of the Commodity Exchange Act (7 U.S.C. 23(a) or (b));

(2) A derivative does not include:

(i) Any consumer, commercial, or other agreement, contract, or transaction that the CFTC and SEC have further defined by joint regulation, interpretation, guidance, or other action as not within the definition of swap, as that term is defined in section 1a(47) of the Commodity Exchange Act (7 U.S.C. 1a(47)), or security-based swap, as that term is defined in section 3(a)(68) of the Exchange Act (15 U.S.C. 78c(a)(68)); or

(ii) Any identified banking product, as defined in section 402(b) of the Legal Certainty for Bank Products Act of 2000 (7 U.S.C. 27(b)), that is subject to section 403(a) of that Act (7 U.S.C. 27a(a)).

(i) *Employee* includes a member of the immediate family of the employee.

(j) *Exchange Act* means the Securities Exchange Act of 1934 (15 U.S.C. 78a *et seq.*).

(k) *Excluded commodity* has the same meaning as in section 1a(19) of the

Commodity Exchange Act (7 U.S.C. 1a(19)).

(l) *FDIC* means the Federal Deposit Insurance Corporation.

(m) *Federal banking agencies* means the Board, the Office of the Comptroller of the Currency, and the FDIC.

(n) *Foreign banking organization* has the same meaning as in section 211.21(o) of the Board's Regulation K (12 CFR 211.21(o)), but does not include a foreign bank, as defined in section 1(b)(7) of the International Banking Act of 1978 (12 U.S.C. 3101(7)), that is organized under the laws of the Commonwealth of Puerto Rico, Guam, American Samoa, the United States Virgin Islands, or the Commonwealth of the Northern Mariana Islands.

(o) *Foreign insurance regulator* means the insurance commissioner, or a similar official or agency, of any country other than the United States that is engaged in the supervision of insurance companies under foreign insurance law.

(p) *General account* means all of the assets of an insurance company except those allocated to one or more separate accounts.

(q) *Insurance company* means a company that is organized as an insurance company, primarily and predominantly engaged in writing insurance or reinsuring risks underwritten by insurance companies, subject to supervision as such by a state insurance regulator or a foreign insurance regulator, and not operated for the purpose of evading the provisions of section 13 of the BHC Act (12 U.S.C. 1851).

(r) *Insured depository institution* has the same meaning as in section 3(c) of the Federal Deposit Insurance Act (12 U.S.C. 1813(c)), but does not include an insured depository institution that is described in section 2(c)(2)(D) of the BHC Act (12 U.S.C. 1841(c)(2)(D)).

(s) *Loan* means any loan, lease, extension of credit, or secured or unsecured receivable that is not a security or derivative.

(t) *Primary financial regulatory agency* has the same meaning as in section 2(12) of the Dodd-Frank Wall Street Reform and Consumer Protection Act (12 U.S.C. 5301(12)).

(u) *Purchase* includes any contract to buy, purchase, or otherwise acquire. For security futures products, purchase includes any contract, agreement, or transaction for future delivery. With respect to a commodity future, purchase includes any contract, agreement, or transaction for future delivery. With respect to a derivative, purchase includes the execution, termination (prior to its scheduled maturity date), assignment, exchange, or similar transfer or conveyance of, or extinguishing of rights or obligations under, a derivative, as the context may require.

(v) *Qualifying foreign banking organization* means a foreign banking organization that qualifies as such under section 211.23(a), (c) or (e) of the Board's Regulation K (12 CFR 211.23(a), (c), or (e)).

(w) *SEC* means the Securities and Exchange Commission.

(x) *Sale* and *sell* each include any contract to sell or otherwise dispose of. For security futures products, such terms include any contract, agreement, or transaction for future delivery. With respect to a commodity future, such terms include any contract, agreement, or transaction for future delivery. With respect to a derivative, such terms include the execution, termination (prior to its scheduled maturity date), assignment, exchange, or similar transfer or conveyance of, or extinguishing of rights or obligations under, a derivative, as the context may require.

(y) *Security* has the meaning specified in section 3(a)(10) of the Exchange Act (15 U.S.C. 78c(a)(10)).

(z) *Security-based swap dealer* has the same meaning as in section 3(a)(71) of the Exchange Act (15 U.S.C. 78c(a)(71)).

(aa) *Security future* has the meaning specified in section 3(a)(55) of the Exchange Act (15 U.S.C. 78c(a)(55)).

(bb) *Separate account* means an account established and maintained by an insurance company in connection with one or more insurance contracts to hold assets that are legally segregated from the insurance company's other assets, under which income, gains, and losses, whether or not realized, from assets allocated to such account, are, in accordance with the applicable contract, credited to or charged against such account without regard to other income, gains, or losses of the insurance company.

(cc) *State* means any State, the District of Columbia, the Commonwealth of Puerto Rico, Guam, American Samoa, the United States Virgin Islands, and the Commonwealth of the Northern Mariana Islands.

(dd) *Subsidiary* has the same meaning as in section 2(d) of the Bank Holding Company Act of 1956 (12 U.S.C. 1841(d)).

(ee) *State insurance regulator* means the insurance commissioner, or a similar official or agency, of a State that is engaged in the supervision of insurance companies under State insurance law.

(ff) *Swap dealer* has the same meaning as in section 1(a)(49) of the Commodity Exchange Act (7 U.S.C. 1a(49)).

Subpart B—Proprietary Trading

§ 44.3 Prohibition on proprietary trading.

(a) *Prohibition.* Except as otherwise provided in this subpart, a banking entity may not engage in proprietary trading. *Proprietary trading* means engaging as principal for the trading account of the banking entity in any purchase or sale of one or more financial instruments.

(b) *Definition of trading account.* (1) Trading account means any account that is used by a banking entity to:

(i) Purchase or sell one or more financial instruments principally for the purpose of:

(A) Short-term resale;

(B) Benefitting from actual or expected short-term price movements;

(C) Realizing short-term arbitrage profits; or

(D) Hedging one or more positions resulting from the purchases or sales of financial instruments described in paragraphs (b)(1)(i)(A), (B), or (C) of this section;

(ii) Purchase or sell one or more financial instruments that are both market risk capital rule covered positions and trading positions (or hedges of other market risk capital rule covered positions), if the banking entity, or any affiliate of the banking entity, is an insured depository institution, bank holding company, or savings and loan holding company, and calculates risk-based capital ratios under the market risk capital rule; or

(iii) Purchase or sell one or more financial instruments for any purpose, if the banking entity:

(A) Is licensed or registered, or is required to be licensed or registered, to engage in the business of a dealer, swap dealer, or security-based swap dealer, to the extent the instrument is purchased or sold in connection with the activities that require the banking entity to be licensed or registered as such; or

(B) Is engaged in the business of a dealer, swap dealer, or security-based swap dealer outside of the United States, to the extent the instrument is purchased or sold in connection with the activities of such business.

(2) *Rebuttable presumption for certain purchases and sales.* The purchase (or sale) of a financial instrument by a banking entity shall be presumed to be for the trading account of the banking entity under paragraph (b)(1)(i) of this section if the banking entity holds the financial instrument for fewer than sixty days or substantially transfers the risk of the financial instrument within sixty days of the purchase (or sale), unless the banking entity can demonstrate, based on all relevant facts and circumstances, that the banking entity did not purchase (or sell) the financial instrument principally for any of the purposes described in paragraph (b)(1)(i) of this section.

(c) *Financial instrument.* (1) *Financial instrument* means:

(i) A security, including an option on a security;

(ii) A derivative, including an option on a derivative; or

(iii) A contract of sale of a commodity for future delivery, or option on a contract of sale of a commodity for future delivery.

(2) A financial instrument does not include:

(i) A loan;

(ii) A commodity that is not:

(A) An excluded commodity (other than foreign exchange or currency);

(B) A derivative;

(C) A contract of sale of a commodity for future delivery; or

(D) An option on a contract of sale of a commodity for future delivery; or

(iii) Foreign exchange or currency.

(d) *Proprietary trading.* Proprietary trading does not include:

(1) Any purchase or sale of one or more financial instruments by a banking entity that arises under a repurchase or reverse repurchase agreement pursuant to which the banking entity has simultaneously agreed, in writing, to both purchase and sell a stated asset, at stated prices, and on stated dates or on demand with the same counterparty;

(2) Any purchase or sale of one or more financial instruments by a banking entity that arises under a transaction in which the banking entity lends or borrows a security temporarily to or from another party pursuant to a written securities lending agreement under which the lender retains the economic interests of an owner of such security, and has the right to terminate the transaction and to recall the loaned security on terms agreed by the parties;

(3) Any purchase or sale of a security by a banking entity for the purpose of liquidity management in accordance with a documented liquidity management plan of the banking entity that:

(i) Specifically contemplates and authorizes the particular securities to be used for liquidity management purposes, the amount, types, and risks of these securities that are consistent with liquidity management, and the liquidity circumstances in which the particular securities may or must be used;

(ii) Requires that any purchase or sale of securities contemplated and authorized by the plan be principally for the purpose of managing the liquidity of the banking entity, and not for the purpose of short-term resale, benefitting from actual or expected short-term price movements, realizing short-term arbitrage profits, or hedging a position taken for such short-term purposes;

(iii) Requires that any securities purchased or sold for liquidity management purposes be highly liquid and limited to securities the market, credit, and other risks of which the banking entity does not reasonably expect to give rise to appreciable profits or losses as a result of short-term price movements;

(iv) Limits any securities purchased or sold for liquidity management purposes, together with any other instruments purchased or sold for such purposes, to an amount that is consistent with the banking entity's near-term funding needs, including deviations from normal operations of the banking entity or any affiliate thereof, as estimated and documented pursuant to methods specified in the plan;

(v) Includes written policies and procedures, internal controls, analysis, and independent testing to ensure that the purchase and sale of securities that are not permitted under §§ 44.6(a) or (b) of this subpart are for the purpose of liquidity management and in accordance with the liquidity management plan described in paragraph (d)(3) of this section; and

(vi) Is consistent with the OCC's supervisory requirements, guidance, and expectations regarding liquidity management;

(4) Any purchase or sale of one or more financial instruments by a banking entity that is a derivatives clearing organization or a clearing agency in connection with clearing financial instruments;

(5) Any excluded clearing activities by a banking entity that is a member of a clearing agency, a member of a derivatives clearing organization, or a member of a designated financial market utility;

(6) Any purchase or sale of one or more financial instruments by a banking entity, so long as:

(i) The purchase (or sale) satisfies an existing delivery obligation of the banking entity or its customers, including to prevent or close out a failure to deliver, in connection with delivery, clearing, or settlement activity; or

(ii) The purchase (or sale) satisfies an obligation of the banking entity in connection with a judicial, administrative, self-regulatory organization, or arbitration proceeding;

(7) Any purchase or sale of one or more financial instruments by a banking entity that is acting solely as agent, broker, or custodian;

(8) Any purchase or sale of one or more financial instruments by a banking entity through a deferred compensation, stock-bonus, profit-sharing, or pension plan of the banking entity that is established and administered in accordance with the law of the United States or a foreign sovereign, if the purchase or sale is made directly or indirectly by the banking entity as trustee for the benefit of persons who are or were employees of the banking entity; or

(9) Any purchase or sale of one or more financial instruments by a banking entity in the ordinary course of collecting a debt previously contracted in good faith, provided that the banking entity divests the financial instrument as soon as practicable, and in no event may the banking entity retain such instrument for longer than such period permitted by the OCC.

(e) *Definition of other terms related to proprietary trading.* For purposes of this subpart:

(1) *Anonymous* means that each party to a purchase or sale is unaware of the identity of the other party(ies) to the purchase or sale.

(2) *Clearing agency* has the same meaning as in section 3(a)(23) of the Exchange Act (15 U.S.C. 78c(a)(23)).

(3) *Commodity* has the same meaning as in section 1a(9) of the Commodity Exchange Act (7 U.S.C. 1a(9)), except that a commodity does not include any security;

(4) *Contract of sale of a commodity for future delivery* means a contract of sale (as that term is defined in section 1a(13) of the Commodity Exchange Act (7 U.S.C. 1a(13)) for future delivery (as that term is defined in section 1a(27) of the Commodity Exchange Act (7 U.S.C. 1a(27))).

(5) *Derivatives clearing organization* means:

(i) A derivatives clearing organization registered under section 5b of the Commodity Exchange Act (7 U.S.C. 7a–1);

(ii) A derivatives clearing organization that, pursuant to CFTC regulation, is exempt from the registration requirements under section 5b of the Commodity Exchange Act (7 U.S.C. 7a–1); or

(iii) A foreign derivatives clearing organization that, pursuant to CFTC regulation, is permitted to clear for a foreign board of trade that is registered with the CFTC.

(6) *Exchange*, unless the context otherwise requires, means any designated contract market, swap execution facility, or foreign board of trade registered with the CFTC, or, for purposes of securities or security-based swaps, an exchange, as defined under section 3(a)(1) of the Exchange Act (15 U.S.C. 78c(a)(1)), or security-based swap execution facility, as defined under section 3(a)(77) of the Exchange Act (15 U.S.C. 78c(a)(77)).

(7) *Excluded clearing activities* means:

(i) With respect to customer transactions cleared on a derivatives clearing organization, a clearing agency, or a designated financial market utility, any purchase or sale necessary to correct trading errors made by or on behalf of a customer provided that such purchase or sale is conducted in accordance with, for transactions cleared on a derivatives clearing organization, the Commodity Exchange Act, CFTC regulations, and the rules or procedures of the derivatives clearing organization, or, for transactions cleared on a clearing agency, the rules or procedures of the clearing agency, or, for transactions cleared on a designated financial market utility that is neither a derivatives clearing organization nor a clearing agency, the rules or procedures of the designated financial market utility;

(ii) Any purchase or sale in connection with and related to the management of a default or threatened imminent default of a customer provided that such purchase or sale is conducted in accordance with, for transactions cleared on a derivatives clearing organization, the Commodity Exchange Act, CFTC regulations, and the rules or procedures of the derivatives clearing organization, or, for transactions cleared on a clearing agency, the rules or procedures of the clearing agency, or, for transactions cleared on a designated financial market utility that is neither a derivatives clearing organization nor a clearing agency, the rules or procedures of the designated financial market utility;

(iii) Any purchase or sale in connection with and related to the management of a default or threatened imminent default of a member of a clearing agency, a member of a derivatives clearing organization, or a member of a designated financial market utility;

(iv) Any purchase or sale in connection with and related to the management of the default or threatened default of a clearing agency, a derivatives clearing organization, or a designated financial market utility; and

(v) Any purchase or sale that is required by the rules or procedures of a clearing agency, a derivatives clearing organization, or a designated financial market utility to mitigate the risk to the clearing agency, derivatives clearing organization, or designated financial market utility that would result from the clearing by a member of security-based swaps that reference the member or an affiliate of the member.

(8) *Designated financial market utility* has the same meaning as in section 803(4) of the Dodd-Frank Act (12 U.S.C. 5462(4)).

(9) *Issuer* has the same meaning as in section 2(a)(4) of the Securities Act of 1933 (15 U.S.C. 77b(a)(4)).

(10) *Market risk capital rule covered position and trading position* means a financial instrument that is both a covered position and a trading position, as those terms are respectively defined:

(i) In the case of a banking entity that is a bank holding company, savings and loan holding company, or insured depository institution, under the market risk capital rule that is applicable to the banking entity; and

(ii) In the case of a banking entity that is affiliated with a bank holding company or savings and loan holding company, other than a banking entity to which a market risk capital rule is applicable, under the market risk capital rule that is applicable to the affiliated bank holding company or savings and loan holding company.

(11) *Market risk capital rule* means the market risk capital rule that is contained in subpart F of 12 CFR part 3, 12 CFR parts 208 and 225, or 12 CFR part 324, as applicable.

(12) *Municipal security* means a security that is a direct obligation of or issued by, or an obligation guaranteed as to principal or interest by, a State or any political subdivision thereof, or any agency or instrumentality of a State or any political subdivision thereof, or any municipal corporate instrumentality of one or more States or political subdivisions thereof.

(13) *Trading desk* means the smallest discrete unit of organization of a banking entity that purchases or sells financial instruments for the trading account of the banking entity or an affiliate thereof.

§ 44.4 Permitted underwriting and market making-related activities.

(a) *Underwriting activities*—(1) *Permitted underwriting activities.* The prohibition contained in § 44.3(a) does not apply to a banking entity's underwriting activities conducted in accordance with this paragraph (a).

(2) *Requirements.* The underwriting activities of a banking entity are permitted under paragraph (a)(1) of this section only if:

(i) The banking entity is acting as an underwriter for a distribution of securities and the trading desk's underwriting position is related to such distribution;

(ii) The amount and type of the securities in the trading desk's underwriting position are designed not to exceed the reasonably expected near term demands of clients, customers, or counterparties, and reasonable efforts are made to sell or otherwise reduce the underwriting position within a reasonable period, taking into account the liquidity, maturity, and depth of the market for the relevant type of security;

(iii) The banking entity has established and implements, maintains, and enforces an internal compliance program required by subpart D of this part that is reasonably designed to ensure the banking entity's compliance with the requirements of paragraph (a) of this section, including reasonably designed written policies and procedures, internal controls, analysis and independent testing identifying and addressing:

(A) The products, instruments or exposures each trading desk may purchase, sell, or manage as part of its underwriting activities;

(B) Limits for each trading desk, based on the nature and amount of the trading desk's underwriting activities, including the reasonably expected near term demands of clients, customers, or counterparties, on the:

(*1*) Amount, types, and risk of its underwriting position;

(*2*) Level of exposures to relevant risk factors arising from its underwriting position; and

(*3*) Period of time a security may be held;

(C) Internal controls and ongoing monitoring and analysis of each trading desk's compliance with its limits; and

(D) Authorization procedures, including escalation procedures that require review and approval of any trade that would exceed a trading desk's limit(s), demonstrable analysis of the basis for any temporary or permanent increase to a trading desk's limit(s), and independent review of such demonstrable analysis and approval;

(iv) The compensation arrangements of persons performing the activities described in this paragraph (a) are designed not to reward or incentivize prohibited proprietary trading; and

(v) The banking entity is licensed or registered to engage in the activity described in this paragraph (a) in accordance with applicable law.

(3) *Definition of distribution.* For purposes of this paragraph (a), a *distribution* of securities means:

(i) An offering of securities, whether or not subject to registration under the Securities Act of 1933, that is distinguished from ordinary trading transactions by the presence of special selling efforts and selling methods; or

(ii) An offering of securities made pursuant to an effective registration statement under the Securities Act of 1933.

(4) *Definition of underwriter.* For purposes of this paragraph (a), *underwriter* means:

(i) A person who has agreed with an issuer or selling security holder to:

(A) Purchase securities from the issuer or selling security holder for distribution;

(B) Engage in a distribution of securities for or on behalf of the issuer or selling security holder; or

(C) Manage a distribution of securities for or on behalf of the issuer or selling security holder; or

(ii) A person who has agreed to participate or is participating in a distribution of such securities for or on behalf of the issuer or selling security holder.

(5) *Definition of selling security holder.* For purposes of this paragraph (a), *selling security holder* means any person, other than an issuer, on whose behalf a distribution is made.

(6) *Definition of underwriting position.* For purposes of this paragraph (a), *underwriting position* means the long or short positions in one or more securities held by a banking entity or its affiliate, and managed by a particular trading desk, in connection with a particular distribution of securities for which such banking entity or affiliate is acting as an underwriter.

(7) *Definition of client, customer, and counterparty.* For purposes of this paragraph (a), the terms *client, customer, and counterparty*, on a collective or individual basis, refer to market participants that may transact with the banking entity in connection with a particular distribution for which the banking entity is acting as underwriter.

(b) *Market making-related activities*—(1) *Permitted market making-related activities.* The prohibition contained in § 44.3(a) does not apply to a banking entity's market making-related activities conducted in accordance with this paragraph (b).

(2) *Requirements.* The market making-related activities of a banking entity are permitted under paragraph (b)(1) of this section only if:

(i) The trading desk that establishes and manages the financial exposure routinely stands ready to purchase and sell one or more types of financial instruments related to its financial exposure and is willing and available to quote, purchase and sell, or otherwise enter into long and short positions in those types of financial instruments for its own account, in commercially reasonable amounts and throughout market cycles on a basis appropriate for the liquidity, maturity, and depth of the market for the relevant types of financial instruments;

(ii) The amount, types, and risks of the financial instruments in the trading desk's market-maker inventory are designed not to exceed, on an ongoing basis, the reasonably expected near term demands of clients, customers, or counterparties, based on:

(A) The liquidity, maturity, and depth of the market for the relevant types of financial instrument(s); and

(B) Demonstrable analysis of historical customer demand, current inventory of financial instruments, and market and other factors regarding the amount, types, and risks, of or associated with financial instruments in which the trading desk makes a market, including through block trades;

(iii) The banking entity has established and implements, maintains, and enforces an internal compliance program required by subpart D of this part that is reasonably designed to ensure the banking entity's compliance with the requirements of paragraph (b) of this section, including reasonably designed written policies and procedures, internal controls, analysis and independent testing identifying and addressing:

(A) The financial instruments each trading desk stands ready to purchase and sell in accordance with paragraph (b)(2)(i) of this section;

(B) The actions the trading desk will take to demonstrably reduce or otherwise significantly mitigate promptly the risks of its financial exposure consistent with the limits required under paragraph (b)(2)(iii)(C) of this section; the products, instruments, and exposures each trading desk may use for risk management purposes; the techniques and strategies each trading desk may use to manage the risks of its market making-related activities and inventory; and the process, strategies, and personnel responsible for ensuring that the actions taken by the trading desk to mitigate these risks are and continue to be effective;

(C) Limits for each trading desk, based on the nature and amount of the trading desk's market making-related activities, that address the factors prescribed by paragraph (b)(2)(ii) of this section, on:

(*1*) The amount, types, and risks of its market-maker inventory;

(*2*) The amount, types, and risks of the products, instruments, and exposures the trading desk may use for risk management purposes;

(*3*) The level of exposures to relevant risk factors arising from its financial exposure; and

(*4*) The period of time a financial instrument may be held;

(D) Internal controls and ongoing monitoring and analysis of each trading desk's compliance with its limits; and

(E) Authorization procedures, including escalation procedures that require review and approval of any trade that would exceed a trading desk's limit(s), demonstrable analysis that the basis for any temporary or permanent increase to a trading desk's limit(s) is consistent with the requirements of this paragraph (b), and independent review of such demonstrable analysis and approval;

(iv) To the extent that any limit identified pursuant to paragraph (b)(2)(iii)(C) of this section is exceeded, the trading desk takes action to bring the trading desk into compliance with the limits as promptly as possible after the limit is exceeded;

(v) The compensation arrangements of persons performing the activities described in this paragraph (b) are designed not to reward or incentivize prohibited proprietary trading; and

(vi) The banking entity is licensed or registered to engage in activity described in this paragraph (b) in accordance with applicable law.

(3) *Definition of client, customer, and counterparty.* For purposes of paragraph (b) of this section, the terms *client, customer, and counterparty,* on a collective or individual basis refer to market participants that make use of the banking entity's market making-related services by obtaining such services, responding to quotations, or entering into a continuing relationship with respect to such services, provided that:

(i) A trading desk or other organizational unit of another banking entity is not a client, customer, or counterparty of the trading desk if that other entity has trading assets and liabilities of $50 billion or more as measured in accordance with §44.20(d)(1) of subpart D, unless:

(A) The trading desk documents how and why a particular trading desk or other organizational unit of the entity should be treated as a client, customer, or counterparty of the trading desk for purposes of paragraph (b)(2) of this section; or

(B) The purchase or sale by the trading desk is conducted anonymously on an exchange or similar trading facility that permits trading on behalf of a broad range of market participants.

(4) *Definition of financial exposure.* For purposes of this paragraph (b), *financial exposure* means the aggregate risks of one or more financial instruments and any associated loans, commodities, or foreign exchange or currency, held by a banking entity or its affiliate and managed by a particular trading desk as part of the trading desk's market making-related activities.

(5) *Definition of market-maker inventory.* For the purposes of this paragraph (b), *market-maker inventory* means all of the positions in the financial instruments for which the trading desk stands ready to make a market in accordance with paragraph (b)(2)(i) of this section, that are managed by the trading desk, including the trading desk's open positions or exposures arising from open transactions.

§ 44.5 Permitted risk-mitigating hedging activities.

(a) *Permitted risk-mitigating hedging activities.* The prohibition contained in § 44.3(a) does not apply to the risk-mitigating hedging activities of a banking entity in connection with and related to individual or aggregated positions, contracts, or other holdings of the banking entity and designed to reduce the specific risks to the banking entity in connection with and related to such positions, contracts, or other holdings.

(b) *Requirements.* The risk-mitigating hedging activities of a banking entity are permitted under paragraph (a) of this section only if:

(1) The banking entity has established and implements, maintains and enforces an internal compliance program required by subpart D of this part that is reasonably designed to ensure the banking entity's compliance with the requirements of this section, including:

(i) Reasonably designed written policies and procedures regarding the positions, techniques and strategies that may be used for hedging, including documentation indicating what positions, contracts or other holdings a particular trading desk may use in its risk-mitigating hedging activities, as well as position and aging limits with respect to such positions, contracts or other holdings;

(ii) Internal controls and ongoing monitoring, management, and authorization procedures, including relevant escalation procedures; and

(iii) The conduct of analysis, including correlation analysis, and independent testing designed to ensure that the positions, techniques and strategies that may be used for hedging may reasonably be expected to demonstrably reduce or otherwise significantly mitigate the specific, identifiable risk(s) being hedged, and such correlation analysis demonstrates that the hedging activity demonstrably reduces or otherwise significantly mitigates the specific, identifiable risk(s) being hedged;

(2) The risk-mitigating hedging activity:

(i) Is conducted in accordance with the written policies, procedures, and internal controls required under this section;

(ii) At the inception of the hedging activity, including, without limitation, any adjustments to the hedging activity, is designed to reduce or otherwise significantly mitigate and demonstrably reduces or otherwise significantly mitigates one or more specific, identifiable risks, including market risk, counterparty or other credit risk, currency or foreign exchange risk, interest rate risk, commodity price risk, basis risk, or similar risks, arising in connection with and related to identified positions, contracts, or other holdings of the banking entity, based upon the facts and circumstances of the identified underlying and hedging positions, contracts or other holdings and the risks and liquidity thereof;

(iii) Does not give rise, at the inception of the hedge, to any significant new or additional risk that is not itself hedged contemporaneously in accordance with this section;

(iv) Is subject to continuing review, monitoring and management by the banking entity that:

(A) Is consistent with the written hedging policies and procedures required under paragraph (b)(1) of this section;

(B) Is designed to reduce or otherwise significantly mitigate and demonstrably reduces or otherwise significantly mitigates the specific, identifiable risks that develop over time from the risk-mitigating hedging activities undertaken under this section and the underlying positions, contracts, and other holdings of the banking entity, based upon the facts and circumstances of the underlying and hedging positions, contracts and other holdings of the banking entity and the risks and liquidity thereof; and

(C) Requires ongoing recalibration of the hedging activity by the banking entity to ensure that the hedging activity satisfies the requirements set out in paragraph (b)(2) of this section and is not prohibited proprietary trading; and

(3) The compensation arrangements of persons performing risk-mitigating hedging activities are designed not to reward or incentivize prohibited proprietary trading.

(c) *Documentation requirement*—(1) A banking entity must comply with the requirements of paragraphs (c)(2) and (3) of this section with respect to any purchase or sale of financial instruments made in reliance on this section for risk-mitigating hedging purposes that is:

(i) Not established by the specific trading desk establishing or responsible for the underlying positions, contracts, or other holdings the risks of which the hedging activity is designed to reduce;

(ii) Established by the specific trading desk establishing or responsible for the underlying positions, contracts, or other holdings the risks of which the purchases or sales are designed to reduce, but that is effected through a financial instrument, exposure, technique, or strategy that is not specifically identified in the trading desk's written policies and procedures established under paragraph (b)(1) of this section or under §44.4(b)(2)(iii)(B) of this subpart as a product, instrument, exposure, technique, or strategy such trading desk may use for hedging; or

(iii) Established to hedge aggregated positions across two or more trading desks.

(2) In connection with any purchase or sale identified in paragraph (c)(1) of this section, a banking entity must, at a minimum, and contemporaneously with the purchase or sale, document:

(i) The specific, identifiable risk(s) of the identified positions, contracts, or other holdings of the banking entity that the purchase or sale is designed to reduce;

(ii) The specific risk-mitigating strategy that the purchase or sale is designed to fulfill; and

(iii) The trading desk or other business unit that is establishing and responsible for the hedge.

(3) A banking entity must create and retain records sufficient to demonstrate compliance with the requirements of this paragraph (c) for a period that is no less than five years in a form that allows the banking entity to promptly produce such records to the OCC on request, or such longer period as required under other law or this part.

§44.6 Other permitted proprietary trading activities.

(a) *Permitted trading in domestic government obligations.* The prohibition contained in §44.3(a) does not apply to the purchase or sale by a banking entity of a financial instrument that is:

(1) An obligation of, or issued or guaranteed by, the United States;

(2) An obligation, participation, or other instrument of, or issued or guaranteed by, an agency of the United States, the Government National Mortgage Association, the Federal National Mortgage Association, the Federal Home Loan Mortgage Corporation, a Federal Home Loan Bank, the Federal Agricultural Mortgage Corporation or a Farm Credit System institution chartered under and subject to the provisions of the Farm Credit Act of 1971 (12 U.S.C. 2001 *et seq.*);

(3) An obligation of any State or any political subdivision thereof, including any municipal security; or

(4) An obligation of the FDIC, or any entity formed by or on behalf of the FDIC for purpose of facilitating the disposal of assets acquired or held by the FDIC in its corporate capacity or as conservator or receiver under the Federal Deposit Insurance Act or Title II of the Dodd-Frank Wall Street Reform and Consumer Protection Act.

(b) *Permitted trading in foreign government obligations*—(1) *Affiliates of foreign banking entities in the United States.* The prohibition contained in § 44.3(a) does not apply to the purchase or sale of a financial instrument that is an obligation of, or issued or guaranteed by, a foreign sovereign (including any multinational central bank of which the foreign sovereign is a member), or any agency or political subdivision of such foreign sovereign, by a banking entity, so long as:

(i) The banking entity is organized under or is directly or indirectly controlled by a banking entity that is organized under the laws of a foreign sovereign and is not directly or indirectly controlled by a top-tier banking entity that is organized under the laws of the United States;

(ii) The financial instrument is an obligation of, or issued or guaranteed by, the foreign sovereign under the laws of which the foreign banking entity referred to in paragraph (b)(1)(i) of this section is organized (including any multinational central bank of which the foreign sovereign is a member), or any agency or political subdivision of that foreign sovereign; and

(iii) The purchase or sale as principal is not made by an insured depository institution.

(2) *Foreign affiliates of a U.S. banking entity.* The prohibition contained in § 44.3(a) does not apply to the purchase or sale of a financial instrument that is an obligation of, or issued or guaranteed by, a foreign sovereign (including any multinational central bank of which the foreign sovereign is a member), or any agency or political subdivision of that foreign sovereign, by a foreign entity that is owned or controlled by a banking entity organized or established under the laws of the United States or any State, so long as:

(i) The foreign entity is a foreign bank, as defined in section 211.2(j) of the Board's Regulation K (12 CFR 211.2(j)), or is regulated by the foreign sovereign as a securities dealer;

(ii) The financial instrument is an obligation of, or issued or guaranteed by, the foreign sovereign under the laws of which the foreign entity is organized (including any multinational central bank of which the foreign sovereign is a member), or any agency or political subdivision of that foreign sovereign; and

(iii) The financial instrument is owned by the foreign entity and is not financed by an affiliate that is located in the United States or organized under the laws of the United States or of any State.

(c) *Permitted trading on behalf of customers*—(1) *Fiduciary transactions.* The prohibition contained in § 44.3(a) does not apply to the purchase or sale of financial instruments by a banking entity acting as trustee or in a similar fiduciary capacity, so long as:

(i) The transaction is conducted for the account of, or on behalf of, a customer; and

(ii) The banking entity does not have or retain beneficial ownership of the financial instruments.

(2) *Riskless principal transactions.* The prohibition contained in § 44.3(a) does not apply to the purchase or sale of financial instruments by a banking entity acting as riskless principal in a transaction in which the banking entity, after receiving an order to purchase (or sell) a financial instrument from a customer, purchases (or sells) the financial instrument for its own account to offset a contemporaneous sale to (or purchase from) the customer.

(d) *Permitted trading by a regulated insurance company.* The prohibition contained in § 44.3(a) does not apply to the purchase or sale of financial instruments by a banking entity that is an insurance company or an affiliate of an insurance company if:

(1) The insurance company or its affiliate purchases or sells the financial instruments solely for:

(i) The general account of the insurance company; or

(ii) A separate account established by the insurance company;

(2) The purchase or sale is conducted in compliance with, and subject to, the

insurance company investment laws, regulations, and written guidance of the State or jurisdiction in which such insurance company is domiciled; and

(3) The appropriate Federal banking agencies, after consultation with the Financial Stability Oversight Council and the relevant insurance commissioners of the States and foreign jurisdictions, as appropriate, have not jointly determined, after notice and comment, that a particular law, regulation, or written guidance described in paragraph (d)(2) of this section is insufficient to protect the safety and soundness of the covered banking entity, or the financial stability of the United States.

(e) *Permitted trading activities of foreign banking entities.* (1) The prohibition contained in §44.3(a) does not apply to the purchase or sale of financial instruments by a banking entity if:

(i) The banking entity is not organized or directly or indirectly controlled by a banking entity that is organized under the laws of the United States or of any State;

(ii) The purchase or sale by the banking entity is made pursuant to paragraph (9) or (13) of section 4(c) of the BHC Act; and

(iii) The purchase or sale meets the requirements of paragraph (e)(3) of this section.

(2) A purchase or sale of financial instruments by a banking entity is made pursuant to paragraph (9) or (13) of section 4(c) of the BHC Act for purposes of paragraph (e)(1)(ii) of this section only if:

(i) The purchase or sale is conducted in accordance with the requirements of paragraph (e) of this section; and

(ii)(A) With respect to a banking entity that is a foreign banking organization, the banking entity meets the qualifying foreign banking organization requirements of section 211.23(a), (c) or (e) of the Board's Regulation K (12 CFR 211.23(a), (c) or (e)), as applicable; or

(B) With respect to a banking entity that is not a foreign banking organization, the banking entity is not organized under the laws of the United States or of any State and the banking entity, on a fully-consolidated basis, meets at least two of the following requirements:

(*1*) Total assets of the banking entity held outside of the United States exceed total assets of the banking entity held in the United States;

(*2*) Total revenues derived from the business of the banking entity outside of the United States exceed total revenues derived from the business of the banking entity in the United States; or

(*3*) Total net income derived from the business of the banking entity outside of the United States exceeds total net income derived from the business of the banking entity in the United States.

(3) A purchase or sale by a banking entity is permitted for purposes of this paragraph (e) if:

(i) The banking entity engaging as principal in the purchase or sale (including any personnel of the banking entity or its affiliate that arrange, negotiate or execute such purchase or sale) is not located in the United States or organized under the laws of the United States or of any State;

(ii) The banking entity (including relevant personnel) that makes the decision to purchase or sell as principal is not located in the United States or organized under the laws of the United States or of any State;

(iii) The purchase or sale, including any transaction arising from risk-mitigating hedging related to the instruments purchased or sold, is not accounted for as principal directly or on a consolidated basis by any branch or affiliate that is located in the United States or organized under the laws of the United States or of any State;

(iv) No financing for the banking entity's purchases or sales is provided, directly or indirectly, by any branch or affiliate that is located in the United States or organized under the laws of the United States or of any State; and

(v) The purchase or sale is not conducted with or through any U.S. entity, other than:

(A) A purchase or sale with the foreign operations of a U.S. entity if no personnel of such U.S. entity that are located in the United States are involved in the arrangement, negotiation, or execution of such purchase or sale;

(B) A purchase or sale with an unaffiliated market intermediary acting as principal, provided the purchase or sale is promptly cleared and settled through a clearing agency or derivatives clearing organization acting as a central counterparty; or

(C) A purchase or sale through an unaffiliated market intermediary acting as agent, provided the purchase or sale is conducted anonymously on an exchange or similar trading facility and is promptly cleared and settled through a clearing agency or derivatives clearing organization acting as a central counterparty.

(4) For purposes of this paragraph (e), a U.S. entity is any entity that is, or is controlled by, or is acting on behalf of, or at the direction of, any other entity that is, located in the United States or organized under the laws of the United States or of any State.

(5) For purposes of this paragraph (e), a U.S. branch, agency, or subsidiary of a foreign banking entity is considered to be located in the United States; however, the foreign bank that operates or controls that branch, agency, or subsidiary is not considered to be located in the United States solely by virtue of operating or controlling the U.S. branch, agency, or subsidiary.

(6) For purposes of this paragraph (e), *unaffiliated market intermediary* means an unaffiliated entity, acting as an intermediary, that is:

(i) A broker or dealer registered with the SEC under section 15 of the Exchange Act or exempt from registration or excluded from regulation as such;

(ii) A swap dealer registered with the CFTC under section 4s of the Commodity Exchange Act or exempt from registration or excluded from regulation as such;

(iii) A security-based swap dealer registered with the SEC under section 15F of the Exchange Act or exempt from registration or excluded from regulation as such; or

(iv) A futures commission merchant registered with the CFTC under section 4f of the Commodity Exchange Act or exempt from registration or excluded from regulation as such.

§44.7 Limitations on permitted proprietary trading activities.

(a) No transaction, class of transactions, or activity may be deemed permissible under §§44.4 through 44.6 if the transaction, class of transactions, or activity would:

(1) Involve or result in a material conflict of interest between the banking entity and its clients, customers, or counterparties;

(2) Result, directly or indirectly, in a material exposure by the banking entity to a high-risk asset or a high-risk trading strategy; or

(3) Pose a threat to the safety and soundness of the banking entity or to the financial stability of the United States.

(b) *Definition of material conflict of interest.* (1) For purposes of this section, a material conflict of interest between a banking entity and its clients, customers, or counterparties exists if the banking entity engages in any transaction, class of transactions, or activity that would involve or result in the banking entity's interests being materially adverse to the interests of its client, customer, or counterparty with respect to such transaction, class of transactions, or activity, and the banking entity has not taken at least one of the actions in paragraph (b)(2) of this section.

(2) Prior to effecting the specific transaction or class or type of transactions, or engaging in the specific activity, the banking entity:

(i) *Timely and effective disclosure.* (A) Has made clear, timely, and effective disclosure of the conflict of interest, together with other necessary information, in reasonable detail and in a manner sufficient to permit a reasonable client, customer, or counterparty to meaningfully understand the conflict of interest; and

(B) Such disclosure is made in a manner that provides the client, customer, or counterparty the opportunity to negate, or substantially mitigate, any materially adverse effect on the client, customer, or counterparty created by the conflict of interest; or

(ii) *Information barriers.* Has established, maintained, and enforced information barriers that are memorialized in written policies and procedures, such as physical separation of personnel, or functions, or limitations on types of activity, that are reasonably designed, taking into consideration the nature of the banking entity's business, to prevent the conflict of interest from involving or resulting in a materially adverse effect on a client, customer, or counterparty. A banking entity may not rely on such information barriers if, in the case of any specific transaction, class or type of transactions or activity, the banking entity knows or should reasonably know that, notwithstanding the banking entity's establishment of information barriers, the conflict of interest may involve or result in a materially adverse effect on a client, customer, or counterparty.

(c) *Definition of high-risk asset and high-risk trading strategy.* For purposes of this section:

(1) *High-risk asset* means an asset or group of related assets that would, if held by a banking entity, significantly increase the likelihood that the banking entity would incur a substantial financial loss or would pose a threat to the financial stability of the United States.

(2) *High-risk trading strategy* means a trading strategy that would, if engaged in by a banking entity, significantly increase the likelihood that the banking entity would incur a substantial financial loss or would pose a threat to the financial stability of the United States.

§§ 44.8–44.9 [Reserved]

Subpart C—Covered Funds Activities and Investments

§ 44.10 Prohibition on acquiring or retaining an ownership interest in and having certain relationships with a covered fund.

(a) *Prohibition.* (1) Except as otherwise provided in this subpart, a banking entity may not, as principal, directly or indirectly, acquire or retain any ownership interest in or sponsor a covered fund.

(2) Paragraph (a)(1) of this section does not include acquiring or retaining an ownership interest in a covered fund by a banking entity:

(i) Acting solely as agent, broker, or custodian, so long as;

(A) The activity is conducted for the account of, or on behalf of, a customer; and

(B) The banking entity and its affiliates do not have or retain beneficial ownership of such ownership interest;

(ii) Through a deferred compensation, stock-bonus, profit-sharing, or pension plan of the banking entity (or an affiliate thereof) that is established and administered in accordance with the law of the United States or a foreign sovereign, if the ownership interest is held or controlled directly or indirectly by the banking entity as trustee for the benefit of persons who are or were employees of the banking entity (or an affiliate thereof);

(iii) In the ordinary course of collecting a debt previously contracted in good faith, provided that the banking entity divests the ownership interest as soon as practicable, and in no event may the banking entity retain such ownership interest for longer than such period permitted by the OCC; or

(iv) On behalf of customers as trustee or in a similar fiduciary capacity for a customer that is not a covered fund, so long as:

(A) The activity is conducted for the account of, or on behalf of, the customer; and

(B) The banking entity and its affiliates do not have or retain beneficial ownership of such ownership interest.

(b) *Definition of covered fund.* (1) Except as provided in paragraph (c) of this section, covered fund means:

(i) An issuer that would be an investment company, as defined in the Investment Company Act of 1940 (15 U.S.C. 80a–1 *et seq.*), *but for* section 3(c)(1) or 3(c)(7) of that Act (15 U.S.C. 80a–3(c)(1) or (7));

(ii) Any commodity pool under section 1a(10) of the Commodity Exchange Act (7 U.S.C. 1a(10)) for which:

(A) The commodity pool operator has claimed an exemption under 17 CFR 4.7; or

(B)(*1*) A commodity pool operator is registered with the CFTC as a commodity pool operator in connection with the operation of the commodity pool;

(*2*) Substantially all participation units of the commodity pool are owned by qualified eligible persons under 17 CFR 4.7(a)(2) and (3); and

(*3*) Participation units of the commodity pool have not been publicly offered to persons who are not qualified eligible persons under 17 CFR 4.7(a)(2) and (3); or

(iii) For any banking entity that is, or is controlled directly or indirectly by a banking entity that is, located in or organized under the laws of the United States or of any State, an entity that:

(A) Is organized or established outside the United States and the ownership interests of which are offered and sold solely outside the United States;

(B) Is, or holds itself out as being, an entity or arrangement that raises money from investors primarily for the purpose of investing in securities for resale or other disposition or otherwise trading in securities; and

(C)(*1*) Has as its sponsor that banking entity (or an affiliate thereof); or

(*2*) Has issued an ownership interest that is owned directly or indirectly by that banking entity (or an affiliate thereof).

(2) An issuer shall not be deemed to be a covered fund under paragraph (b)(1)(iii) of this section if, were the issuer subject to U.S. securities laws, the issuer could rely on an exclusion or exemption from the definition of "investment company" under the Investment Company Act of 1940 (15 U.S.C. 80a–1 *et seq.*) other than the exclusions contained in section 3(c)(1) and 3(c)(7) of that Act.

(3) For purposes of paragraph (b)(1)(iii) of this section, a U.S. branch, agency, or subsidiary of a foreign banking entity is located in the United States; however, the foreign bank that operates or controls that branch, agency, or subsidiary is not considered to be located in the United States solely by virtue of operating or controlling the U.S. branch, agency, or subsidiary.

(c) Notwithstanding paragraph (b) of this section, unless the appropriate Federal banking agencies, the SEC, and the CFTC jointly determine otherwise, a covered fund does not include:

(1) *Foreign public funds.* (i) Subject to paragraphs (ii) and (iii) below, an issuer that:

(A) Is organized or established outside of the United States;

(B) Is authorized to offer and sell ownership interests to retail investors in the issuer's home jurisdiction; and

(C) Sells ownership interests predominantly through one or more public offerings outside of the United States.

(ii) With respect to a banking entity that is, or is controlled directly or indirectly by a banking entity that is, located in or organized under the laws of the United States or of any State and any issuer for which such banking entity acts as sponsor, the sponsoring banking entity may not rely on the exemption in paragraph (c)(1)(i) of this section for such issuer unless ownership interests in the issuer are sold predominantly to persons other than:

(A) Such sponsoring banking entity;

(B) Such issuer;

(C) Affiliates of such sponsoring banking entity or such issuer; and

(D) Directors and employees of such entities.

(iii) For purposes of paragraph (c)(1)(i)(C) of this section, the term "public offering" means a distribution (as defined in § 44.4(a)(3) of subpart B) of securities in any jurisdiction outside the United States to investors, including retail investors, provided that:

(A) The distribution complies with all applicable requirements in the jurisdiction in which such distribution is being made;

(B) The distribution does not restrict availability to investors having a minimum level of net worth or net investment assets; and

(C) The issuer has filed or submitted, with the appropriate regulatory authority in such jurisdiction, offering disclosure documents that are publicly available.

(2) *Wholly-owned subsidiaries.* An entity, all of the outstanding ownership interests of which are owned directly or indirectly by the banking entity (or an affiliate thereof), except that:

(i) Up to five percent of the entity's outstanding ownership interests, less any amounts outstanding under paragraph (c)(2)(ii) of this section, may be held by employees or directors of the banking entity or such affiliate (including former employees or directors if their ownership interest was acquired while employed by or in the service of the banking entity); and

(ii) Up to 0.5 percent of the entity's outstanding ownership interests may be held by a third party if the ownership interest is acquired or retained by the third party for the purpose of establishing corporate separateness or addressing bankruptcy, insolvency, or similar concerns.

(3) *Joint ventures.* A joint venture between a banking entity or any of its affiliates and one or more unaffiliated persons, provided that the joint venture:

(i) Is comprised of no more than 10 unaffiliated co-venturers;

(ii) Is in the business of engaging in activities that are permissible for the banking entity or affiliate, other than investing in securities for resale or other disposition; and

(iii) Is not, and does not hold itself out as being, an entity or arrangement that raises money from investors primarily for the purpose of investing in securities for resale or other disposition or otherwise trading in securities.

(4) *Acquisition vehicles.* An issuer:

(i) Formed solely for the purpose of engaging in a *bona fide* merger or acquisition transaction; and

(ii) That exists only for such period as necessary to effectuate the transaction.

(5) *Foreign pension or retirement funds.* A plan, fund, or program providing pension, retirement, or similar benefits that is:

(i) Organized and administered outside the United States;

(ii) A broad-based plan for employees or citizens that is subject to regulation as a pension, retirement, or similar plan under the laws of the jurisdiction in which the plan, fund, or program is organized and administered; and

(iii) Established for the benefit of citizens or residents of one or more foreign sovereigns or any political subdivision thereof.

(6) *Insurance company separate accounts.* A separate account, provided that no banking entity other than the insurance company participates in the account's profits and losses.

(7) *Bank owned life insurance.* A separate account that is used solely for the purpose of allowing one or more banking entities to purchase a life insurance policy for which the banking entity or entities is beneficiary, provided that no banking entity that purchases the policy:

(i) Controls the investment decisions regarding the underlying assets or holdings of the separate account; or

(ii) Participates in the profits and losses of the separate account other than in compliance with applicable supervisory guidance regarding bank owned life insurance.

(8) *Loan securitizations*—(i) *Scope.* An issuing entity for asset-backed securities that satisfies all the conditions of this paragraph (c)(8) and the assets or holdings of which are comprised solely of:

(A) Loans as defined in §44.2(s) of subpart A;

(B) Rights or other assets designed to assure the servicing or timely distribution of proceeds to holders of such securities and rights or other assets that are related or incidental to purchasing or otherwise acquiring and holding the loans, provided that each asset meets the requirements of paragraph (c)(8)(iii) of this section;

(C) Interest rate or foreign exchange derivatives that meet the requirements of paragraph (c)(8)(iv) of this section; and

(D) Special units of beneficial interest and collateral certificates that meet the requirements of paragraph (c)(8)(v) of this section.

(ii) *Impermissible assets.* For purposes of this paragraph (c)(8), the assets or holdings of the issuing entity shall not include any of the following:

(A) A security, including an asset-backed security, or an interest in an equity or debt security other than as permitted in paragraph (c)(8)(iii) of this section;

(B) A derivative, other than a derivative that meets the requirements of paragraph (c)(8)(iv) of this section; or

(C) A commodity forward contract.

(iii) *Permitted securities.* Notwithstanding paragraph (c)(8)(ii)(A) of this section, the issuing entity may hold securities if those securities are:

(A) Cash equivalents for purposes of the rights and assets in paragraph (c)(8)(i)(B) of this section; or

(B) Securities received in lieu of debts previously contracted with respect to the loans supporting the asset-backed securities.

(iv) *Derivatives*. The holdings of derivatives by the issuing entity shall be limited to interest rate or foreign exchange derivatives that satisfy all of the following conditions:

(A) The written terms of the derivative directly relate to the loans, the asset-backed securities, or the contractual rights of other assets described in paragraph (c)(8)(i)(B) of this section; and

(B) The derivatives reduce the interest rate and/or foreign exchange risks related to the loans, the asset-backed securities, or the contractual rights or other assets described in paragraph (c)(8)(i)(B) of this section.

(v) *Special units of beneficial interest and collateral certificates*. The assets or holdings of the issuing entity may include collateral certificates and special units of beneficial interest issued by a special purpose vehicle, provided that:

(A) The special purpose vehicle that issues the special unit of beneficial interest or collateral certificate meets the requirements in this paragraph (c)(8);

(B) The special unit of beneficial interest or collateral certificate is used for the sole purpose of transferring to the issuing entity for the loan securitization the economic risks and benefits of the assets that are permissible for loan securitizations under this paragraph (c)(8) and does not directly or indirectly transfer any interest in any other economic or financial exposure;

(C) The special unit of beneficial interest or collateral certificate is created solely to satisfy legal requirements or otherwise facilitate the structuring of the loan securitization; and

(D) The special purpose vehicle that issues the special unit of beneficial interest or collateral certificate and the issuing entity are established under the direction of the same entity that initiated the loan securitization.

(9) *Qualifying asset-backed commercial paper conduits*. (i) An issuing entity for asset-backed commercial paper that satisfies all of the following requirements:

(A) The asset-backed commercial paper conduit holds only:

(*1*) Loans and other assets permissible for a loan securitization under paragraph (c)(8)(i) of this section; and

(*2*) Asset-backed securities supported solely by assets that are permissible for loan securitizations under paragraph (c)(8)(i) of this section and acquired by the asset-backed commercial paper conduit as part of an initial issuance either directly from the issuing entity of the asset-backed securities or directly from an underwriter in the distribution of the asset-backed securities;

(B) The asset-backed commercial paper conduit issues only asset-backed securities, comprised of a residual interest and securities with a legal maturity of 397 days or less; and

(C) A regulated liquidity provider has entered into a legally binding commitment to provide full and unconditional liquidity coverage with respect to all of the outstanding asset-backed securities issued by the asset-backed commercial paper conduit (other than any residual interest) in the event that funds are required to redeem maturing asset-backed securities.

(ii) For purposes of this paragraph (c)(9), a regulated liquidity provider means:

(A) A depository institution, as defined in section 3(c) of the Federal Deposit Insurance Act (12 U.S.C. 1813(c));

(B) A bank holding company, as defined in section 2(a) of the Bank Holding Company Act of 1956 (12 U.S.C. 1841(a)), or a subsidiary thereof;

(C) A savings and loan holding company, as defined in section 10a of the Home Owners' Loan Act (12 U.S.C. 1467a), provided all or substantially all of the holding company's activities are permissible for a financial holding company under section 4(k) of the Bank Holding Company Act of 1956 (12 U.S.C. 1843(k)), or a subsidiary thereof;

(D) A foreign bank whose home country supervisor, as defined in § 211.21(q) of the Board's Regulation K (12 CFR

211.21(q)), has adopted capital standards consistent with the Capital Accord for the Basel Committee on banking Supervision, as amended, and that is subject to such standards, or a subsidiary thereof; or

(E) The United States or a foreign sovereign.

(10) *Qualifying covered bonds*—(i) *Scope*. An entity owning or holding a dynamic or fixed pool of loans or other assets as provided in paragraph (c)(8) of this section for the benefit of the holders of covered bonds, provided that the assets in the pool are comprised solely of assets that meet the conditions in paragraph (c)(8)(i) of this section.

(ii) *Covered bond*. For purposes of this paragraph (c)(10), a covered bond means:

(A) A debt obligation issued by an entity that meets the definition of foreign banking organization, the payment obligations of which are fully and unconditionally guaranteed by an entity that meets the conditions set forth in paragraph (c)(10)(i) of this section; or

(B) A debt obligation of an entity that meets the conditions set forth in paragraph (c)(10)(i) of this section, provided that the payment obligations are fully and unconditionally guaranteed by an entity that meets the definition of foreign banking organization and the entity is a wholly-owned subsidiary, as defined in paragraph (c)(2) of this section, of such foreign banking organization.

(11) *SBICs and public welfare investment funds*. An issuer:

(i) That is a small business investment company, as defined in section 103(3) of the Small Business Investment Act of 1958 (15 U.S.C. 662), or that has received from the Small Business Administration notice to proceed to qualify for a license as a small business investment company, which notice or license has not been revoked; or

(ii) The business of which is to make investments that are:

(A) Designed primarily to promote the public welfare, of the type permitted under paragraph (11) of section 5136 of the Revised Statutes of the United States (12 U.S.C. 24), including the welfare of low- and moderate-income communities or families (such as providing housing, services, or jobs); or

(B) Qualified rehabilitation expenditures with respect to a qualified rehabilitated building or certified historic structure, as such terms are defined in section 47 of the Internal Revenue Code of 1986 or a similar State historic tax credit program.

(12) *Registered investment companies and excluded entities*. An issuer:

(i) That is registered as an investment company under section 8 of the Investment Company Act of 1940 (15 U.S.C. 80a–8), or that is formed and operated pursuant to a written plan to become a registered investment company as described in § 44.20(e)(3) of subpart D and that complies with the requirements of section 18 of the Investment Company Act of 1940 (15 U.S.C. 80a–18);

(ii) That may rely on an exclusion or exemption from the definition of "investment company" under the Investment Company Act of 1940 (15 U.S.C. 80a–1 *et seq.*) other than the exclusions contained in section 3(c)(1) and 3(c)(7) of that Act; or

(iii) That has elected to be regulated as a business development company pursuant to section 54(a) of that Act (15 U.S.C. 80a–53) and has not withdrawn its election, or that is formed and operated pursuant to a written plan to become a business development company as described in § 44.20(e)(3) of subpart D and that complies with the requirements of section 61 of the Investment Company Act of 1940 (15 U.S.C. 80a–60).

(13) *Issuers in conjunction with the FDIC's receivership or conservatorship operations*. An issuer that is an entity formed by or on behalf of the FDIC for the purpose of facilitating the disposal of assets acquired in the FDIC's capacity as conservator or receiver under the Federal Deposit Insurance Act or Title II of the Dodd-Frank Wall Street Reform and Consumer Protection Act.

(14) *Other excluded issuers*. (i) Any issuer that the appropriate Federal banking agencies, the SEC, and the CFTC jointly determine the exclusion of which is consistent with the purposes of section 13 of the BHC Act.

(ii) A determination made under paragraph (c)(14)(i) of this section will be promptly made public.

(d) *Definition of other terms related to covered funds.* For purposes of this subpart:

(1) *Applicable accounting standards* means U.S. generally accepted accounting principles, or such other accounting standards applicable to a banking entity that the OCC determines are appropriate and that the banking entity uses in the ordinary course of its business in preparing its consolidated financial statements.

(2) *Asset-backed security* has the meaning specified in Section 3(a)(79) of the Exchange Act (15 U.S.C. 78c(a)(79).

(3) *Director* has the same meaning as provided in section 215.2(d)(1) of the Board's Regulation O (12 CFR 215.2(d)(1)).

(4) *Issuer* has the same meaning as in section 2(a)(22) of the Investment Company Act of 1940 (15 U.S.C. 80a–2(a)(22)).

(5) *Issuing entity* means with respect to asset-backed securities the special purpose vehicle that owns or holds the pool assets underlying asset-backed securities and in whose name the asset-backed securities supported or serviced by the pool assets are issued.

(6) *Ownership interest*—(i) *Ownership interest* means any equity, partnership, or other similar interest. An "other similar interest" means an interest that:

(A) Has the right to participate in the selection or removal of a general partner, managing member, member of the board of directors or trustees, investment manager, investment adviser, or commodity trading advisor of the covered fund (excluding the rights of a creditor to exercise remedies upon the occurrence of an event of default or an acceleration event);

(B) Has the right under the terms of the interest to receive a share of the income, gains or profits of the covered fund;

(C) Has the right to receive the underlying assets of the covered fund after all other interests have been redeemed and/or paid in full (excluding the rights of a creditor to exercise remedies upon the occurrence of an event of default or an acceleration event);

(D) Has the right to receive all or a portion of excess spread (the positive difference, if any, between the aggregate interest payments received from the underlying assets of the covered fund and the aggregate interest paid to the holders of other outstanding interests);

(E) Provides under the terms of the interest that the amounts payable by the covered fund with respect to the interest could be reduced based on losses arising from the underlying assets of the covered fund, such as allocation of losses, write-downs or charge-offs of the outstanding principal balance, or reductions in the amount of interest due and payable on the interest;

(F) Receives income on a pass-through basis from the covered fund, or has a rate of return that is determined by reference to the performance of the underlying assets of the covered fund; or

(G) Any synthetic right to have, receive, or be allocated any of the rights in paragraphs (d)(6)(i)(A) through (F) of this section.

(ii) *Ownership interest* does not include: *Restricted profit interest.* An interest held by an entity (or an employee or former employee thereof) in a covered fund for which the entity (or employee thereof) serves as investment manager, investment adviser, commodity trading advisor, or other service provider so long as:

(A) The sole purpose and effect of the interest is to allow the entity (or employee or former employee thereof) to share in the profits of the covered fund as performance compensation for the investment management, investment advisory, commodity trading advisory, or other services provided to the covered fund by the entity (or employee or former employee thereof), provided that the entity (or employee or former employee thereof) may be obligated under the terms of such interest to return profits previously received;

(B) All such profit, once allocated, is distributed to the entity (or employee or former employee thereof) promptly after being earned or, if not so distributed, is retained by the covered fund for the sole purpose of establishing a reserve amount to satisfy contractual obligations with respect to subsequent losses of the covered fund and such undistributed profit of the entity (or employee or former employee thereof) does not share in the subsequent investment gains of the covered fund;

(C) Any amounts invested in the covered fund, including any amounts paid by the entity (or employee or former employee thereof) in connection with obtaining the restricted profit interest, are within the limits of § 44.12 of this subpart; and

(D) The interest is not transferable by the entity (or employee or former employee thereof) except to an affiliate thereof (or an employee of the banking entity or affiliate), to immediate family members, or through the intestacy, of the employee or former employee, or in connection with a sale of the business that gave rise to the restricted profit interest by the entity (or employee or former employee thereof) to an unaffiliated party that provides investment management, investment advisory, commodity trading advisory, or other services to the fund.

(7) *Prime brokerage transaction* means any transaction that would be a covered transaction, as defined in section 23A(b)(7) of the Federal Reserve Act (12 U.S.C. 371c(b)(7)), that is provided in connection with custody, clearance and settlement, securities borrowing or lending services, trade execution, financing, or data, operational, and administrative support.

(8) *Resident of the United States* means a person that is a "U.S. person" as defined in rule 902(k) of the SEC's Regulation S (17 CFR 230.902(k)).

(9) *Sponsor* means, with respect to a covered fund:

(i) To serve as a general partner, managing member, or trustee of a covered fund, or to serve as a commodity pool operator with respect to a covered fund as defined in (b)(1)(ii) of this section;

(ii) In any manner to select or to control (or to have employees, officers, or directors, or agents who constitute) a majority of the directors, trustees, or management of a covered fund; or

(iii) To share with a covered fund, for corporate, marketing, promotional, or other purposes, the same name or a variation of the same name.

(10) *Trustee.* (i) For purposes of paragraph (d)(9) of this section and § 44.11 of subpart C, a trustee does not include:

(A) A trustee that does not exercise investment discretion with respect to a covered fund, including a trustee that is subject to the direction of an unaffiliated named fiduciary who is not a trustee pursuant to section 403(a)(1) of the Employee's Retirement Income Security Act (29 U.S.C. 1103(a)(1)); or

(B) A trustee that is subject to fiduciary standards imposed under foreign law that are substantially equivalent to those described in paragraph (d)(10)(i)(A) of this section;

(ii) Any entity that directs a person described in paragraph (d)(10)(i) of this section, or that possesses authority and discretion to manage and control the investment decisions of a covered fund for which such person serves as trustee, shall be considered to be a trustee of such covered fund.

§ 44.11 Permitted organizing and offering, underwriting, and market making with respect to a covered fund.

(a) *Organizing and offering a covered fund in general.* Notwithstanding § 44.10(a) of this subpart, a banking entity is not prohibited from acquiring or retaining an ownership interest in, or acting as sponsor to, a covered fund in connection with, directly or indirectly, organizing and offering a covered fund, including serving as a general partner, managing member, trustee, or commodity pool operator of the covered fund and in any manner selecting or controlling (or having employees, officers, directors, or agents who constitute) a majority of the directors, trustees, or management of the covered fund, including any necessary expenses for the foregoing, only if:

(1) The banking entity (or an affiliate thereof) provides *bona fide* trust, fiduciary, investment advisory, or commodity trading advisory services;

(2) The covered fund is organized and offered only in connection with the provision of *bona fide* trust, fiduciary, investment advisory, or commodity trading advisory services and only to persons that are customers of such services of the banking entity (or an affiliate thereof), pursuant to a written plan or similar documentation outlining how the banking entity or such affiliate intends to provide advisory or similar services to its customers

through organizing and offering such fund;

(3) The banking entity and its affiliates do not acquire or retain an ownership interest in the covered fund except as permitted under § 44.12 of this subpart;

(4) The banking entity and its affiliates comply with the requirements of § 44.14 of this subpart;

(5) The banking entity and its affiliates do not, directly or indirectly, guarantee, assume, or otherwise insure the obligations or performance of the covered fund or of any covered fund in which such covered fund invests;

(6) The covered fund, for corporate, marketing, promotional, or other purposes:

(i) Does not share the same name or a variation of the same name with the banking entity (or an affiliate thereof); and

(ii) Does not use the word "bank" in its name;

(7) No director or employee of the banking entity (or an affiliate thereof) takes or retains an ownership interest in the covered fund, except for any director or employee of the banking entity or such affiliate who is directly engaged in providing investment advisory, commodity trading advisory, or other services to the covered fund at the time the director or employee takes the ownership interest; and

(8) The banking entity:

(i) Clearly and conspicuously discloses, in writing, to any prospective and actual investor in the covered fund (such as through disclosure in the covered fund's offering documents):

(A) That "any losses in [such covered fund] will be borne solely by investors in [the covered fund] and not by [the banking entity] or its affiliates; therefore, [the banking entity's] losses in [such covered fund] will be limited to losses attributable to the ownership interests in the covered fund held by [the banking entity] and any affiliate in its capacity as investor in the [covered fund] or as beneficiary of a restricted profit interest held by [the banking entity] or any affiliate";

(B) That such investor should read the fund offering documents before investing in the covered fund;

(C) That the "ownership interests in the covered fund are not insured by the FDIC, and are not deposits, obligations of, or endorsed or guaranteed in any way, by any banking entity" (unless that happens to be the case); and

(D) The role of the banking entity and its affiliates and employees in sponsoring or providing any services to the covered fund; and

(ii) Complies with any additional rules of the appropriate Federal banking agencies, the SEC, or the CFTC, as provided in section 13(b)(2) of the BHC Act, designed to ensure that losses in such covered fund are borne solely by investors in the covered fund and not by the covered banking entity and its affiliates.

(b) *Organizing and offering an issuing entity of asset-backed securities.* (1) Notwithstanding § 44.10(a) of this subpart, a banking entity is not prohibited from acquiring or retaining an ownership interest in, or acting as sponsor to, a covered fund that is an issuing entity of asset-backed securities in connection with, directly or indirectly, organizing and offering that issuing entity, so long as the banking entity and its affiliates comply with all of the requirements of paragraph (a)(3) through (8) of this section.

(2) For purposes of this paragraph (b), organizing and offering a covered fund that is an issuing entity of asset-backed securities means acting as the securitizer, as that term is used in section 15G(a)(3) of the Exchange Act (15 U.S.C. 78*o*–11(a)(3)) of the issuing entity, or acquiring or retaining an ownership interest in the issuing entity as required by section 15G of that Act (15 U.S.C.78*o*–11) and the implementing regulations issued thereunder.

(c) *Underwriting and market making in ownership interests of a covered fund.* The prohibition contained in § 44.10(a) of this subpart does not apply to a banking entity's underwriting activities or market making-related activities involving a covered fund so long as:

(1) Those activities are conducted in accordance with the requirements of § 44.4(a) or § 44.4(b) of subpart B, respectively;

(2) With respect to any banking entity (or any affiliate thereof) that: Acts

as a sponsor, investment adviser or commodity trading advisor to a particular covered fund or otherwise acquires and retains an ownership interest in such covered fund in reliance on paragraph (a) of this section; acquires and retains an ownership interest in such covered fund and is either a securitizer, as that term is used in section 15G(a)(3) of the Exchange Act (15 U.S.C. 78o–11(a)(3)), or is acquiring and retaining an ownership interest in such covered fund in compliance with section 15G of that Act (15 U.S.C.78o–11) and the implementing regulations issued thereunder each as permitted by paragraph (b) of this section; or, directly or indirectly, guarantees, assumes, or otherwise insures the obligations or performance of the covered fund or of any covered fund in which such fund invests, then in each such case any ownership interests acquired or retained by the banking entity and its affiliates in connection with underwriting and market making related activities for that particular covered fund are included in the calculation of ownership interests permitted to be held by the banking entity and its affiliates under the limitations of §44.12(a)(2)(ii) and §44.12(d) of this subpart; and

(3) With respect to any banking entity, the aggregate value of all ownership interests of the banking entity and its affiliates in all covered funds acquired and retained under §44.11 of this subpart, including all covered funds in which the banking entity holds an ownership interest in connection with underwriting and market making related activities permitted under this paragraph (c), are included in the calculation of all ownership interests under §44.12(a)(2)(iii) and §44.12(d) of this subpart.

§44.12 Permitted investment in a covered fund.

(a) *Authority and limitations on permitted investments in covered funds.* (1) Notwithstanding the prohibition contained in §44.10(a) of this subpart, a banking entity may acquire and retain an ownership interest in a covered fund that the banking entity or an affiliate thereof organizes and offers pursuant to §44.11, for the purposes of:

(i) *Establishment.* Establishing the fund and providing the fund with sufficient initial equity for investment to permit the fund to attract unaffiliated investors, subject to the limits contained in paragraphs (a)(2)(i) and (iii) of this section; or

(ii) *De minimis investment.* Making and retaining an investment in the covered fund subject to the limits contained in paragraphs (a)(2)(ii) and (iii) of this section.

(2) *Investment limits*—(i) *Seeding period.* With respect to an investment in any covered fund made or held pursuant to paragraph (a)(1)(i) of this section, the banking entity and its affiliates:

(A) Must actively seek unaffiliated investors to reduce, through redemption, sale, dilution, or other methods, the aggregate amount of all ownership interests of the banking entity in the covered fund to the amount permitted in paragraph (a)(2)(i)(B) of this section; and

(B) Must, no later than 1 year after the date of establishment of the fund (or such longer period as may be provided by the Board pursuant to paragraph (e) of this section), conform its ownership interest in the covered fund to the limits in paragraph (a)(2)(ii) of this section;

(ii) *Per-fund limits.* (A) Except as provided in paragraph (a)(2)(ii)(B) of this section, an investment by a banking entity and its affiliates in any covered fund made or held pursuant to paragraph (a)(1)(ii) of this section may not exceed 3 percent of the total number or value of the outstanding ownership interests of the fund.

(B) An investment by a banking entity and its affiliates in a covered fund that is an issuing entity of asset-backed securities may not exceed 3 percent of the total fair market value of the ownership interests of the fund measured in accordance with paragraph (b)(3) of this section, unless a greater percentage is retained by the banking entity and its affiliates in compliance with the requirements of section 15G of the Exchange Act (15 U.S.C. 78*o*–11) and the implementing regulations issued thereunder, in which case the investment by the banking entity and its affiliates in the covered fund may not exceed the amount, number, or value of ownership interests of the fund required under section 15G of the Exchange Act and the implementing regulations issued thereunder.

(iii) *Aggregate limit.* The aggregate value of all ownership interests of the banking entity and its affiliates in all covered funds acquired or retained under this section may not exceed 3 percent of the tier 1 capital of the banking entity, as provided under paragraph (c) of this section, and shall be calculated as of the last day of each calendar quarter.

(iv) *Date of establishment.* For purposes of this section, the date of establishment of a covered fund shall be:

(A) *In general.* The date on which the investment adviser or similar entity to the covered fund begins making investments pursuant to the written investment strategy for the fund;

(B) *Issuing entities of asset-backed securities.* In the case of an issuing entity of asset-backed securities, the date on which the assets are initially transferred into the issuing entity of asset-backed securities.

(b) *Rules of construction*—(1) *Attribution of ownership interests to a covered banking entity.* (i) For purposes of paragraph (a)(2) of this section, the amount and value of a banking entity's permitted investment in any single covered fund shall include any ownership interest held under § 44.12 directly by the banking entity, including any affiliate of the banking entity.

(ii) *Treatment of registered investment companies, SEC-regulated business development companies and foreign public funds.* For purposes of paragraph (b)(1)(i) of this section, a registered investment company, SEC-regulated business development companies or foreign public fund as described in § 44.10(c)(1) of this subpart will not be considered to be an affiliate of the banking entity so long as the banking entity:

(A) Does not own, control, or hold with the power to vote 25 percent or more of the voting shares of the company or fund; and

(B) Provides investment advisory, commodity trading advisory, administrative, and other services to the company or fund in compliance with the limitations under applicable regulation, order, or other authority.

(iii) *Covered funds.* For purposes of paragraph (b)(1)(i) of this section, a covered fund will not be considered to be an affiliate of a banking entity so long as the covered fund is held in compliance with the requirements of this subpart.

(iv) *Treatment of employee and director investments financed by the banking entity.* For purposes of paragraph (b)(1)(i) of this section, an investment by a director or employee of a banking entity who acquires an ownership interest in his or her personal capacity in a covered fund sponsored by the banking entity will be attributed to the banking entity if the banking entity, directly or indirectly, extends financing for the purpose of enabling the director or employee to acquire the ownership interest in the fund and the financing is used to acquire such ownership interest in the covered fund.

(2) *Calculation of permitted ownership interests in a single covered fund.* Except as provided in paragraph (b)(3) or (4), for purposes of determining whether an investment in a single covered fund complies with the restrictions on ownership interests under paragraphs (a)(2)(i)(B) and (a)(2)(ii)(A) of this section:

(i) The aggregate number of the outstanding ownership interests held by the banking entity shall be the total number of ownership interests held under this section by the banking entity in a covered fund divided by the total number of ownership interests held by all entities in that covered fund, as of the last day of each calendar quarter (both measured without regard to committed funds not yet called for investment);

(ii) The aggregate value of the outstanding ownership interests held by the banking entity shall be the aggregate fair market value of all investments in and capital contributions made to the covered fund by the banking entity, divided by the value of all investments in and capital contributions made to that covered fund by all entities, as of the last day of each calendar quarter (all measured without regard to committed funds not yet called for investment). If fair market value cannot be determined, then the value shall be the historical cost basis of all investments in and contributions made by the banking entity to the covered fund;

(iii) For purposes of the calculation under paragraph (b)(2)(ii) of this section, once a valuation methodology is chosen, the banking entity must calculate the value of its investment and the investments of all others in the covered fund in the same manner and according to the same standards.

(3) *Issuing entities of asset-backed securities.* In the case of an ownership interest in an issuing entity of asset-backed securities, for purposes of determining whether an investment in a single covered fund complies with the restrictions on ownership interests under paragraphs (a)(2)(i)(B) and (a)(2)(ii)(B) of this section:

(i) For securitizations subject to the requirements of section 15G of the Exchange Act (15 U.S.C. 78o–11), the calculations shall be made as of the date and according to the valuation methodology applicable pursuant to the requirements of section 15G of the Exchange Act (15 U.S.C. 78o–11) and the implementing regulations issued thereunder; or

(ii) For securitization transactions completed prior to the compliance date of such implementing regulations (or as to which such implementing regulations do not apply), the calculations shall be made as of the date of establishment as defined in paragraph (a)(2)(iv)(B) of this section or such earlier date on which the transferred assets have been valued for purposes of transfer to the covered fund, and thereafter only upon the date on which additional securities of the issuing entity of asset-backed securities are priced for purposes of the sales of ownership interests to unaffiliated investors.

(iii) For securitization transactions completed prior to the compliance date of such implementing regulations (or as to which such implementing regulations do not apply), the aggregate value of the outstanding ownership interests in the covered fund shall be the fair market value of the assets transferred to the issuing entity of the securitization and any other assets otherwise held by the issuing entity at such time, determined in a manner that is consistent with its determination of the fair market value of those assets for financial statement purposes.

(iv) For purposes of the calculation under paragraph (b)(3)(iii) of this section, the valuation methodology used to calculate the fair market value of the ownership interests must be the same for both the ownership interests held by a banking entity and the ownership interests held by all others in the covered fund in the same manner and according to the same standards.

(4) *Multi-tier fund investments*—(i) *Master-feeder fund investments.* If the principal investment strategy of a covered fund (the "feeder fund") is to invest substantially all of its assets in another single covered fund (the "master fund"), then for purposes of the investment limitations in paragraphs (a)(2)(i)(B) and (a)(2)(ii) of this section, the banking entity's permitted investment in such funds shall be measured only by reference to the value of the master fund. The banking entity's permitted investment in the master fund shall include any investment by the banking entity in the master fund, as well as the banking entity's pro-rata share of any ownership interest of the master fund that is held through the feeder fund; and

(ii) *Fund-of-funds investments.* If a banking entity organizes and offers a covered fund pursuant to § 44.11 of this subpart for the purpose of investing in other covered funds (a "fund of funds") and that fund of funds itself invests in another covered fund that the banking entity is permitted to own, then the banking entity's permitted investment in that other fund shall include any investment by the banking entity in that other fund, as well as the banking entity's pro-rata share of any ownership interest of the fund that is held through the fund of funds. The investment of the banking entity may not represent more than 3 percent of the amount or value of any single covered fund.

(c) *Aggregate permitted investments in all covered funds.* (1) For purposes of paragraph (a)(2)(iii) of this section, the aggregate value of all ownership interests held by a banking entity shall be the sum of all amounts paid or contributed by the banking entity in connection with acquiring or retaining an ownership interest in covered funds (together with any amounts paid by the entity (or employee thereof) in connection with obtaining a restricted profit interest under § 44.10(d)(6)(ii) of this subpart), on a historical cost basis.

(2) *Calculation of tier 1 capital.* For purposes of paragraph (a)(2)(iii) of this section:

(i) *Entities that are required to hold and report tier 1 capital.* If a banking entity is required to calculate and report tier 1 capital, the banking entity's tier 1 capital shall be equal to the amount of tier 1 capital of the banking entity as of the last day of the most recent calendar quarter, as reported to its primary financial regulatory agency; and

(ii) If a banking entity is not required to calculate and report tier 1 capital, the banking entity's tier 1 capital shall be determined to be equal to:

(A) In the case of a banking entity that is controlled, directly or indirectly, by a depository institution that calculates and reports tier 1 capital, be equal to the amount of tier 1 capital reported by such controlling depository institution in the manner described in paragraph (c)(2)(i) of this section;

(B) In the case of a banking entity that is not controlled, directly or indirectly, by a depository institution that calculates and reports tier 1 capital:

(1) Bank holding company subsidiaries. If the banking entity is a subsidiary of a bank holding company or company that is treated as a bank holding company, be equal to the amount of tier 1 capital reported by the top-tier affiliate of such covered banking entity that calculates and reports tier 1 capital in the manner described in paragraph (c)(2)(i) of this section; and

(2) Other holding companies and any subsidiary or affiliate thereof. If the banking entity is not a subsidiary of a bank holding company or a company that is treated as a bank holding company, be equal to the total amount of shareholders' equity of the top-tier affiliate within such organization as of the last day of the most recent calendar quarter that has ended, as determined under applicable accounting standards.

(iii) *Treatment of foreign banking entities*—(A) *Foreign banking entities.* Except as provided in paragraph (c)(2)(iii)(B) of this section, with respect to a banking entity that is not itself, and is not controlled directly or indirectly by, a banking entity that is located or organized under the laws of the United States or of any State, the tier 1 capital of the banking entity shall be the consolidated tier 1 capital of the entity as calculated under applicable home country standards.

(B) *U.S. affiliates of foreign banking entities.* With respect to a banking entity that is located or organized under the laws of the United States or of any State and is controlled by a foreign banking entity identified under paragraph (c)(2)(iii)(A) of this section, the banking entity's tier 1 capital shall be as calculated under paragraphs (c)(2)(i) or (ii) of this section.

(d) *Capital treatment for a permitted investment in a covered fund.* For purposes of calculating compliance with the applicable regulatory capital requirements, a banking entity shall deduct from the banking entity's tier 1 capital (as determined under paragraph (c)(2) of this section) the greater of:

(1) The sum of all amounts paid or contributed by the banking entity in connection with acquiring or retaining an ownership interest (together with any amounts paid by the entity (or employee thereof) in connection with obtaining a restricted profit interest under § 44.10(d)(6)(ii) of subpart C), on a historical cost basis, plus any earnings received; and

(2) The fair market value of the banking entity's ownership interests in the covered fund as determined under paragraph (b)(2)(ii) or (b)(3) of this section (together with any amounts paid by the entity (or employee thereof) in connection with obtaining a restricted profit interest under § 44.10(d)(6)(ii) of subpart C), if the banking entity accounts for the profits (or losses) of the fund investment in its financial statements.

(e) *Extension of time to divest an ownership interest.* (1) Upon application by a banking entity, the Board may extend the period under paragraph (a)(2)(i) of this section for up to 2 additional years if the Board finds that an extension would be consistent with safety and soundness and not detrimental to the public interest. An application for extension must:

(i) Be submitted to the Board at least 90 days prior to the expiration of the applicable time period;

(ii) Provide the reasons for application, including information that addresses the factors in paragraph (e)(2) of this section; and

(iii) Explain the banking entity's plan for reducing the permitted investment in a covered fund through redemption, sale, dilution or other methods as required in paragraph (a)(2) of this section.

(2) *Factors governing Board determinations.* In reviewing any application under paragraph (e)(1) of this section, the Board may consider all the facts and circumstances related to the permitted investment in a covered fund, including:

(i) Whether the investment would result, directly or indirectly, in a material exposure by the banking entity to high-risk assets or high-risk trading strategies;

(ii) The contractual terms governing the banking entity's interest in the covered fund;

(iii) The date on which the covered fund is expected to have attracted sufficient investments from investors unaffiliated with the banking entity to enable the banking entity to comply with the limitations in paragraph (a)(2)(i) of this section;

(iv) The total exposure of the covered banking entity to the investment and the risks that disposing of, or maintaining, the investment in the covered fund may pose to the banking entity and the financial stability of the United States;

(v) The cost to the banking entity of divesting or disposing of the investment within the applicable period;

(vi) Whether the investment or the divestiture or conformance of the investment would involve or result in a material conflict of interest between the banking entity and unaffiliated parties, including clients, customers or counterparties to which it owes a duty;

(vi) The banking entity's prior efforts to reduce through redemption, sale, dilution, or other methods its ownership interests in the covered fund, including activities related to the marketing of interests in such covered fund;

(viii) Market conditions; and

(ix) Any other factor that the Board believes appropriate.

(3) *Authority to impose restrictions on activities or investment during any extension period.* The Board may impose such conditions on any extension approved under paragraph (e)(1) of this section as the Board determines are necessary or appropriate to protect the safety and soundness of the banking entity or the financial stability of the United States, address material conflicts of interest or other unsound banking practices, or otherwise further the purposes of section 13 of the BHC Act and this part.

(4) *Consultation.* In the case of a banking entity that is primarily regulated by another Federal banking agency, the SEC, or the CFTC, the Board will consult with such agency prior to acting on an application by the banking entity for an extension under paragraph (e)(1) of this section.

§ 44.13 Other permitted covered fund activities and investments.

(a) *Permitted risk-mitigating hedging activities.* (1) The prohibition contained in § 44.10(a) of this subpart does not apply with respect to an ownership interest in a covered fund acquired or retained by a banking entity that is designed to demonstrably reduce or otherwise significantly mitigate the specific, identifiable risks to the banking entity in connection with a compensation arrangement with an employee of the banking entity or an affiliate thereof that directly provides investment advisory, commodity trading advisory or other services to the covered fund.

(2) *Requirements.* The risk-mitigating hedging activities of a banking entity are permitted under this paragraph (a) only if:

(i) The banking entity has established and implements, maintains and enforces an internal compliance program required by subpart D of this part that is reasonably designed to ensure the banking entity's compliance with the requirements of this section, including:

(A) Reasonably designed written policies and procedures; and

(B) Internal controls and ongoing monitoring, management, and authorization procedures, including relevant escalation procedures; and

(ii) The acquisition or retention of the ownership interest:

(A) Is made in accordance with the written policies, procedures and internal controls required under this section;

(B) At the inception of the hedge, is designed to reduce or otherwise significantly mitigate and demonstrably reduces or otherwise significantly mitigates one or more specific, identifiable risks arising in connection with the compensation arrangement with the employee that directly provides investment advisory, commodity trading advisory, or other services to the covered fund;

(C) Does not give rise, at the inception of the hedge, to any significant new or additional risk that is not itself hedged contemporaneously in accordance with this section; and

(D) Is subject to continuing review, monitoring and management by the banking entity.

(iii) The compensation arrangement relates solely to the covered fund in which the banking entity or any affiliate has acquired an ownership interest pursuant to this paragraph and such compensation arrangement provides that any losses incurred by the banking entity on such ownership interest will be offset by corresponding decreases in amounts payable under such compensation arrangement.

(b) *Certain permitted covered fund activities and investments outside of the United States.* (1) The prohibition contained in § 44.10(a) of this subpart does not apply to the acquisition or retention of any ownership interest in, or the sponsorship of, a covered fund by a banking entity only if:

(i) The banking entity is not organized or directly or indirectly controlled by a banking entity that is organized under the laws of the United States or of one or more States;

(ii) The activity or investment by the banking entity is pursuant to paragraph (9) or (13) of section 4(c) of the BHC Act;

(iii) No ownership interest in the covered fund is offered for sale or sold to a resident of the United States; and

(iv) The activity or investment occurs solely outside of the United States.

(2) An activity or investment by the banking entity is pursuant to paragraph (9) or (13) of section 4(c) of the BHC Act for purposes of paragraph (b)(1)(ii) of this section only if:

(i) The activity or investment is conducted in accordance with the requirements of this section; and

(ii)(A) With respect to a banking entity that is a foreign banking organization, the banking entity meets the qualifying foreign banking organization requirements of section 211.23(a), (c) or (e) of the Board's Regulation K (12 CFR 211.23(a), (c) or (e)), as applicable; or

(B) With respect to a banking entity that is not a foreign banking organization, the banking entity is not organized under the laws of the United States or of one or more States and the banking entity, on a fully-consolidated basis, meets at least two of the following requirements:

(*1*) Total assets of the banking entity held outside of the United States exceed total assets of the banking entity held in the United States;

(*2*) Total revenues derived from the business of the banking entity outside of the United States exceed total revenues derived from the business of the banking entity in the United States; or

(*3*) Total net income derived from the business of the banking entity outside of the United States exceeds total net income derived from the business of the banking entity in the United States.

(3) An ownership interest in a covered fund is not offered for sale or sold to a resident of the United States for purposes of paragraph (b)(1)(iii) of this section only if it is sold or has been sold pursuant to an offering that does not target residents of the United States.

(4) An activity or investment occurs solely outside of the United States for purposes of paragraph (b)(1)(iv) of this section only if:

(i) The banking entity acting as sponsor, or engaging as principal in the acquisition or retention of an ownership interest in the covered fund, is not itself, and is not controlled directly or indirectly by, a banking entity that is located in the United States or organized under the laws of the United States or of any State;

(ii) The banking entity (including relevant personnel) that makes the decision to acquire or retain the ownership interest or act as sponsor to the covered fund is not located in the United States or organized under the laws of the United States or of any State;

(iii) The investment or sponsorship, including any transaction arising from risk-mitigating hedging related to an ownership interest, is not accounted for as principal directly or indirectly on a consolidated basis by any branch or affiliate that is located in the United States or organized under the laws of the United States or of any State; and

(iv) No financing for the banking entity's ownership or sponsorship is provided, directly or indirectly, by any branch or affiliate that is located in the United States or organized under the laws of the United States or of any State.

(5) For purposes of this section, a U.S. branch, agency, or subsidiary of a foreign bank, or any subsidiary thereof, is located in the United States; however, a foreign bank of which that branch, agency, or subsidiary is a part is not considered to be located in the United States solely by virtue of operation of the U.S. branch, agency, or subsidiary.

(c) *Permitted covered fund interests and activities by a regulated insurance company.* The prohibition contained in §44.10(a) of this subpart does not apply to the acquisition or retention by an insurance company, or an affiliate thereof, of any ownership interest in, or the sponsorship of, a covered fund only if:

(1) The insurance company or its affiliate acquires and retains the ownership interest solely for the general account of the insurance company or for one or more separate accounts established by the insurance company;

(2) The acquisition and retention of the ownership interest is conducted in compliance with, and subject to, the insurance company investment laws, regulations, and written guidance of the State or jurisdiction in which such insurance company is domiciled; and

(3) The appropriate Federal banking agencies, after consultation with the Financial Stability Oversight Council and the relevant insurance commissioners of the States and foreign jurisdictions, as appropriate, have not jointly determined, after notice and comment, that a particular law, regulation, or written guidance described in paragraph (c)(2) of this section is insufficient to protect the safety and soundness of the banking entity, or the financial stability of the United States.

§44.14 Limitations on relationships with a covered fund.

(a) *Relationships with a covered fund.* (1) Except as provided for in paragraph (a)(2) of this section, no banking entity that serves, directly or indirectly, as the investment manager, investment adviser, commodity trading advisor, or sponsor to a covered fund, that organizes and offers a covered fund pursuant to §44.11 of this subpart, or that continues to hold an ownership interest in accordance with §44.11(b) of this subpart, and no affiliate of such entity, may enter into a transaction with the covered fund, or with any other covered fund that is controlled by such covered fund, that would be a covered transaction as defined in section 23A of the Federal Reserve Act (12 U.S.C. 371c(b)(7)), as if such banking entity and the affiliate thereof were a member bank and the covered fund were an affiliate thereof.

(2) Notwithstanding paragraph (a)(1) of this section, a banking entity may:

(i) Acquire and retain any ownership interest in a covered fund in accordance with the requirements of §44.11, §44.12, or §44.13 of this subpart; and

(ii) Enter into any prime brokerage transaction with any covered fund in which a covered fund managed, sponsored, or advised by such banking entity (or an affiliate thereof) has taken an ownership interest, if:

(A) The banking entity is in compliance with each of the limitations set forth in §44.11 of this subpart with respect to a covered fund organized and offered by such banking entity (or an affiliate thereof);

(B) The chief executive officer (or equivalent officer) of the banking entity certifies in writing annually to the OCC (with a duty to update the certification if the information in the certification materially changes) that the banking entity does not, directly or indirectly, guarantee, assume, or otherwise insure the obligations or performance of the covered fund or of any covered fund in which such covered fund invests; and

(C) The Board has not determined that such transaction is inconsistent with the safe and sound operation and condition of the banking entity.

(b) *Restrictions on transactions with covered funds.* A banking entity that serves, directly or indirectly, as the investment manager, investment adviser, commodity trading advisor, or sponsor to a covered fund, or that organizes and offers a covered fund pursuant to § 44.11 of this subpart, or that continues to hold an ownership interest in accordance with § 44.11(b) of this subpart, shall be subject to section 23B of the Federal Reserve Act (12 U.S.C. 371c–1), as if such banking entity were a member bank and such covered fund were an affiliate thereof.

(c) *Restrictions on prime brokerage transactions.* A prime brokerage transaction permitted under paragraph (a)(2)(ii) of this section shall be subject to section 23B of the Federal Reserve Act (12 U.S.C. 371c–1) as if the counterparty were an affiliate of the banking entity.

§ 44.15 Other limitations on permitted covered fund activities and investments.

(a) No transaction, class of transactions, or activity may be deemed permissible under §§ 44.11 through 44.13 of this subpart if the transaction, class of transactions, or activity would:

(1) Involve or result in a material conflict of interest between the banking entity and its clients, customers, or counterparties;

(2) Result, directly or indirectly, in a material exposure by the banking entity to a high-risk asset or a high-risk trading strategy; or

(3) Pose a threat to the safety and soundness of the banking entity or to the financial stability of the United States.

(b) *Definition of material conflict of interest.* (1) For purposes of this section, a material conflict of interest between a banking entity and its clients, customers, or counterparties exists if the banking entity engages in any transaction, class of transactions, or activity that would involve or result in the banking entity's interests being materially adverse to the interests of its client, customer, or counterparty with respect to such transaction, class of transactions, or activity, and the banking entity has not taken at least one of the actions in paragraph (b)(2) of this section.

(2) Prior to effecting the specific transaction or class or type of transactions, or engaging in the specific activity, the banking entity:

(i) *Timely and effective disclosure.* (A) Has made clear, timely, and effective disclosure of the conflict of interest, together with other necessary information, in reasonable detail and in a manner sufficient to permit a reasonable client, customer, or counterparty to meaningfully understand the conflict of interest; and

(B) Such disclosure is made in a manner that provides the client, customer, or counterparty the opportunity to negate, or substantially mitigate, any materially adverse effect on the client, customer, or counterparty created by the conflict of interest; or

(ii) *Information barriers.* Has established, maintained, and enforced information barriers that are memorialized in written policies and procedures, such as physical separation of personnel, or functions, or limitations on types of activity, that are reasonably designed, taking into consideration the nature of the banking entity's business, to prevent the conflict of interest from involving or resulting in a materially adverse effect on a client, customer, or counterparty. A banking entity may not rely on such information barriers if, in the case of any specific transaction, class or type of transactions or activity, the banking entity knows or should reasonably know that, notwithstanding the banking entity's establishment of information barriers, the conflict of interest may involve or result in a materially adverse effect on a client, customer, or counterparty.

(c) *Definition of high-risk asset and high-risk trading strategy.* For purposes of this section:

(1) *High-risk asset* means an asset or group of related assets that would, if held by a banking entity, significantly increase the likelihood that the banking entity would incur a substantial financial loss or would pose a threat to the financial stability of the United States.

(2) *High-risk trading strategy* means a trading strategy that would, if engaged in by a banking entity, significantly increase the likelihood that the banking entity would incur a substantial financial loss or would pose a threat to the financial stability of the United States.

§ 44.16 Ownership of interests in and sponsorship of issuers of certain collateralized debt obligations backed by trust-preferred securities.

(a) The prohibition contained in § 44.10(a)(1) does not apply to the ownership by a banking entity of an interest in, or sponsorship of, any issuer if:

(1) The issuer was established, and the interest was issued, before May 19, 2010;

(2) The banking entity reasonably believes that the offering proceeds received by the issuer were invested primarily in Qualifying TruPS Collateral; and

(3) The banking entity acquired such interest on or before December 10, 2013 (or acquired such interest in connection with a merger with or acquisition of a banking entity that acquired the interest on or before December 10, 2013).

(b) For purposes of this § 44.16, *Qualifying TruPS Collateral* shall mean any trust preferred security or subordinated debt instrument issued prior to May 19, 2010 by a depository institution holding company that, as of the end of any reporting period within 12 months immediately preceding the issuance of such trust preferred security or subordinated debt instrument, had total consolidated assets of less than $15,000,000,000 or issued prior to May 19, 2010 by a mutual holding company.

(c) Notwithstanding paragraph (a)(3) of this section, a banking entity may act as a market maker with respect to the interests of an issuer described in paragraph (a) of this section in accordance with the applicable provisions of §§ 44.4 and 44.11.

(d) Without limiting the applicability of paragraph (a) of this section, the Board, the FDIC and the OCC will make public a non-exclusive list of issuers that meet the requirements of paragraph (a). A banking entity may rely on the list published by the Board, the FDIC and the OCC.

[79 FR 5227, Jan. 31, 2014]

§§ 44.17–44.19 [Reserved]

Subpart D—Compliance Program Requirement; Violations

§ 44.20 Program for compliance; reporting

(a) *Program requirement.* Each banking entity shall develop and provide for the continued administration of a compliance program reasonably designed to ensure and monitor compliance with the prohibitions and restrictions on proprietary trading and covered fund activities and investments set forth in section 13 of the BHC Act and this part. The terms, scope and detail of the compliance program shall be appropriate for the types, size, scope and complexity of activities and business structure of the banking entity.

(b) *Contents of compliance program.* Except as provided in paragraph (f) of this section, the compliance program required by paragraph (a) of this section, at a minimum, shall include:

(1) Written policies and procedures reasonably designed to document, describe, monitor and limit trading activities subject to subpart B (including those permitted under §§ 44.3 to 44.6 of subpart B), including setting, monitoring and managing required limits set out in §§ 44.4 and 44.5, and activities and investments with respect to a covered fund subject to subpart C (including those permitted under §§ 44.11 through 44.14 of subpart C) conducted by the banking entity to ensure that

all activities and investments conducted by the banking entity that are subject to section 13 of the BHC Act and this part comply with section 13 of the BHC Act and this part;

(2) A system of internal controls reasonably designed to monitor compliance with section 13 of the BHC Act and this part and to prevent the occurrence of activities or investments that are prohibited by section 13 of the BHC Act and this part;

(3) A management framework that clearly delineates responsibility and accountability for compliance with section 13 of the BHC Act and this part and includes appropriate management review of trading limits, strategies, hedging activities, investments, incentive compensation and other matters identified in this part or by management as requiring attention;

(4) Independent testing and audit of the effectiveness of the compliance program conducted periodically by qualified personnel of the banking entity or by a qualified outside party;

(5) Training for trading personnel and managers, as well as other appropriate personnel, to effectively implement and enforce the compliance program; and

(6) Records sufficient to demonstrate compliance with section 13 of the BHC Act and this part, which a banking entity must promptly provide to the OCC upon request and retain for a period of no less than 5 years or such longer period as required by the OCC.

(c) *Additional standards.* In addition to the requirements in paragraph (b) of this section, the compliance program of a banking entity must satisfy the requirements and other standards contained in appendix B, if:

(1) The banking entity engages in proprietary trading permitted under subpart B and is required to comply with the reporting requirements of paragraph (d) of this section;

(2) The banking entity has reported total consolidated assets as of the previous calendar year end of $50 billion or more or, in the case of a foreign banking entity, has total U.S. assets as of the previous calendar year end of $50 billion or more (including all subsidiaries, affiliates, branches and agencies of the foreign banking entity operating, located or organized in the United States); or

(3) The OCC notifies the banking entity in writing that it must satisfy the requirements and other standards contained in appendix B to this part.

(d) *Reporting requirements under appendix A to this part.* (1) A banking entity engaged in proprietary trading activity permitted under subpart B shall comply with the reporting requirements described in appendix A, if:

(i) The banking entity (other than a foreign banking entity as provided in paragraph (d)(1)(ii) of this section) has, together with its affiliates and subsidiaries, trading assets and liabilities (excluding trading assets and liabilities involving obligations of or guaranteed by the United States or any agency of the United States) the average gross sum of which (on a worldwide consolidated basis) over the previous consecutive four quarters, as measured as of the last day of each of the four prior calendar quarters, equals or exceeds the threshold established in paragraph (d)(2) of this section;

(ii) In the case of a foreign banking entity, the average gross sum of the trading assets and liabilities of the combined U.S. operations of the foreign banking entity (including all subsidiaries, affiliates, branches and agencies of the foreign banking entity operating, located or organized in the United States and excluding trading assets and liabilities involving obligations of or guaranteed by the United States or any agency of the United States) over the previous consecutive four quarters, as measured as of the last day of each of the four prior calendar quarters, equals or exceeds the threshold established in paragraph (d)(2) of this section; or

(iii) The OCC notifies the banking entity in writing that it must satisfy the reporting requirements contained in appendix A.

(2) The threshold for reporting under paragraph (d)(1) of this section shall be $50 billion beginning on June 30, 2014; $25 billion beginning on April 30, 2016; and $10 billion beginning on December 31, 2016.

(3) Frequency of reporting: Unless the OCC notifies the banking entity in

writing that it must report on a different basis, a banking entity with $50 billion or more in trading assets and liabilities (as calculated in accordance with paragraph (d)(1) of this section) shall report the information required by appendix A for each calendar month within 30 days of the end of the relevant calendar month; beginning with information for the month of January 2015, such information shall be reported within 10 days of the end of each calendar month. Any other banking entity subject to appendix A shall report the information required by appendix A for each calendar quarter within 30 days of the end of that calendar quarter unless the OCC notifies the banking entity in writing that it must report on a different basis.

(e) *Additional documentation for covered funds.* Any banking entity that has more than $10 billion in total consolidated assets as reported on December 31 of the previous two calendar years shall maintain records that include:

(1) Documentation of the exclusions or exemptions other than sections 3(c)(1) and 3(c)(7) of the Investment Company Act of 1940 relied on by each fund sponsored by the banking entity (including all subsidiaries and affiliates) in determining that such fund is not a covered fund;

(2) For each fund sponsored by the banking entity (including all subsidiaries and affiliates) for which the banking entity relies on one or more of the exclusions from the definition of covered fund provided by § 44.10(c)(1), § 44.10(c)(5), § 44.10(c)(8), § 44.10(c)(9), or § 44.10(c)(10) of subpart C, documentation supporting the banking entity's determination that the fund is not a covered fund pursuant to one or more of those exclusions;

(3) For each seeding vehicle described in § 44.10(c)(12)(i) or (iii) of subpart C that will become a registered investment company or SEC-regulated business development company, a written plan documenting the banking entity's determination that the seeding vehicle will become a registered investment company or SEC-regulated business development company; the period of time during which the vehicle will operate as a seeding vehicle; and the banking entity's plan to market the vehicle to third-party investors and convert it into a registered investment company or SEC-regulated business development company within the time period specified in § 44.12(a)(2)(i)(B) of subpart C;

(4) For any banking entity that is, or is controlled directly or indirectly by a banking entity that is, located in or organized under the laws of the United States or of any State, if the aggregate amount of ownership interests in foreign public funds that are described in § 44.10(c)(1) of subpart C owned by such banking entity (including ownership interests owned by any affiliate that is controlled directly or indirectly by a banking entity that is located in or organized under the laws of the United States or of any State) exceeds $50 million at the end of two or more consecutive calendar quarters, beginning with the next succeeding calendar quarter, documentation of the value of the ownership interests owned by the banking entity (and such affiliates) in each foreign public fund and each jurisdiction in which any such foreign public fund is organized, calculated as of the end of each calendar quarter, which documentation must continue until the banking entity's aggregate amount of ownership interests in foreign public funds is below $50 million for two consecutive calendar quarters; and

(5) For purposes of paragraph (e)(4) of this section, a U.S. branch, agency, or subsidiary of a foreign banking entity is located in the United States; however, the foreign bank that operates or controls that branch, agency, or subsidiary is not considered to be located in the United States solely by virtue of operating or controlling the U.S. branch, agency, or subsidiary.

(f) *Simplified programs for less active banking entities*—(1) *Banking entities with no covered activities.* A banking entity that does not engage in activities or investments pursuant to subpart B or subpart C (other than trading activities permitted pursuant to § 44.6(a) of subpart B) may satisfy the requirements of this section by establishing the required compliance program prior to becoming engaged in such activities or making such investments (other than trading activities permitted pursuant to § 44.6(a) of subpart B).

(2) *Banking entities with modest activities.* A banking entity with total consolidated assets of $10 billion or less as reported on December 31 of the previous two calendar years that engages in activities or investments pursuant to subpart B or subpart C (other than trading activities permitted under § 44.6(a) of subpart B) may satisfy the requirements of this section by including in its existing compliance policies and procedures appropriate references to the requirements of section 13 of the BHC Act and this part and adjustments as appropriate given the activities, size, scope and complexity of the banking entity.

§ 44.21 Termination of activities or investments; penalties for violations.

(a) Any banking entity that engages in an activity or makes an investment in violation of section 13 of the BHC Act or this part, or acts in a manner that functions as an evasion of the requirements of section 13 of the BHC Act or this part, including through an abuse of any activity or investment permitted under subparts B or C, or otherwise violates the restrictions and requirements of section 13 of the BHC Act or this part, shall, upon discovery, promptly terminate the activity and, as relevant, dispose of the investment.

(b) Whenever the OCC finds reasonable cause to believe any banking entity has engaged in an activity or made an investment in violation of section 13 of the BHC Act or this part, or engaged in any activity or made any investment that functions as an evasion of the requirements of section 13 of the BHC Act or this part, the OCC may take any action permitted by law to enforce compliance with section 13 of the BHC Act and this part, including directing the banking entity to restrict, limit, or terminate any or all activities under this part and dispose of any investment.

Appendix A to Part 44—Reporting and Recordkeeping Requirements for Covered Trading Activities

I. Purpose

a. This appendix sets forth reporting and recordkeeping requirements that certain banking entities must satisfy in connection with the restrictions on proprietary trading set forth in subpart B ("proprietary trading restrictions"). Pursuant to § 44.20(d), this appendix generally applies to a banking entity that, together with its affiliates and subsidiaries, has significant trading assets and liabilities. These entities are required to (i) furnish periodic reports to the OCC regarding a variety of quantitative measurements of their covered trading activities, which vary depending on the scope and size of covered trading activities, and (ii) create and maintain records documenting the preparation and content of these reports. The requirements of this appendix must be incorporated into the banking entity's internal compliance program under § 44.20 and Appendix B.

b. The purpose of this appendix is to assist banking entities and the OCC in:

(i) Better understanding and evaluating the scope, type, and profile of the banking entity's covered trading activities;

(ii) Monitoring the banking entity's covered trading activities;

(iii) Identifying covered trading activities that warrant further review or examination by the banking entity to verify compliance with the proprietary trading restrictions;

(iv) Evaluating whether the covered trading activities of trading desks engaged in market making-related activities subject to § 44.4(b) are consistent with the requirements governing permitted market making-related activities;

(v) Evaluating whether the covered trading activities of trading desks that are engaged in permitted trading activity subject to §§ 44.4, 44.5, or 44.6(a)-(b) (i.e., underwriting and market making-related related activity, risk-mitigating hedging, or trading in certain government obligations) are consistent with the requirement that such activity not result, directly or indirectly, in a material exposure to high-risk assets or high-risk trading strategies;

(vi) Identifying the profile of particular covered trading activities of the banking entity, and the individual trading desks of the banking entity, to help establish the appropriate frequency and scope of examination by the OCC of such activities; and

(vii) Assessing and addressing the risks associated with the banking entity's covered trading activities.

c. The quantitative measurements that must be furnished pursuant to this appendix are *not* intended to serve as a dispositive tool for the identification of permissible or impermissible activities.

d. In order to allow banking entities and the Agencies to evaluate the effectiveness of these metrics, banking entities must collect and report these metrics for all trading desks beginning on the dates established in §44.20 of the final rule. The Agencies will review the data collected and revise this collection requirement as appropriate based on a review of the data collected prior to September 30, 2015.

e. In addition to the quantitative measurements required in this appendix, a banking entity may need to develop and implement other quantitative measurements in order to effectively monitor its covered trading activities for compliance with section 13 of the BHC Act and this part and to have an effective compliance program, as required by §44.20 and Appendix B to this part. The effectiveness of particular quantitative measurements may differ based on the profile of the banking entity's businesses in general and, more specifically, of the particular trading desk, including types of instruments traded, trading activities and strategies, and history and experience (e.g., whether the trading desk is an established, successful market maker or a new entrant to a competitive market). In all cases, banking entities must ensure that they have robust measures in place to identify and monitor the risks taken in their trading activities, to ensure that the activities are within risk tolerances established by the banking entity, and to monitor and examine for compliance with the proprietary trading restrictions in this part.

f. On an ongoing basis, banking entities must carefully monitor, review, and evaluate all furnished quantitative measurements, as well as any others that they choose to utilize in order to maintain compliance with section 13 of the BHC Act and this part. All measurement results that indicate a heightened risk of impermissible proprietary trading, including with respect to otherwise-permitted activities under §§44.4 through 44.6(a) and (b), or that result in a material exposure to high-risk assets or high-risk trading strategies, must be escalated within the banking entity for review, further analysis, explanation to the OCC, and remediation, where appropriate. The quantitative measurements discussed in this appendix should be helpful to banking entities in identifying and managing the risks related to their covered trading activities.

II. Definitions

The terms used in this appendix have the same meanings as set forth in §§44.2 and 44.3. In addition, for purposes of this appendix, the following definitions apply:

Calculation period means the period of time for which a particular quantitative measurement must be calculated.

Comprehensive profit and loss means the net profit or loss of a trading desk's material sources of trading revenue over a specific period of time, including, for example, any increase or decrease in the market value of a trading desk's holdings, dividend income, and interest income and expense.

Covered trading activity means trading conducted by a trading desk under §§44.4, 44.5, 44.6(a), or 44.6(b). A banking entity may include trading under §§44.3(d), 44.6(c), 44.6(d) or 44.6(e).

Measurement frequency means the frequency with which a particular quantitative metric must be calculated and recorded.

Trading desk means the smallest discrete unit of organization of a banking entity that purchases or sells financial instruments for the trading account of the banking entity or an affiliate thereof.

III. Reporting and Recordkeeping of Quantitative Measurements

a. Scope of Required Reporting

General scope. Each banking entity made subject to this part by §44.20 must furnish the following quantitative measurements for each trading desk of the banking entity, calculated in accordance with this appendix:

- Risk and Position Limits and Usage;
- Risk Factor Sensitivities;
- Value-at-Risk and Stress VaR;
- Comprehensive Profit and Loss Attribution;
- Inventory Turnover;
- Inventory Aging; and
- Customer-Facing Trade Ratio

b. Frequency of Required Calculation and Reporting

A banking entity must calculate any applicable quantitative measurement for each trading day. A banking entity must report each applicable quantitative measurement to the OCC on the reporting schedule established in §44.20 unless otherwise requested by the OCC. All quantitative measurements for any calendar month must be reported within the time period required by §44.20.

c. Recordkeeping

A banking entity must, for any quantitative measurement furnished to the OCC pursuant to this appendix and §44.20(d), create and maintain records documenting the preparation and content of these reports, as well as such information as is necessary to permit the OCC to verify the accuracy of such reports, for a period of 5 years from the end of the calendar year for which the measurement was taken.

IV. QUANTITATIVE MEASUREMENTS

a. Risk-Management Measurements

1. Risk and Position Limits and Usage

i. *Description:* For purposes of this appendix, Risk and Position Limits are the constraints that define the amount of risk that a trading desk is permitted to take at a point in time, as defined by the banking entity for a specific trading desk. Usage represents the portion of the trading desk's limits that are accounted for by the current activity of the desk. Risk and position limits and their usage are key risk management tools used to control and monitor risk taking and include, but are not limited, to the limits set out in §44.4 and §44.5. A number of the metrics that are described below, including "Risk Factor Sensitivities" and "Value-at-Risk and Stress Value-at-Risk," relate to a trading desk's risk and position limits and are useful in evaluating and setting these limits in the broader context of the trading desk's overall activities, particularly for the market making activities under §44.4(b) and hedging activity under §44.5. Accordingly, the limits required under §44.4(b)(2)(iii) and §44.5(b)(1)(i) must meet the applicable requirements under §44.4(b)(2)(iii) and §44.5(b)(1)(i) and also must include appropriate metrics for the trading desk limits including, at a minimum, the "Risk Factor Sensitivities" and "Value-at-Risk and Stress Value-at-Risk" metrics except to the extent any of the "Risk Factor Sensitivities" or "Value-at-Risk and Stress Value-at-Risk" metrics are demonstrably ineffective for measuring and monitoring the risks of a trading desk based on the types of positions traded by, and risk exposures of, that desk.

ii. *General Calculation Guidance:* Risk and Position Limits must be reported in the format used by the banking entity for the purposes of risk management of each trading desk. Risk and Position Limits are often expressed in terms of risk measures, such as VaR and Risk Factor Sensitivities, but may also be expressed in terms of other observable criteria, such as net open positions. When criteria other than VaR or Risk Factor Sensitivities are used to define the Risk and Position Limits, both the value of the Risk and Position Limits and the value of the variables used to assess whether these limits have been reached must be reported.

iii. *Calculation Period:* One trading day.

iv. *Measurement Frequency:* Daily.

2. Risk Factor Sensitivities

i. *Description:* For purposes of this appendix, Risk Factor Sensitivities are changes in a trading desk's Comprehensive Profit and Loss that are expected to occur in the event of a change in one or more underlying variables that are significant sources of the trading desk's profitability and risk.

ii. *General Calculation Guidance:* A banking entity must report the Risk Factor Sensitivities that are monitored and managed as part of the trading desk's overall risk management policy. The underlying data and methods used to compute a trading desk's Risk Factor Sensitivities will depend on the specific function of the trading desk and the internal risk management models employed. The number and type of Risk Factor Sensitivities that are monitored and managed by a trading desk, and furnished to the OCC, will depend on the explicit risks assumed by the trading desk. In general, however, reported Risk Factor Sensitivities must be sufficiently granular to account for a preponderance of the expected price variation in the trading desk's holdings.

A. Trading desks must take into account any relevant factors in calculating Risk Factor Sensitivities, including, for example, the following with respect to particular asset classes:

- *Commodity derivative positions:* risk factors with respect to the related commodities set out in 17 CFR 20.2, the maturity of the positions, volatility and/or correlation sensitivities (expressed in a manner that demonstrates any significant non-linearities), and the maturity profile of the positions;
- *Credit positions:* risk factors with respect to credit spreads that are sufficiently granular to account for specific credit sectors and market segments, the maturity profile of the positions, and risk factors with respect to interest rates of all relevant maturities;
- *Credit-related derivative positions:* risk factor sensitivities, for example credit spreads, shifts (parallel and non-parallel) in credit spreads—volatility, and/or correlation sensitivities (expressed in a manner that demonstrates any significant non-linearities), and the maturity profile of the positions;
- *Equity derivative positions:* risk factor sensitivities such as equity positions, volatility, and/or correlation sensitivities (expressed in a manner that demonstrates any significant non-linearities), and the maturity profile of the positions;
- *Equity positions:* risk factors for equity prices and risk factors that differentiate between important equity market sectors and segments, such as a small capitalization equities and international equities;
- *Foreign exchange derivative positions:* risk factors with respect to major currency pairs and maturities, exposure to interest rates at relevant maturities, volatility, and/or correlation sensitivities (expressed in a manner that demonstrates any significant non-linearities), as well as the maturity profile of the positions; and
- *Interest rate positions, including interest rate derivative positions:* risk factors with respect to major interest rate categories and maturities and volatility and/or correlation sensitivities (expressed in a manner that

demonstrates any significant non-linearities), and shifts (parallel and non-parallel) in the interest rate curve, as well as the maturity profile of the positions.

B. The methods used by a banking entity to calculate sensitivities to a common factor shared by multiple trading desks, such as an equity price factor, must be applied consistently across its trading desks so that the sensitivities can be compared from one trading desk to another.

iii. *Calculation Period:* One trading day.

iv. *Measurement Frequency:* Daily.

3. Value-at-Risk and Stress Value-at-Risk

i. *Description:* For purposes of this appendix, Value-at-Risk ("VaR") is the commonly used percentile measurement of the risk of future financial loss in the value of a given set of aggregated positions over a specified period of time, based on current market conditions. For purposes of this appendix, Stress Value-at-Risk ("Stress VaR") is the percentile measurement of the risk of future financial loss in the value of a given set of aggregated positions over a specified period of time, based on market conditions during a period of significant financial stress.

ii. *General Calculation Guidance:* Banking entities must compute and report VaR and Stress VaR by employing generally accepted standards and methods of calculation. VaR should reflect a loss in a trading desk that is expected to be exceeded less than one percent of the time over a one-day period. For those banking entities that are subject to regulatory capital requirements imposed by a Federal banking agency, VaR and Stress VaR must be computed and reported in a manner that is consistent with such regulatory capital requirements. In cases where a trading desk does not have a standalone VaR or Stress VaR calculation but is part of a larger aggregation of positions for which a VaR or Stress VaR calculation is performed, a VaR or Stress VaR calculation that includes only the trading desk's holdings must be performed consistent with the VaR or Stress VaR model and methodology used for the larger aggregation of positions.

iii. *Calculation Period:* One trading day.

iv. *Measurement Frequency:* Daily.

b. Source-of-Revenue Measurements

1. Comprehensive Profit and Loss Attribution

i. *Description:* For purposes of this appendix, Comprehensive Profit and Loss Attribution is an analysis that attributes the daily fluctuation in the value of a trading desk's positions to various sources. First, the daily profit and loss of the aggregated positions is divided into three categories: (i) profit and loss attributable to a trading desk's existing positions that were also positions held by the trading desk as of the end of the prior day ("existing positions"); (ii) profit and loss attributable to new positions resulting from the current day's trading activity ("new positions"); and (iii) residual profit and loss that cannot be specifically attributed to existing positions or new positions. The sum of (i), (ii), and (iii) must equal the trading desk's comprehensive profit and loss at each point in time. In addition, profit and loss measurements must calculate volatility of comprehensive profit and loss (i.e., the standard deviation of the trading desk's one-day profit and loss, in dollar terms) for the reporting period for at least a 30-, 60- and 90-day lag period, from the end of the reporting period, and any other period that the banking entity deems necessary to meet the requirements of the rule.

A. The comprehensive profit and loss associated with existing positions must reflect changes in the value of these positions on the applicable day. The comprehensive profit and loss from existing positions must be further attributed, as applicable, to changes in (i) the specific Risk Factors and other factors that are monitored and managed as part of the trading desk's overall risk management policies and procedures; and (ii) any other applicable elements, such as cash flows, carry, changes in reserves, and the correction, cancellation, or exercise of a trade.

B. The comprehensive profit and loss attributed to new positions must reflect commissions and fee income or expense and market gains or losses associated with transactions executed on the applicable day. New positions include purchases and sales of financial instruments and other assets/liabilities and negotiated amendments to existing positions. The comprehensive profit and loss from new positions may be reported in the aggregate and does not need to be further attributed to specific sources.

C. The portion of comprehensive profit and loss that cannot be specifically attributed to known sources must be allocated to a residual category identified as an unexplained portion of the comprehensive profit and loss. Significant unexplained profit and loss must be escalated for further investigation and analysis.

ii. *General Calculation Guidance:* The specific categories used by a trading desk in the attribution analysis and amount of detail for the analysis should be tailored to the type and amount of trading activities undertaken by the trading desk. The new position attribution must be computed by calculating the difference between the prices at which instruments were bought and/or sold and the prices at which those instruments are marked to market at the close of business on that day multiplied by the notional or principal amount of each purchase or sale. Any fees, commissions, or other payments received (paid) that are associated with transactions executed on that day must be added (subtracted) from such difference. These factors must be measured consistently over time to facilitate historical comparisons.

iii. *Calculation Period:* One trading day.

iv. *Measurement Frequency:* Daily.

c. Customer-Facing Activity Measurements

1. Inventory Turnover

i. *Description:* For purposes of this appendix, Inventory Turnover is a ratio that measures the turnover of a trading desk's inventory. The numerator of the ratio is the absolute value of all transactions over the reporting period. The denominator of the ratio is the value of the trading desk's inventory at the beginning of the reporting period.

ii. *General Calculation Guidance:* For purposes of this appendix, for derivatives, other than options and interest rate derivatives, value means gross notional value, for options, value means delta adjusted notional value, and for interest rate derivatives, value means 10-year bond equivalent value.

iii. *Calculation Period:* 30 days, 60 days, and 90 days.

iv. *Measurement Frequency:* Daily.

2. Inventory Aging

i. *Description:* For purposes of this appendix, Inventory Aging generally describes a schedule of the trading desk's aggregate assets and liabilities and the amount of time that those assets and liabilities have been held. Inventory Aging should measure the age profile of the trading desk's assets and liabilities.

ii. *General Calculation Guidance:* In general, Inventory Aging must be computed using a trading desk's trading activity data and must identify the value of a trading desk's aggregate assets and liabilities. Inventory Aging must include two schedules, an asset-aging schedule and a liability-aging schedule. Each schedule must record the value of assets or liabilities held over all holding periods. For derivatives, other than options, and interest rate derivatives, value means gross notional value, for options, value means delta adjusted notional value and, for interest rate derivatives, value means 10-year bond equivalent value.

iii. *Calculation Period:* One trading day.

iv. *Measurement Frequency:* Daily.

3. Customer-Facing Trade Ratio—Trade Count Based and Value Based

i. *Description:* For purposes of this appendix, the Customer-Facing Trade Ratio is a ratio comparing (i) the transactions involving a counterparty that is a customer of the trading desk to (ii) the transactions involving a counterparty that is not a customer of the trading desk. A trade count based ratio must be computed that records the number of transactions involving a counterparty that is a customer of the trading desk and the number of transactions involving a counterparty that is not a customer of the trading desk. A value based ratio must be computed that records the value of transactions involving a counterparty that is a customer of the trading desk and the value of transactions involving a counterparty that is not a customer of the trading desk.

ii. *General Calculation Guidance:* For purposes of calculating the Customer-Facing Trade Ratio, a counterparty is considered to be a customer of the trading desk if the counterparty is a market participant that makes use of the banking entity's market making-related services by obtaining such services, responding to quotations, or entering into a continuing relationship with respect to such services. However, a trading desk or other organizational unit of another banking entity would not be a client, customer, or counterparty of the trading desk if the other entity has trading assets and liabilities of $50 billion or more as measured in accordance with §44.20(d)(1) unless the trading desk documents how and why a particular trading desk or other organizational unit of the entity should be treated as a client, customer, or counterparty of the trading desk. Transactions conducted anonymously on an exchange or similar trading facility that permits trading on behalf of a broad range of market participants would be considered transactions with customers of the trading desk. For derivatives, other than options, and interest rate derivatives, value means gross notional value, for options, value means delta adjusted notional value, and for interest rate derivatives, value means 10-year bond equivalent value.

iii. *Calculation Period:* 30 days, 60 days, and 90 days.

iv. *Measurement Frequency:* Daily.

Appendix B to Part 44—Enhanced Minimum Standards for Compliance Programs

I. Overview

Section 44.20(c) requires certain banking entities to establish, maintain, and enforce an enhanced compliance program that includes the requirements and standards in this Appendix as well as the minimum written policies and procedures, internal controls, management framework, independent testing, training, and recordkeeping provisions outlined in §44.20. This Appendix sets forth additional minimum standards with respect to the establishment, oversight, maintenance, and enforcement by these banking entities of an enhanced internal compliance program for ensuring and monitoring compliance with the prohibitions and restrictions on proprietary trading and covered fund activities and investments set forth in section 13 of the BHC Act and this part.

a. This compliance program must:

1. Be reasonably designed to identify, document, monitor, and report the permitted trading and covered fund activities and investments of the banking entity; identify, monitor and promptly address the risks of these covered activities and investments and potential areas of noncompliance; and prevent activities or investments prohibited by, or that do not comply with, section 13 of the BHC Act and this part;

2. Establish and enforce appropriate limits on the covered activities and investments of the banking entity, including limits on the size, scope, complexity, and risks of the individual activities or investments consistent with the requirements of section 13 of the BHC Act and this part;

3. Subject the effectiveness of the compliance program to periodic independent review and testing, and ensure that the entity's internal audit, corporate compliance and internal control functions involved in review and testing are effective and independent;

4. Make senior management, and others as appropriate, accountable for the effective implementation of the compliance program, and ensure that the board of directors and chief executive officer (or equivalent) of the banking entity review the effectiveness of the compliance program; and

5. Facilitate supervision and examination by the Agencies of the banking entity's permitted trading and covered fund activities and investments.

II. ENHANCED COMPLIANCE PROGRAM

a. *Proprietary Trading Activities.* A banking entity must establish, maintain and enforce a compliance program that includes written policies and procedures that are appropriate for the types, size, and complexity of, and risks associated with, its permitted trading activities. The compliance program may be tailored to the types of trading activities conducted by the banking entity, and must include a detailed description of controls established by the banking entity to reasonably ensure that its trading activities are conducted in accordance with the requirements and limitations applicable to those trading activities under section 13 of the BHC Act and this part, and provide for appropriate revision of the compliance program before expansion of the trading activities of the banking entity. A banking entity must devote adequate resources and use knowledgeable personnel in conducting, supervising and managing its trading activities, and promote consistency, independence and rigor in implementing its risk controls and compliance efforts. The compliance program must be updated with a frequency sufficient to account for changes in the activities of the banking entity, results of independent testing of the program, identification of weaknesses in the program, and changes in legal, regulatory or other requirements.

1. *Trading Desks:* The banking entity must have written policies and procedures governing each trading desk that include a description of:

i. The process for identifying, authorizing and documenting financial instruments each trading desk may purchase or sell, with separate documentation for market making-related activities conducted in reliance on §44.4(b) and for hedging activity conducted in reliance on §44.5;

ii. A mapping for each trading desk to the division, business line, or other organizational structure that is responsible for managing and overseeing the trading desk's activities;

iii. The mission (*i.e.*, the type of trading activity, such as market-making, trading in sovereign debt, etc.) and strategy (*i.e.*, methods for conducting authorized trading activities) of each trading desk;

iv. The activities that the trading desk is authorized to conduct, including (i) authorized instruments and products, and (ii) authorized hedging strategies, techniques and instruments;

v. The types and amount of risks allocated by the banking entity to each trading desk to implement the mission and strategy of the trading desk, including an enumeration of material risks resulting from the activities in which the trading desk is authorized to engage (including but not limited to price risks, such as basis, volatility and correlation risks, as well as counterparty credit risk). Risk assessments must take into account both the risks inherent in the trading activity and the strength and effectiveness of controls designed to mitigate those risks;

vi. How the risks allocated to each trading desk will be measured;

vii. Why the allocated risks levels are appropriate to the activities authorized for the trading desk;

viii. The limits on the holding period of, and the risk associated with, financial instruments under the responsibility of the trading desk;

ix. The process for setting new or revised limits, as well as escalation procedures for granting exceptions to any limits or to any policies or procedures governing the desk, the analysis that will be required to support revising limits or granting exceptions, and the process for independently reviewing and documenting those exceptions and the underlying analysis;

x. The process for identifying, documenting and approving new products, trading strategies, and hedging strategies;

xi. The types of clients, customers, and counterparties with whom the trading desk may trade; and

xii. The compensation arrangements, including incentive arrangements, for employees associated with the trading desk, which may not be designed to reward or incentivize prohibited proprietary trading or excessive or imprudent risk-taking.

2. *Description of risks and risk management processes:* The compliance program for the banking entity must include a comprehensive description of the risk management program for the trading activity of the banking entity. The compliance program must also include a description of the governance, approval, reporting, escalation, review and other processes the banking entity will use to reasonably ensure that trading activity is conducted in compliance with section 13 of the BHC Act and this part. Trading activity in similar financial instruments should be subject to similar governance, limits, testing, controls, and review, unless the banking entity specifically determines to establish different limits or processes and documents those differences. Descriptions must include, at a minimum, the following elements:

i. A description of the supervisory and risk management structure governing all trading activity, including a description of processes for initial and senior-level review of new products and new strategies;

ii. A description of the process for developing, documenting, testing, approving and reviewing all models used for valuing, identifying and monitoring the risks of trading activity and related positions, including the process for periodic independent testing of the reliability and accuracy of those models;

iii. A description of the process for developing, documenting, testing, approving and reviewing the limits established for each trading desk;

iv. A description of the process by which a security may be purchased or sold pursuant to the liquidity management plan, including the process for authorizing and monitoring such activity to ensure compliance with the banking entity's liquidity management plan and the restrictions on liquidity management activities in this part;

v. A description of the management review process, including escalation procedures, for approving any temporary exceptions or permanent adjustments to limits on the activities, positions, strategies, or risks associated with each trading desk; and

vi. The role of the audit, compliance, risk management and other relevant units for conducting independent testing of trading and hedging activities, techniques and strategies.

3. *Authorized risks, instruments, and products.* The banking entity must implement and enforce limits and internal controls for each trading desk that are reasonably designed to ensure that trading activity is conducted in conformance with section 13 of the BHC Act and this part and with the banking entity's written policies and procedures. The banking entity must establish and enforce risk limits appropriate for the activity of each trading desk. These limits should be based on probabilistic and non-probabilistic measures of potential loss (*e.g.*, Value-at-Risk and notional exposure, respectively), and measured under normal and stress market conditions. At a minimum, these internal controls must monitor, establish and enforce limits on:

i. The financial instruments (including, at a minimum, by type and exposure) that the trading desk may trade;

ii. The types and levels of risks that may be taken by each trading desk; and

iii. The types of hedging instruments used, hedging strategies employed, and the amount of risk effectively hedged.

4. *Hedging policies and procedures.* The banking entity must establish, maintain, and enforce written policies and procedures regarding the use of risk-mitigating hedging instruments and strategies that, at a minimum, describe:

i. The positions, techniques and strategies that each trading desk may use to hedge the risk of its positions;

ii. The manner in which the banking entity will identify the risks arising in connection with and related to the individual or aggregated positions, contracts or other holdings of the banking entity that are to be hedged and determine that those risks have been properly and effectively hedged;

iii. The level of the organization at which hedging activity and management will occur;

iv. The manner in which hedging strategies will be monitored and the personnel responsible for such monitoring;

v. The risk management processes used to control unhedged or residual risks; and

vi. The process for developing, documenting, testing, approving and reviewing all hedging positions, techniques and strategies permitted for each trading desk and for the banking entity in reliance on §44.5.

5. *Analysis and quantitative measurements.* The banking entity must perform robust analysis and quantitative measurement of its trading activities that is reasonably designed to ensure that the trading activity of each trading desk is consistent with the banking entity's compliance program; monitor and assist in the identification of potential and actual prohibited proprietary trading activity; and prevent the occurrence of prohibited proprietary trading. Analysis and models used to determine, measure and limit

risk must be rigorously tested and be reviewed by management responsible for trading activity to ensure that trading activities, limits, strategies, and hedging activities do not understate the risk and exposure to the banking entity or allow prohibited proprietary trading. This review should include periodic and independent back-testing and revision of activities, limits, strategies and hedging as appropriate to contain risk and ensure compliance. In addition to the quantitative measurements reported by any banking entity subject to Appendix A to this part, each banking entity must develop and implement, to the extent appropriate to facilitate compliance with this part, additional quantitative measurements specifically tailored to the particular risks, practices, and strategies of its trading desks. The banking entity's analysis and quantitative measurements must incorporate the quantitative measurements reported by the banking entity pursuant to Appendix A (if applicable) and include, at a minimum, the following:

i. Internal controls and written policies and procedures reasonably designed to ensure the accuracy and integrity of quantitative measurements;

ii. Ongoing, timely monitoring and review of calculated quantitative measurements;

iii. The establishment of numerical thresholds and appropriate trading measures for each trading desk and heightened review of trading activity not consistent with those thresholds to ensure compliance with section 13 of the BHC Act and this part, including analysis of the measurement results or other information, appropriate escalation procedures, and documentation related to the review; and

iv. Immediate review and compliance investigation of the trading desk's activities, escalation to senior management with oversight responsibilities for the applicable trading desk, timely notification to the OCC, appropriate remedial action (*e.g.*, divesting of impermissible positions, cessation of impermissible activity, disciplinary actions), and documentation of the investigation findings and remedial action taken when quantitative measurements or other information, considered together with the facts and circumstances, or findings of internal audit, independent testing or other review suggest a reasonable likelihood that the trading desk has violated any part of section 13 of the BHC Act or this part.

6. *Other Compliance Matters*. In addition to the requirements specified above, the banking entity's compliance program must:

i. Identify activities of each trading desk that will be conducted in reliance on exemptions contained in §§44.4 through 44.6, including an explanation of:

A. How and where in the organization the activity occurs; and

B. Which exemption is being relied on and how the activity meets the specific requirements for reliance on the applicable exemption;

ii. Include an explanation of the process for documenting, approving and reviewing actions taken pursuant to the liquidity management plan, where in the organization this activity occurs, the securities permissible for liquidity management, the process for ensuring that liquidity management activities are not conducted for the purpose of prohibited proprietary trading, and the process for ensuring that securities purchased as part of the liquidity management plan are highly liquid and conform to the requirements of this part;

iii. Describe how the banking entity monitors for and prohibits potential or actual material exposure to high-risk assets or high-risk trading strategies presented by each trading desk that relies on the exemptions contained in §§44.3(d)(3), and 44.4 through 44.6, which must take into account potential or actual exposure to:

A. Assets whose values cannot be externally priced or, where valuation is reliant on pricing models, whose model inputs cannot be externally validated;

B. Assets whose changes in value cannot be adequately mitigated by effective hedging;

C. New products with rapid growth, including those that do not have a market history;

D. Assets or strategies that include significant embedded leverage;

E. Assets or strategies that have demonstrated significant historical volatility;

F. Assets or strategies for which the application of capital and liquidity standards would not adequately account for the risk; and

G. Assets or strategies that result in large and significant concentrations to sectors, risk factors, or counterparties;

iv. Establish responsibility for compliance with the reporting and recordkeeping requirements of subpart B and §44.20; and

v. Establish policies for monitoring and prohibiting potential or actual material conflicts of interest between the banking entity and its clients, customers, or counterparties.

7. *Remediation of violations*. The banking entity's compliance program must be reasonably designed and established to effectively monitor and identify for further analysis any trading activity that may indicate potential violations of section 13 of the BHC Act and this part and to prevent actual violations of section 13 of the BHC Act and this part. The compliance program must describe procedures for identifying and remedying violations of section 13 of the BHC Act and this part, and must include, at a minimum, a requirement to promptly document, address and remedy any violation of section 13 of the BHC Act or this part, and document all proposed and actual remediation efforts. The

compliance program must include specific written policies and procedures that are reasonably designed to assess the extent to which any activity indicates that modification to the banking entity's compliance program is warranted and to ensure that appropriate modifications are implemented. The written policies and procedures must provide for prompt notification to appropriate management, including senior management and the board of directors, of any material weakness or significant deficiencies in the design or implementation of the compliance program of the banking entity.

b. *Covered Fund Activities or Investments.* A banking entity must establish, maintain and enforce a compliance program that includes written policies and procedures that are appropriate for the types, size, complexity and risks of the covered fund and related activities conducted and investments made, by the banking entity.

1. Identification of covered funds. The banking entity's compliance program must provide a process, which must include appropriate management review and independent testing, for identifying and documenting covered funds that each unit within the banking entity's organization sponsors or organizes and offers, and covered funds in which each such unit invests. In addition to the documentation requirements for covered funds, as specified under §44.20(e), the documentation must include information that identifies all pools that the banking entity sponsors or has an interest in and the type of exemption from the Commodity Exchange Act (whether or not the pool relies on section 4.7 of the regulations under the Commodity Exchange Act), and the amount of ownership interest the banking entity has in those pools.

2. Identification of covered fund activities and investments. The banking entity's compliance program must identify, document and map each unit within the organization that is permitted to acquire or hold an interest in any covered fund or sponsor any covered fund and map each unit to the division, business line, or other organizational structure that will be responsible for managing and overseeing that unit's activities and investments.

3. Explanation of compliance. The banking entity's compliance program must explain how:

i. The banking entity monitors for and prohibits potential or actual material conflicts of interest between the banking entity and its clients, customers, or counterparties related to its covered fund activities and investments;

ii. The banking entity monitors for and prohibits potential or actual transactions or activities that may threaten the safety and soundness of the banking entity related to its covered fund activities and investments; and

iii. The banking entity monitors for and prohibits potential or actual material exposure to high-risk assets or high-risk trading strategies presented by its covered fund activities and investments, taking into account potential or actual exposure to:

A. Assets whose values cannot be externally priced or, where valuation is reliant on pricing models, whose model inputs cannot be externally validated;

B. Assets whose changes in values cannot be adequately mitigated by effective hedging;

C. New products with rapid growth, including those that do not have a market history;

D. Assets or strategies that include significant embedded leverage;

E. Assets or strategies that have demonstrated significant historical volatility;

F. Assets or strategies for which the application of capital and liquidity standards would not adequately account for the risk; and

G. Assets or strategies that expose the banking entity to large and significant concentrations with respect to sectors, risk factors, or counterparties;

4. Description and documentation of covered fund activities and investments. For each organizational unit engaged in covered fund activities and investments, the banking entity's compliance program must document:

i. The covered fund activities and investments that the unit is authorized to conduct;

ii. The banking entity's plan for actively seeking unaffiliated investors to ensure that any investment by the banking entity conforms to the limits contained in §44.12 or registered in compliance with the securities laws and thereby exempt from those limits within the time periods allotted in§44.12; and

iii. How it complies with the requirements of subpart C.

5. Internal Controls. A banking entity must establish, maintain, and enforce internal controls that are reasonably designed to ensure that its covered fund activities or investments comply with the requirements of section 13 of the BHC Act and this part and are appropriate given the limits on risk established by the banking entity. These written internal controls must be reasonably designed and established to effectively monitor and identify for further analysis any covered fund activity or investment that may indicate potential violations of section 13 of the BHC Act or this part. The internal controls must, at a minimum require:

i. Monitoring and limiting the banking entity's individual and aggregate investments in covered funds;

ii. Monitoring the amount and timing of seed capital investments for compliance with the limitations under subpart C (including but not limited to the redemption, sale or disposition requirements) of § 44.12, and the effectiveness of efforts to seek unaffiliated investors to ensure compliance with those limits;

iii. Calculating the individual and aggregate levels of ownership interests in one or more covered fund required by § 44.12;

iv. Attributing the appropriate instruments to the individual and aggregate ownership interest calculations above;

v. Making disclosures to prospective and actual investors in any covered fund organized and offered or sponsored by the banking entity, as provided under § 44.11(a)(8);

vi. Monitoring for and preventing any relationship or transaction between the banking entity and a covered fund that is prohibited under § 44.14, including where the banking entity has been designated as the sponsor, investment manager, investment adviser, or commodity trading advisor to a covered fund by another banking entity; and

vii. Appropriate management review and supervision across legal entities of the banking entity to ensure that services and products provided by all affiliated entities comply with the limitation on services and products contained in § 44.14.

6. Remediation of violations. The banking entity's compliance program must be reasonably designed and established to effectively monitor and identify for further analysis any covered fund activity or investment that may indicate potential violations of section 13 of the BHC Act or this part and to prevent actual violations of section 13 of the BHC Act and this part. The banking entity's compliance program must describe procedures for identifying and remedying violations of section 13 of the BHC Act and this part, and must include, at a minimum, a requirement to promptly document, address and remedy any violation of section 13 of the BHC Act or this part, including § 44.21, and document all proposed and actual remediation efforts. The compliance program must include specific written policies and procedures that are reasonably designed to assess the extent to which any activity or investment indicates that modification to the banking entity's compliance program is warranted and to ensure that appropriate modifications are implemented. The written policies and procedures must provide for prompt notification to appropriate management, including senior management and the board of directors, of any material weakness or significant deficiencies in the design or implementation of the compliance program of the banking entity.

III. Responsibility and Accountability for the Compliance Program

a. A banking entity must establish, maintain, and enforce a governance and management framework to manage its business and employees with a view to preventing violations of section 13 of the BHC Act and this part. A banking entity must have an appropriate management framework reasonably designed to ensure that: appropriate personnel are responsible and accountable for the effective implementation and enforcement of the compliance program; a clear reporting line with a chain of responsibility is delineated; and the compliance program is reviewed periodically by senior management. The board of directors (or equivalent governance body) and senior management should have the appropriate authority and access to personnel and information within the organizations as well as appropriate resources to conduct their oversight activities effectively.

1. Corporate governance. The banking entity must adopt a written compliance program approved by the board of directors, an appropriate committee of the board, or equivalent governance body, and senior management.

2. Management procedures. The banking entity must establish, maintain, and enforce a governance framework that is reasonably designed to achieve compliance with section 13 of the BHC Act and this part, which, at a minimum, provides for:

i. The designation of appropriate senior management or committee of senior management with authority to carry out the management responsibilities of the banking entity for each trading desk and for each organizational unit engaged in covered fund activities;

ii. Written procedures addressing the management of the activities of the banking entity that are reasonably designed to achieve compliance with section 13 of the BHC Act and this part, including:

A. A description of the management system, including the titles, qualifications, and locations of managers and the specific responsibilities of each person with respect to the banking entity's activities governed by section 13 of the BHC Act and this part; and

B. Procedures for determining compensation arrangements for traders engaged in underwriting or market making-related activities under § 44.4 or risk-mitigating hedging activities under § 44.5 so that such compensation arrangements are designed not to reward or incentivize prohibited proprietary trading and appropriately balance risk and financial results in a manner that does not encourage employees to expose the banking entity to excessive or imprudent risk.

3. Business line managers. Managers with responsibility for one or more trading desks of the banking entity are accountable for the effective implementation and enforcement of the compliance program with respect to the applicable trading desk(s).

4. Board of directors, or similar corporate body, and senior management. The board of directors, or similar corporate body, and senior management are responsible for setting and communicating an appropriate culture of compliance with section 13 of the BHC Act and this part and ensuring that appropriate policies regarding the management of trading activities and covered fund activities or investments are adopted to comply with section 13 of the BHC Act and this part. The board of directors or similar corporate body (such as a designated committee of the board or an equivalent governance body) must ensure that senior management is fully capable, qualified, and properly motivated to manage compliance with this part in light of the organization's business activities and the expectations of the board of directors. The board of directors or similar corporate body must also ensure that senior management has established appropriate incentives and adequate resources to support compliance with this part, including the implementation of a compliance program meeting the requirements of this appendix into management goals and compensation structures across the banking entity.

5. *Senior management.* Senior management is responsible for implementing and enforcing the approved compliance program. Senior management must also ensure that effective corrective action is taken when failures in compliance with section 13 of the BHC Act and this part are identified. Senior management and control personnel charged with overseeing compliance with section 13 of the BHC Act and this part should review the compliance program for the banking entity periodically and report to the board, or an appropriate committee thereof, on the effectiveness of the compliance program and compliance matters with a frequency appropriate to the size, scope, and risk profile of the banking entity's trading activities and covered fund activities or investments, which shall be at least annually.

6. *CEO attestation.* Based on a review by the CEO of the banking entity, the CEO of the banking entity must, annually, attest in writing to the OCC that the banking entity has in place processes to establish, maintain, enforce, review, test and modify the compliance program established under this Appendix and §44.20 of this part in a manner reasonably designed to achieve compliance with section 13 of the BHC Act and this part. In the case of a U.S. branch or agency of a foreign banking entity, the attestation may be provided for the entire U.S. operations of the foreign banking entity by the senior management officer of the United States operations of the foreign banking entity who is located in the United States.

IV. Independent Testing

a. Independent testing must occur with a frequency appropriate to the size, scope, and risk profile of the banking entity's trading and covered fund activities or investments, which shall be at least annually. This independent testing must include an evaluation of:

1. The overall adequacy and effectiveness of the banking entity's compliance program, including an analysis of the extent to which the program contains all the required elements of this appendix;

2. The effectiveness of the banking entity's internal controls, including an analysis and documentation of instances in which such internal controls have been breached, and how such breaches were addressed and resolved; and

3. The effectiveness of the banking entity's management procedures.

b. A banking entity must ensure that independent testing regarding the effectiveness of the banking entity's compliance program is conducted by a qualified independent party, such as the banking entity's internal audit department, compliance personnel or risk managers independent of the organizational unit being tested, outside auditors, consultants, or other qualified independent parties. A banking entity must promptly take appropriate action to remedy any significant deficiencies or material weaknesses in its compliance program and to terminate any violations of section 13 of the BHC Act or this part.

V. Training

Banking entities must provide adequate training to personnel and managers of the banking entity engaged in activities or investments governed by section 13 of the BHC Act or this part, as well as other appropriate supervisory, risk, independent testing, and audit personnel, in order to effectively implement and enforce the compliance program. This training should occur with a frequency appropriate to the size and the risk profile of the banking entity's trading activities and covered fund activities or investments.

VI. Recordkeeping

Banking entities must create and retain records sufficient to demonstrate compliance and support the operations and effectiveness of the compliance program. A banking entity must retain these records for a period that is no less than 5 years or such longer period as required by the OCC in a form that allows it to promptly produce such records to the OCC on request.

PART 45—MARGIN AND CAPITAL REQUIREMENTS FOR COVERED SWAP ENTITIES

Sec.
45.1 Authority, purpose, scope, exemptions and compliance dates.

45.2 Definitions.
45.3 Initial margin.
45.4 Variation margin.
45.5 Netting arrangements, minimum transfer amount, and satisfaction of collecting and posting requirements.
45.6 Eligible collateral.
45.7 Segregation of collateral.
45.8 Initial margin models and standardized amounts.
45.9 Cross-border application of margin requirements.
45.10 Documentation of margin matters.
45.11 Special rules for affiliates.
45.12 Capital.
APPENDIX A TO PART 45—STANDARDIZED MINIMUM INITIAL MARGIN REQUIREMENTS FOR NON-CLEARED SWAPS AND NON-CLEARED SECURITY-BASED SWAPS
APPENDIX B TO PART 45—MARGIN VALUES FOR ELIGIBLE NONCASH MARGIN COLLATERAL

AUTHORITY: 7 U.S.C. 6s(e), 12 U.S.C. 1 *et seq.*, 12 U.S.C. 93a, 161, 481, 1818, 3907, 3909, 5412(b)(2)(B), and 15 U.S.C. 78o–10(e).

SOURCE: 80 FR 74898, 74910, Nov. 30, 2015, unless otherwise noted.

EDITORIAL NOTE: Nomenclature changes to part 45 appear at 80 FR 74898, 74910, Nov. 30, 2015.

§45.1 Authority, purpose, scope, exemptions and compliance dates.

(a) *Authority.* This part is issued under the authority of 7 U.S.C. 6s(e), 12 U.S.C. 1 *et seq.*, 93a, 161, 481, 1818, 3907, 3909, 5412(b)(2)(B), and 15 U.S.C. 78o–10(e).

(b) *Purpose.* Section 4s of the Commodity Exchange Act of 1936 (7 U.S.C. 6s) and section 15F of the Securities Exchange Act of 1934 (15 U.S.C. 78o–10) require the OCC to establish capital and margin requirements for any for any national bank or subsidiary thereof, Federal savings association or subsidiary thereof, or Federal branch or agency of a foreign bank that is registered as a swap dealer, major swap participant, security-based swap dealer, or major security-based swap participant with respect to all non-cleared swaps and non-cleared security-based swaps. This regulation implements section 4s of the Commodity Exchange Act of 1936 and section 15F of the Securities Exchange Act of 1934 by defining terms used in the statute and related terms, establishing capital and margin requirements, and explaining the statutes' requirements.

(c) *Scope.* This part establishes minimum capital and margin requirements for each covered swap entity subject to this part with respect to all non-cleared swaps and non-cleared security-based swaps. This part applies to any non-cleared swap or non-cleared security-based swap entered into by a covered swap entity on or after the relevant compliance date set forth in paragraph (e) of this section. Nothing in this part is intended to prevent a covered swap entity from collecting margin in amounts greater than are required under this part.

(d) *Exemptions*—(1) *Swaps.* The requirements of this part (except for §45.12) shall not apply to a non-cleared swap if the counterparty:

(i) Qualifies for an exception from clearing under section 2(h)(7)(A) of the Commodity Exchange Act of 1936 (7 U.S.C. 2(h)(7)(A)) and implementing regulations;

(ii) Qualifies for an exemption from clearing under a rule, regulation, or order that the Commodity Futures Trading Commission issued pursuant to its authority under section 4(c)(1) of the Commodity Exchange Act of 1936 (7 U.S.C. 6(c)(1)) concerning cooperative entities that would otherwise be subject to the requirements of section 2(h)(1)(A) of the Commodity Exchange Act of 1936 (7 U.S.C. 2(h)(1)(A)); or

(iii) Satisfies the criteria in section 2(h)(7)(D) of the Commodity Exchange Act of 1936 (7 U.S.C. 2(h)(7)(D)) and implementing regulations.

(2) *Security-based swaps.* The requirements of this part (except for §45.12) shall not apply to a non-cleared security-based swap if the counterparty:

(i) Qualifies for an exception from clearing under section 3C(g)(1) of the Securities Exchange Act of 1934 (15 U.S.C. 78c–3(g)(1)) and implementing regulations; or

(ii) Satisfies the criteria in section 3C(g)(4) of the Securities Exchange Act of 1934 (15 U.S.C. 78c–3(g)(4)) and implementing regulations.

(e) *Compliance dates.* Covered swap entities shall comply with the minimum margin requirements of this part on or before the following dates for non-cleared swaps and non-cleared security-based swaps entered into on or after the following dates:

(1) September 1, 2016 with respect to the requirements in § 45.3 for initial margin and § 45.4 for variation margin for any non-cleared swaps and non-cleared security-based swaps, where both:

(i) The covered swap entity combined with all its affiliates; and

(ii) Its counterparty combined with all its affiliates, have an average daily aggregate notional amount of non-cleared swaps, non-cleared security-based swaps, foreign exchange forwards and foreign exchange swaps for March, April and May 2016 that exceeds $3 trillion, where such amounts are calculated only for business days; and

(iii) In calculating the amounts in paragraphs (e)(1)(i) and (ii) of this section, an entity shall count the average daily aggregate notional amount of a non-cleared swap, a non-cleared security-based swap, a foreign exchange forward or a foreign exchange swap between the entity and an affiliate only one time, and shall not count a swap or security-based swap that is exempt pursuant to paragraph (d) of this section.

(2) March 1, 2017 with respect to the requirements in § 45.4 for variation margin for any other covered swap entity with respect to non-cleared swaps and non-cleared security-based swaps entered into with any other counterparty.

(3) September 1, 2017 with respect to the requirements in § 45.3 for initial margin for any non-cleared swaps and non-cleared security-based swaps, where both:

(i) The covered swap entity combined with all its affiliates; and

(ii) Its counterparty combined with all its affiliates, have an average daily aggregate notional amount of non-cleared swaps, non-cleared security-based swaps, foreign exchange forwards and foreign exchange swaps for March, April and May 2017 that exceeds $2.25 trillion, where such amounts are calculated only for business days; and

(iii) In calculating the amounts in paragraphs (e)(3)(i) and (ii) of this section, an entity shall count the average daily aggregate notional amount of a non-cleared swap, a non-cleared security-based swap, a foreign exchange forward or a foreign exchange swap between the entity and an affiliate only one time, and shall not count a swap or security-based swap that is exempt pursuant to paragraph (d) of this section.

(4) September 1, 2018 with respect to the requirements in § 45.3 for initial margin for any non-cleared swaps and non-cleared security-based swaps, where both:

(i) The covered swap entity combined with all its affiliates; and

(ii) Its counterparty combined with all its affiliates, have an average daily aggregate notional amount of non-cleared swaps, non-cleared security-based swaps, foreign exchange forwards and foreign exchange swaps for March, April and May 2018 that exceeds $1.5 trillion, where such amounts are calculated only for business days; and

(iii) In calculating the amounts in paragraphs (e)(4)(i) and (ii) of this section, an entity shall count the average daily aggregate notional amount of a non-cleared swap, a non-cleared security-based swap, a foreign exchange forward or a foreign exchange swap between the entity and an affiliate only one time, and shall not count a swap or security-based swap that is exempt pursuant to paragraph (d) of this section.

(5) September 1, 2019 with respect to the requirements in § 45.3 for initial margin for any non-cleared swaps and non-cleared security-based swaps, where both:

(i) The covered swap entity combined with all its affiliates; and

(ii) Its counterparty combined with all its affiliates, have an average daily aggregate notional amount of non-cleared swaps, non-cleared security-based swaps, foreign exchange forwards and foreign exchange swaps for March, April and May 2019 that exceeds $0.75 trillion, where such amounts are calculated only for business days; and

(iii) In calculating the amounts in paragraphs (e)(5)(i) and (ii) of this section, an entity shall count the average daily aggregate notional amount of a non-cleared swap, a non-cleared security-based swap, a foreign exchange forward or a foreign exchange swap between the entity and an affiliate only one time, and shall not count a swap or security-based swap that is exempt pursuant to paragraph (d) of this section.

(6) September 1, 2020 with respect to the requirements in § 45.3 for initial margin for any other covered swap entity with respect to non-cleared swaps and non-cleared security-based swaps entered into with any other counterparty.

(7) For purposes of determining the date on which a non-cleared swap or a non-cleared security-based swap was entered into, a Covered Swap Entity will not take into account amendments to the non-cleared swap or the non-cleared security-based swap that were entered into solely to comply with the requirements of part 47, subpart I of part 252 or part 382 of Title 12, as applicable.

(f) Once a covered swap entity must comply with the margin requirements for non-cleared swaps and non-cleared security-based swaps with respect to a particular counterparty based on the compliance dates in paragraph (e) of this section, the covered swap entity shall remain subject to the requirements of this part with respect to that counterparty.

(g)(1) If a covered swap entity's counterparty changes its status such that a non-cleared swap or non-cleared security-based swap with that counterparty becomes subject to stricter margin requirements under this part (such as if the counterparty's status changes from a financial end user without material swaps exposure to a financial end user with material swaps exposure), then the covered swap entity shall comply with the stricter margin requirements for any non-cleared swap or non-cleared security-based swap entered into with that counterparty after the counterparty changes its status.

(2) If a covered swap entity's counterparty changes its status such that a non-cleared swap or non-cleared security-based swap with that counterparty becomes subject to less strict margin requirements under this part (such as if the counterparty's status changes from a financial end user with material swaps exposure to a financial end user without material swaps exposure), then the covered swap entity may comply with the less strict margin requirements for any non-cleared swap or non-cleared security-based swap entered into with that counterparty after the counterparty changes its status as well as for any outstanding non-cleared swap or non-cleared security-based swap entered into after the applicable compliance date in paragraph (e) of this section and before the counterparty changed its status.

[80 FR 74898, 74910, Nov. 30, 2015, as amended at 80 FR 74910, 74923, Nov. 30, 2015; 83 FR 50811, Oct. 10, 2018]

§ 45.2 Definitions.

Affiliate. A company is an affiliate of another company if:

(1) Either company consolidates the other on financial statements prepared in accordance with U.S. Generally Accepted Accounting Principles, the International Financial Reporting Standards, or other similar standards;

(2) Both companies are consolidated with a third company on a financial statement prepared in accordance with such principles or standards;

(3) For a company that is not subject to such principles or standards, if consolidation as described in paragraph (1) or (2) of this definition would have occurred if such principles or standards had applied; or

(4) The OCC has determined that a company is an affiliate of another company, based on OCC's conclusion that either company provides significant support to, or is materially subject to the risks or losses of, the other company.

Bank holding company has the meaning specified in section 2 of the Bank Holding Company Act of 1956 (12 U.S.C. 1841).

Broker has the meaning specified in section 3(a)(4) of the Securities Exchange Act of 1934 (15 U.S.C. 78c(a)(4)).

Business day means any day other than a Saturday, Sunday, or legal holiday.

Clearing agency has the meaning specified in section 3(a)(23) of the Securities Exchange Act of 1934 (15 U.S.C. 78c(a)(23)).

Company means a corporation, partnership, limited liability company, business trust, special purpose entity, association, or similar organization.

Counterparty means, with respect to any non-cleared swap or non-cleared security-based swap to which a person is a party, each other party to such non-cleared swap or non-cleared security-based swap.

Covered swap entity means any national bank or subsidiary thereof, Federal savings association or subsidiary thereof, or Federal branch or agency of a foreign bank that is a swap entity, or any other entity that the OCC determines.

Cross-currency swap means a swap in which one party exchanges with another party principal and interest rate payments in one currency for principal and interest rate payments in another currency, and the exchange of principal occurs on the date the swap is entered into, with a reversal of the exchange of principal at a later date that is agreed upon when the swap is entered into.

Currency of settlement means a currency in which a party has agreed to discharge payment obligations related to a non-cleared swap, a non-cleared security-based swap, a group of non-cleared swaps, or a group of non-cleared security-based swaps subject to a master agreement at the regularly occurring dates on which such payments are due in the ordinary course.

Day of execution means the calendar day at the time the parties enter into a non-cleared swap or non-cleared security-based swap, provided:

(1) If each party is in a different calendar day at the time the parties enter into the non-cleared swap or non-cleared security-based swap, the day of execution is deemed the latter of the two dates; and

(2) If a non-cleared swap or non-cleared security-based swap is:

(i) Entered into after 4:00 p.m. in the location of a party; or

(ii) Entered into on a day that is not a business day in the location of a party, then the non-cleared swap or non-cleared security-based swap is deemed to have been entered into on the immediately succeeding day that is a business day for both parties, and both parties shall determine the day of execution with reference to that business day.

Dealer has the meaning specified in section 3(a)(5) of the Securities Exchange Act of 1934 (15 U.S.C. 78c(a)(5)).

Depository institution has the meaning specified in section 3(c) of the Federal Deposit Insurance Act (12 U.S.C. 1813(c)).

Derivatives clearing organization has the meaning specified in section 1a(15) of the Commodity Exchange Act of 1936 (7 U.S.C. 1a(15)).

Eligible collateral means collateral described in § 45.6.

Eligible master netting agreement means a written, legally enforceable agreement provided that:

(1) The agreement creates a single legal obligation for all individual transactions covered by the agreement upon an event of default following any stay permitted by paragraph (2) of this definition, including upon an event of receivership, conservatorship, insolvency, liquidation, or similar proceeding, of the counterparty;

(2) The agreement provides the covered swap entity the right to accelerate, terminate, and close-out on a net basis all transactions under the agreement and to liquidate or set-off collateral promptly upon an event of default, including upon an event of receivership, conservatorship, insolvency, liquidation, or similar proceeding, of the counterparty, provided that, in any such case:

(i) Any exercise of rights under the agreement will not be stayed or avoided under applicable law in the relevant jurisdictions, other than:

(A) In receivership, conservatorship, or resolution under the Federal Deposit Insurance Act (12 U.S.C. 1811 *et seq.*), Title II of the Dodd-Frank Wall Street Reform and Consumer Protection Act (12 U.S.C. 5381 *et seq.*), the Federal Housing Enterprises Financial Safety and Soundness Act of 1992, as amended (12 U.S.C. 4617), or the Farm Credit Act of 1971, as amended (12 U.S.C. 2183 and 2279cc), or laws of foreign jurisdictions that are substantially similar to the U.S. laws referenced in this paragraph (2)(i)(A) in order to facilitate the orderly resolution of the defaulting counterparty; or

(B) Where the agreement is subject by its terms to, or incorporates, any of the laws referenced in paragraph (2)(i)(A) of this definition; and

(ii) The agreement may limit the right to accelerate, terminate, and close-out on a net basis all transactions under the agreement and to liquidate or set-off collateral promptly upon an event of default of the counterparty to the extent necessary for the counterparty to comply with the requirements of part 47, subpart I of part 252 or part 382 of Title 12, as applicable;

(3) The agreement does not contain a walkaway clause (that is, a provision that permits a non-defaulting counterparty to make a lower payment than it otherwise would make under the agreement, or no payment at all, to a defaulter or the estate of a defaulter, even if the defaulter or the estate of the defaulter is a net creditor under the agreement); and

(4) A covered swap entity that relies on the agreement for purposes of calculating the margin required by this part must:

(i) Conduct sufficient legal review to conclude with a well-founded basis (and maintain sufficient written documentation of that legal review) that:

(A) The agreement meets the requirements of paragraph (2) of this definition; and

(B) In the event of a legal challenge (including one resulting from default or from receivership, conservatorship, insolvency, liquidation, or similar proceeding), the relevant court and administrative authorities would find the agreement to be legal, valid, binding, and enforceable under the law of the relevant jurisdictions; and

(ii) Establish and maintain written procedures to monitor possible changes in relevant law and to ensure that the agreement continues to satisfy the requirements of this definition.

Financial end user means:

(1) Any counterparty that is not a swap entity and that is:

(i) A bank holding company or an affiliate thereof; a savings and loan holding company; a U.S. intermediate holding company established or designated for purposes of compliance with 12 CFR 252.153; or a nonbank financial institution supervised by the Board of Governors of the Federal Reserve System under Title I of the Dodd-Frank Wall Street Reform and Consumer Protection Act (12 U.S.C. 5323);

(ii) A depository institution; a foreign bank; a Federal credit union or State credit union as defined in section 2 of the Federal Credit Union Act (12 U.S.C. 1752(1) & (6)); an institution that functions solely in a trust or fiduciary capacity as described in section 2(c)(2)(D) of the Bank Holding Company Act (12 U.S.C. 1841(c)(2)(D)); an industrial loan company, an industrial bank, or other similar institution described in section 2(c)(2)(H) of the Bank Holding Company Act (12 U.S.C. 1841(c)(2)(H));

(iii) An entity that is state-licensed or registered as:

(A) A credit or lending entity, including a finance company; money lender; installment lender; consumer lender or lending company; mortgage lender, broker, or bank; motor vehicle title pledge lender; payday or deferred deposit lender; premium finance company; commercial finance or lending company; or commercial mortgage company; except entities registered or licensed solely on account of financing the entity's direct sales of goods or services to customers;

(B) A money services business, including a check casher; money transmitter; currency dealer or exchange; or money order or traveler's check issuer;

(iv) A regulated entity as defined in section 1303(20) of the Federal Housing Enterprises Financial Safety and Soundness Act of 1992, as amended (12 U.S.C. 4502(20)) or any entity for which the Federal Housing Finance Agency or its successor is the primary federal regulator;

(v) Any institution chartered in accordance with the Farm Credit Act of 1971, as amended, 12 U.S.C. 2001 *et seq.*, that is regulated by the Farm Credit Administration;

(vi) A securities holding company; a broker or dealer; an investment adviser as defined in section 202(a) of the Investment Advisers Act of 1940 (15 U.S.C. 80b–2(a)); an investment company registered with the U.S. Securities and Exchange Commission under the Investment Company Act of 1940 (15 U.S.C. 80a–1 *et seq.*); or a company that has elected to be regulated as a business development company pursuant to section 54(a) of the Investment Company Act of 1940 (15 U.S.C. 80a–53(a));

(vii) A private fund as defined in section 202(a) of the Investment Advisers Act of 1940 (15 U.S.C. 80–b–2(a)); an entity that would be an investment company under section 3 of the Investment Company Act of 1940 (15 U.S.C. 80a–3) but for section 3(c)(5)(C); or an entity that is deemed not to be an investment company under section 3 of the Investment Company Act of 1940 pursuant to Investment Company Act Rule 3a–7 (17 CFR 270.3a–7) of the U.S. Securities and Exchange Commission;

(viii) A commodity pool, a commodity pool operator, or a commodity trading advisor as defined, respectively, in section 1a(10), 1a(11), and 1a(12) of the Commodity Exchange Act of 1936 (7 U.S.C. 1a(10), 1a(11), and 1a(12)); a floor broker, a floor trader, or introducing broker as defined, respectively, in 1a(22), 1a(23) and 1a(31) of the Commodity Exchange Act of 1936 (7 U.S.C. 1a(22), 1a(23), and 1a(31)); or a futures commission merchant as defined in 1a(28) of the Commodity Exchange Act of 1936 (7 U.S.C. 1a(28));

(ix) An employee benefit plan as defined in paragraphs (3) and (32) of section 3 of the Employee Retirement Income and Security Act of 1974 (29 U.S.C. 1002);

(x) An entity that is organized as an insurance company, primarily engaged in writing insurance or reinsuring risks underwritten by insurance companies, or is subject to supervision as such by a State insurance regulator or foreign insurance regulator;

(xi) An entity, person or arrangement that is, or holds itself out as being, an entity, person, or arrangement that raises money from investors, accepts money from clients, or uses its own money primarily for the purpose of investing or trading or facilitating the investing or trading in loans, securities, swaps, funds or other assets for resale or other disposition or otherwise trading in loans, securities, swaps, funds or other assets; or

(xii) An entity that would be a financial end user described in paragraph (1) of this definition or a swap entity, if it were organized under the laws of the United States or any State thereof.

(2) The term "financial end user" does not include any counterparty that is:

(i) A sovereign entity;

(ii) A multilateral development bank;

(iii) The Bank for International Settlements;

(iv) An entity that is exempt from the definition of financial entity pursuant to section 2(h)(7)(C)(iii) of the Commodity Exchange Act of 1936 (7 U.S.C. 2(h)(7)(C)(iii)) and implementing regulations; or

(v) An affiliate that qualifies for the exemption from clearing pursuant to section 2(h)(7)(D) of the Commodity Exchange Act of 1936 (7 U.S.C. 2(h)(7)(D)) or section 3C(g)(4) of the Securities Exchange Act of 1934 (15 U.S.C. 78c–3(g)(4)) and implementing regulations.

Foreign bank means an organization that is organized under the laws of a foreign country and that engages directly in the business of banking outside the United States.

Foreign exchange forward has the meaning specified in section 1a(24) of the Commodity Exchange Act of 1936 (7 U.S.C. 1a(24)).

Foreign exchange swap has the meaning specified in section 1a(25) of the Commodity Exchange Act of 1936 (7 U.S.C. 1a(25)).

Initial margin means the collateral as calculated in accordance with § 45.8 that is posted or collected in connection with a non-cleared swap or non-cleared security-based swap.

Initial margin collection amount means:

(1) In the case of a covered swap entity that does not use an initial margin model, the amount of initial margin with respect to a non-cleared swap or non-cleared security-based swap that is required under appendix A of this part; and

(2) In the case of a covered swap entity that uses an initial margin model pursuant to § 45.8, the amount of initial margin with respect to a non-cleared swap or non-cleared security-based swap that is required under the initial margin model.

Initial margin model means an internal risk management model that:

(1) Has been developed and designed to identify an appropriate, risk-based amount of initial margin that the covered swap entity must collect with respect to one or more non-cleared swaps or non-cleared security-based swaps to which the covered swap entity is a party; and

(2) Has been approved by the OCC pursuant to § 45.8.

Initial margin threshold amount means an aggregate credit exposure of $50 million resulting from all non-cleared swaps and non-cleared security-based swaps between a covered swap entity and its affiliates, and a counterparty and its affiliates. For purposes of this calculation, an entity shall not count a swap or security-based swap that is exempt pursuant to § 45.1(d).

Major currency means:

(1) United States Dollar (USD);

(2) Canadian Dollar (CAD);

(3) Euro (EUR);

(4) United Kingdom Pound (GBP);

(5) Japanese Yen (JPY);

(6) Swiss Franc (CHF);

(7) New Zealand Dollar (NZD);

(8) Australian Dollar (AUD);

(9) Swedish Kronor (SEK);

(10) Danish Kroner (DKK);

(11) Norwegian Krone (NOK); or

(12) Any other currency as determined by the OCC.

Margin means initial margin and variation margin.

Market intermediary means a securities holding company; a broker or dealer; a futures commission merchant as defined in 1a(28) of the Commodity Exchange Act of 1936 (7 U.S.C. 1a(28)); a swap dealer as defined in section 1a(49) of the Commodity Exchange Act of 1936 (7 U.S.C. 1a(49)); or a security-based swap dealer as defined in section 3(a)(71) of the Securities Exchange Act of 1934 (15 U.S.C. 78c(a)(71)).

Material swaps exposure for an entity means that an entity and its affiliates have an average daily aggregate notional amount of non-cleared swaps, non-cleared security-based swaps, foreign exchange forwards, and foreign exchange swaps with all counterparties for June, July, and August of the previous calendar year that exceeds $8 billion, where such amount is calculated only for business days. An entity shall count the average daily aggregate notional amount of a non-cleared swap, a non-cleared security-based swap, a foreign exchange forward or a foreign exchange swap between the entity and an affiliate only one time. For purposes of this calculation, an entity shall not count a swap or security-based swap that is exempt pursuant to § 45.1(d).

Multilateral development bank means the International Bank for Reconstruction and Development, the Multilateral Investment Guarantee Agency, the International Finance Corporation, the Inter-American Development Bank, the Asian Development Bank, the African Development Bank, the European Bank for Reconstruction and Development, the European Investment Bank, the European Investment Fund, the Nordic Investment Bank, the Caribbean Development Bank, the Islamic Development Bank, the Council of Europe Development Bank, and any other entity that provides financing for national or regional development in which the U.S. government is a shareholder or contributing member or which the OCC determines poses comparable credit risk.

Non-cleared security-based swap means a security-based swap that is not, directly or indirectly, submitted to and cleared by a clearing agency registered with the U.S. Securities and Exchange Commission pursuant to section 17A of the Securities Exchange Act of 1934 (15 U.S.C. 78q–1) or by a clearing agency that the U.S. Securities and Exchange Commission has exempted from registration by rule or order pursuant to section 17A of the Securities Exchange Act of 1934 (15 U.S.C. 78q–1).

Non-cleared swap means a swap that is not cleared by a derivatives clearing organization registered with the Commodity Futures Trading Commission pursuant to section 5b(a) of the Commodity Exchange Act of 1936 (7 U.S.C. 7a–1(a)) or by a clearing organization that the Commodity Futures Trading Commission has exempted from registration by rule or order pursuant to section 5b(h) of the Commodity Exchange Act of 1936 (7 U.S.C. 7a–1(h)).

Prudential regulator has the meaning specified in section 1a(39) of the Commodity Exchange Act of 1936 (7 U.S.C. 1a(39)).

Savings and loan holding company has the meaning specified in section 10(n) of the Home Owners' Loan Act (12 U.S.C. 1467a(n)).

Securities holding company has the meaning specified in section 618 of the Dodd-Frank Wall Street Reform and Consumer Protection Act (12 U.S.C. 1850a).

Security-based swap has the meaning specified in section 3(a)(68) of the Securities Exchange Act of 1934 (15 U.S.C. 78c(a)(68)).

Sovereign entity means a central government (including the U.S. government) or an agency, department, ministry, or central bank of a central government.

State means any State, commonwealth, territory, or possession of the United States, the District of Columbia, the Commonwealth of Puerto Rico, the Commonwealth of the Northern Mariana Islands, American Samoa, Guam, or the United States Virgin Islands.

Subsidiary. A company is a subsidiary of another company if:

(1) The company is consolidated by the other company on financial statements prepared in accordance with U.S. Generally Accepted Accounting Principles, the International Financial Reporting Standards, or other similar standards;

(2) For a company that is not subject to such principles or standards, if consolidation as described in paragraph (1) of this definition would have occurred if such principles or standards had applied; or

(3) The OCC has determined that the company is a subsidiary of another company, based on OCC's conclusion that either company provides significant support to, or is materially subject to the risks of loss of, the other company.

Swap has the meaning specified in section 1a(47) of the Commodity Exchange Act of 1936 (7 U.S.C. 1a(47)).

Swap entity means a person that is registered with the Commodity Futures Trading Commission as a swap dealer or major swap participant pursuant to the Commodity Exchange Act of 1936 (7 U.S.C. 1 *et seq.*), or a person that is registered with the U.S. Securities and Exchange Commission as a security-based swap dealer or a major security-based swap participant pursuant to the Securities Exchange Act of 1934 (15 U.S.C. 78a *et seq.*).

U.S. Government-sponsored enterprise means an entity established or chartered by the U.S. government to serve public purposes specified by federal statute but whose debt obligations are not explicitly guaranteed by the full faith and credit of the U.S. government.

Variation margin means collateral provided by one party to its counterparty to meet the performance of its obligations under one or more non-cleared swaps or non-cleared security-based swaps between the parties as a result of a change in value of such obligations since the last time such collateral was provided.

Variation margin amount means the cumulative mark-to-market change in value to a covered swap entity of a non-cleared swap or non-cleared security-based swap, as measured from the date it is entered into (or, in the case of a non-cleared swap or non-cleared security-based swap that has a positive or negative value to a covered swap entity on the date it is entered into, such positive or negative value plus any cumulative mark-to-market change in value to the covered swap entity of a non-cleared swap or non-cleared security-based swap after such date), less the value of all variation margin previously collected, plus the value of all variation margin previously posted with respect to such non-cleared swap or non-cleared security-based swap.

[80 FR 74898, 74910, Nov. 30, 2015, as amended at 80 FR 74911, Nov. 30, 2015; 83 FR 50811, Oct. 10, 2018]

§ 45.3 Initial margin.

(a) *Collection of margin.* A covered swap entity shall collect initial margin with respect to any non-cleared swap or non-cleared security-based swap from a counterparty that is a financial end user with material swaps exposure or that is a swap entity in an amount that is no less than the greater of:

(1) Zero; or

(2) The initial margin collection amount for such non-cleared swap or non-cleared security-based swap *less* the initial margin threshold amount

(not including any portion of the initial margin threshold amount already applied by the covered swap entity or its affiliates to other non-cleared swaps or non-cleared security-based swaps with the counterparty or its affiliates), as applicable.

(b) *Posting of margin.* A covered swap entity shall post initial margin with respect to any non-cleared swap or non-cleared security-based swap to a counterparty that is a financial end user with material swaps exposure. Such initial margin shall be in an amount at least as large as the covered swap entity would be required to collect under paragraph (a) of this section if it were in the place of the counterparty.

(c) *Timing.* A covered swap entity shall comply with the initial margin requirements described in paragraphs (a) and (b) of this section on each business day, for a period beginning on or before the business day following the day of execution and ending on the date the non-cleared swap or non-cleared security-based swap terminates or expires.

(d) *Other counterparties.* A covered swap entity is not required to collect or post initial margin with respect to any non-cleared swap or non-cleared security-based swap described in § 45.1(d). For any other non-cleared swap or non-cleared security-based swap between a covered swap entity and a counterparty that is neither a financial end user with a material swaps exposure nor a swap entity, the covered swap entity shall collect initial margin at such times and in such forms and such amounts (if any), that the covered swap entity determines appropriately addresses the credit risk posed by the counterparty and the risks of such non-cleared swap or non-cleared security-based swap.

§ 45.4 Variation margin.

(a) *General.* After the date on which a covered swap entity enters into a non-cleared swap or non-cleared security-based swap with a swap entity or financial end user, the covered swap entity shall collect variation margin equal to the variation margin amount from the counterparty to such non-cleared swap or non-cleared security-based swap when the amount is positive and post variation margin equal to the variation margin amount to the counterparty to such non-cleared swap or non-cleared security-based swap when the amount is negative.

(b) *Timing.* A covered swap entity shall comply with the variation margin requirements described in paragraph (a) of this section on each business day, for a period beginning on or before the business day following the day of execution and ending on the date the non-cleared swap or non-cleared security based swap terminates or expires.

(c) *Other counterparties.* A covered swap entity is not required to collect or post variation margin with respect to any non-cleared swap or non-cleared security-based swap described in § 45.1(d). For any other non-cleared swap or non-cleared security-based swap between a covered swap entity and a counterparty that is neither a financial end user nor a swap entity, the covered swap entity shall collect variation margin at such times and in such forms and such amounts (if any), that the covered swap entity determines appropriately addresses the credit risk posed by the counterparty and the risks of such non-cleared swap or non-cleared security-based swap.

§ 45.5 Netting arrangements, minimum transfer amount, and satisfaction of collecting and posting requirements.

(a) *Netting arrangements.* (1) For purposes of calculating and complying with the initial margin requirements of § 45.3 using an initial margin model as described in § 45.8, or with the variation margin requirements of § 45.4, a covered swap entity may net non-cleared swaps or non-cleared security-based swaps in accordance with this subsection.

(2) To the extent that one or more non-cleared swaps or non-cleared security-based swaps are executed pursuant to an eligible master netting agreement between a covered swap entity and its counterparty that is a swap entity or financial end user, a covered swap entity may calculate and comply with the applicable requirements of this part on an aggregate net basis with respect to all non-cleared swaps and non-cleared security-based swaps

governed by such agreement, subject to paragraph (a)(3) of this section.

(3)(i) Except as permitted in paragraph (a)(3)(ii) of this section, if an eligible master netting agreement covers non-cleared swaps and non-cleared security-based swaps entered into on or after the applicable compliance date set forth in § 45.1(e) or (g), all the non-cleared swaps and non-cleared security-based swaps covered by that agreement are subject to the requirements of this part and included in the aggregate netting portfolio for the purposes of calculating and complying with the margin requirements of this part.

(ii) An eligible master netting agreement may identify one or more separate netting portfolios that independently meet the requirements in paragraph (1) of the definition of "Eligible master netting agreement" in § 45.2 and to which collection and posting of margin applies on an aggregate net basis separate from and exclusive of any other non-cleared swaps or non-cleared security-based swaps covered by the eligible master netting agreement. Any such netting portfolio that contains any non-cleared swap or non-cleared security-based swap entered into on or after the applicable compliance date set forth in § 45.1(e) or (g) is subject to the requirements of this part. Any such netting portfolio that contains only non-cleared swaps or non-cleared security-based swaps entered into before the applicable compliance date is not subject to the requirements of this part.

(4) If a covered swap entity cannot conclude after sufficient legal review with a well-founded basis that the netting agreement described in this section meets the definition of eligible master netting agreement set forth in § 45.2, the covered swap entity must treat the non-cleared swaps and non-cleared security based swaps covered by the agreement on a gross basis for the purposes of calculating and complying with the requirements of this part to collect margin, but the covered swap entity may net those non-cleared swaps and non-cleared security-based swaps in accordance with paragraphs (a)(1) through (3) of this section for the purposes of calculating and complying with the requirements of this part to post margin.

(b) *Minimum transfer amount.* Notwithstanding § 45.3 or § 45.4, a covered swap entity is not required to collect or post margin pursuant to this part with respect to a particular counterparty unless and until the combined amount of initial margin and variation margin that is required pursuant to this part to be collected or posted and that has not yet been collected or posted with respect to the counterparty is greater than $500,000.

(c) *Satisfaction of collecting and posting requirements.* A covered swap entity shall not be deemed to have violated its obligation to collect or post margin from or to a counterparty under § 45.3, § 45.4, or § 45.6(e) if:

(1) The counterparty has refused or otherwise failed to provide or accept the required margin to or from the covered swap entity; and

(2) The covered swap entity has:

(i) Made the necessary efforts to collect or post the required margin, including the timely initiation and continued pursuit of formal dispute resolution mechanisms, or has otherwise demonstrated upon request to the satisfaction of the OCC that it has made appropriate efforts to collect or post the required margin; or

(ii) Commenced termination of the non-cleared swap or non-cleared security-based swap with the counterparty promptly following the applicable cure period and notification requirements.

§ 45.6 Eligible collateral.

(a) *Non-cleared swaps and non-cleared security-based swaps with a swap entity.* For a non-cleared swap or non-cleared security-based swap with a swap entity, a covered swap entity shall collect initial margin and variation margin required pursuant to this part solely in the form of the following types of collateral:

(1) Immediately available cash funds that are denominated in:

(i) U.S. dollars or another major currency; or

(ii) The currency of settlement for the non-cleared swap or non-cleared security-based swap;

(2) With respect to initial margin only:

(i) A security that is issued by, or unconditionally guaranteed as to the timely payment of principal and interest by, the U.S. Department of the Treasury;

(ii) A security that is issued by, or unconditionally guaranteed as to the timely payment of principal and interest by, a U.S. government agency (other than the U.S. Department of Treasury) whose obligations are fully guaranteed by the full faith and credit of the United States government;

(iii) A security that is issued by, or fully guaranteed as to the payment of principal and interest by, the European Central Bank or a sovereign entity that is assigned no higher than a 20 percent risk weight under the capital rules applicable to the covered swap entity as set forth in § 45.12;

(iv) A publicly traded debt security issued by, or an asset-backed security fully guaranteed as to the payment of principal and interest by, a U.S. Government-sponsored enterprise that is operating with capital support or another form of direct financial assistance received from the U.S. government that enables the repayments of the U.S. Government-sponsored enterprise's eligible securities;

(v) A publicly traded debt security that meets the terms of 12 CFR part 1 and is issued by a U.S. Government-sponsored enterprise not operating with capital support or another form of direct financial assistance from the U.S. government, and is not an asset-backed security;

(vi) A security that is issued by, or fully guaranteed as to the payment of principal and interest by, the Bank for International Settlements, the International Monetary Fund, or a multilateral development bank;

(vii) A security solely in the form of:

(A) Publicly traded debt not otherwise described in paragraph (a)(2) of this section that meets the terms of 12 CFR part 1 and is not an asset-backed security;

(B) Publicly traded common equity that is included in:

(*1*) The Standard & Poor's Composite 1500 Index or any other similar index of liquid and readily marketable equity securities as determined by the OCC; or

(*2*) An index that a covered swap entity's supervisor in a foreign jurisdiction recognizes for purposes of including publicly traded common equity as initial margin under applicable regulatory policy, if held in that foreign jurisdiction;

(viii) Securities in the form of redeemable securities in a pooled investment fund representing the security-holder's proportional interest in the fund's net assets and that are issued and redeemed only on the basis of the market value of the fund's net assets prepared each business day after the security-holder makes its investment commitment or redemption request to the fund, if:

(A) The fund's investments are limited to the following:

(*1*) Securities that are issued by, or unconditionally guaranteed as to the timely payment of principal and interest by, the U.S. Department of the Treasury, and immediately-available cash funds denominated in U.S. dollars; or

(*2*) Securities denominated in a common currency and issued by, or fully guaranteed as to the payment of principal and interest by, the European Central Bank or a sovereign entity that is assigned no higher than a 20 percent risk weight under the capital rules applicable to the covered swap entity as set forth in § 45.12, and immediately-available cash funds denominated in the same currency; and

(B) Assets of the fund may not be transferred through securities lending, securities borrowing, repurchase agreements, reverse repurchase agreements, or other means that involve the fund having rights to acquire the same or similar assets from the transferee; or

(ix) Gold.

(b) *Non-cleared swaps and non-cleared security-based swaps with a financial end user*. For a non-cleared swap or non-cleared security-based swap with a financial end user, a covered swap entity shall collect and post initial margin and variation margin required pursuant to this part solely in the form of the following types of collateral:

(1) Immediately available cash funds that are denominated in:

(i) U.S. dollars or another major currency; or

(ii) The currency of settlement for the non-cleared swap or non-cleared security-based swap;

(2) A security that is issued by, or unconditionally guaranteed as to the timely payment of principal and interest by, the U.S. Department of the Treasury;

(3) A security that is issued by, or unconditionally guaranteed as to the timely payment of principal and interest by, a U.S. government agency (other than the U.S. Department of Treasury) whose obligations are fully guaranteed by the full faith and credit of the United States government;

(4) A security that is issued by, or fully guaranteed as to the payment of principal and interest by, the European Central Bank or a sovereign entity that is assigned no higher than a 20 percent risk weight under the capital rules applicable to the covered swap entity as set forth in § 45.12;

(5) A publicly traded debt security issued by, or an asset-backed security fully guaranteed as to the payment of principal and interest by, a U.S. Government-sponsored enterprise that is operating with capital support or another form of direct financial assistance received from the U.S. government that enables the repayments of the U.S. Government-sponsored enterprise's eligible securities;

(6) A publicly traded debt security that meets the terms of 12 CFR part 1 and is issued by a U.S. Government-sponsored enterprise not operating with capital support or another form of direct financial assistance from the U.S. government, and is not an asset-backed security;

(7) A security that is issued by, or fully guaranteed as to the payment of principal and interest by, the Bank for International Settlements, the International Monetary Fund, or a multilateral development bank;

(8) A security solely in the form of:

(i) Publicly traded debt not otherwise described in this paragraph (b) that meets the terms of 12 CFR part 1 and is not an asset-backed security;

(ii) Publicly traded common equity that is included in:

(A) The Standard & Poor's Composite 1500 Index or any other similar index of liquid and readily marketable equity securities as determined by the OCC; or

(B) An index that a covered swap entity's supervisor in a foreign jurisdiction recognizes for purposes of including publicly traded common equity as initial margin under applicable regulatory policy, if held in that foreign jurisdiction;

(9) Securities in the form of redeemable securities in a pooled investment fund representing the security-holder's proportional interest in the fund's net assets and that are issued and redeemed only on the basis of the market value of the fund's net assets prepared each business day after the security-holder makes its investment commitment or redemption request to the fund, if:

(i) The fund's investments are limited to the following:

(A) Securities that are issued by, or unconditionally guaranteed as to the timely payment of principal and interest by, the U.S. Department of the Treasury, and immediately-available cash funds denominated in U.S. dollars; or

(B) Securities denominated in a common currency and issued by, or fully guaranteed as to the payment of principal and interest by, the European Central Bank or a sovereign entity that is assigned no higher than a 20 percent risk weight under the capital rules applicable to the covered swap entity as set forth in § 45.12, and immediately-available cash funds denominated in the same currency; and

(ii) Assets of the fund may not be transferred through securities lending, securities borrowing, repurchase agreements, reverse repurchase agreements, or other means that involve the fund having rights to acquire the same or similar assets from the transferee; or

(10) Gold.

(c)(1) The value of any eligible collateral collected or posted to satisfy margin requirements pursuant to this part is subject to the sum of the following discounts, as applicable:

(i) An 8 percent discount for variation margin collateral denominated in a currency that is not the currency of settlement for the non-cleared swap or non-cleared security-based swap, except for immediately available cash funds denominated in U.S. dollars or another major currency;

(ii) An 8 percent discount for initial margin collateral denominated in a currency that is not the currency of settlement for the non-cleared swap or non-cleared security-based swap, except for eligible types of collateral denominated in a single termination currency designated as payable to the non-posting counterparty as part of the eligible master netting agreement; and

(iii) For variation and initial margin non-cash collateral, the discounts described in appendix B of this part.

(2) The value of variation margin or initial margin collateral is computed as the product of the cash or market value of the eligible collateral asset times one minus the applicable discounts pursuant to paragraph (c)(1) of this section expressed in percentage terms. The total value of all variation margin or initial margin collateral is calculated as the sum of those values for each eligible collateral asset.

(d) Notwithstanding paragraphs (a) and (b) of this section, eligible collateral for initial margin and variation margin required by this part does not include a security issued by:

(1) The party or an affiliate of the party pledging such collateral;

(2) A bank holding company, a savings and loan holding company, a U.S. intermediate holding company established or designated for purposes of compliance with 12 CFR 252.153, a foreign bank, a depository institution, a market intermediary, a company that would be any of the foregoing if it were organized under the laws of the United States or any State, or an affiliate of any of the foregoing institutions; or

(3) A nonbank financial institution supervised by the Board of Governors of the Federal Reserve System under Title I of the Dodd-Frank Wall Street Reform and Consumer Protection Act (12 U.S.C. 5323).

(e) A covered swap entity shall monitor the market value and eligibility of all collateral collected and posted to satisfy the minimum initial margin and minimum variation margin requirements of this part. To the extent that the market value of such collateral has declined, the covered swap entity shall promptly collect or post such additional eligible collateral as is necessary to maintain compliance with the margin requirements of this part. To the extent that the collateral is no longer eligible, the covered swap entity shall promptly collect or post sufficient eligible replacement collateral to comply with the margin requirements of this part.

(f) A covered swap entity may collect or post initial margin and variation margin that is required by §45.3(d) or §45.4(c) or that is not required pursuant to this part in any form of collateral.

[80 FR 74898, 74910, Nov. 30, 2015, as amended at 80 FR 74911, Nov. 30, 2015]

§45.7 Segregation of collateral.

(a) A covered swap entity that posts any collateral other than for variation margin with respect to a non-cleared swap or a non-cleared security-based swap shall require that all funds or other property other than variation margin provided by the covered swap entity be held by one or more custodians that are not the covered swap entity or counterparty and not affiliates of the covered swap entity or the counterparty.

(b) A covered swap entity that collects initial margin required by §45.3(a) with respect to a non-cleared swap or a non-cleared security-based swap shall require that such initial margin be held by one or more custodians that are not the covered swap entity or counterparty and not affiliates of the covered swap entity or the counterparty.

(c) For purposes of paragraphs (a) and (b) of this section, the custodian must act pursuant to a custody agreement that:

(1) Prohibits the custodian from rehypothecating, repledging, reusing, or otherwise transferring (through securities lending, securities borrowing, repurchase agreement, reverse repurchase agreement or other means) the collateral held by the custodian, except that cash collateral may be held in a general deposit account with the custodian if the funds in the account are used to purchase an asset described in §45.6(a)(2) or (b), such asset is held in compliance with this §45.7, and such

purchase takes place within a time period reasonably necessary to consummate such purchase after the cash collateral is posted as initial margin; and

(2) Is a legal, valid, binding, and enforceable agreement under the laws of all relevant jurisdictions, including in the event of bankruptcy, insolvency, or a similar proceeding.

(d) Notwithstanding paragraph (c)(1) of this section, a custody agreement may permit the posting party to substitute or direct any reinvestment of posted collateral held by the custodian, provided that, with respect to collateral collected by a covered swap entity pursuant to § 45.3(a) or posted by a covered swap entity pursuant to § 45.3(b), the agreement requires the posting party to:

(1) Substitute only funds or other property that would qualify as eligible collateral under § 45.6, and for which the amount net of applicable discounts described in appendix B of this part would be sufficient to meet the requirements of § 45.3; and

(2) Direct reinvestment of funds only in assets that would qualify as eligible collateral under § 45.6, and for which the amount net of applicable discounts described in appendix B of this part would be sufficient to meet the requirements of § 45.3.

§ 45.8 Initial margin models and standardized amounts.

(a) *Standardized amounts.* Unless a covered swap entity's initial margin model conforms to the requirements of this section, the covered swap entity shall calculate the amount of initial margin required to be collected or posted for one or more non-cleared swaps or non-cleared security-based swaps with a given counterparty pursuant to § 45.3 on a daily basis pursuant to appendix A of this part.

(b) *Use of initial margin models.* A covered swap entity may calculate the amount of initial margin required to be collected or posted for one or more non-cleared swaps or non-cleared security-based swaps with a given counterparty pursuant to § 45.3 on a daily basis using an initial margin model only if the initial margin model meets the requirements of this section.

(c) *Requirements for initial margin model.* (1) A covered swap entity must obtain the prior written approval of the OCC before using any initial margin model to calculate the initial margin required in this part.

(2) A covered swap entity must demonstrate that the initial margin model satisfies all of the requirements of this section on an ongoing basis.

(3) A covered swap entity must notify the OCC in writing 60 days prior to:

(i) Extending the use of an initial margin model that the OCC has approved under this section to an additional product type;

(ii) Making any change to any initial margin model approved by the OCC under this section that would result in a material change in the covered swap entity's assessment of initial margin requirements; or

(iii) Making any material change to modeling assumptions used by the initial margin model.

(4) The OCC may rescind its approval of the use of any initial margin model, in whole or in part, or may impose additional conditions or requirements if the OCC determines, in its sole discretion, that the initial margin model no longer complies with this section.

(d) *Quantitative requirements.* (1) The covered swap entity's initial margin model must calculate an amount of initial margin that is equal to the potential future exposure of the non-cleared swap, non-cleared security-based swap or netting portfolio of non-cleared swaps or non-cleared security-based swaps covered by an eligible master netting agreement. Potential future exposure is an estimate of the one-tailed 99 percent confidence interval for an increase in the value of the non-cleared swap, non-cleared security-based swap or netting portfolio of non-cleared swaps or non-cleared security-based swaps due to an instantaneous price shock that is equivalent to a movement in all material underlying risk factors, including prices, rates, and spreads, over a holding period equal to the shorter of ten business days or the maturity of the non-cleared swap, non-cleared security-based swap or netting portfolio.

(2) All data used to calibrate the initial margin model must be based on an

equally weighted historical observation period of at least one year and not more than five years and must incorporate a period of significant financial stress for each broad asset class that is appropriate to the non-cleared swaps and non-cleared security-based swaps to which the initial margin model is applied.

(3) The covered swap entity's initial margin model must use risk factors sufficient to measure all material price risks inherent in the transactions for which initial margin is being calculated. The risk categories must include, but should not be limited to, foreign exchange or interest rate risk, credit risk, equity risk, and commodity risk, as appropriate. For material exposures in significant currencies and markets, modeling techniques must capture spread and basis risk and must incorporate a sufficient number of segments of the yield curve to capture differences in volatility and imperfect correlation of rates along the yield curve.

(4) In the case of a non-cleared cross-currency swap, the covered swap entity's initial margin model need not recognize any risks or risk factors associated with the fixed, physically-settled foreign exchange transaction associated with the exchange of principal embedded in the non-cleared cross-currency swap. The initial margin model must recognize all material risks and risk factors associated with all other payments and cash flows that occur during the life of the non-cleared cross-currency swap.

(5) The initial margin model may calculate initial margin for a non-cleared swap or non-cleared security-based swap or a netting portfolio of non-cleared swaps or non-cleared security-based swaps covered by an eligible master netting agreement. It may reflect offsetting exposures, diversification, and other hedging benefits for non-cleared swaps and non-cleared security-based swaps that are governed by the same eligible master netting agreement by incorporating empirical correlations within the following broad risk categories, provided the covered swap entity validates and demonstrates the reasonableness of its process for modeling and measuring hedging benefits: Commodity, credit, equity, and foreign exchange or interest rate. Empirical correlations under an eligible master netting agreement may be recognized by the initial margin model within each broad risk category, but not across broad risk categories.

(6) If the initial margin model does not explicitly reflect offsetting exposures, diversification, and hedging benefits between subsets of non-cleared swaps or non-cleared security-based swaps within a broad risk category, the covered swap entity must calculate an amount of initial margin separately for each subset within which such relationships are explicitly recognized by the initial margin model. The sum of the initial margin amounts calculated for each subset of non-cleared swaps and non-cleared security-based swaps within a broad risk category will be used to determine the aggregate initial margin due from the counterparty for the portfolio of non-cleared swaps and non-cleared security-based swaps within the broad risk category.

(7) The sum of the initial margin amounts calculated for each broad risk category will be used to determine the aggregate initial margin due from the counterparty.

(8) The initial margin model may not permit the calculation of any initial margin collection amount to be offset by, or otherwise take into account, any initial margin that may be owed or otherwise payable by the covered swap entity to the counterparty.

(9) The initial margin model must include all material risks arising from the nonlinear price characteristics of option positions or positions with embedded optionality and the sensitivity of the market value of the positions to changes in the volatility of the underlying rates, prices, or other material risk factors.

(10) The covered swap entity may not omit any risk factor from the calculation of its initial margin that the covered swap entity uses in its initial margin model unless it has first demonstrated to the satisfaction of the OCC that such omission is appropriate.

(11) The covered swap entity may not incorporate any proxy or approximation used to capture the risks of the

covered swap entity's non-cleared swaps or non-cleared security-based swaps unless it has first demonstrated to the satisfaction of the OCC that such proxy or approximation is appropriate.

(12) The covered swap entity must have a rigorous and well-defined process for re-estimating, re-evaluating, and updating its internal margin model to ensure continued applicability and relevance.

(13) The covered swap entity must review and, as necessary, revise the data used to calibrate the initial margin model at least annually, and more frequently as market conditions warrant, to ensure that the data incorporate a period of significant financial stress appropriate to the non-cleared swaps and non-cleared security-based swaps to which the initial margin model is applied.

(14) The level of sophistication of the initial margin model must be commensurate with the complexity of the non-cleared swaps and non-cleared security-based swaps to which it is applied. In calculating an initial margin collection amount, the initial margin model may make use of any of the generally accepted approaches for modeling the risk of a single instrument or portfolio of instruments.

(15) The OCC may in its sole discretion require a covered swap entity using an initial margin model to collect a greater amount of initial margin than that determined by the covered swap entity's initial margin model if the OCC determines that the additional collateral is appropriate due to the nature, structure, or characteristics of the covered swap entity's transaction(s), or is commensurate with the risks associated with the transaction(s).

(e) *Periodic review.* A covered swap entity must periodically, but no less frequently than annually, review its initial margin model in light of developments in financial markets and modeling technologies, and enhance the initial margin model as appropriate to ensure that the initial margin model continues to meet the requirements for approval in this section.

(f) *Control, oversight, and validation mechanisms.* (1) The covered swap entity must maintain a risk control unit that reports directly to senior management and is independent from the business trading units.

(2) The covered swap entity's risk control unit must validate its initial margin model prior to implementation and on an ongoing basis. The covered swap entity's validation process must be independent of the development, implementation, and operation of the initial margin model, or the validation process must be subject to an independent review of its adequacy and effectiveness. The validation process must include:

(i) An evaluation of the conceptual soundness of (including developmental evidence supporting) the initial margin model;

(ii) An ongoing monitoring process that includes verification of processes and benchmarking by comparing the covered swap entity's initial margin model outputs (estimation of initial margin) with relevant alternative internal and external data sources or estimation techniques. The benchmark(s) must address the chosen model's limitations. When applicable, the covered swap entity should consider benchmarks that allow for non-normal distributions such as historical and Monte Carlo simulations. When applicable, validation shall include benchmarking against observable margin standards to ensure that the initial margin required is not less than what a derivatives clearing organization or a clearing agency would require for similar cleared transactions; and

(iii) An outcomes analysis process that includes backtesting the initial margin model. This analysis must recognize and compensate for the challenges inherent in back-testing over periods that do not contain significant financial stress.

(3) If the validation process reveals any material problems with the initial margin model, the covered swap entity must promptly notify the OCC of the problems, describe to the OCC any remedial actions being taken, and adjust the initial margin model to ensure an appropriately conservative amount of required initial margin is being calculated.

(4) The covered swap entity must have an internal audit function independent of business-line management and the risk control unit that at least annually assesses the effectiveness of the controls supporting the covered swap entity's initial margin model measurement systems, including the activities of the business trading units and risk control unit, compliance with policies and procedures, and calculation of the covered swap entity's initial margin requirements under this part. At least annually, the internal audit function must report its findings to the covered swap entity's board of directors or a committee thereof.

(g) *Documentation.* The covered swap entity must adequately document all material aspects of its initial margin model, including the management and valuation of the non-cleared swaps and non-cleared security-based swaps to which it applies, the control, oversight, and validation of the initial margin model, any review processes and the results of such processes.

(h) *Escalation procedures.* The covered swap entity must adequately document internal authorization procedures, including escalation procedures, that require review and approval of any change to the initial margin calculation under the initial margin model, demonstrable analysis that any basis for any such change is consistent with the requirements of this section, and independent review of such demonstrable analysis and approval.

§ 45.9 Cross-border application of margin requirements.

(a) *Transactions to which this rule does not apply.* The requirements of §§ 45.3 through 45.8 and §§ 45.10 through 45.12 shall not apply to any foreign non-cleared swap or foreign non-cleared security-based swap of a foreign covered swap entity.

(b) For purposes of this section, a *foreign non-cleared swap* or *foreign non-cleared security-based swap* is any non-cleared swap or non-cleared security-based swap with respect to which neither the counterparty to the foreign covered swap entity nor any party that provides a guarantee of either party's obligations under the non-cleared swap or non-cleared security-based swap is:

(1) An entity organized under the laws of the United States or any State (including a U.S. branch, agency, or subsidiary of a foreign bank) or a natural person who is a resident of the United States;

(2) A branch or office of an entity organized under the laws of the United States or any State; or

(3) A swap entity that is a subsidiary of an entity that is organized under the laws of the United States or any State.

(c) For purposes of this section, a *foreign covered swap entity* is any covered swap entity that is not:

(1) An entity organized under the laws of the United States or any State, including a U.S. branch, agency, or subsidiary of a foreign bank;

(2) A branch or office of an entity organized under the laws of the United States or any State; or

(3) An entity that is a subsidiary of an entity that is organized under the laws of the United States or any State.

(d) *Transactions for which substituted compliance determination may apply*—(1) *Determinations and reliance.* For non-cleared swaps and non-cleared security-based swaps entered into by covered swap entities described in paragraph (d)(3) of this section, a covered swap entity may satisfy the provisions of this part by complying with the foreign regulatory framework for non-cleared swaps and non-cleared security-based swaps that the prudential regulators jointly, conditionally or unconditionally, determine by public order satisfy the corresponding requirements of §§ 45.3 through 45.8 and §§ 45.10 through 45.12.

(2) *Standard.* In determining whether to make a determination under paragraph (d)(1) of this section, the prudential regulators will consider whether the requirements of such foreign regulatory framework for non-cleared swaps and non-cleared security-based swaps applicable to such covered swap entities are comparable to the otherwise applicable requirements of this part and appropriate for the safe and sound operation of the covered swap entity, taking into account the risks associated with non-cleared swaps and non-cleared security-based swaps.

(3) *Covered swap entities eligible for substituted compliance.* A covered swap

entity may rely on a determination under paragraph (d)(1) of this section only if:

(i) The covered swap entity's obligations under the non-cleared swap or non-cleared security-based swap do not have a guarantee from:

(A) An entity organized under the laws of the United States or any State (other than a U.S. branch or agency of a foreign bank) or a natural person who is a resident of the United States; or

(B) A branch or office of an entity organized under the laws of the United States or any State; and

(ii) The covered swap entity is:

(A) A foreign covered swap entity;

(B) A U.S. branch or agency of a foreign bank; or

(C) An entity that is not organized under the laws of the United States or any State and is a subsidiary of a depository institution, Edge corporation, or agreement corporation.

(4) *Compliance with foreign margin collection requirement.* A covered swap entity satisfies its requirement to post initial margin under § 45.3(b) by posting to its counterparty initial margin in the form and amount, and at such times, that its counterparty is required to collect pursuant to a foreign regulatory framework, provided that the counterparty is subject to the foreign regulatory framework and the prudential regulators have made a determination under paragraph (d)(1) of this section, unless otherwise stated in that determination, and the counterparty's obligations under the non-cleared swap or non-cleared security-based swap do not have a guarantee from:

(i) An entity organized under the laws of the United States or any State (including a U.S. branch, agency, or subsidiary of a foreign bank) or a natural person who is a resident of the United States; or

(ii) A branch or office of an entity organized under the laws of the United States or any State.

(e) *Requests for determinations.* (1) A covered swap entity described in paragraph (d)(3) of this section may request that the prudential regulators make a determination pursuant to this section. A request for a determination must include a description of:

(i) The scope and objectives of the foreign regulatory framework for non-cleared swaps and non-cleared security-based swaps;

(ii) The specific provisions of the foreign regulatory framework for non-cleared swaps and non-cleared security-based swaps that govern:

(A) The scope of transactions covered;

(B) The determination of the amount of initial margin and variation margin required and how that amount is calculated;

(C) The timing of margin requirements;

(D) Any documentation requirements;

(E) The forms of eligible collateral;

(F) Any segregation and rehypothecation requirements; and

(G) The approval process and standards for models used in calculating initial margin and variation margin;

(iii) The supervisory compliance program and enforcement authority exercised by a foreign financial regulatory authority or authorities in such system to support its oversight of the application of the non-cleared swap or non-cleared security-based swap regulatory framework and how that framework applies to the non-cleared swaps or non-cleared security-based swaps of the covered swap entity; and

(iv) Any other descriptions and documentation that the prudential regulators determine are appropriate.

(2) A covered swap entity described in paragraph (d)(3) of this section may make a request under this section only if the non-cleared swap or non-cleared security-based swap activities of the covered swap entity are directly supervised by the authorities administering the foreign regulatory framework for non-cleared swaps and non-cleared security-based swaps.

(f) *Segregation unavailable.* Sections 45.3(b) and 45.7 do not apply to a non-cleared swap or non-cleared security-based swap entered into by:

(1) A foreign branch of a covered swap entity that is a depository institution; or

(2) A covered swap entity that is not organized under the laws of the United States or any State and is a subsidiary

of a depository institution, Edge corporation, or agreement corporation, if:

(i) Inherent limitations in the legal or operational infrastructure in the foreign jurisdiction make it impracticable for the covered swap entity and the counterparty to post any form of eligible initial margin collateral recognized pursuant to §45.6(b) in compliance with the segregation requirements of §45.7;

(ii) The covered swap entity is subject to foreign regulatory restrictions that require the covered swap entity to transact in the non-cleared swap or non-cleared security-based swap with the counterparty through an establishment within the foreign jurisdiction and do not accommodate the posting of collateral for the non-cleared swap or non-cleared security-based swap outside the jurisdiction;

(iii) The counterparty to the non-cleared swap or non-cleared security-based swap is not, and the counterparty's obligations under the non-cleared swap or non-cleared security-based swap do not have a guarantee from:

(A) An entity organized under the laws of the United States or any State (including a U.S. branch, agency, or subsidiary of a foreign bank) or a natural person who is a resident of the United States; or

(B) A branch or office of an entity organized under the laws of the United States or any State;

(iv) The covered swap entity collects initial margin for the non-cleared swap or non-cleared security-based swap in accordance with §45.3(a) in the form of cash pursuant to §45.6(b)(1), and posts and collects variation margin in accordance with §45.4(a) in the form of cash pursuant to §45.6(b)(1); and

(v) The OCC provides the covered swap entity with prior written approval for the covered swap entity's reliance on this paragraph (f) for the foreign jurisdiction.

(g) *Guarantee* means an arrangement pursuant to which one party to a non-cleared swap or non-cleared security-based swap has rights of recourse against a third-party guarantor, with respect to its counterparty's obligations under the non-cleared swap or non-cleared security-based swap. For these purposes, a party to a non-cleared swap or non-cleared security-based swap has rights of recourse against a guarantor if the party has a conditional or unconditional legally enforceable right to receive or otherwise collect, in whole or in part, payments from the guarantor with respect to its counterparty's obligations under the non-cleared swap or non-cleared security-based swap. In addition, any arrangement pursuant to which the guarantor has a conditional or unconditional legally enforceable right to receive or otherwise collect, in whole or in part, payments from any other third party guarantor with respect to the counterparty's obligations under the non-cleared swap or non-cleared security-based swap, such arrangement will be deemed a guarantee of the counterparty's obligations under the non-cleared swap or non-cleared security-based swap by the other guarantor.

§45.10 Documentation of margin matters.

A covered swap entity shall execute trading documentation with each counterparty that is either a swap entity or financial end user regarding credit support arrangements that:

(a) Provides the covered swap entity and its counterparty with the contractual right to collect and post initial margin and variation margin in such amounts, in such form, and under such circumstances as are required by this part; and

(b) Specifies:

(1) The methods, procedures, rules, and inputs for determining the value of each non-cleared swap or non-cleared security-based swap for purposes of calculating variation margin requirements; and

(2) The procedures by which any disputes concerning the valuation of non-cleared swaps or non-cleared security-based swaps, or the valuation of assets collected or posted as initial margin or variation margin, may be resolved; and

(c) Describes the methods, procedures, rules, and inputs used to calculate initial margin for non-cleared swaps and non-cleared security based swaps entered into between the covered swap entity and the counterparty.

§ 45.11 Special rules for affiliates.

(a) *Affiliates.* This part applies to a non-cleared swap or non-cleared security-based swap of a covered swap entity with its affiliate, unless the swap or security-based swap is excluded from coverage under § 45.1(d) or as otherwise provided in this section. To the extent of any inconsistency between this section and any other provision of this part, this section will apply.

(b) *Initial margin*—(1) *Posting of initial margin.* The requirement for a covered swap entity to post initial margin under § 45.3(b) does not apply with respect to any non-cleared swap or non-cleared security-based swap with a counterparty that is an affiliate. A covered swap entity shall calculate the amount of initial margin that would be required to be posted to an affiliate that is a financial end user with material swaps exposure pursuant to § 45.3(b) and provide documentation of such amount to each affiliate on a daily basis.

(2) *Initial margin threshold amount.* For purposes of calculating the amount of initial margin to be collected from an affiliate counterparty in accordance with § 45.3(a) or calculating the amount of initial margin that would have been posted to an affiliate counterparty in accordance with paragraph (b)(1) of this section, the initial margin threshold amount is an aggregate credit exposure of $20 million resulting from all non-cleared swaps and non-cleared security-based swaps between the covered swap entity and that affiliate. For purposes of this calculation, an entity shall not count a non-cleared swap or non-cleared security-based swap that is exempt pursuant to § 45.1(d).

(c) *Variation margin.* A covered swap entity shall collect and post variation margin with respect to a non-cleared swap or non-cleared security-based swap with any counterparty that is an affiliate as provided in § 45.4.

(d) *Custodian for non-cash collateral.* To the extent that a covered swap entity collects initial margin required by § 45.3(a) from an affiliate with respect to any non-cleared swap or non-cleared security-based swap in the form of collateral other than cash collateral, the custodian for such collateral may be the covered swap entity or an affiliate of the covered swap entity.

(e) *Model holding period and netting*—(1) *Model holding period.* For any non-cleared swap or non-cleared security-based swap (or netting portfolio) between a covered swap entity and an affiliate that would be subject to the clearing requirements of section 2(h)(1)(A) of the Commodity Exchange Act of 1936 or section 3C(a)(1) of the Securities Exchange Act of 1934 but for an exemption under section 2(h)(7)(C)(iii) or (D) or section 4(c)(1) of the Commodity Exchange Act of 1936 or regulations of the Commodity Futures Trading Commission or section 3C(g)(4) of the Securities Exchange Act of 1934 or regulations of the U.S. Securities and Exchange Commission, the covered swap entity's initial margin model calculation as described in § 45.8(d)(1) may use a holding period equal to the shorter of five business days or the maturity of the non-cleared swap or non-cleared security-based swap (or netting portfolio).

(2) *Netting arrangements.* Any netting portfolio that contains any non-cleared swap or non-cleared security-based swap with a model holding period equal to the shorter of five business days or the maturity of the non-cleared swap or non-cleared security-based swap pursuant to paragraph (e)(1) of this section must be identified and separate from any other netting portfolio for purposes of calculating and complying with the initial margin requirements of this part.

(f) *Standardized amounts.* If a covered swap entity's initial margin model does not conform to the requirements of § 45.8, the covered swap entity shall calculate the amount of initial margin required to be collected for one or more non-cleared swaps or non-cleared security-based swaps with a given affiliate counterparty pursuant to section § 45.3 on a daily basis pursuant to appendix A with the gross initial margin multiplied by 0.7.

§ 45.12 Capital.

A covered swap entity shall comply with:

(a) In the case of a covered swap entity that is a national bank or Federal savings association, the minimum capital requirements as generally provided 12 CFR part 3.

(b) In the case of a covered swap entity that is a Federal branch or agency of a foreign bank, the capital adequacy guidelines applicable as generally provided under 12 CFR 28.14.

[80 FR 74911, Nov. 30, 2015]

APPENDIX A TO PART 45—STANDARDIZED MINIMUM INITIAL MARGIN REQUIREMENTS FOR NON-CLEARED SWAPS AND NON—CLEARED SECURITY-BASED SWAPS

TABLE A—STANDARDIZED MINIMUM GROSS INITIAL MARGIN REQUIREMENTS FOR NON-CLEARED SWAPS AND NON-CLEARED SECURITY-BASED SWAPS[1]

Asset Class	Gross initial margin (% of notional exposure)
Credit: 0–2 year duration	2
Credit: 2–5 year duration	5
Credit: 5+ year duration	10
Commodity	15
Equity	15
Foreign Exchange/Currency	6
Cross Currency Swaps: 0–2 year duration	1
Cross-Currency Swaps: 2–5 year duration	2
Cross-Currency Swaps: 5+ year duration	4
Interest Rate: 0–2 year duration	1
Interest Rate: 2–5 year duration	2
Interest Rate: 5+ year duration	4
Other	15

[1] The initial margin amount applicable to multiple non-cleared swaps or non-cleared security-based swaps subject to an eligible master netting agreement that is calculated according to Appendix A will be computed as follows:

Initial Margin=0.4xGross Initial Margin +0.6x NGRxGross Initial Margin

where;

Gross Initial Margin = the sum of the product of each non-cleared swap's or non-cleared security-based swap's effective notional amount and the gross initial margin requirement for all non-cleared swaps and non-cleared security-based swaps subject to the eligible master netting agreement;

and

NGR = the net-to-gross ratio (that is, the ratio of the net current replacement cost to the gross current replacement cost). In calculating NGR, the gross current replacement cost equals the sum of the replacement cost for each non-cleared swap and non-cleared security-based swap subject to the eligible master netting agreement for which the cost is positive. The net current replacement cost equals the total replacement cost for all non-cleared swaps and non-cleared security-based swaps subject to the eligible master netting agreement. In cases where the gross replacement cost is zero, the NGR should be set to 1.0.

APPENDIX B TO PART 45—MARGIN VALUES FOR ELIGIBLE NONCASH MARGIN COLLATERAL.

TABLE B—MARGIN VALUES FOR ELIGIBLE NONCASH MARGIN COLLATERAL

Asset class	Discount (%)
Eligible government and related (e.g., central bank, multilateral development bank, GSE securities identified in § 45.6(a)(2)(iv) or (b)(5) debt: residual maturity less than one-year	0.5
Eligible government and related (e.g., central bank, multilateral development bank, GSE securities identified in § 45.6(a)(2)(iv) or (b)(5) debt: residual maturity between one and five years	2.0
Eligible government and related (e.g., central bank, multilateral development bank, GSE securities identified in § 45.6(a)(2)(iv) or (b)(5) debt: residual maturity greater than five years	4.0
Eligible GSE debt securities not identified in § 45.6(a)(2)(iv) or (b)(5): residual maturity less than one-year	1.0
Eligible GSE debt securities not identified in § 45.6(a)(2)(iv) or (b)(5): residual maturity between one and five years:	4.0
Eligible GSE debt securities not identified in § 45.6(a)(2)(iv) or (b)(5): residual maturity greater than five years:	8.0
Other eligible publicly traded debt: residual maturity less than one-year	1.0
Other eligible publicly traded debt: residual maturity between one and five years	4.0
Other eligible publicly traded debt: residual maturity greater than five years	8.0
Equities included in S&P 500 or related index	15.0
Equities included in S&P 1500 Composite or related index but not S&P 500 or related index	25.0
Gold	15.0

[1] The discount to be applied to an eligible investment fund is the weighted average discount on all assets within the eligible investment fund at the end of the prior month. The weights to be applied in the weighted average should be calculated as a fraction of the fund's total market value that is invested in each asset with a given discount amount. As an example, an eligible investment fund that is comprised solely of $100 of 91 day Treasury bills and $100 of 3 year US Treasury bonds would receive a discount of (100/200)*0.5+(100/200)*2.0=(0.5)*0.5+(0.5)*2.0=1.25 percent.

PART 46—ANNUAL STRESS TEST

Sec.
46.1 Authority and purpose.
46.2 Definitions.
46.3 Applicability.
46.4 Reservation of authority.
46.5 Annual stress test.
46.6 Stress test methodologies and practices.
46.7 Reports to the Office of the Comptroller of the Currency and the Federal Reserve Board.
46.8 Publication of disclosures.

AUTHORITY: 12 U.S.C. 93a; 1463(a)(2); 5365(i)(2); and 5412(b)(2)(B).

SOURCE: 77 FR 61246, Oct. 9, 2012, unless otherwise noted.

§ 46.1 Authority and purpose.

(a) *Authority*. 12 U.S.C. 93a; 12 U.S.C. 1463(a)(2); 12 U.S.C. 5365(i)(2); 12 U.S.C. 5412(b)(2)(B).

(b) *Purpose*. This part implements 12 U.S.C. 5365(i)(2), which requires a national bank or Federal savings association with total consolidated assets of more than $10 billion to conduct an annual stress test and establishes a definition of stress test, methodologies for conducting stress tests, and reporting and disclosure requirements.

§ 46.2 Definitions.

For purposes of this part, the following definitions apply:

$10 to $50 billion covered institution means a national bank or Federal savings association with average total consolidated assets, calculated as required under this part, that are greater than $10 billion but less than $50 billion.

$50 billion or over covered institution means a national bank or Federal savings association with average total consolidated assets, calculated as required under this part, that are not less than $50 billion.

Call Report means the Consolidated Report of Condition and Income.

Covered institution means a $10 to $50 billion covered institution or a $50 billion or over covered institution.

Federal savings association has the same meaning as in 12 U.S.C. 1813(b)(2).

Planning horizon means a set period of time over which the impact of the scenarios is assessed.

Pre-provision net revenue means the sum of net interest income and non-interest income less expenses before adjusting for loss provisions.

Scenarios means sets of conditions that affect the U.S. economy or the financial condition of a covered institution that the OCC annually determines are appropriate for use in the stress tests under this part, including, but not limited to, baseline, adverse, and severely adverse scenarios.

Stress test means a process to assess the potential impact of scenarios on the consolidated earnings, losses, and capital of a covered institution over the planning horizon, taking into account the covered institution's current condition, risks, exposures, strategies, and activities.

[77 FR 61246, Oct. 9, 2012, as amended at 83 FR 7953, Feb. 23, 2018]

§ 46.3 Applicability.

(a) *Measurement of average total consolidated assets for a covered institution*. A covered institution's average total consolidated assets is calculated as the average of the covered institution's total consolidated assets, as reported on the covered institution's Call Reports, for the four most recent consecutive quarters. If the covered institution has not filed a Call Report for each of the four most recent consecutive quarters, the covered institution's average total consolidated assets is calculated as the average of the covered institution's total consolidated assets, as reported on the covered institution's Call Reports, for the most recent one or more consecutive quarters. The date on which a national bank or Federal savings association becomes a covered institution shall be the as-of date of the most recent Call Report used in the calculation of the average.

(b) *Covered institutions that become subject to stress testing requirements*. A national bank or Federal savings association that becomes a $10 to $50 billion covered institution on or before March 31 of a given year shall conduct its first annual stress test under this part in the next calendar year after the date the national bank or Federal savings association becomes a $10 to $50 billion covered institution, unless that time is extended by the OCC in writing. A national bank or Federal savings association that becomes a $10 to $50 billion covered institution after March 31 of a given year shall conduct its first annual stress test under this part in the second calendar year after the calendar year in which the national bank or Federal savings association becomes a $10 to $50 billion covered institution, unless that time is extended by the OCC in writing.

(c) *Ceasing to be a covered institution or changing categories.* (1) A covered institution shall remain subject to the stress test requirements based on its applicable category, as defined in § 46.2, unless and until total consolidated assets of the covered institution falls below the relevant size threshold for each of four consecutive quarters as reported by the covered institution's most recent Call Reports. The calculation shall be effective on the "as of" date of the fourth consecutive Call Report.

(2) Notwithstanding paragraph (c)(1) of this section, a national bank or Federal savings association that becomes a $50 billion or over covered institution, whether by migrating from being a $10 to $50 billion covered institution or by directly becoming a $50 billion or over covered institution, after September 30 of a calendar year must comply with the requirements applicable to a $50 billion or over covered institution beginning on January 1 of the third calendar year after the national bank or Federal savings association becomes a $50 billion or over covered institution, unless that time is extended by the OCC in writing. A national bank or Federal savings association that becomes a $50 billion or over covered institution on or before September 30 of a calendar year must comply with the requirements applicable to a $50 billion or over covered institution beginning on January 1 of the second calendar year after the national bank or Federal savings association becomes a $50 billion or over covered institution, unless that time is extended by the OCC in writing.

(d) *Covered institution under bank holding company subject to annual stress test requirements.* (1) Notwithstanding the requirements applicable to a $10 to $50 billion covered institution under this part, a $10 to $50 billion covered institution that is controlled by a bank holding company or savings and loan holding company that is subject to annual stress test requirements pursuant to applicable regulations of the Board of Governors of the Federal Reserve System may elect to conduct its stress test under this part pursuant to the requirements applicable to a $50 billion or over covered institution.

(2) Any $10 to $50 billion covered institution that elects to apply the requirements of a $50 billion or over covered institution under this paragraph shall remain subject to the requirements applicable to a $50 billion or over covered institution until otherwise approved by the OCC.

[77 FR 61246, Oct. 9, 2012, as amended at 79 FR 71633, Dec. 3, 2014; 83 FR 7953, Feb. 23, 2018]

§ 46.4 Reservation of authority.

(a) *Generally.* The OCC may require a national bank or Federal savings association not otherwise subject to this part to comply with the stress test requirements of this part. With respect to any national bank or Federal savings association subject to the stress test requirements of this part pursuant to § 46.3(a), the OCC may modify or delay some or all of the requirements of this part which include:

(1) *Timing of stress test.* The OCC may accelerate or extend any specified deadline for stress testing, reporting, or publication of disclosures of the stress test results.

(2) *Stress tests.* The OCC may require additional stress tests not otherwise required by this part or may require or permit different or additional analytical techniques and methods, different scenarios, or different assumptions, as appropriate for the covered institution to use in meeting the stress test requirements of this part. In addition, the OCC may specify a different as-of date for any or all categories of financial data used by the stress test.

(3) *Reporting and disclosures.* The OCC may modify the reporting date or any reporting requirement of a report required by this part, or may require any additional reports relating to stress testing as may be appropriate. The OCC may delay or otherwise modify

the publication requirements of this part if the disclosure of stress test results under this part would not provide sufficiently meaningful or useful information to the public. In addition, the OCC may require different or additional disclosures not otherwise required by this part, if the existing disclosures do not adequately address one or more material elements of the stress test.

(b) *Factors considered.* Any exercise of authority under this section by the OCC will be in writing and will consider the nature and level of the activities, complexity, risks, operations, and regulatory capital of the national bank or Federal savings association, in addition to any other relevant factors.

(c) *Notice and comment procedures.* In making a determination under paragraph (a) of this section, the OCC will apply notice and response procedures, in the same manner and to the same extent as the notice and response procedures in 12 CFR 3.404.

[77 FR 61246, Oct. 9, 2012, as amended at 79 FR 11313, Feb. 28, 2014]

§ 46.5 Annual stress test.

Each covered institution must conduct the annual stress test under this part subject to the following requirements:

(a) *Financial data.* A covered institution must use financial data as of December 31 of the previous calendar year.

(b) *Scenarios provided by the OCC.* In conducting the stress test under this part, each covered institution must use the scenarios provided by the OCC. The scenarios provided by the OCC will reflect a minimum of three sets of economic and financial conditions, including baseline, adverse, and severely adverse scenarios. The OCC will provide a description of the scenarios required to be used by each covered institution no later than February 15 of that calendar year.

(c) *Significant trading activities.* The OCC may require a covered institution with significant trading activities, as determined by the OCC, to include trading and counterparty components in its adverse and severely adverse scenarios. The trading and counterparty position data to be used in this component will be as of a date between October 1 of the previous calendar year and March 1 of that calendar year in which the stress test is performed, and the OCC will communicate a description of the component to the covered institution no later than March 1 of that calendar year.

(d) *Use of stress test results.* The board of directors and senior management of each covered institution must consider the results of the stress tests conducted under this section in the normal course of business, including but not limited to the covered institution's capital planning, assessment of capital adequacy, and risk management practices.

[83 FR 7953, Feb. 23, 2018]

§ 46.6 Stress test methodologies and practices.

(a) *Potential impact on capital.* During each quarter of the planning horizon, a covered institution shall estimate the following for each scenario required to be used:

(1) Pre-provision net revenues, losses, loan loss provisions, and net income, and

(2) The potential impact on the covered institution's regulatory capital levels and ratios applicable to the covered institution under 12 CFR part 3 or part 167, as applicable, and any other capital ratios specified by the OCC, incorporating the effects of any capital actions over the planning horizon and maintenance by the covered institution of an allowance for loan losses appropriate for credit exposures throughout the planning horizon. Until December 31, 2015, or such other date specified by the OCC, a covered institution is not required to calculate its risk-based capital requirements using the internal ratings-based and advanced measurement approaches as set forth in 12 CFR part 3, subpart E.

(b) *Planning horizon.* A covered institution must use a minimum planning horizon of at least nine quarters, beginning with the first day of the period covered by the stress tests.

(c) *Controls and oversight of stress test processes.* (1) The senior management of the covered institution must establish and maintain a system of controls, oversight, and documentation, including policies and procedures, designed to ensure that the stress test processes used by the covered institution satisfy the requirements in this part. These policies and procedures must, at a minimum, describe the covered institution's stress test practices and methodologies, and processes for validating and updating the covered institution's stress test practices and methodologies consistent with applicable laws, regulations, and supervisory guidance.

(2) The board of directors of the covered institution, or a committee thereof, shall approve and review the policies and procedures of the covered institution's stress testing processes as frequently as economic conditions or the condition of the institution may warrant, but no less than annually. The board of directors and senior management must be provided with a summary of the stress test results.

[77 FR 61246, Oct. 9, 2012, as amended at 79 FR 71633, Dec. 3, 2014]

§ 46.7 Reports to the Office of the Comptroller of the Currency and the Federal Reserve Board.

(a) *$10 to $50 billion covered institution.* A $10 to $50 billion covered institution must report to the OCC and to the Board of Governors of the Federal Reserve System, on or before July 31, the results of the stress test in the manner and form specified by the OCC.

(b) *$50 billion or over covered institution.* A $50 billion or over covered institution must report to the OCC and to the Board of Governors of the Federal Reserve System, on or before April 5, the results of the stress test in the manner and form specified by the OCC.

(c) *Confidentiality of Reports.* As provided by § 4.32(b) of this title, the report required under this section is non-public OCC information because it is deemed to be a record created or obtained by the OCC in connection with the OCC's performance of its responsibilities, such as a record concerning supervision, licensing, regulations, and examination, of a national bank, a Federal savings association, a bank holding company, a savings and loan holding company, or an affiliate. The report is the property of the OCC and unauthorized disclosure of the report is generally prohibited pursuant to § 4.37 of this part.

[77 FR 61246, Oct. 9, 2012, as amended at 79 FR 71633, Dec. 3, 2014; 83 FR 7953, Feb. 23, 2018]

§ 46.8 Publication of disclosures.

(a) *Publication date.* (1) *$50 billion or over covered institution.* A $50 billion or over covered institution must publish a summary of the results of its annual stress test in the period starting June 15 and ending July 15 provided:

(i) Unless the OCC determines otherwise, if the $50 billion or over covered institution is a consolidated subsidiary of a bank holding company or savings and loan holding company subject to supervisory stress tests conducted by the Board of Governors of the Federal Reserve System pursuant to 12 CFR part 252, then within the June 15 to July 15 period such covered institution may not publish the required summary of its annual stress test earlier than the date that the Board of Governors of the Federal Reserve System publishes the supervisory stress test results of the covered bank's parent holding company.

(ii) If the Board of Governors of the Federal Reserve System publishes the supervisory stress test results of the covered institution's parent holding company prior to June 15, then such covered institution may publish its stress test results prior to June 15, but no later than July 15, through actual publication by the covered institution or through publication by the parent holding company pursuant to paragraph (b) of this section.

(2) *$10 to $50 billion covered institution.* A $10 to $50 billion covered institution must publish a summary of the results of its annual stress test in the period starting October 15 and ending October 31.

(b) *Publication method.* The summary required under this section may be published on the covered institution's Web site or in any other forum that is reasonably accessible to the public. A covered institution controlled by a bank holding company that is required to conduct an annual company-run stress test under applicable regulations of the Board of Governors of the Federal Reserve System will be deemed to have satisfied the publication requirement of this section when the bank holding company publicly discloses summary results of its annual stress test in satisfaction of the requirements of applicable regulations of the Board of Governors of the Federal Reserve System, unless the OCC determines that the disclosures at the holding company level do not adequately capture the potential impact of the scenarios on the capital of the covered institution.

(c) *Information to be disclosed in the summary.* The information disclosed shall, at a minimum, include—

(1) A description of the types of risks included in the stress test under this part;

(2) A summary description of the methodologies used in the stress test;

(3) Estimates of aggregate losses, pre-provision net revenue, provisions for loan and lease losses, net income, and pro forma capital ratios (including regulatory and any other capital ratios specified by the OCC); and

(4) An explanation of the most significant causes of the changes in regulatory capital ratios.

(d) *Disclosure of estimates for the planning horizon.* (1) The disclosure of the estimates of aggregate losses, pre-provision net revenue, provisions for loan and lease losses, net income, and pro forma capital ratios (including regulatory and any other capital ratios specified by the OCC), as required by paragraph (b) of this section, must reflect the estimated cumulative effects, as well as the estimated capital ratios, at the end of the planning horizon for the severely adverse scenario.

(2) With respect to the capital ratio disclosure required in paragraph (d)(1) of this section, the disclosure must also include the value at the beginning of the planning horizon, and the minimum over the planning horizon of the estimated quarter-end values of each ratio.

[77 FR 61246, Oct. 9, 2012, as amended at 79 FR 71634, Dec. 3, 2014; 83 FR 7954, Feb. 23, 2018]

PART 47—MANDATORY CONTRACTUAL STAY REQUIREMENTS FOR QUALIFIED FINANCIAL CONTRACTS

Sec.
47.1 Authority and purpose.
47.2 Definitions.
47.3 Applicability.
47.4 U.S. special resolution regimes.
47.5 Insolvency proceedings.
47.6 Approval of enhanced creditor protection conditions.
47.7 Foreign bank multi-branch master agreements.
47.8 Exclusion of certain QFCs.

AUTHORITY: 12 U.S.C. 1, 93a, 481, 1462a, 1463, 1464, 1467a, 1818, 1828, 1831n, 1831o, 1831p–1, 1831w, 1835, 3102(b), 3108(a), 5412(b)(2)(B), (D)–(F).

SOURCE: 82 FR 56662, Nov. 29, 2017, unless otherwise noted.

§ 47.1 Authority and purpose.

(a) *Authority.* 12 U.S.C. 1, 93a, 1462a, 1463, 1464, 1467a, 1818, 1828, 1831n, 1831p–1, 1831w, 1835, 3102(b), 3108(a), 5412(b)(2)(B), (D)–(F).

(b) *Purpose.* The purpose of this part is to promote the safety and soundness of federally chartered or licensed institutions by mitigating the potential destabilizing effects of the resolution of a global systemically important banking entity on an affiliate that is a covered bank (as defined by this part) by requiring covered banks to include in financial contracts covered by this part certain mandatory contractual provisions relating to stays on acceleration and close out rights and transfer rights.

§ 47.2 Definitions.

As used in this part:

Affiliate means an affiliate as defined in 12 U.S.C. 1841(k) (Bank Holding Company Act).

Central counterparty (CCP) means a counterparty (for example, a clearing house) that facilitates trades between counterparties in one or more financial markets by either guaranteeing trades or novating contracts.

Chapter 11 proceeding means a proceeding under Chapter 11 of Title 11, United States Code (11 U.S.C. 1101–74).

Consolidated affiliate means an affiliate of another company that:

(1) Either consolidates the other company, or is consolidated by the other company, on financial statements prepared in accordance with U.S. Generally Accepted Accounting Principles, the International Financial Reporting Standards, or other similar standards;

(2) Is, along with the other company, consolidated with a third company on a financial statement prepared in accordance with principles or standards referenced in paragraph (1) of this definition; or

(3) For a company that is not subject to principles or standards referenced in paragraph (1) of this definition, if consolidation as described in paragraph (1) or (2) of this definition would have occurred if such principles or standards had applied.

Control has the same meaning as in 12 U.S.C. 1841 (Bank Holding Company Act).

Covered entity has the same meaning as in §252.82(a) of this title (Federal Reserve Board Regulation YY) (12 CFR 252.82).

Covered FSI has the same meaning as in §382.2(b) of this title (Federal Deposit Insurance Corporation) (12 CFR 382.2(b)).

Default right (1) Means, with respect to a QFC, any:

(i) Right of a party, whether contractual or otherwise (including, without limitation, rights incorporated by reference to any other contract, agreement, or document, and rights afforded by statute, civil code, regulation, and common law), to liquidate, terminate, cancel, rescind, or accelerate such agreement or transactions thereunder, set off or net amounts owing in respect thereto (except rights related to same-day payment netting), exercise remedies in respect of collateral or other credit support or property related thereto (including the purchase and sale of property), demand payment or delivery thereunder or in respect thereof (other than a right or operation of a contractual provision arising solely from a change in the value of collateral or margin or a change in the amount of an economic exposure), suspend, delay, or defer payment or performance thereunder, or modify the obligations of a party thereunder, or any similar rights; and

(ii) Right or contractual provision that alters the amount of collateral or margin that must be provided with respect to an exposure thereunder, including by altering any initial amount, threshold amount, variation margin, minimum transfer amount, the margin value of collateral, or any similar amount, that entitles a party to demand the return of any collateral or margin transferred by it to the other party or a custodian or that modifies a transferee's right to reuse collateral or margin (if such right previously existed), or any similar rights, in each case, other than a right or operation of a contractual provision arising solely from a change in the value of collateral or margin or a change in the amount of an economic exposure;

(2) With respect to §47.5, does not include any right under a contract that allows a party to terminate the contract on demand or at its option at a specified time, or from time to time, without the need to show cause.

FDI Act proceeding means a proceeding that commences upon the Federal Deposit Insurance Corporation being appointed as conservator or receiver under section 11 of the Federal Deposit Insurance Act (12 U.S.C. 1821).

FDI Act stay period means, in connection with an FDI Act proceeding, the period of time during which a party to a QFC with a party that is subject to an FDI Act proceeding may not exercise any right that the party that is not subject to an FDI Act proceeding has to terminate, liquidate, or net such QFC, in accordance with section 11(e) of the Federal Deposit Insurance Act (12 U.S.C. 1821(e)) and any implementing regulations.

Financial counterparty means a person that is:

(1)(i) A bank holding company or an affiliate thereof; a savings and loan holding company as defined in section 10(n) of the Home Owners' Loan Act (12 U.S.C. 1467a(n)); a U.S. intermediate holding company that is established or designated for purposes of compliance with §252.153 of this title (Federal Reserve Board Regulation YY) (12 CFR 252.153); or a nonbank financial company supervised by the Federal Reserve

Board under Title II of the Dodd-Frank Wall Street Reform and Consumer Protection Act (12 U.S.C. 5323);

(ii) A depository institution as defined in section 3(c) of the Federal Deposit Insurance Act (12 U.S.C. 1813(c)); an organization that is organized under the laws of a foreign country and that engages directly in the business of banking outside the United States; a Federal credit union or State credit union as defined in section 2 of the Federal Credit Union Act (12 U.S.C. 1752(1) and (6)); an institution that functions solely in a trust or fiduciary capacity as described in section 2(c)(2)(D) of the Bank Holding Company Act (12 U.S.C. 1841(c)(2)(D)); an industrial loan company, an industrial bank, or other similar institution described in section 2(c)(2)(H) of the Bank Holding Company Act (12 U.S.C. 1841(c)(2)(H));

(iii) An entity that is state-licensed or registered as:

(A) A credit or lending entity, including a finance company, money lender; installment lender; consumer lender or lending company; mortgage lender, broker, or bank; motor vehicle title pledge lender; payday or deferred deposit lender; premium finance company; commercial finance or lending company; or commercial mortgage company; except entities registered or licensed solely on account of financing the entity's direct sales of goods or services to customers;

(B) A money services business, including a check casher; money transmitter; currency dealer or exchange; or money order or traveler's check issuer;

(iv) A regulated entity as defined in section 1303(20) of the Federal Housing Enterprises Financial Safety and Soundness Act of 1992, as amended (12 U.S.C. 4502(20)) or any entity for which the Federal Housing Finance Agency or its successor is the primary federal regulator;

(v) Any institution chartered in accordance with the Farm Credit Act of 1971, as amended (12 U.S.C. 2002 *et seq.*), that is regulated by the Farm Credit Administration;

(vi) Any entity registered with the Commodity Futures Trading Commission as a swap dealer or major swap participant pursuant to the Commodity Exchange Act of 1936 (7 U.S.C. 1 *et seq.*), or an entity that is registered with the U.S. Securities and Exchange Commission as a security-based swap dealer or a major security-based swap participant pursuant to the Securities Exchange Act of 1934 (15 U.S.C. 78a *et seq.*);

(vii) A securities holding company, with the meaning specified in section 618 of the Dodd-Frank Wall Street Reform and Consumer Protection Act (12 U.S.C. 1850a); a broker or dealer as defined in sections 3(a)(4) and 3(a)(5) of the Securities Exchange Act of 1934 (15 U.S.C. 78c(a)(4)–(5)); an investment adviser as defined in section 202(a) of the Investment Advisers Act of 1940 (15 U.S.C. 80b–2(a)); an investment company registered with the U.S. Securities and Exchange Commission under the Investment Company Act of 1940 (15 U.S.C. 80a–1 *et seq.*); or a company that has elected to be regulated as a business development company pursuant to section 54(a) of the Investment Company Act of 1940 (15 U.S.C. 80a–53(a));

(viii) A private fund as defined in section 202(a) of the Investment Advisers Act of 1940 (15 U.S.C. 80–b–2(a)); an entity that would be an investment company under section 3 of the Investment Company Act of 1940 (15 U.S.C. 80a–3) but for section 3(c)(5)(C); or an entity that is deemed not to be an investment company under section 3 of the Investment Company Act of 1940 pursuant to Investment Company Act Rule 3a–7 (17 CFR 270.3a–7) of the U.S. Securities and Exchange Commission;

(ix) A commodity pool, a commodity pool operator, or a commodity trading advisor as defined, respectively, in sections 1a(10), 1a(11), and 1a(12) of the Commodity Exchange Act of 1936 (7 U.S.C. 1a(10), 1a(11), and 1a(12)); a floor broker, a floor trader, or introducing broker as defined, respectively, in sections 1a(22), 1a(23) and 1a(31) of the Commodity Exchange Act of 1936 (7 U.S.C. 1a(22), 1a(23), and 1a(31)); or a futures commission merchant as defined in section 1a(28) of the Commodity Exchange Act of 1936 (7 U.S.C. 1a(28));

(x) An employee benefit plan as defined in paragraphs (3) and (32) of section 3 of the Employee Retirement Income and Security Act of 1974 (29 U.S.C. 1002);

(xi) An entity that is organized as an insurance company, primarily engaged in writing insurance or reinsuring risks underwritten by insurance companies, or is subject to supervision as such by a State insurance regulator or foreign insurance regulator; or

(xii) An entity that would be a financial counterparty described in paragraphs (1)(i)–(xi) of this definition, if the entity were organized under the laws of the United States or any state thereof.

(2) The term "financial counterparty" does not include any counterparty that is:

(i) A sovereign entity;

(ii) A multilateral development bank; or

(iii) The Bank for International Settlements.

Financial market utility (FMU) means any person, regardless of the jurisdiction in which the person is located or organized, that manages or operates a multilateral system for the purpose of transferring, clearing, or settling payments, securities, or other financial transactions among financial institutions or between financial institutions and the person, but does not include:

(1) Designated contract markets, registered futures associations, swap data repositories, and swap execution facilities registered under the Commodity Exchange Act (7 U.S.C. 1 *et seq.*), or national securities exchanges, national securities associations, alternative trading systems, security-based swap data repositories, and swap execution facilities registered under the Securities Exchange Act of 1934 (15 U.S.C. 78a *et seq.*), solely by reason of their providing facilities for comparison of data respecting the terms of settlement of securities or futures transactions effected on such exchange or by means of any electronic system operated or controlled by such entities, provided that the exclusions in paragraph (1) of this definition apply only with respect to the activities that require the entity to be so registered; or

(2) Any broker, dealer, transfer agent, or investment company, or any futures commission merchant, introducing broker, commodity trading advisor, or commodity pool operator, solely by reason of functions performed by such institution as part of brokerage, dealing, transfer agency, or investment company activities, or solely by reason of acting on behalf of a FMU or a participant therein in connection with the furnishing by the FMU of services to its participants or the use of services of the FMU by its participants, provided that services performed by such institution do not constitute critical risk management or processing functions of the FMU.

Investment advisory contract means any contract or agreement whereby a person agrees to act as investment adviser to or to manage any investment or trading account of another person.

Master agreement means a QFC of the type set forth in section 210(c)(8)(D)(ii)(XI), (iii)(IX), (iv)(IV), (v)(V), or (vi)(V) of Title II of the Dodd-Frank Wall Street Reform and Consumer Protection Act (12 U.S.C. 5390(c)(8)(D)(ii)(XI), (iii)(IX), (iv)(IV), (v)(V), or (vi)(V)) or a master agreement that the Federal Deposit Insurance Corporation determines by regulation is a QFC pursuant to section 210(c)(8)(D)(i) of Title II of the Dodd-Frank Wall Street Reform and Consumer Protection Act (12 U.S.C. 5390(c)(8)(D)(i)).

Person includes an individual, bank, corporation, partnership, trust, association, joint venture, pool, syndicate, sole proprietorship, unincorporated organization, or any other form of entity.

Qualified financial contract (QFC) has the same meaning as in section 210(c)(8)(D) of Title II of the Dodd-Frank Wall Street Reform and Consumer Protection Act (12 U.S.C. 5390(c)(8)(D)).

Retail customer or counterparty means a customer or counterparty that is:

(1) An individual;

(2) A business customer, but solely if and to the extent that:

(i) The national bank, Federal savings association, or Federal branch or agency manages its transactions with the business customer, including deposits, unsecured funding, and credit facility and liquidity facility transactions, in the same way it manages its transactions with individuals;

(ii) Transactions with the business customer have liquidity risk characteristics that are similar to comparable transactions with individuals; and

(iii) The total aggregate funding raised from the business customer is less than $1.5 million; or

(3) A living or testamentary trust that:

(i) Is solely for the benefit of natural persons;

(ii) Does not have a corporate trustee; and

(iii) Terminates within 21 years and 10 months after the death of grantors or beneficiaries of the trust living on the effective date of the trust or within 25 years, if applicable under state law.

Small financial institution means a company that:

(1) Is organized as a bank, as defined in section 3(a) of the Federal Deposit Insurance Act (12 U.S.C. 1813(a)), the deposits of which are insured by the Federal Deposit Insurance Corporation; a savings association, as defined in section 3(b) of the Federal Deposit Insurance Act (12 U.S.C. 1813(b)), the deposits of which are insured by the Federal Deposit Insurance Corporation; a farm credit system institution chartered under the Farm Credit Act of 1971 (12 U.S.C. 2002 *et seq.*); or an insured Federal credit union or State-chartered credit union under the Federal Credit Union Act (12 U.S.C. 1751 *et seq.*); and

(2) Has total assets of $10,000,000,000 or less on the last day of the company's most recent fiscal year.

State means any state, commonwealth, territory, or possession of the United States, the District of Columbia, the Commonwealth of Puerto Rico, the Commonwealth of the Northern Mariana Islands, American Samoa, Guam, or the United States Virgin Islands.

Subsidiary of a covered bank means any operating subsidiary of a national bank, Federal savings association, or Federal branch or agency as defined in § 5.34 of this chapter (national banks), or § 5.38 of this chapter (Federal savings associations), or any other entity owned or controlled by the covered bank that would be a subsidiary under 12 U.S.C. 1841 (Bank Holding Company Act).

U.S. agency has the same meaning as the term "agency" in 12 U.S.C. 3101(1).

U.S. branch has the same meaning as the term "branch" in 12 U.S.C. 3101(3).

U.S. special resolution regimes means the Federal Deposit Insurance Act (12 U.S.C. 1811–1835a) and regulations promulgated thereunder and Title II of the Dodd-Frank Wall Street Reform and Consumer Protection Act (12 U.S.C. 5381–5394) and regulations promulgated thereunder.

§ 47.3 Applicability.

(a) *General requirement.* A covered bank must ensure that each covered QFC conforms to the requirements of §§ 47.4 and 47.5.

(b) *Covered bank*—(1) *Generally.* For purposes of this part, a covered bank is:

(i) A national bank or Federal savings association that has more than $700 billion in total assets as reported on the national bank's or Federal savings association's most recent Consolidated Reports of Condition and Income (Call Report);

(ii) A national bank or Federal savings association that is a subsidiary of a global systemically important bank holding company that has been designated pursuant to § 252.82 of this title (Federal Reserve Board Regulation YY) (12 CFR 252.82);

(iii) A national bank or Federal savings association that is a subsidiary of a global systemically important foreign banking organization that has been designated pursuant to § 252.87 of this title (Federal Reserve Board Regulation YY) (12 CFR 252.87); or

(iv) A Federal branch or agency, as defined in subpart B of this chapter (governing Federal branches and agencies), of a global systemically important foreign banking organization that has been designated pursuant to § 252.87 of this title (Federal Reserve Board Regulation YY) (12 CFR 252.87).

(2) *Subsidiary of a covered bank.* This part applies to a subsidiary of a covered bank as provided under paragraph (b)(1) of this section. Specifically, the covered bank is required to ensure that a covered QFC to which the subsidiary of a covered bank is a party (as a direct counterparty or a support provider) satisfies the requirements of §§ 47.4 and

47.5 in the same manner and to the same extent applicable to the covered bank.

(3) *Subsidiaries not included as covered banks.* Notwithstanding paragraphs (b)(1) and (2) of this section, a covered bank does not include:

(i) A subsidiary that is owned by a covered bank in satisfaction of debt previously contracted in good faith pursuant to section 5137 of the Revised Statutes (12 U.S.C. 29) (national bank) or section 5(c) of the Home Owners' Loan Act (12 U.S.C. 1464) (Federal savings association);

(ii) A portfolio concern, as defined under 13 CFR 107.50, that is controlled by a small business investment company, as defined in section 103(3) of the Small Business Investment Act of 1958 (15 U.S.C. 662) (national banks), or under section 5(c) of the Home Owners' Loan Act (12 U.S.C. 1464(c)) (Federal savings associations);

(iii) A subsidiary that is owned pursuant to paragraph (7) of section 5136 of the Revised Statutes (12 U.S.C. 24(Seventh)), or paragraph (11) of section 5136 of the Revised Statutes (12 U.S.C. 24(Eleventh)) (national banks), or § 5.59 of this chapter (12 CFR 5.59) (Federal savings associations) designed primarily to promote the public welfare, including the welfare of low- and moderate-income communities or families (such as providing housing, services or jobs).

(c) *Covered QFCs.* For purposes of this part, a covered QFC is:

(1) With respect to a covered bank that is a covered bank on January 1, 2018, an in-scope QFC that the covered bank:

(i) Enters, executes, or otherwise becomes a party to on or after January 1, 2019; or

(ii) Entered, executed, or otherwise became a party to before January 1, 2019, if the covered bank, or any affiliate that is a covered entity, covered bank, or covered FSI, also enters, executes, or otherwise becomes a party to a QFC with the same person or a consolidated affiliate of the same person on or after January 1, 2019.

(2) With respect to a covered bank that becomes a covered bank after January 1, 2018, an in-scope QFC that the covered bank:

(i) Enters, executes or otherwise becomes a party to on or after the later of the date the covered bank first becomes a covered bank and January 1, 2019; or

(ii) Entered, executed, or otherwise became a party to before the date identified in paragraph (c)(2)(i) of this section with respect to the covered bank, if the covered bank or any affiliate that is a covered entity, covered bank, or covered FSI, also enters, executes, or otherwise becomes a party to a QFC with the same person or consolidated affiliate of the same person on or after the date identified in paragraph (c)(2)(i) of this section with respect to the covered bank.

(d) *In-scope QFCs.* An in-scope QFC is a QFC that explicitly:

(1) Restricts the transfer of a QFC (or any interest or obligation in or under, or any property securing, the QFC) from a covered bank; or

(2) Provides one or more default rights with respect to a QFC that may be exercised against a covered bank.

(e) *Rules of construction.* For purposes of this part:

(1) A covered bank does not become a party to a QFC solely by acting as agent with respect to the QFC; and

(2) The exercise of a default right with respect to a covered QFC includes the automatic or deemed exercise of the default right pursuant to the terms of the QFC or other arrangement.

(f) *Initial applicability of requirements for covered QFCs.* (1) With respect to each of its covered QFCs, a covered bank that is a covered bank on January 1, 2018, must conform the covered QFC to the requirements of this part by:

(i) January 1, 2019, if each party to the covered QFC is a covered entity, covered bank, or covered FSI;

(ii) July 1, 2019, if each party to the covered QFC (other than the covered bank) is a financial counterparty that is not a covered entity, covered bank, or covered FSI; or

(iii) January 1, 2020, if a party to the covered QFC (other than the covered bank) is not described in paragraphs (f)(1)(i) or (f)(1)(ii) of this section, or if, notwithstanding paragraph (f)(1)(ii) of this section, a party to the covered

QFC (other than the covered bank) is a small financial institution.

(2) With respect to each of its covered QFCs, a covered bank that is not a covered bank on January 1, 2018, must conform the covered QFC to the requirements of this part by:

(i) The first day of the calendar quarter immediately following one year after the date the covered bank first becomes a covered bank if each party to the covered QFC is a covered entity, covered bank, or covered FSI;

(ii) The first day of the calendar quarter immediately following 18 months from the date the covered bank first becomes a covered bank if each party to the covered QFC (other than the covered bank) is a financial counterparty that is not a covered entity, covered bank, or covered FSI; or

(iii) The first day of the calendar quarter immediately following two years from the date the covered bank first becomes a covered bank if a party to the covered QFC (other than the covered bank) is not described in paragraphs (f)(2)(i) or (f)(2)(ii) of this section, or if, notwithstanding paragraph (f)(2)(ii) of this section, a party to the covered QFC (other than the covered bank) is a small financial institution.

§ 47.4 U.S. special resolution regimes.

(a) *Covered QFCs not required to be conformed.* (1) Notwithstanding § 47.3, a covered bank is not required to conform a covered QFC to the requirements of this section if:

(i) The covered QFC designates, in the manner described in paragraph (a)(2) of this section, the U.S. special resolution regimes as part of the law governing the QFC; and

(ii) Each party to the covered QFC, other than the covered bank, is:

(A) An individual that is domiciled in the United States, including any State;

(B) A company that is incorporated in or organized under the laws of the United States or any State;

(C) A company the principal place of business of which is located in the United States, including any State; or

(D) A U.S. branch or U.S. agency.

(2) A covered QFC designates the U.S. special resolution regimes as part of the law governing the QFC if the covered QFC:

(i) Explicitly provides that the covered QFC is governed by the laws of the United States or a state of the United States; and

(ii) Does not explicitly provide that one or both of the U.S. special resolution regimes, or a broader set of laws that includes a U.S. special resolution regime, is excluded from the laws governing the covered QFC.

(b) *Provisions required.* A covered QFC must explicitly provide that:

(1) In the event the covered bank becomes subject to a proceeding under a U.S. special resolution regime, the transfer of the covered QFC (and any interest and obligation in or under, and any property securing, the covered QFC) from the covered bank will be effective to the same extent as the transfer would be effective under the U.S. special resolution regime if the covered QFC (and any interest and obligation in or under, and any property securing, the covered QFC) were governed by the laws of the United States or a state of the United States; and

(2) In the event the covered bank or an affiliate of the covered bank becomes subject to a proceeding under a U.S. special resolution regime, default rights with respect to the covered QFC that may be exercised against the covered bank are permitted to be exercised to no greater extent than the default rights could be exercised under the U.S. special resolution regime if the covered QFC were governed by the laws of the United States or a state of the United States.

(c) *Relevance of creditor protection provisions.* The requirements of this section apply notwithstanding paragraphs (d), (f), and (h) of § 47.5.

§ 47.5 Insolvency proceedings.

(a) *Covered QFCs not required to be conformed.* Notwithstanding § 47.3, a covered bank is not required to conform a covered QFC to the requirements of this section if the covered QFC:

(1) Does not explicitly provide any default right with respect to the covered QFC that is related, directly or indirectly, to an affiliate of the direct party becoming subject to a receivership, insolvency, liquidation, resolution, or similar proceeding; and

(2) Does not explicitly prohibit the transfer of a covered affiliate credit enhancement, any interest or obligation in or under the covered affiliate credit enhancement, or any property securing the covered affiliate credit enhancement to a transferee upon or following an affiliate of the direct party becoming subject to a receivership, insolvency, liquidation, resolution, or similar proceeding or would prohibit such a transfer only if the transfer would result in the supported party being the beneficiary of the credit enhancement in violation of any law applicable to the supported party.

(b) *General prohibitions.* (1) A covered QFC may not permit the exercise of any default right with respect to the covered QFC that is related, directly or indirectly, to an affiliate of the direct party becoming subject to a receivership, insolvency, liquidation, resolution, or similar proceeding.

(2) A covered QFC may not prohibit the transfer of a covered affiliate credit enhancement, any interest or obligation in or under the covered affiliate credit enhancement, or any property securing the covered affiliate credit enhancement to a transferee upon or following an affiliate of the direct party becoming subject to a receivership, insolvency, liquidation, resolution, or similar proceeding unless the transfer would result in the supported party being the beneficiary of the credit enhancement in violation of any law applicable to the supported party.

(c) *Definitions relevant to the general prohibitions*—(1) *Direct party. Direct party* means a covered entity, covered bank, or covered FSI that is a party to the direct QFC.

(2) *Direct QFC. Direct QFC* means a QFC that is not a credit enhancement, provided that, for a QFC that is a master agreement that includes an affiliate credit enhancement as a supplement to the master agreement, the direct QFC does not include the affiliate credit enhancement.

(3) *Affiliate credit enhancement. Affiliate credit enhancement* means a credit enhancement that is provided by an affiliate of a party to the direct QFC that the credit enhancement supports.

(d) *General creditor protections.* Notwithstanding paragraph (b) of this section, a covered direct QFC and covered affiliate credit enhancement that supports the covered direct QFC may permit the exercise of a default right with respect to the covered QFC that arises as a result of:

(1) The direct party becoming subject to a receivership, insolvency, liquidation, resolution, or similar proceeding;

(2) The direct party not satisfying a payment or delivery obligation pursuant to the covered QFC or another contract between the same parties that gives rise to a default right in the covered QFC; or

(3) The covered affiliate support provider or transferee not satisfying a payment or delivery obligation pursuant to a covered affiliate credit enhancement that supports the covered direct QFC.

(e) *Definitions relevant to the general creditor protections*—(1) *Covered direct QFC. Covered direct QFC* means a direct QFC to which a covered entity, covered bank, or covered FSI is a party.

(2) *Covered affiliate credit enhancement. Covered affiliate credit enhancement* means an affiliate credit enhancement in which a covered entity, covered bank, or covered FSI is the obligor of the credit enhancement.

(3) *Covered affiliate support provider. Covered affiliate support provider* means, with respect to a covered affiliate credit enhancement, the affiliate of the direct party that is obligated under the covered affiliate credit enhancement and is not a transferee.

(4) *Supported party. Supported party* means, with respect to a covered affiliate credit enhancement and the direct QFC that the covered affiliate credit enhancement supports, a party that is a beneficiary of the covered affiliate support provider's obligation under the covered affiliate credit enhancement.

(f) *Additional creditor protections for supported QFCs.* Notwithstanding paragraph (b) of this section, with respect to a covered direct QFC that is supported by a covered affiliate credit enhancement, the covered direct QFC and the covered affiliate credit enhancement may permit the exercise of a default right after the stay period that is related, directly or indirectly, to the covered affiliate support provider becoming subject to a receivership, insolvency, liquidation, resolution, or similar proceeding if:

(1) The covered affiliate support provider that remains obligated under the covered affiliate credit enhancement becomes subject to a receivership, insolvency, liquidation, resolution, or similar proceeding other than a Chapter 11 proceeding;

(2) Subject to paragraph (h) of this section, the transferee, if any, becomes subject to a receivership, insolvency, liquidation, resolution, or similar proceeding;

(3) The covered affiliate support provider does not remain, and a transferee does not become, obligated to the same, or substantially similar, extent as the covered affiliate support provider was obligated immediately prior to entering the receivership, insolvency, liquidation, resolution, or similar proceeding with respect to:

(i) The covered affiliate credit enhancement;

(ii) All other covered affiliate credit enhancements provided by the covered affiliate support provider in support of other covered direct QFCs between the direct party and the supported party under the covered affiliate credit enhancement referenced in paragraph (f)(3)(i) of this section; and

(iii) All covered affiliate credit enhancements provided by the covered affiliate support provider in support of covered direct QFCs between the direct party and affiliates of the supported party referenced in paragraph (f)(3)(ii) of this section; or

(4) In the case of a transfer of the covered affiliate credit enhancement to a transferee:

(i) All of the ownership interests of the direct party directly or indirectly held by the covered affiliate support provider are not transferred to the transferee; or

(ii) Reasonable assurance has not been provided that all or substantially all of the assets of the covered affiliate support provider (or net proceeds therefrom), excluding any assets reserved for the payment of costs and expenses of administration in the receivership, insolvency, liquidation, resolution, or similar proceeding, will be transferred or sold to the transferee in a timely manner.

(g) *Definitions relevant to the additional creditor protections for supported QFCs*—(1) *Stay period. Stay period* means, with respect to a receivership, insolvency, liquidation, resolution, or similar proceeding, the period of time beginning on the commencement of the proceeding and ending at the later of 5:00 p.m. (eastern time) on the business day following the date of the commencement of the proceeding and 48 hours after the commencement of the proceeding.

(2) *Business day. Business day* means a day on which commercial banks in the jurisdiction the proceeding is commenced are open for general business (including dealings in foreign exchange and foreign currency deposits).

(3) *Transferee. Transferee* means a person to whom a covered affiliate credit enhancement is transferred upon the covered affiliate support provider entering a receivership, insolvency, liquidation, resolution, or similar proceeding or thereafter as part of the resolution, restructuring, or reorganization involving the covered affiliate support provider.

(h) *Creditor protections related to FDI Act proceedings.* Notwithstanding paragraphs (b), (d), and (f) of this section, with respect to a covered direct QFC that is supported by a covered affiliate credit enhancement, the covered direct QFC and the covered affiliate credit enhancement may permit the exercise of a default right that is related, directly or indirectly, to the covered affiliate support provider becoming subject to FDI Act proceedings:

(1) After the FDI Act stay period, if the covered affiliate credit enhancement is not transferred pursuant to section 11(e)(9)–(e)(10) of Federal Deposit Insurance Act (12 U.S.C. 1821(e)(9)–(e)(10)) and any regulations promulgated thereunder; or

(2) During the FDI Act stay period, if the default right may only be exercised so as to permit the supported party under the covered affiliate credit enhancement to suspend performance with respect to the supported party's obligations under the covered direct QFC to the same extent as the supported party would be entitled to do if

the covered direct QFC were with the covered affiliate support provider and were treated in the same manner as the covered affiliate credit enhancement.

(i) *Prohibited terminations.* A covered QFC must require, after an affiliate of the direct party has become subject to a receivership, insolvency, liquidation, resolution, or similar proceeding:

(1) The party seeking to exercise a default right to bear the burden of proof that the exercise is permitted under the covered QFC; and

(2) Clear and convincing evidence or a similar or higher burden of proof to exercise a default right.

§47.6 Approval of enhanced creditor protection conditions.

(a) *Protocol compliance.* (1) Unless the OCC determines otherwise based on the specific facts and circumstances, a covered QFC is deemed to comply with this part if it is amended by the universal protocol or the U.S. protocol.

(2) A covered QFC will be deemed to be amended by the universal protocol for purposes of paragraph (a)(1) of this section notwithstanding the covered QFC being amended by one or more Country Annexes, as the term is defined in the universal protocol.

(3) For purposes of paragraphs (a)(1) and (2) of this section:

(i) The *universal protocol* means the ISDA 2015 Universal Resolution Stay Protocol, including the Securities Financing Transaction Annex and Other Agreements Annex, published by the International Swaps and Derivatives Association, Inc., as of May 3, 2016, and minor or technical amendments thereto;

(ii) The *U.S. protocol* means a protocol that is the same as the universal protocol other than as provided in paragraphs (a)(3)(ii)(A)–(F) of this section.

(A) The provisions of Section 1 of the attachment to the universal protocol may be limited in their application to a covered entity, covered bank, or covered FSI and may be limited with respect to resolutions under the Identified Regimes, as those regimes are identified by the universal protocol;

(B) The provisions of Section 2 of the attachment to the universal protocol may be limited in their application to a covered entity, covered bank, or covered FSI;

(C) The provisions of Section 4(b)(i)(A) of the attachment to the universal protocol must not apply with respect to U.S. special resolution regimes;

(D) The provision of Section 4(b) of the attachment to the universal protocol may only be effective to the extent that the covered QFC affected by an adherent's election thereunder would continue to meet the requirements of this part;

(E) The provisions of Section 2(k) of the attachment to the universal protocol must not apply; and

(F) The U.S. protocol may include minor and technical differences from the universal protocol and differences necessary to conform the U.S. protocol to the differences described in paragraphs (a)(3)(ii)(A)–(E) of this section;

(iii) Amended by the universal protocol or the U.S. protocol, with respect to covered QFCs between adherents to the protocol, includes amendments through incorporation of the terms of the protocol (by reference or otherwise) into the covered QFC; and

(iv) The *attachment to the universal protocol* means the attachment that the universal protocol identifies as "ATTACHMENT to the ISDA 2015 UNIVERSAL RESOLUTION STAY PROTOCOL."

(b) *Proposal of enhanced creditor protection conditions.* (1) A covered bank may request that the OCC approve as compliant with the requirements of §§47.4 and 47.5 proposed provisions of one or more forms of covered QFCs, or proposed amendments to one or more forms of covered QFCs, with enhanced creditor protection conditions.

(2) Enhanced creditor protection conditions means a set of limited exemptions to the requirements of §47.5(b) that are different than that of paragraphs (d), (f), and (h) of §47.5.

(3) A covered bank making a request under paragraph (b)(1) of this section must provide:

(i) An analysis of the proposal that addresses each consideration in paragraph (d) of this section;

(ii) A written legal opinion verifying that proposed provisions or amendments would be valid and enforceable under applicable law of the relevant jurisdictions, including, in the case of proposed amendments, the validity and enforceability of the proposal to amend the covered QFCs; and

(iii) Any other relevant information that the OCC requests.

(c) *OCC approval.* The OCC may approve, subject to any conditions or commitments the OCC may set, a proposal by a covered bank under paragraph (b) of this section if the proposal, as compared to a covered QFC that contains only the limited exemptions in paragraphs of (d), (f), and (h) of § 47.5 or that is amended as provided under paragraph (a) of this section, would promote the safety and soundness of federally chartered or licensed institutions by mitigating the potential destabilizing effects of the resolution of a global significantly important banking entity that is an affiliate of the covered bank, at least to the same extent.

(d) *Considerations.* In reviewing a proposal under this section, the OCC may consider all facts and circumstances related to the proposal, including:

(1) Whether, and the extent to which, the proposal would reduce the resiliency of such covered banks during distress or increase the impact on U.S. financial stability were one or more of the covered banks to fail;

(2) Whether, and the extent to which, the proposal would materially decrease the ability of a covered bank, or an affiliate of a covered bank, to be resolved in a rapid and orderly manner in the event of the financial distress or failure of the covered bank, or an affiliate of a covered bank, that is required to submit a resolution plan;

(3) Whether, and the extent to which, the set of conditions or the mechanism in which they are applied facilitates, on an industry-wide basis, contractual modifications to remove impediments to resolution and increase market certainty, transparency, and equitable treatment with respect to the default rights of non-defaulting parties to a covered QFC;

(4) Whether, and the extent to which, the proposal applies to existing and future transactions;

(5) Whether, and the extent to which, the proposal would apply to multiple forms of QFCs or multiple covered banks or an affiliates of covered banks;

(6) Whether the proposal would permit a party to a covered QFC that is within the scope of the proposal to adhere to the proposal with respect to only one or a subset of covered banks or an affiliates of covered banks;

(7) With respect to a supported party, the degree of assurance the proposal provides to the supported party that the material payment and delivery obligations of the covered affiliate credit enhancement and the covered direct QFC it supports will continue to be performed after the covered affiliate support provider enters a receivership, insolvency, liquidation, resolution, or similar proceeding;

(8) The presence, nature, and extent of any provisions that require a covered affiliate support provider or transferee to meet conditions other than material payment or delivery obligations to its creditors;

(9) The extent to which the supported party's overall credit risk to the direct party may increase if the enhanced creditor protection conditions are not met and the likelihood that the supported party's credit risk to the direct party would decrease or remain the same if the enhanced creditor protection conditions are met; and

(10) Whether the proposal provides the counterparty with additional default rights or other rights.

§ 47.7 Foreign bank multi-branch master agreements.

(a) *Treatment of foreign bank multi-branch master agreements.* With respect to a Federal branch or agency of a global systemically important foreign banking organization, a foreign bank multi-branch master agreement that is a covered QFC solely because the master agreement permits agreements or transactions that are QFCs to be entered into at one or more Federal branches or agencies of the global systemically important foreign banking organization will be considered a covered QFC for purposes of this part only with respect to such agreements or transactions booked at such Federal branches or agencies.

(b) *Definition of foreign bank multi-branch master agreements.* A *foreign bank multi-branch master agreement* means a master agreement that permits a Federal branch or agency and another place of business of a foreign bank that is outside the United States to enter transactions under the agreement.

§47.8 Exclusion of certain QFCs.

(a) *Exclusion of QFCs with FMUs.* Notwithstanding §47.3, a covered bank is not required to conform to the requirements of this part a covered QFC to which:

(1) A CCP is party; or

(2) Each party (other than the covered bank) is an FMU.

(b) *Exclusion of certain covered entity and covered FSI QFCs.* If a covered QFC is also a covered QFC under part 382 or 252, subpart I, of this title that an affiliate of the covered bank is also required to conform pursuant to part 382 or 252, subpart I, of this title and the covered bank is:

(1) The affiliate credit enhancement provider with respect to the covered QFC, then the covered bank is required to conform the credit enhancement to the requirements of this part but is not required to conform the direct QFC to the requirements of this part; or

(2) The direct party to which the excluded bank is the affiliate credit enhancement provider, then the covered bank is required to conform the direct QFC to the requirements of this part but is not required to conform the credit enhancement to the requirements of this part.

(c) *Exclusion of certain contracts.* Notwithstanding §47.3, a covered bank is not required to conform the following types of contracts or agreements to the requirements of this part:

(1) An investment advisory contract that:

(i) Is with a retail customer or counterparty;

(ii) Does not explicitly restrict the transfer of the contract (or any QFC entered into pursuant thereto or governed thereby, or any interest or obligation in or under, or any property securing, any such QFC or the contract) from the covered bank except as necessary to comply with section 205(a)(2) of the Investment Advisers Act of 1940 (15 U.S.C. 80b–5(a)(2)); and

(iii) Does not explicitly provide a default right with respect to the contract or any QFC entered pursuant thereto or governed thereby.

(2) A warrant that:

(i) Evidences a right to subscribe to or otherwise acquire a security of the covered bank or an affiliate of the covered bank; and

(ii) Was issued prior to January 1, 2018.

(d) *Exemption by order.* The OCC may exempt by order one or more covered banks from conforming one or more contracts or types of contracts to one or more of the requirements of this part after considering:

(1) The potential impact of the exemption on the ability of the covered bank, or affiliates of the covered bank, to be resolved in a rapid and orderly manner in the event of the financial distress or failure of the entity that is required to submit a resolution plan;

(2) The burden the exemption would relieve; and

(3) Any other factor the OCC deems relevant.

PART 48—RETAIL FOREIGN EXCHANGE TRANSACTIONS

Sec.

48.1 Authority, purpose, and scope.
48.2 Definitions.
48.3 Prohibited transactions.
48.4 Supervisory non-objection.
48.5 Application and closing out of offsetting long and short positions.
48.6 Disclosure.
48.7 Recordkeeping.
48.8 Capital requirements.
48.9 Margin requirements.
48.10 Required reporting to customers.
48.11 Unlawful representations.
48.12 Authorization to trade.
48.13 Trading and operational standards.
48.14 Supervision.
48.15 Notice of transfers.
48.16 Customer dispute resolution.
48.17 Reservation of authority.

AUTHORITY: 7 U.S.C. 27 *et seq.*; 12 U.S.C. 1 *et seq.*, 24, 93a, 161, 1461 *et seq.*, 1462a, 1463, 1464, 1813(q), 1818, 1831o, 3101 *et seq.*, 3102, 3106a, 3108, and 5412.

SOURCE: 76 FR 41384, July 14, 2011, unless otherwise noted.

§48.1 Authority, purpose, and scope.

(a) *Authority*—(1) *National banks.* A national bank may offer or enter into retail foreign exchange transactions. A national bank offering or entering into retail foreign exchange transactions must comply with the requirements of this part.

(2) *Federal savings associations.* A Federal savings association may offer or enter into retail foreign exchange transactions. A Federal savings association offering or entering into retail foreign exchange transactions must comply with the requirements of this part as if each reference to a national bank were a reference to a Federal savings association.

(b) *Purpose.* This part establishes rules applicable to retail foreign exchange transactions engaged in by national banks and applies on or after the effective date.

(c) *Scope.* Except as provided in paragraph (d) of this section, this part applies to national banks.

(d) *International applicability.* Sections 48.3 and 48.5 to 48.16 do not apply to retail foreign exchange transactions between a foreign branch of a national bank and a non-U.S. customer. With respect to those transactions, the foreign branch remains subject to any disclosure, recordkeeping, capital, margin, reporting, business conduct, documentation, and other requirements of foreign law applicable to the branch.

[76 FR 41384, July 14, 2011, as amended at 76 FR 56096, Sept. 12, 2011]

§ 48.2 Definitions.

In addition to the definitions in this section, for purposes of this part, the following terms have the same meaning as in the Commodity Exchange Act: "Affiliated person of a futures commission merchant"; "associated person"; "contract of sale"; "commodity"; "eligible contract participant"; "futures commission merchant"; "future delivery"; "option"; "security"; and "security futures product".

Affiliate has the same meaning as in section 2(k) of the Bank Holding Company Act of 1956 (12 U.S.C. 1841(k)).

Commodity Exchange Act means the Commodity Exchange Act (7 U.S.C. 1 *et seq.*).

Federal savings association means a Federal savings association or Federal savings bank chartered under section 5 of the Home Owners' Loan Act (12 U.S.C. 1464) or an operating subsidiary thereof.

Forex means foreign exchange.

Identified banking product has the same meaning as in section 401(b) of the Legal Certainty for Bank Products Act of 2000 (7 U.S.C. 27(b)).

Institution-affiliated party or *IAP* has the same meaning as in section 3(u)(1), (2), or (3) of the Federal Deposit Insurance Act (12 U.S.C. 1813(u)(1), (2), or (3)).

Introducing broker means any person that solicits or accepts orders from a retail forex customer in connection with retail forex transactions.

National bank means:

(1) A national bank;

(2) A Federal branch or agency of a foreign bank, each as defined in 12 U.S.C. 3101; and

(3) An operating subsidiary of a national bank or an operating subsidiary of a Federal branch or agency of a foreign bank.

Related person, when used in reference to a retail forex counterparty, means:

(1) Any general partner, officer, director, or owner of 10 percent or more of the capital stock of the retail forex counterparty;

(2) An associated person or employee of the retail forex counterparty, if the retail forex counterparty is not a national bank;

(3) An IAP of the retail forex counterparty, if the retail forex counterparty is a national bank; and

(4) A relative or spouse of any of the foregoing persons, or a relative of such spouse, who shares the same home as any of the foregoing persons.

Retail foreign exchange dealer means any person other than a retail forex customer that is, or that offers to be, the counterparty to a retail forex transaction, except for a person described in item (aa), (bb), (cc)(AA), (dd), or (ff) of section 2(c)(2)(B)(i)(II) of the Commodity Exchange Act (7 U.S.C. 2(c)(2)(B)(i)(II)).

Retail forex account means the account of a retail forex customer, established with a national bank, in which retail forex transactions with the national bank as counterparty are undertaken, or the account of a retail forex customer that is established in order to enter into such transactions.

Retail forex account agreement means the contractual agreement between a national bank and a retail forex customer that contains the terms governing the customer's retail forex account with the national bank.

Retail forex business means engaging in one or more retail forex transactions with the intent to derive income from those transactions, either directly or indirectly.

Retail forex counterparty includes, as appropriate:

(1) A national bank;

(2) A retail foreign exchange dealer;

(3) A futures commission merchant; and

(4) An affiliated person of a futures commission merchant.

Retail forex customer means a customer that is not an eligible contract participant, acting on his, her, or its own behalf and engaging in retail forex transactions.

Retail forex obligation means an obligation of a retail forex customer with respect to a retail forex transaction, including trading losses, fees, spreads, charges, and commissions.

Retail forex proprietary account means: A retail forex account carried on the books of a national bank for one of the following persons; a retail forex account of which 10 percent or more is owned by one of the following persons; or a retail forex account of which an aggregate of 10 percent or more of which is owned by more than one of the following persons:

(1) The national bank;

(2) An officer, director, or owner of 10 percent or more of the capital stock of the national bank; or

(3) An employee of the national bank, whose duties include:

(i) The management of the national bank's business;

(ii) The handling of the national bank's retail forex transactions;

(iii) The keeping of records, including without limitation the software used to make or maintain those records, pertaining to the national bank's retail forex transactions; or

(iv) The signing or co-signing of checks or drafts on behalf of the national bank;

(4) A spouse or minor dependent living in the same household as any of the foregoing persons; or

(5) An affiliate of the national bank.

Retail forex transaction means an agreement, contract, or transaction in foreign currency, other than an identified banking product or a part of an identified banking product, that is offered or entered into by a national bank with a person that is not an eligible contract participant and that is:

(1) A contract of sale of a commodity for future delivery or an option on such a contract;

(2) An option, other than an option executed or traded on a national securities exchange registered pursuant to section 6(a) of the Securities Exchange Act of 1934 (15 U.S.C. 78(f)(a)); or

(3) Offered or entered into on a leveraged or margined basis, or financed by a national bank, its affiliate, or any person acting in concert with the national bank or its affiliate on a similar basis, other than:

(i) A security that is not a security futures product as defined in section 1a(47) of the Commodity Exchange Act (7 U.S.C. 1a(47)); or

(ii) A contract of sale that:

(A) Results in actual delivery within two days; or

(B) Creates an enforceable obligation to deliver between a seller and buyer that have the ability to deliver and accept delivery, respectively, in connection with their line of business; or

(iii) An agreement, contract, or transaction that the OCC determines is not functionally or economically similar to:

(A) A contract of sale of a commodity for future delivery or an option on such a contract; or

(B) An option, other than an option executed or traded on a national securities exchange registered pursuant to section 6(a) of the Securities Exchange Act of 1934 (15 U.S.C. 78(f)(a)).

[76 FR 41384, July 14, 2011, as amended at 76 FR 56096, Sept. 12, 2011]

§48.3 Prohibited transactions.

(a) *Fraudulent conduct prohibited.* No national bank or its IAPs may, directly or indirectly, in or in connection with any retail forex transaction:

(1) Cheat or defraud or attempt to cheat or defraud any person;

(2) Willfully make or cause to be made to any person any false report or statement or cause to be entered for any person any false record; or

(3) Willfully deceive or attempt to deceive any person by any means whatsoever.

(b) *Acting as counterparty and exercising discretion prohibited.* If a national bank can cause retail forex transactions to be effected for a retail forex customer without the retail forex customer's specific authorization, then neither the national bank nor its affiliates may act as the counterparty for any retail forex transaction with that retail forex customer.

§ 48.4 Supervisory non-objection.

(a) *Supervisory non-objection required.* Before commencing a retail forex business, a national bank must provide the OCC with prior notice and obtain from the OCC a written supervisory non-objection.

(b) *Requirements for obtaining supervisory non-objection.* (1) In order to obtain a written supervisory non-objection, a national bank must:

(i) Establish to the satisfaction of the OCC that the national bank has established and implemented written policies, procedures, and risk measurement and management systems and controls for the purpose of ensuring that it conducts retail forex transactions in a safe and sound manner and in compliance with this part; and

(ii) Provide such other information as the OCC may require.

(2) The information provided under paragraph (b)(1) of this section must include, without limitation, information regarding:

(i) Customer due diligence, including without limitation credit evaluations, customer appropriateness, and "know your customer" documentation;

(ii) New product approvals;

(iii) The haircuts that the national bank will apply to noncash margin as provided in § 48.9(b)(2); and

(iv) Conflicts of interest.

(c) *Treatment of existing retail forex businesses.* A national bank that is engaged in a retail forex business on July 15, 2011 or September 12, 2011 for Federal savings associations, may continue to do so for up to six months, subject to an extension of time by the OCC, if it requests the supervisory non-objection required by paragraph (a) of this section within 30 days of July 15, 2011 or September 12, 2011 for Federal savings associations, and submits the information required to be submitted under paragraph (b) of this section.

(d) *Compliance with the Commodity Exchange Act.* A national bank that is engaged in a retail forex business on July 15, 2011 or September 12, 2011 for Federal savings associations and complies with paragraph (c) of this section will be deemed, during the six-month or extended period described in paragraph (c) of this section, to be acting pursuant to a rule or regulation described in section 2(c)(2)(E)(ii)(I) of the Commodity Exchange Act (7 U.S.C. 2(c)(2)(E)(ii)(I)).

[76 FR 41384, July 14, 2011, as amended at 76 FR 56096, Sept. 12, 2011]

§ 48.5 Application and closing out of offsetting long and short positions.

(a) *Application of purchases and sales.* Any national bank that—

(1) Engages in a retail forex transaction involving the purchase of any currency for the account of any retail forex customer when the account of such retail forex customer at the time of such purchase has an open retail forex transaction for the sale of the same currency;

(2) Engages in a retail forex transaction involving the sale of any currency for the account of any retail forex customer when the account of such retail forex customer at the time of such sale has an open retail forex transaction for the purchase of the same currency;

(3) Purchases a put or call option involving foreign currency for the account of any retail forex customer when the account of such retail forex customer at the time of such purchase has a short put or call option position with the same underlying currency, strike price, and expiration date as that purchased; or

(4) Sells a put or call option involving foreign currency for the account of any retail forex customer when the account of such retail forex customer at

the time of such sale has a long put or call option position with the same underlying currency, strike price, and expiration date as that sold must:

(i) Immediately apply such purchase or sale against such previously held opposite transaction; and

(ii) Promptly furnish such retail forex customer with a statement showing the financial result of the transactions involved and the name of any introducing broker to the account.

(b) *Close-out against oldest open position.* In all instances in which the short or long position in a customer's retail forex account immediately prior to an offsetting purchase or sale is greater than the quantity purchased or sold, the national bank must apply such offsetting purchase or sale to the oldest portion of the previously held short or long position.

(c) *Transactions to be applied as directed by customer.* Notwithstanding paragraphs (a) and (b) of this section, to the extent the national bank allows retail forex customers to use other methods of offsetting retail forex transactions, the offsetting transaction must be applied as directed by a retail forex customer's specific instructions. These instructions may not be made by the national bank or an IAP of the national bank.

§ 48.6 Disclosure.

(a) *Risk disclosure statement required.* No national bank may open or maintain open an account that will engage in retail forex transactions for a retail forex customer unless the national bank has furnished the retail forex customer with a separate written disclosure statement containing only the language set forth in paragraph (d) of this section and the disclosures required by paragraphs (e) and (f) of this section.

(b) *Acknowledgment of risk disclosure statement required.* The national bank must receive from the retail forex customer a written acknowledgment signed and dated by the customer that the customer received and understood the written disclosure statement required by paragraph (a) of this section.

(c) *Placement of risk disclosure statement.* The disclosure statement may be attached to other documents as the initial page(s) of such documents and as the only material on such page(s).

(d) *Content of risk disclosure statement.* The language set forth in the written disclosure statement required by paragraph (a) of this section is as follows:

RISK DISCLOSURE STATEMENT

Retail forex transactions involve the leveraged trading of contracts denominated in foreign currency with [name of entity] as your counterparty. Because of the leverage and the other risks disclosed here, you can rapidly lose all of the funds or property you pledge to [name of entity] as margin for retail forex trading. You may lose more than you pledge as margin.

If your margin falls below the required amount, and you fail to provide the required additional margin, [name of entity] is required to liquidate your retail forex transactions. [Name of entity] cannot apply your retail forex losses to any of your assets or liabilities at [name of entity] other than funds or property that you have pledged as margin for retail forex transactions. However, if you lose more money than you have pledged as margin, [name of entity] may seek to recover that deficiency in an appropriate forum, such as a court of law.

You should be aware of and carefully consider the following points before determining whether retail forex trading is appropriate for you.

(1) Trading is not on a regulated market or exchange—[name of entity] is your trading counterparty and has conflicting interests. The retail forex transaction you are entering into is not conducted on an interbank market nor is it conducted on a futures exchange subject to regulation as a designated contract market by the Commodity Futures Trading Commission. The foreign currency trades you transact are trades with [name of entity] as the counterparty. When you sell, [name of entity] is the buyer. When you buy, [name of entity] is the seller. As a result, when you lose money trading, [name of entity] is making money on such trades, in addition to any fees, commissions, or spreads [name of entity] may charge.

(2) An electronic trading platform for retail foreign currency transactions is not an exchange. It is an electronic connection for accessing [name of entity]. The terms of availability of such a platform are governed only by your contract with [name of entity]. Any trading platform that you may use to enter into off-exchange foreign currency transactions is only connected to [name of entity]. You are accessing that trading platform only to transact with [name of entity]. You are not trading with any other entities or customers of [name of entity] by accessing such platform. The availability and operation of any such platform, including the

consequences of the unavailability of the trading platform for any reason, is governed only by the terms of your account agreement with [name of entity].

(3) You may be able to offset or liquidate any trading positions only through [name of national bank] because the transactions are not made on an exchange or regulated contract market, and [name of entity] may set its own prices. Your ability to close your transactions or offset positions is limited to what [name of entity] will offer to you, as there is no other market for these transactions. [Name of entity] may offer any prices it wishes, including prices derived from outside sources or not in its discretion. [Name of entity] may establish its prices by offering spreads from third-party prices, but it is under no obligation to do so or to continue to do so. [Name of entity] may offer different prices to different customers at any point in time on its own terms. The terms of your account agreement alone govern the obligations [name of entity] has to you to offer prices and offer offset or liquidating transactions in your account and make any payments to you. The prices offered by [name of entity] may or may not reflect prices available elsewhere at any exchange, interbank, or other market for foreign currency.

(4) Paid solicitors may have undisclosed conflicts. [Name of entity] may compensate introducing brokers for introducing your account in ways that are not disclosed to you. Such paid solicitors are not required to have, and may not have, any special expertise in trading and may have conflicts of interest based on the method by which they are compensated. You should thoroughly investigate the manner in which all such solicitors are compensated and be very cautious in granting any person or entity authority to trade on your behalf. You should always consider obtaining dated written confirmation of any information you are relying on from [name of entity] in making any trading or account decisions.

(5) Retail forex transactions are not insured by the Federal Deposit Insurance Corporation.

(6) Retail forex transactions are not a deposit in, or guaranteed by, [name of entity].

(7) Retail forex transactions are subject to investment risks, including possible loss of all amounts invested.

Finally, you should thoroughly investigate any statements by [name of entity] that minimize the importance of, or contradict, any of the terms of this risk disclosure. These statements may indicate sales fraud.

This brief statement cannot, of course, disclose all the risks and other aspects of trading off-exchange foreign currency with [name of entity].

I hereby acknowledge that I have received and understood this risk disclosure statement.

____

Date

____

Signature of Customer

(e)(1) *Disclosure of profitable accounts ratio.* Immediately following the language set forth in paragraph (d) of this section, the statement required by paragraph (a) of this section must include, for each of the most recent four calendar quarters during which the national bank maintained retail forex customer accounts:

(i) The total number of retail forex customer accounts maintained by the national bank over which the national bank does not exercise investment discretion;

(ii) The percentage of such accounts that were profitable for retail forex customer accounts during the quarter; and

(iii) The percentage of such accounts that were not profitable for retail forex customer accounts during the quarter.

(2) The national bank's statement of profitable trades must include the following legend: "Past performance is not necessarily indicative of future results." Each national bank must provide, upon request, to any retail forex customer or prospective retail forex customer the total number of retail forex accounts maintained by the national bank for which the national bank does not exercise investment discretion, the percentage of such accounts that were profitable, and the percentage of such accounts that were not profitable for each calendar quarter during the most recent five-year period during which the national bank maintained such accounts.

(f) *Disclosure of fees and other charges.* Immediately following the language required by paragraph (e) of this section, the statement required by paragraph (a) of this section must include:

(1) The amount of any fee, charge, spread, or commission that the national bank may impose on the retail forex customer in connection with a retail forex account or retail forex transaction;

(2) An explanation of how the national bank will determine the amount of such fees, charges, spreads, or commissions; and

(3) The circumstances under which the national bank may impose such fees, charges, spreads, or commissions.

(g) *Future disclosure requirements.* If, with regard to a retail forex customer, the national bank changes any fee, charge, or commission required to be disclosed under paragraph (f) of this section, then the national bank must mail or deliver to the retail forex customer a notice of the changes at least 15 days prior to the effective date of the change.

(h) *Form of disclosure requirements.* The disclosures required by this section must be clear and conspicuous and designed to call attention to the nature and significance of the information provided.

(i) *Other disclosure requirements unaffected.* This section does not relieve a national bank from any other disclosure obligation it may have under applicable law.

[76 FR 41384, July 14, 2011, as amended at 76 FR 56096, Sept. 12, 2011]

§48.7 Recordkeeping.

(a) *General rule.* A national bank engaging in retail forex transactions must keep full, complete, and systematic records, together with all pertinent data and memoranda, pertaining to its retail forex business, including the following 6 types of records:

(1) *Retail forex account records.* For each retail forex account:

(i) The name and address of the person for whom the account is carried or introduced and the principal occupation or business of the person;

(ii) The name of any other person guaranteeing the account or exercising trading control with respect to the account;

(iii) The establishment or termination of the account;

(iv) A means to identify the person that has solicited and is responsible for the account;

(v) The funds in the account, net of any commissions and fees;

(vi) The account's net profits and losses on open trades;

(vii) The funds in the account plus or minus the net profits and losses on open trades, adjusted for the net option value in the case of open options positions;

(viii) Financial ledger records that show all charges against and credits to the account, including deposits, withdrawals, and transfers, and charges or credits resulting from losses or gains on closed transactions; and

(ix) A list of all retail forex transactions executed for the account, with the details specified in paragraph (a)(2) of this section.

(2) *Retail forex transaction records.* For each retail forex transaction:

(i) The date and time the national bank received the order;

(ii) The price at which the national bank placed the order, or, in the case of an option, the premium that the retail forex customer paid;

(iii) The customer account identification information;

(iv) The currency pair;

(v) The size or quantity of the order;

(vi) Whether the order was a buy or sell order;

(vii) The type of order, if the order was not a market order;

(viii) The size and price at which the order is executed, or in the case of an option, the amount of the premium paid for each option purchased, or the amount credited for each option sold;

(ix) For options, whether the option is a put or call, expiration date, quantity, underlying contract for future delivery or underlying physical, strike price, and details of the purchase price of the option, including premium, mark-up, commission, and fees; and

(x) For futures, the delivery date; and

(xi) If the order was made on a trading platform:

(A) The price quoted on the trading platform when the order was placed, or, in the case of an option, the premium quoted;

(B) The date and time the order was transmitted to the trading platform; and

(C) The date and time the order was executed.

(3) *Price changes on a trading platform.* If a trading platform is used, daily logs showing each price change on the platform, the time of the change to the nearest second, and the trading volume at that time and price.

(4) *Methods or algorithms.* Any method or algorithm used to determine the bid or asked price for any retail forex

transaction or the prices at which customer orders are executed, including, but not limited to, any markups, fees, commissions or other items which affect the profitability or risk of loss of a retail forex customer's transaction.

(5) *Daily records* which show for each business day complete details of:

(i) All retail forex transactions that are futures transactions executed on that day, including the date, price, quantity, market, currency pair, delivery date, and the person for whom such transaction was made;

(ii) All retail forex transactions that are option transactions executed on that day, including the date, whether the transaction involved a put or call, the expiration date, quantity, currency pair, delivery date, strike price, details of the purchase price of the option, including premium, mark-up, commission and fees, and the person for whom the transaction was made; and

(iii) All other retail forex transactions executed on that day for such account, including the date, price, quantity, currency and the person for whom such transaction was made.

(6) *Other records.* Written acknowledgments of receipt of the risk disclosure statement required by § 48.6(b), offset instructions pursuant to § 48.5(c), records required under paragraphs (b) through (f) of this section, trading cards, signature cards, street books, journals, ledgers, payment records, copies of statements of purchase, and all other records, data, and memoranda that have been prepared in the course of the national bank's retail forex business.

(b) *Ratio of profitable accounts.* (1) With respect to its active retail forex customer accounts over which it did not exercise investment discretion and that are not retail forex proprietary accounts open for any period of time during the quarter, a national bank must prepare and maintain on a quarterly basis (calendar quarter):

(i) A calculation of the percentage of such accounts that were profitable;

(ii) A calculation of the percentage of such accounts that were not profitable; and

(iii) Data supporting the calculations described in paragraphs (b)(1)(i) and (ii) of this section.

(2) In calculating whether a retail forex account was profitable or not profitable during the quarter, the national bank must compute the realized and unrealized gains or losses on all retail forex transactions carried in the retail forex account at any time during the quarter, subtract all fees, commissions, and any other charges posted to the retail forex account during the quarter, and add any interest income and other income or rebates credited to the retail forex account during the quarter. All deposits and withdrawals of funds made by the retail forex customer during the quarter must be excluded from the computation of whether the retail forex account was profitable or not profitable during the quarter. Computations that result in a zero or negative number must be considered a retail forex account that was not profitable. Computations that result in a positive number must be considered a retail forex account that was profitable.

(3) A retail forex account must be considered "active" for purposes of paragraph (b)(1) of this section if and only if for the relevant calendar quarter a retail forex transaction was executed in that account or the retail forex account contained an open position resulting from a retail forex transaction.

(c) *Records related to violations of law.* A national bank engaging in retail forex transactions must make a record of all communications received by the national bank or its IAPs concerning facts giving rise to possible violations of law related to the national bank's retail forex business. The record must contain: The name of the complainant, if provided; the date of the communication; the relevant agreement, contract, or transaction; the substance of the communication; the name of the person that received the communication; and the final disposition of the matter.

(d) *Records for noncash margin.* A national bank must maintain a record of all noncash margin collected pursuant to § 48.9. The record must show separately for each retail forex customer:

(1) A description of the securities or property received;

(2) The name and address of such retail forex customer;

(3) The dates when the securities or property were received;

(4) The identity of the depositories or other places where such securities or property are segregated or held, if applicable;

(5) The dates in which the national bank placed or removed such securities or property into or from such depositories; and

(6) The dates of return of such securities or property to such retail forex customer, or other disposition thereof, together with the facts and circumstances of such other disposition.

(e) *Order Tickets.* (1) Except as provided in paragraph (e)(2) of this section, immediately upon the receipt of a retail forex transaction order, a national bank must prepare an order ticket for the order (whether unfulfilled, executed, or canceled). The order ticket must include:

(i) Account identification (account or customer name with which the retail forex transaction was effected);

(ii) Order number;

(iii) Type of order (market order, limit order, or subject to special instructions);

(iv) Date and time, to the nearest minute, that the retail forex transaction order was received (as evidenced by time-stamp or other timing device);

(v) Time, to the nearest minute, that the retail forex transaction order was executed; and

(vi) Price at which the retail forex transaction was executed.

(2) *Post-execution allocation of bunched orders.* Specific identifiers for retail forex accounts included in bunched orders need not be recorded at time of order placement or upon report of execution as required under paragraph (e)(1) of this section if the following requirements are met:

(i) The national bank placing and directing the allocation of an order eligible for post-execution allocation has been granted written investment discretion with regard to participating customer accounts and makes the following information available to retail forex customers upon request:

(A) The general nature of the post-execution allocation methodology the national bank will use;

(B) Whether the national bank has any interest in accounts that may be included with customer accounts in bunched orders eligible for post-execution allocation; and

(C) Summary or composite data sufficient for that customer to compare the customer's results with those of other comparable customers and, if applicable, any account in which the national bank has an interest.

(ii) Post-execution allocations are made as soon as practicable after the entire transaction is executed;

(iii) Post-execution allocations are fair and equitable, with no account or group of accounts receiving consistently favorable or unfavorable treatment; and

(iv) The post-execution allocation methodology is sufficiently objective and specific to permit the OCC to verify the fairness of the allocations using that methodology.

(f) *Record of monthly statements and confirmations.* A national bank must retain a copy of each monthly statement and confirmation required by § 48.10.

(g) *Form of record and manner of maintenance.* The records required by this section must clearly and accurately reflect the information required and provide an adequate basis for the audit of the information. A national bank must create and maintain audio recordings of oral orders and oral offset instructions. Record maintenance may include the use of automated or electronic records provided that the records are easily retrievable and readily available for inspection.

(h) *Length of maintenance.* A national bank must keep each record required by this section for at least five years from the date the record is created.

§ 48.8 Capital requirements.

A national bank offering or entering into retail forex transactions must be well capitalized as defined by 12 CFR part 6.

§ 48.9 Margin requirements.

(a) *Margin required.* A national bank engaging, or offering to engage, in retail forex transactions must collect from each retail forex customer an amount of margin not less than:

(1) Two percent of the notional value of the retail forex transaction for major currency pairs and 5 percent of the notional value of the retail forex transaction for all other currency pairs;

(2) For short options, 2 percent for major currency pairs and 5 percent for all other currency pairs of the notional value of the retail forex transaction, plus the premium received by the retail forex customer; or

(3) For long options, the full premium charged and received by the national bank.

(b)(1) *Form of margin.* Margin collected under paragraph (a) of this section or pledged by a retail forex customer for retail forex transactions must be in the form of cash or the following financial instruments:

(i) Obligations of the United States and obligations fully guaranteed as to principal and interest by the United States;

(ii) General obligations of any State or of any political subdivision thereof;

(iii) General obligations issued or guaranteed by any enterprise, as defined in 12 U.S.C. 4502(10);

(iv) Certificates of deposit issued by an insured depository institution, as defined in section 3(c)(2) of the Federal Deposit Insurance Act (12 U.S.C. 1813(c)(2));

(v) Commercial paper;

(vi) Corporate notes or bonds;

(vii) General obligations of a sovereign nation;

(viii) Interests in money market mutual funds; and

(ix) Such other financial instruments as the OCC deems appropriate.

(2) *Haircuts.* A national bank must establish written policies and procedures that include:

(i) Haircuts for noncash margin collected under this section; and

(ii) Annual evaluation, and, if appropriate, modification, of the haircuts.

(c) *Separate margin account.* Margin collected by the national bank from a retail forex customer for retail forex transactions or pledged by a retail forex customer for retail forex transactions must be placed into a separate account.

(d) *Margin calls; liquidation of position.* (1) For each retail forex customer, at least once per day, a national bank must:

(i) Mark the value of the retail forex customer's open retail forex positions to market;

(ii) Mark the value of the margin collected under this section from the retail forex customer to market; and

(iii) Determine whether, based on the marks in paragraphs (d)(1)(i) and (ii) of this section, the national bank has collected margin from the retail forex customer sufficient to satisfy the requirements of this section.

(2) If, pursuant to paragraph (d)(1)(iii) of this section, the national bank determines that it has not collected margin from the retail forex customer sufficient to satisfy the requirements of this section then, within a reasonable period of time, the national bank must either:

(i) Collect margin from the retail forex customer sufficient to satisfy the requirements of this section; or

(ii) Liquidate the retail forex customer's retail forex transactions.

(e) *Set-off prohibited.* A national bank may not:

(1) Apply a retail forex customer's retail forex obligations against any funds or other asset of the retail forex customer other than margin in the separate margin account described in paragraph (c) of this section;

(2) Apply a retail forex customer's retail forex obligations to increase the amount owed by the retail forex customer to the national bank under any loan; or

(3) Collect the margin required under this section by use of any right of set-off.

§ 48.10 Required reporting to customers.

(a) *Monthly statements.* Each national bank must promptly furnish to each retail forex customer, as of the close of the last business day of each month or as of any regular monthly date selected, except for accounts in which there are neither open positions at the end of the statement period nor any changes to the account balance since the prior statement period but, in any event, not less frequently than once every three months, a statement that clearly shows:

(1) For each retail forex customer:

(i) The open retail forex transactions with prices at which acquired;

(ii) The net unrealized profits or losses in all open retail forex transactions marked to the market;

(iii) Any money, securities, or other property in the separate margin account required by §48.9(c); and

(iv) A detailed accounting of all financial charges and credits to the retail forex customer's retail forex accounts during the monthly reporting period, including: Money, securities, or property received from or disbursed to such customer; realized profits and losses; and fees, charges, spreads, and commissions.

(2) For each retail forex customer engaging in retail forex transactions that are options:

(i) All such options purchased, sold, exercised, or expired during the monthly reporting period, identified by underlying retail forex transaction or underlying currency, strike price, transaction date, and expiration date;

(ii) The open option positions carried for such customer and arising as of the end of the monthly reporting period, identified by underlying retail forex transaction or underlying currency, strike price, transaction date, and expiration date;

(iii) All such option positions marked to the market and the amount each position is in the money, if any;

(iv) Any money, securities, or other property in the separate margin account required by §48.9(c); and

(v) A detailed accounting of all financial charges and credits to the retail forex customer's retail forex accounts during the monthly reporting period, including: Money, securities, or property received from or disbursed to such customer; realized profits and losses; premiums and mark-ups; and fees, charges, and commissions.

(b) *Confirmation statement*. Each national bank must, not later than the next business day after any retail forex transaction, send:

(1) To each retail forex customer, a written confirmation of each retail forex transaction caused to be executed by it for the customer, including offsetting transactions executed during the same business day and the rollover of an open retail forex transaction to the next business day;

(2) To each retail forex customer engaging in forex option transactions, a written confirmation of each forex option transaction, containing at least the following information:

(i) The retail forex customer's account identification number;

(ii) A separate listing of the actual amount of the premium, as well as each markup thereon, if applicable, and all other commissions, costs, fees, and other charges incurred in connection with the forex option transaction;

(iii) The strike price;

(iv) The underlying retail forex transaction or underlying currency;

(v) The final exercise date of the forex option purchased or sold; and

(vi) The date that the forex option transaction was executed.

(3) To each retail forex customer engaging in forex option transactions, upon the expiration or exercise of any option, a written confirmation statement thereof, which statement must include the date of such occurrence, a description of the option involved, and, in the case of exercise, the details of the retail forex or physical currency position that resulted therefrom including, if applicable, the final trading date of the retail forex transaction underlying the option.

(c) Notwithstanding paragraph (b) of this section, a retail forex transaction that is caused to be executed for a pooled investment vehicle that engages in retail forex transactions need be confirmed only to the operator of such pooled investment vehicle.

(d) *Controlled accounts*. With respect to any account controlled by any person other than the retail forex customer for whom such account is carried, each national bank must promptly furnish in writing to such other person the information required by paragraphs (a) and (b) of this section.

(e) *Introduced accounts*. Each statement provided pursuant to the provisions of this section must, if applicable, show that the account for which the national bank was introduced by an introducing broker and the name of the introducing broker.

§ 48.11 Unlawful representations.

(a) *No implication or representation of limiting losses.* No national bank engaged in retail foreign exchange transactions or its IAPs may imply or represent that it will, with respect to any retail customer forex account, for or on behalf of any person:

(1) Guarantee such person or account against loss;

(2) Limit the loss of such person or account; or

(3) Not call for or attempt to collect margin as established for retail forex customers.

(b) *No implication of representation of engaging in prohibited acts.* No national bank or its IAPs may in any way imply or represent that it will engage in any of the acts or practices described in paragraph (a) of this section.

(c) *No Federal government endorsement.* No national bank or its IAPs may represent or imply in any manner whatsoever that any retail forex transaction or retail forex product has been sponsored, recommended, or approved by the OCC, the Federal government, or any agency thereof.

(d) *Assuming or sharing of liability from bank error.* This section does not prevent a national bank from assuming or sharing in the losses resulting from the national bank's error or mishandling of a retail forex transaction.

(e) *Certain guaranties unaffected.* This section does not affect any guarantee entered into prior to the effective date of this part, but this section does apply to any extension, modification, or renewal thereof entered into after such date.

§ 48.12 Authorization to trade.

(a) *Specific authorization required.* No national bank may directly or indirectly effect a retail forex transaction for the account of any retail forex customer unless, before the retail forex transaction occurs, the retail forex customer specifically authorized the national bank to effect the retail forex transaction.

(b) *Requirements for specific authorization.* A retail forex transaction is "specifically authorized" for purposes of this section if the retail forex customer specifies:

(1) The precise retail forex transaction to be effected;

(2) The exact amount of the foreign currency to be purchased or sold; and

(3) In the case of an option, the identity of the foreign currency or contract that underlies the option.

§ 48.13 Trading and operational standards.

(a) *Internal rules, procedures, and controls required.* A national bank engaging in retail forex transactions must establish and implement internal policies, procedures, and controls designed, at a minimum, to:

(1) Ensure, to the extent reasonable, that each retail forex transaction that is executable at or near the price that the national bank has quoted to the retail forex customer is entered for execution before any retail forex transaction for:

(i) A proprietary account;

(ii) An account for which a related person may originate orders without the prior specific consent of the account owner, if the related person has gained knowledge of the retail forex customer's order prior to the transmission of an order for a proprietary account;

(iii) An account in which a related person has an interest, if the related person has gained knowledge of the retail forex customer's order prior to the transmission of an order for a proprietary account; or

(iv) An account in which a related person may originate orders without the prior specific consent of the account owner, if the related person has gained knowledge of the retail forex customer's order prior to the transmission of an order for a proprietary account;

(2) Prevent national-bank related persons from placing orders, directly or indirectly, with another person in a manner designed to circumvent the provisions of paragraph (a)(1) of this section; and

(3) Fairly and objectively establish settlement prices for retail forex transactions.

(b) *Disclosure of retail forex transactions.* No national bank engaging in retail forex transactions may disclose that an order of another person is being held by the national bank, unless the disclosure is necessary to the effective execution of such order or the disclosure is made at the request of the OCC.

(c) *Handling of retail forex accounts of related persons of retail forex counterparties.* No national bank engaging in retail forex transactions may knowingly handle the retail forex account of an employee of another retail forex counterparty's retail forex business unless the national bank:

(1) Receives written authorization from a person designated by the other retail forex counterparty with responsibility for the surveillance over the account pursuant to paragraph (a)(2) of this section;

(2) Prepares immediately upon receipt of an order for the account a written record of the order, including the account identification and order number, and records thereon to the nearest minute, by time-stamp or other timing device, the date and time the order was received; and

(3) Transmits on a regular basis to the other retail forex counterparty copies of all statements for the account and of all written records prepared upon the receipt of orders for the account pursuant to paragraph (c)(2) of this section.

(d) *Related person of national bank establishing account at another retail forex counterparty.* No related person of a national bank working in the national bank's retail forex business may have an account, directly or indirectly, with another retail forex counterparty unless the other retail forex counterparty:

(1) Receives written authorization to open and maintain the account from a person designated by the national bank with responsibility for the surveillance over the account pursuant to paragraph (a)(2) of this section; and

(2) Transmits on a regular basis to the national bank copies of all statements for the account and of all written records prepared by the other retail forex counterparty upon receipt of orders for the account pursuant to paragraph (a)(2) of this section.

(e) *Prohibited trading practices.* No national bank engaging in retail forex transactions may:

(1) Enter into a retail forex transaction, to be executed pursuant to a market or limit order at a price that is not at or near the price at which other retail forex customers, during that same time period, have executed retail forex transactions with the national bank;

(2) Adjust or alter prices for a retail forex transaction after the transaction has been confirmed to the retail forex customer;

(3) Provide to a retail forex customer a new bid price for a retail forex transaction that is higher than its previous bid without providing a new asked price that is also higher than its previous asked price by a similar amount;

(4) Provide to a retail forex customer a new bid price for a retail forex transaction that is lower than its previous bid without providing a new asked price that is also lower than its previous asked price by a similar amount; or

(5) Establish a new position for a retail forex customer (except one that offsets an existing position for that retail forex customer) where the national bank holds outstanding orders of other retail forex customers for the same currency pair at a comparable price.

§48.14 Supervision.

(a) *Supervision by the national bank.* A national bank engaging in retail forex transactions must diligently supervise the handling by its officers, employees, and agents (or persons occupying a similar status or performing a similar function) of all retail forex accounts carried, operated, or advised by at the national bank and all activities of its officers, employees, and agents (or persons occupying a similar status or performing a similar function) relating to its retail forex business.

(b) *Supervision by officers, employees, or agents.* An officer, employee, or agent of a national bank must diligently supervise his or her subordinates' handling of all retail forex accounts at the national bank and all the subordinates' activities relating to the national bank's retail forex business.

§48.15 Notice of transfers.

(a) *Prior notice generally required.* Except as provided in paragraph (b) of this section, a national bank must provide a retail forex customer with 30 days' prior notice of any assignment of any position or transfer of any account of the retail forex customer. The notice must include a statement that the retail forex customer is not required to accept the proposed assignment or transfer and may direct the national bank to liquidate the positions of the retail forex customer or transfer the account to a retail forex counterparty of the retail forex customer's selection.

(b) *Exceptions.* The requirements of paragraph (a) of this section do not apply to transfers:

(1) Requested by the retail forex customer;

(2) Made by the Federal Deposit Insurance Corporation as receiver or conservator under the Federal Deposit Insurance Act; or

(3) Otherwise authorized by applicable law.

(c) *Obligations of transferee national bank.* A national bank to which retail forex accounts or positions are assigned or transferred under paragraph (a) of this section must provide to the affected retail forex customers the risk disclosure statements and forms of acknowledgment required by this part and receive the required signed acknowledgments within 60 days of such assignments or transfers. This requirement does not apply if the national bank has clear written evidence that the retail forex customer has received and acknowledged receipt of the required disclosure statements.

§ 48.16 Customer dispute resolution.

(a) *Voluntary submission of claims to dispute or settlement procedures.* No national bank may enter into any agreement or understanding with a retail forex customer in which the customer agrees, prior to the time a claim or grievance arises, to submit such claim or grievance to any settlement procedure unless the following conditions are satisfied:

(1) Signing the agreement is not a condition for the customer to use the services offered by the national bank.

(2) If the agreement is contained as a clause or clauses of a broader agreement, the customer separately endorses the clause or clauses.

(3) The agreement advises the retail forex customer that, at such time as the customer notifies the national bank that the customer intends to submit a claim to arbitration, or at such time the national bank notifies the customer of its intent to submit a claim to arbitration, the customer will have the opportunity to choose a person qualified in dispute resolution to conduct the proceeding.

(4) The agreement must acknowledge that the national bank will pay any incremental fees that may be assessed in connection with the dispute resolution, unless it is determined in the proceeding that the retail forex customer has acted in bad faith in initiating the proceeding.

(5) The agreement must include the following language printed in large boldface type:

Two forums exist for the resolution of disputes related to retail forex transactions: civil court litigation and arbitration conducted by a private organization. The opportunity to settle disputes by arbitration may in some cases provide benefits to customers, including the ability to obtain an expeditious and final resolution of disputes without incurring substantial cost. Each customer must individually examine the relative merits of arbitration and consent to this arbitration agreement must be voluntary.

By signing this agreement, you: (1) May be waving your right to sue in a court of law; and (2) are agreeing to be bound by arbitration of any claims or counterclaims that you or [name of entity] may submit to arbitration under this agreement. In the event a dispute arises, you will be notified if [name of entity] intends to submit the dispute to arbitration.

You need not sign this agreement to open or maintain a retail forex account with [name of entity].

(b) *Election of forum.* (1) Within 10 business days after receipt of notice from the retail forex customer that the customer intends to submit a claim to arbitration, the national bank must provide the customer with a list of persons qualified in dispute resolution.

(2) The customer must, within 45 days after receipt of such list, notify the national bank of the person selected. The customer's failure to provide such notice must give the national bank the right to select a person from the list.

(c) *Enforceability*. A dispute settlement procedure may require parties using the procedure to agree, under applicable state law, submission agreement, or otherwise, to be bound by an award rendered in the procedure if the agreement to submit the claim or grievance to the procedure complies with paragraph (a) of this section or the agreement to submit the claim or grievance to the procedure was made after the claim or grievance arose. Any award so rendered by the procedure will be enforceable in accordance with applicable law.

(d) *Time limits for submission of claims*. The dispute settlement procedure used by the parties may not include any unreasonably short limitation period foreclosing submission of a customer's claims or grievances or counterclaims.

(e) *Counterclaims*. A procedure for the settlement of a retail forex customer's claims or grievances against a national bank or employee thereof may permit the submission of a counterclaim in the procedure by a person against whom a claim or grievance is brought if the counterclaim:

(1) Arises out of the transaction or occurrence that is the subject of the retail forex customer's claim or grievance; and

(2) Does not require for adjudication the presence of essential witnesses, parties, or third persons over which the settlement process lacks jurisdiction.

[76 FR 41384, July 14, 2011, as amended at 76 FR 56097, Sept. 12, 2011]

§ 48.17 Reservation of authority.

The OCC may modify the disclosure, recordkeeping, capital and margin, reporting, business conduct, documentation, or other standards or requirements under this part for a specific retail forex transaction or a class of retail forex transactions if the OCC determines that the modification is consistent with safety and soundness and the protection of retail forex customers.

PART 49 [RESERVED]

PART 50—LIQUIDITY RISK MEASUREMENT STANDARDS

Subpart A—General Provisions

Sec.
50.1 Purpose and applicability.
50.2 Reservation of authority.
50.3 Definitions.
50.4 Certain operational requirements.

Subpart B—Liquidity Coverage Ratio

50.10 Liquidity coverage ratio.

Subpart C—High-Quality Liquid Assets

50.20 High-quality liquid asset criteria.
50.21 High-quality liquid asset amount.
50.22 Requirements for eligible high-quality liquid assets.

Subpart D—Total Net Cash Outflow

50.30 Total net cash outflow amount.
50.31 Determining maturity.
50.32 Outflow amounts.
50.33 Inflow amounts.

Subpart E—Liquidity Coverage Shortfall

50.40 Liquidity coverage shortfall: Supervisory framework.

Subpart F—Transitions

50.50 Transitions.

AUTHORITY: 12 U.S.C. 1 *et seq.*, 93a, 481, 1818, 1828, and 1462 *et seq.*

SOURCE: 79 FR 61523, 61538, Oct. 10, 2014, unless otherwise noted.

Subpart A—General Provisions

§ 50.1 Purpose and applicability.

(a) *Purpose*. This part establishes a minimum liquidity standard for certain national banks and Federal savings associations on a consolidated basis, as set forth herein.

(b) *Applicability*. (1) A national bank or Federal savings association is subject to the minimum liquidity standard and other requirements of this part if:

(i) It has total consolidated assets equal to $250 billion or more, as reported on the most recent year-end Consolidated Reports of Condition and Income;

(ii) It has total consolidated on-balance sheet foreign exposure at the most recent year-end equal to $10 billion or more (where total on-balance sheet foreign exposure equals total cross-border claims less claims with a head office or guarantor located in another country plus redistributed guaranteed amounts to the country of the head office or guarantor plus local country claims on local residents plus revaluation gains on foreign exchange and derivative transaction products, calculated in accordance with the Federal Financial Institutions Examination Council (FFIEC) 009 Country Exposure Report);

(iii) It is a depository institution that has total consolidated assets equal to $10 billion or more, as reported on the most recent year-end Consolidated Report of Condition and Income and is a consolidated subsidiary of one of the following:

(A) A covered depository institution holding company that has total consolidated assets equal to $250 billion or more, as reported on the most recent year-end Consolidated Financial Statements for Holding Companies reporting form (FR Y–9C), or, if the covered depository institution holding company is not required to report on the FR Y–9C, its estimated total consolidated assets as of the most recent year-end, calculated in accordance with the instructions to the FR Y–9C;

(B) A depository institution that has total consolidated assets equal to $250 billion or more, as reported on the most recent year-end Consolidated Report of Condition and Income; or

(C) A covered depository institution holding company or depository institution that has consolidated total on-balance sheet foreign exposure at the most recent year-end equal to $10 billion or more (where total on-balance sheet foreign exposure equals total cross-border claims less claims with a head office or guarantor located in another country plus redistributed guaranteed amounts to the country of the head office or guarantor plus local country claims on local residents plus revaluation gains on foreign exchange and derivative transaction products, calculated in accordance with the Federal Financial Institutions Examination Council (FFIEC) 009 Country Exposure Report); or

(iv) The OCC has determined that application of this part is appropriate in light of the national bank's or Federal savings association's asset size, level of complexity, risk profile, scope of operations, affiliation with foreign or domestic covered entities, or risk to the financial system.

(2) Subject to the transition periods set forth in subpart F of this part:

(i) A national bank or Federal savings association that is subject to the minimum liquidity standard and other requirements of this part under paragraph (b)(1) of this section on September 30, 2014, must comply with the requirements of this part beginning on January 1, 2015;

(ii) A national bank or Federal savings association that becomes subject to the minimum liquidity standard and other requirements of this part under paragraphs (b)(1)(i) through (iii) of this section after September 30, 2014, must comply with the requirements of this part beginning on April 1 of the year in which the national bank or Federal savings association becomes subject to the minimum liquidity standard and other requirements of this part, except:

(A) From April 1 to December 31 of the year in which the national bank or Federal savings association becomes subject to the minimum liquidity standard and other requirements of this part, the national bank or Federal savings association must calculate and maintain a liquidity coverage ratio monthly, on each calculation date that is the last business day of the applicable calendar month; and

(B) Beginning January 1 of the year after the first year in which the national bank or Federal savings association becomes subject to the minimum liquidity standard and other requirements of this part under paragraph (b)(1) of this section, and thereafter, the national bank or Federal savings association must calculate and maintain a liquidity coverage ratio on each calculation date; and

(iii) A national bank or Federal savings association that becomes subject to the minimum liquidity standard and other requirements of this part under paragraph (b)(1)(iv) of this section after September 30, 2014, must comply with the requirements of this part subject to a transition period specified by the OCC.

(3) This part does not apply to:

(i) A bridge financial company as defined in 12 U.S.C. 5381(a)(3), or a subsidiary of a bridge financial company;

(ii) A new depository institution or a bridge depository institution, as defined in 12 U.S.C. 1813(i); or

(iii) A Federal branch or agency as defined by 12 CFR 28.11.

(4) A national bank or Federal savings association subject to a minimum liquidity standard under this part shall remain subject until the OCC determines in writing that application of this part to the national bank or Federal savings association is not appropriate in light of the national bank's or Federal savings association's asset size, level of complexity, risk profile, scope of operations, affiliation with foreign or domestic covered entities, or risk to the financial system.

(5) In making a determination under paragraphs (b)(1)(iv) or (4) of this section, the OCC will apply notice and response procedures in the same manner and to the same extent as the notice and response procedures in 12 CFR 3.404.

[79 FR 61523, 61538, Oct. 10, 2014, as amended at 79 FR 61538, Oct. 10, 2014]

§ 50.2 Reservation of authority.

(a) The OCC may require a national bank or Federal savings association to hold an amount of high-quality liquid assets (HQLA) greater than otherwise required under this part, or to take any other measure to improve the national bank's or Federal savings association's liquidity risk profile, if the OCC determines that the national bank's or Federal savings association's liquidity requirements as calculated under this part are not commensurate with the national bank's or Federal savings association's liquidity risks. In making determinations under this section, the OCC will apply notice and response procedures as set forth in 12 CFR 3.404.

(b) Nothing in this part limits the authority of the OCC under any other provision of law or regulation to take supervisory or enforcement action, including action to address unsafe or unsound practices or conditions, deficient liquidity levels, or violations of law.

§ 50.3 Definitions.

For the purposes of this part:

Affiliated depository institution means with respect to a national bank or Federal savings association that is a depository institution, another depository institution that is a consolidated subsidiary of a bank holding company or savings and loan holding company of which the national bank or Federal savings association is also a consolidated subsidiary.

Asset exchange means a transaction in which, as of the calculation date, the counterparties have previously exchanged non-cash assets, and have each agreed to return such assets to each other at a future date. Asset exchanges do not include secured funding and secured lending transactions.

Bank holding company is defined in section 2 of the Bank Holding Company Act of 1956, as amended (12 U.S.C. 1841 *et seq.*).

Brokered deposit means any deposit held at the national bank or Federal savings association that is obtained, directly or indirectly, from or through the mediation or assistance of a deposit broker as that term is defined in section 29 of the Federal Deposit Insurance Act (12 U.S.C. 1831f(g)), and includes a reciprocal brokered deposit and a brokered sweep deposit.

Brokered sweep deposit means a deposit held at the national bank or Federal savings association by a customer or counterparty through a contractual feature that automatically transfers to the national bank or Federal savings association from another regulated financial company at the close of each business day amounts identified under the agreement governing the account from which the amount is being transferred.

Calculation date means any date on which a national bank or Federal savings association calculates its liquidity coverage ratio under § 50.10.

Client pool security means a security that is owned by a customer of the national bank or Federal savings association that is not an asset of the national bank or Federal savings association, regardless of a national bank's or Federal savings association's hypothecation rights with respect to the security.

Collateralized deposit means:

(1) A deposit of a public sector entity held at the national bank or Federal savings association that is secured under applicable law by a lien on assets owned by the national bank or Federal savings association and that gives the depositor, as holder of the lien, priority over the assets in the event the national bank or Federal savings association enters into receivership, bankruptcy, insolvency, liquidation, resolution, or similar proceeding; or

(2) A deposit of a fiduciary account held at the national bank or Federal savings association for which the national bank or Federal savings association is a fiduciary and sets aside assets owned by the national bank or Federal savings association as security under 12 CFR 9.10 (national bank) or 12 CFR 150.300 through 150.320 (Federal savings associations) and that gives the depositor priority over the assets in the event the national bank or Federal savings association enters into receivership, bankruptcy, insolvency, liquidation, resolution, or similar proceeding.

Committed means, with respect to a credit facility or liquidity facility, that under the terms of the legally binding written agreement governing the facility:

(1) The national bank or Federal savings association may not refuse to extend credit or funding under the facility; or

(2) The national bank or Federal savings association may refuse to extend credit under the facility (to the extent permitted under applicable law) only upon the satisfaction or occurrence of one or more specified conditions not including change in financial condition of the borrower, customary notice, or administrative conditions.

Company means a corporation, partnership, limited liability company, depository institution, business trust, special purpose entity, association, or similar organization.

Consolidated subsidiary means a company that is consolidated on the balance sheet of a national bank or Federal savings association or other company under GAAP.

Controlled subsidiary means, with respect to a company or a national bank or Federal savings association, a consolidated subsidiary or a company that otherwise meets the definition of "subsidiary" in section 2(d) of the Bank Holding Company Act of 1956 (12 U.S.C. 1841(d)).

Covered depository institution holding company means a top-tier bank holding company or savings and loan holding company domiciled in the United States other than:

(1) A top-tier savings and loan holding company that is:

(i) A grandfathered unitary savings and loan holding company as defined in section 10(c)(9)(A) of the Home Owners' Loan Act (12 U.S.C. 1461 *et seq.*); and

(ii) As of June 30 of the previous calendar year, derived 50 percent or more of its total consolidated assets or 50 percent of its total revenues on an enterprise-wide basis (as calculated under GAAP) from activities that are not financial in nature under section 4(k) of the Bank Holding Company Act (12 U.S.C. 1842(k));

(2) A top-tier depository institution holding company that is an insurance underwriting company; or

(3)(i) A top-tier depository institution holding company that, as of June 30 of the previous calendar year, held 25 percent or more of its total consolidated assets in subsidiaries that are insurance underwriting companies (other than assets associated with insurance for credit risk); and

(ii) For purposes of paragraph 3(i) of this definition, the company must calculate its total consolidated assets in accordance with GAAP, or if the company does not calculate its total consolidated assets under GAAP for any regulatory purpose (including compliance with applicable securities laws), the company may estimate its total consolidated assets, subject to review and adjustment by the Board of Governors of the Federal Reserve System.

Covered nonbank company means a designated company that the Board of Governors of the Federal Reserve System has required by rule or order to comply with the requirements of 12 CFR part 249.

Credit facility means a legally binding agreement to extend funds if requested at a future date, including a general working capital facility such as a revolving credit facility for general corporate or working capital purposes. A credit facility does not include a legally binding written agreement to extend funds at a future date to a counterparty that is made for the purpose of refinancing the debt of the counterparty when it is unable to obtain a primary or anticipated source of funding. *See liquidity facility.*

Customer short position means a legally binding written agreement pursuant to which the customer must deliver to the national bank or Federal savings association a non-cash asset that the customer has already sold.

Deposit means "deposit" as defined in section 3(*l*) of the Federal Deposit Insurance Act (12 U.S.C. 1813(*l*)) or an equivalent liability of the national bank or Federal savings association in a jurisdiction outside of the United States.

Depository institution is defined in section 3(c) of the Federal Deposit Insurance Act (12 U.S.C. 1813(c)).

Depository institution holding company means a bank holding company or savings and loan holding company.

Deposit insurance means deposit insurance provided by the Federal Deposit Insurance Corporation under the Federal Deposit Insurance Act (12 U.S.C. 1811 *et seq.*).

Derivative transaction means a financial contract whose value is derived from the values of one or more underlying assets, reference rates, or indices of asset values or reference rates. Derivative contracts include interest rate derivative contracts, exchange rate derivative contracts, equity derivative contracts, commodity derivative contracts, credit derivative contracts, forward contracts, and any other instrument that poses similar counterparty credit risks. Derivative contracts also include unsettled securities, commodities, and foreign currency exchange transactions with a contractual settlement or delivery lag that is longer than the lesser of the market standard for the particular instrument or five business days. A derivative does not include any identified banking product, as that term is defined in section 402(b) of the Legal Certainty for Bank Products Act of 2000 (7 U.S.C. 27(b)), that is subject to section 403(a) of that Act (7 U.S.C. 27a(a)).

Designated company means a company that the Financial Stability Oversight Council has determined under section 113 of the Dodd-Frank Act (12 U.S.C. 5323) shall be supervised by the Board of Governors of the Federal Reserve System and for which such determination is still in effect.

Dodd-Frank Act means the Dodd-Frank Wall Street Reform and Consumer Protection Act, Public Law 111–203, 124 Stat. 1376 (2010).

Eligible HQLA means a high-quality liquid asset that meets the requirements set forth in § 50.22.

Fair value means fair value as determined under GAAP.

Financial sector entity means an investment adviser, investment company, pension fund, non-regulated fund, regulated financial company, or identified company.

Foreign withdrawable reserves means a national bank's or Federal savings association's balances held by or on behalf of the national bank or Federal savings association at a foreign central bank that are not subject to restrictions on the national bank's or Federal savings association's ability to use the reserves.

GAAP means generally accepted accounting principles as used in the United States.

High-quality liquid asset (HQLA) means an asset that is a level 1 liquid asset, level 2A liquid asset, or level 2B liquid asset, in accordance with the criteria set forth in § 50.20.

HQLA amount means the HQLA amount as calculated under § 50.21.

Identified company means any company that the OCC has determined should be treated for the purposes of this part the same as a regulated financial company, investment company, non-regulated fund, pension fund, or investment adviser, based on activities similar in scope, nature, or operations to those entities.

Individual means a natural person, and does not include a sole proprietorship.

Investment adviser means a company registered with the SEC as an investment adviser under the Investment Advisers Act of 1940 (15 U.S.C. 80b–1 *et seq.*) or foreign equivalents of such company.

Investment company means a person or company registered with the SEC under the Investment Company Act of 1940 (15 U.S.C. 80a–1 *et seq.*) or foreign equivalents of such persons or companies.

Liquid and readily-marketable has the meaning given the term in 12 CFR 249.3.

Liquidity facility means a legally binding written agreement to extend funds at a future date to a counterparty that is made for the purpose of refinancing the debt of the counterparty when it is unable to obtain a primary or anticipated source of funding. A liquidity facility includes an agreement to provide liquidity support to asset-backed commercial paper by lending to, or purchasing assets from, any structure, program or conduit in the event that funds are required to repay maturing asset-backed commercial paper. Liquidity facilities exclude facilities that are established solely for the purpose of general working capital, such as revolving credit facilities for general corporate or working capital purposes. If a facility has characteristics of both credit and liquidity facilities, the facility must be classified as a liquidity facility. *See credit facility*.

Multilateral development bank means the International Bank for Reconstruction and Development, the Multilateral Investment Guarantee Agency, the International Finance Corporation, the Inter-American Development Bank, the Asian Development Bank, the African Development Bank, the European Bank for Reconstruction and Development, the European Investment Bank, the European Investment Fund, the Nordic Investment Bank, the Caribbean Development Bank, the Islamic Development Bank, the Council of Europe Development Bank, and any other entity that provides financing for national or regional development in which the U.S. government is a shareholder or contributing member or which the OCC determines poses comparable risk.

Municipal obligation means an obligation of:

(1) A state or any political subdivision thereof; or

(2) Any agency or instrumentality of a state or any political subdivision thereof.

Non-regulated fund means any hedge fund or private equity fund whose investment adviser is required to file SEC Form PF (Reporting Form for Investment Advisers to Private Funds and Certain Commodity Pool Operators and Commodity Trading Advisors), other than a small business investment company as defined in section 102 of the Small Business Investment Act of 1958 (15 U.S.C. 661 *et seq.*).

Nonperforming exposure means an exposure that is past due by more than 90 days or nonaccrual.

Operational deposit means unsecured wholesale funding or a collateralized deposit that is necessary for the national bank or Federal savings association to provide operational services as an independent third-party intermediary, agent, or administrator to the wholesale customer or counterparty providing the unsecured wholesale funding or collateralized deposit. In order to recognize a deposit as an operational deposit for purposes of this part, a national bank or Federal savings association must comply with the requirements of § 50.4(b) with respect to that deposit.

Operational services means the following services, provided they are performed as part of cash management, clearing, or custody services:

(1) Payment remittance;

(2) Administration of payments and cash flows related to the safekeeping of investment assets, not including the purchase or sale of assets;

(3) Payroll administration and control over the disbursement of funds;

(4) Transmission, reconciliation, and confirmation of payment orders;

(5) Daylight overdraft;

(6) Determination of intra-day and final settlement positions;

(7) Settlement of securities transactions;

(8) Transfer of capital distributions and recurring contractual payments;

(9) Customer subscriptions and redemptions;

(10) Scheduled distribution of customer funds;

(11) Escrow, funds transfer, stock transfer, and agency services, including payment and settlement services, payment of fees, taxes, and other expenses; and

(12) Collection and aggregation of funds.

Pension fund means an employee benefit plan as defined in paragraphs (3) and (32) of section 3 of the Employee Retirement Income and Security Act of 1974 (29 U.S.C. 1001 *et seq.*), a "governmental plan" (as defined in 29 U.S.C. 1002(32)) that complies with the tax deferral qualification requirements provided in the Internal Revenue Code, or any similar employee benefit plan established under the laws of a foreign jurisdiction.

Public sector entity means a state, local authority, or other governmental subdivision below the U.S. sovereign entity level.

Publicly traded means, with respect to an equity security, that the equity security is traded on:

(1) Any exchange registered with the SEC as a national securities exchange under section 6 of the Securities Exchange Act of 1934 (15 U.S.C. 78f); or

(2) Any non-U.S.-based securities exchange that:

(i) Is registered with, or approved by, a national securities regulatory authority; and

(ii) Provides a liquid, two-way market for the security in question.

Qualifying master netting agreement means a written, legally enforceable agreement provided that:

(1) The agreement creates a single legal obligation for all individual transactions covered by the agreement upon an event of default following any stay permitted by paragraph (2) of this definition, including upon an event of receivership, conservatorship, insolvency, liquidation, or similar proceeding, of the counterparty;

(2) The agreement provides the national bank or Federal savings association the right to accelerate, terminate, and close-out on a net basis all transactions under the agreement and to liquidate or set-off collateral promptly upon an event of default, including upon an event of receivership, conservatorship, insolvency, liquidation, or similar proceeding, of the counterparty, provided that, in any such case:

(i) Any exercise of rights under the agreement will not be stayed or avoided under applicable law in the relevant jurisdictions, other than:

(A) In receivership, conservatorship, or resolution under the Federal Deposit Insurance Act, Title II of the Dodd-Frank Act, or under any similar insolvency law applicable to GSEs, or laws of foreign jurisdictions that are substantially similar to the U.S. laws referenced in this paragraph (2)(i)(A) in order to facilitate the orderly resolution of the defaulting counterparty; or

(B) Where the agreement is subject by its terms to, or incorporates, any of the laws referenced in paragraph (2)(i)(A) of this definition; and

(ii) The agreement may limit the right to accelerate, terminate, and close-out on a net basis all transactions under the agreement and to liquidate or set-off collateral promptly upon an event of default of the counterparty to the extent necessary for the counterparty to comply with the requirements of part 47, subpart I of part 225, or part 382 of this title, as applicable;

Reciprocal brokered deposit means a brokered deposit that a national bank or Federal savings association receives through a deposit placement network on a reciprocal basis, such that:

(1) For any deposit received, the national bank or Federal savings association (as agent for the depositors) places the same amount with other depository institutions through the network; and

(2) Each member of the network sets the interest rate to be paid on the entire amount of funds it places with other network members.

Regulated financial company means:

(1) A depository institution holding company or designated company;

(2) A company included in the organization chart of a depository institution holding company on the Form FR Y–6, as listed in the hierarchy report of the

depository institution holding company produced by the National Information Center (NIC) Web site,[2] provided that the top-tier depository institution holding company is subject to a minimum liquidity standard under 12 CFR part 249;

(3) A depository institution; foreign bank; credit union; industrial loan company, industrial bank, or other similar institution described in section 2 of the Bank Holding Company Act of 1956, as amended (12 U.S.C. 1841 *et seq.*); national bank, state member bank, or state non-member bank that is not a depository institution;

(4) An insurance company;

(5) A securities holding company as defined in section 618 of the Dodd-Frank Act (12 U.S.C. 1850a); broker or dealer registered with the SEC under section 15 of the Securities Exchange Act (15 U.S.C. 78o); futures commission merchant as defined in section 1a of the Commodity Exchange Act of 1936 (7 U.S.C. 1 *et seq.*); swap dealer as defined in section 1a of the Commodity Exchange Act (7 U.S.C. 1a); or security-based swap dealer as defined in section 3 of the Securities Exchange Act (15 U.S.C. 78c);

(6) A designated financial market utility, as defined in section 803 of the Dodd-Frank Act (12 U.S.C. 5462); and

(7) Any company not domiciled in the United States (or a political subdivision thereof) that is supervised and regulated in a manner similar to entities described in paragraphs (1) through (6) of this definition (e.g., a foreign banking organization, foreign insurance company, foreign securities broker or dealer or foreign financial market utility).

(8) A regulated financial company does not include:

(i) U.S. government-sponsored enterprises;

(ii) Small business investment companies, as defined in section 102 of the Small Business Investment Act of 1958 (15 U.S.C. 661 *et seq.*);

(iii) Entities designated as Community Development Financial Institutions (CDFIs) under 12 U.S.C. 4701 *et seq.* and 12 CFR part 1805; or

(iv) Central banks, the Bank for International Settlements, the International Monetary Fund, or multilateral development banks.

Reserve Bank balances means:

(1) Balances held in a master account of the national bank or Federal savings association at a Federal Reserve Bank, less any balances that are attributable to any respondent of the national bank or Federal savings association if the national bank or Federal savings association is a correspondent for a pass-through account as defined in section 204.2(l) of Regulation D (12 CFR 204.2(l));

(2) Balances held in a master account of a correspondent of the national bank or Federal savings association that are attributable to the national bank or Federal savings association if the national bank or Federal savings association is a respondent for a pass-through account as defined in section 204.2(l) of Regulation D;

(3) "Excess balances" of the national bank or Federal savings association as defined in section 204.2(z) of Regulation D (12 CFR 204.2(z)) that are maintained in an "excess balance account" as defined in section 204.2(aa) of Regulation D (12 CFR 204.2(aa)) if the national bank or Federal savings association is an excess balance account participant; or

(4) "Term deposits" of the national bank or Federal savings association as defined in section 204.2(dd) of Regulation D (12 CFR 204.2(dd)) if such term deposits are offered and maintained pursuant to terms and conditions that:

(i) Explicitly and contractually permit such term deposits to be withdrawn upon demand prior to the expiration of the term, or that

(ii) Permit such term deposits to be pledged as collateral for term or automatically-renewing overnight advances from the Federal Reserve Bank.

Retail customer or counterparty means a customer or counterparty that is:

(1) An individual;

(2) A business customer, but solely if and to the extent that:

(i) The national bank or Federal savings association manages its transactions with the business customer, including deposits, unsecured funding,

[2] *http://www.ffiec.gov/nicpubweb/nicweb/NicHome.aspx.*

and credit facility and liquidity facility transactions, in the same way it manages its transactions with individuals;

(ii) Transactions with the business customer have liquidity risk characteristics that are similar to comparable transactions with individuals; and

(iii) The total aggregate funding raised from the business customer is less than $1.5 million; or

(3) A living or testamentary trust that:

(i) Is solely for the benefit of natural persons;

(ii) Does not have a corporate trustee; and

(iii) Terminates within 21 years and 10 months after the death of grantors or beneficiaries of the trust living on the effective date of the trust or within 25 years, if applicable under state law.

Retail deposit means a demand or term deposit that is placed with the national bank or Federal savings association by a retail customer or counterparty, other than a brokered deposit.

Retail mortgage means a mortgage that is primarily secured by a first or subsequent lien on one-to-four family residential property.

Savings and loan holding company means a savings and loan holding company as defined in section 10 of the Home Owners' Loan Act (12 U.S.C. 1467a).

SEC means the Securities and Exchange Commission.

Secured funding transaction means any funding transaction that is subject to a legally binding agreement as of the calculation date and gives rise to a cash obligation of the national bank or Federal savings association to a counterparty that is secured under applicable law by a lien on assets owned by the national bank or Federal savings association, which gives the counterparty, as holder of the lien, priority over the assets in the event the national bank or Federal savings association enters into receivership, bankruptcy, insolvency, liquidation, resolution, or similar proceeding. Secured funding transactions include repurchase transactions, loans of collateral to the national bank's or Federal savings association's customers to effect short positions, other secured loans, and borrowings from a Federal Reserve Bank.

Secured lending transaction means any lending transaction that is subject to a legally binding agreement of the calculation date and gives rise to a cash obligation of a counterparty to the national bank or Federal savings association that is secured under applicable law by a lien on assets owned by the counterparty, which gives the national bank or Federal savings association, as holder of the lien, priority over the assets in the event the counterparty enters into receivership, bankruptcy, insolvency, liquidation, resolution, or similar proceeding, including reverse repurchase transactions and securities borrowing transactions.

Securities Exchange Act means the Securities Exchange Act of 1934 (15 U.S.C. 78a *et seq.*).

Sovereign entity means a central government (including the U.S. government) or an agency, department, ministry, or central bank of a central government.

Special purpose entity means a company organized for a specific purpose, the activities of which are significantly limited to those appropriate to accomplish a specific purpose, and the structure of which is intended to isolate the credit risk of the special purpose entity.

Stable retail deposit means a retail deposit that is entirely covered by deposit insurance and:

(1) Is held by the depositor in a transactional account; or

(2) The depositor that holds the account has another established relationship with the national bank or Federal savings association such as another deposit account, a loan, bill payment services, or any similar service or product provided to the depositor that the national bank or Federal savings association demonstrates to the satisfaction of the OCC would make deposit withdrawal highly unlikely during a liquidity stress event.

Structured security means a security whose cash flow characteristics depend upon one or more indices or that has embedded forwards, options, or other derivatives or a security where an investor's investment return and the issuer's payment obligations are contingent on, or highly sensitive to, changes in the value of underlying assets, indices, interest rates, or cash flows.

Structured transaction means a secured transaction in which repayment of obligations and other exposures to the transaction is largely derived, directly or indirectly, from the cash flow generated by the pool of assets that secures the obligations and other exposures to the transaction.

Two-way market means a market where there are independent bona fide offers to buy and sell so that a price reasonably related to the last sales price or current bona fide competitive bid and offer quotations can be determined within one day and settled at that price within a relatively short time frame conforming to trade custom.

U.S. government-sponsored enterprise means an entity established or chartered by the Federal government to serve public purposes specified by the United States Congress, but whose debt obligations are not explicitly guaranteed by the full faith and credit of the United States government.

Unsecured wholesale funding means a liability or general obligation of the national bank or Federal savings association to a wholesale customer or counterparty that is not secured under applicable law by a lien on assets owned by the national bank or Federal savings association, including a wholesale deposit.

Wholesale customer or counterparty means a customer or counterparty that is not a retail customer or counterparty.

Wholesale deposit means a demand or term deposit that is provided by a wholesale customer or counterparty.

[79 FR 61523, 61538, Oct. 10, 2014, as amended at 79 FR 78294, Dec. 30, 2014; 82 FR 56669, Nov. 29, 2017; 83 FR 44454, Aug. 31, 2018]

§ 50.4 Certain operational requirements.

(a) *Qualifying master netting agreements.* In order to recognize an agreement as a qualifying master netting agreement as defined in § 50.3, a national bank or Federal savings association must:

(1) Conduct sufficient legal review to conclude with a well-founded basis (and maintain sufficient written documentation of that legal review) that:

(i) The agreement meets the requirements of the definition of qualifying master netting agreement in § 50.3; and

(ii) In the event of a legal challenge (including one resulting from default or from receivership, bankruptcy, insolvency, liquidation, resolution, or similar proceeding) the relevant judicial and administrative authorities would find the agreement to be legal, valid, binding, and enforceable under the law of the relevant jurisdictions; and

(2) Establish and maintain written procedures to monitor possible changes in relevant law and to ensure that the agreement continues to satisfy the requirements of the definition of qualifying master netting agreement in § 50.3.

(b) *Operational deposits.* In order to recognize a deposit as an operational deposit as defined in § 50.3:

(1) The related operational services must be performed pursuant to a legally binding written agreement, and:

(i) The termination of the agreement must be subject to a minimum 30 calendar-day notice period; or

(ii) As a result of termination of the agreement or transfer of services to a third-party provider, the customer providing the deposit would incur significant contractual termination costs or switching costs (switching costs include significant technology, administrative, and legal service costs incurred in connection with the transfer of the operational services to a third-party provider);

(2) The deposit must be held in an account designated as an operational account;

(3) The customer must hold the deposit at the national bank or Federal savings association for the primary purpose of obtaining the operational services provided by the national bank or Federal savings association;

(4) The deposit account must not be designed to create an economic incentive for the customer to maintain excess funds therein through increased revenue, reduction in fees, or other offered economic incentives;

(5) The national bank or Federal savings association must demonstrate that the deposit is empirically linked to the operational services and that it has a methodology that takes into account the volatility of the average balance for identifying any excess amount, which must be excluded from the operational deposit amount;

(6) The deposit must not be provided in connection with the national bank's or Federal savings association's provision of prime brokerage services, which, for the purposes of this part, are a package of services offered by the national bank or Federal savings association whereby the national bank or Federal savings association, among other services, executes, clears, settles, and finances transactions entered into by the customer or a third-party entity on behalf of the customer (such as an executing broker), and where the national bank or Federal savings association has a right to use or rehypothecate assets provided by the customer, including in connection with the extension of margin and other similar financing of the customer, subject to applicable law, and includes operational services provided to a non-regulated fund; and

(7) The deposits must not be for arrangements in which the national bank or Federal savings association (as correspondent) holds deposits owned by another depository institution bank (as respondent) and the respondent temporarily places excess funds in an overnight deposit with the national bank or Federal savings association.

Subpart B—Liquidity Coverage Ratio

§ 50.10 Liquidity coverage ratio.

(a) *Minimum liquidity coverage ratio requirement.* Subject to the transition provisions in subpart F of this part, a national bank or Federal savings association must calculate and maintain a liquidity coverage ratio that is equal to or greater than 1.0 on each business day in accordance with this part. A national bank or Federal savings association must calculate its liquidity coverage ratio as of the same time on each business day (elected calculation time). The national bank or Federal savings association must select this time by written notice to the OCC prior to the effective date of this rule. The national bank or Federal savings association may not thereafter change its elected calculation time without prior written approval from the OCC.

(b) *Calculation of the liquidity coverage ratio.* A national bank's or Federal savings association's liquidity coverage ratio equals:

(1) The national bank's or Federal savings association's HQLA amount as of the calculation date, calculated under subpart C of this part; *divided by*

(2) The national bank's or Federal savings association's total net cash outflow amount as of the calculation date, calculated under subpart D of this part.

Subpart C—High-Quality Liquid Assets

§ 50.20 High-quality liquid asset criteria.

(a) *Level 1 liquid assets.* An asset is a level 1 liquid asset if it is one of the following types of assets:

(1) Reserve Bank balances;

(2) Foreign withdrawable reserves;

(3) A security that is issued by, or unconditionally guaranteed as to the timely payment of principal and interest by, the U.S. Department of the Treasury;

(4) A security that is issued by, or unconditionally guaranteed as to the timely payment of principal and interest by, a U.S. government agency (other than the U.S. Department of the Treasury) whose obligations are fully and explicitly guaranteed by the full faith and credit of the U.S. government, provided that the security is liquid and readily-marketable;

(5) A security that is issued by, or unconditionally guaranteed as to the timely payment of principal and interest by, a sovereign entity, the Bank for International Settlements, the International Monetary Fund, the European Central Bank, European Community, or a multilateral development bank, that is:

(i) Assigned a zero percent risk weight under subpart D of (12 CFR part 3) as of the calculation date;

(ii) Liquid and readily-marketable;

(iii) Issued or guaranteed by an entity whose obligations have a proven record as a reliable source of liquidity in repurchase or sales markets during stressed market conditions; and

(iv) Not an obligation of a financial sector entity and not an obligation of a consolidated subsidiary of a financial sector entity; or

(6) A security issued by, or unconditionally guaranteed as to the timely payment of principal and interest by, a sovereign entity that is not assigned a zero percent risk weight under subpart D of (12 CFR part 3), where the sovereign entity issues the security in its own currency, the security is liquid and readily-marketable, and the national bank or Federal savings association holds the security in order to meet its net cash outflows in the jurisdiction of the sovereign entity, as calculated under subpart D of this part.

(b) *Level 2A liquid assets.* An asset is a level 2A liquid asset if the asset is liquid and readily-marketable and is one of the following types of assets:

(1) A security issued by, or guaranteed as to the timely payment of principal and interest by, a U.S. government-sponsored enterprise, that is investment grade under 12 CFR part 1 as of the calculation date, provided that the claim is senior to preferred stock; or

(2) A security that is issued by, or guaranteed as to the timely payment of principal and interest by, a sovereign entity or multilateral development bank that is:

(i) Not included in level 1 liquid assets;

(ii) Assigned no higher than a 20 percent risk weight under subpart D of (12 CFR part 3) as of the calculation date;

(iii) Issued or guaranteed by an entity whose obligations have a proven record as a reliable source of liquidity in repurchase or sales markets during stressed market conditions, as demonstrated by:

(A) The market price of the security or equivalent securities of the issuer declining by no more than 10 percent during a 30 calendar-day period of significant stress, or

(B) The market haircut demanded by counterparties to secured lending and secured funding transactions that are collateralized by the security or equivalent securities of the issuer increasing by no more than 10 percentage points during a 30 calendar-day period of significant stress; and

(iv) Not an obligation of a financial sector entity, and not an obligation of a consolidated subsidiary of a financial sector entity.

(c) *Level 2B liquid assets.* An asset is a level 2B liquid asset if the asset is liquid and readily-marketable and is one of the following types of assets:

(1) A corporate debt security that is:

(i) Investment grade under 12 CFR part 1 as of the calculation date;

(ii) Issued or guaranteed by an entity whose obligations have a proven record as a reliable source of liquidity in repurchase or sales markets during stressed market conditions, as demonstrated by:

(A) The market price of the corporate debt security or equivalent securities of the issuer declining by no more than 20 percent during a 30 calendar-day period of significant stress, or

(B) The market haircut demanded by counterparties to secured lending and secured funding transactions that are collateralized by the corporate debt security or equivalent securities of the issuer increasing by no more than 20 percentage points during a 30 calendar-day period of significant stress; and

(iii) Not an obligation of a financial sector entity and not an obligation of a consolidated subsidiary of a financial sector entity;

(2) A publicly traded common equity share that is:

(i) Included in:

(A) The Russell 1000 Index; or

(B) An index that a national bank's or Federal savings association's supervisor in a foreign jurisdiction recognizes for purposes of including equity shares in level 2B liquid assets under applicable regulatory policy, if the share is held in that foreign jurisdiction;

(ii) Issued in:

(A) U.S. dollars; or

(B) The currency of a jurisdiction where the national bank or Federal savings association operates and the national bank or Federal savings association holds the common equity share in order to cover its net cash outflows in that jurisdiction, as calculated under subpart D of this part;

(iii) Issued by an entity whose publicly traded common equity shares have a proven record as a reliable source of liquidity in repurchase or sales markets during stressed market conditions, as demonstrated by:

(A) The market price of the security or equivalent securities of the issuer declining by no more than 40 percent during a 30 calendar-day period of significant stress, or

(B) The market haircut demanded by counterparties to securities borrowing and lending transactions that are collateralized by the publicly traded common equity shares or equivalent securities of the issuer increasing by no more than 40 percentage points, during a 30 calendar day period of significant stress;

(iv) Not issued by a financial sector entity and not issued by a consolidated subsidiary of a financial sector entity;

(v) If held by a depository institution, is not acquired in satisfaction of a debt previously contracted (DPC); and

(vi) If held by a consolidated subsidiary of a depository institution, the depository institution can include the publicly traded common equity share in its level 2B liquid assets only if the share is held to cover net cash outflows of the depository institution's consolidated subsidiary in which the publicly traded common equity share is held, as calculated by the national bank or Federal savings association under subpart D of this part; or

(3) A municipal obligation that is investment grade under 12 CFR part 1 as of the calculation date.

[79 FR 61523, 61538, Oct. 10, 2014, as amended at 83 FR 44454, Aug. 31, 2018]

§ 50.21 High-quality liquid asset amount.

(a) *Calculation of the HQLA amount.* As of the calculation date, a national bank's or Federal savings association's HQLA amount equals:

(1) The level 1 liquid asset amount; plus

(2) The level 2A liquid asset amount; plus

(3) The level 2B liquid asset amount; minus

(4) The greater of:

(i) The unadjusted excess HQLA amount; and

(ii) The adjusted excess HQLA amount.

(b) *Calculation of liquid asset amounts*—(1) *Level 1 liquid asset amount.* The level 1 liquid asset amount equals the fair value of all level 1 liquid assets held by the national bank or Federal savings association as of the calculation date that are eligible HQLA, less the amount of the reserve balance requirement under section 204.5 of Regulation D (12 CFR 204.5).

(2) *Level 2A liquid asset amount.* The level 2A liquid asset amount equals 85 percent of the fair value of all level 2A liquid assets held by the national bank or Federal savings association as of the calculation date that are eligible HQLA.

(3) *Level 2B liquid asset amount.* The level 2B liquid asset amount equals 50 percent of the fair value of all level 2B liquid assets held by the national bank or Federal savings association as of the calculation date that are eligible HQLA.

(c) *Calculation of the unadjusted excess HQLA amount.* As of the calculation date, the unadjusted excess HQLA amount equals:

(1) The level 2 cap excess amount; *plus*

(2) The level 2B cap excess amount.

(d) *Calculation of the level 2 cap excess amount.* As of the calculation date, the level 2 cap excess amount equals the greater of:

(1) The level 2A liquid asset amount plus the level 2B liquid asset amount minus 0.6667 times the level 1 liquid asset amount; and

(2) 0.

(e) *Calculation of the level 2B cap excess amount.* As of the calculation date, the level 2B excess amount equals the greater of:

(1) The level 2B liquid asset amount minus the level 2 cap excess amount minus 0.1765 times the sum of the level 1 liquid asset amount and the level 2A liquid asset amount; and

(2) 0.

(f) *Calculation of adjusted liquid asset amounts*—(1) *Adjusted level 1 liquid asset amount.* A national bank's or Federal savings association's adjusted level 1 liquid asset amount equals the fair value of all level 1 liquid assets that would be eligible HQLA and would be held by the national bank or Federal savings association upon the unwind of any secured funding transaction (other than a collateralized deposit), secured lending transaction, asset exchange, or collateralized derivatives transaction that matures within 30 calendar days of the calculation date where the national bank or Federal savings association will provide an asset that is eligible HQLA and the counterparty will provide an asset that will be eligible HQLA; less the amount of the reserve balance requirement under section 204.5 of Regulation D (12 CFR 204.5).

(2) *Adjusted level 2A liquid asset amount.* A national bank's or Federal savings association's adjusted level 2A liquid asset amount equals 85 percent of the fair value of all level 2A liquid assets that would be eligible HQLA and would be held by the national bank or Federal savings association upon the unwind of any secured funding transaction (other than a collateralized deposit), secured lending transaction, asset exchange, or collateralized derivatives transaction that matures within 30 calendar days of the calculation date where the national bank or Federal savings association will provide an asset that is eligible HQLA and the counterparty will provide an asset that will be eligible HQLA.

(3) *Adjusted level 2B liquid asset amount.* A national bank's or Federal savings association's adjusted level 2B liquid asset amount equals 50 percent of the fair value of all level 2B liquid assets that would be eligible HQLA and would be held by the national bank or Federal savings association upon the unwind of any secured funding transaction (other than a collateralized deposit), secured lending transaction, asset exchange, or collateralized derivatives transaction that matures within 30 calendar days of the calculation date where the national bank or Federal savings association will provide an asset that is eligible HQLA and the counterparty will provide an asset that will be eligible HQLA.

(g) *Calculation of the adjusted excess HQLA amount.* As of the calculation date, the adjusted excess HQLA amount equals:

(1) The adjusted level 2 cap excess amount; *plus*

(2) The adjusted level 2B cap excess amount.

(h) *Calculation of the adjusted level 2 cap excess amount.* As of the calculation date, the adjusted level 2 cap excess amount equals the greater of:

(1) The adjusted level 2A liquid asset amount plus the adjusted level 2B liquid asset amount minus 0.6667 times the adjusted level 1 liquid asset amount; and

(2) 0.

(i) *Calculation of the adjusted level 2B excess amount.* As of the calculation date, the adjusted level 2B excess liquid asset amount equals the greater of:

(1) The adjusted level 2B liquid asset amount minus the adjusted level 2 cap excess amount minus 0.1765 times the sum of the adjusted level 1 liquid asset amount and the adjusted level 2A liquid asset amount; and

(2) 0.

§ 50.22 Requirements for eligible high-quality liquid assets.

(a) *Operational requirements for eligible HQLA.* With respect to each asset that is eligible for inclusion in a national bank's or Federal savings association's HQLA amount, a national bank or Federal savings association must meet all of the following operational requirements:

(1) The national bank or Federal savings association must demonstrate the operational capability to monetize the HQLA by:

(i) Implementing and maintaining appropriate procedures and systems to monetize any HQLA at any time in accordance with relevant standard settlement periods and procedures; and

(ii) Periodically monetizing a sample of HQLA that reasonably reflects the composition of the national bank's or Federal savings association's eligible HQLA, including with respect to asset type, maturity, and counterparty characteristics;

(2) The national bank or Federal savings association must implement policies that require eligible HQLA to be under the control of the management

function in the national bank or Federal savings association that is charged with managing liquidity risk, and this management function must evidence its control over the HQLA by either:

(i) Segregating the HQLA from other assets, with the sole intent to use the HQLA as a source of liquidity; or

(ii) Demonstrating the ability to monetize the assets and making the proceeds available to the liquidity management function without conflicting with a business or risk management strategy of the national bank or Federal savings association;

(3) The fair value of the eligible HQLA must be reduced by the outflow amount that would result from the termination of any specific transaction hedging eligible HQLA;

(4) The national bank or Federal savings association must implement and maintain policies and procedures that determine the composition of its eligible HQLA on each calculation date, by:

(i) Identifying its eligible HQLA by legal entity, geographical location, currency, account, or other relevant identifying factors as of the calculation date;

(ii) Determining that eligible HQLA meet the criteria set forth in this section; and

(iii) Ensuring the appropriate diversification of the eligible HQLA by asset type, counterparty, issuer, currency, borrowing capacity, or other factors associated with the liquidity risk of the assets; and

(5) The national bank or Federal savings association must have a documented methodology that results in a consistent treatment for determining that the national bank's or Federal savings association's eligible HQLA meet the requirements set forth in this section.

(b) *Generally applicable criteria for eligible HQLA.* A national bank's or Federal savings association's eligible HQLA must meet all of the following criteria:

(1) The assets are unencumbered in accordance with the following criteria:

(i) The assets are free of legal, regulatory, contractual, or other restrictions on the ability of the national bank or Federal savings association to monetize the assets; and

(ii) The assets are not pledged, explicitly or implicitly, to secure or to provide credit enhancement to any transaction, but the assets may be considered unencumbered if the assets are pledged to a central bank or a U.S. government-sponsored enterprise where:

(A) Potential credit secured by the assets is not currently extended to the national bank or Federal savings association or its consolidated subsidiaries; and

(B) The pledged assets are not required to support access to the payment services of a central bank;

(2) The asset is not:

(i) A client pool security held in a segregated account; or

(ii) An asset received from a secured funding transaction involving client pool securities that were held in a segregated account;

(3) For eligible HQLA held in a legal entity that is a U.S. consolidated subsidiary of a national bank or Federal savings association:

(i) If the U.S. consolidated subsidiary is subject to a minimum liquidity standard under this part, the national bank or Federal savings association may include the eligible HQLA of the U.S. consolidated subsidiary in its HQLA amount up to:

(A) The amount of net cash outflows of the U.S. consolidated subsidiary calculated by the U.S. consolidated subsidiary for its own minimum liquidity standard under this part; *plus*

(B) Any additional amount of assets, including proceeds from the monetization of assets, that would be available for transfer to the top-tier national bank or Federal savings association during times of stress without statutory, regulatory, contractual, or supervisory restrictions, including sections 23A and 23B of the Federal Reserve Act (12 U.S.C. 371c and 12 U.S.C. 371c–1) and Regulation W (12 CFR part 223); and

(ii) If the U.S. consolidated subsidiary is not subject to a minimum liquidity standard under this part, the national bank or Federal savings association may include the eligible HQLA of the U.S. consolidated subsidiary in its HQLA amount up to:

(A) The amount of the net cash outflows of the U.S. consolidated subsidiary as of the 30th calendar day after the calculation date, as calculated by the national bank or Federal savings association for the national bank's or Federal savings association's minimum liquidity standard under this part; *plus*

(B) Any additional amount of assets, including proceeds from the monetization of assets, that would be available for transfer to the top-tier national bank or Federal savings association during times of stress without statutory, regulatory, contractual, or supervisory restrictions, including sections 23A and 23B of the Federal Reserve Act (12 U.S.C. 371c and 12 U.S.C. 371c–1) and Regulation W (12 CFR part 223);

(4) For HQLA held by a consolidated subsidiary of the national bank or Federal savings association that is organized under the laws of a foreign jurisdiction, the national bank or Federal savings association may include the eligible HQLA of the consolidated subsidiary organized under the laws of a foreign jurisdiction in its HQLA amount up to:

(i) The amount of net cash outflows of the consolidated subsidiary as of the 30th calendar day after the calculation date, as calculated by the national bank or Federal savings association for the national bank's or Federal savings association's minimum liquidity standard under this part; *plus*

(ii) Any additional amount of assets that are available for transfer to the top-tier national bank or Federal savings association during times of stress without statutory, regulatory, contractual, or supervisory restrictions;

(5) The national bank or Federal savings association must not include as eligible HQLA any assets, or HQLA resulting from transactions involving an asset that the national bank or Federal savings association received with rehypothecation rights, if the counterparty that provided the asset or the beneficial owner of the asset has a contractual right to withdraw the assets without an obligation to pay more than de minimis remuneration at any time during the 30 calendar days following the calculation date; and

(6) The national bank or Federal savings association has not designated the assets to cover operational costs.

(c) *Maintenance of U.S. eligible HQLA.* A national bank or Federal savings association is generally expected to maintain as eligible HQLA an amount and type of eligible HQLA in the United States that is sufficient to meet its total net cash outflow amount in the United States under subpart D of this part.

Subpart D—Total Net Cash Outflow

§ 50.30 Total net cash outflow amount.

(a) *Calculation of total net cash outflow amount.* As of the calculation date, a national bank's or Federal savings association's total net cash outflow amount equals:

(1) The sum of the outflow amounts calculated under § 50.32(a) through (l); *minus*

(2) The lesser of:

(i) The sum of the inflow amounts calculated under § 50.33(b) through (g); and

(ii) 75 percent of the amount calculated under paragraph (a)(1) of this section; *plus*

(3) The maturity mismatch add-on as calculated under paragraph (b) of this section.

(b) *Calculation of maturity mismatch add-on.* (1) For purposes of this section:

(i) The net cumulative maturity outflow amount for any of the 30 calendar days following the calculation date is equal to the sum of the outflow amounts for instruments or transactions identified in § 50.32(g), (h)(1), (h)(2), (h)(5), (j), (k), and (l) that have a maturity date prior to or on that calendar day *minus* the sum of the inflow amounts for instruments or transactions identified in § 50.33(c), (d), (e), and (f) that have a maturity date prior to or on that calendar day.

(ii) The net day 30 cumulative maturity outflow amount is equal to, as of the 30th day following the calculation date, the sum of the outflow amounts for instruments or transactions identified in § 50.32(g), (h)(1), (h)(2), (h)(5), (j), (k), and (l) that have a maturity date 30 calendar days or less from the calculation date *minus* the sum of the inflow amounts for instruments or transactions identified in § 50.33(c), (d), (e), and (f) that have a maturity date 30 calendar days or less from the calculation date.

(2) As of the calculation date, a national bank's or Federal savings association's maturity mismatch add-on is equal to:

(i) The greater of:

(A) 0; and

(B) The largest net cumulative maturity outflow amount as calculated under paragraph (b)(1)(i) of this section for any of the 30 calendar days following the calculation date; *minus*

(ii) The greater of:

(A) 0; and

(B) The net day 30 cumulative maturity outflow amount as calculated under paragraph (b)(1)(ii) of this section.

(3) Other than the transactions identified in §50.32(h)(2), (h)(5), or (j) or §50.33(d) or (f), the maturity of which is determined under §50.31(a), transactions that have no maturity date are not included in the calculation of the maturity mismatch add-on.

§50.31 Determining maturity.

(a) For purposes of calculating its liquidity coverage ratio and the components thereof under this subpart, a national bank or Federal savings association shall assume an asset or transaction matures:

(1) With respect to an instrument or transaction subject to §50.32, on the earliest possible contractual maturity date or the earliest possible date the transaction could occur, taking into account any option that could accelerate the maturity date or the date of the transaction as follows:

(i) If an investor or funds provider has an option that would reduce the maturity, the national bank or Federal savings association must assume that the investor or funds provider will exercise the option at the earliest possible date;

(ii) If an investor or funds provider has an option that would extend the maturity, the national bank or Federal savings association must assume that the investor or funds provider will not exercise the option to extend the maturity;

(iii) If the national bank or Federal savings association has an option that would reduce the maturity of an obligation, the national bank or Federal savings association must assume that the national bank or Federal savings association will exercise the option at the earliest possible date, except if either of the following criteria are satisfied, in which case the maturity of the obligation for purposes of this part will be the original maturity date at issuance:

(A) The original maturity of the obligation is greater than one year and the option does not go into effect for a period of 180 days following the issuance of the instrument; or

(B) The counterparty is a sovereign entity, a U.S. government-sponsored enterprise, or a public sector entity.

(iv) If the national bank or Federal savings association has an option that would extend the maturity of an obligation it issued, the national bank or Federal savings association must assume the national bank or Federal savings association will not exercise that option to extend the maturity; and

(v) If an option is subject to a contractually defined notice period, the national bank or Federal savings association must determine the earliest possible contractual maturity date regardless of the notice period.

(2) With respect to an instrument or transaction subject to §50.33, on the latest possible contractual maturity date or the latest possible date the transaction could occur, taking into account any option that could extend the maturity date or the date of the transaction as follows:

(i) If the borrower has an option that would extend the maturity, the national bank or Federal savings association must assume that the borrower will exercise the option to extend the maturity to the latest possible date;

(ii) If the borrower has an option that would reduce the maturity, the national bank or Federal savings association must assume that the borrower will not exercise the option to reduce the maturity;

(iii) If the national bank or Federal savings association has an option that would reduce the maturity of an instrument or transaction, the national bank or Federal savings association must assume the national bank or Federal savings association will not exercise the option to reduce the maturity;

(iv) If the national bank or Federal savings association has an option that would extend the maturity of an instrument or transaction, the national bank or Federal savings association must assume the national bank or Federal savings association will exercise the option to extend the maturity to the latest possible date; and

(v) If an option is subject to a contractually defined notice period, the national bank or Federal savings association must determine the latest possible contractual maturity date based on the borrower using the entire notice period.

(3) With respect to a transaction subject to § 50.33(f)(1)(iii) through (vii) (secured lending transactions) or § 50.33(f)(2)(ii) through (x) (asset exchanges), to the extent the transaction is secured by collateral that has been pledged in connection with either a secured funding transaction or asset exchange that has a remaining maturity of 30 calendar days or less as of the calculation date, the maturity date is the later of the maturity date determined under paragraph (a)(2) of this section for the secured lending transaction or asset exchange or the maturity date determined under paragraph (a)(1) of this section for the secured funding transaction or asset exchange for which the collateral has been pledged.

(4) With respect to a transaction that has no maturity date, is not an operational deposit, and is subject to the provisions of § 50.32(h)(2), (h)(5), (j), or (k) or § 50.33(d) or (f), the maturity date is the first calendar day after the calculation date. Any other transaction that has no maturity date and is subject to the provisions of § 50.32 must be considered to mature within 30 calendar days of the calculation date.

(5) With respect to a transaction subject to the provisions of § 50.33(g), on the date of the next scheduled calculation of the amount required under applicable legal requirements for the protection of customer assets with respect to each broker-dealer segregated account, in accordance with the national bank's or Federal savings association's normal frequency of recalculating such requirements.

(b) [Reserved]

§ 50.32 Outflow amounts.

(a) *Retail funding outflow amount.* A national bank's or Federal savings association's retail funding outflow amount as of the calculation date includes (regardless of maturity or collateralization):

(1) 3 percent of all stable retail deposits held at the national bank or Federal savings association;

(2) 10 percent of all other retail deposits held at the national bank or Federal savings association;

(3) 20 percent of all deposits placed at the national bank or Federal savings association by a third party on behalf of a retail customer or counterparty that are not brokered deposits, where the retail customer or counterparty owns the account and the entire amount is covered by deposit insurance;

(4) 40 percent of all deposits placed at the national bank or Federal savings association by a third party on behalf of a retail customer or counterparty that are not brokered deposits, where the retail customer or counterparty owns the account and where less than the entire amount is covered by deposit insurance; and

(5) 40 percent of all funding from a retail customer or counterparty that is not:

(i) A retail deposit;

(ii) A brokered deposit provided by a retail customer or counterparty; or

(iii) A debt instrument issued by the national bank or Federal savings association that is owned by a retail customer or counterparty (see paragraph (h)(2)(ii) of this section).

(b) *Structured transaction outflow amount.* If the national bank or Federal savings association is a sponsor of a structured transaction where the issuing entity is not consolidated on the national bank's or Federal savings association's balance sheet under GAAP, the structured transaction outflow amount for each such structured transaction as of the calculation date is the greater of:

(1) 100 percent of the amount of all debt obligations of the issuing entity

that mature 30 calendar days or less from such calculation date and all commitments made by the issuing entity to purchase assets within 30 calendar days or less from such calculation date; and

(2) The maximum contractual amount of funding the national bank or Federal savings association may be required to provide to the issuing entity 30 calendar days or less from such calculation date through a liquidity facility, a return or repurchase of assets from the issuing entity, or other funding agreement.

(c) *Net derivative cash outflow amount.* The net derivative cash outflow amount as of the calculation date is the sum of the net derivative cash outflow amount for each counterparty. The net derivative cash outflow amount does not include forward sales of mortgage loans and any derivatives that are mortgage commitments subject to paragraph (d) of this section. The net derivative cash outflow amount for a counterparty is the sum of:

(1) The amount, if greater than zero, of contractual payments and collateral that the national bank or Federal savings association will make or deliver to the counterparty 30 calendar days or less from the calculation date under derivative transactions other than transactions described in paragraph (c)(2) of this section, less the contractual payments and collateral that the national bank or Federal savings association will receive from the counterparty 30 calendar days or less from the calculation date under derivative transactions other than transactions described in paragraph (c)(2) of this section, provided that the derivative transactions are subject to a qualifying master netting agreement; and

(2) The amount, if greater than zero, of contractual principal payments that the national bank or Federal savings association will make to the counterparty 30 calendar days or less from the calculation date under foreign currency exchange derivative transactions that result in the full exchange of contractual cash principal payments in different currencies within the same business day, less the contractual principal payments that the national bank or Federal savings association will receive from the counterparty 30 calendar days or less from the calculation date under foreign currency exchange derivative transactions that result in the full exchange of contractual cash principal payments in different currencies within the same business day.

(d) *Mortgage commitment outflow amount.* The mortgage commitment outflow amount as of a calculation date is 10 percent of the amount of funds the national bank or Federal savings association has contractually committed for its own origination of retail mortgages that can be drawn upon 30 calendar days or less from such calculation date.

(e) *Commitment outflow amount.* (1) A national bank's or Federal savings association's commitment outflow amount as of the calculation date includes:

(i) Zero percent of the undrawn amount of all committed credit and liquidity facilities extended by a national bank or Federal savings association that is a depository institution to an affiliated depository institution that is subject to a minimum liquidity standard under this part;

(ii) 5 percent of the undrawn amount of all committed credit and liquidity facilities extended by the national bank or Federal savings association to retail customers or counterparties;

(iii) 10 percent of the undrawn amount of all committed credit facilities extended by the national bank or Federal savings association to a wholesale customer or counterparty that is not a financial sector entity or a consolidated subsidiary thereof, including a special purpose entity (other than those described in paragraph (e)(1)(viii) of this section) that is a consolidated subsidiary of such wholesale customer or counterparty;

(iv) 30 percent of the undrawn amount of all committed liquidity facilities extended by the national bank or Federal savings association to a wholesale customer or counterparty that is not a financial sector entity or a consolidated subsidiary thereof, including a special purpose entity (other than those described in paragraph (e)(1)(viii) of this section) that is a consolidated subsidiary of such wholesale customer or counterparty;

(v) 50 percent of the undrawn amount of all committed credit and liquidity facilities extended by the national bank or Federal savings association to depository institutions, depository institution holding companies, and foreign banks, but excluding commitments described in paragraph (e)(1)(i) of this section;

(vi) 40 percent of the undrawn amount of all committed credit facilities extended by the national bank or Federal savings association to a financial sector entity or a consolidated subsidiary thereof, including a special purpose entity (other than those described in paragraph (e)(1)(viii) of this section) that is a consolidated subsidiary of a financial sector entity, but excluding other commitments described in paragraph (e)(1)(i) or (v) of this section;

(vii) 100 percent of the undrawn amount of all committed liquidity facilities extended by the national bank or Federal savings association to a financial sector entity or a consolidated subsidiary thereof, including a special purpose entity (other than those described in paragraph (e)(1)(viii) of this section) that is a consolidated subsidiary of a financial sector entity, but excluding other commitments described in paragraph (e)(1)(i) or (v) of this section and liquidity facilities included in paragraph (b)(2) of this section;

(viii) 100 percent of the undrawn amount of all committed credit and liquidity facilities extended to a special purpose entity that issues or has issued commercial paper or securities (other than equity securities issued to a company of which the special purpose entity is a consolidated subsidiary) to finance its purchases or operations, and excluding liquidity facilities included in paragraph (b)(2) of this section; and

(ix) 100 percent of the undrawn amount of all other committed credit or liquidity facilities extended by the national bank or Federal savings association.

(2) For the purposes of this paragraph (e), the undrawn amount of a committed credit facility or committed liquidity facility is the entire unused amount of the facility that could be drawn upon within 30 calendar days of the calculation date under the governing agreement, less the amount of level 1 liquid assets and the amount of level 2A liquid assets securing the facility.

(3) For the purposes of this paragraph (e), the amount of level 1 liquid assets and level 2A liquid assets securing a committed credit or liquidity facility is the fair value of level 1 liquid assets and 85 percent of the fair value of level 2A liquid assets that are required to be pledged as collateral by the counterparty to secure the facility, provided that:

(i) The assets pledged upon a draw on the facility would be eligible HQLA; and

(ii) The national bank or Federal savings association has not included the assets as eligible HQLA under subpart C of this part as of the calculation date.

(f) *Collateral outflow amount.* The collateral outflow amount as of the calculation date includes:

(1) *Changes in financial condition.* 100 percent of all additional amounts of collateral the national bank or Federal savings association could be contractually required to pledge or to fund under the terms of any transaction as a result of a change in the national bank's or Federal savings association's financial condition;

(2) *Derivative collateral potential valuation changes.* 20 percent of the fair value of any collateral securing a derivative transaction pledged to a counterparty by the national bank or Federal savings association that is not a level 1 liquid asset;

(3) *Potential derivative valuation changes.* The absolute value of the largest 30-consecutive calendar day cumulative net mark-to-market collateral outflow or inflow realized during the preceding 24 months resulting from derivative transaction valuation changes;

(4) *Excess collateral.* 100 percent of the fair value of collateral that:

(i) The national bank or Federal savings association could be required by contract to return to a counterparty because the collateral pledged to the national bank or Federal savings association exceeds the current collateral requirement of the counterparty under the governing contract;

(ii) Is not segregated from the national bank's or Federal savings association's other assets such that it cannot be rehypothecated; and

(iii) Is not already excluded as eligible HQLA by the national bank or Federal savings association under § 50.22(b)(5);

(5) *Contractually required collateral.* 100 percent of the fair value of collateral that the national bank or Federal savings association is contractually required to pledge to a counterparty and, as of such calculation date, the national bank or Federal savings association has not yet pledged;

(6) *Collateral substitution.* (i) Zero percent of the fair value of collateral pledged to the national bank or Federal savings association by a counterparty where the collateral qualifies as level 1 liquid assets and eligible HQLA and where, under the contract governing the transaction, the counterparty may replace the pledged collateral with other assets that qualify as level 1 liquid assets, without the consent of the national bank or Federal savings association;

(ii) 15 percent of the fair value of collateral pledged to the national bank or Federal savings association by a counterparty, where the collateral qualifies as level 1 liquid assets and eligible HQLA and where, under the contract governing the transaction, the counterparty may replace the pledged collateral with assets that qualify as level 2A liquid assets, without the consent of the national bank or Federal savings association;

(iii) 50 percent of the fair value of collateral pledged to the national bank or Federal savings association by a counterparty where the collateral qualifies as level 1 liquid assets and eligible HQLA and where under, the contract governing the transaction, the counterparty may replace the pledged collateral with assets that qualify as level 2B liquid assets, without the consent of the national bank or Federal savings association;

(iv) 100 percent of the fair value of collateral pledged to the national bank or Federal savings association by a counterparty where the collateral qualifies as level 1 liquid assets and eligible HQLA and where, under the contract governing the transaction, the counterparty may replace the pledged collateral with assets that do not qualify as HQLA, without the consent of the national bank or Federal savings association;

(v) Zero percent of the fair value of collateral pledged to the national bank or Federal savings association by a counterparty where the collateral qualifies as level 2A liquid assets and eligible HQLA and where, under the contract governing the transaction, the counterparty may replace the pledged collateral with assets that qualify as level 1 or level 2A liquid assets, without the consent of the national bank or Federal savings association;

(vi) 35 percent of the fair value of collateral pledged to the national bank or Federal savings association by a counterparty where the collateral qualifies as level 2A liquid assets and eligible HQLA and where, under the contract governing the transaction, the counterparty may replace the pledged collateral with assets that qualify as level 2B liquid assets, without the consent of the national bank or Federal savings association;

(vii) 85 percent of the fair value of collateral pledged to the national bank or Federal savings association by a counterparty where the collateral qualifies as level 2A liquid assets and eligible HQLA and where, under the contract governing the transaction, the counterparty may replace the pledged collateral with assets that do not qualify as HQLA, without the consent of the national bank or Federal savings association;

(viii) Zero percent of the fair value of collateral pledged to the national bank or Federal savings association by a counterparty where the collateral qualifies as level 2B liquid assets and eligible HQLA and where, under the contract governing the transaction, the counterparty may replace the pledged collateral with other assets that qualify as HQLA, without the consent of the national bank or Federal savings association; and

(ix) 50 percent of the fair value of collateral pledged to the national bank or Federal savings association by a counterparty where the collateral qualifies as level 2B liquid assets and eligible HQLA and where, under the contract governing the transaction, the counterparty may replace the pledged collateral with assets that do not qualify as HQLA, without the consent of the national bank or Federal savings association.

(g) *Brokered deposit outflow amount for retail customers or counterparties.* The brokered deposit outflow amount for retail customers or counterparties as of the calculation date includes:

(1) 100 percent of all brokered deposits at the national bank or Federal savings association provided by a retail customer or counterparty that are not described in paragraphs (g)(5) through (9) of this section and which mature 30 calendar days or less from the calculation date;

(2) 10 percent of all brokered deposits at the national bank or Federal savings association provided by a retail customer or counterparty that are not described in paragraphs (g)(5) through (9) of this section and which mature later than 30 calendar days from the calculation date;

(3) 20 percent of all brokered deposits at the national bank or Federal savings association provided by a retail customer or counterparty that are not described in paragraphs (g)(5) through (9) of this section and which are held in a transactional account with no contractual maturity date, where the entire amount is covered by deposit insurance;

(4) 40 percent of all brokered deposits at the national bank or Federal savings association provided by a retail customer or counterparty that are not described in paragraphs (g)(5) through (9) of this section and which are held in a transactional account with no contractual maturity date, where less than the entire amount is covered by deposit insurance;

(5) 10 percent of all reciprocal brokered deposits at the national bank or Federal savings association provided by a retail customer or counterparty, where the entire amount is covered by deposit insurance;

(6) 25 percent of all reciprocal brokered deposits at the national bank or Federal savings association provided by a retail customer or counterparty, where less than the entire amount is covered by deposit insurance;

(7) 10 percent of all brokered sweep deposits at the national bank or Federal savings association provided by a retail customer or counterparty:

(i) That are deposited in accordance with a contract between the retail customer or counterparty and the national bank or Federal savings association, a controlled subsidiary of the national bank or Federal savings association, or a company that is a controlled subsidiary of the same top-tier company of which the national bank or Federal savings association is a controlled subsidiary; and

(ii) Where the entire amount of the deposits is covered by deposit insurance;

(8) 25 percent of all brokered sweep deposits at the national bank or Federal savings association provided by a retail customer or counterparty:

(i) That are not deposited in accordance with a contract between the retail customer or counterparty and the national bank or Federal savings association, a controlled subsidiary of the national bank or Federal savings association, or a company that is a controlled subsidiary of the same top-tier company of which the national bank or Federal savings association is a controlled subsidiary; and

(ii) Where the entire amount of the deposits is covered by deposit insurance; and

(9) 40 percent of all brokered sweep deposits at the national bank or Federal savings association provided by a retail customer or counterparty where less than the entire amount of the deposit balance is covered by deposit insurance.

(h) *Unsecured wholesale funding outflow amount.* A national bank's or Federal savings association's unsecured wholesale funding outflow amount, for all transactions that mature within 30 calendar days or less of the calculation date, as of the calculation date includes:

(1) For unsecured wholesale funding that is not an operational deposit and

is not provided by a financial sector entity or consolidated subsidiary of a financial sector entity:

(i) 20 percent of all such funding, where the entire amount is covered by deposit insurance and the funding is not a brokered deposit;

(ii) 40 percent of all such funding, where:

(A) Less than the entire amount is covered by deposit insurance; or

(B) The funding is a brokered deposit;

(2) 100 percent of all unsecured wholesale funding that is not an operational deposit and is not included in paragraph (h)(1) of this section, including:

(i) Funding provided by a company that is a consolidated subsidiary of the same top-tier company of which the national bank or Federal savings association is a consolidated subsidiary; and

(ii) Debt instruments issued by the national bank or Federal savings association, including such instruments owned by retail customers or counterparties;

(3) 5 percent of all operational deposits, other than operational deposits that are held in escrow accounts, where the entire deposit amount is covered by deposit insurance;

(4) 25 percent of all operational deposits not included in paragraph (h)(3) of this section; and

(5) 100 percent of all unsecured wholesale funding that is not otherwise described in this paragraph (h).

(i) *Debt security buyback outflow amount.* A national bank's or Federal savings association's debt security buyback outflow amount for debt securities issued by the national bank or Federal savings association that mature more than 30 calendar days after the calculation date and for which the national bank or Federal savings association or a consolidated subsidiary of the national bank or Federal savings association is the primary market maker in such debt securities includes:

(1) 3 percent of all such debt securities that are not structured securities; and

(2) 5 percent of all such debt securities that are structured securities.

(j) *Secured funding and asset exchange outflow amount.* (1) A national bank's or Federal savings association's secured funding outflow amount, for all transactions that mature within 30 calendar days or less of the calculation date, as of the calculation date includes:

(i) Zero percent of all funds the national bank or Federal savings association must pay pursuant to secured funding transactions, to the extent that the funds are secured by level 1 liquid assets;

(ii) 15 percent of all funds the national bank or Federal savings association must pay pursuant to secured funding transactions, to the extent that the funds are secured by level 2A liquid assets;

(iii) 25 percent of all funds the national bank or Federal savings association must pay pursuant to secured funding transactions with sovereign entities, multilateral development banks, or U.S. government-sponsored enterprises that are assigned a risk weight of 20 percent under subpart D of (12 CFR part 3), to the extent that the funds are not secured by level 1 or level 2A liquid assets;

(iv) 50 percent of all funds the national bank or Federal savings association must pay pursuant to secured funding transactions, to the extent that the funds are secured by level 2B liquid assets;

(v) 50 percent of all funds received from secured funding transactions that are customer short positions where the customer short positions are covered by other customers' collateral and the collateral does not consist of HQLA; and

(vi) 100 percent of all other funds the national bank or Federal savings association must pay pursuant to secured funding transactions, to the extent that the funds are secured by assets that are not HQLA.

(2) If an outflow rate specified in paragraph (j)(1) of this section for a secured funding transaction is greater than the outflow rate that the national bank or Federal savings association is required to apply under paragraph (h) of this section to an unsecured wholesale funding transaction that is not an operational deposit with the same counterparty, the national bank or Federal savings association may apply to the secured funding transaction the

outflow rate that applies to an unsecured wholesale funding transaction that is not an operational deposit with that counterparty, except in the case of:

(i) Secured funding transactions that are secured by collateral that was received by the national bank or Federal savings association under a secured lending transaction or asset exchange, in which case the national bank or Federal savings association must apply the outflow rate specified in paragraph (j)(1) of this section for the secured funding transaction; and

(ii) Collateralized deposits that are operational deposits, in which case the national bank or Federal savings association may apply to the operational deposit amount, as calculated in accordance with § 50.4(b), the operational deposit outflow rate specified in paragraph (h)(3) or (4) of this section, as applicable, if such outflow rate is lower than the outflow rate specified in paragraph (j)(1) of this section.

(3) A national bank's or Federal savings association's asset exchange outflow amount, for all transactions that mature within 30 calendar days or less of the calculation date, as of the calculation date includes:

(i) Zero percent of the fair value of the level 1 liquid assets the national bank or Federal savings association must post to a counterparty pursuant to asset exchanges, not described in paragraphs (j)(3)(x) through (xiii) of this section, where the national bank or Federal savings association will receive level 1 liquid assets from the asset exchange counterparty;

(ii) 15 percent of the fair value of the level 1 liquid assets the national bank or Federal savings association must post to a counterparty pursuant to asset exchanges, not described in paragraphs (j)(3)(x) through (xiii) of this section, where the national bank or Federal savings association will receive level 2A liquid assets from the asset exchange counterparty;

(iii) 50 percent of the fair value of the level 1 liquid assets the national bank or Federal savings association must post to a counterparty pursuant to asset exchanges, not described in paragraphs (j)(3)(x) through (xiii) of this section, where the national bank or Federal savings association will receive level 2B liquid assets from the asset exchange counterparty;

(iv) 100 percent of the fair value of the level 1 liquid assets the national bank or Federal savings association must post to a counterparty pursuant to asset exchanges, not described in paragraphs (j)(3)(x) through (xiii) of this section, where the national bank or Federal savings association will receive assets that are not HQLA from the asset exchange counterparty;

(v) Zero percent of the fair value of the level 2A liquid assets that national bank or Federal savings association must post to a counterparty pursuant to asset exchanges, not described in paragraphs (j)(3)(x) through (xiii) of this section, where national bank or Federal savings association will receive level 1 or level 2A liquid assets from the asset exchange counterparty;

(vi) 35 percent of the fair value of the level 2A liquid assets the national bank or Federal savings association must post to a counterparty pursuant to asset exchanges, not described in paragraphs (j)(3)(x) through (xiii) of this section, where the national bank or Federal savings association will receive level 2B liquid assets from the asset exchange counterparty;

(vii) 85 percent of the fair value of the level 2A liquid assets the national bank or Federal savings association must post to a counterparty pursuant to asset exchanges, not described in paragraphs (j)(3)(x) through (xiii) of this section, where the national bank or Federal savings association will receive assets that are not HQLA from the asset exchange counterparty;

(viii) Zero percent of the fair value of the level 2B liquid assets the national bank or Federal savings association must post to a counterparty pursuant to asset exchanges, not described in paragraphs (j)(3)(x) through (xiii) of this section, where the national bank or Federal savings association will receive HQLA from the asset exchange counterparty; and

(ix) 50 percent of the fair value of the level 2B liquid assets the national bank or Federal savings association must post to a counterparty pursuant to asset exchanges, not described in paragraphs (j)(3)(x) through (xiii) of this section, where the national bank or Federal savings association will receive assets that are not HQLA from the asset exchange counterparty;

(x) Zero percent of the fair value of the level 1 liquid assets the national bank or Federal savings association will receive from a counterparty pursuant to an asset exchange where the national bank or Federal savings association has rehypothecated the assets posted by the asset exchange counterparty, and, as of the calculation date, the assets will not be returned to the national bank or Federal savings association within 30 calendar days;

(xi) 15 percent of the fair value of the level 2A liquid assets the national bank or Federal savings association will receive from a counterparty pursuant to an asset exchange where the national bank or Federal savings association has rehypothecated the assets posted by the asset exchange counterparty, and, as of the calculation date, the assets will not be returned to the national bank or Federal savings association within 30 calendar days;

(xii) 50 percent of the fair value of the level 2B liquid assets the national bank or Federal savings association will receive from a counterparty pursuant to an asset exchange where the national bank or Federal savings association has rehypothecated the assets posted by the asset exchange counterparty, and, as of the calculation date, the assets will not be returned to the national bank or Federal savings association within 30 calendar days; and

(xiii) 100 percent of the fair value of the non-HQLA the national bank or Federal savings association will receive from a counterparty pursuant to an asset exchange where the national bank or Federal savings association has rehypothecated the assets posted by the asset exchange counterparty, and, as of the calculation date, the assets will not be returned to the national bank or Federal savings association within 30 calendar days.

(k) *Foreign central bank borrowing outflow amount.* A national bank's or Federal savings association's foreign central bank borrowing outflow amount is, in a foreign jurisdiction where the national bank or Federal savings association has borrowed from the jurisdiction's central bank, the outflow amount assigned to borrowings from central banks in a minimum liquidity standard established in that jurisdiction. If the foreign jurisdiction has not specified a central bank borrowing outflow amount in a minimum liquidity standard, the foreign central bank borrowing outflow amount must be calculated in accordance with paragraph (j) of this section.

(l) *Other contractual outflow amount.* A national bank's or Federal savings association's other contractual outflow amount is 100 percent of funding or amounts, with the exception of operating expenses of the national bank or Federal savings association (such as rents, salaries, utilities, and other similar payments), payable by the national bank or Federal savings association to counterparties under legally binding agreements that are not otherwise specified in this section.

(m) *Excluded amounts for intragroup transactions.* The outflow amounts set forth in this section do not include amounts arising out of transactions between:

(1) The national bank or Federal savings association and a consolidated subsidiary of the national bank or Federal savings association; or

(2) A consolidated subsidiary of the national bank or Federal savings association and another consolidated subsidiary of the national bank or Federal savings association.

§ 50.33 Inflow amounts.

(a) The inflows in paragraphs (b) through (g) of this section do not include:

(1) Amounts the national bank or Federal savings association holds in operational deposits at other regulated financial companies;

(2) Amounts the national bank or Federal savings association expects, or is contractually entitled to receive, 30 calendar days or less from the calculation date due to forward sales of mortgage loans and any derivatives that are mortgage commitments subject to § 50.32(d);

(3) The amount of any credit or liquidity facilities extended to the national bank or Federal savings association;

(4) The amount of any asset that is eligible HQLA and any amounts payable to the national bank or Federal savings association with respect to that asset;

(5) Any amounts payable to the national bank or Federal savings association from an obligation of a customer or counterparty that is a nonperforming asset as of the calculation date or that the national bank or Federal savings association has reason to expect will become a nonperforming exposure 30 calendar days or less from the calculation date; and

(6) Amounts payable to the national bank or Federal savings association with respect to any transaction that has no contractual maturity date or that matures after 30 calendar days of the calculation date (as determined by § 50.31).

(b) *Net derivative cash inflow amount.* The net derivative cash inflow amount as of the calculation date is the sum of the net derivative cash inflow amount for each counterparty. The net derivative cash inflow amount does not include amounts excluded from inflows under paragraph (a)(2) of this section. The net derivative cash inflow amount for a counterparty is the sum of:

(1) The amount, if greater than zero, of contractual payments and collateral that the national bank or Federal savings association will receive from the counterparty 30 calendar days or less from the calculation date under derivative transactions other than transactions described in paragraph (b)(2) of this section, less the contractual payments and collateral that the national bank or Federal savings association will make or deliver to the counterparty 30 calendar days or less from the calculation date under derivative transactions other than transactions described in paragraph (b)(2) of this section, provided that the derivative transactions are subject to a qualifying master netting agreement; and

(2) The amount, if greater than zero, of contractual principal payments that the national bank or Federal savings association will receive from the counterparty 30 calendar days or less from the calculation date under foreign currency exchange derivative transactions that result in the full exchange of contractual cash principal payments in different currencies within the same business day, less the contractual principal payments that the national bank or Federal savings association will make to the counterparty 30 calendar days or less from the calculation date under foreign currency exchange derivative transactions that result in the full exchange of contractual cash principal payments in different currencies within the same business day.

(c) *Retail cash inflow amount.* The retail cash inflow amount as of the calculation date includes 50 percent of all payments contractually payable to the national bank or Federal savings association from retail customers or counterparties.

(d) *Unsecured wholesale cash inflow amount.* The unsecured wholesale cash inflow amount as of the calculation date includes:

(1) 100 percent of all payments contractually payable to the national bank or Federal savings association from financial sector entities, or from a consolidated subsidiary thereof, or central banks; and

(2) 50 percent of all payments contractually payable to the national bank or Federal savings association from wholesale customers or counterparties that are not financial sector entities or consolidated subsidiaries thereof, provided that, with respect to revolving credit facilities, the amount of the existing loan is not included in the unsecured wholesale cash inflow amount and the remaining undrawn balance is included in the outflow amount under § 50.32(e)(1).

(e) *Securities cash inflow amount.* The securities cash inflow amount as of the calculation date includes 100 percent of all contractual payments due to the national bank or Federal savings association on securities it owns that are not eligible HQLA.

(f) *Secured lending and asset exchange cash inflow amount.* (1) A national bank's or Federal savings association's secured lending cash inflow amount as of the calculation date includes:

(i) Zero percent of all contractual payments due to the national bank or Federal savings association pursuant to secured lending transactions, including margin loans extended to customers, to the extent that the payments are secured by collateral that has been rehypothecated in a transaction and, as of the calculation date, will not be returned to the national bank or Federal savings association within 30 calendar days;

(ii) 100 percent of all contractual payments due to the national bank or Federal savings association pursuant to secured lending transactions not described in paragraph (f)(1)(vii) of this section, to the extent that the payments are secured by assets that are not eligible HQLA, but are still held by the national bank or Federal savings association and are available for immediate return to the counterparty at any time;

(iii) Zero percent of all contractual payments due to the national bank or Federal savings association pursuant to secured lending transactions not described in paragraphs (f)(1)(i) or (ii) of this section, to the extent that the payments are secured by level 1 liquid assets;

(iv) 15 percent of all contractual payments due to the national bank or Federal savings association pursuant to secured lending transactions not described in paragraphs (f)(1)(i) or (ii) of this section, to the extent that the payments are secured by level 2A liquid assets;

(v) 50 percent of all contractual payments due to the national bank or Federal savings association pursuant to secured lending transactions not described in paragraphs (f)(1)(i) or (ii) of this section, to the extent that the payments are secured by level 2B liquid assets;

(vi) 100 percent of all contractual payments due to the national bank or Federal savings association pursuant to secured lending transactions not described in paragraphs (f)(1)(i), (ii), or (vii) of this section, to the extent that the payments are secured by assets that are not HQLA; and

(vii) 50 percent of all contractual payments due to the national bank or Federal savings association pursuant to collateralized margin loans extended to customers, not described in paragraph (f)(1)(i) of this section, provided that the loans are secured by assets that are not HQLA.

(2) A national bank's or Federal savings association's asset exchange inflow amount as of the calculation date includes:

(i) Zero percent of the fair value of assets the national bank or Federal savings association will receive from a counterparty pursuant to asset exchanges, to the extent that the asset received by the national bank or Federal savings association from the counterparty has been rehypothecated in a transaction and, as of the calculation date, will not be returned to the national bank or Federal savings association within 30 calendar days;

(ii) Zero percent of the fair value of level 1 liquid assets the national bank or Federal savings association will receive from a counterparty pursuant to asset exchanges, not described in paragraph (f)(2)(i) of this section, where the national bank or Federal savings association must post level 1 liquid assets to the asset exchange counterparty;

(iii) 15 percent of the fair value of level 1 liquid assets the national bank or Federal savings association will receive from a counterparty pursuant to asset exchanges, not described in paragraph (f)(2)(i) of this section, where the national bank or Federal savings association must post level 2A liquid assets to the asset exchange counterparty;

(iv) 50 percent of the fair value of level 1 liquid assets the national bank or Federal savings association will receive from counterparty pursuant to asset exchanges, not described in paragraph (f)(2)(i) of this section, where the national bank or Federal savings association must post level 2B liquid assets to the asset exchange counterparty;

(v) 100 percent of the fair value of level 1 liquid assets the national bank or Federal savings association will receive from a counterparty pursuant to asset exchanges, not described in paragraph (f)(2)(i) of this section, where the national bank or Federal savings association must post assets that are not HQLA to the asset exchange counterparty;

(vi) Zero percent of the fair value of level 2A liquid assets the national bank or Federal savings association will receive from a counterparty pursuant to asset exchanges, not described in paragraph (f)(2)(i) of this section, where the national bank or Federal savings association must post level 1 or level 2A liquid assets to the asset exchange counterparty;

(vii) 35 percent of the fair value of level 2A liquid assets the national bank or Federal savings association will receive from a counterparty pursuant to asset exchanges, not described in paragraph (f)(2)(i) of this section, where the national bank or Federal savings association must post level 2B liquid assets to the asset exchange counterparty;

(viii) 85 percent of the fair value of level 2A liquid assets the national bank or Federal savings association will receive from a counterparty pursuant to asset exchanges, not described in paragraph (f)(2)(i) of this section, where the national bank or Federal savings association must post assets that are not HQLA to the asset exchange counterparty;

(ix) Zero percent of the fair value of level 2B liquid assets the national bank or Federal savings association will receive from a counterparty pursuant to asset exchanges, not described in paragraph (f)(2)(i) of this section, where the national bank or Federal savings association must post assets that are HQLA to the asset exchange counterparty; and

(x) 50 percent of the fair value of level 2B liquid assets the national bank or Federal savings association will receive from a counterparty pursuant to asset exchanges, not described in paragraph (f)(2)(i) of this section, where the national bank or Federal savings association must post assets that are not HQLA to the asset exchange counterparty.

(g) *Broker-dealer segregated account inflow amount.* A national bank's or Federal savings association's broker-dealer segregated account inflow amount is the fair value of all assets released from broker-dealer segregated accounts maintained in accordance with statutory or regulatory requirements for the protection of customer trading assets, provided that the calculation of the broker-dealer segregated account inflow amount, for any transaction affecting the calculation of the segregated balance (as required by applicable law), shall be consistent with the following:

(1) In calculating the broker-dealer segregated account inflow amount, the national bank or Federal savings association must calculate the fair value of the required balance of the customer reserve account as of 30 calendar days from the calculation date by assuming that customer cash and collateral positions have changed consistent with the outflow and inflow calculations required under §§ 50.32 and 50.33.

(2) If the fair value of the required balance of the customer reserve account as of 30 calendar days from the calculation date, as calculated consistent with the outflow and inflow calculations required under §§ 50.32 and 50.33, is less than the fair value of the required balance as of the calculation date, the difference is the segregated account inflow amount.

(3) If the fair value of the required balance of the customer reserve account as of 30 calendar days from the calculation date, as calculated consistent with the outflow and inflow calculations required under §§ 50.32 and 50.33, is more than the fair value of the required balance as of the calculation date, the segregated account inflow amount is zero.

(h) *Other cash inflow amounts.* A national bank's or Federal savings association's inflow amount as of the calculation date includes zero percent of other cash inflow amounts not included in paragraphs (b) through (g) of this section.

(i) *Excluded amounts for intragroup transactions.* The inflow amounts set forth in this section do not include amounts arising out of transactions between:

(1) The national bank or Federal savings association and a consolidated subsidiary of the national bank or Federal savings association; or

(2) A consolidated subsidiary of the national bank or Federal savings association and another consolidated subsidiary of the national bank or Federal savings association.

Subpart E—Liquidity Coverage Shortfall

§ 50.40 Liquidity coverage shortfall: Supervisory framework.

(a) *Notification requirements.* A national bank or Federal savings association must notify the OCC on any business day when its liquidity coverage ratio is calculated to be less than the minimum requirement in § 50.10.

(b) *Liquidity plan.* (1) For the period during which a national bank or Federal savings association must calculate a liquidity coverage ratio on the last business day of each applicable calendar month under subpart F of this part, if the national bank's or Federal savings association's liquidity coverage ratio is below the minimum requirement in § 50.10 for any calculation date that is the last business day of the applicable calendar month, or if the OCC has determined that the national bank or Federal savings association is otherwise materially noncompliant with the requirements of this part, the national bank or Federal savings association must promptly consult with the OCC to determine whether the national bank or Federal savings association must provide to the OCC a plan for achieving compliance with the minimum liquidity requirement in § 50.10 and all other requirements of this part.

(2) For the period during which a national bank or Federal savings association must calculate a liquidity coverage ratio each business day under subpart F of this part, if a national bank's or Federal savings association's liquidity coverage ratio is below the minimum requirement in § 50.10 for three consecutive business days, or if the OCC has determined that the national bank or Federal savings association is otherwise materially noncompliant with the requirements of this part, the national bank or Federal savings association must promptly provide to the OCC a plan for achieving compliance with the minimum liquidity requirement in § 50.10 and all other requirements of this part.

(3) The plan must include, as applicable:

(i) An assessment of the national bank's or Federal savings association's liquidity position;

(ii) The actions the national bank or Federal savings association has taken and will take to achieve full compliance with this part, including:

(A) A plan for adjusting the national bank's or Federal savings association's risk profile, risk management, and funding sources in order to achieve full compliance with this part; and

(B) A plan for remediating any operational or management issues that contributed to noncompliance with this part;

(iii) An estimated time frame for achieving full compliance with this part; and

(iv) A commitment to report to the OCC no less than weekly on progress to achieve compliance in accordance with the plan until full compliance with this part is achieved.

(c) *Supervisory and enforcement actions.* The OCC may, at its discretion, take additional supervisory or enforcement actions to address noncompliance with the minimum liquidity standard and other requirements of this part.

Subpart F—Transitions

§ 50.50 Transitions.

(a) Covered depository institution holding companies with $700 billion or more in total consolidated assets or $10 trillion or more in assets under custody. For any depository institution holding company that has total consolidated assets equal to $700 billion or more, as reported on the company's most recent Consolidated Financial Statements for Holding Companies (FR Y–9C), or $10 trillion or more in assets under custody, as reported on the company's most recent Banking Organization Systemic Risk Report (FR Y–15), and any depository institution that is a consolidated subsidiary of such depository institution holding company that has total consolidated assets equal to $10 billion or more, as reported on the most recent year-end Consolidated Report of Condition and Income:

(1) Beginning January 1, 2015, through June 30, 2015, the national bank or Federal savings association must calculate and maintain a liquidity coverage ratio monthly, on each calculation date that is the last business day of the applicable calendar

month, in accordance with this part, that is equal to or greater than 0.80.

(2) Beginning July 1, 2015 through December 31, 2015, the national bank or Federal savings association must calculate and maintain a liquidity coverage ratio on each calculation date in accordance with this part that is equal to or greater than 0.80.

(3) Beginning January 1, 2016, through December 31, 2016, the national bank or Federal savings association must calculate and maintain a liquidity coverage ratio on each calculation date in accordance with this part that is equal to or greater than 0.90.

(4) On January 1, 2017, and thereafter, the national bank or Federal savings association must calculate and maintain a liquidity coverage ratio on each calculation date that is equal to or greater than 1.0.

(b) *Other national banks and Federal savings associations.* For any national bank or Federal savings association subject to a minimum liquidity standard under this part not described in paragraph (a) of this section:

(1) Beginning January 1, 2015, through December 31, 2015, the national bank or Federal savings association must calculate and maintain a liquidity coverage ratio monthly, on each calculation date that is the last business day of the applicable calendar month, in accordance with this part, that is equal to or greater than 0.80.

(2) Beginning January 1, 2016, through June 30, 2016, the national bank or Federal savings association must calculate and maintain a liquidity coverage ratio monthly, on each calculation date that is the last business day of the applicable calendar month, in accordance with this part, that is equal to or greater than 0.90.

(3) Beginning July 1, 2016, through December 31, 2016, the national bank or Federal savings association must calculate and maintain a liquidity coverage ratio on each calculation date in accordance with this part that is equal to or greater than 0.90.

(4) On January 1, 2017, and thereafter, the national bank or Federal savings association must calculate and maintain a liquidity coverage ratio on each calculation date that is equal to or greater than 1.0.

PART 51—RECEIVERSHIPS FOR UNINSURED NATIONAL BANKS

Sec.
51.1 Purpose and scope.
51.2 Appointment of receiver.
51.3 Notice of appointment of receiver.
51.4 Claims.
51.5 Order of priorities.
51.6 Administrative expenses of receiver.
51.7 Powers and duties of receiver; disposition of fiduciary and custodial accounts.
51.8 Payment of claims and dividends to shareholders.
51.9 Termination of receivership.

AUTHORITY: 12 U.S.C. 16, 93a, 191–200, 481, 482, 1831c, and 1867.

SOURCE: 81 FR 92602, Dec. 20, 2016, unless otherwise noted.

§ 51.1 Purpose and scope.

(a) *Purpose.* This part sets out procedures for receiverships of national banks conducted by the Office of the Comptroller of the Currency (OCC) under the receivership provisions of the National Bank Act (NBA). These receivership provisions apply to national banks that are not insured by the Federal Deposit Insurance Corporation (FDIC).

(b) *Scope.* This part applies to the appointment of a receiver for uninsured national banks (uninsured banks) and the operation of a receivership after appointment of a receiver for an uninsured bank under 12 U.S.C. 191.[31]

§ 51.2 Appointment of receiver.

(a) *In general.* The Comptroller of the Currency (Comptroller) may appoint any person, including the OCC or another government agency, as receiver for an uninsured bank. The receiver performs its duties under the direction of the Comptroller and serves at the will of the Comptroller. The Comptroller may require the receiver to post a bond or other security. The receiver, with the approval of the Comptroller, may employ such staff and enter into contracts for professional services as are necessary to carry out the receivership.

(b) *Grounds for appointment.* The Comptroller may appoint a receiver for

[31] This part does not apply to receiverships for uninsured Federal branches or uninsured Federal agencies.

an uninsured bank based on any of the grounds specified in 12 U.S.C. 191(a).

(c) *Judicial review.* If the Comptroller appoints a receiver for an uninsured bank, the bank may seek judicial review of the appointment as provided in 12 U.S.C. 191(b).

§51.3 Notice of appointment of receiver.

Upon appointment of a receiver for an uninsured bank, the OCC will provide notice to the public of the receivership, including by publication in a newspaper of general circulation for three consecutive months. The notice of the receivership will provide instructions for creditors and other claimants seeking to submit claims with the receiver for the uninsured bank.

§51.4 Claims.

(a) *Submission of claims for consideration by the OCC.* (1) Persons who have claims against the receivership for an uninsured bank may present such claims, along with supporting documentation, for consideration by the OCC. The OCC will determine the validity and approve the amounts of such claims.

(2) The OCC will establish a date by which any person seeking to present a claim against the uninsured bank for consideration by the OCC must present their claim for determination. The deadline for filing such claims will not be less than 30 days after the end of the three-month notice period in §51.3.

(3) The OCC will allow any claim against the uninsured bank received on or before the deadline for presenting claims if such claim is established to the OCC's satisfaction by the information on the uninsured bank's books and records or otherwise submitted. The OCC may disallow any portion of any claim by a creditor or claim of a security, preference, set-off, or priority which is not established to the satisfaction of the OCC.

(b) *Submission of claims to a court.* Persons with claims against an uninsured bank in receivership may present their claims to a court of competent jurisdiction for adjudication. Such persons must submit a copy of any final judgment received from the court to the OCC, to participate in ratable dividends along with other proved claims.

(c) *Right of set-off.* If a person with a claim against an uninsured bank in receivership also has an obligation owed to the bank, the claim and obligation will be set off against each other and only the net balance remaining after set-off shall be considered as a claim, provided such set-off is otherwise legally valid.

§51.5 Order of priorities.

The OCC will pay receivership expenses and proved claims against the uninsured bank in receivership in the following order of priority:

(a) Administrative expenses of the receiver;

(b) Unsecured creditors of the uninsured bank, including secured creditors to the extent their claim exceeds their valid and enforceable security interest;

(c) Creditors of the uninsured bank, if any, whose claims are subordinated to general creditor claims; and

(d) Shareholders of the uninsured bank.

§51.6 Administrative expenses of receiver.

(a) *Priority of administrative expenses.* All administrative expenses of the receiver for an uninsured bank shall be paid out of the assets of the bank in receivership before payment of claims against the receivership.

(b) *Scope of administrative expenses.* Administrative expenses of the receiver for an uninsured bank include those expenses incurred by the receiver in maintaining banking operations during the receivership, to preserve assets of the uninsured bank, while liquidating or otherwise resolving the affairs of the uninsured bank. Such expenses include pre-receivership and post-receivership obligations that the receiver determines are necessary and appropriate to facilitate the orderly liquidation or other resolution of the uninsured bank in receivership.

(c) *Types of administrative expenses.* Administrative expenses for the receiver of an uninsured bank include:

(1) Salaries, costs, and other expenses of the receiver and its staff, and costs

of contracts entered into by the receiver for professional services relating to performing receivership duties; and

(2) Expenses necessary for the operation of the uninsured bank, including wages and salaries of employees, expenses for professional services, contractual rent pursuant to an existing lease or rental agreement, and payments to third-party or affiliated service providers, that in the opinion of the receiver are of benefit to the receivership, until the date the receiver repudiates, terminates, cancels, or otherwise discontinues the applicable contract.

§51.7 Powers and duties of receiver; disposition of fiduciary and custodial accounts.

(a) *Marshalling of assets.* In resolving the affairs of an uninsured bank in receivership, the receiver:

(1) Takes possession of the books, records and other property and assets of the uninsured bank, including the value of collateral pledged by the uninsured bank to the extent it exceeds valid and enforceable security interests of a claimant;

(2) Collects all debts, dues and claims belonging to the uninsured bank, including claims remaining after set-off;

(3) Sells or compromises all bad or doubtful debts, subject to approval by a court of competent jurisdiction;

(4) Sells the real and personal property of the uninsured bank, subject to approval by a court of competent jurisdiction, on such terms as the court shall direct; and

(5) Deposits all receivership funds collected from the liquidation of the uninsured bank in an account designated by the OCC.

(b) *Disposition of fiduciary and custodial accounts.* The receiver for an uninsured bank closes the bank's fiduciary and custodial appointments and accounts or transfers some or all of such accounts to successor fiduciaries and custodians, in accordance with 12 CFR 9.16, and other applicable Federal law.

(c) *Other powers.* The receiver for an uninsured bank may exercise other rights, privileges, and powers authorized for receivers of national banks under the NBA and the common law of receiverships as applied by the courts to receiverships of national banks conducted under the NBA.

(d) *Reports to OCC.* The receiver for an uninsured bank shall make periodic reports to the OCC on the status and proceedings of the receivership.

(e) *Receiver subject to removal; modification of fees.* (1) The Comptroller may remove and replace the receiver for an uninsured bank if, in the Comptroller's discretion, the receiver is not conducting the receivership in accordance with applicable Federal laws or regulations or fails to comply with decisions of the Comptroller with respect to the conduct of the receivership or claims against the receivership.

(2) The Comptroller may reduce the fees of the receiver for an uninsured bank if, in the Comptroller's discretion, the Comptroller finds the performance of the receiver to be deficient, or the fees of the receiver to be excessive, unreasonable, or beyond the scope of the work assigned to the receiver.

§51.8 Payment of claims and dividends to shareholders.

(a) *Claims.* (1) After the administrative expenses of the receivership have been paid, the OCC shall make ratable dividends from time to time of available receivership funds according to the priority described in §51.5, based on the claims that have been proved to the OCC's satisfaction or adjudicated in a court of competent jurisdiction.

(2) Dividend payments to creditors and other claimants of an uninsured bank will be made solely from receivership funds, if any, paid to the OCC by the receiver after payment of the expenses of the receiver.

(b) *Fiduciary and custodial assets.* Assets held by an uninsured bank in a fiduciary or custodial capacity, as designated on the bank's books and records, will not be considered as part of the bank's general assets and liabilities held in connection with its other business, and will not be considered a source for payment of unrelated claims of creditors and other claimants.

(c) *Timing of dividends.* The payment of dividends, if any, under paragraph (a) of this section, on proved or adjudicated claims will be made periodically, at the discretion of the OCC, as the receiver liquidates the assets of the uninsured bank.

(d) *Distribution to shareholders.* After all administrative expenses of the receiver and proved claims of creditors of the uninsured bank have been paid in full, to the extent there are receivership assets to make such payments, any remaining proceeds shall be paid to the shareholders, or their legal representatives, in proportion to their stock ownership.

§ 51.9 Termination of receivership.

If there are assets remaining after full payment of the expenses of the receiver and all claims of creditors for an uninsured bank and all fiduciary accounts of the bank have been closed or transferred to a successor fiduciary and fiduciary powers surrendered, the Comptroller shall call a meeting of the shareholders of the uninsured bank, as provided in 12 U.S.C. 197, for the shareholders to decide the manner in which the liquidation will continue. The liquidation may continue by:

(a) Continuing the receivership of the uninsured bank under the direction of the Comptroller; or

(b) Ending the receivership and oversight by the Comptroller and replacing the receiver with a liquidating agent to proceed to liquidate the remaining assets of the uninsured bank for the benefit of the shareholders, as set out in 12 U.S.C. 197.

PARTS 52–99 [RESERVED]

PART 100—RULES APPLICABLE TO SAVINGS ASSOCIATIONS

AUTHORITY: 12 U.S.C. 1462a, 1463, 5412(b)(2)(B), 5414(b)(2).

SOURCE: 76 FR 48956, Aug. 9, 2011, unless otherwise noted.

§ 100.1 Certain regulations superseded.

Effective on July 21, 2011, section 312(b)(2)(B) of the Dodd-Frank Wall Street Reform and Consumer Protection Act (Pub. L. 111–203, 124 Stat. 1376 (2010)) (12 U.S.C. 5412(b)(2)(B)) transferred rulemaking authority of the Office of Thrift Supervision (OTS) relating to all savings associations, both state and Federal to the OCC. The regulations set forth in parts 1 through 197 of this chapter I applying to Federal savings associations and state savings associations, as those terms are defined in section 3(b) of the Federal Deposit Insurance Act (12 U.S.C. 1813(b)), supersede corresponding regulations set forth in parts 500 through 591 of chapter V of the Code of Federal Regulations that were applicable to such entities prior to July 21, 2011.

[76 FR 48956, Aug. 9, 2011, as amended at 80 FR 28479, May 18, 2015]

§ 100.2 Waiver authority.

The Comptroller of the Currency may, for good cause and to the extent permitted by statute, waive the applicability of any provision of parts 1 through 197 of this chapter I, as applicable, with respect to Federal savings associations.

[76 FR 48956, Aug. 9, 2011, as amended at 80 FR 28479, May 18, 2015]

PARTS 101–107 [RESERVED]

PART 108—REMOVALS, SUSPENSIONS, AND PROHIBITIONS WHERE A CRIME IS CHARGED OR PROVEN

Sec.
108.1 Scope.
108.2 Definitions.
108.3 Issuance of Notice or Order.
108.4 Contents and service of the Notice or Order.
108.5 Petition for hearing.
108.6 Initiation of hearing.
108.7 Conduct of hearings.
108.8 Default.
108.9 Rules of evidence.
108.10 Burden of persuasion.
108.11 Relevant considerations.
108.12 Proposed findings and conclusions and recommended decision.
108.13 Decision of the OCC.
108.14 Miscellaneous.

AUTHORITY: 12 U.S.C. 1464, 1818, 5412(b)(2)(B).

SOURCE: 76 FR 48956, Aug. 9, 2011, unless otherwise noted.

§ 108.1 Scope.

The rules in this part apply to hearings, which are exempt from the adjudicative provisions of the Administrative Procedure Act, afforded to any officer, director, or other person participating in the conduct of the affairs of a Federal savings association, Federal savings association subsidiary, or affiliate service corporation, where such person has been suspended or removed from office or prohibited from further participation in the conduct of the affairs of one of the aforementioned entities by a Notice or Order served by the OCC upon the grounds set forth in section 8(g) of the Federal Deposit Insurance Act, (12 U.S.C. 1818(g)).

§ 108.2 Definitions.

As used in this part—

(a) The term *OCC* means the Office of the Comptroller of the Currency.

(b) [Reserved]

(c) The term *Notice* means a Notice of Suspension or Notice of Prohibition issued by the OCC pursuant to section 8(g) of the Federal Deposit Insurance Act.

(d) The term *Order* means an Order of Removal or Order of Prohibition issued by the OCC pursuant to section 8(g) of the Federal Deposit Insurance Act.

(e) The term *association* means a Federal savings association within the meaning of section 2(5) of the Home Owners' Loan Act of 1933, as amended, 12 U.S.C. 1462(5) ("HOLA"), Federal savings association subsidiary and an affiliate service corporation within the meaning of section 8(b)(8) of the Federal Deposit Insurance Act, as amended, 12 U.S.C. 1818(b)(8) ("FDIA").

(f) The term *subject individual* means a person served with a Notice or Order.

(g) The term *petitioner* means a subject individual who has filed a petition for informal hearing under this part.

§ 108.3 Issuance of Notice or Order.

(a) The OCC may issue and serve a Notice upon an officer, director, or other person participating in the conduct of the affairs of an association, where the individual is charged in any information, indictment, or complaint with the commission of or participation in a crime involving dishonesty or breach of trust that is punishable by imprisonment for a term exceeding one year under state or Federal law, if the OCC, upon due deliberation, determines that continued service or participation by the individual may pose a threat to the interests of the association's depositors or may threaten to impair public confidence in the association. The Notice shall remain in effect until the information, indictment, or complaint is finally disposed of or until terminated by the OCC.

(b) The OCC may issue and serve an Order upon a subject individual against whom a judgment of conviction, or an agreement to enter a pretrial diversion or other similar program has been rendered, where such judgment is not subject to further appellate review, and the OCC, upon the deliberation, has determined that continued service or participation by the subject individual may pose a threat to the interests of the association's depositors or may threaten to impair public confidence in the association.

§ 108.4 Contents and service of the Notice or Order.

(a) The Notice or Order shall set forth the basis and facts in support of the OCC's issuance of such Notice or Order, and shall inform the subject individual of his right to a hearing, in accordance with this part, for the purpose of determining whether the Notice or Order should be continued, terminated, or otherwise modified.

(b) The OCC shall serve a copy of the Notice or Order upon the subject individual and the related association in the manner set forth in § 109.11 of this chapter.

(c) Upon receipt of the Notice or Order, the subject individual shall immediately comply with the requirements thereof.

§ 108.5 Petition for hearing.

(a) To obtain a hearing, the subject individual must file two copies of a petition with the OCC within 30 days of being served with the Notice or Order.

(b) The petition filed under this section shall admit or deny specifically each allegation in the Notice or Order, unless the petitioner is without knowledge or information, in which case the petition shall so state and the statement shall have the effect of a denial. Any allegation not denied shall be deemed to be admitted. When a petitioner intends in good faith to deny only a part of or to qualify an allegation, he shall specify so much of it as is true and shall deny only the remainder.

(c) The petition shall state whether the petitioner is requesting termination or modification of the Notice or Order, and shall state with particularity how the petitioner intends to show that his continued service to or participation in the conduct of the affairs of the association would not, or is not likely to, pose a threat to the interests of the association's depositors or to impair public confidence in the association.

§ 108.6 Initiation of hearing.

(a) Within 10 days of the filing of a petition for hearing, the OCC shall notify the petitioner of the time and place fixed for hearing, and it shall designate one or more OCC employees to serve as presiding officer.

(b) The hearing shall be scheduled to be held no later than 30 days from the date the petition was filed, unless the time is extended at the request of the petitioner.

(c) A petitioner may appear personally or through counsel, but if represented by counsel, said counsel is required to comply with § 109.6 of this chapter.

(d) A representative(s) of the OCC's Enforcement and Compliance Division also may attend the hearing and participate therein as a party.

§ 108.7 Conduct of hearings.

(a) Hearings provided by this section are not subject to the adjudicative provisions of the Administrative Procedure Act (5 U.S.C. 554–557). The presiding officer is, however, authorized to exercise all of the powers enumerated in § 109.5 of this chapter.

(b) Witnesses may be presented, within time limits specified by the presiding officer, provided that at least 10 days prior to the hearing date, the party presenting the witnesses furnishes the presiding officer and the opposing party with a list of such witnesses and a summary of the proposed testimony. However, the requirement for furnishing such a witness list and summary of testimony shall not apply to the presentation of rebuttal witnesses. The presiding officer may ask questions of any witness, and each party shall have an opportunity to cross-examine any witness presented by an opposing party.

(c) Upon the request of either the petitioner or a representative of the Enforcement and Compliance Division, the record shall remain open for a period of 5 business days following the hearing, during which time the parties may make any additional submissions for the record. Thereafter, the record shall be closed.

(d) Following the introduction of all evidence, the petitioner and the representative of the Enforcement and Compliance Division shall have an opportunity for oral argument; however, the parties may jointly waive the right to oral argument, and, in lieu thereof, elect to submit written argument.

(e) All oral testimony and oral argument shall be recorded, and transcripts made available to the petitioner upon payment of the cost thereof. A copy of the transcript shall be sent directly to the presiding officer, who shall have authority to correct the record *sua sponte* or upon the motion of any party.

(f) The parties may, in writing, jointly waive an oral hearing and instead elect a hearing upon a written record in which all evidence and argument would be submitted to the presiding officer in documentary form and statements of individuals would be made by affidavit.

§ 108.8 Default.

If the subject individual fails to file a petition for a hearing, or fails to appear at a hearing, either in person or by attorney, or fails to submit a written argument where oral argument has been waived pursuant to § 108.7(d) or (f) of this part, the Notice shall remain in effect until the information, indictment, or complaint is finally disposed of and the Order shall remain in effect until terminated by the OCC.

§ 108.9 Rules of evidence.

(a) Formal rules of evidence shall not apply to a hearing, but the presiding officer may limit the introduction of irrelevant, immaterial, or unduly repetitious evidence.

(b) All matters officially noticed by the presiding officer shall appear on the record.

§ 108.10 Burden of persuasion.

The petitioner has the burden of showing, by a preponderance of the evidence, that his or her continued service to or participation in the conduct of the affairs of the association does not, or is not likely to, pose a threat to the interests of the association's depositors or threaten to impair public confidence in the association.

§ 108.11 Relevant considerations.

(a) In determining whether the petitioner has shown that his or her continued service to or participation in the conduct of the affairs of the association would not, or is not likely to, pose a threat to the interests of the association's depositors or threaten to impair public confidence in the association, in order to decide whether the Notice or Order should be continued, terminated, or otherwise modified, the OCC will consider:

(1) The nature and extent of the petitioner's participation in the affairs of the association;

(2) The nature of the offense with which the petitioner has been charged;

(3) The extent of the publicity accorded the indictment and trial; and

(4) Such other relevant factors as may be entered on the record.

(b) When considering a request for the termination or modification of a Notice, the OCC will not consider the ultimate guilt or innocence of the petitioner with respect to the criminal charge that is outstanding.

(c) When considering a request for the termination or modification of an Order which has been issued following a final judgment of conviction against a subject individual, the OCC will not collaterally review such final judgment of conviction.

§ 108.12 Proposed findings and conclusions and recommended decision.

(a) Within 30 days after completion of oral argument or the submission of written argument where oral argument has been waived, the presiding officer shall file with and certify to the OCC for decision the entire record of the hearing, which shall include a recommended decision, the Notice or Order, and all other documents filed in connection with the hearing.

(b) The recommended decision shall contain:

(1) A statement of the issue(s) presented,

(2) A statement of findings and conclusions, and the reasons or basis therefor, on all material issues of fact, law, or discretion presented on the record, and

(3) An appropriate recommendation as to whether the suspension, removal, or prohibition should be continued, modified, or terminated.

§ 108.13 Decision of the OCC.

(a) Within 30 days after the recommended decision has been certified to the OCC, the OCC shall issue a final decision.

(b) The OCC's final decision shall contain a statement of the basis therefor. The OCC may satisfy this requirement where it adopts the recommended decision of the presiding officer upon finding that the recommended decision satisfies the requirements of § 109.38 of this chapter.

(c) The OCC shall serve upon the petitioner and the representative of the Enforcement and Compliance Division a copy of the OCC's final decision and the related recommended decision.

§ 108.14 Miscellaneous.

The provisions of §§ 109.10, 109.11, and 109.12 of this chapter shall apply to proceedings under this part.

PART 109—RULES OF PRACTICE AND PROCEDURE IN ADJUDICATORY PROCEEDINGS

Subpart A—Uniform Rules of Practice and Procedure

Sec.
109.1 Scope.

109.2 Rules of construction.
109.3 Definitions.
109.4 Authority of the Comptroller.
109.5 Authority of the administrative law judge.
109.6 Appearance and practice in adjudicatory proceedings.
109.7 Good faith certification.
109.8 Conflicts of interest.
109.9 Ex parte communications.
109.10 Filing of papers.
109.11 Service of papers.
109.12 Construction of time limits.
109.13 Change of time limits.
109.14 Witness fees and expenses.
109.15 Opportunity for informal settlement.
109.16 OCC's right to conduct examination.
109.17 Collateral attacks on adjudicatory proceeding.
109.18 Commencement of proceeding and contents of notice.
109.19 Answer.
109.20 Amended pleadings.
109.21 Failure to appear.
109.22 Consolidation and severance of actions.
109.23 Motions.
109.24 Scope of document discovery.
109.25 Request for document discovery from parties.
109.26 Document subpoenas to nonparties.
109.27 Deposition of witness unavailable for hearing.
109.28 Interlocutory review.
109.29 Summary disposition.
109.30 Partial summary disposition.
109.31 Scheduling and prehearing conferences.
109.32 Prehearing submissions.
109.33 Public hearings.
109.34 Hearing subpoenas.
109.35 Conduct of hearings.
109.36 Evidence.
109.37 Post-hearing filings.
109.38 Recommended decision and filing of record.
109.39 Exceptions to recommended decision.
109.40 Review by the Comptroller.
109.41 Stays pending judicial review.

Subpart B—Local Rules

109.100 Scope.
109.101 Appointment of Office of Financial Institution Adjudication.
109.102 Discovery.
109.103 Civil money penalties.
109.104 Additional procedures.

Subparts C–D [Reserved]

AUTHORITY: 5 U.S.C. 504, 554–557; 12 U.S.C. 1464, 1467, 1467a, 1468, 1817, 1818, 1820(k), 1829(e), 1832, 1884, 1972, 3349, 4717, 5412(b)(2)(B); 15 U.S.C. 78(l), 78o–5, 78u–2, 1639e; 28 U.S.C. 2461 note; 31 U.S.C. 5321; and 42 U.S.C. 4012a.

SOURCE: 76 FR 48957, Aug. 9, 2011, unless otherwise noted.

Subpart A—Uniform Rules of Practice and Procedure

§ 109.1 Scope.

This subpart prescribes Uniform Rules of practice and procedure with regard to Federal savings associations applicable to adjudicatory proceedings as to which hearings on the record are provided for by the following statutory provisions:

(a) Cease-and-desist proceedings under section 8(b) of the Federal Deposit Insurance Act (FDIA) (12 U.S.C. 1818(b));

(b) Removal and prohibition proceedings under section 8(e) of the FDIA (12 U.S.C. 1818(e));

(c) Change-in-control proceedings under section 7(j)(4) of the FDIA (12 U.S.C. 1817(j)(4)) to determine whether the OCC should issue an order to approve or disapprove a person's proposed acquisition of an institution;

(d) Proceedings under section 15C(c)(2) of the Securities Exchange Act of 1934 (Exchange Act) (15 U.S.C. 78o–5), to impose sanctions upon any government securities broker or dealer or upon any person associated or seeking to become associated with a government securities broker or dealer for which the OCC is the appropriate agency.

(e) Assessment of civil money penalties by the OCC against institutions, institution-affiliated parties, and certain other persons for which it is the appropriate agency for any violation of:

(1) Section 5 of the Home Owners' Loan Act (HOLA) or any regulation or order issued thereunder, pursuant to 12 U.S.C. 1464 (d), (s) and (v);

(2) Section 9 of the HOLA or any regulation or order issued thereunder, pursuant to 12 U.S.C. 1467(d);

(3) Section 10 of the HOLA, pursuant to 12 U.S.C. 1467a (i) and (r);

(4) Any provisions of the Change in Bank Control Act, any regulation or order issued thereunder or certain unsafe or unsound practices or breaches of fiduciary duty, pursuant to 12 U.S.C. 1817(j)(16);

(5) Sections 22(h) and 23 of the Federal Reserve Act, or any regulation issued thereunder or certain unsafe or unsound practices or breaches of fiduciary duty, pursuant to 12 U.S.C. 1468;

(6) Certain provisions of the Exchange Act, pursuant to section 21B of the Exchange Act (15 U.S.C. 78u–2);

(7) Section 1120 of Financial Institutions Reform, Recovery and Enforcement Act of 1989 (12 U.S.C. 3349), or any order or regulation issued thereunder;

(8) The terms of any final or temporary order issued or enforceable pursuant to section 8 of the FDIA or of any written agreement executed by the OCC, the terms of any conditions imposed in writing by the OCC in connection with the grant of an application or request, certain unsafe or unsound practices or breaches of fiduciary duty, or any law or regulation not otherwise provided herein pursuant to 12 U.S.C. 1818(i)(2);

(9) Any provision of law referenced in section 102 of the Flood Disaster Protection Act of 1973 (42 U.S.C. 4012a(f)) or any order or regulation issued thereunder; and

(10) Any provision of law referenced in 31 U.S.C. 5321 or any order or regulation issued thereunder;

(f) Remedial action under section 102 of the Flood Disaster Protection Act of 1973 (42 U.S.C. 4012a(g));

(g) Proceedings under section 10(k) of the FDIA (12 U.S.C. 1820(k)) to impose penalties on senior examiners for violation of post-employment prohibitions; and

(h) This subpart also applies to all other adjudications required by statute to be determined on the record after opportunity for an agency hearing, unless otherwise specifically provided for in the Local Rules.

(i) [Reserved]

§ 109.2 Rules of construction.

For purposes of this subpart:

(a) Any term in the singular includes the plural, and the plural includes the singular, if such use would be appropriate;

(b) Any use of a masculine, feminine, or neuter gender encompasses all three, if such use would be appropriate;

(c) The term *counsel* includes a non-attorney representative; and

(d) Unless the context requires otherwise, a party's counsel of record, if any, may, on behalf of that party, take any action required to be taken by the party.

§ 109.3 Definitions.

For purposes of this subpart, unless explicitly stated to the contrary:

(a) *Administrative law judge* means one who presides at an administrative hearing under authority set forth at 5 U.S.C. 556.

(b) *Adjudicatory proceeding* means a proceeding conducted pursuant to these rules and leading to the formulation of a final order other than a regulation.

(c) *Decisional employee* means any member of the OCC's or administrative law judge's staff who has not engaged in an investigative or prosecutorial role in a proceeding and who may assist the OCC or the administrative law judge, respectively, in preparing orders, recommended decisions, decisions, and other documents under the Uniform Rules.

(d) *Comptroller* means the Comptroller of the Currency or his or her designee.

(e) *Enforcement Counsel* means any individual who files a notice of appearance as counsel on behalf of the OCC in an adjudicatory proceeding.

(f) *Final order* means an order issued by the OCC with or without the consent of the affected institution or the institution-affiliated party that has become final, without regard to the pendency of any petition for reconsideration or review.

(g) *Institution* includes any Federal savings association as that term is defined in section 3(b) of the FDIA (12 U.S.C. 1813(b)).

(h) *Institution-affiliated party* means any institution-affiliated party as that term is defined in section 3(u) of the FDIA (12 U.S.C. 1813(u)).

(i) *Local Rules* means those rules found in subpart B of this part.

(j) *OCC* means the Office of the Comptroller of the Currency.

(k) *Office of Financial Institution Adjudication* (OFIA) means the executive body charged with overseeing the administration of administrative enforcement proceedings for the OCC, the

Board of Governors of the Federal Reserve Board, the Federal Deposit Insurance Corporation, and the National Credit Union Administration.

(l) *Party* means the OCC and any person named as a party in any notice.

(m) *Person* means an individual, sole proprietor, partnership, corporation, unincorporated association, trust, joint venture, pool, syndicate, agency or other entity or organization, including an institution as defined in paragraph (g) of this section.

(n) *Respondent* means any party other than the OCC.

(o) *Uniform Rules* means those rules in subpart A of this part.

(p) *Violation* includes any action (alone or with another or others) for or toward causing, bringing about, participating in, counseling, or aiding or abetting a violation.

§ 109.4 Authority of the Comptroller.

The Comptroller may, at any time during the pendency of a proceeding perform, direct the performance of, or waive performance of, any act which could be done or ordered by the administrative law judge.

§ 109.5 Authority of the administrative law judge.

(a) *General rule.* All proceedings governed by this part shall be conducted in accordance with the provisions of chapter 5 of title 5 of the United States Code. The administrative law judge shall have all powers necessary to conduct a proceeding in a fair and impartial manner and to avoid unnecessary delay.

(b) *Powers.* The administrative law judge shall have all powers necessary to conduct the proceeding in accordance with paragraph (a) of this section, including the following powers:

(1) To administer oaths and affirmations;

(2) To issue subpoenas, subpoenas *duces tecum*, and protective orders, as authorized by this part, and to quash or modify any such subpoenas and orders;

(3) To receive relevant evidence and to rule upon the admission of evidence and offers of proof;

(4) To take or cause depositions to be taken as authorized by this subpart;

(5) To regulate the course of the hearing and the conduct of the parties and their counsel;

(6) To hold scheduling and/or pre-hearing conferences as set forth in § 109.31 of this subpart;

(7) To consider and rule upon all procedural and other motions appropriate in an adjudicatory proceeding, provided that only the Comptroller shall have the power to grant any motion to dismiss the proceeding or to decide any other motion that results in a final determination of the merits of the proceeding;

(8) To prepare and present to the Comptroller a recommended decision as provided herein;

(9) To recuse himself or herself by motion made by a party or on his or her own motion;

(10) To establish time, place and manner limitations on the attendance of the public and the media for any public hearing; and

(11) To do all other things necessary and appropriate to discharge the duties of a presiding officer.

§ 109.6 Appearance and practice in adjudicatory proceedings.

(a) *Appearance before the OCC or an administrative law judge*—(1) *By attorneys.* Any member in good standing of the bar of the highest court of any state, commonwealth, possession, territory of the United States, or the District of Columbia may represent others before the OCC if such attorney is not currently suspended or debarred from practice before the OCC.

(2) *By non-attorneys.* An individual may appear on his or her own behalf; a member of a partnership may represent the partnership; a duly authorized officer, director, or employee of any government unit, agency, institution, corporation or authority may represent that unit, agency, institution, corporation or authority if such officer, director, or employee is not currently suspended or debarred from practice before the OCC.

(3) *Notice of appearance.* Any individual acting as counsel on behalf of a party, including the Comptroller, shall file a notice of appearance with OFIA at or before the time that individual submits papers or otherwise appears on

behalf of a party in the adjudicatory proceeding. The notice of appearance must include a written declaration that the individual is currently qualified as provided in paragraph (a)(1) or (a)(2) of this section and is authorized to represent the particular party. By filing a notice of appearance on behalf of a party in an adjudicatory proceeding, the counsel agrees and represents that he or she is authorized to accept service on behalf of the represented party and that, in the event of withdrawal from representation, he or she will, if required by the administrative law judge, continue to accept service until new counsel has filed a notice of appearance or until the represented party indicates that he or she will proceed on a *pro se* basis.

(b) *Sanctions.* Dilatory, obstructionist, egregious, contemptuous or contumacious conduct at any phase of any adjudicatory proceeding may be grounds for exclusion or suspension of counsel from the proceeding.

§ 109.7 Good faith certification.

(a) *General requirement.* Every filing or submission of record following the issuance of a notice shall be signed by at least one counsel of record in his or her individual name and shall state that counsel's address and telephone number. A party who acts as his or her own counsel shall sign his or her individual name and state his or her address and telephone number on every filing or submission of record.

(b) *Effect of signature.* (1) The signature of counsel or a party shall constitute a certification that: the counsel or party has read the filing or submission of record; to the best of his or her knowledge, information, and belief formed after reasonable inquiry, the filing or submission of record is well-grounded in fact and is warranted by existing law or a good faith argument for the extension, modification, or reversal of existing law; and the filing or submission of record is not made for any improper purpose, such as to harass or to cause unnecessary delay or needless increase in the cost of litigation.

(2) If a filing or submission of record is not signed, the administrative law judge shall strike the filing or submission of record, unless it is signed promptly after the omission is called to the attention of the pleader or movant.

(c) *Effect of making oral motion or argument.* The act of making any oral motion or oral argument by any counsel or party constitutes a certification that to the best of his or her knowledge, information, and belief formed after reasonable inquiry, his or her statements are well-grounded in fact and are warranted by existing law or a good faith argument for the extension, modification, or reversal of existing law, and are not made for any improper purpose, such as to harass or to cause unnecessary delay or needless increase in the cost of litigation.

§ 109.8 Conflicts of interest.

(a) *Conflict of interest in representation.* No person shall appear as counsel for another person in an adjudicatory proceeding if it reasonably appears that such representation may be materially limited by that counsel's responsibilities to a third person or by the counsel's own interests. The administrative law judge may take corrective measures at any stage of a proceeding to cure a conflict of interest in representation, including the issuance of an order limiting the scope of representation or disqualifying an individual from appearing in a representative capacity for the duration of the proceeding.

(b) *Certification and waiver.* If any person appearing as counsel represents two or more parties to an adjudicatory proceeding or also represents a non-party on a matter relevant to an issue in the proceeding, counsel must certify in writing at the time of filing the notice of appearance required by § 109.6(a):

(1) That the counsel has personally and fully discussed the possibility of conflicts of interest with each such party and non-party; and

(2) That each such party and non-party waives any right it might otherwise have had to assert any known conflicts of interest or to assert any non-material conflicts of interest during the course of the proceeding.

§ 109.9 Ex parte communications.

(a) *Definition*—(1) *Ex parte communication* means any material oral or written communication relevant to the merits of an adjudicatory proceeding that was neither on the record nor on reasonable prior notice to all parties that takes place between:

(i) An interested person outside the OCC (including such person's counsel); and

(ii) The administrative law judge handling that proceeding, the Comptroller, or a decisional employee.

(2) *Exception.* A request for status of the proceeding does not constitute an *ex parte* communication.

(b) *Prohibition of ex parte communications.* From the time the notice is issued by the Comptroller until the date that the Comptroller issues the final decision pursuant to § 109.40(c) of this subpart:

(1) No interested person outside the OCC shall make or knowingly cause to be made an *ex parte* communication to the Comptroller, the administrative law judge, or a decisional employee; and

(2) The Comptroller, administrative law judge, or decisional employee shall not make or knowingly cause to be made to any interested person outside the OCC any *ex parte* communication.

(c) *Procedure upon occurrence of ex parte communication.* If an ex parte communication is received by the administrative law judge, the Comptroller or other person identified in paragraph (a) of this section, that person shall cause all such written communications (or, if the communication is oral, a memorandum stating the substance of the communication) to be placed on the record of the proceeding and served on all parties. All other parties to the proceeding shall have an opportunity, within ten days of receipt of service of the ex parte communication to file responses thereto and to recommend any sanctions, in accordance with paragraph (d) of this section, that they believe to be appropriate under the circumstances.

(d) *Sanctions.* Any party or his or her counsel who makes a prohibited *ex parte* communication, or who encourages or solicits another to make any such communication, may be subject to any appropriate sanction or sanctions imposed by the Comptroller or the administrative law judge including, but not limited to, exclusion from the proceedings and an adverse ruling on the issue which is the subject of the prohibited communication.

(e) *Separation-of-functions.* Except to the extent required for the disposition of *ex parte* matters as authorized by law, the administrative law judge may not consult a person or party on any matter relevant to the merits of the adjudication, unless on notice and opportunity for all parties to participate. An employee or agent engaged in the performance of investigative or prosecuting functions for the OCC in a case may not, in that or a factually related case, participate or advise in the decision, recommended decision, or agency review of the recommended decision under § 109.40 of this subpart, except as witness or counsel in public proceedings.

§ 109.10 Filing of papers.

(a) *Filing.* Any papers required to be filed, excluding documents produced in response to a discovery request pursuant to §§ 109.25 and 109.26 of this subpart, shall be filed with the OFIA, except as otherwise provided.

(b) *Manner of filing.* Unless otherwise specified by the Comptroller or the administrative law judge, filing may be accomplished by:

(1) Personal service;

(2) Delivering the papers to a reliable commercial courier service, overnight delivery service, or to the U.S. Post Office for Express Mail delivery;

(3) Mailing the papers by first class, registered, or certified mail; or

(4) Transmission by electronic media, only if expressly authorized, and upon any conditions specified, by the Comptroller or the administrative law judge. All papers filed by electronic media shall also concurrently be filed in accordance with paragraph (c) of this section as to form.

(c) *Formal requirements as to papers filed*—(1) *Form.* All papers filed must set forth the name, address, and telephone number of the counsel or party making the filing and must be accompanied by a certification setting forth when and how service has been made on all other parties. All papers filed must be double-spaced and printed or typewritten on 8½ × 11 inch paper, and must be clear and legible.

(2) *Signature.* All papers must be dated and signed as provided in § 109.7 of this subpart.

(3) *Caption.* All papers filed must include at the head thereof, or on a title page, the name of the OCC and of the filing party, the title and docket number of the proceeding, and the subject of the particular paper.

(4) *Number of copies.* Unless otherwise specified by the Comptroller, or the administrative law judge, an original and one copy of all documents and papers shall be filed, except that only one copy of transcripts of testimony and exhibits shall be filed.

§ 109.11 Service of papers.

(a) *By the parties.* Except as otherwise provided, a party filing papers shall serve a copy upon the counsel of record for all other parties to the proceeding so represented, and upon any party not so represented.

(b) *Method of service.* Except as provided in paragraphs (c)(2) and (d) of this section, a serving party shall use one or more of the following methods of service:

(1) Personal service;

(2) Delivering the papers to a reliable commercial courier service, overnight delivery service, or to the U.S. Post Office for Express Mail delivery;

(3) Mailing the papers by first class, registered, or certified mail; or

(4) Transmission by electronic media, only if the parties mutually agree. Any papers served by electronic media shall also concurrently be served in accordance with the requirements of § 109.10(c) of this subpart as to form.

(c) *By the Comptroller or the administrative law judge.* (1) All papers required to be served by the Comptroller or the administrative law judge upon a party who has appeared in the proceeding through a counsel of record, shall be served by any means specified in paragraph (b) of this section.

(2) If a party has not appeared in the proceeding in accordance with § 109.6 of this subpart, the Comptroller or the administrative law judge shall make service by any of the following methods:

(i) By personal service;

(ii) If the person to be served is an individual, by delivery to a person of suitable age and discretion at the physical location where the individual resides or works;

(iii) If the person to be served is a corporation or other association, by delivery to an officer, managing or general agent, or to any other agent authorized by appointment or by law to receive service and, if the agent is one authorized by statute to receive service and the statute so requires, by also mailing a copy to the party;

(iv) By registered or certified mail addressed to the person's last known address; or

(v) By any other method reasonably calculated to give actual notice.

(d) *Subpoenas.* Service of a subpoena may be made:

(1) By personal service;

(2) If the person to be served is an individual, by delivery to a person of suitable age and discretion at the physical location where the individual resides or works;

(3) By delivery to an agent, which in the case of a corporation or other association, is delivery to an officer, managing or general agent, or to any other agent authorized by appointment or by law to receive service and, if the agent is one authorized by statute to receive service and the statute so requires, by also mailing a copy to the party;

(4) By registered or certified mail addressed to the person's last known address; or

(5) By any other method reasonably calculated to give actual notice.

(e) *Area of service.* Service in any state, territory, possession of the United States, or the District of Columbia, on any person or company doing business in any state, territory, possession of the United States, or the District of Columbia, or on any person as otherwise provided by law, is effective without regard to the place where the hearing is held, provided that if service is made on a foreign bank in connection with an action or proceeding involving one or more of its branches or agencies located in any state, territory, possession of the

United States, or the District of Columbia, service shall be made on at least one branch or agency so involved.

§ 109.12 Construction of time limits.

(a) *General rule.* In computing any period of time prescribed by this subpart, the date of the act or event that commences the designated period of time is not included. The last day so computed is included unless it is a Saturday, Sunday, or Federal holiday. When the last day is a Saturday, Sunday, or Federal holiday, the period runs until the end of the next day that is not a Saturday, Sunday, or Federal holiday. Intermediate Saturdays, Sundays, and Federal holidays are included in the computation of time. However, when the time period within which an act is to be performed is ten days or less, not including any additional time allowed for in paragraph (c) of this section, intermediate Saturdays, Sundays, and Federal holidays are not included.

(b) *When papers are deemed to be filed or served.* (1) Filing and service are deemed to be effective:

(i) In the case of personal service or same day commercial courier delivery, upon actual service;

(ii) In the case of overnight commercial delivery service, U.S. Express mail delivery, or first class, registered, or certified mail, upon deposit in or delivery to an appropriate point of collection; or

(iii) In the case of transmission by electronic media, as specified by the authority receiving the filing, in the case of filing, and as agreed among the parties, in the case of service.

(2) The effective filing and service dates specified in paragraph (b)(1) of this section may be modified by the Comptroller or administrative law judge in the case of filing or by agreement of the parties in the case of service.

(c) *Calculation of time for service and filing of responsive papers.* Whenever a time limit is measured by a prescribed period from the service of any notice or paper, the applicable time limits are calculated as follows:

(1) If service is made by first class, registered, or certified mail, add three calendar days to the prescribed period;

(2) If service is made by express mail or overnight delivery service, add one calendar day to the prescribed period; or

(3) If service is made by electronic media transmission, add one calendar day to the prescribed period, unless otherwise determined by the Comptroller or the administrative law judge in the case of filing, or by agreement among the parties in the case of service.

§ 109.13 Change of time limits.

Except as otherwise provided by law, the administrative law judge may, for good cause shown, extend the time limits prescribed by the Uniform Rules or any notice or order issued in the proceedings. After the referral of the case to the Comptroller pursuant to § 109.38 of this subpart, the Comptroller may grant extensions of the time limits for good cause shown. Extensions may be granted at the motion of a party or on the Comptroller's or the administrative law judge's own motion after notice and opportunity to respond is afforded all non-moving parties.

§ 109.14 Witness fees and expenses.

Witnesses subpoenaed for testimony or deposition shall be paid the same fees for attendance and mileage as are paid in the United States district courts in proceedings in which the United States is a party, provided that, in the case of a discovery subpoena addressed to a party, no witness fees or mileage need be paid. Fees for witnesses shall be tendered in advance by the party requesting the subpoena, except that fees and mileage need not be tendered in advance where the OCC is the party requesting the subpoena. The OCC shall not be required to pay any fees to, or expenses of, any witness not subpoenaed by the OCC.

§ 109.15 Opportunity for informal settlement.

Any respondent may, at any time in the proceeding, unilaterally submit to Enforcement Counsel written offers or proposals for settlement of a proceeding, without prejudice to the rights of any of the parties. No such offer or proposal shall be made to any

OCC representative other than Enforcement Counsel. Submission of a written settlement offer does not provide a basis for adjourning or otherwise delaying all or any portion of a proceeding under this part. No settlement offer or proposal, or any subsequent negotiation or resolution, is admissible as evidence in any proceeding.

§ 109.16 OCC's right to conduct examination.

Nothing contained in this subpart limits in any manner the right of the OCC to conduct any examination, inspection, or visitation of any institution or institution-affiliated party, or the right of the OCC to conduct or continue any form of investigation authorized by law.

§ 109.17 Collateral attacks on adjudicatory proceeding.

If an interlocutory appeal or collateral attack is brought in any court concerning all or any part of an adjudicatory proceeding, the challenged adjudicatory proceeding shall continue without regard to the pendency of that court proceeding. No default or other failure to act as directed in the adjudicatory proceeding within the times prescribed in this subpart shall be excused based on the pendency before any court of any interlocutory appeal or collateral attack.

§ 109.18 Commencement of proceeding and contents of notice.

(a) *Commencement of proceeding.* (1)(i) Except for change-in-control proceedings under section 7(j)(4) of the FDIA (12 U.S.C. 1817(j)(4)), a proceeding governed by this subpart is commenced by issuance of a notice by the Comptroller.

(ii) The notice must be served by the Comptroller upon the respondent and given to any other appropriate financial institution supervisory authority where required by law.

(iii) The notice must be filed with the OFIA.

(2) Change-in control proceedings under section 7(j)(4) of the FDIA (12 U.S.C. 1817(j)(4)) commence with the issuance of an order by the Comptroller.

(b) *Contents of notice.* The notice must set forth:

(1) The legal authority for the proceeding and for the OCC's jurisdiction over the proceeding;

(2) A statement of the matters of fact or law showing that the OCC is entitled to relief;

(3) A proposed order or prayer for an order granting the requested relief;

(4) The time, place, and nature of the hearing as required by law or regulation;

(5) The time within which to file an answer as required by law or regulation;

(6) The time within which to request a hearing as required by law or regulation; and

(7) The answer and/or request for a hearing shall be filed with OFIA.

§ 109.19 Answer.

(a) *When.* Within 20 days of service of the notice, respondent shall file an answer as designated in the notice. In a civil money penalty proceeding, respondent shall also file a request for a hearing within 20 days of service of the notice.

(b) *Content of answer.* An answer must specifically respond to each paragraph or allegation of fact contained in the notice and must admit, deny, or state that the party lacks sufficient information to admit or deny each allegation of fact. A statement of lack of information has the effect of a denial. Denials must fairly meet the substance of each allegation of fact denied; general denials are not permitted. When a respondent denies part of an allegation, that part must be denied and the remainder specifically admitted. Any allegation of fact in the notice which is not denied in the answer must be deemed admitted for purposes of the proceeding. A respondent is not required to respond to the portion of a notice that constitutes the prayer for relief or proposed order. The answer must set forth affirmative defenses, if any, asserted by the respondent.

(c) *Default*—(1) *Effect of failure to answer.* Failure of a respondent to file an answer required by this section within the time provided constitutes a waiver of his or her right to appear and contest the allegations in the notice. If no timely answer is filed, Enforcement Counsel may file a motion for entry of an order of default. Upon a finding that no good cause has been shown for the failure to file a timely answer, the administrative law judge shall file with the Comptroller a recommended decision containing the findings and the relief sought in the notice. Any final order issued by the Comptroller based upon a respondent's failure to answer is deemed to be an order issued upon consent.

(2) *Effect of failure to request a hearing in civil money penalty proceedings.* If respondent fails to request a hearing as required by law within the time provided, the notice of assessment constitutes a final and unappealable order.

§ 109.20 Amended pleadings.

(a) *Amendments.* The notice or answer may be amended or supplemented at any stage of the proceeding. The respondent must answer an amended notice within the time remaining for the respondent's answer to the original notice, or within ten days after service of the amended notice, whichever period is longer, unless the Comptroller or administrative law judge orders otherwise for good cause.

(b) *Amendments to conform to the evidence.* When issues not raised in the notice or answer are tried at the hearing by express or implied consent of the parties, they will be treated in all respects as if they had been raised in the notice or answer, and no formal amendments are required. If evidence is objected to at the hearing on the ground that it is not within the issues raised by the notice or answer, the administrative law judge may admit the evidence when admission is likely to assist in adjudicating the merits of the action and the objecting party fails to satisfy the administrative law judge that the admission of such evidence would unfairly prejudice that party's action or defense upon the merits. The administrative law judge may grant a continuance to enable the objecting party to meet such evidence.

§ 109.21 Failure to appear.

Failure of a respondent to appear in person at the hearing or by a duly authorized counsel constitutes a waiver of respondent's right to a hearing and is deemed an admission of the facts as alleged and consent to the relief sought in the notice. Without further proceedings or notice to the respondent, the administrative law judge shall file with the Comptroller a recommended decision containing the findings and the relief sought in the notice.

§ 109.22 Consolidation and severance of actions.

(a) *Consolidation.* (1) On the motion of any party, or on the administrative law judge's own motion, the administrative law judge may consolidate, for some or all purposes, any two or more proceedings, if each such proceeding involves or arises out of the same transaction, occurrence or series of transactions or occurrences, or involves at least one common respondent or a material common question of law or fact, unless such consolidation would cause unreasonable delay or injustice.

(2) In the event of consolidation under paragraph (a)(1) of this section, appropriate adjustment to the prehearing schedule must be made to avoid unnecessary expense, inconvenience, or delay.

(b) *Severance.* The administrative law judge may, upon the motion of any party, sever the proceeding for separate resolution of the matter as to any respondent only if the administrative law judge finds that:

(1) Undue prejudice or injustice to the moving party would result from not severing the proceeding; and

(2) Such undue prejudice or injustice would outweigh the interests of judicial economy and expedition in the complete and final resolution of the proceeding.

§ 109.23 Motions.

(a) *In writing.* (1) Except as otherwise provided herein, an application or request for an order or ruling must be made by written motion.

(2) All written motions must state with particularity the relief sought and must be accompanied by a proposed order.

(3) No oral argument may be held on written motions except as otherwise directed by the administrative law judge. Written memoranda, briefs, affidavits

or other relevant material or documents may be filed in support of or in opposition to a motion.

(b) *Oral motions.* A motion may be made orally on the record unless the administrative law judge directs that such motion be reduced to writing.

(c) *Filing of motions.* Motions must be filed with the administrative law judge, but upon the filing of the recommended decision, motions must be filed with the Comptroller.

(d) *Responses.* (1) Except as otherwise provided herein, within ten days after service of any written motion, or within such other period of time as may be established by the administrative law judge or the Comptroller, any party may file a written response to a motion. The administrative law judge shall not rule on any oral or written motion before each party has had an opportunity to file a response.

(2) The failure of a party to oppose a written motion or an oral motion made on the record is deemed a consent by that party to the entry of an order substantially in the form of the order accompanying the motion.

(e) *Dilatory motions.* Frivolous, dilatory or repetitive motions are prohibited. The filing of such motions may form the basis for sanctions.

(f) *Dispositive motions.* Dispositive motions are governed by §§ 109.29 and 109.30 of this subpart.

§ 109.24 Scope of document discovery.

(a) *Limits on discovery.* (1) Subject to the limitations set out in paragraphs (b), (c), and (d) of this section, a party to a proceeding under this subpart may obtain document discovery by serving a written request to produce documents. For purposes of a request to produce documents, the term "documents" may be defined to include drawings, graphs, charts, photographs, recordings, data stored in electronic form, and other data compilations from which information can be obtained, or translated, if necessary, by the parties through detection devices into reasonably usable form, as well as written material of all kinds.

(2) Discovery by use of deposition is governed by § 109.102 of this part.

(3) Discovery by use of interrogatories is not permitted.

(b) *Relevance.* A party may obtain document discovery regarding any matter, not privileged, that has material relevance to the merits of the pending action. Any request to produce documents that calls for irrelevant material, that is unreasonable, oppressive, excessive in scope, unduly burdensome, or repetitive of previous requests, or that seeks to obtain privileged documents will be denied or modified. A request is unreasonable, oppressive, excessive in scope or unduly burdensome if, among other things, it fails to include justifiable limitations on the time period covered and the geographic locations to be searched, the time provided to respond in the request is inadequate, or the request calls for copies of documents to be delivered to the requesting party and fails to include the requestor's written agreement to pay in advance for the copying, in accordance with § 109.25 of this subpart.

(c) *Privileged matter.* Privileged documents are not discoverable. Privileges include the attorney-client privilege, work-product privilege, any government's or government agency's deliberative-process privilege, and any other privileges the Constitution, any applicable act of Congress, or the principles of common law provide.

(d) *Time limits.* All discovery, including all responses to discovery requests, shall be completed at least 20 days prior to the date scheduled for the commencement of the hearing, except as provided in the Local Rules. No exceptions to this time limit shall be permitted, unless the administrative law judge finds on the record that good cause exists for waiving the requirements of this paragraph.

§ 109.25 Request for document discovery from parties.

(a) *General rule.* Any party may serve on any other party a request to produce for inspection any discoverable documents that are in the possession, custody, or control of the party upon whom the request is served. The request must identify the documents to be produced either by individual item or by category, and must describe each item and category with reasonable particularity. Documents must be produced as they are kept in the usual course of business or must be organized to correspond with the categories in the request.

(b) *Production or copying.* The request must specify a reasonable time, place, and manner for production and performing any related acts. In lieu of inspecting the documents, the requesting party may specify that all or some of the responsive documents be copied and the copies delivered to the requesting party. If copying of fewer than 250 pages is requested, the party to whom the request is addressed shall bear the cost of copying and shipping charges. If a party requests 250 pages or more of copying, the requesting party shall pay for the copying and shipping charges. Copying charges are the current per-page copying rate imposed under 12 CFR 4.17 for requests under the Freedom of Information Act (5 U.S.C. 552). The party to whom the request is addressed may require payment in advance before producing the documents.

(c) *Obligation to update responses.* A party who has responded to a discovery request with a response that was complete when made is not required to supplement the response to include documents thereafter acquired, unless the responding party learns that:

(1) The response was materially incorrect when made; or

(2) The response, though correct when made, is no longer true and a failure to amend the response is, in substance, a knowing concealment.

(d) *Motions to limit discovery.* (1) Any party that objects to a discovery request may, within ten days of being served with such request, file a motion in accordance with the provisions of §109.23 of this subpart to revoke or otherwise limit the request. If an objection is made to only a portion of an item or category in a request, the portion objected to shall be specified. Any objections not made in accordance with this paragraph and §109.23 of this subpart are waived.

(2) The party who served the request that is the subject of a motion to revoke or limit may file a written response within five days of service of the motion. No other party may file a response.

(e) *Privilege.* At the time other documents are produced, the producing party must reasonably identify all documents withheld on the grounds of privilege and must produce a statement of the basis for the assertion of privilege. When similar documents that are protected by deliberative process, attorney-work-product, or attorney-client privilege are voluminous, these documents may be identified by category instead of by individual document. The administrative law judge retains discretion to determine when the identification by category is insufficient.

(f) *Motions to compel production.* (1) If a party withholds any documents as privileged or fails to comply fully with a discovery request, the requesting party may, within ten days of the assertion of privilege or of the time the failure to comply becomes known to the requesting party, file a motion in accordance with the provisions of §109.23 of this subpart for the issuance of a subpoena compelling production.

(2) The party who asserted the privilege or failed to comply with the request may file a written response to a motion to compel within five days of service of the motion. No other party may file a response.

(g) *Ruling on motions.* After the time for filing responses pursuant to this section has expired, the administrative law judge shall rule promptly on all motions filed pursuant to this section. If the administrative law judge determines that a discovery request, or any of its terms, calls for irrelevant material, is unreasonable, oppressive, excessive in scope, unduly burdensome, or repetitive of previous requests, or seeks to obtain privileged documents, he or she may deny or modify the request, and may issue appropriate protective orders, upon such conditions as justice may require. The pendency of a motion to strike or limit discovery or to compel production is not a basis for staying or continuing the proceeding, unless otherwise ordered by the administrative law judge. Notwithstanding any other provision in this part, the administrative law judge may not release, or order a party to produce, documents withheld on grounds of privilege if the party has stated to the administrative law judge its intention to file a timely motion for interlocutory review of the administrative law judge's order to produce the documents, and until the motion for interlocutory review has been decided.

(h) *Enforcing discovery subpoenas.* If the administrative law judge issues a subpoena compelling production of documents by a party, the subpoenaing party may, in the event of noncompliance and to the extent authorized by applicable law, apply to any appropriate United States district court for an order requiring compliance with the subpoena. A party's right to seek court enforcement of a subpoena shall not in any manner limit the sanctions that may be imposed by the administrative law judge against a party who fails to produce subpoenaed documents.

§ 109.26 Document subpoenas to nonparties.

(a) *General rules.* (1) Any party may apply to the administrative law judge for the issuance of a document discovery subpoena addressed to any person who is not a party to the proceeding. The application must contain a proposed document subpoena and a brief statement showing the general relevance and reasonableness of the scope of documents sought. The subpoenaing party shall specify a reasonable time, place, and manner for making production in response to the document subpoena.

(2) A party shall only apply for a document subpoena under this section within the time period during which such party could serve a discovery request under § 109.24(d) of this subpart. The party obtaining the document subpoena is responsible for serving it on the subpoenaed person and for serving copies on all parties. Document subpoenas may be served in any state, territory, or possession of the United States, the District of Columbia, or as otherwise provided by law.

(3) The administrative law judge shall promptly issue any document subpoena requested pursuant to this section. If the administrative law judge determines that the application does not set forth a valid basis for the issuance of the subpoena, or that any of its terms are unreasonable, oppressive, excessive in scope, or unduly burdensome, he or she may refuse to issue the subpoena or may issue it in a modified form upon such conditions as may be consistent with the Uniform Rules.

(b) *Motion to quash or modify.* (1) Any person to whom a document subpoena is directed may file a motion to quash or modify such subpoena, accompanied by a statement of the basis for quashing or modifying the subpoena. The movant shall serve the motion on all parties, and any party may respond to such motion within ten days of service of the motion.

(2) Any motion to quash or modify a document subpoena must be filed on the same basis, including the assertion of privilege, upon which a party could object to a discovery request under § 109.25(d) of this subpart, and during the same time limits during which such an objection could be filed.

(c) *Enforcing document subpoenas.* If a subpoenaed person fails to comply with any subpoena issued pursuant to this section or any order of the administrative law judge which directs compliance with all or any portion of a document subpoena, the subpoenaing party or any other aggrieved party may, to the extent authorized by applicable law, apply to an appropriate United States district court for an order requiring compliance with so much of the document subpoena as the administrative law judge has not quashed or modified. A party's right to seek court enforcement of a document subpoena shall in no way limit the sanctions that may be imposed by the administrative law judge on a party who induces a failure to comply with subpoenas issued under this section.

§ 109.27 Deposition of witness unavailable for hearing.

(a) *General rules.* (1) If a witness will not be available for the hearing, a party may apply in accordance with the procedures set forth in paragraph (a)(2) of this section, to the administrative law judge for the issuance of a subpoena, including a subpoena *duces tecum*, requiring the attendance of the witness at a deposition. The administrative law judge may issue a deposition subpoena under this section upon showing that:

(i) The witness will be unable to attend or may be prevented from attending the hearing because of age, sickness or infirmity, or will otherwise be unavailable;

(ii) The witness' unavailability was not procured or caused by the subpoenaing party;

(iii) The testimony is reasonably expected to be material; and

(iv) Taking the deposition will not result in any undue burden to any other party and will not cause undue delay of the proceeding.

(2) The application must contain a proposed deposition subpoena and a brief statement of the reasons for the issuance of the subpoena. The subpoena must name the witness whose deposition is to be taken and specify the time and place for taking the deposition. A deposition subpoena may require the witness to be deposed at any place within the country in which that witness resides or has a regular place of employment or such other convenient place as the administrative law judge shall fix.

(3) Any requested subpoena that sets forth a valid basis for its issuance must be promptly issued, unless the administrative law judge on his or her own motion, requires a written response or requires attendance at a conference concerning whether the requested subpoena should be issued.

(4) The party obtaining a deposition subpoena is responsible for serving it on the witness and for serving copies on all parties. Unless the administrative law judge orders otherwise, no deposition under this section shall be taken on fewer than ten days' notice to the witness and all parties. Deposition subpoenas may be served in any state, territory, possession of the United States, or the District of Columbia, on any person or company doing business in any state, territory, possession of the United States, or the District of Columbia, or as otherwise permitted by law.

(b) *Objections to deposition subpoenas.* (1) The witness and any party who has not had an opportunity to oppose a deposition subpoena issued under this section may file a motion with the administrative law judge to quash or modify the subpoena prior to the time for compliance specified in the subpoena, but not more than ten days after service of the subpoena.

(2) A statement of the basis for the motion to quash or modify a subpoena issued under this section must accompany the motion. The motion must be served on all parties.

(c) *Procedure upon deposition.* (1) Each witness testifying pursuant to a deposition subpoena must be duly sworn, and each party shall have the right to examine the witness. Objections to questions or documents must be in short form, stating the grounds for the objection. Failure to object to questions or documents is not deemed a waiver except where the ground for the objection might have been avoided if the objection had been timely presented. All questions, answers, and objections must be recorded.

(2) Any party may move before the administrative law judge for an order compelling the witness to answer any questions the witness has refused to answer or submit any evidence the witness has refused to submit during the deposition.

(3) The deposition must be subscribed by the witness, unless the parties and the witness, by stipulation, have waived the signing, or the witness is ill, cannot be found, or has refused to sign. If the deposition is not subscribed by the witness, the court reporter taking the deposition shall certify that the transcript is a true and complete transcript of the deposition.

(d) *Enforcing subpoenas.* If a subpoenaed person fails to comply with any order of the administrative law judge which directs compliance with all or any portion of a deposition subpoena under paragraph (b) or (c)(2) of this section, the subpoenaing party or other aggrieved party may, to the extent authorized by applicable law, apply to an appropriate United States district court for an order requiring compliance with the portions of the subpoena that the administrative law judge has ordered enforced. A party's right to seek court enforcement of a deposition subpoena in no way limits the sanctions that may be imposed by the administrative law judge on a party who fails to comply with or procures a failure to comply with, a subpoena issued under this section.

§ 109.28 Interlocutory review.

(a) *General rule.* The Comptroller may review a ruling of the administrative law judge prior to the certification of the record to the Comptroller only in accordance with the procedures set forth in this section and § 109.23 of this subpart.

(b) *Scope of review.* The Comptroller may exercise interlocutory review of a ruling of the administrative law judge if the Comptroller finds that:

(1) The ruling involves a controlling question of law or policy as to which substantial grounds exist for a difference of opinion;

(2) Immediate review of the ruling may materially advance the ultimate termination of the proceeding;

(3) Subsequent modification of the ruling at the conclusion of the proceeding would be an inadequate remedy; or

(4) Subsequent modification of the ruling would cause unusual delay or expense.

(c) *Procedure.* Any request for interlocutory review shall be filed by a party with the administrative law judge within ten days of his or her ruling and shall otherwise comply with § 109.23 of this subpart. Any party may file a response to a request for interlocutory review in accordance with § 109.23(d) of this subpart. Upon the expiration of the time for filing all responses, the administrative law judge shall refer the matter to the Comptroller for final disposition.

(d) *Suspension of proceeding.* Neither a request for interlocutory review nor any disposition of such a request by the Comptroller under this section suspends or stays the proceeding unless otherwise ordered by the administrative law judge or the Comptroller.

§ 109.29 Summary disposition.

(a) *In general.* The administrative law judge shall recommend that the Comptroller issue a final order granting a motion for summary disposition if the undisputed pleaded facts, admissions, affidavits, stipulations, documentary evidence, matters as to which official notice may be taken, and any other evidentiary materials properly submitted in connection with a motion for summary disposition show that:

(1) There is no genuine issue as to any material fact; and

(2) The moving party is entitled to a decision in its favor as a matter of law.

(b) *Filing of motions and responses.* (1) Any party who believes that there is no genuine issue of material fact to be determined and that he or she is entitled to a decision as a matter of law may move at any time for summary disposition in its favor of all or any part of the proceeding. Any party, within 20 days after service of such a motion, or within such time period as allowed by the administrative law judge, may file a response to such motion.

(2) A motion for summary disposition must be accompanied by a statement of the material facts as to which the moving party contends there is no genuine issue. Such motion must be supported by documentary evidence, which may take the form of admissions in pleadings, stipulations, depositions, investigatory depositions, transcripts, affidavits and any other evidentiary materials that the moving party contends support his or her position. The motion must also be accompanied by a brief containing the points and authorities in support of the contention of the moving party. Any party opposing a motion for summary disposition must file a statement setting forth those material facts as to which he or she contends a genuine dispute exists. Such opposition must be supported by evidence of the same type as that submitted with the motion for summary disposition and a brief containing the points and authorities in support of the contention that summary disposition would be inappropriate.

(c) *Hearing on motion.* At the request of any party or on his or her own motion, the administrative law judge may hear oral argument on the motion for summary disposition.

(d) *Decision on motion.* Following receipt of a motion for summary disposition and all responses thereto, the administrative law judge shall determine whether the moving party is entitled to summary disposition. If the administrative law judge determines that summary disposition is warranted, the administrative law judge shall submit a recommended decision to that effect to the Comptroller. If the administrative law judge finds that no party is entitled to summary disposition, he or she shall make a ruling denying the motion.

§ 109.30 Partial summary disposition.

If the administrative law judge determines that a party is entitled to summary disposition as to certain claims only, he or she shall defer submitting a recommended decision as to those claims. A hearing on the remaining issues must be ordered. Those claims for which the administrative law judge has determined that summary disposition is warranted will be addressed in the recommended decision filed at the conclusion of the hearing.

§ 109.31 Scheduling and prehearing conferences.

(a) *Scheduling conference.* Within 30 days of service of the notice or order commencing a proceeding or such other time as parties may agree, the administrative law judge shall direct counsel for all parties to meet with him or her in person at a specified time and place prior to the hearing or to confer by telephone for the purpose of scheduling the course and conduct of the proceeding. This meeting or telephone conference is called a "scheduling conference." The identification of potential witnesses, the time for and manner of discovery, and the exchange of any prehearing materials including witness lists, statements of issues, stipulations, exhibits and any other materials may also be determined at the scheduling conference.

(b) *Prehearing conferences.* The administrative law judge may, in addition to the scheduling conference, on his or her own motion or at the request of any party, direct counsel for the parties to meet with him or her (in person or by telephone) at a prehearing conference to address any or all of the following:

(1) Simplification and clarification of the issues;

(2) Stipulations, admissions of fact, and the contents, authenticity and admissibility into evidence of documents;

(3) Matters of which official notice may be taken;

(4) Limitation of the number of witnesses;

(5) Summary disposition of any or all issues;

(6) Resolution of discovery issues or disputes;

(7) Amendments to pleadings; and

(8) Such other matters as may aid in the orderly disposition of the proceeding.

(c) *Transcript.* The administrative law judge, in his or her discretion, may require that a scheduling or prehearing conference be recorded by a court reporter. A transcript of the conference and any materials filed, including orders, becomes part of the record of the proceeding. A party may obtain a copy of the transcript at its expense.

(d) *Scheduling or prehearing orders.* At or within a reasonable time following the conclusion of the scheduling conference or any prehearing conference, the administrative law judge shall serve on each party an order setting forth any agreements reached and any procedural determinations made.

§ 109.32 Prehearing submissions.

(a) Within the time set by the administrative law judge, but in no case later than 14 days before the start of the hearing, each party shall serve on every other party, his or her:

(1) Prehearing statement;

(2) Final list of witnesses to be called to testify at the hearing, including name and address of each witness and a short summary of the expected testimony of each witness;

(3) List of the exhibits to be introduced at the hearing along with a copy of each exhibit; and

(4) Stipulations of fact, if any.

(b) *Effect of failure to comply.* No witness may testify and no exhibits may be introduced at the hearing if such witness or exhibit is not listed in the prehearing submissions pursuant to paragraph (a) of this section, except for good cause shown.

§ 109.33 Public hearings.

(a) *General rule.* All hearings shall be open to the public, unless the Comptroller, in the Comptroller's discretion, determines that holding an open hearing would be contrary to the public interest. Within 20 days of service of the notice or, in the case of change-in-control proceedings under section 7(j)(4) of the FDIA (12 U.S.C. 1817(j)(4)), within 20 days from service of the hearing order, any respondent may file with the Comptroller a request for a private hearing, and any party may file a reply to such a request. A party must serve on the administrative law judge a copy of any request or reply the party files with the Comptroller. The form of, and procedure for, these requests and replies are governed by § 109.23 of this subpart. A party's failure to file a request or a reply constitutes a waiver of any objections regarding whether the hearing will be public or private.

(b) *Filing document under seal.* Enforcement Counsel, in his or her discretion, may file any document or part of a document under seal if disclosure of the document would be contrary to the public interest. The administrative law judge shall take all appropriate steps to preserve the confidentiality of such documents or parts thereof, including closing portions of the hearing to the public.

§ 109.34 Hearing subpoenas.

(a) *Issuance.* (1) Upon application of a party showing general relevance and reasonableness of scope of the testimony or other evidence sought, the administrative law judge may issue a subpoena or a subpoena duces tecum requiring the attendance of a witness at the hearing or the production of documentary or physical evidence at the hearing. The application for a hearing subpoena must also contain a proposed subpoena specifying the attendance of a witness or the production of evidence from any state, territory, or possession of the United States, the District of Columbia, or as otherwise provided by law at any designated place where the hearing is being conducted. The party making the application shall serve a copy of the application and the proposed subpoena on every other party.

(2) A party may apply for a hearing subpoena at any time before the commencement of a hearing. During a hearing, a party may make an application for a subpoena orally on the record before the administrative law judge.

(3) The administrative law judge shall promptly issue any hearing subpoena requested pursuant to this section. If the administrative law judge determines that the application does not set forth a valid basis for the issuance of the subpoena, or that any of its terms are unreasonable, oppressive, excessive in scope, or unduly burdensome, he or she may refuse to issue the subpoena or may issue it in a modified form upon any conditions consistent with this subpart. Upon issuance by the administrative law judge, the party making the application shall serve the subpoena on the person named in the subpoena and on each party.

(b) *Motion to quash or modify.* (1) Any person to whom a hearing subpoena is directed or any party may file a motion to quash or modify the subpoena, accompanied by a statement of the basis for quashing or modifying the subpoena. The movant must serve the motion on each party and on the person named in the subpoena. Any party may respond to the motion within ten days of service of the motion.

(2) Any motion to quash or modify a hearing subpoena must be filed prior to the time specified in the subpoena for compliance, but not more than ten days after the date of service of the subpoena upon the movant.

(c) *Enforcing subpoenas.* If a subpoenaed person fails to comply with any subpoena issued pursuant to this section or any order of the administrative law judge which directs compliance with all or any portion of a document subpoena, the subpoenaing party or any other aggrieved party may seek enforcement of the subpoena pursuant to § 109.26(c) of this subpart.

§ 109.35 Conduct of hearings.

(a) *General rules.* (1) Hearings shall be conducted so as to provide a fair and expeditious presentation of the relevant disputed issues. Each party has the right to present its case or defense by oral and documentary evidence and to conduct such cross examination as may be required for full disclosure of the facts.

(2) *Order of hearing.* Enforcement Counsel shall present its case-in-chief first, unless otherwise ordered by the administrative law judge, or unless otherwise expressly specified by law or regulation. Enforcement Counsel shall be the first party to present an opening statement and a closing statement, and may make a rebuttal statement after the respondent's closing statement. If there are multiple respondents, respondents may agree among themselves as to their order of presentation of their cases, but if they do not agree the administrative law judge shall fix the order.

(3) *Examination of witnesses.* Only one counsel for each party may conduct an examination of a witness, except that in the case of extensive direct examination, the administrative law judge may permit more than one counsel for the party presenting the witness to conduct the examination. A party may have one counsel conduct the direct examination and another counsel conduct re-direct examination of a witness, or may have one counsel conduct the cross examination of a witness and another counsel conduct the re-cross examination of a witness.

(4) *Stipulations.* Unless the administrative law judge directs otherwise, all stipulations of fact and law previously agreed upon by the parties, and all documents, the admissibility of which have been previously stipulated, will be admitted into evidence upon commencement of the hearing.

(b) *Transcript.* The hearing must be recorded and transcribed. The reporter will make the transcript available to any party upon payment by that party to the reporter of the cost of the transcript. The administrative law judge may order the record corrected, either upon motion to correct, upon stipulation of the parties, or following notice to the parties upon the administrative law judge's own motion.

§ 109.36 Evidence.

(a) *Admissibility.* (1) Except as is otherwise set forth in this section, relevant, material, and reliable evidence that is not unduly repetitive is admissible to the fullest extent authorized by the APA and other applicable law.

(2) Evidence that would be admissible under the Federal Rules of Evidence is admissible in a proceeding conducted pursuant to this subpart.

(3) Evidence that would be inadmissible under the Federal Rules of Evidence may not be deemed or ruled to be inadmissible in a proceeding conducted pursuant to this subpart if such evidence is relevant, material, reliable and not unduly repetitive.

(b) *Official notice.* (1) Official notice may be taken of any material fact which may be judicially noticed by a United States district court and any material information in the official public records of any Federal or state government agency.

(2) All matters officially noticed by the administrative law judge or Comptroller shall appear on the record.

(3) If official notice is requested or taken of any material fact, the parties, upon timely request, shall be afforded an opportunity to object.

(c) *Documents.* (1) A duplicate copy of a document is admissible to the same extent as the original, unless a genuine issue is raised as to whether the copy is in some material respect not a true and legible copy of the original.

(2) Subject to the requirements of paragraph (a) of this section, any document, including a report of examination, supervisory activity, inspection or visitation, prepared by the appropriate Federal banking agency, as defined in section 3(q) of the FDIA (12 U.S.C. 1813(q)), or state regulatory agency, is admissible either with or without a sponsoring witness.

(3) Witnesses may use existing or newly created charts, exhibits, calendars, calculations, outlines or other graphic material to summarize, illustrate, or simplify the presentation of testimony. Such materials may, subject to the administrative law judge's discretion, be used with or without being admitted into evidence.

(d) *Objections.* (1) Objections to the admissibility of evidence must be timely made and rulings on all objections must appear on the record.

(2) When an objection to a question or line of questioning propounded to a witness is sustained, the examining counsel may make a specific proffer on the record of what he or she expected

to prove by the expected testimony of the witness, either by representation of counsel or by direct interrogation of the witness.

(3) The administrative law judge shall retain rejected exhibits, adequately marked for identification, for the record, and transmit such exhibits to the Comptroller.

(4) Failure to object to admission of evidence or to any ruling constitutes a waiver of the objection.

(e) *Stipulations*. The parties may stipulate as to any relevant matters of fact or the authentication of any relevant documents. Such stipulations must be received in evidence at a hearing, and are binding on the parties with respect to the matters therein stipulated.

(f) *Depositions of unavailable witnesses*. (1) If a witness is unavailable to testify at a hearing, and that witness has testified in a deposition to which all parties in a proceeding had notice and an opportunity to participate, a party may offer as evidence all or any part of the transcript of the deposition, including deposition exhibits, if any.

(2) Such deposition transcript is admissible to the same extent that testimony would have been admissible had that person testified at the hearing, provided that if a witness refused to answer proper questions during the depositions, the administrative law judge may, on that basis, limit the admissibility of the deposition in any manner that justice requires.

(3) Only those portions of a deposition received in evidence at the hearing constitute a part of the record.

§ 109.37 Post-hearing filings.

(a) *Proposed findings and conclusions and supporting briefs*. (1) Using the same method of service for each party, the administrative law judge shall serve notice upon each party, that the certified transcript, together with all hearing exhibits and exhibits introduced but not admitted into evidence at the hearing, has been filed. Any party may file with the administrative law judge proposed findings of fact, proposed conclusions of law, and a proposed order within 30 days following service of this notice by the administrative law judge or within such longer period as may be ordered by the administrative law judge.

(2) Proposed findings and conclusions must be supported by citation to any relevant authorities and by page references to any relevant portions of the record. A post-hearing brief may be filed in support of proposed findings and conclusions, either as part of the same document or in a separate document. Any party who fails to file timely with the administrative law judge any proposed finding or conclusion is deemed to have waived the right to raise in any subsequent filing or submission any issue not addressed in such party's proposed finding or conclusion.

(b) *Reply briefs*. Reply briefs may be filed within 15 days after the date on which the parties' proposed findings, conclusions, and order are due. Reply briefs must be strictly limited to responding to new matters, issues, or arguments raised in another party's papers. A party who has not filed proposed findings of fact and conclusions of law or a post-hearing brief may not file a reply brief.

(c) *Simultaneous filing required*. The administrative law judge shall not order the filing by any party of any brief or reply brief in advance of the other party's filing of its brief.

§ 109.38 Recommended decision and filing of record.

(a) *Filing of recommended decision and record*. Within 45 days after expiration of the time allowed for filing reply briefs under § 109.37(b) of this subpart, the administrative law judge shall file with and certify to the Comptroller, for decision, the record of the proceeding. The record must include the administrative law judge's recommended decision, recommended findings of fact, recommended conclusions of law, and proposed order; all prehearing and hearing transcripts, exhibits, and rulings; and the motions, briefs, memoranda, and other supporting papers filed in connection with the hearing. The administrative law judge shall serve upon each party the recommended decision, findings, conclusions, and proposed order.

(b) *Filing of index*. At the same time the administrative law judge files with and certifies to the Comptroller for final determination the record of the proceeding, the administrative law judge shall furnish to the Comptroller a certified index of the entire record of the proceeding. The certified index shall include, at a minimum, an entry for each paper, document or motion filed with the administrative law judge in the proceeding, the date of the filing, and the identity of the filer. The certified index shall also include an exhibit index containing, at a minimum, an entry consisting of exhibit number and title or description for: Each exhibit introduced and admitted into evidence at the hearing; each exhibit introduced but not admitted into evidence at the hearing; each exhibit introduced and admitted into evidence after the completion of the hearing; and each exhibit introduced but not admitted into evidence after the completion of the hearing.

§ 109.39 Exceptions to recommended decision.

(a) *Filing exceptions.* Within 30 days after service of the recommended decision, findings, conclusions, and proposed order under § 109.38 of this subpart, a party may file with the Comptroller written exceptions to the administrative law judge's recommended decision, findings, conclusions or proposed order, to the admission or exclusion of evidence, or to the failure of the administrative law judge to make a ruling proposed by a party. A supporting brief may be filed at the time the exceptions are filed, either as part of the same document or in a separate document.

(b) *Effect of failure to file or raise exceptions.* (1) Failure of a party to file exceptions to those matters specified in paragraph (a) of this section within the time prescribed is deemed a waiver of objection thereto.

(2) No exception need be considered by the Comptroller if the party taking exception had an opportunity to raise the same objection, issue, or argument before the administrative law judge and failed to do so.

(c) *Contents.* (1) All exceptions and briefs in support of such exceptions must be confined to the particular matters in, or omissions from, the administrative law judge's recommendations to which that party takes exception.

(2) All exceptions and briefs in support of exceptions must set forth page or paragraph references to the specific parts of the administrative law judge's recommendations to which exception is taken, the page or paragraph references to those portions of the record relied upon to support each exception, and the legal authority relied upon to support each exception.

§ 109.40 Review by the Comptroller.

(a) *Notice of submission to the Comptroller.* When the Comptroller determines that the record in the proceeding is complete, the Comptroller shall serve notice upon the parties that the proceeding has been submitted to the Comptroller for final decision.

(b) *Oral argument before the Comptroller.* Upon the initiative of the Comptroller or on the written request of any party filed with the Comptroller within the time for filing exceptions, the Comptroller may order and hear oral argument on the recommended findings, conclusions, decision, and order of the administrative law judge. A written request by a party must show good cause for oral argument and state reasons why arguments cannot be presented adequately in writing. A denial of a request for oral argument may be set forth in the Comptroller's final decision. Oral argument before the Comptroller must be on the record.

(c) *Comptroller's final decision.* (1) Decisional employees may advise and assist the Comptroller in the consideration and disposition of the case. The final decision of the Comptroller will be based upon review of the entire record of the proceeding, except that the Comptroller may limit the issues to be reviewed to those findings and conclusions to which opposing arguments or exceptions have been filed by the parties.

(2) The Comptroller shall render a final decision within 90 days after notification of the parties that the case has been submitted for final decision, or 90 days after oral argument, whichever is later, unless the Comptroller orders that the action or any aspect thereof be remanded to the administrative law judge for further proceedings. Copies of

the final decision and order of the Comptroller shall be served upon each party to the proceeding, upon other persons required by statute, and, if directed by the Comptroller or required by statute, upon any appropriate state or Federal supervisory authority.

§ 109.41 Stays pending judicial review.

The commencement of proceedings for judicial review of a final decision and order of the OCC may not, unless specifically ordered by the Comptroller or a reviewing court, operate as a stay of any order issued by the Comptroller. The Comptroller may, in its discretion, and on such terms as it finds just, stay the effectiveness of all or any part of its order pending a final decision on a petition for review of the order.

Subpart B—Local Rules

§ 109.100 Scope.

The rules and procedures in this subpart B shall apply to those proceedings covered by subpart A of this part. In addition, subpart A of this part and this subpart shall apply to adjudicatory proceedings for which hearings on the record are provided for by the following statutory provisions:

(a) Proceedings under section 10(a)(2)(D) of the HOLA (12 U.S.C. 1467a(a)(2)(D)) to determine whether any person directly or indirectly exercises a controlling influence over the management or policies of a savings association or any other company; and

(b) [Reserved]

(c) Proceedings under section 15(c)(4) of the Securities and Exchange Act of 1934 (15 U.S.C. 78o(c)(4)) (Exchange Act) to determine whether any Federal savings association or person subject to the jurisdiction of the OCC pursuant to section 12(i) of the Exchange Act (15 U.S.C. 78 *l* (i)) has failed to comply with the provisions of sections 12, 13, 14(a), 14(c), 14(d) or 14(f) of the Exchange Act.

§ 109.101 Appointment of Office of Financial Institution Adjudication.

Unless otherwise directed by the OCC, all hearings under subpart A of this part and this subpart shall be conducted by administrative law judges under the direction of the Office of Financial Institution Adjudication.

§ 109.102 Discovery.

(a) *In general.* A party may take the deposition of an expert, or of a person, including another party, who has direct knowledge of matters that are non-privileged, relevant and material to the proceeding and where there is a need for the deposition. The deposition of experts shall be limited to those experts who are expected to testify at the hearing.

(b) *Notice.* A party desiring to take a deposition shall give reasonable notice in writing to the deponent and to every other party to the proceeding. The notice must state the time and place for taking the deposition and the name and address of the person to be deposed.

(c) *Time limits.* A party may take depositions at any time after the commencement of the proceeding, but no later than ten days before the scheduled hearing date, except with permission of the administrative law judge for good cause shown.

(d) *Conduct of the deposition.* The witness must be duly sworn, and each party shall have the right to examine the witness with respect to all non-privileged, relevant and material matters of which the witness has factual, direct and personal knowledge. Objections to questions or exhibits shall be in short form, stating the grounds for objection. Failure to object to questions or exhibits is not a waiver except where the grounds for the objection might have been avoided if the objection had been timely presented. The court reporter shall transcribe or otherwise record the witness's testimony, as agreed among the parties.

(e) *Protective orders.* At any time after notice of a deposition has been given, a party may file a motion for the issuance of a protective order. Such protective order may prohibit, terminate, or limit the scope or manner of the taking of a deposition. The administrative law judge shall grant such protective order upon a showing of sufficient grounds, including that the deposition:

(1) Is unreasonable, oppressive, excessive in scope, or unduly burdensome;

(2) Involves privileged, investigative, trial preparation, irrelevant or immaterial matters; or

(3) Is being conducted in bad faith or in such manner as to unreasonably annoy, embarrass, or oppress the deponent.

(f) *Fees.* Deposition witnesses, including expert witnesses, shall be paid the same expenses in the same manner as are paid witnesses in the district courts of the United States in proceedings in which the United States Government is a party. Expenses in accordance with this paragraph shall be paid by the party seeking to take the deposition.

(g) *Deposition subpoenas*—(1) *Issuance.* At the request of a party, the administrative law judge shall issue a subpoena requiring the attendance of a witness at a deposition. The attendance of a witness may be required from any place in any state or territory that is subject to the jurisdiction of the United States or as otherwise permitted by law.

(2) *Service.* The party requesting the subpoena must serve it on the person named therein or upon that person's counsel, by any of the methods identified in §109.11(d) of this part. The party serving the subpoena must file proof of service with the administrative law judge.

(3) *Motion to quash.* A person named in the subpoena or a party may file a motion to quash or modify the subpoena. A statement of the reasons for the motion must accompany it and a copy of the motion must be served on the party that requested the subpoena. The motion must be made prior to the time for compliance specified in the subpoena and not more than ten days after the date of service of the subpoena, or if the subpoena is served within 15 days of the hearing, within five days after the date of service.

(4) *Enforcement of deposition subpoena.* Enforcement of a deposition subpoena shall be in accordance with the procedures of §109.27(d) of this part.

§ 109.103 Civil money penalties.

(a) *Assessment.* In the event of consent, or if upon the record developed at the hearing the OCC finds that any of the grounds specified in the notice issued pursuant to §109.18 of this part have been established, the OCC may serve an order of assessment of civil money penalty upon the party concerned. The assessment order shall be effective immediately upon service or upon such other date as may be specified therein and shall remain effective and enforceable until it is stayed, modified, terminated, or set aside by the OCC or by a reviewing court.

(b) *Payment.* (1) Civil penalties assessed pursuant to subpart A of this part and this subpart B are payable and to be collected within 60 days after the issuance of the notice of assessment, unless the OCC fixes a different time for payment where it determines that the purpose of the civil money penalty would be better served thereby; however, if a party has made a timely request for a hearing to challenge the assessment of the penalty, the party may not be required to pay such penalty until the OCC has issued a final order of assessment following the hearing. In such instances, the penalty shall be paid within 60 days of service of such order unless the OCC fixes a different time for payment. Notwithstanding the foregoing, the OCC may seek to attach the party's assets or to have a receiver appointed to secure payment of the potential civil money penalty or other obligation in advance of the hearing in accordance with section 8(i)(4) of the FDIA (12 U.S.C. 1818(i)(4)).

(2) Checks in payment of civil penalties shall be made payable to the Treasurer of the United States and sent to the OCC. Upon receipt, the OCC shall forward the check to the Treasury of the United States.

(c) *Maximum amount of civil money penalties*—(1) *Statutory formula.* The OCC is required by statute to annually adjust for inflation the maximum amount of each civil money penalty within its jurisdiction to administer. The inflation adjustment is calculated by multiplying the maximum dollar amount of the civil money penalty for the previous calendar year by the cost-of-living inflation adjustment multiplier provided annually by the Office of Management and Budget and rounding the total to the nearest dollar.

(2) *Notice of inflation adjustments.* The OCC will publish notice in the FEDERAL REGISTER of the maximum penalties which may be assessed on an annual basis on, or before, January 15 of each

calendar year based on the formula in paragraph (a) of this section, for penalties assessed on, or after, the date of publication of the most recent notice related to conduct occurring on or after November 2, 2015.

[76 FR 48957, Aug. 9, 2011, as amended at 77 FR 66534, Nov. 6, 2012; 77 FR 76356, Dec. 28, 2012; 81 FR 43027, July 1, 2016; 82 FR 8587, Jan. 27, 2017; 83 FR 1518, Jan. 12, 2018]

§ 109.104 Additional procedures.

(a) *Replies to exceptions.* Replies to written exceptions to the administrative law judge's recommended decision, findings, conclusions or proposed order pursuant to § 109.39 of this part shall be filed within 10-days of the date such written exceptions were required to be filed.

(b) *Motions.* All motions shall be filed with the administrative law judge and an additional copy shall be filed with the OCC Hearing Clerk who receives adjudicatory filings; provided, however, that once the administrative law judge has certified the record to the Comptroller pursuant to § 109.38 of this part, all motions must be filed with the Comptroller to the attention of the Hearing Clerk within the 10-day period following the filing of exceptions allowed for the filing of replies to exceptions. Responses to such motions filed in a timely manner with the Comptroller, other than motions for oral argument before the Comptroller, shall be allowed pursuant to the procedures at § 109.23(d) of this part. No response is required for the Comptroller to make a determination on a motion for oral argument.

(c) *Authority of administrative law judge.* In addition to the powers listed in § 109.5 of this part, the administrative law judge shall have the authority to deny any dispositive motion and shall follow the procedures set forth for motions for summary disposition at § 109.29 of this part and partial summary disposition at § 109.30 of this part in making determinations on such motions.

(d) *Notification of submission of proceeding to the Comptroller.* Upon the expiration of the time for filing any exceptions, any replies to such exceptions or any motions and any ruling thereon, and after receipt of certified record, the OCC shall notify the parties within ten days of the submission of the proceeding to the Comptroller for final determination.

(e) *Extensions of time for final determination.* The Comptroller may, *sua sponte,* extend the time for final determination by signing an order of extension of time within the 90-day time period and notifying the parties of such extension thereafter.

(f) *Service upon the OCC.* Service of any document upon the OCC shall be made by filing with the Hearing Clerk, in addition to the individuals and/or offices designated by the OCC in its Notice issued pursuant to § 109.18 of this part, or such other means reasonably suited to provide notice of the person and/or offices designated to receive filings.

(g) *Filings with the Comptroller.* An additional copy of all materials required or permitted to be filed with or referred to the administrative law judge pursuant to subpart A and B of this part shall be filed with the Hearing Clerk. This rule shall not apply to the transcript of testimony and exhibits adduced at the hearing or to proposed exhibits submitted in advance of the hearing pursuant to an order of the administrative law judge under § 109.32 of this part. Materials required or permitted to be filed with or referred to the Comptroller pursuant to subparts A and B of this part shall be filed with the Comptroller, to the attention of the Hearing Clerk.

(h) *Presence of cameras and other recording devices.* The use of cameras and other recording devices, other than those used by the court reporter, shall be prohibited and excluded from the proceedings.

Subparts C–D [Reserved]

PARTS 110–111 [RESERVED]

PART 112—RULES FOR INVESTIGATIVE PROCEEDINGS AND FORMAL EXAMINATION PROCEEDINGS

Sec.

112.1 Scope of part.
112.2 Definitions.
112.3 Confidentiality of proceedings.

112.4 Transcripts.
112.5 Rights of witnesses.
112.6 Obstruction of the proceedings.
112.7 Subpoenas.

AUTHORITY: 12 U.S.C. 1462a, 1463, 1464, 1467, 1467a, 1813, 1817(j), 1818(n), 1820(c), 5412(b)(2)(B); 15 U.S.C. 78*l*.

SOURCE: 76 FR 48970, Aug. 9, 2011, unless otherwise noted.

§ 112.1 Scope of part.

This part prescribes rules of practice and procedure applicable to the conduct of formal examination proceedings with respect to Federal savings associations and their affiliates under section 5(d)(1)(B) of the HOLA, as amended, 12 U.S.C. 1464(d)(1)(B) or section 7(j)(15) of the Federal Deposit Insurance Act, as amended, 12 U.S.C. 1817(j)(15) ("FDIA"), section 8(n) of the FDIA, 12 U.S.C. 1818(n), or section 10(c) of the FDIA, 12 U.S.C. 1820(c). This part does not apply to adjudicatory proceedings as to which hearings are required by statute, the rules for which are contained in part 109 of this chapter.

§ 112.2 Definitions.

As used in this part:

(a) *OCC* means the Office of the Comptroller of the Currency;

(b) [Reserved]

(c) *Formal examination proceeding* means the administration of oaths and affirmations, taking and preserving of testimony, requiring the production of books, papers, correspondence, memoranda, and all other records, the issuance of subpoenas, and all related activities in connection with examination of savings associations and their affiliates conducted pursuant to section 5(d)(1)(B) of the HOLA, section 7(j)(15) of the FDIA, section 8(n) of the FDIA or section 10(c) of the FDIA; and

(d) *Designated representative* means the person or persons empowered by the OCC to conduct an investigative proceeding or a formal examination proceeding.

§ 112.3 Confidentiality of proceedings.

All formal examination proceedings shall be private and, unless otherwise ordered by the OCC, all investigative proceedings shall also be private. Unless otherwise ordered or permitted by the OCC, or required by law, and except as provided in §§ 112.4 and 112.5, the entire record of any investigative proceeding or formal examination proceeding, including the resolution of the OCC or its delegate(s) authorizing the proceeding, the transcript of such proceeding, and all documents and information obtained by the designated representative(s) during the course of said proceedings shall be confidential.

§ 112.4 Transcripts.

Transcripts or other recordings, if any, of investigative proceedings or formal examination proceedings shall be prepared solely by an official reporter or by any other person or means authorized by the designated representative. A person who has submitted documentary evidence or given testimony in an investigative proceeding or formal examination proceeding may procure a copy of his own documentary evidence or transcript of his own testimony upon payment of the cost thereof; *provided*, that a person seeking a transcript of his own testimony must file a written request with the OCC's Director for Enforcement and Compliance stating the reason he desires to procure such transcript, and said persons may for good cause deny such request. In any event, any witness (or his counsel) shall have the right to inspect the transcript of the witness' own testimony.

§ 112.5 Rights of witnesses.

(a) Any person who is compelled or requested to furnish documentary evidence or give testimony at an investigative proceeding or formal examination proceeding shall have the right to examine, upon request, the OCC resolution authorizing such proceeding. Copies of such resolution shall be furnished, for their retention, to such persons only with the written approval of the OCC.

(b) Any witness at an investigative proceeding or formal examination proceeding may be accompanied and advised by an attorney personally representing that witness.

(1) Such attorney shall be a member in good standing of the bar of the highest court of any state, Commonwealth, possession, territory, or the District of

Columbia, who has not been suspended or debarred from practice by the bar of any such political entity or before the OCC in accordance with the provisions of part 19 of this chapter and has not been excluded from the particular investigative proceeding or formal examination proceeding in accordance with paragraph (b)(3) of this section.

(2) Such attorney may advise the witness before, during, and after the taking of his testimony and may briefly question the witness, on the record, at the conclusion of his testimony, for the sole purpose of clarifying any of the answers the witness has given. During the taking of the testimony of a witness, such attorney may make summary notes solely for his use in representing his client. All witnesses shall be sequestered, and, unless permitted in the discretion of the designated representative, no witness or accompanying attorney may be permitted to be present during the taking of testimony of any other witness called in such proceeding. Neither attorney(s) for the association(s) that are the subjects of the investigative proceedings or formal examination proceedings, nor attorneys for any other interested persons, shall have any right to be present during the testimony of any witness not personally being represented by such attorney.

(3) The OCC, for good cause, may exclude a particular attorney from further participation in any investigation in which the OCC has found the attorney to have engaged in dilatory, obstructionist, egregious, contemptuous or contumacious conduct. The person conducting an investigation may report to the OCC instances of apparently dilatory, obstructionist, egregious, contemptuous or contumacious conduct on the part of an attorney. After due notice to the attorney, the OCC may take such action as the circumstances warrant based upon a written record evidencing the conduct of the attorney in that investigation or such other or additional written or oral presentation as the OCC may permit or direct.

§ 112.6 Obstruction of the proceedings.

The designated representative shall report to the Comptroller any instances where any witness or counsel has engaged in dilatory, obstructionist, or contumacious conduct or has otherwise violated any provision of this part during the course of an investigative proceeding or formal examination proceeding; and the OCC may take such action as the circumstances warrant, including the exclusion of counsel from further participation in such proceeding.

§ 112.7 Subpoenas.

(a) *Service.* Service of a subpoena in connection with any investigative proceeding or formal examination proceeding shall be effected in the following manner:

(1) *Service upon a natural person.* Service of a subpoena upon a natural person may be effected by handing it to such person; by leaving it at his office with the person in charge thereof, or, if there is no one in charge, by leaving it in a conspicuous place therein; by leaving it at his dwelling place or usual place of abode with some person of suitable age and discretion then residing therein; by mailing it to him by registered or certified mail or by an express delivery service at his last known address; or by any method whereby actual notice is given to him.

(2) *Service upon other persons.* When the person to be served is not a natural person, service of the subpoena may be effected by handing the subpoena to a registered agent for service, or to any officer, director, or agent in charge of any office of such person; by mailing it to any such representative by registered or certified mail or by an express delivery service at his last known address; or by any method whereby actual notice is given to such person.

(b) *Motions to quash.* Any person to whom a subpoena is directed may, prior to the time specified therein for compliance, but in no event more than 10 days after the date of service of such subpoena, apply to the Deputy Chief Counsel or his designee to quash or modify such subpoena, accompanying such application with a statement of the reasons therefor. The Deputy Chief Counsel or his designee, as appropriate, may:

(1) Deny the application;

(2) Quash or revoke the subpoena;

(3) Modify the subpoena; or

(4) Condition the granting of the application on such terms as the Deputy Chief Counsel or his designee determines to be just, reasonable, and proper.

(c) *Attendance of witnesses.* Subpoenas issued in connection with an investigative proceeding or formal examination proceeding may require the attendance and/or testimony of witnesses from any state or territory of the United States and the production by such witnesses of documentary or other tangible evidence at any designated place where the proceeding is being (or is to be) conducted. Foreign nationals are subject to such subpoenas if such service is made upon a duly authorized agent located in the United States.

(d) *Witness fees and mileage.* Witnesses summoned in any proceeding under this part shall be paid the same fees and mileage that are paid witnesses in the district courts of the United States. Such fees and mileage need not be tendered when the subpoena is issued on behalf of the OCC by any of its designated representatives.

PARTS 113–127 [RESERVED]

PART 128—NONDISCRIMINATION REQUIREMENTS

Sec.

128.1 Definitions.
128.2 Nondiscrimination in lending and other services.
128.3 Nondiscrimination in applications.
128.4 Nondiscriminatory advertising.
128.5 Equal Housing Lender Poster.
128.6 Loan application register.
128.7 Nondiscrimination in employment.
128.8 Complaints.
128.9 Guidelines relating to nondiscrimination in lending.
128.10 Supplementary guidelines.
128.11 Nondiscriminatory appraisal and underwriting.

AUTHORITY: 12 U.S.C. 1464, 5412(b)(2)(B).

SOURCE: 76 FR 48978, August 9, 2011, unless otherwise noted.

§ 128.1 Definitions.

As used in this part 128—

(a) *Application.* For purposes of this part, an application for a loan or other service is as defined in Regulation C, 12 CFR 203.2(b).

(b) *Savings association.* The term "savings association" means any Federal savings association as defined in 12 U.S.C. 1813(b)(2).

(c) *Dwelling.* The term "dwelling" means a residential structure (whether or not it is attached to real property) located in a state of the United States of America, the District of Columbia, or the Commonwealth of Puerto Rico. The term includes an individual condominium unit, cooperative unit, or mobile or manufactured home.

§ 128.2 Nondiscrimination in lending and other services.

(a) No savings association may deny a loan or other service, or discriminate in the purchase of loans or securities or discriminate in fixing the amount, interest rate, duration, application procedures, collection or enforcement procedures, or other terms or conditions of such loan or other service on the basis of the age or location of the dwelling, or on the basis of the race, color, religion, sex, handicap, familial status (having one or more children under the age of 18), marital status, age (provided the person has the capacity to contract) or national origin of:

(1) An applicant or joint applicant;

(2) Any person associated with an applicant or joint applicant regarding such loan or other service, or with the purposes of such loan or other service;

(3) The present or prospective owners, lessees, tenants, or occupants of the dwelling(s) for which such loan or other service is to be made or given;

(4) The present or prospective owners, lessees, tenants, or occupants of other dwellings in the vicinity of the dwelling(s) for which such loan or other service is to be made or given.

(b) A savings association shall consider without prejudice the combined income of joint applicants for a loan or other service.

(c) No savings association may discriminate against an applicant for a loan or other service on any prohibited basis (as defined in 12 CFR 202.2(z) and 24 CFR part 100).

NOTE TO § 128.2: *See also*, § 128.9(b) and (c).

§ 128.3 Nondiscrimination in applications.

(a) No savings association may discourage, or refuse to allow, receive, or consider, any application, request, or inquiry regarding a loan or other service, or discriminate in imposing conditions upon, or in processing, any such application, request, or inquiry on the basis of the age or location of the dwelling, or on the basis of the race, color, religion, sex, handicap, familial status (having one or more children under the age of 18), marital status, age (provided the person has the capacity to contract), national origin, or other characteristics prohibited from consideration in § 128.2(c) of this part, of the prospective borrower or other person, who:

(1) Makes application for any such loan or other service;

(2) Requests forms or papers to be used to make application for any such loan or other service; or

(3) Inquires about the availability of such loan or other service.

(b) A savings association shall inform each inquirer of his or her right to file a written loan application, and to receive a copy of the association's underwriting standards.

NOTE TO § 128.3: *See also,* § 128.9(a) through (d).

§ 128.4 Nondiscriminatory advertising.

No savings association may directly or indirectly engage in any form of advertising that implies or suggests a policy of discrimination or exclusion in violation of title VIII of the Civil Rights Acts of 1968, the Equal Credit Opportunity Act, or this part 128. Advertisements for any loan for the purpose of purchasing, constructing, improving, repairing, or maintaining a dwelling or any loan secured by a dwelling shall include a facsimile of the following logotype and legend:

§ 128.5 Equal Housing Lender Poster.

(a) Each savings association shall post and maintain one or more Equal Housing Lender Posters, the text of which is prescribed in paragraph (b) of this section, in the lobby of each of its offices in a prominent place or places readily apparent to all persons seeking loans. The poster shall be at least 11 by 14 inches in size, and the text shall be easily legible. It is recommended that savings associations post a Spanish language version of the poster in offices serving areas with a substantial Spanish-speaking population.

(b) The text of the Equal Housing Lender Poster shall be as follows:

We Do Business In Accordance With Federal Fair Lending Laws.

UNDER THE FEDERAL FAIR HOUSING ACT, IT IS ILLEGAL, ON THE BASIS OF RACE, COLOR, NATIONAL ORIGIN, RELIGION, SEX, HANDICAP, OR FAMILIAL STATUS (HAVING CHILDREN UNDER THE AGE OF 18) TO:

[ ] Deny a loan for the purpose of purchasing, constructing, improving, repairing or maintaining a dwelling or to deny any loan secured by a dwelling; or

[ ] Discriminate in fixing the amount, interest rate, duration, application procedures, or other terms or conditions of such a loan or in appraising property.

IF YOU BELIEVE YOU HAVE BEEN DISCRIMINATED AGAINST, YOU SHOULD:

SEND A COMPLAINT TO:

Assistant Secretary for Fair Housing and Equal Opportunity, Department of Housing and Urban Development, Washington, DC 20410.

For processing under the Federal Fair Housing Act

AND TO:

[Insert contact information for appropriate Federal regulator]

For processing under applicable Regulations.

UNDER THE EQUAL CREDIT OPPORTUNITY ACT, IT IS ILLEGAL TO

DISCRIMINATE IN ANY CREDIT TRANSACTION:

[ ] On the basis of race, color, national origin, religion, sex, marital status, or age;

[ ] Because income is from public assistance; or

[ ] Because a right has been exercised under the Consumer Credit Protection Act.

IF YOU BELIEVE YOU HAVE BEEN DISCRIMINATED AGAINST, YOU SHOULD SEND A COMPLAINT TO:

[Insert contact information for appropriate Federal regulator]

§ 128.6 Loan application register.

Savings associations and other lenders required to file Home Mortgage Disclosure Act Loan Application Registers with the OCC in accordance with 12 CFR part 203 must enter the reason for denial, using the codes provided in 12 CFR part 203, with respect to all loan denials.

§ 128.7 Nondiscrimination in employment.

(a) No savings association shall, because of an individual's race, color, religion, sex, or national origin:

(1) Fail or refuse to hire such individual;

(2) Discharge such individual;

(3) Otherwise discriminate against such individual with respect to such individual's compensation, promotion, or the terms, conditions, or privileges of such individual's employment; or

(4) Discriminate in admission to, or employment in, any program of apprenticeship, training, or retraining, including on-the-job training.

(b) No savings association shall limit, segregate, or classify its employees in any way which would deprive or tend to deprive any individual of employment opportunities or otherwise adversely affect such individual's status as an employee because of such individual's race, color, religion, sex, or national origin.

(c) No savings association shall discriminate against any employee or applicant for employment because such employee or applicant has opposed any employment practice made unlawful by Federal, state, or local law or regulation or because he has in good faith made a charge of such practice or testified, assisted, or participated in any manner in an investigation, proceeding, or hearing of such practice by any lawfully constituted authority.

(d) No savings association shall print or publish or cause to be printed or published any notice or advertisement relating to employment by such savings association indicating any preference, limitation, specification, or discrimination based on race, color, religion, sex, or national origin.

(e) This regulation shall not apply in any case in which the Federal Equal Employment Opportunities law is made inapplicable by the provisions of section 2000e–1 or sections 2000e–2(e) through (j) of title 42, United States Code.

(f) Any violation of the following laws or regulations by a savings association shall be deemed to be a violation of this part 128:

(1) The Equal Employment Opportunity Act, as amended, 42 U.S.C. 2000e–2000h–2, and Equal Employment Opportunity Commission (EEOC) regulations at 29 CFR part 1600;

(2) The Age Discrimination in Employment Act, 29 U.S.C. 621–633, and EEOC and Department of Labor regulations;

(3) Office of Federal Contract Compliance Programs (OFCCP) regulations at 41 CFR part 60;

(4) The Veterans Employment and Readjustment Act of 1972, 38 U.S.C. 2011–2012, and the Vietnam Era Veterans Readjustment Adjustment Assistance Act of 1974, 38 U.S.C. 2021–2026;

(5) The Rehabilitation Act of 1973, 29 U.S.C. 701 *et seq.*; and

(6) The Immigration and Nationality Act, 8 U.S.C. 1324b, and INS regulations at 8 CFR part 274a.

§ 128.8 Complaints.

Complaints alleging violations of the Fair Housing Act by a savings association shall be referred to the Assistant Secretary for Fair Housing and Equal Opportunity, U.S. Department of Housing and Urban Development, Washington, DC 20410 for processing under the Fair Housing Act, and to the appropriate Federal regulator for processing under applicable regulations. Complaints regarding discrimination in employment by a savings association should be referred to the Equal Employment Opportunity Commission, Washington, DC 20506 and a copy, for information only, sent to the appropriate Federal regulator.

§ 128.9 Guidelines relating to nondiscrimination in lending.

(a) *General.* Fair housing and equal opportunity in home financing is a policy of the United States established by Federal statutes and Presidential orders and proclamations. In furtherance of the Federal civil rights laws and the economical home financing purposes of the statutes administered by the OCC, the OCC has adopted, in part 128 of this chapter, nondiscrimination regulations that, among other things, prohibit arbitrary refusals to consider loan applications on the basis of the age or location of a dwelling, and prohibit discrimination based on race, color, religion, sex, handicap, familial status (having one or more children under the age of 18), marital status, age (provided the person has the capacity to contract), or national origin in fixing the amount, interest rate, duration, application procedures, collection or enforcement procedures, or other terms or conditions of housing related loans. Such discrimination is also prohibited in the purchase of loans and securities. This section provides supplementary guidelines to aid savings associations in developing and implementing nondiscriminatory lending policies. Each savings association should reexamine its underwriting standards at least annually in order to ensure equal opportunity.

(b) *Loan underwriting standards.* The basic purpose of the nondiscrimination regulations is to require that every applicant be given an equal opportunity to obtain a loan. Each loan applicant's creditworthiness should be evaluated on an individual basis without reference to presumed characteristics of a group. The use of lending standards which have no economic basis and which are discriminatory in effect is a violation of law even in the absence of an actual intent to discriminate. However, a standard which has a discriminatory effect is not necessarily improper if its use achieves a genuine business need which cannot be achieved by means which are not discriminatory in effect or less discriminatory in effect.

(c) *Discriminatory practices*—(1) *Discrimination on the basis of sex or marital status.* The Civil Rights Act of 1968 and the National Housing Act prohibit discrimination in lending on the basis of sex. The Equal Credit Opportunity Act, in addition to this prohibition, forbids discrimination on the basis of marital status. Refusing to lend to, requiring higher standards of creditworthiness of, or imposing different requirements on, members of one sex or individuals of one marital status, is discrimination based on sex or marital status. Loan underwriting decisions must be based on an applicant's credit history and present and reasonably foreseeable economic prospects, rather than on the basis of assumptions regarding comparative differences in creditworthiness between married and unmarried individuals, or between men and women.

(2) *Discrimination on the basis of language.* Requiring fluency in the English language as a prerequisite for obtaining a loan may be a discriminatory practice based on national origin.

(3) *Income of husbands and wives.* A practice of discounting all or part of either spouse's income where spouses apply jointly is a violation of section 527 of the National Housing Act. As with other income, when spouses apply jointly for a loan, the determination as to whether a spouse's income qualifies for credit purposes should depend upon a reasonable evaluation of his or her past, present, and reasonably foreseeable economic circumstances. Information relating to child-bearing intentions of a couple or an individual may not be requested.

(4) *Supplementary income.* Lending standards which consider as effective only the non-overtime income of the primary wage-earner may result in discrimination because they do not take account of variations in employment patterns among individuals and families. The favored method of loan underwriting reasonably evaluates the credit worthiness of each applicant based on a

realistic appraisal of his or her own past, present, and foreseeable economic circumstances. The determination as to whether primary income or additional income qualifies as effective for credit purposes should depend upon whether such income may reasonably be expected to continue through the early period of the mortgage risk. Automatically discounting other income from bonuses, overtime, or part-time employment, will cause some applicants to be denied financing without a realistic analysis of their credit worthiness. Since statistics show that minority group members and low- and moderate-income families rely more often on such supplemental income, the practice may be racially discriminatory in effect, as well as artificially restrictive of opportunities for home financing.

(5) *Applicant's prior history*. Loan decisions should be based upon a realistic evaluation of all pertinent factors respecting an individual's creditworthiness, without giving undue weight to any one factor. The savings association should, among other things, take into consideration that:

(i) In some instances, past credit difficulties may have resulted from discriminatory practices;

(ii) A policy favoring applicants who previously owned homes may perpetuate prior discrimination;

(iii) A current, stable earnings record may be the most reliable indicator of credit-worthiness, and entitled to more weight than factors such as educational level attained;

(iv) Job or residential changes may indicate upward mobility; and

(v) Preferring applicants who have done business with the lender can perpetuate previous discriminatory policies.

(6) *Income level or racial composition of area*. Refusing to lend or lending on less favorable terms in particular areas because of their racial composition is unlawful. Refusing to lend, or offering less favorable terms (such as interest rate, downpayment, or maturity) to applicants because of the income level in an area can discriminate against minority group persons.

(7) *Age and location factors*. Sections 128.2, 128.11, and 128.3 of this chapter prohibit loan denials based upon the age or location of a dwelling. These restrictions are intended to prohibit use of unfounded or unsubstantiated assumptions regarding the effect upon loan risk of the age of a dwelling or the physical or economic characteristics of an area. Loan decisions should be based on the present market value of the property offered as security (including consideration of specific improvements to be made by the borrower) and the likelihood that the property will retain an adequate value over the term of the loan. Specific factors which may negatively affect its short-range future value (up to 3–5 years) should be clearly documented. Factors which in some cases may cause the market value of a property to decline are recent zoning changes or a significant number of abandoned homes in the immediate vicinity of the property. However, not all zoning changes will cause a decline in property values, and proximity to abandoned buildings may not affect the market value of a property because of rehabilitation programs or affirmative lending programs, or because the cause of abandonment is unrelated to high risk. Proper underwriting considerations include the condition and utility of the improvements, and various physical factors such as street conditions, amenities such as parks and recreation areas, availability of public utilities and municipal services, and exposure to flooding and land faults. However, arbitrary decisions based on age or location are prohibited, since many older, soundly constructed homes provide housing opportunities which may be precluded by an arbitrary lending policy.

(8) *Fair Housing Act (title VIII, Civil Rights Act of 1968, as amended)*. Savings associations must comply with all regulations promulgated by the Department of Housing and Urban Development to implement the Fair Housing Act, found at 24 CFR parts 100 through 125, except that they shall use the Equal Housing Lender logo and poster prescribed by OCC regulations at 12 CFR 128.4 and 128.5 rather than the Equal Housing Opportunity logo and poster required by 24 CFR part 110.

(d) *Marketing practices.* Savings associations should review their advertising and marketing practices to ensure that their services are available without discrimination to the community they serve. Discrimination in lending is not limited to loan decisions and underwriting standards; a savings association does not meet its obligations to the community or implement its equal lending responsibility if its marketing practices and business relationships with developers and real estate brokers improperly restrict its clientele to segments of the community. A review of marketing practices could begin with an examination of an association's loan portfolio and applications to ascertain whether, in view of the demographic characteristics and credit demands of the community in which the institution is located, it is adequately serving the community on a nondiscriminatory basis. The OCC will systematically review marketing practices where evidence of discrimination in lending is discovered.

§ 128.10 Supplementary guidelines.

The policy statement found at 12 CFR 128.9 supplements this part and should be read together with this part. Refer also to the HUD Fair Housing regulations at 24 CFR parts 100 through 125, Federal Reserve Regulation B at 12 CFR part 202, and Federal Reserve Regulation C at 12 CFR part 203.

§ 128.11 Nondiscriminatory appraisal and underwriting.

(a) *Appraisal.* No savings association may use or rely upon an appraisal of a dwelling which the savings association knows, or reasonably should know, is discriminatory on the basis of the age or location of the dwelling, or is discriminatory per se or in effect under the Fair Housing Act of 1968 or the Equal Credit Opportunity Act.

(b) *Underwriting.* Each savings association shall have clearly written, nondiscriminatory loan underwriting standards, available to the public upon request, at each of its offices. Each association shall, at least annually, review its standards, and business practices implementing them, to ensure equal opportunity in lending.

NOTE TO § 128.11: *See also,* § 128.9(b), (c)(6), and (c)(7).

PARTS 129–140 [RESERVED]

PART 141—DEFINITIONS FOR REGULATIONS AFFECTING FEDERAL SAVINGS ASSOCIATIONS

Sec.

141.1 When do the definitions in this part apply?
141.2 Act.
141.5 Commercial paper.
141.7 Corporate debt security.
141.8 Debit card.
141.10 Dwelling unit.
141.11 Federal savings association.
141.14 Home.
141.15 Improved nonresidential real estate.
141.16 Improved residential real estate.
141.18 Interim Federal savings association.
141.19 Interim state savings association.
141.20 Loans.
141.21 Nonresidential real estate.
141.22 [Reserved]
141.23 Residential real estate.
141.25 Single-family dwelling.
141.26 Surplus.
141.27 Unimproved real estate.
141.28 Withdrawal value of a savings account.

AUTHORITY: 12 U.S.C. 1462a, 1463, 1464, 5412(b)(2)(B).

SOURCE: 76 FR 48990, Aug. 9, 2011, unless otherwise noted.

§ 141.1 When do the definitions in this part apply?

The definitions in this part and in 12 CFR part 161 apply throughout parts 100 through 199 of this chapter, unless another definition is specifically provided.

§ 141.2 Act.

The term *Act* means the Home Owners' Loan Act of 1933, as amended.

§ 141.5 Commercial paper.

The term *commercial paper* means any note, draft, or bill of exchange which arises out of a current transaction or the proceeds of which have been or are to be used for current transactions, and which has a maturity at the time of issuance of not exceeding nine months, exclusive of days of grace, or any renewal thereof the maturity of which is likewise limited.

§ 141.7 Corporate debt security.

The term *corporate debt security* means a marketable obligation, evidencing the indebtedness of any corporation in the form of a bond, note and/or debenture which is commonly regarded as a debt security and is not predominantly speculative in nature. A security is marketable if it may be sold with reasonable promptness at a price which corresponds reasonably to its fair value.

§ 141.8 Debit card.

The term *debit card* means a card that enables an accountholder to obtain access to a savings account for the purpose of making withdrawals or of transferring funds to a third party by non-transferable order or authorization.

§ 141.10 Dwelling unit.

The term *dwelling unit* means the unified combination of rooms designed for residential use by one family, other than a single-family dwelling.

§ 141.11 Federal savings association.

The term *Federal savings association* means a Federal savings association or Federal savings bank chartered under section 5 of the Act.

§ 141.14 Home.

The term *home* means real estate comprising a single-family dwelling(s) or a dwelling unit(s) for four or fewer families in the aggregate.

§ 141.15 Improved nonresidential real estate.

The term *improved nonresidential real estate* means nonresidential real estate:

(a) Containing a permanent structure(s) constituting at least 25 percent of its value; or

(b) Containing improvements which make it usable by a business or industrial enterprise; or

(c) Used, or to be used within a reasonable time, for commercial farming, excluding hobby and vacation property.

§ 141.16 Improved residential real estate.

The term *improved residential real estate* means residential real estate containing offsite or other improvements sufficient to make the property ready for primarily residential construction, and real estate in the process of being improved by a building or buildings to be constructed or in the process of construction for primarily residential use.

§ 141.18 Interim Federal savings association.

The term *interim Federal savings association* means a Federal savings association chartered by the OCC or the OTS under section 5 of the Act to facilitate the acquisition of 100 percent of the voting shares of an existing Federal stock savings association or other insured stock savings association by a newly formed company or an existing savings and loan holding company or to facilitate any other transaction the OCC may approve.

§ 141.19 Interim state savings association.

The term *interim state savings association* means a savings association, other than a Federal savings association, the accounts of which are insured by the FDIC to facilitate the acquisition of 100 percent of the voting shares of an existing Federal stock savings association or other insured stock savings association by a newly formed company or an existing savings and loan holding company or to facilitate any other transaction the OCC may approve.

§ 141.20 Loans.

The term *loans* means obligations and extensions or advances of credit; and any reference to a loan or investment includes an interest in such a loan or investment.

§ 141.21 Nonresidential real estate.

The terms *nonresidential real estate or nonresidential real property* mean real estate that is not *residential real estate,* as that term is defined in § 141.23 of this part.

§ 141.22 [Reserved]

§ 141.23 Residential real estate.

The terms *residential real estate or residential real property* mean:

(a) Homes (including a dwelling unit in a multi-family residential property such as a condominium or a cooperative);

(b) Combinations of homes and business property (*i.e.*, a home used in part for business);

(c) Other real estate used for primarily residential purposes other than a home (but which may include homes);

(d) Combinations of such real estate and business property involving only minor business use (*i.e.*, where no more than 20 percent of the total appraised value of the real estate is attributable to the business use);

(e) Farm residences and combinations of farm residences and commercial farm real estate;

(f) Property to be improved by the construction of such structures; or

(g) Leasehold interests in the above real estate.

§ 141.25 Single-family dwelling.

The term *single-family dwelling* means a structure designed for residential use by one family, or a unit so designed, whose owner owns, directly or through a non-profit cooperative housing organization, an undivided interest in the underling real estate, including property owned in common with others which contributes to the use and enjoyment of the structure or unit.

§ 141.26 Surplus.

The term *surplus* means undistributed earnings held as unallocated reserves for general corporate use.

§ 141.27 Unimproved real estate.

The term *unimproved real estate* means real estate that will be improved, as defined in § 141.15 or § 141.16 of this part.

§ 141.28 Withdrawal value of a savings account.

The term *withdrawal value of a savings account* means the amount invested in a savings account plus earnings credited thereto, less lawful deductions therefrom.

PART 142 [RESERVED]

PART 143—FEDERAL SAVINGS ASSOCIATIONS—GRANDFATHERED AUTHORITY

AUTHORITY: 12 U.S.C. 1462a, 1463, 1464, 1467a, 2901 *et seq.*, 5412(b)(2)(B).

SOURCE: 76 FR 48991, Aug. 9, 2011, unless otherwise noted.

§ 143.12 Grandfathered authority.

(a) A Federal savings bank formerly chartered or designated as a mutual savings bank under state law may exercise any authority it was authorized to exercise as a mutual savings bank under state law at the time of its conversion from a state mutual savings bank to a Federal or other state charter. Except to the extent such authority may be exercised by Federal savings associations not enjoying grandfathered rights hereunder, such authority may be exercised only to the degree authorized under state law at the time of such conversion. Unless otherwise determined by the OTS prior to July 21, 2011 or by the OCC an association, in the exercise of grandfathered authority, may continue to follow applicable state laws and regulations in effect at the time of such conversion.

(b) A Federal savings association that acquires, or has acquired, a Federal savings bank by merger or consolidation may itself exercise any grandfathered rights enjoyed by the disappearing institution, whether such rights were obtained directly through conversion or through merger or consolidation. The extent of the grandfathered rights of a Federal savings association that disappeared prior to the effective date of this section shall be determined exclusively pursuant to this section.

(c) This section shall not be construed to prevent the exercise by a Federal savings association enjoying grandfathered rights hereunder of authority that is available under the applicable state law only upon the occurrence of specific preconditions, such as the attainment of a particular future date or specified level of regulatory capital, which have not occurred at the time of conversion from a state mutual savings bank, provided they occur thereafter.

(d) This section shall not be construed to permit the exercise of any particular authority on a more liberal basis than is allowable under the most liberal construction of either state or Federal law or regulation.

PART 144—FEDERAL MUTUAL SAVINGS ASSOCIATIONS—COMMUNICATION BETWEEN MEMBERS

AUTHORITY: 12 U.S.C. 1462a, 1463, 1464, 1467a, 2901 *et seq.*, 5412(b)(2)(B).

SOURCE: 76 FR 48995, Aug. 9, 2011, unless otherwise noted.

§ 144.8 Communication between members of a Federal mutual savings association.

(a) *Right of communication with other members.* A member of a Federal mutual savings association has the right to communicate, as prescribed in paragraph (b) of this section, with other members of the Federal savings association regarding any matter related to the Federal savings association's affairs, except for "improper" communications, as defined in paragraph (c) of this section. The association may not defeat that right by redeeming a savings member's savings account in the Federal mutual savings association.

(b) *Member communication procedures.* If a member of a Federal mutual savings association desires to communicate with other members, the following procedures shall be followed:

(1) The member shall give the Federal mutual savings association a written request to communicate;

(2) If the proposed communication is in connection with a meeting of the Federal savings association's members, the request shall be given at least thirty days before the annual meeting or 10 days before a special meeting;

(3) The request shall contain—

(i) The member's full name and address;

(ii) The nature and extent of the member's interest in the Federal savings association at the time the information is given;

(iii) A copy of the proposed communication; and

(iv) If the communication is in connection with a meeting of the members, the date of the meeting;

(4) The Federal savings association shall reply to the request within either—

(i) Fourteen days;

(ii) Ten days, if the communication is in connection with the annual meeting; or

(iii) Three days, if the communication is in connection with a special meeting;

(5) The reply shall provide either—

(i) The number of the Federal savings association's members and the estimated reasonable cost to the Federal savings association of mailing to them the proposed communication; or

(ii) Notification that the Federal savings association has determined not to mail the communication because it is "improper", as defined in paragraph (c) of this section;

(6) After receiving the amount of the estimated costs of mailing and sufficient copies of the communication, the Federal savings association shall mail the communication to all members, by a class of mail specified by the requesting member, either—

(i) Within fourteen days;

(ii) Within seven days, if the communication is in connection with the annual meeting;

(iii) As soon as practicable before the meeting, if the communication is in connection with a special meeting; or

(iv) On a later date specified by the member;

(7) If the Federal savings association refuses to mail the proposed communication, it shall return the requesting member's materials together with a written statement of the specific reasons for refusal, and shall simultaneously send to the appropriate OCC licensing office two copies each of the requesting member's materials, the Federal savings association's written statement, and any other relevant material. The materials shall be sent within:

(i) Fourteen days,

(ii) Ten days if the communication is in connection with the annual meeting, or

(iii) Three days, if the communication is in connection with a special meeting, after the Federal savings association receives the request for communication.

(c) *Improper communication.* A communication is an "improper communication" if it contains material which:

(1) At the time and in the light of the circumstances under which it is made:

(i) Is false or misleading with respect to any material fact; or

(ii) Omits a material fact necessary to make the statements therein not false or misleading, or necessary to correct a statement in an earlier communication on the same subject which has become false or misleading;

(2) Relates to a personal claim or a personal grievance, or is solicitous of personal gain or business advantage by or on behalf of any party;

(3) Relates to any matter, including a general economic, political, racial, religious, social, or similar cause, that is not significantly related to the business of the Federal savings association or is not within the control of the Federal savings association; or

(4) Directly or indirectly and without expressed factual foundation:

(i) Impugns character, integrity, or personal reputation,

(ii) Makes charges concerning improper, illegal, or immoral conduct, or

(iii) Makes statements impugning the stability and soundness of the Federal savings association.

PART 145—FEDERAL SAVINGS ASSOCIATIONS—OPERATIONS

Sec.

145.1 General authority.
145.2 [Reserved]
145.16 Public deposits, depositaries, and fiscal agents.
145.17 Funds transfer services.
145.92 Branch offices.
145.101 Fiscal agency.
145.121 Indemnification of directors, officers and employees.

AUTHORITY: 12 U.S.C. 1462a, 1463, 1464, 1828, 5412(b)(2)(B).

SOURCE: 76 FR 48999, Aug. 9, 2011, unless otherwise noted.

§ 145.1 General authority.

A Federal savings association may exercise all authority granted it by the Home Owners' Loan Act of 1933 ("Act"), 12 U.S.C. 1464, as amended, and its charter and bylaws, whether or not implemented specifically by OCC regulations, subject to the limitations and interpretations contained in this part.

§ 145.2 [Reserved]

§ 145.16 Public deposits, depositaries, and fiscal agents.

(a) *Definitions.* As used in this section—

(1) *Moneys* includes *monies* and has the same meaning it has in applicable state law;

(2) *State law* includes actions by a governmental body which has a charter adopted under the constitution of the state with provisions respecting deposits of public money of that body;

(3) *Surety* means surety under real and/or personal suretyship, and includes guarantor; and

(4) Terms in paragraph (b) of this section have the meanings they have under applicable state law.

(b) *Authority to act as surety for public deposits.* (1) A Federal savings association that is a deposit association may give bond or security for deposit in it of public moneys or investment in it by a governmental unit if required to do so by state law, either as an alternative condition or otherwise, regardless of the amount required. Any bond or security may be given and any substitution or increase thereof may be made under this section at any time.

(2) If state law requires as a condition of such deposit or investment that the Federal savings association or its bond or security, or any combination thereof, be surety for or with respect to other deposits or instruments, whether of that depositor or investor or of any other(s), and whether in the Federal savings association or in any other institution(s) having, when the investments or deposits were made, insurance by the Federal Deposit Insurance Corporation, the same shall become, or if the state law is self-executing shall be, such surety.

(c) *Depositaries and fiscal agents.* Subject to regulation of the United States Treasury Department, a Federal savings association may serve as a depositary for Federal taxes, as a Treasury tax and loan depositary, or as a depositary of public money and fiscal agent of the Government or any other instrumentality thereof when designated for that purpose by such instrumentality and approved by the OCC, and may satisfy any requirement in connection therewith, including maintaining accounts described in §§ 161.33, 161.52, 161.53, and 161.54 of this chapter; pledging collateral; and performing the services outlined in 31 CFR 202.3(b) or any section that supersedes or amends § 202.3(b).

§ 145.17 Funds transfer services.

A Federal savings association is authorized to transfer, with or without fee, its customers' funds from any account (including a line of credit) of the customer at the Federal savings association or at another financial intermediary to third parties or other accounts of the customer on the customer's order or authorization by any mechanism or device, including cashier's checks, conforming with applicable laws and established commercial practices.

§ 145.92 Branch offices.

(a) *Definition.* A branch office of a Federal savings association ("you") is any office other than your home office, agency office, administrative office, data processing office, or an electronic means or facility under part 155 of this chapter.

(b) *Branching.* Subject to the application and notice requirements at § 5.31 of this chapter, you may branch in any state or states of the United States and its territories unless the location would violate:

(1) Section 5(r) of the HOLA (12 U.S.C. 1464(r));

(2) Section 10(e)(3) of the HOLA (12 U.S.C. 1467a(e)(3)); or

(3) Section 13(k)(4) of the FDIA (12 U.S.C. 1823(k)(4)).

(c) *Preemption.* This exercise of the OCC's authority is preemptive of any state law purporting to address the subject of branching by a Federal savings association.

[76 FR 48999, Aug. 9, 2011, as amended at 80 FR 28480, May 18, 2015]

§ 145.101 Fiscal agency.

A Federal savings association designated fiscal agent by the Secretary of the Treasury or with OCC approval by another instrumentality of the United States, shall, as such, perform such reasonable duties and exercise only such powers and privileges as the Secretary of the Treasury or such instrumentality may prescribe.

§ 145.121 Indemnification of directors, officers and employees.

A Federal savings association shall indemnify its directors, officers, and employees in accordance with the following requirements:

(a) *Definitions and rules of construction.* (1) Definitions for purposes of this section.

(i) *Action.* The term "action" means any judicial or administrative proceeding, or threatened proceeding, whether civil, criminal, or otherwise, including any appeal or other proceeding for review;

(ii) *Court.* The term "court" includes, without limitation, any court to which or in which any appeal or any proceeding for review is brought.

(iii) *Final judgment.* The term "final judgment" means a judgment, decree, or order which is not appealable or as to which the period for appeal has expired with no appeal taken.

(iv) *Settlement.* The term "settlement" includes entry of a judgment by consent or confession or a plea of guilty or *nolo contendere.*

(2) References in this section to any individual or other person, including any association, shall include legal representatives, successors, and assigns thereof.

(b) *General.* Subject to paragraphs (c) and (g) of this section, a Federal savings association shall indemnify any person against whom an action is brought or threatened because that person is or was a director, officer, or employee of the association, for:

(1) Any amount for which that person becomes liable under a judgment if such action; and

(2) Reasonable costs and expenses, including reasonable attorney's fees, actually paid or incurred by that person in defending or settling such action, or in enforcing his or her rights under

this section if he or she attains a favorable judgment in such enforcement action.

(c) *Requirements.* (1) Indemnification shall be made to such person under paragraph (b) of this section only if:

(i) Final judgment on the merits is in his or her favor; or

(ii) In case of:

(A) Settlement,

(B) Final judgment against him or her, or

(C) Final judgment in his or her favor, other than on the merits, if a majority of the disinterested directors of the Federal savings association determine that he or she was acting in good faith within the scope of his or her employment or authority as he or she could reasonably have perceived it under the circumstances and for a purpose he or she could reasonably have believed under the circumstances was in the best interests of the savings association or its members.

(2) However, no indemnification shall be made unless the association gives the OCC at least 60 days' notice of its intention to make such indemnification. Such notice shall state the facts on which the action arose, the terms of any settlement, and any disposition of the action by a court. Such notice, a copy thereof, and a certified copy of the resolution containing the required determination by the board of directors shall be sent to the association's supervisory office, which shall promptly acknowledge receipt thereof. The notice period shall run from the date of such receipt. No such indemnification shall be made if the OCC advises the association in writing, within such notice period, the OCC's objection thereto.

(d) *Insurance.* A Federal savings association may obtain insurance to protect it and its directors, officers, and employees from potential losses arising from claims against any of them for alleged wrongful acts, or wrongful acts, committed in their capacity as directors, officers, or employees. However, no Federal savings association may obtain insurance which provides for payment of losses of any person incurred as a consequence of his or her willful or criminal misconduct.

(e) *Payment of expenses.* If a majority of the directors of a Federal savings association concludes that, in connection with an action, any person ultimately may become entitled to indemnification under this section, the directors may authorize payment of reasonable costs and expenses, including reasonable attorneys' fees, arising from the defense or settlement of such action. Nothing in this paragraph (e) shall prevent the directors of the savings association from imposing such conditions on a payment of expenses as they deem warranted and in the interests of the savings association. Before making advance payment of expenses under this paragraph (e), the savings association shall obtain an agreement that the savings association will be repaid if the person on whose behalf payment is made is later determined not to be entitled to such indemnification.

(f) *Exclusiveness of provisions.* No Federal savings association shall indemnify any person referred to in paragraph (b) of this section or obtain insurance referred to in paragraph (d) of the section other than in accordance with this section. However, an association which has a bylaw in effect relating to indemnification of its personnel shall be governed solely by that bylaw, except that its authority to obtain insurance shall be governed by paragraph (d) of this section.

(g) The indemnification provided for in paragraph (b) of this section is subject to and qualified by 12 U.S.C. 1821(k).

PARTS 146–149 [RESERVED]

PART 150—FIDUCIARY POWERS OF FEDERAL SAVINGS ASSOCIATIONS

Sec.

150.10 What regulations govern the fiduciary operations of Federal savings associations?
150.20 What are fiduciary powers?
150.30 What fiduciary capacities does this part cover?
150.40 When do I have investment discretion?
150.50 What is a fiduciary account?
150.60 What other definitions apply to this part?

Subpart A—Obtaining Fiduciary Powers

150.70 Must I obtain OCC approval or file a notice before I exercise fiduciary powers?

Subpart B—Exercising Fiduciary Powers

150.130 How may I conduct multi-state operations?
150.135 How do I determine which state's laws apply to my operations?
150.136 To what extent do state laws apply to my fiduciary operations?
150.140 Must I adopt and follow written policies and procedures in exercising fiduciary powers?

FIDUCIARY PERSONNEL AND FACILITIES

150.150 Who is responsible for the exercise of fiduciary powers?
150.160 What personnel and facilities may I use to perform fiduciary services?
150.170 May my other departments or affiliates use fiduciary personnel and facilities to perform other services?
150.180 May I perform fiduciary services for, or purchase fiduciary services from, another association or entity?
150.190 Must fiduciary officers and employees be bonded?

REVIEW OF A FIDUCIARY ACCOUNT

150.200 Must I review a prospective account before I accept it?
150.210 Must I conduct another review of an account after I accept it?
150.220 Are any other account reviews required?

CUSTODY AND CONTROL OF ASSETS

150.230 Who must maintain custody or control of assets in a fiduciary account?
150.240 May I hold investments of a fiduciary account off-premises?
150.245 When is a fiduciary not required to maintain custody or control of fiduciary assets?
150.250 Must I keep fiduciary assets separate from other assets?

INVESTING FUNDS OF A FIDUCIARY ACCOUNT

150.260 How may I invest funds of a fiduciary account?

FUNDS AWAITING INVESTMENT OR DISTRIBUTION

150.290 What must I do with fiduciary funds awaiting investment or distribution?
150.300 Where may I deposit fiduciary funds awaiting investment or distribution?
150.310 What if the FDIC does not insure the deposits?
150.320 What is acceptable collateral for uninsured deposits?

RESTRICTIONS ON SELF DEALING

150.330 Are there investments in which I may not invest funds of a fiduciary account?
150.340 May I exercise rights to purchase additional stock or fractional shares of my stock or obligations or the stock or obligations of my affiliates?
150.350 May I lend, sell, or transfer assets of a fiduciary account if I have an interest in the transaction?
150.360 May I make a loan to a fiduciary account that is secured by an interest in the assets of the account?
150.370 May I sell assets or lend money between fiduciary accounts?

COMPENSATION, GIFTS, AND BEQUESTS

150.380 May I earn compensation for acting in a fiduciary capacity?
150.390 May my officer or employee retain compensation for acting as a co-fiduciary?
150.400 May my fiduciary officer or employee accept a gift or bequest?

RECORDKEEPING REQUIREMENTS

150.410 What records must I keep?
150.420 How long must I keep these records?
150.430 Must I keep fiduciary records separate and distinct from other records?

AUDIT REQUIREMENTS

150.440 When do I have to audit my fiduciary activities?
150.450 What standards govern the conduct of the audit?
150.460 Who may conduct an audit?
150.470 Who directs the conduct of the audit?
150.480 How do I report the results of the audit?

Subpart C—Depositing Securities With State Authorities

150.490 When must I deposit securities with state authorities?
150.500 How much must I deposit if I administer fiduciary assets in more than one state?
150.510 What must I do if state authorities refuse my deposit?

Subpart D—Terminating Fiduciary Activities Receivership or Liquidation

150.520 What happens if I am placed in receivership or voluntary liquidation?

SURRENDER OF FIDUCIARY POWERS

150.530 How do I surrender fiduciary powers?
150.540 When will the OCC terminate my fiduciary powers?
150.550 May I recover my deposit from state authorities?

REVOCATION OF FIDUCIARY POWERS

150.560 When may the OCC revoke my fiduciary powers?
150.570 What procedures govern the revocation?

Subpart E—Activities Exempt From This Part

150.580 When may I conduct fiduciary activities without obtaining OCC approval?
150.590 What standards must I observe when acting in exempt fiduciary capacities?
150.600 How may funds be invested when I act in an exempt fiduciary capacity?
150.610 What disclosures must I make when acting in exempt fiduciary capacities?
150.620 May I receive compensation for acting in exempt fiduciary capacities?

AUTHORITY: 12 U.S.C. 1462a, 1463, 1464, 5412(b)(2)(B).

SOURCE: 76 FR 49003, Aug. 9, 2011, unless otherwise noted.

§ 150.10 What regulations govern the fiduciary operations of Federal savings associations?

A Federal savings association ("you") must conduct its fiduciary operations in accordance with 12 U.S.C. 1464(n) and this part.

§ 150.20 What are fiduciary powers?

Fiduciary powers are the authority that the OCC permits you to exercise under 12 U.S.C. 1464(n).

§ 150.30 What fiduciary capacities does this part cover?

You are subject to this part if you act in a fiduciary capacity, except as described in subpart E of this part. You act in a fiduciary capacity when you act in any of the following capacities:

(a) Trustee.

(b) Executor.

(c) Administrator.

(d) Registrar of stocks and bonds.

(e) Transfer agent.

(f) Assignee.

(g) Receiver.

(h) Guardian or conservator of the estate of a minor, an incompetent person, an absent person, or a person over whose estate a court has taken jurisdiction, other than under bankruptcy or insolvency laws.

(i) A fiduciary in a relationship established under a state law that is substantially similar to the Uniform Gifts to Minors Act or the Uniform Transfers to Minors Act as published by the American Law Institute.

(j) Investment adviser, if you receive a fee for your investment advice.

(k) Any capacity in which you have investment discretion on behalf of another.

(l) Any other similar capacity that the OCC may authorize under 12 U.S.C. 1464(n).

§ 150.40 When do I have investment discretion?

(a) *General.* You have investment discretion when you have, with respect to a fiduciary account, the sole or shared authority to determine what securities or other assets to purchase or sell on behalf of that account. It does not matter whether you have exercised this authority.

(b) *Delegations.* You retain investment discretion if you delegate investment discretion to another. You also have investment discretion if you receive delegated authority to exercise investment discretion from another.

§ 150.50 What is a fiduciary account?

A fiduciary account is an account that you administer acting in a fiduciary capacity.

§ 150.60 What other definitions apply to this part?

Activities ancillary to your fiduciary business include advertising, marketing, or soliciting fiduciary business, contacting existing or potential customers, answering questions and providing information to customers related to their accounts, acting as liaison between you and your customer (for example, forwarding requests for distribution, changes in investment objectives, forms, or funds received from the customer), and inspecting or maintaining custody of fiduciary assets or holding title to real property. This list is illustrative and not comprehensive. Other activities may also be "ancillary activities" for purposes of this definition.

Affiliate has the same meaning as in 12 U.S.C. 221a(b). For purposes of this part, substitute the term "Federal savings association" for the term "member bank" whenever it appears in 12 U.S.C. 221a(b).

Applicable law means the law of a state or other jurisdiction governing your fiduciary relationships, any Federal law governing those relationships, the terms of the instrument governing a fiduciary relationship, and any court order pertaining to the relationship.

Fiduciary activities include accepting a fiduciary appointment, executing fiduciary-related documents, providing investment advice for a fee regarding fiduciary assets, or making discretionary decisions regarding investment or distribution of assets.

Fiduciary officers and employees means the officers and employees of a Federal savings association to whom the board of directors or its designee has assigned functions involving the exercise of the association's fiduciary powers.

Subpart A—Obtaining Fiduciary Powers

§ 150.70 Must I obtain OCC approval or file a notice before I exercise fiduciary powers?

Except for fiduciary activities subject solely to subpart E, you should refer to 12 CFR 5.26 to determine if you must obtain OCC approval or file a notice with the OCC before you exercise fiduciary powers. A Federal savings association may not exercise fiduciary powers unless it obtains prior approval from the OCC to the extent required under 12 CFR 5.26.

[80 FR 28480, May 18, 2015]

Subpart B—Exercising Fiduciary Powers

§ 150.130 How may I conduct multistate operations?

(a) *Conducting fiduciary activities in more than one state.* You may conduct fiduciary activities in any state, subject to the application and notice requirements in § 5.26 of this chapter.

(b) *Serving customers in more than one state.* When you conduct fiduciary activities in a state:

(1) You may market your fiduciary services to, and act as a fiduciary for, customers located in any state, may act as a fiduciary for relationships that include property located in other states, and may act as a testamentary trustee for a testator located in other states.

(2) You may establish or utilize an office in any state to perform activities that are ancillary to your fiduciary business.

[76 FR 49003, Aug. 9, 2011, as amended at 80 FR 28480, May 18, 2015]

§ 150.135 How do I determine which state's laws apply to my operations?

(a) The state laws that apply to you by virtue of 12 U.S.C. 1464(n) are the laws of the states in which you conduct fiduciary activities. For each individual state, you may conduct fiduciary activities in the capacity of trustee, executor, administrator, guardian, or in any other fiduciary capacity the state permits for its state banks, trust companies, or other corporations that compete with Federal savings associations in the state.

(b) For each fiduciary relationship, the state referred to in 12 U.S.C. 1464(n) is the state in which you conduct fiduciary activities for that relationship.

§ 150.136 To what extent do state laws apply to my fiduciary operations?

(a) *Application of state law.* To enhance safety and soundness and to enable Federal savings associations to conduct their fiduciary activities in accordance with the best practices of thrift institutions in the United States (by efficiently delivering fiduciary services to the public free from undue regulatory duplication and burden), the OCC intends to give Federal savings associations maximum flexibility to exercise their fiduciary powers in accordance with a uniform scheme of Federal regulation. Accordingly, Federal savings associations may exercise fiduciary powers as authorized under Federal law, including this part, without regard to state laws that purport to regulate or otherwise affect their fiduciary activities, except to the extent provided in 12 U.S.C. 1464(n) (state laws regarding scope of fiduciary powers, access to examination reports regarding trust activities, deposits of securities, oaths and affidavits, and capital) or in paragraph (c) of this section. For purposes of this section, "state law" includes any state statute, regulation, ruling, order, or judicial decision.

(b) *Illustrative examples.* Examples of state laws that are preempted by the HOLA and this section include those regarding:

(1) Registration and licensing;

(2) Recordkeeping;

(3) Advertising and marketing;

(4) The ability of a Federal savings association conducting fiduciary activities to maintain an action or proceeding in state court; and

(5) Fiduciary-related fees.

(c) *State laws that are not preempted.* State laws of the following types are not preempted to the extent that they only incidentally affect the fiduciary operations of Federal savings associations or are otherwise consistent with the purposes of paragraph (a) of this section:

(1) Contract and commercial law;

(2) Real property law;

(3) Tort law;

(4) Criminal law;

(5) Probate law; and

(6) Any other law that the OCC, upon review, finds:

(i) Furthers a vital state interest; and

(ii) Either has only an incidental effect on fiduciary operations or is not otherwise contrary to the purposes expressed in paragraph (a) of this section.

§ 150.140 Must I adopt and follow written policies and procedures in exercising fiduciary powers?

You must adopt and follow written policies and procedures adequate to maintain your fiduciary activities in compliance with applicable law. Among other relevant matters, the policies and procedures should address, where appropriate, the following areas:

(a) Your brokerage placement practices.

(b) Your methods for ensuring that your fiduciary officers and employees do not use material inside information in connection with any decision or recommendation to purchase or sell any security.

(c) Your methods for preventing self-dealing and conflicts of interest.

(d) Your selection and retention of legal counsel who is ready and available to advise you and your fiduciary officers and employees on fiduciary matters.

(e) Your investment of funds held as fiduciary, including short-term investments and the treatment of fiduciary funds awaiting investment or distribution.

Fiduciary Personnel and Facilities

§ 150.150 Who is responsible for the exercise of fiduciary powers?

The exercise of your fiduciary powers must be managed by or under the direction of your board of directors. In discharging its responsibilities, the board may assign any function related to the exercise of fiduciary powers to any director, officer, employee, or committee of directors, officers, or employees.

§ 150.160 What personnel and facilities may I use to perform fiduciary services?

You may use your qualified personnel and facilities or an affiliate's qualified personnel and facilities to perform services related to the exercise of fiduciary powers.

§ 150.170 May my other departments or affiliates use fiduciary personnel and facilities to perform other services?

Your other departments or affiliates may use fiduciary officers, employees, and facilities to perform services unrelated to the exercise of fiduciary powers, to the extent not prohibited by applicable law.

§ 150.180 May I perform fiduciary services for, or purchase fiduciary services from, another association or entity?

You may perform services related to the exercise of fiduciary powers for another association or other entity under a written agreement. You may also purchase services related to the exercise of fiduciary powers from another association or other entity under a written agreement.

§ 150.190 Must fiduciary officers and employees be bonded?

You must obtain an adequate bond for all fiduciary officers and employees.

REVIEW OF A FIDUCIARY ACCOUNT

§ 150.200 Must I review a prospective account before I accept it?

Before accepting a prospective fiduciary account, you must review it to determine whether you can properly administer the account.

§ 150.210 Must I conduct another review of an account after I accept it?

After you accept a fiduciary account for which you have investment discretion, you must conduct a prompt review of all assets of the account to evaluate whether they are appropriate, individually and collectively, for the account.

§ 150.220 Are any other account reviews required?

At least once every calendar year, you must conduct a review of all assets of each fiduciary account for which you have investment discretion. In this review, you must evaluate whether the assets are appropriate, individually and collectively, for the account.

CUSTODY AND CONTROL OF ASSETS

§ 150.230 Who must maintain custody or control of assets in a fiduciary account?

You must place assets of fiduciary accounts in the joint custody or control of not fewer than two fiduciary officers or employees designated for that purpose by the board of directors.

§ 150.240 May I hold investments of a fiduciary account off-premises?

You may hold the investments of a fiduciary account off-premises, if this practice is consistent with applicable law, and you maintain adequate safeguards and controls.

§ 150.245 When is a fiduciary not required to maintain custody or control of fiduciary assets?

If you are deemed a fiduciary based solely on your capacity as investment advisor, as that capacity is defined in § 9.101(a) of this chapter, and have no other fiduciary capacity as enumerated in § 150.30, you are not required to maintain custody or control of fiduciary assets as set forth in § 150.220 or § 150.240.

[82 FR 8109, Jan. 23, 2017]

§ 150.250 Must I keep fiduciary assets separate from other assets?

You must keep the assets of fiduciary accounts separate from your other assets. You must also keep the assets of each fiduciary account separate from all other accounts, or you must identify the investments as the property of a particular account, except as provided in § 150.260.

INVESTING FUNDS OF A FIDUCIARY ACCOUNT

§ 150.260 How may I invest funds of a fiduciary account?

(a) *General.* You must invest funds of a fiduciary account in a manner consistent with applicable law.

(b) *Collective investment funds.* (1) You may invest funds of a fiduciary account in a collective investment fund, including a collective investment fund that you have established. In establishing and administering such funds, you must comply with 12 CFR 9.18.

(2) If you must file a document with the OCC under 12 CFR 9.18, the OCC may review such documents for compliance with this part and other laws and regulations.

(3) "Bank" and "national bank" as used in 12 CFR 9.18 shall be deemed to include a Federal savings association.

FUNDS AWAITING INVESTMENT OR DISTRIBUTION

§ 150.290 What must I do with fiduciary funds awaiting investment or distribution?

If you have investment discretion or discretion over distributions for a fiduciary account which contains funds awaiting investment or distribution, you must ensure that those funds do not remain uninvested and undistributed any longer than is reasonable for the proper management of the account and consistent with applicable law. You also must obtain a rate of return for those funds that is consistent with applicable law.

§ 150.300 Where may I deposit fiduciary funds awaiting investment or distribution?

(a) *Self deposits.* You may deposit funds of a fiduciary account that are awaiting investment or distribution in your other departments, unless prohibited by applicable law.

(b) *Affiliate deposits.* You may also deposit funds of a fiduciary account that are awaiting investment or distribution with an affiliated insured depository institution, unless prohibited by applicable law.

§ 150.310 What if the FDIC does not insure the deposits?

If the FDIC does not insure the entire amount of a self deposit, you must set aside collateral as security. If the FDIC does not insure the entire amount of an affiliate deposit, you or your affiliate must set aside collateral as security. The market value of the collateral must at all times equal or exceed the amount of the uninsured fiduciary funds. You must place the collateral under the control of appropriate fiduciary officers and employees.

§ 150.320 What is acceptable collateral for uninsured deposits?

Any of the following is acceptable collateral for self deposits or affiliate deposits under § 150.310:

(a) Direct obligations of the United States, or other obligations fully guaranteed by the United States as to principal and interest.

(b) Readily marketable securities of the classes in which state-chartered corporate fiduciaries are permitted to invest fiduciary funds under applicable state law.

(c) Other readily marketable securities as the OCC may determine.

(d) Surety bonds, to the extent they provide adequate security, unless prohibited by applicable law.

(e) Any other assets that qualify under applicable state law as appropriate security for deposits of fiduciary funds.

RESTRICTIONS ON SELF DEALING

§ 150.330 Are there investments in which I may not invest funds of a fiduciary account?

You may not invest funds of a fiduciary account for which you have investment discretion in the following assets, unless authorized by applicable law:

(a) The stock or obligations of, or assets acquired from, you or any of your directors, officers, or employees.

(b) The stock or obligations of, or assets acquired from, your affiliates or any of their directors, officers, or employees.

(c) The stock or obligations of, or assets acquired from, other individuals or organizations if you have an interest in the individual or organization that might affect the exercise of your best judgment.

§ 150.340 May I exercise rights to purchase additional stock or fractional shares of my stock or obligations or the stock or obligations of my affiliates?

If the retention of investments in your stock or obligations or the stock or obligations of an affiliate in fiduciary accounts is consistent with applicable law, you may do either of the following:

(a) Exercise rights to purchase additional stock (or securities convertible into additional stock) when these rights are offered *pro rata* to stockholders.

(b) Purchase fractional shares to complement fractional shares acquired through the exercise of rights or through the receipt of a stock dividend resulting in fractional share holdings.

§ 150.350 May I lend, sell, or transfer assets of a fiduciary account if I have an interest in the transaction?

(a) *General restriction.* Except as provided in paragraph (b) of this section, you may not lend, sell, or otherwise transfer assets of a fiduciary account for which you have investment discretion to yourself or any of your directors, officers, or employees; to your affiliates or any of their directors, officers, or employees; or to other individuals or organizations with whom you have an interest that might affect the exercise of your best judgment.

(b) *Exceptions*—(1) *Funds for which you have investment discretion.* You may lend, sell or otherwise transfer assets of a fiduciary account for which you have investment discretion to yourself or any of your directors, officers, or employees; to your affiliates or any of their directors, officers, or employees; or to other individuals or organizations with whom you have an interest that might affect the exercise of your best judgment, if you meet one of the following conditions:

(i) The transaction is authorized by applicable law.

(ii) Legal counsel advises you in writing that you have incurred, in your fiduciary capacity, a contingent or potential liability. Upon the sale or transfer of assets, you must reimburse the fiduciary account in cash in an amount equal to the greater of book or market value of the assets.

(iii) The transaction is permitted under 12 CFR 9.18(b)(8)(iii) for defaulted fixed-income investments.

(iv) The OCC requires you to do so.

(2) *Funds held as trustee.* You may make loans of funds held in trust to any of your directors, officers, or employees if the funds are held in an employee benefit plan and the loan is made in accordance with the exemptions found at section 408 of the Employee Retirement Income Security Act of 1974 (29 U.S.C. 1108).

§ 150.360 May I make a loan to a fiduciary account that is secured by an interest in the assets of the account?

You may make a loan to a fiduciary account that is secured by an interest in the assets of the account, if the transaction is fair to the account and is not prohibited by applicable law.

§ 150.370 May I sell assets or lend money between fiduciary accounts?

You may sell assets or lend money between fiduciary accounts, if the transaction is fair to both accounts and is not prohibited by applicable law.

Compensation, Gifts, and Bequests

§ 150.380 May I earn compensation for acting in a fiduciary capacity?

If the amount of your compensation for acting in a fiduciary capacity is not set or governed by applicable law, you may charge a reasonable fee for your services.

§ 150.390 May my officer or employee retain compensation for acting as a co-fiduciary?

You may not permit your officers or employees to retain any compensation for acting as a co-fiduciary with you in the administration of a fiduciary account, except with the specific approval of your board of directors.

§ 150.400 May my fiduciary officer or employee accept a gift or bequest?

You may not permit any fiduciary officer or employee to accept a bequest or gift of fiduciary assets, unless the bequest or gift is directed or made by a relative of the officer or employee or is specifically approved by your board of directors.

Recordkeeping Requirements

§ 150.410 What records must I keep?

You must keep adequate records for all fiduciary accounts. For example, you must keep documents on the establishment and termination of each fiduciary account.

§ 150.420 How long must I keep these records?

You must keep fiduciary records for three years after the termination of the account or the termination of any litigation relating to the account, whichever is later.

§ 150.430 Must I keep fiduciary records separate and distinct from other records?

You must keep fiduciary records separate and distinct from your other records.

Audit Requirements

§ 150.440 When do I have to audit my fiduciary activities?

(a) *Annual audit.* If you do not use a continuous audit system described in paragraph (b) of this section, then you must arrange for a suitable audit of all significant fiduciary activities at least once during each calendar year.

(b) *Continuous audit.* Instead of an annual audit, you may adopt a continuous audit system. Under a continuous audit system, you must arrange for a discrete audit of each significant fiduciary activity (*i.e.*, on an activity-by-activity basis) at an interval commensurate with the nature and risk of that activity. Some fiduciary activities may receive audits at intervals greater or less than one year, as appropriate.

§ 150.450 What standards govern the conduct of the audit?

Auditors must follow generally accepted standards for attestation engagements and other standards established by the OCC. An audit must ascertain whether your internal control policies and procedures provide reasonable assurance of three things:

(a) You are administering fiduciary activities in accordance with applicable law.

(b) You are properly safeguarding fiduciary assets.

(c) You are accurately recording transactions in appropriate accounts in a timely manner.

§ 150.460 Who may conduct an audit?

Internal auditors, external auditors, or other qualified persons who are responsible only to the board of directors, may conduct an audit.

§ 150.470 Who directs the conduct of the audit?

Your fiduciary audit committee directs the conduct of the audit. Your fiduciary audit committee may consist of a committee of your directors or an audit committee of an affiliate. There are two restrictions on who may serve on the committee:

(a) Your officers and officers of an affiliate who participate significantly in administering your fiduciary activities may not serve on the audit committee.

(b) A majority of the members of the audit committee may not serve on any committee to which the board of directors has delegated power to manage and control your fiduciary activities.

§ 150.480 How do I report the results of the audit?

(a) *Annual audit.* If you conduct an annual audit, you must note the results of the audit (including significant actions taken as a result of the audit) in the minutes of the board of directors.

(b) *Continuous audit.* If you adopt a continuous audit system, you must note the results of all discrete audits conducted since the last audit report (including significant actions taken as a result of the audits) in the minutes of the board of directors at least once during each calendar year.

Subpart C—Depositing Securities With State Authorities

§ 150.490 When must I deposit securities with state authorities?

You must deposit securities with a state's authorities or, if applicable, a Federal Home Loan Bank under § 150.510, if you meet all of the following:

(a) You are located in the state.

(b) You act as a private or court-appointed trustee.

(c) The law of the state requires corporations acting in a fiduciary capacity to deposit securities with state authorities for the protection of private or court trusts.

§ 150.500 How much must I deposit if I administer fiduciary assets in more than one state?

If you administer fiduciary assets in more than one state, you must compute the amount of deposit required for each state on the basis of fiduciary assets that you administer primarily from offices located in that state.

§ 150.510 What must I do if state authorities refuse my deposit?

If state authorities refuse to accept your deposit under § 150.490, you must deposit the securities with the Federal Home Loan Bank of which you are a member. The Federal Home Loan Bank will hold the securities for the protection of private or court trusts to the same extent as if the securities had been deposited with state authorities.

Subpart D—Terminating Fiduciary Activities Receivership or Liquidation

§ 150.520 What happens if I am placed in receivership or voluntary liquidation?

If the OCC appoints a conservator or receiver, or if you place yourself in voluntary liquidation, the receiver, conservator, or liquidating agent must promptly close or transfer all fiduciary accounts to a substitute fiduciary, in accordance with OCC instructions and the orders of the court having jurisdiction.

SURRENDER OF FIDUCIARY POWERS

§ 150.530 How do I surrender fiduciary powers?

If you want to surrender your fiduciary powers, you must file a certified copy of a resolution of your board of directors evidencing that intent. You must file the resolution with the appropriate OCC licensing office.

§ 150.540 When will the OCC terminate my fiduciary powers?

If, after appropriate investigation, the OCC is satisfied that you have been discharged from all fiduciary duties, the appropriate OCC licensing office will issue a written notice indicating that you are no longer authorized to exercise fiduciary powers.

§ 150.550 May I recover my deposit from state authorities?

Upon issuance of the OCC written notice under § 150.540, you may recover any securities deposited with state authorities, or a Federal Home Loan Bank, under subpart C of this part.

REVOCATION OF FIDUCIARY POWERS

§ 150.560 When may the OCC revoke my fiduciary powers?

The OCC may revoke your fiduciary powers if it determines that you have done any of the following:

(a) Exercised those fiduciary powers unlawfully or unsoundly.

(b) Failed to exercise those fiduciary powers for five consecutive years.

(c) Otherwise failed to follow the requirements of this part.

§ 150.570 What procedures govern the revocation?

The procedures for revocation of fiduciary powers are set forth in 12 U.S.C. 1464(n)(10). The OCC will conduct the hearing required under 12 U.S.C. 1464(n)(10)(B) under part 109 of this chapter.

Subpart E—Activities Exempt From This Part

§ 150.580 When may I conduct fiduciary activities without obtaining OCC approval?

Subject to the requirements of this subpart E, you do not need OCC approval under subpart B if you conduct fiduciary activities in the following fiduciary capacities:

(a) Trustee of a trust created or organized in the United States and forming part of a stock bonus, pension, or profit-sharing plan qualifying for specific tax treatment under section 401(d) of the Internal Revenue Code of 1954 (26 U.S.C. 401(d)).

(b) Trustee or custodian of a Individual Retirement Account within the meaning of section 408(a) of the Internal Revenue Code of 1954 (26 U.S.C. 408(a)).

§ 150.590 What standards must I observe when acting in exempt fiduciary capacities?

You must observe principles of sound fiduciary administration, including those related to recordkeeping and segregation of assets.

§ 150.600 How may funds be invested when I act in an exempt fiduciary capacity?

If you act in an exempt fiduciary capacity under § 150.580, the funds of the fiduciary account may be invested only in the following:

(a) Your accounts, deposits, obligations, or securities.

(b) Other assets as the customer may direct, provided you do not exercise any investment discretion and do not directly or indirectly provide any investment advice for the fiduciary account.

§ 150.610 What disclosures must I make when acting in exempt fiduciary capacities?

(a) If you act in an exempt fiduciary capacity under § 150.580 and fiduciary investments are not limited to accounts or deposits insured by the FDIC, you must include the following language in bold type on the first page of any contract documents:

(b) Funds invested pursuant to this agreement are not insured by the FDIC merely because the trustee or custodian is a Federal savings association the accounts of which are covered by such insurance. Only investments in the accounts of a Federal savings association are insured by the FDIC, subject to its rules and regulations.

§ 150.620 May I receive compensation for acting in exempt fiduciary capacities?

You may receive reasonable compensation.

PART 151—RECORDKEEPING AND CONFIRMATION REQUIREMENTS FOR SECURITIES TRANSACTIONS

Sec.
151.10 What does this part do?
151.20 Must I comply with this part?
151.30 What requirements apply to all transactions?
151.40 What definitions apply to this part?

Subpart A—Recordkeeping Requirements

151.50 What records must I maintain for securities transactions?
151.60 How must I maintain my records?

Subpart B—Content and Timing of Notice

151.70 What type of notice must I provide when I effect a securities transaction for a customer?
151.80 How do I provide a registered broker-dealer confirmation?
151.90 How do I provide a written notice?
151.100 What are the alternate notice requirements?
151.120 May I charge a fee for a notice?

Subpart C—Settlement of Securities Transactions

151.130 When must I settle a securities transaction?

Subpart D—Securities Trading Policies and Procedures

151.140 What policies and procedures must I maintain and follow for securities transactions?
151.150 How do my officers and employees file reports of personal securities trading transactions?

AUTHORITY: 12 U.S.C. 1462a, 1463, 1464, 5412(b)(2)(B).

SOURCE: 76 FR 49008, Aug. 9, 2011, unless otherwise noted.

§ 151.10 What does this part do?

This part establishes recordkeeping and confirmation requirements that apply when a Federal savings association ("you") effects certain securities transactions for customers.

§ 151.20 Must I comply with this part?

(a) *General.* Except as provided under paragraph (b) of this section, you must comply with this part when:

(1) You effect a securities transaction for a customer.

(2) You effect a transaction in government securities.

(3) You effect a transaction in municipal securities and are not registered as a municipal securities dealer with the SEC.

(4) You effect a securities transaction as fiduciary. You also must comply with 12 CFR part 150 when you effect such a transaction.

(b) *Exceptions*—(1) *Small number of transactions.* You are not required to comply with §§ 151.50(b) through (d) (recordkeeping) and 151.140(a) through (c) (policies and procedures), if you effected an average of fewer than 500 securities transactions per year for customers over the three prior calendar years. You may exclude transactions in government securities when you calculate this average.

(2) *Government securities.* If you effect fewer than 500 government securities brokerage transactions per year, you are not required to comply with § 151.50 (recordkeeping) for those transactions. This exception does not apply to government securities dealer transactions. *See* 17 CFR 404.4(a).

(3) *Municipal securities.* If you are registered with the SEC as a "municipal securities dealer," as defined in 15 U.S.C. 78c(a)(30) (*see* 15 U.S.C. 78o–4),

you are not required to comply with this part when you conduct municipal securities transactions.

(4) *Foreign branches.* You are not required to comply with this part when you conduct a transaction at your foreign branch.

(5) *Transactions by registered broker-dealers.* You are not required to comply with this part for securities transactions effected by a registered broker-dealer, if the registered broker-dealer directly provides the customer with a confirmation. These transactions include a transaction effected by your employee who also acts as an employee of a registered broker-dealer ("dual employee").

§ 151.30 What requirements apply to all transactions?

You must effect all transactions, including transactions excepted under § 151.20, in a safe and sound manner. You must maintain effective systems of records and controls regarding your customers' securities transactions. These systems must clearly and accurately reflect all appropriate information and provide an adequate basis for an audit.

§ 151.40 What definitions apply to this part?

Asset-backed security means a security that is primarily serviced by the cash flows of a discrete pool of receivables or other financial assets, either fixed or revolving, that by their terms convert into cash within a finite time period. *Asset-backed security* includes any rights or other assets designed to ensure the servicing or timely distribution of proceeds to the security holders.

Common or collective investment fund means any fund established under 12 CFR 150.260(b) or 12 CFR 9.18.

Completion of the transaction means:

(1) If the customer purchases a security through or from you, except as provided in paragraph (2) of this definition, the time the customer pays you any part of the purchase price. If payment is made by a bookkeeping entry, the time you make the bookkeeping entry for any part of the purchase price.

(2) If the customer purchases a security through or from you and pays for the security before you request payment or notify the customer that payment is due, the time you deliver the security to or into the account of the customer.

(3) If the customer sells a security through or to you, except as provided in paragraph (4) of this definition, the time the customer delivers the security to you. If you have custody of the security at the time of sale, the time you transfer the security from the customer's account.

(4) If the customer sells a security through or to you and delivers the security to you before you request delivery or notify the customer that delivery is due, the time you pay the customer or pay into the customer's account.

Customer means a person or account, including an agency, trust, estate, guardianship, or other fiduciary account for which you effect a securities transaction. *Customer* does not include a broker or dealer, or you when you: act as a broker or dealer; act as a fiduciary with investment discretion over an account; are a trustee that acts as the shareholder of record for the purchase or sale of securities; or are the issuer of securities that are the subject of the transaction.

Debt security means any security, such as a bond, debenture, note, or any other similar instrument that evidences a liability of the issuer (including any security of this type that is convertible into stock or a similar security). *Debt security* also includes a fractional or participation interest in these debt securities. *Debt security* does not include securities issued by an investment company registered under the Investment Company Act of 1940, 15 U.S.C. 80a–1, *et seq.*

Government security means:

(1) A security that is a direct obligation of, or an obligation that is guaranteed as to principal and interest by, the United States;

(2) A security that is issued or guaranteed by a corporation in which the United States has a direct or indirect interest if the Secretary of the Treasury has designated the security for exemption as necessary or appropriate in

the public interest or for the protection of investors;

(3) A security issued or guaranteed as to principal and interest by a corporation if a statute specifically designates, by name, the corporation's securities as exempt securities within the meaning of the laws administered by the SEC; or

(4) Any put, call, straddle, option, or privilege on a government security described in this definition, other than a put, call, straddle, option, or privilege:

(i) That is traded on one or more national securities exchanges; or

(ii) For which quotations are disseminated through an automated quotation system operated by a registered securities association.

Investment discretion means the same as under 12 CFR 150.40(a).

Investment company plan means any plan under which:

(1) A customer purchases securities issued by an open-end investment company or unit investment trust registered under the Investment Company Act of 1940, making the payments directly to, or made payable to, the registered investment company, or the principal underwriter, custodian, trustee, or other designated agent of the registered investment company; or

(2) A customer sells securities issued by an open-end investment company or unit investment trust registered under the Investment Company Act of 1940 under:

(i) An individual retirement or individual pension plan qualified under the Internal Revenue Code; or

(ii) A contractual or systematic agreement under which the customer purchases at the applicable public offering price, or redeems at the applicable redemption price, securities in specified amounts (calculated in security units or dollars) at specified time intervals, and stating the commissions or charges (or the means of calculating them) that the customer will pay in connection with the purchase.

Municipal security means:

(1) A security that is a direct obligation of, or an obligation guaranteed as to principal or interest by, a state or any political subdivision, or any agency or instrumentality of a state or any political subdivision.

(2) A security that is a direct obligation of, or an obligation guaranteed as to principal or interest by, any municipal corporate instrumentality of one or more states; or

(3) A security that is an industrial development bond.

Periodic plan means a written document that authorizes you to act as agent to purchase or sell for a customer a specific security or securities (other than securities issued by an open end investment company or unit investment trust registered under the Investment Company Act of 1940). The written document must authorize you to purchase or sell in specific amounts (calculated in security units or dollars) or to the extent of dividends and funds available, at specific time intervals, and must set forth the commission or charges to be paid by the customer or the manner of calculating them.

SEC means the Securities and Exchange Commission.

Security means any note, stock, treasury stock, bond, debenture, certificate of interest or participation in any profit-sharing agreement or in any oil, gas, or other mineral royalty or lease, any collateral-trust certificate, preorganization certificate or subscription, transferable share, investment contract, voting-trust certificate, and any put, call, straddle, option, or privilege on any security or group or index of securities (including any interest therein or based on the value thereof), or, in general, any instrument commonly known as a "security'; or any certificate of interest or participation in, temporary or interim certificate for, receipt for, or warrant or right to subscribe to or purchase, any of the foregoing.

Security does not include currency; any note, draft, bill of exchange, or banker's acceptance which has a maturity at the time of issuance of less than nine months, exclusive of days of grace, or any renewal thereof, the maturity of which is likewise limited; a deposit or share account in a Federal or state chartered depository institution; a loan participation; a letter of credit or other form of bank indebtedness incurred in the ordinary course of business; units of a collective investment fund; interests in a variable amount (master) note of a borrower of prime credit; U.S. Savings Bonds; or any other instrument the OCC determines does not constitute a security for purposes of this part.

Sweep account means any prearranged, automatic transfer or sweep of funds above a certain dollar level from a deposit account to purchase a security or securities, or any prearranged, automatic redemption or sale of a security or securities when a deposit account drops below a certain level with the proceeds being transferred into a deposit account.

[76 FR 49008, Aug. 9, 2011, as amended at 82 FR 8110, Jan. 23, 2017]

Subpart A—Recordkeeping Requirements

§ 151.50 What records must I maintain for securities transactions?

If you effect securities transactions for customers, you must maintain all of the following records for at least three years:

(a) *Chronological records.* You must maintain an itemized daily record of each purchase and sale of securities in chronological order, including:

(1) The account or customer name for which you effected each transaction;

(2) The name and amount of the securities;

(3) The unit and aggregate purchase or sale price;

(4) The trade date; and

(5) The name or other designation of the registered broker-dealer or other person from whom you purchased the securities or to whom you sold the securities.

(b) *Account records.* You must maintain account records for each customer reflecting:

(1) Purchases and sales of securities;

(2) Receipts and deliveries of securities;

(3) Receipts and disbursements of cash; and

(4) Other debits and credits pertaining to transactions in securities.

(c) *Memorandum (order ticket).* You must make and keep current a memorandum (order ticket) of each order or any other instruction given or received for the purchase or sale of securities (whether executed or not), including:

(1) The account or customer name for which you effected each transaction;

(2) Whether the transaction was a market order, limit order, or subject to special instructions;

(3) The time the trader received the order;

(4) The time the trader placed the order with the registered broker-dealer, or if there was no registered broker-dealer, the time the trader executed or cancelled the order;

(5) The price at which the trader executed the order;

(6) The name of the registered broker-dealer you used.

(d) *Record of registered broker-dealers.* You must maintain a record of all registered broker-dealers that you selected to effect securities transactions and the amount of commissions that you paid or allocated to each registered broker-dealer during each calendar year.

(e) *Notices.* You must maintain a copy of the written notice required under subpart B of this part.

§ 151.60 How must I maintain my records?

(a) *In general.* The records required by § 151.50 must clearly and accurately reflect the information required and provide an adequate basis for the audit of the information. Record maintenance may include the use of automated or electronic records provided the records are easily retrievable, readily available for inspection, and capable of being reproduced in a hard copy.

(b) *Use of third party.* You may contract with third-party service providers to maintain the records required by this section, provided that you maintain effective oversight of the third-party vendor to ensure records meet the requirements of § 150.50 and this section.

[82 FR 8110, Jan. 23, 2017]

Subpart B—Content and Timing of Notice

§ 151.70 What type of notice must I provide when I effect a securities transaction for a customer?

If you effect a securities transaction for a customer, you must give or send the customer the registered broker-dealer confirmation described at § 151.80, or the written notice described at § 151.90. For certain types of transactions, you may elect to provide the alternate notices described in § 151.100.

§ 151.80 How do I provide a registered broker-dealer confirmation?

(a) If you elect to satisfy § 151.70 by providing the customer with a registered broker-dealer confirmation, you must provide the confirmation by having the registered broker-dealer send the confirmation directly to the customer or by sending a copy of the registered broker-dealer's confirmation to the customer within one business day after you receive it.

(b) Unless you have determined remuneration in a written agreement with the customer, if you have received or will receive remuneration from any source, including the customer, in connection with the transaction, you must provide a statement of the source and amount of the remuneration in addition to the registered broker-dealer confirmation described in paragraph (a) of this section.

[76 FR 49008, Aug. 9, 2011, as amended at 82 FR 8110, Jan. 23, 2017]

§ 151.90 How do I provide a written notice?

If you elect to satisfy § 151.70 by providing the customer a written notice, you must give or send the written notice at or before the completion of the securities transaction. You must include all of the following information in a written notice:

(a) Your name and the customer's name.

(b) The capacity in which you acted (for example, as agent).

(c) The date and time of execution of the securities transaction (or a statement that you will furnish this information within a reasonable time after the customer's written request), and the identity, price, and number of shares or units (or principal amount in the case of debt securities) of the security the customer purchased or sold.

(d) The name of the person from whom you purchased or to whom you sold the security, or a statement that you will furnish this information within a reasonable time after the customer's written request.

(e) The amount of any remuneration that you have received or will receive from the customer in connection with the transaction unless the remuneration paid by the customer is determined under a written agreement, other than on a transaction basis.

(f) The source and amount of any other remuneration you have received or will receive in connection with the transaction. If, in the case of a purchase, you were not participating in a distribution, or in the case of a sale, were not participating in a tender offer, the written notice may state whether you have or will receive any other remuneration and state that you will furnish the source and amount of the other remuneration within a reasonable time after the customer's written request.

(g) That you are not a member of the Securities Investor Protection Corporation, if that is the case. This does not apply to a transaction in shares of a registered open-end investment company or unit investment trust if the customer sends funds or securities directly to, or receives funds or securities directly from, the registered open-end investment company or unit investment trust, its transfer agent, its custodian, or a designated broker or dealer who sends the customer either a confirmation or the written notice in this section.

(h) Additional disclosures. You must provide all of the additional disclosures described in the following chart for transactions involving certain debt securities:

If you effect a transaction involving . . .	You must provide the following additional information in your written notice . . .
(1) A debt security subject to redemption before maturity	A statement that the issuer may redeem the debt security in whole or in part before maturity, that the redemption could affect the represented yield, and that additional redemption information is available upon request.

If you effect a transaction involving . . .	You must provide the following additional information in your written notice . . .
(2) A debt security that you effected exclusively on the basis of a dollar price.	(i) The dollar price at which you effected the transaction; and (ii) The yield to maturity calculated from the dollar price. You do not have to disclose the yield to maturity if: (A) The issuer may extend the maturity date of the security with a variable interest rate; or (B) The security is an asset-backed security that represents an interest in, or is secured by, a pool of receivables or other financial assets that are subject continuously to prepayment.
(3) A debt security that you effected on basis of yield	(i) The yield at which the transaction, including the percentage amount and its characterization (e.g., current yield, yield to maturity, or yield to call). If you effected the transaction at yield to call, you must indicate the type of call, the call date, and the call price; (ii) The dollar price calculated from that yield; and (iii) The yield to maturity and the represented yield, if you effected the transaction on a basis other than yield to maturity and the yield to maturity is lower than the represented yield. You are not required to disclose this information if: (A) The issuer may extend the maturity date of the security with a variable interest rate; or (B) The security is an asset-backed security that represents an interest in, or is secured by, a pool of receivables or other financial assets that are subject continuously to prepayment.
(4) A debt security that is an asset-backed security that represents an interest in, or is secured by, a pool of receivables or other financial assets that are subject continuously to prepayment.	(i) A statement that the actual yield of the asset-backed security may vary according to the rate at which the underlying receivables or other financial assets are prepaid; and (ii) A statement that you will furnish information concerning the factors that affect yield (including at a minimum estimated yield, weighted average life, and the prepayment assumptions underlying yield) upon the customer's written request.
(5) A debt security, other than a government security	A statement that the security is unrated by a nationally recognized statistical rating organization, if that is the case.

§ 151.100 What are the alternate notice requirements?

You may elect to satisfy § 151.70 by providing the alternate notices described in the following chart for certain types of transactions.

If you effect a securities transaction . . .	Then you may elect to . . .
(a) For or with the account of a customer under a periodic plan, sweep account, or investment company plan.	Give or send to the customer within five business days after the end of each quarterly period a written statement disclosing: (1) Each purchase and redemption that you effected for or with, and each dividend or distribution that you credited to or reinvested for, the customer's account during the period; (2) The date of each transaction; (3) The identity, number, and price of any securities that the customer purchased or redeemed in each transaction; (4) The total number of shares of the securities in the customer's account; (5) Any remuneration that you received or will receive in connection with the transaction; and (6) That you will give or send the registered broker-dealer confirmation described in § 151.80 or the written notice described in § 151.90 within a reasonable time after the customer's written request.
(b) For or with the account of a customer in shares of an open-ended management company registered under the Investment Company Act of 1940 that holds itself out as a money market fund and attempts to maintain a stable net asset value per share.	Give or send to the customer the written statement described at paragraph (a) of this section on a monthly basis. You may not use the alternate notice, however, if you deduct sales loads upon the purchase or redemption of shares in the money market fund.
(c) For an account for which you do not exercise investment discretion, and for which you and the customer have agreed in writing to an arrangement concerning the time and content of the written notice.	Give or send to the customer a written notice at the agreed-upon time and with the agreed-upon content, and include a statement that you will furnish the registered broker-dealer confirmation described in § 151.80 or the written notice described in § 151.90 within a reasonable time after the customer's written request.

If you effect a securities transaction . . .	Then you may elect to . . .
(d) For an account for which you exercise investment discretion other than in an agency capacity, excluding common or collective investment funds.	Give or send the registered broker-dealer confirmation described in § 151.80 or the written notice described in § 151.90 within a reasonable time after a written request by the person with the power to terminate the account or, if there is no such person, any person holding a vested beneficial interest in the account.
(e) For an account in which you exercise investment discretion in an agency capacity.	Give or send each customer a written itemized statement specifying the funds and securities in your custody or possession and all debits, credits, and transactions in the customer's account. You must provide this information to the customer not less than once every three months. You must give or send the registered broker-dealer confirmation described in § 151.80 or the written notice described in § 151.90 within a reasonable time after a customer's written request.
(f) For a common or collective investment fund	(1) Give or send to a customer who invests in the fund a copy of the annual financial report of the fund, or (2) Notify the customer that a copy of the report is available and that you will furnish the report within a reasonable time after a written request by a person to whom a regular periodic accounting would ordinarily be rendered with respect to each participating account.

§ 151.120 May I charge a fee for a notice?

You may not charge a fee for providing a notice required under this subpart B, except that you may charge a reasonable fee for the notices provided under §§ 151.100(a), (d), and (e).

Subpart C—Settlement of Securities Transactions

§ 151.130 When must I settle a securities transaction?

(a) You may not effect or enter into a contract for the purchase or sale of a security that provides for payment of funds and delivery of securities later than the latest of:

(1) The number of business days in the standard settlement cycle followed by registered broker dealers in the United States after the date of the contract. The number of business days in the standard settlement cycle shall be determined by reference to paragraph (a) of SEC Rule 15c6–1, 17 CFR 240.15c6–1(a);

(2) The fourth business day after the contract, if the contract involves the sale for cash of securities that are priced after 4:30 p.m. Eastern Standard Time on the date the securities are priced and are sold by an issuer to an underwriter under a firm commitment underwritten offering registered under the Securities Act of 1933, 15 U.S.C. 77a, *et seq.*, or are sold by you to an initial purchaser participating in the offering;

(3) Such time as the SEC may specify pursuant to an order of exemption in accordance with paragraph (b)(2) of SEC Rule 15c6–1; or

(4) Such time as the parties expressly agree at the time of the transaction. The parties to a contract are deemed to have expressly agreed to an alternate date for payment of funds and delivery of securities at the time of the transaction for a contract for the sale for cash of securities under a firm commitment offering, if the managing underwriter and the issuer have agreed to the date for all securities sold under the offering and the parties to the contract have not expressly agreed to another date for payment of funds and delivery of securities at the time of the transaction.

(b) The deadlines in paragraph (a) of this section do not apply to the purchase or sale of limited partnership interests that are not listed on an exchange or for which quotations are not disseminated through an automated quotation system of a registered securities association.

[76 FR 49008, Aug. 9, 2011, as amended at 83 FR 26349, June 7, 2018]

Subpart D—Securities Trading Policies and Procedures

§ 151.140 What policies and procedures must I maintain and follow for securities transactions?

If you effect securities transactions for customers, you must maintain and follow policies and procedures that meet all of the following requirements:

(a) Your policies and procedures must assign responsibility for the supervision of all officers or employees who:

(1) Transmit orders to, or place orders with, registered broker-dealers;

(2) Execute transactions in securities for customers; or

(3) Process orders for notice or settlement purposes, or perform other back office functions for securities transactions that you effect for customers. Policies and procedures for personnel described in this paragraph (a)(3) must provide supervision and reporting lines that are separate from supervision and reporting lines for personnel described in paragraphs (a)(1) and (2) of this section.

(b) Your policies and procedures must provide for the fair and equitable allocation of securities and prices to accounts when you receive orders for the same security at approximately the same time and you place the orders for execution either individually or in combination.

(c) Your policies and procedures must provide for securities transactions in which you act as agent for the buyer and seller (crossing of buy and sell orders) on a fair and equitable basis to the parties to the transaction, where permissible under applicable law.

(d) Your policies and procedures must require your officers and employees to file the personal securities trading reports described at § 151.150, if the officer or employee:

(1) Makes investment recommendations or decisions for the accounts of customers;

(2) Participates in the determination of these recommendations or decisions; or

(3) In connection with their duties, obtains information concerning which securities you intend to purchase, sell, or recommend for purchase or sale.

§ 151.150 How do my officers and employees file reports of personal securities trading transactions?

An officer or employee described in § 151.140(d) must report all personal transactions in securities made by or on behalf of the officer or employee if he or she has a beneficial interest in the security.

(a) *Contents and filing of report.* The officer or employee must file the report with you no later than 30 calendar days after the end of each calendar quarter. The report must include the following information:

(1) The date of each transaction, the title and number of shares, the interest rate and maturity date (if applicable), and the principal amount of each security involved.

(2) The nature of each transaction (i.e., purchase, sale, or other type of acquisition or disposition).

(3) The price at which each transaction was effected.

(4) The name of the broker, dealer, or other intermediary effecting the transaction.

(5) The date the officer or employee submitted the report.

(b) *Report not required for certain transactions.* Your officer or employee is not required to report a transaction if:

(1) He or she has no direct or indirect influence or control over the account for which the transaction was effected or over the securities held in that account;

(2) The transaction was in shares issued by an open-end investment company registered under the Investment Company Act of 1940;

(3) The transaction was in direct obligations of the government of the United States;

(4) The transaction was in bankers' acceptances, bank certificates of deposit, commercial paper or high quality short term debt instruments, including repurchase agreements; or

(5) The officer or employee had an aggregate amount of purchases and sales of $10,000 or less during the calendar quarter.

(c) *Alternate report.* When you act as an investment adviser to an investment company registered under the Investment Company Act of 1940, an officer or employee that is an "access person" may fulfill his or her reporting requirements under this section by filing with you the "access person" personal securities trading report required by SEC Rule 17j–1(d), 17 CFR 270.17j–1(d).

PARTS 152–154 [RESERVED]

PART 155—ELECTRONIC OPERATIONS OF FEDERAL SAVINGS ASSOCIATIONS

Sec.
155.100 Scope.
155.200 Use of electronic means and facilities.
155.210 Requirements for using electronic means and facilities.

AUTHORITY: 12 U.S.C. 1462a, 1463, 1464, 5412(b)(2)(B).

SOURCE: 82 FR 8110, Jan. 23, 2017, unless otherwise noted.

§ 155.100 Scope.

This part describes how a Federal savings association may provide products and services through electronic means and facilities.

§ 155.200 Use of electronic means and facilities.

(a) *General.* A Federal savings association may use, or participate with others to use, electronic means or facilities to perform any function, or provide any product or service, as part of an authorized activity. Electronic means or facilities include, but are not limited to, automated teller machines, automated loan machines, personal computers, the internet, telephones, and other similar electronic devices.

(b) *Other.* To optimize the use of resources, a Federal savings association may market and sell, or participate with others to market and sell, electronic capacities and by-products to third-parties, if the savings association acquired or developed these capacities and by-products in good faith as part of providing financial services.

§ 155.210 Requirements for using electronic means and facilities.

To use electronic means and facilities under this subpart, a Federal savings association's management must:

(a) Identify, assess, and mitigate potential risks and establish prudent internal controls; and

(b) Implement security measures designed to ensure secure operations. Such measures must be adequate to:

(1) Prevent unauthorized access to the savings association's records and its customers' records;

(2) Prevent financial fraud through the use of electronic means or facilities; and

(3) Comply with applicable security devices requirements of part 168 of this chapter.

PART 156 [RESERVED]

PART 157—DEPOSITS

Sec.
157.1 What does this part do?
157.10 What authorities govern the issuance of deposit accounts by a Federal savings association?
157.11 To what extent does Federal law preempt state laws?
157.12–157.13 [Reserved]
157.14 What interest rate may I pay on accounts?
157.15 Who owns a deposit account?
157.20 What records should I maintain on deposit activities?

AUTHORITY: 12 U.S.C. 1462a, 1463, 1464, 5412(b)(2)(B).

SOURCE: 76 FR 49025, Aug. 9, 2011, unless otherwise noted.

§ 157.1 What does this part do?

This part applies to the deposit activities of Federal savings associations.

§ 157.10 What authorities govern the issuance of deposit accounts by Federal savings associations?

A Federal savings association ("you") may raise funds through accounts and may issue evidence of accounts under section 5(b)(1) of the HOLA (12 U.S.C. 1464(b)(1)), your charter, and this part. Additionally, 12 CFR parts 204 and 230 apply to your deposit activities.

§ 157.11 To what extent does Federal law preempt deposit-related state laws?

State law applies to the deposit activities of Federal savings associations and their subsidiaries to the same extent and in the same manner that those laws apply to national banks and their subsidiaries.

§§ 157.12–157.13 [Reserved]

§ 157.14 What interest rate may I pay on accounts?

(a) You may pay interest at any rate or anticipated rate of return on accounts, either in deposit or in share form, as provided in your charter and the account's terms.

(b) You may pay fixed or variable rates. If you pay a variable rate, you must base it on a schedule, index, or formula that you specify in the account's terms.

§ 157.15 Who owns a deposit account?

You may treat the holder of record as the account owner, even if you receive contrary notice, until you transfer the account on your records.

§ 157.20 What records should I maintain on deposit activities?

You should establish and maintain deposit documentation practices and records that demonstrate that you appropriately administer and monitor deposit-related activities. Your records should adequately evidence ownership, balances, and all transactions involving each account. You may maintain records on deposit activities in any format that is consistent with standard business practices.

PARTS 158–159 [RESERVED]

PART 160—LENDING AND INVESTMENT

Sec.

160.1 General.
160.2 Applicability of law.
160.3 Definitions.
160.30 General lending and investment powers of Federal savings associations.
160.31 Election regarding categorization of loans or investments and related calculations.
160.32 Pass-through investments.
160.33 Late charges.
160.34 Prepayments.
160.35 Adjustments to home loans.
160.36 De minimis investments.
160.40 Commercial paper and corporate debt securities.
160.41 Leasing.
160.42 State and local government obligations.
160.43 Foreign assistance investments.
160.50 Letters of credit and other independent undertakings—authority.
160.60 Suretyship and guaranty.
160.100 Real estate lending standards; purpose and scope.
160.101 Real estate lending standards.
160.110 Most favored lender usury preemption.
160.120 Letters of credit and other independent undertakings to pay against documents.
160.121 Investment in state housing corporations.
160.130 Prohibition on loan procurement fees.
160.160 Asset classification.
160.170 Records for lending transactions.
160.172 Re-evaluation of real estate owned.
160.210 [Reserved]
160.220 [Reserved]

AUTHORITY: 12 U.S.C. 1462a, 1463, 1464, 1467a, 1701j–3, 1828, 3803, 3806, 5412(b)(2)(B); 42 U.S.C. 4106.

SOURCE: 76 FR 49030, Aug. 9, 2011, unless otherwise noted.

§ 160.1 General.

(a) *Authority and scope.* This part is being issued by the OCC under its general rulemaking and supervisory authority under the Home Owners' Loan Act (HOLA), 12 U.S.C. 1462 *et seq.*

(b) *General lending standards.* Each savings association is expected to conduct its lending and investment activities prudently. Each association should use lending and investment standards that are consistent with safety and soundness, ensure adequate portfolio diversification and are appropriate for the size and condition of the institution, the nature and scope of its operations, and conditions in its lending market. Each association should adequately monitor the condition of its portfolio and the adequacy of any collateral securing its loans.

§ 160.2 Applicability of law.

State law applies to the lending activities of Federal savings associations and their subsidiaries to the same extent and in the same manner that those laws apply to national banks and their subsidiaries.

§ 160.3 Definitions.

For purposes of this part and any determination under 12 U.S.C. 1467a(m):

Consumer loans include loans for personal, family, or household purposes and loans reasonably incident thereto, and may be made as either open-end or closed-end consumer credit (as defined at 12 CFR 226.2(a)(10) and (20)). Consumer loans do not include credit extended in connection with credit card loans, bona fide overdraft loans, and other loans that the savings association has designated as made under investment or lending authority other than section 5(c)(2)(D) of the HOLA.

Credit card is any card, plate, coupon book, or other single credit device that may be used from time to time to obtain credit.

Credit card account is a credit account established in conjunction with the issuance of, or the extension of credit through, a credit card. This term includes loans made to consolidate credit card debt, including credit card debt held by other lenders, and participation certificates, securities and similar instruments secured by credit card receivables.

Home loans include any loans made on the security of a home (including a dwelling unit in a multi-family residential property such as a condominium or a cooperative), combinations of homes and business property (*i.e.*, a home used in part for business), farm residences, and combinations of farm residences and commercial farm real estate.

Investment grade means a security that meets the creditworthiness standards described in 12 U.S.C. 1831e.

Loan commitment includes a loan in process, a letter of credit, or any other commitment to extend credit.

Real estate loan, for purposes of this part, is a loan for which the savings association substantially relies upon a security interest in real estate given by the borrower as a condition of making the loan. A loan is made on the security of real estate if:

(1) The security property is real estate pursuant to the law of the state in which the property is located;

(2) The security interest of the Federal savings association may be enforced as a real estate mortgage or its equivalent pursuant to the law of the state in which the property is located;

(3) The security property is capable of separate appraisal; and

(4) With regard to a security property that is a leasehold or other interest for a period of years, the term of the interest extends, or is subject to extension or renewal at the option of the Federal savings association for a term of at least five years following the maturity of the loan.

Small business includes a small business concern or entity as defined by section 3(a) of the Small Business Act, 15 U.S.C. 632(a), and implemented by the regulations of the Small Business Administration at 13 CFR part 121.

Small business loans and *loans to small businesses* include any loan to a small business as defined in this section; or a loan that does not exceed $2 million (including a group of loans to one borrower) and is for commercial, corporate, business, or agricultural purposes.

[76 FR 49030, Aug. 9, 2011, as amended at 77 FR 35258, June 13, 2012]

§ 160.30 General lending and investment powers of Federal savings associations.

Pursuant to section 5(c) of the Home Owners' Loan Act (''HOLA''), 12 U.S.C. 1464(c), a Federal savings association may make, invest in, purchase, sell, participate in, or otherwise deal in (including brokerage or warehousing) all loans and investments allowed under section 5(c) of the HOLA including, without limitation, the following loans, extensions of credit, and investments, subject to the limitations indicated and any such terms, conditions, or limitations as may be prescribed from time to time by the OCC by policy directive, order, or regulation:

LENDING AND INVESTMENT POWERS CHART

Category	Statutory authorization [1]	Statutory investment limitations (Endnotes contain applicable regulatory limitations)
Bankers' bank stock	5(c)(4)(E)	Same terms as applicable to national banks.
Business development credit corporations	5(c)(4)(A)	The lesser of .5% of total outstanding loans or $250,000.
Commercial loans	5(c)(2)(A)	20% of total assets, provided that amounts in excess of 10% of total assets may be used only for small business loans.
Commercial paper and corporate debt securities.	5(c)(2)(D)	Up to 35% of total assets. [2] [3]
Community development loans and equity investments.	5(c)(3)(A)	5% of total assets, provided equity investments do not exceed 2% of total assets. [4]
Construction loans without security	5(c)(3)(C)	In the aggregate, the greater of total capital or 5% of total assets.
Consumer loans	5(c)(2)(D)	Up to 35% of total assets. [2] [5]
Credit card loans or loans made through credit card accounts.	5(c)(1)(T)	None. [6]
Deposits in insured depository institutions	5(c)(1)(G)	None. [6]
Education loans	5(c)(1)(U)	None. [6]
Federal government and government-sponsored enterprise securities and instruments.	5(c)(1)(C), 5(c)(1)(D), 5(c)(1)(E), 5(c)(1)(F).	None. [6]
Finance leasing	5(c)(1)(B), 5(c)(2)(A), 5(c)(2)(B), 5(c)(2)(D).	Based on purpose and property financed. [7]
Foreign assistance investments	5(c)(4)(C)	1% of total assets. [8]
General leasing	5(c)(2)(C)	10% of assets. [7]
Home improvement loans	5(c)(1)(J)	None. [6]
Home (residential) loans [9]	5(c)(1)(B)	None. [6] [10]
HUD-insured or guaranteed investments	5(c)(1)(O)	None. [6]
Insured loans	5(c)(1)(I), 5(c)(1)(K)	None. [6]
Liquidity investments	5(c)(1)(M)	None. [6]
Loans secured by deposit accounts	5(c)(1)(A)	None. [6] [11]
Loans to financial institutions, brokers, and dealers.	5(c)(1)(L)	None. [6] [12]
Manufactured home loans	5(c)(1)(J)	None. [6] [13]
Mortgage-backed securities	5(c)(1)(R)	None. [6]
National Housing Partnership Corporation and related partnerships and joint ventures.	5(c)(1)(N)	None. [6]
New markets venture capital companies	5(c)(4)(F)	5% of total capital.
Nonconforming loans	5(c)(3)(B)	5% of total assets.
Nonresidential real property loans	5(c)(2)(B)	400% of total capital. [14]
Open-end management investment companies [15].	5(c)(1)(Q)	None. [6]
Rural business investment companies	7 U.S.C. 2009cc–9	Five percent of total capital.
Service corporations	5(c)(4)(B)	3% of total assets, as long as any amounts in excess of 2% of total assets further community, inner city, or community development purposes. [16]
Small business investment companies	15 U.S.C. 682(b)(2)	5% of total capital.
Small business-related securities	5(c)(1)(S)	None. [6]
State and local government obligations	5(c)(1)(H)	None for general obligations. Per issuer limitation of 10% of capital for other obligations. [6] [17]
State housing corporations	5(c)(1)(P)	None. [6] [18]
Transaction account loans, including overdrafts.	5(c)(1)(A)	None. [6] [19]

Endnotes

[1] All references are to section 5 of the Home Owners' Loan Act (12 U.S.C. 1464) unless otherwise indicated.

[2] For purposes of determining a Federal savings association's percentage of assets limitation, investment in commercial paper and corporate debt securities must be aggregated with the Federal savings association's investment in consumer loans.

[3] A Federal savings association may invest in commercial paper and corporate debt securities, which includes corporate debt securities convertible into stock, subject to the provisions of § 160.40 of this part. Amounts in excess of 30% of assets, in the aggregate, may be invested only in obligations purchased by the association directly from the original obligor and for which no finder's or referral fees have been paid.

[4] The 2% of assets limitation is a sublimit for investments within the overall 5% of assets limitation on community development loans and investments. The qualitative standards for such loans and investments are set forth in HOLA section 5(c)(3)(A) (formerly 5(c)(3)(B)), as explained in an opinion of the Office of Thrift Supervision Chief Counsel dated May 10, 1995.

[5] Amounts in excess of 30% of assets, in the aggregate, may be invested only in loans made by the association directly to the original obligor and for which no finder's or referral fees have been paid. A Federal savings association may include loans to dealers in consumer goods to finance inventory and floor planning in the total investment made under this section.

[6] While there is no statutory limit on certain categories of loans and investments, including credit card loans, home improvement loans, education loans, and deposit account loans, the OCC may establish an individual limit on such loans or investments if the association's concentration in such loans or investments presents a safety and soundness concern.

[7] A Federal savings association may engage in leasing activities subject to the provisions of § 160.41 of this part.

[8] This 1% of assets limitation applies to the aggregate outstanding investments made under the Foreign Assistance Act and in the capital of the Inter-American Savings and Loan Bank. Such investments may be made subject to the provisions of § 160.43 of this part.

[9] A home (or residential) loan includes loans secured by one-to-four family dwellings, multi-family residential property, and loans secured by a unit or units of a condominium or housing cooperative.

[10] A Federal savings association may make home loans subject to the provisions of §§ 160.33, 160.34, and 160.35 of this part.

[11] Loans secured by savings accounts and other time deposits may be made without limitation, provided the Federal savings association obtains a lien on, or a pledge of, such accounts. Such loans may not exceed the withdrawable amount of the account.

[12] A Federal savings association may only invest in these loans if they are secured by obligations of, or by obligations fully guaranteed as to principal and interest by, the United States or any of its agencies or instrumentalities, the borrower is a financial institution insured by the Federal Deposit Insurance Corporation or is a broker or dealer registered with the Securities and Exchange Commission, and the market value of the securities for each loan at least equals the amount of the loan at the time it is made.

[13] If the wheels and axles of the manufactured home have been removed and it is permanently affixed to a foundation, a loan secured by a combination of a manufactured home and developed residential lot on which it sits may be treated as a home loan.

[14] Without regard to any limitations of this part, a Federal savings association may make or invest in the fully insured or guaranteed portion of nonresidential real estate loans insured or guaranteed by the Economic Development Administration, the Farmers Home Administration, or the Small Business Administration. Unguaranteed portions of guaranteed loans must be aggregated with uninsured loans when determining an association's compliance with the 400% of capital limitation for other real estate loans.

[15] This authority is limited to investments in open-end management investment companies that are registered with the Securities and Exchange Commission under the Investment Company Act of 1940. The portfolio of the investment company must be restricted by the company's investment policy (changeable only if authorized by shareholder vote) solely to investments that a Federal savings association may, without limitation as to percentage of assets, invest in, sell, redeem, hold, or otherwise deal in. Separate and apart from this authority, a Federal savings association may make pass-through investments to the extent authorized by § 160.32 of this part.

[16] A Federal savings association may invest in service corporations subject to the provisions of § 5.59 of this chapter.

[17] This category includes obligations issued by any state, territory, or possession of the United States or political subdivision thereof (including any agency, corporation, or instrumentality of a state or political subdivision), subject to § 160.42 of this part.

[18] A Federal savings association may invest in state housing corporations subject to the provisions of § 160.121 of this part.

[19] Payments on accounts in excess of the account balance (overdrafts) on commercial deposit or transaction accounts shall be considered commercial loans for purposes of determining the association's percentage of assets limitation.

[76 FR 49030, Aug. 9, 2011, as amended at 80 FR 28480, May 18, 2015]

§ 160.31 Election regarding categorization of loans or investments and related calculations.

(a) If a loan or other investment is authorized under more than one section of the HOLA, as amended, or this part, a Federal savings association may designate under which section the loan or investment has been made. Such a loan or investment may be apportioned among appropriate categories, and may be moved, in whole or part, from one category to another. A loan commitment shall be counted as an investment and included in total assets of a Federal savings association for purposes of calculating compliance with HOLA section 5(c)'s investment limitations only to the extent that funds have been advanced and not repaid pursuant to the commitment.

(b) Loans or portions of loans sold to a third party shall be included in the calculation of a percentage-of-assets or percentage-of-capital investment limitation only to the extent they are sold with recourse.

(c) A Federal savings association may make a loan secured by an assignment of loans to the extent that it could, under applicable law and regulations, make or purchase the underlying assigned loans.

§ 160.32 Pass-through investments.

(a) A Federal savings association ("you") may make pass-through investments. A pass-through investment occurs when you invest in an entity ("company") that engages only in activities that you may conduct directly and the investment meets the requirements of this section. If an investment is authorized under both this section and some other provision of law, you may designate under which authority or authorities the investment is made. When making a pass-through investment, you must comply with all the statutes and regulations that would apply if you were engaging in the activity directly. For example, your proportionate share of the company's assets will be aggregated with the assets you hold directly in calculating investment limits (*e.g.*, no more than 400% of total capital may be invested in nonresidential real property loans).

(b) Your pass-through investments are subject to the requirements and filing procedures of 12 CFR 5.58.

[76 FR 49030, Aug. 9, 2011, as amended at 80 FR 28480, May 18, 2015]

§ 160.33 Late charges.

A Federal savings association may include in a home loan contract a provision authorizing the imposition of a late charge with respect to the payment of any delinquent periodic payment. With respect to any loan made after July 31, 1976, on the security of a home occupied or to be occupied by the borrower, no late charge, regardless of form, shall be assessed or collected by a Federal savings association, unless any billing, coupon, or notice the Federal savings association may provide regarding installment payments due on the loan discloses the date after which the charge may be assessed. A Federal savings association may not impose a late charge more than one time for late payment of the same installment, and any installment payment made by the borrower shall be applied to the longest outstanding installment due. A Federal savings association shall not assess a late charge as to any payment received by it within fifteen days after the due date of such payment. No form of such late charge permitted by this paragraph shall be considered as interest to the Federal savings association and the Federal savings association shall not deduct late charges from the regular periodic installment payments on the loan, but must collect them as such from the borrower.

§ 160.34 Prepayments.

Any prepayment on a real estate loan must be applied directly to reduce the principal balance on the loan unless the loan contract or the borrower specifies otherwise. Subject to the terms of the loan contract, a Federal savings association may impose a fee for any prepayment of a loan.

§ 160.35 Adjustments to home loans.

(a) For any home loan secured by borrower-occupied property, or property to be occupied by the borrower, adjustments to the interest rate, payment, balance, or term to maturity must comply with the limitations of this section and the disclosure and notice requirements of 560.210 until superseding regulations are issued by the Consumer Financial Protection Bureau.

(b) Adjustments to the interest rate shall correspond directly to the movement of an index satisfying the requirements of paragraph (d) of this section. A Federal savings association also may increase the interest rate pursuant to a formula or schedule that specifies the amount of the increase, the time at which it may be made, and which is set forth in the loan contract. A Federal savings association may decrease the interest rate at any time.

(c) Adjustments to the payment and the loan balance that do not reflect an interest-rate adjustment may be made if:

(1) The adjustments reflect a change in an index that may be used pursuant to paragraph (d) of this section;

(2) In the case of a payment adjustment, the adjustment reflects a change in the loan balance or is made pursuant to a formula, or to a schedule specifying the percentage or dollar change in the payment as set forth in the loan contract; or

(3) In the case of an open-end line-of-credit loan, the adjustment reflects an advance taken by the borrower under the line-of-credit and is permitted by the loan contract.

(d)(1) Any index used must be readily available and independently verifiable. If set forth in the loan contract, an association may use any combination of indices, a moving average of index values, or more than one index during the term of a loan.

(2) Except as provided in paragraph (d)(3) of this section, any index used must be a national or regional index.

(3) A Federal savings association may use an index not satisfying the requirements of paragraph (d)(2) of this section 30 days after filing a notice unless, within that 30-day period, the OCC has notified the association that the notice presents supervisory concerns or raises significant issues of law or policy. If the OCC provides such notice to the Federal savings association, the Federal savings association may not use

that index unless it applies for and receives the OCC's prior written approval.

[76 FR 49030, Aug. 9, 2011, as amended at 80 FR 28480, May 18, 2015]

§ 160.36 De minimis investments.

A Federal savings association may invest in the aggregate up to the greater of 1% of its total capital or $250,000 in community development investments of the type permitted for a national bank under 12 CFR part 24.

§ 160.40 Commercial paper and corporate debt securities.

Pursuant to HOLA section 5(c)(2)(D), a Federal savings association may invest in, sell, or hold commercial paper and corporate debt securities subject to the provisions of this section.

(a) *Limitations.* (1) Commercial paper must be:

(i) Investment grade as of the date of purchase; or

(ii) Guaranteed by a company having outstanding paper that meets the standard set forth in paragraph (a)(1)(i) of this section.

(2) Corporate debt securities must be:

(i) Securities that may be sold with reasonable promptness at a price that corresponds reasonably to their fair value; and

(ii) Investment grade.

(3) A Federal savings association's total investment in the commercial paper and corporate debt securities of any one issuer, or issued by any one person or entity affiliated with such issuer, together with other loans, shall not exceed the general lending limitations contained in § 32.3(a) of this chapter.

(4) Investments in corporate debt securities convertible into stock are subject to the following additional limitations:

(i) The purchase of securities convertible into stock at the option of the issuer is prohibited;

(ii) At the time of purchase, the cost of such securities must be written down to an amount that represents the investment value of the securities considered independently of the conversion feature; and

(iii) Federal savings associations are prohibited from exercising the conversion feature.

(5) A Federal savings association shall maintain information in its files adequate to demonstrate that it has exercised prudent judgment in making investments under this section.

(b) Notwithstanding the limitations contained in this section, the OCC may permit investment in corporate debt securities of another savings association in connection with the purchase or sale of a branch office or in connection with a supervisory merger or acquisition.

(c) *Underwriting.* Before committing to acquire any investment security, a Federal savings association must determine whether the investment is safe and sound and suitable for the association. The Federal savings association must consider, as appropriate, the interest rate, credit, liquidity, price, transaction, and other risks associated with the investment activity. The Federal savings association must also determine that the issuer has adequate resources and the willingness to provide for all required payments on its obligations in a timely manner.

[76 FR 49030, Aug. 9, 2011, as amended at 77 FR 35258, June 13, 2012; 77 FR 37283, June 21, 2012]

§ 160.41 Leasing.

(a) *Permissible activities.* Subject to the limitations of this section, a Federal savings association may engage in leasing activities. These activities include becoming the legal or beneficial owner of tangible personal property or real property for the purpose of leasing such property, obtaining an assignment of a lessor's interest in a lease of such property, and incurring obligations incidental to its position as the legal or beneficial owner and lessor of the leased property.

(b) *Definitions.* For the purposes of this section:

(1) The term *net lease* means a lease under which the Federal savings association will not, directly or indirectly, provide or be obligated to provide for:

(i) The servicing, repair or maintenance of the leased property during the lease term;

(ii) The purchasing of parts and accessories for the leased property, except that improvements and additions to the leased property may be leased to the lessee upon its request in accordance with the full-payout requirements of paragraph (c)(2)(i) of this section;

(iii) The loan of replacement or substitute property while the leased property is being serviced;

(iv) The purchasing of insurance for the lessee, except where the lessee has failed to discharge a contractual obligation to purchase or maintain insurance; or

(v) The renewal of any license, registration, or filing for the property unless such action by the Federal savings association is necessary to protect its interest as an owner or financier of the property.

(2) The term *full-payout lease* means a lease transaction in which any unguaranteed portion of the estimated residual value relied on by the association to yield the return of its full investment in the leased property, plus the estimated cost of financing the property over the term of the lease, does not exceed 25% of the original cost of the property to the lessor. In general, a lease will qualify as a full-payout lease if the scheduled payments provide at least 75% of the principal and interest payments that a lessor would receive if the finance lease were structured as a market-rate loan.

(3) The term *realization of investment* means that a Federal savings association that enters into a lease financing transaction must reasonably expect to realize the return of its full investment in the leased property, plus the estimated cost of financing the property over the term of the lease from:

(i) Rentals;

(ii) Estimated tax benefits, if any; and

(iii) The estimated residual value of the property at the expiration of the term of the lease.

(c) *Finance leasing*—(1) *Investment limits.* A Federal savings association may exercise its authority under HOLA sections 5(c)(1)(B) (residential real estate loans), 5(c)(2)(A) (commercial, business, corporate or agricultural loans), 5(c)(2)(B) (nonresidential real estate loans), and 5(c)(2)(D) (consumer loans) by conducting leasing activities that are the functional equivalent of loans made under those HOLA sections. These activities are commonly referred to as financing leases. Such financing leases are subject to the same investment limits that apply to loans made under those sections. For example, a financing lease of tangible personal property made to a natural person for personal, family or household purposes is subject to all limitations applicable to the amount of a Federal savings association's investment in consumer loans. A financing lease made for commercial, corporate, business, or agricultural purposes is subject to all limitations applicable to the amount of a Federal savings association's investment in commercial loans. A financing lease of residential or nonresidential real property is subject to all limitations applicable to the amount of a Federal savings association's investment in these types of real estate loans.

(2) *Functional equivalent of lending.* To qualify as the functional equivalent of a loan:

(i) The lease must be a net, full-payout lease representing a non-cancelable obligation of the lessee, notwithstanding the possible early termination of the lease;

(ii) The portion of the estimated residual value of the property relied upon by the lessor to satisfy the requirements of a full-payout lease must be reasonable in light of the nature of the leased property and all relevant circumstances so that realization of the lessor's full investment plus the cost of financing the property depends primarily on the creditworthiness of the lessee, and not on the residual market value of the leased property; and

(iii) At the termination of a financing lease, either by expiration or default, property acquired must be liquidated or released on a net basis as soon as practicable. Any property held in anticipation of re-leasing must be reevaluated and recorded at the lower of fair market value or book value.

(d) *General leasing.* Pursuant to section 5(c)(2)(C) of the HOLA, a Federal savings association may invest in tangible personal property, including vehicles, manufactured homes, machinery, equipment, or furniture, for the purpose of leasing that property. In contrast to financing leases, lease investments made under this authority need not be the functional equivalent of loans.

(e) *Leasing salvage powers.* If, in good faith, a Federal savings association believes that there has been an unanticipated change in conditions that threatens its financial position by significantly increasing its exposure to loss, it may:

(1) As the owner and lessor, take reasonable and appropriate action to salvage or protect the value of the property or its interest arising under the lease;

(2) As the assignee of a lessor's interest in a lease, become the owner and lessor of the leased property pursuant to its contractual right, or take any reasonable and appropriate action to salvage or protect the value of the property or its interest arising under the lease; or

(3) Include any provisions in a lease, or make any additional agreements, to protect its financial position or investment in the circumstances set forth in paragraphs (e)(1) and (e)(2) of this section.

§ 160.42 State and local government obligations.

(a) Pursuant to HOLA section 5(c)(1)(H), a Federal savings association may invest in obligations issued by any state, territory, possession, or political subdivision thereof ("governmental entity"), subject to appropriate underwriting and the following conditions:

	Aggregate limitation	Per-issuer limitation
(1) General obligations	None	None.
(2) Other obligations of a governmental entity (*e.g.*, revenue bonds) if the issuer has an adequate capacity to meet financial commitments under the security for the projected life of the asset or exposure. An issuer has an adequate capacity to meet financial commitments if the risk of default by the obligor is low and the full and timely repayment of principal and interest is expected.	None	10% of the institution's total capital.
(3) Obligations of a governmental entity that do not qualify under any other paragraph but are approved by the OCC.	As approved by the OCC	10% of the institution's total capital.

(b) *What is a political subdivision? Political subdivision* means a county, city, town, or other municipal corporation, a public authority, or a publicly-owned entity that is an instrumentality of a state or a municipal corporation.

(c) *What is a general obligation of a state or political subdivision?* A *general obligation* is an obligation that is guaranteed by the full faith and credit of a state or political subdivision that has the power to tax. Indirect payments, such as through a special fund, may qualify as general obligations if a state or political subdivision with taxing authority has unconditionally agreed to provide funds to cover payments.

(d) For all securities, the institution must consider, as appropriate, the interest rate, credit, liquidity, price, transaction, and other risks associated with the investment activity and determine that such investment is appropriate for the institution. The institution must also determine that the obligor has adequate resources and willingness to provide for all required payments on its obligations in a timely manner.

[76 FR 49030, Aug. 9, 2011, as amended at 77 FR 35258, June 13, 2012]

§ 160.43 Foreign assistance investments.

Pursuant to HOLA section 5(c)(4)(C), a Federal savings association may make foreign assistance investments in an aggregate amount not to exceed one percent of its assets, subject to the following conditions:

(a) For any investment made under the Foreign Assistance Act, the loan agreement shall specify what constitutes an event of default, and provide that upon default in payment of principal or interest under such agreement, the entire amount of outstanding indebtedness thereunder shall become immediately due and payable, at the lender's option. Additionally, the contract of guarantee shall cover

100% of any loss of investment thereunder, except for any portion of the loan arising out of fraud or misrepresentation for which the party seeking payment is responsible, and provide that the guarantor shall pay for any such loss in U.S. dollars within a specified reasonable time after the date of application for payment.

(b) To make any investments in the share capital and capital reserve of the Inter-American Savings and Loan Bank, a Federal savings association must be adequately capitalized and have adequate allowances for loan and lease losses. The Federal savings association's aggregate investment in such capital or capital reserve, including the amount of any obligations undertaken to provide said Bank with reserve capital in the future (call-able capital), must not, as a result of such investment, exceed the lesser of one-quarter of 1% of its assets or $100,000.

§ 160.50 Letters of credit and other independent undertakings—authority.

A Federal savings association may issue letters of credit and may issue such other independent undertakings as are approved by the OCC, subject to the restrictions in § 160.120.

§ 160.60 Suretyship and guaranty.

Pursuant to section 5(b)(2) of the HOLA, a Federal savings association may enter into a repayable suretyship or guaranty agreement, subject to the conditions in this section.

(a) *What is a suretyship or guaranty agreement?* Under a suretyship, a Federal savings association is bound with its principal to pay or perform an obligation to a third person. Under a guaranty agreement, a Federal savings association agrees to satisfy the obligation of the principal only if the principal fails to pay or perform.

(b) *What requirements apply to suretyship and guaranty agreements under this section?* A Federal savings association may enter into a suretyship or guaranty agreement under this section, subject to each of the following requirements:

(1) The Federal savings association must limit its obligations under the agreement to a fixed dollar amount and a specified duration.

(2) The Federal savings association's performance under the agreement must create an authorized loan or other investment.

(3) The Federal savings association must treat its obligation under the agreement as a loan to the principal for purposes of 12 CFR part 32 and § 163.43 of this chapter.

(4) The Federal savings association must take and maintain a perfected security interest in collateral sufficient to cover its total obligation under the agreement.

(c) *What collateral is sufficient?* (1) The Federal savings association must take and maintain a perfected security interest in real estate or marketable securities equal to at least 110 percent of its obligation under the agreement, except as provided in paragraph (c)(2) of this section.

(i) If the collateral is real estate, the Federal savings association must establish the value by a signed appraisal or evaluation in accordance with part 34, subpart C of this chapter. In determining the value of the collateral, the Federal savings association must factor in the value of any existing senior mortgages, liens or other encumbrances on the property, except those held by the principal to the suretyship or guaranty agreement.

(ii) If the collateral is marketable securities, the Federal savings association must be authorized to invest in that security taken as collateral. The Federal savings association must ensure that the value of the security is 110 percent of the obligation at all times during the term of agreement.

(2) The Federal savings association may take and maintain a perfected security interest in collateral which is at all times equal to at least 100 percent of its obligation, if the collateral is:

(i) Cash;

(ii) Obligations of the United States or its agencies;

(iii) Obligations fully guarantied by the United States or its agencies as to principal and interest; or

(iv) Notes, drafts, or bills of exchange or bankers' acceptances that are eligible for rediscount or purchase by a Federal Reserve Bank.

[76 FR 49030, Aug. 9, 2011, as amended at 77 FR 37283, June 21, 2012; 79 FR 28401, May 16, 2014]

§ 160.100 Real estate lending standards; purpose and scope.

This section, and § 160.101 of this subpart, issued pursuant to section 304 of the Federal Deposit Insurance Corporation Improvement Act of 1991, 12 U.S.C. 1828(o), prescribe standards for real estate lending to be used by Federal savings associations and all their includable subsidiaries, as defined in 12 CFR 3.22(a)(8)(iv) or 167.1, as applicable, over which the savings associations exercise control, in adopting internal real estate lending policies.

[76 FR 49030, Aug. 9, 2011, as amended at 79 FR 11313, Feb. 28, 2014]

§ 160.101 Real estate lending standards.

(a) Each Federal savings association shall adopt and maintain written policies that establish appropriate limits and standards for extensions of credit that are secured by liens on or interests in real estate, or that are made for the purpose of financing permanent improvements to real estate.

(b)(1) Real estate lending policies adopted pursuant to this section must:

(i) Be consistent with safe and sound banking practices;

(ii) Be appropriate to the size of the institution and the nature and scope of its operations; and

(iii) Be reviewed and approved by the savings association's board of directors at least annually.

(2) The lending policies must establish:

(i) Loan portfolio diversification standards;

(ii) Prudent underwriting standards, including loan-to-value limits, that are clear and measurable;

(iii) Loan administration procedures for the savings association's real estate portfolio; and

(iv) Documentation, approval, and reporting requirements to monitor compliance with the savings association's real estate lending policies.

(c) Each Federal savings association must monitor conditions in the real estate market in its lending area to ensure that its real estate lending policies continue to be appropriate for current market conditions.

(d) The real estate lending policies adopted pursuant to this section should reflect consideration of the Interagency Guidelines for Real Estate Lending Policies established by the Federal bank and thrift supervisory agencies.

Appendix to § 160.101—Interagency Guidelines for Real Estate Lending Policies

The agencies' regulations require that each insured depository institution adopt and maintain a written policy that establishes appropriate limits and standards for all extensions of credit that are secured by liens on or interests in real estate or made for the purpose of financing the construction of a building or other improvements.[1] These guidelines are intended to assist institutions in the formulation and maintenance of a real estate lending policy that is appropriate to the size of the institution and the nature and scope of its individual operations, as well as satisfies the requirements of the regulation.

Each institution's policies must be comprehensive, and consistent with safe and sound lending practices, and must ensure that the institution operates within limits and according to standards that are reviewed and approved at least annually by the board of directors. Real estate lending is an integral part of many institutions' business plans and, when undertaken in a prudent manner, will not be subject to examiner criticism.

Loan Portfolio Management Considerations

The lending policy should contain a general outline of the scope and distribution of the institution's credit facilities and the manner in which real estate loans are made, serviced, and collected. In particular, the institution's policies on real estate lending should:

- Identify the geographic areas in which the institution will consider lending.
- Establish a loan portfolio diversification policy and set limits for real estate loans by type and geographic market (*e.g.*, limits on higher risk loans).
- Identify appropriate terms and conditions by type of real estate loan.

[1] The agencies have adopted a uniform rule on real estate lending. See 12 CFR part 365 (FDIC); 12 CFR part 208, subpart C (Board); 12 CFR part 34, subpart D and 12 CFR 160.100–160.101 (OCC).

• Establish loan origination and approval procedures, both generally and by size and type of loan.

• Establish prudent underwriting standards that are clear and measurable, including loan-to-value limits, that are consistent with these supervisory guidelines.

• Establish review and approval procedures for exception loans, including loans with loan-to-value percentages in excess of supervisory limits.

• Establish loan administration procedures, including documentation, disbursement, collateral inspection, collection, and loan review.

• Establish real estate appraisal and evaluation programs.

• Require that management monitor the loan portfolio and provide timely and adequate reports to the board of directors.

The institution should consider both internal and external factors in the formulation of its loan policies and strategic plan. Factors that should be considered include:

• The size and financial condition of the institution.

• The expertise and size of the lending staff.

• The need to avoid undue concentrations of risk.

• Compliance with all real estate related laws and regulations, including the Community Reinvestment Act, anti-discrimination laws, and for savings associations, the Qualified Thrift Lender test.

• Market conditions.

The institution should monitor conditions in the real estate markets in its lending area so that it can react quickly to changes in market conditions that are relevant to its lending decisions. Market supply and demand factors that should be considered include:

• Demographic indicators, including population and employment trends.

• Zoning requirements.

• Current and projected vacancy, construction, and absorption rates.

• Current and projected lease terms, rental rates, and sales prices, including concessions.

• Current and projected operating expenses for different types of projects.

• Economic indicators, including trends and diversification of the lending area.

• Valuation trends, including discount and direct capitalization rates.

Underwriting Standards

Prudently underwritten real estate loans should reflect all relevant credit factors, including:

• The capacity of the borrower, or income from the underlying property, to adequately service the debt.

• The value of the mortgaged property.

• The overall creditworthiness of the borrower.

• The level of equity invested in the property.

• Any secondary sources of repayment.

• Any additional collateral or credit enhancements (such as guarantees, mortgage insurance or takeout commitments).

The lending policies should reflect the level of risk that is acceptable to the board of directors and provide clear and measurable underwriting standards that enable the institution's lending staff to evaluate these credit factors. The underwriting standards should address:

• The maximum loan amount by type of property.

• Maximum loan maturities by type of property.

• Amortization schedules.

• Pricing structure for different types of real estate loans.

• Loan-to-value limits by type of property.

For development and construction projects, and completed commercial properties, the policy should also establish, commensurate with the size and type of the project or property:

• Requirements for feasibility studies and sensitivity and risk analyses (*e.g.*, sensitivity of income projections to changes in economic variables such as interest rates, vacancy rates, or operating expenses).

• Minimum requirements for initial investment and maintenance of hard equity by the borrower (*e.g.*, cash or unencumbered investment in the underlying property).

• Minimum standards for net worth, cash flow, and debt service coverage of the borrower or underlying property.

• Standards for the acceptability of and limits on non-amortizing loans.

• Standards for the acceptability of and limits on the use of interest reserves.

• Pre-leasing and pre-sale requirements for income-producing property.

• Pre-sale and minimum unit release requirements for non-income-producing property loans.

• Limits on partial recourse or nonrecourse loans and requirements for guarantor support.

• Requirements for takeout commitments.

• Minimum covenants for loan agreements.

Loan Administration

The institution should also establish loan administration procedures for its real estate portfolio that address:

• Documentation, including:

Type and frequency of financial statements, including requirements for verification of information provided by the borrower;

Type and frequency of collateral evaluations (appraisals and other estimates of value).

• Loan closing and disbursement.
• Payment processing.
• Escrow administration.
• Collateral administration.
• Loan payoffs.
• Collections and foreclosure, including:
Delinquency follow-up procedures;
Foreclosure timing;
Extensions and other forms of forbearance;
Acceptance of deeds in lieu of foreclosure.
• Claims processing (*e.g.*, seeking recovery on a defaulted loan covered by a government guaranty or insurance program).
• Servicing and participation agreements.

Supervisory Loan-to-Value Limits

Institutions should establish their own internal loan-to-value limits for real estate loans. These internal limits should not exceed the following supervisory limits:

Loan category	Loan-to-value limit (percent)
Raw land	65
Land development	75
Construction:	
Commercial, multifamily,[1] and other nonresidential	80
1- to 4-family residential	85
Improved property	85
Owner-occupied 1- to 4-family and home equity	([2])

[1] Multifamily construction includes condominiums and cooperatives.
[2] A loan-to-value limit has not been established for permanent mortgage or home equity loans on owner-occupied, 1- to 4-family residential property. However, for any such loan with a loan-to-value ratio that equals or exceeds 90 percent at origination, an institution should require appropriate credit enhancement in the form of either mortgage insurance or readily marketable collateral.

The supervisory loan-to-value limits should be applied to the underlying property that collateralizes the loan. For loans that fund multiple phases of the same real estate project (*e.g.*, a loan for both land development and construction of an office building), the appropriate loan-to-value limit is the limit applicable to the final phase of the project funded by the loan; however, loan disbursements should not exceed actual development or construction outlays. In situations where a loan is fully cross-collateralized by two or more properties or is secured by a collateral pool of two or more properties, the appropriate maximum loan amount under supervisory loan-to-value limits is the sum of the value of each property, less senior liens, multiplied by the appropriate loan-to-value limit for each property. To ensure that collateral margins remain within the supervisory limits, lenders should redetermine conformity whenever collateral substitutions are made to the collateral pool.

In establishing internal loan-to-value limits, each lender is expected to carefully consider the institution-specific and market factors listed under "Loan Portfolio Management Considerations," as well as any other relevant factors, such as the particular subcategory or type of loan. For any subcategory of loans that exhibits greater credit risk than the overall category, a lender should consider the establishment of an internal loan-to-value limit for that subcategory that is lower than the limit for the overall category.

The loan-to-value ratio is only one of several pertinent credit factors to be considered when underwriting a real estate loan. Other credit factors to be taken into account are highlighted in the "Underwriting Standards" section above. Because of these other factors, the establishment of these supervisory limits should not be interpreted to mean that loans at these levels will automatically be considered sound.

Loans in Excess of the Supervisory Loan-to-Value Limits

The agencies recognize that appropriate loan-to-value limits vary not only among categories of real estate loans but also among individual loans. Therefore, it may be appropriate in individual cases to originate or purchase loans with loan-to-value ratios in excess of the supervisory loan-to-value limits, based on the support provided by other credit factors. Such loans should be identified in the institutions' records, and their aggregate amount reported at least quarterly to the institution's board of directors. (*see* additional reporting requirements described under "Exceptions to the General Policy.") The aggregate amount of all loans in excess of the supervisory loan-to-value limits should not exceed 100 percent of total capital.[2] Moreover, within the aggregate

[2] For the state member banks, the term "total capital" means "total risk-based capital" as defined in Appendix A to 12 CFR part 208. For insured state non-member banks, "total capital" refers to that term described in table I of Appendix A to 12 CFR part 325. For national banks, the term "total capital" is defined at 12 CFR 3.2(e). For savings associations, the term "total capital" as described in part 167 of this chapter.

limit, total loans for all commercial, agricultural, multifamily or other non-1-to-4 family residential properties should not exceed 30 percent of total capital. An institution will come under increased supervisory scrutiny as the total of such loans approaches these levels.

In determining the aggregate amount of such loans, institutions should: (a) Include all loans secured by the same property if any one of those loans exceeds the supervisory loan-to-value limits; and (b) include the recourse obligation of any such loan sold with recourse. Conversely, a loan should no longer be reported to the directors as part of aggregate totals when reduction in principal or senior liens, or additional contribution of collateral or equity (*e.g.*, improvements to the real property securing the loan), bring the loan-to-value ratio into compliance with supervisory limits.

Excluded Transactions

The agencies also recognize that there are a number of lending situations in which other factors significantly outweigh the need to apply the supervisory loan-to-value limits.

These include:

• Loans guaranteed or insured by the U.S. government or its agencies, provided that the amount of the guaranty or insurance is at least equal to the portion of the loan that exceeds the supervisory loan-to-value limit.

• Loans backed by the full faith and credit of a state government, provided that the amount of the assurance is at least equal to the portion of the loan that exceeds the supervisory loan-to-value limit.

• Loans guaranteed or insured by a state, municipal or local government, or an agency thereof, provided that the amount of the guaranty or insurance is at least equal to the portion of the loan that exceeds the supervisory loan-to-value limit, and provided that the lender has determined that the guarantor or insurer has the financial capacity and willingness to perform under the terms of the guaranty or insurance agreement.

• Loans that are to be sold promptly after origination, without recourse, to a financially responsible third party.

• Loans that are renewed, refinanced, or restructured without the advancement of new funds or an increase in the line of credit (except for reasonable closing costs), or loans that are renewed, refinanced, or restructured in connection with a workout situation, either with or without the advancement of new funds, where consistent with safe and sound banking practices and part of a clearly defined and well-documented program to achieve orderly liquidation of the debt, reduce risk of loss, or maximize recovery on the loan.

• Loans that facilitate the sale of real estate acquired by the lender in the ordinary course of collecting a debt previously contracted in good faith.

• Loans for which a lien on or interest in real property is taken as additional collateral through an abundance of caution by the lender (*e.g.*, the institution takes a blanket lien on all or substantially all of the assets of the borrower, and the value of the real property is low relative to the aggregate value of all other collateral).

• Loans, such as working capital loans, where the lender does not rely principally on real estate as security and the extension of credit is not used to acquire, develop, or construct permanent improvements on real property.

• Loans for the purpose of financing permanent improvements to real property, but not secured by the property, if such security interest is not required by prudent underwriting practice.

Exceptions to the General Lending Policy

Some provision should be made for the consideration of loan requests from creditworthy borrowers whose credit needs do not fit within the institution's general lending policy. An institution may provide for prudently underwritten exceptions to its lending policies, including loan-to-value limits, on a loan-by-loan basis. However, any exceptions from the supervisory loan-to-value limits should conform to the aggregate limits on such loans discussed above.

The board of directors is responsible for establishing standards for the review and approval of exception loans. Each institution should establish an appropriate internal process for the review and approval of loans that do not conform to its own internal policy standards. The approval of any such loan should be supported by a written justification that clearly sets forth all of the relevant credit factors that support the underwriting decision. The justification and approval documents for such loans should be maintained as a part of the permanent loan file. Each institution should monitor compliance with its real estate lending policy and individually report exception loans of a significant size to its board of directors.

The cross-references in the first paragraph of this footnote were originally adopted in an interagency rulemaking and are out of date as a result of revisions to capital rules implementing the Basel III Capital Framework. *See* 57 FR 63889 (December 31, 1992). For national banks and Federal savings associations, the term "total capital" is defined at 12 CFR 3.2, 3.2(e), or 167.5, as applicable. *See* 78 FR 62018 (October 11, 2013).

Supervisory Review of Real Estate Lending Policies and Practices

The real estate lending policies of institutions will be evaluated by examiners during the course of their examinations to determine if the policies are consistent with safe and sound lending practices, these guidelines, and the requirements of the regulation. In evaluating the adequacy of the institution's real estate lending policies and practices, examiners will take into consideration the following factors:

- The nature and scope of the institution's real estate lending activities.
- The size and financial condition of the institution.
- The quality of the institution's management and internal controls.
- The expertise and size of the lending and loan administration staff.
- Market conditions.

Lending policy exception reports will also be reviewed by examiners during the course of their examinations to determine whether the institutions' exceptions are adequately documented and appropriate in light of all of the relevant credit considerations. An excessive volume of exceptions to an institution's real estate lending policy may signal a weakening of its underwriting practices, or may suggest a need to revise the loan policy.

Definitions

For the purposes of these Guidelines:

Construction loan means an extension of credit for the purpose of erecting or rehabilitating buildings or other structures, including any infrastructure necessary for development.

Extension of credit or loan means:

(1) The total amount of any loan, line of credit, or other legally binding lending commitment with respect to real property; and

(2) The total amount, based on the amount of consideration paid, of any loan, line of credit, or other legally binding lending commitment acquired by a lender by purchase, assignment, or otherwise.

Improved property loan means an extension of credit secured by one of the following types of real property:

(1) Farmland, ranchland or timberland committed to ongoing management and agricultural production;

(2) 1- to 4-family residential property that is not owner-occupied;

(3) Residential property containing five or more individual dwelling units;

(4) Completed commercial property; or

(5) Other income-producing property that has been completed and is available for occupancy and use, except income-producing owner-occupied 1- to 4-family residential property.

Land development loan means an extension of credit for the purpose of improving unimproved real property prior to the erection of structures. The improvement of unimproved real property may include the laying or placement of sewers, water pipes, utility cables, streets, and other infrastructure necessary for future development.

Loan origination means the time of inception of the obligation to extend credit (*i.e.*, when the last event or prerequisite, controllable by the lender, occurs causing the lender to become legally bound to fund an extension of credit).

Loan-to-value or *loan-to-value ratio* means the percentage or ratio that is derived at the time of loan origination by dividing an extension of credit by the total value of the property(ies) securing or being improved by the extension of credit plus the amount of any readily marketable collateral and other acceptable collateral that secures the extension of credit. The total amount of all senior liens on or interests in such property(ies) should be included in determining the loan-to-value ratio. When mortgage insurance or collateral is used in the calculation of the loan-to-value ratio, and such credit enhancement is later released or replaced, the loan-to-value ratio should be recalculated.

Other acceptable collateral means any collateral in which the lender has a perfected security interest that has a quantifiable value, and is accepted by the lender in accordance with safe and sound lending practices. Other acceptable collateral should be appropriately discounted by the lender consistent with the lender's usual practices for making loans secured by such collateral. Other acceptable collateral includes, among other items, unconditional irrevocable standby letters of credit for the benefit of the lender.

Owner-occupied, when used in conjunction with the term *1- to 4-family residential property* means that the owner of the underlying real property occupies at least one unit of the real property as a principal residence of the owner.

Readily marketable collateral means insured deposits, financial instruments, and bullion in which the lender has a perfected interest. Financial instruments and bullion must be salable under ordinary circumstances with reasonable promptness at a fair market value determined by quotations based on actual transactions, on an auction or similarly available daily bid and ask price market. Readily marketable collateral should be appropriately discounted by the lender consistent with the lender's usual practices for making loans secured by such collateral.

Value means an opinion or estimate, set forth in an appraisal or evaluation, whichever may be appropriate, of the market value of real property, prepared in accordance with the agency's appraisal regulations and guidance. For loans to purchase an existing property, the term "value" means the lesser of the actual acquisition cost or the estimate of value.

1- to 4-family residential property means property containing fewer than five individual dwelling units, including manufactured homes permanently affixed to the underlying property (when deemed to be real property under state law).

[76 FR 49030, Aug. 9, 2011, as amended at 79 FR 11313, Feb. 28, 2014]

§ 160.110 Most favored lender usury preemption for all savings associations.

(a) *Definition.* The term "interest" as used in 12 U.S.C. 1463(g) includes any payment compensating a creditor or prospective creditor for an extension of credit, making available of a line of credit, or any default or breach by a borrower of a condition upon which credit was extended. It includes, among other things, the following fees connected with credit extension or availability: numerical periodic rates, late fees, not sufficient funds (NSF) fees, overlimit fees, annual fees, cash advance fees, and membership fees. It does not ordinarily include appraisal fees, premiums and commissions attributable to insurance guaranteeing repayment of any extension of credit, finders' fees, fees for document preparation or notarization, or fees incurred to obtain credit reports.

(b) *Authority.* A savings association located in a state may charge interest at the maximum rate permitted to any state-chartered or licensed lending institution by the law of that state. If state law permits different interest charges on specified classes of loans, a Federal savings association making such loans is subject only to the provisions of state law relating to that class of loans that are material to the determination of the permitted interest. For example, a Federal savings association may lawfully charge the highest rate permitted to be charged by a state-licensed small loan company, without being so licensed, but subject to state law limitations on the size of loans made by small loan companies. State supervisors determine the degree to which state-chartered savings associations must comply with state laws other than those imposing restrictions on interest, as defined in paragraph (a) of this section.

(c) *Effect on state definitions of interest.* The Federal definition of the term "interest" in paragraph (a) of this section does not change how interest is defined by the individual states (nor how the state definition of interest is used) solely for purposes of state law. For example, if late fees are not "interest" under state law where a savings association is located but state law permits its most favored lender to charge late fees, then a savings association located in that state may charge late fees to its intrastate customers. The savings association may also charge late fees to its interstate customers because the fees are interest under the Federal definition of interest and an allowable charge under state law where the savings association is located. However, the late fees would not be treated as interest for purposes of evaluating compliance with state usury limitations because state law excludes late fees when calculating the maximum interest that lending institutions may charge under those limitations.

§ 160.120 Letters of credit and other independent undertakings to pay against documents.

(a) *General authority.* A Federal savings association may issue and commit to issue letters of credit within the scope of applicable laws or rules of practice recognized by law. It may also issue other independent undertakings within the scope of such laws or rules of practice recognized by law, that have been approved by the OCC (approved undertaking).[1] Under such letters of credit and approved undertakings, the savings association's obligation to honor depends upon the presentation of specified documents and

[1] Samples of laws or rules of practice applicable to letters of credit and other independent undertakings include, but are not limited to: the applicable version of Article 5 of the Uniform Commercial Code (UCC) (1962, as amended 1990) or revised Article 5 of the UCC (as amended 1995) (available from West Publishing Co.); the Uniform Customs and Practice for Documentary Credits (International Chamber of Commerce (ICC) Publication No. 500) (available from ICC Publishing, Inc.; the United Nations Convention

Continued

not upon nondocumentary conditions or resolution of questions of fact or law at issue between the account party and the beneficiary. A savings association may also confirm or otherwise undertake to honor or purchase specified documents upon their presentation under another person's independent undertaking within the scope of such laws or rules.

(b) *Safety and soundness considerations*—(1) *Terms.* As a matter of safe and sound banking practice, Federal savings associations that issue letters of credit or approved undertakings should not be exposed to undue risk. At a minimum, savings associations should consider the following:

(i) The independent character of the letter of credit or approved undertaking should be apparent from its terms (such as terms that subject it to laws or rules providing for its independent character);

(ii) The letter of credit or approved undertaking should be limited in amount;

(iii) The letter of credit or approved undertaking should:

(A) Be limited in duration; or

(B) Permit the savings association to terminate the letter of credit or approved undertaking, either on a periodic basis (consistent with the savings association's ability to make any necessary credit assessments) or at will upon either notice or payment to the beneficiary; or

(C) Entitle the savings association to cash collateral from the account party on demand (with a right to accelerate the customer's obligations, as appropriate); and

(iv) The savings association either should be fully collateralized or have a post-honor right of reimbursement from its customer or from another issuer of a letter of credit or an independent undertaking. Alternatively, if the savings association's undertaking is to purchase documents of title, securities, or other valuable documents, it should obtain a first priority right to realize on the documents if the savings association is not otherwise to be reimbursed.

(2) *Additional considerations in special circumstances.* Certain letters of credit and approved undertakings require particular protections against credit, operational, and market risk:

(i) In the event that the undertaking is to honor by delivery of an item of value other than money, the savings association should ensure that market fluctuations that affect the value of the item will not cause the savings association to assume undue market risk;

(ii) In the event that the undertaking provides for automatic renewal, the terms for renewal should allow the savings association to make any necessary credit assessment prior to renewal;

(iii) In the event that a savings association issues an undertaking for its own account, the underlying transaction for which it is issued must be within the savings association's authority and comply with any safety and soundness requirements applicable to that transaction.

(3) *Operational expertise.* The savings association should possess operational expertise that is commensurate with the sophistication of its letter of credit or independent undertaking activities.

(4) *Documentation.* The savings association must accurately reflect its letters of credit or approved undertakings in its records, including any acceptance or deferred payment or other absolute obligation arising out of its contingent undertaking.

§ 160.121 Investment in state housing corporations.

(a) Any Federal savings association to the extent it has legal authority to do so, may make investments in, commitments to invest in, loans to, or commitments to lend to any state housing corporation; provided, that such obligations or loans are secured directly, or indirectly through a fiduciary, by a first lien on improved real estate which is insured under the National Housing Act, as amended, and that in the event of default, the holder

---

on Independent Guarantees and Standby Letters of Credit (adopted by the U.N. General Assembly in 1995 and signed by the U.S. in 1997) (available from the U.N. Commission on International Trade Law); and the Uniform Rules for Bank-to-Bank Reimbursements Under Documentary Credits (ICC Publication No. 525) (available from ICC Publishing, Inc.).

of such obligations or loans has the right directly, or indirectly through a fiduciary, to subject to the satisfaction of such obligations or loans the real estate described in the first lien, or the insurance proceeds.

(b) Any Federal savings association that is adequately capitalized may, to the extent it has legal authority to do so, invest in obligations (including loans) of, or issued by, any state housing corporation incorporated in the state in which such savings association has its home or a branch office; provided (except with respect to loans), that:

(1) The obligations are investment grade; or

(2) The obligations are approved by the OCC. The aggregate outstanding direct investment in obligations under paragraph (b) of this section shall not exceed the amount of the Federal savings association's total capital.

(c) Each state housing corporation in which a savings association invests under the authority of paragraph (b) of this section shall agree, before accepting any such investment (including any loan or loan commitment), to make available at any time to the OCC such information as the OCC may consider to be necessary to ensure that investments are properly made under this section.

[76 FR 49030, Aug. 9, 2011, as amended at 77 FR 35259, June 13, 2012]

§ 160.130 Prohibition on loan procurement fees.

If you are a director, officer, or other natural person having the power to direct the management or policies of a Federal savings association, you must not receive, directly or indirectly, any commission, fee, or other compensation in connection with the procurement of any loan made by the savings association or a subsidiary of the savings association.

§ 160.160 Asset classification.

(a)(1) Each savings association must evaluate and classify its assets on a regular basis in a manner consistent with, or reconcilable to, the asset classification system used by the OCC.

(2) In connection with the examination of a savings association or its affiliates, OCC examiners may identify problem assets and classify them, if appropriate. The association must recognize such examiner classifications in its subsequent reports to the OCC.

(b) Based on the evaluation and classification of its assets, each savings association shall establish adequate valuation allowances or charge-offs, as appropriate, consistent with generally accepted accounting principles and the practices of the Federal banking agencies.

§ 160.170 Records for lending transactions.

In establishing and maintaining its records pursuant to § 163.170 of this chapter, each Federal savings association and service corporation should establish and maintain loan documentation practices that:

(a) Ensure that the institution can make an informed lending decision and can assess risk on an ongoing basis;

(b) Identify the purpose and all sources of repayment for each loan, and assess the ability of the borrower(s) and any guarantor(s) to repay the indebtedness in a timely manner;

(c) Ensure that any claims against a borrower, guarantor, security holders, and collateral are legally enforceable;

(d) Demonstrate appropriate administration and monitoring of its loans; and

(e) Take into account the size and complexity of its loans.

§ 160.172 Re-evaluation of real estate owned.

A Federal savings association shall appraise each parcel of real estate owned at the earlier of in-substance foreclosure or at the time of the savings association's acquisition of such property, and at such times thereafter as dictated by prudent management policy; such appraisals shall be consistent with the requirements of part 34, subpart C of this chapter. The Comptroller or his or her designee may require subsequent appraisals if, in his or her discretion, such subsequent appraisal is necessary under the particular circumstances. The foregoing requirement shall not apply to any parcel of real estate that is sold and reacquired less than 12 months subsequent to the most recent appraisal made pursuant to this part. A dated, signed copy of each report of appraisal made pursuant to any provisions of this part shall be retained in the savings association's records.

[76 FR 49030, Aug. 9, 2011, as amended at 79 FR 28401, May 16, 2014]

§ 160.210 [Reserved]

§ 160.220 [Reserved]

PART 161—DEFINITIONS FOR REGULATIONS AFFECTING ALL SAVINGS ASSOCIATIONS

Sec.
161.1 When do the definitions in this part apply?
161.2 Account.
161.3 Accountholder.
161.4 Affiliate.
161.5 Affiliated person.
161.6 Audit period.
161.7 Appropriate Federal banking agency.
161.8 [Reserved]
161.9 Certificate account.
161.10 Comptroller
161.12 Consumer credit.
161.14 Controlling person.
161.15 Corporation.
161.16 Demand accounts.
161.18 Director.
161.19 Financial institution.
161.24 Immediate family.
161.26 Land loan.
161.27 Low-rent housing.
161.28 Money Market Deposit Accounts.
161.29 Negotiable Order of Withdrawal Accounts.
161.30 Nonresidential construction loan.
161.31 Nonwithdrawable account.
161.33 Note account.
161.34 OCC.
161.35 Officer.
161.37 Parent company; subsidiary.
161.38 Political subdivision.
161.39 Principal office.
161.40 Public unit.
161.41 [Reserved]
161.42 Savings account.
161.43 Savings association.
161.44 Security.
161.45 Service corporation.
161.50 State.
161.51 Subordinated debt security.
161.52 Tax and loan account.
161.53 United States Treasury General Account.
161.54 United States Treasury Time Deposit Open Account.
161.55 With recourse.

AUTHORITY: 12 U.S.C. 1462a, 1463, 1464, 1467a, 5412(b)(2)(B).

SOURCE: 76 FR 49043, Aug. 9, 2011, unless otherwise noted.

§ 161.1 When do the definitions in this part apply?

The definitions in this part and in 12 CFR part 141 apply throughout parts 100–199 of this chapter, unless another definition is specifically provided.

§ 161.2 Account.

The term *account* means any savings account, demand account, certificate account, tax and loan account, note account, United States Treasury general account or United States Treasury time deposit-open account, whether in the form of a deposit or a share, held by an accountholder in a savings association.

§ 161.3 Accountholder.

The term *accountholder* means the holder of an account or accounts in a savings association insured by the Deposit Insurance Fund. The term does not include the holder of any subordinated debt security or any mortgage-backed bond issued by the savings association.

§ 161.4 Affiliate.

The term *affiliate* of a savings association, unless otherwise defined, means any corporation, business trust, association, or other similar organization:

(a) Of which a savings association, directly or indirectly, owns or controls either a majority of the voting shares or more than 50 per centum of the number of shares voted for the election of its directors, trustees, or other persons exercising similar functions at the preceding election, or controls in any manner the election of a majority of its directors, trustees, or other persons exercising similar functions; or

(b) Of which control is held, directly or indirectly through stock ownership or in any other manner, by the shareholders of a savings association who own or control either a majority of the shares of such savings association or more than 50 per centum of the number of shares voted for the election of directors of such savings association at the preceding election, or by trustees for the benefit of the shareholders of any such savings association; or

(c) Of which a majority of its directors, trustees, or other persons exercising similar functions are directors of any one savings association.

§ 161.5 Affiliated person.

The term *affiliated person* of a savings association means the following:

(a) A director, officer, or controlling person of such association;

(b) A spouse of a director, officer, or controlling person of such association;

(c) A member of the immediate family of a director, officer, or controlling person of such association, who has the same home as such person or who is a director or officer of any subsidiary of such association or of any holding company affiliate of such association;

(d) Any corporation or organization (other than the savings association or a corporation or organization through which the savings association operates) of which a director, officer or the controlling person of such association:

(1) Is chief executive officer, chief financial officer, or a person performing similar functions;

(2) Is a general partner;

(3) Is a limited partner who, directly or indirectly either alone or with his or her spouse and the members of his or her immediate family who are also affiliated persons of the association, owns an interest of 10 percent or more in the partnership (based on the value of his or her contribution) or who, directly or indirectly with other directors, officers, and controlling persons of such association and their spouses and their immediate family members who are also affiliated persons of the association, owns an interest of 25 percent or more in the partnership; or

(4) Directly or indirectly either alone or with his or her spouse and the members of his or her immediate family who are also affiliated persons of the association, owns or controls 10 percent or more of any class of equity securities or owns or controls, with other directors, officers, and controlling persons of such association and their spouses and their immediate family members who are also affiliated persons of the association, 25 percent or more of any class of equity securities; and

(5) Any trust or other estate in which a director, officer, or controlling person of such association or the spouse of such person has a substantial beneficial interest or as to which such person or his or her spouse serves as trustee or in a similar fiduciary capacity.

§ 161.6 Audit period.

The *audit period* of a savings association means the twelve month period (or other period in the case of a change in audit period) covered by the annual audit conducted to satisfy § 163.170 of this chapter.

§ 161.7 Appropriate Federal banking agency.

The term *appropriate Federal banking agency* means appropriate Federal banking agency as that term is defined in 12 U.S.C. 1813(q).

§ 161.8 [Reserved]

§ 161.9 Certificate account.

The term *certificate account* means a savings account evidenced by a certificate that must be held for a fixed or minimum term.

§ 161.10 Comptroller.

The term *Comptroller* means the Comptroller of the Currency.

§ 161.12 Consumer credit.

The term *consumer credit* means credit extended to a natural person for personal, family, or household purposes, including loans secured by liens on real estate and chattel liens secured by mobile homes and leases of personal property to consumers that may be considered the functional equivalent of loans on personal security: *Provided*, the savings association relies substantially upon other factors, such as the general credit standing of the borrower, guaranties, or security other than the real estate or mobile home, as the primary security for the loan. Appropriate evidence to demonstrate justification for such reliance should be retained in a savings association's files. Among the types of credit included within this term are consumer loans; educational loans; unsecured loans for real property alteration, repair or improvement, or for the equipping of real property; loans in the nature of overdraft protection; and credit extended in connection with credit cards.

§ 161.14 Controlling person.

The term *controlling person* of a savings association means any person or entity which, either directly or indirectly, or acting in concert with one or more other persons or entities, owns, controls, or holds with power to vote, or holds proxies representing, ten percent or more of the voting shares or rights of such savings association; or controls in any manner the election or appointment of a majority of the directors of such savings association. However, a director of a savings association will not be deemed to be a controlling person of such savings association based upon his or her voting, or acting in concert with other directors in voting, proxies:

(a) Obtained in connection with an annual solicitation of proxies, or

(b) Obtained from savings account holders and borrowers if such proxies are voted as directed by a majority vote of the entire board of directors of such association, or of a committee of such directors if such committee's composition and authority are controlled by a majority vote of the entire board and if its authority is revocable by such a majority.

§ 161.15 Corporation.

The terms *Corporation* and *FDIC* mean the Federal Deposit Insurance Corporation.

§ 161.16 Demand accounts.

The term *demand accounts* means non-interest-bearing demand deposits that are subject to check or to withdrawal or transfer on negotiable or transferable order to the savings association and that are permitted to be issued by statute, regulation, or otherwise and are payable on demand.

§ 161.18 Director.

(a) The term *director* means any director, trustee, or other person performing similar functions with respect to any organization whether incorporated or unincorporated. Such term does not include an advisory director, honorary director, director emeritus, or similar person, unless the person is otherwise performing functions similar to those of a director.

(b) [Reserved]

§ 161.19 Financial institution.

The term *financial institution* has the same meaning as the term *depository institution* set forth in 12 U.S.C. 1813(c)(1).

§ 161.24 Immediate family.

The term *immediate family* of any natural person means the following (whether by the full or half blood or by adoption):

(a) Such person's spouse, father, mother, children, brothers, sisters, and grandchildren;

(b) The father, mother, brothers, and sisters of such person's spouse; and

(c) The spouse of a child, brother, or sister of such person.

§ 161.26 Land loan.

The term *land loan* means a loan:

(a) Secured by real estate upon which all facilities and improvements have been completely installed, as required by local regulations and practices, so that it is entirely prepared for the erection of structures;

(b) To finance the purchase of land and the accomplishment of all improvements required to convert it to developed building lots; or

(c) Secured by land upon which there is no structure.

§ 161.27 Low-rent housing.

The term *low-rent housing* means real estate which is, or which is being constructed, remodeled, rehabilitated, modernized, or renovated to be, the subject of an annual contributions contract for low-rent housing under the provisions of the United States Housing Act of 1937, as amended.

§ 161.28 Money Market Deposit Accounts.

(a) Money Market Deposit Accounts (MMDAs) offered by Federal savings associations in accordance with 12 U.S.C. 1464(b)(1) and by state-chartered savings associations in accordance with applicable state law are savings accounts on which interest may be paid if issued subject to the following limitations:

(1) The savings association shall reserve the right to require at least seven days' notice prior to withdrawal or transfer of any funds in the account; and

(2)(i) The depositor is authorized by the savings association to make no more than six transfers per calendar month or statement cycle (or similar period) of at least four weeks by means of preauthorized, automatic, telephonic, or data transmission agreement, order, or instruction to another account of the depositor at the same savings association to the savings association itself, or to a third party.

(ii) Savings associations may permit holders of MMDAs to make unlimited transfers for the purpose of repaying loans (except overdraft loans on the depositor's demand account) and associated expenses at the same savings association (as originator or servicer), to make unlimited transfers of funds from this account to another account of the same depositor at the same savings association or to make unlimited payments directly to the depositor from the account when such transfers or payments are made by mail, messenger, automated teller machine, or in person, or when such payments are made by telephone (via check mailed to the depositor).

(3) In order to ensure that no more than the number of transfers specified in paragraph (a)(2)(i) of this section are made, a savings association must either:

(i) Prevent transfers of funds in excess of the limitations; or

(ii) Adopt procedures to monitor those transfers on an after-the-fact basis and contact customers who exceed the limits on more than an occasional basis. For customers who continue to violate those limits after being contacted by the depository savings association the depository savings association must either place funds in another account that the depositor is eligible to maintain or take away the account's transfer and draft capacities.

(iii) Insured savings association at their option, may use on a consistent basis either the date on a check or the date it is paid in determining whether the transfer limitations within the specified interval are exceeded.

(b) Federal savings associations may offer MMDAs to any depositor, and state-chartered savings associations may offer MMDAs to any depositor not inconsistent with applicable state law.

§ 161.29 Negotiable Order of Withdrawal Accounts.

(a) Negotiable Order of Withdrawal (NOW) accounts are savings accounts authorized by 12 U.S.C. 1832 on which the savings association reserves the right to require at least seven days' notice prior to withdrawal or transfer of any funds in the account.

(b) For purposes of 12 U.S.C. 1832:

(1) An organization shall be deemed "operated primarily for religious, philanthropic, charitable, educational, or other similar purposes and * * * not * * * for profit" if it is described in sections 501(c)(3) through (13), 501(c)(19), or 528 of the Internal Revenue Code; and

(2) The funds of a sole proprietorship or unincorporated business owned by a husband and wife shall be deemed beneficially owned by "one or more individuals."

§ 161.30 Nonresidential construction loan.

The term *nonresidential construction loan* means a loan for construction of other than one or more dwelling units.

§ 161.31 Nonwithdrawable account.

The term *nonwithdrawable account* means an account which by the terms of the contract of the accountholder with the savings association or by provisions of state law cannot be paid to the accountholder until all liabilities, including other classes of share liability of the savings association have been fully liquidated and paid upon the winding up of the savings association is referred to as a *nonwithdrawable account*.

§ 161.33 Note account.

The term *note account* means a note, subject to the right of immediate call, evidencing funds held by depositories electing the note option under applicable United States Treasury Department regulations. Note accounts are not savings accounts or savings deposits.

§ 161.34 OCC.

The term *OCC* means Office of the Comptroller of the Currency.

§ 161.35 Officer.

The term *Officer* means the president, any vice-president (but not an assistant vice-president, second vice-president, or other vice president having authority similar to an assistant or second vice-president), the secretary, the treasurer, the comptroller, and any other person performing similar functions with respect to any organization whether incorporated or unincorporated. The term *officer* also includes the chairman of the board of directors if the chairman is authorized by the charter or by-laws of the organization to participate in its operating management or if the chairman in fact participates in such management.

§ 161.37 Parent company; subsidiary.

The term *parent company* means any company which directly or indirectly controls any other company or companies. The term *subsidiary* means any company which is owned or controlled directly or indirectly by a person, and includes any service corporation owned in whole or in part by a savings association, or a subsidiary of such service corporation.

§ 161.38 Political subdivision.

The term *political subdivision* includes any subdivision of a public unit, any principal department of such public unit:

(a) The creation of which subdivision or department has been expressly authorized by state statute,

(b) To which some functions of government have been delegated by state statute, and

(c) To which funds have been allocated by statute or ordinance for its exclusive use and control. It also includes drainage, irrigation, navigation, improvement, levee, sanitary, school or power districts and bridge or port authorities and other special districts created by state statute or compacts between the states. Excluded from the term are subordinate or nonautonomous divisions, agencies or boards within principal departments.

§ 161.39 Principal office.

The term *principal office* means the home office of a savings association established as such in conformity with the laws under which the savings association is organized.

§ 161.40 Public unit.

The term *public unit* means the United States, any state of the United States, the District of Columbia, any territory of the United States, Puerto Rico, the Virgin Islands, any county, any municipality or any political subdivision thereof.

§ 161.41 [Reserved]

§ 161.42 Savings account.

The term *savings account* means any withdrawable account, except a demand account as defined in § 161.16 of this chapter, a tax and loan account, a note account, a United States Treasury general account, or a United States Treasury time deposit-open account.

§ 161.43 Savings association.

The term *savings association* means a savings association as defined in section 3 of the Federal Deposit Insurance Act, the deposits of which are insured by the Corporation. It includes a Federal savings association or Federal savings bank, chartered under section 5 of the Act, or a building and loan, savings and loan, or homestead association, or a cooperative bank (other than a cooperative bank which is a state bank as defined in section 3(a)(2) of the Federal Deposit Insurance Act) organized and operating according to the laws of the state in which it is chartered or organized, or a corporation (other than a bank as defined in section 3(a)(1) of the Federal Deposit Insurance Act) that the Board of Directors of the Federal Deposit Insurance Corporation and the Comptroller jointly determine to be operating substantially in the same manner as a savings association.

§ 161.44 Security.

The term *security* means any non-withdrawable account, note, stock, treasury stock, bond, debenture, evidence of indebtedness, certificate of interest or participation in any profit-sharing agreement, collateral-trust certificate, preorganization certificate or subscription, transferable share, investment contract, voting-trust certificate, or, in general, any interest or instrument commonly known as a *security*, or any certificate of interest or participation in, temporary or interim certificate for, receipt for, guarantee of, or warrant or right to subscribe to or purchase, any of the foregoing, except that a *security* shall not include an account or deposit insured by the Federal Deposit Insurance Corporation.

§ 161.45 Service corporation.

The term *service corporation* has the meaning set forth in § 5.59(d)(4) of this chapter.

[80 FR 28480, May 18, 2015]

§ 161.50 State.

The term *state* means a state, the District of Columbia, Guam, Puerto Rico, and the Virgin Islands of the United States.

§ 161.51 Subordinated debt security.

The term *subordinated debt security* means any unsecured note, debenture, or other debt security issued by a savings association and subordinated on liquidation to all claims having the same priority as account holders or any higher priority.

§ 161.52 Tax and loan account.

The term *tax and loan account* means an account, the balance of which is subject to the right of immediate withdrawal, established for receipt of payments of Federal taxes and certain United States obligations. Such accounts are not savings accounts or savings deposits.

§ 161.53 United States Treasury General Account.

The term *United States Treasury General Account* means an account maintained in the name of the United States Treasury the balance of which is subject to the right of immediate withdrawal, except in the case of the closure of the member, and in which a zero balance may be maintained. Such accounts are not savings accounts or savings deposits.

§ 161.54 United States Treasury Time Deposit Open Account.

The term *United States Treasury Time Deposit Open Account* means a non-interest-bearing account maintained in the name of the United States Treasury which may not be withdrawn prior to the expiration of 30 days' written notice from the United States Treasury, or such other period of notice as the Treasury may require. Such accounts are not savings accounts or savings deposits.

§ 161.55 With recourse.

(a) The term *with recourse* means, in connection with the sale of a loan or a participation interest in a loan, an agreement or arrangement under which the purchaser is to be entitled to receive from the seller a sum of money or thing of value, whether tangible or intangible (including any substitution), upon default in payment of any loan involved or any part thereof or to withhold or to have withheld from the seller a sum of money or anything of value by way of security against default. The recourse liability resulting from a sale with recourse shall be the total book value of any loan sold with recourse less:

(1) The amount of any insurance or guarantee against loss in the event of default provided by a third party,

(2) The amount of any loss to be borne by the purchaser in the event of default, and

(3) The amount of any loss resulting from a recourse obligation entered on the books and records of the savings association.

(b) The term *with recourse* does not include loans or interests therein where the agreement of sale provides for the savings association directly or indirectly:

(1) To hold or retain a subordinate interest in a specified percentage of the loans or interests; or

(2) To guarantee against loss up to a specified percentage of the loans or interests, which specified percentage shall not exceed ten percent of the outstanding balance of the loans or interests at the time of sale: *Provided*, That the savings association designates adequate reserves for the subordinate interest or guarantee.

(c) This definition does not apply for purposes of determining the capital adequacy requirements under 12 CFR part 3 or part 167, as applicable.

[76 FR 49043, Aug. 9, 2011, as amended at 79 FR 11313, Feb. 28, 2014]

PART 162—ACCOUNTING AND DISCLOSURE STANDARDS

AUTHORITY: 12 U.S.C. 1463, 5412(b)(2)(B).

§ 162.1 Accounting and disclosure standards.

A Federal savings association shall follow U.S. generally accepted accounting principles (GAAP) and the disclosure standards included therein when complying with all applicable regulations, unless otherwise required by statute, regulation, or the OCC.

[82 FR 8110, Jan. 23, 2017]

PART 163—SAVINGS ASSOCIATIONS—OPERATIONS

Subpart A—Accounts

Sec.
163.4 [Reserved]
163.5 Securities: Statement of non-insurance.

Subpart B—Operation and Structure

163.27 Advertising.
163.33 Directors, officers, and employees.
163.36 Tying restriction exception.
163.39 Employment contracts.
163.47 Pension plans.

Subpart C—Securities and Borrowings

163.74 Mutual capital certificates.
163.76 Offers and sales of securities at an office of a Federal savings association.
163.80 Borrowing limitations.

Subparts D–E [Reserved]

Subpart F—Financial Management Policies

163.170 Examinations and audits; appraisals; establishment and maintenance of records.
163.171 [Reserved]
163.172 Financial derivatives.
163.176 Interest-rate-risk-management procedures.

Subpart G—Reporting and Bonding

163.180 Suspicious Activity Reports and other reports and statements.
163.200 Conflicts of interest.
163.201 Corporate opportunity.

AUTHORITY: 12 U.S.C. 1462a, 1463, 1464, 1467a, 1817, 1820, 1828, 1831o, 3806, 5101 *et seq.*, 5412(b)(2)(B); 31 U.S.C. 5318; 42 U.S.C. 4106.

SOURCE: 76 FR 49047, Aug. 9, 2011, unless otherwise noted.

Subpart A—Accounts

§ 163.4 [Reserved]

§ 163.5 Securities: Statement of non-insurance.

Every security issued by a Federal savings association must include in its provisions a clear statement that the security is not insured by the Federal Deposit Insurance Corporation.

Subpart B—Operation and Structure

§ 163.27 Advertising.

No Federal savings association shall use advertising (which includes print or broadcast media, displays or signs, stationery, and all other promotional materials), or make any representation which is inaccurate in any particular or which in any way misrepresents its services, contracts, investments, or financial condition.

§ 163.33 Directors, officers, and employees.

(a) *Directors*—(1) *Requirements*. The composition of the board of directors of a Federal savings association must be in accordance with the following requirements:

(i) A majority of the directors must not be salaried officers or employees of the savings association or of any subsidiary thereof.

(ii) Not more than two of the directors may be members of the same immediate family.

(iii) Not more than one director may be an attorney with a particular law firm.

(2) *Prospective application.* In the case of an association whose board of directors does not conform with any requirement set forth in paragraph (a)(1) of this section as of October 5, 1983, this paragraph (a) shall not prohibit the uninterrupted service, including re-election and re-appointment, of any person serving on the board of directors at that date.

(b) [Reserved]

§ 163.36 Tying restriction exception.

For applicable rules, see regulations of the Board of Governors of the Federal Reserve System.

§ 163.39 Employment contracts.

(a) *General.* A Federal savings association may enter into an employment contract with its officers and other employees only in accordance with the requirements of this section. All employment contracts shall be in writing and shall be approved specifically by an association's board of directors. An association shall not enter into an employment contract with any of its officers or other employees if such contract would constitute an unsafe or unsound practice. The making of such an employment contract would be an unsafe or unsound practice if such contract could lead to material financial loss or damage to the association or could interfere materially with the exercise by the members of its board of directors of their duty or discretion provided by law, charter, bylaw or regulation as to the employment or termination of employment of an officer or employee of the association. This may occur, depending upon the circumstances of the case, where an employment contract provides for an excessive term.

(b) *Required provisions.* Each employment contract shall provide that:

(1) The Federal savings association's board of directors may terminate the officer or employee's employment at any time, but any termination by the association's board of directors other than termination for cause, shall not prejudice the officer or employee's right to compensation or other benefits under the contract. The officer or employee shall have no right to receive compensation or other benefits for any period after termination for cause. Termination for cause shall include termination because of the officer or employee's personal dishonesty, incompetence, willful misconduct, breach of fiduciary duty involving personal profit, intentional failure to perform stated duties, willful violation of any law, rule, or regulation (other than traffic violations or similar offenses) or final cease-and-desist order, or material breach of any provision of the contract.

(2) If the officer or employee is suspended and/or temporarily prohibited from participating in the conduct of the association's affairs by a notice served under section 8(e)(3) or (g)(1) of the Federal Deposit Insurance Act (12 U.S.C. 1818(e)(3) and (g)(1)), the association's obligations under the contract shall be suspended as of the date of service unless stayed by appropriate proceedings. If the charges in the notice are dismissed, the association may in its discretion (i) pay the officer or employee all or part of the compensation withheld while its contract obligations were suspended, and (ii) reinstate (in whole or in part) any of its obligations which were suspended.

(3) If the officer or employee is removed and/or permanently prohibited from participating in the conduct of the association's affairs by an order issued under section 8(e)(4) or (g)(1) of the Federal Deposit Insurance Act (12 U.S.C. 1818(e)(4) or (g)(1)), all obligations of the association under the contract shall terminate as of the effective date of the order, but vested rights of the contracting parties shall not be affected.

(4) If the savings association is in default (as defined in section 3(x)(1) of the Federal Deposit Insurance Act), all obligations under the contract shall terminate as of the date of default, but this paragraph (b)(4) shall not affect any vested rights of the contracting parties: *Provided,* that this paragraph

(b)(4) need not be included in an employment contract if prior written approval is secured from the Comptroller or his or her designee.

(5) All obligations under the contract shall be terminated, except to the extent determined that continuation of the contract is necessary for the continued operation of the association;

(i) By the Comptroller, or his or her designee, at the time the Federal Deposit Insurance Corporation enters into an agreement to provide assistance to or on behalf of the association under the authority contained in 13(c) of the Federal Deposit Insurance Act; or

(ii)(A) By the Comptroller or his or her designee, at the time the Comptroller, or his or her designee approves a supervisory merger to resolve problems related to operation of the association or when the association is determined by the Comptroller to be in an unsafe or unsound condition.

(B) Any rights of the parties that have already vested, however, shall not be affected by such action.

§ 163.47 Pension plans.

(a) *General.* No Federal savings association or service corporation thereof shall sponsor an employee pension plan which, because of unreasonable costs or any other reason, could lead to material financial loss or damage to the sponsor. For purposes of this section, an employee pension plan is defined in section 3(2) of the Employee Retirement Income Security Act of 1974, as amended. The prospective obligation or liability of a plan sponsor to each plan participant shall be stated in or determinable from the plan, and, for a defined benefit plan, shall also be based upon an actuarial estimate of future experience under the plan.

(b) *Funding.* Actuarial cost methods permitted under the Employee Retirement Income Security Act of 1974 and the Internal Revenue Code of 1954, as amended, shall be used to determine plan funding.

(c) *Plan amendment.* A plan may be amended to provide reasonable annual cost-of-living increases to retired participants: *Provided,* That

(1) Any such increase shall be for a period and amount determined by the sponsor's board of directors, but in no event shall it exceed the annual increase in the Consumer Price Index published by the Bureau of Labor Statistics; and

(2) No increase shall be granted unless:

(i) Anticipated charges to net income for future periods have first been found by such board of directors to be reasonable and are documented by appropriate resolution and supporting analysis; and

(ii) The increase will not reduce the association's regulatory capital below its regulatory capital requirement.

(d) *Termination.* The plan shall permit the sponsor's board of directors and its successors to terminate such plan. Notice of intent to terminate shall be filed with the OCC at least 60 days prior to the proposed termination date.

(e) *Records.* Each Federal savings association or service corporation maintaining a plan not subject to recordkeeping and reporting requirements of the Employee Retirement Income Security Act of 1974, and the Internal Revenue Code of 1954, as amended, shall establish and maintain records containing the following:

(1) Plan description;

(2) Schedule of participants and beneficiaries;

(3) Schedule of participants and beneficiaries' rights and obligations;

(4) Plan's financial statements; and

(5) Except for defined contribution plans, an opinion signed by an enrolled actuary (as defined by the Employee Retirement Income Security Act of 1974) affirming that actuarial assumptions in the aggregate are reasonable, take into account the plan's experience and expectations, and represent the actuary's best estimate of the plan's projected experiences.

Subpart C—Securities and Borrowings

§ 163.74 Mutual capital certificates.

(a) *General.* No savings association that is in the mutual form shall issue mutual capital certificates pursuant to this section or amend the terms of such certificates unless it has obtained written approval of the appropriate Federal banking agency. No approval shall be granted unless the proposed issuance of the mutual capital certificates and the form and manner of filing of the application are in accordance with the provisions of this section.

(b) *Eligibility Requirements.* The appropriate Federal banking agency will consider and process an application for approval of the issuance of mutual capital certificates pursuant to this section only if the issuance is authorized by applicable law and regulation and is not inconsistent with any provision of the applicant's charter, constitution or bylaws.

(c) *Application form; supporting information.* An application for approval of the issuance of mutual capital certificates pursuant to this section shall be in the form prescribed by the appropriate Federal banking agency. Such application and instructions may be obtained from the appropriate Federal banking agency. Information and exhibits shall be furnished in support of the application in accordance with such instructions, setting forth all of the terms and provisions relating to the proposed issue and showing that all of the requirements of this section have been or will be met.

(d) *Charter amendment.* No application for approval of the issuance of mutual capital certificates pursuant to this section may be filed unless the amendment to the mutual association's charter, constitution or bylaws or other actions conferring such authority shall have been approved pursuant to the procedures and requirements set forth in the mutual association's charter, constitution or bylaws, or as may otherwise be required by applicable law.

(e) *Filing requirements.* The application for issuance of mutual capital certificates shall be publicly filed with the appropriate Federal banking agency.

(f) *Supervisory objection.* No application or approval of the issuance of mutual capital certificates pursuant to this section shall be approved if, in the opinion of the appropriate Federal banking agency, the policies, condition, or operation of the applicant afford a basis for supervisory objection to the application.

(g) *Limitation on offering period.* Following the date of the approval of the application by the appropriate Federal banking agency, the association shall have an offering period of not more than one year in which to complete the sale of the mutual capital certificates issued pursuant to this section. The appropriate Federal banking agency may in its discretion extend such offering period if a written request showing good cause for such extension is filed with it not later than 30 days before the expiration of such offering period or any extension thereof.

(h) *Reports.* Within 30 days after completion of the sale of mutual capital certificates issued pursuant to this section, the association shall transmit to the appropriate Federal banking agency a written report stating the total dollar amount of securities sold, and the amount of net proceeds received by the association, and within 90 days it shall transmit a written report stating the number of purchasers.

(i) *Requirements as to mutual capital certificates*—(1) *Form of certificate.* Each mutual capital certificate and any governing agreement evidencing a mutual capital certificate issued by an association pursuant to this section:

(i) Shall bear on its face, in bold-face type, the following legend: "This security is not a savings account or a deposit and it is not insured by the United States or any agency or fund of the United States"; and

(ii) Shall clearly state that the certificate is subject to the requirements of § 163.74(i)(2).

(2) *Legal requirements.* Mutual capital certificates issued pursuant to this section shall:

(i) Be subordinate to all claims against the association having the same priority as savings accounts, savings certificates, debt obligations or any higher priority;

(ii) Not be eligible for use as collateral for any loan made by the issuing association;

(iii) Constitute a claim in liquidation not exceeding the face value plus accrued dividends of the certificates, on the general reserves, surplus and undivided profits of the association remaining after the payment in full of all savings accounts, savings certificates and debt obligations;

(iv) Be entitled to the payment of dividends, which may be fixed, variable, participating, or cumulative, or any combination thereof, only if, when and as declared by the association's board of directors out of funds legally available for that purpose, provided that no dividend may be declared or paid without the approval of the appropriate Federal banking agency if such payment would cause the association to fail to meet its regulatory capital requirements under 12 CFR part 3 or part 167, as applicable, if a Federal savings association, or 12 CFR part 324 or part 390, subpart Z, as applicable, if a state savings association, and provided further that no dividend may be paid if such payment would constitute a violation of 12 U.S.C. 1828(b);

(v) Not be redeemable, except: where the dollar weighted average term of each issue of mutual capital certificates to be redeemed is seven years or more and redemption is to be made pursuant to a redemption schedule; in the event of a merger, consolidation or reorganization approved by the appropriate Federal banking agency; or where the funds for redemption are raised by the issuance of mutual capital certificates approved pursuant to this section, or in conjunction with the issuance of capital stock pursuant to part 192 of this chapter: *Provided*, that mandatory redemption shall not be required; that mutual capital certificates shall not be redeemable on the demand or at the option of the holder; and that mutual capital certificates shall not receive, benefit from, be credited with or otherwise be entitled to or due payments in or for redemption if such payments would cause the association to fail to meet its regulatory capital requirements under 12 CFR part 3 or part 167, as applicable, if a Federal savings association, or 12 CFR part 324 or part 390, subpart Z, as applicable, if a state savings association; *And Provided further*, for the purposes of this paragraph (i)(2)(v), the "dollar weighted average term" of an issue of mutual capital certificates shall be the sum of the products calculated for each year that the mutual capital certificates in the issue have been redeemed or are scheduled to be redeemed. Each product shall be calculated by multiplying the number of years of each mutual capital certificate of a given term by a fraction, the numerator of which shall be the total dollar amount of each mutual capital certificate in the issue with the same term and the denominator of which shall be the total dollar amount of mutual capital certificates in the entire issue;

(vi) Not have preemptive rights;

(vii) Not have voting rights, except that an association may provide for voting rights if:

(A) The savings association fails to pay dividends for a minimum of three consecutive dividend periods, and then the holders of the class or classes of mutual capital certificates granted such voting rights, and voting as a single class, with one vote for each outstanding certificate, may elect by a majority vote a maximum of one-third of the association's board of directors, the directors so elected to serve until the next annual meeting of the association succeeding the payment of all current and past dividends;

(B) Any merger, consolidation, or reorganization (except in a supervisory case) is sought to be authorized, where the issuing association is not the survivor, provided that the regulatory capital of the resulting association available for payment of any class of mutual capital certificate on liquidation is less than the regulatory capital available for such class prior to the merger, consolidation, or reorganization;

(C) Action is sought to be authorized which would create any class of mutual capital certificates having a preference or priority over an outstanding class or classes of mutual capital certificates;

(D) Any action is sought to be authorized which would adversely change the specific terms of any class of mutual capital certificates;

(E) Action is sought to be authorized which would increase the number of a class of mutual capital certificates, or the number of a class of mutual capital certificates ranking prior to or on parity with another class of mutual capital certificates; or

(F) Action is sought which would authorize the issuance of an additional class or classes of mutual capital certificates without the association having met specific financial standards;

(viii) Not constitute an obligation of the association and shall confer no rights which would give rise to any claim of or action for default;

(ix) Not be convertible into any account, security, or interest, except that mutual capital certificates may be surrendered in exchange for preferred stock issued in connection with the conversion of the issuing savings association to the stock form pursuant to part 192 of this chapter, provided that the preferred stock shall have substantially the same voting rights, designations, preferences and relative, participating optional, or other special rights, and qualifications, limitations, and restrictions, as the mutual capital certificates exchanged for the preferred stock.

(x) Provide for charging of losses after the exhaustion of all other items in the regulatory capital account.

[76 FR 49047, Aug. 9, 2011, as amended at 79 FR 11314, Feb. 28, 2014]

§ 163.76 Offers and sales of securities at an office of a Federal savings association.

(a) A Federal saving association may not offer or sell debt or equity securities issued by the association or an affiliate of the association at an office of the association; except that equity securities issued by the association or an affiliate in connection with the association's conversion from the mutual to stock form of organization in a conversion approved pursuant to part 192 of this chapter may be offered and sold at the association's offices: *Provided*, That:

(1) The OCC does not object on supervisory grounds to the offer and sale of the securities at the offices of the association;

(2) No commissions, bonuses, or comparable payments are paid to any employee of the savings association or its affiliates or to any other person in connection with the sale of securities at an office of a savings association; except that compensation and commissions consistent with industry norms may be paid to securities personnel of registered broker-dealers;

(3) No offers or sales are made by tellers or at the teller counter, or by comparable persons at comparable locations;

(4) Sales activity is conducted in a segregated or separately identifiable area of the savings association's offices apart from the area accessible to the general public for the purposes of making or withdrawing deposits;

(5) Offers and sales are made only by regular, full-time employees of the savings association or by securities personnel who are subject to supervision by a registered broker-dealer;

(6) An acknowledgment, in the form set forth in paragraph (c) of this section, is signed by any customer to whom the security is sold in the savings association's offices prior to the sale of any such securities;

(7) A legend that the security is not a deposit or account and is not Federally insured or guaranteed appears conspicuously on the security and in all offering documents and advertisements for the securities; the legend must state in bold or other prominent type at least as large as other textual type in the document that "This security is not a deposit or account and is not Federally insured or guaranteed"; and

(8) The savings association will be in compliance with its current capital requirements upon completion of the conversion stock offering.

(b) Securities sales practices, advertisements, and other sales literature used in connection with offers and sales of securities by Federal savings associations shall be subject to § 197.10 of this chapter.

(c) Offers and sales of securities of a savings association or its affiliates in any office of the savings association must use a one-page, unambiguous, certification in substantially the following form:

FORM OF CERTIFICATION

I ACKNOWLEDGE THAT THIS SECURITY IS NOT A DEPOSIT OR ACCOUNT AND IS NOT FEDERALLY INSURED, AND IS NOT GUARANTEED BY [*insert name of savings association*] OR BY THE FEDERAL GOVERNMENT.

If anyone asserts that this security is Federally insured or guaranteed, or is as safe as an insured deposit, I should call the Office of the Comptroller of the Currency].

I further certify that, before purchasing the [*description of security being offered*] of [*name of issuer, name of savings association and affiliation to issuer (if different)*], I received an offering circular.

The offering circular that I received contains disclosure concerning the nature of the security being offered and describes the risks involved in the investment, including:

[*List briefly the principal risks involved and cross reference certain specified pages of the offering circular where a more complete description of the risks is made.*]

Signature: ____________________

Date: ____________________

(d) For purposes of this section, an "office" of an association means any premises used by the association that are identified to the public through advertising or signage using the association's name, trade name, or logo.

§ 163.80 Borrowing limitations.

(a) *General.* Except as the appropriate Federal banking agency otherwise may permit by advice in writing, a savings association may borrow only in accordance with the provisions of this section.

(b) *Amount of borrowing.* A savings association may borrow up to the amount authorized by the laws under which the savings association operates.

(c) *Security.* An association may give security for borrowings subject to any requirements imposed by the appropriate Federal banking agency or the FDIC regarding notice of default on borrowings and any FDIC right of first refusal to purchase collateral.

(d) *Required statement for all securities evidencing outside borrowings.* Each security shall bear on its face, in a prominent place, the following legend:

This security is not a savings account or a deposit and it is not insured by the United States or any agency or fund of the United States.

(e) *Filing requirements for outside borrowings with maturities in excess of one year.* (1) Unless the savings association meets its capital requirement under 12 CFR part 3 or part 167, as applicable if a Federal savings association or 12 CFR part 324 or part 390, subpart Z, as applicable, if a state savings association it shall, at least ten business days prior to issuance, file a notice of intent to issue securities evidencing such borrowings with the appropriate OCC licensing office if a Federal savings association, or with the appropriate regional director of the FDIC if a state savings association. Such notice shall contain a summary of the items of the security, including:

(i) Principal amount of the securities;

(ii) Anticipated interest rate range and price range at which the securities are to be sold;

(iii) Minimum denomination;

(iv) Stated and average effective maturity;

(v) Mandatory and optional prepayment provisions;

(vi) Description, amount, and maintenance of collateral if any;

(vii) Trustee provisions if any;

(viii) Events of default and remedies of default;

(ix) Any provisions which restrict, conditionally or otherwise, the operations of the association.

(2) The appropriate Federal banking agency shall have 10 business days after receipt of such filing to object to the issuance of such securities. The appropriate Federal banking agency shall object if the terms or covenants of the proposed issue place unreasonable burdens on, or control over, the operations of the association. If no objection is taken, the savings association shall have 120 calendar days within which to issue such securities.

(f) *Note accounts.* For purposes of this section, note accounts are not borrowings.

[76 FR 49047, Aug. 9, 2011, as amended at 79 FR 11314, Feb. 28, 2014]

Subparts D–E [Reserved]

Subpart F—Financial Management Policies

§ 163.170 Examinations and audits; appraisals; establishment and maintenance of records.

(a) *Examinations and audits.* Each Federal savings association and affiliate thereof shall be examined periodically, and may be examined at any time, by the OCC, with appraisals when deemed advisable, in accordance with general policies from time to time established by the OCC. The costs, as computed by the OCC, of any examinations made by it, including office analysis, overhead, per diem, travel expense, other supervision by the OCC, and other indirect costs, shall be paid by the savings associations examined, except that in the case of service corporations of Federal savings associations the cost of examinations, as determined by the OCC, shall be paid by the service corporations. Payments shall be made in accordance with a schedule of annual assessments based upon each savings association's total assets and of rates for examiner time in amounts determined by the OCC.

(b) *Appraisals.* (1) Unless otherwise ordered by the OCC, appraisal of real estate by the OCC in connection with any examination or audit of a savings association, affiliate, or service corporation shall be made by an appraiser, or by appraisers, selected by the OCC. The cost of such appraisal shall promptly be paid by such savings association, affiliate, or service corporation direct to such appraiser or appraisers upon receipt by the savings association, affiliate, or service corporation of a statement of such cost as approved by the OCC. A copy of the report of each appraisal made by the OCC pursuant to any of the foregoing provisions of this section shall be furnished to the savings association, affiliate, or service corporation, as appropriate within a reasonable time, not to exceed 90 days, following the completion of such appraisals and the filing of a report thereof by the appraiser, or appraisers, with the OCC.

(2) The OCC may obtain at any time, at its expense, such appraisals of any of the assets, including the security therefore, of a savings association, affiliate, or service corporation as the OCC deems appropriate.

(c) *Establishment and maintenance of records.* To enable the OCC to examine Federal savings associations and affiliates and audit savings associations, affiliates, and service corporations pursuant to the provisions of paragraph (a) of this section, each savings association, affiliate, and service corporation shall establish and maintain such accounting and other records as will provide an accurate and complete record of all business it transacts. This includes, without limitation, establishing and maintaining such other records as are required by statute or any other regulation to which the savings association, affiliate, or service corporation is subject. The documents, files, and other material or property comprising said records shall at all times be available for such examination and audit wherever any of said records, documents, files, material, or property may be.

(d) *Change in location of records.* A Federal savings association shall not transfer the location of any of its general accounting or control records, or the maintenance thereof, from its home office to a branch or service office, or from a branch or service office to its home office or to another branch or service office unless prior to the date of transfer its board of directors has:

(1) By resolution authorized the transfer or maintenance; and

(2) Sent a certified copy of the resolution to the OCC.

(e) *Use of data processing services for maintenance of records.* A Federal savings association which determines to maintain any of its records by means of data processing services shall so notify the OCC in writing, at least 90 days prior to the date on which such maintenance of records will begin. Such notification shall include identification of the records to be maintained by data processing services and a statement as to the location at which such records will be maintained. Any contract, agreement, or arrangement made by a savings association pursuant to which data processing services are to be performed for such savings association shall be in writing and shall expressly provide that the records to be maintained by such services shall at all times be available for examination and audit.

§ 163.171 [Reserved]

§ 163.172 Financial derivatives.

(a) *Definition.* A financial derivative is a financial contract whose value depends on the value of one or more underlying assets, indices, or reference rates. The most common types of financial derivatives are futures, forward contracts, options, and swaps. A mortgage derivative security, such as a collateralized mortgage obligation or a real estate mortgage investment conduit, is not a financial derivative under this section.

(b) *Permissible financial derivatives transactions.* A Federal savings association may engage in a transaction involving a financial derivative if the savings association is authorized to invest in the assets underlying the financial derivative, the transaction is safe and sound, and the requirements in paragraphs (c) through (e) of this section are met. In general, a Federal savings association that engages in a transaction involving a financial derivative should do so to reduce its risk exposure.

(c) *Board of directors' responsibilities.* (1) A Federal savings association's board of directors is responsible for effective oversight of financial derivatives activities.

(2) Before a savings association may engage in any transaction involving a financial derivative, your board of directors must establish written policies and procedures governing authorized financial derivatives. The board of directors should review applicable guidance issued by the OCC on establishing a sound risk management program.

(3) The board of directors must periodically review:

(i) Compliance with the policies and procedures established under paragraph (c)(2) of this section; and

(ii) The adequacy of these policies and procedures to ensure that they continue to be appropriate to the nature and scope of the savings association's operations and existing market conditions.

(4) The board of directors must ensure that management establishes an adequate system of internal controls for transactions involving financial derivatives.

(d) *Management responsibilities.* (1) The management of a Federal savings association is responsible for daily oversight and management of financial derivatives activities. The management of a Federal savings association must implement the policies and procedures established by the board of directors and must establish a system of internal controls. This system of internal controls should, at a minimum, provide for periodic reporting to the board of directors and management, segregation of duties, and internal review procedures.

(2) Management must ensure that financial derivatives activities are conducted in a safe and sound manner and should review applicable guidance issued by the OCC on implementing a sound risk management program.

(e) *Recordkeeping requirement.* A Federal savings association must maintain records adequate to demonstrate compliance with this section and with its board of directors' policies and procedures on financial derivatives.

[76 FR 49047, Aug. 9, 2011, as amended at 82 FR 8110, Jan. 23, 2017]

§ 163.176 Interest-rate-risk-management procedures.

Federal savings associations shall take the following actions:

(a) The board of directors or a committee thereof shall review the savings association's interest-rate-risk exposure and devise a policy for the savings association's management of that risk.

(b) The board of directors shall formally adopt a policy for the management of interest-rate risk. The management of the savings association shall establish guidelines and procedures to ensure that the board's policy is successfully implemented.

(c) The management of the savings association shall periodically report to the board of directors regarding implementation of the savings association's policy for interest-rate-risk management and shall make that information available upon request to the OCC.

(d) The savings association's board of directors shall review the results of operations at least quarterly and shall make such adjustments as it considers necessary and appropriate to the policy for interest-rate-risk management, including adjustments to the authorized acceptable level of interest-rate risk.

Subpart G—Reporting and Bonding

§ 163.180 Suspicious Activity Reports and other reports and statements.

(a) [Reserved]

(b) *False or misleading statements or omissions.* No savings association or director, officer, agent, employee, affiliated person, or other person participating in the conduct of the affairs of such association nor any person filing or seeking approval of any application shall knowingly:

(1) Make any written or oral statement to the appropriate Federal banking agency or to an agent, representative or employee of the appropriate Federal banking agency that is false or misleading with respect to any material fact or omits to state a material fact concerning any matter within the jurisdiction of the appropriate Federal banking agency or

(2) Make any such statement or omission to a person or organization auditing a savings association or otherwise preparing or reviewing its financial statements concerning the accounts, assets, management condition, ownership, safety, or soundness, or other affairs of the association.

(c) [Reserved]

(d) *Suspicious Activity Reports*—(1) *Purpose and scope.* This paragraph (d) ensures that savings associations and service corporations file a Suspicious Activity Report when they detect a known or suspected violation of Federal law or a suspicious transaction related to a money laundering activity or a violation of the Bank Secrecy Act.

(2) *Definitions.* For the purposes of this paragraph (d):

(i) *FinCEN* means the Financial Crimes Enforcement Network of the Department of the Treasury.

(ii) *Institution-affiliated party* means any institution-affiliated party as that term is defined in sections 3(u) and 8(b)(9) of the Federal Deposit Insurance Act (12 U.S.C. 1813(u) and 1818(b)(9)).

(iii) *SAR* means a Suspicious Activity Report.

(3) *SARs required.* A savings association or service corporation shall file a SAR with the appropriate Federal law enforcement agencies and the Department of the Treasury on the form prescribed by the appropriate Federal banking agency and in accordance with the form's instructions, by sending a completed SAR to FinCEN in the following circumstances:

(i) *Insider abuse involving any amount.* Whenever the savings association or service corporation detects any known or suspected Federal criminal violation, or pattern of criminal violations, committed or attempted against the savings association or service corporation or involving a transaction or transactions conducted through the savings association or service corporation, where the savings association or service corporation believes that it was either an actual or potential victim of a criminal violation, or series of criminal violations, or that it was used to facilitate a criminal transaction, and it has a substantial basis for identifying one of its directors, officers, employees, agents or other institution-affiliated parties as having committed or aided in the commission of a criminal act, regardless of the amount involved in the violation.

(ii) *Violations aggregating $5,000 or more where a suspect can be identified.* Whenever the savings association or service corporation detects any known or suspected Federal criminal violation, or pattern of criminal violations, committed or attempted against the savings association or service corporation or involving a transaction or transactions conducted through the savings association or service corporation and involving or aggregating $5,000 or more in funds or other assets, where the savings association or service corporation believes that it was either an actual or potential victim of a criminal violation or series of criminal violations, or that it was used to facilitate a criminal transaction, and it has a substantial basis for identifying a possible suspect or group of suspects. If it is determined prior to filing this report that the identified suspect or group of suspects has used an alias, then information regarding the true identity of the suspect or group of suspects, as well as alias identifiers, such as drivers' license or social security numbers, addresses and telephone numbers, must be reported.

(iii) *Violations aggregating $25,000 or more regardless of potential suspects.* Whenever the savings association or service corporation detects any known or suspected Federal criminal violation, or pattern of criminal violations, committed or attempted against the savings association or service corporation or involving a transaction or transactions conducted through the savings association or service corporation and involving or aggregating $25,000 or more in funds or other assets, where the savings association or service corporation believes that it was either an actual or potential victim of a criminal violation or series of criminal violations, or that it was used to facilitate a criminal transaction, even though there is no substantial basis for identifying a possible suspect or group of suspects.

(iv) *Transactions aggregating $5,000 or more that involve potential money laundering or violations of the Bank Secrecy Act.* Any transaction (which for purposes of this paragraph (d)(3)(iv) means a deposit, withdrawal, transfer between accounts, exchange of currency, loan, extension of credit, purchase or sale of any stock, bond, certificate of deposit, or other monetary instrument or investment security, or any other payment, transfer, or delivery by, through, or to a financial institution, by whatever means effected) conducted or attempted by, at or through the savings association or service corporation and involving or aggregating $5,000 or more in funds or other assets, if the savings association or service corporation knows, suspects, or has reason to suspect that:

(A) The transaction involves funds derived from illegal activities or is intended or conducted in order to hide or disguise funds or assets derived from illegal activities (including, without limitation, the ownership, nature, source, location, or control of such funds or assets) as part of a plan to violate or evade any law or regulation or to avoid any transaction reporting requirement under Federal law;

(B) The transaction is designed to evade any regulations promulgated under the Bank Secrecy Act; or

(C) The transaction has no business or apparent lawful purpose or is not the sort in which the particular customer would normally be expected to engage, and the institution knows of no reasonable explanation for the transaction after examining the available facts, including the background and possible purpose of the transaction.

(4) *Service corporations.* When a service corporation is required to file a SAR under paragraph (d)(3) of this section, either the service corporation or a savings association that wholly or partially owns the service corporation may file the SAR.

(5) *Time for reporting.* A savings association or service corporation is required to file a SAR no later than 30 calendar days after the date of initial detection of facts that may constitute a basis for filing a SAR. If no suspect was identified on the date of detection of the incident requiring the filing, a savings association or service corporation may delay filing a SAR for an additional 30 calendar days to identify a suspect. In no case shall reporting be delayed more than 60 calendar days after the date of initial detection of a reportable transaction. In situations involving violations requiring immediate attention, such as when a reportable violation is ongoing, the savings association or service corporation shall immediately notify, by telephone, an appropriate law enforcement authority and the appropriate Federal banking agency in addition to filing a timely SAR.

(6) *Reports to state and local authorities.* A savings association or service corporation is encouraged to file a copy of the SAR with state and local law enforcement agencies where appropriate.

(7) *Exception.* A savings association or service corporation need not file a SAR for a robbery or burglary committed or attempted that is reported to appropriate law enforcement authorities.

(8) *Retention of records.* A savings association or service corporation shall maintain a copy of any SAR filed and the original or business record equivalent of any supporting documentation for a period of five years from the date of the filing of the SAR. Supporting documentation shall be identified and maintained by the savings association or service corporation as such, and shall be deemed to have been filed with the SAR. A savings association or service corporation shall make all supporting documentation available to appropriate law enforcement agencies upon request. A savings association or

service corporation shall make all supporting documentation available to the appropriate Federal banking agency, FinCEN, or any Federal, state, or local law enforcement agency, or any Federal regulatory authority that examines the savings association or service corporation for compliance with the Bank Secrecy Act, or any state regulatory authority administering a state law that requires the savings association or service corporation to comply with the Bank Secrecy Act or otherwise authorizes the state authority to ensure that the institution complies with the Bank Secrecy Act, upon request.

(9) *Notification to board of directors*—(i) *Generally*. Whenever a savings association (or a service corporation in which the savings association has an ownership interest) files a SAR pursuant to this paragraph (d), the management of the savings association or service corporation shall promptly notify its board of directors, or a committee of directors or executive officers designated by the board of directors to receive notice.

(ii) *Suspect is a director or executive officer*. If the savings association or service corporation files a SAR pursuant to this paragraph (d) and the suspect is a director or executive officer, the savings association or service corporation may not notify the suspect, pursuant to 31 U.S.C. 5318(g)(2), but shall notify all directors who are not suspects.

(10) *Compliance*. Failure to file a SAR in accordance with this section and the instructions may subject the savings association or service corporation, its directors, officers, employees, agents, or other institution-affiliated parties to supervisory action.

(11) *Obtaining SARs*. A savings association or service corporation may obtain SARs and the instructions from the appropriate Federal banking agency.

(12) *Confidentiality of SARs*. A SAR, and any information that would reveal the existence of a SAR, are confidential, and shall not be disclosed except as authorized in this paragraph (d)(12).

(i) *Prohibition on disclosure by savings associations or service corporations*—(A) *General rule*. No savings association or service corporation, and no director, officer, employee, or agent of a savings association or service corporation, shall disclose a SAR or any information that would reveal the existence of a SAR. Any savings association or service corporation, and any director, officer, employee, or agent of any savings association or service corporation that is subpoenaed or otherwise requested to disclose a SAR, or any information that would reveal the existence of a SAR, shall decline to produce the SAR or such information, citing this section and 31 U.S.C. 5318(g)(2)(A)(i), and shall notify the following of any such request and the response thereto:

(A) Director, Litigation Division, Office of the Comptroller of the Currency or the appropriate FDIC region, as appropriate and

(B) The Financial Crimes Enforcement Network (FinCEN).

(ii) *Rules of construction*. Provided that no person involved in any reported suspicious transaction is notified that the transaction has been reported, paragraph (d)(1) of this section shall not be construed as prohibiting:

(A) The disclosure by a savings association or service corporation, or any director, officer, employee or agent of a savings association or service corporation of:

(*1*) A SAR, or any information that would reveal the existence of a SAR, to FinCEN or the appropriate Federal banking agency or any Federal, state, or local law enforcement agency; or any Federal regulatory authority that examines the savings association or service corporation for compliance with the Bank Secrecy Act, or any state regulatory authority administering a state law that requires compliance with the Bank Secrecy Act or otherwise authorizes the state authority to ensure that the institution complies with the Bank Secrecy Act; or

(*2*) The underlying facts, transactions, and documents upon which a SAR is based, including, but not limited to, disclosures:

(*i*) To another financial institution, or any director, officer, employee or agent of a financial institution, for the preparation of a joint SAR; or (*ii*) In connection with certain employment references or termination notices, to the full extent authorized in 31 U.S.C. 5318(g)(2)(B); or

(B) The sharing by a savings association or service corporation, or any director, officer, employee, or agent of a savings association or service corporation, of a SAR, or any information that would reveal the existence of a SAR, within the corporate organizational structure of the savings association or service corporation, for purposes consistent with title II of the Bank Secrecy Act as determined by regulation or in guidance.

(iii) *Prohibition on disclosure by the appropriate Federal banking agency.* The appropriate Federal banking agency will not, and no officer, employee or agent of appropriate Federal banking agency shall disclose a SAR, or any information that would reveal the existence of a SAR, except as necessary to fulfill official duties consistent with title II of the Bank Secrecy Act. For purposes of this section, "official duties" shall not include the disclosure of a SAR, or any information that would reveal the existence of a SAR, in response to a request for use in a private legal proceeding or in response to a request for disclosure of non-public information under 12 CFR 4.33 or 12 CFR part 309, as appropriate.

(iv) *Limitation on liability.* A savings association or service corporation and any director, officer, employee or agent of a savings association or service corporation that makes a voluntary disclosure of any possible violation of law or regulation to a government agency or makes a disclosure pursuant to this section or any other authority, including a disclosure made jointly with another institution, shall be protected from liability for any such disclosure, or for failure to provide notice of such disclosure to any person identified in the disclosure, or both, to the full extent provided by 31 U.S.C. 5318(g)(3).

(13) *Safe harbor.* The safe harbor provision of 31 U.S.C. 5318(g), which exempts any financial institution that makes a disclosure of any possible violation of law or regulation from liability under any law or regulation of the United States, or any constitution, law or regulation of any state or political subdivision, covers all reports of suspected or known criminal violations and suspicious activities to law enforcement and financial institution supervisory authorities, including supporting documentation, regardless of whether such reports are filed pursuant to this paragraph (d), or are filed on a voluntary basis.

(e) *Adjustable-rate mortgage indices*—(1) *Reporting obligation.* Upon the request of a Federal Home Loan Bank, all savings associations within the jurisdiction of that Federal Home Loan Bank shall report the data items set forth in paragraph (e)(2) of this section for the Federal Home Loan Bank to use in calculating and publishing an adjustable-rate mortgage index.

(2) *Data to be reported.* For purposes of paragraph (e)(1) of this section, the term "data items" means the data items previously collected from the monthly Thrift Financial Report or Consolidated Reports of Condition and Income, as appropriate, and such data items as may be altered, amended, or substituted by the requesting Federal Home Loan Bank.

(3) *Applicable indices.* For the purpose of this reporting requirement, the term "adjustable-rate mortgage index" means any of the adjustable-rate mortgage indices calculated and published by a Federal Home Loan Bank or the Federal Home Loan Bank Board on or before August 9, 1989.

[76 FR 49047, Aug. 9, 2011, as amended at 82 FR 8111, Jan. 23, 2017]

EDITORIAL NOTE: At 76 FR 49047, Aug. 9, 2011, § 163.180 was added; however, there are two paragraphs (d)(12)(i)(A).

§ 163.200 Conflicts of interest.

If you are a director, officer, or employee of a Federal savings association, or have the power to direct its management or policies, or otherwise owe a fiduciary duty to a Federal savings association:

(a) You must not advance your own personal or business interests, or those of others with whom you have a personal or business relationship, at the expense of the savings association; and

(b) You must, if you have an interest in a matter or transaction before the board of directors:

(1) Disclose to the board all material nonprivileged information relevant to the board's decision on the matter or transaction, including:

(i) The existence, nature and extent of your interests; and

(ii) The facts known to you as to the matter or transaction under consideration;

(2) Refrain from participating in the board's discussion of the matter or transaction; and

(3) Recuse yourself from voting on the matter or transaction (if you are a director).

§ 163.201 Corporate opportunity.

(a) If you are a director or officer of a Federal savings association, or have the power to direct its management or policies, or otherwise owe a fiduciary duty to a Federal savings association, you must not take advantage of corporate opportunities belonging to the savings association.

(b) A corporate opportunity belongs to a Federal savings association if:

(1) The opportunity is within the corporate powers of the savings association or a subsidiary of the savings association; and

(2) The opportunity is of present or potential practical advantage to the savings association, either directly or through its subsidiary.

(c) The OCC will not deem you to have taken advantage of a corporate opportunity belonging to the Federal savings association if a disinterested and independent majority of the savings association's board of directors, after receiving a full and fair presentation of the matter, rejected the opportunity as a matter of sound business judgment.

PART 165—PROMPT CORRECTIVE ACTION

Sec.

165.1–165.7 [Reserved]
165.8 Procedures for reclassifying a Federal savings association based on criteria other than capital.
165.9 Order to dismiss a director or senior executive officer.
165.10 [Reserved]

AUTHORITY: 12 U.S.C. 1831o, 5412(b)(2)(B).

SOURCE: 76 FR 49065, Aug. 9, 2011, unless otherwise noted.

§§ 165.1–165.7 [Reserved]

§ 165.8 Procedures for reclassifying a Federal savings association based on criteria other than capital.

(a) *Reclassification based on unsafe or unsound condition or practice*—(1) *Issuance of notice of proposed reclassification*—(i) *Grounds for reclassification*. (A) Pursuant to 12 CFR 6.4(d), the OCC may reclassify a well capitalized Federal savings association as adequately capitalized or subject an adequately capitalized or undercapitalized institution to the supervisory actions applicable to the next lower capital category if:

(*1*) The OCC determines that the savings association is in an unsafe or unsound condition; or

(*2*) The OCC deems the savings association to be engaged in an unsafe or unsound practice and not to have corrected the deficiency.

(B) Any action pursuant to this paragraph (a)(1)(i) shall hereinafter be referred to as "reclassification."

(ii) *Prior notice to institution*. Prior to taking action pursuant to 12 CFR 6.4(d), the OCC shall issue and serve on the Federal savings association a written notice of the OCC's intention to reclassify the savings association.

(2) *Contents of notice*. A notice of intention to reclassify a Federal savings association based on unsafe or unsound condition shall include:

(i) A statement of the savings association's capital measures and capital levels and the category to which the savings association would be reclassified;

(ii) The reasons for reclassification of the savings association;

(iii) The date by which the savings association subject to the notice of reclassification may file with the OCC a written appeal of the proposed reclassification and a request for a hearing, which shall be at least 14 calendar days from the date of service of the notice unless the OCC determines that a shorter period is appropriate in light of the financial condition of the savings association or other relevant circumstances.

(3) *Response to notice of proposed reclassification.* A Federal savings association may file a written response to a notice of proposed reclassification within the time period set by the OCC. The response should include:

(i) An explanation of why the savings association is not in unsafe or unsound condition or otherwise should not be reclassified; and

(ii) Any other relevant information, mitigating circumstances, documentation, or other evidence in support of the position of the savings association or company regarding the reclassification.

(4) *Failure to file response.* Failure by a Federal savings association to file, within the specified time period, a written response with the OCC to a notice of proposed reclassification shall constitute a waiver of the opportunity to respond and shall constitute consent to the reclassification.

(5) *Request for hearing and presentation of oral testimony or witnesses.* The response may include a request for an informal hearing before the OCC or its designee under this section. If the Federal savings association desires to present oral testimony or witnesses at the hearing, the savings association shall include a request to do so with the request for an informal hearing. A request to present oral testimony or witnesses shall specify the names of the witnesses and the general nature of their expected testimony. Failure to request a hearing shall constitute a waiver of any right to a hearing, and failure to request the opportunity to present oral testimony or witnesses shall constitute a waiver of any right to present oral testimony or witnesses.

(6) *Order for informal hearing.* Upon receipt of a timely written request that includes a request for a hearing, the OCC shall issue an order directing an informal hearing to commence no later than 30 days after receipt of the request, unless the OCC allows further time at the request of the Federal savings association. The hearing shall be held in Washington, DC or at such other place as may be designated by the OCC, before a presiding officer(s) designated by the OCC to conduct the hearing.

(7) *Hearing procedures.* (i) The Federal savings association shall have the right to introduce relevant written materials and to present oral argument at the hearing. The savings association may introduce oral testimony and present witnesses only if expressly authorized by the OCC or the presiding officer(s). Neither the provisions of the Administrative Procedure Act (5 U.S.C. 554–557) governing adjudications required by statute to be determined on the record nor parts 19 or 109 of this chapter apply to an informal hearing under this section unless the OCC orders that such procedures shall apply.

(ii) The informal hearing shall be recorded and a transcript furnished to the savings association upon request and payment of the cost thereof. Witnesses need not be sworn, unless specifically requested by a party or the presiding officer(s). The presiding officer(s) may ask questions of any witness.

(iii) The presiding officer(s) may order that the hearing be continued for a reasonable period (normally five business days) following completion of oral testimony or argument to allow additional written submissions to the hearing record.

(8) *Recommendation of presiding officers.* Within 20 calendar days following the date the hearing and the record on the proceeding are closed, the presiding officer(s) shall make a recommendation to the OCC on the reclassification.

(9) *Time for decision.* Not later than 60 calendar days after the date the record is closed or the date of the response in a case where no hearing was requested, the OCC will decide whether to reclassify the Federal savings association and notify the savings association of the OCC's decision.

(b) *Request for rescission of reclassification.* Any Federal savings association that has been reclassified under this section, may, upon a change in circumstances, request in writing that the OCC reconsider the reclassification, and may propose that the reclassification be rescinded and that any directives issued in connection with the reclassification be modified, rescinded, or removed. Unless otherwise ordered by the OCC, the savings association shall remain subject to the reclassification and to any directives issued in connection with that reclassification while such request is pending before the OCC.

[76 FR 49065, Aug. 9, 2011, as amended at 78 FR 62281, Oct. 11, 2013]

§ 165.9 Order to dismiss a director or senior executive officer.

(a) *Service of notice.* When the OCC issues and serves a directive on a Federal savings association pursuant to subpart B of part 6 of this chapter requiring the savings association to dismiss any director or senior executive officer under section 38(f)(2)(F)(ii) of the FDI Act, the OCC shall also serve a copy of the directive, or the relevant portions of the directive where appropriate, upon the person to be dismissed.

(b) *Response to directive*—(1) *Request for reinstatement.* A director or senior executive officer who has been served with a directive under paragraph (a) of this section (Respondent) may file a written request for reinstatement. The request for reinstatement shall be filed within 10 calendar days of the receipt of the directive by the Respondent, unless further time is allowed by the OCC at the request of the Respondent.

(2) *Contents of request; informal hearing.* The request for reinstatement should include reasons why the Respondent should be reinstated, and may include a request for an informal hearing before the OCC or its designee under this section. If the Respondent desires to present oral testimony or witnesses at the hearing, the Respondent shall include a request to do so with the request for an informal hearing. The request to present oral testimony or witnesses shall specify the names of the witnesses and the general nature of their expected testimony. Failure to request a hearing shall constitute a waiver of any right to a hearing and failure to request the opportunity to present oral testimony or witnesses shall constitute a waiver of any right or opportunity to present oral testimony or witnesses.

(3) *Effective date.* Unless otherwise ordered by the OCC, the dismissal shall remain in effect while a request for reinstatement is pending.

(c) *Order for informal hearing.* Upon receipt of a timely written request from a Respondent for an informal hearing on the portion of a directive requiring a Federal savings association to dismiss from office any director or senior executive officer, the OCC shall issue an order directing an informal hearing to commence no later than 30 days after receipt of the request, unless the Respondent requests a later date. The hearing shall be held in Washington, DC, or at such other place as may be designated by the OCC, before a presiding officer(s) designated by the OCC to conduct the hearing.

(d) *Hearing procedures.* (1) A Respondent may appear at the hearing personally or through counsel. A Respondent shall have the right to introduce relevant written materials and to present oral argument. A Respondent may introduce oral testimony and present witnesses only if expressly authorized by the OCC or the presiding officer(s). Neither the provisions of the Administrative Procedure Act governing adjudications required by statute to be determined on the record nor parts 19 or 109 of this chapter apply to an informal hearing under this section unless the OCC orders that such procedures shall apply.

(2) The informal hearing shall be recorded and a transcript furnished to the Respondent upon request and payment of the cost thereof. Witnesses need not be sworn, unless specifically requested by a party or the presiding officer(s). The presiding officer(s) may ask questions of any witness.

(3) The presiding officer(s) may order that the hearing be continued for a reasonable period (normally five business days) following completion of oral testimony or argument to allow additional written submissions to the hearing record.

(e) *Standard for review.* A Respondent shall bear the burden of demonstrating that his or her continued employment by or service with the Federal savings association would materially strengthen the savings association's ability:

(1) To become adequately capitalized, to the extent that the directive was

issued as a result of the savings association's capital level or failure to submit or implement a capital restoration plan; and

(2) To correct the unsafe or unsound condition or unsafe or unsound practice, to the extent that the directive was issued as a result of classification of the savings association based on supervisory criteria other than capital, pursuant to section 38(g) of the FDI Act.

(f) *Recommendation of presiding officers.* Within 20 calendar days following the date the hearing and the record on the proceeding are closed, the presiding officer(s) shall make a recommendation to the OCC concerning the Respondent's request for reinstatement with the Federal savings association.

(g) *Time for decision.* Not later than 60 calendar days after the date the record is closed or the date of the response in a case where no hearing has been requested, the OCC shall grant or deny the request for reinstatement and notify the Respondent of the OCC's decision. If the OCC denies the request for reinstatement, the OCC shall set forth in the notification the reasons for the OCC's action.

[76 FR 49065, Aug. 9, 2011, as amended at 78 FR 62281, Oct. 11, 2013]

§ 165.10 [Reserved]

PART 167—CAPITAL

Subpart A—Scope

Sec.
167.0 Scope.

Subpart B—Regulatory Capital Requirements

167.1 Definitions.
167.2 Minimum regulatory capital requirement.
167.3 Individual minimum capital requirements.
167.4 Capital directives.
167.5 Components of capital.
167.6 Risk-based capital credit risk-weight categories.
167.8 Leverage ratio.
167.9 Tangible capital requirement.
167.10 Consequences of failure to meet capital requirements.
167.11 Reservation of authority.
167.12 Purchased credit card relationships, servicing assets, intangible assets (other than purchased credit card relationships and servicing assets), credit-enhancing interest-only strips, and deferred tax assets.
167.14–167.19 [Reserved]

APPENDIXES A–C TO PART 167 [RESERVED]

AUTHORITY: 12 U.S.C. 1462, 1462a, 1463, 1464, 1467a, 1828 (note), 5412(b)(2)(B).

SOURCE: 76 FR 49070, Aug. 9, 2011, unless otherwise noted.

Subpart A—Scope

§ 167.0 Scope.

(a) This part prescribes the minimum regulatory capital requirements for Federal savings associations. Subpart B of this part applies to all Federal savings associations, except as described in paragraph (b) of this section.

(b)(1) A Federal savings association that uses appendix C of this part must comply with the minimum qualifying criteria for internal risk measurement and management processes for calculating risk-based capital requirements, utilize the methodologies for calculating risk-based capital requirements, and make the required disclosures described in that appendix.

(2) Subpart B of this part does not apply to the computation of risk-based capital requirements by a Federal savings association that uses appendix C of this part. However, these savings associations:

(i) Must compute the components of capital under § 167.5, subject to the modifications in sections 11 and 12 of appendix C of this part.

(ii) Must meet the leverage ratio requirement at §§ 167.2(a)(2) and 167.8 with tier 1 capital, as computed under sections 11 and 12 of appendix C of this part.

(iii) Must meet the tangible capital requirement described at §§ 167.2(a)(3) and 167.9.

(iv) Are subject to §§ 167.3 (individual minimum capital requirement), 167.4 (capital directives); and 167.10 (consequences of failure to meet capital requirements).

(v) Are subject to the reservations of authority at § 167.11, which supplement the reservations of authority at section 1 of appendix C of this part.

(c) [Reserved]

Subpart B—Regulatory Capital Requirements

§ 167.1 Definitions.

For the purposes of this subpart:

Adjusted total assets. The term *adjusted total assets* means:

(1) A Federal savings association's total assets as that term is defined in this section;

(2) Plus the prorated assets of any includable subsidiary in which the savings association has a minority ownership interest that is not consolidated under GAAP;

(3) Minus:

(i) Assets not included in the applicable capital standard except for those subject to paragraphs (3)(ii) and (3)(iii) of this definition;

(ii) Investments in any includable subsidiary in which a savings association has a minority interest; and

(iii) Investments in any subsidiary subject to consolidation under paragraph (2)(ii) of this definition.

Asset-backed commercial paper program. The term *asset-backed commercial paper program* (ABCP program) means a program that primarily issues commercial paper that has received a credit rating from an NRSRO and that is backed by assets or other exposures held in a bankruptcy-remote special purpose entity. The term *sponsor* of an ABCP program means a Federal savings association that:

(1) Establishes an ABCP program;

(2) Approves the sellers permitted to participate in an ABCP program;

(3) Approves the asset pools to be purchased by an ABCP program; or

(4) Administers the ABCP program by monitoring the assets, arranging for debt placement, compiling monthly reports, or ensuring compliance with the program documents and with the program's credit and investment policy.

Cash items in the process of collection. The term *cash items in the process of collection* means checks or drafts in the process of collection that are drawn on another depository institution, including a central bank, and that are payable immediately upon presentation; U.S. Government checks that are drawn on the United States Treasury or any other U.S. Government or Government-sponsored agency and that are payable immediately upon presentation; broker's security drafts and commodity or bill-of-lading drafts payable immediately upon presentation; and unposted debits.

Commitment. The term commitment means any arrangement that obligates a Federal savings association to:

(1) Purchase loans or securities;

(2) Extend credit in the form of loans or leases, participations in loans or leases, overdraft facilities, revolving credit facilities, home equity lines of credit, eligible ABCP liquidity facilities, or similar transactions.

Common stockholders' equity. The term *common stockholders' equity* means common stock, common stock surplus, retained earnings, and adjustments for the cumulative effect of foreign currency translation, less net unrealized losses on available-for-sale equity securities with readily determinable fair values.

Conditional guarantee. The term *conditional guarantee* means a contingent obligation of the United States Government or its agencies, the validity of which to the beneficiary is dependent upon some affirmative action— *e.g.*, servicing requirements—on the part of the beneficiary of the guarantee or a third party.

Credit derivative. The term *credit derivative* means a contract that allows one party (the protection purchaser) to transfer the credit risk of an asset or off-balance sheet credit exposure to another party (the protection provider). The value of a credit derivative is dependent, at least in part, on the credit performance of a "referenced asset."

Credit-enhancing interest-only strip. (1) The term *credit-enhancing interest-only strip* means an on-balance sheet asset that, in form or in substance:

(i) Represents the contractual right to receive some or all of the interest due on transferred assets; and

(ii) Exposes the Federal savings association to credit risk directly or indirectly associated with the transferred assets that exceeds its *pro rata* share of the savings association's claim on the assets whether through subordination provisions or other credit enhancement techniques.

(2) The OCC reserves the right to identify other cash flows or related interests as a credit-enhancing interest-only strip. In determining whether a particular interest cash flow functions as a credit-enhancing interest-only strip, The OCC will consider the economic substance of the transaction.

Credit-enhancing representations and warranties. (1) The term *credit-enhancing representations and warranties* means representations and warranties that are made or assumed in connection with a transfer of assets (including loan servicing assets) and that obligate a Federal savings association to protect investors from losses arising from credit risk in the assets transferred or loans serviced.

(2) Credit-enhancing representations and warranties include promises to protect a party from losses resulting from the default or nonperformance of another party or from an insufficiency in the value of the collateral.

(3) Credit-enhancing representations and warranties do not include:

(i) Early-default clauses and similar warranties that permit the return of, or premium refund clauses covering, qualifying mortgage loans for a period not to exceed 120 days from the date of transfer. These warranties may cover only those loans that were originated within one year of the date of the transfer;

(ii) Premium refund clauses covering assets guaranteed, in whole or in part, by the United States government, a United States government agency, or a United States government-sponsored enterprise, provided the premium refund clause is for a period not to exceed 120 days from the date of transfer; or

(iii) Warranties that permit the return of assets in instances of fraud, misrepresentation or incomplete documentation.

Depository institution. The term *domestic depository institution* means a financial institution that engages in the business of banking; that is recognized as a bank by the bank supervisory or monetary authorities of the country of its incorporation and the country of its principal banking operations; that receives deposits to a substantial extent in the regular course of business; and that has the power to accept demand deposits. In the United States, this definition encompasses all Federally insured offices of commercial banks, mutual and stock savings banks, savings or building and loan associations (stock and mutual), cooperative banks, credit unions, and international banking facilities of domestic depository institutions. Bank holding companies and savings and loan holding companies are excluded from this definition. For the purposes of assigning risk weights, the differentiation between OECD depository institutions and non-OECD depository institutions is based on the country of incorporation. Claims on branches and agencies of foreign banks located in the United States are to be categorized on the basis of the parent bank's country of incorporation.

Direct credit substitute. The term *direct credit substitute* means an arrangement in which a Federal savings association assumes, in form or in substance, credit risk associated with an on- or off-balance sheet asset or exposure that was not previously owned by the savings association (third-party asset) and the risk assumed by the savings association exceeds the *pro rata* share of the savings association's interest in the third-party asset. If a savings association has no claim on the third-party asset, then the savings association's assumption of any credit risk is a direct credit substitute. Direct credit substitutes include:

(1) Financial standby letters of credit that support financial claims on a third party that exceed a savings association's *pro rata* share in the financial claim;

(2) Guarantees, surety arrangements, credit derivatives, and similar instruments backing financial claims that exceed a savings association's *pro rata* share in the financial claim;

(3) Purchased subordinated interests that absorb more than their *pro rata* share of losses from the underlying assets;

(4) Credit derivative contracts under which the savings association assumes more than its *pro rata* share of credit risk on a third-party asset or exposure;

(5) Loans or lines of credit that provide credit enhancement for the financial obligations of a third party;

(6) Purchased loan servicing assets if the servicer is responsible for credit losses or if the servicer makes or assumes credit-enhancing representations and warranties with respect to the loans serviced. Servicer cash advances as defined in this section are not direct credit substitutes;

(7) Clean-up calls on third party assets. However, clean-up calls that are 10 percent or less of the original pool balance and that are exercisable at the option of the savings association are not direct credit substitutes; and

(8) Liquidity facilities that provide support to asset-backed commercial paper (other than eligible ABCP liquidity facilities).

Eligible ABCP liquidity facility. The term *eligible ABCP liquidity facility* means a liquidity facility that supports asset-backed commercial paper, in form or in substance, and that meets the following criteria:

(1)(i) At the time of the draw, the liquidity facility must be subject to an asset quality test that precludes funding against assets that are 90 days or more past due or in default; and

(ii) If the assets that the liquidity facility is required to fund against are assets or exposures that have received a credit rating by a NRSRO at the time of the inception of the facility, the facility can be used to fund only those assets or exposures that are rated investment grade by an NRSRO at the time of funding; or

(2) If the assets that are funded under the liquidity facility do not meet the criteria described in paragraph (1) of this definition, the assets must be guaranteed, conditionally or unconditionally, by the United States Government, its agencies, or the central government of an OECD country.

Eligible Federal savings association. (1) The term *eligible Federal savings association* means a Federal savings association with respect to which the Comptroller of the Currency has determined, on the basis of information available at the time, that:

(i) The savings association's management appears to be competent;

(ii) The savings association, as certified by its Board of Directors, is in substantial compliance with all applicable statutes, regulations, orders and written agreements and directives; and

(iii) The savings association's management, as certified by its Board of Directors, has not engaged in insider dealing, speculative practices, or any other activities that have or may jeopardize the association's safety and soundness or contributed to impairing the association's capital.

(2) Federal savings associations, for purposes of this paragraph, will be deemed to be eligible unless the Comptroller makes a determination otherwise or notifies the savings association of its intent to conduct either an informal or formal examination to determine eligibility and provides written notification thereof to the savings association.

Equity investments. (1) The term *equity investments* includes investments in equity securities and real property that would be considered an equity investment under GAAP.

(2)(i) The term *equity securities* means any:

(A) Stock, certificate of interest of participation in any profit-sharing agreement, collateral trust certificate or subscription, preorganization certificate or subscription, transferable share, investment contract, or voting trust certificate; or

(B) In general, any interest or instrument commonly known as an equity security; or

(C) Loans having profit sharing features which GAAP would reclassify as equity securities; or

(D) Any security immediately convertible at the option of the holder without payment of substantial additional consideration into such a security; or

(E) Any security carrying any warrant or right to subscribe to or purchase such a security; or

(F) Any certificate of interest or participation in, temporary or Interim certificate for, or receipt for any of the foregoing or any partnership interest; or

(G) Investments in equity securities and loans or advances to and guarantees issued on behalf of partnerships or joint ventures in which a Federal savings association holds an interest in real property under GAAP.

(ii) The term *equity securities* does not include investments in a subsidiary as that term is defined in this section, equity investments that are permissible for national banks, ownership interests in pools of assets that are risk-weighted in accordance with § 167.6(a)(1)(vi) of this part, or the stock of Federal Home Loan Banks or Federal Reserve Banks.

(3) For purposes of this part, the term *equity investments in real property* does not include interests in real property that are primarily used or intended to be used by the savings association, its subsidiaries, or its affiliates as offices or related facilities for the conduct of its business.

(4) In addition, for purposes of this part, the term *equity investments in real property* does not include interests in real property that are acquired in satisfaction of a debt previously contracted in good faith or acquired in sales under judgments, decrees, or mortgages held by the savings association, provided that the property is not intended to be held for real estate investment purposes but is expected to be disposed of within five years or a longer period approved by the OCC.

Exchange rate contracts. The term *exchange rate contracts* includes cross-currency interest rate swaps; forward foreign exchange rate contracts; currency options purchased; and any similar instrument that, in the opinion of the OCC, may give rise to similar risks.

Face amount. The term *face amount* means the notational principal, or face value, amount of an off-balance sheet item or the amortized cost of an on-balance sheet asset.

Financial asset. The term *financial asset* means cash or other monetary instrument, evidence of debt, evidence of an ownership interest in an entity, or a contract that conveys a right to receive or exchange cash or another financial instrument from another party.

Financial standby letter of credit. The term *financial standby letter of credit* means a letter of credit or similar arrangement that represents an irrevocable obligation to a third-party beneficiary:

(1) To repay money borrowed by, or advanced to, or for the account of, a second party (the account party); or

(2) To make payment on behalf of the account party, in the event that the account party fails to fulfill its obligation to the beneficiary.

Includable subsidiary. The term *includable subsidiary* means a subsidiary of a Federal savings association that is:

(1) Engaged solely in activities not impermissible for a national bank;

(2) Engaged in activities not permissible for a national bank, but only if acting solely as agent for its customers and such agency position is clearly documented in the savings association's files;

(3) Engaged solely in mortgage-banking activities;

(4)(i) Itself an insured depository institution or a company the sole investment of which is an insured depository institution, and

(ii) Was acquired by the parent savings association prior to May 1, 1989; or

(5) A subsidiary of any savings association existing as a savings association on August 9, 1989 that

(i) Was chartered prior to October 15, 1982, as a savings bank or a cooperative bank under state law, or

(ii) Acquired its principal assets from an association that was chartered prior to October 15, 1982, as a savings bank or a cooperative bank under state law.

Intangible assets. The term *intangible assets* means assets considered to be intangible assets under GAAP. These assets include, but are not limited to, goodwill, core deposit premiums, purchased credit card relationships, favorable leaseholds, and servicing assets (mortgage and non-mortgage). Interest-only strips receivable and other nonsecurity financial instruments are not intangible assets under this definition.

Interest-rate contracts. The term *interest-rate contracts* includes single currency interest-rate swaps; basis swaps; forward rate agreements; interest-rate options purchased; forward forward deposits accepted; and any other instrument that, in the opinion of the OCC, may give rise to similar risks, including when-issued securities.

Liquidity facility. The term *liquidity facility* means a legally binding commitment to provide liquidity support to asset-backed commercial paper by lending to, or purchasing assets from any structure, program or conduit in the event that funds are required to repay maturing asset-backed commercial paper.

Mortgage-related securities. The term *mortgage-related securities* means any mortgage-related qualifying securities under section 3(a)(41) of the Securities Exchange Act of 1934, 15 U.S.C. 78c(a)(41), *Provided,* That the rating requirements of that section shall not be considered for purposes of this definition.

Nationally recognized statistical rating organization (NRSRO). The term *nationally recognized statistical rating organization* means an entity recognized by the Division of Market Regulation of the Securities and Exchange Commission (Commission) as a nationally recognized statistical rating organization for various purposes, including the Commission's uniform net capital requirements for brokers and dealers.

OECD-based country. The term *OECD-based country* means a member of that grouping of countries that are full members of the Organization for Economic Cooperation and Development (OECD) plus countries that have concluded special lending arrangements with the International Monetary Fund (IMF) associated with the IMF's General Arrangements to Borrow. This term excludes any country that has rescheduled its external sovereign debt within the previous five years. A rescheduling of external sovereign debt generally would include any renegotiation of terms arising from a country's inability or unwillingness to meet its external debt service obligations, but generally would not include renegotiations of debt in the normal course of business, such as a renegotiation to allow the borrower to take advantage of a decline in interest rates or other change in market conditions.

Original maturity. The term *original maturity* means, with respect to a commitment, the earliest date after a commitment is made on which the commitment is scheduled to expire (*i.e.*, it will reach its stated maturity and cease to be binding on either party), *Provided,* That either:

(1) The commitment is not subject to extension or renewal and will actually expire on its stated expiration date; or

(2) If the commitment is subject to extension or renewal beyond its stated expiration date, the stated expiration date will be deemed the original maturity only if the extension or renewal must be based upon terms and conditions independently negotiated in good faith with the customer at the time of the extension or renewal and upon a new, *bona fide* credit analysis utilizing current information on financial condition and trends.

Performance-based standby letter of credit. The term *performance-based standby letter of credit* means any letter of credit, or similar arrangement, however named or described, which represents an irrevocable obligation to the beneficiary on the part of the issuer to make payment on account of any default by a third party in the performance of a nonfinancial or commercial obligation. Such letters of credit include arrangements backing subcontractors' and suppliers' performance, labor and materials contracts, and construction bids.

Perpetual preferred stock. The term *perpetual preferred stock* means preferred stock without a fixed maturity date that cannot be redeemed at the option of the holder, and that has no other provisions that will require future redemption of the issue. For purposes of these instruments, preferred stock that can be redeemed at the option of the holder is deemed to have an "original maturity" of the earliest possible date on which it may be so redeemed. Cumulative perpetual preferred stock is preferred stock where the dividends accumulate from one period to the next. Noncumulative perpetual preferred stock is preferred stock where the unpaid dividends are not carried over to subsequent dividend periods.

Problem institution. The term *problem institution* means a Federal savings association that, at the time of its acquisition, merger, purchase of assets or other business combination with or by another savings association:

(1) Was subject to special regulatory controls by its primary Federal or state regulatory authority;

(2) Posed particular supervisory concerns to its primary Federal or state regulatory authority; or

(3) Failed to meet its regulatory capital requirement immediately before the transaction.

Prorated assets. The term *prorated assets* means the total assets (as determined in the most recently available GAAP report but in no event more than one year old) of a subsidiary (including those subsidiaries where the savings association has a minority interest) multiplied by the Federal savings association's percentage of ownership of that subsidiary.

Qualifying mortgage loan. (1) The term *qualifying mortgage loan* means a loan that:

(i) Is fully secured by a first lien on a one-to four-family residential property;

(ii) Is underwritten in accordance with prudent underwriting standards, including standards relating the ratio of the loan amount to the value of the property (LTV ratio). *See* appendix to 12 CFR 160.101. A nonqualifying mortgage loan that is paid down to an appropriate LTV ratio (calculated using value at origination) may become a qualifying loan if it meets all other requirements of this definition;

(iii) Maintains an appropriate LTV ratio based on the amortized principal balance of the loan; and

(iv) Is performing and is not more than 90 days past due.

(2) If a Federal savings association holds the first and junior lien(s) on a residential property and no other party holds an intervening lien, the transaction is treated as a single loan secured by a first lien for the purposes of determining the LTV ratio and the appropriate risk weight under § 167.6(a).

(3) A loan to an individual borrower for the construction of the borrower's home may be included as a qualifying mortgage loan.

(4) A loan that meets the requirements of this section prior to modification on a permanent or trial basis under the U.S. Department of Treasury's Home Affordable Mortgage Program may be included as a *qualifying mortgage loan*, so long as the loan is not 90 days or more past due.

Qualifying multifamily mortgage loan. (1) The term *qualifying multifamily mortgage loan* means a loan secured by a first lien on multifamily residential properties consisting of 5 or more dwelling units, provided that:

(i) The amortization of principal and interest occurs over a period of not more than 30 years;

(ii) The original minimum maturity for repayment of principal on the loan is not less than seven years;

(iii) When considering the loan for placement in a lower risk-weight category, all principal and interest payments have been made on a timely basis in accordance with its terms for the preceding year;

(iv) The loan is performing and not 90 days or more past due;

(v) The loan is made by the Federal savings association in accordance with prudent underwriting standards; and

(vi) If the interest rate on the loan does not change over the term of the loan:

(A) The current loan balance amount does not exceed 80 percent of the value of the property securing the loan; and

(B) For the property's most recent fiscal year, the ratio of annual net operating income generated by the property (before payment of any debt service on the loan) to annual debt service on the loan is not less than 120 percent, or in the case of cooperative or other not-for-profit housing projects, the property generates sufficient cash flows to provide comparable protection to the institution; or

(vii) If the interest rate on the loan changes over the term of the loan:

(A) The current loan balance amount does not exceed 75 percent of the value of the property securing the loan; and

(B) For the property's most recent fiscal year, the ratio of annual net operating income generated by the property (before payment of any debt service on the loan) to annual debt service on the loan is not less than 115 percent, or in the case of cooperative or other not-for-profit housing projects, the property generates sufficient cash flows to provide comparable protection to the institution.

(2) The term *qualifying multifamily mortgage loan* also includes a multifamily mortgage loan that on March

18, 1994 was a first mortgage loan on an existing property consisting of 5–36 dwelling units with an initial loan-to-value ratio of not more than 80% where an average annual occupancy rate of 80% or more of total units had existed for at least one year, and continues to meet these criteria.

(3) For purposes of paragraphs (1)(vi) and (vii) of this definition, the term *value of the property* means, at origination of a loan to purchase a multifamily property: the lower of the purchase price or the amount of the initial appraisal, or if appropriate, the initial evaluation. In cases not involving the purchase of a multifamily loan, the *value of the property* is determined by the most current appraisal, or if appropriate, the most current evaluation.

(4) In cases where a borrower refinances a loan on an existing property, as an alternative to paragraphs (1)(iii), (vi), and (vii) of this definition:

(i) All principal and interest payments on the loan being refinanced have been made on a timely basis in accordance with the terms of that loan for the preceding year; and

(ii) The net income on the property for the preceding year would support timely principal and interest payments on the new loan in accordance with the applicable debt service requirement.

Qualifying residential construction loan. (1) The term *qualifying residential construction loan*, also referred to as a residential bridge loan, means a loan made in accordance with sound lending principles satisfying the following criteria:

(i) The builder must have substantial project equity in the home construction project;

(ii) The residence being constructed must be a 1–4 family residence sold to a home purchaser;

(iii) The lending Federal savings association must obtain sufficient documentation from a permanent lender (which may be the construction lender) demonstrating that:

(A) The home buyer intends to purchase the residence; and

(B) Has the ability to obtain a permanent qualifying mortgage loan sufficient to purchase the residence;

(iv) The home purchaser must have made a substantial earnest money deposit;

(v) The construction loan must not exceed 80 percent of the sales price of the residence;

(vi) The construction loan must be secured by a first lien on the lot, residence under construction, and other improvements;

(vii) The lending thrift must retain sufficient undisbursed loan funds throughout the construction period to ensure project completion;

(viii) The builder must incur a significant percentage of direct costs (*i.e.*, the actual costs of land, labor, and material) before any drawdown on the loan;

(ix) If at any time during the life of the construction loan any of the criteria of this rule are no longer satisfied, the association must immediately recategorize the loan at a 100 percent risk-weight and must accurately report the loan in the association's next quarterly Consolidated Reports of Condition and Income (Call Report) or Thrift Financial Report (TFR), as appropriate;

(x) The home purchaser must intend that the home will be owner-occupied;

(xi) The home purchaser(s) must be an individual(s), not a partnership, joint venture, trust corporation, or any other entity (including an entity acting as a sole proprietorship) that is purchasing the home(s) for speculative purposes; and

(xii) The loan must be performing and not more than 90 days past due.

(2) The documentation for each loan and home sale must be sufficient to demonstrate compliance with the criteria in paragraph (1) of this definition. The OCC retains the discretion to determine that any loans not meeting sound lending principles must be placed in a higher risk-weight category. The OCC also reserves the discretion to modify these criteria on a case-by-case basis provided that any such modifications are not inconsistent with the safety and soundness objectives of this definition.

Qualifying securities firm. The term *qualifying securities firm* means:

(1) A securities firm incorporated in the United States that is a broker-dealer that is registered with the Securities and Exchange Commission (SEC) and that complies with the SEC's net capital regulations (17 CFR 240.15c3(1)); and

(2) A securities firm incorporated in any other OECD-based country, if the Federal savings association is able to demonstrate that the securities firm is subject to consolidated supervision and regulation (covering its subsidiaries, but not necessarily its parent organizations) comparable to that imposed on depository institutions in OECD countries. Such regulation must include risk-based capital requirements comparable to those imposed on depository institutions under the Accord on International Convergence of Capital Measurement and Capital Standards (1988, as amended in 1998).

Reciprocal holdings of depository institution instruments. The term *reciprocal holdings of depository institution instruments* means cross-holdings or other formal or informal arrangements in which two or more depository institutions swap, exchange, or otherwise agree to hold each other's capital instruments. This definition does not include holdings of capital instruments issued by other depository institutions that were taken in satisfaction of debts previously contracted, provided that the reporting Federal savings association has not held such instruments for more than five years or a longer period approved by the OCC.

Recourse. The term *recourse* means a Federal savings association's retention, in form or in substance, of any credit risk directly or indirectly associated with an asset it has sold (in accordance with GAAP) that exceeds a *pro rata* share of that savings association's claim on the asset. If a savings association has no claim on an asset it has sold, then the retention of any credit risk is recourse. A recourse obligation typically arises when a savings association transfers assets in a sale and retains an explicit obligation to repurchase assets or to absorb losses due to a default on the payment of principal or interest or any other deficiency in the performance of the underlying obligor or some other party. Recourse may also exist implicitly if a savings association provides credit enhancement beyond any contractual obligation to support assets it has sold. Recourse obligations include:

(1) Credit-enhancing representations and warranties made on transferred assets;

(2) Loan servicing assets retained pursuant to an agreement under which the savings association will be responsible for losses associated with the loans serviced. Servicer cash advances as defined in this section are not recourse obligations;

(3) Retained subordinated interests that absorb more than their *pro rata* share of losses from the underlying assets;

(4) Assets sold under an agreement to repurchase, if the assets are not already included on the balance sheet;

(5) Loan strips sold without contractual recourse where the maturity of the transferred portion of the loan is shorter than the maturity of the commitment under which the loan is drawn;

(6) Credit derivatives that absorb more than the savings association's pro rata share of losses from the transferred assets;

(7) Clean-up calls on assets the savings association has sold. However, clean-up calls that are 10 percent or less of the original pool balance and that are exercisable at the option of the savings association are not recourse arrangements; and

(8) Liquidity facilities that provide support to asset-backed commercial paper (other than eligible ABCP liquidity facilities).

Replacement cost. The term *replacement cost* means, with respect to interest rate and exchange-rate contracts, the loss that would be incurred in the event of a counterparty default, as measured by the net cost of replacing the contract at the current market value. If default would result in a theoretical profit, the replacement value is considered to be zero. This mark-to-market process must incorporate changes in both interest rates and counterparty credit quality.

Residential properties. The term *residential properties* means houses, condominiums, cooperative units, and manufactured homes. This definition does not include boats or motor homes, even if used as a primary residence, or timeshare properties.

Residual characteristics. The term *residual characteristics* means interests similar to a multi-class pay-through obligation representing the excess cash flow generated from mortgage collateral over the amount required for the issue's debt service and ongoing administrative expenses or interests presenting similar degrees of interest-rate/prepayment risk and principal loss risks.

Residual interest. (1) The term *residual interest* means any on-balance sheet asset that:

(i) Represents an interest (including a beneficial interest) created by a transfer that qualifies as a sale (in accordance with GAAP) of financial assets, whether through a securitization or otherwise; and

(ii) Exposes a Federal savings association to credit risk directly or indirectly associated with the transferred asset that exceeds a *pro rata* share of that savings association's claim on the asset, whether through subordination provisions or other credit enhancement techniques.

(2) Residual interests generally include credit-enhancing interest-only strips, spread accounts, cash collateral accounts, retained subordinated interests (and other forms of overcollateralization), and similar assets that function as a credit enhancement.

(3) Residual interests further include those exposures that, in substance, cause the savings association to retain the credit risk of an asset or exposure that had qualified as a residual interest before it was sold.

(4) Residual interests generally do not include assets purchased from a third party. However, a credit-enhancing interest-only strip that is acquired in any asset transfer is a residual interest.

Risk participation. The term *risk participation* means a participation in which the originating party remains liable to the beneficiary for the full amount of an obligation (*e.g.*, a direct credit substitute), notwithstanding that another party has acquired a participation in that obligation.

Risk-weighted assets. The term *risk-weighted assets* means the sum total of risk-weighted on-balance sheet assets and the total of risk-weighted off-balance sheet credit equivalent amounts. These assets are calculated in accordance with § 167.6 of this part.

Securitization. The term *securitization* means the pooling and repackaging by a special purpose entity of assets or other credit exposures that can be sold to investors. *Securitization* includes transactions that create stratified credit risk positions whose performance is dependent upon an underlying pool of credit exposures, including loans and commitments.

Servicer cash advance. The term *servicer cash advance* means funds that a residential mortgage servicer advances to ensure an uninterrupted flow of payments, including advances made to cover foreclosure costs or other expenses to facilitate the timely collection of the loan. A servicer cash advance is not a recourse obligation or a direct credit substitute if:

(1) The servicer is entitled to full reimbursement and this right is not subordinated to other claims on the cash flows from the underlying asset pool; or

(2) For any one loan, the servicer's obligation to make nonreimbursable advances is contractually limited to an insignificant amount of the outstanding principal amount on that loan.

State. The term *state* means any one of the several states of the United States of America, the District of Columbia, Puerto Rico, and the territories and possessions of the United States.

Structured financing program. The term *structured financing program* means a program where receivable interests and asset-or mortgage-backed securities issued by multiple participants are purchased by a special purpose entity that repackages those exposures into securities that can be sold to investors. Structured financing programs allocate credit risk, generally, between the participants and credit enhancement provided to the program.

Subsidiary. The term *subsidiary* means any corporation, partnership, business trust, joint venture, association or similar organization in which a Federal savings association directly or indirectly holds an ownership interest and the assets of which are consolidated with those of the Federal savings association for purposes of reporting under GAAP. Generally, these are majority-owned subsidiaries.[1] This definition does not include ownership interests that were taken in satisfaction of debts previously contracted, provided that the reporting association has not held the interest for more than five years or a longer period approved by the OCC.

Tier 1 capital. The term *Tier 1 capital* means core capital as computed in accordance with § 167.5(a) of this part.

Tier 2 capital. The term *Tier 2 capital* means supplementary capital as computed in accordance with § 167.5 of this part.

Total assets. The term *total assets* means total assets as would be required to be reported for consolidated entities on period-end reports filed with the OCC in accordance with GAAP.

Traded position. The term *traded position* means a position retained, assumed, or issued in connection with a securitization that is rated by a NRSRO, where there is a reasonable expectation that, in the near future, the rating will be relied upon by:

(1) Unaffiliated investors to purchase the security; or

(2) An unaffiliated third party to enter into a transaction involving the position, such as a purchase, loan, or repurchase agreement.

Unconditionally cancelable. The term *unconditionally cancelable* means, with respect to a commitment-type lending arrangement, that the Federal savings association may, at any time, with or without cause, refuse to advance funds or extend credit under the facility. In the case of home equity lines of credit, the savings association is deemed able to unconditionally cancel the commitment if it can, at its option, prohibit additional extensions of credit, reduce the line, and terminate the commitment to the full extent permitted by relevant Federal law.

United States Government or its agencies. The term *United States Government or its agencies* means an instrumentality of the U.S. Government whose debt obligations are fully and explicitly guaranteed as to the timely payment of principal and interest by the full faith and credit of the United States Government.

United States Government-sponsored agency or corporation. The term *United States Government-sponsored agency or corporation* means an agency or corporation originally established or chartered to serve public purposes specified by the United States Congress but whose obligations are not explicitly guaranteed by the full faith and credit of the United States Government.

§ 167.2 Minimum regulatory capital requirement.

(a) To meet its regulatory capital requirement a Federal savings association must satisfy each of the following capital standards:

(1) *Risk-based capital requirement.* (i) A Federal savings association's minimum risk-based capital requirement shall be an amount equal to 8% of its risk-weighted assets as measured under § 167.6 of this part.

(ii) A Federal savings association may not use supplementary capital to satisfy this requirement in an amount greater than 100% of its core capital as defined in § 167.5 of this part.

(2) *Leverage ratio requirement.* (i) A Federal savings association's minimum leverage ratio requirement shall be the amount set forth in § 167.8 of this part.

(ii) A Federal savings association must satisfy this requirement with core capital as defined in § 167.5(a) of this part.

(3) *Tangible capital requirement.* (i) A Federal savings association's minimum tangible capital requirement shall be the amount set forth in § 167.9 of this part.

(ii) A Federal savings association must satisfy this requirement with

[1] The OCC reserves the right to review a Federal savings association's investment in a subsidiary on a case-by-case basis. If the OCC determines that such investment is more appropriately treated as an equity security or an ownership interest in a subsidiary, it will make such determination regardless of the percentage of ownership held by the savings association.

tangible capital as defined in § 167.9 of this part in an amount not less than 1.5% of its adjusted total assets.

(b) [Reserved]

(c) Federal savings associations are expected to maintain compliance with all of these standards at all times.

§ 167.3 Individual minimum capital requirements.

(a) *Purpose and scope.* The rules and procedures specified in this section apply to the establishment of an individual minimum capital requirement for a Federal savings association that varies from the risk-based capital requirement, the leverage ratio requirement or the tangible capital requirement that would otherwise apply to the savings association under this part.

(b) *Appropriate considerations for establishing individual minimum capital requirements.* Minimum capital levels higher than the risk-based capital requirement, the leverage ratio requirement or the tangible capital requirement required under this part may be appropriate for individual savings associations. Increased individual minimum capital requirements may be established upon a determination that the savings association's capital is or may become inadequate in view of its circumstances. For example, higher capital levels may be appropriate for:

(1) A Federal savings association receiving special supervisory attention;

(2) A Federal savings association that has or is expected to have losses resulting in capital inadequacy;

(3) A Federal savings association that has a high degree of exposure to interest rate risk, prepayment risk, credit risk, concentration of credit risk, certain risks arising from nontraditional activities, or similar risks; or a high proportion of off-balance sheet risk, especially standby letters of credit;

(4) A Federal savings association that has poor liquidity or cash flow;

(5) A Federal savings association growing, either internally or through acquisitions, at such a rate that supervisory problems are presented that are not dealt with adequately by other OCC regulations or other guidance;

(6) A Federal savings association that may be adversely affected by the activities or condition of its holding company, affiliate(s), subsidiaries, or other persons or savings associations with which it has significant business relationships, including concentrations of credit;

(7) A Federal savings association with a portfolio reflecting weak credit quality or a significant likelihood of financial loss, or that has loans in nonperforming status or on which borrowers fail to comply with repayment terms;

(8) A Federal savings association that has inadequate underwriting policies, standards, or procedures for its loans and investments; or

(9) A Federal savings association that has a record of operational losses that exceeds the average of other, similarly situated savings associations; has management deficiencies, including failure to adequately monitor and control financial and operating risks, particularly the risks presented by concentrations of credit and nontraditional activities; or has a poor record of supervisory compliance.

(c) *Standards for determination of appropriate individual minimum capital requirements.* The appropriate minimum capital level for an individual Federal savings association cannot be determined solely through the application of a rigid mathematical formula or wholly objective criteria. The decision is necessarily based, in part, on subjective judgment grounded in agency expertise. The factors to be considered in the determination will vary in each case and may include, for example:

(1) The conditions or circumstances leading to the determination that a higher minimum capital requirement is appropriate or necessary for the savings association;

(2) The exigency of those circumstances or potential problems;

(3) The overall condition, management strength, and future prospects of the savings association and, if applicable, its holding company, subsidiaries, and affiliates;

(4) The savings association's liquidity, capital and other indicators of financial stability, particularly as compared with those of similarly situated savings associations; and

(5) The policies and practices of the savings association's directors, officers, and senior management as well as the internal control and internal audit systems for implementation of such adopted policies and practices.

(d) *Procedures*—(1) *Notification.* When the OCC determines that a minimum capital requirement is necessary or appropriate for a particular Federal savings association, it shall notify the savings association in writing of its proposed individual minimum capital requirement; the schedule for compliance with the new requirement; and the specific causes for determining that the higher individual minimum capital requirement is necessary or appropriate for the savings association.

(2) *Response.* (i) The response shall include any information that the Federal savings association wants the OCC to consider in deciding whether to establish or to amend an individual minimum capital requirement for the savings association, what the individual capital requirement should be, and, if applicable, what compliance schedule is appropriate for achieving the required capital level. The response of the savings association must be in writing and must be delivered to the OCC within 30 days after the date on which the notification was received. The OCC may extend the time period for good cause. The time period for response by the insured savings association may be shortened for good cause:

(A) When, in the opinion of the OCC, the condition of the savings association so requires, and the OCC informs the savings association of the shortened response period in the notice;

(B) With the consent of the savings association; or

(C) When the savings association already has advised the OCC that it cannot or will not achieve its applicable minimum capital requirement.

(ii) Failure to respond within 30 days, or such other time period as may be specified by the OCC, may constitute a waiver of any objections to the proposed individual minimum capital requirement or to the schedule for complying with it, unless the OCC has provided an extension of the response period for good cause.

(3) *Decision.* After expiration of the response period, the OCC shall decide whether or not the OCC believes the proposed individual minimum capital requirement should be established for the Federal savings association, or whether that proposed requirement should be adopted in modified form, based on a review of the savings association's response and other relevant information. The OCC's decision shall address comments received within the response period from the savings association and shall state the level of capital required, the schedule for compliance with this requirement, and any specific remedial action the savings association could take to eliminate the need for continued applicability of the individual minimum capital requirement. The OCC shall provide the savings association with a written decision on the individual minimum capital requirement, addressing the substantive comments made by the savings association and setting forth the decision and the basis for that decision. Upon receipt of this decision by the savings association, the individual minimum capital requirement becomes effective and binding upon the savings association. This decision represents final agency action.

(4) *Failure to comply.* Failure to satisfy an individual minimum capital requirement, or to meet any required incremental additions to capital under a schedule for compliance with such an individual minimum capital requirement, shall constitute a legal basis for issuing a capital directive pursuant to § 167.4 of this part.

(5) *Change in circumstances.* If, after a decision is made under paragraph (d)(3) of this section, there is a change in the circumstances affecting the savings association's capital adequacy or its ability to reach its required minimum capital level by the specified date, the OCC may amend the individual minimum capital requirement or the savings association's schedule for such compliance. The OCC may decline to consider a savings association's request for such changes that are not based on a significant change in circumstances or that are repetitive or frivolous. Pending the OCC's reexamination of the original decision, that original decision and any

compliance schedule established thereunder shall continue in full force and effect.

§ 167.4 Capital directives.

(a) *Issuance of a Capital Directive*—(1) *Purpose.* (i) In addition to any other action authorized by law, the OCC may issue a capital directive to a Federal savings association that does not have an amount of capital satisfying its minimum capital requirement. Issuance of such a capital directive may be based on a Federal savings association's noncompliance with the risk-based capital requirement, the leverage ratio requirement, the tangible capital requirement, or individual minimum capital requirement established under this part, by a written agreement under 12 U.S.C. 1464(s), or as a condition for approval of an application. A capital directive may order a Federal savings association to:

(A) Achieve its minimum capital requirement by a specified date;

(B) Adhere to the compliance schedule for achieving its individual minimum capital requirement;

(C) Submit and adhere to a capital plan acceptable to the OCC describing the means and a time schedule by which the savings association shall reach its required capital level;

(D) Take other action, including but not limited to, reducing the savings association's assets or its rate of liability growth, or imposing restrictions on the savings association's payment of dividends, in order to cause the savings association to reach its required capital level;

(E) Take any action authorized under § 167.10(e); or

(F) Take a combination of any of these actions.

(ii) A capital directive issued under this section, including a plan submitted pursuant to a capital directive, is enforceable under 12 U.S.C. 1818 in the same manner and to the same extent as an effective and outstanding cease and desist order which has become final under 12 U.S.C. 1818.

(2) *Notice of intent to issue capital directive.* The OCC will determine whether to initiate the process of issuing a capital directive. The OCC will notify a Federal savings association in writing by registered mail of its intention to issue a capital directive. The notice will state:

(i) The reasons for issuance of the capital directive and

(ii) The proposed contents of the capital directive.

(3) *Response to notice of intent.* (i) A Federal savings association may respond to the notice of intent by submitting its own compliance plan, or may propose an alternative plan. The response should also include any information that the savings association wishes the OCC to consider in deciding whether to issue a capital directive. The response must be in writing and be delivered within 30 days after the receipt of the notices. Such response must be filed in accordance with §§ 116.30 and 116.40 of this chapter. In its discretion, the OCC may extend the time period for the response for good cause. The OCC may, for good cause, shorten the 30-day time period for response by the insured savings association:

(A) When, in the opinion of the OCC, the condition of the savings association so requires, and the OCC informs the savings association of the shortened response period in the notice;

(B) With the consent of the savings association; or

(C) When the savings association already has advised the OCC that it cannot or will not achieve its applicable minimum capital requirement.

(ii) Failure to respond within 30 days of receipt, or such other time period as may be specified by the OCC, may constitute a waiver of any objections to the capital directive unless the OCC grants an extension of the time period for good cause.

(4) *Decision.* After the closing date of the Federal savings association's response period, or upon receipt of the savings association's response, if earlier, the OCC shall consider the savings association's response and may seek additional information or clarification of the response. Thereafter, the OCC will determine whether or not to issue a capital directive and, if one is to be issued, whether it should be as originally proposed or in modified form.

(5) *Service and effectiveness.* (i) Upon issuance, a capital directive will be

served upon the Federal savings association. It will include or be accompanied by a statement of reasons for its issuance and shall address the responses received during the response period.

(ii) A capital directive shall become effective upon the expiration of 30 days after service upon the savings association, unless the OCC determines that a shorter effective period is necessary either on account of the public interest or in order to achieve the capital directive's purpose. If the savings association has consented to issuance of the capital directive, it may become effective immediately. A capital directive shall remain in effect and enforceable unless, and then only to the extent that, it is stayed, modified, or terminated by the OCC.

(6) *Change in circumstances.* Upon a change in circumstances, a Federal savings association may submit a request to the OCC to reconsider the terms of the capital directive or consider changes in the savings association's capital plan issued under a directive for the savings association to achieve its minimum capital requirement. If the OCC believes such a change is warranted, the OCC may modify the savings association's capital requirement or may refuse to make such modification if it determines that there are not significant changes in circumstances. Pending a decision on reconsideration, the capital directive and capital plan shall continue in full force and effect.

(b) *Relation to other administrative actions.* The OCC —

(1) May consider a Federal savings association's progress in adhering to any capital plan required under this section whenever such savings association or any affiliate of such savings association (including any company which controls such savings association) seeks approval for any proposal that would have the effect of diverting earnings, diminishing capital, or otherwise impeding such savings association's progress in meeting its minimum capital requirement; and

(2) May disapprove any proposal referred to in paragraph (b)(1) of this section if the OCC determines that the proposal would adversely affect the ability of the savings association on a current or pro forma basis to satisfy its capital requirement.

§ 167.5 Components of capital.

(a) *Core Capital.* (1) The following elements,[2] less the amount of any deductions pursuant to paragraph (a)(2) of this section, comprise a Federal savings association's core capital:

(i) Common stockholders' equity (including retained earnings);

(ii) Noncumulative perpetual preferred stock and related surplus;[3]

(iii) Minority interests in the equity accounts of the subsidiaries that are fully consolidated.

(iv) Nonwithdrawable accounts and pledged deposits of mutual savings associations (excluding any treasury shares held by the savings association) meeting the criteria of regulations and memoranda of the OCC to the extent that such accounts or deposits have no fixed maturity date, cannot be withdrawn at the option of the accountholder, and do not earn interest that carries over to subsequent periods;

(v) [Reserved]

(2) *Deductions from core capital.* (i) Intangible assets, as defined in § 167.1 of this part, are deducted from assets and capital in computing core capital, except as otherwise provided by § 167.12 of this part.

(ii) Servicing assets that are not includable in core capital pursuant to § 167.12 of this part are deducted from assets and capital in computing core capital.

---

[2] Stock issues where the dividend is reset periodically based on current market conditions and the savings association's current credit rating, including but not limited to, auction rate, money market or remarketable preferred stock, are assigned to supplementary capital, regardless of cumulative or noncumulative characteristics.

[3] Stock issued by subsidiaries that may not be counted by the parent savings association on the Call Report or TFR, as appropriate, likewise shall not be considered in calculating capital. For example, preferred stock issued by a Federal savings association or a subsidiary that is, in effect, collateralized by assets of the savings association or one of its subsidiaries shall not be included in capital. Similarly, common stock with mandatorily redeemable provisions is not includable in core capital.

(iii) Credit-enhancing interest-only strips that are not includable in core capital under §167.12 of this part are deducted from assets and capital in computing core capital.

(iv) Investments, both equity and debt, in subsidiaries that are not includable subsidiaries (including those subsidiaries where the savings association has a minority ownership interest) are deducted from assets and, thus core capital except as provided in paragraphs (a)(2)(v) and (a)(2)(vi) of this section.

(v) If a Federal savings association has any investments (both debt and equity) in one or more subsidiaries engaged in any activity that would not fall within the scope of activities in which includable subsidiaries may engage, it must deduct such investments from assets and, thus, core capital in accordance with this paragraph (a)(2)(v). The savings association must first deduct from assets and, thus, core capital the amount by which any investments in such subsidiary(ies) exceed the amount of such investments held by the savings association as of April 12, 1989. Next the savings association must deduct from assets and, thus, core capital, the savings association's investments in and extensions of credit to the subsidiary on the date as of which the savings association's capital is being determined.

(vi) If a Federal savings association holds a subsidiary (either directly or through a subsidiary) that is itself a domestic depository institution, the OCC may, in its sole discretion upon determining that the amount of core capital that would be required would be higher if the assets and liabilities of such subsidiary were consolidated with those of the parent savings association than the amount that would be required if the parent savings association's investment were deducted pursuant to paragraphs (a)(2)(iv) and (a)(2)(v) of this section, consolidate the assets and liabilities of that subsidiary with those of the parent savings association in calculating the capital adequacy of the parent savings association, regardless of whether the subsidiary would otherwise be an includable subsidiary as defined in §167.1 of this part.

(vii) Deferred tax assets that are not includable in core capital pursuant to §167.12 of this part are deducted from assets and capital in computing core capital.

(b) *Supplementary Capital.* Supplementary capital counts towards a Federal savings association's total capital up to a maximum of 100% of the savings association's core capital. The following elements comprise a Federal savings association's supplementary capital:

(1) *Permanent Capital Instruments.* (i) Cumulative perpetual preferred stock and other perpetual preferred stock[4] issued pursuant to regulations and memoranda of the OCC;

(ii) Mutual capital certificates issued pursuant to regulations and memoranda of the OCC;

(iii) Nonwithdrawable accounts and pledged deposits (excluding any treasury shares held by the savings association) meeting the criteria of 12 CFR 161.42 to the extent that such instruments are not included in core capital under paragraph (a) of this section;

(iv) Perpetual subordinated debt issued pursuant to regulations and memoranda of the OCC; and

(v) Mandatory convertible subordinated debt (capital notes) issued pursuant to regulations and memoranda of the OCC.

(2) *Maturing Capital Instruments.* (i) Subordinated debt issued pursuant to regulations and memoranda of the OCC;

(ii) Intermediate-term preferred stock issued pursuant to regulations and memoranda of the OCC and any related surplus:

(iii) Mandatory convertible subordinated debt (commitment notes) issued pursuant to regulations and memoranda of the OCC; and

(iv) Mandatorily redeemable preferred stock that was issued before July 23, 1985 or issued pursuant to regulations and memoranda of the Office of Thrift Supervision and approved in writing by the FSLIC for inclusion as regulatory capital before or after issuance.

[4] Other public disclosure requirements continue to apply—for example, Federal securities law and regulatory reporting requirements.

(3) *Transition rules for maturing capital instruments*—(i) [Reserved]

(ii) A Federal savings association issuing maturing capital instruments after November 7, 1989, may choose, subject to paragraph (b)(3)(ii)(C) of this section, to include such instruments pursuant to either paragraph (b)(3)(ii)(A) or (b)(3)(ii)(B) of this section.

(A) At the beginning of each of the last five years of the life of the maturing capital instrument, the amount that is eligible to be included as supplementary capital is reduced by 20% of the original amount of that instrument (net of redemptions).[5]

(B) Only the aggregate amount of maturing capital instruments that mature in any one year during the seven years immediately prior to an instrument's maturity that does not exceed 20% of an institution's capital will qualify as supplementary capital.

(C) Once a Federal savings association selects either paragraph (b)(3)(ii)(A) or (b)(3)(ii)(B) of this section for the issuance of a maturing capital instrument, it must continue to elect that option for all subsequent issuances of maturing capital instruments for as long as there is a balance outstanding of such issuances. Only when such issuances have all been repaid and the savings association has no balance of such issuances outstanding may the savings association elect the other option.

(4) *Allowance for loan and lease losses.* Allowance for loan and lease losses established under regulations and memoranda of the OCC to a maximum of 1.25 percent of risk-weighted assets.[6]

[5] Capital instruments may be redeemed prior to maturity and without the prior approval of the OCC, as long as the instruments are redeemed with the proceeds of, or replaced by, a like amount of a similar or higher quality capital instrument. However, the OCC must be notified in writing at least 30 days in advance of such redemption.

[6] *See* Security Guidelines, II.B. and III.D. Further, the Agencies note that, in addition to contractual obligations to a financial institution, a service provider may be required to implement its own comprehensive information security program in accordance with the Safeguards Rule promulgated by the Federal Trade Commission ("FTC"), 16 CFR part 314.

(5) *Unrealized gains on equity securities.* Up to 45 percent of unrealized gains on available-for-sale equity securities with readily determinable fair values may be included in supplementary capital. Unrealized gains are unrealized holding gains, net of unrealized holding losses, before income taxes, calculated as the amount, if any, by which fair value exceeds historical cost. The OCC may disallow such inclusion in the calculation of supplementary capital if the OCC determines that the equity securities are not prudently valued.

(c) *Total capital.* (1) A Federal savings association's total capital equals the sum of its core capital and supplementary capital (to the extent that such supplementary capital does not exceed 100% of its core capital).

(2) The following assets, in addition to assets required to be deducted elsewhere in calculating core capital, are deducted from assets for purposes of determining total capital:

(i) Reciprocal holdings of depository institution capital instruments; and

(ii) All equity investments.

§ 167.6 Risk-based capital credit risk-weight categories.

(a) *Risk-weighted assets.* Risk-weighted assets equal risk-weighted on-balance sheet assets (computed under paragraph (a)(1) of this section), plus risk-weighted off-balance sheet activities (computed under paragraph (a)(2) of this section), plus risk-weighted recourse obligations, direct credit substitutes, and certain other positions (computed under paragraph (b) of this section). Assets not included (*i.e.*, deducted from capital) for purposes of calculating capital under § 167.5 are not included in calculating risk-weighted assets.

(1) *On-balance sheet assets.* Except as provided in paragraph (b) of this section, risk-weighted on-balance sheet assets are computed by multiplying the on-balance sheet asset amounts times the appropriate risk-weight categories. The risk-weight categories are:

(i) *Zero percent Risk Weight (Category 1).* (A) Cash, including domestic and foreign currency owned and held in all offices of a Federal savings association or in transit. Any foreign currency held by a Federal savings association must be converted into U.S. dollar equivalents;

(B) Securities issued by and other direct claims on the U.S. Government or its agencies (to the extent such securities or claims are unconditionally backed by the full faith and credit of the United States Government) or the central government of an OECD country;

(C) Notes and obligations issued by either the Federal Savings and Loan Insurance Corporation or the Federal Deposit Insurance Corporation and backed by the full faith and credit of the United States Government;

(D) Deposit reserves at, claims on, and balances due from Federal Reserve Banks;

(E) The book value of paid-in Federal Reserve Bank stock;

(F) That portion of assets that is fully covered against capital loss and/or yield maintenance agreements by the Federal Savings and Loan Insurance Corporation or any successor agency.

(G) That portion of assets directly and unconditionally guaranteed by the United States Government or its agencies, or the central government of an OECD country.

(H) Claims on, and claims guaranteed by, a qualifying securities firm that are collateralized by cash on deposit in the savings association or by securities issued or guaranteed by the United States Government or its agencies, or the central government of an OECD country. To be eligible for this risk weight, the savings association must maintain a positive margin of collateral on the claim on a daily basis, taking into account any change in a savings association's exposure to the obligor or counterparty under the claim in relation to the market value of the collateral held in support of the claim.

(ii) *20 percent Risk Weight (Category 2).* (A) Cash items in the process of collection;

(B) That portion of assets collateralized by the current market value of securities issued or guaranteed by the United States government or its agencies, or the central government of an OECD country;

(C) That portion of assets conditionally guaranteed by the United States Government or its agencies, or the central government of an OECD country;

(D) Securities (not including equity securities) issued by and other claims on the U.S. Government or its agencies which are not backed by the full faith and credit of the United States Government;

(E) Securities (not including equity securities) issued by, or other direct claims on, United States Government-sponsored agencies;

(F) That portion of assets guaranteed by United States Government-sponsored agencies;

(G) That portion of assets collateralized by the current market value of securities issued or guaranteed by United States Government-sponsored agencies;

(H) Claims on, and claims guaranteed by, a qualifying securities firm, subject to the following conditions:

(*1*) A qualifying securities firm must have a long-term issuer credit rating, or a rating on at least one issue of long-term unsecured debt, from a NRSRO. The rating must be in one of the three highest investment grade categories used by the NRSRO. If two or more NRSROs assign ratings to the qualifying securities firm, the savings association must use the lowest rating to determine whether the rating requirement of this paragraph is met. A qualifying securities firm may rely on the rating of its parent consolidated company, if the parent consolidated company guarantees the claim.

(*2*) A collateralized claim on a qualifying securities firm does not have to comply with the rating requirements under paragraph (a)(1)(ii)(H)(*1*) of this section if the claim arises under a contract that:

(*i*) Is a reverse repurchase/repurchase agreement or securities lending/borrowing transaction executed using standard industry documentation;

(*ii*) Is collateralized by debt or equity securities that are liquid and readily marketable;

(*iii*) Is marked-to-market daily;

(*iv*) Is subject to a daily margin maintenance requirement under the standard industry documentation; and (*v*) Can be liquidated, terminated or accelerated immediately in bankruptcy or similar proceeding, and the security or collateral agreement will not be stayed or avoided under applicable law of the relevant jurisdiction. For example, a claim is exempt from the automatic stay in bankruptcy in the United States if it arises under a securities contract or a repurchase agreement subject to section 555 or 559 of the Bankruptcy Code (11 U.S.C. 555 or 559), a qualified financial contract under section 11(e)(8) of the Federal Deposit Insurance Act (12 U.S.C. 1821(e)(8)), or a netting contract between or among financial institutions under sections 401–407 of the Federal Deposit Insurance Corporation Improvement Act of 1991 (12 U.S.C. 4401–4407), or Regulation EE (12 CFR part 231).

(*3*) If the securities firm uses the claim to satisfy its applicable capital requirements, the claim is not eligible for a risk weight under this paragraph (a)(1)(ii)(H);

(I) Claims representing general obligations of any public-sector entity in an OECD country, and that portion of any claims guaranteed by any such public-sector entity;

(J) [Reserved]

(K) Balances due from and all claims on domestic depository institutions. This includes demand deposits and other transaction accounts, savings deposits and time certificates of deposit, Federal funds sold, loans to other depository institutions, including overdrafts and term Federal funds, holdings of the savings association's own discounted acceptances for which the account party is a depository institution, holdings of bankers acceptances of other institutions and securities issued by depository institutions, except those that qualify as capital;

(L) The book value of paid-in Federal Home Loan Bank stock;

(M) Deposit reserves at, claims on and balances due from the Federal Home Loan Banks;

(N) Assets collateralized by cash held in a segregated deposit account by the reporting savings association;

(O) Claims on, or guaranteed by, official multilateral lending institutions or regional development institutions in which the United States Government is a shareholder or contributing member;[7]

(P) That portion of assets collateralized by the current market value of securities issued by official multilateral lending institutions or regional development institutions in which the United States Government is a shareholder or contributing member.

(Q) All claims on depository institutions incorporated in an OECD country, and all assets backed by the full faith and credit of depository institutions incorporated in an OECD country. This includes the credit equivalent amount of participations in commitments and standby letters of credit sold to other depository institutions incorporated in an OECD country, but only if the originating bank remains liable to the customer or beneficiary for the full amount of the commitment or standby letter of credit. Also included in this category are the credit equivalent amounts of risk participations in bankers' acceptances conveyed to other depository institutions incorporated in an OECD country. However, bank-issued securities that qualify as capital of the issuing bank are not included in this risk category;

(R) Claims on, or guaranteed by depository institutions other than the central bank, incorporated in a non-OECD country, with a remaining maturity of one year or less;

(S) That portion of local currency claims conditionally guaranteed by central governments of non-OECD countries, to the extent the savings association has local currency liabilities in that country.

(iii) *50 percent Risk Weight (Category 3).* (A) Revenue bonds issued by any public-sector entity in an OECD country for which the underlying obligor is a public-sector entity, but which are repayable solely from the revenues generated from the project financed through the issuance of the obligations;

[7] These institutions include, but are not limited to, the International Bank for Reconstruction and Development (World Bank), the Inter-American Development Bank, the Asian Development Bank, the African Development Bank, the European Investments Bank, the International Monetary Fund and the Bank for International Settlements.

(B) Qualifying mortgage loans and qualifying multifamily mortgage loans;

(C) Privately-issued mortgage-backed securities (*i.e.*, those that do not carry the guarantee of a government or government sponsored entity) representing an interest in qualifying mortgage loans or qualifying multifamily mortgage loans. If the security is backed by qualifying multifamily mortgage loans, the savings association must receive timely payments of principal and interest in accordance with the terms of the security. Payments will generally be considered timely if they are not 30 days past due;

(D) Qualifying residential construction loans as defined in § 167.1 of this part.

(iv) *100 percent Risk Weight (Category 4).* All assets not specified above or deducted from calculations of capital pursuant to § 167.5 of this part, including, but not limited to:

(A) Consumer loans;

(B) Commercial loans;

(C) Home equity loans;

(D) Non-qualifying mortgage loans;

(E) Non-qualifying multifamily mortgage loans;

(F) Residential construction loans;

(G) Land loans;

(H) Nonresidential construction loans;

(I) Obligations issued by any state or any political subdivision thereof for the benefit of a private party or enterprise where that party or enterprise, rather than the issuing state or political subdivision, is responsible for the timely payment of principal and interest on the obligations, *e.g.*, industrial development bonds;

(J) Debt securities not otherwise described in this section;

(K) Investments in fixed assets and premises;

(L) Certain nonsecurity financial instruments including servicing assets and intangible assets includable in core capital under § 167.12 of this part;

(M) Interest-only strips receivable, other than credit-enhancing interest-only strips;

(N)–(O) [Reserved]

(P) That portion of equity investments not deducted pursuant to § 167.5 of this part;

(Q) The prorated assets of subsidiaries (except for the assets of includable, fully consolidated subsidiaries) to the extent such assets are included in adjusted total assets;

(R) All repossessed assets or assets that are more than 90 days past due; and

(S) Equity investments that the OCC determines have the same risk characteristics as foreclosed real estate by the savings association;

(T) Equity investments permissible for a national bank.

(v) [Reserved]

(vi) *Indirect ownership interests in pools of assets.* Assets representing an indirect holding of a pool of assets, *e.g.*, mutual funds, are assigned to risk-weight categories under this section based upon the risk weight that would be assigned to the assets in the portfolio of the pool. An investment in shares of a mutual fund whose portfolio consists primarily of various securities or money market instruments that, if held separately, would be assigned to different risk-weight categories, generally is assigned to the risk-weight category appropriate to the highest risk-weighted asset that the fund is permitted to hold in accordance with the investment objectives set forth in its prospectus. The savings association may, at its option, assign the investment on a pro rata basis to different risk-weight categories according to the investment limits in its prospectus. In no case will an investment in shares in any such fund be assigned to a total risk weight less than 20 percent. If the savings association chooses to assign investments on a pro rata basis, and the sum of the investment limits of assets in the fund's prospectus exceeds 100 percent, the savings association must assign the highest pro rata amounts of its total investment to the higher risk categories. If, in order to maintain a necessary degree of short-term liquidity, a fund is permitted to hold an insignificant amount of its assets in short-term, highly liquid securities of superior credit quality that do not qualify for a preferential risk weight, such securities will generally be disregarded in determining the risk-weight category into which the savings association's holding in the overall fund should be assigned. The prudent use of hedging instruments by a mutual fund to reduce the risk of its assets will not increase the risk weighting of the mutual fund investment. For example, the use of hedging instruments by a mutual fund to reduce the interest rate risk of its government bond portfolio will not increase the risk weight of that fund above the 20 percent category. Nonetheless, if the fund engages in any activities that appear speculative in nature or has any other characteristics that are inconsistent with the preferential risk-weighting assigned to the fund's assets, holdings in the fund will be assigned to the 100 percent risk-weight category.

(2) *Off-balance sheet items.* Except as provided in paragraph (b) of this section, risk-weighted off-balance sheet items are determined by the following two-step process. First, the face amount of the off-balance sheet item must be multiplied by the appropriate credit conversion factor listed in this paragraph (a)(2). This calculation translates the face amount of an off-balance sheet exposure into an on-balance sheet credit-equivalent amount. Second, the credit-equivalent amount must be assigned to the appropriate risk-weight category using the criteria regarding obligors, guarantors, and collateral listed in paragraph (a)(1) of this section, *provided* that the maximum risk weight assigned to the credit-equivalent amount of an interest-rate or exchange-rate contract is 50 percent. The following are the credit conversion factors and the off-balance sheet items to which they apply.

(i) *100 percent credit conversion factor (Group A).*

(A) [Reserved]

(B) Risk participations purchased in bankers' acceptances;

(C) [Reserved]

(D) Forward agreements and other contingent obligations with a certain draw down, *e.g.*, legally binding agreements to purchase assets at a specified future date. On the date an institution enters into a forward agreement or similar obligation, it should convert the principal amount of the assets to be purchased at 100 percent as of that date and then assign this amount to the risk-weight category appropriate to the obligor or guarantor of the item, or the nature of the collateral;

(E) Indemnification of customers whose securities the savings association has lent as agent. If the customer is not indemnified against loss by the savings association, the transaction is excluded from the risk-based capital calculation. When a savings association lends its own securities, the transaction is treated as a loan. When a savings association lends its own securities or is acting as agent, agrees to indemnify a customer, the transaction is assigned to the risk weight appropriate to the obligor or collateral that is delivered to the lending or indemnifying institution or to an independent custodian acting on their behalf.

(ii) *50 percent credit conversion factor (Group B).* (A) Transaction-related contingencies, including, among other things, performance bonds and performance-based standby letters of credit related to a particular transaction;

(B) Unused portions of commitments (including home equity lines of credit and eligible ABCP liquidity facilities) with an original maturity exceeding one year except those listed in paragraph (a)(2)(v) of this section. For eligible ABCP liquidity facilities, the resulting credit equivalent amount is assigned to the risk category appropriate to the assets to be funded by the liquidity facility based on the assets or the obligor, after considering any collateral or guarantees, or external credit ratings under paragraph (b)(3) of this section, if applicable; and

(C) Revolving underwriting facilities, note issuance facilities, and similar arrangements pursuant to which the savings association's customer can issue short-term debt obligations in its own name, but for which the savings association has a legally binding commitment to either:

(*1*) Purchase the obligations the customer is unable to sell by a stated date; or

(*2*) Advance funds to its customer, if the obligations cannot be sold.

(iii) *20 percent credit conversion factor (Group C).* Trade-related contingencies, *i.e.*, short-term, self-liquidating instruments used to finance the movement of goods and collateralized by the underlying shipment. A commercial letter of credit is an example of such an instrument.

(iv) *10 percent credit conversion factor (Group D).* Unused portions of eligible ABCP liquidity facilities with an original maturity of one year or less. The resulting credit equivalent amount is assigned to the risk category appropriate to the assets to be funded by the liquidity facility based on the assets or the obligor, after considering any collateral or guarantees, or external credit ratings under paragraph (b)(3) of this section, if applicable;

(v) *Zero percent credit conversion factor (Group E).* (A) Unused portions of commitments with an original maturity of one year or less, except for eligible ABCP liquidity facilities;

(B) Unused commitments with an original maturity greater than one year, if they are unconditionally cancelable at any time at the option of the savings association and the savings association has the contractual right to make, and in fact does make, either:

(*1*) A separate credit decision based upon the borrower's current financial condition before each drawing under the lending facility; or

(*2*) An annual (or more frequent) credit review based upon the borrower's current financial condition to determine whether or not the lending facility should be continued; and

(C) The unused portion of retail credit card lines or other related plans that are unconditionally cancelable by the savings association in accordance with applicable law.

(vi) *Off-balance sheet contracts; interest-rate and foreign exchange rate contracts (Group F)*—(A) *Calculation of credit equivalent amounts.* The credit equivalent amount of an off-balance sheet interest rate or foreign exchange rate contract that is not subject to a qualifying bilateral netting contract in accordance with paragraph (a)(2)(vi)(B) of this section is equal to the sum of the current credit exposure, *i.e.*, the replacement cost of the contract, and the potential future credit exposure of the off-balance sheet rate contract. The calculation of credit equivalent amounts is measured in U.S. dollars, regardless of the currency or currencies specified in the off-balance sheet rate contract.

(*1*) *Current credit exposure.* The current credit exposure of an off-balance sheet rate contract is determined by the mark-to-market value of the contract. If the mark-to-market value is positive, then the current credit exposure equals that mark-to-market value. If the mark-to-market value is zero or negative, then the current exposure is zero. In determining its current credit exposure for multiple off-balance sheet rate contracts executed with a single counterparty, a Federal savings association may net positive and negative mark-to-market values of off-balance sheet rate contracts if subject to a bilateral netting contract as provided in paragraph (a)(2)(vi)(B) of this section.

(*2*) *Potential future credit exposure.* The potential future credit exposure of an off-balance sheet rate contract, including a contract with a negative mark-to-market value, is estimated by multiplying the notional principal[8] by a credit conversion factor. Federal savings associations, subject to examiner review, should use the effective rather than the apparent or stated notional amount in this calculation. The conversion factors are:[9]

Remaining maturity	Interest rate contracts (percents)	Foreign exchange rate contracts (percents)
One year or less	0.0	1.0

[8] For purposes of calculating potential future credit exposure for foreign exchange contracts and other similar contracts, in which notional principal is equivalent to cash flows, total notional principal is defined as the net receipts to each party falling due on each value date in each currency.

[9] No potential future credit exposure is calculated for single currency interest rate swaps in which payments are made based upon two floating rate indices, so-called floating/floating or basis swaps; the credit equivalent amount is measured solely on the basis of the current credit exposure.

Remaining maturity	Interest rate contracts (percents)	Foreign exchange rate contracts (percents)
Over one year	0.5	5.0

(B) *Off-balance sheet rate contracts subject to bilateral netting contracts.* In determining its current credit exposure for multiple off-balance sheet rate contracts executed with a single counterparty, a Federal savings association may net off-balance sheet rate contracts subject to a bilateral netting contract by offsetting positive and negative mark-to-market values, provided that:

(*1*) The bilateral netting contract is in writing;

(*2*) The bilateral netting contract creates a single legal obligation for all individual off-balance sheet rate contracts covered by the bilateral netting contract. In effect, the bilateral netting contract provides that the savings association has a single claim or obligation either to receive or pay only the net amount of the sum of the positive and negative mark-to-market values on the individual off-balance sheet rate contracts covered by the bilateral netting contract. The single legal obligation for the net amount is operative in the event that a counterparty, or a counterparty to whom the bilateral netting contract has been validly assigned, fails to perform due to any of the following events: default, insolvency, bankruptcy, or other similar circumstances;

(*3*) The Federal savings association obtains a written and reasoned legal opinion(s) representing, with a high degree of certainty, that in the event of a legal challenge, including one resulting from default, insolvency, bankruptcy or similar circumstances, the relevant court and administrative authorities would find the savings association's exposure to be the net amount under:

(*i*) The law of the jurisdiction in which the counterparty is chartered or the equivalent location in the case of noncorporate entities, and if a branch of the counterparty is involved, then also under the law of the jurisdiction in which the branch is located;

(*ii*) The law that governs the individual off-balance sheet rate contracts covered by the bilateral netting contract; and

(*iii*) The law that governs the bilateral netting contract;

(*4*) The savings association establishes and maintains procedures to monitor possible changes in relevant law and to ensure that the bilateral netting contract continues to satisfy the requirements of this section; and

(*5*) The savings association maintains in its files documentation adequate to support the netting of an off-balance sheet rate contract.[10]

(C) *Walkaway clause.* A bilateral netting contract that contains a walkaway clause is not eligible for netting for purposes of calculating the current credit exposure amount. The term "walkaway clause" means a provision in a bilateral netting contract that permits a nondefaulting counterparty to make a lower payment than it would make otherwise under the bilateral netting contract, or no payment at all, to a defaulter or the estate of a defaulter, even if the defaulter or the estate of the defaulter is a net creditor under the bilateral netting contract.

(D) *Risk weighting.* Once the savings association determines the credit equivalent amount for an off-balance

[10] By netting individual off-balance sheet rate contracts for the purpose of calculating its credit equivalent amount, a Federal savings association represents that documentation adequate to support the netting of an off-balance sheet rate contract is in the savings association's files and available for inspection by the OCC. Upon determination by the OCC that a Federal savings association's files are inadequate or that a bilateral netting contract may not be legally enforceable under any one of the bodies of law described in paragraphs (a)(2)(vi)(B)(*3*)(*i*) through (*iii*) of this section, the underlying individual off-balance sheet rate contracts may not be netted for the purposes of this section.

sheet rate contract, that amount is assigned to the risk-weight category appropriate to the counterparty, or, if relevant, to the nature of any collateral or guarantee. Collateral held against a netting contract is not recognized for capital purposes unless it is legally available for all contracts included in the netting contract. However, the maximum risk weight for the credit equivalent amount of such off-balance sheet rate contracts is 50 percent.

(E) *Exceptions*. The following off-balance sheet rate contracts are not subject to the above calculation, and therefore, are not part of the denominator of a Federal savings association's risk-based capital ratio:

(*1*) A foreign exchange rate contract with an original maturity of 14 calendar days or less; and

(*2*) Any interest rate or foreign exchange rate contract that is traded on an exchange requiring the daily payment of any variations in the market value of the contract.

(*3*) If a Federal savings association has multiple overlapping exposures (such as a program-wide credit enhancement and a liquidity facility) to an ABCP program that is not consolidated for risk-based capital purposes, the savings association is not required to hold duplicative risk-based capital under this part against the overlapping position. Instead, the savings association should apply to the overlapping position the applicable risk-based capital treatment that results in the highest capital charge.

(b) *Recourse obligations, direct credit substitutes, and certain other positions*—(1) *In general*. Except as otherwise permitted in this paragraph (b), to determine the risk-weighted asset amount for a recourse obligation or a direct credit substitute (but not a residual interest):

(i) Multiply the full amount of the credit-enhanced assets for which the savings association directly or indirectly retains or assumes credit risk by a 100 percent conversion factor. (For a direct credit substitute that is an on-balance sheet asset (e.g., a purchased subordinated security), a Federal savings association must use the amount of the direct credit substitute and the full amount of the asset its supports, *i.e.*, all the more senior positions in the structure); and

(ii) Assign this credit equivalent amount to the risk-weight category appropriate to the obligor in the underlying transaction, after considering any associated guarantees or collateral. Paragraph (a)(1) of this section lists the risk-weight categories.

(2) *Residual interests*. Except as otherwise permitted under this paragraph (b), a Federal savings association must maintain risk-based capital for residual interests as follows:

(i) *Credit-enhancing interest-only strips*. After applying the concentration limit under § 167.12(e)(2) of this part, a saving association must maintain risk-based capital for a credit-enhancing interest-only strip equal to the remaining amount of the strip (net of any existing associated deferred tax liability), even if the amount of risk-based capital that must be maintained exceeds the full risk-based capital requirement for the assets transferred. Transactions that, in substance, result in the retention of credit risk associated with a transferred credit-enhancing interest-only strip are treated as if the strip was retained by the savings association and was not transferred.

(ii) *Other residual interests*. A saving association must maintain risk-based capital for a residual interest (excluding a credit-enhancing interest-only strip) equal to the face amount of the residual interest (net of any existing associated deferred tax liability), even if the amount of risk-based capital that must be maintained exceeds the full risk-based capital requirement for the assets transferred. Transactions that, in substance, result in the retention of credit risk associated with a transferred residual interest are treated as if the residual interest was retained by the savings association and was not transferred.

(iii) *Residual interests and other recourse obligations*. Where a Federal savings association holds a residual interest (including a credit-enhancing interest-only strip) and another recourse obligation in connection with the same transfer of assets, the savings association must maintain risk-based capital equal to the greater of:

(A) The risk-based capital requirement for the residual interest as calculated under paragraph (b)(2)(i) through (ii) of this section; or

(B) The full risk-based capital requirement for the assets transferred, subject to the low-level recourse rules under paragraph (b)(7) of this section.

(3) *Ratings-based approach*—(i) *Calculation.* A Federal savings association may calculate the risk-weighted asset amount for an eligible position described in paragraph (b)(3)(ii) of this section by multiplying the face amount of the position by the appropriate risk weight determined in accordance with Table A or B of this section.

NOTE: Stripped mortgage-backed securities or other similar instruments, such as interest-only and principal-only strips, that are not credit enhancing must be assigned to the 100% risk-weight category.

TABLE A

Long term rating category	Risk weight (In percent)
Highest or second highest investment grade	20
Third highest investment grade	50
Lowest investment grade	100
One category below investment grade	200

TABLE B

Short term rating category	Risk weight (In percent)
Highest investment grade	20
Second highest investment grade	50
Lowest investment grade	100

(ii) *Eligibility*—(A) *Traded positions.* A position is eligible for the treatment described in paragraph (b)(3)(i) of this section, if:

(*1*) The position is a recourse obligation, direct credit substitute, residual interest, or asset- or mortgage-backed security and is not a credit-enhancing interest-only strip;

(*2*) The position is a traded position; and

(*3*) The NRSRO has rated a long term position as one grade below investment grade or better or a short term position as investment grade. If two or more NRSROs assign ratings to a traded position, the savings association must use the lowest rating to determine the appropriate risk-weight category under paragraph (b)(3)(i) of this section.

(B) *Non-traded positions.* A position that is not traded is eligible for the treatment described in paragraph (b)(3)(i) of this section if:

(*1*) The position is a recourse obligation, direct credit substitute, residual interest, or asset- or mortgage-backed security extended in connection with a securitization and is not a credit-enhancing interest-only strip;

(*2*) More than one NRSRO rate the position;

(*3*) All of the NRSROs that provide a rating rate a long term position as one grade below investment grade or better or a short term position as investment grade. If the NRSROs assign different ratings to the position, the savings association must use the lowest rating to determine the appropriate risk-weight category under paragraph (b)(3)(i) of this section;

(*4*) The NRSROs base their ratings on the same criteria that they use to rate securities that are traded positions; and

(*5*) The ratings are publicly available.

(C) *Unrated senior positions.* If a recourse obligation, direct credit substitute, residual interest, or asset- or mortgage-backed security is not rated by an NRSRO, but is senior or preferred in all features to a traded position (including collateralization and maturity), the savings association may risk-weight the face amount of the senior position under paragraph (b)(3)(i) of this section, based on the rating of the traded position, subject to supervisory guidance. The savings association must satisfy the OCC that this treatment is appropriate. This paragraph (b)(3)(i)(C) applies only if the traded position provides substantive credit support to the unrated position until the unrated position matures.

(4) *Certain positions that are not rated by NRSROs*—(i) *Calculation.* A Federal savings association may calculate the risk-weighted asset amount for eligible position described in paragraph (b)(4)(ii) of this section based on the savings association's determination of the credit rating of the position. To risk-weight the asset, the savings association must multiply the face amount of the position by the appropriate risk weight determined in accordance with Table C of this section.

TABLE C

Rating category	Risk weight (In percent)
Investment grade	100
One category below investment grade	200

(ii) *Eligibility*. A position extended in connection with a securitization is eligible for the treatment described in paragraph (b)(4)(i) of this section if it is not rated by an NRSRO, is not a residual interest, and meets the one of the three alternative standards described in paragraph (b)(4)(ii)(A), (B), or (C) below of this section:

(A) *Position rated internally*. A direct credit substitute, but not a purchased credit-enhancing interest-only strip, is eligible for the treatment described under paragraph (b)(4)(i) of this section, if the position is assumed in connection with an asset-backed commercial paper program sponsored by the savings association. Before it may rely on an internal credit risk rating system, the saving association must demonstrate to the OCC's satisfaction that the system is adequate. Adequate internal credit risk rating systems typically:

(*1*) Are an integral part of the savings association's risk management system that explicitly incorporates the full range of risks arising from the savings association's participation in securitization activities;

(*2*) Link internal credit ratings to measurable outcomes, such as the probability that the position will experience any loss, the expected loss on the position in the event of default, and the degree of variance in losses in the event of default on that position;

(*3*) Separately consider the risk associated with the underlying loans or borrowers, and the risk associated with the structure of the particular securitization transaction;

(*4*) Identify gradations of risk among "pass" assets and other risk positions;

(*5*) Use clear, explicit criteria to classify assets into each internal rating grade, including subjective factors;

(*6*) Employ independent credit risk management or loan review personnel to assign or review the credit risk ratings;

(*7*) Include an internal audit procedure to periodically verify that internal risk ratings are assigned in accordance with the savings association's established criteria;

(*8*) Monitor the performance of the assigned internal credit risk ratings over time to determine the appropriateness of the initial credit risk rating assignment, and adjust individual credit risk ratings or the overall internal credit risk rating system, as needed; and

(*9*) Make credit risk rating assumptions that are consistent with, or more conservative than, the credit risk rating assumptions and methodologies of NRSROs.

(B) *Program ratings*. (*1*) A recourse obligation or direct credit substitute, but not a residual interest, is eligible for the treatment described in paragraph (b)(4)(i) of this section, if the position is retained or assumed in connection with a structured finance program and an NRSRO has reviewed the terms of the program and stated a rating for positions associated with the program. If the program has options for different combinations of assets, standards, internal or external credit enhancements and other relevant factors, and the NRSRO specifies ranges of rating categories to them, the savings association may apply the rating category applicable to the option that corresponds to the savings association's position.

(*2*) To rely on a program rating, the savings association must demonstrate to the OCC's satisfaction that the credit risk rating assigned to the program meets the same standards generally used by NRSROs for rating traded positions. The savings association must also demonstrate to the OCC's satisfaction that the criteria underlying the assignments for the program are satisfied by the particular position.

(*3*) If a Federal savings association participates in a securitization sponsored by another party, the OCC may authorize the savings association to use this approach based on a program rating obtained by the sponsor of the program.

(C) *Computer program*. A recourse obligation or direct credit substitute, but not a residual interest, is eligible for the treatment described in paragraph (b)(4)(i) of this section, if the position is extended in connection with a structured financing program and the savings association uses an acceptable credit assessment computer program to determine the rating of the position. An NRSRO must have developed the computer program and the savings association must demonstrate to the OCC's satisfaction that the ratings under the program correspond credibly and reliably with the rating of traded positions.

(5) *Alternative capital computation for small business obligations*—(i) *Definitions.* For the purposes of this paragraph (b)(5):

(A) *Qualified Federal savings association* means a savings association that:

(*1*) Is well capitalized as defined in § 165.4 of this chapter without applying the capital treatment described in this paragraph (b)(5); or

(*2*) Is adequately capitalized as defined in § 165.4 of this chapter without applying the capital treatment described in this paragraph (b)(5) and has received written permission from the OCC to apply that capital treatment.

(B) *Small business* means a business that meets the criteria for a small business concern established by the Small Business Administration in 13 CFR 121 pursuant to 15 U.S.C. 632.

(ii) *Capital requirement.* Notwithstanding any other provision of this paragraph (b), with respect to a transfer of a small business loan or lease of personal property with recourse that is a sale under GAAP, a qualified Federal savings association may elect to include only the amount of its recourse in its risk-weighted assets. To qualify for this election, the savings association must establish and maintain a reserve under GAAP sufficient to meet the reasonable estimated liability of the savings association under the recourse obligation.

(iii) *Aggregate amount of recourse.* The total outstanding amount of recourse retained by a qualified Federal savings association with respect to transfers of small business loans and leases of personal property and included in the risk-weighted assets of the savings association as described in paragraph (b)(5)(ii) of this section, may not exceed 15 percent of the association's total capital computed under § 167.5(c).

(iv) *Federal savings association that ceases to be a qualified Federal savings association or that exceeds aggregate limits.* If a Federal savings association ceases to be a qualified savings association or exceeds the aggregate limit described in paragraph (b)(5)(iii) of this section, the savings association may continue to apply the capital treatment described in paragraph (b)(5)(ii) of this section to transfers of small business loans and leases of personal property that occurred when the association was a qualified savings association and did not exceed the limit.

(v) *Prompt corrective action not affected.* (A) A Federal savings association shall compute its capital without regard to this paragraph (b)(5) of this section for purposes of prompt corrective action (12 U.S.C. 1831o), unless the savings association is adequately or well capitalized without applying the capital treatment described in this paragraph (b)(5) and would be well capitalized after applying that capital treatment.

(B) A Federal savings association shall compute its capital requirement without regard to this paragraph (b)(5) for the purposes of applying 12 U.S.C. 1831o(g), regardless of the association's capital level.

(6) *Risk participations and syndications of direct credit substitutes.* A Federal savings association must calculate the risk-weighted asset amount for a risk participation in, or syndication of, a direct credit substitute as follows:

(i) If a Federal savings association conveys a risk participation in a direct credit substitute, the savings association must convert the full amount of the assets that are supported by the direct credit substitute to a credit equivalent amount using a 100 percent conversion factor. The savings association must assign the *pro rata* share of the credit equivalent amount that was conveyed through the risk participation to the lower of: The risk-weight category appropriate to the obligor in the underlying transaction, after considering any associated guarantees or collateral; or the risk-weight category appropriate to the party acquiring the participation. The savings association must assign the *pro rata* share of the credit equivalent amount that was not participated out to the risk-weight category appropriate to the obligor, after considering any associated guarantees or collateral.

(ii) If a Federal savings association acquires a risk participation in a direct credit substitute, the savings association must multiply its *pro rata* share of the direct credit substitute by the full amount of the assets that are supported by the direct credit substitute, and convert this amount to a credit equivalent amount using a 100 percent conversion factor. The savings association must assign the resulting credit equivalent amount to the risk-weight category appropriate to the obligor in the underlying transaction, after considering any associated guarantees or collateral.

(iii) If the Federal savings association holds a direct credit substitute in the form of a syndication where each savings association or other participant is obligated only for its *pro rata* share of the risk and there is no recourse to the originating party, the savings association must calculate the credit equivalent amount by multiplying only its *pro rata* share of the assets supported by the direct credit substitute by a 100 percent conversion factor. The savings association must assign the resulting credit equivalent amount to the risk-weight category appropriate to the obligor in the underlying transaction after considering any associated guarantees or collateral.

(7) *Limitations on risk-based capital requirements*—(i) *Low-level exposure rule.* If the maximum contractual exposure to loss retained or assumed by a Federal savings association is less than the effective risk-based capital requirement, as determined in accordance with this paragraph (b), for the assets supported by the savings association's position, the risk-based capital requirement is limited to the savings association's contractual exposure less any recourse liability account established in accordance with GAAP. This limitation does not apply when a Federal savings association provides credit enhancement beyond any contractual obligation to support assets it has sold.

(ii) *Mortgage-related securities or participation certificates retained in a mortgage loan swap.* If a Federal savings association holds a mortgage-related security or a participation certificate as a result of a mortgage loan swap with recourse, it must hold risk-based capital to support the recourse obligation and that percentage of the mortgage-related security or participation certificate that is not covered by the recourse obligation. The total amount of risk-based capital required for the security (or certificate) and the recourse obligation is limited to the risk-based capital requirement for the underlying loans, calculated as if the savings association continued to hold these loans as an on-balance sheet asset.

(iii) *Related on-balance sheet assets.* If an asset is included in the calculation of the risk-based capital requirement under this paragraph (b) and also appears as an asset on the savings association's balance sheet, the savings association must risk-weight the asset only under this paragraph (b), except in the case of loan servicing assets and similar arrangements with embedded recourse obligations or direct credit substitutes. In that case, the savings association must separately risk-weight the on-balance sheet servicing asset and the related recourse obligations and direct credit substitutes under this section, and incorporate these amounts into the risk-based capital calculation.

(8) *Obligations of subsidiaries.* If a Federal savings association retains a recourse obligation or assumes a direct credit substitute on the obligation of a subsidiary that is not an includable subsidiary, and the recourse obligation or direct credit substitute is an equity or debt investment in that subsidiary under GAAP, the face amount of the recourse obligation or direct credit substitute is deducted for capital under §§ 167.5(a)(2) and 167.9(c). All other recourse obligations and direct credit substitutes retained or assumed by a Federal savings association on the obligations of an entity in which the savings association has an equity investment are risk-weighted in accordance with this paragraph (b).

§ 167.8 Leverage ratio.

(a) The minimum leverage capital requirement for a Federal savings association assigned a composite rating of

1, as defined in § 116.3 of this chapter, shall consist of a ratio of core capital to adjusted total assets of 3 percent. These generally are strong associations that are not anticipating or experiencing significant growth and have well-diversified risks, including no undue interest rate risk exposure, excellent asset quality, high liquidity, and good earnings.

(b) For all Federal savings associations not meeting the conditions set forth in paragraph (a) of this section, the minimum leverage capital requirement shall consist of a ratio of core capital to adjusted total assets of 4 percent. Higher capital ratios may be required if warranted by the particular circumstances or risk profiles of an individual Federal savings association. In all cases, Federal savings associations should hold capital commensurate with the level and nature of all risks, including the volume and severity of problem loans, to which they are exposed.

§ 167.9 Tangible capital requirement.

(a) Federal savings associations shall have and maintain tangible capital in an amount equal to at least 1.5% of adjusted total assets.

(b) The following elements, less the amount of any deductions pursuant to paragraph (c) of this section, comprise a Federal savings association's tangible capital:

(1) Common stockholders' equity (including retained earnings);

(2) Noncumulative perpetual preferred stock and related earnings;

(3) Nonwithdrawable accounts and pledged deposits that would qualify as core capital under § 167.5 of this part; and

(4) Minority interests in the equity accounts of fully consolidated subsidiaries.

(c) *Deductions from tangible capital.* In calculating tangible capital, a Federal savings association must deduct from assets, and, thus, from capital:

(1) Intangible assets (as defined in § 167.1) except for mortgage servicing assets to the extent they are includable in tangible capital under § 167.12, and credit enhancing interest-only strips and deferred tax assets not includable in tangible capital under § 167.12.

(2) Investments, both equity and debt, in subsidiaries that are not includable subsidiaries (including those subsidiaries where the savings association has a minority ownership interest), except as provided in paragraphs (c)(3) and (c)(4) of this section.

(3) If a Federal savings association has any investments (both debt and equity) in one or more subsidiary(ies) engaged in any activity that would not fall within the scope of activities in which includable subsidiaries may engage, it must deduct such investments from assets and, thus, tangible capital in accordance with this paragraph (c)(3). The savings association must first deduct from assets and, thus, capital the amount by which any investments in such a subsidiary(ies) exceed the amount of such investments held by the savings association. Next, the savings association must deduct from assets and, thus, tangible capital the savings association's investments in and extensions of credit to the subsidiary on the date as of which the savings association's capital is being determined.

(4) If a savings association holds a subsidiary (either directly or through a subsidiary) that is itself a domestic depository institution the OCC may, in its sole discretion upon determining that the amount of tangible capital that would be required would be higher if the assets and liabilities of such subsidiary were consolidated with those of the parent savings association than the amount that would be required if the parent savings association's investment were deducted pursuant to paragraphs (c)(2) and (c)(3) of this section, consolidate the assets and liabilities of that subsidiary with those of the parent savings association in calculating the capital adequacy of the parent savings association, regardless of whether the subsidiary would otherwise be an includable subsidiary as defined in § 167.1 of this part.

§ 167.10 Consequences of failure to meet capital requirements.

(a) *Capital plans.* (1) [Reserved]

(2) The OCC shall require any Federal savings association not in compliance with capital standards to submit a capital plan that:

(i) Addresses the savings association's need for increased capital;

(ii) Describes the manner in which the savings association will increase capital so as to achieve compliance with capital standards;

(iii) Specifies types and levels of activities in which the savings association will engage;

(iv) Requires any increase in assets to be accompanied by increase in tangible capital not less in percentage amount than the leverage limit then applicable;

(v) Requires any increase in assets to be accompanied by an increase in capital not less in percentage amount than required under the risk-based capital standard then applicable; and

(vi) Is acceptable to the Comptroller.

(3) To be acceptable to the Comptroller under this section, a plan must, in addition to satisfying all of the requirements set forth in paragraphs (a)(2)(i) through (a)(2)(v) of this section, contain a certification that while the plan is under review by the OCC, the savings association will not, without the prior written approval of the OCC:

(i) Grow beyond net interest credited;

(ii) Make any capital distributions; or

(iii) Act inconsistently with any other limitations on activities established by statute, regulation or by the OCC in supervisory guidance for Federal savings associations not meeting capital standards.

(4) If the plan submitted to the Comptroller under paragraph (a)(2) of this section is not approved by the Comptroller, the savings association shall immediately and without any further action, be subject to the following restrictions:

(i) It may not increase its assets beyond the amount held on the day it receives written notice of the Comptroller's disapproval of the plan; and

(ii) It must comply with any other restrictions or limitations set forth in the written notice of the Comptroller's disapproval of the plan.

(b) The Comptroller shall:

(1) Prohibit any asset growth by any Federal savings association not in compliance with capital standards, *except* as provided in paragraph (d) of this section; and

(2) Require any Federal savings association not in compliance with capital standards to comply with a capital directive issued by the Comptroller which may include the restrictions contained in paragraph (e) of this section and any other restrictions the Comptroller determines appropriate.

(c) A Federal savings association that wishes to obtain an exemption from the sanctions provided in paragraph (b)(2) of this section must file a request for exemption with the OCC. Such request must include a capital plan that satisfies the requirements of paragraph (a)(2) of this section.

(d) The Comptroller may permit any Federal savings association that is subject to paragraph (b) of this section to increase its assets in an amount not exceeding the amount of net interest credited to the savings association's deposit liabilities, if:

(1) The savings association obtains the Comptroller's prior approval;

(2) Any increase in assets is accompanied by an increase in tangible capital in an amount not less than 3% of the increase in assets;

(3) Any increase in assets is accompanied by an increase in capital not less in percentage amount than required under the risk-based capital standards then applicable;

(4) Any increase in assets is invested in low-risk assets; and

(5) The savings association's ratio of core capital to total assets is not less than the ratio existing on January 1, 1991.

(e) If a Federal savings association fails to meet the risk-based capital requirement, the leverage ratio requirement, or the tangible capital requirement established under this part, the Comptroller may, through enforcement proceedings or otherwise, require such savings association to take one or more of the following corrective actions:

(1) Increase the amount of its regulatory capital to a specified level or levels;

(2) Convene a meeting or meetings with the supervision staff of the OCC for the purpose of accomplishing the objectives of this section;

(3) Reduce the rate of earnings that may be paid on savings accounts;

(4) Limit the receipt of deposits to those made to existing accounts;

(5) Cease or limit the issuance of new accounts of any or all classes or categories, except in exchange for existing accounts;

(6) Cease or limit lending or the making of a particular type or category of loan;

(7) Cease or limit the purchase of loans or the making of specified other investments;

(8) Limit operational expenditures to specified levels;

(9) Increase liquid assets and maintain such increased liquidity at specified levels; or

(10) Take such other action or actions as the Comptroller may deem necessary or appropriate for the safety and soundness of the savings association, or depositors or investors in the savings association.

(f) The Comptroller shall treat as an unsafe and unsound practice any material failure by a Federal savings association to comply with any plan, regulation, written agreement undertaken under this section or order or directive issued to comply with the requirements of this part.

§ 167.11 Reservation of authority.

(a) *Transactions for purposes of evasion.* The Comptroller may disregard any transaction entered into primarily for the purpose of reducing the minimum required amount of regulatory capital or otherwise evading the requirements of this part.

(b) *Average versus period-end figures.* The OCC reserves the right to require a Federal savings association to compute its capital ratios on the basis of average, rather than period-end, assets when the OCC determines appropriate to carry out the purposes of this part.

(c)(1) *Reservation of authority.* Notwithstanding the definitions of core and supplementary capital in § 167.5 of this part, the OCC may find that a particular type of purchased intangible asset or capital instrument constitutes or may constitute core or supplementary capital, and may permit one or more Federal savings associations to include all or a portion of such intangible asset or funds obtained through such capital instrument as core or supplementary capital, permanently or on a temporary basis, for the purposes of compliance with this part or for any other purposes. Similarly, the OCC may find that a particular asset or core or supplementary capital component has characteristics or terms that diminish its contribution to a Federal savings association's ability to absorb losses, and the OCC may require the discounting or deduction of such asset or component from the computation of core, supplementary, or total capital.

(2) Notwithstanding § 167.6 of this part, the OCC will look to the substance of a transaction and may find that the assigned risk weight for any asset, or credit equivalent amount or credit conversion factor for any off-balance sheet item does not appropriately reflect the risks imposed on the savings association. The OCC may require the savings association to apply another risk-weight, credit equivalent amount, or credit conversion factor that the OCC deems appropriate.

(3) The OCC may find that the capital treatment for an exposure to a transaction not subject to consolidation on the savings association's balance sheet does not appropriately reflect the risks imposed on the savings association. Accordingly, the OCC may require the savings association to treat the transaction as if it were consolidated on the savings association's balance sheet. The OCC will look to the substance of and risk associated with the transaction as well as other relevant factors in determining whether to require such treatment and in calculating risk based capital as the OCC deems appropriate.

(4) If this part does not specifically assign a risk weight, credit equivalent amount, or credit conversion factor, the OCC may assign any risk weight, credit equivalent amount, or credit conversion factor that it deems appropriate. In making this determination, the OCC will consider the risks associated with the asset or off-balance sheet item as well as other relevant factors.

(d) In making a determination under this paragraph (c) of this section, the OCC will notify the savings association of the determination and solicit a response from the savings association. After review of the response by the savings association, the OCC shall issue a final supervisory decision regarding the determination made under paragraph (c) of this section.

§ 167.12 Purchased credit card relationships, servicing assets, intangible assets (other than purchased credit card relationships and servicing assets), credit-enhancing interest-only strips, and deferred tax assets.

(a) *Scope.* This section prescribes the maximum amount of purchased credit card relationships, serving assets, intangible assets (other than purchased credit card relationships and servicing assets), credit-enhancing interest-only strips, and deferred tax assets that Federal savings associations may include in calculating tangible and core capital.

(b) *Computation of core and tangible capital.* (1) Purchased credit card relationships may be included (that is, not deducted) in computing core capital in accordance with the restrictions in this section, but must be deducted in computing tangible capital.

(2) In accordance with the restrictions in this section, mortgage servicing assets may be included in computing core and tangible capital and nonmortgage servicing assets may be included in core capital.

(3) Intangible assets, as defined in § 167.1 of this part, other than purchased credit card relationships described in paragraph (b)(1) of this section, servicing assets described in paragraph (b)(2) of this section, and core deposit intangibles described in paragraph (g)(3) of this section, are deducted in computing tangible and core capital, subject to paragraph (e)(3)(ii) of this section.

(4) Credit-enhancing interest-only strips may be included (that is not deducted) in computing core capital subject to the restrictions of this section, and may be included in tangible capital in the same amount.

(5) Deferred tax assets may be included (that is not deducted) in computing core capital subject to the restrictions of paragraph (h) of this section, and may be included in tangible capital in the same amount.

(c) *Market valuations.* The OCC reserves the authority to require any Federal savings association to perform an independent market valuation of assets subject to this section on a case-by-case basis or through the issuance of policy guidance. An independent market valuation, if required, shall be conducted in accordance with any policy guidance issued by the OCC. A required valuation shall include adjustments for any significant changes in original valuation assumptions, including changes in prepayment estimates or attrition rates. The valuation shall determine the current fair value of assets subject to this section. This independent market valuation may be conducted by an independent valuation expert evaluating the reasonableness of the internal calculations and assumptions used by the association in conducting its internal analysis. The association shall calculate an estimated fair value for assets subject to this section at least quarterly regardless of whether an independent valuation expert is required to perform an independent market valuation.

(d) *Value limitation.* For purposes of calculating core capital under this part (but not for financial statement purposes), purchased credit card relationships and servicing assets must be valued at the lesser of:

(1) 90 percent of their fair value determined in accordance with paragraph (c) of this section; or

(2) 100 percent of their remaining unamortized book value determined in accordance with the instructions for the Call Report or TFR, as appropriate.

(e) *Core capital limitations*—(1) *Servicing assets and purchased credit card relationships.* (i) The maximum aggregate amount of servicing assets and purchased credit card relationships that may be included in core capital is limited to the lesser of:

(A) 100 percent of the amount of core capital; or

(B) The amount of servicing assets and purchased credit card relationships determined in accordance with paragraph (d) of this section.

(ii) In addition to the aggregate limitation in paragraph (e)(1)(i) of this section, a sublimit applies to purchased credit card relationships and non mortgage-related serving assets. The maximum allowable amount of these two types of assets combined is limited to the lesser of:

(A) 25 percent the amount of core capital; and

(B) The amount of purchased credit card relationships and non mortgage-related servicing assets determined in accordance with paragraph (d) of this section.

(2) *Credit-enhancing interest-only strips*. The maximum aggregate amount of credit-enhancing interest-only strips that may be included in core capital is limited to 25 percent of the amount of core capital. Purchased and retained credit-enhancing interest-only strips, on a non-tax adjusted basis, are included in the total amount that is used for purposes of determining whether a Federal savings association exceeds the core capital limit.

(3) *Computation*. (i) For purposes of computing the limits and sublimits in paragraphs (e) and (h) of this section, core capital is computed before the deduction of disallowed servicing assets, disallowed purchased credit card relationships, disallowed credit-enhancing interest-only strips (purchased and retained), and disallowed deferred tax assets.

(ii) A Federal savings association may elect to deduct the following items on a basis net of deferred tax liabilities:

(A) Disallowed servicing assets;

(B) Goodwill such that only the net amount must be deducted from Tier 1 capital;

(C) Disallowed credit-enhancing interest only strips (both purchased and retained); and

(D) Other intangible assets arising from non-taxable business combinations. A deferred tax liability that is specifically related to an intangible asset (other than purchased credit card relationships) arising from a non-taxable business combination may be netted against this intangible asset. The net amount of the intangible asset must be deducted from Tier 1 capital.

(iii) Deferred tax liabilities that are netted in accordance with paragraph (e)(3)(ii) of this section cannot also be netted against deferred tax assets when determining the amount of deferred tax assets that are dependent upon future taxable income.

(f) *Tangible capital limitation*. The maximum amount of mortgage servicing assets that may be included in tangible capital shall be the same amount includable in core capital in accordance with the limitations set by paragraph (e) of this section. All non-mortgage servicing assets are deducted in computing tangible capital.

(g) *Exemption for certain subsidiaries*—(1) *Exemption standard*. An association holding purchased mortgage servicing rights in separately capitalized, non-includable subsidiaries may submit an application for approval by the OCC for an exemption from the deductions and limitations set forth in this section. The deductions and limitations will apply to such purchased mortgage servicing rights, however, if the OCC determines that:

(i) The thrift and subsidiary are not conducting activities on an arm's length basis; or

(ii) The exemption is not consistent with the association's safe and sound operation.

(2) *Applicable requirements*. If the OCC determines to grant or to permit the continuation of an exemption under paragraph (h)(1) of this section, the association receiving the exemption must ensure the following:

(i) The association's investments in, and extensions of credit to, the subsidiary are deducted from capital when calculating capital under this part;

(ii) Extensions of credit and other transactions with the subsidiary are conducted in compliance with the rules for covered transactions with affiliates set forth in sections 23A and 23B of the Federal Reserve Act, as applied to thrifts; and

(iii) Any contracts entered into by the subsidiary include a written disclosure indicating that the subsidiary is not a bank or Federal savings association; the subsidiary is an organization separate and apart from any bank or Federal savings association; and the obligations of the subsidiary are not backed or guaranteed by any bank or Federal savings association and are not insured by the FDIC.

(h) *Treatment of deferred tax assets.* For purposes of calculating Tier 1 capital under this part (but not for financial statement purposes) deferred tax assets are subject to the conditions, limitations, and restrictions described in this section.

(1) Tier 1 capital limitations. (i) The maximum allowable amount of deferred tax assets net of any valuation allowance that are dependent upon future taxable income will be limited to the lesser of:

(A) The amount of deferred tax assets that are dependent upon future taxable income that is expected to be realized within one year of the calendar quarter-end date, based on a projected future taxable income for that year; or

(B) Ten percent of the amount of Tier 1 capital that exists before the deduction of any disallowed servicing assets, any disallowed purchased credit card relationships, any disallowed credit-enhancing interest-only strips, and any disallowed deferred tax assets.

(ii) For purposes of this limitation, all existing temporary differences should be assumed to fully reverse at the calendar quarter-end date. The recorded amount of deferred tax assets that are dependent upon future taxable income, net of any valuation allowance for deferred tax assets, in excess of this limitation will be deducted from assets and from equity capital for purposes of determining Tier 1 capital under this part. The amount of deferred tax assets that can be realized from taxes paid in prior carryback years and from the reversal of existing taxable temporary differences generally would not be deducted from assets and from equity capital.

(iii) Notwithstanding paragraph (h)(1)(B)(ii) of this section, the amount of carryback potential that may be considered in calculating the amount of deferred tax assets that a Federal savings association that is part of a consolidated group (for tax purposes) may include in Tier 1 capital may not exceed the amount which the association could reasonably expect to have refunded by its parent.

(2) Projected future taxable income. Projected future taxable income should not include net operating loss carryforwards to be used within one year of the most recent calendar quarter-end date or the amount of existing temporary differences expected to reverse within that year. Projected future taxable income should include the estimated effect of tax planning strategies that are expected to be implemented to realize tax carryforwards that will otherwise expire during that year. Future taxable income projections for the current fiscal year (adjusted for any significant changes that have occurred or are expected to occur) may be used when applying the capital limit at an interim calendar quarter-end date rather than preparing a new projection each quarter.

(3) *Unrealized holding gains and losses on available-for-sale debt securities.* The deferred tax effects of any unrealized holding gains and losses on available-for-sale debt securities may be excluded from the determination of the amount of deferred tax assets that are dependent upon future taxable income and the calculation of the maximum allowable amount of such assets. If these deferred tax effects are excluded, this treatment must be followed consistently over time.

§§ 167.14–167.19 [Reserved]

APPENDIXES A–C TO PART 167 [RESERVED]

PART 168—SECURITY PROCEDURES

Sec.

168.1 Authority, purpose, and scope.
168.2 Designation of security officer.
168.3 Security program.
168.4 Report.
168.5 Protection of customer information.

AUTHORITY: 12 U.S.C. 1462a, 1463, 1464, 1467a, 1828, 1831p–1, 1881–1884, 5412(b)(2)(B); 15 U.S.C. 1681s and 1681w; 15 U.S.C. 6801 and 6805(b)(1).

SOURCE: 76 FR 49129, Aug. 9, 2011, unless otherwise noted.

§ 168.1 Authority, purpose, and scope.

(a) This part is issued under section 3 of the Bank Protection Act of 1968 (12 U.S.C 1882), sections 501 and 505(b)(1) of the Gramm-Leach-Bliley Act (15 U.S.C. 6801 and 6805(b)(1)), and sections 621 and

628 of the Fair Credit Reporting Act (15 U.S.C. 1681s and 1681w). This part is applicable to Federal savings associations. It requires each Federal savings association to adopt appropriate security procedures to discourage robberies, burglaries, and larcenies and to assist in the identification and prosecution of persons who commit such acts. Section 168.5 of this part is applicable to Federal savings associations and their subsidiaries (except brokers, dealers, persons providing insurance, investment companies, and investment advisers). Section 168.5 of this part requires covered institutions to establish and implement appropriate administrative, technical, and physical safeguards to protect the security, confidentiality, and integrity of customer information.

(b) It is the responsibility of a Federal savings association's board of directors to comply with this regulation and ensure that a written security program for the association's main office and branches is developed and implemented.

§ 168.2 Designation of security officer.

Within 30 days after the effective date of insurance of accounts, the board of directors of each Federal savings association shall designate a security officer who shall have the authority, subject to the approval of the board of directors, to develop, within a reasonable time but no later than 180 days, and to administer a written security program for each of the association's offices.

§ 168.3 Security program.

(a) *Contents of security program.* The security program shall:

(1) Establish procedures for opening and closing for business and for the safekeeping of all currency, negotiable securities, and similar valuables at all times;

(2) Establish procedures that will assist in identifying persons committing crimes against the association and that will preserve evidence that may aid in their identification and prosecution. Such procedures may include, but are not limited to:

(i) Maintaining a camera that records activity in the office;

(ii) Using identification devices, such as prerecorded serial-numbered bills, or chemical and electronic devices; and

(iii) Retaining a record of any robbery, burglary, or larceny committed against the association;

(3) Provide for initial and periodic training of officers and employees in their responsibilities under the security program and in proper employee conduct during and after a burglary, robbery, or larceny; and

(4) Provide for selecting, testing, operating and maintaining appropriate security devices, as specified in paragraph (b) of this section.

(b) *Security devices.* Each savings association shall have, at a minimum, the following security devices:

(1) A means of protecting cash and other liquid assets, such as a vault, safe, or other secure space;

(2) A lighting system for illuminating, during the hours of darkness, the area around the vault, if the vault is visible from outside the office;

(3) Tamper-resistant locks on exterior doors and exterior windows that may be opened;

(4) An alarm system or other appropriate device for promptly notifying the nearest responsible law enforcement officers of an attempted or perpetrated robbery or burglary; and

(5) Such other devices as the security officer determines to be appropriate, taking into consideration:

(i) The incidence of crimes against financial institutions in the area;

(ii) The amount of currency and other valuables exposed to robbery, burglary, or larceny;

(iii) The distance of the office from the nearest responsible law enforcement officers;

(iv) The cost of the security devices;

(v) Other security measures in effect at the office; and

(vi) The physical characteristics of the structure of the office and its surroundings.

§ 168.4 Report.

The security officer for each Federal savings association shall report at least annually to the association's board of directors on the implementation, administration, and effectiveness of the security program.

§ 168.5 Protection of customer information.

Federal savings associations and their subsidiaries (except brokers, dealers, persons providing insurance, investment companies, and investment advisers) must comply with the Interagency Guidelines Establishing Information Security Standards set forth in appendix B to part 30 of this chapter. Supplement A to appendix B to part 30 of this chapter provides interpretive guidance.

[76 FR 49129, Aug. 9, 2011, as amended at 79 FR 54549, Sept. 11, 2014]

PART 169—PROXIES

Sec.
169.1 Definitions.
169.2 Form of proxies.
169.3 Holders of proxies.
169.4 Proxy soliciting material.

AUTHORITY: Section 2, 48 Stat. 128, as amended (12 U.S.C. 1462); section 3, as added by section 301, 103 Stat. 278 (12 U.S.C. 1462a); section 4, as added by section 301, 103 Stat. 280 (12 U.S.C. 1463), 5412(b)(2)(B).

SOURCE: 76 FR 49129, Aug. 9, 2011, unless otherwise noted.

§ 169.1 Definitions.

As used in this part:

(a) *Security holder*. (1) The term *security holder* means any person having the right to vote in the affairs of a savings association by virtue of:

(i) Ownership of any security of the association or

(ii) Any indebtedness to the association.

(2) For purposes of this part, the term *security holder* shall include any account holder having the right to vote in the affairs of a mutual savings association.

(b) *Person*. The term *person* includes, in addition to natural persons, corporations, partnerships, pension funds, profit-sharing funds, trusts, and any other group of associated persons of whatever nature.

(c) *Proxy*. The term *proxy* includes every form of authorization by which a person is, or may be deemed to be, designated to act for the security holder in the exercise of his or her voting rights in the affairs of a savings association. Such an authorization may take the form of failure to dissent or object.

(d) *Solicit; solicitation*. (1) The terms *solicit* and *solicitation* refer to:

(i) Any request for a proxy whether or not accompanied by or included in a form of proxy;

(ii) Any request to execute, not execute, or revoke a proxy; or

(iii) The furnishing of a form of proxy or other communication to security holders under circumstances reasonably calculated to result in the procurement, withholding, or revocation of a proxy.

(2) The terms do not apply, however, to the furnishing of a form of proxy to a security holder upon the request of such security holder or to the performance by any person of ministerial acts on behalf of a person soliciting a proxy.

§ 169.2 Form of proxies.

Every form of proxy shall conform to the following requirements:

(a) The proxy shall be revocable at will by the person giving it. The power to revoke may not be conditioned on any event or occurrence or be otherwise limited; except that, in the case of a proxy relating to capital stock if such proxy is coupled with an interest, states such fact on its face, and is valid under the laws of the state in which it is to be exercised, such proxy may be made irrevocable to the extent permitted by such state law.

(b) The proxy may not be part of any other document or instrument (such as an account card).

(c) The proxy shall be clearly labeled "Revocable Proxy" in boldface type (at least as large as 18 point).

§ 169.3 Holders of proxies.

No proxy of a mutual savings association with a term greater than eleven months or solicited at the expense of the association may designate as holder anyone other than the board of directors [trustees] as a whole, or a committee appointed by a majority of such board.

§ 169.4 Proxy soliciting material.

No solicitation of a proxy shall be made by means of any statement, form of proxy, notice of meeting, or other communication, written or oral, which:

(a) Solicits any undated or postdated proxy;

(b) Solicits any proxy that provides that it shall be deemed to be dated as of any date subsequent to the date on which it is signed by the security holder; or

(c)(1) Contains any statement that is false or misleading with respect to any material fact, or

(2) Omits to state any material fact:

(i) Necessary in order to make the statements therein not false or misleading or

(ii) Necessary to correct any statement in any earlier communication with respect to the solicitation of a proxy for the same meeting or subject matter that has subsequently become false or misleading.

PARTS 170–189 [RESERVED]

PART 190—PREEMPTION OF STATE USURY LAWS

Sec.

190.1 Authority, purpose, and scope.
190.2 Definitions.
190.3 Operation.
190.4 Federally-related residential manufactured housing loans—consumer protection provisions.
190.100 Status of Interpretations issued under Public Law 96–161.
190.101 State criminal usury statutes.

AUTHORITY: 12 U.S.C. 1735f–7a, 5412(b)(2)(B).

SOURCE: 76 FR 49151, Aug. 9, 2011, unless otherwise noted.

§ 190.1 Authority, purpose, and scope.

(a) *Authority.* This part contains regulations issued under section 501 of the Depository Institutions Deregulation and Monetary Control Act of 1980, Public Law 96–221, 94 Stat. 161.

(b) *Purpose and scope.* The purpose of this permanent preemption of state interest-rate ceilings applicable to Federally-related residential mortgage loans is to ensure that the availability of such loans is not impeded in states having restrictive interest limitations. This part applies to loans, mortgages, credit sales, and advances, secured by first liens on residential real property, stock in residential cooperative housing corporations, or residential manufactured homes as defined in § 190.2 of this part.

§ 190.2 Definitions.

For the purposes of this part, the following definitions apply:

(a) *Loans* mean any loans, mortgages, credit sales, or advances.

(b) *Federally-related loans* include any loan:

(1) Made by any lender whose deposits or accounts are insured by any agency of the Federal government;

(2) Made by any lender regulated by any agency of the Federal government;

(3) Made by any lender approved by the Secretary of Housing and Urban Development for participation in any mortgage insurance program under the National Housing Act;

(4) Made in whole or in part by the Secretary of Housing and Urban Development; insured, guaranteed, supplemented, or assisted in any way by the Secretary or any officer or agency of the Federal government, or made under or in connection with a housing or urban development program administered by the Secretary, or a housing or related program administered by any other such officer or agency;

(5) Eligible for purchase by the Federal National Mortgage Association, the Government National Mortgage Association, or the Federal Home Loan Mortgage Corporation, or made by any financial institution from which the loan could be purchased by the Federal Home Loan Mortgage Corporation; or

(6) Made in whole or in part by any entity which:

(i) Regularly extends, or arranges for the extension of, credit payable by agreement in more than four installments or for which the payment of a finance charge is or may be required; and

(ii) Makes or invests in residential real property loans, including loans secured by first liens on residential manufactured homes that aggregate more than $1,000,000 per year; except that the latter requirement shall not apply to such an entity selling residential manufactured homes and providing financing for such sales through loans or credit sales secured by first liens on residential manufactured homes, if the entity has an arrangement to sell such loans or credit sales in whole or in part, or where such loans or credit sales are sold in whole or in part, to a lender or other institution otherwise included in this section.

(c) *Loans which are secured by first liens on real estate* means loans on the security of any instrument (whether a mortgage, deed of trust, or land contract) which makes the interest in real estate (whether in fee, or in a leasehold or subleasehold extending, or renewable, automatically or at the option of the holder or the lender, for a period of at least 5 years beyond the maturity of the loan) specific security for the payment of the obligation secured by the instrument: *Provided,* That the instrument is of such a nature that, in the event of default, the real estate described in the instrument could be subjected to the satisfaction of the obligation with the same priority as a first mortgage of a first deed of trust in the jurisdiction where the real estate is located.

(d) *Loans secured by first liens on stock in a residential cooperative housing corporation* means loans on the security of:

(1) A first security interest in stock or a membership certificate issued to a tenant stockholder or resident member by a cooperative housing organization; and

(2) An assignment of the borrower's interest in the proprietary lease or occupancy agreement issued by such organization.

(e) *Loans secured by first liens on residential manufactured homes* means a loan made pursuant to an agreement by which the party extending the credit acquires a security interest in the residential manufactured home which will have priority over any conflicting security interest.

(f) *Residential real property* means real estate improved or to be improved by a structure or structures designed primarily for dwelling, as opposed to commercial use.

(g) *Residential manufactured home* shall mean a manufactured home as defined in the National Manufactured Home Construction and Safety Standards Act, 42 U.S.C. 5402(6), which is or will be used as a residence.

(h) *State* means the several states, Puerto Rico, the District of Columbia, Guam, the Trust Territories of the Pacific Islands, the Northern Mariana Islands, and the Virgin Islands, except as provided in section 501(a)(2)(B) of the Depository Institutions Deregulation and Monetary Control Act of 1980, Public Law 96–221, 94 Stat. 161.

§190.3 Operation.

(a) The provisions of the constitution or law of any state expressly limiting the rate or amount of interest, discount points, finance charges, or other charges which may be charged, taken, received, or reserved shall not apply to any Federally-related loan:

(1) Made after March 31, 1980; and

(2) Secured by a first lien on:

(i) Residential real property;

(ii) Stock in a residential cooperative housing corporation when the loan is used to finance the acquisition of such stock; or

(iii) A residential manufactured home: *Provided,* That the loan so secured contains the consumer safeguards required by §190.4 of this part;

(b) The provisions of paragraph (a) of this section shall apply to loans made in any state on or before the date (after April 1, 1980 and prior to April 1, 1983) on which the state adopts a law or certifies that the voters of such state have voted in favor of any law, constitutional or otherwise, which states explicitly and by its terms that such state does not want the provisions of paragraph (a) of this section to apply with respect to loans made in such state, except that—

(1) The provisions of paragraph (a) of this section shall apply to any loan which is made after such date pursuant to a commitment therefore which was entered into during the period beginning on April 1, 1980, and ending on the date the state takes such action;

(2) The provisions of paragraph (a) of this section shall apply to any rollover of a loan which loan was made, or committed to be made, during the period beginning on April 1, 1980, and ending on the date the state takes such action, if the mortgage document or loan note provided that the interest rate to the original borrower could be changed through the use of such a rollover; and

(3) At any time after the date of adoption of these regulations, any state may adopt a provision of law placing limitations on discount points or such other charges on any loan described in this part.

(c) Nothing in this section preempts limitations in state laws on prepayment charges, attorneys' fees, late charges or other provisions designed to protect borrowers.

§ 190.4 Federally-related residential manufactured housing loans—consumer protection provisions.

(a) *Definitions.* As used in this section:

(1) *Prepayment.* A "prepayment" occurs upon—

(i) Refinancing or consolidation of the indebtedness;

(ii) Actual prepayment of the indebtedness by the debtor, whether voluntarily or following acceleration of the payment obligation by the creditor; or

(iii) The entry of a judgment for the indebtedness in favor of the creditor.

(2) *Actuarial method.* The term *actuarial method* means the method of allocating payments made on a debt between the outstanding balance of the obligation and the finance charge pursuant to which a payment is applied first to the accumulated finance charge and any remainder is subtracted from, or any deficiency is added to, the outstanding balance of the obligation.

(3) *Precomputed Finance Charge.* The term *precomputed finance charge* means interest or a time/price differential as computed by the add-on or discount method. Precomputed finance charges do not include loan fees, points, finder's fees, or similar charges.

(4) *Creditor.* The term *creditor* means any entity covered by this part, including those which regularly extend or arrange for the extension of credit and assignees that are creditors under section 501(a)(1)(C)(v) of the Depository Institutions Deregulation and Monetary Control Act of 1980.

(b) *General.* (1) The provisions of the constitution or the laws of any state expressly limiting the rate or amount of interest, discount points, finance charges, or other charges which may be charged, taken, received, or reserved shall not apply to any loan, mortgage, credit sale, or advance which is secured by a first lien on a residential mobile home if a creditor covered by this part complies with the consumer protection regulations of this section.

(2) *Relation to state law.* (i) In making loans or credit sales subject to this section, creditors shall comply with state and Federal law in accordance with the following:

(A) *State law regulating matters not covered by this section.* When state law regulating matters not covered by this section is otherwise applicable to a loan or credit sale subject to this section, creditors shall comply with such state law provisions.

(B) *State law regulating matters covered by this section.* Creditors need comply only with the provisions of this section, unless the OCC determines that an otherwise applicable state law regulating matters covered by this section provides greater protection to consumers. Such determinations shall be published in the FEDERAL REGISTER and shall operate prospectively.

(ii) Any interested party may petition the OCC for a determination that state law requirements are more protective of consumers than the provisions of this section. Petitions shall include:

(A) A copy of the state law to be considered;

(B) Copies of any relevant judicial, regulatory, or administrative interpretations of the state law; and

(C) An opinion or memorandum from the state Attorney General or other appropriate state official having primary enforcement responsibilities for the subject state law provision, indicating how the state law to be considered offers greater protection to consumers than the OCC's regulation.

(c) *Refund of precomputed finance charge.* In the event the entire indebtedness is prepaid, the unearned portion of the precomputed finance charge shall be refunded to the debtor. This refund shall be in an amount not less than the amount which would be refunded if the unearned precomputed finance charge were calculated in accordance with the actuarial method, except that the debtor shall not be entitled to a refund which, is less than one dollar. The unearned portion of the precomputed finance charge is, at the option of the creditor, either:

(1) That portion of the precomputed finance charge which is allocable to all unexpired payment periods as originally scheduled, or if deferred, as deferred. A payment period shall be deemed unexpired if prepayment is made within 15 days after the payment period's scheduled due date. The unearned precomputed finance charge is the total of that which would have been earned for each such period had the loan not been precomputed, by applying to unpaid balances of principal, according to the actuarial method, an annual percentage rate based on those charges which are considered precomputed finance charges in this section, assuming that all payments were made as originally scheduled, or as deferred, if deferred. The creditor, at its option, may round this annual percentage rate to the nearest one-quarter of one percent; or

(2) The total precomputed finance charge less the earned precomputed finance charge. The earned precomputed finance charge shall be determined by applying an annual percentage rate based on the total precomputed finance charge (as that term is defined in this section), under the actuarial method, to the unpaid balances for the actual time those balances were unpaid up to the date of prepayment. If a late charge or deferral fee has been collected, it shall be treated as a payment.

(d) *Prepayment penalties.* A debtor may prepay in full or in part the unpaid balance of the loan at any time without penalty. The right to prepay shall be disclosed in the loan contract in type larger than that used for the body of the document.

(e) *Balloon payments*—(1) *Federal savings associations.* Federal savings association creditors may enter into agreements with debtors which provide for non-amortized and partially-amortized loans on residential manufactured homes, and such loans shall be governed by the provisions of this section and 12 CFR 560.220 until superseding regulations are issued by the Consumer Financial Protection Bureau regarding the Alternative Mortgage Transactions Parity Act.

(2) *Other creditors.* All other creditors may enter into agreements with debtors which provide for non-amortized and partially-amortized loans on residential manufactured homes to the extent authorized by applicable Federal or state law or regulation.

(f) *Late charges.* (1) No late charge may be assessed, imposed, or collected unless provided for by written contract between the creditor and debtor.

(2) To the extent that applicable state law does not provide for a longer period of time, no late charge may be collected on an installment which is paid in full on or before the 15th day after its scheduled or deferred due date even though an earlier maturing installment or a late charge on an earlier installment may not have been paid in full. For purposes of assessing late charges, payments received are deemed to be applied first to current installments.

(3) A late charge may be imposed only once on an installment; however, no such charge may be collected for a late installment which has been deferred.

(4) To the extent that applicable state law does not provide for a lower charge or a longer grace period, a late charge on any installment not paid in full on or before the 15th day after its scheduled or deferred due date may not exceed five percent of the unpaid amount of the installment.

(5) If, at any time after imposition of a late charge, the lender provides the borrower with written notice regarding amounts claimed to be due but unpaid, the notice shall separately state the total of all late charges claimed.

(6) Interest after the final scheduled maturity date may not exceed the maximum rate otherwise allowable under state law for such contracts, and if such interest is charged, no separate late charge may be made on the final scheduled installment.

(g) *Deferral fees.* (1) With respect to mobile home credit transactions containing precomputed finance charges, agreements providing for deferral of all or part of one or more installments shall be in writing, signed by the parties, and

(i) Provide, to the extent that applicable state law does not provide for a lower charge, for a charge not exceeding one percent of each installment or part thereof for each month from the date when such installment was due to the date when it is agreed to become payable and proportionately for a part of each month, counting each day as 1/30th of a month;

(ii) Incorporate by reference the transaction to which the deferral applied;

(iii) Disclose each installment or part thereof in the amount to be deferred, the date or dates originally payable, and the date or dates agreed to become payable: and

(iv) Set forth the fact of the deferral charge, the dollar amount of the charge for each installment to be deferred, and the total dollar amount to be paid by the debtor for the privilege of deferring payment.

(2) No term of a writing executed by the debtor shall constitute authority for a creditor unilaterally to grant a deferral with respect to which a charge is to be imposed or collected.

(3) The deferral period is that period of time in which no payment is required or made by reason of the deferral.

(4) Payments received with respect to deferred installments shall be deemed to be applied first to deferred installments.

(5) A charge may not be collected for the deferral of an installment or any part thereof if, with respect to that installment, a refinancing or consolidation agreement is concluded by the parties, or a late charge has been imposed or collected, unless such late charge is refunded to the borrower or credited to the deferral charge.

(h) *Notice before repossession, foreclosure, or acceleration.* (1) Except in the case of abandonment or other extreme circumstances, no action to repossess or foreclose, or to accelerate payment of the entire outstanding balance of the obligation, may be taken against the debtor until 30 days after the creditor sends the debtor a notice of default in the form set forth in paragraph (h)(2) of this section. Such notice shall be sent by registered or certified mail with return receipt requested. In the case of default on payments, the sum stated in the notice may only include payments in default and applicable late or deferral charges. If the debtor cures the default within 30 days of the postmark of the notice and subsequently defaults a second time, the creditor shall again give notice as described in this paragraph (h)(1). The debtor is not entitled to notice of default more than twice in any one-year period.

(2) The notice in the following form shall state the nature of the default, the action the debtor must take to cure the default, the creditor's intended actions upon failure of the debtor to cure the default, and the debtor's right to redeem under state law.

To:

Date: , 20

Notice of Default and Right To Cure Default

Name, address, and telephone number of creditor

Account number, if any

Brief identification of credit transaction

You are now in default on this credit transaction. You have a right to correct this default within 30 days from the postmarked date of this notice.

If you correct the default, you may continue with the contract as though you did not default. Your default consists of:

Describe default alleged

Cure of default: Within 30 days from the postmarked date of this notice, you may cure your default by (describe the acts necessary for cure, including, if applicable, the amount of payment required, including itemized delinquency or deferral charges).

Creditor's rights: If you do not correct your default in the time allowed, we may exercise our rights against you under the law by (describe action creditor intends to take).

If you have any questions, write (the creditor) at the above address or call (creditor's designated employee) at (telephone number) between the hours of and on (state days of week).

If this default was caused by your failure to make a payment or payments, and you want to pay by mail, please send a check or money order; do not send cash.

§ 190.100 Status of Interpretations issued under Public Law 96–161.

The OCC continues to adhere to the views expressed in the formal Interpretations issued under the authority of section 105(c) of Public Law 96–161, 93 Stat. 1233 (1979). These interpretations, which relate to the temporary preemption of state interest ceilings contained in Public Law 96–161, may be found at 45 FR 2840 (Jan. 15, 1980); 45 FR 6165 (Jan. 25, 1980); 45 FR 8000 (Feb. 6, 1980); 45 FR 15921 (Mar. 12, 1980).

§ 190.101 State criminal usury statutes.

(a) Section 501 provides that "the provisions of the constitution or laws of any state expressly limiting the rate or amount of interest, discount points, finance charges, or other charges shall not apply to any" Federally-related loan secured by a first lien on residential real property, a residential manufactured home, or all the stock allocated to a dwelling unit in a residential housing cooperative. 12 U.S.C. 1735f–7 note (Supp. IV 1980). The question has arisen as to whether the Federal statute preempts a state law which deems it a criminal offense to charge interest at a rate in excess of that specified in the state law.

(b) Section 501 preempts all state laws which expressly limit the rate or amount of interest chargeable on a Federally-related residential first mortgage. It does not matter whether the statute in question imposes criminal or civil sanctions; section 501, by its terms, preempts "any" state law which imposes a ceiling on interest rates. The wording of the Federal statute clearly expresses an intent to displace all direct state law restraints on interest. Any state law that conflicts with this Congressional purpose must yield.

PART 191—PREEMPTION OF STATE DUE-ON-SALE LAWS

Sec.

191.1 Authority, purpose, and scope.
191.2 Definitions.
191.3 Loans originated by Federal savings associations.
191.4 Loans originated by lenders other than Federal savings associations.
191.5 Limitation on exercise of due-on-sale clauses.
191.6 Interpretations.

AUTHORITY: 12 U.S.C. 1464, 1701j–3, and 5412(b)(2)(B).

SOURCE: 76 FR 49154, Aug. 9, 2011, unless otherwise noted.

§ 191.1 Authority, purpose, and scope.

(a) *Authority.* This part contains regulations issued under section 5 of the Home Owners' Loan Act of 1933, as amended, and under section 341 of the Garn-St Germain Depository Institutions Act of 1982, Public Law 97–320, 96 Stat. 1469, 1505–1507.

(b) *Purpose and scope.* The purpose of this permanent preemption of state prohibitions on the exercise of due-on-sale clauses by all lenders, whether Federally- or state-chartered, is to reaffirm the authority of Federal savings associations to enforce due-on-sale clauses, and to confer on other lenders generally comparable authority with respect to the exercise of such clauses. This part applies to all real property loans, and all lenders making such loans, as those terms are defined in § 191.2 of this part.

§ 191.2 Definitions.

For the purposes of this part, the following definitions apply:

(a) *Assumed* includes transfers of real property subject to a real property loan by assumptions, installment land sales contracts, wraparound loans, contracts for deed, transfers subject to the mortgage or similar lien, and other like transfers. "Completed credit application" has the same meaning as completed application for credit as provided in § 202.2(f) of this title.

(b) *Due-on-sale clause* means a contract provision which authorizes the lender, at its option, to declare immediately due and payable sums secured by the lender's security instrument upon a sale of transfer of all or any part of the real property securing the loan without the lender's prior written consent. For purposes of this definition, a *sale or transfer* means the conveyance of real property of any right, title or interest therein, whether legal or equitable, whether voluntary or involuntary, by outright sale, deed, installment sale contract, land contract,

contract for deed, leasehold interest with a term greater than three years, lease-option contract or any other method of conveyance of real property interests.

(c) *Federal savings association* has the same meaning as provided in § 141.11 of this chapter.

(d) *Federal credit union* means a credit union chartered under the Federal Credit Union Act.

(e) *Home* has the same meaning as provided in § 141.14 of this chapter.

(f) *Savings association* has the same meaning as provided in § 161.43 of this chapter.

(g) *Lender* means a person or government agency making a real property loan, including without limitation, individuals, Federal savings associations, state-chartered savings associations, national banks, state-chartered banks and state-chartered mutual savings banks, Federal credit unions, state-chartered credit unions, mortgage banks, insurance companies and finance companies which make real property loans, manufactured-home retailers who extend credit, agencies of the Federal government, any lender approved by the Secretary of Housing and Urban Development for participation in any mortgage insurance program under the National Housing Act, and any assignee or transferee, in whole or part, of any such persons or agencies.

(h) *Loan secured by a lien on real property* means a loan on the security of any instrument (whether a mortgage, deed or trust, or land contract) which makes the interest in real property (whether in fee, or in a leasehold or subleasehold) specific security for the payment of the obligation secured by the instrument.

(i) *Loan secured by a lien on stock in a residential cooperative housing corporation* means a loan on the security of:

(1) A security interest in stock or a membership certificate issued to a tenant stockholder or resident member by a cooperative housing organization; and

(2) An assignment of the borrower's interest in the proprietary lease or occupancy agreement issued by such organization.

(j) *Loan secured by a lien on a residential manufactured home, whether real or personal property,* means a loan made pursuant to an agreement by which the party extending the credit acquires a security interest in the residential manufactured home.

(k) *Loan originated by* a Federal savings association or other lender means any loan for which the lender makes the first advance of credit thereunder, *Provided,* That such lender then held a beneficial interest in the loan, whether as to the whole loan or a portion thereof, and whether or not the loan is later held by or transferred to another lender.

(l) *Real property loan* means any loan, mortgage, advance or credit sale secured by a lien on real property, the stock or membership certificate allocated to a dwelling unit in a cooperative housing corporation, or a residential manufactured home, whether real or personal property.

(m) *Residential manufactured home* has the same meaning as provided in § 190.2(g) of this chapter.

(n) *Reverse mortgage* means an instrument that provides for one or more payments to a homeowner based on accumulated equity. The lender may make payment directly, through the purchase of an annuity through an insurance company, or in any other manner. The loan may be due either on a specific date or when a specified event occurs, such as the sale of the property or the death of the borrower.

(o) *State* means the several states, Puerto Rico, the District of Columbia, Guam, the Trust Territory of the Pacific Islands, the Northern Mariana Islands, the Virgin Islands, and American Samoa.

(p)(1) A *window-period loan* means a real property loan, not originated by a Federal savings association, which was made or assumed during a window-period created by state law and subject to that law, which loan was recorded, at the time of origination or assumption, before October 15, 1982, or within 60 days thereafter (December 14, 1982).

(2) The window-period begins on:

(i) The date a state adopted a law (by means of a constitutional provision or statute) prohibiting the unrestricted exercise of due-on-sale clauses upon outright transfers of property securing loans subject to the state law creating the window-period, or the effective date of a constitutional or statutory provision so adopted, whichever is later; or

(ii) The date on which the highest court of the state rendered a decision prohibiting such unrestricted exercise (or if the highest court has not so decided, the date on which the next highest appellate court rendered a decision resulting in a final judgment which applies statewide), and ends on the earlier of the date such state law prohibition terminated under state law or October 15, 1982.

(3) Categories of state law which create window-periods by prohibiting the unrestricted exercise of due-on-sale clauses upon outright transfers of property securing loans subject to such state law restrictions include laws or judicial decisions which permit the lender to exercise its option under a due-on-sale clause only where:

(i) The lender's security interest or the likelihood of repayment is impaired; or

(ii) The lender is required to accept an assumption of the existing loan without an interest-rate change or with an interest-rate change below the market interest rate currently being offered by the lender on similar loans secured by similar property at the time of the transfer.

§ 191.3 Loans originated by Federal savings associations.

(a) With regard to any real property loan originated or to be originated by a Federal savings association, as a matter of contract between it and the borrower, a Federal savings association continues to have the power to include a due-on-sale clause in its loan instrument.

(b) Except as otherwise provided in § 191.5 of this part with respect to any such loan made on the security of a home occupied or to be occupied by the borrower, exercise by any lender of a due-on-sale clause in a loan originated by a Federal savings association shall be exclusively governed by the terms of the loan contract, and all rights and remedies of the lender and borrower shall at all times be fixed and governed by that contract.

§ 191.4 Loans originated by lenders other than Federal savings associations.

(a) With regard to any real property loan originated by a lender other than a Federal savings association, as a matter of contract between it and the borrower, the lender has the power to include a due on sale clause in its loan instrument.

(b) Except as otherwise provided in paragraph (c) of this section and § 191.5 of this part, the exercise of due-on-sale clauses in loans originated by lenders other than Federal savings associations shall be governed exclusively by the terms of the loan contract, and all rights and remedies of the lender and the borrower shall be fixed and governed by that contract.

(c)(1) In the case of a window-period loan, the provisions of paragraph (b) of this section shall apply only in the case of a sale or transfer of the property subject to the real property loan and only if such sale or transfer occurs on or after October 15, 1985: *Provided*, That:

(i) With respect to real property loans originated in a state by lenders other than national banks, Federal savings associations, and Federal credit unions, a state may otherwise regulate such contracts by state law enacted prior to October 16, 1985, in which case paragraph (b) of this section shall apply only if such state law so provides; and

(ii) With respect to real property loans originated by national banks and Federal credit unions, the OCC or the National Credit Union Administration Board, respectively, may otherwise regulate such contracts by regulations promulgated prior to October 16, 1985, in which case paragraph (b) of this section shall apply only if such regulation so provides.

(2) A lender may not exercise its options pursuant to a due-on-sale clause contained in a window-period loan in the case of a sale or transfer of property securing such loan where the sale or transfer occurred prior to October 15, 1982.

(d)(1) Prior to the sale or transfer of property securing a window-period loan subject to the provisions of paragraph (c) of this section.

(i) Any lender in the business of making real property loans may require any successor or transferee of the borrower to supply credit information customarily required by the lender in connection with credit applications, to complete its customary credit application, and to meet customary credit standards applied by such lender, at the date of sale or transfer, to the lender's similar loans secured by similar property.

(ii) Any lender not in the business of making loans may require any successor or transferee of the borrower to meet credit standards customarily applied by other similarly situated lenders or sellers in the geographic market within which the transaction occurs, for similar loans secured by similar property, prior to the lender's consent to the transfer.

(2) The lender may exercise a due-on-sale clause in a window-period loan if:

(i) The successor or transferee of the borrower fails to meet the lender's credit standards as set forth in paragraphs (b)(1)(i) and (b)(1)(ii) of this section; or

(ii) Upon transfer of the security property and not later than fifteen days after written request by the lender, the successor or transferee of the borrower fails to provide information requested by the lender pursuant to paragraph (d)(1)(i) or (d)(1)(ii) of this section, to determine whether such successor or transferee of the borrower meets the lender's customary credit standards.

(3) The lender shall, within thirty days of receipt of a completed credit application and any other related information provided by the successor or transferee of the borrower, determine whether such successor or transferee meets the customary credit standards of the lender and provide written notice to the successor or transferee of its decision, and the reasons in the event of a disapproval. Failure of the lender to provide such notice shall preclude the lender from exercise of its due-on-sale clause upon the sale or transfer of the property securing the loan.

(4) The lender's right to exercise a due-on-sale clause pursuant to this paragraph (d)(4) is in addition to any other rights afforded the lender by state law regulating window-period loans with regard to the exercise of due-on-sale clauses and loan assumptions.

§ 191.5 Limitation on exercise of due-on-sale clauses.

(a) *General.* Except as provided in § 191.4(c) and (d)(4) of this part, due-on-sale practices of Federal savings associations and other lenders shall be governed exclusively by the OCC's regulations, in preemption of and without regard to any limitations imposed by state law on either their inclusion or exercise including, without limitation, state law prohibitions against restraints on alienation, prohibitions against penalties and forfeitures, equitable restrictions and state law dealing with equitable transfers.

(b) *Specific limitations.* With respect to any loan on the security of a home occupied or to be occupied by the borrower,

(1) A lender shall not (except with regard to a reverse mortgage) exercise its option pursuant to a due-on-sale clause upon:

(i) The creation of a lien or other encumbrance subordinate to the lender's security instrument which does not relate to a transfer of rights of occupancy in the property: *Provided,* That such lien or encumbrance is not created pursuant to a contract for deed;

(ii) The creation of a purchase-money security interest for household appliances;

(iii) A transfer by devise, descent, or operation of law on the death of a joint tenant or tenant by the entirety;

(iv) The granting of a leasehold interest which has a term of three years or less and which does not contain an option to purchase (that is, either a lease of more than three years or a lease with an option to purchase will allow the exercise of a due-on-sale clause);

(v) A transfer, in which the transferee is a person who occupies or will occupy the property, which is:

(A) A transfer to a relative resulting from the death of the borrower;

(B) A transfer where the spouse or child(ren) becomes an owner of the property; or

(C) A transfer resulting from a decree of dissolution of marriage, legal separation agreement, or from an incidental property settlement agreement by which the spouse becomes an owner of the property; or

(vi) A transfer into an inter vivos trust in which the borrower is and remains the beneficiary and occupant of the property, unless, as a condition precedent to such transfer, the borrower refuses to provide the lender with reasonable means acceptable to the lender by which the lender will be assured of timely notice of any subsequent transfer of the beneficial interest or change in occupancy.

(2) A lender shall not impose a prepayment penalty or equivalent fee when the lender or party acting on behalf of the lender.

(i) Declares by written notice that the loan is due pursuant to a due-on-sale clause or

(ii) Commences a judicial or nonjudicial foreclosure proceeding to enforce a due-on-sale clause or to seek payment in full as a result of invoking such clause.

(3) A lender shall not impose a prepayment penalty or equivalent fee when the lender or party acting on behalf of the lender fails to approve within 30 days the completed credit application of a qualified transferee of the security property to assume the loan in accordance with the terms of the loan, and thereafter the borrower transfers the security property to such transferee and prepays the loan in full within 120 days after receipt by the lender of the completed credit application. For purposes of this paragraph (b)(3), a *qualified transferee* is a person who qualifies for the loan under the lender's applicable underwriting standards and who occupies or will occupy the security property.

(4) A lender waives its option to exercise a due-on-sale clause as to a specific transfer if, before the transfer, the lender and the existing borrower's prospective successor in interest agree in writing that the successor in interest will be obligated under the terms of the loan and that interest on sums secured by the lender's security interest will be payable at a rate the lender shall request. Upon such agreement and resultant waiver, a lender shall release the existing borrower from all obligations under the loan instruments, and the lender is deemed to have made a new loan to the existing borrower's successor in interest. The waiver and release apply to all loans secured by homes occupied by borrowers made by a Federal savings association after July 31, 1976, and to all loans secured by homes occupied by borrowers made by other lenders after the effective date of this regulation.

(5) Nothing in paragraph (b)(1) of this section shall be construed to restrict a lender's right to enforce a due-on-sale clause upon the subsequent occurrence of any event which disqualifies a transfer for a previously-applicable exception under that paragraph (b)(1).

(c) *Policy considerations.* Paragraph (b) of this section does not prohibit a lender from requiring, as a condition to an assumption, continued maintenance of mortgage insurance by the existing borrower's successor in interest, whether by endorsement of the existing policy or by entrance into a new contract of insurance.

§ 191.6 Interpretations.

The OCC periodically will publish Interpretations under section 341 of the Garn-St Germain Depository Institutions Act of 1982, Public Law 97–320, 96 Stat. 1469, 1505–1507, in the FEDERAL REGISTER in response to written requests sent to the OCC.

PART 192—CONVERSIONS FROM MUTUAL TO STOCK FORM

Sec.
192.5 What does this part do?
192.10 May I form a holding company as part of my conversion?
192.15 May I form a charitable organization as part of my conversion?
192.20 May I acquire another insured stock depository institution as part of my conversion?
192.25 What definitions apply to this part?

Subpart A—Standard Conversions

PRIOR TO CONVERSION

192.100 What must I do before a conversion?
192.105 What information must I include in my business plan?
192.110 Who must review my business plan?

192.115 How will the appropriate Federal banking agency review my business plan?
192.120 May I discuss my plans to convert with others?

PLAN OF CONVERSION

192.125 Must my board of directors adopt a plan of conversion?
192.130 What must I include in my plan of conversion?
192.135 How do I notify my members that my board of directors approved a plan of conversion?
192.140 May I amend my plan of conversion?

FILING REQUIREMENTS

192.150 What must I include in my application for conversion?
192.155 How do I file my application for conversion?
192.160 May I keep portions of my application for conversion confidential?
192.165 How do I amend my application for conversion?

NOTICE OF FILING OF APPLICATION AND COMMENT PROCESS

192.180 How do I notify the public that I filed an application for conversion?
192.185 How may a person comment on my application for conversion?

AGENCY REVIEW OF THE APPLICATION FOR CONVERSION

192.200 What actions may the appropriate Federal banking agency take on my application?
192.205 May a court review the appropriate Federal banking agency's final action on my conversion?

VOTE BY MEMBERS

192.225 Must I submit the plan of conversion to my members for approval?
192.230 Who is eligible to vote?
192.235 How must I notify my members of the meeting?
192.240 What must I submit to the appropriate Federal banking agency after the members' meeting?

PROXY SOLICITATION

192.250 Who must comply with these proxy solicitation provisions?
192.255 What must the form of proxy include?
192.260 May I use previously executed proxies?
192.265 How may I use proxies executed under this part?
192.270 What must I include in my proxy statement?
192.275 Filing How do I file revised proxy materials?
192.280 Must I mail a member's proxy solicitation material?
192.285 What solicitations are prohibited?
192.290 What will the appropriate Federal banking agency do if a solicitation violates these prohibitions?
192.295 Will the appropriate Federal banking agency require me to re-solicit proxies?

OFFERING CIRCULAR

192.300 What must happen before the appropriate Federal banking agency declares my offering circular effective?
192.305 When may I distribute the offering circular?
192.310 When must I file a post-effective amendment to the offering circular?

OFFERS AND SALES OF STOCK

192.320 Who has priority to purchase my conversion shares?
192.325 When may I offer to sell my conversion shares?
192.330 How do I price my conversion shares?
192.335 How do I sell my conversion shares?
192.340 What sales practices are prohibited?
192.345 How may a subscriber pay for my conversion shares?
192.350 Must I pay interest on payments for conversion shares?
192.355 What subscription rights must I give to each eligible account holder and each supplemental eligible account holder?
192.360 Are my officers, directors, and their associates eligible account holders?
192.365 May other voting members purchase conversion shares in the conversion?
192.370 Does the appropriate Federal banking agency limit the aggregate purchases by officers, directors, and their associates?
192.375 How do I allocate my conversion shares if my shares are oversubscribed?
192.380 May my employee stock ownership plan purchase conversion shares?
192.385 May I impose any purchase limitations?
192.390 Must I provide a purchase preference to persons in my local community?
192.395 What other conditions apply when I offer conversion shares in a community offering, a public offering, or both?

COMPLETION OF THE OFFERING

192.400 When must I complete the sale of my stock?
192.405 How do I extend the offering period?

COMPLETION OF THE CONVERSION

192.420 When must I complete my conversion?
192.425 Who may terminate the conversion?
192.430 What happens to my old charter?

192.435 What happens to my corporate existence after conversion?
192.440 What voting rights must I provide to stockholders after the conversion?
192.445 What must I provide my savings account holders?

LIQUIDATION ACCOUNT

192.450 What is a liquidation account?
192.455 What is the initial balance of the liquidation account?
192.460 How do I determine the initial balances of liquidation sub-accounts?
192.465 Do account holders retain any voting rights based on their liquidation subaccounts?
192.470 Must I adjust liquidation sub-accounts?
192.475 What is a liquidation?
192.480 Does the liquidation account affect my net worth?
192.485 What provision must I include in my new Federal charter?

POST-CONVERSION

192.500 What management stock benefit plans may I implement?
192.505 May my directors, officers, and their associates freely trade shares?
192.510 May I repurchase shares after conversion?
192.515 What information must I provide to the appropriate Federal banking agency before I repurchase my shares?
192.520 May I declare or pay dividends after I convert?
192.525 Who may acquire my shares after I convert?
192.530 What other requirements apply after I convert?

CONTRIBUTIONS TO CHARITABLE ORGANIZATIONS

192.550 May I donate conversion shares or conversion proceeds to a charitable organization?
192.555 How do my members approve a charitable contribution?
192.560 How much may I contribute to a charitable organization?
192.565 What must the charitable organization include in its organizational documents?
192.570 How do I address conflicts of interest involving my directors?
192.575 What other requirements apply to charitable organizations?

Subpart B—Voluntary Supervisory Conversions

192.600 What does this subpart do?
192.605 How may I conduct a voluntary supervisory conversion?
192.610 Do my members have rights in a voluntary supervisory conversion?

ELIGIBILITY

192.625 When is a savings association eligible for a voluntary supervisory conversion?
192.630 When is a state-chartered savings bank eligible for a voluntary supervisory conversion?

PLAN OF SUPERVISORY CONVERSION

192.650 What must I include in my plan of voluntary supervisory conversion?

VOLUNTARY SUPERVISORY CONVERSION APPLICATION

192.660 What must I include in my voluntary supervisory conversion application?

APPROPRIATE FEDERAL BANKING AGENCY REVIEW OF THE VOLUNTARY SUPERVISORY CONVERSION APPLICATION

192.670 Will the appropriate Federal banking agency approve my voluntary supervisory conversion application?
192.675 What conditions will the appropriate Federal banking agency impose on an approval?

OFFERS AND SALES OF STOCK

192.680 How do I sell my shares?

POST-CONVERSION

192.690 Who may not acquire additional shares after the voluntary supervisory conversion?

AUTHORITY: 12 U.S.C. 1462a, 1463, 1464, 1467a, 2901, 5412(b)(2)(B); 15 U.S.C. 78c, 78*l*, 78m, 78n, 78w.

SOURCE: 76 FR 49156, Aug. 9, 2011, unless otherwise noted.

§ 192.5 What does this part do?

(a) *General*. This part governs how a savings association (''you'') may convert from the mutual to the stock form of ownership. Subpart A of this part governs standard mutual-to-stock conversions. Subpart B of this part governs voluntary supervisory mutual-to-stock conversions. This part supersedes all inconsistent charter and bylaw provisions of Federal savings associations converting to stock form.

(b) *Prescribed forms*. You must use the forms prescribed under this part and provide such information as the appropriate Federal banking agency may require under the forms by regulation or otherwise. The forms required under this part include: Form AC (Application for Conversion); Form PS (Proxy

Statement); Form OC (Offering Circular); and Form OF (Order Form). Forms are available on the OCC's web site at *http://www.occ.gov*.

(c) *Waivers*. The appropriate Federal banking agency may waive any requirement of this part or a provision in any prescribed form. To obtain a waiver, you must file a written request with the appropriate Federal banking agency that:

(1) Specifies the requirement(s) or provision(s) you want the appropriate Federal banking agency to waive;

(2) Demonstrates that the waiver is equitable; is not detrimental to you, your account holders, or other savings associations; and is not contrary to the public interest; and

(3) Includes an opinion of counsel demonstrating that applicable law does not conflict with the requirement or provision.

§ 192.10 May I form a holding company as part of my conversion.

You may convert to the stock form of ownership as part of a transaction where you organize a holding company to acquire all of your shares upon their issuance. In such a transaction, your holding company will offer rights to purchase its shares instead of your shares. Regulations of the Board of Governors of the Federal Reserve System address holding company application requirements.

§ 192.15 May I form a charitable organization as part of my conversion?

When you convert to the stock form, you may form a charitable organization. Your contributions to the charitable organization are governed by the requirements of §§ 192.550 through 192.575.

§ 192.20 May I acquire another insured stock depository institution as part of my conversion?

When you convert to stock form, you may acquire for cash or stock another insured depository institution that is already in the stock form of ownership.

§ 192.25 What definitions apply to this part?

The following definitions apply to this part and the forms prescribed under this part:

Acting in concert has the same meaning as in § 5.50(d)(2) of this chapter. The rebuttable presumptions of § 5.50(f)(2) of this chapter, other than § 5.50(f)(2)(ii)(A) and (B) of this chapter, apply to the share purchase limitations at §§ 192.355 through 192.395.

Affiliate of, or a person *affiliated with*, a specified person is a person that directly or indirectly, through one or more intermediaries, controls, is controlled by, or is under common control with the specified person.

Associate of a person is:

(1) A corporation or organization (other than you or your majority-owned subsidiaries), if the person is a senior officer or partner, or beneficially owns, directly or indirectly, 10 percent or more of any class of equity securities of the corporation or organization.

(2) A trust or other estate, if the person has a substantial beneficial interest in the trust or estate or is a trustee or fiduciary of the trust or estate. For purposes of §§ 192.370, 192.380, 192.385, 192.390, 192.395 and 192.505, a person who has a substantial beneficial interest in your tax-qualified or non-tax-qualified employee stock benefit plan, or who is a trustee or a fiduciary of the plan, is not an associate of the plan. For the purposes of § 192.370, your tax-qualified employee stock benefit plan is not an associate of a person.

(3) Any person who is related by blood or marriage to such person and:

(i) Who lives in the same home as the person; or

(ii) Who is your director or senior officer, or a director or senior officer of your holding company or your subsidiary.

Association members or *members* are persons who, under applicable law, are eligible to vote at the meeting on conversion.

Control (including *controlling*, *controlled by*, and *under common control with*) means the direct or indirect power to direct or exercise a controlling influence over the management and policies of a person, whether through the ownership of voting securities, by contract, or otherwise as described in § 5.50 of this chapter.

Eligibility record date is the date for determining eligible account holders. The eligibility record date must be at least one year before the date your board of directors adopts the plan of conversion.

Eligible account holders are any persons holding qualifying deposits on the eligibility record date.

IRS is the Internal Revenue Service.

Local community includes:

(1) Every county, parish, or similar governmental subdivision in which you have a home or branch office;

(2) Each county's, parish's, or subdivision's metropolitan statistical area;

(3) All zip code areas in your Community Reinvestment Act assessment area; and

(4) Any other area or category you set out in your plan of conversion, as approved by the appropriate Federal banking agency.

Offer, offer to sell, or *offer for sale* is an attempt or offer to dispose of, or a solicitation of an offer to buy, a security or interest in a security for value. Preliminary negotiations or agreements with an underwriter, or among underwriters who are or will be in privity of contract with you, are not offers, offers to sell, or offers for sale.

Person is an individual, a corporation, a partnership, an association, a joint-stock company, a limited liability company, a trust, an unincorporated organization, or a government or political subdivision of a government.

Proxy soliciting material includes a proxy statement, form of proxy, or other written or oral communication regarding the conversion.

Purchase or *buy* includes every contract to acquire a security or interest in a security for value.

Qualifying deposit is the total balance in an account holder's savings accounts at the close of business on the eligibility or supplemental eligibility record date. Your plan of conversion may provide that only savings accounts with total deposit balances of $50 or more will qualify.

Sale or *sell* includes every contract to dispose of a security or interest in a security for value. An exchange of securities in a merger or acquisition approved by the appropriate Federal banking agency is not a sale.

Savings account is any withdrawable account as defined in § 161.42 of this chapter, including a demand account as defined in § 161.16 of this chapter.

Solicitation and *solicit* is a request for a proxy, whether or not accompanied by or included in a form of proxy; a request to execute, not execute, or revoke a proxy; or the furnishing of a form of proxy or other communication reasonably calculated to cause your members to procure, withhold, or revoke a proxy. Solicitation or solicit does not include providing a form of proxy at the unsolicited request of a member, the acts required to mail communications for members, or ministerial acts performed on behalf of a person soliciting a proxy.

Subscription offering is the offering of shares through nontransferable subscription rights to:

(1) Eligible account holders under § 192.355;

(2) Tax-qualified employee stock ownership plans under § 192.380;

(3) Supplemental eligible account holders under § 192.355; and

(4) Other voting members under § 192.365.

Supplemental eligibility record date is the date for determining supplemental eligible account holders. The supplemental eligibility record date is the last day of the calendar quarter before the appropriate Federal banking agency approves your conversion and will only occur if such agency has not approved your conversion within 15 months after the eligibility record date.

Supplemental eligible account holders are any persons, except your officers, directors, and their associates, holding qualifying deposits on the supplemental eligibility record date.

Tax-qualified employee stock benefit plan is any defined benefit plan or defined contribution plan, such as an employee stock ownership plan, stock bonus plan, profit-sharing plan, or other plan, and a related trust, that is qualified under section 401 of the Internal Revenue Code (26 U.S.C. 401).

Underwriter is any person who purchases any securities from you with a view to distributing the securities, offers or sells securities for you in connection with the securities' distribution, or participates or has a direct or indirect participation in the direct or indirect underwriting of any such undertaking. Underwriter does not include a person whose interest is limited to a usual and customary distributor's or seller's commission from an underwriter or dealer.

[76 FR 49156, Aug. 9, 2011, as amended at 80 FR 28480, May 18, 2015]

Subpart A—Standard Conversions

PRIOR TO CONVERSION

§ 192.100 What must I do before a conversion?

(a) Your board, or a subcommittee of your board, must meet with the appropriate Federal banking agency before you pass your plan of conversion. The meeting may occur at the appropriate Federal banking agency or your offices at your option. At that meeting you must provide the appropriate Federal banking agency with a written strategic plan that outlines the objectives of the proposed conversion and the intended use of the conversion proceeds.

(b) You should also consult with the appropriate Federal banking agency before you file your application for conversion. The appropriate Federal banking agency will discuss the information that you must include in the application for conversion, general issues that you may confront in the conversion process, and any other pertinent issues.

§ 192.105 What information must I include in my business plan?

(a) Prior to filing an application for conversion, you must adopt a business plan reflecting your intended plans for deployment of the proposed conversion proceeds. Your business plan is required, under § 192.150, to be included in your conversion application. At a minimum, your business plan must address:

(1) Your projected operations and activities for three years following the conversion. You must describe how you will deploy the conversion proceeds at the converted savings association (and holding company, if applicable), what opportunities are available to reasonably achieve your planned deployment of conversion proceeds in your proposed market areas, and how your deployment will provide a reasonable return on investment commensurate with investment risk, investor expectations, and industry norms, by the final year of the business plan. You must include three years of projected financial statements. The business plan must provide that the converted savings association must retain at least 50 percent of the net conversion proceeds. The appropriate Federal banking agency may require that a larger percentage of proceeds remain in the institution.

(2) Your plan for deploying conversion proceeds to meet credit and lending needs in your proposed market areas. The appropriate Federal banking agencies strongly discourage business plans that provide for a substantial investment in mortgage securities or other securities, except as an interim measure to facilitate orderly, prudent deployment of proceeds during the three years following the conversion, or as part of a properly managed leverage strategy.

(3) The risks associated with your plan for deployment of conversion proceeds, and the effect of this plan on management resources, staffing, and facilities.

(4) The expertise of your management and board of directors, or that you have planned for adequate staffing and controls to prudently manage the growth, expansion, new investment, and other operations and activities proposed in your business plan.

(b) You may not project returns of capital or special dividends in any part of the business plan. A newly converted company may not plan on stock repurchases in the first year of the business plan.

§ 192.110 Who must review my business plan?

(a) Your chief executive officer and members of the board of directors must review, and at least two-thirds of your board of directors must approve, the business plan.

(b) Your chief executive officer and at least two-thirds of the board of directors must certify that the business plan accurately reflects the intended plans for deployment of conversion proceeds, and that any new initiatives reflected in the business plan are reasonably achievable. You must submit these certifications with your business plan, as part of your conversion application under § 192.150.

§ 192.115 How will the appropriate Federal banking agency review my business plan?

(a) The appropriate Federal banking agency will review your business plan to determine that it demonstrates a safe and sound deployment of conversion proceeds, as part of its review of your conversion application. In making its determination, the appropriate Federal banking agency will consider how you have addressed the applicable factors of § 192.105. No single factor will be determinative.

(b) If you are a Federal savings association, you must file your business plan with the appropriate OCC licensing office. If you are a state savings association, you must file your business plan with the appropriate FDIC region. The appropriate Federal banking agency may request additional information, if necessary, to support its determination under paragraph (a) of this section. You must file your business plan as a confidential exhibit to the Form AC.

(c) If the appropriate Federal banking agency approves your application for conversion and you complete your conversion, you must operate within the parameters of your business plan. You must obtain the prior written approval of the appropriate Federal banking agency for any material deviations from your business plan.

§ 192.120 May I discuss my plans to convert with others?

(a) You may discuss information about your conversion with individuals that you authorize to prepare documents for your conversion.

(b) Except as permitted under paragraph (a) of this section, you must keep all information about your conversion confidential until your board of directors adopts your plan of conversion.

(c) If you violate this section, the appropriate Federal banking agency may require you to take remedial action. For example, the appropriate Federal banking agency may require you to take any or all of the following actions:

(1) Publicly announce that you are considering a conversion;

(2) Set an eligibility record date acceptable to the appropriate Federal banking agency;

(3) Limit the subscription rights of any person who violates or aids a violation of this section; or

(4) Take any other action to assure that your conversion is fair and equitable.

PLAN OF CONVERSION

§ 192.125 Must my board of directors adopt a plan of conversion?

Prior to filing an application for conversion, your board of directors must adopt a plan of conversion that conforms to §§ 192.320 through 192.485 and 192.505. Your board of directors must adopt the plan by at least a two-thirds vote. Your plan of conversion is required, under § 192.150, to be included in your conversion application.

§ 192.130 What must I include in my plan of conversion?

You must include the information included in §§ 192.320 through 192.485 and 192.505 in your plan of conversion. The appropriate Federal banking agency may require you to delete or revise any provision in your plan of conversion if it determines the provision is inequitable; is detrimental to you, your account holders, or other savings associations; or is contrary to public interest.

§ 192.135 How do I notify my members that my board of directors approved a plan of conversion?

(a) *Notice.* You must promptly notify your members that your board of directors adopted a plan of conversion and that a copy of the plan is available for the members' inspection in your home office and in your branch offices. You must mail a letter to each member or publish a notice in the local newspaper in every local community where you have an office. You may also issue a press release. The appropriate Federal banking agency may require broader publication, if necessary, to ensure adequate notice to your members.

(b) *Contents of notice.* You may include any of the following statements and descriptions in your letter, notice, or press release.

(1) Your board of directors adopted a proposed plan to convert from a mutual to a stock savings institution.

(2) You will send your members a proxy statement with detailed information on the proposed conversion before you convene a members' meeting to vote on the conversion.

(3) Your members will have an opportunity to approve or disapprove the proposed conversion at a meeting. At least a majority of the eligible votes must approve the conversion.

(4) You will not vote existing proxies to approve or disapprove the conversion. You will solicit new proxies for voting on the proposed conversion.

(5) The appropriate Federal banking agency, and in the case of a state-chartered savings association, the appropriate state regulator, must approve the conversion before the conversion will be effective. Your members will have an opportunity to file written comments, including objections and materials supporting the objections, with the appropriate Federal banking agency.

(6) The IRS must issue a favorable tax ruling, or a tax expert must issue an appropriate tax opinion, on the tax consequences of your conversion before the appropriate Federal banking agency will approve the conversion. The ruling or opinion must indicate the conversion will be a tax-free reorganization.

(7) The appropriate Federal banking agency, and in the case of a state-chartered savings association, the appropriate state regulator, might not approve the conversion, and the IRS or a tax expert might not issue a favorable tax ruling or tax opinion.

(8) Savings account holders will continue to hold accounts in the converted savings association with the same dollar amounts, rates of return, and general terms as existing deposits. FDIC will continue to insure the accounts.

(9) Your conversion will not affect borrowers' loans, including the amount, rate, maturity, security, and other contractual terms.

(10) Your business of accepting deposits and making loans will continue without interruption.

(11) Your current management and staff will continue to conduct current services for depositors and borrowers under current policies and in existing offices.

(12) You may continue to be a member of the Federal Home Loan Bank System.

(13) You may substantively amend your proposed plan of conversion before the members' meeting.

(14) You may terminate the proposed conversion.

(15) After the appropriate Federal banking agency, and in the case of a state-chartered savings association, the appropriate state regulator, approves the proposed conversion, you will send proxy materials providing additional information. After you send proxy materials, members may telephone or write to you with additional questions.

(16) The proposed record date for determining the eligible account holders who are entitled to receive subscription rights to purchase your shares.

(17) A brief description of the circumstances under which supplemental eligible account holders will receive subscription rights to purchase your shares.

(18) A brief description of how voting members may participate in the conversion.

(19) A brief description of how directors, officers, and employees will participate in the conversion.

(20) A brief description of the proposed plan of conversion.

(21) The par value (if any) and approximate number of shares you will issue and sell in the conversion.

(c) *Other requirements.* (1) You may not solicit proxies, provide financial statements, describe the benefits of conversion, or estimate the value of your shares upon conversion in the letter, notice, or press release.

(2) If you respond to inquiries about the conversion, you may address only the matters listed in paragraph (b) of this section.

§ 192.140 May I amend my plan of conversion?

You may amend your plan of conversion before you solicit proxies. After you solicit proxies, you may amend your plan of conversion only if the appropriate Federal banking agency concurs.

FILING REQUIREMENTS

§ 192.150 What must I include in my application for conversion?

(a) Your application for conversion must include all of the following information.

(1) Your plan of conversion.

(2) Pricing materials meeting the requirements of § 192.200(b).

(3) Proxy soliciting materials under § 192.270, including:

(i) A preliminary proxy statement with signed financial statements;

(ii) A form of proxy meeting the requirements of § 192.255; and

(iii) Any additional proxy soliciting materials, including press releases, personal solicitation instructions, radio or television scripts that you plan to use or furnish to your members, and a legal opinion indicating that any marketing materials comply with all applicable securities laws.

(4) An offering circular described in § 192.300.

(5) The documents and information required by Form AC. You may obtain Form AC from the appropriate Federal banking agency.

(6) Where indicated, written consents, signed and dated, of any accountant, attorney, investment banker, appraiser, or other professional who prepared, reviewed, passed upon, or certified any statement, report, or valuation for use. *See* Form AC, instruction B(7).

(7) Your business plan, submitted as a separately bound, confidential exhibit. *See* § 192.160.

(8) Any additional information that the appropriate Federal banking agency requests.

(b) The appropriate Federal banking agency will not accept for filing, and will return, any application for conversion that is improperly executed, materially deficient, substantially incomplete, or that provides for unreasonable conversion expenses.

§ 192.155 How do I file my application for conversion?

If you are a Federal savings association, you must file an original and at least one conformed copy of Form AC with the appropriate OCC licensing office. If you are a state savings association, you must file all copies of your application with the appropriate FDIC region.

§ 192.160 May I keep portions of my application for conversion confidential?

(a) The appropriate Federal banking agency makes all filings under this part available to the public, but may keep portions of your application for conversion confidential under paragraph (b) of this section.

(b) You may request that the appropriate Federal banking agency keep portions of your application confidential. To do so, you must separately bind and clearly designate as "confidential" any portion of your application for conversion that you deem confidential. You must provide a written statement specifying the grounds supporting your request for confidentiality. The appropriate Federal banking agency will not treat as confidential the portion of your application describing how you plan to meet your Community Reinvestment Act (CRA) objectives. The CRA portion of your application may not incorporate by reference information contained in the confidential portion of your application.

(c) The appropriate Federal banking agency will determine whether confidential information must be made available to the public under 5 U.S.C. 552 and part 4 of this chapter or 12 CFR 309. The appropriate Federal banking agency will advise you before it makes information you designated as "confidential" available to the public.

§ 192.165 How do I amend my application for conversion?

To amend your application for conversion, you must:

(a) File an amendment with an appropriate facing sheet;

(b) Number each amendment consecutively;

(c) Respond to all issues raised by the appropriate Federal banking agency; and

(d) Demonstrate that the amendment conforms to all applicable regulations.

NOTICE OF FILING OF APPLICATION AND COMMENT PROCESS

§ 192.180 How do I notify the public that I filed an application for conversion?

(a) You must publish a public notice of the application in accordance with the procedures in § 5.8 of this chapter. You must simultaneously prominently post the notice in your home office and all branch offices.

(b) Promptly after publication, you must file any public notice and an affidavit of publication from each publisher. If you are a Federal savings association, you must file the affidavit and two copies of any public notice with the appropriate OCC licensing office. If you are a state savings association, you must file all copies with the appropriate FDIC region.

(c) If the appropriate Federal banking agency does not accept your application for conversion under § 192.200 and requires you to file a new application, you must publish and post a new notice and allow an additional 30 days for comment.

[76 FR 49156, Aug. 9, 2011, as amended at 80 FR 28481, May 18, 2015]

§ 192.185 How may a person comment on my application for conversion?

Commenters may submit comments on your application in accordance with the procedures in § 5.10 of this chapter. A commenter must file the original and one copy of any comments with the appropriate OCC licensing office for Federal savings association applications and with the appropriate FDIC region for state savings association applications.

[76 FR 49156, Aug. 9, 2011, as amended at 80 FR 28481, May 18, 2015]

AGENCY REVIEW OF THE APPLICATION FOR CONVERSION

§ 192.200 What actions may the appropriate Federal banking agency take on my application?

(a) The appropriate Federal banking agency may approve your application for conversion only if:

(1) Your conversion complies with this part;

(2) You will meet your regulatory capital requirements under 12 CFR part 3, part 324, or part 390, subpart Z, as applicable after the conversion; and

(3) Your conversion will not result in a taxable reorganization under the Internal Revenue Code of 1986, as amended.

(b) The appropriate Federal banking agency will review the appraisal required by § 192.150(a)(2) in determining whether to approve your application. The appropriate Federal banking agency will review the appraisal under the following requirements.

(1) Independent persons experienced and expert in corporate appraisal, and acceptable to the appropriate Federal banking agency, must prepare the appraisal report.

(2) An affiliate of the appraiser may serve as an underwriter or selling agent, if you ensure that the appraiser is separate from the underwriter or selling agent affiliate and the underwriter or selling agent affiliate does not make recommendations or affect the appraisal.

(3) The appraiser may not receive any fee in connection with the conversion other than for appraisal services.

(4) The appraisal report must include a complete and detailed description of

the elements of the appraisal, a justification for the appraisal methodology, and sufficient support for the conclusions.

(5) If the appraisal is based on a capitalization of your pro forma income, it must indicate the basis for determining the income to be derived from the sale of shares, and demonstrate that the earnings multiple used is appropriate, including future earnings growth assumptions.

(6) If the appraisal is based on a comparison of your shares with outstanding shares of existing stock associations, the existing stock associations must be reasonably comparable in size, market area, competitive conditions, risk profile, profit history, and expected future earnings.

(7) The appropriate Federal banking agency may decline to process the application for conversion and deem it materially deficient or substantially incomplete if the initial appraisal report is materially deficient or substantially incomplete.

(8) You may not represent or imply that the appropriate Federal banking agency approved the appraisal.

(c) The appropriate Federal banking agency will review your compliance record under part 195 of this chapter and your business plan to determine how you will serve the convenience and needs of your communities after the conversion.

(1) Based on this review, the appropriate Federal banking agency may approve your application, deny your application, or approve your application on the condition that you will improve your CRA performance or that you will address the particular credit or lending needs of the communities that you will serve.

(2) The appropriate Federal banking agency may deny your application if your business plan does not demonstrate that your proposed use of conversion proceeds will help you to meet the credit and lending needs of the communities that you will serve.

(d) The appropriate Federal banking agency may request that you amend your application if further explanation is necessary, material is missing, or material must be corrected.

(e) The appropriate Federal banking agency will deny your application if the application does not meet the requirements of this subpart, unless The appropriate Federal banking agency waives the requirement under § 192.5(c).

[76 FR 49156, Aug. 9, 2011, as amended at 79 FR 11317, Feb. 28, 2014]

§ 192.205 May a court review the appropriate Federal banking agency's final action on my conversion?

(a) Any person aggrieved by the appropriate Federal banking agency's final action on your application for conversion may ask the court of appeals of the United States for the circuit in which the principal office or residence of such person is located, or the U.S. Court of Appeals for the District of Columbia Circuit, to review the action under 12 U.S.C. 1464(i)(2)(B).

(b) To obtain court review of the action, this statute requires the aggrieved person to file a written petition requesting that the court modify, terminate, or set aside the final appropriate Federal banking agency action. The aggrieved person must file the petition with the court within the later of 30 days after the appropriate Federal agency publishes notice of its final action in the FEDERAL REGISTER or 30 days after you mail the proxy statement to your members under § 192.235.

VOTE BY MEMBERS

§ 192.225 Must I submit the plan of conversion to my members for approval?

(a) After the appropriate Federal banking agency approves your plan of conversion, you must submit your plan of conversion to your members for approval. You must obtain this approval at a meeting of your members, which may be a special or annual meeting, unless you are a state-chartered savings association and state law requires you to obtain approval at an annual meeting.

(b) Your members must approve your plan of conversion by a majority of the total outstanding votes, unless you are a state-chartered savings association and state law prescribes a higher percentage.

(c) Your members may vote in person or by proxy.

(d) You may notify eligible account holders or supplemental eligible account holders who are not voting members of your proposed conversion. You may include only the information in §192.135 in your notice.

§ 192.230 Who is eligible to vote?

You determine members' eligibility to vote by setting a voting record date. You must set a voting record date that is not more than 60 days nor less than 20 days before your meeting, unless you are a state-chartered savings association and state law requires a different voting record date.

§ 192.235 How must I notify my members of the meeting?

(a) You must notify your members of the meeting to consider your conversion by sending the members a proxy statement cleared by the appropriate Federal banking agency.

(b) You must notify your members 20 to 45 days before your meeting, unless you are a state-chartered savings association and state law requires a different notice period.

(c) You must also notify each beneficial holder of an account held in a fiduciary capacity:

(1) If you are a Federal savings association, and the name of the beneficial holder is disclosed on your records; or

(2) If you are a state-chartered association and the beneficial holder possesses voting rights under state law.

§ 192.240 What must I submit after the members' meeting?

(a) Promptly after the members' meeting, you must file all of the following information with the appropriate OCC licensing office if you are a Federal savings association, and with the appropriate FDIC region if you are a state savings association.

(1) A certified copy of each adopted resolution on the conversion.

(2) The total votes eligible to be cast.

(3) The total votes represented in person or by proxy.

(4) The total votes cast in favor of and against each matter.

(5) The percentage of votes necessary to approve each matter.

(6) An opinion of counsel that you conducted the members' meeting in compliance with all applicable state or Federal laws and regulations.

(b) Promptly after completion of the conversion, you must submit an opinion of counsel that you complied with all laws applicable to the conversion.

PROXY SOLICITATION

§ 192.250 Who must comply with these proxy solicitation provisions?

(a) You must comply with these proxy solicitation provisions when you provide proxy solicitation material to members for the meeting to vote on your plan of conversion.

(b) Your members must comply with these proxy solicitation provisions when they provide proxy solicitation materials to members for the meeting to vote on your conversion, pursuant to §192.280, except where:

(1) The member solicits 50 people or fewer and does not solicit proxies on your behalf; or

(2) The member solicits proxies through newspaper advertisements after your board of directors adopts the plan of conversion. Any newspaper advertisements may include only the following information:

(i) Your name;

(ii) The reason for the advertisement;

(iii) The proposal or proposals to be voted upon;

(iv) Where a member may obtain a copy of the proxy solicitation material; and

(v) A request for your members to vote at the meeting.

§ 192.255 What must the form of proxy include?

The form of proxy must include all of the following:

(a) A statement in bold face type stating that management is soliciting the proxy.

(b) Blank spaces where the member must date and sign the proxy.

(c) Clear and impartial identification of each matter or group of related matters that members will vote upon. You must include any proposed charitable contribution as an item to be voted on separately.

(d) The phrase "Revocable Proxy" in bold face type (at least 18 point).

(e) A description of any charter or state law requirement that restricts or conditions votes by proxy.

(f) An acknowledgment that the member received a proxy statement before he or she signed the form of proxy.

(g) The date, time, and the place of the meeting, when available.

(h) A way for the member to specify by ballot whether he or she approves or disapproves of each matter that members will vote upon.

(i) A statement that management will vote the proxy in accordance with the member's specifications.

(j) A statement in bold face type indicating how management will vote the proxy if the member does not specify a choice for a matter.

§ 192.260 May I use previously executed proxies?

You may not use previously executed proxies for the plan of conversion vote. If members consider your plan of conversion at an annual meeting, you may vote proxies obtained through other proxy solicitations only on matters not related to your plan of conversion.

§ 192.265 How may I use proxies executed under this part?

You may vote a proxy obtained under this part on matters that are incidental to the conduct of the meeting. You may not vote a proxy obtained under this subpart at any meeting other than the meeting (or any adjournment of the meeting) to vote on your plan of conversion.

§ 192.270 What must I include in my proxy statement?

(a) *Content requirements.* You must prepare your proxy statement in compliance with this part and Form PS.

(b) *Other requirements.* (1) The appropriate Federal banking agency will review your proxy solicitation material when it reviews the application for conversion and will clear the proxy solicitation material.

(2) You must provide a cleared written proxy statement to your members before or at the same time you provide any other soliciting material. You must mail cleared proxy solicitation material to your members within ten days after the appropriate Federal banking agency clears the solicitation.

§ 192.275 How do I file revised proxy materials?

(a) You must file revised proxy materials as an amendment to your application for conversion. *See* § 192.155 for where to file.

(b) To revise your proxy solicitation materials, you must file:

(1) Seven copies of your revised proxy materials as required by Form PS;

(2) Seven copies of your revised form of proxy, if applicable; and

(3) Seven copies of any additional proxy solicitation material subject to § 192.270.

(c) You must mark four of the seven required copies to clearly indicate changes from the prior filing.

(d) You must file seven definitive copies of all proxy solicitation material, in the form in which you furnish the material to your members. You must file no later than the date that you send or give the proxy solicitation material to your members. You must indicate the date that you will release the materials.

(e) Unless the appropriate Federal banking agency requests you to do so, you do not have to file copies of replies to inquiries from your members or copies of communications that merely request members to sign and return proxy forms.

§ 192.280 Must I mail a member's proxy solicitation material?

(a) You must mail the member's cleared proxy solicitation material if:

(1) Your board of directors adopted a plan of conversion;

(2) A member requests in writing that you mail the proxy solicitation material;

(3) The appropriate Federal banking agency has cleared the member's proxy solicitation; and

(4) The member agrees to defray your reasonable expenses.

(b) As soon as practicable after you receive a request under paragraph (a) of this section, you must mail or otherwise furnish the following information to the member:

(1) The approximate number of members that you solicited or will solicit,

or the approximate number of members of any group of account holders that the member designates; and

(2) The estimated cost of mailing the proxy solicitation material for the member.

(c) You must mail cleared proxy solicitation material to the designated members promptly after the member furnishes the materials, envelopes (or other containers), and postage (or payment for postage) to you.

(d) You are not responsible for the content of a member's proxy solicitation material.

(e) A member may furnish other members its own proxy solicitation material, cleared by the appropriate Federal banking agency, subject to the rules in this section.

§ 192.285 What solicitations. are prohibited?

(a) *False or misleading statements.* (1) No one may use proxy solicitation material for the members' meeting if the material contains any statement which, considering the time and the circumstances of the statement:

(i) Is false or misleading with respect to any material fact;

(ii) Omits any material fact that is necessary to make the statements not false or misleading; or

(iii) Omits any material fact that is necessary to correct a statement in an earlier communication that has become false or misleading.

(2) No one may represent or imply that the appropriate Federal banking agency determined that the proxy solicitation material is accurate, complete, not false or not misleading, or passed upon the merits of or approved any proposal.

(b) *Other prohibited solicitations.* No person may solicit:

(1) An undated or post-dated proxy;

(2) A proxy that states it will be dated after the date it is signed by a member;

(3) A proxy that is not revocable at will by the member; or

(4) A proxy that is part of another document or instrument.

§ 192.290 What will the appropriate Federal banking agency do if a solicitation violates these prohibitions?

(a) If a solicitation violates § 192.285, the appropriate Federal banking agency may require remedial measures, including:

(1) Correction of the violation by a retraction and a new solicitation;

(2) Rescheduling the members' meeting; or

(3) Any other actions necessary to ensure a fair vote.

(b) The appropriate Federal banking agency may also bring an enforcement action against the violator.

§ 192.295 Will the appropriate Federal banking agency require me to re-solicit proxies?

If you amend your application for conversion, the appropriate Federal banking agency may require you to resolicit proxies for your members' meeting as a condition of approval of the amendment.

OFFERING CIRCULAR

§ 192.300 What must happen before the appropriate Federal banking agency declares my offering circular effective?

(a) You must prepare and file your offering circular with the Securities and Corporate Practices Division of the OCC if you are a Federal savings association and with the appropriate FDIC region if you are a state savings association, in compliance with this part and Form OC and, where applicable, part 197 of this chapter. File your offering circular in accordance with the procedures in section 192.155.

(b) You must condition your stock offering upon member approval of your plan of conversion.

(c) The appropriate Federal banking agency will review the Form OC and may comment on the included disclosures and financial statements.

(d) You must file any revised offering circular, final offering circular, and any post-effective amendment to the final offering circular in accordance with the procedures in section 192.155.

(e) The appropriate Federal banking agency will not approve the adequacy or accuracy of the offering circular or the disclosures.

(f) After you satisfactorily address the appropriate Federal banking agency's concerns, you must request the appropriate Federal banking agency to declare your Form OC effective for a time period. The time period may not exceed the maximum time period for the completion of the sale of all of your shares under §192.400.

§ 192.305 When may I distribute the offering circular?

(a) You may distribute a preliminary offering circular at the same time as or after you mail the proxy statement to your members.

(b) You may not distribute an offering circular until the appropriate Federal banking agency declares it effective. You must distribute the offering circular in accordance with this part.

(c) You must distribute your offering circular to persons listed in your plan of conversion within 10 days after the appropriate Federal banking agency declares it effective.

§ 192.310 When must I file a post-effective amendment to the offering circular?

(a) You must file a post-effective amendment to the offering circular with the appropriate Federal banking agency when a material event or change of circumstance occurs.

(b) After the appropriate Federal banking agency declares the post-effective amendment effective, you must immediately deliver the amendment to each person who subscribed for or ordered shares in the offering.

(c) Your post-effective amendment must indicate that each person may increase, decrease, or rescind their subscription or order.

(d) The post-effective offering period must remain open no less than 10 days nor more than 20 days, unless the appropriate Federal banking agency approves a longer rescission period.

OFFERS AND SALES OF STOCK

§ 192.320 Who has priority to purchase my conversion shares?

You must offer to sell your shares in the following order:

(a) Eligible account holders.

(b) Tax-qualified employee stock ownership plans.

(c) Supplemental eligible account holders.

(d) Other voting members who have subscription rights.

(e) Your community, your community and the general public, or the general public.

§ 192.325 When may I offer to sell my conversion shares?

(a) You may offer to sell your conversion shares after the appropriate Federal banking agency approves your conversion, clears your proxy statement, and declares your offering circular effective.

(b) The offer may commence at the same time you start the proxy solicitation of your members.

§ 192.330 How do I price my conversion shares?

(a) You must sell your conversion shares at a uniform price per share and at a total price that is equal to the estimated pro forma market value of your shares after you convert.

(b) The maximum price must be no more than 15 percent above the midpoint of the estimated price range in your offering circular.

(c) The minimum price must be no more than 15 percent below the midpoint of the estimated price range in your offering circular.

(d) If the appropriate Federal banking agency permits, you may increase the maximum price of conversion shares sold. The maximum price, as adjusted, must be no more than 15 percent above the maximum price computed under paragraph (b) of this section.

(e) The maximum price must be between $5 and $50 per share.

(f) You must include the estimated price in any preliminary offering circular.

§ 192.335 How do I sell my conversion shares?

(a) You must distribute order forms to all eligible account holders, supplemental eligible account holders, and other voting members to enable them to subscribe for the conversion shares they are permitted under the plan of conversion. You may either send the order forms with your offering circular or after you distribute your offering circular.

(b) You may sell your conversion shares in a community offering, a public offering, or both. You may begin the community offering, the public offering, or both at any time during the subscription offering or upon conclusion of the subscription offering.

(c) You may pay underwriting commissions (including underwriting discounts). The appropriate Federal banking agency may object to the payment of unreasonable commissions. You may reimburse an underwriter for accountable expenses in a subscription offering if the public offering is limited. If no public offering occurs, you may pay an underwriter a consulting fee. The appropriate Federal banking agency may object to the payment of unreasonable consulting fees.

(d) If you conduct the community offering, the public offering, or both at the same time as the subscription offering, you must fill all subscription orders first.

(e) You must prepare your order form in compliance with this part and Form OF.

§ 192.340 What sales practices are prohibited?

(a) In connection with offers, sales, or purchases of conversion shares under this part, you and your directors, officers, agents, or employees may not:

(1) Employ any device, scheme, or artifice to defraud;

(2) Obtain money or property by means of any untrue statement of a material fact or any omission of a material fact necessary to make the statements, in light of the circumstances under which they were made, not misleading; or

(3) Engage in any act, transaction, practice, or course of business that operates or would operate as a fraud or deceit upon a purchaser or seller.

(b) During your conversion, no person may:

(1) Transfer, or enter into any agreement or understanding to transfer, the legal or beneficial ownership of subscription rights for your conversion shares or the underlying securities to the account of another;

(2) Make any offer, or any announcement of an offer, to purchase any of your conversion shares from anyone but you; or

(3) Knowingly acquire more than the maximum purchase allowable under your plan of conversion.

(c) The restrictions in paragraphs (b)(1) and (b)(2) of this section do not apply to offers for more than 10 percent of any class of conversion shares by:

(1) An underwriter or a selling group, acting on your behalf, that makes the offer with a view toward public resale; or

(2) One or more of your tax-qualified employee stock ownership plans so long as the plan or plans do not beneficially own more than 25 percent of any class of your equity securities in the aggregate.

(d) If any person is found to have violated the restrictions in paragraphs (b)(1) and (b)(2) of this section, they may face prosecution or other legal action.

§ 192.345 How may a subscriber pay for my conversion shares?

(a) A subscriber may purchase conversion shares with cash, by a withdrawal from a savings account, or a withdrawal from a certificate of deposit. If a subscriber purchases shares by a withdrawal from a certificate of deposit, you may not assess a penalty for the withdrawal.

(b) You may not extend credit to any person to purchase your conversion shares.

§ 192.350 Must I pay interest on payments for conversion shares?

(a) You must pay interest from the date you receive a payment for conversion shares until the date you complete or terminate the conversion. You must pay interest at no less than your passbook rate for amounts paid in cash, check, or money order.

(b) If a subscriber withdraws money from a savings account to purchase conversion shares, you must pay interest on the payment until you complete or terminate the conversion as if the withdrawn amount remained in the account.

(c) If a depositor fails to maintain the applicable minimum balance requirement because he or she withdraws money from a certificate of deposit to purchase conversion shares, you may cancel the certificate and pay interest at no less than your passbook rate on any remaining balance.

§ 192.355 What subscription rights must I give to each eligible account holder and each supplemental eligible account holder?

(a) You must give each eligible account holder subscription rights to purchase conversion shares in an amount equal to the greater of:

(1) The maximum purchase limitation established for the community offering or the public offering under § 192.395;

(2) One-tenth of one percent of the total stock offering; or

(3) Fifteen times the following number: The total number of conversion shares that you will issue, multiplied by the following fraction. The numerator is the total qualifying deposit of the eligible account holder. The denominator is the total qualifying deposits of all eligible account holders. You must round down the product of this multiplied fraction to the next whole number.

(b) You must give subscription rights to purchase shares to each supplemental eligible account holder in the same amount as described in paragraph (a) of this section, except that you must compute the fraction described in paragraph (a)(3) of this section as follows: The numerator is the total qualifying deposit of the supplemental eligible account holder. The denominator is the total qualifying deposits of all supplemental eligible account holders.

§ 192.360 Are my officers, directors, and their associates eligible account holders?

Your officers, directors, and their associates may be eligible account holders. However, if an officer, director, or his or her associate receives subscription rights based on increased deposits in the year before the eligibility record date, you must subordinate subscription rights for these deposits to subscription rights exercised by other eligible account holders.

§ 192.365 May other voting members purchase conversion shares in the conversion?

(a) You must give rights to purchase your conversion shares in the conversion to voting members who are neither eligible account holders nor supplemental eligible account holders. You must allocate rights to each voting member that are equal to the greater of:

(1) The maximum purchase limitation established for the community offering and the public offering under § 192.395; or

(2) One-tenth of one percent of the total stock offering.

(b) You must subordinate the voting members' rights to the rights of eligible account holders, tax-qualified employee stock ownership plans, and supplemental eligible account holders.

§ 192.370 Does the appropriate Federal banking agency limit the aggregate purchases by officers, directors, and their associates?

(a) When you convert, your officers, directors, and their associates may not purchase, in the aggregate, more than the following percentage of your total stock offering:

Institution size	Officer and director purchases (percent)
$50,000,000 or less	35
$50,000,001–100,000,000	34
$100,000,001–150,000,000	33
$150,000,001–200,000,000	32
$200,000,001–250,000,000	31
$250,000,001–300,000,000	30
$300,000,001–350,000,000	29
$350,000,001–400,000,000	28
$400,000,001–450,000,000	27
$450,000,001–500,000,000	26
Over $500,000,000	25

(b) The purchase limitations in this section do not apply to shares held in tax-qualified employee stock benefit plans that are attributable to your officers, directors, and their associates.

§ 192.375 How do I allocate my conversion shares if my shares are oversubscribed?

(a) If your conversion shares are oversubscribed by your eligible account holders, you must allocate shares among the eligible account holders so that each, to the extent possible, may purchase 100 shares.

(b) If your conversion shares are oversubscribed by your supplemental eligible account holders, you must allocate shares among the supplemental eligible account holders so that each, to the extent possible, may purchase 100 shares.

(c) If a person is an eligible account holder and a supplemental eligible account holder, you must include the eligible account holder's allocation in determining the number of conversion shares that you may allocate to the person as a supplemental eligible account holder.

(d) For conversion shares that you do not allocate under paragraphs (a) and (b) of this section, you must allocate the shares among the eligible or supplemental eligible account holders equitably, based on the amounts of qualifying deposits. You must describe this method of allocation in your plan of conversion.

(e) If shares remain after you have allocated shares as provided in paragraphs (a) and (b) of this section, and if your voting members oversubscribe, you must allocate your conversion shares among those members equitably. You must describe the method of allocation in your plan of conversion.

§ 192.380 May my employee stock ownership plan purchase conversion shares?

(a) Your tax-qualified employee stock ownership plan may purchase up to 10 percent of the total offering of your conversion shares.

(b) If the appropriate Federal banking agency approves a revised stock valuation range as described in § 192.330(e), and the final conversion stock valuation range exceeds the former maximum stock offering range, you may allocate conversion shares to your tax-qualified employee stock ownership plan, up to the 10 percent limit in paragraph (a) of this section.

(c) If your tax-qualified employee stock ownership plan is not able to or chooses not to purchase stock in the offering, it may, with prior appropriate Federal banking agency approval and appropriate disclosure in your offering circular, purchase stock in the open market, or purchase authorized but unissued conversion shares.

(d) You may include stock contributed to a charitable organization in the conversion in the calculation of the total offering of conversion shares under paragraphs (a) and (b) of this section, unless the appropriate Federal banking agency objects on supervisory grounds.

§ 192.385 May I impose any purchase limitations?

(a) You may limit the number of shares that any person, group of associated persons, or persons otherwise acting in concert, may subscribe to up to five percent of the total stock sold.

(b) If you set a limit of five percent under paragraph (a) of this section, you may modify that limit with appropriate Federal banking agency approval to provide that any person, group of associated persons, or persons otherwise acting in concert subscribing for five percent, may purchase between five and ten percent as long as the aggregate amount that the subscribers purchase does not exceed 10 percent of the total stock offering.

(c) You may require persons exercising subscription rights to purchase a minimum number of conversion shares. The minimum number of shares must equal the lesser of the number of shares obtained by a $500 subscription or 25 shares.

(d) In setting purchase limitations under this section, you may not aggregate conversion shares attributed to a person in your tax-qualified employee stock ownership plan with shares purchased directly by, or otherwise attributable to, that person.

§ 192.390 Must I provide a purchase preference to persons in my local community?

(a) In your subscription offering, you may give a purchase preference to eligible account holders, supplemental eligible account holders, and voting members residing in your local community.

(b) In your community offering, you must give a purchase preference to natural persons residing in your local community.

§ 192.395 What other conditions apply when I offer conversion shares in a community offering, a public offering, or both?

(a) You must offer and sell your stock to achieve a widespread distribution of the stock.

(b) If you offer shares in a community offering, a public offering, or both, you must first fill orders for your stock up to a maximum of two percent of the conversion stock on a basis that will promote a widespread distribution of stock. You must allocate any remaining shares on an equal number of shares per order basis until you fill all orders.

COMPLETION OF THE OFFERING

§ 192.400 When must I complete the sale of my stock?

You must complete all sales of your stock within 45 calendar days after the last day of the subscription period, unless the offering is extended under § 192.405.

§ 192.405 How do I extend the offering period?

(a) You must request, in writing, an extension of any offering period.

(b) The appropriate Federal banking agency may grant extensions of time to sell your shares. The appropriate Federal banking agency will not grant any single extension of more than 90 days.

(c) If the appropriate Federal banking agency grants your request for an extension of time, you must provide a post-effective amendment to the offering circular under § 192.310 to each person who subscribed for or ordered stock. Your amendment must indicate that the appropriate Federal banking agency extended the offering period and that each person who subscribed for or ordered stock may increase, decrease, or rescind their subscription or order within the time remaining in the extension period.

COMPLETION OF THE CONVERSION

§ 192.420 When must I complete my conversion?

(a) In your plan of conversion, you must set a date by which the conversion must be completed. This date must not be more than 24 months from the date that your members approve the plan of conversion. The date, once set, may not be extended by you or by the appropriate Federal banking agency. You must terminate the conversion if it is not completed by that date.

(b) Your conversion is complete on the date that you accept the offers for your stock.

§ 192.425 Who may terminate the conversion?

(a) Your members may terminate the conversion by failing to approve the conversion at your members' meeting.

(b) You may terminate the conversion before your members' meeting.

(c) You may terminate the conversion after the members' meeting only if the appropriate Federal banking agency concurs.

§ 192.430 What happens to my old charter?

(a) If you are a Federally chartered mutual savings association or savings bank, and you convert to a Federally chartered stock savings association or savings bank, you must apply to the OCC to amend your charter and bylaws consistent with § 5.22 of this chapter, as part of your application for conversion. You may only include OCC pre-approved anti-takeover provisions in your amended charter and bylaws. *See* § 5.22(g)(7).

(b) If you are a Federally chartered mutual savings association or savings bank and you convert to a state-chartered stock savings association under this part, you must surrender your charter to the OCC for cancellation promptly after the state issues your charter. You must promptly file a copy of your new state stock charter with the FDIC.

(c) If you are a state-chartered mutual savings association or savings bank, and you convert to a Federally chartered stock savings association or savings bank, you must apply to the OCC for a new charter and bylaws consistent with § 5.22 of this chapter. You may only include OCC pre-approved anti-takeover provisions in your charter and bylaws. *See* § 5.22(g)(7).

(d) Your new or amended charter must require you to establish and maintain a liquidation account for eligible and supplemental eligible account holders under § 192.450.

[76 FR 49156, Aug. 9, 2011, as amended at 80 FR 28481, May 18, 2015]

§ 192.435 What happens to my corporate existence after conversion?

Your corporate existence will continue following your conversion, unless you convert to a state-chartered stock savings association and state law prescribes otherwise.

§ 192.440 What voting rights must I provide to stockholders after the conversion?

You must provide your stockholders with exclusive voting rights, except as provided in § 192.445(c).

§ 192.445 What must I provide my savings account holders?

(a) You must provide each savings account holder, without payment, a withdrawable savings account or accounts in the same amount and under the same terms and conditions as their accounts before your conversion.

(b) You must provide a liquidation account for each eligible and supplemental eligible account holder under § 192.450.

(c) If you are a state-chartered savings association and state law requires you to provide voting rights to savings account holders or borrowers, your charter must:

(1) Limit these voting rights to the minimum required by state law; and

(2) Require you to solicit proxies from the savings account holders and borrowers in the same manner that you solicit proxies from your stockholders.

LIQUIDATION ACCOUNT

§ 192.450 What is a liquidation account?

(a) A liquidation account represents the potential interest of eligible account holders and supplemental eligible account holders in your net worth at the time of conversion. You must maintain a sub-account to reflect the interest of each account holder.

(b) Before you may provide a liquidation distribution to common stockholders, you must give a liquidation distribution to those eligible account holders and supplemental eligible account holders who hold savings accounts from the time of conversion until liquidation.

(c) You may not record the liquidation account in your financial statements. You must disclose the liquidation account in the footnotes to your financial statements.

§ 192.455 What is the initial balance of the liquidation account?

The initial balance of the liquidation account is your net worth in the statement of financial condition included in the final offering circular.

§ 192.460 How do I determine the initial balances of liquidation sub-accounts?

(a)(1) You determine the initial sub-account balance for a savings account held by an eligible account holder by multiplying the initial balance of the liquidation account by the following fraction: The numerator is the qualifying deposit in the savings account expressed in dollars on the eligibility record date. The denominator is total qualifying deposits of all eligible account holders on that date.

(2) You determine the initial sub-account balance for a savings account held by a supplemental eligible account holder by multiplying the initial balance of the liquidation account by the following fraction: The numerator is the qualifying deposit in the savings account expressed in dollars on the supplemental eligibility record date. The denominator is total qualifying deposits of all supplemental eligible account holders on that date.

(3) If an account holder holds a savings account on the eligibility record date and a separate savings account on the supplemental eligibility record date, you must compute separate sub-accounts for the qualifying deposits in the savings account on each record date.

(b) You may not increase the initial sub-account balances. You must decrease the initial balance under § 192.470 as depositors reduce or close their accounts.

§ 192.465 Do account holders retain any voting rights based on their liquidation sub-accounts?

Eligible account holders or supplemental eligible account holders do not retain any voting rights based on their liquidation sub-accounts.

§ 192.470 Must I adjust liquidation sub-accounts?

(a)(1) You must reduce the balance of an eligible account holder's or supplemental eligible account holder's sub-account if the deposit balance in the account holder's savings account at the close of business on any annual closing date, which for purposes of this section is your fiscal year end, after the relevant eligibility record dates is less than:

(i) The deposit balance in the account holder's savings account at the close of business on any other annual closing date after the relevant eligibility record date; or

(ii) The qualifying deposits in the account holder's savings account on the relevant eligibility record date.

(2) The reduction must be proportionate to the reduction in the deposit balance.

(b) If you reduce the balance of a liquidation sub-account, you may not subsequently increase it if the deposit balance increases.

(c) You are not required to adjust the liquidation account and sub-account balances at each annual closing date if you maintain sufficient records to make the computations if a liquidation subsequently occurs.

(d) You must maintain the liquidation sub-account for each account holder as long as the account holder maintains an account with the same social security number.

(e) If there is a complete liquidation, you must provide each account holder with a liquidation distribution in the amount of the sub-account balance.

§ 192.475 What is a liquidation?

(a) A liquidation is a sale of your assets and settlement of your liabilities with the intent to cease operations and close. Upon liquidation, you must return your charter to the governmental agency that issued it. The government agency must cancel your charter.

(b) A merger, consolidation, or similar combination or transaction with another depository institution, is not a liquidation. If you are involved in such a transaction, the surviving institution must assume the liquidation account.

§ 192.480 Does the liquidation account affect my net worth?

The liquidation account does not affect your net worth.

§ 192.485 What provision must I include in my new Federal charter?

If you convert to Federal stock form, you must include the following provision in your new charter: "Liquidation Account. Under appropriate Federal banking agency regulations, the association must establish and maintain a liquidation account for the benefit of its savings account holders as of ________. If the association undergoes a complete liquidation, it must comply with appropriate Federal banking agency regulations with respect to the amount and priorities on liquidation of each of the savings account holder's interests in the liquidation account. A savings account holder's interest in the liquidation account does not entitle the savings account holder to any voting rights."

POST-CONVERSION

§ 192.500 What management stock benefit plans may I implement?

(a) During the 12 months after your conversion, you may implement a stock option plan (Option Plan), an employee stock ownership plan or other tax-qualified employee stock benefit plan (collectively, ESOP), and a management recognition plan (MRP), provided you meet all of the following requirements.

(1) You disclose the plans in your proxy statement and offering circular and indicate in your offering circular that there will be a separate shareholder vote on the Option Plan and the MRP at least six months after the conversion. No shareholder vote is required to implement the ESOP. Your ESOP must be tax-qualified.

(2) Your Option Plan does not encompass more than ten percent of the number of shares that you issued in the conversion.

(3)(i) Your ESOP and MRP do not encompass, in the aggregate, more than ten percent of the number of shares that you issued in the conversion. If you have tangible capital of ten percent or more following the conversion, the appropriate Federal banking agency may permit your ESOP and MRP to encompass, in the aggregate, up to 12 percent of the number of shares issued in the conversion; and

(ii) Your MRP does not encompass more than three percent of the number of shares that you issued in the conversion. If you have tangible capital of ten percent or more after the conversion, the appropriate Federal banking agency may permit your MRP to encompass up to four percent of the number of shares that you issued in the conversion.

(4) No individual receives more than 25 percent of the shares under any plan.

(5) Your directors who are not your officers do not receive more than five percent of the shares of your MRP or Option Plan individually, or 30 percent of any such plan in the aggregate.

(6) Your shareholders approve each of the Option Plan and the MRP by a majority of the total votes eligible to be cast at a duly called meeting before you establish or implement the plan. You may not hold this meeting until six months after your conversion.

(7) When you distribute proxies or related material to shareholders in connection with the vote on a plan, you state that the plan complies with the appropriate Federal banking agency's regulations and that the appropriate Federal banking agency does not endorse or approve the plan in any way. You may not make any written or oral representations to the contrary.

(8) You do not grant stock options at less than the market price at the time of grant.

(9) You do not fund the Option Plan or the MRP at the time of the conversion.

(10) Your plan does not begin to vest earlier than one year after shareholders approve the plan, and does not vest at a rate exceeding 20 percent per year.

(11) Your plan permits accelerated vesting only for disability or death, or if you undergo a change of control.

(12) Your plan provides that your executive officers or directors must exercise or forfeit their options in the event the institution becomes critically undercapitalized (as defined in 12 CFR 6.4 or 324.403, as applicable), is subject to appropriate Federal banking agency enforcement action, or receives a capital directive under 12 CFR part 6, subpart B or 12 CFR 308.201, as applicable.

(13) You file a copy of the proposed Option Plan or MRP with the appropriate Federal banking agency and certify to such agency that the plan approved by the shareholders is the same plan that you filed with, and disclosed in, the proxy materials distributed to shareholders in connection with the vote on the plan.

(14) You file the plan and the certification with the appropriate Federal banking agency within five calendar days after your shareholders approve the plan.

(b) You may provide dividend equivalent rights or dividend adjustment rights to allow for stock splits or other adjustments to your stock in your ESOP, MRP, and Option Plan.

(c) The restrictions in paragraph (a) of this section do not apply to plans implemented more than 12 months after the conversion, provided that materials pertaining to any shareholder vote regarding such plans are not distributed within the 12 months after the conversion. If a plan adopted in conformity with paragraph (a) of this section is amended more than 12 months following your conversion, your shareholders must ratify any material deviations to the requirements in paragraph (a).

[76 FR 49156, Aug. 9, 2011, as amended at 79 FR 11317, Feb. 28, 2014]

§ 192.505 May my directors, officers, and their associates freely trade shares?

(a) Directors and officers who purchase conversion shares may not sell the shares for one year after the date of purchase, except that in the event of the death of the officer or director, the successor in interest may sell the shares.

(b) You must include notice of the restriction described in paragraph (a) of this section on each certificate of stock that a director or officer purchases during the conversion or receives in connection with a stock dividend, stock split, or otherwise with respect to such restricted shares.

(c) You must instruct your stock transfer agent about the transfer restrictions in this section.

(d) For three years after you convert, your officers, directors, and their associates may purchase your stock only from a broker or dealer registered with the Securities and Exchange Commission. However, your officers, directors, and their associates may engage in a negotiated transaction involving more than one percent of your outstanding stock, and may purchase stock through any of your management or employee stock benefit plans.

§ 192.510 May I repurchase shares after conversion?

(a) You may not repurchase your shares in the first year after the conversion except:

(1) In extraordinary circumstances, you may make open market repurchases of up to five percent of your outstanding stock in the first year after the conversion if you file a notice under § 192.515(a) and the appropriate Federal banking agency does not disapprove your repurchase. The appropriate Federal banking agency will not approve such repurchases unless the repurchase meets the standards in § 192.515(c), and the repurchase is consistent with paragraph (c) of this section.

(2) You may repurchase qualifying shares of a director or conduct an appropriate Federal banking agency- approved repurchase pursuant to an offer made to all shareholders of your association.

(3) Repurchases to fund management recognition plans that have been ratified by shareholders do not count toward the repurchase limitations in this section. Repurchases in the first year to fund such plans require prior written notification to the appropriate Federal banking agency.

(4) Purchases to fund tax qualified employee stock benefit plans do not count toward the repurchase limitations in this section.

(b) After the first year, you may repurchase your shares, subject to all other applicable regulatory and supervisory restrictions and paragraph (c) of this section.

(c) All stock repurchases are subject to the following restrictions.

(1) You may not repurchase your shares if the repurchase will reduce your regulatory capital below the amount required for your liquidation account under § 192.450. You must comply with the capital distribution requirements at § 5.55 of this chapter.

(2) The restrictions on share repurchases apply to a charitable organization under § 192.550. You must aggregate purchases of shares by the charitable organization with your repurchases.

[76 FR 49156, Aug. 9, 2011, as amended at 80 FR 28481, May 18, 2015]

§ 192.515 What information must I provide to the appropriate Federal banking agency before I repurchase my shares?

(a) To repurchase stock in the first year following conversion, other than repurchases under § 192.510(a)(3) or (a)(4), you must file a written notice with the appropriate OCC licensing office if you are a Federal savings association and with the appropriate FDIC region if you are a state savings association. You must provide the following information:

(1) Your proposed repurchase program;

(2) The effect of the repurchases on your regulatory capital; and

(3) The purpose of the repurchases and, if applicable, an explanation of the extraordinary circumstances necessitating the repurchases.

(b) You must file your notice with the appropriate OCC licensing office if you are a Federal savings association and with the appropriate regional director of the FDIC if you are a state savings association at least ten days before you begin your repurchase program.

(c) You may not repurchase your shares if the appropriate Federal banking agency objects to your repurchase program. The appropriate Federal banking agency will not object to your repurchase program if:

(1) Your repurchase program will not adversely affect your financial condition;

(2) You submit sufficient information to evaluate your proposed repurchases;

(3) You demonstrate extraordinary circumstances and a compelling and valid business purpose for the share repurchases; and

(4) Your repurchase program would not be contrary to other applicable regulations.

§ 192.520 May I declare or pay dividends after I convert?

You may declare or pay a dividend on your shares after you convert if:

(a) The dividend will not reduce your regulatory capital below the amount required for your liquidation account under § 192.450;

(b) You comply with all capital requirements under 12 CFR part 3 or part 167, as applicable after you declare or pay dividends;

(c) You comply with the capital distribution requirements under § 5.55 of this chapter; and

(d) You do not return any capital, other than ordinary dividends, to purchasers during the term of the business plan submitted with the conversion.

[76 FR 49156, Aug. 9, 2011, as amended at 79 FR 11317, Feb. 28, 2014; 80 FR 28481, May 18, 2015]

§ 192.525 Who may acquire my shares after I convert?

(a) For three years after you convert, no person may, directly or indirectly, acquire or offer to acquire the beneficial ownership of more than ten percent of any class of your equity securities without the appropriate Federal banking agency's prior written approval. If a person violates this prohibition, you may not permit the person to vote shares in excess of ten percent, and may not count the shares in excess of ten percent in any shareholder vote.

(b) A person acquires beneficial ownership of more than ten percent of a class of shares when he or she holds any combination of your stock or revocable or irrevocable proxies under circumstances that give rise to a conclusive control determination or rebuttable control determination under § 5.50 of this chapter. The appropriate Federal banking agency will presume that a person has acquired shares if the acquiror entered into a binding written agreement for the transfer of shares. For purposes of this section, an offer is made when it is communicated. An offer does not include non-binding expressions of understanding or letters of intent regarding the terms of a potential acquisition.

(c) Notwithstanding the restrictions in this section:

(1) Paragraphs (a) and (b) of this section do not apply to any offer with a view toward public resale made exclusively to you, to the underwriters, or to a selling group acting on your behalf.

(2) Unless the appropriate Federal banking agency objects in writing, any person may offer or announce an offer to acquire up to one percent of any class of shares. In computing the one percent limit, the person must include all of his or her acquisitions of the same class of shares during the prior 12 months.

(3) A corporation whose ownership is, or will be, substantially the same as your ownership may acquire or offer to acquire more than ten percent of your common stock, if it makes the offer or acquisition more than one year after you convert.

(4) One or more of your tax-qualified employee stock benefit plans may acquire your shares, if the plan or plans do not beneficially own more than 25 percent of any class of your shares in the aggregate.

(5) An acquiror does not have to file a separate application to obtain the appropriate Federal banking agency's approval under paragraph (a) of this section, if the acquiror files an application under § 5.50 of this chapter that specifically addresses the criteria listed under paragraph (d) of this section and you do not oppose the proposed acquisition.

(d) The appropriate Federal banking agency may deny an application under paragraph (a) of this section if the proposed acquisition:

(1) Is contrary to the purposes of this part;

(2) Is manipulative or deceptive;

(3) Subverts the fairness of the conversion;

(4) Is likely to injure you;

(5) Is inconsistent with your plan to meet the credit and lending needs of your proposed market area;

(6) Otherwise violates laws or regulations; or

(7) Does not prudently deploy your conversion proceeds.

[76 FR 49156, Aug. 9, 2011, as amended at 80 FR 28481, May 18, 2015]

§ 192.530 What other requirements apply after I convert?

After you convert, you must:

(a) Promptly register your shares under the Securities Exchange Act of 1934 (15 U.S.C. 78a–78jj, as amended). You may not deregister the shares for three years.

(b) Encourage and assist a market maker to establish and to maintain a market for your shares. A market maker for a security is a dealer who:

(1) Regularly publishes bona fide competitive bid and offer quotations for the security in a recognized inter-dealer quotation system;

(2) Furnishes bona fide competitive bid and offer quotations for the security on request; or

(3) May effect transactions for the security in reasonable quantities at quoted prices with other brokers or dealers.

(c) Use your best efforts to list your shares on a national or regional securities exchange or on the National Association of Securities Dealers Automated Quotation system.

(d) File all post-conversion reports that the appropriate Federal banking agency requires.

Contributions to Charitable Organizations

§ 192.550 May I donate conversion shares or conversion proceeds to a charitable organization?

You may contribute some of your conversion shares or proceeds to a charitable organization if:

(a) Your plan of conversion provides for the proposed contribution;

(b) Your members approve the proposed contribution; and

(c) The IRS either has approved, or approves within two years after formation, the charitable organization as a tax-exempt charitable organization under the Internal Revenue Code.

§ 192.555 How do my members approve a charitable contribution?

At the meeting to consider your conversion, your members must separately approve by at least a majority of the total eligible votes, a contribution of conversion shares or proceeds. If you are in mutual holding company form and adding a charitable contribution as part of a second step stock conversion, you must also have your minority shareholders separately approve the charitable contribution by a majority of their total eligible votes.

§ 192.560 How much may I contribute to a charitable organization?

You may contribute a reasonable amount of conversion shares or proceeds to a charitable organization, if your contribution will not exceed limits for charitable deductions under the Internal Revenue Code and the appropriate Federal banking agency does not object on supervisory grounds. If you are a well-capitalized savings association, the appropriate Federal banking agency generally will not object if you contribute an aggregate amount of eight percent or less of the conversion shares or proceeds.

§ 192.565 What must the charitable organization include in its organizational documents?

The charitable organization's charter (or trust agreement) and gift instrument must provide that:

(a) The charitable organization's primary purpose is to serve and make grants in your local community;

(b) As long as the charitable organization controls shares, it must vote those shares in the same ratio as all other shares voted on each proposal considered by your shareholders;

(c) For at least five years after its organization, one seat on the charitable organization's board of directors (or board of trustees) is reserved for an independent director (or trustee) from your local community. This director may not be your officer, director, or employee, or your affiliate's officer, director, or employee, and should have experience with local community charitable organizations and grant making; and

(d) For at least five years after its organization, one seat on the charitable organization's board of directors (or board of trustees) is reserved for a director from your board of directors or the board of directors of an acquiror or resulting institution in the event of a merger or acquisition of your organization.

§ 192.570 How do I address conflicts of interest involving my directors?

(a) A person who is your director, officer, or employee, or a person who has the power to direct your management or policies, or otherwise owes a fiduciary duty to you (for example, holding company directors) and who will serve as an officer, director, or employee of the charitable organization, is subject to § 163.200 of this chapter. *See* Form AC (Exhibit 9) for further information on operating plans and conflict of interest plans.

(b) Before your board of directors may adopt a plan of conversion that includes a charitable organization, you must identify your directors that will serve on the charitable organization's board. These directors may not participate in your board's discussions concerning contributions to the charitable organization, and may not vote on the matter.

§ 192.575 What other requirements apply to charitable organizations?

(a) The charitable organization's charter (or trust agreement) and the gift instrument for the contribution must provide that:

(1) The appropriate Federal banking agency may examine the charitable organization at the charitable organization's expense;

(2) The charitable organization must comply with all supervisory directives that the appropriate Federal banking agency imposes;

(3) The charitable organization must annually provide the appropriate Federal banking agency with a copy of the annual report that the charitable organization submitted to the IRS;

(4) The charitable organization must operate according to written policies adopted by its board of directors (or board of trustees), including a conflict of interest policy; and

(5) The charitable organization may not engage in self-dealing, and must comply with all laws necessary to maintain its tax-exempt status under the Internal Revenue Code.

(b) You must include the following legend in the stock certificates of shares that you contribute to the charitable organization or that the charitable organization otherwise acquires: "The board of directors must consider the shares that this stock certificate represents as voted in the same ratio as all other shares voted on each proposal considered by the shareholders, as long as the shares are controlled by the charitable organization."

(c) As long as the charitable organization controls shares, you must consider those shares as voted in the same ratio as all of the shares voted on each proposal considered by your shareholders.

(d) After you complete your stock offering, you must submit copies of the following documents to the appropriate OCC licensing office in accordance with part 192.155, or if you are a state savings association, with the appropriate FDIC region: the charitable organization's charter and bylaws (or trust agreement), operating plan (within six months after your stock offering), conflict of interest policy, and the gift instrument for your contributions of either stock or cash to the charitable organization.

Subpart B—Voluntary Supervisory Conversions

§ 192.600 What does this subpart do?

(a) You must comply with this subpart to engage in a voluntary supervisory conversion. This subpart applies to all voluntary supervisory conversions under sections 5(i)(1), (i)(2), and (p) of the Home Owners' Loan Act

(HOLA), 12 U.S.C. 1464(i)(1), (i)(2), and (p).

(b) Subpart A of this part also applies to a voluntary supervisory conversion, unless a requirement is clearly inapplicable.

§ 192.605 How may I conduct a voluntary supervisory conversion?

(a) You may sell your shares or the shares of a holding company to the public under the requirements of subpart A of this part.

(b) You may convert to stock form by merging into an interim Federal-or state-chartered stock association.

(c) You may sell your shares directly to an acquiror, who may be a person, company, depository institution, or depository institution holding company.

(d) You may merge or consolidate with an existing or newly created depository institution. The merger or consolidation must be authorized by, and is subject to, other applicable laws and regulations.

§ 192.610 Do my members have rights in a voluntary supervisory conversion?

Your members do not have the right to approve or participate in a voluntary supervisory conversion, and will not have any legal or beneficial ownership interests in the converted association, unless the appropriate Federal banking agency provides otherwise. Your members may have interests in a liquidation account, if one is established.

ELIGIBILITY

§ 192.625 When is a savings association eligible for a voluntary supervisory conversion?

(a) If you are an insured savings association, you may be eligible to convert under this subpart if:

(1) You are significantly undercapitalized (or you are undercapitalized and a standard conversion that would make you adequately capitalized is not feasible) and you will be a viable entity following the conversion;

(2) Severe financial conditions threaten your stability and a conversion is likely to improve your financial condition;

(3) FDIC will assist you under section 13 of the Federal Deposit Insurance Act, 12 U.S.C. 1823; or

(4) You are in receivership and a conversion will assist you.

(b) You will be a viable entity following the conversion if you satisfy all of the following:

(1) You will be adequately capitalized as a result of the conversion;

(2) You, your proposed conversion, and your acquiror(s) comply with applicable supervisory policies;

(3) The transaction is in your best interest, and the best interest of the Deposit Insurance Fund and the public; and

(4) The transaction will not injure or be detrimental to you, the Deposit Insurance Fund, or the public interest.

§ 192.630 When is a state-chartered savings bank eligible for a voluntary supervisory conversion.

If you are a state-chartered savings bank you may be eligible to convert to a Federal stock savings bank under this subpart if:

(a) FDIC certifies under section 5(o)(2)(C) of the HOLA that severe financial conditions threaten your stability and that the voluntary supervisory conversion is likely to improve your financial condition; or

(b) You meet the following conditions:

(1) Your liabilities exceed your assets, as calculated under generally accepted accounting principles, assuming you are a going concern; and

(2) You will issue a sufficient amount of permanent capital stock to meet your applicable FDIC capital requirement immediately upon completion of the conversion, or FDIC determines that you will achieve an acceptable capital level within an acceptable time period.

PLAN OF SUPERVISORY CONVERSION

§ 192.650 What must I include in my plan of voluntary supervisory conversion?

A majority of your board of directors must adopt a plan of voluntary supervisory conversion. You must include all of the following information in your plan of voluntary supervisory conversion.

(a) Your name and address.

(b) The name, address, date and place of birth, and social security number of each proposed purchaser of conversion shares and a description of that purchaser's relationship to you.

(c) The title, per-unit par value, number, and per-unit and aggregate offering price of shares that you will issue.

(d) The number and percentage of shares that each investor will purchase.

(e) The aggregate number and percentage of shares that each director, officer, and any affiliates or associates of the director or officer will purchase.

(f) A description of any liquidation account.

(g) Certified copies of all resolutions of your board of directors relating to the conversion.

VOLUNTARY SUPERVISORY CONVERSION APPLICATION

§ 192.660 What must I include in my voluntary supervisory conversion application?

You must include all of the following information and documents in a voluntary supervisory conversion application to the appropriate OCC licensing office if you are a Federal savings association and to the appropriate FDIC region if you are a state savings association under this subpart:

(a) *Eligibility.* (1) Evidence establishing that you meet the eligibility requirements under § 192.625 or § 192.630.

(2) An opinion of qualified, independent counsel or an independent, certified public accountant regarding the tax consequences of the conversion, or an IRS ruling indicating that the transaction qualifies as a tax-free reorganization.

(3) An opinion of independent counsel indicating that applicable state law authorizes the voluntary supervisory conversion, if you are a state-chartered savings association converting to state stock form.

(b) *Plan of conversion.* A plan of voluntary supervisory conversion that complies with § 192.650.

(c) *Business plan.* A business plan that complies with § 192.105, when required by the appropriate Federal banking agency.

(d) *Financial data.* (1) Your most recent audited financial statements and Consolidated Reports of Condition and Income or Thrift Financial Report, as appropriate. You must explain how your current capital levels make you eligible to engage in a voluntary supervisory conversion under § 192.625 or § 192.630.

(2) A description of your estimated conversion expenses.

(3) Evidence supporting the value of any non-cash asset contributions. Appraisals must be acceptable to the appropriate Federal banking agency and the non-cash asset must meet all other appropriate Federal banking agency policy guidelines.

(4) Pro forma financial statements that reflect the effects of the transaction. You must identify your tangible, core, and risk-based capital levels and show the adjustments necessary to compute the capital levels. You must prepare your pro forma statements in conformance with the appropriate Federal banking agency regulations and policy.

(e) *Proposed documents.* (1) Your proposed charter and bylaws.

(2) Your proposed stock certificate form.

(f) *Agreements.* (1) A copy of any agreements between you and proposed purchasers.

(2) A copy and description of all existing and proposed employment contracts. You must describe the term, salary, and severance provisions of the contract, the identity and background of the officer or employee to be employed, and the amount of any conversion shares to be purchased by the officer or employee or his or her affiliates or associates.

(g) *Related applications.* (1) All filings required under the securities offering rules of parts 192 and 197 of this chapter.

(2) Any required Control Act notice, rebuttal submission under § 5.50 of this chapter, or copies of any Holding Company Act Applications, including prior-conduct certifications under Regulatory Bulletin 20.

(3) A subordinated debt application, if applicable.

(4) Applications for permission to organize a stock association and for approval of a merger, if applicable, and a copy of any application for Federal Home Loan Bank membership or FDIC insurance of accounts, if applicable.

(5) A statement describing any other applications required under Federal or state banking laws for all transactions related to your conversion, copies of all dispositive documents issued by regulatory authorities relating to the applications, and, if requested by the appropriate Federal banking agency, copies of the applications and related documents.

(h) *Waiver request.* A description of any of the features of your application that do not conform to the requirements of this subpart, including any request for waiver of these requirements.

[76 FR 49156, Aug. 9, 2011, as amended at 80 FR 28481, May 18, 2015]

APPROPRIATE FEDERAL BANKING AGENCY REVIEW OF THE VOLUNTARY SUPERVISORY CONVERSION APPLICATION

§ 192.670 Will the appropriate Federal banking agency approve my voluntary supervisory conversion application?

The appropriate Federal banking agency will generally approve your application to engage in a voluntary supervisory conversion unless it determines:

(a) You do not meet the eligibility requirements for a voluntary supervisory conversion under § 192.625 or § 192.630 or because the proceeds from the sale of your conversion stock, less the expenses of the conversion, would be insufficient to satisfy any applicable viability requirement;

(b) The transaction is detrimental to or would cause potential injury to you or the Deposit Insurance Fund or is contrary to the public interest;

(c) You or your acquiror, or the controlling parties or directors and officers of you or your acquiror, have engaged in unsafe or unsound practices in connection with the voluntary supervisory conversion; or

(d) You fail to justify an employment contract incidental to the conversion, or the employment contract will be an unsafe or unsound practice or represent a sale of control. In a voluntary supervisory conversion, the appropriate Federal banking agency generally will not approve employment contracts of more than one year for your existing management.

§ 192.675 What conditions will the appropriate Federal banking agency impose on an approval?

(a) The appropriate Federal banking agency will condition approval of a voluntary supervisory conversion application on all of the following.

(1) You must complete the conversion stock sale within three months after the appropriate Federal banking agency approves your application. The appropriate Federal banking agency may grant an extension for good cause.

(2) You must comply with all filing requirements of parts 192 and 197 of this chapter.

(3) You must submit an opinion of independent legal counsel indicating that the sale of your shares complies with all applicable state securities law requirements.

(4) You must comply with all applicable laws, rules, and regulations.

(5) You must satisfy any other requirements or conditions the appropriate Federal banking agency may impose.

(b) The appropriate Federal banking agency may condition approval of a voluntary supervisory conversion application on either of the following:

(1) You must satisfy any conditions and restrictions the appropriate Federal banking agency imposes to prevent unsafe or unsound practices, to protect the Deposit Insurance Fund and the public interest, and to prevent potential injury or detriment to you before and after the conversion. The appropriate Federal banking agency may impose these conditions and restrictions on you (before and after the conversion) or, as appropriate, your acquiror, controlling parties, or your directors and officers; or

(2) You must infuse a larger amount of capital, if necessary, for safety and soundness reasons.

OFFERS AND SALES OF STOCK

§ 192.680 How do I sell my shares?

If you convert under this subpart, you must offer and sell your shares under part 197 of this chapter.

POST-CONVERSION

§ 192.690 Who may not acquire additional shares after the voluntary supervisory conversion?

For three years after the completion of a voluntary supervisory conversion, neither you nor your controlling shareholder(s) may acquire shares from minority shareholders without the appropriate Federal banking agency's prior approval.

PART 195—COMMUNITY REINVESTMENT

Subpart A—General

Sec.

195.11 Authority, purposes, and scope.
195.12 Definitions.

Subpart B—Standards for Assessing Performance

195.21 Performance tests, standards, and ratings, in general.
195.22 Lending test.
195.23 Investment test.
195.24 Service test.
195.25 Community development test for wholesale or limited purpose savings associations.
195.26 Small savings association performance standards.
195.27 Strategic plan.
195.28 Assigned ratings.
195.29 Effect of CRA performance on applications.

Subpart C—Records, Reporting, and Disclosure Requirements

195.41 Assessment area delineation.
195.42 Data collection, reporting, and disclosure.
195.43 Content and availability of public file.
195.44 Public notice by savings associations.
195.45 Publication of planned examination schedule.

APPENDIX A TO PART 195—RATINGS
APPENDIX B TO PART 195—CRA NOTICE

AUTHORITY: 12 U.S.C. 1462a, 1463, 1464, 1814, 1816, 1828(c), 2901 through 2908, and 5412(b)(2)(B).

SOURCE: 76 FR 49179, Aug. 9, 2011, unless otherwise noted.

Subpart A—General

§ 195.11 Authority, purposes, and scope.

(a) *Authority.* This part is issued under the Community Reinvestment Act of 1977 (CRA), as amended (12 U.S.C. 2901 *et seq.*); section 5, as amended, and sections 3, and 4, as added, of the Home Owners' Loan Act of 1933 (12 U.S.C. 1462a, 1463, and 1464); and sections 4, 6, and 18(c), as amended of the Federal Deposit Insurance Act (12 U.S.C. 1814, 1816, 1828(c)).

(b) *Purposes.* In enacting the CRA, the Congress required each appropriate Federal financial supervisory agency to assess an institution's record of helping to meet the credit needs of the local communities in which the institution is chartered, consistent with the safe and sound operation of the institution, and to take this record into account in the agency's evaluation of an application for a deposit facility by the institution. This part is intended to carry out the purposes of the CRA by:

(1) Establishing the framework and criteria by which the appropriate Federal banking agency assesses a savings association's record of helping to meet the credit needs of its entire community, including low- and moderate-income neighborhoods, consistent with the safe and sound operation of the savings association; and

(2) Providing that the appropriate Federal banking agency takes that record into account in considering certain applications.

(c) *Scope*—(1) *General.* This part applies to all savings associations except as provided in paragraph (c)(2) of this section.

(2) *Certain special purpose savings associations.* This part does not apply to special purpose savings associations that do not perform commercial or retail banking services by granting credit to the public in the ordinary course of business, other than as incident to their specialized operations. These associations include banker's banks, as defined in 12 U.S.C. 24 (Seventh), and associations that engage only in one or

more of the following activities: Providing cash management controlled disbursement services or serving as correspondent associations, trust companies, or clearing agents.

§ 195.12 Definitions.

For purposes of this part, the following definitions apply:

(a) *Affiliate* means any company that controls, is controlled by, or is under common control with another company. The term "control" has the meaning given to that term in 12 U.S.C. 1841(a)(2), and a company is under common control with another company if both companies are directly or indirectly controlled by the same company.

(b) *Area median income* means:

(1) The median family income for the MSA, if a person or geography is located in an MSA, or for the metropolitan division, if a person or geography is located in an MSA that has been subdivided into metropolitan divisions; or

(2) The statewide nonmetropolitan median family income, if a person or geography is located outside an MSA.

(c) *Assessment area* means a geographic area delineated in accordance with § 195.41.

(d) *Automated teller machine (ATM)* means an automated, unstaffed banking facility owned or operated by, or operated exclusively for, the savings association at which deposits are received, cash dispersed, or money lent.

(e) [Reserved]

(f) *Branch* means a staffed banking facility authorized as a branch, whether shared or unshared, including, for example, a mini-branch in a grocery store or a branch operated in conjunction with any other local business or nonprofit organization.

(g) *Community development* means:

(1) Affordable housing (including multifamily rental housing) for low or moderate-income individuals;

(2) Community services targeted to low- or moderate-income individuals;

(3) Activities that promote economic development by financing businesses or farms that meet the size eligibility standards of the Small Business Administration's Development Company or Small Business Investment Company programs (13 CFR 121.301) or have gross annual revenues of $1 million or less; or

(4) Activities that revitalize or stabilize—

(i) Low- or moderate-income geographies;

(ii) Designated disaster areas; or

(iii) Distressed or underserved, nonmetropolitan middle-income geographies designated by the appropriate Federal banking agency based on—

(A) Rates of poverty, unemployment, and population loss; or

(B) Population size, density, and dispersion. Activities revitalize and stabilize geographies designated based on population size, density, and dispersion if they help to meet essential community needs, including needs of low- and moderate-income individuals.

(h) *Community development loan* means a loan that:

(1) Has as its primary purpose community development; and

(2) Except in the case of a wholesale or limited purpose savings association:

(i) Has not been reported or collected by the savings association or an affiliate for consideration in the savings association's assessment as a home mortgage, small business, small farm, or consumer loan, unless the loan is for a multifamily dwelling (as defined in § 1003.2(n) of this title); and

(ii) Benefits the savings association's assessment area(s) or a broader statewide or regional area that includes the savings association's assessment area(s).

(i) *Community development service* means a service that:

(1) Has as its primary purpose community development;

(2) Is related to the provision of financial services; and

(3) Has not been considered in the evaluation of the savings association's retail banking services under § 195.24(d).

(j) *Consumer loan* means a loan to one or more individuals for household, family, or other personal expenditures. A consumer loan does not include a home mortgage, small business, or small farm loan. Consumer loans include the following categories of loans:

(1) *Motor vehicle loan*, which is a consumer loan extended for the purchase of and secured by a motor vehicle;

(2) *Credit card loan*, which is a line of credit for household, family, or other personal expenditures that is accessed by a borrower's use of a "credit card," as this term is defined in § 1026.2 of this title;

(3) *Other secured consumer loan*, which is a secured consumer loan that is not included in one of the other categories of consumer loans; and

(4) *Other unsecured consumer loan*, which is an unsecured consumer loan that is not included in one of the other categories of consumer loans.

(k) *Geography* means a census tract delineated by the United States Bureau of the Census in the most recent decennial census.

(l) *Home mortgage loan* means a closed-end mortgage loan or an open-end line of credit as these terms are defined under § 1003.2 of this title and that is not an excluded transaction under § 1003.3(c)(1) through (10) and (13) of this title.

(m) *Income level* includes:

(1) *Low-income*, which means an individual income that is less than 50 percent of the area median income or a median family income that is less than 50 percent in the case of a geography.

(2) *Moderate-income*, which means an individual income that is at least 50 percent and less than 80 percent of the area median income or a median family income that is at least 50 and less than 80 percent in the case of a geography.

(3) *Middle-income*, which means an individual income that is at least 80 percent and less than 120 percent of the area median income or a median family income that is at least 80 and less than 120 percent in the case of a geography.

(4) *Upper-income*, which means an individual income that is 120 percent or more of the area median income or a median family income that is 120 percent or more in the case of a geography.

(n) *Limited purpose savings association* means a savings association that offers only a narrow product line (such as credit card or motor vehicle loans) to a regional or broader market and for which a designation as a limited purpose savings association is in effect, in accordance with § 195.25(b).

(o) *Loan location*. A loan is located as follows:

(1) A consumer loan is located in the geography where the borrower resides;

(2) A home mortgage loan is located in the geography where the property to which the loan relates is located; and

(3) A small business or small farm loan is located in the geography where the main business facility or farm is located or where the loan proceeds otherwise will be applied, as indicated by the borrower.

(p) *Loan production office* means a staffed facility, other than a branch, that is open to the public and that provides lending-related services, such as loan information and applications.

(q) *Metropolitan division* means a metropolitan division as defined by the Director of the Office of Management and Budget.

(r) *MSA* means a metropolitan statistical area as defined by the Director of the Office of Management and Budget.

(s) *Nonmetropolitan area* means any area that is not located in an MSA.

(t) *Qualified investment* means a lawful investment, deposit, membership share, or grant that has as its primary purpose community development.

(u) *Small savings association*—(1) *Definition. Small savings association* means a savings association that, as of December 31 of either of the prior two calendar years, had assets of less than $1.284 billion. *Intermediate small savings association* means a small savings association with assets of at least $321 million as of December 31 of both of the prior two calendar years and less than $1.284 billion as of December 31 of either of the prior two calendar years.

(2) *Adjustment*. The dollar figures in paragraph (u)(1) of this section shall be adjusted annually and published by the OCC based on the year-to-year change in the average of the Consumer Price Index for Urban Wage Earners and Clerical Workers, not seasonally adjusted, for each twelve-month period ending in November, with rounding to the nearest million.

(v) *Small business loan* means a loan included in "loans to small businesses" as defined in the instructions for preparation of the Thrift Financial Report

(TFR) or Consolidated Reports of Condition and Income (Call Report), as appropriate.

(w) *Small farm loan* means a loan included in "loans to small farms" as defined in the instructions for preparation of the TFR or Call Report, as appropriate.

(x) *Wholesale savings association* means a savings association that is not in the business of extending home mortgage, small business, small farm, or consumer loans to retail customers, and for which a designation as a wholesale savings association is in effect, in accordance with § 195.25(b).

[76 FR 49179, Aug. 9, 2011, as amended at 76 FR 79530, Dec. 22, 2011; 77 FR 75523, Dec. 21, 2012; 80 FR 81164, Dec. 29, 2015; 82 FR 55742, Nov. 24, 2017; 83 FR 66603, Dec. 27, 2018]

Subpart B—Standards for Assessing Performance

§ 195.21 Performance tests, standards, and ratings, in general.

(a) *Performance tests and standards.* The appropriate Federal banking agency assesses the CRA performance of a savings association in an examination as follows:

(1) *Lending, investment, and service tests.* The appropriate Federal banking agency applies the lending, investment, and service tests, as provided in §§ 195.22 through 195.24, in evaluating the performance of a savings association, except as provided in paragraphs (a)(2), (a)(3), and (a)(4) of this section.

(2) *Community development test for wholesale or limited purpose savings associations.* The appropriate Federal banking agency applies the community development test for a wholesale or limited purpose savings association, as provided in § 195.25, except as provided in paragraph (a)(4) of this section.

(3) *Small savings association performance standards.* The appropriate Federal banking agency applies the small savings association performance standards as provided in § 195.26 in evaluating the performance of a small savings association or a savings association that was a small savings association during the prior calendar year, unless the savings association elects to be assessed as provided in paragraphs (a)(1), (a)(2), or (a)(4) of this section. The savings association may elect to be assessed as provided in paragraph (a)(1) of this section only if it collects and reports the data required for other savings associations under § 195.42.

(4) *Strategic plan.* The appropriate Federal banking agency evaluates the performance of a savings association under a strategic plan if the savings association submits, and the appropriate Federal banking agency approves, a strategic plan as provided in § 195.27.

(b) *Performance context.* The appropriate Federal banking agency applies the tests and standards in paragraph (a) of this section and also considers whether to approve a proposed strategic plan in the context of:

(1) Demographic data on median income levels, distribution of household income, nature of housing stock, housing costs, and other relevant data pertaining to a savings association's assessment area(s);

(2) Any information about lending, investment, and service opportunities in the savings association's assessment area(s) maintained by the savings association or obtained from community organizations, state, local, and tribal governments, economic development agencies, or other sources;

(3) The savings association's product offerings and business strategy as determined from data provided by the savings association;

(4) Institutional capacity and constraints, including the size and financial condition of the savings association, the economic climate (national, regional, and local), safety and soundness limitations, and any other factors that significantly affect the savings association's ability to provide lending, investments, or services in its assessment area(s);

(5) The savings association's past performance and the performance of similarly situated lenders;

(6) The savings association's public file, as described in § 195.43, and any written comments about the savings association's CRA performance submitted to the savings association or the appropriate Federal banking agency; and

(7) Any other information deemed relevant by the appropriate Federal banking agency.

(c) *Assigned ratings.* The appropriate Federal banking agency assigns to a savings association one of the following four ratings pursuant to § 195.28 and appendix A of this part: "outstanding"; "satisfactory"; "needs to improve"; or "substantial noncompliance," as provided in 12 U.S.C. 2906(b)(2). The rating assigned by the appropriate Federal banking agency reflects the savings association's record of helping to meet the credit needs of its entire community, including low- and moderate-income neighborhoods, consistent with the safe and sound operation of the savings association.

(d) *Safe and sound operations.* This part and the CRA do not require a savings association to make loans or investments or to provide services that are inconsistent with safe and sound operations. To the contrary, the appropriate Federal banking agency anticipates savings associations can meet the standards of this part with safe and sound loans, investments, and services on which the savings associations expect to make a profit. Savings associations are permitted and encouraged to develop and apply flexible underwriting standards for loans that benefit low- or moderate-income geographies or individuals, only if consistent with safe and sound operations.

(e) *Low-cost education loans provided to low-income borrowers.* In assessing and taking into account the record of a savings association under this part, the appropriate Federal banking agency considers, as a factor, low-cost education loans originated by the savings association to borrowers, particularly in its assessment area(s), who have an individual income that is less than 50 percent of the area median income. For purposes of this paragraph, "low-cost education loans" means any education loan, as defined in section 140(a)(7) of the Truth in Lending Act (15 U.S.C. 1650(a)(7)) (including a loan under a state or local education loan program), originated by the savings association for a student at an "institution of higher education," as that term is generally defined in sections 101 and 102 of the Higher Education Act of 1965 (20 U.S.C. 1001 and 1002) and the implementing regulations published by the U.S. Department of Education, with interest rates and fees no greater than those of comparable education loans offered directly by the U.S. Department of Education. Such rates and fees are specified in section 455 of the Higher Education Act of 1965 (20 U.S.C. 1087e).

(f) *Activities in cooperation with minority- or women-owned financial institutions and low-income credit unions.* In assessing and taking into account the record of a nonminority-owned and nonwomen-owned savings association under this part, the appropriate Federal banking agency considers as a factor capital investment, loan participation, and other ventures undertaken by the savings association in cooperation with minority- and women-owned financial institutions and low-income credit unions. Such activities must help meet the credit needs of local communities in which the minority- and women-owned financial institutions and low-income credit unions are chartered. To be considered, such activities need not also benefit the savings association's assessment area(s) or the broader statewide or regional area that includes the savings association's assessment area(s).

§ 195.22 Lending test.

(a) *Scope of test.* (1) The lending test evaluates a savings association's record of helping to meet the credit needs of its assessment area(s) through its lending activities by considering a savings association's home mortgage, small business, small farm, and community development lending. If consumer lending constitutes a substantial majority of a savings association's business, the appropriate Federal banking agency will evaluate the savings association's consumer lending in one or more of the following categories: motor vehicle, credit card, other secured, and other unsecured loans. In addition, at a savings association's option, the appropriate Federal banking agency will evaluate one or more categories of consumer lending, if the savings association has collected and maintained, as required in § 195.42(c)(1), the data for each category that the savings association elects to have the appropriate Federal banking agency evaluate.

(2) The appropriate Federal banking agency considers originations and purchases of loans. The appropriate Federal banking agency will also consider any other loan data the savings association may choose to provide, including data on loans outstanding, commitments and letters of credit.

(3) A savings association may ask the appropriate Federal banking agency to consider loans originated or purchased by consortia in which the savings association participates or by third parties in which the savings association has invested only if the loans meet the definition of community development loans and only in accordance with paragraph (d) of this section. The appropriate Federal banking agency will not consider these loans under any criterion of the lending test except the community development lending criterion.

(b) *Performance criteria.* The appropriate Federal banking agency evaluates a savings association's lending performance pursuant to the following criteria:

(1) *Lending activity.* The number and amount of the savings association's home mortgage, small business, small farm, and consumer loans, if applicable, in the savings association's assessment area(s);

(2) *Geographic distribution.* The geographic distribution of the savings association's home mortgage, small business, small farm, and consumer loans, if applicable, based on the loan location, including:

(i) The proportion of the savings association's lending in the savings association's assessment area(s);

(ii) The dispersion of lending in the savings association's assessment area(s); and

(iii) The number and amount of loans in low-, moderate-, middle-, and upper-income geographies in the savings association's assessment area(s);

(3) *Borrower characteristics.* The distribution, particularly in the savings association's assessment area(s), of the savings association's home mortgage, small business, small farm, and consumer loans, if applicable, based on borrower characteristics, including the number and amount of:

(i) Home mortgage loans to low-, moderate-, middle-, and upper-income individuals;

(ii) Small business and small farm loans to businesses and farms with gross annual revenues of $1 million or less;

(iii) Small business and small farm loans by loan amount at origination; and

(iv) Consumer loans, if applicable, to low-, moderate-, middle-, and upper-income individuals;

(4) *Community development lending.* The savings association's community development lending, including the number and amount of community development loans, and their complexity and innovativeness; and

(5) *Innovative or flexible lending practices.* The savings association's use of innovative or flexible lending practices in a safe and sound manner to address the credit needs of low- or moderate-income individuals or geographies.

(c) *Affiliate lending.* (1) At a savings association's option, the appropriate Federal banking agency will consider loans by an affiliate of the savings association, if the savings association provides data on the affiliate's loans pursuant to § 195.42.

(2) The appropriate Federal banking agency considers affiliate lending subject to the following constraints:

(i) No affiliate may claim a loan origination or loan purchase if another institution claims the same loan origination or purchase; and

(ii) If a savings association elects to have the appropriate Federal banking agency consider loans within a particular lending category made by one or more of the savings association's affiliates in a particular assessment area, the savings association shall elect to have the appropriate Federal banking agency consider, in accordance with paragraph (c)(1) of this section, all the loans within that lending category in that particular assessment area made by all of the savings association's affiliates.

(3) The appropriate Federal banking agency does not consider affiliate lending in assessing a savings association's performance under paragraph (b)(2)(i) of this section.

(d) *Lending by a consortium or a third party.* Community development loans originated or purchased by a consortium in which the savings association participates or by a third party in which the savings association has invested:

(1) Will be considered, at the savings association's option, if the savings association reports the data pertaining to these loans under § 195.42(b)(2); and

(2) May be allocated among participants or investors, as they choose, for purposes of the lending test, except that no participant or investor:

(i) May claim a loan origination or loan purchase if another participant or investor claims the same loan origination or purchase; or

(ii) May claim loans accounting for more than its percentage share (based on the level of its participation or investment) of the total loans originated by the consortium or third party.

(e) *Lending performance rating.* The appropriate Federal banking agency rates a savings association's lending performance as provided in appendix A of this part.

[76 FR 49179, Aug. 9, 2011, as amended at 82 FR 55742, Nov. 24, 2017]

§ 195.23 Investment test.

(a) *Scope of test.* The investment test evaluates a savings association's record of helping to meet the credit needs of its assessment area(s) through qualified investments that benefit its assessment area(s) or a broader statewide or regional area that includes the savings association's assessment area(s).

(b) *Exclusion.* Activities considered under the lending or service tests may not be considered under the investment test.

(c) *Affiliate investment.* At a savings association's option, the appropriate Federal banking agency will consider, in its assessment of a savings association's investment performance, a qualified investment made by an affiliate of the savings association, if the qualified investment is not claimed by any other institution.

(d) *Disposition of branch premises.* Donating, selling on favorable terms, or making available on a rent-free basis a branch of the savings association that is located in a predominantly minority neighborhood to a minority depository institution or women's depository institution (as these terms are defined in 12 U.S.C. 2907(b)) will be considered as a qualified investment.

(e) *Performance criteria.* The appropriate Federal banking agency evaluates the investment performance of a savings association pursuant to the following criteria:

(1) The dollar amount of qualified investments;

(2) The innovativeness or complexity of qualified investments;

(3) The responsiveness of qualified investments to credit and community development needs; and

(4) The degree to which the qualified investments are not routinely provided by private investors.

(f) *Investment performance rating.* The appropriate Federal banking agency rates a savings association's investment performance as provided in appendix A of this part.

§ 195.24 Service test.

(a) *Scope of test.* The service test evaluates a savings association's record of helping to meet the credit needs of its assessment area(s) by analyzing both the availability and effectiveness of a savings association's systems for delivering retail banking services and the extent and innovativeness of its community development services.

(b) *Area(s) benefitted.* Community development services must benefit a savings association's assessment area(s) or a broader statewide or regional area that includes the savings association's assessment area(s).

(c) *Affiliate service.* At a savings association's option, the appropriate Federal banking agency will consider, in its assessment of a savings association's service performance, a community development service provided by an affiliate of the savings association, if the community development service is not claimed by any other institution.

(d) *Performance criteria—retail banking services.* The appropriate Federal banking agency evaluates the availability and effectiveness of a savings association's systems for delivering retail banking services, pursuant to the following criteria:

(1) The current distribution of the savings association's branches among low-, moderate-, middle-, and upper-income geographies;

(2) In the context of its current distribution of the savings association's branches, the savings association's record of opening and closing branches, particularly branches located in low- or moderate-income geographies or primarily serving low- or moderate-income individuals;

(3) The availability and effectiveness of alternative systems for delivering retail banking services (*e.g.*, ATMs, ATMs not owned or operated by or exclusively for the savings association, banking by telephone or computer, loan production offices, and bank-at-work or bank-by-mail programs) in low- and moderate-income geographies and to low- and moderate-income individuals; and

(4) The range of services provided in low-, moderate-, middle-, and upper-income geographies and the degree to which the services are tailored to meet the needs of those geographies.

(e) *Performance criteria—community development services.* The appropriate Federal banking agency evaluates community development services pursuant to the following criteria:

(1) The extent to which the savings association provides community development services; and

(2) The innovativeness and responsiveness of community development services.

(f) *Service performance rating.* The appropriate Federal banking agency rates a savings association's service performance as provided in appendix A of this part.

§ 195.25 Community development test for wholesale or limited purpose savings associations.

(a) *Scope of test.* The appropriate Federal banking agency assesses a wholesale or limited purpose savings association's record of helping to meet the credit needs of its assessment area(s) under the community development test through its community development lending, qualified investments, or community development services.

(b) *Designation as a wholesale or limited purpose savings association.* In order to receive a designation as a wholesale or limited purpose savings association, a savings association shall file a request, in writing, with the appropriate Federal banking agency, at least three months prior to the proposed effective date of the designation. If the appropriate Federal banking agency approves the designation, it remains in effect until the savings association requests revocation of the designation or until one year after the appropriate Federal banking agency notifies the savings association that the appropriate Federal banking agency has revoked the designation on its own initiative.

(c) *Performance criteria.* The appropriate Federal banking agency evaluates the community development performance of a wholesale or limited purpose savings association pursuant to the following criteria:

(1) The number and amount of community development loans (including originations and purchases of loans and other community development loan data provided by the savings association, such as data on loans outstanding, commitments, and letters of credit), qualified investments, or community development services;

(2) The use of innovative or complex qualified investments, community development loans, or community development services and the extent to which the investments are not routinely provided by private investors; and

(3) The savings association's responsiveness to credit and community development needs.

(d) *Indirect activities.* At a savings association's option, the appropriate Federal banking agency will consider in its community development performance assessment:

(1) Qualified investments or community development services provided by an affiliate of the savings association, if the investments or services are not claimed by any other institution; and

(2) Community development lending by affiliates, consortia and third parties, subject to the requirements and limitations in § 195.22(c) and (d).

(e) *Benefit to assessment area(s)*—(1) *Benefit inside assessment area(s).* The appropriate Federal banking agency considers all qualified investments, community development loans, and community development services that benefit areas within the savings association's assessment area(s) or a broader statewide or regional area that includes the savings association's assessment area(s).

(2) *Benefit outside assessment area(s).* The appropriate Federal banking agency considers the qualified investments, community development loans, and community development services that benefit areas outside the savings association's assessment area(s), if the savings association has adequately addressed the needs of its assessment area(s).

(f) *Community development performance rating.* The appropriate Federal banking agency rates a savings association's community development performance as provided in appendix A of this part.

§ 195.26 Small savings association performance standards.

(a) *Performance criteria*—(1) *Small savings associations that are not intermediate small savings associations.* The appropriate Federal banking agency evaluates the record of a small savings association that is not, or that was not during the prior calendar year, an intermediate small savings association, of helping to meet the credit needs of its assessment area(s) pursuant to the criteria set forth in paragraph (b) of this section.

(2) *Intermediate small savings associations.* The appropriate Federal banking agency evaluates the record of a small savings association that is, or that was during the prior calendar year, an intermediate small savings association, of helping to meet the credit needs of its assessment area(s) pursuant to the criteria set forth in paragraphs (b) and (c) of this section.

(b) *Lending test.* A small savings association's lending performance is evaluated pursuant to the following criteria:

(1) The savings association's loan-to-deposit ratio, adjusted for seasonal variation, and, as appropriate, other lending-related activities, such as loan originations for sale to the secondary markets, community development loans, or qualified investments;

(2) The percentage of loans and, as appropriate, other lending-related activities located in the savings association's assessment area(s);

(3) The savings association's record of lending to and, as appropriate, engaging in other lending-related activities for borrowers of different income levels and businesses and farms of different sizes;

(4) The geographic distribution of the savings association's loans; and

(5) The savings association's record of taking action, if warranted, in response to written complaints about its performance in helping to meet credit needs in its assessment area(s).

(c) *Community development test.* An intermediate small savings association's community development performance also is evaluated pursuant to the following criteria:

(1) The number and amount of community development loans;

(2) The number and amount of qualified investments;

(3) The extent to which the savings association provides community development services; and

(4) The savings association's responsiveness through such activities to community development lending, investment, and services needs.

(d) *Small savings association performance rating.* The appropriate Federal banking agency rates the performance of a savings association evaluated under this section as provided in appendix A of this part.

§ 195.27 Strategic plan.

(a) *Alternative election.* The appropriate Federal banking agency will assess a savings association's record of helping to meet the credit needs of its assessment area(s) under a strategic plan if:

(1) The savings association has submitted the plan to the appropriate Federal banking agency as provided for in this section;

(2) The appropriate Federal banking agency has approved the plan;

(3) The plan is in effect; and

(4) The savings association has been operating under an approved plan for at least one year.

(b) *Data reporting.* The appropriate Federal banking agency's approval of a plan does not affect the savings association's obligation, if any, to report data as required by § 195.42.

(c) *Plans in general*—(1) *Term.* A plan may have a term of no more than five years, and any multi-year plan must include annual interim measurable goals under which the appropriate Federal banking agency will evaluate the savings association's performance.

(2) *Multiple assessment areas.* A savings association with more than one assessment area may prepare a single plan for all of its assessment areas or one or more plans for one or more of its assessment areas.

(3) *Treatment of affiliates.* Affiliated institutions may prepare a joint plan if the plan provides measurable goals for each institution. Activities may be allocated among institutions at the institutions' option, provided that the same activities are not considered for more than one institution.

(d) *Public participation in plan development.* Before submitting a plan to the appropriate Federal banking agency for approval, a savings association shall:

(1) Informally seek suggestions from members of the public in its assessment area(s) covered by the plan while developing the plan;

(2) Once the savings association has developed a plan, formally solicit public comment on the plan for at least 30 days by publishing notice in at least one newspaper of general circulation in each assessment area covered by the plan; and

(3) During the period of formal public comment, make copies of the plan available for review by the public at no cost at all offices of the savings association in any assessment area covered by the plan and provide copies of the plan upon request for a reasonable fee to cover copying and mailing, if applicable.

(e) *Submission of plan.* The savings association shall submit its plan to the appropriate Federal banking agency at least three months prior to the proposed effective date of the plan. The savings association shall also submit with its plan a description of its informal efforts to seek suggestions from members of the public, any written public comment received, and, if the plan was revised in light of the comment received, the initial plan as released for public comment.

(f) *Plan content*—(1) *Measurable goals.* (i) A savings association shall specify in its plan measurable goals for helping to meet the credit needs of each assessment area covered by the plan, particularly the needs of low- and moderate-income geographies and low- and moderate-income individuals, through lending, investment, and services, as appropriate.

(ii) A savings association shall address in its plan all three performance categories and, unless the savings association has been designated as a wholesale or limited purpose savings association, shall emphasize lending and lending-related activities. Nevertheless, a different emphasis, including a focus on one or more performance categories, may be appropriate if responsive to the characteristics and credit needs of its assessment area(s), considering public comment and the savings association's capacity and constraints, product offerings, and business strategy.

(2) *Confidential information.* A savings association may submit additional information to the appropriate Federal banking agency on a confidential basis, but the goals stated in the plan must be sufficiently specific to enable the public and the appropriate Federal banking agency to judge the merits of the plan.

(3) *Satisfactory and outstanding goals.* A savings association shall specify in its plan measurable goals that constitute "satisfactory" performance. A plan may specify measurable goals that constitute "outstanding" performance. If a savings association submits, and the appropriate Federal banking agency approves, both "satisfactory" and "outstanding" performance goals, the appropriate Federal banking agency will consider the savings association eligible for an "outstanding" performance rating.

(4) *Election if satisfactory goals not substantially met.* A savings association

may elect in its plan that, if the savings association fails to meet substantially its plan goals for a satisfactory rating, the appropriate Federal banking agency will evaluate the savings association's performance under the lending, investment, and service tests, the community development test, or the small savings association performance standards, as appropriate.

(g) *Plan approval*—(1) *Timing.* The appropriate Federal banking agency will act upon a plan within 60 calendar days after it receives the complete plan and other material required under paragraph (e) of this section. If the appropriate Federal banking agency fails to act within this time period, the plan shall be deemed approved unless the appropriate Federal banking agency extends the review period for good cause.

(2) *Public participation.* In evaluating the plan's goals, the appropriate Federal banking agency considers the public's involvement in formulating the plan, written public comment on the plan, and any response by the savings association to public comment on the plan.

(3) *Criteria for evaluating plan.* The appropriate Federal banking agency evaluates a plan's measurable goals using the following criteria, as appropriate:

(i) The extent and breadth of lending or lending-related activities, including, as appropriate, the distribution of loans among different geographies, businesses and farms of different sizes, and individuals of different income levels, the extent of community development lending, and the use of innovative or flexible lending practices to address credit needs;

(ii) The amount and innovativeness, complexity, and responsiveness of the savings association's qualified investments; and

(iii) The availability and effectiveness of the savings association's systems for delivering retail banking services and the extent and innovativeness of the savings association's community development services.

(h) *Plan amendment.* During the term of a plan, a savings association may request the appropriate Federal banking agency to approve an amendment to the plan on grounds that there has been a material change in circumstances. The savings association shall develop an amendment to a previously approved plan in accordance with the public participation requirements of paragraph (d) of this section.

(i) *Plan assessment.* The appropriate Federal banking agency approves the goals and assesses performance under a plan as provided for in appendix A of this part.

§ 195.28 Assigned ratings.

(a) *Ratings in general.* Subject to paragraphs (b) and (c) of this section, the appropriate Federal banking agency assigns to a savings association a rating of "outstanding," "satisfactory," "needs to improve," or "substantial noncompliance" based on the savings association's performance under the lending, investment and service tests, the community development test, the small savings association performance standards, or an approved strategic plan, as applicable.

(b) *Lending, investment, and service tests.* The appropriate Federal banking agency assigns a rating for a savings association assessed under the lending, investment, and service tests in accordance with the following principles:

(1) A savings association that receives an "outstanding" rating on the lending test receives an assigned rating of at least "satisfactory";

(2) A savings association that receives an "outstanding" rating on both the service test and the investment test and a rating of at least "high satisfactory" on the lending test receives an assigned rating of "outstanding"; and

(3) No savings association may receive an assigned rating of "satisfactory" or higher unless it receives a rating of at least "low satisfactory" on the lending test.

(c) *Effect of evidence of discriminatory or other illegal credit practices.* (1) The appropriate Federal banking agency's evaluation of a savings association's CRA performance is adversely affected by evidence of discriminatory or other illegal credit practices in any geography by the savings association or in any assessment area by any affiliate whose loans have been considered as part of the savings association's lending performance. In connection with any type of lending activity described in § 195.22(a), evidence of discriminatory or other credit practices that violate an applicable law, rule, or regulation includes, but is not limited to:

(i) Discrimination against applicants on a prohibited basis in violation, for example, of the Equal Credit Opportunity Act or the Fair Housing Act;

(ii) Violations of the Home Ownership and Equity Protection Act;

(iii) Violations of section 5 of the Federal Trade Commission Act;

(iv) Violations of section 8 of the Real Estate Settlement Procedures Act; and

(v) Violations of the Truth in Lending Act provisions regarding a consumer's right of rescission.

(2) In determining the effect of evidence of practices described in paragraph (c)(1) of this section on the savings association's assigned rating, the appropriate Federal banking agency considers the nature, extent, and strength of the evidence of the practices; the policies and procedures that the savings association (or affiliate, as applicable) has in place to prevent the practices; any corrective action that the savings association (or affiliate, as applicable) has taken or has committed to take, including voluntary corrective action resulting from self-assessment; and any other relevant information.

§ 195.29 Effect of CRA performance on applications.

(a) *CRA performance.* Among other factors, the appropriate Federal banking agency takes into account the record of performance under the CRA of each applicant savings association, and for applications under section 10(e) of the Home Owners' Loan Act (12 U.S.C. 1467a(e)), of each proposed subsidiary savings association, in considering an application for:

(1) The establishment of a domestic branch or other facility that would be authorized to take deposits;

(2) The relocation of the main office or a branch;

(3) The merger or consolidation with or the acquisition of the assets or assumption of the liabilities of an insured depository institution requiring appropriate Federal banking agency approval under the Bank Merger Act (12 U.S.C. 1828(c));

(4) A Federal thrift charter; and

(5) Acquisitions subject to section 10(e) of the Home Owners' Loan Act (12 U.S.C. 1467a(e)).

(b) *Charter application.* An applicant for a Federal thrift charter shall submit with its application a description of how it will meet its CRA objectives. The appropriate Federal banking agency takes the description into account in considering the application and may deny or condition approval on that basis.

(c) *Interested parties.* The appropriate Federal banking agency takes into account any views expressed by interested parties that are submitted in accordance with the applicable comment procedures in considering CRA performance in an application listed in paragraphs (a) and (b) of this section.

(d) *Denial or conditional approval of application.* A savings association's record of performance may be the basis for denying or conditioning approval of an application listed in paragraph (a) of this section.

(e) *Insured depository institution.* For purposes of this section, the term "insured depository institution" has the meaning given to that term in 12 U.S.C. 1813.

Subpart C—Records, Reporting, and Disclosure Requirements

§ 195.41 Assessment area delineation.

(a) *In general.* A savings association shall delineate one or more assessment areas within which the appropriate Federal banking agency evaluates the savings association's record of helping to meet the credit needs of its community. The appropriate Federal banking agency does not evaluate the savings association's delineation of its assessment area(s) as a separate performance criterion, but the appropriate Federal banking agency reviews the delineation for compliance with the requirements of this section.

(b) *Geographic area(s) for wholesale or limited purpose savings associations.* The assessment area(s) for a wholesale or limited purpose savings association must consist generally of one or more

MSAs or metropolitan divisions (using the MSA or metropolitan division boundaries that were in effect as of January 1 of the calendar year in which the delineation is made) or one or more contiguous political subdivisions, such as counties, cities, or towns, in which the savings association has its main office, branches, and deposit-taking ATMs.

(c) *Geographic area(s) for other savings associations.* The assessment area(s) for a savings association other than a wholesale or limited purpose savings association must:

(1) Consist generally of one or more MSAs or metropolitan divisions (using the MSA or metropolitan division boundaries that were in effect as of January 1 of the calendar year in which the delineation is made) or one or more contiguous political subdivisions, such as counties, cities, or towns; and

(2) Include the geographies in which the savings association has its main office, its branches, and its deposit-taking ATMs, as well as the surrounding geographies in which the savings association has originated or purchased a substantial portion of its loans (including home mortgage loans, small business and small farm loans, and any other loans the savings association chooses, such as those consumer loans on which the savings association elects to have its performance assessed).

(d) *Adjustments to geographic area(s).* A savings association may adjust the boundaries of its assessment area(s) to include only the portion of a political subdivision that it reasonably can be expected to serve. An adjustment is particularly appropriate in the case of an assessment area that otherwise would be extremely large, of unusual configuration, or divided by significant geographic barriers.

(e) *Limitations on the delineation of an assessment area.* Each savings association's assessment area(s):

(1) Must consist only of whole geographies;

(2) May not reflect illegal discrimination;

(3) May not arbitrarily exclude low- or moderate-income geographies, taking into account the savings association's size and financial condition; and

(4) May not extend substantially beyond an MSA boundary or beyond a state boundary unless the assessment area is located in a multistate MSA. If a savings association serves a geographic area that extends substantially beyond a state boundary, the savings association shall delineate separate assessment areas for the areas in each state. If a savings association serves a geographic area that extends substantially beyond an MSA boundary, the savings association shall delineate separate assessment areas for the areas inside and outside the MSA.

(f) *Savings associations serving military personnel.* Notwithstanding the requirements of this section, a savings association whose business predominantly consists of serving the needs of military personnel or their dependents who are not located within a defined geographic area may delineate its entire deposit customer base as its assessment area.

(g) *Use of assessment area(s).* The appropriate Federal banking agency uses the assessment area(s) delineated by a savings association in its evaluation of the savings association's CRA performance unless the appropriate Federal banking agency determines that the assessment area(s) do not comply with the requirements of this section.

§ 195.42 Data collection, reporting, and disclosure.

(a) *Loan information required to be collected and maintained.* A savings association, except a small savings association, shall collect, and maintain in machine readable form (as prescribed by the appropriate Federal banking agency) until the completion of its next CRA examination, the following data for each small business or small farm loan originated or purchased by the savings association:

(1) A unique number or alpha-numeric symbol that can be used to identify the relevant loan file;

(2) The loan amount at origination;

(3) The loan location; and

(4) An indicator whether the loan was to a business or farm with gross annual revenues of $1 million or less.

(b) *Loan information required to be reported.* A savings association, except a small savings association or a savings association that was a small savings association during the prior calendar year, shall report annually by March 1 to the appropriate Federal banking agency in machine readable form (as prescribed by the agency) the following data for the prior calendar year:

(1) *Small business and small farm loan data.* For each geography in which the savings association originated or purchased a small business or small farm loan, the aggregate number and amount of loans:

(i) With an amount at origination of $100,000 or less;

(ii) With amount at origination of more than $100,000 but less than or equal to $250,000;

(iii) With an amount at origination of more than $250,000; and

(iv) To businesses and farms with gross annual revenues of $1 million or less (using the revenues that the savings association considered in making its credit decision);

(2) *Community development loan data.* The aggregate number and aggregate amount of community development loans originated or purchased; and

(3) *Home mortgage loans.* If the savings association is subject to reporting under part 1003 of this title, the location of each home mortgage loan application, origination, or purchase outside the MSAs in which the savings association has a home or branch office (or outside any MSA) in accordance with the requirements of part 1003 of this title.

(c) *Optional data collection and maintenance*—(1) *Consumer loans.* A savings association may collect and maintain in machine readable form (as prescribed by the appropriate Federal banking agency) data for consumer loans originated or purchased by the savings association for consideration under the lending test. A savings association may maintain data for one or more of the following categories of consumer loans: Motor vehicle, credit card, other secured, and other unsecured. If the savings association maintains data for loans in a certain category, it shall maintain data for all loans originated or purchased within that category. The savings association shall maintain data separately for each category, including for each loan:

(i) A unique number or alpha-numeric symbol that can be used to identify the relevant loan file;

(ii) The loan amount at origination or purchase;

(iii) The loan location; and

(iv) The gross annual income of the borrower that the savings association considered in making its credit decision.

(2) *Other loan data.* At its option, a savings association may provide other information concerning its lending performance, including additional loan distribution data.

(d) *Data on affiliate lending.* A savings association that elects to have the appropriate Federal banking agency consider loans by an affiliate, for purposes of the lending or community development test or an approved strategic plan, shall collect, maintain, and report for those loans the data that the savings association would have collected, maintained, and reported pursuant to paragraphs (a), (b), and (c) of this section had the loans been originated or purchased by the savings association. For home mortgage loans, the savings association shall also be prepared to identify the home mortgage loans reported under part 1003 of this title by the affiliate.

(e) *Data on lending by a consortium or a third-party.* A savings association that elects to have the appropriate Federal banking agency consider community development loans by a consortium or third party, for purposes of the lending or community development tests or an approved strategic plan, shall report for those loans the data that the savings association would have reported under paragraph (b)(2) of this section had the loans been originated or purchased by the savings association.

(f) *Small savings associations electing evaluation under the lending, investment, and service tests.* A savings association that qualifies for evaluation under the small savings association performance standards but elects evaluation under the lending, investment, and service tests shall collect, maintain, and report the data required for other savings associations pursuant to paragraphs (a) and (b) of this section.

(g) *Assessment area data.* A savings association, except a small savings association or a savings association that was a small savings association during the prior calendar year, shall collect and report to the appropriate Federal banking agency by March 1 of each year a list for each assessment area showing the geographies within the area.

(h) *CRA Disclosure Statement.* The appropriate Federal banking agency prepares annually for each savings association that reports data pursuant to this section a CRA Disclosure Statement that contains, on a state-by-state basis:

(1) For each county (and for each assessment area smaller than a county) with a population of 500,000 persons or fewer in which the savings association reported a small business or small farm loan:

(i) The number and amount of small business and small farm loans reported as originated or purchased located in low-, moderate-, middle-, and upper-income geographies;

(ii) A list grouping each geography according to whether the geography is low-, moderate-, middle-, or upper-income;

(iii) A list showing each geography in which the savings association reported a small business or small farm loan; and

(iv) The number and amount of small business and small farm loans to businesses and farms with gross annual revenues of $1 million or less;

(2) For each county (and for each assessment area smaller than a county) with a population in excess of 500,000 persons in which the savings association reported a small business or small farm loan:

(i) The number and amount of small business and small farm loans reported as originated or purchased located in geographies with median income relative to the area median income of less than 10 percent, 10 or more but less than 20 percent, 20 or more but less than 30 percent, 30 or more but less than 40 percent, 40 or more but less than 50 percent, 50 or more but less than 60 percent, 60 or more but less than 70 percent, 70 or more but less than 80 percent, 80 or more but less than 90 percent, 90 or more but less than 100 percent, 100 or more but less than 110 percent, 110 or more but less than 120 percent, and 120 percent or more;

(ii) A list grouping each geography in the county or assessment area according to whether the median income in the geography relative to the area median income is less than 10 percent, 10 or more but less than 20 percent, 20 or more but less than 30 percent, 30 or more but less than 40 percent, 40 or more but less than 50 percent, 50 or more but less than 60 percent, 60 or more but less than 70 percent, 70 or more but less than 80 percent, 80 or more but less than 90 percent, 90 or more but less than 100 percent, 100 or more but less than 110 percent, 110 or more but less than 120 percent, and 120 percent or more;

(iii) A list showing each geography in which the savings association reported a small business or small farm loan; and

(iv) The number and amount of small business and small farm loans to businesses and farms with gross annual revenues of $1 million or less;

(3) The number and amount of small business and small farm loans located inside each assessment area reported by the savings association and the number and amount of small business and small farm loans located outside the assessment area(s) reported by the savings association; and

(4) The number and amount of community development loans reported as originated or purchased.

(i) *Aggregate disclosure statements.* The appropriate Federal banking agency, in conjunction with the Board of Governors of the Federal Reserve System and the Federal Deposit Insurance Corporation or the OCC, as appropriate, prepares annually, for each MSA or metropolitan division (including an MSA or metropolitan division that crosses a state boundary) and the nonmetropolitan portion of each state, an aggregate disclosure statement of small business and small farm lending by all institutions subject to reporting under this part or parts 25, 228, or 345 of this title. These disclosure statements indicate, for each geography, the number and amount of all small business and small farm loans originated or purchased by reporting institutions, except that the appropriate Federal banking agency may adjust the form of the disclosure if necessary, because of special circumstances, to protect the privacy of a borrower or the competitive position of an institution.

(j) *Central data depositories*. The appropriate Federal banking agency makes the aggregate disclosure statements, described in paragraph (i) of this section, and the individual savings association CRA Disclosure Statements, described in paragraph (h) of this section, available to the public at central data depositories. The appropriate Federal banking agency publishes a list of the depositories at which the statements are available.

[76 FR 49179, Aug. 9, 2011, as amended at 80 FR 81164, Dec. 29, 2015; 82 FR 55742, Nov. 24, 2017]

§ 195.43 Content and availability of public file.

(a) *Information available to the public*. A savings association shall maintain a public file that includes the following information:

(1) All written comments received from the public for the current year and each of the prior two calendar years that specifically relate to the savings association's performance in helping to meet community credit needs, and any response to the comments by the savings association, if neither the comments nor the responses contain statements that reflect adversely on the good name or reputation of any persons other than the savings association or publication of which would violate specific provisions of law;

(2) A copy of the public section of the savings association's most recent CRA Performance Evaluation prepared by the appropriate Federal banking agency. The savings association shall place this copy in the public file within 30 business days after its receipt from the appropriate Federal banking agency;

(3) A list of the savings association's branches, their street addresses, and geographies;

(4) A list of branches opened or closed by the savings association during the current year and each of the prior two calendar years, their street addresses, and geographies;

(5) A list of services (including hours of operation, available loan and deposit products, and transaction fees) generally offered at the savings association's branches and descriptions of material differences in the availability or cost of services at particular branches, if any. At its option, a savings association may include information regarding the availability of alternative systems for delivering retail banking services (*e.g.*, ATMs, ATMs not owned or operated by or exclusively for the savings association, banking by telephone or computer, loan production offices, and bank-at-work or bank-by-mail programs);

(6) A map of each assessment area showing the boundaries of the area and identifying the geographies contained within the area, either on the map or in a separate list; and

(7) Any other information the savings association chooses.

(b) *Additional information available to the public*—(1) *Savings associations other than small savings associations*. A savings association, except a small savings association or a savings association that was a small savings association during the prior calendar year, shall include in its public file the following information pertaining to the savings association and its affiliates, if applicable, for each of the prior two calendar years:

(i) If the savings association has elected to have one or more categories of its consumer loans considered under the lending test, for each of these categories, the number and amount of loans:

(A) To low-, moderate-, middle-, and upper-income individuals;

(B) Located in low-, moderate-, middle-, and upper-income census tracts; and

(C) Located inside the savings association's assessment area(s) and outside the savings association's assessment area(s); and

(ii) The savings association's CRA Disclosure Statement. The savings association shall place the statement in the public file within three business days of its receipt from the appropriate Federal banking agency.

(2) *Savings associations required to report Home Mortgage Disclosure Act (HMDA) data.* A savings association required to report home mortgage loan data pursuant part 1003 of this title shall include in its public file a written notice that the institution's HMDA Disclosure Statement may be obtained on the Consumer Financial Protection Bureau's (Bureau's) Web site at *www.consumerfinance.gov/hmda.* In addition, a savings association that elected to have the appropriate Federal banking agency consider the mortgage lending of an affiliate shall include in its public file the name of the affiliate and a written notice that the affiliate's HMDA Disclosure Statement may be obtained at the Bureau's Web site. The savings association shall place the written notice(s) in the public file within three business days after receiving notification from the Federal Financial Institutions Examination Council of the availability of the disclosure statement(s).

(3) *Small savings associations.* A small savings association or a savings association that was a small savings association during the prior calendar year shall include in its public file:

(i) The savings association's loan-to-deposit ratio for each quarter of the prior calendar year and, at its option, additional data on its loan-to-deposit ratio; and

(ii) The information required for other savings associations by paragraph (b)(1) of this section, if the savings association has elected to be evaluated under the lending, investment, and service tests.

(4) *Savings associations with strategic plans.* A savings association that has been approved to be assessed under a strategic plan shall include in its public file a copy of that plan. A savings association need not include information submitted to the appropriate Federal banking agency on a confidential basis in conjunction with the plan.

(5) *Savings associations with less than satisfactory ratings.* A savings association that received a less than satisfactory rating during its most recent examination shall include in its public file a description of its current efforts to improve its performance in helping to meet the credit needs of its entire community. The savings association shall update the description quarterly.

(c) *Location of public information.* A savings association shall make available to the public for inspection upon request and at no cost the information required in this section as follows:

(1) At the main office and, if an interstate savings association, at one branch office in each state, all information in the public file; and

(2) At each branch:

(i) A copy of the public section of the savings association's most recent CRA Performance Evaluation and a list of services provided by the branch; and

(ii) Within five calendar days of the request, all the information in the public file relating to the assessment area in which the branch is located.

(d) *Copies.* Upon request, a savings association shall provide copies, either on paper or in another form acceptable to the person making the request, of the information in its public file. The savings association may charge a reasonable fee not to exceed the cost of copying and mailing (if applicable).

(e) *Updating.* Except as otherwise provided in this section, a savings association shall ensure that the information required by this section is current as of April 1 of each year.

[76 FR 49179, Aug. 9, 2011, as amended at 80 FR 81164, Dec. 29, 2015; 82 FR 55742, Nov. 24, 2017]

§ 195.44 Public notice by savings associations.

A savings association shall provide in the public lobby of its main office and each of its branches the appropriate public notice set forth in appendix B of this part. Only a branch of a savings association having more than one assessment area shall include the bracketed material in the notice for branch offices. Only a savings association that is an affiliate of a holding company shall include the last two sentences of the notices.

§ 195.45 Publication of planned examination schedule.

The appropriate Federal banking agency publishes at least 30 days in advance of the beginning of each calendar quarter a list of savings associations scheduled for CRA examinations in that quarter.

APPENDIX A TO PART 195—RATINGS

(a) *Ratings in general.* (1) In assigning a rating, the appropriate Federal banking agency evaluates a savings association's performance under the applicable performance criteria in this part, in accordance with §§195.21 and 195.28. This includes consideration of low-cost education loans provided to low-income borrowers and activities in cooperation with minority- or women-owned financial institutions and low-income credit unions, as well as adjustments on the basis of evidence of discriminatory or other illegal credit practices.

(2) A savings association's performance need not fit each aspect of a particular rating profile in order to receive that rating, and exceptionally strong performance with respect to some aspects may compensate for weak performance in others. The savings association's overall performance, however, must be consistent with safe and sound banking practices and generally with the appropriate rating profile as follows.

(b) *Savings associations evaluated under the lending, investment, and service tests*—(1) *Lending performance rating.* The appropriate Federal banking agency assigns each savings association's lending performance one of the five following ratings.

(i) *Outstanding.* The appropriate Federal banking agency rates a savings association's lending performance "outstanding" if, in general, it demonstrates:

(A) Excellent responsiveness to credit needs in its assessment area(s), taking into account the number and amount of home mortgage, small business, small farm, and consumer loans, if applicable, in its assessment area(s);

(B) A substantial majority of its loans are made in its assessment area(s);

(C) An excellent geographic distribution of loans in its assessment area(s);

(D) An excellent distribution, particularly in its assessment area(s), of loans among individuals of different income levels and businesses (including farms) of different sizes, given the product lines offered by the savings association;

(E) An excellent record of serving the credit needs of highly economically disadvantaged areas in its assessment area(s), low-income individuals, or businesses (including farms) with gross annual revenues of $1 million or less, consistent with safe and sound operations;

(F) Extensive use of innovative or flexible lending practices in a safe and sound manner to address the credit needs of low- or moderate-income individuals or geographies; and

(G) It is a leader in making community development loans.

(ii) *High satisfactory.* The appropriate Federal banking agency rates a savings association's lending performance "high satisfactory" if, in general, it demonstrates:

(A) Good responsiveness to credit needs in its assessment area(s), taking into account the number and amount of home mortgage, small business, small farm, and consumer loans, if applicable, in its assessment area(s);

(B) A high percentage of its loans are made in its assessment area(s);

(C) A good geographic distribution of loans in its assessment area(s);

(D) A good distribution, particularly in its assessment area(s), of loans among individuals of different income levels and businesses (including farms) of different sizes, given the product lines offered by the savings association;

(E) A good record of serving the credit needs of highly economically disadvantaged areas in its assessment area(s), low-income individuals, or businesses (including farms) with gross annual revenues of $1 million or less, consistent with safe and sound operations;

(F) Use of innovative or flexible lending practices in a safe and sound manner to address the credit needs of low- or moderate-income individuals or geographies; and

(G) It has made a relatively high level of community development loans.

(iii) *Low satisfactory.* The appropriate Federal banking agency rates a savings association's lending performance "low satisfactory" if, in general, it demonstrates:

(A) Adequate responsiveness to credit needs in its assessment area(s), taking into account the number and amount of home mortgage, small business, small farm, and consumer loans, if applicable, in its assessment area(s);

(B) An adequate percentage of its loans are made in its assessment area(s);

(C) An adequate geographic distribution of loans in its assessment area(s);

(D) An adequate distribution, particularly in its assessment area(s), of loans among individuals of different income levels and businesses (including farms) of different sizes, given the product lines offered by the savings association;

(E) An adequate record of serving the credit needs of highly economically disadvantaged areas in its assessment area(s), low-income individuals, or businesses (including farms) with gross annual revenues of $1 million or less, consistent with safe and sound operations;

(F) Limited use of innovative or flexible lending practices in a safe and sound manner to address the credit needs of low- or moderate-income individuals or geographies; and

(G) It has made an adequate level of community development loans.

(iv) *Needs to improve.* The appropriate Federal banking agency rates a savings association's lending performance "needs to improve" if, in general, it demonstrates:

(A) Poor responsiveness to credit needs in its assessment area(s), taking into account the number and amount of home mortgage, small business, small farm, and consumer loans, if applicable, in its assessment area(s);

(B) A small percentage of its loans are made in its assessment area(s);

(C) A poor geographic distribution of loans, particularly to low- or moderate-income geographies, in its assessment area(s);

(D) A poor distribution, particularly in its assessment area(s), of loans among individuals of different income levels and businesses (including farms) of different sizes, given the product lines offered by the savings association;

(E) A poor record of serving the credit needs of highly economically disadvantaged areas in its assessment area(s), low-income individuals, or businesses (including farms) with gross annual revenues of $1 million or less, consistent with safe and sound operations;

(F) Little use of innovative or flexible lending practices in a safe and sound manner to address the credit needs of low- or moderate-income individuals or geographies; and

(G) It has made a low level of community development loans.

(v) *Substantial noncompliance.* The appropriate Federal banking agency rates a savings association's lending performance as being in "substantial noncompliance" if, in general, it demonstrates:

(A) A very poor responsiveness to credit needs in its assessment area(s), taking into account the number and amount of home mortgage, small business, small farm, and consumer loans, if applicable, in its assessment area(s);

(B) A very small percentage of its loans are made in its assessment area(s);

(C) A very poor geographic distribution of loans, particularly to low- or moderate-income geographies, in its assessment area(s);

(D) A very poor distribution, particularly in its assessment area(s), of loans among individuals of different income levels and businesses (including farms) of different sizes, given the product lines offered by the savings association;

(E) A very poor record of serving the credit needs of highly economically disadvantaged areas in its assessment area(s), low-income individuals, or businesses (including farms) with gross annual revenues of $1 million or less, consistent with safe and sound operations;

(F) No use of innovative or flexible lending practices in a safe and sound manner to address the credit needs of low- or moderate-income individuals or geographies; and

(G) It has made few, if any, community development loans.

(2) *Investment performance rating.* The appropriate Federal banking agency assigns each savings association's investment performance one of the five following ratings.

(i) *Outstanding.* The appropriate Federal banking agency rates a savings association's investment performance "outstanding" if, in general, it demonstrates:

(A) An excellent level of qualified investments, particularly those that are not routinely provided by private investors, often in a leadership position;

(B) Extensive use of innovative or complex qualified investments; and

(C) Excellent responsiveness to credit and community development needs.

(ii) *High satisfactory.* The appropriate Federal banking agency rates a savings association's investment performance "high satisfactory" if, in general, it demonstrates:

(A) A significant level of qualified investments, particularly those that are not routinely provided by private investors, occasionally in a leadership position;

(B) Significant use of innovative or complex qualified investments; and

(C) Good responsiveness to credit and community development needs.

(iii) *Low satisfactory.* The appropriate Federal banking agency rates a savings association's investment performance "low satisfactory" if, in general, it demonstrates:

(A) An adequate level of qualified investments, particularly those that are not routinely provided by private investors, although rarely in a leadership position;

(B) Occasional use of innovative or complex qualified investments; and

(C) Adequate responsiveness to credit and community development needs.

(iv) *Needs to improve.* The appropriate Federal banking agency rates a savings association's investment performance "needs to improve" if, in general, it demonstrates:

(A) A poor level of qualified investments, particularly those that are not routinely provided by private investors;

(B) Rare use of innovative or complex qualified investments; and

(C) Poor responsiveness to credit and community development needs.

(v) *Substantial noncompliance.* The appropriate Federal banking agency rates a savings association's investment performance as being in "substantial noncompliance" if, in general, it demonstrates:

(A) Few, if any, qualified investments, particularly those that are not routinely provided by private investors;

(B) No use of innovative or complex qualified investments; and

(C) Very poor responsiveness to credit and community development needs.

(3) *Service performance rating.* The appropriate Federal banking agency assigns each savings association's service performance one of the five following ratings.

(i) *Outstanding.* The appropriate Federal banking agency rates a savings association's service performance "outstanding" if, in general, the savings association demonstrates:

(A) Its service delivery systems are readily accessible to geographies and individuals of different income levels in its assessment area(s);

(B) To the extent changes have been made, its record of opening and closing branches has improved the accessibility of its delivery systems, particularly in low- or moderate-income geographies or to low- or moderate-income individuals;

(C) Its services (including, where appropriate, business hours) are tailored to the convenience and needs of its assessment area(s), particularly low- or moderate-income geographies or low- or moderate-income individuals; and

(D) It is a leader in providing community development services.

(ii) *High satisfactory.* The appropriate Federal banking agency rates a savings association's service performance "high satisfactory" if, in general, the savings association demonstrates:

(A) Its service delivery systems are accessible to geographies and individuals of different income levels in its assessment area(s);

(B) To the extent changes have been made, its record of opening and closing branches has not adversely affected the accessibility of its delivery systems, particularly in low- and moderate-income geographies and to low- and moderate-income individuals;

(C) Its services (including, where appropriate, business hours) do not vary in a way that inconveniences its assessment area(s), particularly low- and moderate-income geographies and low- and moderate-income individuals; and

(D) It provides a relatively high level of community development services.

(iii) *Low satisfactory.* The appropriate Federal banking agency rates a savings association's service performance "low satisfactory" if, in general, the savings association demonstrates:

(A) Its service delivery systems are reasonably accessible to geographies and individuals of different income levels in its assessment area(s);

(B) To the extent changes have been made, its record of opening and closing branches has generally not adversely affected the accessibility of its delivery systems, particularly in low- and moderate-income geographies and to low- and moderate-income individuals;

(C) Its services (including, where appropriate, business hours) do not vary in a way that inconveniences its assessment area(s), particularly low- and moderate-income geographies and low- and moderate-income individuals; and

(D) It provides an adequate level of community development services.

(iv) *Needs to improve.* The appropriate Federal banking agency rates a savings association's service performance "needs to improve" if, in general, the savings association demonstrates:

(A) Its service delivery systems are unreasonably inaccessible to portions of its assessment area(s), particularly to low- or moderate-income geographies or to low- or moderate-income individuals;

(B) To the extent changes have been made, its record of opening and closing branches has adversely affected the accessibility of its delivery systems, particularly in low- or moderate-income geographies or to low- or moderate-income individuals;

(C) Its services (including, where appropriate, business hours) vary in a way that inconveniences its assessment area(s), particularly low- or moderate-income geographies or low- or moderate-income individuals; and

(D) It provides a limited level of community development services.

(v) *Substantial noncompliance.* The appropriate Federal banking agency rates a savings association's service performance as being in "substantial noncompliance" if, in general, the savings association demonstrates:

(A) Its service delivery systems are unreasonably inaccessible to significant portions of its assessment area(s), particularly to low- or moderate-income geographies or to low- or moderate-income individuals;

(B) To the extent changes have been made, its record of opening and closing branches has significantly adversely affected the accessibility of its delivery systems, particularly in low- or moderate-income geographies or to low- or moderate-income individuals;

(C) Its services (including, where appropriate, business hours) vary in a way that significantly inconveniences its assessment area(s), particularly low- or moderate-income geographies or low- or moderate-income individuals; and

(D) It provides few, if any, community development services.

(c) *Wholesale or limited purpose savings associations.* The appropriate Federal banking agency assigns each wholesale or limited purpose savings association's community development performance one of the four following ratings.

(1) *Outstanding.* The appropriate Federal banking agency rates a wholesale or limited

purpose savings association's community development performance "outstanding" if, in general, it demonstrates:

(i) A high level of community development loans, community development services, or qualified investments, particularly investments that are not routinely provided by private investors;

(ii) Extensive use of innovative or complex qualified investments, community development loans, or community development services; and

(iii) Excellent responsiveness to credit and community development needs in its assessment area(s).

(2) *Satisfactory*. The appropriate Federal banking agency rates a wholesale or limited purpose savings association's community development performance "satisfactory" if, in general, it demonstrates:

(i) An adequate level of community development loans, community development services, or qualified investments, particularly investments that are not routinely provided by private investors;

(ii) Occasional use of innovative or complex qualified investments, community development loans, or community development services; and

(iii) Adequate responsiveness to credit and community development needs in its assessment area(s).

(3) *Needs to improve*. The appropriate Federal banking agency rates a wholesale or limited purpose savings association's community development performance as "needs to improve" if, in general, it demonstrates:

(i) A poor level of community development loans, community development services, or qualified investments, particularly investments that are not routinely provided by private investors;

(ii) Rare use of innovative or complex qualified investments, community development loans, or community development services; and

(iii) Poor responsiveness to credit and community development needs in its assessment area(s).

(4) *Substantial noncompliance*. The appropriate Federal banking agency rates a wholesale or limited purpose savings association's community development performance in "substantial noncompliance" if, in general, it demonstrates:

(i) Few, if any, community development loans, community development services, or qualified investments, particularly investments that are not routinely provided by private investors;

(ii) No use of innovative or complex qualified investments, community development loans, or community development services; and

(iii) Very poor responsiveness to credit and community development needs in its assessment area(s).

(d) *Savings associations evaluated under the small savings association performance standard*—(1) *Lending test ratings*. (i) *Eligibility for a satisfactory lending test rating*. The appropriate Federal banking agency rates a small savings association's lending performance "satisfactory" if, in general, the savings association demonstrates:

(A) A reasonable loan-to-deposit ratio (considering seasonal variations) given the savings association's size, financial condition, the credit needs of its assessment area(s), and taking into account, as appropriate, other lending-related activities such as loan originations for sale to the secondary markets and community development loans and qualified investments;

(B) A majority of its loans and, as appropriate, other lending-related activities, are in its assessment area;

(C) A distribution of loans to and, as appropriate, other lending-related activities for individuals of different income levels (including low- and moderate-income individuals) and businesses and farms of different sizes that is reasonable given the demographics of the savings association's assessment area(s);

(D) A record of taking appropriate action, when warranted, in response to written complaints, if any, about the savings association's performance in helping to meet the credit needs of its assessment area(s); and

(E) A reasonable geographic distribution of loans given the savings association's assessment area(s).

(ii) *Eligibility for an "outstanding" lending test rating*. A small savings association that meets each of the standards for a "satisfactory" rating under this paragraph and exceeds some or all of those standards may warrant consideration for a lending test rating of "outstanding."

(iii) *Needs to improve or substantial noncompliance ratings*. A small savings association may also receive a lending test rating of "needs to improve" or "substantial noncompliance" depending on the degree to which its performance has failed to meet the standard for a "satisfactory" rating.

(2) *Community development test ratings for intermediate small savings associations*—(i) *Eligibility for a satisfactory community development test rating*. The appropriate Federal banking agency rates an intermediate small savings association's community development performance "satisfactory" if the savings association demonstrates adequate responsiveness to the community development needs of its assessment area(s) through community development loans, qualified investments, and community development services. The adequacy of the savings association's response will depend on its capacity for such community development activities, its assessment area's need for such community development activities, and the availability of

such opportunities for community development in the savings association's assessment area(s).

(ii) *Eligibility for an outstanding community development test rating.* The appropriate Federal banking agency rates an intermediate small savings association's community development performance "outstanding" if the savings association demonstrates excellent responsiveness to community development needs in its assessment area(s) through community development loans, qualified investments, and community development services, as appropriate, considering the savings association's capacity and the need and availability of such opportunities for community development in the savings association's assessment area(s).

(iii) *Needs to improve or substantial noncompliance ratings.* An intermediate small savings association may also receive a community development test rating of "needs to improve" or "substantial noncompliance" depending on the degree to which its performance has failed to meet the standards for a "satisfactory" rating.

(3) *Overall rating*—(i) *Eligibility for a satisfactory overall rating.* No intermediate small savings association may receive an assigned overall rating of "satisfactory" unless it receives a rating of at least "satisfactory" on both the lending test and the community development test.

(ii) *Eligibility for an outstanding overall rating.* (A) An intermediate small savings association that receives an "outstanding" rating on one test and at least "satisfactory" on the other test may receive an assigned overall rating of "outstanding."

(B) A small savings association that is not an intermediate small savings association that meets each of the standards for a "satisfactory" rating under the lending test and exceeds some or all of those standards may warrant consideration for an overall rating of "outstanding." In assessing whether a savings association's performance is "outstanding," the appropriate Federal banking agency considers the extent to which the savings association exceeds each of the performance standards for a "satisfactory" rating and its performance in making qualified investments and its performance in providing branches and other services and delivery systems that enhance credit availability in its assessment area(s).

(iii) *Needs to improve or substantial noncompliance overall ratings.* A small savings association may also receive a rating of "needs to improve" or "substantial noncompliance" depending on the degree to which its performance has failed to meet the standards for a "satisfactory" rating.

(e) *Strategic plan assessment and rating*—(1) *Satisfactory goals.* The appropriate Federal banking agency approves as "satisfactory" measurable goals that adequately help to meet the credit needs of the savings association's assessment area(s).

(2) *Outstanding goals.* If the plan identifies a separate group of measurable goals that substantially exceed the levels approved as "satisfactory," the appropriate Federal banking agency will approve those goals as "outstanding."

(3) *Rating.* The appropriate Federal banking agency assesses the performance of a savings association operating under an approved plan to determine if the savings association has met its plan goals:

(i) If the savings association substantially achieves its plan goals for a satisfactory rating, the appropriate Federal banking agency will rate the savings association's performance under the plan as "satisfactory."

(ii) If the savings association exceeds its plan goals for a satisfactory rating and substantially achieves its plan goals for an outstanding rating, the appropriate Federal banking agency will rate the savings association's performance under the plan as "outstanding."

(iii) If the savings association fails to meet substantially its plan goals for a satisfactory rating, the appropriate Federal banking agency will rate the savings association as either "needs to improve" or "substantial noncompliance," depending on the extent to which it falls short of its plan goals, unless the savings association elected in its plan to be rated otherwise, as provided in §195.27(f)(4).

APPENDIX B TO PART 195—CRA NOTICE

(a) *Notice for main offices and, if an interstate savings association, one branch office in each state.*

COMMUNITY REINVESTMENT ACT NOTICE

Under the Federal Community Reinvestment Act (CRA), the [Office of the Comptroller of the Currency (OCC) or Federal Deposit Insurance Corporation (FDIC)] evaluates our record of helping to meet the credit needs of this community consistent with safe and sound operations. The [OCC or FDIC] also takes this record into account when deciding on certain applications submitted by us.

Your involvement is encouraged.

You are entitled to certain information about our operations and our performance under the CRA, including, for example, information about our branches, such as their location and services provided at them; the public section of our most recent CRA Performance Evaluation, prepared by the [OCC or FDIC]; and comments received from the public relating to our performance in helping to meet community credit needs, as well as our responses to those comments. You may review this information today.

At least 30 days before the beginning of each quarter, the [OCC or FDIC] publishes a nationwide list of the savings associations that are scheduled for CRA examination in that quarter. This list is available from the [OCC Deputy Comptroller (address) or FDIC appropriate regional director (address)]. You may send written comments about our performance in helping to meet community credit needs to (name and address of official at savings association) and the [OCC Deputy Comptroller (address) or FDIC appropriate regional director (address)]. Your letter, together with any response by us, will be considered by the [OCC or FDIC] in evaluating our CRA performance and may be made public.

You may ask to look at any comments received by the [OCC Deputy Comptroller or FDIC appropriate regional director]. You may also request from the [OCC Deputy Comptroller or FDIC appropriate regional director] an announcement of our applications covered by the CRA filed with the [OCC or FDIC]. We are an affiliate of (name of holding company), a savings and loan holding company. You may request from the (title of responsible official), Federal Reserve Bank of ______ (address) an announcement of applications covered by the CRA filed by savings and loan holding companies.

(b) *Notice for branch offices.*

COMMUNITY REINVESTMENT ACT NOTICE

Under the Federal Community Reinvestment Act (CRA), the [Office of the Comptroller of the Currency (OCC) or Federal Deposit Insurance Corporation (FDIC)] evaluates our record of helping to meet the credit needs of this community consistent with safe and sound operations. The [OCC or FDIC] also takes this record into account when deciding on certain applications submitted by us.

Your involvement is encouraged.

You are entitled to certain information about our operations and our performance under the CRA. You may review today the public section of our most recent CRA evaluation, prepared by the [OCC or FDIC] and a list of services provided at this branch. You may also have access to the following additional information, which we will make available to you at this branch within five calendar days after you make a request to us: (1) A map showing the assessment area containing this branch, which is the area in which the [OCC or FDIC] evaluates our CRA performance in this community; (2) information about our branches in this assessment area; (3) a list of services we provide at those locations; (4) data on our lending performance in this assessment area; and (5) copies of all written comments received by us that specifically relate to our CRA performance in this assessment area, and any responses we have made to those comments. If we are operating under an approved strategic plan, you may also have access to a copy of the plan.

[If you would like to review information about our CRA performance in other communities served by us, the public file for our entire savings association is available at (name of office located in state), located at (address).]

At least 30 days before the beginning of each quarter, the [OCC or FDIC] publishes a nationwide list of the savings associations that are scheduled for CRA examination in that quarter. This list is available from the [OCC Deputy Comptroller (address) or FDIC appropriate regional office (address)]. You may send written comments about our performance in helping to meet community credit needs to (name and address of official at savings association) and the [OCC or FDIC]. Your letter, together with any response by us, will be considered by the [OCC or FDIC] in evaluating our CRA performance and may be made public.

You may ask to look at any comments received by the [OCC Deputy Comptroller or FDIC appropriate regional director]. You may also request an announcement of our applications covered by the CRA filed with the [OCC Deputy Comptroller or FDIC appropriate regional director]. We are an affiliate of (name of holding company), a savings and loan holding company. You may request from the (title of responsible official), Federal Reserve Bank of ______ (address) an announcement of applications covered by the CRA filed by savings and loan holding companies.

PARTS 196–199 [RESERVED]

FINDING AIDS

A list of CFR titles, subtitles, chapters, subchapters and parts and an alphabetical list of agencies publishing in the CFR are included in the CFR Index and Finding Aids volume to the Code of Federal Regulations which is published separately and revised annually.

Table of CFR Titles and Chapters
Alphabetical List of Agencies Appearing in the CFR
List of CFR Sections Affected

Table of CFR Titles and Chapters

(Revised as of January 1, 2019)

Title 1—General Provisions

I Administrative Committee of the Federal Register (Parts 1—49)

II Office of the Federal Register (Parts 50—299)

III Administrative Conference of the United States (Parts 300—399)

IV Miscellaneous Agencies (Parts 400—599)

VI National Capital Planning Commission (Parts 600—699)

Title 2—Grants and Agreements

SUBTITLE A—OFFICE OF MANAGEMENT AND BUDGET GUIDANCE FOR GRANTS AND AGREEMENTS

I Office of Management and Budget Governmentwide Guidance for Grants and Agreements (Parts 2—199)

II Office of Management and Budget Guidance (Parts 200—299)

SUBTITLE B—FEDERAL AGENCY REGULATIONS FOR GRANTS AND AGREEMENTS

III Department of Health and Human Services (Parts 300—399)

IV Department of Agriculture (Parts 400—499)

VI Department of State (Parts 600—699)

VII Agency for International Development (Parts 700—799)

VIII Department of Veterans Affairs (Parts 800—899)

IX Department of Energy (Parts 900—999)

X Department of the Treasury (Parts 1000—1099)

XI Department of Defense (Parts 1100—1199)

XII Department of Transportation (Parts 1200—1299)

XIII Department of Commerce (Parts 1300—1399)

XIV Department of the Interior (Parts 1400—1499)

XV Environmental Protection Agency (Parts 1500—1599)

XVIII National Aeronautics and Space Administration (Parts 1800—1899)

XX United States Nuclear Regulatory Commission (Parts 2000—2099)

XXII Corporation for National and Community Service (Parts 2200—2299)

XXIII Social Security Administration (Parts 2300—2399)

XXIV Department of Housing and Urban Development (Parts 2400—2499)

XXV National Science Foundation (Parts 2500—2599)

XXVI National Archives and Records Administration (Parts 2600—2699)

Title 2—Grants and Agreements—Continued

Chap.	
XXVII	Small Business Administration (Parts 2700—2799)
XXVIII	Department of Justice (Parts 2800—2899)
XXIX	Department of Labor (Parts 2900—2999)
XXX	Department of Homeland Security (Parts 3000—3099)
XXXI	Institute of Museum and Library Services (Parts 3100—3199)
XXXII	National Endowment for the Arts (Parts 3200—3299)
XXXIII	National Endowment for the Humanities (Parts 3300—3399)
XXXIV	Department of Education (Parts 3400—3499)
XXXV	Export-Import Bank of the United States (Parts 3500—3599)
XXXVI	Office of National Drug Control Policy, Executive Office of the President (Parts 3600—3699)
XXXVII	Peace Corps (Parts 3700—3799)
LVIII	Election Assistance Commission (Parts 5800—5899)
LIX	Gulf Coast Ecosystem Restoration Council (Parts 5900—5999)

Title 3—The President

I	Executive Office of the President (Parts 100—199)

Title 4—Accounts

I	Government Accountability Office (Parts 1—199)

Title 5—Administrative Personnel

I	Office of Personnel Management (Parts 1—1199)
II	Merit Systems Protection Board (Parts 1200—1299)
III	Office of Management and Budget (Parts 1300—1399)
IV	Office of Personnel Management and Office of the Director of National Intelligence (Parts 1400—1499)
V	The International Organizations Employees Loyalty Board (Parts 1500—1599)
VI	Federal Retirement Thrift Investment Board (Parts 1600—1699)
VIII	Office of Special Counsel (Parts 1800—1899)
IX	Appalachian Regional Commission (Parts 1900—1999)
XI	Armed Forces Retirement Home (Parts 2100—2199)
XIV	Federal Labor Relations Authority, General Counsel of the Federal Labor Relations Authority and Federal Service Impasses Panel (Parts 2400—2499)
XVI	Office of Government Ethics (Parts 2600—2699)
XXI	Department of the Treasury (Parts 3100—3199)
XXII	Federal Deposit Insurance Corporation (Parts 3200—3299)
XXIII	Department of Energy (Parts 3300—3399)
XXIV	Federal Energy Regulatory Commission (Parts 3400—3499)
XXV	Department of the Interior (Parts 3500—3599)
XXVI	Department of Defense (Parts 3600—3699)

Chap.	
XXVIII	Department of Justice (Parts 3800—3899)
XXIX	Federal Communications Commission (Parts 3900—3999)
XXX	Farm Credit System Insurance Corporation (Parts 4000—4099)
XXXI	Farm Credit Administration (Parts 4100—4199)
XXXIII	Overseas Private Investment Corporation (Parts 4300—4399)
XXXIV	Securities and Exchange Commission (Parts 4400—4499)
XXXV	Office of Personnel Management (Parts 4500—4599)
XXXVI	Department of Homeland Security (Parts 4600—4699)
XXXVII	Federal Election Commission (Parts 4700—4799)
XL	Interstate Commerce Commission (Parts 5000—5099)
XLI	Commodity Futures Trading Commission (Parts 5100—5199)
XLII	Department of Labor (Parts 5200—5299)
XLIII	National Science Foundation (Parts 5300—5399)
XLV	Department of Health and Human Services (Parts 5500—5599)
XLVI	Postal Rate Commission (Parts 5600—5699)
XLVII	Federal Trade Commission (Parts 5700—5799)
XLVIII	Nuclear Regulatory Commission (Parts 5800—5899)
XLIX	Federal Labor Relations Authority (Parts 5900—5999)
L	Department of Transportation (Parts 6000—6099)
LII	Export-Import Bank of the United States (Parts 6200—6299)
LIII	Department of Education (Parts 6300—6399)
LIV	Environmental Protection Agency (Parts 6400—6499)
LV	National Endowment for the Arts (Parts 6500—6599)
LVI	National Endowment for the Humanities (Parts 6600—6699)
LVII	General Services Administration (Parts 6700—6799)
LVIII	Board of Governors of the Federal Reserve System (Parts 6800—6899)
LIX	National Aeronautics and Space Administration (Parts 6900—6999)
LX	United States Postal Service (Parts 7000—7099)
LXI	National Labor Relations Board (Parts 7100—7199)
LXII	Equal Employment Opportunity Commission (Parts 7200—7299)
LXIII	Inter-American Foundation (Parts 7300—7399)
LXIV	Merit Systems Protection Board (Parts 7400—7499)
LXV	Department of Housing and Urban Development (Parts 7500—7599)
LXVI	National Archives and Records Administration (Parts 7600—7699)
LXVII	Institute of Museum and Library Services (Parts 7700—7799)
LXVIII	Commission on Civil Rights (Parts 7800—7899)
LXIX	Tennessee Valley Authority (Parts 7900—7999)
LXX	Court Services and Offender Supervision Agency for the District of Columbia (Parts 8000—8099)
LXXI	Consumer Product Safety Commission (Parts 8100—8199)
LXXIII	Department of Agriculture (Parts 8300—8399)

Title 5—Administrative Personnel—Continued

Chap.

LXXIV Federal Mine Safety and Health Review Commission (Parts 8400—8499)

LXXVI Federal Retirement Thrift Investment Board (Parts 8600—8699)

LXXVII Office of Management and Budget (Parts 8700—8799)

LXXX Federal Housing Finance Agency (Parts 9000—9099)

LXXXIII Special Inspector General for Afghanistan Reconstruction (Parts 9300—9399)

LXXXIV Bureau of Consumer Financial Protection (Parts 9400—9499)

LXXXVI National Credit Union Administration (Parts 9600—9699)

XCVII Department of Homeland Security Human Resources Management System (Department of Homeland Security—Office of Personnel Management) (Parts 9700—9799)

XCVIII Council of the Inspectors General on Integrity and Efficiency (Parts 9800—9899)

XCIX Military Compensation and Retirement Modernization Commission (Parts 9900—9999)

C National Council on Disability (Parts 10000—10049)

CI National Mediation Board (Part 10101)

Title 6—Domestic Security

I Department of Homeland Security, Office of the Secretary (Parts 1—199)

X Privacy and Civil Liberties Oversight Board (Parts 1000—1099)

Title 7—Agriculture

SUBTITLE A—OFFICE OF THE SECRETARY OF AGRICULTURE (PARTS 0—26)

SUBTITLE B—REGULATIONS OF THE DEPARTMENT OF AGRICULTURE

I Agricultural Marketing Service (Standards, Inspections, Marketing Practices), Department of Agriculture (Parts 27—209)

II Food and Nutrition Service, Department of Agriculture (Parts 210—299)

III Animal and Plant Health Inspection Service, Department of Agriculture (Parts 300—399)

IV Federal Crop Insurance Corporation, Department of Agriculture (Parts 400—499)

V Agricultural Research Service, Department of Agriculture (Parts 500—599)

VI Natural Resources Conservation Service, Department of Agriculture (Parts 600—699)

VII Farm Service Agency, Department of Agriculture (Parts 700—799)

VIII Grain Inspection, Packers and Stockyards Administration (Federal Grain Inspection Service), Department of Agriculture (Parts 800—899)

Chap.	
IX	Agricultural Marketing Service (Marketing Agreements and Orders; Fruits, Vegetables, Nuts), Department of Agriculture (Parts 900—999)
X	Agricultural Marketing Service (Marketing Agreements and Orders; Milk), Department of Agriculture (Parts 1000—1199)
XI	Agricultural Marketing Service (Marketing Agreements and Orders; Miscellaneous Commodities), Department of Agriculture (Parts 1200—1299)
XIV	Commodity Credit Corporation, Department of Agriculture (Parts 1400—1499)
XV	Foreign Agricultural Service, Department of Agriculture (Parts 1500—1599)
XVI	Rural Telephone Bank, Department of Agriculture (Parts 1600—1699)
XVII	Rural Utilities Service, Department of Agriculture (Parts 1700—1799)
XVIII	Rural Housing Service, Rural Business-Cooperative Service, Rural Utilities Service, and Farm Service Agency, Department of Agriculture (Parts 1800—2099)
XX	Local Television Loan Guarantee Board (Parts 2200—2299)
XXV	Office of Advocacy and Outreach, Department of Agriculture (Parts 2500—2599)
XXVI	Office of Inspector General, Department of Agriculture (Parts 2600—2699)
XXVII	Office of Information Resources Management, Department of Agriculture (Parts 2700—2799)
XXVIII	Office of Operations, Department of Agriculture (Parts 2800—2899)
XXIX	Office of Energy Policy and New Uses, Department of Agriculture (Parts 2900—2999)
XXX	Office of the Chief Financial Officer, Department of Agriculture (Parts 3000—3099)
XXXI	Office of Environmental Quality, Department of Agriculture (Parts 3100—3199)
XXXII	Office of Procurement and Property Management, Department of Agriculture (Parts 3200—3299)
XXXIII	Office of Transportation, Department of Agriculture (Parts 3300—3399)
XXXIV	National Institute of Food and Agriculture (Parts 3400—3499)
XXXV	Rural Housing Service, Department of Agriculture (Parts 3500—3599)
XXXVI	National Agricultural Statistics Service, Department of Agriculture (Parts 3600—3699)
XXXVII	Economic Research Service, Department of Agriculture (Parts 3700—3799)
XXXVIII	World Agricultural Outlook Board, Department of Agriculture (Parts 3800—3899)
XLI	[Reserved]
XLII	Rural Business-Cooperative Service and Rural Utilities Service, Department of Agriculture (Parts 4200—4299)

Title 8—Aliens and Nationality

Chap.	
I	Department of Homeland Security (Immigration and Naturalization) (Parts 1—499)
V	Executive Office for Immigration Review, Department of Justice (Parts 1000—1399)

Title 9—Animals and Animal Products

I	Animal and Plant Health Inspection Service, Department of Agriculture (Parts 1—199)
II	Grain Inspection, Packers and Stockyards Administration (Packers and Stockyards Programs), Department of Agriculture (Parts 200—299)
III	Food Safety and Inspection Service, Department of Agriculture (Parts 300—599)

Title 10—Energy

I	Nuclear Regulatory Commission (Parts 0—199)
II	Department of Energy (Parts 200—699)
III	Department of Energy (Parts 700—999)
X	Department of Energy (General Provisions) (Parts 1000—1099)
XIII	Nuclear Waste Technical Review Board (Parts 1300—1399)
XVII	Defense Nuclear Facilities Safety Board (Parts 1700—1799)
XVIII	Northeast Interstate Low-Level Radioactive Waste Commission (Parts 1800—1899)

Title 11—Federal Elections

I	Federal Election Commission (Parts 1—9099)
II	Election Assistance Commission (Parts 9400—9499)

Title 12—Banks and Banking

I	Comptroller of the Currency, Department of the Treasury (Parts 1—199)
II	Federal Reserve System (Parts 200—299)
III	Federal Deposit Insurance Corporation (Parts 300—399)
IV	Export-Import Bank of the United States (Parts 400—499)
V	(Parts 500—599) [Reserved]
VI	Farm Credit Administration (Parts 600—699)
VII	National Credit Union Administration (Parts 700—799)
VIII	Federal Financing Bank (Parts 800—899)
IX	Federal Housing Finance Board (Parts 900—999)
X	Bureau of Consumer Financial Protection (Parts 1000—1099)
XI	Federal Financial Institutions Examination Council (Parts 1100—1199)
XII	Federal Housing Finance Agency (Parts 1200—1299)
XIII	Financial Stability Oversight Council (Parts 1300—1399)

Title 12—Banks and Banking—Continued

Chap.

Chap.	
XIV	Farm Credit System Insurance Corporation (Parts 1400—1499)
XV	Department of the Treasury (Parts 1500—1599)
XVI	Office of Financial Research (Parts 1600—1699)
XVII	Office of Federal Housing Enterprise Oversight, Department of Housing and Urban Development (Parts 1700—1799)
XVIII	Community Development Financial Institutions Fund, Department of the Treasury (Parts 1800—1899)

Title 13—Business Credit and Assistance

I	Small Business Administration (Parts 1—199)
III	Economic Development Administration, Department of Commerce (Parts 300—399)
IV	Emergency Steel Guarantee Loan Board (Parts 400—499)
V	Emergency Oil and Gas Guaranteed Loan Board (Parts 500—599)

Title 14—Aeronautics and Space

I	Federal Aviation Administration, Department of Transportation (Parts 1—199)
II	Office of the Secretary, Department of Transportation (Aviation Proceedings) (Parts 200—399)
III	Commercial Space Transportation, Federal Aviation Administration, Department of Transportation (Parts 400—1199)
V	National Aeronautics and Space Administration (Parts 1200—1299)
VI	Air Transportation System Stabilization (Parts 1300—1399)

Title 15—Commerce and Foreign Trade

	Subtitle A—Office of the Secretary of Commerce (Parts 0—29)
	Subtitle B—Regulations Relating to Commerce and Foreign Trade
I	Bureau of the Census, Department of Commerce (Parts 30—199)
II	National Institute of Standards and Technology, Department of Commerce (Parts 200—299)
III	International Trade Administration, Department of Commerce (Parts 300—399)
IV	Foreign-Trade Zones Board, Department of Commerce (Parts 400—499)
VII	Bureau of Industry and Security, Department of Commerce (Parts 700—799)
VIII	Bureau of Economic Analysis, Department of Commerce (Parts 800—899)
IX	National Oceanic and Atmospheric Administration, Department of Commerce (Parts 900—999)
XI	National Technical Information Service, Department of Commerce (Parts 1100—1199)

Title 15—Commerce and Foreign Trade—Continued

Chap.

XIII East-West Foreign Trade Board (Parts 1300—1399)

XIV Minority Business Development Agency (Parts 1400—1499)

SUBTITLE C—REGULATIONS RELATING TO FOREIGN TRADE AGREEMENTS

XX Office of the United States Trade Representative (Parts 2000—2099)

SUBTITLE D—REGULATIONS RELATING TO TELECOMMUNICATIONS AND INFORMATION

XXIII National Telecommunications and Information Administration, Department of Commerce (Parts 2300—2399) [Reserved]

Title 16—Commercial Practices

I Federal Trade Commission (Parts 0—999)

II Consumer Product Safety Commission (Parts 1000—1799)

Title 17—Commodity and Securities Exchanges

I Commodity Futures Trading Commission (Parts 1—199)

II Securities and Exchange Commission (Parts 200—399)

IV Department of the Treasury (Parts 400—499)

Title 18—Conservation of Power and Water Resources

I Federal Energy Regulatory Commission, Department of Energy (Parts 1—399)

III Delaware River Basin Commission (Parts 400—499)

VI Water Resources Council (Parts 700—799)

VIII Susquehanna River Basin Commission (Parts 800—899)

XIII Tennessee Valley Authority (Parts 1300—1399)

Title 19—Customs Duties

I U.S. Customs and Border Protection, Department of Homeland Security; Department of the Treasury (Parts 0—199)

II United States International Trade Commission (Parts 200—299)

III International Trade Administration, Department of Commerce (Parts 300—399)

IV U.S. Immigration and Customs Enforcement, Department of Homeland Security (Parts 400—599) [Reserved]

Title 20—Employees' Benefits

I Office of Workers' Compensation Programs, Department of Labor (Parts 1—199)

II Railroad Retirement Board (Parts 200—399)

III Social Security Administration (Parts 400—499)

Title 20—Employees' Benefits—Continued

Chap.	
IV	Employees' Compensation Appeals Board, Department of Labor (Parts 500—599)
V	Employment and Training Administration, Department of Labor (Parts 600—699)
VI	Office of Workers' Compensation Programs, Department of Labor (Parts 700—799)
VII	Benefits Review Board, Department of Labor (Parts 800—899)
VIII	Joint Board for the Enrollment of Actuaries (Parts 900—999)
IX	Office of the Assistant Secretary for Veterans' Employment and Training Service, Department of Labor (Parts 1000—1099)

Title 21—Food and Drugs

I	Food and Drug Administration, Department of Health and Human Services (Parts 1—1299)
II	Drug Enforcement Administration, Department of Justice (Parts 1300—1399)
III	Office of National Drug Control Policy (Parts 1400—1499)

Title 22—Foreign Relations

I	Department of State (Parts 1—199)
II	Agency for International Development (Parts 200—299)
III	Peace Corps (Parts 300—399)
IV	International Joint Commission, United States and Canada (Parts 400—499)
V	Broadcasting Board of Governors (Parts 500—599)
VII	Overseas Private Investment Corporation (Parts 700—799)
IX	Foreign Service Grievance Board (Parts 900—999)
X	Inter-American Foundation (Parts 1000—1099)
XI	International Boundary and Water Commission, United States and Mexico, United States Section (Parts 1100—1199)
XII	United States International Development Cooperation Agency (Parts 1200—1299)
XIII	Millennium Challenge Corporation (Parts 1300—1399)
XIV	Foreign Service Labor Relations Board; Federal Labor Relations Authority; General Counsel of the Federal Labor Relations Authority; and the Foreign Service Impasse Disputes Panel (Parts 1400—1499)
XV	African Development Foundation (Parts 1500—1599)
XVI	Japan-United States Friendship Commission (Parts 1600—1699)
XVII	United States Institute of Peace (Parts 1700—1799)

Title 23—Highways

I	Federal Highway Administration, Department of Transportation (Parts 1—999)

Chap.

II National Highway Traffic Safety Administration and Federal Highway Administration, Department of Transportation (Parts 1200—1299)

III National Highway Traffic Safety Administration, Department of Transportation (Parts 1300—1399)

Title 24—Housing and Urban Development

SUBTITLE A—OFFICE OF THE SECRETARY, DEPARTMENT OF HOUSING AND URBAN DEVELOPMENT (PARTS 0—99)

SUBTITLE B—REGULATIONS RELATING TO HOUSING AND URBAN DEVELOPMENT

I Office of Assistant Secretary for Equal Opportunity, Department of Housing and Urban Development (Parts 100—199)

II Office of Assistant Secretary for Housing-Federal Housing Commissioner, Department of Housing and Urban Development (Parts 200—299)

III Government National Mortgage Association, Department of Housing and Urban Development (Parts 300—399)

IV Office of Housing and Office of Multifamily Housing Assistance Restructuring, Department of Housing and Urban Development (Parts 400—499)

V Office of Assistant Secretary for Community Planning and Development, Department of Housing and Urban Development (Parts 500—599)

VI Office of Assistant Secretary for Community Planning and Development, Department of Housing and Urban Development (Parts 600—699) [Reserved]

VII Office of the Secretary, Department of Housing and Urban Development (Housing Assistance Programs and Public and Indian Housing Programs) (Parts 700—799)

VIII Office of the Assistant Secretary for Housing—Federal Housing Commissioner, Department of Housing and Urban Development (Section 8 Housing Assistance Programs, Section 202 Direct Loan Program, Section 202 Supportive Housing for the Elderly Program and Section 811 Supportive Housing for Persons With Disabilities Program) (Parts 800—899)

IX Office of Assistant Secretary for Public and Indian Housing, Department of Housing and Urban Development (Parts 900—1699)

XII Office of Inspector General, Department of Housing and Urban Development (Parts 2000—2099)

XV Emergency Mortgage Insurance and Loan Programs, Department of Housing and Urban Development (Parts 2700—2799) [Reserved]

XX Office of Assistant Secretary for Housing—Federal Housing Commissioner, Department of Housing and Urban Development (Parts 3200—3899)

XXIV Board of Directors of the HOPE for Homeowners Program (Parts 4000—4099) [Reserved]

XXV Neighborhood Reinvestment Corporation (Parts 4100—4199)

Title 25—Indians

Chap.

I Bureau of Indian Affairs, Department of the Interior (Parts 1—299)

II Indian Arts and Crafts Board, Department of the Interior (Parts 300—399)

III National Indian Gaming Commission, Department of the Interior (Parts 500—599)

IV Office of Navajo and Hopi Indian Relocation (Parts 700—899)

V Bureau of Indian Affairs, Department of the Interior, and Indian Health Service, Department of Health and Human Services (Part 900—999)

VI Office of the Assistant Secretary, Indian Affairs, Department of the Interior (Parts 1000—1199)

VII Office of the Special Trustee for American Indians, Department of the Interior (Parts 1200—1299)

Title 26—Internal Revenue

I Internal Revenue Service, Department of the Treasury (Parts 1—End)

Title 27—Alcohol, Tobacco Products and Firearms

I Alcohol and Tobacco Tax and Trade Bureau, Department of the Treasury (Parts 1—399)

II Bureau of Alcohol, Tobacco, Firearms, and Explosives, Department of Justice (Parts 400—699)

Title 28—Judicial Administration

I Department of Justice (Parts 0—299)

III Federal Prison Industries, Inc., Department of Justice (Parts 300—399)

V Bureau of Prisons, Department of Justice (Parts 500—599)

VI Offices of Independent Counsel, Department of Justice (Parts 600—699)

VII Office of Independent Counsel (Parts 700—799)

VIII Court Services and Offender Supervision Agency for the District of Columbia (Parts 800—899)

IX National Crime Prevention and Privacy Compact Council (Parts 900—999)

XI Department of Justice and Department of State (Parts 1100—1199)

Title 29—Labor

SUBTITLE A—OFFICE OF THE SECRETARY OF LABOR (PARTS 0—99)

SUBTITLE B—REGULATIONS RELATING TO LABOR

I National Labor Relations Board (Parts 100—199)

Title 29—Labor—Continued

Chap.

II Office of Labor-Management Standards, Department of Labor (Parts 200—299)

III National Railroad Adjustment Board (Parts 300—399)

IV Office of Labor-Management Standards, Department of Labor (Parts 400—499)

V Wage and Hour Division, Department of Labor (Parts 500—899)

IX Construction Industry Collective Bargaining Commission (Parts 900—999)

X National Mediation Board (Parts 1200—1299)

XII Federal Mediation and Conciliation Service (Parts 1400—1499)

XIV Equal Employment Opportunity Commission (Parts 1600—1699)

XVII Occupational Safety and Health Administration, Department of Labor (Parts 1900—1999)

XX Occupational Safety and Health Review Commission (Parts 2200—2499)

XXV Employee Benefits Security Administration, Department of Labor (Parts 2500—2599)

XXVII Federal Mine Safety and Health Review Commission (Parts 2700—2799)

XL Pension Benefit Guaranty Corporation (Parts 4000—4999)

Title 30—Mineral Resources

I Mine Safety and Health Administration, Department of Labor (Parts 1—199)

II Bureau of Safety and Environmental Enforcement, Department of the Interior (Parts 200—299)

IV Geological Survey, Department of the Interior (Parts 400—499)

V Bureau of Ocean Energy Management, Department of the Interior (Parts 500—599)

VII Office of Surface Mining Reclamation and Enforcement, Department of the Interior (Parts 700—999)

XII Office of Natural Resources Revenue, Department of the Interior (Parts 1200—1299)

Title 31—Money and Finance: Treasury

SUBTITLE A—OFFICE OF THE SECRETARY OF THE TREASURY (PARTS 0—50)

SUBTITLE B—REGULATIONS RELATING TO MONEY AND FINANCE

I Monetary Offices, Department of the Treasury (Parts 51—199)

II Fiscal Service, Department of the Treasury (Parts 200—399)

IV Secret Service, Department of the Treasury (Parts 400—499)

V Office of Foreign Assets Control, Department of the Treasury (Parts 500—599)

VI Bureau of Engraving and Printing, Department of the Treasury (Parts 600—699)

VII Federal Law Enforcement Training Center, Department of the Treasury (Parts 700—799)

Chap.

Chap.	
VIII	Office of Investment Security, Department of the Treasury (Parts 800—899)
IX	Federal Claims Collection Standards (Department of the Treasury—Department of Justice) (Parts 900—999)
X	Financial Crimes Enforcement Network, Department of the Treasury (Parts 1000—1099)

Title 32—National Defense

	SUBTITLE A—DEPARTMENT OF DEFENSE
I	Office of the Secretary of Defense (Parts 1—399)
V	Department of the Army (Parts 400—699)
VI	Department of the Navy (Parts 700—799)
VII	Department of the Air Force (Parts 800—1099)
	SUBTITLE B—OTHER REGULATIONS RELATING TO NATIONAL DEFENSE
XII	Defense Logistics Agency (Parts 1200—1299)
XVI	Selective Service System (Parts 1600—1699)
XVII	Office of the Director of National Intelligence (Parts 1700—1799)
XVIII	National Counterintelligence Center (Parts 1800—1899)
XIX	Central Intelligence Agency (Parts 1900—1999)
XX	Information Security Oversight Office, National Archives and Records Administration (Parts 2000—2099)
XXI	National Security Council (Parts 2100—2199)
XXIV	Office of Science and Technology Policy (Parts 2400—2499)
XXVII	Office for Micronesian Status Negotiations (Parts 2700—2799)
XXVIII	Office of the Vice President of the United States (Parts 2800—2899)

Title 33—Navigation and Navigable Waters

I	Coast Guard, Department of Homeland Security (Parts 1—199)
II	Corps of Engineers, Department of the Army, Department of Defense (Parts 200—399)
IV	Saint Lawrence Seaway Development Corporation, Department of Transportation (Parts 400—499)

Title 34—Education

	SUBTITLE A—OFFICE OF THE SECRETARY, DEPARTMENT OF EDUCATION (PARTS 1—99)
	SUBTITLE B—REGULATIONS OF THE OFFICES OF THE DEPARTMENT OF EDUCATION
I	Office for Civil Rights, Department of Education (Parts 100—199)
II	Office of Elementary and Secondary Education, Department of Education (Parts 200—299)
III	Office of Special Education and Rehabilitative Services, Department of Education (Parts 300—399)

Chap.

IV Office of Career, Technical and Adult Education, Department of Education (Parts 400—499)

V Office of Bilingual Education and Minority Languages Affairs, Department of Education (Parts 500—599) [Reserved]

VI Office of Postsecondary Education, Department of Education (Parts 600—699)

VII Office of Educational Research and Improvement, Department of Education (Parts 700—799) [Reserved]

SUBTITLE C—REGULATIONS RELATING TO EDUCATION

XI (Parts 1100—1199) [Reserved]

XII National Council on Disability (Parts 1200—1299)

Title 35 [Reserved]

Title 36—Parks, Forests, and Public Property

I National Park Service, Department of the Interior (Parts 1—199)

II Forest Service, Department of Agriculture (Parts 200—299)

III Corps of Engineers, Department of the Army (Parts 300—399)

IV American Battle Monuments Commission (Parts 400—499)

V Smithsonian Institution (Parts 500—599)

VI [Reserved]

VII Library of Congress (Parts 700—799)

VIII Advisory Council on Historic Preservation (Parts 800—899)

IX Pennsylvania Avenue Development Corporation (Parts 900—999)

X Presidio Trust (Parts 1000—1099)

XI Architectural and Transportation Barriers Compliance Board (Parts 1100—1199)

XII National Archives and Records Administration (Parts 1200—1299)

XV Oklahoma City National Memorial Trust (Parts 1500—1599)

XVI Morris K. Udall Scholarship and Excellence in National Environmental Policy Foundation (Parts 1600—1699)

Title 37—Patents, Trademarks, and Copyrights

I United States Patent and Trademark Office, Department of Commerce (Parts 1—199)

II U.S. Copyright Office, Library of Congress (Parts 200—299)

III Copyright Royalty Board, Library of Congress (Parts 300—399)

IV National Institute of Standards and Technology, Department of Commerce (Parts 400—599)

Title 38—Pensions, Bonuses, and Veterans' Relief

I Department of Veterans Affairs (Parts 0—199)

II Armed Forces Retirement Home (Parts 200—299)

Title 39—Postal Service

Chap.	
I	United States Postal Service (Parts 1—999)
III	Postal Regulatory Commission (Parts 3000—3099)

Title 40—Protection of Environment

I	Environmental Protection Agency (Parts 1—1099)
IV	Environmental Protection Agency and Department of Justice (Parts 1400—1499)
V	Council on Environmental Quality (Parts 1500—1599)
VI	Chemical Safety and Hazard Investigation Board (Parts 1600—1699)
VII	Environmental Protection Agency and Department of Defense; Uniform National Discharge Standards for Vessels of the Armed Forces (Parts 1700—1799)
VIII	Gulf Coast Ecosystem Restoration Council (Parts 1800—1899)

Title 41—Public Contracts and Property Management

	SUBTITLE A—FEDERAL PROCUREMENT REGULATIONS SYSTEM [NOTE]
	SUBTITLE B—OTHER PROVISIONS RELATING TO PUBLIC CONTRACTS
50	Public Contracts, Department of Labor (Parts 50–1—50–999)
51	Committee for Purchase From People Who Are Blind or Severely Disabled (Parts 51–1—51–99)
60	Office of Federal Contract Compliance Programs, Equal Employment Opportunity, Department of Labor (Parts 60–1—60–999)
61	Office of the Assistant Secretary for Veterans' Employment and Training Service, Department of Labor (Parts 61–1—61–999)
62—100	[Reserved]
	SUBTITLE C—FEDERAL PROPERTY MANAGEMENT REGULATIONS SYSTEM
101	Federal Property Management Regulations (Parts 101–1—101–99)
102	Federal Management Regulation (Parts 102–1—102–299)
103—104	[Reserved]
105	General Services Administration (Parts 105–1—105–999)
109	Department of Energy Property Management Regulations (Parts 109–1—109–99)
114	Department of the Interior (Parts 114–1—114–99)
115	Environmental Protection Agency (Parts 115–1—115–99)
128	Department of Justice (Parts 128–1—128–99)
129—200	[Reserved]
	SUBTITLE D—OTHER PROVISIONS RELATING TO PROPERTY MANAGEMENT [RESERVED]
	SUBTITLE E—FEDERAL INFORMATION RESOURCES MANAGEMENT REGULATIONS SYSTEM [RESERVED]
	SUBTITLE F—FEDERAL TRAVEL REGULATION SYSTEM
300	General (Parts 300–1—300–99)
301	Temporary Duty (TDY) Travel Allowances (Parts 301–1—301–99)

Title 41—Public Contracts and Property Management—Continued

Chap.

302 Relocation Allowances (Parts 302-1—302-99)

303 Payment of Expenses Connected with the Death of Certain Employees (Part 303-1—303-99)

304 Payment of Travel Expenses from a Non-Federal Source (Parts 304-1—304-99)

Title 42—Public Health

I Public Health Service, Department of Health and Human Services (Parts 1—199)

II—III [Reserved]

IV Centers for Medicare & Medicaid Services, Department of Health and Human Services (Parts 400—699)

V Office of Inspector General-Health Care, Department of Health and Human Services (Parts 1000—1099)

Title 43—Public Lands: Interior

SUBTITLE A—OFFICE OF THE SECRETARY OF THE INTERIOR (PARTS 1—199)

SUBTITLE B—REGULATIONS RELATING TO PUBLIC LANDS

I Bureau of Reclamation, Department of the Interior (Parts 400—999)

II Bureau of Land Management, Department of the Interior (Parts 1000—9999)

III Utah Reclamation Mitigation and Conservation Commission (Parts 10000—10099)

Title 44—Emergency Management and Assistance

I Federal Emergency Management Agency, Department of Homeland Security (Parts 0—399)

IV Department of Commerce and Department of Transportation (Parts 400—499)

Title 45—Public Welfare

SUBTITLE A—DEPARTMENT OF HEALTH AND HUMAN SERVICES (PARTS 1—199)

SUBTITLE B—REGULATIONS RELATING TO PUBLIC WELFARE

II Office of Family Assistance (Assistance Programs), Administration for Children and Families, Department of Health and Human Services (Parts 200—299)

III Office of Child Support Enforcement (Child Support Enforcement Program), Administration for Children and Families, Department of Health and Human Services (Parts 300—399)

IV Office of Refugee Resettlement, Administration for Children and Families, Department of Health and Human Services (Parts 400—499)

Title 45—Public Welfare—Continued

Chap.

V Foreign Claims Settlement Commission of the United States, Department of Justice (Parts 500—599)

VI National Science Foundation (Parts 600—699)

VII Commission on Civil Rights (Parts 700—799)

VIII Office of Personnel Management (Parts 800—899)

IX Denali Commission (Parts 900—999)

X Office of Community Services, Administration for Children and Families, Department of Health and Human Services (Parts 1000—1099)

XI National Foundation on the Arts and the Humanities (Parts 1100—1199)

XII Corporation for National and Community Service (Parts 1200—1299)

XIII Administration for Children and Families, Department of Health and Human Services (Parts 1300—1399)

XVI Legal Services Corporation (Parts 1600—1699)

XVII National Commission on Libraries and Information Science (Parts 1700—1799)

XVIII Harry S. Truman Scholarship Foundation (Parts 1800—1899)

XXI Commission of Fine Arts (Parts 2100—2199)

XXIII Arctic Research Commission (Parts 2300—2399)

XXIV James Madison Memorial Fellowship Foundation (Parts 2400—2499)

XXV Corporation for National and Community Service (Parts 2500—2599)

Title 46—Shipping

I Coast Guard, Department of Homeland Security (Parts 1—199)

II Maritime Administration, Department of Transportation (Parts 200—399)

III Coast Guard (Great Lakes Pilotage), Department of Homeland Security (Parts 400—499)

IV Federal Maritime Commission (Parts 500—599)

Title 47—Telecommunication

I Federal Communications Commission (Parts 0—199)

II Office of Science and Technology Policy and National Security Council (Parts 200—299)

III National Telecommunications and Information Administration, Department of Commerce (Parts 300—399)

IV National Telecommunications and Information Administration, Department of Commerce, and National Highway Traffic Safety Administration, Department of Transportation (Parts 400—499)

V The First Responder Network Authority (Parts 500—599)

Title 48—Federal Acquisition Regulations System

Chap.

Chap.	
1	Federal Acquisition Regulation (Parts 1—99)
2	Defense Acquisition Regulations System, Department of Defense (Parts 200—299)
3	Department of Health and Human Services (Parts 300—399)
4	Department of Agriculture (Parts 400—499)
5	General Services Administration (Parts 500—599)
6	Department of State (Parts 600—699)
7	Agency for International Development (Parts 700—799)
8	Department of Veterans Affairs (Parts 800—899)
9	Department of Energy (Parts 900—999)
10	Department of the Treasury (Parts 1000—1099)
12	Department of Transportation (Parts 1200—1299)
13	Department of Commerce (Parts 1300—1399)
14	Department of the Interior (Parts 1400—1499)
15	Environmental Protection Agency (Parts 1500—1599)
16	Office of Personnel Management, Federal Employees Health Benefits Acquisition Regulation (Parts 1600—1699)
17	Office of Personnel Management (Parts 1700—1799)
18	National Aeronautics and Space Administration (Parts 1800—1899)
19	Broadcasting Board of Governors (Parts 1900—1999)
20	Nuclear Regulatory Commission (Parts 2000—2099)
21	Office of Personnel Management, Federal Employees Group Life Insurance Federal Acquisition Regulation (Parts 2100—2199)
23	Social Security Administration (Parts 2300—2399)
24	Department of Housing and Urban Development (Parts 2400—2499)
25	National Science Foundation (Parts 2500—2599)
28	Department of Justice (Parts 2800—2899)
29	Department of Labor (Parts 2900—2999)
30	Department of Homeland Security, Homeland Security Acquisition Regulation (HSAR) (Parts 3000—3099)
34	Department of Education Acquisition Regulation (Parts 3400—3499)
51	Department of the Army Acquisition Regulations (Parts 5100—5199)
52	Department of the Navy Acquisition Regulations (Parts 5200—5299)
53	Department of the Air Force Federal Acquisition Regulation Supplement (Parts 5300—5399) [Reserved]
54	Defense Logistics Agency, Department of Defense (Parts 5400—5499)
57	African Development Foundation (Parts 5700—5799)
61	Civilian Board of Contract Appeals, General Services Administration (Parts 6100—6199)
99	Cost Accounting Standards Board, Office of Federal Procurement Policy, Office of Management and Budget (Parts 9900—9999)

Title 49—Transportation

Chap.

SUBTITLE A—OFFICE OF THE SECRETARY OF TRANSPORTATION (PARTS 1—99)

SUBTITLE B—OTHER REGULATIONS RELATING TO TRANSPORTATION

I Pipeline and Hazardous Materials Safety Administration, Department of Transportation (Parts 100—199)

II Federal Railroad Administration, Department of Transportation (Parts 200—299)

III Federal Motor Carrier Safety Administration, Department of Transportation (Parts 300—399)

IV Coast Guard, Department of Homeland Security (Parts 400—499)

V National Highway Traffic Safety Administration, Department of Transportation (Parts 500—599)

VI Federal Transit Administration, Department of Transportation (Parts 600—699)

VII National Railroad Passenger Corporation (AMTRAK) (Parts 700—799)

VIII National Transportation Safety Board (Parts 800—999)

X Surface Transportation Board (Parts 1000—1399)

XI Research and Innovative Technology Administration, Department of Transportation (Parts 1400—1499) [Reserved]

XII Transportation Security Administration, Department of Homeland Security (Parts 1500—1699)

Title 50—Wildlife and Fisheries

I United States Fish and Wildlife Service, Department of the Interior (Parts 1—199)

II National Marine Fisheries Service, National Oceanic and Atmospheric Administration, Department of Commerce (Parts 200—299)

III International Fishing and Related Activities (Parts 300—399)

IV Joint Regulations (United States Fish and Wildlife Service, Department of the Interior and National Marine Fisheries Service, National Oceanic and Atmospheric Administration, Department of Commerce); Endangered Species Committee Regulations (Parts 400—499)

V Marine Mammal Commission (Parts 500—599)

VI Fishery Conservation and Management, National Oceanic and Atmospheric Administration, Department of Commerce (Parts 600—699)

Alphabetical List of Agencies Appearing in the CFR

(Revised as of January 1, 2019)

Agency	CFR Title, Subtitle or Chapter
Administrative Conference of the United States	1, III
Advisory Council on Historic Preservation	36, VIII
Advocacy and Outreach, Office of	7, XXV
Afghanistan Reconstruction, Special Inspector General for	5, LXXXIII
African Development Foundation	22, XV
Federal Acquisition Regulation	48, 57
Agency for International Development	2, VII; 22, II
Federal Acquisition Regulation	48, 7
Agricultural Marketing Service	7, I, IX, X, XI
Agricultural Research Service	7, V
Agriculture, Department of	2, IV; 5, LXXIII
Advocacy and Outreach, Office of	7, XXV
Agricultural Marketing Service	7, I, IX, X, XI
Agricultural Research Service	7, V
Animal and Plant Health Inspection Service	7, III; 9, I
Chief Financial Officer, Office of	7, XXX
Commodity Credit Corporation	7, XIV
Economic Research Service	7, XXXVII
Energy Policy and New Uses, Office of	2, IX; 7, XXIX
Environmental Quality, Office of	7, XXXI
Farm Service Agency	7, VII, XVIII
Federal Acquisition Regulation	48, 4
Federal Crop Insurance Corporation	7, IV
Food and Nutrition Service	7, II
Food Safety and Inspection Service	9, III
Foreign Agricultural Service	7, XV
Forest Service	36, II
Grain Inspection, Packers and Stockyards Administration	7, VIII; 9, II
Information Resources Management, Office of	7, XXVII
Inspector General, Office of	7, XXVI
National Agricultural Library	7, XLI
National Agricultural Statistics Service	7, XXXVI
National Institute of Food and Agriculture	7, XXXIV
Natural Resources Conservation Service	7, VI
Operations, Office of	7, XXVIII
Procurement and Property Management, Office of	7, XXXII
Rural Business-Cooperative Service	7, XVIII, XLII
Rural Development Administration	7, XLII
Rural Housing Service	7, XVIII, XXXV
Rural Telephone Bank	7, XVI
Rural Utilities Service	7, XVII, XVIII, XLII
Secretary of Agriculture, Office of	7, Subtitle A
Transportation, Office of	7, XXXIII
World Agricultural Outlook Board	7, XXXVIII
Air Force, Department of	32, VII
Federal Acquisition Regulation Supplement	48, 53
Air Transportation Stabilization Board	14, VI
Alcohol and Tobacco Tax and Trade Bureau	27, I
Alcohol, Tobacco, Firearms, and Explosives, Bureau of	27, II
AMTRAK	49, VII
American Battle Monuments Commission	36, IV
American Indians, Office of the Special Trustee	25, VII
Animal and Plant Health Inspection Service	7, III; 9, I

Agency	CFR Title, Subtitle or Chapter
Appalachian Regional Commission	5, IX
Architectural and Transportation Barriers Compliance Board	36, XI
Arctic Research Commission	45, XXIII
Armed Forces Retirement Home	5, XI
Army, Department of	32, V
Engineers, Corps of	33, II; 36, III
Federal Acquisition Regulation	48, 51
Bilingual Education and Minority Languages Affairs, Office of	34, V
Blind or Severely Disabled, Committee for Purchase from People Who Are	41, 51
Broadcasting Board of Governors	22, V
Federal Acquisition Regulation	48, 19
Career, Technical, and Adult Education, Office of	34, IV
Census Bureau	15, I
Centers for Medicare & Medicaid Services	42, IV
Central Intelligence Agency	32, XIX
Chemical Safety and Hazardous Investigation Board	40, VI
Chief Financial Officer, Office of	7, XXX
Child Support Enforcement, Office of	45, III
Children and Families, Administration for	45, II, III, IV, X, XIII
Civil Rights, Commission on	5, LXVIII; 45, VII
Civil Rights, Office for	34, I
Council of the Inspectors General on Integrity and Efficiency	5, XCVIII
Court Services and Offender Supervision Agency for the District of Columbia	5, LXX
Coast Guard	33, I; 46, I; 49, IV
Coast Guard (Great Lakes Pilotage)	46, III
Commerce, Department of	2, XIII; 44, IV; 50, VI
Census Bureau	15, I
Economic Analysis, Bureau of	15, VIII
Economic Development Administration	13, III
Emergency Management and Assistance	44, IV
Federal Acquisition Regulation	48, 13
Foreign-Trade Zones Board	15, IV
Industry and Security, Bureau of	15, VII
International Trade Administration	15, III; 19, III
National Institute of Standards and Technology	15, II; 37, IV
National Marine Fisheries Service	50, II, IV
National Oceanic and Atmospheric Administration	15, IX; 50, II, III, IV, VI
National Technical Information Service	15, XI
National Telecommunications and Information Administration	15, XXIII; 47, III, IV
National Weather Service	15, IX
Patent and Trademark Office, United States	37, I
Secretary of Commerce, Office of	15, Subtitle A
Commercial Space Transportation	14, III
Commodity Credit Corporation	7, XIV
Commodity Futures Trading Commission	5, XLI; 17, I
Community Planning and Development, Office of Assistant Secretary for	24, V, VI
Community Services, Office of	45, X
Comptroller of the Currency	12, I
Construction Industry Collective Bargaining Commission	29, IX
Consumer Financial Protection Bureau	5, LXXXIV; 12, X
Consumer Product Safety Commission	5, LXXI; 16, II
Copyright Royalty Board	37, III
Corporation for National and Community Service	2, XXII; 45, XII, XXV
Cost Accounting Standards Board	48, 99
Council on Environmental Quality	40, V
Court Services and Offender Supervision Agency for the District of Columbia	5, LXX; 28, VIII
Customs and Border Protection	19, I
Defense Contract Audit Agency	32, I
Defense, Department of	2, XI; 5, XXVI; 32, Subtitle A; 40, VII
Advanced Research Projects Agency	32, I
Air Force Department	32, VII

Agency	CFR Title, Subtitle or Chapter
Army Department	32, V; 33, II; 36, III; 48, 51
Defense Acquisition Regulations System	48, 2
Defense Intelligence Agency	32, I
Defense Logistics Agency	32, I, XII; 48, 54
Engineers, Corps of	33, II; 36, III
National Imagery and Mapping Agency	32, I
Navy Department	32, VI; 48, 52
Secretary of Defense, Office of	2, XI; 32, I
Defense Contract Audit Agency	32, I
Defense Intelligence Agency	32, I
Defense Logistics Agency	32, XII; 48, 54
Defense Nuclear Facilities Safety Board	10, XVII
Delaware River Basin Commission	18, III
Denali Commission	45, IX
Disability, National Council on	5, C; 34, XII
District of Columbia, Court Services and Offender Supervision Agency for the	5, LXX; 28, VIII
Drug Enforcement Administration	21, II
East-West Foreign Trade Board	15, XIII
Economic Analysis, Bureau of	15, VIII
Economic Development Administration	13, III
Economic Research Service	7, XXXVII
Education, Department of	2, XXXIV; 5, LIII
Bilingual Education and Minority Languages Affairs, Office of	34, V
Career, Technical, and Adult Education, Office of	34, IV
Civil Rights, Office for	34, I
Educational Research and Improvement, Office of	34, VII
Elementary and Secondary Education, Office of	34, II
Federal Acquisition Regulation	48, 34
Postsecondary Education, Office of	34, VI
Secretary of Education, Office of	34, Subtitle A
Special Education and Rehabilitative Services, Office of	34, III
Educational Research and Improvement, Office of	34, VII
Election Assistance Commission	2, LVIII; 11, II
Elementary and Secondary Education, Office of	34, II
Emergency Oil and Gas Guaranteed Loan Board	13, V
Emergency Steel Guarantee Loan Board	13, IV
Employee Benefits Security Administration	29, XXV
Employees' Compensation Appeals Board	20, IV
Employees Loyalty Board	5, V
Employment and Training Administration	20, V
Employment Policy, National Commission for	1, IV
Employment Standards Administration	20, VI
Endangered Species Committee	50, IV
Energy, Department of	2, IX; 5, XXIII; 10, II, III, X
Federal Acquisition Regulation	48, 9
Federal Energy Regulatory Commission	5, XXIV; 18, I
Property Management Regulations	41, 109
Energy, Office of	7, XXIX
Engineers, Corps of	33, II; 36, III
Engraving and Printing, Bureau of	31, VI
Environmental Protection Agency	2, XV; 5, LIV; 40, I, IV, VII
Federal Acquisition Regulation	48, 15
Property Management Regulations	41, 115
Environmental Quality, Office of	7, XXXI
Equal Employment Opportunity Commission	5, LXII; 29, XIV
Equal Opportunity, Office of Assistant Secretary for	24, I
Executive Office of the President	3, I
Environmental Quality, Council on	40, V
Management and Budget, Office of	2, Subtitle A; 5, III, LXXVII; 14, VI; 48, 99
National Drug Control Policy, Office of	2, XXXVI; 21, III
National Security Council	32, XXI; 47, 2

Agency	CFR Title, Subtitle or Chapter
Presidential Documents	3
Science and Technology Policy, Office of	32, XXIV; 47, II
Trade Representative, Office of the United States	15, XX
Export-Import Bank of the United States	2, XXXV; 5, LII; 12, IV
Family Assistance, Office of	45, II
Farm Credit Administration	5, XXXI; 12, VI
Farm Credit System Insurance Corporation	5, XXX; 12, XIV
Farm Service Agency	7, VII, XVIII
Federal Acquisition Regulation	48, 1
Federal Aviation Administration	14, I
Commercial Space Transportation	14, III
Federal Claims Collection Standards	31, IX
Federal Communications Commission	5, XXIX; 47, I
Federal Contract Compliance Programs, Office of	41, 60
Federal Crop Insurance Corporation	7, IV
Federal Deposit Insurance Corporation	5, XXII; 12, III
Federal Election Commission	5, XXXVII; 11, I
Federal Emergency Management Agency	44, I
Federal Employees Group Life Insurance Federal Acquisition Regulation	48, 21
Federal Employees Health Benefits Acquisition Regulation	48, 16
Federal Energy Regulatory Commission	5, XXIV; 18, I
Federal Financial Institutions Examination Council	12, XI
Federal Financing Bank	12, VIII
Federal Highway Administration	23, I, II
Federal Home Loan Mortgage Corporation	1, IV
Federal Housing Enterprise Oversight Office	12, XVII
Federal Housing Finance Agency	5, LXXX; 12, XII
Federal Housing Finance Board	12, IX
Federal Labor Relations Authority	5, XIV, XLIX; 22, XIV
Federal Law Enforcement Training Center	31, VII
Federal Management Regulation	41, 102
Federal Maritime Commission	46, IV
Federal Mediation and Conciliation Service	29, XII
Federal Mine Safety and Health Review Commission	5, LXXIV; 29, XXVII
Federal Motor Carrier Safety Administration	49, III
Federal Prison Industries, Inc.	28, III
Federal Procurement Policy Office	48, 99
Federal Property Management Regulations	41, 101
Federal Railroad Administration	49, II
Federal Register, Administrative Committee of	1, I
Federal Register, Office of	1, II
Federal Reserve System	12, II
Board of Governors	5, LVIII
Federal Retirement Thrift Investment Board	5, VI, LXXVI
Federal Service Impasses Panel	5, XIV
Federal Trade Commission	5, XLVII; 16, I
Federal Transit Administration	49, VI
Federal Travel Regulation System	41, Subtitle F
Financial Crimes Enforcement Network	31, X
Financial Research Office	12, XVI
Financial Stability Oversight Council	12, XIII
Fine Arts, Commission of	45, XXI
Fiscal Service	31, II
Fish and Wildlife Service, United States	50, I, IV
Food and Drug Administration	21, I
Food and Nutrition Service	7, II
Food Safety and Inspection Service	9, III
Foreign Agricultural Service	7, XV
Foreign Assets Control, Office of	31, V
Foreign Claims Settlement Commission of the United States	45, V
Foreign Service Grievance Board	22, IX
Foreign Service Impasse Disputes Panel	22, XIV
Foreign Service Labor Relations Board	22, XIV
Foreign-Trade Zones Board	15, IV
Forest Service	36, II
General Services Administration	5, LVII; 41, 105

Agency	CFR Title, Subtitle or Chapter
Contract Appeals, Board of	48, 61
Federal Acquisition Regulation	48, 5
Federal Management Regulation	41, 102
Federal Property Management Regulations	41, 101
Federal Travel Regulation System	41, Subtitle F
General	41, 300
Payment From a Non-Federal Source for Travel Expenses	41, 304
Payment of Expenses Connected With the Death of Certain Employees	41, 303
Relocation Allowances	41, 302
Temporary Duty (TDY) Travel Allowances	41, 301
Geological Survey	30, IV
Government Accountability Office	4, I
Government Ethics, Office of	5, XVI
Government National Mortgage Association	24, III
Grain Inspection, Packers and Stockyards Administration	7, VIII; 9, II
Gulf Coast Ecosystem Restoration Council	2, LIX; 40, VIII
Harry S. Truman Scholarship Foundation	45, XVIII
Health and Human Services, Department of	2, III; 5, XLV; 45, Subtitle A
Centers for Medicare & Medicaid Services	42, IV
Child Support Enforcement, Office of	45, III
Children and Families, Administration for	45, II, III, IV, X, XIII
Community Services, Office of	45, X
Family Assistance, Office of	45, II
Federal Acquisition Regulation	48, 3
Food and Drug Administration	21, I
Indian Health Service	25, V
Inspector General (Health Care), Office of	42, V
Public Health Service	42, I
Refugee Resettlement, Office of	45, IV
Homeland Security, Department of	2, XXX; 5, XXXVI; 6, I; 8, I
Coast Guard	33, I; 46, I; 49, IV
Coast Guard (Great Lakes Pilotage)	46, III
Customs and Border Protection	19, I
Federal Emergency Management Agency	44, I
Human Resources Management and Labor Relations Systems	5, XCVII
Immigration and Customs Enforcement Bureau	19, IV
Transportation Security Administration	49, XII
HOPE for Homeowners Program, Board of Directors of	24, XXIV
Housing and Urban Development, Department of	2, XXIV; 5, LXV; 24, Subtitle B
Community Planning and Development, Office of Assistant Secretary for	24, V, VI
Equal Opportunity, Office of Assistant Secretary for	24, I
Federal Acquisition Regulation	48, 24
Federal Housing Enterprise Oversight, Office of	12, XVII
Government National Mortgage Association	24, III
Housing—Federal Housing Commissioner, Office of Assistant Secretary for	24, II, VIII, X, XX
Housing, Office of, and Multifamily Housing Assistance Restructuring, Office of	24, IV
Inspector General, Office of	24, XII
Public and Indian Housing, Office of Assistant Secretary for	24, IX
Secretary, Office of	24, Subtitle A, VII
Housing—Federal Housing Commissioner, Office of Assistant Secretary for	24, II, VIII, X, XX
Housing, Office of, and Multifamily Housing Assistance Restructuring, Office of	24, IV
Immigration and Customs Enforcement Bureau	19, IV
Immigration Review, Executive Office for	8, V
Independent Counsel, Office of	28, VII
Independent Counsel, Offices of	28, VI
Indian Affairs, Bureau of	25, I, V
Indian Affairs, Office of the Assistant Secretary	25, VI

Agency	CFR Title, Subtitle or Chapter
Indian Arts and Crafts Board	25, II
Indian Health Service	25, V
Industry and Security, Bureau of	15, VII
Information Resources Management, Office of	7, XXVII
Information Security Oversight Office, National Archives and Records Administration	32, XX
Inspector General	
Agriculture Department	7, XXVI
Health and Human Services Department	42, V
Housing and Urban Development Department	24, XII, XV
Institute of Peace, United States	22, XVII
Inter-American Foundation	5, LXIII; 22, X
Interior, Department of	2, XIV
American Indians, Office of the Special Trustee	25, VII
Endangered Species Committee	50, IV
Federal Acquisition Regulation	48, 14
Federal Property Management Regulations System	41, 114
Fish and Wildlife Service, United States	50, I, IV
Geological Survey	30, IV
Indian Affairs, Bureau of	25, I, V
Indian Affairs, Office of the Assistant Secretary	25, VI
Indian Arts and Crafts Board	25, II
Land Management, Bureau of	43, II
National Indian Gaming Commission	25, III
National Park Service	36, I
Natural Resource Revenue, Office of	30, XII
Ocean Energy Management, Bureau of	30, V
Reclamation, Bureau of	43, I
Safety and Enforcement Bureau, Bureau of	30, II
Secretary of the Interior, Office of	2, XIV; 43, Subtitle A
Surface Mining Reclamation and Enforcement, Office of	30, VII
Internal Revenue Service	26, I
International Boundary and Water Commission, United States and Mexico, United States Section	22, XI
International Development, United States Agency for	22, II
Federal Acquisition Regulation	48, 7
International Development Cooperation Agency, United States	22, XII
International Joint Commission, United States and Canada	22, IV
International Organizations Employees Loyalty Board	5, V
International Trade Administration	15, III; 19, III
International Trade Commission, United States	19, II
Interstate Commerce Commission	5, XL
Investment Security, Office of	31, VIII
James Madison Memorial Fellowship Foundation	45, XXIV
Japan–United States Friendship Commission	22, XVI
Joint Board for the Enrollment of Actuaries	20, VIII
Justice, Department of	2, XXVIII; 5, XXVIII; 28, I, XI; 40, IV
Alcohol, Tobacco, Firearms, and Explosives, Bureau of	27, II
Drug Enforcement Administration	21, II
Federal Acquisition Regulation	48, 28
Federal Claims Collection Standards	31, IX
Federal Prison Industries, Inc.	28, III
Foreign Claims Settlement Commission of the United States	45, V
Immigration Review, Executive Office for	8, V
Independent Counsel, Offices of	28, VI
Prisons, Bureau of	28, V
Property Management Regulations	41, 128
Labor, Department of	2, XXIX; 5, XLII
Employee Benefits Security Administration	29, XXV
Employees' Compensation Appeals Board	20, IV
Employment and Training Administration	20, V
Employment Standards Administration	20, VI
Federal Acquisition Regulation	48, 29
Federal Contract Compliance Programs, Office of	41, 60

Agency	CFR Title, Subtitle or Chapter
Federal Procurement Regulations System	41, 50
Labor-Management Standards, Office of	29, II, IV
Mine Safety and Health Administration	30, I
Occupational Safety and Health Administration	29, XVII
Public Contracts	41, 50
Secretary of Labor, Office of	29, Subtitle A
Veterans' Employment and Training Service, Office of the Assistant Secretary for	41, 61; 20, IX
Wage and Hour Division	29, V
Workers' Compensation Programs, Office of	20, I, VII
Labor-Management Standards, Office of	29, II, IV
Land Management, Bureau of	43, II
Legal Services Corporation	45, XVI
Libraries and Information Science, National Commission on	45, XVII
Library of Congress	36, VII
Copyright Royalty Board	37, III
U.S. Copyright Office	37, II
Local Television Loan Guarantee Board	7, XX
Management and Budget, Office of	5, III, LXXVII; 14, VI; 48, 99
Marine Mammal Commission	50, V
Maritime Administration	46, II
Merit Systems Protection Board	5, II, LXIV
Micronesian Status Negotiations, Office for	32, XXVII
Military Compensation and Retirement Modernization Commission	5, XCIX
Millennium Challenge Corporation	22, XIII
Mine Safety and Health Administration	30, I
Minority Business Development Agency	15, XIV
Miscellaneous Agencies	1, IV
Monetary Offices	31, I
Morris K. Udall Scholarship and Excellence in National Environmental Policy Foundation	36, XVI
Museum and Library Services, Institute of	2, XXXI
National Aeronautics and Space Administration	2, XVIII; 5, LIX; 14, V
Federal Acquisition Regulation	48, 18
National Agricultural Library	7, XLI
National Agricultural Statistics Service	7, XXXVI
National and Community Service, Corporation for	2, XXII; 45, XII, XXV
National Archives and Records Administration	2, XXVI; 5, LXVI; 36, XII
Information Security Oversight Office	32, XX
National Capital Planning Commission	1, IV, VI
National Counterintelligence Center	32, XVIII
National Credit Union Administration	5, LXXXVI; 12, VII
National Crime Prevention and Privacy Compact Council	28, IX
National Drug Control Policy, Office of	2, XXXVI; 21, III
National Endowment for the Arts	2, XXXII
National Endowment for the Humanities	2, XXXIII
National Foundation on the Arts and the Humanities	45, XI
National Geospatial-Intelligence Agency	32, I
National Highway Traffic Safety Administration	23, II, III; 47, VI; 49, V
National Imagery and Mapping Agency	32, I
National Indian Gaming Commission	25, III
National Institute of Food and Agriculture	7, XXXIV
National Institute of Standards and Technology	15, II; 37, IV
National Intelligence, Office of Director of	5, IV; 32, XVII
National Labor Relations Board	5, LXI; 29, I
National Marine Fisheries Service	50, II, IV
National Mediation Board	5, CI; 29, X
National Oceanic and Atmospheric Administration	15, IX; 50, II, III, IV, VI
National Park Service	36, I
National Railroad Adjustment Board	29, III
National Railroad Passenger Corporation (AMTRAK)	49, VII
National Science Foundation	2, XXV; 5, XLIII; 45, VI
Federal Acquisition Regulation	48, 25
National Security Council	32, XXI

Agency	CFR Title, Subtitle or Chapter
National Security Council and Office of Science and Technology Policy	47, II
National Technical Information Service	15, XI
National Telecommunications and Information Administration	15, XXIII; 47, III, IV, V
National Transportation Safety Board	49, VIII
Natural Resources Conservation Service	7, VI
Natural Resource Revenue, Office of	30, XII
Navajo and Hopi Indian Relocation, Office of	25, IV
Navy, Department of	32, VI
Federal Acquisition Regulation	48, 52
Neighborhood Reinvestment Corporation	24, XXV
Northeast Interstate Low-Level Radioactive Waste Commission	10, XVIII
Nuclear Regulatory Commission	2, XX; 5, XLVIII; 10, I
Federal Acquisition Regulation	48, 20
Occupational Safety and Health Administration	29, XVII
Occupational Safety and Health Review Commission	29, XX
Ocean Energy Management, Bureau of	30, V
Oklahoma City National Memorial Trust	36, XV
Operations Office	7, XXVIII
Overseas Private Investment Corporation	5, XXXIII; 22, VII
Patent and Trademark Office, United States	37, I
Payment From a Non-Federal Source for Travel Expenses	41, 304
Payment of Expenses Connected With the Death of Certain Employees	41, 303
Peace Corps	2, XXXVII; 22, III
Pennsylvania Avenue Development Corporation	36, IX
Pension Benefit Guaranty Corporation	29, XL
Personnel Management, Office of	5, I, XXXV; 5, IV; 45, VIII
Human Resources Management and Labor Relations Systems, Department of Homeland Security	5, XCVII
Federal Acquisition Regulation	48, 17
Federal Employees Group Life Insurance Federal Acquisition Regulation	48, 21
Federal Employees Health Benefits Acquisition Regulation	48, 16
Pipeline and Hazardous Materials Safety Administration	49, I
Postal Regulatory Commission	5, XLVI; 39, III
Postal Service, United States	5, LX; 39, I
Postsecondary Education, Office of	34, VI
President's Commission on White House Fellowships	1, IV
Presidential Documents	3
Presidio Trust	36, X
Prisons, Bureau of	28, V
Privacy and Civil Liberties Oversight Board	6, X
Procurement and Property Management, Office of	7, XXXII
Public Contracts, Department of Labor	41, 50
Public and Indian Housing, Office of Assistant Secretary for	24, IX
Public Health Service	42, I
Railroad Retirement Board	20, II
Reclamation, Bureau of	43, I
Refugee Resettlement, Office of	45, IV
Relocation Allowances	41, 302
Research and Innovative Technology Administration	49, XI
Rural Business-Cooperative Service	7, XVIII, XLII
Rural Development Administration	7, XLII
Rural Housing Service	7, XVIII, XXXV
Rural Telephone Bank	7, XVI
Rural Utilities Service	7, XVII, XVIII, XLII
Safety and Environmental Enforcement, Bureau of	30, II
Saint Lawrence Seaway Development Corporation	33, IV
Science and Technology Policy, Office of	32, XXIV
Science and Technology Policy, Office of, and National Security Council	47, II
Secret Service	31, IV
Securities and Exchange Commission	5, XXXIV; 17, II

Agency	CFR Title, Subtitle or Chapter
Selective Service System	32, XVI
Small Business Administration	2, XXVII; 13, I
Smithsonian Institution	36, V
Social Security Administration	2, XXIII; 20, III; 48, 23
Soldiers' and Airmen's Home, United States	5, XI
Special Counsel, Office of	5, VIII
Special Education and Rehabilitative Services, Office of	34, III
State, Department of	2, VI; 22, I; 28, XI
Federal Acquisition Regulation	48, 6
Surface Mining Reclamation and Enforcement, Office of	30, VII
Surface Transportation Board	49, X
Susquehanna River Basin Commission	18, VIII
Tennessee Valley Authority	5, LXIX; 18, XIII
Trade Representative, United States, Office of	15, XX
Transportation, Department of	2, XII; 5, L
Commercial Space Transportation	14, III
Emergency Management and Assistance	44, IV
Federal Acquisition Regulation	48, 12
Federal Aviation Administration	14, I
Federal Highway Administration	23, I, II
Federal Motor Carrier Safety Administration	49, III
Federal Railroad Administration	49, II
Federal Transit Administration	49, VI
Maritime Administration	46, II
National Highway Traffic Safety Administration	23, II, III; 47, IV; 49, V
Pipeline and Hazardous Materials Safety Administration	49, I
Saint Lawrence Seaway Development Corporation	33, IV
Secretary of Transportation, Office of	14, II; 49, Subtitle A
Transportation Statistics Bureau	49, XI
Transportation, Office of	7, XXXIII
Transportation Security Administration	49, XII
Transportation Statistics Bureau	49, XI
Travel Allowances, Temporary Duty (TDY)	41, 301
Treasury, Department of the	2, X;5, XXI; 12, XV; 17, IV; 31, IX
Alcohol and Tobacco Tax and Trade Bureau	27, I
Community Development Financial Institutions Fund	12, XVIII
Comptroller of the Currency	12, I
Customs and Border Protection	19, I
Engraving and Printing, Bureau of	31, VI
Federal Acquisition Regulation	48, 10
Federal Claims Collection Standards	31, IX
Federal Law Enforcement Training Center	31, VII
Financial Crimes Enforcement Network	31, X
Fiscal Service	31, II
Foreign Assets Control, Office of	31, V
Internal Revenue Service	26, I
Investment Security, Office of	31, VIII
Monetary Offices	31, I
Secret Service	31, IV
Secretary of the Treasury, Office of	31, Subtitle A
Truman, Harry S. Scholarship Foundation	45, XVIII
United States and Canada, International Joint Commission	22, IV
United States and Mexico, International Boundary and Water Commission, United States Section	22, XI
U.S. Copyright Office	37, II
Utah Reclamation Mitigation and Conservation Commission	43, III
Veterans Affairs, Department of	2, VIII; 38, I
Federal Acquisition Regulation	48, 8
Veterans' Employment and Training Service, Office of the Assistant Secretary for	41, 61; 20, IX
Vice President of the United States, Office of	32, XXVIII
Wage and Hour Division	29, V
Water Resources Council	18, VI
Workers' Compensation Programs, Office of	20, I, VII
World Agricultural Outlook Board	7, XXXVIII

List of CFR Sections Affected

All changes in this volume of the Code of Federal Regulations (CFR) that were made by documents published in the FEDERAL REGISTER since January 1, 2014 are enumerated in the following list. Entries indicate the nature of the changes effected. Page numbers refer to FEDERAL REGISTER pages. The user should consult the entries for chapters, parts and subparts as well as sections for revisions.

For changes to this volume of the CFR prior to this listing, consult the annual edition of the monthly List of CFR Sections Affected (LSA). The LSA is available at *www.govinfo.gov*. For changes to this volume of the CFR prior to 2001, see the "List of CFR Sections Affected, 1949–1963, 1964–1972, 1973–1985, and 1986–2000" published in 11 separate volumes. The "List of CFR Sections Affected 1986–2000" is available at *www.govinfo.gov*.

2014

12 CFR

79 FR Page

Chapter I

1.2 (a)(1) revised; (j)(4) amended 11309
3 Footnotes 5 through 29 redesignated as footnotes 9 through 33; interim 78293
3.1 (d)(4) amended 57740
3.2 Amended 44123, 57740
Amended; interim 78293
3.10 (c)(4) revised 57740
3.121 CFR correction 51471
3.172 (d) added 57743
3.173 (a) introductory text revised; (c) and Table 13 added 57743
3.202 CFR correction 51471
4 Authority citation revised 11309
4.4 Amended 15641
4.7 (b)(1)(iii)(A) revised 11309
4.14 (c) amended 15641
4.15 (b)(1), (e)(2) and (g) amended 15641
4.17 (c) amended 15641
4.18 (a)(1) and (b) amended 15641
4.34 (a) amended 15641
5.2 (c) amended 15641
5.3 (d)(1) revised; (g)(1) amended 11309
5.13 (f) corrected; CFR correction 35279

12 CFR—Continued

79 FR Page

Chapter I—Continued

5.20 (i)(5)(i) and (ii) corrected; CFR correction 36387
5.34 (d)(2) amended 11310
(e)(5)(v)(R) footnote 1 amended 15641
(e)(5)(vi)(C) corrected; CFR correction 36387
5.36 (c)(2) amended 11310
5.39 (d)(10) amended 11310
5.46 (e)(1) amended 11310
5.47 Revised 11310, 75421
6.4 (c)(1)(iv) revised; eff. 1-1-18 24539
7.2000 (c) footnote 2 amended 15641
8.2 (a) introductory text and (4) revised 38772
8.8 Revised 38772
10.2 (c) amended 15641
11.3 (a)(1) amended 15641
14 Authority citation revised 28398
14.10 Revised 28398
14.20 (f)(1)(ii) and (j) redesignated as (f)(1)(iii) and (k); new (f)(1)(ii) and (j) added; (f)(1)(i), new (iii), (2) and (i) amended 28398
14.30 (a) introductory text, (1), (b) introductory text, (1), (3) introductory text and (i) revised 28398
14.40 (a)(1), (2), (b) introductory text and (1) revised; (c)(4)(i), (5) and (d) amended 28398
14.50 Amended 28399

12 CFR—Continued

79 FR Page

Chapter I—Continued
14.60 Amended 28399
14 Appendix A revised 28399
16.15 (d) amended 11312
16.17 (a) amended 15641
19.100 Amended 15641
21 Authority citation revised 28399
21.21 (b) and (c) redesignated as (c) and (d); new (b) added; (a), new (c)(1), 2 and (d)(2) amended 28399
23.2 (b)(1) revised 11312
23.6 Corrected; CFR correction 36387
24.2 (b)(1) and (2) revised 11312
24.5 (a)(2) and (b)(1) amended 15641
25.12 (u)(1) revised 77853
26 Authority citation revised 28399
26.1 (a) and (c) amended 28399
26.2 (a)(2) and (j)(1)(vi) amended 28399
26.4 (i) and (j) added 28399
26.6 (c) revised 28399
26.8 Amended 28399
28.14 (b) amended 11312
30 Authority citation revised 54543
30.1 (a) and (b) amended 54543
30.2 Amended 54543
30.3 Heading revised; amended; (a) and (b) amended 54543
30.4 (a) through (e) amended 54543
30.5 Amended; (a)(1) and (2) amended 54544
30.6 Amended; (a) and (b) amended 54544
30 Appendices A, B and C amended 54544
Appendix D added 54545
Appendices C and D corrected 74595
32.2 (i), (m)(1), (s) and (u) amended 11312
32.3 (d)(2)(i)(A) amended 11312
32.4 (a)(2) amended 11312
32.9 (b)(1)(i)(C)(*1*)(*i*), (iii), (c)(1)(i)(A)(*1*) and (iii) amended 11312
34 Authority citation revised 15641, 28400
34.41 (a) revised; (b) introductory text amended 28400
34.42 (f)(1) amended 28400
34.43 (f) removed 28400
34.44 (a) amended 28400
34.61—34.62 (Subpart D) Appendix A amended 11312
34.81 (a)(1) and (2) revised 11313
34.101—34.105 (Subpart F) Removed 15641
34.201—34.203 (Subpart G) Appendix C amended 78298

12 CFR—Continued

79 FR Page

Chapter I—Continued
35 Authority citation revised 28400
35.1 (b) and (c) revised 28400
35.2 (a)(2)(ii) and (4) revised 28400
35.11 (e) revised; (j)(2)(iv) amended 28400
37.7 Corrected; CFR correction 36387
40 Removed 15641
41 Authority citation revised 28400
41.1—41.3 (Subpart A) Removed 28400
41.20—41.28 (Subpart C) Removed 28400
41.30—41.32 (Subpart D) Removed 28400
41.40—41.43 (Subpart E) Removed 28400
41.80—41.83 (Subpart I) Heading revised 28400
41.82 Removed 28400
41.83 Revised 28400
41.90 (a), (b)(5) and (8) revised; (b)(9) and (10) redesignated as (b)(10) and (11); new (b)(9) added 28400
41.91 (a) revised; (b)(3) added 28401
41.92 Added 28401
41 Appendices C and E removed; Appendix J amended 28401
43 Added; eff. 2-23-15 77764
Authority citation added; eff. 2-23-15 77764
43.1 Added; eff. 2-23-15 77764
44 Added; nomenclature change 5804
44.1 Added 5804
44.16 Added; interim 5227
46 Policy statement 14153
Authority citation revised 71633
46.3 (c) revised; eff. 1-2-15 71633
46.4 (c) amended 11313
46.5 (a), (b) and (c) revised; eff. 1-2-15 71633
46.6 (a)(2) revised; eff. 1-2-15 71633
46.7 (a) and (b) revised; eff. 1-2-15 71633
46.8 (a)(1) and (2) revised; eff. 1-2-15 71634
50 Added; nomenclature changes 61538
Authority citation added 61538
50.1 (b)(1)(iii) revised; (b)(3)(i) and (ii) amended; (b)(3)(iii) added 61538
50.3 Amended; interim 78294
116.5 (f) amended 11313
133 Removed 28401

12 CFR—Continued

79 FR Page

Chapter I—Continued

136 Removed 28401
143.3 (c)(2)(iii) amended 11313
145.93 (b)(3)(i) amended 11313
145.95 (b)(1)(i) amended 11313
159.3 (j) and (2) amended 11313
159.13 (c) amended 11313
160 Authority citation revised 28401
160.60 (c)(1)(i) amended 28401
160.100 Amended 11313
160.101 Footnote 2 revised 11313
160.172 Amended 28401
161.55 (c) amended 11313
163 Authority citation revised 28401
163.74 (i)(2)(iv) and (v) amended 11314
163.80 (e)(1) amended 11314
163.81 Revised 11314
163.141 (b) and (d) amended 11317
163.142 Amended 11317
163.143 (a)(3), (b)(1) and (2) amended 11317
163.146 (a) amended 11317
163.177 Removed 28401
163.560 (a)(1) and (3) amended 11317
164 Removed 28401
168.5 Amended 54549
170 Removed 54549
171 Removed 28401
192.200 (a)(2) amended 11317
192.500 (a)(12) amended 11317
192.520 (b) amended 11317
195.12 (u)(1) revised 77854
196 Removed 28401

2015

12 CFR

80 FR Page

Chapter I

3.2 Amended 41415
3.10 (c) introductory text revised 41415
3.22 (b)(1)(iii) revised 41415
3.100 (b)(1)(ii) revised 41415
3.122 (c)(9) and (10) redesignated as (c)(10) and (11); (a)(3), (b)(1), (3), (5), (c)(1), (2), (5), (6), new (10), new (11) and (i)(5) revised; (b)(2)(iii) and new (c)(9) added 41415
3.131 (d)(5)(ii) and (iii) revised; (e)(3)(vi) amended 41416
3.132 Table 1, (d)(2)(iv)(C), (7)(iv)(B) and (9)(ii) amended; (c)(1), (2) and (d)(5)(iii)(B) revised 41417

12 CFR—Continued

80 FR Page

Chapter I—Continued

3.133 (b)(3)(i)(B), (4)(ii) and (c)(4)(ii) amended; (c)(3)(iii) added 41417
3.136 (e)(2)(i) and (ii) amended 41417
3.172 (d) revised 41417
3.173 (a) introductory text redesignated as (a)(1) and revised; (a)(2) and (3) added; Table 6 and Table 9 amended 41418
4 Authority citation revised 28414
4.5 Revised 28414
4.18 (b) amended 28414
5 Authority citation revised 28414
5.1 Revised 28414
5.2—5.13 (Subpart A) Revised 28414
5.20 Revised 28418
5.21 Added 28421
5.22 Added 28425
5.23 Added 28430
5.24 Revised 28432
5.25 Added 28433
5.26 Revised 28433
5.30 Revised 28435
5.31 Added 28436
5.32 Heading revised; (d)(4) added; (h)(2) amended 28437
5.33 Revised 28437
5.34 Revised 28444
5.35 Revised 28448
5.36 Heading revised; (d)(1), (2), (e) introductory text and (g)(1) amended 28449
5.37 Revised 28449
5.38 Added 28450
5.39 Heading revised; (i)(1)(i), (ii) and (2) amended 28452
5.40 Revised 28452
5.42 Revised 28453
5.45 Added 28453
5.46 Revised 28454
5.47 (g)(2)(ii) footnote 2 redesignated as footnote 4 28455
5.48 Revised 28455
5.50 Revised 28456
5.51 Revised 28460
5.52 Revised 28462
5.53 Revised 28462
5.55 Added 28463
5.56 Added 28464
5.58 Added 28466
5.59 Added 28467
5.60—5.67 (Subpart E) Heading revised 28470
5.64 (c)(3) amended 28470
7 Heading and authority citation revised 28470

12 CFR—Continued

80 FR Page

Chapter I—Continued

7.1000—7.1021 (Subpart A) Heading revised 28470
7.1000 Revised 28470
7.1003 Heading revised 28471
7.1004 Heading revised 28471
7.1005 Heading revised 28471
7.1006 Heading revised 28471
7.1007 Heading revised 28471
7.1008 Heading revised 28471
7.1012 Heading revised 28471
7.1014 Heading revised 28471
7.1015 Heading revised 28471
7.1016 Heading revised 28471
7.1018 Heading revised 28471
7.1020 Heading revised 28471
7.2000—7.2024 (Subpart B) Heading revised 28471
7.2000 Footnote 2 amended 28471
7.3000—7.3001 (Subpart C) Heading revised 28471
7.3000 Heading revised 28471
7.3001 Revised 28471
7.4000 Heading revised 28472
7.4001 Heading revised 28472
7.4003 Amended 28472
7.4005 Heading revised 28472
7.4007 Heading revised 28472
7.4008 Heading revised 28472
7.5000—7.5010 (Subpart E) Heading revised 28472
14.10 (b) amended 28472
22 Revised 43240
22.5 Revised 43243
22.9 (b) revised 43244
22 Appendices A and B revised 43244
24.5 (a)(2) amended 28472
24 Appendix 1 revised 28472
Appendix 1 corrected 31463, 34039
25.12 (h)(2)(i), (j)(2) and (l) amended; (u)(1) revised 81164
25.42 (b)(3), (d) and (i) amended 81164
25.43 (b)(2) amended 81164
32 Authority citation revised 28479
32.2 (g)(1)(iv) amended 28479
32.3 (d)(2) revised 28479
32.7 (b) introductory text amended 28479
34 Authority citation revised 32679
34.84 Removed 28479
34.201—34.203 (Subpart G) Appendix C amended 73945
34.210—34.216 (Subpart H) Added 32679
45 Added; nomenclature changes; eff. 4-1-16 74910
45.1 (a), (b) and (c) added; eff. 4-1-16 74910

12 CFR—Continued

80 FR Page

Chapter I—Continued

(d) added; interim; eff. 4-1-16 74923
45.2 Amended; eff. 4-1-16 74911
45.6 Amended; eff. 4-1-16 74911
45.12 Added; eff. 4-1-16 74911
100.1 Amended 28479
100.2 Amended 28479
116 Removed 28479
143 Heading and authority citation revised 28479
143.1 Removed 28479
143.2 Removed 28479
143.3 Removed 28479
143.4 Removed 28479
143.5 Removed 28479
143.6 Removed 28479
143.7 Removed 28479
143.8 Removed 28479
143.9 Removed 28479
143.10 Removed 28479
143.11 Removed 28479
143.14 Removed 28479
144 Authority citation revised 28479
Heading revised 28480
144.1 Undesignated center heading and section removed 28480
144.2 Removed 28480
144.4 Removed 28480
144.5 Removed 28480
144.6 Removed 28480
144.7 Removed 28480
145.91 Removed 28480
145.92 (b) amended 28480
145.93 Removed 28480
145.95 Removed 28480
145.96 Removed 28480
146 Removed 28480
150.70 Revised 28480
150.80 Removed 28480
150.90 Removed 28480
150.100 Removed 28480
150.110 Removed 28480
150.120 Removed 28480
150.125 Removed 28480
150.130 (a) amended 28480
152 Removed 28480
159 Removed 28480
160.30 Footnote 16 amended 28480
160.32 (b) revised; (c) removed 28480
160.35 (d)(3) amended 28480
160.37 Removed 28480
161 Authority citation revised 28480
161.45 Revised 28480
162.4 (b) amended 28480
163.1 Removed 28480
163.22 Removed 28480
163.76 (c) amended; (d) reinstated; CFR correction 79460

12 CFR—Continued

80 FR Page

Chapter I—Continued
163.81 Removed 28480
163.140—163.146 (Subpart E) Removed 28480
163.550—163.590 (Subpart H) Removed 28480
172 Removed 43245
174 Removed 28480
192 Authority citation revised 28480
192.25 Amended 28480
192.180 (a) amended 28481
192.185 Amended 28481
192.430 (a) and (c) amended 28481
192.510 (c)(1) amended 28481
192.520 (c) amended 28481
192.525 (b) and (c)(5) amended 28481
192.660 (g)(2) amended 28481
193.101 (c) amended 28481
195.12 (h)(2)(i), (j)(2) and (l) amended; (u)(1) revised 81164
195.42 (b)(3) and (d) amended 81164
195.43 (b)(2) amended 81164

2016

12 CFR

81 FR Page

Chapter I
4 Authority citation revised 10068
Regulation at 81 FR 10068 confirmed; eff. 1-17-17 90951
4.6 Revised; interim 10068
Regulation at 81 FR 10068 confirmed; eff. 1-17-17 90951
4.7 Revised; interim 10068
Regulation at 81 FR 10068 confirmed; eff. 1-17-17 90951
4.11 (b)(4) removed; interim 94244
4.12 (a), (b)(3) and (5) revised; (b)(8), (9) and (d) amended; (b)(10) removed; interim 94244
4.14 Heading, (a) and (c) revised; (b) amended; interim 94244
4.15 (b)(1), (2)(i) introductory text, (c)(2), (4), (d)(1) and (4) revised; (f)(1) amended; (f)(4) and (h) added; interim 94245
4.17 (b)(6) revised; (c)(1) amended; interim 94245
4.18 (a) and (b) amended; interim 94246
7 Authority citation revised 96360
7.1022 Added; eff. 4-1-17 96360
7.1023 Added; eff. 4-1-17 96360
19 Authority citation revised 43026
19.240 Revised; interim 43026
25 Policy statement 48506
30.1 (a) amended 66800

12 CFR—Continued

81 FR Page

Chapter I—Continued
30.2 Amended 66800
30.3 (a) amended 66800
30 Appendix E added 66800
34 Policy statement 75315
34.201—34.203 (Subpart G) Appendix C amended 86254
45.1 Regulation at 80 FR 74923 confirmed 50613
51 Added; eff. 1-19-17 92602
109 Authority citation revised 43027
109.103 (c) revised; (d) removed; interim 43027
195 Policy statement 48506

2017

12 CFR

82 FR Page

Chapter I
3.2 Amended 56661
3.300 (b)(4), (d)(1) and table 10 revised; (b)(5) added 55315
5.8 (b) amended 8103
5.20 (l) redesignated as (l)(1); (b), (c), new (l)(1) heading and (2) added 8103
5.21 (j)(3)(i)(B), (ii), (iii) and (4) amended 8103
5.22 (j)(2)(iii) amended 8103
5.33 (i), (n)(2)(iii) introductory text, (B) and (o)(3)(i) amended 8103
5.45 (g)(4)(i) introductory text amended 8104
5.46 (i)(6) added 8104
5.48 (e)(2)(ii) amended 8104
5.50 (f)(2)(ii)(E) amended 8104
5.53 (c)(1)(iii) and (iv) amended; (c)(1)(v) added; (d)(3)(ii) revised 8104
5.66 Amended 8104
7 Authority citation revised 8104
7.2008 (b) and (c) revised 8104
7.2013 (a) and (b) introductory text revised; (b)(4) amended 8104
8 Authority citation revised 8104
8.6 (c)(3)(iv) revised 8104
9.13 (a) amended 8105
9.14 (a) amended 8105
9.18 (b)(1) and (c)(2) amended 8105
10 Authority citation revised 8105
10.1 Amended; (b) amended 8105
10.2 (a), (b) and (c) amended 8105
11 Authority citation revised 8105
11.1 Revised 8105
11.2 Revised 8105

12 CFR—Continued

82 FR Page

Chapter I—Continued
11.3 (a)(1), (3)(i) and (ii) heading revised; (a)(3)(iii) and (b) amended; (a)(4) removed 8106
11.4 (b) revised 8106
12.1 (c)(1), (2)(iii) and (v) amended 8106
12.2 (g)(3) amended; (i)(3) revised 8106
12.3 (b) amended 8106
12.4 (b) revised 8106
12.7 (d) amended 8107
12.9 (b)(2) amended 8107
12.101 Undesignated center heading and section removed 8107
12.102 Removed 8107
16 Authority citation revised 8107
16.1 (a) revised; (b) and (c) amended 8107
16.2 (b), (c) and (j) removed; (d) through (h) and (k) through (n) redesignated as (b), (c), (d), (f), (g) and (j) through (m); (a), new (b), new (c), new (g), new (j), new (m), (o), (p) and (q) amended; new (e), (h) and (n) added 8107
16.3 (a) introductory text, (b) introductory text and (c) amended 8107
16.4 Amended 8107
16.5 Introductory text, (a), (b) and (e) revised; (f) and (g) amended 8107
16.6 (a) introductory text, (3) and (b) amended; (a)(1) and (5) revised 8107
16.7 Amended; (a) introductory text, (b) and (c) amended 8108
16.8 Amended; (a) and (b) amended 8108
16.9 (a) revised; introductory text, (b), (c) and (d) amended 8108
16.10 Added 8108
16.15 (a), (b), (d) and (e) amended 8108
16.16 (a) amended 8108
16.17 Revised 8108
16.30 (a) revised 8109
16.32 Heading revised; (a) introductory text, (3) and (d) amended 8109
16.33 Revised 8109
18 Removed 8109
19 Authority citation revised 8586
19.240 Revised 8586

12 CFR—Continued

82 FR Page

Chapter I—Continued
25.12 (u)(1) revised 5355, 61144
(g)(3), (4)(ii)(B), (h)(2)(i) and (l) amended; (g)(5) and (j)(3) removed; (j)(4) and (5) redesignated as new (j)(3) and (4) 55742
25.22 (a)(1) amended 55742
25.42 (c)(1) introductory text amended 55742
25.43 (b)(2) revised 55742
31 Authority citation revised 8109
31.1 Revised 8109
31.2 (a) and (b) amended 8109
31.3 Added 8109
31 Appendix B amended 8109
34 Policy statement 49089
34.201—34.203 (Subpart G) Appendix C amended 51974
47 Added 56662
50.3 Amended 56669
109 Authority citation revised 8587
109.103 (c) revised 8587
150.245 Added 8109
151.40 Amended 8110
151.60 Revised 8110
151.80 (b) revised 8110
151.110 Removed 8110
155 Revised 8110
162 Revised 8110
163.41 Removed 8110
163.43 Removed 8110
163.161 Removed 8110
163.172 (a), (c)(2), (3) introductory text, (ii), (4) and (d)(1) amended; (a) heading, (b), (c) heading, (1), (d) heading and (e) revised 8110
163.180 (a) and (c) removed 8111
163.190 Removed 8111
163.191 Removed 8111
193 Removed 8111
194 Removed 8111
195.12 (u)(1) revised 5356, 61144
(g)(3), (4)(iii)(B), (h)(2)(i) and (l) amended; (g)(5) and (j)(3) removed; (j)(4) and (5) redesignated as new (j)(3) and (4) 55742
195.22 (a)(1) amended 55742
195.42 (c)(1) introductory text amended 55742
195.43 (b)(2) revised 55742
197 Removed 8111

2018

12 CFR

83 FR Page

Chapter I

4.6 (b)(1) revised; interim 43965
4.6 Regulation at 83 FR 43965 confirmed 67035
4.7 (b)(1)(i) revised; interim........... 43965
4.7 Regulation at 83 FR 43965 confirmed 67035
12.9 (a) revised 26349
19 Authority citation revised 1518
19 Policy statement...................... 66599
19.240 Revised 1518
25 Technical correction 15298
25.12 (u)(1) revised......................... 66603
30 Appendix E amended; eff. 1-28-19.. 66607
34.42 (e) through (m) redesignated as (f) through (n); new (e) added....................................... 15035
34.43 (a)(11) amended; (a)(12), (b), and (d)(2) revised; (a)(13) added....................................... 15035

12 CFR—Continued

83 FR Page

Chapter I—Continued

34.201—34.203 (Subpart G) Appendix C amended........................... 59274
45.1 (e)(7) added............................. 50811
45.2 Amended................................ 50811
46.2 Amended 7953
46.3 (b) removed; (c), (d), and (e) redesignated as new (b), (c), and (d); new (b) and new (c) revised; new (d) amended 7953
46.5 Revised 7953
46.7 (a) and (b) revised..................... 7953
46.8 (a) revised................................. 7954
50 Authority citation revised........ 44454
50.3 Amended; interim 44454
50.20 (c)(1)(iii) and (2)(vi) amended; (c)(3) added; interim............. 44454
109 Authority citation revised........ 1518
109 Policy statement 66599
109.103 (c) revised 1518

www.ingramcontent.com/pod-product-compliance
Lightning Source LLC
Chambersburg PA
CBHW052054230326
41599CB00054B/1702